KU-166-678

EDITED BY MATTHEW ENGEL

WISDEN

CRICKETERS' ALMANACK

2004

141st EDITION

Published by John Wisden & Co Ltd,
13 Old Aylesfield, Golden Pot,
Alton, Hampshire GU34 4BY

JOHN WISDEN & CO LTD
13 Old Aylesfield, Golden Pot, Alton, Hampshire GU34 4BY
enquiries@johnwisden.co.uk
www.cricinfo.com

WISDEN CRICKETERS' ALMANACK
Editor **Matthew Engel**
Deputy editors **Harriet Monkhouse** and **Hugh Chevallier**
Assistant editor **Paul Coupar**
Contributing editors **Lawrence Booth** and **Rob Smyth**
Chief statistician **Philip Bailey**
Cover designer **Will Webb**
Design consultant **Peter Ward**
Production co-ordinator **Peter Bather**
Chief typesetter **Mike Smith**
Proofreaders **Gordon Burling, Simon Webber** and **Charles Barr**
Advertisement sales **Colin Ackehurst** (020 7565 3150)
Publisher **Christopher Lane**

Typeset in Times New Roman and Univers
by Lazertype (UK) Ltd, Colchester
Printed and bound in Great Britain by Clays Ltd, St Ives plc

Published by John Wisden & Co Ltd 2004

EDITIONS
Cased ISBN 0-947766-83-9 **£35**
Soft cover ISBN 0-947766-84-7 **£35**
Leatherbound ISBN 0-947766-85-5 **£230**

Distributed by Macmillan Distribution Ltd
Distributed in Australia by Hardie Grant Books, Melbourne

A Taste of Wisden 2004

Many a pre-Ashes Test meeting stopped when S. Waugh's name hit the projector screen. Half the team got animated and said "Look, skip… we'll pepper him with the short stuff. It's only a matter of time."

Nasser Hussain on Steve Waugh, page 27

Sponsorship opportunities in the 1970s and 1980s were limited to a car from the local garage and the occasional tryst with a Benson and Hedges cigarette girl. Players were reluctant to share 10% of either.

Paul Kelso on agents in cricket, page 44

Talk about frayed nerves! It looked as though the fat lady had forgotten to turn up.

Robin Marlar on Sussex's first Championship, page 49

For most batsmen around the world he was too fast, too straight, too much. And boy, did he know it.

The Wisden Forty: Shoaib Akhtar, page 92

For the glitzy opening match at Southampton and televised on Sky, the dug-out was a sophisticated affair, all smoked curving glass; for the next game at the Rose Bowl this had become a couple of garden benches.

Hugh Chevallier on the Twenty20 Cup, page 829

Matthew Hayden went to work with a sore back. He wore a heavy vest to keep it warm, and hardly indulged in the sweep shots that have served him so well. Instead he played blissfully, ruthlessly straight.

Chloe Saltau on Hayden's world record, page 1256

There is no false modesty in this book and, for that matter, no genuine modesty either.

Barry Norman on one cricketer's autobiography, page 1575

Had Blowers been at Chester-le-Street – to be unleashed on a new public transport system – the commentary at least might have gone into a fourth day.

Andrew Nickolds on the media, page 1584

LIST OF CONTRIBUTORS

Tanya Aldred
Andy Arlidge
Chris Aspin
Mike Atherton
Philip August
Charlie Austin
Scyld Berry
Edward Bevan
Rahul Bhattacharya
Martin Blake
Paul Bolton
Richard Boock
Stephen Brenkley
Simon Briggs
Robert Brooke
Colin Bryden
Don Cameron
Tony Cozier
John Curtis
Gareth A. Davies
Geoffrey Dean
Ralph Dellor
Norman de Mesquita
Christopher Douglas
Philip Eden
John Etheridge
Colin Evans
Paul Fearn
David Foot
Neville Foulger
Angus Fraser
Nigel Fuller
Andrew Gidley
Julian Guyer
Gideon Haigh
David Hallett
David Hardy
Norman Harris
Jon Henderson
Richard Hobson
Grenville Holland
David Hopps
Nick Hoult
Nasser Hussain
Guy Jackson
Emma John
Abid Ali Kazi
Paul Kelso
Neil Leitch
David Llewellyn
Steven Lynch
John MacKinnon
Neil Manthorp
Robin Marlar
Vic Marks
Trevor Marshallsea
Nick Mason
Mohandas Menon
Eric Midwinter
Andrew Miller
Fazeer Mohammed
R. Mohan
Glenn Moore
Gerald Mortimer
Tony Munro
Brian Murgatroyd
Pat Murphy
Andrew Nickolds
Barry Norman
William A. Powell
Marcus Prior
Andrew Radd
Andrew Ramsey
David Rayvern Allen
Graham Russell
Christian Ryan
Carol Salmon
Chloe Saltau
Andrew Samson
Derek Scott
Utpal Shuvro
Jasmer Singh
Mike Stanger
Rob Steen
John Stern
Pat Symes
Bruce Talbot
Sa'adi Thawfeeq
Gerry Vaidyasekera
Amit Varma
Gordon Vince
Michael Vockins
Mike Walters
John Ward
David Warner
Paul Weaver
Tim Wellock
Simon Wilde
Graeme Wright

Photographers Arif Ali, Dave Allen, Paul Barker, Daniel Berehulak, Hamish Blair, Shaun Botterill, Billy Bowden, Gordon Brooks, Philip Brown, Andy Clark, Finn Connor, Mark Dadswell, Sucheta Das, Arko Datta, Nigel Davies, David Dawson, Patrick Eagar, Stu Forster, Sean Garnsworthy, Michael Goonan, David Gray, Julian Herbert, Mike Hewitt, Mike Hutchings, Matthew Impey, Tom Jenkins, Derrick Jones, Maurice Jones, Fayaz Kabli, Ross Kinnaird, Nick Laham, Clive Mason, Bob McLeod, Graham Morris, Gary Prior, Ben Radford, Rafiqur Rahman, Clive Rose, Tom Shaw, Darren Staples, Michael Steele, Mark Thompson, Steve Watkin, Alex Wong.

Round the World Contributors to the Round the World section are listed after their articles.

Thanks are accorded to the following for checking the scorecards of county and tourist matches: Keith Booth, John Brown, Wally Clarke, Jack Foley, Keith Gerrish, Neil Harris, John Hartridge, Brian Hunt, Vic Isaacs, David Kendix, Tony Kingston, Gordon Lewis, Ray Markham, David Norris, John Potter, Mike Smith, Gerry Stickley, Gordon Stringfellow, David Wainwright, Alan West, Roy Wilkinson, Graham York.

The editor also acknowledges with gratitude assistance from the following: Bill Allen, Farid Bakri, T. Bedells, Gerry Byrne, John Campbell, Stephen Chalke, Marion Collin, Paddy Cramsie, cricketarchive.com, Brian Croudy, Prakash Dahatonde, Gerald de Kock, Frank Duckworth, Robert Eastaway, M. L. Fernando, Ric Finlay, Bill Frindall, Keith Gerrish, Ghulam Mustafa Khan, Ray Goble, Michael Goldfarb, Peter Griffiths, Neil Hallam, Col. Malcolm Havergal, Ed Hawkins, Keith Hayhurst, Brian Heald, Andrew Hignell, Robin Isherwood, Michael Johnson, Frank Keating, Rajesh Kumar, Stephanie Lawrence, Tony Lewis, Nirav Malavi, Rodney Miles, Colin Mills, Ian Morrison, Francis Payne, Mark Pennell, S. Pervez Qaiser, Qamar Ahmed, Mark Ray, Andrew Renshaw, Martin Searby, Mary Small, Richard Spiller, Mike Spurrier, Josef Steen, Mike Vimpany, Chris Walmsley, Alison Ward, Charlie Wat, Francesca Watson, Robert Wood, John Woodcock, Peter Wynne-Thomas and all our colleagues at *Cricinfo*, *The Wisden Cricketer* and *Wisden Cricket Asia*.

The production of *Wisden* would not be possible without the support and co-operation of many other cricket officials, writers and lovers of the game. To them all, many thanks.

PREFACE

A while back I was at the dentist, having one of those one-way conversations you only ever endure in that situation. He was talking of the wonders of fluoride in the water supply, and how it halted tooth decay. "Hang on," I spluttered, when he finally took his fingers out of my mouth. "Isn't that bad for business?" "No," he said. "We don't have to do so many boring fillings. We can be more creative. It gives us time to do better dentistry."

I am not convinced either way on fluoridation, but he struck a chord. When I first became editor of *Wisden* a dozen years ago, the word "internet" was known only to a handful of techies. Since then it has transformed our lives. The change is evident even since I ended my first term as editor in 2000. This year only two among our hundreds of correspondents attempted to file their reports via battered old typewriters rather than electronically.

The internet undoubtedly changes the purpose and role of reference books. It must do. Our associated website, *Cricinfo*, can give squillions of up-to-the-second scores and stats via a few mouse-clicks; any moment it should make available large chunks of all 141 volumes of *Wisden*. The more I thought about it, the more I came to feel this was not a threat but an opportunity: the chance to be more creative, and produce a better book.

Wisden's prime function in the 21st century is still to report the facts, as it has always done. But cricket's devotees are now bombarded with information all the time. Someone has to stand back and try to pick out what really matters. That's our job.

Wisden 2004 is the first product of this rethink. In some ways, *Wisden* has changed too fast for comfort; in a book like this, familiarity breeds content; it should not be the setting for Maoist permanent revolution. But we need to get it right for the new era, and some things had to change quickly.

The most important is that this is a 15-month book. Traditionally, the almanack reported cricket from September to September. Henceforth, the focus will be squarely on each calendar year. To catch up, *Wisden* 2004 is thus a record of cricket from September 2002 to the end of 2003. Unfortunately, the fixture list is not quite that neat. Full reports of tours that spilled into this year will, as before, be in next year's *Wisden*, though we may push the boundaries in future for England tours. This volume does, however, contain full coverage of the tours completed in late 2003 – including Matthew Hayden's world record 380 and England's adventures in Bangladesh and Sri Lanka.

We are also trying to produce both a shorter book – no one wants a 2,000-page *Wisden* – and a more readable one: we are, for instance, trying to abolish lengthy wodges of text in minuscule type. These two aims are, unfortunately, not complementary.

The cover? Oh, yes, the cover. Last summer, I asked every reader I met what they thought. Hardly anyone said they objected in principle to a pictorial cover; but not everyone was happy with *Wisden's* first, which adorned the

2003 edition. We put the problem to Will Webb, the chief cover designer for our new publishing partners Bloomsbury. I believe what has emerged is a brilliant solution, combining the famous elements of a *Wisden* jacket: the yellow, the wanted-poster typeface and the Eric Ravilious woodcut – plus a stylish and timeless quality that readers will come to relish. This year's version may be a bit too Australian for some tastes; but it does sum up 2003.

So, herewith a guide to what lies inside and how it has changed.

Part One – Comment. I commend what I hope is an excellent selection of articles, led by Nasser Hussain's tribute to Steve Waugh. This section also includes our Five Cricketers of the Year. For reasons that should become clear (see Part Three) we are returning to our old rules, choosing the Five primarily on the basis of the previous English season.

Part Two – World View. Simon Wilde gives an overview of the global cricketing year.

Part Three – The Players. For the first time, *Wisden* names its choice of Leading Cricketer in the World, based on worldwide performances in 2003. We also include the Wisden Forty – the No. 1 and his 39 closest rivals – together with reviews of how they fared during the year. This is the start of a feature that we hope will become as permanent and popular as the Five. Alongside that, two old faithfuls have been merged: the listing of Test Cricketers, using the formula devised by Norman Preston in 1942, had become simply untenable in a world with (as I write) 2,384 Test players. The two-column method of listing Births and Deaths dates back to 1870. It has done sterling service, but modern player mobility was turning it into a hopeless jumble of initials and abbreviations. We can tolerate one Mankad V. (who played for W. Ind., Naw., M'tra, Guj., Bengal, Bombay & Raja.) but not hundreds of the blighters. It was time to move on. Births and Deaths is now in two parts. The first lists all Test cricketers; the second other major figures of interest, players and non-players alike.

Part Four – Records. This section has never been and cannot be more than a sampler – a surface-skim of the profundities of the game's statistics. We can no longer detail every Test century ever scored. Our figures are far more up to date than ever before, with Test records taken up to the break in the schedule in late January 2004. And we include a new feature – Series Notes, which pick out the salient features and sequences to guide you through forthcoming fixtures. Updated records can be found on cricinfo.com.

Part Five – English Cricket. This section now begins with an essay by Scyld Berry, calmly assessing the nerve-racking peaks and troughs of England's year. This is followed by profiles of all the players who appeared for England in Tests or one-day internationals during 2003. (I think we remembered them all.) We are not giving full scores for either the National League or the Twenty20, though they can easily be found at www.cricinfo.com/wisden2004. A Martian might question the logic of minimising the most-watched forms of the county game. A cricket follower will understand the difference between instant cricket and the sort that matures the ripest in these pages.

Part Six – Overseas Cricket. Now including, as explained, all tours ending in 2003.

Part Seven – History and Law. The Laws of Cricket are restored after their one-year absence, by popular demand. Dates in Cricket History, an old favourite, is also back, after a 14-year gap. For the first time, we also try to explain the origins of the game and answer the question *Wisden* has always ignored: what is cricket? (Perhaps we'll crack the American market.) I'm grateful to Nick Mason and Peter Wynne-Thomas for their help.

Part Eight – The Wisden Review. A new name encompassing many popular features, such as the Chronicle noting the year's major events (and the ones that may have escaped your notice), the Obituaries, the Book Review (this year by Barry Norman) etc., plus an assessment of the players who retired in 2003 by Angus Fraser.

Part Nine – The Almanack. When *Wisden* began, it was a real almanack, listing quarter days and phases of the moon. We haven't brought those back, but we do include a list of the year's anniversaries, as well as the 2004 fixture list.

To the staff who produced all that, I am immensely grateful. The core editorial team – Hugh Chevallier, Harriet Monkhouse and Paul Coupar – have been brilliant through a difficult year. We pay tribute elsewhere to *Wisden's* late proprietor, Sir Paul Getty, and I must add my thanks here to his successor, his son Mark, to Christopher Lane, the managing director, and to my colleagues on the John Wisden board.

I need to thank hundreds of others too. I hope everyone gets their due on the Contributors page. But I should single out Lawrence Booth and Rob Smyth, for their efforts, especially on the new profiles; Peter Bather and Mike Smith at our typesetters Lazertype, who calmly and efficiently put up with a great deal, and their boss, David Clark, helpful to us over many years, who is retiring; Graeme Wright, for his work on the obituaries and all-round sagacity; Peter Ward, our consultant designer; our new colleagues at Bloomsbury and Macmillan; and our chief statistician Philip Bailey, who has helped take his abstruse branch of science to levels that in other fields win Nobel prizes. Thanks too to our team of proofreaders, Gordon Burling, Simon Webber and Charles Barr. And I thank my family, Hilary, Laurie and Vika, for forbearance above all.

MATTHEW ENGEL
Newton St Margarets, Herefordshire, February 2004.

CONTENTS

Part One
Comment

Part Two
World View

Part Three
The Players

Part Four
Records

Part Five
English Cricket

STATISTICS

INTERNATIONAL CRICKET IN ENGLAND

FRIZZELL COUNTY CHAMPIONSHIP

CHELTENHAM & GLOUCESTER TROPHY

National League

Twenty20 Cup

Career Figures

The Universities

Other Cricket in the British Isles

Part Six

Overseas Cricket

The World Cup

England Test Tours

Other Tours

One-Day International Tournaments

Other Overseas International Cricket

Domestic Cricket

Part Seven
History and Law

Part Eight
The Wisden Review

Part Nine
The Almanack

Opposite: Country-house cricket at Southill Park, Bedfordshire.
Picture by Patrick Eagar.

PART ONE

Comment

NOTES BY THE EDITOR

Let's start by celebrating. In many respects, 2003 was a brilliant year for cricket. It began with a World Cup won by the team that was not merely the best but, quite conceivably, the best there has ever been. It went on to produce a couple of Test series – England v South Africa and Australia v India – that in their different ways might stand comparison with any in history.

Some of cricket's most resonant records were smashed. There was the first official 100mph ball, bowled by Shoaib Akhtar in Cape Town. Then West Indies, cricket's fallen giants, rose from the canvas to pull off Test cricket's biggest-ever successful run-chase and beat mighty Australia. In Perth, Matthew Hayden took perhaps the game's most magical number – the highest individual Test score – to a new peak of 380. Even the poor sad whipping boys from Bangladesh took part in a fantastic Test match, when they came within one wicket of beating Pakistan in remote Multan.

Australia scored their Test runs in 2003 at a phenomenal rate of 4.08 per over. Everywhere, the pace of batting, and the dominance of bat over ball, seemed rather like global warming: terrifying when you contemplate what it means for the fragile ecology of cricket, with bowlers potentially being driven to the edge of extinction, but thoroughly pleasant when contemplated from a deckchair on a summer's afternoon.

In England, the sun really did blaze down, and the much-derided England and Wales Cricket Board (ECB) produced a new tournament – the Twenty20 Cup – that struck the motherlode of public affection for cricket that runs just below the surface crust of apparent indifference.

Arguably, the game has been better run for the past few years than at any time in history. The ECB has been thinking hard and, I believe, creatively about the problems it faces. At the international level, match-fixing has almost certainly not been eradicated from the game, any more than chucking and dissent have. But at least corruption is handled with a sense of urgency and vigour unthinkable less than a decade ago, when the crisis first emerged and the International Cricket Council (ICC) pretended it was not their problem. And with what was either astonishing acuity or luck, the ICC managed to secure a TV deal for the 2003 and 2007 World Cups at the very top of the TV rights market, which was a remarkable piece of business.

Cricket's development strategy is showing gains and, in places far more improbable than Multan, the game appears to be taking a grip. Some of the gains might be overhyped, but the reality is impressive enough. Our Round the World section reports how an Afghan warrior laid down his arms to join in a match. In the United States, the shimmering fairytale castle (so impregnable! But, oh, so full of treasure!) which cricket's rulers keep glimpsing through the mist, Asian migrants are giving cricket a currency it has not had there since the mid 19th-century. More enticing yet, the Chinese government are said to be keen on encouraging this mysterious sport, believing it will teach their people useful virtues. Think of that.

For those of us who already love the game, the year's events provided regular infusions of delight, reinforcing our romance with this strangely bewitching, ineffably complex and maddeningly beautiful pastime. Maddening? Oh, yes. Definitely maddening.

September song

Consider for a moment Britain, and its ambitions to host the great sporting events of the planet. The Olympic Games might come to London in 2012; they might come sometime never. As things stand, England cannot bid for the football World Cup, never mind get it, until 2018 or 2022 at the earliest. Even rugby, with a nuclear family smaller than cricket, is not expected to stage a World Cup final in the British Isles until 2015. And cricket's own World Cup is not expected back until at least 2019.

But wait a minute. Here is – or was – something: a one-day tournament involving the 12 best cricketing nations planned for England this very year: a World Cup in all but name, but shorter and sharper. Surely given all those other schedules, this could be one of the nation's sporting events of the decade?

Well, by the time you read this, it is possible the Champions Trophy will have been shifted or cancelled – a protest by the rest of the cricketing world against England's refusal to go to Zimbabwe. We await developments.

But think about it anyway. There are two ways of regarding this tournament, devised by the ICC in 1998 as a biennial event to raise funds for cricket's development. Either it is a mini-World Cup, a showcase for the game and a wonderful opportunity for the host country, especially one that cannot expect to hold the real World Cup for a generation and is widely thought to have botched their last one. Or it is an abscess – yet another build-up of stinking pus on the fixture list, which should be lanced immediately: the last one, in 2002, ended in farce, and actually failed to attract crowds in Sri Lanka, where people will normally watch grass grow if you sell it to them as a 50-over grass-grow.

Both these views are perfectly tenable. But you cannot hold them simultaneously. Either the tournament is worth staging properly or it is not worth staging at all. In my view, with a little imagination, effort and co-operation, England could have made the Champions Trophy something sensational: a two-week, sell-out showpiece culminating in a cracking final at Lord's.

So what was offered instead? The fixture list at the back of this book may be a guide to a real live event or a historical curiosity; as I write, we don't know. But it's curious enough either way. No games were scheduled for Lord's; the final was sent to The Oval instead. But even The Oval was offering only a tatty old drugget rather than the red carpet; the place is being rebuilt – not for this year, but for the 2005 Ashes Test. England would not even rate the building site short of being in the final: their biggest scheduled fixture, against Sri Lanka, is at the Rose Bowl in Southampton, which cannot cram in as many as the main Test grounds.

All this was put together with a final on September 25, and a reserve date of the 26th, with October rushing towards us. Only one day of major cricket, the last day of a special Essex v Victoria challenge match in 1991 (when it rained) has been staged as late as September 26 in Britain since 1886. The game's masters are putting remarkable faith in the advance of global warming. Remember that England gave up staging one-day finals in early September because of morning dew: by late September, equinoctial gales are another intriguing meteorological possibility. Nightfall will come quickly and there will be no floodlights.

There is also the simple parochial point. The best argument for staging such a tournament in the UK is not the immediate cash: it is for England to win it and invigorate public support for their sport in the way the rugby team did by winning their World Cup in 2003. By September, the top English players are scheduled to have played 11 Test matches and 16 or 17 one-day internationals in six months. They will be knackered. What kind of preparation is that?

There are reasons for all the above, mostly involving contractual commitments. And the ECB can blame various other parts of the alphabet for most of them. It was the ICC who scheduled this tournament for September, as the only month when there is regularly no major cricket anywhere. (There is a good reason for that too – the weather is unsuitable in just about every cricketing country: either early autumn, early spring or the monsoon season.) It was GCC (the Global Cricket Corporation, who own the TV rights) who insisted that the tournament had to be restricted to three grounds. And it was MCC who chose not to make Lord's available.

Then why the hell did England agree to hold the event? Why didn't they wait for 2006 or 2008, giving time for some of the problems to be sorted and offering a decent chance of success? Although the tournament is supposed to happen in September, my understanding is that the ICC would have been very interested in an English midsummer alternative.

Maybe the Trophy will both happen and turn out fine. Perhaps the sun will shine, the crowds will come and the public will be galvanised. But the objective assessment must be that this has all the makings of being somewhere between a squandered opportunity and a total fiasco.

Not the Nine O'Clock News

"The new right-wing military government in South Africa, which seized power yesterday, has announced that apartheid is to be reintroduced. The black population will be stripped of all voting rights and segregation will be reimposed as soon as practicable. The situation in the country was said to be calm and there were no reports of violence. The International Cricket Council has therefore announced that forthcoming tours to the country can go ahead as normal..."

Unthinkable? Which bit is unthinkable? The ICC has made it plain that safety and security are the only legitimate grounds for countries to call off cricket tours. Apartheid South Africa was a very safe place for white men to play cricket against other white men, as anyone who toured there in the 1950s or 60s will tell you. Issues of morality are irrelevant, according to the nine other countries apparently ranged against England on the issue of whether they should play in Zimbabwe. Do the United Cricket Board of South Africa – of all people – really understand what they are saying?

Of course morality has a legitimate role to play in deciding whether or not a cricket tour can take place. Any contrary argument is contemptible, especially in a game that went through the decades of torment caused by apartheid. The ECB's position on whether or not to go to Zimbabwe has been incoherent and inconsistent. But consistency on this subject is probably for the simple-minded.

It is true that it is all too easy to get on a high horse about this. I could have a decent stab at writing a powerful newspaper column arguing the moral case against playing cricket in any place you care to name, however innocuous it might seem. (Even New Zealand has dirty little secrets, you know. The UK certainly has.) But, somewhere in the dust, by no means easy to find, is a line that no decent human being should cross. And I believe the wretched tyranny that is Robert Mugabe's Zimbabwe is now across that line and that no team should tour there.

On the ICC's own miserable terms, Zimbabwe should fail the test. Visiting teams – in their effective house arrest between airport, hotel and cricket ground – would probably be "secure". I doubt if the same could be said for any accompanying journalist with a moderately enquiring mind, or even a curious spectator. If sanctions are invoked against England for refusing to tour such a country, it will be the majority, not the minority, who will have earned themselves the contempt of thoughtful individuals across the globe.

Post-imperial blues

Whatever the outcome of this dispute, it was evident that by early 2004 England had become something close to the pariahs of the cricketing world: undoubtedly the most unpopular member of the class, regarded by the other countries with head-shaking despair if not outright loathing. The ECB would like to believe this is entirely due to the Zimbabwe issue. It is not.

The cynical explanation for the ICC's insistence that the show must go on is simply money. (Either that or sex usually explains why people entrap themselves in ethically indefensible situations.) But in this case Anglophobia appears to be an important factor. It is a little mysterious how the country that gave the game to the world got itself so disliked, but it certainly predates the first Zimbabwe crisis that blew up before and during the 2003 World Cup. It is not personal either: other administrators say they get on well with David Morgan, the present ECB chairman.

It is less than 11 years since international cricket became, organisationally, an entity in its own right rather than an adjunct of the Marylebone Cricket Club. Until then, England and Australia had a veto. Many overseas officials claim that, unlike the Aussies, England have simply not grasped that the world has moved on.

Far from trying to keep politics out of sport, these officials talk in exactly the same terms as European Union politicians when discussing the Brits: too wedded to the old ways, insufficiently *communitaire*. No one side has a monopoly of truth in this dispute, but it is becoming corrosive: instead of a split at the ICC between black and white or between Asia and the others, there have been growing signs of it being England v The Rest of the World.

Less, less

Modern *Wisden* editors generally welcome the cancellation of cricket tours, because there is too much international cricket to cram into this book already. This one is saddened as well as irritated by the surfeit. Writing these notes between 1993 and 2000, when I took a break, I fought hard for the World Test Championship. Be careful what you wish for, as they say.

The Championship was intended to be like a *salwar kameez*, a loose-fitting outfit within which the air could flow. The ICC instead imposed a straitjacket. The promotion of Bangladesh (now universally recognised as a mistake, certainly in the way it was done), the outlawing of one-off Tests, the imposition of too many one-dayers and the proliferation of back-to-back Tests have all made the schedule too onerous for the players and ill-designed to promote the game. The refusal to persevere with the original simple Championship concept (which went wrong only through ICC neglect) means that we have a system probably understood only by its deviser, my friend David Kendix, who is a clever mathematician. It is not a championship; it is a ratings system and it means damn-all to the man on the Clapham or Colombo omnibus, thus defeating the object.

It is right that everyone should play everyone else, if possible. But this schedule elevates one-sided cricket at the expense of the best cricket. As the 2003 England–South Africa series proved, there is nothing – absolutely nothing – in this game to touch a five-Test series between well-matched teams, in which the battle can ebb and flow. Now there are no five-Test series that do not involve England. But who on earth, outside the ICC, ever says "OK, best of two then"? So much time is taken up with bad cricket, there is not enough time for the really good stuff. To compensate, cricket has to think up gimmicks like the Top Team v Rest of the World artifice, proposed for 2005.

Time for a new trophy

England–South Africa matches have in fact been one of the highlights of world cricket ever since South Africa were readmitted. All the Test series have been intensely, sometimes heroically, fought. Yet these encounters, dating back 115 years, still do not have their own trophy to match the Ashes, the Wisden Trophy (England–West Indies), the Worrell Trophy (Australia–West Indies) or the Border-Gavaskar (Australia–India). They should have. It would be a nice gesture, and an appropriate one, if the ECB were to suggest that the Nelson Mandela Trophy should be inaugurated during the 2004-05 tour.

Down with Buggins

A last word on the ICC: it is only the sum of its parts (sometimes minus England). But such an organisation needs leadership. It is no insult to the chief executive, Malcolm Speed, to say that it cannot and should not come from inside the bureaucracy. Under the present system, ICC presidents serve just two-year terms, chosen on Buggins's turn, by countries. South Africa can name whoever they like next. The current president, Ehsan Mani of Pakistan, has the advantage of being an ICC insider from way back. Most of his successors are likely to spend their first year working out what they are meant to do, and the second as a lame duck, preparing to hand over to the next Buggins. The game needs strong leaders with a clear vision for all aspects of cricket and its place in the wider world. They should be chosen on their own merits and should serve four-year terms.

The Great Reform Act

In England a small band calling itself the Cricket Reform Group got considerable publicity last year. This was partly because the ECB has become so ill-regarded that in England the words cricket and reform in close proximity are assumed to be an absolute good thing, and partly because two-fifths of the group's members were former England captains, Mike Atherton and Bob Willis.

Now I like and respect both these men. And the manifesto they issued does contain some entirely valid objectives – fewer professionals, more streamlined management, more money for the recreational game, mergers between minor counties and major ones. Some of their ideas are rather vague, some extraordinarily prescriptive: the fifth round of Championship matches *will* start on June 6; Herefordshire and Shropshire *will* merge with Worcestershire. (Africa was conquered by remote know-alls drawing lines on the map, and the world is still paying the price.)

But if I grasp this manifesto correctly, there are two central proposals. Firstly, the Reform Group wants a premiership, an elite division: six teams with the best players and just ten fixtures each, taking place between Tests with "England players available for all championship matches".

This is a very appealing idea. Unfortunately – unless England are indeed kicked out of world cricket – there is not a hope in hell of the England management allowing the most important players to take part. If they did, although the scheme would reduce the workload of the average professional to a maximum 65 days a year, England's top cricketers would play at least 110 – or getting on for 200 with a busy winter. You'd have loved that, Bob. In reality, the elite teams would be largely second elevens, as Surrey often are already, bulked out by rotating bought-in stars and Australians with Italian grannies, and thus EU qualification. That is not a premiership.

The second idea is that there should be a clear path to the top via recreational cricket, with "non-full-time professionals" participating in the Championship "and taking minimal time off work". Again, this is appealing.

However, the counties, for all their many flaws, have been consistently excellent at picking up the available talent in their region and beyond, and are now investing large sums of money via their academies in trying to nurture it better. I have seen no evidence that the major club leagues are full of players willing and able to supplant the full-time professionals. Indeed, there is considerable evidence to the contrary.

Since 1964 teams representing the pinnacle of the amateur game – minor counties, universities and so on – have met first-class counties 748 times in various one-day cup competitions. They have won 34 of them, a strike-rate of 4.5%. If you take the minor counties and Board XIs alone, representing the top English club players, the figure goes down to 3%. Most of the 97% have been slaughters; many of the rest can be explained as flukes and freaks. Year after year the Minor County averages are dominated by old pros, and our League cricket reports show the clubs making it clear they want recreational competitions to be just that: recreational.

Across the world and the sporting spectrum, elite performers in once-amateur sports are becoming more and more professional; I am gobsmacked that Mike and Bob expect English cricket to be more competitive by becoming more amateur. I love the thought that once again Mr So-and-so might leave his merchant bank on a Wednesday and flay the Aussies on a Thursday. But that is not how modern cricket works – nor modern merchant banks.

Real reform

County cricket does need reform, badly. As Graeme Wright said in this space in 2002, it is "a confederacy of mediocrity"; and as Tim de Lisle said here last year, there are too many competitions and the tables are "a bad joke". But change has to be sensible and well-considered, and not a cover for the secret agenda of making many of the counties wither away. People flail around despairingly trying to find the alchemist's formula for English cricket: Strangle six counties! Abolish the lot and have regions instead! Let's play inter-city cricket! I find their arguments often naïve and sometimes dangerous.

Counties are expected to perform a difficult balancing act, to be successful in their own right, but also to be run primarily for English cricket as a whole. If they nurture a star player, the brighter he shines, the less likely he is to be around to do them any good. This may be compatible with running counties as businesses, but the proposition is a complex one. It is certainly nothing like running a football club, who would never tolerate such compromises.

Things can't go on as they are, though, and everyone knows it. The ECB working party, due to report this spring, seems sure to recommend less cricket (this year's modish nostrum for county cricketers though, curiously, not for international players) and an end to the mad system of three-up and three-down. A slowdown in the present crazed merry-go-round of overseas stars is already scheduled for 2005; some of them are not so much stars as asteroids. In 1991, you still had to be born in Yorkshire to play for them; in 2003 there appeared to be no obligation even to have visited the place. Bulked out with EU passport-holders, Middlesex – *Middlesex!* – last year sometimes fielded only two English-born players.

I would like to see a small-scale experiment with regional cricket as a stepping stone to the top level, though these games would work better as inter-regional Test trials rather than tourist fixtures (these can be very misleading – remember Shane Warne kidding us that he couldn't bowl to Graeme Hick?). Most of all, I want to see a serious redistribution of money from ordinary cricketers to extraordinary ones: rewards for success, not for turning up.

My own (more or less original) contribution to this debate is a proposal to merge two struggling competitions, the County Championship and the National League. There is no reason except habit why first-class cricket and one-day cricket should require different tournaments. A merger would reinvigorate both of them, provide an attractive sponsorship package, make the game far easier to follow and fixtures easier to plot. Above all, it would cut four competitions down to three and make it harder for counties to try in one form of the game and forget the other. It would be a spur to excellence, which the English domestic game badly needs. It is not, however, a magic bullet. Only children believe in magic.

The old moaners and the vegan

The world's cricketers, we are constantly told, have never been fitter. They spend hours in the gym. They receive constant attention from all manner of specialists. Yet they keep falling down. In 13 Test matches in 2003, England had to field 11 different new-ball pairings. As soon as a fast bowler emerged, he collapsed in a heap. Even Australia were not immune and their attack was unusually hard-hit.

The older generation of cricketers have long had an explanation for this. The likes of Sir Alec Bedser and Fred Trueman have moaned for years about the issue, with lots of eye-rolling and "Idunnos" and "inmydays". They have now received improbable support from another all-time great with a very different outlook on life.

Since retiring from cricket, Greg Chappell, who once dickered with conservative politics, has embraced veganism (he prefers the term "pure vegetarianism") and become an animal rights activist. His approach to cricketing fitness is based on reading the works of nutritionists, educational experts and fitness gurus, but they have led him right back to the world of Alec and Fred. "Gymnasiums should be banned," he said in an unguarded moment.

On further questioning, he rowed back, but only a bit. "A lot of what cricketers are doing in the gymnasium is creating problems, not solving them," Chappell said. "Many of the leg machines are incorrectly set up and put pressure on the lower back. For a batsman, too much weight work can have quite drastic effects on movement patterns. Nobody's done any real research on what's right for cricketers. And I believe a lot of what we do is setting players up to be injured. We're going blindly down modern paths and ignoring what's served us so well in the past. The best way for young people to prepare for cricket is by playing cricket."

And you read the papers, you note that yet another quick bowler has done yet another part of his anatomy, and you begin to think Chappell may be on to something.

A time to mourn

On the final day of the Sydney Test this year, Steve Waugh's last day in Test cricket, the Australian players took the field wearing black armbands. There was no obvious reason for this. However, enquiring pressmen were informed it was to mark the death of Brett Lee's grandmother. The crowd were just left puzzled. And it was notable that, on his big day, Waugh chose not to join in.

Now the Lee family has all our sympathy in their loss, and I would never belittle it. But players these days seem to wear black armbands more often than not, and it is time the authorities stamped out this dressing-room indulgence. There were 27,000 people at the SCG that day, all of whom either have lost or will expect to lose their grandmothers. There is a difference between private grief and public grief. Black armbands represent an important tradition: a shared emotion between player and spectator. They should be reserved for the deaths of famous cricketers or major public figures and for national or global tragedies. Otherwise, if a future Flower and Olonga try to draw the world's attention to their nation's plight, people will just assume it concerns one of their team-mates' elderly relatives.

Ground rules

Unfortunately, cricketing authorities are more concerned about stopping what shouldn't be stopped. When England won the Wisden Trophy by beating West Indies at The Oval in 2000, the crowd were welcomed on to the pitch to share a perfect moment of national cricketing joy. A full house cheered, and kids celebrated by playing on the outfield – not football, but cricket. There was not a hint of a problem. Three years later, on the same ground, when England squared the series against South Africa with a tremendous win, the crowd were sent a different message by phalanxes of cold-eyed stewards.

I was in the Peter May stand at the time, as were a large proportion of a substantial crowd. The rostrum was erected with its back to us, and the symbolism was very clear: "This is for telly, not for you. You can go home now." And most people did, deflated, disgruntled and rather insulted.

Thus ends a beautiful English end-of-summer tradition. Of course, it is right to be stern about the players' security. Of course, we cannot go back to the old days of stump-grabbing mayhem. But there is no good reason why, say, ten minutes after play in the final Test of summer, when the players are safely corralled and stewards have had time to cordon off the square, the crowd cannot be allowed on to the outfield. This is an over-zealous ruling by Tim Lamb, the ECB chief executive, and I beseech him to think again. It alienates the people cricket should cherish most.

Initial reaction

It is possible that not every *Wisden* reader will make it through to page 1415, the Sri Lankan domestic scores. This seems a pity, because you might be missing the following:

At FTZ Sports Complex, Katunayake, February 14, 15. **Kurunegala Youth won by an innings and four runs.** Toss: Kurunegala Youth. **Antonians 100** (A. R. R. A. P. W. R. R. K. B. Amunugama 4-39) **and 121** (A. R. R. A. P. W. R. R. K. B. Amunugama 4-34, A. W. Ekanayake 4-18); **Kurunegala Youth 225** (K. G. S. Sirisoma 5-40).

The successful bowler in this game, as we all know, is Amunugama Rajapakse Rajakaruna Abeykoon Panditha Wasalamudiyanse Ralahamilage Ranjith Krishantha Bandara Amunugama – Ranjith to his friends, apparently. With ten initials, he has now established a commanding lead over his nearest rival, A. K. T. D. G. L. A. S. de Silva (I won't spell it out, if you don't mind: I'm getting tired) and the leading international player W. P. U. J. C. Vaas. This is an area where England used to fancy it could hold its own with any other cricketing country, but such stars of yesteryear as J. W. H. T. Douglas, M. E. J. C. Norman and R. I. H. B. Dyer have long been eclipsed by these ex-colonial upstarts. Only the Essex newcomer A. G. A. M. McCoubrey carries on the tradition – and he's Irish.

Amunugama is not a newcomer. As far back as 1990-91 *Wisden* reported him taking match figures of 12 for 91 for Tamil Union against Sebastianites. But in those days he was plain old R. K. B. Amunugama, which just makes me wonder. Is this an elaborate joke, along the lines of Llanfairpwllgwyngyllgogerychwyrndrobwllllantysiliogogogoch? *Wisden's* policy is that players may suppress embarrassing middle names if they wish without fear of being outed by researchers bearing birth certificates, and the reverse should also apply (after all, Bob Willis added the middle name Dylan). But our patience is not infinite. You can call yourself what you like – but not if we have to omit the Laws of Cricket again just to make room.

A returned exile writes

As some readers may know, I returned to edit *Wisden* having spent two years on the heathen shores of the United States. But cricket changes so fast these days that even after a short absence one comes back entirely disorientated.

In a way, the arrival of Twenty20 cricket was the least of it. I am delighted by its success but also remember the initial ecstatic response to 65-over cricket (1963) and 40-over cricket (1969). Actually, Twenty20 went on a bit too long for my own taste. I shall try to hang on for Ten10 or maybe Five5.

Other things were also different. All the county players seemed to have changed, or at least changed counties. Of the few in their familiar place, Matthew Maynard had hair poking out from the back of his cap, and it had either gone completely grey or been dyed blond. Maybe both. Players seem, indeed, an entirely different breed. Last year Alamgir Sheriyar of Kent was injured, having cut his hand while washing up, while Saqlain Mushtaq fell downstairs holding his baby. Such injuries never happened to Lord Harris or D. R. Jardine. Dominic Cork turned out for Derbyshire wearing an Alice band; I am reliably informed that Copson and Pope did not wear Alice bands when they bowled Derbyshire to the Championship in 1936.

In hot weather, the umpires now officiate at county games wearing polo shirts. Since, in the nature of things, not all of them are as svelte as they used to be, and the shirt is sometimes worn over a substantial paunch, it makes them look less like figures of authority and more as if they've wandered in from a game of crazy golf with the grandchildren.

The battle to get players' names on their shirts in the Championship has, surprisingly, largely been won. Unfortunately, my eyes have deteriorated too much in the meantime for them to be any use to me. (It remains mysterious that all spectators who come to a Test match are automatically expected to be able to recognise everyone under their helmets and sunhats; the commentators can't always do it – how can the customers?) And occasionally last summer the terrified cry would go up "The PLO is coming!" Only in county cricket does this refer, not to the Palestine Liberation Organisation, but to the Pitch Liaison Officer.

Meanwhile, squad numbers, Duckworth/Lewis, "overs remaining", "overs per bowler" and the obsessive recording of extras have combined to render scoreboards more incomprehensible than ever.

One ground, however, is offering a potentially vital service. Signs round Trent Bridge say: "Would spectators experiencing any problems please inform an official or steward." Nottinghamshire have always had a reputation as a helpful club, but this is a breakthrough in customer care: "Excuse me, steward. My wife doesn't understand me." "I've got this pain on my left side and the doctor says it's indigestion, but I don't think it is." "The council haven't fixed the holes in the road." Other counties, please copy.

Horse play

Regular readers of our Chronicle feature know that over the past ten years *Wisden* has developed a considerable fascination with exotic reasons for stopping play: boy falling out of tree, rogue hang glider, galloping elk – we've had the lot. On my very first weekend back in England last summer, I went down to the New Forest for a family party.

On the Saturday there was a game – Brockenhurst v Ellingham – being played on a lovely cricket ground on a heavenly afternoon. I settled down to enjoy it but the over after I arrived, a herd of New Forest ponies suddenly galloped out of the woods and on to the outfield around deep extra cover. Wild Horses Stopped Play. I watched a lot of baseball in the US, and loved that too, but somehow only cricket produces stuff like this.

Trying to Melt the Iceman

NASSER HUSSAIN

At the beginning of this year, the cricketing world witnessed a remarkable week in which the people of Sydney poured out their affection towards their beloved son Stephen Waugh.

The members were reportedly queuing as early as four in the morning to get their favourite seats, and the streets outside the ground were gridlocked by eight, not because the enthralling series between India and Australia was coming to its conclusion, but because one man who had meant so much to Australian cricket and Australians in general was donning his dishevelled baggy green cap for the last time.

Steve Waugh was not a cricketing god or a genius, like Tendulkar or Lara, nor even technically brilliant like Rahul Dravid. Like the rest of us, he was human. But a previously unremarkable household in suburban Sydney was definitely given more than its fair share of talent when the Waugh twins, Stephen and Mark, arrived on the scene nearly 39 years ago. Their little games of backyard cricket eventually led to the pair of them playing nearly 300 Tests and scoring nearly 20,000 runs between them. Some would argue that one was given a little bit more talent than the other. As one member of the Barmy Army once said, as he dared to sledge the greatest sledger of them all, "Oy, Stephen, best batsman in the world? You ain't even the best batsman in your family!"

Well, for over a decade Stephen Waugh made himself into the best batsman in the world. He was given two useful cricketing skills at birth: incredible hand–eye co-ordination and the fastest pair of hands of any cricketer I have played against. The rest he has had to work for. He has proved one cricketing cliché during his career: that the higher the level you play, the more it is played in your head. And he was, mentally, the strongest player of his era.

He didn't deal with the short ball particularly well and he moved around the crease a lot as the bowler delivered, staying back and not really transferring all his weight on to the front foot when the ball was pitched up. But, hey, that is the game. Every batsman has weaknesses, and it is up to the player to overcome them and the opposition to exploit them. Waugh overcame his deficiencies because his hand–eye co-ordination meant he could keep the good ones out and put the bad ones away – and because his mental toughness helped him through every situation batting can throw up.

Many a pre-Ashes Test meeting stopped when S. Waugh's name hit the projector screen. Half the team got animated and said "Look, skip, just put in a leg gully and a short leg and we'll pepper him with the short stuff. It's only a matter of time." The other less emotional half, usually the batters and the coach, said "No, pitch it up and try to hit off stump early, because he has a tendency to get his head off-side of the ball a bit, and then there's a chance of him being bowled or lbw." The final thing always said was that, when he first came in, everyone must be on their toes as he loved to push a single and get off strike. Meeting finished. Everyone happy.

Next day, if we were doing really well and had reduced Australia to 300 for three, we would be pleased with ourselves. In comes Waugh, red handkerchief hanging out of pocket, pushes the ball (usually to someone like dopey Gough standing at mid-on) and scampers a single, smiles and stays off strike for a while. This would be followed by a few short balls (which Waugh finds uncomfortable, but never gets out to), and the bowlers begin thinking that they had better start pitching it up. They over-correct and these incredible hands start to caress the ball through the covers. Before you know it, you look up at the scoreboard and he's 30 not out, off and running. Groundhog Day! You've seen it all before, but there seems nothing you can do to stop it happening all over again.

As a player, Waugh was always at his most dangerous when confronted by a real challenge. All his great innings came in the face of adversity. Whether it was a poor wicket, or a poor calf, or a poor press hinting at the waning of his power, he felt most at home in difficult situations. It was as if he believed in his own reputation as the "iceman" and was keen to enhance it. Nothing would give him more pleasure than reading the next day about another gutsy Steve Waugh innings.

I had no real cunning plan but to stall things

There could not have been any more pressure on a cricketer than in January 2003 against England at the SCG. Waugh has since admitted that if he hadn't got runs in that Test it would have been his last. He was not particularly playing well in the series, and looked surprisingly nervous. He came in when Australia were 56 for three and I immediately thought: "Dangerous." Everything I tried to do that day seemed almost pointless. It was as if the script had already been written.

That evening, with Waugh on 98 and the last ball of the day coming up, I ran up to Dawson, told him I had no real cunning plan but to stall things, get Waugh nervous and hope he would make a mistake. Dawson bowled a perfectly good ball and those Waugh hands just flicked it away through the covers with complete disdain.

As a captain, Waugh used the same principles that he did as a player: he made the most of what he was given. Luckily for him, he was given a remarkable collection of batsmen plus three all-time great bowlers in McGrath, Warne and Gillespie. His side played in such a way that they basically took the draw out of the equation. They would score their runs at over four an over, declare early and leave as much time as possible to bowl the opposition out twice. The days of someone like Boycott batting a day for a hundred were gone. The likes of Hayden, Ponting and Gilchrist were scoring centuries in a session, and this attitude was infectious, spreading throughout the team with more compact players, such as Langer, becoming more expansive.

Richie Benaud, a man who should know, believes Waugh's team has produced in the last four or five years the most exhilarating cricket in the history of the game. The three-Test series England played in Sri Lanka

"Mentally the strongest of his era": former England captain Nasser Hussain (*left*) on his Australian counterpart Steve Waugh.

Picture by Patrick Eagar.

recently is how cricket used to be played, but it now seems ever so turgid by comparison. Whether the pace is sustainable, only time will tell. It will depend on the talent available.

Three great captains have taken Australia to where they are now. Allan Border changed the culture by altering Australia's attitude. No longer were they going to be the "let's have a beer after the game" sort of men, but a much more ruthless outfit. That was the most difficult part. He was followed by the more cerebral Mark Taylor, who would quietly stand at first slip influencing the game and, more importantly, influencing some of the gems that were starting to appear in the Australian team, thanks to Border's change in culture. Taylor made sure the Australians wouldn't have to survive just on bravado, but left them with four or five all-time greats who could single-handedly turn a game of cricket. Steve Waugh combined all of this and gave them that final ingredient, belief.

Waugh's one big failure came in India, where they managed to lose a series they had for the taking. I believe that was the only time their attitude let them down. Sometimes in India you just have to sit in: slow the opposition run-rate down, keep the pressure on the likes of Tendulkar, Laxman and Dravid. Stopping them scoring gets the crowds on their backs and creates pressure. However, Australia – in search of their 17th consecutive victory – had an attitude that didn't allow for "sitting in". Waugh kept attacking; enforced the follow-on and before he knew it, found his team batting last, and under pressure themselves. They lost that Test, in Calcutta, and the series. It is a blemish on his record – but it was done for all the right reasons.

I can't say I have ever got to know Steve Waugh well. He never let his guard slip for fear of letting anything penetrate his veneer of inscrutability. The nearest I came to cracking it was in a bar in Adelaide after we had failed to regain the Ashes in 1998-99, when I picked Steve's brain over his attitude to batting. Now for me there is no point in trying to talk to Lara or Tendulkar about things like that; to them it is just natural.

But I have always found Waugh intriguing. How did he make himself so good? He told me that the most important aspect to him was body language. He liked to almost sprint to the crease to emphasise that he was relishing the battle ahead; he liked to give off an aura of aggression. Nothing emphasises this more than when, in Port-of-Spain nine years ago, Waugh stood face to face with one of the greatest fast bowlers of all time, Curtly Ambrose.

Now, here is a man who doesn't play the short ball particularly well, doesn't pull or hook, telling the man who has dismissed him the most in Test cricket to get back to his mark and bowl. Robert Craddock wrote in that year's *Wisden*: Waugh "stood his ground like John Wayne when Ambrose engaged him in a verbal exchange of fire from two metres; the bowler had to be tugged away by Richie Richardson. 'It's Test cricket,' the unrepentant Waugh said afterwards. 'If you want an easy game, go play netball.'" Waugh made 63 not out in that innings and went on to make 200 in the next game, when Australia won by an innings and regained the Worrell Trophy.

Throughout his career, Waugh, almost on purpose, maximised the challenge – whether it be a sore calf, a last-chance-saloon innings, or a fired-up Ambrose – to bring the best out of himself. Basically, for over 20 years he has been playing mind games with himself and the opposition. The crowds did not turn up at Sydney to thank him for his statistics. They came to thank him for his character.

Nasser Hussain captained England 45 times, seven of them in Ashes Tests against Australia led by Waugh. England won one, Australia six.

STEVE WAUGH IN TEST CRICKET

	Tests	*Runs*	*HS*	*100s*	*Avge*	*Wkts*	*BB*	*Avge*	*Ct*
v England	46	3,200	177*	10	58.18	22	5-69	41.54	29
v South Africa	16	1,147	164	2	49.86	17	5-28	15.88	9
v West Indies	32	2,192	200	7	49.81	19	5-92	49.68	19
v New Zealand	23	1,117	151*	2	38.51	14	4-56	29.57	18
v India	18	1,090	150	2	41.92	6	2-36	57.33	12
v Pakistan	20	934	157	3	34.59	6	1-13	68.00	14
v Sri Lanka	8	701	170	3	87.62	8	4-33	10.87	7
v Zimbabwe	3	290	151*	1	145.00	–	–	–	4
v Bangladesh	2	256	156*	2	–	–	–	–	–
In Australia	89	5,710	170	15	47.58	58	5-69	33.56	55
Elsewhere	79	5,217	200	17	55.50	34	5-28	44.05	57
Overall	**168**	**10,927**	**200**	**32**	**51.06**	**92**	**5-28**	**37.44**	**112**

Stumpers or Stoppers?

PAT MURPHY

Usually – in theory at least – the best batsmen and bowlers get picked for England. But with wicket-keepers, even the theory doesn't apply. Over the last few years Alec Stewart has stilled much of the debate over the wicket-keeper's role because he has been England's best all-rounder since Ian Botham.

Batting predominantly at five or six and good enough to score six Test hundreds while keeping wicket, Stewart got better and better as a gloveman through a Stakhanovite application and natural athleticism. He wasn't the most naturally talented of his time but his sheer efficiency was greatly valued. And his runs. Though his batting average was far better when he did not keep wicket (46.70 v 34.92), the difference was not enough in the minds of most selectors to justify expending a place.

Stewart was a spectacular example of cricket's trend towards "multi-skilling". Fast bowlers everywhere have to practise their batting with a brief to hang around in often strokeless defiance, even if the rest of us lose the will to live while watching them. But at least if they keep taking wickets, they can stay in the side. The best wicket-keeper in the country enjoys no such security. He has to bat, and bat well. This is not new: the trend has, however, become much stronger. The effect on the standards of keeping everywhere has been quietly disastrous.

Any competent catcher of the ball can do it standing back

Bob Taylor, the most admired wicket-keeper in the world in the 1970s and 1980s, says he would have no chance of playing for England today. "I was fortunate enough to be around when Ian Botham was at his peak, batting at six. He was such a great all-rounder that they could afford to have me at seven and play four front-line bowlers, in addition to Botham. That, to me, is the ideal balance for a side."

But Taylor was a contemporary of Alan Knott, and his 57 Tests would have been reduced to little more than a handful but for Knott joining his generation's two great rebellions: those instigated by Kerry Packer and the South Africans. When they were competing, Knott's batting was decisive – his average for England was more than double Taylor's: 32.75 v 16.28.

Both were wonderful keepers. Taylor acknowledges Knott's marvellous agility and knack of conjuring up a miraculous catch, even though he stood back too often to the medium-pacers for Taylor's purist tastes. "Wicket-keeping is about standing up, not back," he says, "because any competent catcher of the ball can do it standing back."

Once Taylor had lost his role as perennial reserve wicket-keeper on tour, his shimmering brilliance stood out, but at times he did lose his place due to the superior batting of David Bairstow and Paul Downton. And his own hero was even less fortunate.

When Taylor first played for Derbyshire in 1961, he idolised Keith Andrew of Northamptonshire. He called him "Mr Andrew" when they first met on county duty and the young protégé cherished the pair of gloves Mr Andrew sent him. "He was a master of his trade and it never occurred to me that he wasn't much of a batsman," Taylor says. "I saw him standing up to the brisk medium-pace of Brian Crump and the left-arm spin of George Tribe, who bowled all sorts, and he was an inspiration. You never heard the ball drop into Keith Andrew's hands, he was so deft and unspectacular." This view was shared by almost all Andrew's contemporaries. "Keith was a master craftsman," said Micky Stewart, the future England coach, "like a silvery, smooth, slinky shadow behind the stumps."

In 13 years of first-class cricket Keith Andrew made only three fifties and played just twice for England. Godfrey Evans's flair for the big occasion, his spring-heeled athleticism and knack of scoring vital runs meant he stayed in the England team for more than a decade until he was 38. But Andrew was widely recognised as the superior keeper. Taller than many of his rivals at 5ft 9in, he crouched halfway down, rather than squatting on his haunches in the approved manner. That meant he could cover a lot of ground down the leg side without resorting to the trademark Evans leap that delighted so many press photographers. Andrew accepts why Evans played 91 Tests to his two. "I'm slightly ashamed of my poor batting record. I was a fool not to work at it more. I'd be a much better batsman now, because I wouldn't get a game otherwise for my county, never mind England."

When he played his second Test at Old Trafford in 1963, nine years after the first, Andrew conceded just three byes in a total of 501. More relevantly, England lost by ten wickets. For the next Test, he was replaced by Jim Parks, a batsman who had manufactured himself into a competent performer standing back. "Jim was an excellent fielder anywhere and he could score a hundred going in at six," Andrew recalls. "I'd be lucky if I scratched together 12. No contest and no complaints from me."

So none of this is new. John Woodcock, the former *Wisden* editor, dates it back much further and says that England's No. 1 wicket-keeper of the 1930s, Les Ames, was not the best. He also believes this is a legitimate selection decision.

"George Duckworth was the better keeper, but Les was a wonderful all-round cricketer," says Woodcock. "He was a beautiful fielder, like Stewart and Parks, and they can do the job perfectly well. If you had Warne at one end and Murali at the other, it might be different, you might want the best wicket-keeper. But Clyde Walcott wasn't a specialist keeper and he kept to Ramadhin and Valentine in 1950. It is the practical and sensible thing to do." Ames (Test batting average: 40.56) and Duckworth (14.62) toured Australasia together in both Ashes tours of the 1930s and Duckworth played just one Test out of 12 – in New Zealand, where the opposition was weak enough for Ames to be played safely as a specialist bat.

Nor is this just an English phenomenon. In Australia, the Victorian keeper Darren Berry was picked out by Steve Waugh as unlucky never to play a Test. Yet when the World Cup came, Jimmy Maher was sent as No. 2 to

Three of the best: George Duckworth (*left*), Keith Andrew and Godfrey Evans in Australia, 1954-55. The gloves belonged to the Australian Bert Oldfield, and were given to Andrew.

Picture courtesy of Keith Andrew.

Adam Gilchrist. "What message does that send to the state wicket-keepers?" asked Berry sadly. And he was very scathing about some of his contemporaries elsewhere. Parthiv Patel of India is quite a good keeper, he reckons. "But he missed a chance from Ricky Ponting, who then scored a double ton. They've done the same thing in West Indies and look at some of the keepers they've come up with. They've been atrocious."

Andrew, who went on to be director of coaching at the National Cricket Association, blames the pitches rather than selectors for modern wicket-keeping standards, which he describes as "pathetic".

"The wickets are to blame, they're too benign. Two of the game's skills have been neutered – positive, attacking bowling and wicket-keeping." He acknowledges that Alec Stewart had a great pair of hands, missing little at his peak, but feels he was never fully stretched because turning wickets are a thing of the past.

Andrew's nostalgia for the days when keepers regularly stood up to the stumps strikes a chord with Jack Russell. In 1983, his first full season with Gloucestershire, he took 17 stumpings, a figure he has not matched since. But he has now begun to stand up to the medium-pacers, at the instigation of the Gloucestershire coach John Bracewell. "He told me I'd become a defensive keeper and he was right. I needed to impose myself on the batters by getting in their ears, daring them to get out of their crease. I enjoy being aggressive, rather than just reacting."

Russell's England career embodies the wicket-keeping conundrum. In his first full series, he scored a hundred against the 1989 Australians and, because he was also the best keeper around, seemed certain to be a fixture for the next decade. Yet 18 months later he was dropped: England needed to claw

---

STANDING UP TO BE COUNTED

"It can therefore be laid down as an absolute principle in team selection that the best wicket-keeper, irrespective of all other considerations, must always be chosen..."

MCC Cricket Coaching Book (1952)

"...That remains my philosophy."

Bob Taylor

"Wicket-keeping could go the same way as spin bowling. They don't stand up enough any more and Knotty, one of the all-time greats, didn't help by doing that standing back to the medium-pacers. I used to joke with him that anyone who had an eye for the ball could don the gloves and do it standing back and he'd get mad at me."

Micky Stewart

"Don't waste the wicket-keeping talent we've got in this country by giving the gloves to batters. We'll be paying the penalty 20 years down the line. Go for the stumper ahead of the stopper every time."

Jack Russell

"We don't know if we've got any high-class keepers now because bowlers don't do enough with the ball other than use the big seam on green wickets."

Keith Andrew

"Everyone does it, even the Australians. Rod Marsh was known as 'Irongloves' when he started. He could bat, though."

John Woodcock

---

back a losing series at Adelaide in 1990-91, so an extra bowler was needed. Alec Stewart's superior batting became the panacea whenever England had to retrieve a losing position.

The captain Graham Gooch still defends the decision. "For a long time England have been in the position where four front-line bowlers aren't enough on good wickets. The Australians and the West Indians of the 1980s could get away with just four, because at least two of them would be world-class performers. I had to get the extra bowler in because we were behind in the series and needed more options."

Surprisingly, one man less than happy at the decision was the England coach at the time, Stewart's father, Micky. "I didn't like it early on because Alec and Mike Atherton were a big plus as an opening partnership of contrasting styles, with fine temperaments. Also I thought that Jack Russell would end up getting consistent runs at seven. But the one-off became a pattern over the next few years and we lost that major attribute of a settled opening pair while playing a keeper who wasn't as good as Jack at the time."

He thinks his son improved, though. "I honestly believe that Alec became a better keeper standing back than Jack Russell. Jack was of course a natural and Alec had to work at the job, but there were times when Jack would spill a straightforward catch for some unaccountable reason when standing back. Alec, once he gave as much time to his preparation with the gloves as his batting, was very consistent."

For the past five years, Micky Stewart has scoured Surrey looking for young cricketers to send on to The Oval, men like Rikki Clarke, who made his Test debut in Bangladesh. He has unearthed plenty of talent. "But the one department where I haven't seen anything special is wicket-keeping. We need to keep the role of the specialist keeper to the fore."

Yet the England wicket-keeper no longer gets the specialist coaching batsmen and bowlers expect. Both Alec Stewart and Jack Russell valued hugely the input of Alan Knott before and during every Test, but their successor has to be largely self-motivated in his preparations. What does that tell us about the value placed by the England coaching set-up on the job?

It will be interesting to see just who nails down the place as Stewart's successor. Chris Read of Nottinghamshire was given first crack. But, among the next generation, Russell rates highly both Phil Mustard and Andrew Pratt at Durham, and Simon Guy at Yorkshire. But he says the outstanding English keeper is 34 and has no chance of representing his country any more. "Keith Piper has the most beautiful hands and makes it look so easy. He should've scored enough runs to have made them pick him for England." Which is where we came in...

Pat Murphy covers England cricket for BBC Radio Five Live. He has co-authored five books with three England wicket-keepers – Bob Taylor, Jack Russell and Alec Stewart.

Fortifying the Over-Forties

NICK MASON

When he appeared in the first Lord's Test of 2003, Alec Stewart was already past his 40th birthday. The man who scored 100 in his 100th Test on the Queen Mother's 100th birthday might also have been expected to make himself the 100th player to play in a Test aged 40 or above.

In fact, Stewart was No. 102 – Jimmy Cook of South Africa was the 100th. Stewart might, however, be the last – at least for some time to come. For a cricketer over 40 to be selected for his country, he has always had to be pretty good; nowadays he has to be exceptional. With fielding ability and physical fitness the current watchwords, the adjective "veteran" is being applied ever more readily to sprightly 34-year-olds, and team physios these days have better things to do than strap up creaking joints just to squeeze an extra few Tests from a workhorse in decline.

That said, the statistics have shown no consistent sign that the supply of 40-year-olds is drying up. While the undoubted heyday of the aged Test player lay between 1920 and 1949 (more than half of all the quadragenarians worldwide played their relevant Tests in those three decades), the years since have conformed to no predictable pattern. The 1960s, for example, saw only three Test players in their forties: Tom Graveney and Bert Sutcliffe wound up two distinguished batting careers for England and New Zealand respectively, and Les Jackson was recalled by England for the second of his two Test matches a dozen years after his first.

Yet in the 1990s as many as eight oldies caught the selectors' eyes, from Graham Gooch, who was undroppable when he passed the 40-year milestone and went on to play a further 13 matches for England, to Gordon Greenidge, who had the distinction of completing the shortest quadragenarian Test career on record: the last day of his last Test for West Indies was his 40th birthday, and he was run out for 43 before lunch.

The great majority of the 102 players have been batsmen, whose technique, timing and experience have survived the inevitable decline in physical sharpness, eyesight and reaction speed. Fifty-eight would have been picked for their batting alone, and of the 15 genuine all-rounders in the club nearly all – Walter Hammond, Frank Woolley, Basil D'Oliveira, Warwick Armstrong, for example – were top-class batsmen who also happened to bowl very well, as opposed to the handful, like India's Lala Amarnath and Vinoo Mankad, who would have earned their place simply as bowlers.

Conversely, of the nine wicket-keepers (six Englishmen, three Australians), only Stewart was a genuine Test batsman as well. Among the bowlers ten, surprisingly, were still regularly entrusted with the new ball in their forties (Gubby Allen was probably the fastest of them, Sydney Barnes the deadliest); double that number were out-and-out spinners.

Of the 102, 52 have been Englishmen, led by James Southerton, the long-serving round-arm bowler who was more than ten years older than any other player in the inaugural Melbourne Test in 1877. Sixteen Australians and a dozen South Africans make up the bulk of the rest, though a healthy challenge from the younger ranks has meant that only two Australians born in the 20th century have played a Test in their forties – Bill O'Reilly in the one-off destruction of New Zealand early in 1946 (only later recognised as a Test) and, to his and everyone else's surprise, Bobby Simpson, fully ten years into Test retirement, recalled as captain during the Packer crisis. Steve Waugh was six months short of his 39th birthday when he retired earlier this year. Neither India nor Pakistan have fielded a 40-year-old since the 1950s.

Understandably, Test careers for quadragenarians tend to be short. More than a quarter of the total, 26 players, appeared in only a single Test in their forties, and another 13 played in only two. Against these fly-by-nights, though, there is a select gallery of 21 cricketers who have succeeded in appearing in at least ten Tests after their 40th birthday. Of them Armstrong, W. G. Grace, Ray Illingworth and Simpson were captain in all their Tests over 40, and Freddie Brown in all but one of his.

For some in this list, their latter years represented a genuine late flowering: the remarkable Bert Ironmonger, slow of foot and incompetent of bat, did not win his first cap until he was nearly 47, yet for five years his niggardly left-arm slow-medium was considered almost essential for Australia in their

Going, going… Graham Gooch's hair was disappearing but the runs kept coming. He played 13 Tests after his 40th birthday.

Picture by Patrick Eagar.

Clocking on: Bert Ironmonger in 1928, the year of his Test debut for Australia, aged 46. Clocking off: Wilfred Rhodes in 1930, shortly after playing his last Test for England, aged 52.

Pictures by EMPICS.

home Tests. And Bob Taylor, who celebrated his 40th birthday in the middle of the pivotal Headingley Test match of 1981, went on to complete another 29 as England's wicket-keeper – more than half his Test career – and a record tally of over-40 appearances that might never be beaten.

The only cricketers to come near him on that score are Patsy Hendren and Jack Hobbs, both of whom had truly enviable quadragenarian careers. (Hobbs, let us not forget, scored 98 of his 197 first-class hundreds after his 40th birthday.) Hendren averaged 48.12 in 44 innings and Hobbs, with eight Test centuries and 11 fifties, averaged an astonishing 58.10, a figure even more remarkable considering all but seven of his 27 matches were against Australia. In all, eight of these 21 men had better Test batting averages after their 40th birthday than in their Test careers as a whole, and five of the 12 who regularly bowled also improved their figures, notably Clarrie Grimmett, who took 96 Test wickets in his forties at a cost of only 21.11 each.

If one match could stand as the ultimate memorial to veterans' Test cricket, it would have to be the final, interminable Test in Kingston, Jamaica, in April 1930. England's team in that game (abandoned as a draw after nine days, two of them washed out) was the oldest ever fielded in any international contest. Wilfred Rhodes, in his 53rd year, was completing an epic Test career that had spanned five separate decades; George Gunn, too, was over 50 and three more – Nigel Haig, Ewart Astill and Hendren – were in their forties. And the man of the match – had such fripperies been on the menu in 1930 – would have been Andrew Sandham, whose 325 was then the highest Test score ever made, and who was playing his last game for England at the tender age of 39 years and nine months.

Nick Mason is a sports historian and journalist who was a long-serving executive on the sports desks of The Sunday Times *and* The Guardian. *He is over 40.*

THE BOYS OF THE OLD BRIGADE

Most Tests after 40		Most runs after 40		Most wickets after 40	
R. W. Taylor	30	J. B. Hobbs	2,440	C. V. Grimmett	96
J. B. Hobbs	27	E. H. Hendren	1,912	H. Ironmonger	74
E. H. Hendren	25	T. W. Graveney	1,243	S. F. Barnes	49
T. W. Graveney	19	G. Boycott	999	A. P. Freeman	44
H. Strudwick	17	E. A. B. Rowan	919	L. R. Gibbs	44

The following have played Test cricket after their 40th birthday.

England (52): R. Abel, G. O. B. Allen, W. E. Astill, S. F. Barnes, G. Boycott, F. R. Brown, D. B. Close, M. C. Cowdrey, B. L. D'Oliveira, J. W. H. T. Douglas, H. Elliott, J. E. Emburey, T. Emmett, L. B. Fishlock, A. P. Freeman, C. B. Fry, G. Geary, G. A. Gooch, W. G. Grace, T. W. Graveney, G. Gunn, W. Gunn, N. E. Haig, S. Haigh, W. R. Hammond, E. E. Hemmings, E. H. Hendren, J. B. Hobbs, P. Holmes, R. Illingworth, H. L. Jackson, S. P. Kinneir, James Langridge, H. W. Lee, A. A. Lilley, C. P. Mead, W. Rhodes, J. Southerton, A. J. Stewart, H. Strudwick, H. Sutcliffe, M. W. Tate, R. W. Taylor, F. J. Titmus, E. Tyldesley, C. Washbrook, J. C. White, W. W. Whysall, E. R. Wilson, A. Wood, F. E. Woolley, E. G. Wynyard.

Australia (16): W. W. Armstrong, W. Bardsley, J. McC. Blackham, D. D. Blackie, H. Carter, S. E. Gregory, C. V. Grimmett, H. Ironmonger, C. Kelleway, C. G. Macartney, A. A. Mailey, W. A. Oldfield, W. J. O'Reilly, R. K. Oxenham, V. Y. Richardson, R. B. Simpson.

South Africa (12): C. P. Carter, G. W. A. Chubb, J. M. M. Commaille, S. J. Cook, G. A. Faulkner, O. Henry, B. Mitchell, A. D. Nourse, A. W. Nourse, E. A. B. Rowan, S. J. Snooke, H. W. Taylor.

West Indies (8): N. Betancourt, G. Challenor, L. R. Gibbs, C. G. Greenidge, G. A. Headley, H. H. H. Johnson, C. H. Lloyd, C. A. Wiles.

New Zealand (3): J. C. Alabaster, B. E. Congdon, B. Sutcliffe.

India (6): L. Amarnath, R. J. D. Jamshedji, V. Mankad, V. M. Merchant, C. K. Nayudu, C. Ramaswami.

Pakistan (2): Amir Elahi, Miran Bux.

Sri Lanka (1): D. S. de Silva.

Zimbabwe (2): D. L. Houghton, A. J. Traicos.

Would you rather be an Oaf than a Fool?

GLENN MOORE

For an English cricketer to hit the back-page headlines this June only the most spectacular feats or depraved acts will suffice. Otherwise football will rule, and not just in the red-top tabloids. As far as Kipling was concerned, it was an equal choice:

> ...ye contented your souls
> With the flannelled fools at the wicket or the muddied oafs at the goals.

But it is not equal any more. The oafs will be in Portugal, seeking to win football's European Championship, and while David Beckham's England team remain in contention, the fools will have to perform wonders – or horrors – against New Zealand and West Indies to get any attention at all.

Once, the games coexisted quite happily. Into the 1950s it was possible for men like Willie Watson (Yorkshire and Sunderland) and Arthur Milton (Gloucestershire and Arsenal) to be internationals in both sports. On the day Leicestershire became champions in 1975, Chris Balderstone got to 51 not out against Derbyshire, raced off in a taxi to play for Doncaster Rovers against Brentford and came back next morning to complete his century. Perhaps that was the apogee of the *Boy's Own* ideal. It probably came to a halt 14 years later when Andy Goram, who won 43 caps for Scotland at soccer, was also picked to play for Scotland at cricket (in mid-July) against Allan Border's Australians. He played; and his football club, then Hibernian, fined him for it.

Now, another 15 years on, both games are in perpetual motion. And football, with its uncomplicated nature and rapid drama, dominates the British scene. As a consequence even mundane players in the Premiership are paid £1 million plus a year. Little wonder the successors to Balderstone and Goram are more likely to hang up their whites than their shorts. Last year even Michael Vaughan, the England captain, said he would have done the same had his knees allowed him.

Never again will the world look upon the likes of Colonel Henry Waugh Renny-Tailyour of the Royal Engineers, who in the 1870s batted and bowled for Kent, played in three of the first four FA Cup finals and still had time to slip in a rugby international for Scotland.

Indeed, rugby now appears to have joined football as a threat to cricket. The England team's 2003 World Cup triumph significantly raised the allure of the oval-ball code. Already two potential England cricketers have been lost to the scrum. Liam Botham's decision to play rugby, rather than carry on with Hampshire, stemmed from a desire to be judged on his own merits, rather than by comparison with the epic feats of his father, Ian. His former Newcastle Falcons team-mate, Jonny Wilkinson, simply saw rugby as the better outlet for his talent.

Renaissance man: Henry Renny-Tailyour was a Victorian star at cricket, football and rugby.
Picture courtesy of Kent CCC.

Wilkinson's performances in Australia made him a national hero. But the cupping movement he makes with his hands before each kick at goal might easily have been seen in a slip cordon. Wilkinson's all-round performances for Lord Wandsworth College led to him being described as "outstanding" in both the 1997 and 1998 *Wisdens*. But even then there was mention of his rugby commitments restricting his involvement.

Unlike Renny-Tailyour, he had to make a choice – as did Phil Neville, Manchester United's England international. Neville was a high-class batsman as a schoolboy; when captaining young England teams, he numbered Andrew Flintoff, Vikram Solanki and Gareth Batty among his charges. Jim Cumbes, now chief executive of Lancashire, and a former footballer-cricketer himself, said: "Many of the members at Lancashire who knew him felt he would have gone all the way with cricket. But clearly when Manchester United knock on your door, you go."

It was not, said Neville, quite as simple as that. His elder brother Gary was already at United and loving it. There was one other factor. "One year I played both sports for England," Neville recalled. "In the football I played at Wembley Stadium in front of 50,000. I made my England cricket debut in front of 50 people at a village cricket club." It was a similar reality which drove Neville's United team-mate, Roy Keane, to seek anonymity at the cricketing Old Trafford one afternoon when some indiscretion had the world's press at his door.

English cricket will never know what it lost in Neville, Botham and Wilkinson. It does know what it would have lost had Vaughan been blessed with the same dual ability. Vaughan admitted to the magazine *FHM* that he would have chosen football had the opportunity arisen. "I love football," he said, "but my knees would never have lasted."

Since the interview was part of cricket's attempt to rebrand itself in an attempt to dent football's hold on the youth market this was something of an own goal. Vaughan still follows the game, especially if Sheffield Wednesday are involved, but since becoming England captain he has become cautious on this subject.

Graham Thorpe is less reticent. He was a central midfielder good enough to win three caps for England Schools Under-18s. Unlike his team-mates, who were affiliated to professional clubs, Thorpe was an amateur and, although Brentford showed an interest, a future in cricket seemed more probable. Since none of the footballers went on to play at the highest level, and only a few made a career in the game, it seems he made the right move.

Thorpe, a keen Chelsea fan, has no regrets. He said: "I don't really envy anything about a footballer's life – certainly not the adulation or the pressures of fame the top players have to contend with. I am quite happy with the career I have chosen. I reckon the only advantage they have over us is that their game lasts 90 minutes not five days so they get more time off to work on their golf swings."

That is not just a joke. The time commitment is one of the most significant differences. Cricketers spend a lot more time "playing" their game, even if they are sitting in the pavilion. Footballers train more than they play but, because it is a physically demanding sport, even the training is limited to around three hours a day. This leaves them with a lot of free time on their hands. Too much for many, judging by the game's problems with alcohol, gambling and drugs.

Cricketers are away from their families for much longer. Winter tours last months, and even in the summer they are away half the season. Outside the major competitions, and pre-season tours, footballers are rarely absent for more than a couple of days at a stretch. However, the lack of trust in players' self-discipline means their trips are strictly controlled – they rarely see anything other than airports, hotels and stadiums. Cricketers do sometimes actually visit places. "We get to see far more of the world than they do," said Thorpe. "I've been everywhere from the Khyber Pass to the Victoria Falls with England."

The downside, as Thorpe has himself painfully experienced, is that personal relationships suffer. But the divorce rate is high among both sets of sportsmen: footballers, encouraged by their clubs to settle down, tend to marry younger. And both footballers and cricketers can have their personal business exposed in the tabloids – though footballers will rate bigger headlines.

Another plus of cricketing life, said Thorpe, is the longer career. Few footballers have earned an England comeback at 34, as he did last summer. Traditionally, there have also been greater opportunities for cricketers to forge a rewarding second career in the media. It might be argued that footballers, because of the money they earn, should not need either to play into their late thirties or find future employment. However, football can be a short career and rugby, given the potential for serious injury, even briefer. Many players are poorly advised and others never earn serious money.

Vince Wells and Tony Cottey, for example, chose football first but probably benefited by failing to make the grade. Wells was on Leyton Orient's books, only turning to cricket after being rejected for an apprenticeship; Cottey played three league matches for Swansea as a teenager before being released. Both have forged long and fruitful county careers.

There are other differences, some cultural. The feature in *The Wisden Cricketer*, "Dressing-room read", would not last long in a football magazine. When his first "autobiography" was published, Michael Owen admitted

Phil Neville (*left*) and his brother Gary playing for Lancashire Schools in 1989, before both swapped one Old Trafford for the other.
Picture by Maurice Jones, Bolton Evening News.

he had never actually read a book. Phil Neale, of Lincoln City and Worcestershire, carried a Tolstoy on to the coach for his first football away trip. It went swiftly out of the window. Graham Taylor, his manager, advised him to start watching *Coronation Street* so he would be able to join in conversations. English football is now more cosmopolitan, but the nature of its Anglo-Saxon participants has not changed significantly.

Neale was, though, impressed with the greater fitness, a gap that remains. He also found football to be mentally tougher. There is a casual hardness about the game bred, he feels, by the insecurity that comes from having more time between performances and being one bad tackle away from a broken career.

The cricketer does still have rewards denied to the muddied millionaires. In their peripatetic careers, footballers and, increasingly, rugby players, tend to make acquaintances. Cricketers, living cheek-by-jowl with team-mates and drinking with opponents, do still make friends.

Between 1990 and 1994 Glenn Moore covered cricket for Reuters, The Independent on Sunday *and* The Independent. *Since 1994 he has been* The Independent's *football correspondent.*

Call My Agent

PAUL KELSO

The birth of the sports agent can be traced, so the story goes, to England's 1948-49 tour of South Africa, when Denis Compton handed a suitcase to the journalist, Reg Hayter. It contained hundreds of letters that Compo, a man hardly cut out for admin, could not face opening.

Hayter began ploughing through them and found scores of what would now be called commercial opportunities. Among the invitations to after-dinner speaking engagements and public appearances was an offer of £2,000 to write a column for the *News of the World*. There was also a further letter, written two months later, withdrawing the offer because the paper had not received a reply.

Hayter passed the suitcase on to Bagenal Harvey, a publisher who quickly abandoned books to devote himself to the promotion of sportsmen. Harvey secured the £1,000-a-year Brylcreem contract that put Compton's face and gleaming hair on posters across the country, and happily trousered a 10% fee for himself. His success with Compton had the leading lights of other sports scurrying to his office, among them Fulham footballers Jimmy Hill and Johnny Haynes. Hill was campaigning for an end to football's £20 maximum wage (that was £20 per week, not per minute) and, when he succeeded in 1961, Harvey was well placed to secure Haynes the first £100-a-week contract.

Ever since then, football has dwarfed cricket, where players of limited profile and modest income have presented few opportunities for agents following in Harvey's footsteps. There have been exceptions for exceptional players. The eccentric entrepreneur "Lord" Tim Hudson sparkled briefly, promising to take Ian Botham, the most marketable English cricketer since Compton, to Hollywood and make him the "new Errol Flynn". (Nothing came of it and Hudson, down on his luck, was reduced to living in a caravan adjoining the Cheshire estate he owned in his pomp.) David Gower, meanwhile, is still represented by Jon Holmes, a friend of his and Gary Lineker's from their Leicester days, whose SFX agency grew huge from its provincial roots.

Botham and Gower stood out because they were marketable well beyond the county grounds. For the average county player, however, sponsorship opportunities in the 1970s and 1980s were limited to a car from the local garage and the occasional tryst with a Benson and Hedges cigarette girl. Players were reluctant to share 10% of either.

In the last five years, however, changes to the structure of the domestic game, increased television revenues and more aggressive marketing of the sport have led to an increase in cricket's fortunes. And in sport, where there's brass, there are agents.

There are now more than a dozen agencies representing English cricket's 350-odd middling players. (There are even agents operating outside the first-class structure. For instance, Paul Carrick, a civil servant based in the North-

East, offers overseas professionals to league clubs via his website.) For evidence of their growing influence, you have only to turn to the acknowledgments page of Michael Vaughan's hastily ghosted book, *A Year in the Sun*. There, in a list that includes his parents, his brother and sundry Yorkshire coaches, England's captain thanks the team at International Sports Management for guiding his career thus far. James Anderson, rising star of Vaughan's England, was at it too when he stepped up to receive his award for the 2003 Young Cricketer of the Year at the Cricket Writers' Club annual dinner. "Thanks to everyone at ISM," stuttered the tyro.

When Vaughan had the captaincy thrust upon him much was made of his old-fashioned virtues. He wore an England cap to his first press conference, and his former captain David Byas revealed that Vaughan was known as "the Amateur" at Headingley. In fact Vaughan is far more Player than Gentleman and, along with Anderson, Andrew Flintoff and others, is one of a new generation of English international cricketers benefiting from an unprecedented degree of professionalism in the management both of their careers and their bank accounts.

Vaughan's agent is Andrew "Chubby" Chandler, a modestly talented former European Tour golf professional who realised there were better ways to make money out of other golfers than losing to them, and established ISM. His core business is still golf, a game awash with money. However, Chandler has moved into cricket and established a specialist division headed by the former England batsman Neil Fairbrother, a man with excellent contacts in the Lancashire dressing-room and beyond. As well as Vaughan and Flintoff, ISM represent just a handful of the most marketable and high-profile players, including Muttiah Muralitharan and Marcus Trescothick, reasoning that once you move away from the elite, cricketers make little commercial sense. With the average county pro earning around £50,000 and with limited potential to make more, agents have to represent a lot of players before they can make a decent living.

"If I could put a logo on Freddie's helmet I'd get him £200,000"

"The idea is to have a small group of players you do a real proper job for," says Chandler. "We are starting to see crossover opportunities between cricket and golf, we do pro-am days and have clients out for dinner with the players. There's potential there. The difference between cricket and golf is that cricket's a team game, so I can't put a logo on Freddie's helmet. If I could, I'd get him £200,000. But our cricket broke even in the first year and we'll make some money in the years to come."

Chandler may focus on the elite, but it is among the modest ranks of the game that the growth in player representation is most marked, thanks mainly to the easing of restrictions on overseas cricketers, a rise in the number of players moving counties and the advent of the EU-qualified cricketer. Richard Thompson is chairman of cricket at Surrey CCC and managing director of Merlin Elite, a sports management company, so he is both poacher and gamekeeper and has watched the process at first hand.

"More and more counties are looking for dual-passport players because they are cheaper and cost nothing to develop," says Thompson. "You can have as many as six effectively foreign players in a team now, and the agents are selling these players to clubs. I am constantly getting lists of players from agents via fax and email. I'm sure most players could get by with just a good lawyer advising them, but agents are useful sometimes. In cricket we deal with a lot of fathers, and in some ways I'd rather deal with an agent than a parent."

THE MEN IN THE MIDDLE

A selection of players and the agents who represent them (as at end 2003). These arrangements are subject to regular change.

athletes1 (David Ligertwood)	**ISM ("Chubby" Chandler)**	**SFX (Jon Holmes)**	**Graham Staples**
Gareth Batty	James Anderson	Nasser Hussain	Graham Thorpe
Ian Bell	Andrew Flintoff	Graeme Smith	
Mark Butcher	Matthew Hoggard		
Paul Collingwood	Muttiah Muralitharan		
Ashley Giles	Marcus Trescothick	**WorldTel**	**21st Century Media**
Adam Hollioake	Michael Vaughan	Sachin Tendulkar	Rahul Dravid
Darren Lehmann			
Vikram Solanki			
Chaminda Vaas			

Thompson recently took on Alec Stewart in a non-executive role, but has stuck to representing golfers and footballers rather than cricketers, partly because of the potential conflict of interest, and partly because of money. "The finances of the cricket agent's business are tight," he says. "A senior pro, capped and with six years behind him, will earn on average £50,000, and have a bat and kit deal worth around £10,000. At Surrey we also offer personal player sponsorship deals to companies. For between £10,000 and £15,000 the client gets, say, five personal appearances a year from the player, who will also be around during Oval Test matches and come along and say hello when the sponsor has guests in his box. But even taken together, a cricketer's income is small by the standards of other sports."

Despite the modest returns, there are more agents then ever, and the ECB and the Professional Cricketers' Association have introduced a registration system to ensure that counties deal only with approved agents. Their role remains controversial. In football, agents are blamed for unsettling players and encouraging them to move so the agent can pocket a commission. Cricket remains more stable, largely thanks to the benefit system, but young players are far more restless than they used to be. And when they need a new county, an agent will help them find one. "Youngsters are unlikely to linger in Second Eleven cricket at their first county for more than a season or two now," says Thompson. "At Surrey, the bulk of the home-grown players –

First-class service: agents like David Ligertwood (*left*) even offer a mail-opening service for players on tour. Richard Thompson is both poacher and gamekeeper. *Pictures by Philip Brown and Graham Morris.*

Thorpe, Bicknell, Butcher and Stewart – spent up to four years on the fringes of the first team before nailing down their places. That wouldn't happen now."

Given English cricket's obsession with all things Australian, it comes as no surprise to hear that the man widely considered the best in the business grew up in Adelaide. David Ligertwood, born in Oxford but raised in Australia, played first-class cricket for Surrey and Durham. In 1999, he founded athletes1, a management company with offices in London, Melbourne and Adelaide, and more than 150 cricketers worldwide on its books, including Mark Butcher, Michael Bevan, Stuart MacGill, Chaminda Vaas, Henry Olonga and around 30% of the English game's first-class stock.

Ligertwood says cricketers are commercially viable to his firm for two reasons: volume, and because they offer their clients more than occasional contract advice. "The easy part of representing a player is getting them a county and doing the contract. All you need for that is a few contacts. What we offer the players is the whole deal. We do all their legal work and accounting, financial planning, deal with the taxman, source sponsorship opportunities for them, open their mail when they are on tour. If you sit down with a player and say 'we can save you £10,000 this year and it's going to cost you £1,000', you often find they are interested."

Ligertwood is starting to bring some of the more sophisticated strategies common in other sports into cricket. For example, county salaries are made up of two strands, one for playing and another for promotional work on the county's behalf. One method employed by athletes1 is to separate those streams and siphon the money for the promotional work into a separate company. It is common practice in football where image rights are recognised as one of the key assets a player has, but it is relatively new in cricket.

"These are all pretty straightforward, tax-efficient ways of doing things, but they are just coming into the game in this country," says Ligertwood.

Ligertwood is frank about the marketing opportunities presented by England's current first-class stock. "The game here is not nearly as marketable as it is in Australia. There the players are massive, huge stars, as big as any footballer here. But in England there is so much competition and, unless you are really special, you are not going to make a fortune. International players will have their central contract, a bat deal worth up to £60,000 and then a bit of media work, but it's still a long way off golf.

"Vaughan is marketable because the captain always is. Butcher is fantastic and if he was captain he'd be huge. He's got personality, he's a top bloke and a rounded guy, he plays the guitar, and he's had a bit of sketchy publicity about his personal life. He's easy to market.

"Anderson's all right, but he's done nothing yet apart from dye his hair red. You have to be absolutely outstanding as a bowler to get really big because all the focus is on the batters. Darren Gough, who was the most marketable Englishman since Botham, was only just good enough in a poor side to be worth it, and that was because he had such charisma on top of his ability."

Ligertwood forecasts that for now cricketers' earnings will remain modest compared to golf, tennis and football. "None of the really big agencies, the Octagons and IMGs, have an interest in cricket at the moment, so outside India we've not seen any mega-deals, the sort you get in football where Coke or Pepsi buy up a whole team of players and use them across the board."

He does see richer times ahead, however. In 2002 the ICC approved a change in regulations to allow players to display the name of any sponsor on their bats. Prior to this, only kit manufacturers were permitted to advertise in that space, a rule famously broken by Arjuna Ranatunga who displayed an ad for Sam's Chicken and Ribs at Trent Bridge in 1998. At the moment the space available is restricted to ten square inches on the back of the bat, which is barely visible on a stump cam – and even that is illegal at ICC events such as the World Cup and the Champions' Trophy. Discussions continue, however, and if the players get their way, cricketers' incomes could be transformed. "If you had a large space on the front of the bat you could see players getting up to £200,000 each. If four kit manufacturers can push it up to £60,000, imagine what open competition could do," says Ligertwood. When that day comes, you can be sure no cricketer will ever have to open his own mail again.

Paul Kelso is sports news correspondent of The Guardian.

THE GAFFER, THE GASOMETER, THE GOODBYE: Alec Stewart walks off The Oval in September 2003 after being lbw for 38 in his farewell Test.

Picture by Clive Mason, Getty Images.

CHAIRED...: Steve Waugh receives the adulation of his team-mates and the Sydney crowd in January 2004 after his final Test.

Picture by Matthew Impey.

...AND CHEERED: The Australian newspapers join the chorus.

Picture by Nigel Davies.

FIVE CRICKETERS OF THE YEAR: Andrew Flintoff.

Picture by Graham Morris.

FIVE CRICKETERS OF THE YEAR: Ian Harvey.

Picture by Patrick Eagar.

FIVE CRICKETERS OF THE YEAR: Gary Kirsten

Picture by Patrick Eagar.

FIVE CRICKETERS OF THE YEAR: Graeme Smith.

Picture by Graham Morris.

FIVE CRICKETERS OF THE YEAR: Chris Adams.

Picture by Finn Connor.

The Year of the Martlet

ROBIN MARLAR

Founded in faraway 1839, Sussex is the oldest of the county cricket clubs. But boy, have we been late developers! In the first season, all the matches were lost. Never mind the sea fret at Hove – there was a pall of gloom for 164 years and certainly for the 112 years from 1890, the official start of the County Championship, until 2002.

That was all part of local folklore. Now the discussion has gone from macro to micro: disputing the exact time. At some time between 1.43 p.m. and 1.45 p.m. on September 18, but definitely after lunch on the second day of the last match against lowly Leicestershire, Murray Goodwin, prolific opening batsman from Zimbabwe via Australia, pulled the boundary which took Sussex to the 300 mark, and their sixth bonus point of the game. This put them beyond the reach of their last challengers for the 2003 County Championship, Lancashire, who had thrashed Sussex in the previous match at Old Trafford. Talk about frayed nerves! It looked as though the fat lady had forgotten to turn up.

Thanks to the generous forbearance of their visitors, play was held up for no fewer than eight minutes' rejoicing. Celebrations were instantaneous, wholehearted and prolonged. It was a privilege to be present, especially among so many fellow old sweats. It was a masterstroke to bring down the 105-strong Christ's Hospital marching band, boys and girls, on that last day. It was necessary, too, because the tape of that stirring song, "Sussex By The Sea", was all but worn through. Even now the memory of the blue cassocks and yellow stockings striding the outfield and the crowd singing the chorus

> You may tell them all
> That we stand or fall,
> For Sussex by the sea

can bring a tear to a rheumy old eye. On the next day, handicapped by a collective hangover which only a club with its own pub could generate, Sussex went on to win by an innings, and finish 34 points clear of the field. This was a ready riposte to clever dicks, especially from old rivals Kent, who publicly doubted whether Sussex were the rightful winners.

On no fewer than seven occasions, the Martlets have been second: bridesmaids may share the excitement, the occasion and a slice of cake, but next day they are back where they were. This time, Sussex made it to Buckingham Palace, where by long-established practice, they received their medals from the Duke of Edinburgh, a talented batsman in his day (he hit me for six, anyway) before polo called. It was a double triumph too, because the Sussex women's team also became champions for the first time, and they came to the palace together on a coach from Hove, arriving late enough

Fifty years on: the Sussex team of 1953 who narrowly missed out, with Robin Marlar seated far left, and (*below*) their 2003 successors who made it.

Picture (below) by Finn Connor.

to qualify both teams for bread and water in the dungeon. (Yorkshire also copped both titles in 2001, we discovered – and their coach was even later.) Whatever view you may take of tradition and ceremonial, it was very special to those who had never come close to honours before – not least because so many of those associated with winning the title were already planning the encore.

It had seemed a distant prospect six years earlier, after half a dozen top players had walked out. A sporting banker called Jim May heard me tut-

tutting on telly and rang me up to inform me that, as I had got a big mouth, I had better join him to do something about it. Meanwhile, Tony Pigott, a former stalwart but then at Surrey, was canvassing support for Sussex 2000, which successfully ousted the old committee at the AGM.

At that stage, just stopping the rot, trying to avoid bottom place, was a noble enough ambition. But Pigott and Peter Moores, the executive and captain who were obliged to sort out this mess, were – believe me – not merely dreaming of the Championship but working towards it. Top of the wish list was a new, imported skipper, whose arrival would be a symbol of change. A magnet for others, he would be a recognisable leader to bright young things emerging through the development programme.

It was a Benson and Hedges final that made it obvious that Chris Adams was a future captain of somebody. A class act is easily spotted. In 1993, there had been a fuss over ball-tampering in a county match, and when Derbyshire squared up to Lancashire at Lord's, Wasim Akram let go a beamer from the pavilion end that hit Adams on the shoulder. Intentional or not (and the umpire thought it was), words were exchanged at lunch, Adams not mincing his. He exuded spirit all day. It was the quality most needed on our precious acres. Four years later, we recruited him and never regretted it, even though some thin years still followed. Whatever the results, he brought a glimmer of hope because people wanted to play for him; the spirit and attitude in the club were transformed.

There were times even in 2003 when Sussex reverted to collapse mode. But the collapses became uncharacteristic. The team's mettle was most visible in the crucial ninth win against Middlesex, when Sussex, facing 392, were 107 for six. A locally bred star, Matthew Prior, together with the South African Mark Davis, batting at Nos 7 and 8, saved Sussex with huge innings, and in the process demoralised their old bank holiday rivals. Then Mushtaq Ahmed bowled them out on his way to his 100th wicket.

He was the signing that made all the difference. A match-winner hungry for more and more five and ten-wicket hauls, he was given extra motivation by trading wickets for cash, a feature of cricket even before Sussex were founded. Once given the ball, he was reluctant to let it go. Wonderful to captain, said Adams. Mushtaq had bowled like that when he destroyed England at The Oval in 1996: now he was back to his best. So was James Kirtley, who should have been picked by England when Sussex were in the doldrums. In the final game, Leicestershire were bowled out by another local stalwart who had lived through the bad times, Jason Lewry. By then Mushtaq, like the king in the nursery rhyme, was in the counting house counting out his money – prior to an unexpected resumption of his Test career.

What took Sussex so long? It is possible to argue that they were champion county before everyone else had woken up. That was what I used to hear from George Washer – gas fitter and scorer, a hard man withal, who could continue talking non-stop without ever losing the fag from his lower lip. He insisted Sussex had been champions, according to his equivalent of Duckworth/Lewis, in the 1870s, and took on the formidable Major Rowland Bowen on this subject.

Certainly, they twice came second in Edwardian times, with Fry and Ranji. Then there were three in a row during the frustrating 1930s: in late July 1934, they looked almost certain to be champions, but only won one game out of the last 12. "Short of being a really tip-top team," sniffed *Wisden*. I was personally convinced we were going to win in 1953, David Sheppard's year, until Rupert Webb missed a vital catch behind the stumps at Hastings against Yorkshire. There may be an element of bias here since I was bowling at the time, and had turned an off-break away from the left-hander, Vic Wilson. Anyway, Webb went on to play the father of one of the brides in *Four Weddings and a Funeral*, which some might think constitutes greater glory than any Championship.

In 1981, when John Barclay led arguably the strongest Sussex team, they maddeningly failed to take the last Nottinghamshire wicket in a match which pitted Imran Khan and Garth le Roux against Richard Hadlee and Clive Rice. Afterwards, there was a spirited row about over-rates.

Looking at so many distinguished names, it is clear that Sussex have never lacked for style. That elusive quality is, happily, endemic at Hove. But perhaps Sussex have not always played primarily to win. That, historically, might be the difference between the "southron folk" and the northerners. Why play if not to win? For fun; for friendship; for experience; to explore.

When Chris Adams gave his victor's speech, he said: "We wanted it more than any of the others." He was also kind enough to say that he wanted to share his triumph with all those who had gone before. But perhaps in the past Sussex have not wanted it quite enough. The truth is that only this team has deserved today's congratulations: "Well done, lads."

Robin Marlar was captain of Sussex from 1955 to 1959 and chairman from 1997 to 2000. He was cricket correspondent of the Sunday Times *from 1970 to 1996.*

Sir Paul Getty

Born September 7, 1932

Died April 17, 2003

MATTHEW ENGEL

On a warm September morning last year 1,200 people filled every seat at a memorial service in Westminster Cathedral. The cathedral is the building that the unwary regularly confuse with Westminster Abbey. This is in fact the Byzantine building with a rich, dark brick interior (rather reminiscent of a Belgian railway station) that serves as the mother church for Britain's Roman Catholics.

Many people present remarked that they never knew Paul Getty was a Catholic. But then he led a remarkably multi-faceted life: those who dealt with him in one compartment did not necessarily know anything about the others.

Even at the service there were compartments. For convenience and sociability, various interest groups were put together: most of the cricketers were at the back on the left-hand side. Thus they could easily have been unaware of the politicians, or the actors, or the musicians, or the military men, or the representatives of the dozens of causes that Paul helped.

It was not exactly a cross-section of British life; the upper reaches of the Conservative Party, which he supported lavishly, were decidedly over-represented; the Labour government was invisible. And there were an awful lot of cricket people. But then perhaps none of the other compartments had quite so much cause to be grateful as this game did.

There have been improbable people in cricket before, but none perhaps quite so improbable. He was an American, and generally a taste for cricket, as with Marmite or Christmas pantomime, only touches those exposed to it at an early age. He became not merely a fan but its patron par excellence. No one knows accurately how much Getty largesse cricket received in all: he certainly never did. Some donations – like the one towards the new Mound Stand at Lord's – were well-publicised. Others were very discreet.

Yet he was not a cricket fan in the conventional sense. He never followed all the notes of the music in detail – but he loved the sound they made. Paul was the game's ultimate nostalgist. He revered players whose cricket he could only have glimpsed briefly in grainy old newsreels: Allen and Wyatt and Compton and Miller. He befriended them all, which was a bittersweet pleasure because old cricketers die.

Two of his contributions, however, might outlast all of us, and neither of them was essentially philanthropic. One was the construction of the beautiful ground at his Wormsley estate, in Buckinghamshire, which was pure self-indulgence but an indulgence that has already given pleasure to thousands

Sir Paul Getty: "his passionate romance with cricket enriched and enlivened the game". *Picture by Rex Features.*

of people who have enjoyed heavenly afternoons there. The immediate future of Wormsley is secure and cricket will continue, on a reduced scale, in 2004. Plans for MCC to play there regularly have so far foundered, though it is hard to believe that some kind of long-term arrangement cannot be worked out with someone.

Secondly, there was his ownership of this almanack. He bought John Wisden and Co in 1993. He liked to save threatened British institutions although *Wisden* did not, in the conventional sense, need saving. The book was (and, mercifully, still is) profitable and in no danger of closure. But its ownership situation was messy and unsatisfactory; the company needed love and affection, and got it.

Paul worried no more about the day-to-day running of the company than he did about the lbw law. But in business, as in cricket, he had an instinct for what really mattered. His support, through difficult times, enabled *Wisden* to invest in such fraught areas as the internet. As a result, his proprietorship (which has now passed to his son Mark) has left *Wisden* infinitely stronger, just as his passionate romance with cricket enriched and enlivened the game.

See also Obituaries, page 1541.

Temples of Bumblepuppy

CHRISTOPHER DOUGLAS

House for sale "with own cricket pitch for tea-time fun... £400,000" ran a recent advertisement in the property section of the *Sunday Telegraph*, no doubt causing a few owners of three-bedroomed urban properties to flirt with the idea of a straight swap. It might be, as the ad claimed, "a cricket addict's dream" but given the time and toil involved in maintaining a square – cutting, rolling, scarifying, reseeding it and de-moling the outfield – the dream could be a fretful one.

"House for sale next door to house with own cricket ground" might be a different matter altogether. A stroll to a neighbouring field where everything has been laid on, wicket shaved and rolled, lunch and tea in preparation, showers functioning, all for free and taken care of by someone else would have an appeal few social cricketers could resist.

For about fifty years up until the First World War, that kind of life was available all summer to anyone with the ability and the time to devote themselves to playing cricket. Accommodation with full board was provided for those who wanted it plus, for sought-after players, discreet inducements too. Country-house cricket was not just a cricket lover's dream, it was a freeloader's fantasy.

Of the 10,000 houses referred to by the Country House database perhaps 300 had their own grounds at some point. It could well have been more. In Nottinghamshire a century ago no fewer than 18 houses had the wherewithal to stage matches. In Kent and Sussex the figure was higher still, and you would not have had to ride for more than an hour or two in any direction before reaching a house with its own groundsman and often a retained professional.

At Lord Kingsdown's home, Torry Hill near Maidstone, the family has hosted matches since 1845. It's a rarity now, but falling within a mere ten-mile radius of it a hundred years ago were the cricketing demesnes of Belmont, Bobbing Court, Boxley House, Chilham Castle, Chilston Park, Evington, Gore Court, Highland Court, Hothfield Place, Linton Park, Mote Park, Preston Hall and Sharsted Court. A few staged county games (The Mote still does) and in the case of Belmont, Lord Harris's seat, international sides interrupted their punishing progress around the country to pass an agreeable day or two.

Almost all these houses still stand, but the grounds have been sold, cultivated or buried under the M20. However, the story is far from being one of dereliction and decay. Some of the grounds taken over by local clubs have been improved and extended. At Gore Court in 1998, the Australian women's Test side played a warm-up match. At Mount Ephraim House, a few miles from Torry Hill, one of the most beautifully positioned small grounds in the country was laid out in 1994. The pattern is repeated elsewhere. The somnolent glory of the 19th century can never be recaptured in the 21st, but this rarified form of the game is currently enjoying a revival.

The golden age of country-house cricket began around 1850. It bridged the gap between the game's disreputable past and the respectable age that began with the formalised County Championship. The popular image is of languorous late-Victorians and Edwardians lolling about with wispy moustaches and striped blazers, yet some of the best cricket of the time was played on private grounds. The sports journalist, E. H. D. Sewell, wrote a chapter in one of his five autobiographies about the Rothschilds' house, Ascott, in the 1890s: "To the uninitiated, country-house cricket may savour sometimes of bumblepuppy, of taking things easy… I don't know if there were ever any country houses where such slacking goes on. I don't believe there were."

Nevertheless a certain amount of bumblepuppy did take place. "Champagne lunches are being horribly overdone," wrote H. D. G. Leveson Gower in a *Country Life* piece published in 1924. "Men do not play good cricket on Perrier Jouet… No, give us some big pies, cold chickens, a fine sirloin of English beef, and a round of brawn, washed down by good ale and luscious shandygaff." There must have been quite a few on the other side of the Perrier Jouet versus big pies debate or he wouldn't have felt the need to speak out so strongly, but he was writing at a time when country-house cricket was already in decline.

Lord Harris himself urged amateurs to support their counties instead, so competition among hosts to attract the better players was intense. Leveson Gower (pronounced Loosun Gore – it seems to have been a point of honour among country-house cricketers that the names of both houses and players

Glorious Goodwood: cricket at Goodwood House in Sussex began in 1702 and is still flourishing.

Picture courtesy of the Trustees of the Goodwood Collection.

should only be pronounceable by the initiated) believed the reasons for the decline were fourfold: the First World War, the County Championship, the need for young amateurs to work for a living and finally "insidious beguiling golf".

Even in that era, though, Sir Julien Cahn, who is remembered for batting in a special pair of inflatable pads blown up by a servant with a bicycle pump, offered a range of attractions to his guests in Nottinghamshire, including a famously liberal supply of champagne, sea lions in the lake, a bijou theatre and a substantial collection of cricket books and erotica kept in the library where he died peacefully in 1944.

From a sample selection of a hundred houses staging country-house cricket in 1904, 62 grounds have survived, the majority long since bequeathed, sold or loaned in perpetuity to the local club. You are most likely to be visiting one of these houses themselves now as a member of a wedding party – many are licensed to hold civil ceremonies. You might also be going there as a golfer, a paintballer, a carp fisher, a charismatic evangelist (Mattersey Hall), a trainee osteopath or police officer (Hothfield Place and Bramshill Park).

One of the most prized invitations a century ago was to Newbold Revel in Warwickshire. Now it's a museum of prison life and the cricket ground is used for football by the Prison Service. At the former Hemsted Park, where Alfred Mynn once bowled Kent to victory over England, you can still play cricket but you will be doing so as a pupil of Benenden school for girls. Yet hundreds of old-fashioned games still take place in the shadow of the big house. You can take your pick of architectural styles: Eastnor Castle (Victorian Gothic), Blenheim Palace (Vanbrugh), Petworth House (Jacobean), Penshurst Place (14th-century with Tudor additions), Arundel Castle (Norman), Bamburgh Castle (Saxon origins) and so on.

What is perhaps more surprising is the number of private grounds that continue to function on a version of the Victorian model. Torry Hill, despite a modern pavilion, still stages something like the old-style games and earned an approving mention and photo in the *Sloane Ranger Diary*. The exclusive wandering sides I Zingari and Free Foresters will play a couple of games there this year.

At Highclere in Hampshire, Lord Carnarvon still fields his own XI. Arundel Castle in Sussex is well known for hosting the first match against touring sides. Nearby Goodwood celebrated its 300th season in 2002 with a match played under 1727 rules. Lord Coke of Holkham Hall (Coke pronounced Cook and Holkham pronounced Hokum) runs several games a year at his Palladian pile in Norfolk. The Earl Spencer hosts matches at Althorp (pronounced Althrup) and the Lords Stafford and Vestey do likewise at Swynnerton Park in Staffordshire and Stowell Park in Gloucestershire. The house fields an XI at Petworth in Sussex, Widford in Hertfordshire and Hovingham in Yorkshire, an 18th-century gem which E. W. Swanton reckoned to be the best of all country-house grounds. According to *Wisden*, I Zingari played five games on country-house grounds in 1904 (though other sources say it was more). Ten years ago it was up to six, and this year they are scheduled to play eight.

Cricketing stronghold: Bamburgh Castle in Northumberland.
Picture by Michael Goonan, Scenic Photos.

Nowadays, hosting matches can be expensive and in order to cover the running costs houses such as Hagley Hall, Toddington and Althorp charge rental for some of their games. It's becoming an increasingly popular corporate day, from a few hundred pounds up – cheap by the standards of corporate entertainment – and it offers a lifeline to owners who might otherwise be forced to sell.

There have been many casualties down the years. The Blofelds of Norfolk created a ground at Hoveton (pronounced Hofftun) after the Second World War using German PoW labour, and Henry Blofeld continued to run sides there until the 1970s, when his elder brother inherited the house. Trees are planted on the ground now. Diamond millionaire Solly Joel's house, Maiden Erlegh in Berkshire, is no more and gone too are his ground, stud farm and private racecourse. Ian Botham's one-time agent Tim Hudson briefly created the Birtles Bowl at his house in Cheshire. Now it's just a field. Some famous venues have entered a kind of twilight zone. Sir Julien Cahn had two grounds, one at West Bridgford, still used by local teams but where the pavilion has just escaped a plan to build new houses, and the other at his home, Stanford Hall, later taken over by the Co-op. There has been no cricket there since 1999.

Nevertheless, the impression is that the number of private grounds is on the increase. The late Sir Paul Getty's ground in its silent Buckinghamshire valley at Wormsley with its matching thatched pavilion and scorebox, and its flower-filled marquee, is arguably the most opulent of them all – a temple to bumblepuppy. Guests are sometimes entertained by sky-divers in the tea interval and invited to stroll up to the library to inspect the first editions of Shakespeare and Chaucer. The cricket is often star-studded (touring teams have played quasi-official games here for several years) but fairly amiable. Mark Getty, Sir Paul's heir, is intending to maintain the traditions, but on a more commercial basis.

A notably successful addition is at Brundall in Norfolk where the caravan-park entrepreneur, Stan Biss, set up the Vauxhall Mallards club. It has been thriving for some years, with three league sides, a junior division and the means to host floodlit games. Naturally, some of the newer grounds are scorned as nouveau riche by the grand wandering sides. But the older fortunes were not always gained by entirely honourable means. Lord Harris's great-grandfather acquired Belmont on the proceeds of loot from the sack of Seringapatam, and what is Arundel Castle if not a backhander from one grateful Norman warlord to another?

In other parts of the world, only India comes close to a tradition of private grounds. A dozen or more princely rulers were extravagant patrons. Three successive Maharajas of Patiala were fine players, although India boasted arguably one of the richest and least athletic of all cricket sponsors, the Maharaja of Kashmir. He would wait by the phone in his palace until informed that a wicket had fallen, whereupon he would be driven to his ground, helped into his pads and aided to the middle. His team of bowlers then got to work trying to hit his limply dangling bat and they were backed up by a crack fielding unit whose terrific footwork somehow coaxed the ball across the boundary. The Maharaja never made less than a hundred and once sympathised with Ranjitsinhji for his relatively disappointing record.

Some 30 miles south-west of Sydney the Camden Park ground has been owned by the Macarthur family for six generations. Carved out of a hillside outside Johannesburg is the Oppenheimers' private ground where international sides often begin their tours. Marquees ring the boundary on either side of an imposing three-storey pavilion. The heir to the De Beers billions, Jonathan Oppenheimer, captained a side that beat Nasser Hussain's England tourists in 1999.

Touring sides have fewer anxious moments at Wormsley, Highclere and Arundel. And it is in England where country-house cricket continues to thrive. Like a shoot or a hunt or a ball, a cricket match was and remains an agreeable way for the super rich to throw a party.

For all that, it is not easy to say what constitutes a country-house match. When does a field or even a large garden become a country-house ground? When the owner acquires a title? Or when he lays on a tray of sandwiches and a few cans of lager? Games of no consequence whatever except to those involved are taking place on private properties all over the country. Just as an Englishman's home is his castle, his garden is his Lord's.

Christopher Douglas is the biographer of Douglas Jardine and alter ego of Pod, the feckless fictional county cricketer. An invitation to the net in his garden is much coveted.

FIVE CRICKETERS OF THE YEAR

The Five Cricketers of the Year represent a tradition that dates back in Wisden *to 1889, making this the oldest individual award in cricket. The Five are picked by the editor, and the selection is based, primarily but not exclusively, on the players' influence on the previous English season. No one can be chosen more than once.*

Chris Adams

PAUL WEAVER

The boundary against Leicestershire that finally made Sussex county champions was hit, on September 18, by the opening batsman, Murray Goodwin, a cricketer of great skill and accomplishment. When the innings was finally declared closed, Goodwin was unbeaten on 335, the highest-ever score by a Sussex player. But hardly anyone gave him a second glance. They were too busy embracing the captain, Chris Adams, who had delivered what in Sussex had always been regarded as the Holy Grail: domestic cricket's grandest prize, which had eluded all his predecessors since the club was formed in 1839.

For this reason alone, Adams stands ahead of all Sussex captains now. The princely Ranji and the autocratic C. B. Fry, the inspiring Arthur Gilligan and the elegant, sickly Duleepsinhji, the godly David Sheppard and the maverick Robin Marlar, the imperious, glorious Ted Dexter, the towering Tony Greig and the preposterously enthusiastic John Barclay – they all jostle in his shadow. Sussex, some argue, with forlorn voices and sad, defeated eyes, were champions in 1875. But unofficial pre-1890 championships are fool's gold; now there can be no argument.

CHRISTOPHER JOHN ADAMS was born on May 6, 1970 in the small mining village of Whitwell, close to the Yorkshire border in north Derbyshire. His first cricket was played with his elder brother, David, in their sloping back garden. The two of them played for Staveley CC, where Chris won the open single-wicket competition at the age of 13. The greatest influence on his fledgling career was Benita White, a woman who ran the Chesterfield Cricket Society. Adams first went to her when he was eight and she taught him the rocking-your-teddy-bear-to-sleep technique. "When you hold your bat you've got your arms in a round with your elbows stuck out," she explains. "You rock your bat back and forward as if you're rocking your teddy to sleep." When Adams was finally selected for England he gave her the credit. But by the time he was 16, even though he had played cricket for English Schools, Adams was more interested in rocking centre-forwards. As a tough centre-half he had decided to leave Chesterfield Grammar School and join a footballing training scheme.

Mike Stone, who ran the Derbyshire Cricket Association team, persuaded Adams to take a very different turn: not merely to continue his education but to join the sixth form at Repton, a public school with a long cricketing tradition. There he broke Richard Hutton's run-scoring record; the former Derbyshire captain Guy Willatt took careful note and Kim Barnett, the then captain, visited the school to make him an offer. Adams first played for Derbyshire in 1988 and started to build a reputation as a forceful, at times brutal, middle-order batsman and outstanding fielder. By the mid-1990s, though, he felt his ambitions were being frustrated: by the club, the bowler-friendly pitches and maybe the people around him. His attempts to leave provoked resistance, and a bitter feud at Derby. The club eventually relented, he moved to Sussex, was offered the captaincy and pots of money, and achieved his ambition – selection for the millennium tour of South Africa. It was a disaster. Adams was picked in all five Tests but averaged only 13: "not up to the challenge of Test cricket," said *Wisden* dismissively. There could be no road back.

A bad summer followed. Sussex finished bottom of the second division and Adams got himself into trouble after confrontations with the umpire David Constant and Essex's Danny Law. "I had spent a very difficult winter," Adams recalls. "I came back wanting to fight the world." Thwarted in his main cricketing goal, he might easily have drifted out of the game. But he has a competitive and combative spirit – he is the son of a Yorkshireman, after all – and instead he channelled his aggression creatively and threw himself into the challenges of county cricket. Last season he led Sussex by bold example. "He's not the easiest to play against," grumbled one opposing captain. "He's very aggressive and in your face."

Yet, perversely, Adams was close to despair for much of 2003. "I couldn't have been in a worse state, mentally, in mid-July," he says. "I didn't know where to place my feet, head or hands. If I'm honest I have to say that I hadn't done enough work in pre-season or early season. It was my benefit season and we were also moving house. I had a lot of things on my mind." By July, his confidence destroyed, he decided to return to the nets and hit a thousand balls a day.

It seemed to work. He hit four centuries, three of them against Surrey and Lancashire, the main Championship rivals. Crucially, he scored runs when they were needed. When the batting faltered, as it frequently did between Tony Cottey's spring blossoming and Goodwin's late harvest, he often stood alone. He has matured, both as a player and a man and has found fulfilment. And for a county cricketer, days don't get more fulfilling than September 18.

> "Play halted for eight minutes as the squad did a lap of honour while the county anthem 'Sussex by the Sea' echoed around the ground."
>
> Sussex in 2003, page 719.

Andrew Flintoff

TANYA ALDRED

Did you see it? That Sunday morning at The Oval when, in late-summer sunshine, a blond Apollo destroyed South Africa with a joyful 95.

There always was something about Andrew Flintoff, this amiable giant who carved into the bowling, a farmhand delighting in the coconut shy. His spine-tingling whirl of the bat, exaggerated defensive shot and love of replaying his own strokes in slow-motion made him a crowd favourite and annoyingly impossible for the armchair punter to switch off. For too long, though, he had been a might-do, haunted by back trouble that threatened his bowling career, a comfortably upholstered physique, and inconsistency in the face of the hype that has surrounded every English all-rounder since Ian Botham.

But, in 2003, he became a can-do at last. First, quietly, he was England's best player at the World Cup. Then, explosively, he lit up the second half of the African summer, lifting spirits at Lord's with a bat-smashing 142 in England's grotty defeat, then setting up an improbable win with that wonderful innings at The Oval. There were other cameos in between, too. He walked off with the England man of the series award and averages to flaunt. Not that figures have ever done him justice: they ill-define his threat, his heart and the will of the crowd, gulping on their hasty return from the bars as he makes his jerky, proud way to the crease.

ANDREW FLINTOFF was born on December 6, 1977 in Preston, Lancashire, where he lived until he was 21. His first game came as a six-year-old, when Dutton Forshaw Under-13s were short and he scampered around in a Manchester United tracksuit. At nine he was turning out for Lancashire Under-11s, although he did not get around to watching the first team until he was on the staff: even when they came to play at Blackpool and his brother went to the cricket, he preferred to go to the amusements at the Tower.

The young Flintoff played chess for Lancashire but at secondary school cricket was "for posh lads", so he played football to save face, and kept cricket for the weekends. In search of tougher competition he moved clubs to St Annes, continued playing for Lancashire age-group teams, and at 16 won a three-year county contract. The Old Trafford dressing-room, stuffed with big names, was a daunting place for a teenage beanpole. "I couldn't say anything for about three years," he recalls.

A spell behind the record counter at Woolworths was followed by an England Under-19 trip to the West Indies, where he injured his back again after bowling himself into the ground. The problem remained when, aged 20, he was picked for his Test debut against South Africa. He was greeted coolly in the dressing-room and the reception grew icier when he tried to hit Jacques Kallis over extra-cover for six in his first innings and was caught behind for 17. In the next Test he made a pair and was dropped.

What followed was a helter-skelter ride of injury, disappointment, jubilant innings – like the devastating 135 against Surrey in a NatWest Trophy quarter-final in 2000 – and humiliation, when the England management hinted publicly that Flintoff was overweight. (He followed this up with a match award against Zimbabwe, describing it as "all right for a fat lad".) At the end of a dismal 2001 season, when he had made only two Championship fifties and his love of a good time was threatening to ruin his career, he was given a rocket by his personal management team.

He asked to go to the England Academy that winter but, thanks to a Duncan Fletcher hunch, ended up in India opening the bowling, specialising in Nasser Hussain's version of leg-theory to Sachin Tendulkar. He dates his change in fortunes to that tour – even though, transfixed by Anil Kumble, he was hardly able to make a run. His maiden Test hundred came against New Zealand the following March but the summer of 2002 was botched by indecision over when he should have a hernia operation, and he missed the Ashes Tests that followed. But by the time he came back from the World Cup – he finished as the tournament's most economical bowler – he felt he knew himself and his game.

Batting is getting easier. He is learning to build an innings even when he admits out of touch, and is reining in his instinct to deposit every ball out of the ground. "It has probably taken quite a while longer than I and everyone else hoped," he admits. Now he wants to work on his bowling – which he admits, despite sterling performances for England as the old hand in an inexperienced pace attack, he has not given enough attention. He has his eye on developing a ball that goes out when he wants it to, and taking more Test wickets to correct a puzzlingly high average.

Flintoff is big-hearted, genial, humble, unselfish – and surprisingly shy: he still gnaws his hands in press conferences. He loves the companionship of the game, and can often be found sitting in the Old Trafford dressing-room even when banned from playing for Lancashire by England. He was 15 when John Stanworth, the former Lancashire wicket-keeper who moved on to the coaching staff, first called him Freddie. He has been stalked with cartoon expectations ever since. When he cracked it last season, it was the most heart-warming performance by an English all-rounder since… well, let's not go into that.

Ian Harvey

David Foot

Ian Harvey is one of the great paradoxes of cricket. Spectators get the impression that his bowling is not much more than ordinary medium-pace and Gloucestershire supporters initially wondered why the county used an overseas registration to sign such an innocuous Australian. Yet that has proved, to hundreds of visibly perplexed batsmen, a dangerous assumption. In his five years with them, Gloucestershire, a county without much flamboyance or individual stardom, methodically became the best one-day side in the country and rapidly won five trophies – and Harvey was their match-winner time and again. Few imports have ever been so influential.

Harvey has now chosen to join Yorkshire, a division below Gloucestershire in 2004 in both leagues, but a club where he has the potential to make a huge difference, once again. In the West, he leaves plenty of memories of his freakish sleight-of-hand skills: whether it was his five cheap wickets – four it seemed from different balls – as Glamorgan were beaten in the 2000 Benson and Hedges Cup final; his prized trio of victims – Alec Stewart, Adam Hollioake and Graham Thorpe – in a quarter-final against Surrey a year earlier; or removing Graeme Hick for a duck in the 2003 C&G Trophy final, when a scorching 61 sealed the match award. "He was a top man, funny, unassuming," said a team-mate. "We're devastated that he's leaving us."

IAN JOSEPH HARVEY hardly conforms to the archetype of the big, loquacious Aussie. He is not particularly tall and his self-confidence is hidden beneath a quiet, amiable exterior. He was born in small-town Wonthaggi, Victoria on April 10, 1972 and completed his education at the local Technical College. As a boy he was more interested in tennis than cricket, which he only took up at 14. Then, with his inherently quirky tendency, he started wicket-keeping and represented Victoria at junior level. His coaches suggested he might try bowling instead.

By 1994-95 he was touring New Zealand with the Australian Academy, and the national selectors, eager for reliable all-rounders, were keen to place faith in him as a one-day player. His colleagues liked his equable personality and healthy thirst. They began to call him "Freak", a reference to his adept and at times unorthodox fielding and ability to throw with either arm, another knack acquired from his Academy days. His progress in Australia was sometimes erratic, but the first season he arrived in Bristol – while other Australians were in England winning the World Cup – Harvey made himself the top wicket-taker in the National League.

His batting has been forceful and entertaining – he won the Lawrence Trophy in 2001 for the summer's fastest hundred, from 61 balls against Derbyshire, and last year smashed the first and only Twenty20 Cup century, off 50 balls. Yet it has been Harvey's bowling that stood out, and some of his changes may well be remembered as mould-breaking. He has experimented endlessly with a quiet perseverance. To deliver six boringly similar balls in an over would be anathema to him. In his Academy days he instinctively concluded that subtle variety brought more success – and was more fun – than brute force. Most effective of all is his slower ball. No one these days can hold it back with more cunning. It was to be the Great Deceiver.

"I can't think of any bowler in the present game with quite the same skills, especially in those vital overs at the end of a one-day innings," says Jack Russell, who regards Harvey as the most difficult bowler he has kept to while standing up. "He always carried the element of surprise. When it came to the slower ball, it was fascinating for me to watch the way a succession of batsmen were utterly confused. To me, he's an absolute bag of tricks, slipping in the occasional bouncer and a very good yorker. He was capable of winning a game for us – with bat or ball, quite apart from his brilliant fielding. He could take a game away from any side, or close it down."

With a fetchingly self-deprecating manner, Harvey would ponder his oddball range of deliveries and say: "At my pace I need to do something different and I've three or four variations that I use. The slow one is my most productive." His easy-going temperament has allowed him to withstand those rare liberties from batsmen who take him on. His reputation for bowling successfully at the death is wholly deserved. "It's something I like, even if I'm going for a few runs. I'm aware of the impact of the final overs when the cricket can become very tense. I try not to let it bother me at all – I back myself."

In the 2003 World Cup, having made useful but not especially decisive contributions throughout, he narrowly failed to make the team for the final. He returned to England and had perhaps his most influential season yet. His simple professional approach may be a product of post-30 maturity and growing contentment. Married to Amanda and with two children, Charlotte and Will, he tells you how his lifestyle has changed. Apart from the odd round of golf, family life is now the perfect therapy. He hints that helping to look after the children is as important to him as magically spiriting up that slower ball, like a rabbit, from his concealed pocket.

Gary Kirsten

JON HENDERSON

It has been easy to overlook Gary Kirsten when the game's accolades are being handed out. It is the price, he might reflect, for placing pragmatism above the other, more appealing, qualities to be found in great run-scoring batsmen. Connoisseurs may doubt his right to be called a great batsman in the purest sense, but his status as a great run-maker is beyond question. He demonstrated this once again during a typically acquisitive 2003, when he played the England bowlers with a bat that at times must have appeared broader by some distance than the legal limit.

After a faltering start to the series in England, Kirsten, approaching his 36th birthday, quashed the notion that he was past his retire-by date with one of those merciless bouts of heavy scoring that have characterised his career. The five innings he played in the Second, Fourth and Fifth Tests – injury kept him out of the Third – produced 417 runs, including successive centuries at Lord's and Headingley. No matter that his batting was, as ever, more functional than festive, his runs gave the solid core to South Africa's batting after Graeme Smith's extraordinary form evaporated.

Originally, he planned to retire after the England tour, but he was persuaded that the team's needs and his lingering cricketing ambitions were intertwined.

"I didn't want to leave with the possibility of any regrets," he said. He fancied scoring 20 Test hundreds, and got there in the Durban Test after Christmas, which took him to the edge of the top 20 most prolific scorers in Test history. His 100th Test beckoned in 2004. At the same time, he insisted: "If I wasn't performing, then I would have retired when I originally intended to."

GARY KIRSTEN was born in Cape Town on November 23, 1967, the latest addition to a cricket family even more sprawling than the Pollocks. His late father Noel, brother Paul and half-brothers Andrew and Peter – who made 12 Test appearances – all played at first-class level. Noel, who represented Border from 1947 to 1961, became the Newlands groundsman and for eight of Kirsten's formative cricketing years the family lived at the ground. Kirsten was also a useful rugby, squash and tennis player, but it was cricket, which he started playing "from the moment I could stand", at which he excelled.

He was in the Western Province Under-19 team for three years and played for South Africa Schools in 1985. Duncan Fletcher, the England coach who was an early influence on Kirsten's career, was among the first to spot his qualities. "There are those few players like Gary who have technical faults, but with guts, determination and the will to succeed it's very difficult to put a ceiling on what level of cricket they will play," Fletcher said.

"You always have dreams of trying to hit the ball out of the ground... but I wouldn't have been around very long"

Like many left-handed batsmen, Kirsten is essentially a right-handed person. He writes and plays golf and tennis right-handed. If players like David Gower and Brian Lara have helped to establish a swashbuckling reputation for left-handers, Kirsten is certainly not unique in being a chiseller rather than a chaser. More than anyone, he probably resembles John Edrich, the England opener of the 1960s and 1970s, with his controlled power square with the wicket and unrattled response to playing and missing. Like Edrich, he may not be the most obviously intimidating presence at the crease, but his wicket is prized by opponents more than most.

Kirsten's most monumental effort was a match-saving 275 against England in Durban in 1999-2000. It lasted more than 14 hours, making it the second longest Test innings behind only the sultan of stickability, Hanif Mohammad. Surviving an apparently certain lbw appeal on 33 because Phil Tufnell overstepped, Kirsten never budged thereafter or gave the bowlers a sniff. "That was special," says Kirsten, who has always been happily unrepentant about the way he amasses his runs. "You always have dreams of trying to hit the ball out of the ground, but I think if I had done that my average would have been nearer 20 than 40, and I wouldn't have been around very long." He adds: "I like to focus on batting for as long as possible. There are too many bad days in the game to give it away when things are going your way. And when I get in, I like to score big."

Another by-product of his industrial approach to batting is the idea that he is a man with no hinterland, someone who disappears after one Test match and materialises just in time for the next. In fact Kirsten, whose wife Deborah gave birth to their first child, Joshua, in December, probably has a fuller life than most professional cricketers, particularly since in 2002 helping to found a charity, The Foundation for a Brighter Future, that supports street children in a suburb of Cape Town through getting them to play cricket. One employee of the charity noted: "Gary was busy with his preparations for the World Cup but kept saying, 'I want involvement'. I found it quite unusual for a person of his calibre not wanting to be just a pretty picture." But then being a pretty picture has never been a priority for Kirsten.

Graeme Smith

MIKE ATHERTON

Captaining one's country can be a hard road. Captaining South Africa, one senses, is the hardest road of all. This is a country that still defines itself, to some extent, by sporting success. But that is not enough any more: success must be achieved alongside the fulfilment of the hopes and dreams of all its people, with the long-term prosperity of a much-changed nation in mind.

A year ago these attendant pressures left South African cricket in a mess. An ill-chosen World Cup squad played nervously and, in farcical circumstances, was bundled out of the preliminary stages of the competition. Shaun Pollock was unceremoniously sacked as captain. In advance, half the team had dedicated their imagined World Cup triumph to their former captain Hansie Cronje, who was disgraced before he was killed in a plane crash. South African cricket needed urgent regeneration, and it was to a 22-year-old man, with minimal international experience, that they turned.

The cricketing world was incredulous. When the team began their 2003 tour to England, Graeme Smith was patronised and derided. People said he would have to learn the hard way. When South Africa were thrashed in the NatWest Series final, he did. But then came the Test series and Edgbaston and Lord's. He imposed his will upon England emphatically with compassionless innings of 277, 85 and 259. Never had the tone for a series been set so devastatingly.

Smith took on and crushed all-comers. His body language in the field contrasted sharply with the two England captains on show, Michael Vaughan and Nasser Hussain. Hussain, plainly worried that he had "lost" his team at Edgbaston, veered between a Zen-like calm and indignant intensity. At the end of the game, he resigned. Vaughan, at first, looked lost in his new role. Though six years older than Smith, he seemed like the tyro. His opponent, throughout, gave the impression of confidence, optimism and certainty.

GRAEME CRAIG SMITH was born on February 1, 1981 in Johannesburg, the son of Graham, an electrical engineer, and Janet, a draughtswoman. Two things were ingrained from the start: the traditional middle-class values of thrift and hard work; and the importance of sport. Smith played provincial soccer until 14 and represented his school at rugby. Cricket, though, was always the thing. At the age of 19, Smith scored 187 on his first-class debut and stuck a series of short-, medium- and long-term goals to his fridge; he had achieved the lot within three years. To captain South Africa was the ultimate. "I've been dreaming of this moment all my life," he said when given the job.

At a stroke, Smith's appointment allowed South Africa to leave behind the two issues that have dogged the team. He was only nine when Nelson Mandela was released from jail and spent his teenage years, at King Edward's School in Johannesburg, in a society that had moved on from apartheid. Unlike the previous generation, he had no reason to feel guilty and no need to look back. He was the perfect age to mould a team that could be representative of all South Africans. He was also free of the more recent taint: he had never played with or against Hansie Cronje.

It was apparent that Smith was a remarkable young man. His captaincy was not overly adventurous – it can be placed squarely in the dour tradition of South African captains – but immediately it was clear that he brought his whole being to the job, and that he gave every ounce of energy to his team. Ruthlessness is a necessary quality for a successful captain, and Smith signalled his intentions before the tour with the omission of Lance Klusener, announcing that Klusener was a bad influence on the team and that his ability was on the wane. Such openness came to be Smith's calling card throughout the tour of England. He looked everyone in the eye and said what he thought. (By early 2004, Klusener was back in the side, but Smith's authority was no longer in question.)

During the one-day games in England there were mutterings about Smith's "closed-face" technique and propensity to play across the line, but he soon silenced the doubters, gloriously. The series was not yet halfway through and England were sick of the sight of him and still trying to work out any plan at all. He is leg-side dominant, unlike many other left-handers, but with an ability to cut the ball well outside off stump. Throughout most of the series, England's fielders in the slips waited in vain; by not opening the face he made them redundant.

Only one thing remains for Smith himself to work out. His casual attitude towards sledging and on-field aggression is an anachronism, a throwback to the late 1980s before match referees were brought in to clean up the game. Rightly, he wants to emulate the success of the Australians. He can do it without imitating their worst excesses. If he can find it in himself to pursue his goals alongside his wider responsibilities to the game, he can be the leader that South Africa and international cricket need.

Opposite: V. V. S. Laxman eyes another big score against Australia during the Fourth Test at Sydney, January, 2004. He made 178. *Picture by Nick Laham, Getty Images.*

PART TWO

World View

WORLD CRICKET IN 2003

Back to Bradman

SIMON WILDE

For much of 2003, international cricket followed a predictable pattern, with teams divided into three categories. Australia stood alone in the first as undisputed champions, and Zimbabwe and Bangladesh in the third as an axis of weevils. The other seven sat in the middle, all seemingly capable of beating one another on their day.

The likelihood was that if Australia, Zimbabwe or Bangladesh were involved, the series would be lopsided. Australia faced both of them at home and had no difficulty completing their seventh and eighth clean sweeps under Steve Waugh.

However, by the end of an engrossing Australia–India series which finished tied at 1–1 in the first week of 2004, the picture looked more confused. A vibrant Indian side led unwaveringly by Sourav Ganguly came closer to winning a Test series on Australian soil than any visiting side since Australia became the dominant team in world cricket – a reign that really dates back to their win in the West Indies in 1995.

Waugh, the game's senior statesman, went into international retirement praising India as the equal of any batting side he had seen. Meanwhile, the Border–Gavaskar Trophy – which India retained by dint of victory at home to Australia in 2001 – appeared to have emerged as Test cricket's premier event, a claim no observer of recent Ashes series could dispute. In 14 Tests between the sides since 1996, the score now stood at 6–6.

Worthy runners-up to Australia at the World Cup, India had the right to claim to be the world's second-best team, though further supporting evidence was thin. India played remarkably little cricket in 2003, including just two Tests outside the Australia series, both at home to New Zealand and both drawn. They won no one-day tournament either. Among the failures was

TEST MATCHES IN 2003

Team	*Tests*	*Won*	*Lost*	*Drawn*	*% won*	*% lost*	*% drawn*
Australia	12	8	3	1	**66.66**	25.00	8.33
Pakistan	8	5	1	2	**62.50**	12.50	25.00
South Africa	12	7	3	2	**58.33**	25.00	16.66
England	13	7	3	3	**53.84**	23.07	23.07
West Indies	10	3	5	2	**30.00**	50.00	20.00
India	5	1	1	3	**20.00**	20.00	60.00
Sri Lanka	7	1	1	5	**14.28**	14.28	71.42
New Zealand	6	0	1	5	**0.00**	16.66	83.33
Zimbabwe	6	0	5	1	**0.00**	83.33	16.66
Bangladesh	9	0	9	0	**0.00**	100.00	0.00
Totals	44	32	32	12	72.72	72.72	27.27

another defeat in a final with Australia, in Kolkata, during a triangular also involving New Zealand. Australia, who extended their record sequence of one-day wins under Ricky Ponting's captaincy to 21 in the Caribbean before dead-rubber syndrome and fatigue took hold and they lost three in a row, won the most Tests of any side in the year, their tally of eight boosted by the four demolitions of Bangladesh and Zimbabwe.

After feeble World Cup showings, South Africa and Pakistan regrouped well. South Africa were lifted by the precocious leadership of Graeme Smith, who led from the front in every way after taking over from Shaun Pollock, aged just 22. Opening the batting, he scored a mountain of runs in aggressive style, and was forever geeing up his men in the field if they looked like drifting. His manner suggested that at last South Africa might be ready to shake off their tag as chokers. Smith led them to a 2–2 draw in England and also to victories over Bangladesh away and West Indies at home. The only blemish was a narrow 1–0 defeat in Pakistan; even there, Smith's men came close to drawing a brutally fought series.

Pakistan also turned to a new captain after the World Cup, Rashid Latif replacing Waqar Younis, although within months he was removed in favour of Inzamam-ul-Haq after a disciplinary breach. With Yousuf Youhana deputising once, Pakistan got through four Test captains in the year, which even by their standards was a good effort.

But by following home victories over Bangladesh and South Africa with another in New Zealand, thanks to a brilliant spell of reverse swing by Shoaib Akhtar, Pakistan enjoyed an impressive second half of the year. A crowd of 12,000 (unusual in a country where Test crowds are usually paltry) watched them hold out for a draw against South Africa in Faisalabad to seal the series.

England, the busiest team with 13 Tests, won seven times but, like Australia, got four of them against Zimbabwe and Bangladesh. The way they trounced South Africa in a one-day final at Lord's and twice fought back to level the Test series against them promised much, but the optimism evaporated in both forms of the game in the Sri Lankan heat. Rather than going forward or back, England – under both Nasser Hussain and his successor Michael Vaughan – seemed to be treading water.

TEST MATCHES IN 2003

(excluding Zimbabwe and Bangladesh matches)

Team	*Tests*	*Won*	*Lost*	*Drawn*	*% won*	*% lost*	*% drawn*
South Africa.	10	5	3	2	**50.00**	30.00	20.00
Australia	8	4	3	1	**50.00**	37.50	12.50
Pakistan.	5	2	1	2	**40.00**	20.00	40.00
England.	9	3	3	3	**33.33**	33.33	33.33
West Indies	8	2	5	1	**25.00**	62.50	12.50
India.	5	1	1	3	**20.00**	20.00	60.00
Sri Lanka	7	1	1	5	**14.28**	14.28	71.42
New Zealand	6	0	1	5	**0.00**	16.66	83.33
Totals	29	18	18	11	62.06	62.06	37.93

The same can be said of New Zealand and Sri Lanka. New Zealand, the only established side not to win a Test, enjoyed qualified success in Asia, where they fought tenaciously to draw Test series in Sri Lanka and India. They also won a low-scoring triangular one-day event hosted by Sri Lanka, who seemed to be drifting under the new split captaincy of Hashan Tillekeratne in Tests and Marvan Atapattu in one-dayers – at least until they beat England just before Christmas.

West Indies continued to struggle, despite displays of individual brilliance with the bat, many from Brian Lara in a second spell as captain, and one monumental team effort to score 418 to beat Australia in Antigua. Lara said the team would want to forget 2003.

Even Bangladesh and Zimbabwe found slim cause for hope. Both came within a whisker of a rare Test win: Pakistan had only one wicket to spare when they scraped home against Bangladesh in Multan, while the last West Indies pair, Ridley Jacobs and Fidel Edwards, survived 12 overs to deny Zimbabwe victory in Harare. Zimbabwe had lost their previous 11 Tests and by the end of 2003 Bangladesh's losing streak stood at 20 – sequences that date back to their last series against each other.

The intensity of the schedule continued to cause concern, with boards using their commitment to the ICC Test Championship to fill the calendar. Despite a three-month hiatus for the World Cup, 44 Tests were staged. To cram them in, back-to-back Tests (separated by two or three days) became standard fare. The four-match Australia–India series spanned 34 days, and England and South Africa played five Tests in 47 days. The longer series tended to produce the more compelling cricket and the England–South Africa contest, the only five-match series of the year, was a wonderful advertisement for an endangered product.

Matches were even played out of traditional seasons, including the first-ever Tests in Australia's tropical north, in July. The relentless programme took heaviest toll of fast bowlers, many of whom spent long periods injured. England fielded 11 different new-ball combinations in their 13 Tests. Burnout contributed to Australia's three defeats: all three came in the second of back-to-back Tests, and two followed long spells in the field in the first games because Waugh had enforced the follow-on. Brilliant though it was for West Indies to score 418 to win in Antigua, it was hard to imagine such a thing happening against Australia in normal circumstances (whatever they now were). When India beat them in Adelaide, Australia for various reasons were missing Glenn McGrath, Brett Lee and Shane Warne.

The ICC ordered an inquiry into burnout that was due to report in 2004. But there were several other factors favouring batsmen: good pitches, improved bat technology and the ineffectiveness of the Kookaburra ball once it lost its shine and hardness. All that said, there was a shortage of top-class fast bowlers, and the upshot was batsmen making hay as rarely before.

Including the Test record 380 Matthew Hayden took off Zimbabwe in Perth, there were 14 double-centuries (three by Ricky Ponting, two each by Graeme Smith, Rahul Dravid and Brian Lara) and 99 centuries in all. South Africa's 682 for six at Lord's was their highest-ever score and their 658 for nine against West Indies at Durban the best by any side in South Africa. Australia's 735 for six at Perth was their best at home; New Zealand's 630 for six at Mohali their highest overseas. Runs had not been so cheap since Bradman's day.

It was not just the volume of runs that was striking, but the speed at which they came. Scoring at a rate of 4.08 runs per over, Waugh's Australia beat their own annual record of 3.99 in 2002, ahead of South Africa, who managed a creditable 3.54, their third successive annual increase.

South Africa opened games with first-day scores of 445 for three, 398 for one and 368 for three, but such was the pace of the game that it was hard to know what score might be safe: Australia scored 556 and lost to India

ONE-DAY INTERNATIONALS IN 2003

Team	*ODIs*	*Won*	*Lost*	*Tied*	*NR*	*% won*	*% lost*
Australia	35	30	5	0	0	**85.71**	14.28
Pakistan	33	21	11	0	1	**65.62**	34.37
India	28	16	10	0	2	**61.53**	38.46
South Africa	23	13	8	1	1	**59.09**	36.36
England	25	13	11	0	1	**54.16**	45.83
Sri Lanka	26	13	12	1	0	**50.00**	46.15
West Indies	21	10	10	0	1	**50.00**	50.00
New Zealand	29	12	16	0	1	**42.85**	57.14
Kenya	12	4	8	0	0	**33.33**	66.66
Zimbabwe	23	7	14	0	2	**33.33**	66.66
Holland	6	1	5	0	0	**16.66**	83.33
Canada	6	1	5	0	0	**16.66**	83.33
Bangladesh	21	0	20	0	1	**0.00**	100.00
Namibia	6	0	6	0	0	**0.00**	100.00
Totals	147	141	141	1	5		

For one-day internationals, the % won and lost excludes no results and ties.

in Adelaide while South Africa, after totalling 484, were still easily beaten by England at The Oval. First-innings crease occupation appeared a forgotten gambit.

Hayden's colossal 380 was scored at 87 runs per 100 balls, easily the fastest Test triple-century for which balls faced are known. His tempo for the entire year (75 per 100 balls) matched Bradman's at Leeds in 1930. During the West Indian tour of southern Africa, Lara was on course for the second-fastest Test double-century when he fell for 191 to his 203rd delivery against the hapless Zimbabweans in Bulawayo, while Shivnarine Chanderpaul scored Test cricket's third-fastest hundred off 69 balls against Australia in his native Guyana.

So spare a thought for the poor bowlers. Those with the miserly streak of a McGrath, Warne, Pollock or Muttiah Muralitharan were in short supply, and seamers needed a working knowledge of reverse swing, just as a spinner needed a good wrong 'un, to prosper. A full report on each of the top 40 players in world cricket is in the next section, pages 78–95.

New order? India gave Australia a fright and made a strong claim to be the world's second-best side. Irfan Pathan, a new arrival in the team, feels good.
Picture by Mark Dadswell, Getty Images.

The ICC got tougher on indiscipline. An ugly spat between McGrath and Ramnaresh Sarwan in Antigua appeared the catalyst. McGrath was seen as chief culprit, and Hayden and Waugh also had an exchange with Lara, reinforcing an impression that the Australians might be the best cricketers but not the best sports. The Australian board issued a general warning to its players, who bound themselves to a document concerning the spirit of cricket.

The first indication of the ICC's tougher stance came when referee Mike Procter handed Rashid Latif a ban of five one-day internationals for claiming a catch against Bangladesh that plainly went to ground, an incident that contributed to Latif's subsequent removal from the Pakistan captaincy before a series against South Africa that proved particularly fractious: Clive Lloyd, the referee, issued an unprecedented string of bans.

ICC WORLD TEST CHAMPIONSHIP

(As at January 20, 2004)

		Matches/series	Points	Rating
1	Australia	40	5016	125
2	South Africa	42	4731	113
3	Pakistan	30	3060	102
4	England	45	4548	101
5	India	36	3587	100
6	New Zealand	26	2587	100
7	Sri Lanka	30	2881	96
8	West Indies	42	3441	82
9	Zimbabwe	27	1506	56
10	Bangladesh	28	0	0

ICC WORLD ONE-DAY CHAMPIONSHIP

(As at December 31, 2003)

		Matches	Points	Rating
1	Australia	38	5163	136
2	South Africa	39	4600	118
3	Pakistan	45	5017	111
4	Sri Lanka	36	3844	107
5	England	27	2863	106
6	India	35	3662	105
7	West Indies	28	2829	101
8	New Zealand	33	3192	97
9	Zimbabwe	28	1915	68
10	Kenya	16	451	28
11	Bangladesh	25	0	0

If the schedule was tough on players, it was unforgiving on the elite panel of umpires. The ICC acknowledged the problem by expanding the panel from eight to 11 in April 2003, but it went back down to nine early in 2004.

Forty-nine players made Test debuts: ten of them for England, eight for Pakistan and seven for West Indies. Australia, who introduced only two newcomers in the first three years of the millennium, added Brad Williams and Nathan Bracken. Devon Smith of West Indies and Ed Smith of England took the number of Smiths to play Test cricket to 27, leaving the Joneses – who acquired a tenth member in Richard Jones of New Zealand – far behind. A 28th Smith (but the first Dwayne) came on board for West Indies in the first week of 2004 and celebrated with a century in 93 balls. But that is part of next year's story...

Simon Wilde is cricket correspondent of the Sunday Times, *London.*

Opposite: On top... again. Australian players celebrate winning the World Cup after beating India in the final. *Picture by Graham Morris.*

PART THREE

The Players

The Wisden Forty

The Wisden Forty, including the Leading Cricketer in the World, have been selected by Wisden *as the world's top players on the basis of their class and form shown in all cricket during the calendar year 2003. The selections were made in consultation with many of the game's most experienced writers and commentators. In the end, though, they were* Wisden's *choices, guided by the statistics but not governed by them. The selection panel are no more infallible than any other selectors.*

THE LEADING CRICKETER IN THE WORLD, 2003

Ricky Ponting

GIDEON HAIGH

To concerns about the demoralising and deadening effects of the grind of international cricket, there could be no more effective riposte than Ricky Ponting. Too many games? Too much travel? Bring 'em on! In 2003, tackling every challenge with unfailing enterprise, he set the tempo of the world's best Test and one-day teams – and, in Australia's undefeated World Cup campaign, the tactics too.

Ponting's calendar year featured 11 hundreds, five among 1,154 one-day runs at 46.16, and six in 1,503 Test runs at 100.20, including three that became doubles. Yet as impressive as his run-pile's height was the energy with which it was scaled. Ponting hits his attacking shots hard, his defensive strokes barely less hard, and runs every run as though it might be his last. Even at his most restrained and responsible, he impresses one as barely contained, brimful of confidence, ready any moment to bust loose.

For almost its entirety, the same has been thought of Ponting's career; it has been hampered not by doubts of his ability but by certainties. Born in Tasmania's Prospect, he quickly became it. His grandmother dressed four-year-old Ricky in a T-shirt bearing the legend: "Inside this shirt is an Australian Test cricketer". He had his first equipment deal with Kookaburra at the age of 12, represented his state at 17 and his country at 20; his maiden Test hundred at Headingley in July 1997, when he was 22, suggested not so much a coming man as an arriving and disembarking one.

For the next four years, however, Ponting's career was of the coming-and-going kind. There was more coming than going, as a Test average a tick over 40 from his first 45 Tests suggests, but questions remained about his staying power, except when it was devoted to staying out late: commotions in nightclubs in Calcutta and Sydney tarnished his reputation. Thirty subsequent Tests in which he has averaged 79.73 have answered every interrogatory, plus a few not even asked. His restless cricket intelligence forced him to the forefront of candidates to succeed Steve Waugh as

Ricky Ponting

Photograph: Hamish Blair/Getty Images.

Australian captain; his marriage to Rianna Cantor, an arts/law graduate from University of Wollongong, provided domestic serenity.

Few issues in Australian cricket have caused such public discontent as the cultivation of separate Test and one-day teams. When Waugh's limited-overs mandate was rescinded, one Sydney newspaper ran mug shots of the country's selectors beneath the headline "Wanted: For Incompetence". Some, doubtless, wished their prejudices justified when Ponting was appointed Waugh's one-day successor in February 2002; he did not oblige them. The worst mishap when Australia began their World Cup defence in February 2003 befell them before they took the field, and Ponting so skilfully contained the morale damage from the Shane Warne drug drama that Warne was barely missed. And, with 114 in the first Super Six game against Sri Lanka and 140 not out in the final against India, Ponting was himself Australia's highest scorer of the tournament.

As if to make his own statement about the relationship between the game's two forms, Ponting promptly set about bringing to Test cricket some of his one-day vim. Three Tests against West Indies yielded 523 at 130.75. Series against Bangladesh and Zimbabwe then warmed him up for a rematch with India, who had had Australia's and his measure just under three years earlier: while again more than matching Australia, India had this time to go round

Ponting rather than through him. He sold his wicket not just dearly but, with 242 in Adelaide and 257 in Melbourne, downright exorbitantly.

While Ponting's appointment as Waugh's Test successor was welcomed for restoring the five and one-day leaderships to a single custodian, it reasserted some other old Australian cricket values too: that a team's most complete batsman should bat at No. 3 and that the captain is chosen from a nation's best 11 cricketers. Departures from both customs have been countenanced in recent years – not without sound reason – but Ponting seems to fit as snugly into the traditions of his office as any of his antecedents. And, as for "the grind", Ponting seems quite content for it to continue – preferably with Australia doing most of the grinding.

THE FORTY

MICHAEL BEVAN — Australia

This was just another year in the life of the world's greatest one-day batsman. There was no sign of a Test recall, so Bevan contented himself with giving lesson after lesson in the art of finishing. Most notable were two eerily certain innings to redeem apparently lost causes against England and New Zealand in the World Cup, when he coaxed unprecedented performances out of his tail-end partner Bichel. Almost every innings Bevan played was an imperious study in risk management and, with almost half his innings marked by an asterisk, his average moved back above 55. With the pyjamas on, he was entirely without peer.

2003: 31 one-day internationals: 784 runs @ 65.33.

ANDY BICHEL — Australia

In a team of celebrities, Bichel was an unobtrusive and unpretentious figure, but a winner none the less. His straight-talking seam-up got going with four for 18 in the first VB Series final against England, and after three games in the World Cup, he had 12 wickets at the staggering average of 2.75. But Bichel was knocking on the all-rounder's door too. With Bevan he added 73 against England (having already taken seven for 20), then 97 against New Zealand to transform defeat into victory. An innings of 71 in the Bridgetown Test confirmed Bichel could hold a bat, while every one of his 32 Test wickets was celebrated with the enthusiasm of an ordinary bloke who could not quite believe he was wearing the baggy green.

2003: 9 Tests: 233 runs @ 23.30; 32 wickets @ 33.25.
28 ODI: 243 runs @ 34.71; 38 wickets @ 26.05.

MARK BOUCHER — South Africa

South Africa's obvious choice as wicket-keeper/batsman since February 1998, Boucher remained one of the most familiar – and combative – faces on the international circuit. Once he had got over his failure to score the single against Sri Lanka that would have spared South Africa their humiliating World Cup exit on a rainy night in Durban, Boucher got to work on another productive, consistent year with bat and gloves. He averaged over 30 in both forms of the game, and batted as high as No. 5 in the one-day side; the epitaph "c Boucher b Ntini", meanwhile, was one of the most common scorebook entries in world cricket. In early January 2004, he became the third-most successful wicket-keeper in Test history.

2003: 12 Tests: 520 runs @ 32.50; 38 catches, 5 stumpings.
23 ODI: 372 runs @ 31.00; 42 catches, 1 stumping.

RAHUL DRAVID — India

Just when it looked like the man nicknamed the Wall could not scale any greater heights after a run-laden 2002, Dravid took his batting to another level. It is not easy to stand out in the Indian top six – who by the end of the year were established as cricket's answer to Real Madrid's footballing *galacticos* – but Dravid began India's unusually light Test year with 222 and 73 against New Zealand at Ahmedabad, and finished with a Man of the Series performance in Australia, where his tally of 305 for once out at Adelaide was one of the all-time great performances. Few batsmen anywhere could match his blend of patience, elegance, strokeplay and modesty. Through it all, he remained the backbone of the Indian line-up, as five unbeaten innings out of ten plus an average of over 63 at the World Cup – despite the burden of keeping wicket – confirmed.

2003: 5 Tests: 803 runs @ 100.37.
23 ODI (19 as wicket-keeper): 623 runs @ 41.53. 19 catches as keeper, 2 stumpings.

STEPHEN FLEMING — New Zealand

For most of his career, Fleming had been a legside-oriented David Gower – left-handed, upright, elegant, but with too many failures amid the aesthetics. (Maybe it's something to do with them both being born on April 1.) By the start of the year, however, he had devised a plan to make himself more productively Goweresque, subtly adjusting the position of his top hand to allow more freedom through the off side. A spanking unbeaten 134 against South Africa in the World Cup provided instant reward; scores of 274 and 69, both unbeaten, in the Colombo Test showed that the change was no flash in the one-day pan. There were still failures – five of his 11 Test innings ended in single figures – but 192 against Pakistan at Hamilton suggested he was giving it away less easily than in the past. In a disappointing year for New Zealand, his captaincy and slip catching were as imperturbable as ever.

2003: 6 Tests: 631 runs @ 70.11.
23 ODI: 681 runs @ 34.05.

ANDREW FLINTOFF — England

This was the year people began to take Flintoff seriously. After missing the Ashes with a groin strain, Flintoff was the World Cup's most economical bowler, while his performances with the bat during the English summer were rarely less than bar-emptying. Three consecutive match awards in Bangladesh confirmed that he could play pyjama cricket in his sleep. But it was as a Test batsman that he really opened eyes. A free-hitting 142 in a lost cause at Lord's was followed by a pair of fifties at Headingley and a murderous 95 at The Oval, this time to set up victory. In Sri Lanka, after another bout of subcontinental soul-searching, he added a more subtle shade to his palette, hitting a cathartic 77 during the calamity in Colombo and playing Muttiah Muralitharan with more care than his reputation would suggest. His bang-it-in seam-up remained heartfelt but one-dimensional. Often he was England's best bowler, but rarely had the figures to prove it. A freakish attack of butter-fingers among his team-mates was one explanation; an inability to move his stock delivery away from the right-hander was another. But his value on pitches that demanded graft was underlined by nine wickets at 24.55 in Sri Lanka. By the end of the year, an England team without Flintoff in it seemed unthinkable. *See also Five Cricketers of the Year, page 62.*

2003: 8 Tests: 566 runs @ 40.42; 19 wickets @ 42.78.
20 ODI: 631 runs @ 45.07; 30 wickets @ 18.60.

HERSCHELLE GIBBS — South Africa

Almost everyone got blamed for South Africa's World Cup farrago – from captain to coach to twelfth man to mathematician – but Gibbs was entirely exempt. While his team-mates were weighed down by history and expectation, he floated through the tournament like a butterfly, but with the ability to sting new-ball bowlers with his irrepressible strokeplay. Apart from a humbling spell as he acclimatised to English conditions, it was the same all year. Gibbs had always had the tools; now, by and large, he knew where and when to use them, as he showed with 179 on the first day of the Test series against England at Edgbaston. Yet even that barnstormer could not match his bewitching 228 off 240 balls against Pakistan at Cape Town. To most observers these were calculated, statement-making attacks. To Gibbs they were just hits in the park, the most natural thing in the world – as was his consistently brilliant fielding. And though his talk-first-think-later interviews continued to rub some people up the wrong way, few begrudged Gibbs his status as one of cricket's great entertainers.

2003: 12 Tests: 1,156 runs @ 64.22.
21 ODI: 693 runs @ 40.76.

ADAM GILCHRIST — Australia

Gilchrist went into 2004 in the middle of the biggest slump of his Test career – but, when it comes to the best keeper/batsman in the history of the game, these things are relative. He still averaged nearly 60, and his strike-rate of 93 was miles clear of anyone else. For once, however, most of his best work was done in the shadows. His 94-ball century against England at Sydney hardly registered amid the Waugh fever; ditto his 84-baller against Zimbabwe in Hayden's match at Perth. Similarly, his tone-setting assault in the World Cup final was lost when Ponting went berserk. It was a dismissal – his own – that brought Gilchrist the most headlines, when he sportingly walked in the semi-final against Sri Lanka. He still held more Test catches than anyone else.

2003: 12 Tests: 714 runs @ 59.50; 43 catches, 7 stumpings.
31 ODI: 1,098 runs @ 37.86; 53 catches, 3 stumpings.

JASON GILLESPIE — Australia

With Warne suspended and McGrath injured for long periods, the most deadly support act in world cricket had to become the main man in 2003. Gillespie grew a wild mullet for the occasion but, despite his flair, skill, sweat and more thought than might be obvious, he could not quite locate the door marked "greatness". He was injured quite a lot himself, perhaps because of all the effort involved, and missed most of the World Cup, though not before he had hoodwinked Tendulkar quite gloriously. He could not find an answer to India's batting riches later in the year, but came closer than any of his team-mates. As usual with Gillespie, there were few stand-out performances, just consistent, relentless, bat-jarring excellence – and the perpetual absence of just deserts as another sucker failed to nick that ripping, snarling leg-cutter.

2003: 10 Tests: 145 runs @ 29.00; 41 wickets @ 22.51.
11 ODI: 7 runs (not dismissed); 18 wickets @ 17.61.

MATTHEW HAYDEN — Australia

For Hayden, the last three years have been one long, largely indistinguishable orgy of run-scoring. But one innings ensured that 2003 will always stand out – the Test-record 380 against Zimbabwe at Perth, which fulfilled Steve Waugh's alarmingly prescient remark a year earlier that Hayden would one day pass Brian Lara's 375. Yet when he began the year with a series of unfulfilled starts in the World Cup, it seemed the biggest bully in world cricket had lost some of his ruthlessness. As if. His conversion rate in Tests – five of his eight fifties were turned into hundreds – was indicative of a man still desperately hungry to make up for the lost years of his early international career. For cowering, panting bowlers, it was like facing a batting machine.

2003: 12 Tests: 1,312 runs @ 77.17.
32 ODI: 1,037 runs @ 39.88.

INZAMAM-UL-HAQ — Pakistan

Usually such a reliable and consistent player, Inzamam-ul-Haq blew hot and cold. His World Cup was a disaster – he lost more pounds (23) in a much-publicised pre-tournament diet than he made runs (19) – and he was cast into the wilderness. He returned five months later and hit a superb 138 not out on his home ground at Multan in a face-saving one-wicket win over Bangladesh. Having been out of the squad three weeks earlier, Inzamam was made stand-in captain two days later, and got the job officially barely a fortnight after that; the prodigal son's rehabilitation was complete. By the end of the year, the weight – of body and runs – was back, his Test average had never been higher, and he was expertly shepherding Pakistan to a series victory against New Zealand at Wellington with his old mate Yousuf Youhana.

2003: 7 Tests: 558 runs @ 62.00.
18 ODI: 418 runs @ 34.83.

JACQUES KALLIS — South Africa

For much of the year it was impossible to separate Kallis's public persona from his private. After South Africa lost the final of the one-day series at Lord's, Kallis flew home to Cape Town to be with his father, Henry, who was suffering from cancer and died soon after. It made Kallis's performances in the tournament – at one stage he had hit 329 runs for once out – all the more remarkable, especially after a wretched World Cup. He rejoined the England tour in time for the Third Test and, although his batting was solid rather than spectacular, he still finished the year averaging nearly 50, not to mention nine wickets in the win at Headingley. A riot of centuries against West Indies in the 2003-04 series indicated he was back to his very best. His slip fielding remained world-class.

2003: 8 Tests: 698 runs @ 49.85; 19 wickets @ 38.42.
17 ODI: 595 runs @ 54.09; 14 wickets @ 43.42.

MICHAEL KASPROWICZ — Australia

Restricted almost exclusively to domestic cricket by the excellence of the Australian pace attack, Kasprowicz had the energy, enthusiasm and class to shine in both the Pura Cup and the County Championship. First, he finished the 2002-03 Australian season with 48 first-class wickets – second only to leg-spinner MacGill – for Queensland. Then he flew north to play for Glamorgan, where his tally of 77 Championship scalps – second only to another leg-spinner, Mushtaq Ahmed – included two separate innings hauls of nine wickets against Durham. When Australia did find room for him, his bustling, nippy seamers returned comfortably the most economical analysis on either side during a TVS Cup game with India that yielded 633 runs. Batsmen under-estimated Kasprowicz at their peril.

2003: 2 ODI: did not bat; 2 wickets @ 32.50.

GARY KIRSTEN — South Africa

With the possible exception of his captain, Graeme Smith, Kirsten bore the hardest nose in a hard-nosed team. Still full of left-handed pragmatism and common sense, he oozed competitiveness, particularly during a magnificent, match-winning 130 at Headingley which, for sheer tenacity, put even Smith's twin double-hundreds in the shade. His public dressing-down of a skittish Gibbs at The Oval was wonderfully indicative of his waste-not-want-not attitude to sport. Supposedly in the twilight of his career, Kirsten was more productive than ever: he made more hundreds, and had a higher average, than in any other calendar year. You might not have paid to watch him, but you would certainly have paid to have him in your team. *See also Five Cricketers of the Year, page 64.*

2003: 8 Tests: 889 runs @ 74.08.
6 ODI: 186 runs @ 62.00.

ANIL KUMBLE — India

It was the biggest turnaround of the year. Kumble spent most of the time in the shadow of Harbhajan Singh – he hardly featured in India's run to the World Cup final – and his career seemed to be winding down gently. But Harbhajan lost form, then got injured and, by the end of 2003, Kumble was India's supersub, gunning down Australians by the dozen – and getting the respect that had been absent for much of his 14 years in international cricket. He added more variations, of pace especially, to his splice-rattling top-spinners, and his control was magnificent. At Adelaide, his bowling was overshadowed by Dravid and Laxman, but without Kumble there would have been no famous victory. That match took his tally of wickets in Test wins to 176; no other Indian had even 100.

2003: 4 Tests: 20 runs @ 5.00; 21 wickets @ 36.42.
10 ODI: 66 runs @ 16.50; 13 wickets @ 25.76.

JUSTIN LANGER — Australia

It did not matter to Langer that he spent much of the year in the ample shadow of his opening partner and buddy, Hayden. The archetypal team man, and one of Steve Waugh's most fervent disciples, he simply carried on scoring runs in the selfless cut-and-thrust style he had adopted ever since his Test return at The Oval in 2001. In four Tests in the West Indies he averaged 69. Then, after failing to cash in against Bangladesh and Zimbabwe, he immediately repaid his critics with 121 at Brisbane against India. As the perfect foil to the bigger, brasher Hayden, his role in the team – low-key but loyal – went beyond mere statistics.

2003: 12 Tests: 824 runs @ 41.20.

> "Whatever else changes in cricket, the Don is big business."
>
> David Rayvern Allen on Cricketana, page 1599.

BRIAN LARA — West Indies

Two stats summed up the unique burden that Lara faced: at Johannesburg in December, he became the first man in history to have scored two double-hundreds in Test defeats, and by the end of the year he had scored over 3,700 Test runs when his team lost; no one else anywhere in the world had even made 3,000. He had more on his plate than anyone: star batsman and, later, captain of a poor West Indies side, with an almost tangible expectation every time he walked to the crease. Yet he batted like a man without a care in the world. The warning shot came right at the start: 116 against South Africa in the World Cup opener told everyone that, after his mystery illness, Lara was back. From there, it was one long purple patch. Given the captaincy for the home series with Australia, he fell only 13 runs shy of his miracle series in 1998-99. The Lara calling-card – big hundreds, made at high speed – was there, but perhaps his most important innings was a delicious, unbeaten 80 that won the series with Sri Lanka, when he again had Muralitharan in his pocket. In that, as in so much else, Lara was entirely out on his own.

2003: 10 Tests: 1,344 runs @ 74.66.
21 ODI: 888 runs @ 46.73; no wicket for 15.

V. V. S. LAXMAN — India

At the start of the year, Laxman was not good enough for India's World Cup squad; by the end, as he tormented his favourite victims Australia once more, he was one of the richest, purest sights in world cricket.

Brought back into the fold in October, Laxman meant business from the off: two unbeaten, unusually disciplined innings saved the Mohali Test against New Zealand, then a beautiful 148 at Adelaide helped win one in sensational circumstances. Australian bowlers wondered just where to bowl to him: like Viv Richards, he seemed to be able to choose where he wanted to hit any delivery; everybody else felt like they had been touched by something Very Very Special. And with every wristily sleek stroke the question grew ever more perplexing: how on earth had Dinesh Mongia played in the World Cup ahead of him?

2003: 5 Tests: 595 runs @ 85.00.
8 ODI: 232 runs @ 29.00.

BRETT LEE **Australia**

The sight of Lee steaming in to bowl during the World Cup captured perfectly the panache, adventure and will to win of the Australians. In three Super Six games and a semi-final, Lee took 14 wickets – and never once failed to entertain. He dismantled Sri Lanka's top order twice, finished off New Zealand with a scorching spell of five for three, and claimed a hat-trick – only Australia's third in one-day internationals – against Kenya. His competition haul of 22 wickets was second only to Vaas of Sri Lanka; his calendar tally of 46 in all one-day internationals second to none, and equal to Muralitharan. In Tests, however, he did lose some of his edge: with the old ball against top batsmen on shirtfronts, he had little to offer. In bursts, he remained one of the most destructive fast bowlers on the planet.

2003: 10 Tests: 141 runs @ 17.62; 38 wickets @ 35.02.
24 ODI: 85 runs @ 10.62; 46 wickets @ 20.13.

DARREN LEHMANN **Australia**

His achievements were sandwiched by disgrace and disappointment, but Lehmann's prolific form with the bat compensated in part for years of thumb-twiddling on the periphery of the Australian team. In January 2003, he was banned for five one-day internationals after a racist expletive in the dressing-room was overheard during a game with Sri Lanka at Brisbane. He returned contrite and refreshed and set about booking what looked like a permanent place in Australia's powerful batting line-up: he pummelled West Indies – including a cathartic first Test hundred, five years after his debut – and Bangladesh, and averaged nearly 52 in one-day internationals, where his tidy left-arm spin was an unexpected bonus. But his progress was halted in November by an Achilles injury, and the emergence of Simon Katich and Michael Clarke as middle-order rivals meant that Lehmann ended the year with his career shrouded in uncertainty once more.

2003: 7 Tests: 670 runs @ 74.44; 5 wickets @ 24.80.
16 ODI: 467 runs @ 51.88; 10 wickets @ 20.90.

STUART MacGILL **Australia**

As well as providing respite for batsmen everywhere, the Shane Warne drugs scandal gave MacGill his biggest break yet in a frustrating career. Limited to 18 Test caps in five years by the presence of the only man in the world who bowled more beguiling leg-spin than he did, MacGill got to work immediately, taking 57 wickets in 11 Tests and fading only when the twinkle-toed Indians used their feet to devastating effect. At that point, Australia badly missed Warne's ability to attack without offering regular four-balls. The highlights of a year in which only South Africa's Ntini claimed more Test scalps were a nine-wicket haul in the win at Bridgetown, and three successive five-fors against Bangladesh. Easy pickings or not, MacGill had waited too long to care.

2003: 11 Tests: 10 runs @ 1.11; 57 wickets @ 29.61.

GLENN McGRATH — Australia

After ten years of exploiting it with his peerlessly metronomic fast-medium, McGrath suddenly found himself in a corridor of uncertainty. Injury meant he played in only four of Australia's 12 Tests; in those his strike-rate was a fraction below 100, and his only notable contribution was taking the grumpy-old-man act a bit too far with Ramnaresh Sarwan in Antigua. McGrath's contribution to the World Cup was more worthy, however. His surgical dismantling of improper Namibian techniques was a predictable mismatch. More importantly, it took him just five balls to win the battle of the giants with Tendulkar in the final. How Australia could have done with him when they met the Indians again later in the year.

2003: 4 Tests: 19 runs @ 19.00; 8 wickets @ 35.25.
19 ODI: 6 runs (not dismissed); 29 wickets @ 19.65.

DAMIEN MARTYN — Australia

It was not so much his Test returns that made this a memorable year for Martyn – every one of his nine innings reached 20, none passed 66 – but his part in Australia's World Cup-winning machine. Martyn hit 323 runs in the competition at 64.60, and saved the best until last, compiling an underrated, unbeaten 88 off 84 balls in the final against India and adding an unbroken 234 with Ponting. He was batting with a broken finger, and an operation soon afterwards meant he was unable to pick up a bat again for two months. But he was soon back in the one-day runs, scoring 100, 61 not out and 61 against the hosts in the one-day tournament in India.

2003: 6 Tests: 339 runs @ 42.37; no wicket for 57.
26 ODI: 878 runs @ 58.53; 1 wicket @ 78.00.

MUTTIAH MURALITHARAN — Sri Lanka

It was a disappointing year for Sri Lanka but, for Muralitharan, 2003 was just another step on the road to becoming one of the great phenomena of cricket history. Not everyone approved of his controversial off-spinning action, and the whispers grew louder when his "doosra" (the off-spinner's googly) wrought havoc against England. But there was no escaping the fact that Murali – manic eyes gleaming, mouth open wide at the point of delivery – remained a uniquely absorbing sight. Without him, Sri Lanka would barely have been half the side. He took nearly 44% of their Test wickets, and conceded just 1.80 runs an over to go with his scarcely believable one-day international economy-rate of 3.34. But it was his desire to remain one step ahead of the opposition that underlined his status as one of the all-time greats. When England visited before Christmas, he hit them with a series of unpickable, big-turning wrong 'uns – a masterly response to series defeats in 2000-01 and 2002. Even England's most experienced batsmen said they had never seen anything like it. In the professional era, Murali remained that rarest of breeds – an entertainer, and a highly successful one at that.

2003: 7 Tests: 113 runs @ 16.14; 48 wickets @ 17.68.
24 ODI: 72 runs @ 6.54; 46 wickets @ 15.89.

MUSHTAQ AHMED **Pakistan**

Eyebrows were raised around the counties when Sussex signed Mushtaq Ahmed, aged 32 and in the wilderness with Pakistan; hearts sank everywhere but Hove once he got to work with his leg-breaks and googlies. His competitive instincts were re-vitalised by a tantalising sterling-for-scalps deal. And, arms whirring, seam buzzing in the air, Mushtaq was back to his most mischievous, and the county set – who still handle mystery spin like soap in the bath – had no answer. He was the dominant figure of the domestic summer, and the first man to take 100 first-class wickets since 1998. (Nobody else in the first division even exceeded 60.) More importantly, he was the key factor in Sussex finally winning the County Championship for the first time. Mushtaq got his international recall as a result, and, even though he found South Africa a much tougher proposition, nothing could take the gloss off a sensational year.

2003: 2 Tests: 20 runs @ 20.00; 2 wickets @ 99.50.
1 ODI: did not bat; no wicket for 65.

MAKHAYA NTINI **South Africa**

Ntini's graduation from hit-and-miss scattergun to the most potent weapon in South Africa's arsenal did not get the attention it deserved in 2003. He was the leading wicket-taker in Test cricket with 59, and third in the one-day international list with 45, one behind Brett Lee and Muttiah Muralitharan. Angling the ball in from wide of the crease with a lightning-fast arm action, he provided the perfect foil to Pollock's more measured, probing approach. Ntini could still be expensive, but he was a match-winner too, taking eight against Pakistan at Cape Town, ten – celebrated with an emotional kiss of the turf – against England at Lord's, and nine against West Indies at Johannesburg. An inspiration to South Africa's under-privileged communities, he made his presence felt far beyond the boundary.

2003: 12 Tests: 105 runs @ 21.00; 59 wickets @ 26.54.
23 ODI: 45 runs @ 15.00; 45 wickets @ 18.13.

"Yorkshire collapsed to 93 all out, a defeat that inspired a death threat to the executive board, politely signed by the former member who sent it."

Yorkshire in 2003, page 757.

SHAUN POLLOCK South Africa

The bald statistics say it all: in 11 Tests, Pollock averaged 50 with the bat and 21 with the ball, which is not bad for a man who was dumped as captain after South Africa's World Cup debacle, and who might reasonably have spent the year sulking. Pollock did precisely the opposite, and yet most of his work went largely unnoticed – except by opponents. His jaunty hitting at No. 8 was a tiring bowler's worst nightmare, and his Chinese-torture seamers – every ball drip-dripped on the spot – tested batsmen's faculties to the full. With Pollock, the watchword was parsimony: he rarely hit even 80mph, and at Rawalpindi he bowled the thriftiest ten-over spell in South Africa's one-day history. In an age where batsmen deal in persecution, his economy-rate was outstanding: 2.22 in Tests and 3.51 in one-day internationals. On a flat track he was unhittable; on a feisty one, such as Trent Bridge against England, he was unplayable.

2003: 11 Tests: 452 runs @ 50.22; 45 wickets @ 20.97.
23 ODI: 170 runs @ 18.88; 27 wickets @ 25.77.

RICKY PONTING Australia

See The Leading Cricketer in the World, page 78.

2003: 11 Tests: 1,503 runs @ 100.20; no wicket for 25.
34 ODI: 1,154 runs @ 46.16.

MARK RICHARDSON New Zealand

There were few more self-deprecating, likeable cricketers in the world in 2003 than Richardson – and few more effective Test opening batsmen. He was the archetypal New Zealand anchorman, yet his self-imposed limitations, infused with humour and spirit, were absorbing rather than off-putting. Pigeon-holed – reasonably enough – as a Test player, he was restricted to 11 international innings in the calendar year, but made almost every one of them count, falling for under 40 on only three occasions. His 410-ball 145 at Mohali was typical of his unbending powers of concentration. A late starter in Test cricket, he was, at 32, established as one of the most bankable batsmen in the business. He was also one of a handful in the world who managed to blunt the threat of Murali.

2003: 6 Tests: 555 runs @ 55.50.

KUMAR SANGAKKARA **Sri Lanka**

If Gilchrist was the world's most valuable keeper/batsman, Sangakkara came in a stylish second. His glovework was not always perfect – he often played as a specialist batsman – but he averaged over 40 in Tests with his silken strokeplay at No. 3, and hit successive unbeaten one-day hundreds at Sharjah. Had two flowing Test innings against England not ended with avoidable run-outs, his impact would have been even greater. He remained Sri Lanka's mouthpiece on the field, where a mixture of sharp banter (Oscar Wilde is one of his favourites) and incessant encouragement troubled opposition batsmen and umpires alike.

2003: 7 Tests (3 as wicket-keeper): 412 runs @ 41.20; 9 catches as keeper, 4 stumpings.
26 ODI (15 as wicket-keeper): 695 runs @ 36.57; 19 catches as keeper, 5 stumpings.

VIRENDER SEHWAG **India**

It was the year Sehwag forged his own identity. No longer was he just a Tendulkar doppelgänger; now he was big box-office in his own right. But though he was a year older, Sehwag was not necessarily a year wiser, and he continued to open the innings the only way he knew how. His live-fast-die-young style of batting was exhilarating when it came off, but with the hits came the inevitable misses – most notably during an underwhelming World Cup. Two breathtaking innings, however, stood out: a match-winning 112 in a one-day international at Auckland, when no other Indian reached 25, and a glorious 195 on Boxing Day at Melbourne. For its relentless risk-taking, mass devastation and pure, unbridled talent, this was Sehwag at his most definitive.

2003: 5 Tests: 522 runs @ 52.20; 1 wicket @ 100.00.
27 ODI: 871 runs @ 32.25; 10 wickets @ 30.50.

SHOAIB AKHTAR **Pakistan**

The averages were stunning, particularly in Tests, but you suspect the stat that mattered most to Shoaib Akhtar was the 100.2mph ball he sent hurtling down to Nick Knight during the World Cup. Self-satisfied with breaking cricket's four-minute mile, Shoaib bowled like a drain in the games that mattered as Pakistan tumbled ignominiously out of the competition. In the subsequent fall-out, and with his hubris in danger of going off the scale, Shoaib was advised to "shut up and bowl, mate" by Waqar Younis. When he was not injured or suspended for sledging tailenders or ball-tampering, he did precisely that and more. He made only four Test appearances, but certainly made them count: he was way too hot for South Africa's star-studded top order at Lahore, and scalded New Zealand with a dazzling performance at Wellington. Of his 30 Test wickets, a third were out lbw or bowled without scoring. For most batsmen around the world he was too fast, too straight, too much. And boy, did he know it.

2003: 4 Tests: 17 runs @ 4.25; 30 wickets @ 12.36.
20 ODI: 151 runs @ 18.87; 33 wickets @ 22.93.

GRAEME SMITH — South Africa

It seemed unfair to place the burden on a 22-year-old, but in 2003 Smith exceeded his brief, helping a nation forget the twin traumas of Hansie Cronje's demise and a catastrophic World Cup. The critics scoffed when Smith inherited the South African captaincy from Pollock. But after two innings wins in Bangladesh he set about proving them wrong: scores of 277 at Edgbaston and 259 at Lord's, full of square-jawed defiance and crunching leg-side strokeplay, quickly became part of his country's sporting folklore. Although South Africa ended up drawing in England, then losing in Pakistan, he was back on track with 132 at Johannesburg to help set up a series win over West Indies. If first impressions count, then Smith – articulate, precocious, and so very determined – made them count double. *See also Five Cricketers of the Year, page 67.*

2003: 12 Tests: 1,198 runs @ 63.05; 2 wickets @ 54.50.
19 ODI: 600 runs @ 33.33; no wicket for 53.

HEATH STREAK — Zimbabwe

As Zimbabwe reached a nadir on and off the pitch, Streak's quiet dignity stood out. Some were offended by his refusal to condemn Robert Mugabe's regime, but generally he made the best of an unspeakably bad situation. His captaincy may have been one-dimensional, but he led by example. After the retirement of Andy Flower, Streak invariably stood alone: his bowling was as wholehearted and probing as ever, and his lower-order batting – strong-armed and full of rugged defiance – was a minor sensation. He averaged a shade under 40 in both forms of the game, and scored his maiden Test century. And he did it all with the minimum of fuss. International sport, Streak demonstrated, still had room for the strong, silent type.

2003: 6 Tests: 317 runs @ 39.62; 17 wickets @ 38.29.
23 ODI: 469 runs @ 39.08; 29 wickets @ 26.75.

SACHIN TENDULKAR — India

In whites, an *annus horribilis*; in pyjamas, *mirabilis*. It was hard to know which was greater: the peak he touched in South Africa, or – until he redeemed himself with a consummate double-century at Sydney at the start of 2004 – the trough he entered in Australia. Tendulkar was the player of the World Cup, his genius in full, unfettered glory, displaying all the colours of the cricketing rainbow. His assault on Shoaib Akhtar in India's crunch match with Pakistan acquired immediate fame in his homeland. If his failure in the final – when India needed a miracle from him but got only a mistimed pull – stimulated the begrudgers' juices, his Test-match form drove them to distraction. Statistically and actually, it was the worst year of Tendulkar's Test career: six single-figure scores in nine, and the ignominy of being dropped down the order in the MCG bear pit – a bit like Eliot Ness being taken out of the firing line for his own good. But as Tendulkar's scorching beginning to 2004 showed, the gravity of genius cannot be defied for ever.

2003: 5 Tests: 153 runs @ 17.00; 4 wickets @ 51.25.
21 ODI: 1,141 runs @ 57.05; 3 wickets @ 67.33.

MARCUS TRESCOTHICK — England

On the face of it, Trescothick enjoyed a triumphant year, hammering more runs – 1,003 in Tests – than any of his team-mates and cementing his reputation as England's best top-order batsman in one-day cricket. But the stats did not tell the whole story. Trescothick tended to dazzle only in patches, and although he rarely failed – there were just four single-figure dismissals in 24 Test innings – he rarely turned promising starts into big scores either, falling between 22 and 43 on nine occasions. Trescothick admitted to exhaustion after a long winter, but England would have been a lesser side without him, and he saved his *magnum opus* for their most important Test of the year. Against South Africa at The Oval, Trescothick bludgeoned 219 and 69 not out, crashing 188 runs in boundaries and squaring the series in the process. A century in the next Test, at Dhaka, confirmed that, when the mood took him, he left his contemporaries for dead, with the occasional exceptions of Vaughan and Flintoff. His sporadically volcanic one-day batting erupted with 409 runs in six innings, a summer sequence that included two unbeaten centuries. But the abiding impression was of a naturally gifted cricketer who had not quite come to terms with his talent. Passed over for the Test captaincy at the start of the summer, and his judgment ridiculed after the Headingley bad-light incident, he was dropping straightforward slip catches by the end of the year. Would the real Trescothick please stand up?

2003: 13 Tests: 1,003 runs @ 47.76; no wicket for 10.
25 ODI: 867 runs @ 37.69.

CHAMINDA VAAS — Sri Lanka

His position at the top of the World Cup wicket-taking list went relatively unnoticed, but then that was typical of the left-armer Vaas – the world's best unsung seamer. He played all seven of his Tests on the merciless strips of Sri Lanka and the West Indies, yet chipped in regularly to prevent a Muralitharan monopoly. And he was a model of canny economy in the one-day game, conceding just 3.69 runs an over all year, and going for more than 40 runs in just six of his 23 matches. His hat-trick against Bangladesh

with the first three balls of their World Cup game was unusually dramatic for him. More often, he would be quietly swinging the ball in, sometimes cutting it away, always on the spot, occasionally reaping the harvest.
2003: 7 Tests: 199 runs @ 24.87; 23 wickets @ 28.47.
23 ODI: 149 runs @ 12.41; 34 wickets @ 21.20.

MICHAEL VAUGHAN England

Vaughan began the year with a sublime 183 at Sydney, and by April he was top of the world Test batting rankings. He spent the rest of it trying to justify that tag – and by the end of 2003 he was 13th. In May, Vaughan succeeded Nasser Hussain as one-day captain, and made a flying start, leading England to victory in two one-day series and barely raising his voice once. When Hussain returned to the dressing-room for the Test series with South Africa, he sensed a change of mood and dramatically resigned after one game, plunging Vaughan head first into the deep end. The carefree brilliance that had brought him 156 among the rank and file at Edgbaston was replaced by a series of distracted 20s, and Vaughan the captain went nine Test innings without a half-century. Under the circumstances, a 2–2 draw with South Africa was a mini-triumph. Bangladesh provided temporary respite from the batting blues, but Vaughan did not hint at a return to the heights of 2002 until Kandy, where he followed a first-innings fifty with an epic match-saving 105 in seven and a half hours. Vaughan rated it the best of his ten Test centuries and admitted, for the first time, that he was only just beginning to learn how to compartmentalise his various roles when he was at the crease. His one-day batting, though, waited for a breakthrough which never really came, while his off-spin remained underused and underrated, mainly by himself. As a leader, Vaughan could point to four Test wins to go with three defeats, but his tactical rawness was exposed on a belter in Colombo.
2003: 13 Tests: 958 runs @ 41.65; 1 wicket @ 90.00.
22 ODI: 587 @ 30.89; 2 wickets @ 72.00.

STEVE WAUGH Australia

For a man who has always enjoyed the symbolic gesture, it was appropriate that the final leg of Waugh's 18-year Test marathon should begin and end in his home town of Sydney. A stunning century against England at the SCG, reached triumphantly off the last ball of the second day, heralded for some the end of a glorious career, but Waugh kept going for another year, culminating in an emotional month-long farewell during the epic drawn series with India. In between, he led his side to victory in the Caribbean, and hauled his batting average back over 50 with two ruthless unbeaten centuries against Bangladesh. He finished with a world-record 41 Test wins as captain, and – despite the failure to beat India – a place on the topmost level of Australia's sporting pantheon.
2003: 12 Tests: 876 runs @ 79.63; 2 wickets @ 103.00.

YOUSUF YOUHANA Pakistan

It was business as usual for Yousuf Youhana: loads of runs, very few headlines. He was the world's leading one-day international run-scorer, and averaged a shade under 60 in Tests – but you would never have known it. Youhana was the invisible man of world cricket, with his serene batsmanship only really noticeable right at the end: in a low-scoring Boxing Day Test at Wellington he scored 148 runs for once out, guiding Pakistan to a famous victory. Typically, his performance was overshadowed by Shoaib Akhtar's whirlwind fast bowling.

2003: 6 Tests: 359 runs @ 59.83.
33 ODI: 1,168 runs @ 43.25.

OVERSEAS PLAYERS IN 2003

In 2003, a change to ECB regulations allowed counties to field two overseas cricketers for the first time since the 1980s. It also became easier to replace overseas players either injured or called up by their country. Each county was permitted to register a maximum of four such players: seven used their full quota; only four managed with two.

Derbyshire M. J. Di Venuto (A), C. Z. Harris (NZ), M. Kaif (I), Shahid Afridi (P). *N. J. Astle withdrew unfit before the season.*
Durham M. L. Love (A), D. Pretorius (SA), Shoaib Akhtar (P), J. Srinath (I).
Essex S. A. Brant (A), A. Flower (Z), Mohammad Akram (P).
Glamorgan M. S. Kasprowicz (A), J. P. Maher (A).
Gloucestershire I. G. Butler (NZ), I. J. Harvey (A), J. N. Rhodes (SA), Shoaib Malik (P). *New Zealanders C. Z. Harris, who later played for Derbyshire, and C. D. McMillan appeared in a one-day game v India A; this did not breach the quota of four overseas players as it did not count as a competitive match.*
Hampshire S. M. Katich (A), W. P. U. J. C. Vaas (SL), Wasim Akram (P). *S. K. Warne (A) withdrew before the season when he was banned after failing a drugs test.*
Kent G. S. Blewett (A), Mohammad Sami (P), M. Muralitharan (SL), A. Symonds (A).
Lancashire C. L. Hooper (WI), S. G. Law (A). *Harbhajan Singh (I) withdrew unfit before playing.*
Leicestershire V. C. Drakes (WI), B. J. Hodge (A), V. Sehwag (I).
Middlesex Abdul Razzaq (P), J. H. Dawes (A), Imran Tahir (P), A. A. Noffke (A).
Northamptonshire M. E. K. Hussey (A), A. Nel (SA), D. G. Wright (A).
Nottinghamshire C. L. Cairns (NZ), S. Elworthy (SA), S. C. G. MacGill (A), D. L. Vettori (NZ).
Somerset J. Cox (A), N. A. M. McLean (WI).
Surrey Azhar Mahmood (P), F. A. Rose (WI), Saqlain Mushtaq (P).
Sussex M. W. Goodwin (Z/A), Mushtaq Ahmed (P).
Warwickshire M. W. Clark (A), C. D. Collymore (WI), C. O. Obuya (K), Waqar Younis (P). *S. E. Bond (NZ) withdrew unfit before playing.*
Worcestershire A. J. Hall (SA), M. Hayward (SA), J. M. Kemp (SA).
Yorkshire S. P. Fleming (NZ), D. R. Martyn (A), Yuvraj Singh (I). *M. T. G. Elliott withdrew unfit before playing.*

Scotland R. Dravid (I), C. V. English (SA), J. C. Kent (SA).

BIRTHS AND DEATHS

TEST CRICKETERS

Full list from 1876-77 to January 20, 2004

Abbreviations A: Australia. B: Bangladesh. E: England. I: India. NZ: New Zealand. P: Pakistan. SA: South Africa. SL: Sri Lanka. WI: West Indies. Z: Zimbabwe.

In the Test career column, dates in italics indicate seasons embracing two different years (i.e. non-English seasons). In these cases, only the first year is given, e.g. *1876* for 1876-77.

The totals of Tests played are complete up to January 20, 2004; the totals of one-day internationals are complete up to December 31, 2003.

The forename by which a player is known is underlined if it is not his first name.

Family relationships are indicated by superscript numbers; where the relationship is not immediately apparent from a shared name, see the notes at the end of this section.

	Country	*Born*	*Died*	*Tests*	*Test Career*	*ODIs*
Aamer Malik	P	3.1.1963		14	*1987–1994*	24
Aamir Nazir	P	2.1.1971		6	*1992–1995*	9
Aamir Sohail	P	14.9.1966		47	1992–*1999*	156
Abdul Kadir	P	10.5.1944	12.3.2002	4	*1964*	
Abdul Qadir	P	15.9.1955		67	*1977–1990*	104
Abdul Razzaq	P	2.12.1979		27	*1999–2003*	149
a'Beckett, Edward Lambert	A	11.8.1907	2.6.1989	4	*1928–1931*	
Abel, Robert	E	30.11.1857	10.12.1936	13	1888–1902	
Abid Ali, Syed	I	9.9.1941		29	*1967–1974*	5
Absolom, Charles Alfred	E	7.6.1846	30.7.1889	1	*1878*	
Achong, Ellis Edgar	WI	16.2.1904	29.8.1986	6	*1929–1934*	
Ackerman, Hylton Deon	SA	14.2.1973		4	*1997*	
Adams, Andre Ryan	NZ	17.7.1975		1	*2001*	28
Adams, Christopher John	E	6.5.1970		5	*1999*	5
Adams, James Clive	WI	9.1.1968		54	*1991–2000*	127
Adams, Paul Regan	SA	20.1.1977		44	*1995–2003*	24
Adcock, Neil Amwin Treharne	SA	8.3.1931		26	*1953–1961*	
Adhikari, Hemchandra Ramachandra	I	31.7.1919	25.10.2003	21	*1947–1958*	
Afaq Hussain	P	31.12.1939	25.2.2002	2	*1961–1964*	
Aftab Baloch	P	1.4.1953		2	*1969–1974*	
Aftab Gul	P	31.3.1946		6	*1968*–1971	
Afzaal, Usman	E	9.6.1977		3	2001	
Agarkar, Ajit Bhalchandra	I	4.12.1977		20	*1998–2003*	121
Agha Saadat Ali	P	21.6.1929	26.10.1995	1	*1955*	
Agha Zahid	P	7.1.1953		1	*1974*	
Agnew, Jonathan Philip	E	4.4.1960		3	1984–1985	3
Ahangama, Franklyn <u>Saliya</u>	SL	14.9.1959		3	*1985*	1
Akram Khan	B	1.11.1968		8	*2000–2002*	44
Akram Raza	P	22.11.1964		9	*1989–1994*	49
Alabaster, John Chaloner	NZ	11.7.1930		21	*1955–1971*	
Alamgir Kabir	B	10.1.1981		2	*2002–2003*	
Alderman, Terence Michael	A	12.6.1956		41	1981–*1990*	65
Alexander, Franz Copeland Murray	WI	2.11.1928		25	1957–*1960*	
Alexander, George	A	22.4.1851	6.11.1930	2	1880–*1884*	
Alexander, Harry Houston	A	9.6.1905	15.4.1993	1	*1932*	
Ali, Imtiaz	WI	28.7.1954		1	*1975*	
Ali, Inshan	WI	25.9.1949	24.6.1995	12	*1970–1976*	
Ali, Kabir	E	24.11.1980		1	2003	1
Ali Hussain Rizvi	P	6.1.1974		1	*1997*	
Alim-ud-Din	P	15.12.1930		25	1954–1962	
Ali Naqvi	P	19.3.1977		5	*1997*	

[1] *Father and son(s).* [2] *Brothers.*

	Country	Born	Died	Tests	Test Career	ODIs
Allan, David Walter	WI	5.11.1937		5	*1961*–1966	
Allan, Francis Erskine	A	2.12.1849	9.2.1917	1	*1878*	
Allan, Peter John	A	31.12.1935		1	*1965*	
Allcott, Cyril Francis Walter	NZ	7.10.1896	19.11.1973	6	*1929–1931*	
Allen, David Arthur	E	29.10.1935		39	*1959*–1966	
Allen, *Sir* George Oswald Browning ("Gubby")	E	31.7.1902	29.11.1989	25	1930–*1947*	
Allen, Ian Basil Alston	WI	6.10.1965		2	1991	
Allen, Reginald Charles	A	2.7.1858	2.5.1952	1	*1886*	
Allom, Maurice James Carrick	E	23.3.1906	8.4.1995	5	*1929–1930*	
Allott, Geoffrey Ian	NZ	24.12.1971		10	*1995*–1999	31
Allott, Paul John Walter	E	14.9.1956		13	1981–1985	13
Alok Kapali	B	1.1.1984		14	*2002–2003*	32
Al Sahariar	B	23.4.1978		15	*2000–2003*	29
Amalean, Kaushik Naginda	SL	7.4.1965		2	*1985–1987*	8
[1, 2]**Amarnath,** Mohinder	I	24.9.1950		69	*1969–1987*	85
[1]**Amarnath,** Nanik ("Lala")	I	11.9.1911	5.8.2000	24	*1933–1952*	
[1, 2]**Amarnath,** Surinder	I	30.12.1948		10	*1975–1978*	3
[2]**Amar Singh,** Ladha	I	4.12.1910	20.5.1940	7	1932–1936	
Ambrose, Curtly Elconn Lynwall	WI	21.9.1963		98	*1987*–2000	176
Amerasinghe, Amerasinghe Mudalige Jayantha Gamini	SL	2.2.1954		2	*1983*	
Ames, Leslie Ethelbert George CBE	E	3.12.1905	26.2.1990	47	1929–*1938*	
Aminul Islam	B	2.2.1968		13	*2000–2002*	39
Amir Elahi	I, P	1.9.1908	28.12.1980	6	*1947–1952*	
Amiss, Dennis Leslie MBE	E	7.4.1943		50	1966–1977	18
Amre, Pravin Kalyan	I	14.8.1968		11	*1992–1993*	37
Anderson, James Henry	SA	26.4.1874	11.3.1926	1	*1902*	
Anderson, James Michael	E	30.7.1982		8	2003–*2003*	27
[1]**Anderson,** Robert Wickham	NZ	2.10.1948		9	*1976*–1978	2
[1]**Anderson,** William McDougall	NZ	8.10.1919	21.12.1979	1	*1945*	
Andrew, Keith Vincent	E	15.12.1929		2	*1954*–1963	
Andrews, Bryan	NZ	4.4.1945		2	*1973*	
Andrews, Thomas James Edwin	A	26.8.1890	28.1.1970	16	1921–1926	
Angel, Jo	A	22.4.1968		4	*1992–1994*	3
Anil Dalpat	P	20.9.1963		9	*1983–1984*	15
Ankola, Salil Ashok	I	1.3.1968		1	*1989*	20
Anurasiri, Sangarange Don	SL	25.2.1966		18	*1985–1997*	45
Anwar Hossain Monir	B	31.12.1981		1	*2003*	1
Anwar Hossain Piju	B	10.12.1983		1	*2002*	1
Anwar Hussain	P	16.7.1920	9.10.2002	4	*1952*	
Anwar Khan	P	24.12.1955		1	*1978*	
Appleyard, Robert	E	27.6.1924		9	1954–1956	
[2]**Apte,** Arvindrao Laxmanrao	I	24.10.1934		1	1959	
[2]**Apte,** Madhavrao Laxmanrao	I	5.10.1932		7	*1952*	
Aqib Javed	P	5.8.1972		22	*1988–1998*	163
Archer, Alfred German	E	6.12.1871	15.7.1935	1	*1898*	
[2]**Archer,** Kenneth Alan	A	17.1.1928		5	*1950–1951*	
[2]**Archer,** Ronald Graham	A	25.10.1933		19	*1952–1956*	
Arif Butt	P	17.5.1944		3	*1964*	
Armitage, Thomas	E	25.4.1848	21.9.1922	2	*1876*	
Armstrong, Warwick Windridge	A	22.5.1879	13.7.1947	50	*1901*–1921	
Arnold, Edward George	E	7.11.1876	25.10.1942	10	*1903*–1907	
Arnold, Geoffrey Graham	E	3.9.1944		34	1967–1975	14
Arnold, John	E	30.11.1907	4.4.1984	1	1931	
Arnold, Russel Premakumaran	SL	25.10.1973		43	*1996–2002*	120
Arnott, Kevin John	Z	8.3.1961		4	*1992*	13
Arshad Ayub	I	2.8.1958		13	*1987–1989*	32
Arshad Khan	P	22.3.1971		8	*1997–2000*	48

[1] *Father and son(s).* [2] *Brothers.*

	Country	Born	Died	Tests	Test Career	ODIs
Arthurton, Keith Lloyd Thomas	WI	21.2.1965		33	1988–1995	105
Arun, Bharathi	I	14.12.1962		2	1986	4
Arun Lal	I	1.8.1955		16	1982–1988	13
Asgarali, Nyron Sultan	WI	28.12.1920		2	1957	
Ashfaq Ahmed	P	6.6.1973		1	1993	3
Ashley, William Hare	SA	10.2.1862	14.7.1930	1	1888	
Ashraf Ali	P	22.4.1958		8	1981–1987	16
Asif Iqbal	P	6.6.1943		58	1964–1979	10
Asif Masood	P	23.1.1946		16	1968–1976	7
Asif Mujtaba	P	4.11.1967		25	1986–1996	66
Asim Kamal	P	31.5.1976		2	2003	
Astill, William Ewart	E	1.3.1888	10.2.1948	9	1927–1929	
Astle, Nathan John	NZ	15.9.1971		59	1995–2003	174
Atapattu, Marvan Samson	SL	22.11.1970		68	1990–2003	201
Ata-ur-Rehman	P	28.3.1975		13	1992–1996	30
Atherton, Michael Andrew OBE	E	23.3.1968		115	1989–2001	54
Athey, Charles William Jeffrey	E	27.9.1957		23	1980–1988	31
Atif Rauf	P	3.3.1964		1	1993	
Atiq-uz-Zaman	P	20.7.1975		1	1999	3
[2]**Atkinson,** Denis St Eval	WI	9.8.1926	9.11.2001	22	1948–1957	
[2]**Atkinson,** Eric St Eval	WI	6.11.1927	29.5.1998	8	1957–1958	
Attewell, William	E	12.6.1861	11.6.1927	10	1884–1891	
Austin, Richard Arkwright	WI	5.9.1954		2	1977	1
Azad, Kirtivardhan	I	2.1.1959		7	1980–1983	25
Azam Khan	P	1.3.1969		1	1996	6
Azeem Hafeez	P	29.7.1963		18	1983–1984	15
Azhar Khan	P	7.9.1955		1	1979	
Azhar Mahmood	P	28.2.1975		21	1997–2001	129
Azharuddin, Mohammad	I	8.2.1963		99	1984–1999	334
[2]**Azmat Rana**	P	3.11.1951		1	1979	2
Bacchus, Sheik Faoud Ahamul Fasiel	WI	31.1.1954		19	1977–1981	29
Bacher, Adam Marc	SA	29.10.1973		19	1996–1999	8
Bacher, Aron ("Ali")	SA	24.5.1942		12	1965–1969	
Badani, Hemang Kamal	I	14.11.1976		4	2001	31
Badcock, Clayvel Lindsay	A	10.4.1914	13.12.1982	7	1936–1938	
Badcock, Frederick Theodore	NZ	9.8.1897	19.9.1982	7	1929–1932	
Bahutule, Sairaj Vasant	I	6.1.1973		2	2000–2001	8
Baichan, Leonard	WI	12.5.1946		3	1974–1975	
Baig, Abbas Ali	I	19.3.1939		10	1959–1966	
Bailey, Robert John	E	28.10.1963		4	1988–1989	4
Bailey, Trevor Edward CBE	E	3.12.1923		61	1949–1958	
Bairstow, David Leslie	E	1.9.1951	5.1.1998	4	1979–1980	21
Bakewell, Alfred Harry	E	2.11.1908	23.1.1983	6	1931–1935	
Balaji, Lakshmipathy	I	27.9.1981		2	2003	1
Balaskas, Xenophon Constantine	SA	15.10.1910	12.5.1994	9	1930–1938	
Balderstone, John Christopher	E	16.11.1940	6.3.2000	2	1976	
Bandara, Charitha Malinga	SL	31.12.1979		1	1997	
Bandaratilleke, Mapa Rallage Chandima Niroshan	SL	16.5.1975		7	1997–2001	3
Banerjee, Sarobindu Nath	I	3.10.1911	14.10.1980	1	1948	
Banerjee, Subroto Tara	I	13.2.1969		1	1991	6
Banerjee, Sudangsu Abinash	I	1.11.1917	14.9.1992	1	1948	
Bangar, Sanjay Bapusaheb	I	11.10.1972		12	2001–2002	13
Banks, Omari Ahmed Clemente	WI	17.7.1982		5	2002–2003	3
[2]**Bannerman,** Alexander Chalmers	A	21.3.1854	19.9.1924	28	1878–1893	
[2]**Bannerman,** Charles	A	23.7.1851	20.8.1930	3	1876–1878	
Baptiste, Eldine Ashworth Elderfield	WI	12.3.1960		10	1983–1989	43
Baqa Jilani, Mohammad	I	20.7.1911	2.7.1941	1	1936	

[1] *Father and son(s).* [2] *Brothers.*

	Country	*Born*	*Died*	*Tests*	*Test Career*	*ODIs*
Barber, Richard Trevor	NZ	3.6.1925		1	*1955*	
Barber, Robert William	E	26.9.1935		28	1960–1968	
Barber, Wilfred	E	18.4.1901	10.9.1968	2	1935	
Bardsley, Warren	A	6.12.1882	20.1.1954	41	1909–1926	
Barlow, Edgar John	SA	12.8.1940		30	*1961–1969*	
Barlow, Graham Derek	E	26.3.1950		3	*1976*–1977	6
Barlow, Richard Gorton	E	28.5.1851	31.7.1919	17	*1881–1886*	
Barnes, Sydney Francis	E	19.4.1873	26.12.1967	27	*1901–1913*	
Barnes, Sidney George	A	5.6.1916	16.12.1973	13	1938–1948	
Barnes, William	E	27.5.1852	24.3.1899	21	1880–1890	
Barnett, Benjamin Arthur	A	23.3.1908	29.6.1979	4	1938	
Barnett, Charles John	E	3.7.1910	28.5.1993	20	1933–1948	
Barnett, Kim John	E	17.7.1960		4	1988–1989	1
Barratt, Fred	E	12.4.1894	29.1.1947	5	1929–*1929*	
Barrett, Arthur George	WI	5.4.1942		6	*1970–1974*	
Barrett, John Edward	A	15.10.1866	6.2.1916	2	1890	
Barrington, Kenneth Frank	E	24.11.1930	14.3.1981	82	1955–1968	
Barrow, Ivanhoe Mordred	WI	16.1.1911	2.4.1979	11	*1929*–1939	
Bartlett, Edward Lawson	WI	10.3.1906	21.12.1976	5	1928–*1930*	
Bartlett, Gary Alex	NZ	3.2.1941		10	*1961–1967*	
Barton, Paul Thomas	NZ	9.10.1935		7	*1961–1962*	
Barton, Victor Alexander	E	6.10.1867	23.3.1906	1	*1891*	
Basit Ali	P	13.12.1970		19	*1992–1995*	50
Bates, Willie	E	19.11.1855	8.1.1900	15	*1881–1886*	
Batty, Gareth Jon	E	13.10.1977		4	*2003*	3
Baugh, Carlton Seymour	WI	23.6.1982		3	*2002–2003*	5
Baumgartner, Harold Vane	SA	17.11.1883	8.4.1938	1	*1913*	
Bean, George	E	7.3.1864	16.3.1923	3	*1891*	
Beard, Donald Derek	NZ	14.1.1920	15.7.1982	4	*1951–1955*	
Beard, Graeme Robert	A	19.8.1950		3	*1979*	2
Beaumont, Rolland	SA	4.2.1884	25.5.1958	5	1912–*1913*	
Beck, John Edward Francis	NZ	1.8.1934	23.4.2000	8	*1953–1955*	
Bedi, Bishan Singh	I	25.9.1946		67	*1966*–1979	10
Bedser, *Sir* Alec Victor	E	4.7.1918		51	1946–1955	
Begbie, Denis Warburton	SA	12.12.1914		5	*1948–1949*	
Bell, Alexander John	SA	15.4.1906	1.8.1985	16	1929–1935	
Bell, Matthew David	NZ	25.2.1977		13	*1998–2001*	7
Bell, William	NZ	5.9.1931	23.7.2002	2	*1953*	
[2]**Benaud,** John	A	11.5.1944		3	*1972*	
[2]**Benaud,** Richard OBE	A	6.10.1930		63	*1951–1963*	
Benjamin, Joseph Emmanuel	E	2.2.1961		1	1994	2
Benjamin, Kenneth Charlie Griffith	WI	8.4.1967		26	*1991–1997*	26
Benjamin, Winston Keithroy Matthew	WI	31.12.1964		21	*1987–1994*	85
Bennett, Murray John	A	6.10.1956		3	*1984*–1985	8
Benson, Mark Richard	E	6.7.1958		1	1986	1
Bernard, David Eddison	WI	19.7.1981		1	*2002*	4
Berry, Robert	E	29.1.1926		2	1950	
Best, Carlisle Alonza	WI	14.5.1959		8	*1985–1990*	24
Best, Tino la Bertram	WI	26.8.1981		1	*2002*	
Betancourt, Nelson	WI	4.6.1887	12.10.1947	1	*1929*	
Bevan, Michael Gwyl	A	8.5.1970		18	*1994–1997*	220
Bhandari, Prakash	I	27.11.1935		3	*1954–1956*	
Bharadwaj, Raghvendrarao Vijay	I	15.8.1975		3	*1999*	10
Bhat, Adwai Ragharam	I	16.4.1958		2	*1983*	
Bichel, Andrew John	A	27.8.1970		19	*1996–2003*	61
Bicknell, Martin Paul	E	14.1.1969		4	1993–2003	7
Bikash Ranjan Das	B	14.7.1982		1	*2000*	
Bilby, Grahame Paul	NZ	7.5.1941		2	*1965*	
Binks, James Graham	E	5.10.1935		2	*1963*	

[1] *Father and son(s).* [2] *Brothers.*

	Country	Born	Died	Tests	Test Career	ODIs
Binns, Alfred Phillip	WI	24.7.1929		5	1952–1955	
Binny, Roger Michael Humphrey	I	19.7.1955		27	1979–1986	72
Bird, Morice Carlos	E	25.3.1888	9.12.1933	10	1909–1913	
Birkenshaw, Jack	E	13.11.1940		5	1972–1973	
Birkett, Lionel Sydney	WI	14.4.1905	16.1.1998	4	1930	
Bishop, Ian Raphael	WI	24.10.1967		43	1988–1997	84
Bisset, *Sir* Murray	SA	14.4.1876	24.10.1931	3	1898–1909	
Bissett, George Finlay	SA	5.11.1905	14.11.1965	4	1927	
Black, Marlon Ian	WI	7.6.1975		6	2000–2001	5
Blackham, John McCarthy	A	11.5.1854	28.12.1932	35	1876–1894	
Blackie, Donald Dearness	A	5.4.1882	18.4.1955	3	1928	
Blain, Tony Elston	NZ	17.2.1962		11	1986–1993	38
Blair, Robert William	NZ	23.6.1932		19	1952–1963	
Blakey, Richard John	E	15.1.1967		2	1992	3
Blanckenberg, James Manuel	SA	31.12.1892	d unknown	18	1913–1924	
Bland, Kenneth Colin	SA	5.4.1938		21	1961–1966	
Blewett, Gregory Scott	A	29.10.1971		46	1994–1999	32
Bligh *Hon.* Ivo Francis Walter [later 8th Earl of Darnley]	E	13.3.1859	10.4.1927	4	1882	
Blignaut, Arnoldus Mauritius	Z	1.8.1978		14	2000–2003	38
Blunt, Roger Charles	NZ	3.11.1900	22.6.1966	9	1929–1931	
Blythe, Colin	E	30.5.1879	8.11.1917	19	1901–1909	
Board, John Henry	E	23.2.1867	15.4.1924	6	1898–1905	
Bock, Ernest George	SA	17.9.1908	5.9.1961	1	1935	
Boje, Nico	SA	20.3.1973		21	1999–2002	91
Bolton, Bruce Alfred	NZ	31.5.1935		2	1958	
Bolus, John Brian	E	31.1.1934		7	1963–1963	
Bond, Gerald Edward	SA	5.4.1909	27.8.1965	1	1938	
Bond, Shane Edward	NZ	7.6.1975		10	2001–2002	27
Bonnor, George John	A	25.2.1855	27.6.1912	17	1880–1888	
Boock, Stephen Lewis	NZ	20.9.1951		30	1977–1988	14
Boon, David Clarence	A	29.12.1960		107	1984–1995	181
Booth, Brian Charles MBE	A	19.10.1933		29	1961–1965	
Booth, Major William	E	10.12.1886	1.7.1916	2	1913	
Borde, Chandrakant Gulabrao	I	21.7.1933		55	1958–1969	
Border, Allan Robert	A	27.7.1955		156	1978–1993	273
Bosanquet, Bernard James Tindal	E	13.10.1877	12.10.1936	7	1903–1905	
Bosch, Tertius	SA	14.3.1966	13.2.2000	1	1991	2
Botham, Ian Terence OBE	E	24.11.1955		102	1977–1992	116
Botten, James Thomas	SA	21.6.1938		3	1965	
Boucher, Mark Verdon	SA	3.12.1976		71	1997–2003	160
Bowden, Montague Parker	E	1.11.1865	19.2.1892	2	1888	
Bowes, William Eric	E	25.7.1908	5.9.1987	15	1932–1946	
Bowley, Edward Henry	E	6.6.1890	9.7.1974	5	1929–1929	
Boyce, Keith David	WI	11.10.1943	11.10.1996	21	1970–1975	8
Boycott, Geoffrey OBE	E	21.10.1940		108	1964–1981	36
Boyle, Henry Frederick	A	10.12.1847	21.11.1907	12	1878–1884	
[2]**Bracewell,** Brendon Paul	NZ	14.9.1959		6	1978–1984	1
[2]**Bracewell,** John Garry	NZ	15.4.1958		41	1980–1990	53
Bracken, Nathan Wade	A	12.9.1977		3	2003	17
[1]**Bradburn,** Grant Eric	NZ	26.5.1966		7	1990–2000	11
[1]**Bradburn,** Wynne Pennell	NZ	24.11.1938		2	1963	
Bradley, Walter Morris	E	2.1.1875	19.6.1944	2	1899	
Bradman, *Sir* Donald George	A	27.8.1908	25.2.2001	52	1928–1948	
Brain, David Hayden	Z	4.10.1964		9	1992–1994	23
Brandes, Eddo André	Z	5.3.1963		10	1992–1999	59
Brann, William Henry	SA	4.4.1899	22.9.1953	3	1922	
Braund, Leonard Charles	E	18.10.1875	23.12.1955	23	1901–1907	
Brearley, John Michael OBE	E	28.4.1942		39	1976–1981	25

[1] *Father and son(s).* [2] *Brothers.*

	Country	*Born*	*Died*	*Tests*	*Test Career*	*ODIs*
Brearley, Walter	E	11.3.1876	13.1.1937	4	1905–1912	
Breese, Gareth Rohan	WI	9.1.1976		1	*2002*	
Brennan, Donald Vincent	E	10.2.1920	9.1.1985	2	1951	
Brent, Gary Bazil	Z	13.1.1976		4	*1999–2001*	46
Briant, Gavin Aubrey	Z	11.4.1969		1	*1992*	5
Briggs, John	E	3.10.1862	11.1.1902	33	*1884*–1899	
Bright, Raymond James	A	13.7.1954		25	1977–*1986*	11
Briscoe, Arthur Wellesley	SA	6.2.1911	22.4.1941	2	*1935–1938*	
Broad, Brian Christopher	A	29.9.1957		25	1984–1989	34
Brockwell, William	E	21.1.1865	30.6.1935	7	1893–1899	
Bromfield, Harry Dudley	SA	26.6.1932		9	*1961*–1965	
Bromley, Ernest Harvey	A	2.9.1912	1.2.1967	2	*1932*–1934	
Bromley-Davenport, Hugh Richard	E	18.8.1870	23.5.1954	4	*1895–1898*	
Brookes, Dennis	E	29.10.1915		1	*1947*	
Brown, Alan	E	17.10.1935		2	*1961*	
Brown, David John	E	30.1.1942		26	1965–1969	
Brown, Frederick Richard MBE	E	16.12.1910	24.7.1991	22	1931–1953	
Brown, George	E	6.10.1887	3.12.1964	7	1921–*1922*	
Brown, John Thomas	E	20.8.1869	4.11.1904	8	*1894*–1899	
Brown, Lennox Sidney	SA	24.11.1910	1.9.1983	2	*1931*	
Brown, Simon John Emmerson	E	29.6.1969		1	1996	
Brown, Vaughan Raymond	NZ	3.11.1959		2	*1985*	3
Brown, William Alfred	A	31.7.1912		22	1934–1948	
Browne, Courtney Oswald	WI	7.12.1970		14	*1994–2001*	28
Browne, Cyril Rutherford	WI	8.10.1890	12.1.1964	4	1928–*1929*	
Bruce, William	A	22.5.1864	3.8.1925	14	*1884–1894*	
Bruk-Jackson, Glen Keith	Z	25.4.1969		2	*1993*	1
Buckenham, Claude Percival	E	16.1.1876	23.2.1937	4	*1909*	
Burge, Peter John Parnell	A	17.5.1932	5.10.2001	42	*1954–1965*	
Burger, Christopher George de Villiers	SA	12.7.1935		2	*1957*	
Burgess, Mark Gordon	NZ	17.7.1944		50	*1967–1980*	26
Burke, Cecil	NZ	22.3.1914	4.8.1997	1	*1945*	
Burke, James Wallace	A	12.6.1930	2.2.1979	24	*1950–1958*	
Burke, Sydney Frank	SA	11.3.1934		2	*1961–1964*	
Burmester, Mark Greville	Z	24.1.1968		3	*1992*	8
Burn, Kenneth Edwin	A	17.9.1862	20.7.1956	2	1890	
Burton, Frederick John	A	2.11.1865	25.8.1929	2	*1886–1887*	
Burtt, Thomas Browning	NZ	22.1.1915	24.5.1988	10	*1946–1952*	
Butchart, Iain Peter	Z	9.5.1960		1	*1994*	20
[1]**Butcher,** Alan Raymond	E	7.1.1954		1	1979	1
Butcher, Basil Fitzherbert	WI	3.9.1933		44	*1958*–1969	
[1]**Butcher,** Mark Alan	E	23.8.1972		62	1997–*2003*	
Butcher, Roland Orlando	E	14.10.1953		3	*1980*	3
Butler, Harold James	E	12.3.1913	17.7.1991	2	1947–*1947*	
Butler, Ian Gareth	NZ	24.11.1981		7	*2001–2003*	9
Butler, Lennox Stephen	WI	9.2.1929		1	*1954*	
Butt, Henry Rigden	E	27.12.1865	21.12.1928	3	*1895*	
Butterfield, Leonard Arthur	NZ	29.8.1913	7.7.1999	1	*1945*	
Butts, Clyde Godfrey	WI	8.7.1957		7	*1984–1987*	
Buys, Isaac Daniel	SA	4.2.1895	d unknown	1	*1922*	
Bynoe, Michael Robin	WI	23.2.1941		4	*1958–1966*	
Caddick, Andrew Richard	E	21.11.1968		62	1993–*2002*	54
[1]**Cairns,** Bernard Lance	NZ	10.10.1949		43	*1973–1985*	78
[1]**Cairns,** Christopher Lance	NZ	13.6.1970		56	*1989–2003*	175
Callaway, Sydney Thomas	A	6.2.1868	25.11.1923	3	*1891–1894*	
Callen, Ian Wayne	A	2.5.1955		1	*1977*	5
Calthorpe, *Hon.* Frederick Somerset Gough-	E	27.5.1892	19.11.1935	4	*1929*	

[1] *Father and son(s).* [2] *Brothers.*

	Country	*Born*	*Died*	*Tests*	*Test Career*	*ODIs*
Camacho, George Stephen	WI	15.10.1945		11	*1967–1970*	
[2]**Cameron,** Francis James	WI	22.6.1923	10.6.1994	5	*1948*	
Cameron, Francis James MBE	NZ	1.6.1932		19	*1961*–1965	
Cameron, Horace Brakenridge	SA	5.7.1905	2.11.1935	26	*1927*–1935	
[2]**Cameron,** John Hemsley	WI	8.4.1914	13.2.2000	2	1939	
Campbell, Alistair Douglas Ross	Z	23.9.1972		60	*1992–2002*	188
Campbell, Gregory Dale	A	10.3.1964		4	1989–*1989*	12
Campbell, Sherwin Legay	WI	1.11.1970		52	*1994–2001*	90
Campbell, Thomas	SA	9.2.1882	5.10.1924	5	*1909*–1912	
Capel, David John	E	6.2.1963		15	1987–*1989*	23
Carew, George McDonald	WI	4.6.1910	9.12.1974	4	*1934–1948*	
Carew, Michael Conrad	WI	15.9.1937		19	1963–*1971*	
Carkeek, William	A	17.10.1878	20.2.1937	6	1912	
Carlisle, Stuart Vance	Z	10.5.1972		33	*1994–2003*	98
Carlson, Phillip Henry	A	8.8.1951		2	*1978*	4
Carlstein, Peter Rudolph	SA	28.10.1938		8	*1957–1963*	
Carr, Arthur William	E	21.5.1893	7.2.1963	11	*1922*–1929	
Carr, Donald Bryce OBE	E	28.12.1926		2	*1951*	
Carr, Douglas Ward	E	17.3.1872	23.3.1950	1	1909	
Carter, Claude Pagdett	SA	23.4.1881	8.11.1952	10	1912–1924	
Carter, Hanson	A	15.3.1878	8.6.1948	28	*1907–1921*	
Cartwright, Thomas William MBE	E	22.7.1935		5	1964–1965	
Catterall, Robert Hector	SA	10.7.1900	3.1.1961	24	*1922–1930*	
Cave, Henry Butler	NZ	10.10.1922	15.9.1989	19	1949–1958	
Challenor, George	WI	28.6.1888	30.7.1947	3	1928	
Chandana, Umagiliya Durage Upul	SL	7.5.1972		9	*1998–2003*	106
Chanderpaul, Shivnarine	WI	18.8.1974		71	*1993–2003*	137
Chandrasekhar, Bhagwat Subramanya	I	17.5.1945		58	*1963*–1979	1
Chang, Herbert Samuel	WI	22.7.1952		1	*1978*	
Chapman, Arthur Percy Frank	E	3.9.1900	16.9.1961	26	1924–*1930*	
Chapman, Horace William	SA	30.6.1890	1.12.1941	2	*1913–1921*	
[2]**Chappell,** Gregory Stephen MBE	A	7.8.1948		87	*1970–1983*	74
[2]**Chappell,** Ian Michael	A	26.9.1943		75	*1964–1979*	16
[2]**Chappell,** Trevor Martin	A	21.10.1952		3	1981	20
Chapple, Murray Ernest	NZ	25.7.1930	31.7.1985	14	*1952–1965*	
Charlton, Percie Chater	A	9.4.1867	30.9.1954	2	1890	
Charlwood, Henry Rupert James	E	19.12.1846	6.6.1888	2	*1876*	
Chatfield, Ewen John MBE	NZ	3.7.1950		43	*1974–1988*	114
Chatterton, William	E	27.12.1861	19.3.1913	1	*1891*	
Chauhan, Chetandra Pratap Singh	I	21.7.1947		40	*1969–1980*	7
Chauhan, Rajesh Kumar	I	19.12.1966		21	*1992–1997*	35
Cheetham, John Erskine	SA	26.5.1920	21.8.1980	24	*1948*–1955	
Chevalier, Grahame Anton	SA	9.3.1937		1	*1969*	
Childs, John Henry	E	15.8.1951		2	1988	
Chipperfield, Arthur Gordon	A	17.11.1905	29.7.1987	14	1934–1938	
Chopra, Aakash	I	19.9.1977		6	*2003*	
Chopra, Nikhil	I	26.12.1973		1	*1999*	39
Chowdhury, Nirode Ranjan	I	23.5.1923	14.12.1979	2	*1948–1951*	
[2]**Christiani,** Cyril Marcel	WI	28.10.1913	4.4.1938	4	*1934*	
[2]**Christiani,** Robert Julian	WI	19.7.1920		22	*1947–1953*	
Christopherson, Stanley	E	11.11.1861	6.4.1949	1	1884	
Christy, James Alexander Joseph	SA	12.12.1904	1.2.1971	10	1929–*1931*	
Chubb, Geoffrey Walter Ashton	SA	12.4.1911	28.8.1982	5	1951	
Clark, Edward Winchester	E	9.8.1902	28.4.1982	8	1929–1934	
Clark, Wayne Maxwell	A	19.9.1953		10	*1977–1978*	2
Clarke, Carlos Bertram OBE	WI	7.4.1918	14.10.1993	3	1939	
Clarke, Rikki	E	29.9.1981		2	*2003*	11
Clarke, Sylvester Theophilus	WI	11.12.1954	4.12.1999	11	*1977–1981*	10
Clay, John Charles	E	18.3.1898	12.8.1973	1	1935	

[1] *Father and son(s).* [2] *Brothers.*

	Country	*Born*	*Died*	*Tests*	*Test Career*	*ODIs*
Cleverley, Donald Charles	NZ	23.12.1909	16.2.2004	2	*1931–1945*	
Close, Dennis Brian CBE	E	24.2.1931		22	1949–1976	3
Cochran, John Alexander Kennedy	SA	15.7.1909	15.6.1987	1	*1930*	
Coen, Stanley Keppel	SA	14.10.1902	28.1.1967	2	*1927*	
Colah, Sorabji Hormasji Munchersha	I	22.9.1902	11.9.1950	2	1932–*1933*	
Coldwell, Leonard John	E	10.1.1933	6.8.1996	7	1962–1964	
Colley, David John	A	15.3.1947		3	1972	1
Collinge, Richard Owen	NZ	2.4.1946		35	*1964*–1978	15
Collingwood, Paul David	E	26.5.1976		2	*2003*	42
Collins, Herbert Leslie	A	21.1.1888	28.5.1959	19	*1920*–1926	
Collins, Pedro Tyrone	WI	12.8.1976		19	*1998–2002*	23
Collymore, Corey Dalanelo	WI	21.12.1977		7	*1998–2003*	46
Colquhoun, Ian Alexander	NZ	8.6.1924		2	*1954*	
Commaille, John McIllwaine Moore	SA	21.2.1883	28.7.1956	12	*1909–1927*	
Commins, John Brian	SA	19.2.1965		3	*1994*	
Compton, Denis Charles Scott CBE	E	23.5.1918	23.4.1997	78	1937–*1956*	
Coney, Jeremy Vernon MBE	NZ	21.6.1952		52	*1973–1986*	88
Congdon, Bevan Ernest OBE	NZ	11.2.1938		61	*1964*–1978	11
Coningham, Arthur	A	14.7.1863	13.6.1939	1	*1894*	
Connolly, Alan Norman	A	29.6.1939		29	*1963–1970*	1
Constantine, Learie Nicholas (later Baron Constantine of Maraval & Nelson)	WI	21.9.1901	1.7.1971	18	1928–1939	
Contractor, Nariman Jamshedji	I	7.3.1934		31	*1955–1961*	
Conyngham, Dalton Parry	SA	10.5.1897	7.7.1979	1	*1922*	
Cook, Cecil	E	23.8.1921	4.9.1996	1	1947	
Cook, Frederick James	SA	1870	30.11.1915	1	*1895*	
Cook, Geoffrey	E	9.10.1951		7	*1981–1982*	6
Cook, Nicholas Grant Billson	E	17.6.1956		15	1983–1989	3
Cook, Simon Hewitt	A	29.1.1972		2	*1997*	
Cook, Stephen James	SA	31.7.1953		3	*1992–1993*	4
Cooper, Alfred Henry Cecil	SA	2.9.1893	18.7.1963	1	*1913*	
Cooper, Bransby Beauchamp	A	15.3.1844	7.8.1914	1	*1876*	
[5]**Cooper,** William Henry	A	11.9.1849	5.4.1939	2	*1881–1884*	
Cope, Geoffrey Alan	E	23.2.1947		3	*1977*	2
Copson, William Henry	E	27.4.1908	14.9.1971	3	1939–1947	
Cork, Dominic Gerald	E	7.8.1971		37	1995–2002	32
Corling, Grahame Edward	A	13.7.1941		5	1964	
Cornford, Walter Latter	E	25.12.1900	6.2.1964	4	*1929*	
Cosier, Gary John	A	25.4.1953		18	*1975–1978*	9
Cottam, John Thomas	A	5.9.1867	30.1.1897	1	*1886*	
Cottam, Robert Michael Henry	E	16.10.1944		4	*1968–1972*	
Cotter, Albert	A	3.12.1884	31.10.1917	21	*1903–1911*	
Coulthard, George	A	1.8.1856	22.10.1883	1	*1881*	
Coventry, *Hon.* Charles John	E	26.2.1867	2.6.1929	2	*1888*	
Cowans, Norman George	E	17.4.1961		19	*1982*–1985	23
[1]**Cowdrey,** Christopher Stuart	E	20.10.1957		6	*1984*–1988	3
[1]**Cowdrey,** Michael Colin (later Baron Cowdrey of Tonbridge)	E	24.12.1932	4.12.2000	114	*1954–1974*	1
Cowie, John OBE	NZ	30.3.1912	3.6.1994	9	1937–1949	
Cowper, Robert Maskew	A	5.10.1940		27	1964–1968	
Cox, Joseph Lovell	SA	28.6.1886	4.7.1971	3	*1913*	
Coxon, Alexander	E	18.1.1916		1	1948	
Craig, Ian David	A	12.6.1935		11	*1952–1957*	
Cranston, James	E	9.1.1859	10.12.1904	1	1890	
Cranston, Kenneth	E	20.10.1917		8	1947–1948	
Crapp, John Frederick	E	14.10.1912	15.2.1981	7	1948–*1948*	
Crawford, John Neville	E	1.12.1886	2.5.1963	12	*1905–1907*	
Crawford, William Patrick Anthony	A	3.8.1933		4	1956–*1956*	
Crawley, John Paul	E	21.9.1971		37	1994–*2002*	13

[1] *Father and son.* [2] *Brothers.* [5] *Great-grandfather and great-grandson.*

	Country	*Born*	*Died*	*Tests*	*Test Career*	*ODIs*
Cresswell, George Fenwick	NZ	22.3.1915	10.1.1966	3	1949–*1950*	
Cripps, Godfrey	SA	19.10.1865	27.7.1943	1	*1891*	
Crisp, Robert James	SA	28.5.1911	2.3.1994	9	1935–*1935*	
Crocker, Gary John	Z	16.5.1962		3	*1992*	6
Croft, Colin Everton Hunte	WI	15.3.1953		27	*1976–1981*	19
Croft, Robert Damien Bale	E	25.5.1970		21	1996–2001	50
Cromb, Ian Burns	NZ	25.6.1905	6.3.1984	5	1931–*1931*	
Cronje, Wessel Johannes ("Hansie")	SA	25.9.1969	1.6.2002	68	*1991–1999*	188
[2]**Crowe,** Jeffrey John	NZ	14.9.1958		39	*1982–1989*	75
[2]**Crowe,** Martin David MBE	NZ	22.9.1962		77	*1981–1995*	143
Cuffy, Cameron Eustace	WI	8.2.1970		15	*1994–2002*	41
Cullinan, Daryll John	SA	4.3.1967		70	*1992–2000*	138
Cummins, Anderson Cleophas	WI	7.5.1966		5	*1992–1994*	63
Cunis, Robert Smith	NZ	5.1.1941		20	*1963–1971*	
Curnow, Sydney Harry	SA	16.12.1907	28.7.1986	7	*1930–1931*	
Curtis, Timothy Stephen	E	15.1.1960		5	1988–1989	
Cuttell, Willis Robert	E	13.9.1864	9.12.1929	2	*1898*	
Da Costa, Oscar Constantine	WI	11.9.1907	1.10.1936	5	*1929–1934*	
Dahiya, Vijay	I	10.5.1973		2	*2000*	19
Dale, Adam Craig	A	30.12.1968		2	*1997–1998*	30
Dalton, Eric Londesbrough	SA	2.12.1906	3.6.1981	15	1929–*1938*	
Dani, Hemchandra Tukaram	I	24.5.1933	19.12.1999	1	*1952*	
Daniel, Wayne Wendell	WI	16.1.1956		10	*1975–1983*	18
Danish Kaneria	P	16.12.1980		16	*2000–2003*	9
D'Arcy, John William	NZ	23.4.1936		5	1958	
Darling, Joseph	A	21.11.1870	2.1.1946	34	*1894*–1905	
Darling, Leonard Stuart	A	14.8.1909	24.6.1992	12	*1932–1936*	
Darling, Warrick Maxwell	A	1.5.1957		14	*1977–1979*	18
Das, Shiv Sunder	I	5.11.1977		23	*2000–2001*	4
Dasgupta, Deep	I	7.6.1977		8	*2001*	5
Dassanayake, Pubudu Bathiya	SL	11.7.1970		11	*1993–1994*	16
Davidson, Alan Keith	A	14.6.1929		44	1953–*1962*	
Davies, Eric Quail	SA	26.8.1909	11.11.1976	5	*1935–1938*	
[2]**Davis,** Bryan Allan	WI	2.5.1940		4	*1964*	
[2]**Davis,** Charles Allan	WI	1.1.1944		15	*1968–1972*	
Davis, Heath Te-Ihi-O-Te-Rangi	NZ	30.11.1971		5	1994–*1997*	11
Davis, Ian Charles	A	25.6.1953		15	*1973*–1977	3
Davis, Simon Peter	A	8.11.1959		1	*1985*	39
Davis, Winston Walter	WI	18.9.1958		15	*1982–1987*	35
Dawson, Alan Charles	SA	27.11.1969		2	*2002*	16
Dawson, Edward William	A	13.2.1904	4.6.1979	5	*1927–1929*	
Dawson, Oswald Charles	SA	1.9.1919		9	1947–*1948*	
Dawson, Richard Kevin James	E	4.8.1980		7	*2001–2002*	
de Alwis, Ronald Guy	SL	15.2.1959		11	*1982–1987*	31
Dean, Harry	E	13.8.1884	12.3.1957	3	1912	
Deane, Hubert Gouvaine	SA	21.7.1895	21.10.1939	17	1924–*1930*	
De Caires, Francis Ignatius	WI	12.5.1909	2.2.1959	3	*1929*	
De Courcy, James Harry	A	18.4.1927	20.6.2000	3	1953	
DeFreitas, Phillip Anthony Jason	E	18.2.1966		44	*1986*–1995	103
de Groen, Richard Paul	NZ	5.8.1962		5	*1993–1994*	12
Dekker, Mark Hamilton	Z	5.12.1969		14	*1993–1996*	23
Dell, Anthony Ross	A	6.8.1947		2	*1970–1973*	
de Mel, Ashantha Lakdasa Francis	SL	9.5.1959		17	*1981–1986*	57
Dempster, Charles Stewart	NZ	15.11.1903	14.2.1974	10	*1929–1932*	
Dempster, Eric William	NZ	25.1.1925		5	*1952–1953*	
Denness, Michael Henry	E	1.12.1940		28	1969–1975	12
Denton, David	E	4.7.1874	16.2.1950	11	1905–*1909*	
Depeiza, Cyril Clairmonte	WI	10.10.1927	10.11.1995	5	*1954–1955*	

[1] *Father and son(s).* [2] *Brothers.*

	Country	*Born*	*Died*	*Tests*	*Test Career*	*ODIs*
Desai, Ramakant Bhikaji	I	20.6.1939	27.4.1998	28	*1958–1967*	
de Saram, Samantha Indika	SL	2.9.1973		4	*1999*	15
de Silva, Ashley Matthew	SL	3.12.1963		3	*1992–1993*	4
de Silva, Dandeniyage Somachandra	SL	11.6.1942		12	*1981*–1984	41
de Silva, Ellawalakankanamge Asoka Ranjit	SL	28.3.1956		10	*1985–1990*	28
de Silva, Ginigalgodage Ramba Ajit	SL	12.12.1952		4	*1981–1982*	6
de Silva, Karunakalage Sajeewa Chanaka	SL	11.1.1971		8	*1996–1998*	38
de Silva, Pinnaduwage Aravinda	SL	17.10.1965		93	1984–*2002*	308
de Silva, Sanjeewa Kumara Lanka	SL	29.7.1975		3	*1997*	11
de Silva, Weddikkara Ruwan Sujeewa	SL	7.10.1979		2	*2002*	
de Villiers, Petrus Stephanus ("Fanie")	SA	13.10.1964		18	*1993–1997*	83
Dewdney, David Thomas	WI	23.10.1933		9	*1954–1957*	
Dewes, John Gordon	E	11.10.1926		5	1948–*1950*	
Dexter, Edward Ralph	E	15.5.1935		62	1958–1968	
Dhanraj, Rajindra	WI	6.2.1969		4	*1994–1995*	6
Dharmasena, Handunnettige Deepthi Priyantha Kumar	SL	24.4.1971		30	*1993–2003*	138
Dias, Roy Luke	SL	18.10.1952		20	*1981–1986*	58
Dick, Arthur Edward	NZ	10.10.1936		17	*1961*–1965	
Dickinson, George Ritchie	NZ	11.3.1903	17.3.1978	3	*1929–1931*	
Dighe, Sameer Sudhakar	I	8.10.1968		6	*2000–2001*	23
Dilawar Hussain	I	19.3.1907	26.8.1967	3	*1933*–1936	
Dilley, Graham Roy	E	18.5.1959		41	*1979*–1989	36
Dillon, Mervyn	WI	5.6.1974		38	*1996–2003*	93
Dilshan, Tillekeratne Mudiyanselage	SL	14.10.1976		12	*1999–2003*	24
Dippenaar, Hendrik Human	SA	14.6.1977		24	*1999–2003*	67
Dipper, Alfred Ernest	E	9.11.1885	7.11.1945	1	1921	
Divecha, Ramesh Vithaldas	I	18.10.1927	19.2.2003	5	*1951–1952*	
Dixon, Cecil Donovan	SA	12.2.1891	9.9.1969	1	*1913*	
Dodemaide, Anthony Ian Christopher	A	5.10.1963		10	*1987–1992*	24
Doggart, George Hubert Graham OBE	E	18.7.1925		2	1950	
D'Oliveira, Basil Lewis OBE	E	4.10.1931		44	1966–1972	4
Dollery, Horace Edgar	E	15.10.1914	20.1.1987	4	1947–1950	
Dolphin, Arthur	E	24.12.1885	23.10.1942	1	*1920*	
Donald, Allan Anthony	SA	20.10.1966		72	*1991–2001*	164
Donnan, Henry	A	12.11.1864	13.8.1956	5	*1891*–1896	
Donnelly, Martin Paterson	NZ	17.10.1917	22.10.1999	7	1937–1949	
Dooland, Bruce	A	1.11.1923	8.9.1980	3	*1946–1947*	
Doshi, Dilip Rasiklal	I	22.12.1947		33	*1979–1983*	15
Douglas, John William Henry Tyler	E	3.9.1882	19.12.1930	23	*1911–1924*	
Doull, Simon Blair	NZ	6.8.1969		32	*1992–1999*	42
Dowe, Uton George	WI	29.3.1949		4	*1970–1972*	
Dower, Robert Reid	SA	4.6.1876	15.9.1964	1	*1898*	
Dowling, Graham Thorne OBE	NZ	4.3.1937		39	*1961–1971*	
Downton, Paul Rupert	E	4.4.1957		30	*1980*–1988	28
Drakes, Vasbert Conniel	WI	5.8.1969		12	*2002–2003*	33
Draper, Ronald George	SA	24.12.1926		2	*1949*	
Dravid, Rahul	I	11.1.1973		75	1996–*2003*	214
Druce, Norman Frank	E	1.1.1875	27.10.1954	5	*1897*	
Drum, Christopher James	NZ	10.7.1974		5	*2000–2001*	5
D'Souza, Antao	P	17.1.1939		6	*1958*–1962	
Ducat, Andrew	E	16.2.1886	23.7.1942	1	1921	
Duckworth, Christopher Anthony Russell	SA	22.3.1933		2	*1956*	
Duckworth, George	E	9.5.1901	5.1.1966	24	1924–1936	
Duff, Reginald Alexander	A	17.8.1878	13.12.1911	22	*1901*–1905	
Dujon, Peter Jeffrey Leroy	WI	28.5.1956		81	*1981*–1991	169
Duleepsinhji, Kumar Shri	E	13.6.1905	5.12.1959	12	1929–1931	

[1] *Father and son(s).* [2] *Brothers.*

	Country	*Born*	*Died*	*Tests*	*Test Career*	*ODIs*
Dumbrill, Richard	SA	19.11.1938		5	1965–*1966*	
Duminy, Jacobus Petrus	SA	16.12.1897	31.1.1980	3	*1927*–1929	
Duncan, John Ross Frederick	A	25.3.1944		1	*1970*	
Dunell, Owen Robert	SA	15.7.1856	21.10.1929	2	*1888*	
Dunning, John Angus	NZ	6.2.1903	24.6.1971	4	*1932*–1937	
Dunusinghe, Chamara Iroshan	SL	19.10.1970		5	*1994–1995*	1
Du Preez, John Harcourt	SA	14.11.1942		2	*1966*	
Durani, Salim Aziz	I	11.12.1934		29	*1959–1972*	
Durston, Frederick John	E	11.7.1893	8.4.1965	1	1921	
Du Toit, Jacobus Francois	SA	2.4.1869	10.7.1909	1	*1891*	
Dyer, Dennis Victor	SA	2.5.1914	16.6.1990	3	1947	
Dyer, Gregory Charles	A	16.3.1959		6	*1986–1987*	23
Dymock, Geoffrey	A	21.7.1945		21	*1973–1979*	15
Dyson, John	A	11.6.1954		30	*1977–1984*	29
Eady, Charles John	A	29.10.1870	20.12.1945	2	1896–*1901*	
Ealham, Mark Alan	E	27.8.1969		8	1996–1998	64
Eastwood, Kenneth Humphrey	A	23.11.1935		1	*1970*	
Ebeling, Hans Irvine	A	1.1.1905	12.1.1980	1	1934	
Ebrahim, Dion Digby	Z	7.8.1980		18	*2000–2003*	53
Edgar, Bruce Adrian	NZ	23.11.1956		39	1978–1986	64
Edmonds, Philippe-Henri	E	8.3.1951		51	1975–1987	29
Edrich, John Hugh MBE	E	21.6.1937		77	1963–1976	7
Edrich, William John	E	26.3.1916	24.4.1986	39	1938–*1954*	
Edwards, Fidel Henderson	WI	6.2.1982		7	*2002–2003*	2
Edwards, Graham Neil	NZ	27.5.1955		8	*1976–1980*	6
Edwards, John Dunlop	A	12.6.1860	31.7.1911	3	1888	
Edwards, Richard Martin	WI	3.6.1940		5	*1968*	
Edwards, Ross	A	1.12.1942		20	1972–1975	9
Edwards, Walter John	A	23.12.1949		3	*1974*	1
Ehsanul Haque	B	1.12.1979		1	*2002*	6
Ehtesham-ud-Din	P	4.9.1950		5	*1979*–1982	
Eksteen, Clive Edward	SA	2.12.1966		7	*1993–1999*	6
Elgie, Michael Kelsey	SA	6.3.1933		3	*1961*	
Elliott, Harry	E	2.11.1891	2.2.1976	4	*1927–1933*	
Elliott, Matthew Thomas Gray	A	28.9.1971		20	*1996–1998*	1
Ellison, Richard Mark	E	21.9.1959		11	1984–1986	14
Elworthy, Steven	SA	23.2.1965		4	1998–*2002*	39
Emburey, John Ernest	E	20.8.1952		64	1978–1995	61
Emery, Philip Allen	A	25.6.1964		1	*1994*	1
Emery, Raymond William George	NZ	28.3.1915	18.12.1982	2	*1951*	
Emery, Sidney Hand	A	16.10.1885	7.1.1967	4	1912	
Emmett, George Malcolm	E	2.12.1912	18.12.1976	1	1948	
Emmett, Thomas	E	3.9.1841	30.6.1904	7	*1876–1881*	
Enamul Haque, sen.	B	27.2.1966		10	*2000–2002*	29
Enamul Haque, jun.	B	5.12.1986		2	*2003*	
Endean, William Russell	SA	31.5.1924	28.6.2003	28	1951–*1957*	
Engineer, Farokh Maneksha	I	25.2.1938		46	*1961–1974*	5
Ervine, Sean Michael	Z	6.12.1982		3	2003–*2003*	31
Evans, Alfred John	E	1.5.1889	18.9.1960	1	1921	
Evans, Craig Neil	Z	29.11.1969		3	*1996–2003*	53
Evans, Edwin	A	26.3.1849	2.7.1921	6	*1881*–1886	
Evans, Thomas Godfrey CBE	E	18.8.1920	3.5.1999	91	1946–1959	
Ewing, Gavin Mackie	Z	21.1.1981		1	*2003*	
Fagg, Arthur Edward	E	18.6.1915	13.9.1977	5	1936–1939	
Fahim Muntasir	B	1.11.1980		3	*2001–2002*	3
Fairbrother, Neil Harvey	E	9.9.1963		10	1987–*1992*	75
Fairfax, Alan George	A	16.6.1906	17.5.1955	10	*1928–1930*	

[1] *Father and son(s).* [2] *Brothers.*

	Country	*Born*	*Died*	*Tests*	*Test Career*	*ODIs*
Faisal Iqbal	P	30.12.1981		10	*2000–2002*	17
Fane, Frederick Luther	E	27.4.1875	27.11.1960	14	*1905–1909*	
Farhan Adil	P	25.9.1977		1	*2003*	
Farnes, Kenneth	E	8.7.1911	20.10.1941	15	1934–*1938*	
Farooq Hamid	P	3.3.1945		1	*1964*	
Farrer, William Stephen	SA	8.12.1936		6	*1961–1963*	
Farrimond, William	E	23.5.1903	14.11.1979	4	*1930*–1935	
Farrukh Zaman	P	2.4.1956		1	*1976*	
Faulkner, George Aubrey	SA	17.12.1881	10.9.1930	25	*1905*–1924	
Favell, Leslie Ernest MBE	A	6.10.1929	14.6.1987	19	*1954–1960*	
Fazal Mahmood	P	18.2.1927		34	*1952*–1962	
Fazl-e-Akbar	P	20.10.1980		4	*1997–2000*	2
Fellows-Smith, Jonathan Payn	SA	3.2.1932		4	1960	
Fender, Percy George Herbert	E	22.8.1892	15.6.1985	13	*1920*–1929	
Ferguson, Wilfred	WI	14.12.1917	23.2.1961	8	*1947–1953*	
Fernandes, Maurius Pacheco	WI	12.8.1897	8.5.1981	2	1928–*1929*	
Fernando, Congenige Randhi Dilhara	SL	19.7.1979		14	*2000–2003*	55
Fernando, Ellekutige Rufus Nemesion Susil	SL	19.12.1955		5	*1982–1983*	7
Fernando, Kandana Arachchige Dinusha Manoj	SL	10.8.1979		2	*2003*	1
Fernando, Kandage Hasantha Ruwan Kumara	SL	14.10.1979		2	*2002*	5
Fernando, Thudellage Charitha Buddhika	SL	22.8.1980		9	*2001–2002*	17
Ferris, John James	A, E	21.5.1867	21.11.1900	9	*1886–1891*	
Fichardt, Charles Gustav	SA	20.3.1870	30.5.1923	2	*1891–1895*	
Fielder, Arthur	E	19.7.1877	30.8.1949	6	*1903–1907*	
Findlay, Thaddeus Michael MBE	WI	19.10.1943		10	1969–*1972*	
Fingleton, John Henry Webb OBE	A	28.4.1908	22.11.1981	18	*1931*–1938	
Finlason, Charles Edward	SA	19.2.1860	31.7.1917	1	*1888*	
Fisher, Frederick Eric	NZ	28.7.1924	19.6.1996	1	*1952*	
Fishlock, Laurence Barnard	E	2.1.1907	26.6.1986	4	1936–*1946*	
Flavell, John Alfred	E	15.5.1929		4	1961–1964	
Fleetwood-Smith, Leslie O'Brien	A	30.3.1908	16.3.1971	10	*1935*–1938	
Fleming, Damien William	A	24.4.1970		20	*1994–2000*	88
Fleming, Stephen Paul	NZ	1.4.1973		79	*1993–2003*	207
Fletcher, Keith William Robert OBE	E	20.5.1944		59	1968–*1981*	24
Flintoff, Andrew	E	6.12.1977		29	1998–*2003*	66
Floquet, Claude Eugene	SA	3.11.1884	22.11.1963	1	*1909*	
[2]**Flower,** Andrew	Z	28.4.1968		63	*1992–2002*	213
[2]**Flower,** Grant William	Z	20.12.1970		65	*1992*–2003	209
Flowers, Wilfred	A	7.12.1856	1.11.1926	8	*1884*–1893	
Foley, Henry	NZ	28.1.1906	16.10.1948	1	*1929*	
Ford, Francis Gilbertson Justice	E	14.12.1866	7.2.1940	5	*1894*	
Foster, Frank Rowbotham	E	31.1.1889	3.5.1958	11	*1911*–1912	
Foster, James Savin	E	15.4.1980		7	*2001–2002*	11
Foster, Maurice Linton Churchill	WI	9.5.1943		14	1969–*1977*	2
Foster, Neil Alan	E	6.5.1962		29	1983–1993	48
Foster, Reginald Erskine	E	16.4.1878	13.5.1914	8	*1903*–1907	
Fothergill, Arnold James	E	26.8.1854	1.8.1932	2	*1888*	
Fowler, Graeme	E	20.4.1957		21	1982–*1984*	26
Francis, Bruce Colin	A	18.2.1948		3	1972	
Francis, George Nathaniel	WI	11.12.1897	7.1.1942	10	1928–1933	
Francis, Howard Henry	SA	26.5.1868	7.1.1936	2	*1898*	
Francois, Cyril Matthew	SA	20.6.1897	26.5.1944	5	*1922*	
Frank, Charles Newton	SA	27.1.1891	25.12.1961	3	*1921*	
Frank, William Hughes Bowker	SA	23.11.1872	16.2.1945	1	*1895*	
Franklin, James Edward Charles	NZ	7.11.1980		2	*2000*	24

[1] *Father and son(s).* [2] *Brothers.*

	Country	Born	Died	Tests	Test Career	ODIs
Franklin, Trevor John	NZ	18.3.1962		21	1983–*1990*	3
Fraser, Angus Robert Charles	E	8.8.1965		46	1989–*1998*	42
Frederick, Michael Campbell	WI	6.5.1927		1	*1953*	
Fredericks, Roy Clifton	WI	11.11.1942	5.9.2000	59	*1968–1976*	12
Freeman, Alfred Percy	E	17.5.1888	28.1.1965	12	*1924*–1929	
Freeman, Douglas Linford	NZ	8.9.1914	31.5.1994	2	*1932*	
Freeman, Eric Walter	A	13.7.1944		11	*1967–1969*	
Freer, Frederick Alfred William	A	4.12.1915	2.11.1998	1	*1946*	
French, Bruce Nicholas	E	13.8.1959		16	1986–*1987*	13
Friend, Travis John	Z	7.1.1981		12	*2001*–2003	47
Fry, Charles Burgess	E	25.4.1872	7.9.1956	26	*1895*–1912	
Fuller, Edward Russell Henry	SA	2.8.1931		7	*1952–1957*	
Fuller, Richard Livingston	SA	30.1.1913	3.5.1987	1	*1934*	
Fullerton, George Murray	SA	8.12.1922	19.11.2002	7	1947–1951	
Funston, Kenneth James	SA	3.12.1925		18	*1952–1957*	
Furlonge, Hammond Allan	WI	19.6.1934		3	*1954–1955*	
Gadkari, Chandrasekhar Vaman	I	3.2.1928	11.1.1998	6	*1952–1954*	
[1]**Gaekwad,** Anshuman Dattajirao	I	23.9.1952		40	*1974–1984*	15
[1]**Gaekwad,** Dattajirao Krishnarao	I	27.10.1928		11	1952–*1960*	
Gaekwad, Hiralal Ghasulal	I	29.8.1923	2.1.2003	1	*1952*	
Gallage, Indika Sanjeewa	SL	22.11.1975		1	*1999*	3
Gallian, Jason Edward Riche	E	25.6.1971		3	1995–*1995*	
Gallichan, Norman	NZ	3.6.1906	25.3.1969	1	1937	
Gamsy, Dennis	SA	17.2.1940		2	*1969*	
Gandhi, Devang Jayant	I	6.9.1971		4	*1999*	3
Gandotra, Ashok	I	24.11.1948		2	*1969*	
Ganesh, Doddanarasiah	I	30.6.1973		4	*1996*	1
Ganga, Daren	WI	14.1.1979		28	*1998–2003*	28
Ganguly, Sourav Chandidas	I	8.7.1972		72	1996–*2003*	235
Gannon, John Bryant	A	8.2.1947		3	*1977*	
Ganteaume, Andrew Gordon	WI	22.1.1921		1	*1947*	
Garner, Joel MBE	WI	16.12.1952		58	*1976–1986*	98
Garrett, Thomas William	A	26.7.1858	6.8.1943	19	*1876–1887*	
Garrick, Leon Vivian	WI	11.11.1976		1	*2000*	3
Gaskin, Berkeley Bertram McGarrell	WI	21.3.1908	1.5.1979	2	*1947*	
Gatting, Michael William OBE	E	6.6.1957		79	*1977–1994*	92
Gaunt, Ronald Arthur	A	26.2.1934		3	*1957–1963*	
Gavaskar, Sunil Manohar	I	10.7.1949		125	*1970–1986*	108
Gay, Leslie Hewitt	E	24.3.1871	1.11.1949	1	*1894*	
Gayle, Christopher Henry	WI	21.9.1979		37	*1999–2003*	83
Geary, George	E	9.7.1893	6.3.1981	14	1924–1934	
Gedye, Sidney Graham	NZ	2.5.1929		4	*1963–1964*	
Gehrs, Donald Raeburn Algernon	A	29.11.1880	25.6.1953	6	*1903–1910*	
Germon, Lee Kenneth	NZ	4.11.1968		12	*1995–1996*	37
Ghavri, Karsan Devjibhai	I	28.2.1951		39	*1974–1980*	19
Ghazali, Mohammad Ebrahim Zainuddin	P	15.6.1924	26.4.2003	2	1954	
Ghorpade, Jayasinghrao Mansinghrao	I	2.10.1930	29.3.1978	8	*1952*–1959	
Ghulam Abbas	P	1.5.1947		1	1967	
Ghulam Ahmed	I	4.7.1922	28.10.1998	22	*1948–1958*	
Gibb, Paul Antony	E	11.7.1913	7.12.1977	8	*1938–1946*	
Gibbs, Glendon Lionel	WI	27.12.1925	21.2.1979	1	*1954*	
Gibbs, Herschelle Herman	SA	23.2.1974		56	*1996–2003*	138
Gibbs, Lancelot Richard	WI	29.9.1934		79	*1957–1975*	3
Gibson, Ottis Delroy	WI	16.3.1969		2	1995–*1998*	15
Giddins, Edward Simon Hunter	E	20.7.1971		4	1999–2000	
[2]**Giffen,** George	A	27.3.1859	29.11.1927	31	*1881*–1896	
[2]**Giffen,** Walter Frank	A	20.9.1861	28.6.1949	3	*1886–1891*	
Gifford, Norman MBE	E	30.3.1940		15	1964–1973	2

[1] *Father and son(s).* [2] *Brothers.*

	Country	*Born*	*Died*	*Tests*	*Test Career*	*ODIs*
Gilbert, David Robert	A	29.12.1960		9	1985–*1986*	14
Gilchrist, Adam Craig	A	14.11.1971		51	*1999–2003*	177
Gilchrist, Roy	WI	28.6.1934	18.7.2001	13	1957–*1958*	
Giles, Ashley Fraser	E	19.3.1973		30	1998–*2003*	35
Gillespie, Jason Neil	A	19.4.1975		49	*1996–2003*	57
Gillespie, Stuart Ross	NZ	2.3.1957		1	*1985*	19
[2]**Gilligan,** Alfred Herbert Harold	E	29.6.1896	5.5.1978	4	*1929*	
[2]**Gilligan,** Arthur Edward Robert	E	23.12.1894	5.9.1976	11	*1922–1924*	
Gilmour, Gary John	A	26.6.1951		15	*1973–1976*	5
Gimblett, Harold	E	19.10.1914	30.3.1978	3	1936–1939	
Gladstone Morais, George	WI	14.1.1901	19.5.1978	1	*1929*	
Gladwin, Clifford	E	3.4.1916	10.4.1988	8	1947–1949	
Gleeson, John William	A	14.3.1938		29	*1967*–1972	
Gleeson, Robert Anthony	SA	6.12.1873	27.9.1919	1	*1895*	
Glover, George Keyworth	SA	13.5.1870	15.11.1938	1	*1895*	
Goddard, John Douglas Claude OBE	WI	21.4.1919	26.8.1987	27	*1947*–1957	
Goddard, Thomas William	E	1.10.1900	22.5.1966	8	1930–1939	
Goddard, Trevor Leslie	SA	1.8.1931		41	1955–*1969*	
Gomes, Hilary Angelo	WI	13.7.1953		60	1976–*1986*	83
Gomez, Gerald Ethridge	WI	10.10.1919	6.8.1996	29	1939–*1953*	
Gooch, Graham Alan OBE	E	23.7.1953		118	1975–*1994*	125
Goodwin, Murray William	Z	11.12.1972		19	*1997*–2000	71
Goonatillake, Hettiarachige Mahes	SL	16.8.1952		5	*1981–1982*	6
Gopalan, Morappakam Joysam	I	6.6.1909	21.12.2003	1	*1933*	
Gopinath, Coimbatarao Doraikannu	I	1.3.1930		8	*1951–1959*	
Gordon, Norman	SA	6.8.1911		5	*1938*	
Gough, Darren	E	18.9.1970		58	1994–2003	121
Gover, Alfred Richard MBE	E	29.2.1908	7.10.2001	4	1936–1946	
Gower, David Ivon OBE	E	1.4.1957		117	1978–1992	114
[2]**Grace,** Edward Mills	E	28.11.1841	20.5.1911	1	1880	
[2]**Grace,** George Frederick	E	13.12.1850	22.9.1880	1	1880	
[2]**Grace,** William Gilbert (W.G.)	E	18.7.1848	23.10.1915	22	1880–1899	
Graham, Henry	A	22.11.1870	7.2.1911	6	1893–1896	
Graham, Robert	SA	16.9.1877	21.4.1946	2	*1898*	
[2]**Grant,** George Copeland	WI	9.5.1907	26.10.1978	12	*1930–1934*	
[2]**Grant,** Rolph Stewart	WI	15.12.1909	18.10.1977	7	*1934*–1939	
Graveney, Thomas William OBE	E	16.6.1927		79	1951–1969	
Gray, Anthony Hollis	WI	23.5.1963		5	*1986*	25
Gray, Evan John	NZ	18.11.1954		10	1983–*1988*	10
Greatbatch, Mark John	NZ	11.12.1963		41	*1987–1996*	84
Greenhough, Thomas	E	9.11.1931		4	1959–1960	
Greenidge, Alvin Ethelbert	WI	20.8.1956		6	*1977–1978*	1
Greenidge, Cuthbert Gordon MBE	WI	1.5.1951		108	*1974–1990*	128
Greenidge, Geoffrey Alan	WI	26.5.1948		5	*1971–1972*	
Greenwood, Andrew	E	20.8.1847	12.2.1889	2	*1876*	
[2]**Gregory,** David William	A	15.4.1845	4.8.1919	3	*1876–1878*	
[1, 2]**Gregory,** Edward James	A	29.5.1839	22.4.1899	1	*1876*	
Gregory, Jack Morrison	A	14.8.1895	7.8.1973	24	*1920–1928*	
Gregory, Ross Gerald	A	28.2.1916	10.6.1942	2	*1936*	
[1]**Gregory,** Sydney Edward	A	14.4.1870	1.8.1929	58	1890–1912	
[2]**Greig,** Anthony William	E	6.10.1946		58	1972–1977	22
[2]**Greig,** Ian Alexander	E	8.12.1955		2	1982	
Grell, Mervyn George	WI	18.12.1899	11.1.1976	1	*1929*	
Grieve, Basil Arthur Firebrace	E	28.5.1864	19.11.1917	2	*1888*	
Grieveson, Ronald Eustace	SA	24.8.1909	24.7.1998	2	*1938*	
Griffin, Geoffrey Merton	SA	12.6.1939		2	1960	
Griffith, Adrian Frank Gordon	WI	19.11.1971		14	*1996*–2000	9
Griffith, Charles Christopher	WI	14.12.1938		28	*1959–1968*	
Griffith, Herman Clarence	WI	1.12.1893	18.3.1980	13	1928–1933	

[1] *Father and son(s).* [2] *Brothers.*

	Country	Born	Died	Tests	Test Career	ODIs
Griffith, Stewart Cathie CBE	E	16.6.1914	7.4.1993	3	*1947–1948*	
Grimmett, Clarence Victor	A	25.12.1891	2.5.1980	37	*1924–1935*	
Gripper, Trevor Raymond	Z	28.12.1975		18	*1999–2003*	8
Groube, Thomas Underwood	A	2.9.1857	5.8.1927	1	1880	
Grout, Arthur Theodore Wallace	A	30.3.1927	9.11.1968	51	*1957–1965*	
Guard, Ghulam Mustafa	I	12.12.1925	13.3.1978	2	*1958–1959*	
Guest, Colin Ernest John	A	7.10.1937		1	*1962*	
Guha, Subrata	I	31.1.1946	5.11.2003	4	1967–*1969*	
Guillen, Simpson Clairmonte	WI, NZ	24.9.1924		8	*1951–1955*	
Gul Mahomed	I, P	15.10.1921	8.5.1992	9	1946–*1956*	
Gunasekera, Yohan	SL	8.11.1957		2	*1982*	3
Gunawardene, Dihan Avishka	SL	26.5.1977		3	*1998–2000*	45
Guneratne, Roshan Punyajith Wijesinghe	SL	26.1.1962		1	*1982*	
[2]**Gunn,** George	E	13.6.1879	29.6.1958	15	*1907–1929*	
[2]**Gunn,** John Richmond	E	19.7.1876	21.8.1963	6	*1901*–1905	
Gunn, William	E	4.12.1858	29.1.1921	11	*1886*–1899	
[2]**Gupte,** Balkrishna Pandharinath	I	30.8.1934		3	*1960–1964*	
[2]**Gupte,** Subhashchandra Pandharinath	I	11.12.1929	31.5.2002	36	*1951–1961*	
Gursharan Singh	I	8.3.1963		1	*1989*	1
Gurusinha, Asanka Pradeep	SL	16.9.1966		41	*1985–1996*	147
Guy, John William	NZ	29.8.1934		12	*1955–1961*	
Habib, Aftab	E	7.2.1972		2	1999	
Habibul Bashar	B	17.8.1972		26	*2000–2003*	42
[1, 2]**Hadlee,** Dayle Robert	NZ	6.1.1948		26	1969–*1977*	11
[1, 2]**Hadlee,** *Sir* Richard John	NZ	3.7.1951		86	*1972*–1990	115
[1]**Hadlee,** Walter Arnold CBE	NZ	4.6.1915		11	1937–*1950*	
Hafeez, Abdul (see Kardar)						
Haig, Nigel Esmé	E	12.12.1887	27.10.1966	5	1921–*1929*	
Haigh, Schofield	E	19.3.1871	27.2.1921	11	*1898*–1912	
Hall, Alfred Ewart	SA	23.1.1896	1.1.1964	7	*1922–1930*	
Hall, Andrew James	SA	31.7.1975		10	*2001–2003*	43
Hall, Glen Gordon	SA	24.5.1938	26.6.1987	1	*1964*	
Hall, Wesley Winfield	WI	12.9.1937		48	*1958–1968*	
Halliwell, Ernest Austin	SA	7.9.1864	2.10.1919	8	*1891–1902*	
Hallows, Charles	E	4.4.1895	10.11.1972	2	1921–1928	
Halse, Clive Gray	SA	28.2.1935	28.5.2002	3	*1963*	
Hamence, Ronald Arthur	A	25.11.1915		3	*1946–1947*	
Hamilton, Gavin Mark	E	16.9.1974		1	*1999*	5
Hammond, Jeffrey Roy	A	19.4.1950		5	*1972*	1
Hammond, Walter Reginald	E	19.6.1903	1.7.1965	85	*1927–1946*	
Hampshire, John Harry	E	10.2.1941		8	1969–1975	3
[2]**Hands,** Philip Albert Myburgh	SA	18.3.1890	27.4.1951	7	*1913*–1924	
[2]**Hands,** Reginald Harry Myburgh	SA	26.7.1888	20.4.1918	1	*1913*	
[1, 2]**Hanif Mohammad**	P	21.12.1934		55	*1952–1969*	
Hanley, Martin Andrew	SA	10.11.1918	2.6.2000	1	*1948*	
Hannan Sarkar	B	1.12.1982		12	*2002–2003*	16
Hanumant Singh	I	29.3.1939		14	*1963–1969*	
Harbhajan Singh	I	3.7.1980		36	*1997–2003*	82
Hardikar, Manohar Shankar	I	8.2.1936	4.2.1995	2	*1958*	
Hardinge, Harold Thomas William	E	25.2.1886	8.5.1965	1	1921	
[1]**Hardstaff,** Joseph	E	9.11.1882	2.4.1947	5	*1907*	
[1]**Hardstaff,** Joseph, jun.	E	3.7.1911	1.1.1990	23	1935–1948	
Harford, Noel Sherwin	NZ	30.8.1930	30.3.1981	8	*1955*–1958	
Harford, Roy Ivan	NZ	30.5.1936		3	*1967*	
Harmison, Stephen James	E	23.10.1978		12	2002–*2003*	6
Haroon Rashid	P	25.3.1953		23	*1976–1982*	12
Harper, Roger Andrew	WI	17.3.1963		25	*1983–1993*	105

[1] *Father and son(s).* [2] *Brothers.*

	Country	Born	Died	Tests	Test Career	ODIs
[1]**Harris,** Chris Zinzan	NZ	20.11.1969		23	*1992–2001*	238
Harris, *Lord* George Robert Canning	E	3.2.1851	24.3.1932	4	*1878*–1884	
[1]**Harris,** Parke Gerald Zinzan	NZ	18.7.1927	1.12.1991	9	*1955–1964*	
Harris, Roger Meredith	NZ	27.7.1933		2	*1958*	
Harris, Terence Anthony	SA	27.8.1916	7.3.1993	3	1947–*1948*	
Harry, John	A	1.8.1857	27.10.1919	1	*1894*	
[2]**Hart,** Matthew Norman	NZ	16.5.1972		14	*1993–1995*	13
[2]**Hart,** Robert Garry	NZ	2.12.1974		11	*2001–2003*	2
Hartigan, Gerald Patrick Desmond	SA	30.12.1884	7.1.1955	5	1912–*1913*	
Hartigan, Roger Joseph	A	12.12.1879	7.6.1958	2	*1907*	
Hartkopf, Albert Ernst Victor	A	28.12.1889	20.5.1968	1	*1924*	
Hartland, Blair Robert	NZ	22.10.1966		9	*1991*–1994	16
Hartley, John Cabourn	E	15.11.1874	8.3.1963	2	*1905*	
[2]**Harvey,** Mervyn Roye	A	29.4.1918	18.3.1995	1	*1946*	
Harvey, Robert Lyon	SA	14.9.1911	20.7.2000	2	*1935*	
[2]**Harvey,** Robert Neil MBE	A	8.10.1928		79	*1947–1962*	
Harvinder Singh	I	23.12.1977		3	*1997–2001*	16
Hasan Raza	P	11.3.1982		5	*1996–2002*	16
Haseeb Ahsan	P	15.7.1939		12	*1957–1961*	
Hasibul Hussain	B	3.6.1977		5	*2000–2001*	31
Haslam, Mark James	NZ	26.9.1972		4	*1992–1995*	1
Hassett, Arthur Lindsay MBE	A	28.8.1913	16.6.1993	43	1938–1953	
Hastings, Brian Frederick	NZ	23.3.1940		31	*1968–1975*	11
Hathorn, Christopher Maitland Howard	SA	7.4.1878	17.5.1920	12	*1902–1910*	
Hathurusinghe, Upul Chandika	SL	13.9.1968		26	*1990–1998*	35
Hawke, *Lord* Martin Bladen	E	16.8.1860	10.10.1938	5	*1895–1898*	
Hawke, Neil James Napier	A	27.6.1939	25.12.2000	27	*1962*–1968	
Hayden, Matthew Lawrence	A	29.10.1971		50	*1993–2003*	80
Hayes, Ernest George	E	6.11.1876	2.12.1953	5	*1905*–1912	
Hayes, Frank Charles	E	6.12.1946		9	1973–1976	6
Hayes, John Arthur	NZ	11.1.1927		15	*1950*–1958	
Haynes, Desmond Leo	WI	15.2.1956		116	*1977–1993*	238
Hayward, Mornantau	SA	6.3.1977		14	*1999–2002*	21
Hayward, Thomas Walter	E	29.3.1871	19.7.1939	35	*1895*–1909	
Hazare, Vijay Samuel	I	11.3.1915		30	1946–*1952*	
Hazlitt, Gervys Rignold	A	4.9.1888	30.10.1915	9	*1907*–1912	
[3]**Headley,** Dean Warren	E	27.1.1970		15	1997–1999	13
[3]**Headley,** George Alphonso MBE	WI	30.5.1909	30.11.1983	22	*1929–1953*	
[3]**Headley,** Ronald George Alphonso	WI	29.6.1939		2	1973	1
Healy, Ian Andrew	A	30.4.1964		119	*1988–1999*	168
[2]**Hearne,** Alec	E	22.7.1863	16.5.1952	1	*1891*	
[1, 2]**Hearne,** Frank	E, SA	23.11.1858	14.7.1949	6	*1888–1895*	
[1]**Hearne,** George Alfred Lawrence	SA	27.3.1888	13.11.1978	3	*1922*–1924	
[2]**Hearne,** George Gibbons	E	7.7.1856	13.2.1932	1	*1891*	
Hearne, John Thomas	E	3.5.1867	17.4.1944	12	*1891*–1899	
Hearne, John William	E	11.2.1891	14.9.1965	24	*1911*–1926	
Hegg, Warren Kevin	E	23.2.1968		2	*1998*	
Heine, Peter Samuel	SA	28.6.1928		14	1955–*1961*	
Hemmings, Edward Ernest	E	20.2.1949		16	1982–*1990*	33
Henderson, Claude William	SA	14.6.1972		7	*2001–2002*	4
Henderson, Matthew	NZ	2.8.1895	17.6.1970	1	*1929*	
Hendren, Elias Henry ("Patsy")	E	5.2.1889	4.10.1962	51	*1920–1934*	
Hendrick, Michael	E	22.10.1948		30	1974–1981	22
Hendriks, John Leslie	WI	21.12.1933		20	*1961*–1969	
Hendry, Hunter Scott Thomas Laurie	A	24.5.1895	16.12.1988	11	1921–*1928*	
Henry, Omar	SA	23.1.1952		3	*1992*	3
Herath, Herath Mudiyanselage Rangana Keerthi Bandara	SL	19.3.1978		3	*1999–2000*	

[1] *Father and son.* [2] *Brothers.* [3] *Grandfather, father and son.*

	Country	*Born*	*Died*	*Tests*	*Test Career*	*ODIs*
Heseltine, Christopher	E	26.11.1869	13.6.1944	2	*1895*	
Hettiarachchi, Dinuka	SL	15.7.1976		1	*2000*	
Hibbert, Paul Anthony	A	23.7.1952		1	*1977*	
Hick, Graeme Ashley	E	23.5.1966		65	1991–*2000*	120
Higgs, James Donald	A	11.7.1950		22	*1977–1980*	
Higgs, Kenneth	E	14.1.1937		15	1965–1968	
Hilditch, Andrew Mark Jefferson	A	20.5.1956		18	*1978–1985*	8
Hill, Allen	E	14.11.1843	29.8.1910	2	*1876*	
Hill, Arthur James Ledger	E	26.7.1871	6.9.1950	3	*1895*	
Hill, Clement	A	18.3.1877	5.9.1945	49	1896–*1911*	
Hill, John Charles	A	25.6.1923	11.8.1974	3	1953–*1954*	
Hilton, Malcolm Jameson	E	2.8.1928	8.7.1990	4	1950–*1951*	
Hime, Charles Frederick William	SA	24.10.1869	6.12.1940	1	*1895*	
Hindlekar, Dattaram Dharmaji	I	1.1.1909	30.3.1949	4	1936–1946	
Hinds, Ryan O'Neal	WI	17.2.1981		4	*2001–2002*	11
Hinds, Wavell Wayne	WI	7.9.1976		38	*1999–2003*	83
Hirst, George Herbert	E	7.9.1871	10.5.1954	24	*1897*–1909	
Hirwani, Narendra Deepchand	I	18.10.1968		17	*1987–1996*	18
Hitch, John William	E	7.5.1886	7.7.1965	7	*1911*–1921	
Hoad, Edward Lisle Goldsworthy	WI	29.1.1896	5.3.1986	4	1928–1933	
Hoare, Desmond Edward	A	19.10.1934		1	*1960*	
Hobbs, *Sir* John Berry	E	16.12.1882	21.12.1963	61	*1907*–1930	
Hobbs, Robin Nicholas Stuart	E	8.5.1942		7	1967–1971	
Hodges, John Robart	A	11.8.1855	d unknown	2	*1876*	
Hogan, Tom George	A	23.9.1956		7	*1982–1983*	16
Hogg, George Bradley	A	6.2.1971		4	*1996–2003*	38
Hogg, Rodney Malcolm	A	5.3.1951		38	*1978–1984*	71
Hoggard, Matthew James	E	31.12.1976		22	2000–*2003*	20
Hohns, Trevor Victor	A	23.1.1954		7	*1988*–1989	
Holder, Roland Irwin Christopher	WI	22.12.1967		11	*1996–1998*	37
Holder, Vanburn Alonza	WI	8.10.1945		40	1969–*1978*	12
Holding, Michael Anthony	WI	16.2.1954		60	*1975–1986*	102
Hole, Graeme Blake	A	6.1.1931	14.2.1990	18	*1950–1954*	
Holford, David Anthony Jerome	WI	16.4.1940		24	1966–*1976*	
Holland, Robert George	A	19.10.1946		11	*1984–1985*	2
Hollies, William Eric	E	5.6.1912	16.4.1981	13	*1934*–1950	
[2]**Hollioake,** Adam John	E	5.9.1971		4	1997–*1997*	35
[2]**Hollioake,** Benjamin Caine	E	11.11.1977	23.3.2002	2	1997–1998	20
Holmes, Errol Reginald Thorold	E	21.8.1905	16.8.1960	5	*1934*–1935	
Holmes, Percy	E	25.11.1886	3.9.1971	7	1921–1932	
Holt, John Kenneth Constantine	WI	12.8.1923	3.6.1997	17	*1953–1958*	
Hondo, Douglas Tafadzwa	Z	7.7.1979		3	*2001*–2003	30
Hone, Leland	E	30.1.1853	31.12.1896	1	*1878*	
Hookes, David William	A	3.5.1955	19.1.2004	23	*1976–1985*	39
Hooper, Carl Llewellyn	WI	15.12.1966		102	*1987–2002*	227
Hopkins, Albert John Young	A	3.5.1874	25.4.1931	20	*1901*–1909	
Hopwood, John Leonard	E	30.10.1903	15.6.1985	2	1934	
Horan, Thomas Patrick	A	8.3.1854	16.4.1916	15	*1876–1884*	
Hordern, Herbert Vivian	A	10.2.1883	17.6.1938	7	*1910–1911*	
Hornby, Albert Neilson	E	10.2.1847	17.12.1925	3	*1878*–1884	
[2]**Horne,** Matthew Jeffery	NZ	5.12.1970		35	*1996–2002*	50
[2]**Horne,** Philip Andrew	NZ	21.1.1960		4	*1986–1990*	4
Hornibrook, Percival Mitchell	A	27.7.1899	25.8.1976	6	*1928*–1930	
Horton, Martin John	E	21.4.1934		2	1959	
Hough, Kenneth William	NZ	24.10.1928		2	*1958*	
Houghton, David Laud	Z	23.6.1957		22	*1992–1997*	63
Howard, Anthony Bourne	WI	27.8.1946		1	*1971*	
Howard, Nigel David	E	18.5.1925	31.5.1979	4	*1951*	

[1] *Father and son(s).* [2] *Brothers.*

	Country	Born	Died	Tests	Test Career	ODIs
[2]**Howarth,** Geoffrey Philip OBE	NZ	29.3.1951		47	1974–1984	70
[2]**Howarth,** Hedley John	NZ	25.12.1943		30	1969–1976	9
Howell, Henry	E	29.11.1890	9.7.1932	5	1920–1924	
Howell, William Peter	A	29.12.1869	14.7.1940	18	1897–1903	
Howorth, Richard	E	26.4.1909	2.4.1980	5	1947–1947	
Huckle, Adam George	Z	21.9.1971		8	1997–1998	19
Hudson, Andrew Charles	SA	17.3.1965		35	1991–1997	89
Hughes, Kimberley John	A	26.1.1954		70	1977–1984	97
Hughes, Mervyn Gregory	A	23.11.1961		53	1985–1993	33
[2]**Humayun Farhat**	P	24.1.1981		1	2000	5
Humphries, Joseph	E	19.5.1876	7.5.1946	3	1907	
Hunt, William Alfred	A	26.8.1908	30.12.1983	1	1931	
Hunte, *Sir* Conrad Cleophas	WI	9.5.1932	3.12.1999	44	1957–1966	
Hunte, Errol Ashton Clairmore	WI	3.10.1905	26.6.1967	3	1929	
Hunter, Joseph	E	3.8.1855	4.1.1891	5	1884	
Hurst, Alan George	A	15.7.1950		12	1973–1979	8
Hurwood, Alexander	A	17.6.1902	26.9.1982	2	1930	
Hussain, Nasser	E	28.3.1968		91	1989–2003	88
Hutchings, Kenneth Lotherington	E	7.12.1882	3.9.1916	7	1907–1909	
Hutchinson, Philip	SA	25.1.1862	30.9.1925	2	1888	
[1]**Hutton,** *Sir* Leonard	E	23.6.1916	6.9.1990	79	1937–1954	
[1]**Hutton,** Richard Anthony	E	6.9.1942		5	1971	
Hylton, Leslie George	WI	29.3.1905	17.5.1955	6	1934–1939	
Ibadulla, Khalid	P	20.12.1935		4	1964–1967	
Ibrahim, Khanmohammad Cassumbhoy	I	26.1.1919		4	1948	
Iddon, John	E	8.1.1902	17.4.1946	5	1934–1935	
Igglesden, Alan Paul	E	8.10.1964		3	1989–1993	4
Ijaz Ahmed, sen.	P	20.9.1968		60	1986–2000	250
Ijaz Ahmed, jun.	P	2.2.1969		2	1995	2
Ijaz Butt	P	10.3.1938		8	1958–1962	
Ijaz Faqih	P	24.3.1956		5	1980–1987	27
Ikin, John Thomas	E	7.3.1918	15.9.1984	18	1946–1955	
Illingworth, Raymond CBE	E	8.6.1932		61	1958–1973	3
Illingworth, Richard Keith	E	23.8.1963		9	1991–1995	25
Ilott, Mark Christopher	E	27.8.1970		5	1993–1995	
[2]**Imran Farhat**	P	20.5.1982		8	2000–2003	9
Imran Khan	P	25.11.1952		88	1971–1991	175
Imran Nazir	P	16.12.1981		8	1998–2002	57
Imtiaz Ahmed	P	5.1.1928		41	1952–1962	
Indrajitsinhji, Kumar Shri	I	15.6.1937		4	1964–1969	
Insole, Douglas John CBE	E	18.4.1926		9	1950–1957	
Intikhab Alam	P	28.12.1941		47	1959–1976	4
Inverarity, Robert John	A	31.1.1944		6	1968–1972	
Inzamam-ul-Haq	P	3.3.1970		91	1992–2003	302
Iqbal Qasim	P	6.8.1953		50	1976–1988	15
Irani, Jamshed Khudadad	I	18.8.1923	25.2.1982	2	1947	
Irani, Ronald Charles	E	26.10.1971		3	1996–1999	31
Iredale, Francis Adams	A	19.6.1867	15.4.1926	14	1894–1899	
Irfan Fazil	P	2.11.1981		1	1999	1
Ironmonger, Herbert	A	7.4.1882	1.6.1971	14	1928–1932	
Ironside, David Ernest James	SA	2.5.1925		3	1953	
Irvine, Brian Lee	SA	9.3.1944		4	1969	
Israr Ali	P	1.5.1927		4	1952–1959	
Iverson, John Brian	A	27.7.1915	24.10.1973	5	1950	
Jack, Steven Douglas	SA	4.8.1970		2	1994	2
Jackman, Robin David	E	13.8.1945		4	1980–1982	15

[1] *Father and son(s).* [2] *Brothers.*

	Country	Born	Died	Tests	Test Career	ODIs
Jackson, Archibald Alexander	A	5.9.1909	16.2.1933	8	*1928–1930*	
Jackson, *Sir* Francis Stanley	E	21.11.1870	9.3.1947	20	1893–1905	
Jackson, Herbert Leslie	E	5.4.1921		2	1949–1961	
Jacobs, Ridley Detamore	WI	26.11.1967		57	*1998–2003*	128
Jadeja, Ajaysinhji	I	1.2.1971		15	*1992–1999*	196
[1]**Jahangir Khan,** Mohammad	I	1.2.1910	23.7.1988	4	1932–1936	
Jai, Laxmidas Purshottamdas	I	1.4.1902	29.1.1968	1	*1933*	
Jaisimha, Motganhalli Laxmanarsu	I	3.3.1939	7.7.1999	39	1959–*1970*	
Jalal-ud-Din	P	12.6.1959		6	*1982–1985*	8
James, Kenneth Cecil	NZ	12.3.1904	21.8.1976	11	*1929–1932*	
James, Stephen Peter	E	7.9.1967		2	1998	
James, Wayne Robert	Z	27.8.1965		4	*1993–1994*	11
Jameson, John Alexander	E	30.6.1941		4	1971–*1973*	3
Jamshedji, Rustomji Jamshedji Dorabji	I	18.11.1892	5.4.1976	1	*1933*	
Jardine, Douglas Robert	E	23.10.1900	18.6.1958	22	1928–*1933*	
Jarman, Barrington Noel	A	17.2.1936		19	*1959–1968*	
Jarvis, Arthur Harwood	A	19.10.1860	15.11.1933	11	*1884–1894*	
Jarvis, Malcolm Peter	Z	6.12.1955		5	*1992–1994*	12
Jarvis, Paul William	E	29.6.1965		9	*1987–1992*	16
Jarvis, Terrence Wayne	NZ	29.7.1944		13	*1964–1972*	
Javed Akhtar	P	21.11.1940		1	1962	
Javed Burki	P	8.5.1938		25	*1960–1969*	
Javed Miandad	P	12.6.1957		124	*1976–1993*	233
Javed Omar	B	25.11.1976		19	*2000–2003*	28
Jayantilal, Kenia	I	13.1.1948		1	*1970*	
Jayasekera, Rohan Stanley Amarasiriwardene	SL	7.12.1957		1	*1981*	2
Jayasuriya, Sanath Teran	SL	30.6.1969		83	*1990–2003*	308
Jayawardene, Denagamage Proboth Mahela de Silva	SL	27.5.1977		54	*1997–2003*	148
Jayawardene, Hewasandatchige Asiri Prasanna Wishvanath	SL	9.10.1979		3	*2000–2002*	3
Jeganathan, Sridharan	SL	11.7.1951	14.5.1996	2	*1982*	5
Jenkins, Roland Oliver	E	24.11.1918	21.7.1995	9	*1948*–1952	
Jenner, Terrence James	A	8.9.1944		9	*1970–1975*	1
Jennings, Claude Burrows	A	5.6.1884	20.6.1950	6	1912	
Jessop, Gilbert Laird	E	19.5.1874	11.5.1955	18	1899–1912	
John, Vinothen Bede	SL	27.5.1960		6	*1982*–1984	45
Johnson, Clement Lecky	SA	31.3.1871	31.5.1908	1	*1895*	
Johnson, David Jude	I	16.10.1971		2	*1996*	
Johnson, Hophnie Hobah Hines	WI	13.7.1910	24.6.1987	3	*1947*–1950	
Johnson, Ian William OBE	A	8.12.1917	9.10.1998	45	*1945–1956*	
Johnson, Leonard Joseph	A	18.3.1919	20.4.1977	1	*1947*	
Johnson, Neil Clarkson	Z	24.1.1970		13	*1998*–2000	48
Johnson, Richard Leonard	E	29.12.1974		3	2003–*2003*	10
Johnson, Tyrell Fabian	WI	10.1.1917	5.4.1985	1	1939	
Johnston, William Arras	A	26.2.1922		40	*1947–1954*	
Jones, Andrew Howard	NZ	9.5.1959		39	*1986–1994*	87
Jones, Arthur Owen	E	16.8.1872	21.12.1914	12	1899–1909	
Jones, Charles Ernest Llewellyn	WI	3.11.1902	10.12.1959	4	*1929–1934*	
Jones, Dean Mervyn	A	24.3.1961		52	*1983–1992*	164
Jones, Ernest	A	30.9.1869	23.11.1943	19	*1894–1902*	
[1]**Jones,** Ivor Jeffrey	E	10.12.1941		15	*1963–1967*	
Jones, Prior Erskine Waverley	WI	6.6.1917	21.11.1991	9	*1947–1951*	
Jones, Richard Andrew	NZ	22.10.1973		1	*2003*	5
Jones, Samuel Percy	A	1.8.1861	14.7.1951	12	*1881–1887*	
[1]**Jones,** Simon Philip	E	25.12.1978		2	2002–*2002*	
Joseph, David Rolston Emmanuel	WI	15.11.1969		4	*1998*	
Joshi, Padmanabh Govind	I	27.10.1926	8.1.1987	12	*1951–1960*	

[1] *Father and son(s).* [2] *Brothers.*

	Country	Born	Died	Tests	Test Career	ODIs
Joshi, Sunil Bandacharya	I	6.6.1969		15	1996–*2000*	69
Joslin, Leslie Ronald	A	13.12.1947		1	*1967*	
Julian, Brendon Paul	A	10.8.1970		7	1993–*1995*	25
Julien, Bernard Denis	WI	13.3.1950		24	1973–*1976*	12
Jumadeen, Raphick Rasif	WI	12.4.1948		12	*1971–1978*	
Jupp, Henry	E	19.11.1841	8.4.1889	2	*1876*	
Jupp, Vallance William Crisp	E	27.3.1891	9.7.1960	8	1921–1928	
Jurangpathy, Baba Roshan	SL	25.6.1967		2	*1985–1986*	
Kabir Khan	P	12.4.1974		4	*1994*	10
Kaif, Mohammad	I	1.12.1980		4	*1999–2001*	59
Kallicharran, Alvin Isaac	WI	21.3.1949		66	*1971–1980*	31
Kallis, Jacques Henry	SA	16.10.1975		75	*1995–2003*	185
Kalpage, Ruwan Senani	SL	19.2.1970		11	*1993–1998*	86
[2]**Kaluperuma,** Lalith Wasantha Silva	SL	25.5.1949		2	*1981*	4
[2]**Kaluperuma,** Sanath Mohan Silva	SL	22.10.1961		4	*1983–1987*	2
Kaluwitharana, Romesh Shantha	SL	24.11.1969		44	*1992–2002*	187
Kambli, Vinod Ganpat	I	18.1.1972		17	*1992–1995*	104
Kamran Akmal	P	13.1.1982		4	*2002*	12
Kanhai, Rohan Bholalall	WI	26.12.1935		79	1957–*1973*	7
[1]**Kanitkar,** Hrishikesh Hemant	I	14.11.1974		2	*1999*	34
[1]**Kanitkar,** Hemant Shamsunder	I	8.12.1942		2	*1974*	
Kapil Dev	I	6.1.1959		131	*1978–1993*	225
Kapoor, Aashish Rakesh	I	25.3.1971		4	*1994–1996*	17
Kardar, Abdul Hafeez	I, P	17.1.1925	21.4.1996	26	1946–*1957*	
Karim, Syed Saba	I	14.11.1967		1	*2000*	34
Kartik, Murali	I	11.9.1976		5	*1999–2003*	9
Kasprowicz, Michael Scott	A	10.2.1972		17	*1996–2000*	18
Katich, Simon Mathew	A	21.8.1975		6	2001–*2003*	1
Keeton, William Walter	E	30.4.1905	10.10.1980	2	1934–1939	
Keith, Headley James	SA	25.10.1927	17.11.1997	8	*1952–1956*	
Kelleway, Charles	A	25.4.1886	16.11.1944	26	*1910–1928*	
Kelly, James Joseph	A	10.5.1867	14.8.1938	36	1896–1905	
Kelly, Thomas Joseph Dart	A	3.5.1844	20.7.1893	2	*1876–1878*	
Kemp, Justin Miles	SA	2.10.1977		3	*2000*	14
Kempis, Gustav Adolph	SA	4.8.1865	19.5.1890	1	*1888*	
Kendall, Thomas Kingston	A	24.8.1851	17.8.1924	2	*1876*	
Kennedy, Alexander Stuart	E	24.1.1891	15.11.1959	5	*1922*	
Kennedy, Robert John	NZ	3.6.1972		4	*1995*	7
Kenny, Ramnath Baburao	I	29.9.1930	21.11.1985	5	*1958–1959*	
Kent, Martin Francis	A	23.11.1953		3	1981	5
Kentish, Esmond Seymour Maurice	WI	21.11.1916		2	*1947–1953*	
Kenyon, Donald	E	15.5.1924	12.11.1996	8	*1951*–1955	
Kerr, John Lambert	NZ	28.12.1910		7	1931–1937	
Kerr, Robert Byers	A	16.6.1961		2	*1985*	4
Key, Robert William Trevor	E	12.5.1979		8	2002–2003	2
Khaled Mahmud	B	26.7.1971		12	*2001–2003*	53
Khaled Masud	B	8.2.1976		23	*2000–2003*	69
Khalid Hassan	P	14.7.1937		1	1954	
[1]**Khalid Wazir**	P	27.4.1936		2	1954	
Khan Mohammad	P	1.1.1928		13	*1952–1957*	
Killick, *Rev.* Edgar Thomas	E	9.5.1907	18.5.1953	2	1929	
Kilner, Roy	E	17.10.1890	5.4.1928	9	1924–1926	
King, Collis Llewellyn	WI	11.6.1951		9	1976–1980	18
King, Frank McDonald	WI	8.12.1926	23.12.1990	14	*1952–1955*	
King, John Herbert	E	16.4.1871	18.11.1946	1	1909	
King, Lester Anthony	WI	27.2.1939	9.7.1998	2	*1961–1967*	
King, Reon Dane	WI	6.10.1975		14	*1998–2001*	48
Kinneir, Septimus Paul	E	13.5.1871	16.10.1928	1	*1911*	

[1] *Father and son(s).* [2] *Brothers.*

	Country	*Born*	*Died*	*Tests*	*Test Career*	*ODIs*
Kippax, Alan Falconer	A	25.5.1897	4.9.1972	22	*1924*–1934	
Kirmani, Syed Mujtaba Hussein	I	29.12.1949		88	*1975–1985*	49
[2]**Kirsten,** Gary	SA	23.11.1967		98	*1993–2003*	185
[2]**Kirsten,** Peter Noel	SA	14.5.1955		12	*1991*–1994	40
Kirtley, Robert James	E	10.1.1975		4	2003–*2003*	10
Kishenchand, Gogumal	I	14.4.1925	16.4.1997	5	*1947–1952*	
Kline, Lindsay Francis	A	29.9.1934		13	*1957–1960*	
Klusener, Lance	SA	4.9.1971		48	*1996–2001*	154
Knight, Albert Ernest	E	8.10.1872	25.4.1946	3	*1903*	
Knight, Barry Rolfe	E	18.2.1938		29	*1961*–1969	
Knight, Donald John	E	12.5.1894	5.1.1960	2	1921	
Knight, Nicholas Verity	E	28.11.1969		17	1995–2001	100
Knott, Alan Philip Eric	E	9.4.1946		95	1967–1981	20
Knox, Neville Alexander	E	10.10.1884	3.3.1935	2	1907	
Kotze, Johannes Jacobus	SA	7.8.1879	7.7.1931	3	*1902*–1907	
[2]**Kripal Singh,** Amritsar Govindsingh	I	6.8.1933	23.7.1987	14	*1955–1964*	
Krishnamurthy, Pochiah	I	12.7.1947	28.1.1999	5	*1970*	1
Kuggeleijn, Christopher Mary	NZ	10.5.1956		2	*1988*	16
Kuiper, Adrian Paul	SA	24.8.1959		1	*1991*	25
Kulkarni, Nilesh Moreshwar	I	3.4.1973		3	*1997–2000*	10
Kulkarni, Rajiv Ramesh	I	25.9.1962		3	*1986*	10
Kulkarni, Umesh Narayan	I	7.3.1942		4	*1967*	
Kumar, Vaman Viswanath	I	22.6.1935		2	*1960–1961*	
Kumble, Anil	I	17.10.1970		81	1990–*2003*	246
Kunderan, Budhisagar Krishnappa	I	2.10.1939		18	*1959*–1967	
Kuruppu, Don Sardha Brendon Priyantha	SL	5.1.1962		4	*1986*–1991	54
Kuruppuarachchi, Ajith Kosala	SL	1.11.1964		2	*1985–1986*	
Kuruvilla, Abey	I	8.8.1968		10	*1996–1997*	25
Kuys, Frederick	SA	21.3.1870	12.9.1953	1	*1898*	
Labrooy, Graeme Fredrick	SL	7.6.1964		9	*1986–1990*	44
Laird, Bruce Malcolm	A	21.11.1950		21	*1979–1982*	23
Laker, James Charles	E	9.2.1922	23.4.1986	46	*1947–1958*	
Lakshitha, Materba Kanatha Gamage Chamila Premanath	SL	4.1.1979		2	*2002*	7
Lall Singh	I	16.12.1909	19.11.1985	1	1932	
Lamb, Allan Joseph	E	20.6.1954		79	1982–1992	122
Lamba, Raman	I	2.1.1960	23.2.1998	4	*1986–1987*	32
Lambert, Clayton Benjamin	WI	10.2.1962		5	1991–*1998*	11
Lance, Herbert Roy	SA	6.6.1940		13	*1961–1969*	
Langer, Justin Lee	A	21.11.1970		71	*1992–2003*	8
Langley, Gilbert Roche Andrews	A	14.9.1919	14.5.2001	26	*1951–1956*	
Langridge, James	E	10.7.1906	10.9.1966	8	1933–1946	
Langton, Arthur Chudleigh Beaumont	SA	2.3.1912	27.11.1942	15	1935–*1938*	
Lara, Brian Charles	WI	2.5.1969		102	*1990–2003*	224
Larkins, Wayne	E	22.11.1953		13	*1979–1990*	25
Larsen, Gavin Rolf	NZ	27.9.1962		8	1994–*1995*	121
Larter, John David Frederick	E	24.4.1940		10	1962–1965	
Larwood, Harold MBE	E	14.11.1904	22.7.1995	21	1926–*1932*	
Lashley, Patrick Douglas	WI	11.2.1937		4	*1960*–1966	
Latham, Rodney Terry	NZ	12.6.1961		4	*1991–1992*	33
Lathwell, Mark Nicholas	E	26.12.1971		2	1993	
Laughlin, Trevor John	A	30.1.1951		3	*1977–1978*	6
Laver, Frank Jonas	A	7.12.1869	24.9.1919	15	1899–1909	
Law, Stuart Grant	A	18.10.1968		1	*1995*	54
Lawrence, David Valentine	E	28.1.1964		5	1988–*1991*	1
Lawrence, Godfrey Bernard	SA	31.3.1932		5	*1961*	
Lawry, William Morris	A	11.2.1937		67	1961–*1970*	1

[1] *Father and son(s).* [2] *Brothers.*

	Country	Born	Died	Tests	Test Career	ODIs
Lawson, Geoffrey Francis	A	7.12.1957		46	1980–1989	79
Lawson, Jermaine Jay Charles	WI	13.1.1982		7	2002	6
Laxman, Vangipurappu Venkata Sai	I	1.11.1974		50	1996–2003	58
Leadbeater, Edric	E	15.8.1927		2	1951	
Lee, Brett	A	8.11.1976		37	1999–2003	73
Lee, Henry William	E	26.10.1890	21.4.1981	1	1930	
Lee, Philip Keith	A	15.9.1904	9.8.1980	2	1931–1932	
Lees, Warren Kenneth MBE	NZ	19.3.1952		21	1976–1983	31
Lees, Walter Scott	E	25.12.1875	10.9.1924	5	1905	
Legall, Ralph Archibald	WI	1.12.1925		4	1952	
Leggat, Ian Bruce	NZ	7.6.1930		1	1953	
Leggat, John Gordon	NZ	27.5.1926	9.3.1973	9	1951–1955	
Legge, Geoffrey Bevington	E	26.1.1903	21.11.1940	5	1927–1929	
Lehmann, Darren Scott	A	5.2.1970		15	1997–2003	100
le Roux, Frederick Louis	SA	5.2.1882	22.9.1963	1	1913	
Leslie, Charles Frederick Henry	E	8.12.1861	12.2.1921	4	1882	
Lever, John Kenneth MBE	E	24.2.1949		21	1976–1986	22
Lever, Peter	E	17.9.1940		17	1970–1975	10
Leveson Gower, *Sir* Henry Dudley Gresham	E	8.5.1873	1.2.1954	3	1909	
Levett, William Howard Vincent	E	25.1.1908	30.11.1995	1	1933	
Lewis, Anthony Robert CBE	E	6.7.1938		9	1972–1973	
Lewis, Clairmonte Christopher	E	14.2.1968		32	1990–1996	53
Lewis, Desmond Michael	WI	21.2.1946		3	1970	
Lewis, Percy Tyson	SA	2.10.1884	30.1.1976	1	1913	
Lewis, Rawl Nicholas	WI	5.9.1974		3	1997–1998	16
Leyland, Maurice	E	20.7.1900	1.1.1967	41	1928–1938	
Liaqat Ali Khan	P	21.5.1955		5	1974–1978	3
Liebenberg, Gerhardus Frederick Johannes	SA	7.4.1972		5	1997–1998	4
Lillee, Dennis Keith MBE	A	18.7.1949		70	1970–1983	63
Lilley, Arthur Augustus	E	28.11.1866	17.11.1929	35	1896–1909	
Lillywhite, James	E	23.2.1842	25.10.1929	2	1876	
[1]**Lindsay,** Denis Thomson	SA	4.9.1939		19	1963–1969	
[1]**Lindsay,** John Dixon	SA	8.9.1908	31.8.1990	3	1947	
Lindsay, Nevil Vernon	SA	30.7.1886	2.2.1976	1	1921	
Lindwall, Raymond Russell MBE	A	3.10.1921	22.6.1996	61	1945–1959	
Ling, William Victor Stone	SA	3.10.1891	26.9.1960	6	1921–1922	
Lissette, Allen Fisher	NZ	6.11.1919	24.1.1973	2	1955	
Liyanage, Dulip Kapila	SL	6.6.1972		9	1992–2001	16
Llewellyn, Charles Bennett	SA	26.9.1876	7.6.1964	15	1895–1912	
Lloyd, Clive Hubert OBE	WI	31.8.1944		110	1966–1984	87
Lloyd, David	E	18.3.1947		9	1974–1974	8
Lloyd, Timothy Andrew	E	5.11.1956		1	1984	3
Loader, Peter James	E	25.10.1929		13	1954–1958	
Lock, Alan Charles Ingram	Z	10.9.1962		1	1995	8
Lock, Graham Anthony Richard	E	5.7.1929	29.3.1995	49	1952–1967	
Lockwood, William Henry	E	25.3.1868	26.4.1932	12	1893–1902	
Logie, Augustine Lawrence	WI	28.9.1960		52	1982–1991	158
Lohmann, George Alfred	E	2.6.1865	1.12.1901	18	1886–1896	
Lokuarachchi, Kaushal Samaraweera	SL	20.5.1982		3	2002	5
Love, Hampden Stanley Bray	A	10.8.1895	22.7.1969	1	1932	
Love, Martin Lloyd	A	30.3.1974		5	2002–2003	
Loveridge, Greg Riaka	NZ	15.1.1975		1	1995	
Lowry, Thomas Coleman	NZ	17.2.1898	20.7.1976	7	1929–1931	
Lowson, Frank Anderson	E	1.7.1925	8.9.1984	7	1951–1955	
Loxton, Samuel John Everett	A	29.3.1921		12	1947–1950	
Lucas, Alfred Perry	E	20.2.1857	12.10.1923	5	1878–1884	
Luckhurst, Brian William	E	5.2.1939		21	1970–1974	3

[1] *Father and son(s).* [2] *Brothers.*

	Country	*Born*	*Died*	*Tests*	*Test Career*	*ODIs*
Lundie, Eric Balfour	SA	15.3.1888	12.9.1917	1	*1913*	
Lyons, John James	A	21.5.1863	21.7.1927	14	*1886–1897*	
Lyttelton, *Hon.* Alfred	E	7.2.1857	5.7.1913	4	1880–1884	
McAlister, Peter Alexander	A	11.7.1869	10.5.1938	8	*1903*–1909	
Macartney, Charles George	A	27.6.1886	9.9.1958	35	*1907*–1926	
Macaulay, George Gibson	E	7.12.1897	13.12.1940	8	*1922*–1933	
Macaulay, Michael John	SA	19.4.1939		1	*1964*	
MacBryan, John Crawford William	E	22.7.1892	14.7.1983	1	1924	
McCabe, Stanley Joseph	A	16.7.1910	25.8.1968	39	1930–1938	
McCague, Martin John	E	24.5.1969		3	1993–*1994*	
McCarthy, Cuan Neil	SA	24.3.1929	14.8.2000	15	*1948*–1951	
McConnon, James Edward	E	21.6.1922	26.1.2003	2	1954	
McCool, Colin Leslie	A	9.12.1916	5.4.1986	14	*1945–1949*	
McCormick, Ernest Leslie	A	16.5.1906	28.6.1991	12	*1935*–1938	
McCosker, Richard Bede	A	11.12.1946		25	*1974–1979*	14
McDermott, Craig John	A	14.4.1965		71	*1984–1995*	138
McDonald, Colin Campbell	A	17.11.1928		47	*1951*–1961	
McDonald, Edgar Arthur	A	6.1.1891	22.7.1937	11	*1920–1921*	
McDonnell, Percy Stanislaus	A	13.11.1858	24.9.1896	19	1880–1888	
McEwan, Paul Ernest	NZ	19.12.1953		4	*1979–1984*	17
McGahey, Charles Percy	E	12.2.1871	10.1.1935	2	*1901*	
McGarrell, Neil Christopher	WI	12.7.1972		4	*2000–2001*	17
MacGibbon, Anthony Roy	NZ	28.8.1924		26	*1950*–1958	
MacGill, Stuart Charles Glyndwr	A	25.2.1971		30	*1997–2003*	3
McGirr, Herbert Mendelson	NZ	5.11.1891	14.4.1964	2	*1929*	
McGlew, Derrick John	SA	11.3.1929	9.6.1998	34	1951–*1961*	
McGrath, Anthony	E	6.10.1975		4	2003	10
McGrath, Glenn Donald	A	9.2.1970		95	*1993–2003*	185
MacGregor, Gregor	E	31.8.1869	20.8.1919	8	1890–1893	
McGregor, Spencer Noel	NZ	18.12.1931		25	*1954–1964*	
McIlwraith, John	A	7.9.1857	5.7.1938	1	1886	
McIntyre, Arthur John William	E	14.5.1918		3	1950–1955	
McIntyre, Peter Edward	A	27.4.1966		2	*1994–1996*	
Mackay, Kenneth Donald MBE	A	24.10.1925	13.6.1982	37	1956–*1962*	
McKenzie, Graham Douglas	A	24.6.1941		60	1961–*1970*	1
McKenzie, Neil Douglas	SA	24.11.1975		39	*2000–2003*	59
McKibbin, Thomas Robert	A	10.12.1870	15.12.1939	5	*1894–1897*	
McKinnon, Atholl Henry	SA	20.8.1932	2.12.1983	8	1960–*1966*	
MacKinnon, Francis Alexander	E	9.4.1848	27.2.1947	1	*1878*	
MacLaren, Archibald Campbell	E	1.12.1871	17.11.1944	35	*1894*–1909	
McLaren, John William	A	22.12.1886	17.11.1921	1	*1911*	
Maclean, John Alexander	A	27.4.1946		4	*1978*	2
McLean, Nixon Alexei McNamara	WI	20.7.1973		19	*1997–2000*	45
McLean, Roy Alastair	SA	9.7.1930		40	1951–*1964*	
[2]**McLeod,** Charles Edward	A	24.10.1869	26.11.1918	17	*1894*–1905	
McLeod, Edwin George	NZ	14.10.1900	14.9.1989	1	*1929*	
[2]**McLeod,** Robert William	A	19.1.1868	14.6.1907	6	*1891*–1893	
McMahon, Trevor George	NZ	8.11.1929		5	*1955*	
McMaster, Joseph Emile Patrick	E	16.3.1861	7.6.1929	1	*1888*	
McMillan, Brian Mervin	SA	22.12.1963		38	*1992*–1998	78
McMillan, Craig Douglas	NZ	13.9.1976		48	*1997–2003*	136
McMillan, Quintin	SA	23.6.1904	3.7.1948	13	1929–*1931*	
McMorris, Easton Dudley Ashton St John	WI	4.4.1935		13	*1957*–1966	
McRae, Donald Alexander Noel	NZ	25.12.1912	10.8.1986	1	*1945*	
McShane, Patrick George	A	18.4.1858	11.12.1903	3	*1884–1887*	
McWatt, Clifford Aubrey	WI	1.2.1922	20.7.1997	6	*1953–1954*	
Madan Lal	I	20.3.1951		39	1974–1986	67

[1] *Father and son(s).* [2] *Brothers.*

	Country	*Born*	*Died*	*Tests*	*Test Career*	*ODIs*
Maddocks, Leonard Victor	A	24.5.1926		7	*1954–1956*	
Maddy, Darren Lee	E	23.5.1974		3	*1999–1999*	8
Madondo, Trevor Nyasha	Z	22.11.1976	11.6.2001	3	*1997–2000*	13
Madray, Ivan Samuel	WI	2.7.1934		2	*1957*	
Madugalle, Ranjan Senerath	SL	22.4.1959		21	*1981*–1988	63
Madurasinghe, Madurasinghe Arachchige Wijayasiri Ranjith	SL	30.1.1961		3	1988–*1992*	12
Maguire, John Norman	A	15.9.1956		3	*1983*	23
Mahanama, Roshan Siriwardene	SL	31.5.1966		52	*1985–1997*	213
Mahmood Hussain	P	2.4.1932	25.12.1991	27	*1952*–1962	
Mahwire, Ngonidzashe Blessing	Z	31.7.1982		4	*2002–2003*	
Mailey, Arthur Alfred	A	3.1.1886	31.12.1967	21	*1920*–1926	
[1]**Majid Khan**	P	28.9.1946		63	*1964–1982*	23
Maka, Ebrahim Suleman	I	5.3.1922	d unknown	2	*1952*	
Makepeace, Joseph William Henry	E	22.8.1881	19.12.1952	4	*1920*	
Malcolm, Devon Eugene	E	22.2.1963		40	1989–1997	10
Malhotra, Ashok Omprakash	I	26.1.1957		7	*1981–1984*	20
Mallender, Neil Alan	E	13.8.1961		2	1992	
Mallett, Ashley Alexander	A	13.7.1945		38	1968–1980	9
Malone, Michael Francis	A	9.10.1950		1	1977	10
Maninder Singh	I	13.6.1965		35	*1982–1992*	59
[1]**Manjrekar,** Sanjay Vijay	I	12.7.1965		37	*1987–1996*	74
[1]**Manjrekar,** Vijay Laxman	I	26.9.1931	18.10.1983	55	*1951–1964*	
Manjurul Islam	B	7.11.1979		16	*2000–2003*	34
[1]**Mankad,** Ashok Vinoo	I	12.10.1946		22	*1969–1977*	1
[1]**Mankad,** Mulvantrai Himmatlal ("Vinoo")	I	12.4.1917	21.8.1978	44	1946–*1958*	
Mann, Anthony Longford	A	8.11.1945		4	*1977*	
[1]**Mann,** Francis George CBE	E	6.9.1917	8.8.2001	7	*1948*–1949	
[1]**Mann,** Francis Thomas	E	3.3.1888	6.10.1964	5	*1922*	
Mann, Norman Bertram Fleetwood	SA	28.12.1920	31.7.1952	19	1947–1951	
Mansell, Percy Neville Frank MBE	SA	16.3.1920	9.5.1995	13	1951–1955	
Mansoor Akhtar	P	25.12.1957		19	*1980–1989*	41
Mantri, Madhav Krishnaji	I	1.9.1921		4	*1951–1954*	
[2]**Manzoor Elahi**	P	15.4.1963		6	*1984–1994*	54
Maqsood Ahmed	P	26.3.1925	4.1.1999	16	*1952–1955*	
Marillier, Douglas Anthony	Z	24.4.1978		5	*2000–2001*	48
Markham, Lawrence Anderson	SA	12.9.1924	5.8.2000	1	*1948*	
Marks, Victor James	E	25.6.1955		6	1982–*1983*	34
Marr, Alfred Percy	A	28.3.1862	15.3.1940	1	*1884*	
Marriott, Charles Stowell	E	14.9.1895	13.10.1966	1	1933	
Marsh, Geoffrey Robert	A	31.12.1958		50	*1985–1991*	117
Marsh, Rodney William MBE	A	4.11.1947		96	*1970–1983*	92
Marshall, Hamish John Hamilton	NZ	15.2.1979		1	*2000*	5
Marshall, Malcolm Denzil	WI	18.4.1958	4.11.1999	81	*1978*–1991	136
[2]**Marshall,** Norman Edgar	WI	27.2.1924		1	*1954*	
[2]**Marshall,** Roy Edwin	WI	25.4.1930	27.10.1992	4	*1951*	
Martin, Christopher Stewart	NZ	10.12.1974		11	*2000–2001*	7
Martin, Frank Reginald	WI	12.10.1893	23.11.1967	9	1928–*1930*	
Martin, Frederick	E	12.10.1861	13.12.1921	2	1890–*1891*	
Martin, John Wesley	A	28.7.1931	16.7.1992	8	*1960–1966*	
Martin, John William	E	16.2.1917	4.1.1987	1	1947	
Martin, Peter James	E	15.11.1968		8	1995–1997	20
Martindale, Emmanuel Alfred	WI	25.11.1909	17.3.1972	10	1933–1939	
Martyn, Damien Richard	A	21.10.1971		39	*1992–2003*	133
Marx, Waldemar Frederick Eric	SA	4.7.1895	2.6.1974	3	*1921*	
Masakadza, Hamilton	Z	9.8.1983		7	*2001–2002*	3
Mashrafe bin Mortaza	B	5.10.1983		12	*2001–2003*	12
Mason, John Richard	E	26.3.1874	15.10.1958	5	*1897*	

[1] *Father and son(s).* [2] *Brothers.*

	Country	Born	Died	Tests	Test Career	ODIs
Masood Anwar	P	12.12.1967		1	1990	
Massie, Hugh Hamon	A	11.4.1854	12.10.1938	9	1881–1884	
Massie, Robert Arnold Lockyer	A	14.4.1947		6	1972–1972	3
Matambanadzo, Everton Zvikomborero	Z	13.4.1976		3	1996–1999	7
Matheson, Alexander Malcolm	NZ	27.2.1906	31.12.1985	2	1929–1931	
Mathias, Wallis	P	4.2.1935	1.9.1994	21	1955–1962	
Matsikenyeri, Stuart	Z	3.5.1983		2	2003	13
Matthews, Austin David George	E	3.5.1904	29.7.1977	1	1937	
Matthews, Christopher Darrell	A	22.9.1962		3	1986–1988	
Matthews, Craig Russell	SA	15.2.1965		18	1992–1995	56
Matthews, Gregory Richard John	A	15.12.1959		33	1983–1992	59
Matthews, Thomas James	A	3.4.1884	14.10.1943	8	1911–1912	
Mattis, Everton Hugh	WI	11.4.1957		4	1980	2
May, Peter Barker Howard CBE	E	31.12.1929	27.12.1994	66	1951–1961	
May, Timothy Brian Alexander	A	26.1.1962		24	1987–1994	47
Maynard, Matthew Peter	E	21.3.1966		4	1988–1993	14
Mayne, Edgar Richard	A	2.7.1882	26.10.1961	4	1912–1921	
Mayne, Lawrence Charles	A	23.1.1942		6	1964–1969	
Mbangwa, Mpumelelo	Z	26.6.1976		15	1996–2000	29
Mead, Charles Philip	E	9.3.1887	26.3.1958	17	1911–1928	
Mead, Walter	E	1.4.1868	18.3.1954	1	1899	
Meale, Trevor	NZ	11.11.1928		2	1958	
Meckiff, Ian	A	6.1.1935		18	1957–1963	
Meherhomji, Khershedji Rustomji	I	9.8.1911	10.2.1982	1	1936	
Mehra, Vijay Laxman	I	12.3.1938		8	1955–1963	
Mehrab Hossain	B	22.9.1978		9	2000–2002	18
Meintjes, Douglas James	SA	9.6.1890	17.7.1979	2	1922	
Melle, Michael George	SA	3.6.1930		7	1949–1952	
Melville, Alan	SA	19.5.1910	18.4.1983	11	1938–1948	
Mendis, Louis Rohan Duleep	SL	25.8.1952		24	1981–1988	79
Mendonca, Ivor Leon	WI	13.7.1934		2	1961	
Merchant, Vijay Madhavji	I	12.10.1911	27.10.1987	10	1933–1951	
Merritt, William Edward	NZ	18.8.1908	9.6.1977	6	1929–1931	
Merry, Cyril Arthur	WI	20.1.1911	19.4.1964	2	1933	
Meuleman, Kenneth Douglas	A	5.9.1923		1	1945	
Meuli, Edgar Milton	NZ	20.2.1926		1	1952	
Mhambrey, Paras Laxmikant	I	20.6.1972		2	1996	3
Middleton, James	SA	30.9.1865	23.12.1913	6	1895–1902	
Midwinter, William Evans	A, E	19.6.1851	3.12.1890	12	1876–1886	
Milburn, Barry Douglas	NZ	24.11.1943		3	1968	
Milburn, Colin	E	23.10.1941	28.2.1990	9	1966–1968	
[2]**Milkha Singh,** Amritsar Govindsingh	I	31.12.1941		4	1959–1961	
Miller, Audley Montague	E	19.10.1869	26.6.1959	1	1895	
Miller, Colin Reid	A	6.2.1964		18	1998–2000	
Miller, Geoffrey	E	8.9.1952		34	1976–1984	25
Miller, Keith Ross MBE	A	28.11.1919		55	1945–1956	
Miller, Lawrence Somerville Martin	NZ	31.3.1923	17.12.1996	13	1952–1958	
Miller, Roy	WI	24.12.1924		1	1952	
Milligan, Frank William	E	19.3.1870	31.3.1900	2	1898	
Millman, Geoffrey	E	2.10.1934		6	1961–1962	
Mills, Charles Henry	SA	26.11.1867	26.7.1948	1	1891	
Mills, John Ernest	NZ	3.9.1905	11.12.1972	7	1929–1932	
Milton, Clement Arthur	E	10.3.1928		6	1958–1959	
Milton, *Sir* William Henry	SA	3.12.1854	6.3.1930	3	1888–1891	
Minnett, Roy Baldwin	A	13.6.1888	21.10.1955	9	1911–1912	
Miran Bux	P	20.4.1907	8.2.1991	2	1954	
Mirando, Magina Thilan Thushara	SL	1.3.1981		1	2002	
Misbah-ul-Haq	P	28.5.1974		5	2000–2003	11
Misson, Francis Michael	A	19.11.1938		5	1960–1961	

[1] *Father and son(s).* [2] *Brothers.*

	Country	*Born*	*Died*	*Tests*	*Test Career*	*ODIs*
Mitchell, Arthur	E	13.9.1902	25.12.1976	6	*1933*–1936	
Mitchell, Bruce	SA	8.1.1909	2.7.1995	42	1929–*1948*	
Mitchell, Frank	E, SA	13.8.1872	11.10.1935	5	*1898*–1912	
Mitchell, Thomas Bignall	E	4.9.1902	27.1.1996	5	*1932*–1935	
Mitchell-Innes, Norman Stewart	E	7.9.1914		1	1935	
Modi, Rustomji Sheryar	I	11.11.1924	17.5.1996	10	1946–*1952*	
Mohammad Akram	P	10.9.1974		9	*1995–2000*	23
Mohammad Ashraful	B	9.9.1984		15	*2001–2003*	24
Mohammad Aslam	P	5.1.1920		1	1954	
Mohammad Farooq	P	8.4.1938		7	*1960–1964*	
Mohammad Hafeez	P	17.10.1980		3	*2003*	22
Mohammad Hussain	P	8.10.1976		2	*1996–1998*	14
Mohammad Ilyas	P	19.3.1946		10	*1964–1968*	
Mohammad Munaf	P	2.11.1935		4	*1959–1961*	
Mohammad Nazir	P	8.3.1946		14	*1969–1983*	4
Mohammad Rafiq	B	5.9.1970		8	*2000–2003*	54
Mohammad Ramzan	P	25.12.1970		1	*1997*	
Mohammad Salim	B	15.10.1981		2	*2002*	1
Mohammad Sami	P	24.2.1981		12	*2000–2003*	40
Mohammad Sharif	B	12.12.1985		8	*2000–2001*	8
Mohammad Wasim	P	8.8.1977		18	*1996–2000*	25
Mohammad Zahid	P	2.8.1976		5	*1996–2002*	11
Mohammed, Dave	WI	8.10.1979		1	*2003*	
Mohanty, Debasis Sarbeswar	I	20.7.1976		2	*1997*	45
Mohsin Kamal	P	16.6.1963		9	*1983–1994*	19
Mohsin Khan	P	15.3.1955		48	*1977–1986*	75
[2]**Moin Khan**	P	23.9.1971		67	*1990–2003*	195
Moir, Alexander McKenzie	NZ	17.7.1919	17.6.2000	17	*1950–1958*	
Mold, Arthur Webb	E	27.5.1863	29.4.1921	3	1893	
Moloney, Denis Andrew Robert	NZ	11.8.1910	15.7.1942	3	1937	
Mongia, Nayan Ramlal	I	19.12.1969		44	*1993–2000*	140
Moodie, George Horatio	WI	26.11.1915	8.6.2002	1	*1934*	
Moody, Thomas Masson	A	2.10.1965		8	*1989–1992*	76
Moon, Leonard James	E	9.2.1878	23.11.1916	4	*1905*	
Mooney, Francis Leonard Hugh	NZ	26.5.1921		14	1949–*1953*	
More, Kiran Shankar	I	4.9.1962		49	1986–*1993*	94
Morgan, Ross Winston	NZ	12.2.1941		20	*1964–1971*	
Morkel, Denijs Paul Beck	SA	25.1.1906	6.10.1980	16	*1927–1931*	
Morley, Frederick	E	16.12.1850	28.9.1884	4	1880–*1882*	
Moroney, John	A	24.7.1917	1.7.1999	7	*1949–1951*	
Morris, Arthur Robert MBE	A	19.1.1922		46	*1946–1954*	
Morris, Hugh	E	5.10.1963		3	1991	
Morris, John Edward	E	1.4.1964		3	1990	8
Morris, Samuel	A	22.6.1855	20.9.1931	1	*1884*	
Morrison, Bruce Donald	NZ	17.12.1933		1	*1962*	
Morrison, Daniel Kyle	NZ	3.2.1966		48	*1987–1996*	96
Morrison, John Francis MacLean	NZ	27.8.1947		17	*1973–1981*	18
Mortimore, John Brian	E	14.5.1933		9	*1958*–1964	
Moseley, Ezra Alphonsa	WI	5.1.1958		2	*1989*	9
Moses, Henry	A	13.2.1858	7.12.1938	6	*1886–1894*	
Moss, Alan Edward	E	14.11.1930		9	*1953*–1960	
Moss, Jeffrey Kenneth	A	29.6.1947		1	*1978*	1
Motz, Richard Charles	NZ	12.1.1940		32	*1961*–1969	
Moule, William Henry	A	31.1.1858	24.8.1939	1	1880	
Moxon, Martyn Douglas	E	4.5.1960		10	1986–1989	8
Mubarak, Jehan	SL	10.1.1981		2	*2002*	7
[1]**Mudassar Nazar**	P	6.4.1956		76	*1976–1988*	122
Muddiah, Venatappa Musandra	I	8.6.1929		2	*1959–1960*	
Mufasir-ul-Haq	P	16.8.1944	27.7.1983	1	*1964*	

[1] *Father and son(s).* [2] *Brothers.*

	Country	Born	Died	Tests	Test Career	ODIs
Mullally, Alan David	E	12.7.1969		19	1996–2001	50
Muller, Scott Andrew	A	11.7.1971		2	*1999*	
Munir Malik	P	10.7.1934		3	*1959–1962*	
Munton, Timothy Alan	E	30.7.1965		2	1992	
Muralitharan, Muttiah	SL	17.4.1972		85	*1992–2003*	224
Murdoch, William Lloyd	A, E	18.10.1954	18.2.1911	19	*1876–1891*	
Murphy, Brian Andrew	Z	1.12.1976		11	*1999–2001*	31
Murray, Anton Ronald Andrew	SA	30.4.1922	17.4.1995	10	*1952–1953*	
Murray, Bruce Alexander Grenfell	NZ	18.9.1940		13	*1967–1970*	
Murray, David Anthony	WI	29.9.1950		19	*1977–1981*	10
Murray, Darrin James	NZ	4.9.1967		8	*1994*	1
Murray, Deryck Lance	WI	20.5.1943		62	1963–1980	26
Murray, Junior Randalph	WI	20.1.1968		33	*1992–2001*	55
Murray, John Thomas MBE	E	1.4.1935		21	1961–1967	
Musgrove, Henry Alfred	A	27.11.1860	2.11.1931	1	*1884*	
Mushfiqur Rahman	B	1.1.1980		4	*2000–2003*	14
Mushtaq Ahmed	P	28.6.1970		52	*1989–2003*	144
Mushtaq Ali, Syed	I	17.12.1914		11	*1933–1951*	
[2]**Mushtaq Mohammad**	P	22.11.1943		57	*1958–1978*	10
Mutendera, David Travolta	Z	25.1.1979		1	*2000*	9
Nadeem Abbasi	P	15.4.1964		3	*1989*	
Nadeem Ghauri	P	12.10.1962		1	*1989*	6
[2]**Nadeem Khan**	P	10.12.1969		2	*1992–1998*	2
Nadkarni, Rameshchandra Gangaram	I	4.4.1932		41	*1955–1967*	
Nagamootoo, Mahendra Veeren	WI	9.10.1975		5	2000–*2002*	24
Nagel, Lisle Ernest	A	6.3.1905	23.11.1971	1	*1932*	
Naik, Sudhir Sakharam	I	21.2.1945		3	1974–*1974*	2
Naimur Rahman	B	19.9.1974		8	*2000–2002*	29
Nanan, Rangy	WI	29.5.1953		1	*1980*	
Naoomal Jeoomal	I	17.4.1904	18.7.1980	3	1932–*1933*	
Narasimha Rao, Modireddy Venkateshwar	I	11.8.1954		4	*1978–1979*	
Nash, Dion Joseph	NZ	20.11.1971		32	*1992–2001*	81
Nash, Laurence John	A	2.5.1910	24.7.1986	2	*1931–1936*	
Nasim-ul-Ghani	P	14.5.1941		29	*1957–1972*	1
Naushad Ali	P	1.10.1943		6	*1964*	
Naved Anjum	P	27.7.1963		2	*1989–1990*	13
Naved Ashraf	P	4.9.1974		2	*1998–1999*	
Naved Latif	P	21.2.1976		1	*2001*	11
Navle, Janaradan Gyanoba	I	7.12.1902	7.9.1979	2	1932–*1933*	
Nawaz, Mohamed <u>Naveed</u>	SL	20.9.1973		1	*2002*	3
Nayak, Surendra Vithal	I	20.10.1954		2	1982	4
[2]**Nayudu,** Cottari Kanakaiya	I	31.10.1895	14.11.1967	7	1932–1936	
[2]**Nayudu,** Cottari Subbanna	I	18.4.1914	22.11.2002	11	*1933–1951*	
[1]**Nazar Mohammad**	P	5.3.1921	12.7.1996	5	*1952*	
[2]**Nazir Ali,** Syed	I	8.1.1906	18.2.1975	2	1932–*1933*	
Neblett, James Montague	WI	13.11.1901	28.3.1959	1	*1934*	
Nehra, Ashish	I	29.4.1979		16	*1998–2003*	40
Nel, Andre	SA	15.7.1977		8	*2001–2003*	13
Nel, John Desmond	SA	10.7.1928		6	*1949–1957*	
Newberry, Claude	SA	1889	1.8.1916	4	*1913*	
Newham, William	E	12.12.1860	26.6.1944	1	*1887*	
Newman, *Sir* Jack	NZ	3.7.1902	23.9.1996	3	*1931–1932*	
Newport, Philip John	E	11.10.1962		3	1988–*1990*	
Newson, Edward Serrurier OBE	SA	2.12.1910	24.4.1988	3	*1930–1938*	
Ngam, Mfuneko	SA	29.1.1979		3	*2000*	
Niaz Ahmed	P	11.11.1945	12.4.2000	2	1967–*1968*	
Nichols, Morris Stanley	E	6.10.1900	26.1.1961	14	*1929*–1939	

[1] *Father and son(s).* [2] *Brothers.*

	Country	*Born*	*Died*	*Tests*	*Test Career*	*ODIs*
Nicholson, Frank	SA	17.9.1909	30.7.1982	4	*1935*	
Nicholson, Matthew James	A	2.10.1974		1	*1998*	
Nicolson, John Fairless William	SA	19.7.1899	13.12.1935	3	*1927*	
Nissanka, Ratnayake Arachchige Prabath	SL	25.10.1980		4	*2002*	23
Nissar, Mohammad	I	1.8.1910	11.3.1963	6	1932–1936	
Nitschke, Homesdale Carl	A	14.4.1905	29.9.1982	2	*1931*	
Nkala, Mluleki Luke	Z	1.4.1981		7	2000–*2002*	35
Noble, Montague Alfred	A	28.1.1873	22.6.1940	42	*1897*–1909	
Noblet, Geffery	A	14.9.1916		3	*1949–1952*	
Noreiga, Jack Mollinson	WI	15.4.1936	8.8.2003	4	*1970*	
Norton, Norman Ogilvie	SA	11.5.1881	27.6.1968	1	*1909*	
Nothling, Otto Ernest	A	1.8.1900	26.9.1965	1	*1928*	
[1]**Nourse,** Arthur Dudley	SA	12.11.1910	14.8.1981	34	1935–1951	
[1]**Nourse,** Arthur William ("Dave")	SA	26.1.1878	8.7.1948	45	*1902*–1924	
Ntini, Makhaya	SA	6.7.1977		42	*1997–2003*	85
Nunes, Robert Karl	WI	7.6.1894	22.7.1958	4	1928–*1929*	
Nupen, Eiulf Peter	SA	1.1.1902	29.1.1977	17	*1921–1935*	
Nurse, Seymour MacDonald	WI	10.11.1933		29	*1959–1968*	
Nyalchand, Shah	I	14.9.1919	3.1.1997	1	*1952*	
Oakman, Alan Stanley Myles	E	20.4.1930		2	1956	
O'Brien, Leo Patrick Joseph	A	2.7.1907	13.3.1997	5	*1932–1936*	
O'Brien, *Sir* Timothy Carew	E	5.11.1861	9.12.1948	5	1884–*1895*	
Ochse, Arthur Edward	SA	11.3.1870	11.4.1918	2	*1888*	
Ochse, Arthur Lennox	SA	11.10.1899	5.5.1949	3	*1927*–1929	
O'Connor, Jack	E	6.11.1897	22.2.1977	4	1929–*1929*	
O'Connor, John Denis Alphonsus	A	9.9.1875	23.8.1941	4	*1907*–1909	
O'Connor, Shayne Barry	NZ	15.11.1973		19	*1997–2001*	38
O'Donnell, Simon Patrick	A	26.1.1963		6	1985–*1985*	87
Ogilvie, Alan David	A	3.6.1951		5	*1977*	
O'Keeffe, Kerry James	A	25.11.1949		24	*1970*–1977	2
Old, Christopher Middleton	E	22.12.1948		46	*1972*–1981	32
Oldfield, Norman	E	5.5.1911	19.4.1996	1	1939	
Oldfield, William Albert Stanley MBE	A	9.9.1894	10.8.1976	54	*1920–1936*	
O'Linn, Sidney	SA	5.5.1927		7	1960–*1961*	
Olonga, Henry Khaaba	Z	3.7.1976		30	*1994–2002*	50
O'Neill, Norman Clifford	A	19.2.1937		42	*1958–1964*	
Ontong, Justin Lee	SA	4.1.1980		1	*2001*	16
Oram, Jacob David Philip	NZ	28.7.1978		7	*2002–2003*	49
O'Reilly, William Joseph OBE	A	20.12.1905	6.10.1992	27	*1931–1945*	
Ormond, James	E	20.8.1977		2	2001–*2001*	
O'Sullivan, David Robert	NZ	16.11.1944		11	*1972–1976*	3
Overton, Guy William Fitzroy	NZ	8.6.1919	7.9.1993	3	*1953*	
Owens, Michael Barry	NZ	11.11.1969		8	*1992*–1994	1
Owen-Smith, Harold Geoffrey	SA	18.2.1909	28.2.1990	5	1929	
Oxenham, Ronald Keven	A	28.7.1891	16.8.1939	7	*1928–1931*	
Padgett, Douglas Ernest Vernon	E	20.7.1934		2	1960	
Padmore, Albert Leroy	WI	17.12.1946		2	*1975*–1976	
Page, Milford Laurenson	NZ	8.5.1902	13.2.1987	14	*1929*–1937	
Pai, Ajit Manohar	I	28.4.1945		1	*1969*	
Paine, George Alfred Edward	E	11.6.1908	30.3.1978	4	*1934*	
Pairaudeau, Bruce Hamilton	WI	14.4.1931		13	*1952*–1957	
Palairet, Lionel Charles Hamilton	E	27.5.1870	27.3.1933	2	1902	
Palia, Phiroze Edulji	I	5.9.1910	9.9.1981	2	1932–1936	
Palm, Archibald William	SA	8.6.1901	17.8.1966	1	*1927*	
Palmer, Charles Henry CBE	E	15.5.1919		1	*1953*	
Palmer, George Eugene	A	22.2.1859	22.8.1910	17	1880–1886	
Palmer, Kenneth Ernest MBE	E	22.4.1937		1	*1964*	

[1] *Father and son(s).* [2] *Brothers.*

	Country	Born	Died	Tests	Test Career	ODIs
Pandit, Chandrakant Sitaram.	I	30.9.1961		5	1986–*1991*	36
Parfitt, Peter Howard.	E	8.12.1936		37	*1961*–1972	
Park, Roy Lindsay	A	30.7.1892	23.1.1947	1	*1920*	
Parkar, Ghulam Ahmed	I	25.10.1955		1	1982	10
Parkar, Ramnath Dhondu.	I	31.10.1946	11.8.1999	2	*1972*	
Parker, Charles Warrington Leonard. . .	E	14.10.1882	11.7.1959	1	1921	
Parker, George Macdonald	SA	27.5.1899	1.5.1969	2	1924	
[2]**Parker,** John Morton	NZ	21.2.1951		36	*1972–1980*	24
[2]**Parker,** Norman Murray	NZ	28.8.1948		3	*1976*	1
Parker, Paul William Giles	E	15.1.1956		1	1981	
Parkhouse, William Gilbert Anthony . .	E	12.10.1925	10.8.2000	7	1950–1959	
Parkin, Cecil Harry	E	18.2.1886	15.6.1943	10	*1920*–1924	
Parkin, Durant Clifford	SA	20.2.1873	20.3.1936	1	*1891*	
[1]**Parks,** James Horace	E	12.5.1903	21.11.1980	1	1937	
[1]**Parks,** James Michael.	E	21.10.1931		46	1954–*1967*	
Parore, Adam Craig	NZ	23.1.1971		78	1990–*2001*	179
Parry, Derick Recaldo	WI	22.12.1954		12	*1977–1979*	6
Parsana, Dhiraj Devshibhai	I	2.12.1947		2	*1978*	
Partridge, Joseph Titus	SA	9.12.1932	6.6.1988	11	*1963–1964*	
Pascoe, Leonard Stephen	A	13.2.1950		14	1977–*1981*	29
Passailaigue, Charles Clarence	WI	4.8.1902	7.1.1972	1	*1929*	
Patankar, Chandrakant Trimbak.	I	24.11.1930		1	*1955*	
[1]**Pataudi,** Iftikhar Ali Khan, Nawab of .	E, I	16.3.1910	5.1.1952	6	*1932*–1946	
[1]**Pataudi,** Mansur Ali Khan, Nawab of .	I	5.1.1941		46	*1961–1974*	
Patel, Brijesh Pursuram	I	24.11.1952		21	1974–*1977*	10
Patel, Dipak Narshibhai	NZ	25.10.1958		37	*1986–1996*	75
Patel, Jasubhai Motibhai	I	26.11.1924	12.12.1992	7	*1954–1959*	
Patel, Minal Mahesh	E	7.7.1970		2	1996	
Patel, Parthiv Ajay	I	9.3.1985		13	2002–*2003*	9
Patel, Rashid	I	1.6.1964		1	*1988*	1
Pathan, Irfan Khan	I	27.10.1984		2	*2003*	
Patiala, Maharaja of (Yadavendra Singh)	I	17.1.1913	17.6.1974	1	*1933*	
Patil, Sadashiv Raoji	I	10.10.1933		1	*1955*	
Patil, Sandeep Madhusudan	I	18.8.1956		29	*1979–1984*	45
Patterson, Balfour Patrick	WI	15.9.1961		28	*1985–1992*	59
Payne, Thelston Rodney O'Neale.	WI	13.2.1957		1	*1985*	7
Paynter, Edward	E	5.11.1901	5.2.1979	20	1931–1939	
Peall, Stephen Guy	Z	2.9.1969		4	*1993–1994*	21
Pearse, Charles Ormerod Cato.	SA	10.10.1884	7.5.1953	3	*1910*	
Peate, Edmund	E	2.3.1855	11.3.1900	9	*1881*–1886	
Peebles, Ian Alexander Ross	E	20.1.1908	28.2.1980	13	*1927*–1931	
Peel, Robert.	E	12.2.1857	12.8.1941	20	*1884*–1896	
Pegler, Sidney James	SA	28.7.1888	10.9.1972	16	*1909*–1924	
Pellew, Clarence Everard	A	21.9.1893	9.5.1981	10	*1920–1921*	
Penn, Frank	E	7.3.1851	26.12.1916	1	1880	
Perera, Anhettige Suresh Asanka	SL	16.2.1978		3	1998–*2001*	20
Perera, Panagodage Don Ruchira Laksiri	SL	6.4.1977		8	*1998–2002*	2
Perks, Reginald Thomas David	E	4.10.1911	22.11.1977	2	*1938*–1939	
Perry, Nehemiah Odolphus	WI	16.6.1968		4	*1998–1999*	21
[2]**Pervez Sajjad**	P	30.8.1942		19	*1964–1972*	
Peterson, Robin John	SA	4.8.1979		4	*2002–2003*	13
Petherick, Peter James.	NZ	25.9.1942		6	*1976*	
Petrie, Eric Charlton	NZ	22.5.1927		14	*1955–1965*	
Phadkar, Dattatraya Gajanan.	I	12.12.1925	17.3.1985	31	*1947–1958*	
Philipson, Hylton	E	8.6.1866	4.12.1935	5	*1891–1894*	
Phillip, Norbert	WI	12.6.1948		9	*1977–1978*	1
Phillips, Wayne Bentley	A	1.3.1958		27	*1983–1985*	48
Phillips, Wayne Norman.	A	7.11.1962		1	*1991*	
Philpott, Peter Ian.	A	21.11.1934		8	*1964–1965*	

[1] *Father and son(s).* [2] *Brothers.*

	Country	*Born*	*Died*	*Tests*	*Test Career*	*ODIs*
Pierre, Lancelot Richard	WI	5.6.1921	14.4.1989	1	*1947*	
Pigott, Anthony Charles Shackleton	E	4.6.1958		1	*1983*	
Pilling, Richard	E	5.7.1855	28.3.1891	8	*1881*–1888	
[2]**Pithey,** Anthony John	SA	17.7.1933		17	*1956–1964*	
[2]**Pithey,** David Bartlett	SA	4.10.1936		8	*1963–1966*	
Place, Winston	E	7.12.1914	25.1.2002	3	*1947*	
Playle, William Rodger	NZ	1.12.1938		8	1958–*1962*	
Plimsoll, Jack Bruce	SA	27.10.1917	11.11.1999	1	1947	
Pocock, Blair Andrew	NZ	18.6.1971		15	*1993–1997*	
Pocock, Patrick Ian	E	24.9.1946		25	*1967–1984*	1
Pollard, Richard	E	19.6.1912	16.12.1985	4	1946–1948	
Pollard, Victor	NZ	7.9.1945		32	*1964*–1973	3
[1, 2]**Pollock,** Peter Maclean	SA	30.6.1941		28	*1961–1969*	
[2]**Pollock,** Robert Graeme	SA	27.2.1944		23	*1963–1969*	
[1]**Pollock,** Shaun Maclean	SA	16.7.1973		80	*1995–2003*	203
Ponsford, William Harold MBE	A	19.10.1900	6.4.1991	29	*1924*–1934	
Ponting, Ricky Thomas	A	19.12.1974		75	*1995–2003*	185
Poole, Cyril John	E	13.3.1921	11.2.1996	3	*1951*	
Poore, Matt Beresford	NZ	1.6.1930		14	*1952–1955*	
Poore, Robert Montagu	SA	20.3.1866	14.7.1938	3	*1895*	
Pope, George Henry	E	27.1.1911	29.10.1993	1	1947	
Pope, Roland James	A	18.2.1864	27.7.1952	1	*1884*	
Pothecary, James Edward	SA	6.12.1933		3	1960	
Pougher, Arthur Dick	E	19.4.1865	20.5.1926	1	*1891*	
Powell, Albert William	SA	18.7.1873	11.9.1948	1	*1898*	
Powell, Daren Brentlyle	WI	15.4.1978		4	*2001–2002*	2
Powell, Ricardo Lloyd	WI	16.12.1978		1	*1999*	79
Prabhakar, Manoj	I	15.4.1963		39	*1984–1995*	130
Prasad, Bapu Krishnarao Venkatesh	I	5.8.1969		33	1996–*2001*	161
Prasad, Mannava Sri Kanth	I	24.4.1975		6	*1999*	17
Prasanna, Erapalli Anatharao Srinivas	I	22.5.1940		49	*1961–1978*	
Pretorius, Dewald	SA	6.12.1977		4	*2001*–2003	
Price, John Sidney Ernest	E	22.7.1937		15	*1963*–1972	
Price, Raymond William	Z	12.6.1976		16	*1999–2003*	15
Price, Wilfred Frederick Frank	E	25.4.1902	13.1.1969	1	1938	
Prideaux, Roger Malcolm	E	31.7.1939		3	1968–*1968*	
Priest, Mark Wellings	NZ	12.8.1961		3	1990–*1997*	18
Prince, Ashwell Gavin	SA	28.5.1977		7	*2001–2002*	1
Prince, Charles Frederick Henry	SA	11.9.1874	2.2.1949	1	*1898*	
Pringle, Christopher	NZ	26.1.1968		14	*1990–1994*	64
Pringle, Derek Raymond	E	18.9.1958		30	1982–1992	44
Pringle, Meyrick Wayne	SA	22.6.1966		4	*1991–1995*	17
Procter, Michael John	SA	15.9.1946		7	*1966–1969*	
Promnitz, Henry Louis Ernest	SA	23.2.1904	7.9.1983	2	*1927*	
Pullar, Geoffrey	E	1.8.1935		28	1959–*1962*	
Puna, Narotam	NZ	28.10.1929	7.6.1996	3	*1965*	
Punjabi, Pananmal Hotchand	I	20.9.1921		5	*1954*	
Pushpakumara, Karuppiahyage Ravindra	SL	21.7.1975		23	*1994–2001*	31
Pycroft, Andrew John	Z	6.6.1956		3	*1992*	20
Qaiser Abbas	P	7.5.1982		1	*2000*	
Qasim Omar	P	9.2.1957		26	*1983–1986*	31
Quaife, William George	E	17.3.1872	13.10.1951	7	1899–*1901*	
Quinn, Neville Anthony	SA	21.2.1908	5.8.1934	12	1929–*1931*	
Rabone, Geoffrey Osbourne	NZ	6.11.1921		12	1949–*1954*	
Rackemann, Carl Gray	A	3.6.1960		12	*1982–1990*	52
Radford, Neal Victor	E	7.6.1957		3	1986–*1987*	6

[1] *Father and son(s).* [2] *Brothers.*

	Country	*Born*	*Died*	*Tests*	*Test Career*	*ODIs*
Radley, Clive Thornton	E	13.5.1944		8	*1977–1978*	4
Rae, Allan Fitzroy	WI	30.9.1922		15	*1948–1952*	
Rafiqul Islam	B	7.11.1977		1	*2002*	1
Ragoonath, Suruj	WI	22.3.1968		2	*1998*	
Rai Singh, Kanwar	I	24.2.1922		1	*1947*	
Rajindernath, Vijay	I	7.1.1928	22.11.1989	1	*1952*	
Rajinder Pal	I	18.11.1937		1	*1963*	
Rajin Saleh	B	20.11.1983		5	*2003*	8
Rajput, Lalchand Sitaram	I	18.12.1961		2	*1985*	4
Raju, Sagi Lakshmi Venkatapathy	I	9.7.1969		28	*1989–2000*	53
Ramadhin, Sonny	WI	1.5.1929		43	1950–*1960*	
Raman, Woorkeri Venkat	I	23.5.1965		11	*1987–1996*	27
Ramanayake, Champaka Priyadarshana Hewage	SL	8.1.1965		18	*1987–1993*	62
Ramaswami, Cotar	I	16.6.1896	d unknown	2	1936	
Ramchand, Gulabrai Sipahimalani	I	26.7.1927	8.9.2003	33	1952–*1959*	
Ramesh, Sadagoppan	I	16.10.1975		19	*1998–2001*	24
[2]**Ramiz Raja**	P	14.8.1962		57	*1983–1996*	198
[2]**Ramji,** Ladha	I	2.10.1902	20.12.1948	1	*1933*	
Ramnarine, Dinanath	WI	4.6.1975		12	*1997–2001*	4
Ramprakash, Mark Ravin	E	5.9.1969		52	1991–*2001*	18
Ranasinghe, Anura Nandana	SL	13.10.1956	9.11.1998	2	*1981–1982*	9
[2]**Ranatunga,** Arjuna	SL	1.12.1963		93	*1981–2000*	269
[2]**Ranatunga,** Dammika	SL	12.10.1962		2	*1989*	4
[2]**Ranatunga,** Sanjeeva	SL	25.4.1969		9	*1994–1996*	13
Ranchod, Ujesh	Z	17.5.1969		1	*1992*	3
Randall, Derek William	E	24.2.1951		47	*1976*–1984	49
Rangachari, Commandur Rajagopalachari	I	14.4.1916	9.10.1993	4	*1947–1948*	
Rangnekar, Khanderao Moreshwar	I	27.6.1915	11.10.1984	3	*1947*	
Ranjane, Vasant Baburao	I	22.7.1937		7	*1958–1964*	
Ranjitsinhji, Kumar Shri	E	10.9.1872	2.4.1933	15	1896–1902	
Ransford, Vernon Seymour	A	20.3.1885	19.3.1958	20	*1907–1911*	
Rashid Khan	P	15.12.1959		4	*1981–1984*	29
Rashid Latif	P	14.10.1968		37	1992–*2003*	166
Rathore, Vikram	I	26.3.1969		6	1996–*1996*	7
Ratnayake, Rumesh Joseph	SL	2.1.1964		23	*1982–1991*	70
Ratnayeke, Joseph Ravindran	SL	2.5.1960		22	*1981–1989*	78
Ratra, Ajay	I	13.12.1981		6	*2001*–2002	12
Razdan, Vivek	I	25.8.1969		2	*1989*	3
Read, Christopher Mark Wells	E	10.8.1978		8	1999–*2003*	23
Read, Holcombe Douglas	E	28.1.1910	5.1.2000	1	1935	
Read, John Maurice	E	9.2.1859	17.2.1929	17	1882–1893	
Read, Walter William	E	23.11.1855	6.1.1907	18	*1882*–1893	
Reddy, Bharath	I	12.11.1954		4	1979	3
Redmond, Rodney Ernest	NZ	29.12.1944		1	*1972*	2
Redpath, Ian Ritchie MBE	A	11.5.1941		66	*1963–1975*	5
Reedman, John Cole	A	9.10.1865	25.3.1924	1	*1894*	
Reeve, Dermot Alexander OBE	E	2.4.1963		3	*1991*	29
Rege, Madhusudan Ramachandra	I	18.3.1924		1	*1948*	
Rehman, Sheikh Fazalur	P	11.6.1935		1	*1957*	
Reid, Bruce Anthony	A	14.3.1963		27	*1985–1992*	61
Reid, John Fulton	NZ	3.3.1956		19	*1978–1985*	25
Reid, John Richard OBE	NZ	3.6.1928		58	1949–1965	
Reid, Norman	SA	26.12.1890	6.6.1947	1	*1921*	
Reifer, Floyd Lamonte	WI	23.7.1972		4	*1996–1998*	2
Reiffel, Paul Ronald	A	19.4.1966		35	*1991–1997*	92
Relf, Albert Edward	E	26.6.1874	26.3.1937	13	*1903–1913*	
Renneberg, David Alexander	A	23.9.1942		8	*1966–1967*	

[1] *Father and son.* [2] *Brothers.* [3] *Grandfather and grandson.*

	Country	*Born*	*Died*	*Tests*	*Test Career*	*ODIs*
[2]**Rennie,** Gavin James	Z	12.1.1976		23	*1997–2001*	40
[2]**Rennie,** John Alexander	Z	29.7.1970		4	*1993–1997*	44
Rhodes, Harold James	E	22.7.1936		2	1959	
Rhodes, Jonathan Neil	SA	27.7.1969		52	*1992–2000*	245
Rhodes, Steven John	E	17.6.1964		11	1994–*1994*	9
Rhodes, Wilfred	E	29.10.1877	8.7.1973	58	1899–*1929*	
[2]**Richards,** Alfred Renfrew	SA	14.12.1867	9.1.1904	1	*1895*	
Richards, Barry Anderson	SA	21.7.1945		4	*1969*	
Richards, Clifton James	E	10.8.1958		8	*1986*–1988	22
Richards, *Sir* Isaac Vivian Alexander	WI	7.3.1952		121	*1974*–1991	187
[2]**Richards,** William Henry Matthews	SA	26.3.1862	4.1.1903	1	*1888*	
Richardson, Arthur John	A	24.7.1888	23.12.1973	9	*1924*–1926	
Richardson, David John	SA	16.9.1959		42	*1991–1997*	122
[2]**Richardson,** Derek Walter	E	3.11.1934		1	1957	
Richardson, Mark Hunter	NZ	11.6.1971		28	*2000–2003*	4
[2]**Richardson,** Peter Edward	E	4.7.1931		34	1956–1963	
Richardson, Richard Benjamin	WI	12.1.1962		86	*1983*–1995	224
Richardson, Thomas	E	11.8.1870	2.7.1912	14	1893–*1897*	
[4]**Richardson,** Victor York	A	7.9.1894	29.10.1969	19	*1924–1935*	
Richmond, Thomas Leonard	E	23.6.1890	29.12.1957	1	1921	
Rickards, Kenneth Roy	WI	22.8.1923	21.8.1995	2	*1947–1951*	
Ridgway, Frederick	E	10.8.1923		5	*1951*	
Rigg, Keith Edward	A	21.5.1906	28.2.1995	8	*1930–1936*	
Ring, Douglas Thomas	A	14.10.1918	23.6.2003	13	*1947*–1953	
Ritchie, Gregory Michael	A	23.1.1960		30	*1982–1986*	44
Rixon, Stephen John	A	25.2.1954		13	*1977–1984*	6
Rizwan-uz-Zaman	P	4.9.1961		11	*1981–1988*	3
Roach, Clifford Archibald	WI	13.3.1904	16.4.1988	16	1928–*1934*	
Roberts, Albert William	NZ	20.8.1909	13.5.1978	5	*1929*–1937	
Roberts, Alphonso Theodore	WI	18.9.1937	24.7.1996	1	*1955*	
Roberts, Anderson Montgomery Everton CBE	WI	29.1.1951		47	*1973–1983*	56
Roberts, Andrew Duncan Glenn	NZ	6.5.1947	26.10.1989	7	*1975–1976*	1
Roberts, Lincoln Abraham	WI	4.9.1974		1	*1998*	
Robertson, Gary Keith	NZ	15.7.1960		1	*1985*	10
Robertson, Gavin Ron	A	28.5.1966		4	*1997–1998*	13
Robertson, John Benjamin	SA	5.6.1906	5.7.1985	3	*1935*	
Robertson, John David Benbow	E	22.2.1917	12.10.1996	11	1947–*1951*	
Robertson, William Roderick	A	6.10.1861	24.6.1938	1	*1884*	
Robins, Robert Walter Vivian	E	3.6.1906	12.12.1968	19	1929–1937	
Robinson, Rayford Harold	A	26.3.1914	10.8.1965	1	*1936*	
Robinson, Richard Daryl	A	8.6.1946		3	1977	2
Robinson, Robert Timothy	E	21.11.1958		29	*1984*–1989	26
Rodriguez, William Vicente	WI	25.6.1934		5	*1961–1967*	
Roope, Graham Richard James	E	12.7.1946		21	*1972*–1978	8
Root, Charles Frederick	E	16.4.1890	20.1.1954	3	1926	
Rorke, Gordon Frederick	A	27.6.1938		4	*1958–1959*	
Rose, Brian Charles	E	4.6.1950		9	*1977–1980*	2
Rose, Franklyn Albert	WI	1.2.1972		19	*1996*–2000	27
Rose-Innes, Albert	SA	16.2.1868	22.11.1946	2	*1888*	
Routledge, Thomas William	SA	18.4.1867	9.5.1927	4	*1891–1895*	
[2]**Rowan,** Athol Matthew Burchell	SA	7.2.1921	22.2.1998	15	1947–1951	
[2]**Rowan,** Eric Alfred Burchell	SA	20.7.1909	30.4.1993	26	1935–1951	
Rowe, Charles Gordon	NZ	30.6.1915	9.6.1995	1	*1945*	
Rowe, George Alexander	SA	15.6.1874	8.1.1950	5	*1895–1902*	
Rowe, Lawrence George	WI	8.1.1949		30	*1971–1979*	11
Roy, Ambar	I	5.6.1945	19.9.1997	4	*1969*	
[1]**Roy,** Pankaj	I	31.5.1928	4.2.2001	43	*1951–1960*	

[1] *Father and son(s).* [2] *Brothers.*

	Country	*Born*	*Died*	*Tests*	*Test Career*	*ODIs*
[1]**Roy,** Pranab	I	10.2.1957		2	*1981*	
Royle, Vernon Peter Fanshawe Archer	E	29.1.1854	21.5.1929	1	*1878*	
Rudolph, Jacobus Andries	SA	4.5.1981		11	*2002–2003*	17
Rumsey, Frederick Edward	E	4.12.1935		5	1964–1965	
Rushmere, Mark Weir	SA	7.1.1965		1	*1991*	4
Russell, Albert Charles	E	7.10.1887	23.3.1961	10	*1920–1922*	
Russell, Robert Charles ("Jack")	E	15.8.1963		54	1988–*1997*	40
Russell, William Eric	E	3.7.1936		10	*1961*–1967	
Rutherford, John Walter	A	25.9.1929		1	*1956*	
Rutherford, Kenneth Robert	NZ	26.10.1965		56	*1984–1994*	121
Ryder, John	A	8.8.1889	3.4.1977	20	*1920–1928*	
[2]**Sadiq Mohammad**	P	3.5.1945		41	*1969–1980*	19
[2]**Saeed Ahmed**	P	1.10.1937		41	*1957–1972*	
Saeed Anwar	P	6.9.1968		55	*1990–2001*	247
Saggers, Martin John	E	23.5.1972		1	*2003*	
Saggers, Ronald Arthur	A	15.5.1917	17.3.1987	6	1948–*1949*	
[2]**St Hill,** Edwin Lloyd	WI	9.3.1904	21.5.1957	2	*1929*	
[2]**St Hill,** Wilton H.	WI	6.7.1893	d unknown	3	1928–*1929*	
Salah-ud-Din	P	14.2.1947		5	*1964–1969*	
Saleem Jaffer	P	19.11.1962		14	*1986–1991*	39
Salim Altaf	P	19.4.1944		21	1967–*1978*	6
[2]**Salim Elahi**	P	21.11.1976		13	*1995–2002*	44
Salim Malik	P	16.4.1963		103	*1981–1998*	283
Salim Yousuf	P	7.12.1959		32	*1981–1990*	86
Salisbury, Ian David Kenneth	E	21.1.1970		15	1992–*2000*	4
Salman Butt	P	7.10.1984		1	*2003*	
Samarasekera, Maitipage Athula Rohitha	SL	5.8.1961		4	1988–*1991*	39
[2]**Samaraweera,** Dulip Prasanna	SL	12.2.1972		7	*1993–1994*	5
[2]**Samaraweera,** Thilan Thusara	SL	22.9.1976		14	*2001–2003*	14
Samuels, Marlon Nathaniel	WI	5.1.1981		19	*2000–2002*	53
Samuels, Robert George	WI	13.3.1971		6	*1995–1996*	8
Samuelson, Sivert Vause	SA	21.11.1883	18.11.1958	1	*1909*	
Sandham, Andrew	E	6.7.1890	20.4.1982	14	1921–*1929*	
Sandhu, Balwinder Singh	I	3.8.1956		8	*1982–1983*	22
Sanford, Adam	WI	12.7.1976		9	*2001–2003*	
Sangakkara, Kumar Chokshanada	SL	27.10.1977		33	*2000–2003*	96
Sanghvi, Rahul Laxman	I	3.9.1974		1	*2000*	10
Sanwar Hossain	B	5.8.1973		9	*2001–2003*	27
Saqlain Mushtaq	P	29.12.1976		48	*1995–2003*	169
Sarandeep Singh	I	21.10.1979		3	*2000–2001*	5
Sardesai, Dilip Narayan	I	8.8.1940		30	*1961–1972*	
Sarfraz Nawaz	P	1.12.1948		55	*1968–1983*	45
Sarwan, Ramnaresh Ronnie	WI	23.6.1980		40	*1999–2003*	49
Sarwate, Chandrasekhar Trimbak	I	22.6.1920	23.12.2003	9	1946–*1951*	
Saunders, John Victor	A	21.3.1876	21.12.1927	14	*1901–1907*	
Saxena, Ramesh Chandra	I	20.9.1944		1	1967	
Scarlett, Reginald Osmond	WI	15.8.1934		3	*1959*	
Schofield, Christopher Paul	E	6.10.1978		2	2000	
Schultz, Brett Nolan	SA	26.8.1970		9	*1992–1997*	1
Schultz, Sandford Spence	E	29.8.1857	18.12.1937	1	*1878*	
Schwarz, Reginald Oscar	SA	4.5.1875	18.11.1918	20	*1905*–1912	
[1]**Scott,** Alfred Homer Patrick	WI	29.7.1934		1	*1952*	
Scott, Henry James Herbert	A	26.12.1858	23.9.1910	8	1884–1886	
[1]**Scott,** Oscar Charles	WI	14.8.1892	15.6.1961	8	1928–*1930*	
Scott, Roy Hamilton	NZ	6.3.1917		1	*1946*	
Scott, Verdun John	NZ	31.7.1916	2.8.1980	10	*1945–1951*	
Scotton, William Henry	E	15.1.1856	9.7.1893	15	*1881–1886*	

[1] *Father and son(s).* [2] *Brothers.*

	Country	Born	Died	Tests	Test Career	ODIs
Sealey, Benjamin James	WI	12.8.1899	12.9.1963	1	1933	
Sealy, James Edward Derrick	WI	11.9.1912	3.1.1982	11	*1929*–1939	
Seccull, Arthur William	SA	14.9.1868	20.7.1945	1	*1895*	
Sehwag, Virender	I	20.10.1978		20	*2001–2003*	79
Sekhar, Thirumalai Ananthanpillai	I	28.3.1955		2	*1982*	4
Selby, John	E	1.7.1849	11.3.1894	6	*1876–1881*	
Sellers, Reginald Hugh Durning	A	20.8.1940		1	*1964*	
Selvey, Michael Walter William	E	25.4.1948		3	1976–*1976*	
Sen, Probir Kumar	I	31.5.1926	27.1.1970	14	*1947–1952*	
Senanayake, Charith Panduka	SL	19.12.1962		3	*1990*	7
Sen Gupta, Apoorva Kumar	I	3.8.1939		1	*1958*	
Serjeant, Craig Stanton	A	1.11.1951		12	1977–*1977*	3
Sewell, David Graham	NZ	20.10.1977		1	*1997*	
Seymour, Michael Arthur	SA	5.6.1936		7	*1963–1969*	
Shabbir Ahmed	P	21.4.1976		6	*2003*	16
Shackleton, Derek	E	12.8.1924		7	1950–1963	
Shadab Kabir	P	12.11.1977		5	1996–*2001*	3
Shafiq Ahmed	P	28.3.1949		6	1974–*1980*	3
[2]**Shafqat Rana**	P	10.8.1943		5	*1964–1969*	
Shah, Ali Hassimshah	Z	7.8.1959		3	*1992–1996*	28
Shahid Afridi	P	1.3.1980		14	*1998–2001*	176
Shahid Israr	P	1.3.1950		1	*1976*	
Shahid Mahboob	P	25.8.1962		1	*1989*	10
Shahid Mahmood	P	17.3.1939		1	1962	
Shahid Nazir	P	4.12.1977		8	*1996–1998*	17
Shahid Saeed	P	6.1.1966		1	*1989*	10
Shahriar Hossain	B	1.6.1976		1	*2000*	18
Shakeel Ahmed, sen.	P	12.2.1966		1	*1998*	
Shakeel Ahmed, jun.	P	12.11.1971		3	*1992–1994*	2
Shalders, William Alfred	SA	12.2.1880	18.3.1917	12	*1898*–1907	
Sharma, Ajay Kumar	I	3.4.1964		1	*1987*	31
Sharma, Chetan	I	3.1.1966		23	*1984–1988*	65
Sharma, Gopal	I	3.8.1960		5	*1984–1990*	11
Sharma, Parthasarathy Harishchandra	I	5.1.1948		5	*1974–1976*	2
Sharma, Sanjeev Kumar	I	25.8.1965		2	*1988*–1990	23
Sharp, John	E	15.2.1878	28.1.1938	3	1909	
Sharpe, Duncan Albert	P	3.8.1937		3	*1959*	
Sharpe, John William	E	9.12.1866	19.6.1936	3	1890–*1891*	
Sharpe, Philip John	E	27.12.1936		12	1963–1969	
Shastri, Ravishankar Jayadritha	I	27.5.1962		80	*1980–1992*	150
Shaw, Alfred	E	29.8.1842	16.1.1907	7	*1876–1881*	
[5]**Sheahan,** Andrew Paul	A	30.9.1946		31	*1967–1973*	3
Shepherd, Barry Kenneth	A	23.4.1937	17.9.2001	9	*1962–1964*	
Shepherd, John Neil	WI	9.11.1943		5	1969–*1970*	
Sheppard, *Rt. Rev. Lord* David Stuart	E	6.3.1929		22	1950–*1962*	
Shepstone, George Harold	SA	9.4.1876	3.7.1940	2	*1895–1898*	
Sherwell, Percy William	SA	17.8.1880	17.4.1948	13	*1905–1910*	
Sherwin, Mordecai	E	26.2.1851	3.7.1910	3	*1886*–1888	
Shillingford, Grayson Cleophas	WI	25.9.1944		7	1969–*1971*	
Shillingford, Irvine Theodore	WI	18.4.1944		4	*1976–1977*	2
Shinde, Sadashiv Ganpatrao	I	18.8.1923	22.6.1955	7	1946–1952	
Shivnarine, Sewdatt	WI	13.5.1952		8	*1977–1978*	1
Shoaib Akhtar	P	13.8.1975		29	*1997–2003*	95
Shoaib Malik	P	1.2.1982		5	*2001–2003*	58
[1]**Shoaib Mohammad**	P	8.1.1961		45	*1983–1995*	63
Shodhan, Roshan Harshadlal	I	18.10.1928		3	*1952*	
Shrewsbury, Arthur	E	11.4.1856	19.5.1903	23	*1881*–1893	
Shrimpton, Michael John Froud	NZ	23.6.1940		10	*1962–1973*	
Shuja-ud-Din Butt	P	10.4.1930		19	1954–*1961*	

[1] *Father and son.* [2] *Brothers.* [5] *Great-grandfather and great-grandson.*

	Country	*Born*	*Died*	*Tests*	*Test Career*	*ODIs*
Shukla, Rakesh Chandra	I	4.2.1948		1	*1982*	
Shuter, John	E	9.2.1855	5.7.1920	1	1888	
Shuttleworth, Kenneth	E	13.11.1944		5	*1970*–1971	1
Sibanda, Vusimuzi	Z	10.10.1983		2	*2003*	5
Siddiqui, Iqbal Rashid	I	26.12.1974		1	*2001*	
[1]**Sidebottom,** Arnold	E	1.4.1954		1	1985	
[1]**Sidebottom,** Ryan Jay	E	15.1.1978		1	2001	2
Sidhu, Navjot Singh	I	20.10.1963		51	*1983–1998*	136
Siedle, Ivan Julian	SA	11.1.1903	24.8.1982	18	*1927–1935*	
Sievers, Morris William	A	13.4.1912	10.5.1968	3	*1936*	
Sikander Bakht	P	25.8.1957		26	*1976–1982*	27
Silva, Kelaniyage Jayantha	SL	2.6.1973		7	*1995–1997*	1
Silva, Sampathawaduge Amal Rohitha	SL	12.12.1960		9	*1982*–1988	20
Silverwood, Christopher Eric Wilfred	E	5.3.1975		6	*1996–2002*	7
Simmons, Philip Verant	WI	18.4.1963		26	*1987–1997*	143
Simpson, Robert Baddeley	A	3.2.1936		62	*1957–1977*	2
Simpson, Reginald Thomas	E	27.2.1920		27	*1948–1954*	
Simpson-Hayward, George Hayward	E	7.6.1875	2.10.1936	5	*1909*	
Sims, James Morton	E	13.5.1903	27.4.1973	4	1935–*1936*	
Sinclair, Barry Whitley	NZ	23.10.1936		21	*1962–1967*	
Sinclair, Ian McKay	NZ	1.6.1933		2	*1955*	
Sinclair, James Hugh	SA	16.10.1876	23.2.1913	25	*1895–1910*	
Sinclair, Mathew Stuart	NZ	9.11.1975		20	*1999–2002*	38
Sincock, David John	A	1.2.1942		3	*1964–1965*	
Sinfield, Reginald Albert	E	24.12.1900	17.3.1988	1	1938	
Singh, Charran Kamkaran	WI	27.11.1935		2	*1959*	
Singh, Rabindra Ramanarayan	I	14.9.1963		1	*1998*	136
Singh, Robin	I	1.1.1970		1	*1998*	
Sivaramakrishnan, Laxman	I	31.12.1965		9	*1982–1985*	16
Slack, Wilfred Norris	E	12.12.1954	15.1.1989	3	*1985*–1986	2
Slater, Keith Nichol	A	12.3.1935		1	*1958*	
Slater, Michael Jonathon	A	21.2.1970		74	1993–2001	42
Sleep, Peter Raymond	A	4.5.1957		14	*1978–1989*	
Slight, James	A	20.10.1855	9.12.1930	1	1880	
Smailes, Thomas Francis	E	27.3.1910	1.12.1970	1	1946	
Small, Gladstone Cleophas	E	18.10.1961		17	1986–*1990*	53
Small, Joseph A.	WI	3.11.1892	26.4.1958	3	1928–*1929*	
Small, Milton Aster	WI	12.2.1964		2	*1983*–1984	2
Smith, Alan Christopher CBE	E	25.10.1936		6	*1962*	
Smith, Andrew Michael	E	1.10.1967		1	1997	
Smith, Cameron Wilberforce	WI	29.7.1933		5	*1960–1961*	
Smith, Cedric Ivan James	E	25.8.1906	9.2.1979	5	*1934*–1937	
Smith, *Sir* Charles Aubrey	E	21.7.1863	20.12.1948	1	*1888*	
Smith, Charles James Edward	SA	25.12.1872	27.3.1947	3	*1902*	
[2]**Smith,** Christopher Lyall	E	15.10.1958		8	1983–1986	4
Smith, David Bertram Miller	A	14.9.1884	29.7.1963	2	1912	
Smith, David Mark	E	9.1.1956		2	*1985*	2
Smith, David Robert	E	5.10.1934	17.12.2003	5	*1961*	
Smith, Denis	E	24.1.1907	12.9.1979	2	1935	
Smith, Devon Sheldon	WI	21.10.1981		4	*2002*	3
Smith, Donald Victor	E	14.6.1923		3	1957	
Smith, Dwayne Romel	WI	12.4.1983		2	*2003*	
Smith, Edward Thomas	E	19.7.1977		3	2003	
Smith, Ernest James	E	6.2.1886	31.8.1979	11	*1911–1913*	
Smith, Frank Brunton	NZ	13.3.1922	6.7.1997	4	*1946–1951*	
Smith, Frederick William	SA	31.3.1861	17.4.1914	3	*1888–1895*	
Smith, Graeme Craig	SA	1.2.1981		21	*2001–2003*	38
Smith, Harry	E	21.5.1890	12.11.1937	1	1928	
Smith, Horace Dennis	NZ	8.1.1913	25.1.1986	1	*1932*	

[1] *Father and son(s).* [2] *Brothers.*

	Country	*Born*	*Died*	*Tests*	*Test Career*	*ODIs*
Smith, Ian David Stockley MBE	NZ	28.2.1957		63	*1980–1991*	98
Smith, Michael John Knight OBE	E	30.6.1933		50	1958–1972	
Smith, O'Neil Gordon ("Collie")	WI	5.5.1933	9.9.1959	26	*1954–1958*	
[2]**Smith,** Robin Arnold	E	13.9.1963		62	1988–*1995*	71
Smith, Steven Barry	A	18.10.1961		3	*1983*	28
Smith, Thomas Peter Bromley	E	30.10.1908	4.8.1967	4	1946–*1946*	
Smith, Vivian Ian	SA	23.2.1925		9	1947–*1957*	
Smithson, Gerald Arthur	E	1.11.1926	6.9.1970	2	*1947*	
Snedden, Colin Alexander	NZ	7.1.1918		1	*1946*	
Snedden, Martin Colin	NZ	23.11.1958		25	*1980*–1990	93
Snell, Richard Peter	SA	12.9.1968		5	*1991–1994*	42
[2]**Snooke,** Sibley John	SA	1.2.1881	14.8.1966	26	*1905–1922*	
[2]**Snooke,** Stanley de la Courtte	SA	11.11.1878	6.4.1959	1	1907	
Snow, John Augustine	E	13.10.1941		49	1965–1976	9
Sobers, *Sir* Garfield St Aubrun	WI	28.7.1936		93	*1953–1973*	1
Sohoni, Sriranga Wasudev	I	5.3.1918	19.5.1993	4	1946–*1951*	
Solkar, Eknath Dhondu	I	18.3.1948		27	*1969–1976*	7
Solomon, Joseph Stanislaus	WI	26.8.1930		27	*1958–1964*	
Solomon, William Rodger Thomson	SA	23.4.1872	12.7.1964	1	*1898*	
Sood, Man Mohan	I	6.7.1939		1	*1959*	
Southerton, James	E	16.11.1827	16.6.1880	2	*1876*	
Sparling, John Trevor	NZ	24.7.1938		11	1958–*1963*	
Spearman, Craig Murray	NZ	4.7.1972		19	*1995–2000*	51
Spofforth, Frederick Robert	A	9.9.1853	4.6.1926	18	*1876–1886*	
Spooner, Reginald Herbert	E	21.10.1880	2.10.1961	10	1905–1912	
Spooner, Richard Thompson	E	30.12.1919	20.12.1997	7	*1951*–1955	
Srikkanth, Krishnamachari	I	21.12.1959		43	*1981–1991*	146
Srinath, Javagal	I	31.8.1969		67	*1991–2002*	229
Srinivasan, Thirumalai Echambadi	I	26.10.1950		1	*1980*	2
Stackpole, Keith Raymond MBE	A	10.7.1940		43	*1965–1973*	6
Stanyforth, Ronald Thomas	E	30.5.1892	20.2.1964	4	*1927*	
Staples, Samuel James	E	18.9.1892	4.6.1950	3	*1927*	
Statham, John Brian CBE	E	17.6.1930	10.6.2000	70	*1950*–1965	
Stayers, Sven Conrad	WI	9.6.1937		4	*1961*	
Stead, Gary Raymond	NZ	9.1.1972		5	*1998–1999*	
Steel, Allan Gibson	E	24.9.1858	15.6.1914	13	1880–1888	
Steele, David Stanley OBE	E	29.9.1941		8	1975–1976	1
Stephenson, John Patrick	E	14.3.1965		1	1989	
Stevens, Gavin Byron	A	29.2.1932		4	*1959*	
Stevens, Greville Thomas Scott	E	7.1.1901	19.9.1970	10	*1922–1929*	
Stevenson, Graham Barry	E	16.12.1955		2	*1979–1980*	4
[1]**Stewart,** Alec James OBE	E	8.4.1963		133	*1989*–2003	170
[1]**Stewart,** Michael James OBE	E	16.9.1932		8	1962–*1963*	
Stewart, Robert Burnard	SA	3.9.1856	12.9.1913	1	*1888*	
Steyn, Philippus Jeremia Rudolf	SA	30.6.1967		3	*1994*	1
Stirling, Derek Alexander	NZ	5.10.1961		6	*1984*–1986	6
Stoddart, Andrew Ernest	E	11.3.1863	3.4.1915	16	*1887–1897*	
[2]**Stollmeyer,** Jeffrey Baxter	WI	11.4.1921	10.9.1989	32	1939–*1954*	
[2]**Stollmeyer,** Victor Humphrey	WI	24.1.1916	21.9.1999	1	1939	
Storer, William	E	25.1.1867	28.2.1912	6	*1897*–1899	
[2]**Strang,** Bryan Colin	Z	9.6.1972		26	*1994–2001*	49
[2]**Strang,** Paul Andrew	Z	28.7.1970		24	*1994–2001*	95
Streak, Heath Hilton	Z	16.3.1974		57	*1993–2003*	172
Street, George Benjamin	E	6.12.1889	24.4.1924	1	*1922*	
Stricker, Louis Anthony	SA	26.5.1884	5.2.1960	13	*1909*–1912	
Strudwick, Herbert	E	28.1.1880	14.2.1970	28	*1909*–1926	
Strydom, Pieter Coenraad	SA	10.6.1969		2	*1999*	10
Stuart, Colin Ellsworth Laurie	WI	28.9.1973		6	*2000–2001*	5

[1] *Father and son(s).* [2] *Brothers.*

	Country	Born	Died	Tests	Test Career	ODIs
[2]**Studd,** Charles Thomas	E	2.12.1860	16.7.1931	5	1882–*1882*	
[2]**Studd,** George Brown	E	20.10.1859	13.2.1945	4	*1882*	
Styris, Scott Bernard	NZ	10.7.1975		9	*2001–2003*	70
Su'a, Murphy Logo	NZ	7.11.1966		13	*1991–1994*	12
Subba Row, Raman CBE	E	29.1.1932		13	1958–1961	
Subramanya, Venkataraman	I	16.7.1936		9	*1964–1967*	
Such, Peter Mark	E	12.6.1964		11	1993–1999	
Sugg, Frank Howe	E	11.1.1862	29.5.1933	2	1888	
Sunderam, Gundibali Rama	I	29.3.1930		2	*1955*	
Surendranath	I	4.1.1937		11	*1958–1960*	
Surti, Rusi Framroze	I	25.5.1936		26	*1960–1969*	
Susskind, Manfred John	SA	8.6.1891	9.7.1957	5	1924	
Sutcliffe, Bert MBE	NZ	17.11.1923	20.4.2001	42	*1946*–1965	
Sutcliffe, Herbert	E	24.11.1894	22.1.1978	54	1924–1935	
Swamy, Venkatraman Narayan	I	23.5.1924	1.5.1983	1	*1955*	
Swetman, Roy	E	25.10.1933		11	*1958–1959*	
Symcox, Patrick Leonard	SA	14.4.1960		20	*1993–1998*	80
Taber, Hedley Brian	A	29.4.1940		16	*1966–1969*	
Taberer, Henry Melville	SA	7.10.1870	5.6.1932	1	*1902*	
Tahir Naqqash	P	6.7.1959		15	*1981–1984*	40
Taibu, Tatenda	Z	14.5.1983		12	*2001–2003*	43
Talat Ali Malik	P	29.5.1950		10	*1972–1978*	
Talha Jubair	B	10.12.1985		6	*2002*	6
Tallon, Donald	A	17.2.1916	7.9.1984	21	*1945*–1953	
Tamhane, Narendra Shankar	I	4.8.1931	19.3.2002	21	*1954–1960*	
[2]**Tancred,** Augustus Bernard	SA	20.8.1865	23.11.1911	2	*1888*	
[2]**Tancred,** Louis Joseph	SA	7.10.1876	28.7.1934	14	*1902–1913*	
[2]**Tancred,** Vincent Maximillian	SA	7.7.1875	3.6.1904	1	*1898*	
Tapash Baisya	B	25.12.1982		11	*2002–2003*	26
[2]**Tapscott,** George Lancelot	SA	7.11.1889	13.12.1940	1	*1913*	
[2]**Tapscott,** Lionel Eric	SA	18.3.1894	7.7.1934	2	*1922*	
Tarapore, Keki Khurshedji	I	17.12.1910	15.6.1986	1	*1948*	
Taslim Arif	P	1.5.1954		6	*1979–1980*	2
[1]**Tate,** Frederick William	E	24.7.1867	24.2.1943	1	1902	
[1]**Tate,** Maurice William	E	30.5.1895	18.5.1956	39	1924–1935	
Tattersall, Roy	E	17.8.1922		16	*1950*–1954	
Taufeeq Umar	P	20.6.1981		19	*2001–2003*	17
Tauseef Ahmed	P	10.5.1958		34	*1979–1993*	70
Tavaré, Christopher James	E	27.10.1954		31	1980–1989	29
Tayfield, Hugh Joseph	SA	30.1.1929	24.2.1994	37	*1949*–1960	
Taylor, Alistair Innes	SA	25.7.1925		1	*1956*	
Taylor, Bruce Richard	NZ	12.7.1943		30	*1964*–1973	2
[2]**Taylor,** Daniel	SA	9.1.1887	24.1.1957	2	*1913*	
Taylor, Donald Dougald	NZ	2.3.1923	5.12.1980	3	*1946–1955*	
[2]**Taylor,** Herbert Wilfred	SA	5.5.1889	8.2.1973	42	1912–*1931*	
Taylor, Jaswick Ossie	WI	3.1.1932	13.11.1999	3	*1957–1958*	
Taylor, Jerome Everton	WI	22.6.1984		3	*2002–2003*	1
Taylor, John Morris	A	10.10.1895	12.5.1971	20	*1920*–1926	
Taylor, Jonathan Paul	E	8.8.1964		2	*1992*–1994	1
Taylor, Kenneth	E	21.8.1935		3	1959–1964	
Taylor, Leslie Brian	E	25.10.1953		2	1985	2
Taylor, Mark Anthony	A	27.10.1964		104	*1988–1998*	113
Taylor, Peter Laurence	A	22.8.1956		13	*1986–1991*	83
Taylor, Robert William MBE	E	17.7.1941		57	*1970–1983*	27
Tendulkar, Sachin Ramesh	I	24.4.1973		111	*1989–2003*	321
Tennyson, *Lord* Lionel Hallam	E	7.11.1889	6.6.1951	9	*1913*–1921	
Terbrugge, David John	SA	31.1.1977		6	*1998–2002*	4

[1] *Father and son(s).* [2] *Brothers.*

	Country	*Born*	*Died*	*Tests*	*Test Career*	*ODIs*
Terry, Vivian Paul	E	14.1.1959		2	1984	
Theunissen, Nicolaas Hendrik Christiaan de Jong	SA	4.5.1867	9.11.1929	1	*1888*	
Thomas, Grahame	A	21.3.1938		8	*1964–1965*	
Thomas, John Gregory	E	12.8.1960		5	*1985*–1986	3
Thompson, George Joseph	E	27.10.1877	3.3.1943	6	1909–*1909*	
Thompson, Patterson Ian Chesterfield	WI	26.9.1971		2	*1995–1996*	2
Thoms, George Ronald	A	22.3.1927	29.8.2003	1	*1951*	
Thomson, Alan Lloyd	A	2.12.1945		4	*1970*	1
Thomson, Jeffrey Robert	A	16.8.1950		51	*1972*–1985	50
Thomson, Keith	NZ	26.2.1941		2	*1967*	
Thomson, Nathaniel Frampton Davis	A	29.5.1839	2.9.1896	2	*1876*	
Thomson, Norman Ian	E	23.1.1929		5	*1964*	
Thomson, Shane Alexander	NZ	27.1.1969		19	*1989–1995*	56
Thornton, George	SA	24.12.1867	31.1.1939	1	*1902*	
Thorpe, Graham Paul	E	1.8.1969		83	1993–*2003*	82
Thurlow, Hugh Motley	A	10.1.1903	3.12.1975	1	*1931*	
Tillekeratne, Hashan Prasantha	SL	14.7.1967		80	*1989–2003*	200
Tindill, Eric William Thomas	NZ	18.12.1910		5	1937–*1946*	
Titmus, Frederick John MBE	E	24.11.1932		53	1955–*1974*	2
Tolchard, Roger William	E	15.6.1946		4	*1976*	1
Tomlinson, Denis Stanley	SA	4.9.1910	11.7.1993	1	1935	
Toohey, Peter Michael	A	20.4.1954		15	*1977–1979*	5
Toshack, Ernest Raymond Herbert	A	15.12.1914	11.5.2003	12	*1945*–1948	
[1]**Townsend,** Charles Lucas	E	7.11.1876	17.10.1958	2	1899	
[1]**Townsend,** David Charles Humphery	E	20.4.1912	27.1.1997	3	*1934*	
Townsend, Leslie Fletcher	E	8.6.1903	17.2.1993	4	*1929–1933*	
Traicos, Athanasios John	SA, Z	17.5.1947		7	*1969–1992*	27
Travers, Joseph Patrick Francis	A	10.1.1871	15.9.1942	1	*1901*	
Tremlett, Maurice Fletcher	E	5.7.1923	30.7.1984	3	*1947*	
Trescothick, Marcus Edward	E	25.12.1975		43	2000–*2003*	75
Tribe, George Edward	A	4.10.1920		3	*1946*	
Trim, John	WI	25.1.1915	12.11.1960	4	*1947–1951*	
Trimborn, Patrick Henry Joseph	SA	18.5.1940		4	*1966–1969*	
[2]**Trott,** Albert Edwin	A, E	6.2.1873	30.7.1914	5	*1894–1898*	
[2]**Trott,** George Henry Stevens	A	5.8.1866	10.11.1917	24	1888–*1897*	
Troup, Gary Bertram	NZ	3.10.1952		15	*1976–1985*	22
Trueman, Frederick Sewards OBE	E	6.2.1931		67	1952–1965	
[2]**Trumble,** Hugh	A	12.5.1867	14.8.1938	32	1890–*1903*	
[2]**Trumble,** John William	A	16.9.1863	17.8.1944	7	*1884*–1886	
Trumper, Victor Thomas	A	2.11.1877	28.6.1915	48	1899–*1911*	
Truscott, Peter Bennetts	NZ	14.8.1941		1	*1964*	
[1]**Tuckett,** Lindsay	SA	6.2.1919		9	1947–*1948*	
[1]**Tuckett,** Lindsay Richard	SA	19.4.1885	8.4.1963	1	*1913*	
Tudor, Alex Jeremy	E	23.10.1977		10	*1998–2002*	3
Tuffey, Daryl Raymond	NZ	11.6.1978		18	*1999–2003*	60
Tufnell, Neville Charsley	E	13.6.1887	3.8.1951	1	*1909*	
Tufnell, Philip Clive Roderick	E	29.4.1966		42	*1990*–2001	20
Turnbull, Maurice Joseph Lawson	E	16.3.1906	5.8.1944	9	*1929*–1936	
Turner, Alan	A	23.7.1950		14	1975–*1976*	6
Turner, Charles Thomas Biass	A	16.11.1862	1.1.1944	17	*1886–1894*	
Turner, Glenn Maitland	NZ	26.5.1947		41	*1968–1982*	41
Tushar Imran	B	10.12.1983		3	*2002*	24
Twentyman-Jones, *Sir* Percy Sydney	SA	13.9.1876	8.3.1954	1	*1902*	
Twose, Roger Graham	NZ	17.4.1968		16	*1995*–1999	87
[2]**Tyldesley,** Ernest	E	5.2.1889	5.5.1962	14	1921–*1928*	
[2]**Tyldesley,** John Thomas	E	22.11.1873	27.11.1930	31	*1898*–1909	
Tyldesley, Richard Knowles	E	11.3.1897	17.9.1943	7	1924–1930	
Tylecote, Edward Ferdinando Sutton	E	23.6.1849	15.3.1938	6	*1882*–1886	

[1] *Father and son(s).* [2] *Brothers.*

	Country	*Born*	*Died*	*Tests*	*Test Career*	*ODIs*
Tyler, Edwin James	E	13.10.1864	25.1.1917	1	*1895*	
Tyson, Frank Holmes	E	6.6.1930		17	1954–*1958*	
Ulyett, George	E	21.10.1851	18.6.1898	25	*1876*–1890	
Umar Gul	P	14.4.1984		4	*2003*	15
Umrigar, Pahlanji Ratanji	I	28.3.1926		59	*1948–1961*	
Underwood, Derek Leslie MBE	E	8.6.1945		86	1966–*1981*	26
Upashantha, Kalutarage Eric Amila	SL	10.6.1972		2	*1998*–2002	12
Vaas, Warnakulasuriya Patabendige Ushantha Joseph Chaminda	SL	27.1.1974		71	*1994–2003*	228
Valentine, Alfred Louis	WI	28.4.1930		36	1950–*1961*	
Valentine, Bryan Herbert	E	17.1.1908	2.2.1983	7	*1933–1938*	
Valentine, Vincent Adolphus	WI	4.4.1908	6.7.1972	2	1933	
Vance, Robert Howard	NZ	31.3.1955		4	*1987–1989*	8
van der Bijl, Pieter Gerhard Vintcent	SA	21.10.1907	16.2.1973	5	*1938*	
Van der Merwe, Edward Alexander	SA	9.11.1903	26.2.1971	2	1929–*1935*	
Van der Merwe, Peter Laurence	SA	14.3.1937		15	*1963–1966*	
Vandort, Michael Graydon	SL	19.1.1980		2	*2001–2002*	
Van Jaarsveld, Martin	SA	18.6.1974		4	*2002–2003*	9
Van Ryneveld, Clive Berrange	SA	19.3.1928		19	1951–*1957*	
Varnals, George Derek	SA	24.7.1935		3	*1964*	
Vaughan, Justin Thomas Caldwell	NZ	30.8.1967		6	*1992–1996*	18
Vaughan, Michael Paul	E	29.10.1974		40	*1999–2003*	39
Veivers, Thomas Robert	A	6.4.1937		21	*1963–1966*	
Veletta, Michael Robert John	A	30.10.1963		8	*1987–1989*	20
Vengsarkar, Dilip Balwant	I	6.4.1956		116	*1975–1991*	129
Venkataraghavan, Srinivasaraghavan	I	21.4.1946		57	*1964–1983*	15
Venkataramana, Margashayam	I	24.4.1966		1	*1988*	1
Verity, Hedley	E	18.5.1905	31.7.1943	40	1931–1939	
Vermeulen, Mark Andrew	Z	2.3.1979		7	*2002–2003*	15
Vernon, George Frederick	E	20.6.1856	10.8.1902	1	*1882*	
Vettori, Daniel Luca	NZ	27.1.1979		50	*1996–2003*	120
Viljoen, Dirk Peter	Z	11.3.1977		2	*1997–2000*	53
Viljoen, Kenneth George	SA	14.5.1910	21.1.1974	27	*1930–1948*	
Vincent, Cyril Leverton	SA	16.2.1902	24.8.1968	25	*1927*–1935	
Vincent, Lou	NZ	11.11.1978		15	*2001–2003*	62
Vine, Joseph	E	15.5.1875	25.4.1946	2	*1911*	
Vintcent, Charles Henry	SA	2.9.1866	28.9.1943	3	*1888–1891*	
Viswanath, Gundappa Rangnath	I	12.2.1949		91	*1969–1982*	25
Viswanath, Sadanand	I	29.11.1962		3	*1985*	22
[1]**Vivian,** Graham Ellery	NZ	28.2.1946		5	*1964–1971*	1
[1]**Vivian,** Henry Gifford	NZ	4.11.1912	12.8.1983	7	1931–1937	
Vizianagram, Maharaj Kumar of (*Sir* Vijaya Anand)	I	28.12.1905	2.12.1965	3	1936	
Voce, William	E	8.8.1909	6.6.1984	27	*1929–1946*	
Vogler, Albert Edward Ernest	SA	28.11.1876	9.8.1946	15	*1905–1910*	
Waddington, Abraham	E	4.2.1893	28.10.1959	2	*1920*	
[2]**Wade,** Herbert Frederick	SA	14.9.1905	23.11.1980	10	1935–*1935*	
[2]**Wade,** Walter Wareham	SA	18.6.1914	31.5.2003	11	*1938–1949*	
Wadekar, Ajit Laxman	I	1.4.1941		37	*1966*–1974	2
Wadsworth, Kenneth John	NZ	30.11.1946	19.8.1976	33	1969–*1975*	13
Wainwright, Edward	E	8.4.1865	28.10.1919	5	1893–*1897*	
Waite, John Henry Bickford	SA	19.1.1930		50	1951–*1964*	
Waite, Mervyn George	A	7.1.1911	16.12.1985	2	1938	
Wajahatullah Wasti	P	11.11.1974		6	*1998–1999*	15
Walcott, *Sir* Clyde Leopold	WI	17.1.1926		44	*1947–1959*	
Walcott, Leslie Arthur	WI	18.1.1894	27.2.1984	1	*1929*	

[1] *Father and son(s).* [2] *Brothers.*

	Country	*Born*	*Died*	*Tests*	*Test Career*	*ODIs*
Walker, Brooke Graeme Keith	NZ	25.3.1977		5	*2000–2001*	11
Walker, Maxwell Henry Norman	A	12.9.1948		34	*1972*–1977	17
Walker, Peter Michael	E	17.2.1936		3	1960	
Wall, Thomas Welbourn	A	13.5.1904	26.3.1981	18	*1928*–1934	
Wallace, Philo Alphonso	WI	2.8.1970		7	*1997–1998*	33
Wallace, Walter Mervyn	NZ	19.12.1916		13	1937–*1952*	
Waller, Andrew Christopher	Z	25.9.1959		2	*1996*	39
Walmsley, Kerry Peter	NZ	23.8.1973		3	*1994–2000*	2
Walsh, Courtney Andrew	WI	30.10.1962		132	*1984–2000*	205
Walter, Kenneth Alexander	SA	5.11.1939		2	*1961*	
Walters, Cyril Frederick	E	28.8.1905	23.12.1992	11	1933–1934	
Walters, Francis Henry	A	9.2.1860	1.6.1922	1	*1884*	
Walters, Kevin Douglas MBE	A	21.12.1945		74	*1965–1980*	28
[2]**Waqar Hassan**	P	12.9.1932		21	*1952–1959*	
Waqar Younis	P	16.11.1971		87	*1989–2002*	262
Ward, Alan	E	10.8.1947		5	1969–1976	
Ward, Albert	E	21.11.1865	6.1.1939	7	1893–*1894*	
Ward, Francis Anthony	A	23.2.1906	25.3.1974	4	*1936*–1938	
Ward, Ian James	E	30.9.1972		5	2001	
Ward, John Thomas	NZ	11.3.1937		8	*1963–1967*	
Ward, Thomas Alfred	SA	2.8.1887	16.2.1936	23	1912–1924	
Wardle, John Henry	E	8.1.1923	23.7.1985	28	*1947*–1957	
Warnapura, Bandula	SL	1.3.1953		4	*1981–1982*	12
Warnaweera, Kahakatchchi Patabandige Jayananda	SL	23.11.1960		10	*1985–1994*	6
Warne, Shane Keith	A	13.9.1969		107	*1991–2002*	193
Warner, *Sir* Pelham Francis	E	2.10.1873	30.1.1963	15	*1898*–1912	
Warr, John James	E	16.7.1927		2	*1950*	
Warren, Arnold	E	2.4.1875	3.9.1951	1	1905	
Washbrook, Cyril CBE	E	6.12.1914	27.4.1999	37	1937–1956	
Wasim Akram	P	3.6.1966		104	*1984–2001*	356
Wasim Bari	P	23.3.1948		81	1967–*1983*	51
Wasim Jaffer	I	16.2.1978		7	*1999*–2002	
[2]**Wasim Raja**	P	3.7.1952		57	*1972–1984*	54
Wassan, Atul Satish	I	23.3.1968		4	*1989*–1990	9
Watambwa, Brighton Tonderai	Z	9.6.1977		6	*2000–2001*	
Watkin, Steven Llewellyn	E	15.9.1964		3	1991–1993	4
Watkins, Albert John	E	21.4.1922		15	1948–1952	
Watkins, John Cecil	SA	10.4.1923		15	*1949–1956*	
Watkins, John Russell	A	16.4.1943		1	*1972*	
Watkinson, Michael	E	1.8.1961		4	1995–*1995*	1
Watson, Chester Donald	WI	1.7.1938		7	*1959–1961*	
Watson, Graeme Donald	A	8.3.1945		5	*1966*–1972	2
Watson, William	NZ	31.8.1965		15	1986–*1993*	61
Watson, William James	A	31.1.1931		4	*1954*	
Watson, Willie	E	7.3.1920		23	1951–*1958*	
Watt, Leslie	NZ	17.9.1924	15.11.1996	1	*1954*	
[2]**Waugh,** Mark Edward	A	2.6.1965		128	*1990–2002*	244
[2]**Waugh,** Stephen Rodger	A	2.6.1965		168	*1985–2003*	325
[1, 2]**Wazir Ali,** Syed	I	15.9.1903	17.6.1950	7	1932–1936	
[2]**Wazir Mohammad**	P	22.12.1929		20	*1952–1959*	
Webb, Murray George	NZ	22.6.1947		3	*1970–1973*	
Webb, Peter Neil	NZ	14.7.1957		2	*1979*	5
Webbe, Alexander Josiah	E	16.1.1855	19.2.1941	1	*1878*	
Weekes, *Sir* Everton de Courcy	WI	26.2.1925		48	*1947–1957*	
Weekes, Kenneth Hunnell	WI	24.1.1912	9.2.1998	2	1939	
Weerasinghe, Colombage Don Udesh Sanjeewa	SL	1.3.1968		1	*1985*	
Weir, Gordon Lindsay	NZ	2.6.1908	31.10.2003	11	*1929*–1937	

[1] *Father and son(s).* [2] *Brothers.*

	Country	*Born*	*Died*	*Tests*	*Test Career*	*ODIs*
Wellard, Arthur William	E	8.4.1902	31.12.1980	2	1937–1938	
Wellham, Dirk Macdonald	A	13.3.1959		6	1981–*1986*	17
Wells, Alan Peter	E	2.10.1961		1	1995	1
Wesley, Colin	SA	5.9.1937		3	1960	
Wessels, Kepler Christoffel	A, SA	14.9.1957		40	*1982*–1994	109
Westcott, Richard John	SA	19.9.1927		5	*1953–1957*	
[2]**Wettimuny,** Mithra de Silva	SL	11.6.1951		2	*1982*	1
[2]**Wettimuny,** Sidath	SL	12.8.1956		23	*1981–1986*	35
Wharton, Alan	E	30.4.1923	26.8.1993	1	1949	
Whatmore, Davenell Frederick	A	16.3.1954		7	*1978–1979*	1
Whitaker, John James	E	5.5.1962		1	*1986*	2
White, Anthony Wilbur	WI	20.11.1938		2	*1964*	
White, Craig	E	16.12.1969		30	1994–*2002*	51
White, David John	NZ	26.6.1961		2	*1990*	3
White, David William	E	14.12.1935		2	*1961*	
White, Gordon Charles	SA	5.2.1882	17.10.1918	17	*1905*–1912	
White, John Cornish	E	19.2.1891	2.5.1961	15	1921–*1930*	
Whitelaw, Paul Erskine	NZ	10.2.1910	28.8.1988	2	*1932*	
Whitney, Michael Roy	A	24.2.1959		12	1981–*1992*	38
Whittall, Andrew Richard	Z	28.3.1973		10	*1996–1999*	63
Whittall, Guy James	Z	5.9.1972		46	*1993–2002*	147
Whitty, William James	A	15.8.1886	30.1.1974	14	1909–1912	
Whysall, William Wilfrid	E	31.10.1887	11.11.1930	4	*1924*–1930	
Wickremasinghe, Anguppulige Gamini Dayantha	SL	27.12.1965		3	*1989–1992*	4
Wickremasinghe, Gallage Pramodya . .	SL	14.8.1971		40	*1991–2000*	134
Wiener, Julien Mark	A	1.5.1955		6	*1979*	7
Wight, Claude Vibart	WI	28.7.1902	4.10.1969	2	1928–*1929*	
Wight, George Leslie	WI	28.5.1929	4.1.2004	1	*1952*	
Wijegunawardene, Kapila Indaka Weerakkody	SL	23.11.1964		2	1991–*1991*	26
Wijesuriya, Roger Gerard Christopher Ediriweera	SL	18.2.1960		4	*1981–1985*	8
Wijetunge, Piyal Kashyapa	SL	6.8.1971		1	*1993*	
Wiles, Charles Archibald	WI	11.8.1892	4.11.1957	1	1933	
Wilkinson, Leonard Litton	A	5.11.1916	3.9.2002	3	*1938*	
Willett, Elquemedo Tonito	WI	1.5.1953		5	*1972–1974*	
Willey, Peter	E	6.12.1949		26	1976–1986	26
Williams, Alvadon Basil	WI	21.11.1949		7	*1977–1978*	
Williams, Brad Andrew	A	20.11.1974		3	*2003*	13
Williams, David	WI	4.11.1963		11	*1991–1997*	36
Williams, Ernest Albert Vivian	WI	10.4.1914	13.4.1997	4	1939–*1947*	
Williams, Neil FitzGerald	E	2.7.1962		1	1990	
Williams, Stuart Clayton	WI	12.8.1969		31	*1993–2001*	57
Willis, Robert George Dylan MBE	E	30.5.1949		90	*1970*–1984	64
Willoughby, Charl Myles	SA	3.12.1974		2	*2002*–2003	3
Willoughby, Joseph Thomas	SA	7.11.1874	11.3.1952	2	*1895*	
[2]**Wilson,** Clement Eustace Macro	E	15.5.1875	8.2.1944	2	*1898*	
Wilson, Donald	E	7.8.1937		6	*1963–1970*	
[2]**Wilson,** Evelyn Rockley	E	25.3.1879	21.7.1957	1	*1920*	
Wilson, John William	A	20.8.1921	13.10.1985	1	*1956*	
Wilson, Paul	A	12.1.1972		1	*1997*	11
Wimble, Clarence Skelton	SA	22.4.1861	28.1.1930	1	*1891*	
Winslow, Paul Lyndhurst	SA	21.5.1929		5	*1949*–1955	
Wiseman, Paul John	NZ	4.5.1970		18	*1997–2003*	15
Wishart, Craig Brian	Z	9.1.1974		25	*1995–2003*	89
Wishart, Kenneth Leslie	WI	28.11.1908	18.10.1972	1	*1934*	
Wood, Arthur	E	25.8.1898	1.4.1973	4	1938–1939	
Wood, Barry	E	26.12.1942		12	1972–1978	13

[1] *Father and son(s).* [2] *Brothers.*

	Country	Born	Died	Tests	Test Career	ODIs
Wood, George Edward Charles	E	22.8.1893	18.3.1971	3	1924	
Wood, Graeme Malcolm	A	6.11.1956		59	*1977–1988*	83
Wood, Henry	E	14.12.1853	30.4.1919	4	1888–*1891*	
Wood, Reginald	E	7.3.1860	6.1.1915	1	*1886*	
Woodcock, Ashley James	A	27.2.1947		1	*1973*	1
Woodfull, William Maldon OBE	A	22.8.1897	11.8.1965	35	1926–1934	
Woods, Samuel Moses James	A, E	13.4.1867	30.4.1931	6	1888–*1895*	
Woolley, Frank Edward	E	27.5.1887	18.10.1978	64	1909–1934	
Woolley, Roger Douglas	A	16.9.1954		2	*1982–1983*	4
Woolmer, Robert Andrew	E	14.5.1948		19	1975–1981	6
Worrall, John	A	21.6.1860	17.11.1937	11	*1884*–1899	
Worrell, *Sir* Frank Mortimer Maglinne	WI	1.8.1924	13.3.1967	51	*1947*–1963	
Worthington, Thomas Stanley	E	21.8.1905	31.8.1973	9	*1929–1936*	
Wright, Charles William	E	27.5.1863	10.1.1936	3	*1895*	
Wright, Douglas Vivian Parson	E	21.8.1914	13.11.1998	34	1938–*1950*	
Wright, John Geoffrey MBE	NZ	5.7.1954		82	*1977–1992*	149
Wright, Kevin John	A	27.12.1953		10	*1978–1979*	5
Wyatt, Robert Elliott Storey	E	2.5.1901	20.4.1995	40	*1927–1936*	
Wynne, Owen Edgar	SA	1.6.1919	13.7.1975	6	*1948–1949*	
Wynyard, Edward George	E	1.4.1861	30.10.1936	3	1896–*1905*	
Yadav, Nandlal Shivlal	I	26.1.1957		35	*1979–1986*	7
Yadav, Vijay	I	14.3.1967		1	*1992*	19
Yajurvindra Singh	I	1.8.1952		4	*1976–1979*	
Yallop, Graham Neil	A	7.10.1952		39	*1975–1984*	30
Yardley, Bruce	A	5.9.1947		33	*1977–1982*	7
Yardley, Norman Walter Dransfield	E	19.3.1915	4.10.1989	20	*1938*–1950	
Yashpal Sharma	I	11.8.1954		37	1979–*1983*	42
Yasir Ali	P	15.10.1985		1	*2003*	
Yasir Hameed	P	28.2.1978		7	*2003*	19
[1]**Yograj Singh**	I	25.3.1958		1	*1980*	6
Yohannan, Tinu	I	18.2.1979		3	*2001–2002*	3
Young, Bryan Andrew	NZ	3.11.1964		35	*1993–1998*	74
Young, Harding Isaac	E	5.2.1876	12.12.1964	2	1899	
Young, John Albert	E	14.10.1912	5.2.1993	8	1947–1949	
Young, Richard Alfred	E	16.9.1885	1.7.1968	2	*1907*	
Young, Shaun	A	13.6.1970		1	1997	
[2]**Younis Ahmed**	P	20.10.1947		4	*1969–1986*	2
Younis Khan	P	29.11.1977		28	*1999–2003*	96
Yousuf Youhana	P	27.8.1974		48	*1997–2003*	154
Yuile, Bryan William	NZ	29.10.1941		17	*1962–1969*	
[1]**Yuvraj Singh**	I	12.12.1981		1	*2003*	80
Zaheer Abbas	P	24.7.1947		78	*1969–1985*	62
Zaheer Khan	I	7.10.1978		28	*2000–2003*	77
Zahid Fazal	P	10.11.1973		9	*1990–1995*	19
[2]**Zahoor Elahi**	P	1.3.1971		2	*1996*	14
Zakir Khan	P	3.4.1963		2	*1985–1989*	17
Zoehrer, Timothy Joseph	A	25.9.1961		10	*1985–1986*	22
Zondeki, Monde	SA	25.7.1982		1	2003	5
Zoysa, Demuni Nuwan Tharanga	SL	13.5.1978		24	*1996*–2002	67
Zulch, Johan Wilhelm	SA	2.1.1886	19.5.1924	16	*1909–1921*	
Zulfiqar Ahmed	P	22.11.1926		9	*1952–1956*	
Zulqarnain	P	25.5.1962		3	*1985*	16

See page 138 for an explanation of family relationships not immediately apparent from a shared name.

[1] *Father and son(s).* [2] *Brothers.*

Notes

In the same match, A. and G. G. Hearne played for England; their brother, F. Hearne, for South Africa.
The Waugh brothers are the only instance of Test-playing twins.
P. N. and G. Kirsten are half-brothers.
Azmat Rana is the brother of Shafqat Rana.
Chappell, G. S., Chappell I. M. and Chappell T. M. are the grandsons of V. Y. Richardson.
Cooper, W. H. is the great-grandfather of A. P. Sheahan.
Hanif Mohammad is the brother of Mushtaq Mohammad, Sadiq Mohammad and Wazir Mohammad, and the father of Shoaib Mohammad.
Jahangir Khan, M. is the father of Majid Khan.
Khalid Wazir is the son of S. Wazir Ali.
Majid Khan is the son of M. Jahangir Khan.
Manzoor Elahi is the brother of Salim Elahi and Zahoor Elahi.
Moin Khan is the brother of Nadeem Khan.
Mudassar Nazar is the son of Nazar Mohammad.
Mushtaq Mohammad is the brother of Hanif Mohammad, Sadiq Mohammad and Wazir Mohammad.
Nadeem Khan is the brother of Moin Khan.
Nazar Mohammad is the father of Mudassar Nazar.
Nazir Ali, S. is the brother of S. Wazir Ali.
Pervez Sajjad is the brother of Waqar Hassan.
Ramiz Raja is the brother of Wasim Raja.
Richardson, V. Y. is the grandfather of G. S., I. M. and T. M. Chappell.
Sadiq Mohammad is the brother of Hanif Mohammad, Mushtaq Mohammad and Wazir Mohammad.
Saeed Ahmed is the brother of Younis Ahmed.
Salim Elahi is the brother of Manzoor Elahi and Zahoor Elahi.
Shafqat Rana is the brother of Azmat Rana.
Sheahan, A. P. is the great-grandson of W. H. Cooper.
Shoaib Mohammad is the son of Hanif Mohammad.
Waqar Hassan is the brother of Pervez Sajjad.
Wasim Raja is the brother of Ramiz Raja.
Wazir Ali, S. is the brother of S. Nazir Ali and the father of Khalid Wazir.
Wazir Mohammad is the brother of Hanif Mohammad, Mushtaq Mohammad and Sadiq Mohammad.
Yograj Singh is the father of Yuvraj Singh.
Younis Ahmed is the brother of Saeed Ahmed.
Yuvraj Singh is the son of Yograj Singh.
Zahoor Elahi is the brother of Manzoor Elahi and Salim Elahi.

LIMITED-OVERS INTERNATIONAL CRICKETERS

The following players have appeared for Test-playing countries in limited-overs internationals but had not represented their countries in Test matches by December 31, 2003:

England M. W. Alleyne, I. D. Austin, I. D. Blackwell, A. D. Brown, D. R. Brown, M. V. Fleming, P. J. Franks, I. J. Gould, A. P. Grayson, G. W. Humpage, T. E. Jesty, G. D. Lloyd, J. D. Love, M. A. Lynch, O. A. Shah, M. J. Smith, N. M. K. Smith, J. N. Snape, V. S. Solanki, A. J. Strauss. G. P. Swann, J. O. Troughton, S. D. Udal, C. M. Wells, V. J. Wells.

Australia G. A. Bishop, R. J. Campbell, M. J. Clarke, M. J. Di Venuto, S. F. Graf, B. J. Haddin, I. J. Harvey, N. M. Hauritz, S. Lee, R. J. McCurdy, K. H. MacLeay, J. P. Maher, G. D. Porter, J. D. Siddons, A. M. Stuart, A. Symonds, G. S. Trimble, S. R. Watson, B. E. Young, A. K. Zesers.

South Africa S. Abrahams, D. M. Benkenstein, R. E. Bryson, D. J. Callaghan, D. N. Crookes, J. C. Kent, L. J. Koen, C. K. Langeveldt, P. V. Mpitsang, S. J. Palframan, N. Pothas, C. E. B. Rice, M. J. R. Rindel, D. B. Rundle, T. G. Shaw, E. O. Simons, E. L. R. Stewart, R. Telemachus, M. N. van Wyk, C. J. P. G. van Zyl, H. S. Williams, M. Yachad.

West Indies H. A. G. Anthony, D. Brown, B. St A. Browne, H. R. Bryan, R. S. Gabriel, R. C. Haynes, R. O. Hurley, K. C. B. Jeremy, S. C. Joseph, R. S. Morton, M. R. Pydanna, R. Rampaul, K. F. Semple, C. M. Tuckett, L. R. Williams.

New Zealand M. D. Bailey, B. R. Blair, C. E. Bulfin, T. K. Canning, P. G. Coman, C. D. Cumming, M. W. Douglas, B. G. Hadlee, R. T. Hart, R. L. Hayes, P. A. Hitchcock, L. G. Howell, B. B. McCullum, B. J. McKechnie, E. B. McSweeney, M. J. Mason, J. P. Millmow, K. D. Mills, C. J. Nevin, A. J. Penn, R. G. Petrie, R. B. Reid, S. J. Roberts, L. W. Stott, G. P. Sulzberger, A. R. Tait, M. D. J. Walker, R. J. Webb, J. W. Wilson, W. A. Wisneski.

India A. C. Bedade, A. Bhandari, Bhupinder Singh, sen., G. Bose, V. B. Chandrasekhar, U. Chatterjee, N. A. David, P. Dharmani, G. Gambhir, R. S. Ghai, A. V. Kale, S. C. Khanna, G. K. Khoda, A. R. Khurasiya, T. Kumaran, J. J. Martin, A. Mishra, D. Mongia, S. P. Mukherjee, G. K. Pandey, J. V. Paranjpe, A. K. Patel, Randhir Singh, S. S. Raul, A. M. Salvi, L. R. Shukla, R. P. Singh, R. S. Sodhi, S. Somasunder, S. Sriram, Sudhakar Rao, P. S. Vaidya, J. P. Yadav.

Pakistan Aamer Hameed, Aamer Hanif, Akhtar Sarfraz, Arshad Pervez, Asif Mahmood, Faisal Athar, Ghulam Ali, Haafiz Shahid, Hasan Jamil, Imran Abbas, Iqbal Sikandar, Irfan Bhatti, Javed Qadir, Junaid Zia, Kashif Raza, Mahmood Hamid, Mansoor Rana, Manzoor Akhtar, Maqsood Rana, Masood Iqbal, Moin-ul-Atiq, Mujahid Jamshed, Naeem Ahmed, Naeem Ashraf, Naseer Malik, Naved-ul-Hasan, Parvez Mir, Saadat Ali, Saeed Azad, Sajid Ali, Sajjad Akbar, Salim Pervez, Shahid Anwar, Shakil Khan, Sohail Fazal, Tanvir Mehdi, Wasim Haider, Yasir Arafat, Zafar Iqbal, Zahid Ahmed.

Sri Lanka J. W. H. D. Boteju, D. L. S. de Silva, G. N. de Silva, E. R. Fernando, T. L. Fernando, U. N. K. Fernando, J. C. Gamage, W. C. A. Ganegama, F. R. M. Goonatillake, P. W. Gunaratne, A. A. W. Gunawardene, P. D. Heyn, S. A. Jayasinghe, S. H. U. Karnain, K. M. D. N. Kulasekara, C. Mendis, A. M. N. Munasinghe, H. G. D. Nayanakantha, A. R. M. Opatha, S. P. Pasqual, K. G. Perera, H. S. M. Pieris, S. K. Ranasinghe, N. Ranatunga, N. L. K. Ratnayake, L. P. C. Silva, A. P. B. Tennekoon, M. H. Tissera, D. M. Vonhagt, A. P. Weerakkody, K. Weeraratne, S. R. de S. Wettimuny, R. P. A. H. Wickremaratne.

Zimbabwe R. D. Brown, C. K. Coventry, K. M. Curran, S. G. Davies, K. G. Duers, S. M. Ervine, E. A. Essop-Adam, D. A. G. Fletcher, J. G. Heron, V. R. Hogg, A. J. Mackay, A. Maragwede, G. C. Martin, M. A. Meman, W. Mwayenga, G. A. Paterson, G. E. Peckover, P. W. E. Rawson, B. G. Rogers, R. W. Sims.

Bangladesh Ahmed Kamal, Alam Talukdar, Aminul Islam, jun., Anisur Rahman, Ather Ali Khan, Azhar Hussain, Faruq Ahmed, Faruq Chowdhury, Gazi Ashraf, Ghulam Faruq, Ghulam Nausher, Hafizur Rahman, Harunur Rashid, Jahangir Alam, Jahangir Badshah, Jamaluddin Ahmed, Mafizur Rahman, Mahbubur Rahman, Manjurul Islam Rana, Mazharul Haque, Minhazul Abedin, Moniruzzaman, Morshed Ali Khan, Nafis Iqbal, Nasir Ahmed, Neeyamur Rashid, Nurul Abedin, Rafiqul Alam, Raqibul Hassan, Saiful Islam, Sajjad Ahmed, Samiur Rahman, Shafiuddin Ahmed, Shahidur Rahman, Shariful Haq, Sheikh Salahuddin, Tareq Aziz, Wahidul Gani, Zahid Razzak, Zakir Hassan.

A. C. Gilchrist appeared for Australia in 76 limited-overs internationals before making his Test debut.

BIRTHS AND DEATHS

OTHER CRICKETING NOTABLES

The following list shows the births and deaths of cricketers, and people associated with cricket, who have *not* played in Test matches and are not expected to appear in first-class cricket again.

Criteria for inclusion The following are included: all non-Test players, no longer active, who have either (1) been chosen as one of *Wisden's* Five Cricketers of the Year, or (2) scored 15,000 runs in first-class cricket, or (3) taken 1,000 first-class wickets, or (4) achieved 500 dismissals as a wicket-keeper, or (5) reached *both* 10,000 runs *and* 500 wickets, or (6) achieved 10,000 runs or 500 wickets or 500 dismissals and have never played in the County Championship, or (7) taken 500 wickets or achieved 500 dismissals if their career started in 1969 or later. It also includes (8) the leading players who flourished before the start of Test cricket and (9) all others deemed of sufficient merit or interest for inclusion, either because of their playing skill, their present position, their contribution to the game in whatever capacity or their fame in other walks of life.

Names Where players were normally known by a name other than their first, this is underlined.

Teams Where only one team is listed, this is normally the one for which the player made most first-class appearances. Additional teams are listed only if the player appeared for them in more than 20 first-class matches or if they are especially relevant to their career. School and university teams are not given unless especially relevant (e.g. for the schoolboys chosen as wartime Cricketers of the Year in the 1918 and 1919 *Wisdens*).

Abbreviations The following may not be obvious: ADBP – Agricultural Development Bank of Pakistan. HBFC – House Building Finance Corporation (Pakistan). KRL – Khan Research Laboratories (Pakistan). NBP – National Bank of Pakistan. OFS – Orange Free State (South Africa). PIA – Pakistan International Airlines. PNSC – Pakistan National Shipping Corporation.

	Teams	*Born*	*Died*
Abdur Raqib	Karachi, Habib Bank	18.11.1947	
Ackerman, Hylton Michael	Northants, W. Province	28.4.1947	
Adams, Percy Webster	Cheltenham, Sussex	5.9.1900	28.9.1962
Aird, Ronald MC	Hampshire	4.5.1902	16.8.1986
Secretary of MCC 1953–62; president of MCC 1968–69.			
Aislabie, Benjamin	Surrey	14.1.1774	2.6.1842
Secretary of MCC 1822–42; president of MCC 1823.			
Aitchison, *Rev.* James	Scotland	26.5.1920	13.2.1994
Alcock, Charles William	Secretary of Surrey 1872–1907	2.12.1842	26.2.1907
Editor, Cricket *magazine, 1882–1907. Captain of Wanderers and England football teams.*			
Aleem Dar	Lahore; ICC umpire	6.6.1968	
Alletson, Edwin Boaler	Nottinghamshire	6.3.1884	5.7.1963
Scored 189 in 90 minutes v Sussex at Hove in 1911.			
Alley, William Edward	NSW, Somerset; Test umpire	3.2.1919	
Alleyne, Mark Wayne MBE	Gloucestershire	23.5.1968	
Altham, Harry Surtees CBE	Surrey, Hampshire; historian	30.11.1888	11.3.1965
Coach at Winchester for 30 years; president of MCC 1959–60.			
Andrews, William Harry Russell	Somerset; coach	14.4.1908	9.1.1989
Arlott, Leslie Thomas John OBE	Broadcaster and writer	25.2.1914	14.12.1991
Armstrong, Norman Foster	Leicestershire	22.12.1892	19.1.1990
Arshad Pervez	Sargodha, Habib Bank	1.10.1953	
Ashdown, William Henry	Kent	27.12.1898	15.9.1979
The only cricketer to appear in English first-class cricket before and after the two wars.			
Ashley-Cooper, Frederick Samuel	Historian	22.3.1877	31.1.1932
Ashton, Sir Hubert	Camb. U., Essex; pres MCC *1960–61*	13.2.1898	17.6.1979
Atkinson, Colin Ronald Michael CBE	Somerset	23.7.1931	25.6.1991
Atkinson, Graham	Somerset	29.3.1938	

	Teams	Born	Died
Austin, *Sir* Harold Bruce Gardiner	Barbados	15.7.1877	27.7.1943
Austin, Ian David	Lancashire	30.5.1966	
Aylward, James	Hampshire, All-England	1741	1827
Aymes, Adrian Nigel	Hampshire	4.6.1964	
Bailey, Jack Arthur	Essex; secretary of MCC 1974–87	22.6.1930	
Bainbridge, Philip	Gloucestershire, Durham	16.4.1958	
Baldwin, Herbert George	Surrey; Test umpire	16.3.1893	7.3.1969
Bannister, John David	Warwickshire; writer and broadcaster	23.8.1930	
Barclay, John Robert Troutbeck	Sussex	22.1.1954	
Barker, Gordon	Essex	6.7.1931	
Barling, Thomas Henry	Surrey	1.9.1906	2.1.1993
Bartlett, Hugh Tryon	Sussex	7.10.1914	26.6.1988
Bates, Leonard Ashton	Warwickshire	20.3.1895	11.3.1971
Bates, William Ederick	Yorkshire, Glamorgan	5.3.1884	17.1.1957
Beauclerk, *Rev. Lord* Frederick	Middlesex, Surrey, MCC	8.5.1773	22.4.1850
Bedser, Eric Arthur	Surrey	4.7.1918	
Beldam, George William	Middlesex; photographer	1.5.1868	23.11.1937
Beldam, William ("Silver Billy")	Hambledon, Surrey	5.2.1766	26.2.1862
Bennett, Donald	Middlesex; coach	18.12.1933	
Berry, Leslie George	Leicestershire	28.4.1906	5.2.1985
Berry, Scyld	Writer	28.4.1954	
Bestwick, William	Derbyshire; Test umpire	24.2.1875	2.5.1938
Bird, Harold Dennis MBE	Yorkshire, Leicestershire; Test umpire	19.4.1933	
Blofeld, Henry Calthorpe OBE	Cambridge Univ; broadcaster	23.9.1939	
Bond, John David	Lancashire	6.5.1932	
Booth, Brian Joseph	Leicestershire	3.12.1935	
Booth, Roy	Yorkshire, Worcestershire	1.10.1926	
Boucher, James Chrysostom	Ireland	22.12.1910	25.12.1995
Bowden, Brent Fraser ("Billy")	ICC umpire	11.4.1963	
Bowell, Alexander	Hampshire	27.4.1880	28.8.1957
Bowley, Frederick Lloyd	Worcestershire	9.11.1873	31.5.1943
Box, Thomas	Sussex	7.2.1808	12.7.1876
Boyes, George Stuart	Hampshire	31.3.1899	11.2.1973
Briers, Nigel Edwin	Leicestershire	15.1.1955	
Brittin, Janette Ann	England Women	4.7.1959	
Brooks, Edward William	Surrey	6.7.1898	10.2.1960
Brown, Anthony Stephen	Gloucestershire; administrator	24.6.1936	
Brown, Sydney Maurice	Middlesex	8.12.1917	28.12.1987
Bryan, Godfrey James CBE	Kent	29.12.1902	4.4.1991
The youngest player to hit a County Championship hundred, aged 17 years 247 days.			
Bryan, John Lindsay	Kent, Cambridge Univ	26.5.1896	23.4.1985
Buchanan, John Marshall	Queensland; Australian coach 1999–	5.4.1953	
Bucknor, Stephen Anthony	ICC umpire	31.5.1946	
Umpire of 86 Tests up to January 2004, a record.			
Bull, Frederick George	Essex	2.4.1875	16.9.1910
Buller, John Sydney MBE	Worcestershire; Test umpire	23.8.1909	7.8.1970
Burgess, Graham Iefvion	Somerset; umpire	5.5.1943	
Burns, Neil David	Somerset	19.9.1965	
Burnup, Cuthbert James	Kent	21.11.1875	5.4.1960
Buse, Herbert Francis Thomas	Somerset	5.8.1910	23.2.1992
Buss, Antony	Sussex	1.9.1939	
Buss, Michael Alan	Sussex	24.1.1944	
Byas, David	Yorkshire	26.8.1963	
Cadman, Samuel	Derbyshire	29.1.1877	6.5.1952
Caesar, Julius	Surrey, All-England	25.3.1830	6.3.1878
Calder, Harry Lawton	Cranleigh	24.1.1901	15.9.1995
The youngest-ever and longest-lived Wisden *Cricketer of the Year.*			
Cardus, *Sir* Neville	Writer	3.4.1888	27.2.1975
Carr, John Donald	Middlesex; ECB director of cricket operations	15.6.1963	
Carrick, Phillip	Yorkshire	16.7.1952	11.1.2000

Name	Teams	Born	Died
Chalk, Frederick Gerald Hudson	Kent	7.9.1910	17.2.1943
Chester, Frank	Worcestershire; Test umpire	20.1.1895	8.4.1957
Stood in 48 Tests between 1924 and 1955, a record that lasted until 1992.			
Clark, Belinda Jane	Australia Women	10.9.1970	
Clark, David Graham	Kent; president of MCC 1977–78	27.1.1919	
Clarke, William	Nottinghamshire	24.12.1798	25.8.1856
Founded the All-England XI, Trent Bridge ground.			
Clarkson, Anthony	Somerset; umpire	5.9.1939	
Clift, Patrick Bernard	Leicestershire	14.7.1953	3.9.1996
Cobden, Frank Carroll	Cambridge Univ	14.10.1849	7.12.1932
Decided the 1870 University Match with a last-over hat-trick.			
Coe, Samuel	Leicestershire	3.6.1873	4.11.1955
Collins, Arthur Edward Jeune	Clifton College	18.8.1885	11.11.1914
Made the highest score in any cricket, 628 in a house match in 1899.*			
Compton, Leslie Harry	Middlesex	12.9.1912	27.12.1984
England football international. Brother of Denis Compton.			
Conan Doyle, *Dr Sir* Arthur Ignatius	MCC	22.5.1859	7.7.1930
Creator of Sherlock Holmes; his only victim in first-class cricket was W. G. Grace.			
Connor, Cardigan Adolphus	Hampshire	24.3.1961	
Connor, Clare Joanne	England Women	1.9.1976	
Constable, Bernard	Surrey	19.2.1921	15.5.1997
Constant, David John	Kent, Leicestershire; Test umpire	9.11.1941	
35 seasons on first-class list 1969–2003, a record.			
Cook, Thomas Edwin Reed	Sussex	5.1.1901	15.1.1950
Cooper, Kevin Edwin	Nottinghamshire	27.12.1957	
Cornford, Walter Latter ("Tich")	Sussex	25.12.1900	6.2.1964
Cowley, Nigel Geoffrey	Hampshire; umpire	1.3.1953	
Cox, George, jun.	Sussex	23.8.1911	30.3.1985
Cox, George, sen.	Sussex	29.11.1873	24.3.1949
Cozier, Tony	Broadcaster and writer	10.7.1940	
Croom, Alfred John	Warwickshire	23.5.1896	16.8.1947
Curran, Kevin Malcolm	Zimbabwe, Glos, Northants	7.9.1959	
Cutmore, James Albert	Essex	28.12.1898	30.11.1985
Daft, Richard	Nottinghamshire, All-England	2.11.1835	18.7.1900
Dalmiya, Jagmohan	President of ICC 1997–2000	30.5.1940	
Daniell, John	Somerset	12.12.1878	24.1.1963
Davies, Dai	Glamorgan; Test umpire	26.8.1896	16.7.1976
Davies, Emrys	Glamorgan; Test umpire	27.6.1904	10.11.1975
Davies, Haydn George	Glamorgan	23.4.1912	4.9.1993
Davies, Jack Gale Wilmot OBE	Kent; president of MCC 1985–86	10.9.1911	5.11.1992
Davis, Richard Peter	Kent, Warwicks, Glos, Sussex, Leics	18.3.1966	29.12.2003
Davison, Brian Fettes	Rhodesia, Leics, Tasmania, Gloucestershire	21.12.1946	
Dawkes, George Owen	Leicestershire, Derbyshire	19.7.1920	
Day, Arthur Percival	Kent	10.4.1885	22.1.1969
Dean, James, sen.	Sussex	4.1.1816	25.12.1881
Dennett, George	Gloucestershire	27.4.1880	14.9.1937
Deodhar, *Prof* Dinakar Balwant	Maharashtra	14.1.1892	24.8.1993
Dews, George	Worcestershire	5.6.1921	29.1.2003
Dodds, Thomas Carter ("Dickie")	Essex	29.5.1919	17.9.2001
Dorset, 3rd Duke of	Kent	24.3.1745	19.7.1799
Ambassador to France; organised tour of France 1789, abandoned due to revolution.			
Dudleston, Barry	Leicestershire; Test umpire	16.7.1945	
Dyson, Arnold Herbert	Glamorgan	10.7.1905	7.6.1978
Eagar, Edward Desmond Russell	Glos, Hants, administrator	8.12.1917	13.9.1977
Eagar, Edward Patrick	Photographer	9.3.1944	
East, David Edward	Essex; chief executive, 2000–	27.7.1959	
East, Raymond Eric	Essex	20.6.1947	
Eastman, Lawrence Charles	Essex	3.6.1897	17.4.1941
Edinburgh, *HRH Duke of*	President of MCC twice	10.6.1921	
Edrich, Geoffrey Arthur	Lancashire	13.7.1918	2.1.2004

	Teams	Born	Died
Ehsan Mani	President, ICC 2003–	23.3.1945	
Ekanayake, Ajith Wijeratne	Kurunegala Youth	3.10.1965	
Elliott, Charles Standish MBE	Derbyshire; Test umpire	24.4.1912	1.1.2004
Evans, Jeffrey Howard	Umpire	7.8.1954	
Fearnley, Charles Duncan	Worcestershire; bat-maker	12.4.1940	
"Felix" (Nicholas Wanostrocht)	Kent, Surrey, All-England	4.10.1804	3.9.1876
Batsman, artist, author (Felix on the Bat) *and inventor of the Catapulta bowling machine.*			
Ferguson, William Henry BEM	Scorer	6.6.1880	22.9.1957
Scorer and baggage-master for five Test teams on 43 tours over 52 years and "never lost a bag".			
Ferreira, Anthonie Michal	N. Transvaal, Warwickshire	13.4.1955	
Field, Frank Ernest	Warwickshire	23.9.1874	25.8.1934
Findlay, William	Lancashire	22.6.1880	19.6.1953
Secretary of Surrey 1907–19; secretary of MCC 1926–36.			
Firth, John D'Ewes Evelyn	Winchester, Oxford U, Nottinghamshire	21.1.1900	21.9.1957
Fitzpatrick, Cathryn Lorraine	Australia women	4.3.1968	
Fleming, Matthew Valentine	Kent	12.12.1964	
Fordham, Alan	Northants; ECB official	9.11.1964	
Foster, Henry Knollys	Oxford Univ, Worcestershire	30.10.1873	23.6.1950
Frindall, William Howard	Statistician	3.3.1939	
Frith, David Edward John	Writer	16.3.1937	
Gardner, Fred Charles	Warwickshire	4.6.1922	12.1.1979
Gibbons, Harold Harry Haywood	Worcestershire	8.10.1904	16.2.1973
Gibson, Clement Herbert	Sussex, Cambridge Univ, Argentina	23.8.1900	31.12.1976
Gillingham, *Canon* Frank Hay	Essex; broadcaster	6.9.1875	1.4.1953
Goel, Rajinder	Delhi, Haryana	20.9.1942	
Goonesena, Gamini	Ceylon, Nottinghamshire	16.2.1931	
Gore, Adrian Clements	Eton, Army	14.5.1900	7.6.1990
Gould, Ian James	Middlesex, Sussex; umpire	19.8.1957	
Grace, Mrs Martha	Mother and cricketing mentor of W.G.	18.7.1812	25.7.1884
Grace, William Gilbert	Gloucestershire; son of W.G.	6.7.1874	2.3.1905
Graveney, David Anthony	Gloucestershire, Somerset, Durham	2.1.1953	
Chairman of England selectors 1997–.			
Gray, James Roy	Hampshire	19.5.1926	
Gray, Malcolm Alexander	President of ICC 2000–03	30.5.1940	
Green, David Michael	Lancashire, Gloucestershire	10.11.1939	
Green, *Major* Leonard	Lancashire	1.2.1890	2.3.1963
Gregory, Robert James	Surrey	26.8.1902	6.10.1973
Grieves, Kenneth James	New South Wales, Lancashire	27.8.1925	3.1.1992
Grundy, James	Nottinghamshire	5.3.1824	24.11.1873
Hair, Darrell Bruce	ICC umpire	30.9.1952	
Hall, Louis	Yorkshire	1.11.1852	19.11.1915
Hallam, Albert William	Lancashire, Nottinghamshire	12.11.1869	24.7.1940
Hallam, Maurice Raymond	Leicestershire	10.9.1931	1.1.2000
Hallows, James	Lancashire	14.11.1873	20.5.1910
Hamer, Arnold	Derbyshire	8.12.1916	3.11.1993
Hardie, Brian Ross	Essex	14.1.1950	
Harper, Daryl John	ICC umpire	23.10.1951	
Harris, Charles Bowmar	Nottinghamshire	6.12.1907	8.8.1954
Harris, Michael John ("Pasty")	Middlesex, Notts; umpire	25.5.1944	
Harrison, Leo	Hampshire	8.6.1922	
Hartley, Alfred	Lancashire	11.4.1879	9.10.1918
Hartley, Peter John	Yorkshire, Hampshire; umpire	18.4.1960	
Haygarth, Arthur	Sussex; historian	4.8.1825	1.5.1903
Hayward, Thomas	Cambridgeshire, All-England	21.3.1835	21.7.1876
Hearne, Thomas	Middlesex	4.9.1826	13.5.1900
Hedges, Bernard	Glamorgan	10.11.1927	
Hedges, Lionel Paget	Tonbridge, Kent, Oxford Univ, Glos	13.7.1900	12.1.1933
Henderson, Robert	Surrey	30.3.1865	29.1.1931
Herman, Oswald William	Hampshire; umpire	18.9.1907	24.6.1987
Hewett, Herbert Tremenheere	Somerset	25.5.1864	4.3.1921

	Teams	*Born*	*Died*
Heyhoe-Flint, Rachael	England Women	11.6.1939	
Hide, Mary Edith ("Molly")	England Women	24.10.1913	10.9.1995
Hillyer, William Richard	Kent	5.3.1813	8.1.1861
First cricketer known to have performed the match double, 100 runs and ten wickets, in 1847.			
Hogg, Vincent Richard	Rhodesia/Zim; administrator	3.7.1952	
Holder, John Wakefield	Hampshire; Test umpire	19.3.1945	
Holmes, *Group Captain* Albert John	Sussex	30.6.1899	21.5.1950
Home of the Hirsel, Lord	Middx; President of MCC 1966–67	2.7.1903	9.10.1995
Prime Minister (as Sir Alec Douglas-Home) 1963–64.			
Horner, Norman Frederick	Warwickshire	10.5.1926	24.12.2003
Horton, Henry	Hampshire	18.4.1923	2.11.1998
Howard, Cecil Geoffrey	Middlesex; administrator	14.2.1909	8.11.2002
Hughes, David Paul	Lancashire	13.5.1947	
Hughes, Simon Peter	Middx, Durham; broadcaster	20.12.1959	
Huish, Frederick Henry	Kent	15.11.1869	16.3.1957
Humpage, Geoffrey William	Warwickshire	24.4.1954	
Humphreys, Edward	Kent	24.8.1881	6.11.1949
Humphreys, Walter Alexander	Sussex, Hampshire	28.10.1849	23.3.1924
Hunt, Alma Victor OBE	Scotland, Bermuda	1.10.1910	3.3.1999
"The best cricketer ever to emerge from Bermuda" – Wisden.			
Hunter, David	Yorkshire	23.2.1860	11.1.1927
Hutchinson, James Metcalf	Derbyshire	29.11.1896	7.11.2000
Believed to be the longest-lived first-class cricketer at 103 years 344 days.			
Iddison, Roger	Yorkshire, Lancashire	15.9.1834	19.3.1890
Inchmore, John Darling	Worcestershire	22.2.1949	
Ingleby-Mackenzie, Alexander Colin David	Hampshire	15.9.1933	
President of MCC 1996–98.			
Inman, Clive Clay	Ceylon, Leicestershire	29.1.1936	
Hit 51 in eight minutes for Leicestershire v Nottinghamshire 1965.			
Iqbal Sikander	Karachi, PIA	19.12.1958	
Iremonger, James	Nottinghamshire	5.3.1876	25.3.1956
Jackson, Guy Rolf	Derbyshire	23.6.1896	21.2.1966
Jackson, John	Nottinghamshire, All-England	21.5.1833	4.11.1901
Jackson, Percy Frederick	Worcestershire	11.5.1911	27.4.1999
Jackson, Victor Edward	NSW, Leicestershire	25.10.1916	30.1.1965
James, Cyril Lionel Robert	Writer	4.1.1901	31.5.1989
Jarvis, Kevin Bertram Sidney	Kent	23.4.1953	
Jayasinghe, Stanley	Ceylon, Leicestershire	19.1.1931	
Jeeves, Percy	Warwickshire	5.3.1888	22.7.1916
Jefferies, Stephen Thomas	Hants, Lancs, W. Province	8.12.1959	
Jennings, Raymond Vernon	Transvaal, N. Transvaal	9.8.1954	
Jepson, Arthur	Nottinghamshire; Test umpire	12.7.1915	17.7.1997
Jesty, Trevor Edward	Hampshire, Griqualand W, Surrey, Lancashire; umpire	2.6.1948	
Johnson, Graham William	Kent, Transvaal	8.11.1946	
Johnson, Paul	Nottinghamshire	24.4.1965	
Johnston, Brian Alexander CBE, MC	Broadcaster	24.6.1912	5.1.1994
Jones, Alan MBE	Glamorgan	4.11.1938	
Played once for England v Rest of the World, 1970, regarded at the time as a Test match.			
Jones, Allan Arthur	Sussex, Somerset, Middx, Glam; umpire	9.12.1947	
Jones, Eifion Wyn	Glamorgan	25.6.1942	
Julian, Raymond	Leicestershire; umpire	23.8.1936	
Key, *Sir* Kingsmill James	Surrey	11.10.1864	9.8.1932
Killick, Ernest Harry	Sussex	17.1.1875	29.9.1948
Kilner, Norman	Yorkshire, Warwickshire	21.7.1895	28.4.1979
King, John Barton	Philadelphia	19.10.1873	17.10.1965
"Beyond question the greatest all-round cricketer produced by America." – Wisden.			
Kitchen, Mervyn John	Somerset; Test umpire	1.8.1940	
Knight, Roger David Verdon	Surrey, Gloucestershire, Sussex	6.9.1946	
Secretary of MCC 1994–.			

	Teams	Born	Died
Knott, Charles James	Hampshire	26.11.1914	27.2.2003
Koertzen, Rudolf Eric	ICC umpire	26.3.1949	
Kortright, Charles Jesse	Essex	9.1.1871	12.12.1952
Krikken, Karl Matthew	Derbyshire	9.4.1969	
Kynaston, Roger	Middlesex; Secretary of MCC 1846–58	5.11.1805	21.6.1874
Lacey, Sir Francis Eden	Hants; Secretary of MCC 1898–1926	19.10.1859	26.5.1946
Lamb, Timothy Michael	Middlesex, Northants		
Chief Executive of ECB, 1997–.		24.3.1953	
Lambert, George Edward	Gloucestershire, Somerset	11.5.1918	31.10.1991
Lambert, Robert Hamilton	Ireland	18.7.1874	24.3.1956
Lambert, William	Surrey	1779	19.4.1851
The first batsman to score two hundreds in the same match.			
Lampitt, Stuart Richard	Worcestershire	29.7.1966	
Langford, Brian Anthony	Somerset	17.12.1935	
Langridge, John George MBE	Sussex; Test umpire	10.2.1910	27.6.1999
Lawrence, John	Somerset; coach	29.3.1914	10.12.1988
Leadbeater, Barrie	Yorkshire; umpire	14.8.1943	
Leary, Stuart Edward	Kent	30.4.1933	21.8.1988
Lee, Frank Stanley	Middlesex, Somerset; Test umpire	24.7.1905	30.3.1982
Lee, Garnet Morley	Nottinghamshire, Derbyshire	7.6.1887	29.2.1976
Lee, Peter Granville	Northamptonshire, Lancashire	27.8.1945	
Lefebvre, Roland Philippe	Somerset, Glamorgan, Holland	7.2.1963	
Lenham, Leslie John	Sussex; coach	24.5.1936	
Le Roux, Garth Stirling	Western Province, Sussex	4.9.1955	
Lester, Edward	Yorkshire; scorer	18.2.1923	
Lester, *Dr* John Ashby	Philadelphia	1.8.1871	3.9.1969
Lewis, Claude BEM	Kent; coach and scorer	27.7.1908	26.4.1993
Lilley, Ben	Nottinghamshire	11.2.1895	4.8.1950
Lillywhite, Fred	Sussex	23.7.1829	15.9.1866
Lillywhite, Frederick William	Sussex	13.6.1792	21.8.1854
Livingston, Leonard ("Jock")	NSW, Northamptonshire	3.5.1920	16.1.1998
Livsey, Walter Herbert	Hampshire	23.9.1893	12.9.1978
Llong, Nigel James	Kent; umpire	11.2.1969	
Lloyds, Jeremy William	Somerset, Gloucestershire; umpire	17.11.1954	
Lock, Herbert Christmas	Surrey; groundsman	8.5.1903	19.5.1978
Long, Arnold	Surrey, Sussex	18.12.1940	
Longrigg, Edmund Fallowfield	Somerset	16.4.1906	23.7.1974
Lord, Thomas	Middlesex; founder of Lord's Cricket Ground	23.11.1755	13.1.1832
Love, James Derek	Yorkshire	22.4.1955	
Luckes, Walter Thomas	Somerset	1.1.1901	27.10.1982
Lynch, Monte Alan	Surrey, Gloucestershire	21.5.1958	
Lyon, Beverley Hamilton	Gloucestershire	19.1.1902	22.6.1970
Lyon, Malcolm Douglas	Somerset	22.4.1898	17.2.1964
McCorkell, Neil Thomas	Hampshire	23.3.1912	
McCurdy, Rodney John	Victoria, E. Province	30.12.1959	
McEwan, Kenneth Scott	E. Province, Essex	16.7.1952	
McGilvray, Alan David	NSW; broadcaster	6.12.1909	17.7.1996
McKechnie, Brian John	Otago	6.11.1953	
Represented New Zealand at rugby and cricket (14 one-day internationals).			
MacLaurin of Knebworth, Lord	Chairman of ECB 1997–2002	30.3.1937	
MacLeay, Kenneth Hervey	W. Australia, Somerset	2.4.1959	
Majola, Khaya Eldridge	SA Council of Sport XI	17.5.1953	28.8.2000
Pioneer of non-racial cricket in South Africa.			
Majola, Mongezi Gerald	Chief executive, UCBSA	20.11.1959	
Manning, John Stephen	S. Australia, Northamptonshire	11.6.1923	5.5.1988
Mansoor Rana	Lahore, ADBP	27.12.1962	
Marchant, Francis	Kent	22.5.1864	13.4.1946
Marlar, Robin Geoffrey	Sussex; writer	2.1.1931	
Marner, Peter Thomas	Lancashire, Leicestershire	31.3.1936	
Marsh, Steven Andrew	Kent	27.1.1961	

	Teams	Born	Died
Marshal, Alan	Queensland, Surrey	12.6.1883	23.7.1915
Martin, Sidney Hugh	Worcestershire, Natal	11.1.1909	17.2.1988
Martin-Jenkins, Christopher Dennis Alexander	Writer; broadcaster	20.1.1945	
Maru, Rajesh Jamandass	Hampshire	28.10.1962	
Mayer, Joseph Herbert	Warwickshire	2.3.1902	6.9.1981
Mendis, Gehan Dixon	Sussex, Lancashire	20.4.1955	
Mercer, John	Sussex, Glamorgan; coach and scorer	22.4.1893	31.8.1987
Merriman, Robert Frederick AO	Chmn, Cricket Australia 2001–	22.8.1935	
Metson, Colin Peter	Middlesex, Glamorgan	2.7.1963	
Meyer, Barrie John	Gloucestershire; Test umpire	21.8.1932	
Meyer, Rollo John Oliver OBE	Somerset	15.3.1905	9.3.1991
Millns, David James	Nottinghamshire, Leicestershire	27.2.1965	
Minshull, John	Kent, Surrey	c.1741	Oct 1793
Scorer of first recorded century: 107 for Duke of Dorset's XI v Wrotham, 1769.			
Mohammad Zahid	Bahawalpur, Allied Bank	12.8.1965	
Moles, Andrew James	Warwickshire	12.2.1961	
Moore, Denis Neville	Oxford Univ, Gloucestershire	26.9.1910	2.10.2003
Moore, Richard Henry	Hampshire	14.11.1913	1.3.2002
Moores, Peter	Sussex; coach	18.12.1962	
Morgan, Derek Clifton	Derbyshire	26.2.1929	
Morgan, Frederick David	Chairman of ECB 2003–	6.10.1937	
Mortensen, Ole Henrik	Denmark, Derbyshire	29.1.1958	
Morton, Arthur	Derbyshire	7.5.1883	19.12.1935
Moseley, Hallam Reynold	Somerset	28.5.1948	
Muncer, Bernard Leonard	Middlesex, Glamorgan; coach	23.10.1913	18.1.1982
Murrell, Harry Robert	Kent, Middlesex	19.11.1879	15.8.1952
Murtaza Hussain	Bahawalpur, KRL	20.12.1974	
Mynn, Alfred	Kent, All-England	19.1.1807	1.11.1861
Nash, Malcolm Andrew	Glamorgan	9.5.1945	
Neale, Phillip Anthony	Worcestershire	5.6.1954	
Newman, John Alfred	Hampshire	12.11.1884	21.12.1973
Newstead, John Thomas	Yorkshire	8.9.1877	25.3.1952
Nicholas, Mark Charles Jefford	Hampshire; broadcaster	29.9.1957	
Nicholls, Ronald Bernard	Gloucestershire	4.12.1933	21.7.1994
Norman, Michael Eric John Charles	Northants, Leics	19.1.1933	
Nyren, John	Hampshire	15.12.1764	28.6.1837
Author of The Young Cricketer's Tutor, *1833.*			
Nyren, Richard	Hampshire	1734	25.4.1797
Proprietor Bat & Ball Inn, Broadhalfpenny Down.			
Oakes, Charles	Sussex	10.8.1912	
Oates, Thomas William	Nottinghamshire	9.6.1875	18.6.1949
Oldroyd, Edgar	Yorkshire	1.10.1888	27.12.1964
Ontong, Rodney Craig	Border, Glamorgan, N. Transvaal	9.9.1955	
Ormrod, Joseph Alan	Worcestershire, Lancashire	22.12.1942	
Outschoorn, Ladislaus	Worcestershire	26.9.1918	9.1.1994
Page, John Colin Theodore	Kent; coach	20.5.1930	14.12.1990
Palairet, Richard Cameron North	Somerset; administrator	25.6.1871	11.2.1955
Palmer, Roy	Somerset; Test umpire	12.7.1942	
Pardon, Sydney Herbert	Editor of *Wisden* 1891–1925	23.9.1855	20.11.1925
Parker, John Frederick	Surrey	23.4.1913	27.1.1983
Parks, Henry William	Sussex	18.7.1906	7.5.1984
Parks, Robert James	Hampshire	15.6.1959	
Parr, George	Nottinghamshire, All-England	22.5.1826	23.6.1891
Captain and manager of the All-England XI.			
Parsons, Gordon James	Leicestershire, OFS, Warwickshire	17.10.1959	
Parsons, *Canon* John Henry	Warwickshire	30.5.1890	2.2.1981
Partridge, Norman Ernest	Malvern, Cambridge U., Warwicks	10.8.1900	10.3.1982
Payton, Wilfred Richard Daniel	Nottinghamshire	13.2.1882	2.5.1943
Peach, Herbert Alan	Surrey; coach	6.10.1890	8.10.1961
Pearce, Thomas Neill	Essex; administrator	3.11.1905	10.4.1994

	Teams	Born	Died
Pearson, Frederick	Worcestershire	23.9.1880	10.11.1963
Perkins, Henry	Cambridgeshire; secretary of MCC 1876–97	10.12.1832	6.5.1916
Perrin, Percival Albert	Essex	26.5.1876	20.11.1945
Pienaar, Roy Francois	Transvaal, N. Transvaal, W. Province, Kent	17.7.1961	
Pilch, Fuller	Norfolk, Kent	17.3.1804	1.5.1870
"The best batsman that has ever yet appeared" – Arthur Haygarth, 1862.			
Pilling, Harry	Lancashire	23.2.1943	
Pont, Keith Rupert	Essex; ECB director of development	16.1.1953	
Pooley, Edward	Surrey	13.2.1842	18.7.1907
Popplewell, *Hon. Sir* Oliver Bury	Camb U.; pres MCC 1994–96	15.8.1927	
Pressdee, James Stuart	Glamorgan, NE Transvaal	19.6.1933	
Preston, Kenneth Charles	Essex	22.8.1925	
Preston, Norman MBE	Editor of *Wisden* 1952–80	18.3.1903	6.3.1980
Prichard, Paul John	Essex	7.1.1965	
Pridgeon, Alan Paul	Worcestershire	22.2.1954	
Raees Mohammad	Karachi	24.12.1932	
His four brothers – Hanif, Mushtaq, Sadiq and Wazir – all played Test cricket.			
Rait-Kerr, *Colonel* Rowan Scrope	Europeans; sec. MCC 1936–52	13.4.1891	2.4.1961
Raja Afaq	Rawalpindi, ADBP	15.11.1956	
Rawson, Peter Walter Edward	Zimbabwe, Natal	25.5.1957	
Reeves, William	Essex; Test umpire	22.1.1875	22.3.1944
Relf, Robert Richard	Sussex	1.9.1883	28.4.1965
Revill, Alan Chambers	Derbyshire, Leicestershire	27.3.1923	6.7.1998
Reynolds, Brian Leonard	Northamptonshire	10.6.1932	
Rhodes, Albert Ennion Groucott	Derbyshire; Test umpire	10.10.1916	18.10.1983
Rice, Clive Edward Butler	Transvaal, Nottinghamshire	23.7.1949	
Riches, Norman Vaughan Hurry	Glamorgan	9.6.1883	6.11.1975
Ripley, David	Northamptonshire	13.9.1966	
Roberts, Frederick George	Gloucestershire; umpire	1.4.1862	7.4.1936
Roberts, William Braithwaite	Lancashire, Victory Tests	27.9.1914	24.8.1951
Robertson-Glasgow, Raymond Charles	Somerset; writer	15.7.1901	4.3.1965
Robins, Derrick Harold	Warwickshire; tour promoter	27.6.1914	
Robinson, Ellis Pembroke	Yorkshire, Somerset	10.8.1911	10.11.1998
Robinson, Emmott	Yorkshire; Test umpire	16.11.1883	17.11.1969
Robinson, Mark Andrew	Northamptonshire, Yorkshire, Sussex	23.11.1966	
Robson, Ernest	Somerset	1.5.1870	23.5.1924
Roebuck, Peter Michael	Somerset; writer	6.3.1956	
Rogers, Neville Hamilton	Hampshire	9.3.1918	7.10.2003
Rose, Graham David	Somerset	12.4.1964	
Rotherham, Gerard Alexander	Rugby, Camb. U., Warwicks	28.5.1899	31.1.1985
Ryan, Francis	Hampshire, Glamorgan	14.11.1888	5.1.1954
Saadat Ali	HBFC, Pakistan Railways, United Bank	6.2.1955	
Sainsbury, Peter James	Hampshire	13.6.1934	
Sajid Ali	Karachi, National Bank	1.7.1963	
Sajjad Akbar	PNSC, Sargodha	1.3.1961	
Santall, Frederick Reginald	Warwickshire	12.7.1903	3.11.1950
Santall, Sydney	Warwickshire	10.6.1873	19.3.1957
Saville, Graham John	Essex; coach	5.2.1944	
Scott, Stanley Winckworth	Middlesex	24.3.1854	8.12.1933
Sellers, Arthur Brian MBE	Yorkshire	5.3.1907	20.2.1981
Seymour, James	Kent	25.10.1879	30.9.1930
Shahid Anwar	Lahore, NBP	5.7.1968	
Sharp, George	Northamptonshire; Test umpire	12.3.1950	
Sharp, Harry Philip	Middlesex; scorer	6.10.1917	15.1.1995
Shepherd, David Robert MBE	Gloucestershire; ICC umpire	27.12.1940	
Shepherd, Donald John	Glamorgan	12.8.1927	
Shepherd, Thomas Frederick	Surrey	5.12.1889	13.2.1957
Shipman, Alan Wilfred	Leicestershire	7.3.1901	12.12.1979
Shipston, Frank William	Nottinghamshire	29.7.1906	
Believed to be the oldest living first-class cricketer at end of 2003.			

	Teams	*Born*	*Died*
Shivalkar, Padmakar Kashinath	Bombay	14.4.1940	
Siddons, James Darren	Victoria, S. Australia	25.4.1964	
Silk, Dennis Raoul Whitehall CBE	Somerset	8.10.1931	
President of MCC 1992–94; chairman of TCCB 1994–96.			
Simmons, Jack MBE	Lancashire, Tasmania	28.3.1941	
Simons, Eric Owen	W. Province; S. African coach 2002–	9.3.1962	
Skelding, Alexander	Leicestershire; umpire	5.9.1886	17.4.1960
First-class umpire 1931–1958, when he was 72.			
Smales, Kenneth	Nottinghamshire	15.9.1927	
Small, John, sen.	Hampshire, All-England	19.4.1737	31.12.1826
Smedley, Michael John	Nottinghamshire	28.10.1941	
Smith, Edwin	Derbyshire	2.1.1934	
Smith, Haydon Arthur	Leicestershire	29.3.1901	7.8.1948
Smith, Michael John	Middlesex	4.1.1942	
Smith, Raymond	Essex	10.8.1914	21.2.1996
Smith, Sydney Gordon	Trinidad, Northamptonshire, Auckland	15.1.1881	25.10.1963
Smith, William Charles	Surrey	4.10.1877	15.7.1946
Speed, Malcolm Walter	Chief Executive of ICC 2001–	14.9.1948	
Spencer, Charles Terence	Leicestershire	18.8.1931	
Spencer, John	Sussex	6.10.1949	
Spencer, Thomas William OBE	Kent; Test umpire	22.3.1914	1.11.1995
Squires, Harry Stanley	Surrey	22.2.1909	24.1.1950
Staples, Arthur	Nottinghamshire	4.2.1899	9.9.1965
Steele, John Frederick	Leicestershire, Glamorgan; umpire	23.7.1946	
Stephenson, Franklyn Dacosta	Barbados, Notts, Sussex, OFS	8.4.1959	
Stephenson, Harold William	Somerset	18.7.1920	
Stephenson, Heathfield Harman	Surrey, All-England	3.5.1832	17.12.1896
Captained first English team to Australia, 1861-62; umpired first Test in England, 1880.			
Stephenson, *Lt-Col.* John Robin CBE	Sec. MCC 1987–93	25.2.1931	2.6.2003
Stevens, Edward ("Lumpy")	Hampshire	c.1735	7.9.1819
Stewart, William James	Warwickshire	31.10.1934	
Storey, Stewart James	Surrey; coach	6.1.1941	
Stovold, Andrew Willis	Gloucestershire	19.3.1953	
Studd, *Sir* John Edward Kynaston	Middlesex	26.7.1858	14.1.1944
Lord Mayor of London 1928–29; President of MCC 1930.			
Surridge, Walter Stuart	Surrey	3.9.1917	13.4.1992
Sutcliffe, William Herbert Hobbs	Yorkshire	10.10.1926	16.9.1998
Sutherland, James Alexander	Vic.; ch. exec. Cricket Australia 2001–	14.7.1965	
Suttle, Kenneth George	Sussex	25.8.1928	
Swanton, Ernest William CBE	Middlesex; writer	11.2.1907	22.1.2000
Tahir Rashid	Habib Bank, HBFC	21.11.1960	
Tarrant, Francis Alfred	Victoria, Middlesex	11.12.1880	29.1.1951
Taufel, Simon James Arthur	ICC umpire	21.1.1971	
Taylor, Brian	Essex	19.6.1932	
Taylor, Derief David Samuel	Warwickshire; coach	10.9.1910	10.3.1987
Taylor, Neil Royston	Kent, Sussex	21.7.1959	
Taylor, Tom Launcelot	Cambridge Univ, Yorkshire	25.5.1878	16.3.1960
Tennekoon, Anura Punchi Banda	Sri Lanka	29.10.1946	
Thornton, Charles Inglis	Middlesex	20.3.1850	10.12.1929
Timms, John Edward	Northamptonshire	3.11.1906	18.5.1980
Tissera, Michael Hugh	Sri Lanka	23.3.1939	
Todd, Leslie John	Kent	19.6.1907	20.8.1967
Tompkin, Maurice	Leicestershire	17.2.1919	27.9.1956
Trimble, Samuel Christy	Queensland	16.8.1934	
Tunnicliffe, John	Yorkshire	26.8.1866	11.7.1948
Turner, David Roy	Hampshire	5.2.1949	
Turner, Francis Michael MBE	Leicestershire; administrator	8.8.1934	
Turner, Stuart	Essex	18.7.1943	
Ufton, Derek Gilbert	Kent	31.5.1928	
van der Bijl, Vintcent Adriaan Pieter	Natal, Middx, Transvaal	19.3.1948	

	Teams	*Born*	*Died*
van Geloven, Jack	Leicestershire; umpire	4.1.1934	21.8.2003
van Zyl, Cornelius Johannes Petrus Gerthardus	OFS, Glamorgan	1.10.1961	
Virgin, Roy Thomas	Somerset, Northamptonshire	26.8.1939	
Wade, Thomas Henry	Essex	24.11.1910	25.7.1987
Walden, Frederick Ingram ("Fanny")	Northants; Test umpire	1.3.1888	3.5.1949
Also played football for Tottenham Hotspur, Northampton Town and England; 5ft 2in tall.			
Walker, Willis	Nottinghamshire	24.11.1892	3.12.1991
Walsh, John Edward	Leicestershire	4.12.1912	20.5.1980
Ward, William	Hampshire	24.7.1787	30.6.1849
Scorer of the first double-century: 278 for MCC v Norfolk, 1820.			
Wass, Thomas George	Nottinghamshire	26.12.1873	27.10.1953
Watson, Alexander	Lancashire	4.11.1844	26.10.1920
Watson, Frank	Lancashire	17.9.1898	1.2.1976
Watts, Patrick James	Northamptonshire	16.6.1940	
Webb, Rupert Thomas	Sussex	11.7.1922	
Webber, Roy	Statistician	23.7.1914	14.11.1962
Weigall, Gerald John Villiers	Kent; coach	19.10.1870	17.5.1944
Wells, Bryan Douglas ("Bomber")	Glos, Notts	27.7.1930	
Wells, Colin Mark	Sussex, Derbyshire	3.3.1960	
Wensley, Albert Frederick	Sussex	23.5.1898	17.6.1970
Wheatley, Oswald Stephen CBE	Warwickshire, Glamorgan	28.5.1935	
White, Hon. Luke Robert (Lord Annaly)	Middlesex, Victory Test	15.3.1927	30.9.1990
White, Robert Arthur	Middlesex, Nottinghamshire; umpire	6.10.1936	
Whitehead, Alan Geoffrey Thomas	Somerset; Test umpire	28.10.1940	
Whitehead, Harry	Leicestershire	19.9.1874	14.9.1944
Whitington, Richard Smallpeice	S. Aust., Victory Tests; writer	30.6.1912	13.3.1984
Wight, Peter Bernard	Somerset; umpire	25.6.1930	
Wilkinson, Cyril Theodore Anstruther	Surrey	4.10.1884	16.12.1970
Hockey gold medallist at the 1920 Olympics.			
Willatt, Guy Longfield	Nottinghamshire, Derbyshire	7.5.1918	11.6.2003
Willsher, Edgar	Kent, All-England	22.11.1828	7.10.1885
Wilson, Arthur Edward ("Andy")	Gloucestershire	18.5.1910	29.7.2002
Wilson, Elizabeth Rebecca ("Betty")	Australia Women	21.11.1921	
Wilson, Jeffrey William	Otago	24.10.1973	
Represented New Zealand at rugby and cricket (four one-day internationals).			
Wilson, John Victor	Yorkshire	17.1.1921	
Wilson, Robert Colin	Kent	18.2.1928	
Wisden, John	Sussex	5.9.1826	5.4.1884
"The Little Wonder"; founder of Wisden Cricketers' Almanack, *1864.*			
Wood, Cecil John Burditt	Leicestershire	21.11.1875	5.6.1960
Woodcock, John Charles OBE	Writer; editor of *Wisden* 1981–86	7.8.1926	
Wooller, Wilfred	Glamorgan	20.11.1912	10.3.1997
Woolley, Claud Neville	Northamptonshire; Test umpire	5.5.1886	3.11.1962
Wright, Levi George	Derbyshire	15.6.1862	11.1.1953
Yachad, Mandy	Transvaal	17.11.1960	
Yarnold, Henry ("Hugo")	Worcestershire; Test umpire	6.7.1917	13.8.1974
Young, Douglas Martin	Worcestershire, Gloucestershire	15.4.1924	18.6.1993

CRICKETERS OF THE YEAR, 1889–2004

1889 *Six Great Bowlers of the Year:* J. Briggs, J. J. Ferris, G. A. Lohmann, R. Peel, C. T. B. Turner, S. M. J. Woods.
1890 *Nine Great Batsmen of the Year:* R. Abel, W. Barnes, W. Gunn, L. Hall, R. Henderson, J. M. Read, A. Shrewsbury, F. H. Sugg, A. Ward.
1891 *Five Great Wicket-Keepers:* J. McC. Blackham, G. MacGregor, R. Pilling, M. Sherwin, H. Wood.
1892 *Five Great Bowlers:* W. Attewell, J. T. Hearne, F. Martin, A. W. Mold, J. W. Sharpe.
1893 *Five Batsmen of the Year:* H. T. Hewett, L. C. H. Palairet, W. W. Read, S. W. Scott, A. E. Stoddart.
1894 *Five All-Round Cricketers:* G. Giffen, A. Hearne, F. S. Jackson, G. H. S. Trott, E. Wainwright.
1895 *Five Young Batsmen of the Season:* W. Brockwell, J. T. Brown, C. B. Fry, T. W. Hayward, A. C. MacLaren.
1896 W. G. Grace.
1897 *Five Cricketers of the Season:* S. E. Gregory, A. A. Lilley, K. S. Ranjitsinhji, T. Richardson, H. Trumble.
1898 *Five Cricketers of the Year:* F. G. Bull, W. R. Cuttell, N. F. Druce, G. L. Jessop, J. R. Mason.
1899 *Five Great Players of the Season:* W. H. Lockwood, W. Rhodes, W. Storer, C. L. Townsend, A. E. Trott.
1900 *Five Cricketers of the Season:* J. Darling, C. Hill, A. O. Jones, M. A. Noble, Major R. M. Poore.
1901 *Mr R. E. Foster and Four Yorkshiremen:* R. E. Foster, S. Haigh, G. H. Hirst, T. L. Taylor, J. Tunnicliffe.
1902 L. C. Braund, C. P. McGahey, F. Mitchell, W. G. Quaife, J. T. Tyldesley.
1903 W. W. Armstrong, C. J. Burnup, J. Iremonger, J. J. Kelly, V. T. Trumper.
1904 C. Blythe, J. Gunn, A. E. Knight, W. Mead, P. F. Warner.
1905 B. J. T. Bosanquet, E. A. Halliwell, J. Hallows, P. A. Perrin, R. H. Spooner.
1906 D. Denton, W. S. Lees, G. J. Thompson, J. Vine, L. G. Wright.
1907 J. N. Crawford, A. Fielder, E. G. Hayes, K. L. Hutchings, N. A. Knox.
1908 A. W. Hallam, R. O. Schwarz, F. A. Tarrant, A. E. E. Vogler, T. G. Wass.
1909 *Lord Hawke and Four Cricketers of the Year:* W. Brearley, Lord Hawke, J. B. Hobbs, A. Marshal, J. T. Newstead.
1910 W. Bardsley, S. F. Barnes, D. W. Carr, A. P. Day, V. S. Ransford.
1911 H. K. Foster, A. Hartley, C. B. Llewellyn, W. C. Smith, F. E. Woolley.
1912 *Five Members of the MCC's Team in Australia:* F. R. Foster, J. W. Hearne, S. P. Kinneir, C. P. Mead, H. Strudwick.
1913 John Wisden: Personal Recollections.
1914 M. W. Booth, G. Gunn, J. W. Hitch, A. E. Relf, Hon. L. H. Tennyson.
1915 J. W. H. T. Douglas, P. G. H. Fender, H. T. W. Hardinge, D. J. Knight, S. G. Smith.
1916–17 No portraits appeared.
1918 *School Bowlers of the Year:* H. L. Calder, J. E. D'E. Firth, C. H. Gibson, G. A. Rotherham, G. T. S. Stevens.
1919 *Five Public School Cricketers of the Year:* P. W. Adams, A. P. F. Chapman, A. C. Gore, L. P. Hedges, N. E. Partridge.
1920 *Five Batsmen of the Year:* A. Ducat, E. H. Hendren, P. Holmes, H. Sutcliffe, E. Tyldesley.
1921 P. F. Warner.
1922 H. Ashton, J. L. Bryan, J. M. Gregory, C. G. Macartney, E. A. McDonald.
1923 A. W. Carr, A. P. Freeman, C. W. L. Parker, A. C. Russell, A. Sandham.
1924 *Five Bowlers of the Year:* A. E. R. Gilligan, R. Kilner, G. G. Macaulay, C. H. Parkin, M. W. Tate.
1925 R. H. Catterall, J. C. W. MacBryan, H. W. Taylor, R. K. Tyldesley, W. W. Whysall.
1926 J. B. Hobbs.
1927 G. Geary, H. Larwood, J. Mercer, W. A. Oldfield, W. M. Woodfull.
1928 R. C. Blunt, C. Hallows, W. R. Hammond, D. R. Jardine, V. W. C. Jupp.
1929 L. E. G. Ames, G. Duckworth, M. Leyland, S. J. Staples, J. C. White.
1930 E. H. Bowley, K. S. Duleepsinhji, H. G. Owen-Smith, R. W. V. Robins, R. E. S. Wyatt.

1931 D. G. Bradman, C. V. Grimmett, B. H. Lyon, I. A. R. Peebles, M. J. Turnbull.
1932 W. E. Bowes, C. S. Dempster, James Langridge, Nawab of Pataudi sen., H. Verity.
1933 W. E. Astill, F. R. Brown, A. S. Kennedy, C. K. Nayudu, W. Voce.
1934 A. H. Bakewell, G. A. Headley, M. S. Nichols, L. F. Townsend, C. F. Walters.
1935 S. J. McCabe, W. J. O'Reilly, G. A. E. Paine, W. H. Ponsford, C. I. J. Smith.
1936 H. B. Cameron, E. R. T. Holmes, B. Mitchell, D. Smith, A. W. Wellard.
1937 C. J. Barnett, W. H. Copson, A. R. Gover, V. M. Merchant, T. S. Worthington.
1938 T. W. J. Goddard, J. Hardstaff jun., L. Hutton, J. H. Parks, E. Paynter.
1939 H. T. Bartlett, W. A. Brown, D. C. S. Compton, K. Farnes, A. Wood.
1940 L. N. Constantine, W. J. Edrich, W. W. Keeton, A. B. Sellers, D. V. P. Wright.
1941–46 No portraits appeared.
1947 A. V. Bedser, L. B. Fishlock, V. (M. H.) Mankad, T. P. B. Smith, C. Washbrook.
1948 M. P. Donnelly, A. Melville, A. D. Nourse, J. D. Robertson, N. W. D. Yardley.
1949 A. L. Hassett, W. A. Johnston, R. R. Lindwall, A. R. Morris, D. Tallon.
1950 T. E. Bailey, R. O. Jenkins, John Langridge, R. T. Simpson, B. Sutcliffe.
1951 T. G. Evans, S. Ramadhin, A. L. Valentine, E. D. Weekes, F. M. M. Worrell.
1952 R. Appleyard, H. E. Dollery, J. C. Laker, P. B. H. May, E. A. B. Rowan.
1953 H. Gimblett, T. W. Graveney, D. S. Sheppard, W. S. Surridge, F. S. Trueman.
1954 R. N. Harvey, G. A. R. Lock, K. R. Miller, J. H. Wardle, W. Watson.
1955 B. Dooland, Fazal Mahmood, W. E. Hollies, J. B. Statham, G. E. Tribe.
1956 M. C. Cowdrey, D. J. Insole, D. J. McGlew, H. J. Tayfield, F. H. Tyson.
1957 D. Brookes, J. W. Burke, M. J. Hilton, G. R. A. Langley, P. E. Richardson.
1958 P. J. Loader, A. J. McIntyre, O. G. Smith, M. J. Stewart, C. L. Walcott.
1959 H. L. Jackson, R. E. Marshall, C. A. Milton, J. R. Reid, D. Shackleton.
1960 K. F. Barrington, D. B. Carr, R. Illingworth, G. Pullar, M. J. K. Smith.
1961 N. A. T. Adcock, E. R. Dexter, R. A. McLean, R. Subba Row, J. V. Wilson.
1962 W. E. Alley, R. Benaud, A. K. Davidson, W. M. Lawry, N. C. O'Neill.
1963 D. Kenyon, Mushtaq Mohammad, P. H. Parfitt, P. J. Sharpe, F. J. Titmus.
1964 D. B. Close, C. C. Griffith, C. C. Hunte, R. B. Kanhai, G. S. Sobers.
1965 G. Boycott, P. J. Burge, J. A. Flavell, G. D. McKenzie, R. B. Simpson.
1966 K. C. Bland, J. H. Edrich, R. C. Motz, P. M. Pollock, R. G. Pollock.
1967 R. W. Barber, B. L. D'Oliveira, C. Milburn, J. T. Murray, S. M. Nurse.
1968 Asif Iqbal, Hanif Mohammad, K. Higgs, J. M. Parks, Nawab of Pataudi jun.
1969 J. G. Binks, D. M. Green, B. A. Richards, D. L. Underwood, O. S. Wheatley.
1970 B. F. Butcher, A. P. E. Knott, Majid Khan, M. J. Procter, D. J. Shepherd.
1971 J. D. Bond, C. H. Lloyd, B. W. Luckhurst, G. M. Turner, R. T. Virgin.
1972 G. G. Arnold, B. S. Chandrasekhar, L. R. Gibbs, B. Taylor, Zaheer Abbas.
1973 G. S. Chappell, D. K. Lillee, R. A. L. Massie, J. A. Snow, K. R. Stackpole.
1974 K. D. Boyce, B. E. Congdon, K. W. R. Fletcher, R. C. Fredericks, P. J. Sainsbury.
1975 D. L. Amiss, M. H. Denness, N. Gifford, A. W. Greig, A. M. E. Roberts.
1976 I. M. Chappell, P. G. Lee, R. B. McCosker, D. S. Steele, R. A. Woolmer.
1977 J. M. Brearley, C. G. Greenidge, M. A. Holding, I. V. A. Richards, R. W. Taylor.
1978 I. T. Botham, M. Hendrick, A. Jones, K. S. McEwan, R. G. D. Willis.
1979 D. I. Gower, J. K. Lever, C. M. Old, C. T. Radley, J. N. Shepherd.
1980 J. Garner, S. M. Gavaskar, G. A. Gooch, D. W. Randall, B. C. Rose.
1981 K. J. Hughes, R. D. Jackman, A. J. Lamb, C. E. B. Rice, V. A. P. van der Bijl.
1982 T. M. Alderman, A. R. Border, R. J. Hadlee, Javed Miandad, R. W. Marsh.
1983 Imran Khan, T. E. Jesty, A. I. Kallicharran, Kapil Dev, M. D. Marshall.
1984 M. Amarnath, J. V. Coney, J. E. Emburey, M. W. Gatting, C. L. Smith.
1985 M. D. Crowe, H. A. Gomes, G. W. Humpage, J. Simmons, S. Wettimuny.
1986 P. Bainbridge, R. M. Ellison, C. J. McDermott, N. V. Radford, R. T. Robinson.
1987 J. H. Childs, G. A. Hick, D. B. Vengsarkar, C. A. Walsh, J. J. Whitaker.
1988 J. P. Agnew, N. A. Foster, D. P. Hughes, P. M. Roebuck, Salim Malik.
1989 K. J. Barnett, P. J. L. Dujon, P. A. Neale, F. D. Stephenson, S. R. Waugh.
1990 S. J. Cook, D. M. Jones, R. C. Russell, R. A. Smith, M. A. Taylor.
1991 M. A. Atherton, M. Azharuddin, A. R. Butcher, D. L. Haynes, M. E. Waugh.
1992 C. E. L. Ambrose, P. A. J. DeFreitas, A. A. Donald, R. B. Richardson, Waqar Younis.
1993 N. E. Briers, M. D. Moxon, I. D. K. Salisbury, A. J. Stewart, Wasim Akram.
1994 D. C. Boon, I. A. Healy, M. G. Hughes, S. K. Warne, S. L. Watkin.
1995 B. C. Lara, D. E. Malcolm, T. A. Munton, S. J. Rhodes, K. C. Wessels.
1996 D. G. Cork, P. A. de Silva, A. R. C. Fraser, A. Kumble, D. A. Reeve.

1997 S. T. Jayasuriya, Mushtaq Ahmed, Saeed Anwar, P. V. Simmons, S. R. Tendulkar.
1998 M. T. G. Elliott, S. G. Law, G. D. McGrath, M. P. Maynard, G. P. Thorpe.
1999 I. D. Austin, D. Gough, M. Muralitharan, A. Ranatunga, J. N. Rhodes.
2000 C. L. Cairns, R. Dravid, L. Klusener, T. M. Moody, Saqlain Mushtaq.
Cricketers of the Century D. G. Bradman, G. S. Sobers, J. B. Hobbs, S. K. Warne, I. V. A. Richards.
2001 M. W. Alleyne, M. P. Bicknell, A. R. Caddick, J. L. Langer, D. S. Lehmann.
2002 A. Flower, A. C. Gilchrist, J. N. Gillespie, V. V. S. Laxman, D. R. Martyn.
2003 M. L. Hayden, A. J. Hollioake, N. Hussain, S. M. Pollock, M. P. Vaughan.
2004 C. J. Adams, A. Flintoff, I. J. Harvey, G. Kirsten, G. C. Smith.

Note: From 2000 to 2003 the award was made on the basis of all cricket round the world, not just the English season. This ended in 2004 with the start of *Wisden's* Leading Cricketer in the World award. Jayasuriya in 1997 was chosen for his "influence" on the English season, stemming from the 1996 World Cup.

CRICKETERS OF THE YEAR: AN ANALYSIS

The five players selected to be Cricketers of the Year for 2004 bring the number chosen since selection began in 1889 to 527. They have been chosen from 37 different teams as follows:

Derbyshire	13	Nottinghamshire	25	South Africans	24	Eton College	2
Essex	23	Somerset	17	West Indians	23	Malvern College	1
Glamorgan	10	Surrey	48	New Zealanders	8	Rugby School	1
Gloucestershire	17	Sussex	21	Indians	13	Tonbridge School	1
Hampshire	14	Warwickshire	19	Pakistanis	11	Univ. Coll. School	1
Kent	25	Worcestershire	15	Sri Lankans	4	Uppingham School	1
Lancashire	32	Yorkshire	41	Zimbabweans	1	Winchester College	1
Leicestershire	8	Oxford Univ.	6	Staffordshire	1		
Middlesex	26	Cambridge Univ.	10	Cheltenham College	1		
Northants	13	Australians	68	Cranleigh School	1		

Notes: Schoolboys were chosen in 1918 and 1919 when first-class cricket was suspended due to war. The total of sides comes to 546 because 19 players played regularly for two teams (England excluded) in the year for which they were chosen. John Wisden, listed as a Sussex player, retired 50 years before his posthumous selection.

Types of Players

Of the 527 Cricketers of the Year, 266 are best classified as batsmen, 148 as bowlers, 79 as all-rounders and 34 as wicket-keepers or wicket-keeper/batsmen.

Nationalities

At the time they were chosen, 331 players (62.80%) were qualified to play for England, 79 for Australia, 36 West Indies, 34 South Africa, 14 Pakistan, 14 India, 12 New Zealand, 5 Sri Lanka and 2 Zimbabwe.

Note: Nationalities and teams are not necessarily identical.

Research: Robert Brooke

Opposite: Calm after the storm. Matthew Hayden savours the moment after hitting the highest score in the history of Test cricket: 380 against Zimbabwe. *Picture by Hamish Blair, Getty Images.*

PART FOUR

Records

RECORDS

COMPILED BY PHILIP BAILEY

This section covers
- first-class records to December 31, 2003 (pages 160–198)
- Test records to January 20, 2004, the end of the South Africa v West Indies series (pages 199–237)
- Test records series by series (pages 238–341)
- limited-overs international records to December 31, 2003 (pages 344–355)
- World Cup records (pages 355–359)
- One-day records to September 21, 2003, the end of the season in England (pages 359–361)
- miscellaneous other records to September 21, 2003, the end of the season in England (pages 362–364)

The sequence
- Test series records begin with those involving England, arranged in the order their opponents entered Test cricket (Australia, South Africa, West Indies, New Zealand, India, Pakistan, Sri Lanka, Zimbabwe, Bangladesh). Next come all remaining series involving Australia, then South Africa – and so on until Zimbabwe v Bangladesh records appear on pages 340–341

Notes
- Unless otherwise stated, all records apply only to first-class cricket. This is considered to have started in 1815, after the Napoleonic War
- mid-year seasons taking place outside England are given simply as 2002, 2003, etc.
- (E), (A), (SA), (WI), (NZ), (I), (P), (SL), (Z) or (B) indicates the nationality of a player or the country in which a record was made

See also
- up-to-date Test records on www.cricinfo.com
- Features of 2003 (pages 385–390)
- Overseas Features of 2002-03 and 2003 (pages 948–953)

CONTENTS

FIRST-CLASS RECORDS

BATTING RECORDS

BOWLING RECORDS

ALL-ROUND RECORDS

WICKET-KEEPING RECORDS

FIELDING RECORDS

TEAM RECORDS

TEST RECORDS

BATTING RECORDS

BOWLING RECORDS

ALL-ROUND RECORDS

WICKET-KEEPING RECORDS

FIELDING RECORDS

TEAM RECORDS

PLAYERS

UMPIRES

TEST SERIES

"The Australians paid him their highest compliment: they stopped sledging him."
England in Australia, page 1057.

LIMITED-OVERS INTERNATIONAL RECORDS

WORLD CUP RECORDS

LIST A LIMITED-OVERS RECORDS

MISCELLANEOUS

FIRST-CLASS RECORDS

BATTING RECORDS

HIGHEST INDIVIDUAL INNINGS

In the history of first-class cricket, there have been **142** individual scores of 300 or more:

501*	B. C. Lara	Warwickshire v Durham at Birmingham	1994
499	Hanif Mohammad	Karachi v Bahawalpur at Karachi	1958-59
452*	D. G. Bradman	NSW v Queensland at Sydney	1929-30
443*	B. B. Nimbalkar	Maharashtra v Kathiawar at Poona	1948-49
437	W. H. Ponsford	Victoria v Queensland at Melbourne	1927-28
429	W. H. Ponsford	Victoria v Tasmania at Melbourne	1922-23
428	Aftab Baloch	Sind v Baluchistan at Karachi	1973-74
424	A. C. MacLaren	Lancashire v Somerset at Taunton	1895
405*	G. A. Hick	Worcestershire v Somerset at Taunton	1988
394	Naved Latif	Sargodha v Gujranwala at Gujranwala	2000-01
385	B. Sutcliffe	Otago v Canterbury at Christchurch	1952-53
383	C. W. Gregory	NSW v Queensland at Brisbane	1906-07
380	M. L. Hayden	Australia v Zimbabwe at Perth	2003-04
377	S. V. Manjrekar	Bombay v Hyderabad at Bombay	1990-91
375	B. C. Lara	West Indies v England at St John's	1993-94
369	D. G. Bradman	South Australia v Tasmania at Adelaide	1935-36
366	N. H. Fairbrother	Lancashire v Surrey at The Oval	1990
366	M. V. Sridhar	Hyderabad v Andhra at Secunderabad	1993-94
365*	C. Hill	South Australia v NSW at Adelaide	1900-01
365*	G. S. Sobers	West Indies v Pakistan at Kingston	1957-58
364	L. Hutton	England v Australia at The Oval	1938
359*	V. M. Merchant	Bombay v Maharashtra at Bombay	1943-44
359	R. B. Simpson	NSW v Queensland at Brisbane	1963-64
357*	R. Abel	Surrey v Somerset at The Oval	1899
357	D. G. Bradman	South Australia v Victoria at Melbourne	1935-36
356	B. A. Richards	South Australia v Western Australia at Perth	1970-71
355*	G. R. Marsh	Western Australia v South Australia at Perth	1989-90
355	B. Sutcliffe	Otago v Auckland at Dunedin	1949-50
353	V. V. S. Laxman	Hyderabad v Karnataka at Bangalore	1999-2000
352	W. H. Ponsford	Victoria v NSW at Melbourne	1926-27
350	Rashid Israr	Habib Bank v National Bank at Lahore	1976-77
345	C. G. Macartney	Australians v Nottinghamshire at Nottingham	1921
344*	G. A. Headley	Jamaica v Lord Tennyson's XI at Kingston	1931-32
344	W. G. Grace	MCC v Kent at Canterbury	1876
343*	P. A. Perrin	Essex v Derbyshire at Chesterfield	1904
341	G. H. Hirst	Yorkshire v Leicestershire at Leicester	1905
340*	D. G. Bradman	NSW v Victoria at Sydney	1928-29
340	S. M. Gavaskar	Bombay v Bengal at Bombay	1981-82
340	S. T. Jayasuriya	Sri Lanka v India at Colombo	1997-98
338*	R. C. Blunt	Otago v Canterbury at Christchurch	1931-32
338	W. W. Read	Surrey v Oxford University at The Oval	1888
337*	Pervez Akhtar	Railways v Dera Ismail Khan at Lahore	1964-65
337*	D. J. Cullinan	Transvaal v Northern Transvaal at Johannesburg	1993-94
337	Hanif Mohammad	Pakistan v West Indies at Bridgetown	1957-58
336*	W. R. Hammond	England v New Zealand at Auckland	1932-33
336	W. H. Ponsford	Victoria v South Australia at Melbourne	1927-28
335*	M. W. Goodwin	Sussex v Leicestershire at Hove	2003
334*	M. A. Taylor	Australia v Pakistan at Peshawar	1998-99
334	D. G. Bradman	Australia v England at Leeds	1930
333	K. S. Duleepsinhji	Sussex v Northamptonshire at Hove	1930
333	G. A. Gooch	England v India at Lord's	1990
332	W. H. Ashdown	Kent v Essex at Brentwood	1934

331*	J. D. Robertson	Middlesex v Worcestershire at Worcester	1949
331*	M. E. K. Hussey	Northamptonshire v Somerset at Taunton	2003
329*	M. E. K. Hussey	Northamptonshire v Essex at Northampton	2001
329	Inzamam-ul-Haq	Pakistan v New Zealand at Lahore	2002
325*	H. L. Hendry	Victoria v New Zealanders at Melbourne	1925-26
325	A. Sandham	England v West Indies at Kingston	1929-30
325	C. L. Badcock	South Australia v Victoria at Adelaide	1935-36
324*	D. M. Jones	Victoria v South Australia at Melbourne	1994-95
324	J. B. Stollmeyer	Trinidad v British Guiana at Port-of-Spain	1946-47
324	Waheed Mirza	Karachi Whites v Quetta at Karachi	1976-77
323	A. L. Wadekar	Bombay v Mysore at Bombay	1966-67
323	D. Gandhi	Bengal v Assam at Gauhati	1998-99
322*	M. B. Loye	Northamptonshire v Glamorgan at Northampton	1998
322	E. Paynter	Lancashire v Sussex at Hove	1937
322	I. V. A. Richards	Somerset v Warwickshire at Taunton	1985
321	W. L. Murdoch	NSW v Victoria at Sydney	1881-82
320	R. Lamba	North Zone v West Zone at Bhilai	1987-88
319	Gul Mahomed	Baroda v Holkar at Baroda	1946-47
318*	W. G. Grace	Gloucestershire v Yorkshire at Cheltenham	1876
317	W. R. Hammond	Gloucestershire v Nottinghamshire at Gloucester	1936
317	K. R. Rutherford	New Zealanders v D. B. Close's XI at Scarborough	1986
316*	J. B. Hobbs	Surrey v Middlesex at Lord's	1926
316*	V. S. Hazare	Maharashtra v Baroda at Poona	1939-40
316	R. H. Moore	Hampshire v Warwickshire at Bournemouth	1937
315*	T. W. Hayward	Surrey v Lancashire at The Oval	1898
315*	P. Holmes	Yorkshire v Middlesex at Lord's	1925
315*	A. F. Kippax	NSW v Queensland at Sydney	1927-28
315*	G. A. Hick	Worcestershire v Durham at Worcester	2002
315	M. A. Wagh	Warwickshire v Middlesex at Lord's	2001
314*	C. L. Walcott	Barbados v Trinidad at Port-of-Spain	1945-46
314*	Wasim Jaffer	Mumbai v Saurashtra at Rajkot	1996-97
313*	S. J. Cook	Somerset v Glamorgan at Cardiff	1990
313	H. Sutcliffe	Yorkshire v Essex at Leyton	1932
313	W. V. Raman‡	Tamil Nadu v Goa at Panjim	1988-89
312*	W. W. Keeton	Nottinghamshire v Middlesex at The Oval†	1939
312*	J. M. Brearley	MCC Under-25 v North Zone at Peshawar	1966-67
312	R. Lamba	Delhi v Himachal Pradesh at Delhi	1994-95
312	J. E. R. Gallian	Lancashire v Derbyshire at Manchester	1996
311*	G. M. Turner	Worcestershire v Warwickshire at Worcester	1982
311	J. T. Brown	Yorkshire v Sussex at Sheffield	1897
311	R. B. Simpson	Australia v England at Manchester	1964
311	Javed Miandad	Karachi Whites v National Bank at Karachi	1974-75
310*	J. H. Edrich	England v New Zealand at Leeds	1965
310*	M. E. K. Hussey	Northamptonshire v Gloucestershire at Bristol	2002
310	H. Gimblett	Somerset v Sussex at Eastbourne	1948
309*	S. P. James	Glamorgan v Sussex at Colwyn Bay	2000
309	V. S. Hazare	The Rest v Hindus at Bombay	1943-44
308*	F. M. M. Worrell	Barbados v Trinidad at Bridgetown	1943-44
308*	D. Mongia	Punjab v Jammu and Kashmir at Jullundur	2000-01
307*	T. N. Lazard	Boland v W. Province at Worcester, Cape Province	1993-94
307	M. C. Cowdrey	MCC v South Australia at Adelaide	1962-63
307	R. M. Cowper	Australia v England at Melbourne	1965-66
306*	A. Ducat	Surrey v Oxford University at The Oval	1919
306*	E. A. B. Rowan	Transvaal v Natal at Johannesburg	1939-40
306*	D. W. Hookes	South Australia v Tasmania at Adelaide	1986-87
306	M. H. Richardson	New Zealanders v Zimbabwe A at Kwekwe	2000-01
305*	F. E. Woolley	MCC v Tasmania at Hobart	1911-12
305*	F. R. Foster	Warwickshire v Worcestershire at Dudley	1914
305*	W. H. Ashdown	Kent v Derbyshire at Dover	1935
305*	P. Dharmani	Punjab v Jammu and Kashmir at Ludhiana	1999-2000
304*	A. W. Nourse	Natal v Transvaal at Johannesburg	1919-20

304*	P. H. Tarilton	Barbados v Trinidad at Bridgetown	1919-20
304*	E. D. Weekes	West Indians v Cambridge University at Cambridge	1950
304	R. M. Poore	Hampshire v Somerset at Taunton	1899
304	D. G. Bradman	Australia v England at Leeds	1934
303*	W. W. Armstrong	Australians v Somerset at Bath	1905
303*	Mushtaq Mohammad	Karachi Blues v Karachi University at Karachi	1967-68
303*	Abdul Azeem	Hyderabad v Tamil Nadu at Hyderabad	1986-87
303*	S. Chanderpaul	Guyana v Jamaica at Kingston	1995-96
303*	G. A. Hick	Worcestershire v Hampshire at Southampton	1997
303*	D. J. Sales	Northamptonshire v Essex at Northampton	1999
302*	P. Holmes	Yorkshire v Hampshire at Portsmouth	1920
302*	W. R. Hammond	Gloucestershire v Glamorgan at Bristol	1934
302*	Arjan Kripal Singh‡	Tamil Nadu v Goa at Panjim	1988-89
302*	B. J. Hodge	Leicestershire v Nottinghamshire at Nottingham	2003
302	W. R. Hammond	Gloucestershire v Glamorgan at Newport	1939
302	L. G. Rowe	West Indies v England at Bridgetown	1973-74
301*	E. H. Hendren	Middlesex v Worcestershire at Dudley	1933
301*	V. V. S. Laxman	Hyderabad v Bihar at Jamshedpur	1997-98
301*	P. G. Fulton	Canterbury v Auckland at Christchurch	2002-03
301	W. G. Grace	Gloucestershire v Sussex at Bristol	1896
300*	V. T. Trumper	Australians v Sussex at Hove	1899
300*	F. B. Watson	Lancashire v Surrey at Manchester	1928
300*	Imtiaz Ahmed	PM's XI v Commonwealth XI at Bombay	1950-51
300*	G. K. Khoda	Central Zone v South Zone at Panaji	2000-01
300*	M. L. Love	Queensland v Victoria at Melbourne (Junction Oval)	2003-04
300	J. T. Brown	Yorkshire v Derbyshire at Chesterfield	1898
300	D. C. S. Compton	MCC v N. E. Transvaal at Benoni	1948-49
300	R. Subba Row	Northamptonshire v Surrey at The Oval	1958
300	Ramiz Raja	Allied Bank v Habib Bank at Lahore	1994-95

† *Played at The Oval because Lord's was required for Eton v Harrow.*

‡ *W. V. Raman and Arjan Kripal Singh scored triple-hundreds in the same innings, a unique occurrence.*

DOUBLE-HUNDRED ON DEBUT

227	T. Marsden	Sheffield & Leicester v Nottingham at Sheffield	1826
207	N. F. Callaway†	New South Wales v Queensland at Sydney	1914-15
240	W. F. E. Marx	Transvaal v Griqualand West at Johannesburg	1920-21
200*	A. Maynard	Trinidad v MCC at Port-of-Spain	1934-35
232*	S. J. E. Loxton	Victoria v Queensland at Melbourne	1946-47
215*	G. H. G. Doggart	Cambridge University v Lancashire at Cambridge	1948
202	J. Hallebone	Victoria v Tasmania at Melbourne	1951-52
230	G. R. Viswanath	Mysore v Andhra at Vijayawada	1967-68
260	A. A. Muzumdar	Bombay v Haryana at Faridabad	1993-94
209*	A. Pandey	Madhya Pradesh v Uttar Pradesh at Bhilai	1995-96
210*	D. J. Sales	Northants v Worcestershire at Kidderminster	1996
200*	M. J. Powell	Glamorgan v Oxford University at Oxford	1997

† *In his only first-class innings. He was killed in action in France in 1917.*

TWO SEPARATE HUNDREDS ON DEBUT

148 and 111	A. R. Morris	New South Wales v Queensland at Sydney	1940-41
152 and 102*	N. J. Contractor	Gujarat v Baroda at Baroda	1952-53
132* and 110	Aamer Malik	Lahore A v Railways at Lahore	1979-80

HUNDRED ON DEBUT IN ENGLAND

This does not include players who have previously appeared in first-class cricket outside the British Isles. The following have achieved the feat since 1990. For fuller lists please see earlier *Wisdens*.

116*	J. J. B. Lewis	Essex v Surrey at The Oval	1990
117	J. D. Glendenen	Durham v Oxford University at Oxford	1992
109	J. R. Wileman	Nottinghamshire v Cambridge University at Nottingham	1992
123	A. J. Hollioake†	Surrey v Derbyshire at Ilkeston	1993
101	E. T. Smith	Cambridge University v Glamorgan at Cambridge	1996
110	S. D. Peters	Essex v Cambridge University at Cambridge	1996
210*	D. J. Sales†	Northamptonshire v Worcestershire at Kidderminster	1996
200*	M. J. Powell	Glamorgan v Oxford University at Oxford	1997
104	C. G. Taylor	Gloucestershire v Middlesex at Lord's	2000
107*	R. Clarke	Surrey v Cambridge UCCE at Cambridge	2002
169	J. S. D. Moffat	Cambridge University v Oxford University at Oxford	2002

† *In his second innings.*

TWO DOUBLE-HUNDREDS IN A MATCH

A. E. Fagg	244	202*	Kent v Essex at Colchester	1938

TRIPLE-HUNDRED AND HUNDRED IN A MATCH

G. A. Gooch	333	123	England v India at Lord's	1990

DOUBLE-HUNDRED AND HUNDRED IN A MATCH

C. B. Fry	125	229	Sussex v Surrey at Hove	1900
W. W. Armstrong	157*	245	Victoria v South Australia at Melbourne	1920-21
H. T. W. Hardinge	207	102*	Kent v Surrey at Blackheath	1921
C. P. Mead	113	224	Hampshire v Sussex at Horsham	1921
K. S. Duleepsinhji	115	246	Sussex v Kent at Hastings	1929
D. G. Bradman	124	225	Woodfull's XI v Ryder's XI at Sydney	1929-30
B. Sutcliffe	243	100*	New Zealanders v Essex at Southend	1949
M. R. Hallam	210*	157	Leicestershire v Glamorgan at Leicester	1959
M. R. Hallam	203*	143*	Leicestershire v Sussex at Worthing	1961
Hanumant Singh	109	213*	Rajasthan v Bombay at Bombay	1966-67
Salah-ud-Din	256	102*	Karachi v East Pakistan at Karachi	1968-69
K. D. Walters	242	103	Australia v West Indies at Sydney	1968-69
S. M. Gavaskar	124	220	India v West Indies at Port-of-Spain	1970-71
L. G. Rowe	214	100*	West Indies v New Zealand at Kingston	1971-72
G. S. Chappell	247*	133	Australia v New Zealand at Wellington	1973-74
L. Baichan	216*	102	Berbice v Demerara at Georgetown	1973-74
Zaheer Abbas	216*	156*	Gloucestershire v Surrey at The Oval	1976
Zaheer Abbas	230*	104*	Gloucestershire v Kent at Canterbury	1976
Zaheer Abbas	205*	108*	Gloucestershire v Sussex at Cheltenham	1977
Saadat Ali	141	222	Income Tax v Multan at Multan	1977-78
Talat Ali	214*	104	PIA v Punjab at Lahore	1978-79
Shafiq Ahmad	129	217*	National Bank v MCB at Karachi	1978-79
D. W. Randall	209	146	Nottinghamshire v Middlesex at Nottingham	1979
Zaheer Abbas	215*	150*	Gloucestershire v Somerset at Bath	1981
Qasim Omar	210*	110	MCB v Lahore at Lahore	1982-83
A. I. Kallicharran	200*	117*	Warwickshire v Northants at Birmingham	1984
Rizwan-uz-Zaman	139	217*	PIA v PACO at Lahore	1989-90
G. A. Hick	252*	100*	Worcestershire v Glamorgan at Abergavenny	1990
N. R. Taylor	204	142	Kent v Surrey at Canterbury	1990
N. R. Taylor	111	203*	Kent v Sussex at Hove	1991
W. V. Raman	226	120	Tamil Nadu v Haryana at Faridabad	1991-92
A. J. Lamb	209	107	Northants v Warwicks at Northampton	1992
G. A. Gooch	101	205	Essex v Worcestershire at Worcester	1994

P. A. de Silva	255	116	Kent v Derbyshire at Maidstone	1995
M. C. Mendis	111	200*	Colts CC v Singha SC at Colombo	1995-96
A. M. Bacher	210	112*	Transvaal v Griqualand West at Kimberley	1996-97
H. H. Gibbs	200*	171	South Africans v India A at Nagpur	1996-97
M. L. Hayden	235*	119	Hampshire v Warwickshire at Southampton	1997
G. S. Blewett	169*	213*	Australian XI v England XI at Hobart	1998-99
A. Jadeja	136	202*	Haryana v Saurashtra at Rajkot	1998-99
J. Cox	216	129*	Somerset v Hampshire at Southampton	1999
Mohammad Ramzan	205	102*	Faisalabad v Sargodha at Faisalabad	2000-01
M. W. Goodwin	115	203*	Sussex v Nottinghamshire at Nottingham	2001
D. P. Fulton	208*	104*	Kent v Somerset at Canterbury	2001
B. C. Lara	221	130	West Indies v Sri Lanka at Colombo	2001-02
Minhazul Abedin	210	110	Chittagong v Dhaka at Mymensingh	2001-02
A. T. Rayudu	210	159*	Hyderabad v Andhra at Secunderabad	2002-03
H. H. Kanitkar	112	207*	Maharashtra v Services at Aurangabad	2003-04

TWO SEPARATE HUNDREDS IN A MATCH

Eight times: Zaheer Abbas.
Seven times: W. R. Hammond.
Six times: J. B. Hobbs, G. M. Turner.
Five times: C. B. Fry, G. A. Gooch, R. T. Ponting.
Four times: D. G. Bradman, G. S. Chappell, J. Cox, J. H. Edrich, L. B. Fishlock, T. W. Graveney, C. G. Greenidge, H. T. W. Hardinge, M. L. Hayden, E. H. Hendren, G. A. Hick, Javed Miandad, G. L. Jessop, S. G. Law, H. Morris, M. H. Parmar, P. A. Perrin, M. R. Ramprakash, B. Sutcliffe, H. Sutcliffe.
Three times: C. J. Adams, Agha Zahid, L. E. G. Ames, Basit Ali, G. Boycott, I. M. Chappell, D. C. S. Compton, S. J. Cook, M. C. Cowdrey, D. Denton, P. A. de Silva, K. S. Duleepsinhji, R. E. Foster, R. C. Fredericks, S. M. Gavaskar, W. G. Grace, G. Gunn, M. R. Hallam, Hanif Mohammad, M. J. Harris, T. W. Hayward, V. S. Hazare, D. W. Hookes, L. Hutton, A. Jones, D. M. Jones, P. N. Kirsten, R. B. McCosker, P. B. H. May, M. P. Maynard, C. P. Mead, T. M. Moody, Rizwan-uz-Zaman, R. T. Robinson, A. C. Russell, Sadiq Mohammad, J. T. Tyldesley, K. C. Wessels.

Notes: W. Lambert scored 107 and 157 for Sussex v Epsom at Lord's in 1817, and it was not until W. G. Grace made 130 and 102* for South of the Thames v North of the Thames at Canterbury in 1868 that the feat was repeated.

C. J. B. Wood, 107* and 117* for Leicestershire v Yorkshire at Bradford in 1911, and S. J. Cook, 120* and 131* for Somerset v Nottinghamshire at Nottingham in 1989, are alone in carrying their bats and scoring hundreds in each innings.

FOUR HUNDREDS OR MORE IN SUCCESSION

Six in succession: D. G. Bradman 1938-39; C. B. Fry 1901; M. J. Procter 1970-71.
Five in succession: B. C. Lara 1993-94/1994; E. D. Weekes 1955-56; M. E. K. Hussey 2003.
Four in succession: C. W. J. Athey 1987; M. Azharuddin 1984-85; M. G. Bevan 1990-91; G. S. Blewett 1998-99; A. R. Border 1985; D. G. Bradman 1931-32, 1948/1948-49; D. C. S. Compton 1946-47; N. J. Contractor 1957-58; S. J. Cook 1989; K. S. Duleepsinhji 1931; C. B. Fry 1911; C. G. Greenidge 1986; W. R. Hammond 1936-37, 1945/1946; H. T. W. Hardinge 1913; T. W. Hayward 1906; G. A. Hick 1998; J. B. Hobbs 1920, 1925; D. W. Hookes 1976-77; Ijaz Ahmed, jun. 1994-95; R. S. Kaluwitharana 1996-97; P. N. Kirsten 1976-77; J. G. Langridge 1949; C. G. Macartney 1921; K. S. McEwan 1977; P. B. H. May 1956-57; V. M. Merchant 1941-42; A. Mitchell 1933; Nawab of Pataudi sen. 1931; Rizwan-uz-Zaman 1989-90; L. G. Rowe 1971-72; Pankaj Roy 1962-63; Sadiq Mohammad 1976; Saeed Ahmed 1961-62; E. T. Smith 2003; M. V. Sridhar 1990-91/1991-92; H. Sutcliffe 1931, 1939; S. R. Tendulkar 1994-95; E. Tyldesley 1926; I. J. Ward 2002; W. W. Whysall 1930; F. E. Woolley 1929; Yasir Hameed 2002-03/2003; Younis Khan 1999-2000; Zaheer Abbas 1970-71, 1982-83.

Notes: T. W. Hayward (Surrey v Nottinghamshire and Leicestershire) and D. W. Hookes (South Australia v Queensland and New South Wales) are the only players listed above to score two hundreds in two successive matches. Hayward scored his in six days, June 4-9, 1906.

The most fifties in consecutive innings is ten – by E. Tyldesley in 1926, by D. G. Bradman in the 1947-48 and 1948 seasons and by R. S. Kaluwitharana in 1994-95.

MOST HUNDREDS IN A SEASON

Eighteen: D. C. S. Compton 1947.
Sixteen: J. B. Hobbs 1925.
Fifteen: W. R. Hammond 1938.
Fourteen: H. Sutcliffe 1932.
Thirteen: G. Boycott 1971, D. G. Bradman 1938, C. B. Fry 1901, W. R. Hammond 1933 and 1937, T. W. Hayward 1906, E. H. Hendren 1923, 1927 and 1928, C. P. Mead 1928, H. Sutcliffe 1928 and 1931.

Since 1969 (excluding G. Boycott – above)

Twelve: G. A. Gooch 1990.
Eleven: S. J. Cook 1991, Zaheer Abbas 1976.
Ten: G. A. Hick 1988, H. Morris 1990, M. R. Ramprakash 1995, G. M. Turner 1970, Zaheer Abbas 1981.

Note: The most achieved outside England is eight by D. G. Bradman in Australia (1947-48), D. C. S. Compton (1948-49), R. N. Harvey and A. R. Morris (both 1949-50) in South Africa, M. D. Crowe in New Zealand (1986-87), Asif Mujtaba in Pakistan (1995-96) and V. V. S. Laxman in India (1999-2000).

MOST DOUBLE-HUNDREDS IN A SEASON

Six: D. G. Bradman 1930.
Five: K. S. Ranjitsinhji 1900; E. D. Weekes 1950.
Four: Arun Lal 1986-87; C. B. Fry 1901; W. R. Hammond 1933, 1934; E. H. Hendren 1929-30; V. M. Merchant 1944-45; G. M. Turner 1971-72.
Three: L. E. G. Ames 1933; Arshad Pervez 1977-78; D. G. Bradman 1930-31, 1931-32, 1934, 1935-36, 1936-37, 1938, 1939-40; W. J. Edrich 1947; C. B. Fry 1903, 1904; M. W. Gatting 1994; G. A. Gooch 1994; W. R. Hammond 1928, 1928-29, 1932-33, 1938; J. Hardstaff jun. 1937, 1947; V. S. Hazare 1943-44; E. H. Hendren 1925; J. B. Hobbs 1914, 1926; M. E. K. Hussey 2001; L. Hutton 1949; D. M. Jones 1991-92; A. I. Kallicharran 1982; V. G. Kambli 1992-93; P. N. Kirsten 1980; R. S. Modi 1944-45; D. Mongia 2000-01; Nawab of Pataudi sen. 1933; W. H. Ponsford 1927-28, 1934; W. V. Raman 1988-89; M. R. Ramprakash 1995; K. S. Ranjitsinhji 1901; I. V. A. Richards 1977; R. B. Simpson 1963-64; P. R. Umrigar 1952, 1959; F. B. Watson 1928.

MOST HUNDREDS IN A CAREER

(50 or more)

			Total	100th 100				
		Total	Inns	Season	Inns	400+	300+	200+
1	J. B. Hobbs	197	1,315	1923	821	0	1	16
2	E. H. Hendren	170	1,300	1928-29	740	0	1	22
3	W. R. Hammond	167	1,005	1935	679	0	4	36
4	C. P. Mead	153	1,340	1927	892	0	0	13
5	G. Boycott	151	1,014	1977	645	0	0	10
6	H. Sutcliffe	149	1,088	1932	700	0	1	17
7	F. E. Woolley	145	1,532	1929	1,031	0	1	9
8	L. Hutton	129	814	1951	619	0	1	11
9	G. A. Gooch	128	990	1992-93	820	0	1	13
10	W. G. Grace	126	1,493	1895	1,113	0	3	13
11	D. C. S. Compton	123	839	1952	552	0	1	9
12	**G. A. Hick**	**122**	**748**	**1998**	**597**	**1**	**3**	**14**
12	T. W. Graveney	122	1,223	1964	940	0	0	7
14	D. G. Bradman	117	338	1947-48	295	1	6	37
15	I. V. A. Richards	114	796	1988-89	658	0	1	10

		Total	Total Inns	100th 100 Season	Inns	400+	300+	200+
16	Zaheer Abbas	108	768	1982-83	658	0	0	10
17	A. Sandham	107	1,000	1935	871	0	1	11
	M. C. Cowdrey	107	1,130	1973	1,035	0	1	3
19	T. W. Hayward	104	1,138	1913	1,076	0	1	8
20	G. M. Turner	103	792	1982	779	0	1	10
	J. H. Edrich	103	979	1977	945	0	1	4
22	L. E. G. Ames	102	951	1950	915	0	0	9
	E. Tyldesley	102	961	1934	919	0	0	7
	D. L. Amiss	102	1,139	1986	1,081	0	0	3

E. H. Hendren, D. G. Bradman and I. V. A. Richards scored their 100th hundreds in Australia; G. A. Gooch scored his in India. His record includes his century in South Africa in 1981-82, which is no longer accepted by the ICC. Zaheer Abbas scored his 100th in Pakistan. Zaheer Abbas and G. Boycott did so in Test matches.

Most double-hundreds scored by batsmen not included in the above list:

Sixteen: C. B. Fry. **Fourteen:** C. G. Greenidge, K. S. Ranjitsinhji. **Thirteen:** W. H. Ponsford (including two 400s and two 300s), J. T. Tyldesley. **Twelve:** P. Holmes, Javed Miandad, R. B. Simpson. **Eleven:** J. W. Hearne, V. M. Merchant. **Ten:** S. M. Gavaskar, J. Hardstaff, jun., V. S. Hazare, A. Shrewsbury, R. T. Simpson.

J. W. Hearne	96
C. B. Fry	94
M. W. Gatting	94
C. G. Greenidge	92
A. J. Lamb	89
A. I. Kallicharran	87
W. J. Edrich	86
G. S. Sobers	86
J. T. Tyldesley	86
P. B. H. May	85
R. E. S. Wyatt	85
J. Hardstaff, jun.	83
R. B. Kanhai	83
S. M. Gavaskar	81
M. E. Waugh	**81**
Javed Miandad	80
M. Leyland	80
B. A. Richards	80
C. H. Lloyd	79
S. R. Waugh	**79**
K. F. Barrington	76
J. G. Langridge	76
C. Washbrook	76
H. T. W. Hardinge	75
R. Abel	74
G. S. Chappell	74
D. Kenyon	74
K. S. McEwan	74
Majid Khan	73
Mushtaq Mohammad	72
J. O'Connor	72
W. G. Quaife	72
K. S. Ranjitsinhji	72
D. Brookes	71
M. D. Crowe	71
A. C. Russell	71
A. R. Border	70
D. Denton	69
M. J. K. Smith	69
D. C. Boon	68
R. E. Marshall	68
R. N. Harvey	67
P. Holmes	67
C. L. Hooper	**67**
J. D. Robertson	67
P. A. Perrin	66
M. R. Ramprakash	**66**
K. C. Wessels	66
M. L. Hayden	**65**
S. J. Cook	64
D. S. Lehmann	**64**
T. M. Moody	64
R. G. Pollock	64
R. T. Simpson	64
K. W. R. Fletcher	63
S. G. Law	**63**
R. T. Robinson	63
G. Gunn	62
K. J. Barnett	61
D. L. Haynes	61
J. L. Langer	**61**
R. A. Smith	**61**
V. S. Hazare	60
G. H. Hirst	60
R. B. Simpson	60
P. F. Warner	60
M. G. Bevan	**59**
I. M. Chappell	59
A. L. Hassett	59
W. Larkins	59
A. Shrewsbury	59
J. G. Wright	59
A. E. Fagg	58
P. H. Parfitt	58
W. Rhodes	58
P. N. Kirsten	57
L. B. Fishlock	56
A. Jones	56
M. P. Maynard	**56**
C. A. Milton	56
C. W. J. Athey	55
C. Hallows	55
Hanif Mohammad	55
D. M. Jones	55
S. R. Tendulkar	**55**
D. B. Vengsarkar	55
W. Watson	55
M. A. Atherton	54
M. Azharuddin	54
D. J. Insole	54
W. W. Keeton	54
W. Bardsley	53
B. F. Davison	53
A. E. Dipper	53
D. I. Gower	53
G. L. Jessop	53
H. Morris	53
James Seymour	53
Shafiq Ahmad	53
E. H. Bowley	52
D. B. Close	52
A. Ducat	52
J. E. Morris	52
D. W. Randall	52
E. R. Dexter	51
B. C. Lara	**51**
J. M. Parks	51
W. W. Whysall	51
B. C. Broad	50
G. Cox, jun.	50
H. E. Dollery	50
K. S. Duleepsinhji	50
H. Gimblett	50
N. Hussain	**50**
W. M. Lawry	50
Sadiq Mohammad	50
F. B. Watson	50

Bold type denotes those who have played since the start of 2002-03.

Other Current Players

In addition to the above, the following who have played since the start of 2002-03 have scored 30 or more hundreds.

R. T. Ponting	49	R. Dravid	41	A. Flower	34
J. Cox	48	M. S. Atapattu	40	V. G. Kambli	34
A. J. Stewart	48	D. J. Bicknell	39	V. Rathore	33
S. P. James	47	M. T. G. Elliott	38	M. P. Vaughan	33
Asif Mujtaba	45	Inzamam-ul-Haq	38	A. D. Brown	32
G. Kirsten	45	Sajid Ali	38	M. E. K. Hussey	32
G. P. Thorpe	45	C. J. Adams	37	N. V. Knight	32
G. S. Blewett	43	M. J. Slater	36	S. Chanderpaul	31
P. D. Bowler	42	V. V. S. Laxman	35	P. A. Cottey	30
J. P. Crawley	42	D. R. Martyn	35	Saeed Anwar	30
D. J. Cullinan	41	H. P. Tillekeratne	35	B. F. Smith	30

MOST RUNS IN A SEASON

	Season	*I*	*NO*	*R*	*HS*	*100s*	*Avge*
D. C. S. Compton	1947	50	8	3,816	246	18	90.85
W. J. Edrich	1947	52	8	3,539	267*	12	80.43
T. W. Hayward	1906	61	8	3,518	219	13	66.37
L. Hutton	1949	56	6	3,429	269*	12	68.58
F. E. Woolley	1928	59	4	3,352	198	12	60.94
H. Sutcliffe	1932	52	7	3,336	313	14	74.13
W. R. Hammond	1933	54	5	3,323	264	13	67.81
E. H. Hendren	1928	54	7	3,311	209*	13	70.44
R. Abel	1901	68	8	3,309	247	7	55.15

Notes: 3,000 in a season has been surpassed on 19 other occasions (a full list can be found in *Wisden* 1999 and earlier editions). W. R. Hammond, E. H. Hendren and H. Sutcliffe are the only players to achieve the feat three times. M. J. K. Smith (3,245 in 1959) and W. E. Alley (3,019 in 1961) are the only players except those listed above to have reached 3,000 since World War II.

2,000 RUNS IN A SEASON

(Since reduction of Championship matches in 1969)

Five times: G. A. Gooch 2,746 (1990), 2,559 (1984), 2,324 (1988), 2,208 (1985), 2,023 (1993).
Three times: D. L. Amiss 2,239 (1984), 2,110 (1976), 2,030 (1978); S. J. Cook 2,755† (1991), 2,608 (1990), 2,241 (1989); M. W. Gatting 2,257 (1984), 2,057 (1991), 2,000 (1992); G. A. Hick 2,713 (1988), 2,347 (1990), 2,004 (1986); G. M. Turner 2,416 (1973), 2,379 (1970), 2,101 (1981).
Twice: G. Boycott 2,503 (1971), 2,051 (1970); J. H. Edrich 2,238 (1969), 2,031 (1971); A. I. Kallicharran 2,301 (1984), 2,120 (1982); Zaheer Abbas 2,554 (1976), 2,306 (1981).
Once: M. Azharuddin 2,016 (1991); J. B. Bolus 2,143 (1970); P. D. Bowler 2,044 (1992); B. C. Broad 2,226 (1990); A. R. Butcher 2,116 (1990); C. G. Greenidge 2,035 (1986); M. J. Harris 2,238 (1971); D. L. Haynes 2,346 (1990); M. E. K. Hussey 2,055 (2001); Javed Miandad 2,083 (1981); A. J. Lamb 2,049 (1981); B. C. Lara 2,066 (1994); K. S. McEwan 2,176 (1983); Majid Khan 2,074 (1972); A. A. Metcalfe 2,047 (1990); H. Morris 2,276 (1990); M. R. Ramprakash 2,258 (1995); D. W. Randall 2,151 (1985); I. V. A. Richards 2,161 (1977); R. T. Robinson 2,032 (1984); M. A. Roseberry 2,044 (1992); C. L. Smith 2,000 (1985); R. T. Virgin 2,223 (1970); D. M. Ward 2,072 (1990); M. E. Waugh 2,072 (1990).

Notes: W. G. Grace scored 2,739 runs in 1871 – the first batsman to reach 2,000 runs in a season. He made ten hundreds and twice exceeded 200, with an average of 78.25 in all first-class matches.

† *Highest since the reduction of Championship matches in 1969.*

1,000 RUNS IN A SEASON MOST TIMES

Includes overseas tours and seasons

28 times: W. G. Grace 2,000 (6); F. E. Woolley 3,000 (1), 2,000 (12).
27 times: M. C. Cowdrey 2,000 (2); C. P. Mead 3,000 (2), 2,000 (9).
26 times: G. Boycott 2,000 (3); J. B. Hobbs 3,000 (1), 2,000 (16).
25 times: E. H. Hendren 3,000 (3), 2,000 (12).
24 times: D. L. Amiss 2,000 (3); W. G. Quaife 2,000 (1); H. Sutcliffe 3,000 (3), 2,000 (12).
23 times: A. Jones.
22 times: T. W. Graveney 2,000 (7); W. R. Hammond 3,000 (3), 2,000 (9).
21 times: D. Denton 2,000 (5); J. H. Edrich 2,000 (6); G. A. Gooch 2,000 (5); W. Rhodes 2,000 (2).
20 times: D. B. Close; K. W. R. Fletcher; M. W. Gatting 2,000 (3); G. Gunn; T. W. Hayward 3,000 (2), 2,000 (8); James Langridge 2,000 (1); J. M. Parks 2,000 (3); A. Sandham 2,000 (8); M. J. K. Smith 3,000 (1), 2,000 (5); C. Washbrook 2,000 (2).

Notes: F. E. Woolley reached 1,000 runs in 28 consecutive seasons (1907–1938), C. P. Mead in 27 (1906–1936).

Outside England, 1,000 runs in a season has been reached most times by D. G. Bradman (in 12 seasons in Australia).

Three batsmen have scored 1,000 runs in a season in each of four different countries: G. S. Sobers in West Indies, England, India and Australia; M. C. Cowdrey and G. Boycott in England, South Africa, West Indies and Australia.

HIGHEST AGGREGATES OUTSIDE ENGLAND

	Season	I	NO	R	HS	100s	Avge
In Australia							
D. G. Bradman	1928-29	24	6	1,690	340*	7	93.88
In South Africa							
J. R. Reid	1961-62	30	2	1,915	203	7	68.39
In West Indies							
E. H. Hendren	1929-30	18	5	1,765	254*	6	135.76
In New Zealand							
M. D. Crowe	1986-87	21	3	1,676	175*	8	93.11
In India							
C. G. Borde	1964-65	28	3	1,604	168	6	64.16
In Pakistan							
Saadat Ali	1983-84	27	1	1,649	208	4	63.42
In Sri Lanka							
R. P. Arnold	1995-96	24	3	1,475	217*	5	70.23
In Zimbabwe							
G. W. Flower	1994-95	20	3	983	201*	4	57.82
In Bangladesh							
Minhazul Abedin	2001-02	15	1	1,012	210	3	72.28

Note: In more than one country, the following aggregates of over 2,000 runs have been recorded:

	Season	I	NO	R	HS	100s	Avge
M. Amarnath (P/I/WI)	1982-83	34	6	2,234	207	9	79.78
J. R. Reid (SA/A/NZ)	1961-62	40	2	2,188	203	7	57.57
S. M. Gavaskar (I/P)	1978-79	30	6	2,121	205	10	88.37
R. B. Simpson (I/P/A/WI)	1964-65	34	4	2,063	201	8	68.76
M. H. Richardson (Z/SA/NZ)	2000-01	34	3	2,030	306	4	65.48

LEADING BATSMEN IN AN ENGLISH SEASON

(Qualification: 8 completed innings)

Season	Leading scorer	Runs	Avge	Top of averages	Runs	Avge
1946	D. C. S. Compton	2,403	61.61	W. R. Hammond	1,783	84.90
1947	D. C. S. Compton	3,816	90.85	D. C. S. Compton	3,816	90.85
1948	L. Hutton	2,654	64.73	D. G. Bradman	2,428	89.92
1949	L. Hutton	3,429	68.58	J. Hardstaff	2,251	72.61
1950	R. T. Simpson	2,576	62.82	E. D. Weekes	2,310	79.65
1951	J. D. Robertson	2,917	56.09	P. B. H. May	2,339	68.79
1952	L. Hutton	2,567	61.11	D. S. Sheppard	2,262	64.62
1953	W. J. Edrich	2,557	47.35	R. N. Harvey	2,040	65.80
1954	D. Kenyon	2,636	51.68	D. C. S. Compton	1,524	58.61
1955	D. J. Insole	2,427	42.57	D. J. McGlew	1,871	58.46
1956	T. W. Graveney	2,397	49.93	K. Mackay	1,103	52.52
1957	T. W. Graveney	2,361	49.18	P. B. H. May	2,347	61.76
1958	P. B. H. May	2,231	63.74	P. B. H. May	2,231	63.74
1959	M. J. K. Smith	3,245	57.94	V. L. Manjrekar	755	68.63
1960	M. J. K. Smith	2,551	45.55	R. Subba Row	1,503	55.66
1961	W. E. Alley	3,019	56.96	W. M. Lawry	2,019	61.18
1962	J. H. Edrich	2,482	51.70	R. T. Simpson	867	54.18
1963	J. B. Bolus	2,190	41.32	G. S. Sobers	1,333	47.60
1964	T. W. Graveney	2,385	54.20	K. F. Barrington	1,872	62.40
1965	J. H. Edrich	2,319	62.67	M. C. Cowdrey	2,093	63.42
1966	A. R. Lewis	2,198	41.47	G. S. Sobers	1,349	61.31
1967	C. A. Milton	2,089	46.42	K. F. Barrington	2,059	68.63
1968	B. A. Richards	2,395	47.90	G. Boycott	1,487	64.65
1969	J. H. Edrich	2,238	69.93	J. H. Edrich	2,238	69.93
1970	G. M. Turner	2,379	61.00	G. S. Sobers	1,742	75.73
1971	G. Boycott	2,503	100.12	G. Boycott	2,503	100.12
1972	Majid Khan	2,074	61.00	G. Boycott	1,230	72.35
1973	G. M. Turner	2,416	67.11	G. M. Turner	2,416	67.11
1974	R. T. Virgin	1,936	56.94	C. H. Lloyd	1,458	63.39
1975	G. Boycott	1,915	73.65	R. B. Kanhai	1,073	82.53
1976	Zaheer Abbas	2,554	75.11	Zaheer Abbas	2,554	75.11
1977	I. V. A. Richards	2,161	65.48	G. Boycott	1,701	68.04
1978	D. L. Amiss	2,030	53.42	C. E. B. Rice	1,871	66.82
1979	K. C. Wessels	1,800	52.94	G. Boycott	1,538	102.53
1980	P. N. Kirsten	1,895	63.16	A. J. Lamb	1,797	66.55
1981	Zaheer Abbas	2,306	88.69	Zaheer Abbas	2,306	88.69
1982	A. I. Kallicharran	2,120	66.25	G. M. Turner	1,171	90.07
1983	K. S. McEwan	2,176	64.00	I. V. A. Richards	1,204	75.25
1984	G. A. Gooch	2,559	67.34	C. G. Greenidge	1,069	82.23
1985	G. A. Gooch	2,208	71.22	I. V. A. Richards	1,836	76.50
1986	C. G. Greenidge	2,035	67.83	C. G. Greenidge	2,035	67.83
1987	G. A. Hick	1,879	52.19	M. D. Crowe	1,627	67.79
1988	G. A. Hick	2,713	77.51	R. A. Harper	622	77.75
1989	S. J. Cook	2,241	60.56	D. M. Jones	1,510	88.82
1990	G. A. Gooch	2,746	101.70	G. A. Gooch	2,746	101.70
1991	S. J. Cook	2,755	81.02	C. L. Hooper	1,501	93.81
1992	P. D. Bowler M. A. Roseberry	2,044 2,044	65.93 56.77	Salim Malik	1,184	78.93
1993	G. A. Gooch	2,023	63.21	D. C. Boon	1,437	75.63
1994	B. C. Lara	2,066	89.82	J. D. Carr	1,543	90.76
1995	M. R. Ramprakash	2,258	77.86	M. R. Ramprakash	2,258	77.86
1996	G. A. Gooch	1,944	67.03	S. C. Ganguly	762	95.25
1997	S. P. James	1,775	68.26	G. A. Hick	1,524	69.27
1998	J. P. Crawley	1,851	74.04	J. P. Crawley	1,851	74.04
1999	S. G. Law	1,833	73.32	S. G. Law	1,833	73.32
2000	D. S. Lehmann	1,477	67.13	M. G. Bevan	1,124	74.93

Season	*Leading scorer*	*Runs*	*Avge*	*Top of averages*	*Runs*	*Avge*
2001	M. E. K. Hussey. . . .	2,055	79.03	D. R. Martyn	942	104.66
2002	I. J. Ward	1,759	62.82	R. Dravid	773	96.62
2003	S. G. Law	1,820	91.00	S. G. Law	1,820	91.00

Notes: The highest average recorded in an English season was 115.66 (2,429 runs, 26 innings) by D. G. Bradman in 1938.

In 1953, W. A. Johnston averaged 102.00 from 17 innings, 16 not out.

25,000 RUNS

Dates in italics denote the first half of an overseas season; i.e. *1945* denotes the 1945-46 season.

		Career	*R*	*I*	*NO*	*HS*	*100s*	*Avge*
1	J. B. Hobbs	1905–34	61,237	1,315	106	316*	197	50.65
2	F. E. Woolley	1906–38	58,969	1,532	85	305*	145	40.75
3	E. H. Hendren	1907–38	57,611	1,300	166	301*	170	50.80
4	C. P. Mead	1905–36	55,061	1,340	185	280*	153	47.67
5	W. G. Grace	1865–1908	54,896	1,493	105	344	126	39.55
6	W. R. Hammond. . . .	1920–51	50,551	1,005	104	336*	167	56.10
7	H. Sutcliffe	1919–45	50,138	1,088	123	313	149	51.95
8	G. Boycott.	1962–86	48,426	1,014	162	261*	151	56.83
9	T. W. Graveney.	1948–*71*	47,793	1,223	159	258	122	44.91
10	G. A. Gooch	1973–2000	44,846	990	75	333	128	49.01
11	T. W. Hayward	1893–1914	43,551	1,138	96	315*	104	41.79
12	D. L. Amiss.	1960–87	43,423	1,139	126	262*	102	42.86
13	M. C. Cowdrey	1950–76	42,719	1,130	134	307	107	42.89
14	A. Sandham.	1911–*37*	41,284	1,000	79	325	107	44.82
15	L. Hutton	1934–60	40,140	814	91	364	129	55.51
16	M. J. K. Smith.	1951–75	39,832	1,091	139	204	69	41.84
17	W. Rhodes.	1898–1930	39,802	1,528	237	267*	58	30.83
18	J. H. Edrich.	1956–78	39,790	979	104	310*	103	45.47
19	R. E. S. Wyatt	1923–57	39,405	1,141	157	232	85	40.04
20	D. C. S. Compton. . .	1936–64	38,942	839	88	300	123	51.85
21	E. Tyldesley.	1909–36	38,874	961	106	256*	102	45.46
22	J. T. Tyldesley	1895–1923	37,897	994	62	295*	86	40.66
23	K. W. R. Fletcher . . .	1962–88	37,665	1,167	170	228*	63	37.77
24	C. G. Greenidge	1970–92	37,354	889	75	273*	92	45.88
25	J. W. Hearne	1909–36	37,252	1,025	116	285*	96	40.98
26	L. E. G. Ames	1926–51	37,248	951	95	295	102	43.51
27	D. Kenyon.	1946–67	37,002	1,159	59	259	74	33.63
28	W. J. Edrich.	1934–58	36,965	964	92	267*	86	42.39
29	J. M. Parks	1949–76	36,673	1,227	172	205*	51	34.76
30	M. W. Gatting	1975–98	36,549	861	123	258	94	49.52
31	D. Denton	1894–1920	36,479	1,163	70	221	69	33.37
32	G. H. Hirst	1891–1929	36,323	1,215	151	341	60	34.13
33	I. V. A. Richards. . . .	*1971*–93	36,212	796	63	322	114	49.40
34	A. Jones	1957–83	36,049	1,168	72	204*	56	32.89
35	W. G. Quaife	1894–1928	36,012	1,203	185	255*	72	35.37
36	**G. A. Hick . . . .**	***1983*–2003**	**35,916**	**748**	**72**	**405***	**122**	**53.13**
37	R. E. Marshall	*1945*–72	35,725	1,053	59	228*	68	35.94
38	G. Gunn	1902–32	35,208	1,061	82	220	62	35.96
39	D. B. Close	1949–86	34,994	1,225	173	198	52	33.26
40	Zaheer Abbas.	*1965*–*86*	34,843	768	92	274	108	51.54
41	J. G. Langridge	1928–55	34,380	984	66	250*	76	37.45
42	G. M. Turner	*1964*–*82*	34,346	792	101	311*	103	49.70
43	C. Washbrook	1933–64	34,101	906	107	251*	76	42.67
44	M. Leyland	1920–48	33,660	932	101	263	80	40.50

		Career	*R*	*I*	*NO*	*HS*	*100s*	*Avge*
45	H. T. W. Hardinge. . .	1902–33	33,519	1,021	103	263*	75	36.51
46	R. Abel.	1881–1904	33,124	1,007	73	357*	74	35.46
47	A. I. Kallicharran . . .	*1966*–90	32,650	834	86	243*	87	43.64
48	A. J. Lamb	*1972*–95	32,502	772	108	294	89	48.94
49	C. A. Milton	1948–74	32,150	1,078	125	170	56	33.73
50	J. D. Robertson.	1937–59	31,914	897	46	331*	67	37.50
51	J. Hardstaff, jun. . . .	1930–55	31,847	812	94	266	83	44.35
52	James Langridge. . . .	1924–53	31,716	1,058	157	167	42	35.20
53	K. F. Barrington	1953–68	31,714	831	136	256	76	45.63
54	C. H. Lloyd.	*1963*–86	31,232	730	96	242*	79	49.26
55	Mushtaq Mohammad.	*1956*–85	31,091	843	104	303*	72	42.07
56	C. B. Fry	1892–*1921*	30,886	658	43	258*	94	50.22
57	D. Brookes	1934–59	30,874	925	70	257	71	36.10
58	P. Holmes	1913–35	30,573	810	84	315*	67	42.11
59	R. T. Simpson	*1944*–63	30,546	852	55	259	64	38.32
60	L. G. Berry	1924–51	30,225	1,056	57	232	45	30.25
	K. G. Suttle.	1949–71	30,225	1,064	92	204*	49	31.09
62	P. A. Perrin	1896–1928	29,709	918	91	343*	66	35.92
63	P. F. Warner	1894–1929	29,028	875	75	244	60	36.28
64	R. B. Kanhai	*1954–81*	28,774	669	82	256	83	49.01
65	J. O'Connor	1921–39	28,764	903	79	248	72	34.90
66	Javed Miandad	*1973–93*	28,647	631	95	311	80	53.44
67	T. E. Bailey	1945–67	28,641	1,072	215	205	28	33.42
68	K. J. Barnett	1979–2002	28,593	784	76	239*	61	40.38
69	D. W. Randall	1972–93	28,456	827	81	237	52	38.14
70	E. H. Bowley.	1912–34	28,378	859	47	283	52	34.94
71	B. A. Richards	*1964–82*	28,358	576	58	356	80	54.74
72	G. S. Sobers	*1952*–74	28,315	609	93	365*	86	54.87
73	A. E. Dipper	1908–32	28,075	865	69	252*	53	35.27
74	D. G. Bradman	*1927–48*	28,067	338	43	452*	117	95.14
75	J. H. Hampshire	1961–84	28,059	924	112	183*	43	34.55
76	P. B. H. May	1948–63	27,592	618	77	285*	85	51.00
77	R. T. Robinson.	1978–99	27,571	739	85	220*	63	42.15
78	B. F. Davison	*1967–87*	27,453	766	79	189	53	39.96
79	Majid Khan.	*1961–84*	27,444	700	62	241	73	43.01
80	A. C. Russell.	1908–30	27,358	717	59	273	71	41.57
81	E. G. Hayes	1896–1926	27,318	896	48	276	48	32.21
82	A. E. Fagg	1932–57	27,291	803	46	269*	58	36.05
83	James Seymour	1900–26	27,237	911	62	218*	53	32.08
84	W. Larkins.	1972–95	27,142	842	54	252	59	34.44
85	A. R. Border	*1976–95*	27,131	625	97	205	70	51.38
86	P. H. Parfitt	1956–*73*	26,924	845	104	200*	58	36.33
87	G. L. Jessop	1894–1914	26,698	855	37	286	53	32.63
88	K. S. McEwan	*1972–91*	26,628	705	67	218	74	41.73
89	D. E. Davies	1924–54	26,564	1,032	80	287*	32	27.90
90	**M. E. Waugh. . . . . .**	***1985–2003***	**26,557**	**582**	**74**	**229***	**81**	**52.27**
91	A. Shrewsbury	1875–1902	26,505	813	90	267	59	36.65
92	M. J. Stewart	1954–72	26,492	898	93	227*	49	32.90
93	C. T. Radley	1964–87	26,441	880	134	200	46	35.44
94	D. I. Gower	1975–93	26,339	727	70	228	53	40.08
95	C. E. B. Rice.	*1969–93*	26,331	766	123	246	48	40.95
96	**A. J. Stewart. . . . . .**	**1981–2003**	**26,165**	**734**	**81**	**271***	**48**	**40.06**
97	**R. A. Smith. . . . . . .**	***1980*–2003**	**26,155**	**717**	**87**	**209***	**61**	**41.51**
98	Younis Ahmed	*1961–86*	26,073	762	118	221*	46	40.48
99	P. E. Richardson	1949–65	26,055	794	41	185	44	34.60
100	D. L. Haynes	1976–96	26,030	639	72	255*	61	45.90
101	M. H. Denness.	1959–80	25,886	838	65	195	33	33.48
102	S. M. Gavaskar	*1966*–87	25,834	563	61	340	81	51.46
103	J. W. H. Makepeace. .	1906–30	25,799	778	66	203	43	36.23

		Career	R	I	NO	HS	100s	Avge
104	W. Gunn	1880–1904	25,691	850	72	273	48	33.02
105	W. Watson	1939–64	25,670	753	109	257	55	39.86
106	G. Brown	1908–33	25,649	1,012	52	232*	37	26.71
107	G. M. Emmett	1936–59	25,602	865	50	188	37	31.41
108	J. B. Bolus	1956–75	25,598	833	81	202*	39	34.03
109	W. E. Russell	1956–72	25,525	796	64	193	41	34.87
110	C. W. J. Athey	1976–97	25,453	784	71	184	55	35.69
111	C. J. Barnett	1927–*53*	25,389	821	45	259	48	32.71
112	L. B. Fishlock	1931–52	25,376	699	54	253	56	39.34
113	D. J. Insole	1947–63	25,241	743	72	219*	54	37.61
114	J. M. Brearley	1961–83	25,185	768	102	312*	45	37.81
115	J. Vine	1896–1922	25,171	920	79	202	34	29.92
116	R. M. Prideaux	1958–*74*	25,136	808	75	202*	41	34.29
117	J. H. King	1895–1925	25,122	988	69	227*	34	27.33
118	J. G. Wright	*1975–92*	25,073	636	44	192	59	42.35

Bold type denotes those who have played since the start of 2002-03.

Note: Some works of reference provide career figures which differ from those in this list, owing to the exclusion or inclusion of matches recognised or not recognised as first-class by *Wisden*.

Other Current Players with 20,000 Runs

	Career	R	I	NO	HS	100s	Avge
M. P. Maynard	1985–2003	23,873	617	57	243	56	42.63
S. R. Waugh	*1984–2003*	23,677	540	88	216*	79	52.38
M. R. Ramprakash	1987–2003	23,223	560	70	279*	66	47.39
C. L. Hooper	*1984*–2003	22,341	514	49	236*	67	48.04
S. G. Law	*1988–2003*	21,494	477	51	263	63	50.45
N. Hussain	1987–*2003*	20,106	532	51	207	50	41.80

CAREER AVERAGE OVER 50

(Qualification: 10,000 runs)

Avge		Career	I	NO	R	HS	100s
95.14	D. G. Bradman	*1927–48*	338	43	28,067	452*	117
71.22	V. M. Merchant	*1929–51*	229	43	13,248	359*	44
67.46	Ajay Sharma	*1984–2000*	166	16	10,120	259*	38
65.18	W. H. Ponsford	*1920–34*	235	23	13,819	437	47
64.99	W. M. Woodfull	*1921–34*	245	39	13,388	284	49
60.28	**S. R. Tendulkar**	***1988–2003***	**319**	**31**	**17,363**	**233***	**55**
58.24	A. L. Hassett	*1932–53*	322	32	16,890	232	59
58.19	V. S. Hazare	*1934–66*	365	45	18,621	316*	60
58.05	**R. T. Ponting**	***1992–2003***	**270**	**38**	**13,469**	**257**	**49**
57.45	**M. G. Bevan**	***1989–2003***	**355**	**62**	**16,833**	**216**	**59**
57.35	**R. Dravid**	***1990–2003***	**302**	**43**	**14,855**	**233**	**41**
57.22	A. F. Kippax	*1918–35*	256	33	12,762	315*	43
56.91	**D. S. Lehmann**	***1987–2003***	**376**	**26**	**19,921**	**255**	**64**
56.83	G. Boycott	1962–86	1,014	162	48,426	261*	151
56.55	C. L. Walcott	*1941–63*	238	29	11,820	314*	40
56.37	K. S. Ranjitsinhji	1893–1920	500	62	24,692	285*	72
56.32	**V. V. S. Laxman**	***1992–2003***	**227**	**26**	**11,321**	**353**	**35**
56.22	R. B. Simpson	*1952–77*	436	62	21,029	359	60
56.10	W. R. Hammond	1920–51	1,005	104	50,551	336*	167

Avge		*Career*	*I*	*NO*	*R*	*HS*	*100s*
56.02	M. D. Crowe	*1979–95*	412	62	19,608	299	71
55.51	L. Hutton	1934–60	814	91	40,140	364	129
55.34	E. D. Weekes	*1944*–64	241	24	12,010	304*	36
55.11	S. V. Manjrekar	*1984–97*	217	31	10,252	377	31
54.96	**M. L. Hayden**	***1991–2003***	**396**	**41**	**19,511**	**380**	**65**
54.87	G. S. Sobers	*1952*–74	609	93	28,315	365*	86
54.74	B. A. Richards	*1964–82*	576	58	28,358	356	80
54.67	R. G. Pollock	*1960–86*	437	54	20,940	274	64
54.24	F. M. M. Worrell	*1941*–64	326	49	15,025	308*	39
53.78	R. M. Cowper	*1959–69*	228	31	10,595	307	26
53.67	A. R. Morris	*1940–63*	250	15	12,614	290	46
53.44	Javed Miandad	*1973–93*	631	95	28,647	311	80
53.13	**G. A. Hick**	***1983*–2003**	**748**	**72**	**35,916**	**405***	**122**
52.86	D. B. Vengsarkar	*1975–91*	390	52	17,868	284	55
52.72	**A. Flower**	***1986–2003***	**287**	**54**	**12,284**	**232***	**34**
52.58	**M. E. K. Hussey**	***1994–2003***	**253**	**18**	**12,357**	**331***	**32**
52.38	**S. R. Waugh**	***1984–2003***	**540**	**88**	**23,677**	**216***	**79**
52.32	Hanif Mohammad	*1951–75*	371	45	17,059	499	55
52.27	P. R. Umrigar	*1944–67*	350	41	16,154	252*	49
52.27	**M. E. Waugh**	***1985–2003***	**582**	**74**	**26,557**	**229***	**81**
52.20	G. S. Chappell	*1966–83*	542	72	24,535	247*	74
51.98	M. Azharuddin	*1981–99*	343	38	15,855	226	54
51.95	H. Sutcliffe	1919–45	1,088	123	50,138	313	149
51.85	D. M. Jones	*1981–97*	415	45	19,188	324*	55
51.85	D. C. S. Compton	1936–64	839	88	38,942	300	123
51.54	Zaheer Abbas	*1965–86*	768	92	34,843	274	108
51.53	A. D. Nourse	*1931–52*	269	27	12,472	260*	41
51.46	S. M. Gavaskar	*1966*–87	563	61	25,834	340	81
51.44	W. A. Brown	*1932–49*	284	15	13,838	265*	39
51.38	A. R. Border	*1976–95*	625	97	27,131	205	70
51.14	**Inzamam-ul-Haq**	***1985–2003***	**330**	**50**	**14,320**	**329**	**38**
51.03	**B. C. Lara**	***1987–2003***	**371**	**9**	**18,476**	**501***	**51**
51.00	P. B. H. May	1948–63	618	77	27,592	285*	85
50.98	**S. Chanderpaul**	***1991–2003***	**250**	**41**	**10,656**	**303***	**31**
50.97	**M. S. Atapattu**	***1988–2003***	**287**	**48**	**12,184**	**253***	**40**
50.95	N. C. O'Neill	*1955–67*	306	34	13,859	284	45
50.93	R. N. Harvey	*1946–62*	461	35	21,699	231*	67
50.90	W. M. Lawry	*1955–71*	417	49	18,734	266	50
50.90	A. V. Mankad	*1963–82*	326	71	12,980	265	31
50.80	E. H. Hendren	1907–38	1,300	166	57,611	301*	170
50.72	**J. H. Kallis**	***1993–2003***	**247**	**31**	**10,957**	**200**	**29**
50.65	J. B. Hobbs	1905–34	1,315	106	61,237	316*	197
50.61	**J. L. Langer**	***1991–2003***	**421**	**42**	**19,183**	**274***	**61**
50.58	K. C. Wessels	*1973–99*	539	50	24,738	254	66
50.58	S. J. Cook	*1972–94*	475	57	21,143	313*	64
50.46	**M. L. Love**	***1992–2003***	**264**	**24**	**12,111**	**300***	**28**
50.45	**S. G. Law**	***1988–2003***	**477**	**51**	**21,494**	**263**	**63**
50.22	C. B. Fry	1892–*1921*	658	43	30,886	258*	94

Note: G. A. Headley (*1927*–1954) scored 9,921 runs, average 69.86.

Bold type denotes those who have played since the start of 2002-03.

"As Bichel and Bevan ran off delirious, England stood still. How had this happened?"

The World Cup, page 989.

FASTEST FIFTIES

Minutes			
11	C. I. J. Smith (66)	Middlesex v Gloucestershire at Bristol	1938
13	Khalid Mahmood (56)	Gujranwala v Sargodha at Gujranwala	2000-01
14	S. J. Pegler (50)	South Africans v Tasmania at Launceston	1910-11
14	F. T. Mann (53)	Middlesex v Nottinghamshire at Lord's	1921
14	H. B. Cameron (56)	Transvaal v Orange Free State at Johannesburg	1934-35
14	C. I. J. Smith (52)	Middlesex v Kent at Maidstone	1935

Note: The following fast fifties were scored in contrived circumstances when runs were given from full tosses and long hops to expedite a declaration: C. C. Inman (8 minutes), Leicestershire v Nottinghamshire at Nottingham, 1965; G. Chapple (10 minutes), Lancashire v Glamorgan at Manchester, 1993; T. M. Moody (11 minutes), Warwickshire v Glamorgan at Swansea, 1990; A. J. Stewart (14 minutes), Surrey v Kent at Dartford, 1986; M. P. Maynard (14 minutes), Glamorgan v Yorkshire at Cardiff, 1987.

FASTEST HUNDREDS

Minutes			
35	P. G. H. Fender (113*)	Surrey v Northamptonshire at Northampton	1920
40	G. L. Jessop (101)	Gloucestershire v Yorkshire at Harrogate	1897
40	Ahsan-ul-Haq (100*)	Muslims v Sikhs at Lahore	1923-24
42	G. L. Jessop (191)	Gentlemen of South v Players of South at Hastings	1907
43	A. H. Hornby (106)	Lancashire v Somerset at Manchester	1905
43	D. W. Hookes (107)	South Australia v Victoria at Adelaide	1982-83
44	R. N. S. Hobbs (100)	Essex v Australians at Chelmsford	1975

Notes: The fastest recorded authentic hundred in terms of balls received was scored off 34 balls by D. W. Hookes (above).

Research of the scorebook has shown that P. G. H. Fender scored his hundred from between 40 and 46 balls. He contributed 113 to an unfinished sixth-wicket partnership of 171 in 42 minutes with H. A. Peach.

E. B. Alletson (Nottinghamshire) scored 189 out of 227 runs in 90 minutes against Sussex at Hove in 1911. It has been estimated that his last 139 runs took 37 minutes.

The following fast hundreds were scored in contrived circumstances when full tosses, long hops etc were bowled deliberately to expedite a declaration: G. Chapple (21 minutes), Lancashire v Glamorgan at Manchester, 1993; T. M. Moody (26 minutes), Warwickshire v Glamorgan at Swansea, 1990; S. J. O'Shaughnessy (35 minutes), Lancashire v Leicestershire at Manchester, 1983; C. M. Old (37 minutes), Yorkshire v Warwickshire at Birmingham, 1977; N. F. M. Popplewell (41 minutes), Somerset v Gloucestershire at Bath, 1983.

FASTEST DOUBLE-HUNDREDS

Minutes			
113	R. J. Shastri (200*)	Bombay v Baroda at Bombay	1984-85
120	G. L. Jessop (286)	Gloucestershire v Sussex at Hove	1903
120	C. H. Lloyd (201*)	West Indians v Glamorgan at Swansea	1976
130	G. L. Jessop (234)	Gloucestershire v Somerset at Bristol	1905
131	V. T. Trumper (293)	Australians v Canterbury at Christchurch	1913-14

FASTEST TRIPLE-HUNDREDS

Minutes			
181	D. C. S. Compton (300)	MCC v N. E. Transvaal at Benoni	1948-49
205	F. E. Woolley (305*)	MCC v Tasmania at Hobart	1911-12
205	C. G. Macartney (345)	Australians v Nottinghamshire at Nottingham	1921
213	D. G. Bradman (369)	South Australia v Tasmania at Adelaide	1935-36

MOST RUNS IN A DAY BY ONE BATSMAN

390*	B. C. Lara	Warwickshire v Durham at Birmingham	1994
345	C. G. Macartney	Australians v Nottinghamshire at Nottingham	1921
334	W. H. Ponsford	Victoria v New South Wales at Melbourne	1926-27
333	K. S. Duleepsinhji	Sussex v Northamptonshire at Hove	1930
331*	J. D. Robertson	Middlesex v Worcestershire at Worcester	1949
325*	B. A. Richards	S. Australia v W. Australia at Perth	1970-71

Note: These scores do not necessarily represent the complete innings. See pages 160–162.

There have been another 13 instances of a batsman scoring 300 runs in a day (see *Wisden* 2003, pages 278–279, for full list).

LONGEST INNINGS

Mins			
1,015	R. Nayyar (271)	Himachal Pradesh v Jammu and Kashmir at Chamba	1999-2000
970	Hanif Mohammad (337)	Pakistan v West Indies at Bridgetown	1957-58
	Hanif believes he batted 999 minutes.		
878	G. Kirsten (275)	South Africa v England at Durban	1999-2000
799	S. T. Jayasuriya (340)	Sri Lanka v India at Colombo	1997-98
797	L. Hutton (364)	England v Australia at The Oval	1938

1,000 RUNS IN MAY

	Runs	*Avge*
W. G. Grace, May 9 to May 30, 1895 (22 days)	1,016	112.88
Grace was 46 years old.		
W. R. Hammond, May 7 to May 31, 1927 (25 days)	1,042	74.42
Hammond scored his 1,000th run on May 28, thus equalling Grace's record of 22 days.		
C. Hallows, May 5 to May 31, 1928 (27 days)	1,000	125.00

1,000 RUNS IN APRIL AND MAY

	Runs	*Avge*
T. W. Hayward, April 16 to May 31, 1900	1,074	97.63
D. G. Bradman, April 30 to May 31, 1930	1,001	143.00
On April 30 Bradman was 75 not out.		
D. G. Bradman, April 30 to May 31, 1938	1,056	150.85
Bradman scored 258 on April 30, and his 1,000th run on May 27.		
W. J. Edrich, April 30 to May 31, 1938	1,010	84.16
Edrich was 21 not out on April 30. All his runs were scored at Lord's.		
G. M. Turner, April 24 to May 31, 1973	1,018	78.30
G. A. Hick, April 17 to May 29, 1988	1,019	101.90
Hick scored a record 410 runs in April, and his 1,000th run on May 28.		

MOST RUNS SCORED OFF AN OVER

(All instances refer to six-ball overs)

36	G. S. Sobers	off M. A. Nash, Nottinghamshire v Glamorgan at Swansea (six sixes)	1968
36	R. J. Shastri	off Tilak Raj, Bombay v Baroda at Bombay (six sixes)	1984-85
34	E. B. Alletson	off E. H. Killick, Nottinghamshire v Sussex at Hove (46604446; including two no-balls)	1911
34	F. C. Hayes	off M. A. Nash, Lancashire v Glamorgan at Swansea (646666)	1977
34†	A. Flintoff	off A. J. Tudor, Lancashire v Surrey at Manchester (64444660; including two no-balls)	1998
32	I. T. Botham	off I. R. Snook, England XI v Central Districts at Palmerston North (466466)	1983-84
32	P. W. G. Parker	off A. I. Kallicharran, Sussex v Warwickshire at Birmingham (466664)	1982
32	I. R. Redpath	off N. Rosendorff, Australians v Orange Free State at Bloemfontein (666644)	1969-70
32	C. C. Smart	off G. Hill, Glamorgan v Hampshire at Cardiff (664664)	1935
32	Khalid Mahmood	off Naved Latif, Gujranwala v Sargodha at Gujranwala (666662)	2000-01

† *Altogether 38 runs were scored off this over, the two no-balls counting for two extra runs each under ECB regulations.*

Notes: The following instances have been excluded from the above table because of the bowlers' compliance: 34 – M. P. Maynard off S. A. Marsh, Glamorgan v Kent at Swansea, 1992; 34 – G. Chapple off P. A. Cottey, Lancashire v Glamorgan at Manchester, 1993; 34 – F. B. Touzel off F. J. J. Viljoen, Western Province B v Griqualand West at Kimberley, 1993-94; 32 – C. C. Inman off N. W. Hill, Leicestershire v Nottinghamshire at Nottingham, 1965; 32 – T. E. Jesty off R. J. Boyd-Moss, Hampshire v Northamptonshire at Southampton, 1984; 32 – M. A. Ealham off G. D. Hodgson, Kent v Gloucestershire at Bristol, 1992; 32 – G. Chapple off P. A. Cottey, Lancashire v Glamorgan at Manchester, 1993. Chapple's 34 and 32 came off successive overs from Cottey.

There were 35 runs off an over received by A. T. Reinholds off H. T. Davis, Auckland v Wellington at Auckland 1995-96, but this included six no-balls (counting as two runs each), four byes and only 19 off the bat.

In a Shell Trophy match against Canterbury at Christchurch in 1989-90, R. H. Vance (Wellington), acting on the instructions of his captain, deliberately conceded 77 runs in an over of full tosses which contained 17 no-balls and, owing to the umpire's understandable miscalculation, only five legitimate deliveries.

The greatest number of runs scored off an eight-ball over is 34 (40446664) by R. M. Edwards off M. C. Carew, Governor-General's XI v West Indians at Auckland, 1968-69.

MOST SIXES IN AN INNINGS

16	A. Symonds (254*)	Gloucestershire v Glamorgan at Abergavenny	1995
15	J. R. Reid (296)	Wellington v Northern Districts at Wellington	1962-63
14	Shakti Singh (128)	Himachal Pradesh v Haryana at Dharmsala	1990-91
13	Majid Khan (147*)	Pakistanis v Glamorgan at Swansea	1967
13	C. G. Greenidge (273*)	D. H. Robins' XI v Pakistanis at Eastbourne	1974
13	C. G. Greenidge (259)	Hampshire v Sussex at Southampton	1975
13	G. W. Humpage (254)	Warwickshire v Lancashire at Southport	1982
13	R. J. Shastri (200*)	Bombay v Baroda at Bombay	1984-85
12	Gulfraz Khan (207)	Railways v Universities at Lahore	1976-77
12	I. T. Botham (138*)	Somerset v Warwickshire at Birmingham	1985
12	R. A. Harper (234)	Northamptonshire v Gloucestershire at Northampton	1986
12	D. M. Jones (248)	Australians v Warwickshire at Birmingham	1989
12	U. N. K. Fernando (160)	Sinhalese SC v Sebastianites C and AC at Colombo	1990-91
12	D. N. Patel (204)	Auckland v Northern Districts at Auckland	1991-92
12	W. V. Raman (206)	Tamil Nadu v Kerala at Madras	1991-92
12	G. D. Lloyd (241)	Lancashire v Essex at Chelmsford	1996
12	Wasim Akram (257*)	Pakistan v Zimbabwe at Sheikhupura	1996-97

11	C. K. Nayudu (153)	Hindus v MCC at Bombay	1926-27
11	C. J. Barnett (194)	Gloucestershire v Somerset at Bath	1934
11	R. Benaud (135)	Australians v T. N. Pearce's XI at Scarborough	1953
11	R. Bora (126)	Assam v Tripura at Gauhati	1987-88
11	G. A. Hick (405*)	Worcestershire v Somerset at Taunton	1988
11	A. S. Jayasinghe (183)	Tamil Union v Burgher RC at Colombo	1996-97
11	N. J. Astle (222)	New Zealand v England at Christchurch	2001-02
11	C. L. Hooper (201)	Lancashire v Middlesex at Manchester	2003
11	I. D. Blackwell (247*)	Somerset v Derbyshire at Taunton	2003
11	M. L. Hayden (380)	Australia v Zimbabwe at Perth	2003-04
11	C. M. Spearman (133)	Central Districts v Auckland at Auckland	2003-04

Note: F. B. Touzel (128*) hit 13 sixes for Western Province B v Griqualand West in contrived circumstances at Kimberley in 1993-94.

MOST SIXES IN A MATCH

20	A. Symonds (254*, 76)	Gloucestershire v Glamorgan at Abergavenny	1995
17	W. J. Stewart (155, 125)	Warwickshire v Lancashire at Blackpool	1959

MOST SIXES IN A SEASON

80	I. T. Botham	1985
66	A. W. Wellard	1935
57	A. W. Wellard	1936
57	A. W. Wellard	1938
51	A. W. Wellard	1933
49	I. V. A. Richards	1985
48	A. W. Carr	1925
48	J. H. Edrich	1965
48	A. Symonds	1995

MOST BOUNDARIES IN AN INNINGS

	4s/6s			
72	62/10	B. C. Lara (501*)	Warwickshire v Durham at Birmingham	1994
68	68/–	P. A. Perrin (343*)	Essex v Derbyshire at Chesterfield	1904
65	64/1	A. C. MacLaren (424)	Lancashire v Somerset at Taunton	1895
64	64/–	Hanif Mohammad (499)	Karachi v Bahawalpur at Karachi	1958-59
57	52/5	J. H. Edrich (310*)	England v New Zealand at Leeds	1965
57	52/5	Naved Latif (394)	Sargodha v Gujranwala at Gujranwala	2000-01
55	55/–	C. W. Gregory (383)	NSW v Queensland at Brisbane	1906-07
55	53/2	G. R. Marsh (355*)	W. Australia v S. Australia at Perth	1989-90
55	51/3†	S. V. Manjrekar (377)	Bombay v Hyderabad at Bombay	1990-91
54	53/1	G. H. Hirst (341)	Yorkshire v Leicestershire at Leicester	1905
53	53/–	A. W. Nourse (304*)	Natal v Transvaal at Johannesburg	1919-20
53	45/8	K. R. Rutherford (317)	New Zealanders v D. B. Close's XI at Scarborough	1986
53	51/2	V. V. S. Laxman (353)	Hyderabad v Karnataka at Bangalore	1999-2000
53	52/1	M. W. Goodwin (335*)	Sussex v Leicestershire at Hove	2003
52	47/5	N. H. Fairbrother (366)	Lancashire v Surrey at The Oval	1990
51	51/–	W. G. Grace (344)	MCC v Kent at Canterbury	1876
51	47/4	C. G. Macartney (345)	Australians v Notts at Nottingham	1921
51	50/1	B. B. Nimbalkar (443*)	Maharashtra v Kathiawar at Poona	1948-49
51	49/2	G. A. Hick (315*)	Worcestershire v Durham at Worcester	2002
50	47/–‡	A. Ducat (306*)	Surrey v Oxford U. at The Oval	1919
50	46/4	D. G. Bradman (369)	S. Australia v Tasmania at Adelaide	1935-36
50	35/15	J. R. Reid (296)	Wellington v N. Districts at Wellington	1962-63
50	42/8	I. V. A. Richards (322)	Somerset v Warwickshire at Taunton	1985

† *Plus one five.*
‡ *Plus three fives.*

PARTNERSHIPS OVER 500

577 for 4th	V. S. Hazare (288) and Gul Mahomed (319), Baroda v Holkar at Baroda	1946-47
576 for 2nd	S. T. Jayasuriya (340) and R. S. Mahanama (225), Sri Lanka v India at Colombo	1997-98
574* for 4th	F. M. M. Worrell (255*) and C. L. Walcott (314*), Barbados v Trinidad at Port-of-Spain	1945-46
561 for 1st	Waheed Mirza (324) and Mansoor Akhtar (224*), Karachi Whites v Quetta at Karachi	1976-77
555 for 1st	P. Holmes (224*) and H. Sutcliffe (313), Yorkshire v Essex at Leyton	1932
554 for 1st	J. T. Brown (300) and J. Tunnicliffe (243), Yorkshire v Derbyshire at Chesterfield	1898
502* for 4th	F. M. M. Worrell (308*) and J. D. C. Goddard (218*), Barbados v Trinidad at Bridgetown	1943-44

HIGHEST PARTNERSHIPS FOR EACH WICKET

The following lists include all stands above 400; otherwise the top ten for each wicket.

First Wicket

561	Waheed Mirza and Mansoor Akhtar, Karachi Whites v Quetta at Karachi	1976-77
555	P. Holmes and H. Sutcliffe, Yorkshire v Essex at Leyton	1932
554	J. T. Brown and J. Tunnicliffe, Yorkshire v Derbyshire at Chesterfield	1898
490	E. H. Bowley and J. G. Langridge, Sussex v Middlesex at Hove	1933
464	R. Sehgal and R. Lamba, Delhi v Himachal Pradesh at Delhi	1994-95
459	Wasim Jaffer and S. K. Kulkarni, Mumbai v Saurashtra at Rajkot	1996-97
456	E. R. Mayne and W. H. Ponsford, Victoria v Queensland at Melbourne	1923-24
451*	S. Desai and R. M. H. Binny, Karnataka v Kerala at Chikmagalur	1977-78
431	M. R. J. Veletta and G. R. Marsh, Western Australia v South Australia at Perth	1989-90
428	J. B. Hobbs and A. Sandham, Surrey v Oxford University at The Oval	1926
425*	L. V. Garrick and C. H. Gayle, Jamaica v West Indies B at Montego Bay	2000-01
424	I. J. Siedle and J. F. W. Nicolson, Natal v Orange Free State at Bloemfontein	1926-27
421	S. M. Gavaskar and G. A. Parkar, Bombay v Bengal at Bombay	1981-82
418	Kamal Najamuddin and Khalid Alvi, Karachi v Railways at Karachi	1980-81
413	V. Mankad and Pankaj Roy, India v New Zealand at Madras	1955-56
406*	D. J. Bicknell and G. E. Welton, Notts v Warwickshire at Birmingham	2000
405	C. P. S. Chauhan and M. S. Gupte, Maharashtra v Vidarbha at Poona	1972-73
403	Rizwan-uz-Zaman and Shoaib Mohammad, PIA v Hyderabad at Hyderabad	1999-2000

Second Wicket

576	S. T. Jayasuriya and R. S. Mahanama, Sri Lanka v India at Colombo	1997-98
475	Zahir Alam and L. S. Rajput, Assam v Tripura at Gauhati	1991-92
465*	J. A. Jameson and R. B. Kanhai, Warwicks v Gloucestershire at Birmingham	1974
455	K. V. Bhandarkar and B. B. Nimbalkar, Maharashtra v Kathiawar at Poona	1948-49
451	W. H. Ponsford and D. G. Bradman, Australia v England at The Oval	1934
446	C. C. Hunte and G. S. Sobers, West Indies v Pakistan at Kingston	1957-58
441	C. C. Bradfield and J. D. C. Bryant, Eastern Province v North West at Potchefstroom	2002-03
429*	J. G. Dewes and G. H. G. Doggart, Cambridge U. v Essex at Cambridge	1949
426	Arshad Pervez and Mohsin Khan, Habib Bank v Income Tax at Lahore	1977-78
417	K. J. Barnett and T. A. Tweats, Derbyshire v Yorkshire at Derby	1997
415	A. Jadeja and S. V. Manjrekar, Indians v Bowl XI at Springs	1992-93
403	G. A. Gooch and P. J. Prichard, Essex v Leicestershire at Chelmsford	1990

Third Wicket

467	A. H. Jones and M. D. Crowe, New Zealand v Sri Lanka at Wellington	1990-91
456	Khalid Irtiza and Aslam Ali, United Bank v Multan at Karachi	1975-76
451	Mudassar Nazar and Javed Miandad, Pakistan v India at Hyderabad	1982-83
445	P. E. Whitelaw and W. N. Carson, Auckland v Otago at Dunedin	1936-37
438*	G. A. Hick and T. M. Moody, Worcestershire v Hampshire at Southampton	1997
436*	D. L. Maddy and B. J. Hodge, Leicestershire v Loughborough UCCE at Leicester	2003
436	S. S. Das and S. S. Raul, Orissa v Bengal at Baripada	2001-02
434	J. B. Stollmeyer and G. E. Gomez, Trinidad v British Guiana at Port-of-Spain	1946-47
429*	J. A. Rudolph and H. H. Dippenaar, South Africa v Bangladesh at Chittagong	2003
424*	W. J. Edrich and D. C. S. Compton, Middlesex v Somerset at Lord's	1948
413	D. J. Bicknell and D. M. Ward, Surrey v Kent at Canterbury	1990
410*	R. S. Modi and L. Amarnath, India in England v The Rest at Calcutta	1946-47
409	V. V. S. Laxman and R. Dravid, South Zone v West Zone at Surat	2000-01
406*	R. S. Gavaskar and S. J. Kalyani, Bengal v Tripura at Agartala	1999-2000
405	A. Jadeja and A. S. Kaypee, Haryana v Services at Faridabad	1991-92

Fourth Wicket

577	V. S. Hazare and Gul Mahomed, Baroda v Holkar at Baroda	1946-47
574*	C. L. Walcott and F. M. M. Worrell, Barbados v Trinidad at Port-of-Spain	1945-46
502*	F. M. M. Worrell and J. D. C. Goddard, Barbados v Trinidad at Bridgetown	1943-44
470	A. I. Kallicharran and G. W. Humpage, Warwicks v Lancs at Southport	1982
462*	D. W. Hookes and W. B. Phillips, South Australia v Tasmania at Adelaide	1986-87
448	R. Abel and T. W. Hayward, Surrey v Yorkshire at The Oval	1899
436	S. Abbas Ali and P. K. Dwevedi, Madhya Pradesh v Railways at Indore	1997-98
425*	A. Dale and I. V. A. Richards, Glamorgan v Middlesex at Cardiff	1993
424	I. S. Lee and S. O. Quin, Victoria v Tasmania at Melbourne	1933-34
411	P. B. H. May and M. C. Cowdrey, England v West Indies at Birmingham	1957
410	G. Abraham and P. Balan Pandit, Kerala v Andhra at Palghat	1959-60
402	W. Watson and T. W. Graveney, MCC v British Guiana at Georgetown	1953-54
402	R. B. Kanhai and K. Ibadulla, Warwicks v Notts at Nottingham	1968

Fifth Wicket

464*	M. E. Waugh and S. R. Waugh, New South Wales v Western Australia at Perth	1990-91
405	S. G. Barnes and D. G. Bradman, Australia v England at Sydney	1946-47
401	M. B. Loye and D. Ripley, Northamptonshire v Glamorgan at Northampton	1998
397	W. Bardsley and C. Kelleway, New South Wales v South Australia at Sydney	1920-21
393	E. G. Arnold and W. B. Burns, Worcestershire v Warwickshire at Birmingham	1909
391	A. Malhotra and S. Dogra, Delhi v Services at Delhi	1995-96
385	S. R. Waugh and G. S. Blewett, Australia v South Africa at Johannesburg	1996-97
381	R. Nayyar and V. Sehwag, North Zone v South Zone at Agartala	1999-2000
377*	G. P. Thorpe and M. R. Ramprakash, England XI v South Australia at Adelaide	1998-99
376	V. V. S. Laxman and R. Dravid, India v Australia at Kolkata	2000-01

Sixth Wicket

487*	G. A. Headley and C. C. Passailaigue, Jamaica v Lord Tennyson's XI at Kingston	1931-32
428	W. W. Armstrong and M. A. Noble, Australians v Sussex at Hove	1902
411	R. M. Poore and E. G. Wynyard, Hampshire v Somerset at Taunton	1899
376	R. Subba Row and A. Lightfoot, Northamptonshire v Surrey at The Oval	1958
372*	K. P. Pietersen and J. E. Morris, Nottinghamshire v Derbyshire at Derby	2001
371	V. M. Merchant and R. S. Modi, Bombay v Maharashtra at Bombay	1943-44
365	B. C. Lara and R. D. Jacobs, West Indians v Australia A at Hobart	2000-01
356	W. V. Raman and A. Kripal Singh, Tamil Nadu v Goa at Panjim	1988-89
353	Salah-ud-Din and Zaheer Abbas, Karachi v East Pakistan at Karachi	1968-69
346	J. H. W. Fingleton and D. G. Bradman, Australia v England at Melbourne	1936-37

Seventh Wicket

460	Bhupinder Singh, jun. and P. Dharmani, Punjab v Delhi at Delhi	1994-95
347	D. St E. Atkinson and C. C. Depeiza, West Indies v Australia at Bridgetown	1954-55
344	K. S. Ranjitsinhji and W. Newham, Sussex v Essex at Leyton	1902
340	K. J. Key and H. Philipson, Oxford University v Middlesex at Chiswick Park	1887
336	F. C. W. Newman and C. R. N. Maxwell, Sir J. Cahn's XI v Leicestershire at Nottingham	1935
335	C. W. Andrews and E. C. Bensted, Queensland v New South Wales at Sydney	1934-35
325	G. Brown and C. H. Abercrombie, Hampshire v Essex at Leyton	1913
323	E. H. Hendren and L. F. Townsend, MCC v Barbados at Bridgetown	1929-30
308	Waqar Hassan and Imtiaz Ahmed, Pakistan v New Zealand at Lahore	1955-56
301	C. C. Lewis and B. N. French, Nottinghamshire v Durham at Chester-le-Street	1993

Eighth Wicket

433	V. T. Trumper and A. Sims, A. Sims' Aust. XI v Canterbury at Christchurch	1913-14
313	Wasim Akram and Saqlain Mushtaq, Pakistan v Zimbabwe at Sheikhupura	1996-97
292	R. Peel and Lord Hawke, Yorkshire v Warwickshire at Birmingham	1896
291	R. S. C. Martin-Jenkins and M. J. G. Davis, Sussex v Somerset at Taunton	2002
270	V. T. Trumper and E. P. Barbour, New South Wales v Victoria at Sydney	1912-13
268	S. Sriram and M. R. Srinivas, Tamil Nadu v Punjab at Mohali	2002-03
263	D. R. Wilcox and R. M. Taylor, Essex v Warwickshire at Southend	1946
255	E. A. V. Williams and E. A. Martindale, Barbados v Trinidad at Bridgetown	1935-36
253	N. J. Astle and A. C. Parore, New Zealand v Australia at Perth	2001-02
249*	Shaukat Mirza and Akram Raza, Habib Bank v PNSC at Lahore	1993-94

Ninth Wicket

283	J. Chapman and A. Warren, Derbyshire v Warwickshire at Blackwell	1910
268	J. B. Commins and N. Boje, South Africa A v Mashonaland at Harare	1994-95
251	J. W. H. T. Douglas and S. N. Hare, Essex v Derbyshire at Leyton	1921
249*†	A. S. Srivastava and K. Seth, Madhya Pradesh v Vidarbha at Indore	2000-01
245	V. S. Hazare and N. D. Nagarwalla, Maharashtra v Baroda at Poona	1939-40
244*	Arshad Ayub and M. V. Ramanamurthy, Hyderabad v Bihar at Hyderabad	1986-87
239	H. B. Cave and I. B. Leggat, Central Districts v Otago at Dunedin	1952-53
232	C. Hill and E. Walkley, South Australia v New South Wales at Adelaide	1900-01
231	P. Sen and J. Mitter, Bengal v Bihar at Jamshedpur	1950-51
230	D. A. Livingstone and A. T. Castell, Hampshire v Surrey at Southampton	1962

† 276 unbeaten runs were scored for this wicket in two separate partnerships; after Srivastava retired hurt, Seth and N. D. Hirwani added 27.

Tenth Wicket

307	A. F. Kippax and J. E. H. Hooker, New South Wales v Victoria at Melbourne	1928-29
249	C. T. Sarwate and S. N. Banerjee, Indians v Surrey at The Oval	1946
235	F. E. Woolley and A. Fielder, Kent v Worcestershire at Stourbridge	1909
233	Ajay Sharma and Maninder Singh, Delhi v Bombay at Bombay	1991-92
230	R. W. Nicholls and W. Roche, Middlesex v Kent at Lord's	1899
228	R. Illingworth and K. Higgs, Leicestershire v Northamptonshire at Leicester	1977
218	F. H. Vigar and T. P. B. Smith, Essex v Derbyshire at Chesterfield	1947
214	N. V. Knight and A. Richardson, Warwickshire v Hampshire at Birmingham	2002
211	M. Ellis and T. J. Hastings, Victoria v South Australia at Melbourne	1902-03
196*	Nadim Yousuf and Maqsood Kundi, MCB v National Bank at Lahore	1981-82

UNUSUAL DISMISSALS

Handled the Ball

There have been **49** instances in first-class cricket. The most recent are:

G. A. Gooch	England v Australia at Manchester	1993
A. C. Waller	Mashonaland CD v Mashonaland Under-24 at Harare	1994-95
K. M. Krikken	Derbyshire v Indians at Derby	1996
A. Badenhorst	Eastern Province B v North West at Fochville	1998-99
S. R. Waugh	Australia v India at Chennai	2000-01
M. P. Vaughan	England v India at Bangalore	2001-02
Tushar Imran	Bangladesh A v Jamaica at Spanish Town	2001-02
Al Sahariar	Dhaka v Chittagong at Dhaka	2003-04

Obstructing the Field

There have been **19** instances in first-class cricket. T. Straw of Worcestershire was given out for obstruction v Warwickshire in both 1899 and 1901. The last occurrence in England involved K. Ibadulla of Warwickshire v Hampshire at Coventry in 1963. The most recent are:

Arshad Ali	Sukkur v Quetta at Quetta	1983-84
H. R. Wasu	Vidarbha v Rajasthan at Akola	1984-85
Khalid Javed	Railways v Lahore at Lahore	1985-86
C. Binduhewa	Singha SC v Sinhalese SC at Colombo	1990-91
S. J. Kalyani	Bengal v Orissa at Calcutta	1994-95
R. C. Rupasinghe	Rio v Kurunegala Youth at Colombo	2001-02

Hit the Ball Twice

There have been **20** instances in first-class cricket. The last occurrence in England involved J. H. King of Leicestershire v Surrey at The Oval in 1906. The most recent are:

Aziz Malik	Lahore Division v Faisalabad at Sialkot	1984-85
Javed Mohammad	Multan v Karachi Whites at Sahiwal	1986-87
Shahid Pervez	Jammu and Kashmir v Punjab at Srinagar	1986-87
Ali Naqvi	PNSC v National Bank at Faisalabad	1998-99
A. George	Tamil Nadu v Maharashtra at Pune	1998-99
Maqsood Raza	Lahore Division v PNSC at Sheikhupura	1999-2000

Timed Out

There have been **three** instances in first-class cricket:

H. Yadav	Tripura v Orissa at Cuttack	1997-98
V. C. Drakes	Border v Free State at East London	2002-03
A. J. Harris	Nottinghamshire v Durham UCCE at Nottingham	2003

BOWLING RECORDS

TEN WICKETS IN AN INNINGS

In the history of first-class cricket, there have been **77** instances of a bowler taking all ten wickets in an innings:

	O	*M*	*R*		
E. Hinkly (Kent)				v England at Lord's	1848
*J. Wisden (North)				v South at Lord's	1850
V. E. Walker (England)	43	17	74	v Surrey at The Oval	1859
V. E. Walker (Middlesex)	44.2	5	104	v Lancashire at Manchester	1865
G. Wootton (All England)	31.3	9	54	v Yorkshire at Sheffield	1865
W. Hickton (Lancashire)	36.2	19	46	v Hampshire at Manchester	1870

	O	M	R		
S. E. Butler (Oxford)	24.1	11	38	v Cambridge at Lord's	1871
James Lillywhite (South)	60.2	22	129	v North at Canterbury	1872
A. Shaw (MCC)	36.2	8	73	v North at Lord's	1874
E. Barratt (Players)	29	11	43	v Australians at The Oval	1878
G. Giffen (Australian XI)	26	10	66	v The Rest at Sydney	1883-84
W. G. Grace (MCC)	36.2	17	49	v Oxford University at Oxford	1886
G. Burton (Middlesex)	52.3	25	59	v Surrey at The Oval	1888
†A. E. Moss (Canterbury)	21.3	10	28	v Wellington at Christchurch	1889-90
S. M. J. Woods (Cambridge U.)	31	6	69	v Thornton's XI at Cambridge	1890
T. Richardson (Surrey)	15.3	3	45	v Essex at The Oval	1894
H. Pickett (Essex)	27	11	32	v Leicestershire at Leyton	1895
E. J. Tyler (Somerset)	34.3	15	49	v Surrey at Taunton	1895
W. P. Howell (Australians)	23.2	14	28	v Surrey at The Oval	1899
C. H. G. Bland (Sussex)	25.2	10	48	v Kent at Tonbridge	1899
J. Briggs (Lancashire)	28.5	7	55	v Worcestershire at Manchester	1900
A. E. Trott (Middlesex)	14.2	5	42	v Somerset at Taunton	1900
A. Fielder (Players)	24.5	1	90	v Gentlemen at Lord's	1906
E. G. Dennett (Gloucestershire)	19.4	7	40	v Essex at Bristol	1906
A. E. E. Vogler (E. Province)	12	2	26	v Griqualand W. at Johannesburg	1906-07
C. Blythe (Kent)	16	7	30	v Northants at Northampton	1907
J. B. King (Philadelphia)	18.1	7	53	v Ireland at Haverford‡	1909
A. Drake (Yorkshire)	8.5	0	35	v Somerset at Weston-s-Mare	1914
W. Bestwick (Derbyshire)	19	2	40	v Glamorgan at Cardiff	1921
A. A. Mailey (Australians)	28.4	5	66	v Gloucestershire at Cheltenham	1921
C. W. L. Parker (Glos.)	40.3	13	79	v Somerset at Bristol	1921
T. Rushby (Surrey)	17.5	4	43	v Somerset at Taunton	1921
J. C. White (Somerset)	42.2	11	76	v Worcestershire at Worcester	1921
G. C. Collins (Kent)	19.3	4	65	v Nottinghamshire at Dover	1922
H. Howell (Warwickshire)	25.1	5	51	v Yorkshire at Birmingham	1923
A. S. Kennedy (Players)	22.4	10	37	v Gentlemen at The Oval	1927
G. O. B. Allen (Middlesex)	25.3	10	40	v Lancashire at Lord's	1929
A. P. Freeman (Kent)	42	9	131	v Lancashire at Maidstone	1929
G. Geary (Leicestershire)	16.2	8	18	v Glamorgan at Pontypridd	1929
C. V. Grimmett (Australians)	22.3	8	37	v Yorkshire at Sheffield	1930
A. P. Freeman (Kent)	30.4	8	53	v Essex at Southend	1930
H. Verity (Yorkshire)	18.4	6	36	v Warwickshire at Leeds	1931
A. P. Freeman (Kent)	36.1	9	79	v Lancashire at Manchester	1931
V. W. C. Jupp (Northants)	39	6	127	v Kent at Tunbridge Wells	1932
H. Verity (Yorkshire)	19.4	16	10	v Nottinghamshire at Leeds	1932
T. W. Wall (South Australia)	12.4	2	36	v New South Wales at Sydney	1932-33
T. B. Mitchell (Derbyshire)	19.1	4	64	v Leicestershire at Leicester	1935
J. Mercer (Glamorgan)	26	10	51	v Worcestershire at Worcester	1936
T. W. J. Goddard (Glos.)	28.4	4	113	v Worcestershire at Cheltenham	1937
T. F. Smailes (Yorkshire)	17.1	5	47	v Derbyshire at Sheffield	1939
E. A. Watts (Surrey)	24.1	8	67	v Warwickshire at Birmingham	1939
*W. E. Hollies (Warwickshire)	20.4	4	49	v Notts at Birmingham	1946
J. M. Sims (East)	18.4	2	90	v West at Kingston	1948
T. E. Bailey (Essex)	39.4	9	90	v Lancashire at Clacton	1949
J. K. Graveney (Glos.)	18.4	2	66	v Derbyshire at Chesterfield	1949
R. Berry (Lancashire)	36.2	9	102	v Worcestershire at Blackpool	1953
S. P. Gupte (President's XI)	24.2	7	78	v Combined XI at Bombay	1954-55
J. C. Laker (Surrey)	46	18	88	v Australians at The Oval	1956
J. C. Laker (England)	51.2	23	53	v Australia at Manchester	1956
G. A. R. Lock (Surrey)	29.1	18	54	v Kent at Blackheath	1956
K. Smales (Nottinghamshire)	41.3	20	66	v Gloucestershire at Stroud	1956
P. M. Chatterjee (Bengal)	19	11	20	v Assam at Jorhat	1956-57
J. D. Bannister (Warwickshire)	23.3	11	41	v Comb. Services at Birmingham§	1959
A. J. G. Pearson (Cambridge U.)	30.3	8	78	v Leics at Loughborough	1961
N. I. Thomson (Sussex)	34.2	19	49	v Warwickshire at Worthing	1964
P. J. Allan (Queensland)	15.6	3	61	v Victoria at Melbourne	1965-66

	O	M	R		
I. J. Brayshaw (W. Australia)	17.6	4	44	v Victoria at Perth	1967-68
Shahid Mahmood (Karachi Whites)	25	5	58	v Khairpur at Karachi	1969-70
E. E. Hemmings (International XI)	49.3	14	175	v West Indies XI at Kingston	1982-83
P. Sunderam (Rajasthan)	22	5	78	v Vidarbha at Jodhpur	1985-86
S. T. Jefferies (W. Province)	22.5	7	59	v Orange Free State at Cape Town	1987-88
Imran Adil (Bahawalpur)	22.5	3	92	v Faisalabad at Faisalabad	1989-90
G. P. Wickremasinghe (Sinhalese)	19.2	5	41	v Kalutara at Colombo	1991-92
R. L. Johnson (Middlesex)	18.5	6	45	v Derbyshire at Derby	1994
Naeem Akhtar (Rawalpindi B)	21.3	10	28	v Peshawar at Peshawar	1995-96
A. Kumble (India)	26.3	9	74	v Pakistan at Delhi	1998-99
D. S. Mohanty (East Zone)	19	5	46	v South Zone at Agartala	2000-01

Note: In addition, the following instances were achieved in 12-a-side matches:

	O	M	R		
E. M. Grace (MCC)	32.2	7	69	v Gents of Kent at Canterbury	1862
W. G. Grace (MCC)	46.1	15	92	v Kent at Canterbury	1873
†D. C. S. Hinds (A. B. St Hill's XII)	19.1	6	36	v Trinidad at Port-of-Spain	1900-01

* *J. Wisden and W. E. Hollies achieved the feat without the direct assistance of a fielder. Wisden's ten were all bowled; Hollies bowled seven and had three lbw.*
† *On debut in first-class cricket.* ‡ *Pennsylvania.* § *Mitchells & Butlers Ground.*

OUTSTANDING BOWLING ANALYSES

	O	M	R	W		
H. Verity (Yorkshire)	19.4	16	10	10	v Nottinghamshire at Leeds	1932
G. Elliott (Victoria)	19	17	2	9	v Tasmania at Launceston	1857-58
Ahad Khan (Railways)	6.3	4	7	9	v Dera Ismail Khan at Lahore	1964-65
J. C. Laker (England)	14	12	2	8	v The Rest at Bradford	1950
D. Shackleton (Hampshire)	11.1	7	4	8	v Somerset at Weston-s-Mare	1955
E. Peate (Yorkshire)	16	11	5	8	v Surrey at Holbeck	1883
F. R. Spofforth (Australians)	8.3	6	3	7	v England XI at Birmingham	1884
W. A. Henderson (North-Eastern Transvaal)	9.3	7	4	7	v Orange Free State at Bloemfontein	1937-38
Rajinder Goel (Haryana)	7	4	4	7	v Jammu and Kashmir at Chandigarh	1977-78
V. I. Smith (South Africans)	4.5	3	1	6	v Derbyshire at Derby	1947
S. Cosstick (Victoria)	21.1	20	1	6	v Tasmania at Melbourne	1868-69
Israr Ali (Bahawalpur)	11	10	1	6	v Dacca U. at Bahawalpur	1957-58
A. D. Pougher (MCC)	3	3	0	5	v Australians at Lord's	1896
G. R. Cox (Sussex)	6	6	0	5	v Somerset at Weston-s-Mare	1921
R. K. Tyldesley (Lancashire)	5	5	0	5	v Leicestershire at Manchester	1924
P. T. Mills (Gloucestershire)	6.4	6	0	5	v Somerset at Bristol	1928

MOST WICKETS IN A MATCH

19-90	J. C. Laker	England v Australia at Manchester	1956
17-48†	C. Blythe	Kent v Northamptonshire at Northampton	1907
17-50	C. T. B. Turner	Australians v England XI at Hastings	1888
17-54	W. P. Howell	Australians v Western Province at Cape Town	1902-03
17-56	C. W. L. Parker	Gloucestershire v Essex at Gloucester	1925
17-67	A. P. Freeman	Kent v Sussex at Hove	1922
17-89	W. G. Grace	Gloucestershire v Nottinghamshire at Cheltenham	1877
17-89	F. C. L. Matthews	Nottinghamshire v Northants at Nottingham	1923
17-91	H. Dean	Lancashire v Yorkshire at Liverpool	1913
17-91†	H. Verity	Yorkshire v Essex at Leyton	1933
17-92	A. P. Freeman	Kent v Warwickshire at Folkestone	1932
17-103	W. Mycroft	Derbyshire v Hampshire at Southampton	1876

17-106	G. R. Cox	Sussex v Warwickshire at Horsham	1926
17-106†	T. W. J. Goddard	Gloucestershire v Kent at Bristol	1939
17-119	W. Mead	Essex v Hampshire at Southampton	1895
17-137	W. Brearley	Lancashire v Somerset at Manchester	1905
17-159	S. F. Barnes	England v South Africa at Johannesburg	1913-14
17-201	G. Giffen	South Australia v Victoria at Adelaide	1885-86
17-212	J. C. Clay	Glamorgan v Worcestershire at Swansea	1937

† *Achieved in a single day.*

Note: H. Arkwright took 18-96 for MCC v Gentlemen of Kent in a 12-a-side match at Canterbury in 1861.

There have been 56 instances of a bowler taking 16 wickets in an 11-a-side match, the most recent being 16-119 by M. P. Bicknell for Surrey v Leicestershire at Guildford, 2000.

FOUR WICKETS WITH CONSECUTIVE BALLS

There have been **34** instances in first-class cricket. R. J. Crisp achieved the feat twice, for Western Province in 1931-32 and 1933-34. A. E. Trott took four in four balls and another hat-trick in the same innings for Middlesex v Somerset in 1907, his benefit match. Occurrences since the Second World War:

F. Ridgway	Kent v Derbyshire at Folkestone	1951
A. K. Walker‡	Nottinghamshire v Leicestershire at Leicester	1956
D. Robins†	South Australia v New South Wales at Adelaide	1965-66
S. N. Mohol	President's XI v Combined XI at Poona	1965-66
P. I. Pocock	Surrey v Sussex at Eastbourne	1972
S. S. Saini†	Delhi v Himachal Pradesh at Delhi	1988-89
D. Dias	W. Province (Suburbs) v Central Province at Colombo	1990-91
Ali Gauhar	Karachi Blues v United Bank at Peshawar	1994-95
K. D. James§	Hampshire v Indians at Southampton	1996
G. P. Butcher	Surrey v Derbyshire at The Oval	2000
Fazl-e-Akbar	PIA v Habib Bank at Lahore	2001-02

† *Not all in the same innings.*
‡ *Having bowled Firth with the last ball of the first innings, Walker achieved a unique feat by dismissing Lester, Tompkin and Smithson with the first three balls of the second.*
§ *James also scored a century, a unique double.*

Notes: In their match with England at The Oval in 1863, Surrey lost four wickets in the course of a four-ball over from G. Bennett.

Sussex lost five wickets in the course of the final (six-ball) over of their match with Surrey at Eastbourne in 1972. P. I. Pocock, who had taken three wickets in his previous over, captured four more, taking in all seven wickets with 11 balls, a feat unique in first-class matches. (The eighth wicket fell to a run-out.)

HAT-TRICKS

Double Hat-Trick

Besides Trott's performance, which is mentioned in the preceding section, the following instances are recorded of players having performed the hat-trick twice in the same match, Rao doing so in the same innings.

A. Shaw	Nottinghamshire v Gloucestershire at Nottingham	1884
T. J. Matthews	Australia v South Africa at Manchester	1912
C. W. L. Parker	Gloucestershire v Middlesex at Bristol	1924
R. O. Jenkins	Worcestershire v Surrey at Worcester	1949
J. S. Rao	Services v Northern Punjab at Amritsar	1963-64
Amin Lakhani	Combined XI v Indians at Multan	1978-79

Five Wickets in Six Balls

W. H. Copson	Derbyshire v Warwickshire at Derby	1937
W. A. Henderson	N.E. Transvaal v Orange Free State at Bloemfontein	1937-38
P. I. Pocock	Surrey v Sussex at Eastbourne	1972

Most Hat-Tricks

Seven times: D. V. P. Wright.
Six times: T. W. J. Goddard, C. W. L. Parker.
Five times: S. Haigh, V. W. C. Jupp, A. E. G. Rhodes, F. A. Tarrant.
Four times: R. G. Barlow, A. P. Freeman, J. T. Hearne, J. C. Laker, G. A. R. Lock, G. G. Macaulay, T. J. Matthews, M. J. Procter, T. Richardson, F. R. Spofforth, F. S. Trueman.
Three times: W. M. Bradley, H. J. Butler, S. T. Clarke, W. H. Copson, R. J. Crisp, J. W. H. T. Douglas, J. A. Flavell, G. Giffen, D. W. Headley, K. Higgs, A. Hill, W. A. Humphreys, R. D. Jackman, R. O. Jenkins, A. S. Kennedy, W. H. Lockwood, E. A. McDonald, T. L. Pritchard, J. S. Rao, A. Shaw, J. B. Statham, M. W. Tate, H. Trumble, Wasim Akram, D. Wilson, G. A. Wilson.
Twice (current players only): D. G. Cork, K. J. Dean, Fazl-e-Akbar, D. Gough, A. Kumble, J. D. Lewry, A. Sheriyar, J. Srinath, Waqar Younis.

Hat-Trick on Debut

H. Hay	South Australia v Lord Hawke's XI at Unley, Adelaide	1902-03
H. A. Sedgwick	Yorkshire v Worcestershire at Hull	1906
R. Wooster	Northamptonshire v Dublin University at Northampton	1925
J. C. Treanor	New South Wales v Queensland at Brisbane	1954-55
V. B. Ranjane	Maharashtra v Saurashtra at Poona	1956-57
Arshad Khan	Dacca University v East Pakistan B at Dacca	1957-58
N. Fredrick	Ceylon v Madras at Colombo	1963-64
J. S. Rao	Services v Jammu and Kashmir at Delhi	1963-64
Mehboodullah	Uttar Pradesh v Madhya Pradesh at Lucknow	1971-72
R. O. Estwick	Barbados v Guyana at Bridgetown	1982-83
S. A. Ankola	Maharashtra v Gujarat at Poona	1988-89
J. Srinath	Karnataka v Hyderabad at Secunderabad	1989-90
S. P. Mukherjee	Bengal v Hyderabad at Secunderabad	1989-90
S. M. Harwood	Victoria v Tasmania at Melbourne	2002-03

Notes: R. R. Phillips (Border) took a hat-trick in his first over in first-class cricket (v Eastern Province at Port Elizabeth, 1939-40) having previously played in four matches without bowling.
J. S. Rao took two more hat-tricks in his next match.

250 WICKETS IN A SEASON

	Season	*O*	*M*	*R*	*W*	*Avge*
A. P. Freeman	1928	1,976.1	423	5,489	304	18.05
A. P. Freeman	1933	2,039	651	4,549	298	15.26
T. Richardson	1895‡	1,690.1	463	4,170	290	14.37
C. T. B. Turner	1888†	2,427.2	1,127	3,307	283	11.68
A. P. Freeman	1931	1,618	360	4,307	276	15.60
A. P. Freeman	1930	1,914.3	472	4,632	275	16.84
T. Richardson	1897‡	1,603.4	495	3,945	273	14.45
A. P. Freeman	1929	1,670.5	381	4,879	267	18.27
W. Rhodes	1900	1,553	455	3,606	261	13.81
J. T. Hearne	1896‡	2,003.1	818	3,670	257	14.28
A. P. Freeman	1932	1,565.5	404	4,149	253	16.39
W. Rhodes	1901	1,565	505	3,797	251	15.12

† *Indicates 4-ball overs.* ‡ *5-ball overs.*

Notes: In four consecutive seasons (1928-31), A. P. Freeman took 1,122 wickets, and in eight consecutive seasons (1928-35), 2,090 wickets. In each of these eight seasons he took over 200 wickets.
T. Richardson took 1,005 wickets in four consecutive seasons (1894-97).
In 1896, J. T. Hearne took his 100th wicket as early as June 12. In 1931, C. W. L. Parker did the same and A. P. Freeman obtained his 100th wicket a day later.

LEADING BOWLERS IN AN ENGLISH SEASON

(Qualification: 10 wickets in 10 innings)

Season	*Leading wicket-taker*	*Wkts*	*Avge*	*Top of averages*	*Wkts*	*Avge*
1946	W. E. Hollies	184	15.60	A. Booth	111	11.61
1947	T. W. J. Goddard	238	17.30	J. C. Clay	65	16.44
1948	J. E. Walsh	174	19.56	J. C. Clay	41	14.17
1949	R. O. Jenkins	183	21.19	T. W. J. Goddard	160	19.18
1950	R. Tattersall	193	13.59	R. Tattersall	193	13.59
1951	R. Appleyard	200	14.14	R. Appleyard	200	14.14
1952	J. H. Wardle	177	19.54	F. S. Trueman	61	13.78
1953	B. Dooland	172	16.58	C. J. Knott	38	13.71
1954	B. Dooland	196	15.48	J. B. Statham	92	14.13
1955	G. A. R. Lock	216	14.49	R. Appleyard	85	13.01
1956	D. J. Shepherd	177	15.36	G. A. R. Lock	155	12.46
1957	G. A. R. Lock	212	12.02	G. A. R. Lock	212	12.02
1958	G. A. R. Lock	170	12.08	H. L. Jackson	143	10.99
1959	D. Shackleton	148	21.55	J. B. Statham	139	15.01
1960	F. S. Trueman	175	13.98	J. B. Statham	135	12.31
1961	J. A. Flavell	171	17.79	J. A. Flavell	171	17.79
1962	D. Shackleton	172	20.15	C. Cook	58	17.13
1963	D. Shackleton	146	16.75	C. C. Griffith	119	12.83
1964	D. Shackleton	142	20.40	J. A. Standen	64	13.00
1965	D. Shackleton	144	16.08	H. J. Rhodes	119	11.04
1966	D. L. Underwood	157	13.80	D. L. Underwood	157	13.80
1967	T. W. Cartwright	147	15.52	D. L. Underwood	136	12.39
1968	R. Illingworth	131	14.36	O. S. Wheatley	82	12.95
1969	R. M. H. Cottam	109	21.04	A. Ward	69	14.82
1970	D. J. Shepherd	106	19.16	Majid Khan	11	18.81
1971	L. R. Gibbs	131	18.89	G. G. Arnold	83	17.12
1972	T. W. Cartwright	98	18.64	I. M. Chappell	10	10.60
	B. Stead	98	20.38			
1973	B. S. Bedi	105	17.94	T. W. Cartwright	89	15.84
1974	A. M. E. Roberts	119	13.62	A. M. E. Roberts	119	13.62
1975	P. G. Lee	112	18.45	A. M. E. Roberts	57	15.80
1976	G. A. Cope	93	24.13	M. A. Holding	55	14.38
1977	M. J. Procter	109	18.04	R. A. Woolmer	19	15.21
1978	D. L. Underwood	110	14.49	D. L. Underwood	110	14.49
1979	D. L. Underwood	106	14.85	J. Garner	55	13.83
	J. K. Lever	106	17.30			
1980	R. D. Jackman	121	15.40	J. Garner	49	13.93
1981	R. J. Hadlee	105	14.89	R. J. Hadlee	105	14.89
1982	M. D. Marshall	134	15.73	R. J. Hadlee	61	14.57
1983	J. K. Lever	106	16.28	Imran Khan	12	7.16
	D. L. Underwood	106	19.28			
1984	R. J. Hadlee	117	14.05	R. J. Hadlee	117	14.05
1985	N. V. Radford	101	24.68	R. M. Ellison	65	17.20
1986	C. A. Walsh	118	18.17	M. D. Marshall	100	15.08
1987	N. V. Radford	109	20.81	R. J. Hadlee	97	12.64
1988	F. D. Stephenson	125	18.31	M. D. Marshall	42	13.16
1989	D. R. Pringle	94	18.64	T. M. Alderman	70	15.64
	S. L. Watkin	94	25.09			
1990	N. A. Foster	94	26.61	I. R. Bishop	59	19.05
1991	Waqar Younis	113	14.65	Waqar Younis	113	14.65
1992	C. A. Walsh	92	15.96	C. A. Walsh	92	15.96
1993	S. L. Watkin	92	22.80	Wasim Akram	59	19.27
1994	M. M. Patel	90	22.86	C. E. L. Ambrose	77	14.45
1995	A. Kumble	105	20.40	A. A. Donald	89	16.07

Season	*Leading wicket-taker*	*Wkts*	*Avge*	*Top of averages*	*Wkts*	*Avge*
1996	C. A. Walsh	85	16.84	C. E. L. Ambrose	43	16.67
1997	A. M. Smith	83	17.63	A. A. Donald	60	15.63
1998	C. A. Walsh	106	17.31	V. J. Wells	36	14.27
1999	A. Sheriyar	92	24.70	Saqlain Mushtaq	58	11.37
2000	G. D. McGrath	80	13.21	C. A. Walsh	40	11.42
2001	R. J. Kirtley	75	23.32	G. D. McGrath	40	15.60
2002	M. J. Saggers K. J. Dean	83 83	21.51 23.50	C. P. Schofield	18	18.38
2003	Mushtaq Ahmed	103	24.65	Shoaib Akhtar	34	17.05

100 WICKETS IN A SEASON

(Since reduction of Championship matches in 1969)

Five times: D. L. Underwood 110 (1978), 106 (1979), 106 (1983), 102 (1971), 101 (1969).
Four times: J. K. Lever 116 (1984), 106 (1978), 106 (1979), 106 (1983).
Twice: B. S. Bedi 112 (1974), 105 (1973); T. W. Cartwright 108 (1969), 104 (1971); N. A. Foster 105 (1986), 102 (1991); N. Gifford 105 (1970), 104 (1983); R. J. Hadlee 117 (1984), 105 (1981); P. G. Lee 112 (1975), 101 (1973); M. D. Marshall 134 (1982), 100 (1986); M. J. Procter 109 (1977), 108 (1969); N. V. Radford 109 (1987), 101 (1985); F. J. Titmus 105 (1970), 104 (1971); C. A. Walsh 118 (1986), 106 (1998).
Once: J. P. Agnew 101 (1987); I. T. Botham 100 (1978); A. R. Caddick 105 (1998); K. E. Cooper 101 (1988); R. M. H. Cottam 109 (1969); D. R. Doshi 101 (1980); J. E. Emburey 103 (1983); L. R. Gibbs 131 (1971); R. N. S. Hobbs 102 (1970); Intikhab Alam 104 (1971); R. D. Jackman 121 (1980); A. Kumble 105 (1995); Mushtaq Ahmed 103 (2003); A. M. E. Roberts 119 (1974); P. J. Sainsbury 107 (1971); Sarfraz Nawaz 101 (1975); M. W. W. Selvey 101 (1978); D. J. Shepherd 106 (1970); F. D. Stephenson 125 (1988); Waqar Younis 113 (1991); D. Wilson 102 (1969).

200 WICKETS IN A SEASON MOST TIMES

Eight times: A. P. Freeman (in successive seasons – 1928 to 1935 – including 304 in 1928).
Five times: C. W. L. Parker.
Four times: T. W. J. Goddard.
Three times: J. T. Hearne, G. A. Lohmann, W. Rhodes, T. Richardson, M. W. Tate and H. Verity.

100 WICKETS IN A SEASON MOST TIMES

(Includes overseas tours and seasons)

23 times: W. Rhodes.
20 times: D. Shackleton (in successive seasons – 1949 to 1968).
17 times: A. P. Freeman.
16 times: T. W. J. Goddard, C. W. L. Parker, R. T. D. Perks, F. J. Titmus.
15 times: J. T. Hearne, G. H. Hirst, A. S. Kennedy.

100 WICKETS IN A SEASON OUTSIDE ENGLAND

W		*Season*	*Country*	*R*	*Avge*
116	M. W. Tate	1926-27	India/Ceylon	1,599	13.78
113	Kabir Khan	1998-99	Pakistan	1,706	15.09
107	Ijaz Faqih	1985-86	Pakistan	1,719	16.06
106	C. T. B. Turner	1887-88	Australia	1,441	13.59
106	R. Benaud	1957-58	South Africa	2,056	19.39
105	Murtaza Hussain	1995-96	Pakistan	1,882	17.92
104	S. F. Barnes	1913-14	South Africa	1,117	10.74
104	Sajjad Akbar	1989-90	Pakistan	2,328	22.38
103	Abdul Qadir	1982-83	Pakistan	2,367	22.98

1,500 WICKETS

Dates in italics denote the first half of an overseas season; i.e. *1970* denotes the 1970-71 season.

		Career	*W*	*R*	*Avge*
1	W. Rhodes	1898–1930	4,187	69,993	16.71
2	A. P. Freeman	1914–36	3,776	69,577	18.42
3	C. W. L. Parker	1903–35	3,278	63,817	19.46
4	J. T. Hearne	1888–1923	3,061	54,352	17.75
5	T. W. J. Goddard	1922–52	2,979	59,116	19.84
6	W. G. Grace	1865–1908	2,876	51,545	17.92
7	A. S. Kennedy	1907–36	2,874	61,034	21.23
8	D. Shackleton	1948–69	2,857	53,303	18.65
9	G. A. R. Lock	1946–*70*	2,844	54,709	19.23
10	F. J. Titmus	1949–82	2,830	63,313	22.37
11	M. W. Tate	1912–37	2,784	50,571	18.16
12	G. H. Hirst	1891–1929	2,739	51,282	18.72
13	C. Blythe	1899–1914	2,506	42,136	16.81
14	D. L. Underwood	1963–87	2,465	49,993	20.28
15	W. E. Astill	1906–39	2,431	57,783	23.76
16	J. C. White	1909–37	2,356	43,759	18.57
17	W. E. Hollies	1932–57	2,323	48,656	20.94
18	F. S. Trueman	1949–69	2,304	42,154	18.29
19	J. B. Statham	1950–68	2,260	36,999	16.37
20	R. T. D. Perks	1930–55	2,233	53,770	24.07
21	J. Briggs	1879–1900	2,221	35,431	15.95
22	D. J. Shepherd	1950–72	2,218	47,302	21.32
23	E. G. Dennett	1903–26	2,147	42,571	19.82
24	T. Richardson	1892–1905	2,104	38,794	18.43
25	T. E. Bailey	1945–67	2,082	48,170	23.13
26	R. Illingworth	1951–83	2,072	42,023	20.28
27	N. Gifford	1960–88	2,068	48,731	23.56
	F. E. Woolley	1906–38	2,068	41,066	19.85
29	G. Geary	1912–38	2,063	41,339	20.03
30	D. V. P. Wright	1932–57	2,056	49,307	23.98
31	J. A. Newman	1906–30	2,032	51,111	25.15
32	†A. Shaw	1864–97	2,027	24,580	12.12
33	S. Haigh	1895–1913	2,012	32,091	15.94
34	H. Verity	1930–39	1,956	29,146	14.90
35	W. Attewell	1881–1900	1,951	29,896	15.32
36	J. C. Laker	1946–*64*	1,944	35,791	18.41
37	A. V. Bedser	1939–60	1,924	39,279	20.41
38	W. Mead	1892–1913	1,916	36,388	18.99
39	A. E. Relf	1900–21	1,897	39,724	20.94
40	P. G. H. Fender	1910–36	1,894	47,458	25.05
41	J. W. H. T. Douglas	1901–30	1,893	44,159	23.32
42	J. H. Wardle	1946–*67*	1,846	35,027	18.97
43	G. R. Cox	1895–1928	1,843	42,136	22.86
44	G. A. Lohmann	1884–*97*	1,841	25,295	13.73
45	J. W. Hearne	1909–36	1,839	44,926	24.42
46	G. G. Macaulay	1920–35	1,837	32,440	17.65
47	M. S. Nichols	1924–39	1,833	39,666	21.63
48	J. B. Mortimore	1950–75	1,807	41,904	23.18
	C. A. Walsh	*1981–2000*	1,807	39,233	21.71
50	C. Cook	1946–64	1,782	36,578	20.52
51	R. Peel	1882–99	1,752	28,442	16.23
52	H. L. Jackson	1947–63	1,733	30,101	17.36
53	J. K. Lever	1967–89	1,722	41,772	24.25
54	T. P. B. Smith	1929–52	1,697	45,059	26.55
55	J. Southerton	1854–79	1,681	24,290	14.44
56	A. E. Trott	*1892*–1911	1,674	35,317	21.09

		Career	W	R	Avge
57	A. W. Mold	1889–1901	1,673	26,010	15.54
58	T. G. Wass	1896–1920	1,666	34,092	20.46
59	V. W. C. Jupp	1909–38	1,658	38,166	23.01
60	C. Gladwin	1939–58	1,653	30,265	18.30
61	M. D. Marshall	*1977–95*	1,651	31,548	19.10
62	W. E. Bowes	1928–47	1,639	27,470	16.76
63	A. W. Wellard	1927–50	1,614	39,302	24.35
64	J. E. Emburey	1973–97	1,608	41,958	26.09
65	P. I. Pocock	1964–86	1,607	42,648	26.53
66	N. I. Thomson	1952–72	1,597	32,867	20.58
67	J. Mercer	1919–47	1,591	37,210	23.38
	G. J. Thompson	1897–1922	1,591	30,058	18.89
69	J. M. Sims	1929–53	1,581	39,401	24.92
70	T. Emmett	1866–88	1,571	21,314	13.56
	Intikhab Alam	*1957*–82	1,571	43,474	27.67
72	B. S. Bedi	*1961–81*	1,560	33,843	21.69
73	W. Voce	1927–52	1,558	35,961	23.08
74	A. R. Gover	1928–48	1,555	36,753	23.63
75	T. W. Cartwright	1952–77	1,536	29,357	19.11
	K. Higgs	1958–86	1,536	36,267	23.61
77	James Langridge	1924–53	1,530	34,524	22.56
78	J. A. Flavell	1949–67	1,529	32,847	21.48
79	E. E. Hemmings	1966–95	1,515	44,403	29.30
80	C. F. Root	1910–33	1,512	31,933	21.11
	F. A. Tarrant	*1898–1936*	1,512	26,450	17.49
82	R. K. Tyldesley	1919–35	1,509	25,980	17.21

† *The figures for A. Shaw exclude one wicket for which no analysis is available.*

Note: Some works of reference provide career figures which differ from those in this list, owing to the exclusion or inclusion of matches recognised or not recognised as first-class by *Wisden*.

Current Players with 1,000 Wickets

	Career	W	R	Avge
A. A. Donald	*1985–2003*	1,212	27,515	22.70
P. A. J. DeFreitas	1985–2003	1,205	33,339	27.66
D. E. Malcolm	1984–2003	1,054	31,973	30.33
Wasim Akram	*1984*–2003	1,042	22,549	21.64

ALL-ROUND RECORDS

HUNDRED AND TEN WICKETS IN AN INNINGS

V. E. Walker, England v Surrey at The Oval; 20*, 108, ten for 74, and four for 17 . . 1859
W. G. Grace, MCC v Oxford University at Oxford; 104, two for 60, and ten for 49 . . 1886

Note: E. M. Grace, for MCC v Gentlemen of Kent in a 12-a-side match at Canterbury in 1862, scored 192* and took five for 77 and ten for 69.

DOUBLE-HUNDRED AND 16 WICKETS

G. Giffen, South Australia v Victoria at Adelaide; 271, nine for 96, and seven for 70 . . 1891-92

HUNDRED IN EACH INNINGS AND FIVE WICKETS TWICE

G. H. Hirst, Yorkshire v Somerset at Bath; 111, 117*, six for 70, and five for 45 . . . 1906

HUNDRED IN EACH INNINGS AND TEN WICKETS

B. J. T. Bosanquet, Middlesex v Sussex at Lord's; 103, 100*, three for 75, and eight for 53 1905
F. D. Stephenson, Nottinghamshire v Yorkshire at Nottingham; 111, 117, four for 105, and seven for 117 1988

HUNDRED AND HAT-TRICK

K. D. James, Hampshire v Indians at Southampton. *Unique instance of 100 and four wickets in four balls* 1996
G. Giffen, Australians v Lancashire at Manchester 1884
W. E. Roller, Surrey v Sussex at The Oval. *Unique instance of 200 and hat-trick*... 1885
W. B. Burns, Worcestershire v Gloucestershire at Worcester.......... 1913
V. W. C. Jupp, Sussex v Essex at Colchester.......... 1921
R. E. S. Wyatt, MCC v Ceylon at Colombo 1926-27
L. N. Constantine, West Indians v Northamptonshire at Northampton.......... 1928
D. E. Davies, Glamorgan v Leicestershire at Leicester.......... 1937
V. M. Merchant, Dr C. R. Pereira's XI v Sir Homi Mehta's XI at Bombay 1946-47
M. J. Procter, Gloucestershire v Essex at Westcliff-on-Sea.......... 1972
M. J. Procter, Gloucestershire v Leicestershire at Bristol.......... 1979

SEASON DOUBLES

2,000 Runs and 200 Wickets

1906 G. H. Hirst 2,385 runs and 208 wickets

3,000 Runs and 100 Wickets

1937 J. H. Parks 3,003 runs and 101 wickets

1,000 Runs and 100 Wickets

Sixteen times: W. Rhodes.
Fourteen times: G. H. Hirst.
Ten times: V. W. C. Jupp.
Nine times: W. E. Astill.
Eight times: T. E. Bailey, W. G. Grace, M. S. Nichols, A. E. Relf, F. A. Tarrant, M. W. Tate†, F. J. Titmus, F. E. Woolley.
Seven times: G. E. Tribe.

† *M. W. Tate also scored 1,193 runs and took 116 wickets for MCC in first-class matches on the 1926-27 MCC tour of India and Ceylon.*

Note: R. J. Hadlee (1984) and F. D. Stephenson (1988) are the only players to perform the feat since the reduction of County Championship matches. A complete list of those performing the feat before then will be found on page 202 of the 1982 *Wisden*.

T. E. Bailey (1959) was the last player to achieve 2,000 runs and 100 wickets in a season. M. W. Tate (1925) was the last to reach 1,000 runs and 200 wickets. Full lists can be found in previous *Wisdens*.

Wicket-Keeper's Double

	Season	*R*	*D*		*Season*	*R*	*D*
L. E. G. Ames....	1928	1,919	122	L. E. G. Ames ..	1932	2,482	104
L. E. G. Ames....	1929	1,795	128	J. T. Murray	1957	1,025	104

20,000 RUNS AND 2,000 WICKETS

	Career	*R*	*Avge*	*W*	*Avge*	*Doubles*
W. E. Astill	1906–39	22,731	22.55	2,431	23.76	9
T. E. Bailey	1945–67	28,641	33.42	2,082	23.13	8
W. G. Grace	1865–1908	54,896	39.55	2,876	17.92	8
G. H. Hirst	1891–1929	36,323	34.13	2,739	18.72	14
R. Illingworth	1951–83	24,134	28.06	2,072	20.28	6
W. Rhodes	1898–1930	39,802	30.83	4,187	16.71	16
M. W. Tate	1912–37	21,717	25.01	2,784	18.16	8†
F. J. Titmus	1949–82	21,588	23.11	2,830	22.37	8
F. E. Woolley	1906–38	58,969	40.75	2,068	19.85	8

† *Plus one double overseas (see above).*

Current Player with 10,000 Runs and 1,000 Wickets

	Career	*R*	*Avge*	*W*	*Avge*	*Doubles*
P. A. J. DeFreitas	1985-2003	10,535	22.95	1,205	27.66	–

WICKET-KEEPING RECORDS

MOST DISMISSALS IN AN INNINGS

9 (8ct, 1st)	Tahir Rashid	Habib Bank v PACO at Gujranwala	1992-93
9 (7ct, 2st)	W. R. James*	Matabeleland v Mashonaland CD at Bulawayo	1995-96
8 (all ct)	A. T. W. Grout	Queensland v Western Australia at Brisbane	1959-60
8 (all ct)†	D. E. East	Essex v Somerset at Taunton	1985
8 (all ct)	S. A. Marsh‡	Kent v Middlesex at Lord's	1991
8 (6ct, 2st)	T. J. Zoehrer	Australians v Surrey at The Oval	1993
8 (7ct, 1st)	D. S. Berry	Victoria v South Australia at Melbourne	1996-97
8 (7ct, 1st)	Y. S. S. Mendis	Bloomfield v Kurunegala Youth at Colombo	2000-01
8 (7ct, 1st)	S. Nath§	Assam v Tripura at Guwahati	2001-02

There have been **58** instances of seven dismissals in an innings. R. W. Taylor achieved the feat three times, and S. A. Marsh, K. J. Piper and Wasim Bari twice. One of Marsh's two instances was of eight dismssals – see above. A list can be found in previous *Wisdens*. The most recent occurrences are:

7 (all ct)	C. W. Scott	Durham v Yorkshire at Chester-le-Street	1996
7 (all ct)	Zahid Umar	WAPDA v Habib Bank at Sheikhupura	1997-98
7 (all ct)	K. S. M. Iyer	Vidarbha v Uttar Pradesh at Allahabad	1997-98
7 (all ct)	W. M. Noon	Nottinghamshire v Kent at Nottingham	1999
7 (all ct)	Aamer Iqbal	Pakistan Customs v Karachi Whites at Karachi	1999-2000
7 (all ct)	H. A. P. W. Jayawardene	Sebastianites v Sinhalese at Colombo	1999-2000
7 (all ct)	R. D. Jacobs	West Indies v Australia at Melbourne	2000-01
7 (all ct)	N. D. Burns	Leicestershire v Somerset at Leicester	2001
7 (all ct)	R. J. Turner	Somerset v Northamptonshire at Taunton	2001
7 (all ct)	W. A. Seccombe	Queensland v New South Wales at Brisbane	2001-02
7 (all ct)	M. G. Croy	Otago v Auckland at Auckland	2001-02
7 (all ct)	Wasim Ahmed	Dadu v PWD at Karachi	2002-03
7 (all ct)	S. G. Clingeleffer	Tasmania v Western Australia at Perth	2003-04

* *W. R. James also scored 99 and 99 not out.* † *The first eight wickets to fall.*
‡ *S. A. Marsh also scored 108 not out.* § *On first-class debut.*

WICKET-KEEPERS' HAT-TRICKS

W. H. Brain, Gloucestershire v Somerset at Cheltenham, 1893 – three stumpings off successive balls from C. L. Townsend.
G. O. Dawkes, Derbyshire v Worcestershire at Kidderminster, 1958 – three catches off successive balls from H. L. Jackson.
R. C. Russell, Gloucestershire v Surrey at The Oval, 1986 – three catches off successive balls from C. A. Walsh and D. V. Lawrence (2).

MOST DISMISSALS IN A MATCH

13 (11ct, 2st)	W. R. James*	Matabeleland v Mashonaland CD at Bulawayo . .	1995-96
12 (8ct, 4st)	E. Pooley	Surrey v Sussex at The Oval	1868
12 (9ct, 3st)	D. Tallon	Queensland v New South Wales at Sydney	1938-39
12 (9ct, 3st)	H. B. Taber	New South Wales v South Australia at Adelaide .	1968-69
11 (all ct)	A. Long	Surrey v Sussex at Hove	1964
11 (all ct)	R. W. Marsh	Western Australia v Victoria at Perth	1975-76
11 (all ct)	D. L. Bairstow	Yorkshire v Derbyshire at Scarborough.	1982
11 (all ct)	W. K. Hegg	Lancashire v Derbyshire at Chesterfield	1989
11 (all ct)	A. J. Stewart	Surrey v Leicestershire at Leicester	1989
11 (all ct)	T. J. Nielsen	South Australia v Western Australia at Perth	1990-91
11 (10ct, 1st)	I. A. Healy	Australians v N. Transvaal at Verwoerdburg	1993-94
11 (10ct, 1st)	K. J. Piper	Warwickshire v Derbyshire at Chesterfield	1994
11 (all ct)	D. S. Berry	Victoria v Pakistanis at Melbourne	1995-96
11 (10ct, 1st)	W. A. Seccombe	Queensland v Western Australia at Brisbane	1995-96
11 (all ct)	R. C. Russell	England v South Africa (2nd Test) at Johannesburg	1995-96
11 (10ct, 1st)	D. S. Berry	Victoria v South Australia at Melbourne.	1996-97
11 (all ct)	Wasim Yousufi	Peshawar v Bahawalpur at Peshawar	1997-98
11 (all ct)	Aamer Iqbal	Pakistan Customs v Karachi Whites at Karachi . .	1999-2000
11 (10ct, 1st)	S. Nath†	Assam v Tripura at Guwahati.	2001-02
11 (all ct)	Wasim Ahmed	Dadu v PWD at Karachi	2002-03

* *W. R. James also scored 99 and 99 not out.* † *On first-class debut.*

100 DISMISSALS IN A SEASON

128 (79ct, 49st)	L. E. G. Ames . . .	1929	104 (82ct, 22st)	J. T. Murray	1957
122 (70ct, 52st)	L. E. G. Ames . . .	1928	102 (69ct, 33st)	F. H. Huish	1913
110 (63ct, 47st)	H. Yarnold.	1949	102 (95ct, 7st)	J. T. Murray	1960
107 (77ct, 30st)	G. Duckworth . . .	1928	101 (62ct, 39st)	F. H. Huish	1911
107 (96ct, 11st)	J. G. Binks	1960	101 (85ct, 16st)	R. Booth	1960
104 (40ct, 64st)	L. E. G. Ames . . .	1932	100 (91ct, 9st)	R. Booth	1964

1,000 DISMISSALS

Dates in italics denote the first half of an overseas season; i.e. *1914* denotes the 1914-15 season.

			Career	*M*	*Ct*	*St*
1	1,649	R. W. Taylor	1960–88	639	1,473	176
2	1,527	J. T. Murray	1952–75	635	1,270	257
3	1,497	H. Strudwick.	1902–27	675	1,242	255
4	1,344	A. P. E. Knott	1964–85	511	1,211	133
5	**1,319**	**R. C. Russell**	**1981–2003**	**463**	**1,191**	**128**
6	1,310	F. H. Huish.	1895–1914	497	933	377
7	1,294	B. Taylor	1949–73	572	1,083	211
8	1,253	D. Hunter.	1889–1909	548	906	347
9	1,228	H. R. Butt	1890–1912	550	953	275
10	**1,215**	**S. J. Rhodes**.	**1981–2003**	**423**	**1,095**	**120**

			Career	M	Ct	St
11	1,207	J. H. Board.	1891–*1914*	525	852	355
12	1,206	H. Elliott	1920–47	532	904	302
13	1,181	J. M. Parks.	1949–76	739	1,088	93
14	1,126	R. Booth	1951–70	468	948	178
15	1,121	L. E. G. Ames	1926–51	593	703	418†
16	1,099	D. L. Bairstow.	1970–90	459	961	138
17	1,096	G. Duckworth	1923–47	504	753	343
18	1,082	H. W. Stephenson.	1948–64	462	748	334
19	1,071	J. G. Binks	1955–75	502	895	176
20	1,066	T. G. Evans	1939–69	465	816	250
21	1,046	A. Long.	1960–80	452	922	124
22	1,043	G. O. Dawkes	1937–61	482	895	148
23	1,037	R. W. Tolchard	1965–83	483	912	125
24	1,017	W. L. Cornford	1921–47	496	675	342

Bold type denotes those who have played since the start of 2002-03.

† *Record.*

Other Current Players with 500 Dismissals

		Career	M	Ct	St
877	W. K. Hegg	1986–2003	321	793	84
835	R. J. Blakey	1985–2003	348	778	57
753	A. J. Stewart.	1981–2003	447	721	32
721	P. A. Nixon.	1989–2003	253	669	52
665	R. J. Turner.	1988–2003	225	620	45
593	A. C. Gilchrist	*1992–2003*	139	556	37
585	D. S. Berry.	*1989–2003*	148	537	48
562	Tahir Rashid	*1979–2003*	181	501	61
557	K. M. Krikken	*1988*–2003	214	526	31
536	K. J. Piper	1989–2003	199	502	34
507	Moin Khan.	*1986–2003*	187	452	55

Note: A. J. Stewart's total includes 212 catches taken as a fielder.

FIELDING RECORDS

excluding wicket-keepers

MOST CATCHES IN AN INNINGS

7	M. J. Stewart	Surrey v Northamptonshire at Northampton.	1957
7	A. S. Brown	Gloucestershire v Nottinghamshire at Nottingham. . .	1966

MOST CATCHES IN A MATCH

10	W. R. Hammond†	Gloucestershire v Surrey at Cheltenham	1928
8	W. B. Burns	Worcestershire v Yorkshire at Bradford.	1907
8	F. G. Travers	Europeans v Parsees at Bombay	1923-24
8	A. H. Bakewell	Northamptonshire v Essex at Leyton	1928
8	W. R. Hammond	Gloucestershire v Worcestershire at Cheltenham	1932
8	K. J. Grieves	Lancashire v Sussex at Manchester	1951
8	C. A. Milton	Gloucestershire v Sussex at Hove	1952
8	G. A. R. Lock	Surrey v Warwickshire at The Oval	1957
8	J. M. Prodger	Kent v Gloucestershire at Cheltenham	1961
8	P. M. Walker	Glamorgan v Derbyshire at Swansea	1970
8	Masood Anwar	Rawalpindi v Lahore Division at Rawalpindi	1983-84
8	M. C. J. Ball	Gloucestershire v Yorkshire at Cheltenham	1994
8	J. D. Carr	Middlesex v Warwickshire at Birmingham	1995

† *Hammond also scored a hundred in each innings.*

MOST CATCHES IN A SEASON

78	W. R. Hammond	1928	69	P. M. Walker	1960
77	M. J. Stewart	1957	66	J. Tunnicliffe	1895
73	P. M. Walker	1961	65	W. R. Hammond	1925
71	P. J. Sharpe	1962	65	P. M. Walker	1959
70	J. Tunnicliffe	1901	65	D. W. Richardson	1961
69	J. G. Langridge	1955			

Note: The most catches by a fielder since the reduction of County Championship matches in 1969 is 49 by C. J. Tavaré in 1978.

750 CATCHES

Dates in italics denote the first half of an overseas season; i.e. *1970* denotes the 1970-71 season.

			M				*M*
1,018	F. E. Woolley	1906–38	979	784	J. G. Langridge	1928–55	574
887	W. G. Grace	1865–1908	879	764	W. Rhodes	1898–1930	1,107
830	G. A. R. Lock	1946–*70*	654	758	C. A. Milton	1948–74	620
819	W. R. Hammond	1920–51	634	754	E. H. Hendren	1907–38	833
813	D. B. Close	1949–86	786				

Note: The most catches by a current player is 571 by G. A. Hick (*1983*–2003).

TEAM RECORDS

HIGHEST INNINGS TOTALS

1,107	Victoria v New South Wales at Melbourne	1926-27
1,059	Victoria v Tasmania at Melbourne	1922-23
952-6 dec.	Sri Lanka v India at Colombo	1997-98
951-7 dec.	Sind v Baluchistan at Karachi	1973-74
944-6 dec.	Hyderabad v Andhra at Secunderabad	1993-94
918	New South Wales v South Australia at Sydney	1900-01
912-8 dec.	Holkar v Mysore at Indore	1945-46
912-6 dec.†	Tamil Nadu v Goa at Panjim	1988-89
910-6 dec.	Railways v Dera Ismail Khan at Lahore	1964-65
903-7 dec.	England v Australia at The Oval	1938
887	Yorkshire v Warwickshire at Birmingham	1896
868†	North Zone v West Zone at Bhilai	1987-88
863	Lancashire v Surrey at The Oval	1990
855-6 dec.†	Bombay v Hyderabad at Bombay	1990-91
849	England v West Indies at Kingston	1929-30
843	Australians v Oxford & Cambridge U P & P at Portsmouth	1893
839	New South Wales v Tasmania at Sydney	1898-99
826-4	Maharashtra v Kathiawar at Poona	1948-49
824	Lahore Greens v Bahawalpur at Lahore	1965-66
821-7 dec.	South Australia v Queensland at Adelaide	1939-40
815	New South Wales v Victoria at Sydney	1908-09
811	Surrey v Somerset at The Oval	1899
810-4 dec.	Warwickshire v Durham at Birmingham	1994
807	New South Wales v South Australia at Adelaide	1899-1900
805	New South Wales v Victoria at Melbourne	1905-06
803-4 dec.	Kent v Essex at Brentwood	1934
803	Non-Smokers v Smokers at East Melbourne	1886-87
802-8 dec.	Karachi Blues v Lahore City at Peshawar	1994-95
802	New South Wales v South Australia at Sydney	1920-21
801	Lancashire v Somerset at Taunton	1895

798	Maharashtra v Northern India at Poona	1940-41
793	Victoria v Queensland at Melbourne	1927-28
791-6 dec.	Karnataka v Bengal at Calcutta	1990-91
790-3 dec.	West Indies v Pakistan at Kingston	1957-58
786	New South Wales v South Australia at Adelaide	1922-23
784	Baroda v Holkar at Baroda	1946-47
783-8 dec.	Hyderabad v Bihar at Secunderabad	1986-87
781-7 dec.	Northamptonshire v Nottinghamshire at Northampton	1995
781	Lancashire v Warwickshire at Birmingham	2003
780-8	Punjab v Delhi at Delhi	1994-95
777	Canterbury v Otago at Christchurch	1996-97
775	New South Wales v Victoria at Sydney	1881-82

† *Tamil Nadu's total of 912-6 dec. included 52 penalty runs from their opponents' failure to meet the required bowling rate. North Zone's total of 868 included 68, and Bombay's total of 855-6 dec. included 48.*

Note: The highest total in a team's second innings is 770 by New South Wales v South Australia at Adelaide in 1920-21.

HIGHEST FOURTH-INNINGS TOTALS

654-5	England v South Africa at Durban *After being set 696 to win. The match was left drawn on the tenth day.*	1938-39
604	Maharashtra (*set 959 to win*) v Bombay at Poona	1948-49
576-8	Trinidad (*set 672 to win*) v Barbados at Port-of-Spain	1945-46
572	New South Wales (*set 593 to win*) v South Australia at Sydney	1907-08
529-9	Combined XI (*set 579 to win*) v South Africans at Perth	1963-64
518	Victoria (*set 753 to win*) v Queensland at Brisbane	1926-27
507-7	Cambridge University (*won*) v MCC and Ground at Lord's	1896
506-6	South Australia (*won*) v Queensland at Adelaide	1991-92
502-6	Middlesex (*won*) v Nottinghamshire at Nottingham	1925
502-8	Players (*won*) v Gentlemen at Lord's	1900
500-7	South African Universities (*won*) v Western Province at Stellenbosch	1978-79

Note: In January 2004, after the deadline for this section, Central Province scored 513-9 to beat Southern Province at Kandy. This was the highest winning fourth-innings total, beating Cambridge University's record.

HIGHEST AGGREGATES IN A MATCH

Runs	*Wkts*		
2,376	37	Maharashtra v Bombay at Poona	1948-49
2,078	40	Bombay v Holkar at Bombay	1944-45
1,981	35	England v South Africa at Durban	1938-39
1,945	18	Canterbury v Wellington at Christchurch	1994-95
1,929	39	New South Wales v South Australia at Sydney	1925-26
1,911	34	New South Wales v Victoria at Sydney	1908-09
1,905	40	Otago v Wellington at Dunedin	1923-24

In Britain

Runs	*Wkts*		
1,815	28	Surrey v Somerset at Taunton	2002
1,808	20	Sussex v Essex at Hove	1993
1,795	34	Somerset v Northamptonshire at Taunton	2001
1,723	31	England v Australia at Leeds	1948
1,706	23	Hampshire v Warwickshire at Southampton	1997
1,665	33	Warwickshire v Yorkshire at Birmingham	2002
1,655	25	Derbyshire v Nottinghamshire at Derby	2001
1,650	19	Surrey v Lancashire at The Oval	1990
1,642	29	Nottinghamshire v Kent at Nottingham	1995

Runs	Wkts		
1,641	16	Glamorgan v Worcestershire at Abergavenny	1990
1,614	30	England v India at Manchester	1990
1,614	26	Gloucestershire v Northamptonshire at Bristol	2002
1,606	34	Somerset v Derbyshire at Taunton	1996
1,603	28	England v India at Lord's	1990
1,601	29	England v Australia at Lord's	1930
1,601	35	Kent v Surrey at Canterbury	1995

LOWEST INNINGS TOTALS

12†	Oxford University v MCC and Ground at Oxford	1877
12	Northamptonshire v Gloucestershire at Gloucester	1907
13	Auckland v Canterbury at Auckland	1877-78
13	Nottinghamshire v Yorkshire at Nottingham	1901
14	Surrey v Essex at Chelmsford	1983
15	MCC v Surrey at Lord's	1839
15†	Victoria v MCC at Melbourne	1903-04
15†	Northamptonshire v Yorkshire at Northampton	1908
15	Hampshire v Warwickshire at Birmingham	1922
	Following on, Hampshire scored 521 and won by 155 runs.	
16	MCC and Ground v Surrey at Lord's	1872
16	Derbyshire v Nottinghamshire at Nottingham	1879
16	Surrey v Nottinghamshire at The Oval	1880
16	Warwickshire v Kent at Tonbridge	1913
16	Trinidad v Barbados at Bridgetown	1942-43
16	Border v Natal at East London (first innings)	1959-60
17	Gentlemen of Kent v Gentlemen of England at Lord's	1850
17	Gloucestershire v Australians at Cheltenham	1896
18	The Bs v England at Lord's	1831
18†	Kent v Sussex at Gravesend	1867
18	Tasmania v Victoria at Melbourne	1868-69
18†	Australians v MCC and Ground at Lord's	1896
18	Border v Natal at East London (second innings)	1959-60
19	Sussex v Surrey at Godalming	1830
19†	Sussex v Nottinghamshire at Hove	1873
19	MCC and Ground v Australians at Lord's	1878
19	Wellington v Nelson at Nelson	1885-86
19	Matabeleland v Mashonaland at Harare	2000-01

† *One man absent.*

Note: At Lord's in 1810, The Bs, with one man absent, were dismissed by England for 6.

LOWEST TOTALS IN A MATCH

34	(16 and 18) Border v Natal at East London	1959-60
42	(27 and 15) Northamptonshire v Yorkshire at Northampton	1908

Note: Northamptonshire batted one man short in each innings.

LOWEST AGGREGATE IN A COMPLETED MATCH

Runs	Wkts		
105	31	MCC v Australians at Lord's	1878

Note: The lowest aggregate since 1900 is 157 for 22 wickets, Surrey v Worcestershire at The Oval, 1954.

LARGEST VICTORIES

Largest Innings Victories

Inns and 851 runs:	Railways (910-6 dec.) v Dera Ismail Khan at Lahore	1964-65
Inns and 666 runs:	Victoria (1,059) v Tasmania at Melbourne	1922-23
Inns and 656 runs:	Victoria (1,107) v New South Wales at Melbourne	1926-27
Inns and 605 runs:	New South Wales (918) v South Australia at Sydney	1900-01
Inns and 579 runs:	England (903-7 dec.) v Australia at The Oval	1938
Inns and 575 runs:	Sind (951-7 dec.) v Baluchistan at Karachi	1973-74
Inns and 527 runs:	New South Wales (713) v South Australia at Adelaide	1908-09
Inns and 517 runs:	Australians (675) v Nottinghamshire at Nottingham	1921

Largest Victories by Runs Margin

685 runs:	New South Wales (235 and 761-8 dec.) v Queensland at Sydney	1929-30
675 runs:	England (521 and 342-8 dec.) v Australia at Brisbane	1928-29
638 runs:	New South Wales (304 and 770) v South Australia at Adelaide	1920-21
609 runs:	Muslim Commercial Bank (575 and 282-0 dec.) v WAPDA at Lahore	1977-78
585 runs:	Sargodha (336 and 416) v Lahore Municipal Corporation at Faisalabad	1978-79
573 runs:	Sinhalese SC (395-7 dec. and 350-2 dec.) v Sebastianites C and AC at Colombo	1990-91
571 runs:	Victoria (304 and 649) v South Australia at Adelaide	1926-27
562 runs:	Australia (701 and 327) v England at The Oval	1934
556 runs:	Nondescripts (397-8 dec. and 313-6 dec.) v Matara at Colombo	1998-99

Victory Without Losing a Wicket

Lancashire (166-0 dec. and 66-0) beat Leicestershire by ten wickets at Manchester	1956
Karachi A (277-0 dec.) beat Sind A by an innings and 77 runs at Karachi	1957-58
Railways (236-0 dec. and 16-0) beat Jammu and Kashmir by ten wickets at Srinagar	1960-61
Karnataka (451-0 dec.) beat Kerala by an innings and 186 runs at Chikmagalur	1977-78

Notes: There have been 28 wins by an innings and 400 runs or more, the most recent being an innings and 425 runs by Allied Bank v Dadu at Karachi in 2002-03.

There have been 18 wins by 500 runs or more, the most recent being 533 runs by Chilaw Marians v Rio at Colombo in 2001-02.

There have been 28 wins by a team losing only one wicket, the most recent being by PIA v Hyderabad at Hyderabad in 1999-2000.

TIED MATCHES

Since 1948 a tie has been recognised only when the scores are level with all the wickets down in the fourth innings.

The following are the instances since then:

Hampshire v Kent at Southampton	1950
Sussex v Warwickshire at Hove	1952
Essex v Lancashire at Brentwood	1952
Northamptonshire v Middlesex at Peterborough	1953
Yorkshire v Leicestershire at Huddersfield	1954
Sussex v Hampshire at Eastbourne	1955
Victoria v New South Wales at Melbourne	1956-57
T. N. Pearce's XI v New Zealanders at Scarborough	1958
Essex v Gloucestershire at Leyton	1959
Australia v West Indies (First Test) at Brisbane	1960-61
Bahawalpur v Lahore B at Bahawalpur	1961-62
Hampshire v Middlesex at Portsmouth	1967
England XI v England Under-25 XI at Scarborough	1968
Yorkshire v Middlesex at Bradford	1973
Sussex v Essex at Hove	1974

South Australia v Queensland at Adelaide	1976-77
Central Districts v England XI at New Plymouth	1977-78
Victoria v New Zealanders at Melbourne	1982-83
Muslim Commercial Bank v Railways at Sialkot	1983-84
Sussex v Kent at Hastings	1984
Northamptonshire v Kent at Northampton	1984
Eastern Province B v Boland at Albany SC, Grahamstown	1985-86
Natal B v Eastern Province B at Pietermaritzburg	1985-86
India v Australia (First Test) at Madras	1986-87
Gloucestershire v Derbyshire at Bristol	1987
Bahawalpur v Peshawar at Bahawalpur	1988-89
Wellington v Canterbury at Wellington	1988-89
Sussex v Kent at Hove	1991
Nottinghamshire v Worcestershire at Nottingham	1993
Somerset v West Indies A at Taunton	†2002
Warwickshire v Essex at Birmingham	2003
Worcestershire v Zimbabweans at Worcester	2003

† *Somerset (453) made the highest total to tie a first-class match.*

MATCHES COMPLETED ON FIRST DAY

(Since 1946)

Derbyshire v Somerset at Chesterfield, June 11	1947
Lancashire v Sussex at Manchester, July 12	1950
Surrey v Warwickshire at The Oval, May 16	1953
Somerset v Lancashire at Bath, June 6 (H. F. T. Buse's benefit)	1953
Kent v Worcestershire at Tunbridge Wells, June 15	1960

THE ASHES

"In affectionate remembrance of English cricket which died at The Oval, 29th August, 1882. Deeply lamented by a large circle of sorrowing friends and acquaintances, R.I.P.
N.B. The body will be cremated and the Ashes taken to Australia."

Australia's first victory on English soil over the full strength of England, on August 29, 1882, inspired a young London journalist, Reginald Shirley Brooks, to write this mock "obituary". It appeared in the *Sporting Times*.

Before England's defeat at The Oval, by seven runs, arrangements had already been made for the Hon. Ivo Bligh, afterwards Lord Darnley, to lead a team to Australia. Three weeks later they set out, now with the popular objective of recovering the Ashes. In the event, Australia won the First Test by nine wickets, but with England winning the next two it became generally accepted that they brought back the Ashes.

It was long believed that the real Ashes – a small urn thought to contain the ashes of a bail used in the third match – were presented to Bligh by a group of Melbourne women. In 1998, Lord Darnley's 82-year-old daughter-in-law said they were the remains of her mother-in-law's veil, not a bail. Other evidence suggests a ball. The certain origin of the Ashes, therefore, is the subject of some dispute.

After Lord Darnley's death in 1927, the urn was given to MCC by Lord Darnley's Australian-born widow, Florence. It can be seen in the cricket museum at Lord's, together with a red and gold velvet bag, made specially for it, and the scorecard of the 1882 match.

TEST RECORDS

Note: This section covers all Tests up to January 20, 2004.

BATTING RECORDS

HIGHEST INDIVIDUAL INNINGS

380	M. L. Hayden	Australia v Zimbabwe at Perth	2003-04
375	B. C. Lara	West Indies v England at St John's	1993-94
365*	G. S. Sobers	West Indies v Pakistan at Kingston	1957-58
364	L. Hutton	England v Australia at The Oval	1938
340	S. T. Jayasuriya	Sri Lanka v India at Colombo (RPS)	1997-98
337	Hanif Mohammad	Pakistan v West Indies at Bridgetown	1957-58
336*	W. R. Hammond	England v New Zealand at Auckland	1932-33
334*	M. A. Taylor	Australia v Pakistan at Peshawar	1998-99
334	D. G. Bradman	Australia v England at Leeds	1930
333	G. A. Gooch	England v India at Lord's	1990
329	Inzamam-ul-Haq	Pakistan v New Zealand at Lahore	2002
325	A. Sandham	England v West Indies at Kingston	1929-30
311	R. B. Simpson	Australia v England at Manchester	1964
310*	J. H. Edrich	England v New Zealand at Leeds	1965
307	R. M. Cowper	Australia v England at Melbourne	1965-66
304	D. G. Bradman	Australia v England at Leeds	1934
302	L. G. Rowe	West Indies v England at Bridgetown	1973-74
299*	D. G. Bradman	Australia v South Africa at Adelaide	1931-32
299	M. D. Crowe	New Zealand v Sri Lanka at Wellington	1990-91
291	I. V. A. Richards	West Indies v England at The Oval	1976
287	R. E. Foster	England v Australia at Sydney	1903-04
285*	P. B. H. May	England v West Indies at Birmingham	1957
281	V. V. S. Laxman	India v Australia at Kolkata	2000-01
280*	Javed Miandad	Pakistan v India at Hyderabad	1982-83
278	D. C. S. Compton	England v Pakistan at Nottingham	1954
277	B. C. Lara	West Indies v Australia at Sydney	1992-93
277	G. C. Smith	South Africa v England at Birmingham	2003
275*	D. J. Cullinan	South Africa v New Zealand at Auckland	1998-99
275	G. Kirsten	South Africa v England at Durban	1999-2000
274*	S. P. Fleming	New Zealand v Sri Lanka at Colombo (PSS)	2003
274	R. G. Pollock	South Africa v Australia at Durban	1969-70
274	Zaheer Abbas	Pakistan v England at Birmingham	1971
271	Javed Miandad	Pakistan v New Zealand at Auckland	1988-89
270*	G. A. Headley	West Indies v England at Kingston	1934-35
270	D. G. Bradman	Australia v England at Melbourne	1936-37
268	G. N. Yallop	Australia v Pakistan at Melbourne	1983-84
267*	B. A. Young	New Zealand v Sri Lanka at Dunedin	1996-97
267	P. A. de Silva	Sri Lanka v New Zealand at Wellington	1990-91
266	W. H. Ponsford	Australia v England at The Oval	1934
266	D. L. Houghton	Zimbabwe v Sri Lanka at Bulawayo	1994-95
262*	D. L. Amiss	England v West Indies at Kingston	1973-74
261	F. M. M. Worrell	West Indies v England at Nottingham	1950
260	C. C. Hunte	West Indies v Pakistan at Kingston	1957-58
260	Javed Miandad	Pakistan v England at The Oval	1987
259	G. M. Turner	New Zealand v West Indies at Georgetown	1971-72
259	G. C. Smith	South Africa v England at Lord's	2003
258	T. W. Graveney	England v West Indies at Nottingham	1957
258	S. M. Nurse	West Indies v New Zealand at Christchurch	1968-69
257*	Wasim Akram	Pakistan v Zimbabwe at Sheikhupura	1996-97
257	R. T. Ponting	Australia v India at Melbourne	2003-04
256	R. B. Kanhai	West Indies v India at Calcutta	1958-59
256	K. F. Barrington	England v Australia at Manchester	1964
255*	D. J. McGlew	South Africa v New Zealand at Wellington	1952-53

254	D. G. Bradman	Australia v England at Lord's	1930
251	W. R. Hammond	England v Australia at Sydney	1928-29
250	K. D. Walters	Australia v New Zealand at Christchurch	1976-77
250	S. F. A. F. Bacchus	West Indies v India at Kanpur	1978-79
250	J. L. Langer	Australia v England at Melbourne	2002-03

Note: The highest individual innings for Bangladesh is 145 by Aminul Islam against India at Dhaka in 2000-01.

HUNDRED ON TEST DEBUT

C. Bannerman (165*)	Australia v England at Melbourne	1876-77
W. G. Grace (152)	England v Australia at The Oval	1880
H. Graham (107)	Australia v England at Lord's	1893
†K. S. Ranjitsinhji (154*)	England v Australia at Manchester	1896
†P. F. Warner (132*)	England v South Africa at Johannesburg	1898-99
†R. A. Duff (104)	Australia v England at Melbourne	1901-02
R. E. Foster (287)	England v Australia at Sydney	1903-04
G. Gunn (119)	England v Australia at Sydney	1907-08
†R. J. Hartigan (116)	Australia v England at Adelaide	1907-08
†H. L. Collins (104)	Australia v England at Sydney	1920-21
W. H. Ponsford (110)	Australia v England at Sydney	1924-25
A. A. Jackson (164)	Australia v England at Adelaide	1928-29
†G. A. Headley (176)	West Indies v England at Bridgetown	1929-30
J. E. Mills (117)	New Zealand v England at Wellington	1929-30
Nawab of Pataudi sen. (102)	England v Australia at Sydney	1932-33
B. H. Valentine (136)	England v India at Bombay	1933-34
†L. Amarnath (118)	India v England at Bombay	1933-34
†P. A. Gibb (106)	England v South Africa at Johannesburg	1938-39
S. C. Griffith (140)	England v West Indies at Port-of-Spain	1947-48
A. G. Ganteaume (112)	West Indies v England at Port-of-Spain	1947-48
†J. W. Burke (101*)	Australia v England at Adelaide	1950-51
P. B. H. May (138)	England v South Africa at Leeds	1951
R. H. Shodhan (110)	India v Pakistan at Calcutta	1952-53
B. H. Pairaudeau (115)	West Indies v India at Port-of-Spain	1952-53
†O. G. Smith (104)	West Indies v Australia at Kingston	1954-55
A. G. Kripal Singh (100*)	India v New Zealand at Hyderabad	1955-56
C. C. Hunte (142)	West Indies v Pakistan at Bridgetown	1957-58
C. A. Milton (104*)	England v New Zealand at Leeds	1958
†A. A. Baig (112)	India v England at Manchester	1959
Hanumant Singh (105)	India v England at Delhi	1963-64
Khalid Ibadulla (166)	Pakistan v Australia at Karachi	1964-65
B. R. Taylor (105)	New Zealand v India at Calcutta	1964-65
K. D. Walters (155)	Australia v England at Brisbane	1965-66
J. H. Hampshire (107)	England v West Indies at Lord's	1969
†G. R. Viswanath (137)	India v Australia at Kanpur	1969-70
G. S. Chappell (108)	Australia v England at Perth	1970-71
‡L. G. Rowe (214, 100*)	West Indies v New Zealand at Kingston	1971-72
A. I. Kallicharran (100*)	West Indies v New Zealand at Georgetown	1971-72
R. E. Redmond (107)	New Zealand v Pakistan at Auckland	1972-73
†F. C. Hayes (106*)	England v West Indies at The Oval	1973
†C. G. Greenidge (107)	West Indies v India at Bangalore	1974-75
†L. Baichan (105*)	West Indies v Pakistan at Lahore	1974-75
G. J. Cosier (109)	Australia v West Indies at Melbourne	1975-76
S. Amarnath (124)	India v New Zealand at Auckland	1975-76
Javed Miandad (163)	Pakistan v New Zealand at Lahore	1976-77
†A. B. Williams (100)	West Indies v Australia at Georgetown	1977-78
†D. M. Wellham (103)	Australia v England at The Oval	1981
†Salim Malik (100*)	Pakistan v Sri Lanka at Karachi	1981-82
K. C. Wessels (162)	Australia v England at Brisbane	1982-83
W. B. Phillips (159)	Australia v Pakistan at Perth	1983-84
§M. Azharuddin (110)	India v England at Calcutta	1984-85
D. S. B. P. Kuruppu (201*)	Sri Lanka v New Zealand at Colombo (CCC)	1986-87
†M. J. Greatbatch (107*)	New Zealand v England at Auckland	1987-88

M. E. Waugh (138)	Australia v England at Adelaide	1990-91
A. C. Hudson (163)	South Africa v West Indies at Bridgetown	1991-92
R. S. Kaluwitharana (132*)	Sri Lanka v Australia at Colombo (SSC)	1992-93
D. L. Houghton (121)	Zimbabwe v India at Harare	1992-93
P. K. Amre (103)	India v South Africa at Durban	1992-93
†G. P. Thorpe (114*)	England v Australia at Nottingham	1993
G. S. Blewett (102*)	Australia v England at Adelaide	1994-95
S. C. Ganguly (131)	India v England at Lord's	1996
†Mohammad Wasim (109*)	Pakistan v New Zealand at Lahore	1996-97
Ali Naqvi (115)	Pakistan v South Africa at Rawalpindi	1997-98
Azhar Mahmood (128*)	Pakistan v South Africa at Rawalpindi	1997-98
M. S. Sinclair (214)	New Zealand v West Indies at Wellington	1999-2000
†Younis Khan (107)	Pakistan v Sri Lanka at Rawalpindi	1999-2000
Aminul Islam (145)	Bangladesh v India at Dhaka	2000-01
†H. Masakadza (119)	Zimbabwe v West Indies at Harare	2001
T. T. Samaraweera (103*)	Sri Lanka v India at Colombo (SSC)	2001
Taufeeq Umar (104)	Pakistan v Bangladesh at Multan	2001-02
†Mohammad Ashraful (114)	Bangladesh v Sri Lanka at Colombo (SSC)	2001-02
V. Sehwag (105)	India v South Africa at Bloemfontein	2001-02
L. Vincent (104)	New Zealand v Australia at Perth	2001-02
S. B. Styris (107)	New Zealand v West Indies at St George's	2002
J. A. Rudolph (222*)	South Africa v Bangladesh at Chittagong	2003
‡Yasir Hameed (170, 105)	Pakistan v Bangladesh at Karachi	2003
D. R. Smith (105*)	West Indies v South Africa at Cape Town	2003-04

† *In his second innings of the match.*
‡ *L. G. Rowe and Yasir Hameed are the only batsmen to score a hundred in each innings on debut.*
§ *M. Azharuddin is the only batsman to score hundreds in each of his first three Tests.*

Notes: L. Amarnath and S. Amarnath were father and son.
Ali Naqvi and Azhar Mahmood achieved the feat in the same innings.
Only Bannerman, Houghton and Aminul Islam scored hundreds in their country's first Test.

300 RUNS ON TEST DEBUT

314	L. G. Rowe (214, 100*)	West Indies v New Zealand at Kingston	1971-72
306	R. E. Foster (287, 19)	England v Australia at Sydney	1903-04

DUCK ON TEST DEBUT

(Players with 2,500 Test runs who started with a duck in their first innings.)

†M. S. Atapattu	Sri Lanka v India at Chandigarh	1990-91
M. A. Atherton	England v Australia at Nottingham	1989
K. F. Barrington	England v South Africa at Nottingham	1955
K. W. R. Fletcher	England v Australia at Leeds	1968
H. A. Gomes	West Indies v England at Nottingham	1976
†G. A. Gooch	England v Australia at Birmingham	1975
L. Hutton	England v New Zealand at Lord's	1937
A. P. E. Knott	England v Pakistan at Nottingham	1967
M. Leyland	England v West Indies at The Oval	1928
Majid Khan	Pakistan v Australia at Karachi	1964-65
R. B. Richardson	West Indies v India at Bombay	1983-84
†Saeed Anwar	Pakistan v West Indies at Faisalabad	1990-91
H. W. Taylor	South Africa v Australia at Manchester	1912
H. P. Tillekeratne	Sri Lanka v Australia at Hobart	1989-90
V. T. Trumper	Australia v England at Nottingham	1899
G. M. Turner	New Zealand v West Indies at Auckland	1968-69
G. R. Viswanath	India v Australia at Kanpur	1969-70
Wasim Akram	Pakistan v New Zealand at Auckland	1984-85

† *Made a pair.*

Notes: Atapattu made a duck and a single in his second Test, and another pair in his third.
In his second innings, Viswanath made a hundred (see previous page).

TRIPLE-HUNDRED AND HUNDRED IN A TEST

G. A. Gooch (England)	333 and 123 v India at Lord's	1990

The only instance in first-class cricket. M. A. Taylor (Australia) scored 334 and 92 v Pakistan at Peshawar in 1998-99.*

DOUBLE-HUNDRED AND HUNDRED IN A TEST

K. D. Walters (Australia)	242 and 103 v West Indies at Sydney	1968-69
S. M. Gavaskar (India)	124 and 220 v West Indies at Port-of-Spain	1970-71
†L. G. Rowe (West Indies)	214 and 100* v New Zealand at Kingston	1971-72
G. S. Chappell (Australia)	247* and 133 v New Zealand at Wellington	1973-74
B. C. Lara (West Indies)	221 and 130 v Sri Lanka at Colombo (SSC)	2001-02

† *On Test debut.*

TWO SEPARATE HUNDREDS IN A TEST

Three times: S. M. Gavaskar.
Twice in one series: C. L. Walcott v Australia (1954-55).
Twice: †A. R. Border; G. S. Chappell; ‡P. A. de Silva; G. A. Headley; H. Sutcliffe.
Once: W. Bardsley; D. G. Bradman; I. M. Chappell; D. C. S. Compton; R. Dravid; A. Flower; G. W. Flower; G. A. Gooch; C. G. Greenidge; A. P. Gurusinha; W. R. Hammond; Hanif Mohammad; M. L. Hayden; V. S. Hazare; G. P. Howarth; Javed Miandad; A. H. Jones; D. M. Jones; R. B. Kanhai; G. Kirsten; B. C. Lara; A. Melville; L. R. D. Mendis; B. Mitchell; J. Moroney; A. R. Morris; E. Paynter; §L. G. Rowe; A. C. Russell; R. B. Simpson; G. S. Sobers; A. J. Stewart; G. M. Turner; Wajahatullah Wasti; K. D. Walters; S. R. Waugh; E. D. Weekes; §Yasir Hameed.

† *A. R. Border scored 150* and 153 against Pakistan in 1979-80 to become the first to score 150 in each innings of a Test match.*
‡ *P. A. de Silva scored 138* and 103* against Pakistan in 1996-97 to become the first to score two not out hundreds in a Test match.*
§ *L. G. Rowe's and Yasir Hameed's two hundreds were on Test debut.*

MOST DOUBLE-HUNDREDS

D. G. Bradman (A)	12	**M. S. Atapattu (SL)**	**5**	C. G. Greenidge (WI)	4
W. R. Hammond (E)	7	G. S. Chappell (A)	4	L. Hutton (E)	4
Javed Miandad (P)	6	**R. Dravid**	**4**	Zaheer Abbas (P)	4
B. C. Lara (WI)	**6**	S. M. Gavaskar (I)	4		

MOST HUNDREDS

S. M. Gavaskar (I)	34	R. N. Harvey (A)	21	M. D. Crowe (NZ)	17
S. R. Tendulkar (I)	**32**	K. F. Barrington (E)	20	**M. L. Hayden (A)**	**17**
S. R. Waugh (A)	**32**	P. A. de Silva (SL)	20	**J. L. Langer (A)**	**17**
D. G. Bradman (A)	29	G. A. Gooch (E)	20	D. B. Vengsarkar (I)	17
A. R. Border (A)	27	**G. Kirsten (SA)**	**20**	M. A. Atherton (E)	16
G. S. Sobers (WI)	26	**R. T. Ponting (A)**	**20**	**R. Dravid (I)**	**16**
G. S. Chappell (A)	24	**M. E. Waugh (A)**	**20**	R. B. Richardson (WI)	16
B. C. Lara (WI)	**24**	C. G. Greenidge (WI)	19	H. Sutcliffe (E)	16
I. V. A. Richards (WI)	24	L. Hutton (E)	19	J. B. Hobbs (E)	15
Javed Miandad (P)	23	C. H. Lloyd (WI)	19	**J. H. Kallis (SA)**	**15**
M. Azharuddin (I)	22	M. A. Taylor (A)	19	R. B. Kanhai (WI)	15
G. Boycott (E)	22	D. I. Gower (E)	18	Salim Malik (P)	15
M. C. Cowdrey (E)	22	D. L. Haynes (WI)	18	**A. J. Stewart (E)**	**15**
W. R. Hammond (E)	22	**Inzamam-ul-Haq (P)**	**18**	C. L. Walcott (WI)	15
D. C. Boon (A)	21	D. C. S. Compton (E)	17	K. D. Walters (A)	15

E. D. Weekes (WI)	15	Hanif Mohammad (P)	12	D. M. Jones (A)	11
I. T. Botham (E)	14	Ijaz Ahmed, sen. (P)	12	Saeed Anwar (P)	11
I. M. Chappell (A)	14	A. I. Kallicharran (WI)	12	R. J. Shastri (I)	11
D. J. Cullinan (SA)	14	A. R. Morris (A)	12	**H. P. Tillekeratne (SL)**	**11**
A. J. Lamb (E)	14	**G. P. Thorpe (E)**	**12**	M. W. Gatting (E)	10
M. J. Slater (A)	14	P. R. Umrigar (I)	12	A. L. Hassett (A)	10
G. R. Viswanath (I)	14	J. G. Wright (NZ)	12	G. A. Headley (WI)	10
H. H. Gibbs (SA)	**13**	Zaheer Abbas (P)	12	**S. T. Jayasuriya (SL)**	**10**
C. L. Hooper (WI)	**13**	M. Amarnath (I)	11	**D. P. M. D. Jayawardene (SL)**	**10**
N. Hussain (E)	**13**	D. L. Amiss (E)	11	Mudassar Nazar (P)	10
W. M. Lawry (A)	13	Asif Iqbal (P)	11	Mushtaq Mohammad (P)	10
P. B. H. May (E)	13	**M. S. Atapattu (SL)**	**11**	R. B. Simpson (A)	10
J. H. Edrich (E)	12	**S. C. Ganguly (I)**	**11**	**M. P. Vaughan (E)**	**10**
A. Flower (Z)	**12**	T. W. Graveney (E)	11	**Yousuf Youhana (P)**	**10**

Note: The most hundreds for Bangladesh is **2** by **Habibul Bashar.**

Bold type denotes those who have played Test cricket since the start of 2002-03.

MOST HUNDREDS AGAINST ONE TEAM

19	D. G. Bradman	Australia v England
13	S. M. Gavaskar	India v West Indies
12	J. B. Hobbs	England v Australia
10	G. S. Sobers	West Indies v England
10	S. R. Waugh	Australia v England

CARRYING BAT THROUGH TEST INNINGS

(Figures in brackets show team's total.)

A. B. Tancred	26* (47)	South Africa v England at Cape Town	1888-89
J. E. Barrett	67* (176)†	Australia v England at Lord's	1890
R. Abel	132* (307)	England v Australia at Sydney	1891-92
P. F. Warner	132* (237)†	England v South Africa at Johannesburg	1898-99
W. W. Armstrong	159* (309)	Australia v South Africa at Johannesburg	1902-03
J. W. Zulch	43* (103)	South Africa v England at Cape Town	1909-10
W. Bardsley	193* (383)	Australia v England at Lord's	1926
W. M. Woodfull	30* (66)§	Australia v England at Brisbane	1928-29
W. M. Woodfull	73* (193)‡	Australia v England at Adelaide	1932-33
W. A. Brown	206* (422)	Australia v England at Lord's	1938
L. Hutton	202* (344)	England v West Indies at The Oval	1950
L. Hutton	156* (272)	England v Australia at Adelaide	1950-51
Nazar Mohammad¶	124* (331)	Pakistan v India at Lucknow	1952-53
F. M. M. Worrell	191* (372)	West Indies v England at Nottingham	1957
T. L. Goddard	56* (99)	South Africa v Australia at Cape Town	1957-58
D. J. McGlew	127* (292)	South Africa v New Zealand at Durban	1961-62
C. C. Hunte	60* (131)	West Indies v Australia at Port-of-Spain	1964-65
G. M. Turner	43* (131)	New Zealand v England at Lord's	1969
W. M. Lawry	49* (107)	Australia v India at Delhi	1969-70
W. M. Lawry	60* (116)‡	Australia v England at Sydney	1970-71
G. M. Turner	223* (386)	New Zealand v West Indies at Kingston	1971-72
I. R. Redpath	159* (346)	Australia v New Zealand at Auckland	1973-74
G. Boycott	99* (215)	England v Australia at Perth	1979-80
S. M. Gavaskar	127* (286)	India v Pakistan at Faisalabad	1982-83
Mudassar Nazar¶	152* (323)	Pakistan v India at Lahore	1982-83
S. Wettimuny	63* (144)	Sri Lanka v New Zealand at Christchurch	1982-83
D. C. Boon	58* (103)	Australia v New Zealand at Auckland	1985-86
D. L. Haynes	88* (211)	West Indies v Pakistan at Karachi	1986-87
G. A. Gooch	154* (252)	England v West Indies at Leeds	1991
D. L. Haynes	75* (176)	West Indies v England at The Oval	1991
A. J. Stewart	69* (175)	England v Pakistan at Lord's	1992
D. L. Haynes	143* (382)	West Indies v Pakistan at Port-of-Spain	1992-93

M. H. Dekker	68* (187)	Zimbabwe v Pakistan at Rawalpindi	1993-94
M. A. Atherton	94* (228)	England v New Zealand at Christchurch	1996-97
G. Kirsten	100* (239)	South Africa v Pakistan at Faisalabad	1997-98
M. A. Taylor	169* (350)	Australia v South Africa at Adelaide	1997-98
G. W. Flower	156* (321)	Zimbabwe v Pakistan at Bulawayo	1997-98
Saeed Anwar	188* (316)	Pakistan v India at Calcutta	1998-99
M. S. Atapattu	216* (428)	Sri Lanka v Zimbabwe at Bulawayo	1999-2000
R. P. Arnold	104* (231)	Sri Lanka v Zimbabwe at Harare	1999-2000
Javed Omar	85* (168)†‡	Bangladesh v Zimbabwe at Bulawayo	2000-01

† *On debut.* ‡ *One man absent.* § *Two men absent.* ¶ *Father and son.*

Notes: G. M. Turner (223*) holds the record for the highest score by a player carrying his bat through a Test innings. He is also the youngest player to do so, being 22 years 63 days old when he first achieved the feat (1969).

D. L. Haynes, who is alone in achieving this feat on three occasions, also opened the batting and was last man out in each innings for West Indies v New Zealand at Dunedin, 1979-80.

750 RUNS IN A SERIES

	T	*I*	*NO*	*R*	*HS*	*100s*	*Avge*		
D. G. Bradman	5	7	0	974	334	4	139.14	A v E	1930
W. R. Hammond	5	9	1	905	251	4	113.12	E v A	1928-29
M. A. Taylor	6	11	1	839	219	2	83.90	A v E	1989
R. N. Harvey	5	9	0	834	205	4	92.66	A v SA	1952-53
I. V. A. Richards	4	7	0	829	291	3	118.42	WI v E	1976
C. L. Walcott	5	10	0	827	155	5	82.70	WI v A	1954-55
G. S. Sobers	5	8	2	824	365*	3	137.33	WI v P	1957-58
D. G. Bradman	5	9	0	810	270	3	90.00	A v E	1936-37
D. G. Bradman	5	5	1	806	299*	4	201.50	A v SA	1931-32
B. C. Lara	5	8	0	798	375	2	99.75	WI v E	1993-94
E. D. Weekes	5	7	0	779	194	4	111.28	WI v I	1948-49
†S. M. Gavaskar	4	8	3	774	220	4	154.80	I v WI	1970-71
B. C. Lara	6	10	1	765	179	3	85.00	WI v E	1995
Mudassar Nazar	6	8	2	761	231	4	126.83	P v I	1982-83
D. G. Bradman	5	8	0	758	304	2	94.75	A v E	1934
D. C. S. Compton	5	8	0	753	208	4	94.12	E v SA	1947
‡G. A. Gooch	3	6	0	752	333	3	125.33	E v I	1990

† *Gavaskar's aggregate was achieved in his first Test series.*
‡ *G. A. Gooch is alone in scoring 1,000 runs in Test cricket during an English season with 1,058 runs in 11 innings against New Zealand and India in 1990.*

MOST RUNS IN A CALENDAR YEAR

	T	*I*	*NO*	*R*	*HS*	*100s*	*Avge*	*Year*
I. V. A. Richards (WI)	11	19	0	1,710	291	7	90.00	1976
S. M. Gavaskar (I)	18	27	1	1,555	221	5	59.80	1979
R. T. Ponting (A)	11	18	3	1,503	257	6	100.20	2003
M. P. Vaughan (E)	14	26	2	1,481	197	6	61.70	2002
S. R. Tendulkar (I)	16	26	1	1,392	193	4	55.68	2002
M. L. Hayden (A)	14	25	3	1,391	203	5	63.22	2001
G. R. Viswanath (I)	17	26	3	1,388	179	5	60.34	1979
R. B. Simpson (A)	14	26	3	1,381	311	3	60.04	1964
D. L. Amiss (E)	13	22	2	1,379	262*	5	68.95	1974
R. Dravid (I)	16	26	3	1,357	217	5	59.00	2002
B. C. Lara (WI)	10	19	1	1,344	209	5	74.66	2003
M. L. Hayden (A)	12	21	4	1,312	380	5	77.17	2003
S. M. Gavaskar (I)	18	32	4	1,310	236*	5	46.78	1983

Notes: M. Amarnath reached 1,000 runs in 1983 on May 3.

The only batsman to score 1,000 runs in a year before World War II was C. Hill of Australia: 1,061 in 1902.

MOST RUNS

		T	*I*	*NO*	*R*	*HS*	*100s*	*Avge*
1	A. R. Border (Australia)	156	265	44	11,174	205	27	50.56
2	**S. R. Waugh (Australia)**	**168**	**260**	**46**	**10,927**	**200**	**32**	**51.06**
3	S. M. Gavaskar (India)	125	214	16	10,122	236*	34	51.12
4	**S. R. Tendulkar (India)**	**111**	**180**	**18**	**9,265**	**241***	**32**	**57.19**
5	**B. C. Lara (West Indies)**	**102**	**180**	**5**	**9,157**	**375**	**24**	**52.32**
6	G. A. Gooch (England)	118	215	6	8,900	333	20	42.58
7	Javed Miandad (Pakistan)	124	189	21	8,832	280*	23	52.57
8	I. V. A. Richards (West Indies)	121	182	12	8,540	291	24	50.23
9	**A. J. Stewart (England)**	**133**	**235**	**21**	**8,463**	**190**	**15**	**39.54**
10	D. I. Gower (England)	117	204	18	8,231	215	18	44.25
11	G. Boycott (England)	108	193	23	8,114	246*	22	47.72
12	G. S. Sobers (West Indies)	93	160	21	8,032	365*	26	57.78
13	**M. E. Waugh (Australia)**	**128**	**209**	**17**	**8,029**	**153***	**20**	**41.81**
14	M. A. Atherton (England)	115	212	7	7,728	185*	16	37.69
15	M. C. Cowdrey (England)	114	188	15	7,624	182	22	44.06
16	C. G. Greenidge (West Indies)	108	185	16	7,558	226	19	44.72
17	M. A. Taylor (Australia)	104	186	13	7,525	334*	19	43.49
18	C. H. Lloyd (West Indies)	110	175	14	7,515	242*	19	46.67
19	D. L. Haynes (West Indies)	116	202	25	7,487	184	18	42.29
20	D. C. Boon (Australia)	107	190	20	7,422	200	21	43.65
21	W. R. Hammond (England)	85	140	16	7,249	336*	22	58.45
22	G. S. Chappell (Australia)	87	151	19	7,110	247*	24	53.86
23	**G. Kirsten (South Africa)**	**98**	**170**	**14**	**7,039**	**275**	**20**	**45.12**
24	D. G. Bradman (Australia)	52	80	10	6,996	334	29	99.94
25	L. Hutton (England)	79	138	15	6,971	364	19	56.67
26	D. B. Vengsarkar (India)	116	185	22	6,868	166	17	42.13
27	K. F. Barrington (England)	82	131	15	6,806	256	20	58.67
28	**Inzamam-ul-Haq (Pakistan)**	**91**	**150**	**16**	**6,680**	**329**	**18**	**49.85**
29	**R. Dravid (India)**	**75**	**130**	**16**	**6,546**	**233**	**16**	**57.42**
30	P. A. de Silva (Sri Lanka)	93	159	11	6,361	267	20	42.97
31	R. B. Kanhai (West Indies)	79	137	6	6,227	256	15	47.53
32	M. Azharuddin (India)	99	147	9	6,215	199	22	45.03
33	R. N. Harvey (Australia)	79	137	10	6,149	205	21	48.41
34	G. R. Viswanath (India)	91	155	10	6,080	222	14	41.93
35	R. B. Richardson (West Indies)	86	146	12	5,949	194	16	44.39
36	**R. T. Ponting (Australia)**	**75**	**119**	**15**	**5,821**	**257**	**20**	**55.97**
37	D. C. S. Compton (England)	78	131	15	5,807	278	17	50.06
38	Salim Malik (Pakistan)	103	154	22	5,768	237	15	43.69
39	**C. L. Hooper (West Indies)**	**102**	**173**	**15**	**5,762**	**233**	**13**	**36.46**
40	**G. P. Thorpe (England)**	**83**	**151**	**19**	**5,552**	**200***	**12**	**42.06**
41	**J. H. Kallis (South Africa)**	**75**	**123**	**20**	**5,486**	**189***	**15**	**53.26**
42	M. D. Crowe (New Zealand)	77	131	11	5,444	299	17	45.36
43	**N. Hussain (England)**	**91**	**162**	**14**	**5,430**	**207**	**13**	**36.68**
44	J. B. Hobbs (England)	61	102	7	5,410	211	15	56.94
45	K. D. Walters (Australia)	74	125	14	5,357	250	15	48.26
46	I. M. Chappell (Australia)	75	136	10	5,345	196	14	42.42
47	J. G. Wright (New Zealand)	82	148	7	5,334	185	12	37.82
48	M. J. Slater (Australia)	74	131	7	5,312	219	14	42.83
49	**S. T. Jayasuriya (Sri Lanka)**	**83**	**140**	**13**	**5,258**	**340**	**10**	**41.40**
50	Kapil Dev (India)	131	184	15	5,248	163	8	31.05

Note: The leading aggregates for other countries are:

	T	I	NO	R	HS	100s	Avge
A. Flower (Zimbabwe)	**63**	**112**	**19**	**4,794**	**232***	**12**	**51.54**
Habibul Bashar (Bangladesh)	**26**	**52**	**1**	**1,840**	**108**	**2**	**36.07**

Bold type denotes those who have played Test cricket since the start of 2002-03.

2,500 RUNS

ENGLAND

		T	I	NO	R	HS	100s	Avge
1	G. A. Gooch	118	215	6	8,900	333	20	42.58
2	**A. J. Stewart**	**133**	**235**	**21**	**8,463**	**190**	**15**	**39.54**
3	D. I. Gower	117	204	18	8,231	215	18	44.25
4	G. Boycott	108	193	23	8,114	246*	22	47.72
5	M. A. Atherton	115	212	7	7,728	185*	16	37.69
6	M. C. Cowdrey	114	188	15	7,624	182	22	44.06
7	W. R. Hammond	85	140	16	7,249	336*	22	58.45
8	L. Hutton	79	138	15	6,971	364	19	56.67
9	K. F. Barrington	82	131	15	6,806	256	20	58.67
10	D. C. S. Compton	78	131	15	5,807	278	17	50.06
11	**G. P. Thorpe**	**83**	**151**	**19**	**5,552**	**200***	**12**	**42.06**
12	**N. Hussain**	**91**	**162**	**14**	**5,430**	**207**	**13**	**36.68**
13	J. B. Hobbs	61	102	7	5,410	211	15	56.94
14	I. T. Botham	102	161	6	5,200	208	14	33.54
15	J. H. Edrich	77	127	9	5,138	310*	12	43.54
16	T. W. Graveney	79	123	13	4,882	258	11	44.38
17	A. J. Lamb	79	139	10	4,656	142	14	36.09
18	H. Sutcliffe	54	84	9	4,555	194	16	60.73
19	P. B. H. May	66	106	9	4,537	285*	13	46.77
20	E. R. Dexter	62	102	8	4,502	205	9	47.89
21	M. W. Gatting	79	138	14	4,409	207	10	35.55
22	A. P. E. Knott	95	149	15	4,389	135	5	32.75
23	R. A. Smith	62	112	15	4,236	175	9	43.67
24	**M. A. Butcher**	**62**	**114**	**4**	**3,790**	**173***	**8**	**34.45**
25	D. L. Amiss	50	88	10	3,612	262*	11	46.30
26	A. W. Greig	58	93	4	3,599	148	8	40.43
27	E. H. Hendren	51	83	9	3,525	205*	7	47.63
28	G. A. Hick	65	114	6	3,383	178	6	31.32
29	F. E. Woolley	64	98	7	3,283	154	5	36.07
30	K. W. R. Fletcher	59	96	14	3,272	216	7	39.90
31	**M. E. Trescothick**	**43**	**81**	**7**	**3,175**	**219**	**5**	**42.90**
32	**M. P. Vaughan**	**40**	**71**	**4**	**3,118**	**197**	**10**	**46.53**
33	M. Leyland	41	65	5	2,764	187	9	46.06
34	C. Washbrook	37	66	6	2,569	195	6	42.81

AUSTRALIA

		T	I	NO	R	HS	100s	Avge
1	A. R. Border	156	265	44	11,174	205	27	50.56
2	**S. R. Waugh**	**168**	**260**	**46**	**10,927**	**200**	**32**	**51.06**
3	**M. E. Waugh**	**128**	**209**	**17**	**8,029**	**153***	**20**	**41.81**
4	M. A. Taylor	104	186	13	7,525	334*	19	43.49
5	D. C. Boon	107	190	20	7,422	200	21	43.65
6	G. S. Chappell	87	151	19	7,110	247*	24	53.86
7	D. G. Bradman	52	80	10	6,996	334	29	99.94
8	R. N. Harvey	79	137	10	6,149	205	21	48.41
9	**R. T. Ponting**	**75**	**119**	**15**	**5,821**	**257**	**20**	**55.97**
10	K. D. Walters	74	125	14	5,357	250	15	48.26
11	I. M. Chappell	75	136	10	5,345	196	14	42.42
12	M. J. Slater	74	131	7	5,312	219	14	42.83
13	W. M. Lawry	67	123	12	5,234	210	13	47.15
14	**J. L. Langer**	**71**	**118**	**6**	**5,037**	**250**	**17**	**44.97**
15	R. B. Simpson	62	111	7	4,869	311	10	46.81
16	I. R. Redpath	66	120	11	4,737	171	8	43.45

		T	*I*	*NO*	*R*	*HS*	*100s*	*Avge*
17	**M. L. Hayden**	**50**	**85**	**8**	**4,488**	**380**	**17**	**58.28**
18	K. J. Hughes	70	124	6	4,415	213	9	37.41
19	I. A. Healy	119	182	23	4,356	161*	4	27.39
20	R. W. Marsh	96	150	13	3,633	132	3	26.51
21	D. M. Jones	52	89	11	3,631	216	11	46.55
22	A. R. Morris	46	79	3	3,533	206	12	46.48
23	C. Hill	49	89	2	3,412	191	7	39.21
24	G. M. Wood	59	112	6	3,374	172	9	31.83
25	**A. C. Gilchrist**	**51**	**70**	**13**	**3,169**	**204***	**9**	**55.59**
26	V. T. Trumper	48	89	8	3,163	214*	8	39.04
27	C. C. McDonald	47	83	4	3,107	170	5	39.32
28	A. L. Hassett	43	69	3	3,073	198*	10	46.56
29	K. R. Miller	55	87	7	2,958	147	7	36.97
30	W. W. Armstrong	50	84	10	2,863	159*	6	38.68
31	G. R. Marsh	50	93	7	2,854	138	4	33.18
32	K. R. Stackpole	43	80	5	2,807	207	7	37.42
33	N. C. O'Neill	42	69	8	2,779	181	6	45.55
34	G. N. Yallop	39	70	3	2,756	268	8	41.13
35	S. J. McCabe	39	62	5	2,748	232	6	48.21
36	G. S. Blewett	46	79	4	2,552	214	4	34.02

SOUTH AFRICA

		T	*I*	*NO*	*R*	*HS*	*100s*	*Avge*
1	**G. Kirsten**	**98**	**170**	**14**	**7,039**	**275**	**20**	**45.12**
2	**J. H. Kallis**	**75**	**123**	**20**	**5,486**	**189***	**15**	**53.26**
3	D. J. Cullinan	70	115	12	4,554	275*	14	44.21
4	**H. H. Gibbs**	**56**	**94**	**5**	**4,372**	**228**	**13**	**49.12**
5	W. J. Cronje	68	111	9	3,714	135	6	36.41
6	B. Mitchell	42	80	9	3,471	189*	8	48.88
7	A. D. Nourse	34	62	7	2,960	231	9	53.81
8	H. W. Taylor	42	76	4	2,936	176	7	40.77
9	**S. M. Pollock**	**80**	**112**	**29**	**2,868**	**111**	**2**	**34.55**
10	**M. V. Boucher**	**71**	**96**	**12**	**2,679**	**125**	**4**	**31.89**
11	J. N. Rhodes	52	80	9	2,532	117	3	35.66
12	E. J. Barlow	30	57	2	2,516	201	6	45.74
12	T. L. Goddard	41	78	5	2,516	112	1	34.46

Note: K. C. Wessels scored 2,788 runs in 40 Tests: 1,761 (average 42.95) in 24 Tests for Australia, and 1,027 (average 38.03) in 16 Tests for South Africa.

WEST INDIES

		T	*I*	*NO*	*R*	*HS*	*100s*	*Avge*
1	**B. C. Lara**	**102**	**180**	**5**	**9,157**	**375**	**24**	**52.32**
2	I. V. A. Richards	121	182	12	8,540	291	24	50.23
3	G. S. Sobers	93	160	21	8,032	365*	26	57.78
4	C. G. Greenidge	108	185	16	7,558	226	19	44.72
5	C. H. Lloyd	110	175	14	7,515	242*	19	46.67
6	D. L. Haynes	116	202	25	7,487	184	18	42.29
7	R. B. Kanhai	79	137	6	6,227	256	15	47.53
8	R. B. Richardson	86	146	12	5,949	194	16	44.39
9	**C. L. Hooper**	**102**	**173**	**15**	**5,762**	**233**	**13**	**36.46**
10	**S. Chanderpaul**	**71**	**119**	**15**	**4,546**	**140**	**9**	**43.71**
11	E. D. Weekes	48	81	5	4,455	207	15	58.61

		T	I	NO	R	HS	100s	Avge
12	A. I. Kallicharran	66	109	10	4,399	187	12	44.43
13	R. C. Fredericks	59	109	7	4,334	169	8	42.49
14	F. M. M. Worrell	51	87	9	3,860	261	9	49.48
15	C. L. Walcott	44	74	7	3,798	220	15	56.68
16	P. J. L. Dujon	81	115	11	3,322	139	5	31.94
17	C. C. Hunte	44	78	6	3,245	260	8	45.06
18	H. A. Gomes	60	91	11	3,171	143	9	39.63
19	B. F. Butcher	44	78	6	3,104	209*	7	43.11
20	J. C. Adams	54	90	17	3,012	208*	6	41.26
21	S. L. Campbell	52	93	4	2,882	208	4	32.38
22	**R. R. Sarwan**	**40**	**72**	**5**	**2,641**	**119**	**4**	**39.41**
23	S. M. Nurse	29	54	1	2,523	258	6	47.60

NEW ZEALAND

		T	I	NO	R	HS	100s	Avge
1	M. D. Crowe	77	131	11	5,444	299	17	45.36
2	J. G. Wright	82	148	7	5,334	185	12	37.82
3	**S. P. Fleming**	**79**	**137**	**9**	**4,926**	**274***	**6**	**38.48**
4	**N. J. Astle**	**59**	**101**	**9**	**3,592**	**222**	**9**	**39.04**
5	B. E. Congdon	61	114	7	3,448	176	7	32.22
6	J. R. Reid	58	108	5	3,428	142	6	33.28
7	R. J. Hadlee	86	134	19	3,124	151*	2	27.16
8	G. M. Turner	41	73	6	2,991	259	7	44.64
9	A. H. Jones	39	74	8	2,922	186	7	44.27
10	**C. D. McMillan**	**48**	**80**	**10**	**2,909**	**142**	**6**	**41.55**
11	A. C. Parore	78	128	19	2,865	110	2	26.28
12	**C. L. Cairns**	**56**	**94**	**5**	**2,864**	**126**	**4**	**32.17**
13	B. Sutcliffe	42	76	8	2,727	230*	5	40.10
14	M. G. Burgess	50	92	6	2,684	119*	5	31.20
15	J. V. Coney	52	85	14	2,668	174*	3	37.57
16	G. P. Howarth	47	83	5	2,531	147	6	32.44

INDIA

		T	I	NO	R	HS	100s	Avge
1	S. M. Gavaskar	125	214	16	10,122	236*	34	51.12
2	**S. R. Tendulkar**	**111**	**180**	**18**	**9,265**	**241***	**32**	**57.19**
3	D. B. Vengsarkar	116	185	22	6,868	166	17	42.13
4	**R. Dravid**	**75**	**130**	**16**	**6,546**	**233**	**16**	**57.42**
5	M. Azharuddin	99	147	9	6,215	199	22	45.03
6	G. R. Viswanath	91	155	10	6,080	222	14	41.93
7	Kapil Dev	131	184	15	5,248	163	8	31.05
8	**S. C. Ganguly**	**72**	**120**	**12**	**4,509**	**173**	**11**	**41.75**
9	M. Amarnath	69	113	10	4,378	138	11	42.50
10	R. J. Shastri	80	121	14	3,830	206	11	35.79
11	P. R. Umrigar	59	94	8	3,631	223	12	42.22
12	**V. V. S. Laxman**	**50**	**83**	**10**	**3,460**	**281**	**7**	**47.39**
13	V. L. Manjrekar	55	92	10	3,208	189*	7	39.12
14	N. S. Sidhu	51	78	2	3,202	201	9	42.13
15	C. G. Borde	55	97	11	3,061	177*	5	35.59
16	Nawab of Pataudi jun.	46	83	3	2,793	203*	6	34.91
17	S. M. H. Kirmani	88	124	22	2,759	102	2	27.04
18	F. M. Engineer	46	87	3	2,611	121	2	31.08

PAKISTAN

		T	I	NO	R	HS	100s	Avge
1	Javed Miandad	124	189	21	8,832	280*	23	52.57
2	**Inzamam-ul-Haq**	**91**	**150**	**16**	**6,680**	**329**	**18**	**49.85**
3	Salim Malik	103	154	22	5,768	237	15	43.69
4	Zaheer Abbas	78	124	11	5,062	274	12	44.79
5	Mudassar Nazar	76	116	8	4,114	231	10	38.09
6	Saeed Anwar	55	91	2	4,052	188*	11	45.52
7	Majid Khan	63	106	5	3,931	167	8	38.92
8	Hanif Mohammad	55	97	8	3,915	337	12	43.98
9	Imran Khan	88	126	25	3,807	136	6	37.69
10	Mushtaq Mohammad	57	100	7	3,643	201	10	39.17
11	Asif Iqbal	58	99	7	3,575	175	11	38.85
12	**Yousuf Youhana**	**48**	**78**	**8**	**3,458**	**204***	**10**	**49.40**
13	Ijaz Ahmed, sen.	60	92	4	3,315	211	12	37.67
14	Saeed Ahmed	41	78	4	2,991	172	5	40.41
15	Wasim Akram	104	147	19	2,898	257*	3	22.64
16	Ramiz Raja	57	94	5	2,833	122	2	31.83
17	Aamir Sohail	47	83	3	2,823	205	5	35.28
18	Wasim Raja	57	92	14	2,821	125	4	36.16
19	**Moin Khan**	**67**	**100**	**8**	**2,713**	**137**	**4**	**29.48**
20	Mohsin Khan	48	79	6	2,709	200	7	37.10
21	Shoaib Mohammad	45	68	7	2,705	203*	7	44.34
22	Sadiq Mohammad	41	74	2	2,579	166	5	35.81

SRI LANKA

		T	I	NO	R	HS	100s	Avge
1	P. A. de Silva	93	159	11	6,361	267	20	42.97
2	**S. T. Jayasuriya**	**83**	**140**	**13**	**5,258**	**340**	**10**	**41.40**
3	A. Ranatunga	93	155	12	5,105	135*	4	35.69
4	**H. P. Tillekeratne**	**80**	**125**	**24**	**4,373**	**204***	**11**	**43.29**
5	**M. S. Atapattu**	**68**	**117**	**14**	**3,907**	**223**	**11**	**37.93**
6	**D. P. M. D. Jayawardene**	**54**	**86**	**7**	**3,877**	**242**	**10**	**49.07**
7	R. S. Mahanama	52	89	1	2,576	225	4	29.27

ZIMBABWE

		T	I	NO	R	HS	100s	Avge
1	**A. Flower**	**63**	**112**	**19**	**4,794**	**232***	**12**	**51.54**
2	**G. W. Flower**	**65**	**120**	**5**	**3,412**	**201***	**6**	**29.66**
3	**A. D. R. Campbell**	**60**	**109**	**4**	**2,858**	**103**	**2**	**27.21**

BANGLADESH: The highest aggregate is **1,840** (average 36.07) by **Habibul Bashar** in 26 Tests.

Bold type denotes those who have played Test cricket since the start of 2002-03.

CAREER AVERAGE OVER 50

(Qualification: 20 innings)

Avge		*T*	*I*	*NO*	*R*	*HS*	*100s*
99.94	D. G. Bradman (A)	52	80	10	6,996	334	29
60.97	R. G. Pollock (SA)	23	41	4	2,256	274	7
60.83	G. A. Headley (WI)	22	40	4	2,190	270*	10
60.73	H. Sutcliffe (E)	54	84	9	4,555	194	16
59.23	E. Paynter (E)	20	31	5	1,540	243	4
58.78	**G. C. Smith (SA)**	**21**	**34**	**2**	**1,881**	**277**	**6**
58.67	K. F. Barrington (E)	82	131	15	6,806	256	20
58.61	E. D. Weekes (WI)	48	81	5	4,455	207	15
58.45	W. R. Hammond (E)	85	140	16	7,249	336*	22
58.28	**M. L. Hayden (A)**	**50**	**85**	**8**	**4,488**	**380**	**17**
57.78	G. S. Sobers (WI)	93	160	21	8,032	365*	26
57.42	**R. Dravid (I)**	**75**	**130**	**16**	**6,546**	**233**	**16**
57.19	**S. R. Tendulkar (I)**	**111**	**180**	**18**	**9,265**	**241***	**32**
56.94	J. B. Hobbs (E)	61	102	7	5,410	211	15
56.68	C. L. Walcott (WI)	44	74	7	3,798	220	15
56.67	L. Hutton (E)	79	138	15	6,971	364	19
55.97	**R. T. Ponting (A)**	**75**	**119**	**15**	**5,821**	**257**	**20**
55.59	**A. C. Gilchrist (A)**	**51**	**70**	**13**	**3,169**	**204***	**9**
55.00	E. Tyldesley (E)	14	20	2	990	122	3
54.20	C. A. Davis (WI)	15	29	5	1,301	183	4
54.20	V. G. Kambli (I)	17	21	1	1,084	227	4
53.86	G. S. Chappell (A)	87	151	19	7,110	247*	24
53.81	A. D. Nourse (SA)	34	62	7	2,960	231	9
53.26	**J. H. Kallis (SA)**	**75**	**123**	**20**	**5,486**	**189***	**15**
52.57	Javed Miandad (P)	124	189	21	8,832	280*	23
52.32	**B. C. Lara (WI)**	**102**	**180**	**5**	**9,157**	**375**	**24**
51.62	J. Ryder (A)	20	32	5	1,394	201*	3
51.54	**A. Flower (Z)**	**63**	**112**	**19**	**4,794**	**232***	**12**
51.12	S. M. Gavaskar (I)	125	214	16	10,122	236*	34
51.06	**S. R. Waugh (A)**	**168**	**260**	**46**	**10,927**	**200**	**32**
50.56	A. R. Border (A)	156	265	44	11,174	205	27
50.23	I. V. A. Richards (WI)	121	182	12	8,540	291	24
50.06	D. C. S. Compton (E)	78	131	15	5,807	278	17

Bold type denotes those who have played Test cricket since the start of 2002-03.

FASTEST FIFTIES

Minutes			
28	J. T. Brown	England v Australia at Melbourne	1894-95
29	S. A. Durani	India v England at Kanpur	1963-64
30	E. A. V. Williams	West Indies v England at Bridgetown	1947-48
30	B. R. Taylor	New Zealand v West Indies at Auckland	1968-69
33	C. A. Roach	West Indies v England at The Oval	1933
34	C. R. Browne	West Indies v England at Georgetown	1929-30

The fastest fifties in terms of balls received (where recorded) are:

Balls			
26	I. T. Botham	England v India at Delhi	1981-82
27	Yousuf Youhana	Pakistan v South Africa at Cape Town	2002-03
30	Kapil Dev	India v Pakistan at Karachi (2nd Test)	1982-83
31	W. J. Cronje	South Africa v Sri Lanka at Centurion	1997-98
32	I. V. A. Richards	West Indies v India at Kingston	1982-83
32	I. T. Botham	England v New Zealand at The Oval	1986

Balls			
33	R. C. Fredericks	West Indies v Australia at Perth	1975-76
33	Kapil Dev	India v Pakistan at Karachi	1978-79
33	Kapil Dev	India v England at Manchester	1982
33	A. J. Lamb	England v New Zealand at Auckland	1991-92
33	A. Flintoff	England v New Zealand at Wellington	2001-02

FASTEST HUNDREDS

Minutes			
70	J. M. Gregory	Australia v South Africa at Johannesburg	1921-22
75	G. L. Jessop	England v Australia at The Oval	1902
78	R. Benaud	Australia v West Indies at Kingston	1954-55
80	J. H. Sinclair	South Africa v Australia at Cape Town	1902-03
81	I. V. A. Richards	West Indies v England at St John's	1985-86
86	B. R. Taylor	New Zealand v West Indies at Auckland	1968-69

The fastest hundreds in terms of balls received (where recorded) are:

Balls			
56	I. V. A. Richards	West Indies v England at St John's	1985-86
67	J. M. Gregory	Australia v South Africa at Johannesburg	1921-22
69	S. Chanderpaul	West Indies v Australia at Georgetown	2002-03
71	R. C. Fredericks	West Indies v Australia at Perth	1975-76
74	Majid Khan	Pakistan v New Zealand at Karachi	1976-77
74	Kapil Dev	India v Sri Lanka at Kanpur	1986-87
74	M. Azharuddin	India v South Africa at Calcutta	1996-97
76	G. L. Jessop	England v Australia at The Oval	1902

FASTEST DOUBLE-HUNDREDS

Minutes			
214	D. G. Bradman	Australia v England at Leeds	1930
217	N. J. Astle	New Zealand v England at Christchurch	2001-02
223	S. J. McCabe	Australia v England at Nottingham	1938
226	V. T. Trumper	Australia v South Africa at Adelaide	1910-11
234	D. G. Bradman	Australia v England at Lord's	1930
240	W. R. Hammond	England v New Zealand at Auckland	1932-33
241	S. E. Gregory	Australia v England at Sydney	1894-95
245	D. C. S. Compton	England v Pakistan at Nottingham	1954

The fastest double-hundreds in terms of balls received (where recorded) are:

Balls			
153	N. J. Astle	New Zealand v England at Christchurch	2001-02
211	H. H. Gibbs	South Africa v Pakistan at Cape Town	2002-03
212	A. C. Gilchrist	Australia v South Africa at Johannesburg	2001-02
220	I. T. Botham	England v India at The Oval	1982
229	P. A. de Silva	Sri Lanka v Bangladesh at Colombo (PSS)	2002
231	G. P. Thorpe	England v New Zealand at Christchurch	2001-02
232	C. G. Greenidge	West Indies v England at Lord's	1984
240	C. H. Lloyd	West Indies v India at Bombay	1974-75
241	Zaheer Abbas	Pakistan v India at Lahore	1982-83
242	D. G. Bradman	Australia v England at The Oval	1934
242	I. V. A. Richards	West Indies v Australia at Melbourne	1984-85

FASTEST TRIPLE-HUNDREDS

Minutes			
288	W. R. Hammond	England v New Zealand at Auckland	1932-33
336	D. G. Bradman	Australia v England at Leeds	1930

MOST RUNS SCORED OFF AN OVER

28	B. C. Lara (466444)	off R. J. Peterson	WI v SA at Johannesburg	2003-04
26	C. D. McMillan (444464)	off Younis Khan	NZ v P at Hamilton	2000-01

MOST RUNS IN A DAY

309	D. G. Bradman	Australia v England at Leeds	1930
295	W. R. Hammond	England v New Zealand at Auckland	1932-33
273	D. C. S. Compton	England v Pakistan at Nottingham	1954
271	D. G. Bradman	Australia v England at Leeds	1934

SLOWEST INDIVIDUAL BATTING

0	in 101 minutes	G. I. Allott, New Zealand v South Africa at Auckland	1998-99
5	in 102 minutes	Nawab of Pataudi jun., India v England at Bombay	1972-73
6	in 106 minutes	D. R. Martyn, Australia v South Africa at Sydney	1993-94
7	in 123 minutes	G. Miller, England v Australia at Melbourne	1978-79
9	in 132 minutes	R. K. Chauhan, India v Sri Lanka at Ahmedabad	1993-94
10*	in 133 minutes	T. G. Evans, England v Australia at Adelaide	1946-47
14*	in 165 minutes	D. K. Morrison, New Zealand v England at Auckland	1996-97
18	in 194 minutes	W. R. Playle, New Zealand v England at Leeds	1958
19	in 217 minutes	M. D. Crowe, New Zealand v Sri Lanka at Colombo (SSC)	1983-84
25	in 242 minutes	D. K. Morrison, New Zealand v Pakistan at Faisalabad	1990-91
29*	in 277 minutes	R. C. Russell, England v South Africa at Johannesburg	1995-96
35	in 332 minutes	C. J. Tavaré, England v India at Madras	1981-82
60	in 390 minutes	D. N. Sardesai, India v West Indies at Bridgetown	1961-62
62	in 408 minutes	Ramiz Raja, Pakistan v West Indies at Karachi	1986-87
68	in 458 minutes	T. E. Bailey, England v Australia at Brisbane	1958-59
99	in 505 minutes	M. L. Jaisimha, India v Pakistan at Kanpur	1960-61
105	in 575 minutes	D. J. McGlew, South Africa v Australia at Durban	1957-58
114	in 591 minutes	Mudassar Nazar, Pakistan v England at Lahore	1977-78
146*	in 635 minutes	N. Hussain, England v South Africa at Durban	1999-2000
163	in 720 minutes	Shoaib Mohammad, Pakistan v New Zealand at Wellington	1988-89
201*	in 777 minutes	D. S. B. P. Kuruppu, Sri Lanka v New Zealand at Colombo (CCC)	1986-87
275	in 878 minutes	G. Kirsten, South Africa v England at Durban	1999-2000
337	in 970 minutes	Hanif Mohammad, Pakistan v West Indies at Bridgetown	1957-58

SLOWEST HUNDREDS

557 minutes	Mudassar Nazar, Pakistan v England at Lahore	1977-78
545 minutes	D. J. McGlew, South Africa v Australia at Durban	1957-58
535 minutes	A. P. Gurusinha, Sri Lanka v Zimbabwe at Harare	1994-95
516 minutes	J. J. Crowe, New Zealand v Sri Lanka at Colombo (CCC)	1986-87
500 minutes	S. V. Manjrekar, India v Zimbabwe at Harare	1992-93
488 minutes	P. E. Richardson, England v South Africa at Johannesburg	1956-57

Notes: The slowest hundred for any Test in England is 458 minutes (329 balls) by K. W. R. Fletcher, England v Pakistan, The Oval, 1974.

The slowest double-hundred in a Test was scored in 777 minutes (548 balls) by D. S. B. P. Kuruppu for Sri Lanka v New Zealand at Colombo (CCC), 1986-87, on his debut. It is also the slowest-ever first-class double-hundred.

MOST DUCKS

C. A. Walsh (West Indies) 43; **S. K. Warne (Australia) 27**; C. E. L. Ambrose (West Indies), **M. Dillon (West Indies)** and **G. D. McGrath (Australia) 26**; D. K. Morrison (New Zealand) 24; B. S. Chandrasekhar (India) 23; **M. Muralitharan (Sri Lanka)** and **S. R. Waugh (Australia) 22**; **Waqar Younis (Pakistan) 21**; M. A. Atherton (England) and B. S. Bedi (India) 20.

Bold type denotes those who have played Test cricket since the start of 2002-03.

PARTNERSHIPS OVER 400

576	for 2nd	S. T. Jayasuriya (340)/R. S. Mahanama (225)	SL v I	Colombo (RPS)	1997-98
467	for 3rd	A. H. Jones (186)/M. D. Crowe (299)	NZ v SL	Wellington	1990-91
451	for 2nd	W. H. Ponsford (266)/D. G. Bradman (244)	A v E	The Oval	1934
451	for 3rd	Mudassar Nazar (231)/Javed Miandad (280*)	P v I	Hyderabad	1982-83
446	for 2nd	C. C. Hunte (260)/G. S. Sobers (365*)	WI v P	Kingston	1957-58
429*	for 3rd	J. A. Rudolph (222*)/H. H. Dippenaar (177*)	SA v B	Chittagong	2003
413	for 1st	V. Mankad (231)/Pankaj Roy (173)	I v NZ	Madras	1955-56
411	for 4th	P. B. H. May (285*)/M. C. Cowdrey (154)	E v WI	Birmingham	1957
405	for 5th	S. G. Barnes (234)/D. G. Bradman (234)	A v E	Sydney	1946-47

Note: 415 runs were added for the third wicket for India v England at Madras in 1981-82 by D. B. Vengsarkar (retired hurt), G. R. Viswanath and Yashpal Sharma.

HIGHEST PARTNERSHIPS FOR EACH WICKET

The following lists include all stands above 300; otherwise the top ten for each wicket.

First Wicket

413	V. Mankad (231)/Pankaj Roy (173)	I v NZ	Madras	1955-56
387	G. M. Turner (259)/T. W. Jarvis (182)	NZ v WI	Georgetown	1971-72
382	W. M. Lawry (210)/R. B. Simpson (201)	A v WI	Bridgetown	1964-65
368	G. C. Smith (151)/H. H. Gibbs (228)	SA v P	Cape Town	2002-03
359	L. Hutton (158)/C. Washbrook (195)	E v SA	Johannesburg	1948-49
338	G. C. Smith (277)/H. H. Gibbs (179)	SA v E	Birmingham	2003
335	M. S. Atapattu (207*)/S. T. Jayasuriya (188)	SL v P	Kandy	2000
329	G. R. Marsh (138)/M. A. Taylor (219)	A v E	Nottingham	1989
323	J. B. Hobbs (178)/W. Rhodes (179)	E v A	Melbourne	1911-12
301	G. C. Smith (139)/H. H. Gibbs (192)	SA v WI	Centurion	2003-04

Second Wicket

576	S. T. Jayasuriya (340)/R. S. Mahanama (225)	SL v I	Colombo (RPS)	1997-98
451	W. H. Ponsford (266)/D. G. Bradman (244)	A v E	The Oval	1934
446	C. C. Hunte (260)/G. S. Sobers (365*)	WI v P	Kingston	1957-58
382	L. Hutton (364)/M. Leyland (187)	E v A	The Oval	1938
369	J. H. Edrich (310*)/K. F. Barrington (163)	E v NZ	Leeds	1965
351	G. A. Gooch (196)/D. I. Gower (157)	E v A	The Oval	1985
344*	S. M. Gavaskar (182*)/D. B. Vengsarkar (157*)	I v WI	Calcutta	1978-79
331	R. T. Robinson (148)/D. I. Gower (215)	E v A	Birmingham	1985
315*	H. H. Gibbs (211*)/J. H. Kallis (148*)	SA v NZ	Christchurch	1998-99
301	A. R. Morris (182)/D. G. Bradman (173*)	A v E	Leeds	1948

Third Wicket

467	A. H. Jones (186)/M. D. Crowe (299)	NZ v SL	Wellington	1990-91
451	Mudassar Nazar (231)/Javed Miandad (280*)	P v I	Hyderabad	1982-83
429*	J. A. Rudolph (222*)/H. H. Dippenaar (177*)	SA v B	Chittagong	2003
397	Qasim Omar (206)/Javed Miandad (203*)	P v SL	Faisalabad	1985-86
370	W. J. Edrich (189)/D. C. S. Compton (208)	E v SA	Lord's	1947
352*‡	Ijaz Ahmed, sen. (211)/Inzamam-ul-Haq (200*)	P v SL	Dhaka	1998-99
341	E. J. Barlow (201)/R. G. Pollock (175)	SA v A	Adelaide	1963-64
338	E. D. Weekes (206)/F. M. M. Worrell (167)	WI v E	Port-of-Spain	1953-54
323	Aamir Sohail (160)/Inzamam-ul-Haq (177)	P v WI	Rawalpindi	1997-98
319	A. Melville (189)/A. D. Nourse (149)	SA v E	Nottingham	1947

316†	G. R. Viswanath (222)/Yashpal Sharma (140)	I v E	Madras	1981-82
315	R. T. Ponting (206)/D. S. Lehmann (160)	A v WI	Port-of-Spain	2002-03
308	R. B. Richardson (154)/I. V. A. Richards (178)	WI v A	St John's	1983-84
308	G. A. Gooch (333)/A. J. Lamb (139)	E v I	Lord's	1990
303	I. V. A. Richards (232)/A. I. Kallicharran (97)	WI v E	Nottingham	1976
303	M. A. Atherton (135)/R. A. Smith (175)	E v WI	St John's	1993-94

† 415 runs were scored for this wicket in two separate partnerships; D. B. Vengsarkar retired hurt when he and Viswanath had added 99 runs.
‡ 366 runs were scored for this wicket in two separate partnerships; Inzamam retired ill when he and Ijaz had added 352 runs.

Fourth Wicket

411	P. B. H. May (285*)/M. C. Cowdrey (154)	E v WI	Birmingham	1957
399	G. S. Sobers (226)/F. M. M. Worrell (197*)	WI v E	Bridgetown	1959-60
388	W. H. Ponsford (181)/D. G. Bradman (304)	A v E	Leeds	1934
353	S. R. Tendulkar (241*)/V. V. S. Laxman (178)	I v A	Sydney	2003-04
350	Mushtaq Mohammad (201)/Asif Iqbal (175)	P v NZ	Dunedin	1972-73
336	W. M. Lawry (151)/K. D. Walters (242)	A v WI	Sydney	1968-69
322	Javed Miandad (153*)/Salim Malik (165)	P v E	Birmingham	1992
288	N. Hussain (207)/G. P. Thorpe (138)	E v A	Birmingham	1997
287	Javed Miandad (126)/Zaheer Abbas (168)	P v I	Faisalabad	1982-83
283	F. M. M. Worrell (261)/E. D. Weekes (129)	WI v E	Nottingham	1950

288 runs were scored for this wicket in two separate partnerships for Pakistan v Bangladesh at Multan, 2001-02; Inzamam-ul-Haq retired hurt after adding 123 with Yousuf Youhana, who added a further 165 with Abdul Razzaq.*

Fifth Wicket

405	S. G. Barnes (234)/D. G. Bradman (234)	A v E	Sydney	1946-47
385	S. R. Waugh (160)/G. S. Blewett (214)	A v SA	Johannesburg	1996-97
376	V. V. S. Laxman (281)/R. Dravid (180)	I v A	Kolkata	2000-01
332*	A. R. Border (200*)/S. R. Waugh (157*)	A v E	Leeds	1993
327	J. L. Langer (144)/R. T. Ponting (197)	A v P	Perth	1999-2000
322†	B. C. Lara (213)/J. C. Adams (94)	WI v A	Kingston	1998-99
303	R. Dravid (233)/V. V. S. Laxman (148)	I v A	Adelaide	2003-04
293	C. L. Hooper (233)/S. Chanderpaul (140)	WI v I	Georgetown	2001-02
281	Javed Miandad (163)/Asif Iqbal (166)	P v NZ	Lahore	1976-77
281	S. R. Waugh (199)/R. T. Ponting (104)	A v WI	Bridgetown	1998-99

† 344 runs were scored for this wicket in two separate partnerships; P. T. Collins retired hurt when he and Lara had added 22 runs.

Sixth Wicket

346	J. H. Fingleton (136)/D. G. Bradman (270)	A v E	Melbourne	1936-37
317	D. R. Martyn (133)/A. C. Gilchrist (204*)	A v SA	Johannesburg	2001-02
298*	D. B. Vengsarkar (164*)/R. J. Shastri (121*)	I v A	Bombay	1986-87
281	G. P. Thorpe (200*)/A. Flintoff (137)	E v NZ	Christchurch	2001-02
274*	G. S. Sobers (163*)/D. A. J. Holford (105*)	WI v E	Lord's	1966
272	M. Azharuddin (199)/Kapil Dev (163)	I v SL	Kanpur	1986-87
260*	D. M. Jones (118*)/S. R. Waugh (134*)	A v SL	Hobart	1989-90
254	C. A. Davis (183)/G. S. Sobers (142)	WI v NZ	Bridgetown	1971-72
250	C. H. Lloyd (242*)/D. L. Murray (91)	WI v I	Bombay	1974-75
246*	J. J. Crowe (120*)/R. J. Hadlee (151*)	NZ v SL	Colombo (CCC)	1986-87

Seventh Wicket

347	D. St E. Atkinson (219)/C. C. Depeiza (122).	WI v A	Bridgetown	1954-55
308	Waqar Hassan (189)/Imtiaz Ahmed (209)	P v NZ	Lahore	1955-56
248	Yousuf Youhana (203)/Saqlain Mushtaq (101*) . . .	P v NZ	Christchurch	2000-01
246	D. J. McGlew (255*)/A. R. A. Murray (109)	SA v NZ	Wellington	1952-53
235	R. J. Shastri (142)/S. M. H. Kirmani (102)	I v E	Bombay	1984-85
221	D. T. Lindsay (182)/P. L. van der Merwe (76)	SA v A	Johannesburg	1966-67
217	K. D. Walters (250)/G. J. Gilmour (101).	A v NZ	Christchurch	1976-77
217	V. V. S. Laxman (130)/A. Ratra (115*).	I v WI	St John's	2001-02
197	M. J. K. Smith (96)/J. M. Parks (101*).	E v WI	Port-of-Spain	1959-60
194*	H. P. Tillekeratne (136*)/T. T. Samaraweera (103*) . .	SL v I	Colombo (SSC)	2001

Eighth Wicket

313	Wasim Akram (257*)/Saqlain Mushtaq (79).	P v Z	Sheikhupura	1996-97
253	N. J. Astle (156*)/A. C. Parore (110).	NZ v A	Perth	2001-02
246	L. E. G. Ames (137)/G. O. B. Allen (122)	E v NZ	Lord's	1931
243	R. J. Hartigan (116)/C. Hill (160)	A v E	Adelaide	1907-08
217	T. W. Graveney (165)/J. T. Murray (112).	E v WI	The Oval	1966
173	C. E. Pellew (116)/J. M. Gregory (100)	A v E	Melbourne	1920-21
168	R. Illingworth (107)/P. Lever (88*)	E v I	Manchester	1971
168	H. H. Streak (127*)/A. M. Blignaut (91)	Z v WI	Harare	2003-04
161	M. Azharuddin (109)/A. Kumble (88).	I v SA	Calcutta	1996-97
154	G. J. Bonnor (128)/S. P. Jones (40)	A v E	Sydney	1884-85
154	C. W. Wright (71)/H. R. Bromley-Davenport (84). .	E v SA	Johannesburg	1895-96
154	D. Tallon (92)/R. R. Lindwall (100).	A v E	Melbourne	1946-47

Ninth Wicket

195	M. V. Boucher (78)/P. L. Symcox (108)	SA v P	Johannesburg	1997-98
190	Asif Iqbal (146)/Intikhab Alam (51).	P v E	The Oval	1967
163*	M. C. Cowdrey (128*)/A. C. Smith (69*).	E v NZ	Wellington	1962-63
161	C. H. Lloyd (161*)/A. M. E. Roberts (68)	WI v I	Calcutta	1983-84
161	Zaheer Abbas (82*)/Sarfraz Nawaz (90)	P v E	Lahore	1983-84
154	S. E. Gregory (201)/J. McC. Blackham (74)	A v E	Sydney	1894-95
151	W. H. Scotton (90)/W. W. Read (117).	E v A	The Oval	1884
150	E. A. E. Baptiste (87*)/M. A. Holding (69).	WI v E	Birmingham	1984
149	P. G. Joshi (52*)/R. B. Desai (85)	I v P	Bombay	1960-61
147	Mohammad Wasim (192)/Mushtaq Ahmed (57) . . .	P v Z	Harare	1997-98

Tenth Wicket

151	B. F. Hastings (110)/R. O. Collinge (68*)	NZ v P	Auckland	1972-73
151	Azhar Mahmood (128*)/Mushtaq Ahmed (59)	P v SA	Rawalpindi	1997-98
133	Wasim Raja (71)/Wasim Bari (60*)	P v WI	Bridgetown	1976-77
130	R. E. Foster (287)/W. Rhodes (40*)	E v A	Sydney	1903-04
128	K. Higgs (63)/J. A. Snow (59*).	E v WI	The Oval	1966
127	J. M. Taylor (108)/A. A. Mailey (46*)	A v E	Sydney	1924-25
124	J. G. Bracewell (83*)/S. L. Boock (37).	NZ v A	Sydney	1985-86
120	R. A. Duff (104)/W. W. Armstrong (45*)	A v E	Melbourne	1901-02
118	N. J. Astle (222)/C. L. Cairns (23*).	NZ v E	Christchurch	2001-02
117*	P. Willey (100*)/R. G. D. Willis (24*)	E v WI	The Oval	1980

UNUSUAL DISMISSALS

Handled the Ball

W. R. Endean	South Africa v England at Cape Town	1956-57
A. M. J. Hilditch	Australia v Pakistan at Perth	1978-79
Mohsin Khan	Pakistan v Australia at Karachi	1982-83
D. L. Haynes	West Indies v India at Bombay	1983-84
G. A. Gooch	England v Australia at Manchester	1993
S. R. Waugh	Australia v India at Chennai	2000-01
M. P. Vaughan	England v India at Bangalore	2001-02

Obstructing the Field

L. Hutton	England v South Africa at The Oval	1951

Note: There have been no cases of Hit the Ball Twice or Timed Out in Test cricket.

BOWLING RECORDS

MOST WICKETS IN AN INNINGS

10-53	J. C. Laker	England v Australia at Manchester	1956
10-74	A. Kumble	India v Pakistan at Delhi	1998-99
9-28	G. A. Lohmann	England v South Africa at Johannesburg	1895-96
9-37	J. C. Laker	England v Australia at Manchester	1956
9-51	M. Muralitharan	Sri Lanka v Zimbabwe at Kandy	2001-02
9-52	R. J. Hadlee	New Zealand v Australia at Brisbane	1985-86
9-56	Abdul Qadir	Pakistan v England at Lahore	1987-88
9-57	D. E. Malcolm	England v South Africa at The Oval	1994
9-65	M. Muralitharan	Sri Lanka v England at The Oval	1998
9-69	J. M. Patel	India v Australia at Kanpur	1959-60
9-83	Kapil Dev	India v West Indies at Ahmedabad	1983-84
9-86	Sarfraz Nawaz	Pakistan v Australia at Melbourne	1978-79
9-95	J. M. Noreiga	West Indies v India at Port-of-Spain	1970-71
9-102	S. P. Gupte	India v West Indies at Kanpur	1958-59
9-103	S. F. Barnes	England v South Africa at Johannesburg	1913-14
9-113	H. J. Tayfield	South Africa v England at Johannesburg	1956-57
9-121	A. A. Mailey	Australia v England at Melbourne	1920-21
8-7	G. A. Lohmann	England v South Africa at Port Elizabeth	1895-96
8-11	J. Briggs	England v South Africa at Cape Town	1888-89
8-29	S. F. Barnes	England v South Africa at The Oval	1912
8-29	C. E. H. Croft	West Indies v Pakistan at Port-of-Spain	1976-77
8-31	F. Laver	Australia v England at Manchester	1909
8-31	F. S. Trueman	England v India at Manchester	1952
8-34	I. T. Botham	England v Pakistan at Lord's	1978
8-35	G. A. Lohmann	England v Australia at Sydney	1886-87
8-38	L. R. Gibbs	West Indies v India at Bridgetown	1961-62
8-38	G. D. McGrath	Australia v England at Lord's	1997
8-43†	A. E. Trott	Australia v England at Adelaide	1894-95
8-43	H. Verity	England v Australia at Lord's	1934
8-43	R. G. D. Willis	England v Australia at Leeds	1981
8-45	C. E. L. Ambrose	West Indies v England at Bridgetown	1989-90
8-51	D. L. Underwood	England v Pakistan at Lord's	1974
8-52	V. Mankad	India v Pakistan at Delhi	1952-53
8-53	G. B. Lawrence	South Africa v New Zealand at Johannesburg	1961-62
8-53†	R. A. L. Massie	Australia v England at Lord's	1972
8-53	A. R. C. Fraser	England v West Indies at Port-of-Spain	1997-98
8-55	V. Mankad	India v England at Madras	1951-52
8-56	S. F. Barnes	England v South Africa at Johannesburg	1913-14
8-58	G. A. Lohmann	England v Australia at Sydney	1891-92

8-58	Imran Khan	Pakistan v Sri Lanka at Lahore	1981-82
8-59	C. Blythe	England v South Africa at Leeds	1907
8-59	A. A. Mallett	Australia v Pakistan at Adelaide	1972-73
8-60	Imran Khan	Pakistan v India at Karachi	1982-83
8-61†	N. D. Hirwani	India v West Indies at Madras	1987-88
8-64†	L. Klusener	South Africa v India at Calcutta	1996-97
8-65	H. Trumble	Australia v England at The Oval	1902
8-68	W. Rhodes	England v Australia at Melbourne	1903-04
8-69	H. J. Tayfield	South Africa v England at Durban	1956-57
8-69	Sikander Bakht	Pakistan v India at Delhi	1979-80
8-70	S. J. Snooke	South Africa v England at Johannesburg	1905-06
8-71	G. D. McKenzie	Australia v West Indies at Melbourne	1968-69
8-71	S. K. Warne	Australia v England at Brisbane	1994-95
8-71	A. A. Donald	South Africa v Zimbabwe at Harare	1995-96
8-72	S. Venkataraghavan	India v New Zealand at Delhi	1964-65
8-75†	N. D. Hirwani	India v West Indies at Madras	1987-88
8-75	A. R. C. Fraser	England v West Indies at Bridgetown	1993-94
8-76	E. A. S. Prasanna	India v New Zealand at Auckland	1975-76
8-79	B. S. Chandrasekhar	India v England at Delhi	1972-73
8-81	L. C. Braund	England v Australia at Melbourne	1903-04
8-83	J. R. Ratnayeke	Sri Lanka v Pakistan at Sialkot	1985-86
8-84†	R. A. L. Massie	Australia v England at Lord's	1972
8-84	Harbhajan Singh	India v Australia at Chennai	2000-01
8-85	Kapil Dev	India v Pakistan at Lahore	1982-83
8-86	A. W. Greig	England v West Indies at Port-of-Spain	1973-74
8-86	J. Srinath	India v Pakistan at Calcutta	1998-99
8-87	M. G. Hughes	Australia v West Indies at Perth	1988-89
8-87	M. Muralitharan	Sri Lanka v India at Colombo (SSC)	2001
8-92	M. A. Holding	West Indies v England at The Oval	1976
8-94	T. Richardson	England v Australia at Sydney	1897-98
8-97	C. J. McDermott	Australia v England at Perth	1990-91
8-103	I. T. Botham	England v West Indies at Lord's	1984
8-104†	A. L. Valentine	West Indies v England at Manchester	1950
8-106	Kapil Dev	India v Australia at Adelaide	1985-86
8-107	B. J. T. Bosanquet	England v Australia at Nottingham	1905
8-107	N. A. Foster	England v Pakistan at Leeds	1987
8-109	P. A. Strang	Zimbabwe v New Zealand at Bulawayo	2000-01
8-112	G. F. Lawson	Australia v West Indies at Adelaide	1984-85
8-126	J. C. White	England v Australia at Adelaide	1928-29
8-141	C. J. McDermott	Australia v England at Manchester	1985
8-141	A. Kumble	India v Australia at Sydney	2003-04
8-143	M. H. N. Walker	Australia v England at Melbourne	1974-75
8-164	Saqlain Mushtaq	Pakistan v England at Lahore	2000-01

† *On Test debut.*

Note: The best for Bangladesh is 6-77 by Mohammad Rafiq against South Africa at Dhaka in 2003.

OUTSTANDING BOWLING ANALYSES

	O	*M*	*R*	*W*		
J. C. Laker (E)	51.2	23	53	10	v Australia at Manchester	1956
A. Kumble (I)	26.3	9	74	10	v Pakistan at Delhi	1998-99
G. A. Lohmann (E)	14.2	6	28	9	v South Africa at Johannesburg	1895-96
J. C. Laker (E)	16.4	4	37	9	v Australia at Manchester	1956
G. A. Lohmann (E)	9.4	5	7	8	v South Africa at Port Elizabeth	1895-96
J. Briggs (E)	14.2	5	11	8	v South Africa at Cape Town	1888-89
J. Briggs (E)	19.1	11	17	7	v South Africa at Cape Town	1888-89
M. A. Noble (A)	7.4	2	17	7	v England at Melbourne	1901-02
W. Rhodes (E)	11	3	17	7	v Australia at Birmingham	1902
J. J. C. Lawson (WI)	6.5	4	3	6	v Bangladesh at Dhaka	2002-03
A. E. R. Gilligan (E)	6.3	4	7	6	v South Africa at Birmingham	1924

	O	M	R	W		
S. Haigh (E)	11.4	6	11	6	v South Africa at Cape Town	1898-99
Shoaib Akhtar (P)	8.2	4	11	6	v New Zealand at Lahore	2002
D. L. Underwood (E)	11.6	7	12	6	v New Zealand at Christchurch	1970-71
S. L. V. Raju (I)	17.5	13	12	6	v Sri Lanka at Chandigarh	1990-91
H. J. Tayfield (SA)	14	7	13	6	v New Zealand at Johannesburg	1953-54
C. T. B. Turner (A)	18	11	15	6	v England at Sydney	1886-87
M. H. N. Walker (A)	16	8	15	6	v Pakistan at Sydney	1972-73
E. R. H. Toshack (A)	2.3	1	2	5	v India at Brisbane	1947-48
H. Ironmonger (A)	7.2	5	6	5	v South Africa at Melbourne	1931-32
T. B. A. May (A)	6.5	3	9	5	v West Indies at Adelaide	1992-93
Pervez Sajjad (P)	12	8	5	4	v New Zealand at Rawalpindi	1964-65
K. Higgs (E)	9	7	5	4	v New Zealand at Christchurch	1965-66
P. H. Edmonds (E)	8	6	6	4	v Pakistan at Lord's	1978
J. C. White (E)	6.3	2	7	4	v Australia at Brisbane	1928-29
J. H. Wardle (E)	5	2	7	4	v Australia at Manchester	1953
R. Appleyard (E)	6	3	7	4	v New Zealand at Auckland	1954-55
R. Benaud (A)	3.4	3	0	3	v India at Delhi	1959-60

WICKET WITH FIRST BALL IN TEST CRICKET

	Batsman dismissed			
A. Coningham	A. C. MacLaren	A v E	Melbourne	1894-95
W. M. Bradley	F. Laver	E v A	Manchester	1899
E. G. Arnold	V. T. Trumper	E v A	Sydney	1903-04
G. G. Macaulay	G. A. L. Hearne	E v SA	Cape Town	1922-23
M. W. Tate	M. J. Susskind	E v SA	Birmingham	1924
M. Henderson	E. W. Dawson	NZ v E	Christchurch	1929-30
H. D. Smith	E. Paynter	NZ v E	Christchurch	1932-33
T. F. Johnson	W. W. Keeton	WI v E	The Oval	1939
R. Howorth	D. V. Dyer	E v SA	The Oval	1947
Intikhab Alam	C. C. McDonald	P v A	Karachi	1959-60
R. K. Illingworth	P. V. Simmons	E v WI	Nottingham	1991
N. M. Kulkarni	M. S. Atapattu	I v SL	Colombo (RPS)	1997-98
M. K. G. C. P. Lakshitha	Mohammad Ashraful	SL v B	Colombo (SSC)	2002

HAT-TRICKS

F. R. Spofforth	Australia v England at Melbourne	1878-79
W. Bates	England v Australia at Melbourne	1882-83
J. Briggs	England v Australia at Sydney	1891-92
G. A. Lohmann	England v South Africa at Port Elizabeth	1895-96
J. T. Hearne	England v Australia at Leeds	1899
H. Trumble	Australia v England at Melbourne	1901-02
H. Trumble	Australia v England at Melbourne	1903-04
T. J. Matthews† T. J. Matthews	Australia v South Africa at Manchester	1912
M. J. C. Allom‡	England v New Zealand at Christchurch	1929-30
T. W. J. Goddard	England v South Africa at Johannesburg	1938-39
P. J. Loader	England v West Indies at Leeds	1957
L. F. Kline	Australia v South Africa at Cape Town	1957-58
W. W. Hall	West Indies v Pakistan at Lahore	1958-59
G. M. Griffin	South Africa v England at Lord's	1960
L. R. Gibbs	West Indies v Australia at Adelaide	1960-61
P. J. Petherick‡	New Zealand v Pakistan at Lahore	1976-77
C. A. Walsh§	West Indies v Australia at Brisbane	1988-89
M. G. Hughes§	Australia v West Indies at Perth	1988-89
D. W. Fleming‡	Australia v Pakistan at Rawalpindi	1994-95

S. K. Warne	Australia v England at Melbourne	1994-95
D. G. Cork	England v West Indies at Manchester	1995
D. Gough	England v Australia at Sydney	1998-99
Wasim Akram¶	Pakistan v Sri Lanka at Lahore	1998-99
Wasim Akram¶	Pakistan v Sri Lanka at Dhaka	1998-99
D. N. T. Zoysa	Sri Lanka v Zimbabwe at Harare	1999-2000
Abdul Razzaq	Pakistan v Sri Lanka at Galle	2000
G. D. McGrath	Australia v West Indies at Perth	2000-01
Harbhajan Singh	India v Australia at Kolkata	2000-01
Mohammad Sami	Pakistan v Sri Lanka at Lahore	2001-02
J. J. C. Lawson§	West Indies v Australia at Bridgetown	2002-03
Alok Kapali	Bangladesh v Pakistan at Peshawar	2003

† *T. J. Matthews did the hat-trick in each innings of the same match.*
‡ *On Test debut.*
§ *Not all in the same innings.*
¶ *Wasim Akram did the hat-trick in successive matches.*

FOUR WICKETS IN FIVE BALLS

M. J. C. Allom	England v New Zealand at Christchurch. *On debut, in his eighth over: W-WWW*	1929-30
C. M. Old	England v Pakistan at Birmingham *Sequence interrupted by a no-ball: WW-WW*	1978
Wasim Akram	Pakistan v West Indies at Lahore (*WW-WW*)	1990-91

MOST WICKETS IN A TEST

19-90	J. C. Laker	England v Australia at Manchester	1956
17-159	S. F. Barnes	England v South Africa at Johannesburg	1913-14
16-136†	N. D. Hirwani	India v West Indies at Madras	1987-88
16-137†	R. A. L. Massie	Australia v England at Lord's	1972
16-220	M. Muralitharan	Sri Lanka v England at The Oval	1998
15-28	J. Briggs	England v South Africa at Cape Town	1888-89
15-45	G. A. Lohmann	England v South Africa at Port Elizabeth	1895-96
15-99	C. Blythe	England v South Africa at Leeds	1907
15-104	H. Verity	England v Australia at Lord's	1934
15-123	R. J. Hadlee	New Zealand v Australia at Brisbane	1985-86
15-124	W. Rhodes	England v Australia at Melbourne	1903-04
15-217	Harbhajan Singh	India v Australia at Chennai	2000-01
14-90	F. R. Spofforth	Australia v England at The Oval	1882
14-99	A. V. Bedser	England v Australia at Nottingham	1953
14-102	W. Bates	England v Australia at Melbourne	1882-83
14-116	Imran Khan	Pakistan v Sri Lanka at Lahore	1981-82
14-124	J. M. Patel	India v Australia at Kanpur	1959-60
14-144	S. F. Barnes	England v South Africa at Durban	1913-14
14-149	M. A. Holding	West Indies v England at The Oval	1976
14-149	A. Kumble	India v Pakistan at Delhi	1998-99
14-191	W. P. U. J. C. Vaas	Sri Lanka v West Indies at Colombo (SSC)	2001-02
14-199	C. V. Grimmett	Australia v South Africa at Adelaide	1931-32

† *On Test debut.*

Note: The best for South Africa is 13-165 by H. J. Tayfield against Australia at Melbourne, 1952-53, for Zimbabwe 11-255 by A. G. Huckle v New Zealand at Bulawayo, 1997-98, and for Bangladesh 7-116 by Mohammad Rafiq v Pakistan at Multan, 2003.

MOST BALLS BOWLED IN A TEST

S. Ramadhin (West Indies) sent down 774 balls in 129 overs against England at Birmingham, 1957. It was the most delivered by any bowler in a Test, beating H. Verity's 766 for England against South Africa at Durban, 1938-39. In this match Ramadhin also bowled the most balls (588) in a Test or first-class innings, since equalled by Arshad Ayub, Hyderabad v Madhya Pradesh at Secunderabad, 1991-92.

MOST WICKETS IN A SERIES

	T	*R*	*W*	*Avge*		
S. F. Barnes	4	536	49	10.93	England v South Africa	1913-14
J. C. Laker	5	442	46	9.60	England v Australia	1956
C. V. Grimmett	5	642	44	14.59	Australia v South Africa	1935-36
T. M. Alderman	6	893	42	21.26	Australia v England	1981
R. M. Hogg	6	527	41	12.85	Australia v England	1978-79
T. M. Alderman	6	712	41	17.36	Australia v England	1989
Imran Khan	6	558	40	13.95	Pakistan v India	1982-83
A. V. Bedser	5	682	39	17.48	England v Australia	1953
D. K. Lillee	6	870	39	22.30	Australia v England	1981
M. W. Tate	5	881	38	23.18	England v Australia	1924-25
W. J. Whitty	5	632	37	17.08	Australia v South Africa	1910-11
H. J. Tayfield	5	636	37	17.18	South Africa v England	1956-57
A. E. E. Vogler	5	783	36	21.75	South Africa v England	1909-10
A. A. Mailey	5	946	36	26.27	Australia v England	1920-21
G. D. McGrath	6	701	36	19.47	Australia v England	1997
G. A. Lohmann	3	203	35	5.80	England v South Africa	1895-96
B. S. Chandrasekhar	5	662	35	18.91	India v England	1972-73
M. D. Marshall	5	443	35	12.65	West Indies v England	1988

Notes: The most for New Zealand is 33 by R. J. Hadlee against Australia in 1985-86, for Sri Lanka 30 by M. Muralitharan against Zimbabwe in 2001-02, for Zimbabwe 22 by H. H. Streak against Pakistan in 1994-95, and for Bangladesh 17 by Mohammad Rafiq against Pakistan in 2003 (all in three Tests).

75 WICKETS IN A CALENDAR YEAR

	T	*R*	*W*	*Avge*	*5W/i*	*10W/m*	*Year*
D. K. Lillee (A)	13	1,781	85	20.95	5	2	1981
A. A. Donald (SA)	14	1,571	80	19.63	7	–	1998
M. Muralitharan (SL)	12	1,699	80	21.23	7	4	2001
J. Garner (WI)	15	1,604	77	20.83	4	–	1984
Kapil Dev (I)	18	1,739	75	23.18	5	1	1983
M. Muralitharan (SL)	10	1,463	75	19.50	7	3	2000

MOST WICKETS

		T	*Balls*	*R*	*W*	*Avge*	*5W/i*	*10W/m*
1	C. A. Walsh (West Indies)	132	30,019	12,688	519	24.44	22	3
2	**S. K. Warne (Australia)**	**107**	**29,877**	**12,624**	**491**	**25.71**	**23**	**6**
3	**M. Muralitharan (Sri Lanka)**	**85**	**28,967**	**11,130**	**485**	**22.94**	**39**	**12**
4	Kapil Dev (India)	131	27,740	12,867	434	29.64	23	2
5	R. J. Hadlee (New Zealand)	86	21,918	9,611	431	22.29	36	9
6	**G. D. McGrath (Australia)**	**95**	**22,374**	**9,338**	**430**	**21.71**	**23**	**3**
7	Wasim Akram (Pakistan)	104	22,627	9,779	414	23.62	25	5
8	C. E. L. Ambrose (West Indies)	98	22,103	8,501	405	20.99	22	3
9	I. T. Botham (England)	102	21,815	10,878	383	28.40	27	4
10	**A. Kumble (India)**	**81**	**25,868**	**10,812**	**382**	**28.30**	**23**	**5**
11	M. D. Marshall (West Indies)	81	17,584	7,876	376	20.94	22	4

		T	Balls	R	W	Avge	5W/i	10W/m
12	**Waqar Younis (Pakistan)**	**87**	**16,224**	**8,788**	**373**	**23.56**	**22**	**5**
13	Imran Khan (Pakistan)	88	19,458	8,258	362	22.81	23	6
14	D. K. Lillee (Australia)	70	18,467	8,493	355	23.92	23	7
15	A. A. Donald (South Africa)	72	15,519	7,344	330	22.25	20	3
16	**S. M. Pollock (South Africa)**	**80**	**17,980**	**6,893**	**326**	**21.14**	**16**	**1**
17	R. G. D. Willis (England)	90	17,357	8,190	325	25.20	16	–
18	L. R. Gibbs (West Indies)	79	27,115	8,989	309	29.09	18	2
19	F. S. Trueman (England)	67	15,178	6,625	307	21.57	17	3
20	D. L. Underwood (England)	86	21,862	7,674	297	25.83	17	6
21	C. J. McDermott (Australia)	71	16,586	8,332	291	28.63	14	2
22	B. S. Bedi (India)	67	21,364	7,637	266	28.71	14	1
23	J. Garner (West Indies)	58	13,169	5,433	259	20.97	7	–
24	J. B. Statham (England)	70	16,056	6,261	252	24.84	9	1
25	M. A. Holding (West Indies)	60	12,680	5,898	249	23.68	13	2
26	R. Benaud (Australia)	63	19,108	6,704	248	27.03	16	1
27	G. D. McKenzie (Australia)	60	17,681	7,328	246	29.78	16	3
28	B. S. Chandrasekhar (India)	58	15,963	7,199	242	29.74	16	2
29	A. V. Bedser (England)	51	15,918	5,876	236	24.89	15	5
29	**J. Srinath (India)**	**67**	**15,104**	**7,196**	**236**	**30.49**	**10**	**1**
29	Abdul Qadir (Pakistan)	67	17,126	7,742	236	32.80	15	5
32	G. S. Sobers (West Indies)	93	21,599	7,999	235	34.03	6	–
33	**A. R. Caddick (England)**	**62**	**13,558**	**6,999**	**234**	**29.91**	**13**	**1**
34	**D. Gough (England)**	**58**	**11,821**	**6,503**	**229**	**28.39**	**9**	**–**
34	**W. P. U. J. C. Vaas (Sri Lanka)**	**71**	**15,637**	**6,899**	**229**	**30.12**	**7**	**2**
36	R. R. Lindwall (Australia)	61	13,650	5,251	228	23.03	12	–
37	C. V. Grimmett (Australia)	37	14,513	5,231	216	24.21	21	7
38	M. G. Hughes (Australia)	53	12,285	6,017	212	28.38	7	1
39	**Saqlain Mushtaq (Pakistan)**	**48**	**13,812**	**6,002**	**207**	**28.99**	**13**	**3**
40	A. M. E. Roberts (West Indies)	47	11,135	5,174	202	25.61	11	2
40	J. A. Snow (England)	49	12,021	5,387	202	26.66	8	1
42	J. R. Thomson (Australia)	51	10,535	5,601	200	28.00	8	–

Note: The most wickets for other countries are:

	T	Balls	R	W	Avge	5W/i	10W/m
H. H. Streak (Zimbabwe)	**57**	**12,491**	**5,509**	**197**	**27.96**	**6**	–
Mohammad Rafiq (Bangladesh)	**8**	**2,345**	**997**	**36**	**27.69**	**3**	–

Bold type denotes those who have played Test cricket since the start of 2002-03.

100 WICKETS

ENGLAND

		T	Balls	R	W	Avge	5W/i	10W/m
1	I. T. Botham	102	21,815	10,878	383	28.40	27	4
2	R. G. D. Willis	90	17,357	8,190	325	25.20	16	–
3	F. S. Trueman	67	15,178	6,625	307	21.57	17	3
4	D. L. Underwood	86	21,862	7,674	297	25.83	17	6
5	J. B. Statham	70	16,056	6,261	252	24.84	9	1
6	A. V. Bedser	51	15,918	5,876	236	24.89	15	5
7	**A. R. Caddick**	**62**	**13,558**	**6,999**	**234**	**29.91**	**13**	**1**
8	**D. Gough**	**58**	**11,821**	**6,503**	**229**	**28.39**	**9**	**–**
9	J. A. Snow	49	12,021	5,387	202	26.66	8	1
10	J. C. Laker	46	12,027	4,101	193	21.24	9	3
11	S. F. Barnes	27	7,873	3,106	189	16.43	24	7
12	A. R. C. Fraser	46	10,876	4,836	177	27.32	13	2
13	G. A. R. Lock	49	13,147	4,451	174	25.58	9	3
14	M. W. Tate	39	12,523	4,055	155	26.16	7	1

		T	Balls	R	W	Avge	5W/i	10W/m
15	F. J. Titmus	53	15,118	4,931	153	32.22	7	–
16	J. E. Emburey	64	15,391	5,646	147	38.40	6	–
17	H. Verity	40	11,173	3,510	144	24.37	5	2
18	C. M. Old	46	8,858	4,020	143	28.11	4	–
19	A. W. Greig	58	9,802	4,541	141	32.20	6	2
20	P. A. J. DeFreitas	44	9,838	4,700	140	33.57	4	–
21	G. R. Dilley	41	8,192	4,107	138	29.76	6	–
22	T. E. Bailey	61	9,712	3,856	132	29.21	5	1
23	D. G. Cork	37	7,678	3,906	131	29.81	5	–
24	D. E. Malcolm	40	8,480	4,748	128	37.09	5	2
25	W. Rhodes	58	8,231	3,425	127	26.96	6	1
26	P. H. Edmonds	51	12,028	4,273	125	34.18	2	–
27	D. A. Allen	39	11,297	3,779	122	30.97	4	–
	R. Illingworth	61	11,934	3,807	122	31.20	3	–
29	P. C. R. Tufnell	42	11,288	4,560	121	37.68	5	2
30	J. Briggs	33	5,332	2,095	118	17.75	9	4
31	G. G. Arnold	34	7,650	3,254	115	28.29	6	–
32	G. A. Lohmann	18	3,821	1,205	112	10.75	9	5
33	D. V. P. Wright	34	8,135	4,224	108	39.11	6	1
34	J. H. Wardle	28	6,597	2,080	102	20.39	5	1
35	R. Peel	20	5,216	1,715	101	16.98	5	1
36	C. Blythe	19	4,546	1,863	100	18.63	9	4

AUSTRALIA

		T	Balls	R	W	Avge	5W/i	10W/m
1	**S. K. Warne**	**107**	**29,877**	**12,624**	**491**	**25.71**	**23**	**6**
2	**G. D. McGrath**	**95**	**22,374**	**9,338**	**430**	**21.71**	**23**	**3**
3	D. K. Lillee	70	18,467	8,493	355	23.92	23	7
4	C. J. McDermott	71	16,586	8,332	291	28.63	14	2
5	R. Benaud	63	19,108	6,704	248	27.03	16	1
6	G. D. McKenzie	60	17,681	7,328	246	29.78	16	3
7	R. R. Lindwall	61	13,650	5,251	228	23.03	12	–
8	C. V. Grimmett	37	14,513	5,231	216	24.21	21	7
9	M. G. Hughes	53	12,285	6,017	212	28.38	7	1
10	J. R. Thomson	51	10,535	5,601	200	28.00	8	–
11	**J. N. Gillespie**	**49**	**9,993**	**4,772**	**189**	**25.24**	**7**	**–**
12	A. K. Davidson	44	11,587	3,819	186	20.53	14	2
13	G. F. Lawson	46	11,118	5,501	180	30.56	11	2
14	K. R. Miller	55	10,461	3,906	170	22.97	7	1
	T. M. Alderman	41	10,181	4,616	170	27.15	14	1
16	W. A. Johnston	40	11,048	3,826	160	23.91	7	–
17	**S. C. G. MacGill**	**30**	**8,185**	**4,210**	**147**	**28.63**	**9**	**2**
18	W. J. O'Reilly	27	10,024	3,254	144	22.59	11	3
19	H. Trumble	32	8,099	3,072	141	21.78	9	3
20	**B. Lee**	**37**	**7,380**	**4,401**	**139**	**31.66**	**4**	**–**
21	M. H. N. Walker	34	10,094	3,792	138	27.47	6	–
22	A. A. Mallett	38	9,990	3,940	132	29.84	6	1
23	B. Yardley	33	8,909	3,986	126	31.63	6	1
24	R. M. Hogg	38	7,633	3,503	123	28.47	6	2
25	M. A. Noble	42	7,159	3,025	121	25.00	9	2
26	B. A. Reid	27	6,244	2,784	113	24.63	5	2
27	I. W. Johnson	45	8,780	3,182	109	29.19	3	–
28	P. R. Reiffel	35	6,403	2,804	104	26.96	5	–
29	G. Giffen	31	6,457	2,791	103	27.09	7	1
30	A. N. Connolly	29	7,818	2,981	102	29.22	4	–
31	C. T. B. Turner	17	5,179	1,670	101	16.53	11	2

SOUTH AFRICA

		T	*Balls*	*R*	*W*	*Avge*	*5W/i*	*10W/m*
1	A. A. Donald	72	15,519	7,344	330	22.25	20	3
2	**S. M. Pollock**	**80**	**17,980**	**6,893**	**326**	**21.14**	**16**	**1**
3	H. J. Tayfield	37	13,568	4,405	170	25.91	14	2
4	**J. H. Kallis**	**75**	**10,500**	**4,777**	**158**	**30.23**	**4**	–
5	**M. Ntini**	**42**	**8,489**	**4,494**	**156**	**28.80**	**7**	**1**
6	**P. R. Adams**	**44**	**8,562**	**4,285**	**132**	**32.46**	**4**	**1**
7	T. L. Goddard	41	11,736	3,226	123	26.22	5	–
8	P. M. Pollock	28	6,522	2,806	116	24.18	9	1
9	N. A. T. Adcock	26	6,391	2,195	104	21.10	5	–

WEST INDIES

		T	*Balls*	*R*	*W*	*Avge*	*5W/i*	*10W/m*
1	C. A. Walsh	132	30,019	12,688	519	24.44	22	3
2	C. E. L. Ambrose	98	22,103	8,501	405	20.99	22	3
3	M. D. Marshall	81	17,584	7,876	376	20.94	22	4
4	L. R. Gibbs	79	27,115	8,989	309	29.09	18	2
5	J. Garner	58	13,169	5,433	259	20.97	7	–
6	M. A. Holding	60	12,680	5,898	249	23.68	13	2
7	G. S. Sobers	93	21,599	7,999	235	34.03	6	–
8	A. M. E. Roberts	47	11,135	5,174	202	25.61	11	2
9	W. W. Hall	48	10,421	5,066	192	26.38	9	1
10	I. R. Bishop	43	8,407	3,909	161	24.27	6	–
11	S. Ramadhin	43	13,939	4,579	158	28.98	10	1
12	A. L. Valentine	36	12,953	4,215	139	30.32	8	2
13	**M. Dillon**	**38**	**8,704**	**4,398**	**131**	**33.57**	**2**	–
14	C. E. H. Croft	27	6,165	2,913	125	23.30	3	–
15	**C. L. Hooper**	**102**	**13,794**	**5,635**	**114**	**49.42**	**4**	–
16	V. A. Holder	40	9,095	3,627	109	33.27	3	–

NEW ZEALAND

		T	*Balls*	*R*	*W*	*Avge*	*5W/i*	*10W/m*
1	R. J. Hadlee	86	21,918	9,611	431	22.29	36	9
2	**C. L. Cairns**	**56**	**10,547**	**5,735**	**197**	**29.11**	**12**	**1**
3	D. K. Morrison	48	10,064	5,549	160	34.68	10	–
4	**D. L. Vettori**	**50**	**12,198**	**5,368**	**150**	**35.78**	**7**	**1**
5	B. L. Cairns	43	10,628	4,280	130	32.92	6	1
6	E. J. Chatfield	43	10,360	3,958	123	32.17	3	1
7	R. O. Collinge	35	7,689	3,393	116	29.25	3	–
8	B. R. Taylor	30	6,334	2,953	111	26.60	4	–
9	J. G. Bracewell	41	8,403	3,653	102	35.81	4	1
10	R. C. Motz	32	7,034	3,148	100	31.48	5	–

INDIA

		T	*Balls*	*R*	*W*	*Avge*	*5W/i*	*10W/m*
1	Kapil Dev	131	27,740	12,867	434	29.64	23	2
2	**A. Kumble**	**81**	**25,868**	**10,812**	**382**	**28.30**	**23**	**5**
3	B. S. Bedi	67	21,364	7,637	266	28.71	14	1
4	B. S. Chandrasekhar	58	15,963	7,199	242	29.74	16	2
5	**J. Srinath**	**67**	**15,104**	**7,196**	**236**	**30.49**	**10**	**1**
6	E. A. S. Prasanna	49	14,353	5,742	189	30.38	10	2
7	V. Mankad	44	14,686	5,236	162	32.32	8	2
8	S. Venkataraghavan	57	14,877	5,634	156	36.11	3	1

		T	Balls	R	W	Avge	5W/i	10W/m
9	**Harbhajan Singh** . . .	**36**	**9,647**	**4,299**	**151**	**28.47**	**11**	**2**
	R. J. Shastri	80	15,751	6,185	151	40.96	2	–
11	S. P. Gupte.	36	11,284	4,403	149	29.55	12	1
12	D. R. Doshi	33	9,322	3,502	114	30.71	6	–
13	K. D. Ghavri	39	7,042	3,656	109	33.54	4	–
14	N. S. Yadav	35	8,349	3,580	102	35.09	3	–

PAKISTAN

		T	Balls	R	W	Avge	5W/i	10W/m
1	Wasim Akram	104	22,627	9,779	414	23.62	25	5
2	**Waqar Younis**	**87**	**16,224**	**8,788**	**373**	**23.56**	**22**	**5**
3	Imran Khan	88	19,458	8,258	362	22.81	23	6
4	Abdul Qadir.	67	17,126	7,742	236	32.80	15	5
5	**Saqlain Mushtaq** . .	**48**	**13,812**	**6,002**	**207**	**28.99**	**13**	**3**
6	**Mushtaq Ahmed** . . .	**52**	**12,532**	**6,100**	**185**	**32.97**	**10**	**3**
7	Sarfraz Nawaz	55	13,927	5,798	177	32.75	4	1
8	Iqbal Qasim	50	13,019	4,807	171	28.11	8	2
9	Fazal Mahmood	34	9,834	3,434	139	24.70	13	4
10	Intikhab Alam	47	10,474	4,494	125	35.95	5	2
11	**Shoaib Akhtar**	**29**	**5,139**	**2,763**	**118**	**23.41**	**8**	**2**

SRI LANKA

		T	Balls	R	W	Avge	5W/i	10W/m
1	**M. Muralitharan** . . .	**85**	**28,967**	**11,130**	**485**	**22.94**	**39**	**12**
2	**W. P. U. J. C. Vaas** .	**71**	**15,637**	**6,899**	**229**	**30.12**	**7**	**2**

ZIMBABWE

		T	Balls	R	W	Avge	5W/i	10W/m
1	**H. H. Streak**	**57**	**12,491**	**5,509**	**197**	**27.96**	**6**	–

BANGLADESH: The highest aggregate is **36** wickets, average 27.69, by **Mohammad Rafiq** in 8 Tests.

Bold type denotes those who have played Test cricket since the start of 2002-03.

BEST CAREER AVERAGES

(Qualification: 75 wickets)

Avge		T	W	BB	5W/i	10W/m	SR
10.75	G. A. Lohmann (E)	18	112	9-28	9	5	34.11
16.43	S. F. Barnes (E)	27	189	9-103	24	7	41.65
16.53	C. T. B. Turner (A)	17	101	7-43	11	2	51.27
16.98	R. Peel (E).	20	101	7-31	5	1	51.64
17.75	J. Briggs (E).	33	118	8-11	9	4	45.18
18.41	F. R. Spofforth (A)	18	94	7-44	7	4	44.52
18.56	F. H. Tyson (E).	17	76	7-27	4	1	45.42
18.63	C. Blythe (E)	19	100	8-59	9	4	45.46
20.39	J. H. Wardle (E)	28	102	7-36	5	1	64.67
20.53	A. K. Davidson (A).	44	186	7-93	14	2	62.29
20.94	M. D. Marshall (WI)	81	376	7-22	22	4	46.76
20.97	J. Garner (WI)	58	259	6-56	7	–	50.84
20.99	C. E. L. Ambrose (WI). . .	98	405	8-45	22	3	54.57
21.10	N. A. T. Adcock (SA). . . .	26	104	6-43	5	–	61.45

Avge		*T*	*W*	*BB*	*5W/i*	*10W/m*	*SR*
21.14	**S. M. Pollock (SA)**	**80**	**326**	**7-87**	**16**	**1**	**55.15**
21.24	J. C. Laker (E)	46	193	10-53	9	3	62.31
21.51	G. E. Palmer (A)	17	78	7-65	6	2	57.91
21.57	F. S. Trueman (E)	67	307	8-31	17	3	49.43
21.71	**G. D. McGrath (A)**	**95**	**430**	**8-38**	**23**	**3**	**52.03**
21.78	H. Trumble (A)	32	141	8-65	9	3	57.43
22.25	A. A. Donald (SA)	72	330	8-71	20	3	47.02
22.29	R. J. Hadlee (NZ)	86	431	9-52	36	9	50.85
22.59	W. J. O'Reilly (A)	27	144	7-54	11	3	69.61
22.73	J. V. Saunders (A)	14	79	7-34	6	–	45.12
22.81	Imran Khan (P)	88	362	8-58	23	6	53.75
22.94	**M. Muralitharan (SL)**	**85**	**485**	**9-51**	**39**	**12**	**59.72**
22.97	K. R. Miller (A)	55	170	7-60	7	1	61.53

Bold type denotes those who have played Test cricket since the start of 2002-03.

BEST CAREER STRIKE-RATES

(Qualification: 75 wickets)

SR		*T*	*W*	*Avge*	*BB*	*5W/i*	*10W/m*
34.11	G. A. Lohmann (E)	18	112	10.75	9-28	9	5
41.65	S. F. Barnes (E)	27	189	16.43	9-103	24	7
43.49	**Waqar Younis (P)**	**87**	**373**	**23.56**	**7-76**	**22**	**5**
43.55	**Shoaib Akhtar (P)**	**29**	**118**	**23.41**	**6-11**	**8**	**2**
44.52	F. R. Spofforth (A)	18	94	18.41	7-44	7	4
45.12	J. V. Saunders (A)	14	79	22.73	7-34	6	–
45.18	J. Briggs (E)	33	118	17.75	8-11	9	4
45.42	F. H. Tyson (E)	17	76	18.56	7-27	4	1
45.46	C. Blythe (E)	19	100	18.63	8-59	9	4
46.76	M. D. Marshall (WI)	81	376	20.94	7-22	22	4
47.02	A. A. Donald (SA)	72	330	22.25	8-71	20	3
49.32	C. E. H. Croft (WI)	27	125	23.30	8-29	3	–
49.43	F. S. Trueman (E)	67	307	21.57	8-31	17	3
50.84	J. Garner (WI)	58	259	20.97	6-56	7	–
50.85	R. J. Hadlee (NZ)	86	431	22.29	9-52	36	9
50.92	M. A. Holding (WI)	60	249	23.68	8-92	13	2
51.10	T. Richardson (E)	14	88	25.22	8-94	11	4
51.27	C. T. B. Turner (A)	17	101	16.53	7-43	11	2
51.54	G. A. Faulkner (SA)	25	82	26.58	7-84	4	–
51.62	**D. Gough (E)**	**58**	**229**	**28.39**	**6-42**	**9**	–
51.64	R. Peel (E)	20	101	16.98	7-31	5	1
51.92	B. P. Patterson (WI)	28	93	30.90	5-24	5	–
52.01	D. K. Lillee (A)	70	355	23.92	7-83	23	7
52.03	**G. D. McGrath (A)**	**95**	**430**	**21.71**	**8-38**	**23**	**3**
52.05	A. Cotter (A)	21	89	28.64	7-148	7	–
52.21	I. R. Bishop (WI)	43	161	24.27	6-40	6	–
52.67	J. R. Thomson (A)	51	200	28.00	6-46	8	–
52.87	**J. N. Gillespie (A)**	**49**	**189**	**25.24**	**7-37**	**7**	–
53.09	**B. Lee (A)**	**37**	**139**	**31.66**	**5-47**	**4**	–
53.40	R. G. D. Willis (E)	90	325	25.20	8-43	16	–
53.53	**C. L. Cairns (NZ)**	**56**	**197**	**29.11**	**7-27**	**12**	**1**
53.75	Imran Khan (P)	88	362	22.81	8-58	23	6
54.14	G. O. B. Allen (E)	25	81	29.37	7-80	5	1
54.27	W. W. Hall (WI)	48	192	26.38	7-69	9	1
54.57	C. E. L. Ambrose (WI)	98	405	20.99	8-45	22	3
54.65	Wasim Akram (P)	104	414	23.62	7-119	25	5

Bold type denotes those who have played Test cricket since the start of 2002-03.

ALL-ROUND RECORDS

HUNDRED AND FIVE WICKETS IN AN INNINGS

England					
A. W. Greig	148	6-164	v West Indies	Bridgetown	1973-74
I. T. Botham	103	5-73	v New Zealand	Christchurch	1977-78
I. T. Botham	108	8-34	v Pakistan	Lord's	1978
I. T. Botham	114	6-58 } 7-48 }	v India	Bombay	1979-80
I. T. Botham	149*	6-95	v Australia	Leeds	1981
I. T. Botham	138	5-59	v New Zealand	Wellington	1983-84
Australia					
C. Kelleway	114	5-33	v South Africa	Manchester	1912
J. M. Gregory	100	7-69	v England	Melbourne	1920-21
K. R. Miller	109	6-107	v West Indies	Kingston	1954-55
R. Benaud	100	5-84	v South Africa	Johannesburg	1957-58
South Africa					
J. H. Sinclair	106	6-26	v England	Cape Town	1898-99
G. A. Faulkner	123	5-120	v England	Johannesburg	1909-10
J. H. Kallis	110	5-90	v West Indies	Cape Town	1998-99
J. H. Kallis	139*	5-21	v Bangladesh	Potchefstroom	2002-03
West Indies					
D. St E. Atkinson	219	5-56	v Australia	Bridgetown	1954-55
O. G. Smith	100	5-90	v India	Delhi	1958-59
G. S. Sobers	104	5-63	v India	Kingston	1961-62
G. S. Sobers	174	5-41	v England	Leeds	1966
New Zealand					
B. R. Taylor†	105	5-86	v India	Calcutta	1964-65
India					
V. Mankad	184	5-196	v England	Lord's	1952
P. R. Umrigar	172*	5-107	v West Indies	Port-of-Spain	1961-62
Pakistan					
Mushtaq Mohammad	201	5-49	v New Zealand	Dunedin	1972-73
Mushtaq Mohammad	121	5-28	v West Indies	Port-of-Spain	1976-77
Imran Khan	117	6-98 } 5-82 }	v India	Faisalabad	1982-83
Wasim Akram	123	5-100	v Australia	Adelaide	1989-90
Zimbabwe					
P. A. Strang	106*	5-212	v Pakistan	Sheikhupura	1996-97

† *On debut.*

HUNDRED AND FIVE DISMISSALS IN AN INNINGS

D. T. Lindsay	182	6ct	SA v A	Johannesburg	1966-67
I. D. S. Smith	113*	4ct, 1st	NZ v E	Auckland	1983-84
S. A. R. Silva	111	5ct	SL v I	Colombo (PSS)	1985-86

100 RUNS AND TEN WICKETS IN A TEST

A. K. Davidson	44 80	5-135 6-87	A v WI	Brisbane	1960-61
I. T. Botham	114	6-58 7-48	E v I	Bombay	1979-80
Imran Khan	117	6-98 5-82	P v I	Faisalabad	1982-83

1,000 RUNS AND 100 WICKETS

	Tests	*Runs*	*Wkts*	*Tests for Double*
England				
T. E. Bailey	61	2,290	132	47
†I. T. Botham	102	5,200	383	21
J. E. Emburey	64	1,713	147	46
A. W. Greig	58	3,599	141	37
R. Illingworth	61	1,836	122	47
W. Rhodes	58	2,325	127	44
M. W. Tate	39	1,198	155	33
F. J. Titmus	53	1,449	153	40
Australia				
R. Benaud	63	2,201	248	32
A. K. Davidson	44	1,328	186	34
G. Giffen	31	1,238	103	30
M. G. Hughes	53	1,032	212	52
I. W. Johnson	45	1,000	109	45
R. R. Lindwall	61	1,502	228	38
K. R. Miller	55	2,958	170	33
M. A. Noble	42	1,997	121	27
S. K. Warne	**107**	**2,238**	**491**	**58**
South Africa				
T. L. Goddard	41	2,516	123	36
J. H. Kallis	**75**	**5,486**	**158**	**53**
S. M. Pollock	**80**	**2,868**	**326**	**26**
West Indies				
C. E. L. Ambrose	98	1,439	405	69
†C. L. Hooper	**102**	**5,762**	**114**	**90**
M. D. Marshall	81	1,810	376	49
†G. S. Sobers	93	8,032	235	48
New Zealand				
J. G. Bracewell	41	1,001	102	41
C. L. Cairns	**56**	**2,864**	**197**	**33**
R. J. Hadlee	86	3,124	431	28
D. L. Vettori	**50**	**1,249**	**150**	**47**
India				
Kapil Dev	131	5,248	434	25
A. Kumble	**81**	**1,408**	**382**	**56**
V. Mankad	44	2,109	162	23
R. J. Shastri	80	3,830	151	44
J. Srinath	**67**	**1,009**	**236**	**67**

	Tests	Runs	Wkts	Tests for Double
Pakistan				
Abdul Qadir	67	1,029	236	62
Imran Khan	88	3,807	362	30
Intikhab Alam	47	1,493	125	41
Sarfraz Nawaz	55	1,045	177	55
Waqar Younis	**87**	**1,010**	**373**	**86**
Wasim Akram	104	2,898	414	45
Sri Lanka				
W. P. U. J. C. Vaas	**71**	**1,659**	**229**	**47**
Zimbabwe				
H. H. Streak	**57**	**1,746**	**197**	**40**

Bold type denotes those who have played Test cricket since the start of 2002-03.

† I. T. Botham (120 catches), C. L. Hooper (115) and G. S. Sobers (109) are the only players to have achieved the treble of 1,000 runs, 100 wickets and 100 catches.

WICKET-KEEPING RECORDS

MOST DISMISSALS IN AN INNINGS

7 (all ct)	Wasim Bari	Pakistan v New Zealand at Auckland	1978-79
7 (all ct)	R. W. Taylor	England v India at Bombay	1979-80
7 (all ct)	I. D. S. Smith	New Zealand v Sri Lanka at Hamilton	1990-91
7 (all ct)	R. D. Jacobs	West Indies v Australia at Melbourne	2000-01
6 (all ct)	A. T. W. Grout	Australia v South Africa at Johannesburg	1957-58
6 (all ct)	D. T. Lindsay	South Africa v Australia at Johannesburg	1966-67
6 (all ct)	J. T. Murray	England v India at Lord's	1967
6 (5ct, 1st)	S. M. H. Kirmani	India v New Zealand at Christchurch	1975-76
6 (all ct)	R. W. Marsh	Australia v England at Brisbane	1982-83
6 (all ct)	S. A. R. Silva	Sri Lanka v India at Colombo (SSC)	1985-86
6 (all ct)	R. C. Russell	England v Australia at Melbourne	1990-91
6 (all ct)	R. C. Russell	England v South Africa at Johannesburg	1995-96
6 (all ct)	I. A. Healy	Australia v England at Birmingham	1997
6 (all ct)	A. J. Stewart	England v Australia at Manchester	1997
6 (all ct)	M. V. Boucher	South Africa v Pakistan at Port Elizabeth	1997-98
6 (all ct)	Rashid Latif	Pakistan v Zimbabwe at Bulawayo	1997-98
6 (all ct)	M. V. Boucher	South Africa v Sri Lanka at Cape Town	1997-98
6 (5ct, 1st)	†C. M. W. Read	England v New Zealand at Birmingham	1999

† *On debut.*

MOST STUMPINGS IN AN INNINGS

5	K. S. More	India v West Indies at Madras	1987-88

MOST DISMISSALS IN A TEST

11 (all ct)	R. C. Russell	England v South Africa at Johannesburg	1995-96
10 (all ct)	R. W. Taylor	England v India at Bombay	1979-80
10 (all ct)	A. C. Gilchrist	Australia v New Zealand at Hamilton	1999-2000
9 (8ct, 1st)	G. R. A. Langley	Australia v England at Lord's	1956
9 (all ct)	D. A. Murray	West Indies v Australia at Melbourne	1981-82
9 (all ct)	R. W. Marsh	Australia v England at Brisbane	1982-83
9 (all ct)	S. A. R. Silva	Sri Lanka v India at Colombo (SSC)	1985-86
9 (8ct, 1st)	S. A. R. Silva	Sri Lanka v India at Colombo (PSS)	1985-86
9 (all ct)	D. J. Richardson	South Africa v India at Port Elizabeth	1992-93

9 (all ct)	Rashid Latif	Pakistan v New Zealand at Auckland	1993-94
9 (all ct)	I. A. Healy	Australia v England at Brisbane	1994-95
9 (all ct)	C. O. Browne	West Indies v England at Nottingham	1995
9 (7ct, 2st)	R. C. Russell	England v South Africa at Port Elizabeth	1995-96
9 (8ct, 1st)	M. V. Boucher	South Africa v Pakistan at Port Elizabeth	1997-98
9 (8ct, 1st)	R. D. Jacobs	West Indies v Australia at Melbourne	2000-01

Notes: S. A. R. Silva made 18 dismissals in two successive Tests.

The most stumpings in a match is 6 by K. S. More for India v West Indies at Madras in 1987-88.

J. J. Kelly (8ct) for Australia v England in 1901-02 and L. E. G. Ames (6ct, 2st) for England v West Indies in 1933 were the only wicket-keepers to make eight dismissals in a Test before World War II.

MOST DISMISSALS IN A SERIES

(Played in 5 Tests unless otherwise stated)

28 (all ct)	R. W. Marsh	Australia v England	1982-83
27 (25ct, 2st)	R. C. Russell	England v South Africa	1995-96
27 (25ct, 2st)	I. A. Healy	Australia v England (6 Tests)	1997
26 (23ct, 3st)	J. H. B. Waite	South Africa v New Zealand	1961-62
26 (all ct)	R. W. Marsh	Australia v West Indies (6 Tests)	1975-76
26 (21ct, 5st)	I. A. Healy	Australia v England (6 Tests)	1993
26 (25ct, 1st)	M. V. Boucher	South Africa v England	1998
26 (24ct, 2st)	A. C. Gilchrist	Australia v England	2001
25 (23ct, 2st)	I. A. Healy	Australia v England	1994-95

Notes: S. A. R. Silva made 22 dismissals (21ct, 1st) in three Tests for Sri Lanka v India in 1985-86.

H. Strudwick, with 21 (15ct, 6st) for England v South Africa in 1913-14, was the only wicket-keeper to make as many as 20 dismissals in a series before World War II.

100 DISMISSALS

			T	*Ct*	*St*
1	395	I. A. Healy (Australia)	119	366	29
2	355	R. W. Marsh (Australia)	96	343	12
3	**274**	**M. V. Boucher (South Africa)**	**71**	**264**	**10**
4	270	P. J. L. Dujon (West Indies)	79	265	5
5	269	A. P. E. Knott (England)	95	250	19
6	**241**	**A. J. Stewart (England)**	**82**	**227**	**14**
7	228	Wasim Bari (Pakistan)	81	201	27
8	219	T. G. Evans (England)	91	173	46
9	**214**	**A. C. Gilchrist (Australia)**	**51**	**195**	**19**
10	201	A. C. Parore (New Zealand)	67	194	7
11	198	S. M. H. Kirmani (India)	88	160	38
12	**192**	**R. D. Jacobs (West Indies)**	**57**	**183**	**9**
13	189	D. L. Murray (West Indies)	62	181	8
14	187	A. T. W. Grout (Australia)	51	163	24
15	176	I. D. S. Smith (New Zealand)	63	168	8
16	174	R. W. Taylor (England)	57	167	7
17	165	R. C. Russell (England)	54	153	12
18	152	D. J. Richardson (South Africa)	42	150	2
19	**151**	**A. Flower (Zimbabwe)**	**55**	**142**	**9**
20	**143**	**Moin Khan (Pakistan)**	**64**	**123**	**20**
21	141	J. H. B. Waite (South Africa)	50	124	17
22	130	K. S. More (India)	49	110	20
	130	W. A. Oldfield (Australia)	54	78	52
	130	**Rashid Latif (Pakistan)**	**37**	**119**	**11**

25	112	J. M. Parks (England)	43	101	11
26	107	N. R. Mongia (India)	44	99	8
27	**104**	**R. S. Kaluwitharana (Sri Lanka)**	**44**	**82**	**22**
	104	Salim Yousuf (Pakistan)	32	91	13
29	102	J. R. Murray (West Indies)	33	99	3

Notes: The records for P. J. L. Dujon and J. M. Parks each exclude two catches taken when not keeping wicket in two and three Tests respectively. A. J. Stewart's record excludes 36 catches taken in 51 Tests when not keeping wicket; A. C. Parore's excludes three in 11 Tests, A. Flower's nine in eight Tests and Moin Khan's one in three Tests when not keeping wicket.

The most wicket-keeping dismissals for Bangladesh is **40** (**Khaled Masud** 37ct, 3st in 23 Tests). H. P. Tillekeratne (Sri Lanka) has made 122 dismissals (120ct, 2st) in 80 Tests but only 35 (33ct, 2st) in 12 Tests as wicket-keeper (including one in which he took over during the match).

Bold type denotes those who have played Test cricket since the start of 2002-03.

FIELDING RECORDS

(Excluding wicket-keepers)

MOST CATCHES IN AN INNINGS

5	V. Y. Richardson	Australia v South Africa at Durban	1935-36
5	Yajurvindra Singh	India v England at Bangalore	1976-77
5	M. Azharuddin	India v Pakistan at Karachi	1989-90
5	K. Srikkanth	India v Australia at Perth	1991-92
5	S. P. Fleming	New Zealand v Zimbabwe at Harare	1997-98

MOST CATCHES IN A TEST

7	G. S. Chappell	Australia v England at Perth	1974-75
7	Yajurvindra Singh	India v England at Bangalore	1976-77
7	H. P. Tillekeratne	Sri Lanka v New Zealand at Colombo (SSC)	1992-93
7	S. P. Fleming	New Zealand v Zimbabwe at Harare	1997-98
6	A. Shrewsbury	England v Australia at Sydney	1887-88
6	A. E. E. Vogler	South Africa v England at Durban	1909-10
6	F. E. Woolley	England v Australia at Sydney	1911-12
6	J. M. Gregory	Australia v England at Sydney	1920-21
6	B. Mitchell	South Africa v Australia at Melbourne	1931-32
6	V. Y. Richardson	Australia v South Africa at Durban	1935-36
6	R. N. Harvey	Australia v England at Sydney	1962-63
6	M. C. Cowdrey	England v West Indies at Lord's	1963
6	E. D. Solkar	India v West Indies at Port-of-Spain	1970-71
6	G. S. Sobers	West Indies v England at Lord's	1973
6	I. M. Chappell	Australia v New Zealand at Adelaide	1973-74
6	A. W. Greig	England v Pakistan at Leeds	1974
6	D. F. Whatmore	Australia v India at Kanpur	1979-80
6	A. J. Lamb	England v New Zealand at Lord's	1983
6	G. A. Hick	England v Pakistan at Leeds	1992
6	B. A. Young	New Zealand v Pakistan at Auckland	1993-94
6	J. C. Adams	West Indies v England at Kingston	1993-94
6	S. P. Fleming	New Zealand v Australia at Brisbane	1997-98
6	D. P. M. D. Jayawardene	Sri Lanka v Pakistan at Peshawar	1999-2000
6	M. E. Waugh	Australia v India at Chennai	2000-01
6	V. Sehwag	India v England at Leeds	2002
6	Taufeeq Umar	Pakistan v South Africa at Faisalabad	2003-04

MOST CATCHES IN A SERIES

15	J. M. Gregory	Australia v England	1920-21
14	G. S. Chappell	Australia v England (6 Tests)	1974-75
13	R. B. Simpson	Australia v South Africa	1957-58
13	R. B. Simpson	Australia v West Indies	1960-61
13	B. C. Lara	West Indies v England (6 Tests)	1997-98

100 CATCHES

Ct	*T*		*Ct*	*T*	
181	**128**	**M. E. Waugh (Australia)**	**115**	**102**	**C. L. Hooper (West Indies)**
157	104	M. A. Taylor (Australia)	**112**	**168**	**S. R. Waugh (Australia)**
156	156	A. R. Border (Australia)	110	62	R. B. Simpson (Australia)
136	**102**	**B. C. Lara (West Indies)**	110	85	W. R. Hammond (England)
122	87	G. S. Chappell (Australia)	109	93	G. S. Sobers (West Indies)
122	121	I. V. A. Richards (West Indies)	108	125	S. M. Gavaskar (India)
120	102	I. T. Botham (England)	105	75	I. M. Chappell (Australia)
120	114	M. C. Cowdrey (England)	105	99	M. Azharuddin (India)
117	**79**	**S. P. Fleming (New Zealand)**	103	118	G. A. Gooch (England)

Note: The most catches in the field for other countries are South Africa **83** in 98 Tests (**G. Kirsten**); Pakistan 93 in 124 Tests (Javed Miandad); Sri Lanka **87** in 69 Tests (**H. P. Tillekeratne**); Zimbabwe **60** in 60 Tests (**A. D. R. Campbell**); Bangladesh **12** in 26 Tests (**Habibul Bashar**). Tillekeratne's record excludes 35 dismissals in his Tests as wicket-keeper.

Bold type denotes those who have played Test cricket since the start of 2002-03.

TEAM RECORDS

HIGHEST INNINGS TOTALS

952-6 dec.	Sri Lanka v India at Colombo (RPS)	1997-98
903-7 dec.	England v Australia at The Oval	1938
849	England v West Indies at Kingston	1929-30
790-3 dec.	West Indies v Pakistan at Kingston	1957-58
758-8 dec.	Australia v West Indies at Kingston	1954-55
735-6 dec.	Australia v Zimbabwe at Perth	2003-04
729-6 dec.	Australia v England at Lord's	1930
708	Pakistan v England at The Oval	1987
705-7 dec.	India v Australia at Sydney	2003-04
701	Australia v England at The Oval	1934
699-5	Pakistan v India at Lahore	1989-90
695	Australia v England at The Oval	1930
692-8 dec.	West Indies v England at The Oval	1995
687-8 dec.	West Indies v England at The Oval	1976
682-6 dec.	South Africa v England at Lord's	2003
681-8 dec.	West Indies v England at Port-of-Spain	1953-54
676-7	India v Sri Lanka at Kanpur	1986-87
674-6	Pakistan v India at Faisalabad	1984-85
674	Australia v India at Adelaide	1947-48
671-4	New Zealand v Sri Lanka at Wellington	1990-91
668	Australia v West Indies at Bridgetown	1954-55
660-5 dec.	West Indies v New Zealand at Wellington	1994-95

The highest innings for the countries not mentioned above are:

563-9 dec.	Zimbabwe v West Indies at Harare	2001
400	Bangladesh v India at Dhaka	2000-01

HIGHEST FOURTH-INNINGS TOTALS

To win

418-7	West Indies (needing 418) v Australia at St John's	2002-03
406-4	India (needing 403) v West Indies at Port-of-Spain	1975-76
404-3	Australia (needing 404) v England at Leeds	1948
369-6	Australia (needing 369) v Pakistan at Hobart	1999-2000
362-7	Australia (needing 359) v West Indies at Georgetown	1977-78
348-5	West Indies (needing 345) v New Zealand at Auckland	1968-69
344-1	West Indies (needing 342) v England at Lord's	1984

To tie

347	India v Australia at Madras	1986-87

To draw

654-5	England (needing 696 to win) v South Africa at Durban	1938-39
429-8	India (needing 438 to win) v England at The Oval	1979
423-7	South Africa (needing 451 to win) v England at The Oval	1947
408-5	West Indies (needing 836 to win) v England at Kingston	1929-30

To lose

451	New Zealand (lost by 98 runs) v England at Christchurch	2001-02
445	India (lost by 47 runs) v Australia at Adelaide	1977-78
440	New Zealand (lost by 38 runs) v England at Nottingham	1973
417	England (lost by 45 runs) v Australia at Melbourne	1976-77
411	England (lost by 193 runs) v Australia at Sydney	1924-25
402	Australia (lost by 103 runs) v England at Manchester	1981

MOST RUNS IN A DAY (BOTH SIDES)

588	England (398-6), India (190-0) at Manchester (2nd day)	1936
522	England (503-2), South Africa (19-0) at Lord's (2nd day)	1924
509	Sri Lanka (509-9) v Bangladesh at Colombo (PSS) (2nd day)	2002
508	England (221-2), South Africa (287-6) at The Oval (3rd day)	1935

MOST RUNS IN A DAY (ONE SIDE)

509	Sri Lanka (509-9) v Bangladesh at Colombo (PSS) (2nd day)	2002
503	England (503-2) v South Africa at Lord's (2nd day)	1924
494	Australia (494-6) v South Africa at Sydney (1st day)	1910-11
475	Australia (475-2) v England at The Oval (1st day)	1934
471	England (471-8) v India at The Oval (1st day)	1936
458	Australia (458-3) v England at Leeds (1st day)	1930
455	Australia (455-1) v England at Leeds (2nd day)	1934
450	Australia (450) v South Africa at Johannesburg (1st day)	1921-22

MOST WICKETS IN A DAY

27	England (18-3 to 53 all out and 62) v Australia (60) at Lord's (2nd day)	1888
25	Australia (112 and 48-5) v England (61) at Melbourne (1st day)	1901-02

HIGHEST AGGREGATES IN A TEST

Runs	Wkts			Days played
1,981	35	South Africa v England at Durban	1938-39	10†
1,815	34	West Indies v England at Kingston	1929-30	9‡
1,764	39	Australia v West Indies at Adelaide	1968-69	5
1,753	40	Australia v England at Adelaide	1920-21	6
1,747	25	Australia v India at Sydney	2003-04	5
1,723	31	England v Australia at Leeds	1948	5

† *No play on one day.* ‡ *No play on two days.*

LOWEST INNINGS TOTALS

26	New Zealand v England at Auckland	1954-55
30	South Africa v England at Port Elizabeth	1895-96
30	South Africa v England at Birmingham	1924
35	South Africa v England at Cape Town	1898-99
36	Australia v England at Birmingham	1902
36	South Africa v Australia at Melbourne	1931-32
42	Australia v England at Sydney	1887-88
42	New Zealand v Australia at Wellington	1945-46
42†	India v England at Lord's	1974
43	South Africa v England at Cape Town	1888-89
44	Australia v England at The Oval	1896
45	England v Australia at Sydney	1886-87
45	South Africa v Australia at Melbourne	1931-32
46	England v West Indies at Port-of-Spain	1993-94
47	South Africa v England at Cape Town	1888-89
47	New Zealand v England at Lord's	1958

The lowest innings for the countries not mentioned above are:

51	West Indies v Australia at Port-of-Spain	1998-99
53†	Pakistan v Australia at Sharjah	2002-03
63	Zimbabwe v West Indies at Port-of-Spain	1999-2000
71	Sri Lanka v Pakistan at Kandy	1994-95
87	Bangladesh v West Indies at Dhaka	2002-03

† *Batted one man short.*

FEWEST RUNS IN A FULL DAY'S PLAY

95	Australia (80), Pakistan (15-2) at Karachi (1st day, 5½ hours)	1956-57
104	Pakistan (0-0 to 104-5) v Australia at Karachi (4th day, 5½ hours)	1959-60
106	England (92-2 to 198) v Australia at Brisbane (4th day, 5 hours). *England were dismissed five minutes before the close of play, leaving no time for Australia to start their second innings.*	1958-59
111	South Africa (48-2 to 130-6 dec.), India (29-1) at Cape Town (5th day, 5½ hours)	1992-93
112	Australia (138-6 to 187), Pakistan (63-1) at Karachi (4th day, 5½ hours)	1956-57
115	Australia (116-7 to 165 and 66-5 after following on) v Pakistan at Karachi (4th day, 5½ hours)	1988-89
117	India (117-5) v Australia at Madras (1st day, 5½ hours)	1956-57
117	New Zealand (6-0 to 123-4) v Sri Lanka at Colombo (SSC) (5th day, 5¾ hours)	1983-84

In England

151	England (175-2 to 289), New Zealand (37-7) at Lord's (3rd day, 6 hours)	1978
158	England (211-2 to 369-9) v South Africa at Manchester (5th day, 6 hours)	1998
159	Pakistan (208-4 to 350), England (17-1) at Leeds (3rd day, 6 hours)	1971

LOWEST AGGREGATES IN A COMPLETED TEST

Runs	Wkts			Days played
234	29	Australia v South Africa at Melbourne	1931-32	3†
291	40	England v Australia at Lord's	1888	2
295	28	New Zealand v Australia at Wellington	1945-46	2
309	29	West Indies v England at Bridgetown	1934-35	3
323	30	England v Australia at Manchester	1888	2

† *No play on one day.*

LARGEST VICTORIES

Largest Innings Victories

Inns & 579 runs	England (903-7 dec.) v Australia (201 & 123‡) at The Oval	1938
Inns & 360 runs	Australia (652-7 dec.) v South Africa (159 & 133) at Johannesburg	2001-02
Inns & 336 runs	West Indies (614-5 dec.) v India (124 & 154) at Calcutta	1958-59
Inns & 332 runs	Australia (645) v England (141 & 172) at Brisbane	1946-47
Inns & 324 runs	Pakistan (643) v New Zealand (73 & 246) at Lahore	2002
Inns & 322 runs	West Indies (660-5 dec.) v New Zealand (216 & 122) at Wellington	1994-95
Inns & 310 runs	West Indies (536) v Bangladesh (139 & 87) at Dhaka	2002-03
Inns & 285 runs	England (629) v India (302 & 42†) at Lord's	1974
Inns & 264 runs	Pakistan (546-3 dec.) v Bangladesh (134 & 148) at Multan	2001-02
Inns & 259 runs	Australia (549-7 dec.) v South Africa (158 & 132) at Port Elizabeth	1949-50

‡ *Two men absent in both Australian innings.* † *One man absent in India's second innings.*

Largest Victories by Runs Margin

675 runs	England (521 & 342-8 dec.) v Australia (122 & 66†) at Brisbane	1928-29
562 runs	Australia (701 & 327) v England (321 & 145‡) at The Oval	1934
530 runs	Australia (328 & 578) v South Africa (205 & 171§) at Melbourne	1910-11
425 runs	West Indies (211 & 411-5 dec.) v England (71 & 126) at Manchester	1976
409 runs	Australia (350 & 460-7 dec.) v England (215 & 186) at Lord's	1948
408 runs	West Indies (328 & 448) v Australia (203 & 165) at Adelaide	1979-80
384 runs	Australia (492 & 296-5 dec.) v England (325 & 79) at Brisbane	2002-03
382 runs	Australia (238 & 411) v England (124 & 143) at Adelaide	1894-95
382 runs	Australia (619 & 394-8 dec.) v West Indies (279 & 352) at Sydney	1968-69
377 runs	Australia (267 & 581) v England (190 & 281) at Sydney	1920-21

† *One man absent in Australia's first innings; two men absent in their second.*
‡ *Two men absent in England's first innings; one man absent in their second.*
§ *One man absent in South Africa's second innings.*

TIED TESTS

West Indies (453 & 284) v Australia (505 & 232) at Brisbane	1960-61
Australia (574-7 dec. & 170-5 dec.) v India (397 & 347) at Madras	1986-87

PLAYERS

YOUNGEST TEST PLAYERS

Years	Days			
14	227	Hasan Raza	Pakistan v Zimbabwe at Faisalabad	1996-97
15	124	Mushtaq Mohammad	Pakistan v West Indies at Lahore	1958-59
15	128	Mohammad Sharif	Bangladesh v Zimbabwe at Bulawayo	2000-01
16	189	Aqib Javed	Pakistan v New Zealand at Wellington	1988-89
16	205	S. R. Tendulkar	India v Pakistan at Karachi	1989-90

The previous table should be treated with extreme caution. All birthdates for Bangladesh and Pakistan (after Partition) must be regarded as questionable owing to deficiencies in record-keeping. Hasan Raza's age has been rejected by the Pakistan Cricket Board although no alternative has been offered. Suggestions that Enamul Haque jun. was 16 years 230 days old when he played against England in Dhaka in 2003-04 have been discounted by well-informed local observers, who believe he was 18.

The youngest Test players for countries not mentioned above are:

17	122	J. E. D. Sealy	West Indies v England at Bridgetown	1929-30
17	189	C. D. U. S. Weerasinghe	Sri Lanka v India at Colombo (PSS)	1985-86
17	239	I. D. Craig	Australia v South Africa at Melbourne	1952-53
17	352	H. Masakadza	Zimbabwe v West Indies at Harare	2001
18	10	D. L. Vettori	New Zealand v England at Wellington	1996-97
18	149	D. B. Close	England v New Zealand at Manchester	1949
18	340	P. R. Adams	South Africa v England at Port Elizabeth	1995-96

OLDEST PLAYERS ON TEST DEBUT

Years	*Days*			
49	119	J. Southerton	England v Australia at Melbourne	1876-77
47	284	Miran Bux	Pakistan v India at Lahore	1954-55
46	253	D. D. Blackie	Australia v England at Sydney	1928-29
46	237	H. Ironmonger	Australia v England at Brisbane	1928-29
42	242	N. Betancourt	West Indies v England at Port-of-Spain	1929-30
41	337	E. R. Wilson	England v Australia at Sydney	1920-21
41	27	R. J. D. Jamshedji	India v England at Bombay	1933-34
40	345	C. A. Wiles	West Indies v England at Manchester	1933
40	295	O. Henry	South Africa v India at Durban	1992-93
40	216	S. P. Kinneir	England v Australia at Sydney	1911-12
40	110	H. W. Lee	England v South Africa at Johannesburg	1930-31
40	56	G. W. A. Chubb	South Africa v England at Nottingham	1951
40	37	C. Ramaswami	India v England at Manchester	1936

Note: The oldest Test player on debut for New Zealand was H. M. McGirr, 38 years 101 days, v England at Auckland, 1929-30; for Sri Lanka, D. S. de Silva, 39 years 251 days, v England at Colombo (PSS), 1981-82; for Zimbabwe, A. C. Waller, 37 years 84 days, v England at Bulawayo, 1996-97; for Bangladesh, Enamul Haque, 35 years 58 days, v Zimbabwe at Harare, 2000-01. A. J. Traicos was 45 years 154 days old when he made his debut for Zimbabwe (v India at Harare, 1992-93) having played three Tests for South Africa in 1969-70.

OLDEST TEST PLAYERS

(Age on final day of their last Test match)

Years	*Days*			
52	165	W. Rhodes	England v West Indies at Kingston	1929-30
50	327	H. Ironmonger	Australia v England at Sydney	1932-33
50	320	W. G. Grace	England v Australia at Nottingham	1899
50	303	G. Gunn	England v West Indies at Kingston	1929-30
49	139	J. Southerton	England v Australia at Melbourne	1876-77
47	302	Miran Bux	Pakistan v India at Peshawar	1954-55
47	249	J. B. Hobbs	England v Australia at The Oval	1930
47	87	F. E. Woolley	England v Australia at The Oval	1934
46	309	D. D. Blackie	Australia v England at Adelaide	1928-29
46	206	A. W. Nourse	South Africa v England at The Oval	1924
46	202	H. Strudwick	England v Australia at The Oval	1926
46	41	E. H. Hendren	England v West Indies at Kingston	1934-35
45	304	A. J. Traicos	Zimbabwe v India at Delhi	1992-93
45	245	G. O. B. Allen	England v West Indies at Kingston	1947-48
45	215	P. Holmes	England v India at Lord's	1932
45	140	D. B. Close	England v West Indies at Manchester	1976

100 TEST APPEARANCES

168	**S. R. Waugh (Australia)**	115	M. A. Atherton (England)
156	A. R. Border (Australia)	114	M. C. Cowdrey (England)
133	**A. J. Stewart (England)**	**111**	**S. R. Tendulkar (India)**
132	C. A. Walsh (West Indies)	110	C. H. Lloyd (West Indies)
131	Kapil Dev (India)	108	G. Boycott (England)
128	**M. E. Waugh (Australia)**	108	C. G. Greenidge (West Indies)
125	S. M. Gavaskar (India)	107	D. C. Boon (Australia)
124	Javed Miandad (Pakistan)	**107**	**S. K. Warne (Australia)**
121	I. V. A. Richards (West Indies)	104	M. A. Taylor (Australia)
119	I. A. Healy (Australia)	104	Wasim Akram (Pakistan)
118	G. A. Gooch (England)	103	Salim Malik (Pakistan)
117	D. I. Gower (England)	102	I. T. Botham (England)
116	D. L. Haynes (West Indies)	**102**	**C. L. Hooper (West Indies)**
116	D. B. Vengsarkar (India)	**102**	**B. C. Lara (West Indies)**

Note: The most appearances for South Africa is **98** by **G. Kirsten**, for Sri Lanka 93 by P. A. de Silva and A. Ranatunga, for New Zealand 86 by R. J. Hadlee, for Zimbabwe **65** by **G. W. Flower** and for Bangladesh **26** by **Habibul Bashar**.

Bold type denotes those who have played Test cricket since the start of 2002-03.

MOST CONSECUTIVE TEST APPEARANCES

153	A. R. Border (Australia)	March 1979 to March 1994
107	M. E. Waugh (Australia)	June 1993 to October 2002
106	S. M. Gavaskar (India)	January 1975 to February 1987
87	G. R. Viswanath (India)	March 1971 to February 1983
85	G. S. Sobers (West Indies)	April 1955 to April 1972
84	S. R. Tendulkar (India)	November 1989 to June 2001
75	R. Dravid (India)	June 1996 to January 2004
72	D. L. Haynes (West Indies)	December 1979 to June 1988
71	I. M. Chappell (Australia)	January 1966 to February 1976
70	M. V. Boucher (South Africa)	February 1998 to January 2004
69	M. Azharuddin (India)	April 1989 to February 1999
66	Kapil Dev (India)	October 1978 to December 1984
65	I. T. Botham (England)	February 1978 to March 1984
65	Kapil Dev (India)	January 1985 to March 1994
65	A. P. E. Knott (England)	March 1971 to August 1977

The most consecutive Test appearances for the countries not mentioned above are:

58†	J. R. Reid (New Zealand)	July 1949 to July 1965
56	A. D. R. Campbell (Zimbabwe)	October 1992 to September 2001
53	M. S. Atapattu (Sri Lanka)	June 1997 to July 2002
53	Javed Miandad (Pakistan)	December 1977 to January 1984

† *Complete Test career.*

> “If the decision by the umpires to offer the light was surprising, the decision of the rampant England batsmen to accept it was incredible.”
>
> South Africans in England, page 451.

MOST TESTS AS CAPTAIN

	P	*W*	*L*	*D*
A. R. Border (A)	93	32	22	38*
C. H. Lloyd (WI)	74	36	12	26
S. R. Waugh (A)	**57**	**41**	**9**	**7**
A. Ranatunga (SL)	56	12	19	25
S. P. Fleming (NZ)	**55**	**19**	**16**	**20**
M. A. Atherton (E)	54	13	21	20
W. J. Cronje (SA)	53	27	11	15
I. V. A. Richards (WI)	50	27	8	15
M. A. Taylor (A)	50	26	13	11
G. S. Chappell (A)	48	21	13	14
Imran Khan (P)	48	14	8	26
M. Azharuddin (I)	47	14	14	19
S. M. Gavaskar (I)	47	9	8	30
N. Hussain (E)	**45**	**17**	**15**	**13**
P. B. H. May (E)	41	20	10	11
Nawab of Pataudi jun. (I)	40	9	19	12
R. B. Simpson (A)	39	12	12	15
G. S. Sobers (WI)	39	9	10	20
S. T. Jayasuriya (SL)	**38**	**18**	**12**	**8**
S. C. Ganguly (I)	**37**	**14**	**11**	**12**
G. A. Gooch (E)	34	10	12	12
Javed Miandad (P)	34	14	6	14
Kapil Dev (I)	34	4	7	22*
J. R. Reid (NZ)	34	3	18	13
D. I. Gower (E)	32	5	18	9
J. M. Brearley (E)	31	18	4	9
R. Illingworth (E)	31	12	5	14
I. M. Chappell (A)	30	15	5	10
E. R. Dexter (E)	30	9	7	14
G. P. Howarth (NZ)	30	11	7	12
B. C. Lara (WI)	**30**	**9**	**16**	**5**

* *One match tied.*

Most Tests as captain of other countries:

	P	*W*	*L*	*D*
A. D. R. Campbell (Z)	**21**	**2**	**12**	**7**
Khaled Masud (B)	**10**	**0**	**10**	**0**

Notes: A. R. Border captained Australia in 93 consecutive Tests.

W. W. Armstrong (Australia) captained his country in the most Tests without being defeated: ten matches with eight wins and two draws.

I. T. Botham (England) captained his country in the most Tests without ever winning: 12 matches with eight draws and four defeats.

Bold type denotes those who have been captains since the start of 2002-03.

UMPIRES

MOST TESTS

		First Test	*Last Test*
86	**S. A. Bucknor (West Indies)**	**1988-89**	**2003-04**
78	**D. R. Shepherd (England)**	**1985**	**2003-04**
73	**S. Venkataraghavan (India)**	**1992-93**	**2003-04**
66	H. D. Bird (England)	1973	1996
51	**D. B. Hair (Australia)**	**1991-92**	**2003-04**
48	F. Chester (England)	1924	1955
46	**R. E. Koertzen (South Africa)**	**1992-93**	**2003-04**
42	C. S. Elliott (England)	1957	1974
40	**D. L. Orchard (South Africa)**	**1995-96**	**2003-04**
39	R. S. Dunne (New Zealand)	1988-89	2001-02
37	**D. J. Harper (Australia)**	**1998-99**	**2003-04**
37	**R. B. Tiffin (Zimbabwe)**	**1995-96**	**2003**
36	D. J. Constant (England)	1971	1988
36	S. G. Randell (Australia)	1984-85	1997-98
34	Khizar Hayat (Pakistan)	1979-80	1996-97
33	J. S. Buller (England)	1956	1969
33	A. R. Crafter (Australia)	1978-79	1991-92
32	R. W. Crockett (Australia)	1901-02	1924-25
31	D. Sang Hue (West Indies)	1961-62	1980-81

Bold type indicates umpires who have stood since the start of 2002-03.

SUMMARY OF TESTS

To January 20, 2004

	Opponents	*Tests*	*Won by* E	A	SA	WI	NZ	I	P	SL	Z	B	*Tied*	*Drawn*
England	Australia	**306**	95	125	–	–	–	–	–	–	–	–	–	86
	South Africa	**125**	52	–	25	–	–	–	–	–	–	–	–	48
	West Indies	**126**	31	–	–	52	–	–	–	–	–	–	–	43
	New Zealand	**85**	38	–	–	–	7	–	–	–	–	–	–	40
	India	**91**	33	–	–	–	–	16	–	–	–	–	–	42
	Pakistan	**60**	16	–	–	–	–	–	10	–	–	–	–	34
	Sri Lanka	**15**	7	–	–	–	–	–	–	4	–	–	–	4
	Zimbabwe	**6**	3	–	–	–	–	–	–	–	0	–	–	3
	Bangladesh	**2**	2	–	–	–	–	–	–	–	–	0	–	0
Australia	South Africa	**71**	–	39	15	–	–	–	–	–	–	–	–	17
	West Indies	**99**	–	45	–	32	–	–	–	–	–	–	1	21
	New Zealand	**41**	–	18	–	–	7	–	–	–	–	–	–	16
	India	**64**	–	30	–	–	–	14	–	–	–	–	1	19
	Pakistan	**49**	–	21	–	–	–	–	11	–	–	–	–	17
	Sri Lanka	**13**	–	7	–	–	–	–	–	1	–	–	–	5
	Zimbabwe	**3**	–	3	–	–	–	–	–	–	0	–	–	0
	Bangladesh	**2**	–	2	–	–	–	–	–	–	–	0	–	0
South Africa	West Indies	**15**	–	–	10	2	–	–	–	–	–	–	–	3
	New Zealand	**27**	–	–	15	–	3	–	–	–	–	–	–	9
	India	**14**	–	–	7	–	–	2	–	–	–	–	–	5
	Pakistan	**11**	–	–	5	–	–	–	2	–	–	–	–	4
	Sri Lanka	**13**	–	–	8	–	–	–	–	1	–	–	–	4
	Zimbabwe	**5**	–	–	4	–	–	–	–	–	0	–	–	1
	Bangladesh	**4**	–	–	4	–	–	–	–	–	–	0	–	0
West Indies	New Zealand	**32**	–	–	–	10	7	–	–	–	–	–	–	15
	India	**78**	–	–	–	30	–	10	–	–	–	–	–	38
	Pakistan	**39**	–	–	–	13	–	–	12	–	–	–	–	14
	Sri Lanka	**8**	–	–	–	2	–	–	–	3	–	–	–	3
	Zimbabwe	**6**	–	–	–	4	–	–	–	–	0	–	–	2
	Bangladesh	**2**	–	–	–	2	–	–	–	–	–	0	–	0
New Zealand	India	**44**	–	–	–	–	9	14	–	–	–	–	–	21
	Pakistan	**45**	–	–	–	–	6	–	21	–	–	–	–	18
	Sri Lanka	**20**	–	–	–	–	7	–	–	4	–	–	–	9
	Zimbabwe	**11**	–	–	–	–	5	–	–	–	0	–	–	6
	Bangladesh	**2**	–	–	–	–	2	–	–	–	–	0	–	0
India	Pakistan	**47**	–	–	–	–	–	5	9	–	–	–	–	33
	Sri Lanka	**23**	–	–	–	–	–	8	–	3	–	–	–	12
	Zimbabwe	**9**	–	–	–	–	–	5	–	–	2	–	–	2
	Bangladesh	**1**	–	–	–	–	–	1	–	–	–	0	–	0
Pakistan	Sri Lanka	**28**	–	–	–	–	–	–	13	6	–	–	–	9
	Zimbabwe	**14**	–	–	–	–	–	–	8	–	2	–	–	4
	Bangladesh	**6**	–	–	–	–	–	–	6	–	–	0	–	0
Sri Lanka	Zimbabwe	**13**	–	–	–	–	–	–	–	8	0	–	–	5
	Bangladesh	**3**	–	–	–	–	–	–	–	3	–	0	–	0
Zimbabwe	Bangladesh	**4**	–	–	–	–	–	–	–	–	3	0	–	1
		1,682	277	290	93	147	53	75	92	33	7	0	2	613

	Tests	*Won*	*Lost*	*Drawn*	*Tied*	*% Won*	*Toss Won*
England	816	277	239	300	–	33.94	392
Australia	648	290	175	181	2	44.75	328
South Africa	285	93	101	91	–	32.63	134
West Indies	405	147	118	139	1	36.29	214
New Zealand	307	53	120	134	–	17.26	157
India	371	75	123	172	1	20.21	188
Pakistan	299	92	74	133	–	30.76	140
Sri Lanka	136	33	52	51	–	24.26	73
Zimbabwe	71	7	40	24	–	9.85	42
Bangladesh	26	0	25	1	–	0.00	14

ENGLAND v AUSTRALIA

Series notes: England have won only one Test when the Ashes were still at stake (Birmingham 1997) in the last eight series between the sides… S. K. Warne needs 11 wickets in England to become the first man to take 100 Test wickets in an overseas country… Warne has 132 wickets against England, and needs 36 to break D. K. Lillee's record for Test wickets against one country… Since England last scored 500 in this fixture (Perth, 1986-87), Australia have exceeded 500 on 12 occasions – with five of those 12 in excess of 600… Australia have lost only one (1934) of their last 26 Tests at Lord's, and none of the last 17… In Ashes Tests since 1993, Australia have a conversion-rate of fifties to hundreds of 43% (50 x 100, 65 x 50); England's is 16% (16 x 100; 84 x 50)… In the last four series, Australia have won 15 out of 21 tosses… None of the last 14 Tests between the sides has been drawn… England have lost 14 and won only three of the 22 Tests in which they have put Australia in… Australia have won the last eight series between the sides – an Ashes record – and excluding one-off Tests there have been no drawn series since 1972.

	Captains					
Season	*England*	*Australia*	*T*	*E*	*A*	*D*
1876-77	James Lillywhite	D. W. Gregory	2	1	1	0
1878-79	Lord Harris	D. W. Gregory	1	0	1	0
1880	Lord Harris	W. L. Murdoch	1	1	0	0
1881-82	A. Shaw	W. L. Murdoch	4	0	2	2
1882	A. N. Hornby	W. L. Murdoch	1	0	1	0

THE ASHES

	Captains						
Season	*England*	*Australia*	*T*	*E*	*A*	*D*	*Held by*
1882-83	Hon. Ivo Bligh	W. L. Murdoch	4*	2	2	0	E
1884	Lord Harris[1]	W. L. Murdoch	3	1	0	2	E
1884-85	A. Shrewsbury	T. P. Horan[2]	5	3	2	0	E
1886	A. G. Steel	H. J. H. Scott	3	3	0	0	E
1886-87	A. Shrewsbury	P. S. McDonnell	2	2	0	0	E
1887-88	W. W. Read	P. S. McDonnell	1	1	0	0	E
1888	W. G. Grace[3]	P. S. McDonnell	3	2	1	0	E
1890†	W. G. Grace	W. L. Murdoch	2	2	0	0	E
1891-92	W. G. Grace	J. McC. Blackham	3	1	2	0	A
1893	W. G. Grace[4]	J. McC. Blackham	3	1	0	2	E
1894-95	A. E. Stoddart	G. Giffen[5]	5	3	2	0	E
1896	W. G. Grace	G. H. S. Trott	3	2	1	0	E
1897-98	A. E. Stoddart[6]	G. H. S. Trott	5	1	4	0	A
1899	A. C. MacLaren[7]	J. Darling	5	0	1	4	A
1901-02	A. C. MacLaren	J. Darling[8]	5	1	4	0	A
1902	A. C. MacLaren	J. Darling	5	1	2	2	A
1903-04	P. F. Warner	M. A. Noble	5	3	2	0	E
1905	Hon. F. S. Jackson	J. Darling	5	2	0	3	E
1907-08	A. O. Jones[9]	M. A. Noble	5	1	4	0	A
1909	A. C. MacLaren	M. A. Noble	5	1	2	2	A
1911-12	J. W. H. T. Douglas	C. Hill	5	4	1	0	E
1912	C. B. Fry	S. E. Gregory	3	1	0	2	E
1920-21	J. W. H. T. Douglas	W. W. Armstrong	5	0	5	0	A
1921	Hon. L. H. Tennyson[10]	W. W. Armstrong	5	0	3	2	A
1924-25	A. E. R. Gilligan	H. L. Collins	5	1	4	0	A
1926	A. W. Carr[11]	H. L. Collins[12]	5	1	0	4	E
1928-29	A. P. F. Chapman[13]	J. Ryder	5	4	1	0	E
1930	A. P. F. Chapman[14]	W. M. Woodfull	5	1	2	2	A
1932-33	D. R. Jardine	W. M. Woodfull	5	4	1	0	E
1934	R. E. S. Wyatt[15]	W. M. Woodfull	5	1	2	2	A
1936-37	G. O. B. Allen	D. G. Bradman	5	2	3	0	A
1938†	W. R. Hammond	D. G. Bradman	4	1	1	2	A

	Captains						
Season	*England*	*Australia*	*T*	*E*	*A*	*D*	*Held by*
1946-47	W. R. Hammond[16]	D. G. Bradman	5	0	3	2	A
1948	N. W. D. Yardley	D. G. Bradman	5	0	4	1	A
1950-51	F. R. Brown	A. L. Hassett	5	1	4	0	A
1953	L. Hutton	A. L. Hassett	5	1	0	4	E
1954-55	L. Hutton	I. W. Johnson[17]	5	3	1	1	E
1956	P. B. H. May	I. W. Johnson	5	2	1	2	E
1958-59	P. B. H. May	R. Benaud	5	0	4	1	A
1961	P. B. H. May[18]	R. Benaud[19]	5	1	2	2	A
1962-63	E. R. Dexter	R. Benaud	5	1	1	3	A
1964	E. R. Dexter	R. B. Simpson	5	0	1	4	A
1965-66	M. J. K. Smith	R. B. Simpson[20]	5	1	1	3	A
1968	M. C. Cowdrey[21]	W. M. Lawry[22]	5	1	1	3	A
1970-71†	R. Illingworth	W. M. Lawry[23]	6	2	0	4	E
1972	R. Illingworth	I. M. Chappell	5	2	2	1	E
1974-75	M. H. Denness[24]	I. M. Chappell	6	1	4	1	A
1975	A. W. Greig[25]	I. M. Chappell	4	0	1	3	A
1976-77‡	A. W. Greig	G. S. Chappell	1	0	1	0	—
1977	J. M. Brearley	G. S. Chappell	5	3	0	2	E
1978-79	J. M. Brearley	G. N. Yallop	6	5	1	0	E
1979-80‡	J. M. Brearley	G. S. Chappell	3	0	3	0	—
1980‡	I. T. Botham	G. S. Chappell	1	0	0	1	—
1981	J. M. Brearley[26]	K. J. Hughes	6	3	1	2	E
1982-83	R. G. D. Willis	G. S. Chappell	5	1	2	2	A
1985	D. I. Gower	A. R. Border	6	3	1	2	E
1986-87	M. W. Gatting	A. R. Border	5	2	1	2	E
1987-88‡	M. W. Gatting	A. R. Border	1	0	0	1	—
1989	D. I. Gower	A. R. Border	6	0	4	2	A
1990-91	G. A. Gooch[27]	A. R. Border	5	0	3	2	A
1993	G. A. Gooch[28]	A. R. Border	6	1	4	1	A
1994-95	M. A. Atherton	M. A. Taylor	5	1	3	1	A
1997	M. A. Atherton	M. A. Taylor	6	2	3	1	A
1998-99	A. J. Stewart	M. A. Taylor	5	1	3	1	A
2001	N. Hussain[29]	S. R. Waugh[30]	5	1	4	0	A
2002-03	N. Hussain	S. R. Waugh	5	1	4	0	A
	In Australia		160	54	80	26	
	In England		146	41	45	60	
	Totals		306	95	125	86	

* *The Ashes were awarded in 1882-83 after a series of three matches which England won 2–1. A fourth match was played and this was won by Australia.*
† *The matches at Manchester in 1890 and 1938 and at Melbourne (Third Test) in 1970-71 were abandoned without a ball being bowled and are excluded.*
‡ *The Ashes were not at stake in these series.*

Notes: The following deputised for the official touring captain or were appointed by the home authority for only a minor proportion of the series:

[1]A. N. Hornby (First). [2]W. L. Murdoch (First), H. H. Massie (Third), J. McC. Blackham (Fourth). [3]A. G. Steel (First). [4]A. E. Stoddart (First). [5]J. McC. Blackham (First). [6]A. C. MacLaren (First, Second and Fifth). [7]W. G. Grace (First). [8]H. Trumble (Fourth and Fifth). [9]F. L. Fane (First, Second and Third). [10]J. W. H. T. Douglas (First and Second). [11]A. P. F. Chapman (Fifth). [12]W. Bardsley (Third and Fourth). [13]J. C. White (Fifth). [14]R. E. S. Wyatt (Fifth). [15]C. F. Walters (First). [16]N. W. D. Yardley (Fifth). [17]A. R. Morris (Second). [18]M. C. Cowdrey (First and Second). [19]R. N. Harvey (Second). [20]B. C. Booth (First and Third). [21]T. W. Graveney (Fourth). [22]B. N. Jarman (Fourth). [23]I. M. Chappell (Seventh). [24]J. H. Edrich (Fourth). [25]M. H. Denness (First). [26]I. T. Botham (First and Second). [27]A. J. Lamb (First). [28]M. A. Atherton (Fifth and Sixth). [29]M. A. Atherton (Second and Third). [30]A. C. Gilchrist (Fourth).

HIGHEST INNINGS TOTALS

For England	in England: 903-7 dec. at The Oval	1938
	in Australia: 636 at Sydney	1928-29
For Australia	in England: 729-6 dec. at Lord's	1930
	in Australia: 659-8 dec. at Sydney	1946-47

LOWEST INNINGS TOTALS

For England	in England: 52 at The Oval	1948
	in Australia: 45 at Sydney	1886-87
For Australia	in England: 36 at Birmingham	1902
	in Australia: 42 at Sydney	1887-88

DOUBLE-HUNDREDS

For England (10)

364	L. Hutton at The Oval	1938
287	R. E. Foster at Sydney	1903-04
256	K. F. Barrington at Manchester	1964
251	W. R. Hammond at Sydney	1928-29
240	W. R. Hammond at Lord's	1938
231*	W. R. Hammond at Sydney	1936-37
216*	E. Paynter at Nottingham	1938
215	D. I. Gower at Birmingham	1985
207	N. Hussain at Birmingham	1997
200	W. R. Hammond at Melbourne	1928-29

For Australia (23)

334	D. G. Bradman at Leeds	1930
311	R. B. Simpson at Manchester	1964
307	R. M. Cowper at Melbourne	1965-66
304	D. G. Bradman at Leeds	1934
270	D. G. Bradman at Melbourne	1936-37
266	W. H. Ponsford at The Oval	1934
254	D. G. Bradman at Lord's	1930
250	J. L. Langer at Melbourne	2002-03
244	D. G. Bradman at The Oval	1934
234	S. G. Barnes at Sydney	1946-47
234	D. G. Bradman at Sydney	1946-47
232	D. G. Bradman at The Oval	1930
232	S. J. McCabe at Nottingham	1938
225	R. B. Simpson at Adelaide	1965-66
219	M. A. Taylor at Nottingham	1989
212	D. G. Bradman at Adelaide	1936-37
211	W. L. Murdoch at The Oval	1884
207	K. R. Stackpole at Brisbane	1970-71
206*	W. A. Brown at Lord's	1938
206	A. R. Morris at Adelaide	1950-51
201*	J. Ryder at Adelaide	1924-25
201	S. E. Gregory at Sydney	1894-95
200*	A. R. Border at Leeds	1993

INDIVIDUAL HUNDREDS

For England (212)

12: J. B. Hobbs.
9: D. I. Gower, W. R. Hammond.
8: H. Sutcliffe.
7: G. Boycott, J. H. Edrich, M. Leyland.
5: K. F. Barrington, D. C. S. Compton, M. C. Cowdrey, L. Hutton, F. S. Jackson, A. C. MacLaren.
4: I. T. Botham, B. C. Broad, M. W. Gatting, G. A. Gooch.

3: M. A. Butcher, E. H. Hendren, P. B. H. May, D. W. Randall, A. C. Russell, A. Shrewsbury, G. P. Thorpe, J. T. Tyldesley, M. P. Vaughan, R. A. Woolmer.

2: C. J. Barnett, L. C. Braund, E. R. Dexter, B. L. D'Oliveira, W. J. Edrich, W. G. Grace, G. Gunn, T. W. Hayward, N. Hussain, A. P. E. Knott, B. W. Luckhurst, K. S. Ranjitsinhji, R. T. Robinson, Rev. D. S. Sheppard, R. A. Smith, A. G. Steel, A. E. Stoddart, R. Subba Row, C. Washbrook, F. E. Woolley.

1: R. Abel, L. E. G. Ames, M. A. Atherton, R. W. Barber, W. Barnes, J. Briggs, J. T. Brown, A. P. F. Chapman, M. H. Denness, K. S. Duleepsinhji, K. W. R. Fletcher, R. E. Foster, C. B. Fry, T. W. Graveney, A. W. Greig, W. Gunn, J. Hardstaff, jun., J. W. Hearne, K. L. Hutchings, G. L. Jessop, A. J. Lamb, J. W. H. Makepeace, C. P. Mead, Nawab of Pataudi, sen., E. Paynter, M. R. Ramprakash, W. W. Read, W. Rhodes, C. J. Richards, P. E. Richardson, R. C. Russell, J. Sharp, R. T. Simpson, A. J. Stewart, G. Ulyett, A. Ward, W. Watson.

For Australia (264)

19: D. G. Bradman.

10: S. R. Waugh.

9: G. S. Chappell.

8: A. R. Border, A. R. Morris.

7: D. C. Boon, W. M. Lawry, M. J. Slater.

6: R. N. Harvey, M. A. Taylor, V. T. Trumper, M. E. Waugh, W. M. Woodfull.

5: C. G. Macartney, W. H. Ponsford.

4: W. W. Armstrong, P. J. Burge, I. M. Chappell, S. E. Gregory, A. L. Hassett, C. Hill, S. J. McCabe, R. T. Ponting, K. D. Walters.

3: W. Bardsley, G. S. Blewett, W. A. Brown, H. L. Collins, J. Darling, M. L. Hayden, K. J. Hughes, D. M. Jones, J. L. Langer, P. S. McDonnell, K. R. Miller, K. R. Stackpole, G. M. Wood, G. N. Yallop.

2: S. G. Barnes, B. C. Booth, R. A. Duff, R. Edwards, M. T. G. Elliott, J. H. Fingleton, A. C. Gilchrist, H. Graham, I. A. Healy, F. A. Iredale, R. B. McCosker, C. C. McDonald, G. R. Marsh, D. R. Martyn, W. L. Murdoch, N. C. O'Neill, C. E. Pellew, I. R. Redpath, J. Ryder, R. B. Simpson.

1: C. L. Badcock, C. Bannerman, G. J. Bonnor, J. W. Burke, R. M. Cowper, J. Dyson, G. Giffen, J. M. Gregory, R. J. Hartigan, H. L. Hendry, A. M. J. Hilditch, T. P. Horan, A. A. Jackson, C. Kelleway, A. F. Kippax, R. R. Lindwall, J. J. Lyons, C. L. McCool, C. E. McLeod, R. W. Marsh, G. R. J. Matthews, M. A. Noble, V. S. Ransford, A. J. Richardson, V. Y. Richardson, G. M. Ritchie, H. J. H. Scott, J. M. Taylor, G. H. S. Trott, D. M. Wellham, K. C. Wessels.

RECORD PARTNERSHIPS FOR EACH WICKET

For England

323 for 1st	J. B. Hobbs and W. Rhodes at Melbourne	1911-12
382 for 2nd†	L. Hutton and M. Leyland at The Oval	1938
262 for 3rd	W. R. Hammond and D. R. Jardine at Adelaide	1928-29
288 for 4th	N. Hussain and G. P. Thorpe at Birmingham	1997
206 for 5th	E. Paynter and D. C. S. Compton at Nottingham	1938
215 for 6th	L. Hutton and J. Hardstaff jun. at The Oval	1938
	G. Boycott and A. P. E. Knott at Nottingham	1977
143 for 7th	F. E. Woolley and J. Vine at Sydney	1911-12
124 for 8th	E. H. Hendren and H. Larwood at Brisbane	1928-29
151 for 9th	W. H. Scotton and W. W. Read at The Oval	1884
130 for 10th†	R. E. Foster and W. Rhodes at Sydney	1903-04

For Australia

329 for 1st	G. R. Marsh and M. A. Taylor at Nottingham	1989
451 for 2nd†	W. H. Ponsford and D. G. Bradman at The Oval	1934
276 for 3rd	D. G. Bradman and A. L. Hassett at Brisbane	1946-47
388 for 4th†	W. H. Ponsford and D. G. Bradman at Leeds	1934
405 for 5th†	S. G. Barnes and D. G. Bradman at Sydney	1946-47
346 for 6th†	J. H. Fingleton and D. G. Bradman at Melbourne	1936-37
165 for 7th	C. Hill and H. Trumble at Melbourne	1897-98
243 for 8th†	R. J. Hartigan and C. Hill at Adelaide	1907-08
154 for 9th†	S. E. Gregory and J. McC. Blackham at Sydney	1894-95
127 for 10th†	J. M. Taylor and A. A. Mailey at Sydney	1924-25

† *Record partnership against all countries.*

MOST RUNS IN A SERIES

England in England	732 (average 81.33)	D. I. Gower	1985
England in Australia	905 (average 113.12)	W. R. Hammond	1928-29
Australia in England	974 (average 139.14)	D. G. Bradman	1930
Australia in Australia	810 (average 90.00)	D. G. Bradman	1936-37

TEN WICKETS OR MORE IN A MATCH

For England (38)

13-163 (6-42, 7-121)	S. F. Barnes, Melbourne	1901-02
14-102 (7-28, 7-74)	W. Bates, Melbourne	1882-83
10-105 (5-46, 5-59)	A. V. Bedser, Melbourne	1950-51
14-99 (7-55, 7-44)	A. V. Bedser, Nottingham	1953
11-102 (6-44, 5-58)	C. Blythe, Birmingham	1909
11-176 (6-78, 5-98)	I. T. Botham, Perth	1979-80
10-253 (6-125, 4-128)	I. T. Botham, The Oval	1981
11-74 (5-29, 6-45)	J. Briggs, Lord's	1886
12-136 (6-49, 6-87)	J. Briggs, Adelaide	1891-92
10-148 (5-34, 5-114)	J. Briggs, The Oval	1893
10-215 (3-121, 7-94)	A. R. Caddick, Sydney	2002-03
10-104 (6-77, 4-27)†	R. M. Ellison, Birmingham	1985
10-179 (5-102, 5-77)†	K. Farnes, Nottingham	1934
10-60 (6-41, 4-19)	J. T. Hearne, The Oval	1896
11-113 (5-58, 6-55)	J. C. Laker, Leeds	1956
19-90 (9-37, 10-53)	J. C. Laker, Manchester	1956
10-124 (5-96, 5-28)	H. Larwood, Sydney	1932-33
11-76 (6-48, 5-28)	W. H. Lockwood, Manchester	1902
12-104 (7-36, 5-68)	G. A. Lohmann, The Oval	1886
10-87 (8-35, 2-52)	G. A. Lohmann, Sydney	1886-87
10-142 (8-58, 2-84)	G. A. Lohmann, Sydney	1891-92
12-102 (6-50, 6-52)†	F. Martin, The Oval	1890
11-68 (7-31, 4-37)	R. Peel, Manchester	1888
15-124 (7-56, 8-68)	W. Rhodes, Melbourne	1903-04
10-156 (5-49, 5-107)†	T. Richardson, Manchester	1893
11-173 (6-39, 5-134)	T. Richardson, Lord's	1896
13-244 (7-168, 6-76)	T. Richardson, Manchester	1896
10-204 (8-94, 2-110)	T. Richardson, Sydney	1897-98

11-228 (6-130, 5-98)†	M. W. Tate, Sydney	1924-25
11-88 (5-58, 6-30)	F. S. Trueman, Leeds	1961
11-93 (7-66, 4-27)	P. C. R. Tufnell, The Oval	1997
10-130 (4-45, 6-85)	F. H. Tyson, Sydney	1954-55
10-82 (4-37, 6-45)	D. L. Underwood, Leeds	1972
11-215 (7-113, 4-102)	D. L. Underwood, Adelaide	1974-75
15-104 (7-61, 8-43)	H. Verity, Lord's	1934
10-57 (6-41, 4-16)	W. Voce, Brisbane	1936-37
13-256 (5-130, 8-126)	J. C. White, Adelaide	1928-29
10-49 (5-29, 5-20)	F. E. Woolley, The Oval	1912

For Australia (41)

10-151 (5-107, 5-44)	T. M. Alderman, Leeds	1989
10-239 (4-129, 6-110)	L. O'B. Fleetwood-Smith, Adelaide	1936-37
10-160 (4-88, 6-72)	G. Giffen, Sydney	1891-92
11-82 (5-45, 6-37)†	C. V. Grimmett, Sydney	1924-25
10-201 (5-107, 5-94)	C. V. Grimmett, Nottingham	1930
10-122 (5-65, 5-57)	R. M. Hogg, Perth	1978-79
10-66 (5-30, 5-36)	R. M. Hogg, Melbourne	1978-79
12-175 (5-85, 7-90)†	H. V. Hordern, Sydney	1911-12
10-161 (5-95, 5-66)	H. V. Hordern, Sydney	1911-12
10-164 (7-88, 3-76)	E. Jones, Lord's	1899
11-134 (6-47, 5-87)	G. F. Lawson, Brisbane	1982-83
10-181 (5-58, 5-123)	D. K. Lillee, The Oval	1972
11-165 (6-26, 5-139)	D. K. Lillee, Melbourne	1976-77
11-138 (6-60, 5-78)	D. K. Lillee, Melbourne	1979-80
11-159 (7-89, 4-70)	D. K. Lillee, The Oval	1981
11-85 (7-58, 4-27)	C. G. Macartney, Leeds	1909
11-157 (8-97, 3-60)	C. J. McDermott, Perth	1990-91
12-107 (5-57, 7-50)	S. C. G. MacGill, Sydney	1998-99
10-302 (5-160, 5-142)	A. A. Mailey, Adelaide	1920-21
13-236 (4-115, 9-121)	A. A. Mailey, Melbourne	1920-21
16-137 (8-84, 8-53)†	R. A. L. Massie, Lord's	1972
10-152 (5-72, 5-80)	K. R. Miller, Lord's	1956
13-77 (7-17, 6-60)	M. A. Noble, Melbourne	1901-02
11-103 (5-51, 6-52)	M. A. Noble, Sheffield	1902
10-129 (5-63, 5-66)	W. J. O'Reilly, Melbourne	1932-33
11-129 (4-75, 7-54)	W. J. O'Reilly, Nottingham	1934
10-122 (5-66, 5-56)	W. J. O'Reilly, Leeds	1938
11-165 (7-68, 4-97)	G. E. Palmer, Sydney	1881-82
10-126 (7-65, 3-61)	G. E. Palmer, Melbourne	1882-83
13-148 (6-97, 7-51)	B. A. Reid, Melbourne	1990-91
13-110 (6-48, 7-62)	F. R. Spofforth, Melbourne	1878-79
14-90 (7-46, 7-44)	F. R. Spofforth, The Oval	1882
11-117 (4-73, 7-44)	F. R. Spofforth, Sydney	1882-83
10-144 (4-54, 6-90)	F. R. Spofforth, Sydney	1884-85
12-89 (6-59, 6-30)	H. Trumble, The Oval	1896
10-128 (4-75, 6-53)	H. Trumble, Manchester	1902
12-173 (8-65, 4-108)	H. Trumble, The Oval	1902
12-87 (5-44, 7-43)	C. T. B. Turner, Sydney	1887-88
10-63 (5-27, 5-36)	C. T. B. Turner, Lord's	1888
11-110 (3-39, 8-71)	S. K. Warne, Brisbane	1994-95
11-229 (7-165, 4-64)	S. K. Warne, The Oval	2001

† *On first appearance in England–Australia Tests.*

Note: J. Briggs, J. C. Laker, T. Richardson in 1896, R. M. Hogg, A. A. Mailey, H. Trumble and C. T. B. Turner took ten wickets or more in successive Tests. J. Briggs was omitted, however, from the England team for the first Test match in 1893.

RESULTS ON EACH GROUND

In England

	Matches	*England wins*	*Australia wins*	*Drawn*
The Oval	33	15	6	12
Manchester	27	7	7	13†
Lord's	32	5‡	13	14
Nottingham	19	3	7	9
Leeds	23	7	8	8
Birmingham	11	4	3	4
Sheffield	1	0	1	0

† *Excludes two matches abandoned without a ball bowled.*
‡ *England have won only once (1934) since 1896.*

In Australia

	Matches	*England wins*	*Australia wins*	*Drawn*
Melbourne	52	19	26	7†
Sydney	52	21	24	7
Adelaide	28	8	15	5
Brisbane				
Exhibition Ground	1	1	0	0
Woolloongabba	17	4	9	4
Perth	10	1	6	3

† *Excludes one match abandoned without a ball bowled.*

ENGLAND v SOUTH AFRICA

Series notes: South Africa have failed to win away of their post-isolation series in England, despite leading each time... In their post-readmission Lord's Tests, South Africa have averaged 49.7 runs per wicket and England 21.0... England have won only one of their last 14 Tests in South Africa, ten of which have been drawn... South Africa have failed to win in 12 attempts at The Oval and in five at Birmingham... S. M. Pollock needs 30 wickets to become the first man to take 100 in this fixture... England lead 11–2 in the third Test of a series between the sides.

	Captains					
Season	*England*	*South Africa*	*T*	*E*	*SA*	*D*
1888-89	C. A. Smith[1]	O. R. Dunell[2]	2	2	0	0
1891-92	W. W. Read	W. H. Milton	1	1	0	0
1895-96	Lord Hawke[3]	E. A. Halliwell[4]	3	3	0	0
1898-99	Lord Hawke	M. Bisset	2	2	0	0
1905-06	P. F. Warner	P. W. Sherwell	5	1	4	0
1907	R. E. Foster	P. W. Sherwell	3	1	0	2
1909-10	H. D. G. Leveson Gower[5]	S. J. Snooke	5	2	3	0
1912	C. B. Fry	F. Mitchell[6]	3	3	0	0
1913-14	J. W. H. T. Douglas	H. W. Taylor	5	4	0	1
1922-23	F. T. Mann	H. W. Taylor	5	2	1	2
1924	A. E. R. Gilligan[7]	H. W. Taylor	5	3	0	2
1927-28	R. T. Stanyforth[8]	H. G. Deane	5	2	2	1
1929	J. C. White[9]	H. G. Deane	5	2	0	3
1930-31	A. P. F. Chapman	H. G. Deane[10]	5	0	1	4
1935	R. E. S. Wyatt	H. F. Wade	5	0	1	4
1938-39	W. R. Hammond	A. Melville	5	1	0	4
1947	N. W. D. Yardley	A. Melville	5	3	0	2

Season	England	Captains South Africa	T	E	SA	D
1948-49	F. G. Mann	A. D. Nourse	5	2	0	3
1951	F. R. Brown	A. D. Nourse	5	3	1	1
1955	P. B. H. May	J. E. Cheetham[11]	5	3	2	0
1956-57	P. B. H. May	C. B. van Ryneveld[12]	5	2	2	1
1960	M. C. Cowdrey	D. J. McGlew	5	3	0	2
1964-65	M. J. K. Smith	T. L. Goddard	5	1	0	4
1965	M. J. K. Smith	P. L. van der Merwe	3	0	1	2
1994	M. A. Atherton	K. C. Wessels	3	1	1	1
1995-96	M. A. Atherton	W. J. Cronje	5	0	1	4
1998	A. J. Stewart	W. J. Cronje	5	2	1	2
1999-2000	N. Hussain	W. J. Cronje	5	1	2	2
2003	M. P. Vaughan[13]	G. C. Smith	5	2	2	1
	In South Africa		68	26	16	26
	In England		57	26	9	22
	Totals		125	52	25	48

Notes: The following deputised for the official touring captain or were appointed by the home authority for only a minor proportion of the series:

[1]M. P. Bowden (Second). [2]W. H. Milton (Second). [3]Sir T. C. O'Brien (First). [4]A. R. Richards (Third). [5]F. L. Fane (Fourth and Fifth). [6]L. J. Tancred (Second and Third). [7]J. W. H. T. Douglas (Fourth). [8]G. T. S. Stevens (Fifth). [9]A. W. Carr (Fourth and Fifth). [10]E. P. Nupen (First), H. B. Cameron (Fourth and Fifth). [11]D. J. McGlew (Third and Fourth). [12]D. J. McGlew (Second). [13]N. Hussain (First).

HIGHEST INNINGS TOTALS

For England in England: 604-9 dec. at The Oval . . . 2003
in South Africa: 654-5 at Durban . . . 1938-39

For South Africa in England: 682-6 dec. at Lord's . . . 2003
in South Africa: 572-7 at Durban . . . 1999-2000

LOWEST INNINGS TOTALS

For England in England: 76 at Leeds . . . 1907
in South Africa: 92 at Cape Town . . . 1898-99

For South Africa in England: 30 at Birmingham . . . 1924
in South Africa: 30 at Port Elizabeth . . . 1895-96

DOUBLE-HUNDREDS

For England (5)

243 E. Paynter at Durban . . . 1938-39
219 W. J. Edrich at Durban . . . 1938-39
219 M. E. Trescothick at The Oval . 2003
211 J. B. Hobbs at Lord's . . . 1924
208 D. C. S. Compton at Lord's . . . 1947

For South Africa (6)

277 G. C. Smith at Birmingham . . 2003
275 G. Kirsten at Durban . . . 1999-2000
259 G. C. Smith at Lord's . . . 2003
236 E. A. B. Rowan at Leeds . . . 1951
210 G. Kirsten at Manchester . . . 1998
208 A. D. Nourse at Nottingham . . . 1951

INDIVIDUAL HUNDREDS

For England (102)

7: D. C. S. Compton.
6: W. R. Hammond, H. Sutcliffe.
4: L. Hutton.
3: M. A. Atherton, M. C. Cowdrey, W. J. Edrich, N. Hussain, P. B. H. May, C. P. Mead, E. Paynter, F. E. Woolley.
2: L. E. G. Ames, K. F. Barrington, M. A. Butcher, P. A. Gibb, E. H. Hendren, G. A. Hick, J. B. Hobbs, M. Leyland, A. C. Russell, E. Tyldesley, R. E. S. Wyatt.
1: R. Abel, G. Boycott, L. C. Braund, D. Denton, E. R. Dexter, J. W. H. T. Douglas, F. L. Fane, A. Flintoff, C. B. Fry, T. W. Hayward, A. J. L. Hill, D. J. Insole, F. G. Mann, P. H. Parfitt, J. M. Parks, G. Pullar, W. Rhodes, P. E. Richardson, R. W. V. Robins, R. T. Simpson, M. J. K. Smith, R. H. Spooner, A. J. Stewart, M. W. Tate, G. P. Thorpe, M. E. Trescothick, J. T. Tyldesley, B. H. Valentine, M. P. Vaughan, P. F. Warner, C. Washbrook, A. J. Watkins, H. Wood.

For South Africa (78)

7: B. Mitchell, A. D. Nourse, H. W. Taylor.
5: G. Kirsten.
4: A. Melville.
3: R. H. Catterall, R. A. McLean.
2: K. C. Bland, D. J. Cullinan, E. L. Dalton, H. H. Gibbs, J. H. Kallis, D. J. McGlew, R. G. Pollock, E. A. B. Rowan, G. C. Smith, G. C. White.
1: E. J. Barlow, M. V. Boucher, W. J. Cronje, W. R. Endean, G. A. Faulkner, T. L. Goddard, C. M. H. Hathorn, P. N. Kirsten, L. Klusener, B. M. McMillan, H. G. Owen-Smith, A. J. Pithey, J. N. Rhodes, P. W. Sherwell, I. J. Siedle, J. H. Sinclair, P. G. van der Bijl, K. G. Viljoen, W. W. Wade, J. H. B. Waite, K. C. Wessels, P. L. Winslow.

RECORD PARTNERSHIPS FOR EACH WICKET

For England

359	for 1st	L. Hutton and C. Washbrook at Johannesburg	1948-49
280	for 2nd	P. A. Gibb and W. J. Edrich at Durban	1938-39
370	for 3rd†	W. J. Edrich and D. C. S. Compton at Lord's	1947
197	for 4th	W. R. Hammond and L. E. G. Ames at Cape Town	1938-39
237	for 5th	D. C. S. Compton and N. W. D. Yardley at Nottingham	1947
206*	for 6th	K. F. Barrington and J. M. Parks at Durban	1964-65
115	for 7th	J. W. H. T. Douglas and M. C. Bird at Durban	1913-14
154	for 8th	C. W. Wright and H. R. Bromley-Davenport at Johannesburg	1895-96
99	for 9th	A. Flintoff and S. J. Harmison at The Oval	2003
92	for 10th	A. C. Russell and A. E. R. Gilligan at Durban	1922-23

For South Africa

260	for 1st†	B. Mitchell and I. J. Siedle at Cape Town	1930-31
257	for 2nd	G. C. Smith and G. Kirsten at Lord's	2003
319	for 3rd	A. Melville and A. D. Nourse at Nottingham	1947
214	for 4th	H. W. Taylor and H. G. Deane at The Oval	1929
192	for 5th†	G. Kirsten and M. V. Boucher at Durban	1999-2000
171	for 6th	J. H. B. Waite and P. L. Winslow at Manchester	1955
123	for 7th	H. G. Deane and E. P. Nupen at Durban	1927-28
150	for 8th†	G. Kirsten and M. Zondeki at Leeds	2003
137	for 9th	E. L. Dalton and A. B. C. Langton at The Oval	1935
103	for 10th†	H. G. Owen-Smith and A. J. Bell at Leeds	1929

† *Record partnership against all countries.*

MOST RUNS IN A SERIES

England in England	753 (average 94.12)	D. C. S. Compton	1947
England in South Africa	653 (average 81.62)	E. Paynter	1938-39
South Africa in England	714 (average 79.33)	G. C. Smith	2003
South Africa in South Africa	582 (average 64.66)	H. W. Taylor	1922-23

TEN WICKETS OR MORE IN A MATCH

For England (25)

11-110 (5-25, 6-85)†	S. F. Barnes, Lord's	1912
10-115 (6-52, 4-63)	S. F. Barnes, Leeds	1912
13-57 (5-28, 8-29)	S. F. Barnes, The Oval	1912
10-105 (5-57, 5-48)	S. F. Barnes, Durban	1913-14
17-159 (8-56, 9-103)	S. F. Barnes, Johannesburg	1913-14
14-144 (7-56, 7-88)	S. F. Barnes, Durban	1913-14
12-112 (7-58, 5-54)	A. V. Bedser, Manchester	1951
11-118 (6-68, 5-50)	C. Blythe, Cape Town	1905-06
15-99 (8-59, 7-40)	C. Blythe, Leeds	1907
10-104 (7-46, 3-58)	C. Blythe, Cape Town	1909-10
15-28 (7-17, 8-11)	J. Briggs, Cape Town	1888-89
13-91 (6-54, 7-37)†	J. J. Ferris, Cape Town	1891-92
10-122 (5-60, 5-62)	A. R. C. Fraser, Nottingham	1998
10-207 (7-115, 3-92)	A. P. Freeman, Leeds	1929
12-171 (7-71, 5-100)	A. P. Freeman, Manchester	1929
12-130 (7-70, 5-60)	G. Geary, Johannesburg	1927-28
11-90 (6-7, 5-83)	A. E. R. Gilligan, Birmingham	1924
10-119 (4-64, 6-55)	J. C. Laker, The Oval	1951
15-45 (7-38, 8-7)†	G. A. Lohmann, Port Elizabeth	1895-96
12-71 (9-28, 3-43)	G. A. Lohmann, Johannesburg	1895-96
10-138 (1-81, 9-57)	D. E. Malcolm, The Oval	1994
11-97 (6-63, 5-34)	J. B. Statham, Lord's	1960
12-101 (7-52, 5-49)	R. Tattersall, Lord's	1951
12-89 (5-53, 7-36)	J. H. Wardle, Cape Town	1956-57
10-175 (5-95, 5-80)	D. V. P. Wright, Lord's	1947

For South Africa (8)

11-127 (6-53, 5-74)	A. A. Donald, Johannesburg	1999-2000
11-112 (4-49, 7-63)†	A. E. Hall, Cape Town	1922-23
10-220 (5-75, 5-145)	M. Ntini, Lord's	2003
11-150 (5-63, 6-87)	E. P. Nupen, Johannesburg	1930-31
10-87 (5-53, 5-34)	P. M. Pollock, Nottingham	1965
12-127 (4-57, 8-70)	S. J. Snooke, Johannesburg	1905-06
13-192 (4-79, 9-113)	H. J. Tayfield, Johannesburg	1956-57
12-181 (5-87, 7-94)	A. E. E. Vogler, Johannesburg	1909-10

† *On first appearance in England–South Africa Tests.*

Notes: S. F. Barnes took ten wickets or more in his first five Tests v South Africa and in six of his seven Tests v South Africa. A. P. Freeman and G. A. Lohmann took ten wickets or more in successive matches.

SEVEN WICKETS OR MORE IN AN INNINGS

In addition to those listed above, the following have taken seven wickets or more in an innings:

For England

7-46	A. R. Caddick, Durban	1999-2000	7-39	J. B. Statham, Lord's	1955
7-42	G. A. Lohmann, Cape Town	1895-96			

For South Africa

7-95	W. H. Ashley, Cape Town	1888-89	7-65	S. J. Pegler, Lord's	1912
7-29	G. F. Bissett, Durban	1927-28	8-69	H. J. Tayfield, Durban	1956-57
7-84	G. A. Faulkner, The Oval	1912	7-128	A. E. E. Vogler, Lord's	1907

MOST WICKETS IN A SERIES

England in England	34 (average 8.29)	S. F. Barnes	1912
England in South Africa	49 (average 10.93)	S. F. Barnes	1913-14
South Africa in England	33 (average 19.78)	A. A. Donald	1998
South Africa in South Africa	37 (average 17.18)	H. J. Tayfield	1956-57

ENGLAND v WEST INDIES

Series notes: Six of West Indies' last seven innings in England have totalled 215 or less... West Indies have never lost in eight Tests at Nottingham – England are not playing them there in 2004... Pending the 2003-04 series, Lord's is the only ground, home or away, on which England have a superior head-to-head record: they lead West Indies 6–4... In five Tests at St John's, West Indies have averaged 64.4 runs per wicket and England 29.7... Only one of West Indies' 52 Test wins over England has come in a lost series... West Indies have won their last four Tests at Birmingham... West Indies' five wins at Manchester have all been emphatic: three by an innings, one by ten wickets – and the other by 425 runs.

	Captains					
Season	*England*	*West Indies*	*T*	*E*	*WI*	*D*
1928	A. P. F. Chapman	R. K. Nunes	3	3	0	0
1929-30	Hon. F. S. G. Calthorpe	E. L. G. Hoad[1]	4	1	1	2
1933	D. R. Jardine[2]	G. C. Grant	3	2	0	1
1934-35	R. E. S. Wyatt	G. C. Grant	4	1	2	1
1939	W. R. Hammond	R. S. Grant	3	1	0	2
1947-48	G. O. B. Allen[3]	J. D. C. Goddard[4]	4	0	2	2
1950	N. W. D. Yardley[5]	J. D. C. Goddard	4	1	3	0
1953-54	L. Hutton	J. B. Stollmeyer	5	2	2	1
1957	P. B. H. May	J. D. C. Goddard	5	3	0	2
1959-60	P. B. H. May[6]	F. C. M. Alexander	5	1	0	4

THE WISDEN TROPHY

	Captains						
Season	*England*	*West Indies*	*T*	*E*	*WI*	*D*	*Held by*
1963	E. R. Dexter	F. M. M. Worrell	5	1	3	1	WI
1966	M. C. Cowdrey[7]	G. S. Sobers	5	1	3	1	WI
1967-68	M. C. Cowdrey	G. S. Sobers	5	1	0	4	E
1969	R. Illingworth	G. S. Sobers	3	2	0	1	E
1973	R. Illingworth	R. B. Kanhai	3	0	2	1	WI
1973-74	M. H. Denness	R. B. Kanhai	5	1	1	3	WI

Season	Captains England	West Indies	T	E	WI	D	Held by
1976	A. W. Greig	C. H. Lloyd	5	0	3	2	WI
1980	I. T. Botham	C. H. Lloyd[8]	5	0	1	4	WI
1980-81†	I. T. Botham	C. H. Lloyd	4	0	2	2	WI
1984	D. I. Gower	C. H. Lloyd	5	0	5	0	WI
1985-86	D. I. Gower	I. V. A. Richards	5	0	5	0	WI
1988	J. E. Emburey[9]	I. V. A. Richards	5	0	4	1	WI
1989-90‡	G. A. Gooch[10]	I. V. A. Richards[11]	4	1	2	1	WI
1991	G. A. Gooch	I. V. A. Richards	5	2	2	1	WI
1993-94	M. A. Atherton	R. B. Richardson[12]	5	1	3	1	WI
1995	M. A. Atherton	R. B. Richardson	6	2	2	2	WI
1997-98	M. A. Atherton	B. C. Lara	6	1	3	2	WI
2000	N. Hussain[13]	J. C. Adams	5	3	1	1	E
	In England		70	21	29	20	
	In West Indies		56	10	23	23	
	Totals		126	31	52	43	

† *The Second Test, at Georgetown, was cancelled owing to political pressure and is excluded.*
‡ *The Second Test, at Georgetown, was abandoned without a ball being bowled and is excluded.*

Notes: The following deputised for the official touring captain or were appointed by the home authority for only a minor proportion of the series:

[1]N. Betancourt (Second), M. P. Fernandes (Third), R. K. Nunes (Fourth). [2]R. E. S. Wyatt (Third). [3]K. Cranston (First). [4]G. A. Headley (First), G. E. Gomez (Second). [5]F. R. Brown (Fourth). [6]M. C. Cowdrey (Fourth and Fifth). [7]M. J. K. Smith (First), D. B. Close (Fifth). [8]I. V. A. Richards (Fifth). [9]M. W. Gatting (First), C. S. Cowdrey (Fourth), G. A. Gooch (Fifth). [10]A. J. Lamb (Fourth and Fifth). [11]D. L. Haynes (Third). [12]C. A. Walsh (Fifth). [13]A. J. Stewart (Second).

HIGHEST INNINGS TOTALS

For England in England: 619-6 dec. at Nottingham . . . 1957
in West Indies: 849 at Kingston . . . 1929-30

For West Indies in England: 692-8 dec. at The Oval . . . 1995
in West Indies: 681-8 dec. at Port-of-Spain . . . 1953-54

LOWEST INNINGS TOTALS

For England in England: 71 at Manchester . . . 1976
in West Indies: 46 at Port-of-Spain . . . 1993-94

For West Indies in England: 54 at Lord's . . . 2000
in West Indies: 102 at Bridgetown . . . 1934-35

DOUBLE-HUNDREDS

For England (8)

325 A. Sandham at Kingston . . . 1929-30
285* P. B. H. May at Birmingham . . . 1957
262* D. L. Amiss at Kingston . . . 1973-74
258 T. W. Graveney at Nottingham . . . 1957
205* E. H. Hendren at Port-of-Spain . . . 1929-30
205 L. Hutton at Kingston . . . 1953-54
203 D. L. Amiss at The Oval . . . 1976
202* L. Hutton at The Oval . . . 1950

For West Indies (14)

375	B. C. Lara at St John's	1993-94	223	C. G. Greenidge at Manchester	1984
302	L. G. Rowe at Bridgetown	1973-74	223	G. A. Headley at Kingston	1929-30
291	I. V. A. Richards at The Oval	1976	220	C. L. Walcott at Bridgetown	1953-54
270*	G. A. Headley at Kingston	1934-35	214*	C. G. Greenidge at Lord's	1984
261	F. M. M. Worrell at Nottingham	1950	209*	B. F. Butcher at Nottingham	1966
232	I. V. A. Richards at Nottingham	1976	209	C. A. Roach at Georgetown	1929-30
226	G. S. Sobers at Bridgetown	1959-60	206	E. D. Weekes at Port-of-Spain	1953-54

INDIVIDUAL HUNDREDS

For England (100)

6: M. C. Cowdrey, A. J. Lamb.
5: G. Boycott, G. A. Gooch, T. W. Graveney, L. Hutton.
4: D. L. Amiss, M. A. Atherton.
3: L. E. G. Ames, K. F. Barrington, A. W. Greig, P. B. H. May, R. A. Smith, A. J. Stewart.
2: D. C. S. Compton, E. R. Dexter, E. H. Hendren, P. E. Richardson, A. Sandham, C. Washbrook, P. Willey.
1: A. H. Bakewell, J. H. Edrich, T. G. Evans, K. W. R. Fletcher, G. Fowler, D. I. Gower, S. C. Griffith, W. R. Hammond, J. H. Hampshire, F. C. Hayes, G. A. Hick, J. B. Hobbs, N. Hussain, R. Illingworth, D. R. Jardine, A. P. E. Knott, C. Milburn, J. T. Murray, J. M. Parks, W. Place, M. R. Ramprakash, J. D. Robertson, M. J. K. Smith, D. S. Steele, R. Subba Row, G. P. Thorpe, E. Tyldesley, W. Watson.

For West Indies (111)

10: G. S. Sobers.
8: G. A. Headley, I. V. A. Richards.
7: C. G. Greenidge.
6: B. C. Lara, F. M. M. Worrell.
5: D. L. Haynes, R. B. Kanhai, C. H. Lloyd.
4: R. B. Richardson, C. L. Walcott.
3: R. C. Fredericks, C. L. Hooper, C. C. Hunte, L. G. Rowe, E. D. Weekes.
2: B. F. Butcher, H. A. Gomes, A. I. Kallicharran, S. M. Nurse, A. F. Rae, C. A. Roach, O. G. Smith.
1: J. C. Adams, K. L. T. Arthurton, I. Barrow, C. A. Best, G. M. Carew, S. Chanderpaul, C. A. Davis, P. J. L. Dujon, A. G. Ganteaume, D. A. J. Holford, J. K. Holt, B. D. Julien, C. B. Lambert, K. H. Weekes.

RECORD PARTNERSHIPS FOR EACH WICKET

For England

212 for 1st	C. Washbrook and R. T. Simpson at Nottingham	1950
266 for 2nd	P. E. Richardson and T. W. Graveney at Nottingham	1957
303 for 3rd	M. A. Atherton and R. A. Smith at St John's	1993-94
411 for 4th†	P. B. H. May and M. C. Cowdrey at Birmingham	1957
150 for 5th	A. J. Stewart and G. P. Thorpe at Bridgetown	1993-94
205 for 6th	M. R. Ramprakash and G. P. Thorpe at Bridgetown	1997-98
197 for 7th†	M. J. K. Smith and J. M. Parks at Port-of-Spain	1959-60
217 for 8th	T. W. Graveney and J. T. Murray at The Oval	1966
109 for 9th	G. A. R. Lock and P. I. Pocock at Georgetown	1967-68
128 for 10th	K. Higgs and J. A. Snow at The Oval	1966

For West Indies

298	for 1st†	C. G. Greenidge and D. L. Haynes at St John's	1989-90
287*	for 2nd	C. G. Greenidge and H. A. Gomes at Lord's	1984
338	for 3rd†	E. D. Weekes and F. M. M. Worrell at Port-of-Spain	1953-54
399	for 4th†	G. S. Sobers and F. M. M. Worrell at Bridgetown	1959-60
265	for 5th	S. M. Nurse and G. S. Sobers at Leeds	1966
274*	for 6th†	G. S. Sobers and D. A. J. Holford at Lord's	1966
155*	for 7th‡	G. S. Sobers and B. D. Julien at Lord's	1973
99	for 8th	C. A. McWatt and J. K. Holt at Georgetown	1953-54
150	for 9th	E. A. E. Baptiste and M. A. Holding at Birmingham	1984
70	for 10th	I. R. Bishop and D. Ramnarine at Georgetown	1997-98

† *Record partnership against all countries.*
‡ *231 runs were added for this wicket in two separate partnerships: G. S. Sobers retired ill and was replaced by K. D. Boyce when 155 had been added.*

TEN WICKETS OR MORE IN A MATCH

For England (12)

11-98 (7-44, 4-54)	T. E. Bailey, Lord's	1957
11-110 (8-53, 3-57)	A. R. C. Fraser, Port-of-Spain	1997-98
10-93 (5-54, 5-39)	A. P. Freeman, Manchester	1928
13-156 (8-86, 5-70)	A. W. Greig, Port-of-Spain	1973-74
11-48 (5-28, 6-20)	G. A. R. Lock, The Oval	1957
10-137 (4-60, 6-77)	D. E. Malcolm, Port-of-Spain	1989-90
11-96 (5-37, 6-59)†	C. S. Marriott, The Oval	1933
10-142 (4-82, 6-60)	J. A. Snow, Georgetown	1967-68
10-195 (5-105, 5-90)†	G. T. S. Stevens, Bridgetown	1929-30
11-152 (6-100, 5-52)	F. S. Trueman, Lord's	1963
12-119 (5-75, 7-44)	F. S. Trueman, Birmingham	1963
11-149 (4-79, 7-70)	W. Voce, Port-of-Spain	1929-30

For West Indies (15)

10-127 (2-82, 8-45)	C. E. L. Ambrose, Bridgetown	1989-90
11-84 (5-60, 6-24)	C. E. L. Ambrose, Port-of-Spain	1993-94
10-174 (5-105, 5-69)	K. C. G. Benjamin, Nottingham	1995
11-147 (5-70, 6-77)†	K. D. Boyce, The Oval	1973
11-229 (5-137, 6-92)	W. Ferguson, Port-of-Spain	1947-48
11-157 (5-59, 6-98)†	L. R. Gibbs, Manchester	1963
10-106 (5-37, 5-69)	L. R. Gibbs, Manchester	1966
14-149 (8-92, 6-57)	M. A. Holding, The Oval	1976
10-96 (5-41, 5-55)†	H. H. H. Johnson, Kingston	1947-48
10-92 (6-32, 4-60)	M. D. Marshall, Lord's	1988
11-152 (5-66, 6-86)	S. Ramadhin, Lord's	1950
10-123 (5-60, 5-63)	A. M. E. Roberts, Lord's	1976
11-204 (8-104, 3-100)†	A. L. Valentine, Manchester	1950
10-160 (4-121, 6-39)	A. L. Valentine, The Oval	1950
10-117 (4-43, 6-74)	C. A. Walsh, Lord's	2000

† *On first appearance in England–West Indies Tests.*

Note: F. S. Trueman took ten wickets or more in successive matches.

SEVEN WICKETS OR MORE IN AN INNINGS

In addition to those listed above, the following have taken seven wickets or more in an innings:

For England

7-34	T. E. Bailey, Kingston	1953-54
8-103	I. T. Botham, Lord's	1984
7-43	D. G. Cork, Lord's	1995
8-75	A. R. C. Fraser, Bridgetown	1993-94
7-50	W. E. Hollies, Georgetown	1934-35
7-103	J. C. Laker, Bridgetown	1947-48
7-56	James Langridge, Manchester	1933
7-49	J. A. Snow, Kingston	1967-68

For West Indies

7-69	W. W. Hall, Kingston	1959-60
7-53	M. D. Marshall, Leeds	1984
7-22	M. D. Marshall, Manchester	1988
7-49	S. Ramadhin, Birmingham	1957
7-70	F. M. M. Worrell, Leeds	1957

ENGLAND v NEW ZEALAND

Series notes: The teams' averages for runs per wicket in Tests between the sides are almost identical in England and New Zealand: in 44 Tests at home, England average 36.6 and New Zealand 25.4: in 41 Tests away, England average 36.7 and New Zealand 25.4… England have a 100% record from four Tests against New Zealand at Birmingham, but are not playing them there this summer… England average 46.9 runs per wicket in Tests between the sides at Leeds, more than double New Zealand's 22.8… New Zealand's win at Lord's on their last tour in 1999 was their only victory in 13 attempts… England have lost more Tests to New Zealand at home (four) than away (three)… In the 60 Tests where the team winning the toss have batted, they have won 30 and lost just three… None of the last 15 innings in this fixture has spanned 100 overs – even though two of them exceeded 450… The home team have won only two of the last eight series between the sides… New Zealand have won three of the last six Tests between the sides, having gone 17 matches without a win before that.

	Captains					
Season	*England*	*New Zealand*	*T*	*E*	*NZ*	*D*
1929-30	A. H. H. Gilligan	T. C. Lowry	4	1	0	3
1931	D. R. Jardine	T. C. Lowry	3	1	0	2
1932-33	D. R. Jardine[1]	M. L. Page	2	0	0	2
1937	R. W. V. Robins	M. L. Page	3	1	0	2
1946-47	W. R. Hammond	W. A. Hadlee	1	0	0	1
1949	F. G. Mann[2]	W. A. Hadlee	4	0	0	4
1950-51	F. R. Brown	W. A. Hadlee	2	1	0	1
1954-55	L. Hutton	G. O. Rabone	2	2	0	0
1958	P. B. H. May	J. R. Reid	5	4	0	1
1958-59	P. B. H. May	J. R. Reid	2	1	0	1
1962-63	E. R. Dexter	J. R. Reid	3	3	0	0
1965	M. J. K. Smith	J. R. Reid	3	3	0	0
1965-66	M. J. K. Smith	B. W. Sinclair[3]	3	0	0	3
1969	R. Illingworth	G. T. Dowling	3	2	0	1
1970-71	R. Illingworth	G. T. Dowling	2	1	0	1
1973	R. Illingworth	B. E. Congdon	3	2	0	1
1974-75	M. H. Denness	B. E. Congdon	2	1	0	1
1977-78	G. Boycott	M. G. Burgess	3	1	1	1
1978	J. M. Brearley	M. G. Burgess	3	3	0	0
1983	R. G. D. Willis	G. P. Howarth	4	3	1	0
1983-84	R. G. D. Willis	G. P. Howarth	3	0	1	2
1986	M. W. Gatting	J. V. Coney	3	0	1	2
1987-88	M. W. Gatting	J. J. Crowe[4]	3	0	0	3

Season	England	*Captains* New Zealand	T	E	NZ	D
1990	G. A. Gooch	J. G. Wright	3	1	0	2
1991-92	G. A. Gooch	M. D. Crowe	3	2	0	1
1994	M. A. Atherton	K. R. Rutherford	3	1	0	2
1996-97	M. A. Atherton	L. K. Germon[5]	3	2	0	1
1999	N. Hussain[6]	S. P. Fleming	4	1	2	1
2001-02	N. Hussain	S. P. Fleming	3	1	1	1
	In New Zealand		41	16	3	22
	In England		44	22	4	18
	Totals		85	38	7	40

Notes: The following deputised for the official touring captain or were appointed by the home authority for only a minor proportion of the series:

[1]R. E. S. Wyatt (Second). [2]F. R. Brown (Third and Fourth). [3]M. E. Chapple (First). [4]J. G. Wright (Third). [5]S. P. Fleming (Third). [6]M. A. Butcher (Third).

HIGHEST INNINGS TOTALS

For England in England: 567-8 dec. at Nottingham . . . 1994
in New Zealand: 593-6 dec. at Auckland . . . 1974-75

For New Zealand in England: 551-9 dec. at Lord's . . . 1973
in New Zealand: 537 at Wellington . . . 1983-84

LOWEST INNINGS TOTALS

For England in England: 126 at Birmingham . . . 1999
in New Zealand: 64 at Wellington . . . 1977-78

For New Zealand in England: 47 at Lord's . . . 1958
in New Zealand: 26 at Auckland . . . 1954-55

DOUBLE-HUNDREDS

For England (7)

336* W. R. Hammond at Auckland . . . 1932-33
310* J. H. Edrich at Leeds . . . 1965
227 W. R. Hammond at Christchurch. 1932-33
216 K. W. R. Fletcher at Auckland . . 1974-75
210 G. A. Gooch at Nottingham . . . 1994
206 L. Hutton at The Oval . . . 1949
200* G. P. Thorpe at Christchurch . . . 2001-02

For New Zealand (2)

222 N. J. Astle at Christchurch . . . 2001-02
206 M. P. Donnelly at Lord's . . . 1949

INDIVIDUAL HUNDREDS

For England (86)

4: M. A. Atherton, G. A. Gooch, D. I. Gower, W. R. Hammond, A. J. Stewart.
3: K. F. Barrington, I. T. Botham, J. H. Edrich, L. Hutton, A. J. Lamb, P. B. H. May, G. P. Thorpe.
2: L. E. G. Ames, D. L. Amiss, G. Boycott, D. C. S. Compton, M. C. Cowdrey, K. S. Duleepsinhji, K. W. R. Fletcher, J. Hardstaff, jun., D. W. Randall, H. Sutcliffe.
1: G. O. B. Allen, T. E. Bailey, E. H. Bowley, B. C. Broad, M. H. Denness, E. R. Dexter, B. L. D'Oliveira, W. J. Edrich, A. Flintoff, G. Fowler, M. W. Gatting, A. W. Greig, N. Hussain, B. R. Knight, A. P. E. Knott, G. B. Legge, C. A. Milton, P. H. Parfitt, C. T. Radley, P. E. Richardson, J. D. Robertson, P. J. Sharpe, R. T. Simpson, C. J. Tavaré, C. Washbrook.

For New Zealand (44)

5: M. D. Crowe.
4: J. G. Wright.
3: N. J. Astle, B. E. Congdon, G. P. Howarth.
2: M. G. Burgess, C. S. Dempster, V. Pollard, B. Sutcliffe.
1: J. G. Bracewell, J. V. Coney, J. J. Crowe, M. P. Donnelly, S. P. Fleming, T. J. Franklin, M. J. Greatbatch, W. A. Hadlee, M. J. Horne, A. H. Jones, C. D. McMillan, J. E. Mills, M. L. Page, J. M. Parker, J. R. Reid, K. R. Rutherford, B. W. Sinclair, I. D. S. Smith.

RECORD PARTNERSHIPS FOR EACH WICKET

For England

223 for 1st	G. Fowler and C. J. Tavaré at The Oval	1983
369 for 2nd	J. H. Edrich and K. F. Barrington at Leeds	1965
245 for 3rd	J. Hardstaff jun. and W. R. Hammond at Lord's	1937
266 for 4th	M. H. Denness and K. W. R. Fletcher at Auckland	1974-75
242 for 5th	W. R. Hammond and L. E. G. Ames at Christchurch	1932-33
281 for 6th†	G. P. Thorpe and A. Flintoff at Christchurch	2001-02
149 for 7th	A. P. E. Knott and P. Lever at Auckland	1970-71
246 for 8th†	L. E. G. Ames and G. O. B. Allen at Lord's	1931
163* for 9th†	M. C. Cowdrey and A. C. Smith at Wellington	1962-63
59 for 10th	A. P. E. Knott and N. Gifford at Nottingham	1973

For New Zealand

276 for 1st	C. S. Dempster and J. E. Mills at Wellington	1929-30
241 for 2nd†	J. G. Wright and A. H. Jones at Wellington	1991-92
210 for 3rd	B. A. Edgar and M. D. Crowe at Lord's	1986
155 for 4th	M. D. Crowe and M. J. Greatbatch at Wellington	1987-88
180 for 5th	M. D. Crowe and S. A. Thomson at Lord's	1994
141 for 6th	M. D. Crowe and A. C. Parore at Manchester	1994
117 for 7th	D. N. Patel and C. L. Cairns at Christchurch	1991-92
104 for 8th	D. A. R. Moloney and A. W. Roberts at Lord's	1937
118 for 9th	J. V. Coney and B. L. Cairns at Wellington	1983-84
118 for 10th	N. J. Astle and C. L. Cairns at Christchurch	2001-02

† *Record partnership against all countries.*

TEN WICKETS OR MORE IN A MATCH

For England (8)

11-140 (6-101, 5-39)	I. T. Botham, Lord's	1978
10-149 (5-98, 5-51)	A. W. Greig, Auckland	1974-75
11-65 (4-14, 7-51)	G. A. R. Lock, Leeds	1958
11-84 (5-31, 6-53)	G. A. R. Lock, Christchurch	1958-59
11-147 (4-100, 7-47)†	P. C. R. Tufnell, Christchurch	1991-92
11-70 (4-38, 7-32)†	D. L. Underwood, Lord's	1969
12-101 (6-41, 6-60)	D. L. Underwood, The Oval	1969
12-97 (6-12, 6-85)	D. L. Underwood, Christchurch	1970-71

For New Zealand (5)

10-144 (7-74, 3-70)	B. L. Cairns, Leeds	1983
10-140 (4-73, 6-67)	J. Cowie, Manchester	1937
10-100 (4-74, 6-26)	R. J. Hadlee, Wellington	1977-78
10-140 (6-80, 4-60)	R. J. Hadlee, Nottingham	1986
11-169 (6-76, 5-93)	D. J. Nash, Lord's	1994

† *On first appearance in England–New Zealand Tests.*

Note: D. L. Underwood took 12 wickets in successive matches against New Zealand in 1969 and 1970-71.

SEVEN WICKETS OR MORE IN AN INNINGS

In addition to those listed above, the following have taken seven wickets or more in an innings:

For England

7-63 M. J. Hoggard, Christchurch . . . 2001-02
7-35 G. A. R. Lock, Manchester 1958
7-75 F. S. Trueman, Christchurch . . . 1962-63
7-76 F. E. Woolley, Wellington 1929-30

For New Zealand

7-143 B. L. Cairns, Wellington 1983-84

ENGLAND v INDIA

Series notes: The away side have won only one of the last 17 Tests between these teams... England have batted first in 40 of the 42 Tests against India in which they have won the toss... India have batted first in 43 out of 49... S. R. Tendulkar needs 317 runs to become the second Indian (after S. M. Gavaskar) to score 2,000 runs against one country... India have won their last two Tests at Leeds and have not lost there since 1967... England are unbeaten in seven Tests at Delhi and in six at Kanpur... India have failed to win in 16 Tests at Birmingham, Manchester and Nottingham... In Tests in India, A. Flintoff has been dismissed by three of the last four balls bowled to him by A. Kumble... England have won only five of the last 20 Tests at home to India, drawing 12.

	Captains					
Season	*England*	*India*	*T*	*E*	*I*	*D*
1932	D. R. Jardine	C. K. Nayudu	1	1	0	0
1933-34	D. R. Jardine	C. K. Nayudu	3	2	0	1
1936	G. O. B. Allen	Maharaj of Vizianagram	3	2	0	1
1946	W. R. Hammond	Nawab of Pataudi sen.	3	1	0	2
1951-52	N. D. Howard[1]	V. S. Hazare	5	1	1	3
1952	L. Hutton	V. S. Hazare	4	3	0	1
1959	P. B. H. May[2]	D. K. Gaekwad[3]	5	5	0	0
1961-62	E. R. Dexter	N. J. Contractor	5	0	2	3
1963-64	M. J. K. Smith	Nawab of Pataudi jun.	5	0	0	5
1967	D. B. Close	Nawab of Pataudi jun.	3	3	0	0
1971	R. Illingworth	A. L. Wadekar	3	0	1	2
1972-73	A. R. Lewis	A. L. Wadekar	5	1	2	2
1974	M. H. Denness	A. L. Wadekar	3	3	0	0
1976-77	A. W. Greig	B. S. Bedi	5	3	1	1
1979	J. M. Brearley	S. Venkataraghavan	4	1	0	3
1979-80	J. M. Brearley	G. R. Viswanath	1	1	0	0
1981-82	K. W. R. Fletcher	S. M. Gavaskar	6	0	1	5
1982	R. G. D. Willis	S. M. Gavaskar	3	1	0	2
1984-85	D. I. Gower	S. M. Gavaskar	5	2	1	2
1986	M. W. Gatting[4]	Kapil Dev	3	0	2	1
1990	G. A. Gooch	M. Azharuddin	3	1	0	2
1992-93	G. A. Gooch[5]	M. Azharuddin	3	0	3	0
1996	M. A. Atherton	M. Azharuddin	3	1	0	2
2001-02	N. Hussain	S. C. Ganguly	3	0	1	2
2002	N. Hussain	S. C. Ganguly	4	1	1	2
	In England		45	23	4	18
	In India		46	10	12	24
	Totals.		91	33	16	42

Notes: The 1932 Indian touring team was captained by the Maharaj of Porbandar but he did not play in the Test match.

The following deputised for the official touring captain or were appointed by the home authority for only a minor proportion of the series:

[1]D. B. Carr (Fifth). [2]M. C. Cowdrey (Fourth and Fifth). [3]Pankaj Roy (Second). [4]D. I. Gower (First). [5]A. J. Stewart (Second).

HIGHEST INNINGS TOTALS

For England in England: 653-4 dec. at Lord's 1990
in India: 652-7 dec. at Madras 1984-85

For India in England: 628-8 dec. at Leeds 2002
in India: 591 at Bombay 1992-93

LOWEST INNINGS TOTALS

For England in England: 101 at The Oval 1971
in India: 102 at Bombay 1981-82

For India in England: 42 at Lord's 1974
in India: 83 at Madras 1976-77

DOUBLE-HUNDREDS

For England (9)

333 G. A. Gooch at Lord's 1990
246* G. Boycott at Leeds 1967
217 W. R. Hammond at The Oval . . . 1936
214* D. Lloyd at Birmingham 1974
208 I. T. Botham at The Oval 1982
207 M. W. Gatting at Madras 1984-85
205* J. Hardstaff, jun. at Lord's 1946
201 G. Fowler at Madras 1984-85
200* D. I. Gower at Birmingham 1979

For India (5)

224 V. G. Kambli at Bombay 1992-93
222 G. R. Viswanath at Madras 1981-82
221 S. M. Gavaskar at The Oval 1979
217 R. Dravid at The Oval 2002
203* Nawab of Pataudi, jun. at Delhi . 1963-64

INDIVIDUAL HUNDREDS

For England (83)

5: I. T. Botham, G. A. Gooch.
4: G. Boycott, N. Hussain.
3: K. F. Barrington, M. C. Cowdrey, M. W. Gatting, A. W. Greig, A. J. Lamb, M. P. Vaughan.
2: D. L. Amiss, M. A. Atherton, M. H. Denness, K. W. R. Fletcher, D. I. Gower, T. W. Graveney, W. R. Hammond, L. Hutton, G. Pullar, R. A. Smith.
1: J. P. Crawley, E. R. Dexter, B. L. D'Oliveira, J. H. Edrich, T. G. Evans, G. Fowler, J. Hardstaff, jun., G. A. Hick, R. Illingworth, B. R. Knight, A. R. Lewis, C. C. Lewis, D. Lloyd, B. W. Luckhurst, P. B. H. May, P. H. Parfitt, D. W. Randall, R. T. Robinson, R. C. Russell, Rev. D. S. Sheppard, M. J. K. Smith, C. J. Tavaré, B. H. Valentine, C. F. Walters, A. J. Watkins, C. White, T. S. Worthington.

For India (73)

6: M. Azharuddin, S. R. Tendulkar.
5: D. B. Vengsarkar.
4: S. M. Gavaskar, R. J. Shastri, G. R. Viswanath.
3: R. Dravid, S. C. Ganguly, V. L. Manjrekar, V. M. Merchant, Nawab of Pataudi, jun., P. R. Umrigar.
2: V. S. Hazare, M. L. Jaisimha, Kapil Dev, B. K. Kunderan, Pankaj Roy.
1: A. B. Agarkar, L. Amarnath, A. A. Baig, D. Dasgupta, F. M. Engineer, Hanumant Singh, V. G. Kambli, S. M. H. Kirmani, V. Mankad, Mushtaq Ali, R. G. Nadkarni, S. M. Patil, D. G. Phadkar, V. Sehwag, N. S. Sidhu, Yashpal Sharma.

Notes: G. A. Gooch's match aggregate of 456 (333 and 123) for England at Lord's in 1990 is the record in Test matches and the only instance of a batsman scoring a triple-hundred and a hundred in the same first-class match. His 333 is the highest innings in any match at Lord's.

M. Azharuddin scored hundreds in each of his first three Tests.

RECORD PARTNERSHIPS FOR EACH WICKET

For England

225 for 1st	G. A. Gooch and M. A. Atherton at Manchester	1990
241 for 2nd	G. Fowler and M. W. Gatting at Madras	1984-85
308 for 3rd	G. A. Gooch and A. J. Lamb at Lord's	1990
266 for 4th	W. R. Hammond and T. S. Worthington at The Oval	1936
254 for 5th†	K. W. R. Fletcher and A. W. Greig at Bombay	1972-73
171 for 6th	I. T. Botham and R. W. Taylor at Bombay	1979-80
125 for 7th	D. W. Randall and P. H. Edmonds at Lord's	1982
168 for 8th	R. Illingworth and P. Lever at Manchester	1971
103 for 9th	C. White and M. J. Hoggard at Nottingham	2002
70 for 10th	P. J. W. Allott and R. G. D. Willis at Lord's	1982

For India

213 for 1st	S. M. Gavaskar and C. P. S. Chauhan at The Oval	1979
192 for 2nd	F. M. Engineer and A. L. Wadekar at Bombay	1972-73
316 for 3rd†‡	G. R. Viswanath and Yashpal Sharma at Madras	1981-82
249 for 4th	S. R. Tendulkar and S. C. Ganguly at Leeds	2002
214 for 5th	M. Azharuddin and R. J. Shastri at Calcutta	1984-85
130 for 6th	S. M. H. Kirmani and Kapil Dev at The Oval	1982
235 for 7th†	R. J. Shastri and S. M. H. Kirmani at Bombay	1984-85
128 for 8th	R. J. Shastri and S. M. H. Kirmani at Delhi	1981-82
104 for 9th	R. J. Shastri and Madan Lal at Delhi	1981-82
63 for 10th	A. B. Agarkar and A. Nehra at Lord's	2002

† *Record partnership against all countries.*
‡ *415 runs were added between the fall of the 2nd and 3rd wickets: D. B. Vengsarkar retired hurt when he and Viswanath had added 99 runs.*

TEN WICKETS OR MORE IN A MATCH

For England (7)

10-78 (5-35, 5-43)†	G. O. B. Allen, Lord's	1936
11-145 (7-49, 4-96)†	A. V. Bedser, Lord's	1946
11-93 (4-41, 7-52)	A. V. Bedser, Manchester	1946
13-106 (6-58, 7-48)	I. T. Botham, Bombay	1979-80
11-163 (6-104, 5-59)†	N. A. Foster, Madras	1984-85
10-70 (7-46, 3-24)†	J. K. Lever, Delhi	1976-77
11-153 (7-49, 4-104)	H. Verity, Madras	1933-34

For India (5)

10-177 (6-105, 4-72)	S. A. Durani, Madras	1961-62
10-233 (7-115, 3-118)	A. Kumble, Ahmedabad	2001-02
12-108 (8-55, 4-53)	V. Mankad, Madras	1951-52
10-188 (4-130, 6-58)	Chetan Sharma, Birmingham	1986
12-181 (6-64, 6-117)†	L. Sivaramakrishnan, Bombay	1984-85

† *On first appearance in England–India Tests.*

Note: A. V. Bedser took 11 wickets in a match in each of the first two Tests of his career.

SEVEN WICKETS OR MORE IN AN INNINGS

In addition to those listed above, the following have taken seven wickets or more in an innings:

For England

7-80 G. O. B. Allen, The Oval 1936
8-31 F. S. Trueman, Manchester 1952

For India

7-86 L. Amar Singh, Madras 1933-34
8-79 B. S. Chandrasekhar, Delhi 1972-73

ENGLAND v PAKISTAN

Series notes: In 21 Tests between the sides in Pakistan, the team winning the toss – and the team batting first – have never won... The two are not unrelated: the team winning the toss have batted first in 20 out of 21 in Pakistan... Pakistan have won the last four tosses against England... Only one of the last nine series has been drawn (2001)... Over 80% of the matches in Pakistan have been drawn (17 out of 21), as against 44% in England (17 out of 39)... England lead Pakistan 10–4 when they have lost the toss – but are level at 6–6 when they have won it... Pakistan have not lost a series in England since 1982... England have never lost in five Tests where they have been put in – or in five more where they have put Pakistan in.

	Captains					
Season	*England*	*Pakistan*	*T*	*E*	*P*	*D*
1954	L. Hutton[1]	A. H. Kardar	4	1	1	2
1961-62	E. R. Dexter	Imtiaz Ahmed	3	1	0	2
1962	E. R. Dexter[2]	Javed Burki	5	4	0	1
1967	D. B. Close	Hanif Mohammad	3	2	0	1
1968-69	M. C. Cowdrey	Saeed Ahmed	3	0	0	3
1971	R. Illingworth	Intikhab Alam	3	1	0	2
1972-73	A. R. Lewis	Majid Khan	3	0	0	3
1974	M. H. Denness	Intikhab Alam	3	0	0	3
1977-78	J. M. Brearley[3]	Wasim Bari	3	0	0	3
1978	J. M. Brearley	Wasim Bari	3	2	0	1
1982	R. G. D. Willis[4]	Imran Khan	3	2	1	0
1983-84	R. G. D. Willis[5]	Zaheer Abbas	3	0	1	2
1987	M. W. Gatting	Imran Khan	5	0	1	4
1987-88	M. W. Gatting	Javed Miandad	3	0	1	2
1992	G. A. Gooch	Javed Miandad	5	1	2	2
1996	M. A. Atherton	Wasim Akram	3	0	2	1
2000-01	N. Hussain	Moin Khan	3	1	0	2
2001	N. Hussain[6]	Waqar Younis	2	1	1	0
	In England		39	14	8	17
	In Pakistan		21	2	2	17
	Totals		60	16	10	34

Notes: The following deputised for the official touring captain or were appointed by the home authority for only a minor proportion of the series:

[1]D. S. Sheppard (Second and Third). [2]M. C. Cowdrey (Third). [3]G. Boycott (Third). [4]D. I. Gower (Second). [5]D. I. Gower (Second and Third). [6]A. J. Stewart (Second).

HIGHEST INNINGS TOTALS

For England	in England: 558-6 dec. at Nottingham	1954
	in Pakistan: 546-8 dec. at Faisalabad	1983-84
For Pakistan	in England: 708 at The Oval	1987
	in Pakistan: 569-9 dec. at Hyderabad	1972-73

LOWEST INNINGS TOTALS

For England	in England: 130 at The Oval	1954
	in Pakistan: 130 at Lahore	1987-88
For Pakistan	in England: 87 at Lord's	1954
	in Pakistan: 158 at Karachi	2000-01

DOUBLE-HUNDREDS

For England (2)

278	D. C. S. Compton at Nottingham	1954
205	E. R. Dexter at Karachi	1961-62

For Pakistan (5)

274	Zaheer Abbas at Birmingham	1971
260	Javed Miandad at The Oval	1987
240	Zaheer Abbas at The Oval	1974
205	Aamir Sohail at Manchester	1992
200	Mohsin Khan at Lord's	1982

INDIVIDUAL HUNDREDS

For England (52)

4: K. F. Barrington, P. H. Parfitt.
3: D. L. Amiss, G. Boycott, M. C. Cowdrey, T. W. Graveney.
2: I. T. Botham, E. R. Dexter, M. W. Gatting, D. I. Gower, A. J. Stewart, G. P. Thorpe.
1: M. A. Atherton, C. W. J. Athey, B. C. Broad, D. C. S. Compton, J. P. Crawley, B. L. D'Oliveira, K. W. R. Fletcher, G. A. Gooch, N. V. Knight, A. P. E. Knott, B. W. Luckhurst, C. Milburn, G. Pullar, C. T. Radley, D. W. Randall, R. T. Robinson, R. T. Simpson, R. A. Smith, M. E. Trescothick, M. P. Vaughan.

For Pakistan (43)

4: Salim Malik.
3: Asif Iqbal, Hanif Mohammad, Inzamam-ul-Haq, Javed Burki, Mudassar Nazar, Mushtaq Mohammad.
2: Haroon Rashid, Javed Miandad, Mohsin Khan, Yousuf Youhana, Zaheer Abbas.
1: Aamir Sohail, Abdul Razzaq, Alim-ud-Din, Ijaz Ahmed, sen., Imran Khan, Intikhab Alam, Moin Khan, Nasim-ul-Ghani, Sadiq Mohammad, Saeed Anwar, Wasim Raja.

Note: Three batsmen – Majid Khan, Mushtaq Mohammad and D. L. Amiss – were dismissed for 99 at Karachi, 1972-73: the only instance in Test matches.

RECORD PARTNERSHIPS FOR EACH WICKET

For England

198 for 1st	G. Pullar and R. W. Barber at Dacca	1961-62
248 for 2nd	M. C. Cowdrey and E. R. Dexter at The Oval	1962
267 for 3rd	M. P. Vaughan and G. P. Thorpe at Manchester	2001
188 for 4th	E. R. Dexter and P. H. Parfitt at Karachi	1961-62
192 for 5th	D. C. S. Compton and T. E. Bailey at Nottingham	1954
166 for 6th	G. P. Thorpe and C. White at Lahore	2000-01
167 for 7th	D. I. Gower and V. J. Marks at Faisalabad	1983-84
99 for 8th	P. H. Parfitt and D. A. Allen at Leeds	1962
76 for 9th	T. W. Graveney and F. S. Trueman at Lord's	1962
79 for 10th	R. W. Taylor and R. G. D. Willis at Birmingham	1982

For Pakistan

173 for 1st	Mohsin Khan and Shoaib Mohammad at Lahore	1983-84
291 for 2nd†	Zaheer Abbas and Mushtaq Mohammad at Birmingham	1971
180 for 3rd	Mudassar Nazar and Haroon Rashid at Lahore	1977-78
322 for 4th	Javed Miandad and Salim Malik at Birmingham	1992
197 for 5th	Javed Burki and Nasim-ul-Ghani at Lord's	1962
145 for 6th	Mushtaq Mohammad and Intikhab Alam at Hyderabad	1972-73
112 for 7th	Asif Mujtaba and Moin Khan at Leeds	1996
130 for 8th	Hanif Mohammad and Asif Iqbal at Lord's	1967
190 for 9th†	Asif Iqbal and Intikhab Alam at The Oval	1967
62 for 10th	Sarfraz Nawaz and Asif Masood at Leeds	1974

† *Record partnership against all countries.*

TEN WICKETS OR MORE IN A MATCH

For England (2)

11-83 (6-65, 5-18)†	N. G. B. Cook, Karachi	1983-84
13-71 (5-20, 8-51)	D. L. Underwood, Lord's	1974

For Pakistan (6)

10-194 (5-84, 5-110)	Abdul Qadir, Lahore	1983-84
10-211 (7-96, 3-115)	Abdul Qadir, The Oval	1987
13-101 (9-56, 4-45)	Abdul Qadir, Lahore	1987-88
10-186 (5-88, 5-98)	Abdul Qadir, Karachi	1987-88
12-99 (6-53, 6-46)	Fazal Mahmood, The Oval	1954
10-77 (3-37, 7-40)	Imran Khan, Leeds	1987

† *On first appearance in England–Pakistan Tests.*

SEVEN WICKETS OR MORE IN AN INNINGS

In addition to those listed above, the following have taken seven wickets or more in an innings:

For England

8-34	I. T. Botham, Lord's	1978
7-66	P. H. Edmonds, Karachi	1977-78
8-107	N. A. Foster, Leeds	1987
7-50	C. M. Old, Birmingham	1978
7-56	J. H. Wardle, The Oval	1954

For Pakistan

7-52	Imran Khan, Birmingham	1982
8-164	Saqlain Mushtaq, Lahore	2000-01

ENGLAND v SRI LANKA

Series notes: M. Muralitharan has taken 69 wickets in this fixture, more than twice the next best on either side (W. P. U. J. C. Vaas, with 33)... D. P. M. D. Jayawardene is the leading scorer in this fixture with 877 runs... In Tests between the sides in Sri Lanka, the home side have won six out of eight tosses – but England have lost both matches when they won the toss... The team batting first have won just three and lost eight of the 15 matches... England scored in excess of 500 in their last three Tests at home to Sri Lanka – but have never managed it in 16 innings overseas... England average 44.8 runs per wicket at home, as opposed to 26.4 away... Sri Lanka, by contrast, average more in England (36.3) than at home (33.5).

	Captains					
Season	*England*	*Sri Lanka*	*T*	*E*	*SL*	*D*
1981-82	K. W. R. Fletcher	B. Warnapura	1	1	0	0
1984	D. I. Gower	L. R. D. Mendis	1	0	0	1
1988	G. A. Gooch	R. S. Madugalle	1	1	0	0
1991	G. A. Gooch	P. A. de Silva	1	1	0	0
1992-93	A. J. Stewart	A. Ranatunga	1	0	1	0
1998	A. J. Stewart	A. Ranatunga	1	0	1	0
2000-01	N. Hussain	S. T. Jayasuriya	3	2	1	0
2002	N. Hussain	S. T. Jayasuriya	3	2	0	1
2003-04	M. P. Vaughan	H. P. Tillekeratne	3	0	1	2
	In England		7	4	1	2
	In Sri Lanka		8	3	3	2
	Totals		15	7	4	4

HIGHEST INNINGS TOTALS

For England in England: 545 at Birmingham 2002
in Sri Lanka: 387 at Kandy 2000-01

For Sri Lanka in England: 591 at The Oval 1998
in Sri Lanka: 628-8 dec. at Colombo (SSC) 2003-04

LOWEST INNINGS TOTALS

For England in England: 181 at The Oval 1998
in Sri Lanka: 148 at Colombo (SSC) 2003-04

For Sri Lanka in England: 162 at Birmingham 2002
in Sri Lanka: 81 at Colombo (SSC) 2000-01

DOUBLE-HUNDREDS

For Sri Lanka (2)

213 S. T. Jayasuriya at The Oval . . . 1998 | 201* M. S. Atapattu at Galle 2000-01

Highest score for England: 174 by G. A. Gooch at Lord's, 1991.

INDIVIDUAL HUNDREDS

For England (16)

2: M. A. Butcher, A. J. Stewart, G. P. Thorpe, M. E. Trescothick, M. P. Vaughan.
1: J. P. Crawley, G. A. Gooch, G. A. Hick, N. Hussain, A. J. Lamb, R. A. Smith.

For Sri Lanka (14)

3: D. P. M. D. Jayawardene.
2: M. S. Atapattu, P. A. de Silva.
1: R. P. Arnold, T. M. Dilshan, S. T. Jayasuriya, L. R. D. Mendis, T. T. Samaraweera, S. A. R. Silva, S. Wettimuny.

RECORD PARTNERSHIPS FOR EACH WICKET

For England

168 for 1st	M. E. Trescothick and M. P. Vaughan at Lord's	2002
202 for 2nd	M. E. Trescothick and M. A. Butcher at Birmingham	2002
167 for 3rd	N. Hussain and G. P. Thorpe at Kandy	2000-01
128 for 4th	G. A. Hick and M. R. Ramprakash at The Oval	1998
92 for 5th	M. A. Butcher and A. J. Stewart at Manchester	2002
87 for 6th	A. J. Lamb and R. M. Ellison at Lord's	1984
	A. J. Stewart and C. White at Kandy	2000-01
	A. Flintoff and G. J. Batty at Colombo (SSC)	2003-04
63 for 7th	A. J. Stewart and R. C. Russell at Lord's	1991
102 for 8th	A. J. Stewart and A. F. Giles at Manchester	2002
53 for 9th	M. R. Ramprakash and D. Gough at The Oval	1998
91 for 10th	G. P. Thorpe and M. J. Hoggard at Birmingham	2002

For Sri Lanka

99 for 1st‡	R. S. Mahanama and U. C. Hathurusinghe at Colombo (SSC)	1992-93
92 for 2nd	M. S. Atapattu and K. C. Sangakkara at Galle	2000-01
262 for 3rd†	T. T. Samaraweera and D. P. M. D. Jayawardene at Colombo (SSC)	2003-04
153 for 4th	D. P. M. D. Jayawardene and T. M. Dilshan at Kandy	2003-04
150 for 5th†	S. Wettimuny and L. R. D. Mendis at Lord's	1984
138 for 6th	S. A. R. Silva and L. R. D. Mendis at Lord's	1984
93 for 7th	K. C. Sangakkara and H. D. P. K. Dharmasena at Kandy	2000-01
53 for 8th	H. D. P. K. Dharmasena and W. P. U. J. C. Vaas at Kandy	2000-01
83 for 9th†	H. P. Tillekeratne and M. Muralitharan at Colombo (SSC)	1992-93
64 for 10th	J. R. Ratnayeke and G. F. Labrooy at Lord's	1988

† *Record partnership against all countries.*
‡ *107 runs were scored for Sri Lanka's first wicket at Manchester in 2002, in two partnerships: M. S. Atapattu and R. P. Arnold put on 48 before Atapattu retired hurt, then Arnold and K. C. Sangakkara added a further 59.*

TEN WICKETS OR MORE IN A MATCH

For Sri Lanka (2)

16-220 (7-155, 9-65)	M. Muralitharan at The Oval	1998
11-93 (7-46, 4-47)	M. Muralitharan at Galle	2003-04

Note: The best match figures by an England bowler are 8-95 (5-28, 3-67) by D. L. Underwood at Colombo (PSS), 1981-82.

SEVEN WICKETS OR MORE IN AN INNINGS

In addition to those listed above, the following has taken seven wickets or more in an innings:

For England

7-70 P. A. J. DeFreitas, Lord's 1991

ENGLAND v ZIMBABWE

Series notes: All three of England's victories have been by an innings... Since scoring 376 in their first innings against England, Zimbabwe have failed to reach 300 in ten attempts... In the two Tests between the sides at Lord's, England average 44.3 runs per wicket and Zimbabwe 14.6... Spin bowlers have taken only 1.75 wickets per Test when the sides have met in England (seven in four matches) – and 12.5 per Test in Zimbabwe (25 in two).

	Captains					
Season	*England*	*Zimbabwe*	*T*	*E*	*Z*	*D*
1996-97	M. A. Atherton	A. D. R. Campbell	2	0	0	2
2000	N. Hussain	A. Flower	2	1	0	1
2003	N. Hussain	H. H. Streak	2	2	0	0
	In England		4	3	0	1
	In Zimbabwe		2	0	0	2
	Totals		6	3	0	3

HIGHEST INNINGS TOTALS

For England in England: 472 at Lord's 2003
in Zimbabwe: 406 at Bulawayo 1996-97

For Zimbabwe in England: 285-4 dec. at Nottingham 2000
in Zimbabwe: 376 at Bulawayo 1996-97

LOWEST INNINGS TOTALS

For England in England: 147 at Nottingham 2000
in Zimbabwe: 156 at Harare 1996-97

For Zimbabwe in England: 83 at Lord's 2000
in Zimbabwe: 215 at Harare 1996-97

HIGHEST INDIVIDUAL INNINGS

For England

137 M. A. Butcher at Lord's 2003

For Zimbabwe

148* M. W. Goodwin at Nottingham . 2000

INDIVIDUAL HUNDREDS

For England (7)

2: A. J. Stewart.
1: M. A. Atherton, M. A. Butcher, J. P. Crawley, G. A. Hick, N. Hussain.

For Zimbabwe (2)

1: A. Flower, M. W. Goodwin.

RECORD PARTNERSHIPS FOR EACH WICKET

For England

121 for 1st	M. A. Atherton and M. R. Ramprakash at Nottingham	2000
137 for 2nd	N. V. Knight and A. J. Stewart at Bulawayo	1996-97
68 for 3rd	A. J. Stewart and N. Hussain at Bulawayo	1996-97
149 for 4th	G. A. Hick and A. J. Stewart at Lord's	2000
148 for 5th	N. Hussain and J. P. Crawley at Bulawayo	1996-97
149 for 6th	A. J. Stewart and A. McGrath at Chester-le-Street	2003
66 for 7th	A. McGrath and A. F. Giles at Lord's	2003
32 for 8th	C. P. Schofield and A. R. Caddick at Nottingham	2000
	A. F. Giles and R. L. Johnson at Chester-le-Street	2003
57 for 9th	A. F. Giles and M. J. Hoggard at Lord's	2003
28 for 10th	J. P. Crawley and P. C. R. Tufnell at Bulawayo	1996-97

For Zimbabwe

20 for 1st	D. D. Ebrahim and M. A. Vermeulen at Lord's	2003
127 for 2nd	G. W. Flower and A. D. R. Campbell at Bulawayo	1996-97
129 for 3rd	M. W. Goodwin and N. C. Johnson at Nottingham	2000
122 for 4th	M. W. Goodwin and A. Flower at Nottingham	2000
29 for 5th	A. Flower and A. C. Waller at Bulawayo	1996-97
54 for 6th	S. M. Ervine and T. J. Friend at Chester-le-Street	2003
79 for 7th	A. Flower and P. A. Strang at Bulawayo	1996-97
41 for 8th	A. Flower and H. H. Streak at Bulawayo	1996-97
51 for 9th	T. J. Friend and R. W. Price at Lord's	2003
31 for 10th	B. C. Strang and M. Mbangwa at Lord's	2000

BEST MATCH BOWLING ANALYSES

For England

7-42 (5-15, 2-27)† E. S. H. Giddins, Lord's 2000

For Zimbabwe

7-186 (5-123, 2-63)† P. A. Strang, Bulawayo 1996-97

† *On first appearance in England–Zimbabwe Tests.*

ENGLAND v BANGLADESH

Series notes: England's lowest innings total (295) is higher than Bangladesh's highest (255)... Bangladesh spinners have taken 50% of their side's wickets in this fixture (14 out of 28); England's spinners have managed only 8% (three of 39)... England's average opening partnership is 98.25; Bangladesh's is 8.75.

	Captains					
Season	*England*	*Bangladesh*	*T*	*E*	*B*	*D*
2003-04	M. P. Vaughan	Khaled Mahmud	2	2	0	0

HIGHEST INNINGS TOTALS

For England: 326 at Chittagong 2003-04

For Bangladesh: 255 at Dhaka 2003-04

LOWEST INNINGS TOTALS

For England: 295 at Dhaka 2003-04

For Bangladesh: 138 at Chittagong 2003-04

HIGHEST INDIVIDUAL INNINGS

For England

113 M. E. Trescothick at Dhaka 2003-04

For Bangladesh

58 Habibul Bashar at Dhaka 2003-04

INDIVIDUAL HUNDRED

For England (1)

1: M. E. Trescothick.

HUNDRED PARTNERSHIPS

For England

137 for 1st	M. E. Trescothick and M. P. Vaughan at Dhaka	2003-04
125 for 1st	M. E. Trescothick and M. P. Vaughan at Chittagong	2003-04
138 for 3rd	N. Hussain and G. P. Thorpe at Chittagong	2003-04
116 for 5th	N. Hussain and R. Clarke at Chittagong	2003-04

For Bangladesh

108 for 2nd	Hannan Sarkar and Habibul Bashar at Dhaka	2003-04

BEST MATCH BOWLING ANALYSES

For England

9-79 (5-35, 4-44)†	S. J. Harmison, Dhaka	2003-04

For Bangladesh

5-141 (3-84, 2-57)†	Mohammad Rafiq, Dhaka	2003-04

† *On first appearance in England–Bangladesh Tests.*

"Harris had not expected to bat and, by the time he had strapped on his pads, the fielders were already heading his way."
Nottinghamshire in 2003, page 661.

AUSTRALIA v SOUTH AFRICA

Series notes: South Africa have not beaten Australia in six series since their return from isolation… Australia have won eight of the nine Tests between the teams at Cape Town… In 35 matches where they have won the toss, Australia have won 22 and lost just three… In 71 Tests between the sides, the team winning the toss have batted first 60 times… S. K. Warne is the only bowler in history to have taken 100 South African Test wickets – he has 101 from 18 Tests at 22.35.

	Captains					
Season	*Australia*	*South Africa*	*T*	*A*	*SA*	*D*
1902-03*S*	J. Darling	H. M. Taberer[1]	3	2	0	1
1910-11*A*	C. Hill	P. W. Sherwell	5	4	1	0
1912*E*	S. E. Gregory	F. Mitchell[2]	3	2	0	1
1921-22*S*	H. L. Collins	H. W. Taylor	3	1	0	2
1931-32*A*	W. M. Woodfull	H. B. Cameron	5	5	0	0
1935-36*S*	V. Y. Richardson	H. F. Wade	5	4	0	1
1949-50*S*	A. L. Hassett	A. D. Nourse	5	4	0	1
1952-53*A*	A. L. Hassett	J. E. Cheetham	5	2	2	1
1957-58*S*	I. D. Craig	C. B. van Ryneveld[3]	5	3	0	2
1963-64*A*	R. B. Simpson[4]	T. L. Goddard	5	1	1	3
1966-67*S*	R. B. Simpson	P. L. van der Merwe	5	1	3	1
1969-70*S*	W. M. Lawry	A. Bacher	4	0	4	0
1993-94*A*	A. R. Border	K. C. Wessels[5]	3	1	1	1
1993-94*S*	A. R. Border	K. C. Wessels	3	1	1	1
1996-97*S*	M. A. Taylor	W. J. Cronje	3	2	1	0
1997-98*A*	M. A. Taylor	W. J. Cronje	3	1	0	2
2001-02*A*	S. R. Waugh	S. M. Pollock	3	3	0	0
2001-02*S*	S. R. Waugh	M. V. Boucher	3	2	1	0
	In South Africa		39	20	10	9
	In Australia		29	17	5	7
	In England		3	2	0	1
	Totals		71	39	15	17

S Played in South Africa. A Played in Australia. E Played in England.

Notes: The following deputised for the official touring captain or were appointed by the home authority for only a minor proportion of the series:

[1]J. H. Anderson (Second), E. A. Halliwell (Third). [2]L. J. Tancred (Third). [3]D. J. McGlew (First). [4]R. Benaud (First). [5]W. J. Cronje (Third).

HIGHEST INNINGS TOTALS

For Australia in Australia: 578 at Melbourne . . . 1910-11
in South Africa: 652-7 dec. at Johannesburg . . . 2001-02

For South Africa in Australia: 595 at Adelaide . . . 1963-64
in South Africa: 622-9 dec. at Durban . . . 1969-70

LOWEST INNINGS TOTALS

For Australia in Australia: 111 at Sydney . . . 1993-94
in South Africa: 75 at Durban . . . 1949-50

For South Africa in Australia: 36† at Melbourne . . . 1931-32
in South Africa: 85‡ at Johannesburg . . . 1902-03
85‡ at Cape Town . . . 1902-03

† *Scored 45 in the second innings, giving the smallest aggregate of 81 (12 extras) in Test cricket.*
‡ *In successive innings.*

DOUBLE-HUNDREDS

For Australia (7)

299*	D. G. Bradman at Adelaide	1931-32
226	D. G. Bradman at Brisbane	1931-32
214*	V. T. Trumper at Adelaide	1910-11
214	G. S. Blewett at Johannesburg	1996-97
205	R. N. Harvey at Melbourne	1952-53
204*	A. C. Gilchrist at Johannesburg	2001-02
203	H. L. Collins at Johannesburg	1921-22

For South Africa (5)

274	R. G. Pollock at Durban	1969-70
231	A. D. Nourse at Johannesburg	1935-36
209	R. G. Pollock at Cape Town	1966-67
204	G. A. Faulkner at Melbourne	1910-11
201	E. J. Barlow at Adelaide	1963-64

INDIVIDUAL HUNDREDS

For Australia (77)

8: R. N. Harvey.
4: D. G. Bradman, M. L. Hayden, M. E. Waugh.
3: W. Bardsley, J. H. Fingleton, A. L. Hassett, C. Hill, D. R. Martyn.
2: W. W. Armstrong, R. Benaud, B. C. Booth, A. C. Gilchrist, C. Kelleway, J. L. Langer, C. G. Macartney, S. J. McCabe, J. Moroney, A. R. Morris, R. T. Ponting, M. A. Taylor, V. T. Trumper, S. R. Waugh.
1: G. S. Blewett, W. A. Brown, J. W. Burke, A. G. Chipperfield, H. L. Collins, J. M. Gregory, W. M. Lawry, S. J. E. Loxton, C. C. McDonald, K. E. Rigg, J. Ryder, R. B. Simpson, K. R. Stackpole, W. M. Woodfull.

For South Africa (42)

5: E. J. Barlow, R. G. Pollock.
3: G. A. Faulkner, D. T. Lindsay.
2: G. Kirsten, D. J. McGlew, A. D. Nourse, B. A. Richards, J. H. Sinclair, J. H. B. Waite, J. W. Zulch.
1: K. C. Bland, W. J. Cronje, W. R. Endean, C. N. Frank, H. H. Gibbs, A. C. Hudson, B. L. Irvine, J. H. Kallis, A. W. Nourse, E. A. B. Rowan, S. J. Snooke, K. G. Viljoen.

RECORD PARTNERSHIPS FOR EACH WICKET

For Australia

233 for 1st	J. H. Fingleton and W. A. Brown at Cape Town	1935-36
275 for 2nd	C. C. McDonald and A. L. Hassett at Adelaide	1952-53
242 for 3rd	C. Kelleway and W. Bardsley at Lord's	1912
169 for 4th	M. A. Taylor and M. E. Waugh at Melbourne	1993-94
385 for 5th	S. R. Waugh and G. S. Blewett at Johannesburg	1996-97
317 for 6th	D. R. Martyn and A. C. Gilchrist at Johannesburg	2001-02
160 for 7th	R. Benaud and G. D. McKenzie at Sydney	1963-64
83 for 8th	A. G. Chipperfield and C. V. Grimmett at Durban	1935-36
78 for 9th	D. G. Bradman and W. J. O'Reilly at Adelaide	1931-32
	K. D. Mackay and I. Meckiff at Johannesburg	1957-58
82 for 10th	V. S. Ransford and W. J. Whitty at Melbourne	1910-11

For South Africa

176 for 1st	D. J. McGlew and T. L. Goddard at Johannesburg	1957-58
173 for 2nd	L. J. Tancred and C. B. Llewellyn at Johannesburg	1902-03
341 for 3rd	E. J. Barlow and R. G. Pollock at Adelaide	1963-64
206 for 4th	C. N. Frank and A. W. Nourse at Johannesburg	1921-22
129 for 5th	J. H. B. Waite and W. R. Endean at Johannesburg	1957-58
200 for 6th†	R. G. Pollock and H. R. Lance at Durban	1969-70
221 for 7th	D. T. Lindsay and P. L. van der Merwe at Johannesburg	1966-67
124 for 8th	A. W. Nourse and E. A. Halliwell at Johannesburg	1902-03
85 for 9th	R. G. Pollock and P. M. Pollock at Cape Town	1966-67
74 for 10th	B. M. McMillan and P. L. Symcox at Adelaide	1997-98

† *Record partnership against all countries.*

TEN WICKETS OR MORE IN A MATCH

For Australia (7)

14-199 (7-116, 7-83)	C. V. Grimmett, Adelaide	1931-32
10-88 (5-32, 5-56)	C. V. Grimmett, Cape Town	1935-36
10-110 (3-70, 7-40)	C. V. Grimmett, Johannesburg	1935-36
13-173 (7-100, 6-73)	C. V. Grimmett, Durban	1935-36
11-24 (5-6, 6-18)	H. Ironmonger, Melbourne	1931-32
12-128 (7-56, 5-72)	S. K. Warne, Sydney	1993-94
11-109 (5-75, 6-34)	S. K. Warne, Sydney	1997-98

For South Africa (3)

10-123 (4-80, 6-43)	P. S. de Villiers, Sydney	1993-94
10-116 (5-43, 5-73)	C. B. Llewellyn, Johannesburg	1902-03
13-165 (6-84, 7-81)	H. J. Tayfield, Melbourne	1952-53

Note: C. V. Grimmett took ten wickets or more in three consecutive matches in 1935-36.

SEVEN WICKETS OR MORE IN AN INNINGS

In addition to those listed above, the following have taken seven wickets or more in an innings:

For Australia

7-34 J. V. Saunders, Johannesburg . . . 1902-03

For South Africa

7-91	J. T. Partridge, Sydney	1963-64
7-87	S. M. Pollock, Adelaide	1997-98
7-23	H. J. Tayfield, Durban	1949-50

AUSTRALIA v WEST INDIES

Series notes: There has not been a draw between the sides in the last 20 Tests… West Indies' last seven victories over Australia have come when they have fielded first… B. C. Lara is the only non-Englishman in the top ten Test run-scorers against Australia – he lies eighth with 2,470… West Indies have lost eight of the last ten matches in Australia; before that they lost only four in 21… G. D. McGrath needs three wickets to become the first bowler from any country to take 100 in Tests against West Indies… Of the top 18 bowling analyses in this fixture, 16 were recorded in Australia… Australia have won six of the last eight tosses in the West Indies.

Season	Captains Australia	West Indies	T	A	WI	T	D
1930-31*A*	W. M. Woodfull	G. C. Grant	5	4	1	0	0
1951-52*A*	A. L. Hassett[1]	J. D. C. Goddard[2]	5	4	1	0	0
1954-55*W*	I. W. Johnson	D. St E. Atkinson[3]	5	3	0	0	2

THE FRANK WORRELL TROPHY

Season	Captains Australia	West Indies	T	A	WI	T	D	Held by
1960-61*A*	R. Benaud	F. M. M. Worrell	5	2	1	1	1	A
1964-65*W*	R. B. Simpson	G. S. Sobers	5	1	2	0	2	WI
1968-69*A*	W. M. Lawry	G. S. Sobers	5	3	1	0	1	A
1972-73*W*	I. M. Chappell	R. B. Kanhai	5	2	0	0	3	A
1975-76*A*	G. S. Chappell	C. H. Lloyd	6	5	1	0	0	A
1977-78*W*	R. B. Simpson	A. I. Kallicharran[4]	5	1	3	0	1	WI
1979-80*A*	G. S. Chappell	C. H. Lloyd[5]	3	0	2	0	1	WI
1981-82*A*	G. S. Chappell	C. H. Lloyd	3	1	1	0	1	WI
1983-84*W*	K. J. Hughes	C. H. Lloyd[6]	5	0	3	0	2	WI
1984-85*A*	A. R. Border[7]	C. H. Lloyd	5	1	3	0	1	WI
1988-89*A*	A. R. Border	I. V. A. Richards	5	1	3	0	1	WI
1990-91*W*	A. R. Border	I. V. A. Richards	5	1	2	0	2	WI
1992-93*A*	A. R. Border	R. B. Richardson	5	1	2	0	2	WI
1994-95*W*	M. A. Taylor	R. B. Richardson	4	2	1	0	1	A
1996-97*A*	M. A. Taylor	C. A. Walsh	5	3	2	0	0	A
1998-99*W*	S. R. Waugh	B. C. Lara	4	2	2	0	0	A
2000-01*A*	S. R. Waugh[8]	J. C. Adams	5	5	0	0	0	A
2002-03*W*	S. R. Waugh	B. C. Lara	4	3	1	0	0	A
	In Australia		57	30	18	1	8	
	In West Indies		42	15	14	0	13	
	Totals		99	45	32	1	21	

A Played in Australia. W Played in West Indies.

Notes: The following deputised for the official touring captain or were appointed by the home authority for only a minor proportion of the series:

[1]A. R. Morris (Third). [2]J. B. Stollmeyer (Fifth). [3]J. B. Stollmeyer (Second and Third). [4]C. H. Lloyd (First and Second). [5]D. L. Murray (First). [6]I. V. A. Richards (Second). [7]K. J. Hughes (First and Second). [8]A. C. Gilchrist (Third).

HIGHEST INNINGS TOTALS

For Australia in Australia: 619 at Sydney 1968-69
in West Indies: 758-8 dec. at Kingston 1954-55

For West Indies in Australia: 616 at Adelaide 1968-69
in West Indies: 573 at Bridgetown 1964-65

LOWEST INNINGS TOTALS

For Australia in Australia: 76 at Perth 1984-85
in West Indies: 90 at Port-of-Spain 1977-78

For West Indies in Australia: 78 at Sydney 1951-52
in West Indies: 51 at Port-of-Spain 1998-99

DOUBLE-HUNDREDS

For Australia (9)

242	K. D. Walters at Sydney	1968-69	205	W. M. Lawry at Melbourne	1968-69
223	D. G. Bradman at Brisbane	1930-31	204	R. N. Harvey at Kingston	1954-55
216	D. M. Jones at Adelaide	1988-89	201	R. B. Simpson at Bridgetown	1964-65
210	W. M. Lawry at Bridgetown	1964-65	200	S. R. Waugh at Kingston	1994-95
206	R. T. Ponting at Port-of-Spain	2002-03			

For West Indies (6)

277	B. C. Lara at Sydney	1992-93	213	B. C. Lara at Kingston	1998-99
226	C. G. Greenidge at Bridgetown	1990-91	208	I. V. A. Richards at Melbourne	1984-85
219	D. St E. Atkinson at Bridgetown	1954-55	201	S. M. Nurse at Bridgetown	1964-65

INDIVIDUAL HUNDREDS

For Australia (96)

7: S. R. Waugh.
6: K. D. Walters.
5: G. S. Chappell, I. M. Chappell.
4: W. M. Lawry, K. R. Miller, R. T. Ponting, I. R. Redpath, M. E. Waugh.
3: D. C. Boon, A. R. Border, R. N. Harvey, M. L. Hayden, J. L. Langer.
2: D. G. Bradman, R. M. Cowper, A. L. Hassett, K. J. Hughes, C. C. McDonald, W. H. Ponsford, G. M. Wood.
1: R. G. Archer, R. Benaud, B. C. Booth, G. J. Cosier, J. Dyson, A. C. Gilchrist, I. A. Healy, A. M. J. Hilditch, D. M. Jones, A. F. Kippax, D. S. Lehmann, R. R. Lindwall, R. B. McCosker, A. R. Morris, N. C. O'Neill, W. B. Phillips, C. S. Serjeant, R. B. Simpson, M. J. Slater, K. R. Stackpole, M. A. Taylor, P. M. Toohey, A. Turner, K. C. Wessels.

For West Indies (93)

9: R. B. Richardson.
8: B. C. Lara.
6: H. A. Gomes, C. H. Lloyd.
5: D. L. Haynes, R. B. Kanhai, I. V. A. Richards, C. L. Walcott.
4: C. G. Greenidge, A. I. Kallicharran, G. S. Sobers.
3: B. F. Butcher.
2: S. L. Campbell, S. Chanderpaul, P. J. L. Dujon, D. Ganga, G. A. Headley, S. M. Nurse.
1: F. C. M. Alexander, K. L. T. Arthurton, D. St E. Atkinson, C. C. Depeiza, M. L. C. Foster, R. C. Fredericks, C. L. Hooper, C. C. Hunte, F. R. Martin, L. G. Rowe, R. R. Sarwan, P. V. Simmons, O. G. Smith, J. B. Stollmeyer, E. D. Weekes, A. B. Williams, F. M. M. Worrell.

Note: F. C. M. Alexander and C. C. Depeiza scored the only hundreds of their first-class careers in a Test match.

RECORD PARTNERSHIPS FOR EACH WICKET

For Australia

382 for 1st†	W. M. Lawry and R. B. Simpson at Bridgetown	1964-65
298 for 2nd	W. M. Lawry and I. M. Chappell at Melbourne	1968-69
315 for 3rd†	R. T. Ponting and D. S. Lehmann at Port-of-Spain	2002-03
336 for 4th	W. M. Lawry and K. D. Walters at Sydney	1968-69
281 for 5th	S. R. Waugh and R. T. Ponting at Bridgetown	1998-99
206 for 6th	K. R. Miller and R. G. Archer at Bridgetown	1954-55
134 for 7th	A. K. Davidson and R. Benaud at Brisbane	1960-61
137 for 8th	R. Benaud and I. W. Johnson at Kingston	1954-55
114 for 9th	D. M. Jones and M. G. Hughes at Adelaide	1988-89
97 for 10th	T. G. Hogan and R. M. Hogg at Georgetown	1983-84

For West Indies

250*	for 1st	C. G. Greenidge and D. L. Haynes at Georgetown	1983-84
297	for 2nd	D. L. Haynes and R. B. Richardson at Georgetown	1990-91
308	for 3rd	R. B. Richardson and I. V. A. Richards at St John's	1983-84
198	for 4th	L. G. Rowe and A. I. Kallicharran at Brisbane	1975-76
322	for 5th†‡	B. C. Lara and J. C. Adams at Kingston	1998-99
165	for 6th	R. B. Kanhai and D. L. Murray at Bridgetown	1972-73
347	for 7th†	D. St E. Atkinson and C. C. Depeiza at Bridgetown	1954-55
87	for 8th	P. J. L. Dujon and C. E. L. Ambrose at Port-of-Spain	1990-91
122	for 9th	D. A. J. Holford and J. L. Hendriks at Adelaide	1968-69
56	for 10th	J. Garner and C. E. H. Croft at Brisbane	1979-80

† *Record partnership against all countries.*
‡ *344 runs were added between the fall of the 4th and 5th wickets: P. T. Collins retired hurt when he and Lara had added 22 runs.*

TEN WICKETS OR MORE IN A MATCH

For Australia (15)

10-113 (4-31, 6-82)	M. G. Bevan, Adelaide	1996-97
11-96 (7-46, 4-50)	A. R. Border, Sydney	1988-89
11-222 (5-135, 6-87)†	A. K. Davidson, Brisbane	1960-61
11-183 (7-87, 4-96)†	C. V. Grimmett, Adelaide	1930-31
10-115 (6-72, 4-43)	N. J. N. Hawke, Georgetown	1964-65
10-144 (6-54, 4-90)	R. G. Holland, Sydney	1984-85
13-217 (5-130, 8-87)	M. G. Hughes, Perth	1988-89
11-79 (7-23, 4-56)	H. Ironmonger, Melbourne	1930-31
11-181 (8-112, 3-69)	G. F. Lawson, Adelaide	1984-85
10-127 (7-83, 3-44)	D. K. Lillee, Melbourne	1981-82
10-78 (5-50, 5-28)	G. D. McGrath, Port-of-Spain	1998-99
10-27 (6-17, 4-10)	G. D. McGrath, Brisbane	2000-01
10-159 (8-71, 2-88)	G. D. McKenzie, Melbourne	1968-69
10-113 (5-81, 5-32)	C. R. Miller, Adelaide	2000-01
10-185 (3-87, 7-98)	B. Yardley, Sydney	1981-82

For West Indies (4)

10-120 (6-74, 4-46)	C. E. L. Ambrose, Adelaide	1992-93
10-113 (7-55, 3-58)	G. E. Gomez, Sydney	1951-52
11-107 (5-45, 6-62)	M. A. Holding, Melbourne	1981-82
10-107 (5-69, 5-38)	M. D. Marshall, Adelaide	1984-85

† *On first appearance in Australia–West Indies Tests.*

SEVEN WICKETS OR MORE IN AN INNINGS

In addition to those listed above, the following have taken seven wickets or more in an innings:

For Australia

7-44	I. W. Johnson, Georgetown	1954-55
7-104	S. C. G. MacGill, Sydney	2000-01
7-52	S. K. Warne, Melbourne	1992-93
7-89	M. R. Whitney, Adelaide	1988-89

For West Indies

7-25	C. E. L. Ambrose, Perth	1992-93
7-78	J. J. C. Lawson, St John's	2002-03
7-54	A. M. E. Roberts, Perth	1975-76

AUSTRALIA v NEW ZEALAND

Series notes: New Zealand have never beaten Australia in 16 Tests when they have batted first... The side winning the toss have fielded in 63% of matches between the sides... The teams have never played more than a three-match series... Only one of the 25 victories has been in a losing series... In 22 Tests at home, Australia average 40.8 runs per wicket and New Zealand 28.4... In three Tests at Hobart, Australia average 63.0 and New Zealand 24.7 – but Australia have won only one of the matches... Six of the last ten innings in this fixture have been declared... In the last ten Tests between the sides in Australia, only 14 of a possible 40 innings have been completed... In the last four series between the sides, Australia are unbeaten and have won seven out of 12 Tests... In the same period, New Zealand have won eight out of 12 tosses... The side winning the toss have won only three of the last 19 Tests between these teams... New Zealand bowlers have taken eight of the top ten analyses in this fixture... S. K. Warne holds the record for Test wickets against New Zealand (75 at 25.08).

	Captains					
Season	*Australia*	*New Zealand*	*T*	*A*	*NZ*	*D*
1945-46*N*	W. A. Brown	W. A. Hadlee	1	1	0	0
1973-74*A*	I. M. Chappell	B. E. Congdon	3	2	0	1
1973-74*N*	I. M. Chappell	B. E. Congdon	3	1	1	1
1976-77*N*	G. S. Chappell	G. M. Turner	2	1	0	1
1980-81*A*	G. S. Chappell	G. P. Howarth[1]	3	2	0	1
1981-82*N*	G. S. Chappell	G. P. Howarth	3	1	1	1

TRANS-TASMAN TROPHY

	Captains						
Season	*Australia*	*New Zealand*	*T*	*A*	*NZ*	*D*	*Held by*
1985-86*A*	A. R. Border	J. V. Coney	3	1	2	0	NZ
1985-86*N*	A. R. Border	J. V. Coney	3	0	1	2	NZ
1987-88*A*	A. R. Border	J. J. Crowe	3	1	0	2	A
1989-90*A*	A. R. Border	J. G. Wright	1	0	0	1	A
1989-90*N*	A. R. Border	J. G. Wright	1	0	1	0	NZ
1992-93*N*	A. R. Border	M. D. Crowe	3	1	1	1	NZ
1993-94*A*	A. R. Border	M. D. Crowe[2]	3	2	0	1	A
1997-98*A*	M. A. Taylor	S. P. Fleming	3	2	0	1	A
1999-2000*N*	S. R. Waugh	S. P. Fleming	3	3	0	0	A
2001-02*A*	S. R. Waugh	S. P. Fleming	3	0	0	3	A
	In Australia		22	10	2	10	
	In New Zealand		19	8	5	6	
	Totals		41	18	7	16	

A Played in Australia. N Played in New Zealand.

Notes: The following deputised for the official touring captain: [1]M. G. Burgess (Second). [2]K. R. Rutherford (Second and Third).

HIGHEST INNINGS TOTALS

For Australia in Australia: 607-6 dec. at Brisbane 1993-94
in New Zealand: 552 at Christchurch 1976-77

For New Zealand in Australia: 553-7 dec. at Brisbane 1985-86
in New Zealand: 484 at Wellington........ 1973-74

LOWEST INNINGS TOTALS

For Australia in Australia: 162 at Sydney 1973-74
in New Zealand: 103 at Auckland 1985-86

For New Zealand in Australia: 121 at Perth 1980-81
in New Zealand: 42 at Wellington 1945-46

DOUBLE-HUNDREDS

For Australia (4)

250	K. D. Walters at Christchurch . . .	1976-77	205	A. R. Border at Adelaide	1987-88
247*	G. S. Chappell at Wellington . . .	1973-74	200	D. C. Boon at Perth	1989-90

Highest score for New Zealand: 188 by M. D. Crowe at Brisbane, 1985-86.

INDIVIDUAL HUNDREDS

For Australia (40)

5: A. R. Border.
3: D. C. Boon, G. S. Chappell, J. L. Langer, K. D. Walters.
2: I. M. Chappell, G. R. J. Matthews, M. J. Slater, M. A. Taylor, S. R. Waugh, G. M. Wood.
1: M. T. G. Elliott, A. C. Gilchrist, G. J. Gilmour, M. L. Hayden, I. A. Healy, G. R. Marsh, R. W. Marsh, R. T. Ponting, I. R. Redpath, K. R. Stackpole, M. E. Waugh.

For New Zealand (25)

3: M. D. Crowe.
2: B. E. Congdon, A. H. Jones, G. M. Turner, J. G. Wright.
1: N. J. Astle, C. L. Cairns, J. V. Coney, B. A. Edgar, S. P. Fleming, M. J. Greatbatch, B. F. Hastings, M. J. Horne, J. F. M. Morrison, J. M. Parker, A. C. Parore, J. F. Reid, K. R. Rutherford, L. Vincent.

Note: G. S. and I. M. Chappell each hit two hundreds at Wellington in 1973-74, the only instance of two batsmen on the same side scoring twin hundreds in the same Test.

RECORD PARTNERSHIPS FOR EACH WICKET

For Australia

224 for 1st	J. L. Langer and M. L. Hayden at Brisbane	2001-02
235 for 2nd	M. J. Slater and D. C. Boon at Hobart	1993-94
264 for 3rd	I. M. Chappell and G. S. Chappell at Wellington	1973-74
153 for 4th	M. E. Waugh and S. R. Waugh at Perth	1997-98
213 for 5th	G. M. Ritchie and G. R. J. Matthews at Wellington	1985-86
197 for 6th	A. R. Border and G. R. J. Matthews at Brisbane	1985-86
217 for 7th†	K. D. Walters and G. J. Gilmour at Christchurch	1976-77
135 for 8th	A. C. Gilchrist and B. Lee at Brisbane	2001-02
69 for 9th	I. A. Healy and C. J. McDermott at Perth	1993-94
60 for 10th	K. D. Walters and J. D. Higgs at Melbourne	1980-81

For New Zealand

111	for 1st	M. J. Greatbatch and J. G. Wright at Wellington	1992-93
132	for 2nd	M. J. Horne and A. C. Parore at Hobart	1997-98
224	for 3rd	J. F. Reid and M. D. Crowe at Brisbane	1985-86
229	for 4th	B. E. Congdon and B. F. Hastings at Wellington	1973-74
97	for 5th	S. P. Fleming and C. D. McMillan at Hobart	2001-02
110	for 6th	S. P. Fleming and C. L. Cairns at Wellington	1999-2000
132*	for 7th	J. V. Coney and R. J. Hadlee at Wellington	1985-86
253	for 8th†	N. J. Astle and A. C. Parore at Perth	2001-02
73	for 9th	H. J. Howarth and D. R. Hadlee at Christchurch	1976-77
124	for 10th	J. G. Bracewell and S. L. Boock at Sydney	1985-86

† *Record partnership against all countries.*

TEN WICKETS OR MORE IN A MATCH

For Australia (2)

10-174 (6-106, 4-68)	R. G. Holland, Sydney	1985-86
11-123 (5-51, 6-72)	D. K. Lillee, Auckland	1976-77

For New Zealand (5)

10-106 (4-74, 6-32)	J. G. Bracewell, Auckland	1985-86
15-123 (9-52, 6-71)	R. J. Hadlee, Brisbane	1985-86
11-155 (5-65, 6-90)	R. J. Hadlee, Perth	1985-86
10-176 (5-109, 5-67)	R. J. Hadlee, Melbourne	1987-88
12-149 (5-62, 7-87)	D. L. Vettori, Auckland	1999-2000

SEVEN WICKETS OR MORE IN AN INNINGS

In addition to those listed above, the following have taken seven wickets or more in an innings:

For New Zealand

7-116 R. J. Hadlee, Christchurch. . . . . 1985-86 | 7-89 D. K. Morrison, Wellington. . . . 1992-93

AUSTRALIA v INDIA

Series notes: The team winning the toss have lost six and won only one of the last nine Tests between the teams... India have won three and lost only one of the last six Tests... Before that they had lost five in a row... Australia have not won a series in India since 1969-70, and have won only one live Test in that time... India have never won a series in Australia, and have won only one Test there since 1980-81... India have never won in ten Tests where they have put Australia in... R. T. Ponting averages 108.10 in seven Tests at home to India but only 12.41 in seven Tests away... S. R. Tendulkar is the top-scorer in this fixture with 1,789 runs... The six highest individual scores between the sides have all been scored since the turn of the century.

	Captains						
Season	*Australia*	*India*	*T*	*A*	*I*	*T*	*D*
1947-48*A*	D. G. Bradman	L. Amarnath	5	4	0	0	1
1956-57*I*	I. W. Johnson[1]	P. R. Umrigar	3	2	0	0	1
1959-60*I*	R. Benaud	G. S. Ramchand	5	2	1	0	2
1964-65*I*	R. B. Simpson	Nawab of Pataudi jun.	3	1	1	0	1
1967-68*A*	R. B. Simpson[2]	Nawab of Pataudi jun.[3]	4	4	0	0	0
1969-70*I*	W. M. Lawry	Nawab of Pataudi jun.	5	3	1	0	1
1977-78*A*	R. B. Simpson	B. S. Bedi	5	3	2	0	0
1979-80*I*	K. J. Hughes	S. M. Gavaskar	6	0	2	0	4
1980-81*A*	G. S. Chappell	S. M. Gavaskar	3	1	1	0	1
1985-86*A*	A. R. Border	Kapil Dev	3	0	0	0	3
1986-87*I*	A. R. Border	Kapil Dev	3	0	0	1	2
1991-92*A*	A. R. Border	M. Azharuddin	5	4	0	0	1

THE BORDER-GAVASKAR TROPHY

	Captains							
Season	*Australia*	*India*	*T*	*A*	*I*	*T*	*D*	*Held by*
1996-97*I*	M. A. Taylor	S. R. Tendulkar	1	0	1	0	0	I
1997-98*I*	M. A. Taylor	M. Azharuddin	3	1	2	0	0	I
1999-2000*A*	S. R. Waugh	S. R. Tendulkar	3	3	0	0	0	A
2000-01*I*	S. R. Waugh	S. C. Ganguly	3	1	2	0	0	I
2003-04*A*	S. R. Waugh	S. C. Ganguly	4	1	1	0	2	I
	In Australia		32	20	4	0	8	
	In India		32	10	10	1	11	
	Totals		64	30	14	1	19	

A Played in Australia. I Played in India.

Notes: The following deputised for the official touring captain or were appointed by the home authority for only a minor proportion of the series:

[1]R. R. Lindwall (Second). [2]W. M. Lawry (Third and Fourth). [3]C. G. Borde (First).

HIGHEST INNINGS TOTALS

For Australia in Australia: 674 at Adelaide 1947-48
in India: 574-7 dec. at Madras 1986-87

For India in Australia: 705-7 dec. at Sydney 2003-04
in India: 657-7 dec. at Kolkata 2000-01

LOWEST INNINGS TOTALS

For Australia in Australia: 83 at Melbourne 1980-81
in India: 105 at Kanpur 1959-60

For India in Australia: 58 at Brisbane 1947-48
in India: 135 at Delhi 1959-60

DOUBLE-HUNDREDS

For Australia (8)

257 R. T. Ponting at Melbourne . . 2003-04
242 R. T. Ponting at Adelaide . . . 2003-04
223 J. L. Langer at Sydney 1999-2000
213 K. J. Hughes at Adelaide . . . 1980-81
210 D. M. Jones at Madras 1986-87
204 G. S. Chappell at Sydney 1980-81
203 M. L. Hayden at Chennai 2000-01
201 D. G. Bradman at Adelaide . . 1947-48

For India (4)

281 V. V. S. Laxman at Kolkata 2000-01
241* S. R. Tendulkar at Sydney 2003-04
233 R. Dravid at Adelaide 2003-04
206 R. J. Shastri at Sydney 1991-92

INDIVIDUAL HUNDREDS

For Australia (67)

6: D. C. Boon.
4: A. R. Border, D. G. Bradman, R. N. Harvey, R. T. Ponting, R. B. Simpson.
3: M. L. Hayden, J. L. Langer.
2: I. M. Chappell, R. M. Cowper, K. J. Hughes, D. M. Jones, N. C. O'Neill, M. A. Taylor, S. R. Waugh, G. N. Yallop.

1: S. G. Barnes, J. W. Burke, G. S. Chappell, L. E. Favell, A. C. Gilchrist, A. L. Hassett, S. M. Katich, W. M. Lawry, A. L. Mann, G. R. Marsh, G. R. J. Matthews, T. M. Moody, A. R. Morris, G. M. Ritchie, A. P. Sheahan, K. R. Stackpole, K. D. Walters, M. E. Waugh, G. M. Wood.

For India (50)

8: S. M. Gavaskar.
7: S. R. Tendulkar.
4: V. V. S. Laxman, G. R. Viswanath.
2: M. Amarnath, M. Azharuddin, R. Dravid, V. S. Hazare, V. Mankad, R. J. Shastri, D. B. Vengsarkar.
1: N. J. Contractor, S. C. Ganguly, M. L. Jaisimha, Kapil Dev, S. M. H. Kirmani, N. R. Mongia, Nawab of Pataudi, jun., S. M. Patil, D. G. Phadkar, G. S. Ramchand, V. Sehwag, K. Srikkanth, Yashpal Sharma.

RECORD PARTNERSHIPS FOR EACH WICKET

For Australia

217	for 1st	D. C. Boon and G. R. Marsh at Sydney	1985-86
236	for 2nd	S. G. Barnes and D. G. Bradman at Adelaide	1947-48
222	for 3rd	A. R. Border and K. J. Hughes at Madras	1979-80
178	for 4th	D. M. Jones and A. R. Border at Madras	1986-87
239	for 5th	S. R. Waugh and R. T. Ponting at Adelaide	1999-2000
197	for 6th	M. L. Hayden and A. C. Gilchrist at Mumbai	2000-01
108	for 7th	S. R. Waugh and S. K. Warne at Adelaide	1999-2000
117	for 8th	S. M. Katich and J. N. Gillespie at Sydney	2003-04
133	for 9th	S. R. Waugh and J. N. Gillespie at Kolkata	2000-01
77	for 10th	A. R. Border and D. R. Gilbert at Melbourne	1985-86

For India

192	for 1st	S. M. Gavaskar and C. P. S. Chauhan at Bombay	1979-80
224	for 2nd	S. M. Gavaskar and M. Amarnath at Sydney	1985-86
159	for 3rd	S. M. Gavaskar and G. R. Viswanath at Delhi	1979-80
353	for 4th†	S. R. Tendulkar and V. V. S. Laxman at Sydney	2003-04
376	for 5th†	V. V. S. Laxman and R. Dravid at Kolkata	2000-01
298*	for 6th†	D. B. Vengsarkar and R. J. Shastri at Bombay	1986-87
132	for 7th	V. S. Hazare and H. R. Adhikari at Adelaide	1947-48
127	for 8th	S. M. H. Kirmani and K. D. Ghavri at Bombay	1979-80
81	for 9th	S. R. Tendulkar and K. S. More at Perth	1991-92
94	for 10th	S. M. Gavaskar and N. S. Yadav at Adelaide	1985-86

† *Record partnership against all countries.*

TEN WICKETS OR MORE IN A MATCH

For Australia (12)

11-105 (6-52, 5-53)	R. Benaud, Calcutta	1956-57
12-124 (5-31, 7-93)	A. K. Davidson, Kanpur	1959-60
12-166 (5-99, 7-67)	G. Dymock, Kanpur	1979-80
10-168 (5-76, 5-92)	C. J. McDermott, Adelaide	1991-92
10-103 (5-48, 5-55)	G. D. McGrath, Sydney	1999-2000
10-91 (6-58, 4-33)†	G. D. McKenzie, Madras	1964-65
10-151 (7-66, 3-85)	G. D. McKenzie, Melbourne	1967-68
10-144 (5-91, 5-53)	A. A. Mallett, Madras	1969-70
10-249 (5-103, 5-146)	G. R. J. Matthews, Madras	1986-87
12-126 (6-66, 6-60)	B. A. Reid, Melbourne	1991-92
11-31 (5-2, 6-29)†	E. R. H. Toshack, Brisbane	1947-48
11-95 (4-68, 7-27)	M. R. Whitney, Perth	1991-92

For India (9)

10-194 (5-89, 5-105)	B. S. Bedi, Perth	1977-78
12-104 (6-52, 6-52)	B. S. Chandrasekhar, Melbourne	1977-78
10-130 (7-49, 3-81)	Ghulam Ahmed, Calcutta	1956-57
13-196 (7-123, 6-73)	Harbhajan Singh, Kolkata	2000-01
15-217 (7-133, 8-84)	Harbhajan Singh, Chennai	2000-01
12-279 (8-141, 4-138)	A. Kumble, Sydney	2003-04
11-122 (5-31, 6-91)	R. G. Nadkarni, Madras	1964-65
14-124 (9-69, 5-55)	J. M. Patel, Kanpur	1959-60
10-174 (4-100, 6-74)	E. A. S. Prasanna, Madras	1969-70

† *On first appearance in Australia–India Tests.*

SEVEN WICKETS OR MORE IN AN INNINGS

In addition to those listed above, the following have taken seven wickets or more in an innings:

For Australia

7-72	R. Benaud, Madras	1956-57
7-143	J. D. Higgs, Madras	1979-80
7-38	R. R. Lindwall, Adelaide	1947-48
7-43	R. R. Lindwall, Madras	1956-57

For India

7-98	B. S. Bedi, Calcutta	1969-70
8-106	Kapil Dev, Adelaide	1985-86

AUSTRALIA v PAKISTAN

Series notes: Pakistan have lost their last six Tests against Australia, three by an innings, and two of them by an innings and 20 runs... Australia have won 58% of Tests between the sides in Australia, but only 15% in Pakistan... Pakistan have won none of the 14 Tests played in Australia outside Sydney and Melbourne... Australia have won all four Tests between the teams at Perth... In four Tests at Brisbane, Australia average 59.3 runs per wicket and Pakistan 24.1... Pakistan have won five and lost none of the teams' eight Tests at Karachi... Pakistan have failed to reach 300 in their last eight innings against Australia... In the second Test of a series, Australia lead 8–1 from 15 Tests.

	Captains					
Season	*Australia*	*Pakistan*	*T*	*A*	*P*	*D*
1956-57*P*	I. W. Johnson	A. H. Kardar	1	0	1	0
1959-60*P*	R. Benaud	Fazal Mahmood[1]	3	2	0	1
1964-65*P*	R. B. Simpson	Hanif Mohammad	1	0	0	1
1964-65*A*	R. B. Simpson	Hanif Mohammad	1	0	0	1
1972-73*A*	I. M. Chappell	Intikhab Alam	3	3	0	0
1976-77*A*	G. S. Chappell	Mushtaq Mohammad	3	1	1	1
1978-79*A*	G. N. Yallop[2]	Mushtaq Mohammad	2	1	1	0
1979-80*P*	G. S. Chappell	Javed Miandad	3	0	1	2
1981-82*A*	G. S. Chappell	Javed Miandad	3	2	1	0
1982-83*P*	K. J. Hughes	Imran Khan	3	0	3	0
1983-84*A*	K. J. Hughes	Imran Khan[3]	5	2	0	3
1988-89*P*	A. R. Border	Javed Miandad	3	0	1	2
1989-90*A*	A. R. Border	Imran Khan	3	1	0	2

Season	*Captains* Australia	Pakistan	T	A	P	D
1994-95*P*	M. A. Taylor	Salim Malik	3	0	1	2
1995-96*A*	M. A. Taylor	Wasim Akram	3	2	1	0
1998-99*P*	M. A. Taylor	Aamir Sohail	3	1	0	2
1999-2000*A*	S. R. Waugh	Wasim Akram	3	3	0	0
2002-03*S/U*	S. R. Waugh	Waqar Younis	3	3	0	0
	In Pakistan		20	3	7	10
	In Sri Lanka		1	1	0	0
	In United Arab Emirates		2	2	0	0
	In Australia		26	15	4	7
	Totals		49	21	11	17

A Played in Australia. P Played in Pakistan.
S/U First Test played in Sri Lanka, Second and Third Tests in United Arab Emirates.

Notes: The following deputised for the official touring captain or were appointed by the home authority for only a minor proportion of the series:
[1]Imtiaz Ahmed (Second). [2]K. J. Hughes (Second). [3]Zaheer Abbas (First, Second and Third).

HIGHEST INNINGS TOTALS

For Australia in Australia: 585 at Adelaide 1972-73
in Pakistan: 617 at Faisalabad 1979-80
in Sri Lanka: 467 at Colombo (PSS). 2002-03
in United Arab Emirates: 444 at Sharjah 2002-03

For Pakistan in Australia: 624 at Adelaide 1983-84
in Pakistan: 580-9 dec. at Peshawar 1998-99
in Sri Lanka: 279 at Colombo (PSS) 2002-03
in United Arab Emirates: 221 at Sharjah. 2002-03

LOWEST INNINGS TOTALS

For Australia in Australia: 125 at Melbourne 1981-82
in Pakistan: 80 at Karachi. 1956-57
in Sri Lanka: 127 at Colombo (PSS). 2002-03
in United Arab Emirates: 310 at Sharjah 2002-03

For Pakistan in Australia: 62 at Perth 1981-82
in Pakistan: 134 at Dacca 1959-60
in Sri Lanka: 274 at Colombo (PSS) 2002-03
in United Arab Emirates: 53 at Sharjah 2002-03

DOUBLE-HUNDREDS

For Australia (4)

334* M. A. Taylor at Peshawar 1998-99
268 G. N. Yallop at Melbourne. 1983-84
235 G. S. Chappell at Faisalabad . . . 1979-80
201 G. S. Chappell at Brisbane 1981-82

For Pakistan (3)

237	Salim Malik at Rawalpindi	1994-95
211	Javed Miandad at Karachi	1988-89
210*	Taslim Arif at Faisalabad	1979-80

INDIVIDUAL HUNDREDS

For Australia (57)

6: A. R. Border, G. S. Chappell.
4: M. A. Taylor.
3: J. L. Langer, R. T. Ponting, M. J. Slater, M. E. Waugh, S. R. Waugh, G. N. Yallop.
2: K. J. Hughes, D. M. Jones, R. B. Simpson.
1: J. Benaud, D. C. Boon, I. M. Chappell, G. J. Cosier, I. C. Davis, A. C. Gilchrist, M. L. Hayden, R. B. McCosker, R. W. Marsh, N. C. O'Neill, W. B. Phillips, I. R. Redpath, G. M. Ritchie, A. P. Sheahan, K. D. Walters, K. C. Wessels, G. M. Wood.

For Pakistan (44)

6: Ijaz Ahmed, sen., Javed Miandad.
3: Asif Iqbal, Majid Khan, Mohsin Khan, Saeed Anwar.
2: Aamir Sohail, Hanif Mohammad, Sadiq Mohammad, Salim Malik, Zaheer Abbas.
1: Imran Khan, Inzamam-ul-Haq, Khalid Ibadulla, Mansoor Akhtar, Moin Khan, Mushtaq Mohammad, Qasim Omar, Saeed Ahmed, Taslim Arif, Wasim Akram.

RECORD PARTNERSHIPS FOR EACH WICKET

For Australia

269 for 1st	M. J. Slater and G. S. Blewett at Brisbane	1999-2000
279 for 2nd	M. A. Taylor and J. L. Langer at Peshawar	1998-99
203 for 3rd	G. N. Yallop and K. J. Hughes at Melbourne	1983-84
217 for 4th	G. S. Chappell and G. N. Yallop at Faisalabad	1979-80
327 for 5th	J. L. Langer and R. T. Ponting at Perth	1999-2000
238 for 6th	J. L. Langer and A. C. Gilchrist at Hobart	1999-2000
185 for 7th	G. N. Yallop and G. R. J. Matthews at Melbourne	1983-84
117 for 8th	G. J. Cosier and K. J. O'Keeffe at Melbourne	1976-77
83 for 9th	J. R. Watkins and R. A. L. Massie at Sydney	1972-73
86 for 10th	S. K. Warne and S. A. Muller at Brisbane	1999-2000

For Pakistan

249 for 1st	Khalid Ibadulla and Abdul Kadir at Karachi	1964-65
233 for 2nd	Mohsin Khan and Qasim Omar at Adelaide	1983-84
223* for 3rd	Taslim Arif and Javed Miandad at Faisalabad	1979-80
177 for 4th	Saeed Anwar and Yousuf Youhana at Brisbane	1999-2000
186 for 5th	Javed Miandad and Salim Malik at Adelaide	1983-84
196 for 6th	Salim Malik and Aamir Sohail at Lahore	1994-95
104 for 7th	Intikhab Alam and Wasim Bari at Adelaide	1972-73
111 for 8th	Majid Khan and Imran Khan at Lahore	1979-80
120 for 9th	Saeed Anwar and Mushtaq Ahmed at Rawalpindi	1998-99
87 for 10th	Asif Iqbal and Iqbal Qasim at Adelaide	1976-77

TEN WICKETS OR MORE IN A MATCH

For Australia (5)

10-111 (7-87, 3-24)†	R. J. Bright, Karachi	1979-80
10-135 (6-82, 4-53)	D. K. Lillee, Melbourne	1976-77
11-118 (5-32, 6-86)†	C. G. Rackemann, Perth	1983-84
11-77 (7-23, 4-54)	S. K. Warne, Brisbane	1995-96
11-188 (7-94, 4-94)	S. K. Warne, Colombo (PSS)	2002-03

For Pakistan (6)

11-218 (4-76, 7-142)	Abdul Qadir, Faisalabad	1982-83
13-114 (6-34, 7-80)†	Fazal Mahmood, Karachi	1956-57
12-165 (6-102, 6-63)	Imran Khan, Sydney	1976-77
11-118 (4-69, 7-49)	Iqbal Qasim, Karachi	1979-80
11-125 (2-39, 9-86)	Sarfraz Nawaz, Melbourne	1978-79
11-160 (6-62, 5-98)†	Wasim Akram, Melbourne	1989-90

† *On first appearance in Australia–Pakistan Tests.*

SEVEN WICKETS OR MORE IN AN INNINGS

In addition to those listed above, the following have taken seven wickets or more in an innings:

For Australia

7-75	L. F. Kline, Lahore	1959-60
8-59	A. A. Mallett, Adelaide	1972-73
7-187	B. Yardley, Melbourne	1981-82

AUSTRALIA v SRI LANKA

Series notes: Sri Lanka have never won in Australia – Brisbane is the only ground at which they have avoided defeat… In six Tests in Australia, Sri Lanka average 27.4 runs per wicket and Australia 56.8… In seven Tests in Sri Lanka (pending the 2003-04 series), they average 30.1 and Australia 34.2… Australia have batted first in 11 of the 13 matches between the sides… Sri Lanka have elected to field five times out of seven… Australia have elected to bat first six times out of six – but their only defeat came when they did so, at Kandy… Australia have won both matches at Perth by an innings.

	Captains					
Season	*Australia*	*Sri Lanka*	*T*	*A*	*SL*	*D*
1982-83*S*	G. S. Chappell	L. R. D. Mendis	1	1	0	0
1987-88*A*	A. R. Border	R. S. Madugalle	1	1	0	0
1989-90*A*	A. R. Border	A. Ranatunga	2	1	0	1
1992-93*S*	A. R. Border	A. Ranatunga	3	1	0	2
1995-96*A*	M. A. Taylor	A. Ranatunga[1]	3	3	0	0
1999-2000*S*	S. R. Waugh	S. T. Jayasuriya	3	0	1	2
	In Australia		6	5	0	1
	In Sri Lanka		7	2	1	4
	Totals		13	7	1	5

A Played in Australia. S Played in Sri Lanka.

Note: The following deputised for the official touring captain:
[1]P. A. de Silva (Third).

HIGHEST INNINGS TOTALS

For Australia in Australia: 617-5 dec. at Perth 1995-96
in Sri Lanka: 514-4 dec. at Kandy 1982-83

For Sri Lanka in Australia: 418 at Brisbane 1989-90
in Sri Lanka: 547-8 dec. at Colombo (SSC) 1992-93

LOWEST INNINGS TOTALS

For Australia in Australia: 224 at Hobart 1989-90
in Sri Lanka: 140 at Kandy 1999-2000

For Sri Lanka in Australia: 153 at Perth 1987-88
in Sri Lanka: 164 at Colombo (SSC) 1992-93

DOUBLE-HUNDRED

For Australia (1)

219 M. J. Slater at Perth 1995-96

Highest score for Sri Lanka: 167 by P. A. de Silva at Brisbane, 1989-90.

INDIVIDUAL HUNDREDS

For Australia (16)

3: D. M. Jones, S. R. Waugh.
2: M. A. Taylor.
1: D. C. Boon, A. R. Border, D. W. Hookes, T. M. Moody, R. T. Ponting, M. J. Slater, M. E. Waugh, K. C. Wessels.

For Sri Lanka (7)

2: A. P. Gurusinha.
1: P. A. de Silva, S. T. Jayasuriya, R. S. Kaluwitharana, A. Ranatunga, H. P. Tillekeratne.

RECORD PARTNERSHIPS FOR EACH WICKET

For Australia

228	for 1st	M. J. Slater and M. A. Taylor at Perth	1995-96
170	for 2nd	K. C. Wessels and G. N. Yallop at Kandy	1982-83
158	for 3rd	T. M. Moody and A. R. Border at Brisbane	1989-90
163	for 4th	M. A. Taylor and A. R. Border at Hobart	1989-90
155*	for 5th	D. W. Hookes and A. R. Border at Kandy	1982-83
260*	for 6th	D. M. Jones and S. R. Waugh at Hobart	1989-90
129	for 7th	G. R. J. Matthews and I. A. Healy at Moratuwa	1992-93
107	for 8th	R. T. Ponting and J. N. Gillespie at Kandy	1999-2000
45	for 9th	I. A. Healy and S. K. Warne at Colombo (SSC)	1992-93
49	for 10th	I. A. Healy and M. R. Whitney at Colombo (SSC)	1992-93

For Sri Lanka

110 for 1st	R. S. Mahanama and U. C. Hathurusinghe at Colombo (KS)	1992-93
92 for 2nd	R. S. Mahanama and A. P. Gurusinha at Colombo (SSC)	1992-93
125 for 3rd	S. T. Jayasuriya and S. Ranatunga at Adelaide	1995-96
230 for 4th	A. P. Gurusinha and A. Ranatunga at Colombo (SSC)	1992-93
116 for 5th	H. P. Tillekeratne and A. Ranatunga at Moratuwa	1992-93
96 for 6th	A. P. Gurusinha and R. S. Kaluwitharana at Colombo (SSC)	1992-93
144 for 7th	P. A. de Silva and J. R. Ratnayeke at Brisbane	1989-90
33 for 8th	A. Ranatunga and C. P. H. Ramanayake at Perth	1987-88
46 for 9th	H. D. P. K. Dharmasena and G. P. Wickremasinghe at Perth	1995-96
27 for 10th	P. A. de Silva and C. P. H. Ramanayake at Brisbane	1989-90

BEST MATCH BOWLING ANALYSES

For Australia

8-156 (3-68, 5-88)	M. G. Hughes, Hobart	1989-90

For Sri Lanka

8-157 (5-82, 3-75)	C. P. H. Ramanayake, Moratuwa	1992-93

AUSTRALIA v ZIMBABWE

Series notes: Zimbabwe have won all three tosses – and lost all three matches... Australia average 64.3 runs per wicket and Zimbabwe 26.0... Australia's lowest innings score (403) exceeds Zimbabwe's highest (321)... Zimbabwe do lead 9–0 in one field, though: ducks.

	Captains					
Season	*Australia*	*Zimbabwe*	*T*	*A*	*Z*	*D*
1999-2000*Z*	S. R. Waugh	A. D. R. Campbell	1	1	0	0
2003-04*A*	S. R. Waugh	H. H. Streak	2	2	0	0
	In Australia		2	2	0	0
	In Zimbabwe		1	1	0	0
	Totals		3	3	0	0

A Played in Australia. Z Played in Zimbabwe.

HIGHEST INNINGS TOTALS

For Australia in Australia: 735-6 dec. at Perth 2003-04
in Zimbabwe: 422 at Harare 1999-2000

For Zimbabwe in Australia: 321 at Perth 2003-04
in Zimbabwe: 232 at Harare 1999-2000

LOWEST INNINGS TOTALS

For Australia in Australia: 403 at Sydney 2003-04
in Zimbabwe: 422 at Harare 1999-2000

For Zimbabwe in Australia: 239 at Perth 2003-04
in Zimbabwe: 194 at Harare 1999-2000

DOUBLE-HUNDRED

For Australia (1)

380 M. L. Hayden at Perth 2003-04

Highest score for Zimbabwe: 118 by S. V. Carlisle at Sydney, 2003-04.

INDIVIDUAL HUNDREDS

For Australia (5)

2: M. L. Hayden.
1: A. C. Gilchrist, R. T. Ponting, S. R. Waugh.

For Zimbabwe (1)

1: S. V. Carlisle.

HIGHEST PARTNERSHIPS

For Australia

233	for 6th	M. L. Hayden and A. C. Gilchrist at Perth	2003-04
207	for 4th	M. L. Hayden and S. R. Waugh at Perth	2003-04
151*	for 2nd	M. L. Hayden and R. T. Ponting at Sydney	2003-04
135	for 4th	R. T. Ponting and S. R. Waugh at Sydney	2003-04
114	for 8th	S. R. Waugh and D. W. Fleming at Harare	1999-2000

For Zimbabwe

99	for 3rd	M. A. Vermeulen and S. V. Carlisle at Perth	2003-04

BEST MATCH BOWLING ANALYSES

For Australia

6-90 (0-25, 6-65)	S. M. Katich, Sydney	2003-04

For Zimbabwe

6-184 (6-121, 0-63)	R. W. Price, Sydney	2003-04

AUSTRALIA v BANGLADESH

Series notes: Australia average 87.5 runs per wicket and Bangladesh 18.3... Bangladesh have yet to dismiss Australia in a Test... In both the Tests between the sides, Australia have won the toss, fielded and won by an innings... S. R. Waugh has scored 256 runs against Bangladesh without being dismissed... Australia have taken a wicket every six overs in this fixture, Bangladesh every 24... S. C. G. MacGill has all three five-wicket hauls in this fixture... M. L. Hayden's average against Bangladesh (30.50) is the lowest of the eight nations he has played against.

	Captains					
Season	*Australia*	*Bangladesh*	*T*	*A*	*B*	*D*
2003*A*	S. R. Waugh	Khaled Mahmud	2	2	0	0

A Played in Australia.

HIGHEST INNINGS TOTALS

For Australia: 556-4 dec. at Cairns 2003

For Bangladesh: 295 at Cairns 2003

LOWEST INNINGS TOTALS

For Bangladesh: 97 at Darwin 2003

HIGHEST INDIVIDUAL INNINGS

For Australia

177 D. S. Lehmann at Cairns. 2003

For Bangladesh

76 Hannan Sarkar at Cairns 2003

INDIVIDUAL HUNDREDS

For Australia (5)

2: D. S. Lehmann, S. R. Waugh.
1: M. L. Love.

HUNDRED PARTNERSHIPS

For Australia

141 for 3rd J. L. Langer and D. S. Lehmann at Darwin. 2003
250 for 4th D. S. Lehmann and S. R. Waugh at Cairns 2003
174* for 5th S. R. Waugh and M. L. Love at Cairns 2003

For Bangladesh

108 for 2nd Hannan Sarkar and Habibul Bashar at Cairns 2003

TEN WICKETS OR MORE IN A MATCH

For Australia (1)

10-133 (5-77, 5-56) S. C. G. MacGill at Cairns 2003

Note: The best match figures for Bangladesh are 3-74 (3-74) by Mashrafe bin Mortaza at Darwin, 2003.

SOUTH AFRICA v WEST INDIES

Series notes: West Indies have never won a Test in South Africa, who lead 8–0 in home Tests, but are level at 2–2 away... West Indies trail 7–0 from nine Tests in which they have fielded first, but only 3–2 from six where they have batted first... South Africa have scored over 500 in the first innings of the last four Tests – before that neither side had done so in 11 Tests... South Africa have been bowled out in the second innings in only four of the 15 Tests between the sides; West Indies have been bowled out 12 times... The highest fourth-innings total to win a Test between the sides is 164 for six... J. H. Kallis is the leading run-scorer in this fixture, with 1,464... S. M. Pollock is the leading wicket-taker, with 65... B. C. Lara's 202 is the highest score between these sides – but the next 16 have all been made by South Africans... In two Tests at Centurion, South Africa have averaged 64.8 runs per wicket, more than double West Indies' 25.2.

	Captains					
Season	*South Africa*	*West Indies*	*T*	*SA*	*WI*	*D*
1991-92*W*	K. C. Wessels	R. B. Richardson	1	0	1	0
1998-99*S*	W. J. Cronje	B. C. Lara	5	5	0	0

SIR VIVIAN RICHARDS TROPHY

	Captains						
Season	*South Africa*	*West Indies*	*T*	*SA*	*WI*	*D*	*Held by*
2000-01*W*	S. M. Pollock	C. L. Hooper	5	2	1	2	SA
2003-04*S*	G. C. Smith	B. C. Lara	4	3	0	1	SA
	In South Africa		9	8	0	1	
	In West Indies		6	2	2	2	
	Totals		15	10	2	3	

S Played in South Africa. W Played in West Indies.

HIGHEST INNINGS TOTALS

For South Africa in South Africa: 658-9 dec. at Durban 2003-04
in West Indies: 454 at Bridgetown 2000-01

For West Indies in South Africa: 427 at Cape Town 2003-04
in West Indies: 387 at Bridgetown 2000-01

LOWEST INNINGS TOTALS

For South Africa in South Africa: 195 at Port Elizabeth 1998-99
in West Indies: 141 at Kingston 2000-01

For West Indies in South Africa: 121 at Port Elizabeth 1998-99
in West Indies: 140 at St John's 2000-01

DOUBLE-HUNDREDS

For West Indies (1)

202 B. C. Lara at Johannesburg . . 2003-04

Highest score for South Africa: 192 by H. H. Gibbs at Centurion, 2003-04.

INDIVIDUAL HUNDREDS

For South Africa (22)

5: J. H. Kallis.
3: D. J. Cullinan, H. H. Gibbs, G. Kirsten.
2: M. V. Boucher, G. C. Smith.
1: A. C. Hudson, S. M. Pollock, J. N. Rhodes, J. A. Rudolph.

For West Indies (9)

2: C. H. Gayle, B. C. Lara, R. R. Sarwan.
1: S. Chanderpaul, R. D. Jacobs, D. R. Smith.

RECORD PARTNERSHIPS FOR EACH WICKET

For South Africa

301 for 1st	G. C. Smith and H. H. Gibbs at Centurion	2003-04
146 for 2nd	G. Kirsten and J. H. Kallis at Georgetown	2000-01
251 for 3rd	H. H. Gibbs and J. H. Kallis at Cape Town	2003-04
249 for 4th†	J. H. Kallis and G. Kirsten at Durban	2003-04
115 for 5th	G. Kirsten and J. N. Rhodes at Centurion	1998-99
92 for 6th	J. N. Rhodes and S. M. Pollock at Port Elizabeth	1998-99
92 for 7th	J. H. Kallis and M. V. Boucher at Centurion	1998-99
146 for 8th	M. V. Boucher and J. H. Kallis at Cape Town	2003-04
132 for 9th	S. M. Pollock and A. A. Donald at Bridgetown	2000-01
41 for 10th	R. J. Peterson and M. Ntini at Johannesburg	2003-04

For West Indies

126 for 1st	C. H. Gayle and D. Ganga at Cape Town	2003-04
88 for 2nd	C. H. Gayle and M. N. Samuels at Georgetown	2000-01
160 for 3rd	S. Chanderpaul and B. C. Lara at Durban	1998-99
174 for 4th	R. R. Sarwan and C. H. Gayle at Centurion	2003-04
116 for 5th	B. C. Lara and C. L. Hooper at Bridgetown	2000-01
113 for 6th	R. R. Sarwan and S. Chanderpaul at Durban	2003-04
81 for 7th	R. D. Jacobs and N. A. M. McLean at Centurion	1998-99
65 for 8th	R. D. Jacobs and N. A. M. McLean at Cape Town	1998-99
71 for 9th	R. D. Jacobs and M. Dillon at Port-of-Spain	2000-01
64 for 10th	R. D. Jacobs and M. Dillon at Cape Town	1998-99

BEST MATCH BOWLING ANALYSES

For South Africa

9-94 (5-28, 4-66)	S. M. Pollock, Kingston	2000-01

For West Indies

8-79 (2-28, 6-51)	C. E. L. Ambrose, Port Elizabeth	1998-99

SEVEN WICKETS OR MORE IN AN INNINGS

In addition to those listed above, the following has taken seven wickets or more in an innings:

For West Indies

7-84 F. A. Rose, Durban 1998-99

SOUTH AFRICA v NEW ZEALAND

Series notes: New Zealand have never won a series against South Africa and have never beaten them in 11 home Tests... South Africa average 48.2 runs per wicket away from home, almost double New Zealand's 24.5... All three of New Zealand's victories over South Africa have come when they have won the toss and batted... South Africa have won all three matches between the sides at Durban.

	Captains					
Season	*South Africa*	*New Zealand*	*T*	*SA*	*NZ*	*D*
1931-32*N*	H. B. Cameron	M. L. Page	2	2	0	0
1952-53*N*	J. E. Cheetham	W. M. Wallace	2	1	0	1
1953-54*S*	J. E. Cheetham	G. O. Rabone[1]	5	4	0	1
1961-62*S*	D. J. McGlew	J. R. Reid	5	2	2	1
1963-64*N*	T. L. Goddard	J. R. Reid	3	0	0	3
1994-95*S*	W. J. Cronje	K. R. Rutherford	3	2	1	0
1994-95*N*	W. J. Cronje	K. R. Rutherford	1	1	0	0
1998-99*N*	W. J. Cronje	D. J. Nash	3	1	0	2
2000-01*S*	S. M. Pollock	S. P. Fleming	3	2	0	1
	In New Zealand		11	5	0	6
	In South Africa		16	10	3	3
	Totals		27	15	3	9

N Played in New Zealand. S Played in South Africa.

Note: The following deputised for the official touring captain:
[1]B. Sutcliffe (Fourth and Fifth).

HIGHEST INNINGS TOTALS

For South Africa in South Africa: 471-9 dec. at Bloemfontein ... 2000-01
in New Zealand: 621-5 dec. at Auckland ... 1998-99

For New Zealand in South Africa: 505 at Cape Town ... 1953-54
in New Zealand: 364 at Wellington ... 1931-32

LOWEST INNINGS TOTALS

For South Africa in South Africa: 148 at Johannesburg ... 1953-54
in New Zealand: 223 at Dunedin ... 1963-64

For New Zealand in South Africa: 79 at Johannesburg ... 1953-54
in New Zealand: 138 at Dunedin ... 1963-64

DOUBLE-HUNDREDS

For South Africa (3)

275* D. J. Cullinan at Auckland ... 1998-99
255* D. J. McGlew at Wellington ... 1952-53
211* H. H. Gibbs at Christchurch ... 1998-99

Highest score for New Zealand: 150 by M. S. Sinclair at Port Elizabeth, 2000-01.

INDIVIDUAL HUNDREDS

For South Africa (23)

3: D. J. McGlew.
2: W. J. Cronje, D. J. Cullinan, H. H. Gibbs, J. H. Kallis, R. A. McLean.
1: X. C. Balaskas, J. A. J. Christy, H. H. Dippenaar, W. R. Endean, G. Kirsten, N. D. McKenzie, B. Mitchell, A. R. A. Murray, D. J. Richardson, J. H. B. Waite.

For New Zealand (8)

2: J. R. Reid.
1: P. T. Barton, P. G. Z. Harris, G. O. Rabone, B. W. Sinclair, M. S. Sinclair, H. G. Vivian.

RECORD PARTNERSHIPS FOR EACH WICKET

For South Africa

196	for 1st	J. A. J. Christy and B. Mitchell at Christchurch	1931-32
315*	for 2nd†	H. H. Gibbs and J. H. Kallis at Christchurch	1998-99
183	for 3rd	G. Kirsten and D. J. Cullinan at Auckland	1998-99
145	for 4th	D. J. Cullinan and W. J. Cronje at Wellington	1998-99
141	for 5th	D. J. Cullinan and J. N. Rhodes at Auckland	1998-99
126*	for 6th	D. J. Cullinan and S. M. Pollock at Auckland	1998-99
246	for 7th†	D. J. McGlew and A. R. A. Murray at Wellington	1952-53
136	for 8th	N. D. McKenzie and N. Boje at Port Elizabeth	2000-01
60	for 9th	P. M. Pollock and N. A. T. Adcock at Port Elizabeth	1961-62
47	for 10th	D. J. McGlew and H. D. Bromfield at Port Elizabeth	1961-62

For New Zealand

126	for 1st	G. O. Rabone and M. E. Chapple at Cape Town	1953-54
90	for 2nd	M. J. Horne and N. J. Astle at Auckland	1998-99
94	for 3rd	M. B. Poore and B. Sutcliffe at Cape Town	1953-54
171	for 4th	B. W. Sinclair and S. N. McGregor at Auckland	1963-64
176	for 5th	J. R. Reid and J. E. F. Beck at Cape Town	1953-54
100	for 6th	H. G. Vivian and F. T. Badcock at Wellington	1931-32
84	for 7th	J. R. Reid and G. A. Bartlett at Johannesburg	1961-62
74	for 8th	S. A. Thomson and D. J. Nash at Johannesburg	1994-95
69	for 9th	C. F. W. Allcott and I. B. Cromb at Wellington	1931-32
57	for 10th	S. B. Doull and R. P. de Groen at Johannesburg	1994-95

† *Record partnership against all countries.*

TEN WICKETS OR MORE IN A MATCH

For South Africa (1)

11-196 (6-128, 5-68)†	S. F. Burke, Cape Town	1961-62

† *On first appearance in South Africa–New Zealand Tests.*

Note: The best match figures for New Zealand are 8-134 (3-57, 5-77) by M. N. Hart at Johannesburg, 1994-95.

SEVEN WICKETS OR MORE IN AN INNINGS

In addition to those listed above, the following has taken seven wickets or more in an innings:

For South Africa

8-53 G. B. Lawrence, Johannesburg . . 1961-62

SOUTH AFRICA v INDIA

Series notes: India have never won a Test in South Africa in nine attempts... The side batting first have won none and lost three of the last five... Before that, the side batting first had won the previous five... Neither side has chased more than 163 in the final innings to win this fixture... India have won four of the last five tosses, but none of the matches... India's only two victories over South Africa have come when they won the toss and batted... South Africa average 45.1 runs per wicket when they win the toss, but only 27.2 when they lose it... S. R. Tendulkar needs 52 runs to become the first man to score 1,000 runs in Tests between the sides... In seven Tests against India, S. M. Pollock has taken 35 wickets at 16.85.

	Captains					
Season	*South Africa*	*India*	*T*	*SA*	*I*	*D*
1992-93*S*	K. C. Wessels	M. Azharuddin	4	1	0	3
1996-97*I*	W. J. Cronje	S. R. Tendulkar	3	1	2	0
1996-97*S*	W. J. Cronje	S. R. Tendulkar	3	2	0	1
1999-2000*I*	W. J. Cronje	S. R. Tendulkar	2	2	0	0
2001-02*S*†	S. M. Pollock	S. C. Ganguly	2	1	0	1
	In South Africa		9	4	0	5
	In India		5	3	2	0
	Totals		14	7	2	5

S Played in South Africa. I Played in India.

† *The Third Test at Centurion was stripped of its official status by the ICC after a disciplinary dispute and is excluded.*

HIGHEST INNINGS TOTALS

For South Africa in South Africa: 563 at Bloemfontein 2001-02
in India: 479 at Bangalore 1999-2000

For India in South Africa: 410 at Johannesburg 1996-97
in India: 400-7 dec. at Kanpur 1996-97

LOWEST INNINGS TOTALS

For South Africa in South Africa: 235 at Durban 1996-97
in India: 105 at Ahmedabad 1996-97

For India in South Africa: 66 at Durban 1996-97
in India: 113 at Mumbai 1999-2000

HIGHEST INDIVIDUAL INNINGS

For South Africa

196 H. H. Gibbs at Port Elizabeth . . 2001-02

For India

169 S. R. Tendulkar at Cape Town . . 1996-97

INDIVIDUAL HUNDREDS

For South Africa (13)

3: G. Kirsten.
2: D. J. Cullinan, H. H. Gibbs, L. Klusener.
1: W. J. Cronje, A. C. Hudson, B. M. McMillan, K. C. Wessels.

For India (11)

4: M. Azharuddin.
3: S. R. Tendulkar.
1: P. K. Amre, R. Dravid, Kapil Dev, V. Sehwag.

RECORD PARTNERSHIPS FOR EACH WICKET

For South Africa

236	for 1st	A. C. Hudson and G. Kirsten at Calcutta	1996-97
212	for 2nd	G. Kirsten and D. J. Cullinan at Calcutta	1996-97
130	for 3rd	J. H. Kallis and N. D. McKenzie at Bloemfontein	2001-02
105	for 4th	H. H. Gibbs and H. H. Dippenaar at Port Elizabeth	2001-02
164	for 5th	J. H. Kallis and L. Klusener at Bangalore	1999-2000
112	for 6th	B. M. McMillan and S. M. Pollock at Johannesburg	1996-97
121	for 7th	L. Klusener and M. V. Boucher at Bloemfontein	2001-02
147*	for 8th	B. M. McMillan and L. Klusener at Cape Town	1996-97
60	for 9th	P. S. de Villiers and A. A. Donald at Ahmedabad	1996-97
74	for 10th	B. M. McMillan and A. A. Donald at Durban	1996-97

For India

90	for 1st	V. Rathore and N. R. Mongia at Johannesburg	1996-97
171	for 2nd	D. Dasgupta and R. Dravid at Port Elizabeth	2001-02
54	for 3rd	R. Dravid and S. R. Tendulkar at Johannesburg	1996-97
145	for 4th	R. Dravid and S. C. Ganguly at Johannesburg	1996-97
220	for 5th	S. R. Tendulkar and V. Sehwag at Bloemfontein	2001-02
222	for 6th	S. R. Tendulkar and M. Azharuddin at Cape Town	1996-97
76	for 7th	R. Dravid and J. Srinath at Johannesburg	1996-97
161	for 8th†	M. Azharuddin and A. Kumble at Calcutta	1996-97
80	for 9th	V. V. S. Laxman and A. Kumble at Port Elizabeth	2001-02
52	for 10th	A. B. Agarkar and M. Kartik at Mumbai	1999-2000

† *Record partnership against all countries.*

TEN WICKETS OR MORE IN A MATCH

For South Africa (2)

12-139 (5-55, 7-84)	A. A. Donald, Port Elizabeth	1992-93
10-147 (4-91, 6-56)	S. M. Pollock, Bloemfontein	2001-02

For India (1)

10-153 (5-60, 5-93)	B. K. V. Prasad, Durban	1996-97

SEVEN WICKETS OR MORE IN AN INNINGS

In addition to those listed above, the following has taken seven wickets or more in an innings:

For South Africa

8-64 L. Klusener, Calcutta 1996-97

SOUTH AFRICA v PAKISTAN

Series notes: S. M. Pollock is the top wicket-taker in this fixture, and needs 13 more to become the first man to 50... G. Kirsten is the top-scorer with 838 runs, comfortably ahead of the next-best (Taufeeq Umar: 593)... South Africa have batted first in nine of the 11 Tests between these sides... Both Pakistan's victories came when they lost the toss... Kirsten is the only man to have played in all 11 Tests between the sides... In home Tests, South Africa average 38.4 runs per wicket, almost double Pakistan's 21.2... In away Tests, however, South Africa average 32.0 and Pakistan 34.5... Azhar Mahmood averages 75.71 in six Tests against South Africa – and 16.08 in 15 Tests against everyone else.

	Captains					
Season	*South Africa*	*Pakistan*	*T*	*SA*	*P*	*D*
1994-95*S*	W. J. Cronje	Salim Malik	1	1	0	0
1997-98*P*	W. J. Cronje	Saeed Anwar	3	1	0	2
1997-98*S*	W. J. Cronje[1]	Rashid Latif[2]	3	1	1	1
2002-03*S*	S. M. Pollock	Waqar Younis	2	2	0	0
2003-04*P*	G. C. Smith	Inzamam-ul-Haq[3]	2	0	1	1
	In South Africa		6	4	1	1
	In Pakistan		5	1	1	3
	Totals		11	5	2	4

S Played in South Africa. P Played in Pakistan.

Notes: The following deputised for the official touring captain or were appointed by the home authority for only a minor proportion of the series:

[1]G. Kirsten (First). [2]Aamir Sohail (First and Second). [3]Yousuf Youhana (First).

HIGHEST INNINGS TOTALS

For South Africa in South Africa: 620-7 dec. at Cape Town 2002-03
in Pakistan: 403 at Rawalpindi 1997-98

For Pakistan in South Africa: 329 at Johannesburg 1996-97
in Pakistan: 456 at Rawalpindi 1997-98

LOWEST INNINGS TOTALS

For South Africa in South Africa: 225 at Durban 1997-98
in Pakistan: 214 at Faisalabad 1997-98

For Pakistan in South Africa: 106 at Port Elizabeth 1997-98
in Pakistan: 92 at Faisalabad 1997-98

DOUBLE-HUNDRED

For South Africa (1)

228 H. H. Gibbs at Cape Town 2002-03

Highest score for Pakistan: 136 by Azhar Mahmood at Johannesburg, 1997-98.

INDIVIDUAL HUNDREDS

For South Africa (7)

2: G. Kirsten.
1: H. H. Gibbs, J. H. Kallis, B. M. McMillan, G. C. Smith, P. L. Symcox.

For Pakistan (8)

3: Azhar Mahmood.
2: Taufeeq Umar.
1: Ali Naqvi, Imran Farhat, Saeed Anwar.

RECORD PARTNERSHIPS FOR EACH WICKET

For South Africa

368 for 1st†	G. C. Smith and H. H. Gibbs at Cape Town	2002-03
114 for 2nd	G. Kirsten and J. H. Kallis at Rawalpindi	1997-98
122 for 3rd	G. Kirsten and J. H. Kallis at Durban	2002-03
108 for 4th	H. H. Gibbs and G. Kirsten at Faisalabad	2003-04
90 for 5th	G. Kirsten and J. H. Kallis at Faisalabad	2003-04
157 for 6th	J. N. Rhodes and B. M. McMillan at Johannesburg	1994-95
106 for 7th	S. M. Pollock and D. J. Richardson at Rawalpindi	1997-98
124 for 8th	G. Kirsten and P. L. Symcox at Faisalabad	1997-98
195 for 9th†	M. V. Boucher and P. L. Symcox at Johannesburg	1997-98
71 for 10th	P. S. de Villiers and A. A. Donald at Johannesburg	1994-95

For Pakistan

137 for 1st	Taufeeq Umar and Imran Farhat at Faisalabad	2003-04
116 for 2nd	Taufeeq Umar and Younis Khan at Cape Town	2002-03
121 for 3rd	Taufeeq Umar and Inzamam-ul-Haq at Cape Town	2002-03
93 for 4th	Asif Mujtaba and Inzamam-ul-Haq at Johannesburg	1994-95
99 for 5th	Asim Kamal and Shoaib Malik at Lahore	2003-04
144 for 6th	Inzamam-ul-Haq and Moin Khan at Faisalabad	1997-98
35 for 7th	Salim Malik and Wasim Akram at Johannesburg	1994-95
40 for 8th	Inzamam-ul-Haq and Kabir Khan at Johannesburg	1994-95
80 for 9th	Azhar Mahmood and Shoaib Akhtar at Durban	1997-98
151 for 10th†	Azhar Mahmood and Mushtaq Ahmed at Rawalpindi	1997-98

† *Record partnership against all countries.*

TEN WICKETS OR MORE IN A MATCH

For South Africa (1)

10-108 (6-81, 4-27)†	P. S. de Villiers, Johannesburg	1994-95

For Pakistan (1)

10-133 (6-78, 4-55)	Waqar Younis, Port Elizabeth	1997-98

† *On first appearance in South Africa–Pakistan Tests.*

SEVEN WICKETS OR MORE IN AN INNINGS

In addition to those listed above, the following has taken seven wickets or more in an innings:

For South Africa

7-128 P. R. Adams, Lahore 2003-04

SOUTH AFRICA v SRI LANKA

Series notes: M. Muralitharan has taken eight five-wicket hauls against South Africa – the rest of Sri Lanka have managed one between them... In the second Test of series between the sides, South Africa have won five out of five... Five of the nine victories in this fixture have been by an innings... Sri Lanka have won nine out of 13 tosses... Six of South Africa's eight wins have come when they have lost the toss... Muralitharan has taken 77 wickets in 12 Tests between the sides; he needs 23 more to become the second bowler (after S. K. Warne) to take 100 South African wickets in Tests.

	Captains					
Season	*South Africa*	*Sri Lanka*	*T*	*SA*	*SL*	*D*
1993-94*SL*	K. C. Wessels	A. Ranatunga	3	1	0	2
1997-98*SA*	W. J. Cronje	A. Ranatunga	2	2	0	0
2000*SL*	S. M. Pollock	S. T. Jayasuriya	3	1	1	1
2000-01*SA*	S. M. Pollock	S. T. Jayasuriya	3	2	0	1
2002-03*SA*	S. M. Pollock	S. T. Jayasuriya[1]	2	2	0	0
	In South Africa		7	6	0	1
	In Sri Lanka		6	2	1	3
	Totals		13	8	1	4

SA Played in South Africa. SL Played in Sri Lanka.

Note: The following deputised for the official captain:
[1]M. S. Atapattu (Second).

HIGHEST INNINGS TOTALS

For South Africa in South Africa: 504-7 dec. at Cape Town 2000-01
in Sri Lanka: 495 at Colombo (SSC) 1993-94

For Sri Lanka in South Africa: 323 at Centurion 2002-03
in Sri Lanka: 522 at Galle 2000

LOWEST INNINGS TOTALS

For South Africa in South Africa: 200 at Centurion 1997-98
in Sri Lanka: 231 at Kandy 2000

For Sri Lanka in South Africa: 95 at Cape Town 2000-01
in Sri Lanka: 119 at Colombo (SSC) 1993-94

HIGHEST INDIVIDUAL INNINGS

For South Africa

180 G. Kirsten at Durban 2000-01

For Sri Lanka

167 D. P. M. D. Jayawardene at Galle 2000

INDIVIDUAL HUNDREDS

For South Africa (11)

5: D. J. Cullinan.
1: W. J. Cronje, G. Kirsten, L. Klusener, N. D. McKenzie, S. M. Pollock, J. N. Rhodes.

For Sri Lanka (6)

2: D. P. M. D. Jayawardene.
1: M. S. Atapattu, S. T. Jayasuriya, A. Ranatunga, H. P. Tillekeratne.

RECORD PARTNERSHIPS FOR EACH WICKET

For South Africa

137 for 1st	K. C. Wessels and A. C. Hudson at Colombo (SSC)	1993-94
96 for 2nd	G. Kirsten and J. H. Kallis at Cape Town	2000-01
140 for 3rd	H. H. Gibbs and J. H. Kallis at Centurion	2002-03
116 for 4th	G. Kirsten and W. J. Cronje at Centurion	1997-98
86 for 5th	D. J. Cullinan and M. V. Boucher at Cape Town	2000-01
124 for 6th	L. Klusener and M. V. Boucher at Kandy	2000
132 for 7th	M. V. Boucher and S. M. Pollock at Centurion	2002-03
150 for 8th†	N. D. McKenzie and S. M. Pollock at Centurion	2000-01
45 for 9th	N. Boje and P. R. Adams at Kandy	2000
43 for 10th	L. Klusener and M. Hayward at Kandy	2000

For Sri Lanka

193 for 1st	M. S. Atapattu and S. T. Jayasuriya at Galle	2000
103 for 2nd	S. T. Jayasuriya and R. P. Arnold at Colombo (SSC)	2000
168 for 3rd	K. C. Sangakkara and D. P. M. D. Jayawardene at Durban	2000-01
118 for 4th	R. S. Mahanama and A. Ranatunga at Centurion	1997-98
121 for 5th	P. A. de Silva and A. Ranatunga at Moratuwa	1993-94
103 for 6th	A. Ranatunga and H. P. Tillekeratne at Moratuwa	1993-94
43 for 7th	P. A. de Silva and G. P. Wickremasinghe at Centurion	1997-98
117 for 8th	D. P. M. D. Jayawardene and W. P. U. J. C. Vaas at Galle	2000
48 for 9th	G. P. Wickremasinghe and M. Muralitharan at Cape Town	1997-98
42 for 10th	H. P. Tillekeratne and M. Muralitharan at Centurion	2002-03

† *Record partnership against all countries.*

TEN WICKETS OR MORE IN A MATCH

For Sri Lanka (2)

13-171 (6-87, 7-84)	M. Muralitharan at Galle	2000
11-161 (5-122, 6-39)	M. Muralitharan at Durban	2000-01

Note: The best match figures for South Africa are 9-106 (5-48, 4-58) by B. N. Schultz at Colombo (SSC), 1993-94.

"'I will not speak of that,' Taufeeq Umar seethed through clenched teeth. 'I have no comment.'"

Pakistanis in Zimbabwe and South Africa, page 1159.

SOUTH AFRICA v ZIMBABWE

Series notes: South Africa have a 100% record in three Tests at Harare but drew their only Test at Bulawayo... South Africa average 169.7 runs per wicket when they bat first, as against 46.3 when they field... In Tests between the sides in Zimbabwe, South Africa's average is 62.1 and Zimbabwe's 26.2... Zimbabwe have failed to bowl South Africa out in the last three Tests, and have managed it only twice in five Tests overall... In five Tests against South Africa, G. W. Flower has made 102 runs at an average of 11.33... In three Tests in Zimbabwe, J. H. Kallis averages 503.

	Captains					
Season	*South Africa*	*Zimbabwe*	*T*	*SA*	*Z*	*D*
1995-96*Z*	W. J. Cronje	A. Flower	1	1	0	0
1999-2000*S*	W. J. Cronje	A. D. R. Campbell	1	1	0	0
1999-2000*Z*	W. J. Cronje	A. Flower	1	1	0	0
2001-02*Z*	S. M. Pollock	H. H. Streak	2	1	0	1
	In Zimbabwe		4	3	0	1
	In South Africa		1	1	0	0
	Totals		5	4	0	1

S Played in South Africa. Z Played in Zimbabwe.

HIGHEST INNINGS TOTALS

For South Africa in South Africa: 417 at Bloemfontein 1999-2000
in Zimbabwe: 600-3 dec. at Harare 2001-02

For Zimbabwe in South Africa: 212 at Bloemfontein. 1999-2000
in Zimbabwe: 419-9 dec. at Bulawayo 2001-02

LOWEST INNINGS TOTALS

For South Africa in South Africa: 417 at Bloemfontein 1999-2000
in Zimbabwe: 346 at Harare 1995-96

For Zimbabwe in South Africa: 192 at Bloemfontein. 1999-2000
in Zimbabwe: 102 at Harare. 1999-2000

DOUBLE-HUNDRED

For South Africa (1)

220 G. Kirsten at Harare. 2001-02

Highest score for Zimbabwe: 199* by A. Flower at Harare, 2001-02.

INDIVIDUAL HUNDREDS

For South Africa (7)

3: J. H. Kallis.
1: M. V. Boucher, H. H. Gibbs, A. C. Hudson, G. Kirsten.

For Zimbabwe (2)

2: A. Flower.

RECORD PARTNERSHIPS FOR EACH WICKET

For South Africa

256 for 1st	H. H. Gibbs and G. Kirsten at Harare	2001-02
199 for 2nd	G. Kirsten and J. H. Kallis at Harare	2001-02
181 for 3rd	J. H. Kallis and N. D. McKenzie at Bulawayo	2001-02
100 for 4th	J. H. Kallis and W. J. Cronje at Harare	1999-2000
60 for 5th	A. C. Hudson and J. N. Rhodes at Harare	1995-96
101 for 6th	A. C. Hudson and B. M. McMillan at Harare	1995-96
44 for 7th	M. V. Boucher and L. Klusener at Harare	1999-2000
148 for 8th	M. V. Boucher and S. M. Pollock at Harare	1999-2000
79 for 9th	B. M. McMillan and A. A. Donald at Harare	1995-96
54 for 10th	M. V. Boucher and P. R. Adams at Bloemfontein	1999-2000

For Zimbabwe

152 for 1st	A. D. R. Campbell and D. D. Ebrahim at Bulawayo	2001-02
51 for 2nd	M. H. Dekker and A. D. R. Campbell at Harare	1995-96
29 for 3rd	M. W. Goodwin and N. C. Johnson at Harare	1999-2000
186 for 4th	H. Masakadza and A. Flower at Harare	2001-02
97 for 5th	A. Flower and G. J. Whittall at Harare	1995-96
17 for 6th	A. Flower and G. J. Whittall at Harare	2001-02
47 for 7th	G. J. Whittall and H. H. Streak at Bulawayo	2001-02
43 for 8th	C. B. Wishart and H. H. Streak at Harare	1995-96
75 for 9th	A. Flower and T. J. Friend at Harare	2001-02
47 for 10th	A. Flower and D. T. Hondo at Harare	2001-02

TEN WICKETS OR MORE IN A MATCH

For South Africa (1)

11-113 (3-42, 8-71)† A. A. Donald, Harare 1995-96

Note: The best match figures for Zimbabwe are 5-105 (3-68, 2-37) by A. C. I. Lock at Harare, 1995-96.

† *On first appearance in South Africa–Zimbabwe Tests.*

SOUTH AFRICA v BANGLADESH

Series notes: South Africa have won all four Tests by an innings... South Africa average 86.2 runs per wicket and Bangladesh 18.3... South Africa's lowest score (330) is higher than Bangladesh's highest (252)... Bangladesh have taken an average of only 5.25 wickets per Test... J. H. Kallis has scored 214 runs against Bangladesh without being dismissed... J. A. Rudolph averages 293 in this fixture.

	Captains					
Season	*South Africa*	*Bangladesh*	*T*	*SA*	*B*	*D*
2002-03*S*	S. M. Pollock[1]	Khaled Masud	2	2	0	0
2003*B*	G. C. Smith	Khaled Mahmud	2	2	0	0
	In South Africa		2	2	0	0
	In Bangladesh		2	2	0	0
	Totals		4	4	0	0

S Played in South Africa. B Played in Bangladesh.

Note: The following deputised for the official captain:
[1]M. V. Boucher (First).

HIGHEST INNINGS TOTALS

For South Africa in South Africa: 529-4 dec. at East London 2002-03
in Bangladesh: 470-2 dec. at Chittagong 2003

For Bangladesh in South Africa: 252 at East London 2002-03
in Bangladesh: 237 at Chittagong 2003

LOWEST INNINGS TOTALS

For South Africa in Bangladesh: 330 at Dhaka. 2003

For Bangladesh in South Africa: 107 at Potchefstroom 2002-03
in Bangladesh: 102 at Dhaka 2003

DOUBLE-HUNDREDS

For South Africa (2)

222* J. A. Rudolph at Chittagong. . . . 2003 | 200 G. C. Smith at East London. . . . 2002-03

Highest score for Bangladesh: 75 by Habibul Bashar at Chittagong, 2003.

INDIVIDUAL HUNDREDS

For South Africa (7)

2: G. Kirsten.
1: H. H. Dippenaar, H. H. Gibbs, J. H. Kallis, J. A. Rudolph, G. C. Smith.

HUNDRED PARTNERSHIPS

For South Africa

429*	for 3rd†	J. A. Rudolph and H. H. Dippenaar at Chittagong	2003
272	for 2nd	G. C. Smith and G. Kirsten at East London	2002-03
234	for 3rd	G. Kirsten and J. H. Kallis at Potchefstroom	2002-03
141	for 2nd	H. H. Gibbs and G. Kirsten at Potchefstroom	2002-03
107	for 5th	J. A. Rudolph and M. V. Boucher at Dhaka.	2003

For Bangladesh

131	for 2nd	Javed Omar and Habibul Bashar at Chittagong	2003

† *Record partnership against all countries.*

TEN WICKETS OR MORE IN A MATCH

For South Africa (1)

10-106 (5-37, 5-69) P. R. Adams at Chittagong. 2003

Note: The best match figures for Bangladesh are 6-77 by Mohammad Rafiq at Dhaka, 2003.

WEST INDIES v NEW ZEALAND

Series notes: West Indies have won 12 of the last 15 tosses and 22 out of 32 overall... In seven home Tests outside Bridgetown and Kingston, West Indies have never won... In two Tests at Georgetown, New Zealand average 75.6 runs per wicket and West Indies 64.7.

	Captains					
Season	*West Indies*	*New Zealand*	*T*	*WI*	*NZ*	*D*
1951-52*N*	J. D. C. Goddard	B. Sutcliffe	2	1	0	1
1955-56*N*	D. St E. Atkinson	J. R. Reid[1]	4	3	1	0
1968-69*N*	G. S. Sobers	G. T. Dowling	3	1	1	1
1971-72*W*	G. S. Sobers	G. T. Dowling[2]	5	0	0	5
1979-80*N*	C. H. Lloyd	G. P. Howarth	3	0	1	2
1984-85*W*	I. V. A. Richards	G. P. Howarth	4	2	0	2
1986-87*N*	I. V. A. Richards	J. V. Coney	3	1	1	1
1994-95*N*	C. A. Walsh	K. R. Rutherford	2	1	0	1
1995-96*W*	C. A. Walsh	L. K. Germon	2	1	0	1
1999-2000*N*	B. C. Lara	S. P. Fleming	2	0	2	0
2002*W*	C. L. Hooper	S. P. Fleming	2	0	1	1
	In New Zealand		19	7	6	6
	In West Indies		13	3	1	9
	Totals		32	10	7	15

N Played in New Zealand. W Played in West Indies.

Notes: The following deputised for the official touring captain or were appointed by the home authority for only a minor proportion of the series:
[1]H. B. Cave (First). [2]B. E. Congdon (Third, Fourth and Fifth).

HIGHEST INNINGS TOTALS

For West Indies in West Indies: 564-8 at Bridgetown . . . 1971-72
in New Zealand: 660-5 dec. at Wellington . . . 1994-95

For New Zealand in West Indies: 543-3 dec. at Georgetown . . . 1971-72
in New Zealand: 518-9 dec. at Wellington . . . 1999-2000

LOWEST INNINGS TOTALS

For West Indies in West Indies: 107 at Bridgetown . . . 2002
in New Zealand: 77 at Auckland . . . 1955-56

For New Zealand in West Indies: 94 at Bridgetown . . . 1984-85
in New Zealand: 74 at Dunedin . . . 1955-56

DOUBLE-HUNDREDS

For West Indies (6)

258 S. M. Nurse at Christchurch . . . 1968-69
214 L. G. Rowe at Kingston . . . 1971-72
213 C. G. Greenidge at Auckland . . . 1986-87
208* J. C. Adams at St John's . . . 1995-96
208 S. L. Campbell at Bridgetown . . . 1995-96
204 C. H. Gayle at St George's . . . 2002

For New Zealand (3)

259 G. M. Turner at Georgetown . . . 1971-72
223* G. M. Turner at Kingston . . . 1971-72
214 M. S. Sinclair at Wellington . . . 1999-2000

INDIVIDUAL HUNDREDS

For West Indies (34)

3: D. L. Haynes, L. G. Rowe, E. D. Weekes.
2: J. C. Adams, S. L. Campbell, C. G. Greenidge, A. I. Kallicharran, S. M. Nurse.
1: M. C. Carew, C. A. Davis, R. C. Fredericks, C. H. Gayle, A. F. G. Griffith, C. L. King, B. C. Lara, J. R. Murray, I. V. A. Richards, R. B. Richardson, R. G. Samuels, G. S. Sobers, J. B. Stollmeyer, C. L. Walcott, F. M. M. Worrell.

For New Zealand (23)

3: M. D. Crowe.
2: N. J. Astle, B. E. Congdon, B. F. Hastings, G. M. Turner.
1: M. G. Burgess, J. J. Crowe, B. A. Edgar, S. P. Fleming, R. J. Hadlee, G. P. Howarth, T. W. Jarvis, A. C. Parore, M. S. Sinclair, S. B. Styris, B. R. Taylor, J. G. Wright.

Notes: E. D. Weekes in 1955-56 made three hundreds in consecutive innings.
L. G. Rowe and A. I. Kallicharran each scored hundreds in their first two innings in Test cricket. Rowe is the only batsman to do so in his first match.

RECORD PARTNERSHIPS FOR EACH WICKET

For West Indies

276 for 1st	A. F. G. Griffith and S. L. Campbell at Hamilton	1999-2000
269 for 2nd	R. C. Fredericks and L. G. Rowe at Kingston	1971-72
221 for 3rd	B. C. Lara and J. C. Adams at Wellington	1994-95
162 for 4th	E. D. Weekes and O. G. Smith at Dunedin	1955-56
	C. G. Greenidge and A. I. Kallicharran at Christchurch	1979-80
189 for 5th	F. M. M. Worrell and C. L. Walcott at Auckland	1951-52
254 for 6th	C. A. Davis and G. S. Sobers at Bridgetown	1971-72
143 for 7th	D. St E. Atkinson and J. D. C. Goddard at Christchurch	1955-56
83 for 8th	I. V. A. Richards and M. D. Marshall at Bridgetown	1984-85
70 for 9th	M. D. Marshall and J. Garner at Bridgetown	1984-85
31 for 10th	T. M. Findlay and G. C. Shillingford at Bridgetown	1971-72

For New Zealand

387 for 1st†	G. M. Turner and T. W. Jarvis at Georgetown	1971-72
210 for 2nd	G. P. Howarth and J. J. Crowe at Kingston	1984-85
241 for 3rd	J. G. Wright and M. D. Crowe at Wellington	1986-87
189 for 4th	M. S. Sinclair and N. J. Astle at Wellington	1999-2000
144 for 5th	N. J. Astle and J. T. C. Vaughan at Bridgetown	1995-96
220 for 6th	G. M. Turner and K. J. Wadsworth at Kingston	1971-72
143 for 7th	M. D. Crowe and I. D. S. Smith at Georgetown	1984-85
136 for 8th	B. E. Congdon and R. S. Cunis at Port-of-Spain	1971-72
62* for 9th	V. Pollard and R. S. Cunis at Auckland	1968-69
45 for 10th	D. K. Morrison and R. J. Kennedy at Bridgetown	1995-96

† *Record partnership against all countries.*

TEN WICKETS OR MORE IN A MATCH

For West Indies (2)

11-120 (4-40, 7-80)	M. D. Marshall, Bridgetown	1984-85
13-55 (7-37, 6-18)	C. A. Walsh, Wellington	1994-95

For New Zealand (4)

10-100 (3-73, 7-27)†	C. L. Cairns, Hamilton	1999-2000
10-124 (4-51, 6-73)†	E. J. Chatfield, Port-of-Spain	1984-85
11-102 (5-34, 6-68)†	R. J. Hadlee, Dunedin	1979-80
10-166 (4-71, 6-95)	G. B. Troup, Auckland	1979-80

† *On first appearance in West Indies–New Zealand Tests.*

SEVEN WICKETS OR MORE IN AN INNINGS

In addition to those listed above, the following have taken seven wickets or more in an innings:

For West Indies

7-53 D. St E. Atkinson, Auckland . . . 1955-56

For New Zealand

7-74 B. R. Taylor, Bridgetown 1971-72

WEST INDIES v INDIA

Series notes: The away side have not won this series since 1983-84... The side winning the toss have won only two of the last 13 Tests between the sides... Of the 16 Tests in the last ten years, the team batting second have won only two... Nineteen centuries have been scored in the last eight West Indies–India Tests... These sides have drawn only two of their 17 Test series... All six Tests in Georgetown have been drawn... India have never won in 26 Tests in the Caribbean outside Port-of-Spain... West Indies have won seven out of eight Tests against India in Bridgetown... Eight of the top ten analyses in this fixture have been recorded by spinners.

	Captains					
Season	*West Indies*	*India*	*T*	*WI*	*I*	*D*
1948-49*I*	J. D. C. Goddard	L. Amarnath	5	1	0	4
1952-53*W*	J. B. Stollmeyer	V. S. Hazare	5	1	0	4
1958-59*I*	F. C. M. Alexander	Ghulam Ahmed[1]	5	3	0	2
1961-62*W*	F. M. M. Worrell	N. J. Contractor[2]	5	5	0	0
1966-67*I*	G. S. Sobers	Nawab of Pataudi jun.	3	2	0	1
1970-71*W*	G. S. Sobers	A. L. Wadekar	5	0	1	4
1974-75*I*	C. H. Lloyd	Nawab of Pataudi jun.[3]	5	3	2	0
1975-76*W*	C. H. Lloyd	B. S. Bedi	4	2	1	1
1978-79*I*	A. I. Kallicharran	S. M. Gavaskar	6	0	1	5
1982-83*W*	C. H. Lloyd	Kapil Dev	5	2	0	3
1983-84*I*	C. H. Lloyd	Kapil Dev	6	3	0	3
1987-88*I*	I. V. A. Richards	D. B. Vengsarkar[4]	4	1	1	2
1988-89*W*	I. V. A. Richards	D. B. Vengsarkar	4	3	0	1
1994-95*I*	C. A. Walsh	M. Azharuddin	3	1	1	1
1996-97*W*	C. A. Walsh[5]	S. R. Tendulkar	5	1	0	4
2001-02*W*	C. L. Hooper	S. C. Ganguly	5	2	1	2
2002-03*I*	C. L. Hooper	S. C. Ganguly	3	0	2	1
	In India		40	14	7	19
	In West Indies		38	16	3	19
	Totals		78	30	10	38

I Played in India. W Played in West Indies.

Notes: The following deputised for the official touring captain or were appointed by the home authority for only a minor proportion of the series:

[1]P. R. Umrigar (First), V. Mankad (Fourth), H. R. Adhikari (Fifth). [2]Nawab of Pataudi jun. (Third, Fourth and Fifth). [3]S. Venkataraghavan (Second). [4]R. J. Shastri (Fourth). [5]B. C. Lara (Third).

HIGHEST INNINGS TOTALS

For West Indies in West Indies: 631-8 dec. at Kingston 1961-62
in India: 644-8 dec. at Delhi 1958-59

For India in West Indies: 513-9 dec. at St John's. 2001-02
in India: 644-7 dec. at Kanpur 1978-79

LOWEST INNINGS TOTALS

For West Indies in West Indies: 140 at Bridgetown 1996-97
in India: 127 at Delhi. 1987-88

For India in West Indies: 81 at Bridgetown. 1996-97
in India: 75 at Delhi 1987-88

DOUBLE-HUNDREDS

For West Indies (6)

256 R. B. Kanhai at Calcutta 1958-59
250 S. F. A. F. Bacchus at Kanpur . . 1978-79
242* C. H. Lloyd at Bombay. 1974-75
237 F. M. M. Worrell at Kingston. . . 1952-53
233 C. L. Hooper at Georgetown . . . 2001-02
207 E. D. Weekes at Port-of-Spain . . 1952-53

For India (5)

236* S. M. Gavaskar at Madras 1983-84
220 S. M. Gavaskar at Port-of-Spain . 1970-71
212 D. N. Sardesai at Kingston 1970-71
205 S. M. Gavaskar at Bombay 1978-79
201 N. S. Sidhu at Port-of-Spain . . . 1996-97

INDIVIDUAL HUNDREDS

For West Indies (93)

8: I. V. A. Richards, G. S. Sobers.
7: C. H. Lloyd, E. D. Weekes.
5: S. Chanderpaul, C. G. Greenidge, C. L. Hooper.
4: R. B. Kanhai, C. L. Walcott.
3: A. I. Kallicharran.
2: J. C. Adams, B. F. Butcher, C. A. Davis, R. C. Fredericks, D. L. Haynes, W. W. Hinds, A. L. Logie, A. F. Rae, R. B. Richardson, J. B. Stollmeyer.
1: S. F. A. F. Bacchus, R. J. Christiani, P. J. L. Dujon, H. A. Gomes, G. E. Gomez, J. K. Holt, C. C. Hunte, R. D. Jacobs, B. C. Lara, E. D. A. McMorris, B. H. Pairaudeau, M. N. Samuels, O. G. Smith, J. S. Solomon, A. B. Williams, S. C. Williams, F. M. M. Worrell.

For India (67)

13: S. M. Gavaskar.
6: D. B. Vengsarkar.
4: G. R. Viswanath.
3: M. Amarnath, C. G. Borde, Kapil Dev, D. N. Sardesai, N. S. Sidhu, S. R. Tendulkar, P. R. Umrigar.
2: R. Dravid, V. S. Hazare, V. V. S. Laxman, R. J. Shastri.
1: H. R. Adhikari, M. L. Apte, S. A. Durani, F. M. Engineer, A. D. Gaekwad, S. V. Manjrekar, V. L. Manjrekar, R. S. Modi, Mushtaq Ali, B. P. Patel, M. Prabhakar, A. Ratra, Pankaj Roy, V. Sehwag, E. D. Solkar.

RECORD PARTNERSHIPS FOR EACH WICKET

For West Indies

296	for 1st	C. G. Greenidge and D. L. Haynes at St John's	1982-83
255	for 2nd	E. D. A. McMorris and R. B. Kanhai at Kingston	1961-62
220	for 3rd	I. V. A. Richards and A. I. Kallicharran at Bridgetown	1975-76
267	for 4th	C. L. Walcott and G. E. Gomez at Delhi	1948-49
293	for 5th	C. L. Hooper and S. Chanderpaul at Georgetown	2001-02
250	for 6th	C. H. Lloyd and D. L. Murray at Bombay	1974-75
130	for 7th	C. G. Greenidge and M. D. Marshall at Kanpur	1983-84
124	for 8th	I. V. A. Richards and K. D. Boyce at Delhi	1974-75
161	for 9th†	C. H. Lloyd and A. M. E. Roberts at Calcutta	1983-84
98*	for 10th	F. M. M. Worrell and W. W. Hall at Port-of-Spain	1961-62

For India

201	for 1st	S. B. Bangar and V. Sehwag at Mumbai	2002-03
344*	for 2nd†	S. M. Gavaskar and D. B. Vengsarkar at Calcutta	1978-79
177	for 3rd	N. S. Sidhu and S. R. Tendulkar at Nagpur	1994-95
172	for 4th	G. R. Viswanath and A. D. Gaekwad at Kanpur	1978-79
214	for 5th	S. R. Tendulkar and V. V. S. Laxman at Kolkata	2002-03
170	for 6th	S. M. Gavaskar and R. J. Shastri at Madras	1983-84
217	for 7th	V. V. S. Laxman and A. Ratra at St John's	2001-02
120*	for 8th	R. Dravid and Sarandeep Singh at Georgetown	2001-02
143*	for 9th	S. M. Gavaskar and S. M. H. Kirmani at Madras	1983-84
64	for 10th	J. Srinath and S. L. V. Raju at Mohali	1994-95

† *Record partnership against all countries.*

TEN WICKETS OR MORE IN A MATCH

For West Indies (4)

11-126 (6-50, 5-76)	W. W. Hall, Kanpur	1958-59
11-89 (5-34, 6-55)	M. D. Marshall, Port-of-Spain	1988-89
12-121 (7-64, 5-57)	A. M. E. Roberts, Madras	1974-75
10-101 (6-62, 4-39)	C. A. Walsh, Kingston	1988-89

For India (4)

11-235 (7-157, 4-78)†	B. S. Chandrasekhar, Bombay	1966-67
10-223 (9-102, 1-121)	S. P. Gupte, Kanpur	1958-59
16-136 (8-61, 8-75)†	N. D. Hirwani, Madras	1987-88
10-135 (1-52, 9-83)	Kapil Dev, Ahmedabad	1983-84

† *On first appearance in West Indies–India Tests.*

SEVEN WICKETS OR MORE IN AN INNINGS

In addition to those listed above, the following have taken seven wickets or more in an innings:

For West Indies

8-38	L. R. Gibbs, Bridgetown	1961-62
7-98	L. R. Gibbs, Bombay	1974-75
9-95	J. M. Noreiga, Port-of-Spain	1970-71

For India

7-162	S. P. Gupte, Port-of-Spain	1952-53
7-48	Harbhajan Singh, Mumbai	2002-03
7-159	D. G. Phadkar, Madras	1948-49

WEST INDIES v PAKISTAN

Series notes: The away side have not won this series since 1980-81... Pakistan have batted first in the last five Tests between the sides; before that West Indies batted first in the previous seven... In the last three series West Indies have failed to pass 400; Pakistan have managed it five times... West Indies have won none of their six Tests at Karachi, but are unbeaten in five at Lahore... Pakistan have won none of the nine Tests played in Bridgetown, Kingston and St John's... West Indies have won ten of the last 15 tosses... West Indies average 36.3 runs per wicket at home and 23.3 in Pakistan... Inzamam-ul-Haq has made 840 Test runs against West Indies, and needs 252 to overtake I. V. A. Richards as the top-scorer in this fixture... Pakistan lead 6–1 in the first Test of series between the sides, but West Indies lead 6–3 in the second Test and 4–1 in the third... The best figures in this match were returned by a West Indian (eight for 29 by C. E. H. Croft) but the 12 next-best analyses were all taken by Pakistanis.

	Captains					
Season	*West Indies*	*Pakistan*	*T*	*WI*	*P*	*D*
1957-58*W*	F. C. M. Alexander	A. H. Kardar	5	3	1	1
1958-59*P*	F. C. M. Alexander	Fazal Mahmood	3	1	2	0
1974-75*P*	C. H. Lloyd	Intikhab Alam	2	0	0	2
1976-77*W*	C. H. Lloyd	Mushtaq Mohammad	5	2	1	2
1980-81*P*	C. H. Lloyd	Javed Miandad	4	1	0	3
1986-87*P*	I. V. A. Richards	Imran Khan	3	1	1	1
1987-88*W*	I. V. A. Richards[1]	Imran Khan	3	1	1	1
1990-91*P*	D. L. Haynes	Imran Khan	3	1	1	1
1992-93*W*	R. B. Richardson	Wasim Akram	3	2	0	1
1997-98*P*	C. A. Walsh	Wasim Akram	3	0	3	0
1999-2000*W*	J. C. Adams	Moin Khan	3	1	0	2
2001-02*U*	C. L. Hooper	Waqar Younis	2	0	2	0
	In West Indies		19	9	3	7
	In Pakistan		18	4	7	7
	In United Arab Emirates		2	0	2	0
	Totals		39	13	12	14

P Played in Pakistan. W Played in West Indies. U Played in United Arab Emirates.

Note: The following was appointed by the home authority for only a minor proportion of the series:
[1]C. G. Greenidge (First).

HIGHEST INNINGS TOTALS

For West Indies in West Indies: 790-3 dec. at Kingston 1957-58
in Pakistan: 493 at Karachi 1974-75
in United Arab Emirates: 366 at Sharjah 2001-02

For Pakistan in West Indies: 657-8 dec. at Bridgetown 1957-58
in Pakistan: 471 at Rawalpindi 1997-98
in United Arab Emirates: 493 at Sharjah 2001-02

LOWEST INNINGS TOTALS

For West Indies in West Indies: 127 at Port-of-Spain 1992-93
in Pakistan: 53 at Faisalabad 1986-87
in United Arab Emirates: 171 at Sharjah 2001-02

For Pakistan in West Indies: 106 at Bridgetown 1957-58
in Pakistan: 77 at Lahore 1986-87
in United Arab Emirates: 472 at Sharjah 2001-02

DOUBLE-HUNDREDS

For West Indies (3)

365* G. S. Sobers at Kingston. 1957-58
260 C. C. Hunte at Kingston 1957-58
217 R. B. Kanhai at Lahore. 1958-59

For Pakistan (1)

337 Hanif Mohammad at Bridgetown 1957-58

INDIVIDUAL HUNDREDS

For West Indies (26)

3: D. L. Haynes, C. L. Hooper, C. C. Hunte, G. S. Sobers.
2: I. V. A. Richards.
1: L. Baichan, P. J. L. Dujon, R. C. Fredericks, C. G. Greenidge, W. W. Hinds, B. D. Julien, A. I. Kallicharran, R. B. Kanhai, C. H. Lloyd, I. T. Shillingford, C. L. Walcott, E. D. Weekes.

For Pakistan (30)

3: Inzamam-ul-Haq, Yousuf Youhana.
2: Aamir Sohail, Hanif Mohammad, Javed Miandad, Majid Khan, Mushtaq Mohammad, Wasim Raja, Wazir Mohammad.
1: Asif Iqbal, Ijaz Ahmed, sen., Imran Khan, Imran Nazir, Imtiaz Ahmed, Rashid Latif, Saeed Ahmed, Salim Malik, Shahid Afridi, Younis Khan.

RECORD PARTNERSHIPS FOR EACH WICKET

For West Indies

182	for 1st	R. C. Fredericks and C. G. Greenidge at Kingston	1976-77
446	for 2nd†	C. C. Hunte and G. S. Sobers at Kingston	1957-58
169	for 3rd	D. L. Haynes and B. C. Lara at Port-of-Spain	1992-93
188*	for 4th	G. S. Sobers and C. L. Walcott at Kingston	1957-58
185	for 5th	E. D. Weekes and O. G. Smith at Bridgetown	1957-58
151	for 6th	C. H. Lloyd and D. L. Murray at Bridgetown	1976-77
74	for 7th	S. Chanderpaul and N. A. M. McLean at Georgetown	1999-2000
60	for 8th	C. L. Hooper and A. C. Cummins at St John's	1992-93
61*	for 9th	P. J. L. Dujon and W. K. M. Benjamin at Bridgetown	1987-88
106	for 10th†	C. L. Hooper and C. A. Walsh at St John's	1992-93

For Pakistan

298	for 1st†	Aamir Sohail and Ijaz Ahmed, sen. at Karachi	1997-98
190	for 2nd	Shahid Afridi and Younis Khan at Sharjah	2001-02
323	for 3rd	Aamir Sohail and Inzamam-ul-Haq at Rawalpindi	1997-98
174	for 4th	Shoaib Mohammad and Salim Malik at Karachi	1990-91
88	for 5th	Basit Ali and Inzamam-ul-Haq at St John's	1992-93
206	for 6th	Inzamam-ul-Haq and Abdul Razzaq at Georgetown	1999-2000
128	for 7th‡	Wasim Raja and Wasim Bari at Karachi	1974-75
94	for 8th	Salim Malik and Salim Yousuf at Port-of-Spain	1987-88
96	for 9th	Inzamam-ul-Haq and Nadeem Khan at St John's	1992-93
133	for 10th	Wasim Raja and Wasim Bari at Bridgetown	1976-77

† *Record partnership against all countries.*
‡ *Although Pakistan's seventh wicket added 168 runs against West Indies at Lahore in 1980-81, this comprised two partnerships. Imran Khan added 72* with Abdul Qadir (retired hurt) and a further 96 with Sarfraz Nawaz.*

TEN WICKETS OR MORE IN A MATCH

For Pakistan (4)

12-100 (6-34, 6-66)	Fazal Mahmood, Dacca	1958-59
11-121 (7-80, 4-41)	Imran Khan, Georgetown	1987-88
10-106 (5-35, 5-71)	Mushtaq Ahmed, Peshawar	1997-98
11-110 (6-61, 5-49)	Wasim Akram, St John's	1999-2000

Note: The best match figures for West Indies are 9-95 (8-29, 1-66) by C. E. H. Croft at Port-of-Spain, 1976-77.

WEST INDIES v SRI LANKA

Series notes: B. C. Lara has scored 1,125 runs in Tests between these teams, more than twice the next-best (S. T. Jayasuriya 506)... The team batting first have won only one of the eight Tests between the sides... Only seven of the 30 innings in this fixture have exceeded 300... There have been no away victories... West Indies have lost both matches where they won the toss and batted – and won both where they won the toss and fielded... H. P. Tillekeratne averages 206.00 at home to West Indies, and 11.33 away.

	Captains					
Season	*West Indies*	*Sri Lanka*	*T*	*WI*	*SL*	*D*
1993-94*S*	R. B. Richardson	A. Ranatunga	1	0	0	1
1996-97*W*	C. A. Walsh	A. Ranatunga	2	1	0	1
2001-02*S*	C. L. Hooper	S. T. Jayasuriya	3	0	3	0
2003*W*	B. C. Lara	H. P. Tillekeratne	2	1	0	1
	In West Indies		4	2	0	2
	In Sri Lanka		4	0	3	1
	Totals		8	2	3	3

W Played in West Indies. S Played in Sri Lanka.

HIGHEST INNINGS TOTALS

For West Indies in West Indies: 477-9 dec. at Gros Islet, St Lucia . . . 2003
in Sri Lanka: 448 at Galle . . . 2001-02

For Sri Lanka in West Indies: 354 at Gros Islet, St Lucia . . . 2003
in Sri Lanka: 627-9 dec. at Colombo (SSC) . . . 2001-02

LOWEST INNINGS TOTALS

For West Indies in West Indies: 147 at St Vincent . . . 1996-97
in Sri Lanka: 144 at Galle . . . 2001-02

For Sri Lanka in West Indies: 152 at St John's . . . 1996-97
in Sri Lanka: 190 at Moratuwa . . . 1993-94

> "Antonians 100 (A. R. R. A. P. W. R. R. K. B. Amunuguma 4-39) and 121 (A. R. R. A. P. W. R. R. K. B. Amunuguma 4-34)."
>
> **Cricket in Sri Lanka, page 1415.**

DOUBLE-HUNDREDS

For West Indies (2)

221 B. C. Lara at Colombo (SSC) . . 2001-02 | 209 B. C. Lara at Gros Islet, St Lucia 2003

For Sri Lanka (1)

204* H. P. Tillekeratne at Colombo (SSC) 2001-02

INDIVIDUAL HUNDREDS

For West Indies (6)

5: B. C. Lara.
1: W. W. Hinds.

For Sri Lanka (4)

2: H. P. Tillekeratne.
1: M. S. Atapattu, K. C. Sangakkara.

RECORD PARTNERSHIPS FOR EACH WICKET

For West Indies

160	for 1st	S. L. Campbell and S. C. Williams at St John's	1996-97
80	for 2nd	D. Ganga and R. R. Sarwan at Galle	2001-02
194	for 3rd	R. R. Sarwan and B. C. Lara at Colombo (SSC)	2001-02
153	for 4th	B. C. Lara and C. L. Hooper at Galle	2001-02
84	for 5th	R. B. Richardson and C. L. Hooper at Moratuwa	1993-94
41	for 6th	B. C. Lara and R. D. Jacobs at Kandy	2001-02
136	for 7th	B. C. Lara and O. A. C. Banks at Gros Islet, St Lucia	2003
53	for 8th	R. I. C. Holder and C. E. L. Ambrose at St Vincent	1996-97
13	for 9th	W. K. M. Benjamin and C. E. L. Ambrose at Moratuwa	1993-94
29*	for 10th	O. A. C. Banks and J. E. Taylor at Gros Islet, St Lucia	2003

For Sri Lanka

126*	for 1st	M. S. Atapattu and S. T. Jayasuriya at Gros Islet, St Lucia	2003
109	for 2nd	M. S. Atapattu and K. C. Sangakkara at Galle	2001-02
162	for 3rd	K. C. Sangakkara and D. P. M. D. Jayawardene at Galle	2001-02
110	for 4th	S. T. Jayasuriya and A. Ranatunga at St John's	1996-97
141	for 5th	R. P. Arnold and H. P. Tillekeratne at Colombo (SSC)	2001-02
165	for 6th	H. P. Tillekeratne and T. T. Samaraweera at Colombo (SSC)	2001-02
52	for 7th	K. C. Sangakkara and W. P. U. J. C. Vaas at Kingston	2003
19	for 8th	H. P. Tillekeratne and D. N. T. Zoysa at Colombo (SSC)	2001-02
42	for 9th	H. P. Tillekeratne and M. R. C. N. Bandaratilleke at Colombo (SSC)	2001-02
28	for 10th	W. P. U. J. C. Vaas and R. A. P. Nissanka at Gros Islet, St Lucia	2003

TEN WICKETS OR MORE IN A MATCH

For Sri Lanka (3)

11-170 (6-126, 5-44)	M. Muralitharan, Galle	2001-02
10-135 (4-54, 6-81)	M. Muralitharan, Kandy	2001-02
14-191 (7-120, 7-71)	W. P. U. J. C. Vaas, Colombo (SSC)	2001-02

Note: The best match figures for West Indies are 9-85 (2-28, 7-57) by C. D. Collymore at Kingston, 2003.

WEST INDIES v ZIMBABWE

Series notes: West Indies have never lost a Test to Zimbabwe... The two matches between the sides at Harare are the only ones in which Zimbabwe have not been beaten... Zimbabwe do outscore West Indies in centuries – six to four – but the three highest scores are all by West Indians... C. B. Wishart and A. M. Blignaut have both been out twice in the 90s.

	Captains					
Season	*West Indies*	*Zimbabwe*	*T*	*WI*	*Z*	*D*
1999-2000*W*	J. C. Adams	A. Flower	2	2	0	0
2001*Z*	C. L. Hooper	H. H. Streak	2	1	0	1
2003-04*Z*	B. C. Lara	H. H. Streak	2	1	0	1
	In West Indies		2	2	0	0
	In Zimbabwe		4	2	0	2
	Totals		6	4	0	2

W Played in West Indies. Z Played in Zimbabwe.

HIGHEST INNINGS TOTALS

For West Indies in West Indies: 339 at Kingston 1999-2000
in Zimbabwe: 559-6 dec. at Bulawayo 2001

For Zimbabwe in West Indies: 308 at Kingston 1999-2000
in Zimbabwe: 563-9 dec. at Harare 2001

LOWEST INNINGS TOTALS

For West Indies in West Indies: 147 at Port-of-Spain. 1999-2000
in Zimbabwe: 128 at Bulawayo 2003-04

For Zimbabwe in West Indies: 63 at Port-of-Spain 1999-2000
in Zimbabwe: 104 at Bulawayo. 2003-04

HIGHEST INDIVIDUAL SCORES

For West Indies

191 B. C. Lara at Bulawayo. 2003-04

For Zimbabwe

127* H. H. Streak at Harare 2003-04

INDIVIDUAL HUNDREDS

For West Indies (4)

1: J. C. Adams, C. H. Gayle, C. L. Hooper, B. C. Lara.

For Zimbabwe (6)

1: A. D. R. Campbell, A. Flower, M. W. Goodwin, H. Masakadza, H. H. Streak, M. A. Vermeulen.

RECORD PARTNERSHIPS FOR EACH WICKET

For West Indies

214 for 1st	D. Ganga and C. H. Gayle at Bulawayo	2001
100 for 2nd	D. Ganga and S. Chanderpaul at Harare	2001
52 for 3rd	D. Ganga and B. C. Lara at Harare	2003-04
190 for 4th	B. C. Lara and R. R. Sarwan at Bulawayo	2003-04
100 for 5th	C. L. Hooper and M. N. Samuels at Bulawayo	2001
68 for 6th	S. Chanderpaul and R. D. Jacobs at Harare	2003-04
50 for 7th	R. R. Sarwan and N. C. McGarrell at Harare	2001
	S. Chanderpaul and V. C. Drakes at Harare	2003-04
148 for 8th	J. C. Adams and F. A. Rose at Kingston	1999-2000
26 for 9th	M. Dillon and C. D. Collymore at Bulawayo	2003-04
26 for 10th	W. W. Hinds and C. A. Walsh at Port-of-Spain	1999-2000
	C. D. Collymore and F. H. Edwards at Harare	2003-04

For Zimbabwe

164 for 1st†	D. D. Ebrahim and A. D. R. Campbell at Bulawayo	2001
91 for 2nd	A. D. R. Campbell and H. Masakadza at Harare	2001
169 for 3rd	H. Masakadza and C. B. Wishart at Harare	2001
176 for 4th	M. W. Goodwin and A. Flower at Kingston	1999-2000
42 for 5th	C. B. Wishart and S. Matsikenyeri at Harare	2003-04
79 for 6th	S. Matsikenyeri and T. Taibu at Harare	2003-04
154 for 7th†	H. H. Streak and A. M. Blignaut at Harare	2001
168 for 8th†	H. H. Streak and A. M. Blignaut at Harare	2003-04
34 for 9th	A. M. Blignaut and R. W. Price at Bulawayo	2003-04
54 for 10th	S. V. Carlisle and H. K. Olonga at Kingston	1999-2000

† *Record partnership against all countries.*

TEN WICKETS OR MORE IN A MATCH

For Zimbabwe

10-161 (6-73, 4-88)	R. W. Price at Harare	2003-04

Note: The best match figures for West Indies are 7-50 (4-42, 3-8) by C. E. L. Ambrose at Port-of-Spain, 1999-2000.

WEST INDIES v BANGLADESH

Series notes: The teams are yet to meet in the West Indies... Bangladesh have batted first in both Tests between the sides... Bangladesh have recorded 11 ducks to West Indies' none.

	Captains					
Season	*West Indies*	*Bangladesh*	*T*	*WI*	*B*	*D*
2002-03*B*	R. D. Jacobs	Khaled Masud	2	2	0	0

B Played in Bangladesh.

HIGHEST INNINGS TOTALS

For West Indies: 536 at Dhaka	2002-03
For Bangladesh: 212 at Chittagong	2002-03

LOWEST INNINGS TOTALS

For West Indies: 296 at Chittagong 2002-03

For Bangladesh: 87 at Dhaka 2002-03

HIGHEST INDIVIDUAL INNINGS

For West Indies

119 R. R. Sarwan at Dhaka 2002-03

For Bangladesh

85 Alok Kapali at Chittagong 2002-03

INDIVIDUAL HUNDRED

For West Indies (1)

1: R. R. Sarwan.

HIGHEST PARTNERSHIPS

For West Indies

176 for 4th	R. R. Sarwan and M. N. Samuels at Dhaka	2002-03
131 for 1st	C. H. Gayle and W. W. Hinds at Dhaka	2002-03
99 for 6th	D. Ganga and R. D. Jacobs at Chittagong	2002-03

For Bangladesh

73 for 6th	Alok Kapali and Khaled Masud at Dhaka	2002-03
73 for 7th	Alok Kapali and Enamul Haque at Chittagong	2002-03

BEST BOWLING MATCH ANALYSES

For West Indies

7-27 (1-24, 6-3) J. J. C. Lawson at Dhaka 2002-03

For Bangladesh

6-117 (4-72, 2-45) Tapash Baisya at Chittagong 2002-03

NEW ZEALAND v INDIA

Series notes: The away team have won none of the last 17 Tests between the sides... Five of New Zealand's nine wins over India have come in the second Test of the series... New Zealand have lost only one of the last 11 Tests between the sides... The team batting first have won none of the last 15... In the last series in India the teams averaged 53.4 runs per wicket – more than three times as many as in the last series in New Zealand (16.2)... India are unbeaten in four Tests at Auckland, but have never won in four Tests at Christchurch.

	Captains					
Season	*New Zealand*	*India*	*T*	*NZ*	*I*	*D*
1955-56*I*	H. B. Cave	P. R. Umrigar[1]	5	0	2	3
1964-65*I*	J. R. Reid	Nawab of Pataudi jun.	4	0	1	3
1967-68*N*	G. T. Dowling[2]	Nawab of Pataudi jun.	4	1	3	0
1969-70*I*	G. T. Dowling	Nawab of Pataudi jun.	3	1	1	1
1975-76*N*	G. M. Turner	B. S. Bedi[3]	3	1	1	1
1976-77*I*	G. M. Turner	B. S. Bedi	3	0	2	1
1980-81*N*	G. P. Howarth	S. M. Gavaskar	3	1	0	2
1988-89*I*	J. G. Wright	D. B. Vengsarkar	3	1	2	0
1989-90*N*	J. G. Wright	M. Azharuddin	3	1	0	2
1993-94*N*	K. R. Rutherford	M. Azharuddin	1	0	0	1
1995-96*I*	L. K. Germon	M. Azharuddin	3	0	1	2
1998-99*N*†	S. P. Fleming	M. Azharuddin	2	1	0	1
1999-2000*I*	S. P. Fleming	S. R. Tendulkar	3	0	1	2
2002-03*N*	S. P. Fleming	S. C. Ganguly	2	2	0	0
2003-04*I*	S. P. Fleming	S. C. Ganguly[4]	2	0	0	2
	In India		26	2	10	14
	In New Zealand		18	7	4	7
	Totals		44	9	14	21

I Played in India. N Played in New Zealand.

† The First Test at Dunedin was abandoned without a ball being bowled and is excluded.

Notes: The following deputised for the official touring captain or were appointed by the home authority for a minor proportion of the series:
[1]Ghulam Ahmed (First). [2]B. W. Sinclair (First). [3]S. M. Gavaskar (First). [4]R. Dravid (Second).

HIGHEST INNINGS TOTALS

For New Zealand in New Zealand: 502 at Christchurch 1967-68
in India: 630-6 dec. at Mohali 2003-04

For India in New Zealand: 482 at Auckland 1989-90
in India: 583-7 dec. at Ahmedabad 1999-2000

LOWEST INNINGS TOTALS

For New Zealand in New Zealand: 94 at Hamilton 2002-03
in India: 124 at Hyderabad 1988-89

For India in New Zealand: 81 at Wellington 1975-76
in India: 83 at Mohali 1999-2000

DOUBLE-HUNDREDS

For New Zealand (2)

239 G. T. Dowling at Christchurch. 1967-68
230* B. Sutcliffe at Delhi 1955-56

For India (6)

231 V. Mankad at Madras 1955-56
223 V. Mankad at Bombay...... 1955-56
223 P. R. Umrigar at Hyderabad .. 1955-56
222 R. Dravid at Ahmedabad 2003-04
217 S. R. Tendulkar at Ahmedabad 1999-2000
200* D. N. Sardesai at Bombay ... 1964-65

INDIVIDUAL HUNDREDS

For New Zealand (27)

3: G. T. Dowling, B. Sutcliffe, J. G. Wright.
2: J. R. Reid, G. M. Turner.
1: N. J. Astle, C. L. Cairns, M. D. Crowe, J. W. Guy, G. P. Howarth, A. H. Jones, C. D. McMillan, J. M. Parker, J. F. Reid, M. H. Richardson, I. D. S. Smith, S. B. Styris, B. R. Taylor, L. Vincent.

For India (36)

4: R. Dravid.
3: S. C. Ganguly, V. L. Manjrekar, S. R. Tendulkar.
2: M. Azharuddin, S. M. Gavaskar, V. Mankad, Nawab of Pataudi, jun., Pankaj Roy, D. N. Sardesai.
1: S. Amarnath, C. G. Borde, A. G. Kripal Singh, V. V. S. Laxman, G. S. Ramchand, S. Ramesh, V. Sehwag, N. S. Sidhu, P. R. Umrigar, G. R. Viswanath, A. L. Wadekar.

RECORD PARTNERSHIPS FOR EACH WICKET

For New Zealand

231	for 1st	M. H. Richardson and L. Vincent at Mohali	2003-04
155	for 2nd	G. T. Dowling and B. E. Congdon at Dunedin	1967-68
222*	for 3rd	B. Sutcliffe and J. R. Reid at Delhi	1955-56
160	for 4th	R. G. Twose and C. D. McMillan at Hamilton	1998-99
140	for 5th	C. D. McMillan and A. C. Parore at Hamilton	1998-99
137	for 6th	C. D. McMillan and C. L. Cairns at Wellington	1998-99
163	for 7th	B. Sutcliffe and B. R. Taylor at Calcutta	1964-65
137	for 8th	D. J. Nash and D. L. Vettori at Wellington	1998-99
136	for 9th†	I. D. S. Smith and M. C. Snedden at Auckland	1989-90
61	for 10th	J. T. Ward and R. O. Collinge at Madras	1964-65

For India

413	for 1st†	V. Mankad and Pankaj Roy at Madras	1955-56
204	for 2nd	S. M. Gavaskar and S. Amarnath at Auckland	1975-76
238	for 3rd	P. R. Umrigar and V. L. Manjrekar at Hyderabad	1955-56
281	for 4th	S. R. Tendulkar and S. C. Ganguly at Ahmedabad	1999-2000
182	for 5th	R. Dravid and S. C. Ganguly at Ahmedabad	2003-04
193*	for 6th	D. N. Sardesai and Hanumant Singh at Bombay	1964-65
128	for 7th	S. R. Tendulkar and K. S. More at Napier	1989-90
144	for 8th	R. Dravid and J. Srinath at Hamilton	1998-99
105	for 9th	S. M. H. Kirmani and B. S. Bedi at Bombay	1976-77
		S. M. H. Kirmani and N. S. Yadav at Auckland	1980-81
57	for 10th	R. B. Desai and B. S. Bedi at Dunedin	1967-68

† *Record partnership against all countries.*

TEN WICKETS OR MORE IN A MATCH

For New Zealand (2)

11-58 (4-35, 7-23)	R. J. Hadlee, Wellington	1975-76
10-88 (6-49, 4-39)	R. J. Hadlee, Bombay	1988-89

For India (3)

10-134 (4-67, 6-67)	A. Kumble, Kanpur	1999-2000
11-140 (3-64, 8-76)	E. A. S. Prasanna, Auckland	1975-76
12-152 (8-72, 4-80)	S. Venkataraghavan, Delhi	1964-65

SEVEN WICKETS OR MORE IN AN INNINGS

In addition to those listed above, the following have taken seven wickets or more in an innings:

For New Zealand

7-65 S. B. Doull, Wellington 1998-99

For India

7-128 S. P. Gupte, Hyderabad. 1955-56

NEW ZEALAND v PAKISTAN

Series note: New Zealand have won only one, and lost 12, of 21 Tests against Pakistan when they have batted first... Seven of the last 12 wins in this fixture, and ten of the last 19, have been achieved by sides trailing on first innings... Eight of the nine double-centuries in this fixture have been made by Pakistanis... In two Tests against New Zealand, Shoaib Akhtar has taken 17 wickets at an average of 5.23, with a wicket every 16.52 balls... Seven of the 17 were out for ducks, and nine of the 17 bowled... D. L. Vettori has taken four wickets in three matches at an average of 100.25... New Zealand have failed to win in six Tests at Wellington and six at Karachi... Four of New Zealand's wins have come when they won the toss and fielded: in such games they trail 5–4; in others they trail 16–2.

	Captains					
Season	*New Zealand*	*Pakistan*	*T*	*NZ*	*P*	*D*
1955-56*P*	H. B. Cave	A. H. Kardar	3	0	2	1
1964-65*N*	J. R. Reid	Hanif Mohammad	3	0	0	3
1964-65*P*	J. R. Reid	Hanif Mohammad	3	0	2	1
1969-70*P*	G. T. Dowling	Intikhab Alam	3	1	0	2
1972-73*N*	B. E. Congdon	Intikhab Alam	3	0	1	2
1976-77*P*	G. M. Turner[1]	Mushtaq Mohammad	3	0	2	1
1978-79*N*	M. G. Burgess	Mushtaq Mohammad	3	0	1	2
1984-85*P*	J. V. Coney	Zaheer Abbas	3	0	2	1
1984-85*N*	G. P. Howarth	Javed Miandad	3	2	0	1
1988-89*N*†	J. G. Wright	Imran Khan	2	0	0	2
1990-91*P*	M. D. Crowe	Javed Miandad	3	0	3	0
1992-93*N*	K. R. Rutherford	Javed Miandad	1	0	1	0
1993-94*N*	K. R. Rutherford	Salim Malik	3	1	2	0
1995-96*N*	L. K. Germon	Wasim Akram	1	0	1	0
1996-97*P*	L. K. Germon	Saeed Anwar	2	1	1	0
2000-01*N*	S. P. Fleming	Moin Khan[2]	3	1	1	1
2002*P*‡	S. P. Fleming	Waqar Younis	1	0	1	0
2003-04*N*	S. P. Fleming	Inzamam-ul-Haq	2	0	1	1
	In Pakistan		21	2	13	6
	In New Zealand		24	4	8	12
	Totals		45	6	21	18

N Played in New Zealand. P Played in Pakistan.

† *The First Test at Dunedin was abandoned without a ball being bowled and is excluded.*
‡ *The Second Test at Karachi was cancelled owing to civil disturbances.*

Note: The following deputised for the official touring captain:
[1]J. M. Parker (Third). [2]Inzamam-ul-Haq (Third).

HIGHEST INNINGS TOTALS

For New Zealand in New Zealand: 563 at Hamilton 2003-04
in Pakistan: 482-6 dec. at Lahore 1964-65

For Pakistan in New Zealand: 616-5 dec. at Auckland 1988-89
in Pakistan: 643 at Lahore 2002

LOWEST INNINGS TOTALS

For New Zealand in New Zealand: 93 at Hamilton 1992-93
in Pakistan: 70 at Dacca 1955-56

For Pakistan in New Zealand: 104 at Hamilton 2000-01
in Pakistan: 102 at Faisalabad 1990-91

DOUBLE-HUNDREDS

For New Zealand (1)

204* M. S. Sinclair at Christchurch . . 2000-01

For Pakistan (8)

329 Inzamam-ul-Haq at Lahore 2002
271 Javed Miandad at Auckland 1988-89
209 Imtiaz Ahmed at Lahore 1955-56
206 Javed Miandad at Karachi 1976-77
203* Hanif Mohammad at Lahore . . . 1964-65
203* Shoaib Mohammad at Karachi . . 1990-91
203 Yousuf Youhana at Christchurch 2000-01
201 Mushtaq Mohammad at Dunedin 1972-73

INDIVIDUAL HUNDREDS

For New Zealand (26)

3: J. F. Reid.
2: M. G. Burgess, M. D. Crowe.
1: M. D. Bell, J. V. Coney, B. A. Edgar, S. P. Fleming, M. J. Greatbatch, B. F. Hastings, G. P. Howarth, W. K. Lees, S. N. McGregor, R. E. Redmond, J. R. Reid, M. H. Richardson, B. W. Sinclair, M. S. Sinclair, S. A. Thomson, G. M. Turner, D. L. Vettori, J. G. Wright, B. A. Young.

For Pakistan (48)

7: Javed Miandad.
5: Shoaib Mohammad.
3: Asif Iqbal, Hanif Mohammad, Inzamam-ul-Haq, Majid Khan, Mushtaq Mohammad.
2: Ijaz Ahmed, sen., Sadiq Mohammad, Saeed Anwar, Salim Malik.
1: Basit Ali, Imran Nazir, Imtiaz Ahmed, Mohammad Ilyas, Mohammad Wasim, Moin Khan, Mudassar Nazar, Saeed Ahmed, Saqlain Mushtaq, Waqar Hassan, Younis Khan, Yousuf Youhana, Zaheer Abbas.

Note: Mushtaq and Sadiq Mohammad both hit hundreds at Hyderabad in 1976-77, the fourth time – after the Chappells (thrice) – that brothers had each scored hundreds in the same Test innings.

RECORD PARTNERSHIPS FOR EACH WICKET

For New Zealand

181 for 1st	M. H. Richardson and M. D. Bell at Hamilton	2000-01
195 for 2nd	J. G. Wright and G. P. Howarth at Napier	1978-79
178 for 3rd	B. W. Sinclair and J. R. Reid at Lahore	1964-65
147 for 4th	C. D. McMillan and S. P. Fleming at Hamilton	2000-01
183 for 5th	M. G. Burgess and R. W. Anderson at Lahore	1976-77
145 for 6th	J. F. Reid and R. J. Hadlee at Wellington	1984-85
186 for 7th†	W. K. Lees and R. J. Hadlee at Karachi	1976-77
125 for 8th	S. P. Fleming and D. L. Vettori at Hamilton	2003-04
99 for 9th	D. L. Vettori and D. R. Tuffey at Hamilton	2003-04
151 for 10th†	B. F. Hastings and R. O. Collinge at Auckland	1972-73

For Pakistan

172 for 1st	Ramiz Raja and Shoaib Mohammad at Karachi	1990-91
262 for 2nd	Saeed Anwar and Ijaz Ahmed, sen. at Rawalpindi	1996-97
248 for 3rd	Shoaib Mohammad and Javed Miandad at Auckland	1988-89
350 for 4th†	Mushtaq Mohammad and Asif Iqbal at Dunedin	1972-73
281 for 5th†	Javed Miandad and Asif Iqbal at Lahore	1976-77
217 for 6th†	Hanif Mohammad and Majid Khan at Lahore	1964-65
308 for 7th†	Waqar Hassan and Imtiaz Ahmed at Lahore	1955-56
89 for 8th	Anil Dalpat and Iqbal Qasim at Karachi	1984-85
78 for 9th	Inzamam-ul-Haq and Shoaib Akhtar at Lahore	2002
65 for 10th	Salah-ud-Din and Mohammad Farooq at Rawalpindi	1964-65

† *Record partnership against all countries.*

TEN WICKETS OR MORE IN A MATCH

For New Zealand (1)

11-152 (7-52, 4-100)	C. Pringle, Faisalabad	1990-91

For Pakistan (11)

10-182 (5-91, 5-91)	Intikhab Alam, Dacca	1969-70
11-130 (7-52, 4-78)	Intikhab Alam, Dunedin	1972-73
11-130 (4-64, 7-66)†	Mohammad Zahid, Rawalpindi	1996-97
10-171 (3-115, 7-56)	Mushtaq Ahmed, Christchurch	1995-96
10-143 (4-59, 6-84)	Mushtaq Ahmed, Lahore	1996-97
11-78 (5-48, 6-30)	Shoaib Akhtar, Christchurch	2003-04
10-106 (3-20, 7-86)	Waqar Younis, Lahore	1990-91
12-130 (7-76, 5-54)	Waqar Younis, Faisalabad	1990-91
10-128 (5-56, 5-72)	Wasim Akram, Dunedin	1984-85
11-179 (4-60, 7-119)	Wasim Akram, Wellington	1993-94
11-79 (5-37, 6-42)†	Zulfiqar Ahmed, Karachi	1955-56

† *On first appearance in New Zealand–Pakistan Tests.*

Note: Waqar Younis's performances were in successive matches.

SEVEN WICKETS OR MORE IN AN INNINGS

In addition to those listed above, the following have taken seven wickets or more in an innings:

For New Zealand

7-87 S. L. Boock, Hyderabad 1984-85

For Pakistan

7-99 Mohammad Nazir, Karachi . . . . 1969-70 | 7-74 Pervez Sajjad, Lahore. 1969-70

NEW ZEALAND v SRI LANKA

Series notes: The team batting first have won six and lost only one of the last 15 matches between these teams... New Zealand's three highest individual scores have come against Sri Lanka... S. P. Fleming needs 54 runs, and H. P. Tillekeratne 181, to become the first to score 1,000 in Tests between the teams... Sri Lanka's only victory in New Zealand came at Napier... New Zealand have won only three of the last 15 Tests between these sides, having won four of the first five... Sri Lanka have won none of the five Tests in which they have inserted New Zealand... New Zealand have won the toss in seven of the last nine Tests.

	Captains					
Season	*New Zealand*	*Sri Lanka*	*T*	*NZ*	*SL*	*D*
1982-83*N*	G. P. Howarth	D. S. de Silva	2	2	0	0
1983-84*S*	G. P. Howarth	L. R. D. Mendis	3	2	0	1
1986-87*S*†	J. J. Crowe	L. R. D. Mendis	1	0	0	1
1990-91*N*	M. D. Crowe[1]	A. Ranatunga	3	0	0	3
1992-93*S*	M. D. Crowe	A. Ranatunga	2	0	1	1
1994-95*N*	K. R. Rutherford	A. Ranatunga	2	0	1	1
1996-97*N*	S. P. Fleming	A. Ranatunga	2	2	0	0
1997-98*S*	S. P. Fleming	A. Ranatunga	3	1	2	0
2003*S*	S. P. Fleming	H. P. Tillekeratne	2	0	0	2
	In New Zealand		9	4	1	4
	In Sri Lanka		11	3	3	5
	Totals		20	7	4	9

N Played in New Zealand. S Played in Sri Lanka.

† *The Second and Third Tests were cancelled owing to civil disturbances.*

Note: The following was appointed by the home authority for only a minor proportion of the series:
[1]I. D. S. Smith (Third).

HIGHEST INNINGS TOTALS

For New Zealand in New Zealand: 671-4 at Wellington 1990-91
in Sri Lanka: 515-7 dec. at Colombo (PSS) 2003

For Sri Lanka in New Zealand: 497 at Wellington 1990-91
in Sri Lanka: 483 at Colombo (PSS) 2003

LOWEST INNINGS TOTALS

For New Zealand in New Zealand: 109 at Napier 1994-95
in Sri Lanka: 102 at Colombo (SSC) 1992-93

For Sri Lanka in New Zealand: 93 at Wellington 1982-83
in Sri Lanka: 97 at Kandy 1986-87

DOUBLE-HUNDREDS

For New Zealand (3)

299 M. D. Crowe at Wellington 1990-91
274* S. P. Fleming at Colombo (PSS). 2003
267* B. A. Young at Dunedin 1996-97

For Sri Lanka (2)

267 P. A. de Silva at Wellington . . . . 1990-91 | 201* D. S. B. P. Kuruppu at Colombo (CCC) 1986-87

INDIVIDUAL HUNDREDS

For New Zealand (14)

3: A. H. Jones.
2: M. D. Crowe, S. P. Fleming.
1: J. J. Crowe, R. J. Hadlee, C. D. McMillan, J. F. Reid, K. R. Rutherford, J. G. Wright, B. A. Young.

For Sri Lanka (13)

3: A. P. Gurusinha.
2: P. A. de Silva, R. S. Mahanama, H. P. Tillekeratne.
1: R. L. Dias, D. P. M. D. Jayawardene, R. S. Kaluwitharana, D. S. B. P. Kuruppu.

Note: A. H. Jones and A. P. Gurusinha, on opposing sides, each hit two hundreds at Hamilton in 1990-91, the second time this had happened in Tests, after D. C. S. Compton and A. R. Morris, for England and Australia at Adelaide in 1946-47.

RECORD PARTNERSHIPS FOR EACH WICKET

For New Zealand

161	for 1st	T. J. Franklin and J. G. Wright at Hamilton	1990-91
172	for 2nd	M. H. Richardson and S. P. Fleming at Colombo (PSS)	2003
467	for 3rd†‡	A. H. Jones and M. D. Crowe at Wellington	1990-91
240	for 4th	S. P. Fleming and C. D. McMillan at Colombo (RPS)	1997-98
151	for 5th	K. R. Rutherford and C. Z. Harris at Moratuwa	1992-93
246*	for 6th†	J. J. Crowe and R. J. Hadlee at Colombo (CCC)	1986-87
47	for 7th	D. N. Patel and M. L. Su'a at Dunedin	1994-95
79	for 8th	J. V. Coney and W. K. Lees at Christchurch	1982-83
43	for 9th	A. C. Parore and P. J. Wiseman at Galle	1997-98
52	for 10th	W. K. Lees and E. J. Chatfield at Christchurch	1982-83

For Sri Lanka

102	for 1st	R. S. Mahanama and U. C. Hathurusinghe at Colombo (SSC)	1992-93
138	for 2nd	R. S. Mahanama and A. P. Gurusinha at Moratuwa	1992-93
159*	for 3rd§	S. Wettimuny and R. L. Dias at Colombo (SSC)	1983-84
192	for 4th	A. P. Gurusinha and H. P. Tillekeratne at Dunedin	1994-95
133	for 5th	D. P. M. D. Jayawardene and H. P. Tillekeratne at Colombo (PSS)	2003
109*	for 6th¶	R. S. Madugalle and A. Ranatunga at Colombo (CCC)	1983-84
109	for 6th	D. S. B. P. Kuruppu and R. S. Madugalle at Colombo (PSS)	1986-87
137	for 7th	R. S. Kaluwitharana and W. P. U. J. C. Vaas at Dunedin	1996-97
73	for 8th	H. P. Tillekeratne and G. P. Wickremasinghe at Dunedin	1996-97
31	for 9th	G. F. Labrooy and R. J. Ratnayake at Auckland	1990-91
		S. T. Jayasuriya and R. J. Ratnayake at Auckland	1990-91
71	for 10th	R. S. Kaluwitharana and M. Muralitharan at Colombo (SSC)	1997-98

† *Record partnership against all countries.*
‡ *Record third-wicket partnership in first-class cricket.*
§ *163 runs were added for this wicket in two separate partnerships: S. Wettimuny retired hurt and was replaced by J. R. Ratnayeke when 159 had been added.*
¶ *119 runs were added for this wicket in two separate partnerships: R. S. Madugalle retired hurt and was replaced by D. S. de Silva when 109 had been added.*

TEN WICKETS OR MORE IN A MATCH

For New Zealand (1)

10-102 (5-73, 5-29) R. J. Hadlee, Colombo (CCC) 1983-84

For Sri Lanka (1)

10-90 (5-47, 5-43)† W. P. U. J. C. Vaas, Napier 1994-95

† *On first appearance in New Zealand–Sri Lanka Tests.*

NEW ZEALAND v ZIMBABWE

Series notes: New Zealand have won four of the last five Tests between the sides... The team winning the toss have batted first in the last six matches, and nine of 11 overall... The team batting first have won only two out of 11 Tests between these sides... G. W. Flower is the top-scorer in this fixture, and needs 220 runs to become the first to 1,000.

	Captains					
Season	*New Zealand*	*Zimbabwe*	*T*	*NZ*	*Z*	*D*
1992-93*Z*	M. D. Crowe	D. L. Houghton	2	1	0	1
1995-96*N*	L. K. Germon	A. Flower	2	0	0	2
1997-98*Z*	S. P. Fleming	A. D. R. Campbell	2	0	0	2
1997-98*N*	S. P. Fleming	A. D. R. Campbell	2	2	0	0
2000-01*Z*	S. P. Fleming	H. H. Streak	2	2	0	0
2000-01*N*	S. P. Fleming	H. H. Streak	1	0	0	1
	In New Zealand		5	2	0	3
	In Zimbabwe		6	3	0	3
	Totals		11	5	0	6

N Played in New Zealand. *Z Played in Zimbabwe.*

HIGHEST INNINGS TOTALS

For New Zealand in New Zealand: 487-7 dec. at Wellington 2000-01
in Zimbabwe: 465 at Harare 2000-01

For Zimbabwe in New Zealand: 340-6 dec. at Wellington 2000-01
in Zimbabwe: 461 at Bulawayo 1997-98

LOWEST INNINGS TOTALS

For New Zealand in New Zealand: 251 at Auckland 1995-96
in Zimbabwe: 207 at Harare 1997-98

For Zimbabwe in New Zealand: 170 at Auckland 1997-98
in Zimbabwe: 119 at Bulawayo 2000-01

DOUBLE-HUNDRED

For Zimbabwe (1)

203* G. J. Whittall at Bulawayo 1997-98

Highest score for New Zealand: 157 by M. J. Horne at Auckland, 1997-98.

INDIVIDUAL HUNDREDS

For New Zealand (11)

2: N. J. Astle, C. L. Cairns, M. J. Horne, C. D. McMillan.
1: M. D. Crowe, R. T. Latham, C. M. Spearman.

For Zimbabwe (6)

2: G. W. Flower, G. J. Whittall.
1: K. J. Arnott, D. L. Houghton.

RECORD PARTNERSHIPS FOR EACH WICKET

For New Zealand

214	for 1st	C. M. Spearman and R. G. Twose at Auckland	1995-96
127	for 2nd	R. T. Latham and A. H. Jones at Bulawayo	1992-93
71	for 3rd	A. H. Jones and M. D. Crowe at Bulawayo	1992-93
243	for 4th†	M. J. Horne and N. J. Astle at Auckland	1997-98
222	for 5th†	N. J. Astle and C. D. McMillan at Wellington	2000-01
82*	for 6th	A. C. Parore and L. K. Germon at Hamilton	1995-96
108	for 7th	C. D. McMillan and D. J. Nash at Wellington	1997-98
144	for 8th	C. L. Cairns and D. J. Nash at Harare	2000-01
78	for 9th	A. C. Parore and D. L. Vettori at Bulawayo	2000-01
27	for 10th	C. D. McMillan and S. B. Doull at Auckland	1997-98

For Zimbabwe

156	for 1st	G. J. Rennie and G. W. Flower at Harare	1997-98
107	for 2nd	K. J. Arnott and A. D. R. Campbell at Harare	1992-93
70	for 3rd	A. Flower and G. J. Whittall at Bulawayo	1997-98
130	for 4th	G. J. Rennie and A. Flower at Wellington	2000-01
131	for 5th	A. Flower and G. J. Whittall at Harare	2000-01
151	for 6th	G. J. Whittall and H. H. Streak at Harare	2000-01
91	for 7th	G. J. Whittall and P. A. Strang at Hamilton	1995-96
94	for 8th	A. D. R. Campbell and H. H. Streak at Wellington	1997-98
46	for 9th	G. J. Crocker and M. G. Burmester at Harare	1992-93
40	for 10th	G. J. Whittall and E. Z. Matambanadzo at Bulawayo	1997-98

† *Record partnership against all countries.*

TEN WICKETS OR MORE IN A MATCH

For Zimbabwe (2)

11-255 (6-109, 5-146)	A. G. Huckle, Bulawayo	1997-98
10-158 (8-109, 2-49)	P. A. Strang, Bulawayo	2000-01

Note: The best match figures for New Zealand are 8-85 (4-35, 4-50) by S. B. Doull at Auckland, 1997-98.

NEW ZEALAND v BANGLADESH

Series notes: New Zealand have won both matches by an innings... In both matches, the team winning the toss have bowled first... Bangladesh have yet to bowl New Zealand out... New Zealand have never failed to reach 300; Bangladesh have never reached it... No innings has lasted for 100 overs.

	Captains					
Season	*New Zealand*	*Bangladesh*	*T*	*NZ*	*B*	*D*
2001-02*N*	S. P. Fleming	Khaled Masud	2	2	0	0

N Played in New Zealand.

HIGHEST INNINGS TOTALS

For New Zealand: 365-9 dec. at Hamilton 2001-02

For Bangladesh: 205 at Hamilton 2001-02

LOWEST INNINGS TOTAL

For Bangladesh: 108 at Hamilton 2001-02

HIGHEST INDIVIDUAL INNINGS

For New Zealand

143 M. H. Richardson at Hamilton . . 2001-02

For Bangladesh

61 Habibul Bashar at Hamilton. . . . 2001-02

INDIVIDUAL HUNDREDS

For New Zealand (2)

1: C. D. McMillan, M. H. Richardson.

HIGHEST PARTNERSHIPS

For New Zealand

190 for 5th	M. H. Richardson and C. D. McMillan at Hamilton	2001-02
130 for 4th	S. P. Fleming and C. D. McMillan at Wellington	2001-02
104 for 1st	M. H. Richardson and M. J. Horne at Wellington	2001-02

For Bangladesh

60 for 3rd	Habibul Bashar and Aminul Islam at Hamilton	2001-02

BEST MATCH BOWLING ANALYSES

For New Zealand

8-108 (1-55, 7-53) C. L. Cairns, Hamilton 2001-02

For Bangladesh

3-99 (3-99) Manjurul Islam, Wellington. 2001-02

"As soon as Bangladesh emerged from the pavilion they were mercilessly, predictably and often tediously put to the sword."

Bangladeshis in South Africa, page 1092.

INDIA v PAKISTAN

Series notes: Pending the scheduled 2003-04 series, India have never won a Test in Pakistan in 20 attempts… Over 70% of Tests between these sides have been drawn (33 out of 47)… The last three Tests have all had positive results; before that there were 15 draws out of 16… India have won just one of their last 24 Tests against Pakistan… The team batting second have won none of the last 20 matches in this fixture; before that they had lost just one in 26… India's runs-per-wicket average is exactly the same at home and away to Pakistan: 34.0… Pakistan's, by contrast, is 48.0 at home and 29.6 away… In the last 24 matches, no team have won the toss and lost the match.

Season	*Captains* *India*	*Pakistan*	*T*	*I*	*P*	*D*
1952-53*I*	L. Amarnath	A. H. Kardar	5	2	1	2
1954-55*P*	V. Mankad	A. H. Kardar	5	0	0	5
1960-61*I*	N. J. Contractor	Fazal Mahmood	5	0	0	5
1978-79*P*	B. S. Bedi	Mushtaq Mohammad	3	0	2	1
1979-80*I*	S. M. Gavaskar[1]	Asif Iqbal	6	2	0	4
1982-83*P*	S. M. Gavaskar	Imran Khan	6	0	3	3
1983-84*I*	Kapil Dev	Zaheer Abbas	3	0	0	3
1984-85*P*	S. M. Gavaskar	Zaheer Abbas	2	0	0	2
1986-87*I*	Kapil Dev	Imran Khan	5	0	1	4
1989-90*P*	K. Srikkanth	Imran Khan	4	0	0	4
1998-99*I*	M. Azharuddin	Wasim Akram	2	1	1	0
1998-99*I*†	M. Azharuddin	Wasim Akram	1	0	1	0
	In India		27	5	4	18
	In Pakistan		20	0	5	15
	Totals		47	5	9	33

I Played in India. P Played in Pakistan.

† This Test was part of the Asian Test Championship and was not counted as part of the preceding bilateral series.

Note: The following was appointed by the home authority for only a minor proportion of the series:
[1]G. R. Viswanath (Sixth).

HIGHEST INNINGS TOTALS

For India in India: 539-9 dec. at Madras 1960-61
in Pakistan: 509 at Lahore 1989-90

For Pakistan in India: 487-9 dec. at Madras 1986-87
in Pakistan: 699-5 at Lahore 1989-90

LOWEST INNINGS TOTALS

For India in India: 106 at Lucknow. 1952-53
in Pakistan: 145 at Karachi 1954-55

For Pakistan in India: 116 at Bangalore 1986-87
in Pakistan: 158 at Dacca 1954-55

DOUBLE-HUNDREDS

For India (2)

218 S. V. Manjrekar at Lahore . . . . . 1989-90 | 201 A. D. Gaekwad at Jullundur. . . . 1983-84

For Pakistan (6)

280*	Javed Miandad at Hyderabad	1982-83
235*	Zaheer Abbas at Lahore	1978-79
231	Mudassar Nazar at Hyderabad	1982-83
215	Zaheer Abbas at Lahore	1982-83
210	Qasim Omar at Faisalabad	1984-85
203*	Shoaib Mohammad at Lahore	1989-90

INDIVIDUAL HUNDREDS

For India (32)

5: S. M. Gavaskar, P. R. Umrigar.
4: M. Amarnath.
3: M. Azharuddin, R. J. Shastri.
2: S. V. Manjrekar, D. B. Vengsarkar.
1: C. G. Borde, A. D. Gaekwad, V. S. Hazare, S. M. Patil, R. H. Shodhan, K. Srikkanth, S. R. Tendulkar, G. R. Viswanath.

For Pakistan (43)

6: Mudassar Nazar, Zaheer Abbas.
5: Javed Miandad.
3: Imran Khan, Salim Malik.
2: Aamer Malik, Hanif Mohammad, Saeed Ahmed, Shoaib Mohammad.
1: Alim-ud-Din, Asif Iqbal, Ijaz Faqih, Imtiaz Ahmed, Mohsin Khan, Mushtaq Mohammad, Nazar Mohammad, Qasim Omar, Ramiz Raja, Saeed Anwar, Shahid Afridi, Wasim Raja.

RECORD PARTNERSHIPS FOR EACH WICKET

For India

200 for 1st	S. M. Gavaskar and K. Srikkanth at Madras	1986-87
135 for 2nd	N. S. Sidhu and S. V. Manjrekar at Karachi	1989-90
190 for 3rd	M. Amarnath and Yashpal Sharma at Lahore	1982-83
186 for 4th	S. V. Manjrekar and R. J. Shastri at Lahore	1989-90
200 for 5th	S. M. Patil and R. J. Shastri at Faisalabad	1984-85
143 for 6th	M. Azharuddin and Kapil Dev at Calcutta	1986-87
155 for 7th	R. M. H. Binny and Madan Lal at Bangalore	1983-84
122 for 8th	S. M. H. Kirmani and Madan Lal at Faisalabad	1982-83
149 for 9th†	P. G. Joshi and R. B. Desai at Bombay	1960-61
109 for 10th†	H. R. Adhikari and Ghulam Ahmed at Delhi	1952-53

For Pakistan

162 for 1st	Hanif Mohammad and Imtiaz Ahmed at Madras	1960-61
250 for 2nd	Mudassar Nazar and Qasim Omar at Faisalabad	1984-85
451 for 3rd†	Mudassar Nazar and Javed Miandad at Hyderabad	1982-83
287 for 4th	Javed Miandad and Zaheer Abbas at Faisalabad	1982-83
213 for 5th	Zaheer Abbas and Mudassar Nazar at Karachi	1982-83
207 for 6th	Salim Malik and Imran Khan at Faisalabad	1982-83
154 for 7th	Imran Khan and Ijaz Faqih at Ahmedabad	1986-87
112 for 8th	Imran Khan and Wasim Akram at Madras	1986-87
60 for 9th	Wasim Bari and Iqbal Qasim at Bangalore	1979-80
104 for 10th	Zulfiqar Ahmed and Amir Elahi at Madras	1952-53

† *Record partnership against all countries.*

TEN WICKETS OR MORE IN A MATCH

For India (5)

11-146 (4-90, 7-56)	Kapil Dev, Madras	1979-80
14-149 (4-75, 10-74)	A. Kumble, Delhi	1998-99
10-126 (7-27, 3-99)	Maninder Singh, Bangalore	1986-87
13-131 (8-52, 5-79)†	V. Mankad, Delhi	1952-53
13-132 (5-46, 8-86)	J. Srinath, Calcutta	1998-99

For Pakistan (7)

12-94 (5-52, 7-42)	Fazal Mahmood, Lucknow	1952-53
11-79 (3-19, 8-60)	Imran Khan, Karachi	1982-83
11-180 (6-98, 5-82)	Imran Khan, Faisalabad	1982-83
10-175 (4-135, 6-40)	Iqbal Qasim, Bombay	1979-80
10-187 (5-94, 5-93)†	Saqlain Mushtaq, Chennai	1998-99
10-216 (5-94, 5-122)	Saqlain Mushtaq, Delhi	1998-99
11-190 (8-69, 3-121)	Sikander Bakht, Delhi	1979-80

† *On first appearance in India–Pakistan Tests.*

SEVEN WICKETS OR MORE IN AN INNINGS

In addition to those listed above, the following have taken seven wickets or more in an innings:

For India

7-220 Kapil Dev, Faisalabad . . . . 1982-83 | 8-85 Kapil Dev, Lahore 1982-83

INDIA v SRI LANKA

Series notes: Sri Lanka have never won a Test in India... The team batting first have won none of the last ten Tests between the teams... In 11 Tests between the sides in India, India average 51.0 runs per wicket and Sri Lanka 24.4... S. R. Tendulkar has scored 1,124 runs against Sri Lanka and needs 129 more to overtake P. A. de Silva as the top-scorer in this fixture... Seven of the 11 victories in this fixture have been by an innings... India have batted first in five of the last six – but only won when they fielded first.

	Captains					
Season	*India*	*Sri Lanka*	*T*	*I*	*SL*	*D*
1982-83*I*	S. M. Gavaskar	B. Warnapura	1	0	0	1
1985-86*S*	Kapil Dev	L. R. D. Mendis	3	0	1	2
1986-87*I*	Kapil Dev	L. R. D. Mendis	3	2	0	1
1990-91*I*	M. Azharuddin	A. Ranatunga	1	1	0	0
1993-94*S*	M. Azharuddin	A. Ranatunga	3	1	0	2
1993-94*I*	M. Azharuddin	A. Ranatunga	3	3	0	0
1997-98*S*	S. R. Tendulkar	A. Ranatunga	2	0	0	2
1997-98*I*	S. R. Tendulkar	A. Ranatunga	3	0	0	3
1998-99*S*†	M. Azharuddin	A. Ranatunga	1	0	0	1
2001*S*	S. C. Ganguly	S. T. Jayasuriya	3	1	2	0
	In India		11	6	0	5
	In Sri Lanka		12	2	3	7
	Totals		23	8	3	12

I Played in India. S Played in Sri Lanka.

† *This Test was part of the Asian Test Championship.*

HIGHEST INNINGS TOTALS

For India in India: 676-7 at Kanpur . . . 1986-87
in Sri Lanka: 537-8 dec. at Colombo (RPS) . . . 1997-98

For Sri Lanka in India: 420 at Kanpur . . . 1986-87
in Sri Lanka: 952-6 dec. at Colombo (RPS) . . . 1997-98

LOWEST INNINGS TOTALS

For India in India: 288 at Chandigarh . . . 1990-91
in Sri Lanka: 180 at Galle . . . 2001

For Sri Lanka in India: 82 at Chandigarh . . . 1990-91
in Sri Lanka: 198 at Kandy . . . 1985-86

DOUBLE-HUNDREDS

For Sri Lanka (3)

340 S. T. Jayasuriya at Colombo (RPS) . . . 1997-98
242 D. P. M. D. Jayawardene at Colombo (SSC) . . . 1998-99
225 R. S. Mahanama at Colombo (RPS) . . . 1997-98

Highest score for India: 199 by M. Azharuddin at Kanpur, 1986-87.

INDIVIDUAL HUNDREDS

For India (30)

6: S. R. Tendulkar.
5: M. Azharuddin.
4: N. S. Sidhu.
3: S. C. Ganguly.
2: M. Amarnath, S. M. Gavaskar, V. G. Kambli, D. B. Vengsarkar.
1: R. Dravid, Kapil Dev, S. M. Patil, S. Ramesh.

For Sri Lanka (25)

5: P. A. de Silva.
3: S. T. Jayasuriya, D. P. M. D. Jayawardene, L. R. D. Mendis.
2: M. S. Atapattu, R. S. Mahanama.
1: R. L. Dias, R. S. Madugalle, A. Ranatunga, T. T. Samaraweera, K. C. Sangakkara, S. A. R. Silva, H. P. Tillekeratne.

RECORD PARTNERSHIPS FOR EACH WICKET

For India

171	for 1st	M. Prabhakar and N. S. Sidhu at Colombo (SSC)	1993-94
232	for 2nd	S. Ramesh and R. Dravid at Colombo (SSC)	1998-99
173	for 3rd	M. Amarnath and D. B. Vengsarkar at Nagpur	1986-87
256	for 4th	S. C. Ganguly and S. R. Tendulkar at Mumbai	1997-98
150	for 5th	S. R. Tendulkar and S. C. Ganguly at Colombo (SSC)	1997-98
272	for 6th	M. Azharuddin and Kapil Dev at Kanpur	1986-87
78*	for 7th	S. M. Patil and Madan Lal at Madras	1982-83
70	for 8th	Kapil Dev and L. Sivaramakrishnan at Colombo (PSS)	1985-86
89	for 9th	S. C. Ganguly and A. Kuruvilla at Mohali	1997-98
30	for 10th	Zaheer Khan and B. K. V. Prasad at Colombo (SSC)	2001

For Sri Lanka

159	for 1st	S. Wettimuny and J. R. Ratnayeke at Kanpur	1986-87
576	for 2nd†	S. T. Jayasuriya and R. S. Mahanama at Colombo (RPS)	1997-98
218	for 3rd	S. T. Jayasuriya and P. A. de Silva at Colombo (SSC)	1997-98
216	for 4th	R. L. Dias and L. R. D. Mendis at Kandy	1985-86
144	for 5th‡	R. S. Madugalle and A. Ranatunga at Colombo (SSC)	1985-86
103	for 6th	P. A. de Silva and H. D. P. K. Dharmasena at Mohali	1997-98
194*	for 7th†	H. P. Tillekeratne and T. T. Samaraweera at Colombo (SSC)	2001
48	for 8th	P. A. de Silva and M. Muralitharan at Colombo (SSC)	1997-98
60	for 9th	H. P. Tillekeratne and A. W. R. Madurasinghe at Chandigarh	1990-91
64	for 10th	M. Muralitharan and P. D. R. L. Perera at Kandy	2001

† *Record partnership against all countries.*
‡ *Although Sri Lanka's fifth wicket added 176 runs against India at Colombo (SSC) in 1998-99, this comprised two partnerships. D. P. M. D. Jayawardene added 115* with A. Ranatunga (retired hurt) and a further 61 with H. P. Tillekeratne.*

TEN WICKETS OR MORE IN A MATCH

For India (3)

11-128 (4-69, 7-59)	A. Kumble, Lucknow	1993-94
10-107 (3-56, 7-51)	Maninder Singh, Nagpur	1986-87
11-125 (5-38, 6-87)	S. L. V. Raju, Ahmedabad	1993-94

For Sri Lanka (1)

11-196 (8-87, 3-109)	M. Muralitharan, Colombo (SSC)	2001

INDIA v ZIMBABWE

Series notes: The nine highest individual scores in this fixture were all made at Nagpur or Delhi… Both of Zimbabwe's victories over India have come at Harare… India have won all three matches at Delhi… In two matches at Nagpur, India average 90.6 runs per wicket and Zimbabwe 37.6… The team batting second have won each of the last four Tests between the sides, despite losing the toss on each occasion.

	Captains					
Season	*India*	*Zimbabwe*	*T*	*I*	*Z*	*D*
1992-93*Z*	M. Azharuddin	D. L. Houghton	1	0	0	1
1992-93*I*	M. Azharuddin	D. L. Houghton	1	1	0	0
1998-99*Z*	M. Azharuddin	A. D. R. Campbell	1	0	1	0
2000-01*I*	S. C. Ganguly	H. H. Streak	2	1	0	1
2001*Z*	S. C. Ganguly	H. H. Streak	2	1	1	0
2001-02*I*	S. C. Ganguly	S. V. Carlisle	2	2	0	0
	In India		5	4	0	1
	In Zimbabwe		4	1	2	1
	Totals		9	5	2	2

I Played in India. Z Played in Zimbabwe.

HIGHEST INNINGS TOTALS

For India in India: 609-6 dec. at Nagpur 2000-01
in Zimbabwe: 318 at Bulawayo 2001

For Zimbabwe in India: 503-6 at Nagpur 2000-01
in Zimbabwe: 456 at Harare 1992-93

LOWEST INNINGS TOTALS

For India in India: 354 at Delhi 2001-02
in Zimbabwe: 173 at Harare 1998-99

For Zimbabwe in India: 146 at Delhi 2001-02
in Zimbabwe: 173 at Bulawayo 2001

DOUBLE-HUNDREDS

For India (3)

227 V. G. Kambli at Delhi 1992-93
201* S. R. Tendulkar at Nagpur 2000-01
200* R. Dravid at Delhi 2000-01

For Zimbabwe (1)

232* A. Flower at Nagpur 2000-01

INDIVIDUAL HUNDREDS

For India (12)

3: R. Dravid, S. R. Tendulkar.
2: S. S. Das.
1: S. B. Bangar, S. C. Ganguly, V. G. Kambli, S. V. Manjrekar.

For Zimbabwe (6)

3: A. Flower.
1: A. D. R. Campbell, G. W. Flower, D. L. Houghton.

RECORD PARTNERSHIPS FOR EACH WICKET

For India

79	for 1st	S. S. Das and D. Dasgupta at Nagpur	2001-02
155	for 2nd	S. S. Das and R. Dravid at Nagpur	2000-01
249	for 3rd	R. Dravid and S. R. Tendulkar at Nagpur	2000-01
110*	for 4th	R. Dravid and S. C. Ganguly at Delhi	2000-01
120	for 5th	S. C. Ganguly and V. Sehwag at Delhi	2001-02
171	for 6th	S. R. Tendulkar and S. B. Bangar at Nagpur	2001-02
44	for 7th	R. Dravid and R. R. Singh at Harare	1998-99
72	for 8th	S. S. Dighe and Harbhajan Singh at Bulawayo	2001
19	for 9th	H. K. Badani and J. Srinath at Harare	2001
40	for 10th	J. Srinath and Harbhajan Singh at Harare	1998-99

For Zimbabwe

138	for 1st	G. J. Rennie and C. B. Wishart at Harare	1998-99
106	for 2nd	S. V. Carlisle and A. D. R. Campbell at Nagpur	2001-02
119	for 3rd	S. V. Carlisle and A. D. R. Campbell at Delhi	2000-01
209	for 4th	A. D. R. Campbell and A. Flower at Nagpur	2000-01
96	for 5th	A. Flower and G. W. Flower at Nagpur	2000-01
165	for 6th†	D. L. Houghton and A. Flower at Harare	1992-93
98*	for 7th	A. Flower and H. H. Streak at Nagpur	2000-01
46	for 8th	A. Flower and B. A. Murphy at Delhi	2000-01
59	for 9th	T. J. Friend and R. W. Price at Nagpur	2001-02
97*	for 10th†	A. Flower and H. K. Olonga at Delhi	2000-01

† *Record partnership against all countries.*

BEST MATCH BOWLING ANALYSES

For India

9-141 (4-81, 5-60) J. Srinath, Delhi 2000-01

For Zimbabwe

7-115 (3-69, 4-46) H. H. Streak, Harare 2001

INDIA v BANGLADESH

Series notes: S. R. Tendulkar's fledgling average against Bangladesh (18.00) is his lowest against any country… Spin bowlers have taken 61% of the wickets in this fixture.

	Captains					
Season	*India*	*Bangladesh*	*T*	*I*	*B*	*D*
2000-01*B*	S. C. Ganguly	Naimur Rahman	1	1	0	0

B Played in Bangladesh.

HIGHEST INNINGS TOTALS

For India: 429 at Dhaka 2000-01

For Bangladesh: 400 at Dhaka 2000-01

HIGHEST INDIVIDUAL INNINGS

For India

92 S. B. Joshi at Dhaka. 2000-01

For Bangladesh

145 Aminul Islam at Dhaka. 2000-01

INDIVIDUAL HUNDRED

For Bangladesh (1)

1: Aminul Islam.

HIGHEST PARTNERSHIPS

For India

121 for 7th S. C. Ganguly and S. B. Joshi at Dhaka 2000-01

For Bangladesh

93 for 7th Aminul Islam and Khaled Masud at Dhaka 2000-01

BEST MATCH BOWLING ANALYSES

For India

8-169 (5-142, 3-27) S. B. Joshi, Dhaka 2000-01

For Bangladesh

6-154 (6-132, 0-22) Naimur Rahman, Dhaka 2000-01

PAKISTAN v SRI LANKA

Series notes: Sri Lanka have won the toss in the last five – and ten of the last 12 – Tests between these teams... Six of Pakistan's 13 wins over Sri Lanka have been by an innings – but Sri Lanka have never beaten Pakistan by an innings... Inzamam-ul-Haq has scored 1,313 runs against Sri Lanka and needs 163 to overtake P. A. de Silva as the leading run-scorer in this fixture... Sri Lanka have won only 8% of the matches between the sides in which they have won the toss and batted (one in 13), as against 60% when they have won the toss and fielded (three in five).

	Captains					
Season	*Pakistan*	*Sri Lanka*	*T*	*P*	*SL*	*D*
1981-82*P*	Javed Miandad	B. Warnapura[1]	3	2	0	1
1985-86*P*	Javed Miandad	L. R. D. Mendis	3	2	0	1
1985-86*S*	Imran Khan	L. R. D. Mendis	3	1	1	1
1991-92*P*	Imran Khan	P. A. de Silva	3	1	0	2
1994-95*S*†	Salim Malik	A. Ranatunga	2	2	0	0
1995-96*P*	Ramiz Raja	A. Ranatunga	3	1	2	0
1996-97*S*	Ramiz Raja	A. Ranatunga	2	0	0	2
1998-99*P*‡	Wasim Akram	H. P. Tillekeratne	1	0	0	1
1998-99*B*‡	Wasim Akram	P. A. de Silva	1	1	0	0
1999-2000*P*	Saeed Anwar[2]	S. T. Jayasuriya	3	1	2	0
2000*S*	Moin Khan	S. T. Jayasuriya	3	2	0	1
2001-02*P*‡	Waqar Younis	S. T. Jayasuriya	1	0	1	0
	In Pakistan		17	7	5	5
	In Sri Lanka		10	5	1	4
	In Bangladesh		1	1	0	0
	Totals		28	13	6	9

P Played in Pakistan. S Played in Sri Lanka. B Played in Bangladesh.

† *One Test was cancelled owing to the threat of civil disturbances following a general election.*
‡ *These Tests were part of the Asian Test Championship.*

Note: The following deputised for the official touring captain or were appointed by the home authority for only a minor proportion of the series:
[1]L. R. D. Mendis (Second). [2]Moin Khan (Third).

HIGHEST INNINGS TOTALS

For Pakistan	in Pakistan: 555-3 at Faisalabad	1985-86
	in Sri Lanka: 600-8 dec. at Galle	2000
	in Bangladesh: 594 at Dhaka	1998-99
For Sri Lanka	in Pakistan: 528 at Lahore	2001-02
	in Sri Lanka: 467-5 at Kandy	2000

LOWEST INNINGS TOTALS

For Pakistan	in Pakistan: 182 at Rawalpindi	1999-2000
	in Sri Lanka: 132 at Colombo (CCC)	1985-86
For Sri Lanka	in Pakistan: 149 at Karachi	1981-82
	in Sri Lanka: 71 at Kandy	1994-95

DOUBLE-HUNDREDS

For Pakistan (4)

211	Ijaz Ahmed, sen. at Dhaka	1998-99	203*	Javed Miandad at Faisalabad	1985-86
206	Qasim Omar at Faisalabad	1985-86	200*	Inzamam-ul-Haq at Dhaka	1998-99

For Sri Lanka (2)

230	K. C. Sangakkara at Lahore	2001-02	207*	M. S. Atapattu at Kandy	2000

INDIVIDUAL HUNDREDS

For Pakistan (23)

4: Inzamam-ul-Haq.
3: Salim Malik.
2: Ijaz Ahmed, sen., Saeed Anwar, Wajahatullah Wasti, Younis Khan.
1: Haroon Rashid, Javed Miandad, Mohsin Khan, Moin Khan, Qasim Omar, Ramiz Raja, Wasim Akram, Zaheer Abbas.

For Sri Lanka (20)

8: P. A. de Silva.
2: S. T. Jayasuriya, H. P. Tillekeratne.
1: R. P. Arnold, M. S. Atapattu, R. L. Dias, A. P. Gurusinha, R. S. Kaluwitharana, A. Ranatunga, K. C. Sangakkara, S. Wettimuny.

RECORD PARTNERSHIPS FOR EACH WICKET

For Pakistan

156 for 1st	Wajahatullah Wasti and Shahid Afridi at Lahore	1998-99
151 for 2nd	Mohsin Khan and Majid Khan at Lahore	1981-82
397 for 3rd	Qasim Omar and Javed Miandad at Faisalabad	1985-86
178 for 4th	Wajahatullah Wasti and Yousuf Youhana at Lahore	1998-99
132 for 5th	Salim Malik and Imran Khan at Sialkot	1991-92
124 for 6th	Inzamam-ul-Haq and Younis Khan at Karachi	1999-2000
120 for 7th	Younis Khan and Wasim Akram at Galle	2000
88 for 8th	Moin Khan and Waqar Younis at Karachi	1999-2000
145 for 9th	Younis Khan and Wasim Akram at Rawalpindi	1999-2000
90 for 10th	Wasim Akram and Arshad Khan at Colombo (SSC)	2000

For Sri Lanka

335	for 1st†	M. S. Atapattu and S. T. Jayasuriya at Kandy	2000
217	for 2nd	S. Wettimuny and R. L. Dias at Faisalabad	1981-82
176	for 3rd	U. C. Hathurusinghe and P. A. de Silva at Faisalabad	1995-96
240*	for 4th†	A. P. Gurusinha and A. Ranatunga at Colombo (PSS)	1985-86
143	for 5th	R. P. Arnold and R. S. Kaluwitharana at Lahore	1998-99
121	for 6th	A. Ranatunga and P. A. de Silva at Faisalabad	1985-86
131	for 7th	H. P. Tillekeratne and R. S. Kalpage at Kandy	1994-95
76	for 8th	P. A. de Silva and W. P. U. J. C. Vaas at Colombo (SSC)	1996-97
52	for 9th	P. A. de Silva and R. J. Ratnayake at Faisalabad	1985-86
73	for 10th†	H. P. Tillekeratne and K. S. C. de Silva at Dhaka	1998-99

† *Record partnership against all countries.*

TEN WICKETS OR MORE IN A MATCH

For Pakistan (2)

14-116 (8-58, 6-58)	Imran Khan, Lahore	1981-82
11-119 (6-34, 5-85)	Waqar Younis, Kandy	1994-95

For Sri Lanka (1)

10-148 (4-77, 6-71)	M. Muralitharan, Peshawar	1999-2000

SEVEN WICKETS OR MORE IN AN INNINGS

In addition to those listed above, the following has taken seven wickets or more in an innings:

For Sri Lanka

8-83 J. R. Ratnayeke, Sialkot 1985-86

PAKISTAN v ZIMBABWE

Series notes: Zimbabwe have won the toss in 11 of the 14 Tests between the sides… H. H. Streak needs six Pakistan wickets to become the first Zimbabwean to take 50 wickets against any single country… Pakistan have a worse record at home to Zimbabwe (three wins and one defeat from seven matches) than away (five wins and one defeat from seven)… G. W. Flower needs 39 runs to become the first man to score 1,000 in this fixture… Zimbabwe are the only team with an innings win… The team batting first have won only one of the last eight matches between the sides… Pakistan lead 3–1 in Tests at Harare, but Zimbabwe have a greater runs-per-wicket average there (31.3–28.0).

	Captains					
Season	*Pakistan*	*Zimbabwe*	*T*	*P*	*Z*	*D*
1993-94*P*	Wasim Akram[1]	A. Flower	3	2	0	1
1994-95*Z*	Salim Malik	A. Flower	3	2	1	0
1996-97*P*	Wasim Akram	A. D. R. Campbell	2	1	0	1
1997-98*Z*	Rashid Latif	A. D. R. Campbell	2	1	0	1
1998-99*P*†	Aamir Sohail[2]	A. D. R. Campbell	2	0	1	1
2002-03*Z*	Waqar Younis	A. D. R. Campbell	2	2	0	0
	In Pakistan		7	3	1	3
	In Zimbabwe		7	5	1	1
	Totals		14	8	2	4

P Played in Pakistan. Z Played in Zimbabwe.

† *The Third Test at Faisalabad was abandoned without a ball being bowled and is excluded.*

Notes: The following were appointed by the home authority for only a minor proportion of the series:

[1]Waqar Younis (First). [2]Moin Khan (Second).

HIGHEST INNINGS TOTALS

For Pakistan in Pakistan: 553 at Sheikhupura 1996-97
in Zimbabwe: 403 at Bulawayo. 2002-03

For Zimbabwe in Pakistan: 375 at Sheikhupura 1996-97
in Zimbabwe: 544-4 dec. at Harare. 1994-95

LOWEST INNINGS TOTALS

For Pakistan in Pakistan: 103 at Peshawar 1998-99
in Zimbabwe: 158 at Harare. 1994-95

For Zimbabwe in Pakistan: 133 at Faisalabad 1996-97
in Zimbabwe: 139 at Harare 1994-95

DOUBLE-HUNDREDS

For Pakistan (1)

257* Wasim Akram at Sheikhupura . . 1996-97

For Zimbabwe (1)

201* G. W. Flower at Harare. 1994-95

INDIVIDUAL HUNDREDS

For Pakistan (7)

2: Inzamam-ul-Haq, Yousuf Youhana.
1: Mohammad Wasim, Taufeeq Umar, Wasim Akram.

For Zimbabwe (9)

3: G. W. Flower.
2: A. Flower.
1: M. W. Goodwin, N. C. Johnson, P. A. Strang, G. J. Whittall.

RECORD PARTNERSHIPS FOR EACH WICKET

For Pakistan

95	for 1st	Aamir Sohail and Shoaib Mohammad at Karachi (DS)	1993-94
118*	for 2nd	Shoaib Mohammad and Asif Mujtaba at Lahore	1993-94
180	for 3rd	Taufeeq Umar and Inzamam-ul-Haq at Harare	2002-03
127	for 4th	Younis Khan and Yousuf Youhana at Bulawayo	2002-03
110	for 5th	Yousuf Youhana and Moin Khan at Bulawayo	1997-98
121	for 6th	Yousuf Youhana and Kamran Akmal at Bulawayo	2002-03
120	for 7th	Ijaz Ahmed, sen. and Inzamam-ul-Haq at Harare	1994-95
313	for 8th†	Wasim Akram and Saqlain Mushtaq at Sheikhupura	1996-97
147	for 9th	Mohammad Wasim and Mushtaq Ahmed at Harare	1997-98
50*	for 10th	Yousuf Youhana and Waqar Younis at Lahore	1998-99

For Zimbabwe

48*	for 1st	G. J. Rennie and G. W. Flower at Lahore	1998-99
135	for 2nd†	M. H. Dekker and A. D. R. Campbell at Rawalpindi	1993-94
111	for 3rd	D. D. Ebrahim and G. W. Flower at Harare	2002-03
269	for 4th†	G. W. Flower and A. Flower at Harare	1994-95
277*	for 5th†	M. W. Goodwin and A. Flower at Bulawayo	1997-98
72	for 6th	M. H. Dekker and G. J. Whittall at Rawalpindi	1993-94
131	for 7th	G. W. Flower and P. A. Strang at Sheikhupura	1996-97
110	for 8th	G. J. Whittall and B. C. Strang at Harare	1997-98
87	for 9th†	P. A. Strang and B. C. Strang at Sheikhupura	1996-97
29	for 10th	E. A. Brandes and S. G. Peall at Rawalpindi	1993-94

† *Record partnership against all countries.*

TEN WICKETS OR MORE IN A MATCH

For Pakistan (3)

10-155 (7-66, 3-89)	Saqlain Mushtaq, Bulawayo	2002-03
13-135 (7-91, 6-44)†	Waqar Younis, Karachi (DS)	1993-94
10-106 (6-48, 4-58)	Wasim Akram, Faisalabad	1996-97

Note: The best match figures for Zimbabwe are 9-105 (6-90, 3-15) by H. H. Streak at Harare, 1994-95.

† *On first appearance in Pakistan–Zimbabwe Tests.*

PAKISTAN v BANGLADESH

Series notes: Pakistan are the only team who have conceded a first-innings lead to Bangladesh – twice… Bangladesh have batted first in all six Tests between the sides… Inzamam-ul-Haq averages 253 against Bangladesh in two Tests on his home ground at Multan… Pakistan have only been bowled out three times in six Tests, but have dismissed Bangladesh twice in each game… Yousuf Youhana has scored more runs against Bangladesh than anyone else (503)… Danish Kaneria has taken 34 Bangladesh wickets.

	Captains					
Season	*Pakistan*	*Bangladesh*	*T*	*P*	*B*	*D*
2001-02*P*†	Waqar Younis	Naimur Rahman	1	1	0	0
2001-02*B*	Waqar Younis	Khaled Masud	2	2	0	0
2003*P*	Rashid Latif	Khaled Mahmud	3	3	0	0
	In Pakistan		4	4	0	0
	In Bangladesh		2	2	0	0
	Totals		6	6	0	0

P Played in Pakistan. B Played in Bangladesh.

† *This Test was part of the Asian Test Championship.*

> "Kent were without four front-line bowlers, including Sheriyar, who had cut his hand while washing up."
>
> Surrey in 2003, page 698.

HIGHEST INNINGS TOTALS

For Pakistan in Pakistan: 546-3 dec. at Multan 2001-02
in Bangladesh: 490-9 dec. at Dhaka 2001-02

For Bangladesh in Pakistan: 361 at Peshawar 2003
in Bangladesh: 160 at Dhaka 2001-02

LOWEST INNINGS TOTALS

For Pakistan in Pakistan: 175 at Multan 2003

For Bangladesh in Pakistan: 96 at Peshawar 2003
in Bangladesh: 148 at Chittagong (in both innings) 2001-02

DOUBLE-HUNDRED

For Pakistan (1)

204* Yousuf Youhana at Chittagong . 2001-02

Highest individual score for Bangladesh: 119 by Javed Omar at Peshawar, 2003.

INDIVIDUAL HUNDREDS

For Pakistan (12)

2: Abdul Razzaq, Inzamam-ul-Haq, Yasir Hameed, Yousuf Youhana.
1: Mohammad Hafeez, Saeed Anwar, Taufeeq Umar, Younis Khan.

For Bangladesh (2)

1: Habibul Bashar, Javed Omar.

RECORD PARTNERSHIPS FOR EACH WICKET

For Pakistan

168	for 1st	Saeed Anwar and Taufeeq Umar at Multan	2001-02
134	for 2nd	Mohammad Hafeez and Yasir Hameed at Karachi	2003
80	for 3rd	Taufeeq Umar and Inzamam-ul-Haq at Multan	2001-02
165*	for 4th‡	Yousuf Youhana and Abdul Razzaq at Multan	2001-02
64	for 5th	Yousuf Youhana and Rashid Latif at Peshawar	2003
175	for 6th	Abdul Razzaq and Rashid Latif at Dhaka	2001-02
67	for 7th	Abdul Razzaq and Inzamam-ul-Haq at Dhaka	2001-02
99	for 8th	Yousuf Youhana and Saqlain Mushtaq at Chittagong	2001-02
52	for 9th	Inzamam-ul-Haq and Umar Gul at Multan	2003
18*	for 10th	Yousuf Youhana and Danish Kaneria at Chittagong	2001-02

‡ *A total of 288 runs was added between the fall of Pakistan's third wicket and the end of the innings: Inzamam-ul-Haq retired hurt when he and Yousuf Youhana had added 123 runs.*

For Bangladesh

38	for 1st	Mehrab Hossain and Mohammad Ashraful at Dhaka	2001-02
167	for 2nd†	Javed Omar and Habibul Bashar at Peshawar	2003
130	for 3rd†	Javed Omar and Mohammad Ashraful at Peshawar	2003
111	for 4th	Habibul Bashar and Rajin Saleh at Karachi	2003
69	for 5th	Habibul Bashar and Sanwar Hossain at Chittagong	2001-02
62	for 6th	Rajin Saleh and Khaled Masud at Multan	2003
27	for 7th	Aminul Islam and Khaled Masud at Chittagong	2001-02
45	for 8th	Habibul Bashar and Hasibul Hossain at Multan	2001-02
27	for 9th	Hasibul Hossain and Mohammad Sharif at Multan	2001-02
		Fahim Muntasir and Mohammad Sharif at Dhaka	2001-02
21	for 10th	Khaled Masud and Manjurul Islam at Chittagong	2001-02

† *Record partnership against all countries.*

TEN WICKETS OR MORE IN A MATCH

For Pakistan (2)

12-94 (6-42, 6-52)†	Danish Kaneria, Multan	2001-02
10-80 (6-50, 4-30)	Shoaib Akhtar, Peshawar	2003

Note: The best match figures for Bangladesh are 7-105 (4-37, 3-68) by Khaled Mahmud at Multan, 2003.

† *On first appearance in Pakistan–Bangladesh Tests.*

SEVEN WICKETS OR MORE IN AN INNINGS

In addition to those listed above, the following has taken seven wickets or more in an innings:

For Pakistan

7-77 Danish Kaneria, Dhaka. 2001-02

SRI LANKA v ZIMBABWE

Series notes: Zimbabwe have never beaten Sri Lanka... Sri Lanka have won all seven Tests at home to Zimbabwe, but only one of six away... Sri Lanka are yet to win at Bulawayo, which is the only ground where Zimbabwe average more runs per wicket – 40.1 to Sri Lanka's 34.9... Zimbabwe have lost 80% of matches when they have won the toss (four out of five) but only 50% when they have lost the toss (four/eight)... Zimbabwe passed 300 in their first three innings against Sri Lanka; since then they have managed it only once in 20 innings... Sri Lanka have never been dismissed for under 200 in this fixture... M. Muralitharan has taken more wickets in Tests against Zimbabwe than anyone, and needs 27 more to reach 100.

	Captains					
Season	*Sri Lanka*	*Zimbabwe*	*T*	*SL*	*Z*	*D*
1994-95*Z*	A. Ranatunga	A. Flower	3	0	0	3
1996-97*S*	A. Ranatunga	A. D. R. Campbell	2	2	0	0
1997-98*S*	A. Ranatunga	A. D. R. Campbell	2	2	0	0
1999-2000*Z*	S. T. Jayasuriya	A. Flower	3	1	0	2
2001-02*S*	S. T. Jayasuriya	S. V. Carlisle	3	3	0	0
	In Sri Lanka		7	7	0	0
	In Zimbabwe		6	1	0	5
	Totals		13	8	0	5

S Played in Sri Lanka. Z Played in Zimbabwe.

HIGHEST INNINGS TOTALS

For Sri Lanka in Sri Lanka: 586-6 dec. at Colombo (SSC) 2001-02
in Zimbabwe: 432 at Harare 1999-2000

For Zimbabwe in Sri Lanka: 338 at Kandy 1997-98
in Zimbabwe: 462-9 dec. at Bulawayo 1994-95

LOWEST INNINGS TOTALS

For Sri Lanka in Sri Lanka: 225 at Colombo (SSC). 1997-98
in Zimbabwe: 218 at Bulawayo 1994-95

For Zimbabwe in Sri Lanka: 79 at Galle. 2001-02
in Zimbabwe: 174 at Harare. 1999-2000

DOUBLE-HUNDREDS

For Sri Lanka (2)

223 M. S. Atapattu at Kandy . . . . . . 1997-98 | 216* M. S. Atapattu at Bulawayo . . 1999-2000

For Zimbabwe (1)

266 D. L. Houghton at Bulawayo . . . 1994-95

INDIVIDUAL HUNDREDS

For Sri Lanka (14)

3: M. S. Atapattu.
2: S. Ranatunga, H. P. Tillekeratne.
1: R. P. Arnold, P. A. de Silva, T. M. Dilshan, A. P. Gurusinha, S. T. Jayasuriya, T. T. Samaraweera, K. C. Sangakkara.

For Zimbabwe (4)

2: A. Flower, D. L. Houghton.

RECORD PARTNERSHIPS FOR EACH WICKET

For Sri Lanka

85	for 1st	M. S. Atapattu and S. T. Jayasuriya at Bulawayo.	1999-2000
217	for 2nd	A. P. Gurusinha and S. Ranatunga at Harare	1994-95
140	for 3rd	M. S. Atapattu and P. A. de Silva at Kandy	1997-98
178	for 4th	D. P. M. D. Jayawardene and T. M. Dilshan at Harare	1999-2000
114	for 5th	A. P. Gurusinha and H. P. Tillekeratne at Colombo (SSC)	1996-97
189*	for 6th†	P. A. de Silva and A. Ranatunga at Colombo (SSC).	1997-98
136*	for 7th	T. T. Samaraweera and W. P. U. J. C. Vaas at Colombo (SSC)	2001-02
146	for 8th†	T. T. Samaraweera and U. D. U. Chandana at Galle	2001-02
30	for 9th	R. P. Arnold and G. P. Wickremasinghe at Harare	1999-2000
25	for 10th	H. D. P. K. Dharmasena and M. Muralitharan at Bulawayo	1994-95

For Zimbabwe

153 for 1st	S. V. Carlisle and T. R. Gripper at Galle	2001-02
40 for 2nd	G. J. Rennie and M. W. Goodwin at Colombo (SSC)	1997-98
194 for 3rd†	A. D. R. Campbell and D. L. Houghton at Harare	1994-95
121 for 4th	D. L. Houghton and A. Flower at Bulawayo	1994-95
101 for 5th	M. W. Goodwin and A. Flower at Harare	1999-2000
100 for 6th	D. L. Houghton and W. R. James at Bulawayo	1994-95
125 for 7th	A. Flower and G. J. Whittall at Harare	1999-2000
84 for 8th	D. L. Houghton and J. A. Rennie at Bulawayo	1994-95
43 for 9th	J. A. Rennie and S. G. Peall at Bulawayo	1994-95
35 for 10th	T. J. Friend and H. K. Olonga at Kandy	2001-02

† *Record partnership against all countries.*

TEN WICKETS OR MORE IN A MATCH

For Sri Lanka (2)

12-117 (5-23, 7-94)	M. Muralitharan, Kandy	1997-98
13-115 (9-51, 4-64)	M. Muralitharan, Kandy	2001-02

Note: The best match figures for Zimbabwe are 6-112 (2-28, 4-84) by H. H. Streak at Colombo (SSC), 1997-98.

SEVEN WICKETS OR MORE IN AN INNINGS

In addition to those listed above, the following has taken seven wickets or more in an innings:

For Pakistan

7-116 K. R. Pushpakumara, Harare . . . 1994-95

SRI LANKA v BANGLADESH

Series notes: M. Muralitharan has taken all four five-fors in this fixture... Muralitharan has taken 20 wickets in matches between the sides, nearly three times the next best (T. T. Samaraweera and W. R. S. de Silva, with seven each)... In all three Tests, the team winning the toss have fielded... The teams have never met outside Colombo... D. P. M. D. Jayawardene has made 150 (retired out) and nought in his two innings against Bangladesh.

	Captains					
Season	*Sri Lanka*	*Bangladesh*	*T*	*SL*	*B*	*D*
2001-02*S*†	S. T. Jayasuriya	Naimur Rahman	1	1	0	0
2002*S*	S. T. Jayasuriya	Khaled Masud	2	2	0	0
	Totals		3	3	0	0

S Played in Sri Lanka.

† *This Test was part of the Asian Test Championship.*

HIGHEST INNINGS TOTALS

For Sri Lanka: 555-5 dec. at Colombo (SSC) 2001-02

For Bangladesh: 328 at Colombo (SSC) 2001-02

LOWEST INNINGS TOTALS

For Sri Lanka: 373 at Colombo (SSC). 2002

For Bangladesh: 90 at Colombo (SSC) 2001-02

DOUBLE-HUNDREDS

For Sri Lanka (2)

206 P. A. de Silva at Colombo (PSS). 2002 | 201 M. S. Atapattu at Colombo (SSC) 2001-02

Highest score for Bangladesh: 114 by Mohammad Ashraful at Colombo (SSC), 2001-02.

INDIVIDUAL HUNDREDS

For Sri Lanka (5)

1: M. S. Atapattu, P. A. de Silva, S. T. Jayasuriya, D. P. M. D. Jayawardene, M. G. Vandort.

For Bangladesh (1)

1: Mohammad Ashraful.

HUNDRED PARTNERSHIPS

For Sri Lanka

234 for 5th†	P. A. de Silva and S. T. Jayasuriya at Colombo (PSS)	2002
172 for 2nd	M. G. Vandort and M. N. Nawaz at Colombo (SSC)	2002
171 for 3rd	M. S. Atapattu and D. P. M. D. Jayawardene at Colombo (SSC). . . .	2001-02
150 for 4th	K. C. Sangakkara and P. A. de Silva at Colombo (PSS)	2002
144 for 1st	M. S. Atapattu and S. T. Jayasuriya at Colombo (SSC).	2001-02
127 for 5th	S. T. Jayasuriya and T. T. Samaraweera at Colombo (SSC)	2002
125 for 2nd	M. S. Atapattu and K. C. Sangakkara at Colombo (SSC)	2001-02

For Bangladesh

126 for 5th†	Aminul Islam and Mohammad Ashraful at Colombo (SSC).	2001-02

† *Record partnership against all countries.*

TEN WICKETS OR MORE IN A MATCH

For Sri Lanka (2)

10-111 (5-13, 5-98)	M. Muralitharan, Colombo (SSC)	2001-02
10-98 (5-39, 5-59)	M. Muralitharan, Colombo (PSS).	2002

Note: The best match figures for Bangladesh are 4-144 (4-144) by Enamul Haque at Colombo (PSS), 2002.

ZIMBABWE v BANGLADESH

Series notes: Zimbabwe are the only team against whom Bangladesh have avoided defeat in a Test, due to rain... Zimbabwe have passed 400 in the first innings of all four of their Tests against Bangladesh... The team winning the toss have fielded in all the Tests between the sides.

	Captains					
Season	*Zimbabwe*	*Bangladesh*	*T*	*Z*	*B*	*D*
2000-01*Z*	H. H. Streak	Naimur Rahman	2	2	0	0
2001-02*B*	B. A. Murphy[1]	Naimur Rahman	2	1	0	1
	In Zimbabwe		2	2	0	0
	In Bangladesh		2	1	0	1
	Totals		4	3	0	1

Z Played in Zimbabwe. *B Played in Bangladesh.*

Note: The following deputised for the official touring captain:

[1]S. V. Carlisle (Second).

HIGHEST INNINGS TOTALS

For Zimbabwe in Zimbabwe: 457 at Bulawayo 2000-01
in Bangladesh: 542-7 dec. at Chittagong 2001-02

For Bangladesh in Zimbabwe: 266 at Harare. 2000-01
in Bangladesh: 301 at Chittagong 2001-02

LOWEST INNINGS TOTALS

For Zimbabwe in Zimbabwe: 457 at Bulawayo 2000-01
in Bangladesh: 431 at Dhaka. 2001-02

For Bangladesh in Zimbabwe: 168 at Bulawayo. 2000-01
in Bangladesh: 107 at Dhaka 2001-02

HIGHEST INDIVIDUAL INNINGS

For Zimbabwe

119 G. J. Whittall at Bulawayo. 2000-01

For Bangladesh

108 Habibul Bashar at Chittagong. . . 2001-02

INDIVIDUAL HUNDREDS

For Zimbabwe (4)

1: A. Flower, T. R. Gripper, G. J. Whittall, C. B. Wishart.

For Bangladesh (1)

1: Habibul Bashar.

HUNDRED PARTNERSHIPS

For Zimbabwe

149 for 4th	G. J. Whittall and A. Flower at Bulawayo	2000-01
137 for 6th	C. B. Wishart and D. A. Marillier at Dhaka	2001-02
133 for 6th	G. W. Flower and H. H. Streak at Harare	2000-01
123 for 6th‡	C. B. Wishart and D. A. Marillier at Chittagong	2001-02
120 for 6th	G. W. Flower and H. H. Streak at Bulawayo	2000-01
108 for 8th	H. H. Streak and T. J. Friend at Dhaka	2001-02
108 for 1st	D. D. Ebrahim and T. R. Gripper at Chittagong	2001-02

For Bangladesh

122 for 2nd†	Javed Omar and Habibul Bashar at Chittagong	2001-02
114 for 4th†	Mehrab Hossain and Habibul Bashar at Harare	2000-01
102 for 2nd	Javed Omar and Habibul Bashar at Dhaka	2001-02

† *Record partnership against all countries.*
‡ *189 runs were added for Zimbabwe's sixth wicket in two separate partnerships. A. Flower retired hurt after adding 66* with Wishart.*

BEST MATCH BOWLING ANALYSES

For Zimbabwe

8-104 (4-41, 4-63)	G. W. Flower, Chittagong	2001-02

For Bangladesh

6-81 (6-81)	Manjurul Islam, Bulawayo	2000-01

TEST GROUNDS

in chronological order

	City and Ground	*First Test Match*		*Tests*
1	Melbourne, Melbourne Cricket Ground	March 15, 1877	A v E	96
2	London, Kennington Oval	September 6, 1880	E v A	86
3	Sydney, Sydney Cricket Ground (No. 1)	February 17, 1882	A v E	91
4	Manchester, Old Trafford	July 11, 1884	E v A	68
5	London, Lord's	July 21, 1884	E v A	106
6	Adelaide, Adelaide Oval	December 12, 1884	A v E	62
7	Port Elizabeth, St George's Park	March 12, 1889	SA v E	20
8	Cape Town, Newlands	March 25, 1889	SA v E	36
9	Johannesburg, Old Wanderers	March 2, 1896	SA v E	22
	Now the site of Johannesburg Railway Station.			
10	Nottingham, Trent Bridge	June 1, 1899	E v A	50
11	Leeds, Headingley	June 29, 1899	E v A	64
12	Birmingham, Edgbaston	May 29, 1902	E v A	39
13	Sheffield, Bramall Lane	July 3, 1902	E v A	1
	Sheffield United Football Club have built a stand over the cricket pitch.			
14	Durban, Lord's	January 21, 1910	SA v E	4
	Ground destroyed and built on.			
15	Durban, Kingsmead	January 18, 1923	SA v E	31
16	Brisbane, Exhibition Ground	November 30, 1928	A v E	2
	No longer used for cricket.			

	City and Ground	First Test Match		Tests
17	Christchurch, Lancaster Park	January 10, 1930	NZ v E	38
	Ground also known under sponsors' names; currently Jade Stadium.			
18	Bridgetown, Kensington Oval	January 11, 1930	WI v E	40
19	Wellington, Basin Reserve	January 24, 1930	NZ v E	41
20	Port-of-Spain, Queen's Park Oval	February 1, 1930	WI v E	52
21	Auckland, Eden Park	February 17, 1930	NZ v E	44
22	Georgetown, Bourda	February 21, 1930	WI v E	29
23	Kingston, Sabina Park	April 3, 1930	WI v E	38
24	Brisbane, Woolloongabba	November 27, 1931	A v SA	46
25	Bombay, Gymkhana Ground	December 15, 1933	I v E	1
	No longer used for first-class cricket.			
26	Calcutta (*now Kolkata*), Eden Gardens	January 5, 1934	I v E	32
27	Madras (*now Chennai*), Chepauk (Chidambaram Stadium)	February 10, 1934	I v E	26
28	Delhi, Feroz Shah Kotla	November 10, 1948	I v WI	27
29	Bombay, Brabourne Stadium	December 9, 1948	I v WI	17
	Rarely used for first-class cricket.			
30	Johannesburg, Ellis Park	December 27, 1948	SA v E	6
	Mainly a rugby stadium, no longer used for cricket.			
31	Kanpur, Green Park (Modi Stadium)	January 12, 1952	I v E	18
32	Lucknow, University Ground	October 25, 1952	I v P	1
	Ground destroyed, now partly under a river bed.			
33	Dacca (*now Dhaka*), Dacca (now Bangabandhu) Stadium	January 1, 1955	P v I	14
	Originally in East Pakistan, now Bangladesh.			
34	Bahawalpur, Dring (now Bahawal) Stadium	January 15, 1955	P v I	1
	Still used for first-class cricket.			
35	Lahore, Lawrence Gardens (Bagh-i-Jinnah)	January 29, 1955	P v I	3
	Still used for club and occasional first-class matches.			
36	Peshawar, Services Ground	February 13, 1955	P v I	1
	Superseded by new stadium.			
37	Karachi, National Stadium	February 26, 1955	P v I	36
38	Dunedin, Carisbrook	March 11, 1955	NZ v E	10
39	Hyderabad, Fateh Maidan (Lal Bahadur Stadium)	November 19, 1955	I v NZ	3
40	Madras, Corporation Stadium	January 6, 1956	I v NZ	9
	Superseded by rebuilt Chepauk Stadium.			
41	Johannesburg, Wanderers	December 24, 1956	SA v E	25
42	Lahore, Gaddafi Stadium	November 21, 1959	P v A	34
43	Rawalpindi, Pindi Club Ground	March 27, 1965	P v NZ	1
	Superseded by new stadium.			
44	Nagpur, Vidarbha C.A. Ground	October 3, 1969	I v NZ	7
45	Perth, Western Australian C.A. Ground	December 11, 1970	A v E	31
46	Hyderabad, Niaz Stadium	March 16, 1973	P v E	5
47	Bangalore, Karnataka State C.A. Ground (Chinnaswamy Stadium)	November 22, 1974	I v WI	14
48	Bombay (*now Mumbai*), Wankhede Stadium	January 23, 1975	I v WI	19
49	Faisalabad, Iqbal Stadium	October 16, 1978	P v I	21
50	Napier, McLean Park	February 16, 1979	NZ v P	3
51	Multan, Ibn-e-Qasim Bagh Stadium	December 30, 1980	P v WI	1
52	St John's (Antigua), Recreation Ground	March 27, 1981	WI v E	18
53	Colombo, P. Saravanamuttu Stadium	February 17, 1982	SL v E	9
54	Kandy, Asgiriya Stadium	April 22, 1983	SL v A	16
55	Jullundur, Burlton Park	September 24, 1983	I v P	1
56	Ahmedabad, Gujarat Stadium	November 12, 1983	I v WI	7
57	Colombo, Sinhalese Sports Club Ground	March 16, 1984	SL v NZ	23
58	Colombo, Colombo Cricket Club Ground	March 24, 1984	SL v NZ	3
59	Sialkot, Jinnah Stadium	October 27, 1985	P v SL	4
60	Cuttack, Barabati Stadium	January 4, 1987	I v SL	2
61	Jaipur, Sawai Mansingh Stadium	February 21, 1987	I v P	1

	City and Ground	*First Test Match*		*Tests*
62	Hobart, Bellerive Oval	December 16, 1989	A v SL	6
63	Chandigarh, Sector 16 Stadium	November 23, 1990	I v SL	1
	Superseded by Mohali ground.			
64	Hamilton, Seddon Park	February 22, 1991	NZ v SL	12
	Ground also known under various sponsors' names, including Trust Bank Park; currently Westpac Trust Park.			
65	Gujranwala, Municipal Stadium	December 20, 1991	P v SL	1
66	Colombo, R. Premadasa (Khettarama) Stadium	August 28, 1992	SL v A	5
67	Moratuwa, Tyronne Fernando Stadium	September 8, 1992	SL v A	4
68	Harare, Harare Sports Club	October 18, 1992	Z v I	22
69	Bulawayo, Bulawayo Athletic Club	November 1, 1992	Z v NZ	1
	Superseded by Queens Sports Club ground.			
70	Karachi, Defence Stadium	December 1, 1993	P v Z	1
71	Rawalpindi, Rawalpindi Cricket Stadium	December 9, 1993	P v Z	7
72	Lucknow, K. D. "Babu" Singh Stadium	January 18, 1994	I v SL	1
73	Bulawayo, Queens Sports Club	October 20, 1994	Z v SL	13
74	Mohali, Punjab Cricket Association Stadium	December 10, 1994	I v WI	5
75	Peshawar, Arbab Niaz Stadium	September 8, 1995	P v SL	6
76	Centurion (*formerly Verwoerdburg*), Centurion Park	November 16, 1995	SA v E	8
77	Sheikhupura, Municipal Stadium	October 17, 1996	P v Z	2
78	St Vincent, Arnos Vale	June 20, 1997	WI v SL	1
79	Galle, International Stadium	June 3, 1998	SL v NZ	9
80	Springbok Park, Bloemfontein	October 29, 1999	SA v Z	3
	Ground also known under sponsor's name; currently Goodyear Park.			
81	Multan, Multan Cricket Stadium	August 29, 2001	P v B	2
82	Chittagong, Chittagong Stadium	November 15, 2001	B v Z	5
83	Sharjah, Sharjah Cricket Association Stadium	January 31, 2002	P v WI	4
84	St George's, Queen's Park New Stadium	June 28, 2002	WI v NZ	1
85	East London, Buffalo Park	October 18, 2002	SA v B	1
86	Potchefstroom, North West Cricket Stadium	October 25, 2002	SA v B	1
87	Chester-le-Street, Riverside Ground	June 5, 2003	E v Z	1
88	Gros Islet, St Lucia, Beausejour Stadium	June 20, 2003	WI v SL	1
89	Darwin, Marrara Cricket Ground	July 18, 2003	A v B	1
90	Cairns, Bundaberg Rum Stadium	July 25, 2003	A v B	1

LIMITED-OVERS INTERNATIONAL RECORDS

Matches in this section do not have first-class status.

SUMMARY OF LIMITED-OVERS INTERNATIONALS

1970-71 to December 31, 2003

	Opponents	*Matches*						*Won by*						*Tied*	*NR*
			E	*A*	*SA*	*WI*	*NZ*	*I*	*P*	*SL*	*Z*	*B*	*Ass*		
England	Australia	**77**	31	44	–	–	–	–	–	–	–	–	–	1	1
	South Africa	**27**	10	–	17	–	–	–	–	–	–	–	–	–	–
	West Indies	**61**	26	–	–	32	–	–	–	–	–	–	–	–	3
	New Zealand	**52**	25	–	–	–	23	–	–	–	–	–	–	1	3
	India	**48**	23	–	–	–	–	23	–	–	–	–	–	–	2
	Pakistan	**53**	31	–	–	–	–	–	21	–	–	–	–	–	1
	Sri Lanka	**31**	18	–	–	–	–	–	–	13	–	–	–	–	–
	Zimbabwe	**25**	16	–	–	–	–	–	–	–	8	–	–	–	1
	Bangladesh	**4**	4	–	–	–	–	–	–	–	–	0	–	–	–
	Associates	**7**	7	–	–	–	–	–	–	–	–	–	0	–	–
Australia	South Africa	**56**	–	29	24	–	–	–	–	–	–	–	–	3	–
	West Indies	**105**	–	47	–	55	–	–	–	–	–	–	–	2	1
	New Zealand	**89**	–	61	–	–	25	–	–	–	–	–	–	–	3
	India	**73**	–	44	–	–	–	26	–	–	–	–	–	–	3
	Pakistan	**67**	–	37	–	–	–	–	26	–	–	–	–	1	3
	Sri Lanka	**50**	–	33	–	–	–	–	–	15	–	–	–	–	2
	Zimbabwe	**20**	–	19	–	–	–	–	–	–	1	–	–	–	–
	Bangladesh	**6**	–	6	–	–	–	–	–	–	–	0	–	–	–
	Associates	**8**	–	8	–	–	–	–	–	–	–	–	0	–	–
South Africa	West Indies	**27**	–	–	18	9	–	–	–	–	–	–	–	–	–
	New Zealand	**34**	–	–	22	–	9	–	–	–	–	–	–	–	3
	India	**46**	–	–	28	–	–	16	–	–	–	–	–	–	2
	Pakistan	**41**	–	–	28	–	–	–	13	–	–	–	–	–	–
	Sri Lanka	**34**	–	–	18	–	–	–	–	14	–	–	–	1	1
	Zimbabwe	**18**	–	–	15	–	–	–	–	–	2	–	–	–	1
	Bangladesh	**6**	–	–	6	–	–	–	–	–	–	0	–	–	0
	Associates	**11**	–	–	11	–	–	–	–	–	–	–	0	–	–
West Indies	New Zealand	**36**	–	–	–	22	11	–	–	–	–	–	–	–	3
	India	**76**	–	–	–	46	–	28	–	–	–	–	–	1	1
	Pakistan	**98**	–	–	–	60	–	–	36	–	–	–	–	2	–
	Sri Lanka	**39**	–	–	–	23	–	–	–	15	–	–	–	–	1
	Zimbabwe	**24**	–	–	–	17	–	–	–	–	7	–	–	–	–
	Bangladesh	**7**	–	–	–	5	–	–	–	–	–	0	–	–	2
	Associates	**8**	–	–	–	7	–	–	–	–	–	–	1	–	–
New Zealand	India	**72**	–	–	–	–	33	35	–	–	–	–	–	–	4
	Pakistan	**72**	–	–	–	–	24	–	46	–	–	–	–	1	1
	Sri Lanka	**55**	–	–	–	–	28	–	–	24	–	–	–	1	2
	Zimbabwe	**26**	–	–	–	–	17	–	–	–	7	–	–	1	1
	Bangladesh	**4**	–	–	–	–	4	–	–	–	–	0	–	–	–
	Associates	**5**	–	–	–	–	5	–	–	–	–	–	0	–	–
India	Pakistan	**86**	–	–	–	–	–	30	52	–	–	–	–	–	4
	Sri Lanka	**76**	–	–	–	–	–	40	–	29	–	–	–	–	7
	Zimbabwe	**43**	–	–	–	–	–	33	–	–	8	–	–	2	–
	Bangladesh	**10**	–	–	–	–	–	10	–	–	–	0	–	–	–
	Associates	**16**	–	–	–	–	–	14	–	–	–	–	2	–	–
Pakistan	Sri Lanka	**99**	–	–	–	–	–	–	60	36	–	–	–	1	2
	Zimbabwe	**32**	–	–	–	–	–	–	28	–	2	–	–	1	1
	Bangladesh	**16**	–	–	–	–	–	–	15	–	–	1	–	–	–
	Associates	**12**	–	–	–	–	–	–	12	–	–	–	0	–	–
Sri Lanka	Zimbabwe	**29**	–	–	–	–	–	–	–	22	6	–	–	–	1
	Bangladesh	**10**	–	–	–	–	–	–	–	10	–	0	–	–	–
	Associates	**7**	–	–	–	–	–	–	–	6	–	–	1	–	–
Zimbabwe	Bangladesh	**10**	–	–	–	–	–	–	–	–	10	0	–	–	–
	Associates	**18**	–	–	–	–	–	–	–	–	15	–	1	–	2
Bangladesh	Associates	**9**	–	–	–	–	–	–	–	–	–	2	7	–	–
Associates	Associates	**3**	–	–	–	–	–	–	–	–	–	–	3	–	–
		2,074	191	328	187	276	179	255	309	184	66	3	15	19	62

Note: Current Associate Members of ICC who have played one-day internationals are Canada, East Africa, Holland, Kenya, Namibia, Scotland and United Arab Emirates. Sri Lanka, Zimbabwe and Bangladesh also played one-day internationals before being given Test status; these are not included among the Associates' results.

RESULTS SUMMARY OF LIMITED-OVERS INTERNATIONALS

1970-71 to December 31, 2003 (2,074 matches)

	Matches	*Won*	*Lost*	*Tied*	*No Result*	*% Won (excl. NR)*
South Africa	300	187	102	4	7	64.50
Australia	551	328	203	7	13	61.61
West Indies	481	276	189	5	11	59.25
Pakistan	576	309	249	6	12	55.31
England	385	191	181	2	11	51.33
India	546	255	265	3	23	49.04
Sri Lanka	430	184	227	3	16	44.80
New Zealand	445	179	242	4	20	42.58
Zimbabwe	245	66	168	4	7	28.57
Kenya	64	12	50	–	2	19.35
United Arab Emirates	7	1	6	–	–	14.28
Canada	9	1	8	–	–	11.11
Holland	13	1	12	–	–	7.69
Bangladesh	82	3	77	–	2	3.75
East Africa	3	–	3	–	–	–
Scotland	5	–	5	–	–	–
Namibia	6	–	6	–	–	–

Note: Matches abandoned without a ball bowled are not included. Those called off after play began are counted as official internationals in their own right, even when replayed, according to the ICC's ruling. In the percentages of matches won, ties are counted as half a win.

BATTING RECORDS

MOST RUNS

		M	*I*	*NO*	*R*	*HS*	*100s*	*Avge*
1	**S. R. Tendulkar (India)**	**321**	**312**	**31**	**12,685**	**186***	**36**	**45.14**
2	M. Azharuddin (India)	334	308	54	9,378	153*	7	36.92
3	**Inzamam-ul-Haq (Pakistan)**	**302**	**282**	**42**	**9,356**	**137***	**8**	**38.98**
4	**P. A. de Silva (Sri Lanka)**	**308**	**296**	**30**	**9,284**	**145**	**11**	**34.90**
5	**S. T. Jayasuriya (Sri Lanka)**	**308**	**300**	**13**	**9,172**	**189**	**16**	**31.95**
6	**S. C. Ganguly (India)**	**235**	**227**	**19**	**8,967**	**183**	**22**	**43.11**
7	**Saeed Anwar (Pakistan)**	**247**	**244**	**19**	**8,824**	**194**	**20**	**39.21**
8	D. L. Haynes (West Indies)	238	237	28	8,648	152*	17	41.37
9	M. E. Waugh (Australia)	244	236	20	8,500	173	18	39.35
10	**B. C. Lara (West Indies)**	**224**	**219**	**23**	**8,437**	**169**	**18**	**43.04**
11	S. R. Waugh (Australia)	325	288	58	7,569	120*	3	32.90
12	A. Ranatunga (Sri Lanka)	269	255	47	7,456	131*	4	35.84
13	Javed Miandad (Pakistan)	233	218	41	7,381	119*	8	41.70
14	Salim Malik (Pakistan)	283	256	38	7,170	102	5	32.88
15	**G. Kirsten (South Africa)**	**185**	**185**	**19**	**6,798**	**188***	**13**	**40.95**
16	**A. Flower (Zimbabwe)**	**213**	**208**	**16**	**6,786**	**145**	**4**	**35.34**
17	**R. Dravid (India)**	**214**	**196**	**25**	**6,726**	**153**	**8**	**39.33**
18	I. V. A. Richards (West Indies)	187	167	24	6,721	189*	11	47.00
19	**M. G. Bevan (Australia)**	**220**	**184**	**65**	**6,634**	**108***	**6**	**55.74**
20	**R. T. Ponting (Australia)**	**185**	**181**	**25**	**6,582**	**145**	**15**	**42.19**
21	**M. S. Atapattu (Sri Lanka)**	**201**	**198**	**24**	**6,567**	**132***	**10**	**37.74**
22	Ijaz Ahmed, sen. (Pakistan)	250	232	29	6,564	139*	10	32.33
23	A. R. Border (Australia)	273	252	39	6,524	127*	3	30.62

	M	I	NO	R	HS	100s	Avge
24 J. H. Kallis (South Africa)	**185**	**176**	**31**	**6,497**	**125***	**10**	**44.80**
25 G. W. Flower (Zimbabwe)	**209**	**203**	**18**	**6,277**	**142***	**6**	**33.92**
26 R. B. Richardson (West Indies)	224	217	30	6,249	122	5	33.41
27 D. M. Jones (Australia)	164	161	25	6,068	145	7	44.61

Note: The leading aggregates for other Test-playing countries are:

	M	I	NO	R	HS	100s	Avge
S. P. Fleming (New Zealand)	**207**	**199**	**17**	**5,618**	**134***	**4**	**30.86**
A. J. Stewart (England)	**170**	**162**	**14**	**4,677**	**116**	**4**	**31.60**
Akram Khan (Bangladesh)	**44**	**44**	**2**	**976**	**65**	**0**	**23.23**

Bold type denotes those who have played limited-overs internationals since the start of 2002-03.

BEST CAREER STRIKE-RATES BY BATSMEN

(Runs per 100 balls. Qualification: 500 runs)

SR		Position	M	I	R	Avge
104.88	B. L. Cairns (NZ)	9/8	78	65	987	16.72
101.48	**Shahid Afridi (P)**	**2**	**176**	**171**	**3,887**	**23.70**
100.58	**R. L. Powell (WI)**	**6**	**79**	**72**	**1,550**	**25.40**
99.43	I. D. S. Smith (NZ)	8	98	77	1,055	17.29
95.94	**V. Sehwag (I)**	**2**	**79**	**77**	**2,460**	**34.64**
95.07	Kapil Dev (I)	7/6	225	198	3,783	23.79
92.43	**A. C. Gilchrist (A)**	**2**	**177**	**171**	**5,782**	**35.04**
90.64	**L. Klusener (SA)**	**8/3**	**154**	**124**	**3,381**	**43.34**
90.20	I. V. A. Richards (WI)	4	187	167	6,721	47.00

Note: Position means a batsman's most usual position in the batting order.

Bold type denotes those who have played limited-overs internationals since the start of 2002-03.

HIGHEST INDIVIDUAL INNINGS

194	Saeed Anwar	Pakistan v India at Chennai	1996-97
189*	I. V. A. Richards	West Indies v England at Manchester	1984
189	S. T. Jayasuriya	Sri Lanka v India at Sharjah	2000-01
188*	G. Kirsten	South Africa v UAE at Rawalpindi	1995-96
186*	S. R. Tendulkar	India v New Zealand at Hyderabad	1999-2000
183	S. C. Ganguly	India v Sri Lanka at Taunton	1999
181	I. V. A. Richards	West Indies v Sri Lanka at Karachi	1987-88
175*	Kapil Dev	India v Zimbabwe at Tunbridge Wells	1983
173	M. E. Waugh	Australia v West Indies at Melbourne	2000-01
172*	C. B. Wishart	Zimbabwe v Namibia at Harare	2002-03
171*	G. M. Turner	New Zealand v East Africa at Birmingham	1975
169*	D. J. Callaghan	South Africa v New Zealand at Verwoerdburg	1994-95
169	B. C. Lara	West Indies v Sri Lanka at Sharjah	1995-96
167*	R. A. Smith	England v Australia at Birmingham	1993
161	A. C. Hudson	South Africa v Holland at Rawalpindi	1995-96
159*	D. Mongia	India v Zimbabwe at Guwahati	2001-02
158	D. I. Gower	England v New Zealand at Brisbane	1982-83
154	A. C. Gilchrist	Australia v Sri Lanka at Melbourne	1998-99
153*	I. V. A. Richards	West Indies v Australia at Melbourne	1979-80
153*	M. Azharuddin	India v Zimbabwe at Cuttack	1997-98
153*	S. C. Ganguly	India v New Zealand at Gwalior	1999-2000
153*	C. H. Gayle	West Indies v Zimbabwe at Bulawayo	2003-04
153	B. C. Lara	West Indies v Pakistan at Sharjah	1993-94
153	R. Dravid	India v New Zealand at Hyderabad	1999-2000
153	H. H. Gibbs	South Africa v Bangladesh at Potchefstroom	2002-03
152*	D. L. Haynes	West Indies v India at Georgetown	1988-89

152	C. H. Gayle	West Indies v Kenya at Nairobi	2001
152	S. R. Tendulkar	India v Namibia at Pietermaritzburg	2002-03
151*	S. T. Jayasuriya	Sri Lanka v India at Mumbai	1996-97
150	S. Chanderpaul	West Indies v South Africa at East London	1998-99

Note: The highest individual score for Bangladesh is:

101	Mehrab Hossain	Bangladesh v Zimbabwe at Dhaka	1998-99

MOST HUNDREDS

		Opponents										
Total		*E*	*A*	*SA*	*WI*	*NZ*	*I*	*P*	*SL*	*Z*	*B*	*Ass*
36	**S. R. Tendulkar (India)**	**1**	**7**	**3**	**2**	**4**	–	**2**	**7**	**5**	**0**	**5**
22	**S. C. Ganguly (India)**	**1**	**1**	**3**	**0**	**3**	–	**2**	**4**	**3**	**1**	**4**
20	**Saeed Anwar (Pakistan)**	**0**	**1**	**0**	**2**	**4**	**4**	–	**7**	**2**	**0**	**0**
18	**B. C. Lara (West Indies)**	**1**	**3**	**3**	–	**2**	**0**	**4**	**2**	**1**	**1**	**1**
18	M. E. Waugh (Australia)	1	–	2	3	3	3	1	1	3	0	1
17	D. L. Haynes (West Indies)	2	6	0	–	2	2	4	1	0	–	–
16	**S. T. Jayasuriya (Sri Lanka)**	**2**	**1**	**0**	**0**	**4**	**4**	**3**	–	**1**	**1**	**0**
15	**R. R. Ponting (Australia)**	**2**	–	**1**	**1**	**1**	**4**	**1**	**3**	**1**	**1**	**0**
13	**N. J. Astle (New Zealand)**	**2**	**1**	**1**	**0**	–	**4**	**2**	**0**	**3**	**0**	**0**
13	**G. Kirsten (South Africa)**	**1**	**2**	–	**0**	**2**	**4**	**2**	**0**	**0**	**0**	**2**
12	**H. H. Gibbs (South Africa)**	**0**	**1**	–	**3**	**1**	**2**	**1**	**1**	**1**	**1**	**1**
11	**P. A. de Silva (Sri Lanka)**	**0**	**2**	**0**	**0**	**0**	**3**	**3**	–	**2**	**0**	**1**
11	C. G. Greenidge (West Indies)	0	1	–	–	3	3	2	1	1	–	–
11	I. V. A. Richards (West Indies)	3	3	–	–	1	3	0	1	0	–	–
10	**M. S. Atapattu (Sri Lanka)**	**1**	**1**	**2**	**0**	**0**	**2**	**2**	–	**1**	**0**	**1**
10	Ijaz Ahmed, sen. (Pakistan)	1	1	2	0	0	2	–	1	2	1	0
10	**J. H. Kallis (South Africa)**	**1**	**1**	–	**1**	**3**	**0**	**1**	**2**	**1**	**0**	**0**

Note: Ass = Associate Members.

Bold type denotes those who have played limited-overs internationals since the start of 2002-03. Dashes indicate that a player did not play against the country concerned.

HIGHEST PARTNERSHIP FOR EACH WICKET

258	for 1st	S. C. Ganguly and S. R. Tendulkar	I v K	Paarl	2001-02
331	for 2nd	S. R. Tendulkar and R. Dravid	I v NZ	Hyderabad	1999-2000
237*	for 3rd	R. Dravid and S. R. Tendulkar	I v K	Bristol	1999
275*	for 4th	M. Azharuddin and A. Jadeja	I v Z	Cuttack	1997-98
223	for 5th	M. Azharuddin and A. Jadeja	I v SL	Colombo (RPS)	1997-98
161	for 6th	M. O. Odumbe and A. V. Vadher	K v SL	Southampton	1999
130	for 7th	A. Flower and H. H. Streak	Z v E	Harare	2001-02
119	for 8th	P. R. Reiffel and S. K. Warne	A v SA	Port Elizabeth	1993-94
126*	for 9th	Kapil Dev and S. M. H. Kirmani	I v Z	Tunbridge Wells	1983
106*	for 10th	I. V. A. Richards and M. A. Holding	WI v E	Manchester	1984

BOWLING RECORDS

MOST WICKETS

		M	*Balls*	*R*	*W*	*BB*	*4W/i*	*Avge*
1	**Wasim Akram (Pakistan)**	**356**	**18,186**	**11,812**	**502**	**5-15**	**23**	**23.52**
2	**Waqar Younis (Pakistan)**	**262**	**12,698**	**9,919**	**416**	**7-36**	**27**	**23.84**
3	**M. Muralitharan (Sri Lanka)**	**224**	**12,123**	**7,647**	**343**	**7-30**	**16**	**22.29**
4	**J. Srinath (India)**	**229**	**11,935**	**8,847**	**315**	**5-23**	**10**	**28.08**
5	**A. Kumble (India)**	**246**	**13,137**	**9,303**	**313**	**6-12**	**10**	**29.72**
6	**S. K. Warne (Australia)**	**193**	**10,600**	**7,514**	**291**	**5-33**	**13**	**25.82**

		M	Balls	R	W	BB	4W/i	Avge
7	**Saqlain Mushtaq (Pakistan)**	**169**	**8,770**	**6,275**	**288**	**5-20**	**17**	**21.78**
8	**S. M. Pollock (South Africa)**	**203**	**10,648**	**6,645**	**287**	**6-35**	**14**	**23.15**
9	**W. P. U. J. C. Vaas (Sri Lanka)**	**228**	**11,134**	**7,714**	**285**	**8-19**	**7**	**27.06**
10	**G. D. McGrath (Australia)**	**185**	**9,784**	**6,356**	**284**	**7-15**	**14**	**22.38**
11	**A. A. Donald (South Africa)**	**164**	**8,561**	**5,926**	**272**	**6-23**	**13**	**21.78**
12	Kapil Dev (India)	225	11,202	6,945	253	5-43	4	27.45
13	**S. T. Jayasuriya (Sri Lanka)**	**308**	**11,296**	**9,048**	**251**	**6-29**	**9**	**36.04**
14	C. A. Walsh (West Indies)	205	10,822	6,918	227	5-1	7	30.47
15	C. E. L. Ambrose (West Indies)	176	9,353	5,429	225	5-17	10	24.12
16	**H. H. Streak (Zimbabwe)**	**172**	**8,587**	**6,474**	**212**	**5-32**	**7**	**30.53**
17	C. J. McDermott (Australia)	138	7,461	5,018	203	5-44	5	24.71

Note: The most wickets for other Test-playing countries are:

	M	Balls	R	W	BB	4W/i	Avge
C. Z. Harris (New Zealand)	**238**	**10,313**	**7,374**	**199**	**5-42**	**3**	**37.05**
D. Gough (England)	**121**	**6,589**	**4,694**	**188**	**5-44**	**10**	**24.96**
Khaled Mahmud (Bangladesh)	**53**	**2,322**	**1,997**	**43**	**3-31**	**0**	**46.44**
Mohammad Rafiq (Bangladesh)	**54**	**2,624**	**2,084**	**43**	**3-56**	**0**	**48.46**

Bold type denotes those who have played limited-overs internationals since the start of 2002-03.

BEST CAREER STRIKE-RATES BY BOWLERS

(Balls per wicket. Qualification: 1,500 balls)

SR		M	Balls	W	BB	4W/i	Avge
27.42	**B. Lee (A)**	**73**	**3,757**	**137**	**5-27**	**9**	**21.43**
28.45	**Shoaib Akhtar (P)**	**95**	**4,410**	**155**	**6-16**	**6**	**21.41**
29.38	G. I. Allott (NZ)	31	1,528	52	4-35	4	23.21
29.58	L. S. Pascoe (A)	29	1,568	53	5-30	5	20.11
29.75	**Mohammad Sami (P)**	**40**	**1,934**	**65**	**5-10**	**4**	**22.98**
30.45	**Saqlain Mushtaq (P)**	**169**	**8,770**	**288**	**5-20**	**17**	**21.78**
30.52	**Waqar Younis (P)**	**262**	**12,698**	**416**	**7-36**	**27**	**23.84**

Bold type denotes those who have played limited-overs internationals since the start of 2002-03.

BEST CAREER ECONOMY RATES

(Runs per six balls. Qualification: 50 wickets)

ER		M	Balls	R	W	BB	Avge
3.09	J. Garner (WI)	98	5,330	2,752	146	5-31	18.84
3.28	R. G. D. Willis (E)	64	3,595	1,968	80	4-11	24.60
3.30	R. J. Hadlee (NZ)	115	6,182	3,407	158	5-25	21.56
3.32	M. A. Holding (WI)	102	5,473	3,034	142	5-26	21.36
3.40	A. M. E. Roberts (WI)	56	3,123	1,771	87	5-22	20.35
3.48	C. E. L. Ambrose (WI)	176	9,353	5,429	225	5-17	24.12

BEST BOWLING ANALYSES

8-19	W. P. U. J. C. Vaas	Sri Lanka v Zimbabwe at Colombo (SSC)	2001-02
7-15	G. D. McGrath	Australia v Namibia at Potchefstroom	2002-03
7-20	A. J. Bichel	Australia v England at Port Elizabeth	2002-03
7-30	M. Muralitharan	Sri Lanka v India at Sharjah	2000-01

7-36	Waqar Younis	Pakistan v England at Leeds	2001
7-37	Aqib Javed	Pakistan v India at Sharjah	1991-92
7-51	W. W. Davis	West Indies v Australia at Leeds	1983
6-12	A. Kumble	India v West Indies at Calcutta	1993-94
6-14	G. J. Gilmour	Australia v England at Leeds	1975
6-14	Imran Khan	Pakistan v India at Sharjah	1984-85
6-15	C. E. H. Croft	West Indies v England at St Vincent	1980-81
6-16	Shoaib Akhtar	Pakistan v New Zealand at Karachi	2002
6-18	Azhar Mahmood	Pakistan v West Indies at Sharjah	1999-2000
6-19	H. K. Olonga	Zimbabwe v England at Cape Town	1999-2000
6-20	B. C. Strang	Zimbabwe v Bangladesh at Nairobi (Aga Khan)	1997-98
6-22	F. H. Edwards*	West Indies v Zimbabwe at Harare	2003-04
6-23	A. A. Donald	South Africa v Kenya at Nairobi (Gymkhana)	1996-97
6-23	A. Nehra	India v England at Durban	2002-03
6-23	S. E. Bond	New Zealand v Australia at Port Elizabeth	2002-03
6-25	S. B. Styris	New Zealand v West Indies at Port-of-Spain	2002
6-25	W. P. U. J. C. Vaas	Sri Lanka v Bangladesh at Pietermaritzburg	2002-03
6-26	Waqar Younis	Pakistan v Sri Lanka at Sharjah	1989-90
6-29	B. P. Patterson	West Indies v India at Nagpur	1987-88
6-29	S. T. Jayasuriya	Sri Lanka v England at Moratuwa	1992-93
6-30	Waqar Younis	Pakistan v New Zealand at Auckland	1993-94
6-35	S. M. Pollock	South Africa v West Indies at East London	1998-99
6-35	Abdul Razzaq	Pakistan v Bangladesh at Dhaka	2001-02
6-39	K. H. MacLeay	Australia v India at Nottingham	1983
6-41	I. V. A. Richards	West Indies v India at Delhi	1989-90
6-44	Waqar Younis	Pakistan v New Zealand at Sharjah	1996-97
6-49	L. Klusener	South Africa v Sri Lanka at Lahore	1997-98
6-50	A. H. Gray	West Indies v Australia at Port-of-Spain	1990-91
6-59	Waqar Younis	Pakistan v Australia at Nottingham	2001

* *Edwards is the first bowler to take six wickets on debut.*

Note: The best analyses for other Test-playing countries are:

5-15	M. A. Ealham	England v Zimbabwe at Kimberley	1999-2000
4-36	Saiful Islam	Bangladesh v Sri Lanka at Sharjah	1994-95

HAT-TRICKS

Jalal-ud-Din	Pakistan v Australia at Hyderabad	1982-83
B. A. Reid	Australia v New Zealand at Sydney	1985-86
Chetan Sharma	India v New Zealand at Nagpur	1987-88
Wasim Akram	Pakistan v West Indies at Sharjah	1989-90
Wasim Akram	Pakistan v Australia at Sharjah	1989-90
Kapil Dev	India v Sri Lanka at Calcutta	1990-91
Aqib Javed	Pakistan v India at Sharjah	1991-92
D. K. Morrison	New Zealand v India at Napier	1993-94
Waqar Younis	Pakistan v New Zealand at East London	1994-95
Saqlain Mushtaq†	Pakistan v Zimbabwe at Peshawar	1996-97
E. A. Brandes	Zimbabwe v England at Harare	1996-97
A. M. Stuart	Australia v Pakistan at Melbourne	1996-97
Saqlain Mushtaq	Pakistan v Zimbabwe at The Oval	1999
W. P. U. J. C. Vaas	Sri Lanka v Zimbabwe at Colombo (SSC)	2001-02
Mohammad Sami	Pakistan v West Indies at Sharjah	2001-02
W. P. U. J. C. Vaas‡	Sri Lanka v Bangladesh at Pietermaritzburg	2002-03
B. Lee	Austraia v Kenya at Durban	2002-03
J. M. Anderson	England v Pakistan at The Oval	2003

† *Four wickets in five balls.* ‡ *The first three balls of the match.*

WICKET-KEEPING AND FIELDING RECORDS

MOST DISMISSALS IN AN INNINGS

6 (all ct)	A. C. Gilchrist	Australia v South Africa at Cape Town	1999-2000
6 (all ct)	A. J. Stewart	England v Zimbabwe at Manchester	2000
6 (5ct, 1st)	R. D. Jacobs	West Indies v Sri Lanka at Colombo (RPS)	2001-02
6 (5ct, 1st)	A. C. Gilchrist	Australia v England at Sydney	2002-03
6 (all ct)	A. C. Gilchrist	Australia v Namibia at Potchefstroom	2002-03

MOST DISMISSALS

			M	*Ct*	*St*
1	**293**	**A. C. Gilchrist (Australia)**	**177**	**256**	**37**
2	**260**	**Moin Khan (Pakistan)**	**195**	**192**	**68**
3	**244**	**M. V. Boucher (South Africa)**	**160**	**233**	**11**
4	234	I. A. Healy (Australia)	168	195	39
5	**220**	**Rashid Latif (Pakistan)**	**166**	**182**	**38**
6	**205**	**R. S. Kaluwitharana (Sri Lanka)**	**184**	**131**	**74**
7	204	P. J. L. Dujon (West Indies)	169	183	21
8	**172**	**R. D. Jacobs (West Indies)**	**128**	**145**	**27**
9	165	D. J. Richardson (South Africa)	122	148	17
	165	**A. Flower (Zimbabwe)**	**186**	**133**	**32**
11	**163**	**A. J. Stewart (England)**	**138**	**148**	**15**
12	154	N. R. Mongia (India)	140	110	44
13	136	A. C. Parore (New Zealand)	150	111	25
14	124	R. W. Marsh (Australia)	92	120	4
15	103	Salim Yousuf (Pakistan)	86	81	22

Notes: The most for Bangladesh is **61** (48 ct, 13 st) in 69 matches by **Khaled Masud.**

A. J. Stewart's record excludes 11 catches taken in 32 limited-overs internationals when not keeping wicket; A. C. Parore's excludes 5 in 29; A. Flower's 8 in 27; and R. S. Kaluwitharana's 1 in 3. R. Dravid (India) has made 137 dismissals (126 ct, 11 st) in 214 limited-overs internationals but only 61 (50 ct, 11 st) in 52 as wicket-keeper (including one where he took over during the match).

Bold type denotes those who have played limited-overs internationals since the start of 2002-03

MOST CATCHES IN AN INNINGS

(Excluding wicket-keepers)

5	J. N. Rhodes	South Africa v West Indies at Bombay	1993-94
4	Salim Malik	Pakistan v New Zealand at Sialkot	1984-85
4	S. M. Gavaskar	India v Pakistan at Sharjah	1984-85
4	R. B. Richardson	West Indies v England at Birmingham	1991
4	K. C. Wessels	South Africa v West Indies at Kingston	1991-92
4	M. A. Taylor	Australia v West Indies at Sydney	1992-93
4	C. L. Hooper	West Indies v Pakistan at Durban	1992-93
4	K. R. Rutherford	New Zealand v India at Napier	1994-95
4	P. V. Simmons	West Indies v Sri Lanka at Sharjah	1995-96
4	M. Azharuddin	India v Pakistan at Toronto	1997-98
4	S. R. Tendulkar	India v Pakistan at Dhaka	1997-98
4	R. Dravid	India v West Indies at Toronto	1999-2000
4	G. J. Whittall	Zimbabwe v England at The Oval	2000
4	C. Z. Harris	New Zealand v India at Colombo (RPS)	2001
4	Younis Khan	Pakistan v Zimbabwe at Harare	2002-03
4	M. Kaif	India v Sri Lanka at Johannesburg	2002-03

Note: While fielding as substitute, J. G. Bracewell held 4 catches for New Zealand v Australia at Adelaide, 1980-81.

MOST CATCHES

Ct	M	
156	334	M. Azharuddin (India)
127	273	A. R. Border (Australia)
120	**227**	**C. L. Hooper (West Indies)**
111	325	S. R. Waugh (Australia)
109	213	R. S. Mahanama (Sri Lanka)
108	244	M. E. Waugh (Australia)
105	**245**	**J. N. Rhodes (South Africa)**
102	**308**	**S. T. Jayasuriya (Sri Lanka)**
100	187	I. V. A. Richards (West Indies)

Most catches for other Test-playing countries:

Ct	M	
99	**207**	**S. P. Fleming (New Zealand)**
93	**302**	**Inzamam-ul-Haq (Pakistan)**
83	**209**	**G. W. Flower (Zimbabwe)**
64	120	G. A. Hick (England)
13	39	Aminul Islam (Bangladesh)
13	**54**	**Mohammad Rafiq (Bangladesh)**

Bold type denotes those who have played limited-overs internationals since the start of 2002-03.

TEAM RECORDS

HIGHEST INNINGS TOTALS

398-5	(50 overs)	Sri Lanka v Kenya at Kandy	1995-96
376-2	(50 overs)	India v New Zealand at Hyderabad	1999-2000
373-6	(50 overs)	India v Sri Lanka at Taunton	1999
371-9	(50 overs)	Pakistan v Sri Lanka at Nairobi (Gymkhana)	1996-97
363-3	(50 overs)	South Africa v Zimbabwe at Bulawayo	2001-02
363-7	(55 overs)	England v Pakistan at Nottingham	1992
360-4	(50 overs)	West Indies v Sri Lanka at Karachi	1987-88
359-2	(50 overs)	Australia v India at Johannesburg	2002-03
354-3	(50 overs)	South Africa v Kenya at Cape Town	2001-02
353-5	(50 overs)	India v New Zealand at Hyderabad	2003-04
351-3	(50 overs)	India v Kenya at Paarl	2001-02
349-6	(50 overs)	Australia v New Zealand at Auckland	1999-2000
349-9	(50 overs)	Sri Lanka v Pakistan at Singapore	1995-96
349-9	(50 overs)	New Zealand v India at Rajkot	1999-2000
348-8	(50 overs)	New Zealand v India at Nagpur	1995-96
347-2	(50 overs)	Australia v India at Bangalore	2003-04
347-3	(50 overs)	Kenya v Bangladesh at Nairobi (Gymkhana)	1997-98
347-6	(50 overs)	West Indies v Zimbabwe at Bulawayo	2003-04
344-5	(50 overs)	Pakistan v Zimbabwe at Bulawayo	2002-03
343-5	(50 overs)	Sri Lanka v Australia at Sydney	2002-03
340-2	(50 overs)	Zimbabwe v Namibia at Harare	2002-03

Note: The highest total by Bangladesh is:

272-8	(50 overs)	Bangladesh v Zimbabwe at Bulawayo	2000-01

HIGHEST TOTALS BATTING SECOND

330-7	(49.1 overs)	Australia v South Africa at Port Elizabeth (*Won by 3 wickets*)	2001-02
329	(49.3 overs)	Sri Lanka v West Indies at Sharjah (*Lost by 4 runs*)	1995-96
326-8	(49.3 overs)	India v England at Lord's (*Won by 2 wickets*)	2002
325-5	(47.4 overs)	India v West Indies at Ahmedabad (*Won by 5 wickets*)	2002-03
316-7	(47.5 overs)	India v Pakistan at Dhaka (*Won by 3 wickets*)	1997-98
316-4	(48.5 overs)	Australia v Pakistan at Lahore (*Won by 6 wickets*)	1998-99
315	(49.4 overs)	Pakistan v Sri Lanka at Singapore (*Lost by 34 runs*)	1995-96

HIGHEST MATCH AGGREGATES

664-19	(99.4 overs)	Pakistan v Sri Lanka at Singapore	1995-96
662-17	(99.3 overs)	Sri Lanka v West Indies at Sharjah	1995-96
660-19	(99.5 overs)	Pakistan v Sri Lanka at Nairobi (Gymkhana)	1996-97
656-10	(99.1 overs)	South Africa v Australia at Port Elizabeth	2001-02
655-19	(97 overs)	India v New Zealand at Rajkot	1999-2000
652-12	(100 overs)	Sri Lanka v Kenya at Kandy	1995-96
651-13	(99.3 overs)	England v India at Lord's	2002
650-15	(100 overs)	New Zealand v Australia at Auckland	1999-2000

LOWEST INNINGS TOTALS

36	(18.4 overs)	Canada v Sri Lanka at Paarl	2002-03
38	(15.4 overs)	Zimbabwe v Sri Lanka at Colombo (SSC)	2001-02
43	(19.5 overs)	Pakistan v West Indies at Cape Town	1992-93
45	(40.3 overs)	Canada v England at Manchester	1979
45	(14 overs)	Namibia v Australia at Potchefstroom	2002-03
54	(26.3 overs)	India v Sri Lanka at Sharjah	2000-01
55	(28.3 overs)	Sri Lanka v West Indies at Sharjah	1986-87
63	(25.5 overs)	India v Australia at Sydney	1980-81
64	(35.5 overs)	New Zealand v Pakistan at Sharjah	1985-86
68	(31.3 overs)	Scotland v West Indies at Leicester	1999
69	(28 overs)	South Africa v Australia at Sydney	1993-94
70	(25.2 overs)	Australia v England at Birmingham	1977
70	(26.3 overs)	Australia v New Zealand at Adelaide	1985-86

Note: This section does not take into account those matches in which the number of overs was reduced.

The lowest totals by other Test-playing countries are:

76	(30.1 overs)	Bangladesh v Sri Lanka at Colombo (SSC)	2002
86	(32.4 overs)	England v Australia at Manchester	2001
87	(29.3 overs)	West Indies v Australia at Sydney	1992-93

In January 2004, after the deadline for this section, West Indies were dismissed for 54 by South Africa at Cape Town.

LARGEST VICTORIES

256 runs	Australia (301-6 in 50 overs) v Namibia (45 in 14 overs) at Potchefstroom	2002-03
245 runs	Sri Lanka (299-5 in 50 overs) v India (54 in 26.3 overs) at Sharjah	2000-01
233 runs	Pakistan (320-3 in 50 overs) v Bangladesh (87 in 34.2 overs) at Dhaka	1999-2000
232 runs	Australia (323-2 in 50 overs) v Sri Lanka (91 in 35.5 overs) at Adelaide	1984-85
224 runs	Australia (332-5 in 50 overs) v Pakistan (108 in 36 overs) at Nairobi	2002
217 runs	Pakistan (295-6 in 50 overs) v Sri Lanka (78 in 16.5 overs) at Sharjah	2001-02
208 runs	South Africa (354-3 in 50 overs) v Kenya (146 in 45.3 overs) at Cape Town	2001-02
206 runs	New Zealand (276-7 in 50 overs) v Australia (70 in 26.3 overs) at Adelaide	1985-86
206 runs	Sri Lanka (292-5 in 50 overs) v Holland (86 in 29.3 overs) at Colombo (RPS)	2002
202 runs	England (334-4 in 60 overs) v India (132-3 in 60 overs) at Lord's	1975
202 runs	South Africa (305-8 in 50 overs) v Kenya (103 in 25.1 overs) at Nairobi	1996-97
202 runs	Zimbabwe (325-6 in 50 overs) v Kenya (123 in 36.5 overs) at Dhaka	1998-99
200 runs	India (276 in 49.3 overs) v Bangladesh (76 in 27.3 overs) at Dhaka	2003

By ten wickets: there have been 23 instances of victory by ten wickets.

TIED MATCHES

West Indies (222-5 in 50 overs) v Australia (222-9 in 50 overs) at Melbourne	1983-84
England (226-5 in 55 overs) v Australia (226-8 in 55 overs) at Nottingham	1989
West Indies (186-5 in 39 overs) v Pakistan (186-9 in 39 overs) at Lahore	1991-92
India (126 in 47.4 overs) v West Indies (126 in 41 overs) at Perth	1991-92
Australia (228-7 in 50 overs) v Pakistan (228-9 in 50 overs) at Hobart	1992-93
Pakistan (244-6 in 50 overs) v West Indies (244-5 in 50 overs) at Georgetown	1992-93
India (248-5 in 50 overs) v Zimbabwe (248 in 50 overs) at Indore	1993-94
Pakistan (161-9 in 50 overs) v New Zealand (161 in 49.4 overs) at Auckland	1993-94
Zimbabwe (219-9 in 50 overs) v Pakistan (219 in 49.5 overs) at Harare	1994-95
New Zealand (169-8 in 50 overs) v Sri Lanka (169 in 48 overs) at Sharjah	1996-97
Zimbabwe (236-8 in 50 overs) v India (236 in 49.5 overs) at Paarl	1996-97
New Zealand (237 in 49.4 overs) v England (237-8 in 50 overs) at Napier	1996-97
Zimbabwe (233-8 in 50 overs) v New Zealand (233-9 in 50 overs) at Bulawayo	1997-98
West Indies (173-5 in 30 overs) v Australia (173-7 in 30 overs) at Georgetown	1998-99
Australia (213 in 49.2 overs) v South Africa (213 in 49.4 overs) at Birmingham	1999
Pakistan (196 in 49.4 overs) v Sri Lanka (196 in 49.1 overs) at Sharjah	1999-2000
South Africa (226 in 50 overs) v Australia (226-9 in 50 overs) at Melbourne (CS)	2000
South Africa (259-7 in 50 overs) v Australia (259-9 in 50 overs) at Potchefstroom	2001-02
Sri Lanka (268-9 in 50 overs) v South Africa (229-6 in 45 overs) at Durban (D/L method)	2002-03

OTHER RECORDS

MOST APPEARANCES

356	**Wasim Akram (P)**	**247**	**Saeed Anwar (P)**	**224**	**M. Muralitharan (SL)**
334	M. Azharuddin (I)	**246**	**A. Kumble (I)**	224	R. B. Richardson (WI)
325	S. R. Waugh (A)	**245**	**J. N. Rhodes (SA)**	**220**	**M. G. Bevan (A)**
321	**S. R. Tendulkar (I)**	**238**	**C. Z. Harris (NZ)**	**214**	**R. Dravid (I)**
308	**P. A. de Silva (SL)**	238	D. L. Haynes (WI)	**213**	**A. Flower (Z)**
308	**S. T. Jayasuriya (SL)**	**235**	**S. C. Ganguly (I)**	213	R. S. Mahanama (SL)
302	**Inzamam-ul-Haq (P)**	233	Javed Miandad (P)	**209**	**G. W. Flower (Z)**
283	Salim Malik (P)	**229**	**J. Srinath (I)**	**207**	**S. P. Fleming (NZ)**
273	A. R. Border (A)	**228**	**W. P. U. J. C. Vaas (SL)**	205	C. A. Walsh (WI)
269	A. Ranatunga (SL)	**227**	**C. L. Hooper (WI)**	**203**	**S. M. Pollock (SA)**
262	**Waqar Younis (P)**	225	Kapil Dev (I)	**201**	**M. S. Atapattu (SL)**
250	Ijaz Ahmed, sen. (P)	**224**	**B. C. Lara (WI)**	**200**	**H. P. Tillekeratne (SL)**

Note: The most appearances for other Test-playing countries are **170** by **A. J. Stewart** for England and **69** by **Khaled Masud** for Bangladesh.

Bold type denotes those who have played limited-overs internationals since the start of 2002-03.

MOST APPEARANCES AGAINST ONE TEAM

75	**P. A. de Silva**	**Sri Lanka v Pakistan**	64	Javed Miandad	Pakistan v West Indies
68	**S. T. Jayasuriya**	**Sri Lanka v Pakistan**	**64**	**Wasim Akram**	**Pakistan v West Indies**
67	A. Ranatunga	Sri Lanka v Pakistan	61	A. R. Border	Australia v West Indies
65	D. L. Haynes	West Indies v Pakistan	61	R. B. Richardson	West Indies v Pakistan
64	M. Azharuddin	India v Pakistan	60	S. R. Waugh	Australia v New Zealand
64	D. L. Haynes	West Indies v Australia			

Bold type denotes those who have played limited-overs internationals since the start of 2003-03.

CAPTAINS

England (385 matches; 24 captains)

N. Hussain 56; G. A. Gooch 50; M. A. Atherton 43; **A. J. Stewart 41;** M. W. Gatting 37; R. G. D. Willis 29; J. M. Brearley 25; D. I. Gower 24; A. J. Hollioake 14; **M. P. Vaughan 13;** M. H. Denness 12; I. T. Botham 9; K. W. R. Fletcher 5; J. E. Emburey 4; A. J. Lamb 4; D. B. Close 3; R. Illingworth 3; G. P. Thorpe 3; G. Boycott 2; N. Gifford 2; A. W. Greig 2; **M. E. Trescothick 2;** J. H. Edrich 1; A. P. E. Knott 1.

Australia (551 matches; 16 captains)

A. R. Border 178; S. R. Waugh 106; M. A. Taylor 67; **R. T. Ponting 54;** G. S. Chappell 49; K. J. Hughes 49; I. M. Chappell 11; S. K. Warne 11; I. A. Healy 8; **A. C. Gilchrist 5;** G. R. Marsh 4; G. N. Yallop 4; R. B. Simpson 2; R. J. Bright 1; D. W. Hookes 1; W. M. Lawry 1.

South Africa (300 matches; 6 captains)

W. J. Cronje 138; **S. M. Pollock 90;** K. C. Wessels 52; **G. C. Smith 16;** C. E. B. Rice 3; **M. V. Boucher 1**.

West Indies (481 matches; 16 captains)

I. V. A. Richards 108; R. B. Richardson 87; C. H. Lloyd 81; **B. C. Lara 59; C. L. Hooper 49;** C. A. Walsh 43; J. C. Adams 26; C. G. Greenidge 8; D. L. Haynes 7; **R. D. Jacobs 4;** M. A. Holding 2; R. B. Kanhai 2; D. L. Murray 2; S. L. Campbell 1; P. J. L. Dujon 1; A. I. Kallicharran 1.

New Zealand (445 matches; 16 captains)

S. P. Fleming 147; G. P. Howarth 60; M. D. Crowe 44; K. R. Rutherford 37; L. K. Germon 36; J. G. Wright 31; J. V. Coney 25; J. J. Crowe 16; M. G. Burgess 8; C. D. McMillan 8; G. M. Turner 8; **C. L. Cairns** 7; D. J. Nash 7; B. E. Congdon 6; G. R. Larsen 3; A. H. Jones 2.

India (546 matches; 18 captains)

M. Azharuddin 174; **S. C. Ganguly 106;** Kapil Dev 74; S. R. Tendulkar 73; S. M. Gavaskar 37; D. B. Vengsarkar 18; A. Jadeja 13; K. Srikkanth 13; R. J. Shastri 11; **R. Dravid 9;** S. Venkataraghavan 7; B. S. Bedi 4; A. L. Wadekar 2; M. Amarnath 1; S. M. H. Kirmani 1; A. Kumble 1; **V. Sehwag 1;** G. R. Viswanath 1.

Pakistan (576 matches; 20 captains)

Imran Khan 139; Wasim Akram 110; Javed Miandad 62; **Waqar Younis 62;** Moin Khan 34; Salim Malik 34; **Rashid Latif 25;** Aamir Sohail 22; Ramiz Raja 22; **Inzamam-ul-Haq 14;** Zaheer Abbas 13; Saeed Anwar 10; Asif Iqbal 6; Abdul Qadir 5; Wasim Bari 5; Mushtaq Mohammad 4; Intikhab Alam 3; **Yousuf Youhana 3;** Majid Khan 2; Sarfraz Nawaz 1.

Sri Lanka (430 matches; 11 captains)

A. Ranatunga 193; **S. T. Jayasuriya 118;** L. R. D. Mendis 61; P. A. de Silva 18; R. S. Madugalle 13; **M. S. Atapattu 11;** B. Warnapura 8; A. P. B. Tennekoon 4; R. S. Mahanama 2; D. S. de Silva 1; J. R. Ratnayeke 1.

Zimbabwe (245 matches; 10 captains)

A. D. R. Campbell 86; H. H. Streak 57; A. Flower 52; D. L. Houghton 17; S. V. Carlisle 12; D. A. G. Fletcher 6; A. J. Traicos 6; B. A. Murphy 4; G. J. Whittall 4; G. W. Flower 1.

Bangladesh (82 matches; 7 captains)

Khaled Masud 23; Aminul Islam 16; Akram Khan 15; **Khaled Mahmud 15;** Gazi Ashraf 7; Naimur Rahman 4; Minhazul Abedin 2.

Associate Members (107 matches; 13 captains)

S. O. Tikolo (Kenya) 22; A. Y. Karim (Kenya) 21; M. O. Odumbe (Kenya) 20; **R. P. Lefebvre (Holland) 8;** Sultan M. Zarawani (UAE) 7; **J. V. Harris (Canada) 6; D. B. Kotze (Namibia) 6;** G. Salmond (Scotland) 5; S. W. Lubbers (Holland) 4; B. M. Mauricette (Canada) 3; Harilal R. Shah (East Africa) 3; **T. M. Odoyo (Kenya) 1; L. P. van Troost (Holland) 1**.

Bold type denotes those who have captained in a limited-overs international since the start of 2002-03.

WORLD CUP RECORDS

WORLD CUP FINALS

1975	WEST INDIES (291-8) beat Australia (274) by 17 runs	Lord's
1979	WEST INDIES (286-9) beat England (194) by 92 runs	Lord's
1983	INDIA (183) beat West Indies (140) by 43 runs	Lord's
1987	AUSTRALIA (253-5) beat England (246-8) by seven runs	Calcutta
1992	PAKISTAN (249-6) beat England (227) by 22 runs	Melbourne
1996	SRI LANKA (245-3) beat Australia (241-7) by seven wickets	Lahore
1999	AUSTRALIA (133-2) beat Pakistan (132) by eight wickets	Lord's
2003	AUSTRALIA (359-2) beat India (234) by 125 runs	Johannesburg

TEAM RESULTS

	Rounds reached			*Matches*				
	W	*F*	*SF*	*P*	*W*	*L*	*T*	*NR*
Australia (8)	3	5	5	58	40	17	1	0
West Indies (8)	2	3	4	48	31	16	0	1
England (8)	0	3	5	50	31	18	0	1
India (8)	1	2	4	55	31	23	0	1
Pakistan (8)	1	2	5	53	29	22	0	2
New Zealand (8)	0	0	4	52	28	23	0	1
South Africa (4)	0	0	2	30	19	9	2	0
Sri Lanka (8)	1	1	2	46	17	27	1	1
Zimbabwe (6)	0	0	0	42	8	31	0	3
Kenya (3)	0	0	1	20	5	14	0	1
Bangladesh (2)	0	0	0	11	2	8	0	1
United Arab Emirates (1)	0	0	0	5	1	4	0	0
Canada (2)	0	0	0	9	1	8	0	0
Holland (2)	0	0	0	11	1	10	0	0
East Africa (1)	0	0	0	3	0	3	0	0
Scotland (1)	0	0	0	5	0	5	0	0
Namibia (1)	0	0	0	6	0	6	0	0

The number of tournaments each team has played in is shown in brackets.

BATTING RECORDS

Most Runs

	M	*I*	*NO*	*R*	*HS*	*100s*	*Avge*
S. R. Tendulkar (I)	**33**	**32**	**3**	**1,732**	**152**	**4**	**59.72**
Javed Miandad (P)	33	30	5	1,083	103	1	43.32
P. A. de Silva (SL)	**35**	**32**	**3**	**1,064**	**145**	**2**	**36.68**
I. V. A. Richards (WI)	23	21	5	1,013	181	3	63.31
M. E. Waugh (A)	22	22	3	1,004	130	4	52.84
R. T. Ponting (A)	**28**	**27**	**3**	**998**	**140***	**3**	**41.58**
S. R. Waugh (A)	33	30	10	978	120*	1	48.90
A. Ranatunga (SL)	30	29	8	969	88*	0	46.14
B. C. Lara (WI)	**25**	**25**	**3**	**956**	**116**	**2**	**43.45**
Saeed Anwar (P)	**21**	**21**	**4**	**915**	**113***	**3**	**53.82**

Bold type denotes those who played in the 2002-03 tournament.

Highest Scores

188*	G. Kirsten	South Africa v United Arab Emirates at Rawalpindi	1995-96
183	S. C. Ganguly	India v Sri Lanka at Taunton	1999
181	I. V. A. Richards	West Indies v Sri Lanka at Karachi	1987-88
175*	Kapil Dev	India v Zimbabwe at Tunbridge Wells	1983
172*	C. B. Wishart	Zimbabwe v Namibia at Harare	2002-03
171*	G. M. Turner†	New Zealand v East Africa at Birmingham	1975
161	A. C. Hudson	South Africa v Holland at Rawalpindi	1995-96
152	S. R. Tendulkar	India v Namibia at Pietermaritzburg	2002-03

Highest scores for other Test-playing countries:

145	P. A. de Silva	Sri Lanka v Kenya at Kandy	1995-96
143*	A. Symonds	Australia v Pakistan at Johannesburg	2002-03
137	D. L. Amiss†	England v India at Lord's	1975
119*	Ramiz Raja	Pakistan v New Zealand at Christchurch	1991-92
68*	Minhazul Abedin	Bangladesh v Scotland at Edinburgh	1999

† *Amiss scored 137 and Turner 171* on the opening day of the inaugural World Cup in 1975; both remain national World Cup records.*

Most Hundreds

4, **S. C. Ganguly (I)**, **S. R. Tendulkar (I)** and M. E. Waugh (A); 3, **R. T. Ponting (A)**, Ramiz Raja (P), I. V. A. Richards (WI) and **Saeed Anwar (P)**.

Bold type denotes those who played in the 2002-03 tournament.

Most Runs in a Tournament

673, S. R. Tendulkar (I) 2002-03; 523, S. R. Tendulkar (I) 1995-96; 484, M. E. Waugh (A) 1995-96; 471, G. A. Gooch (E) 1987-88; 465, S. C. Ganguly (I) 2002-03; 461, R. Dravid (I) 1999; 456, M. D. Crowe (NZ) 1991-92.

Highest Partnership for Each Wicket

194	for 1st	Saeed Anwar and Wajahatullah Wasti	P v NZ	Manchester	1999
318	for 2nd	S. C. Ganguly and R. Dravid	I v SL	Taunton	1999
237*	for 3rd	R. Dravid and S. R. Tendulkar	I v K	Bristol	1999
168	for 4th	L. K. Germon and C. Z. Harris	NZ v A	Madras	1995-96
148	for 5th	R. G. Twose and C. L. Cairns	NZ v A	Cardiff	1999
161	for 6th	M. O. Odumbe and A. V. Vadher	K v SL	Southampton	1999
98	for 7th	R. R. Sarwan and R. D. Jacobs	WI v NZ	Port Elizabeth	2002-03
117	for 8th	D. L. Houghton and I. P. Butchart	Z v NZ	Hyderabad (India)	1987-88
126*	for 9th	Kapil Dev and S. M. H. Kirmani	I v Z	Tunbridge Wells	1983
71	for 10th	A. M. E. Roberts and J. Garner	WI v I	Manchester	1983

BOWLING RECORDS

Most Wickets

	O	*R*	*W*	*BB*	*4W/i*	*Avge*
Wasim Akram (P)	**324.3**	**1,311**	**55**	**5-28**	**3**	**23.83**
G. D. McGrath (A)	**245**	**935**	**45**	**7-15**	**2**	**20.77**
J. Srinath (I)	**283.2**	**1,224**	**44**	**4-30**	**2**	**27.81**
A. A. Donald (SA)	**218.5**	**913**	**38**	**4-17**	**2**	**24.02**
W. P. U. J. C. Vaas (SL)	**184**	**754**	**36**	**6-25**	**2**	**20.94**
Imran Khan (P)	169.3	655	34	4-37	2	19.26
S. K. Warne (A)	162.5	624	32	4-29	4	19.50
C. Z. Harris (NZ)	**194.2**	**861**	**32**	**4-7**	**1**	**26.90**
M. Muralitharan (SL)	**187.5**	**693**	**30**	**4-28**	**1**	**23.10**
I. T. Botham (E)	222	762	30	4-31	1	25.40

Bold type denotes those who played in the 2002-03 tournament.

Best Bowling

7-15	G. D. McGrath	Australia v Namibia at Potchefstroom	2002-03
7-20	A. J. Bichel	Australia v England at Port Elizabeth	2002-03
7-51	W. W. Davis	West Indies v Australia at Leeds	1983
6-14	G. J. Gilmour	Australia v England at Leeds	1975
6-39	K. H. MacLeay	Australia v India at Nottingham	1983
6-23	A. Nehra	India v England at Durban	2002-03
6-23	S. E. Bond	New Zealand v Australia at Port Elizabeth	2002-03
6-25	W. P. U. J. C. Vaas	Sri Lanka v Bangladesh at Pietermaritzburg	2002-03

Best analyses for other Test-playing countries:

5-21	P. A. Strang	Zimbabwe v Kenya at Patna	1995-96
5-21	L. Klusener	South Africa v Kenya at Amstelveen	1999
5-28	Wasim Akram	Pakistan v Namibia at Kimberley	2002-03
5-39	V. J. Marks	England v Sri Lanka at Taunton	1983
3-31	Khaled Mahmud	Bangladesh v Pakistan at Northampton	1999

Other Bowling Records

Hat-tricks: Chetan Sharma, India v New Zealand at Nagpur, 1987-88; Saqlain Mushtaq, Pakistan v Zimbabwe at The Oval, 1999; W. P. U. J. C. Vaas, Sri Lanka v Bangladesh at Pietermaritzburg, 2002-03 (the first three balls of the match); B. Lee, Australia v Kenya at Durban, 2002-03.

Most economical bowling: 12–8–6–1; B. S. Bedi, India v East Africa at Leeds, 1975.

Most expensive bowling: 12–1–105–2; M. C. Snedden, New Zealand v England at The Oval, 1983.

Most Wickets in a Tournament

23, W. P. U. J. C. Vaas (SL) 2002-03; 22, B. Lee (A) 2002-03; 21, G. D. McGrath (A) 2002-03; 20, G. I. Allott (NZ) 1999 and S. K. Warne (A) 1999.

WICKET-KEEPING RECORDS

Most Dismissals

A. C. Gilchrist (A)	**35 (33ct, 2st)**	**R. D. Jacobs (WI)**	**22 (21ct, 1st)**
Moin Khan (P)	30 (23ct, 7st)	Wasim Bari (P)	22 (18ct, 4st)
A. J. Stewart (E)	**23 (21ct, 2st)**	I. A. Healy (A)	21 (18ct, 3st)
M. V. Boucher (SA)	**22 (all ct)**	P. J. L. Dujon (WI)	20 (19ct, 1st)

Bold type denotes those who played in the 2002-03 tournament.

Most Dismissals in an Innings

6 (6ct)	A. C. Gilchrist	Australia v Namibia at Potchefstroom	2002-03
5 (5ct)	S. M. H. Kirmani	India v Zimbabwe at Leicester	1983
5 (4ct, 1st)	J. C. Adams	West Indies v Kenya at Pune	1995-96
5 (4ct, 1st)	Rashid Latif	Pakistan v New Zealand at Lahore	1995-96
5 (5ct)	R. D. Jacobs	West Indies v New Zealand at Southampton	1999
5 (4ct, 1st)	N. R. Mongia	India v Zimbabwe at Leicester	1999

Most Dismissals in a Tournament

21, A. C. Gilchrist (A) 2002-03; 17, K. C. Sangakkara (SL) 2002-03; 16, R. Dravid (I) 2002-03, P. J. L. Dujon (WI) 1983 and Moin Khan (P) 1999; 15, D. J. Richardson (SA) 1991-92.

FIELDING RECORDS

Most Catches

18, R. T. Ponting (A); 16, C. L. Cairns (NZ); 15, S. T. Jayasuriya (SL); 14, P. A. de Silva (SL), A. Kumble (I) and S. R. Waugh (A); **13, C. L. Hooper (WI).**

Bold type denotes those who played in the 2002-03 tournament.

MOST APPEARANCES

38, **Wasim Akram (P)**; 35, **P. A. de Silva (SL)**; 34, **J. Srinath (I)**; 33, Javed Miandad (P), **S. R. Tendulkar (I)** and S. R. Waugh (A); 32, **Inzamam-ul-Haq (P)**; 30, M. Azharuddin (I), **A. Flower (Z)** and A. Ranatunga (SL).

Bold type denotes those who played in the 2002-03 tournament.

TEAM RECORDS

Highest Totals

398-5	(50 overs)	Sri Lanka v Kenya at Kandy	1995-96
373-6	(50 overs)	India v Sri Lanka at Taunton	1999
360-4	(50 overs)	West Indies v Sri Lanka at Karachi	1987-88
359-2	(50 overs)	Australia v India at Johannesburg	2002-03
340-2	(50 overs)	Zimbabwe v Namibia at Harare	2002-03
338-5	(60 overs)	Pakistan v Sri Lanka at Swansea	1983
334-4	(60 overs)	England v India at Lord's	1975
333-9	(60 overs)	England v Sri Lanka at Taunton	1983
330-6	(60 overs)	Pakistan v Sri Lanka at Nottingham	1975

Highest totals for other Test-playing countries:

328-3	(50 overs)	South Africa v Holland at Rawalpindi	1995-96
309-5	(60 overs)	New Zealand v East Africa at Birmingham	1975
223-9	(50 overs)	Bangladesh v Pakistan at Northampton	1999

Highest total batting second:

313-7	(49.2)	Sri Lanka v Zimbabwe at New Plymouth	1991-92

Lowest Totals

36	(18.4 overs)	Canada v Sri Lanka at Paarl	2002-03
45	(40.3 overs)	Canada v England at Manchester	1979
45	(14 overs)	Namibia v Australia at Potchefstroom	2002-03
68	(31.3 overs)	Scotland v West Indies at Leicester	1999
74	(40.2 overs)	Pakistan v England at Adelaide	1991-92
84	(17.4 overs)	Namibia v Pakistan at Kimberley	2002-03
86	(37.2 overs)	Sri Lanka v West Indies at Manchester	1975
93	(36.2 overs)	England v Australia at Leeds	1975
93	(35.2 overs)	West Indies v Kenya at Pune	1995-96
94	(52.3 overs)	East Africa v England at Birmingham	1975

Highest Aggregate

652-12	(100 overs)	Sri Lanka v Kenya at Kandy	1995-96

RESULTS

Largest Victories

10 wkts	India beat East Africa at Leeds	1975
10 wkts	West Indies beat Zimbabwe at Birmingham	1983
10 wkts	West Indies beat Pakistan at Melbourne	1991-92
10 wkts	South Africa beat Kenya at Potchefstroom	2002-03
10 wkts	Sri Lanka beat Bangladesh at Pietermaritzburg	2002-03
10 wkts	South Africa beat Bangladesh at Bloemfontein	2002-03
256 runs	Australia beat Namibia at Potchefstroom	2002-03
202 runs	England beat India at Lord's	1975

Narrowest Victories

1 wkt	West Indies beat Pakistan at Birmingham	1975
1 wkt	Pakistan beat West Indies at Lahore	1987-88
1 run	Australia beat India at Madras	1987-88
1 run	Australia beat India at Brisbane	1991-92

Ties

Australia v South Africa at Birmingham	1999
South Africa v Sri Lanka (D/L method) at Durban	2002-03

LIST A LIMITED-OVERS RECORDS

List A is a concept, introduced by the Association of Cricket Statisticians and Historians, intended to provide an approximate equivalent in one-day cricket of first-class status. List A games comprise:

(a) Limited-overs internationals.
(b) Other international matches (e.g. A-team internationals).
(c) Premier domestic limited-overs tournaments in Test-playing countries.
(d) Official tourist matches against the main first-class teams (e.g. counties, states, provinces and national Board XIs).

The following matches are excluded:

(a) Matches originally scheduled as less than 40 overs per side (e.g. Twenty20 games).
(b) World Cup warm-up games.
(c) Tourist matches against teams outside the major domestic competitions (e.g. universities).
(d) Festival games and pre-season friendlies.

Note: This section covers one-day cricket to the end of the 2003 season in England.

BATTING RECORDS

HIGHEST INDIVIDUAL INNINGS

268	A. D. Brown	Surrey v Glamorgan at The Oval	2002
222*	R. G. Pollock	Eastern Province v Border at East London	1974-75
206	A. I. Kallicharran	Warwickshire v Oxfordshire at Birmingham	1984
203	A. D. Brown	Surrey v Hampshire at Guildford	1997
202*	A. Barrow	Natal v SA African XI at Durban	1975-76
201	V. J. Wells	Leicestershire v Berkshire at Leicester	1996

MOST RUNS

	Career	*M*	*I*	*NO*	*R*	*HS*	*100s*	*Avge*
G. A. Gooch	1973–1997	614	601	48	22,211	198*	44	40.16
G. A. Hick	***1983*–2003**	**569**	**552**	**82**	**19,833**	**172***	**37**	**42.19**
I. V. A. Richards	*1973*–1993	500	466	61	16,995	189*	26	41.96
C. G. Greenidge	1970–1992	440	436	33	16,349	186*	33	40.56
S. R. Tendulkar	***1989–2003***	**401**	**390**	**45**	**15,980**	**186***	**46**	**46.31**
A. J. Lamb	*1972*–1995	484	463	63	15,658	132*	19	39.14
D. L. Haynes	*1976–1996*	419	416	44	15,651	152*	28	42.07
K. J. Barnett	**1979–2003**	**525**	**498**	**54**	**15,532**	**136**	**17**	**34.98**

Bold type denotes those who have played since the start of 2002-03.

HIGHEST PARTNERSHIP FOR EACH WICKET

326*	for 1st	Ghulam Ali/Sohail Jaffer, PIA v ADBP at Sialkot	2000-01
331	for 2nd	S. R. Tendulkar/R. Dravid, India v New Zealand at Hyderabad	1999-2000
309*	for 3rd	T. S. Curtis/T. M. Moody, Worcestershire v Surrey at The Oval	1994
275*	for 4th	M. Azharuddin/A. Jadeja, India v Zimbabwe at Cuttack	1997-98
267*	for 5th	Minhazul Abedin/Khaled Mahmud, Bangladeshis v Bahawalpur at Karachi	1997-98
226	for 6th	N. J. Llong/M. V. Fleming, Kent v Cheshire at Bowdon	1999
170	for 7th	D. R. Brown/A. F. Giles, Warwickshire v Essex at Birmingham	2003
203	for 8th	Shahid Iqbal/Haaris Ayaz, Karachi Whites v Hyderabad at Karachi	1998-99
130	for 9th	C. P. Schofield/G. I. Maiden, Lancashire v India A at Blackpool	2003
106*	for 10th	I. V. A. Richards/M. A. Holding, West Indies v England at Manchester	1984

BOWLING RECORDS

BEST BOWLING ANALYSES

8-15	R. L. Sanghvi	Delhi v Himachal Pradesh at Una	1997-98
8-19	W. P. U. J. C. Vaas	Sri Lanka v Zimbabwe at Colombo	2001-02
8-21	M. A. Holding	Derbyshire v Sussex at Hove	1988
8-26	K. D. Boyce	Essex v Lancashire at Manchester	1971
8-31	D. L. Underwood	Kent v Scotland at Edinburgh	1987

MOST WICKETS

	Career	*M*	*B*	*R*	*W*	*BB*	*4W/i*	*Avge*
Wasim Akram	***1984*–2003**	**594**	**29,719**	**19,303**	**881**	**5-10**	**46**	**21.91**
A. A. Donald	***1985–2002***	**450**	**22,508**	**14,685**	**678**	**6-15**	**38**	**21.65**
J. K. Lever	1968–1990	481	23,208	13,278	674	5-8	34	19.70
Waqar Younis	***1988*–2003**	**410**	**19,745**	**15,037**	**672**	**7-36**	**44**	**22.37**
J. E. Emburey	1975–2000	536	26,399	16,811	647	5-23	26	25.98
I. T. Botham	1973–1993	470	22,899	15,264	612	5-27	18	24.94

Bold type denotes those who have played since the start of 2002-03.

WICKET-KEEPING AND FIELDING RECORDS

MOST DISMISSALS IN AN INNINGS

8 (5ct, 3st)	S. J. Palframan	Boland v Easterns at Paarl	1997-98
8 (all ct)	D. J. Pipe	Worcestershire v Hertfordshire at Hertford	2001
8 (all ct)	D. J. S. Taylor	Somerset v Combined Universities at Taunton	1982
7 (6ct, 1st)	M. K. P. B. Kularatne	Galle v Colts at Colombo	2001-02
7 (all ct)	I. Mitchell	Border v Western Province at East London	1998-99
7 (4ct, 3st)	Rizwan Umar	Sargodha v Bahawalpur at Sargodha	1991-92
7 (all ct)	A. J. Stewart	Surrey v Glamorgan at Swansea	1994
7 (6ct, 1st)	R. W. Taylor	Derbyshire v Lancashire at Manchester	1975

MOST CATCHES IN AN INNINGS IN THE FIELD

5	Hasnain Raza	Bahawalpur v Pakistan Customs at Karachi	2002-03
5	K. C. Jackson	Boland v Natal at Durban	1995-96
5	A. J. Kourie	Transvaal v Western Province at Johannesburg	1979-80
5	V. J. Marks	Combined Universities v Kent at Oxford	1976
5	Mohammad Ramzan	PNSC v PIA at Karachi	1998-99
5	J. N. Rhodes	South Africa v West Indies at Bombay	1993-94
5	J. M. Rice	Hampshire v Warwickshire at Southampton	1978
5	Amit Sharma	Punjab v Jammu and Kashmir at Ludhiana	1999-2000
5	J. W. Wilson	Otago v Auckland at Dunedin	1993-94
5	B. E. Young	South Australia v Tasmania at Launceston	2001-02

TEAM RECORDS

HIGHEST INNINGS TOTALS

438-5	(50 overs)	Surrey v Glamorgan at The Oval	2002
429	(49.5 overs)	Glamorgan v Surrey at The Oval	2002
424-5	(50 overs)	Buckinghamshire v Suffolk at Dinton	2002
413-4	(60 overs)	Somerset v Devon at Torquay	1990
409-6	(50 overs)	Trinidad & Tobago v North Windward Islands at Kingston	2001-02
408-4	(50 overs)	KRL v Sialkot at Sialkot	2002-03
406-5	(60 overs)	Leicestershire v Berkshire at Leicester	1996
404-3	(60 overs)	Worcestershire v Devon at Worcester	1987
401-7	(50 overs)	Gloucestershire v Buckinghamshire at Wing	2003

LOWEST INNINGS TOTALS

23	(19.4 overs)	Middlesex v Yorkshire at Leeds	1974
30	(20.4 overs)	Chittagong v Sylhet at Dhaka	2002-03
34	(21.1 overs)	Saurashtra v Mumbai at Mumbai	1999-2000
36	(25.4 overs)	Leicestershire v Sussex at Leicester	1973
36	(18.4 overs)	Canada v Sri Lanka at Paarl	2002-03
38	(15.4 overs)	Zimbabwe v Sri Lanka at Colombo	2001-02
39	(26.4 overs)	Ireland v Sussex at Hove	1985

MISCELLANEOUS RECORDS

LARGE ATTENDANCES

Test Series

943,000	Australia v England (5 Tests)	1936-37
In England		
549,650	England v Australia (5 Tests)	1953

Test Matches

†‡465,000	India v Pakistan, Calcutta	1998-99
350,534	Australia v England, Melbourne (Third Test)	1936-37

Note: Attendance at India v England at Calcutta in 1981-82 may have exceeded 350,000.

In England		
158,000+	England v Australia, Leeds	1948
137,915	England v Australia, Lord's	1953

Test Match Day

‡100,000	India v Pakistan, Calcutta (first four days)	1998-99
90,800	Australia v West Indies, Melbourne (Fifth Test, second day)	1960-61

Other First-Class Matches in England

93,000	England v Australia, Lord's (Fourth Victory Match, 3 days)	1945
80,000+	Surrey v Yorkshire, The Oval (3 days)	1906
78,792	Yorkshire v Lancashire, Leeds (3 days)	1904
76,617	Lancashire v Yorkshire, Manchester (3 days)	1926

Limited-Overs Internationals

‡100,000	India v South Africa, Calcutta	1993-94
‡100,000	India v West Indies, Calcutta	1993-94
‡100,000	India v West Indies, Calcutta	1994-95
‡100,000	India v Sri Lanka, Calcutta (World Cup semi-final)	1995-96
‡100,000	India v Australia, Kolkata	2003-04
‡90,000	India v Pakistan, Calcutta	1986-87
‡90,000	India v South Africa, Calcutta	1991-92
87,182	England v Pakistan, Melbourne (World Cup final)	1991-92
86,133	Australia v West Indies, Melbourne	1983-84

† *Estimated.*
‡ *No official attendance figures were issued for these games, but capacity at Calcutta (now Kolkata) is believed to have reached 100,000 following rebuilding in 1993.*

LORD'S CRICKET GROUND

Lord's and the Marylebone Cricket Club were founded in London in 1787. The Club has enjoyed an uninterrupted career since that date, but there have been three grounds known as Lord's. The first (1787–1810) was situated where Dorset Square now is; the second (1809–13), at North Bank, had to be abandoned owing to the cutting of the Regent's Canal; and the third, opened in 1814, is the present one at St John's Wood. It was not until 1866 that the freehold of Lord's was secured by MCC. The present pavilion was erected in 1890 at a cost of £21,000.

HIGHEST INDIVIDUAL SCORES MADE AT LORD'S

333	G. A. Gooch	England v India	1990
316*	J. B. Hobbs	Surrey v Middlesex	1926
315*	P. Holmes	Yorkshire v Middlesex	1925
315	M. A. Wagh	Warwickshire v Middlesex	2001

Notes: The longest innings in a first-class match at Lord's was played by S. Wettimuny (636 minutes, 190 runs) for Sri Lanka v England, 1984. Wagh batted for 630 minutes.

HIGHEST TOTALS AT LORD'S

First-Class Matches

729-6 dec.	Australia v England	1930
682-6 dec.	South Africa v England	2003
665	West Indians v Middlesex	1939
653-4 dec.	England v India	1990
652-8 dec.	West Indies v England	1973

Minor Match

735-9 dec.	MCC and Ground v Wiltshire	1888

BIGGEST HIT AT LORD'S

The only known instance of a batsman hitting a ball over the present pavilion at Lord's occurred when A. E. Trott, appearing for MCC against Australians on July 31, August 1, 2, 1899, drove M. A. Noble so far and high that the ball struck a chimney pot and fell behind the building.

MINOR CRICKET

HIGHEST INDIVIDUAL SCORES

628*	A. E. J. Collins, Clark's House v North Town at Clifton College. *A junior house match. His innings of 6 hours 50 minutes was spread over four afternoons*	1899
566	C. J. Eady, Break-o'-Day v Wellington at Hobart	1901-02
515	D. R. Havewalla, B. B. and C. I. Railways v St Xavier's at Bombay	1933-34
506*	J. C. Sharp, Melbourne GS v Geelong College at Melbourne	1914-15
502*	Chaman Lal, Mehandra Coll., Patiala v Government Coll., Rupar at Patiala	1956-57
485	A. E. Stoddart, Hampstead v Stoics at Hampstead	1886
475*	Mohammad Iqbal, Muslim Model HS v Islamia HS, Sialkot at Lahore	1958-59
466*	G. T. S. Stevens, Beta v Lambda (University College School house match) at Neasden	1919
459	J. A. Prout, Wesley College v Geelong College at Geelong	1908-09

Note: The highest score in a Minor County match is 323* by F. E. Lacey for Hampshire v Norfolk at Southampton in 1887; the highest in the Minor Counties Championship is 282 by E. Garnett for Berkshire v Wiltshire at Reading in 1908.

HIGHEST PARTNERSHIP

664* for 3rd	V. G. Kambli and S. R. Tendulkar, Sharadashram Vidyamandir School v St Xavier's High School at Bombay	1987-88

Note: Kambli was 16 years old, Tendulkar 14. Tendulkar made his Test debut 21 months later.

RECORD HIT

The Rev. W. Fellows, while at practice on the Christ Church ground at Oxford in 1856, drove a ball bowled by Charles Rogers 175 yards from hit to pitch.

THROWING THE CRICKET BALL

140 yards 2 feet, Robert Percival, on the Durham Sands racecourse, Co. Durham	c1882
140 yards 9 inches, Ross Mackenzie, at Toronto	1872
140 yards, "King Billy" the Aborigine, at Clermont, Queensland	1872

Note: Extensive research by David Rayvern Allen has shown that these traditional records are probably authentic, if not necessarily wholly accurate. Modern competitions have failed to produce similar distances although Ian Pont, the Essex all-rounder who also played baseball, was reported to have thrown 138 yards in Cape Town in 1981. There have been speculative reports attributing throws of 150 yards or more to figures as diverse as the South African Test player Colin Bland, the Latvian javelin thrower Janis Lusis, who won a gold medal for the Soviet Union in the 1968 Olympics, and the British sprinter Charley Ransome. The definitive record is still awaited.

COUNTY CHAMPIONSHIP

MOST APPEARANCES

762	W. Rhodes	Yorkshire	1898–1930
707	F. E. Woolley	Kent	1906–1938
668	C. P. Mead	Hampshire	1906–1936
617	N. Gifford	Worcestershire (484), Warwickshire (133)	1960–1988
611	W. G. Quaife	Warwickshire	1895–1928
601	G. H. Hirst	Yorkshire	1891–1921

MOST CONSECUTIVE APPEARANCES

423	K. G. Suttle	Sussex	1954–1969
412	J. G. Binks	Yorkshire	1955–1969

Notes: J. Vine made 417 consecutive appearances for Sussex in all first-class matches (399 of them in the Championship) between July 1900 and September 1914.

J. G. Binks did not miss a Championship match for Yorkshire between making his debut in June 1955 and retiring at the end of the 1969 season.

UMPIRES

MOST COUNTY CHAMPIONSHIP APPEARANCES

570	T. W. Spencer	1950–1980	**485**	**D. J. Constant**	**1969–2003**
531	F. Chester	1922–1955	483	P. B. Wight	1966–1995
516	H. G. Baldwin	1932–1962	461	J. Moss	1899–1929
488	**A. G. T. Whitehead**	**1970–2003**	452	A. Skelding	1931–1958

MOST SEASONS ON FIRST-CLASS LIST

35	**D. J. Constant**	**1969–2003**	28	F. Chester	1922–1955
34	**A. G. T. Whitehead**	**1970–2003**	27	J. Moss	1899–1929
31	K. E. Palmer	1972–2002	26	W. A. J. West	1896–1925
31	T. W. Spencer	1950–1980	25	H. G. Baldwin	1932–1962
30	R. Julian	1972–2001	25	A. Jepson	1960–1984
30	P. B. Wight	1966–1995	25	J. G. Langridge	1956–1980
29	H. D. Bird	1970–1998	25	B. J. Meyer	1973–1997

Bold type denotes umpires who stood in the 2003 season.

"For South Africa, the psychological damage of watching ball after ball sail over the rope was as telling as the runs themselves; for the first time all series, Graeme Smith looked lost."

South Africans in England, page 456.

WOMEN'S TEST RECORDS

Amended by MARION COLLIN to the end of the 2003 season in England

HIGHEST INDIVIDUAL INNINGS

214	M. Raj	India v England at Taunton	2002
209*	K. L. Rolton	Australia v England at Leeds	2001
204	K. E. Flavell	New Zealand v England at Scarborough	1996
204	M. A. J. Goszko	Australia v England at Shenley Park	2001
200	J. Broadbent	Australia v England at Guildford	1998
193	D. A. Annetts	Australia v England at Collingham	1987
190	S. Agarwal	India v England at Worcester	1986
189	E. A. Snowball	England v New Zealand at Christchurch	1934-35
179	R. Heyhoe-Flint	England v Australia at The Oval	1976
177	S. C. Taylor	England v South Africa at Shenley Park	2003
176*	K. L. Rolton	Australia v England at Worcester	1998

1,000 RUNS IN A CAREER

R	*T*	
1,935	27	J. A. Brittin (England)
1,594	22	R. Heyhoe-Flint (England)
1,301	19	D. A. Hockley (New Zealand)
1,164	18	C. A. Hodges (England)
1,110	13	S. Agarwal (India)
1,078	12	E. Bakewell (England)
1,007	14	M. E. Maclagan (England)

BEST BOWLING ANALYSES

8-53	N. David	India v England at Jamshedpur	1995-96
7-6	M. B. Duggan	England v Australia at Melbourne	1957-58
7-7	E. R. Wilson	Australia v England at Melbourne	1957-58
7-10	M. E. Maclagan	England v Australia at Brisbane	1934-35
7-18	A. Palmer	Australia v England at Brisbane	1934-35
7-24	L. Johnston	Australia v New Zealand at Melbourne	1971-72
7-34	G. E. McConway	England v India at Worcester	1986
7-41	J. A. Burley	New Zealand v England at The Oval	1966
7-51	L. C. Pearson	England v Australia at Sydney	2002-03
7-61	E. Bakewell	England v West Indies at Birmingham	1979

11 WICKETS IN A MATCH

11-16	E. R. Wilson	Australia v England at Melbourne	1957-58
11-63	J. Greenwood	England v West Indies at Canterbury	1979
11-107	L. C. Pearson	England v Australia at Sydney	2002-03

50 WICKETS IN A CAREER

W	*T*	
77	17	M. B. Duggan (England)
68	11	E. R. Wilson (Australia)
63	20	D. F. Edulji (India)
60	14	M. E. Maclagan (England)
60	19	S. Kulkarni (India)
57	16	R. H. Thompson (Australia)
55	15	J. Lord (New Zealand)
50	12	E. Bakewell (England)

SIX DISMISSALS IN AN INNINGS

8 (6ct, 2st)	L. Nye	England v New Zealand at New Plymouth	1991-92
6 (2ct, 4st)	B. A. Brentnall	New Zealand v South Africa at Johannesburg	1971-72

EIGHT DISMISSALS IN A MATCH

9 (8ct, 1st)	C. Matthews	Australia v India at Adelaide	1990-91
8 (6ct, 2st)	L. Nye	England v New Zealand at New Plymouth	1991-92

25 DISMISSALS IN A CAREER

		T	*Ct*	*St*
58	C. Matthews (Australia)	20	46	12
36	S. A. Hodges (England)	11	19	17
28	B. A. Brentnall (New Zealand)	10	16	12

HIGHEST INNINGS TOTALS

569-6 dec.	Australia v England at Guildford	1998
525	Australia v India at Ahmedabad	1983-84
517-8	New Zealand v England at Scarborough	1996
503-5 dec.	England v New Zealand at Christchurch	1934-35

LOWEST INNINGS TOTALS

35	England v Australia at Melbourne	1957-58
38	Australia v England at Melbourne	1957-58
44	New Zealand v England at Christchurch	1934-35
47	Australia v England at Brisbane	1934-35

Opposite: Written all over his face. Marcus Trescothick reaches his first double-hundred, against South Africa at The Oval. *Picture by Patrick Eagar*

PART FIVE

English Cricket

THE ENGLAND TEAM IN 2003

Good housekeeping

SCYLD BERRY

In 2003, England's cricket was a neat semi-detached house. One or two other countries could boast grander structures with more inspiring façades, but anyone who could remember England's cricket – often dilapidated and shambolic – over the previous couple of decades would not have complained. It was well-kept, middle-of-the-range, and inhabited by manifestly decent and thoughtful people.

The tidiness of the frontage disguised the fact that a change of tenant took place in mid-year. It had been Nasser Hussain's house but in two separate stages Michael Vaughan took over as one-day and Test captain. It says much for the good sense of those concerned that the household rapidly settled down again. But above all, it was thanks to the steady hand of the housekeeper or – if the image would suit Duncan Fletcher better – the janitor, who ensured continuity. The neighbours' curtains twitched as they looked for signs of rows and disruption, but the appearance of stability remained.

Hussain, 35 just after the tournament ended, had long intended to resign as England's one-day captain after the World Cup, and when a day's rain in Bulawayo meant that England were knocked out, this passionate man (a thousand miles away in Port Elizabeth at the time) saw no reason to alter his mind. One-day cricket had never been his forte, hence his prickliness on the subject of whether he should bat at No. 3. He was also drained by the furore over Zimbabwe when the discussions, about whether England should play their qualifying match in Harare or not, went to the eleventh hour and beyond. But Hussain intended to carry on as Test captain, he said, until such time as the new one-day captain had got his feet under the table.

This scheme, however, did not quite work out as planned. England's first assignment was the two-Test series at home to Zimbabwe: this turned out to be a formality, as the tourists had probably the weakest batting side that any Test country has brought to England, which made no sort of trial of the transitional arrangements. Rather unexpectedly, England then won – under their new one-day captain Vaughan – both the NatWest Challenge against Pakistan 2–1, and the three-way NatWest Series. As this involved, after an initial loss to Zimbabwe, three victories in four internationals against South Africa, the achievement was rightly hailed as speedy rebuilding after the World Cup. Nick Knight, Andrew Caddick, Alec Stewart and Hussain himself had all gone, but able replacements were immediately slotted in.

So when England's Test team regrouped for the first of the five Test matches against South Africa, the dynamics had changed more rapidly than anyone had suspected. Hussain had been away for the month of one-day cricket in midsummer. When he returned, he found that everyone was

Goodbye to all that: after a fraught World Cup and a terrible Test at Edgbaston against South Africa, Nasser Hussain resigns as England captain.

Picture by Graham Morris.

managing fairly well without him. A selfish captain – which is how some still characterised Hussain, based on knowledge of his youth rather than his cricketing maturity – would have carried on. England bowled poorly in the First Test at Edgbaston, but on a flat pitch that was nothing new, and another big hundred from Vaughan's bat saw them through to a draw. Hussain had taken over almost exactly four years before, only to end his first Test series – just before Fletcher took over as coach – by losing to New Zealand 2–1 and being booed on the Oval balcony. Nothing would have been easier, or more tempting, than for Hussain to have stayed on for the rest of the series against South Africa, hoping for his team to spark again so that he could retire as England's Test captain on a far more triumphant note at The Oval.

Hussain did not take that easy option. Spurred on by the media who wanted to see a new face as captain if only for the sake of change, he asked Vaughan on the last day at Edgbaston if he was ready to take over as Test captain as well, without his form being affected. When Vaughan said yes, Hussain went to the chairman of selectors David Graveney. Hussain had noticed that his team had moved on; he could not revert to his barking, hectoring style of keeping everyone up to the mark after Vaughan had introduced his quieter, more consensual style which expected every player to do his duty without being told. The Hussain–Fletcher combination had worked so well for England because they were complementary, the one passionate, the other more measured. Now captain and coach were more of a kind. But, after a heavy defeat by South Africa the following week at Lord's, redeemed only by Andrew Flintoff's hitting, this chemistry also showed signs of working.

The series-levelling victory at Trent Bridge owed a great deal to winning the toss on a pitch that broke up, but England still had to pull together. The first-innings hundreds by Hussain and Mark Butcher were vital in initiating the new era: after a polite but no more than warm reception at Lord's following his resignation, the Nottingham crowd greeted Hussain's century with the popular acclamation that was his due for being England's best captain in the post-Brearley era. It matched the applause for Alec Stewart's hundred at Old Trafford against West Indies in 2000, and for Mike Atherton's at The Oval the same season. They were all heartfelt displays of public gratitude for former England captains who have done their best in circumstances that have not always been favourable.

The change in leadership could not disguise the fact that some things about the modern England team remain the same no matter who the captain is: firstly, the absence of an attacking spinner; secondly, the lack of a match-winning fast bowler (although Darren Gough and Caddick as a pair were as good as one); and, thirdly, the unending succession of injuries to the fast bowlers they do have. This was the first year that England had a full-time medical officer, Dr Peter Gregory, but the differences were not readily apparent. It was still utterly predictable that whatever pace attack England picked for one Test, the same bowlers would not be in a fit state for the following match. The disruption can hardly be overestimated. Yet the coach, and captain, continued to minimise the impact – except in the Headingley Test, where for the second successive season England's seam attack bowled their worst in the most helpful conditions.

It was typical that Caddick should have been announced as unfit a week ahead of the series against Zimbabwe in May; and that a simple leg injury should involve so many complications that he was out for the rest of the year. More understandably, Simon Jones spent the whole year recovering from the torn cruciates in his right knee. Gough gave up trying to get his right knee fit for Test cricket again and, after the Lord's Test against South Africa, announced he was going to concentrate on one-day internationals. Richard Johnson made an encouraging six-wicket debut against Zimbabwe in the inaugural Test at Chester-le-Street – and duly missed the South African series. There was never any danger that James Anderson, the one-day discovery of the winter, would have to wait for his Test debut, and he managed the complete series against South Africa before he – and Flintoff – missed the series in Bangladesh. There in the autumn Vaughan stamped his mark on the new era by forcing England's fitness levels up to their highest yet, but it did not stop the fast bowlers falling over like flies.

Some more fortunate constants applied too. One was the stability of the top-order batting. Vaughan, Butcher and Marcus Trescothick all had productive years, as indeed did Hussain. In his first four Tests as captain, Vaughan kept getting out after playing himself in, perhaps going too hard at the ball with the intent to show who was boss. A brilliant attacking innings of 81 not out to see England home on a turning pitch at Dhaka took him over that psychological hurdle; and an Athertonian innings of 105 saved the Second Test against Sri Lanka in Kandy. His captaincy, essentially conventional and defensive, became more inventive with regard to field placings in Sri Lanka; and he never asked too much of his bowlers, as Hussain occasionally did when setting 8–1 fields.

Trescothick, and the whole England team, saved their best for the Oval Test against South Africa. In the ongoing absence of any match-winning bowler, the team turned on a collective effort that was nothing short of magnificent. It was Stewart's final game for England, and two of his oldest Surrey colleagues – Graham Thorpe and Martin Bicknell – made sure that he went out on a triumphant note. Nothing seemed less likely after a dazzling hundred by Herschelle Gibbs on the opening day, but inch by inch England clawed their way back. Bicknell supplied old-fashioned line and length; Trescothick and Thorpe constructed a substantial cake, then Flintoff sprayed icing everywhere to put England on top. Steve Harmison at long last translated his promise into performance by taking four for 33 on a still true pitch, before England knocked off the runs in style. The victory had to rank alongside the ones over West Indies in 1991 and 2000 as the best England have achieved at The Oval outside Ashes series.

The team turned on a collective effort that was nothing short of magnificent

John Crawley, Robert Key and Ed Smith were tried as fifth batsman during the year but none came near to filling the position in the way that Thorpe did. He had been more often out than in the England side since his back injury in mid-1998; he had not had the best of summers with Surrey. But his private life was apparently less turbulent at last, and his cricketing revival gave England's batting a formidable look. However, even Thorpe was unable to repeat his previous success in Sri Lanka: Muttiah Muralitharan's new leg-break saw to that.

Flintoff was declared England's Man of the Series against South Africa, and there was considerable evidence to suggest that the prodigy was settling down. By the end of the year, though, the jury was still out on the question of whether he was just a No. 7 hitter or had the capacity – above all the nous – to turn himself into a No. 6 batsman. The South African attack, almost entirely fast-medium, was too one-dimensional to prove anything one way or the other. The most encouraging sign came in the final Test of the year at Colombo when, after some unintelligent back-foot prodding mixed with aimless swiping in the two previous games, Flintoff buckled down to bat against the Sri Lankan spinners, working the ball around yet occasionally calling on his massive strength.

Facing the future: Michael Vaughan begins his reign as Test captain at Lord's.
Picture by Patrick Eagar.

Flintoff was also England's most accurate and economical bowler, and often the fastest too, as he banged the ball in short of a length. With a little more artfulness, he would have cashed in on all the balls that forced the batsman into back-foot defence by pitching the odd one up, but he himself admitted that he was a slow learner. The possibilities were evident when out of nowhere, on the flattest of pitches in Kandy, he dismissed a well-set Tillekeratne Dilshan with a rip-snorting bouncer that seamed in sharply and gloved the batsman. Not since Gough in his prime had England possessed a bowler who could make something happen in those conditions.

For the rest of the bowling, Fletcher's plan was for Anderson, Harmison and Jones to take the field together, with Flintoff in support. The England pace attack would then have everything: the both-ways swing of Anderson, the bounce of Harmison and the speed of Jones. Such a house might be des-res indeed.

Unfortunately, the back garden was messier than the building: the behind-the-scenes arrangements were not nearly so neat and orderly. The chaotic mass of committees was simplified to the extent that Fletcher reported to the ECB No. 2, John Carr, but the chain of command and responsibility other than that was as obscure as ever.

Scyld Berry is cricket correspondent of the Sunday Telegraph.

ENGLAND PLAYERS IN 2003

The following 35 players appeared for England in Tests and one-day internationals in the calendar year 2003. All statistics refer to the full year not the 2003 season.

KABIR ALI

Worcestershire

A young seamer could not ask for a better venue to get started, but Headingley's damp was worse than usual: Kabir's first one-day international, against Zimbabwe, was rained off before he could take the field. And although he struck with his fifth ball in Tests at the same ground, this time against South Africa, he soon lost the confidence of his captain, and was left out at The Oval amid mutterings about excess girth. Asian and good-looking, and with a well-publicised website (www.kabirali.com – "Professional cricketer and model"), Kabir epitomised the new breed of England cricketer, not least perhaps in that he appeared not quite good enough. Though his bowling had some of Waqar Younis's old virtues, Kabir was well short of his pace.

2003: 1 Test: 10 runs @ 5.00; 5 wickets @ 27.20
1 ODI: did not bat or bowl.

JAMES ANDERSON

Lancashire

The magic ultimately faded a little, but few players have acquired the Midas touch as quickly. After being summoned from the Academy to join the senior squad for the VB Series, the 20-year-old Anderson was soon bowling like an old pro to return figures of 10–6–12–1 against Australia at Adelaide. Four wickets destroyed Pakistan on a balmy World Cup evening at Cape Town, and not even a crucially wayward over during the defeat by Australia could dampen the enthusiasm. Anderson was seen as both a saviour and sexy: his chameleon-like coiffures led to the fancy that here was cricket's answer to David Beckham. Five wickets on Test debut against Zimbabwe at Lord's further enhanced his reputation, as did a hat-trick, England's first in one-day cricket, against Pakistan at The Oval. Anderson's eventual tally of 41 one-day wickets in 2003 was bettered only by Lee, Muralitharan and Ntini. But as expectations increased, his Test returns went the other way. A buffeting from Graeme Smith – not to mention a mid-pitch shoulder charge – was a harsh dose of reality for the boy from Burnley Thirds, and his opening bursts against South Africa often felt like exercises in damage limitation. England used the excuse of a knee niggle to give Anderson a much-needed breather from the Bangladesh Test series, but he cut a peripheral figure in Sri Lanka after twisting an ankle playing squash. A wicketless return during the Third Test at Colombo was a disappointing end to a year that had probably begun too well for his own good. There remained some doubt about whether he was being over-bowled or over-cosseted, not having played enough to learn resilience ("Burned out?" said Mike Selvey. "He's never been burned in.") And, though he retained a beautiful swing bowler's action, purists noted that Anderson was looking at his feet rather than down the track.

2003: 8 Tests: 45 runs @ 22.50; 26 wickets @ 34.84.
24 ODI: 21 runs @ 4.20; 41 wickets @ 22.53.

GARETH BATTY — Worcestershire

When you come perilously close to drowning, which Batty did while body-surfing in the Indian Ocean in November, being out of your depth on the field is less of a worry. But, after a promising start, he was struck down by Croft/Salisbury syndrome: he batted spunkily down the order, and was even promoted to No. 6 in the final Test in Sri Lanka, but posed little genuine wicket-taking threat. His absence of natural drift away from the right-hander made it hard for him to acquire the off-spinner's extra dimension of hitting the outside edge. In Sri Lanka, on helpful pitches, every scalp took more than 20 overs to arrive.

2003: 4 Tests: 136 runs @ 22.66; 8 wickets @ 63.00.
1 ODI: did not bat; 1 wicket @ 35.00.

MARTIN BICKNELL — Surrey

After a world-record 114 Tests between appearances, Bicknell was brought in to sex down England's young, over-exuberant seam attack for the last two Tests against South Africa. His was a comeback in three phases: instant success, then toil as the unique demands of Test cricket took their toll on his 34-year-old limbs, and finally glory on his home ground at The Oval, where his nous was central to England's series-levelling victory. Workhorses of the world united in approval. There was a peculiar acceptance that this was a two-off comeback, and he was duly omitted from England's winter tour parties a few days later. But it was just possible it was not his last hurrah: there were signs of repentance inside the England camp about the 114 lost opportunities. After all, here was a bowler genuinely capable of making the ball swing both ways.

2003: 2 Tests: 19 runs @ 6.33; 10 wickets @ 28.00.

IAN BLACKWELL — Somerset

Blackwell's eat-drink-and-be-merry philosophy of cricket was always going to bring problems at the very highest level and, despite adequate performances, he was dumped by England after the World Cup on suspicion of not being committed enough. He was ignored all summer but then recalled to the one-day squad for the tour of the subcontinent after showing devastating late-season county batting form. For England, his batting was racked by binary demons in the VB Series and never really recovered: his downfall at Dambulla – courtesy of a reckless cut shot – was typical of an unfulfilled year. His gentle left-arm spinners were innocuous yet also consistently economical.

2003: 12 ODI: 70 runs @ 8.75; 7 wickets @ 36.71.

MARK BUTCHER

Surrey

It was a year of two halves. In the first seven Tests Butcher averaged 63; in the last six just 26. He began with a century at Sydney to redeem a poor Ashes tour, and was in delicious touch throughout the English summer – his other two centuries were also match-winners. In many ways it was a return to the old Butcher. Gone was the sobriety of 2002; in its place came a roguish charmer who sucked you in then often betrayed your trust with a loose stroke. His fielding was even more infuriating, and he was shifted out of the slips in Sri Lanka. Butcher also drew the short straw by failing against Bangladesh – there's always one – and though he scrapped hard in Sri Lanka, it was a struggle for him, as for everyone else. At Kandy, Butcher became only the second man to be stumped twice in a Test since 1956. When called upon to bowl, notably against Zimbabwe at Lord's, Butcher showed he can boomerang the ball dangerously in the right conditions: at the end of the year, his career strike-rate in Tests was better than Harmison's. He did make the World Cup, but only in the commentary box. Despite a maiden limited-overs hundred for Surrey, that elusive one-day international debut looked as far away as ever.

2003: 13 Tests: 979 runs @ 44.50; 5 wickets @ 25.80.

ANDREW CADDICK

Somerset

A year that started with a bang and – at long last – a maiden ten-wicket haul in the Sydney Test fizzled out just as Caddick was set to clamber into the top five of England's all-time wicket-taking list. A stress fracture of the right foot was followed by the recurrence of an old back problem, and Caddick sat out the rest of the year as younger men fought over his wickets instead. When he was fit, Caddick remained the attack leader, with his experience and economy, his height and hustle. No one else in the side would have been capable of taking seven Australian wickets in an innings. But it was still hard to love him. At the World Cup, he made the mistake of riling India with some loose pre-match comments and was promptly hammered by Tendulkar in a game England lost. And his final role was to be ignored by Hussain at a crucial stage of the next match, against Australia, despite already having claimed four wickets in the innings. Dangerous, yet fragile – this was Caddick to the core.

2003: 1 Test: 15 runs @ 7.50; 10 wickets @ 21.50.
11 ODI: 64 runs @ 21.33; 17 wickets @ 22.58.

RIKKI CLARKE **Surrey**

Clarke's heady rise from the fringes of Surrey's First XI to the England one-day team and ultimately the Test side was typical of the new English fashion for fast-tracking. At the age of 21 and with just 11 Championship games on his CV, he was picked against Pakistan and duly took a wicket with his first ball. The delivery, however, was a long-hop, and the feeling lingered that his bowling was more rickety fourth-change than genuine all-rounder – though he had some interesting changes of pace and in Sri Lanka got significantly quicker. But his batting was a different matter – a half-century in his second Test at Chittagong was full of maturity – and his fielding at backward point superb.
2003: 2 Tests: 96 runs @ 32.00; 4 wickets @ 15.00.
11 ODI: 66 runs @ 13.20; 7 wickets @ 31.42.

PAUL COLLINGWOOD **Durham**

For someone who missed almost all of the English summer with a dislocated shoulder, the rest of Collingwood's year could scarcely have gone any better.

He was one of the few stars of England's World Cup campaign, and come the winter was a senior player in the one-day side, having been given the crucial position of No. 4 – the finisher's natural habitat. His status as teacher's pet was such that he was awarded a 12-month central contract before his first Test cap. He showed why with two gutsy performances against Muralitharan in Sri Lanka. With his superb fielding under the helmet, the conviction that he was made of the right stuff was growing.
2003: 2 Tests: 89 runs @ 22.25; no wickets for 37.
15 ODI: 411 runs @ 45.66; 3 wickets @ 24.00.

JOHN CRAWLEY **Hampshire**

Crawley was dumped after the Ashes tour despite averaging 47.10 in the eight Tests since his recall the previous summer. But his contribution to England's victory at Sydney – a painstaking unbeaten 35 off 142 balls in the first innings – summed up his problem: there was a hare in there somewhere, as county bowlers would confirm, but at Test level the angst-ridden tortoise won out.
2003: 1 Test: 43 runs @ 43.00.

RICHARD DAWSON **Yorkshire**

Combative at county level, off-spinner Dawson was eaten alive in the big, bad, real world of Australia. Having started that series with purpose and gumption, he looked tired and out of his depth by the end – on a Sydney pitch usually tailor-made for spinners he took just one for 113, and his main contribution was to bowl the final over of the second day, when Steve Waugh completed his unforgettable hundred. By the end of the summer, Dawson was struggling to make the Yorkshire team. A bowling arm that went beyond perpendicular, making his head fall away, seemed to be creating technical problems all round.

2003: 1 Test: 14 runs @ 7.00; 1 wicket @ 113.00

ANDREW FLINTOFF — Lancashire

See *The Wisden Forty* (page 81).

ASHLEY GILES — Warwickshire

Giles was called many things in 2003: the King of Spain (there was a rogue "A" on some county mugs), a wheelie-bin, useless, and finally heroic, after his batting saved the First Test in Sri Lanka. Giles got his first Test fifties against Zimbabwe, but in his day job he laboured badly. He used the Bangladesh tour to remodel his action, trying to get closer to the stumps with a straighter approach and, after Chittagong, he had taken just ten wickets in eight Tests. Then, in Sri Lanka, he took 16 in the next two; his series tally of 18 was double England's next best, his year's tally second only to Harmison and, whether people liked it or not, Giles ended 2003 once again England's undisputed No. 1 spinner. It may be that his new action was most effective not in improving Giles's bowling, but in improving his own belief in it.

2003: 11 Tests: 317 runs @ 22.64; 28 wickets @ 43.57.
13 ODI: 64 runs @ 16.00; 9 wickets @ 40.00.

DARREN GOUGH — Yorkshire

After a winter's recuperation, Gough was back to his old, ebullient self in the one-day game: grinning, experimenting, grabbing wickets – and doing it all at less than four an over. His performance in the final of the NatWest Series was one of his very best. But his return to the Test side, after two years of injury and self-imposed exile, was a disaster. Gough was made to look pedestrian by Graeme Smith, took a solitary wicket in two games, and duly announced his retirement at Test level. He was, however, still available for one-day cricket and was shocked by his winter omission. The selectors assured him that his career was not necessarily over, but the boyish grin was replaced by the scowl of a fading veteran. Maybe his move to Essex for 2004 will be rejuvenating.

2003: 2 Tests: 49 runs @ 16.33; 1 wicket @ 215.00.
10 ODI: 14 runs, not out; 14 wickets @ 22.42.

STEVE HARMISON — Durham

England's leading Test wicket-taker of 2003 had an enigmatic year. When he was good, he was very good, but searing spells were often sandwiched by three or four anodyne ones. For someone rumoured to be resistant to advice, however, Harmison seemed very responsive to the kick up the backside: after being dropped for the Fourth Test against South Africa at Headingley, he stormed back at The Oval with the most significant spell of his life. And then, far more paradoxically, a man labelled as both lazy and a bad traveller saved England from disaster by taking nine wickets in extreme conditions in Dhaka. Then, just as he was starting to seem indispensable, he got injured again. Harmison began the year modestly, as a non-playing member of the World Cup squad and a first-change who could not consistently deploy all the tools at his disposal, although he did add a spectacular final flourish to the inaugural Test on his home ground in Durham. But, with an average of 13 against Zimbabwe and Bangladesh and 43 against the rest, he finished 2003 with plenty to prove.

2003: 8 Tests: 64 runs @ 8.00; 31 wickets @ 24.25.
4 ODI: 7 runs @ 7.00; 1 wicket @ 162.00.

MATTHEW HOGGARD — Yorkshire

Hoggard, having been the heir apparent to Gough and Caddick for at least 18 months, slipped back into the pack. With an influx of new seamers catching the eye – either through debut six-fors or sexy haircuts – Hoggard's old-fashioned virtues made him something of a forgotten man. He began 2003 with a redemption of sorts for a humbling Ashes tour, at Sydney, but faded into the background as a non-playing member of the World Cup squad. After missing most of the English summer with a knee injury (he played only one Test, working Zimbabwe over in comfortingly dank conditions at Lord's) Hoggard returned to take the Man of the Series award in Bangladesh, although that was as much for lasting the course as anything. He was then dropped after one, largely impotent, performance in Sri Lanka; the public explanation from the usually reticent England coach Duncan Fletcher – "Hoggard struggles a bit when it does not swing" – was worth about ten letters from his heart-on-sleeve Australian counterpart John Buchanan. Prevailing wisdom by now had Hoggard not as the new Gough or Caddick, but as the new Phil DeFreitas: a handful at home when it moves around; anodyne away when it does not. A genuine in-swinger might help.

2003: 5 Tests: 31 runs @ 10.33; 18 wickets @ 26.22.
2 ODI: 5 runs @ 2.50; no wicket for 71.00.

NASSER HUSSAIN — Essex

Most people, as they edge towards retirement, prefer to take things a bit easier. But the quiet life is never an option for an England captain, and 2003 contained enough tumult for a whole career. Worn down by yet another Ashes debacle, Hussain went out of the frying pan and into the fire with a shocker of a World Cup. He was haunted by the Zimbabwe crisis, proved hardly able to buy a run, and his hunch of bowling Anderson ahead of Caddick against Australia cost England dear. Within hours of the team's exit, he announced his retirement from one-day internationals. Then, after a chastening First Test against South Africa, came his resignation as Test captain – English cricket's biggest JFK moment for many a year (where were you when you heard the news?). Hussain probably looked forward to slipping back into the crowd as just another batsman. Some chance. At Lord's he dropped a sitter from Graeme Smith – it cost 251 runs – and his almost blood-curdling cry when he was suckered in the second innings led many to suggest he was mentally shot. He responded at Trent Bridge with a trademark what-do-you-make-of-that century, showing again that he is one of the best rough-track bullies around, but at Headingley his soft dismissal by Jacques Rudolph – after which he lingered at the crease, transfixed by his fate – was pivotal. Given all that had gone on, it felt strangely appropriate that he should miss England's Oval frolic through injury. He was back for the tour of the subcontinent, but his only significant contribution in Sri Lanka was an old-school outburst at Muralitharan, which allegedly involved the words "cheat", "chucker" and some colourful adjectives for clarification. By the end of the year, Collingwood's cool countenance looked a more likely fashion accessory for 2004 than Hussain's passion.

2003: 11 Tests: 711 runs @ 37.42.
10 ODI: 127 runs @ 14.11.

RONNIE IRANI — Essex

Irani's trials and tribulations up and down the batting order mirrored England's chaotic one-day winter of 2002-03. Whether it was at No. 3, 8 or 9, he enjoyed little success, and struggled on true surfaces to make incisions with his honest but transparent medium-pace. Force of personality carried him further than he might otherwise have gone. His greatest achievement was to develop a cult following among the Australian crowds during the VB Series with some impromptu aerobic sessions on the boundary, while his well-publicised love of alternative medical treatments amused the local press. But the callisthenics and homoeopathy could not hide the truth: at international level, enthusiasm and a smile were not enough. Irani was discarded for the English summer, when a troublesome knee plunged his future as an all-rounder into serious doubt.

2003: 8 ODI: 67 runs @ 11.16; 7 wickets @ 40.57.

RICHARD JOHNSON — Somerset

A Test bowling average of 17 was not to be sniffed at, but Johnson was never quite able to shake off the accusation that his successes had come a little too easily. He began with two wickets in his first over and six for 33 on Test debut against Zimbabwe at Chester-le-Street – not to mention a wicket with his second ball in one-day internationals – and then came off the bench to knock down nine Bangladeshis at Chittagong. When he floundered in his first serious tester on a Galle belter, the critics stirred, but he was not the only England seamer to find life hard in Sri Lanka. The net result was that Johnson ended the year as he had begun it: as an often-wounded infantryman in England's jostling army of seam bowlers.

2003: 3 Tests: 59 runs @ 14.75; 16 wickets @ 17.18.
10 ODI: 16 runs @ 5.33; 11 wickets @ 21.72.

ROBERT KEY — Kent

Despite modest statistical returns, Key came back from Australia in credit after showing plenty of courage and resourcefulness in Test cricket's hottest kitchen. But a penchant for getting out to medium-pace trundlers did not bode well for a series against Zimbabwe; and he was duly dropped after scores of 18 (a rough decision) and four. In his two one-day appearances Key looked a fish out of water – which he was: a robust, hard-handed opener asked to pick the gaps in the middle order.

2003: 3 Tests: 39 runs @ 9.75.
2 ODI: 11 runs @ 5.50.

JAMES KIRTLEY — Sussex

Few people can ever have scratched an itch as exquisitely as Kirtley did last year. After being England's perennial twelfth man for the first half of the summer, he torpedoed South Africa at Trent Bridge with six second-innings wickets to grab the match award and the headlines. After reality bit at Headingley, Kirtley missed the final Test of the summer through injury – and a few days later was left out of the winter Test squads altogether, though he was paid the hush money of a one-day place. In this age of fragile fast bowlers, however, a tour party is a bit like a call for a sharp single from Denis Compton: a basis for negotiation. Kirtley, called up as cover, jumped right to the front of the queue for the final two Tests in Sri Lanka. He performed zealously, but his action remained the subject of whispers.

2003: 4 Tests: 32 runs @ 5.33; 19 wickets @ 29.52.
1 ODI: did not bat; 2 wickets @ 16.50.

NICK KNIGHT — Warwickshire

Having waited seven long years to play in a World Cup, Knight had a tournament that was a microcosm of England's: it never really got going. He had started to run out of steam after a fine VB Series, and found a string of weird and wonderful ways to lose his wicket, including a needless run-out against India. At times he looked torn between dashing and dropping anchor; with Trescothick having taken possession of the long handle, Knight moulded himself into a kind of finisher-opener. Yet his most noteworthy act was passive – facing the first recorded 100mph delivery, from Shoaib Akhtar. He announced his retirement after the World Cup, and probably deserved more of a fanfare than he received: Knight's final average (40.41) was the highest of any Englishman to play 20 one-day internationals.

2003: 11 ODI: 339 runs @ 30.81.

ANTHONY McGRATH — Yorkshire

McGrath's selection for the First Test against Zimbabwe in May fell into the category marked "hunch". Like Vaughan and Trescothick before him, McGrath's domestic record was modest – his first-class batting average for Yorkshire was barely 30 – but the hunch seemed to pay off when his first two Tests brought him two gutsy half-centuries and three bonus wickets with his apologetic dobbers. But he failed to dominate even against Zimbabwe, or take the chance to convert his starts into centuries. And the doubts about his capacity against stronger attacks grew when he was promoted from No. 7 in the Test side to No. 4 in the one-day team: one half-century in nine NatWest innings was hardly compelling. He was bounced out by Dewald Pretorious in the Edgbaston Test, and dropped after two failures at Lord's. But McGrath continued to be picked for one-day squads, suggesting coach Duncan Fletcher had not given up on this hunch yet.

2003: 4 Tests: 201 runs @ 40.20; 4 wickets @ 14.00.
10 ODI: 143 runs @ 20.42; 2 wickets @ 63.00.

CHRIS READ — Nottinghamshire

For most of the year, and without a hint of arrogance, Read oozed the conviction that right here, right now, this was his time. Not even an untimely broken finger could stop his second coming as an England player more than three years after his first and, after a classily unobtrusive display in the one-day games at home, there were some loud calls for him to gatecrash Stewart's farewell summer as a Test player. He eventually filled the biggest gloves in English cricket for the tour of the subcontinent. Then the problems began. Read's wicket-keeping remained tidy but, in this Gilchristian age, that was not enough. Despite a feisty willingness to counter-attack, his output with the bat was minimal. By the end of the Sri Lanka series he had been demoted to No. 8, a vulnerable position for a modern wicket-keeper.

2003: 5 Tests: 125 runs @ 20.83; 15 catches, 2 stumpings.
14 ODI: 84 runs @ 21.00; 21 catches.

MARTIN SAGGERS — Kent

It was all over in a flash. When Flintoff had to withdraw from the Test series in Bangladesh, Saggers replaced him, though he was a very different kind of player: no batsman and a pitch-kissing swing bowler. He got his chance to play in Chittagong, and even got to lead England off the field – albeit for some spectacular fielding – before flying home less than a month after his arrival. But as holiday souvenirs go, his Test bowling average was not bad, even if that did only represent three Bangladeshi wickets.

2003: 1 Test: 1 run @ 1.00; 3 wickets @ 20.66.

OWAIS SHAH — Middlesex

His chances were limited, but Shah did little to persuade the selectors that he could yet rise above talented-underachiever status. His preferred mode

of dismissal during the VB Series – one lazy chip against the spinners after another – hardly helped, and by the time the English summer arrived, he had slipped out of sight.
2003: 2 ODI: 47 runs @ 23.50.

ED SMITH  Kent

At the start of the summer, Smith would not have made an England C team, but after an outrageous run of form for Kent – five centuries in six Championship innings in July – he was picked to face South Africa, amid more focus on his double-first from Cambridge University than his batting. He began with a stylish 64, but he soon reminded some observers of another Cambridge man, Crawley, as he began to struggle outside off stump. When he failed on the belting pitch at The Oval, his time seemed up, though the selectors did offer the winter sweetener of an England A place.
2003: 3 Tests: 87 runs @ 17.40.

VIKRAM SOLANKI Worcestershire

Solanki's second coming as a one-day batsman was a typically infuriating mixture of wrist and waste. More than three years after the most recent of his eight one-day internationals, Solanki made a solid start against Pakistan, before producing a string of innings that were either all or nothing, but more usually nothing. There was a sparkling, if vulnerable, hundred against South Africa at The Oval, and an enterprising half-century at Lord's, but otherwise Solanki's shot-selection was as flawed as it had been on the tour to southern Africa in 1999-2000. In the field, he could be electric at backward point, but it was his inconsistency with the bat that stood out. In 13 innings, he failed to pass 12 on nine occasions, and three failures in Bangladesh, of all places, looked like the final straw.
2003: 13 ODI: 277 runs @ 23.08.

ALEC STEWART Surrey

Stewart could hardly have scripted the end to his England career any better: draped in the Cross of St George, on his home ground, celebrating an England victory. But for much of the year he had to fight for his right to party. There was a serious clamour on more than one occasion for him to abdicate his role behind the stumps in favour of Read. He began the year with the last of the great Stewart cameos: a delightful 86-ball 71 that was central to England's victory at Sydney. He could not resist one last summer of Test cricket, but before that he found a new lease of life in one-day cricket: pushed back up to No. 4 or 5 in the World Cup, he contributed strongly in three of his four innings. Stewart hung up his pyjamas after that, and following a self-satisfying performance against Zimbabwe, announced that the South African series would be his last. The knives were out when he made seven and nought in England's heavy defeat at Lord's, but a vital 72 in England's win at Trent Bridge – combined with largely immaculate glovework all year – secured his big farewell. There was no fairytale century, though, and Stewart's average rested at a tantalising 39.54. At long last, England had lost their only world-class all-rounder since the retirement of Ian Botham – just as the nation hailed the arrival of another in Flintoff.

2003: 8 Tests: 385 runs @ 35.00; 21 catches, 1 stumping.
11 ODI: 287 runs @ 28.70; 12 catches, 2 stumpings.

ANDREW STRAUSS — Middlesex

Two factors spoiled Strauss's chance of making more of his call-up for the one-day tour of the subcontinent. One was Solanki, who was given every chance to establish himself at the top of the order in Bangladesh. The other was the Sri Lankan monsoon. After playing himself into the side by top-scoring in a warm-up game at Moratuwa, Strauss's only innings came during the collective disaster at Dambulla. Rain in Colombo meant he would have to wait to show whether he can complement organisation with flair. If he can do that, then as captain of Middlesex, he could be a frontrunner in the Future England Captain stakes.

2003: 1 ODI: 3 runs @ 3.00.

GRAHAM THORPE — Surrey

Thorpe's year did not get going until September, and he was in no mood to hang around. After some bitter personal problems and a string of newspaper confessionals in which he revealed that he had been suffering from depression, Thorpe's return was one of the highlights of England's year. Confronted with a big South African total on his home ground at The Oval, he hit 124 runs of comforting class and put on 268 with Trescothick. England won and Thorpe, in his first Test for nearly 14 months, was clasped to the bosom of the cricketing fraternity once more. But in Sri Lanka he could not repeat the heroics of 2000-01, mainly because of Muralitharan's doosra. Murali got him five times out of six in the Tests, and Thorpe admitted that he had run out of ideas. From a man who remained England's best player of spin, this was a worrying admission. But the middle order still felt safer for his return.

2003: 6 Tests: 443 runs @ 44.30.

MARCUS TRESCOTHICK — Somerset

See *The Wisden Forty* (page 93).

JIM TROUGHTON **Warwickshire**

After leapfrogging his Warwickshire team-mate Ian Bell into the England side, Troughton was unable to transfer his belligerence in four-day Championship cricket to the one-day international stage, where bowlers were quick to seize on a weakness against the short ball. His fielding in the covers was spell-binding, but in the absence of anything to write home about with the bat, journalists everywhere kept bringing up his grandfather, Patrick, who once starred as BBC TV's *Doctor Who*.
2003: 6 ODI: 36 runs @ 9.00.

MICHAEL VAUGHAN **Yorkshire**

See *The Wisden Forty* (page 94).

CRAIG WHITE **Yorkshire**

Not for the first time in his England career, White's stock rose considerably in his absence. He began the year by missing the final Ashes Test, and ended it by missing England's trip to the subcontinent – where his canny reverse swing and fleet-footed strokeplay would have been crucial – because of an ongoing side problem, which precluded him from bowling. That injury did relent long enough to allow White to make a solid contribution to England's World Cup campaign as a thrifty second-change. But his pace had gone and, with it apparently, his Test career.
2003: 5 ODI: 79 runs @ 26.33; 9 wickets @ 19.88.

FEATURES OF 2003

Double-Hundreds (29)

335*†‡	M. W. Goodwin	Sussex v Leicestershire at Hove.
331*†‡	M. E. K. Hussey	Northamptonshire v Somerset at Taunton.
302*†‡	B. J. Hodge	Leicestershire v Nottinghamshire at Nottingham.
279*‡	M. R. Ramprakash	Surrey v Nottinghamshire at Whitgift School.
277‡	G. C. Smith	South Africa v England (First Test) at Birmingham.
273†	M. L. Love	Durham v Hampshire at Chester-le-Street.
264‡	M. E. K. Hussey	Northamptonshire v Gloucestershire at Gloucester.
259‡	G. C. Smith	South Africa v England (Second Test) at Lord's.
247*	I. D. Blackwell	Somerset v Derbyshire at Taunton.
238	D. R. Martyn	Yorkshire v Gloucestershire at Leeds.
236*	J. W. M. Dalrymple	Oxford University v Cambridge University at Cambridge.
236*	S. G. Law	Lancashire v Warwickshire at Manchester.
229*§	D. L. Maddy	Leicestershire v Loughborough UCCE at Leicester.
223*	R. J. Blakey	Yorkshire v Northamptonshire at Leeds.
222	P. A. Jaques	Northamptonshire v Yorkshire at Northampton.
221	K. P. Pietersen	Nottinghamshire v Warwickshire at Birmingham.
219	M. E. Trescothick	England v South Africa (Fifth Test) at The Oval.
218	Wasim Jaffer	India A v Warwickshire at Birmingham.
213‡	E. T. Smith	Kent v Warwickshire at Canterbury.
210‡	M. W. Goodwin	Sussex v Essex at Colchester.
207	M. J. Wood	Yorkshire v Somerset at Taunton.
206	N. Hussain	Essex v Kent at Chelmsford.
205‡	M. R. Ramprakash	Surrey v Loughborough UCCE at The Oval.
203‡	E. T. Smith	Kent v Lancashire at Blackpool.
202*‡§	B. J. Hodge	Leicestershire v Loughborough UCCE at Leicester.
201*	A. Flower	Essex v Surrey at The Oval.
201	C. L. Hooper	Lancashire v Middlesex at Manchester.
200*	D. J. Sales	Northamptonshire v Derbyshire at Derby.
200	J. H. Kallis	South Africans v Derbyshire at Derby.

† *County record.*
‡ *Goodwin, Hodge, Hussey, Ramprakash, E. T. Smith and G. C. Smith each scored two double-hundreds.*
§ *Maddy and Hodge scored double-hundreds in the same innings.*

Three or More Hundreds in Successive Innings

M. E. K. Hussey (Northamptonshire)	100	v Hampshire at Southampton;
	331*	v Somerset at Taunton;
	115	v Derbyshire at Derby;
	187	v Durham at Northampton;
	147	v Glamorgan at Cardiff.
E. T. Smith (Kent)	149 } 113 }	v Nottinghamshire at Maidstone;
	203	v Lancashire at Blackpool;
	108	v Essex at Canterbury.
C. L. Hooper (Lancashire)	201	v Middlesex at Manchester;
	114	v Surrey at Manchester;
	177	v Warwickshire at Birmingham.
M. B. Loye (Lancashire)	137	v Middlesex at Manchester;
	102	v Warwickshire at Birmingham;
	144	v Sussex at Manchester.

Hundred in Each Innings of a Match

C. J. Adams	140	190	Sussex v Lancashire at Hove.
M. J. Powell	125	142	Glamorgan v Worcestershire at Cardiff.
J. N. Rhodes	103	102	Gloucestershire v Durham at Bristol.
E. T. Smith	149	113	Kent v Nottinghamshire at Maidstone.
R. J. Warren	123	113*	Nottinghamshire v Middlesex at Lord's.

Carrying Bat through Completed Innings

J. N. Batty	154*	Surrey (337) v Lancashire at Manchester.
D. P. Fulton	94*	Kent (284) v Essex at Canterbury.
J. E. R. Gallian	112*	Nottinghamshire (211) v Surrey at Nottingham.
M. W. Goodwin	118*	Sussex (251) v Lancashire at Manchester.
A. Singh	83*	Worcestershire (212) v Gloucestershire at Worcester.

Hundred before Lunch

M. A. Carberry	109*	Kent v Cambridge UCCE at Cambridge (1st day).
B. J. Hodge	67* to 175*	Leicestershire v Loughborough UCCE at Leicester (2nd day).
C. L. Hooper	26* to 135*	Lancashire v Middlesex at Manchester (2nd day).
W. I. Jefferson	125*	Essex v Cambridge UCCE at Cambridge (1st day).
S. G. Law	41* to 142*	Lancashire v Middlesex at Manchester (2nd day).
N. Peng	103*	Durham v Durham UCCE at Durham (1st day).
M. J. Prior	9* to 133*	Sussex v Nottinghamshire at Horsham (2nd day).

Fastest Hundred

D. R. Martyn (238) . . . . 65 balls   Yorkshire v Gloucestershire at Leeds.

Fastest Double-Hundred

D. R. Martyn (238)	128 balls	Yorkshire v Gloucestershire at Leeds.
I. D. Blackwell (247*)	134 balls	Somerset v Derbyshire at Taunton.

Four Sixes in Successive Balls

Shoaib Malik (60). . .   off R. K. J. Dawson, Gloucestershire v Yorkshire at Cheltenham.

Most Sixes in an Innings

11	I. D. Blackwell (247*)	Somerset v Derbyshire at Taunton.
11	C. L. Hooper (201)	Lancashire v Middlesex at Manchester.
8	A. Flintoff (154)	Lancashire v Kent at Canterbury.
8	C. L. Hooper (177)	Lancashire v Warwickshire at Birmingham.
7	D. R. Martyn (238)	Yorkshire v Gloucestershire at Leeds.
7	G. G. Wagg (74)	Warwickshire v India A at Birmingham.

Most Runs in Boundaries in an Innings

214 (52 x 4, 1 x 6)	M. W. Goodwin (335*)	Sussex v Leicestershire at Hove.
202 (46 x 4, 3 x 6)	B. J. Hodge (302*)	Leicestershire v Nottinghamshire at Nottingham.

First to 1,000 Runs

E. T. Smith (Kent) on July 15.

Longest Innings

Mins
651 M. E. K. Hussey (331*) . . . Northamptonshire v Somerset at Taunton.

An Hour without Scoring a Run

Mins
62 M. P. Vaughan (156). . . . . . England v South Africa (First Test) at Birmingham (on 12*).

Unusual Dismissal

Timed Out
A. J. Harris. . . . . Nottinghamshire v Durham UCCE at Nottingham.
The third instance in first-class cricket.

First-Wicket Partnership of 100 in Each Innings

104 113 N. V. Knight/I. J. L. Trott, Warwickshire v Nottinghamshire at Birmingham.

Highest Partnerships

First Wicket
338 G. C. Smith/H. H. Gibbs, South Africa v England (First Test) at Birmingham.
258 M. A. Carberry/R. W. T. Key, Kent v Cambridge UCCE at Cambridge.

Second Wicket
281 J. K. Maunders/B. J. Hodge, Leicestershire v Surrey at Leicester.
268 M. E. K. Hussey/P. A. Jaques, Northamptonshire v Durham at Northampton.
259 M. J. Chilton/M. B. Loye, Lancashire v Middlesex at Manchester.
257 G. C. Smith/G. Kirsten, South Africa v England (Second Test) at Lord's.

Third Wicket
436*† D. L. Maddy/B. J. Hodge, Leicestershire v Loughborough UCCE at Leicester.
282 M. B. Loye/S. G. Law, Lancashire v Surrey at The Oval.
268 M. E. Trescothick/G. P. Thorpe, England v South Africa (Fifth Test) at The Oval.
267 M. W. Goodwin/C. J. Adams, Sussex v Leicestershire at Hove.
263 J. W. M. Dalrymple/N. Millar, Oxford University v Cambridge University at Cambridge.

Fourth Wicket
330† M. J. Wood/D. R. Martyn, Yorkshire v Gloucestershire at Leeds.
282 S. G. Law/C. L. Hooper, Lancashire v Middlesex at Manchester.
278 B. J. Hodge/P. A. Nixon, Leicestershire v Nottinghamshire at Nottingham.
273 K. P. Pietersen/C. L. Cairns, Nottinghamshire v Warwickshire at Birmingham.
267 E. T. Smith/M. J. Walker, Kent v Warwickshire at Canterbury.
264 S. G. Law/M. J. Chilton, Lancashire v Middlesex at Lord's.

Fifth Wicket
360† S. G. Law/C. L. Hooper, Lancashire v Warwickshire at Birmingham.
247 S. G. Law/C. L. Hooper, Lancashire v Leicestershire at Leicester.

Sixth Wicket
260 M. E. K. Hussey/G. L. Brophy, Northamptonshire v Gloucestershire at Gloucester.
242* M. E. K. Hussey/T. M. B. Bailey, Northamptonshire v Somerset at Taunton.
228 S. G. Law/G. Chapple, Lancashire v Warwickshire at Manchester.

Eighth Wicket
150 G. Kirsten/M. Zondeki, South Africa v England (Fourth Test) at Leeds.

Tenth Wicket

163† I. D. Blackwell/N. A. M. McLean, Somerset v Derbyshire at Taunton.
107 M. R. Ramprakash/Saqlain Mushtaq, Surrey v Nottinghamshire at Whitgift School.
106 M. J. G. Davis/B. V. Taylor, Sussex v Middlesex at Hove.

† *County record.*

Eight Wickets in an Innings (9)

9-36	M. S. Kasprowicz	Glamorgan v Durham at Cardiff.
9-45	M. S. Kasprowicz	Glamorgan v Durham at Chester-le-Street.
9-79	P. R. Adams.	South Africans v Kent at Canterbury.
8-49	Mohammad Akram	Essex v Surrey at The Oval.
8-53	Kabir Ali.	Worcestershire v Yorkshire at Scarborough (*before lunch*).
8-58	Kabir Ali.	Worcestershire v Derbyshire at Worcester.
8-64	Mohammad Sami	Kent v Nottinghamshire at Maidstone.
8-80	S. P. Kirby.	Yorkshire v Somerset at Taunton.
8-106	J. D. Lewry	Sussex v Leicestershire at Hove.

Twelve Wickets in a Match (4)

15-114	Mohammad Sami	Kent v Nottinghamshire at Maidstone.
13-110	M. S. Kasprowicz	Glamorgan v Durham at Chester-le-Street.
13-154	S. P. Kirby.	Yorkshire v Somerset at Taunton.
12-244	Mushtaq Ahmed	Sussex v Nottinghamshire at Horsham.

Hat-Tricks (4)

J. M. Anderson	Lancashire v Essex at Manchester.
S. R. G. Francis.	Somerset v Loughborough UCCE at Taunton.
J. D. Middlebrook	Essex v Kent at Canterbury.
J. Ormond	Surrey v Middlesex at Guildford.

100 Wickets

Mushtaq Ahmed (Sussex) on September 17.

Outstanding Spells of Bowling

Wkts/Balls		
8 in 38	Mohammad Sami	Kent v Nottinghamshire at Maidstone.
6 in 12	M. Muralitharan	Kent v Nottinghamshire at Nottingham.

Six Wicket-Keeping Dismissals in an Innings

6 ct.	R. J. Blakey	Yorkshire v Glamorgan at Leeds.
6 ct.	G. O. Jones	Kent v Essex at Canterbury.
6 ct.	R. J. Turner	Somerset v Derbyshire at Taunton.

Nine Wicket-Keeping Dismissals in a Match

8 ct, 1 st . . .	R. J. Turner	Somerset v Derbyshire at Taunton.

Six Catches in a Match in the Field

M. J. Powell.	Northamptonshire v Durham at Northampton.

No Byes Conceded in Total of 500 or More

J. N. Batty. . . . . Surrey v Lancashire (599) at The Oval.
J. N. Batty. . . . . Surrey v Kent (535) at Canterbury.
J. S. Foster . . . . Essex v Leicestershire (600-7 dec.) at Southend.
J. S. Foster . . . . Essex v Sussex (612) at Colchester.
D. C. Nash . . . . Middlesex v Surrey (568) at Lord's.
L. D. Sutton . . . . . . Derbyshire v Durham (501-8 dec.) at Derby.
R. J. Turner . . . . Somerset v Worcestershire (538) at Bath.
R. J. Turner . . . . Somerset v Yorkshire (512) at Taunton.

Highest Innings Totals

781 . . . . Lancashire v Warwickshire at Birmingham.
734-5 dec. . . . . Lancashire v Middlesex at Manchester.
705-9 dec.† . . . . Somerset v Hampshire at Taunton.
693 . . . . Surrey v Nottinghamshire at Whitgift School.
682-6 dec. . . . . South Africa v England (Second Test) at Lord's.
681-5 dec. . . . . Northamptonshire v Somerset at Taunton.
673-8 dec. . . . . Yorkshire v Northamptonshire at Leeds.
663-9 dec. . . . . Surrey v Loughborough UCCE at The Oval.
647-5 dec. . . . . Northamptonshire v Derbyshire at Derby.
646 . . . . Nottinghamshire v Warwickshire at Birmingham.
636-4 dec. . . . . Leicestershire v Surrey at Leicester.
622-8 dec. . . . . Northamptonshire v Gloucestershire at Gloucester.
620-7 dec. . . . . Middlesex v Leicestershire at Southgate.
619-7 dec. . . . . Sussex v Nottinghamshire at Horsham.
614-4 dec. . . . . Sussex v Leicestershire at Hove.
612 . . . . Sussex v Essex at Colchester.
611-9 dec. . . . . Gloucestershire v Somerset at Taunton.
604-9 dec. . . . . England v South Africa (Fifth Test) at The Oval.
602-6 dec. . . . . Kent v Lancashire at Blackpool.
600-7 dec. . . . . Leicestershire v Essex at Southend.

† *County record.*

Lowest Innings Total

56 . . . . Somerset v Durham at Chester-le-Street.

Highest Fourth-Innings Totals

425 . . . . Warwickshire v Surrey at Birmingham (set 561).

Match Aggregate of 1,500 Runs

1,568-29 . . . . Middlesex (620-7 dec. and 166-2) v Leicestershire (447 and 335) at Southgate.
1,515-22 . . . . Lancashire (734-5 dec.) v Middlesex (544 and 237-7) at Manchester.

Four Individual Hundreds in an Innings

Surrey (663-9 dec.) v Loughborough UCCE at The Oval:
M. R. Ramprakash (205), A. J. Hollioake (121*), J. N. Batty (123), M. P. Bicknell (103*).
Lancashire (734-5 dec.) v Middlesex at Manchester:
M. J. Chilton (125), M. B. Loye (137), S. G. Law (144), C. L. Hooper (201).
Lancashire (781) v Warwickshire at Birmingham:
M. J. Chilton (121), M. B. Loye (102), S. G. Law (168), C. L. Hooper (177).

Six Individual Fifties in an Innings

Nottinghamshire (542) v Durham UCCE at Nottingham:
D. J. Bicknell (62), J. E. R. Gallian (126*), U. Afzaal (52), K. P. Pietersen (58), B. M. Shafayat (105), C. M. W. Read (94*).
Lancashire (503-6 dec.) v Leicestershire at Liverpool:
M. J. Chilton (108), I. J. Sutcliffe (55), M. B. Loye (54), S. G. Law (82), C. L. Hooper (74), A. Flintoff (71*).
Somerset (705-9 dec.) v Hampshire at Taunton:
N. J. Edwards (160), J. D. C. Bryant (73), T. Webley (59), I. D. Blackwell (189), A. W. Laraman (52), R. J. Turner (67*).
Hampshire (580) v Derbyshire at Derby:
D. A. Kenway (68), J. H. K. Adams (60), S. M. Katich (122), J. P. Crawley (59), J. R. C. Hamblin (96), S. D. Udal (57).

Victory after Following On

Hampshire (185 and 449) beat Glamorgan (437 and 104) by 93 runs at Southampton.

Tied Matches

Warwickshire (446-7 dec. and forfeited second innings) v Essex (66-0 dec. and 380) at Birmingham.
Worcestershire (262 and 247) v Zimbabweans (334 and 175) at Worcester.

Most Extras in an Innings

	b	*l-b*	*w*	*n-b*	
68	18	21	0	29	Leicestershire (636-4 dec.) v Surrey at Leicester.
67	8	5	6	48	Lancashire (781) v Warwickshire at Birmingham.
64	25	21	5	13	South Africa (682-6 dec.) v England (Second Test) at Lord's.
64	16	13	5	30	Surrey (693) v Nottinghamshire at Whitgift School.
62	12	7	1	42	Hampshire (580) v Derbyshire at Derby.
61	14	27	3	17	England (472) v Zimbabwe (First Test) at Lord's.

Career Aggregate Milestones

20,000 runs . . . . S. G. Law.
10,000 runs . . . . J. E. R. Gallian, W. K. Hegg, R. C. Irani, J. H. Kallis, D. A. Leatherdale, R. R. Montgomerie, A. Symonds, W. P. C. Weston.
500 wickets . . . . A. M. Smith.

FIRST-CLASS AVERAGES, 2003

BATTING

(Qualification: 8 completed innings)

† *Left-handed batsman.*

		M	*I*	*NO*	*R*	*HS*	*100s*	*50s*	*Avge*	*Ct/St*
1	S. G. Law (*Lancs*)	16	24	4	1,820	236*	7	6	91.00	17
2	†M. E. K. Hussey (*Northants*)	14	21	2	1,697	331*	6	5	89.31	17
3	†G. C. Smith (*South Africans*)	8	13	1	980	277	3	2	81.66	6
4	M. R. Ramprakash (*Surrey*)	15	23	4	1,444	279*	6	2	76.00	7
5	A. Flintoff (*Lancs & England*)	10	14	1	942	154	3	5	72.46	7
6	†G. Kirsten (*South Africans*)	7	12	2	713	130	2	4	71.30	5
7	C. L. Hooper (*Lancs*)	14	20	2	1,219	201	6	3	67.72	15
8	B. J. Hodge (*Leics*)	16	26	2	1,495	302*	5	3	62.29	12
9	†M. A. Butcher (*Surrey & England*)	14	20	1	1,162	144	4	5	61.15	17
10	†S. M. Katich (*Hants*)	13	22	3	1,143	143*	4	6	60.15	15
11	M. L. Love (*Durham*)	7	13	0	778	273	1	4	59.84	8
12	M. W. Goodwin (*Sussex*)	17	29	3	1,545	335*	4	5	59.42	12
13	J. N. Rhodes (*Glos*)	15	27	5	1,293	151*	5	7	58.77	7
14	N. D. McKenzie (*South Africans*)	6	11	3	470	105*	1	3	58.75	2
15	†P. A. Jaques (*Northants*)	16	25	1	1,409	222	5	6	58.70	9
16	Wasim Jaffer (*India A*)	6	9	0	522	218	1	3	58.00	2
17	J. N. Batty (*Surrey*)	12	22	5	968	168*	3	4	56.94	32/2
18	†G. P. Thorpe (*Surrey & England*)	13	20	2	1,019	156	2	7	56.61	9
19	M. J. Wood (*Yorks*)	17	33	6	1,432	207	5	3	53.03	8
20	E. T. Smith (*Kent & England*)	18	30	1	1,534	213	7	3	52.89	15
21	J. H. Kallis (*South Africans*)	5	9	0	471	200	1	2	52.33	6
22	S. V. Carlisle (*Zimbabweans*)	6	9	0	469	157	2	1	52.11	2
23	†M. E. Trescothick (*Somerset & England*)	11	18	2	826	219	1	7	51.62	17
24	K. P. Pietersen (*Notts*)	16	30	0	1,546	221	4	11	51.53	17
25	†A. J. Strauss (*Middx*)	18	33	3	1,529	155	4	8	50.96	6
26	M. B. Loye (*Lancs*)	15	22	1	1,062	144	5	2	50.57	4
27	†I. D. Blackwell (*Somerset*)	15	26	3	1,160	247*	3	2	50.43	7
28	M. J. Chilton (*Lancs*)	17	25	2	1,154	125	6	3	50.17	15
29	C. White (*Yorks*)	10	16	3	644	173*	2	3	49.53	4
30	†M. J. Di Venuto (*Derbys*)	16	31	0	1,520	150	5	8	49.03	25
31	M. J. Prior (*Sussex*)	16	24	3	1,006	153*	4	3	47.90	28
32	†A. Flower (*Essex*)	17	29	3	1,244	201*	2	7	47.84	17
33	V. Sehwag (*Leics*)	6	10	0	478	137	2	1	47.80	4
34	B. F. Smith (*Worcs*)	18	29	2	1,289	110	2	12	47.74	4
35	J. E. R. Gallian (*Notts*)	13	24	3	1,002	126*	4	5	47.71	16
36	†S. G. Koenig (*Middx*)	16	27	3	1,140	166*	1	7	47.50	3
37	A. Symonds (*Kent*)	10	16	2	659	121	2	4	47.07	6
38	D. R. Brown (*Warwicks*)	16	26	4	1,028	140*	3	7	46.72	10
39	M. P. Maynard (*Glam*)	16	28	0	1,297	142	5	4	46.32	11
40	N. Hussain (*Essex & England*)	11	19	2	783	206	2	3	46.05	3
41	P. A. Cottey (*Sussex*)	15	25	0	1,149	188	3	7	45.96	8
42	A. W. Laraman (*Somerset*)	13	18	5	597	148*	1	3	45.92	5
43	R. J. Warren (*Notts*)	9	18	2	734	123	3	2	45.87	9/2
44	M. A. Wagh (*Warwicks*)	16	30	3	1,228	138	3	7	45.48	15
45	†I. J. Sutcliffe (*Lancs*)	12	17	2	681	109	1	4	45.40	13
46	J. Cox (*Somerset*)	15	27	3	1,087	160	3	5	45.29	10
47	M. A. Vermeulen (*Zimbabweans*)	6	11	1	451	198	1	3	45.10	4
48	N. Pothas (*Hants*)	13	20	2	809	146*	2	4	44.94	38/2
49	I. J. Harvey (*Glos*)	6	12	3	404	128*	1	1	44.88	4

		M	I	NO	R	HS	100s	50s	Avge	Ct/St
50	D. J. Sales (*Northants*)	16	23	2	942	200*	2	4	44.85	13
51	G. O. Jones (*Kent*)	18	27	5	985	108*	2	7	44.77	54/5
52	G. W. Flower (*Zimbabweans*)	6	10	1	399	130	1	2	44.33	7
53	†N. V. Knight (*Warwicks*)	14	26	3	1,012	146	3	5	44.00	11
54	†M. J. Walker (*Kent*)	17	27	3	1,051	150	3	4	43.79	22
55	†J. L. Sadler (*Leics*)	7	11	1	434	145	2	1	43.40	5
56	O. A. Shah (*Middx*)	18	30	2	1,206	147	3	6	43.07	11
57	S. S. Das (*India A*)	7	10	0	428	125	1	3	42.80	8
58	A. J. Stewart (*Surrey & England*)	13	18	1	727	98	0	7	42.76	36/1
59	A. G. R. Loudon (*Durham UCCE & Kent*)	6	11	1	427	172	1	1	42.70	4
60	D. L. Maddy (*Leics*)	17	29	3	1,110	229*	1	6	42.69	15
61	M. J. Powell (*Glam*)	17	30	1	1,234	198	4	3	42.55	14
62	A. McGrath (*Yorks & England*)	14	23	3	850	127*	1	7	42.50	8
63	I. J. L. Trott (*Warwicks*)	10	18	0	763	134	2	5	42.38	4
64	H. H. Gibbs (*South Africans*)	8	14	0	590	183	2	1	42.14	6
65	†J. O. Troughton (*Warwicks*)	12	20	2	748	129*	3	2	41.55	5
66	†M. J. Lumb (*Yorks*)	17	27	2	1,038	115*	2	7	41.52	7
67	S. D. Peters (*Worcs*)	18	30	1	1,177	165	2	9	40.58	15
68	†P. J. Franks (*Notts*)	16	26	8	729	123*	2	1	40.50	9
69	T. R. Ambrose (*Sussex*)	15	26	3	931	93*	0	9	40.47	29/7
70	†B. L. Hutton (*Middx*)	18	30	6	961	107	4	1	40.04	17
71	M. P. Bicknell (*Surrey & England*)	14	15	4	440	141	2	0	40.00	4
71	†N. J. Edwards (*Somerset*)	5	9	0	360	160	1	1	40.00	1
73	J. W. M. Dalrymple (*Oxford UCCE & Middx*)	7	11	2	357	236*	1	0	39.66	6
74	D. C. Nash (*Middx*)	17	26	7	752	113	2	2	39.57	42/3
75	R. Clarke (*Surrey*)	11	16	2	551	139	2	1	39.35	10
76	†E. C. Joyce (*Middx*)	18	30	4	1,023	117	3	4	39.34	7
77	L. D. Sutton (*Derbys*)	16	30	5	982	127	2	2	39.28	26/2
78	†S. P. Fleming (*Yorks*)	7	14	2	469	98	0	3	39.08	13
79	M. Burns (*Somerset*)	18	32	3	1,133	118*	2	8	39.06	15
80	†J. K. Maunders (*Leics*)	12	22	2	777	171	2	3	38.85	3
81	A. J. Hollioake (*Surrey*)	14	19	1	688	122	2	3	38.22	11
82	M. P. Vaughan (*Yorks & England*)	10	18	2	609	156	2	1	38.06	3
83	A. K. D. Gray (*Yorks*)	9	13	2	415	104	1	1	37.72	12
84	G. Chapple (*Lancs*)	16	21	3	679	132*	2	3	37.72	8
85	R. J. Turner (*Somerset*)	16	26	9	641	139*	1	3	37.70	65/5
86	R. W. T. Key (*Kent & England*)	14	22	2	754	140	2	1	37.70	13
87	D. P. Fulton (*Kent*)	11	19	1	674	94*	0	5	37.44	4
88	R. A. Smith (*Hants*)	10	15	1	522	92	0	5	37.28	9
89	†I. J. Ward (*Surrey*)	15	24	1	856	158	3	2	37.21	8
90	J. J. B. Lewis (*Durham*)	18	34	2	1,188	124	1	11	37.12	5
91	Azhar Mahmood (*Surrey*)	11	14	2	445	98	0	4	37.08	17
92	R. S. C. Martin-Jenkins (*Sussex*)	16	25	3	811	121*	1	5	36.86	7
93	M. A. Ealham (*Kent*)	17	25	0	911	101	1	7	36.44	18
94	†R. C. Russell (*Glos*)	11	16	4	436	78*	0	3	36.33	33/4
95	M. V. Boucher (*South Africans*)	8	11	1	360	89	0	3	36.00	21/1
96	†M. A. Carberry (*Kent*)	14	24	1	824	137	1	6	35.82	2
97	C. J. Adams (*Sussex*)	16	27	0	966	190	4	2	35.77	18
98	A. Habib (*Essex*)	13	22	1	738	151	2	4	35.14	9
99	T. H. C. Hancock (*Glos*)	12	21	0	720	97	0	5	34.28	13
100	M. J. Powell (*Warwicks*)	12	22	0	754	110	1	6	34.27	4
101	†U. Afzaal (*Notts*)	9	15	1	477	161*	1	2	34.07	3
101	P. D. Bowler (*Somerset*)	9	15	1	477	92	0	5	34.07	11
103	W. I. Jefferson (*Essex*)	14	27	4	781	125*	1	5	33.95	12
104	H. H. Dippenaar (*South Africans*)	7	11	1	339	92	0	3	33.90	4
105	J. P. Crawley (*Hants*)	16	27	1	878	93	0	8	33.76	5
106	†W. P. C. Weston (*Glos*)	15	27	1	877	179	2	2	33.73	10
107	†D. L. Hemp (*Glam*)	12	21	3	607	85*	0	5	33.72	5

		M	*I*	*NO*	*R*	*HS*	*100s*	*50s*	*Avge*	*Ct/St*
108	R. R. Montgomerie (*Sussex*)	17	29	2	908	105	1	7	33.62	24
109	G. A. Hick (*Worcs*)	13	23	3	670	155	1	3	33.50	19
	Waqar Younis (*Warwicks*)	8	13	5	268	61	0	2	33.50	1
111	C. M. Spearman (*Glos*)	15	27	0	903	103	1	7	33.44	15
112	†D. J. Bicknell (*Notts*)	16	29	1	936	81	0	9	33.42	4
113	†G. J. Pratt (*Durham*)	18	33	1	1,055	150	1	8	32.96	11
114	D. D. J. Robinson (*Essex*)	11	20	2	592	89	0	4	32.88	7
115	A. F. Giles (*Warwicks & England*)	12	18	1	556	96	0	4	32.70	2
116	I. D. K. Salisbury (*Surrey*)	14	18	4	455	101*	1	1	32.50	6
117	Saqlain Mushtaq (*Surrey*)	14	15	2	421	69	0	4	32.38	4
118	D. I. Stevens (*Leics*)	11	19	0	615	149	1	6	32.36	12
119	A. J. Hall (*Worcs & South Africans*)	11	16	2	445	104	1	3	31.78	11
120	T. Taibu (*Zimbabweans*)	6	10	2	254	57	0	1	31.75	17/2
121	†P. N. Weekes (*Middx*)	18	29	5	760	102*	1	4	31.66	20
122	R. C. Irani (*Essex*)	13	20	1	597	102*	1	4	31.42	4
123	G. S. Blewett (*Kent*)	7	12	0	377	71	0	3	31.41	7
124	W. K. Hegg (*Lancs*)	16	20	7	404	61*	0	1	31.07	46/3
125	†C. P. Schofield (*Lancs*)	9	12	2	310	66	0	2	31.00	9
126	C. M. W. Read (*Notts*)	13	23	3	619	94*	0	4	30.95	32/3
127	C. L. Cairns (*Notts*)	13	23	2	645	104	1	4	30.71	7
128	M. G. N. Windows (*Glos*)	16	29	0	890	150	1	5	30.68	11
129	†J. P. Maher (*Glam*)	8	16	0	491	95	0	4	30.68	7
130	†T. Webley (*Cambridge UCCE & Somerset*)	9	16	2	428	104	1	2	30.57	3
131	I. R. Bell (*Warwicks*)	17	30	2	854	107	1	5	30.50	5
132	Kadeer Ali (*Worcs*)	8	14	0	426	99	0	3	30.42	2
133	W. S. Kendall (*Hants*)	9	13	0	391	114	1	1	30.07	6
134	G. R. Napier (*Essex*)	15	24	8	480	89*	0	2	30.00	3
	V. Atri (*Loughborough UCCE & Notts*)	5	10	2	240	82*	0	2	30.00	3
136	†J. A. Rudolph (*South Africans*)	8	13	0	389	92	0	4	29.92	6
137	J. D. C. Bryant (*Somerset*)	14	24	2	658	109*	1	2	29.90	8
138	Abdul Razzaq (*Middx*)	8	11	0	328	81	0	3	29.81	2
139	N. Peng (*Durham*)	15	25	0	743	158	2	2	29.72	12
140	R. D. B. Croft (*Glam*)	17	29	4	739	122	1	4	29.56	9
141	T. R. Ward (*Leics*)	9	15	0	443	168	1	1	29.53	7
142	†M. A. Wallace (*Glam*)	17	29	0	856	121	2	3	29.51	49/2
143	†P. A. Nixon (*Leics*)	17	27	4	676	113*	1	3	29.39	50/2
144	R. K. J. Dawson (*Yorks*)	12	18	2	467	77	0	2	29.18	11
145	A. P. R. Gidman (*Glos*)	8	16	2	407	68	0	2	29.07	7
146	J. N. Snape (*Leics*)	16	23	6	494	54	0	2	29.05	8
147	A. Singh (*Worcs*)	16	27	1	754	105	1	4	29.00	6
	M. M. Betts (*Warwicks*)	10	14	2	348	73	0	2	29.00	2
149	D. A. Kenway (*Hants*)	16	28	1	760	115	2	3	28.14	14
150	†V. J. Craven (*Yorks*)	6	11	1	281	47	0	0	28.10	0
151	R. J. Blakey (*Yorks*)	13	19	2	468	223*	1	0	27.52	32/1
152	P. S. Jones (*Somerset*)	8	12	2	273	63	0	2	27.30	2
153	S. D. Udal (*Hants*)	16	24	6	488	60*	0	3	27.11	5
154	D. D. Ebrahim (*Zimbabweans*)	6	11	1	271	68	0	3	27.10	4
155	Mushtaq Ahmed (*Sussex*)	16	19	2	456	60	0	3	26.82	3
156	A. I. Gait (*Derbys*)	13	25	0	664	110	1	4	26.56	10
157	V. S. Solanki (*Worcs*)	15	23	1	584	79	0	4	26.54	24
158	J. S. Foster (*Essex*)	17	26	0	689	85	0	4	26.50	49/2
159	†J. H. K. Adams (*Loughborough UCCE, Hants & British Us*)	13	26	1	661	107	1	3	26.44	6
160	A. G. Wharf (*Glam*)	16	27	9	475	79	0	2	26.38	7
161	J. M. Kemp (*Worcs*)	6	11	0	290	90	0	1	26.36	9
162	T. W. Roberts (*Northants*)	7	10	0	263	83	0	2	26.30	7
163	R. S. Ferley (*Durham UCCE, British Us & Kent*)	10	14	4	262	78*	0	2	26.20	5

		M	I	NO	R	HS	100s	50s	Avge	Ct/St
164	R. L. Johnson (*Somerset & England*)	11	15	3	314	118	1	0	26.16	5
165	M. J. G. Davis (*Sussex*)	11	12	2	259	168	1	0	25.90	4
166	†J. W. Cook (*Northants*)	14	22	2	517	85	0	3	25.85	3
167	G. J. Muchall (*Durham*)	13	25	1	620	121	2	3	25.83	5
168	A. Nel (*Northants*)	13	13	3	258	42	0	0	25.80	4
169	S. J. Rhodes (*Worcs*)	11	14	2	309	81*	0	2	25.75	38/2
170	A. D. Brown (*Surrey*)	14	21	2	484	74	0	5	25.47	12
171	M. C. J. Ball (*Glos*)	10	15	3	304	75	0	2	25.33	12
172	M. S. Kasprowicz (*Glam*)	15	26	4	556	78	0	2	25.27	7
173	A. Dale (*Glam*)	15	27	1	657	123	1	2	25.26	12
174	A. D. Mascarenhas (*Hants*)	17	26	2	600	100*	1	2	25.00	7
175	G. E. Welton (*Notts*)	12	23	0	572	99	0	5	24.86	6
176	N. R. C. Dumelow (*Derbys*)	10	17	3	347	75	0	3	24.78	2
177	M. J. Wood (*Somerset*)	12	23	1	536	100	1	3	24.36	1
178	†I. D. Fisher (*Glos*)	10	12	3	219	71	0	1	24.33	4
179	A. P. Grayson (*Essex*)	10	18	2	388	90	0	3	24.25	5
180	†J. M. Dakin (*Essex*)	11	19	2	411	59	0	2	24.17	2
181	T. M. B. Bailey (*Northants*)	14	19	3	384	101*	1	0	24.00	29/6
181	G. D. Bridge (*Durham*)	8	13	3	240	50	0	1	24.00	7
183	T. Frost (*Warwicks*)	13	21	1	477	84	0	4	23.85	33/2
184	Kabir Ali (*Worcs & England*)	14	20	4	381	84*	0	2	23.81	2
185	A. J. Swann (*Lancs*)	10	15	0	355	137	1	1	23.66	14
186	A. Khan (*Kent*)	8	10	0	236	78	0	1	23.60	1
187	K. J. Innes (*Sussex*)	8	12	4	188	103*	1	0	23.50	1
188	M. A. Gough (*Durham*)	13	25	0	584	73	0	4	23.36	8
189	B. M. Shafayat (*Notts*)	13	23	0	533	105	1	3	23.17	3
190	D. G. Cork (*Derbys*)	16	29	3	593	92	0	3	22.80	11
191	J. Ormond (*Surrey*)	13	15	5	226	47	0	0	22.60	2
192	S. Elworthy (*Notts*)	5	8	0	179	52	0	1	22.37	3
193	R. J. Kirtley (*Sussex & England*)	13	17	7	223	40*	0	0	22.30	5
194	M. Kaif (*Derbys*)	8	15	0	332	87	0	1	22.13	5
195	†P. Mustard (*Durham*)	13	23	1	486	70*	0	1	22.09	42/3
196	G. J. Batty (*Worcs*)	18	28	4	529	60	0	3	22.04	14
197	J. Hughes (*Glam*)	10	17	0	372	73	0	2	21.88	10
198	M. J. Powell (*Northants*)	16	25	2	494	64	0	4	21.47	32
199	P. A. J. DeFreitas (*Leics*)	16	25	2	493	103	1	2	21.43	6
200	C. G. Taylor (*Glos*)	4	8	0	171	45	0	0	21.37	3
201	G. P. Swann (*Northants*)	9	13	1	256	69	0	2	21.33	9
202	V. J. Wells (*Durham*)	12	21	1	420	106	1	2	21.00	11
202	R. M. Khan (*Derbys*)	9	16	0	336	76	0	2	21.00	3
204	†S. A. Selwood (*Derbys*)	9	17	1	333	88	0	2	20.81	3
205	D. Gough (*Yorks & England*)	9	13	1	248	83	0	2	20.66	2
206	G. Welch (*Derbys*)	15	27	6	429	54	0	2	20.42	3
207	J. D. Middlebrook (*Essex*)	16	25	1	484	82*	0	2	20.16	7
208	†J. D. Francis (*Loughborough UCCE, British Us & Hants*)	10	19	0	369	65	0	2	19.42	6
209	M. W. Alleyne (*Glos*)	8	13	3	193	32*	0	0	19.30	9
210	R. A. White (*Loughborough UCCE, Northants & British Us*)	7	14	0	261	76	0	2	18.64	4
211	C. T. Tremlett (*Hants*)	10	13	2	199	43	0	0	18.09	5
212	†J. D. Lewry (*Sussex*)	12	15	3	215	70	0	1	17.91	4
213	G. M. Fellows (*Yorks*)	6	8	0	142	53	0	1	17.75	1
214	J. Lewis (*Glos*)	14	18	4	248	47	0	0	17.71	3
215	N. M. K. Smith (*Warwicks*)	6	8	0	138	57	0	1	17.25	2
216	†N. A. M. McLean (*Somerset*)	17	23	4	318	76	0	1	16.73	2
217	†J. C. Tredwell (*Kent*)	13	19	3	267	36	0	0	16.68	15
218	†I. J. Thomas (*Glam*)	7	11	0	182	53	0	1	16.54	8
219	Shoaib Akhtar (*Durham*)	7	14	2	197	37	0	0	16.41	0
220	K. P. Dutch (*Somerset*)	7	10	0	161	61	0	1	16.10	9
221	M. J. Saggers (*Kent*)	15	20	5	240	47	0	0	16.00	3

		M	I	NO	R	HS	100s	50s	Avge	Ct/St
222	C. B. Keegan (*Middx*)	17	20	3	270	36*	0	0	15.88	5
223	M. S. Mason (*Worcs*)	15	20	4	250	52	0	1	15.62	2
224	S. J. Cook (*Middx*)	12	17	3	211	65	0	1	15.07	5
225	D. P. Ostler (*Warwicks*)	5	8	0	119	58	0	1	14.87	3
226	C. W. G. Bassano (*Derbys*)	12	22	3	277	53*	0	2	14.57	7
227	†Yuvraj Singh (*Yorks*)	7	12	2	145	56	0	1	14.50	12
228	D. R. Law (*Durham*)	6	10	1	127	74	0	1	14.11	1
229	N. C. Phillips (*Durham*)	13	22	5	239	39	0	0	14.05	9
230	D. R. Hewson (*Derbys*)	9	16	0	222	57	0	1	13.87	4
231	†R. J. Sidebottom (*Yorks*)	9	11	2	122	28	0	0	13.55	4
232	D. S. Harrison (*Glam*)	16	25	5	271	66	0	1	13.55	3
233	D. D. Masters (*Leics*)	17	23	3	269	119	1	0	13.45	4
234	S. R. G. Francis (*Somerset*)	10	13	2	133	44	0	0	12.09	2
235	A. Richardson (*Warwicks*)	14	19	5	158	47	0	0	11.28	1
236	C. E. W. Silverwood (*Yorks*)	12	18	4	152	53	0	1	10.85	2
237	P. J. McMahon (*Oxford UCCE & Notts*)	6	9	0	93	30	0	0	10.33	3
238	P. J. Martin (*Lancs*)	14	12	0	120	23	0	0	10.00	8
239	G. J. Smith (*Notts*)	13	21	3	172	42	0	0	9.55	4
240	S. C. G. MacGill (*Notts*)	11	18	6	112	27	0	0	9.33	2
241	S. M. Guy (*Yorks*)	6	8	0	73	26	0	0	9.12	16/2
242	A. Sheriyar (*Kent*)	15	20	9	97	18*	0	0	8.81	3
243	S. J. Harmison (*Durham & England*)	11	14	5	78	14*	0	0	8.66	2
244	J. T. A. Bruce (*Hants*)	8	11	3	68	21*	0	0	8.50	3
245	S. P. Kirby (*Yorks*)	14	18	4	113	33	0	0	8.07	5
246	N. Killeen (*Durham*)	11	18	4	110	26	0	0	7.85	2
247	M. Hayward (*Worcs*)	16	21	5	123	28	0	0	7.68	5
248	Mohammad Ali (*Derbys*)	10	17	3	101	31	0	0	7.21	1
249	†K. J. Dean (*Derbys*)	16	24	3	148	30*	0	0	7.04	4
250	C. E. Shreck (*Notts*)	11	15	6	51	19	0	0	5.66	1
251	S. A. Brant (*Essex*)	11	14	6	37	23	0	0	4.62	3
252	†J. A. Tomlinson (*British Us & Hants*)	8	13	5	27	10	0	0	3.37	2
253	A. J. Harris (*Notts*)	10	12	1	37	16*	0	0	3.36	2

BOWLING

(Qualification: 10 wickets in 10 innings)

		Style	O	M	R	W	BB	5W/i	Avge
1	Shoaib Akhtar (*Durham*)	RF	183	40	580	34	4-9	0	17.05
2	B. J. Phillips (*Northants*)	RFM	149	47	400	21	4-45	0	19.04
3	R. J. Sidebottom (*Yorks*)	LFM	222.2	37	710	35	7-97	2	20.28
4	M. S. Kasprowicz (*Glam*)	RFM	572.3	140	1,629	77	9-36	4	21.15
5	M. S. Mason (*Worcs*)	RFM	439.3	128	1,144	53	6-68	2	21.58
6	S. M. Pollock (*South Africans*)	RFM	198	61	480	22	6-39	1	21.81
7	J. M. Kemp (*Worcs*)	RM	102.1	17	319	14	5-48	1	22.78
8	M. Hayward (*Worcs*)	RF	427.3	83	1,533	67	5-46	2	22.88
9	G. P. Swann (*Northants*)	OB	238.2	37	759	33	7-33	3	23.00
10	I. J. Harvey (*Glos*)	RM	195.2	54	625	27	4-43	0	23.14
11	Kabir Ali (*Worcs & England*)	RFM	415.2	72	1,552	67	8-53	3	23.16
12	V. J. Wells (*Durham*)	RM	164.4	36	515	22	4-16	0	23.40
13	Waqar Younis (*Warwicks*)	RFM	244.2	39	917	39	5-40	3	23.51
14	A. J. Hall (*Worcs & South Africans*)	RFM	293.4	70	823	35	3-10	0	23.51
15	A. M. Smith (*Glos*)	LFM	329.5	91	898	38	5-70	1	23.63
16	A. McGrath (*Yorks & England*)	RM	134.1	21	403	17	3-16	0	23.70
17	J. F. Brown (*Northants*)	OB	647	188	1,565	66	7-69	4	23.71
18	P. A. J. DeFreitas (*Leics*)	RM	540.3	154	1,443	60	7-51	4	24.05
19	G. J. Smith (*Notts*)	LFM	356.1	78	1,227	51	5-42	3	24.05

		Style	O	M	R	W	BB	5W/i	Avge
20	J. Lewis (*Glos*)	RFM	551.2	142	1,800	74	7-117	5	24.32
21	C. E. W. Silverwood (*Yorks*)	RF	351.4	73	1,177	48	5-63	2	24.52
22	Mushtaq Ahmed (*Sussex*)	LBG	836.3	163	2,539	103	7-85	10	24.65
23	M. J. Saggers (*Kent*)	RFM	450	97	1,441	58	5-42	2	24.84
24	M. J. Cawdron (*Northants*)	RM	142.3	31	504	20	6-87	1	25.20
25	J. W. Cook (*Northants*)	RM	162.3	46	479	19	5-31	1	25.21
26	R. L. Johnson (*Somerset & England*)	RFM	364.1	85	1,077	42	6-33	2	25.64
27	G. J. Batty (*Worcs*)	OB	574.4	142	1,575	60	6-88	1	26.25
28	S. P. Kirby (*Yorks*)	RF	463	80	1,769	67	8-80	5	26.40
29	G. Keedy (*Lancs*)	SLA	555.5	126	1,593	60	6-68	5	26.55
30	J. D. Lewry (*Sussex*)	LFM	337.2	73	1,118	42	8-106	3	26.61
31	M. A. Ealham (*Kent*)	RM	357.5	106	1,013	38	6-35	3	26.65
32	R. J. Kirtley (*Sussex & England*)	RFM	529.1	127	1,662	62	6-26	3	26.80
33	S. J. Harmison (*Durham & England*)	RF	349.2	97	1,002	37	4-33	0	27.08
34	D. G. Cork (*Derbys*)	RFM	444.1	99	1,363	50	6-28	3	27.26
35	I. D. Fisher (*Glos*)	SLA	225.1	50	767	28	5-30	3	27.39
36	J. M. Dakin (*Essex*)	RM	352.3	79	1,099	40	5-86	1	27.47
37	M. P. Bicknell (*Surrey & England*)	RFM	444.4	110	1,391	50	5-42	3	27.82
38	D. L. Maddy (*Leics*)	RM	297.1	59	1,002	36	5-49	1	27.83
39	G. Welch (*Derbys*)	RM	483.3	121	1,476	53	6-102	2	27.84
40	J. Ormond (*Surrey*)	RFM	392.1	74	1,428	51	6-34	3	28.00
41	P. R. Adams (*South Africans*)	SLC	130.3	21	425	15	9-79	1	28.33
42	N. A. M. McLean (*Somerset*)	RFM	551.3	115	1,872	65	5-43	3	28.80
43	M. J. Hoggard (*Yorks & England*)	RFM	225.3	57	606	21	7-49	1	28.85
44	B. V. Taylor (*Sussex*)	RFM	244.1	69	681	23	4-42	0	29.60
45	R. D. B. Croft (*Glam*)	OB	731.5	192	1,928	65	6-71	5	29.66
46	J. M. Anderson (*Lancs & England*)	RFM	332.5	72	1,232	41	5-61	3	30.04
47	S. A. Brant (*Essex*)	LFM	344.5	77	1,117	37	6-45	1	30.18
48	C. L. Hooper (*Lancs*)	OB	366.2	86	912	30	6-51	2	30.40
49	C. B. Keegan (*Middx*)	RFM	585.4	121	1,925	63	6-114	3	30.55
50	Azhar Mahmood (*Surrey*)	RFM	283.5	52	1,097	35	5-78	1	31.34
51	J. H. Dawes (*Middx*)	RFM	331.4	58	1,071	34	5-46	1	31.50
52	P. J. Martin (*Lancs*)	RFM	432.1	99	1,295	41	5-54	1	31.58
53	J. Wood (*Lancs*)	RFM	222.4	32	854	27	3-17	0	31.62
54	D. S. Harrison (*Glam*)	RM	366	84	1,284	40	5-80	1	32.10
55	S. D. Udal (*Hants*)	OB	436.4	87	1,350	42	4-50	0	32.14
56	A. D. Mascarenhas (*Hants*)	RFM	489.1	150	1,287	40	6-55	1	32.17
57	A. Symonds (*Kent*)	RM/OB	152	26	517	16	3-38	0	32.31
58	P. J. McMahon (*Oxford UCCE & Notts*)	OB	203.4	51	595	18	4-59	0	33.05
59	A. Sheriyar (*Kent*)	LFM	374.3	76	1,257	38	5-65	1	33.07
60	D. Pretorius (*Durham & S. Africans*)	RFM	206	31	863	26	4-15	0	33.19
61	Saqlain Mushtaq (*Surrey*)	OB	471	100	1,364	41	5-46	3	33.26
62	A. G. Wharf (*Glam*)	RM	432.3	72	1,734	52	4-53	0	33.34
63	S. C. G. MacGill (*Notts*)	LBG	412.2	73	1,408	42	6-117	2	33.52
64	S. R. G. Francis (*Somerset*)	RFM	328.1	72	1,179	35	4-47	0	33.68
65	C. T. Tremlett (*Hants*)	RFM	248.4	48	929	27	6-51	1	34.40
66	S. M. Katich (*Hants*)	SLC	160.4	29	591	17	4-21	0	34.76
67	J. D. Middlebrook (*Essex*)	OB	593	87	1,979	56	6-123	3	35.33
68	L. E. Plunkett (*Durham*)	RFM	164	34	672	19	5-53	1	35.36
69	D. R. Brown (*Warwicks*)	RFM	377.5	81	1,274	36	5-72	2	35.38
70	G. Chapple (*Lancs*)	RFM	494.2	90	1,744	49	6-98	2	35.59
71	A. Nel (*Northants*)	RFM	422.3	99	1,292	36	5-47	1	35.88
72	C. E. Dagnall (*Leics*)	RM	295.5	70	1,005	28	5-66	1	35.89
73	A. A. Noffke (*Middx*)	RFM	245.4	52	754	21	5-52	1	35.90
74	M. C. J. Ball (*Glos*)	OB	378.3	99	1,008	28	5-104	1	36.00
75	N. Killeen (*Durham*)	RFM	290	70	946	26	7-70	1	36.38
76	M. A. Wagh (*Warwicks*)	OB	193.3	28	730	20	7-222	1	36.50
77	I. D. K. Salisbury (*Surrey*)	LBG	371.1	60	1,224	33	4-116	0	37.09
78	I. D. Blackwell (*Somerset*)	SLA	466.4	111	1,336	36	5-65	2	37.11

		Style	O	M	R	W	BB	5W/i	Avge
79	N. G. Hatch (*Durham*)	RM	149.4	28	484	13	3-66	0	37.23
80	M. M. Betts (*Warwicks*)	RFM	240.2	30	970	26	5-43	1	37.30
81	Mohammad Ali (*Derbys*)	LFM	221	36	1,060	28	4-79	0	37.85
82	M. Ntini (*South Africans*)	RF	222.2	40	910	24	5-75	2	37.91
83	C. E. Shreck (*Notts*)	RFM	227.1	46	878	23	5-100	1	38.17
84	P. N. Weekes (*Middx*)	OB	451.1	85	1,355	35	4-55	0	38.71
85	S. J. Cook (*Middx*)	RFM	332.2	78	1,048	27	4-42	0	38.81
86	K. J. Dean (*Derbys*)	LFM	445.3	108	1,593	41	4-39	0	38.85
87	K. P. Pietersen (*Notts*)	OB	108.4	18	428	11	4-31	0	38.90
88	A. D. Mullally (*Hants*)	LFM	229.1	55	664	17	3-31	0	39.05
89	M. Burns (*Somerset*)	RM	153.5	29	514	13	3-35	0	39.53
90	N. C. Phillips (*Durham*)	OB	408.4	63	1,513	38	5-144	1	39.81
91	A. Richardson (*Warwicks*)	RFM	453	104	1,314	33	4-37	0	39.81
92	G. D. Bridge (*Durham*)	SLA	289	59	996	25	4-47	0	39.84
93	J. C. Tredwell (*Kent*)	OB	329.4	73	1,125	28	4-48	0	40.17
94	R. S. C. Martin-Jenkins (*Sussex*)	RFM	364	82	1,258	31	3-9	0	40.58
95	A. W. Laraman (*Somerset*)	RFM	279.5	58	979	24	3-20	0	40.79
96	D. A. Cosker (*Glam*)	SLA	264.5	67	695	17	3-49	0	40.88
97	R. Clarke (*Surrey*)	RFM	164.1	22	709	17	4-21	0	41.70
98	P. J. Franks (*Notts*)	RFM	296	49	1,177	28	4-62	0	42.03
99	P. S. Jones (*Somerset*)	RFM	204.3	27	930	22	5-42	1	42.27
100	C. P. Schofield (*Lancs*)	LBG	187.1	37	636	15	4-64	0	42.40
101	D. D. Masters (*Leics*)	RFM	425.3	85	1,581	37	5-53	1	42.72
102	R. S. Ferley (*Durham UCCE, British Us & Kent*)	SLA	259	44	1,032	24	4-76	0	43.00
103	N. R. C. Dumelow (*Derbys*)	OB	214.5	43	776	18	5-78	2	43.11
104	D. Gough (*Yorks & England*)	RFM	271.1	55	866	20	3-40	0	43.30
105	J. T. A. Bruce (*Hants*)	RFM	196	39	829	19	3-42	0	43.63
106	J. W. M. Dalrymple (*Oxford UCCE & Middx*)	OB	172.1	27	529	12	5-49	1	44.08
107	G. R. Napier (*Essex*)	RM	379.3	60	1,506	33	5-66	1	45.63
108	A. M. Davies (*Durham*)	RFM	149	35	509	11	2-34	0	46.27
109	J. A. Tomlinson (*British Us & Hants*)	LM	171.5	22	794	17	6-63	1	46.70
110	A. Khan (*Kent*)	RFM	165	16	797	17	4-65	0	46.88
111	C. G. Greenidge (*Northants*)	RFM	230.4	25	1,039	22	3-33	0	47.22
112	Abdul Razzaq (*Middx*)	RFM	202.4	28	761	16	3-69	0	47.56
113	A. Flintoff (*Lancs & England*)	RFM	232	57	727	15	2-47	0	48.46
114	R. K. J. Dawson (*Yorks*)	OB	241.5	47	840	17	3-119	0	49.41
115	M. A. Harrity (*Worcs*)	LFM	166.5	37	549	11	4-39	0	49.90
116	B. J. Trott (*Kent*)	RFM	150.3	27	649	13	4-73	0	49.92
117	C. L. Cairns (*Notts*)	RFM	184	31	755	15	3-59	0	50.33
118	M. J. G. Davis (*Sussex*)	OB	237	46	761	15	3-44	0	50.73
119	A. F. Giles (*Warwicks & England*)	SLA	374.5	62	1,146	22	5-115	1	52.09
120	A. K. D. Gray (*Yorks*)	OB	233.2	51	692	13	3-43	0	53.23
121	A. P. Palladino (*Cambridge UCCE & Essex*)	RM	162	31	594	11	6-41	1	54.00
122	A. J. Harris (*Notts*)	RFM	208.5	31	850	15	4-23	0	56.66

The following bowlers took ten wickets but bowled in fewer than ten innings:

	Style	O	M	R	W	BB	5W/i	Avge
M. Muralitharan (*Kent*)	OB	178	41	447	33	6-36	4	13.54
Mohammad Sami (*Kent*)	RF	89.1	17	357	18	8-64	2	19.83
D. T. Hondo (*Zimbabweans*)	RFM	94	23	312	15	5-26	1	20.80
M. K. Munday (*Oxford UCCE*)	LB	80	8	305	14	5-83	1	21.78
H. H. Streak (*Zimbabweans*)	RFM	123.3	38	263	12	4-64	0	21.91
S. D. Thomas (*Glam*)	RFM	82.1	8	293	13	4-47	0	22.53
Wasim Akram (*Hants*)	LFM	167.3	44	503	20	3-31	0	25.15
D. E. Malcolm (*Leics*)	RFM	94	22	358	14	5-40	1	25.57
E. S. H. Giddins (*Hants*)	RFM	98.5	18	336	13	4-88	0	25.84
A. Bhandari (*India A*)	RFM	119.2	23	424	16	6-38	2	26.50

	Style	O	M	R	W	BB	5W/i	Avge
J. H. Kallis (*South Africans*)	RFM	131.3	29	412	15	6-54	1	27.46
Mohammad Akram (*Essex*)	RFM	145	31	560	20	8-49	2	28.00
I. G. Butler (*Glos*)	RF	124	24	478	17	4-74	0	28.11
D. R. Law (*Durham*)	RFM	103.3	15	353	12	4-30	0	29.41
S. I. Mahmood (*Lancs*)	RF	109	16	444	15	5-37	1	29.60
G. M. Andrew (*Somerset*)	RFM	78	13	310	10	3-14	0	31.00
S. Elworthy (*Notts*)	RFM	160.1	22	627	20	5-71	1	31.35
A. M. Blignaut (*Zimbabweans*)	RFM	130.5	21	487	15	4-89	0	32.46
S. A. Khalid (*Worcs*)	OB	90.5	14	334	10	4-131	0	33.40
J. E. Bishop (*Durham UCCE, British Us & Essex*)	LFM	87.1	10	369	11	4-111	0	33.54
J. A. R. Blain (*Northants*)	RFM	87.1	7	449	13	5-84	1	34.53
P. M. R. Havell (*Derbys*)	RFM	106.4	18	498	14	4-129	0	35.57
L. Balaji (*India A*)	RFM	137	32	430	12	3-58	0	35.83
A. Mishra (*India A*)	LB	134	22	468	13	5-183	1	36.00
M. A. Sheikh (*Warwicks*)	RM	181.5	43	553	15	4-60	0	36.86
M. Kartik (*India A*)	SLA	135.5	27	400	10	4-112	0	40.00
V. C. Drakes (*Leics*)	RFM	143.1	33	463	11	3-58	0	42.09
M. S. Panesar (*Northants*)	SLA	161.2	30	557	13	3-92	0	42.84
T. J. Murtagh (*Surrey & British Us*)	RFM	146.5	17	615	12	4-130	0	51.25
A. J. Tudor (*Surrey*)	RFM	144	24	532	10	3-56	0	53.20

BOWLING STYLES

LB	Leg-breaks (2)	**RF**	Right-arm fast (9)
LBG	Leg-breaks and googlies (4)	**RFM**	Right-arm fast medium (71)
LFM	Left-arm fast medium (12)	**RM**	Right-arm medium (20)
LM	Left-arm medium (1)	**SLA**	Slow left-arm (9)
OB	Off-breaks (23)	**SLC**	Slow left-arm chinamen (2)

Note: The total comes to 153, because A. Symonds has two styles of bowling.

EDITORS OF WISDEN, 1864–2004

W. H. Crockford* and W. H. Knight*	1864–1869
W. H. Knight*	1870–1879
George H. West*	1880–1886
Charles F. Pardon	1887–1890
Sydney H. Pardon	1891–1925
C. Stewart Caine	1926–1933
Sydney J. Southerton	1934–1935
Wilfrid H. Brookes	1936–1939
Haddon Whitaker	1940–1943
Hubert Preston	1944–1951
Norman Preston	1952–1980
John Woodcock	1981–1986
Graeme Wright	1987–1992, 2001–2002
Matthew Engel	1993–2000, 2004–
Tim de Lisle	2003

* *Exact dates and roles unconfirmed.*

INDIVIDUAL SCORES OF 100 AND OVER

There were 305 three-figure innings in 178 first-class matches in 2003, four more than in 2002 when 177 first-class matches were played. Of these, 29 were double-hundreds, compared with 22 in 2002. The list includes 238 hundreds hit in the County Championship, compared with 240 in 2002.

S. G. Law (7)
169 Lancs v Surrey, The Oval
198 Lancs v Middx, Lord's
236* Lancs v Warwicks, Manchester
186 Lancs v Leics, Leicester
144 Lancs v Middx, Manchester
168 Lancs v Warwicks, Birmingham
163* Lancs v Sussex, Manchester

E. T. Smith (7)
103 Kent v Middx, Canterbury
135 Kent v Surrey, The Oval
149 } Kent v Notts, Maidstone
113 }
203 Kent v Lancs, Blackpool
108 Kent v Essex, Canterbury
213 Kent v Warwicks, Canterbury

M. J. Chilton (6)
119 Lancs v Middx, Lord's
106 Lancs v Essex, Manchester
108 Lancs v Leics, Liverpool
114 Lancs v Kent, Blackpool
125 Lancs v Middx, Manchester
121 Lancs v Warwicks, Birmingham

C. L. Hooper (6)
101 Lancs v Durham UCCE, Durham
128* Lancs v Kent, Blackpool
117 Lancs v Leics, Leicester
201 Lancs v Middx, Manchester
114 Lancs v Surrey, Manchester
177 Lancs v Warwicks, Birmingham

M. E. K. Hussey (6)
264 Northants v Glos, Gloucester
100 Northants v Hants, Southampton
331* Northants v Somerset, Taunton
115 Northants v Derbys, Derby
187 Northants v Durham, Northampton
147 Northants v Glam, Cardiff

M. R. Ramprakash (6)
205 Surrey v Loughborough UCCE, The Oval
152 Surrey v Leics, The Oval
110 Surrey v Middx, Lord's
182* Surrey v Warwicks, Birmingham
104 Surrey v Sussex, Hove
279* Surrey v Notts, Whitgift School

M. J. Di. Venuto (5)
121 Derbys v Glam, Derby
150 Derbys v Durham, Chester-le-Street
148 Derbys v Glos, Derby
143 Derbys v Durham, Derby
116 Derbys v Northants, Derby

B. J. Hodge (5)
202* Leics v Loughborough UCCE, Leicester
128 Leics v Warwicks, Leicester
112 Leics v Middx, Southgate
157 Leics v Surrey, Leicester
302* Leics v Notts, Nottingham

P. A. Jaques (5)
149* Northants v Worcs, Worcester
222 Northants v Yorks, Northampton
109 Northants v Durham, Chester-le-Street
123 Northants v Derbys, Derby
147 Northants v Durham, Northampton

M. B. Loye (5)
126 Lancs v Surrey, The Oval
113 Lancs v Notts, Manchester
137 Lancs v Middx, Manchester
102 Lancs v Warwicks, Birmingham
144 Lancs v Sussex, Manchester

M. P. Maynard (5)
142 Glam v Derbys, Derby
112 Glam v Hants, Cardiff
101 Glam v Somerset, Cardiff
129 Glam v Hants, Southampton
102 Glam v Durham, Chester-le-Street

J. N. Rhodes (5)
128 Glos v Northants, Northampton
151* Glos v Hants, Southampton
137 Glos v Derbys, Bristol
103 } Glos v Durham, Bristol
102 }

M. J. Wood (5)
157 Yorks v Northants, Leeds
207 Yorks v Somerset, Taunton
155 Yorks v Hants, Scarborough
126 Yorks v Glam, Colwyn Bay
116 Yorks v Glos, Leeds

C. J. Adams (4)
107 Sussex v Surrey, Hove
140 } Sussex v Lancs, Hove
190 }
102 Sussex v Leics, Hove

M. A. Butcher (4)
137 England v Zimbabwe, Lord's
144 Surrey v Kent, The Oval
118 Surrey v Warwicks, Birmingham
106 England v South Africa, Nottingham

J. E. R. Gallian (4)
126* Notts v Durham UCCE, Nottingham
112* Notts v Surrey, Nottingham
106 Notts v Kent, Maidstone
116 Notts v Middx, Lord's

M. W. Goodwin (4)
148 Sussex v Notts, Nottingham
210 Sussex v Essex, Colchester
118* Sussex v Lancs, Manchester
335* Sussex v Leics, Hove

B. L. Hutton (4)
107 Middx v Essex, Lord's
101 Middx v Surrey, Lord's
102* Middx v Warwicks, Southgate
107 Middx v Lancs, Manchester

S. M. Katich (4)
135 Hants v Durham, Southampton
143* Hants v Yorks, Scarborough
117 Hants v Northants, Southampton
122 Hants v Derbys, Derby

K. P. Pietersen (4)
166 Notts v Sussex, Horsham
221 Notts v Warwicks, Birmingham
139 Notts v Sussex, Nottingham
100 Notts v Kent, Nottingham

M. J. Powell (4)
125 } Glam v Worcs, Cardiff
142 }
146 Glam v Yorks, Colwyn Bay
198 Glam v Durham, Chester-le-Street

M. J. Prior (4)
133 Sussex v Notts, Horsham
100 Sussex v Warwicks, Hove
153* Sussex v Essex, Colchester
148 Sussex v Middx, Hove

A. J. Strauss (4)
100* Middx v Lancs, Lord's
147 Middx v Leics, Southgate
155 Middx v Lancs, Manchester
138 Middx v Sussex, Hove

J. N. Batty (3)
123 Surrey v Loughborough UCCE, The Oval
168* Surrey v Essex, Chelmsford
154* Surrey v Lancs, Manchester

I. D. Blackwell (3)
140 Somerset v Northants, Taunton
189 Somerset v Hants, Taunton
247* Somerset v Derbys, Taunton

D. R. Brown (3)
120 Warwicks v Essex, Birmingham
113 Warwicks v Middx, Southgate
140* Warwicks v Lancs, Birmingham

P. A. Cottey (3)
188 Sussex v Warwicks, Hove
107 Sussex v Essex, Arundel
147 Sussex v Leics, Leicester

J. Cox (3)
126 Somerset v Derbys, Derby
127* Somerset v Hants, Southampton
160 Somerset v Worcs, Bath

A. Flintoff (3)
111 Lancs v Middx, Lord's
154 Lancs v Kent, Canterbury
142 England v South Africa, Lord's

E. C. Joyce (3)
117 Middx v Essex, Chelmsford
102 Middx v Leics, Southgate
107 Middx v Warwicks, Birmingham

N. V. Knight (3)
103* Warwicks v Surrey, The Oval
146 Warwicks v Notts, Birmingham
122* Warwicks v Leics, Birmingham

O. A. Shah (3)
101* Middx v Zimbabweans, Shenley Park
147 Middx v Lancs, Manchester
140 Middx v Sussex, Hove

G. C. Smith (3)
152 South Africans v Somerset, Taunton
277 South Africa v England, Birmingham
259 South Africa v England, Lord's

J. O. Troughton (3)
129* Warwicks v Essex, Birmingham
105 Warwicks v Sussex, Birmingham
120 Warwicks v Kent, Birmingham

M. A. Wagh (3)
136 Warwicks v Surrey, The Oval
138 Warwicks v Leics, Leicester
116 Warwicks v Essex, Chelmsford

M. J. Walker (3)
106 Kent v Warwicks, Birmingham
150 Kent v Lancs, Blackpool
121 Kent v Warwicks, Canterbury

I. J. Ward (3)
158 Surrey v Lancs, The Oval
135 Surrey v Sussex, The Oval
104 Surrey v Middx, Lord's

R. J. Warren (3)
114* Notts v Sussex, Nottingham
123 } Notts v Middx, Lord's
113* }

M. P. Bicknell (2)
103* Surrey v Loughborough UCCE, The Oval
141 Surrey v Essex, Chelmsford

G. L. Brophy (2)
102* Northants v Cambridge UCCE, Cambridge
152* Northants v Glos, Gloucester

M. Burns (2)
118* Somerset v Loughborough UCCE, Taunton
106 Somerset v Glam, Cardiff

S. V. Carlisle (2)
157 Zimbabweans v Worcs, Worcester
137 Zimbabweans v Middx, Shenley Park

G. Chapple (2)
132* Lancs v Essex, Chelmsford
132 Lancs v Warwicks, Manchester

R. Clarke (2)
127* Surrey v Lancs, The Oval
139 Surrey v Leics, Leicester

A. Flower (2)
127 Essex v Leics, Southend
201* Essex v Surrey, The Oval

P. J. Franks (2)
123* Notts v Leics, Leicester
100* Notts v Lancs, Nottingham

H. H. Gibbs (2)
179 South Africa v England, Birmingham
183 South Africa v England, The Oval

A. Habib (2)
102* Essex v Cambridge UCCE, Cambridge
151 Essex v Notts, Nottingham

A. J. Hollioake (2)
121* Surrey v Loughborough UCCE, The Oval
122 Surrey v Warwicks, The Oval

N. Hussain (2)
206 Essex v Kent, Chelmsford
116 England v South Africa, Nottingham

G. O. Jones (2)
104 Kent v Leics, Canterbury
108* Kent v Essex, Chelmsford

D. A. Kenway (2)
115 Hants v Glos, Southampton
100 Hants v Somerset, Taunton

R. W. T. Key (2)
129 Kent v Cambridge UCCE, Cambridge
140 Kent v Notts, Maidstone

G. Kirsten (2)
108 South Africa v England, Lord's
130 South Africa v England, Leeds

M. J. Lumb (2)
115* Yorks v Hants, Southampton
105 Yorks v Durham, Leeds

J. K. Maunders (2)
171 Leics v Surrey, Leicester
129 Leics v Kent, Leicester

G. J. Muchall (2)
101* Durham v Durham UCCE, Durham
121 Durham v India A, Chester-le-Street

D. C. Nash (2)
103* Middx v Leics, Southgate
113 Middx v Kent, Lord's

N. Peng (2)
158 Durham v Durham UCCE, Durham
133 Durham v Glam, Cardiff

S. D. Peters (2)
165 Worcs v Somerset, Bath
103 Worcs v Somerset, Worcester

N. Pothas (2)
146* Hants v Worcs, Worcester
121 Hants v Glam, Southampton

J. L. Sadler (2)
145 Leics v Surrey, Leicester
145 Leics v Sussex, Hove

D. J. Sales (2)
125 Northants v Somerset, Taunton
200* Northants v Derbys, Derby

V. Sehwag (2)
137 Leics v Notts, Leicester
130 Leics v Middx, Southgate

B. F. Smith (2)
104 Worcs v Hants, Worcester
110 Worcs v Yorks, Worcester

S. Sriram (2)
115 India A v Surrey, The Oval
104* India A v Warwicks, Birmingham

L. D. Sutton (2)
120 Derbys v Glam, Derby
127 Derbys v Yorks, Leeds

A. Symonds (2)
103* Kent v Notts, Maidstone
121 Kent v Surrey, Canterbury

G. P. Thorpe (2)
156 Surrey v Sussex, The Oval
124 England v South Africa, The Oval

I. J. L. Trott (2)
134 Warwicks v Sussex, Birmingham
126 Warwicks v Lancs, Birmingham

M. P. Vaughan (2)
103 Yorks v Northants, Northampton
156 England v South Africa, Birmingham

M. A. Wallace (2)
117 Glam v Durham, Cardiff
121 Glam v Durham, Chester-le-Street

W. P. C. Weston (2)
100 Glos v Hants, Southampton
179 Glos v Somerset, Taunton

C. White (2)
173* Yorks v Derbys, Derby
135* Yorks v Durham, Chester-le-Street

The following each played one three-figure innings:

J. H. K. Adams, 107, Loughborough UCCE v Somerset, Taunton; U. Afzaal, 161*, Notts v India A, Nottingham; Arfan Akram, 110, Cambridge UCCE v Kent, Cambridge.
H. K. Badani, 133, India A v Durham, Chester-le-Street; T. M. B. Bailey, 101*, Northants v Somerset, Taunton; I. R. Bell, 107, Warwicks v Sussex, Birmingham; R. J. Blakey, 223*, Yorks v Northants, Leeds; J. D. C. Bryant, 109*, Somerset v Loughborough UCCE, Taunton.
C. L. Cairns, 104, Notts v Warwicks, Birmingham; M. A. Carberry, 137, Kent v Cambridge UCCE, Cambridge; E. J. M. Cowan, 137*, British Universities v Zimbabweans, Birmingham; R. D. B. Croft, 122, Glam v Somerset, Cardiff.
A. Dale, 123, Glam v Hants, Southampton; J. W. M. Dalrymple, 236*, Oxford U. v Cambridge U., Cambridge; S. S. Das, 125, India A v Durham, Chester-le-Street; M. J. G. Davis, 168, Sussex v Middx, Hove; P. A. J. DeFreitas, 103, Leics v Sussex, Leicester.
M. A. Ealham, 101, Kent v Essex, Chelmsford; N. J. Edwards, 160, Somerset v Hants, Taunton.
G. W. Flower, 130, Zimbabweans v British Universities, Birmingham.
A. I. Gait, 110, Derbys v Somerset, Taunton; G. Gambhir, 130*, India A v Surrey, The Oval; R. S. Gavaskar, 139*, India A v Notts, Nottingham; A. K. D. Gray, 104, Yorks v Somerset, Taunton.
A. J. Hall, 104, Worcs v Somerset, Bath; I. J. Harvey, 128*, Glos v Somerset, Taunton; G. A. Hick, 155, Worcs v Derbys, Derby.
K. J. Innes, 103*, Sussex v Notts, Horsham; R. C. Irani, 102*, Essex v Cambridge UCCE, Cambridge.
W. I. Jefferson, 125*, Essex v Cambridge UCCE, Cambridge; R. L. Johnson, 118, Somerset v Glos, Bristol.
J. H. Kallis, 200, South Africans v Derbys, Derby; W. S. Kendall, 114, Hants v Oxford UCCE, Oxford; S. G. Koenig, 166*, Middx v Oxford UCCE, Oxford.
A. W. Laraman, 148*, Somerset v Glos, Taunton; J. J. B. Lewis, 124, Durham v Yorks, Leeds; A. G. R. Loudon, 172, Durham UCCE v Durham, Durham; M. L. Love, 273, Durham v Hants, Chester-le-Street.
A. McGrath, 127*, Yorks v Glam, Colwyn Bay; N. D. McKenzie, 105*, South Africans v Kent, Canterbury; D. L. Maddy, 229*, Leics v Loughborough UCCE, Leicester; S. J. Marshall, 126*, Cambridge U. v Oxford U., Cambridge; R. S. C. Martin-Jenkins, 121*, Sussex v Notts, Nottingham; D. R. Martyn, 238, Yorks v Glos, Leeds; A. D. Mascarenhas, 100*, Hants v Glam, Cardiff; D. D. Masters, 119, Leics v Sussex, Hove; N. Millar, 108, Oxford U. v Cambridge U., Cambridge; R. R. Montgomerie, 105, Sussex v Notts, Horsham.
P. A. Nixon, 113*, Leics v Kent, Canterbury.
P. A. Patel, 129, India A v Yorks, Leeds; D. E. Paynter, 146, Northants v Cambridge UCCE, Cambridge; D. J. Pipe, 104*, Worcs v Hants, Southampton; M. J. Powell, 110, Warwicks v Kent, Canterbury; G. J. Pratt, 150, Durham v Northants, Chester-le-Street.
A. T. Rayudu, 101*, India A v Surrey, The Oval.

I. D. K. Salisbury, 101*, Surrey v Leics, The Oval; J. J. Sayers, 122, Oxford UCCE v Hants, Oxford; B. M. Shafayat, 105, Notts v Durham UCCE, Nottingham; A. Singh, 105, Worcs v Somerset, Bath; C. M. Spearman, 103, Glos v Hants, Bristol; D. I. Stevens, 149, Leics v Essex, Southend; S. D. Stubbings, 103, Derbys v Glos, Bristol; I. J. Sutcliffe, 109, Lancs v Essex, Manchester; A. J. Swann, 137, Lancs v Durham UCCE, Durham.

M. E. Trescothick, 219, England v South Africa, The Oval; R. J. Turner, 139*, Somerset v Loughborough UCCE, Taunton.

M. A. Vermeulen, 198, Zimbabweans v Sussex, Hove.

T. R. Ward, 168, Leics v Essex, Southend; Wasim Jaffer, 218, India A v Warwicks, Birmingham; T. Webley, 104, Cambridge UCCE v Northants, Cambridge; P. N. Weekes, 102*, Middx v Zimbabweans, Shenley Park; V. J. Wells, 106, Durham v Derbys, Derby; R. M. S. Weston, 129, Middx v Zimbabweans, Shenley Park; M. G. N. Windows, 150, Glos v Northants, Gloucester; M. J. Wood, 100, Somerset v Northants, Taunton.

FASTEST HUNDREDS BY BALLS

Balls	*Mins*		
65	93	D. R. Martyn	Yorks v Glos, Leeds
73	78	B. M. Shafayat	Notts v Durham UCCE, Nottingham
75	95	R. L. Johnson	Somerset v Glos, Bristol
75	95	K. P. Pietersen	Notts v Sussex, Horsham
78	120	A. D. Mascarenhas	Hants v Glam, Cardiff
80	111	O. A. Shah	Middx v Zimbabweans, Shenley Park
81	92	A. Symonds	Kent v Notts, Maidstone
86	132	M. J. Prior	Sussex v Essex, Colchester
86	134	B. J. Hodge	Leics v Surrey, Leicester
87	110	A. J. Hollioake	Surrey v Loughborough UCCE, The Oval
89	115	M. Burns	Somerset v Loughborough UCCE, Taunton
89	124	T. R. Ward	Leics v Essex, Southend
90	133	I. J. Harvey	Glos v Somerset, Taunton
91	100	M. P. Bicknell	Surrey v Loughborough UCCE, The Oval
92	114	V. Sehwag	Leics v Middx, Southgate
93	99	N. Peng	Durham v Durham UCCE, Durham
93	146	I. D. Blackwell	Somerset v Derbys, Taunton
95	131	J. O. Troughton	Warwicks v Kent, Birmingham
96	140	A. Flintoff	Lancs v Kent, Canterbury
96	117	E. T. Smith	Kent v Notts, Maidstone
97	123	M. P. Maynard	Glam v Durham, Chester-le-Street
98	159	K. P. Pietersen	Notts v Kent, Nottingham
99	141	A. Symonds	Kent v Surrey, Canterbury

The fastest hundred in terms of minutes not in the above list was by W. I. Jefferson (107 minutes, 101 balls), Essex v Cambridge UCCE at Cambridge.

... AND THE SLOWEST

Balls	*Mins*		
290	356	E. C. Joyce	Middx v Essex, Chelmsford
267	297	I. J. Sutcliffe	Lancs v Essex, Manchester
266	317	J. E. R. Gallian	Notts v Kent, Maidstone
265	313	J. J. B. Lewis	Durham v Yorks, Leeds

"Told his figures were Yorkshire's best for 36 years, Kirby was uncharacteristically dumbstruck."

Somerset in 2003, page 682.

TEN WICKETS IN A MATCH

There were 22 instances of bowlers taking ten or more wickets in first-class cricket in 2003, four fewer than in 2002. The list includes 20 in the County Championship.

Mushtaq Ahmed (5)
12-244, Sussex v Notts, Horsham; 11-140, Sussex v Warwicks, Hove; 10-189, Sussex v Leics, Leicester; 11-173, Sussex v Lancs, Hove; 10-225, Sussex v Middx, Hove.

D. G. Cork (2)
10-67, Derbys v Hants, Southampton; 10-127, Derbys v Somerset, Taunton.

M. S. Kasprowicz (2)
11-77, Glam v Durham, Cardiff; 13-110, Glam v Durham, Chester-le-Street.

S. P. Kirby (2)
13-154, Yorks v Somerset, Taunton; 10-183, Yorks v Glos, Cheltenham.

The following each took ten wickets in a match on one occasion:

P. R. Adams, 11-140, South Africans v Kent, Canterbury.
R. D. B. Croft, 10-147, Glam v Northants, Cardiff.
P. A. J. DeFreitas, 10-113, Leics v Notts, Nottingham; N. R. C. Dumelow, 10-160, Derbys v Northants, Northampton.
I. D. Fisher, 10-123, Glos v Durham, Bristol.
G. Keedy, 10-167, Lancs v Sussex, Manchester.
J. Lewis, 11-183, Glos v Derbys, Bristol; J. D. Lewry, 10-124, Sussex v Essex, Arundel.
Mohammad Akram, 10-142, Essex v Surrey, The Oval; Mohammad Sami, 15-114, Kent v Notts, Maidstone.
M. Ntini, 10-220, South Africa v England, Lord's.

ICC REFEREES' PANEL

In 1991, the International Cricket Council formed a panel of referees to enforce its Code of Conduct for Tests and one-day internationals, to impose penalties for slow over-rates, breaches of the Code and other ICC regulations, and to support the umpires in upholding the conduct of the game.

In March 2002, the ICC launched an elite panel of five referees, on two-year full-time contracts, to act as its independent representatives in all international cricket. The chief referee was R. S. Madugalle (Sri Lanka), supported by C. H. Lloyd (West Indies), M. J. Procter (South Africa), Wasim Raja (Pakistan) and G. R. Viswanath (India). The five had played 286 Test matches between them.

The ICC also named a supplementary panel of referees, to provide cover during busy periods of the international calendar and during major tournaments. This consisted of B. C. Broad (England), A. M. Ebrahim (Zimbabwe), G. F. Labrooy (Sri Lanka), D. T. Lindsay (South Africa), J. F. M. Morrison (New Zealand), E. A. S. Prasanna (India), Sultan Rana (Pakistan) and Raqibul Hassan (Bangladesh). Ebrahim was added to the supplementary panel during 2003. Both panels were sponsored by Emirates Airline for three years from July 2002.

THE ZIMBABWEANS IN ENGLAND, 2003

REVIEW BY SIMON BRIGGS

Less than three months after England's failure to fulfil their World Cup fixture in Harare, a party of Zimbabwean cricketers arrived at Gatwick. As their visit represented something of a political hot potato, the England and Wales Cricket Board shared a common aim with its team: to get through this awkward little tour without suffering too much embarrassment.

Though the mandarins came under far more pressure than the players, both would emerge largely unscathed. The Zimbabwean captain, Heath Streak, was leading a painfully inexperienced squad: only Grant Flower had scored a Test hundred. Streak thus had rather less ammunition than Kate Hoey, the Labour MP and former Minister for Sport.

"The Zimbabwe Cricket Union have [President] Mugabe as their patron," Hoey wrote in the *Daily Telegraph* on April 19. "Yet on May 22 at Lord's, the most famous ground in the world, England will play against a country soaked in the blood of men, women and children who have done nothing other than stand up for the freedoms and rights that we in this country take for granted."

Hoey's invective served as a rallying cry for the Stop The Tour campaign, which was soon claiming the support of around 100 MPs. Yet only a handful of them attended the first day's demonstrations outside the Grace Gates, where the most recognisable figure was the serial agitator Peter Tatchell. The game suffered two low-key interruptions in the afternoon, when a couple of Tatchell's comrades wandered on to the pitch with placards. And that was about as rough as things got for the ECB.

Crucially, the Stop The Tour movement went unsupported by the two political parties who could have given it legitimacy. One was the ruling British Labour Party, whose cabinet minister Tessa Jowell approved the tour in a letter to the ECB. The other was the Zimbabwean opposition party, the Movement for Democratic Change (MDC), who seemed to view cricket as a useful tool for redirecting the British media's attention towards Mugabe's outrages. The US-led war against Iraq, which preceded the tour, meant that the plight of millions of Zimbabweans facing food shortages had gone largely unreported.

After the May 22 demonstration at Lord's, the Stop The Tour protest dropped almost out of sight, and *The Times* newspaper took over. One of its correspondents, Owen Slot, took a particularly hard line on the selection of the Zimbabwean squad – which he argued was politically vetted – and savaged the smooth-talking Peter Chingoka, the chairman of the Zimbabwe Cricket Union, for his constant dissembling. "When the conversation strays to topics anywhere beyond bat and ball," Slot wrote, "this is a squad that is either frightened or incapable of talking truthfully."

Slot was right, of course, but it was not entirely the players' fault. The treatment of Andy Flower and Henry Olonga, who were reprimanded after

THE ZIMBABWEAN TOURING PARTY

Standing: S. Cloete (*analyst*), D. D. Ebrahim, B. G. Rogers, D. T. Hondo, D. A. Marillier, M. A. Vermeulen, T. J. Friend, S. M. Ervine, M. L. Nkala, V. Sibanda, B. I. Robinson (*physiotherapist*), L. Banda (*communications manager*). *Seated:* M. A. Meman (*manager*), S. V. Carlisle, G. W. Flower, H. H. Streak (*captain*), T. Taibu (*vice-captain*), A. M. Blignaut, R. W. Price, G. R. Marsh (*coach*).

Picture by Graham Morris.

their brave black-armband protest at the start of the World Cup and announced their retirements from international cricket when Zimbabwe were knocked out, made it clear that dissenters would not be tolerated. Flower himself admitted that he had talked a number of team-mates out of emulating him, arguing that: "If everybody took the same stand, you would run the serious risk of eliminating most of the side in one fell swoop. From what I understand, the MDC would not be in favour of such drastic action."

Without Flower in particular, Zimbabwe proved to be a soft touch on the field. Their bowling was often respectable, thanks to Streak's exemplary leadership, but they simply could not make any runs. In two Tests and five completed one-day internationals, they passed 200 on just three occasions, with a top score of only 253. Their one worthwhile win – a four-wicket triumph over England in the NatWest Series opener – was underpinned by the only meaningful innings of any quality, Grant Flower's unbeaten 96. They were even thrashed by Ireland.

THE RED, WHITE AND BLUE-WASH

There have been 17 series in which England have won both/all the Tests. Six were series of two or three Tests against Australia and South Africa in the 19th century. Occurrences since then:

	Captain	*Tests*	*Opponents*
1912	C. B. Fry	3	South Africa
1928	A. P. F. Chapman	3	West Indies
1954-55	L. Hutton	2	New Zealand
1959	P. B. H. May/M. C. Cowdrey	5	India
1962-63	E. R. Dexter	3	New Zealand
1965	M. J. K. Smith	3	New Zealand
1967	D. B. Close	3	India
1974	M. H. Denness	3	India
1978	J. M. Brearley	3	New Zealand
2003	**N. Hussain**	**2**	**Zimbabwe**
2003-04	**M. P. Vaughan**	**2**	**Bangladesh**

England cashed in on Zimbabwe's naivety. For the first time in 25 years, they won every Test in a series – even if the series was only two games long. And with Darren Gough, Andrew Caddick and Andrew Flintoff unavailable through injury, they were able to blood a few novices of their own.

Much of the pre-publicity focused on the artfully styled head and shoulders of James Anderson, the emerging poster boy of English cricket, who followed up an encouraging World Cup by taking five for 73 at Lord's on his Test debut. But there were also debuts for the Yorkshire captain, Anthony McGrath, who became the first Englishman since David Gower to score fifties in his first two Test innings, and the Somerset paceman Richard Johnson. After numerous near misses with England over the previous eight years, Johnson finally won selection for the Second Test at Chester-le-Street. He was soon making up for lost time, finding himself on a hat-trick in his first over, and finishing the innings with six for 33.

At the end of that humiliating match, which they lost by an innings and 69 runs, Zimbabwe's downward slide continued with the removal of opening

Sharing the load: Richard Johnson (*left*), playing his first Test, was one of a trio of inexperienced England bowlers to pick up six wickets at the Riverside. Steve Harmison (*right*) and James Anderson were the other two.

Picture by Patrick Eagar.

batsman Mark Vermeulen from the tour. There appeared to be nothing politically motivated about this move: instead, Vermeulen was being punished for what the team management described as a series of petty indisciplines.

It quickly emerged that Vermeulen had had a reputation for being a hothead ever since his schooldays, when he once reacted to a bad lbw decision by walking off with the stumps. If there was a last straw for the officials on this tour, it came after close of play on the Friday of the Second Test, when Vermeulen refused to take the bus with the rest of the team from the ground to their nearby hotel. His solitary mood may be partly explained by the fact that he had just completed a rare and unenviable feat: bagging a pair on the same day of a Test match.

England finished the series in contrastingly upbeat mode, both in the dressing-room and the executives' offices. But the sting in the tail was still to come. After the Harare shemozzle, the ZCU were hardly going to fulfil their summer obligations without asking the ECB for a few assurances in return, notably over England's scheduled visit to Zimbabwe in November 2004. The board had no alternative but to commit but, as the Zimbabwe crisis deepened at the end of 2003, the chances of England actually going, barring a change of regime, looked increasingly remote.

THE ENGLAND SQUAD FOR THE LORD'S TEST AGAINST ZIMBABWE

Back row: R. W. T. Key, M. J. Hoggard, J. M. Anderson, S. J. Harmison, R. J. Kirtley, A. McGrath. *Middle row:* M. N. Ashton (*team analyst*), K. A. Russell (*physiotherapist*), A. Flintoff, A. R. Caddick. A. F. Giles, N. P. Stockill (*physiologist*), P. A. Neale (*operations manager*). *Front row:* M. E. Trescothick, A. J. Stewart, D. A. G. Fletcher (*coach*), N. Hussain (*captain*), M. A. Butcher, M. P. Vaughan.

Picture by Tom Shaw, Getty Images.

ZIMBABWEAN TOURING PARTY

H. H. Streak (Matabeleland) (*captain*), T. Taibu (Mashonaland) (*vice-captain*), A. M. Blignaut (Mashonaland), S. V. Carlisle (Mashonaland), D. D. Ebrahim (Mashonaland), S. M. Ervine (Midlands), G. W. Flower (Mashonaland), T. J. Friend (Midlands), D. T. Hondo (Mashonaland), D. A. Marillier (Midlands), M. L. Nkala (Matabeleland), R. W. Price (Midlands), B. G. Rogers (Matabeleland), V. Sibanda (Midlands), M. A. Vermeulen (Matabeleland).

Nkala, Rogers and Sibanda left after the Test series. Vermeulen was sent home for disciplinary reasons, and Carlisle withdrew from the NatWest Series squad through injury. They were replaced for the one-day games by G. B. Brent (Manicaland), C. K. Coventry (Matabeleland), S. Matsikenyeri (Manicaland), W. Mwayenga (Mashonaland) and R. W. Sims (Manicaland).

Coach: G. R. Marsh. *Manager:* M. A. Meman. *Bowling coach:* R. M. Hogg. *Physiotherapist:* B. I. Robinson.

ZIMBABWEAN TOUR RESULTS

Test matches – Played 2: Lost 2.
First-class matches – Played 6: Won 1, Lost 2, Drawn 2, Tied 1.
Win – British Universities.
Losses – England (2).
Draws – Sussex, Middlesex.
Tie – Worcestershire.
One-day internationals – Played 6: Won 1, Lost 4, No result 1. *Win* – England. *Losses* – South Africa (3), England. *No result* – England.
Other non-first-class matches – Played 5: Won 3, Lost 2. *Wins* – Ireland, Somerset, Essex. *Losses* – Ireland, Hampshire.

TEST MATCH AVERAGES

ENGLAND – BATTING AND FIELDING

	T	*I*	*NO*	*R*	*HS*	*100s*	*50s*	*Avge*	*Ct*
†M. A. Butcher	2	2	0	184	137	1	0	92.00	3
A. McGrath	2	2	0	150	81	0	2	75.00	2
A. F. Giles	2	2	0	102	52	0	2	51.00	1
†M. E. Trescothick	2	2	0	102	59	0	1	51.00	6
A. J. Stewart	2	2	0	94	68	0	1	47.00	2
N. Hussain	2	2	0	37	19	0	0	18.50	1
M. P. Vaughan	2	2	0	28	20	0	0	14.00	0
R. W. T. Key	2	2	0	22	18	0	0	11.00	3
S. J. Harmison	2	2	0	11	11	0	0	5.50	0

Played in two Tests: †J. M. Anderson 4*, 12* (1 ct). Played in one Test: M. J. Hoggard 19 (1 ct); R. L. Johnson 24.

† *Left-handed batsman.*

BOWLING

	Style	*O*	*M*	*R*	*W*	*BB*	*5W/i*	*Avge*
A. McGrath	RM	6	1	16	3	3-16	0	5.33
M. A. Butcher	RM	19.5	2	77	5	4-60	0	15.40
S. J. Harmison	RF	58.5	16	148	9	4-55	0	16.44
R. L. Johnson	RFM	34	11	100	6	6-33	1	16.66
M. J. Hoggard	RFM	33	13	59	3	3-24	0	19.66
J. M. Anderson	RFM	64	18	223	11	5-73	1	20.27

Also bowled: A. F. Giles (SLA) 34–11–67–2.

ZIMBABWE – BATTING AND FIELDING

	T	*I*	*NO*	*R*	*HS*	*100s*	*50s*	*Avge*	*Ct*
T. J. Friend	2	4	1	108	65*	0	1	36.00	0
D. D. Ebrahim	2	4	0	135	68	0	2	33.75	2
T. Taibu	2	4	0	86	31	0	0	21.50	5
R. W. Price	2	4	1	56	26	0	0	18.66	0
S. V. Carlisle	2	4	0	63	28	0	0	15.75	0
M. A. Vermeulen	2	4	0	62	61	0	1	15.50	2
G. W. Flower	2	4	0	53	26	0	0	13.25	1
†S. M. Ervine	2	4	0	42	34	0	0	10.50	3
†A. M. Blignaut	2	4	0	34	13	0	0	8.50	0
H. H. Streak	2	4	0	28	11	0	0	7.00	1
D. T. Hondo.	2	4	2	9	5*	0	0	4.50	1

† *Left-handed batsman.*

BOWLING

	Style	*O*	*M*	*R*	*W*	*BB*	*5W/i*	*Avge*
H. H. Streak	RFM	71.1	20	163	7	4-64	0	23.28
A. M. Blignaut	RFM	49.1	8	191	5	3-96	0	38.20
D. T. Hondo	RFM	36	5	143	3	3-98	0	47.66

Also bowled: S. M. Ervine (RM) 25–5–112–2; G. W. Flower (SLA) 2–0–8–0; T. J. Friend (RFM) 17–2–75–1; R. W. Price (SLA) 60–15–149–2.

ZIMBABWEAN TOUR AVERAGES – FIRST-CLASS MATCHES

BATTING AND FIELDING

	M	*I*	*NO*	*R*	*HS*	*100s*	*50s*	*Avge*	*Ct/St*
S. V. Carlisle	6	9	0	469	157	2	1	52.11	2
M. A. Vermeulen	6	11	1	451	198	1	3	45.10	4
G. W. Flower	6	10	1	399	130	1	2	44.33	7
T. Taibu	6	10	2	254	57	0	1	31.75	17/2
T. J. Friend	4	6	1	151	65*	0	1	30.20	1
D. D. Ebrahim	6	11	1	271	68	0	3	27.10	4
†S. M. Ervine	5	8	2	161	57*	0	1	26.83	5
H. H. Streak	5	7	0	127	51	0	1	18.14	1
†A. M. Blignaut	5	8	1	114	42	0	0	16.28	2
R. W. Price	5	7	2	68	26	0	0	13.60	1
D. T. Hondo.	4	7	3	41	24*	0	0	10.25	1
†B. G. Rogers	3	4	0	11	6	0	0	2.75	0

Played in two matches: D. A. Marillier 1, 0 (4 ct); M. L. Nkala 0. Played in one match: V. Sibanda 0 (1 ct).

† *Left-handed batsman.*

BOWLING

	Style	*O*	*M*	*R*	*W*	*BB*	*5W/i*	*Avge*
D. T. Hondo	RFM	94	23	312	15	5-26	1	20.80
G. W. Flower	SLA	40.5	7	129	6	3-25	0	21.50
H. H. Streak	RFM	123.3	38	263	12	4-64	0	21.91
A. M. Blignaut	RFM	130.5	21	487	15	4-89	0	32.46
R. W. Price	SLA	156.3	34	431	8	2-47	0	53.87
T. J. Friend	RFM	67	6	357	6	2-42	0	59.50

Also bowled: S. M. Ervine (RM) 79–16–343–4; D. A. Marillier (OB) 17–4–65–2; M. L. Nkala (RFM) 46–13–182–0; B. G. Rogers (OB) 3–0–8–0; V. Sibanda (RM) 5–1–34–0.

Note: Matches in this section which were not first-class are signified by a dagger.

BRITISH UNIVERSITIES v ZIMBABWEANS

At Birmingham, May 3, 4, 5. Zimbabweans won by ten wickets. Toss: British Universities.

The Zimbabweans got their tour off to an untroubled start – both on and off the pitch. After rain had limited the first day to just 38 overs, the Universities were blown away by the dreadlocked medium-pacer Hondo, who struck four times in three overs as the last eight wickets tumbled for only 29. The Zimbabweans stuttered in turn to 183 for seven but then took control thanks to an eighth-wicket stand of 138 between Flower and Streak. Only an impressive unbeaten 137 off 148 balls from Ed Cowan, an Oxford Brookes student who had represented Australia Under-19s, stood in the Zimbabweans' way after that, and victory was completed late on the third day of four. On the opening morning, the expected anti-tour protest failed to get off the ground: perhaps deterred by the poor weather, only seven people turned up.

Close of play: First day, British Universities 92-2 (Francis 19, Cowan 6); Second day, Zimbabweans 302-7 (Flower 112, Streak 38).

British Universities

*J. H. K. Adams (*Loughborough*) c Taibu b Blignaut	42	– c Marillier b Streak	26
D. B. Taylor (*Durham*) c Marillier b Hondo	16	– c Blignaut b Hondo	27
J. D. Francis (*Loughborough*) c Taibu b Hondo	26	– c Taibu b Hondo	5
E. J. M. Cowan (*Oxford Brookes*) c Carlisle b Blignaut	20	– not out	137
R. A. White (*Loughborough*) lbw b Hondo	0	– run out	7
†I. Dawood (*Leeds Metropolitan*) c Vermeulen b Streak	12	– lbw b Blignaut	5
R. S. Ferley (*Durham*) lbw b Hondo	0	– lbw b Blignaut	14
J. E. Bishop (*Durham*) c Taibu b Hondo	0	– c Marillier b Streak	4
T. J. Murtagh (*St Mary's UC*) c Flower b Marillier	12	– c Ebrahim b Streak	10
J. A. Tomlinson (*Cardiff*) c Blignaut b Marillier	3	– c Marillier b Blignaut	5
T. Mees (*Oxford Brookes*) not out	0	– c sub b Blignaut	10
B 2, l-b 8, n-b 5	15	L-b 2, w 7, n-b 4	13
1/25 (2) 2/80 (1) 3/117 (3) 4/117 (4) 5/117 (5) 6/117 (7) 7/119 (8) 8/138 (9) 9/146 (10) 10/146 (6)	146	1/54 (2) 2/60 (3) 3/66 (1) 4/83 (5) 5/100 (6) 6/123 (7) 7/179 (8) 8/193 (9) 9/231 (10) 10/263 (11)	263

Bowling: *First Innings*—Streak 22.1–10–27–1; Blignaut 19–3–51–2; Ervine 6–2–22–0; Hondo 13–5–26–5; Marillier 3–0–10–2. *Second Innings*—Streak 16–4–33–3; Blignaut 21.4–4–89–4; Hondo 14–4–49–2; Marillier 14–4–55–0; Flower 8–0–35–0.

Zimbabweans

D. D. Ebrahim lbw b Mees	4	– not out	9
M. A. Vermeulen c Dawood b Tomlinson	51	– not out	28
S. V. Carlisle c Dawood b Ferley	54		
G. W. Flower c Dawood b Bishop	130		
B. G. Rogers b Ferley	1		
†T. Taibu lbw b Bishop	17		
S. M. Ervine c White b Ferley	9		
D. A. Marillier c Cowan b Bishop	1		
*H. H. Streak lbw b Mees	51		
A. M. Blignaut not out	34		
D. T. Hondo c Dawood b Murtagh	8		
B 1, l-b 2, w 2, n-b 11	16		
1/10 (1) 2/105 (2) 3/114 (3) 4/122 (5) 5/169 (6) 6/182 (7) 7/183 (8) 8/321 (9) 9/349 (4) 10/376 (11)	376	(no wkt)	37

Bowling: *First Innings*—Mees 23–3–84–2; Tomlinson 20–4–64–1; Bishop 14–2–70–3; Murtagh 14–4–59–1; Ferley 24–3–81–3; Adams 2–0–12–0; Cowan 1–0–3–0. *Second Innings*—Mees 2–0–28–0; Tomlinson 1.4–0–9–0.

Umpires: R. Palmer and K. Shuttleworth.

WORCESTERSHIRE v ZIMBABWEANS

At Worcester, May 9, 10, 11, 12. Tied. Toss: Worcestershire. County debut: A. J. Hall.

Kabir Ali took the last two Zimbabwean wickets in the space of three balls to earn Worcestershire a thrilling and unlikely tie. After straining his back earlier in the match, Streak had emerged with a runner and lifted the Zimbabweans from the depths of 128 for eight to the verge of victory. But with the scores level, he edged Kabir to third slip and the last man Hondo was bowled shouldering arms. On the opening day, Solanki had taken advantage of some ring-rusty bowling before he became one of five victims for the keeper Taibu – who had played club cricket for Worcester Norton Taverners in 2002 – as the last eight wickets fell for 92. Taibu later proved an able batting partner for Carlisle, who finally made a first-class century outside southern Africa and eventually faced 374 balls for his 157. Worcestershire struggled second time round on a pitch of uneven bounce, but the Zimbabweans soon slipped to 55 for five in pursuit of a modest 176. A run-a-ball 42 from Blignaut started the recovery, but another collapse of three wickets for nine runs swung the game Worcestershire's way to set up the climax.

Close of play: First day, Zimbabweans 69-3 (Carlisle 29, Rogers 1); Second day, Zimbabweans 296-8 (Carlisle 139, Hondo 4); Third day, Worcestershire 247.

Worcestershire

S. D. Peters b Blignaut	18	– c Carlisle b Hondo	63
A. Singh c Flower b Blignaut	14	– c Taibu b Friend	35
V. S. Solanki st Taibu b Price	74	– c Flower b Friend	5
*B. F. Smith c Taibu b Hondo	53	– lbw b Hondo	18
Kadeer Ali c Taibu b Hondo	10	– c Taibu b Blignaut	14
A. J. Hall c Taibu b Flower	34	– c Price b Flower	68
G. J. Batty b Hondo	0	– c Friend b Flower	12
†D. J. Pipe c and b Flower	15	– st Taibu b Price	6
Kabir Ali run out	0	– b Flower	0
M. S. Mason not out	4	– c Flower b Price	9
M. A. Harrity c Taibu b Price	16	– not out	0
B 6, l-b 11, w 1, n-b 6	24	B 4, l-b 2, w 3, n-b 8	17
1/40 (2) 2/41 (1) 3/170 (3) 4/187 (5) 5/188 (4) 6/188 (7) 7/237 (6) 8/241 (9) 9/241 (8) 10/262 (11)	262	1/63 (2) 2/106 (3) 3/131 (4) 4/132 (1) 5/173 (5) 6/199 (7) 7/235 (6) 8/236 (9) 9/247 (10) 10/247 (8)	247

Bowling: *First Innings*—Blignaut 13–2–46–2; Streak 2–0–11–0; Hondo 13–4–53–3; Friend 6–0–54–0; Price 19.5–3–64–2; Flower 7–2–17–2. *Second Innings*—Blignaut 18–3–86–1; Hondo 18–5–41–2; Friend 7–1–42–2; Price 25.4–10–47–2; Flower 11–3–25–3.

Zimbabweans

D. D. Ebrahim run out	0	– c Solanki b Kabir Ali	15
M. A. Vermeulen c Solanki b Kabir Ali	11	– c Pipe b Harrity	0
S. V. Carlisle st Pipe b Batty	157	– c Pipe b Kabir Ali	23
G. W. Flower c Peters b Mason	18	– c Solanki b Batty	26
B. G. Rogers c Peters b Harrity	4	– b Kabir Ali	0
†T. Taibu c Pipe b Kabir Ali	57	– c Pipe b Hall	8
A. M. Blignaut c Hall b Kabir Ali	2	– c Smith b Batty	42
T. J. Friend c Hall b Batty	39	– b Batty	4
R. W. Price c Solanki b Hall	5	– (10) not out	7
D. T. Hondo not out	24	– (11) b Kabir Ali	0
*H. H. Streak absent hurt		– (9) c Peters b Kabir Ali	37
B 1, l-b 10, n-b 6	17	B 1, l-b 9, w 1, n-b 2	13
1/0 (1) 2/12 (2) 3/58 (4) 4/73 (5) 5/178 (6) 6/180 (7) 7/267 (8) 8/278 (9) 9/334 (3)	334	1/10 (2) 2/20 (1) 3/43 (3) 4/43 (5) 5/55 (6) 6/119 (7) 7/128 (4) 8/128 (8) 9/175 (9) 10/175 (11)	175

Bowling: *First Innings*—Kabir Ali 28–8–89–3; Harrity 28–7–66–1; Mason 25–10–66–1; Hall 26–7–58–1; Batty 19.2–8–44–2. *Second Innings*—Kabir Ali 15–2–48–5; Harrity 7–0–29–1; Mason 13–7–18–0; Hall 13–5–38–1; Batty 14–4–32–3.

Umpires: N. G. Cowley and R. A. Kettleborough.

SUSSEX v ZIMBABWEANS

At Hove, May 15, 16, 17, 18. Drawn. Toss: Zimbabweans. First-class debut: A. J. Hodd.

The Sussex director of cricket, Peter Moores, was forced to defend his team selection after widespread criticism of the decision to rest seven of the players who had just taken part in the Championship game against Warwickshire. The critics felt that fielding a weakened side was disrespectful to the tourists, but Moores countered that the attack boasted over 800 first-class wickets and the batsmen more than 20,000 runs, while the only debutant was the 19-year-old Andrew Hodd, who kept wicket tidily. He might have added that Sussex were being captained by the former Zimbabwe star, Goodwin. The dismal weather meant only 171 overs were possible anyway. Hove can never have staged a more low-key tour match, although history was made on the third day after floodlights were used – with permission from the ECB – for the first time in a first-class match in England. The best cricket, and the best weather, was on the first day, when Vermeulen, Zimbabwe's powerfully built opener, struck a six and 33 fours, the majority timed sublimely between backward point and mid-off, on his way to a career-best 198. But the Zimbabweans lost their last eight wickets for 78, as the innings was ravaged by Hutchison in only his fourth first-class appearance for Sussex. There was time for Zuiderent to make an attractive 50 before bad light caused an early abandonment.

Close of play: First day, Zimbabweans 317-4 (Vermeulen 194); Second day, No play; Third day, Zimbabweans 374-7 (Ervine 39, Blignaut 2).

Zimbabweans

D. D. Ebrahim c Hodd b Taylor	14
M. A. Vermeulen c Hodd b Innes	198
S. V. Carlisle c Montgomerie b Davis	35
G. W. Flower c Goodwin b Hutchison	64
†T. Taibu c Zuiderent b Hutchison	0
S. M. Ervine not out	57
D. A. Marillier c Yardy b Taylor	0
*H. H. Streak c Goodwin b Innes	11
A. M. Blignaut b Hutchison	2
M. L. Nkala c Montgomerie b Lewry	0
R. W. Price b Hutchison	0
B 1, l-b 5, w 1, n-b 7	14
1/33 (1) 2/147 (3) 3/317 (4) 4/317 (5) 5/322 (2) 6/325 (7) 7/362 (8) 8/374 (9) 9/393 (10) 10/395 (11)	395

Bowling: Lewry 22–2–98–1; Taylor 30–9–64–2; Hutchison 22.5–5–94–4; Innes 24–7–57–2; Davis 17–4–58–1; Yardy 5–0–10–0; Hopkinson 2–0–8–0.

Sussex

R. R. Montgomerie c Ervine b Streak	24
M. H. Yardy run out	18
*M. W. Goodwin b Blignaut	49
B. Zuiderent c Taibu b Ervine	50
C. D. Hopkinson not out	7
K. J. Innes not out	6
L-b 6, w 2, n-b 17	25
1/55 (1) 2/63 (2) 3/155 (3) 4/168 (4)	(4 wkts) 179

P. M. Hutchison, M. J. G. Davis, †A. J. Hodd, B. V. Taylor and J. D. Lewry did not bat.

Bowling: Blignaut 10–1–24–1; Nkala 9–2–35–0; Streak 12.1–4–29–1; Ervine 11–3–56–1; Price 6–0–29–0.

Umpires: M. J. Harris and P. Willey.

ENGLAND v ZIMBABWE

First npower Test

PAUL COUPAR

At Lord's, May 22, 23, 24. England won by an innings and 92 runs. Toss: Zimbabwe. Test debuts: J. M. Anderson, A. McGrath; S. M. Ervine.

Zimbabwe arrived at Lord's with one player likely to have made the England side (Streak), and seven successive Test defeats behind them. They left having lost 19 wickets in a day – and the match inside three.

England's crushing win – by an innings and 92 runs – was competent rather than compelling: the exception was a dazzling spell on the third afternoon, when Zimbabwe's first innings crumbled and James Anderson sent stumps cartwheeling to become the first England bowler since Dominic Cork in 1995 to take a five-for on debut. But the true value of any performance was hard to judge: by the end, wickets and runs against Zimbabwe were beginning to look like a devalued currency.

Despite a pitch showing some fresh shoots, England excluded a seamer – James Kirtley – from their eleven, and included a spinner, Giles. After showing hints of the Midas touch in one-day matches over the winter, Anderson was a certainty to replace the injured Andrew Caddick. But the choice of the Yorkshire captain, Anthony McGrath, was a bolt from the blue. His selection maintained Duncan Fletcher's reputation for picking batsmen in spite rather than because of their career average. McGrath's was under 30.

From the start, the match never felt like the opening Test of a summer. The usual buzz of anticipation was replaced by the chatter of 6,000 schoolkids let in free to fill seats. And the first-morning gossip was not about cricket, but political protest. The anti-Mugabe campaigner Peter Tatchell had threatened to deliver "chaos and mayhem". Instead there were around 100 demonstrators outside the Grace Gates ("Tim Lamb is

Flying start: although James Anderson took an outstanding five for 73 on debut in the Lord's Test, his figures were bettered by two other England debutants during the summer.

Picture by Patrick Eagar.

Mugabe's Lord Haw-Haw" said one placard), two dignified pitch-invaders and a double-decker bus full of cheerful-looking Zimbabwean exiles. The Zimbabwe question, the great saga of England's winter, slowly faded from public view.

Like the protest, the first day was underwhelming. Early-morning rain and a damp outfield delayed the start until just after noon, and provided ideal conditions for Zimbabwe's seamers when Streak chose to bowl. Streak himself got the ball to swing and jag; Vaughan fenced his way to a painful 42-ball eight; and for one deceptive hour England were not on top. But Zimbabwe bowled too wide. It might have been different had Butcher not survived a convincing shout for leg-before from Hondo on ten, and a chance at slip on 36. Unruffled by these escapes, neat in defence and punchy on the counter-attack, he changed the tone of the innings.

On the second day Zimbabwe paid for their indiscipline on the first. The pitch eased, Butcher went on to 137, full of cuts and drives as crisp as a pippin, and the last four wickets added a spirit-sapping 130. McGrath marked his debut with a composed 69, helping England to 472, well above par in the conditions.

The third day was one of the longest in Test history (seven hours 39 minutes), and 19 wickets fell, but it was a hollow sort of epic. Zimbabwe simply rolled over. Against an attack that provided too much width, they contrived to stagger to 120 for five by lunch, Ebrahim managing a frisky 68 which combined crunching drives and streaky edges. Hoggard seemed to have recovered some of the swing and self-belief that had leached away during a winter in Australia, but after lunch he was dramatically upstaged by Anderson, who bowled less well but with more spectacular results.

Anderson's debut was enigmatic. He began his Test career by conceding 17 runs off his first over, but came back with a maiden, followed by a wicket maiden. On the third morning he looked as threatening as a pet moggy; in the afternoon he smashed the stumps of Streak and Friend with successive full-pitched balls that slanted in towards middle and hit off, then finished by removing Blignaut and Hondo: the last four wickets in 14 balls. His nervous smile looked like that of an apprentice magician, delighted with the result but unsure exactly how he'd managed it.

After the swift end to their first innings, Zimbabwe followed on 325 behind. Vermeulen blasted 61 at the top of the order and Friend 43 at the bottom, both enjoying the liberty that comes with having nothing to lose. But in the best batting conditions of the match nine wickets fell in 42 overs, as England claimed the extra half-hour. Butcher and McGrath took seven wickets between them with swinging dobbers, and in the process rubbed some of the sheen off Anderson's achievements. This was a little *too* easy.

Man of the Match: M. A. Butcher. *Attendance:* 60,938; *receipts* £926,715.

Close of play: First day, England 184-3 (Butcher 52, Key 11); Second day, Zimbabwe 48-1 (Ebrahim 40, Carlisle 4).

England

M. E. Trescothick c Ervine b Blignaut	59
M. P. Vaughan b Streak	8
M. A. Butcher c Vermeulen b Price	137
*N. Hussain c Hondo b Friend	19
R. W. T. Key c Taibu b Streak	18
†A. J. Stewart c Taibu b Streak	26
A. McGrath b Ervine	69
A. F. Giles b Blignaut	52
S. J. Harmison c Ebrahim b Ervine	0
M. J. Hoggard c Ebrahim b Blignaut	19
J. M. Anderson not out	4
B 14, l-b 27, w 3, n-b 17	61
1/45 (2) 2/121 (1) 3/165 (4) 4/204 (5) 5/274 (6) 6/342 (3) 7/408 (7) 8/408 (9) 9/465 (10) 10/472 (8)	472

Bowling: Streak 37–9–99–3; Blignaut 26.1–4–96–3; Hondo 14–4–45–0; Ervine 22–5–95–2; Friend 13–2–49–1; Price 20–6–44–1; Flower 1–0–3–0.

Zimbabwe

D. D. Ebrahim c McGrath b Butcher	68	– c Key b Harmison	6
M. A. Vermeulen b Anderson	1	– c Trescothick b Butcher	61
S. V. Carlisle c Trescothick b Hoggard	11	– lbw b Butcher	24
G. W. Flower c Key b Hoggard	3	– c Trescothick b Harmison	26
†T. Taibu c Hoggard b Harmison	25	– c Butcher b McGrath	16
S. M. Ervine lbw b Hoggard	4	– c Trescothick b McGrath	4
*H. H. Streak b Anderson	10	– lbw b McGrath	11
A. M. Blignaut c Butcher b Anderson	3	– b Butcher	6
T. J. Friend b Anderson	0	– c Giles b Butcher	43
R. W. Price not out	7	– c Trescothick b Giles	26
D. T. Hondo b Anderson	0	– not out	0
B 5, l-b 1, w 1, n-b 8	15	B 1, l-b 6, w 3	10
1/20 (2) 2/64 (3) 3/79 (4) 4/104 (1) 5/109 (6) 6/129 (5) 7/133 (7) 8/133 (9) 9/147 (8) 10/147 (11)	147	1/11 (1) 2/91 (2) 3/95 (3) 4/128 (5) 5/132 (6) 6/150 (7) 7/158 (8) 8/168 (4) 9/219 (10) 10/233 (9)	233

Bowling: *First Innings*—Hoggard 18–8–24–3; Anderson 16–4–73–5; Harmison 16–5–36–1; Butcher 5–2–8–1. *Second Innings*—Anderson 15–4–65–0; Hoggard 15–5–35–0; Harmison 12–4–35–2; Giles 8–2–15–1; Butcher 12.5–0–60–4; McGrath 6–1–16–3.

Umpires: S. A. Bucknor (West Indies) and D. L. Orchard (South Africa).
Third umpire: N. A. Mallender. Referee: C. H. Lloyd (West Indies).

MIDDLESEX v ZIMBABWEANS

At Shenley Park, May 30, 31, June 1, 2. Drawn. Toss: Middlesex. First-class debut: C. T. Peploe.

On an easy-paced pitch and with both sides resting strike bowlers, the match produced 1,360 runs – including four centuries and 15 scores above 40 – for the loss of just 17 wickets. The game began with centuries for Weston, granted a rare first-team opportunity, and Weekes, plus a near-miss from Michael Brown, Middlesex's 23-year-old third-choice keeper. The Zimbabweans easily avoided the follow-on thanks to Carlisle's 137, and declared behind before Shah took full advantage of the conditions to score his first hundred of the season and help add 222 to Middlesex's first-innings lead of 115. Set 338 in 68 overs, the Zimbabweans at one stage lost five for 53 before Taibu and Flower steered them to the draw that had looked inevitable all along.

Close of play: First day, Middlesex 330-5 (Weekes 30, Brown 0); Second day, Zimbabweans 176-2 (Carlisle 39, Flower 30); Third day, Middlesex 86-1 (Strauss 36, Shah 0).

Middlesex

*A. J. Strauss c Taibu b Ervine	0	– c Flower b Price	49
R. M. S. Weston c Sibanda b Friend	129	– lbw b Friend	41
O. A. Shah c Ebrahim b Friend	68	– not out	101
B. L. Hutton c Vermeulen b Price	2	– not out	19
E. C. Joyce run out	80		
P. N. Weekes not out	102		
†M. J. Brown c Ervine b Flower	98		
S. J. Cook not out	9		
B 7, l-b 10, w 6, n-b 5	28	L-b 7, w 3, n-b 2	12
1/0 (1) 2/148 (3) 3/151 (4) 4/246 (2) 5/317 (5) 6/500 (7) (6 wkts dec.)	516	1/74 (2) 2/148 (1) (2 wkts dec.)	222

T. A. Hunt, C. T. Peploe and T. F. Bloomfield did not bat.

Bowling: *First Innings*—Ervine 27–5–102–1; Nkala 25–9–79–0; Friend 28–3–121–2; Price 38–6–111–1; Sibanda 5–1–34–0; Flower 12.5–2–44–1; Rogers 3–0–8–0. *Second Innings*—Friend 9–0–65–1; Nkala 12–2–68–0; Ervine 10–1–51–0; Price 7–0–31–1.

Zimbabweans

D. D. Ebrahim c Peploe b Weekes	30	– c Weekes b Peploe	64
M. A. Vermeulen b Hunt	59	– c Brown b Hunt	42
S. V. Carlisle c Hutton b Bloomfield	137		
G. W. Flower c Brown b Peploe	65	– (7) not out	43
*†T. Taibu not out	49	– (6) not out	37
S. M. Ervine not out	32	– (4) b Weekes	21
B. G. Rogers (did not bat)		– (3) c Bloomfield b Hunt	6
V. Sibanda (did not bat)		– (5) b Weekes	0
B 7, l-b 10, w 5, n-b 7	29	B 2, l-b 2, n-b 4	8
1/96 (1) 2/101 (2) 3/274 (4) 4/351 (3) (4 wkts dec.)	401	1/87 (2) 2/93 (3) 3/126 (4) 4/126 (5) 5/140 (1) (5 wkts)	221

R. W. Price, T. J. Friend and M. L. Nkala did not bat.

Bowling: *First Innings*—Bloomfield 24–4–82–1; Cook 18–6–49–0; Weekes 23–4–79–1; Hunt 15–3–68–1; Peploe 14–2–61–1; Hutton 11–4–34–0; Joyce 3–1–11–0. *Second Innings*—Bloomfield 7–0–31–0; Cook 6–1–17–0; Hutton 5–2–22–0; Hunt 7–1–28–2; Weekes 19–5–38–2; Peploe 17–3–58–1; Shah 2–0–14–0; Joyce 2–0–9–0.

Umpires: M. Dixon and J. H. Hampshire.

ENGLAND v ZIMBABWE

Second npower Test

STEPHEN BRENKLEY

At Chester-le-Street, June 5, 6, 7. England won by an innings and 69 runs. Toss: England. Test debut: R. L. Johnson.

England's first new Test venue for 101 years – and the 87th in all Test cricket – produced an occasion that the contest failed to match. The organisation at the Riverside ground was meticulous but not oppressive; the setting in the shadow of 14th-century Lumley Castle had a charm unlike anything seen before at an English Test ground; and it was clear throughout that the North-East wanted and deserved to stage regular international cricket.

If there was a criticism, it was that the attendance on the first two days did not match expectations. Not until the climax on the third day did the temporary stands brim with spectators. The explanation was probably simple: inaugural Test or not, the area's fervent sporting public was not deluded by the quality of the competition.

BEST BOWLING ON TEST DEBUT FOR ENGLAND

7-37	†J. J. Ferris v South Africa at Cape Town (second innings)	1891-92
7-43	D. G. Cork v West Indies at Lord's (second innings)	1995
7-46	J. K. Lever v India at Delhi	1976-77
7-49	A. V. Bedser v India at Lord's	1946
7-56	James Langridge v West Indies at Manchester (second innings)	1933
7-103	J. C. Laker v West Indies at Bridgetown	1947-48
6-33	**R. L. Johnson v Zimbabwe at Chester-le-Street**	**2003**
6-34	**R. J. Kirtley v South Africa at Nottingham** (second innings)	**2003**
6-43	G. H. T. Simpson-Hayward v South Africa at Johannesburg	1909-10
6-50	F. Martin v Australia at The Oval	1890
6-52	F. Martin v Australia at The Oval (second innings)	1890
6-54	†J. J. Ferris v South Africa at Cape Town	1891-92

All instances are in the first innings unless stated otherwise.

† *Ferris had previously played eight Tests for Australia.*

Although Streak bowled with admirable control and there was some belated resistance on the third afternoon, too many of Zimbabwe's players lacked method or gumption, or both. England took comprehensive advantage, and although there was a puncture in the middle of their innings, it was painlessly repaired, and they sent Zimbabwe to their ninth consecutive Test defeat.

For England, Richard Johnson made his debut in place of the injured Hoggard, nine years after first entering the national consciousness by taking ten wickets in an innings for Middlesex. His analysis here was eye-catching too, if not quite as spectacular, and he instantly found a good length and some accurate in-swing. Helped by two wickets in his first over, he followed Anderson at Lord's in claiming a five-wicket haul in his first Test. His eventual figures of six for 33 were the sixth-best by an Englishman on Test debut (not counting Ferris – see above).

On a pitch as low and slow as expected, only Butcher in the England top order looked fluent, and when Hondo produced a golden spell on the first afternoon to take three wickets in 11 balls, England were in a spot of trouble at 156 for five. They were eased calmly out of it by Stewart and McGrath, whose partnership of 149 equalled

Beneath the battlements: the Riverside, home to Durham for eight years, became the first new Test venue in England for over a century.

Picture by Patrick Eagar.

the record for any England wicket against Zimbabwe. The calls for Stewart to be jettisoned had, if anything, grown louder since the victory at Lord's. He responded with clean-cut defiance, as might have been expected. Each of his 11 fours seemed to be designed to make his point, while his 68 lifted his Test aggregate to 8,281 runs, ahead of David Gower (8,231) and behind only Graham Gooch (8,900) on England's all-time list.

Meanwhile, McGrath again looked at home by making his second half-century in his second Test. He was playing well enough to make the Riverside's first Test hundred when he pushed at one away from his body. With Giles also making a second consecutive fifty and Johnson enjoying himself, England's last five wickets contributed 260.

But when Johnson's name was announced in the field, the spectators greeted his introduction silently: they wanted the local boy, Harmison, to share the new ball. The equivalent of just over a session later, Johnson was accorded a hero's return. His first ball in Test cricket was a menacing yorker that almost sneaked through. Before the over was out, however, he was on a hat-trick. Vermeulen misjudged an in-swinger and Carlisle was understandably beaten by another brutal yorker. Only Taibu displayed any semblance of purpose. There were seven lbws, a Test record for a single innings; the technology did suggest some umpiring errors, but the lack of batting proficiency against persistent bowling was more culpable.

Zimbabwe could hardly do worse in following on and in the event gave a capacity third-day crowd the best of both worlds. The entertainment, comprising Zimbabwean resistance and inevitable English victory, went on into the late afternoon. Ebrahim concentrated fiercely and made a half-century, while Friend indulged in some unfettered hitting towards the end.

Anderson, who seemed like an old hand in his second Test, was given every opportunity by Hussain to take another five-wicket haul. He was denied by Harmison who, to the delight of the crowd, finished off the match and the series by bouncing out Price and yorking Hondo. For the first time since the 1985 Ashes, England had won successive Tests by an innings. It was a happy omen for future Tests here. Unlike the last new ground – Bramall Lane, Sheffield, used in 1902 but never again – the Riverside looked here to stay.

Man of the Match: R. L. Johnson. *Attendance*: 25,878; *receipts* £569,159.

Men of the Series: England – M. A. Butcher; Zimbabwe – H. H. Streak.

Close of play: First day, England 298-5 (Stewart 67, McGrath 68); Second day, Zimbabwe 41-1 (Ebrahim 22, Carlisle 19).

England

M. E. Trescothick c Taibu b Price	43
M. P. Vaughan c Ervine b Streak	20
M. A. Butcher b Hondo	47
*N. Hussain c Taibu b Hondo	18
R. W. T. Key c Flower b Hondo	4
†A. J. Stewart lbw b Streak	68
A. McGrath c Taibu b Blignaut	81
A. F. Giles c Ervine b Streak	50
R. L. Johnson c Streak b Blignaut	24
S. J. Harmison c Vermeulen b Streak	11
J. M. Anderson not out	12
B 1, l-b 5, w 7, n-b 25	38
1/49 (2) 2/109 (1) 3/146 (3) 4/152 (5) 5/156 (4) 6/305 (6) 7/324 (7) 8/356 (9) 9/390 (10) 10/416 (8)	416

Bowling: Streak 34.1–11–64–4; Blignaut 23–4–95–2; Hondo 22–1–98–3; Ervine 3–0–17–0; Price 40–9–105–1; Friend 4–0–26–0; Flower 1–0–5–0.

"Bowlers and spectators alike began to forget there was an existence without Graeme Smith at the centre of it."

South Africans in England, page 444.

Zimbabwe

D. D. Ebrahim lbw b Anderson	6	– lbw b Harmison	55
M. A. Vermeulen lbw b Johnson	0	– c McGrath b Anderson	0
S. V. Carlisle lbw b Johnson	0	– c Key b Anderson	28
G. W. Flower c Trescothick b Anderson	8	– b Anderson	16
†T. Taibu lbw b Johnson	31	– c Butcher b Giles	14
S. M. Ervine c Stewart b Johnson	0	– b Harmison	34
T. J. Friend lbw b Johnson	0	– not out	65
*H. H. Streak lbw b Johnson	4	– run out	3
A. M. Blignaut c Anderson b Harmison	13	– c Hussain b Anderson	12
R. W. Price lbw b Harmison	17	– c Stewart b Harmison	6
D. T. Hondo not out	5	– b Harmison	4
B 5, l-b 3, n-b 2	10	B 6, l-b 10	16
1/3 (2) 2/3 (3) 3/11 (1) 4/18 (4) 5/23 (6) 6/31 (7) 7/35 (8) 8/48 (9) 9/73 (5) 10/94 (10)	94	1/5 (2) 2/65 (3) 3/102 (1) 4/113 (4) 5/131 (5) 6/185 (6) 7/202 (8) 8/223 (9) 9/244 (10) 10/253 (11)	253

Bowling: *First Innings*—Anderson 10–2–30–2; Johnson 12–4–33–6; Harmison 9.1–3–22–2; Giles 1–0–1–0. *Second Innings*—Anderson 23–8–55–4; Johnson 22–7–67–0; Harmison 21.4–4–55–4; Giles 25–9–51–1; Butcher 2–0–9–0.

Umpires: D. B. Hair (Australia) and D. L. Orchard (South Africa).
Third umpire: P. Willey. Referee: C. H. Lloyd (West Indies).

†IRELAND v ZIMBABWEANS

At Belfast, June 13. Ireland won by ten wickets. Toss: Ireland.

Ireland pulled off their first win over a touring Test side since 1969, when they famously dismissed West Indies for 25. This victory, at the Civil Service Ground, Stormont, was almost as convincing. After their bowlers had made short work of the Zimbabwean batting, Ireland's openers reached the target of 183 with staggering ease and more than 16 overs to spare. Their captain, Jason Molins, cracked 107 from 101 balls with 14 fours and two sixes, while Jeremy Bray, a 19-year-old import from Sydney, finished with a more patient 67. Earlier, the Zimbabweans had recovered from 12 for three, but Matsikenyeri was stumped off Andrew White for 50, Ebrahim was bowled for a painstaking 52 from 152 balls and the innings fell away. Six Zimbabweans were out in single figures. Their preparations for the NatWest Series could not have got off to a more humiliating start.

Zimbabweans

D. A. Marillier b Mooney	0
D. D. Ebrahim b McCallan	52
C. K. Coventry b Mooney	4
R. W. Sims c Molins b Neely	0
S. Matsikenyeri st O'Brien b White	50
*†T. Taibu c Armstrong b Botha	35
S. M. Ervine run out	0
T. J. Friend c O'Brien b Neely	22
G. B. Brent c and b Botha	0
D. T. Hondo not out	5
W. Mwayenga c Armstrong b Neely	1
B 1, l-b 6, w 5, n-b 1	13
1/0 (1) 2/11 (3) 3/12 (4) 4/108 (5) 5/132 (2) 6/133 (7) 7/170 (8) 8/171 (9) 9/178 (6) 10/182 (11) (49.5 overs)	182

Bowling: Mooney 8–2–19–2; Neely 9.5–0–30–3; Armstrong 6–0–25–0; Botha 9–0–39–2; White 9–0–36–1; McCallan 8–1–26–1.

Ireland

*J. A. M. Molins not out	107
J. P. Bray not out	67
B 1, w 1, n-b 7	9
(no wkt, 33.4 overs)	183

A. C. Botha, †N. J. O'Brien, P. G. Gillespie, W. K. McCallan, D. Joyce, A. R. White, P. J. K. Mooney, C. M. Armstrong and G. J. Neely did not bat.

Bowling: Hondo 7–2–37–0; Mwayenga 4–1–22–0; Brent 7–1–28–0; Marillier 4–0–26–0; Friend 5–0–35–0; Ervine 2–0–15–0; Sims 3.4–0–17–0; Matsikenyeri 1–0–2–0.

Umpires: J. Boomer and T. Henry.

†IRELAND v ZIMBABWEANS

At Eglinton, June 15. Zimbabweans won by eight wickets. Toss: Ireland.

A solid all-round display from the Zimbabweans prevented a repeat of their shock defeat two days earlier, but their eight-wicket win could have been even more convincing. After choosing to make first use of ideal batting conditions, Ireland lost Molins, the centurion at Belfast, to a mistimed pull to mid-on from the third ball of the innings and were quickly reduced to 36 for five by Streak and Blignaut, who both missed the previous match. A careful 56 from Peter Gillespie helped Ireland to 196 and respectability, but any hopes of a fightback with the ball were dashed by a second-wicket stand of 82 between Ebrahim and Carlisle.

Ireland

*J. A. M. Molins c Hondo b Streak	0
J. P. Bray c Taibu b Streak	9
A. C. Botha c Taibu b Streak	8
†N. J. O'Brien c Flower b Blignaut	2
P. G. Gillespie c Ebrahim b Hondo	56
W. K. McCallan c Taibu b Blignaut	1
D. Joyce c Streak b Hondo	29
A. R. White run out	14
P. J. K. Mooney c Marillier b Price	31
C. M. Armstrong not out	13
G. J. Neely c and b Hondo	1
L-b 7, w 16, n-b 9	32
1/0 (1) 2/15 (3) 3/21 (4) 4/34 (2) 5/36 (6) 6/75 (7) 7/112 (8) 8/174 (9) 9/185 (5) 10/196 (11) (48.4 overs)	196

Bowling: Streak 10–2–29–3; Blignaut 6–0–32–2; Brent 9–3–15–0; Hondo 9.4–0–53–3; Price 8–0–36–1; Marillier 6–0–24–0.

Zimbabweans

D. A. Marillier c Molins b White	23
D. D. Ebrahim not out	81
S. V. Carlisle c and b Mooney	49
G. W. Flower not out	31
B 2, l-b 2, w 7, n-b 4	15
1/52 (1) 2/134 (3) (2 wkts, 40.1 overs)	199

*H. H. Streak, †T. Taibu, S. Matsikenyeri, A. M. Blignaut, G. B. Brent, R. W. Price and D. T. Hondo did not bat.

Bowling: Mooney 7–0–29–1; Neely 8–0–38–0; Botha 8–0–32–0; White 7–1–40–1; McCallan 7.1–0–37–0; Armstrong 3–0–19–0.

Umpires: E. Cooke and C. McElwee.

†SOMERSET v ZIMBABWEANS

At Taunton, June 17. Zimbabweans won by three runs. Toss: Zimbabweans.

The Somerset all-rounder Keith Dutch completed an extraordinary double when he was run out at the non-striker's end backing up yet again, two days after suffering the same fate in a National League match against Scotland. Once again, it was after a deflection by the bowler, on this occasion. Streak. Until then, Somerset were on course at 262 for three, and Dutch, off 82 balls, and Bowler had both made 93. But two more run-outs followed and, with five needed to win, Durston could only manage a single from the final delivery. Zimbabwe were grateful for a racy stand of 134 between Carlisle and Matsikenyeri, whose 66 came off just 62 deliveries.

Zimbabweans

D. A. Marillier b Francis . . . 15
D. D. Ebrahim c and b Francis . . . 8
S. V. Carlisle c Jones b Durston . . . 119
G. W. Flower c and b Dutch . . . 29
A. M. Blignaut c Burns b Blackwell . . . 10
S. Matsikenyeri b Jones . . . 66
*H. H. Streak b Andrew . . . 12
G. B. Brent run out . . . 6
†T. Taibu not out . . . 3
R. W. Price b Jones . . . 1
W. Mwayenga not out . . . 4
L-b 3, w 5, n-b 4 . . . 12

1/13 (2) 2/46 (1) 3/96 (4) 4/113 (5) 5/247 (3) 6/265 (6) 7/271 (7) 8/277 (8) 9/281 (10) (9 wkts, 50 overs) 285

Bowling: Francis 10–0–56–2; Andrew 7–0–63–1; Jones 10–0–40–2; Blackwell 10–0–46–1; Dutch 7–0–37–1; Durston 6–0–40–1.

Somerset

P. D. Bowler st Taibu b Marillier . . . 93
†C. M. Gazzard lbw b Streak . . . 2
J. D. C. Bryant b Price . . . 27
K. P. Dutch run out . . . 93
I. D. Blackwell run out . . . 30
*M. Burns c Price b Brent . . . 6
M. J. Wood run out . . . 1
W. J. Durston not out . . . 1
G. M. Andrew not out . . . 1
L-b 12, w 15, n-b 1 . . . 28

1/12 (2) 2/85 (3) 3/219 (1) 4/262 (4) 5/270 (6) 6/275 (7) 7/280 (5) (7 wkts, 50 overs) 282

P. S. Jones and S. R. G. Francis did not bat.

Bowling: Streak 10–2–31–1; Blignaut 10–1–64–0; Brent 10–0–52–1; Mwayenga 4–0–23–0; Price 9–0–52–1; Marillier 4–0–31–1; Flower 3–0–17–0.

Umpires: R. J. Bailey and T. E. Jesty.

†HAMPSHIRE v ZIMBABWEANS

At Southampton, June 19. Hampshire won by 16 runs. Toss: Zimbabweans.

An unbroken stand of 108 in 13 overs between Kenway and Mascarenhas took the game beyond the Zimbabweans' reach, before Giddins finished them off with the ball. But Zimbabwe only had themselves to blame. After choosing to bowl on a benign pitch, they dropped catches, conceded 19 wides, and leaked 21 from the final over, delivered by Ervine. Marillier gave the Zimbabweans a sound footing in reply, but wickets fell regularly.

Hampshire

J. R. C. Hamblin c Taibu b Hondo . . . 4
D. A. Kenway not out . . . 120
W. S. Kendall st Taibu b Price . . . 20
L. R. Prittipaul lbw b Ervine . . . 0
*R. A. Smith c Hondo b Flower . . . 28
N. Pothas c Ebrahim b Marillier . . . 16
A. D. Mascarenhas not out . . . 50
L-b 3, w 19, n-b 2 . . . 24

1/14 (1) 2/85 (3) 3/86 (4) 4/136 (5) 5/154 (6) (5 wkts, 50 overs) 262

S. D. Udal, †I. Brunnschweiler, A. D. Mullally and E. S. H. Giddins did not bat.

Bowling: Blignaut 8–0–43–0; Hondo 9–2–33–1; Brent 3–0–31–0; Ervine 10–0–66–1; Price 10–2–37–1; Marillier 5–1–23–1; Flower 5–0–26–1.

Zimbabweans

D. A. Marillier b Udal	54	G. B. Brent b Mascarenhas	0
C. K. Coventry c Hamblin b Mascarenhas	2	R. W. Price b Giddins	3
D. D. Ebrahim b Giddins	5	D. T. Hondo not out	0
*†T. Taibu c Pothas b Hamblin	29	B 3, l-b 13, w 9	25
G. W. Flower c Kendall b Giddins	22		
S. Matsikenyeri b Mullally	38	1/10 (2) 2/19 (3) 3/87 (4) (49.1 overs)	246
S. M. Ervine c Prittipaul b Mullally	24	4/111 (1) 5/145 (5)	
A. M. Blignaut c Brunnschweiler b Giddins	44	6/183 (6) 7/199 (7)	
		8/203 (9) 9/243 (10) 10/246 (8)	

Bowling: Giddins 9.1–2–33–4; Mascarenhas 9–1–48–2; Mullally 10–0–44–2; Hamblin 4–0–17–1; Prittipaul 7–1–36–0; Udal 10–0–52–1.

Umpires: N. L. Bainton and M. J. Kitchen.

†ESSEX v ZIMBABWEANS

At Chelmsford, June 22. Zimbabweans won by five wickets. Toss: Zimbabweans. County debut: A. P. Palladino.

This battle of the Flower brothers was a triumph for Zimbabwe's Grant as his polished unbeaten 60 brought about victory with 11 overs to spare. Earlier, Andy underlined his class with a half-century before becoming the second of four run-out casualties in the Essex innings. Price, the left-arm spinner, had already undermined the top order by capturing three wickets during a five-over spell costing just six runs.

Essex

N. Hussain run out	21	A. P. Palladino run out	0
D. D. J. Robinson c Taibu b Price	37	J. B. Grant not out	4
R. S. Bopara c Taibu b Friend	18		
A. Habib lbw b Price	0	L-b 7, w 3, n-b 1	11
R. C. Irani c Ebrahim b Price	1		
*†A. Flower run out	52	1/56 (1) 2/68 (2) (9 wkts, 50 overs)	189
J. D. Middlebrook not out	42	3/68 (4) 4/70 (5)	
N. A. Denning c Ebrahim b Streak	2	5/118 (3) 6/154 (6)	
S. A. Brant run out	1	7/168 (8) 8/183 (9) 9/183 (10)	

Bowling: Streak 10–3–25–1; Blignaut 8–1–44–0; Ervine 4–1–17–0; Price 10–1–20–3; Friend 10–2–47–1; Marillier 8–0–29–0.

Zimbabweans

D. A. Marillier lbw b Grant	30	†T. Taibu not out	12
D. D. Ebrahim c Middlebrook b Palladino	8	L-b 2, w 5, n-b 3	10
T. J. Friend b Middlebrook	44		
G. W. Flower not out	60	1/13 (2) 2/77 (1) (5 wkts, 39 overs)	193
R. W. Sims c Flower b Palladino	18	3/91 (3) 4/123 (5)	
S. Matsikenyeri c Flower b Grant	11	5/138 (6)	

*H. H. Streak, A. M. Blignaut, R. W. Price and S. M. Ervine did not bat.

Bowling: Brant 8–1–39–0; Palladino 8–0–45–2; Grant 7–0–36–2; Denning 7–1–34–0; Middlebrook 7–0–27–1; Bopara 2–0–10–0.

Umpires: M. J. Harris and R. T. Robinson.

Zimbabwe's matches against England and South Africa in the NatWest Series (June 26–July 10) appear on pages 466–476.

THE SOUTH AFRICANS IN ENGLAND, 2003

REVIEW BY JOHN ETHERIDGE

Five unpredictable and action-laden Test matches, all squeezed into less than seven weeks, gave South Africa's third series in England since readmission an almost non-stop rush of excitement. The buzz started when South Africa scorched to 398 for one on the opening day of the First Test, and finished with England completing a staggering comeback in the Fifth. There was scarcely time to pause for breath.

Although South Africa dominated large chunks of the series they will ultimately judge their tour as one of frustration and lack of fulfilment, if not exactly failure. Undoubtedly they played the more consistent cricket, and the final result – a 2–2 draw – gave little clue as to how the matches actually unfolded. More revealing was the number of runs each team averaged per wicket: 44.30 for South Africa, but just 35.81 for England. Graeme Smith, at the age of 22 and on his first major tour as captain, was left to ponder how his side failed to win the rubber by a convincing margin.

Rain probably deprived them of a win in the First Test, although they achieved a victory of sorts when the opposition captain, Nasser Hussain, decided to resign immediately afterwards. They won the Second overwhelmingly, but England drew level after winning a crucial toss in the Third. In the Fourth, at Headingley, South Africa hauled themselves to an unlikely victory after England surrendered at least three positions of superiority, prompting Hussain's replacement, Michael Vaughan, to criticise his players for a lack of ruthlessness. Going into the last match, South Africa could easily have been leading 4–0 rather than 2–1.

Instead, Vaughan and England were somehow able to level the series in an astonishing match at The Oval. At 345 for two shortly before the close on the first day, South Africa's position seemed unassailable. But, perhaps because of their own complacency and certainly because of English skill and resolve, the balance of power in the game swung to such an extent that England eventually won by nine wickets.

So South Africa's tour, like their previous two, ended without victory in the Test series, though they were ahead every time. They were also thrashed by England in the final of the one-day NatWest Series (a triangular tournament, with Zimbabwe the makeweights). But despite failing in their principal objective, the tourists made many friends. Their Test squad was more demographically representative than any since their readmission, with six non-whites among the 16 originally chosen. They also played more adventurous cricket than much of that offered by recent South African teams, and they certainly succeeded in their stated aim of embracing the public and being more accessible. Smith and the coach Eric Simons wanted the squad to have greater pride in representing their country, and to take on a more ambassadorial role. Consequently, players were often to be seen signing autographs half an hour after the end of play, none more frequently than Smith himself.

Smith, who succeeded Shaun Pollock as captain in the wake of South Africa's ignominious, mathematically challenged exit from the World Cup, became the towering figure of the tour. Alec Stewart, who had been around a bit and was old enough to be Smith's father, described him as "the most impressive 22-year-old I have ever seen". Few would disagree.

His influence was felt even before the squad left home when, on his personal recommendation, the popular all-rounder Lance Klusener was omitted. Popular, that is, in most places except the South African dressing-room. Smith regarded Klusener as a divisive influence and had the confidence to go public with his views. Among those to criticise the decision was the former South African coach Bob Woolmer, and Klusener himself was so incensed that he threatened legal action. But Smith remained firm.

Indeed his single-mindedness was awe-inspiring. Even as a young teenager, Smith had made no secret of his ambition to captain his country, and while most teenagers might pin up a picture of the latest pop princess, Smith stuck a list of his watchwords to the family fridge in Johannesburg: "Brave. Strong. Calm. Confident. Enjoy." This was a young man with a sense of destiny and his thirst for knowledge was unquenchable. He read books about leadership and newspaper clippings about his opposite number; he sought out Mike Brearley and they had dinner together. However, their methods were completely different: the cerebral Brearley brought to the job the mind of the trained psychoanalyst; Smith was all about pounding handclaps, meaningful stares and plenty of verbal intimidation.

Smith also used a British sports psychologist, Michael Finnigan, and was not afraid to admit his importance. While many teams are secretive about such men, as though their presence suggests mental weakness, Smith asked Finnigan to sit alongside him at two press conferences. This captain was anything but mentally weak, publicly criticising England for "arrogance" after their one-day victory. When Hussain referred to him during a media conference before the Edgbaston Test as "wotsisname", he first expressed irritation, then imposed an authority so crushing that no one on the field in the first two Tests is likely to forget his name as long as they live. Smith scored 277, 85 and 259.

At the time, only Don Bradman (three times), Walter Hammond (twice) and Vinod Kambli of India had scored double-centuries in successive Tests. On the eve of the series, Smith had taken his batsmen out for dinner and came up with the maxim "Never Satisfied". Hundreds were not enough; he wanted big ones. However, after treading on his stumps for 35 in the first innings of the Third Test, he failed to reach 20 in the rest of the series. Perhaps those who questioned his technique and said the face of his bat was too closed for success in international cricket had a point after all.

But it would be wrong to portray South Africa's tour as a one-man show. When available, their experienced major players all made telling contributions. Gary Kirsten followed a century at Lord's with one at Headingley which, on a malevolent pitch, was arguably more important than

Doubling up: the four batsmen to have hit double-hundreds in successive Tests: this page, Don Bradman (*left*), and Wally Hammond; far page, Vinod Kambli (*left*) and Graeme Smith. In December 2003, Ricky Ponting became the fifth.
Pictures by Getty Images, EMPICS and Patrick Eagar.

either of Smith's double-hundreds. When an arm injury kept him out of the match at Trent Bridge (played on an even more awkward surface) South Africa were beaten. Jacques Kallis also missed games – the first two Tests – after he returned home to be with his dying father. Kallis had scored prodigiously in the NatWest Series and although his batting never hit those heights when he returned, he swerved and swung England towards defeat at Headingley, ending with a second-innings six for 54, his best in Tests. That performance was well timed because Pollock, who would surely have been devastating in the conditions, had travelled home for the birth of his first child. In the four Tests he played, Pollock was, as usual, the most economical bowler on either side, as well as playing a couple of major innings. Meanwhile, Makhaya Ntini added firepower, removing five of England's top seven with the short ball during the victory at Lord's, and taking ten in the match. But the various absences meant South Africa's strongest team did not take the field until the decisive last Test when, ironically, they produced their sloppiest performance.

Herschelle Gibbs, who also fielded brilliantly, completed an intimidating top three and book-ended his series with dazzling centuries in the first and last Tests. And wicket-keeper Mark Boucher averaged nearly 39 at No. 6 or 7 (his keeping was untidy and he often fumbled the ball – except when a batsman had actually edged it). But in between they struggled:

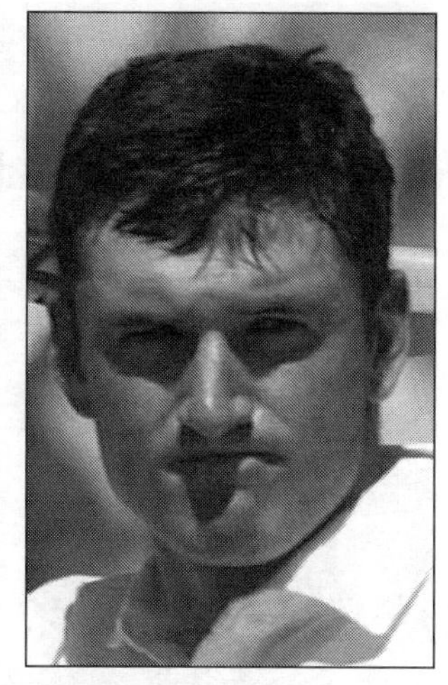

South Africa's middle order was an area of distinct vulnerability throughout. Jacques Rudolph, for instance, played in all five Tests but endured a wretched time.

But the lower order regularly made up the deficit, most notably at Headingley, where Monde Zondeki scored 59 on his debut and, in the second innings, Andrew Hall, the closest to a like-for-like replacement for Klusener, plundered 99 not out from No. 8. Hall had a curious summer, constantly nipping off to help Worcestershire reach the C&G Final (he had signed for the county after initially being left out of the Test squad), and sandwiching his one telling innings between four disasters. But his Headingley rampage knocked the spirit out of England and helped put South Africa 2–1 up.

England's bowling that Sunday morning was nothing short of disgraceful and their morale visibly disintegrated. Their eventual defeat at Leeds prompted the usual cries for the restructuring of domestic cricket and plenty of self-analysis. Marcus Trescothick and Mark Butcher were widely condemned for going off for bad light on the Friday evening when they had been pummelling the bowling. Typical of the cautious, old pro, don't-risk-what-you've-got mentality, echoed the critics. Then, after the match, Vaughan was attacked by several officials from the shires for suggesting the county game was the reason English Test players lacked ruthlessness and mental toughness. England were in a mess and there was much talk of how the momentum (a watchword of the series) was with South Africa as they approached the decisive Oval Test.

At 345 for two, that momentum seemed unstoppable. But Vaughan's side, in common with many recent England teams, rallied when at their lowest

Not with a whimper... Alec Stewart – who had announced that the Fifth Test, at his home ground, The Oval, would be his last – is chaired from the field after England's thrilling nine-wicket win.

Picture by Patrick Eagar.

ebb. He was the latest captain to discover England's infuriating capacity for lurching from ineptitude to brilliance on an almost daily basis. He was not the only one flummoxed: the Cricket Reform Group – an assortment led by Bob Willis, Mike Atherton and Michael Parkinson – were left launching their manifesto for dismantling the current format of county cricket at the very moment England were heading towards a historic win. Plenty of journalists, whose pens had been dripping with vitriol four days earlier, were forced into some serious back-tracking. The England team do that to people.

Vaughan had not been thrown in at the deep end so much as tossed into the Pacific without a life-jacket. He discovered he was being given the job while chomping a bacon butty in a downcast Edgbaston dressing-room and, in these days of back-to-back Tests, had little more than 48 hours to prepare to lift his side at Lord's. He failed. Although he had proved a popular and effective leader in the one-day series, at times he looked overawed by the demands of Test captaincy and allowed the game to drift without sufficient intervention or animation. His relaxed, unflustered demeanour certainly contrasted with Hussain's Mr Angry, heart-on-the-sleeve style. But Vaughan insisted he would not change, and rejected all suggestions that he was too soft for a job the Prime Minister described as harder than his.

After making 156 in the First Test, when Hussain was still in charge, Vaughan's form with the bat dipped alarmingly. Others did their best to make up: five more England batsmen hit centuries. Hussain, who kept his place despite suggestions that his wallow in self-pity at Lord's disrupted the rest of the team, scored a redeeming and warmly received hundred in the next match, at Trent Bridge; Butcher was England's most consistent batsman (but dropped five catches); and Trescothick was chiefly responsible for the heart-lifting win at The Oval. In the same match, Thorpe made a hundred in his first Test for 14 months. Andrew Flintoff, with a strong-arm century in a lost cause at Lord's, a brace of fifties at Headingley and, most importantly, a pulverising and wholly demoralising 95 at The Oval, showed he is at least the batting half of becoming the new Ian Botham.

Flintoff also bowled most overs for England, but his wickets cost 59 apiece. And he was not the only one who lacked a cutting edge. Eight fast bowlers who were or could have been chosen were injured for all or part of the series. A debutant, James Kirtley, and a stopgap, Martin Bicknell, took advantage of helpful pitches but otherwise England's best bowling average was 39.86 from James Anderson, who took just 15 wickets in five Tests. At times, as Smith and Gibbs marched on, a run-out looked the best hope of a breakthrough. And Darren Gough, who had bust a gut (not to mention a knee) to grab wickets on flat pitches in the past, through force of personality as much as anything else, retired from Test cricket after two ineffectual matches.

Alec Stewart also said goodbye, having announced before the First Test that he would retire from international cricket at the end of the summer. He kept his place despite averaging just 22 with the bat and was therefore granted his wish of a valedictory tour of the English Test grounds. He finally departed, aged 40 years and five months, collar up and bearing jaunty, on his home patch at The Oval, at the end of a match that provided a mind-boggling conclusion to a series full of wild fluctuations and engrossing cricket.

SOUTH AFRICAN TOURING PARTY

G. C. Smith (Western Province) (*captain*), M. V. Boucher (Border) (*vice-captain*), P. R. Adams (Western Province), H. H. Dippenaar (Free State), H. H. Gibbs (Western Province), A. J. Hall (Easterns), J. H. Kallis (Western Province), G. Kirsten (Western Province), N. D. McKenzie (Northerns), M. Ntini (Border), R. J. Peterson (Eastern Province), S. M. Pollock (KwaZulu-Natal), D. Pretorius (Free State), J. A. Rudolph (Northerns), T. L. Tsolekile (Western Province), C. M. Willoughby (Western Province), M. Zondeki (Border).

N. Boje (Free State), A. C. Dawson (Western Province), C. K. Langeveldt (Boland), A. Nel (Easterns), M. van Jaarsveld (Northerns) and M. N. van Wyk (Free State) left after the one-day tournament, when Kirsten, Peterson, Tsolekile, Willoughby and Zondeki arrived for the first-class programme. McKenzie was unable to play in the one-day tournament due to a back injury, so Dippenaar (originally selected for the first-class leg only) was called up early as cover; Hall, who was originally to be released after the one-day games, stayed on for the first-class leg.

Coach: E. O. Simons. *Manager:* Goolam Rajah. *Assistant coach:* C. J. P. G. van Zyl. *Physiotherapist:* S. Jabaar. *Fitness trainer:* A. le Roux. *Computer analyst:* G. Obermeyer. *Communications manager:* G. de Kock.

THE SOUTH AFRICAN TOURING PARTY

Back row: A. le Roux (*fitness trainer*), R. J. Peterson, A. J. Hall, H. H. Dippenaar, J. A. Rudolph, N. D. McKenzie, T. L. Tsolekile, G. Obermeyer (*computer analyst*). *Middle row:* S. Jabaar (*physiotherapist*), P. R. Adams, M. Zondeki, D. Pretorius, C. M. Willoughby, M. Ntini, H. H. Gibbs, C. J. G. P. van Zyl (*assistant coach*). *Front row:* S. M. Pollock, Goolam Rajah (*manager*), E. O. Simons (*coach*), G. C. Smith (*captain*), M. V. Boucher (*vice-captain*), G. Kirsten.

Picture by Tom Shaw, Getty Images.

SOUTH AFRICAN TOUR RESULTS

Test matches – Played 5: Won 2, Lost 2, Drawn 1.
First-class matches – Played 9: Won 3, Lost 2, Drawn 4.
Wins – England (2), Kent.
Losses – England (2).
Draws – England, Somerset, India A, Derbyshire.
One-day internationals – Played 7: Won 4, Lost 3. *Wins* – England, Zimbabwe (3). *Losses* – England (3).
Other non-first class matches – Played 4: Won 3, No result 1. *Wins* – Ireland, Sussex, Worcestershire. *No result* – Northamptonshire.

TEST MATCH AVERAGES

ENGLAND – BATTING AND FIELDING

	T	*I*	*NO*	*R*	*HS*	*100s*	*50s*	*Avge*	*Ct/St*
†M. E. Trescothick	5	10	2	487	219	1	3	60.87	3
A. Flintoff	5	8	0	423	142	1	3	52.87	0
†M. A. Butcher	5	9	1	406	106	1	3	50.75	4
N. Hussain	4	8	1	293	116	1	1	41.85	0
M. P. Vaughan	5	10	0	318	156	1	0	31.80	2
†J. M. Anderson	5	8	7	27	21*	0	0	27.00	1
A. J. Stewart	5	8	0	182	72	0	1	22.75	14/1
A. F. Giles	4	6	0	116	41	0	0	19.33	1
E. T. Smith	3	5	0	87	64	0	1	17.40	5
S. J. Harmison	4	6	2	29	14	0	0	7.25	0
R. J. Kirtley	2	4	0	16	11	0	0	4.00	2

Played in two Tests: M. P. Bicknell 4, 15, 0 (2 ct); D. Gough 1, 34, 14 (1 ct); A. McGrath 34, 4, 13 (1 ct). Played in one Test: Kabir Ali 1, 9; †G. P. Thorpe 124 (1 ct).

† *Left-handed batsman.*

BOWLING

	Style	*O*	*M*	*R*	*W*	*BB*	*5W/i*	*Avge*
R. J. Kirtley	RFM	98.5	32	259	13	6-34	1	19.92
Kabir Ali	RFM	36	5	136	5	3-80	0	27.20
M. P. Bicknell	RFM	93	22	280	10	4-84	0	28.00
J. M. Anderson	RFM	161.5	35	598	15	5-102	1	39.86
S. J. Harmison	RF	129.2	26	413	9	4-33	0	45.88
A. Flintoff	RFM	182	44	592	10	2-55	0	59.20
A. F. Giles	SLA	142	15	502	7	2-45	0	71.71

Also bowled: M. A. Butcher (RM) 11–1–52–0; D. Gough (RFM) 53–9–215–1; A. McGrath (RM) 11–0–40–1; M. P. Vaughan (OB) 19–2–63–1.

SOUTH AFRICA – BATTING AND FIELDING

	T	I	NO	R	HS	100s	50s	Avge	Ct/St
†G. C. Smith	5	9	0	714	277	2	1	79.33	3
S. M. Pollock	4	6	3	205	66*	0	2	68.33	6
†G. Kirsten	4	7	0	462	130	2	2	66.00	4
H. H. Gibbs	5	9	0	478	183	2	0	53.11	5
M. V. Boucher	5	8	1	271	68	0	2	38.71	17/1
H. H. Dippenaar	3	5	1	143	92	0	1	35.75	0
N. D. McKenzie	3	6	0	190	90	0	1	31.66	0
J. H. Kallis	3	6	0	188	66	0	1	31.33	1
A. J. Hall	4	7	2	121	99*	0	1	24.20	7
M. Ntini	5	6	3	59	32*	0	0	19.66	0
†J. A. Rudolph	5	9	0	132	55	0	1	14.66	4
P. R. Adams	3	4	1	42	15	0	0	14.00	6

Played in three Tests: D. Pretorius 9, 8. Played in one Test: M. Zondeki 59, 7; †R. J. Peterson and †C. M. Willoughby did not bat.

† *Left-handed batsman.*

BOWLING

	Style	O	M	R	W	BB	5W/i	Avge
S. M. Pollock	RFM	177	57	420	17	6-39	1	24.70
J. H. Kallis	RFM	113.3	25	362	14	6-54	1	25.85
A. J. Hall	RFM	144.4	29	430	16	3-18	0	26.87
M. Ntini	RF	196.2	34	814	23	5-75	2	35.39
D. Pretorius	RF	70	12	298	5	4-115	0	59.60

Also bowled: P. R. Adams (SLC) 69.4–10–238–4; R. J. Peterson (SLA) 35–12–90–1; J. A. Rudolph (LBG) 8–2–29–1; C. M. Willoughby (LFM) 20–7–46–0; M. Zondeki (RFM) 4.5–0–25–0.

SOUTH AFRICAN TOUR AVERAGES – FIRST-CLASS MATCHES

BATTING AND FIELDING

	M	I	NO	R	HS	100s	50s	Avge	Ct/St
†G. C. Smith	8	13	1	980	277	3	2	81.66	6
†G. Kirsten	7	12	2	713	130	2	4	71.30	5
S. M. Pollock	5	7	3	241	66*	0	2	60.25	6
N. D. McKenzie	6	11	3	470	105*	1	3	58.75	2
J. H. Kallis	5	9	0	471	200	1	2	52.33	6
H. H. Gibbs	8	14	0	590	183	2	1	42.14	6
M. V. Boucher	8	11	1	360	89	0	3	36.00	21/1
H. H. Dippenaar	7	11	1	339	92	0	3	33.90	4
†J. A. Rudolph	8	13	0	389	92	0	4	29.92	6
†R. J. Peterson	5	5	2	78	33	0	0	26.00	2
A. J. Hall	4	7	2	121	99*	0	1	24.20	7
P. R. Adams	6	5	2	64	22*	0	0	21.33	7
M. Ntini	6	7	3	64	32*	0	0	16.00	0

Played in six matches: D. Pretorius 0, 9, 8 (1 ct). Played in four matches: M. Zondeki 12*, 59, 7 (1 ct); †C. M. Willoughby did not bat (1 ct). Played in two matches: T. L. Tsolekile 90 (2 ct).

† *Left-handed batsman.*

BOWLING

	Style	O	M	R	W	BB	5W/i	Avge
S. M. Pollock	RFM	198	61	480	22	6-39	1	21.81
A. J. Hall	RFM	144.4	29	430	16	3-18	0	26.87
J. H. Kallis	RFM	131.3	29	412	15	6-54	1	27.46
C. M. Willoughby	LFM	79	23	220	8	3-31	0	27.50
P. R. Adams	SLC	130.3	21	425	15	9-79	1	28.33
M. Zondeki	RFM	63.5	8	281	9	5-64	1	31.22
M. Ntini	RF	222.2	40	910	24	5-75	2	37.91
R. J. Peterson	SLA	116.2	28	381	7	3-58	0	54.42
D. Pretorius	RF	127	18	546	10	4-115	0	54.60

Also bowled: J. A. Rudolph (LBG) 24–5–82–1.

Note: Matches in this section which were not first-class are signified by a dagger.

†IRELAND v SOUTH AFRICANS

At Clontarf, June 18. South Africans won by 132 runs. Toss: South Africans.

Ireland had crushed Zimbabwe by ten wickets the week before but this was a total reversion to the normal order of things. Although most of the South Africans had not played for more than a month, and then in Dhaka, they soon got used to Dublin. Each of the top four cantered at close to a run a ball, before a late flurry from van Jaarsveld and Pollock. A total of 294 was off Ireland's radar and their innings dribbled to a close in less than 40 overs. Seven South Africans turned their arm over, Ntini with most success.

South Africans

*G. C. Smith c Armstrong b White	61
H. H. Gibbs c Mooney b Botha	33
H. H. Dippenaar c O'Brien b Armstrong	76
J. A. Rudolph c Bray b Botha	54
M. van Jaarsveld c Joyce b Neely	23
†M. V. Boucher run out	6
S. M. Pollock c McCallan b Neely	16
A. C. Dawson c Gillespie b Neely	5
P. R. Adams not out	1
C. K. Langeveldt not out	0
L-b 7, w 3, n-b 9	19
1/55 (2) 2/131 (1) 3/234 (3) 4/249 (4) 5/268 (5) 6/271 (6) 7/293 (7) 8/293 (8) (8 wkts, 50 overs)	294

M. Ntini did not bat.

Bowling: Mooney 9–1–47–0; Neely 7–1–40–3; Botha 9–1–66–2; Armstrong 10–0–54–1; McCallan 8–0–47–0; White 7–0–33–1.

Ireland

*J. A. M. Molins c Pollock b Langeveldt	27
J. P. Bray c Boucher b Ntini	11
A. C. Botha b Ntini	16
†N. J. O'Brien run out	31
P. G. Gillespie c van Jaarsveld b Ntini	1
W. K. McCallan c van Jaarsveld b Dawson	5
D. Joyce lbw b Adams	0
A. R. White lbw b van Jaarsveld	29
P. J. K. Mooney c Rudolph b Adams	8
C. M. Armstrong not out	14
G. J. Neely lbw b van Jaarsveld	0
B 1, l-b 4, w 4, n-b 11	20
1/45 (1) 2/53 (2) 3/89 (3) 4/94 (5) 5/108 (6) 6/108 (4) 7/114 (7) 8/130 (8) 9/162 (9) 10/162 (11) (37.5 overs)	162

Bowling: Pollock 7–0–39–0; Dawson 8–4–25–1; Langeveldt 6–1–23–1; Ntini 6–0–21–3; Adams 6–1–25–2; Smith 3–0–13–0; van Jaarsveld 1.5–0–11–2.

Umpires: S. Daultrey and R. O'Reilly.

†SUSSEX v SOUTH AFRICANS

At Hove, June 20 (day/night). South Africans won by 153 runs. Toss: South Africans.

Dippenaar was to make little impression on more important days, but a crowd of 3,000 saw glimpses of his undoubted talent. A straight-driven four off the penultimate delivery of the innings completed a century in 89 balls, although his first fifty – which included a dropped chance on 12 – contained only three boundaries. He opened his shoulders later as the tourists rattled to an intimidating 267 on a typically slow Hove pitch. Sussex were never in the contest after Langeveldt and Ntini destroyed their top order with the new ball; only Chris Adams, who blazed away briefly, offered resistance. By then a section of the crowd were content to concentrate on cheerful banter with the ebullient Ntini in the outfield.

South Africans

*G. C. Smith c Goodwin b Hopkinson	31
H. H. Gibbs lbw b Martin-Jenkins	31
M. van Jaarsveld lbw b Innes	46
J. A. Rudolph c Prior b Mushtaq Ahmed	19
H. H. Dippenaar not out	101
†M. V. Boucher run out	5
S. M. Pollock b Davis	10
A. J. Hall c Lewry b Martin-Jenkins	3
P. R. Adams not out	1
L-b 8, w 12	20
1/66 (1) 2/66 (2) 3/105 (4) 4/187 (3) 5/204 (6) 6/238 (7) 7/256 (8) (7 wkts, 50 overs)	267

C. K. Langeveldt and M. Ntini did not bat.

Bowling: Lewry 8–1–40–0; Innes 7–0–47–1; Hopkinson 6–1–36–1; Martin-Jenkins 10–0–34–2; Mushtaq Ahmed 10–0–48–1; Davis 9–0–54–1.

Sussex

R. R. Montgomerie b Ntini	17
M. H. Yardy b Langeveldt	12
M. W. Goodwin b Langeveldt	0
*C. J. Adams c Dippenaar b Adams	32
R. S. C. Martin-Jenkins c and b Langeveldt	9
†M. J. Prior c Boucher b Hall	3
C. D. Hopkinson c and b Adams	2
K. J. Innes not out	13
M. J. G. Davis c Boucher b Adams	7
Mushtaq Ahmed c Boucher b Hall	0
J. D. Lewry c Boucher b Ntini	11
L-b 1, w 3, n-b 4	8
1/27 (2) 2/27 (3) 3/55 (1) 4/69 (5) 5/78 (6) 6/81 (7) 7/88 (4) 8/99 (9) 9/100 (10) 10/114 (11) (30.5 overs)	114

Bowling: Pollock 6–0–22–0; Ntini 6.5–2–26–2; Langeveldt 6–0–30–3; Hall 6–2–16–2; Adams 6–1–19–3.

Umpires: R. J. Bailey and G. Sharp.

†NORTHAMPTONSHIRE v SOUTH AFRICANS

At Northampton, June 22. No result. Toss: South Africans.

A spectacular thunderstorm washed out the match at an interesting stage: Northamptonshire needed 185 from 35 overs, with nine wickets left and Hussey hitting his stride. The two-paced pitch showed occasional erratic bounce – Kallis was out to a ball that kicked from a length – which was not what the South Africans wanted with internationals approaching. They were struggling at 70 for three before Boucher and Pollock, promoted up the order, came to the rescue. A fine pick-up and throw by Morne van Wyk at mid-off then ran out Jaques at the start of Northamptonshire's reply.

South Africans

*G. C. Smith c Bailey b Cawdron	24	N. Boje not out	10
H. H. Gibbs b Wright	15		
J. H. Kallis c Sales b Cawdron	3	L-b 14, w 9, n-b 2	25
†M. V. Boucher c Hussey b Swann	69		
S. M. Pollock c sub b Swann	53	1/27 (2) 2/34 (3) (6 wkts, 50 overs)	229
M. N. van Wyk not out	17	3/70 (1) 4/175 (5)	
M. van Jaarsveld b Wright	13	5/185 (4) 6/206 (7)	

A. C. Dawson, A. J. Hall and M. Ntini did not bat.

Bowling: Wright 10–1–40–2; Cawdron 10–1–36–2; Anderson 9–0–43–0; Cook 9–0–31–0; Brown 2–0–14–0; Swann 10–0–51–2.

Northamptonshire

M. J. Powell not out	11
P. A. Jaques run out	0
*M. E. K. Hussey not out	27
W 5, n-b 2	7
1/2 (2) (1 wkt, 15 overs)	45

J. W. Cook, D. J. Sales, G. P. Swann, †T. M. B. Bailey, D. G. Wright, R. S. G. Anderson, M. J. Cawdron and J. F. Brown did not bat.

Bowling: Pollock 6–1–19–0; Ntini 5–1–12–0; Hall 2–1–5–0; Kallis 2–0–9–0.

Umpires: P. J. Hartley and A. A. Jones.

†At Wormsley, June 23. **South Africans won by 50 runs.** Toss: South Africans. **South Africans 276-6** (50 overs) (G. C. Smith 67, H. H. Gibbs 52, J. H. Kallis 81); **Sir Paul Getty's XI 226-9** (50 overs) (C. J. L. Rogers 67, K. P. Pietersen 50).

Not part of the official tour programme. Martin van Jaarsveld, one of the South African tourists, played for Sir Paul Getty's XI.

†WORCESTERSHIRE v SOUTH AFRICANS

At Worcester, June 25. South Africans won by 69 runs. Toss: South Africans. County debut: J. M. Kemp.

The South Africans were relieved to go into the imminent NatWest Series with a comfortable win and no broken bones. Their top three were all rapped painfully on the hands as the ball popped off a length, but Smith and Kallis hung in and a late attack by Rudolph ensured an imposing total. Hayward, who had shunned the touring party in favour of Worcestershire, bowled with plenty of pace but little direction and conceded nearly seven an over. Worcestershire's other South African Test player, Justin Kemp (a replacement for Hall, who had been called up by the opposition) was more successful, smashing an explosive 77 on his county debut, including three sixes in one Boje over. But once Pollock broke a stand of 97 in 17 overs with Leatherdale, the last five wickets subsided for just 11.

South Africans

*G. C. Smith c Kabir Ali b Khalid	65	M. van Jaarsveld not out	13
H. H. Gibbs c Peters b Hayward	27	L-b 3, w 16, n-b 3	22
J. H. Kallis c Adshead b Kabir Ali	66		
J. A. Rudolph not out	48	1/52 (2) 2/151 (1) (4 wkts, 50 overs)	261
†M. V. Boucher c Batty b Kabir Ali	20	3/221 (3) 4/246 (5)	

S. M. Pollock, N. Boje, A. J. Hall, A. C. Dawson and M. Ntini did not bat.

Bowling: Kabir Ali 10–2–49–2; Hayward 10–0–66–1; Kemp 10–0–47–0; Khalid 10–0–45–1; Batty 10–0–51–0.

Worcestershire

S. D. Peters c van Jaarsveld b Hall	10
S. C. Moore b Ntini	0
Kadeer Ali c Smith b Boje	29
*B. F. Smith c Kallis b Hall	0
J. M. Kemp lbw b Pollock	77
D. A. Leatherdale c Rudolph b Kallis	38
G. J. Batty c sub b Dawson	11
Kabir Ali c Smith b Dawson	4
†S. J. Adshead b Dawson	5
S. A. Khalid b Dawson	0
M. Hayward not out	1
L-b 8, w 7, n-b 2	17
1/0 (2) 2/30 (1) 3/30 (4) 4/66 (3) 5/163 (5) 6/181 (6) 7/182 (7) 8/191 (9) 9/191 (10) 10/192 (8)	(45 overs) 192

Bowling: Pollock 8–2–18–1; Ntini 10–0–43–1; Hall 8–1–30–2; Dawson 8–0–26–4; Boje 7–1–44–1; Kallis 4–0–23–1.

Umpires: N. G. Cowley and I. J. Gould.

South Africa's matches against England and Zimbabwe in the NatWest Series (June 28–July 12) appear on pages 466–476.

SOMERSET v SOUTH AFRICANS

At Taunton, July 15, 16, 17. Drawn. Toss: South Africans. County debut: G. M. Gilder.

After a high-profile thrashing in the one-day final at Lord's, South Africa began the first-class leg of their tour with a low-key draw. Smith gave a hint of the relentless batting to come in the Tests with a well-made 152, taking advantage of Somerset's depleted attack. And in the battle for the last Test batting spot, McKenzie, who scored 148 in two unbeaten innings, and Dippenaar, with 68 in the second, remained locked together. Despite two first-innings declarations, a rain-affected match deteriorated into a meaningless draw, Smith opting for extended batting practice and leaving Somerset to score an implausible 327 in 35 overs. Somerset, desperate for seam bowlers, introduced Gary Gilder, a 29-year-old former Natal player with an EU passport. The accuracy of his left-arm swing, rather than any tangible success, earned him further appearances over the summer.

Close of play: First day, Somerset 38-0 (Wood 18, Bryant 17); Second day, South Africans 126-2 (Dippenaar 52, McKenzie 14).

South Africans

*G. C. Smith c Andrews b Parsons	152	– (6) not out	26
H. H. Gibbs b Jones	4	– c Gazzard b Jones	17
G. Kirsten c Durston b Blackwell	66	– (1) c Gilder b Durston	42
H. H. Dippenaar c Blackwell b Durston	17	– (3) c Durston b Gilder	68
N. D. McKenzie not out	66	– (4) not out	82
R. J. Peterson not out	2	– (5) c Gazzard b Parsons	6
B 6, l-b 8, w 1, n-b 4	19	N-b 4	4
1/10 (2) 2/173 (3) 3/213 (4) 4/312 (1)	(4 wkts dec.) 326	1/36 (2) 2/99 (1) 3/172 (3) 4/200 (5)	(4 wkts dec.) 245

†T. L. Tsolekile, P. R. Adams, D. Pretorius, C. M. Willoughby and M. Zondeki did not bat.

Bowling: *First Innings*—Gilder 12–2–45–0; Jones 13–2–61–1; Andrew 10–1–54–0; Laraman 10–2–43–0; Durston 17–4–60–1; Blackwell 8–3–26–1; Parsons 8–2–23–1. *Second Innings*—Gilder 13–0–56–1; Jones 10–1–45–1; Andrews 11–2–31–0; Laraman 3–1–8–0; Durston 15–3–42–1; Parsons 10–0–37–1; Wood 4–0–26–0.

Somerset

M. J. Wood lbw b Willoughby	55	– c Tsolekile b Zondeki	9
J. D. C. Bryant b Zondeki	39	– b Pretorius	27
K. A. Parsons c Gibbs b Zondeki	1	– lbw b Willoughby	2
*M. Burns c Pretorius b Willoughby	35		
I. D. Blackwell c Willoughby b Zondeki	19		
A. W. Laraman not out	41		
†C. M. Gazzard c Tsolekile b Zondeki	27	– (5) not out	35
W. J. Durston c Smith b Zondeki	8	– (4) not out	30
L-b 7, w 2, n-b 11	20	W 3, n-b 3	6
1/100 (1) 2/104 (2) 3/122 (3) 4/144 (5) 5/185 (4) 6/235 (7) 7/245 (8)	(7 wkts dec.) 245	1/16 (1) 2/25 (3) 3/59 (2)	(3 wkts) 109

G. M. Andrew, G. M. Gilder and P. S. Jones did not bat.

Bowling: *First Innings*—Pretorius 15–1–93–0; Willoughby 17–7–38–2; Zondeki 11–0–64–5; Adams 4–0–22–0; Peterson 4–0–21–0. *Second Innings*—Pretorius 9–0–42–1; Zondeki 6–2–20–1; Willoughby 7–1–31–1; Peterson 2–0–12–0; Adams 1–0–4–0.

Umpires: J. W. Holder and N. J. Llong.

INDIA A v SOUTH AFRICANS

At Arundel, July 19, 20, 21. Drawn. Toss: India A.

South Africa coach Eric Simons was left scratching his head at the end of this dull draw, admitting that all seven of his specialist bowlers were still in contention for the First Test three days later. Pollock aside, there was little to choose between those on show here: one looked just as tame as the next on a spirit-sapping pitch. Simons admitted the team was missing Nantie Hayward, who had opted for county cricket instead. The spirit of the spectators was tested too, as the match ground on. Jaffer top-scored for India A but the dash of sparkle came during Gambhir's twinkle-toed 64; Pollock, on his return from five days' pre-paternity leave in Durban, took three wickets in seven deliveries. In reply, Gibbs began to find form and each of South Africa's top four totted up around three hours at the crease. With five full international batsmen in the India A line-up, and the pitch still as pristine as the castle grounds, there was never much chance of a result.

Close of play: First day, India A 319; Second day, South Africans 342-5 (Dippenaar 4, Pollock 0).

India A

*S. S. Das c Boucher b Pollock	33	– b Pollock	15
G. Gambhir c Kirsten b Peterson	64	– c Boucher b Zondeki	18
Wasim Jaffer c Smith b Pretorius	90	– c and b Peterson	54
H. K. Badani c Boucher b Zondeki	23	– not out	58
A. T. Rayudu lbw b Pretorius	32	– not out	4
†P. A. Patel b Pretorius	8		
A. Mishra b Pollock	25		
M. Kartik c Dippenaar b Ntini	16		
I. K. Pathan c Smith b Pollock	6		
A. Bhandari not out	1		
A. M. Salvi b Pollock	0		
W 5, n-b 16	21	B 4, l-b 3, n-b 4	11
1/93 (2) 2/144 (1) 3/195 (4) 4/251 (5) 5/261 (6) 6/272 (3) 7/304 (8) 8/318 (9) 9/319 (7) 10/319 (11)	319	1/35 (1) 2/36 (2) 3/137 (3)	(3 wkts) 160

Bowling: *First Innings*—Pollock 15–2–46–4; Ntini 19–5–70–1; Pretorius 16–3–41–3; Zondeki 14–2–58–1; Peterson 20–2–87–1; Rudolph 5–1–17–0. *Second Innings*—Pollock 6–2–14–1; Ntini 7–1–26–0; Zondeki 8–2–31–1; Peterson 14–4–45–1; Pretorius 6–2–22–0; Rudolph 2–0–15–0.

South Africans

G. C. Smith lbw b Pathan	79	M. Zondeki not out	12
H. H. Gibbs c Patel b Kartik	79	M. Ntini c and b Pathan	5
G. Kirsten run out	75		
J. A. Rudolph c Patel b Salvi	83	B 1, l-b 11, n-b 13	25
H. H. Dippenaar c sub b Salvi	37		—
*†M. V. Boucher b Salvi	0	1/150 (2) 2/164 (1) 3/335 (3)	463
S. M. Pollock b Bhandari	36	4/341 (4) 5/341 (6) 6/394 (7)	
R. J. Peterson c Das b Pathan	32	7/445 (5) 8/445 (9)	
D. Pretorius c Patel b Salvi	0	9/445 (8) 10/463 (11)	

Bowling: Salvi 29–7–92–4; Bhandari 18–3–65–1; Kartik 29–5–120–1; Pathan 28.4–3–83–3; Mishra 16–0–88–0; Rayudu 1–0–3–0.

Umpires: M. J. Kitchen and A. G. T. Whitehead.

ENGLAND v SOUTH AFRICA

First npower Test

RICHARD HOBSON

At Birmingham, July 24, 25, 26, 27, 28. Drawn. Toss: South Africa.

After their emphatic victory in the NatWest Series final, England went into this game convinced they were strong favourites to add greater success in the Tests. But the turnaround could not have been swifter or much more severe. Smith and Gibbs dominated the opening proceedings with a record first-wicket partnership of 338, and Hussain felt so powerless to stop them that he resigned as the England captain as soon as the match was over. Vaughan, having struck his eighth Test hundred in 14 months, was duly installed as his successor. He had only two full days to impose a semblance of authority before the Second Test at Lord's.

In a game of three captains, both Hussain and Vaughan were forced to defer to Graeme Smith, leading South Africa at the age of 22 going on 35. If he was a little cautious on the final day, when he could have shown more urgency to press for a positive finish, the rest of the proceedings were a personal triumph. His 277 in the first innings, spanning 373 balls and a minute over nine hours, with 35 fours, was the highest individual Test score for his country. He and Gibbs became the second pair to build two triple-century stands at the highest level: Bradman and Ponsford managed it twice against England in 1934. And his match aggregate of 362 runs was South Africa's biggest-ever, passing the 309 amassed by Bruce Mitchell at The Oval in 1947.

Hussain's opinion that South Africa were "there for the taking" was made to look extremely unwise. His comments only served to rouse the touring side, all too happy to be cast as underdogs. They had made purposeful use of the 12 days after the one-day final, drafting in a sports psychologist to re-establish positive thought and adjusting their methods in a pair of first-class matches. England, meanwhile, missed the youthful vigour that had made the limited-overs tournament such a breeze. As soon as the squad assembled in Birmingham, Hussain – who had ceded the one-day leadership to Vaughan after the World Cup – realised that things had moved on. It was no longer his team.

The man who had spent the previous four years barking out instructions presented an uncharacteristically timid, even cowed figure as Gibbs, having taken 25 balls to get off the mark, and Smith began to dominate. They struck 165 during a balmy and barmy afternoon session alone. Duncan Fletcher suggested that the England bowlers were still in one-day mode – an open goal for those who felt the coach should have allowed Flintoff and Anderson, both contracted players, to appear for Lancashire in a Championship game at Blackpool the week before. For Anderson, the new boy wonder

Driven: Graeme Smith punches with a characteristically closed face of the bat as he moves relentlessly towards 277 at Edgbaston.

Picture by Patrick Eagar.

with his red mohican haircut, it was a particularly chastening experience: his 13 overs on the first day cost six runs each. But he was not alone in feeding Smith's strengths through the leg side or allowing Gibbs to swing his arms.

Gough, too, endured a torrid return in his first Test appearance for nearly two years. That he was here at all spoke volumes for the character which underpinned his recovery from a career-threatening knee injury. But the old spring in his delivery was missing and it fell to Vaughan to split the openers after more than five hours. Gibbs, having survived three sharp chances, succumbed to a cunning trap when he pulled a long hop – his 236th ball – to deep mid-wicket. Just a few minutes earlier he and Smith had overtaken the previous best opening partnership against England, 329 by Mark Taylor and Geoff Marsh for Australia at Trent Bridge in 1989. To complete a harrowing day for the hosts, Trescothick fractured the tip of his right index finger while fielding at slip.

Even by the standards of the frenetic modern game, a total of 398 for one by the close represented some achievement, and the rate of scoring meant that South Africa were not completely disheartened by the loss of the entire second day to rain. It meant a total refund of £547,000 for the 18,000 would-be spectators, though the ECB reclaimed the money on insurance. Sadly, there was no similar recovery mechanism for the bowlers. Smith, strong-shouldered and ruthlessly efficient, simply continued on the third morning where he left off on Thursday night, completing his second double-hundred (in his 11th Test) and then taking fresh guard, intent on grinding the bowlers to dust. He was entitled to feel fatigued when he eventually slogged Giles to the leg-side boundary.

The declaration arrived not long afterwards, leaving England 395 to avoid the follow-on. They made it, but only just, and thanks largely to Vaughan. Becalmed on 12 for 62 minutes and 41 balls during a compelling personal battle with Pollock, he went on to drive and pull with the style and sure judgment of length that had elevated him to the ranks of the world-class batsmen in Australia the previous winter. His 156 came in 415 minutes from 286 balls. Hussain, though, seemed distracted in shouldering arms to Pollock and too many batsmen chipped in instead of providing lengthy support.

England were still 21 short of their initial objective on the final morning, with three wickets remaining, yet a touch of aggression from Giles meant just ten balls were needed to ensure that South Africa would have to bat again. When they did there was little urgency from anybody bar Smith – 85 from 70 balls – and no promotion for a Boucher or Pollock to add gusto. England were never likely to attempt a nominal target of 321 from 65 overs and South Africa lacked the penetration to make sufficient inroads before rain and bad light curtailed proceedings. Hussain, by then, had come to his decision.

Man of the Match: G. C. Smith. *Attendance:* 57,029; *receipts* £1,338,247.

Close of play: First day, South Africa 398-1 (Smith 178, Kirsten 26); Second day, No play; Third day, England 25-0 (Trescothick 14, Vaughan 4); Fourth day, England 374-7 (Giles 9).

South Africa

First innings		Second innings	
*G. C. Smith c Anderson b Giles	277	– b Giles	85
H. H. Gibbs c Butcher b Vaughan	179	– b Anderson	9
G. Kirsten c Stewart b Giles	44	– c McGrath b Harmison	1
H. H. Dippenaar c Butcher b Gough	22	– not out	28
J. A. Rudolph c Gough b Harmison	10	– st Stewart b Giles	8
†M. V. Boucher not out	15		
S. M. Pollock not out	24		
B 8, l-b 11, n-b 4	23	L-b 2, n-b 1	3
1/338 (2) 2/438 (3) 3/514 (4) 4/552 (5) 5/556 (1) (5 wkts dec.)	594	1/30 (2) 2/32 (3) 3/114 (1) 4/134 (5) (4 wkts dec.)	134

R. J. Peterson, D. Pretorius, C. M. Willoughby and M. Ntini did not bat.

Bowling: *First Innings*—Anderson 16–2–92–0; Gough 25–6–88–1; Flintoff 25–6–97–0; Harmison 27–2–104–1; Giles 42–2–153–2; Butcher 2–0–15–0; Vaughan 8–0–26–1. *Second Innings*—Harmison 6–0–34–1; Anderson 10–1–37–1; Giles 8–0–45–2; Flintoff 2–0–16–0.

England

First innings		Second innings	
M. E. Trescothick b Ntini	31	– not out	52
M. P. Vaughan c Boucher b Pretorius	156	– c Pollock b Peterson	22
M. A. Butcher lbw b Ntini	13		
*N. Hussain lbw b Pollock	1	– (3) not out	23
A. McGrath c Rudolph b Pretorius	34		
†A. J. Stewart b Pretorius	38		
A. Flintoff lbw b Pretorius	40		
A. F. Giles b Pollock	41		
D. Gough c Rudolph b Ntini	1		
S. J. Harmison b Ntini	0		
J. M. Anderson not out	0		
B 19, l-b 6, w 11, n-b 17	53	B 8, l-b 5	13
1/66 (1) 2/132 (3) 3/133 (4) 4/222 (5) 5/306 (2) 6/311 (6) 7/374 (7) 8/398 (9) 9/398 (10) 10/408 (8)	408	1/72 (2) (1 wkt)	110

Bowling: *First Innings*—Pollock 27.4–10–51–2; Ntini 28–8–114–4; Willoughby 20–7–46–0; Pretorius 25–2–115–4; Peterson 22–9–57–0. *Second Innings*—Pollock 7–3–6–0; Ntini 4–0–38–0; Peterson 13–3–33–1; Pretorius 10–6–20–0.

Umpires: D. J. Harper (Australia) and S. Venkataraghavan (India).
Third umpire: J. W. Lloyds. Referee: R. S. Madugalle (Sri Lanka).

ENGLAND v SOUTH AFRICA

Second npower Test

MATTHEW ENGEL

At Lord's, July 31, August 1, 2, 3. South Africa won by an innings and 92 runs. Toss: South Africa.

The new smiling face of English cricket, which Michael Vaughan presented to the cameras in the Long Room on the eve of the game, lasted less than 24 hours – indeed only about 65 hours from the moment he was handed the captaincy when Hussain resigned on the Monday night. Normally, even England captains get a honeymoon longer than that. But by Thursday lunchtime, England were in crisis for the second Test in succession. And this time there was no escape.

South Africa won massively, having scored 682 for six, smashed the record for their highest total and inflicted on England their biggest-ever first-innings deficit – 509, five more than at Brisbane in 1946-47. Throughout the game, Vaughan retained something close to a smile, though it presumably represented bemusement (unless, frighteningly for England, it was gormlessness). Hussain's grim-visaged pent-up fury would have been more appropriate.

The disaster was, at least in part, attributable to the unplanned handover, and the brutal scheduling of Tests with only two days in between. England were too distracted to absorb the lessons of Edgbaston and evolve a plan to combat Smith's relentless, but not infallible, batting. By the end of this game a man being patronised ten days earlier as a young inadequate was being compared to Bradman – indeed he had surpassed him by scoring 259, five more than the Don's 73-year-old record for an overseas player in a Lord's Test, and reaching 621 in the two games, which was beyond even Bradman.

England's first-day batting certainly was gormless. They were put in, though Vaughan would have batted anyway: there was cloud cover but nothing beyond normal first-day juice in the pitch. The teams were identical to Edgbaston except for South Africa preferring Hall to Willoughby as their fourth seamer and Adams to Peterson as the spinner. In the event, Adams was hardly required in the first innings. Nor did anyone miss Pretorius, who limped off with a thigh injury: England's batsmen did the bowlers' work for them, as if their mindset had not adjusted after their overwhelming one-day triumph here just 19 days earlier. They nearly all looked at home but got out needlessly, the mood typified by the top-edged hook that did for Vaughan on 33. For no good reason, England crashed to 118 for nine.

The last pair, Gough and Anderson, had some fun. Their 55 was the highest stand of the innings, an oddity last achieved for England 133 Tests earlier, by Phil DeFreitas and David Lawrence at Trent Bridge against West Indies in 1991. But the spectators' cheers were more ironic than delighted, and if there were a trace of happiness left in Vaughan's smile, it was wiped out when Smith was dropped horribly by Hussain at cover on eight. By the close, South Africa were 151 for one.

Hook, line and sinker: at Lord's, Nasser Hussain top-edges Makhaya Ntini to Mark Boucher, leaving England 208 for four and on their way to defeat. Five of Ntini's ten wickets came from hooks or pulls.

Picture by Patrick Eagar.

England's bowlers trudged on to the field on Friday like men wearing signs saying "Hit me". Smith obliged. His opening stand with Gibbs was worth 133; he put on 257 with the uncompromising and unflashy deflector Kirsten, then 123 with Dippenaar. At 3.02 on the second afternoon, Smith reached 500 for the series, only eight days after it had begun. Night fell again, and he was still there, Brian Lara's 375 apparently at risk. By then bowlers and spectators alike began to forget there was ever an existence without Smith at the centre of it.

The interminability of his innings had a drawback for him – observers began to sniff out his technique, which involved biffing anything straightish into the leg side and keeping the face closed to avoid nicks. A line outside off stump had possibilities. But as the weather grew hotter, the pitch ever blander and their spirits weaker, England had no way of executing a plan even if they had one: the old-new pairing of Gough and Anderson, so hyped during the one-day series, was a disaster (except with the bat). Both were knackered: Anderson by overwork; Gough, terminally, by the passing years. And what chances came were mostly dropped, four in all. Stewart, who had a ghastly game, could at least be absolved of eight of the byes, which came when he was off with an eye injury and McGrath deputised.

After nine hours (or maybe years) and 34 minutes, 370 balls and 34 fours, Smith was bowled by Anderson for 259. South Africa improved their highest total against England for the second match running, but Smith declared, kindly, just short of the wholly demoralising 700 mark and England, in their second innings, batted far better than in their first. No one ever imagined they could save the game but they did put down markers for the weeks ahead. Butcher and Hussain put on 126, and later came

Flintoff, who finally played the sensational innings in front of an English Test crowd that he had long threatened. He smashed 142 off 146 balls, with 18 fours and five sixes, crashing the ball with a power that may even have surpassed Ian Botham and enchanted a packed house (who feared they would watch only another collapse). Just as importantly, he dispelled the panic in the England camp. It was the highest score by a No. 7 in a Lord's Test, beating Les Ames's 137 against New Zealand in 1931. The less quantifiable Lord's thrill-factor matched that of the late Ben Hollioake's one-day flourish against Australia in 1997.

Flintoff finally took one liberty too many against Adams, but it was Ntini who had done the real damage, becoming the first South African to take ten wickets in a Lord's Test. This was just reward for Ntini's pace and zest, though he was helped by the tightness of the other bowlers and the looseness of the batting – half his wickets came from misjudged pulls, hooks and swats. But as South Africa celebrated, England were calming down: at the height of the panic on Saturday morning, it had been assumed that their old guard would all be despatched – Gough took the hint and retired from Tests, but both Hussain and Stewart lived to fight again.

Men of the Match: G. C. Smith and M. Ntini.

Attendance: 80,118; *receipts* £2,887,800.

Close of play: First day, South Africa 151-1 (Smith 80, Kirsten 9); Second day, South Africa 412-2 (Smith 214, Dippenaar 11); Third day, England 129-2 (Butcher 33, Hussain 36).

England

First innings		Second innings	
M. E. Trescothick b Ntini	6	– c Adams b Ntini	23
*M. P. Vaughan c sub (N. D. McKenzie) b Ntini	33	– c Pollock b Hall	29
M. A. Butcher c Hall b Pollock	19	– c Kirsten b Hall	70
N. Hussain b Hall	14	– c Boucher b Ntini	61
A. McGrath c Kirsten b Hall	4	– c Boucher b Pollock	13
†A. J. Stewart c Adams b Ntini	7	– c Hall b Ntini	0
A. Flintoff c Adams b Ntini	11	– st Boucher b Adams	142
A. F. Giles c Pollock b Hall	7	– c Pollock b Ntini	23
D. Gough c Adams b Pollock	34	– c Adams b Pollock	14
S. J. Harmison b Ntini	0	– c Hall b Ntini	7
J. M. Anderson not out	21	– not out	4
B 5, l-b 3, w 1, n-b 3, p 5	17	B 6, l-b 5, w 3, n-b 17	31
1/11 (1) 2/35 (3) 3/73 (4) 4/77 (5) 5/85 (2) 6/96 (6) 7/109 (8) 8/112 (7) 9/118 (10) 10/173 (9)	173	1/52 (2) 2/60 (1) 3/186 (3) 4/208 (4) 5/208 (6) 6/208 (5) 7/297 (8) 8/344 (9) 9/371 (10) 10/417 (7)	417

Bowling: *First Innings*—Pollock 14.4–5–28–2; Ntini 17–3–75–5; Pretorius 4–0–20–0; Hall 10–4–18–3; Adams 3–0–19–0. *Second Innings*—Pollock 29–7–105–2; Ntini 31–5–145–5; Hall 24–6–66–2; Adams 20.1–1–74–1; Pretorius 3–0–16–0.

South Africa

*G. C. Smith b Anderson	259
H. H. Gibbs b Harmison	49
G. Kirsten b McGrath	108
H. H. Dippenaar c Butcher b Giles	92
J. A. Rudolph c Stewart b Flintoff	26
†M. V. Boucher b Anderson	68
S. M. Pollock not out	10
A. J. Hall not out	6
B 25, l-b 21, w 5, n-b 13	64
1/133 (2) 2/390 (3) 3/513 (1) 4/580 (5) 5/630 (4) 6/672 (6) (6 wkts dec.)	682

P. R. Adams, D. Pretorius and M. Ntini did not bat.

Bowling: Gough 28–3–127–0; Anderson 27–6–90–2; Harmison 22–3–103–1; Flintoff 40–10–115–1; Giles 43–5–142–1; Butcher 6–1–19–0; McGrath 11–0–40–1.

Umpires: S. A. Bucknor (West Indies) and D. B. Hair (Australia).
Third umpire: P. Willey. Referee: R. S. Madugalle (Sri Lanka).

KENT v SOUTH AFRICANS

At Canterbury, August 7, 8, 9. South Africans won by 101 runs. Toss: South Africans.

Paul Adams achieved the best-ever figures by a South African touring England by taking nine for 79 to settle the match. He stole the limelight from Kent's acting-captain Ed Smith, just selected by England – but Smith was the one Kent player to elude him. Adams had an ordinary, indeed expensive, first spell in the Kent second innings and, at 125 for one, Carberry and Smith were cruising. Then Smith was caught off a leading edge against Peterson, which led to Adams being recalled to the attack. Bowling down the Nackington Road slope, he sent back eight batsmen in 14.3 overs between tea and the close, four to sharp close catches. On a dusting pitch in extreme heat, Adams put aside his tendency towards an overfull length and got the ball to grip and bite, baffling an inexperienced Kent middle order and decisively re-establishing himself over Peterson as the team's No. 1 spinner. The match had begun in drama too: Kallis, welding muscle and finesse, hit all bar one of his first 50 runs in boundaries, overshadowing McKenzie, who had made 105 when Boucher declared. McKenzie's aggregate in three first-class innings on tour stood at 253 without being out. Loudon, the captain of Durham University, then batted with style and confidence in bright sunshine to score his maiden fifty for Kent. But Rudolph and Dippenaar extended the lead before Adams took over. The last two wickets came in successive balls, leaving him on a hat-trick of a kind for the Trent Bridge Test.

Close of play: First day, Kent 47-2 (Key 14, Banes 10); Second day, South Africans 145-4 (Dippenaar 53, Peterson 1).

South Africans

First innings		Second innings	
G. Kirsten retired hurt	40	(8) not out	28
H. H. Gibbs c Banes b Sheriyar	4	b Saggers	8
J. H. Kallis c Jones b Sheriyar	77	b Saggers	6
H. H. Dippenaar c Key b Trott	1	c Jones b Tredwell	69
N. D. McKenzie not out	105	b Ferley	5
J. A. Rudolph c Saggers b Loudon	92	(1) c Loudon b Tredwell	65
R. J. Peterson (did not bat)		(6) c Smith b Ferley	33
*†M. V. Boucher (did not bat)		(7) b Tredwell	0
P. R. Adams (did not bat)		not out	22
B 4, l-b 2	6	B 2, l-b 4, w 1	7
1/22 (2) 2/67 (4) 3/146 (3) 4/325 (6) (4 wkts dec.)	325	1/17 (2) 2/45 (3) 3/135 (1) 4/140 (5) 5/188 (6) 6/190 (7) 7/197 (4) (7 wkts dec.)	243

C. M. Willoughby and M. Zondeki did not bat.

In the first innings Kirsten retired hurt at 44.

Bowling: *First Innings*—Saggers 14–6–43–0; Sheriyar 15–5–44–2; Trott 12–4–62–1; Ferley 11–0–68–0; Tredwell 8–1–50–0; Loudon 10.3–1–52–1. *Second Innings*—Saggers 12–3–34–2; Sheriyar 12–2–70–0; Trott 4–0–23–0; Tredwell 17–0–75–3; Ferley 10–0–35–2.

Kent

First innings		Second innings	
M. A. Carberry c McKenzie b Willoughby	5	c Dippenaar b Adams	75
R. W. T. Key c sub b Kallis	47	b Adams	49
*E. T. Smith c Boucher b Zondeki	7	c and b Peterson	27
M. J. Banes b Willoughby	15	b Adams	24
A. G. R. Loudon c Kallis b Adams	63	not out	30
†G. O. Jones c Dippenaar b Peterson	50	lbw b Adams	6
J. C. Tredwell b Adams	0	c and b Adams	4
R. S. Ferley run out	10	c Dippenaar b Adams	4
M. J. Saggers c Zondeki b Peterson	10	c Kallis b Adams	1
A. Sheriyar c Rudolph b Peterson	8	c Rudolph b Adams	1
B. J. Trott not out	2	lbw b Adams	0
B 1, l-b 3, w 1, n-b 13	18	L-b 1, w 4, n-b 6	11
1/15 (1) 2/24 (3) 3/65 (4) 4/107 (2) 5/194 (6) 6/195 (7) 7/210 (8) 8/225 (9) 9/233 (5) 10/235 (10)	235	1/72 (2) 2/125 (3) 3/185 (4) 4/186 (1) 5/194 (6) 6/198 (7) 7/208 (8) 8/228 (9) 9/232 (10) 10/232 (11)	232

Bowling: *First Innings*—Willoughby 13–2–50–2; Zondeki 12–2–38–1; Kallis 11–4–24–1; Adams 21–5–61–2; Peterson 16.2–2–58–3. *Second Innings*—Willoughby 8–2–24–0; Zondeki 8–0–45–0; Kallis 7–0–26–0; Adams 22.5–4–79–9; Peterson 19–8–48–1; Rudolph 4–0–9–0.

Umpires: R. K. Illingworth and G. Sharp.

ENGLAND v SOUTH AFRICA

Third npower Test

PAUL WEAVER

At Nottingham, August 14, 15, 16, 17, 18. England won by 70 runs. Toss: England. Test debuts: R. J. Kirtley, E. T. Smith.

Having been roundly outplayed in the opening two Tests, losing a captain in the process, England travelled to Trent Bridge in the midst of a not unfamiliar crisis. Once again, the entire structure of English cricket, as well as the make-up of the Test team, was the subject of heated debate, so when four champions of the shires were selected it looked as though the county game, as well as the England side, was on trial.

Darren Gough had retired from Tests after Lord's, McGrath was dropped and four uncapped players – Gareth Batty, Glen Chapple, James Kirtley and Ed Smith – joined the nine survivors in a squad of 13. Batty and Chapple (whose seasonal bowling average of 37 made him a puzzling choice, anyway) missed out, so Kirtley, after several near misses, and Smith won their first caps. For South Africa, Kallis, after his father's funeral, returned instead of Pretorius, but Kirsten, having injured his arm at Canterbury, had to be replaced by McKenzie. Their captain Graeme Smith, having scored 621 runs in his first three innings of the series, had planned to relax before the match with a break in the Kent countryside. But at 22 he discovered he was too young to get insurance for a hire car.

He was thwarted at the toss too, when Vaughan called right. It was an important slice of luck, given a crazy-paving pitch that started poor and got worse, and Butcher and Hussain showed impressive application to put England on top. Butcher's 106 was the joy of the day, though he was fortunate to survive a convincing lbw appeal from Pollock before he had scored. He took 160 balls to reach his third century in six Tests and the timing of his driving was remarkable on a pitch showing early signs of treachery. But it was Hussain's cathartic hundred – a riposte to those who claimed he should have been dropped for his introverted moping at Lord's – that received the more moving ovation from the packed stands. Bashfully, he raised his bat time and again before the cheers subsided from those anxious to recognise the combative qualities of the former captain.

Ed Smith also batted fluently, though both he and Hussain fell quickly on the second day before Stewart stopped the rot, driving powerfully off his legs and through the covers on his way to 72. England were finally bowled out for 445.

Their satisfaction was soon blended with the enormous relief that washed around Trent Bridge when Graeme Smith went back to a good-length ball from Flintoff, trod on his stumps and was on his way for 35. This relative failure sliced his series average to 164. It was a cameo by Smith's previous standards but he had spent enough time on the pitch to call it, at close of play on the second day, the worst Test wicket he had seen. Those with more experience might have thought that overdramatic but even Stewart, with 130 Tests behind him, admitted to having a "nightmare" knowing how far back to stand while keeping.

Torpedo alley: Graeme Smith survives – just. He called the Trent Bridge wicket the worst Test pitch he had seen.

Picture by Patrick Eagar.

The ball continued to seam and occasionally scuttle on day three, when South Africa were bowled out for 362, a first-innings deficit of 83 which might have been more if England had bowled straighter. Kirtley started the morning with a spring in his step, sprinting in to take wickets with the fifth and sixth deliveries of the day, Rudolph caught behind, then Dippenaar lbw. But England's momentum stalled. Kirtley should have had three wickets in five balls when Kallis offered a straightforward catch to Stewart; South Africa would have been 89 for five with the follow-on beckoning. Although Kallis made only 12 more runs, England had failed to thrust home the advantage. McKenzie, supported by the scampering Boucher, and Pollock, rescued the innings. Among the bowlers, Anderson recovered from a poor start to take five for 102.

At 44 for five on the fourth morning, England were losing the match. With the pitch misbehaving more frequently, no one was quite sure how big a lead they would need to avoid defeat, but this looked nowhere near enough. However, Hussain again proved his skill on dodgy pitches and a violent cameo from Flintoff helped stretch the advantage to 201. Hall, with swing and seam movement, proved a handful but it was Pollock's accuracy that provided most problems. He finished with six for 39.

As South Africa began their pursuit of 202 on the fourth evening, the match was delicately and dramatically poised. That soon changed. Once again it was Kirtley who gave England the impetus of winners: first Smith tried to work an in-swinger into the leg side, getting more bat on it than umpire Harper suspected when he upheld the lbw appeal, and then Rudolph went to Kirtley's next ball but one. When Gibbs spooned a pull to mid-on and was soon followed back by two colleagues, the close, and a chance to regroup, could not come quickly enough for South Africa.

But any doubts that the break would cost England the initiative evaporated in the morning sunshine. The 139 South Africa still needed was always going to be difficult with five wickets standing, and Kirtley made it impossible. Swinging the ball both ways and bowling the odd shooter, he wrapped things up before lunch and ended the innings with six for 34 and a beaming smile. He and Ed Smith had played well in a thrilling match to level the series at 1–1: this was a good Test for county cricket, as well as for England.

Man of the Match: R. J. Kirtley. *Attendance:* 57,829; *receipts* £1,176,601.

Close of play: First day, England 296-3 (Hussain 108, Smith 40); Second day, South Africa 84-2 (Rudolph 11, Kallis 11); Third day, England 0-1 (Vaughan 0); Fourth day, South Africa 63-5 (McKenzie 6, Boucher 9).

England

M. E. Trescothick c Boucher b Hall	24	– c Adams b Pollock	0
*M. P. Vaughan c Gibbs b Pollock	1	– c Boucher b Pollock	5
M. A. Butcher c Boucher b Ntini	106	– b Hall	8
N. Hussain lbw b Pollock	116	– lbw b Pollock	30
E. T. Smith c Boucher b Kallis	64	– lbw b Hall	0
†A. J. Stewart c Smith b Adams	72	– c Boucher b Kallis	5
A. Flintoff c Pollock b Hall	0	– c Gibbs b Pollock	30
A. F. Giles b Hall	22	– c Boucher b Pollock	21
R. J. Kirtley c Smith b Ntini	1	– c Boucher b Ntini	3
S. J. Harmison c Pollock b Adams	14	– not out	2
J. M. Anderson not out	0	– lbw b Pollock	2
B 9, l-b 8, w 4, n-b 4	25	B 4, l-b 5, n-b 3	12
1/7 (2) 2/29 (1) 3/218 (3) 4/322 (4) 5/334 (5) 6/347 (7) 7/388 (8) 8/408 (9) 9/440 (6) 10/445 (10)	445	1/0 (1) 2/17 (2) 3/39 (3) 4/39 (5) 5/44 (6) 6/76 (4) 7/91 (7) 8/114 (9) 9/114 (8) 10/118 (11)	118

Bowling: *First Innings*—Pollock 36–18–65–2; Ntini 33–3–137–2; Hall 24–6–88–3; Kallis 27–7–92–1; Adams 26.3–7–46–2. *Second Innings*—Pollock 17.4–4–39–6; Ntini 13–5–28–1; Kallis 10–2–36–1; Hall 6–2–6–2.

South Africa

*G. C. Smith hit wkt b Flintoff	35	– lbw b Kirtley	5
H. H. Gibbs b Harmison	19	– c Giles b Harmison	28
J. A. Rudolph c Stewart b Kirtley	15	– lbw b Kirtley	0
J. H. Kallis b Anderson	27	– b Anderson	13
H. H. Dippenaar lbw b Kirtley	0	– c Smith b Anderson	1
N. D. McKenzie c Trescothick b Anderson	90	– b Kirtley	11
†M. V. Boucher lbw b Flintoff	48	– c Stewart b Kirtley	52
S. M. Pollock c Kirtley b Anderson	62	– b Flintoff	0
A. J. Hall b Anderson	15	– c Trescothick b Kirtley	0
P. R. Adams b Anderson	13	– c and b Kirtley	15
M. Ntini not out	4	– not out	3
B 4, l-b 19, w 3, n-b 8	34	L-b 2, n-b 1	3
1/56 (2) 2/66 (1) 3/88 (3) 4/88 (5) 5/132 (4) 6/261 (6) 7/284 (7) 8/309 (9) 9/337 (10) 10/362 (8)	362	1/22 (1) 2/28 (3) 3/40 (2) 4/41 (5) 5/50 (4) 6/71 (6) 7/80 (8) 8/81 (9) 9/126 (10) 10/131 (7)	131

Bowling: *First Innings*—Anderson 27.5–4–102–5; Kirtley 31–8–80–2; Flintoff 33–8–91–2; Harmison 17–3–42–1; Giles 10–3–24–0; Vaughan 1–1–0–0. *Second Innings*—Kirtley 16.2–7–34–6; Flintoff 17–4–54–1; Harmison 11–2–24–1; Anderson 12–4–17–2.

Umpires: D. B. Hair (Australia) and D. J. Harper (Australia).
Third umpire: N. A. Mallender. Referee: R. S. Madugalle (Sri Lanka).

ENGLAND v SOUTH AFRICA

Fourth npower Test

NEIL MANTHORP

At Leeds, August 21, 22, 23, 24, 25. South Africa won by 191 runs. Toss: South Africa. Test debuts: Kabir Ali; M. Zondeki.

Seldom, if ever, can an England team have contrived to lose after seeing their opponents sagging so sorrowfully: South Africa were cut and bloodied, and most sides in England's position would have won in three and a half days. Or less. In the immediate aftermath of the defeat, Vaughan launched a scathing attack on the county system, saying it produced too many players who were soft and bored and lacked the killer instinct. This match certainly lent weight to his argument. Not that South Africa's remarkable and rousing fightback should be diminished for that.

At 21 for four in the 15th over, the South Africans were in disarray. Their captain Graeme Smith, who later admitted he had hoped to avoid having to choose, finally opted to bat, backing his top six to battle through the morning against England's five seamers until the tricky conditions eased. But Smith himself started the collapse with a nasty swat at the fourth ball of the game, and Martin Bicknell, playing his third Test ten years (and a record 115 matches) after his second, bowled a metronomic line and length to snare two early victims. Even a fifth-wicket stand of 95 between the most composed batsman of the match, Kirsten, and the stylish left-hander, Rudolph, seemed insufficient when South Africa slumped again, this time to 142 for seven.

But England then exposed their embarrassing inability to land the killer punch for the first of three times in the match. Monde Zondeki, on his Test debut and with no batting record to speak of in 16 previous first-class games, made a heroic 59, while Kirsten chiselled his way to an 18th Test century. By playing the line down which the ball was first released, Zondeki survived where others had edged: Headingley's typically awkward pitch and the cloudy skies meant the ball was doing too much for him and Zondeki played and missed an extraordinary 33 times. Yet he remained calm and determined, and there was a steady supply of poor balls which he drove straight or through the covers. Early on the second day, he and Kirsten equalled South Africa's record eighth-wicket stand of 150 (set by Neil McKenzie and Shaun Pollock against Sri Lanka at Centurion in 2000-01), before Ntini – who really isn't supposed to be able to bat – compounded England's frustration by crashing a brisk 32. South Africa reached a very healthy 342, of which the last three wickets had contributed 200.

England's second faux pas was even greater than their first. Not having the nous to dismiss a tailender was one thing; deliberately surrendering an advantage for fear of

---

LONG TIME, NO SEE. . .

The longest break in an England Test career since the Second World War.

Years	*Days*		*From*	*To*
11	348	H. L. Jackson	3rd Test v NZ, 1949	3rd Test v A, 1961
11	230	D. Shackleton	1st Test v I, 1951-52	2nd Test v WI, 1963
10	**16**	**M. P. Bicknell**	**5th Test v A, 1993**	**4th Test v SA, 2003**
8	284	D. B. Close	3rd Test v P, 1967	1st Test v WI, 1976
8	192	K. V. Andrew	1st Test v P, 1954-55	1st Test v WI, 1963
8	181	W. Larkins	6th Test v P, 1981	1st Test v WI, 1989-90
8	100	W. G. A. Parkhouse	2nd Test v NZ, 1950-51	3rd Test v I, 1959
8	18	P. I. Pocock	3rd Test v WI, 1976	4th Test v WI, 1984

Research: Robert Brooke

losing it naturally was quite another. After adding 83 together before tea on the second day, Butcher, and to a lesser degree Trescothick, were so dominant as they looted 54 in ten brutal overs after the break, that South Africa's bowlers – already minus the injured Zondeki – were left shell shocked. England were 164 for one and flying.

If the decision by umpires Billy Bowden and Simon Taufel to offer the light was surprising, the decision of the rampant batsmen to accept it was incredible. Trescothick was the man who said yes and he justified his choice by claiming that a new batsman might struggle in light that was barely below bright sunshine. But there was no new batsman. It was negative thinking at its English worst.

During the unscheduled 30-minute break, Smith spoke "a few harsh words" and regrouped his wayward bowlers, and with an air of grim predictability both batsmen were dismissed by Kallis within eight overs of the restart, Trescothick to a breathtaking one-handed return catch, Butcher to a thin edge.

On the third day, the South African bowlers were discipline personified but the key to unlocking the innings was provided by a man who had never bowled in a Test before.

LEFT STRANDED

Scores of 99 not out in Test cricket.

G. Boycott England v Australia at Perth 1979-80
Boycott carried his bat; R. G. D. Willis was last man out for 0 and England lost.

S. R. Waugh Australia v England at Perth 1994-95
Stranded when his twin brother, runner for the injured C. J. McDermott, attempted an unlikely single.

A. J. Tudor England v New Zealand at Birmingham. 1999
Record score by England night-watchman; his partner, G. P. Thorpe, dominated the scoring as England neared victory.

S. M. Pollock South Africa v Sri Lanka at Centurion. 2002-03
See page 1135.

A. J. Hall South Africa v England at Leeds 2003

While waiting for the second new ball, Smith turned to the exciting but rarely seen leg-spin of Rudolph. His second delivery was a beauty, dipping late and teasing Hussain into a premature drive and a critical return catch. The tail then folded quickly, with the last five wickets adding just 68, despite Flintoff's aggressive and entertaining 55.

The pitch had been moody and unpredictable from the very beginning and it became no easier, so South Africa's lead of 35 was always likely to be important. Kirsten battled harder than ever to boost it with a courageous 60 that was comfortably as valuable as his century. He simply smiled when a good-length ball flew past his nose, never allowing his even temperament to be unsettled, and Kallis and McKenzie took the cue from their patient team-mate, batting with visible determination. But the game could still have twisted either way on the fourth morning, when the tourists resumed on 164 for five, a lead of 199.

However, Boucher batted with flair and aggression to disrupt England's fragile attack, before Hall ripped into them like a ravenous lion. He cut and pulled the barrage of long-hops that came his way and in barely an hour had dragged the match well beyond England's grasp. When the last man, Pretorius, was bowled by a shooter, Hall became only the fifth man to score an unbeaten 99 in Tests. He had faced just 87 deliveries.

England's target was of academic interest. They could not score 401, they knew it and they batted like they knew it. Butcher showed class, again, but failed to push on when well set, and Flintoff bashed a second half-century of the match. But Kallis completed a crushing victory with classic, fast away-swingers that earned him career-best figures for both an innings (six for 54) and a match (nine for 92). And the South Africans did it all without Shaun Pollock, who had returned home to Durban for the birth of his first child. Here was good news, even for England: given the Test record of the Pollock dynasty, their own heirs might be pleased to know that he had a daughter, Jemma.

Man of the Match: G. Kirsten. *Attendance:* 57,996; *receipts* £1,104,973.

Close of play: First day, South Africa 260-7 (Kirsten 109, Zondeki 50); Second day, England 197-3 (Hussain 14, Smith 0); Third day, South Africa 164-5 (McKenzie 17, Boucher 2); Fourth day, England 165-5 (Butcher 57, Flintoff 45).

South Africa

*G. C. Smith c Stewart b Kirtley	2	lbw b Bicknell	14
H. H. Gibbs c Stewart b Bicknell	0	lbw b Kirtley	2
G. Kirsten c Bicknell b Ali	130	lbw b Ali	60
J. H. Kallis c Vaughan b Bicknell	6	c Stewart b Kirtley	41
N. D. McKenzie c Stewart b Ali	4	c Bicknell b Flintoff	38
J. A. Rudolph lbw b Ali	55	c Smith b Anderson	10
†M. V. Boucher c Vaughan b Flintoff	16	c Stewart b Flintoff	39
A. J. Hall c Smith b Flintoff	0	not out	99
M. Zondeki c Butcher b Anderson	59	b Bicknell	7
M. Ntini not out	32	lbw b Ali	8
D. Pretorius c Stewart b Kirtley	9	b Kirtley	8
L-b 20, w 2, n-b 7	29	B 7, l-b 24, n-b 8	39
1/2 (1) 2/2 (2) 3/16 (4) 4/21 (5) 5/116 (6) 6/142 (7) 7/142 (8) 8/292 (9) 9/316 (3) 10/342 (11)	342	1/9 (2) 2/31 (1) 3/128 (4) 4/139 (3) 5/160 (6) 6/219 (5) 7/232 (7) 8/281 (9) 9/311 (10) 10/365 (11)	365

Bowling: *First Innings*—Kirtley 29.4–10–74–2; Bicknell 27–11–50–2; Ali 22–3–80–3; Anderson 18–7–63–1; Flintoff 18–5–55–2. *Second Innings*—Kirtley 21.5–7–71–3; Bicknell 22–3–75–2; Flintoff 22–5–63–2; Anderson 16–4–56–1; Ali 14–2–56–2; Vaughan 5–1–13–0.

England

M. E. Trescothick c and b Kallis	59	c Gibbs b Ntini	4
*M. P. Vaughan b Ntini	15	c Gibbs b Kallis	21
M. A. Butcher c Boucher b Kallis	77	c Hall b Kallis	61
N. Hussain c and b Rudolph	42	lbw b Kallis	6
E. T. Smith c Boucher b Kallis	0	c Smith b Hall	7
†A. J. Stewart c Hall b Pretorius	15	c Boucher b Ntini	7
A. Flintoff b Ntini	55	c Hall b Kallis	50
M. P. Bicknell b Ntini	4	c Boucher b Kallis	15
Kabir Ali c Boucher b Hall	1	c Kirsten b Kallis	9
R. J. Kirtley c Boucher b Hall	1	c Kirsten b Hall	11
J. M. Anderson not out	0	not out	0
B 2, l-b 17, w 6, n-b 13	38	L-b 9, w 2, n-b 7	18
1/27 (2) 2/169 (1) 3/193 (3) 4/197 (5) 5/239 (6) 6/261 (4) 7/289 (8) 8/293 (9) 9/307 (10) 10/307 (7)	307	1/11 (1) 2/44 (2) 3/62 (4) 4/81 (5) 5/95 (6) 6/169 (3) 7/182 (7) 8/189 (8) 9/206 (9) 10/209 (10)	209

Bowling: *First Innings*—Pretorius 19–1–100–1; Ntini 20.2–4–62–3; Hall 24–3–77–2; Zondeki 1.5–0–10–0; Kallis 20.1–7–38–3; Rudolph 2–1–1–1. *Second Innings*—Ntini 11–2–40–2; Hall 21.4–3–64–2; Pretorius 9–3–27–0; Kallis 17–4–54–6; Zondeki 3–0–15–0.

Umpires: B. F. Bowden (New Zealand) and S. J. A. Taufel (Australia).
Third umpire: P. Willey. Referee: R. S. Madugalle (Sri Lanka).

DERBYSHIRE v SOUTH AFRICANS

At Derby, August 28, 29, 30. Drawn. Toss: South Africans. County debut: P. M. R. Havell.

The match, even more likely to be an extended net for the tourists after the first day was washed out, was overshadowed by Derbyshire politics, with word that both the captain, Dominic Cork, and coach, Adrian Pierson, were on their way out. The South Africans carried on serenely, opting for extended batting practice between the Fourth and Fifth Tests, as Kallis scored his first double-century, in an innings at once commanding and pleasing to watch. It lasted seven hours six minutes, 305 balls and included 27 fours and a six. Thami Tsolekile, the reserve wicket-keeper, came close to a maiden century and Paul Havell, who played one first-class match for Sussex in 2001, made a good impression with the ball for Derbyshire, bowling brisk seamers.

Close of play: First day, No play; Second day, South Africans 317-5 (Kallis 141, Tsolekile 16).

South Africans

*G. C. Smith lbw b Havell	9	R. J. Peterson not out	5
J. A. Rudolph lbw b Gunter	17		
J. H. Kallis c Bassano b Dumelow	200	B 8, l-b 8, n-b 8	24
N. D. McKenzie c Sutton b Havell	22		—
H. H. Dippenaar lbw b Havell	4	1/13 (1) 2/50 (2) (7 wkts dec.)	460
M. V. Boucher lbw b Havell	89	3/106 (4) 4/111 (5)	
†T. L. Tsolekile c Bassano b Dumelow	90	5/272 (6) 6/441 (3) 7/460 (7)	

P. R. Adams, D. Pretorius and C. M. Willoughby did not bat.

Bowling: Dean 24–7–87–0; Havell 29–6–129–4; Gunter 18–3–81–1; Welch 28–8–82–0; Dumelow 14.1–4–65–2.

Derbyshire

A. I. Gait c McKenzie b Willoughby	2	G. Welch not out	15
S. D. Stubbings c Kallis b Pretorius	44	B 1, l-b 1, w 1, n-b 6	9
R. M. Khan c Kallis b Willoughby	14		—
C. W. G. Bassano c Kallis b Willoughby	6	1/26 (1) 2/55 (3) (4 wkts dec.)	136
*†L. D. Sutton not out	46	3/63 (4) 4/86 (2)	

D. R. Hewson, N. R. C. Dumelow, N. E. L. Gunter, K. J. Dean and P. M. R. Havell did not bat.

Bowling: Pretorius 11–0–50–1; Willoughby 14–4–31–3; Adams 12–2–21–0; Peterson 6–0–20–0; Rudolph 5–2–12–0.

Umpires: N. G. Cowley and J. F. Steele.

ENGLAND v SOUTH AFRICA

Fifth npower Test

HUGH CHEVALLIER

At The Oval, September 4, 5, 6, 7, 8. England won by nine wickets. Toss: South Africa.

At the start of the second day, bookies were offering 40 to one against an England win – not quite the 500 to one that tempted Rod Marsh and Dennis Lillee at Headingley in 1981, but an indication of the mountain England climbed to claim this epic. South Africa had lost a wicket to the last ball of the first day but, even at 362 for four, a huge score beckoned, and with it victory in the series. That wicket turned out to be the fulcrum on which the match pivoted. From then on, England produced far the sharper cricket. They were especially ruthless in the morning sessions, plundering five wickets for 70 on the second day, hitting 106 without loss on the third and 102 for two on the fourth before scattering the tail to the four winds on the last. On this sublime pitch, South Africa's 484 simply wasn't enough. Only once before in a Test in England, when Arthur Morris and Don Bradman triumphed at Headingley in 1948, had a first-innings total of 450 or more led to defeat.

It was not just the delicious reversal of fortune that made this a classic: there were myriad subplots to intrigue and absorb a packed house for five days. Alec Stewart, at the age of 40 and in his record 133rd and avowedly final Test appearance for England, wrapped himself in the cross of St George for the last time, at least on a cricket pitch. Thorpe, back from the wilderness only because another of Nasser Hussain's brittle bones was broken, achieved redemption with a beautiful hundred. And Bicknell, strutting his stuff on the big stage, hinted at what he might have done as a regular Test cricketer. Huge roars from the crowd regularly filled the air at the exploits of these three, Surrey stalwarts all.

NO SAFETY IN NUMBERS

Teams who batted first in a Test, scored 450 and lost.

586	Australia (586 and 166) lost to England† (325 and 437) at Sydney	1894-95
556	Australia (556 and 196) lost to India (523 and 233-6) at Adelaide	2003-04
526	West Indies (526-7 dec. and 92-2 dec.) lost to England (404 and 215-3) at Port-of-Spain	1967-68
520	Australia (520 and 209) lost to South Africa (435 and 297-4) at Melbourne	1952-53
519	England (519 and 257) lost to Australia (491 and 287-5) at Melbourne	1928-29
496	England (496 and 365-8 dec.) lost to Australia (458 and 404-3) at Leeds	1948
490	Australia (490 and 146) lost to West Indies (329 and 311-9) at Bridgetown	1998-99
484	**South Africa (484 and 229) lost to England (604-9 dec. and 110-1) at The Oval**	**2003**

† *Followed on.*

As Graeme Smith walked out that first, late-summer morning, he could have been forgiven a glow of confidence. More luck with the Edgbaston weather and the Trent Bridge toss, and he might have been contemplating a 5–0 whitewash. And his fortunes seemed to have changed now: a full-strength team for the first time in the series, a psychological edge after England's Headingley implosion, an important toss and a forecast of three fine days and two wet.

On a pitch aching to give up its runs, Gibbs was first to make hay in the September sunshine, crafting a big, full-blooded hundred bursting with drives and cuts. When he reached three figures, he had studded his tenth Test century with 20 fours and a six; only Flintoff, 18 months earlier in Christchurch, had hit more in boundaries en route to a Test century. Gibbs had reason to spurn ones and twos: in the morning, he had run out his captain, though Smith later had the grace to say he did not back up far enough. It hardly mattered, as Gibbs and Kirsten revelled in the conditions, adding 227 untroubled runs for the second wicket. True, both fell in the last session as Giles gained reward for perseverance, to be followed by McKenzie to the day's last gasp, but South Africa held the match in an iron grip.

It was loosened on the second morning, when they could – and should – have taken the game beyond England. More of what had gone before would have done the job, but England bowled with heart, fielded with zest, and South Africa floundered. There were two early wickets – which meant three had gone for 23 – but Kallis and Pollock looked as safe as houses. They had taken the score well past 400 when disaster struck. Inside 28 balls England's morning lurched from the good to the miraculous: Giles ran out Kallis with a fluky deflection on to the non-striker's stumps, Hall fell for a single, and Adams was beaten by Butcher's throw from the deep. But with the score 432 for

Off the middle: at The Oval, Marcus Trescothick crashes one of 34 boundaries during his first double-hundred.

Picture by Patrick Eagar.

nine, was it all too late? Once the resourceful Pollock eked 52 from the last wicket, the door seemed firmly shut.

Gloom-mongers pointed out that England needed 285 to avoid the follow-on, and had adopted an I-told-you-so air when Thorpe, whose last three Test innings against South Africa were ducks, joined Trescothick at 78 for two. But the next five hours left the pessimists squirming. Neither batsman gave a genuine chance as runs came thick, fast and handsome. Thorpe, who likened the occasion to a second debut after dropping out of international cricket 14 months earlier, did what he had done first time round and hit a hundred. Even Pollock, who became the 19th bowler to 300 Test wickets – and at 20.45 the one with the lowest average – when he whipped out Vaughan, came in for uncharacteristic stick during the partnership of 268.

BEATING THE ODDS

Best available odds against an England victory with London bookmakers on each morning of the match:

First day:	7-2	Fourth day:	11-2*
Second day:	40-1	Fifth day:	8-13
Third day:	10-1		

* *The draw was 1-6 on the fourth morning.*

Source: Racing Post

A deafening cheer greeted Stewart, collar up, as he strode through the South Africans' generous guard of honour. Several bat twiddles and knee squats later, he was slotting the ball between the fielders – though not for as long as the crowd wanted. On 38, he played across a straight ball, and a career totalling 8,463 runs at a shade under 40 was almost over. Cue more rapturous applause. Trescothick, meanwhile, was in consummate touch. Recently upbraided for a susceptibility outside off (and for the bad-light nonsense at Headingley), he silenced his critics with a glorious hundred later converted into a maiden double; his best shot was the leave. He faced 374 balls, batted nine and a half hours, and swatted 32 fours and two sixes before holing out for 219. Yet despite these riches, there was a danger the innings would peter out as the South Africans' had. Early on the fourth morning, England, eight down, led by a gossamer 18. With the forecast predicting that the tail-end of Hurricane Fabian would drown The Oval – and with the pitch as immaculate as Stewart's whites – the sensible money was on a draw.

Flintoff treated that logic with utter disdain. Beefy shots flashed from his bat as if it had been Ian Botham's; he hit cleanly, he hit hard and he hit often; 85 came from his last 72 balls. If there was an occasional slog-sweep, it disappeared for six, and the only thing agricultural about his innings was the assured way he farmed the strike: Harmison's contribution to a stand of 99 was a level-headed three. For South Africa, the psychological damage of watching ball after ball sail over the rope was as telling as the runs themselves; for the first time all series, Graeme Smith looked lost.

Shortly before lunch, Vaughan declared 120 ahead. England had bowled decently on the first day, but without fire. Now the South Africans wilted in the heat. Harmison subtly honed his "They don't like it up 'em" technique and deservedly reaped dividends. Bicknell slanted two away-swingers across Rudolph, then bowled a majestic in-swinger, unwisely ignored. By the close – and still no rain to speak of – South Africa, effectively 65 for six, had nowhere to hide.

The noisy fifth-day crowd craved victory, yet hankered for drama. They had to make do with the win. The South African lower order keeled over feebly against more lion-hearted bowling, and England, finding it all very easy, tore to their target at nearly five an over. The massive victory allowed Stewart to end his Test career – which also numbered 54 defeats – as he began it, on the winning side.

Man of the Match: M. E. Trescothick. *Attendance:* 80,000; *receipts* £1,600,000.

Men of the Series: England – A. Flintoff; South Africa – G. C. Smith.

Close of play: First day, South Africa 362-4 (Kallis 32); Second day, England 165-2 (Trescothick 64, Thorpe 28); Third day, England 502-7 (Flintoff 10, Bicknell 0); Fourth day, South Africa 185-6 (Boucher 22, Pollock 19).

South Africa

*G. C. Smith run out	18	– lbw b Bicknell	19
H. H. Gibbs b Giles	183	– c Stewart b Anderson	9
G. Kirsten lbw b Giles	90	– c Trescothick b Harmison	29
J. H. Kallis run out	66	– lbw b Harmison	35
N. D. McKenzie c Stewart b Anderson	9	– lbw b Flintoff	38
J. A. Rudolph lbw b Bicknell	0	– b Bicknell	8
†M. V. Boucher c Stewart b Bicknell	8	– c Stewart b Bicknell	25
S. M. Pollock not out	66	– c Thorpe b Harmison	43
A. J. Hall lbw b Flintoff	1	– c Smith b Bicknell	0
P. R. Adams run out	1	– not out	13
M. Ntini b Anderson	11	– c Smith b Harmison	1
B 12, l-b 10, w 4, n-b 5	31	B 1, l-b 7, n-b 1	9
1/63 (1) 2/290 (3) 3/345 (2) 4/362 (5) 5/365 (6) 6/385 (7) 7/419 (4) 8/421 (9) 9/432 (10) 10/484 (11)	484	1/24 (2) 2/34 (1) 3/92 (3) 4/93 (4) 5/118 (6) 6/150 (5) 7/193 (7) 8/193 (9) 9/215 (8) 10/229 (11)	229

Bowling: *First Innings*—Bicknell 20–3–71–2; Anderson 25–6–86–2; Harmison 27–8–73–0; Giles 29–3–102–2; Flintoff 19–4–88–1; Vaughan 5–0–24–0; Butcher 3–0–18–0. *Second Innings*—Bicknell 24–5–84–4; Anderson 10–1–55–1; Harmison 19.2–8–33–4; Giles 10–2–36–0; Flintoff 6–2–13–1.

England

M. E. Trescothick c Rudolph b Ntini	219	– not out	69
*M. P. Vaughan c Gibbs b Pollock	23	– c Boucher b Kallis	13
M. A. Butcher lbw b Hall	32	– not out	20
G. P. Thorpe b Kallis	124		
E. T. Smith lbw b Hall	16		
†A. J. Stewart lbw b Pollock	38		
A. Flintoff b Adams	95		
A. F. Giles c Hall b Kallis	2		
M. P. Bicknell lbw b Pollock	0		
S. J. Harmison not out	6		
J. M. Anderson not out	0		
B 11, l-b 18, w 9, n-b 11	49	L-b 4, n-b 4	8
1/28 (2) 2/78 (3) 3/346 (4) 4/379 (5) 5/480 (6) 6/489 (1) 7/502 (8) 8/502 (9) 9/601 (7)	(9 wkts dec.) 604	1/47 (2)	(1 wkt) 110

Bowling: *First Innings*—Pollock 39–10–111–3; Ntini 31–4–129–1; Hall 35–5–111–2; Kallis 34–5–117–2; Adams 17–2–79–1; Rudolph 6–1–28–0. *Second Innings*—Pollock 6–0–15–0; Ntini 8–0–46–0; Kallis 5.2–0–25–1; Adams 3–0–20–0.

Umpires: S. J. A. Taufel (Australia) and S. Venkataraghavan (India).
Third umpire: J. W. Lloyds. Referee: R. S. Madugalle (Sri Lanka).

THE PAKISTANIS IN ENGLAND, 2003

REVIEW BY LAWRENCE BOOTH

This was an international tour of high speed, but low relevance. The Pakistanis were in and out in little more than a fortnight, during which they played four warm-up games and three one-day internationals, the NatWest Challenge, a competition introduced at the request of Duncan Fletcher, who was concerned at his players' lack of one-day nous. Both teams had skulked disappointedly away from the World Cup in South Africa three months earlier, and though Pakistan had not in modern times been short of one-day match practice, England were now also intent on ensuring that they would not be accused of that mistake before the 2007 event.

The Challenge was a new competition won by a new captain leading a new team. And thanks to murderous batting from Marcus Trescothick, *Boy's Own* bowling from James Anderson, and an ounce of luck, the reshaped team under Michael Vaughan were able to kickstart his captaincy with a trophy.

Pakistan were in the process of rebuilding too, having dropped eight senior players after an even more harrowing World Cup. Even so, the 12 they picked here still started the series with an average of 71 one-day caps each. Only Darren Gough in the England squad could beat that figure. In the event, England were thankful for the experience of one of their older troupers: Trescothick smashed 212 runs – more than twice as many as his nearest rival, Mohammad Hafeez – with a strike-rate of 94, and settled the series with a century at Lord's. England's fielding, though, was boosted by the new brigade, and looked sharper than it had for years. The players even looked as if they were enjoying themselves.

PAKISTANI TOURING PARTY

Rashid Latif (Allied Bank) (*captain*), Azhar Mahmood (Islamabad/PIA), Bilal Asad (Allied Bank), Danish Kaneria (Habib Bank), Faisal Athar (PWD), Imran Nazir (National Bank), Misbah-ul-Haq (KRL), Mohammad Hafeez (Sargodha), Mohammad Sami (National Bank), Shabbir Ahmed (National Bank), Shoaib Akhtar (KRL), Shoaib Malik (PIA), Umar Gul (PIA), Yasir Hameed (PIA), Younis Khan (Habib Bank), Yousuf Youhana (ZTBL).

Abdul Razzaq (ZTBL), not named in the original party, was called up from a stint as an overseas player for Middlesex.

Coach: Javed Miandad. *Manager:* Haroon Rashid. *Doctor:* Riaz Ahmed. *Trainer:* Dr Tauseef Razzaq. *Media manager:* Samiul Hasan.

PAKISTANI TOUR RESULTS

One-day internationals – Played 3: Won 1, Lost 2.
Other non-first-class matches – Played 4: Won 3, Lost 1. *Wins* – Scotland, Northamptonshire, Leicestershire. *Loss* – Essex.

Note: Matches in this section were not first-class.

SCOTLAND v PAKISTANIS

At Hamilton Crescent, Glasgow, June 7. Pakistanis won by one wicket. Toss: Pakistanis. First-team debut: K. J. Coetzer.

Having already defeated three counties in the National League, Scotland came within a whisker of some full-scale giant-killing. But the Pakistanis, thanks to a fine all-round performance from Shoaib Malik – who took three for 17 with his off-spin and then hit the game's only fifty – clung on by their fingertips. Scotland began disastrously, stumbling to five for two when the Indian Test player Dravid fell first ball. But they recovered through a gutsy 36 from their opener, Williamson, who added 47 with Scotland's lesser-known import, the South African Jon Kent. Maiden then rounded off the innings with an enterprising 31 from 39 balls. The Pakistanis' reply also started shakily, but Imran Nazir steadied things with 38, before Shoaib kept a cool head to guide the tourists home.

Scotland

R. R. Watson c Younis Khan b Shabbir Ahmed	2
J. G. Williamson st Rashid Latif b Shoaib Malik	36
R. Dravid c Rashid Latif b Shabbir Ahmed	0
J. C. Kent c Rashid Latif b Bilal Asad	27
†C. J. O. Smith b Shoaib Malik	26
I. M. Stanger c Younis Khan b Shoaib Malik	0
K. J. Coetzer c Rashid Latif b Danish Kaneria	5
*C. M. Wright lbw b Shabbir Ahmed	7
G. I. Maiden lbw b Mohammad Hafeez	31
P. J. C. Hoffmann c Rashid Latif b Danish Kaneria	9
R. M. Haq not out	3
B 1, l-b 7, w 11, n-b 4	23
1/5 (1) 2/5 (3) 3/52 (4) 4/95 (2) 5/95 (6) 6/112 (5) 7/118 (7) 8/132 (8) 9/153 (10) 10/169 (9) (45.1 overs)	169

Bowling: Shabbir Ahmed 10–1–41–3; Umar Gul 7–1–19–0; Danish Kaneria 10–0–49–2; Mohammad Hafeez 2.1–0–8–1; Bilal Asad 3–0–17–1; Younis Khan 3–0–10–0; Shoaib Malik 10–3–17–3.

Pakistanis

Imran Nazir lbw b Wright	38
Mohammad Hafeez c Williamson b Hoffmann	5
Yasir Hameed c Watson b Kent	6
Yousuf Youhana c Smith b Kent	13
Younis Khan c Smith b Wright	3
Shoaib Malik not out	52
Bilal Asad c Kent b Stanger	8
*†Rashid Latif run out	26
Shabbir Ahmed lbw b Wright	2
Umar Gul lbw b Watson	0
Danish Kaneria not out	5
L-b 6, w 2, n-b 4	12
1/9 (2) 2/18 (3) 3/52 (1) 4/60 (5) 5/102 (4) 6/121 (7) 7/157 (8) 8/164 (9) 9/165 (10) (9 wkts, 47 overs)	170

Bowling: Hoffmann 10–3–22–1; Kent 10–0–40–2; Stanger 10–0–28–1; Wright 10–1–42–3; Haq 2–0–15–0; Maiden 2–0–10–0; Watson 3–0–7–1.

Umpires: J. B. Anderson and J. Thallon.

ESSEX v PAKISTANIS

At Chelmsford, June 9 (day/night). Essex won by 50 runs. Toss: Essex. First-team debuts: A. N. Cook, N. A. Denning.

Thanks to a magnificent innings from Flower – one of just four capped players in the side – Essex won with something to spare. He survived a difficult chance in the covers before scoring, went to a canny century with just nine fours, and received eye-catching support from Foster and Bopara. Napier then struck twice in his third over, and Nick Denning picked up a wicket with his first delivery at senior level, as the Pakistanis struggled. Not even an entertaining 82 from 89 balls from Yasir Hameed could save them. A crowd of more than 4,000 watched the first game under Essex's newly installed floodlights.

Essex

W. I. Jefferson c Yasir Hameed b Mohammad Sami . 16
A. Flower not out 115
†J. S. Foster c Younis Khan b Shoaib Malik . 56
M. L. Pettini b Shoaib Akhtar 18
R. S. Bopara c Imran Nazir b Shoaib Malik . 46
G. R. Napier c Mohammad Sami b Shoaib Akhtar . 3
*A. P. Grayson b Mohammad Sami 1
A. N. Cook not out 0
B 9, l-b 4, w 13, n-b 3 29

1/28 (1) 2/118 (3) 3/163 (4) 4/258 (5) 5/265 (6) 6/284 (7) (6 wkts, 50 overs) 284

J. D. Middlebrook, N. A. Denning and J. B. Grant did not bat.

Bowling: Shoaib Akhtar 10–1–47–2; Mohammad Sami 10–0–54–2; Shabbir Ahmed 5–0–24–0; Bilal Asad 2–0–11–0; Danish Kaneria 10–0–58–0; Shoaib Malik 7–0–38–2; Mohammad Hafeez 6–0–39–0.

Pakistanis

Imran Nazir c sub b Napier 3
Bilal Asad lbw b Denning 34
*Yousuf Youhana lbw b Napier 0
Younis Khan c Middlebrook b Denning . 16
†Yasir Hameed c Pettini b Grant 82
Shoaib Malik run out 35
Mohammad Hafeez run out 2
Shoaib Akhtar c Jefferson b Grayson . . . 11
Mohammad Sami b Bopara 20
Shabbir Ahmed c Middlebrook b Bopara 23
Danish Kaneria not out 0
L-b 4, w 4 8

1/20 (1) 2/20 (3) 3/52 (4) 4/72 (2) 5/140 (6) 6/142 (7) 7/188 (5) 8/190 (8) 9/232 (10) 10/234 (9) (46.1 overs) 234

Bowling: Napier 9–1–35–2; Grant 8–0–48–1; Denning 9–0–48–2; Bopara 7.1–0–28–2; Middlebrook 6–0–38–0; Grayson 7–0–33–1.

Umpires: N. L. Bainton and B. Dudleston.

NORTHAMPTONSHIRE v PAKISTANIS

At Northampton, June 11. Pakistanis won by 62 runs. Toss: Pakistanis. County debut: D. G. Wright.

After two less-than-convincing performances, the Pakistanis showed signs of progress in every department to overcome Northamptonshire with some ease – despite a defiant innings from Sales. Last out for 104 off 109 balls after reaching his century with his third six, he was unable to repair the damage done by Mohammad Sami, who removed both openers in a pacy spell with the new ball. Earlier, Imran Nazir lit up the batting for Pakistan, striking a six and 12 fours in a run-a-ball 66. He dominated an opening stand of 116, before Younis Khan and Yasir Hameed also hit similar scores against a Northamptonshire attack led for the first time by Damien Wright, a right-arm seamer from Tasmania signed as a temporary overseas replacement for Andre Nel, who had been called up by South Africa.

Pakistanis

Imran Nazir c Powell b Anderson 66
Mohammad Hafeez lbw b Swann 38
Younis Khan c Swann b Anderson 69
Yasir Hameed run out 62
Shoaib Akhtar c and b Wright 5
Misbah-ul-Haq b Cawdron 18
Bilal Asad c Wright b Cawdron 4
Shoaib Malik not out 7
Mohammad Sami not out 1
L-b 7, w 16, n-b 5 28

1/116 (2) 2/126 (1) 3/252 (3) 4/268 (5) 5/268 (4) 6/274 (7) 7/291 (6) (7 wkts, 50 overs) 298

*†Rashid Latif and Umar Gul did not bat.

Bowling: Wright 10–1–49–1; Cawdron 10–0–70–2; Greenidge 5–0–56–0; Anderson 10–0–43–2; Swann 10–0–41–1; Cook 5–0–32–0.

Northamptonshire

*M. E. K. Hussey c Rashid Latif b Mohammad Sami	1
M. J. Powell b Mohammad Sami	7
P. A. Jaques c Yasir Hameed b Umar Gul	29
D. J. Sales st Rashid Latif b Mohammad Hafeez	104
J. W. Cook b Shoaib Malik	45
G. P. Swann c Mohammad Hafeez b Umar Gul	5
†T. M. B. Bailey b Umar Gul	0
R. S. G. Anderson lbw b Shoaib Malik	0
D. G. Wright b Shoaib Akhtar	18
M. J. Cawdron b Shoaib Akhtar	3
C. G. Greenidge not out	0
B 5, l-b 5, w 11, n-b 3	24
1/10 (1) 2/43 (2) 3/47 (3) 4/153 (5) 5/170 (6) 6/170 (7) 7/171 (8) 8/210 (9) 9/221 (10) 10/236 (4) (45.3 overs)	236

Bowling: Shoaib Akhtar 10–1–34–2; Mohammad Sami 8–0–35–2; Umar Gul 10–0–73–3; Mohammad Hafeez 9.3–1–32–1; Shoaib Malik 8–0–52–2.

Umpires: B. Dudleston and I. J. Gould.

LEICESTERSHIRE v PAKISTANIS

At Leicester, June 14. Pakistanis won by five wickets. Toss: Leicestershire.

The Pakistanis made short work of a potentially awkward target in their final warm-up game before the NatWest Challenge. They could even afford to give away 43 in extras, and later shrugged off a brief crisis in which they lost four wickets for 19. Mohammad Hafeez made a crisp half-century before his departure prompted the wobble. Younis Khan and Rashid Latif then added 81 runs in ten overs, as an array of elegant strokes took the Pakistanis to victory with 19 balls to spare. Hodge had a fine all-round game, first hitting an unbeaten 47 – Leicestershire's best – and then seizing three for 19 in six overs of off-spin.

Leicestershire

J. K. Maunders b Mohammad Hafeez	25
V. Sehwag c Rashid Latif b Umar Gul	19
*D. L. Maddy lbw b Abdul Razzaq	15
D. I. Stevens c Shoaib Akhtar b Shabbir Ahmed	40
B. J. Hodge not out	47
T. R. Ward b Abdul Razzaq	28
J. N. Snape lbw b Abdul Razzaq	0
†P. A. Nixon c Imran Nazir b Abdul Razzaq	13
D. D. Masters not out	1
B 4, l-b 12, w 19, n-b 8	43
1/53 (2) 2/82 (3) 3/86 (1) 4/134 (4) 5/199 (6) 6/199 (7) 7/225 (8) (7 wkts, 50 overs)	231

M. J. A. Whiley and J. O. Grove did not bat.

Bowling: Shoaib Akhtar 10–0–44–0; Shabbir Ahmed 8–0–44–1; Umar Gul 10–0–31–1; Abdul Razzaq 10–0–55–4; Mohammad Hafeez 10–1–26–1; Younis Khan 2–0–15–0.

Pakistanis

Imran Nazir b Whiley	30
Mohammad Hafeez c Maddy b Hodge	54
Yasir Hameed lbw b Snape	48
Yousuf Youhana c and b Hodge	3
Younis Khan not out	45
Misbah-ul-Haq c Nixon b Hodge	3
*†Rashid Latif not out	40
B 1, w 8	9
1/51 (1) 2/132 (2) 3/138 (4) 4/144 (3) 5/151 (6) (5 wkts, 46.5 overs)	232

Shoaib Akhtar, Abdul Razzaq, Shabbir Ahmed and Umar Gul did not bat.

Bowling: Whiley 7–0–54–1; Grove 8–2–21–0; Masters 9.5–0–52–0; Snape 10–0–39–1; Sehwag 5–0–35–0; Hodge 6–1–19–3; Maddy 1–0–11–0.

Umpires: N. J. Llong and J. F. Steele.

THE NATWEST CHALLENGE

LAWRENCE BOOTH

ENGLAND v PAKISTAN

First One-Day International

At Manchester, June 17 (day/night). Pakistan won by two wickets. Toss: England. One-day international debuts: R. Clarke, A. McGrath, J. O. Troughton.

A see-sawing, low-scoring thriller finally went Pakistan's way after some inspired bowling from Anderson and Gough late on gave England hope. Cruising at 116 for one in pursuit of 205, Pakistan nearly made a mess of it. Vaughan ran out Yousuf Youhana, Anderson returned after an early pasting to claim three wickets, and when Gough struck twice in five balls, it was 194 for eight. But Abdul Razzaq found a nerveless ally in Mohammad Sami and pulled the winning runs with four balls to spare. Without a patient 69 from the opener, Mohammad Hafeez, things might have been different. Earlier, England had struggled on a slow pitch after a whippet-like start from Trescothick and Solanki, one of six players who were not part of England's last one-day team, against Australia in the World Cup just over three months earlier. From the side that trudged off from that let-down, Knight, Hussain, Stewart, Caddick and White had apparently gone from one-day internationals for ever, and Collingwood was injured. Vaughan, the new captain, could see a big score beckoning at 152 for four in the 32nd over, but Flintoff picked out deep square leg, and Rikki Clarke was bowled second ball by the thrifty Shoaib Malik. Clarke made amends when he dismissed Imran Nazir with a long-hop to become the first Englishman since Geoff Arnold in 1972 to take a wicket with his first ball in one-day internationals. England, though, had left their fightback a little too late. More than a thousand Pakistani supporters surged on to the outfield as the winning run was being scored in a display of the kind of over-exuberance cricket was hoping it had quashed. ECB officials considered extra security measures and renewed their call to the government to make pitch invasions a criminal offence. Seven of their security men were diverted from crowd control by the urgent necessity of ejecting one of cricket's most experienced photographers, Graham Morris, who was taking a picture of the sunset from the press box roof.

Man of the Match: Mohammad Hafeez. *Attendance:* 18,208; *receipts* £441,902.

England

Batsman	Runs	Balls
M. E. Trescothick c Rashid Latif b Mohammad Sami	18	(25)
V. S. Solanki b Mohammad Hafeez	36	(36)
*M. P. Vaughan c Rashid Latif b Umar Gul	27	(34)
J. O. Troughton c Rashid Latif b Umar Gul	6	(8)
A. Flintoff c Yasir Hameed b Abdul Razzaq	39	(55)
A. McGrath c Mohammad Sami b Shoaib Malik	33	(75)
R. Clarke b Shoaib Malik	0	(2)
†C. M. W. Read c Imran Nazir b Shoaib Malik	5	(17)
A. F. Giles run out	3	(9)
D. Gough not out	14	(30)
J. M. Anderson not out	6	(14)
L-b 6, w 6, n-b 5	17	
(9 wkts, 50 overs)	204	

1/45 (1) 2/64 (2) 3/96 (4) 4/106 (3) 5/152 (5) 6/152 (7) 7/164 (8) 8/169 (9) 9/194 (6)

15 overs: 96-3

Bowling: Azhar Mahmood 7–0–24–0; Mohammad Sami 10–2–52–1; Mohammad Hafeez 10–0–41–1; Umar Gul 7–0–33–2; Abdul Razzaq 6–0–22–1; Shoaib Malik 10–2–26–3.

> "'It's a mental thing', said Derbyshire's coach Adrian Pierson, 'We are in a dark hole and we have to find the light'."
>
> Derbyshire in 2003, page 506.

Pakistan

Batting	R	B
Imran Nazir c Solanki b Clarke	33	(56)
Mohammad Hafeez c Clarke b Anderson	69	(112)
Yasir Hameed c McGrath b Giles	23	(44)
Yousuf Youhana run out	8	(10)
Younis Khan b Anderson	0	(2)
Shoaib Malik c Clarke b Gough	24	(26)
Azhar Mahmood c Troughton b Gough	16	(18)
*†Rashid Latif lbw b Anderson	1	(2)
Abdul Razzaq not out	12	(9)
Mohammad Sami not out	7	(17)
L-b 9, w 6	15	
(8 wkts, 49.2 overs)	208	

1/60 (1) 2/116 (3) 3/139 (4) 4/139 (5) 5/158 (2) 6/181 (6) 7/188 (8) 8/194 (7) 15 overs: 54-0

Umar Gul did not bat.

Bowling: Anderson 10–0–59–3; Gough 10–1–38–2; Flintoff 10–2–23–0; Giles 10–0–29–1; Clarke 7.2–0–41–1; Vaughan 2–0–9–0.

Umpires: D. B. Hair (Australia) and D. R. Shepherd.
Third umpire: P. Willey. Referee: G. R. Viswanath (India).

ENGLAND v PAKISTAN

Second One-Day International

At The Oval, June 20. England won by seven wickets. Toss: Pakistan.

A hat-trick from Anderson and a brutal *tour de force* from Trescothick catapulted England to victory in just 22 overs. Pakistan lost Imran Nazir to the first ball of the match – one of four golden ducks in the innings – and slumped to 80 for six before Yousuf Youhana and Azhar Mahmood added a face-saving 72. At 185 for seven, Pakistan were just breathing, but Anderson then claimed England's first hat-trick in 373 one-day internationals. Abdul Razzaq drove to mid-off, Shoaib Akhtar edged behind and Mohammad Sami was bowled middle and off by a yorker verging on a full toss. It was not just a statistic; it was the culmination of perhaps Anderson's most promising bowling performance yet. For Pakistan, the punishment was far from over. Trescothick needed 11 balls to get off the mark, but then, in a ferocious display of cover-driving and upper-cutting, left Pakistan for dead, to say nothing of his opening partner, Solanki. By the time he top-edged a pull in the 12th over, Trescothick had bludgeoned 86 off 55 balls – with 16 fours and two sixes – from a total of 109. Deprived of the strike, Solanki's share was a mere eight. Flintoff supplied a strongarm 26, leaving the patient Solanki unbeaten on 40 – and Pakistan's bowlers licking their wounds.

Man of the Match: M. E. Trescothick. *Attendance*: 18,104; *receipts* £586,491.

Pakistan

Batting	R	B
Imran Nazir lbw b Anderson	0	(1)
Mohammad Hafeez lbw b Flintoff	14	(27)
Yasir Hameed b Gough	28	(56)
Yousuf Youhana not out	75	(102)
Younis Khan c Read b Gough	0	(1)
Shoaib Malik run out	2	(12)
*†Rashid Latif c Solanki b McGrath	3	(11)
Azhar Mahmood c Solanki b Clarke	30	(39)
Abdul Razzaq c Trescothick b Anderson	17	(16)
Shoaib Akhtar c Read b Anderson	0	(1)
Mohammad Sami b Anderson	0	(1)
B 1, l-b 1, w 11, n-b 3	16	
(44 overs)	185	

1/0 (1) 2/37 (2) 3/61 (3) 4/61 (5) 5/73 (6) 6/80 (7) 7/152 (8) 8/185 (9) 9/185 (10) 10/185 (11) 15 overs: 50-2

Bowling: Anderson 9–2–27–4; Gough 7–1–28–2; Flintoff 8–1–36–1; McGrath 10–1–40–1; Giles 5–0–22–0; Clarke 5–0–30–1.

England

M. E. Trescothick c Rashid Latif b Abdul Razzaq	86	(55)	A. Flintoff not out	26	(13)
V. S. Solanki not out	40	(49)	B 4, l-b 4, w 14, n-b 5	27	
*M. P. Vaughan c Younis Khan b Shoaib Akhtar	10	(14)	1/109 (1) (3 wkts, 22 overs)	189	
J. O. Troughton c Rashid Latif b Shoaib Akhtar	0	(6)	2/143 (3) 3/147 (4) 15 overs: 131-1		

A. McGrath, R. Clarke, †C. M. W. Read, A. F. Giles, D. Gough and J. M. Anderson did not bat.

Bowling: Shoaib Akhtar 9–0–69–2; Mohammad Sami 3–0–25–0; Azhar Mahmood 3–0–35–0; Mohammad Hafeez 2–0–19–0; Abdul Razzaq 5–0–33–1.

Umpires: D. B. Hair (Australia) and N. A. Mallender.
Third umpire: J. W. Lloyds. Referee: G. R. Viswanath (India).

ENGLAND v PAKISTAN

Third One-Day International

At Lord's, June 22. England won by four wickets. Toss: England.

An emphatic flick for six by Trescothick sealed the series with nine balls to spare, but England's road to victory was littered with several accidents and near-misses. Chasing a below-par 230, they were progressing smoothly at 129 for two. But Troughton needlessly launched Shoaib Malik to long-off, and Mohammad Hafeez struck three times in three overs with his subtly varied off-breaks. With 76 still required, Read dug in at Trescothick's side, though both were lucky to come through a maniacal spell of extra-fast bowling from Shoaib Akhtar. Trescothick was dropped by Rashid Latif – high and bullet-like to his left – on 93, while Read somehow survived a convincing shout for leg-before, and was twice a whisker from being bowled. But Trescothick hung on to complete his fifth one-day international century – his third at Lord's – from 142 balls, and Read was still with him at the end. Pakistan had left themselves too much to do after their top order struggled in damp conditions against the thudding accuracy of Flintoff, whose first seven overs cost only nine. But Abdul Razzaq changed the complexion of the innings with a daring 64 from 53 balls. It was not quite enough.

Man of the Match: M. E. Trescothick.

Man of the Series: M. E. Trescothick. *Attendance*: 27,078; *receipts* £750,846.

Pakistan

Mohammad Hafeez c Clarke b Gough	19	(41)	Azhar Mahmood not out	20	(15)
Imran Nazir c Vaughan b Flintoff	8	(26)	Shoaib Akhtar not out	0	(0)
Yasir Hameed c and b Flintoff	5	(12)	L-b 15, w 6, n-b 1	22	
Yousuf Youhana c Read b Clarke	5	(21)			
Younis Khan c McGrath b Anderson	63	(87)	1/29 (2) (7 wkts, 50 overs)	229	
Shoaib Malik c Read b Flintoff	23	(46)	2/38 (1) 3/44 (3) 4/61 (4)		
Abdul Razzaq c Trescothick b Flintoff	64	(53)	5/117 (6) 6/165 (5) 7/225 (7) 15 overs: 46-3		

*†Rashid Latif and Mohammad Sami did not bat.

Bowling: Anderson 10–1–52–1; Gough 10–1–45–1; Flintoff 10–2–32–4; Clarke 6–0–29–1; McGrath 5–0–21–0; Giles 9–0–35–0.

England

M. E. Trescothick not out	108	(145)	R. Clarke c Rashid Latif b Mohammad Hafeez	4	(8)
V. S. Solanki c Rashid Latif b Mohammad Sami	12	(15)	†C. M. W. Read not out	25	(40)
*M. P. Vaughan c Mohammad Hafeez b Azhar Mahmood	29	(41)	B 8, l-b 7, w 4, n-b 8	27	
J. O. Troughton c Shoaib Akhtar b Shoaib Malik	20	(26)			
A. Flintoff c Mohammad Sami b Mohammad Hafeez	4	(13)	1/24 (2) (6 wkts, 48.3 overs)	231	
A. McGrath st Rashid Latif b Mohammad Hafeez	2	(11)	2/89 (3) 3/129 (4) 4/143 (5) 5/147 (6) 6/154 (7)	15 overs: 71-1	

A. F. Giles, D. Gough and J. M. Anderson did not bat.

Bowling: Shoaib Akhtar 10–1–40–0; Mohammad Sami 9–0–50–1; Abdul Razzaq 7–1–28–0; Azhar Mahmood 6.3–0–41–1; Shoaib Malik 7–0–26–1; Mohammad Hafeez 9–0–31–3.

Umpires: D. B. Hair (Australia) and P. Willey.
Third umpire: N. A. Mallender. Referee: G. R. Viswanath (India).

Figures in brackets are balls received.

INTERNATIONAL UMPIRES' PANEL

In 1993, the International Cricket Council formed an international umpires' panel, containing at least two officials from each full member of ICC. A third-country umpire from this panel stood with a "home" umpire, not necessarily from the panel, in every Test from February 1994 onwards.

In March 2002, an elite panel of eight umpires (contracted to the ICC for two years at a time) was appointed after consultation with the Test captains, who assess umpires' performances after every match. Two elite umpires were expected to stand in all Tests from April 2002, and at least one in every one-day international. A supporting panel of international umpires was created to provide cover if the Test schedule became unusually crowded, and to provide a second umpire in one-day internationals. The ICC also appointed specialist third umpires to give rulings from TV replays. The panels were sponsored by Emirates Airlines for three years from July 2002.

The elite panel was expanded from eight to 11 in April 2003. At the end of 2003, the following umpires were on the elite panel: B. F. Bowden (New Zealand), S. A. Bucknor (West Indies), E. A. R. de Silva (Sri Lanka), D. B. Hair (Australia), D. J. Harper (Australia), R. E. Koertzen (South Africa), D. L. Orchard (South Africa), D. R. Shepherd (England), S. J. A. Taufel (Australia), R. B. Tiffin (Zimbabwe) and S. Venkataraghavan (India). Bowden, Hair and Taufel were the three added in April 2003. In April 2004, Venkataraghavan was due to retire, de Silva, Orchard and Tiffin were not offered new contracts, and Aleem Dar (Pakistan) and N. A. Mallender (England) were to be promoted from the international panel.

The international panel in 2003 consisted of A. F. M. Akhtaruddin (Bangladesh), Aleem Dar (Pakistan), K. C. Barbour (Zimbabwe), D. B. Cowie (New Zealand), S. J. Davis (Australia), B. R. Doctrove (West Indies), K. Hariharan (India), A. L. Hill (New Zealand), I. L. Howell (South Africa), A. V. Jayaprakash (India), B. G. Jerling (South Africa), Mahbubur Rahman (Bangladesh), N. A. Mallender (England), P. Manuel (Sri Lanka), Nadeem Ghauri (Pakistan), E. A. Nicholls (West Indies), P. D. Parker (Australia), I. D. Robinson (Zimbabwe), T. H. Wijewardene (Sri Lanka) and P. Willey (England). The specialist third umpires were Asad Rauf (Pakistan), G. A. Baxter (New Zealand), J. W. Lloyds (England), B. E. W. Morgan (West Indies), R. L. Parry (Australia), Showkatur Rahman (Bangladesh), M. G. Silva (Sri Lanka), I. Sivaram (India) and G. B. Cuddumbey (South Africa). During 2003, Davis, Hill and Robinson were promoted from the third umpire list to the main international panel, along with Parker, who was not previously on either, and M. A. Esat (Zimbabwe) left the panel. Baxter, Cuddumbey, Morgan and Parry joined the third umpire list and S. Wadvalla (South Africa) left.

THE NATWEST SERIES, 2003

JULIAN GUYER

A series against South Africa and Zimbabwe was never likely to set the British sporting public's pulse racing. But, after an uncertain start, England's cricket certainly did. Not only did they lift the trophy – always an important consideration however much talk there is of future planning – but the team enjoyed a number of individual successes that seemed to have helpful implications for the long run-up to the 2007 World Cup.

The dormant talent of Vikram Solanki came to life, while Andrew Flintoff indicated that nous was finally joining forces with natural ability. Meanwhile, Darren Gough and James Anderson cemented an effective new-ball partnership that had been established during England's NatWest Challenge triumph over Pakistan.

The compact format of the competition helped England too. There was not much time to brood on setbacks before a fresh challenge confronted Michael Vaughan's zestful side. England might have lost a leader in Nasser Hussain, who resigned after the World Cup, but somehow, under Vaughan, it always seemed as if a "glad confident morning" were just around the corner, a mood that, within weeks, would have profound implications for the Test captaincy as well as the one-day leadership.

Never was this new sense of optimism better demonstrated than in the second game of the series at The Oval, where, in Vaughan's absence, England faced South Africa just two days after losing to a weak Zimbabwe side. South Africa had made 264 for six, but England knocked off the runs in truly thrilling fashion, thanks to hundreds from Marcus Trescothick and Solanki. In 23 previous one-day internationals, no England batsman had scored a century against South Africa. Now, like the buses on the Harleyford Road, two came along at once.

Problems, however, remained. The absence of Paul Collingwood, who was injured, and Graham Thorpe, who was omitted, left the team short of a batsman who could finish an innings. Chris Read, whose wicket-keeping was uniformly excellent, was a gutsy contributor with the bat, but the middle-order experiments with Robert Key and Jim Troughton both failed.

By contrast, Jacques Kallis, the rock of South Africa's line-up, made batting look absurdly easy. He started the series with successive hundreds and might have had three in a row but for the excellence of Jacques Rudolph during a match-winning stand against England at Old Trafford. His competition tally of 329 at an average of 109.66 was 98 runs clear of his nearest rival, Trescothick. Kallis's performances were all the more remarkable for taking place against the backdrop of his father's unsuccessful battle against cancer back home in Cape Town.

But South Africa were less than the sum of their parts. They were newly arrived in the country, and their young captain, Graeme Smith, still seemed uncertain about the correct strategy in English conditions. Sometimes, it was as if he were talking his top order into failure. Herschelle Gibbs's return of 117 runs in seven innings – including an unbeaten 93 – summed up their problems, while South Africa's dismal total of 107 in the final was more reminiscent of a lopsided domestic showpiece in September than a one-day international in July. Eight of the nine completed matches were won by the side batting second, including – contrary to conventional wisdom – the two floodlit ones.

Zimbabwe's stirring victory in the competition opener at Trent Bridge offered hope of a genuinely three-cornered fight. This quickly proved illusory, although their captain, Heath Streak, never let his standards slip. His performance against England at Bristol, when he responded to his own side's score of 92 by taking four quick wickets, was typical, and his conduct in difficult circumstances was exemplary.

The same could not be be said for some of the tournament's arrangements. Once again, the two visiting teams were made to play on successive days, while England were not. ECB officials muttered darkly that England had been similarly ill-treated abroad, which had a certain playground logic about it.

Notes: Matches in this section were not first-class.
Figures in brackets are balls received.

ENGLAND v ZIMBABWE

At Nottingham, June 26. Zimbabwe won by four wickets. Zimbabwe 5 pts, England 1 pt. Toss: Zimbabwe. One-day international debuts: R. L. Johnson, R. W. T. Key.

Zimbabwe were indebted to Grant Flower for ending a run of nine one-day defeats by England stretching back nearly three years. Flower made a composed unbeaten 96 to rescue Zimbabwe from the depths of 15 for four as they chased what seemed to be a modest 192 for victory. He was well supported by the 20-year-old Matsikenyeri, who rode his luck to make a career-best 44 in a crucial stand of 96, before Ervine settled nerves with a brisk, undefeated 26. Earlier, England struggled against Zimbabwe's slow bowlers, who took two for 64 from 24 overs between them, with Price outstanding. Gough and the debutant Richard Johnson then made up for the absence of Anderson, who was being rested, by taking four wickets in the first ten overs, only for Zimbabwe to belie their status as the tournament whipping-boys and complete a well-earned win with two overs to spare.

Man of the Match: G. W. Flower. *Attendance:* 11,455; *receipts* £297,436.

England

M. E. Trescothick c Flower b Streak	38	(38)
V. S. Solanki c Ebrahim b Streak	1	(3)
*M. P. Vaughan c Taibu b Ervine	13	(22)
R. W. T. Key b Price	11	(37)
A. Flintoff c Blignaut b Marillier	53	(90)
A. McGrath run out	14	(42)
R. Clarke b Blignaut	23	(38)
†C. M. W. Read c Brent b Blignaut	23	(32)
R. L. Johnson not out	0	(0)
A. F. Giles not out	1	(1)
B 2, l-b 2, w 7, n-b 3	14	
1/9 (2) (8 wkts, 50 overs)	191	

2/56 (3) 3/57 (1) 4/104 (4) 5/134 (6) 6/144 (5) 7/190 (8) 8/190 (7)

15 overs: 80-3

D. Gough did not bat.

Bowling: Streak 9–1–30–2; Blignaut 8–0–53–2; Ervine 8–1–26–1; Friend 1–0–14–0; Price 10–2–20–1; Marillier 10–0–30–1; Flower 4–0–14–0.

Zimbabwe

D. A. Marillier c Clarke b Gough	0	(5)
D. D. Ebrahim c Flintoff b Johnson	1	(7)
T. J. Friend c Clarke b Gough	5	(15)
G. W. Flower not out	96	(152)
†T. Taibu c Solanki b Johnson	4	(9)
S. Matsikenyeri c Clarke b Johnson	44	(55)
*H. H. Streak run out	7	(21)
S. M. Ervine not out	26	(25)
L-b 1, w 10, n-b 1	12	
1/2 (2) 2/3 (1) 3/8 (3) 4/15 (5) 5/111 (6) 6/143 (7) (6 wkts, 48 overs)	195	
15 overs: 39-4		

A. M. Blignaut, R. W. Price and G. B. Brent did not bat.

Bowling: Gough 10–2–40–2; Johnson 10–1–32–3; Flintoff 10–2–24–0; Clarke 3–0–13–0; Giles 9–0–50–0; McGrath 6–0–35–0.

Umpires: S. J. A. Taufel (Australia) and P. Willey.
Third umpire: N. A. Mallender. Referee: C. H. Lloyd (West Indies).

ENGLAND v SOUTH AFRICA

At The Oval, June 28. England won by six wickets. England 5 pts, South Africa 1 pt. Toss: South Africa.

Rarely can two England one-day batsmen have played as well together as Trescothick and Solanki. Both men made blistering hundreds to hurry England to victory with more than four overs to spare, while their opening stand of 200 was an England record, surpassing the 193 put on by Gooch and Athey against New Zealand at Old Trafford in 1986. Solanki was caught behind off a Pollock no-ball on 21, but then unfurled an array of wristy, attacking strokes, and needed just 101 deliveries to complete his maiden one-day international century. Trescothick, England's stand-in captain after Vaughan withdrew on the morning of the match because of a back injury, reached his sixth one-day hundred from 110. Not even a mini-collapse of three wickets for three runs could dampen English spirits, and Flintoff finished things off in style with a murderous 32. In perfect batting conditions, South Africa's below-par total of 264 was built around a steady 107 from Kallis, and received some late impetus from Hall, who hit the first five balls of Gough's final over for four.

Man of the Match: V. S. Solanki. *Attendance:* 17,799; *receipts* £554,998.

South Africa

*G. C. Smith b Anderson	15	(25)
H. H. Gibbs b Anderson	5	(5)
J. H. Kallis b Flintoff	107	(133)
J. A. Rudolph run out	20	(35)
†M. V. Boucher b Flintoff	55	(64)
M. van Jaarsveld b Flintoff	13	(23)
S. M. Pollock not out	12	(7)
A. J. Hall not out	23	(8)
L-b 11, w 3	14	
1/5 (2) 2/33 (1) 3/72 (4) 4/183 (5) 5/221 (6) 6/240 (3) (6 wkts, 50 overs)	264	
15 overs: 60-2		

N. Boje, A. C. Dawson and M. Ntini did not bat.

Bowling: Anderson 10–1–54–2; Gough 10–1–61–0; Flintoff 10–1–46–3; Johnson 10–1–39–0; Giles 8–0–38–0; McGrath 2–0–15–0.

England

*M. E. Trescothick not out	114	(125)
V. S. Solanki c Kallis b Ntini	106	(108)
R. W. T. Key c Boucher b Ntini	0	(1)
A. McGrath c Boucher b Kallis	0	(7)
A. Flintoff b Hall	32	(21)
J. O. Troughton not out	5	(14)
L-b 3, w 4, n-b 1	8	
1/200 (2) 2/202 (3) 3/203 (4) 4/247 (5) (4 wkts, 45.5 overs)	265	
15 overs: 93-0		

†C. M. W. Read, A. F. Giles, R. L. Johnson, D. Gough and J. M. Anderson did not bat.

Bowling: Pollock 8–0–41–0; Ntini 10–0–56–2; Kallis 9–0–54–1; Hall 8.5–0–49–1; Boje 5–0–31–0; Dawson 5–0–31–0.

Umpires: S. J. A. Taufel (Australia) and D. R. Shepherd.
Third umpire: J. W. Lloyds. Referee: C. H. Lloyd (West Indies).

SOUTH AFRICA v ZIMBABWE

At Canterbury, June 29. South Africa won by 46 runs. South Africa 5 pts, Zimbabwe 1 pt. Toss: Zimbabwe.

Kallis's second hundred of the weekend, his tenth in one-day internationals and a career-best, proved the difference between the teams, although the outcome might well have been different had Hondo not missed a tough caught-and-bowled chance when Kallis had 21. After completing his century from 137 balls, Kallis scored a further 25 runs from only ten deliveries to build on some good work from the combative Hall, who had revived his team's faltering innings with a dashing 56 that included three sixes. Zimbabwe were up with the rate during a second-wicket stand of 109 between Ebrahim and the clean-striking Friend, but when Hall bowled Friend for 82, the rest of the batting subsided tamely. Earlier, there had been an unusual climax to the South African innings when, with one ball to go, the umpires removed Blignaut from the attack for bowling his second full toss above waist-height, a no-ball which Kallis swatted for six. The over, which cost 20 in all, was completed by Hondo.

Man of the Match: J. H. Kallis. *Attendance:* 5,518; *receipts* £80,849.

South Africa

*G. C. Smith lbw b Hondo	7	(21)
H. H. Gibbs b Blignaut	5	(9)
J. H. Kallis not out	125	(147)
J. A. Rudolph c Flower b Price	32	(45)
A. J. Hall c Flower b Ervine	56	(51)
†M. V. Boucher b Hondo	17	(21)
S. M. Pollock not out	12	(9)
L-b 4, w 11, n-b 3	18	
1/7 (2) 2/29 (1) 3/84 (4) 4/175 (5) 5/220 (6) (5 wkts, 50 overs)	272	
15 overs: 48-2		

M. van Jaarsveld, N. Boje, A. C. Dawson and M. Ntini did not bat.

Bowling: Streak 10–1–50–0; Blignaut 8.5–1–66–1; Hondo 9.1–3–29–2; Price 8–1–37–1; Ervine 5–0–39–1; Marillier 4–0–19–0; Flower 5–0–28–0.

Zimbabwe

Batting	R	(B)
D. A. Marillier c Boucher b Ntini.	3	(12)
D. D. Ebrahim c Smith b Boje. . .	40	(68)
T. J. Friend b Hall.	82	(93)
G. W. Flower c Dawson b Kallis .	27	(43)
S. Matsikenyeri run out	5	(15)
A. M. Blignaut c van Jaarsveld b Hall .	6	(10)
*H. H. Streak c Hall b Dawson . .	5	(6)
S. M. Ervine c Smith b Pollock . .	11	(15)
†T. Taibu not out.	18	(27)
R. W. Price b Hall.	8	(6)
D. T. Hondo not out.	12	(7)
L-b 2, w 5, n-b 2.	9	
(9 wkts, 50 overs)	226	

1/3 (1) 2/112 (2) 3/146 (3) 4/158 (5) 5/170 (6) 6/176 (7) 7/178 (4) 8/200 (8) 9/212 (10) 15 overs: 47-1

Bowling: Pollock 10–1–35–1; Ntini 10–1–44–1; Hall 9–0–38–3; Dawson 8–0–47–1; Boje 7–0–30–1; Kallis 6–0–30–1.

Umpires: B. F. Bowden (New Zealand) and N. A. Mallender.
Third umpire: P. Willey. Referee: C. H. Lloyd (West Indies).

ENGLAND v ZIMBABWE

At Leeds, July 1. No result. England 3 pts, Zimbabwe 3 pts. Toss: Zimbabwe. One-day international debut: Kabir Ali.

Both captains expressed their frustration with the competition rules after rain ruined a match that had already been reduced to the bare minimum of 25 overs a side by the weather. Play finally got under way at 3.50 p.m., but after less than 17 overs it rained again and, under ICC regulations, this meant the game had to be abandoned. This was especially unfortunate for Kabir Ali: handed his debut, he never took the field. In the play that was possible, England collapsed to 32 for four in typically testing Headingley conditions, before two local favourites, Vaughan and McGrath, gave the home crowd a little solace with an unbroken stand of 49.

Attendance: 7,593; *receipts* £170,947.

England

Batting	R	(B)
M. E. Trescothick c Flower b Streak .	3	(8)
V. S. Solanki c Flower b Streak . .	8	(9)
†C. M. W. Read run out	1	(4)
*M. P. Vaughan not out	35	(45)
A. Flintoff c Friend b Blignaut . .	6	(12)
A. McGrath not out.	15	(21)
B 2, l-b 5, w 6	13	
(4 wkts, 16.3 overs)	81	

1/11 (2) 2/12 (1) 3/13 (3) 4/32 (5) 7 overs: 29-3

J. O. Troughton, Kabir Ali, R. L. Johnson, D. Gough and J. M. Anderson did not bat.

Bowling: Streak 4–0–13–2; Hondo 4–0–16–0; Blignaut 4–0–14–1; Ervine 3–0–20–0; Brent 1–0–4–0; Friend 0.3–0–7–0.

Zimbabwe

D. A. Marillier, D. D. Ebrahim, T. J. Friend, G. W. Flower, †T. Taibu, S. Matsikenyeri, *H. H. Streak, S. M. Ervine, A. M. Blignaut, D. T. Hondo and G. B. Brent.

Umpires: S. J. A. Taufel (Australia) and D. R. Shepherd.
Third umpire: J. W. Lloyds. Referee: C. H. Lloyd (West Indies).

ENGLAND v SOUTH AFRICA

At Manchester, July 3 (day/night). South Africa won by seven wickets. South Africa 5 pts, England 1 pt. Toss: England.

Kallis's bid to become only the fourth player to make hundreds in three successive one-day internationals (after his team-mate Gibbs and the Pakistanis Zaheer Abbas and Saeed Anwar) narrowly failed. But few of his team-mates were complaining after he and Rudolph overturned the notion that batting under lights is a disadvantage. Kallis had to be content with an unbeaten 82 off 105 balls, which took his average for the tournament to an astonishing 314, and a match-winning stand of 145 with Rudolph, whose undefeated 71 off 101 was every bit as accomplished. On a day when the stretch of Warwick Road running outside the ground was officially renamed in honour of Brian Statham, the late England and Lancashire fast bowler, Pollock produced an opening spell of 7–4–5–1 of which Statham would surely have approved. England's innings had stagnated after the departure of Trescothick, before Read and Giles gave them some hope with a brisk eighth-wicket stand of 47.

Man of the Match: J. H. Kallis. *Attendance:* 18,575; *receipts* £447,357.

England

M. E. Trescothick c Boje b van Jaarsveld	60	(92)
V. S. Solanki c Boucher b Ntini	4	(9)
*M. P. Vaughan c Boucher b Pollock	3	(4)
A. McGrath st Boucher b Boje	52	(98)
A. Flintoff c Smith b Kallis	12	(27)
J. O. Troughton c Gibbs b Ntini	5	(22)
†C. M. W. Read not out	30	(27)
R. L. Johnson b Ntini	10	(6)
A. F. Giles not out	20	(18)
B 4, l-b 10, w 10, n-b 3	27	
1/4 (2) 2/7 (3) 3/121 (1) 4/140 (4) 5/162 (5) 6/162 (6) 7/176 (8) (7 wkts, 50 overs)	223	
15 overs: 48-2		

D. Gough and J. M. Anderson did not bat.

Bowling: Pollock 10–4–21–1; Ntini 8–0–38–3; Hall 7–0–43–0; Langeveldt 6–0–25–0; Boje 10–0–46–1; van Jaarsveld 5–1–18–1; Kallis 4–1–18–1.

South Africa

*G. C. Smith b Anderson	22	(34)
H. H. Gibbs run out	1	(7)
A. J. Hall b Flintoff	29	(40)
J. H. Kallis not out	82	(105)
J. A. Rudolph not out	71	(101)
L-b 11, w 9, n-b 2	22	
1/24 (2) 2/37 (1) 3/82 (3) (3 wkts, 47.3 overs)	227	
15 overs: 71-2		

†M. V. Boucher, S. M. Pollock, M. van Jaarsveld, N. Boje, C. K. Langeveldt and M. Ntini did not bat.

Bowling: Anderson 7–0–37–1; Gough 10–0–38–0; Flintoff 9.3–2–33–1; Johnson 7–0–30–0; Giles 9–0–51–0; Vaughan 5–0–27–0.

Umpires: B. F. Bowden (New Zealand) and N. A. Mallender.
Third umpire: P. Willey. Referee: C. H. Lloyd (West Indies).

SOUTH AFRICA v ZIMBABWE

At Cardiff, July 5. South Africa won by nine wickets. South Africa 6 pts. Toss: South Africa.

The match was all but over as a contest when Zimbabwe's fragile top order failed to come to terms with a lively pitch after being put in to bat. Streak showed what was possible with a defiant, hard-hitting half-century, but a total of 174 was never likely to trouble South Africa. In their reply, Streak was convinced he had the out-of-form Gibbs caught behind for nought, but umpire Willey was unmoved and Gibbs went on to regain his touch with an unbeaten 93 off 96 balls. One of his two sixes, a back-foot force over cover off the medium-pace of Friend, showed that he had lost none of his audacity. Smith ground down the bowling at the other end, and after the pair had put on 154 at five an over, van Jaarsveld helped complete the formalities with more than 15 overs in hand.

Man of the Match: H. H. Gibbs. *Attendance:* 2,574; *receipts* £32,849.

Zimbabwe

D. D. Ebrahim c Boucher b Kallis	20	(49)
D. A. Marillier c Rudolph b Ntini	4	(19)
T. J. Friend b Langeveldt	12	(20)
G. W. Flower b Hall	26	(49)
†T. Taibu lbw b Adams	19	(31)
S. Matsikenyeri c Rudolph b Hall	1	(12)
*H. H. Streak b Kallis	54	(72)
S. M. Ervine c Boucher b Kallis	18	(26)
A. M. Blignaut not out	13	(15)
R. W. Price not out	3	(7)
L-b 1, w 2, n-b 1	4	
1/11 (2) 2/36 (3) 3/38 (1) 4/67 (5) 5/80 (6) 6/92 (4) 7/144 (8) 8/167 (7) (8 wkts, 50 overs)	174	
15 overs: 36-2		

D. T. Hondo did not bat.

Bowling: Pollock 10–3–23–0; Ntini 10–2–36–1; Langeveldt 6–0–22–1; Kallis 10–0–47–3; Adams 8–0–26–1; Hall 6–2–19–2.

South Africa

*G. C. Smith c Taibu b Ervine	58	(99)
H. H. Gibbs not out	93	(96)
M. van Jaarsveld not out	8	(12)
L-b 4, w 11, n-b 1	16	
1/154 (1) (1 wkt, 34.2 overs)	175	
15 overs: 65-0		

A. J. Hall, J. H. Kallis, J. A. Rudolph, S. M. Pollock, P. R. Adams, †M. V. Boucher, C. K. Langeveldt and M. Ntini did not bat.

Bowling: Streak 6–1–16–0; Hondo 5–0–22–0; Blignaut 5–0–40–0; Marillier 3–0–20–0; Price 9–1–33–0; Friend 4–0–27–0; Ervine 2.2–0–13–1.

Umpires: S. J. A. Taufel (Australia) and P. Willey.
Third umpire: J. W. Lloyds. Referee: C. H. Lloyd (West Indies).

ENGLAND v ZIMBABWE

At Bristol, July 6. England won by six wickets. England 6 pts. Toss: England. One-day international debut: C. K. Coventry.

Complicated calculations about bonus points were rendered irrelevant as England ended Zimbabwe's hopes of reaching the final in merciless fashion. Inserted on a surface which offered far too much movement and bounce to the pace bowlers, Zimbabwe were bundled out for 92 in fewer than half their overs. Had not Vaughan shown a lack of ruthlessness by replacing Gough, who had taken four wickets in his first eight overs, with the ineffectual Harmison, Zimbabwe might have struggled to make as many as that. But the brevity of their innings meant there was still life in the surface when their turn came to bowl, and Streak exploited the conditions masterfully to take four wickets for no runs in 16 balls. But Flintoff, who had already picked up three for 13, restored order with a quickfire unbeaten 47 in 37 balls, characteristically ending the match with a six. The whole game was finished in less than 43 overs.

Man of the Match: A. Flintoff. *Attendance:* 12,393; *receipts* £289,092.

Zimbabwe

Batsman	Runs	Balls
D. D. Ebrahim c Trescothick b Gough	7	(22)
C. K. Coventry c Vaughan b Anderson	3	(10)
T. J. Friend c Read b Gough	4	(4)
G. W. Flower c Read b Gough	1	(21)
†T. Taibu c Trescothick b Johnson	5	(15)
S. Matsikenyeri b Flintoff	26	(35)
*H. H. Streak c Read b Gough	5	(5)
S. M. Ervine c Clarke b Johnson	0	(11)
A. M. Blignaut c Clarke b Flintoff	17	(21)
R. W. Price c Read b Flintoff	0	(4)
D. T. Hondo not out	0	(5)
B 1, l-b 3, w 16, n-b 4	24	
(24.5 overs)	92	

1/14 (2) 2/14 (1) 3/20 (3) 4/34 (5) 5/39 (4) 6/45 (7) 7/51 (8) 8/84 (6) 9/84 (10) 10/92 (9)   15 overs: 47-6

Bowling: Anderson 5–0–15–1; Gough 9–1–26–4; Johnson 5–0–16–2; Harmison 3–0–18–0; Flintoff 2.5–1–13–3.

England

Batsman	Runs	Balls
M. E. Trescothick c Friend b Streak	8	(11)
V. S. Solanki c Taibu b Streak	7	(23)
R. L. Johnson c Coventry b Streak	0	(2)
*M. P. Vaughan not out	11	(34)
A. McGrath c Flower b Streak	1	(5)
A. Flintoff not out	47	(37)
B 2, l-b 2, w 12, n-b 5	21	
(4 wkts, 17.5 overs)	95	

1/20 (1) 2/20 (3) 3/22 (2) 4/25 (5)   15 overs: 67-4

R. Clarke, †C. M. W. Read, D. Gough, S. J. Harmison and J. M. Anderson did not bat.

Bowling: Streak 9–3–21–4; Hondo 3–0–14–0; Blignaut 5.5–0–56–0.

Umpires: B. F. Bowden (New Zealand) and N. A. Mallender.
Third umpire: J. W. Lloyds. Referee: C. H. Lloyd (West Indies).

ENGLAND v SOUTH AFRICA

At Birmingham, July 8 (day/night). England won by four wickets. England 6 pts. Toss: South Africa.

The dress rehearsal for the final was also the match of the tournament. Set a modest 199 to win, England collapsed to 30 for three, before Vaughan, at last transferring his commandingly stylish Test form to the one-day arena with a career-best 83, and Flintoff shared a memorable century stand in 104 balls. Clarke, relishing the limelight, then made a 34-ball 37 that was rich in promise to set up victory with 11 overs to spare. South Africa had talked up their desire to score some valuable psychological points ahead of the final, and their aggressive approach was clear when Smith took 19 off Anderson's first over. Anderson later responded with a spell of three for none in nine balls to derail the innings, but it was Flintoff who removed the dangerman Kallis with a superlative diving catch in the floating-slip position. Tottering at 104 for seven halfway through their innings, South Africa managed to bat out their overs thanks to spirited knocks from van Jaarsveld and Adams. But it was not quite enough, and there was worse news for South Africa when Boje, on as a substitute fielder, broke a shin bone after falling awkwardly.

Man of the Match: A. Flintoff. *Attendance:* 20,504; *receipts* £523,819.

South Africa

Batsman	Runs	Balls
*G. C. Smith c McGrath b Flintoff	45	(39)
H. H. Gibbs c Clarke b Gough	2	(8)
J. H. Kallis c Flintoff b Johnson	15	(26)
A. J. Hall lbw b Johnson	3	(3)
J. A. Rudolph c McGrath b Anderson	16	(36)
†M. V. Boucher c Trescothick b Anderson	13	(25)
M. van Jaarsveld lbw b McGrath	45	(69)
S. M. Pollock c Flintoff b Anderson	0	(3)
P. R. Adams not out	33	(71)
A. Nel c Flintoff b Anderson	1	(2)
M. Ntini not out	10	(19)
L-b 6, w 8, n-b 1	15	
(9 wkts, 50 overs)	198	

1/28 (2) 2/65 (1) 3/67 (3) 4/74 (4) 5/99 (6) 6/104 (5) 7/104 (8) 8/175 (7) 9/177 (10)   15 overs: 74-4

Bowling: Anderson 10–2–38–4; Gough 10–3–29–1; Johnson 8–1–34–2; Flintoff 9–0–47–1; Giles 10–0–29–0; McGrath 3–0–15–1.

England

M. E. Trescothick c Hall b Pollock	8	(15)
V. S. Solanki c Nel b Ntini	2	(11)
*M. P. Vaughan lbw b Hall	83	(115)
A. McGrath b Kallis	11	(17)
A. Flintoff c Adams b Ntini	54	(40)
R. Clarke lbw b Adams	37	(34)
†C. M. W. Read not out	0	(2)
A. F. Giles not out	0	(0)
L-b 1, w 3	4	
1/11 (2) 2/11 (1) 3/30 (4) 4/130 (5) 5/194 (3) 6/198 (6)	(6 wkts, 39 overs) 199	
	15 overs: 65-3	

R. L. Johnson, D. Gough and J. M. Anderson did not bat.

Bowling: Pollock 6–1–15–1; Ntini 6–0–30–2; Kallis 6–0–43–1; Nel 8–1–38–0; Adams 6–0–44–1; Hall 7–0–28–1.

Umpires: S. J. A. Taufel (Australia) and D. R. Shepherd.
Third umpire: P. Willey. Referee: C. H. Lloyd (West Indies).

SOUTH AFRICA v ZIMBABWE

At Southampton, July 10. South Africa won by seven wickets. South Africa 6 pts. Toss: Zimbabwe.

The first international match staged in the majestic surroundings of the Rose Bowl was watched by a pleasingly large crowd. Unfortunately, many of them were still stuck in the traffic jam that clogged the one access road to the ground as Zimbabwe's top order caved in once more, this time to Ntini, who struck four times in his first six overs. The Zimbabwean coach Geoff Marsh had criticised English pitches the previous day – whether he was justified or not, his batsmen were again unable to cope with one, and provided a succession of catches behind the wicket as the ball shifted around. But from 74 for six, Streak engineered a minor recovery and reached a bloody-minded half-century off the last ball of the innings. Hondo removed Gibbs and van Jaarsveld in his first two overs to suggest Zimbabwe might make a game of it, but a third-wicket stand of 137 between Smith and Rudolph, both making 69, eased South Africa home with more than 14 overs left.

Man of the Match: M. Ntini. *Attendance:* 6,821; *receipts* £132,223.

Zimbabwe

G. W. Flower c Boucher b Ntini	1	(4)
D. D. Ebrahim c Boucher b Nel	27	(56)
T. J. Friend c van Jaarsveld b Ntini	4	(6)
†T. Taibu b Ntini	0	(1)
S. M. Ervine c Pollock b Ntini	17	(35)
S. Matsikenyeri c Boucher b Nel	7	(20)
R. W. Sims c Boucher b Pollock	24	(60)
*H. H. Streak not out	50	(90)
A. M. Blignaut b Adams	1	(6)
R. W. Price not out	17	(25)
W 22, n-b 3	25	
1/11 (1) 2/18 (3) 3/18 (4) 4/49 (5) 5/68 (6) 6/74 (2) 7/128 (7) 8/129 (9)	(8 wkts, 50 overs) 173	
	15 overs: 58-4	

D. T. Hondo did not bat.

Bowling: Pollock 10–1–40–1; Ntini 10–1–45–4; Nel 10–3–33–2; Hall 10–2–25–0; Adams 10–1–30–1.

South Africa

*G. C. Smith c Ebrahim b Friend.	69	(80)
H. H. Gibbs b Hondo	2	(5)
M. van Jaarsveld c Taibu b Hondo	5	(11)
J. A. Rudolph not out.	69	(97)
†M. V. Boucher not out	13	(22)
B 3, l-b 4, w 6, n-b 3 . .	16	
1/2 (2) (3 wkts, 35.2 overs)	174	
2/8 (3) 3/145 (1) 15 overs: 56-2		

H. H. Dippenaar, A. J. Hall, S. M. Pollock, P. R. Adams, A. Nel and M. Ntini did not bat.

Bowling: Streak 7–1–27–0; Hondo 7–2–25–2; Blignaut 6–0–31–0; Price 7.2–0–33–0; Sims 3–0–18–0; Friend 5–0–33–1.

Umpires: B. F. Bowden (New Zealand) and D. R. Shepherd.
Third umpire: N. A. Mallender. Referee: C. H. Lloyd (West Indies).

QUALIFYING TABLE

	Played	*Won*	*Lost*	*No result*	*Bonus Points*	*Points*	*Net run-rate*
South Africa	6	4	2	0	3	23	0.48
England	6	3	2	1	4	22	0.82
Zimbabwe	6	1	4	1	1	9	–1.37

Win = 5 pts; no result = 3 pts. One bonus point awarded either to the winning team for achieving victory with a run-rate 1.25 times that of the opposition or to the losing team for denying the winners a bonus point. Net run-rate is calculated by subtracting runs conceded per over from runs scored per over.

FINAL

ENGLAND v SOUTH AFRICA

At Lord's, July 12. England won by seven wickets. Toss: England. One-day international debut: M. N. van Wyk.

England, demonstrating a ruthlessness many felt beyond them, inflicted a record-breaking defeat upon South Africa in an unexpectedly – and gruesomely – one-sided final. In their first one-day appearance at Lord's, South Africa were asked to bat and were promptly bowled out for 107, the lowest score in 34 one-day internationals at the ground. Not one of their batsmen reached 20.

The obvious conclusion, that the toss decided the match, was unfair on the head groundsman, Mick Hunt, who produced a pitch which had a little moisture to start with, but displayed even bounce throughout. The fault lay instead with a sequence of flat-footed strokes from South Africa, some of them batting on the Lord's slope for the first time. Read benefited to the tune of five catches, while England's discipline with the ball was exemplified by Gough, whose opening burst of seven overs cost just nine runs.

In the circumstances, the 50 conceded by Anderson felt almost indecently expensive, but he was the only man to bowl his full quota, and he took three wickets, including the ball of the innings – a full-length off-cutter that came back sharply to bowl the debutant Morne van Wyk. The wicket that symbolised England's dominance, however, was that of Kallis, who came into the match with a tournament average of 164.50, but was out for a 12-ball nought when he edged Gough through to Read. Kallis flew home to Cape Town immediately after the game to be with his dying father.

The South African innings lasted just 32.1 overs, and England's reply was even quicker. After Trescothick edged to slip in the second over, Solanki overcame a cautious start to hit a 58-ball half-century and take England to the brink of victory with the help of Vaughan. Both men fell in successive overs, but McGrath and Flintoff supplied the finishing touches.

At the end of the match Smith gathered his players around him on the outfield, a sight more usually associated with winning teams. He told his players to "remember the hurt" of this defeat. It was a neat way of converting humiliation into motivation and, as far as England were concerned, it worked all too quickly.

Man of the Match: D. Gough. *Attendance:* 26,369; *receipts* £800,407.
Man of the Series: A. Flintoff.

South Africa

Batsman	Runs	Balls
*G. C. Smith c Trescothick b Anderson	7	(7)
H. H. Gibbs c Read b Gough	9	(25)
M. N. van Wyk b Anderson	17	(20)
J. H. Kallis c Read b Gough	0	(12)
J. A. Rudolph c Read b Flintoff	19	(40)
†M. V. Boucher c Read b Johnson	11	(31)
M. van Jaarsveld c and b Giles	11	(20)
S. M. Pollock c Read b Flintoff	18	(22)
A. J. Hall c Vaughan b Anderson	0	(4)
A. Nel lbw b Giles	1	(11)
M. Ntini not out	0	(4)
L-b 1, w 10, n-b 3	14	
(32.1 overs)	107	

1/10 (1) 2/30 (2) 3/39 (3) 4/43 (4) 5/75 (5) 6/75 (6) 7/102 (7) 8/103 (9) 9/107 (10) 10/107 (8) 15 overs: 56-4

Bowling: Anderson 10–0–50–3; Gough 7–2–9–2; Flintoff 6.1–0–18–2; Johnson 6–1–26–1; Giles 3–2–3–2.

England

Batsman	Runs	Balls
M. E. Trescothick c Hall b Ntini	0	(9)
V. S. Solanki b Hall	50	(58)
*M. P. Vaughan c Ntini b Nel	30	(29)
A. McGrath not out	15	(15)
A. Flintoff not out	6	(13)
L-b 1, w 7, n-b 2	10	
(3 wkts, 20.2 overs)	111	

1/1 (1) 2/88 (3) 3/89 (2) 15 overs: 87-1

R. Clarke, †C. M. W. Read, A. F. Giles, R. L. Johnson, D. Gough and J. M. Anderson did not bat.

Bowling: Pollock 5–1–17–0; Ntini 5–1–24–1; Kallis 3–0–33–0; Nel 5–0–22–1; Hall 2.2–0–14–1.

Umpires: S. J. A. Taufel (Australia) and N. A. Mallender.
Third umpire: J. W. Lloyds. Referee: C. H. Lloyd (West Indies).

INDIA A IN ENGLAND, 2003

In a summer that lingers in the memory for sunshine and warmth, the Indian tourists were cruelly dogged by rain. Their one-day matches went unscathed – and they went unbeaten – but it was a different matter for their first-class fixtures.

Four of the seven were severely disrupted, though the clouds at Nottingham did at least have a silver lining when they forced the captains into mutual forfeits, and the agreed target proved well within the Indians' range. It was their only first-class win, though they were in no danger of defeat in the other six, and against Durham and Surrey they held much the upper hand.

The coach for the tour was Sandeep Patil, the former Indian Test batsman who guided Kenya to the semi-finals of the World Cup just three months earlier. That achievement had prompted speculation that he would succeed John Wright as national coach, and so Patil, who had held the post for a few months in 1996, was under almost as much scrutiny as his squad.

The party he brought was an experienced one, with 12 of the 16 having represented India at Test or one-day level. And they were given plenty of incentive to perform: Patil made it clear that anyone who shone on this six-week tour would have an excellent chance of stepping up to the senior side. Competition among the openers was especially keen since Sanjay Bangar's place in the Test team was looking vulnerable, while Virender Sehwag was not guaranteed an opening slot.

Leading the pack of aspirants was the captain, Shiv Sunder Das, with 23 Tests to his name. He began the first-class games with a hundred against Durham and remained reliable, though he did not quite sparkle as he might have wished. Four others opened at one stage or another, and although there were decent scores from them all, no one did enough to get the nod when in October the selectors did indeed plump for a new opener. Aakash Chopra, ruled out of this tour with a knee injury, was chosen.

Part of the problem for the batsmen was that it was impossible to judge just what their runs were worth. "We were very happy with our itinerary," Patil said, "but disappointed that few sides put out strong teams. We would have liked to have played an England A team to test ourselves." It was a familiar, valid gripe: none of the counties put out full-strength teams, and Surrey, capable of fielding 11 internationals, selected five youngsters to make their first-class debuts. Even at Arundel, against the touring South African side, the match was treated as an extended net session.

Given the weakness of the opposition, it was important that the Indians avoided defeat, which they did. And there were several positives to emerge from the visit. The wicket-keeper, Parthiv Patel, still only 18, hit his maiden first-class hundred, against Yorkshire, while Ambati Rayudu, even younger at 17, confirmed what a huge prospect he is with wristy, elegant performances against Nottinghamshire and Surrey. Meanwhile, Rohan Gavaskar looked as though he were emerging from the shadow of his illustrious father – and in January 2004 was called up to the senior one-day side for the VB Series in

Australia. Run-scoring generally was a strength, and only one member of the squad, Vijay Bharadwaj, would look back at the tour as an opportunity missed.

The bowling – inevitably subject to the same caveat as the batting – perhaps achieved slightly less. Amit Bhandari, a right-arm seamer, was most penetrative, though an 18-year-old, the brisk left-armer Irfan Pathan, caught the eye with nine (admittedly expensive) wickets. There were high hopes for the leg-spinner Amit Mishra, but the conditions did not always favour him – or the left-arm spinner Murali Kartik – and Patil would have struggled to draw meaningful conclusions from their combined 270 overs.

Overall, despite a spate of injuries, the squad performed well as a unit, banana skins were avoided, and there were none of the discipline problems that had plagued West Indies A the previous year. All that was really missing was a proper commitment to the tour on the part of the counties and the ECB. That, it seems, is asking too much.

INDIA A TOURING PARTY

S. S. Das (Orissa) (*captain*), H. K. Badani (Tamil Nadu), L. Balaji (Tamil Nadu), A. Bhandari (Delhi), R. V. Bharadwaj (Karnataka), G. Gambhir (Delhi), R. S. Gavaskar (Bengal), M. Kartik (Railways), A. Mishra (Haryana), S. S. Parab (Baroda), P. A. Patel (Gujarat), I. K. Pathan (Baroda), A. T. Rayudu (Hyderabad), A. M. Salvi (Mumbai), S. Sriram (Tamil Nadu), Wasim Jaffer (Mumbai).

Badani captained India A in their one-day matches.

Coach: S. M. Patil. *Manager:* S. Chakraborty. *Physiotherapist:* V. Dhaga.

INDIA A TOUR RESULTS

First-class matches – Played 7: Won 1, Drawn 6.
Win – Nottinghamshire.
Draws – Durham, Yorkshire, Surrey, South Africans, Glamorgan, Warwickshire.
Non first-class matches – Played 4: Won 4. *Wins* – British Universities, Leicestershire, Lancashire, Gloucestershire.

INDIA A TOUR AVERAGES – FIRST-CLASS MATCHES

BATTING

	M	*I*	*NO*	*R*	*HS*	*100s*	*50s*	*Avge*	*Ct/St*
†S. Sriram	3	4	1	322	115	2	1	107.33	0
A. T. Rayudu	5	7	4	262	101*	1	1	87.33	1
†P. A. Patel	7	7	3	238	129	1	0	59.50	15/3
Wasim Jaffer	6	9	0	522	218	1	3	58.00	2
†G. Gambhir	4	6	1	277	130*	1	1	55.40	2
†H. K. Badani	5	7	2	248	133	1	1	49.60	5
S. S. Das	7	10	0	428	125	1	3	42.80	8
A. Mishra	6	5	1	89	52*	0	1	22.25	1
A. Bhandari	7	4	3	12	5*	0	0	12.00	1
L. Balaji	6	4	0	29	14	0	0	7.25	1
†I. K. Pathan	5	4	2	8	6	0	0	4.00	2

Played in four matches: †M. Kartik (1 ct); A. M. Salvi 0, 0, 0 (1 ct). Played in three matches: R. V. Bharadwaj 7, 1, 12* (2 ct); †R. S. Gavaskar 139*, 16, 61 (1 ct). Played in two matches: S. S. Parab 4, 0, 90.

† *Left-handed batsman.*

BOWLING

	Style	*O*	*M*	*R*	*W*	*BB*	*5W/i*	*Avge*
A. Bhandari	RFM	119.2	23	424	16	6-38	2	26.50
A. M. Salvi	RM	87	25	267	9	4-92	0	29.66
L. Balaji	RFM	137	32	430	12	3-58	0	35.83
A. Mishra	LB	134	22	468	13	5-183	1	36.00
M. Kartik	SLA	135.5	27	400	10	4-112	0	40.00
I. K. Pathan	LFM	124	28	394	9	4-60	0	43.77

Also bowled: H. K. Badani (SLA) 1–1–0–0; R. V. Bharadwaj (OB) 3–0–13–0; G. Gambhir (LB) 1–0–3–0; R. S. Gavaskar (SLA) 6–3–10–0; A. T. Rayudu (OB) 3–0–13–0; S. Sriram (SLA) 11–2–43–0.

Note: Matches in this section which were not first-class are signified with a dagger.

†At Durham, June 25. **India A won by eight wickets.** Toss: British Universities. **British Universities 221-9** (50 overs) (R. A. White 52, J. D. Francis 40, M. L. Pettini 34, R. S. Ferley 35*; A. Mishra 4-41); **India A 224-2** (42.3 overs) (G. Gambhir 128*, R. S. Gavaskar 41, H. K. Badani 33*).

DURHAM v INDIA A

At Chester-le-Street, June 27, 28, 29, 30. Drawn. Toss: Durham.

By way of explanation for his side's reluctance to take risks, Sandeep Patil, the India A coach, revealed that the Test selectors were on the look-out for an opening batsman. A docile pitch scarcely helped, and it was a merciful relief for the 66 paying spectators when rain ended the dour fare an over after lunch on the fourth day. Four of India A's top five had played Test cricket (though the only household name at the Riverside was not actually playing: Durham paraded their new overseas recruit, Shoaib Akhtar, at tea on the first day). Two of those with Test experience, Das and Badani, made determined centuries as India A batted for five sessions. Durham then scored even more slowly, though it provided invaluable experience for Muchall, who showed great patience against high-class slow bowling from left-armer Murali Kartik and leg-spinner Amit Mishra to compile his third first-class hundred.

Close of play: First day, India A 275-3 (Badani 43, Patel 21); Second day, Durham 94-1 (Gough 25, Muchall 41); Third day, India A 3-0 (Das 3, Gambhir 0).

India A

*S. S. Das c Wells b Hunter	125	– c Pratt b Hatch	31
Wasim Jaffer c Lewis b Hunter	43	– (3) b Hatch	15
G. Gambhir c Mustard b Hatch	35	– (2) b Davies	4
H. K. Badani st Mustard b Gough	133		
†P. A. Patel c Pratt b Hatch	21	– not out	15
A. T. Rayudu c Wells b Phillips	25	– (4) not out	29
M. Kartik c Hatch b Phillips	50		
A. Mishra c Lewis b Phillips	10		
L. Balaji st Mustard b Phillips	14		
A. Bhandari not out	5		
I. K. Pathan not out	0		
B 8, l-b 10, n-b 3	21	L-b 1	1
1/122 (2) 2/202 (3) 3/212 (1) 4/275 (5) 5/346 (6) 6/402 (4) 7/455 (8) 8/467 (7) 9/477 (9) (9 wkts dec.)	482	1/16 (2) 2/47 (1) 3/52 (3) (3 wkts)	95

Bowling: *First Innings*—Hatch 33–5–77–2; Hunter 18–2–55–2; Davies 31–6–104–0; Muchall 12–1–49–0; Wells 16–3–41–0; Phillips 34–4–126–4; Gough 3–1–12–1. *Second Innings*—Hatch 12–2–23–2; Davies 8–3–16–1; Hunter 6–1–21–0; Phillips 4–0–16–0; Wells 3–0–18–0.

Durham

*J. J. B. Lewis b Bhandari	20
M. A. Gough st Patel b Mishra	56
G. J. Muchall c Patel b Mishra	121
G. J. Pratt c sub b Kartik	10
N. Peng c Patel b Kartik	5
V. J. Wells c Pathan b Mishra	1
†P. Mustard c Rayudu b Kartik	2
I. D. Hunter c Gambhir b Kartik	44
N. C. Phillips b Balaji	19
A. M. Davies not out	9
N. G. Hatch not out	3
B 4, l-b 10, w 2, n-b 27	43
1/36 (1) 2/175 (2) 3/204 (4) 4/232 (5) 5/240 (3) 6/241 (6) 7/244 (7) 8/310 (8) 9/327 (9)	(9 wkts dec.) 333

Bowling: Balaji 18–3–45–1; Pathan 19–6–37–0; Bhandari 8–0–37–1; Kartik 45–10–112–4; Mishra 32–7–85–3; Gambhir 1–0–3–0.

Umpires: A. Hill and G. Sharp.

NOTTINGHAMSHIRE v INDIA A

At Nottingham, July 2, 3, 4. India A won by seven wickets. Toss: Nottinghamshire. First-class debut: A. C. Thomas. County debut: D. L. Vettori.

India A showed off their batting prowess by scampering to a target of 340 runs with oceans of time to spare. On the shower-interrupted first day, Afzaal responded to being dropped from the Championship side by making an unbeaten hundred. The second day was washed out, but on the third he went to a career-best 161 not out – sharing a stand of 160 with Clough, who hit a maiden fifty – before Franks generously agreed a declaration and mutual forfeits, giving India A a minimum of 86 overs. They lost two early wickets, but thereafter their batsmen held sway. Gavaskar, son of the Indian legend, Sunil, strode out with some aggressive shots, including 17 fours and four sixes. Parab also sparkled before the 17-year-old Ambati Rayudu revealed why many rate him so highly. All took advantage of a short boundary and some feeble bowling; Vettori, on his Nottinghamshire debut, cost more than seven an over.

Close of play: First day, Nottinghamshire 265-3 (Afzaal 114, Clough 39); Second day, No play.

Nottinghamshire

D. J. Bicknell c Bhandari b Balaji	52
G. E. Welton b Balaji	25
U. Afzaal not out	161
B. M. Shafayat c Wasim Jaffer b Kartik	6
G. D. Clough b Pathan	55
D. L. Vettori c Patel b Kartik	10
L-b 13, w 1, n-b 16	30
1/51 (2) 2/140 (1) 3/154 (4) 4/314 (5) 5/339 (6)	(5 wkts dec.) 339

R. J. Logan, *P. J. Franks, †A. C. Thomas, A. J. Harris and C. E. Shreck did not bat.

Bowling: Balaji 25–2–94–2; Bhandari 18–1–68–0; Pathan 20–8–72–1; Kartik 27.5–5–64–2; Bharadwaj 3–0–13–0; Gavaskar 2–0–9–0; Rayudu 1–0–6–0.

Nottinghamshire forfeited their second innings.

India A

India A forfeited their first innings.

*S. S. Das c Thomas b Harris	18	R. S. Gavaskar not out	139
Wasim Jaffer b Shreck	0	L-b 7, w 1, n-b 15	23
S. S. Parab b Vettori	90		
A. T. Rayudu not out	71	1/19 (2) 2/21 (1) 3/169 (3) (3 wkts)	341

†P. A. Patel, M. Kartik, R. V. Bharadwaj, L. Balaji, I. K. Pathan and A. Bhandari did not bat.

Bowling: Harris 9–3–21–1; Shreck 14–2–51–1; Vettori 14–0–104–1; Logan 14–1–79–0; Franks 11–0–49–0; Clough 5–0–23–0; Shafayat 1–0–3–0; Bicknell 0.3–0–4–0.

Umpires: N. L. Bainton and V. A. Holder.

†At Leicester, July 6. **India A won by four wickets.** Toss: Leicestershire. **Leicestershire 262-3** (50 overs) (P. A. Nixon 76, D. I. Stevens 101*, T. R. Ward 45); **India A 263-6** (44.3 overs) (G. Gambhir 74, H. K. Badani 111*; D. D. Masters 3-71).

YORKSHIRE v INDIA A

At Leeds, July 9, 10, 11. Drawn. Toss: Yorkshire.

Yorkshire took little interest in this fixture, fielding a weak team – in marked contrast to an India A side that contained nine players with full international experience – and barely promoting it, so that a mere sprinkling of spectators turned up. Wiping out a first-innings deficit of 90, Yorkshire batted throughout the final day as the game limped to an inevitable draw, with neither side making any attempt at a positive result. Lumb enhanced his reputation with a fifty in each innings, but the highlight was a maiden first-class century for 18-year-old wicket-keeper/batsman Parthiv Patel, whose 129 from 146 balls contained 22 elegant boundaries, the majority well-executed ground shots through the off side.

Close of play: First day, India A 29-1 (Wasim Jaffer 22, Gambhir 5); Second day, Yorkshire 27-1 (Wood 6, Craven 11).

Yorkshire

C. R. Taylor lbw b Pathan	13	– c Das b Bhandari	4
*M. J. Wood b Bhandari	5	– c Patel b Kartik	88
V. J. Craven c Kartik b Pathan	27	– b Kartik	46
M. J. Lumb c Badani b Mishra	65	– c Wasim Jaffer b Balaji	56
G. M. Fellows lbw b Pathan	17	– c Patel b Balaji	11
C. White c Gavaskar b Mishra	31	– not out	21
†R. J. Blakey c and b Balaji	1	– b Kartik	20
A. K. D. Gray c Badani b Mishra	15	– not out	34
T. T. Bresnan c Patel b Pathan	52		
P. J. Swanepoel lbw b Mishra	1		
N. D. Thornicroft not out	1		
B 6, l-b 7, w 2, n-b 3	18	B 8, l-b 6, n-b 2	16
1/10 (2) 2/41 (1) 3/60 (3) 4/109 (5) 5/161 (4) 6/162 (7) 7/178 (6) 8/223 (8) 9/244 (10) 10/246 (9)	246	1/5 (1) 2/88 (3) 3/192 (4) 4/214 (2) 5/214 (5) 6/249 (7) (6 wkts dec.)	296

Bowling: *First Innings*—Balaji 16–4–52–1; Bhandari 16–5–51–1; Pathan 15.2–3–60–4; Mishra 21–5–42–4; Kartik 9–2–28–0. *Second Innings*—Balaji 19–6–51–2; Bhandari 12–4–36–1; Påthan 17–4–73–0; Kartik 25–5–76–3; Mishra 16–2–45–0; Gavaskar 4–3–1–0; Badani 1–1–0–0.

India A

*S. S. Das c Blakey b Bresnan	2	L. Balaji lbw b Gray	3
Wasim Jaffer lbw b Bresnan	67	I. K. Pathan not out	2
G. Gambhir run out	26		
H. K. Badani run out	17	B 2, l-b 6, n-b 1	9
†P. A. Patel c Blakey b Wood	129		—
R. S. Gavaskar c Fellows b Bresnan	16	1/7 (1) 2/91 (2) 3/112 (4) (8 wkts dec.)	336
M. Kartik c Gray b Fellows	13	4/113 (3) 5/173 (6)	
A. Mishra not out	52	6/228 (7) 7/297 (5) 8/310 (9)	

A. Bhandari did not bat.

Bowling: Thornicroft 14–2–57–0; Bresnan 21.1–4–88–3; Swanepoel 17–5–59–0; Gray 26–8–64–1; Craven 3–0–14–0; Fellows 5–1–21–1; Lumb 1–0–7–0; Wood 6–0–18–1.

Umpires: G. I. Burgess and R. K. Illingworth.

†At Blackpool, July 13. **India A won by one wicket.** Toss: India A. **Lancashire 191** (47 overs) (C. P. Schofield 69*, G. I. Maiden 62; A. M. Salvi 3-38, I. K. Pathan 4-19, L. Balaji 3-37); **India A 192-9** (44.4 overs) (Extras 30; S. I. Mahmood 3-28).

Lancashire had slipped to 61 for eight before Schofield and Maiden, each making their highest one-day score, added 130. In reply, India A lost their ninth wicket at 155, but the last pair – Pathan and Salvi – constructed the highest partnership of the innings to see them home. Seven Indian batsmen reached 17, but none passed 23.

SURREY v INDIA A

At The Oval, July 15, 16, 17. Drawn. Toss: Surrey. First-class debuts: J. G. E. Benning, J. Dernbach, N. C. Saker, B. J. M. Scott, M. J. Todd.

Surrey's young hopefuls – five were making their first-class debuts – soon discovered they were out of their depth against a touring team beginning to hit their stride. Surrey fell woefully short of setting a challenging target, and then found their opponents rather more successful with the bat. Clarke bowled a few good spells, while teenagers Neil Saker and South Africa-born Jade Dernbach also impressed, though not as much as the Indians. At 17 years 134 days, Dernbach became the youngest Surrey debutant since David Smith played against Cambridge University in 1973 when 11 days younger. Rayudu, another 17-year-old, scored a stylish century at a run a ball, upstaging earlier hundreds by Gambhir and Sriram, and helping the tourists to a first-innings lead of 289. But it counted for nothing when rain stole the entire last day.

Close of play: First day, India A 235-2 (Sriram 92, Gambhir 43); Second day, Surrey 39-0 (Newman 6, Batty 27).

Surrey

*S. A. Newman c Salvi b Bhandari	27	– not out	6
†J. N. Batty c Patel b Bhandari	24	– not out	27
N. Shahid c Gambhir b Bhandari	0		
R. Clarke c Patel b Balaji	38		
A. D. Brown c Patel b Salvi	0		
J. G. E. Benning c Das b Mishra	22		
B. J. M. Scott c Das b Bhandari	16		
T. J. Murtagh c Patel b Bhandari	12		
M. J. Todd not out	6		
N. C. Saker c Das b Salvi	5		
J. Dernbach c Das b Salvi	3		
L-b 4, w 2, n-b 14	20	L-b 2, w 1, n-b 3	6
	—		—
1/55 (1) 2/55 (3) 3/73 (2) 4/75 (5) 5/122 (4) 6/144 (7) 7/144 (6) 8/158 (8) 9/164 (10) 10/173 (11)	173	(no wkt)	39

Bowling: *First Innings*—Salvi 12–3–49–3; Balaji 9–2–50–1; Bhandari 15–4–54–5; Mishra 8–4–16–1. *Second Innings*—Salvi 4–1–7–0; Bhandari 3–0–20–0; Balaji 3–0–8–0; Mishra 2–0–2–0.

India A

*S. S. Das lbw b Todd	74
Wasim Jaffer c Batty b Dernbach	21
S. Sriram c Batty b Clarke	115
G. Gambhir not out	130
R. V. Bharadwaj c Shahid b Clarke	7
A. T. Rayudu not out	101
B 2, l-b 5, w 3, n-b 4	14
1/48 (2) 2/150 (1) 3/276 (3) 4/291 (5)	(4 wkts dec.) 462

†P. A. Patel, A. Mishra, L. Balaji, A. M. Salvi and A. Bhandari did not bat.

Bowling: Murtagh 17.5–0–81–0; Saker 15–1–76–0; Dernbach 13–3–74–1; Clarke 18–5–36–2; Benning 5–0–42–0; Todd 14–0–92–1; Shahid 9–1–42–0; Brown 2–0–7–0; Newman 1–0–5–0.

Umpires: J. H. Evans and S. A. Garratt.

At Arundel, July 19, 20, 21. INDIA A drew with SOUTH AFRICANS (see South African tour section).

GLAMORGAN v INDIA A

At Swansea, July 24, 25, 26. Drawn. Toss: India A.

With almost half the playing time lost to rain – and Croft's suggestion of a manufactured run-chase declined – India A drew their fifth first-class game out of six. On the first day, at 142 for two, the Indians seemed set for a healthy total, but then Croft dismissed Gavaskar as part of a burst of three for three, and his wicket was the catalyst for a spectacular collapse in which eight batsmen fell for 23. In only his third first-class game of the season, Darren Thomas swung the ball appreciably in helpful conditions and grabbed four for four in 12 balls. But Glamorgan also found batting difficult, and the Indian pace attack occasionally extracted alarming lift, reducing them to 55 for four. Then Shaw and Wallace, Glamorgan's former No. 1 wicket-keeper and his successor, inched them toward parity. Once they departed, though, the innings folded quickly. Bhandari took six for 38, the best figures of the tour for India A. Rain, a constant companion for the tourists, returned on the last day, and the match petered out.

Close of play: First day, India A 149-6 (Patel 1); Second day, Glamorgan 104-4 (Shaw 27, Wallace 24).

India A

*S. S. Das c Cosker b Harrison	14		
S. S. Parab c Croft b Harrison	4	– (1) c Powell b Harrison	0
S. Sriram c Powell b Croft	62		
R. S. Gavaskar c Parkin b Croft	61		
R. V. Bharadwaj lbw b Parkin	1	– (3) not out	12
H. K. Badani lbw b Croft	0		
†P. A. Patel b S. D. Thomas	5	– (2) not out	14
A. Mishra b S. D. Thomas	2		
L. Balaji lbw b S. D. Thomas	7		
A. Bhandari not out	3		
A. M. Salvi b S. D. Thomas	0		
B 4, l-b 1, w 1	6	L-b 1	1
1/7 (2) 2/26 (1) 3/142 (4) 4/145 (5) 5/146 (6) 6/149 (3) 7/155 (7) 8/162 (8) 9/165 (9) 10/165 (11)	165	1/0 (1)	(1 wkt) 27

Bowling: *First Innings*—S. D. Thomas 13–1–47–4; Harrison 13–5–27–2; Parkin 9–3–19–1; Croft 20–3–55–3; Cosker 5–1–12–0. *Second Innings*—Harrison 4–2–9–1; Parkin 3–2–3–0; Cosker 2–0–11–0; S. D. Thomas 1–0–3–0.

Glamorgan

I. J. Thomas c Das b Bhandari	10
J. Hughes c Bharadwaj b Salvi	15
D. D. Cherry b Balaji	9
M. J. Powell c Bharadwaj b Bhandari	0
A. D. Shaw c Patel b Balaji	33
†M. A. Wallace b Balaji	29
D. A. Cosker c Badani b Bhandari	1
S. D. Thomas b Bhandari	0
D. S. Harrison c Mishra b Bhandari	7
*R. D. B. Croft not out	12
O. T. Parkin b Bhandari	2
B 8, l-b 6, w 2, n-b 6	22
1/22 (2) 2/33 (1) 3/35 (4) 4/55 (3) 5/111 (5) 6/117 (7) 7/117 (8) 8/117 (6) 9/136 (9) 10/140 (11)	140

Bowling: Salvi 16–6–22–1; Balaji 16–3–58–3; Bhandari 13.2–3–38–6; Mishra 4–2–7–0; Sriram 1–0–1–0.

Umpires: M. Dixon and R. Palmer.

†At Cheltenham, July 28. **India A won by 69 runs.** Toss: India A. **India A 262-8** (50 overs) (S. Sriram 50, H. K. Badani 48, R. S. Gavaskar 34, A. T. Rayudu 54; I. D. Fisher 3-45); **Gloucestershire 193** (44.2 overs) (C. Z. Harris 65, Shoaib Malik 36; I. K. Pathan 3-38, M. Kartik 3-44).

WARWICKSHIRE v INDIA A

At Birmingham, July 30, 31, August 1, 2. Drawn. Toss: India A. First-class debut: I. J. Westwood.

India A finished their tour unbeaten thanks to a double-century from Wasim Jaffer, though they were outplayed by a depleted Warwickshire side for most of the first three days. On an underprepared pitch so green it was indistinguishable from the rest of the square, the Indians bowled too short, and Warwickshire made untroubled progress to an imposing total, their highest without a century. The most entertaining innings came from Wagg, whose 74 from 52 balls included seven sixes, six from the leg-spin of Mishra. In reply, India A reached 117 for one before Bell's intelligent out-swing destroyed the middle order: he took four wickets, and Wagg two, as the Indians lost six for 11. Powell enforced the follow-on, but Jaffer had the last word. He struck 38 fours and a six, faced 269 balls, batted five and a half hours and shared a second-wicket stand of 247 in just 45 overs with Sriram.

Close of play: First day, Warwickshire 302-4 (Bell 71, Frost 30); Second day, India A 5-0 (Das 5, Wasim Jaffer 0); Third day, India A 70-0 (Das 22, Wasim Jaffer 32).

Warwickshire

*M. J. Powell lbw b Mishra	68
I. J. Westwood b Bhandari	19
I. J. L. Trott c Patel b Balaji	78
I. R. Bell c Badani b Salvi	75
D. P. Ostler c Das b Balaji	10
†T. Frost st Patel b Mishra	76
M. A. Sheikh c sub b Mishra	42
C. O. Obuya not out	36
G. G. Wagg c Badani b Mishra	74
M. M. Betts st Patel b Mishra	21
N. M. Carter b Pathan	0
B 2, l-b 13, w 17, n-b 6	38
1/54 (2) 2/137 (1) 3/180 (3) 4/213 (5) 5/310 (4) 6/392 (6) 7/401 (7) 8/496 (9) 9/534 (10) 10/537 (11)	537

Bowling: Salvi 26–8–97–1; Pathan 24–4–69–1; Bhandari 16–3–55–1; Balaji 31–12–72–2; Mishra 35–2–183–5; Sriram 10–2–42–0; Rayudu 1–0–4–0.

India A

*S. S. Das c Powell b Bell	51	– c and b Obuya	65
Wasim Jaffer b Betts	14	– lbw b Sheikh	218
S. Sriram c Bell b Wagg	41	– not out	104
H. K. Badani lbw b Bell	3	– not out	14
A. T. Rayudu c Frost b Wagg	0		
†P. A. Patel not out	46		
A. Mishra b Bell	0		
I. K. Pathan c Ostler b Bell	0		
L. Balaji c Frost b Betts	5		
A. Bhandari c Powell b Sheikh	3		
A. M. Salvi b Sheikh	0		
B 8, w 1, n-b 9	18	B 4, l-b 19, w 3, n-b 22	48
1/27 (2) 2/117 (3) 3/121 (1) 4/124 (5) 5/124 (4) 6/124 (7) 7/128 (8) 8/166 (9) 9/181 (10) 10/181 (11)	181	1/151 (1) 2/398 (2) (2 wkts dec.)	449

Bowling: *First Innings*—Betts 11–3–34–2; Carter 11–4–36–0; Sheikh 12.5–4–30–2; Wagg 9–2–61–2; Bell 9–4–12–4. *Second Innings*—Betts 15–3–51–0; Sheikh 18–2–69–1; Carter 12–3–43–0; Obuya 18–0–96–1; Trott 12–1–47–0; Bell 9–1–49–0; Westwood 8–0–57–0; Powell 3–0–14–0.

Umpires: R. J. Bailey and B. Leadbeater.

HONOURS' LIST, 2003-04

In 2003-04, the following were decorated for their services to cricket:

Queen's Birthday Honours, 2003: D. S. English (services to charity) MBE, A. J. Stewart (Surrey and England) OBE.

Queen's Birthday Honours (Australia), 2003: W. J. Foreman (cricket and Australian Rules football commentator; services to sport) AM, J. R. Mitchell (services to sports administration, especially at Melbourne Cricket Club and Ground) AM, N. C. O'Neill (New South Wales and Australia) OAM, P. I. Philpott (New South Wales and Australia) OAM, D. L. Richards (former chief executive of the ICC; services to cricket) OAM, Sir G. S. Sobers (Barbados, South Australia, Nottinghamshire and West Indies) AO, A. H. Stacey (services to cricket as player, coach and administrator) OAM, S. R. Waugh (New South Wales and Australia) AO.

New Year's Honours, 2004: M. W. Alleyne (Gloucestershire and England) MBE.

Australia Day Honours, 2004: C. L. Fitzpatrick (Australia Women; services to women's cricket) OAM. S. R. Waugh, the recently retired Test captain, was named Australian of the Year by the National Australia Day Council for his services to sport, humanitarian causes and charity.

FRIZZELL COUNTY CHAMPIONSHIP, 2003

Mushtaq Ahmed

The end of the 2003 County Championship engendered more delight than any in years when the oldest and perhaps best-loved of all the counties finally won the title. **Sussex** became champions on a late summer's afternoon at Hove before a packed house of their own supporters, 164 years after the club's foundation, 113 years after the official start of the Championship and just three years after winning the wooden spoon and beginning what *Wisden* called "serious soul-searching".

The real soul-searching had come three years before that: another bottom-place season, preceded by a members' revolt which brought in a new regime – led on the playing side by coach Peter Moores and captain Chris Adams – committed to modernising the club and ending its reputation for dozy, if often disputatious, charm.

Yet very few people saw Sussex coming. They had been promoted to the first division at the end of 2001 and finished one place above the relegation zone in 2002. Most people, inside and outside The Oval, assumed that, for the fourth time in five years, **Surrey** would be champions again. They had assembled a squad so powerful that they were able to shake off the depredations of England selectors with equanimity and indeed were most embarrassed on the rare occasions when they were at full strength: at various times, some of the country's most distinguished batsmen, including Mark Butcher and Graham Thorpe, were excluded when available for selection, leaving their rivals aghast.

And for most of the season all seemed in order: Surrey won their fifth game out of nine on July 12, when they had a 26-point lead. But Sussex began breathing down their necks after a sequence of four wins in June and July. As the sun grew hotter and the wickets drier, their leg-spinner Mushtaq Ahmed established himself as the most influential player in the competition. Sussex failed to finish Surrey off when the teams met at Hove on July 30, despite dominating the exchanges – it was the only home game they did not win – and there was a sense that the weight of history, power and money would be far too much for them in the end.

COUNTY CHAMPIONSHIP TABLE

Division One	*Matches*	*Won*	*Lost*	*Drawn*	*Tied*	*Bonus Points* *Batting*	*Bonus Points* *Bowling*	*Penalty*	*Points*
1 – Sussex (**6**)	16	10	4	2	0	62	47	0	257
2 – Lancashire (**4**)	16	6	2	8	0	64	43	0	223
3 – Surrey (**1**)	16	6	3	7	0	63	44	0	219
4 – Kent (**3**)	16	6	5	5	0	47	47	0	198
5 – Warwickshire (**2**)	16	4	5	6	1	50	37	2.50	171.50
6 – Middlesex (*2*)	16	3	3	10	0	46	41	0	169
7 – Essex (*1*)	16	3	5	7	1	34	45	0	156
8 – Nottinghamshire (*3*)	16	2	8	6	0	36	45	1	132
9 – Leicestershire (**5**)	16	1	6	9	0	36	40	0.50	125.50

Division Two	*Matches*	*Won*	*Lost*	*Drawn*	*Tied*	*Bonus Points* *Batting*	*Bonus Points* *Bowling*	*Penalty*	*Points*
1 – Worcestershire (*4*)	16	10	1	5	0	42	44	0.25	245.75
2 – Northamptonshire (*7*)	16	10	2	4	0	45	44	8	237
3 – Gloucestershire (*8*)	16	5	2	9	0	38	46	0	190
4 – Yorkshire (**9**)	16	4	5	7	0	54	47	1.50	183.50
5 – Glamorgan (*5*)	16	5	5	6	0	45	45	1	183
6 – Durham (*9*)	16	5	7	4	0	31	43	0.75	159.25
7 – Somerset (**8**)	16	4	8	4	0	41	44	0	157
8 – Hampshire (**7**)	16	2	6	8	0	36	44	0	140
9 – Derbyshire (*6*)	16	2	11	3	0	30	44	0	114

2002 positions are shown in brackets: Division One in bold, Division Two in italic.

Win = 14 pts; draw = 4 pts; tie = 7 pts.

Northamptonshire had eight points deducted for a poor pitch. All other penalties were for slow over-rates.

But in late August Surrey faltered badly. They made Leicestershire follow on 335 behind, but could not win the game, and then went down to two stunning defeats at Old Trafford and Canterbury, where Kent beat them by an innings and 155 in three days. While they were enduring that horror, Sussex were pulling off the most extraordinary win of the season, achieving a seven-wicket win at Hove, having been 107 for six in their first innings facing a Middlesex total of 392. That put them top.

Sussex lost their penultimate game, at Old Trafford, which left their conquerors, Lancashire, as their last plausible challengers. All that did was to allow Sussex to complete their triumph memorably in front of their own enchanted supporters, rather than amid polite applause hundreds of miles from home. They thus became the 14th different champions since the competition was formally constituted in 1890, leaving Somerset, Northamptonshire, Gloucestershire (whose titles in the days of the Graces were all unofficial), and the newcomers Durham as the only counties still waiting.

Lancashire, 69 years after their own last outright Championship, came second, 34 points behind, after a season dominated by sensational performances from their batsmen, mainly the overseas stars Stuart Law and Carl Hooper. Surrey finished with three successive defeats, their worst run since 1995, and came third, by their standards a sad end to Adam Hollioake's brilliant seven-year reign as captain and a position that, under current rules, fails to offer any prize money.

Kent did not win any games in the first half of their programme but won six of their last eight, five of them inside three days. Their batsman Ed Smith put together a sensational run of centuries that saw him elevated (less successfully) into the England team. And, given infinite time, they would surely have beaten Lancashire at Blackpool in a match, unfortunately televised, played on the most ludicrously bland wicket of the summer. **Warwickshire** failed to get their act together – their captain, their young hopefuls and their imports all struggled for form – and they settled, not very contentedly, in mid-table.

Middlesex, making their debut in the first division with a largely unknown team after the loss of Angus Fraser and Phil Tufnell, finished more happily in sixth place. But, with the absurd three-up, three-down system still in force, **Essex** and **Nottinghamshire** dropped straight back down into the second division a year after being promoted. Essex won only once before September, and Nottinghamshire went without a single win between April 21 (their opening game) and September 20 (their last). That was still enough to lift them above **Leicestershire**, relegated for the first time after failing to win at all until the penultimate match.

Worcestershire and **Gloucestershire**, the last teams who have never appeared in the first division, will be there in 2004, the fifth season of the two-division competition. Worcestershire went up as champions after an acrimonious end to the season when they declared behind in the final match against their rivals for the second division title, **Northamptonshire**, thus depriving their opponents of a bowling point and ensuring they could not be overtaken. Northamptonshire had irritated several opponents and the ECB by preparing pitches deemed to be too favourable to their spinners, and in this game pushed their luck too far and were docked eight points anyway.

Both teams should have been happier. Worcestershire, getting the best out of their overseas bowlers and the eccentricities of their own pitch, won ten of their last 13 games. Northamptonshire, after a terrible start, revelled in the sunshine and built their own sequence of six successive wins – the spinners, Jason Brown and Graeme Swann, had their successes even when other clubs prepared the wickets. Gloucestershire had a tougher time but went up on the final day of the season: they evaded defeat against their last rivals for promotion, **Yorkshire**, who thus found themselves condemned to a second successive season without even the chance to compete for the Championship they dominated for so many decades.

Glamorgan faded into fifth, despite two magnificent wins over **Durham** in both of which their Australian fast bowler Michael Kasprowicz took nine wickets in an innings. Durham themselves were sixth, losing their last three games and, with them, their outside chance of promotion. **Somerset** started with three wins out of five, then sank into oblivion, **Hampshire** were worse, and **Derbyshire** picked up a record 13th wooden spoon – unlucky for both their captain, Dominic Cork, and coach, Adrian Pierson, who will now be employed elsewhere.

The flaws in the divisional system, with a third of the counties going up and down every year, became increasingly obvious as the season wore on and were a subject for discussion at an ECB working party, meeting over the winter to try to refettle domestic cricket for the 2006 season. There was also widespread alarm at the workings of the liberal rules on overseas player registration, which led to counties shipping cricketers in and out with a frequency that left team-mates and spectators equally bewildered. The situation was compounded by the growing popularity of the "EU-player", mostly Australians or South Africans with close enough European ancestry to qualify for a British or other European Union passport, making it legally difficult or impossible for Lord's to restrict their employment.

On the plus side, attendances rose from their low base, from 505,202 to 530,938. Popular interest was piqued by warm, dry weather, in the spring and then again after midsummer; perhaps by spillover from the success of the Twenty20 Cup; and by the popular, and unexpected, triumph for Sussex.

Pre-season betting (best available prices): *Division One* – 5-6 Surrey; 7-1 Lancashire; 8-1 Warwickshire; 14-1 Nottinghamshire; 16-1 Kent; 20-1 Leicestershire; 33-1 Essex; 40-1 Middlesex and SUSSEX.

Division Two – 3-1 Yorkshire; 4-1 WORCESTERSHIRE; 6-1 Hampshire; 15-2 Somerset; 12-1 Gloucestershire; 14-1 Glamorgan; 16-1 Northamptonshire; 25-1 Derbyshire; 50-1 Durham.

Prize money

Division One
£105,000 for winners: SUSSEX.
£50,000 for runners-up: LANCASHIRE.

Division Two
£40,000 for winners: WORCESTERSHIRE.
£25,000 for runners-up: NORTHAMPTONSHIRE.

Winners of each match (both divisions): £2,000.

SUMMARY OF RESULTS, 2003

DIVISION ONE

	Essex	Kent	Lancashire	Leicestershire	Middlesex	Nottinghamshire	Surrey	Sussex	Warwickshire
Essex	–	D	D	D	D	W	L	L	L
Kent	W	–	L	D	D	W	W	L	W
Lancashire	D	D	–	W	D	D	W	W	D
Leicestershire	D	W	L	–	D	D	D	L	D
Middlesex	D	L	D	W	–	D	D	W	D
Nottinghamshire	L	L	W	D	L	–	L	D	W
Surrey	L	W	D	D	D	W	–	W	D
Sussex	W	W	W	W	W	W	D	–	W
Warwickshire	T	D	L	W	W	D	L	W	–

DIVISION TWO

	Derbyshire	Durham	Glamorgan	Gloucestershire	Hampshire	Northamptonshire	Somerset	Worcestershire	Yorkshire
Derbyshire	–	D	D	L	L	L	D	L	L
Durham	W	–	L	D	W	L	W	D	W
Glamorgan	W	W	–	L	D	L	W	D	D
Gloucestershire	W	W	D	–	D	L	W	D	D
Hampshire	L	D	W	D	–	L	L	L	D
Northamptonshire	W	W	L	D	W	–	W	W	D
Somerset	W	W	W	D	D	D	–	L	L
Worcestershire	W	W	W	W	D	D	W	–	W
Yorkshire	L	L	D	D	D	W	W	L	–

Home teams listed on left, away teams across top; results are for home teams.

W = Won, L = Lost, D = Drawn, T = Tied.

Leaders: *Division One* – from April 21 Nottinghamshire; May 12 Warwickshire; May 17 Surrey; August 22 Sussex; August 29 Surrey; September 8 Sussex. Sussex became champions on September 18.
Division Two – from April 20 Yorkshire; April 26 Gloucestershire; May 24 Somerset; June 7 Worcestershire; July 11 Northamptonshire; July 18 Worcestershire. Worcestershire became champions on September 18.

Bottom place: *Division One* – from April 21 Kent, Leicestershire and Sussex; April 26 Sussex; May 3 Kent; May 24 Leicestershire; July 28 Nottinghamshire; September 20 Leicestershire.
Division Two – from April 21 Durham; May 24 Northamptonshire; June 7 Hampshire; June 30 Derbyshire.

Scoring of Points

(*a*) For a win, 14 points plus any points scored in the first innings.

(*b*) In a tie, each side scores seven points, plus any points scored in the first innings.

(*c*) In a drawn match, each side scores four points, plus any points scored in the first innings (see also paragraph (*f*)).

(*d*) If the scores are equal in a drawn match, the side batting in the fourth innings scores seven points, plus any points scored in the first innings, and the opposing side scores four points plus any points scored in the first innings.

(*e*) First-innings points (awarded only for performances in the first 130 overs of each first innings and retained whatever the result of the match).

(i) A maximum of five batting points to be available: 200 to 249 runs – 1 point; 250 to 299 runs – 2 points; 300 to 349 runs – 3 points; 350 to 399 runs – 4 points; 400 runs or over – 5 points. Penalty runs awarded within the first 130 overs of each first innings count towards the award of bonus points.

(ii) A maximum of three bowling points to be available: 3 to 5 wickets taken – 1 point; 6 to 8 wickets taken – 2 points; 9 to 10 wickets taken – 3 points.

(*f*) If play starts when less than eight hours' playing time remains and a one-innings match is played, no first-innings points shall be scored. The side winning on the one innings scores 14 points. In a tie, each side scores seven points. In a drawn match, each side scores four points. If the scores are equal in a drawn match, the side batting in the second innings scores seven points and the opposing side scores four points.

(*g*) If a match is abandoned without a ball being bowled, each side scores four points.

(*h*) The side which has the highest aggregate of points shall be the Champion County of their respective Division. Should any sides in the Championship table be equal on points, the following tie-breakers will be applied in the order stated: most wins, fewest losses, team achieving most points in head-to-head contests between teams level on points, most wickets taken, most runs scored. At the end of the season, the top three teams from the second division will be promoted and the bottom three teams from the first division will be relegated.

(*i*) The minimum over-rate to be achieved by counties will be 16 overs per hour. Overs will be calculated at the end of the match and penalties applied on a match-by-match basis. For each over (ignoring fractions) that a side has bowled short of the target number, 0.25 points will be deducted from their Championship total.

(*j*) A county which is adjudged to have prepared a pitch unfit for four-day first-class cricket will have 22 points deducted. A county adjudged to have prepared a poor pitch will have eight points deducted. This penalty will rise to 12 points if the county has prepared a poor or unfit pitch within the previous 12 months.

Under ECB playing conditions, two extras were scored for every no-ball bowled whether scored off or not, and one for every wide. Any runs scored off the bat were credited to the batsman, while byes and leg-byes were counted as no-balls or wides, as appropriate, in accordance with Law 24.13, in addition to the initial penalty.

CONSTITUTION OF COUNTY CHAMPIONSHIP

At least four possible dates have been given for the start of county cricket in England. The first, patchy, references began in 1825. The earliest mention in any cricket publication is in 1864 and eight counties have come to be regarded as first-class from that date, including Cambridgeshire, who dropped out after 1871. For many years, the County Championship was considered to have started in 1873, when regulations governing qualification first applied; indeed, a special commemorative stamp was issued by the Post Office in 1973. However, the Championship was not formally organised until 1890 and before then champions were proclaimed by the press; sometimes publications differed in their views and no definitive list of champions can start before that date. Eight teams contested the 1890 competition – Gloucestershire, Kent, Lancashire, Middlesex, Nottinghamshire, Surrey, Sussex and Yorkshire. Somerset joined in the following year, and in 1895 the Championship began to acquire something of its modern shape when Derbyshire, Essex, Hampshire, Leicestershire and Warwickshire were added. At that point MCC officially recognised the competition's existence. Worcestershire, Northamptonshire and Glamorgan were admitted to the Championship in 1899, 1905 and 1921 respectively and are regarded as first-class from these dates. An invitation in 1921 to Buckinghamshire to enter the Championship was declined, owing to the lack of necessary playing facilities, and an application by Devon in 1948 was unsuccessful. Durham were admitted to the Championship in 1992 and were granted first-class status prior to their pre-season tour of Zimbabwe.

In 2000, the Championship was split for the first time into two divisions, on the basis of counties' standings in the 1999 competition. From 2000 onwards, the bottom three teams in Division One were relegated at the end of the season, and the top three teams in Division Two promoted.

COUNTY CHAMPIONS

The title of champion county is unreliable before 1890. In 1963, *Wisden* formally accepted the list of champions "most generally selected" by contemporaries, as researched by the late Rowland Bowen (See *Wisden 1959*, pp 91–98). This appears to be the most accurate available list but has no official status. The county champions from 1864 to 1889 were, according to Bowen: 1864 Surrey; 1865 Nottinghamshire; 1866 Middlesex; 1867 Yorkshire; 1868 Nottinghamshire; 1869 Nottinghamshire and Yorkshire; 1870 Yorkshire; 1871 Nottinghamshire; 1872 Nottinghamshire;

1873 Gloucestershire and Nottinghamshire; 1874 Gloucestershire; 1875 Nottinghamshire; 1876 Gloucestershire; 1877 Gloucestershire; 1878 undecided; 1879 Lancashire and Nottinghamshire; 1880 Nottinghamshire; 1881 Lancashire; 1882 Lancashire and Nottinghamshire; 1883 Nottinghamshire; 1884 Nottinghamshire; 1885 Nottinghamshire; 1886 Nottinghamshire; 1887 Surrey; 1888 Surrey; 1889 Lancashire, Nottinghamshire and Surrey.

Official champions

1890	Surrey
1891	Surrey
1892	Surrey
1893	Yorkshire
1894	Surrey
1895	Surrey
1896	Yorkshire
1897	Lancashire
1898	Yorkshire
1899	Surrey
1900	Yorkshire
1901	Yorkshire
1902	Yorkshire
1903	Middlesex
1904	Lancashire
1905	Yorkshire
1906	Kent
1907	Nottinghamshire
1908	Yorkshire
1909	Kent
1910	Kent
1911	Warwickshire
1912	Yorkshire
1913	Kent
1914	Surrey
1919	Yorkshire
1920	Middlesex
1921	Middlesex
1922	Yorkshire
1923	Yorkshire
1924	Yorkshire
1925	Yorkshire
1926	Lancashire
1927	Lancashire
1928	Lancashire
1929	Nottinghamshire
1930	Lancashire
1931	Yorkshire
1932	Yorkshire
1933	Yorkshire
1934	Lancashire
1935	Yorkshire
1936	Derbyshire
1937	Yorkshire
1938	Yorkshire
1939	Yorkshire
1946	Yorkshire
1947	Middlesex
1948	Glamorgan
1949	Middlesex
	Yorkshire
1950	Lancashire
	Surrey
1951	Warwickshire
1952	Surrey
1953	Surrey
1954	Surrey
1955	Surrey
1956	Surrey
1957	Surrey
1958	Surrey
1959	Yorkshire
1960	Yorkshire
1961	Hampshire
1962	Yorkshire
1963	Yorkshire
1964	Worcestershire
1965	Worcestershire
1966	Yorkshire
1967	Yorkshire
1968	Yorkshire
1969	Glamorgan
1970	Kent
1971	Surrey
1972	Warwickshire
1973	Hampshire
1974	Worcestershire
1975	Leicestershire
1976	Middlesex
1977	Middlesex
	Kent
1978	Kent
1979	Essex
1980	Middlesex
1981	Nottinghamshire
1982	Middlesex
1983	Essex
1984	Essex
1985	Middlesex
1986	Essex
1987	Nottinghamshire
1988	Worcestershire
1989	Worcestershire
1990	Middlesex
1991	Essex
1992	Essex
1993	Middlesex
1994	Warwickshire
1995	Warwickshire
1996	Leicestershire
1997	Glamorgan
1998	Leicestershire
1999	Surrey
2000	Surrey
2001	Yorkshire
2002	Surrey
2003	Sussex

Notes: Since the Championship was constituted in 1890 it has been won outright as follows: Yorkshire 30 times, Surrey 18, Middlesex 10, Lancashire 7, Essex and Kent 6, Warwickshire and Worcestershire 5, Nottinghamshire 4, Glamorgan and Leicestershire 3, Hampshire 2, Derbyshire and Sussex 1. Durham, Gloucestershire, Northamptonshire and Somerset have never won.

The title has been shared three times since 1890, involving Middlesex twice, Kent, Lancashire, Surrey and Yorkshire.

Wooden Spoons: since the major expansion of the Championship from nine teams to 14 in 1895, the counties have finished outright bottom as follows: Derbyshire 13; Northamptonshire and Somerset 11; Glamorgan 9; Nottinghamshire and Sussex 8; Gloucestershire and Leicestershire 7; Worcestershire 6; Hampshire 5; Durham 4; Warwickshire 3; Essex and Kent 2; Yorkshire 1. Lancashire, Middlesex and Surrey have never finished bottom. Leicestershire have also shared bottom place twice, once with Hampshire and once with Somerset.

From 1977 to 1983 the Championship was sponsored by Schweppes, from 1984 to 1998 by Britannic Assurance, from 1999 to 2000 by PPP healthcare, in 2001 by CricInfo, and from 2002 by Frizzell.

COUNTY CHAMPIONSHIP – FINAL POSITIONS, 1890–2003

	Derbyshire	Essex	Glamorgan	Gloucestershire	Hampshire	Kent	Lancashire	Leicestershire	Middlesex	Northamptonshire	Nottinghamshire	Somerset	Surrey	Sussex	Warwickshire	Worcestershire	Yorkshire
1890	–	–	–	6	–	3	2	–	7	–	5	–	1	8	–	–	3
1891	–	–	–	9	–	5	2	–	3	–	4	5	1	7	–	–	8
1892	–	–	–	7	–	7	4	–	5	–	2	3	1	9	–	–	6
1893	–	–	–	9	–	4	2	–	3	–	6	8	5	7	–	–	1
1894	–	–	–	9	–	4	4	–	3	–	7	6	1	8	–	–	2
1895	5	9	–	4	10	14	2	12	6	–	12	8	1	11	6	–	3
1896	7	5	–	10	8	9	2	13	3	–	6	11	4	14	12	–	1
1897	14	3	–	5	9	12	1	13	8	–	10	11	2	6	7	–	4
1898	9	5	–	3	12	7	6	13	2	–	8	13	4	9	9	–	1
1899	15	6	–	9	10	8	4	13	2	–	10	13	1	5	7	12	3
1900	13	10	–	7	15	3	2	14	7	–	5	11	7	3	6	12	1
1901	15	10	–	14	7	7	3	12	2	–	9	12	6	4	5	11	1
1902	10	13	–	14	15	7	5	11	12	–	3	7	4	2	6	9	1
1903	12	8	–	13	14	8	4	14	1	–	5	10	11	2	7	6	3
1904	10	14	–	9	15	3	1	7	4	–	5	12	11	6	7	13	2
1905	14	12	–	8	16	6	2	5	11	13	10	15	4	3	7	8	1
1906	16	7	–	9	8	1	4	15	11	11	5	11	3	10	6	14	2
1907	16	7	–	10	12	8	6	11	5	15	1	14	4	13	9	2	2
1908	14	11	–	10	9	2	7	13	4	15	8	16	3	5	12	6	1
1909	15	14	–	16	8	1	2	13	6	7	10	11	5	4	12	8	3
1910	15	11	–	12	6	1	4	10	3	9	5	16	2	7	14	13	8
1911	14	6	–	12	11	2	4	15	3	10	8	16	5	13	1	9	7
1912	12	15	–	11	6	3	4	13	5	2	8	14	7	10	9	16	1
1913	13	15	–	9	10	1	8	14	6	4	5	16	3	7	11	12	2
1914	12	8	–	16	5	3	11	13	2	9	10	15	1	6	7	14	4
1919	9	14	–	8	7	2	5	9	13	12	3	5	4	11	15	–	1
1920	16	9	–	8	11	5	2	13	1	14	7	10	3	6	12	15	4
1921	12	15	17	7	6	4	5	11	1	13	8	10	2	9	16	14	3
1922	11	8	16	13	6	4	5	14	7	15	2	10	3	9	12	17	1
1923	10	13	16	11	7	5	3	14	8	17	2	9	4	6	12	15	1
1924	17	15	13	6	12	5	4	11	2	16	6	8	3	10	9	14	1
1925	14	7	17	10	9	5	3	12	6	11	4	15	2	13	8	16	1
1926	11	9	8	15	7	3	1	13	6	16	4	14	5	10	12	17	2
1927	5	8	15	12	13	4	1	7	9	16	2	14	6	10	11	17	3
1928	10	16	15	5	12	2	1	9	8	13	3	14	6	7	11	17	4
1929	7	12	17	4	11	8	2	9	6	13	1	15	10	4	14	16	2
1930	9	6	11	2	13	5	1	12	16	17	4	13	8	7	15	10	3
1931	7	10	15	2	12	3	6	16	11	17	5	13	8	4	9	14	1
1932	10	14	15	13	8	3	6	12	10	16	4	7	5	2	9	17	1
1933	6	4	16	10	14	3	5	17	12	13	8	11	9	2	7	15	1
1934	3	8	13	7	14	5	1	12	10	17	9	15	11	2	4	16	5
1935	2	9	13	15	16	10	4	6	3	17	5	14	11	7	8	12	1
1936	1	9	16	4	10	8	11	15	2	17	5	7	6	14	13	12	3
1937	3	6	7	4	14	12	9	16	2	17	10	13	8	5	11	15	1
1938	5	6	16	10	14	9	4	15	2	17	12	7	3	8	13	11	1
1939	9	4	13	3	15	5	6	17	2	16	12	14	8	10	11	7	1
1946	15	8	6	5	10	6	3	11	2	16	13	4	11	17	14	8	1
1947	5	11	9	2	16	4	3	14	1	17	11	11	6	9	15	7	7
1948	6	13	1	8	9	15	5	11	3	17	14	12	2	16	7	10	4
1949	15	9	8	7	16	13	11	17	1	6	11	9	5	13	4	3	1
1950	5	17	11	7	12	9	1	16	14	10	15	7	1	13	4	6	3
1951	11	8	5	12	9	16	3	15	7	13	17	14	6	10	1	4	2

	Derbyshire	Durham	Essex	Glamorgan	Gloucestershire	Hampshire	Kent	Lancashire	Leicestershire	Middlesex	Northamptonshire	Nottinghamshire	Somerset	Surrey	Sussex	Warwickshire	Worcestershire	Yorkshire
1952	4	–	10	7	9	12	15	3	6	5	8	16	17	1	13	10	14	2
1953	6	–	12	10	6	14	16	3	3	5	11	8	17	1	2	9	15	12
1954	3	–	15	4	13	14	11	10	16	7	7	5	17	1	9	6	11	2
1955	8	–	14	16	12	3	13	9	6	5	7	11	17	1	4	9	15	2
1956	12	–	11	13	3	6	16	2	17	5	4	8	15	1	9	14	9	7
1957	4	–	5	9	12	13	14	6	17	7	2	15	8	1	9	11	16	3
1958	5	–	6	15	14	2	8	7	12	10	4	17	3	1	13	16	9	11
1959	7	–	9	6	2	8	13	5	16	10	11	17	12	3	15	4	14	1
1960	5	–	6	11	8	12	10	2	17	3	9	16	14	7	4	15	13	1
1961	7	–	6	14	5	1	11	13	9	3	16	17	10	15	8	12	4	2
1962	7	–	9	14	4	10	11	16	17	13	8	15	6	5	12	3	2	1
1963	17	–	12	2	8	10	13	15	16	6	7	9	3	11	4	4	14	1
1964	12	–	10	11	17	12	7	14	16	6	3	15	8	4	9	2	1	5
1965	9	–	15	3	10	12	5	13	14	6	2	17	7	8	16	11	1	4
1966	9	–	16	14	15	11	4	12	8	12	5	17	3	7	10	6	2	1
1967	6	–	15	14	17	12	2	11	2	7	9	15	8	4	13	10	5	1
1968	8	–	14	3	16	5	2	6	9	10	13	4	12	15	17	11	7	1
1969	16	–	6	1	2	5	10	15	14	11	9	8	17	3	7	4	12	13
1970	7	–	12	2	17	10	1	3	15	16	14	11	13	5	9	7	6	4
1971	17	–	10	16	8	9	4	3	5	6	14	12	7	1	11	2	15	13
1972	17	–	5	13	3	9	2	15	6	8	4	14	11	12	16	1	7	10
1973	16	–	8	11	5	1	4	12	9	13	3	17	10	2	15	7	6	14
1974	17	–	12	16	14	2	10	8	4	6	3	15	5	7	13	9	1	11
1975	15	–	7	9	16	3	5	4	1	11	8	13	12	6	17	14	10	2
1976	15	–	6	17	3	12	14	16	4	1	2	13	7	9	10	5	11	8
1977	7	–	6	14	3	11	1	16	5	1	9	17	4	14	8	10	13	12
1978	14	–	2	13	10	8	1	12	6	3	17	7	5	16	9	11	15	4
1979	16	–	1	17	10	12	5	13	6	14	11	9	8	3	4	15	2	7
1980	9	–	8	13	7	17	16	15	10	1	12	3	5	2	4	14	11	6
1981	12	–	5	14	13	7	9	16	8	4	15	1	3	6	2	17	11	10
1982	11	–	7	16	15	3	13	12	2	1	9	4	6	5	8	17	14	10
1983	9	–	1	15	12	3	7	12	4	2	6	14	10	8	11	5	16	17
1984	12	–	1	13	17	15	5	16	4	3	11	2	7	8	6	9	10	14
1985	13	–	4	12	3	2	9	14	16	1	10	8	17	6	7	15	5	11
1986	11	–	1	17	2	6	8	15	7	12	9	4	16	3	14	12	5	10
1987	6	–	12	13	10	5	14	2	3	16	7	1	11	4	17	15	9	8
1988	14	–	3	17	10	15	2	9	8	7	12	5	11	4	16	6	1	13
1989	6	–	2	17	9	6	15	4	13	3	5	11	14	12	10	8	1	16
1990	12	–	2	8	13	3	16	6	7	1	11	13	15	9	17	5	4	10
1991	3	–	1	12	13	9	6	8	16	15	10	4	17	5	11	2	6	14
1992	5	18	1	14	10	15	2	12	8	11	3	4	9	13	7	6	17	16
1993	15	18	11	3	17	13	8	13	9	1	4	7	5	6	10	16	2	12
1994	17	16	6	18	12	13	9	10	2	4	5	3	11	7	8	1	15	13
1995	14	17	5	16	6	13	18	4	7	2	3	11	9	12	15	1	10	8
1996	2	18	5	10	13	14	4	15	1	9	16	17	11	3	12	8	7	6
1997	16	17	8	1	7	14	2	11	10	4	15	13	12	8	18	4	3	6
1998	10	14	18	12	4	6	11	2	1	17	15	16	9	5	7	8	13	3
1999	9	8	12	14	18	7	5	2	3	16	13	17	4	1	11	10	15	6
2000	**9**	**8**	*2*	*3*	*4*	**7**	**6**	**2**	**4**	*8*	*1*	*7*	**5**	**1**	*9*	*6*	*5*	**3**
2001	*9*	*8*	**9**	**8**	*4*	*2*	**3**	**6**	**5**	*5*	**7**	*7*	**2**	**4**	*1*	*3*	*6*	**1**
2002	*6*	*9*	*1*	*5*	*8*	**7**	**3**	**4**	**5**	*2*	*7*	*3*	**8**	**1**	**6**	**2**	*4*	**9**
2003	*9*	*6*	**7**	*5*	*3*	*8*	**4**	**2**	**9**	**6**	*2*	**8**	*7*	**3**	**1**	**5**	*1*	*4*

Note: For the 2000–2003 Championships, Division One placings are shown in bold, Division Two in italic.

MATCH RESULTS, 1864–2003

County	*Years of Play*	*Played*	*Won*	*Lost*	*Drawn*	*Tied*	*% Won*
Derbyshire	1871–87; 1895–2003	2,339	581	866	891	1	24.83
Durham	1992–2003	204	34	112	58	0	16.66
Essex	1895–2003	2,301	666	673	956	6	28.94
Glamorgan	1921–2003	1,835	410	622	803	0	22.34
Gloucestershire	1870–2003	2,575	763	950	860	2	29.63
Hampshire	1864–85; 1895–2003	2,410	625	829	952	4	25.93
Kent	1864–2003	2,699	974	809	911	5	36.08
Lancashire	1865–2003	2,774	1,032	579	1,160	3	37.20
Leicestershire	1895–2003	2,268	517	821	929	1	22.79
Middlesex	1864–2003	2,478	916	627	930	5	36.96
Northamptonshire	1905–2003	2,036	508	706	819	3	24.95
Nottinghamshire	1864–2003	2,608	783	710	1,114	1	30.02
Somerset	1882–85; 1891–2003	2,309	547	920	839	3	23.68
Surrey	1864–2003	2,855	1,136	628	1,087	4	39.78
Sussex	1864–2003	2,748	772	949	1,021	6	28.09
Warwickshire	1895–2003	2,281	625	658	996	2	27.40
Worcestershire	1899–2003	2,223	567	762	892	2	25.50
Yorkshire	1864–2003	2,876	1,271	506	1,097	2	44.19
Cambridgeshire	1864–69; 1871	19	8	8	3	0	42.10
		20,919	12,735	12,735	8,159	25	

Notes: Matches abandoned without a ball bowled are wholly excluded.

Counties participated in the years shown, except that there were no matches in the years 1915–18 and 1940–45; Hampshire did not play inter-county matches in 1868–69, 1871–74 and 1879; Worcestershire did not take part in the Championship in 1919.

COUNTY CHAMPIONSHIP STATISTICS FOR 2003

		For			*Against*		
County	*Runs*	*Wickets*	*Avge*	*Runs*	*Wickets*	*Avge*	*RPF*
Derbyshire (*9*)	7,468	285	26.20	7,862	226	34.78	0.75
Durham (*6*)	7,333	280	26.18	7,454	242	30.80	0.85
Essex (**7**)	7,525	251	29.98	8,512	236	36.06	0.83
Glamorgan (*5*)	8,608	268	32.11	8,107	261	31.06	1.03
Gloucestershire (*3*)	8,072	243	33.21	7,811	254	30.75	1.08
Hampshire (*8*)	7,446	243	30.64	7,915	222	35.65	0.85
Kent (**4**)	8,286	235	35.25	7,950	271	29.33	1.20
Lancashire (**2**)	8,893	190	46.80	8,647	259	33.38	1.40
Leicestershire (**9**)	7,987	244	32.73	8,706	216	40.30	0.81
Middlesex (**6**)	8,313	233	35.67	8,538	210	40.65	0.87
Northamptonshire (*2*)	7,656	199	38.47	7,426	257	28.89	1.33
Nottinghamshire (**8**)	8,364	281	29.76	8,138	204	39.89	0.74
Somerset (*7*)	8,103	260	31.16	8,451	244	34.63	0.89
Surrey (**3**)	9,149	213	42.95	8,752	245	35.72	1.20
Sussex (**1**)	9,302	231	40.26	8,677	276	31.43	1.28
Warwickshire (**5**)	9,078	260	34.91	8,977	221	40.61	0.85
Worcestershire (*1*)	7,478	241	31.02	7,232	288	25.11	1.23
Yorkshire (*4*)	7,907	229	34.52	7,813	254	30.75	1.12
	146,968	4,386	33.50	146,968	4,386	33.50	

2003 Championship positions are shown in brackets; Division One in bold, Division Two in italic.

Relative performance factor (RPF) is determined by dividing the average runs scored per wicket by the average runs conceded per wicket.

RUNS SCORED PER 100 BALLS IN THE COUNTY CHAMPIONSHIP, 2003

County	*Run-rate/ 100 balls*	*County*	*Run-rate/ 100 balls*
Derbyshire (*9*)	53.08	Middlesex (**6**)	54.53
Durham (*6*)	54.09	Northamptonshire (*2*)	60.08
Essex (**7**)	56.32	Nottinghamshire (**8**)	58.81
Glamorgan (*5*)	59.21	Somerset (*7*)	58.68
Gloucestershire (*3*)	55.28	Surrey (**3**)	67.17
Hampshire (*8*)	56.07	Sussex (**1**)	60.33
Kent (**4**)	61.33	Warwickshire (**5**)	61.36
Lancashire (**2**)	60.57	Worcestershire (*1*)	57.39
Leicestershire (**9**)	59.50	Yorkshire (*4*)	59.77
		2003 average rate	58.52

2003 Championship positions are shown in brackets: Division One in bold, Division Two in italic.

ECB PITCHES TABLE OF MERIT

First-Class Matches, Under-19 & Women's Tests and UCCE Matches

		Points	*Matches*	*Average in 2003*	*Average in 2002*
1	Surrey (1)	125	11	5.68	5.33
2	Middlesex (3)	130	12	5.42	5.14
3	Somerset (5)	115	11	5.23	5.00
4	Kent (4)	90	9	5.00	5.10
5	Gloucestershire (2)	89	9	4.94	5.19
6	Lancashire (6)	77	8	4.81	4.95
7	Derbyshire (17)	94	10	4.70	4.05
8	Sussex (11)	103	11	4.68	4.45
9	Essex (12)	83	9	4.61	4.33
10	Glamorgan (8)	90	10	4.50	4.68
11	Warwickshire (15)	98	11	4.45	4.27
12	Durham (13)	88	10	4.40	4.30
13	Hampshire (18)	66	8	4.13	3.83
14	Nottinghamshire (7)	88	11	4.00	4.73
14	Yorkshire (16)	88	11	4.00	4.25
16	Worcestershire (10)	78	10	3.90	4.56
17	Leicestershire (14)	70	9	3.89	4.28
18	Northamptonshire (9)	60	8	3.75	4.60
	Durham UCCE	50	5	5.00	5.00
	Bradford/Leeds UCCE	38	4	4.75	5.00
	Cambridge UCCE	66	7	4.71	4.80
	Oxford UCCE	41	5	4.10	5.29
	Loughborough UCCE	16	2	4.00	5.00

ECB PITCHES TABLE OF MERIT

One-Day Matches

		Points	Matches	Average in 2003	Average in 2002
1	Surrey (2)	144	13	5.54	5.15
2	Somerset (3)	141	13	5.42	5.03
3	Middlesex (5)	172	16	5.38	4.78
4	Essex (15)	146	14	5.21	4.22
5	Warwickshire (10)	128	13	4.92	4.64
6	Yorkshire (18)	108	11	4.91	3.69
7	Glamorgan (11)	137	14	4.89	4.50
8	Lancashire (6)	156	16	4.88	4.71
9	Sussex (14)	146	15	4.87	4.32
10	Kent (7)	126	13	4.85	4.70
11	Gloucestershire (4)	135	14	4.82	4.88
12	Leicestershire (8=)	144	15	4.80	4.67
13	Durham (12)	100	11	4.55	4.42
14	Derbyshire (17)	108	12	4.50	3.85
15	Scotland (–)	89	10	4.45	–
16	Nottinghamshire (1)	131	15	4.37	5.17
17	Northamptonshire (8=)	122	14	4.36	4.67
18	Worcestershire (16)	127	15	4.23	4.05
19	Hampshire (13)	126	15	4.20	4.33

In both tables 2002 positions are shown in brackets. Each umpire in a game marks the pitch on the following scale of merit: 6 – very good; 5 – good; 4 – above average; 3 – below average; 2 – poor; 1 – unfit.

The tables, provided by the ECB, cover major matches, including Tests, Under-19 internationals, women's internationals and UCCE games, played on grounds under the county or UCCE's jurisdiction. Middlesex pitches at Lord's are the responsibility of MCC.

The ECB points out that the tables of merit are not a direct assessment of the groundsmen's ability. Marks may be affected by many factors including weather, soil conditions and the resources available.

PROFESSIONAL CRICKETERS' ASSOCIATION AWARDS

At the Professional Cricketers' Association annual dinner in September 2003, Mushtaq Ahmed was named NatWest Player of the Year and won the Reg Hayter Cup for his role in Sussex's triumphant Championship campaign. Kabir Ali of Worcestershire won the John Arlott Cup for the Costcutter PCA Young Player of the Year, for the second season running. Alec Stewart, who had recently announced his retirement, received an ECB Special Merit Award. Ed Smith of Kent won the Slazenger Sheer Instinct Award for his run of six centuries in seven innings. For the third year running, Neil Mallender received the Umpire of the Year award and Glamorgan won the MCC Spirit of Cricket Award. Mick Hunt of Lord's was the Mitsubishi Motors PCA Groundsman of the Year. The Power Cricket PCA in the Community Award went to NatWest Cricket Initiative with the Princes Trust, a series of volunteer programmes for young disadvantaged people. The npower Special Merit Award went to Stuart Robertson for his work on Twenty20 Cricket.

DERBYSHIRE

The Cork flies off

GERALD MORTIMER

The preliminaries were uneasy, as the captain Dominic Cork said publicly that Adrian Pierson was not his choice of coach. The aftermath was worse. By the end of a deplorable season, Pierson was not Derbyshire's choice either, and Cork had left the County Ground after 16 years on the staff.

Seven Championship victories in 2002 had encouraged Derbyshire to believe promotion was feasible. Instead, the county slid to the bottom of the table. A run of seven consecutive Championship defeats was their worst since 1921 and, among three innings defeats, the thrashing by Northamptonshire was their heaviest in 28 years.

For the most part, the County Ground felt embattled. Those who talked of chopping a first-class county or six continued to see Derbyshire as prime candidates for the cull, and the conspiracy theories were encouraged in late June when the pitch for the Twenty20 game against Nottinghamshire attracted a suspended points penalty. Only a week later they saw what they considered an outrageous turner at Northampton go unpunished. That decision – "a complete joke" according to Pierson – prompted anger and an empty threat to withdraw co-operation from pitch inspectors.

In the same period, Derbyshire missed out on the semi-finals of the Twenty20 in a one-run defeat, during which Leicestershire's Brad Hodge, having completed a catch, carried the ball over the boundary in celebration. Cork called Hodge a "cheat" and dismissed the ECB's handling of the episode as "pathetic". Cork narrowly escaped suspension, but it was an undignified episode.

This gloomy summer was the logical conclusion to a decade of turmoil. At least, everyone hopes it is a conclusion. For 2004, the former Worcestershire and Zimbabwe coach Dave Houghton was appointed director of cricket. And after Houghton failed to confirm that he wanted him as captain, Cork asked to be released, and joined Lancashire. So when Karl Krikken, one of the best wicket-keepers in the game and certainly the noisiest, announced his retirement, the last links were broken with the team that won the 1993 Benson and Hedges Cup. For seasons, too many of that side's best players had been spread around the other counties.

However, the wide margin of Derbyshire's two Championship wins, against Yorkshire and Hampshire, suggested they had more talent than they routinely displayed. In the C&G Trophy they beat Glamorgan and Surrey in magnificent style before narrowly failing against Gloucestershire in the semi-final at Bristol. There was a sense of purpose not always evident in the Championship, or during an indifferent National League campaign.

But across the season, too few of the squad played to potential. No county won fewer than Derbyshire's 30 batting points. Michael Di Venuto, who succeeds Cork as captain, was the one feared batsman, but his 1,520 Championship runs constituted more than a fifth of Derbyshire's total. He badly needed a reliable opening partner: Andrew Gait still looked vulnerable to early movement; Steve Selwood, who battled gamely in an unaccustomed role, missed the end of the summer through injury; and, ludicrously, Steve Stubbings, a capped opener who scored 1,024 runs in 2001, did not appear in the Championship until September, after which he hit 306 in three games. Otherwise, Luke Sutton, vice-captain for 2004, was the most consistent batsman, falling just 18 short of becoming the first Derbyshire wicket-keeper since William Storer in 1901 to reach 1,000 first-class runs. Reservations persist about his keeping but, dedicated and intelligent cricketer that he is, he will continue to work on it.

Graeme Welch

Before the season, Cork had wanted Kim Barnett, recently paid off by Gloucestershire, to return as player-coach and strengthen the line-up. He found no support from the committee, which was hardly surprising, given the acrimonious nature of Barnett's departure in 1999. But the stated reason – that Barnett would inhibit the progress of younger batsmen – was made to look ridiculous. Nor could a flurry of overseas players make up the shortfall. New Zealand batsman Nathan Astle never arrived because of injury; Pakistani Test all-rounder Shahid Afridi wanted only to hit everything out of sight; and Mohammad Kaif of India was happier in one-day cricket, where he played some lovely innings. It was hard to see the point of bringing in the New Zealand all-rounder Chris Harris for the last four National League games.

The bowling was held together by Graeme Welch. Like Welch, Cork took 50 wickets, showing his determination by playing with a chipped bone in his ankle for half the summer. Inevitably, his effectiveness was reduced. Kevin Dean found swing more elusive than in 2002, Mohammad Ali was expensive and, disappointingly, the slow left-armer Lian Wharton was released.

Houghton has much to do, as a total of 12 Championship wins in four seasons confirms. It is not just on the field that improvement is needed: the club needs a clearer sense of direction. Too many of the committee are only enthusiastic followers and none of them has played the first-class game, so the body lacks cricket knowledge. Over the winter, work began on a new cricket centre and in 2004 Derbyshire will have Academy status. But in both cases most other counties have got there first. Captaincy problems over many years have stemmed from failures of management. Irrespective of his merits as captain, Cork is yet another talented player to leave.

DERBYSHIRE RESULTS

All first-class matches – Played 17: Won 2, Lost 11, Drawn 4.
County Championship matches – Played 16: Won 2, Lost 11, Drawn 3.

Frizzell County Championship, 9th in Division 2; Cheltenham & Gloucester Trophy, s-f; National Cricket League, 6th in Division 2; Twenty20 Cup, 3rd in North Group.

COUNTY CHAMPIONSHIP AVERAGES

BATTING AND FIELDING

Cap		*M*	*I*	*NO*	*R*	*HS*	*100s*	*50s*	*Avge*	*Ct/St*
	Hasan Adnan	2	4	1	189	84	0	2	63.00	1
2001	S. D. Stubbings	3	6	0	306	103	1	2	51.00	1
2000	M. J. Di Venuto§	16	31	0	1,520	150	5	8	49.03	25
2002	L. D. Sutton	15	29	4	936	127	2	2	37.44	25/2
	A. I. Gait	12	24	0	662	110	1	4	27.58	10
	N. R. C. Dumelow	9	17	3	347	75	0	3	24.78	2
1993	D. G. Cork	16	29	3	593	92	0	3	22.80	11
	M. Kaif§	8	15	0	332	87	0	1	22.13	5
	R. M. Khan	8	15	0	322	76	0	2	21.46	3
	S. A. Selwood	9	17	1	333	88	0	2	20.81	3
2001	G. Welch	14	26	5	414	54	0	2	19.71	3
	Shahid Afridi§	3	6	0	92	67	0	1	15.33	0
2002	C. W. G. Bassano	11	21	3	271	53*	0	2	15.05	5
	D. R. Hewson	8	16	0	222	57	0	1	13.87	4
	L. J. Wharton	6	9	5	46	30	0	0	11.50	4
	T. Lungley	5	8	1	80	29	0	0	11.42	2
	P. M. R. Havell	3	6	5	10	7*	0	0	10.00	2
	Mohammad Ali	10	17	3	101	31	0	0	7.21	1
1998	K. J. Dean	15	24	3	148	30*	0	0	7.04	4

Also batted: N. E. L. Gunter (2 matches) 9*, 20*; K. M. Krikken (cap 1992) (1 match) 14, 1 (1 ct).

§ *Overseas player.*

BOWLING

	O	*M*	*R*	*W*	*BB*	*5W/i*	*Avge*
G. Welch	455.3	113	1,394	53	6-102	2	26.30
D. G. Cork	444.1	99	1,363	50	6-28	3	27.26
K. J. Dean	421.3	101	1,506	41	4-39	0	36.73
P. M. Havell	77.4	12	369	10	3-34	0	36.90
Mohammad Ali	221	36	1,060	28	4-79	0	37.85
N. R. C. Dumelow	200.4	39	711	16	5-78	2	44.43

Also bowled: M. J. Di Venuto 6–0–23–0; N. E. L. Gunter 27.1–2–153–3; D. R. Hewson 4–0–14–0; M. Kaif 4–1–21–1; R. M. Khan 3–1–13–0; T. Lungley 66.2–6–350–7; S. A. Selwood 7–0–28–0; Shahid Afridi 54.4–15–147–4; L. J. Wharton 115–24–364–9.

COUNTY RECORDS

Highest score for:	274	G. Davidson v Lancashire at Manchester	1896
Highest score against:	343*	P. A. Perrin (Essex) at Chesterfield	1904
Best bowling for:	10-40	W. Bestwick v Glamorgan at Cardiff	1921
Best bowling against:	10-45	R. L. Johnson (Middlesex) at Derby	1994
Highest total for:	645	v Hampshire at Derby	1898
Highest total against:	662	by Yorkshire at Chesterfield	1898
Lowest total for:	16	v Nottinghamshire at Nottingham	1879
Lowest total against:	23	by Hampshire at Burton upon Trent	1958

DERBYSHIRE DIRECTORY

ADDRESS

County Ground, Nottingham Road, Derby DE21 6DA (01332 383211; fax 01332 290251; email post@dccc.org.uk). **Website** www.dccc.org.uk.

GROUND

Derby: 1 mile E of town centre, to the N of Pentagon Island roundabout where A61 and A52 cross. Nearest station: Derby (1¼ miles).

OFFICIALS

Captain 2003 – D. G. Cork; 2004 – M. J. Di Venuto
First-team coach 2003 – A. R. K. Pierson
Director of cricket 2004 – D. L. Houghton
Director of academy K. M. Krikken
President D. K. Amott
Chairman G. T. Bowring
Chief executive J. T. Smedley
Head groundsman N. Godrich
Scorer J. M. Brown

PLAYERS

Players expected to reappear in 2004

	Former counties	*Country*	*Born*	*Birthplace*
Bassano Christopher Warwick Godfrey		A (EU)	11.9.1975	*East London, SA*
Dean Kevin James		E	16.10.1975	†*Derby*
Di Venuto Michael James	Sussex	A	12.12.1973	*Hobart*
Dumelow Nathan Robert Charles		E	30.4.1981	†*Derby*
Gait Andrew Ian		SA (EU)	19.12.1978	*Bulawayo, Zim.*
Gunter Neil Edward Lloyd		E	12.5.1981	*Basingstoke*
Hasan Adnan		P (EU)	15.5.1975	*Lahore*
Havell Paul Matthew Roger	Sussex	A (EU)	4.7.1980	*Melbourne*
Hewson Dominic Robert	Glos	E	3.10.1974	*Cheltenham*
Khan Rawait Mahmood		E	5.3.1982	*Birmingham*
Lungley Tom		E	25.7.1979	†*Derby*
Mohammad Ali		P (EU)	8.11.1973	*Bahawalpur*
Selwood Steven Andrew		E	24.11.1979	*Barnet*
Stubbings Stephen David		E	31.3.1978	*Huddersfield*
Sutton Luke David	Somerset	E	4.10.1976	*Keynsham*
Welch Graeme	Warwicks	E	21.3.1972	*Durham*

Players due to join in 2004

Botha Anthony Greyvensteyn		SA (EU)	17.11.1976	*Pretoria*
Bryant James Douglas Campbell	Somerset	SA (EU)	4.2.1976	*Durban*
Wright Damien Geoffrey	Northants	A	25.7.1975	*Casino*

† *Born in Derbyshire.*

DERBYSHIRE v GLAMORGAN

At Derby, April 18, 19, 20, 21. Drawn. Derbyshire 12 pts, Glamorgan 11 pts. Toss: Derbyshire. County debut: Shahid Afridi.

A healthy Good Friday crowd basking in ideal weather saw Di Venuto reproduce the form that made him the country's second-heaviest run-scorer in 2002 and give Derbyshire an authoritative start. The last four wickets more than doubled the score with Sutton leading the way, and the advantage swung further to Derbyshire when Glamorgan staggered to 71 for five on the interrupted second day. A typically eloquent hundred by Maynard, who added 182 in 30 overs with Croft, pulled Glamorgan back into the match. But their bowling was weakened in the second innings because Thomas had been stretchered off with a knee injury in the first, and Cork set Glamorgan a steep target of 314 in 69 overs. Dale hung in at one end but nobody stayed long at the other, and the seventh wicket fell with 12 overs to go. However, Kasprowicz and Wharf survived.

Close of play: First day, Derbyshire 356-8 (Sutton 77, Dean 12); Second day, Glamorgan 181-5 (Maynard 85, Croft 52); Third day, Derbyshire 189-5 (Cork 28, Sutton 13).

Derbyshire

First innings		Second innings	
A. I. Gait c James b Wharf	0	(2) b Wharf	6
M. J. Di Venuto c Wallace b Thomas	121	(1) lbw b Croft	61
C. W. G. Bassano b Wharf	0	c Dale b Croft	52
S. A. Selwood c Wallace b Thomas	20	lbw b Croft	10
Shahid Afridi c Kasprowicz b Thomas	14	c Maynard b Croft	1
*D. G. Cork c Kasprowicz b Croft	37	b Wharf	31
†L. D. Sutton c Dale b Croft	120	not out	37
G. Welch c Dale b Thomas	37	not out	25
Mohammad Ali b Croft	31		
K. J. Dean b Wharf	20		
L. J. Wharton not out	8		
B 5, l-b 7	12	B 7, l-b 4, w 5, n-b 6	22
1/9 (1) 2/9 (3) 3/56 (4) 4/72 (5) 5/165 (6) 6/204 (2) 7/284 (8) 8/337 (9) 9/382 (10) 10/420 (7)	420	1/32 (2) 2/108 (1) 3/136 (4) 4/144 (5) 5/149 (3) 6/193 (6)	(6 wkts dec.) 245

Bonus points – Derbyshire 5, Glamorgan 3 (130 overs: 405-9).

Bowling: *First Innings*—Kasprowicz 32.2–13–94–0; Wharf 23–2–83–3; Davies 4–2–23–0; Thomas 19.4–4–69–4; Croft 52.4–11–128–3; Dale 4–1–11–0. *Second Innings*—Kasprowicz 11–1–39–0; Wharf 26–4–87–2; Davies 10–0–47–0; Croft 31–10–61–4.

Glamorgan

First innings		Second innings	
*S. P. James lbw b Dean	1	lbw b Cork	14
A. Dale c Cork b Mohammad Ali	13	c Dean b Wharton	92
D. L. Hemp b Dean	7	c sub b Welch	7
M. J. Powell b Mohammad Ali	12	lbw b Cork	37
M. P. Maynard c Gait b Mohammad Ali	142	c Di Venuto b Shahid Afridi	9
†M. A. Wallace lbw b Wharton	6	c Di Venuto b Shahid Afridi	16
R. D. B. Croft c Wharton b Mohammad Ali	79	b Cork	6
M. S. Kasprowicz c Di Venuto b Cork	41	not out	13
A. G. Wharf b Shahid Afridi	16	not out	19
A. P. Davies c Cork b Shahid Afridi	9		
S. D. Thomas not out	9		
L-b 5, n-b 12	17	B 9, l-b 3, n-b 28	40
1/3 (1) 2/19 (3) 3/25 (2) 4/38 (4) 5/71 (6) 6/253 (7) 7/291 (5) 8/332 (9) 9/342 (10) 10/352 (8)	352	1/32 (1) 2/52 (3) 3/119 (4) 4/154 (5) 5/201 (6) 6/201 (2) 7/216 (7)	(7 wkts) 253

Bonus points – Glamorgan 4, Derbyshire 3.

Bowling: *First Innings*—Cork 24.2–5–83–1; Dean 17–3–65–2; Mohammad Ali 17–3–79–4; Welch 16–3–66–0; Wharton 6–0–25–1; Shahid Afridi 10–2–29–2. *Second Innings*—Cork 14–1–61–3; Dean 6–2–22–0; Welch 8–4–10–1; Mohammad Ali 8–0–56–0; Shahid Afridi 22.4–6–69–2; Wharton 10–3–23–1.

Umpires: D. J. Constant and I. J. Gould.

At Derby, April 23, 24, 25 (not first-class). **Drawn.** Toss: Derbyshire. **Derbyshire 511-5 dec.** (A. I. Gait 54, Shahid Afridi 59, S. A. Selwood 157, D. R. Hewson 153); **Bradford/Leeds UCCE 108-5**.

Selwood and Hewson put on 297 for the fourth wicket.

DERBYSHIRE v SOMERSET

At Derby, April 30, May 1, 2, 3. Drawn. Derbyshire 7 pts, Somerset 11 pts. Toss: Somerset.

Somerset were denied their deserts on the last afternoon as the skies darkened and Derbyshire took the light, effectively seven wickets down and still ten runs behind Somerset's first innings. Bad light and rain had already interrupted the first day and the last, while the third was washed out. On the first morning, Johnson took three early wickets in ten balls to push Derbyshire into trouble, and their innings lacked substance, a problem that would become familiar. Caddick, in his only first-class match of the season, took four wickets. In reply, Burns attacked vigorously before the close, then Cox settled resolutely for five and a half hours, scoring his first century in his last 44 innings for Somerset and Tasmania. Cork took five wickets, though the persevering Welch deserved better than two for 64. Gait batted solidly on the final day but Derbyshire ended the match grateful for the stoppages.

Close of play: First day, Somerset 60-2 (Trescothick 15); Second day, Derbyshire 38-0 (Di Venuto 24, Gait 14); Third day, No play.

Derbyshire

A. I. Gait c Turner b Caddick	41	– (2) lbw b Caddick	63
M. J. Di Venuto b Johnson	17	– (1) lbw b Caddick	36
C. W. G. Bassano c Dutch b Johnson	0	– c Bryant b Dutch	0
S. A. Selwood c Turner b Johnson	0	– c Turner b McLean	18
D. R. Hewson c Cox b Caddick	37	– c Dutch b McLean	13
Shahid Afridi b McLean	4	– c Trescothick b Caddick	6
†L. D. Sutton c Trescothick b Laraman	38	– not out	23
*D. G. Cork c Turner b Johnson	25	– retired not out	6
G. Welch c Dutch b Caddick	14	– not out	9
Mohammad Ali c Trescothick b Caddick	0		
K. J. Dean not out	1		
L-b 7, n-b 6	13	B 4, l-b 12, w 1, n-b 6	23
1/20 (2) 2/20 (3) 3/22 (4) 4/94 (1) 5/101 (6) 6/105 (5) 7/151 (8) 8/188 (9) 9/188 (10) 10/190 (7)	190	1/80 (1) 2/81 (3) 3/115 (4) 4/139 (2) 5/150 (6) 6/154 (5)	(6 wkts) 197

Bonus points – Somerset 3.

In the second innings Cork retired at 176 due to family illness.

Bowling: *First Innings*—McLean 14–5–32–1; Johnson 15–4–47–4; Caddick 17–1–66–4; Laraman 6.1–0–38–1. *Second Innings*—McLean 19–4–66–2; Johnson 10.1–3–25–0; Caddick 21–7–44–3; Dutch 9–1–29–1; Laraman 4–0–15–0; Bowler 1–0–2–0.

Somerset

P. D. Bowler c Sutton b Dean	1	N. A. M. McLean b Welch	15
M. E. Trescothick c and b Welch	69	A. R. Caddick b Mohammad Ali	1
*M. Burns lbw b Cork	40		
J. Cox c Sutton b Cork	126	B 12, l-b 17, w 3, n-b 26	58
J. D. C. Bryant c Welch b Cork	26		
A. W. Laraman c Dean b Cork	24	1/1 (1) 2/60 (3) 3/154 (2)	397
†R. J. Turner not out	32	4/240 (5) 5/330 (6) 6/337 (4)	
K. P. Dutch c Gait b Cork	4	7/340 (9) 8/342 (8)	
R. L. Johnson c Gait b Mohammad Ali	1	9/347 (11) 10/397 (10)	

Bonus points – Somerset 4, Derbyshire 3.

Turner, when 0, retired hurt at 330-5 and resumed at 347.

Bowling: Cork 37–11–74–5; Dean 21–6–90–1; Welch 24.1–7–64–2; Mohammad Ali 18–1–118–2; Shahid Afridi 12–5–22–0.

Umpires: M. R. Benson and A. A. Jones.

At Leeds, May 9, 10, 11, 12. DERBYSHIRE beat YORKSHIRE by 166 runs.

At Chester-le-Street, May 21, 22, 23, 24. DERBYSHIRE lost to DURHAM by 30 runs.

DERBYSHIRE v WORCESTERSHIRE

At Derby, May 30, 31, June 1. Worcestershire won by nine wickets. Worcestershire 21 pts, Derbyshire 3 pts. Toss: Worcestershire.

A 122nd first-class century by Hick put him level at No. 12 in the all-time list with Tom Graveney, who was present to watch one of Hick's more domineering innings. He drove and pulled with such authority that 120 of his 155 came in boundaries. Derbyshire's attack was summarily dismissed, and Mohammad Ali's left-arm pace was treated savagely: he conceded more than ten an over. Although openers Gait and Di Venuto put on 83 in reply, Derbyshire collapsed to Worcestershire's overseas-bred seam bowlers, who probed their flawed technique, Hayward's pace proving too much for the tail. It was no better when Derbyshire followed on, until a determined partnership between Cork and Welch prolonged the match into a third day. But Worcestershire used only 100 minutes of it in completing their fourth consecutive victory in all competitions. They climbed to third in the second division, continuing their recovery from a rain-blighted early season; Derbyshire, meanwhile, were heading in the opposite direction.

Close of play: First day, Derbyshire 24-0 (Gait 9, Di Venuto 13); Second day, Derbyshire 185-6 (Cork 44, Welch 36).

Worcestershire

S. D. Peters b Mohammad Ali	47	– not out	25
A. Singh b Cork	50	– c Dean b Mohammad Ali	21
G. A. Hick c Khan b Mohammad Ali	155	– not out	1
*B. F. Smith lbw b Mohammad Ali	0		
V. S. Solanki c Hewson b Dean	6		
A. J. Hall lbw b Dean	0		
G. J. Batty c Dumelow b Dean	4		
†S. J. Rhodes c Sutton b Welch	29		
Kabir Ali not out	19		
M. S. Mason c Dumelow b Mohammad Ali	4		
M. Hayward b Cork	1		
B 4, l-b 13, w 10, n-b 32	59	N-b 4	4
1/106 (2) 2/125 (1) 3/125 (4) 4/172 (5) 5/172 (6) 6/222 (7) 7/332 (8) 8/348 (3) 9/367 (10) 10/374 (11)	374	1/50 (2)	(1 wkt) 51

Bonus points – Worcestershire 4, Derbyshire 3.

Bowling: *First Innings*—Cork 24.1–9–70–2; Dean 21–7–41–3; Welch 26–6–81–1; Mohammad Ali 12–0–124–4; Dumelow 9–1–41–0. *Second Innings*—Cork 3–0–22–0; Dean 2–0–16–0; Mohammad Ali 1.5–0–10–1; Dumelow 1–0–3–0.

Derbyshire

A. I. Gait c Rhodes b Mason	50	– (2) b Batty	18
M. J. Di Venuto c Smith b Mason	54	– (1) lbw b Ali	4
R. M. Khan c Hayward b Mason	2	– c Ali b Hayward	32
S. A. Selwood b Hayward	17	– lbw b Ali	11
D. R. Hewson c Rhodes b Hall	0	– c Hick b Ali	4
†L. D. Sutton c Rhodes b Hall	3	– lbw b Hall	25
*D. G. Cork c Rhodes b Hayward	24	– b Hayward	52
G. Welch c Singh b Hall	9	– not out	51
N. R. C. Dumelow b Hayward	5	– c Rhodes b Hayward	6
Mohammad Ali not out	3	– c Solanki b Mason	5
K. J. Dean b Hayward	0	– b Hayward	21
B 1, l-b 4, w 3, n-b 4	12	B 8, l-b 3, w 1, n-b 4	16
1/83 (2) 2/93 (3) 3/113 (1) 4/114 (5) 5/118 (6) 6/159 (7) 7/170 (4) 8/171 (8) 9/179 (9) 10/179 (11)	179	1/5 (1) 2/48 (2) 3/71 (4) 4/75 (3) 5/82 (5) 6/111 (6) 7/203 (7) 8/211 (9) 9/216 (10) 10/245 (11)	245

Bonus points – Worcestershire 3.

Bowling: *First Innings*—Hayward 16.5–4–53–4; Ali 9–3–35–0; Mason 10–1–27–3; Batty 9–2–31–0; Hall 12–0–28–3. *Second Innings*—Ali 11–0–60–3; Mason 19–4–54–1; Batty 9–1–29–1; Hall 10–3–24–1; Hayward 14–1–67–4.

Umpires: T. E. Jesty and J. W. Lloyds.

At Swansea, June 4, 5, 6, 7. DERBYSHIRE lost to GLAMORGAN by an innings and 70 runs.

At Northampton, June 27, 28, 29. DERBYSHIRE lost to NORTHAMPTONSHIRE by 180 runs.

DERBYSHIRE v YORKSHIRE

At Derby, July 2, 3, 4, 5. Yorkshire won by ten wickets. Yorkshire 22 pts, Derbyshire 3 pts. Toss: Derbyshire.

Derbyshire ended a bad week in turmoil. Cork heard he would face the ECB's disciplinary committee for calling Brad Hodge a "cheat" after a Twenty20 match at Leicester; the club complained about "serial inconsistencies" when the pitch panel cleared the Northampton wicket on which Derbyshire had been spun out earlier in the week; and this failure against Yorkshire completed the club's worst Championship run since 1932 – five consecutive defeats. After Cork put Yorkshire in, White scored a majestic 173 not out, adding 195 with Lumb (dropped on 63), and 96 for the last wicket with Kirby. Cork, playing through an ankle injury, managed only 15 overs, throwing a heavy load on Dean and Welch, who bowled 77 between them. Derbyshire's reply was pathetic. Against aggressive bowling by Kirby and Sidebottom, eight wickets fell for 22 in 16 overs and, despite some enterprise from Dumelow, the follow-on was inevitable. Di Venuto, the patient Kaif and the tail at least did enough to make Yorkshire bat again.

Close of play: First day, Yorkshire 314-7 (White 102, Bresnan 6); Second day, Derbyshire 80-8 (Lungley 4, Dumelow 20); Third day, Derbyshire 238-5 (Kaif 76, Cork 26).

Yorkshire

*M. J. Wood c Bassano b Welch	35	– not out	21
S. P. Fleming lbw b Welch	13	– not out	42
Yuvraj Singh lbw b Cork	6		
M. J. Lumb c Kaif b Welch	93		
R. J. Blakey lbw b Dean	0		
C. White not out	173		
†S. M. Guy lbw b Welch	0		
A. K. D. Gray c Sutton b Welch	14		
T. T. Bresnan c Sutton b Welch	19		
R. J. Sidebottom c Bassano b Dean	2		
S. P. Kirby c Di Venuto b Lungley	33		
B 5, l-b 14, w 3, n-b 34	56	L-b 3, n-b 2	5
1/25 (2) 2/44 (3) 3/75 (1) 4/78 (5) 5/273 (4) 6/273 (7) 7/299 (8) 8/339 (9) 9/348 (10) 10/444 (11)	444		(no wkt) 68

Bonus points – Yorkshire 5, Derbyshire 3 (130 overs: 443-9).

Bowling: *First Innings*—Dean 36–7–113–2; Welch 41–13–102–6; Cork 15–5–34–1; Lungley 16.4–1–84–1; Dumelow 21–3–90–0; Hewson 1–0–2–0. *Second Innings*—Cork 7–0–20–0; Dean 7–3–12–0; Welch 3.3–0–20–0; Dumelow 3–0–13–0.

Derbyshire

A. I. Gait c Guy b Sidebottom	17	– (2) c Gray b Bresnan	6
M. J. Di Venuto c Yuvraj Singh b Kirby	27	– (1) c Yuvraj Singh b Sidebottom	74
C. W. G. Bassano lbw b Kirby	0	– c White b Kirby	7
M. Kaif b Kirby	0	– c Gray b Kirby	87
D. R. Hewson c Fleming b Sidebottom	0	– c sub b Gray	8
†L. D. Sutton c Guy b Sidebottom	5	– run out	35
*D. G. Cork lbw b Bresnan	1	– c Sidebottom b Kirby	35
T. Lungley lbw b Sidebottom	6	– lbw b Bresnan	1
G. Welch b Sidebottom	0	– c Guy b Sidebottom	54
N. R. C. Dumelow not out	60	– b Sidebottom	25
K. J. Dean b Sidebottom	0	– not out	30
B 1, l-b 9, n-b 2	12	B 5, l-b 11, p 5	21
1/33 (2) 2/33 (3) 3/35 (4) 4/47 (5) 5/52 (1) 6/55 (7) 7/55 (6) 8/55 (9) 9/128 (8) 10/128 (11)	128	1/38 (2) 2/71 (3) 3/106 (1) 4/115 (5) 5/201 (6) 6/250 (7) 7/257 (8) 8/263 (4) 9/315 (10) 10/383 (9)	383

Bonus points – Yorkshire 3.

Bowling: *First Innings*—Kirby 12–5–31–3; Sidebottom 13.4–6–38–6; Bresnan 9–4–14–1; Gray 7–1–25–0; Yuvraj Singh 1–0–10–0. *Second Innings*—Kirby 30–5–85–3; Sidebottom 22.3–5–73–3; Bresnan 25–5–63–2; Gray 43–10–125–1; White 7–2–16–0; Yuvraj Singh 1–1–0–0.

Umpires: M. R. Benson and R. Palmer.

DERBYSHIRE v GLOUCESTERSHIRE

At Derby, July 9, 10, 11. Gloucestershire won by five wickets. Gloucestershire 19 pts, Derbyshire 3 pts. Toss: Derbyshire.

Batting without confidence or application, Derbyshire again rolled over in their first innings. A total of 89 was their lowest since 1998: "It's a mental thing," said their coach Adrian Pierson, "We are in a dark hole and we have to find the light." Well though Lewis bowled, it was an inadequate batting performance, and Spearman almost matched Derbyshire's total by himself, driving fluently and pulling fiercely, as Gloucestershire coped easily enough with a pitch that gave the umpires no worries. A lead of 188 looked decisive when Derbyshire slumped to 39 for three. However, Di Venuto fought back gloriously, with his third century of the season, helped by Sutton, who shrugged off a hamstring injury to battle tenaciously for 81. Sutton's hopes of a century came to an improbable end when the last man, Mohammad Ali, wandered off to prod the pitch before the umpire called "Over" and was run out because the ball was not dead. After some early alarms, Rhodes steered Gloucestershire to their target of 169. As Derbyshire's run got worse, the precedents got fewer: not since 1922 had they suffered six successive defeats.

Close of play: First day, Gloucestershire 214-6 (Gidman 21, Ball 4); Second day, Derbyshire 226-4 (Di Venuto 116, Sutton 38).

Derbyshire

A. I. Gait c Taylor b Lewis	12	– (2) c Windows b Smith	3
M. J. Di Venuto b Lewis	17	– (1) c and b Ball	148
C. W. G. Bassano c Ball b Lewis	3	– lbw b Harvey	3
M. Kaif c Pope b Harvey	12	– lbw b Harvey	6
D. R. Hewson c Pope b Gidman	8	– lbw b Harvey	39
†L. D. Sutton c Gidman b Harvey	5	– not out	81
G. Welch lbw b Lewis	3	– lbw b Ball	0
*D. G. Cork b Lewis	0	– b Ball	39
N. R. C. Dumelow c Ball b Harvey	0	– c Spearman b Ball	5
K. J. Dean c Spearman b Lewis	6	– lbw b Smith	1
Mohammad Ali not out	14	– run out	2
B 4, l-b 5	9	B 17, l-b 9, w 3	29
1/16 (1) 2/28 (3) 3/37 (2) 4/51 (4) 5/57 (6) 6/69 (7) 7/69 (5) 8/69 (8) 9/73 (9) 10/89 (10)	89	1/21 (2) 2/24 (3) 3/39 (4) 4/145 (5) 5/264 (1) 6/268 (7) 7/318 (8) 8/342 (9) 9/349 (10) 10/356 (11)	356

Bonus points – Gloucestershire 3.

Bowling: *First Innings*—Lewis 11–0–48–6; Smith 11–6–14–0; Harvey 13–6–18–3; Gidman 1–1–0–1. *Second Innings*—Lewis 29–7–91–0; Smith 25–5–72–2; Ball 34–11–65–4; Harvey 24–7–58–3; Gidman 10–1–44–0.

Gloucestershire

*C. M. Spearman c Gait b Dean	85	– (2) lbw b Dean	0
W. P. C. Weston b Welch	28	– (1) c Di Venuto b Dean	6
C. G. Taylor c Sutton b Mohammad Ali	1	– c Hewson b Welch	16
J. N. Rhodes lbw b Cork	6	– not out	62
M. G. N. Windows lbw b Cork	20	– lbw b Welch	0
A. P. R. Gidman c Sutton b Dean	25	– b Cork	41
I. J. Harvey c Di Venuto b Mohammad Ali	27	– not out	21
M. C. J. Ball not out	34		
†S. P. Pope b Cork	1		
J. Lewis b Cork	13		
A. M. Smith b Welch	15		
B 5, l-b 6, w 1, n-b 10	22	L-b 14, n-b 11	25
1/53 (2) 2/60 (3) 3/101 (4) 4/158 (1) 5/158 (5) 6/202 (7) 7/230 (6) 8/231 (9) 9/257 (10) 10/277 (11)	277	1/4 (2) 2/15 (1) 3/52 (3) 4/52 (5) 5/121 (6)	(5 wkts) 171

Bonus points – Gloucestershire 2, Derbyshire 3.

Bowling: *First Innings*—Cork 27–3–75–4; Dean 22–4–85–2; Welch 19.2–6–45–2; Mohammad Ali 16–2–60–2; Dumelow 2–1–1–0. *Second Innings*—Cork 13–3–47–1; Dean 8.4–2–42–2; Welch 11–1–36–2; Mohammad Ali 7–0–32–0.

Umpires: B. Dudleston and I. J. Gould.

At Worcester, July 15, 16, 17, 18. DERBYSHIRE lost to WORCESTERSHIRE by an innings and 42 runs.

DERBYSHIRE v DURHAM

At Derby, July 24, 25, 26, 27. Drawn. Derbyshire 10 pts, Durham 10 pts. Toss: Derbyshire. Championship debut: N. E. L. Gunter.

After seven successive Championship defeats, Derbyshire's worst sequence since a run of 18 in 1920 and 1921, a draw provided some relief. Having been put in, Durham, with only 12 batting points from nine games, helped themselves against poor bowling. Lewis became Cork's 700th first-class victim, but Peng, who had not reached a Championship fifty for a year, and Wells, with his first century for Durham, added 197, a county record for the fifth wicket. After the second day was washed out, Di Venuto and his new opening partner Selwood responded in kind, their own 197 bettering half Derbyshire's completed first-class innings so far in 2003. Even more remarkably in such a poor batting side, Di Venuto became the first in the country to 1,000 Championship runs. After Durham left a challenging target of 251 in 55 overs, Selwood again batted well but Lungley and the debutant Neil Gunter had to block out the last ten overs, grateful that Shoaib Akhtar was absent.

Close of play: First day, Durham 434-7 (Mustard 33, Plunkett 24); Second day, No play; Third day, Derbyshire 287-4 (Bassano 19, Sutton 12).

Durham

	First innings		Second innings	
*J. J. B. Lewis c Sutton b Cork	77	–	not out	41
M. A. Gough c Cork b Gunter	36	–	c Kaif b Gunter	31
G. J. Muchall c Kaif b Wharton	9	–	c Di Venuto b Dean	0
G. J. Pratt c Di Venuto b Gunter	4	–	not out	33
N. Peng lbw b Wharton	99			
V. J. Wells c and b Lungley	106			
†P. Mustard not out	70			
G. D. Bridge lbw b Lungley	4			
L. E. Plunkett b Dean	29			
N. Killeen not out	13			
L-b 23, w 5, n-b 26	54		L-b 3, w 2	5
1/110 (2) 2/120 (3) 3/133 (4) 4/162 (1) 5/359 (6) 6/389 (5) 7/398 (8) 8/475 (9)	(8 wkts dec.) 501		1/52 (2) 2/53 (3)	(2 wkts dec.) 110

N. G. Hatch did not bat.

Bonus points – Durham 5, Derbyshire 2.

Bowling: *First Innings*—Cork 20.5–3–92–1; Dean 31–5–138–1; Lungley 14.4–0–91–2; Gunter 13.1–2–48–2; Wharton 27–4–103–2; Khan 2–1–6–0. *Second Innings*—Dean 6–1–29–1; Gunter 6–0–57–1; Cork 1.1–0–10–0; Di Venuto 1–0–11–0.

"The *Ottawa Citizen* proclaimed 'Spunky Canadians Beat Top-Ranking Bangladesh', thus showing everything is relative."

The World Cup, page 966.

Derbyshire

S. A. Selwood c and b Bridge	62	– (2) b Gough	88
M. J. Di Venuto lbw b Plunkett	143	– (1) lbw b Plunkett	8
M. Kaif c Gough b Bridge	31	– c Mustard b Killeen	7
R. M. Khan c Gough b Killeen	7	– c Muchall b Hatch	23
C. W. G. Bassano not out	44	– c Mustard b Hatch	0
†L. D. Sutton c Wells b Killeen	20	– run out	36
*D. G. Cork not out	39	– c Killeen b Gough	1
T. Lungley (did not bat)		– not out	10
N. E. L. Gunter (did not bat)		– not out	9
B 1, l-b 6, n-b 8	15	B 7, l-b 15	22
1/197 (1) 2/241 (2) 3/255 (4) 4/255 (3) 5/302 (6)	(5 wkts dec.) 361	1/8 (1) 2/15 (3) 3/64 (4) 4/72 (5) 5/176 (6) 6/178 (2) 7/179 (7)	(7 wkts) 204

K. J. Dean and L. J. Wharton did not bat.

Bonus points – Derbyshire 4, Durham 1.

Bowling: *First Innings*—Plunkett 16–1–67–1; Hatch 14–1–70–0; Killeen 26–4–94–2; Wells 4–0–23–0; Bridge 33–10–100–2. *Second Innings*—Plunkett 8–0–41–1; Killeen 12–2–28–1; Hatch 10–2–29–2; Bridge 18–3–61–0; Gough 7.4–3–23–2.

Umpires: M. J. Kitchen and N. J. Llong.

At Southampton, August 13, 14. DERBYSHIRE beat HAMPSHIRE by an innings and 43 runs.

DERBYSHIRE v NORTHAMPTONSHIRE

At Derby, August 20, 21, 22. Northamptonshire won by an innings and 231 runs. Northamptonshire 22 pts, Derbyshire 1 pt. Toss: Northamptonshire.

Northamptonshire were so dominant, and their opponents so spineless, that the match ended in Derbyshire's most comprehensive innings defeat since 1975, in the famous match at Buxton when Lancashire caught them on a snow-affected wicket. After Derbyshire's first innings disintegrated, any questions about the slow pitch were soon answered as Hussey, Jaques and Sales batted with increasing momentum. Meanwhile, Cork retreated to long leg on the second morning, leaving Welch to captain the side. With Derbyshire's morale at rock bottom, Sales just helped himself and reached his fifth double-century with authority in just 217 balls. By the late afternoon, Northamptonshire had piled up the highest score against Derbyshire since Nottinghamshire's 661 on this ground in 1901; Hussey's declaration, at 647 for five, was an act of mercy. The deficit was a mountainous 509, and even a fifth century of the summer from Di Venuto failed to avert a rout, the prelude to the committee's refusal to continue with Cork as captain or Adrian Pierson as coach. To add to the misery, Selwood's season was ended when a ball from Nel broke his wrist. Northamptonshire were left almost certain of promotion; Derbyshire remained bottom.

Close of play: First day, Northamptonshire 224-1 (Hussey 103, Jaques 99); Second day, Derbyshire 66-0 (Di Venuto 34, Selwood 31).

Derbyshire

S. A. Selwood c Roberts b Nel	1	– (2) retired hurt	33
M. J. Di Venuto b Nel	0	– (1) b Brown	116
R. M. Khan b Greenidge	76	– c Powell b Brown	8
M. Kaif c Sales b Cook	31	– lbw b Cawdron	14
C. W. G. Bassano b Cook	1	– c Bailey b Brown	0
†L. D. Sutton b Cawdron	0	– b Brown	56
*D. G. Cork c Jaques b Cook	1	– c Powell b Nel	12
G. Welch b Cook	3	– c Roberts b Greenidge	8
N. R. C. Dumelow c Bailey b Greenidge	15	– not out	6
K. J. Dean lbw b Greenidge	0	– b Greenidge	1
Mohammad Ali not out	1	– b Greenidge	0
B 1, l-b 2, w 2, n-b 4	9	B 7, l-b 5, w 2, n-b 10	24
1/1 (2) 2/4 (1) 3/83 (4) 4/88 (5) 5/95 (6) 6/96 (7) 7/109 (8) 8/133 (9) 9/133 (10) 10/138 (3)	138	1/99 (3) 2/132 (4) 3/135 (5) 4/220 (1) 5/249 (6) 6/264 (7) 7/272 (8) 8/278 (10) 9/278 (11)	278

Bonus points – Northamptonshire 3.

In the second innings Selwood retired hurt at 75.

Bowling: *First Innings*—Nel 15–5–40–2; Greenidge 10.3–2–33–3; Cawdron 9–2–27–1; Cook 15–6–35–4. *Second Innings*—Nel 20–6–57–1; Greenidge 17.4–1–75–3; Cook 6–0–33–0; Brown 42–16–60–4; Cawdron 14–1–41–1.

Northamptonshire

*M. E. K. Hussey run out	115
T. W. Roberts lbw b Dean	12
P. A. Jaques b Dean	123
D. J. Sales not out	200
M. J. Powell c Khan b Dean	50
J. W. Cook c Welch b Dean	85
†T. M. B. Bailey not out	22
B 15, l-b 1, w 4, n-b 20	40
1/28 (2) 2/261 (3) 3/274 (1) 4/413 (5) 5/609 (6)	(5 wkts dec.) 647

M. J. Cawdron, A. Nel, C. G. Greenidge and J. F. Brown did not bat.

Bonus points – Northamptonshire 5, Derbyshire 1 (130 overs: 597-4).

Bowling: Cork 21.1–0–83–0; Dean 30.5–3–145–4; Mohammad Ali 23.3–3–118–0; Welch 25–2–112–0; Dumelow 26–1–131–0; Khan 1–0–7–0; Selwood 7–0–28–0; Di Venuto 2–0–7–0.

Umpires: V. A. Holder and A. G. T. Whitehead.

At Derby, August 28, 29, 30. DERBYSHIRE drew with SOUTH AFRICANS (see South African tour section).

At Bristol, September 3, 4, 5, 6. DERBYSHIRE lost to GLOUCESTERSHIRE by 20 runs.

At Taunton, September 10, 11, 12, 13. DERBYSHIRE lost to SOMERSET by 27 runs.

DERBYSHIRE v HAMPSHIRE

At Derby, September 17, 18, 19, 20. Hampshire won by ten wickets. Hampshire 22 pts, Derbyshire 6 pts. Toss: Hampshire.

Hampshire, inspired by Hamblin and Tomlinson, two of their least experienced players, dodged the wooden spoon, leaving Derbyshire bottom for the second time in three years. Derbyshire's 11th Championship defeat began with Cork, having apparently lost the captaincy, requesting his release, which was provisionally granted. He played little part – a slapdash 20 and four expensive overs – before succumbing to a hamstring strain. Gait continued his late flurry of runs and there was another impressive contribution from Hasan Adnan, until he became one of Hamblin's six first-innings victims. Hamblin had never taken more than one in an innings in the Championship before, and after another commanding performance from Katich, he then took Hampshire galloping towards a lead of 263 with a career-best 96. Derbyshire's bowling was wearily ineffectual as the last four wickets added 214. In the second-innings, Di Venuto passed 1,500 runs for the season, but Sutton fell 18 short of becoming the first Derbyshire wicket-keeper to reach 1,000 since 1901. Tomlinson's career-best bowling left Hampshire needing only 27 to win.

Close of play: First day, Hampshire 76-0 (Kenway 38, Adams 32); Second day, Hampshire 458-6 (Hamblin 61, Mascarenhas 17); Third day, Derbyshire 160-4 (Gait 5, Sutton 14).

Derbyshire

First innings		Second innings	
A. I. Gait c Prittipaul b Hamblin	63	– (2) c Pothas b Tomlinson	71
M. J. Di Venuto c Pothas b Hamblin	35	– (1) c Pothas b Tomlinson	52
R. M. Khan c Katich b Hamblin	6	– b Bruce	58
S. D. Stubbings c Prittipaul b Udal	30	– lbw b Bruce	8
Hasan Adnan b Hamblin	84	– b Udal	14
†L. D. Sutton c Bruce b Hamblin	17	– c Katich b Mascarenhas	30
*D. G. Cork c Tomlinson b Bruce	20	– (9) not out	1
G. Welch lbw b Udal	14	– (7) b Tomlinson	17
N. R. C. Dumelow c Katich b Hamblin	1	– (8) c Prittipaul b Tomlinson	19
Mohammad Ali c Bruce b Udal	18	– c and b Tomlinson	0
P. M. R. Havell not out	0	– b Tomlinson	0
B 1, l-b 8, w 5, n-b 15	29	B 6, l-b 7, n-b 6	19
1/82 (2) 2/112 (3) 3/117 (1) 4/180 (4) 5/213 (6) 6/252 (7) 7/298 (8) 8/298 (5) 9/307 (9) 10/317 (10)	317	1/71 (1) 2/90 (4) 3/108 (5) 4/160 (3) 5/215 (6) 6/260 (2) 7/288 (8) 8/289 (7) 9/289 (10) 10/289 (11)	289

Bonus points – Derbyshire 3, Hampshire 3.

In the second innings Gait, when 5, retired hurt at 36 and resumed at 160.

Bowling: *First Innings*—Mascarenhas 14–4–38–0; Tomlinson 13–2–58–0; Bruce 13–4–54–1; Hamblin 22–3–93–6; Udal 19.3–2–52–3; Katich 3–0–13–0. *Second Innings*—Mascarenhas 16–5–43–1; Tomlinson 19.1–6–63–6; Bruce 14–3–60–2; Hamblin 6–1–30–0; Udal 29–14–50–1; Katich 11–5–30–0.

Hampshire

First innings		Second innings	
D. A. Kenway lbw b Mohammad Ali	68	– not out	16
J. H. K. Adams b Havell	60	– not out	10
S. M. Katich c Havell b Welch	122		
*J. P. Crawley lbw b Welch	59		
L. R. Prittipaul lbw b Welch	18		
†N. Pothas c Khan b Havell	4		
J. R. C. Hamblin b Dumelow	96		
A. D. Mascarenhas c Sutton b Welch	21		
S. D. Udal c Gait b Mohammad Ali	57		
J. T. A. Bruce c Di Venuto b Havell	12		
J. A. Tomlinson not out	1		
B 12, l-b 7, w 1, n-b 42	62	N-b 2	2
1/138 (1) 2/142 (2) 3/295 (4) 4/346 (3) 5/365 (5) 6/366 (6) 7/478 (8) 8/542 (7) 9/577 (9) 10/580 (10)	580		(no wkt) 28

Bonus points – Hampshire 5, Derbyshire 3.

Bowling: *First Innings*—Cork 4–0–28–0; Welch 41–7–163–4; Mohammad Ali 36–4–166–2; Dumelow 26–9–75–1; Havell 20.4–1–129–3. *Second Innings*—Welch 2.2–0–18–0; Dumelow 2–0–10–0.

Umpires: J. W. Holder and G. Sharp.

DURHAM

The Rickshaw at the Riverside

TIM WELLOCK

Eleven years after becoming a first-class county, Durham achieved one of their most burning ambitions in 2003 when the Riverside became the eighth English ground to stage a Test match – and the first newcomer to the list in 101 years. The success of the occasion was followed a month later by the shock resignation of the chairman who had done so much to bring it about.

In almost four years in charge, Bill Midgley had overseen an improvement in the financial situation and continued the development of the ground to Test standard. It culminated in the installation of 2,000 extra permanent seats, paid for by a private development in the opposite corner of the ground. This new health club had not been part of the original plans, which angered some members, and when Midgley felt complaints had become personal insults, he walked out.

This sad coda to the club's greatest week epitomised a year of highs and lows. On the field, the highlights were a double over Yorkshire, who had never previously lost to Durham in the Championship, a county-record 273 by the Australian, Martin Love, against Hampshire, and excitement generated for half a season by the world's fastest bowler, Shoaib Akhtar, otherwise known as the "Rawalpindi Express". After his arrival in late June, Shoaib clearly paced himself, prompting one member to call him the "Rawalpindi Rickshaw", but his final statistics were impressive. He took 34 Championship wickets at 17.05 and was due to return for 2004.

In the end, Durham finished fourth from bottom in both second divisions which, in the Championship at least, represented a significant improvement. Their tally of Championship wins rose to five from one – and the wooden spoon – in 2002. With three games left, all against fellow contenders, Durham had a good chance of promotion. But they lost all three, each time failing to reach 250 in the first innings. Across the season, they made a first-innings total of more than 350 only three times, which was again inadequate.

For 2004, the county announced that Love, who was twice called away by Australian Test commitments, would be replaced as their other overseas player by the South African opening batsman Herschelle Gibbs. In a significant change to their home-grown policy, Durham also signed Jamaican-born Gareth Breese, an off-spinning all-rounder with one Test cap for West Indies and an EU passport. "We have a policy of encouraging local talent, but there are areas we need to strengthen and we decided we're prepared to go down the EU route to do it," said coach, Martyn Moxon.

Shoaib arrived as a replacement for Dewald Pretorius, a seamer who made a good impression before being summoned in June to join the touring South Africans. Love, Durham's other first-choice overseas player, turned up in late May after touring the West Indies with Australia, broke his thumb a week later, and recovered just in time to fly out to face Bangladesh in July. His replacement in the early weeks was the Indian seam bowler Javagal Srinath, who looked jaded and announced he would be retiring from first-class cricket. And in August, Shoaib was called up by Pakistan to play Bangladesh. The upshot of the to-ing and fro-ing was that Durham fielded two overseas players in only three of their first 13 Championship matches.

Shoaib Akhtar

The homegrown contributions were also patchy. Captain Jon Lewis hit form in the first half of the season, after a poor 2002, and 21-year-old Gary Pratt passed 1,000 first-class runs for the first time, as well as averaging over 42 in the National League. Pratt aside, the young batsmen again fell below expectations. Nicky Peng and Gordon Muchall failed to turn talent into consistent results. But the greatest disappointment, not least to himself, was Michael Gough, once captain of England Under-19. After an excellent closing half in 2002, he averaged just 23.77 in the Championship and announced in September that he would not be fulfilling the final year of his contract because he had stopped enjoying the game.

Vince Wells, signed from Leicestershire to add some experience, had an indifferent season and subsequently retired. The search for more runs meant the highly rated wicket-keeper Andrew Pratt was dropped, in the hope that the fearless strokeplay of 20-year-old Phil Mustard would prove more productive. Initially, Mustard did well, but as his runs dried up his wicket-keeping also suffered. Crucially, Paul Collingwood dislocated his shoulder in a pre-season match, ruling him out for four months. And when Mark Davies suffered a collapsed lung in the same match, it seemed the cruel run of injuries in 2002 would continue unabated.

The bowling showed little progress. Neil Killeen joined with Shoaib to rout Somerset for 56, the lowest first-class total against Durham, and later took a career-best seven for 70 during the innings victory over Hampshire. But otherwise he continued to look more of a one-day bowler. Eighteen-year-old Liam Plunkett generated pace and movement as he took five for 53 against Yorkshire on his Championship debut; an improvement could be seen in Steve Harmison when released by England; and Graeme Bridge grabbed his belated chance to prove himself a better all-round prospect than fellow-spinner Nicky Phillips, who was released. But only Shoaib took more than 30 Championship wickets. For Durham, success on the field seems tantalisingly just out of reach.

DURHAM RESULTS

All first-class matches – Played 18: Won 5, Lost 7, Drawn 6.
County Championship matches – Played 16: Won 5, Lost 7, Drawn 4.

Frizzell County Championship, 6th in Division 2; Cheltenham & Gloucester Trophy, 4th round; National Cricket League, 7th in Division 2; Twenty20 Cup, 5th in North Group.

COUNTY CHAMPIONSHIP AVERAGES, BATTING AND FIELDING

Cap		*M*	*I*	*NO*	*R*	*HS*	*100s*	*50s*	*Avge*	*Ct/St*
2001	M. L. Love§	7	13	0	778	273	1	4	59.84	8
1998	J. J. B. Lewis	16	31	2	1,104	124	1	10	38.06	3
	G. J. Pratt	16	31	1	949	150	1	7	31.63	9
1998	P. D. Collingwood	4	7	1	169	68	0	2	28.16	4
2001	N. Peng	13	23	0	580	133	1	2	25.21	11
	G. D. Bridge	8	13	3	240	50	0	1	24.00	7
	M. A. Gough	11	22	0	523	73	0	3	23.77	7
	P. Mustard	12	22	1	484	70*	0	1	23.04	41/1
	V. J. Wells	11	20	1	419	106	1	2	22.05	9
	L. E. Plunkett	6	11	4	139	40*	0	0	19.85	2
	G. J. Muchall	11	22	0	379	74	0	3	17.22	4
	Shoaib Akhtar§	7	14	2	197	37	0	0	16.41	0
2001	A. Pratt	4	7	2	79	27	0	0	15.80	12
2001	N. C. Phillips	11	20	4	211	39	0	0	13.18	7
1999	S. J. Harmison	5	6	3	38	14*	0	0	12.66	2
	J. Srinath§	3	5	3	24	13*	0	0	12.00	1
	A. M. Davies	4	7	2	55	21	0	0	11.00	0
	D. Pretorius§	4	7	3	32	16	0	0	8.00	3
1999	N. Killeen	10	18	4	110	26	0	0	7.85	2
2001	D. R. Law	5	9	1	53	35	0	0	6.62	0
	N. G. Hatch	4	4	1	13	5	0	0	4.33	0

Also batted: J. A. Lowe (1 match) 80, 0; I. Pattison (1 match) 62; A. M. Thorpe (2 matches) 35, 11, 4.

§ *Overseas player.*

BOWLING

	O	*M*	*R*	*W*	*BB*	*5W/i*	*Avge*
Shoaib Akhtar	183	40	580	34	4-9	0	17.05
D. Pretorius	79	13	317	16	4-15	0	19.81
V. J. Wells	145.4	33	456	22	4-16	0	20.72
S. J. Harmison	161.1	55	441	19	4-50	0	23.21
D. R. Law	76.3	10	256	11	4-30	0	23.27
L. E. Plunkett	150	27	636	18	5-53	1	35.33
N. Killeen	267	63	848	23	7-70	1	36.86
A. M. Davies	110	26	389	10	2-34	0	38.90
G. D. Bridge	289	59	996	25	4-47	0	39.84
N. C. Phillips	326.4	50	1,200	30	5-144	1	40.00

Also bowled: P. D. Collingwood 61.1–7–228–4; M. A. Gough 9.4–3–35–2; N. G. Hatch 104.4–21–384–9; G. J. Muchall 37.2–7–144–4; I. Pattison 5.4–3–7–1; G. J. Pratt 1–0–5–0; J. Srinath 84–24–226–6.

COUNTY RECORDS

Highest score for:	273	M. L. Love v Hampshire at Chester-le-Street	2003
Highest score against:	501*	B. C. Lara (Warwickshire) at Birmingham	1994
Best bowling for:	9-64	M. M. Betts v Northamptonshire at Northampton	1997
Best bowling against:	8-22	D. Follett (Middlesex) at Lord's	1996
Highest total for:	645-6 dec.	v Middlesex at Lord's	2002
Highest total against:	810-4 dec.	by Warwickshire at Birmingham	1994
Lowest total for:	67	v Middlesex at Lord's	1996
Lowest total against:	56	by Somerset at Chester-le-Street	2003

DURHAM DIRECTORY

ADDRESS

County Ground, Riverside, Chester-le-Street, County Durham DH3 3QR (0191 387 1717; fax 0191 387 1616; email james.bailey.durham@ecb.co.uk). **Website** www.durhamccc.org.uk.

GROUND

Chester-le-Street (Riverside): ¼ mile W of town centre between A167 and A1(M). Entrance is from roundabout off A167. Nearest station: Chester-le-Street (1 mile).

OFFICIALS

Captain J. J. B. Lewis
Head coach M. D. Moxon
President 2003 – M. Pratt
Chairman 2003 – D. W. Midgley; 2004 – R. Jackson
Chief executive D. Harker
Director of cricket G. Cook
Head groundsman D. Measor
Scorer B. Hunt

PLAYERS

Players expected to reappear in 2004

	Former counties	*Country*	*Born*	*Birthplace*
Bridge Graeme David		E	4.9.1980	†*Sunderland*
***Collingwood** Paul David		‡E	26.5.1976	†*Shotley Bridge*
Davies Anthony Mark		E	4.10.1980	†*Stockton-on-Tees*
***Harmison** Stephen James		E	23.10.1978	*Ashington*
Killeen Neil		E	17.10.1975	†*Shotley Bridge*
Lewis Jonathan James Benjamin	Essex	E	21.5.1970	*Isleworth*
Lowe James Adam		E	4.11.1982	*Bury St Edmunds*
Muchall Gordon James		E	2.11.1982	*Newcastle upon Tyne*
Mustard Philip		E	8.10.1982	†*Sunderland*
Pattison Ian		E	5.5.1982	†*Ryhope*
Peng Nicky		E	18.9.1982	*Newcastle upon Tyne*
Plunkett Liam Edward		E	6.4.1985	*Middlesbrough*
Pratt Andrew		E	4.3.1975	†*Helmington Row*
Pratt Gary Joseph		E	22.12.1981	†*Bishop Auckland*
***Shoaib Akhtar**	Somerset	P	13.8.1975	*Rawalpindi*

Players due to join in 2004

***Breese** Gareth Rohan		WI (EU)	9.1.1976	*Montego Bay, Jamaica*
***Gibbs** Herschelle Herman		SA	23.2.1974	*Cape Town*
***Hamilton** Gavin Mark	Yorks	E/SCO	16.9.1974	*Broxburn*

* *Test player.* † *Born in Durham* ‡ *12-month ECB contract.*

At Taunton, April 23, 24, 25, 26. DURHAM lost to SOMERSET by six wickets.

DURHAM v GLOUCESTERSHIRE

At Chester-le-Street, April 30, May 1, 2, 3. Drawn. Durham 7 pts, Gloucestershire 10 pts. Toss: Gloucestershire. Championship debut: D. Pretorius.

On a bland pitch, Gloucestershire's county-circuit stalwarts outbowled Durham's internationals, but were denied by Jon Lewis – and the loss of more than a day to rain. With nearly nine overs left and Durham 149 for five, nine short of avoiding an innings defeat, Gloucestershire still had the faintest glimmer. Lewis, who held his team together with dogged fifties in each innings, was removed but the wicket came too late and Durham reached safety. Dewald Pretorius completed a trio of Test bowlers in the Durham line-up, but it was Law who was the pick on the first day, as Gloucestershire slipped from 194 for three to 243 for eight. However, Russell expertly supervised the addition of 98 for the last two wickets, which seemed to deflate Durham, and they replied feebly. After they followed on 158 behind, Gough dominated an opening stand of 118, Durham's biggest since 1999, before the jitters set in again.

Close of play: First day, Gloucestershire 285-9 (Russell 31, Smith 0); Second day, Durham 129-7 (Srinath 10, Phillips 0); Third day, No play.

Gloucestershire

C. M. Spearman lbw b Srinath	4
W. P. C. Weston c Lewis b Law	40
T. H. C. Hancock c A. Pratt b Law	59
J. N. Rhodes c A. Pratt b Pretorius	60
M. G. N. Windows c G. J. Pratt b Wells	44
*M. W. Alleyne lbw b Law	21
†R. C. Russell b Law	65
I. D. Fisher lbw b Phillips	0
R. J. Sillence b Phillips	0
J. Lewis b Harmison	10
A. M. Smith not out	17
B 4, l-b 13, w 2, n-b 2	21
1/10 (1) 2/65 (2) 3/148 (3) 4/194 (4) 5/234 (6) 6/240 (5) 7/243 (8) 8/243 (9) 9/276 (10) 10/341 (7)	341

Bonus points – Gloucestershire 3, Durham 3.

Bowling: Harmison 30–11–58–1; Srinath 24–6–64–1; Pretorius 20–5–94–1; Law 18.2–5–30–4; Wells 13–3–28–1; Phillips 14–4–50–2.

Durham

*J. J. B. Lewis c Spearman b Smith	54	– c Weston b Sillence	55
M. A. Gough c Fisher b Lewis	2	– c Weston b Smith	73
G. J. Pratt c Alleyne b Smith	0	– c Weston b Smith	0
V. J. Wells b Lewis	0	– c Russell b Smith	1
N. Peng c and b Alleyne	37	– c sub b Sillence	10
D. R. Law c Sillence b Alleyne	2	– b Lewis	2
†A. Pratt b Smith	13	– not out	8
J. Srinath b Lewis	10	– not out	0
N. C. Phillips c Russell b Sillence	27		
D. Pretorius lbw b Sillence	16		
S. J. Harmison not out	7		
L-b 5, n-b 10	15	B 1, l-b 1, n-b 8	10
1/3 (2) 2/4 (3) 3/5 (4) 4/80 (5) 5/84 (6) 6/118 (7) 7/123 (1) 8/129 (8) 9/166 (9) 10/183 (10)	183	1/118 (2) 2/118 (3) 3/130 (4) 4/143 (5) 5/149 (6) 6/155 (1)	(6 wkts) 159

Bonus points – Gloucestershire 3.

Bowling: *First Innings*—Lewis 17–4–32–3; Smith 24–5–64–3; Sillence 15.3–2–52–2; Alleyne 8–1–30–2. *Second Innings*—Lewis 17.5–6–48–1; Smith 12–7–14–3; Sillence 17–4–46–2; Alleyne 7–1–38–0; Fisher 12–8–11–0.

Umpires: B. Leadbeater and A. G. T. Whitehead.

At Durham, May 9, 10, 11. DURHAM drew with DURHAM UCCE.

DURHAM v WORCESTERSHIRE

At Stockton-on-Tees, May 14, 15, 16, 17. Drawn. Durham 7 pts, Worcestershire 9 pts. Toss: Worcestershire. Championship debut: A. J. Hall.

With the groundsman at the Riverside preparing for Durham's inaugural Test, the county returned to Stockton for the first time since 1999. Only 148 overs were squeezed into the first three days, and the morning session was lost on the last, but the captains conspired, leaving Durham a target of 250 in 67 overs. At tea, they needed only 115 from 32, with nine wickets left and Muchall batting superbly. But when Lewis fell immediately after the interval, the rot set in. Five wickets fell in four overs, with Muchall skying a hook on 74, and Durham ended up grateful when the rain returned. During the match, Srinath announced his first-class retirement, but he wavered later. He jolted briefly to life during a spell of three for none in 11 balls, but otherwise ambled in like a man ready for a rest. Smith was his first victim in Worcestershire's only innings, hoisting a catch to fine leg after a fluent 81, before Kabir Ali thrashed a career-best 84.

Close of play: First day, Worcestershire 156-3 (Smith 39, Solanki 0); Second day, Durham 146-3 (Lewis 66, Phillips 1); Third day, No play.

Worcestershire

S. D. Peters lbw b Harmison	62
A. Singh run out	16
G. A. Hick c Phillips b Law	30
*B. F. Smith c Harmison b Srinath	81
V. S. Solanki c A. Pratt b Srinath	52
A. J. Hall b Srinath	0
G. J. Batty c Muchall b Wells	18
†S. J. Rhodes lbw b Harmison	1
Kabir Ali not out	84
M. S. Mason b Wells	0
M. Hayward b Harmison	28
L-b 18, w 1, n-b 4	23
1/18 (2) 2/70 (3) 3/149 (1) 4/250 (4) 5/254 (6) 6/255 (5) 7/258 (8) 8/334 (7) 9/346 (10) 10/395 (11)	395

Bonus points – Worcestershire 4, Durham 3.

Bowling: Harmison 29–14–69–3; Srinath 27–10–70–3; Wells 14–2–58–2; Law 22–2–100–1; Phillips 15–0–80–0.

Worcestershire forfeited their second innings.

Durham

	First innings		Second innings	
*J. J. B. Lewis not out	66	–	lbw b Hall	43
M. A. Gough b Hayward	22	–	c Hick b Ali	1
G. J. Muchall c Rhodes b Hayward	0	–	c Singh b Hall	74
G. J. Pratt c Hick b Batty	38	–	c Rhodes b Batty	4
N. C. Phillips not out	1			
J. Srinath (did not bat)		–	(5) c Peters b Batty	1
V. J. Wells (did not bat)		–	(6) st Rhodes b Batty	0
N. Peng (did not bat)		–	(7) lbw b Hall	0
D. R. Law (did not bat)		–	(8) not out	0
†A. Pratt (did not bat)		–	(9) not out	0
B 2, l-b 1, n-b 16	19		B 8, l-b 11, w 1, n-b 8	28
1/41 (2) 2/41 (3) 3/140 (4)	(3 wkts dec.) 146		1/3 (2) 2/135 (1) 3/148 (4) 4/150 (3) 5/150 (6) 6/151 (7) 7/151 (5)	(7 wkts) 151

S. J. Harmison did not bat.

Bonus point – Worcestershire 1.

Bowling: *First Innings*—Hayward 10–1–34–2; Ali 9–0–44–0; Hall 3–0–21–0; Mason 8–4–21–0; Batty 11–5–23–1. *Second Innings*—Hayward 5–0–32–0; Ali 8–0–37–1; Batty 16–6–34–3; Mason 5–0–19–0; Hall 6–2–10–3.

Umpires: A. A. Jones and M. J. Kitchen.

DURHAM v DERBYSHIRE

At Chester-le-Street, May 21, 22, 23, 24. Durham won by 30 runs. Durham 20 pts, Derbyshire 4 pts. Toss: Durham.

Di Venuto rose like a colossus above some shambolic batting, but still failed to save Derbyshire. On the second day, when Durham lost their last four first-innings wickets for 16, and no other Derbyshire batsman managed more than 20, Di Venuto eased dreamy back-foot drives down the ground and made 150 of his side's 244. His scorching first fifty came in 42 balls. Then, in just 24 overs on day three, Durham's second innings disintegrated from 106 for two – a lead of 179 – to 149 all out, Welch's accuracy and persistence rewarded with five for 60. Chasing 223, and with Gait ill, Derbyshire opened with the out-of-form Shahid Afridi. He thrashed 14 off the first over he faced, reached fifty off 37 balls and crashed four sixes in his 67. Cork maintained the rumbustious approach, and Derbyshire began the last day needing 64, with four wickets left. But Cork was too frenzied on the resumption, edging a wild drive, and, between showers, Pretorius cleaned up, taking three for 13 in less than six overs. The win was Durham's first in the Championship since their last game against Derbyshire, in July 2002.

Close of play: First day, Durham 296-6 (Wells 61, A. Pratt 5); Second day, Durham 16-0 (Lewis 0, Gough 15); Third day, Derbyshire 159-6 (Cork 48, Dean 1).

Durham

*J. J. B. Lewis b Wharton	52	– b Welch	32
M. A. Gough c Sutton b Mohammad Ali	12	– c sub b Dean	17
M. L. Love c Cork b Welch	54	– c Wharton b Mohammad Ali	41
G. J. Muchall b Welch	0	– c Selwood b Mohammad Ali	9
G. J. Pratt lbw b Welch	62	– c Sutton b Welch	2
V. J. Wells c Gait b Dean	61	– c Cork b Welch	15
D. R. Law c Wharton b Mohammad Ali	3	– b Cork	7
†A. Pratt c Di Venuto b Dean	5	– lbw b Cork	3
N. C. Phillips b Dean	15	– c Wharton b Welch	4
N. Killeen not out	0	– lbw b Welch	0
D. Pretorius b Dean	0	– not out	1
L-b 29, w 1, n-b 23	53	L-b 14, n-b 4	18
1/34 (2) 2/137 (3) 3/137 (4) 4/137 (1) 5/263 (5) 6/279 (7) 7/301 (6) 8/312 (8) 9/317 (9) 10/317 (11)	317	1/22 (2) 2/70 (1) 3/106 (3) 4/108 (5) 5/110 (4) 6/132 (7) 7/136 (8) 8/146 (6) 9/146 (10) 10/149 (9)	149

Bonus points – Durham 3, Derbyshire 3.

Bowling: *First Innings*—Cork 19–2–65–0; Dean 20.4–11–41–4; Welch 21–10–53–3; Mohammad Ali 14–2–49–2; Shahid Afridi 10–2–27–0; Wharton 16–3–48–1; Di Venuto 3–0–5–0. *Second Innings*—Cork 23–8–49–2; Dean 10–5–19–1; Welch 26.4–5–60–5; Wharton 3–1–5–0; Mohammad Ali 4–3–2–2.

"When Middlesex's wicket-keeper, Nash, became their tenth bowler his figures were omitted from the board, with a note at the top reading: 'Sorry Nashy – no more room'."

Middlesex in 2003, page 642.

Derbyshire

A. I. Gait c A. Pratt b Killeen	5	– (7) b Phillips	10
M. J. Di Venuto lbw b Law	150	– (1) lbw b Pretorius	4
S. A. Selwood c A. Pratt b Pretorius	20	– c Love b Wells	8
D. R. Hewson b Pretorius	9	– c Love b Wells	10
†L. D. Sutton b Phillips	9	– c A. Pratt b Law	10
Shahid Afridi c G. J. Pratt b Phillips	0	– (2) c Phillips b Wells	67
*D. G. Cork c Love b Phillips	0	– (6) c A. Pratt b Pretorius	52
G. Welch c Wells b Pretorius	20	– (9) not out	23
Mohammad Ali c Lewis b Pretorius	1	– (10) c Love b Pretorius	4
K. J. Dean run out	15	– (8) c A. Pratt b Phillips	1
L. J. Wharton not out	0	– c Gough b Pretorius	1
B 2, l-b 2, n-b 11	15	L-b 1, w 1	2
1/11 (1) 2/81 (3) 3/97 (4) 4/130 (5) 5/130 (6) 6/131 (7) 7/174 (8) 8/182 (9) 9/236 (10) 10/244 (2)	244	1/4 (1) 2/49 (3) 3/61 (4) 4/92 (2) 5/130 (5) 6/151 (7) 7/164 (8) 8/164 (6) 9/172 (10) 10/192 (11)	192

Bonus points – Derbyshire 1, Durham 3.

Bowling: *First Innings*—Pretorius 17–2–96–4; Killeen 20–5–49–1; Law 9.3–1–35–1; Phillips 31–8–60–3. *Second Innings*—Pretorius 12.2–1–49–4; Killeen 9–1–60–0; Wells 6–1–13–3; Phillips 13–0–49–2; Law 4–0–20–1.

Umpires: J. H. Evans and P. J. Hartley.

At Leeds, May 30, 31, June 1. DURHAM beat YORKSHIRE by 167 runs.

At Southampton, June 4, 5, 6, 7. DURHAM drew with HAMPSHIRE.

At Chester-le-Street, June 27, 28, 29, 30. DURHAM drew with INDIA A (see India A tour section).

At Worcester, July 2, 3, 4. DURHAM lost to WORCESTERSHIRE by 31 runs.

DURHAM v NORTHAMPTONSHIRE

At Chester-le-Street, July 9, 10, 11. Northamptonshire won by eight wickets. Northamptonshire 20 pts, Durham 6 pts. Toss: Durham.

Brown gave Northamptonshire their fourth win in a row. Late on the third morning, Durham led by 75, with no second-innings wickets down, but after fellow off-spinner Swann exposed the middle order, Brown's flatter trajectory and immaculate control brought a career-best seven for 69, on a pitch offering modest help. It was the first time a spinner had taken seven wickets in an innings in the Riverside's eight-year history. Left 205 to chase, Northamptonshire raced to 180 for two, claimed the extra half-hour, and did the rest in the blink of an eye. Jaques, cutting strongly throughout, followed his first-innings century with 81. On the first day, Gary Pratt had made a magnificent 150 for Durham – his maiden first-class hundred – but there was little support as Cawdron moved the ball in to the right-handers, claiming four of his six victims lbw. After the match, Durham's chairman, Bill Midgley, resigned, citing personal attacks by members.

Close of play: First day, Durham 325-9 (Plunkett 38, Hatch 3); Second day, Northamptonshire 320-8 (Phillips 9, Cawdron 10).

Durham

*J. J. B. Lewis lbw b Cawdron	7	– lbw b Swann	21
M. A. Gough lbw b Cawdron	9	– c Jaques b Brown	53
G. J. Muchall c Bailey b Cawdron	22	– lbw b Swann	1
G. J. Pratt lbw b Cawdron	150	– c Bailey b Brown	5
N. Peng c Powell b Brown	18	– c Hussey b Brown	36
V. J. Wells lbw b Cawdron	30	– b Brown	10
†P. Mustard c Bailey b Phillips	16	– run out	49
Shoaib Akhtar c Bailey b Wright	18	– c Bailey b Brown	8
L. E. Plunkett not out	38	– b Brown	0
N. C. Phillips c and b Cawdron	6	– not out	9
N. G. Hatch b Wright	5	– c Powell b Brown	3
L-b 2, w 2, n-b 4	8	L-b 4	4
1/11 (1) 2/18 (2) 3/49 (3) 4/119 (5) 5/178 (6) 6/202 (7) 7/236 (8) 8/308 (4) 9/318 (10) 10/327 (11)	327	1/70 (1) 2/74 (2) 3/80 (3) 4/84 (4) 5/100 (6) 6/171 (5) 7/179 (8) 8/187 (9) 9/189 (7) 10/199 (11)	199

Bonus points – Durham 3, Northamptonshire 3.

Bowling: *First Innings*—Wright 27.3–5–86–2; Cawdron 20–3–87–6; Phillips 19–2–58–1; Brown 30–10–53–1; Cook 5–2–15–0; Swann 13–4–26–0. *Second Innings*—Wright 14–3–37–0; Cawdron 2–0–17–0; Phillips 7–1–29–0; Brown 23.4–3–69–7; Swann 13–1–43–2.

Northamptonshire

*M. E. K. Hussey c Mustard b Shoaib Akhtar	43	– (2) not out	72
M. J. Powell lbw b Hatch	6	– (1) c Phillips b Hatch	7
P. A. Jaques c Peng b Phillips	109	– c sub b Muchall	81
J. W. Cook c Mustard b Phillips	18	– not out	32
D. J. Sales c Plunkett b Hatch	33		
G. P. Swann c Peng b Shoaib Akhtar	13		
†T. M. B. Bailey c Wells b Plunkett	39		
D. G. Wright c Plunkett b Wells	27		
B. J. Phillips not out	9		
M. J. Cawdron b Shoaib Akhtar	11		
J. F. Brown b Hatch	0		
B 2, l-b 4, n-b 8	14	L-b 4, n-b 10	14
1/10 (2) 2/102 (1) 3/147 (4) 4/190 (5) 5/208 (6) 6/232 (3) 7/293 (8) 8/302 (7) 9/321 (10) 10/322 (11)	322	1/9 (1) 2/165 (3)	(2 wkts) 206

Bonus points – Northamptonshire 3, Durham 3.

Bowling: *First Innings*—Shoaib Akhtar 19–7–49–3; Hatch 21.4–6–66–3; Plunkett 19–5–78–1; Wells 14–2–31–1; Phillips 33–5–92–2. *Second Innings*—Shoaib Akhtar 6–1–25–0; Hatch 7–1–39–1; Wells 4–0–14–0; Plunkett 6–2–44–0; Phillips 11.1–0–54–0; Muchall 4–1–26–1.

Umpires: J. H. Evans and J. W. Holder.

DURHAM v YORKSHIRE

At Chester-le-Street, July 15, 16, 17, 18. Durham won by three wickets. Durham 20 pts, Yorkshire 8 pts. Toss: Yorkshire.

Durham turned a riveting match on its head to complete their first-ever Championship double. After Yorkshire took a first-innings lead of 121, the turning point came during the 29 gloomy overs the rain allowed on day three: Shoaib Akhtar grabbed three wickets in 11 balls, as Yorkshire

PROGRESS CHECK...

Durham's first Championship win against each of the other counties:

	First win	*Attempt*
Derbyshire	1994	3rd
Essex	1993	2nd
Glamorgan	1992	1st
Gloucestershire	1994	3rd
Hampshire	1995	5th
Kent	1997	7th
Lancashire	Never	10 games so far
Leicestershire	Never	11 games so far
Middlesex	1998	7th
Northamptonshire	1994	3rd
Nottinghamshire	1995	4th
Somerset	1992	1st
Surrey	2000	9th
Sussex	2001	10th
Warwickshire	1993	2nd
Worcestershire	2001	9th
Yorkshire	2003	11th

Research: Philip Bailey

---

lost six for 101. The rest succumbed swiftly on the final day and, chasing 251, Durham batted solidly, before Shoaib smashed 14 off 11 balls to finish the job with seven and a half overs left. On the day his Test recall was announced, Darren Gough managed just one expensive wicket. Shoaib had a curious match, roaring back after four short and wicketless spells on the first day to polish off the Yorkshire tail in 11 energetic overs the next morning. During that burst he clashed with Kirby, who responded to a beamer by flinging down his helmet and marching up to him. At the other end, White stood firm to make 135 not out.

Close of play: First day, Yorkshire 340-6 (White 82, Gray 60); Second day, Yorkshire 2-0 (Wood 1, Fleming 1); Third day, Yorkshire 103-6 (White 30, Gray 4).

Yorkshire

M. J. Wood c Peng b Harmison	18	– lbw b Harmison	10
S. P. Fleming c and b Harmison	10	– c Mustard b Wells	38
*A. McGrath c Pratt b Wells	86	– c Pratt b Shoaib Akhtar	3
M. J. Lumb c and b Bridge	43	– c Pratt b Shoaib Akhtar	5
Yuvraj Singh c Mustard b Hatch	7	– c Mustard b Shoaib Akhtar	0
C. White not out	135	– lbw b Wells	30
†S. M. Guy c Mustard b Wells	3	– b Harmison	7
A. K. D. Gray c Gough b Shoaib Akhtar	60	– c Mustard b Shoaib Akhtar	11
D. Gough c Mustard b Shoaib Akhtar	4	– c Gough b Wells	0
R. J. Sidebottom c Peng b Shoaib Akhtar	12	– not out	18
S. P. Kirby c Peng b Bridge	17	– c Gough b Harmison	1
B 12, l-b 28, w 1, n-b 12	53	B 4, l-b 2	6
1/28 (2) 2/39 (1) 3/160 (4) 4/167 (5) 5/191 (3) 6/197 (7) 7/340 (8) 8/346 (9) 9/382 (10) 10/448 (11)	448	1/11 (1) 2/32 (3) 3/40 (4) 4/40 (5) 5/72 (2) 6/86 (7) 7/104 (6) 8/104 (9) 9/128 (8) 10/129 (11)	129

Bonus points – Yorkshire 5, Durham 3.

Bowling: *First Innings*—Shoaib Akhtar 25–6–87–3; Harmison 29–7–92–2; Hatch 21–3–79–1; Wells 20–10–41–2; Bridge 34–9–109–2. *Second Innings*—Harmison 10.3–2–45–3; Wells 9–3–20–3; Shoaib Akhtar 10–2–38–4; Hatch 6–1–20–0; Bridge 1–1–0–0.

Durham

*J. J. B. Lewis lbw b Kirby	7	– c Fleming b Sidebottom	41
M. A. Gough c Yuvraj Singh b Gough	54	– c Yuvraj Singh b Kirby	38
G. J. Muchall c Guy b Kirby	8	– c Fleming b Sidebottom	30
G. J. Pratt c Gray b Sidebottom	51	– b Kirby	14
V. J. Wells c Fleming b Gray	42	– (6) b Gough	17
N. Peng c Guy b Sidebottom	8	– (5) b Gray	30
†P. Mustard c Guy b McGrath	32	– run out	34
G. D. Bridge lbw b Kirby	50	– not out	1
Shoaib Akhtar c Wood b Kirby	25	– not out	14
N. G. Hatch b Gray	4		
S. J. Harmison not out	14		
B 9, l-b 5, n-b 18	32	B 13, l-b 11, n-b 8	32
1/13 (1) 2/27 (3) 3/102 (4) 4/175 (5) 5/177 (2) 6/210 (6) 7/240 (7) 8/284 (9) 9/300 (10) 10/327 (8)	327	1/57 (2) 2/97 (1) 3/117 (4) 4/172 (5) 5/172 (3) 6/229 (6) 7/232 (7)	(7 wkts) 251

Bonus points – Durham 3, Yorkshire 3.

Bowling: *First Innings*—Gough 18–2–77–1; Kirby 20–3–93–4; Sidebottom 17–0–67–2; McGrath 8–3–31–1; Gray 9–1–45–2. *Second Innings*—Gough 19.3–6–68–1; Kirby 21–5–54–2; Sidebottom 16–2–57–2; McGrath 11–1–18–0; Gray 12–2–30–1.

Umpires: A. Clarkson and A. A. Jones.

At Derby, July 24, 25, 26, 27. DURHAM drew with DERBYSHIRE.

DURHAM v SOMERSET

At Chester-le-Street, July 30, 31, August 1. Durham won by 318 runs. Durham 20 pts, Somerset 3 pts. Toss: Durham. County debut: T. Webley. Championship debut: W. J. Durston.

Two blistering spells by Shoaib Akhtar handed Durham an extraordinary win. On the third morning, he helped wreck Somerset's first innings with four wickets in 14 balls. In the afternoon, after Durham had spurned the follow-on and extended their lead to 374, he snatched three in an over: Cox gloved to the keeper, Burns was pinned by a shooter, and debutant Tom Webley fended a fearsome delivery to short leg. Somerset were soon one for four and then eight for six. They quickly crumbled to 56 all out, the lowest first-class total against Durham, and the lowest of the first-class season; the biggest partnership was the last, 17. Despite some variable bounce, it was a pathetic effort. Killeen bowled with zip and, like Shoaib, took four wickets. On the rain-shortened first day, wicket-keeper Turner twisted his ankle but Somerset did well to reduce Durham to 164 for five, under the eye of their chief executive, Peter Anderson, who had recently threatened to sack ten players. But Durham recovered patiently on day two, and then Shoaib took over. It was Durham's first Championship win over Somerset since their inaugural season in 1992.

Close of play: First day, Durham 164-5 (Peng 6, Mustard 11); Second day, Somerset 83-4 (Burns 25, Laraman 0).

LOWEST FIRST-CLASS TOTALS AGAINST DURHAM

56	**Somerset at Chester-le-Street**	**2003**
67	Durham UCCE at Chester-le-Street	2001
73	Oxford University at Oxford	1994
85	Surrey at Chester-le-Street	2000

Durham

*J. J. B. Lewis b McLean	2	– c Durston b Jones	25
M. A. Gough c Durston b Johnson	19	– (8) c Bryant b McLean	0
G. J. Muchall b Jones	65	– (2) c Johnson b Laraman	20
G. J. Pratt b Blackwell	51	– c sub b McLean	41
N. Peng c Bryant b Johnson	58	– (3) lbw b Laraman	1
V. J. Wells b Jones	3	– (5) b Jones	5
†P. Mustard c and b McLean	31	– (6) c Johnson b Durston	37
G. D. Bridge b McLean	42	– (7) b Jones	8
Shoaib Akhtar c Webley b Burns	26	– (10) not out	5
N. Killeen c Burns b Laraman	26	– (9) b Jones	11
A. M. Davies not out	3	– lbw b Jones	5
B 5, l-b 10, w 2, n-b 2	19	B 3, l-b 3, n-b 4	10
1/2 (1) 2/53 (2) 3/141 (3) 4/143 (4) 5/146 (6) 6/207 (7) 7/285 (5) 8/285 (8) 9/339 (10) 10/345 (9)	345	1/40 (1) 2/46 (2) 3/49 (3) 4/56 (5) 5/137 (4) 6/139 (6) 7/141 (8) 8/157 (9) 9/162 (7) 10/168 (11)	168

Bonus points – Durham 3, Somerset 3.

Bowling: *First Innings*—McLean 22–8–56–3; Johnson 28–0–109–2; Jones 22–5–76–2; Laraman 18–4–45–1; Blackwell 20–6–33–1; Durston 2–0–7–0; Burns 3.1–2–4–1. *Second Innings*—McLean 10–2–28–2; Johnson 4–1–18–0; Laraman 8–2–26–2; Jones 9.5–2–42–5; Burns 4–0–19–0; Blackwell 3–0–13–0; Durston 6–1–16–1.

Somerset

J. Cox lbw b Wells	29	– (2) c Mustard b Shoaib Akhtar	1
J. D. C. Bryant c Mustard b Davies	5	– (1) c Mustard b Killeen	0
*M. Burns not out	35	– lbw b Shoaib Akhtar	0
T. Webley lbw b Wells	6	– c Peng b Shoaib Akhtar	0
I. D. Blackwell c Wells b Bridge	14	– c Mustard b Killeen	6
A. W. Laraman c sub b Shoaib Akhtar	9	– b Shoaib Akhtar	0
†R. J. Turner c Mustard b Shoaib Akhtar	7	– lbw b Davies	6
W. J. Durston c Bridge b Shoaib Akhtar	4	– c Mustard b Killeen	6
R. L. Johnson c Mustard b Shoaib Akhtar	0	– run out	12
P. S. Jones b Wells	25	– not out	9
N. A. M. McLean b Wells	0	– c Wells b Killeen	14
B 2, l-b 1, n-b 2	5	N-b 2	2
1/33 (2) 2/35 (1) 3/47 (4) 4/77 (5) 5/92 (6) 6/100 (7) 7/106 (8) 8/106 (9) 9/139 (10) 10/139 (11)	139	1/1 (2) 2/1 (3) 3/1 (4) 4/1 (1) 5/2 (6) 6/8 (5) 7/20 (7) 8/32 (8) 9/39 (9) 10/56 (11)	56

Bonus points – Durham 3.

Bowling: *First Innings*—Shoaib Akhtar 14–4–39–4; Killeen 11–2–28–0; Davies 12–4–36–1; Wells 10–4–16–4; Muchall 3–1–9–0; Bridge 2–0–8–1. *Second Innings*—Shoaib Akhtar 7–2–9–4; Killeen 9.4–2–30–4; Davies 3–1–17–1.

Umpires: I. J. Gould and V. A. Holder.

At Cardiff, August 13, 14, 15, 16. DURHAM lost to GLAMORGAN by eight wickets.

DURHAM v HAMPSHIRE

At Chester-le-Street, August 20, 21, 22, 23. Durham won by an innings and 115 runs. Durham 22 pts, Hampshire 4 pts. Toss: Durham.

At lunch on the first day the match was evenly balanced, with Durham 114 for three. Thereafter, it was one-way traffic. Love and Pratt plundered 52 from the next seven overs, and Love sailed on remorselessly, running the deep-cover sweeper ragged during a seven-and-a-half-hour 273. It was Durham's highest first-class score, beating Love's own 251 at Lord's in 2002. Among his 38 fours and two sixes from 364 balls came only one mistake, a miscued pull on 46 that fell just short of fine leg. Pratt hit 66 and the third-highest scorer was Extras with 36, but Durham still managed 515, their biggest total at the Riverside. Love was last out, dancing down the pitch. Hampshire seemed overawed by his monumental effort and once an opening stand of 50 was broken, they twice subsided meekly. First time round, Francis and Pothas provided the only application in a fifth-wicket stand of 81; when they followed on, Killeen's sustained accuracy – and some compliant batsmen – won him seven for 70, his first five-wicket haul in four years. Durham rose to third in the second division table.

Close of play: First day, Durham 388-7 (Love 181, Killeen 0); Second day, Hampshire 88-4 (Francis 12, Pothas 5); Third day, Hampshire 125-5 (Pothas 26, Mascarenhas 2).

Durham

*J. J. B. Lewis c Pothas b Mullally	11
N. Peng c Pothas b Mascarenhas	30
M. L. Love b Udal	273
P. D. Collingwood c Smith b Tomlinson	9
G. J. Pratt lbw b Mascarenhas	66
A. M. Thorpe c Adams b Udal	35
†P. Mustard c Vaas b Mullally	4
G. D. Bridge lbw b Mascarenhas	23
N. Killeen c Pothas b Mullally	16
A. M. Davies c Pothas b Vaas	11
N. G. Hatch not out	1
B 11, l-b 13, n-b 12	36
1/25 (1) 2/62 (2) 3/73 (4) 4/234 (5) 5/315 (6) 6/320 (7) 7/378 (8) 8/445 (9) 9/489 (10) 10/515 (3)	515

Bonus points – Durham 5, Hampshire 3 (130 overs: 510-9).

Bowling: Vaas 27–2–115–1; Mullally 29–3–121–3; Mascarenhas 32–9–71–3; Tomlinson 18–0–105–1; Udal 16.5–3–50–2; Katich 9–1–29–0.

Hampshire

J. H. K. Adams c Mustard b Davies	21	– c Mustard b Killeen	36
*J. P. Crawley c Collingwood b Bridge	29	– c Collingwood b Killeen	4
S. M. Katich lbw b Davies	16	– b Killeen	2
R. A. Smith lbw b Collingwood	1	– lbw b Hatch	49
J. D. Francis c Peng b Collingwood	65	– c Mustard b Killeen	6
†N. Pothas c Peng b Bridge	50	– b Davies	47
A. D. Mascarenhas lbw b Hatch	12	– b Davies	10
S. D. Udal b Bridge	10	– c Love b Killeen	5
W. P. U. J. C. Vaas c Love b Bridge	0	– not out	1
A. D. Mullally c Mustard b Collingwood	0	– lbw b Killeen	14
J. A. Tomlinson not out	0	– c Lewis b Killeen	10
B 1, l-b 4, n-b 2	7	B 4, l-b 1	5
1/50 (1) 2/66 (3) 3/67 (4) 4/80 (2) 5/161 (6) 6/190 (7) 7/203 (8) 8/211 (5) 9/211 (9) 10/211 (10)	211	1/8 (2) 2/18 (3) 3/63 (1) 4/79 (5) 5/117 (4) 6/158 (6) 7/159 (7) 8/163 (8) 9/177 (10) 10/189 (11)	189

Bonus points – Hampshire 1, Durham 3.

Bowling: *First Innings*—Killeen 15–8–30–0; Hatch 18–4–57–1; Collingwood 16.1–4–38–3; Davies 18–5–34–2; Bridge 24–6–47–4. *Second Innings*—Davies 19–7–49–2; Killeen 20.2–6–70–7; Hatch 7–3–24–1; Collingwood 7–2–23–0; Bridge 8–2–18–0.

Umpires: N. A. Mallender and R. Palmer.

At Northampton, September 3, 4, 5. DURHAM lost to NORTHAMPTONSHIRE by an innings and 85 runs.

At Bristol, September 10, 11, 12, 13. DURHAM lost to GLOUCESTERSHIRE by 126 runs.

DURHAM v GLAMORGAN

At Chester-le-Street, September 17, 18, 19. Glamorgan won by 369 runs. Glamorgan 18 pts (after 1 pt penalty), Durham 3.5 pts (after 0.5 pt penalty). Toss: Glamorgan.

For the second time this season Kasprowicz sliced through Durham with nine wickets in an innings. His nine for 45 to win the game was the second-best of the 2003 Championship (behind his nine for 36 at Cardiff), and it took to 35 his tally in his last three first-class matches against Durham. No one had taken two nine-fors in an English season since Jim Laker in his heroic year of 1956. The easy-paced pitch offered just enough seam movement to reward his hostility and accuracy – five batsmen were bowled, two lbw and two caught behind – and he was twice on a hat-trick, albeit against demoralised batsmen. The win was Glamorgan's biggest ever in terms of runs (beating 332 against the New Zealanders at Swansea in 1937) but it still failed to win them

NINE PLUS NINE

Bowlers taking nine or more wickets in an innings twice in a season since the Second World War:

T. P. B. Smith (Essex)	9-117 and 9-108	1948
J. H. Wardle (Yorkshire)	9-48 and 9-25	1954
J. C. Laker (Surrey and England)	10-88, 9-37* and 10-53*	1956
R. W. Blair (Wellington)	9-75 and 9-72	1956-57
Abdul Qadir (Habib Bank)	9-49 and 9-82	1982-83
M. S. Kasprowicz (Glamorgan)	**9-36 and 9-45**	**2003**

* *In same match: England v Australia at Manchester.*

promotion, and it had been much closer after the first innings. Wallace hit a second hundred of the season but received scant support, and Durham conceded a lead of only 23. But they haemorrhaged 239 on the second afternoon – prompting Lewis to gather his players for a dressing down – and the match slipped away. Maynard hit 46 of his first fifty in boundaries, going on to a 97-ball hundred, Powell played with effortless power, and together they put on a glorious 231 in 33 overs, until Maynard hit his wicket after being pinned on the helmet by Shoaib Akhtar. Wallace had already been out hit wicket when he slipped attempting to run. (The oddity of two hit-wickets in an innings had not occurred in first-class cricket since 1992-93, when Mickey Arthur and Omar Henry of Orange Free State were victims against Eastern Province at Bloemfontein. The last occurrence in England was at Folkestone in 1966, involving two Gloucestershire Test players, Arthur Milton and David Allen.) Glamorgan declared with a lead of 487 – and then Croft handed the ball to Kasprowicz.

Close of play: First day, Durham 142-4 (Pratt 58, Wells 16); Second day, Glamorgan 296-4 (Powell 156).

Glamorgan

First Innings		Second Innings	
J. P. Maher b Davies	63	c Love b Wells	24
†M. A. Wallace c Mustard b Killeen	121	hit wkt b Shoaib Akhtar	4
A. Dale c Collingwood b Wells	1	c Bridge b Killeen	0
M. J. Powell c Wells b Davies	5	b Davies	198
M. P. Maynard lbw b Killeen	12	hit wkt b Shoaib Akhtar	102
D. L. Hemp run out	36	c Collingwood b Shoaib Akhtar	3
*R. D. B. Croft c and b Bridge	5	c Mustard b Shoaib Akhtar	4
A. G. Wharf c Wells b Bridge	0	b Bridge	4
S. D. Thomas b Bridge	7	not out	69
M. S. Kasprowicz b Wells	4	not out	34
D. S. Harrison not out	0		
B 7, l-b 6, w 1, n-b 2	16	B 12, l-b 8, n-b 2	22
1/127 (1) 2/154 (3) 3/171 (4) 4/213 (5) 5/222 (2) 6/249 (7) 7/249 (8) 8/260 (6) 9/266 (9) 10/270 (10)	270	1/5 (2) 2/10 (3) 3/65 (1) 4/296 (5) 5/322 (6) 6/334 (7) 7/345 (8) 8/371 (4)	(8 wkts dec.) 464

Bonus points – Glamorgan 2, Durham 3.

Bowling: *First Innings*—Shoaib Akhtar 7–1–19–0; Killeen 16–6–59–2; Davies 16–5–52–2; Collingwood 10–1–49–0; Wells 12.4–3–52–2; Bridge 9–3–26–3. *Second Innings*—Shoaib Akhtar 17–1–84–4; Killeen 14–2–61–1; Davies 15–0–95–1; Wells 7–0–45–1; Collingwood 4–0–21–0; Bridge 26–0–138–1.

Durham

First Innings		Second Innings	
*J. J. B. Lewis c Maher b Kasprowicz	0	c Wallace b Kasprowicz	0
N. Peng c Wallace b Kasprowicz	9	c Powell b Harrison	16
M. L. Love c Wallace b Harrison	0	lbw b Kasprowicz	4
P. D. Collingwood c Wallace b Harrison	50	not out	21
G. J. Pratt c Hemp b Wharf	59	c Wallace b Kasprowicz	7
V. J. Wells not out	58	lbw b Kasprowicz	0
†P. Mustard c Maher b Kasprowicz	5	b Kasprowicz	5
G. D. Bridge c Hemp b Wharf	10	b Kasprowicz	0
Shoaib Akhtar c Dale b Wharf	0	b Kasprowicz	37
N. Killeen b Kasprowicz	8	b Kasprowicz	0
A. M. Davies c Wallace b Thomas	21	b Kasprowicz	14
B 1, l-b 12, w 2, n-b 12	27	L-b 6, n-b 8	14
1/0 (1) 2/9 (3) 3/11 (2) 4/113 (4) 5/146 (5) 6/155 (7) 7/180 (8) 8/180 (9) 9/199 (10) 10/247 (11)	247	1/4 (1) 2/20 (2) 3/28 (3) 4/36 (5) 5/36 (6) 6/42 (7) 7/44 (8) 8/82 (9) 9/82 (10) 10/118 (11)	118

Bonus points – Durham 1, Glamorgan 3.

Bowling: *First Innings*—Kasprowicz 22–3–65–4; Harrison 11–1–57–2; Thomas 8.3–0–37–1; Wharf 12–0–66–3; Croft 5–2–9–0. *Second Innings*—Kasprowicz 12.5–2–45–9; Harrison 8–2–38–1; Wharf 4–0–29–0.

Umpires: M. J. Harris and N. J. Llong.

ESSEX

Oh, no! Yo-yo!

NIGEL FULLER

"If we are relegated, it will mean we have played badly." That was the straightforward stance adopted by the head coach, Graham Gooch, at the start of the season. Five months later, defeat by Warwickshire did indeed mean relegation for Essex, who had now yo-yoed up or down in all four years of the two-division Championship. And Gooch did not shy away from the earlier comment. "We all have to hold up our hands – and that includes me and the rest of the coaching staff – and share responsibility for what has happened," he said. "The simple truth is that we underperformed."

Failure by the top order was the biggest handicap. Essex managed just four Championship centuries all summer, fewer than any other county, and only three times did they achieve maximum batting points. Two of their three victories came against Nottinghamshire, who were also relegated, and the third in the last match of the summer against what was effectively a Surrey Second XI. In that game, Andy Flower hit his second hundred, an unbeaten double, to take his Championship aggregate to 1,153 runs. This was nearly 500 more than Will Jefferson, his nearest rival, which explains the problem.

Not that Nasser Hussain let his county down. His retirement from England's one-day side gave him time for five Championship matches – his most since 1999 – and his presence certainly added steel; he totalled 453 runs, including a double-hundred against Kent. (Hussain also hit majestic form in the National League, where he made successive scores of 144 not out, 98 and 161 not out.) Aftab Habib was the other Championship centurion, his 151 bringing victory at Trent Bridge, though he was so out of touch towards the end of the summer that he was dropped. So too were Jefferson, whose encouraging form of the previous season soon evaporated, and Darren Robinson, another star of 2002. When Robinson was recalled, he had to be stretchered off at Colchester with a serious groin injury; a few days later, he was told his contract would not be renewed. James Foster also had a lean year. Competent rather than outstanding behind the stumps, he let himself down with the bat, several times getting out on the threshold of a substantial score.

The bowling was very ordinary, lacking the cutting edge and staying power that in halcyon days was provided by John Lever and Neil Foster. The news, in early February, that Essex had signed Darren Gough was not just a PR coup – although Gough helped the show along by arriving in a helicopter – it was a chance to plug a substantial gap in the side. Scott Brant, a 20-year-old left-armer born in Zimbabwe but now playing for Queensland, turned in promising performances with the new ball before a knee injury cut short his season in July. An arthritic knee condition also prevented the skipper, Ronnie

Irani, from bowling a single ball after late May. Following surgery in September, he was advised to play on only as a batsman. With Jon Dakin also missing several games through injury, it was no wonder opposing batsmen were able to gorge themselves: all told, Essex conceded 18 hundreds. The off-spinner, James Middlebrook, took most wickets, with 52 – including a hat-trick at Canterbury – but he bowled 180 more overs than anyone else and averaged over 36. The only bowler to grab ten in a match was the Pakistan seamer, Mohammad Akram, signed as Brant's replacement for the final four games. Against a weakened Surrey, he took two for 93 and eight for 49, the best figures of Essex's summer.

Andy Flower

Three victories in the last four fixtures allowed Essex to finish a gratifying third in the National League after they were flirting with the drop a month before. But early elimination in the C&G, plus failure to make much impact in the Twenty20 Cup, did not suggest a major revival in one-day cricket. However, there was nothing mediocre about the crowds (and the cash they generated) for the floodlit Twenty20 clashes with Kent and Middlesex. Both played to packed houses, and another big crowd turned out for the day/nighter against Pakistan. These three Chelmsford games brought in a total of around £150,000, confirming the wisdom of installing permanent floodlighting earlier in the year.

Essex are far from re-establishing themselves as a potent force, but there are at least some encouraging signs. Gough should add some excitement. A British passport means Flower, who signed for another two years, is no longer considered an overseas player – allowing Essex to recruit the 23-year-old Pakistan leg-spinner, Danish Kaneria, to join Brant as the imports for 2004. Meanwhile, Graham Napier looks to be developing into a quality all-rounder, adding a yard of pace with the ball and displaying more maturity with the bat, and teenage seam bowler Tony Palladino marked his second Championship appearance with six for 41 against Kent. Unfortunately, he suffered a badly dislocated shoulder after diving trying to prevent a boundary in the next match against Sussex, and was forced to miss the rest of the season.

But it was Alastair Cook, another teenager, who made the biggest impression. A tall, left-handed batsman, he was thrust into opening for the last three Championship games – and responded with a fifty in each. Like his team-mate Ravinder Bopara, Cook was selected for England's Under-19 World Cup squad over the winter, and both should play a significant part in Essex's future.

ESSEX RESULTS

All first-class matches – Played 17: Won 3, Lost 5, Drawn 8, Tied 1.
County Championship matches – Played 16: Won 3, Lost 5, Drawn 7, Tied 1.

Frizzell County Championship, 7th in Division 1; Cheltenham & Gloucester Trophy, 4th round; National Cricket League, 3rd in Division 1; Twenty20 Cup, 5th in South Group.

COUNTY CHAMPIONSHIP AVERAGES

BATTING AND FIELDING

Cap		*M*	*I*	*NO*	*R*	*HS*	*100s*	*50s*	*Avge*	*Ct/St*
1989	N. Hussain	5	9	1	453	206	1	2	56.62	2
	A. N. Cook	3	6	1	239	84	0	3	47.80	3
2002	A. Flower§	16	28	3	1,153	201*	2	6	46.12	17
	M. L. Pettini	3	5	1	172	78	0	2	43.00	3
	R. S. Bopara	4	7	3	163	48	0	0	40.75	3
1989	J. P. Stephenson	3	5	1	137	75*	0	2	34.25	0
2003	G. R. Napier	15	24	8	480	89*	0	2	30.00	3
2002	A. Habib	12	20	0	599	151	1	4	29.95	9
1997	D. D. J. Robinson	10	19	2	503	83	0	3	29.58	5
	A. J. Clarke	3	4	1	87	41	0	0	29.00	1
2002	W. I. Jefferson	13	26	3	656	62	0	5	28.52	10
2001	J. S. Foster	16	25	0	648	85	0	4	25.92	45/2
1994	R. C. Irani	12	18	0	450	87	0	4	25.00	4
2003	J. M. Dakin	10	17	1	390	59	0	2	24.37	2
1996	A. P. Grayson	9	16	2	287	71	0	2	20.50	5
2003	J. D. Middlebrook	15	24	1	468	82*	0	2	20.34	6
	R. N. ten Doeschate	2	4	0	48	31	0	0	12.00	1
2003	S. A. Brant§	10	14	6	37	23	0	0	4.62	3
	Mohammad Akram§	4	6	1	19	10	0	0	3.80	0
	J. B. Grant	3	4	1	11	4	0	0	3.66	1

Also batted J. E. Bishop (1 match) 21; A. G. A. M. McCoubrey (2 matches) 1, 0, 0*; A. C. McGarry (1 match) 4*; A. P. Palladino (3 matches) 5, 7*, 8; Z. K. Sharif (1 match) 0 (1 ct).

§ *Overseas player.*

BOWLING

	O	*M*	*R*	*W*	*BB*	*5W/i*	*Avge*
J. M. Dakin	330.3	74	1,049	39	5-86	1	26.89
Mohammad Akram	145	31	560	20	8-49	2	28.00
S. A. Brant	325.5	70	1,060	36	6-45	1	29.44
J. D. Middlebrook	559.3	79	1,889	52	6-123	3	36.32
G. R. Napier	379.3	60	1,506	33	5-66	1	45.63

Also bowled: J. E. Bishop 29–4–101–1; R. S. Bopara 30–3–122–2; A. J. Clarke 59–13–205–7; A. N. Cook 2–0–11–0; A. Flower 8.3–0–24–1; J. B. Grant 39.2–3–181–7; A. P. Grayson 133–22–432–8; A. Habib 2.4–0–10–1; R. C. Irani 87–28–223–8; A. G. A. M. McCoubrey 24.1–3–142–3; A. C. McGarry 25.3–3–89–0; A. P. Palladino 75–21–215–7; D. D. J. Robinson 5.5–0–40–1; Z. K. Sharif 17–1–103–3; J. P. Stephenson 42–8–162–3; R. N. ten Doeschate 24–3–122–0.

COUNTY RECORDS

Highest score for:	343*	P. A. Perrin v Derbyshire at Chesterfield	1904
Highest score against:	332	W. H. Ashdown (Kent) at Brentwood	1934
Best bowling for:	10-32	H. Pickett v Leicestershire at Leyton	1895
Best bowling against:	10-40	E. G. Dennett (Gloucestershire) at Bristol	1906
Highest total for:	761-6 dec.	v Leicestershire at Chelmsford	1990
Highest total against:	803-4 dec.	by Kent at Brentwood	1934
Lowest total for:	30	v Yorkshire at Leyton	1901
Lowest total against:	14	by Surrey at Chelmsford	1983

ESSEX DIRECTORY

ADDRESS

County Ground, New Writtle Street, Chelmsford CM2 0PG (01245 252420; fax 01245 254030; email greg.lansdowne.essex@ecb.co.uk). **Website** www.essexcricket.org.uk.

GROUNDS

Chelmsford: ¼ mile S of town centre at junction of A138 Parkway and A12 New London Road. Entrance in New Writtle Street. Nearest station: Chelmsford (½ mile).

Southend-on-Sea: 1 mile E of town centre between A13 and seafront. Take R into Lifstan Road and then R into Southchurch Road. Nearest station: Southend East (½ mile).

Colchester: ½ mile S of town centre in Lower Castle Park. From A133 Cowdray Avenue R into Catchpool Road and then straight on into Sportsway. Nearest stations: Colchester or Colchester Town (both ¾ mile).

OFFICIALS

Club captain N. Hussain
Team captain R. C. Irani
Head coach G. A. Gooch
President D. J. Insole
Chairman N. R. A. Hilliard
Chief executive D. E. East
Chairman, cricket committee G. J. Saville
Head groundsman S. Kerrison
Scorer D. J. Norris

PLAYERS

Players expected to reappear in 2004

	Former counties	*Country*	*Born*	*Birthplace*
Bishop Justin Edward		E	4.1.1982	*Bury St Edmunds*
Bopara Ravinder Singh		E	4.5.1985	*Forest Gate*
Brant Scott Andrew		A	26.1.1983	*Harare, Zim*
Clarke Andrew John		E	9.11.1975	*†Brentwood*
Cook Alastair Nathan		E	25.12.1984	*Gloucester*
Denning Nicholas Alexander		E	3.10.1978	*Ascot*
***Flower** Andrew		Z (EU)	28.4.1968	*Cape Town, SA*
***Foster** James Savin		E	15.4.1980	*Whipps Cross*
Grayson Adrian Paul	Yorks	E	31.3.1971	*Ripon*
***Habib** Aftab	Middx, Leics	E	7.2.1972	*Reading*
***Hussain** Nasser		‡E	28.3.1968	*Madras, India*
***Irani** Ronald Charles	Lancs	E	26.10.1971	*Leigh*
Jefferson William Ingleby		E	25.10.1979	*Derby*
McCoubrey Adrian George Agustus Mathew		E	3.4.1980	*Ballymena*
Middlebrook James Daniel	Yorks	E	13.5.1977	*Leeds*
Napier Graham Richard		E	6.1.1980	*†Colchester*
Palladino Antonio Paul		E	29.6.1983	*London*
Pettini Mark Lewis		E	7.8.1983	*Brighton*
Sharif Zoheb Khalid		E	22.2.1983	*Leytonstone*
***Stephenson** John Patrick	Essex, Hants	E	14.3.1965	*†Stebbing*
ten Doeschate Ryan Neil		SA (EU/NL)	30.6.1980	*Port Elizabeth*

Players due to join in 2004

***Danish Kaneria**		P	16.12.1980	*Karachi*
***Gough** Darren	Yorks	E	18.9.1970	*Barnsley*

** Test player. † Born in Essex. ‡ 12-month ECB contract.*

At Cambridge, April 12, 13, 14. ESSEX drew with CAMBRIDGE UCCE.

ESSEX v MIDDLESEX

At Chelmsford, April 18, 19, 20, 21. Drawn. Essex 12 pts, Middlesex 8 pts. Toss: Middlesex. Championship debuts: S. A. Brant; J. H. Dawes.

Middlesex, trailing by 188 on first innings, eked out a draw. In their second innings, the top six all reached 40, Koenig setting the standard with a steady 94. Joyce reached a responsible hundred from 290 balls in 356 minutes – the slowest of the whole summer by either reckoning – and had guaranteed safety when he was last out playing on to Robinson, whose maiden first-class wicket came ten years after his debut. Earlier, Middlesex were undone by Dakin on a moist opening-day pitch. Essex fared better, and after bad light stole half the second day, a boisterous innings from Dakin – he galloped from ten to 50 in 17 balls with four sixes – took them past 400. Middlebrook took five wickets for Essex for the first time, and if Jefferson had caught Dawes first ball, they would have needed a feasible 240 from 33 overs for victory.

Close of play: First day, Essex 164-4 (Middlebrook 4, Habib 0); Second day, Essex 356-7 (Foster 32, Dakin 10); Third day, Middlesex 251-4 (Joyce 11, Abdul Razzaq 13).

Middlesex

*A. J. Strauss c Robinson b Dakin	1	– lbw b Middlebrook	40
S. G. Koenig c Foster b Irani	42	– c Foster b Dakin	94
O. A. Shah run out	13	– c Habib b Grayson	46
†D. C. Nash lbw b Dakin	0	– c Robinson b Grayson	42
E. C. Joyce lbw b Dakin	28	– b Robinson	117
Abdul Razzaq c Foster b Irani	0	– c Habib b Middlebrook	81
P. N. Weekes lbw b Brant	31	– lbw b Brant	0
B. L. Hutton not out	45	– c Flower b Middlebrook	23
S. J. Cook lbw b Dakin	22	– lbw b Middlebrook	0
C. B. Keegan st Foster b Middlebrook	24	– c Grayson b Middlebrook	0
J. H. Dawes c Jefferson b Middlebrook	2	– not out	32
L-b 4, n-b 2	6	B 6, l-b 4, w 6, n-b 4	20
1/1 (1) 2/24 (3) 3/24 (4) 4/82 (2) 5/84 (6) 6/86 (5) 7/124 (7) 8/169 (9) 9/206 (10) 10/214 (11)	214	1/65 (1) 2/174 (3) 3/191 (2) 4/233 (4) 5/384 (6) 6/385 (7) 7/422 (8) 8/422 (9) 9/427 (10) 10/495 (5)	495

Bonus points – Middlesex 1, Essex 3.

Bowling: *First Innings*—Brant 13–2–50–1; Dakin 18–3–57–4; McGarry 9–1–48–0; Irani 14–4–43–2; Middlebrook 5–0–12–2. *Second Innings*—Brant 23–6–60–1; Dakin 26–11–56–1; Irani 13–4–39–0; Middlebrook 57–11–172–5; Grayson 34–5–107–2; McGarry 16.3–2–41–0; Flower 1.3–0–3–0; Robinson 1.5–0–7–1.

Essex

D. D. J. Robinson b Cook	83	– not out	23
W. I. Jefferson b Dawes	56	– not out	18
A. P. Grayson c Nash b Abdul Razzaq	7		
A. Flower c Shah b Cook	7		
J. D. Middlebrook c Weekes b Keegan	36		
A. Habib lbw b Weekes	34		
*R. C. Irani lbw b Abdul Razzaq	69		
†J. S. Foster b Keegan	32		
J. M. Dakin c Dawes b Abdul Razzaq	52		
S. A. Brant lbw b Keegan	0		
A. C. McGarry not out	4		
L-b 10, n-b 12	22		
1/104 (2) 2/128 (3) 3/148 (4) 4/163 (1) 5/215 (5) 6/291 (6) 7/320 (7) 8/356 (8) 9/356 (10) 10/402 (9)	402		(no wkt) 41

Bonus points – Essex 5, Middlesex 3.

Bowling: *First Innings*—Dawes 22–6–69–1; Keegan 23–3–106–3; Cook 22–3–105–2; Weekes 16–3–39–1; Abdul Razzaq 23.3–5–69–3; Joyce 1–0–4–0. *Second Innings*—Dawes 4–0–10–0; Keegan 4–1–16–0; Strauss 1–0–15–0.

Umpires: M. R. Benson and T. E. Jesty.

At Birmingham, April 23, 24, 25, 26. ESSEX tied with WARWICKSHIRE.

At Leicester, April 30, May 1, 2, 3. ESSEX drew with LEICESTERSHIRE.

At Manchester, May 14, 15, 16, 17. ESSEX drew with LANCASHIRE.

ESSEX v SURREY

At Chelmsford, May 21, 22, 23, 24. Surrey won by 258 runs. Surrey 21 pts, Essex 5 pts. Toss: Essex.

The summit of Essex's ambition was always a draw once they had been set 506 on the last day, but their hopes were scuppered by Ormond, who expertly dismantled their top order. Habib and Foster provided stout resistance during a century stand until the reintroduction of Ormond accounted for both, and pointed the way for the spinners to seal victory. The opening day began perfectly for Essex when their seam attack exploited a damp pitch to reduce Surrey to 51 for five. However, thanks to Bicknell, scoring his second Championship century 17 years after his debut, Surrey were able to reach 376. He went to a career-best 141. There was no holding Bicknell now, and a burst of three wickets in 14 balls had Essex reeling at 17 for four. They too rallied before Batty took the game beyond them with his career-best. Hollioake opted not to declare at tea on the third day – when the lead was already 426 – and, despite losing 16 overs to rain, Surrey ran out comfortable winners.

Close of play: First day, Surrey 337-8 (Bicknell 117, Saqlain Mushtaq 25); Second day, Surrey 7-0 (Ward 6, Batty 1); Third day, Surrey 381-7 (Batty 168, Salisbury 9).

Surrey

I. J. Ward lbw b Brant	0	– b Dakin	49
†J. N. Batty c Foster b Dakin	7	– not out	168
M. R. Ramprakash c Foster b Napier	10	– c Flower b Napier	1
G. P. Thorpe c Foster b Napier	52	– c Foster b Napier	3
A. D. Brown lbw b Napier	4	– c Jefferson b Middlebrook	64
*A. J. Hollioake lbw b Napier	10	– c Robinson b Middlebrook	51
Azhar Mahmood b Brant	77	– c sub b Napier	16
M. P. Bicknell c and b Dakin	141	– c Foster b Napier	13
I. D. K. Salisbury run out	30	– not out	9
Saqlain Mushtaq b Brant	30		
J. Ormond not out	9		
L-b 4, n-b 2	6	L-b 7	7
1/0 (1) 2/8 (2) 3/27 (3) 4/31 (5) 5/51 (6) 6/162 (4) 7/168 (7) 8/258 (9) 9/360 (10) 10/376 (8)	376	1/102 (1) 2/120 (3) 3/124 (4) 4/209 (5) 5/303 (6) 6/339 (7) 7/368 (8) (7 wkts dec.)	381

Bonus points – Surrey 4, Essex 3.

Bowling: *First Innings*—Brant 29–4–94–3; Dakin 20.3–5–96–2; Napier 24–4–82–4; Irani 9–2–31–0; Middlebrook 9–0–38–0; Grayson 8–1–31–0. *Second Innings*—Brant 19–5–62–0; Dakin 17–2–55–1; Napier 21–0–124–4; Middlebrook 26–0–117–2; Grayson 4–0–16–0.

Essex

D. D. J. Robinson lbw b Ormond	5	– lbw b Ormond	41
W. I. Jefferson c Batty b Bicknell	11	– lbw b Ormond	3
A. P. Grayson c Batty b Bicknell	1	– c Batty b Ormond	19
A. Flower c sub b Azhar Mahmood	51	– c Batty b Azhar Mahmood	6
A. Habib lbw b Bicknell	0	– c Batty b Ormond	61
*R. C. Irani c Ramprakash b Azhar Mahmood	42	– (7) c sub b Saqlain Mushtaq	9
†J. S. Foster c Azhar Mahmood b Bicknell	38	– (6) lbw b Ormond	42
J. M. Dakin c Azhar Mahmood b Ormond	59	– c Azhar Mahmood b Saqlain Mushtaq	15
J. D. Middlebrook c Batty b Ormond	29	– b Salisbury	13
G. R. Napier c Saqlain Mushtaq b Salisbury	5	– not out	15
S. A. Brant not out	0	– c sub b Salisbury	0
L-b 5, n-b 6	11	L-b 11, n-b 12	23
1/7 (1) 2/8 (3) 3/17 (2) 4/17 (5) 5/99 (6) 6/132 (4) 7/179 (7) 8/243 (9) 9/252 (8) 10/252 (10)	252	1/16 (2) 2/44 (3) 3/69 (4) 4/69 (1) 5/188 (6) 6/197 (7) 7/205 (5) 8/225 (8) 9/247 (9) 10/247 (11)	247

Bonus points – Essex 2, Surrey 3.

Bowling: *First Innings*—Bicknell 19–5–67–4; Ormond 19–3–68–3; Saqlain Mushtaq 19–2–65–0; Azhar Mahmood 11–2–39–2; Salisbury 3.1–1–8–1. *Second Innings*—Bicknell 15–6–37–0; Ormond 22–3–82–5; Azhar Mahmood 12–1–72–1; Saqlain Mushtaq 11–2–42–2; Salisbury 2.2–1–3–2.

Umpires: G. I. Burgess and M. J. Kitchen.

At Nottingham, May 30, 31, June 1. ESSEX beat NOTTINGHAMSHIRE by 268 runs.

At Lord's, June 4, 5, 6, 7. ESSEX drew with MIDDLESEX.

At Chelmsford, June 9. ESSEX beat PAKISTANIS by 50 runs (see Pakistani tour section).

At Chelmsford, June 22. ESSEX lost to ZIMBABWEANS by five wickets (see Zimbabwean tour section).

ESSEX v KENT

At Chelmsford, June 27, 28, 29, 30. Drawn. Essex 12 pts, Kent 10 pts. Toss: Kent. Championship debut: Mohammad Sami.

In the previous three and a half years, Hussain had totalled 140 Championship runs with a highest score of 34. Available because he had retired from international one-day cricket, but still the Test captain, he batted throughout the second day before departing early next morning for 206. He faced 351 balls in seven hours 40 minutes, hit 29 fours – including several glorious cover-drives – and shared century stands with Robinson and Habib. Between them, they helped Essex establish a lead of 133 after Kent had batted enterprisingly on the first day, despite Middlebrook finding turn. As the game wore on, however, the pitch became slower and lower, and Ealham and Jones batted Kent to safety. Half the last day was lost to rain, though they would probably have survived without disruption. Essex, already facing an injury crisis among their bowlers, lost Grant after he broke down with a groin strain on the first morning.

Close of play: First day, Essex 7-0 (Robinson 3, Hussain 4); Second day, Essex 423-5 (Hussain 192, Middlebrook 23); Third day, Kent 278-5 (Ealham 85, Jones 22).

Kent

*D. P. Fulton b Middlebrook	93	– c Flower b Middlebrook	33
M. A. Carberry lbw b Brant	50	– c Flower b Middlebrook	8
E. T. Smith lbw b Brant	0	– c Habib b Napier	0
A. Symonds c Brant b Middlebrook	37	– b Napier	39
M. J. Walker c Habib b Middlebrook	20	– lbw b Bishop	65
M. A. Ealham c Hussain b Middlebrook	34	– c Brant b Napier	101
†G. O. Jones run out	84	– not out	108
J. C. Tredwell c Habib b Middlebrook	16	– c Brant b Flower	20
Mohammad Sami c sub b Middlebrook	2	– c Flower b Habib	1
A. Sheriyar not out	18		
B. J. Trott lbw b Brant	12		
L-b 6, w 1, n-b 8	15	B 17, l-b 17, w 3, n-b 4	41
1/138 (2) 2/138 (3) 3/191 (4) 4/214 (5) 5/215 (1) 6/278 (6) 7/302 (8) 8/340 (9) 9/351 (7) 10/381 (11)	381	1/27 (2) 2/28 (3) 3/72 (1) 4/108 (4) 5/235 (5) 6/335 (6) 7/402 (8) 8/416 (9)	(8 wkts dec.) 416

Bonus points – Kent 4, Essex 3.

Bowling: *First Innings*—Brant 24.4–2–107–3; Napier 21–3–79–0; Grant 4.2–1–13–0; Bishop 9–1–53–0; Middlebrook 34–8–123–6. *Second Innings*—Brant 20–0–75–0; Napier 27–4–90–3; Middlebrook 47–7–138–2; Bishop 20–3–48–1; Flower 7–0–21–1; Habib 2.4–0–10–1.

Essex

D. D. J. Robinson lbw b Ealham	47
N. Hussain lbw b Ealham	206
†J. S. Foster c Jones b Sheriyar	44
A. Flower c Smith b Tredwell	13
A. Habib b Sheriyar	77
*R. C. Irani b Sheriyar	0
J. D. Middlebrook c Jones b Sheriyar	39
G. R. Napier lbw b Tredwell	19
J. E. Bishop b Mohammad Sami	21
S. A. Brant not out	6
J. B. Grant c Ealham b Mohammad Sami	4
B 1, l-b 3, w 2, n-b 32	38
1/114 (1) 2/189 (3) 3/202 (4) 4/376 (5) 5/376 (6) 6/458 (7) 7/460 (2) 8/487 (8) 9/510 (9) 10/514 (11)	514

Bonus points – Essex 5, Kent 2 (130 overs: 503-8).

Bowling: Mohammad Sami 28.4–3–150–2; Sheriyar 30–5–73–4; Tredwell 34–4–119–2; Trott 14–3–60–0; Symonds 6–0–31–0; Ealham 16–2–65–2; Carberry 3–0–12–0.

Umpires: B. Dudleston and I. J. Gould.

ESSEX v LANCASHIRE

At Chelmsford, July 2, 3, 4, 5. Drawn. Essex 8 pts, Lancashire 8 pts. Toss: Lancashire. First-class debut: R. N. ten Doeschate.

An overcautious approach from Hegg probably cost Lancashire the match. Though already 337 ahead, Hegg delayed his declaration on the final morning for another 50 minutes and 11 overs. Later, as time ran out, Hooper claimed Essex's ninth wicket – the sixth for his teasing off-spin – but Brant and Napier survived the two remaining balls. On the rain-affected first day, only Law, who spent six seasons at Chelmsford, batted with authority on a damp, green-tinged pitch. Essex also struggled, owing much to Hussain after Martin struck twice in the opening over, and the teams achieved near-parity on first innings. Brant then swung the ball enough to take a wicket in each of his first three overs as Lancashire lurched to 13 for three, then 30 for four. But, inspired by a hundred from Chapple, the middle order staged a fine recovery. Essex were set a notional 394, though their real target was to see out a minimum 83 overs. Foster was fined £400 and severely reprimanded by Essex after verbally abusing a spectator in his anger at being dismissed for a duck on the first day.

Close of play: First day, Essex 6-2 (Hussain 6, Flower 0); Second day, Essex 178-7 (Dakin 1, Napier 1); Third day, Lancashire 327-7 (Chapple 101, Hegg 38).

Lancashire

J. J. Haynes b Brant	12 – c Foster b Brant	0
A. J. Swann lbw b Brant	7 – lbw b Napier	16
M. B. Loye c Grayson b Dakin	5 – b Brant	0
S. G. Law c ten Doeschate b Brant	80 – c Foster b Brant	4
M. J. Chilton c Foster b Brant	0 – c Foster b Middlebrook	70
C. L. Hooper b Dakin	18 – c Grayson b Middlebrook	50
G. Chapple lbw b Middlebrook	31 – not out	132
C. P. Schofield not out	35 – c Middlebrook b Dakin	38
*†W. K. Hegg lbw b Dakin	6 – not out	61
P. J. Martin lbw b Middlebrook	12	
S. I. Mahmood b Middlebrook	5	
L-b 6, w 1	7	L-b 8, w 2, n-b 2 12
1/11 (2) 2/22 (3) 3/30 (1) 4/34 (5) 5/66 (6) 6/148 (7) 7/168 (4) 8/179 (9) 9/212 (10) 10/218 (11)	218	1/1 (1) 2/3 (3) 3/13 (4) 4/30 (2) 5/109 (6) 6/188 (5) 7/252 (8) (7 wkts dec.) 383

Bonus points – Lancashire 1, Essex 3.

Bowling: *First Innings*—Brant 18–7–39–4; Dakin 16–2–55–3; Napier 12–3–40–0; ten Doeschate 5–1–27–0; Middlebrook 15.2–2–47–3; Grayson 1–0–4–0. *Second Innings*—Brant 18–3–67–3; Dakin 22–2–97–1; Napier 14–2–43–1; ten Doeschate 9–1–42–0; Middlebrook 28–3–93–2; Grayson 9–0–33–0.

Essex

A. P. Grayson b Martin	0 – lbw b Mahmood	17
N. Hussain c Haynes b Chapple	54 – lbw b Hooper	31
†J. S. Foster c Haynes b Martin	0 – c Martin b Hooper	5
A. Flower lbw b Hooper	46 – c Law b Hooper	49
A. Habib b Chapple	19 – c Law b Hooper	69
*R. C. Irani b Martin	19 – b Chapple	9
J. D. Middlebrook c and b Schofield	9 – c Hegg b Hooper	21
J. M. Dakin c Schofield b Martin	18 – lbw b Schofield	3
G. R. Napier c Hegg b Hooper	5 – not out	0
R. N. ten Doeschate st Hegg b Hooper	6 – c Swann b Hooper	5
S. A. Brant not out	1 – not out	1
B 2, l-b 4, w 1, n-b 24	31	B 7, l-b 1, n-b 18 26
1/0 (1) 2/0 (3) 3/90 (2) 4/128 (5) 5/162 (4) 6/170 (6) 7/177 (7) 8/196 (9) 9/202 (8) 10/208 (10)	208	1/29 (1) 2/56 (2) 3/57 (3) 4/170 (4) 5/195 (6) 6/219 (5) 7/230 (7) 8/230 (8) 9/235 (10) (9 wkts) 236

Bonus points – Essex 1, Lancashire 3.

Bowling: *First Innings*—Martin 21–8–60–4; Chapple 13–3–44–2; Mahmood 10–1–67–0; Hooper 16.5–7–30–3; Schofield 1–0–1–1. *Second Innings*—Martin 18–4–50–0; Chapple 19–3–58–1; Mahmood 9–2–39–1; Hooper 32–13–51–6; Schofield 10–2–30–1.

Umpires: A. Clarkson and J. W. Holder.

At Arundel, July 9, 10, 11, 12. ESSEX lost to SUSSEX by six wickets.

ESSEX v LEICESTERSHIRE

At Southend, July 23, 24, 25, 26. Drawn. Essex 9 pts, Leicestershire 12 pts. Toss: Leicestershire. Championship debuts: A. P. Palladino, A. G. A. M. McCoubrey.

Before the last day's play, Irani offered a deal: Essex, 329 behind but with four wickets left, would declare if a realistic fourth-innings target could be agreed. With further rain forecast, he never expected a positive answer, and Leicestershire, without a win and propping up the table, refused, preferring to chase 14 wickets – and the safety-net of a draw – to ten and the risk of defeat. On the opening day, Stevens and Ward, who skipped to an 88-ball hundred, enjoyed themselves on a placid pitch against a severely weakened attack, allowing Maddy to declare at 600 late next morning. Rash strokes contributed to Essex's poor response, before Flower, who went to his first hundred of the summer, and Foster turned things around. Rain then washed out all but an hour of the third day, prompting Irani's offer. Middlebrook, with his highest Essex score, ensured a fourth batting point, but could not save the follow-on. Essex, however, helped by the return of rain in the last session, survived with ease.

Close of play: First day, Leicestershire 471-5 (Ward 103); Second day, Essex 227-5 (Flower 115, Palladino 5); Third day, Essex 271-6 (Flower 125, Middlebrook 28).

Leicestershire

J. K. Maunders c Foster b Middlebrook	44
D. I. Stevens c and b Sharif	149
*D. L. Maddy lbw b Sharif	41
B. J. Hodge c Flower b Sharif	74
T. R. Ward lbw b McCoubrey	168
†P. A. Nixon lbw b Middlebrook	30
J. N. Snape not out	52
D. D. Masters b Middlebrook	8
L-b 18, w 8, n-b 8	34
1/108 (1) 2/184 (3) 3/314 (2) 4/350 (4) 5/471 (6) 6/591 (5) 7/600 (8)	(7 wkts dec.) 600

C. E. Dagnall, M. J. A. Whiley and R. M. Amin did not bat.

Bonus points – Leicestershire 5, Essex 1 (130 overs: 591-5).

Bowling: Napier 22–3–115–0; McCoubrey 16–2–102–1; Middlebrook 41.5–6–150–3; Palladino 28–8–76–0; Sharif 17–1–103–3; Bopara 7–0–36–0.

Essex

W. I. Jefferson lbw b Dagnall	7	– not out 54
R. S. Bopara c Maunders b Amin	18	
A. Flower c Nixon b Whiley	127	– not out 39
A. Habib c Nixon b Maddy	7	
*R. C. Irani b Maddy	9	
†J. S. Foster b Hodge	50	
A. P. Palladino b Dagnall	5	
J. D. Middlebrook not out	82	– (2) c Ward b Dagnall 13
G. R. Napier b Maddy	17	
Z. K. Sharif lbw b Maddy	0	
A. G. A. M. McCoubrey c Whiley b Masters	1	
L-b 6, w 4, n-b 18	28	B 1, l-b 1, w 1, n-b 2 5
1/13 (1) 2/68 (2) 3/87 (4) 4/97 (5) 5/215 (6) 6/227 (7) 7/291 (3) 8/346 (9) 9/346 (10) 10/351 (11)	351	1/16 (2) (1 wkt) 111

Bonus points – Essex 4, Leicestershire 3.

Bowling: *First Innings*—Dagnall 22–5–58–2; Whiley 19–3–62–1; Masters 18.2–4–53–1; Amin 23–3–82–1; Maddy 17–9–42–4; Hodge 9–2–35–1; Snape 5–2–13–0. *Second Innings*—Masters 9–5–17–0; Maddy 6–3–8–0; Amin 11.1–2–38–0; Dagnall 5–2–13–1; Whiley 3–0–8–0; Snape 8–2–19–0; Hodge 4–1–6–0.

Umpires: I. J. Gould and N. A. Mallender.

At Canterbury, July 30, 31, August 1. ESSEX lost to KENT by 55 runs.

ESSEX v SUSSEX

At Colchester, August 20, 21, 22. Sussex won by an innings and 120 runs. Sussex 22 pts, Essex 5 pts. Toss: Sussex.

Sussex moved top of the Championship with their eighth win, achieved with four sessions to spare. Victory came when Taylor captured the last four wickets for 18 in 30 balls. A double-century opening stand had laid Sussex's foundations, though Goodwin and Montgomerie were dropped in the slips by Jefferson – both off the unlucky Napier – before the score had passed 50. Goodwin went on to 210, batting two minutes over six hours, facing 270 deliveries and striking 30 fours and two sixes; Prior reached an 86-ball hundred with successive sixes (again off Napier); and Lewry made 70. All three were career-bests. Hostile, full-length bowling earned Mohammad Akram five wickets, but Sussex still made their highest total against Essex. The openers gave Essex a confident start, and Flower also batted well, but the innings subsided as the pitch deteriorated. Needing 329 to avoid an innings defeat, Essex failed again, despite a second fifty from Jefferson. On the opening day, Palladino was stretchered off after dislocating his shoulder trying to save a four from Goodwin.

Close of play: First day, Sussex 521-8 (Prior 104, Lewry 37); Second day, Essex 23-0 (Robinson 11, Jefferson 6).

Sussex

Batsman	Runs
R. R. Montgomerie b Palladino	97
M. W. Goodwin b Mohammad Akram	210
P. A. Cottey run out	23
*C. J. Adams b Mohammad Akram	0
†T. R. Ambrose c Flower b Mohammad Akram	4
R. S. C. Martin-Jenkins c Foster b Middlebrook	10
M. J. Prior not out	153
M. J. G. Davis b Mohammad Akram	8
Mushtaq Ahmed b Mohammad Akram	0
J. D. Lewry c sub b Middlebrook	70
B. V. Taylor b Dakin	3
L-b 9, n-b 20, p 5	34
	612

1/202 (1) 2/270 (3) 3/270 (4) 4/303 (5) 5/325 (6) 6/438 (2) 7/452 (8) 8/454 (9) 9/595 (10) 10/612 (11)

Bonus points – Sussex 5, Essex 3.

Bowling: Mohammad Akram 29–2–130–5; Dakin 20–1–120–1; Napier 24–5–149–0; Palladino 16–6–40–1; Middlebrook 26–1–126–2; Robinson 4–0–33–0.

Essex

Batsman	First innings		Second innings	
D. D. J. Robinson c Cottey b Mushtaq Ahmed	64	–	run out	12
W. I. Jefferson c Goodwin b Mushtaq Ahmed	55	–	c and b Martin-Jenkins	59
A. Flower c Ambrose b Lewry	50	–	c Prior b Mushtaq Ahmed	32
A. Habib lbw b Mushtaq Ahmed	0	–	b Mushtaq Ahmed	11
*R. C. Irani c Adams b Taylor	3	–	c Ambrose b Taylor	38
†J. S. Foster c Montgomerie b Davis	31	–	lbw b Mushtaq Ahmed	3
J. M. Dakin lbw b Davis	6	–	c Goodwin b Taylor	7
J. D. Middlebrook c Lewry b Martin-Jenkins	33	–	c Davis b Taylor	5
G. R. Napier c Prior b Mushtaq Ahmed	34	–	not out	21
Mohammad Akram not out	0	–	lbw b Taylor	10
A. P. Palladino absent hurt		–	absent hurt	
L-b 5, n-b 2	7		B 2, l-b 3, n-b 6	11
	283			209

First innings: 1/101 (2) 2/144 (1) 3/144 (4) 4/163 (5) 5/208 (3) 6/214 (6) 7/219 (7) 8/281 (9) 9/283 (8)

Second innings: 1/24 (1) 2/109 (2) 3/123 (3) 4/130 (4) 5/164 (6) 6/164 (5) 7/172 (8) 8/185 (7) 9/209 (10)

Bonus points – Essex 2, Sussex 3.

Bowling: *First Innings*—Lewry 12–4–46–1; Taylor 17–3–52–1; Mushtaq Ahmed 25–2–87–4; Martin-Jenkins 11.5–2–32–1; Davis 12–0–61–2. *Second Innings*—Taylor 16.3–6–50–4; Lewry 8–1–28–0; Mushtaq Ahmed 28–7–83–3; Davis 4–1–13–0; Martin-Jenkins 12–4–30–1.

Umpires: A. Clarkson and N. J. Llong.

ESSEX v NOTTINGHAMSHIRE

At Chelmsford, September 3, 4, 5. Essex won by nine wickets. Essex 20 pts, Nottinghamshire 5 pts. Toss: Nottinghamshire. First-class debut: A. N. Cook.

Essex won with more than a day to spare, sent Nottinghamshire into the second division and maintained their own slim chances of staying up. The only Nottinghamshire player to show stomach for the fight was Gallian, who followed a steady first-innings 65 with over five and a half hours' resistance in the second before he was ninth out. Too many of his colleagues threw away their wickets with wretched strokes on a blameless pitch. A last-wicket stand of 63 between Dakin and Clarke saw Essex to a useful first-innings lead. Clarke, playing his first Championship game of the summer and with his contract up for renewal, then undermined Nottinghamshire with a spell of three for seven in 31 balls, and Essex were eventually left needing 154. With Alastair Cook, an 18-year-old left-hander from Bedford School, underlining his potential with some fine drives and pulls, they made them with ease. This was Essex's second Championship success, after winning at Trent Bridge in June.

Close of play: First day, Essex 77-2 (Flower 33, Pettini 20); Second day, Nottinghamshire 71-2 (Gallian 28, Warren 10).

Nottinghamshire

First innings		Second innings	
D. J. Bicknell c Cook b Mohammad Akram	8	b Mohammad Akram	3
*J. E. R. Gallian c Irani b Clarke	65	c Clarke b Middlebrook	79
†C. M. W. Read b Dakin	5	c Foster b Clarke	27
R. J. Warren c Foster b Clarke	41	c Foster b Clarke	15
K. P. Pietersen b Dakin	2	c Foster b Clarke	11
C. L. Cairns b Dakin	70	c Pettini b Clarke	5
B. M. Shafayat c Foster b Mohammad Akram	3	c Foster b Dakin	10
P. J. Franks not out	49	c Flower b Middlebrook	23
P. J. McMahon c Foster b Clarke	0	lbw b Napier	1
S. C. G. MacGill b Napier	9	not out	12
C. E. Shreck c Foster b Dakin	19	c Pettini b Napier	4
B 5, l-b 6, n-b 2	13	B 4, l-b 8, w 2	14
1/14 (1) 2/19 (3) 3/72 (4) 4/79 (5) 5/177 (6) 6/190 (7) 7/218 (2) 8/218 (9) 9/242 (10) 10/284 (11)	284	1/5 (1) 2/49 (3) 3/90 (4) 4/102 (5) 5/108 (6) 6/129 (7) 7/173 (8) 8/188 (9) 9/192 (2) 10/204 (11)	204

Bonus points – Nottinghamshire 2, Essex 3.

Bowling: *First Innings*—Mohammad Akram 23–7–65–2; Dakin 16.5–3–53–4; Napier 17–5–42–1; Clarke 16–3–70–3; Middlebrook 5–0–43–0. *Second Innings*—Mohammad Akram 22–7–56–1; Dakin 18–6–30–1; Napier 19.4–5–56–2; Clarke 19–6–34–4; Middlebrook 8–3–16–2.

Essex

First innings		Second innings	
W. I. Jefferson lbw b Cairns	1	c Gallian b McMahon	38
A. N. Cook lbw b Shreck	13	not out	69
A. Flower c McMahon b Shreck	53	not out	45
M. L. Pettini c Franks b Shreck	20		
*R. C. Irani c Gallian b MacGill	51		
†J. S. Foster c Cairns b McMahon	58		
G. R. Napier c Pietersen b McMahon	5		
J. D. Middlebrook c Pietersen b Cairns	34		
J. M. Dakin c Gallian b McMahon	47		
Mohammad Akram c and b McMahon	0		
A. J. Clarke not out	32		
B 4, l-b 9, w 2, n-b 6	21	N-b 2	2
1/2 (1) 2/31 (2) 3/89 (4) 4/118 (3) 5/170 (5) 6/175 (7) 7/234 (8) 8/268 (6) 9/272 (10) 10/335 (9)	335	1/80 (1)	(1 wkt) 154

Bonus points – Essex 3, Nottinghamshire 3.

Bowling: *First Innings*—Cairns 22–4–89–2; Shreck 22–9–67–3; Franks 11–5–28–0; MacGill 24–3–79–1; McMahon 27.5–7–59–4. *Second Innings*—Cairns 4–2–11–0; Shreck 6–1–21–0; MacGill 12–4–47–0; McMahon 7.1–2–54–1; Franks 5–1–21–0.

Umpires: M. J. Harris and P. J. Hartley.

ESSEX v WARWICKSHIRE

At Chelmsford, September 11, 12, 13, 14. Warwickshire won by nine wickets. Warwickshire 22 pts, Essex 5 pts. Toss: Warwickshire.

One or other of these teams was almost certain to be the third to slide into Division Two, and it became clear well before Wagh completed a resounding Warwickshire victory with a straight-driven six off Middlebrook that it would be Essex. Earlier on the fourth day, in 24 devastating balls, Waqar Younis had seized five for 12 as Essex nose-dived from 279 for four to 302 all out. Conditions had certainly helped the seamers on the much-interrupted first day, and by the 30th over Essex were 73 for seven. Stephenson and the tailenders produced a spirited recovery, but as the pitch eased and the bowling proved wayward, Warwickshire soon established a commanding position. Wagh hit a brisk hundred and received useful support from almost everyone, including Brown, who passed 1,000 runs for the season for the first time. Two young players, Cook and Pettini, reinforced the good impressions they had already made when Essex batted again, 247 adrift, but Waqar proved far too much for the lower order.

Close of play: First day, Essex 249-9 (Stephenson 69, Mohammad Akram 5); Second day, Warwickshire 456-7 (Brown 67, Waqar Younis 14); Third day, Essex 257-4 (Pettini 67, Foster 11).

Essex

W. I. Jefferson lbw b Brown	33	– c Brown b Wagh	62
A. N. Cook lbw b Collymore	0	– b Wagh	55
A. Flower run out	13	– c Piper b Wagh	28
M. L. Pettini b Collymore	0	– c Knight b Wagh	78
*R. C. Irani c Wagh b Waqar Younis	9	– c Knight b Brown	18
†J. S. Foster b Richardson	15	– c Piper b Waqar Younis	23
J. D. Middlebrook b Richardson	1	– b Waqar Younis	0
G. R. Napier c Wagh b Brown	48	– not out	3
J. P. Stephenson not out	75	– c Knight b Waqar Younis	10
A. J. Clarke c Troughton b Richardson	41	– b Waqar Younis	6
Mohammad Akram lbw b Waqar Younis	6	– b Waqar Younis	3
B 6, l-b 3, n-b 6	15	B 4, l-b 4, n-b 8	16
1/0 (2) 2/17 (3) 3/17 (4) 4/46 (5) 5/63 (6) 6/73 (1) 7/73 (7) 8/179 (8) 9/238 (10) 10/256 (11)	256	1/122 (2) 2/137 (1) 3/188 (3) 4/223 (5) 5/279 (6) 6/279 (7) 7/281 (4) 8/292 (9) 9/298 (10) 10/302 (11)	302

Bonus points – Essex 2, Warwickshire 3.

Bowling: *First Innings*—Waqar Younis 15.2–3–69–2; Collymore 16–3–60–2; Richardson 20–6–51–3; Brown 9–3–41–2; Wagh 6–1–26–0. *Second Innings*—Waqar Younis 25.1–4–77–5; Collymore 11–2–57–0; Wagh 41–9–111–4; Richardson 16–7–25–0; Troughton 1–0–4–0; Brown 14–5–20–1.

Warwickshire

*M. J. Powell lbw b Middlebrook	30	– c Middlebrook b Mohammad Akram	10
N. V. Knight st Foster b Middlebrook	64	– not out	24
M. A. Wagh c Foster b Middlebrook	116	– not out	23
I. J. L. Trott lbw b Middlebrook	65		
I. R. Bell lbw b Stephenson	13		
J. O. Troughton c Jefferson b Mohammad Akram	28		
D. R. Brown lbw b Napier	77		
†K. J. Piper c Foster b Napier	24		
Waqar Younis not out	45		
A. Richardson lbw b Napier	0		
C. D. Collymore c Foster b Middlebrook	1		
B 5, l-b 6, w 1, n-b 28	40	B 1, l-b 1, n-b 2	4
1/65 (1) 2/172 (2) 3/255 (3) 4/281 (5) 5/335 (4) 6/361 (6) 7/421 (8) 8/488 (7) 9/488 (10) 10/503 (11)	503	1/22 (1)	(1 wkt) 61

Bonus points – Warwickshire 5, Essex 3.

Bowling: *First Innings*—Mohammad Akram 24–0–151–1; Napier 19–2–80–3; Clarke 10–1–50–0; Middlebrook 48.3–8–154–5; Stephenson 8–0–46–1; Cook 2–0–11–0. *Second Innings*—Mohammad Akram 5–1–16–1; Middlebrook 7.4–2–29–0; Napier 3–0–14–0.

Umpires: J. H. Hampshire and G. Sharp.

At The Oval, September 17, 18, 19. ESSEX beat SURREY by eight wickets.

DATES OF FORMATION OF FIRST-CLASS COUNTIES

		Present Club		
County	*First known organisation*	*Original date*	*Reorganisation, if substantial*	*First-class status from*
Derbyshire	1870	1870	–	1871
Durham	1874	1882	1991	1992
Essex	By 1790	1876	–	1895
Glamorgan	1861	1888	–	1921
Gloucestershire	1863	1871	–	1870
Hampshire	1849	1863	1879	1864
Kent	1842	1859	1870	1864
Lancashire	1864	1864	–	1865
Leicestershire	By 1820	1879	–	1895
Middlesex	1863	1864	–	1864
Northamptonshire	1820†	1878	–	1905
Nottinghamshire	1841	1841	1866	1864
Somerset	1864	1875	–	1882
Surrey	1845	1845	–	1864
Sussex	1836	1839	1857	1864
Warwickshire	1826	1882	–	1895
Worcestershire	1844	1865	–	1899
Yorkshire	1861	1863	1891	1864

Note: Derbyshire lost first-class status from 1888 to 1894, Hampshire between 1886 and 1894 and Somerset between 1886 and 1890.

† Town club.

GLAMORGAN

Missed Opportunities

EDWARD BEVAN

This was a season that might have been one of far greater success for Glamorgan. Inconsistency was the biggest problem, as Robert Croft admitted at the end of his first season as captain.

The year got off to a tricky start, as Croft had not been the first choice: he was appointed only after the opening Championship game, when Steve James's troublesome knee ruled him out for the rest of the summer. (It later forced him to retire.) And the team never quite acquired a sense of momentum though they were always on the fringe of the second division promotion race. As in 2002, Glamorgan finished fifth; this time, though, they were, tantalisingly, only seven points behind Gloucestershire, who claimed the third promotion place.

After winning their first five matches, Glamorgan did have hopes of retaining their National League title. But one win from the next six – which included a controversial game at New Road, where Glamorgan were convinced Worcestershire should have been penalised six runs for a slow over-rate – ended their challenge, and they finished fifth. Among the missed opportunities was the floodlit game at Sophia Gardens when Leicestershire, chasing 227, stumbled to 52 for five, yet won off the last ball. Glamorgan's slump in the National League coincided with their inability to adapt to Twenty20 cricket: they won only once and could not even defend a total of 193 against Somerset. They also exited the C&G in the fourth round after losing at home to Derbyshire.

Glamorgan's 45 batting points were bettered only by Yorkshire in the second division, yet they struggled to build commanding first-innings totals. They often seemed to rely on the middle and late order, as in their first Championship win of the season at Northampton, where the last two wickets added 80 in a low-scoring game. Two more victories by mid-July kept them in the hunt for promotion, but then, at Southampton a week later, came the defining moment of their season. By the end of the second day, Hampshire, after following on, trailed by 138 with six wickets left – and maximum points appeared a formality. But Hampshire added another 335 and, on an uneven last-day wicket, Glamorgan were routed for 104. As it turned out, a win in that game would have secured promotion, though there were other occasions when earlier declarations, or a bit more luck, might have ensured victory.

Matthew Maynard, who turned 37 before the season started, belied his years and again topped the batting. His fifth century of the summer, at Chester-le-Street, was his 51st for Glamorgan, one short of the county record held by Alan Jones and Hugh Morris. Michael Powell also played consistently well, scoring 1,234 first-class runs, plus 597 in the National League. He hit a hundred in each innings against Worcestershire and just missed a maiden double against county opposition in the 369-run victory – Glamorgan's biggest ever in terms of runs – at Chester-le-Street.

Michael Kasprowicz

Maynard and Powell kept the middle order ticking, but finding a settled opening pair proved more difficult. The Australian Jimmy Maher was re-signed for the second half of the season, but failed to match the consistency of 2001. For the final three games Mark Wallace went in first and hit encouraging form, but it is asking much of a wicket-keeper to open, especially after a day or more behind the stumps. David Hemp ended the season far better than he started, and the move from No. 3 to No. 6 did wonders for his assurance. While Wallace and Croft both prospered in the Championship, Adrian Dale's form slumped, and he was happy neither opening nor at No. 3.

Three bowlers passed fifty wickets. The Australian seamer, Michael Kasprowicz, took pride of place with 77 at 21.15, making him the leading wicket-taker after Sussex's Mushtaq Ahmed. He also grabbed nine wickets in an innings twice – both times against Durham – to emulate Johnnie Clay's achievement for the county in 1937. All told, Kasprowicz had taken 35 wickets at 8.34 in his last three Championship matches against Durham. His 556 runs at just over 25 also gave him credence as an all-rounder.

At 33, Croft bowled as well as at any time in his career, five times taking five wickets in an innings, and by November he found himself unexpectedly out in Sri Lanka to bolster England's struggling spin attack. Having got there, he was ignored and soon decided he was finally done with the vagaries of England selection. Alex Wharf, free from the heel injury that had restricted him to just seven Championship games in two years, enjoyed his best season, with 52 victims. David Harrison, a 22-year-old all-rounder, captured 40 wickets in his first full season, and his omission from the ECB Academy puzzled many locally. Simon Jones, having missed the entire season, *was* chosen – the first step in his comeback. Dean Cosker, not helped by the prevalence of seamer-friendly pitches, managed 17 wickets with his left-arm spin in the National League – and fielded superbly.

In the winter, Steve James was forced to bow to reality after several operations, and announced his retirement. He will be much missed in a team searching for men to rely on. But the county continues, commendably, to pursue local talent. Recognition of this came when all-rounder Adam Harrison, 18-year-old brother of David, won an England Under-19 cap.

GLAMORGAN RESULTS

All first-class matches – Played 17: Won 5, Lost 5, Drawn 7.
County Championship matches – Played 16: Won 5, Lost 5, Drawn 6.

Frizzell County Championship, 5th in Division 2; Cheltenham & Gloucester Trophy, 4th round; National Cricket League, 5th in Division 1; Twenty20 Cup, 6th in Midlands/Wales/West Group.

COUNTY CHAMPIONSHIP AVERAGES

BATTING AND FIELDING

Cap		*M*	*I*	*NO*	*R*	*HS*	*100s*	*50s*	*Avge*	*Ct/St*
1987	M. P. Maynard	16	28	0	1,297	142	5	4	46.32	11
2000	M. J. Powell	16	29	1	1,234	198	4	3	44.07	12
1994	D. L. Hemp	12	21	3	607	85*	0	5	33.72	5
2001	J. P. Maher§	8	16	0	491	95	0	4	30.68	7
2003	M. A. Wallace.	16	28	0	827	121	2	3	29.53	49/2
1992	R. D. B. Croft.	16	28	3	727	122	1	4	29.08	8
1997	S. D. Thomas	4	7	2	145	69*	0	1	29.00	1
2000	A. G. Wharf.	16	27	9	475	79	0	2	26.38	7
2002	M. S. Kasprowicz§ .	15	26	4	556	78	0	2	25.27	7
1992	A. Dale	15	27	1	657	123	1	2	25.26	12
	J. Hughes.	9	16	0	357	73	0	2	22.31	10
	I. J. Thomas	6	10	0	172	53	0	1	17.20	8
2000	D. A. Cosker.	8	11	6	79	42	0	0	15.80	6
	D. S. Harrison.	15	24	5	264	66	0	1	13.89	3

Also batted: A. P. Davies (3 matches) 9, 19*, 4 (1 ct); S. P. James (cap 1992) (1 match) 1, 14 (1 ct).

§ *Overseas player.*

BOWLING

	O	*M*	*R*	*W*	*BB*	*5W/i*	*Avge*
M. S. Kasprowicz	572.3	140	1,629	77	9-36	4	21.15
R. D. B. Croft.	711.5	189	1,873	62	6-71	5	30.20
A. G. Wharf.	432.3	72	1,734	52	4-53	0	33.34
D. S. Harrison.	349	77	1,248	37	5-80	1	33.72
D. A. Cosker	257.5	66	672	17	3-49	0	39.52

Also bowled: A. Dale 48–9–159–3; A. P. Davies 46–8–225–2; J. P. Maher 1–0–2–0; M. P. Maynard 2–0–2–0; S. D. Thomas 68.1–7–243–9.

COUNTY RECORDS

Highest score for:	309*	S. P. James v Sussex at Colwyn Bay	2000
Highest score against:	322*	M. B. Loye (Northamptonshire) at Northampton. .	1998
Best bowling for:	10-51	J. Mercer v Worcestershire at Worcester	1936
Best bowling against:	10-18	G. Geary (Leicestershire) at Pontypridd	1929
Highest total for:	718-3 dec.	v Sussex at Colwyn Bay	2000
Highest total against:	712	by Northamptonshire at Northampton.	1998
Lowest total for:	22	v Lancashire at Liverpool	1924
Lowest total against:	33	by Leicestershire at Ebbw Vale	1965

GLAMORGAN DIRECTORY

ADDRESS

Sophia Gardens, Cardiff CF11 9XR (029 2040 9380; fax 029 2040 9390; email gccc@ecb.co.uk). **Website** www. glamorgancricket.com.

GROUNDS

Cardiff (Sophia Gardens): 1 mile NW of city centre between A4119 and River Taff. From city centre take A4119 over the Taff Bridge and filter R into Cathedral Road, then R into Sophia Close. Nearest station: Cardiff Central (1 mile).

Colwyn Bay: Situated in Rhos-on-Sea. From A55 (signposted Rhos-on-Sea), take B5115 Brompton Avenue, continuing on Llandudno Road, then R into Church Road and R into Penrhyn Avenue for ground on R. Nearest station: Colwyn Bay (1½ miles).

Swansea (St Helen's): 1 mile W of city centre on A4067 Oystermouth Road, which becomes Mumbles Road. Then R into Gorse Lane for St Helen's Ground. Nearest station: Swansea (1½ miles).

OFFICIALS

Captain 2003 – S. P. James; 2004 – R. D. B. Croft
First-team coach J. Derrick
President A. R. Lewis
Chairman 2003 – G. Elias; 2004 – R. P. Russell
Chief executive M. J. Fatkin
Cricket secretary Mrs C. L. Watkin
Head groundsman L. A. Smith
Scorer G. N. Lewis

PLAYERS

Players expected to reappear in 2004

	Former counties	*Country*	*Born*	*Birthplace*
Cherry Daniel David		E	7.2.1980	†*Newport*
Cosker Dean Andrew		E	7.1.1978	*Weymouth*
***Croft** Robert Damien Bale		E	25.5.1970	†*Morriston*
Dale Adrian		E	24.10.1968	*Germiston, SA*
Davies Andrew Philip		E	7.11.1976	†*Neath*
Harrison David Stuart		E	30.7.1981	†*Newport*
Hemp David Lloyd	Warwicks	E	8.11.1970	*Hamilton, Bermuda*
Hughes Jonathan		E	30.6.1981	†*Pontypridd*
***Jones** Simon Philip		E	25.12.1978	†*Morriston*
***Kasprowicz** Michael Scott	Essex, Leics	A	10.2.1972	*Brisbane*
Maher James Patrick		A	27.2.1974	*Innisfail*
***Maynard** Matthew Peter		E	21.3.1966	*Oldham*
Powell Michael John		E	3.2.1977	†*Abergavenny*
Shaw Adrian David		E	17.2.1972	†*Neath*
Thomas Ian James		E	9.5.1979	†*Newport*
Thomas Stuart Darren		E	25.1.1975	†*Morriston*
Wallace Mark Alexander		E	19.11.1981	†*Abergavenny*
Wharf Alexander George	Yorks, Notts	E	4.6.1975	*Bradford*

* *Test player.* † *Born in Wales.*

At Cardiff, April 12, 13, 14 (not first-class). **Drawn.** Toss: Glamorgan. **Glamorgan 434** (S. P. James 81, M. J. Powell 52, M. P. Maynard 92, M. A. Wallace 55, S. D. Thomas 57) **and 306-5 dec.** (D. L. Hemp 54, M. J. Powell 55, M. P. Maynard 101); **Cardiff UCCE 222** (J. Cook 79; D. S. Harrison 4-42).

At Derby, April 18, 19, 20, 21. GLAMORGAN drew with DERBYSHIRE.

GLAMORGAN v HAMPSHIRE

At Cardiff, April 23, 24, 25, 26. Drawn. Glamorgan 11 pts, Hampshire 11 pts. Toss: Hampshire.

On a Sophia Gardens shirtfront, the loss of nearly two days' play killed off the game. When the rain relented both teams easily managed maximum batting points, Hampshire making 531 against an attack well below full strength. After Crawley and Smith had laid the foundations with a second-wicket stand of 123, Mascarenhas flogged the weary Glamorgan attack, blazing a 78-ball century. His second fifty came from just 20 balls, and he and Udal added 105 in only 11 overs. Most of the third day was lost, but there was time for Maynard to strike Tremlett for five successive fours before hoisting him over the pavilion for a huge six. Tremlett emerged from the assault having conceded 44 in two overs. On the fourth day, Maynard completed his second Championship century in two games.

Close of play: First day, Hampshire 381-5 (Pothas 81, Mascarenhas 17); Second day, Glamorgan 128-2 (Hemp 41, Powell 7); Third day, Glamorgan 288-3 (Powell 74, Maynard 63).

Hampshire

D. A. Kenway c Cosker b Wharf	19
*J. P. Crawley b Wharf	65
R. A. Smith c Wallace b Harrison	92
W. S. Kendall lbw b Harrison	32
A. C. Morris c Harrison b Davies	46
†N. Pothas c Wallace b Wharf	87
A. D. Mascarenhas not out	100
Wasim Akram c Davies b Harrison	23
S. D. Udal not out	32
B 7, l-b 11, w 1, n-b 16	35
1/24 (1) 2/147 (2) 3/210 (4) 4/223 (3) 5/345 (5) 6/387 (6) 7/426 (8)	(7 wkts dec.) 531

C. T. Tremlett and A. D. Mullally did not bat.

Bonus points – Hampshire 5, Glamorgan 2.

Bowling: Wharf 28–4–134–3; Davies 17–3–96–1; Cosker 21–1–63–0; Harrison 20–4–87–3; Croft 30.5–5–119–0; Dale 5–3–14–0.

Glamorgan

I. J. Thomas c Kendall b Mascarenhas	41
A. Dale c Pothas b Tremlett	16
D. L. Hemp b Mullally	57
M. J. Powell b Wasim Akram	85
M. P. Maynard c Udal b Tremlett	112
†M. A. Wallace lbw b Tremlett	37
*R. D. B. Croft not out	15
D. S. Harrison not out	6
B 2, l-b 8, w 1, n-b 32	43
1/40 (2) 2/109 (1) 3/159 (3) 4/325 (4) 5/367 (5) 6/400 (6)	(6 wkts) 412

A. G. Wharf, A. P. Davies and D. A. Cosker did not bat.

Bonus points – Glamorgan 5, Hampshire 2.

Bowling: Wasim Akram 20–4–82–1; Mullally 22–5–81–1; Tremlett 22–7–101–3; Udal 27–5–93–0; Mascarenhas 19.3–9–45–1.

Umpires: N. G. Cowley and P. Willey.

GLAMORGAN v GLOUCESTERSHIRE

At Cardiff, May 9, 10, 11, 12. Gloucestershire won by six wickets. Gloucestershire 22 pts, Glamorgan 2 pts. Toss: Gloucestershire. County debut: I. G. Butler.

Gloucestershire won in the end but only after stumbling over the last hurdle. Having examined the damp green pitch, they chose to field and were quickly vindicated when Glamorgan slipped to 87 for eight in the 29th over, Lewis and the other seamers making full use of helpful conditions. The wicket had eased by the time Gloucestershire began their reply in the afternoon and they reached 400 – a lead of 261, which was hard on Harrison whose efforts brought a career-best five for 80. When Glamorgan started the last day still 191 behind, with three second-innings wickets down, defeat looked close to inevitable. But Harrison kept fighting, this time with the bat. He defied the bowlers for two and a half hours and his maiden fifty; with Kasprowicz, he added 140 for the ninth wicket as Glamorgan batted deep into the afternoon session. But they could not hold out long enough and Gloucestershire sped to their target of 95 in only 15 overs.

Close of play: First day, Gloucestershire 217-3 (Rhodes 39, Butler 1); Second day, Gloucestershire 232-4 (Butler 2, Windows 1); Third day, Glamorgan 70-3 (Hemp 12, Davies 0).

Glamorgan

First innings		Second innings	
I. J. Thomas b Smith	1	– c Russell b Butler	13
A. Dale b Butler	8	– c Alleyne b Lewis	17
D. L. Hemp c Russell b Smith	1	– c Russell b Lewis	34
M. J. Powell c Spearman b Lewis	4	– lbw b Lewis	19
M. P. Maynard run out	31	– (6) c Windows b Butler	43
†M. A. Wallace c Russell b Lewis	0	– (7) b Smith	31
*R. D. B. Croft lbw b Butler	4	– (8) c and b Alleyne	14
D. S. Harrison c Alleyne b Lewis	16	– (9) c Russell b Smith	66
M. S. Kasprowicz c Smith b Lewis	22	– (10) b Lewis	78
A. G. Wharf c Windows b Lewis	25	– (11) not out	0
A. P. Davies not out	19	– (5) b Butler	4
L-b 2, n-b 6	8	B 1, l-b 12, w 7, n-b 16	36
1/5 (1) 2/9 (3) 3/16 (4) 4/18 (2) 5/19 (6) 6/30 (7) 7/57 (5) 8/87 (8) 9/102 (9) 10/139 (10)	139	1/30 (1) 2/41 (2) 3/69 (4) 4/103 (3) 5/103 (5) 6/173 (7) 7/196 (8) 8/203 (6) 9/343 (10) 10/355 (9)	355

Bonus points – Gloucestershire 3.

Bowling: *First Innings*—Lewis 19.2–4–61–5; Smith 9–4–24–2; Butler 12–1–45–2; Alleyne 2–1–7–0. *Second Innings*—Smith 19.5–2–91–2; Butler 25–7–90–3; Lewis 29–11–88–4; Alleyne 9–0–44–1; Fisher 7–2–29–0.

Gloucestershire

First innings		Second innings	
C. M. Spearman c Thomas b Harrison	75	– c Kasprowicz b Wharf	39
W. P. C. Weston lbw b Harrison	49	– c Thomas b Wharf	17
T. H. C. Hancock c Powell b Kasprowicz	24	– c Dale b Wharf	13
J. N. Rhodes lbw b Harrison	47	– not out	14
I. G. Butler b Harrison	13		
M. G. N. Windows c Wallace b Harrison	63	– (5) c Maynard b Davies	0
*M. W. Alleyne lbw b Wharf	20	– (6) not out	6
†R. C. Russell c Maynard b Kasprowicz	16		
I. D. Fisher not out	7		
J. Lewis not out	37		
B 5, l-b 23, w 5, n-b 16	49	L-b 2, n-b 4	6
1/137 (1) 2/145 (2) 3/207 (3) 4/227 (4) 5/264 (5) 6/311 (7) 7/349 (8) 8/351 (6)	(8 wkts dec.) 400	1/33 (2) 2/71 (3) 3/78 (1) 4/84 (5)	(4 wkts) 95

A. M. Smith did not bat.

Bonus points – Gloucestershire 5, Glamorgan 2.

Bowling: *First Innings*—Kasprowicz 29–3–111–2; Harrison 24.4–4–80–5; Davies 12–3–37–0; Wharf 28–4–93–1; Dale 3–0–11–0; Croft 19–5–40–0. *Second Innings*—Kasprowicz 3–0–24–0; Harrison 4–0–19–0; Wharf 5–0–28–3; Davies 3–0–22–1.

Umpires: P. J. Hartley and G. Sharp.

At Taunton, May 14, 15, 16, 17. GLAMORGAN lost to SOMERSET by an innings and 143 runs.

At Leeds, May 21, 22, 23, 24. GLAMORGAN drew with YORKSHIRE.

At Northampton, May 30, 31, June 1. GLAMORGAN beat NORTHAMPTONSHIRE by 55 runs.

GLAMORGAN v DERBYSHIRE

At Swansea, June 4, 5, 6, 7. Glamorgan won by an innings and 70 runs. Glamorgan 21 pts, Derbyshire 4 pts. Toss: Glamorgan. County debut: M. Kaif.

Despite rain cutting 145 overs from the first three days, Derbyshire fell well short of a draw. They began the last morning 205 behind with 12 wickets in hand, but stumbled to 15 for five in their second innings, and lost before tea. The pitch was at its best during Glamorgan's innings, when Croft and Cosker put on 81 for the last wicket, before spinning their way to nine victims as the strip grew slower and took turn. After following on 186 behind, Derbyshire's top order caved in against the pace of Kasprowicz and Wharf, and only a half-century partnership for the sixth wicket between Sutton and Welch avoided complete humiliation. Cork did not bat because of an Achilles injury, which he did not want to aggravate before Derbyshire's C&G quarter-final the following week.

Close of play: First day, No play; Second day, Derbyshire 7-0 (Gait 4, Di Venuto 3); Third day, Derbyshire 190-8 (Lungley 15, Dean 5).

Glamorgan

A. Dale lbw b Lungley	43
J. Hughes c and b Cork	69
D. L. Hemp c Sutton b Lungley	9
M. J. Powell lbw b Lungley	23
M. P. Maynard c Hewson b Lungley	35
†M. A. Wallace c Sutton b Dean	35
*R. D. B. Croft c Lungley b Dean	84
D. S. Harrison c Gait b Welch	4
M. S. Kasprowicz b Dean	19
A. G. Wharf c Sutton b Cork	15
D. A. Cosker not out	12
B 4, l-b 17, n-b 26	47
1/82 (1) 2/92 (3) 3/126 (4) 4/176 (2) 5/216 (5) 6/258 (6) 7/263 (8) 8/282 (9) 9/314 (10) 10/395 (7)	395

Bonus points – Glamorgan 4, Derbyshire 3.

Bowling: Cork 21–5–71–2; Dean 22.5–4–84–3; Welch 25–7–78–1; Lungley 20–3–101–4; Wharton 9–2–40–0.

Derbyshire

A. I. Gait b Croft	23	– (2) c Wallace b Wharf	0
M. J. Di Venuto c Maynard b Croft	29	– (1) lbw b Kasprowicz	0
C. W. G. Bassano lbw b Croft	8	– c Wallace b Kasprowicz	0
M. Kaif c Dale b Cosker	13	– lbw b Wharf	6
D. R. Hewson c Hughes b Croft	18	– c Wallace b Wharf	3
†L. D. Sutton lbw b Kasprowicz	28	– b Cosker	29
G. Welch c Wallace b Croft	16	– c Dale b Croft	31
T. Lungley c Cosker b Croft	20	– b Cosker	29
*D. G. Cork c Powell b Cosker	18	– absent hurt	
K. J. Dean lbw b Cosker	15	– (9) c Wallace b Croft	5
L. J. Wharton not out	0	– (10) not out	0
B 8, l-b 5, n-b 8	21	B 6, l-b 2, w 1, n-b 4	13
1/49 (1) 2/57 (3) 3/78 (2) 4/89 (4) 5/107 (5) 6/131 (7) 7/159 (6) 8/181 (9) 9/209 (10) 10/209 (8)	209	1/0 (1) 2/2 (2) 3/2 (3) 4/8 (4) 5/15 (5) 6/68 (6) 7/98 (7) 8/116 (9) 9/116 (8)	116

Bonus points – Derbyshire 1, Glamorgan 3.

Bowling: *First Innings*—Kasprowicz 15–4–43–1; Croft 30.3–9–71–6; Wharf 7–2–21–0; Harrison 4–0–12–0; Cosker 19–3–49–3. *Second Innings*—Kasprowicz 7–2–14–2; Wharf 7–3–12–3; Harrison 4–1–5–0; Croft 18–5–39–2; Cosker 14.5–5–38–2.

Umpires: J. F. Steele and A. G. T. Whitehead.

GLAMORGAN v WORCESTERSHIRE

At Cardiff, June 27, 28, 29, 30. Drawn. Glamorgan 9 pts, Worcestershire 10 pts. Toss: Glamorgan. First-class debut: S. C. Moore. Championship debuts: S. J. Adshead, J. M. Kemp, S. A. Khalid.

The efforts of Powell, who hit a hundred in each innings and scored almost half the runs Glamorgan made off the bat, might have been better rewarded had Croft declared earlier and given his bowlers more time. As it was, Worcestershire made no attempt to score 309 for victory and batted out the last 80 overs. Their captain, Smith, explained that he had five regular players missing, and that he was unwilling to take a chance on a pitch of low bounce. Earlier, Powell had arrived with Glamorgan six for two in the second over, but he counter-attacked well, hitting 11 fours in his first fifty. One of Worcestershire's four Championship debutants, Steve Adshead, a wicket-keeper hurriedly recruited from Shropshire, then helped their last five wickets double the total. As Powell again attacked with relish, Croft allowed Glamorgan's second innings to run until just before midday on the final morning.

Close of play: First day, Glamorgan 228-7 (Powell 116, Kasprowicz 8); Second day, Worcestershire 315-8 (Adshead 58, Khalid 10); Third day, Glamorgan 311-8 (Kasprowicz 7, Wharf 6).

Glamorgan

A. Dale lbw b Hayward	0	– c Batty b Mason	1
J. Hughes lbw b Mason	1	– c Ali b Batty	41
D. L. Hemp c Adshead b Mason	15	– run out	63
M. J. Powell b Hayward	125	– st Adshead b Kemp	142
M. P. Maynard c Kemp b Mason	9	– b Kemp	0
†M. A. Wallace c Moore b Kemp	9	– c Adshead b Kemp	3
*R. D. B. Croft run out	36	– b Khalid	17
D. S. Harrison c Moore b Hayward	11	– lbw b Kemp	4
M. S. Kasprowicz b Mason	19	– b Kemp	35
A. G. Wharf b Hayward	17	– not out	32
D. A. Cosker not out	2	– not out	1
B 2, l-b 21, w 1, n-b 2	26	B 14, l-b 7, w 2, n-b 4	27
1/0 (1) 2/6 (2) 3/31 (3) 4/75 (5) 5/103 (6) 6/187 (7) 7/210 (8) 8/251 (9) 9/251 (4) 10/270 (10)	270	1/9 (1) 2/60 (2) 3/208 (3) 4/209 (5) 5/217 (6) 6/281 (7) 7/291 (4) 8/300 (8) 9/364 (9) (9 wkts dec.)	366

Bonus points – Glamorgan 2, Worcestershire 3.

Bowling: *First Innings*—Hayward 21.2–4–71–4; Mason 21–7–69–4; Kemp 13–2–40–1; Batty 17–4–47–0; Khalid 6–0–20–0. *Second Innings*—Hayward 19–2–74–0; Mason 20–4–69–1; Kemp 17–0–48–5; Batty 30–6–100–1; Khalid 22–7–54–1.

Worcestershire

S. D. Peters c Wallace b Kasprowicz	2	– c Hughes b Croft	32
A. Singh b Kasprowicz	38	– lbw b Kasprowicz	0
Kadeer Ali b Kasprowicz	15	– b Kasprowicz	53
*B. F. Smith b Cosker	32	– c and b Cosker	44
J. M. Kemp b Wharf	14	– lbw b Kasprowicz	3
S. C. Moore c Hemp b Harrison	24	– not out	28
G. J. Batty c Hughes b Croft	49	– st Wallace b Cosker	2
†S. J. Adshead c Kasprowicz b Wharf	63	– not out	3
M. S. Mason b Cosker	52		
S. A. Khalid lbw b Wharf	13		
M. Hayward not out	0		
B 2, l-b 8, w 5, n-b 6, p 5	26	B 5, l-b 2, w 1, n-b 2	10
1/12 (1) 2/58 (3) 3/59 (2) 4/85 (5) 5/135 (4) 6/135 (6) 7/207 (7) 8/291 (9) 9/323 (8) 10/328 (10)	328	1/3 (2) 2/53 (1) 3/104 (3) 4/110 (5) 5/153 (4) 6/165 (7)	(6 wkts) 175

Bonus points – Worcestershire 3, Glamorgan 3.

Bowling: *First Innings*—Kasprowicz 21–5–38–3; Wharf 16.5–1–76–3; Harrison 10–3–23–1; Cosker 19–1–56–2; Croft 28–4–99–1; Dale 3–0–21–0. *Second Innings*—Kasprowicz 16–4–35–3; Harrison 11–2–32–0; Croft 23.4–9–54–1; Cosker 19–7–34–2; Wharf 10–4–13–0.

Umpires: P. J. Hartley and J. W. Holder.

GLAMORGAN v SOMERSET

At Cardiff, July 9, 10, 11, 12. Glamorgan won by 110 runs. Glamorgan 20 pts, Somerset 4 pts. Toss: Glamorgan.

Once again Glamorgan's late order did an unfair share of the batting in the first innings and rescued their side. This was the sixth time in eight completed Championship first innings that the county's last five wickets had added more than the first five. In fact, the last four wickets added 235, more than twice as many as the first six managed. Croft led the way from No. 7, hitting his fourth first-class hundred. He remained unruffled when about 200 seagulls, looking for their own tea after the players had taken theirs, stopped play for several minutes. Blackwell took three for four in 25 balls with his left-arm spin, but Glamorgan's decision to play just one spinner was soon vindicated when the bounce became increasingly variable, and their seamers removed Somerset for 233. Then, against an attack missing Francis, who suffered a side strain in the first innings, Maynard eased to a century and helped stretch Glamorgan's lead of 116 to 423. Despite Burns lasting three and a quarter hours for his 106, there was never much chance of Somerset batting 151 overs for a draw. Victory left Glamorgan in the slipstream of the three top second division counties, ten points behind leaders Northamptonshire.

Close of play: First day, Glamorgan 337-9 (Croft 111, Harrison 18); Second day, Glamorgan 113-3 (Maher 42, Maynard 32); Third day, Somerset 129-3 (Cox 17, Burns 23).

Glamorgan

J. P. Maher c and b Blackwell	21	– c Bowler b Dutch	62
J. Hughes lbw b McLean	1	– lbw b Burns	16
A. Dale c Turner b Blackwell	13	– c Burns b Dutch	7
M. J. Powell c Turner b Blackwell	14	– c Bowler b Dutch	1
M. P. Maynard lbw b McLean	37	– lbw b Burns	101
†M. A. Wallace c Bowler b McLean	20	– c Turner b McLean	26
*R. D. B. Croft c Bryant b McLean	122	– c Turner b McLean	17
S. D. Thomas c Dutch b Laraman	25	– b McLean	4
M. S. Kasprowicz c Cox b Dutch	24	– c Turner b McLean	0
A. G. Wharf c sub b McLean	45	– lbw b Laraman	39
D. S. Harrison not out	18	– not out	12
L-b 6, w 1, n-b 2	9	B 8, l-b 3, w 1, n-b 10	22
1/9 (2) 2/34 (1) 3/35 (3) 4/52 (4) 5/93 (6) 6/114 (5) 7/163 (8) 8/203 (9) 9/307 (10) 10/349 (7)	349	1/39 (2) 2/56 (3) 3/68 (4) 4/164 (1) 5/223 (5) 6/233 (6) 7/251 (8) 8/251 (9) 9/260 (7) 10/307 (10)	307

Bonus points – Glamorgan 3, Somerset 3.

Bowling: *First Innings*—McLean 23.1–4–79–5; Francis 5.5–1–20–0; Dutch 31.1–9–100–1; Blackwell 35–6–93–3; Laraman 12–4–43–1; Burns 2–0–8–0. *Second Innings*—McLean 25–4–84–4; Burns 18–3–61–2; Dutch 16–3–56–3; Blackwell 19–6–65–0; Laraman 4.4–0–30–1.

Somerset

P. D. Bowler c Wallace b Wharf	5	– c Wallace b Thomas	49
M. J. Wood c Powell b Thomas	5	– lbw b Croft	26
J. D. C. Bryant lbw b Thomas	20	– b Kasprowicz	7
J. Cox c Hughes b Kasprowicz	24	– c Maynard b Wharf	24
*M. Burns c Wallace b Kasprowicz	50	– run out	106
I. D. Blackwell c Wallace b Harrison	82	– b Wharf	10
A. W. Laraman lbw b Kasprowicz	0	– c Wallace b Wharf	21
†R. J. Turner c Croft b Kasprowicz	1	– c Wallace b Kasprowicz	9
K. P. Dutch b Wharf	22	– c Thomas b Croft	30
N. A. M. McLean lbw b Harrison	0	– lbw b Wharf	18
S. R. G. Francis not out	0	– not out	2
B 4, l-b 4, w 4, n-b 12	24	B 6, l-b 1, n-b 4	11
1/7 (1) 2/37 (2) 3/38 (3) 4/102 (4) 5/163 (5) 6/163 (7) 7/169 (8) 8/205 (9) 9/206 (10) 10/233 (6)	233	1/44 (2) 2/81 (3) 3/102 (1) 4/144 (4) 5/164 (6) 6/228 (7) 7/247 (8) 8/263 (5) 9/294 (10) 10/313 (9)	313

Bonus points – Somerset 1, Glamorgan 3.

Bowling: *First Innings*—Kasprowicz 19–6–53–4; Wharf 15–3–55–2; Thomas 12–0–41–2; Harrison 10.4–1–52–2; Croft 3–0–24–0. *Second Innings*—Kasprowicz 35–11–91–2; Wharf 26–5–90–4; Thomas 13–3–36–1; Croft 28.5–5–74–2; Harrison 7–1–15–0.

Umpires: T. E. Jesty and N. J. Llong.

At Southampton, July 15, 16, 17, 18. GLAMORGAN lost to HAMPSHIRE by 93 runs.

At Swansea, July 24, 25, 26. GLAMORGAN drew with INDIA A (see India A tour section).

At Worcester, July 31, August 1, 2, 3. GLAMORGAN lost to WORCESTERSHIRE by 14 runs.

GLAMORGAN v DURHAM

At Cardiff, August 13, 14, 15, 16. Glamorgan won by eight wickets. Glamorgan 22 pts, Durham 6 pts. Toss: Durham.

On a slow, lifeless pitch, and with an old, scuffed ball, Kasprowicz destroyed Durham and ended with Glamorgan's best figures since 1936. At tea on the third day, Durham led by 30 runs, with only one second-innings wicket down. But by bowling fast and straight, pitching the ball up and primarily allowing it to reverse-swing, Kasprowicz then whipped out nine batsmen – including

NINE OR MORE WICKETS IN AN INNINGS FOR GLAMORGAN

10-51	J. Mercer v Worcestershire at Worcester	1936
9-36	**M. S. Kasprowicz v Durham at Cardiff (Sophia Gardens)**	**2003**
9-43	J. S. Pressdee v Yorkshire at Swansea	1965
9-45	**M. S. Kasprowicz v Durham at Chester-le-Street**	**2003**
9-47	D. J. Shepherd v Northamptonshire at Cardiff (Arms Park).	1954
9-48	D. J. Shepherd v Yorkshire at Swansea	1965
9-49	A. E. Cordle v Leicestershire at Colwyn Bay	1969
9-54	J. C. Clay v Northamptonshire at Llanelli	1935
9-56	M. A. Nash v Hampshire at Basingstoke	1975
9-59	J. C. Clay v Essex at Westcliff	1937
9-60	O. S. Wheatley v Sussex at Ebbw Vale	1968
9-62	B. L. Muncer v Essex at Brentwood	1948
9-66	J. C. Clay v Worcestershire at Swansea	1937
9-93	A. Nash v Sussex at Swansea	1922
9-97	B. L. Muncer v Surrey at Cardiff (Arms Park)	1947

The previous best figures at Sophia Gardens were 9-57 by P. I. Pocock for Surrey against Glamorgan in 1979.

Research: Andrew Hignell

four lbw and three bowled – in 64 balls; Durham lost eight for 38 as their players scrambled to pad up in time. Kasprowicz's final figures of nine for 36 were the best of the season and the second-best ever for Glamorgan. Earlier, the bowlers had toiled. Two young batsmen both reached Championship-best scores: Peng hit 133 for Durham but received little support as Croft's accuracy and flight undid several well-set batsmen; Wallace received more assistance and helped give Glamorgan a lead of 89. Kasprowicz's dazzling burst left them chasing just 86 to win, and they breezed home, jumping to third in the table.

Close of play: First day, Durham 353-8 (Phillips 38); Second day, Glamorgan 331-6 (Wallace 94); Third day, Glamorgan 74-2 (Dale 13, Powell 11).

Durham

	First Innings		Second Innings	
*J. J. B. Lewis	c Wallace b Kasprowicz	13	lbw b Kasprowicz	68
M. A. Gough	c Hughes b Wharf	30	c and b Cosker	25
M. L. Love	c Wallace b Croft	38	lbw b Kasprowicz	36
G. J. Pratt	b Croft	36	c Maynard b Kasprowicz	18
N. Peng	b Cosker	133	lbw b Kasprowicz	0
V. J. Wells	b Croft	1	lbw b Kasprowicz	0
†P. Mustard	lbw b Croft	0	c Hughes b Kasprowicz	3
G. D. Bridge	c Maher b Croft	49	b Kasprowicz	3
N. C. Phillips	b Kasprowicz	39	b Kasprowicz	6
N. Killeen	not out	0	b Kasprowicz	4
A. M. Davies	c Wallace b Croft	1	not out	0
	B 1, l-b 8, n-b 6	15	L-b 9, n-b 2	11
	1/28 (1) 2/51 (2) 3/124 (3) 4/133 (4) 5/141 (6) 6/141 (7) 7/237 (8) 8/353 (5) 9/354 (9) 10/355 (11)	355	1/61 (2) 2/119 (3) 3/136 (1) 4/136 (5) 5/136 (6) 6/144 (7) 7/160 (8) 8/165 (4) 9/169 (10) 10/174 (9)	174

Bonus points – Durham 4, Glamorgan 3.

Bowling: *First Innings*—Kasprowicz 24–10–41–2; Wharf 17–1–76–1; Harrison 15–5–55–0; Dale 4–0–26–0; Croft 35.1–12–98–6; Cosker 22–9–50–1. *Second Innings*—Kasprowicz 20.2–6–36–9; Croft 26–10–53–0; Wharf 7–1–28–0; Harrison 4–0–15–0; Cosker 8–1–31–1; Maher 1–0–2–0.

Glamorgan

	First Innings		Second Innings	
J. P. Maher	c Pratt b Killeen	8	c Mustard b Phillips	35
J. Hughes	b Bridge	39	lbw b Davies	11
A. Dale	c Pratt b Phillips	66	not out	14
M. J. Powell	c Peng b Phillips	14	not out	19
M. P. Maynard	lbw b Bridge	70		
†M. A. Wallace	lbw b Phillips	117		
*R. D. B. Croft	lbw b Bridge	25		
A. G. Wharf	lbw b Bridge	50		
M. S. Kasprowicz	b Phillips	24		
D. S. Harrison	c and b Phillips	6		
D. A. Cosker	not out	3		
	B 7, l-b 14, w 1	22	B 4, l-b 3	7
	1/17 (1) 2/65 (2) 3/112 (4) 4/161 (3) 5/245 (5) 6/331 (7) 7/383 (6) 8/421 (8) 9/437 (9) 10/444 (10)	444	1/34 (2) 2/52 (1)	(2 wkts) 86

Bonus points – Glamorgan 5, Durham 2 (130 overs: 435-8).

Bowling: *First Innings*—Killeen 17–4–50–1; Davies 21–4–77–0; Wells 10–3–26–0; Bridge 38–10–114–4; Phillips 44.5–8–144–5; Gough 2–0–12–0. *Second Innings*—Killeen 2–0–17–0; Davies 6–0–29–1; Phillips 6.1–0–27–1; Pratt 1–0–5–0; Bridge 1–0–1–0.

Umpires: M. R. Benson and J. F. Steele.

At Bristol, August 19, 20, 21, 22. GLAMORGAN drew with GLOUCESTERSHIRE.

GLAMORGAN v YORKSHIRE

At Colwyn Bay, August 25, 26, 27, 28. Drawn. Glamorgan 12 pts, Yorkshire 12 pts. Toss: Glamorgan.

Indifferent light and an undefeated century from McGrath – told to score runs in county cricket after being dropped by England – frustrated Glamorgan. In the 33rd over of the final day, Yorkshire were 89 for five and still 291 behind; victory seemed within touching distance. But the light soon deteriorated, denying Croft the use of his quicker bowlers for the last 60 overs. As the spinners wheeled away on a placid pitch, McGrath and Dawson, who eked out 22 in 34 overs, showed a broad bat and Yorkshire held out. Earlier, both teams reached 400 in their first innings. Powell kept cover-point busy during his 146 for Glamorgan, on a first day that ended with the dominant batsmen accepting the light and losing nine overs. Only Silverwood hammered some life from the pitch, taking four for 56. Wood and McGrath then booked in too, dragging Yorkshire within 44. On the third afternoon, Powell and Hemp extended Glamorgan's lead, but too slowly as it turned out. Powell fell 15 runs short of becoming the first Glamorgan batsman to score twin hundreds in a match twice in a season.

Close of play: First day, Glamorgan 380-7 (Wharf 31, Kasprowicz 33); Second day, Yorkshire 291-4 (Wood 124, Kirby 4); Third day, Glamorgan 270-4 (Powell 81, Hemp 54).

Glamorgan

First innings		Second innings	
J. P. Maher c Fleming b Silverwood	53	– lbw b Gough	0
†M. A. Wallace lbw b Kirby	31	– c Gray b Dawson	61
A. Dale lbw b Silverwood	0	– c Blakey b Yuvraj Singh	47
M. J. Powell c Silverwood b Yuvraj Singh	146	– b Dawson	85
M. P. Maynard c Blakey b Silverwood	32	– c Gray b Dawson	3
D. L. Hemp b Kirby	25	– not out	85
*R. D. B. Croft lbw b Silverwood	0	– b Gough	5
A. G. Wharf c Blakey b Gray	79	– not out	23
M. S. Kasprowicz c Dawson b McGrath	51		
D. S. Harrison lbw b McGrath	1		
D. A. Cosker not out	5		
B 9, l-b 10, n-b 24	43	B 7, l-b 4, w 6, n-b 10	27
1/82 (2) 2/85 (3) 3/102 (1) 4/162 (5) 5/280 (6) 6/284 (7) 7/323 (4) 8/460 (8) 9/461 (10) 10/466 (9)	466	1/2 (1) 2/118 (2) 3/144 (3) 4/158 (5) 5/277 (4) 6/292 (7)	(6 wkts dec.) 336

Bonus points – Glamorgan 5, Yorkshire 3.

Bowling: *First Innings*—Gough 20–3–73–0; Kirby 26–1–158–2; Silverwood 19–2–56–4; Dawson 17–4–70–0; Gray 18–2–45–1; McGrath 10–2–37–2; Yuvraj Singh 4–1–8–1. *Second Innings*—Gough 14–2–33–2; Kirby 5–0–30–0; Dawson 34–7–119–3; Silverwood 9–1–46–0; Yuvraj Singh 12.5–1–65–1; Gray 2–0–11–0; McGrath 6–0–21–0.

Yorkshire

First innings		Second innings	
M. J. Wood c Dale b Croft	126	– lbw b Kasprowicz	0
S. P. Fleming c Dale b Croft	61	– lbw b Cosker	16
*A. McGrath c Powell b Cosker	92	– not out	127
M. J. Lumb b Croft	5	– lbw b Croft	1
Yuvraj Singh b Cosker	2	– c Cosker b Croft	6
S. P. Kirby c Croft b Cosker	11		
†R. J. Blakey lbw b Kasprowicz	36	– (6) lbw b Kasprowicz	0
A. K. D. Gray not out	48	– (7) c Wallace b Croft	13
R. K. J. Dawson c Powell b Harrison	7	– (8) lbw b Croft	22
C. E. W. Silverwood b Kasprowicz	9	– (9) not out	2
D. Gough b Kasprowicz	12		
B 4, l-b 9	13	B 4, l-b 2	6
1/104 (2) 2/259 (3) 3/280 (4) 4/285 (5) 5/295 (1) 6/307 (6) 7/380 (7) 8/389 (9) 9/406 (10) 10/422 (11)	422	1/6 (1) 2/45 (2) 3/58 (4) 4/78 (5) 5/89 (6) 6/124 (7) 7/188 (8)	(7 wkts) 193

Bonus points – Yorkshire 5, Glamorgan 3.

Bowling: *First Innings*—Kasprowicz 19.2–5–60–3; Wharf 7–0–35–0; Cosker 39–8–109–3; Croft 37–4–125–3; Harrison 16–2–67–1; Dale 10–3–13–0. *Second Innings*—Kasprowicz 8–1–30–2; Harrison 4–0–13–0; Croft 42–14–80–4; Cosker 38–17–62–1; Maynard 2–0–2–0.

Umpires: J. H. Hampshire and A. A. Jones.

GLAMORGAN v NORTHAMPTONSHIRE

At Cardiff, September 10, 11, 12, 13. Northamptonshire won by 20 runs. Northamptonshire 20 pts, Glamorgan 4 pts. Toss: Northamptonshire.

On the last afternoon, Cosker, Glamorgan's No. 11, joined Hemp at the fall of the ninth wicket, with 99 still needed for victory and their promotion hopes hanging by a thread. When Cosker played fatally back to Brown's off-spin, they were just 21 short. Two dropped catches off Hussey on the first day proved costly for Glamorgan: he went on to drive his way to a fifth consecutive first-class century (100, 331*, 115, 187, 147). Croft finally lured him down the pitch, taking five wickets on a strip that showed increasing turn and bounce. But his fellow off-spinner Swann showed impressive control for Northamptonshire and they took a first-innings lead of 116. In the second innings, Croft ended Hussey's awesome run (he reached a mere 50), thus depriving him of the chance to equal C. B. Fry, Bradman and Mike Procter on six successive centuries; instead, he emulated Everton Weekes and Brian Lara, which is distinguished enough company (see page 164). Croft took his match figures to ten for 147, but he could not stop Northamptonshire's last pair, Nel and the renowned rabbit Brown, cracking 58 in less than nine overs. Although Glamorgan's last pair did even better it was not good enough.

Close of play: First day, Glamorgan 20-0 (Maher 9, Wallace 10); Second day, Northamptonshire 80-2 (Hussey 22, Sales 52); Third day, Glamorgan 167-4 (Maynard 46, Hemp 15).

Northamptonshire

*M. E. K. Hussey b Croft	147	– (2) c Maynard b Croft	50
T. W. Roberts c Wallace b Wharf	41	– (1) c Wallace b Kasprowicz	6
P. A. Jaques lbw b Croft	28	– c and b Wharf	0
D. J. Sales lbw b Croft	17	– lbw b Kasprowicz	52
M. J. Powell lbw b Cosker	3	– c Wallace b Wharf	1
J. W. Cook c Maher b Croft	3	– lbw b Croft	37
†T. M. B. Bailey lbw b Kasprowicz	11	– c Maynard b Croft	7
G. P. Swann lbw b Kasprowicz	0	– c Wallace b Wharf	39
M. J. Cawdron lbw b Croft	5	– c and b Croft	1
A. Nel b Kasprowicz	19	– c Kasprowicz b Croft	42
J. F. Brown not out	19	– not out	9
B 6, n-b 20	26	B 9, l-b 2, n-b 10	21
1/95 (2) 2/142 (3) 3/184 (4) 4/219 (5) 5/222 (6) 6/253 (7) 7/253 (8) 8/260 (9) 9/287 (10) 10/319 (1)	319	1/6 (1) 2/7 (3) 3/80 (4) 4/85 (5) 5/134 (2) 6/154 (7) 7/181 (6) 8/199 (9) 9/207 (8) 10/265 (10)	265

Bonus points – Northamptonshire 3, Glamorgan 3.

Bowling: *First Innings*—Kasprowicz 20–2–58–3; Wharf 13–2–83–1; Harrison 9–2–47–0; Cosker 11–4–32–1; Croft 28.3–6–93–5. *Second Innings*—Kasprowicz 13–3–41–2; Wharf 16–2–83–3; Harrison 4–3–12–0; Cosker 22–5–64–0; Croft 24.1–12–54–5.

Glamorgan

J. P. Maher c Hussey b Cawdron	29	– st Bailey b Brown	35
†M. A. Wallace lbw b Cawdron	10	– run out	38
A. Dale c Hussey b Cook	24	– c Roberts b Swann	16
M. J. Powell c Roberts b Swann	40	– b Brown	11
M. P. Maynard c Powell b Swann	48	– c and b Swann	78
D. L. Hemp lbw b Swann	29	– not out	85
*R. D. B. Croft c Powell b Brown	1	– b Cook	31
A. G. Wharf c Sales b Brown	4	– b Cook	4
M. S. Kasprowicz not out	12	– c Bailey b Cook	0
D. S. Harrison b Swann	0	– b Cook	4
D. A. Cosker lbw b Swann	0	– lbw b Brown	42
B 2, l-b 3, w 1	6	B 10, l-b 5, n-b 2	17
1/20 (2) 2/53 (1) 3/86 (3) 4/141 (4) 5/170 (5) 6/171 (7) 7/187 (8) 8/203 (6) 9/203 (10) 10/203 (11)	203	1/63 (1) 2/88 (2) 3/91 (3) 4/136 (4) 5/222 (5) 6/271 (7) 7/279 (8) 8/279 (9) 9/283 (10) 10/361 (11)	361

Bonus points – Glamorgan 1, Northamptonshire 3.

Bowling: *First Innings*—Nel 12.3–3–24–0; Cawdron 11.3–2–58–2; Brown 24–8–56–2; Cook 7–2–23–1; Swann 16–4–37–5. *Second Innings*—Nel 1–0–7–0; Cawdron 14–3–48–0; Cook 20–5–66–4; Hussey 3–0–9–0; Brown 62.2–24–100–3; Swann 47–8–116–2.

Umpires: N. G. Cowley and B. Dudleston.

At Chester-le-Street, September 17, 18, 19. GLAMORGAN beat DURHAM by 369 runs.

CRICKET SOCIETY AWARDS, 2003

Samit Patel of Nottinghamshire won the Cricket Society's Most Promising Young Cricketer Award, and Glamorgan's Australian player Mike Kasprowicz won the Wetherell award for the outstanding all-rounder in the first-class game. The Sir John Hobbs Jubilee Memorial Prize for the outstanding Under-16 schoolboy went to Ben Wright of Cowbridge Comprehensive School, Glamorgan, who also, uniquely, won the A. A. Thomson Fielding Prize for the best schoolboy fielder. The best schools all-rounder was Wian Potgieter of Merchiston Castle School. The Most Promising Young Woman Cricketer of the Year was Yorkshire opening bowler Kathryn Doherty. The 2003 Don Rowan Memorial Trophy, for primary schools promoting cricket, was given to Loughborough School in Brixton, and the Christopher Box-Grainger Memorial Trophy for schools promoting cricket to under-privileged children went to Lansdowne School in Stockwell. The Perry-Lewis/Kershaw Trophy to the Society XI Player best representing the spirit of Society cricket was won jointly by Bill Allen and Tony Warrington.

GLOUCESTERSHIRE

A touch of cold steel, Cap'n Mainwaring

GRAHAM RUSSELL

Some perceived a thickening in the players' waistlines, and the evidence of their birthdates was incontrovertible. Everyone seemed to agree Gloucestershire were cricket's Dad's Army. The soubriquet amused the dressing-room as they celebrated victory over Worcestershire in the C&G final. It was their sixth one-day trophy in five years. Given that they also won promotion to Division One of the Championship, finished runners-up in the National League and reached the semi-finals of the Twenty20, they could afford to laugh. They bore all the hallmarks of a mature side knowing exactly what was required of them.

There was truth, though, in the gibe about age. Of the team that swept Worcestershire aside at Lord's, only Jon Lewis and Alex Gidman were under 30. And before stumps were drawn on the season, two leading lights had announced they were off: South African Jonty Rhodes into retirement and Ian Harvey, the Australian, to Yorkshire, it ultimately turned out. Three others, Mark Alleyne, Jack Russell and Mike Smith, took long-standing back problems with them into the winter. Alleyne – captain for the past seven years – had to cope with personal loss of form in 2003 and eventually moved at least partially upstairs to the job of head coach. The plan was that he would stay on to lead the side in one-day cricket, with Craig Spearman expected to replace him as captain of the Championship side.

The change was precipitated by the departure of John Bracewell, director of cricket and the architect of Gloucestershire's rise to one-day glory. In the spring, rumours had linked him with the post of Sri Lankan coach, but he finally got the job of running the national team of his own country, New Zealand. It was fitting reward for a job well done at Bristol. Bracewell made his mark the moment he arrived in 1998, revolutionising the county's approach to fitness, discipline and dress, and adopting a horses-for-courses selection policy, which saw capped players dropped. To get things right as he saw them – and results bore him out – he trod on toes, seeing off a dressing-room rebellion in 2002. Having established Gloucestershire as the premier one-day outfit in the country, he left behind a remarkable record. But old warhorses cannot keep galloping for ever. His successor faces formidable problems.

Every county needs to establish at least one new player a year and in 2003 Gloucestershire's was Gidman. Given a regular middle-order place when Alleyne dropped himself, he seized his chance. Aged 22, and allying a tall man's reach, an ease at the crease and promising medium-pace – which together secured him a National Academy place – he averaged 29 from eight Championship matches, though his contribution to the shorter game was especially telling. There is a confidence to his game, but so there was with

Jon Lewis

Chris Taylor, who in 2000 announced himself with a debut century at Lord's. In 2003, he hardly got a look in: four first-class games and a few one-day appearances behind the stumps when Russell was injured and his deputy Stephen Pope judged not good enough. Russell, now 40, returns for 2004 but not Pope: Stephen Adshead, late of Leicestershire and Worcestershire, took his place.

The arrival of Philip Weston from Worcestershire gave the top order some solidity. He opened with Spearman – who acted as captain for around half the season – and both averaged a respectable 33. Weston hit 179 on a Taunton shirt-front, but 46 against his old county in the Lord's final was more satisfying. Matt Windows maintained his close-season fitness by training with a woman boxer, but never quite punched his weight. Despite playing 16 Championship matches, he failed to reach the 1,000-run benchmark.

The overseas players more than earned their keep. The season stretched Rhodes more than he expected, but enthusiasm pushed the aches aside and he comfortably topped the batting with 1,293 at 58. Even more difficult to replicate will be the explosive, intense skills that Harvey brought to the one-day side. He was the match-winner: a cerebral bowler and a sharp, gambling, bat.

Harvey missed the early summer and was with Australia for a month mid-season. Money was tight for short-term replacements but Bracewell knew where to turn. First came Ian Butler, a 21-year-old New Zealander capable of 90mph. A brewery sponsored his stay to the tune of a litre and a half of lager and £150 per wicket – and he went home with £2,550. As a non-drinker, though, he donated the lager to his colleagues. They could also toast Shoaib Malik, the second teetotal import, who handed on the champagne that came as recognition for steering Gloucestershire through a tricky C&G semi-final with Derbyshire. Shoaib, an off-spinning all-rounder, returns in 2004.

It was a better year for Martyn Ball; reliability personified in the slips, he seized 28 wickets with his off-spin. A good year, too, for the seamer, Jon Lewis, who after two quiet summers stormed back with 74 wickets, more than any other home-bred bowler. Repositioning his front foot worked wonders, and shifted the pressure away from his back and on to the batsman. Life will be harder for everyone in 2004. Unlike the Walmington-on-Sea Home Guard, this cast cannot go on with triumphant repeats indefinitely.

GLOUCESTERSHIRE RESULTS

All first-class matches – Played 16: Won 5, Lost 2, Drawn 9.
County Championship matches – Played 16: Won 5, Lost 2, Drawn 9.

Frizzell County Championship, 3rd in Division 2; Cheltenham & Gloucester Trophy, winners; National Cricket League, 2nd in Division 1; Twenty20 Cup, semi-finalists.

COUNTY CHAMPIONSHIP AVERAGES

BATTING AND FIELDING

Cap		*M*	*I*	*NO*	*R*	*HS*	*100s*	*50s*	*Avge*	*Ct/St*
	J. N. Rhodes§	15	27	5	1,293	151*	5	7	58.77	7
1999	I. J. Harvey§	6	12	3	404	128*	1	1	44.88	4
1985	R. C. Russell	11	16	4	436	78*	0	3	36.33	33/4
1998	T. H. C. Hancock	12	21	0	720	97	0	5	34.28	13
	W. P. C. Weston	15	27	1	877	179	2	2	33.73	10
2002	C. M. Spearman	15	27	0	903	103	1	7	33.44	15
1998	M. G. N. Windows	16	29	0	890	150	1	5	30.68	11
	A. P. R. Gidman	8	16	2	407	68	0	2	29.07	7
1996	M. C. J. Ball	10	15	3	304	75	0	2	25.33	12
	I. D. Fisher	10	12	3	219	71	0	1	24.33	4
2001	C. G. Taylor	4	8	0	171	45	0	0	21.37	3
	Shoaib Malik§	2	4	0	80	60	0	1	20.00	0
	R. J. Sillence	4	5	0	98	42	0	0	19.60	1
1990	M. W. Alleyne	8	13	3	193	32*	0	0	19.30	9
1998	J. Lewis	14	18	4	248	47	0	0	17.71	3
	S. P. Pope	5	8	3	65	17*	0	0	13.00	10/1
1995	A. M. Smith	11	14	7	58	17*	0	0	8.28	1
	I. G. Butler§	4	5	0	20	13	0	0	4.00	0

Also batted: J. M. M. Averis (cap 2001) (4 matches) 8, 0, 4* (1 ct); M. A. Hardinges (2 matches) 17, 10*, 0 (1 ct).

§ *Overseas player.*

BOWLING

	O	*M*	*R*	*W*	*BB*	*5W/i*	*Avge*
I. J. Harvey	195.2	54	625	27	4-43	0	23.14
A. M. Smith	329.5	91	898	38	5-70	1	23.63
J. Lewis	551.2	142	1,800	74	7-117	5	24.32
I. D. Fisher	225.1	50	767	28	5-30	3	27.39
I. G. Butler	124	24	478	17	4-74	0	28.11
M. C. J. Ball	378.3	99	1,008	28	5-104	1	36.00

Also bowled: M. W. Alleyne 133–32–460–9; J. M. M. Averis 107.2–30–298–9; A. P. R. Gidman 104–20–441–5; T. H. C. Hancock 5–0–22–0; M. A. Hardinges 27–9–118–3; Shoaib Malik 66–19–146–5; R. J. Sillence 100.5–15–408–9; C. G. Taylor 11–0–48–0; W. P. C. Weston 2–0–10–0.

COUNTY RECORDS

Highest score for:	318*	W. G. Grace v Yorkshire at Cheltenham	1876
Highest score against:	310*	M. E. K. Hussey (Northamptonshire) at Bristol	2002
Best bowling for:	10-40	E. G. Dennett v Essex at Bristol	1906
Best bowling against:	10-66	A. A. Mailey (Australians) at Cheltenham	1921
	10-66	K. Smales (Nottinghamshire) at Stroud	1956
Highest total for:	653-6 dec.	v Glamorgan at Bristol	1928
Highest total against:	774-7 dec.	by Australians at Bristol	1948
Lowest total for:	17	v Australians at Cheltenham	1896
Lowest total against:	12	by Northamptonshire at Gloucester	1907

GLOUCESTERSHIRE DIRECTORY

ADDRESS

County Ground, Nevil Road, Bristol BS7 9EJ (0117 910 8000; fax 0117 924 1193; email jane.lobb@glosccc.co.uk). **Website** www.gloscricket.co.uk.

GROUNDS

Bristol (Nevil Road) 2 miles NW of city centre between A38 and M32 junction 2 via B4469 on Muller Road, L into Ralph Road, L then immediate R into Kennington Avenue then L into Nevil Road. Nearest stations: Montpelier (¾ mile), Bristol Parkway (2½ miles) and Temple Meads (2 miles).

Cheltenham (College): 1 mile S of town centre off A46 Bath Road in Thirlestaine Road. Signposted Cricket Festival from both M5 junctions. Nearest station: Cheltenham Spa (1 mile).

Gloucester (Archdeacon Meadow): ½ mile NW of city centre on A417 in St Oswald's Road S of railway line. Nearest station: Gloucester (½ mile).

OFFICIALS

Club captain M. W. Alleyne
Director of cricket 2003 – J. G. Bracewell
Head coach 2004 – M. W. Alleyne
Director of development A. W. Stovold
President G. F. Collis
Chairman A. H. Haines
Chief executive T. E. M. Richardson
Chairman, cricket committee A. S. Brown
Head groundsman S. Williams
Scorer K. T. Gerrish

PLAYERS

Players expected to reappear in 2004

	Former counties	*Country*	*Born*	*Birthplace*
Alleyne Mark Wayne		E	23.5.1968	*Tottenham*
Averis James Maxwell Michael		E	28.5.1974	†*Bristol*
Ball Martyn Charles John		E	26.4.1970	†*Bristol*
Bressington Alastair Nigel		E	28.11.1979	†*Bristol*
Fisher Ian Douglas	Yorks	E	31.3.1976	*Bradford*
Gidman Alexander Peter Richard		E	22.6.1981	*High Wycombe*
Hancock Timothy Harold Coulter		E	20.4.1972	*Reading*
Hardinges Mark Andrew		E	5.2.1978	†*Gloucester*
Lewis Jonathan		E	26.8.1975	*Aylesbury*
***Russell** Robert Charles ("Jack")		E	15.8.1963	†*Stroud*
***Shoaib Malik**		P	1.2.1982	*Sialkot*
Sillence Roger John		E	29.6.1977	*Salisbury*
***Smith** Andrew Michael		E	1.10.1967	*Dewsbury*
***Spearman** Craig Murray		NZ (EU)	4.7.1972	*Auckland*
Taylor Christopher Glyn		E	27.9.1976	†*Bristol*
Weston William Philip Christopher	Worcs	E	16.6.1973	*Durham*
Windows Matthew Guy Newman		E	5.4.1973	†*Bristol*

* *Test player.* † *Born in Gloucestershire.*

Player due to join in 2004

Adshead Stephen John	Leics, Worcs	E	29.1.1980	*Redditch*

At Bristol, April 12, 13, 14. **Drawn.** Toss: Gloucestershire. **Gloucestershire 381** (M. W. Alleyne 90, I. D. Fisher 92) **and 347-4 dec.** (T. H. C. Hancock 60, M. G. N. Windows 104, J. N. Rhodes 101); **Bradford/Leeds UCCE 217** (R. J. Sillence 6-65) **and 72-3**.

First-team debut: S. P. Pope. County debut: J. N. Rhodes.

GLOUCESTERSHIRE v SOMERSET

At Bristol, April 18, 19, 20, 21. Gloucestershire won by eight runs. Gloucestershire 18 pts, Somerset 5 pts. Toss: Gloucestershire. County debut: W. P. C. Weston. Championship debuts: J. N. Rhodes; J. D. C. Bryant.

By mid-afternoon on the first day, with Gloucestershire dismissed for 203 and Somerset gasping at 36 for six, the big crowd were already wondering how they would spend the rest of the Easter weekend. But the match somehow lasted four days, and enthralling, switchback cricket it was. After Lewis had blazed through Somerset's top order, Johnson reshaped the game with a maiden century from No. 8. Initially he played and missed like so many others, but when he took control the hitting was clean, and the punishment savage: Johnson's 118 took 95 balls with 19 fours and four sixes. One Alleyne over cost 25. Batting again, Gloucestershire were five down and only 69 ahead, before Somerset ran up against Russell. Having earlier passed Jack Board's record of 1,016 dismissals for Gloucestershire, he showed stubborn concentration with the bat, lasting five and a half hours and 252 balls for an unbeaten 78. Still, his efforts looked in vain when Somerset were strolling towards their target of 283 on the last day. But from 204 for three they crumbled, leaving their first-innings saviour Johnson stranded on 11.

Close of play: First day, Somerset 175-6 (Turner 33, Johnson 106); Second day, Gloucestershire 209-5 (Windows 53, Russell 25); Third day, Somerset 99-2 (Bowler 38, Cox 9).

Gloucestershire

First innings		Second innings	
C. M. Spearman c Burns b McLean	8	(2) c Turner b Johnson	8
W. P. C. Weston lbw b Laraman	12	(1) b McLean	12
T. H. C. Hancock b McLean	33	c Turner b McLean	44
J. N. Rhodes c Bowler b Johnson	42	b Blackwell	55
M. G. N. Windows c Bowler b Francis	10	c Burns b McLean	78
*M. W. Alleyne c Turner b Francis	19	lbw b McLean	0
†R. C. Russell c Blackwell b Francis	11	not out	78
I. D. Fisher c Bowler b Burns	15	c Trescothick b McLean	18
R. J. Sillence b Johnson	42	b Laraman	40
J. Lewis not out	1	c sub b Laraman	8
A. M. Smith c Turner b Johnson	0	c Bryant b Laraman	1
L-b 7, w 1, n-b 2	10	B 12, l-b 10, n-b 4	26
1/16 (1) 2/25 (2) 3/92 (4) 4/108 (5) 5/117 (3) 6/138 (7) 7/143 (6) 8/198 (9) 9/202 (8) 10/203 (11)	203	1/20 (2) 2/28 (1) 3/113 (4) 4/147 (3) 5/155 (6) 6/258 (5) 7/282 (8) 8/348 (9) 9/360 (10) 10/368 (11)	368

Bonus points – Gloucestershire 1, Somerset 3.

Bowling: *First Innings*—McLean 13–1–43–2; Johnson 13.2–3–27–3; Francis 20–7–65–3; Laraman 13–4–54–1; Blackwell 1–1–0–0; Burns 2–0–7–1. *Second Innings*—McLean 35–9–87–5; Johnson 33–8–84–1; Francis 22–2–79–0; Laraman 21–7–45–3; Blackwell 19–7–46–1; Burns 3–1–5–0.

Somerset

P. D. Bowler lbw b Lewis	0	– lbw b Smith	50
M. E. Trescothick b Smith	0	– c Russell b Smith	10
*M. Burns b Lewis	1	– lbw b Lewis	25
J. Cox c Russell b Lewis	11	– lbw b Alleyne	67
J. D. C. Bryant c Russell b Lewis	19	– c Russell b Alleyne	31
†R. J. Turner not out	59	– (7) c Alleyne b Sillence	15
A. W. Laraman c Russell b Lewis	0	– (8) b Sillence	23
R. L. Johnson b Lewis	118	– (9) not out	11
I. D. Blackwell b Smith	31	– (6) c Russell b Alleyne	0
N. A. M. McLean c Spearman b Fisher	9	– c Russell b Smith	3
S. R. G. Francis c Fisher b Sillence	34	– c Weston b Sillence	1
L-b 5, n-b 2	7	B 10, l-b 10, w 4, n-b 14	38
1/0 (1) 2/0 (2) 3/8 (3) 4/17 (4) 5/36 (5) 6/36 (7) 7/192 (8) 8/236 (9) 9/247 (10) 10/289 (11)	289	1/18 (2) 2/74 (3) 3/124 (1) 4/204 (4) 5/204 (6) 6/229 (5) 7/237 (7) 8/262 (8) 9/271 (10) 10/274 (11)	274

Bonus points – Somerset 2, Gloucestershire 3.

Bowling: *First Innings*—Lewis 21–4–58–6; Smith 16–1–64–2; Alleyne 6–3–37–0; Sillence 6.2–0–54–1; Fisher 16–6–71–1. *Second Innings*—Lewis 23–8–40–1; Smith 28–8–69–3; Sillence 18–2–55–3; Alleyne 27–4–77–3; Fisher 6–2–13–0.

Umpires: G. I. Burgess and P. J. Hartley.

At Northampton, April 23, 24, 25, 26. GLOUCESTERSHIRE drew with NORTHAMPTONSHIRE.

At Chester-le-Street, April 30, May 1, 2, 3. GLOUCESTERSHIRE drew with DURHAM.

At Cardiff, May 9, 10, 11, 12. GLOUCESTERSHIRE beat GLAMORGAN by six wickets.

GLOUCESTERSHIRE v HAMPSHIRE

At Bristol, May 14, 15, 16, 17. Drawn. Gloucestershire 10 pts, Hampshire 9 pts. Toss: Hampshire.

Late on the second afternoon the weather forced the players off, and they never returned. After winning the toss, Crawley had put safety first, scoring just three in the opening 85 minutes and ending up with 69 at a run an over. Katich had no such inhibitions. He hit 96 before misjudging Fisher's left-arm spin to end a second-wicket stand of 142 with Crawley. In reply, Gloucestershire's openers put on a brisk 141, with Spearman going on to a sixth century in 21 Championship matches, and their position looked strong at 316 for four when the weather took over. Gloucestershire had now lost six days to rain during their first five matches. Despite the soggy start, they remained top of the second division.

Close of play: First day, Hampshire 351-6 (Mascarenhas 13, Udal 6); Second day, Gloucestershire 316-4 (Rhodes 57, Alleyne 18); Third day, No play.

Hampshire

D. A. Kenway c Weston b Smith 8
*J. P. Crawley c Alleyne b Butler 69
S. M. Katich b Fisher 96
R. A. Smith c Windows b Lewis 0
W. S. Kendall c Russell b Butler 69
†N. Pothas c Russell b Lewis 63
A. D. Mascarenhas c Spearman b Butler. 14
S. D. Udal retired hurt 6
C. T. Tremlett not out 10
A. D. Mullally b Lewis 0
J. A. Tomlinson c Russell b Lewis 6
B 4, l-b 10, w 2, n-b 12 28

1/11 (1) 2/153 (3) 3/168 (4) 369
4/213 (2) 5/316 (5) 6/342 (6)
7/352 (7) 8/353 (10) 9/369 (11)

Bonus points – Hampshire 4, Gloucestershire 3.

Udal retired hurt at 351.

Bowling: Lewis 29.5–12–80–4; Smith 19–4–50–1; Butler 23–7–80–3; Alleyne 19–5–58–0; Fisher 22–2–87–1.

Gloucestershire

W. P. C. Weston c Katich b Mascarenhas 61
C. M. Spearman c Kenway b Katich . . . 103
T. H. C. Hancock run out 47
J. N. Rhodes not out 57
M. G. N. Windows c Kenway b Katich . 21
*M. W. Alleyne not out 18
L-b 5, n-b 4 9

1/141 (1) 2/216 (3) (4 wkts) 316
3/217 (2) 4/253 (5)

†R. C. Russell, I. D. Fisher, I. G. Butler, J. Lewis and A. M. Smith did not bat.

Bonus points – Gloucestershire 3, Hampshire 1.

Bowling: Mullally 22–5–67–0; Tremlett 12–3–35–0; Mascarenhas 20–5–74–1; Tomlinson 9–0–62–0; Katich 20–2–73–2.

Umpires: M. R. Benson and D. J. Constant.

At Worcester, May 21, 22, 23, 24. GLOUCESTERSHIRE lost to WORCESTERSHIRE by 111 runs.

GLOUCESTERSHIRE v NORTHAMPTONSHIRE

At Gloucester, June 4, 5, 6, 7. Northamptonshire won by an innings and 54 runs. Northamptonshire 22 pts, Gloucestershire 2 pts. Toss: Northamptonshire.

A flat wicket and massive concentration – the home coach John Bracewell called it "awesome" – helped Hussey continue the punishment he had inflicted upon Gloucestershire during his unbeaten 310 at Bristol in August 2002. Unhurried and largely untroubled, he was on 264 when, with both feet off the ground, he hooked to deep square leg. Having dominated for six minutes short of ten hours, Hussey had faced 436 balls and hit 35 fours and two sixes. By then it was mid-afternoon on the second day, and he and Brophy had added 260 for the sixth wicket. Brophy went on to 152 not out as Northamptonshire piled up 622 before declaring. Gloucestershire's regular openers were both missing with injuries but their deputies, Taylor and Hancock, took the score to 96 when four wickets tumbled without a run added. After following on, Windows and Russell spat defiance with a seventh-wicket stand of 175, but when Russell tickled a catch behind, Nel mopped up the tail with 20 minutes to spare, completing match figures of eight for 134.

Close of play: First day, Northamptonshire 348-5 (Hussey 169, Brophy 6); Second day, Gloucestershire 109-4 (Rhodes 10, Gidman 2); Third day, Gloucestershire 66-1 (Hancock 18, Butler 4).

Northamptonshire

*M. E. K. Hussey c Hancock b Lewis	264	A. Nel b Ball	0
D. E. Paynter b Butler	5	C. G. Greenidge not out	3
P. A. Jaques lbw b Ball	75	B 13, l-b 6, w 6, n-b 29	54
J. W. Cook b Smith	1		—
D. J. Sales c Russell b Butler	46	1/32 (2) 2/158 (3) (8 wkts dec.)	622
M. J. Powell c Russell b Butler	19	3/172 (4) 4/286 (5)	
†G. L. Brophy not out	152	5/328 (6) 6/588 (1)	
B. J. Phillips b Ball	3	7/612 (8) 8/612 (9)	

J. F. Brown did not bat.

Bonus points – Northamptonshire 5, Gloucestershire 1 (130 overs: 481-5).

Bowling: Lewis 35.5–6–145–1; Smith 25–5–63–1; Butler 28–2–130–3; Ball 44–6–149–3; Gidman 17–1–76–0; Taylor 9–0–40–0.

Gloucestershire

C. G. Taylor b Nel	45	– run out	31
T. H. C. Hancock lbw b Greenidge	44	– c Brophy b Nel	18
M. G. N. Windows lbw b Greenidge	0	– (4) c Hussey b Brown	150
J. N. Rhodes lbw b Nel	24	– (5) b Brown	4
*M. W. Alleyne c Brophy b Nel	0	– (6) c Brophy b Greenidge	8
A. P. R. Gidman c Powell b Phillips	20	– (7) c Sales b Brown	8
†R. C. Russell lbw b Nel	22	– (8) c Brophy b Phillips	63
M. C. J. Ball b Brown	53	– (9) b Nel	1
J. Lewis c Greenidge b Nel	5	– (10) not out	11
I. G. Butler run out	0	– (3) c Powell b Brown	7
A. M. Smith not out	0	– c Brophy b Nel	4
B 3, l-b 3, w 3, n-b 8	17	B 12, l-b 6, w 5, n-b 10	33
	—		—
1/96 (2) 2/96 (3) 3/96 (1) 4/96 (5) 5/146 (4) 6/146 (6) 7/218 (7) 8/222 (8) 9/225 (10) 10/230 (9)	230	1/61 (1) 2/66 (2) 3/93 (3) 4/97 (5) 5/126 (6) 6/147 (7) 7/322 (8) 8/322 (4) 9/324 (9) 10/338 (11)	338

Bonus points – Gloucestershire 1, Northamptonshire 3.

Bowling: *First Innings*—Nel 28.1–11–47–5; Greenidge 19–1–80–2; Brown 26–8–63–1; Phillips 13–4–34–1. *Second Innings*—Nel 32.1–6–87–3; Greenidge 14–1–59–1; Phillips 16–5–32–1; Brown 49–20–106–4; Cook 6–4–10–0; Paynter 6–1–26–0.

Umpires: N. J. Llong and J. W. Lloyds.

At Southampton, June 27, 28, 29, 30. GLOUCESTERSHIRE drew with HAMPSHIRE.

At Taunton, July 2, 3, 4, 5. GLOUCESTERSHIRE drew with SOMERSET.

At Derby, July 9, 10, 11. GLOUCESTERSHIRE beat DERBYSHIRE by five wickets.

GLOUCESTERSHIRE v WORCESTERSHIRE

At Cheltenham, July 23, 24, 25, 26. Drawn. Gloucestershire 9 pts, Worcestershire 12 pts. Toss: Gloucestershire. County debut: Shoaib Malik.

Last-day showers rescued Gloucestershire. When the rain arrived with 43 overs left they were hanging on desperately, five wickets down and 35 short of making the opposition bat again. With the pitch losing its early bounce, the defiance was led by Weston, a former Worcestershire player, and Jonty Rhodes, who batted a shade over two and a half hours for a determined and unbeaten 58. On the first day, the greatest resistance to Worcestershire's bowlers came where they least expected it, with No. 11 Lewis top-scoring with a bravado-filled 47; on the second, off-spinning all-rounder Shoaib Malik took two for eight during his first spell for Gloucestershire, but patient batting from Worcestershire's middle order put them in control. A washout on the third set up the attritional conclusion.

Close of play: First day, Worcestershire 48-1 (Singh 22, Batty 8); Second day, Worcestershire 392-7 (Rhodes 42, Ali 15); Third day, No play.

Gloucestershire

W. P. C. Weston c Solanki b Hall	28	– (2) c Rhodes b Ali	25
*C. M. Spearman c Rhodes b Hayward	12	– (1) b Ali	0
J. N. Rhodes c Rhodes b Mason	19	– not out	58
M. G. N. Windows lbw b Ali	23	– lbw b Hall	12
A. P. R. Gidman c Rhodes b Hayward	12	– c Hayward b Batty	13
Shoaib Malik c Batty b Mason	20	– c Singh b Batty	0
M. A. Hardinges c Hall b Hayward	17	– not out	10
M. C. J. Ball c Singh b Batty	29		
†S. P. Pope not out	17		
J. M. M. Averis c Rhodes b Batty	8		
J. Lewis c Solanki b Mason	47		
B 2, l-b 10, w 5, n-b 22	39	B 4, l-b 3, n-b 8	15
1/26 (2) 2/69 (1) 3/85 (3) 4/117 (4) 5/117 (5) 6/157 (7) 7/178 (6) 8/199 (8) 9/213 (10) 10/271 (11)	271	1/0 (1) 2/50 (2) 3/96 (4) 4/115 (5) 5/115 (6)	(5 wkts) 133

Bonus points – Gloucestershire 2, Worcestershire 3.

Bowling: *First Innings*—Ali 17–2–64–1; Hayward 17–3–77–3; Hall 14–6–29–1; Mason 16.1–7–48–3; Batty 8–0–41–2; Solanki 1–1–0–0. *Second Innings*—Ali 12–2–43–2; Hayward 7–2–17–0; Mason 8–4–23–0; Batty 8–1–19–2; Hall 6–2–24–1.

Worcestershire

S. D. Peters c Gidman b Averis	14
A. Singh b Shoaib Malik	50
G. J. Batty c Averis b Hardinges	24
G. A. Hick c Ball b Shoaib Malik	9
*B. F. Smith c Pope b Lewis	92
V. S. Solanki lbw b Averis	35
A. J. Hall lbw b Averis	73
†S. J. Rhodes c Gidman b Lewis	63
Kabir Ali c Ball b Shoaib Malik	34
M. S. Mason not out	3
M. Hayward c Rhodes b Lewis	0
B 12, l-b 12, n-b 18	42
1/33 (1) 2/83 (3) 3/102 (4) 4/103 (2) 5/186 (6) 6/294 (7) 7/354 (5) 8/434 (9) 9/439 (8) 10/439 (11)	439

Bonus points – Worcestershire 5, Gloucestershire 3.

Bowling: Lewis 29–3–136–3; Averis 34–13–84–3; Hardinges 8–0–60–1; Shoaib Malik 35–10–76–3; Ball 14–2–43–0; Gidman 4–0–16–0.

Umpires: A. Clarkson and V. A. Holder.

At Cheltenham, July 28. GLOUCESTERSHIRE lost to INDIA A by 69 runs (see India A tour section).

GLOUCESTERSHIRE v YORKSHIRE

At Cheltenham, July 30, 31, August 1, 2. Drawn. Gloucestershire 9 pts, Yorkshire 8 pts. Toss: Gloucestershire.

With only 56 overs bowled on the first two days, and neither captain wanting to risk losing to a promotion rival, the match petered out. As Gloucestershire eyed a last-day declaration, Spearman hit a polished 94 and Shoaib Malik blazed past fifty with four successive straightish sixes off

Dawson on to and over the festival marquees. He was stumped next ball (making the over 06666W) and Spearman, captain while Mark Alleyne rested a back injury, declared. But it was too late. Wood, his opposite number, refused to take up the challenge of scoring 322 at seven an over against an attack with three spinners. Bad weather dogged the first two days, and Gloucestershire did not finish their first innings till the third. Between showers, Kirby took six for 101, reward for his fiery pace. A bittersweet subplot came from Yorkshire's struggling all-rounder, Hamilton. After a terrible start – he survived big lbw shouts from each of the first three balls – he batted with growing assurance to reach 68. But he had still not recovered enough confidence to bowl, and was not picked for another first-class game all season.

Close of play: First day, Gloucestershire 33-2 (Hancock 16, Windows 15); Second day, Gloucestershire 201-6 (Russell 17, Fisher 10); Third day, Yorkshire 226.

Gloucestershire

*C. M. Spearman b Silverwood	0	– c White b Kirby	94
W. P. C. Weston c Guy b Kirby	0	– (7) not out	0
T. H. C. Hancock c Guy b Silverwood	35	– (2) b Kirby	21
M. G. N. Windows b Kirby	73	– (3) c Hamilton b Kirby	57
A. P. R. Gidman c Guy b Craven	43	– (4) c Wood b Kirby	14
Shoaib Malik c Fleming b Kirby	0	– (5) st Guy b Dawson	60
†R. C. Russell not out	35	– (6) c Dawson b Gray	18
I. D. Fisher c Fleming b Kirby	18		
M. C. J. Ball c Gray b Kirby	24		
J. M. M. Averis c and b Kirby	0		
A. M. Smith c Fleming b Dawson	0		
B 10, l-b 6, w 3, n-b 16	35	B 2, l-b 4, n-b 14	20
1/0 (1) 2/4 (2) 3/84 (3) 4/153 (4) 5/153 (6) 6/184 (5) 7/214 (8) 8/260 (9) 9/260 (10) 10/263 (11)	263	1/38 (2) 2/170 (3) 3/198 (1) 4/221 (4) 5/260 (6) 6/284 (5) (6 wkts dec.)	284

Bonus points – Gloucestershire 2, Yorkshire 3.

Bowling: *First Innings*—Silverwood 22–3–81–2; Kirby 24–4–101–6; Craven 12–5–37–1; Gray 8–2–22–0; Dawson 3.5–1–6–1. *Second Innings*—Silverwood 13–2–48–0; Kirby 13–2–82–4; Dawson 12–0–77–1; Craven 1–0–12–0; Gray 10–2–59–1.

Yorkshire

C. White c Russell b Smith	4		
S. P. Fleming c Russell b Smith	0	– lbw b Shoaib Malik	16
V. J. Craven lbw b Averis	7	– not out	20
M. J. Lumb c Russell b Ball	37	– not out	4
G. M. Hamilton c Gidman b Shoaib Malik	68		
†S. M. Guy lbw b Ball	8		
A. K. D. Gray c sub b Ball	23		
*M. J. Wood not out	15	– (1) lbw b Fisher	33
R. K. J. Dawson c Ball b Averis	15		
C. E. W. Silverwood c Hancock b Fisher	15		
S. P. Kirby lbw b Fisher	0		
B 5, l-b 9, w 2, n-b 18	34	B 2	2
1/3 (2) 2/16 (1) 3/16 (3) 4/107 (4) 5/119 (6) 6/175 (5) 7/175 (7) 8/195 (9) 9/226 (10) 10/226 (11)	226	1/43 (2) 2/55 (1) (2 wkts)	75

Bonus points – Yorkshire 1, Gloucestershire 3.

Bowling: *First Innings*—Smith 15–3–32–2; Averis 12–2–26–2; Gidman 4–1–16–0; Shoaib Malik 19–3–60–1; Fisher 8–0–31–2; Ball 21–6–47–3. *Second Innings*—Smith 5–1–18–0; Averis 2–0–3–0; Ball 13–2–29–0; Shoaib Malik 12–6–10–1; Fisher 8–3–13–1.

Umpires: T. E. Jesty and N. A. Mallender.

GLOUCESTERSHIRE v GLAMORGAN

At Bristol, August 19, 20, 21, 22. Drawn. Gloucestershire 9 pts, Glamorgan 10 pts. Toss: Glamorgan.

On a pitch too low for either batsmen or bowlers, the result was stalemate. Only Maynard played fluently: en route to 85 on the opening day, he hit 46 of his first 50 in sparkling boundaries. Otherwise, batsmen toiled. After Lewis cleaned up the Glamorgan tail, Gloucestershire had a hard time scoring against Croft, who bowled 43 accurate overs on the second day broken only by lunch and tea, and was into his sixth before conceding a run. Even the normally belligerent Harvey took 74 balls to reach double figures. Powell's watchful 90 helped Glamorgan build a lead of 359 by the last morning but, with both sides chasing promotion, Croft chose not to risk a declaration. Left to survive most of the final day, Gloucestershire ended up seven down, Hancock and Gidman (who lasted 38 overs) making their second fifties of the match. Russell's 1,311th dismissal – Maher stumped down the leg side – put him fifth in the all-time list.

Close of play: First day, Glamorgan 314-6 (Hemp 64, Croft 19); Second day, Gloucestershire 237-7 (Gidman 63, Ball 1); Third day, Glamorgan 276-9 (Kasprowicz 16, Harrison 33).

Glamorgan

J. P. Maher st Russell b Harvey	16	– c and b Lewis	11
I. J. Thomas c and b Ball	24	– lbw b Harvey	13
A. Dale c Hancock b Averis	32	– lbw b Averis	27
M. J. Powell lbw b Ball	42	– lbw b Lewis	90
M. P. Maynard c Lewis b Ball	85	– c and b Ball	33
D. L. Hemp not out	69	– c Weston b Harvey	31
†M. A. Wallace c Gidman b Lewis	8	– c Russell b Lewis	0
*R. D. B. Croft c Weston b Lewis	21	– c Spearman b Harvey	11
A. G. Wharf lbw b Lewis	0	– c Rhodes b Ball	3
M. S. Kasprowicz b Lewis	4	– c Hancock b Ball	25
D. S. Harrison b Lewis	0	– not out	39
B 4, l-b 9, w 1, n-b 16	30	L-b 2, n-b 6	8
1/33 (1) 2/75 (2) 3/105 (3) 4/178 (4) 5/257 (5) 6/268 (7) 7/318 (8) 8/318 (9) 9/322 (10) 10/331 (11)	331	1/14 (2) 2/42 (1) 3/91 (3) 4/156 (5) 5/200 (4) 6/204 (7) 7/224 (8) 8/227 (9) 9/229 (6) 10/291 (10)	291

Bonus points – Glamorgan 3, Gloucestershire 3.

Bowling: *First Innings*—Lewis 26.5–10–66–5; Averis 26–8–75–1; Harvey 21–6–42–1; Gidman 13–4–52–0; Ball 22–10–63–3; Hancock 4–0–20–0. *Second Innings*—Lewis 20–6–66–3; Harvey 19–5–54–3; Ball 37.3–7–100–3; Gidman 4–0–27–0; Averis 9–1–42–1.

Gloucestershire

*C. M. Spearman b Kasprowicz	1	– (2) c sub b Harrison	37
W. P. C. Weston c Thomas b Kasprowicz	42	– (1) c Wallace b Harrison	12
T. H. C. Hancock c Wallace b Wharf	64	– c Thomas b Croft	53
J. N. Rhodes lbw b Wharf	7	– lbw b Wharf	57
M. G. N. Windows c Croft b Harrison	26	– c Thomas b Croft	9
A. P. R. Gidman c Wallace b Wharf	68	– not out	50
I. J. Harvey c Wharf b Croft	13	– c and b Croft	16
†R. C. Russell lbw b Croft	12	– lbw b Croft	8
M. C. J. Ball b Wharf	8	– not out	10
J. M. M. Averis not out	4		
J. Lewis c Harrison b Kasprowicz	8		
B 3, l-b 5, n-b 2	10	B 5, l-b 14, w 1, n-b 8	28
1/6 (1) 2/99 (2) 3/115 (4) 4/130 (3) 5/149 (5) 6/196 (7) 7/232 (8) 8/243 (6) 9/250 (9) 10/263 (11)	263	1/48 (1) 2/55 (2) 3/180 (4) 4/180 (3) 5/193 (5) 6/221 (7) 7/255 (8)	(7 wkts) 280

Bonus points – Gloucestershire 2, Glamorgan 3.

Bowling: *First Innings*—Kasprowicz 27.1–5–75–3; Wharf 21–7–53–4; Croft 43–16–82–2; Harrison 13–4–45–1. *Second Innings*—Kasprowicz 27–5–65–0; Wharf 18–2–89–1; Harrison 17–5–46–2; Croft 32–10–61–4.

Umpires: G. I. Burgess and B. Dudleston.

GLOUCESTERSHIRE v DERBYSHIRE

At Bristol, September 3, 4, 5, 6. Gloucestershire won by 20 runs. Gloucestershire 21 pts, Derbyshire 5 pts. Toss: Derbyshire. Championship debut: P. M. R. Havell.

After four hard-fought days, Derbyshire needed 21 off 17 balls, with one wicket left. But Sutton swished and missed, and Gloucestershire were back in the promotion race, five and a half points behind third-placed Yorkshire. It was Lewis's wicket-to-wicket seam bowling and Fisher's controlled left-arm spin which put them there: on another sluggish pitch, they took 19 wickets. Rhodes also battled hard. Dropped on 29, he took 141 balls to reach fifty on the first day, but drives then started to flow as he moved toward 137. On the next day he announced this season would be his last before retiring. In reply, Stubbings stiffened Derbyshire's batting in his first Championship match for 13 months. He blunted Lewis's cutting edge, hitting two fours and a six to reach his hundred, but ended the third day in hospital after being hit in the face while fielding. Spearman led Gloucestershire's drive towards a declaration before leaving Derbyshire the whole last day to make 290. Stubbings returned to aid Di Venuto's resistance but Gloucestershire squeezed home.

Close of play: First day, Gloucestershire 331-5 (Rhodes 121, Fisher 21); Second day, Derbyshire 234-6 (Stubbings 52, Cork 5); Third day, Gloucestershire 209-8 (Ball 22, Pope 14).

Gloucestershire

*C. M. Spearman lbw b Welch	21	(2) c Sutton b Havell	87
W. P. C. Weston c Gait b Havell	34	(1) lbw b Welch	6
T. H. C. Hancock c Sutton b Cork	8	lbw b Havell	15
J. N. Rhodes c Di Venuto b Dean	137	run out	2
M. G. N. Windows c Sutton b Havell	49	c Sutton b Havell	8
A. P. R. Gidman lbw b Havell	46	b Dumelow	17
I. D. Fisher c Di Venuto b Dean	24	lbw b Welch	10
M. C. J. Ball c Stubbings b Welch	26	not out	22
R. J. Sillence lbw b Cork	13	c Sutton b Welch	3
J. Lewis lbw b Welch	8		
†S. P. Pope not out	0	(10) not out	14
B 1, l-b 17, w 3, n-b 14	35	B 9, l-b 9, w 1, n-b 6	25
1/41 (1) 2/58 (3) 3/78 (2) 4/174 (5) 5/273 (6) 6/346 (7) 7/361 (4) 8/391 (8) 9/401 (10) 10/401 (9)	401	1/34 (1) 2/90 (3) 3/94 (4) 4/111 (5) 5/132 (2) 6/156 (7) 7/162 (6) 8/171 (9) (8 wkts dec.)	209

Bonus points – Gloucestershire 4 pts, Derbyshire 2 pts (130 overs: 399-8).

Bowling: *First Innings*—Dean 27–7–98–2; Welch 36–8–95–3; Cork 27.5–7–75–2; Havell 30–8–95–3; Dumelow 8–3–8–0; Hewson 3–0–12–0. *Second Innings*—Cork 11–4–37–0; Welch 18–8–37–3; Dean 9–2–32–0; Dumelow 16–6–51–1; Havell 12–3–34–3.

Derbyshire

A. I. Gait c Pope b Lewis	10	– (2) c Pope b Sillence	12
M. J. Di Venuto c Windows b Fisher	75	– (1) b Fisher	80
R. M. Khan b Lewis	39	– c Gidman b Lewis	10
S. D. Stubbings c Weston b Lewis	103	– c Ball b Lewis	63
D. R. Hewson lbw b Lewis	0	– c Hancock b Fisher	13
†L. D. Sutton c Pope b Lewis	34	– b Lewis	41
K. J. Dean b Fisher	1	– (10) c Hancock b Lewis	2
*D. G. Cork c Weston b Lewis	10	– (7) c Spearman b Fisher	19
G. Welch lbw b Lewis	1	– (8) st Pope b Fisher	6
N. R. C. Dumelow c Hancock b Fisher	24	– (9) lbw b Fisher	11
P. M. R. Havell not out	0	– not out	2
B 4, l-b 7, w 1, n-b 12	24	B 1, l-b 3, w 2, n-b 4	10
1/38 (1) 2/115 (2) 3/145 (3) 4/145 (5) 5/217 (6) 6/218 (7) 7/241 (8) 8/254 (9) 9/299 (10) 10/321 (4)	321	1/22 (2) 2/46 (3) 3/155 (1) 4/182 (5) 5/194 (4) 6/230 (7) 7/238 (8) 8/253 (9) 9/256 (10) 10/269 (6)	269

Bonus points – Derbyshire 3, Gloucestershire 3.

Bowling: *First Innings*—Lewis 27.2–3–117–7; Sillence 20–3–81–0; Gidman 3–2–1–0; Ball 20–6–45–0; Fisher 23–8–66–3. *Second Innings*—Lewis 26.2–9–66–4; Sillence 10–2–42–1; Gidman 12–4–30–0; Ball 22–7–54–0; Fisher 19–2–73–5.

Umpires: N. J. Llong and N. A. Mallender.

GLOUCESTERSHIRE v DURHAM

At Bristol, September 10, 11, 12, 13. Gloucestershire won by 126 runs. Gloucestershire 21 pts, Durham 4 pts. Toss: Gloucestershire.

Two centuries from Rhodes and ten wickets from Fisher helped Gloucestershire elbow Durham aside in the race for the last remaining promotion spot. The win set up a do-or-die contest against Yorkshire in their final match. On a bone-dry, turning wicket, Hancock's 97 and nimble footwork and cheeky improvisation from Rhodes (bowled by a Shoaib Akhtar no-ball on 14) put Gloucestershire on top. Durham then fell to Fisher, who varied his flight to take five for 30 against tentative batsmen. Love was more certain, except when he neared three figures – he almost emulated Rhodes but was out for 98 and 97. Despite a lead of 156, Gloucestershire chose not to impose the follow-on. Instead, they batted Durham out of the game, led by Rhodes, who admitted feeling emotional as he approached a second hundred in his last game in Gloucestershire. Hopes of a three-day win were thwarted as Love and Pratt added 101 for the fourth wicket, but Fisher cleared up with his third successive five-for.

Close of play: First day, Durham 2-0 (Lewis 0, Muchall 0); Second day, Gloucestershire 53-2 (Hancock 14, Ball 0); Third day, Durham 171-4 (Love 49, Peng 15).

> "The real financial winners were the lawyers, who were rarely out of the action and, unlike the players, never succumbed to fatigue."
>
> **The World Cup, page 957.**

Gloucestershire

W. P. C. Weston c Mustard b Shoaib Akhtar	12	– (2) c Bridge b Shoaib Akhtar	7
*C. M. Spearman lbw b Bridge	59	– (1) b Shoaib Akhtar	28
T. H. C. Hancock b Collingwood	97	– c Peng b Plunkett	32
J. N. Rhodes c Peng b Phillips	103	– (5) st Mustard b Bridge	102
M. G. N. Windows c Mustard b Phillips	28	– (6) c Bridge b Plunkett	12
I. J. Harvey b Bridge	29	– (7) c Mustard b Shoaib Akhtar	41
†R. C. Russell b Bridge	5	– (8) not out	34
I. D. Fisher c Mustard b Shoaib Akhtar	18	– (9) not out	12
M. A. Hardinges lbw b Bridge	0		
M. C. J. Ball b Shoaib Akhtar	3	– (4) b Shoaib Akhtar	8
J. Lewis not out	0		
B 8, l-b 10, n-b 2	20	B 7, l-b 5	12
1/14 (1) 2/109 (2) 3/240 (3) 4/293 (5) 5/322 (4) 6/347 (7) 7/360 (6) 8/360 (9) 9/373 (8) 10/374 (10)	374	1/29 (2) 2/52 (1) 3/67 (4) 4/100 (3) 5/122 (6) 6/195 (7) 7/258 (5)	(7 wkts dec.) 288

Bonus points – Gloucestershire 4, Durham 3.

Bowling: *First Innings*—Shoaib Akhtar 14–3–30–3; Plunkett 12–3–53–0; Collingwood 8–0–36–1; Phillips 43–9–139–2; Bridge 32–8–98–4. *Second Innings*—Shoaib Akhtar 17–3–48–4; Plunkett 16–3–54–2; Phillips 8–2–51–0; Bridge 21–1–96–1; Collingwood 5–0–27–0.

Durham

*J. J. B. Lewis lbw b Lewis	16	– b Hardinges	28
G. J. Muchall c Russell b Lewis	1	– b Lewis	11
M. L. Love st Russell b Fisher	98	– c Spearman b Fisher	97
P. D. Collingwood lbw b Lewis	11	– c Harvey b Lewis	0
G. J. Pratt c Spearman b Hardinges	1	– st Russell b Fisher	62
N. Peng lbw b Harvey	0	– c Russell b Fisher	38
†P. Mustard c and b Fisher	31	– c Windows b Fisher	7
G. D. Bridge c Spearman b Fisher	5	– absent hurt	
Shoaib Akhtar st Russell b Fisher	34	– (8) c Harvey b Fisher	14
L. E. Plunkett c Ball b Fisher	0	– (9) not out	40
N. C. Phillips not out	11	– (10) c Hardinges b Lewis	5
L-b 4, n-b 6	10	B 4, l-b 6, w 2, n-b 4	16
1/11 (2) 2/32 (1) 3/56 (4) 4/57 (5) 5/84 (6) 6/159 (7) 7/170 (3) 8/173 (8) 9/173 (10) 10/218 (9)	218	1/42 (1) 2/42 (2) 3/42 (4) 4/143 (5) 5/220 (6) 6/227 (7) 7/252 (8) 8/278 (3) 9/318 (10)	318

Bonus points – Durham 1, Gloucestershire 3.

Bowling: *First Innings*—Lewis 19–7–52–3; Harvey 13–4–41–1; Hardinges 10–5–28–1; Ball 10–2–63–0; Fisher 9.1–1–30–5. *Second Innings*—Lewis 20.3–5–64–3; Harvey 13–5–58–0; Hardinges 9–4–30–1; Ball 26–7–63–0; Fisher 26–5–93–5.

Umpires: T. E. Jesty and A. A. Jones.

At Leeds, September 17, 18, 19, 20. GLOUCESTERSHIRE drew with YORKSHIRE.

HAMPSHIRE

Thin times for Terry's assortment

PAT SYMES

Hampshire followers will not look back at 2003 with affection. The county did scrape promotion to the first division of the National League, but otherwise it was one of the poorest seasons since the Second World War. While the Rose Bowl continued to emerge like a butterfly from a chrysalis of development, few believed the team worthy of it.

The plans had started to go wrong the previous winter, after the county's former playing stalwart, Paul Terry, was brought back from Perth to become the manager instead of the dismissed Jimmy Cook. Robin Smith stood down as captain after presiding over years of declining fortunes, and the plan was for Shane Warne to take over. But in February Warne was banned for a year by an Australian anti-doping committee for taking a prohibited diuretic, which scuppered that idea – and blew a gaping hole in the playing ranks.

Less than a fortnight before the season, John Crawley was persuaded to take on the captaincy for 12 months, with Warne pencilled in for 2004. The search for a high-profile overseas player eventually led to Wasim Akram, just short of his 37th birthday and out of county cricket since 1998. By May 7, when Hampshire went out of the C&G Trophy, to Sussex, it was clear that Terry had a major task on his hands if he was to weld ageing senior professionals – some signed on their reputations rather than their potential – and unproven youngsters into a cohesive unit.

Success in the National League could not quite conceal the alarming deficiencies exposed in the first-class game. For the second successive season, Hampshire won just two of their 16 Championship matches, finally avoiding the wooden spoon during the last game. Only Simon Katich reached 1,000 first-class runs, with an average of 60.15 – yet another fringe Australian setting an example that his English team-mates could not match. Crawley, unable to retain an England place and weighed down by the burden of captaincy, failed to make a first-class century for the first time since 1990, his debut year. Smith, beset by injuries, also never made a hundred. Nic Pothas, steady behind the stumps, managed a couple, and might have made his 1,000 runs but for a hamstring injury. But Derek Kenway, Will Kendall, Jimmy Adams and John Francis all scorned numerous opportunities.

At times, the bowling was little short of chaotic. Wasim, debilitated by illness, was past his best, and his brutal treatment by Chris Adams in the C&G Trophy defeat by Sussex was one of the Rose Bowl's sadder sights. He retired in mid-season, to be briefly replaced – no more productively – by the Sri Lankan, Chaminda Vaas. This retirement was followed by those of the unlucky spin bowler, Charlie van der Gucht, his career ruined by a car accident, and Ed Giddins, who played only three first-class matches before going into terminal dispute with the club over his fitness. Dimitri

Nic Pothas

Mascarenhas, outstanding in the National League where he took 34 wickets – more than anyone else – was perhaps the only player apart from Katich to enhance his reputation. No bowler took more than Mascarenhas's 39 Championship wickets, while the loyal Shaun Udal played through a shoulder injury – later requiring surgery – as the only front-line spinner. Alan Mullally and Chris Tremlett both struggled to be fit.

Hampshire failed in the Twenty20 Cup, finishing bottom of their group. It was left to the National League to provide solace, but even here Hampshire did it the hard way: a glorious mid-season burst of ten wins from 11 games was almost thrown away when they lost their last four, limping over the line and into the first division.

The Rose Bowl itself was perhaps the star of the season. It drew national attention when it staged the high-profile televised opener of the Twenty20 (when Hampshire did manage a victory over Sussex), slightly less when it staged its first one-day international, South Africa against Zimbabwe – bound to be the first of many. Just as important financially, there were concerts by Blue, Darius and the Royal Philharmonic. Such extracurricular activity may prove the club's salvation: with so much money being sunk into the project, they reported an operating loss of £1.1m for the year ending October 2002; the next set of figures were expected to be almost as bleak.

Robin Smith called it a day in 2003, on the eve of his 40th birthday, ending a Hampshire era. In his prime, there were few better batsmen in the world, and his efforts for the county were just as emphatic: his 18,984 put him ninth on the county's list of run-scorers. He won everything bar the Championship in Mark Nicholas's team, and while the thumping square cuts and drives were still there, they came less frequently in the last four of his 22 years. Hampshire suffered another setback when John Francis, nurtured through the youth system and regarded as a fine prospect, rejected a new contract and joined his brother Simon at Somerset.

Katich also declined to return for 2004. But in December, there appeared a glimmer of optimism when it was announced that Michael Clarke, perhaps the most exciting young batsman in Australia, had been signed to play alongside Warne, which is an enticing prospect. If nothing goes wrong this time.

HAMPSHIRE RESULTS

All first-class matches – Played 17: Won 2, Lost 6, Drawn 9.
County Championship matches – Played 16: Won 2, Lost 6, Drawn 8.

Frizzell County Championship, 8th in Division 2; Cheltenham & Gloucester Trophy, 3rd round; National Cricket League, 3rd in Division 2; Twenty20 Cup, 6th in South Group.

COUNTY CHAMPIONSHIP AVERAGES

BATTING AND FIELDING

Cap		*M*	*I*	*NO*	*R*	*HS*	*100s*	*50s*	*Avge*	*Ct/St*
2003	S. M. Katich§	13	22	3	1,143	143*	4	6	60.15	15
	J. R. C. Hamblin	4	6	2	219	96	0	2	54.75	0
2003	N. Pothas	13	20	2	809	146*	2	4	44.94	38/2
	L. R. Prittipaul	3	5	1	167	56*	0	1	41.75	5
1985	R. A. Smith	10	15	1	522	92	0	5	37.28	9
2002	J. P. Crawley	16	27	1	878	93	0	8	33.76	5
1992	S. D. Udal	15	23	5	488	60*	0	3	27.11	5
2001	D. A. Kenway	15	26	1	657	115	2	2	26.28	13
1998	A. D. Mascarenhas	16	25	1	584	100*	1	2	24.33	7
1999	W. S. Kendall	8	12	0	277	69	0	1	23.08	6
	J. H. K. Adams	9	18	1	361	60	0	2	21.23	6
	J. D. Francis	6	11	0	211	65	0	1	19.18	6
	C. T. Tremlett	10	13	2	199	43	0	0	18.09	5
	W. P. U. J. C. Vaas§	3	6	2	64	35	0	0	16.00	2
	I. Brunnschweiler	3	4	0	58	34	0	0	14.50	6
	Wasim Akram§	5	7	1	55	23	0	0	9.16	0
	J. T. A. Bruce	7	11	3	68	21*	0	0	8.50	2
2000	A. D. Mullally	8	10	3	38	14	0	0	5.42	2
	E. S. H. Giddins	3	4	1	10	10	0	0	3.33	0
	J. A. Tomlinson	7	11	5	19	10	0	0	3.16	2

Also batted: R. J. E. Hindley (1 match) 8, 68*; A. C. Morris (cap 2001) (1 match) 46.

§ *Overseas player.*

BOWLING

	O	*M*	*R*	*W*	*BB*	*5W/i*	*Avge*
Wasim Akram	167.3	44	503	20	3-31	0	25.15
E. S. H. Giddins	98.5	18	336	13	4-88	0	25.84
A. D. Mascarenhas	467.1	144	1,222	39	6-55	1	31.33
C. T. Tremlett	248.4	48	929	27	6-51	1	34.40
S. M. Katich	160.4	29	591	17	4-21	0	34.76
S. D. Udal	408.2	82	1,242	34	4-69	0	36.52
A. D. Mullally	229.1	55	664	17	3-31	0	39.05
J. A. Tomlinson	150.1	18	721	16	6-63	1	45.06
J. T. A. Bruce	163	29	726	16	3-42	0	45.37

Also bowled: J. R. C. Hamblin 41–4–185–6; R. J. E. Hindley 9–0–46–0; W. S. Kendall 8–2–34–0; D. A. Kenway 2–0–9–1; L. R. Prittipaul 28–2–131–4; W. P. U. J. C. Vaas 94–18–310–8.

COUNTY RECORDS

Highest score for:	316	R. H. Moore v Warwickshire at Bournemouth	1937
Highest score against:	303*	G. A. Hick (Worcestershire) at Southampton	1997
Best bowling for:	9-25	R. M. H. Cottam v Lancashire at Manchester	1965
Best bowling against:	10-46	W. Hickton (Lancashire) at Manchester	1870
Highest total for:	672-7 dec.	v Somerset at Taunton	1899
Highest total against:	742	by Surrey at The Oval	1909
Lowest total for:	15	v Warwickshire at Birmingham	1922
Lowest total against:	23	by Yorkshire at Middlesbrough	1965

HAMPSHIRE DIRECTORY

ADDRESS

The Rose Bowl, Botley Road, West End, Southampton SO30 3XH (023 8047 2002; fax 023 8047 2122; email enquiries@rosebowlplc.com). **Website** www.hampshire.cricinfo.com.

GROUND

Southampton (The Rose Bowl): 2$$ miles NE of city centre from M27 junction 7 then A334 Charles Watts Way. Turn L Tollbar Way B3342 and L Botley Road B3035 for entrance. Nearest stations: Hedge End (2 miles) and Southampton Airport/Parkway (2 miles).

OFFICIALS

Captain 2003 – J. P. Crawley; 2004 – S. K. Warne
Director of cricket T. M. Tremlett
First-team manager V. P. Terry
President A. C. D. Ingleby-Mackenzie
Chairman R. G. Bransgrove
Managing director N. S. Pike
Chairman, members committee R. J. Treherne
Head groundsman N. Gray
Scorer V. H Isaacs

PLAYERS

Players expected to reappear in 2004

	Former counties	*Country*	*Born*	*Birthplace*
Adams James Henry Kenneth		E	23.9.1980	†*Winchester*
Bruce James Thomas Anthony		E	17.12.1979	*Hammersmith*
Clapp Dominic Adrian	Sussex	E	25.5.1980	*Southport*
***Crawley** John Paul	Lancs	E	21.9.1971	*Maldon*
Hamblin James Rupert Christopher		E	16.8.1978	*Pembury*
Hindley Richard James Edward		E	25.4.1975	†*Portsmouth*
Kendall William Salwey		E	18.12.1973	*Wimbledon*
Kenway Derek Anthony		E	12.6.1978	*Fareham*
Mascarenhas Adrian Dimitri		E	30.10.1977	*Chiswick*
***Mullally** Alan David	Hants, Leics	E	12.7.1969	*Southend-on-Sea*
Pothas Nic		SA (EU)	18.11.1973	*Johannesburg*
Prittipaul Lawrence Roland		E	19.10.1979	†*Portsmouth*
Thorburn Mark		E	11.8.1978	*Bath*
Tomlinson James Andrew		E	12.6.1982	†*Winchester*
Tremlett Christopher Timothy		E	2.9.1981	†*Southampton*
Udal Shaun David		E	18.3.1969	†*Farnborough*
***Warne** Shane Keith		A	13.9.1969	*Ferntree Gully*

Players due to join in 2004

Brown Michael James	Middx	E	9.2.1980	*Burnley*
Clarke Michael John		A	2.4.1981	*Liverpool, NSW*
Taylor Billy Victor	Sussex	E	11.1.1977	†*Southampton*

* *Test player.* † *Born in Hampshire.*

At Worcester, April 18, 19, 20, 21. HAMPSHIRE drew with WORCESTERSHIRE.

At Cardiff, April 23, 24, 25, 26. HAMPSHIRE drew with GLAMORGAN.

HAMPSHIRE v YORKSHIRE

At Southampton, April 30, May 1, 2, 3. Drawn. Hampshire 7 pts, Yorkshire 9 pts. Toss: Hampshire. County debut: S. M. Katich.

Rain ruined any chance of Yorkshire repeating the crushing victory of their opening fixture. The first morning and the whole of days three and four were washed out, but between the showers, Yorkshire had secured a powerful position. Crawley, in his first home match as captain, had no hesitation in fielding first and was vindicated when Yorkshire struggled to 128 for seven. But with calm authority, Lumb began a recovery and, with Gough blasting an aggressive 72, including three sixes, the pair added 126. Lumb's unbeaten 115 lasted almost five and a half hours. Its value soon became clear, as Kirby took three wickets in 14 balls, and Hampshire slumped to 64 for six. Pothas diligently averted the follow-on but the rain soon returned with a vengeance. On the second afternoon, the scoreboards stuck for some time on 111 due to electrical problems, causing Hampshire, still trying to avoid the follow-on, some confusion – and general regret that umpire Shepherd was not officiating.

Close of play: First day, Yorkshire 174-7 (Lumb 60, Gough 30); Second day, Yorkshire 23-0 (Wood 8, Vaughan 10); Third day, No play.

Yorkshire

M. J. Wood c Pothas b Mullally	5	– not out	8
M. P. Vaughan b Wasim Akram	1	– not out	10
*A. McGrath c Udal b Tremlett	15		
M. J. Lumb not out	115		
†R. J. Blakey c Pothas b Mullally	24		
G. M. Fellows c Kenway b Mullally	0		
R. K. J. Dawson lbw b Udal	10		
C. E. W. Silverwood c Smith b Udal	0		
D. Gough c Pothas b Katich	72		
R. J. Sidebottom lbw b Wasim Akram	9		
S. P. Kirby lbw b Wasim Akram	0		
B 1, l-b 15, n-b 26	42	L-b 1, n-b 4	5
1/1 (2) 2/15 (1) 3/49 (3) 4/82 (5) 5/84 (6) 6/128 (7) 7/128 (8) 8/254 (9) 9/289 (10) 10/293 (11)	293		(no wkt) 23

Bonus points – Yorkshire 2, Hampshire 3.

Bowling: *First Innings*—Wasim Akram 19.1–6–64–3; Mullally 22–5–31–3; Mascarenhas 13–3–41–0; Tremlett 16–2–71–1; Udal 13–2–47–2; Katich 9–2–23–1. *Second Innings*—Wasim Akram 4–2–7–0; Mullally 4–1–15–0.

Hampshire

D. A. Kenway b Kirby	10
*J. P. Crawley b Silverwood	1
S. M. Katich run out	17
R. A. Smith c Blakey b Kirby	30
W. S. Kendall c Lumb b Sidebottom	1
†N. Pothas not out	44
A. D. Mascarenhas lbw b Kirby	1
Wasim Akram b Sidebottom	18
S. D. Udal c Lumb b Dawson	31
C. T. Tremlett c Vaughan b Dawson	2
A. D. Mullally c Blakey b McGrath	8
B 6, l-b 2, n-b 4	12
1/2 (2) 2/21 (3) 3/53 (1) 4/60 (5) 5/60 (4) 6/64 (7) 7/107 (8) 8/154 (9) 9/162 (10) 10/175 (11)	175

Bonus points – Yorkshire 3.

Bowling: Gough 14–5–28–0; Silverwood 9–2–34–1; Kirby 11–3–19–3; Sidebottom 14–3–44–2; Dawson 7–2–23–2; McGrath 4.5–0–19–1.

Umpires: A. Clarkson and G. Sharp.

At Oxford, May 9, 10, 11. HAMPSHIRE drew with OXFORD UCCE.

At Bristol, May 14, 15, 16, 17. HAMPSHIRE drew with GLOUCESTERSHIRE.

HAMPSHIRE v SOMERSET

At Southampton, May 21, 22, 23, 24. Somerset won by six wickets. Somerset 20 pts, Hampshire 3 pts. Toss: Somerset. First-class debut: G. M. Andrew. Championship debut: J. T. A. Bruce.

McLean and Francis returned to their old club and forced a comfortable Somerset victory. McLean, Hampshire's overseas player in 1998 and 1999, took eight wickets and was at times a yard quicker than any other bowler, while Francis, released at the end of 2001, grabbed five. However, in difficult batting conditions, Somerset's match-winner was Cox. He showed patience and impeccable technique when the wicket was at its most unpredictable, steering them out of a first-innings crisis at 30 for three, and remained unbeaten for nearly seven and a half vigilant hours. McLean and Francis then proved ruthlessly effective and along with Gareth Andrew, a sharpish seam bowler, they forced Hampshire, who never came to terms with the variable bounce, to follow on 179 behind. Kenway led some stronger resistance in the second innings, grafting nearly six hours for 94 on the third day, only to be out to his first ball on the fourth. Somerset stumbled in pursuit of a small target before Blackwell biffed them to victory.

Close of play: First day, Somerset 224-6 (Cox 101, Dutch 30); Second day, Hampshire 123-7 (Udal 5, Tremlett 3); Third day, Hampshire 239-6 (Kenway 94, Udal 16).

Somerset

P. D. Bowler b Tremlett	3		
M. J. Wood lbw b Tremlett	18	– (1) lbw b Mascarenhas	4
*M. Burns c Kendall b Mullally	7	– (5) c Pothas b Bruce	17
J. Cox not out	127	– lbw b Bruce	8
J. D. C. Bryant run out	18	– (3) not out	39
I. D. Blackwell c and b Udal	19	– not out	41
†R. J. Turner b Katich	11	– (2) c Pothas b Mascarenhas	13
K. P. Dutch c Katich b Mascarenhas	61		
G. M. Andrew lbw b Katich	7		
N. A. M. McLean c and b Mascarenhas	16		
S. R. G. Francis c Kendall b Katich	0		
B 1, l-b 14, n-b 6	21	B 2, n-b 4	6
1/7 (1) 2/18 (3) 3/30 (2) 4/82 (5) 5/137 (6) 6/162 (7) 7/277 (8) 8/288 (9) 9/307 (10) 10/308 (11)	308	1/17 (1) 2/20 (2) 3/35 (4) 4/59 (5)	(4 wkts) 128

Bonus points – Somerset 3, Hampshire 3.

Bowling: *First Innings*—Mullally 30–11–67–1; Tremlett 12–2–28–2; Udal 15–3–36–1; Mascarenhas 32–11–75–2; Bruce 15–3–39–0; Katich 12.5–1–48–3. *Second Innings*—Mullally 7–2–13–0; Mascarenhas 11–3–37–2; Bruce 11–3–32–2; Udal 7–2–17–0; Katich 3.5–0–27–0.

Hampshire

D. A. Kenway lbw b McLean	3 – c Turner b McLean	94
*J. P. Crawley lbw b McLean	0 – c Turner b Francis	2
S. M. Katich lbw b Francis	24 – c Turner b Burns	4
R. A. Smith b McLean	0 – b Andrew	55
W. S. Kendall c Dutch b Andrew	49 – c Dutch b McLean	33
†N. Pothas c Bowler b Andrew	34 – lbw b Burns	13
A. D. Mascarenhas c McLean b Andrew	0 – c Dutch b Burns	10
S. D. Udal b McLean	5 – c Blackwell b Francis	34
C. T. Tremlett c Bowler b Francis	4 – b McLean	43
A. D. Mullally not out	4 – lbw b McLean	0
J. T. A. Bruce c Burns b Francis	0 – not out	5
L-b 6	6 B 1, l-b 6, n-b 6	13
1/1 (2) 2/6 (1) 3/6 (4) 4/38 (3) 5/114 (5) 6/115 (6) 7/116 (7) 8/125 (8) 9/125 (9) 10/129 (11)	129 1/10 (2) 2/18 (3) 3/107 (4) 4/171 (5) 5/188 (6) 6/202 (7) 7/239 (1) 8/270 (8) 9/271 (10) 10/306 (9)	306

Bonus points – Somerset 3.

Bowling: *First Innings*—McLean 15–7–31–4; Francis 17.5–11–24–3; Andrew 9–1–30–3; Blackwell 10–4–27–0; Burns 4–1–11–0. *Second Innings*—McLean 28.5–7–64–4; Francis 30–12–81–2; Andrew 17–5–55–1; Burns 24–5–64–3; Blackwell 9–6–19–0; Dutch 6–1–16–0.

Umpires: B. Dudleston and J. W. Lloyds.

HAMPSHIRE v DURHAM

At Southampton, June 4, 5, 6, 7. Drawn. Hampshire 12 pts, Durham 7 pts. Toss: Hampshire. First-class debut: J. A. Lowe.

After rain wiped out the third day, Hampshire needed 18 Durham wickets on the last to force their first win of the season. They got 17 of them, but Durham's last pair, Phillips and the injured Pretorius, held out for the final 15 balls. Durham, plagued by injuries in 2002, were already without several key players and a cruel run continued when Pretorius bowled only four overs before tearing his hamstring. Katich drove his way to a first Hampshire century and his team-mates milked the depleted attack. In reply to 456, the 20-year-old opener James Lowe, a recruit from Northallerton who opted for Durham rather than Yorkshire, peppered the off side for 80 on his debut, but Hampshire's international bowlers quickly whittled through the rest. Durham followed on 221 behind. Wasim Akram and Katich, bowling chinamen, found even less resistance second time round – until the end. Hampshire slipped to the bottom of the table, level with Derbyshire.

Close of play: First day, Hampshire 238-4 (Katich 101, Pothas 53); Second day, Durham 107-2 (Lowe 41, Pratt 17); Third day, No play.

Hampshire

D. A. Kenway c Mustard b Law	8
*J. P. Crawley lbw b Law	29
S. M. Katich b Phillips	135
R. A. Smith c Muchall b Law	5
W. S. Kendall run out	33
†N. Pothas c sub b Plunkett	79
A. D. Mascarenhas lbw b Phillips	92
Wasim Akram b Phillips	0
S. D. Udal not out	60
A. D. Mullally c sub b Phillips	0
E. S. H. Giddins c Mustard b Law	0
B 4, l-b 7, n-b 4	15
1/36 (1) 2/45 (2) 3/61 (4) 4/151 (5) 5/284 (6) 6/330 (3) 7/332 (8) 8/455 (7) 9/455 (10) 10/456 (11)	456

Bonus points – Hampshire 5, Durham 2 (130 overs: 408-7).

Bowling: Pretorius 4–2–9–0; Plunkett 28–7–109–1; Killeen 28–7–57–0; Law 22.4–2–71–4; Muchall 18–3–70–0; Phillips 36–7–129–4.

Durham

*J. J. B. Lewis c Pothas b Giddins	44	– c Katich b Mascarenhas	8
J. A. Lowe lbw b Wasim Akram	80	– c Smith b Giddins	0
G. J. Muchall lbw b Udal	0	– lbw b Katich	16
G. J. Pratt lbw b Mullally	43	– st Pothas b Katich	30
N. Peng b Mullally	0	– c Smith b Katich	7
D. R. Law c Pothas b Mullally	0	– lbw b Wasim Akram	0
†P. Mustard b Wasim Akram	15	– c Kendall b Udal	30
L. E. Plunkett not out	10	– lbw b Wasim Akram	0
N. C. Phillips b Wasim Akram	10	– not out	31
N. Killeen c Kendall b Giddins	0	– c Smith b Wasim Akram	10
D. Pretorius b Giddins	12	– not out	0
B 1, l-b 12, n-b 8	21	L-b 5	5
1/79 (1) 2/80 (3) 3/175 (4) 4/175 (5) 5/175 (6) 6/179 (2) 7/194 (7) 8/208 (9) 9/223 (10) 10/235 (11)	235	1/0 (2) 2/14 (1) 3/52 (4) 4/59 (3) 5/62 (6) 6/62 (5) 7/63 (8) 8/107 (7) 9/136 (10)	(9 wkts) 137

Bonus points – Durham 1, Hampshire 3.

Bowling: *First Innings*—Wasim Akram 25–7–53–3; Giddins 17–4–51–3; Mullally 21–4–57–3; Mascarenhas 4–1–9–0; Udal 19–3–40–1; Katich 2–0–12–0. *Second Innings*—Mascarenhas 6–1–13–1; Giddins 10–2–29–1; Katich 16–9–39–3; Wasim Akram 14–2–44–3; Mullally 2–0–3–0; Udal 4–2–4–1.

Umpires: G. I. Burgess and D. J. Constant.

At Southampton, June 19. HAMPSHIRE beat ZIMBABWEANS by 16 runs (see Zimbabwean tour section).

HAMPSHIRE v GLOUCESTERSHIRE

At Southampton, June 27, 28, 29, 30. Drawn. Hampshire 10 pts, Gloucestershire 7 pts. Toss: Gloucestershire. First-class debut: S. P. Pope.

Hampshire dominated the first two days, only to see Gloucestershire come close to pinching the match. By the end, Hampshire were seven wickets down and clinging on for a draw, having failed to get anywhere near a target of 283 in 55 overs. If the morning session of the last day had not been washed out, they would probably have lost. On the first, Gloucestershire batted indifferently on a seaming wicket, and in reply, Kenway scored his first Championship century in almost two years. After two days, Gloucestershire were still 95 behind, with eight second-innings wickets left. But Rhodes and the more dogged Weston hit centuries of contrasting style and helped them not only recover, but take a position of supremacy. As the wicket wore and the bounce became more erratic, the rain, a perky fifty by Katich and an hour of defiance at the death by Udal, saved Hampshire. Umpire Allan Jones was locked in the Rose Bowl overnight on the second evening after sharing fish and chips in a camper van belonging to his colleague Alan Whitehead.

Close of play: First day, Hampshire 17-0 (Kenway 6, Crawley 11); Second day, Gloucestershire 50-2 (Weston 24); Third day, Gloucestershire 382-9 (Rhodes 134).

Gloucestershire

*C. M. Spearman b Wasim Akram	4	– (2) c Pothas b Giddins	20
W. P. C. Weston b Mascarenhas	39	– (1) c Pothas b Giddins	100
C. G. Taylor lbw b Giddins	24	– (4) c Smith b Udal	31
J. N. Rhodes lbw b Giddins	11	– (5) not out	151
M. G. N. Windows c Pothas b Wasim Akram	3	– (6) lbw b Mascarenhas	40
A. P. R. Gidman b Mullally	16	– (7) c Pothas b Mascarenhas	17
I. J. Harvey c Katich b Mascarenhas	20	– (8) b Udal	10
M. C. J. Ball b Mullally	4	– (9) st Pothas b Katich	7
†S. P. Pope c Smith b Wasim Akram	14	– (10) run out	4
J. Lewis c Smith b Mascarenhas	14	– (11) c Pothas b Wasim Akram	26
A. M. Smith not out	7	– (3) b Mascarenhas	4
B 4, l-b 16, w 1, n-b 8	29	B 3, l-b 9, w 5	17
1/14 (1) 2/70 (2) 3/90 (4) 4/99 (5) 5/99 (3) 6/140 (6) 7/144 (7) 8/146 (8) 9/177 (10) 10/185 (9)	185	1/41 (2) 2/50 (3) 3/112 (4) 4/208 (1) 5/283 (6) 6/314 (7) 7/345 (8) 8/372 (9) 9/382 (10) 10/427 (11)	427

Bonus points – Hampshire 3.

Bowling: *First Innings*—Wasim Akram 16.5–8–31–3; Giddins 14–2–41–2; Mascarenhas 19–7–48–3; Mullally 17–6–45–2. *Second Innings*—Wasim Akram 24.3–5–75–1; Giddins 21–5–79–2; Mullally 9.1–1–34–0; Mascarenhas 29–12–79–3; Udal 25–6–84–2; Katich 16–4–44–1; Kendall 5–1–20–0.

Hampshire

D. A. Kenway b Ball	115	– c Taylor b Harvey	12
*J. P. Crawley b Lewis	15	– b Harvey	5
S. M. Katich b Gidman	61	– c Pope b Harvey	52
R. A. Smith b Gidman	50	– lbw b Ball	16
W. S. Kendall lbw b Harvey	22	– c Windows b Harvey	2
†N. Pothas b Lewis	21	– c Windows b Ball	14
A. D. Mascarenhas c Pope b Harvey	21	– c Taylor b Ball	29
S. D. Udal c Rhodes b Smith	5	– not out	16
Wasim Akram b Harvey	0	– not out	4
A. D. Mullally not out	0		
E. S. H. Giddins b Harvey	0		
B 6, l-b 10, w 4	20	B 1, l-b 7, w 1, n-b 2	11
1/29 (2) 2/162 (3) 3/247 (4) 4/260 (1) 5/299 (6) 6/311 (5) 7/330 (7) 8/330 (8) 9/330 (9) 10/330 (11)	330	1/10 (2) 2/31 (1) 3/58 (4) 4/87 (5) 5/110 (3) 6/112 (6) 7/149 (7)	(7 wkts) 161

Bonus points – Hampshire 3, Gloucestershire 3.

Bowling: *First Innings*—Lewis 25–7–86–2; Smith 21–12–44–1; Harvey 18.2–2–73–4; Ball 17–2–65–1; Gidman 15–5–46–2. *Second Innings*—Lewis 12–1–49–0; Harvey 16–8–43–4; Smith 8–3–25–0; Gidman 1–0–12–0; Ball 18–9–24–3.

Umpires: A. A. Jones and A. G. T. Whitehead.

At Northampton, July 2, 3, 4. HAMPSHIRE lost to NORTHAMPTONSHIRE by seven wickets.

HAMPSHIRE v GLAMORGAN

At Southampton, July 15, 16, 17, 18. Hampshire won by 93 runs. Hampshire 17 pts, Glamorgan 8 pts. Toss: Glamorgan. First-class debut: R. J. E. Hindley.

This was the first time ever that Glamorgan had lost after imposing the follow-on, and the first time that Hampshire had followed on and won since 1922. The match could not compete with that famous victory, when Hampshire beat Warwickshire after making 15 in their first innings, but was sensational nonetheless. For two days Glamorgan dominated a Hampshire side in apparent disarray: Smith, Udal and Mullally were injured, Wasim Akram had just left because of ill health and Giddins was in dispute with the club. It showed, as Kasprowicz ran through some half-hearted batting on a pitch of variable bounce, after Dale and Maynard had made untroubled centuries for Glamorgan. At the start of the third day Hampshire were still 138 behind with six wickets left. But the match was then transformed. After pulling a hamstring on 52, Pothas smashed a century; Mascarenhas scored 75 more carefully; and Richard Hindley cracked an unbeaten 68. The day before the game, Hindley, a 28-year-old off-spinner for Havant CC but otherwise unemployed, had been painting his mother's office. Requiring 198 in just over a day, Glamorgan could not cope with the bounce found by Tremlett, whose six for 51 was a career-best and gave Hampshire their first win of the season.

Close of play: First day, Glamorgan 436-9 (Wharf 16, Cosker 6); Second day, Hampshire 114-4 (Francis 6); Third day, Glamorgan 33-3 (Cosker 2).

Glamorgan

J. P. Maher hit wkt b Tomlinson	30	– c Crawley b Tremlett	9
J. Hughes c and b Mascarenhas	4	– c Crawley b Tremlett	7
A. Dale c Kenway b Katich	123	– (9) c Katich b Tremlett	3
M. J. Powell c Kenway b Katich	44	– (5) c sub b Bruce	4
M. P. Maynard c Pothas b Tremlett	129	– (6) lbw b Tremlett	3
†M. A. Wallace b Katich	0	– (3) b Bruce	11
*R. D. B. Croft c Francis b Mascarenhas	28	– (8) c Katich b Tremlett	12
M. S. Kasprowicz c Pothas b Tremlett	24	– (10) c Katich b Mascarenhas	14
A. G. Wharf not out	16	– (11) not out	10
D. S. Harrison c Pothas b Tremlett	0	– (7) c sub b Tremlett	9
D. A. Cosker c Katich b Mascarenhas	7	– (4) lbw b Bruce	6
B 3, l-b 4, w 3, n-b 22	32	N-b 16	16
1/7 (2) 2/69 (1) 3/158 (4) 4/287 (3) 5/287 (6) 6/360 (7) 7/407 (8) 8/424 (5) 9/430 (10) 10/437 (11)	437	1/16 (1) 2/21 (2) 3/33 (3) 4/39 (5) 5/46 (6) 6/50 (4) 7/74 (7) 8/79 (8) 9/94 (9) 10/104 (10)	104

Bonus points – Glamorgan 5, Hampshire 3.

Bowling: *First Innings*—Mascarenhas 20.1–4–50–3; Tremlett 22–5–72–3; Tomlinson 20–2–89–1; Bruce 17–3–86–0; Hindley 9–0–46–0; Katich 17–2–87–3. *Second Innings*—Tremlett 16–3–51–6; Mascarenhas 5.2–2–11–1; Bruce 10–1–42–3.

"Graham Gooch, the 49-year-old Essex coach, fielded for seven overs as a sub in Jefferson's sweater, which reached his knees."

Lancashire in 2003, page 604.

Hampshire

D. A. Kenway b Wharf	26	– b Croft	24
J. H. K. Adams c Wallace b Kasprowicz	21	– c Wallace b Croft	21
S. M. Katich c Maynard b Kasprowicz	4	– c Wharf b Croft	53
*J. P. Crawley c Hughes b Croft	24	– st Wallace b Croft	9
J. D. Francis c Wallace b Croft	27	– c Wallace b Wharf	40
†N. Pothas lbw b Kasprowicz	2	– c Croft b Harrison	121
A. D. Mascarenhas c Maher b Harrison	16	– lbw b Kasprowicz	75
R. J. E. Hindley c Wallace b Harrison	8	– not out	68
C. T. Tremlett c Wharf b Kasprowicz	22	– c Maher b Kasprowicz	6
J. T. A. Bruce not out	21	– c Wallace b Kasprowicz	10
J. A. Tomlinson b Kasprowicz	0	– c Wallace b Croft	1
L-b 4, w 2, n-b 8	14	B 9, l-b 6, n-b 6	21
1/40 (2) 2/48 (3) 3/58 (1) 4/93 (4) 5/102 (6) 6/126 (5) 7/137 (8) 8/140 (7) 9/169 (9) 10/185 (11)	185	1/40 (2) 2/55 (1) 3/75 (4) 4/114 (3) 5/194 (5) 6/343 (6) 7/394 (7) 8/420 (9) 9/432 (10) 10/449 (11)	449

Bonus points – Glamorgan 3.

Bowling: *First Innings*—Kasprowicz 22.5–10–48–5; Wharf 10–1–31–1; Harrison 15–3–51–2; Croft 26–8–51–2. *Second Innings*—Kasprowicz 28–8–103–3; Wharf 17–4–68–1; Harrison 10–0–81–1; Cosker 14–1–65–0; Croft 38.3–9–117–5.

Umpires: M. J. Kitchen and R. Palmer.

At Scarborough, July 23, 24, 25, 26. HAMPSHIRE drew with YORKSHIRE.

HAMPSHIRE v NORTHAMPTONSHIRE

At Southampton, July 31, August 1, 2, 3. Northamptonshire won by five wickets. Northamptonshire 17 pts, Hampshire 5 pts. Toss: Northamptonshire.

In baking sunshine Northamptonshire breezed to their target of 330, equalling the county record of six successive Championship wins (achieved in 1909, 1955, 1958 and 1995). As they eased home with 12 overs left, Crawley's tempting declaration was made to look too generous, but he was let down by his attack. With Mullally left out, Hampshire lacked guile and potency on an easy-paced pitch, allowing Hussey and Sales to add a match-winning 159 for the third wicket. The second day had been lost to rain, but Hampshire – and Katich in particular – had dominated the first and third. Katich followed a fluent first-innings century by hatching the plan that saw fellow Australian Hussey caught cheaply at leg gully, then taking four for 21 with his chinamen. Building on a lead of 102, he and Crawley gathered runs at will on the third evening in an unbroken stand of 131, before Crawley, desperate for a win, chose a declaration that kept the match alive.

Close of play: First day, Northamptonshire 76-0 (Hussey 13, Roberts 56); Second day, No play; Third day, Northamptonshire 23-0 (Roberts 9, Hussey 11).

Hampshire

D. A. Kenway c Powell b Greenidge	6	– lbw b Brown	46
J. H. K. Adams c Hussey b Shantry	32	– hit wkt b Nel	12
S. M. Katich c Powell b Nel	117	– not out	79
*J. P. Crawley c Roberts b Greenidge	8	– not out	81
J. D. Francis lbw b Brown	4		
J. R. C. Hamblin c Brophy b Brown	4		
A. D. Mascarenhas c Powell b Shantry	31		
S. D. Udal c Hussey b Brown	16		
†I. Brunnschweiler lbw b Nel	3		
C. T. Tremlett c Brophy b Shantry	29		
J. T. A. Bruce not out	7		
B 1, w 2, n-b 18	21	L-b 1, n-b 8	9
1/7 (1) 2/64 (2) 3/87 (4) 4/97 (5) 5/134 (6) 6/195 (7) 7/222 (8) 8/225 (9) 9/244 (3) 10/278 (10)	278	1/19 (2) 2/96 (1) (2 wkts dec.)	227

Bonus points – Hampshire 2, Northamptonshire 3.

Bowling: *First Innings*—Nel 21–4–79–2; Greenidge 15–1–74–2; Shantry 11.4–2–44–3; Brown 26–7–80–3. *Second Innings*—Nel 13.2–2–47–1; Greenidge 10–2–53–0; Shantry 7–2–42–0; Brown 13–2–58–1; White 3–0–26–0.

Northamptonshire

*M. E. K. Hussey c Katich b Tremlett	13	– (2) c Tremlett b Bruce	100
T. W. Roberts c Adams b Tremlett	60	– (1) c Brunnschweiler b Tremlett	10
P. A. Jaques c Kenway b Tremlett	9	– c Francis b Udal	34
D. J. Sales c Brunnschweiler b Katich	16	– lbw b Bruce	75
M. J. Powell lbw b Katich	31	– not out	47
R. A. White lbw b Katich	12	– c Brunnschweiler b Udal	27
†G. L. Brophy c Francis b Katich	0	– not out	2
A. J. Shantry c Francis b Udal	0		
C. G. Greenidge b Udal	6		
A. Nel not out	5		
J. F. Brown c Adams b Udal	0		
B 6, l-b 2, w 2, n-b 14	24	B 12, l-b 7, n-b 16	35
1/76 (1) 2/89 (2) 3/103 (3) 4/150 (4) 5/157 (5) 6/157 (7) 7/160 (8) 8/162 (6) 9/176 (9) 10/176 (11)	176	1/24 (1) 2/87 (3) 3/246 (4) 4/251 (2) 5/318 (6) (5 wkts)	330

Bonus points – Hampshire 3.

Bowling: *First Innings*—Tremlett 13–4–49–3; Mascarenhas 14–3–49–0; Bruce 7–1–37–0; Udal 13.3–7–12–3; Katich 8–1–21–4. *Second Innings*—Tremlett 20–4–54–1; Mascarenhas 16.4–5–28–0; Udal 34–5–114–2; Katich 10–0–56–0; Bruce 13–1–59–2.

Umpires: A. A. Jones and J. F. Steele.

HAMPSHIRE v DERBYSHIRE

At Southampton, August 13, 14. Derbyshire won by an innings and 43 runs. Derbyshire 20 pts, Hampshire 3 pts. Toss: Hampshire. Championship debut: W. P. U. J. C. Vaas.

The bottom clubs in the second division failed to take the match beyond tea on the second day. Despite some early seam movement, only poor batting could explain the loss of 16 wickets on the first day and 14 on the second. Cork began by taking six for 28 – his best in eight seasons – with his bustling fast-medium. Then, as Derbyshire's innings was threatening to fade as fast as Hampshire's had, he hit an aggressive 40 from No. 7. Dumelow followed Cork's lead, smashing

75 from No. 9, and 226 were filched for the last five wickets. Behind by 198, Hampshire showed little inclination to make a fight of it. Losing eight wickets between lunch and tea to the accuracy of Cork (who took ten in a match for the fourth time) and Welch, they were saved from even quicker defeat by Katich's doggedness and some late blows by Tremlett. Despite the win, Derbyshire remained bottom, five points behind Hampshire.

Close of play: First day, Derbyshire 185-6 (Bassano 33).

Hampshire

First innings		Second innings	
D. A. Kenway c Di Venuto b Welch	17	lbw b Dean	11
J. H. K. Adams c Bassano b Dean	8	lbw b Cork	0
S. M. Katich lbw b Cork	7	not out	48
*J. P. Crawley c Di Venuto b Cork	49	(7) b Welch	16
J. D. Francis c Sutton b Cork	11	(4) c Di Venuto b Cork	3
A. D. Mascarenhas c Sutton b Welch	0	(5) b Cork	6
S. D. Udal lbw b Cork	0	(6) c Kaif b Welch	12
W. P. U. J. C. Vaas c Bassano b Welch	1	c Kaif b Dumelow	2
†I. Brunnschweiler lbw b Cork	16	lbw b Cork	5
C. T. Tremlett not out	22	c Cork b Welch	30
J. T. A. Bruce b Cork	0	b Welch	1
B 2, l-b 2, n-b 8	12	B 5, l-b 6, w 2, n-b 8	21
1/14 (2) 2/27 (3) 3/36 (1) 4/99 (5) 5/100 (6) 6/101 (7) 7/104 (4) 8/104 (8) 9/143 (9) 10/143 (11)	143	1/11 (1) 2/11 (2) 3/17 (4) 4/24 (5) 5/55 (6) 6/79 (7) 7/98 (8) 8/103 (9) 9/153 (10) 10/155 (11)	155

Bonus points – Derbyshire 3.

Bowling: *First Innings*—Cork 14.5–6–28–6; Dean 11–3–31–1; Welch 14–4–50–3; Gunter 5–0–30–0. *Second Innings*—Cork 12–1–39–4; Dean 10–1–40–1; Welch 9.3–2–27–4; Gunter 3–0–18–0; Dumelow 8–2–20–1.

Derbyshire

Batsman	Runs
S. A. Selwood c Katich b Mascarenhas	29
M. J. Di Venuto c Brunnschweiler b Vaas	20
R. M. Khan b Vaas	0
M. Kaif lbw b Vaas	36
C. W. G. Bassano lbw b Vaas	39
†L. D. Sutton c Brunnschweiler b Udal	18
*D. G. Cork lbw b Udal	40
G. Welch b Mascarenhas	27
N. R. C. Dumelow lbw b Mascarenhas	75
N. E. L. Gunter not out	20
K. J. Dean lbw b Mascarenhas	12
B 2, l-b 14, w 1, n-b 8	25
1/27 (2) 2/27 (3) 3/87 (4) 4/91 (1) 5/115 (6) 6/185 (7) 7/199 (5) 8/290 (8) 9/311 (9) 10/341 (11)	341

Bonus points – Derbyshire 3, Hampshire 3.

Bowling: Vaas 26–8–82–4; Tremlett 19–1–80–0; Mascarenhas 26.3–11–45–4; Udal 17–3–63–2; Bruce 7–0–55–0.

Umpires: J. H. Hampshire and J. W. Lloyds.

"Under a hot sun and in front of a crammed stadium, Tendulkar played an astounding innings."

The World Cup, page 988.

At Chester-le-Street, August 20, 21, 22, 23. HAMPSHIRE lost to DURHAM by an innings and 115 runs.

At Taunton, August 26, 27, 28, 29. HAMPSHIRE drew with SOMERSET.

HAMPSHIRE v WORCESTERSHIRE

At Southampton, September 3, 4, 5, 6. Worcestershire won by 101 runs. Worcestershire 21 pts, Hampshire 5 pts. Toss: Worcestershire.

On an awkward first-morning pitch Worcestershire, despite starting 87 points ahead of Hampshire, were in a spot of bother at 106 for four after Tomlinson had extracted life and lift from short of a length. But Kemp made a steadying 90 and the reserve wicket-keeper James Pipe, in his first Championship appearance of the season, grabbed his chance. He reached his maiden first-class century with two thumping pulls, and later completed eight dismissals. Accurate bowling then gave Worcestershire a 99-run first-innings lead, which Kadeer Ali and Solanki helped stretch to 412. Hampshire, second-bottom in the table, aimed for the victory but their hopes withered when Crawley, without a Championship hundred since April 2002, got an inside edge after an uninhibited 88. By then, defeat for Durham at Northampton had already confirmed Worcestershire's promotion. Kabir Ali, released by England, replaced Harrity at lunch on the second day; Batty, also in the original squad for the Oval Test, replaced Khalid and took seven wickets with his combative off-spin.

Close of play: First day, Hampshire 4-0 (Kenway 3, Adams 0); Second day, Worcestershire 50-0 (Peters 21, Hick 26); Third day, Hampshire 91-2 (Kenway 35, Crawley 2).

Worcestershire

S. D. Peters c Adams b Mascarenhas	87	– c Pothas b Tomlinson	23
G. A. Hick c Prittipaul b Tomlinson	21	– lbw b Mascarenhas	42
Kadeer Ali c Prittipaul b Mascarenhas	6	– c Pothas b Vaas	79
*B. F. Smith c Pothas b Tomlinson	16	– c and b Vaas	11
V. S. Solanki c Pothas b Tomlinson	8	– c Pothas b Vaas	77
J. M. Kemp c Kenway b Prittipaul	90	– c Kenway b Udal	33
†D. J. Pipe not out	104	– (8) b Udal	0
G. J. Batty c Pothas b Prittipaul	1	– (7) c Mascarenhas b Udal	0
M. S. Mason c Mascarenhas b Prittipaul	0	– (10) not out	2
M. A. Harrity c Prittipaul b Tremlett	0		
M. Hayward c Pothas b Tremlett	25		
Kabir Ali (did not bat)		– (9) c Kenway b Udal	20
B 3, l-b 2, w 1	6	L-b 11, w 7, n-b 8	26
1/55 (2) 2/77 (3) 3/98 (4) 4/106 (5) 5/179 (1) 6/316 (6) 7/323 (8) 8/323 (9) 9/330 (10) 10/364 (11)	364	1/53 (1) 2/87 (2) 3/107 (4) 4/243 (5) 5/256 (3) 6/259 (7) 7/264 (8) 8/302 (9) 9/313 (6) (9 wkts dec.)	313

S. A. Khalid did not bat.

Bonus points – Worcestershire 4, Hampshire 3.

Bowling: *First Innings*—Tremlett 21.4–5–78–2; Vaas 19–1–71–0; Tomlinson 17–1–69–3; Mascarenhas 18–7–54–2; Udal 8–1–38–0; Katich 9–1–32–0; Prittipaul 7–1–17–3. *Second Innings*—Tremlett 7–1–32–0; Vaas 22–7–42–3; Mascarenhas 18–4–54–1; Tomlinson 15–2–61–1; Udal 21.5–2–69–4; Prittipaul 4–0–13–0; Katich 5–0–31–0.

Hampshire

D. A. Kenway c Pipe b Mason	3	– c Pipe b Mason	44
J. H. K. Adams c Pipe b Hayward	3	– c Kemp b Hayward	6
S. M. Katich c Kabir Ali b Batty	70	– run out	42
*J. P. Crawley c Pipe b Hayward	35	– b Batty	88
L. R. Prittipaul c Peters b Kabir Ali	19	– c Pipe b Kabir Ali	35
†N. Pothas c and b Batty	7	– c Hick b Mason	3
A. D. Mascarenhas c Pipe b Mason	24	– b Mason	16
S. D. Udal c Peters b Kabir Ali	50	– c Pipe b Batty	29
W. P. U. J. C. Vaas c Mason b Batty	35	– not out	25
C. T. Tremlett run out	0	– st Pipe b Batty	0
J. A. Tomlinson not out	0	– c Kemp b Batty	0
B 6, l-b 8, w 3, n-b 2	19	B 4, l-b 8, w 7, n-b 4	23
1/9 (2) 2/9 (1) 3/73 (4) 4/107 (5) 5/136 (6) 6/167 (3) 7/189 (7) 8/241 (8) 9/256 (10) 10/265 (9)	265	1/12 (2) 2/89 (3) 3/121 (1) 4/213 (5) 5/225 (6) 6/251 (4) 7/251 (7) 8/301 (8) 9/305 (10) 10/311 (11)	311

Bonus points – Hampshire 2, Worcestershire 3.

Bowling: *First Innings*—Hayward 18–4–50–2; Mason 19–5–47–2; Harrity 9–4–26–0; Batty 26–8–77–3; Kabir Ali 11–1–40–2; Kemp 4–0–11–0. *Second Innings*—Kabir Ali 16–1–60–1; Hayward 17–1–69–1; Batty 34.2–10–94–4; Mason 18–3–66–3; Kemp 3–1–10–0.

Umpires: J. H. Evans and J. F. Steele.

At Derby, September 17, 18, 19, 20. HAMPSHIRE beat DERBYSHIRE by ten wickets.

WOMBWELL CRICKET LOVERS' SOCIETY AWARDS, 2003

Mushtaq Ahmed, the Pakistan leg-spinner who bowled Sussex to their first County Championship, was voted George Spofforth Cricketer of the Year by members of the Wombwell Cricket Lovers' Society. Chris Adams of Sussex was named Brian Sellers County Captain of the Year. Other award-winners were: C. B. Fry Young Cricketer of the Year – Graeme Smith of South Africa; Arthur Wood Wicket-Keeper of the Year – Geraint Jones of Kent; Les Bailey Most Promising Youngster for Yorkshire – Michael Lumb; Learie Constantine Award for Best Fielder in the C&G Final – Jonty Rhodes of Gloucestershire. Ted Umbers Services to Yorkshire Cricket – Geoff Holmes & Vivian Stone, for their fundraising bookstand at Headingley. The J. M. Kilburn Cricket Writer of the Year and Jack Fingleton Commentator of the Year awards were not made.

KENT

The boys of late summer

ANDREW GIDLEY

No county could have been more excited about their prospects for 2003 than Kent. A good pre-season build-up gave them every reason to hope they could improve on their third place in the last two Championships. But in early July – halfway through the season – Kent were still looking for a first-class win. Their proud status as one of the two counties who had never been in the second division of either the Championship or the National League seemed doomed: they were in the bottom three of both first divisions. They were also out of the C&G Trophy and Twenty20 Cup.

"It was shaping up as the worst season in our history," admitted the captain, David Fulton. But the second half of the season saw a transformation. Kent won six of their eight remaining Championship games to finish fourth, and avoided the drop in the League – while Leicestershire, the only other side with a perfect first-division record, went down in both.

Kent's pre-season planning and preparation were scuppered by injuries to key players: Fulton himself, spinner Min Patel and seamer Amjad Khan. Patel underwent a major back operation just before the season, and never appeared for the first team. A week before the opening game, Fulton was hit on the right eye by a 90mph delivery from a bowling machine. The blow scarred his retina and threatened his career – but he returned by the end of May, having regained half his sight in the damaged eye, to score 674 first-class runs. Meanwhile, shin problems sidelined Khan for three months.

Kent had engaged Greg Blewett to strengthen the batting until his fellow-Australian, Andrew Symonds, returned from the Caribbean, but, in their own words, "kept their powder dry" regarding a second overseas signing. In the end, Blewett stayed alongside Symonds until Pakistan pace bowler Mohammad Sami arrived in June. Sami left early, after twisting his ankle, but Kent had a trump card to play. They recruited the world's No. 1 spinner, Muttiah Muralitharan of Sri Lanka, with one objective: first-division survival. The investment paid off handsomely. Murali returned 33 wickets in just five Championship matches, though he was less effective in the National League.

The real turning point was Maidstone Festival Week in July, where Kent broke their Championship duck with a three-day win over Nottinghamshire, thanks to 15 wickets from Sami – in what was to be his final appearance – and twin hundreds from Ed Smith. Against Essex and Surrey, Smith had recorded an intriguing sequence of 0, 0, 135 and 0; his next innings was a maiden one-day hundred against Glamorgan. Then came 149 and 113 at Maidstone, followed by 203 against Lancashire at Blackpool and 108 – out of 189 – against Essex at Canterbury, to match Frank Woolley, the last Kent player to score four first-class hundreds in a row, in 1929.

Smith, the first player to reach 1,000 first-class runs in the English summer, batted his way to a Test call-up, announced as he led Kent against the South Africans. He followed team-mate Rob Key on to the international stage; later, wicket-keeper Geraint Jones and Martin Saggers were named as England winter tourists. Saggers collected 58 first-class wickets for Kent during the season, and his late inclusion, replacing Andrew Flintoff, provided a great deal of local satisfaction; he took his first Test wickets in Chittagong, at the age of 31.

Ed Smith

Jones was the find of the summer. Kent had been swayed by financial considerations when they preferred him to the experienced Paul Nixon, but he soon caught the eye with both bat and gloves. Almost 1,000 first-class runs, nearly 60 dismissals, and two National League records – most dismissals in a season, and equal most in an innings – made for a highly impressive first full season, which earned him a county cap, and the nod from the England selectors seeking an understudy to Chris Read.

Matthew Walker passed 1,000 first-class runs for the first time in his tenth season. Mark Ealham, who led the side while Fulton was absent, put in some good all-round performances in his benefit season, before defecting to Nottinghamshire, who offered him a contract for three years rather than Kent's one. There has been an Ealham – Mark or his father Alan – in the Kent team for 32 of the past 38 seasons, and it will feel almost as much the end of an era as the loss of the last Cowdrey. Three imports from other counties – former Surrey batsman Michael Carberry, ex-Worcestershire pace bowler Alamgir Sheriyar, and Peter Trego from Somerset – had mixed starts to their Canterbury careers, but two young slow bowlers, off-spinner James Tredwell and left-armer Robert Ferley, made good strides; Tredwell did enough to be included in the National Academy's winter squad.

In August, Kent were awarded a £500,000 interest-free loan by the county council to redevelop the Ames Levett Sports Centre and secure ECB County Academy status. Former Kent wicket-keeper Simon Willis was appointed the new academy's director. But in November, Willis was named coaching co-ordinator, taking over responsibility for the first team from Ian Brayshaw, who returned to Australia after two years with the county. Willis was to share coaching duties with another ex-keeper, Paul Farbrace, who took on the academy, and youth coach Chris Stone, in what the county presented as "an all-Kent team".

KENT RESULTS

All first-class matches – Played 18: Won 6, Lost 6, Drawn 6.
County Championship matches – Played 16: Won 6, Lost 5, Drawn 5.

Frizzell County Championship, 4th in Division 1; Cheltenham & Gloucester Trophy, 4th round; National Cricket League, 6th in Division 1; Twenty20 Cup, 3rd in South Group.

COUNTY CHAMPIONSHIP AVERAGES

BATTING AND FIELDING

Cap		*M*	*I*	*NO*	*R*	*HS*	*100s*	*50s*	*Avge*	*Ct/St*
2001	E. T. Smith	13	22	0	1,352	213	7	1	61.45	9
1999	A. Symonds§	10	16	2	659	121	2	4	47.07	6
2003	G. O. Jones	16	24	4	886	108*	2	6	44.30	50/5
2000	M. J. Walker	16	25	2	927	150	3	3	40.30	22
1998	D. P. Fulton	11	19	1	674	94*	0	5	37.44	4
1992	M. A. Ealham	16	24	0	847	101	1	6	35.29	18
2001	R. W. T. Key	10	17	2	507	140	1	1	33.80	9
	G. S. Blewett§	6	10	0	319	71	0	3	31.90	7
	M. A. Carberry	12	21	1	607	92	0	5	30.35	2
	A. Khan	7	10	0	236	78	0	1	23.60	1
	J. C. Tredwell	11	16	2	263	36	0	0	18.78	14
2001	M. J. Saggers	13	18	5	229	47	0	0	17.61	2
	A. Sheriyar	13	18	9	88	18*	0	0	9.77	3
	R. S. Ferley	5	4	1	24	14*	0	0	8.00	4
2003	M. Muralitharan§	5	7	0	49	15	0	0	7.00	1
	B. J. Trott	6	8	3	35	12*	0	0	7.00	2
	Mohammad Sami§	3	4	0	19	16	0	0	4.75	0

Also batted: A. G. R. Loudon (2 matches) 8, 0, 9 (2 ct); P. D. Trego (1 match) 13 (1 ct).

§ *Overseas player.*

BOWLING

	O	*M*	*R*	*W*	*BB*	*5W/i*	*Avge*
M. Muralitharan	178	41	447	33	6-36	4	13.54
Mohammad Sami	89.1	17	357	18	8-64	2	19.83
M. J. Saggers	396	81	1,294	54	5-42	2	23.96
M. A. Ealham	350.5	103	998	38	6-35	3	26.26
R. S. Ferley	128.2	30	429	14	4-76	0	30.64
A. Sheriyar	325.3	66	1,042	33	5-65	1	31.57
A. Symonds	152	26	517	16	3-38	0	32.31
A. Khan	145	15	704	17	4-65	0	41.41
J. C. Tredwell	278.4	59	962	23	4-48	0	41.82
B. J. Trott	134.3	23	564	12	4-73	0	47.00

Also bowled: G. S. Blewett 34–7–121–2; M. A. Carberry 23–2–94–1; R. W. T. Key 0.4–0–4–0; E. T. Smith 3–1–14–0; P. D. Trego 13–0–69–2; M. J. Walker 9–0–51–0.

COUNTY RECORDS

Highest score for:	332	W. H. Ashdown v Essex at Brentwood	1934
Highest score against:	344	W. G. Grace (MCC) at Canterbury	1876
Best bowling for:	10-30	C. Blythe v Northamptonshire at Northampton	1907
Best bowling against:	10-48	C. H. G. Bland (Sussex) at Tonbridge	1899
Highest total for:	803-4 dec.	v Essex at Brentwood	1934
Highest total against:	676	by Australians at Canterbury	1921
Lowest total for:	18	v Sussex at Gravesend	1867
Lowest total against:	16	by Warwickshire at Tonbridge	1913

KENT DIRECTORY

ADDRESS

St Lawrence Ground, Old Dover Road, Canterbury CT1 3NZ (01227 456886; fax 01227 762168; email kent@ecb.co.uk). **Website** www.kentccc.com.

GROUNDS

Canterbury (St Lawrence Ground): 1 mile SE of city centre in Old Dover Road. Well signposted from A2 junction at Bridge. Nearest stations: Canterbury East (1 mile) and Canterbury West (1½ miles).

Maidstone (The Mote): 1 mile SE of town centre in Willow Way. From Upper Stone Street, L into Waterloo Street, R into St Philips Avenue and then L into Lower Road for Willow Way. Nearest stations: Maidstone East (1 mile) and Maidstone West (1¼ miles).

Tunbridge Wells (Nevill Ground): ¼ mile E of town centre. From A21 junction with A26 Quarry Hill Road at Mount Ephraim take L on A267 then L into Warwick Gate for Nevill Gate. Nearest station: Tunbridge Wells (¾ mile).

Beckenham: ¼ mile off A21 towards Bromley, R into A2015 Beckenham Hill Road, R Stumps Hill and then R into Worsley Bridge Road. Nearest stations: Lower Sydenham and Beckenham Junction (both ½ mile).

OFFICIALS

Captain D. P. Fulton
Coaching co-ordinator S. C. Willis
President 2003 – R. H. B. Neame
2004 – B. W. Luckhurst
Chairman C. F. Openshaw
Chief executive P. E. Millman
Chairman, cricket committee M. H. Denness
Head groundsman M. Grantham
Scorer J. C. Foley

PLAYERS

Players expected to reappear in 2004

	Former counties	*Country*	*Born*	*Birthplace*
Carberry Michael Alexander	Surrey	E	29.9.1980	*Croydon*
Dennington Matthew John		E	16.10.1982	*Durban, SA*
Ferley Robert Steven		E	4.2.1982	*Norwich*
Fulton David Paul		E	15.11.1971	*Lewisham*
Jones Geraint Owen		E	14.7.1976	*Kundiawa, Papua NG*
***Key** Robert William Trevor		E	12.5.1979	*East Dulwich*
Khan Amjad		DEN (EU)	14.10.1980	*Copenhagen*
Loudon Alexander Guy Rushworth		E	6.9.1980	*Westminster*
***Mohammad Sami**		P	24.2.1981	*Karachi*
***Patel** Minal Mahesh		E	7.7.1970	*Bombay, India*
***Saggers** Martin John	Durham	E	23.5.1972	*King's Lynn*
Sheriyar Alamgir	Leics, Worcs	E	15.11.1973	*Birmingham*
***Smith** Edward Thomas		E	19.7.1977	†*Pembury*
Symonds Andrew	Glos	A	9.6.1975	*Birmingham, England*
Tredwell James Cullum		E	27.2.1982	†*Ashford*
Walker Matthew Jonathan		E	2.1.1974	†*Gravesend*

Players due to join in 2004

Stiff David Alexander		E	20.10.1984	*Dewsbury*

* *Test player.* † *Born in Kent.*

At Cambridge, April 18, 19, 20. KENT drew with CAMBRIDGE UCCE.

KENT v LEICESTERSHIRE

At Canterbury, April 23, 24, 25, 26. Drawn. Kent 8 pts, Leicestershire 9 pts. Toss: Kent. First-class debuts: D. S. Brignull, J. L. Sadler. County debuts: D. D. Masters, J. N. Snape.

Two wicket-keepers defined this game. Nixon had just returned to Leicestershire after three years with Kent, who had plumped for the younger Jones instead. His very first match brought Nixon back to Canterbury, and he took revenge in a five-hour hundred, which made him the first player to score first-class centuries for and against Kent at Canterbury, and gave Leicestershire a slight first-innings advantage. Next day, however, Jones counter-attacked with a maiden hundred, lasting just three and a half hours; he reached the milestone in 150 balls, when a potential catch on the long-leg boundary turned into his second six. Jones's efforts left Leicestershire with 387 to get on the last day. Rain and bad light wiped out most of the morning session; in the afternoon Nixon made another fifty, while Brandy scored his first, and after tea Snape and DeFreitas dug in to ensure the draw. Ealham led Kent after Fulton sustained a serious eye injury in pre-season net practice with a bowling machine.

Close of play: First day, Leicestershire 101-3 (Maddy 20, Nixon 29); Second day, Kent 147-4 (Walker 24, Ealham 40); Third day, Kent 411.

Kent

Batsman	First innings		Second innings	
M. A. Carberry	c Snape b Dagnall	55	c Nixon b Brignull	36
R. W. T. Key	lbw b Dagnall	25	c Nixon b DeFreitas	18
E. T. Smith	run out	3	lbw b DeFreitas	8
G. S. Blewett	c Nixon b Dagnall	57	c Nixon b DeFreitas	0
M. J. Walker	c Nixon b Brignull	1	lbw b DeFreitas	38
*M. A. Ealham	run out	17	b Brignull	82
†G. O. Jones	lbw b Maddy	38	c Maddy b Snape	104
J. C. Tredwell	c Stevens b Brignull	9	c Sadler b Dagnall	31
A. Khan	c Nixon b Masters	23	c Snape b Dagnall	11
M. J. Saggers	b Maddy	9	c Stevens b Snape	47
A. Sheriyar	not out	0	not out	8
	B 1, l-b 5, n-b 2	8	B 10, l-b 14, w 2, n-b 2	28
	1/43 (2) 2/52 (3) 3/100 (1) 4/103 (5) 5/158 (4) 6/170 (6) 7/205 (8) 8/227 (7) 9/245 (9) 10/245 (10)	245	1/54 (2) 2/64 (3) 3/66 (1) 4/68 (4) 5/169 (5) 6/233 (6) 7/291 (8) 8/309 (9) 9/397 (7) 10/411 (10)	411

Bonus points – Kent 1, Leicestershire 3.

Bowling: *First Innings*—DeFreitas 13–1–60–0; Masters 17–5–47–1; Dagnall 14–4–43–3; Brignull 11–4–30–2; Maddy 13.2–2–59–2. *Second Innings*—Masters 16–4–83–0; Dagnall 27–4–95–2; Brignull 17–3–42–2; DeFreitas 28–7–69–4; Maddy 20–4–63–0; Stevens 4–0–9–0; Snape 9.2–2–26–2.

"The Bangladeshis may have been guilty of an unfamiliar sin – overconfidence."
The World Cup, page 967.

Leicestershire

T. R. Ward c Tredwell b Ealham	29	– c Ealham b Khan	22
J. L. Sadler b Saggers	4	– lbw b Saggers	0
D. L. Maddy c Key b Blewett	63	– lbw b Khan	4
D. I. Stevens lbw b Ealham	4	– lbw b Sheriyar	45
†P. A. Nixon not out	113	– c Walker b Saggers	53
D. G. Brandy c Jones b Khan	9	– c Ealham b Sheriyar	52
J. N. Snape c Jones b Saggers	0	– not out	26
*P. A. J. DeFreitas c Jones b Saggers	5	– not out	34
D. D. Masters c Sheriyar b Tredwell	15		
C. E. Dagnall lbw b Sheriyar	0		
D. S. Brignull lbw b Saggers	1		
B 6, l-b 11, n-b 10	27	B 5, l-b 4, n-b 10	19
1/40 (2) 2/40 (1) 3/48 (4) 4/169 (3) 5/196 (6) 6/199 (7) 7/211 (8) 8/259 (9) 9/259 (10) 10/270 (11)	270	1/1 (2) 2/14 (3) 3/27 (1) 4/102 (4) 5/154 (5) 6/202 (6)	(6 wkts) 255

Bonus points – Leicestershire 2, Kent 3.

Bowling: *First Innings*—Saggers 24–4–75–4; Sheriyar 20–4–72–1; Ealham 20–9–36–2; Khan 17–4–61–1; Blewett 8–5–6–1; Tredwell 4–2–3–1. *Second Innings*—Saggers 17–3–60–2; Khan 14–1–77–2; Ealham 8–1–28–0; Sheriyar 14–3–44–2; Tredwell 12–7–21–0; Blewett 5–2–16–0.

Umpires: G. I. Burgess and M. J. Harris.

At Hove, April 30, May 1, 2. KENT lost to SUSSEX by 133 runs.

KENT v MIDDLESEX

At Canterbury, May 14, 15, 16, 17. Drawn. Kent 12 pts, Middlesex 8 pts. Toss: Kent. County debut: B. W. Gannon.

Middlesex conceded a three-figure first-innings lead for the fourth time in four Championship matches. But rain, which washed out nearly 130 overs of this game, ensured they remained fourth and Kent bottom of the first division. The opening day's highlight was a 138-run stand between Smith and Blewett. Then, in one over from Dawes, Blewett was caught by Koenig, diving on the boundary, and Smith reached his century – then promptly hit to gully. Jones struck another impressive fifty, before Hutton batted more than three hours in reply. His dismissal next morning triggered a swift collapse. For the second match running, Middlesex followed on over 250 behind – and for the second time running, Strauss and Koenig responded with an opening stand of 176. Both just missed centuries, but their batting, and frequent weather breaks, frustrated Kent.

Close of play: First day, Kent 291-4 (Walker 10, Ealham 3); Second day, Middlesex 135-5 (Hutton 61, Nash 10); Third day, Middlesex 61-0 (Strauss 32, Koenig 24).

Kent

M. A. Carberry c Nash b Keegan	53
R. W. T. Key lbw b Dawes	36
E. T. Smith c Hutton b Dawes	103
G. S. Blewett c Koenig b Dawes	60
M. J. Walker c Keegan b Dawes	32
*M. A. Ealham lbw b Keegan	32
†G. O. Jones c Hutton b Weekes	52
J. C. Tredwell c and b Weekes	36
M. J. Saggers c Hutton b Weekes	16
A. Sheriyar not out	12
B. J. Trott b Weekes	2
B 13, l-b 12, w 4, n-b 9	38
1/66 (2) 2/132 (1) 3/270 (4) 4/274 (3) 5/319 (5) 6/380 (6) 7/412 (7) 8/452 (9) 9/455 (8) 10/472 (11)	472

Bonus points – Kent 5, Middlesex 3 (130 overs: 455-9).

Bowling: Dawes 28–2–90–4; Keegan 28–8–72–2; Gannon 23–4–102–0; Hutton 7–1–45–0; Imran Tahir 20–5–68–0; Weekes 28–6–70–4.

Middlesex

*A. J. Strauss run out	3	– c Ealham b Tredwell	93
S. G. Koenig b Saggers	42	– c Walker b Trott	96
O. A. Shah c Walker b Trott	5	– c Walker b Tredwell	21
B. L. Hutton c Sheriyar b Saggers	74	– c Blewett b Trott	5
E. C. Joyce b Saggers	0	– not out	15
P. N. Weekes lbw b Trott	3	– not out	1
†D. C. Nash lbw b Saggers	12		
C. B. Keegan c Tredwell b Ealham	19		
Imran Tahir c Key b Ealham	29		
J. H. Dawes c Ealham b Tredwell	16		
B. W. Gannon not out	1		
B 5, l-b 7, w 1, n-b 4	17	B 1, l-b 13, n-b 4	18
1/3 (1) 2/8 (3) 3/105 (2) 4/119 (5) 5/122 (6) 6/150 (4) 7/154 (7) 8/203 (8) 9/212 (9) 10/221 (10)	221	1/176 (1) 2/212 (3) 3/230 (2) 4/245 (4)	(4 wkts) 249

Bonus points – Middlesex 1, Kent 3.

Bowling: *First Innings*—Saggers 23–9–48–4; Trott 20–4–68–2; Sheriyar 14–0–69–0; Ealham 11–4–21–2; Tredwell 2.4–0–2–1; Blewett 1–0–1–0. *Second Innings*—Saggers 12–2–42–0; Trott 16.3–3–52–2; Tredwell 24–6–70–2; Sheriyar 11–0–31–0; Ealham 4–0–18–0; Carberry 4–1–22–0.

Umpires: J. H. Evans and J. W. Lloyds.

At Birmingham, May 21, 22, 23, 24. KENT drew with WARWICKSHIRE.

KENT v LANCASHIRE

At Canterbury, May 30, 31, June 1, 2. Lancashire won by 75 runs. Lancashire 20 pts, Kent 5 pts. Toss: Lancashire.

Flintoff, deemed unfit for England because of a trapped nerve in his shoulder, showed little sign of discomfort. Lancashire had struggled to 52 for five as Ealham took four for 11; Flintoff's riposte was to hit his first ball from Ealham for six. A blistering array of strokes brought him eight sixes in all, and 17 fours, as he ran up 154 in 158 balls; Chapple helped him add 179. Flintoff offered two chances before Ealham finally got him, completing his first five-wicket haul in nearly two years. Jones responded with 92 out of a 128-run stand with Ealham, but Kent eventually faced a target of 415. The last day started 75 minutes late, dismaying Lancashire who had endured four rain-affected draws. But despite stout resistance, especially from Ealham, they achieved their first Championship win of 2003 – and their first at Canterbury since 1936. Kent suffered a further blow when their captain, Fulton, chipped his thumb, in his first-class comeback after a serious eye injury.

Close of play: First day, Kent 12-0 (Fulton 7, Carberry 4); Second day, Lancashire 94-2 (Loye 52, Law 28); Third day, Kent 123-4 (Walker 15, Saggers 0).

Lancashire

A. J. Swann lbw b Saggers	8	– (2) c Walker b Saggers	4
M. J. Chilton c Tredwell b Ealham	10	– (1) b Trott	5
M. B. Loye c Jones b Ealham	27	– c Smith b Sheriyar	86
S. G. Law c Jones b Ealham	0	– c Carberry b Saggers	67
C. L. Hooper lbw b Ealham	0	– c Smith b Tredwell	48
A. Flintoff c Tredwell b Ealham	154	– c Smith b Tredwell	43
G. Chapple run out	66	– c and b Trott	3
*†W. K. Hegg not out	37	– c Trott b Tredwell	35
P. J. Martin c and b Tredwell	2	– c Jones b Tredwell	8
S. I. Mahmood lbw b Sheriyar	34	– run out	16
G. Keedy c Blewett b Sheriyar	0	– not out	4
B 2, l-b 5, n-b 2	9	B 4, l-b 9, n-b 2	15
1/8 (1) 2/43 (2) 3/43 (4) 4/43 (5) 5/52 (3) 6/231 (7) 7/284 (6) 8/295 (9) 9/347 (10) 10/347 (11)	347	1/5 (1) 2/19 (2) 3/155 (3) 4/188 (4) 5/252 (6) 6/257 (7) 7/269 (5) 8/295 (9) 9/322 (10) 10/334 (8)	334

Bonus points – Lancashire 3, Kent 3.

Bowling: *First Innings*—Saggers 22–3–100–1; Trott 9–3–35–0; Sheriyar 20.2–6–70–2; Ealham 23–8–54–5; Tredwell 16–3–48–1; Blewett 7–0–33–0. *Second Innings*—Saggers 13–2–36–2; Trott 16–1–67–2; Sheriyar 19–3–58–1; Ealham 15–3–44–0; Tredwell 26.5–4–112–4; Carberry 2–0–4–0.

Kent

*D. P. Fulton lbw b Martin	11	– c Hooper b Mahmood	37
M. A. Carberry c Hooper b Mahmood	38	– c Chilton b Chapple	0
E. T. Smith b Chapple	26	– c and b Keedy	56
G. S. Blewett b Keedy	0	– c Flintoff b Keedy	7
M. J. Walker b Keedy	11	– b Keedy	52
M. A. Ealham b Keedy	43	– (7) c Hooper b Martin	79
†G. O. Jones c Martin b Mahmood	92	– (8) c Flintoff b Keedy	31
J. C. Tredwell c Hegg b Martin	16	– (9) lbw b Chapple	16
M. J. Saggers b Keedy	12	– (6) lbw b Chapple	14
A. Sheriyar c Chapple b Keedy	4	– c Hegg b Chapple	5
B. J. Trott not out	0	– not out	12
L-b 9, w 1, n-b 4	14	B 14, l-b 10, w 2, n-b 4	30
1/16 (1) 2/56 (3) 3/57 (4) 4/85 (2) 5/91 (5) 6/219 (7) 7/241 (8) 8/262 (9) 9/266 (10) 10/267 (6)	267	1/15 (2) 2/79 (1) 3/92 (4) 4/121 (3) 5/156 (6) 6/200 (5) 7/279 (8) 8/319 (7) 9/324 (10) 10/339 (9)	339

Bonus points – Kent 2, Lancashire 3.

Bowling: *First Innings*—Martin 20–8–52–2; Chapple 15–4–43–1; Mahmood 12–1–40–2; Keedy 23.1–4–99–5; Hooper 7–1–24–0. *Second Innings*—Martin 28–3–95–1; Chapple 21.2–5–66–4; Keedy 29–5–79–4; Mahmood 6–0–20–1; Hooper 19–2–55–0.

Umpires: G. I. Burgess and J. W. Holder.

KENT v SUSSEX

At Tunbridge Wells, June 4, 5, 6, 7. Sussex won by 191 runs. Sussex 20 pts, Kent 5 pts. Toss: Sussex. Championship debut: A. G. R. Loudon.

Kent had high hopes of a first Championship victory – they had won their last three games at Tunbridge Wells, and Symonds was back from Australia's Caribbean tour. Instead, they failed to exploit the breaks they got, and conceded their second comprehensive defeat to Sussex in five weeks. Twice Martin-Jenkins guided Sussex out of trouble, with his third and fourth successive half-centuries. But the key was Mushtaq Ahmed, who took nine for 126 in the match despite suspected food poisoning – after his fourth five-wicket return in as many games, he was so ill he returned to the team hotel, where he was attended by Kent's doctor. Mushtaq's bowling had good support from Kirtley, who arrived on the second afternoon after his omission from England's side in the Chester-le-Street Test. A flight from Newcastle and a fast car from Gatwick got him on to the field at 3.30, replacing nominated stand-in Hutchison. Sussex eventually set a target of 323 in 75 overs, but Kent still had no answer to Mushtaq.

Close of play: First day, Sussex 142-5 (Martin-Jenkins 12, Hutchison 5); Second day, Kent 188-5 (Loudon 2, Ealham 2); Third day, Sussex 188-5 (Martin-Jenkins 45, Prior 0).

Sussex

R. R. Montgomerie b Sheriyar	13	– (2) lbw b Saggers	0
M. W. Goodwin run out	35	– (1) run out	58
P. A. Cottey lbw b Sheriyar	0	– lbw b Symonds	52
*C. J. Adams c Ealham b Sheriyar	62	– lbw b Sheriyar	4
T. R. Ambrose c Walker b Blewett	11	– lbw b Symonds	17
R. S. C. Martin-Jenkins c Tredwell b Symonds	67	– c Jones b Sheriyar	84
P. M. Hutchison b Ealham	18		
†M. J. Prior c Symonds b Saggers	23	– (7) c and b Tredwell	45
K. J. Innes c and b Sheriyar	30	– (8) b Tredwell	0
Mushtaq Ahmed c Jones b Saggers	43	– (9) c Loudon b Sheriyar	9
J. D. Lewry not out	0	– (11) not out	1
R. J. Kirtley (did not bat)		– (10) c Jones b Sheriyar	0
B 2, l-b 5, w 2	9	B 3, l-b 12, w 1	16
1/21 (1) 2/25 (3) 3/79 (2) 4/104 (5) 5/136 (4) 6/174 (7) 7/205 (8) 8/249 (6) 9/311 (9) 10/311 (10)	311	1/1 (2) 2/112 (3) 3/117 (1) 4/131 (4) 5/184 (5) 6/273 (7) 7/273 (8) 8/284 (9) 9/285 (10) 10/286 (6)	286

Bonus points – Sussex 3, Kent 3.

Bowling: *First Innings*—Saggers 24.1–6–76–2; Sheriyar 24–6–49–4; Ealham 20–8–63–1; Blewett 5–0–21–1; Tredwell 12–0–65–0; Symonds 10–2–30–1. *Second Innings*—Saggers 20–4–62–1; Sheriyar 23.5–1–93–4; Ealham 10–2–37–0; Symonds 10–1–25–2; Tredwell 10–2–37–2; Blewett 2–0–17–0.

Kent

M. A. Carberry c Cottey b Kirtley	23	– b Mushtaq Ahmed	40
G. S. Blewett b Innes	46	– c Prior b Lewry	0
E. T. Smith lbw b Kirtley	13	– c Montgomerie b Lewry	40
A. Symonds c Innes b Mushtaq Ahmed	54	– lbw b Mushtaq Ahmed	1
M. J. Walker c Ambrose b Mushtaq Ahmed	30	– c Prior b Lewry	7
A. G. R. Loudon c Ambrose b Mushtaq Ahmed	8	– (8) lbw b Martin-Jenkins	0
*M. A. Ealham c Martin-Jenkins b Mushtaq Ahmed	9	– lbw b Martin-Jenkins	3
†G. O. Jones not out	46	– (6) c Lewry b Martin-Jenkins	22
J. C. Tredwell lbw b Kirtley	16	– c Montgomerie b Mushtaq Ahmed	11
M. J. Saggers b Kirtley	2	– not out	0
A. Sheriyar lbw b Mushtaq Ahmed	7	– c Goodwin b Mushtaq Ahmed	4
B 11, l-b 10	21	L-b 1, w 2	3
1/74 (1) 2/84 (2) 3/90 (3) 4/180 (4) 5/180 (5) 6/198 (7) 7/203 (6) 8/238 (9) 9/250 (10) 10/275 (11)	275	1/0 (2) 2/65 (3) 3/66 (4) 4/83 (5) 5/99 (1) 6/110 (7) 7/110 (8) 8/127 (6) 9/127 (9) 10/131 (11)	131

Bonus points – Kent 2, Sussex 3.

Bowling: *First Innings*—Lewry 11–4–19–0; Hutchison 5–0–27–0; Martin-Jenkins 10–3–26–0; Kirtley 21–4–84–4; Innes 9–1–28–1; Mushtaq Ahmed 17.2–3–70–5. *Second Innings*—Kirtley 9–2–29–0; Lewry 11–2–36–3; Mushtaq Ahmed 20.4–7–56–4; Martin-Jenkins 7–3–9–3.

Umpires: I. J. Gould and D. R. Shepherd.

At Chelmsford, June 27, 28, 29, 30. KENT drew with ESSEX.

At The Oval, July 2, 3, 4, 5. KENT lost to SURREY by 186 runs.

KENT v NOTTINGHAMSHIRE

At Maidstone, July 9, 10, 11. Kent won by 287 runs. Kent 21 pts, Nottinghamshire 3 pts. Toss: Kent. Championship debut: D. L. Vettori.

After four draws and four defeats, Kent broke their Championship duck in breathtaking style. Pakistan pace bowler Mohammad Sami claimed 15 for 114, the best match analysis for Kent since 1939, when Doug Wright took 16 at Bath. Sami's genuinely pacy action extracted the best out of The Mote's batsman-friendly pitch – but sadly he injured his ankle, to end his county career after 19 days. Kent's other hero was Ed Smith, who scored twin hundreds, beginning with 149 in 143 balls on a spectacular opening day, when his side scored nearly six an over. Before the close, Sami took three wickets in an over, and he grabbed five more in the morning for a career-best eight for 64, all eight coming in 38 balls. Despite a lead of 206, Fulton waived the follow-on, allowing Smith to feast again on a poor Nottinghamshire attack. This time, he added 233 with Key, who scored his first Championship hundred of the season after a disappointing run with England, and 120 with Symonds, whose unbeaten 103 needed only 81 balls. The declaration set Nottinghamshire a notional target of 625. Gallian batted six hours, but fell during another burst from Sami, who wrapped up the last five wickets in 14 balls and received a second standing ovation as he led his team-mates off.

Close of play: First day, Nottinghamshire 137-5 (Bicknell 31, Cairns 11); Second day, Nottinghamshire 29-2 (Gallian 11).

Kent

*D. P. Fulton c Warren b Harris	6	– c Warren b Smith	18
R. W. T. Key run out	31	– st Warren b Vettori	140
E. T. Smith c Pietersen b Franks	149	– c Vettori b Cairns	113
A. Symonds c Warren b Vettori	8	– not out	103
M. J. Walker c Welton b Vettori	0	– not out	11
M. A. Ealham c Gallian b Vettori	5		
†G. O. Jones c Gallian b Franks	82		
J. C. Tredwell b Smith	16		
R. S. Ferley not out	14		
Mohammad Sami c Franks b Smith	16		
A. Sheriyar c Franks b Vettori	0		
B 5, l-b 3, w 1, n-b 26	35	B 6, l-b 11, w 2, n-b 14	33
1/11 (1) 2/98 (2) 3/112 (4) 4/112 (5) 5/121 (6) 6/299 (7) 7/312 (3) 8/336 (8) 9/360 (10) 10/362 (11)	362	1/22 (1) 2/255 (3) 3/375 (2) (3 wkts dec.)	418

Bonus points – Kent 4, Nottinghamshire 3.

Bowling: *First Innings*—Smith 13–0–58–2; Harris 9–0–55–1; Franks 10–0–51–2; Logan 6–0–48–0; Vettori 14.3–2–74–4; Pietersen 6–0–39–0; Cairns 3–0–29–0. *Second Innings*—Smith 12–0–55–1; Harris 14–4–62–0; Cairns 12–2–43–1; Franks 12–1–53–0; Vettori 20–0–124–1; Pietersen 7.3–0–48–0; Gallian 3–0–16–0.

Nottinghamshire

*J. E. R. Gallian c Jones b Ferley	51	– (2) c Tredwell b Mohammad Sami. 106
G. E. Welton c Symonds b Ferley	17	– (1) lbw b Mohammad Sami 15
D. J. Bicknell not out	37	– b Mohammad Sami 0
†R. J. Warren c Jones b Mohammad Sami	1	– lbw b Tredwell 23
A. J. Harris lbw b Mohammad Sami	0	– (11) b Mohammad Sami 0
K. P. Pietersen c Key b Mohammad Sami	6	– (5) c Smith b Symonds 62
C. L. Cairns b Mohammad Sami	19	– (6) b Ealham 58
P. J. Franks b Mohammad Sami	0	– (7) b Mohammad Sami 45
D. L. Vettori c Jones b Mohammad Sami	0	– (8) c Walker b Mohammad Sami 0
R. J. Logan c Tredwell b Mohammad Sami	4	– (9) not out 5
G. J. Smith b Mohammad Sami	1	– (10) c Jones b Mohammad Sami 2
B 1, l-b 9, n-b 10	20	B 1, l-b 11, w 7, n-b 2 21
1/63 (2) 2/106 (1) 3/113 (4) 4/113 (5) 5/121 (6) 6/146 (7) 7/146 (8) 8/146 (9) 9/150 (10) 10/156 (11)	156	1/27 (1) 2/29 (3) 3/80 (4) 4/158 (5) 5/249 (6) 6/330 (7) 7/330 (8) 8/331 (2) 9/333 (10) 10/337 (11) 337

Bonus points – Kent 3.

Bowling: *First Innings*—Mohammad Sami 14.1–3–64–8; Sheriyar 6–3–17–0; Ferley 19–6–39–2; Ealham 5–1–17–0; Tredwell 5–2–9–0. *Second Innings*—Mohammad Sami 21.2–8–50–7; Sheriyar 13–2–40–0; Ferley 21–6–70–0; Ealham 13–4–39–1; Tredwell 21–5–84–1; Symonds 12–0–42–1.

Umpires: A. Clarkson and A. A. Jones.

At Blackpool, July 15, 16, 17, 18. KENT drew with LANCASHIRE.

KENT v ESSEX

At Canterbury, July 30, 31, August 1. Kent won by 55 runs. Kent 17 pts, Essex 3 pts. Toss: Kent.

Sri Lankan off-spinner Muralitharan, Mohammad Sami's replacement, celebrated his first-class debut for Kent by helping them pull ahead of relegation rivals Essex. Having finished wicketless for the first time in a Championship innings (including his two seasons with Lancashire), he rewarded Kent's investment at the second attempt with six for 61 to secure victory before tea on the third day. Kent were bolstered by Smith's fourth successive first-class hundred – his sixth in eight innings in all cricket – when Kent's next best contribution was 18 from no-balls. Seventeen wickets fell on the first day, six to Palladino, who found excellent swing and seam movement in his second Championship match. Neither side managed a batting point. Fulton carried his bat through Kent's second innings but missed his century, thanks to a hat-trick from Middlebrook which, split between two overs, almost went unnoticed. Chasing 291, Essex were kept in the hunt by Flower, who denied Kent for four hours before he was ninth out, playing on to Sheriyar. Jones was awarded his county cap on the second day, after taking six catches.

Close of play: First day, Essex 164-7 (Napier 8, Palladino 1); Second day, Essex 24-1 (Robinson 15, Palladino 2).

Kent

*D. P. Fulton c Flower b Grant	12	– not out	94
R. W. T. Key lbw b Palladino	6	– (4) c Foster b McCoubrey	4
E. T. Smith c Flower b Palladino	108	– c Flower b Grant	32
M. A. Carberry c and b Grant	6	– (2) c Foster b Napier	36
M. J. Walker c Jefferson b McCoubrey	8	– c Flower b Napier	23
M. A. Ealham c Foster b Palladino	3	– c Jefferson b Grant	8
†G. O. Jones b Palladino	5	– c Irani b Grant	31
A. Khan c Irani b Palladino	12	– c Jefferson b Middlebrook	17
M. J. Saggers c Foster b Palladino	4	– lbw b Middlebrook	4
M. Muralitharan c Robinson b Middlebrook	4	– lbw b Middlebrook	1
A. Sheriyar not out	0	– b Middlebrook	0
B 2, w 1, n-b 18	21	B 8, l-b 4, n-b 22	34
1/8 (2) 2/21 (1) 3/33 (4) 4/65 (5) 5/102 (6) 6/128 (7) 7/164 (8) 8/170 (9) 9/187 (3) 10/189 (10)	189	1/48 (2) 2/103 (3) 3/115 (4) 4/169 (5) 5/181 (6) 6/237 (7) 7/266 (8) 8/282 (9) 9/284 (10) 10/284 (11)	284

Bonus points – Essex 3.

Bowling: *First Innings*—Grant 10–2–63–2; Palladino 15–5–41–6; Napier 5–1–23–0; McCoubrey 5–0–33–1; Middlebrook 5.3–0–27–1. *Second Innings*—Grant 15–0–61–3; Palladino 16–2–58–0; Napier 16.5–4–68–2; Middlebrook 30.2–5–78–4; McCoubrey 3.1–1–7–1.

Essex

D. D. J. Robinson c Jones b Ealham	25	– b Khan	42
W. I. Jefferson c Jones b Khan	4	– c Walker b Muralitharan	5
A. Flower c Jones b Ealham	39	– (4) b Sheriyar	83
A. Habib c Muralitharan b Ealham	5	– (5) b Muralitharan	14
*R. C. Irani c Jones b Khan	52	– (6) b Khan	14
†J. S. Foster c Jones b Saggers	0	– (7) lbw b Muralitharan	31
J. D. Middlebrook b Khan	15	– (8) c Walker b Muralitharan	5
G. R. Napier c and b Khan	16	– (9) lbw b Muralitharan	5
A. P. Palladino not out	7	– (3) b Saggers	8
J. B. Grant lbw b Ealham	1	– b Muralitharan	4
A. G. A. M. McCoubrey c Jones b Ealham	0	– not out	0
B 5, l-b 2, n-b 12	19	B 4, l-b 7, w 1, n-b 12	24
1/14 (2) 2/75 (3) 3/82 (1) 4/95 (4) 5/107 (6) 6/146 (7) 7/159 (5) 8/174 (8) 9/175 (10) 10/183 (11)	183	1/20 (2) 2/51 (3) 3/63 (1) 4/118 (5) 5/141 (6) 6/188 (7) 7/194 (8) 8/221 (9) 9/235 (4) 10/235 (10)	235

Bonus points – Kent 3.

Bowling: *First Innings*—Saggers 13–5–29–1; Khan 15–0–65–4; Sheriyar 2–0–15–0; Ealham 17–8–26–5; Muralitharan 22–9–41–0. *Second Innings*—Saggers 15–4–40–1; Khan 11–2–61–2; Ealham 12–3–32–0; Muralitharan 28.1–6–61–6; Sheriyar 14–6–30–1.

Umpires: N. G. Cowley and M. J. Kitchen.

At Canterbury, August 7, 8, 9. KENT lost to SOUTH AFRICANS by 101 runs (see South African tour section).

At Lord's, August 13, 14, 15, 16. KENT beat MIDDLESEX by eight wickets.

At Nottingham, August 20, 21. KENT beat NOTTINGHAMSHIRE by nine wickets.

KENT v SURREY

At Canterbury, September 4, 5, 6. Kent won by an innings and 155 runs. Kent 22 pts, Surrey 3 pts. Toss: Kent.

Kent's fifth win in six Championship matches effectively ended Surrey's hopes of retaining their title. It was achieved in spectacular style too: their biggest victory over Surrey since 1902 and Surrey's first innings defeat in five years. On their previous visit to Canterbury, in 2002, they had successfully chased 410 to win; this time, 410 was their first-innings deficit after a humiliating batting display. Surrey were 30 for four inside an hour against Saggers and Khan, and collapsed completely in 29 overs. They did little better second time round. Ormond and Rose, a stand-in for Saqlain Mushtaq, delayed the inevitable with a flurry of boundaries, but it was all over 45 minutes into the third morning. Muralitharan took his aggregate for Kent to 27 wickets in four games. On the first day, Carberry just missed a hundred against his old county. He and Fulton gave Kent their best Championship start in 2003; once they fell, shortly after lunch, Symonds hit 18 fours and a six to reach 121 off 123 balls, and aggressive half-centuries from Ealham and Jones swept Kent past 500.

Close of play: First day, Kent 435-5 (Ealham 80, Jones 26); Second day, Surrey 169-7 (Salisbury 3, Ormond 6).

Kent

*D. P. Fulton c Batty b Rose	71
M. A. Carberry c Batty b Rose	92
A. G. R. Loudon lbw b Murtagh	9
A. Symonds st Batty b Salisbury	121
M. J. Walker c Brown b Clarke	25
M. A. Ealham lbw b Murtagh	93
†G. O. Jones c Batty b Murtagh	53
R. S. Ferley c Clarke b Rose	4
A. Khan c Batty b Clarke	25
M. J. Saggers not out	10
M. Muralitharan c Ramprakash b Murtagh	5
L-b 11, n-b 16	27
1/160 (2) 2/175 (1) 3/191 (3) 4/262 (5) 5/368 (4) 6/451 (6) 7/472 (8) 8/506 (7) 9/528 (9) 10/535 (11)	535

Bonus points – Kent 5, Surrey 3.

Bowling: Ormond 10–0–48–0; Rose 28–8–101–3; Murtagh 27.2–2–130–4; Clarke 21–1–95–2; Hollioake 7–1–35–0; Salisbury 27–4–115–1.

Surrey

I. J. Ward b Saggers	2	– b Muralitharan	53
†J. N. Batty b Saggers	28	– lbw b Ealham	17
M. R. Ramprakash b Saggers	4	– lbw b Saggers	15
N. Shahid lbw b Saggers	4	– c Fulton b Saggers	1
A. D. Brown c Fulton b Khan	2	– b Muralitharan	40
R. Clarke c Jones b Khan	26	– c Loudon b Muralitharan	13
*A. J. Hollioake lbw b Khan	3	– st Jones b Ferley	6
I. D. K. Salisbury c Walker b Muralitharan	16	– lbw b Saggers	7
J. Ormond b Symonds	1	– c Walker b Muralitharan	32
F. A. Rose c Ferley b Muralitharan	1	– c Saggers b Ferley	36
T. J. Murtagh not out	17	– not out	12
B 5, l-b 5, w 1, n-b 10	21	B 8, l-b 13, n-b 2	23
1/6 (1) 2/19 (3) 3/27 (4) 4/30 (5) 5/64 (2) 6/78 (6) 7/79 (7) 8/99 (9) 9/100 (10) 10/125 (8)	125	1/23 (2) 2/62 (3) 3/68 (4) 4/112 (1) 5/144 (6) 6/155 (7) 7/159 (5) 8/183 (8) 9/215 (9) 10/255 (10)	255

Bonus points – Kent 3.

Bowling: *First Innings*—Saggers 10–1–40–4; Khan 11–0–50–3; Muralitharan 4.5–2–11–2; Symonds 3–0–14–1. *Second Innings*—Saggers 14–5–37–3; Symonds 10–3–36–0; Ealham 6–1–17–1; Khan 4–0–11–0; Muralitharan 25–5–90–4; Ferley 11–2–43–2.

Umpires: I. J. Gould and G. Sharp.

At Leicester, September 10, 11, 12. KENT lost to LEICESTERSHIRE by ten wickets.

KENT v WARWICKSHIRE

At Canterbury, September 17, 18, 19. Kent won by an innings and 70 runs. Kent 22 pts, Warwickshire 3 pts. Toss: Kent.

Kent's campaign concluded on a glorious September evening with their sixth victory in eight games. It put them fourth, one place above Warwickshire, who lost 17 wickets during an eventful third day. Ealham polished off their first innings with four in 13 balls, in his best return for four years. When Warwickshire followed on, Powell produced his only first-class hundred of the season, in his last innings as captain, and big hitting by Piper and Carter briefly delayed Kent. Earlier, Smith had converted his eighth fifty in the 2003 Championship into his seventh century, which became a career-best 213, featuring 26 fours in 343 balls and 429 minutes. He was the first to score two double-hundreds for Kent in a season since Aravinda de Silva in 1995, and passed 1,500 runs en route. He and Walker, who reached 1,000 runs for the first time, doubled Kent's total with 267, a county fourth-wicket record against Warwickshire, before both fell to an unlikely destroyer. Trott's career had previously brought him four wickets for 396; on the second day, his unpretentious out-swing produced a spell of seven for 28 in 8.1 overs either side of lunch.

Close of play: First day, Kent 379-3 (Smith 121, Walker 50); Second day, Warwickshire 200-3 (Trott 52, Bell 37).

Kent

Batsman	Runs
*D. P. Fulton c Piper b Richardson	51
R. W. T. Key lbw b Brown	54
E. T. Smith c Wagh b Trott	213
A. Symonds c and b Wagh	88
M. J. Walker c Piper b Trott	121
†G. O. Jones c Piper b Trott	0
M. A. Ealham c Piper b Trott	30
J. C. Tredwell lbw b Trott	4
R. S. Ferley c Piper b Trott	4
A. Khan lbw b Trott	7
M. J. Saggers not out	0
B 6, l-b 12, n-b 4	22
1/95 (2) 2/123 (1) 3/267 (4) 4/534 (5) 5/534 (6) 6/553 (3) 7/570 (8) 8/585 (7) 9/593 (10) 10/594 (9)	594

Bonus points – Kent 5, Warwickshire 1 (130 overs: 477-3).

Bowling: Collymore 24–2–71–0; Carter 18–1–90–0; Richardson 26–4–87–1; Brown 24–6–80–1; Wagh 30–2–122–1; Bell 16–3–53–0; Trott 11.1–2–39–7; Troughton 7–0–34–0.

Warwickshire

Batsman	First innings		Second innings	
*M. J. Powell c Tredwell b Ealham	61	–	c Key b Tredwell	110
N. V. Knight c Ferley b Ealham	25	–	c Walker b Symonds	1
M. A. Wagh c Jones b Saggers	6	–	b Symonds	0
I. J. L. Trott c Jones b Saggers	53	–	c Walker b Ealham	7
I. R. Bell c Jones b Symonds	54	–	c Jones b Ealham	0
J. O. Troughton lbw b Ealham	26	–	c Jones b Ferley	20
D. R. Brown c Ferley b Symonds	0	–	c Key b Tredwell	21
†K. J. Piper b Ealham	3	–	run out	39
N. M. Carter c Saggers b Ealham	15	–	lbw b Ferley	38
A. Richardson c Walker b Ealham	0	–	c and b Ferley	7
C. D. Collymore not out	0	–	not out	10
B 4, l-b 8, n-b 12	24		N-b 4	4
1/55 (2) 2/87 (3) 3/112 (1) 4/203 (4) 5/249 (5) 6/249 (7) 7/251 (6) 8/256 (8) 9/256 (10) 10/267 (9)	267		1/10 (2) 2/16 (3) 3/45 (4) 4/55 (5) 5/123 (6) 6/157 (1) 7/180 (7) 8/236 (8) 9/240 (9) 10/257 (10)	257

Bonus points – Warwickshire 2, Kent 3.

Bowling: *First Innings*—Saggers 15–2–67–2; Khan 15–0–70–0; Ealham 15.5–7–35–6; Tredwell 8–2–19–0; Symonds 12–2–42–2; Ferley 5–1–22–0. *Second Innings*—Saggers 7–0–19–0; Symonds 10–4–24–2; Ferley 14.4–2–45–3; Ealham 13–2–52–2; Khan 7–1–32–0; Tredwell 17–1–85–2.

Umpires: P. J. Hartley and N. A. Mallender.

LANCASHIRE

Supremacy of the Law

COLIN EVANS

Dark clouds hung over Lancashire, even though they finished Championship runners-up for the fourth time in six seasons. Eleven days were lost to the weather, badly affecting four matches they had the better of, while the sun seemed to shine constantly for the eventual winners, Sussex. Jack Simmons, the club chairman, joked grimly about relocating to the South Coast, and though relocation did become a possibility before the year was out, Lancashire were not thinking of going that far.

Frustration also burned deeply over suggestions that Sussex's triumph stemmed from a greater team ethic. "Nonsense," said captain Warren Hegg. "I have played in several successful Lancashire sides, and the spirit in this dressing-room is the best of the lot."

Mainly because of the weather, Lancashire had to wait until early June for their first Championship win, though they had hit form immediately, amassing 599 in their very first innings, against reigning champions Surrey. Later in the summer, with their batsmen wreaking havoc and left-arm spinner Gary Keedy revelling in the heat and dust, they kept the title tussle alive until the final round. And even an outside observer could detect the team bonding. Stuart Law claimed: "I'm ready to go to work at 7.30 a.m. – the missus asks why so early, but it's just that I can't wait to get there."

But solely blaming the weather for another near-miss is simplistic. Other factors were involved, including a delayed declaration at Chelmsford, where Lancashire were intent on giving "nowt", and two home draws on flat pitches: at Blackpool, where they were outplayed by Kent, and at Old Trafford, where Middlesex comfortably staved off defeat after being flayed for 734 for five, a ground record. Two weeks later Lancashire made 781 at Edgbaston, the third-highest total in their history. Both innings featured centuries from the same four batsmen – Mark Chilton, Mal Loye, Law and Carl Hooper, all of whom topped 1,000 Championship runs to make this Lancashire's Year of the Bat. Law, with 1,820 at 91, was the most prolific scorer in the country. Iain Sutcliffe might have been the fifth to reach 1,000 but for injuries, and there were 28 Championship centuries in all.

Bolstered by huge totals, Keedy was encouraged to attack, and took 60 wickets in 12 matches, when he had expected to play second fiddle to Indian off-spin maestro Harbhajan Singh. Harbhajan never made it because of a finger injury; instead, Lancashire kept Hooper, the former West Indian captain originally signed as a stand-in, who quickly established himself and, especially in partnership with Law, laid on a rare feast of runs. Law, who won the club's player of the year award, was due back in 2004 and was applying for British citizenship, which would make him an "England" player after that. Hooper also agreed to return.

Stuart Law

The side that finished the season had an average age of 31 and included two overseas stars and four imports from other counties – and in October, Lancashire added 32-year-old Dominic Cork on a three-year contract. Yet they did not abandon their commitment to home-grown youth. Sajid Mahmood, a lively seamer from Bolton, won a place in the England Academy; Cheshire batsman Mark Currie made a promising Championship debut; all-rounder Kyle Hogg would surely have played a lot more but for illness; and the leg-spinner Chris Schofield figured in half the Championship programme, though Keedy and Hooper provided most of the spin bowling. Another promising youngster was Australian Steven Crook, who has English parents.

Lancashire also showed signs of returning to the one-day heights, but lost their fifth semi-final in four years in a roller-coaster C&G clash at Worcester, where Loye was left high and not merely dry but dehydrated after scoring a century in intense heat. Another Loye century, against his old club Northamptonshire, clinched the National League's second-division title, Lancashire's first trophy since 1999. The new Twenty20 Cup worked well for Lancashire in terms of crowds, with a massive turnout at Old Trafford for the only Roses fixture of the season; luckily, this tournament took place in perfect weather, though after crushing Yorkshire that midsummer evening, Lancashire played pretty abjectly.

Overall it was a nearly, nearly season, but one with so many memorable moments: Andrew Flintoff, defying stomach and shoulder problems and bringing Lord's to its feet with a mesmerising 111 against Middlesex to foreshadow his Test century on the same ground; James Anderson grabbing a hat-trick including the then England captain Nasser Hussain; Law winning a battle of wills with Mushtaq Ahmed at Old Trafford; Hooper toying with the Surrey attack... At the end of the season, Law said: "I think we are on the verge of something very special."

This year will mark the 70th anniversary of Lancashire's last outright County Championship. The next success may have to hurry if the title is ever to come back to Old Trafford. In November, Manchester City Council offered Lancashire the chance to leave the ancient ground, their home for exactly twice as long, for a new site on the east side of Manchester, close to the stadium built for the 2002 Commonwealth Games and now occupied by Manchester City Football Club. A feasibility study was ordered. The club's executive claimed the move would cure their financial problems and give them a purpose-built stadium, rather than a famous but outdated one.

LANCASHIRE RESULTS

All first-class matches – Played 17: Won 6, Lost 2, Drawn 9.
County Championship matches – Played 16: Won 6, Lost 2, Drawn 8.

Frizzell County Championship, 2nd in Division 1; Cheltenham & Gloucester Trophy, s-f; National Cricket League, winners in Division 2; Twenty20 Cup, 4th in North Group

COUNTY CHAMPIONSHIP AVERAGES

BATTING AND FIELDING

Cap		*M*	*I*	*NO*	*R*	*HS*	*100s*	*50s*	*Avge*	*Ct/St*
1998	A. Flintoff	5	6	1	519	154	2	2	103.80	7
2002	S. G. Law§.	16	24	4	1,820	236*	7	6	91.00	17
2003	C. L. Hooper§.	13	19	2	1,118	201	5	3	65.76	14
2003	M. B. Loye.	15	22	1	1,062	144	5	2	50.57	4
2002	M. J. Chilton	16	24	2	1,065	125	6	2	48.40	12
2003	I. J. Sutcliffe.	12	17	2	681	109	1	4	45.40	13
1994	G. Chapple.	16	21	3	679	132*	2	3	37.72	8
	K. W. Hogg	5	5	0	158	53	0	1	31.60	1
1989	W. K. Hegg	16	20	7	404	61*	0	1	31.07	46/3
2002	C. P. Schofield	8	11	2	263	66	0	2	29.22	8
2002	A. J. Swann	9	14	0	218	57	0	1	15.57	13
	S. I. Mahmood	4	4	0	57	34	0	0	14.25	0
2003	J. Wood	9	8	2	67	30	0	0	11.16	2
1994	P. J. Martin.	14	12	0	120	23	0	0	10.00	8
2000	G. Keedy	12	10	6	16	6	0	0	4.00	4

Also batted: J. M. Anderson (4 matches) 3*, 0*, 9* (3 ct); M. R. Currie (1 match) 56, 13 (1 ct); S. P. Crook (1 match) 27 (1 ct); J. J. Haynes (1 match) 12, 0 (2 ct).

§ *Overseas player.*

BOWLING

	O	*M*	*R*	*W*	*BB*	*5W/i*	*Avge*
G. Keedy	531.5	125	1,532	60	6-68	5	25.53
J. M. Anderson	107	19	411	15	5-61	1	27.40
C. L. Hooper.	348.2	83	870	30	6-51	2	29.00
P. J. Martin	432.1	99	1,295	41	5-54	1	31.58
J. Wood	222.4	32	854	27	3-17	0	31.62
G. Chapple	494.2	90	1,744	49	6-98	2	35.59
C. P. Schofield.	151.1	26	562	11	3-14	0	51.09

Also bowled: M. J. Chilton 39–8–94–0; S. P. Crook 13.1–1–58–2; A. Flintoff 50–13–135–5; K. W. Hogg 97–22–370–7; S. G. Law 7–0–29–0; M. B. Loye 4–0–16–1; S. I. Mahmood 71–9–331–6; I. J. Sutcliffe 4–1–11–1; A. J. Swann 5–0–22–0.

COUNTY RECORDS

Highest score for:	424	A. C. MacLaren v Somerset at Taunton	1895
Highest score against:	315*	T. W. Hayward (Surrey) at The Oval	1898
Best bowling for:	10-46	W. Hickton v Hampshire at Manchester	1870
Best bowling against:	10-40	G. O. B. Allen (Middlesex) at Lord's	1929
Highest total for:	863	v Surrey at The Oval	1990
Highest total against:	707-9 dec.	by Surrey at The Oval	1990
Lowest total for:	25	v Derbyshire at Manchester	1871
Lowest total against:	22	by Glamorgan at Liverpool	1924

LANCASHIRE DIRECTORY

ADDRESS

County Cricket Ground, Old Trafford, Manchester M16 0PX (0161 282 4000; fax 0161 282 4100; email enquiries@lccc.co.uk). **Website** www.lccc.co.uk.

GROUNDS

Manchester (Old Trafford): 2 miles SW of city centre on E side of A56 in Old Trafford close to Manchester United football ground, entrance in Talbot Road. Nearest stations: Old Trafford (MetroLink Tram) (adjacent) and Manchester Piccadilly (2½ miles).

Liverpool: 4 miles SE of city centre between A561 and River Mersey. From A562 Speke Road continue on A561 Speke Boulevard, R on Garston Way for Aigburth Road. Nearest station: Aigburth (½ mile).

OFFICIALS

Captain W. K. Hegg
Cricket manager M. Watkinson
President J. F. Blackledge
Chairman J. Simmons
Chief executive J. Cumbes
Chairman, cricket committee G. Ogden
Head groundsman P. Marron
Scorer A. West

PLAYERS

Players expected to reappear in 2004

	Former counties	*Country*	*Born*	*Birthplace*
***Anderson** James Michael		‡E	30.7.1982	†*Burnley*
Chapple Glen		E	23.1.1974	*Skipton*
Chilton Mark James		E	2.10.1976	*Sheffield*
Crook Steven Paul		A (EU)	28.5.1983	*Modbury*
Currie Mark Robert		E	22.9.1979	†*Manchester*
***Flintoff** Andrew		‡E	6.12.1977	†*Preston*
Haynes Jamie Jonathan		E	5.7.1974	*Bristol*
***Hegg** Warren Kevin		E	23.2.1968	†*Whitefield*
Hogg Kyle William		E	2.7.1983	*Birmingham*
***Hooper** Carl Llewellyn	Kent	WI	15.12.1966	*Georgetown, Guyana*
Horton Paul James		E	20.9.1982	*Sydney, Aus.*
Keedy Gary	Yorks	E	27.11.1974	*Wakefield*
***Law** Stuart Grant	Essex	A	18.10.1968	*Herston*
Loye Malachy Bernard	Northants	E	27.9.1972	*Northampton*
Mahmood Sajid Iqbal		E	21.12.1981	†*Bolton*
***Martin** Peter James		E	15.11.1968	†*Accrington*
Newby Oliver James		E	26.8.1984	†*Blackburn*
Rees Timothy Martyn		E	4.9.1984	*Loughborough*
***Schofield** Christopher Paul		E	6.10.1978	†*Rochdale*
Sutcliffe Iain John	Leics	E	20.12.1974	*Leeds*
Swann Alec James	Northants	E	26.10.1976	*Northampton*
Wood John	Durham	E	22.7.1970	*Crofton*
Yates Gary		E	20.9.1967	†*Ashton-under-Lyne*

Player due to join in 2004

***Cork** Dominic Gerald	Derbys	E	7.8.1971	*Newcastle-under-Lyme*

* *Test player.* † *Born in Lancashire.* ‡ *12-month ECB contract.*

At The Oval, April 18, 19, 20, 21. LANCASHIRE drew with SURREY.

LANCASHIRE v NOTTINGHAMSHIRE

At Manchester, April 23, 24, 25, 26. Drawn. Lancashire 11 pts, Nottinghamshire 9 pts. Toss: Lancashire.

Loye, signed from Northamptonshire during the close season, became the first player to score centuries in his first two games for Lancashire. He followed up 126 at The Oval with 113 here – surviving an lbw appeal from Harris on 99. But he was almost beaten to three figures by Flintoff, batting at No. 6 to accommodate Loye and another new signing, Sutcliffe. Arriving when Loye was on 60, Flintoff looked lean and fit after a diet of vegetable soup and cranberry juice – and cracked 97 off 130 balls. Elworthy, the South African seamer who played at Old Trafford in 1996, enjoyed his return, finishing with five wickets when his old club lost their last five for 14. Bad weather cut deeply into the last three days of the match, allowing barely 100 overs, in which Cairns and Read ensured against the threat of the follow-on with defiant fifties.

Close of play: First day, Lancashire 354; Second day, Nottinghamshire 113-3 (Bicknell 30, Cairns 51); Third day, No play.

Lancashire

A. J. Swann c Read b Elworthy	15	– lbw b Smith	7
I. J. Sutcliffe c and b Elworthy	42	– not out	17
M. B. Loye c Afzaal b Elworthy	113	– c Cairns b Smith	7
S. G. Law c Shafayat b Franks	6	– not out	8
M. J. Chilton c Gallian b Elworthy	14		
A. Flintoff c Read b Pietersen	97		
G. Chapple b Smith	28		
C. P. Schofield b Smith	3		
*†W. K. Hegg b Elworthy	0		
P. J. Martin lbw b Smith	1		
J. M. Anderson not out	0		
B 1, l-b 9, w 7, n-b 18	35	N-b 2	2
1/54 (1) 2/77 (2) 3/104 (4) 4/156 (5) 5/293 (6) 6/340 (7) 7/351 (8) 8/353 (3) 9/354 (10) 10/354 (9)	354	1/17 (1) 2/31 (3)	(2 wkts) 41

Bonus points – Lancashire 4, Nottinghamshire 3.

Bowling: *First Innings*—Smith 19–4–50–3; Harris 25–5–87–0; Elworthy 24.1–6–71–5; Franks 16–1–74–1; Gallian 7–3–17–0; Pietersen 9–0–33–1; Shafayat 2–0–12–0. *Second Innings*—Elworthy 6–0–13–0; Harris 4.4–0–20–0; Smith 8–4–8–2.

Nottinghamshire

D. J. Bicknell c Hegg b Martin	30
*J. E. R. Gallian lbw b Anderson	0
U. Afzaal c Hegg b Chapple	6
K. P. Pietersen lbw b Martin	19
C. L. Cairns c Hegg b Martin	57
B. M. Shafayat c and b Martin	18
†C. M. W. Read lbw b Martin	57
P. J. Franks c Chilton b Flintoff	5
S. Elworthy c Martin b Anderson	30
G. J. Smith c Swann b Chapple	19
A. J. Harris not out	16
B 11, l-b 5, w 2	18
1/1 (2) 2/11 (3) 3/44 (4) 4/113 (1) 5/126 (5) 6/155 (6) 7/173 (8) 8/238 (7) 9/240 (9) 10/275 (10)	275

Bonus points – Nottinghamshire 2, Lancashire 3.

Bowling: Anderson 20–2–76–2; Chapple 18.3–3–51–2; Martin 19–3–54–5; Flintoff 11–4–23–1; Schofield 13–0–52–0; Law 1–0–3–0.

Umpires: J. H. Evans and A. G. T. Whitehead.

At Lord's, May 9, 10, 11, 12. LANCASHIRE drew with MIDDLESEX.

LANCASHIRE v ESSEX

At Manchester, May 14, 15, 16, 17. Drawn. Lancashire 11 pts, Essex 8 pts. Toss: Essex. County debut: C. L. Hooper.

Anderson's meteoric rise continued when he had Robinson caught at gully and the England captain, Hussain, lbw with the last two balls of one over, and then had Jefferson caught behind edging his next delivery. It took a moment to sink in. "I didn't think much about it until someone shouted 'That's a hat-trick, isn't it?'" he said. Removing Hussain first ball possibly sealed his place in the Test squad announced on the final day. "He didn't say anything, just gave me a wry smile," said Anderson. Aged 20, he was believed to be the youngest Lancashire player to claim a hat-trick (though the precise birthdate of Jack Bullough, who achieved one at Derby in 1914, has eluded researchers) and was undoubtedly the first since Mike Watkinson in 1992. Later, Sutcliffe scored his first, painstaking, hundred for the county. Chilton emulated him, but Hooper, signed the day before the match to fill in for Harbhajan Singh, had a quiet debut, and Lancashire were frustrated again in their fourth rain-affected draw. Graham Gooch, the 49-year-old Essex coach, fielded for seven overs as a sub in Jefferson's sweater, which reached his knees. The crowd cheered his every move – not that he made many.

Close of play: First day, Lancashire 127-1 (Sutcliffe 50, Loye 33); Second day, Essex 41-2 (Hussain 13, Flower 16); Third day, No play.

Essex

D. D. J. Robinson c Swann b Anderson	11	– c Hegg b Anderson	8
W. I. Jefferson c Hegg b Anderson	19	– b Martin	3
N. Hussain lbw b Anderson	0	– not out	13
A. Flower lbw b Martin	25	– b Chapple	16
A. P. Grayson c Sutcliffe b Martin	13	– not out	1
*R. C. Irani c Swann b Martin	0		
†J. S. Foster c Anderson b Hooper	57		
J. D. Middlebrook lbw b Keedy	12		
G. R. Napier c Martin b Anderson	40		
S. A. Brant c Chilton b Hooper	23		
J. B. Grant not out	2		
B 2, l-b 6, n-b 5	13	L-b 1	1
1/34 (1) 2/34 (3) 3/35 (2) 4/67 (5) 5/67 (6) 6/82 (4) 7/95 (8) 8/152 (9) 9/194 (7) 10/215 (10)	215	1/12 (2) 2/14 (1) 3/41 (4)	(3 wkts) 42

Bonus points – Essex 1, Lancashire 3.

Bowling: *First Innings*—Anderson 15–1–67–4; Martin 12–3–32–3; Chapple 13–3–40–0; Chilton 4–0–10–0; Keedy 5–0–24–1; Hooper 8.5–3–34–2. *Second Innings*—Anderson 7–3–11–1; Martin 7–2–12–1; Chapple 4.3–0–18–1; Keedy 1–1–0–0.

Lancashire

A. J. Swann lbw b Irani	33
I. J. Sutcliffe lbw b Middlebrook	109
M. B. Loye lbw b Irani	33
S. G. Law c and b Irani	6
M. J. Chilton c Napier b Middlebrook	106
C. L. Hooper c Middlebrook b Grayson	8
G. Chapple c Foster b Middlebrook	1
*†W. K. Hegg c Napier b Irani	23
P. J. Martin c Middlebrook b Grant	23
G. Keedy c Foster b Grant	0
J. M. Anderson not out	9
B 3, l-b 6, w 3, n-b 12	24
1/44 (1) 2/128 (3) 3/146 (4) 4/229 (2) 5/245 (6) 6/255 (7) 7/303 (8) 8/338 (9) 9/343 (10) 10/375 (5)	375

Bonus points – Lancashire 4, Essex 3 (130 overs: 366-9).

Bowling: Brant 11–3–36–0; Napier 16–1–73–0; Irani 32–13–59–4; Middlebrook 40.1–11–86–3; Grant 10–0–44–2; Grayson 24–6–68–1.

Umpires: J. W. Holder and B. Leadbeater.

At Durham, May 21, 22, 23. LANCASHIRE drew with DURHAM UCCE.

At Canterbury, May 30, 31, June 1, 2. LANCASHIRE beat KENT by 75 runs.

LANCASHIRE v LEICESTERSHIRE

At Liverpool, June 4, 5, 6, 7. Lancashire won by ten wickets. Lancashire 22 pts, Leicestershire 5 pts. Toss: Lancashire. Championship debut: J. K. Maunders.

With Lancashire still expecting Harbhajan Singh, the Indian spinner, this seemed to be Hooper's last Championship match, but he was just warming up as they steamrollered Leicestershire at Aigburth. The top six of Lancashire's powerful batting line-up all passed 50, led by Chilton, who scored his third century in four Championship games, and his first since resuming his opening position. Hooper struck 74 from 88 balls, then Flintoff, ruled out for England by a bad shoulder, smashed 71 in 55. In reply, Maddy and Stevens batted purposefully but their side still had to follow on. Sehwag, who had been hit in the face when fielding, ended an unfortunate match by running himself out risking a second to Chilton at third man. Maddy resisted for a couple of hours, but Hooper and Keedy patiently worked their way through the innings. Lancashire's victory cut Surrey's lead to six points.

Close of play: First day, Lancashire 210-1 (Chilton 87, Loye 53); Second day, Leicestershire 117-4 (Maddy 27, Stevens 0); Third day, Leicestershire 130-5 (Maddy 18).

Lancashire

M. J. Chilton lbw b Brignull	108	– not out	16
I. J. Sutcliffe c Maddy b Masters	55	– not out	5
M. B. Loye c Stevens b Dagnall	54		
S. G. Law c Nixon b Maddy	82		
C. L. Hooper c Stevens b Maddy	74		
A. Flintoff not out	71		
G. Chapple c Masters b Brignull	15		
*†W. K. Hegg not out	23		
B 5, l-b 5, w 5, n-b 6	21	B 1, l-b 2	3
1/104 (2) 2/211 (3) 3/254 (1) 4/377 (4) 5/394 (5) 6/436 (7) (6 wkts dec.)	503	(no wkt)	24

P. J. Martin, G. Keedy and S. I. Mahmood did not bat.

Bonus points – Lancashire 5, Leicestershire 2.

Bowling: *First Innings*—DeFreitas 31–9–73–0; Dagnall 28–8–81–1; Masters 17–3–68–1; Brignull 21.4–3–113–2; Maddy 15–1–84–2; Sehwag 1–0–1–0; Snape 11–1–48–0; Hodge 2–0–10–0; Stevens 1–0–15–0. *Second Innings*—Sehwag 4.2–0–10–0; Snape 4–0–11–0.

Leicestershire

J. K. Maunders c Flintoff b Mahmood	16	– (2) c Hegg b Hooper	39
V. Sehwag c Hooper b Chapple	30	– (4) run out	5
D. L. Maddy c Law b Keedy	85	– st Hegg b Hooper	48
B. J. Hodge lbw b Martin	26	– (5) lbw b Hooper	14
D. D. Masters c Sutcliffe b Martin	0	– (6) c Loye b Hooper	0
D. I. Stevens c Law b Chapple	65	– (7) c Law b Keedy	6
J. N. Snape b Keedy	31	– (8) c Sutcliffe b Keedy	26
†P. A. Nixon c Hegg b Chapple	0	– (1) b Keedy	32
*P. A. J. DeFreitas c Chilton b Mahmood	16	– c Martin b Keedy	9
D. S. Brignull c Chapple b Keedy	5	– b Hooper	6
C. E. Dagnall not out	5	– not out	0
B 4, l-b 5, w 5, n-b 21	35	B 10, l-b 5, n-b 12	27
1/41 (1) 2/59 (2) 3/105 (4) 4/116 (5) 5/238 (3) 6/246 (6) 7/246 (8) 8/294 (9) 9/303 (7) 10/314 (10)	314	1/81 (1) 2/83 (2) 3/99 (4) 4/126 (5) 5/130 (6) 6/147 (7) 7/191 (3) 8/199 (8) 9/208 (9) 10/212 (10)	212

Bonus points – Leicestershire 3, Lancashire 3.

Bowling: *First Innings*—Martin 20–2–71–2; Chapple 21–4–66–3; Mahmood 19–3–91–2; Keedy 24.4–12–43–3; Hooper 9–1–34–0. *Second Innings*—Chapple 12–1–57–0; Mahmood 4–1–21–0; Hooper 26.4–7–52–5; Martin 1–0–6–0; Keedy 29–7–61–4.

Umpires: P. J. Hartley and V. A. Holder.

At Chelmsford, July 2, 3, 4, 5. LANCASHIRE drew with ESSEX.

At Blackpool, July 13. LANCASHIRE lost to INDIA A by one wicket (see India A tour section).

LANCASHIRE v KENT

At Blackpool, July 15, 16, 17, 18. Drawn. Lancashire 9 pts, Kent 12 pts. Toss: Kent.

Lancashire bemoaned England's decision to insist that Flintoff and Anderson should be rested. While Flintoff commentated on TV and Anderson batted in a charity game, Kent stroked their way to 602, a Stanley Park record, in stifling heat. Smith, whose maiden double-century was his fourth hundred in five Championship innings, became the first batsman to 1,000 first-class runs, hitting a six and 35 fours in 257 balls and 307 minutes. "Form is capricious," he said. "You have to cash in." On a benign pitch with a fast outfield, Walker and Ealham cashed in too. Chilton responded with his fourth century of 2003 – doubling his first-class total. On a lively final morning, Lancashire lost their last three for 18 and, following on, their first three for 12, against Saggers. Then Hooper, a Kent player in the 1990s, produced arguably the game's best innings, a blend of staunch defence and occasional aggression lasting nearly five hours but including four sixes. A frustrated Fulton finally called it a day, and said: "It was a pleasure to play with him but today it was a pain in the arse to play against him."

Close of play: First day, Kent 384-4 (Walker 92, Ealham 18); Second day, Lancashire 130-2 (Chilton 52, Hooper 52); Third day, Lancashire 347-7 (Hegg 5, Martin 8).

Kent

*D. P. Fulton c Swann b Hooper	47	J. C. Tredwell not out	3
R. W. T. Key c Hegg b Martin	1		
E. T. Smith b Hooper	203	B 1, l-b 13, w 5, n-b 8	27
A. Symonds c Hegg b Chapple	10		
M. J. Walker c Chapple b Hooper	150	1/5 (2) 2/127 (1) (6 wkts dec.)	602
M. A. Ealham c Schofield b Loye	95	3/150 (4) 4/346 (3)	
†G. O. Jones not out	66	5/488 (5) 6/586 (6)	

R. S. Ferley, M. J. Saggers and A. Sheriyar did not bat.

Bonus points – Kent 5, Lancashire 1 (130 overs: 458-4).

Bowling: Martin 26–4–82–1; Chapple 27–8–64–1; Wood 21–1–101–0; Hooper 51–10–147–3; Mahmood 11–1–53–0; Schofield 15–1–86–0; Chilton 13–2–36–0; Swann 3–0–11–0; Loye 2–0–8–1.

Lancashire

M. J. Chilton c Key b Tredwell	114	– c Jones b Saggers	2
A. J. Swann lbw b Ferley	2	– c Jones b Saggers	1
M. B. Loye c Key b Ferley	13	– lbw b Ealham	33
C. L. Hooper c Smith b Saggers	60	– (5) not out	128
S. G. Law b Tredwell	29	– (4) lbw b Saggers	0
C. P. Schofield b Saggers	66	– c Smith b Symonds	40
G. Chapple c Jones b Sheriyar	33	– c Jones b Tredwell	9
*†W. K. Hegg not out	10	– not out	16
P. J. Martin lbw b Sheriyar	18		
J. Wood lbw b Saggers	0		
S. I. Mahmood hit wkt b Sheriyar	2		
B 8, l-b 10	18	B 4, l-b 7, n-b 4	15
1/6 (2) 2/30 (3) 3/143 (4) 4/203 (5) 5/256 (1) 6/330 (7) 7/334 (6) 8/361 (9) 9/362 (10) 10/365 (11)	365	1/3 (2) 2/4 (1) 3/12 (4) 4/55 (3) 5/127 (6) 6/163 (7) (6 wkts)	244

Bonus points – Lancashire 4, Kent 3.

Bowling: *First Innings*—Saggers 20–1–93–3; Sheriyar 19–6–63–3; Ferley 14–4–51–2; Ealham 14–4–46–0; Symonds 13–3–30–0; Tredwell 25–8–64–2. *Second Innings*—Saggers 12–3–31–3; Sheriyar 13–2–35–0; Ealham 12–4–31–1; Ferley 16–7–30–0; Tredwell 18–4–64–1; Symonds 13–4–42–1.

Umpires: M. J. Harris and N. A. Mallender.

LANCASHIRE v WARWICKSHIRE

At Manchester, July 23, 24, 25, 26. Drawn. Lancashire 12 pts, Warwickshire 7.75 pts (after 0.25 pt penalty). Toss: Lancashire.

Yet again a full day was lost to rain, depriving Lancashire of a likely win. A magnificent double-century from Law and an explosive all-round display from Chapple ultimately counted for little, though Chapple was named in the Nottingham Test squad a fortnight later. Law's first hundred came off 137 balls, as he and Hooper batted in deteriorating light on the first evening to win control. Next day, he advanced to 236 in 292 balls and a minute over eight hours, with 32 fours and two sixes – but was outshone by Chapple's second century of the season, underlining the faith Lancashire had shown in moving him up the order. Together they added 228 in three hours: at one point Chapple battered 20 runs off four balls from Smith. After lunch, Chapple's hostile bowling had Warwickshire eight down and still 396 behind. But rain and more determined batting allowed them to escape comfortably enough.

Close of play: First day, Lancashire 384-5 (Law 150, Chapple 37); Second day, Warwickshire 192-8 (Brown 31, Waqar Younis 8); Third day, No play.

Lancashire

A. J. Swann c Brown b Carter	15
I. J. Sutcliffe b Brown	86
M. B. Loye lbw b Brown	14
S. G. Law not out	236
M. J. Chilton c Frost b Waqar Younis	30
C. L. Hooper c Brown b Carter	35
G. Chapple b Smith	132
*†W. K. Hegg not out	7
B 8, l-b 6, w 6	20
1/37 (1) 2/85 (3) 3/134 (2) 4/212 (5) 5/314 (6) 6/542 (7)	(6 wkts dec.) 575

P. J. Martin, J. Wood and G. Keedy did not bat.

Bonus points – Lancashire 5, Warwickshire 2.

Bowling: Waqar Younis 24–5–79–1; Carter 24–1–133–2; Richardson 29–3–112–0; Brown 30–7–117–2; Smith 15–0–97–1; Bell 7–0–23–0.

Warwickshire

*M. J. Powell b Martin	28	– b Chapple	21
N. V. Knight c Hegg b Wood	27	– b Wood	56
M. A. Wagh c Swann b Chapple	1	– not out	76
I. R. Bell c Hegg b Chapple	48	– c Law b Martin	28
J. O. Troughton c Hegg b Hooper	16	– c Swann b Martin	4
†T. Frost c Hegg b Chapple	7	– not out	3
D. R. Brown not out	52		
N. M. K. Smith c Hegg b Hooper	10		
N. M. Carter c Law b Chapple	4		
Waqar Younis c Wood b Keedy	22		
A. Richardson c Swann b Wood	4		
B 4, l-b 8, w 5, n-b 19	36	B 6, l-b 1, n-b 16	23
1/34 (2) 2/35 (3) 3/65 (1) 4/98 (5) 5/134 (6) 6/137 (4) 7/163 (8) 8/179 (9) 9/251 (10) 10/255 (11)	255	1/76 (1) 2/91 (2) 3/163 (4) 4/183 (5)	(4 wkts) 211

Bonus points – Warwickshire 2, Lancashire 3.

Bowling: *First Innings*—Martin 17–1–55–1; Chapple 21–4–82–4; Wood 8–1–33–2; Keedy 22–12–31–1; Hooper 13–3–42–2. *Second Innings*—Martin 18.4–5–57–2; Wood 9–1–26–1; Keedy 24–3–74–0; Chapple 9–1–34–1; Hooper 12–4–13–0.

Umpires: N. G. Cowley and G. Sharp.

At Leicester, July 30, 31, August 1, 2. LANCASHIRE beat LEICESTERSHIRE by seven wickets.

At Hove, August 14, 15, 16, 17. LANCASHIRE lost to SUSSEX by 252 runs.

LANCASHIRE v MIDDLESEX

At Manchester, August 21, 22, 23, 24. Drawn. Lancashire 10 pts, Middlesex 10 pts. Toss: Lancashire.

This game epitomised Lancashire's Year of the Bat. But it ended in their eighth draw and a frowning footnote from their manager, Mike Watkinson, who said: "If ever we needed a pitch to help us it was this one." He got a close look on the last day, standing in at square leg until a reserve official arrived, after umpire Hartley broke his wrist: Watkinson immediately rejected an over-exuberant stumping appeal from his players. Lancashire's total of 734 for five declared was (briefly) their third-highest ever, their best on home soil, and the highest conceded by Middlesex. Not since 1904 had Lancashire boasted four centurions in the same innings, though the same quartet – Chilton, Loye, Law and Hooper – repeated the feat a fortnight later. Law and Hooper both scored more than 100 runs in the morning session on the second day. Hooper became only the second batsman, after Mark Ramprakash in June, to claim hundreds against all 18 first-class

HIGHEST FIRST-INNINGS TOTALS BY TEAMS WHO FOLLOWED ON

544	**Middlesex v Lancashire (734-5 dec.) at Manchester (drawn)**	**2003**
468	Victoria v New South Wales (815) at Sydney (lost by six wickets)	1908-09
465	Middlesex v Durham (645-6 dec.) at Lord's (drawn)	2002
454	India v West Indies (631) at Delhi (drawn)	1948-49
452	Derbyshire v Nottinghamshire (661) at Derby (drawn)	1901
447	**Leicestershire v Middlesex (620-7 dec.) at Southgate (lost by eight wickets)**	**2003**
442	Sussex v Gloucestershire (608-7 dec.) at Cheltenham (lost by seven wickets)	1934
432	**Matabeleland v Manicaland (650-8 dec.) at Bulawayo (lost by three wickets)**	**2002-03**
432	England v Australia (641-4 dec.) at The Oval (lost by an innings and 25 runs)	2001
430	Essex v Northamptonshire (633-6 dec.) at Northampton (lost by ten wickets)	2001

This does not include cases where the follow-on was available but not enforced.

Research: Philip Bailey

---

counties; in all, he scored 201 in 193 balls and 284 minutes, and hit 15 fours and 11 sixes, pulling one on to the players' balcony. Middlesex were almost as voracious, with Strauss batting flawlessly during the game's third double-century stand, and reached their highest total against Lancashire, becoming the first team in history to follow on after passing 500. On the last day, they lost their seventh second-innings wicket when just eight runs ahead, with 40 minutes left, but safely batted out time.

Close of play: First day, Lancashire 363-3 (Law 41, Hooper 26); Second day, Middlesex 156-1 (Strauss 99, Shah 34); Third day, Middlesex 484-6 (Hutton 91, Nash 7).

Lancashire

M. J. Chilton b Abdul Razzaq	125
I. J. Sutcliffe c Hutton b Dawes	4
M. B. Loye c Nash b Abdul Razzaq	137
S. G. Law run out	144
C. L. Hooper c Joyce b Keegan	201
C. P. Schofield not out	58
G. Chapple not out	21
B 8, l-b 13, w 1, n-b 22	44
1/24 (2) 2/283 (1) 3/304 (3) 4/586 (4) 5/699 (5)	(5 wkts dec.) 734

*†W. K. Hegg, P. J. Martin, J. Wood and G. Keedy did not bat.

Bonus points – Lancashire 5, Middlesex 1 (130 overs: 509-3)

Bowling: Dawes 30–5–125–1; Keegan 34–6–124–1; Abdul Razzaq 29–1–170–2; Dalrymple 24–3–96–0; Hutton 1–1–0–0; Weekes 33–5–145–0; Joyce 11–1–53–0.

Middlesex

*A. J. Strauss c Keedy b Martin	155	– c Schofield b Hooper	63
S. G. Koenig c Sutcliffe b Schofield	13	– (9) not out	16
O. A. Shah b Keedy	147	– lbw b Martin	15
B. L. Hutton c sub b Keedy	107	– (2) c Chilton b Keedy	10
E. C. Joyce b Hooper	3	– (4) c sub b Hooper	41
Abdul Razzaq c Martin b Keedy	22	– c Hegg b Hooper	25
P. N. Weekes c Hegg b Martin	24	– not out	26
†D. C. Nash c Hooper b Chapple	15	– (5) c and b Hooper	23
J. W. M. Dalrymple b Keedy	17	– (8) c sub b Keedy	0
C. B. Keegan b Keedy	18		
J. H. Dawes not out	0		
B 4, l-b 9, n-b 10	23	B 7, l-b 7, n-b 4	18
1/59 (2) 2/294 (1) 3/338 (3) 4/343 (5) 5/374 (6) 6/450 (7) 7/508 (4) 8/508 (8) 9/543 (10) 10/544 (9)	544	1/29 (2) 2/61 (3) 3/107 (1) 4/157 (5) 5/176 (4) 6/197 (6) 7/198 (8)	(7 wkts) 237

Bonus points – Middlesex 5, Lancashire 1 (130 overs: 441-5)

Bowling: *First Innings*—Martin 17–6–44–2; Chapple 19–0–71–1; Keedy 52–10–188–5; Schofield 34–5–120–1; Hooper 26–9–53–1; Wood 13–1–43–0; Law 3–0–12–0. *Second Innings*—Martin 9–3–17–1; Wood 4–0–21–0; Keedy 29–8–76–2; Chapple 6–1–18–0; Hooper 18–3–51–4; Schofield 11–2–34–0; Law 1–0–6–0.

Umpires: P. J. Hartley and G. Sharp.
(M. Watkinson and M. Dixon deputised for Hartley on the fourth day.)

LANCASHIRE v SURREY

At Manchester, August 26, 27, 28, 29. Lancashire won by eight wickets. Lancashire 20 pts, Surrey 6 pts. Toss: Surrey. Championship debut: M. R. Currie.

Surrey's hold on the title was considerably loosened by their first defeat of the season. They won the toss, were bolstered by a fine 154 from Batty – the first Surrey player to carry his bat against Lancashire since Tom Hayward in 1907 – and later benefited from a brave decision by umpire Leadbeater, who recalled Brown after giving him out on three, when he realised the ball had been caught off his helmet. But by then Hooper had wrested the initiative in a remarkable stand with Keedy. Hooper was 49 and Lancashire 75 behind when the ninth wicket fell, but he audaciously farmed the bowling to reach 114; Keedy contributed a single as they added 79 in 83 minutes. With their captain, Hollioake, off the field feeling unwell, Surrey looked rudderless. Keedy was a key figure again on the next, rain-shortened, day, claiming four for four in 12 balls, which gave him 14 in four innings – a sharp contrast with Saqlain Mushtaq, wicketless for the same stretch. Lancashire needed only 135 on the last day, and won just after lunch. Although Surrey regained top place (Sussex had skipped a round), they left looking anything but champion.

Close of play: First day, Surrey 330-9 (Batty 152); Second day, Lancashire 341; Third day, Surrey 137-8 (Saqlain Mushtaq 11, Ormond 6).

Surrey

I. J. Ward c Hegg b Martin	10	– c Chilton b Martin	3
†J. N. Batty not out	154	– c Law b Martin	0
G. P. Thorpe lbw b Chapple	57	– c Hegg b Wood	38
R. Clarke st Hegg b Keedy	11	– lbw b Chapple	1
A. D. Brown c Sutcliffe b Keedy	1	– b Keedy	61
*A. J. Hollioake b Martin	0	– (7) c Law b Keedy	8
Azhar Mahmood c Hegg b Keedy	63	– (6) c Martin b Keedy	8
I. D. K. Salisbury c Currie b Schofield	5	– c Hegg b Keedy	0
Saqlain Mushtaq c Hegg b Wood	11	– c Keedy b Martin	11
J. Ormond b Wood	0	– run out	7
T. J. Murtagh b Martin	5	– not out	0
B 8, l-b 6, n-b 6	20	L-b 1	1
1/10 (1) 2/114 (3) 3/143 (4) 4/147 (5) 5/148 (6) 6/261 (7) 7/298 (8) 8/329 (9) 9/330 (10) 10/337 (11)	337	1/1 (2) 2/10 (1) 3/23 (4) 4/93 (3) 5/108 (6) 6/119 (7) 7/119 (8) 8/122 (5) 9/137 (9) 10/138 (10)	138

Bonus points – Surrey 3, Lancashire 3.

Bowling: *First Innings*—Martin 14.4–2–54–3; Chapple 21–4–87–1; Hooper 18–6–38–0; Wood 15–4–64–2; Keedy 24–9–62–3; Schofield 10–2–18–1. *Second Innings*—Martin 12–5–20–3; Chapple 7–1–24–1; Keedy 14.1–1–57–4; Wood 7–0–29–1; Hooper 3–0–7–0.

Lancashire

M. J. Chilton b Murtagh	27	– not out	33
I. J. Sutcliffe c Hollioake b Azhar Mahmood	8	– c Batty b Azhar Mahmood	47
M. R. Currie c Azhar Mahmood b Ormond	56	– c and b Salisbury	13
S. G. Law c Brown b Salisbury	67	– not out	35
C. L. Hooper c Salisbury b Azhar Mahmood	114		
C. P. Schofield lbw b Salisbury	0		
G. Chapple c Azhar Mahmood b Ormond	1		
*†W. K. Hegg c Ormond b Azhar Mahmood	19		
P. J. Martin c Clarke b Azhar Mahmood	8		
J. Wood b Salisbury	6		
G. Keedy not out	1		
B 8, l-b 7, w 3, n-b 16	34	B 2, l-b 1, n-b 4	7
1/18 (2) 2/60 (1) 3/169 (4) 4/175 (3) 5/178 (6) 6/183 (7) 7/221 (8) 8/251 (9) 9/262 (10) 10/341 (5)	341	1/69 (2) 2/92 (3)	(2 wkts) 135

Bonus points – Lancashire 3, Surrey 3.

Bowling: *First Innings*—Ormond 20–3–70–2; Azhar Mahmood 24.2–3–76–4; Murtagh 5–1–26–1; Saqlain Mushtaq 20–2–58–0; Clarke 6–0–26–0; Salisbury 19–2–70–3. *Second Innings*—Ormond 5–1–25–0; Azhar Mahmood 7–1–28–1; Saqlain Mushtaq 13–3–49–0; Salisbury 5–0–19–1; Brown 0.4–0–11–0.

Umpires: A. Clarkson and B. Leadbeater.

At Birmingham, September 3, 4, 5, 6. LANCASHIRE beat WARWICKSHIRE by an innings and 145 runs.

LANCASHIRE v SUSSEX

At Manchester, September 10, 11, 12, 13. Lancashire won by an innings and 19 runs. Lancashire 22 pts, Sussex 4 pts. Toss: Lancashire.

Sussex arrived at Old Trafford hoping to clinch the Championship against the one side who could realistically stop them. Instead, they lost by an innings, and left still needing six points for the title. Lancashire also had the better of the personal duel between Law, the country's leading run-scorer, and Mushtaq Ahmed, the top wicket-taker bidding for his 100th victim. Law scored just four singles in an hour at the height of their battle – but still completed his seventh century of the season, while Mushtaq remained stranded on 99 wickets. It was a compelling match, despite two washed-out half-days. Law and Loye, who scored his third consecutive first-class hundred, added 241 to put Sussex on the back foot – dropping a bowling point for the first time in 2003. Then Wood smashed a hole in their defences, grabbing three for two in nine balls. Goodwin was felled by a bouncer from Martin on 87, but continued after on-field treatment and carried his bat before having seven stitches over his eye, and Mushtaq scored an entertaining fifty. But they followed on and the last word fell to Keedy, who collected ten wickets where Mushtaq found none. "I think we concentrated too much on getting points rather than playing our normal game," said Adams. "We gave them a good hiding," said Keedy.

Close of play: First day, Lancashire 225-2 (Loye 110, Law 65); Second day, Lancashire 368-5 (Law 131); Third day, Sussex 21-2 (Adams 19, Cottey 0).

Lancashire

M. J. Chilton c Ambrose b Taylor 6
I. J. Sutcliffe c Davis b Lewry 38
M. B. Loye c Montgomerie b Martin-Jenkins . 144
S. G. Law not out 163
C. L. Hooper lbw b Lewry 33
C. P. Schofield b Taylor 1
G. Chapple b Lewry 14
*†W. K. Hegg not out 26
B 4, l-b 12, w 1, n-b 8 25

1/21 (1) 2/66 (2) 3/307 (3) 4/363 (5) 5/368 (6) 6/414 (7) (6 wkts dec.) 450

P. J. Martin, J. Wood and G. Keedy did not bat.

Bonus points – Lancashire 5, Sussex 2.

Bowling: Lewry 26.3–3–125–3; Taylor 35–8–114–2; Martin-Jenkins 23–7–73–1; Mushtaq Ahmed 37–6–99–0; Davis 5–1–23–0.

Sussex

M. W. Goodwin not out . . . . 118 – (6) lbw b Keedy 57
R. R. Montgomerie lbw b Keedy . . . . 10 – (1) lbw b Martin 2
P. A. Cottey c Chapple b Wood . . . . 40 – (4) c sub b Keedy 32
*C. J. Adams c Chapple b Wood . . . . 1 – (2) c Law b Wood 35
†T. R. Ambrose b Wood . . . . 0 – c Sutcliffe b Wood 2
R. S. C. Martin-Jenkins c Hegg b Keedy . . . . . 2 – (7) b Martin 6
M. J. Prior c Law b Keedy . . . . 2 – (8) c Schofield b Keedy 10
M. J. G. Davis c Law b Keedy . . . . 2 – (9) c Sutcliffe b Keedy 11
Mushtaq Ahmed c Chilton b Hooper . . . . 54 – (10) c and b Schofield 16
J. D. Lewry b Hooper . . . . 2 – (11) not out 7
B. V. Taylor c Schofield b Keedy . . . . 0 – (3) lbw b Keedy 0
B 9, l-b 3, n-b 8 . . . . 20 L-b 2 2

1/28 (2) 2/122 (3) 3/126 (4) 4/126 (5) 5/143 (6) 6/147 (7) 7/157 (8) 8/238 (9) 9/240 (10) 10/251 (11) 251

1/20 (1) 2/21 (3) 3/61 (2) 4/67 (5) 5/73 (4) 6/96 (7) 7/125 (8) 8/146 (6) 9/164 (10) 10/180 (9) 180

Bonus points – Sussex 2, Lancashire 3.

Bowling: *First Innings*—Martin 15–4–40–0; Chapple 15–2–54–0; Keedy 28–5–106–5; Wood 9–3–17–3; Hooper 5–0–17–2; Schofield 1–0–5–0. *Second Innings*—Martin 20–7–43–2; Wood 14–4–27–2; Keedy 32–6–61–5; Hooper 17–3–33–0; Schofield 4–0–14–1.

Umpires: J. W. Lloyds and A. G. T. Whitehead.

At Nottingham, September 17, 18, 19, 20. LANCASHIRE lost to NOTTINGHAMSHIRE by 233 runs.

COUNTY BENEFITS AWARDED FOR 2004

Durham	J. J. B. Lewis.
Essex	Essex Academy.
Glamorgan	Glamorgan CCC.
Hampshire	Hampshire Youth Trust.
Kent	M. M. Patel.
Lancashire	G. Chapple.
Leicestershire	P. A. J. DeFreitas.
Nottinghamshire	P. Johnson (Testimonial).
Somerset	K. A. Parsons.
Surrey	A. J. Hollioake.
Sussex	K. Greenfield (Testimonial).
Warwickshire	N. V. Knight.
Worcestershire	T. M. Moody.
Yorkshire	C. E. W. Silverwood.

LEICESTERSHIRE

The year of disarray

NEVILLE FOULGER

After a winter of discontent and departures, it was a summer of disillusion and disarray for Leicestershire. Relegated from the top flight for the first time in both County Championship and National League, they were bombarded from all directions.

In a hot, dry summer, Leicestershire managed to lose well over 1,000 overs to the weather. The gamble of going for two overseas batsmen, rather than at least one front-line bowler, soon blew up in their faces when 40-year-old Devon Malcolm suffered a knee injury that required surgery, and bowled only 62 Championship overs, for six wickets, before retiring. No one looked likely to come through and replace him. Then, to rub salt into the wounds, Virender Sehwag, the brilliant young Indian opening batsman signed along with Australian Brad Hodge, left in July with a recurring back problem.

The only brief respite during this most miserable of seasons came in the new Twenty20 Cup. Leicestershire won all five group games, playing to full houses in their three matches at Grace Road. But at Trent Bridge on finals day, they failed to produce, losing the first semi to Warwickshire. By the end of the season, it hardly required 20-20 vision to see Leicestershire had major problems to address if they were to have any hope of recapturing the glory days of the late 1990s, when they won the Championship twice.

One step they took to tackle the discord was converting to Industrial and Provident Society status and electing a six-man board, rather than a 13-man committee, to run the club from October 2003. The board created a novel set-up more akin to football than a cricket club. The new chairman, Neil Davidson, announced that former captain and general manager James Whitaker was returning as director of cricket after a year away, with Zimbabwean Gus Mackay promoted to operations manager. But there was no chief executive: Kevin Hill, one of the chief proponents of the reforms, departed after only a year in the job. This suggested Davidson himself would wield a good deal of power.

"The board has been elected to make a difference," Davidson said, "and we see these appointments as important building blocks. Whitaker's loyalties lie firmly with Leicestershire and his track record as captain demonstrates he has the credentials to get the best out of players and put the club back where it belongs, in the first division of both competitions."

Inevitably, the previous winter's contentious departures of Neil Burns and Carl Crowe (not offered contracts), Vince Wells (sacked as captain) and Iain Sutcliffe (who decided to join Lancashire) had their impact. Burns and Crowe took their complaints to an industrial tribunal; the issue dragged on throughout the summer and was settled out of court in September. This was widely interpreted as an effective victory for the players and an embarrassing climbdown for the county, whose internal procedures were exposed as inadequate, and dubious under modern employment law.

Phil DeFreitas

The case cast a cloud over the summer. One had to feel sorry for Phil DeFreitas, still a class act at 37. Not only did he captain the team; much of the time, he carried them on his shoulders. Without Malcolm, DeFreitas was too often a one-man attack. His haul of 58 Championship wickets at 24.15 spoke volumes for his ability and stamina. Nobody else came close. Darren Maddy took 36 wickets, David Masters, signed from Kent, 34. With Jeremy Snape under-used in the four-day game – in 15 appearances, he bowled only 158 overs for ten wickets – Leicestershire struggled to bowl sides out twice. They had to wait until the last home fixture for their only Championship win, when they crushed Kent by ten wickets in seamer-friendly conditions. It typified Leicestershire's inconsistency and inability to produce under pressure that, two days later, Kent routed them for 98 in the National League when a win would have kept them in the first division.

There were a few encouraging signs that things could improve. After a slow start, Hodge blossomed into a batsman of genuine quality in both forms of the game. In the Championship, he scored nearly 1,300 runs with four centuries, including a county-record 302 not out at Trent Bridge. He was the club's highest run-scorer in the National League and the nation's highest in the Twenty20 Cup, where he scored three fifties. Hodge agreed a new contract for 2004.

Maddy, now a genuine all-rounder, was second-highest scorer in the Championship with 881 and, like Hodge, helped himself to a double-century against Loughborough to boost his first-class runs above 1,000. John Maunders and John Sadler, both young left-handers, emerged in the later stages. Maunders established himself as an opener, scoring 171 against Surrey and 129 against Kent, and Sadler also made two centuries in his last five innings.

If the county were to claw their way back, they had much work to do. DeFreitas, awarded a benefit after all his wanderings, was to continue as captain and hoped for a much better summer, with more players contributing. That was the very least the county's disgruntled supporters had a right to expect.

LEICESTERSHIRE RESULTS

All first-class matches – Played 17: Won 2, Lost 6, Drawn 9.
County Championship matches – Played 16: Won 1, Lost 6, Drawn 9.

Frizzell County Championship, 9th in Division 1; Cheltenham & Gloucester Trophy, q-f; National Cricket League, 7th in Division 1; Twenty20 Cup, s-f.

COUNTY CHAMPIONSHIP AVERAGES

BATTING AND FIELDING

Cap		*M*	*I*	*NO*	*R*	*HS*	*100s*	*50s*	*Avge*	*Ct/St*
2003	B. J. Hodge§	15	25	1	1,293	302*	4	3	53.87	10
2003	V. Sehwag§	6	10	0	478	137	2	1	47.80	4
	J. L. Sadler	6	10	1	410	145	2	1	45.55	5
	J. K. Maunders	12	22	2	777	171	2	3	38.85	3
1996	D. L. Maddy	16	28	2	881	98	0	6	33.88	14
2002	D. I. Stevens	11	19	0	615	149	1	6	32.36	12
1994	P. A. Nixon	16	27	4	676	113*	1	3	29.39	46/2
2001	T. R. Ward	8	14	0	409	168	1	1	29.21	4
	J. N. Snape	15	23	6	494	54	0	2	29.05	8
1986	P. A. J. DeFreitas	15	25	2	493	103	1	2	21.43	6
	D. G. Brandy	5	9	2	148	52	0	1	21.14	1
	C. E. Dagnall	10	11	5	103	23*	0	0	17.16	0
	D. S. Brignull	3	4	0	58	46	0	0	14.50	0
	D. D. Masters	16	23	3	269	119	1	0	13.45	4
	V. C. Drakes§	5	7	1	57	18	0	0	9.50	1
	M. J. A. Whiley	5	6	2	29	16	0	0	7.25	1
2001	D. E. Malcolm	3	4	0	27	14	0	0	6.75	0
	R. M. Amin	5	7	2	30	11	0	0	6.00	0

Also batted: R. J. Cunliffe (1 match) 0; G. W. Walker (2 matches) 4*, 21 (1 ct); L. J. Wright (1 match) 0, 11*.

§ *Overseas player.*

BOWLING

	O	*M*	*R*	*W*	*BB*	*5W/i*	*Avge*
P. A. J. DeFreitas	528.3	151	1,401	58	7-51	4	24.15
D. L. Maddy	297.1	59	1,002	36	5-49	1	27.83
C. E. Dagnall	295.5	70	1,005	28	5-66	1	35.89
V. C. Drakes	143.1	33	463	11	3-58	0	42.09
D. D. Masters	399.5	78	1,476	34	5-53	1	43.41
J. N. Snape	157.3	21	622	10	3-108	0	62.20

Also bowled: R. M. Amin 146.1–24–601–8; D. G. Brandy 7–1–47–0; D. S. Brignull 68.4–14–235–7; B. J. Hodge 49–5–239–4; D. E. Malcolm 62–15–230–6; J. K. Maunders 9–1–38–0; J. L. Sadler 0.5–0–20–0; V. Sehwag 34.2–4–153–0; D. I. Stevens 23–5–71–1; G. W. Walker 29–3–111–1; M. J. A. Whiley 117.3–14–562–7; L. J. Wright 19–0–95–0.

COUNTY RECORDS

Highest score for:	302*	B. J. Hodge v Nottinghamshire at Nottingham	2003
Highest score against:	341	G. H. Hirst (Yorkshire) at Leicester	1905
Best bowling for:	10-18	G. Geary v Glamorgan at Pontypridd	1929
Best bowling against:	10-32	H. Pickett (Essex) at Leyton	1895
Highest total for:	701-4 dec.	v Worcestershire at Worcester	1906
Highest total against:	761-6 dec.	by Essex at Chelmsford	1990
Lowest total for:	25	v Kent at Leicester	1912
Lowest total against:	24	by Glamorgan at Leicester	1971
	24	by Oxford University at Oxford	1985

LEICESTERSHIRE DIRECTORY

ADDRESS

County Ground, Grace Road, Leicester LE2 8AD (0116 283 2128; fax 0116 244 0363; email enquiries@leicestershireccc.co.uk). **Website** www.leicestershireccc.co.uk.

GROUNDS

Leicester (Grace Road): 2 miles S of city centre close to A426. From Aylestone Road, turn L into Park Hill Drive or Duncan Road and then first L into Curzon Road. Nearest station: Leicester (2 miles).

Oakham: ¼ mile from town centre. From town, turn L into B668 Station Road then L into Kilburn Road for Oakham School entrance in Station Road. Nearest station: Oakham (¼ mile).

OFFICIALS

Captain P. A. J. DeFreitas
Head coach P. Whitticase
Chairman R. C. N. Davidson
Director of Cricket J. J. Whitaker
Operations manager A. J. Mackay
Head groundsmen A. Ward and A. Whiteman
Scorer G. A. York

PLAYERS

Players expected to reappear in 2004

	Former counties	*Country*	*Born*	*Birthplace*
Brandy Damian Gareth		E	14.9.1981	*Highgate*
Brignull David Stephen		E	27.11.1981	*Forest Gate*
Dagnall Charles Edward	Warwicks	E	10.7.1976	*Bury*
***DeFreitas** Phillip Anthony Jason	Leics, Lancs, Derbys	E	18.2.1966	*Scotts Head, Dominica*
Hodge Bradley John	Durham	A	29.12.1974	*Sandringham*
***Maddy** Darren Lee		E	23.5.1974	†*Leicester*
Masters David Daniel	Kent	E	22.4.1978	*Chatham*
Maunders John Kenneth	Middx	E	4.4.1981	*Ashford, Middlesex*
New Thomas James		E	18.1.1985	*Sutton-in-Ashfield*
Nixon Paul Andrew	Leics, Kent	E	21.10.1970	*Carlisle*
Sadler John Leonard	Yorks	E	19.11.1981	*Dewsbury*
Snape Jeremy Nicholas	Northants, Glos	E	27.4.1973	*Stoke-on-Trent*
Stevens Darren Ian		E	30.4.1976	†*Leicester*
Walker George William		E	12.5.1984	*Norwich*

Players due to join in 2004

Dakin Jonathan Michael	Leics, Essex	E	28.2.1973	*Hitchin*
Kruger Garnett John-Peter		SA	5.1.1977	*Port Elizabeth*
Robinson Darren David John	Essex	E	2.3.1973	*Braintree*

* *Test player.* † *Born in Leicestershire.*

At Canterbury, April 23, 24, 25, 26. LEICESTERSHIRE drew with KENT.

LEICESTERSHIRE v ESSEX

At Leicester, April 30, May 1, 2, 3. Drawn. Leicestershire 8 pts, Essex 7 pts. Toss: Essex.

Even with almost two days lost to the weather there might have been a positive outcome. Leicestershire were challenged to score 179 off 30 overs – perhaps easy enough in midsummer. But on a pitch of uneven bounce and untrustworthy pace they never came close, and with five wickets down for 94 runs were hanging on for the draw. It was a low-scoring match throughout with only Stephenson and Stevens getting to 50; the England captain Hussain perished for six and 26 as the seamers dominated. He felt perished in the field too, wearing a woolly hat to keep warm. Dakin, on his return against his former county, scored a valuable 33 and then dismantled Leicestershire's first innings with four wickets, while Dagnall claimed his first five-wicket haul for Leicestershire, with Hussain one of his victims, as Essex hurried to 191 for nine before declaring, in a bold if ultimately vain attempt to snatch victory.

Close of play: First day, Leicestershire 114-3 (Stevens 33, Nixon 7); Second day, Leicestershire 185-7 (DeFreitas 8); Third day, No play.

Essex

D. D. J. Robinson c Masters b Malcolm	4	– b Malcolm	7
W. I. Jefferson lbw b DeFreitas	32	– lbw b Dagnall	43
N. Hussain c Maddy b DeFreitas	6	– c Nixon b Dagnall	26
A. Flower lbw b Masters	14	– (5) c Maddy b Dagnall	20
A. Habib c Stevens b Dagnall	35	– (6) lbw b Masters	15
*A. P. Grayson lbw b Masters	0	– (8) not out	14
†J. S. Foster c Nixon b Masters	0	– (9) c Nixon b Malcolm	23
J. M. Dakin c Nixon b DeFreitas	33	– (7) c Ward b Dagnall	15
J. P. Stephenson c Ward b Maddy	50	– (10) lbw b Malcolm	1
G. R. Napier not out	0	– (4) lbw b Dagnall	19
S. A. Brant c Nixon b Maddy	0		
B 3, l-b 9, w 2	14	L-b 7, w 1	8
1/9 (1) 2/37 (3) 3/44 (2) 4/77 (4) 5/87 (6) 6/91 (5) 7/91 (7) 8/188 (8) 9/188 (9) 10/188 (11)	188	1/13 (1) 2/75 (2) 3/82 (3) 4/129 (4) 5/131 (6) 6/153 (7) 7/186 (9) 8/188 (10) 9/191 (5)	(9 wkts dec.) 191

Bonus points – Leicestershire 3.

In the second innings Flower, when 17, retired hurt at 100 and resumed at 188.

Bowling: *First Innings*—DeFreitas 18–8–34–3; Malcolm 10–3–39–1; Dagnall 16–4–49–1; Maddy 9.3–4–19–2; Masters 8–3–31–3; Stevens 1–0–4–0. *Second Innings*—DeFreitas 11–1–43–0; Malcolm 9–3–31–3; Dagnall 16.5–3–66–5; Snape 3–1–13–0; Masters 7–1–31–1.

> "James Anderson's nervous smile looked like that of an apprentice magician, delighted with the result but unsure exactly how he'd managed it."
>
> Zimbabweans in England, page 417.

Leicestershire

T. R. Ward c Foster b Stephenson	44	– c Flower b Dakin	1
D. L. Maddy b Dakin	16	– not out	39
B. J. Hodge lbw b Brant	5	– c Jefferson b Brant	19
D. I. Stevens c Habib b Dakin	65	– b Grayson	8
†P. A. Nixon lbw b Dakin	10	– c Jefferson b Dakin	17
D. G. Brandy b Stephenson	21	– (7) not out	6
J. N. Snape b Dakin	2		
*P. A. J. DeFreitas lbw b Brant	8	– (6) c Habib b Brant	5
D. D. Masters not out	8		
C. E. Dagnall lbw b Brant	0		
D. E. Malcolm c Jefferson b Brant	7		
L-b 13, w 2	15	B 4, l-b 5	9
1/34 (2) 2/39 (3) 3/105 (1) 4/124 (5) 5/158 (4) 6/165 (7) 7/185 (6) 8/185 (8) 9/185 (10) 10/201 (11)	201	1/1 (1) 2/34 (3) 3/57 (4) 4/87 (5) 5/94 (6)	(5 wkts) 104

Bonus points – Leicestershire 1, Essex 3.

Bowling: *First Innings*—Brant 22.1–7–54–4; Dakin 24–6–64–4; Stephenson 19–6–55–2; Napier 3–0–15–0. *Second Innings*—Brant 10–2–24–2; Dakin 6.1–1–16–2; Napier 6–0–30–0; Stephenson 1–0–10–0; Grayson 2–0–15–1.

Umpires: D. J. Constant and J. W. Holder.

LEICESTERSHIRE v LOUGHBOROUGH UCCE

At Leicester, May 9, 10, 11. Leicestershire won by an innings and 35 runs. Toss: Loughborough UCCE.

Loughborough, who had moved up to first-class status in April, suffered their first defeat, after draws with Somerset and Surrey. On a good pitch, their potentially strong line-up failed to come to terms with the extra pace of 40-year-old Malcolm, with only Sharif (born on Malcolm's 20th birthday) passing 30 first time round. Then their bowlers were put to the sword by Maddy and Hodge, who both hit double centuries in an unbroken stand of 436, the joint sixth-highest for the third wicket in all first-class cricket (see page 179). Maddy batted 318 minutes, hitting 38 fours and a six from 258 balls; Hodge contributed 34 fours in 290 balls and 310 minutes. The student batsmen did themselves more justice in their second innings, when Adams and Nash added 94, and Sharif scored another half-century, but they were beaten four overs into the last afternoon. Malcolm took eight wickets in the match, and Hodge claimed three with some useful off-spin.

Close of play: First day, Leicestershire 202-2 (Maddy 72, Hodge 67); Second day, Loughborough UCCE 184-4 (Nash 53, Sharif 4).

Loughborough UCCE

R. A. White c Hodge b Malcolm	20	– c Ward b Malcolm	24
*J. H. K. Adams b Grove	3	– c Maddy b Hodge	78
J. D. Francis lbw b Masters	7	– lbw b Malcolm	4
V. Atri b DeFreitas	14	– c Brandy b Snape	14
C. D. Nash b DeFreitas	30	– c Nixon b Masters	60
Z. K. Sharif c Nixon b Masters	64	– c Nixon b Brandy	67
R. E. King c Ward b Malcolm	1	– lbw b Malcolm	1
†L. J. Goddard c Nixon b Malcolm	0	– lbw b Hodge	17
P. D. Lewis lbw b Malcolm	2	– c Ward b Hodge	2
J. E. Anyon c Hodge b Malcolm	0	– c sub b Brandy	21
R. A. G. Cummins not out	2	– not out	0
L-b 2, w 1, n-b 8	11	B 2, l-b 6, w 3, n-b 9	20
1/15 (2) 2/31 (1) 3/44 (3) 4/77 (5) 5/92 (4) 6/104 (7) 7/110 (8) 8/114 (9) 9/130 (10) 10/154 (6)	154	1/44 (1) 2/48 (3) 3/85 (4) 4/179 (2) 5/198 (5) 6/201 (7) 7/240 (8) 8/244 (9) 9/303 (10) 10/308 (6)	308

Bowling: *First Innings*—Grove 8–2–21–1; Malcolm 16–6–40–5; DeFreitas 12–3–42–2; Masters 10.4–3–49–2. *Second Innings*—Grove 12–1–43–0; Malcolm 16–1–88–3; Masters 15–4–56–1; Snape 20–4–47–1; Hodge 19–7–35–3; Sadler 7–1–20–0; Brandy 1.3–0–11–2.

Leicestershire

T. R. Ward c Goddard b Lewis	34
J. L. Sadler b Lewis	24
D. L. Maddy not out	229
B. J. Hodge not out	202
L-b 6, w 2	8
1/52 (2) 2/61 (1) (2 wkts dec.)	497

D. G. Brandy, †P. A. Nixon, J. N. Snape, *P. A. J. DeFreitas, D. D. Masters, J. O. Grove and D. E. Malcolm did not bat.

Bowling: Anyon 21–2–104–0; King 14.3–3–85–0; Cummins 22–5–92–0; Lewis 21–2–96–2; Nash 13–3–66–0; Sharif 10–2–41–0; Adams 2–0–7–0.

Umpires: A. A. Jones and P. Willey.

At The Oval, May 14, 15, 16, 17. LEICESTERSHIRE drew with SURREY.

LEICESTERSHIRE v MIDDLESEX

At Leicester, May 21, 22, 23, 24. Drawn. Leicestershire 7 pts, Middlesex 8 pts. Toss: Leicestershire.

Leicestershire slipped to the bottom of the first division through their fourth soggy draw, although 13 wickets fell in 62 overs on the opening day. Dagnall injured his ankle in a warm-up, so Masters was summoned from Second Eleven duty at Trent Bridge – to take a wicket in his first over. It was damp and overcast, the ball swung and seamed prodigiously, and Middlesex should have been out for much less than 201. They were 93 for seven at lunch, after Maddy took four wickets in 15 balls, but were let off the hook, and the tail stole a batting point. Leicestershire's reply was virtually a mirror image. Keegan and Cook reduced them to 86 for six, but Snape, with the game's only fifty, and Brignull shared the biggest stand, 73 for the ninth wicket, so Leicestershire narrowly missed a point themselves. The weather continued to play havoc, however: more than two days were lost overall, and no result could be contrived.

Close of play: First day, Leicestershire 19-3 (Hodge 4, Stevens 4); Second day, Leicestershire 136-8 (Snape 28, Brignull 16); Third day, Leicestershire 167-8 (Snape 40, Brignull 29).

Middlesex

*A. J. Strauss c Snape b DeFreitas	28	– c DeFreitas b Brignull	25
S. G. Koenig lbw b Masters	18	– lbw b Maddy	18
O. A. Shah c Nixon b Masters	28	– c Nixon b DeFreitas	9
B. L. Hutton lbw b Maddy	3	– not out	41
E. C. Joyce lbw b Maddy	0	– c Masters b Stevens	23
P. N. Weekes lbw b Whiley	29	– lbw b Masters	6
†D. C. Nash c Stevens b Maddy	3	– not out	11
S. J. Cook c Sehwag b Maddy	2		
A. A. Noffke c Nixon b Masters	40		
C. B. Keegan lbw b Maddy	32		
Imran Tahir not out	1		
B 2, l-b 4, w 5, n-b 6	17	L-b 6, w 1, n-b 2	9
1/33 (1) 2/66 (2) 3/81 (3) 4/82 (5) 5/83 (4) 6/89 (7) 7/93 (8) 8/146 (6) 9/195 (9) 10/201 (10)	201	1/39 (1) 2/56 (3) 3/56 (2) 4/99 (5) 5/117 (6) (5 wkts dec.)	142

Bonus points – Middlesex 1, Leicestershire 3.

Bowling: *First Innings*—DeFreitas 14–4–37–1; Whiley 6–0–54–1; Brignull 11–3–22–0; Maddy 13.1–1–49–5; Masters 10–2–33–3. *Second Innings*—DeFreitas 16–7–35–1; Brignull 8–1–28–1; Maddy 10–2–29–1; Masters 6–1–12–1; Stevens 3–1–5–1; Whiley 6.5–2–27–0.

Leicestershire

V. Sehwag c Strauss b Keegan	10
R. J. Cunliffe c Nash b Noffke	0
D. L. Maddy c Nash b Keegan	0
B. J. Hodge b Keegan	22
D. I. Stevens c Weekes b Cook	29
†P. A. Nixon c Nash b Cook	17
J. N. Snape c Cook b Keegan	54
*P. A. J. DeFreitas lbw b Cook	9
D. D. Masters c Weekes b Cook	0
D. S. Brignull b Keegan	46
M. J. A. Whiley not out	0
L-b 6, w 1, n-b 4	11
1/1 (2) 2/2 (3) 3/15 (1) 4/63 (5) 5/71 (4) 6/86 (6) 7/112 (8) 8/112 (9) 9/185 (7) 10/198 (10)	198

Bonus points – Middlesex 3.

Bowling: Noffke 24–4–89–1; Keegan 18–4–61–5; Cook 18–4–42–4.

Umpires: A. Clarkson and J. H. Hampshire.

At Liverpool, June 4, 5, 6, 7. LEICESTERSHIRE lost to LANCASHIRE by ten wickets.

At Leicester, June 14. LEICESTERSHIRE lost to PAKISTANIS by five wickets (see Pakistani tour section).

LEICESTERSHIRE v NOTTINGHAMSHIRE

At Leicester, June 27, 28, 29, 30. Drawn. Leicestershire 8 pts, Nottinghamshire 10 pts. Toss: Nottinghamshire. County debut: R. M. Amin.

Yet again rain had the last word, but the gloom lifted a little thanks to some high-class performances. The highlight was a breathtaking century – his first for Leicestershire – from the Indian opener, Sehwag. He reached three figures in 104 balls between tea and the close on the second day. Sumptuous strokeplay brought him almost three-quarters of the runs scored while he was at the crease; Sehwag caressed the ball through the covers off front and back foot, square cut ferociously and flicked beautifully to the mid-wicket boundary. But his colleagues let him down; when he was third out, at 188, the rest went for 55 on a benign pitch. Earlier, Nottinghamshire wriggled free from 123 for five against some limp bowling. Franks led the rescue with a maiden century, adding 149 with Pietersen, who bludgeoned 88, which he followed with 95, off 89 balls, in the second innings. Gallian set a target of 402, but a last-day washout made it academic.

Close of play: First day, Nottinghamshire 90-3 (Warren 32, Pietersen 0); Second day, Leicestershire 159-2 (Sehwag 121, Hodge 6); Third day, Leicestershire 5-1 (Maunders 0).

Nottinghamshire

G. E. Welton b Masters	41	– (2) c Stevens b Dagnall	86
*J. E. R. Gallian c Hodge b DeFreitas	5	– (1) b Dagnall	5
D. J. Bicknell c Maddy b DeFreitas	1	– c Nixon b Maddy	38
†R. J. Warren c Maunders b Masters	40	– (6) c Nixon b Dagnall	11
K. P. Pietersen lbw b Amin	88	– (4) c Nixon b Dagnall	95
C. L. Cairns b DeFreitas	5	– (5) not out	41
P. J. Franks not out	123	– c DeFreitas b Masters	21
G. D. Clough c Maddy b Hodge	0	– not out	1
G. J. Smith b DeFreitas	2		
A. J. Harris c Hodge b Maddy	3		
S. C. G. MacGill c Snape b Maddy	2		
B 8, l-b 7, w 1	16	B 6, l-b 9, w 3, n-b 2	20
1/9 (2) 2/11 (3) 3/89 (1) 4/104 (4) 5/123 (6) 6/272 (5) 7/277 (8) 8/291 (9) 9/310 (10) 10/326 (11)	326	1/5 (1) 2/62 (3) 3/211 (4) 4/270 (2) 5/290 (6) 6/311 (7)	(6 wkts dec.) 318

Bonus points – Nottinghamshire 3, Leicestershire 3.

Bowling: *First Innings*—DeFreitas 30–9–68–4; Dagnall 19–5–69–0; Maddy 17.5–7–52–2; Masters 20–7–58–2; Amin 14–3–40–1; Snape 4–0–11–0; Stevens 1–0–1–0; Hodge 4–0–12–1. *Second Innings*—DeFreitas 10–3–23–0; Dagnall 16–4–61–4; Amin 13–1–90–0; Masters 12–2–62–1; Maddy 7–2–15–1; Snape 6–2–22–0; Sehwag 3–1–30–0.

Leicestershire

J. K. Maunders b Smith	3	– (2) not out	0
V. Sehwag c Smith b Harris	137		
D. L. Maddy lbw b Franks	23		
B. J. Hodge b Smith	13		
D. I. Stevens c Warren b Smith	4		
†P. A. Nixon st Warren b MacGill	5		
J. N. Snape b Smith	0		
*P. A. J. DeFreitas c Warren b MacGill	5		
D. D. Masters not out	25	– (1) lbw b Harris	5
C. E. Dagnall c Warren b Franks	0		
R. M. Amin lbw b MacGill	1		
B 7, l-b 17, w 1, n-b 2	27		
1/30 (1) 2/114 (3) 3/188 (2) 4/193 (4) 5/196 (5) 6/196 (7) 7/201 (8) 8/217 (6) 9/220 (10) 10/243 (11)	243	1/5 (1)	(1 wkt) 5

Bonus points – Leicestershire 1, Nottinghamshire 3.

Bowling: *First Innings*—Smith 20–8–40–4; Harris 18–2–64–1; Franks 11–0–47–2; Clough 4–0–20–0; MacGill 12–2–44–3; Pietersen 1–0–4–0. *Second Innings*—Smith 2–0–3–0; Harris 1.5–1–2–1.

Umpires: J. H. Evans and T. E. Jesty.

LEICESTERSHIRE v WARWICKSHIRE

At Leicester, July 2, 3, 4, 5. Drawn. Leicestershire 10 pts, Warwickshire 8 pts (after 1 pt penalty). Toss: Warwickshire.

The best efforts of DeFreitas and Hodge failed to secure Leicestershire's first Championship win. Chasing 287 in 61 overs, they started badly until Hodge put them on track with his first Championship century, adding 130 with Nixon. When both fell in successive overs, Leicestershire settled for the draw. On a slow pitch of variable bounce, they should have taken a bigger first-innings lead. They were 21 behind Warwickshire with three down; then Maddy was out for 98 and there was an instant collapse. In the second innings, Leicestershire had to endure a stand of

224 between Wagh, who produced a superb array of shots, and Bell. They used ten bowlers, but it took a direct hit from Sehwag to part them. Next morning, DeFreitas struck five times in an unbroken 16-over spell to earn his best return in two years and a plausible target. Warwickshire's star recruit, Waqar Younis, managed only three wickets in all, but a maiden Championship fifty put a smile on his face; Warwickshire were less happy to lose a full point for a slow over-rate.

Close of play: First day, Leicestershire 72-1 (Maunders 18, Maddy 10); Second day, Leicestershire 215-3 (Maddy 88); Third day, Warwickshire 261-3 (Wagh 123, Knight 5).

Warwickshire

First innings		Second innings	
*M. J. Powell b DeFreitas	0	lbw b DeFreitas	11
N. V. Knight b Whiley	66	(5) c Sehwag b DeFreitas	33
M. A. Wagh c Sehwag b Masters	35	c Nixon b DeFreitas	138
I. R. Bell lbw b Masters	0	run out	93
I. J. L. Trott b Maddy	23	(2) lbw b Dagnall	9
†T. Frost c Nixon b Masters	11	c DeFreitas b Masters	17
D. R. Brown c Sehwag b Whiley	5	lbw b DeFreitas	5
N. M. K. Smith c Hodge b Masters	4	c Stevens b DeFreitas	8
M. M. Betts c Hodge b Masters	20	not out	16
Waqar Younis c Stevens b Snape	52	b DeFreitas	0
A. Richardson not out	16	c Snape b Masters	10
B 6, l-b 8, w 1, n-b 6	21	B 4, l-b 8, w 3, n-b 6	21
1/0 (1) 2/78 (3) 3/78 (4) 4/120 (5) 5/142 (2) 6/146 (6) 7/154 (8) 8/167 (7) 9/193 (9) 10/253 (10)	253	1/16 (1) 2/20 (2) 3/244 (4) 4/300 (3) 5/305 (5) 6/317 (7) 7/331 (6) 8/336 (8) 9/336 (10) 10/361 (11)	361

Bonus points – Warwickshire 2, Leicestershire 3.

Bowling: *First Innings*—DeFreitas 13–9–22–1; Dagnall 12–3–46–0; Whiley 17–3–76–2; Masters 17–4–53–5; Maddy 12–3–36–1; Snape 3–0–5–1; Sehwag 1–0–1–0. *Second Innings*—DeFreitas 31–10–78–6; Dagnall 19–5–60–1; Masters 14.5–3–60–2; Maddy 9–1–32–0; Whiley 10–1–49–0; Maunders 3–1–10–0; Stevens 3–0–15–0; Snape 4–1–20–0; Hodge 3–0–16–0; Sehwag 3–1–9–0.

Leicestershire

First innings		Second innings	
J. K. Maunders c Frost b Betts	64	b Waqar Younis	2
V. Sehwag b Betts	30	b Richardson	40
D. L. Maddy lbw b Waqar Younis	98	st Frost b Waqar Younis	0
B. J. Hodge lbw b Bell	7	b Richardson	128
D. I. Stevens b Betts	7	lbw b Richardson	3
†P. A. Nixon c sub b Brown	11	run out	36
J. N. Snape lbw b Brown	4	not out	5
*P. A. J. DeFreitas c Wagh b Betts	45	not out	6
D. D. Masters lbw b Brown	0		
C. E. Dagnall run out	23		
M. J. A. Whiley not out	0		
B 7, l-b 15, n-b 17	39	B 2, l-b 13, n-b 6	21
1/42 (2) 2/198 (1) 3/215 (4) 4/232 (3) 5/234 (5) 6/244 (7) 7/259 (6) 8/267 (9) 9/328 (10) 10/328 (8)	328	1/2 (1) 2/20 (3) 3/77 (2) 4/93 (5) 5/223 (6) 6/230 (4)	(6 wkts) 241

Bonus points – Leicestershire 3, Warwickshire 3.

Bowling: *First Innings*—Waqar Younis 22–2–75–1; Betts 21.2–1–88–4; Richardson 21–6–44–0; Brown 18–3–53–3; Smith 4–0–36–0; Bell 2–1–10–1. *Second Innings*—Waqar Younis 9–1–60–2; Betts 12–2–53–0; Brown 13–2–47–0; Richardson 17–5–29–3; Bell 8–0–33–0; Smith 1.3–0–4–0.

Umpires: G. I. Burgess and M. J. Kitchen.

At Leicester, July 6. LEICESTERSHIRE lost to INDIA A by four wickets (see India A tour section).

At Southgate, July 9, 10, 11, 12. LEICESTERSHIRE lost to MIDDLESEX by eight wickets.

LEICESTERSHIRE v SUSSEX

At Leicester, July 15, 16, 17, 18. Sussex won by five wickets. Sussex 21 pts, Leicestershire 5 pts. Toss: Leicestershire.

This game offered an insight into why something special was happening for Sussex as the summer turned scorching. They were aggressively efficient in everything they did, and their fourth win in a row closed the gap with leaders Surrey to just five points. Mushtaq Ahmed was magical, taking ten wickets for the third time in the season. He started with five in his first 12 overs: a back problem had ruled out Sehwag, and no batsman could cope with his wiles until DeFreitas scored his tenth first-class century, in 116 balls, pushing the total past 300. For Sussex, Cottey dug in, scoring his third hundred in four innings while batting six and a half hours. He and Prior eased Sussex into the lead before DeFreitas completed his own five-wicket return. But Mushtaq was soon back in action, thriving on hard work: he bowled nearly 75 overs in all, and ensured that Sussex needed only 163 for victory. Cottey led the way with another fifty.

Close of play: First day, Sussex 51-0 (Goodwin 34, Montgomerie 13); Second day, Sussex 340-5 (Cottey 137, Prior 68); Third day, Leicestershire 186-5 (Ward 21, Snape 10).

Leicestershire

J. K. Maunders lbw b Kirtley	0	– lbw b Mushtaq Ahmed	27
D. I. Stevens st Ambrose b Mushtaq Ahmed	51	– lbw b Mushtaq Ahmed	50
D. L. Maddy lbw b Mushtaq Ahmed	30	– c Martin-Jenkins b Innes	40
B. J. Hodge c Montgomerie b Mushtaq Ahmed	47	– lbw b Kirtley	18
T. R. Ward lbw b Mushtaq Ahmed	4	– c Prior b Mushtaq Ahmed	50
†P. A. Nixon b Mushtaq Ahmed	4	– lbw b Mushtaq Ahmed	11
J. N. Snape b Kirtley	36	– run out	20
*P. A. J. DeFreitas b Martin-Jenkins	103	– c Goodwin b Martin-Jenkins	8
D. D. Masters run out	0	– c Ambrose b Martin-Jenkins	0
C. E. Dagnall not out	15	– c Cottey b Mushtaq Ahmed	15
R. M. Amin b Martin-Jenkins	0	– not out	6
B 1, l-b 22, w 5, n-b 2	30	B 1, l-b 9, w 3	13
1/0 (1) 2/60 (3) 3/107 (2) 4/123 (5) 5/127 (6) 6/154 (4) 7/250 (7) 8/251 (9) 9/320 (8) 10/320 (11)	320	1/70 (1) 2/93 (2) 3/128 (4) 4/150 (3) 5/162 (6) 6/225 (5) 7/234 (8) 8/234 (9) 9/237 (7) 10/258 (10)	258

Bonus points – Leicestershire 3, Sussex 3.

Bowling: *First Innings*—Kirtley 21–6–68–2; Lewry 6–1–18–0; Martin-Jenkins 13.5–1–66–2; Mushtaq Ahmed 33–4–93–5; Innes 12–1–52–0. *Second Innings*—Kirtley 22–7–72–1; Martin-Jenkins 25–9–53–2; Mushtaq Ahmed 41.5–18–96–5; Innes 7–1–27–1.

Sussex

M. W. Goodwin lbw b DeFreitas	34	– (2) b Masters	11
R. R. Montgomerie b DeFreitas	52	– (1) b Amin	28
P. A. Cottey c Nixon b DeFreitas	147	– b Amin	58
*C. J. Adams lbw b DeFreitas	0	– lbw b Maddy	16
†T. R. Ambrose b Dagnall	2	– b Snape	25
R. S. C. Martin-Jenkins lbw b Dagnall	7	– not out	6
M. J. Prior c Hodge b Maddy	96	– not out	4
K. J. Innes not out	14		
Mushtaq Ahmed st Nixon b Amin	21		
R. J. Kirtley c Maunders b Amin	0		
J. D. Lewry c Snape b DeFreitas	0		
B 15, l-b 16, w 2, n-b 10	43	B 10, l-b 2, w 2, n-b 4	18
1/58 (1) 2/161 (2) 3/161 (4) 4/187 (5) 5/215 (6) 6/370 (3) 7/382 (7) 8/415 (9) 9/415 (10) 10/416 (11)	416	1/30 (2) 2/48 (1) 3/96 (4) 4/156 (5) 5/158 (3)	(5 wkts) 166

Bonus points – Sussex 4, Leicestershire 2 (130 overs: 388-7).

Bowling: *First Innings*—Dagnall 30–10–87–2; Masters 27–5–89–0; Amin 19–5–50–2; Maddy 17–1–70–1; Snape 4–0–10–0; DeFreitas 29.5–10–55–5; Maunders 5–0–12–0; Stevens 5–1–11–0; Hodge 1–0–1–0. *Second Innings*—DeFreitas 2.4–0–5–0; Dagnall 2–0–20–0; Masters 8.2–1–31–1; Amin 11–1–41–2; Maddy 7–0–23–1; Hodge 6–0–28–0; Snape 1.5–0–6–1.

Umpires: P. J. Hartley and J. F. Steele.

At Southend, July 23, 24, 25, 26. LEICESTERSHIRE drew with ESSEX.

LEICESTERSHIRE v LANCASHIRE

At Leicester, July 30, 31, August 1, 2. Lancashire won by seven wickets. Lancashire 22 pts, Leicestershire 4 pts. Toss: Leicestershire.

Leicestershire's inability to post a formidable first-innings total was again their undoing. After their innings dwindled away, they could only stand and watch as Law and Hooper conducted a batting masterclass. They added 247 – two short of Lancashire's fifth-wicket record – in 210 minutes, an awesome partnership of dazzling strokes and effortless power. Hooper reached a hundred with his fourth six; Law hit two sixes and 25 fours in his 60th century, before he played across the line on 186, close to a second consecutive double. Amid Leicestershire's gloom, DeFreitas's bowling shone like a beacon. He sent down 41 overs, taking six for 88, and home supporters only wished he could bowl at both ends. A lead of 220 gave the visitors total control. Though Stevens hit his fifth fifty in a row since being promoted to open, and Maunders made a career-best 75, Lancashire needed only 68, and knocked them off inside 21 overs – while DeFreitas claimed another three wickets.

Close of play: First day, Lancashire 28-2 (Keedy 4); Second day, Lancashire 332-4 (Law 150, Hooper 88); Third day, Leicestershire 156-2 (Maunders 56, Hodge 33).

Leicestershire

J. K. Maunders c Hooper b Martin	21	– run out	75
D. I. Stevens c Hooper b Chapple	54	– c Swann b Keedy	50
D. L. Maddy lbw b Wood	19	– lbw b Keedy	14
B. J. Hodge c Hegg b Wood	5	– c Hooper b Chapple	38
T. R. Ward c Swann b Keedy	20	– c Hegg b Chapple	0
†P. A. Nixon c Swann b Martin	19	– c Hooper b Martin	33
J. N. Snape c Wood b Keedy	27	– c Hegg b Wood	36
*P. A. J. DeFreitas c Hegg b Keedy	57	– c Hegg b Wood	0
D. D. Masters not out	10	– c Hegg b Wood	1
R. M. Amin c Loye b Wood	1	– not out	6
D. E. Malcolm c Hogg b Keedy	3	– b Chapple	14
B 6, l-b 3, n-b 14	23	L-b 5, w 1, n-b 14	20
1/32 (1) 2/65 (3) 3/73 (4) 4/103 (5) 5/146 (2) 6/146 (6) 7/220 (7) 8/243 (8) 9/244 (10) 10/259 (11)	259	1/76 (2) 2/106 (3) 3/161 (4) 4/161 (5) 5/200 (1) 6/246 (6) 7/247 (8) 8/257 (9) 9/262 (7) 10/287 (11)	287

Bonus points – Leicestershire 2, Lancashire 3.

Bowling: *First Innings*—Martin 17–1–77–2; Chapple 15–4–53–1; Wood 16–3–59–3; Hogg 10–3–29–0; Hooper 6–2–15–0; Keedy 9.4–3–17–4. *Second Innings*—Martin 26–11–51–1; Chapple 23–4–84–3; Wood 10–1–42–3; Keedy 21–4–59–2; Hooper 8–1–25–0; Hogg 5–1–21–0.

Lancashire

M. J. Chilton c Nixon b DeFreitas	14	– b DeFreitas	9
A. J. Swann b Malcolm	7	– c Nixon b DeFreitas	1
G. Keedy c Nixon b DeFreitas	6		
M. B. Loye lbw b DeFreitas	45	– (3) not out	21
S. G. Law lbw b Maddy	186	– (4) c Nixon b DeFreitas	15
C. L. Hooper c Stevens b DeFreitas	117	– (5) not out	20
G. Chapple c Nixon b DeFreitas	8		
*†W. K. Hegg c DeFreitas b Masters	27		
K. W. Hogg c Maddy b DeFreitas	12		
J. Wood not out	8		
P. J. Martin c Ward b Masters	19		
B 7, l-b 16, w 5, n-b 2	30	L-b 2	2
1/20 (1) 2/28 (2) 3/44 (3) 4/137 (4) 5/384 (6) 6/400 (7) 7/413 (5) 8/435 (9) 9/459 (8) 10/479 (11)	479	1/5 (2) 2/10 (1) 3/28 (4)	(3 wkts) 68

Bonus points – Lancashire 5, Leicestershire 2 (130 overs: 450-8).

Bowling: *First Innings*—DeFreitas 41–14–88–6; Malcolm 27–5–102–1; Maddy 15–3–56–1; Masters 31.2–4–107–2; Amin 12–1–68–0; Hodge 1–0–7–0; Snape 8–1–28–0. *Second Innings*—DeFreitas 10.2–5–24–3; Masters 9–0–36–0; Amin 1–0–6–0.

Umpires: J. W. Lloyds and R. Palmer.

At Birmingham, August 14, 15, 16. LEICESTERSHIRE lost to WARWICKSHIRE by eight wickets.

LEICESTERSHIRE v SURREY

At Leicester, August 21, 22, 23, 24. Drawn. Leicestershire 6 pts, Surrey 12 pts. Toss: Surrey.

Leicestershire finally discovered their lost resilience, earning an honourable draw after following on 335 behind, and sowing seeds of doubt about Surrey's title challenge. On a bland pitch, Surrey had to change tack on the last afternoon, donating runs in a desperate bid to unearth a win. Earlier, a century and career-best bowling from Clarke gave them an awesome first-innings lead, but

Leicestershire turned the tide with three big hundreds. Hodge's happened to be the county's thousandth in first-class cricket, while two young left-handers, Maunders and Sadler, scored the first of their careers. Maunders batted eight and a half hours, and his stand of 281 with Hodge was eight short of the county's second-wicket record; after his dismissal, the runs gifted by Ward and Thorpe inflated the total to the fourth highest in Leicestershire history. Finally, Surrey were set an impossible 302 in a maximum 37 overs, and dropped to second place for the first time since May. But the draw did little for Leicestershire's hopes of first division survival.

Close of play: First day, Surrey 349-4 (Clarke 90, Saqlain Mushtaq 0); Second day, Leicestershire 127-7 (Nixon 16, Drakes 9); Third day, Leicestershire 348-2 (Maunders 126, Sadler 6).

Surrey

I. J. Ward lbw b Maddy	59	– run out	23
†J. N. Batty c Maddy b DeFreitas	50	– lbw b DeFreitas	30
M. R. Ramprakash c sub b Maddy	55		
G. P. Thorpe c Nixon b Snape	87	– (3) not out	52
R. Clarke c Nixon b Snape	139	– (4) not out	3
Saqlain Mushtaq lbw b Drakes	13		
*A. J. Hollioake b Drakes	21		
Azhar Mahmood retired hurt	30		
I. D. K. Salisbury not out	24		
J. Ormond c Nixon b Snape	0		
T. J. Murtagh c Maddy b Drakes	6		
B 8, l-b 2, w 1, n-b 6	17	L-b 7, n-b 2	9
1/93 (2) 2/145 (1) 3/178 (3) 4/347 (4) 5/378 (6) 6/420 (7) 7/456 (5) 8/481 (10) 9/501 (11)	501	1/32 (1) 2/89 (2) (2 wkts)	117

Bonus points – Surrey 5 pts, Leicestershire 2 pts (130 overs: 481-8).

In the first innings Azhar Mahmood retired hurt at 481-7.

Bowling: *First Innings*—DeFreitas 29–10–87–1; Drakes 21.1–2–85–3; Dagnall 23–3–88–0; Maddy 14–1–40–2; Masters 16–0–78–0; Snape 30–6–108–3; Hodge 1–0–5–0. *Second Innings*—DeFreitas 9–2–31–1; Drakes 8–1–41–0; Masters 6–1–19–0; Dagnall 3–0–14–0; Brandy 2–1–5–0.

Leicestershire

J. K. Maunders c Batty b Ormond	12	– c Batty b Salisbury	171
D. L. Maddy lbw b Murtagh	12	– c Batty b Clarke	20
B. J. Hodge b Clarke	20	– c Batty b Salisbury	157
J. L. Sadler b Clarke	31	– c Hollioake b Thorpe	145
J. N. Snape c and b Clarke	10		
†P. A. Nixon lbw b Salisbury	30	– (5) not out	44
D. G. Brandy b Murtagh	4	– (6) not out	31
*P. A. J. DeFreitas b Murtagh	4		
V. C. Drakes run out	10		
C. E. Dagnall not out	22		
D. D. Masters c Ward b Clarke	1		
B 4, l-b 4, n-b 2	10	B 18, l-b 21, n-b 29	68
1/24 (1) 2/30 (2) 3/58 (3) 4/89 (4) 5/98 (5) 6/108 (7) 7/112 (8) 8/129 (9) 9/153 (6) 10/166 (11)	166	1/49 (2) 2/330 (3) 3/465 (1) 4/588 (4) (4 wkts dec.)	636

Bonus points – Surrey 3.

Bowling: *First Innings*—Ormond 9–1–30–1; Murtagh 16–2–68–3; Saqlain Mushtaq 8–4–18–0; Clarke 12.1–4–21–4; Salisbury 13–5–21–1. *Second Innings*—Ormond 25–5–91–0; Murtagh 18–2–62–0; Saqlain Mushtaq 26–8–57–0; Clarke 18–3–82–1; Salisbury 25–5–92–2; Hollioake 9–0–39–0; Azhar Mahmood 14–3–37–0; Ward 12–0–64–0; Thorpe 11–1–73–1.

Umpires: D. J. Constant and N. G. Cowley.

At Nottingham, August 26, 27, 28, 29. LEICESTERSHIRE drew with NOTTINGHAMSHIRE.

LEICESTERSHIRE v KENT

At Leicester, September 10, 11, 12. Leicestershire won by ten wickets. Leicestershire 19 pts, Kent 3 pts. Toss: Leicestershire.

Leicestershire's first and only Championship win of the season arrived far too late to save them from relegation but did at least prevent the ignominy of finishing winless for the first time in their history. Having waited so long, they completed victory in double-quick time: the entire match lasted less than 180 overs, though more than a day was lost to rain. Kent had won all four Championship games since Muralitharan joined them and, despite a century from Maunders – his second in three innings – must have expected a fifth success when Murali clocked up six more wickets. But, on the remarkable third day, Kent lost 19 wickets for 276 in 81.5 overs. Their highest score was 35 from Walker after they followed on. Leicestershire's battery of fast-medium bowlers enjoyed themselves in conditions favouring both seam and swing, and the openers needed just five runs to seal the overdue victory.

Close of play: First day, Leicestershire 151-6 (Maunders 76, Snape 0); Second day, Kent 23-1 (Fulton 7, Smith 0).

Leicestershire

J. K. Maunders c Walker b Khan	129	– not out	2
D. L. Maddy c Jones b Sheriyar	1	– not out	1
B. J. Hodge c Walker b Ealham	31		
J. L. Sadler c Ealham b Muralitharan	20		
T. R. Ward c Smith b Saggers	15		
†P. A. Nixon c Ealham b Muralitharan	3		
C. E. Dagnall lbw b Muralitharan	0		
J. N. Snape not out	45		
*P. A. J. DeFreitas st Jones b Muralitharan	8		
V. C. Drakes c Ealham b Muralitharan	18		
D. D. Masters c Fulton b Muralitharan	3		
B 3, l-b 8, w 1, n-b 10	22	N-b 2	2
1/16 (2) 2/71 (3) 3/111 (4) 4/132 (5) 5/139 (6) 6/139 (7) 7/232 (1) 8/261 (9) 9/291 (10) 10/295 (11)	295	(no wkt)	5

Bonus points – Leicestershire 2, Kent 3.

Bowling: *First Innings*—Saggers 15–2–63–1; Sheriyar 10–1–48–1; Khan 15–2–67–1; Symonds 7–2–23–0; Ealham 13–2–32–1; Muralitharan 22.1–4–51–6. *Second Innings*—Walker 1–0–1–0; Key 0.4–0–4–0.

Kent

*D. P. Fulton c Hodge b Drakes	13	– c Hodge b Dagnall	21
R. W. T. Key b DeFreitas	11	– b Dagnall	15
E. T. Smith b Drakes	21	– c Nixon b Maddy	30
A. Symonds lbw b DeFreitas	2	– c Nixon b Masters	0
M. J. Walker c Nixon b Dagnall	24	– c Nixon b Masters	35
M. A. Ealham lbw b Dagnall	13	– lbw b DeFreitas	1
†G. O. Jones lbw b Dagnall	9	– lbw b DeFreitas	1
A. Khan lbw b Maddy	0	– b Drakes	17
M. J. Saggers c Snape b Maddy	4	– not out	26
M. Muralitharan run out	12	– c Sadler b Masters	0
A. Sheriyar not out	4	– c Masters b Maddy	11
L-b 9, n-b 8	17	L-b 10, n-b 2	12
1/23 (2) 2/41 (1) 3/58 (4) 4/62 (3) 5/95 (6) 6/109 (7) 7/110 (8) 8/110 (5) 9/122 (10) 10/130 (9)	130	1/33 (2) 2/58 (1) 3/59 (4) 4/87 (3) 5/88 (6) 6/104 (7) 7/124 (8) 8/140 (5) 9/140 (10) 10/169 (11)	169

Bonus points – Leicestershire 3.

Bowling: *First Innings*—DeFreitas 16–5–44–2; Drakes 15–4–29–2; Masters 6–2–5–0; Dagnall 9–1–37–3; Maddy 3.3–2–6–2. *Second Innings*—DeFreitas 11–3–16–2; Drakes 9–2–33–1; Maddy 10.5–1–43–2; Dagnall 6–1–23–2; Masters 9–0–44–3.

Umpires: V. A. Holder and P. Willey.

At Hove, September 17, 18, 19. LEICESTERSHIRE lost to SUSSEX by an innings and 55 runs.

THE DUCKWORTH/LEWIS METHOD

In 1997, the ECB's one-day competitions adopted a new method to revise targets in interrupted games, devised by Frank Duckworth of the Royal Statistical Society and Tony Lewis of the University of the West of England. The method was gradually taken up by other countries and, in 1999, the ICC decided to incorporate it into the standard playing conditions for one-day internationals.

The system aims to preserve any advantage that one team has established before the interruption. It uses the idea that teams have two resources from which they make runs – an allocated number of overs, and ten wickets. It also takes into account when the interruption occurs, because of the different scoring-rates typical of different stages of an innings. Traditional run-rate calculations relied only on the overs available, and ignored wickets lost.

After modifications, the system now uses one table with 50 rows, covering matches of any length up to 50 overs, and ten columns, from nought to nine wickets down. Each figure in the table gives the percentage of the total runs in an innings that would, on average, be scored with a certain number of overs left and wickets lost.

If overs are lost, the table is used to calculate the percentage of runs the team would be expected to score in those missing overs. This is obtained by reading off the figure for the number of overs left and wickets down when play stops and subtracting from it the corresponding figure for the number of overs remaining when it resumes.

If the suspension of play occurs between innings, and the second team's allocation of overs is reduced, then their target is obtained by calculating the appropriate percentage for the reduced number of overs with all ten wickets standing. For instance, if the second team's innings halves from 50 overs to 25, the table shows that they still have 66.5% of their resources left, so have to beat two-thirds of the first team's total rather than half.

If the first innings is complete and the second innings is interrupted or prematurely terminated, the score to be beaten is reduced by the percentage of the innings lost. In the World Cup match between South Africa and Sri Lanka at Durban on March 3, 2003, South Africa's run-chase was ended by rain after 45 overs, when they were 229 for six. The Duckworth/Lewis tables showed that, with five overs left and four wickets standing, South Africa has used 85.7% of their run-scoring resources, and 14.3% remained unused. Multiplying Sri Lanka's 50-over total, 268, by 85.7% produced a figure of 229.67. This was rounded down to 229 to give the par score (the runs needed to tie), and the target to win became par plus one – 230 in 45 overs. Under old-fashioned average run-rate per over, the target would have been 242; South Africa benefited because they had preserved wickets into the final stages. (If they had lost one more wicket, par would have been 233; one fewer, 226). As South Africa had equalled par exactly, the match was tied, the points were split, and they failed to qualify for the Super Six stage of the tournament.

The system also covers interruptions to the first innings, multiple interruptions and innings terminated by rain. The tables were revised slightly in September 2002, taking account of rising scoring-rates; the average 50-over total in a one-day international is now taken to be 235, rather than 225.

A new version known as "Professional Edition" was introduced into one-day internationals from October 1, 2003. Based on a more advanced mathematical formula (it is entirely computerised), in effect it adjusts the tables to make allowance for the different scoring-rates that emerge in matches with above-average first-innings scores. The former version, now known as "Standard Edition", continues to operate below international level.

MIDDLESEX

After the Phil Tufnell Show...

NORMAN DE MESQUITA

For the third year running, August was the cruellest month for Middlesex. In August 2001, their chance of promotion disappeared; in 2002 it almost did, until salvaged by a vital win at Worcester. In 2003, Middlesex entered August unbeaten, their first-division status seemingly safe. Then the annual blight struck again: with two losses and a draw, they became dependent on others slipping up. Luckily, Essex obliged.

When Phil Tufnell suddenly decided to leave, two days before the start of the season, to join a TV celebrity game show – which he won – the bowling looked weak, and survival was never going to be easy. But Middlesex supporters thought that, with a strong batting line-up, high-scoring draws would be the order of the day and that would be enough to survive under the current points system.

In the event, it was the batting that disappointed far too often (especially on the last day at Edgbaston and in the second innings at Hove) and maximum batting points were earned only three times; these included the match at Old Trafford when, after Lancashire scored 734, 544 was not enough to avoid the follow-on. One thing the team did show – an advance on previous years – was a notable fighting spirit, which saw them rebound from poor first-innings performances to salvage draws at Chelmsford and Canterbury and against Warwickshire at Southgate.

Overseas players contributed far too little to the cause, particularly Abdul Razzaq. He played seven of the first ten Championship matches, with breaks for one-day internationals in Sri Lanka and England. In those seven games, he passed 50 just three times and took only 14 wickets at 42 apiece. Then he was recalled by Pakistan again, to prepare for their Tests against Bangladesh – but when they chose to blood youngsters instead, he returned for the match at Old Trafford and took two for 170, only to be told that he was to be released from his contract, because he was not match-fit. Somehow, he never seemed to adjust to the rigours of county cricket. The Australian Ashley Noffke looked short of practice when he arrived from the Caribbean tour in mid-May, and was unable to find his rhythm, taking only 21 wickets at 36 in seven matches before going home with a back problem. He originally agreed to return for a third year, but withdrew through injury – and, less than two months before the start of the 2004 season, Middlesex had no overseas players in place. During Noffke's absence last year, Middlesex signed his fellow-Queenslander, Joe Dawes, who showed commendable enthusiasm, though 32 wickets at 32 each is less than one would hope for from an overseas player. A brief appearance by Pakistani leg-spinner Imran Tahir produced one wicket for 196 runs in three first-class games. There was no doubt that the pressing need for 2004 was for a fast bowler or spinner of international stature – preferably both.

In February, Middlesex announced they had signed two South Africans: Nantie Hayward, undeniably fast but discarded by Worcestershire, and Lance Klusener, an explosive all-rounder towards the end of his career.

Chad Keegan

One big plus was Chad Keegan, the team's best bowler, who improved all aspects of his game, collected 63 first-class wickets, and was named player of the year along with Andrew Strauss, the captain. Strauss scored 1,529 first-class runs at nearly 51, to win a place as a one-day player on England's winter tours. While everyone connected with the county was delighted, the team would sorely miss him if he were to become an England regular. Once again, Owais Shah flattered to deceive in the Championship, with two half-centuries in the first three matches; he then went until mid-August before passing fifty again. Ben Hutton had a golden June and David Nash an equally productive July, and their runs were often scored at a vital stage of the game. Ed Joyce occasionally showed his undoubted potential but needs to find consistency. Sven Koenig was unable to recapture the reliability he showed in 2002 and there were too few significant opening partnerships.

Strauss tended to overbowl Noffke and Dawes, but this was probably because the back-up seam bowling was so ineffective. In Tufnell's absence, Paul Weekes was the only spinner until Jamie Dalrymple came down from Oxford, but his 35 wickets cost 38 runs each. With the bat, Weekes passed fifty only four times in the Championship but, opening the innings in the National League, hit seven fifties and a century. At last, Middlesex improved their one-day form. Promotion in the League was just one win away when the batting subsided on the last day of the season, at Chester-le-Street; there was no coming back from 27 for seven.

County coach John Emburey said he was satisfied that his five-year plan was on track and expressed confidence that Middlesex would be challenging for the Championship by 2005. His hopes were boosted by several highly promising youngsters waiting in the wings. Middlesex signed 19-year-old Boyd Rankin from Northern Ireland, who is 6ft 7in and could perhaps be the fast bowler they so desperately need. Another Irishman, 16-year-old Eoin Morgan from Dublin, was already in the Second Eleven. There is also Nick Compton, who looked so good at the end of the previous season; unfortunately, he missed 2003 with a groin problem. Signings from other counties included seamers Melvyn Betts from Warwickshire and Paul Hutchison from Sussex, and wicket-keeper Ben Scott, returning from Surrey.

MIDDLESEX RESULTS

All first-class matches – Played 18: Won 3, Lost 3, Drawn 12.
County Championship matches – Played 16: Won 3, Lost 3, Drawn 10.

Frizzell County Championship, 6th in Division 1; Cheltenham & Gloucester Trophy, q-f; National Cricket League, 4th in Division 2; Twenty20 Cup, 4th in South Group.

COUNTY CHAMPIONSHIP AVERAGES

BATTING AND FIELDING

Cap		*M*	*I*	*NO*	*R*	*HS*	*100s*	*50s*	*Avge*	*Ct/St*
2001	A. J. Strauss	16	29	2	1,401	155	4	7	51.88	6
2000	D. C. Nash	16	24	7	713	113	2	2	41.94	40/3
2003	B. L. Hutton	16	27	5	913	107	4	1	41.50	15
2002	S. G. Koenig	15	26	2	974	96	0	7	40.58	3
2000	O. A. Shah	16	27	1	964	147	2	4	37.07	11
2002	E. C. Joyce	16	27	3	881	117	3	2	36.70	7
2002	Abdul Razzaq§	8	11	0	328	81	0	3	29.81	2
1993	P. N. Weekes	16	26	3	633	75	0	4	27.52	18
2003	A. A. Noffke§	7	7	1	134	40	0	0	22.33	2
2003	C. B. Keegan	16	19	3	244	36*	0	0	15.25	5
2003	S. J. Cook	10	15	2	190	65	0	1	14.61	5
2003	J. H. Dawes§	9	12	5	97	32*	0	0	13.85	3
	J. W. M. Dalrymple	6	10	1	121	33*	0	0	13.44	3
2001	T. F. Bloomfield	3	4	1	19	9*	0	0	6.33	1

Also batted: B. W. Gannon (1 match) 1*; Imran Tahir§ (3 matches) 0, 29, 1*; C. T. Peploe (1 match) 0*, 13 (1 ct); R. M. S. Weston (cap 2001) (1 match) 31, 6.

§ *Overseas player.*

BOWLING

	O	*M*	*R*	*W*	*BB*	*5W/i*	*Avge*
J. H. Dawes	304.4	47	1,008	32	5-46	1	31.50
C. B. Keegan	563.5	113	1,898	60	6-114	3	31.63
S. J. Cook	281.2	62	929	27	4-42	0	34.40
A. A. Noffke	245.4	52	754	21	5-52	1	35.90
P. N. Weekes	373.1	59	1,157	28	4-70	0	41.32
Abdul Razzaq	202.4	28	761	16	3-69	0	47.56

Also bowled: T. F. Bloomfield 54.4–4–257–6; J. W. M. Dalrymple 128–16–437–6; B. W. Gannon 23–4–102–0; B. L. Hutton 67–8–307–5; Imran Tahir 59–13–196–1; E. C. Joyce 49–5–198–2; S. G. Koenig 5–0–19–1; D. C. Nash 5–0–25–0; C. T. Peploe 34–4–120–0; O. A. Shah 9–0–41–0; A. J. Strauss 6–0–42–1.

COUNTY RECORDS

Highest score for:	331*	J. D. Robertson v Worcestershire at Worcester	1949
Highest score against:	316*	J. B. Hobbs (Surrey) at Lord's	1926
Best bowling for:	10-40	G. O. B. Allen v Lancashire at Lord's	1929
Best bowling against:	9-38	R. C. Robertson-Glasgow (Somerset) at Lord's	1924
Highest total for:	642-3 dec.	v Hampshire at Southampton	1923
Highest total against:	734-5 dec.	by Lancashire at Manchester	2003
Lowest total for:	20	v MCC at Lord's	1864
Lowest total against:	31	by Gloucestershire at Bristol	1924
	31	by Glamorgan at Cardiff	1997

MIDDLESEX DIRECTORY

ADDRESS

Lord's Cricket Ground, London NW8 8QN (020 7289 1300; fax 020 7289 5831; email enquiries@middlesexccc.com). **Website** www.middlesexccc.com.

GROUNDS

Lord's: in St John's Wood, just W of Regent's Park, accessed from A41 or A5 via St John's Wood Road. Nearest station: St John's Wood (Jubilee Line Underground) (½ mile).

Southgate: ¼ mile SW of town centre. At Betstyle Circus continue on A1003 Waterfall Road for ground on L side opposite Christ Church. Nearest stations: Southgate (Piccadilly Line Underground) (¾ mile) and New Southgate (1 mile).

Richmond: ¾ mile NW of town centre in Old Deer Park in Kew Road A307, S of Kew Gardens. Nearest station: Richmond (District Line Underground) (¾ mile).

Shenley: 1½ miles E of Radlett town centre located in Radlett Lane between A5183 and B5378. Ground adjoins Shenley Park. Nearest station: Radlett (1½ miles).

OFFICIALS

Captain A. J. Strauss
Head coach J. E. Emburey
President A. E. Moss
Chairman P. H. Edmonds
Secretary/chief executive V. J. Codrington
Chairman, cricket committee D. Bennett
Head groundsmen M. Hunt (Lord's)
S. Martin (Southgate)
Scorer M. J. Smith

PLAYERS

Players expected to reappear in 2004

	Former counties	*Country*	*Born*	*Birthplace*
Bloomfield Timothy Francis		E	31.5.1973	†*Ashford*
Cook Simon James		E	15.1.1977	*Oxford*
Dalrymple James William Murray		E	21.1.1981	*Nairobi, Kenya*
Hutton Benjamin Leonard		E	29.1.1977	*Johannesburg, SA*
Joyce Edmund Christopher		IRE (EU)	22.9.1978	*Dublin*
Keegan Chad Blake		E	30.7.1979	*Sandton, SA*
Koenig Sven Gaetan		SA (EU)	9.12.1973	*Durban*
Nash David Charles		E	19.1.1978	*Chertsey*
Noffke Ashley Allan		A	30.4.1977	*Nambour*
Peploe Christopher Thomas		E	26.4.1981	*Hammersmith*
Shah Owais Alam		E	22.10.1978	*Karachi, Pak.*
Strauss Andrew John		E	2.3.1977	*Johannesburg, SA*
Weekes Paul Nicholas		E	8.7.1969	*Hackney*

Players due to join in 2004

Betts Melvyn Morris	Durham, Warwicks	E	26.3.1975	*Sacriston*
***Hayward** Mornantau	Worcestershire	SA	6.3.1977	*Uitenhage*
Hutchison Paul Michael	Yorks, Sussex	E	9.6.1977	*Leeds*
***Klusener** Lance	Nottinghamshire	SA	4.9.1971	*Durban*
Scott Ben James Matthew	Surrey	E	4.8.1981	*Isleworth*
Trott Benjamin James	Somerset, Kent	E	14.3.1975	*Wellington*

* *Test player.* † *Born in Middlesex.*

At Oxford, April 12, 13, 14. MIDDLESEX drew with OXFORD UCCE.

At Chelmsford, April 18, 19, 20, 21. MIDDLESEX drew with ESSEX.

MIDDLESEX v SUSSEX

At Lord's, April 23, 24, 25, 26. Middlesex won by three wickets. Middlesex 17 pts, Sussex 4 pts. Toss: Sussex.

Just as at Chelmsford, the Middlesex batsmen showed a marked improvement second time round – and on this occasion, their determined display on a tense final day produced victory. The first two days saw 29 wickets fall, despite time lost to rain, and the most productive partnership for either side came from Sussex's last pair, Kirtley and Lewry, who put on 67 in 16 overs. That gave Sussex a batting point and an eventual first-innings lead of 123, after a woeful performance by Middlesex when only Koenig passed 17. Keegan was briefly reprieved when a ball from Kirtley grazed his off stump, disturbing the bails without removing them. Though they lost wickets steadily themselves, Sussex left a formidable target of 328. More rain fell, but there was never any hurry. Strauss and Shah built a solid platform of 117 on the third day; the rest did their job, and the winning runs came with a session to spare.

Close of play: First day, Middlesex 79-4 (Koenig 35, Joyce 4); Second day, Sussex 194-9 (Kirtley 22, Lewry 2); Third day, Middlesex 136-2 (Strauss 64).

Sussex

R. R. Montgomerie c Nash b Keegan	20	– (2) b Keegan	2
M. W. Goodwin c Shah b Dawes	16	– (1) lbw b Dawes	23
P. A. Cottey lbw b Dawes	0	– b Cook	38
*C. J. Adams c and b Weekes	26	– lbw b Abdul Razzaq	12
T. R. Ambrose b Cook	51	– lbw b Dawes	35
R. S. C. Martin-Jenkins c Hutton b Dawes	13	– lbw b Weekes	50
†M. J. Prior c Abdul Razzaq b Weekes	11	– lbw b Keegan	4
K. J. Innes st Nash b Weekes	15	– c Hutton b Keegan	1
Mushtaq Ahmed c Nash b Keegan	9	– c Nash b Keegan	2
R. J. Kirtley not out	20	– not out	25
J. D. Lewry c Hutton b Abdul Razzaq	45	– c Nash b Dawes	8
L-b 11, n-b 2	13	L-b 4	4
1/37 (2) 2/41 (1) 3/41 (3) 4/92 (4) 5/132 (6) 6/138 (5) 7/154 (7) 8/168 (8) 9/172 (9) 10/239 (11)	239	1/24 (1) 2/28 (2) 3/63 (4) 4/79 (3) 5/123 (5) 6/132 (7) 7/136 (8) 8/146 (9) 9/186 (6) 10/204 (11)	204

Bonus points – Sussex 1, Middlesex 3.

Bowling: *First Innings*—Dawes 22–4–58–3; Keegan 19–4–49–2; Cook 13–2–42–1; Abdul Razzaq 9.1–0–43–1; Weekes 10–1–36–3. *Second Innings*—Dawes 15.1–3–47–3; Keegan 21–8–36–4; Abdul Razzaq 11–0–55–1; Cook 10–0–45–1; Hutton 2–0–10–0; Weekes 3–1–7–1.

Middlesex

*A. J. Strauss c Prior b Kirtley	10	– lbw b Kirtley	83
S. G. Koenig lbw b Kirtley	43	– c Prior b Lewry	7
O. A. Shah b Lewry	1	– lbw b Innes	61
†D. C. Nash b Martin-Jenkins	17	– b Mushtaq Ahmed	29
S. J. Cook b Mushtaq Ahmed	5	– (9) not out	22
E. C. Joyce lbw b Kirtley	8	– (5) lbw b Kirtley	49
Abdul Razzaq lbw b Lewry	3	– (6) lbw b Kirtley	11
P. N. Weekes run out	0	– (7) lbw b Kirtley	33
B. L. Hutton lbw b Mushtaq Ahmed	2	– (8) not out	11
C. B. Keegan c Prior b Mushtaq Ahmed	8		
J. H. Dawes not out	3		
B 1, l-b 4, w 1, n-b 10	16	B 8, l-b 11, w 1, n-b 4	24
1/24 (1) 2/29 (3) 3/69 (4) 4/74 (5) 5/92 (6) 6/97 (7) 7/97 (2) 8/98 (8) 9/109 (10) 10/116 (9)	116	1/19 (2) 2/136 (3) 3/165 (1) 4/200 (4) 5/225 (6) 6/287 (7) 7/288 (5)	(7 wkts) 330

Bonus points – Sussex 3.

Bowling: *First Innings*—Lewry 17–8–34–2; Kirtley 16–3–51–3; Mushtaq Ahmed 10.3–4–16–3; Martin-Jenkins 5–2–10–1. *Second Innings*—Lewry 25–4–50–1; Kirtley 33–10–87–4; Mushtaq Ahmed 28.4–6–97–1; Martin-Jenkins 10–2–42–0; Innes 10–2–35–1.

Umpires: B. Dudleston and V. A. Holder.

MIDDLESEX v LANCASHIRE

At Lord's, May 9, 10, 11, 12. Drawn. Middlesex 8 pts, Lancashire 12 pts. Toss: Lancashire. Championship debut: Imran Tahir.

Painstaking centuries by Law, who batted more than seven hours, and Chilton, plus a spectacular one by Flintoff – his tenth, at a run a ball, with four sixes and two changes of bat – ensured Lancashire the full benefit of batting first in perfect conditions. Middlesex battled to avoid the follow-on, and failed, despite a fine 81 by Shah. As the pitch grew more responsive to spin, Keedy did most of the damage: he removed the last five for 23 in 49 balls. But, yet again, Middlesex salvaged the game in their second innings when Strauss and Koenig shared an unbroken stand of 176 in 60 overs. Their determination and the rain, which wiped out nearly half the playing time over the last two days, made sure of the draw.

Close of play: First day, Lancashire 366-3 (Law 143, Chilton 106); Second day, Middlesex 163-4 (Joyce 8, Weekes 10); Third day, Middlesex 89-0 (Strauss 50, Koenig 35).

Lancashire

A. J. Swann c Nash b Dawes	45
I. J. Sutcliffe lbw b Keegan	27
M. B. Loye c Hutton b Imran Tahir	30
S. G. Law c and b Bloomfield	198
M. J. Chilton lbw b Dawes	119
A. Flintoff b Weekes	111
G. Chapple not out	7
*†W. K. Hegg c Shah b Dawes	9
B 7, l-b 9, w 1, n-b 2	19
1/38 (2) 2/97 (3) 3/120 (1) 4/384 (5) 5/519 (4) 6/556 (6) 7/565 (8)	(7 wkts dec.) 565

J. M. Anderson, P. J. Martin and G. Keedy did not bat.

Bonus points – Lancashire 5, Middlesex 1 (130 overs: 453-4).

Bowling: Dawes 30.3–5–82–3; Keegan 27–4–120–1; Bloomfield 21–2–101–1; Imran Tahir 39–8–128–1; Weekes 27–0–91–1; Hutton 6–0–13–0; Joyce 2–0–14–0.

Middlesex

*A. J. Strauss c Flintoff b Anderson	6	– not out 100
S. G. Koenig c Hegg b Keedy	34	– not out 71
O. A. Shah c Chilton b Flintoff	81	
†D. C. Nash lbw b Anderson	13	
E. C. Joyce c Flintoff b Chapple	53	
P. N. Weekes c Swann b Keedy	39	
B. L. Hutton c Flintoff b Keedy	33	
Imran Tahir c Chapple b Keedy	0	
C. B. Keegan lbw b Keedy	21	
J. H. Dawes not out	1	
T. F. Bloomfield c Chilton b Keedy	1	
B 4, l-b 10, w 2, n-b 6	22	B 5 5
1/13 (1) 2/94 (2) 3/137 (4) 4/147 (3) 5/225 (5) 6/253 (6) 7/253 (8) 8/299 (9) 9/300 (7) 10/304 (11)	304	(no wkt) 176

Bonus points – Middlesex 3, Lancashire 3.

Bowling: *First Innings*—Anderson 19–3–90–2; Martin 16–3–52–0; Chapple 17–2–63–1; Flintoff 3–0–17–1; Keedy 22.2–5–68–6. *Second Innings*—Martin 12–3–25–0; Chapple 10–4–24–0; Flintoff 4–2–6–0; Keedy 23–2–82–0; Anderson 11–1–34–0.

Umpires: M. J. Harris and J. F. Steele.

At Canterbury, May 14, 15, 16, 17. MIDDLESEX drew with KENT.

At Leicester, May 21, 22, 23, 24. MIDDLESEX drew with LEICESTERSHIRE.

At Shenley Park, May 30, 31, June 1, 2. MIDDLESEX drew with ZIMBABWEANS (see Zimbabwean tour section).

MIDDLESEX v ESSEX

At Lord's, June 4, 5, 6, 7. Drawn. Middlesex 11 pts, Essex 7 pts. Toss: Essex.

The absence of a second spinner, and Strauss's reluctance to turn to Weekes, meant Middlesex drew a match they should have won. Essex had followed on 197 behind and, though rain cost 76 overs on the third day, were 60 adrift and six down early on the last afternoon. They should not have been allowed to recover, but they did, thanks largely to Bopara and Middlebrook. It was Bopara's second rescue act: he had batted three hours in the first innings, when he and Napier doubled the Essex total from a miserable 78 for eight. After a rain-delayed start, Grayson, acting-captain because Irani was injured, put Middlesex in. Within an hour, Dakin reduced them to 23 for three, on his way to the first five-wicket return of a ten-year career. But Hutton knuckled down for nearly six hours, sharing century stands with Joyce and Abdul Razzaq, and Middlesex earned four batting points for the first time in this campaign.

Close of play: First day, Middlesex 178-4 (Hutton 69, Abdul Razzaq 15); Second day, Essex 95-8 (Bopara 15, Napier 6); Third day, Essex 21-0 (Robinson 13, Jefferson 3).

Middlesex

*A. J. Strauss lbw b Dakin	11
S. G. Koenig c Foster b Dakin	0
O. A. Shah c Jefferson b Dakin	4
B. L. Hutton c Foster b Dakin	107
E. C. Joyce c and b Bopara	69
Abdul Razzaq b Dakin	54
P. N. Weekes not out	51
†D. C. Nash b Brant	1
A. A. Noffke lbw b Brant	8
S. J. Cook b Napier	20
C. B. Keegan b Middlebrook	21
L-b 12, w 5	17
1/4 (2) 2/8 (3) 3/23 (1) 4/151 (5) 5/254 (4) 6/261 (6) 7/272 (8) 8/282 (9) 9/324 (10) 10/363 (11)	363

Bonus points – Middlesex 4, Essex 3.

Bowling: Brant 31–10–67–2; Dakin 35–10–86–5; Napier 24–5–74–1; Bopara 15–1–61–1; Middlebrook 16.1–1–63–1.

Essex

D. D. J. Robinson c Nash b Keegan	7	b Keegan	13
W. I. Jefferson c Nash b Noffke	22	lbw b Abdul Razzaq	30
*A. P. Grayson c Nash b Noffke	0	c Nash b Cook	69
A. Flower c Nash b Keegan	11	c Nash b Cook	3
A. Habib b Abdul Razzaq	15	b Abdul Razzaq	2
†J. S. Foster c Shah b Cook	11	c Weekes b Noffke	15
R. S. Bopara run out	48	not out	40
J. M. Dakin lbw b Cook	5	c Joyce b Cook	24
J. D. Middlebrook c Strauss b Cook	1	lbw b Cook	52
G. R. Napier c Keegan b Noffke	44	not out	3
S. A. Brant not out	0		
L-b 2	2	B 5, l-b 9, n-b 4	18
1/29 (2) 2/29 (3) 3/37 (1) 4/46 (4) 5/62 (5) 6/70 (6) 7/76 (8) 8/78 (9) 9/157 (10) 10/166 (7)	166	1/21 (1) 2/65 (2) 3/70 (4) 4/75 (5) 5/129 (6) 6/137 (3) 7/165 (8) 8/265 (9)	(8 wkts) 269

Bonus points – Middlesex 3.

Bowling: *First Innings*—Noffke 18–6–39–3; Keegan 16.1–3–56–2; Cook 16–7–33–3; Abdul Razzaq 13–0–34–1; Weekes 2–1–2–0. *Second Innings*—Noffke 25–5–81–1; Keegan 20–4–52–1; Abdul Razzaq 20–3–40–2; Cook 18–4–54–4; Hutton 3–2–1–0; Weekes 6–2–14–0; Joyce 3–0–13–0.

Umpires: N. G. Cowley and N. A. Mallender.

MIDDLESEX v SURREY

At Lord's, June 27, 28, 29, 30. Drawn. Middlesex 10 pts, Surrey 12 pts. Toss: Middlesex.

Once again, Middlesex could thank Strauss and Koenig, who had another big second-innings opening partnership, and the weather, which washed out half the last day. A first-innings lead of 198 had given Surrey high hopes of a win, and they might have come much closer but for a strange performance by Stewart, who spent nearly four hours making 87 when fast scoring was required. He ran a single off the first ball in eight of the last ten overs. Ward scored his second successive hundred, and Ramprakash, spurred on by a hostile reception from his old club's supporters, batted determinedly to become the first man to complete centuries against all 18

HUNDREDS AGAINST MOST COUNTIES

18	*Hundred against 18th county*	
M. R. Ramprakash	**2003**	
C. L. Hooper	**2003**	
17	*Hundred against 17th county*	*Missing county*
G. M. Turner	1979	Never played Durham.
I. V. A. Richards	1981	HS v Durham 62* in five innings.
B. C. Broad	1991	HS v Durham 26 in four innings.
G. A. Gooch	1992	Never played Essex.
C. J. Tavaré	1992	HS v Middlesex 81 in 45 innings.
T. S. Curtis	1993	HS v Worcs 8 in two innings.
W. Larkins	1995	Never played Durham.
M. W. Gatting	1996	Never played Middlesex.
G. A. Hick	1996	Never played Worcestershire.
N. R. Taylor	1997	Never played Kent.
S. G. Law	**2003**	**HS v Essex 80 in three innings.**
C. J. Adams	**2003**	**HS v Northamptonshire 84 in 20 innings.**

48 other batsmen have scored centuries against 16 counties.
There were only 17 counties before Durham gained first-class status in 1992.

Research: Philip Bailey.

---

counties (Carl Hooper emulated him in August). But he also took his time – five and a half hours. Middlesex bowled well, and Strauss set excellent defensive fields, but Surrey's superior talent should have found a way. Strauss won only his second toss in this Championship season but, at 110 for four after lunch, Middlesex looked to be struggling. Then Hutton batted superbly, hitting four sixes in a second successive century, and had excellent support from the later order.

Close of play: First day, Middlesex 311-7 (Nash 22, Noffke 2); Second day, Surrey 274-3 (Ramprakash 68, Saqlain Mushtaq 0); Third day, Middlesex 74-0 (Strauss 42, Koenig 29).

Middlesex

*A. J. Strauss c Hollioake b Saqlain Mushtaq	47	– c Butcher b Salisbury	95
S. G. Koenig c Saqlain Mushtaq b Bicknell	22	– c Thorpe b Hollioake	89
O. A. Shah c Stewart b Bicknell	31	– not out	7
B. L. Hutton b Salisbury	101	– not out	5
E. C. Joyce lbw b Bicknell	0		
Abdul Razzaq c Stewart b Bicknell	29		
P. N. Weekes c Stewart b Bicknell	39		
†D. C. Nash not out	36		
A. A. Noffke b Ormond	23		
S. J. Cook lbw b Ormond	0		
C. B. Keegan b Ormond	20		
B 8, l-b 7, w 7	22	B 10, n-b 12	22
1/59 (2) 2/92 (1) 3/110 (3) 4/110 (5) 5/148 (6) 6/256 (7) 7/305 (4) 8/340 (9) 9/340 (10) 10/370 (11)	370	1/186 (1) 2/202 (2) (2 wkts dec.)	218

Bonus points – Middlesex 4, Surrey 3.

Bowling: *First Innings*—Bicknell 35–7–92–5; Ormond 28.2–3–103–3; Tudor 13–5–43–0; Saqlain Mushtaq 24–5–66–1; Salisbury 9–2–21–1; Butcher 2–0–12–0; Hollioake 4–0–18–0. *Second Innings*—Bicknell 8–0–33–0; Ormond 12–2–53–0; Tudor 12–2–45–0; Salisbury 17–2–60–1; Saqlain Mushtaq 2–1–1–0; Hollioake 6.3–1–15–1; Ward 0.3–0–1–0.

Surrey

I. J. Ward c Shah b Weekes	104	I. D. K. Salisbury b Cook	17
M. A. Butcher c Koenig b Abdul Razzaq	44	J. Ormond not out	1
M. R. Ramprakash c Hutton b Cook	110		
G. P. Thorpe c Nash b Abdul Razzaq	46	L-b 23, w 3, n-b 14	40
Saqlain Mushtaq c Keegan b Weekes	69		
†A. J. Stewart c Joyce b Weekes	87	1/89 (2) 2/193 (1) 3/270 (4)	568
*A. J. Hollioake b Noffke	10	4/352 (3) 5/413 (5) 6/444 (7)	
A. J. Tudor b Abdul Razzaq	30	7/497 (8) 8/535 (9)	
M. P. Bicknell c Nash b Joyce	10	9/562 (10) 10/568 (6)	

Bonus points – Surrey 5, Middlesex 2 (130 overs: 445-6).

Bowling: Noffke 37–5–134–1; Keegan 31–6–102–0; Abdul Razzaq 29–4–95–3; Joyce 11–3–25–1; Cook 28–4–101–2; Weekes 32.2–7–88–3.

Umpires: G. I. Burgess and N. J. Llong.

MIDDLESEX v LEICESTERSHIRE

At Southgate, July 9, 10, 11, 12. Middlesex won by eight wickets. Middlesex 22 pts, Leicestershire 7 pts. Toss: Middlesex.

On a pitch offering the bowlers no help, and in great heat, the match generated 1,568 runs, a record for Middlesex. Some suggested their first innings dragged on too long but, as Leicestershire missed saving the follow-on by only 24 runs, the tactics were justified. Strauss led from the front: with 163 needed for victory at a run a ball, he scored 73 off 67, and Middlesex got home with three overs to spare. This followed 147 from Strauss on the opening day, backed up by hundreds from Joyce and Nash. But of the five centuries in the match, by far the most spectacular was Sehwag's. He batted magnificently for 130 in 111 balls, striking 20 fours and four sixes – one shattering a pavilion window. It looked ridiculously easy. However, Keegan claimed three victims in 12 balls, and improved his career-best for the third time in 2003. Hodge delayed Middlesex on the final day for century No. 5, but Strauss had the last word. This was Middlesex's only full haul of points in the season. Only two members of the Middlesex team, Nash and Weekes, were born in the UK, a statistic repeated in two further Championship games in 2003.

Close of play: First day, Middlesex 382-5 (Joyce 81, Weekes 17); Second day, Leicestershire 221-3 (Masters 9, Hodge 4); Third day, Leicestershire 148-2 (Maddy 74, Hodge 57).

Middlesex

*A. J. Strauss c Nixon b Amin	147	– (2) not out	73
S. G. Koenig c Maddy b Masters	20		
O. A. Shah c Nixon b Masters	16	– st Nixon b Amin	20
B. L. Hutton b Hodge	40		
E. C. Joyce b Snape	102	– (4) not out	29
Abdul Razzaq c Nixon b Masters	25		
P. N. Weekes c Maddy b DeFreitas	75	– (1) b Whiley	29
†D. C. Nash not out	103		
J. W. M. Dalrymple not out	33		
B 7, l-b 3, w 15, n-b 34	59	L-b 12, w 3	15
1/33 (2) 2/96 (3) 3/185 (4) 4/277 (1) 5/324 (6) 6/432 (5) 7/523 (7)	(7 wkts dec.) 620	1/51 (1) 2/84 (3)	(2 wkts) 166

A. A. Noffke and C. B. Keegan did not bat.

Bonus points – Middlesex 5, Leicestershire 2 (130 overs: 486-6).

Bowling: *First Innings*—DeFreitas 24–5–75–1; Masters 26–6–81–3; Whiley 27.4–4–118–0; Maddy 11–1–32–0; Amin 34–8–137–1; Snape 17–0–83–1; Hodge 5–2–18–1; Sehwag 16–1–66–0. *Second Innings*—DeFreitas 3–0–19–0; Masters 3–0–17–0; Whiley 5–0–32–1; Amin 8–0–49–1; Sehwag 2–0–10–0; Snape 2–0–17–0; Maddy 1–0–10–0.

Leicestershire

J. K. Maunders c and b Keegan	55	– c Nash b Noffke	0
V. Sehwag c Koenig b Keegan	130	– c Nash b Noffke	13
D. L. Maddy c and b Keegan	4	– b Weekes	94
D. D. Masters c Weekes b Keegan	23	– (9) b Dalrymple	4
B. J. Hodge c Nash b Keegan	52	– (4) b Noffke	112
D. I. Stevens lbw b Abdul Razzaq	25	– (5) c Shah b Weekes	0
†P. A. Nixon not out	52	– (6) lbw b Keegan	34
J. N. Snape c Hutton b Dalrymple	3	– (7) not out	40
*P. A. J. DeFreitas lbw b Keegan	46	– (8) c Hutton b Keegan	0
R. M. Amin c Weekes b Noffke	5	– b Abdul Razzaq	11
M. J. A. Whiley c Joyce b Weekes	6	– lbw b Keegan	3
L-b 7, n-b 39	46	B 7, l-b 9, n-b 8	24
1/197 (2) 2/206 (1) 3/209 (3) 4/296 (4) 5/297 (5) 6/332 (6) 7/337 (8) 8/413 (9) 9/422 (10) 10/447 (11)	447	1/0 (1) 2/31 (2) 3/207 (3) 4/207 (5) 5/247 (4) 6/292 (6) 7/292 (8) 8/297 (9) 9/326 (10) 10/335 (11)	335

Bonus points – Leicestershire 5, Middlesex 3.

Bowling: *First Innings*—Noffke 29–7–74–1; Keegan 29–4–114–6; Weekes 18–1–65–1; Abdul Razzaq 27–6–113–1; Dalrymple 14–1–73–1; Joyce 1–0–1–0. *Second Innings*—Noffke 20–5–48–3; Abdul Razzaq 15–2–54–1; Dalrymple 15–3–45–1; Keegan 23–10–66–3; Weekes 25–2–98–2; Hutton 2–0–8–0.

Umpires: G. Sharp and A. G. T. Whitehead.

MIDDLESEX v WARWICKSHIRE

At Southgate, July 15, 16, 17, 18. Drawn. Middlesex 8 pts, Warwickshire 12 pts. Toss: Warwickshire.

Although the Southgate pitch was less docile than the previous week, this was a good toss to win: it was something of a surprise when Warwickshire were 100 for five shortly after lunch. But Frost and Brown added 209 for the sixth wicket – a county record against Middlesex, as was 90 for the ninth wicket between Giles and Betts. Giles, who had asked the England management for permission to play, just missed his fourth century but secured Warwickshire maximum batting points for the first time since May. Middlesex again frustrated their supporters, throwing wickets away with injudicious strokes (none more than the one Abdul Razzaq played at his first ball); only Nash, at No. 9, reached 40. Following on, however, Hutton and Koenig batted with discipline to preserve Middlesex's unbeaten record. Koenig fell in the nineties for the third time in 2003, but Hutton completed his third hundred in four matches off the last ball.

Close of play: First day, Warwickshire 315-7 (Giles 4, Smith 1); Second day, Middlesex 58-2 (Koenig 10, Shah 5); Third day, Middlesex 244-8 (Nash 29, Noffke 6).

Warwickshire

*M. J. Powell b Hutton	8
N. V. Knight b Keegan	11
M. A. Wagh c Joyce b Noffke	0
I. R. Bell c Shah b Abdul Razzaq	31
J. O. Troughton c and b Noffke	37
†T. Frost c Nash b Noffke	84
D. R. Brown b Keegan	113
A. F. Giles c Abdul Razzaq b Keegan	96
N. M. K. Smith c Weekes b Hutton	30
M. M. Betts c Nash b Weekes	38
A. Richardson not out	9
L-b 20, n-b 19	39
1/14 (2) 2/15 (3) 3/45 (1) 4/67 (4) 5/100 (5) 6/309 (7) 7/309 (6) 8/386 (9) 9/476 (10) 10/496 (8)	496

Bonus points – Warwickshire 5, Middlesex 2 (130 overs: 433-8).

Bowling: Noffke 32–8–92–3; Keegan 34.4–9–125–3; Hutton 13–3–53–2; Abdul Razzaq 21–6–71–1; Dalrymple 16–2–53–0; Weekes 23–6–60–1; Joyce 4–0–17–0; Shah 1–0–5–0.

Middlesex

*A. J. Strauss c Troughton b Giles	37	– c Wagh b Betts	23
S. G. Koenig c Powell b Richardson	35	– b Giles	96
J. W. M. Dalrymple lbw b Brown	0	– c Brown b Betts	0
O. A. Shah b Richardson	31		
B. L. Hutton c Frost b Smith	38	– (4) not out	102
E. C. Joyce b Giles	29	– (5) not out	22
Abdul Razzaq c Betts b Giles	0		
P. N. Weekes lbw b Giles	10		
†D. C. Nash not out	44		
A. A. Noffke c Knight b Richardson	7		
C. B. Keegan c Wagh b Richardson	0		
B 12, l-b 3, w 2, n-b 12	29	L-b 9, n-b 29	38
1/51 (1) 2/52 (3) 3/110 (4) 4/123 (2) 5/177 (6) 6/177 (7) 7/201 (5) 8/211 (8) 9/252 (10) 10/260 (11)	260	1/50 (1) 2/56 (3) 3/215 (2)	(3 wkts) 281

Bonus points – Middlesex 2, Warwickshire 3.

Bowling: *First Innings*—Betts 15–2–63–0; Richardson 19.1–5–37–4; Brown 5–2–8–1; Giles 30–7–90–4; Smith 20–5–47–1. *Second Innings*—Richardson 12–1–52–0; Betts 12–2–44–2; Brown 19–5–45–0; Giles 28–4–78–1; Troughton 5–0–47–0; Knight 4–3–6–0.

Umpires: T. E. Jesty and B. Leadbeater.

At Guildford, July 23, 24, 25, 26. MIDDLESEX drew with SURREY.

At Nottingham, July 30, 31, August 1, 2. MIDDLESEX beat NOTTINGHAMSHIRE by four wickets.

MIDDLESEX v KENT

At Lord's, August 13, 14, 15, 16. Kent won by eight wickets. Kent 22 pts, Middlesex 7 pts. Toss: Middlesex.

Middlesex went down to their first Championship defeat in the first division – all the more galling after they had won the toss and gained only their second set of maximum batting points. The last time, against Leicestershire, Nash had contributed a century; he made a more important one here, rescuing his side from 190 for seven as Cook helped him add 125. Kent ended the second day 122 behind, with four wickets left. Then came arguably Middlesex's worst day of the season. With Khan making a career-best 78, the remaining batsmen added another 192 to give Kent a 70-run lead. If the bowling had been poor, the Middlesex batting was worse: Saggers accelerated the slide with three strikes in 18 balls, and Muralitharan finished with nine wickets on his first-class debut at Lord's. Kent needed 96 to win, a formality completed shortly after lunch.

Close of play: First day, Middlesex 364-8 (Nash 104, Keegan 21); Second day, Kent 285-6 (Ealham 5, Khan 2); Third day, Middlesex 141-6 (Weekes 38, Dalrymple 20).

Middlesex

*A. J. Strauss c Jones b Khan	12 – c Jones b Saggers	9
S. G. Koenig c Ealham b Muralitharan	57 – lbw b Khan	0
O. A. Shah b Khan	0 – c Jones b Saggers	12
B. L. Hutton c Jones b Saggers	17 – c Jones b Sheriyar	3
E. C. Joyce b Muralitharan	43 – lbw b Saggers	17
P. N. Weekes lbw b Muralitharan	11 – c Jones b Muralitharan	51
†D. C. Nash run out	113 – c Ealham b Muralitharan	23
J. W. M. Dalrymple c Walker b Muralitharan	5 – c Symonds b Muralitharan	28
S. J. Cook lbw b Saggers	65 – c Walker b Muralitharan	0
C. B. Keegan not out	36 – c and b Symonds	2
J. H. Dawes b Muralitharan	18 – not out	0
B 1, l-b 8, w 3, n-b 18	30 B 1, l-b 13, w 2, n-b 4	20
1/31 (1) 2/35 (3) 3/58 (4) 4/119 (2) 5/149 (6) 6/160 (5) 7/190 (8) 8/315 (9) 9/381 (7) 10/407 (11)	407 1/8 (2) 2/25 (3) 3/28 (1) 4/48 (5) 5/69 (4) 6/108 (7) 7/154 (8) 8/154 (9) 9/165 (10) 10/165 (6)	165

Bonus points – Middlesex 5, Kent 3.

Bowling: *First Innings*—Saggers 26–3–95–2; Khan 17–1–100–2; Sheriyar 15–6–40–0; Ealham 15–3–42–0; Muralitharan 38–4–103–5; Symonds 4–1–18–0. *Second Innings*—Saggers 17–4–31–3; Khan 7–2–38–1; Muralitharan 21.2–8–38–4; Sheriyar 4–2–6–1; Symonds 11–0–27–1; Ealham 9–7–11–0.

Kent

*D. P. Fulton c Cook b Dalrymple	86 – b Dawes	2
R. W. T. Key b Cook	40 – not out	45
M. A. Carberry lbw b Dawes	49 – c Nash b Keegan	4
A. Symonds b Keegan	71 – not out	41
M. J. Walker lbw b Weekes	17	
M. A. Ealham lbw b Dawes	58	
†G. O. Jones c Nash b Keegan	2	
A. Khan lbw b Dawes	78	
M. J. Saggers b Cook	44	
M. Muralitharan c Shah b Dalrymple	12	
A. Sheriyar not out	0	
B 1, l-b 13, w 4, n-b 2	20 B 4	4
1/64 (2) 2/172 (3) 3/218 (1) 4/272 (5) 5/276 (4) 6/282 (7) 7/415 (6) 8/422 (8) 9/471 (10) 10/477 (9)	477 1/4 (1) 2/23 (3)	(2 wkts) 96

Bonus points – Kent 5, Middlesex 2 (130 overs: 440-8).

Bowling: *First Innings*—Dawes 32–3–119–3; Keegan 35–8–92–2; Cook 26.2–3–113–2; Weekes 19–1–64–1; Dalrymple 25–3–75–2. *Second Innings*—Dawes 5–1–12–1; Keegan 6–1–20–1; Cook 2–0–18–0; Joyce 1–0–4–0; Weekes 5.2–1–23–0; Dalrymple 5–0–15–0.

Umpires: R. Palmer and A. G. T. Whitehead.

At Manchester, August 21, 22, 23, 24. MIDDLESEX drew with LANCASHIRE.

At Birmingham, August 26, 27, 28, 29. MIDDLESEX lost to WARWICKSHIRE by 31 runs.

At Hove, September 5, 6, 7, 8. MIDDLESEX lost to SUSSEX by seven wickets.

MIDDLESEX v NOTTINGHAMSHIRE

At Lord's, September 10, 11, 12, 13. Drawn. Middlesex 10 pts, Nottinghamshire 11 pts. Toss: Nottinghamshire.

With rain culling 101 overs, a positive result always looked elusive, but Nottinghamshire, already relegated, might have made a game of it. They decided against and, with Middlesex not wanting to risk defeat in the quest for survival, the draw became inevitable. The final day's cricket was possibly the most pointless either county has played, though a scoreboard operator added a touch of humour. When Nash became the tenth Middlesex bowler (it would have been 11, but Bloomfield was injured) his figures were omitted on the board, with a note at the top reading: "Sorry Nashy – no more room." Nottinghamshire started the day 83 ahead, and batted on and on, apparently with two objectives: a second century of the match for Warren, and the season's fastest hundred for Pietersen. Strauss's first-ever wicket stopped him at 68 in 57 balls, but Warren achieved his target, assisted by some very occasional bowling. The ultimate nonsense came when he scored his last two runs off Keegan, a right-arm quickie bowling slow left-arm.

Close of play: First day, Nottinghamshire 316-5 (Warren 100, Read 16); Second day, Middlesex 9-0 (Strauss 1, Koenig 4); Third day, Nottinghamshire 48-0 (Bicknell 30, Gallian 12).

Nottinghamshire

D. J. Bicknell c Nash b Bloomfield	35	– lbw b Dawes	42
*J. E. R. Gallian c Strauss b Dawes	73	– c Dalrymple b Joyce	116
B. M. Shafayat c Nash b Hutton	5	– c sub b Weekes	6
R. J. Warren lbw b Keegan	123	– not out	113
K. P. Pietersen c Joyce b Weekes	70	– b Strauss	68
C. L. Cairns run out	1		
†C. M. W. Read st Nash b Dalrymple	16	– not out	3
P. J. Franks b Weekes	1		
S. C. G. MacGill c Weekes b Dalrymple	0		
P. J. McMahon b Keegan	7	– (6) c Nash b Koenig	30
C. E. Shreck not out	4		
B 6, l-b 11, w 5, n-b 4	26	B 10, l-b 10, w 1, n-b 8	29
1/70 (1) 2/106 (3) 3/146 (2) 4/274 (5) 5/275 (6) 6/317 (7) 7/320 (8) 8/321 (9) 9/346 (4) 10/361 (10)	361	1/86 (1) 2/115 (3) 3/234 (2) 4/345 (5) 5/397 (6) (5 wkts dec.)	407

Bonus points – Nottinghamshire 4, Middlesex 3.

Bowling: *First Innings*—Dawes 28–3–93–1; Keegan 25–2–105–2; Bloomfield 6.4–1–25–1; Hutton 5–1–26–1; Weekes 23.2–3–72–2; Joyce 3–0–18–0; Dalrymple 7–2–5–2. *Second Innings*—Dawes 13–2–47–1; Keegan 13–2–37–0; Weekes 23–6–32–1; Dalrymple 20–2–71–0; Hutton 10–0–70–0; Joyce 7–1–23–1; Shah 8–0–36–0; Strauss 5–0–27–1; Koenig 5–0–19–1; Nash 5–0–25–0.

Middlesex

*A. J. Strauss c and b Cairns	15
S. G. Koenig lbw b Shreck	13
B. L. Hutton c Pietersen b MacGill	20
O. A. Shah c Warren b Franks	87
E. C. Joyce c Read b Cairns	14
P. N. Weekes c MacGill b Franks	38
†D. C. Nash not out	53
J. W. M. Dalrymple c Pietersen b MacGill	26
C. B. Keegan lbw b MacGill	17
J. H. Dawes b Cairns	14
T. F. Bloomfield lbw b MacGill	0
B 3, l-b 5, w 11, n-b 10	29
1/28 (1) 2/43 (2) 3/85 (3) 4/121 (5) 5/197 (6) 6/230 (4) 7/274 (8) 8/304 (9) 9/325 (10) 10/326 (11)	326

Bonus points – Middlesex 3, Nottinghamshire 3.

Bowling: Cairns 30–8–101–3; Shreck 14–5–36–1; Franks 12–3–54–2; MacGill 33–6–98–4; McMahon 5–0–29–0.

Umpires: M. J. Kitchen and N. A. Mallender.

NORTHAMPTONSHIRE

Imported steel

ANDREW RADD

By recruiting Kepler Wessels as manager, Northamptonshire sought to forge a new, hard-nosed and excuse-free ethos, after two disastrous seasons. Wessels arrived from Eastern Province with a formidable reputation as a blunt disciple of the work ethic. His appointment was a kill-or-cure remedy.

His task seemed gargantuan: in their first Championship match, against Yorkshire, Northamptonshire suffered their heaviest first-class defeat since 1921. Yet five months later, the county's supporters were celebrating promotion in both the Championship and National League. Second place in both competitions hugely exceeded expectations. Among ten Championship wins came a record-equalling run of six in succession.

The influence of the southern hemisphere on Northamptonshire's cricket was evident throughout – uncomfortably so for those who craved a local flavour to the team. The South African Wessels looked on approvingly as Mike Hussey, the captain, and Phil Jaques, born in New South Wales to English parents, scored 4,729 runs between them in the two league competitions – more than 44% of the total scored off the bat. Hussey's decision, announced in September, to sit out the next English summer dismayed officials and supporters, and no wonder. At Taunton in August, he hit an unbeaten 331, beating his own 329 not out as Northamptonshire's highest score, and became only the third batsman – after Wally Hammond and Graeme Hick – to make three Championship triple-hundreds. Hussey's total of 820 runs in the National League was also a county record, while in the Twenty20 Cup he demonstrated that thoughtful shot selection and urgent running were more effective than empty-headed slogging.

Jaques, spotted in Sydney Grade cricket, proved only slightly less prolific. But his future remained uncertain. Although he signed a three-year deal in November, by then Jaques had already played for New South Wales in 2003-04, which compromised his status as an ECB-qualified player. Northamptonshire resolved to mount a legal challenge. They also strengthened their batting by signing Usman Afzaal from Nottinghamshire.

Of the other batsmen, only David Sales (the captain for 2004) even approached 1,000 first-class runs. Mark Powell and Rob White – the two youngsters who burst through in late 2002 – endured frustrating seasons. Powell's close catching helped him hold his place for most of the Championship games; White played only three, and found himself overtaken by Tim Roberts, Kettering-born but formerly of Lancashire, who forced his way into a job after a string of big scores in local league cricket.

As in 2000, Championship promotion owed much to the off-spin of Jason Brown and Graeme Swann. Then, they took 98 wickets at less than 25; three years later, it was 98 at under 23. Brown proved the Championship's most successful England-qualified spinner, and his control made him a force to be reckoned with on all surfaces. However, the Northampton pitches were usually prepared with slow bowlers in mind: none of the last six Championship matches at Wantage Road – of which Northamptonshire won five – reached a fourth day. All season the county flirted with the eight-point penalty for a "poor" pitch that was finally imposed in September during the title decider against Worcestershire. A repeat in 2004 will mean 12 points docked.

Jason Brown

Other than the South African fast bowler Andre Nel, none of the seamers managed more than 21 Championship wickets. After a poor start, Nel ended his first county season as a crowd favourite through his wholehearted and aggressive approach – a little too aggressive for some, as he frequently extended his follow-through to deliver an observation or two. But he lacked a regular new-ball partner. Carl Greenidge, the county's outstanding seamer in 2002, was often out of sorts, though 20-year-old Adam Shantry, a left-armer from the Academy, made a promising debut. Nel, like Hussey, was unavailable for 2004. Two of Wessels's compatriots were signed instead: Martin van Jaarsveld and Johann Louw.

All the bowlers were well supported by Toby Bailey behind the stumps. Gerry Brophy was twice preferred in an effort to bolster the batting: for one of those games, against Gloucestershire, Northamptonshire fielded five players of Australian or South African origin. Only Powell was born inside the county boundary. The "League of Nations" tag, dating back to the cosmopolitan Northamptonshire teams of the 1950s, was appropriate once again. This, together with the pitch policy, created a sense in some quarters that the club were more concerned with their short-term interests than the greater good of English cricket. This was reinforced when the chief executive, Steve Coverdale, said in a TV interview that Northamptonshire supporters were more concerned with the county than with England.

The close season brought dramatic personnel changes. Vice-captain Tony Penberthy, injured for much of the summer, was controversially released. Nick Cook declined a new contract as technical support manager (effectively No. 2 to Wessels) and – most significantly and surprisingly – Coverdale himself left the club to seek "a new challenge". Appointed in 1985, Coverdale, still not 50, was the longest-serving senior administrator on the circuit and only the third post-war incumbent in charge at the County Ground. The sudden end to this bastion of stability added to the sense that this apparently successful club was more fearful than elated.

NORTHAMPTONSHIRE RESULTS

All first-class matches – Played 17: Won 10, Lost 3, Drawn 4.
County Championship matches – Played 16: Won 10, Lost 2, Drawn 4.

Frizzell County Championship, 2nd in Division 2; Cheltenham & Gloucester Trophy, 3rd round; National Cricket League, 2nd in Division 2; Twenty20 Cup, 4th in Midlands/Wales/West Group.

COUNTY CHAMPIONSHIP AVERAGES

BATTING AND FIELDING

Cap		*M*	*I*	*NO*	*R*	*HS*	*100s*	*50s*	*Avge*	*Ct/St*
2001	M. E. K. Hussey§	14	21	2	1,697	331*	6	5	89.31	17
2003	P. A. Jaques	16	25	1	1,409	222	5	6	58.70	9
1999	D. J. Sales	16	23	2	942	200*	2	4	44.85	13
	G. L. Brophy	6	10	3	289	152*	1	1	41.28	11
	T. W. Roberts	7	10	0	263	83	0	2	26.30	7
2003	J. W. Cook	14	22	2	517	85	0	3	25.85	3
	A. Nel§	13	13	3	258	42	0	0	25.80	4
2003	T. M. B. Bailey	14	19	3	384	101*	1	0	24.00	29/6
1999	G. P. Swann	9	13	1	256	69	0	2	21.33	9
	M. J. Powell	15	23	2	427	60	0	3	20.33	29
	B. J. Phillips	7	8	2	119	48*	0	0	19.83	1
	R. A. White	3	6	0	110	55	0	1	18.33	1
2000	J. F. Brown	13	12	6	91	38	0	0	15.16	2
	M. J. Cawdron	6	6	0	63	24	0	0	10.50	1
	C. G. Greenidge	7	6	2	32	13	0	0	8.00	2
	M. S. Panesar	5	6	3	15	6*	0	0	5.00	3

Also batted: R. S. G. Anderson (1 match) 13; J. A. R. Blain (3 matches) 1*, 5; D. E. Paynter (2 matches) 50, 2, 5; A. L. Penberthy (cap 1994) (1 match) 32*; A. J. Shantry (2 matches) 38*, 0 (1 ct); D. G. Wright§ (2 matches) 46, 27 (1 ct).

§ *Overseas player.*

BOWLING

	O	*M*	*R*	*W*	*BB*	*5W/i*	*Avge*
B. J. Phillips	149	47	400	21	4-45	0	19.04
J. F. Brown	617	180	1,469	65	7-69	4	22.60
G. P. Swann	238.2	37	759	33	7-33	3	23.00
M. J. Cawdron	142.3	31	504	20	6-87	1	25.20
J. W. Cook	162.3	46	479	19	5-31	1	25.21
A. Nel	422.3	99	1,292	36	5-47	1	35.88
J. A. R. Blain	62.2	3	366	10	5-84	1	36.60
M. S. Panesar	131.2	24	447	11	3-92	0	40.63
C. G. Greenidge	205.3	23	927	20	3-33	0	46.35

Also bowled: R. S. G. Anderson 10–1–67–0; T. M. B. Bailey 1–0–3–0; M. E. K. Hussey 14–2–52–1; P. A. Jaques 4–0–25–0; D. E. Paynter 6–1–26–0; A. L. Penberthy 11–4–26–0; M. J. Powell 2–0–12–0; T. W. Roberts 4–0–4–0; D. J. Sales 1–0–4–0; A. J. Shantry 31.4–9–113–6; R. A. White 7–0–61–1; D. G. Wright 73.5–19–194–7.

COUNTY RECORDS

Highest score for:	331*	M. E. K. Hussey v Somerset at Taunton	2003
Highest score against:	333	K. S. Duleepsinhji (Sussex) at Hove	1930
Best bowling for:	10-127	V. W. C. Jupp v Kent at Tunbridge Wells	1932
Best bowling against:	10-30	C. Blythe (Kent) at Northampton	1907
Highest total for:	781-7 dec.	v Nottinghamshire at Northampton	1995
Highest total against:	670-9 dec.	by Sussex at Hove	1921
Lowest total for:	12	v Gloucestershire at Gloucester	1907
Lowest total against:	33	by Lancashire at Northampton	1977

NORTHAMPTONSHIRE DIRECTORY

ADDRESS

County Ground, Wantage Road, Northampton NN1 4TJ (01604 514455; fax 01604 514488; email post@nccc.co.uk). **Website** www.nccc.co.uk.

GROUNDS

Northampton (County Ground): 2 miles NE of town centre between A45 and A43. Turn L off Wellingborough Road A4500 at Abington Avenue. Nearest station: Northampton (2¼ miles).

Luton (Wardown Park): 1¼ miles N of town centre between A6 New Bedford Road and Old Bedford Road at junction with Stockingstone Road. Nearest station: Luton (1 mile).

Milton Keynes (Campbell Park): Located E of the centre and 1 mile from junction 14 of M1. The ground is on E side of Campbell Park. Turns S off H6 (A509) near V10 (A4146). Nearest station: Milton Keynes Central (1 mile). *Possible National League fixture.*

OFFICIALS

Captain 2003 – M. E. K. Hussey; 2004 – D. J. Sales
First-team coach K. C. Wessels
Director of academy D. J. Capel
President L. A. Wilson
Chairman S. G. Schanschieff
Chief executive 2003 – S. P. Coverdale
Chairman, cricket committee J. A. Scopes
Head groundsman 2003 – D. Bates
2004 – P. Marshall
Scorer A. C. Kingston

PLAYERS

Players expected to reappear in 2004

	Former counties	*Country*	*Born*	*Birthplace*
Anderson Ricaldo Sherman Glenroy	Essex	E	22.9.1976	*Hammersmith*
Bailey Tobin Michael Barnaby		E	28.8.1976	†*Kettering*
Brophy Gerard Louis		SA (EU)	26.11.1975	*Welkom*
Brown Jason Fred		E	10.10.1974	*Newcastle-under-Lyme*
Cawdron Michael John.	Glos	E	7.10.1974	*Luton*
Cook Jeffrey William		E	2.2.1972	*Sydney, Aus.*
Greenidge Carl Gary	Surrey	E	20.4.1978	*Basingstoke*
Huggins Thomas Benjamin		E	6.3.1983	*Peterborough*
‡**Jaques** Philip Anthony		A (EU)	3.5.1979	*Wollongong*
***Nel** Andre.		SA	15.7.1977	*Germiston*
Panesar Mudhsuden Singh.		E	25.4.1982	*Luton*
Phillips Ben James.	Kent	E	30.9.1974	*Lewisham*
Powell Mark John		E	4.11.1980	†*Northampton*
Roberts Timothy William	Lancs	E	4.3.1978	†*Kettering*
Sales David John		E	3.12.1977	*Carshalton*
Shantry Adam John.		E	13.11.1982	*Bristol*
Swann Graeme Peter		E	24.3.1979	†*Northampton*
White Robert Allan		E	15.10.1979	*Chelmsford*

Players due to join in 2004

***Afzaal** Usman	Notts	E	9.6.1977	*Rawalpindi, Pak.*
Jones Philip Steffan	Somerset	E	9.2.1974	*Llanelli*
Louw Johann		SA	12.4.1979	*Cape Town*
***van Jaarsveld** Martin		SA	18.6.1974	*Klerksdorp*

* *Test player.* † *Born in Northamptonshire.* ‡ *Eligibility in dispute, February 2004.*

At Leeds, April 18, 19, 20. NORTHAMPTONSHIRE lost to YORKSHIRE by an innings and 343 runs.

NORTHAMPTONSHIRE v GLOUCESTERSHIRE

At Northampton, April 23, 24, 25, 26. Drawn. Northamptonshire 9 pts, Gloucestershire 12 pts. Toss: Northamptonshire.

With a day and a half's play lost to rain the match was reduced to a battle for bonus points, though a maiden Championship century from Rhodes ensured some late entertainment. The pitch, scrubbed at both ends, offered help to spinners almost from the start – "it did turn, but not unduly" was the verdict of ECB inspector Chris Broad – and Northamptonshire reached a serviceable 352. No play was possible after lunch on the second or third days, but Rhodes and Windows brought a little sparkle to the last with a stand of 157 in only 25 overs. Enjoying an animated tussle with his fellow South African Nel, Rhodes hit 128 at a run a ball as Northamptonshire's spinners – Panesar and Swann – proved even less effective in helpful conditions than their Gloucestershire counterparts Ball and Fisher. Bailey took over from Northamptonshire's acting-captain when Sales was taken ill on the last day.

Close of play: First day, Northamptonshire 338-8 (Bailey 30, Nel 39); Second day, Gloucestershire 61-1 (Spearman 35, Hancock 3); Third day, Gloucestershire 114-1 (Spearman 68, Hancock 23).

Northamptonshire

First innings		Second innings	
M. J. Powell c Russell b Ball	60	– c Russell b Ball	13
D. E. Paynter lbw b Fisher	50	– b Averis	2
P. A. Jaques c Hancock b Fisher	14	– c and b Ball	11
J. W. Cook lbw b Ball	10	– not out	21
*D. J. Sales c Russell b Alleyne	59		
G. L. Brophy c Hancock b Fisher	32	– (5) not out	10
G. P. Swann c Hancock b Ball	1		
†T. M. B. Bailey c Rhodes b Averis	38		
R. S. G. Anderson b Ball	13		
A. Nel c Russell b Ball	39		
M. S. Panesar not out	5		
B 2, l-b 7, n-b 22	31	B 3, l-b 1, n-b 8	12
1/126 (2) 2/144 (1) 3/148 (3) 4/164 (4) 5/253 (5) 6/253 (6) 7/257 (7) 8/275 (9) 9/338 (10) 10/352 (8)	352	1/3 (2) 2/27 (3) 3/44 (1)	(3 wkts) 69

Bonus points – Northamptonshire 4, Gloucestershire 3.

Bowling: *First Innings*—Averis 19.2–5–46–1; Sillence 9–1–60–0; Alleyne 8–3–12–1; Fisher 36–6–121–3; Ball 40–9–104–5. *Second Innings*—Averis 5–1–22–1; Sillence 5–1–18–0; Ball 8–6–4–2; Fisher 5–0–19–0; Hancock 1–0–2–0.

Gloucestershire

C. M. Spearman c Swann b Nel	69
W. P. C. Weston c Powell b Panesar	13
T. H. C. Hancock b Swann	59
J. N. Rhodes c Cook b Swann	128
M. G. N. Windows c Powell b Panesar	35
*M. W. Alleyne not out	32
†R. C. Russell not out	31
B 14, l-b 10, n-b 12	36
1/52 (2) 2/128 (1) 3/173 (3) 4/330 (4) 5/331 (5)	(5 wkts dec.) 403

I. D. Fisher, M. C. J. Ball, R. J. Sillence and J. M. M. Averis did not bat.

Bonus points – Gloucestershire 5, Northamptonshire 1.

Bowling: Nel 30–7–84–1; Anderson 10–1–67–0; Panesar 45–9–135–2; Swann 21–2–76–2; Jaques 1–0–17–0.

Umpires: I. J. Gould and A. A. Jones.

At Worcester, April 30, May 1, 2, 3. NORTHAMPTONSHIRE drew with WORCESTERSHIRE.

At Cambridge, May 9, 10, 11. NORTHAMPTONSHIRE lost to CAMBRIDGE UCCE by four wickets.

NORTHAMPTONSHIRE v YORKSHIRE

At Northampton, May 14, 15, 16, 17. Drawn. Northamptonshire 12 pts, Yorkshire 10 pts. Toss: Yorkshire. First-class debut: T. T. Bresnan.

A week before the opening Test against Zimbabwe, Vaughan heartened England supporters with his first century for Yorkshire since the final match of 2001. He passed both 50 and 100 with sixes, but needed to be at his watchful best to counter an outstanding display of controlled off-spin by Brown, who sent down 38 overs unchanged from the Abington Avenue end. Vaughan and McGrath – also called up by England – added 142 together. Northamptonshire replied strongly through Jaques and Hussey, the two Australian-born left-handers putting on 189. On a good pitch, Jaques, who could not make the New South Wales side over the winter, preyed on anything off-line, and five and three-quarter hours of efficient batting brought him 222 off 301 balls, including two sixes and 26 fours. The second day included several dropped chances and he escaped twice after reaching his second successive Championship hundred. No play was possible on the third day, and on the fourth Vaughan enjoyed a gentle net, hitting five fours in an over off Hussey.

Close of play: First day, Yorkshire 360-9 (Dawson 50, Hoggard 9); Second day, Northamptonshire 311-2 (Jaques 183, Cook 24); Third day, No play.

Yorkshire

M. J. Wood c Hussey b Blain	15	– lbw b Panesar	33
M. P. Vaughan lbw b Brown	103	– not out	64
*A. McGrath c and b Panesar	51	– not out	0
M. J. Lumb c Nel b Panesar	46		
†R. J. Blakey b Brown	8		
G. M. Fellows lbw b Brown	18		
T. T. Bresnan lbw b Brown	7		
R. K. J. Dawson b Panesar	77		
A. K. D. Gray lbw b Blain	25		
R. J. Sidebottom c Bailey b Nel	0		
M. J. Hoggard not out	21		
L-b 2, n-b 26	28	N-b 12	12
1/31 (1) 2/173 (3) 3/189 (2) 4/207 (5) 5/249 (6) 6/271 (4) 7/273 (7) 8/339 (9) 9/345 (10) 10/399 (8)	399	1/105 (1)	(1 wkt) 109

Bonus points – Yorkshire 4, Northamptonshire 3.

Bowling: *First Innings*—Nel 26–7–84–1; Blain 13–0–75–2; Penberthy 11–4–26–0; Brown 46–18–99–4; Panesar 31.1–6–113–3. *Second Innings*—Blain 8–0–54–0; Cook 5–2–11–0; Hussey 3–0–32–0; Powell 2–0–12–0; Panesar 1.1–1–0–1.

Northamptonshire

*M. E. K. Hussey c Lumb b Gray	65
M. J. Powell c Bresnan b Hoggard	5
P. A. Jaques lbw b Hoggard	222
J. W. Cook c and b Sidebottom	29
D. J. Sales c Dawson b Hoggard	2
A. L. Penberthy not out	32
†T. M. B. Bailey lbw b Sidebottom	7
M. S. Panesar not out	3
B 15, l-b 6, n-b 16	37
1/23 (2) 2/212 (1) 3/346 (4) 4/353 (5) 5/366 (3) 6/382 (7)	(6 wkts dec.) 402

A. Nel, J. A. R. Blain and J. F. Brown did not bat.

Bonus points – Northamptonshire 5, Yorkshire 2.

Bowling: Hoggard 29–6–74–3; Sidebottom 23–4–66–2; Bresnan 12.2–3–43–0; Dawson 27–3–105–0; Gray 24–4–66–1; McGrath 4–0–22–0; Vaughan 1–0–5–0.

Umpires: N. J. Llong and R. Palmer.

NORTHAMPTONSHIRE v GLAMORGAN

At Northampton, May 30, 31, June 1. Glamorgan won by 55 runs. Glamorgan 19 pts, Northamptonshire 5 pts. Toss: Glamorgan.

Northamptonshire's plan to prepare a more seamer-friendly pitch backfired as the Glamorgan attack, led splendidly by Kasprowicz, ensured victory within three days. Kasprowicz was rarely out of the action: he contributed usefully with the bat in both innings; ripped out his three fellow Australian-born players, Hussey, Jaques and Cook, in the space of seven balls on the second morning; and was even more hostile as Northamptonshire set about scoring 228 to win in a day and a half, a task they approached with unnecessary haste and insufficient care. The run-out of Mark Powell, answering Jaques's call for the sharpest of singles, summed up the rash approach. Earlier, Glamorgan had won a closely fought and absorbing battle for first-innings lead, but when they slumped to 140 for eight in their second innings – only 147 ahead – the match looked to have swung decisively against them. Croft, Kasprowicz and Wharf eked out 80 priceless runs for the last two wickets, however, and Glamorgan never relinquished the initiative.

Close of play: First day, Northamptonshire 70-0 (Hussey 24, White 37); Second day, Glamorgan 71-4 (Hughes 34, Maynard 6).

Glamorgan

A. Dale c Powell b Nel	37	– c Hussey b Greenidge	2
J. Hughes b Nel	24	– lbw b Greenidge	73
D. L. Hemp c Jaques b Phillips	4	– lbw b Nel	9
M. J. Powell lbw b Brown	29	– b Phillips	8
M. P. Maynard c Greenidge b Brown	26	– (6) c Powell b Phillips	11
†M. A. Wallace lbw b Brown	32	– (7) lbw b Nel	3
*R. D. B. Croft c Nel b Phillips	34	– (8) not out	50
D. S. Harrison c Brown b Cook	33	– (9) st Bailey b Brown	1
M. S. Kasprowicz c Sales b Brown	21	– (10) c Bailey b Nel	23
A. G. Wharf c Bailey b Phillips	5	– (11) c Sales b Nel	17
D. A. Cosker not out	1	– (5) c Powell b Phillips	0
L-b 11, w 2, n-b 10	23	L-b 4, w 2, n-b 17	23
1/48 (2) 2/57 (3) 3/112 (4) 4/114 (1) 5/173 (5) 6/174 (6) 7/225 (8) 8/259 (9) 9/263 (7) 10/269 (10)	269	1/13 (1) 2/22 (3) 3/62 (4) 4/65 (5) 5/93 (6) 6/101 (7) 7/139 (2) 8/140 (9) 9/190 (10) 10/220 (11)	220

Bonus points – Glamorgan 2, Northamptonshire 3.

Bowling: *First Innings*—Nel 24–4–86–2; Greenidge 15–3–65–0; Phillips 15.3–7–33–3; Cook 8–1–22–1; Brown 23–7–52–4. *Second Innings*—Nel 25–8–57–4; Greenidge 12–0–72–2; Cook 4–1–10–0; Phillips 18–4–59–3; Brown 7–3–18–1.

Northamptonshire

*M. E. K. Hussey c Wallace b Kasprowicz	39	– c Cosker b Kasprowicz	14
R. A. White c Croft b Wharf	55	– b Kasprowicz	14
P. A. Jaques c Hemp b Kasprowicz	0	– c Wallace b Kasprowicz	59
J. W. Cook lbw b Kasprowicz	0	– c Powell b Croft	6
D. J. Sales c Wallace b Harrison	23	– c Wallace b Harrison	6
M. J. Powell lbw b Cosker	55	– run out	15
†T. M. B. Bailey c Hemp b Harrison	2	– lbw b Kasprowicz	2
B. J. Phillips c Dale b Croft	23	– b Kasprowicz	16
C. G. Greenidge b Harrison	13	– c Hughes b Kasprowicz	0
A. Nel c Hughes b Harrison	24	– c Wharf b Harrison	14
J. F. Brown not out	0	– not out	12
B 4, l-b 8, w 2, n-b 14	28	L-b 4, n-b 10	14
1/97 (1) 2/101 (3) 3/101 (4) 4/113 (2) 5/161 (5) 6/169 (7) 7/224 (6) 8/224 (8) 9/255 (9) 10/262 (10)	262	1/37 (2) 2/40 (1) 3/70 (4) 4/85 (5) 5/120 (6) 6/126 (3) 7/137 (7) 8/137 (9) 9/152 (8) 10/172 (10)	172

Bonus points – Northamptonshire 2, Glamorgan 3.

Bowling: *First Innings*—Kasprowicz 24–4–77–3; Harrison 24.3–8–64–4; Wharf 16–4–44–1; Croft 18–4–32–1; Dale 3–0–16–0; Cosker 10–4–17–1. *Second Innings*—Kasprowicz 23–3–72–6; Harrison 6.1–0–19–2; Wharf 8–2–41–0; Croft 15–5–34–1; Cosker 1–0–2–0.

Umpires: M. R. Benson and N. A. Mallender.

At Gloucester, June 4, 5, 6, 7. NORTHAMPTONSHIRE beat GLOUCESTERSHIRE by an innings and 54 runs.

At Northampton, June 11. NORTHAMPTONSHIRE lost to PAKISTANIS by 62 runs (see Pakistani tour section).

At Northampton, June 22. NORTHAMPTONSHIRE v SOUTH AFRICANS. No result (see South African tour section).

NORTHAMPTONSHIRE v DERBYSHIRE

At Northampton, June 27, 28, 29. Northamptonshire won by 180 runs. Northamptonshire 18 pts, Derbyshire 3 pts. Toss: Northamptonshire.

Having been publicly told by coach Kepler Wessels to shape up, Swann produced a career-best seven for 33 and spun Northamptonshire to a comfortable victory. But the pitch was the main talking point. From the first session, it turned appreciably and showed uneven bounce, although an ECB panel ruled that it was only "below average" with no deduction of points necessary. Derbyshire – no strangers to point deductions themselves – bridled at this decision, described by their coach Adrian Pierson as a "complete joke". Hussey and Jaques coped best, using their feet effectively against the spinners, though Dumelow still managed the first two five-wicket hauls of his career with his off-breaks. He also top-scored in Derbyshire's first innings, hitting three sixes in a pugnacious half-century, but his team-mates were found wanting against Brown's off-spin. After Northamptonshire stretched their lead to 286, Derbyshire crumbled again. Swann, who did not bowl in the first innings, took the last six wickets in eight overs either side of lunch on the third day. An ankle injury prevented Cork bowling at all.

Close of play: First day, Derbyshire 46-3 (Kaif 17, Sutton 11); Second day, Derbyshire 0-0 (Di Venuto 0, Gait 0).

Northamptonshire

First innings		Second innings	
*M. E. K. Hussey st Sutton b Dumelow	59	– c Sutton b Dumelow	28
M. J. Powell b Dean	6	– st Sutton b Welch	5
P. A. Jaques c Di Venuto b Dumelow	60	– lbw b Kaif	57
J. W. Cook c Di Venuto b Wharton	10	– c Di Venuto b Dumelow	21
D. J. Sales c Di Venuto b Dumelow	20	– lbw b Dumelow	33
G. P. Swann b Wharton	0	– c Cork b Welch	19
B. J. Phillips c Cork b Dumelow	4	– lbw b Dumelow	4
†T. M. B. Bailey lbw b Wharton	9	– run out	40
A. Nel not out	23	– c Dean b Welch	23
M. S. Panesar c Cork b Wharton	0	– b Dumelow	1
J. F. Brown b Dumelow	2	– not out	2
B 8, l-b 2	10	B 6, l-b 4	10
1/36 (2) 2/116 (1) 3/127 (3) 4/161 (4) 5/161 (6) 6/161 (5) 7/172 (7) 8/180 (8) 9/184 (10) 10/203 (11)	203	1/19 (2) 2/60 (1) 3/100 (3) 4/124 (4) 5/168 (5) 6/174 (7) 7/174 (6) 8/204 (9) 9/209 (10) 10/243 (8)	243

Bonus points – Northamptonshire 1, Derbyshire 3.

Bowling: *First Innings*—Welch 7–3–28–0; Dean 8–2–18–1; Lungley 2–0–15–0; Wharton 24–7–50–4; Dumelow 23.4–4–82–5. *Second Innings*—Welch 17–3–55–3; Wharton 20–4–70–0; Dumelow 23–2–78–5; Dean 5–2–9–0; Kaif 4–1–21–1.

Derbyshire

First innings		Second innings	
A. I. Gait run out	7	– (2) c Swann b Brown	29
M. J. Di Venuto c Powell b Nel	10	– (1) lbw b Brown	29
C. W. G. Bassano lbw b Brown	1	– not out	17
M. Kaif c Swann b Nel	28	– c Sales b Swann	0
†L. D. Sutton st Bailey b Panesar	25	– lbw b Brown	3
*D. G. Cork b Brown	16	– c Jaques b Swann	2
G. Welch st Bailey b Brown	0	– c Hussey b Swann	7
T. Lungley c Swann b Brown	7	– c Bailey b Swann	0
N. R. C. Dumelow not out	52	– b Swann	11
K. J. Dean c Jaques b Nel	3	– c Panesar b Swann	2
L. J. Wharton b Nel	1	– c Panesar b Swann	1
B 4, l-b 6	10	B 1, l-b 4	5
1/13 (1) 2/18 (2) 3/22 (3) 4/60 (4) 5/81 (6) 6/87 (7) 7/97 (5) 8/141 (8) 9/150 (10) 10/160 (11)	160	1/57 (2) 2/58 (1) 3/61 (4) 4/72 (5) 5/75 (6) 6/85 (7) 7/85 (8) 8/99 (9) 9/103 (10) 10/106 (11)	106

Bonus points – Northamptonshire 3.

Bowling: *First Innings*—Nel 17–1–52–4; Phillips 3–1–8–0; Brown 23–6–39–4; Panesar 10–2–51–1. *Second Innings*—Nel 6–1–19–0; Phillips 5–0–19–0; Brown 21–5–30–3; Swann 15.1–2–33–7.

Umpires: A. Clarkson and M. J. Harris.

NORTHAMPTONSHIRE v HAMPSHIRE

At Northampton, July 2, 3, 4. Northamptonshire won by seven wickets. Northamptonshire 18 pts, Hampshire 3 pts. Toss: Northamptonshire. Championship debut: D. G. Wright.

Hampshire lost in just over two days' playing time and reached the halfway point of their Championship campaign winless. Inevitably, given the controversy surrounding the previous match at Wantage Road, the pitch came under close scrutiny. But although 13 wickets fell on the first day, and no one managed a fifty in the entire match, little blame could be apportioned to the surface, and much to poor batting. Two players making Championship debuts for Northamptonshire – Damien

Wright, a Tasmanian all-rounder, and the former Gloucestershire seamer Michael Cawdron – began Hampshire's slide to 125 all out. But despite Hampshire missing four front-line seam bowlers, Northamptonshire struggled too, at least until a last-wicket stand of 77. Mascarenhas took six for 55, his best for two years. Trailing by 93, Hampshire again fell well short of 200, despite some dogged resistance from Katich and Francis. Northamptonshire completed their third successive victory in the extra half-hour on the third evening and rose into the promotion places.

Close of play: First day, Northamptonshire 20-3 (Jaques 14, Cawdron 0); Second day, Northamptonshire 163-9 (Phillips 30, Brown 7).

Hampshire

D. A. Kenway c Wright b Cawdron	5	– c Sales b Cawdron	3
*J. P. Crawley c Sales b Cawdron	21	– lbw b Wright	16
S. M. Katich c Jaques b Cawdron	11	– lbw b Brown	36
R. A. Smith c Bailey b Phillips	41	– b Wright	28
J. D. Francis c Bailey b Swann	8	– c Powell b Cawdron	36
W. S. Kendall c Swann b Wright	4	– lbw b Phillips	3
†N. Pothas c Sales b Wright	0	– c Bailey b Phillips	5
A. D. Mascarenhas c Hussey b Swann	11	– c Cook b Swann	28
S. D. Udal c Bailey b Swann	12	– c Bailey b Cawdron	14
J. T. A. Bruce c Powell b Brown	4	– c Bailey b Wright	6
J. A. Tomlinson not out	0	– not out	1
L-b 2, n-b 6	8	B 2, l-b 1	3
1/7 (1) 2/23 (3) 3/83 (2) 4/84 (4) 5/94 (6) 6/94 (7) 7/107 (8) 8/114 (5) 9/125 (10) 10/125 (9)	125	1/19 (1) 2/19 (2) 3/71 (4) 4/89 (3) 5/92 (6) 6/100 (7) 7/151 (8) 8/171 (5) 9/174 (9) 10/179 (10)	179

Bonus points – Northamptonshire 3.

Bowling: *First Innings*—Wright 16–6–33–2; Cawdron 13–5–25–3; Phillips 6–2–27–1; Brown 15–5–27–1; Swann 3.1–0–11–3. *Second Innings*—Wright 16.2–5–38–3; Cawdron 19–7–58–3; Phillips 10–6–15–2; Swann 12–3–24–1; Brown 15–3–41–1.

Northamptonshire

*M. E. K. Hussey c Pothas b Bruce	4	– (2) lbw b Tomlinson	18
M. J. Powell c Kendall b Bruce	0	– (1) not out	38
P. A. Jaques lbw b Mascarenhas	15	– c Pothas b Tomlinson	0
J. W. Cook c Kenway b Mascarenhas	0	– c Katich b Tomlinson	25
M. J. Cawdron c Pothas b Mascarenhas	24		
D. J. Sales c Pothas b Mascarenhas	6	– (5) not out	5
G. P. Swann c Katich b Mascarenhas	10		
D. G. Wright c Pothas b Mascarenhas	46		
†T. M. B. Bailey lbw b Bruce	11		
B. J. Phillips not out	48		
J. F. Brown lbw b Udal	38		
B 2, l-b 4, n-b 10	16	L-b 1	1
1/0 (2) 2/5 (1) 3/8 (4) 4/21 (3) 5/35 (6) 6/51 (7) 7/72 (5) 8/116 (9) 9/141 (8) 10/218 (11)	218	1/44 (2) 2/44 (3) 3/72 (4)	(3 wkts) 87

Bonus points – Northamptonshire 1, Hampshire 3.

Bowling: *First Innings*—Mascarenhas 25–6–55–6; Bruce 21–6–72–3; Udal 16.4–4–49–1; Tomlinson 6–1–35–0; Katich 1–0–1–0. *Second Innings*—Mascarenhas 6–1–18–0; Bruce 5–0–24–0; Tomlinson 5–0–37–3; Udal 4.4–0–7–0.

Umpires: T. E. Jesty and A. G. T. Whitehead.

At Chester-le-Street, July 9, 10, 11. NORTHAMPTONSHIRE beat DURHAM by eight wickets.

NORTHAMPTONSHIRE v SOMERSET

At Northampton, July 23, 24. Northamptonshire won by an innings and 61 runs. Northamptonshire 20 pts, Somerset 3 pts. Toss: Northamptonshire. Championship debuts: A. J. Shantry; G. M. Gilder. County debut: T. W. Roberts.

Somerset capitulated, handing Northamptonshire a fifth successive victory, but once again the pitch attracted controversy. Although reported by the umpires for offering too much turn on the opening day, no points were deducted by the ECB inspector Peter Walker. That decision had much to do with Somerset's abject batting, which convinced Walker that he was watching "one side at the top of their form and another at the bottom". Replying to 325, Somerset proved equally fragile against both seam and spin, losing 18 wickets on the second day. In their first innings no batsman managed more than 22 as Adam Shantry, a 20-year-old left-arm fast bowler, took three wickets in five balls on Championship debut. Somerset followed on, and once a dogged fifth-wicket stand of 83 had been broken, Brown quickly wrapped up the match with five wickets in nine overs. Earlier, the Kettering-born batsman Tim Roberts hit an aggressive 83. Roberts, who had played briefly for Lancashire before working as a teacher, was offered match terms in response to a brilliant run of form in local club cricket. Blackwell took five wickets with his left-arm spin.

Close of play: First day, Somerset 26-2 (Wood 3, Cox 9).

Northamptonshire

Batsman	Runs
*M. E. K. Hussey b Blackwell	20
T. W. Roberts st Turner b Blackwell	83
P. A. Jaques c Turner b Blackwell	41
D. J. Sales b Blackwell	38
M. J. Powell run out	18
†T. M. B. Bailey lbw b Jones	0
G. P. Swann c Burns b Jones	44
B. J. Phillips c Turner b Blackwell	12
A. J. Shantry not out	38
A. Nel b McLean	22
J. F. Brown c Burns b Jones	1
L-b 8	8
1/62 (1) 2/131 (3) 3/170 (2) 4/191 (4) 5/192 (6) 6/232 (5) 7/252 (8) 8/262 (7) 9/322 (10) 10/325 (11)	325

Bonus points – Northamptonshire 3, Somerset 3.

Bowling: McLean 15–2–51–1; Gilder 4–0–32–0; Jones 17.1–2–61–3; Blackwell 38–6–96–5; Dutch 16–3–62–0; Burns 3–0–15–0.

Somerset

Batsman	First innings		Second innings	
P. D. Bowler c Bailey b Phillips	14	–	(8) c Jaques b Brown	8
M. J. Wood c Powell b Nel	10	–	(1) c Shantry b Phillips	6
J. D. C. Bryant b Phillips	0	–	c Bailey b Phillips	15
J. Cox lbw b Nel	22	–	c Jaques b Brown	24
*M. Burns run out	15	–	c Phillips b Brown	55
I. D. Blackwell lbw b Shantry	5	–	c Hussey b Nel	40
†R. J. Turner not out	10	–	(2) lbw b Phillips	0
K. P. Dutch c Powell b Shantry	0	–	(7) c Powell b Brown	7
N. A. M. McLean c Nel b Shantry	0	–	c Roberts b Brown	0
P. S. Jones b Brown	8	–	b Brown	8
G. M. Gilder c Sales b Nel	12	–	not out	0
			B 2, l-b 3	5
1/15 (1) 2/15 (3) 3/46 (4) 4/47 (2) 5/66 (5) 6/66 (6) 7/66 (8) 8/66 (9) 9/81 (10) 10/96 (11)	96		1/2 (2) 2/9 (1) 3/32 (3) 4/59 (4) 5/142 (6) 6/142 (5) 7/157 (7) 8/157 (9) 9/165 (8) 10/168 (10)	168

Bonus points – Northamptonshire 3.

Bowling: *First Innings*—Nel 13.2–2–51–3; Phillips 11–6–20–2; Brown 7–3–17–1; Shantry 5–3–8–3. *Second Innings*—Nel 16–4–48–1; Phillips 11–3–21–3; Shantry 8–2–19–0; Brown 22.1–7–42–6; Swann 6–0–33–0.

Umpires: D. J. Constant and P. Willey.

At Southampton, July 31, August 1, 2, 3. NORTHAMPTONSHIRE beat HAMPSHIRE by five wickets.

At Taunton, August 14, 15, 16, 17. NORTHAMPTONSHIRE drew with SOMERSET.

At Derby, August 20, 21, 22. NORTHAMPTONSHIRE beat DERBYSHIRE by an innings and 231 runs.

NORTHAMPTONSHIRE v DURHAM

At Northampton, September 3, 4, 5. Northamptonshire won by an innings and 85 runs. Northamptonshire 22 pts, Durham 2 pts. Toss: Durham.

Relegated in 2001 and third from the bottom in 2002, Northamptonshire made sure of promotion this time with another straightforward win featuring major contributions from their three Australian-born regulars. The innocuous-looking medium-pace of Cook made deep inroads into Durham's first innings, only Collingwood offering much resistance as his team-mates squandered first use of a blameless pitch. Then Hussey, dropped on 39, and Jaques added 268 at four an over to consolidate Northamptonshire's powerful position. In glorious second-day sunshine Sales looked set to become the third century-maker, hitting an aggressive 79 before missing a sweep at Phillips. By the declaration, Bridge had conceded 180 runs, the most by a Durham bowler in a first-class innings. Durham went in again on the second evening facing a daunting deficit of 348, and defeat was almost inevitable. At 111 for one, some cricket on the last day – a rarity at Northampton in 2003 – looked possible, but wickets fell regularly to begin with, and then in a clatter, Brown and Swann taking the last four in seven deliveries.

Close of play: First day, Northamptonshire 166-1 (Hussey 62, Jaques 102); Second day, Durham 50-0 (Lewis 10, Muchall 40).

Durham

*J. J. B. Lewis c Powell b Nel	0	– b Greenidge	22
G. J. Muchall c Bailey b Hussey	23	– c Powell b Cook	62
M. L. Love c Powell b Cook	25	– c Roberts b Brown	84
P. D. Collingwood c Swann b Cook	68	– c Sales b Swann	10
G. J. Pratt lbw b Nel	26	– c Hussey b Brown	5
A. M. Thorpe lbw b Brown	11	– c Powell b Swann	4
†P. Mustard c Jaques b Cook	10	– c Powell b Brown	35
G. D. Bridge not out	12	– not out	33
Shoaib Akhtar c Nel b Brown	9	– c Hussey b Brown	0
N. C. Phillips b Cook	1	– lbw b Brown	0
N. Killeen lbw b Cook	0	– c Powell b Swann	0
B 1, l-b 4	5	B 2, l-b 6	8
1/0 (1) 2/40 (3) 3/52 (2) 4/125 (5) 5/152 (6) 6/168 (4) 7/168 (7) 8/181 (9) 9/188 (10) 10/190 (11)	190	1/79 (1) 2/111 (2) 3/123 (4) 4/154 (5) 5/183 (6) 6/211 (3) 7/262 (7) 8/262 (9) 9/262 (10) 10/263 (11)	263

Bonus points – Northamptonshire 3.

Bowling: *First Innings*—Nel 15–3–39–2; Greenidge 10–3–41–0; Cook 9.3–2–31–5; Hussey 3–1–5–1; Brown 19–4–46–2; Swann 4–0–23–0. *Second Innings*—Nel 12–2–52–0; Greenidge 10–2–26–1; Brown 34–8–90–5; Swann 24.3–5–77–3; Cook 8–2–10–1.

Northamptonshire

*M. E. K. Hussey b Bridge	187	G. P. Swann not out	50
T. W. Roberts c Pratt b Shoaib Akhtar	0	A. Nel not out	22
P. A. Jaques b Bridge	147	B 8, l-b 6	14
D. J. Sales lbw b Phillips	79		
M. J. Powell c Mustard b Shoaib Akhtar	10	1/1 (2) 2/269 (3) (7 wkts dec.)	538
J. W. Cook lbw b Bridge	12	3/396 (4) 4/427 (5)	
†T. M. B. Bailey c Muchall b Phillips	17	5/440 (1) 6/453 (6) 7/489 (7)	

C. G. Greenidge and J. F. Brown did not bat.

Bonus points – Northamptonshire 5, Durham 2.

Bowling: Shoaib Akhtar 21–3–91–2; Killeen 20–5–59–0; Bridge 42–6–180–3; Phillips 35.2–3–160–2; Collingwood 11–0–34–0.

Umpires: J. H. Hampshire and B. Leadbeater.

At Cardiff, September 10, 11, 12, 13. NORTHAMPTONSHIRE beat GLAMORGAN by 20 runs.

NORTHAMPTONSHIRE v WORCESTERSHIRE

At Northampton, September 17, 18, 19. Northamptonshire won by 92 runs. Northamptonshire 8 pts (after 8 pt penalty), Worcestershire 3 pts. Toss: Northamptonshire.

To scattered boos from the home supporters, Worcestershire made sure of the second division title with a calculating declaration. With both teams already promoted, Northamptonshire needed at least 17 points to have a chance of being champions; by closing their first innings at the fall of the eighth wicket (thus denying Northamptonshire a final bowling point), Worcestershire kept their opponents' maximum to 16. It prompted Northamptonshire's coach Kepler Wessels to complain that the spirit of the game had been lost in the modern era. His counterpart at Worcestershire, Tom Moody, saw it differently: with an extra £15,000 in prize money at stake, he said, "the bottom line is to win the division". However, some thought Northamptonshire were in no position to invoke the spirit of cricket. These evidently included the ECB pitch panel who ruled that the wicket had helped spinners excessively and inflicted the eight-point deduction the county had flirted with all season. Wessels pointed out that Northamptonshire scored 379 in their second innings, which he thought reflected either well on the pitch or badly on the future of English spin bowling. His team at least had the satisfaction of inflicting Worcestershire's first Championship defeat of the season. The surface was dry and dusty on the first day, with signs of scuffing at the ends, and Worcestershire were able to keep Northamptonshire under 200 thanks to Batty – who bowled with excellent control in the first innings – and fellow off-spinner Shaftab Khalid, a 20-year-old named in the winter Academy squad. Then, with Worcestershire still 24 behind, came the controversial declaration, after which Northamptonshire knuckled down to the business of winning the game. Worcestershire were left an unlikely 404 for victory in two days; in the event, they lasted just two sessions.

Close of play: First day, Worcestershire 139-6 (Leatherdale 7, Pipe 2); Second day, Northamptonshire 379-9 (Cawdron 18, Brown 2).

Northamptonshire

*M. E. K. Hussey run out	4	– (2) c Pipe b Batty	79
T. W. Roberts c Hick b Hayward	6	– (1) c Hick b Hayward	0
P. A. Jaques c Pipe b Khalid	29	– c Mason b Khalid	39
D. J. Sales lbw b Batty	32	– c Peters b Khalid	29
G. L. Brophy lbw b Batty	25	– b Khalid	60
J. W. Cook b Khalid	57	– c Leatherdale b Batty	31
G. P. Swann c Hayward b Batty	1	– (8) c Solanki b Khalid	69
†T. M. B. Bailey c Pipe b Khalid	13	– (7) b Hayward	22
M. J. Cawdron c and b Batty	4	– b Mason	18
M. S. Panesar not out	6	– run out	0
J. F. Brown b Hayward	6	– not out	2
B 5, l-b 8	13	B 12, l-b 14, w 2, n-b 2	30
1/6 (2) 2/10 (1) 3/73 (3) 4/75 (4) 5/126 (5) 6/130 (7) 7/153 (8) 8/170 (9) 9/184 (6) 10/196 (11)	196	1/0 (1) 2/62 (3) 3/108 (4) 4/207 (5) 5/248 (2) 6/263 (6) 7/339 (7) 8/368 (8) 9/369 (10) 10/379 (9)	379

Bonus points – Worcestershire 3.

Bowling: *First Innings*—Mason 11–3–19–0; Hayward 11.3–0–41–2; Batty 32–11–53–4; Khalid 21–1–70–3. *Second Innings*—Hayward 10–2–37–2; Mason 11.4–3–28–1; Batty 24–4–94–2; Khalid 28–5–131–4; Hick 21–5–63–0.

Worcestershire

S. D. Peters b Swann	69	– b Panesar	50
G. A. Hick c Brophy b Cook	0	– lbw b Cawdron	4
Kadeer Ali b Swann	6	– b Brown	30
*B. F. Smith b Swann	34	– b Panesar	53
V. S. Solanki st Bailey b Swann	17	– b Panesar	0
D. A. Leatherdale b Swann	20	– c Swann b Brown	61
G. J. Batty c Hussey b Panesar	1	– c and b Brown	20
†D. J. Pipe not out	13	– c sub b Brown	35
M. S. Mason b Swann	8	– st Bailey b Swann	27
S. A. Khalid (did not bat)		– c Swann b Brown	8
M. Hayward (did not bat)		– not out	8
B 1, l-b 3	4	B 4, l-b 11	15
1/4 (2) 2/37 (3) 3/109 (1) 4/124 (4) 5/133 (5) 6/134 (7) 7/164 (6) 8/172 (9)	(8 wkts dec.) 172	1/7 (2) 2/80 (3) 3/88 (1) 4/88 (5) 5/181 (4) 6/223 (7) 7/242 (6) 8/285 (9) 9/298 (10) 10/311 (8)	311

Bonus points – Northamptonshire 2.

Bowling: *First Innings*—Cawdron 4–0–22–0; Cook 5–3–8–1; Swann 18.3–5–66–6; Brown 11–1–35–0; Panesar 17–4–37–1. *Second Innings*—Cawdron 7–2–15–1; Cook 6–2–14–0; Brown 20.5–1–89–5; Swann 19–2–86–1; Panesar 24–2–92–3.

Umpires: A. Clarkson and R. Palmer.

NOTTINGHAMSHIRE

And when they were down, they were down

PAUL FEARN

Nottinghamshire embarked on their first foray into the upper echelon of the County Championship with considerable enthusiasm and expectation. So impressive had been their run of form at the back end of the previous summer that predictions of a top-three finish were not uncommon.

When the season began brightly – a good home win over Warwickshire and a solid draw at Lancashire made them Championship leaders at the end of April – such talk appeared justified. But what followed was in such stark contrast to Nottinghamshire's promotion run in 2003, when they lost only one of their last ten matches, that it beggared belief the same squad of players were responsible. They dropped into the relegation zone in late May and never escaped; it was not until the very last game that they achieved their second victory.

The batting rolled over with alarming ease and regularity. August saw two spectacular collapses at Trent Bridge. On the final morning against Middlesex, they lost their remaining five wickets in the first five overs, when any decent lower-order runs could have set up a winning opportunity. This was eclipsed by a spineless display against Muttiah Muralitharan, who rattled through their last six in 12 balls, enabling Kent to wrap up victory on the second afternoon. But the nadir of Nottinghamshire's miserable batting year had come in May against Essex: an abject capitulation for 79 all out. The total was actually a relief: it had been eight for seven.

Batting statistics do not make it obvious why the team struggled so severely. The prolific Kevin Pietersen plundered over 1,500 first-class runs, captain Jason Gallian completed 1,000 in the final game, while Paul Franks, a much-improved batsman, and new signing Russell Warren both averaged more than 40 – though Warren played only half the season.

Individuals played their parts; the problem was that they played them as individuals. Seldom was a clutch of top-order batsmen in form at the same time, and an inability to forge lengthy, let alone meaningful, partnerships cost Nottinghamshire dear. They were also let down by Usman Afzaal, who had completed 1,000 runs in each of the previous three seasons. His form and average dipped so dramatically that he played only seven Championship games, passing 50 once in 13 attempts. Chris Read's availability was interrupted first by injury and then by England duty, and the potentially exhilarating duo of Chris Cairns and Bilal Shafayat performed well below par.

The lack of runs often gave the bowlers little to go at but, in truth, the attack could be held just as culpable for failing to give their batsmen competitive targets to chase. With the exception of Greg Smith, who claimed another 50 wickets with unerring and lively left-armers, it was a sorry season for the seamers. Lacking in penetration, accuracy and discipline, they seldom looked likely to bowl a side out twice, and very rarely did.

Cairns barely bowled until July, and did not approach anything like his usual form with the ball until the closing weeks, while the normally ebullient Franks suffered a crisis of confidence and lacked direction. Australian leg-spinner Stuart MacGill escaped blame, claiming 42 wickets in 11 games; unlike 2002, when he proved so effective, he was given virtually no opportunity to attack with the security of a large lead. The only other vaguely bright spot came from the Cornishman, Charlie Shreck, whose elevation from Minor Counties cricket produced accuracy to shame more experienced team-mates and earned him a two-year deal. The most acute decline was seen in Andrew Harris. His whole-hearted displays had earned him 63 Championship wickets as Nottinghamshire won promotion, but he seemed to have misplaced his ability to swing the ball and finished with only ten scalps in eight Championship games.

Kevin Pietersen

In one-day cricket, early exits in the Twenty20 Cup and C&G knockout, and a failure to mount a serious promotion bid in the National League, meant the season was effectively over in June. Nottinghamshire were consistently inconsistent in the League, alternating wins and losses for nine consecutive matches in the later stages. Cairns usually captained the team in the shorter game, and at times led admirably with the bat, scoring six unbeaten, match-winning half-centuries. Read, who was called up for England's one-day side, played some fine innings in the League, where he averaged 75; Pietersen, with 776 League runs, threatened Clive Rice's club record of 814.

Towards the end of the summer, divisions were showing in the beleaguered dressing-room. Pietersen publicly implied that he was carrying the team and that, coupled with an openly expressed desire to leave a year before the end of his contract, infuriated his team-mates. He chose to warm up without them for the final fixtures. Afzaal's loss of form was compounded by his attitude and he was told he could go, which he did, gracelessly and vociferously, to Northamptonshire. For 2004, Nottinghamshire raided Australia for their overseas players: MacGill was due to return alongside the Test batsman Damien Martyn, with Michael Hussey's highly rated younger brother, David, covering Martyn's expected absences. Wicket-keeper David Alleyne joined from Middlesex as cover for the resurgent Read, opener Anurag Singh came from Worcestershire, while Kent all-rounder Mark Ealham and Yorkshireman Ryan Sidebottom, both former Test players, bolstered the seam attack.

NOTTINGHAMSHIRE RESULTS

All first-class matches – Played 18: Won 3, Lost 9, Drawn 6.
County Championship matches – Played 16: Won 2, Lost 8, Drawn 6.

Frizzell County Championship, 8th in Division 1; Cheltenham & Gloucester Trophy, 4th round; National Cricket League, 5th in Division 2; Twenty20 Cup, 6th in North Group.

COUNTY CHAMPIONSHIP AVERAGES

BATTING AND FIELDING

Cap		*M*	*I*	*NO*	*R*	*HS*	*100s*	*50s*	*Avge*	*Ct/St*
2002	K. P. Pietersen	15	29	0	1,488	221	4	10	51.31	16
	R. J. Warren	9	18	2	734	123	3	2	45.87	9/2
1999	P. J. Franks	14	25	8	729	123*	2	1	42.88	9
1998	J. E. R. Gallian	12	23	2	876	116	3	5	41.71	15
2000	D. J. Bicknell	14	27	1	822	81	0	7	31.61	4
1993	C. L. Cairns§	13	23	2	645	104	1	4	30.71	7
1999	C. M. W. Read	12	22	2	525	93	0	3	26.25	26/3
	G. E. Welton	11	22	0	547	99	0	5	24.86	6
	S. Elworthy§	4	7	0	159	52	0	1	22.71	3
2000	U. Afzaal	7	13	0	264	72	0	1	20.30	2
	B. M. Shafayat	11	21	0	422	97	0	3	20.09	3
1995	W. M. Noon	2	4	1	38	25	0	0	12.66	7
	R. J. Logan	2	4	2	23	13*	0	0	11.50	0
2001	G. J. Smith	12	20	3	168	42	0	0	9.88	4
	P. J. McMahon	2	4	0	38	30	0	0	9.50	2
2002	S. C. G. MacGill§	11	18	6	112	27	0	0	9.33	2
	C. E. Shreck	9	14	6	51	19	0	0	6.37	1
	V. Atri	2	4	0	15	5	0	0	3.75	3
2000	A. J. Harris	8	11	1	37	16*	0	0	3.70	1

Also batted: G. D. Clough (2 matches) 0, 1*, 16 (1 ct); M. N. Malik (2 matches) 30*, 15, 10; S. R. Patel (1 match) 9, 55 (1 ct); D. L. Vettori§ (1 match) 0, 0 (1 ct).

§ *Overseas player.*

BOWLING

	O	*M*	*R*	*W*	*BB*	*5W/i*	*Avge*
G. J. Smith	346.1	75	1,205	50	5-42	3	24.10
S. Elworthy	134.1	17	534	16	5-71	1	33.37
S. C. G. MacGill	412.2	73	1,408	42	6-117	2	33.52
C. E. Shreck	191.1	40	745	21	5-100	1	35.47
P. J. Franks	265.2	45	1,070	25	4-62	0	42.80
C. L. Cairns	184	31	755	15	3-59	0	50.33
A. J. Harris	189.5	26	806	10	2-98	0	80.60

Also bowled: G. D. Clough 20–0–96–1; J. E. R. Gallian 29–6–91–1; R. J. Logan 14–1–94–0; P. J. McMahon 40–9–142–5; M. N. Malik 57–7–227–3; S. R. Patel 8–5–10–0; K. P. Pietersen 86.3–10–383–6; B. M. Shafayat 9–0–71–0; D. L. Vettori 34.3–2–198–5.

COUNTY RECORDS

Highest score for:	312*	W. W. Keeton v Middlesex at The Oval	1939
Highest score against:	345	C. G. Macartney (Australians) at Nottingham	1921
Best bowling for:	10-66	K. Smales v Gloucestershire at Stroud	1956
Best bowling against:	10-10	H. Verity (Yorkshire) at Leeds	1932
Highest total for:	739-7 dec.	v Leicestershire at Nottingham	1903
Highest total against:	781-7 dec.	by Northamptonshire at Northampton	1995
Lowest total for:	13	v Yorkshire at Nottingham	1901
Lowest total against:	16	by Derbyshire at Nottingham	1879
	16	by Surrey at The Oval	1880

NOTTINGHAMSHIRE DIRECTORY

ADDRESS

County Cricket Ground, Trent Bridge, Nottingham NG2 6AG (0115 982 3000; fax 0115 945 5730; email marketing.notts@ecb.co.uk). **Website** www.nottsccc.co.uk.

GROUNDS

Nottingham (Trent Bridge): 1½ miles S of city centre in West Bridgford S of bridge over River Trent at junction of A52 Grantham Road and A6011 Radcliffe Road and Bridgford Road. Nearest station: Nottingham (1 mile).

Cleethorpes: 1½ miles S of town centre and ¼ mile from seafront. From A1098 Isaacs Hill turn R into St Peter's Avenue, R into Highgate, L into Thrunscoe Road, then cross into Hardys Road and L into Chichester Road. Nearest station: Cleethorpes (1½ miles).

OFFICIALS

Captain J. E. R. Gallian
Director of cricket M. Newell
President 2003 – The Rt Hon. K. Clarke
Chairman 2003 – A. Bocking
Chief executive D. G. Collier
Chairman, cricket committee S. E. Foster
Head groundsman S. Birks
Scorer G. Stringfellow

PLAYERS

Players expected to reappear in 2004

	Former counties	*Country*	*Born*	*Birthplace*
Atri Vikram		E	9.3.1983	*Hull*
Bicknell Darren John	Surrey	E	24.6.1967	*Guildford*
Clough Gareth David	Yorks	E	23.5.1978	*Leeds*
Franks Paul John		E	3.2.1979	†*Mansfield*
***Gallian** Jason Edward Riche	Lancs	E	25.6.1971	*Sydney, Aus.*
Harris Andrew James	Derbys	E	26.6.1973	*Ashton-under-Lyne*
Logan Richard James	Northants	E	28.1.1980	*Stone*
***MacGill** Stuart Charles Glyndwr	Somerset	A	25.2.1971	*Mount Lawley*
McMahon Paul Joseph		E	12.3.1983	*Wigan*
Noon Wayne Michael	Northants	E	5.2.1971	*Grimsby*
Patel Samit Rohit		E	30.11.1984	*Leicester*
Pietersen Kevin Peter		SA (EU)	27.6.1980	*Pietermaritzberg*
Randall Stephen John		E	9.6.1980	†*Nottingham*
***Read** Christopher Mark Wells	Glos	E	10.8.1978	*Paignton*
Shafayat Bilal Mustapha		E	10.7.1984	†*Nottingham*
Shreck Charles Edward		E	6.1.1978	*Truro*
Smith Gregory James		SA (EU)	30.10.1971	*Pretoria*
Smith William Rew		E	28.9.1982	*Luton*
Thomas Aaron Courteney		E	6.5.1985	*Edmonton*
Warren Russell John	Northants	E	10.9.1971	*Northampton*

Players due to join in 2004

Alleyne David	Middx	E	17.4.1976	*York*
***Ealham** Mark Alan	Kent	E	27.8.1969	*Willesborough*
Hussey David John		A	15.7.1977	*Morley (WA)*
***Martyn** Damien Richard	Leics, Yorks	A	21.10.1971	*Darwin*
***Sidebottom** Ryan Jay	Yorks	E	15.1.1978	*Huddersfield*
Singh Anurag	Warwicks, Worcs	E	9.9.1975	*Kanpur, India*

* *Test player.* † *Born in Nottinghamshire.*

NOTTINGHAMSHIRE v DURHAM UCCE

At Nottingham, April 12, 13, 14. Nottinghamshire won by an innings and 168 runs. Toss: Durham UCCE. First-class debuts: C. E. Shreck; D. O. Brown, L. M. Daggett, M. A. P. Dale, W. T. D. Hanson, S. R. Polley. County debut: S. Elworthy. UCCE debuts: W. R. Smith, D. B. Taylor.

The students were comfortably outclassed, and Shafayat made an early bid for the fastest hundred of the season – 73 balls – but the most remarkable incident was only the third case of a player being timed out in first-class cricket. Nottinghamshire were delaying the declaration for Read's century, but No. 10 Charlie Shreck lasted just three balls on first-class debut. Harris, nursing a groin strain, had not expected to bat and, by the time he had strapped on his pads, and raced part-way down the pavilion steps, the fielders were heading his way – he had already exceeded the three minutes now allowed for players to arrive at the crease under Law 31. Earlier, the students had struggled against Harris as a bowler, though Delroy Taylor – who had represented Jamaica against Lancashire in a 1996 pre-season friendly – managed four hours of unconvincing resistance. Nottinghamshire cruised past 500 and Pietersen's accurate off-spin brought him career-best figures and victory in seven sessions.

Close of play: First day, Nottinghamshire 199-1 (Gallian 126, Afzaal 1); Second day, Durham UCCE 141-6 (Brown 28, Bishop 10).

Durham UCCE

First innings		Second innings	
A. J. Maiden c Read b Smith	0	– run out	35
D. B. Taylor b Franks	82	– c Read b Franks	1
*A. G. R. Loudon c Read b Elworthy	12	– b Franks	48
W. R. Smith lbw b Harris	28	– c Read b Pietersen	0
M. A. P. Dale c Afzaal b Harris	5	– c and b Pietersen	8
R. S. Ferley b Pietersen	9	– c Read b Shreck	1
D. O. Brown c Harris b Elworthy	0	– c sub b Elworthy	31
J. E. Bishop b Elworthy	0	– lbw b Pietersen	50
S. R. Polley lbw b Harris	9	– c Read b Shafayat	2
†W. T. D. Hanson b Harris	0	– not out	9
L. M. Daggett not out	2	– c Gallian b Pietersen	1
B 1, l-b 4, w 3, n-b 10	18	L-b 7, w 2, n-b 14	23
1/0 (1) 2/23 (3) 3/67 (4) 4/78 (5) 5/119 (6) 6/120 (7) 7/120 (8) 8/152 (9) 9/152 (10) 10/165 (2)	165	1/10 (2) 2/81 (3) 3/87 (4) 4/92 (1) 5/99 (5) 6/109 (6) 7/150 (7) 8/171 (9) 9/205 (8) 10/209 (11)	209

Bowling: *First Innings*—Smith 10–3–22–1; Elworthy 14–4–40–3; Shreck 7–0–28–0; Harris 10–2–23–4; Franks 8.4–1–33–1; Pietersen 8–3–14–1. *Second Innings*—Elworthy 12–1–53–1; Franks 11–3–25–2; Pietersen 14.1–5–31–4; Shreck 15–4–54–1; Afzaal 4–2–14–0; Shafayat 6–2–22–1; Gallian 2–0–3–0.

Nottinghamshire

D. J. Bicknell c Hanson b Bishop	62
*J. E. R. Gallian retired hurt	126
U. Afzaal st Hanson b Ferley	52
K. P. Pietersen st Hanson b Ferley	58
B. M. Shafayat c Bishop b Ferley	105
†C. M. W. Read not out	94
P. J. Franks run out	0
S. Elworthy b Bishop	20
G. J. Smith c Ferley b Bishop	4
C. E. Shreck lbw b Bishop	0
A. J. Harris timed out	0
B 1, l-b 3, w 1, n-b 16	21
1/198 (1) 2/291 (3) 3/332 (4) 4/444 (5) 5/445 (7) 6/528 (8) 7/542 (9) 8/542 (10) 9/542 (11)	542

Gallian retired hurt at 199.

Bowling: Bishop 23.5–3–111–4; Daggett 25–6–91–0; Dale 4–0–32–0; Polley 9–0–50–0; Loudon 9–0–69–0; Ferley 25–3–133–3; Brown 4–0–52–0.

Umpires: G. I. Burgess and J. W. Lloyds.

NOTTINGHAMSHIRE v WARWICKSHIRE

At Nottingham, April 18, 19, 20, 21. Nottinghamshire won by three wickets. Nottinghamshire 19.25 pts (after 0.75 pt penalty), Warwickshire 3.75 pts (after 0.25 pt penalty). Toss: Warwickshire. County debut: M. W. Clark. Championship debut: C. E. Shreck.

After a tense tussle, Nottinghamshire prevailed on their first division debut. The opening day saw 410 runs and 15 wickets under clear skies on a good pitch. For Warwickshire, only Wagh used the conditions, driving crisply, before Shreck, a 6ft 7in Cornish seamer on a three-month trial, wound the innings up with four in 28 balls. Nottinghamshire fared little better, losing three quick wickets before Cairns steadied the ship with Bicknell. The precocious Shafayat played some beautiful, wristy leg-side shots, and it was a shock when he missed his century. Resuming 127 behind, Warwickshire got back into the game when their last four added 220, thanks to a defiant 94 from acting-captain Giles. Nottinghamshire needed 264 in a day and a half, and were already on course when Warwickshire's Western Australian seamer Michael Clark strained his groin – this was to be his only county game. The bustling Betts snatched four for nought in 15 balls either side of lunch, but Read and Franks saw their side home.

Close of play: First day, Nottinghamshire 188-5 (Shafayat 37, Read 34); Second day, Warwickshire 162-5 (Ostler 58, Brown 3); Third day, Nottinghamshire 122-3 (Bicknell 52, Pietersen 4).

Warwickshire

First innings		Second innings	
N. V. Knight c Read b Smith	1	c Bicknell b Elworthy	41
†T. Frost c Pietersen b Franks	17	c Cairns b Smith	0
M. A. Wagh c Read b Elworthy	73	c Pietersen b Smith	14
I. R. Bell c Cairns b Elworthy	32	b Shreck	11
J. O. Troughton c Gallian b Franks	16	c Bicknell b Shreck	24
D. P. Ostler b Elworthy	0	b Smith	58
D. R. Brown c and b Shreck	7	b Smith	52
*A. F. Giles c Elworthy b Shreck	38	c Pietersen b Elworthy	94
M. M. Betts c Read b Shreck	5	not out	56
M. W. Clark not out	2	c Read b Smith	2
A. Richardson c Pietersen b Shreck	0	c Gallian b Franks	13
B 1, l-b 8, w 6, n-b 16	31	B 1, l-b 14, n-b 10	25
1/1 (1) 2/72 (2) 3/125 (3) 4/153 (4) 5/153 (6) 6/157 (5) 7/188 (7) 8/208 (9) 9/218 (8) 10/222 (11)	222	1/2 (2) 2/54 (3) 3/58 (1) 4/81 (4) 5/140 (5) 6/170 (6) 7/299 (7) 8/341 (8) 9/356 (10) 10/390 (11)	390

Bonus points – Warwickshire 1, Nottinghamshire 3.

Bowling: *First Innings*—Elworthy 19–5–68–3; Smith 13–2–55–1; Franks 17–6–57–2; Shreck 9.4–1–33–4. *Second Innings*—Elworthy 29–0–117–2; Smith 26–6–98–5; Franks 8.2–1–65–1; Shreck 14–1–76–2; Pietersen 2–0–19–0.

Nottinghamshire

First innings		Second innings	
D. J. Bicknell c Frost b Brown	61	c sub b Betts	81
*J. E. R. Gallian lbw b Betts	2	lbw b Richardson	9
U. Afzaal c Frost b Clark	1	c Bell b Giles	43
K. P. Pietersen c Ostler b Clark	0	(5) lbw b Betts	54
C. L. Cairns b Richardson	44	(6) b Betts	7
B. M. Shafayat c Frost b Brown	97	(7) c Brown b Betts	1
†C. M. W. Read c Frost b Richardson	49	(8) not out	20
P. J. Franks not out	39	(9) not out	25
S. Elworthy c Frost b Brown	4	(4) c Brown b Clark	0
G. J. Smith c Brown b Richardson	35		
C. E. Shreck b Richardson	0		
B 1, l-b 9, w 1, n-b 6	17	B 6, l-b 10, w 6, n-b 2	24
1/9 (2) 2/15 (3) 3/15 (4) 4/94 (5) 5/121 (1) 6/227 (7) 7/291 (6) 8/295 (9) 9/349 (10) 10/349 (11)	349	1/14 (2) 2/109 (3) 3/110 (4) 4/209 (5) 5/210 (1) 6/216 (7) 7/219 (6)	(7 wkts) 264

Bonus points – Nottinghamshire 3, Warwickshire 3.

Bowling: *First Innings*—Betts 16–3–76–1; Clark 15–2–71–2; Richardson 22.5–8–85–4; Brown 19–4–61–3; Giles 12–1–46–0. *Second Innings*—Clark 18–5–39–1; Betts 16.2–2–49–4; Richardson 24–7–59–1; Brown 16–1–42–0; Giles 26–1–59–1.

Umpires: N. G. Cowley and B. Leadbeater.

At Manchester, April 23, 24, 25, 26. NOTTINGHAMSHIRE drew with LANCASHIRE.

NOTTINGHAMSHIRE v SURREY

At Nottingham, May 9, 10, 11. Surrey won by an innings and six runs. Surrey 21 pts, Nottinghamshire 3.75 pts (after 0.25 pt penalty). Toss: Nottinghamshire.

Nottinghamshire started this game at the top of the table, but the reigning champions, Surrey, gave them a reality check: a resounding defeat 70 minutes into day three. For the home side, only Gallian demonstrated application on a tricky pitch against an accurate, aggressive seam attack. He brought up their single batting point with a straight six and finished unbeaten on 112 – the first player to carry his bat for Nottinghamshire since he himself did it nearly five years before. After tea, the 40-year-old Stewart proved he still had plenty of class in a dismissive 98 from 70 balls with a flurry of boundaries. Fifteen wickets fell on the first day, but the pitch was pronounced innocent, and next day Azhar Mahmood was merciless, matching Stewart's score in 95 balls as Surrey constructed a formidable lead. Martin Bicknell trapped his brother in the first over of Nottinghamshire's second innings, and the attack carried on from there.

Close of play: First day, Surrey 159-5 (Saqlain Mushtaq 0, Hollioake 1); Second day, Nottinghamshire 94-6 (Franks 12, Elworthy 9).

Nottinghamshire

D. J. Bicknell c Butcher b Azhar Mahmood	29	– lbw b Bicknell	0
*J. E. R. Gallian not out	112	– lbw b Bicknell	28
G. E. Welton c Butcher b Azhar Mahmood	0	– c Bicknell b Ormond	4
U. Afzaal b Butcher	16	– c Butcher b Ormond	0
B. M. Shafayat c Ramprakash b Azhar Mahmood	8	– c Stewart b Ormond	10
†C. M. W. Read b Ormond	22	– c Azhar Mahmood b Bicknell	26
P. J. Franks c Stewart b Ormond	0	– c Brown b Azhar Mahmood	25
S. Elworthy c Stewart b Tudor	0	– c Azhar Mahmood b Bicknell	52
G. J. Smith c Azhar Mahmood b Ormond	1	– c Ramprakash b Bicknell	2
A. J. Harris c Stewart b Ormond	0	– lbw b Azhar Mahmood	3
C. E. Shreck c Stewart b Ormond	5	– not out	16
B 4, l-b 9, w 5	18	L-b 4, n-b 6	10
1/42 (1) 2/48 (3) 3/83 (4) 4/96 (5) 5/155 (6) 6/177 (7) 7/178 (8) 8/179 (9) 9/185 (10) 10/211 (11)	211	1/0 (1) 2/15 (3) 3/15 (4) 4/35 (5) 5/71 (2) 6/76 (6) 7/128 (7) 8/131 (9) 9/138 (10) 10/176 (8)	176

Bonus points – Nottinghamshire 1, Surrey 3.

Bowling: *First Innings*—Bicknell 16–4–41–0; Tudor 16–1–58–1; Azhar Mahmood 16–4–46–3; Ormond 18.4–5–45–5; Butcher 2–0–8–1. *Second Innings*—Bicknell 25.5–8–83–5; Ormond 8–0–26–3; Azhar Mahmood 16–3–59–2; Butcher 1–0–4–0.

Surrey

M. A. Butcher c Read b Elworthy	0	M. P. Bicknell not out	33
I. J. Ward c Franks b Smith	3	J. Ormond c Afzaal b Smith	5
M. R. Ramprakash c Smith b Shreck	38		
†A. J. Stewart b Smith	98	B 5, l-b 8, n-b 10	23
A. D. Brown c Elworthy b Smith	9		
Saqlain Mushtaq c Read b Harris	24	1/0 (1) 2/4 (2) 3/147 (4)	393
*A. J. Hollioake b Elworthy	35	4/157 (3) 5/157 (5) 6/202 (7)	
Azhar Mahmood c Read b Elworthy	98	7/251 (6) 8/333 (9)	
A. J. Tudor c Read b Gallian	27	9/365 (8) 10/393 (11)	

Bonus points – Surrey 4, Nottinghamshire 3.

Bowling: Elworthy 21–2–136–3; Smith 22.1–4–81–4; Shreck 12–1–81–1; Harris 12–1–75–1; Gallian 5–0–7–1.

Umpires: J. W. Holder and T. E. Jesty.

At Horsham, May 21, 22, 23, 24. NOTTINGHAMSHIRE lost to SUSSEX by ten wickets.

NOTTINGHAMSHIRE v ESSEX

At Nottingham, May 30, 31, June 1. Essex won by 268 runs. Essex 18 pts, Nottinghamshire 3 pts. Toss: Essex.

Record books were thumbed as Nottinghamshire plummeted to eight for seven – four runs short of the lowest first-class total in history, and five short of their own worst in 1901. They had barely avoided that ignominy at 19 for nine. But two unlikely heroes appeared in Malik and MacGill, who thumped 60 in six overs, raising Malik's best score from 18 to 30. They even avoided the follow-on – thanks to Essex's own miserable batting earlier on, when they scraped a point only

---

WHAT DID YOU SAY THE SCORE WAS?

Lowest scores at the fall of the seventh wicket in first-class history:

0	MCC and Ground (16) v Surrey at Lord's	1872
4	Leicestershire (28) v Australians at Leicester	1899
4	Northamptonshire (60) v Kent at Northampton	1907
6	Gloucestershire (36) v Yorkshire at Sheffield	1903
6	Kerala (27) v Mysore at Bangalore	1963-64
7	Tasmania (18) v Victoria at Melbourne	1868-69
8	Oxford University (12) v MCC and Ground at Oxford	1877
8	MCC and Ground (139) v Lancashire at Lord's	1890
8	Somerset (35) v Middlesex at Lord's	1899
8	Leicestershire (37-8) v Gloucestershire at Ashby-de-la-Zouch	1922
8	Surrey (14) v Essex at Chelmsford	1983
8	**Nottinghamshire (79) v Essex at Nottingham**	**2003**
9	Oxford University (32) v MCC and Ground at Lord's	1867
9	Cambridge University (31) v Lancashire at Manchester	1882
9	Yorkshire (48) v Australians at Leeds	1893
9	Southern Punjab (22) v Northern India at Amritsar	1934-35
9	Essex (13-7) v Kent at Blackheath	1951
9	Glamorgan (24) v Leicestershire at Leicester	1971

Final innings totals in brackets.

Note: This list is believed to be exhaustive but it is possible that some early instances are unknown in cases where no scorebooks or match reports survive.

Research: Philip Bailey.

through the ninth-wicket pair, Dakin and Napier, adding 88. That satisfied ECB pitch liaison officer Peter Walker that the wicket was "up to speed", though he wouldn't comment on the batting – and he left before Nottinghamshire lowered the standard. Their top eight scored six between them; Dakin was twice on a hat-trick, and Brant claimed a career-best six scalps. Still the wickets tumbled, with Essex three down again by the close. Although the ball swung, conditions were far from impossible. Next day, Habib scored 151 in four hours, his highest for Essex, and added 178 with Foster, a sixth-wicket record between these teams. A target of 484 was far beyond Nottinghamshire. They suffered their third consecutive defeat as another of Essex's uncapped attack, Napier, took five for the first time.

Close of play: First day, Essex 39-3 (Grayson 13, Flower 9); Second day, Nottinghamshire 58-1 (Gallian 28, Afzaal 14).

Essex

D. D. J. Robinson c Gallian b Smith	9	– c Noon b Malik	4
W. I. Jefferson c Noon b Smith	0	– lbw b Harris	10
*A. P. Grayson c Pietersen b Harris	27	– b Smith	20
A. Flower lbw b Smith	4	– (5) lbw b Malik	32
A. Habib c Gallian b MacGill	31	– (6) lbw b MacGill	151
†J. S. Foster run out	12	– (7) lbw b Pietersen	85
R. S. Bopara run out	9	– (8) not out	15
J. M. Dakin not out	44	– (9) lbw b MacGill	4
J. D. Middlebrook lbw b MacGill	0	– (4) lbw b MacGill	3
G. R. Napier c Noon b Smith	57	– c Welton b MacGill	15
S. A. Brant b Smith	0	– c Cairns b MacGill	0
B 1, l-b 2, w 1, n-b 6	10	L-b 12, n-b 8	20
1/1 (2) 2/10 (1) 3/20 (4) 4/64 (3) 5/82 (5) 6/94 (6) 7/114 (7) 8/115 (9) 9/203 (10) 10/203 (11)	203	1/5 (1) 2/23 (2) 3/26 (4) 4/47 (3) 5/125 (5) 6/303 (7) 7/331 (6) 8/337 (9) 9/359 (10) 10/359 (11)	359

Bonus points – Essex 1, Nottinghamshire 3.

Bowling: *First Innings*—Smith 18–6–42–5; Harris 20–2–68–1; Malik 15–3–43–0; MacGill 13–3–41–2; Gallian 2–1–6–0. *Second Innings*—Smith 16–2–79–1; Malik 18–3–58–2; Harris 16–1–75–1; MacGill 30.2–3–118–5; Pietersen 11–5–17–1.

Nottinghamshire

G. E. Welton c Foster b Brant	1	– lbw b Dakin	11
*J. E. R. Gallian c Flower b Dakin	0	– lbw b Brant	42
U. Afzaal lbw b Dakin	3	– lbw b Napier	33
K. P. Pietersen b Dakin	0	– c Grayson b Middlebrook	18
B. M. Shafayat lbw b Brant	1	– c Bopara b Napier	21
C. L. Cairns lbw b Brant	1	– b Middlebrook	39
†W. M. Noon c Grayson b Dakin	0	– lbw b Napier	13
G. J. Smith b Brant	0	– c Robinson b Middlebrook	0
M. N. Malik not out	30	– (10) c Foster b Napier	15
A. J. Harris b Brant	4	– (9) lbw b Napier	4
S. C. G. MacGill c Middlebrook b Brant	27	– not out	8
B 9, l-b 3	12	B 9, l-b 2	11
1/2 (1) 2/2 (2) 3/2 (4) 4/7 (5) 5/7 (3) 6/7 (7) 7/8 (8) 8/15 (6) 9/19 (10) 10/79 (11)	79	1/31 (1) 2/90 (3) 3/96 (2) 4/116 (4) 5/150 (5) 6/184 (6) 7/184 (8) 8/188 (7) 9/200 (9) 10/215 (10)	215

Bonus points – Essex 3.

Bowling: *First Innings*—Brant 8.5–3–45–6; Dakin 8–2–22–4. *Second Innings*—Brant 16–7–30–1; Dakin 19–8–42–1; Middlebrook 16–2–64–3; Napier 18–5–66–5; Bopara 3–2–2–0.

Umpires: I. J. Gould and J. F. Steele.

At Birmingham, June 4, 5, 6, 7. NOTTINGHAMSHIRE drew with WARWICKSHIRE.

At Leicester, June 27, 28, 29, 30. NOTTINGHAMSHIRE drew with LEICESTERSHIRE.

At Nottingham, July 2, 3, 4. NOTTINGHAMSHIRE lost to INDIA A by seven wickets (see India A tour section).

At Maidstone, July 9, 10, 11. NOTTINGHAMSHIRE lost to KENT by 287 runs.

NOTTINGHAMSHIRE v SUSSEX

At Nottingham, July 25, 26, 27, 28. Drawn. Nottinghamshire 8 pts, Sussex 12 pts. Toss: Sussex.

Sussex arrived looking for a fifth consecutive Championship win, which would have lifted them over Surrey to the top of the table, but rain washed out the first day and they finally had to settle for maximum bonus points when Nottinghamshire rallied on the final afternoon. The toss looked crucial on a slow pitch. Goodwin scored an effortless hundred, and was particularly brutal on short deliveries, while Martin-Jenkins smashed the attack to all parts on the third morning: Sussex added 142 in just 22 overs before declaring. A belligerent 139 from Pietersen failed to save the follow-on and, when Gallian fell first ball, the signs were ominous. But Warren halted the slide with his maiden hundred for Nottinghamshire, sharing century partnerships with Bicknell and Pietersen, whose 81 in 76 balls took him past 1,000 runs. Pietersen was on course for a second hundred until, looking for his sixth six, he gifted part-time off-spinner Montgomerie the second wicket of his career.

Close of play: First day, No play; Second day, Sussex 355-4 (Yardy 18, Martin-Jenkins 35); Third day, Nottinghamshire 289-7 (Pietersen 138, Clough 11).

Sussex

M. W. Goodwin b Clough	148
R. R. Montgomerie c Read b Cairns	32
P. A. Cottey c Harris b Franks	53
*C. J. Adams c Franks b Harris	46
M. H. Yardy c Read b Harris	47
R. S. C. Martin-Jenkins not out	121
†M. J. Prior c Clough b Franks	17
K. J. Innes not out	6
L-b 6, w 5, n-b 16	27
1/60 (2) 2/197 (3) 3/295 (4) 4/297 (1) 5/434 (5) 6/474 (7)	(6 wkts dec.) 497

Mushtaq Ahmed, R. J. Kirtley and P. M. Hutchison did not bat.

Bonus points – Sussex 5, Nottinghamshire 2.

Bowling: Harris 28–5–98–2; Shreck 28–4–109–0; Cairns 18–5–63–1; Franks 19–3–102–2; Clough 16–0–76–1; Pietersen 4–0–43–0.

Nottinghamshire

D. J. Bicknell c Prior b Kirtley	15	– c Montgomerie b Kirtley	75
*J. E. R. Gallian b Kirtley	6	– lbw b Kirtley	0
G. E. Welton c Yardy b Kirtley	12	– c Cottey b Hutchison	8
R. J. Warren c Cottey b Martin-Jenkins	42	– not out	114
K. P. Pietersen c Adams b Kirtley	139	– c and b Montgomerie	81
C. L. Cairns c Prior b Martin-Jenkins	1	– not out	7
†C. M. W. Read c Montgomerie b Mushtaq Ahmed	0		
P. J. Franks c Yardy b Hutchison	43		
G. D. Clough c Adams b Mushtaq Ahmed	16		
A. J. Harris b Kirtley	1		
C. E. Shreck not out	0		
B 3, l-b 12, n-b 6	21	B 4, l-b 2	6
1/16 (1) 2/35 (2) 3/46 (3) 4/127 (4) 5/139 (6) 6/140 (7) 7/254 (8) 8/290 (5) 9/296 (10) 10/296 (9)	296	1/1 (2) 2/34 (3) 3/144 (1) 4/275 (5) (4 wkts dec.)	291

Bonus points – Nottinghamshire 2, Sussex 3.

Bowling: *First Innings*—Kirtley 23–9–60–5; Hutchison 17–5–60–1; Mushtaq Ahmed 28.5–2–87–2; Yardy 5–0–14–0; Martin-Jenkins 14–1–60–2. *Second Innings*—Kirtley 11–4–32–2; Hutchison 16–2–66–1; Yardy 13–2–50–0; Mushtaq Ahmed 9–2–41–0; Martin-Jenkins 12–2–43–0; Cottey 9–1–44–0; Montgomerie 3–0–9–1.

Umpires: J. H. Hampshire and A. G. T. Whitehead.

NOTTINGHAMSHIRE v MIDDLESEX

At Nottingham, July 30, 31, August 1, 2. Middlesex won by four wickets. Middlesex 19 pts, Nottinghamshire 5 pts. Toss: Nottinghamshire. Championship debut: V. Atri.

An 18-ball spell on the final morning kept Nottinghamshire at the foot of the table. Losing their last five for no runs meant the difference between setting Middlesex a challenging run-chase, with MacGill, just back from routing Bangladesh in Australia, in threatening form on a spin-friendly surface, and the actual target of 146, which caused only the odd scare. The pitch offered variable bounce, making it tricky to score. Nottinghamshire attempted to take the initiative, and Pietersen scored his tenth half-century of 2003. But they were undone by Noffke, who ripped the heart out of their batting for season's-best figures. Smith, briefly labelled Eddie Hemmings on the scoreboard, and MacGill, who landed at Heathrow a few hours before the game, soon retaliated, and kept the Middlesex lead down to 24. At the close of the third day the match was delicately poised: Nottinghamshire were 136 ahead, with Cairns and Read sharing a crucial partnership. Then Dawes and Keegan swept them away, leaving Trent Bridge members thoroughly demoralised.

Close of play: First day, Nottinghamshire 249-9 (MacGill 1); Second day, Middlesex 198-6 (Nash 18, Noffke 0); Third day, Nottinghamshire 160-5 (Cairns 32, Read 38).

> "Hayward bowled fast, but was wilder than a Karoo ostrich."
>
> Pakistanis in South Africa and Zimbabwe, page 1157.

Nottinghamshire

First Innings		Second Innings	
D. J. Bicknell c and b Dawes	39	lbw b Keegan	2
G. E. Welton lbw b Keegan	1	c Weekes b Keegan	69
V. Atri c Nash b Noffke	5	c Nash b Dawes	2
R. J. Warren b Noffke	33	c Nash b Dawes	9
K. P. Pietersen c and b Noffke	67	b Dawes	1
*C. L. Cairns lbw b Cook	14	c Weekes b Dawes	41
†C. M. W. Read c Joyce b Weekes	26	c Nash b Keegan	38
P. J. Franks c Nash b Noffke	28	c Weekes b Dawes	0
G. J. Smith b Noffke	27	not out	0
S. C. G. MacGill not out	5	b Keegan	0
C. E. Shreck c Weekes b Keegan	1	c Nash b Keegan	0
L-b 4, n-b 4	8	B 2, l-b 3, n-b 2	7
1/2 (2) 2/13 (3) 3/67 (1) 4/98 (4) 5/119 (6) 6/188 (5) 7/202 (7) 8/246 (9) 9/249 (8) 10/254 (11)	254	1/13 (1) 2/49 (3) 3/67 (4) 4/73 (5) 5/94 (2) 6/169 (6) 7/169 (8) 8/169 (7) 9/169 (10) 10/169 (11)	169

Bonus points – Nottinghamshire 2, Middlesex 3.

Bowling: *First Innings*—Noffke 21–5–52–5; Keegan 19.3–4–71–2; Cook 16–4–49–1; Dawes 15–2–59–1; Joyce 2–0–8–0; Weekes 8–2–11–1. *Second Innings*—Noffke 9.4–3–33–0; Keegan 12.3–3–39–5; Cook 13–5–38–0; Dawes 18–6–46–5; Weekes 3.2–1–8–0.

Middlesex

First Innings		Second Innings	
*A. J. Strauss c Atri b Smith	29	c Read b Cairns	6
S. G. Koenig lbw b MacGill	75	c Pietersen b Cairns	10
O. A. Shah c Read b MacGill	13	c Pietersen b MacGill	41
B. L. Hutton lbw b MacGill	16	lbw b Shreck	29
E. C. Joyce c Read b Cairns	36	lbw b MacGill	14
P. N. Weekes st Read b MacGill	0	c Welton b Smith	11
†D. C. Nash c Warren b Franks	36	not out	14
A. A. Noffke b Smith	20	not out	18
S. J. Cook not out	19		
C. B. Keegan b Smith	4		
J. H. Dawes c Read b Smith	9		
B 7, l-b 8, n-b 6	21	B 1, l-b 1, w 1	3
1/54 (1) 2/82 (3) 3/120 (4) 4/155 (2) 5/159 (6) 6/187 (5) 7/246 (7) 8/246 (8) 9/250 (10) 10/278 (11)	278	1/9 (1) 2/26 (2) 3/81 (4) 4/87 (3) 5/114 (6) 6/116 (5)	(6 wkts) 146

Bonus points – Middlesex 2, Nottinghamshire 3.

Bowling: *First Innings*—Smith 19.4–6–57–4; Shreck 16–7–31–0; Cairns 18–3–61–1; MacGill 30–8–78–4; Franks 15–1–36–1. *Second Innings*—Smith 15–5–37–1; Cairns 10–1–43–2; Franks 3–2–2–0; MacGill 18.1–4–48–2; Shreck 4–1–14–1.

Umpires: A. Clarkson and D. J. Constant.

At Whitgift School, August 13, 14, 15. NOTTINGHAMSHIRE lost to SURREY by an innings and 211 runs.

NOTTINGHAMSHIRE v KENT

At Nottingham, August 20, 21. Kent won by nine wickets. Kent 18 pts, Nottinghamshire 3 pts. Toss: Nottinghamshire.

It hardly seemed possible that Nottinghamshire's season could get any worse. However, this two-day loss, completed inside five sessions, plumbed new depths. Perhaps distracted by the criticism over the Test pitch a week earlier, both sides batted as if demons lurked beneath the surface. Twenty wickets fell on the first day, though Pietersen demonstrated it was far from unplayable. He hit Muralitharan's single over for a four and two sixes, and reached his hundred in 98 balls without a hint of carelessness – until he was caught on the boundary off the next delivery. The only other batsman to last as long was Ealham, who pushed Kent ahead in a crucial seventh-wicket stand with Khan. Bicknell and Welton gave Nottinghamshire's second innings a more solid start, before Muralitharan tore them apart with six wickets in 12 balls. His bowling was intelligent, but without any vicious turn – still they buckled under the pressure.

Close of play: First day, Kent 242.

Nottinghamshire

D. J. Bicknell c Walker b Saggers	5	– st Jones b Muralitharan	46
V. Atri b Saggers	5	– c Key b Saggers	3
G. E. Welton lbw b Khan	7	– c Jones b Ealham	43
K. P. Pietersen c Carberry b Saggers	100	– lbw b Symonds	13
B. M. Shafayat lbw b Symonds	23	– lbw b Symonds	0
*C. L. Cairns lbw b Symonds	0	– c Ealham b Muralitharan	6
†C. M. W. Read c Key b Ealham	5	– lbw b Muralitharan	0
P. J. Franks lbw b Symonds	17	– not out	5
G. J. Smith b Saggers	0	– c Walker b Muralitharan	0
S. C. G. MacGill not out	7	– b Muralitharan	0
C. E. Shreck lbw b Saggers	0	– b Muralitharan	0
L-b 2, n-b 6	8	B 4, l-b 5, w 1	10
1/6 (1) 2/17 (2) 3/17 (3) 4/73 (5) 5/73 (6) 6/92 (7) 7/151 (8) 8/154 (9) 9/177 (4) 10/177 (11)	177	1/13 (2) 2/92 (3) 3/110 (4) 4/110 (5) 5/119 (6) 6/119 (7) 7/124 (1) 8/124 (9) 9/124 (10) 10/126 (11)	126

Bonus points – Kent 3.

Bowling: *First Innings*—Saggers 13.5–2–42–5; Khan 8–2–41–1; Sheriyar 2–0–24–0; Ealham 7–4–14–1; Symonds 9–2–38–3; Muralitharan 1–0–16–0. *Second Innings*—Saggers 7–4–20–1; Khan 4–0–31–0; Muralitharan 15.3–3–36–6; Ealham 6–1–18–1; Symonds 7–2–12–2.

Kent

*D. P. Fulton c Franks b Cairns	43	– c Atri b Shreck	11
R. W. T. Key b Cairns	7	– not out	46
M. A. Carberry c Franks b Smith	5	– not out	8
A. Symonds lbw b Franks	1		
M. J. Walker c Read b Shreck	11		
M. A. Ealham lbw b Cairns	83		
†G. O. Jones c Atri b Smith	0		
A. Khan c Welton b Shreck	46		
M. J. Saggers b MacGill	3		
M. Muralitharan c Bicknell b MacGill	15		
A. Sheriyar not out	4		
B 8, l-b 9, w 1, n-b 6	24		
1/26 (2) 2/41 (3) 3/50 (4) 4/63 (5) 5/118 (1) 6/121 (7) 7/194 (8) 8/210 (9) 9/234 (6) 10/242 (10)	242	1/51 (1)	(1 wkt) 65

Bonus points – Kent 1, Nottinghamshire 3.

Bowling: *First Innings*—Smith 11–1–47–2; Cairns 14–2–59–3; Franks 11–2–36–1; Shreck 13–0–55–2; MacGill 11.3–2–28–2. *Second Innings*—Smith 4–0–21–0; Cairns 4–0–14–0; Franks 3–0–20–0; Shreck 2.3–0–10–1.

Umpires: J. W. Holder and J. F. Steele.

NOTTINGHAMSHIRE v LEICESTERSHIRE

At Nottingham, August 26, 27, 28, 29. Drawn. Nottinghamshire 8 pts, Leicestershire 12 pts. Toss: Nottinghamshire.

When rain, which had wiped out the third day, cost another 25 minutes before lunch on the last, Leicestershire led by 211, with Hodge on 285. Perhaps the news that Warwickshire had won, making this almost certainly a battle for the wooden spoon, swung it. DeFreitas gave Hodge his chance before pushing for a first Championship win. In 15 minutes, Hodge reached Leicestershire's maiden triple-century, and only the second at Trent Bridge, after fellow-Australian Charles Macartney's 345 in 1921. Driving classically at anything of full or decent length, he was equally dismissive of the short delivery, peppering the square boundaries, with three sixes and 46 fours in 280 balls and 362 minutes. None of the bowlers had an answer, but Shreck attacked the other end to collect his first five-wicket haul. Earlier, DeFreitas had picked up seven, using all his wiles on a flat track after Nottinghamshire's highest opening stand of the Championship season to date. The delayed declaration looked less of a gamble when Nottinghamshire slumped to 29 for four, but Cairns and Read rallied and the chance of a result dribbled away.

Close of play: First day, Nottinghamshire 257-6 (Shafayat 56, Franks 24); Second day, Leicestershire 376-4 (Hodge 220, Brandy 16); Third day, No play.

TRIPLE-CENTURIES FOR FIRST-CLASS COUNTIES

	Total	*First 300*	*Most recent*
Northamptonshire	**6**	**1958**	**2003**
Yorkshire	6	1897	1932
Gloucestershire	5	1876	1939
Lancashire	5	1895	1996
Surrey	5	1888	1926
Worcestershire	4	1982	2002
Somerset	3	1948	1990
Warwickshire	3	1914	2001
Hampshire	2	1899	1937
Kent	2	1934	1935
Middlesex	2	1933	1949
Sussex	**2**	**1930**	**2003**
Essex	1	1904	1904
Glamorgan	1	2000	2000
Leicestershire	**1**	**2003**	**2003**
Nottinghamshire	1	1939	1939
Derbyshire	0	–	–
Durham	0	–	–

Nottinghamshire

D. J. Bicknell c Nixon b Maddy	59	– c DeFreitas b Drakes	1
G. E. Welton c Hodge b DeFreitas	60	– lbw b DeFreitas	0
R. J. Warren lbw b DeFreitas	5	– c DeFreitas b Drakes	4
K. P. Pietersen lbw b DeFreitas	0	– b DeFreitas	16
B. M. Shafayat c Brandy b DeFreitas	68	– c Sadler b Masters	13
*C. L. Cairns lbw b Maddy	15	– lbw b DeFreitas	75
†C. M. W. Read c Sadler b Maddy	16	– lbw b Drakes	65
P. J. Franks c Nixon b DeFreitas	36	– not out	32
R. J. Logan lbw b DeFreitas	1	– not out	13
S. C. G. MacGill c Walker b DeFreitas	0		
C. E. Shreck not out	0		
B 9, l-b 2, w 1, n-b 18	30	B 1, l-b 8, w 1, n-b 12	22
1/132 (1) 2/136 (2) 3/136 (4) 4/145 (3) 5/164 (6) 6/216 (7) 7/285 (8) 8/289 (9) 9/289 (10) 10/290 (5)	290	1/1 (1) 2/1 (2) 3/27 (4) 4/29 (3) 5/72 (5) 6/180 (7) 7/205 (6)	(7 wkts dec.) 241

Bonus points – Nottinghamshire 2, Leicestershire 3.

Bowling: *First Innings*—DeFreitas 26.4–9–51–7; Drakes 29–9–80–0; Maddy 23–3–62–3; Masters 14–6–29–0; Brandy 2–0–21–0; Walker 7–0–18–0; Snape 5–1–18–0. *Second Innings*—DeFreitas 17–3–62–3; Drakes 15–4–58–3; Masters 11–2–52–1; Maddy 10.4–2–48–0; Walker 3–2–1–0; Brandy 1–0–11–0.

Leicestershire

J. K. Maunders lbw b Shreck	33
D. L. Maddy b Shreck	9
B. J. Hodge not out	302
J. L. Sadler lbw b Shreck	2
†P. A. Nixon lbw b MacGill	65
D. G. Brandy st Read b MacGill	19
J. N. Snape c Franks b Shreck	48
*P. A. J. DeFreitas c MacGill b Shreck	0
V. C. Drakes not out	4
B 12, l-b 11, w 2, n-b 16	41
1/45 (2) 2/54 (1) 3/60 (4) 4/338 (5) 5/385 (6) 6/497 (7) 7/498 (8)	(7 wkts dec.) 523

D. D. Masters and G. W. Walker did not bat.

Bonus points – Leicestershire 5, Nottinghamshire 2.

Bowling: Cairns 22–1–109–0; Franks 22–2–98–0; Shreck 25–6–100–5; Logan 8–1–46–0; MacGill 27–2–135–2; Shafayat 1–0–12–0.

Umpires: M. R. Benson and G. Sharp.

At Chelmsford, September 3, 4, 5. NOTTINGHAMSHIRE lost to ESSEX by nine wickets.

At Lord's, September 10, 11, 12, 13. NOTTINGHAMSHIRE drew with MIDDLESEX.

NOTTINGHAMSHIRE v LANCASHIRE

At Nottingham, September 17, 18, 19, 20. Nottinghamshire won by 233 runs. Nottinghamshire 21 pts, Lancashire 4 pts. Toss: Lancashire. Championship debut: S. R. Patel.

Lancashire started with an outside chance of the title, whereas Nottinghamshire's last Championship victory was in the opening round. But they ripped up the formbook, ran out comfortable winners and eased themselves off the bottom of the table. From the moment Hegg made the baffling decision to concede first use of a decent-looking pitch on an unseasonably sunny day, Lancashire were on the back foot. Bicknell and Gallian took full advantage with 165, Nottinghamshire's biggest opening stand in the 2003 Championship. Once word filtered through on the second day that Sussex were champions, Lancashire lost heart – or ten of their players did. After Gallian waived the follow-on, Chapple bowled 29 overs unchanged either side of lunch on the third day, claiming a season's-best six wickets. When he took a breather, Franks hammered his second century – following the first in June – and then seized three wickets in six balls. MacGill followed up, before Smith, returning from injury, finished things off with his 50th Championship victim. Lancashire remained runners-up despite the defeat.

Close of play: First day, Lancashire 3-0 (Chilton 3, Sutcliffe 0); Second day, Nottinghamshire 16-1 (Bicknell 11, Read 2); Third day, Lancashire 6-0 (Chilton 3, Sutcliffe 1).

Nottinghamshire

First innings		Second innings	
D. J. Bicknell b Wood	75	– c Hooper b Chapple	53
*J. E. R. Gallian c Keedy b Hogg	83	– lbw b Chapple	2
†C. M. W. Read c Hegg b Wood	9	– lbw b Chapple	2
R. J. Warren b Wood	75	– c Hegg b Chapple	0
K. P. Pietersen c Hegg b Hooper	52	– b Chapple	37
B. M. Shafayat lbw b Martin	22	– c Hegg b Chapple	26
S. R. Patel c sub b Keedy	9	– c Law b Hogg	55
P. J. Franks b Chapple	14	– not out	100
G. J. Smith not out	8	– c Law b Sutcliffe	9
S. C. G. MacGill b Chapple	4	– not out	16
B 3, l-b 6, w 3, n-b 8, p 5	25	B 8, l-b 6, n-b 5	19
1/165 (1) 2/175 (2) 3/183 (3) 4/270 (5) 5/318 (6) 6/342 (7) 7/360 (4) 8/362 (8) 9/376 (10) (9 wkts dec.)	376	1/8 (2) 2/16 (3) 3/22 (4) 4/85 (1) 5/116 (5) 6/151 (6) 7/228 (7) 8/264 (9) (8 wkts dec.)	319

A. J. Harris did not bat.

Bonus points – Nottinghamshire 4, Lancashire 3.

Bowling: *First Innings*—Martin 21–4–66–1; Chapple 23–2–78–2; Hogg 13–2–71–1; Wood 19–4–80–3; Keedy 15–2–51–1; Hooper 9–2–16–1. *Second Innings*—Martin 8.5–0–55–0; Chapple 33–8–98–6; Wood 11–1–43–0; Keedy 16–4–40–0; Hogg 9–0–50–1; Sutcliffe 4–1–11–1; Loye 2–0–8–0.

Lancashire

First innings		Second innings	
M. J. Chilton b Smith	7	– c Read b MacGill	27
I. J. Sutcliffe c Read b Smith	37	– b Franks	65
M. B. Loye lbw b Smith	9	– lbw b Franks	28
S. G. Law c Bicknell b Smith	51	– b Franks	3
C. L. Hooper lbw b Smith	11	– lbw b Franks	0
K. W. Hogg c Shafayat b MacGill	46	– b MacGill	53
G. Chapple c Patel b Harris	25	– lbw b MacGill	0
*†W. K. Hegg lbw b Franks	11	– c Gallian b Smith	12
P. J. Martin c Read b Franks	4	– c Pietersen b Smith	16
G. Keedy not out	1	– (11) not out	2
J. Wood lbw b MacGill	3	– (10) c Gallian b MacGill	20
B 2, l-b 9, w 1, n-b 2	14	B 1, l-b 9, w 1, n-b 6	17
1/8 (1) 2/36 (3) 3/109 (2) 4/124 (4) 5/147 (5) 6/186 (7) 7/211 (6) 8/211 (8) 9/216 (9) 10/219 (11)	219	1/54 (1) 2/134 (3) 3/137 (2) 4/137 (5) 5/168 (4) 6/169 (7) 7/194 (6) 8/211 (9) 9/239 (10) 10/243 (8)	243

Bonus points – Lancashire 1, Nottinghamshire 3.

Bowling: *First Innings*—Smith 20–7–61–5; MacGill 14.4–2–52–2; Franks 17–7–36–2; Harris 15–2–59–1. *Second Innings*—Smith 19.2–3–61–2; Franks 18–5–62–4; MacGill 22–4–67–4; Harris 6–1–33–0; Patel 8–5–10–0.

Umpires: I. J. Gould and J. H. Hampshire.

SOMERSET

Easy pitch, hard times

DAVID FOOT

It is an embarrassing reflection of the season that one claws for compensations: the ironic fact that Somerset scored more than 700 runs in an innings for the first time, that they created a new last-wicket record – an apposite metaphor for upside-down form – and that Ian Blackwell produced some of the most dynamic batting since the days when Richards and Botham, in daring tandem, rearranged the Taunton groundsman's bijou vegetable garden with their brutal blows.

Only two years before, Somerset had finished second in the Championship table, higher than ever before. It led to ecstatic predictions about the club's upward pattern, an attitude rapidly made redundant as Somerset suffered double relegation in 2002. And they ended 2003 with only Hampshire and Derbyshire below them in the Championship. They were also the least successful county in the National League; Scotland alone propped them up.

Overall, Somerset's batting was loose and careless, too much of the bowling wayward and the fielding, historically of varying quality, involved too many dropped catches. The members were restive and for the second successive season the chief executive, Peter Anderson, strode into action to placate them. After a miserable two-day defeat against Northamptonshire, he sent an unequivocal improve-or-you're-out letter to ten players, a first warning with a view to possible dismissal. It had little obvious impact: having won three times in the Championship by late May, Somerset failed to repeat the trick until the last match.

As the season petered out, the inquest began. Kevin Shine, the head coach, inevitably found himself criticised by supporters, but Anderson placed the blame primarily on the players. He said pointedly: "If guns are blazing, there is no shame in losing. If our players show no fight, then there is." Although the threatened mass clearout never materialised, four were not offered new terms. Michael Burns offered to stand down as captain but, after the club failed to lure Ian Ward from Surrey, he stayed on, to try and learn from the "harsh lessons" of his first season in charge.

In partial mitigation, it could be argued that the county suffered for producing England players. Marcus Trescothick played only four Championship games. Injury rather than England deprived them of Andrew Caddick, but his problems with a fractured foot opened the international door for another Somerset seamer, Richard Johnson, who made his Test debut against Zimbabwe before succumbing to injury himself. Without him, Somerset were missing a lively and integral part of their attack.

Blackwell's wonderfully uncomplicated batting rightly earned him selection for England's winter one-day squad. After a moderate start, the Derbyshire exile, thick of forearm and superficially rustic in demeanour, lifted sagging spirits in the closing weeks, when he zoomed past his career-best score in three home Championship matches in succession. The run climaxed triumphantly in a thoroughly memorable 247 against his old club in the season's last game. In terms of balls faced, this blitz was the fastest officially recorded double-hundred by an Englishman. The sustained excellence of his timing mocked any disparaging hint of slogging.

Ian Blackwell

Blackwell passed 1,000 home Championship runs for the first time and, from a modest position at No. 6, topped Somerset's averages. Burns and Jamie Cox also reached 1,000 first-class runs, though much less spectacularly. Aaron Laraman, from Middlesex, impressed once or twice, and there was an encouraging century from Neil Edwards, a talented young Cornishman.

Somerset's seamers struggled – with the placid pitch, with their length and line and with injuries. Johnson missed seven games, Caddick, after one match in April, was out for the rest of the season and back problems forced Matt Bulbeck into retirement. Nixon McLean, who carried both a hamstring problem and often the rest of the attack, took 62 Championship wickets. He was by some distance the pick. A lack of balance was too often apparent. Blackwell wheeled away for 416 Championship overs and took 30 wickets with his left-arm spin; off-spinner Keith Dutch took just eight wickets in seven matches.

The easy-paced Taunton pitch was regularly debated. Ever since the 1930s most of the compliments about the wicket have come from batsmen. Certainly in recent years it has often offered little to bowlers, while the fast outfield and short boundaries helped produce sky-high totals. In August, Northamptonshire ran up 681 for five and Mike Hussey helped himself to a triple-hundred; later that month, Somerset themselves made a county-record 705 against Hampshire. For 2004, Phil Frost, the groundsman, was expected to make adjustments to redress the balance between bat and ball.

The signing of Ricky Ponting, the World Cup-winning captain, who hit seven centuries in 11 Tests in 2002-03, was another sign of intent. He is a player capable of restoring morale on both sides of the boundary, but international commitments mean Ponting's role may be largely symbolic. For Somerset supporters a more potent symbol may have been Viv Richards's return to the ground, which he once departed amid such acrimony. He opened the ground's Priory Bridge Road gates, which have been named after him. He and Botham (now an unpaid marketing consultant for the county) are embraced once again: it can't be all bad.

SOMERSET RESULTS

All first-class matches – Played 17: Won 4, Lost 8, Drawn 5.
County Championship matches – Played 16: Won 4, Lost 8, Drawn 4.

Frizzell County Championship, 7th in Division 2; Cheltenham & Gloucester Trophy, 4th round; National Cricket League, 9th in Division 2; Twenty20 Cup, 5th in Midlands/Wales/West Group.

COUNTY CHAMPIONSHIP AVERAGES

BATTING AND FIELDING

Cap		*M*	*I*	*NO*	*R*	*HS*	*100s*	*50s*	*Avge*	*Ct/St*
2001	I. D. Blackwell	13	24	2	1,066	247*	3	1	48.45	6
	A. W. Laraman	11	17	4	556	148*	1	3	42.76	4
1999	J. Cox§	14	26	2	999	160	3	4	41.62	10
	N. J. Edwards	5	9	0	360	160	1	1	40.00	1
1999	M. E. Trescothick	4	6	0	237	70	0	3	39.50	8
1999	M. Burns	16	29	2	897	106	1	7	33.22	14
1995	P. D. Bowler	8	13	1	372	92	0	4	31.00	11
1994	R. J. Turner	15	25	8	502	81*	0	3	29.52	61/4
2001	P. S. Jones	7	12	2	273	63	0	2	27.30	2
2001	R. L. Johnson	9	14	3	290	118	1	0	26.36	4
	J. D. C. Bryant	12	21	1	483	73	0	2	24.15	8
	M. J. Wood	11	21	1	472	100	1	2	23.60	1
	T. Webley	6	11	1	208	59	0	1	20.80	3
2003	N. A. M. McLean§	16	23	4	318	76	0	1	16.73	2
2001	K. P. Dutch	7	10	0	161	61	0	1	16.10	9
	S. R. G. Francis	9	13	2	133	44	0	0	12.09	0
	G. M. Andrew	3	5	0	36	11	0	0	7.20	1

Also batted: A. R. Caddick (cap 1992) (1 match) 1; W. J. Durston (1 match) 4, 6 (2 ct); C. M. Gazzard (2 matches) 2, 4, 41 (3 ct); G. M. Gilder (2 matches) 12, 0*, 7*; J. C. Hildreth (1 match) 9, 0; P. C. L. Holloway (cap 1997) (1 match) 30, 11; K. A. Parsons (cap 1999) (1 match) 4, 6 (1 ct); A. V. Suppiah (1 match) 16.

§ *Overseas player.*

BOWLING

	O	*M*	*R*	*W*	*BB*	*5W/i*	*Avge*
G. M. Andrew	57	10	225	10	3-14	0	22.50
R. L. Johnson	310.1	70	918	34	5-64	1	27.00
N. A. M. McLean	521.3	113	1,732	62	5-43	3	27.93
A. W. Laraman	252.5	55	846	24	3-20	0	35.25
S. R. G. Francis	302.1	66	1,091	30	4-94	0	36.36
M. Burns	153.5	29	514	13	3-35	0	39.53
I. D. Blackwell	416	91	1,223	30	5-96	1	40.76
P. S. Jones	181.3	24	824	20	5-42	1	41.20

Also bowled: P. D. Bowler 1–0–2–0; J. D. C. Bryant 1–0–8–0; A. R. Caddick 38–8–110–7; J. Cox 1–0–8–0; W. J. Durston 8–1–23–1; K. P. Dutch 126.1–25–428–8; N. J. Edwards 18.5–1–71–0; G. M. Gilder 4–0–32–0; K. A. Parsons 14.4–3–63–2; A. V. Suppiah 11–1–44–1; T. Webley 6–1–26–0; M. J. Wood 1.1–0–6–0.

COUNTY RECORDS

Highest score for:	322	I. V. A. Richards v Warwickshire at Taunton	1985
Highest score against:	424	A. C. MacLaren (Lancashire) at Taunton	1895
Best bowling for:	10-49	E. J. Tyler v Surrey at Taunton	1895
Best bowling against:	10-35	A. Drake (Yorkshire) at Weston-super-Mare	1914
Highest total for:	705-9 dec.	v Hampshire at Taunton	2003
Highest total against:	811	by Surrey at The Oval	1899
Lowest total for:	25	v Gloucestershire at Bristol	1947
Lowest total against:	22	by Gloucestershire at Bristol	1920

SOMERSET DIRECTORY

ADDRESS

County Ground, St James's Street, Taunton TA1 1JT (01823 272946; fax 01823 332395; email info@somersetcountycc.co.uk). **Website** www.somersetcountycc.co.uk.

GROUNDS

Taunton: ¼ mile N of town centre in St James's Street. From A358 or A38 follow signs for town centre and cricket ground. Nearest station: Taunton (½ mile).

Bath: ¼ mile from city centre in William Street adjoining Bath RFC. From Great Pulteney Street take L into William Street for main entrance, or access by foot via towpath from River Avon. Nearest station: Bath Spa (½ mile).

OFFICIALS

Captain M. Burns
First-team coach K. J. Shine
President 2003 – M. F. Hill; 2004 – R. Kerslake
Chairman C. G. Clarke
Chief executive P. W. Anderson
Chairman, cricket committee V. J. Marks
Head groundsman P. Frost
Scorer G. A. Stickley

PLAYERS

Players expected to reappear in 2004

	Former counties	*Country*	*Born*	*Birthplace*
Andrew Gareth Mark		E	27.12.1983	†*Yeovil*
Blackwell Ian David	Derbys	E	10.6.1978	*Chesterfield*
Bowler Peter Duncan	Leics, Derbys	E	30.7.1963	*Plymouth*
Burns Michael	Warwicks	E	6.2.1969	*Barrow-in-Furness*
***Caddick** Andrew Richard		E	21.11.1968	*Christchurch, NZ*
Cox Jamie		A	15.10.1969	*Burnie*
Durston Wesley John		E	6.10.1980	†*Taunton*
Dutch Keith Philip	Middx	E	21.3.1973	*Harrow*
Edwards Neil James		E	14.10.1983	*Treliske*
Francis Simon Richard George	Hants	E	15.8.1978	*Bromley*
Gazzard Carl Matthew		E	15.4.1982	*Penzance*
Hildreth James Charles		E	9.9.1984	*Milton Keynes*
***Johnson** Richard Leonard	Middx	E	29.12.1974	*Chertsey*
Laraman Aaron William	Middx	E	10.1.1979	*Enfield*
***McLean** Nixon Alexei McNamara	Hants	WI	20.7.1973	*Stubbs, St Vincent*
Parsons Keith Alan		E	2.5.1973	†*Taunton*
Parsons Michael		E	26.11.1984	†*Taunton*
Suppiah Arul Vivasvan		E	30.8.1983	*Kuala Lumpur, Malaysia*
***Trescothick** Marcus Edward		‡E	25.12.1975	†*Keynsham*
Turner Robert Julian		E	25.11.1967	*Malvern*
Webley Thomas		E	2.3.1983	*Bristol*
Wood Matthew James		E	30.9.1980	*Exeter*

Players due to join in 2004

Francis John Daniel	Hants	E	13.11.1980	*Bromley*
***Ponting** Ricky Thomas		A	19.12.1974	*Launceston*

* *Test player.* † *Born in Somerset.* ‡ *12-month ECB contract.*

SOMERSET v LOUGHBOROUGH UCCE

At Taunton, April 12, 13, 14. Drawn. Toss: Somerset. First-class debuts: J. E. Anyon, R. A. G. Cummins, L. J. Goddard, R. E. King. County debuts: J. D. C. Bryant, A. W. Laraman, N. A. M. McLean. UCCE debut: Z. K. Sharif.

Loughborough battled to a draw in their opening match after becoming the fourth English university team raised to first-class status. Although their bowlers managed only four wickets in 158 overs, and were hit to all corners of the ground – plus a few outside it – their top six, all of whom had played first-class cricket for counties, were good enough to save the game. On a flat pitch, South African-born James Bryant trotted to a brisk century as Somerset hurried to a first-day declaration. But despite facing a more menacing attack, Loughborough were able to respond in kind, with a hundred from James Adams of Hampshire and a declaration of their own. Blackwell, selected and dropped by England over the winter, winkled out five wickets in a 27-over spell, then made a pulverising 46-ball 75, as Somerset blazed to 427 for one in their second innings, at more than five an over. However the pitch remained too good and despite a hat-trick from Simon Francis – who had earlier removed his brother, John – Loughborough went home happy.

Close of play: First day, Loughborough UCCE 79-1 (Adams 35, Francis 26); Second day, Somerset 160-0 (Bowler 73, Turner 84).

Somerset

P. D. Bowler c Goddard b Anyon	21	– c White b Wigley	84
P. C. L. Holloway lbw b Anyon	96		
*M. Burns c Anyon b Nash	83	– not out	118
J. Cox not out	88		
J. D. C. Bryant not out	109		
†R. J. Turner (did not bat)		– (2) retired hurt	139
I. D. Blackwell (did not bat)		– (4) not out	75
L-b 5, w 1, n-b 10	16	B 2, l-b 2, w 1, n-b 6	11
1/58 (1) 2/188 (3) 3/224 (2) (3 wkts dec.)	413	1/191 (1) (1 wkt dec.)	427

A. W. Laraman, R. L. Johnson, N. A. M. McLean and S. R. G. Francis did not bat.

In the second innings Turner retired hurt at 307.

Bowling: *First Innings*—Wigley 17–1–98–0; Anyon 16–4–59–2; Cummins 11–1–86–0; King 12–1–61–0; Nash 8–0–46–1; Sharif 16–0–58–0. *Second Innings*—Wigley 15–2–87–1; Anyon 14–2–73–0; King 11–0–59–0; Cummins 13–3–71–0; Sharif 7–0–42–0; Nash 6–0–28–0; White 11–0–62–0; Adams 1–0–1–0.

Loughborough UCCE

R. A. White b Johnson	9	– c Johnson b McLean	1
*J. H. K. Adams c Turner b Francis	107	– c Turner b McLean	17
J. D. Francis lbw b Johnson	39	– c and b Francis	20
V. Atri b Blackwell	32	– not out	57
C. D. Nash b Blackwell	49	– c Burns b Francis	20
Z. K. Sharif c Laraman b Blackwell	41	– c Turner b Francis	0
R. E. King c Francis b Blackwell	17	– lbw b Francis	0
†L. J. Goddard not out	23	– (9) not out	8
D. H. Wigley st Turner b Blackwell	9	– (8) c Turner b McLean	6
B 1, l-b 6, w 2, n-b 10	19	B 1, n-b 2	3
1/10 (1) 2/96 (3) 3/193 (4) 4/211 (2) 5/281 (5) 6/308 (6) 7/313 (7) 8/345 (9) (8 wkts dec.)	345	1/4 (1) 2/35 (2) 3/60 (3) 4/90 (5) 5/90 (6) 6/90 (7) 7/104 (8) (7 wkts)	132

J. E. Anyon and R. A. G. Cummins did not bat.

Bowling: *First Innings*—Johnson 20–4–59–2; McLean 18–0–91–0; Laraman 14–0–82–0; Francis 12–4–41–1; Blackwell 27.4–11–65–5. *Second Innings*—McLean 12–2–49–3; Francis 14–2–47–4; Cox 1–0–7–0; Blackwell 15–6–22–0; Bowler 3–0–6–0.

Umpires: J. H. Evans and R. Palmer.

At Bristol, April 18, 19, 20, 21. SOMERSET lost to GLOUCESTERSHIRE by eight runs.

SOMERSET v DURHAM

At Taunton, April 23, 24, 25, 26. Somerset won by six wickets. Somerset 17 pts, Durham 2.75 pts (after 0.25 pt penalty). Toss: Durham. County debuts: J. Srinath, V. J. Wells.

Johnson twice undermined Durham with his muscular fast-medium, blasted the winning runs as rain clouds loomed and gave the England selectors an early-season prod. Let down by much of their batting, Somerset's success was never a formality, although Durham's batsmen were at times worse. Lewis was the exception, and he grafted for the first of two fifties as their first innings crumbled in 59 overs. However, Somerset also lost five wickets cheaply on the opening day, and only Trescothick, who hit 52 of his 60 in meaty boundaries, boosted the total. After Durham again succumbed cheaply, Bowler, in the conscientious role he fills best, and Bryant steadied Somerset's pursuit of 195. More reliable slip catching would have removed them both. With a downpour threatening and 24 needed, Johnson was promoted and he settled things emphatically with three consecutive sixes off Phillips's off-spin. Turner held eight catches in the match, one of them athletically brilliant.

Close of play: First day, Somerset 126-5 (Bryant 12, Turner 0); Second day, Durham 153-5 (Law 35, A. Pratt 19); Third day, Somerset 75-2 (Bowler 30, Cox 8).

Durham

First innings		Second innings	
*J. J. B. Lewis c Turner b Francis	78	b Francis	50
M. A. Gough c Turner b Johnson	14	c Burns b Johnson	4
G. J. Pratt lbw b Johnson	8	lbw b Johnson	21
V. J. Wells c Trescothick b McLean	7	c Turner b Francis	9
N. Peng c Turner b Johnson	15	c Turner b McLean	4
D. R. Law c Turner b Johnson	4	b McLean	35
†A. Pratt b Johnson	23	c Burns b Johnson	27
N. C. Phillips c Trescothick b Laraman	6	c Dutch b McLean	4
N. Killeen c Laraman b Francis	20	c Turner b Johnson	0
J. Srinath not out	0	not out	13
S. J. Harmison c Bryant b Francis	0	c Turner b Francis	2
L-b 2, n-b 8	10	L-b 1, n-b 10	11
1/24 (2) 2/40 (3) 3/66 (4) 4/96 (5) 5/100 (6) 6/134 (7) 7/147 (8) 8/180 (1) 9/185 (9) 10/185 (11)	185	1/6 (2) 2/36 (3) 3/53 (4) 4/66 (5) 5/112 (1) 6/153 (6) 7/165 (7) 8/165 (8) 9/165 (9) 10/180 (11)	180

Bonus points – Somerset 3.

Bowling: *First Innings*—McLean 17–4–44–1; Johnson 16–1–64–5; Francis 15–4–49–3; Laraman 11–2–26–1. *Second Innings*—McLean 14–4–50–3; Johnson 19–5–52–4; Francis 12.4–3–41–3; Burns 6–3–13–0; Laraman 2–1–3–0; Dutch 5–0–20–0.

> "The oddity of two hit-wickets in an innings had not occurred in England since 1966."
>
> Durham in 2003, page 525.

Somerset

P. D. Bowler c Srinath b Killeen	25	– not out	67
M. E. Trescothick c Phillips b Wells	60	– c A. Pratt b Killeen	28
*M. Burns lbw b Wells	17	– b Killeen	0
J. Cox lbw b Srinath	0	– c A. Pratt b Harmison	10
J. D. C. Bryant b Srinath	13	– c A. Pratt b Phillips	51
S. R. G. Francis b Wells	0		
†R. J. Turner not out	27		
K. P. Dutch b Harmison	4		
A. W. Laraman c A. Pratt b Harmison	1		
R. L. Johnson run out	7	– (6) not out	23
N. A. M. McLean b Harmison	0		
B 5, l-b 5, w 1, n-b 6	17	B 1, l-b 6, w 1, n-b 10	18
1/91 (2) 2/100 (1) 3/100 (4) 4/125 (3) 5/125 (6) 6/130 (5) 7/151 (8) 8/153 (9) 9/169 (10) 10/171 (11)	171	1/50 (2) 2/54 (3) 3/82 (4) 4/171 (5)	(4 wkts) 197

Bonus points – Durham 3.

Bowling: *First Innings*—Srinath 17–4–46–2; Harmison 20.4–7–49–3; Killeen 12–4–31–1; Wells 11–0–35–3. *Second Innings*—Srinath 16–4–46–0; Harmison 15–8–25–1; Killeen 14–2–57–2; Wells 5–1–19–0; Phillips 5.4–1–43–1.

Umpires: J. W. Lloyds and G. Sharp.

At Derby, April 30, May 1, 2, 3. SOMERSET drew with DERBYSHIRE.

SOMERSET v GLAMORGAN

At Taunton, May 14, 15, 16, 17. Somerset won by an innings and 143 runs. Somerset 22 pts, Glamorgan 3 pts. Toss: Somerset.

From the moment McLean found Thomas's edge with the fifth ball of the game, Glamorgan never really looked up for a fight. McLean backed up Burns's decision to bowl first on a pitch with a green tinge, finding bounce and a little movement to take five for 43. In reply, Trescothick bucked the pattern of uncertainty at the crease, thumping 70 off 74 balls. There was no play after tea on the second day, and only 24 overs on the third, but between the breaks, Somerset batted as if keen to make good the previous summer's shortcomings. Bowler hit 92 at his own poised pace, Burns also reached sight of a century, and Laraman hurried excitingly to fifty by the shortest route. After Somerset declared 276 ahead, only the weather looked likely to thwart them and Glamorgan, frail once again, capitulated in 44 overs in their second innings.

Close of play: First day, Somerset 161-1 (Bowler 51, Burns 21); Second day, Somerset 394-6 (Turner 12, Laraman 0); Third day, Glamorgan 29-1 (Dale 15, Hemp 12).

Glamorgan

I. J. Thomas c Trescothick b McLean	0	– (2) c Turner b Johnson	1
A. Dale c Bryant b McLean	40	– (1) c Burns b McLean	15
D. L. Hemp c Cox b McLean	2	– c Turner b McLean	36
M. J. Powell c Trescothick b Laraman	7	– lbw b Laraman	16
M. P. Maynard lbw b McLean	34	– (6) c Bowler b Francis	30
J. Hughes c Turner b Francis	2	– (5) c Turner b McLean	5
†M. A. Wallace b Blackwell	26	– b Laraman	4
*R. D. B. Croft lbw b Laraman	46	– c Blackwell b Laraman	0
D. S. Harrison c Turner b Johnson	0	– c Turner b Johnson	6
M. S. Kasprowicz c Turner b McLean	13	– not out	11
A. G. Wharf not out	8	– c Turner b Johnson	2
B 8, n-b 14	22	B 4, l-b 2, w 1	7
1/0 (1) 2/6 (3) 3/15 (4) 4/70 (5) 5/95 (2) 6/99 (6) 7/140 (7) 8/141 (9) 9/182 (10) 10/200 (8)	200	1/2 (2) 2/41 (1) 3/58 (3) 4/64 (5) 5/80 (4) 6/88 (7) 7/92 (8) 8/111 (9) 9/127 (6) 10/133 (11)	133

Bonus points – Glamorgan 1, Somerset 3.

Bowling: *First Innings*—McLean 17–6–43–5; Johnson 17–7–23–1; Laraman 10–2–46–2; Francis 14–2–61–1; Blackwell 5–0–19–1. *Second Innings*—McLean 12–4–38–3; Johnson 14–3–36–3; Francis 12–5–33–1; Laraman 6–2–20–3.

Somerset

P. D. Bowler c Wharf b Dale	92
M. E. Trescothick c Dale b Wharf	70
*M. Burns b Dale	82
J. Cox lbw b Wharf	29
J. D. C. Bryant lbw b Dale	30
I. D. Blackwell b Harrison	42
†R. J. Turner not out	32
A. W. Laraman not out	61
B 6, l-b 17, w 1, n-b 14	38
1/121 (2) 2/249 (3) 3/290 (1) 4/316 (4) 5/373 (6) 6/390 (5) (6 wkts dec.)	476

R. L. Johnson, N. A. M. McLean and S. R. G. Francis did not bat.

Bonus points – Somerset 5, Glamorgan 2.

Bowling: Kasprowicz 30–9–103–0; Wharf 22–3–113–2; Harrison 27–3–116–1; Croft 23–5–92–0; Dale 12–2–29–3.

Umpires: A. Clarkson and A. G. T. Whitehead.

At Southampton, May 21, 22, 23, 24. SOMERSET beat HAMPSHIRE by six wickets.

SOMERSET v WORCESTERSHIRE

At Bath, June 4, 5, 6, 7. Worcestershire won by nine wickets. Worcestershire 22 pts, Somerset 3 pts. Toss: Worcestershire.

A disappointing Bath festival for Somerset partisans went wrong from the opening day when Worcestershire showed a collective disdain for their attack. Benefiting from dropped catches, they went on to amass 538, with three hundreds: Peters, who got off the mark with an ominous six, scored an attractive career-best 165, though fellow-opener Singh beat him to a century, while Hall was quicker yet as he pulled and swept to three figures. Hick had also looked set for another of his massive innings at Somerset's expense but chipped meekly to mid-wicket for 71. Somerset were daunted by the total and forced to follow on. They began the last day 156 behind with three second-innings wickets down, but Cox, almost the only voice of resolve, and Burns edged them into a small lead. Batty took six for 88 as the pitch, so bland at the start, began to take spin. Worcestershire dashed to victory in the last hour and replaced Somerset as leaders.

Close of play: First day, Worcestershire 422-5 (Hall 30, Batty 22); Second day, Somerset 19-0 (Holloway 6, Wood 6); Third day, Somerset 144-3 (Cox 35, Burns 33).

Worcestershire

S. D. Peters b Francis	165		
A. Singh c Cox b Dutch	105	– c Bryant b Francis	15
G. A. Hick c Parsons b Blackwell	71	– not out	29
*B. F. Smith st Turner b Blackwell	2		
V. S. Solanki b McLean	10	– (1) not out	20
A. J. Hall lbw b Parsons	104		
G. J. Batty b Francis	26		
†S. J. Rhodes lbw b Blackwell	22		
Kabir Ali c Turner b Blackwell	0		
M. A. Harrity not out	2		
M. Hayward c Turner b Parsons	4		
L-b 17, w 2, n-b 8	27	N-b 4	4
1/201 (2) 2/320 (3) 3/326 (4) 4/353 (5) 5/383 (1) 6/432 (7) 7/524 (6) 8/532 (8) 9/533 (9) 10/538 (11)	538	1/21 (2)	(1 wkt) 68

Bonus points – Worcestershire 5, Somerset 2 (130 overs: 526-7).

Bowling: *First Innings*—McLean 21–1–105–1; Francis 30–5–112–2; Parsons 14.4–3–63–2; Burns 8–0–25–0; Blackwell 45–8–131–4; Dutch 15–1–85–1. *Second Innings*—Francis 4–0–40–1; Blackwell 3.1–0–28–0.

Somerset

P. C. L. Holloway c Rhodes b Ali	30	– lbw b Ali	11
M. J. Wood c Singh b Hayward	8	– c Solanki b Batty	32
J. D. C. Bryant c Smith b Batty	28	– c Rhodes b Harrity	12
J. Cox lbw b Hall	37	– lbw b Hall	160
*M. Burns c Hick b Hall	6	– c Solanki b Hall	57
I. D. Blackwell lbw b Batty	28	– c sub b Batty	10
†R. J. Turner c Smith b Batty	23	– lbw b Batty	10
K. A. Parsons c Hick b Hayward	4	– c Singh b Batty	6
K. P. Dutch c Rhodes b Ali	17	– c Hick b Batty	1
N. A. M. McLean not out	35	– not out	9
S. R. G. Francis lbw b Ali	4	– c sub b Batty	1
L-b 1, w 1, n-b 16	18	B 4, l-b 14, w 9, n-b 26, p 5	58
1/40 (2) 2/42 (1) 3/115 (3) 4/123 (4) 5/138 (5) 6/169 (6) 7/182 (8) 8/188 (7) 9/220 (9) 10/238 (11)	238	1/37 (1) 2/66 (2) 3/68 (3) 4/247 (5) 5/282 (6) 6/334 (7) 7/356 (4) 8/356 (8) 9/365 (9) 10/367 (11)	367

Bonus points – Somerset 1, Worcestershire 3.

Bowling: *First Innings*—Ali 13.4–1–68–3; Hayward 15–5–56–2; Harrity 8–3–20–0; Batty 22–8–66–3; Hall 7–1–27–2. *Second Innings*—Hayward 15–2–49–0; Ali 19–4–75–1; Batty 39.1–8–88–6; Harrity 20–2–69–1; Hall 23–7–63–2.

Umpires: M. R. Benson and J. W. Holder.

At Taunton, June 17. SOMERSET lost to ZIMBABWEANS by three runs (see Zimbabwean tour section).

SOMERSET v YORKSHIRE

At Taunton, June 27, 28, 29, 30. Yorkshire won by ten wickets. Yorkshire 21.75 pts (after 0.25 pt penalty), Somerset 5 pts. Toss: Yorkshire.

The memorable performances all belonged to Yorkshire, and Kirby's was the most memorable of all. On a true pitch, he bent his back to take a match-winning 13 for 154, Yorkshire's best figures since Ray Illingworth spun his way to 14 for 64 against Gloucestershire in 1967. Nothing much went right for Somerset after they were put in, and they were 64 for six before being partially rescued by Turner and the tail. Yorkshire's reply of 512 determined the course of the game: a diligent, well-made double-hundred from Wood, an especially attractive 98 by Fleming, out to a fine running catch, and a maiden century by Gray built a lead of 237. Wood batted seven hours and 300 balls with 27 fours and a six. Kirby then finished in great style, grabbing eight second-innings wickets. Told his figures were Yorkshire's best for 36 years, he was uncharacteristically dumbstruck: "I don't know what to say. I am quite stunned by that." Earlier in the match, some of his more pithy comments to batsmen brought a quiet word of caution from umpire Steele.

Close of play: First day, Somerset 275; Second day, Yorkshire 409-6 (Wood 207, Gray 44); Third day, Somerset 213-6 (Blackwell 13, Laraman 1).

Somerset

P. D. Bowler c Fleming b Silverwood	0	– c Yuvraj Singh b Kirby	58
M. J. Wood c Yuvraj Singh b Kirby	16	– c White b Silverwood	1
J. D. C. Bryant b Kirby	7	– c Fleming b Yuvraj Singh	45
J. Cox lbw b Kirby	0	– lbw b Kirby	39
*M. Burns lbw b Kirby	0	– c White b Kirby	39
I. D. Blackwell c Guy b Silverwood	19	– c Guy b Kirby	23
†R. J. Turner not out	81	– c Yuvraj Singh b Kirby	4
A. W. Laraman b Sidebottom	36	– not out	39
N. A. M. McLean c Yuvraj Singh b Silverwood	5	– c Gray b Kirby	35
P. S. Jones b Kirby	39	– b Kirby	0
S. R. G. Francis c Wood b Sidebottom	44	– c Yuvraj Singh b Kirby	6
L-b 11, w 1, n-b 16	28	B 5, l-b 4, w 2, n-b 6	17
1/0 (1) 2/19 (3) 3/19 (4) 4/19 (5) 5/40 (2) 6/64 (6) 7/137 (8) 8/144 (9) 9/204 (10) 10/275 (11)	275	1/11 (2) 2/98 (1) 3/128 (3) 4/191 (5) 5/194 (4) 6/210 (7) 7/236 (6) 8/296 (9) 9/296 (10) 10/306 (11)	306

Bonus points – Somerset 2, Yorkshire 3.

Bowling: *First Innings*—Silverwood 14–3–46–3; Kirby 16–1–74–5; Sidebottom 18–3–74–2; Gray 8–1–34–0; White 9–1–21–0; Lumb 2–0–15–0. *Second Innings*—Silverwood 15–6–76–1; Kirby 24.4–5–80–8; White 5–0–27–0; Sidebottom 18–3–49–0; Gray 10–3–22–0; Yuvraj Singh 11–1–43–1.

Yorkshire

*M. J. Wood c Bowler b Francis	207	– not out	30
S. P. Fleming c Jones b Blackwell	98	– not out	40
Yuvraj Singh c Burns b McLean	5		
M. J. Lumb c Turner b McLean	5		
R. J. Blakey c Turner b Francis	13		
C. White run out	6		
†S. M. Guy c Bowler b McLean	16		
A. K. D. Gray c Cox b Francis	104		
C. E. W. Silverwood b Jones	22		
R. J. Sidebottom b Blackwell	16		
S. P. Kirby not out	0		
L-b 10, w 2, n-b 8	20	L-b 1	1
1/165 (2) 2/176 (3) 3/188 (4) 4/219 (5) 5/254 (6) 6/297 (7) 7/413 (1) 8/483 (9) 9/512 (10) 10/512 (8)	512	(no wkt)	71

Bonus points – Yorkshire 5, Somerset 3.

Bowling: *First Innings*—McLean 25–5–87–3; Francis 28.2–3–111–3; Laraman 23–4–82–0; Jones 22–1–135–1; Burns 3–1–14–0; Blackwell 27–6–73–2. *Second Innings*—McLean 4–1–22–0; Francis 6–2–18–0; Jones 3–0–30–0.

Umpires: N. G. Cowley and J. F. Steele.

SOMERSET v GLOUCESTERSHIRE

At Taunton, July 2, 3, 4, 5. Drawn. Somerset 12 pts, Gloucestershire 8 pts. Toss: Somerset. Championship debut: C. M. Gazzard.

After three days of fluctuating and often absorbing cricket, Gloucestershire batted on in their second innings to leave Somerset an unrealistic target of 363 in 51 overs. But the visitors had fought back impressively from a gaping first-innings deficit and their captain, Alleyne, argued that the pitch was still too flat and easy-paced to allow their neighbours any last-day liberties. The match had already produced much to admire. Replying to Gloucestershire's 228, Laraman hit a maiden first-class century, followed by some Caribbean fireworks from McLean. But a splendid 179 by Weston and an unbeaten hundred from Harvey helped Gloucestershire turn a first-innings deficit of 249 into a lead of 362. The county's 611 for nine declared was their highest total in a second innings. Bowlers toiled throughout, though Smith, economical as ever, managed six wickets in the match for Gloucestershire.

Close of play: First day, Somerset 100-2 (Bryant 29, Cox 56); Second day, Gloucestershire 31-0 (Weston 27, Spearman 2); Third day, Gloucestershire 436-5 (Harvey 69, Alleyne 29).

Gloucestershire

First innings		Second innings	
C. M. Spearman b McLean	54	(2) lbw b McLean	3
W. P. C. Weston c Gazzard b Laraman	19	(1) b Laraman	179
C. G. Taylor c Turner b Francis	23	c Cox b McLean	0
J. N. Rhodes c Turner b Laraman	50	c Turner b Burns	49
M. G. N. Windows lbw b Laraman	19	c Turner b Laraman	89
*M. W. Alleyne b Burns	10	(7) lbw b McLean	29
I. J. Harvey c Gazzard b McLean	28	(6) not out	128
M. C. J. Ball lbw b Burns	0	c Dutch b Suppiah	75
†S. P. Pope c Turner b Burns	8	c Cox b Dutch	7
J. Lewis c Cox b McLean	5	st Turner b Dutch	14
A. M. Smith not out	0	not out	8
L-b 8, w 2, n-b 2	12	B 6, l-b 8, w 2, n-b 14	30
1/57 (2) 2/83 (1) 3/127 (3) 4/172 (4) 5/175 (5) 6/197 (6) 7/209 (8) 8/213 (7) 9/222 (10) 10/228 (9)	228	1/37 (2) 2/41 (3) 3/117 (4) 4/315 (5) 5/368 (1) 6/436 (7) 7/576 (8) 8/584 (9) 9/600 (10) (9 wkts dec.)	611

Bonus points – Gloucestershire 1, Somerset 3.

Bowling: *First Innings*—McLean 16–2–68–3; Francis 16–2–73–1; Laraman 18–8–44–3; Burns 11.4–4–35–3. *Second Innings*—Francis 32–2–147–0; Burns 31–7–105–1; Dutch 28–7–60–2; McLean 30–2–139–3; Laraman 26–3–102–2; Suppiah 11–1–44–1.

Somerset

First innings		Second innings	
M. J. Wood c Ball b Harvey	10	not out	49
C. M. Gazzard b Smith	2	b Smith	4
J. D. C. Bryant c Pope b Smith	29	lbw b Smith	15
J. Cox c Pope b Harvey	69	c Lewis b Alleyne	28
*M. Burns b Smith	66	not out	6
†R. J. Turner lbw b Smith	7		
A. W. Laraman not out	148		
K. P. Dutch c Harvey b Lewis	15		
A. V. Suppiah c Alleyne b Lewis	16		
N. A. M. McLean c Windows b Ball	76		
S. R. G. Francis c Windows b Lewis	19		
B 7, l-b 7, w 2, n-b 4	20	L-b 3, n-b 10	13
1/10 (2) 2/12 (1) 3/101 (3) 4/113 (4) 5/136 (6) 6/244 (5) 7/259 (8) 8/331 (9) 9/432 (10) 10/477 (11)	477	1/6 (2) 2/38 (3) 3/76 (4) (3 wkts)	115

Bonus points – Somerset 5, Gloucestershire 3 (130 overs: 472-9).

Bowling: *First Innings*—Lewis 28–6–107–3; Smith 31–10–67–4; Harvey 27–6–103–2; Alleyne 28–6–116–0; Ball 19–2–70–1. *Second Innings*—Lewis 9–2–37–0; Smith 11–5–19–2; Ball 13–5–20–0; Alleyne 6–2–18–1; Weston 2–0–10–0; Taylor 2–0–8–0.

Umpires: J. H. Evans and J. H. Hampshire.

At Cardiff, July 9, 10, 11, 12. SOMERSET lost to GLAMORGAN by 110 runs.

At Taunton, July 15, 16, 17. SOMERSET drew with SOUTH AFRICANS (see South African tour section).

At Northampton, July 23, 24. SOMERSET lost to NORTHAMPTONSHIRE by an innings and 61 runs.

At Chester-le-Street, July 30, 31, August 1. SOMERSET lost to DURHAM by 318 runs.

SOMERSET v NORTHAMPTONSHIRE

At Taunton, August 14, 15, 16, 17. Drawn. Somerset 10 pts, Northamptonshire 12 pts. Toss: Somerset. Championship debut: N. J. Edwards.

While Somerset's form – five defeats in six Championship matches – was grim, Northamptonshire's was glorious – six straight wins – and their confidence plain during a formidable first innings. So the result represented a small triumph for Somerset although, given the conditions, a draw was always predictable. The pitch could not have been more amiable, or the outfield faster, and as usual Hussey accumulated without flamboyance or obvious risk. He batted nine minutes short of 11 hours and faced 471 balls for a county-record 331 not out, including 38 fours and five sixes. Three of his 13 Championship centuries since his arrival at Northampton in 2001 had now been converted into triples, and three more into doubles. However, one member of the Somerset party did show menace with the ball: their coach, Kevin Shine, hit his seamer Gary Gilder on the head in the nets and the resulting dizziness prevented Gilder bowling. Hundreds from Sales and Bailey pushed Northamptonshire towards 681 for five declared, a lead of 205. Blackwell's first century of the season had already helped Somerset to 476 in their first innings; in their second, Wood, with limited scope and success in 2003, became the game's fifth centurion.

Close of play: First day, Somerset 374-7 (Gazzard 15, Jones 12); Second day, Northamptonshire 322-2 (Hussey 144, Sales 84); Third day, Somerset 26-0 (Wood 14, Edwards 10).

Somerset

M. J. Wood c Hussey b Cawdron	30	– b Cawdron	100
N. J. Edwards c Powell b Nel	9	– lbw b Greenidge	10
*M. Burns b Greenidge	28	– c Bailey b Cawdron	13
J. Cox b Nel	30	– retired hurt	64
T. Webley b Brown	32	– not out	41
I. D. Blackwell b Nel	140	– c Bailey b Greenidge	38
A. W. Laraman c Bailey b Greenidge	70	– not out	8
†C. M. Gazzard c Bailey b Cook	41		
P. S. Jones c Hussey b Brown	63		
N. A. M. McLean b Greenidge	16		
G. M. Gilder not out	7		
B 1, l-b 6, w 1, n-b 2	10	L-b 5, n-b 13	18
1/23 (2) 2/59 (1) 3/77 (3) 4/106 (4) 5/160 (5) 6/343 (6) 7/347 (7) 8/449 (9) 9/457 (8) 10/476 (10)	476	1/30 (2) 2/63 (3) 3/169 (1) 4/267 (6)	(4 wkts) 292

Bonus points – Somerset 5, Northamptonshire 3.

In the second innings Cox retired hurt at 218.

Bowling: *First Innings*—Nel 31–10–113–3; Greenidge 28.2–4–111–3; Cawdron 18–3–80–1; Cook 18–7–47–1; Brown 31–5–118–2. *Second Innings*—Nel 18–3–53–0; Greenidge 17–2–74–2; Brown 26–6–81–0; Cawdron 11–3–26–2; Cook 10–3–28–0; Jaques 3–0–8–0; Hussey 5–1–6–0; Roberts 4–0–4–0; Sales 1–0–4–0; Bailey 1–0–3–0.

Northamptonshire

*M. E. K. Hussey not out	331
T. W. Roberts b Blackwell	45
P. A. Jaques c Gazzard b Burns	38
D. J. Sales b Blackwell	125
M. J. Powell c Burns b Blackwell	3
J. W. Cook c Cox b Jones	15
†T. M. B. Bailey not out	101
B 6, l-b 11, n-b 6	23
1/84 (2) 2/169 (3) 3/390 (4) 4/416 (5) 5/439 (6)	(5 wkts dec.) 681

C. G. Greenidge, M. J. Cawdron, A. Nel and J. F. Brown did not bat.

Bonus points – Northamptonshire 5, Somerset 1 (130 overs: 501-5).

Bowling: McLean 26–3–99–0; Jones 34–3–162–1; Blackwell 53–4–206–3; Laraman 24–1–91–0; Burns 18–1–53–1; Edwards 8–0–35–0; Webley 5–1–10–0; Cox 1–0–8–0.

Umpires: G. I. Burgess and P. J. Hartley.

At Worcester, August 20, 21, 22. SOMERSET lost to WORCESTERSHIRE by eight wickets.

SOMERSET v HAMPSHIRE

At Taunton, August 26, 27, 28, 29. Drawn. Somerset 12 pts, Hampshire 10 pts. Toss: Somerset.

Another flat Taunton pitch produced another draw, but not before Somerset had created a piece of history: 705 for nine beat their previous highest first-class total, 675 for nine against the same county 79 years earlier at Bath. Neil Edwards, a 19-year-old left-handed Cornishman playing only his third Championship match, made a resolute 160 and was compared by his coach, Kevin Shine, to the former England batsman Chris Broad. Meanwhile, Blackwell's 189 in 211 balls superseded his career-best set in the last home game: again his timing and fiery strokeplay were exceptional and he punished the bowling mercilessly. Burns had chosen to field first, only to watch his attack bowl poorly and allow Kenway to complete a conscientious hundred for Hampshire. But once Blackwell had finished, their 395 looked paltry. Overnight rain ruled out 45 overs at the start of the final day and the match dwindled to a draw.

Close of play: First day, Hampshire 300-7 (Smith 7, Udal 3); Second day, Somerset 338-4 (Webley 30, Blackwell 27); Third day, Hampshire 4-0 (Kenway 0, Adams 4).

Hampshire

D. A. Kenway c Edwards b Johnson	100	– c Turner b McLean	8
J. H. K. Adams b McLean	14	– b Blackwell	50
*J. P. Crawley c Blackwell b McLean	60	– c Blackwell b McLean	1
R. A. Smith not out	56		
†N. Pothas b Jones	21		
L. R. Prittipaul c Burns b Johnson	39	– (4) not out	56
A. D. Mascarenhas lbw b Blackwell	5		
J. R. C. Hamblin c Turner b Johnson	31	– (5) not out	53
S. D. Udal b Jones	30		
C. T. Tremlett c Laraman b Jones	12		
J. A. Tomlinson c Turner b Jones	0		
L-b 17, n-b 10	27	L-b 4, w 1, n-b 4	9
1/35 (2) 2/175 (1) 3/195 (3) 4/219 (5) 5/234 (7) 6/293 (8) 7/300 (6) 8/364 (9) 9/388 (10) 10/395 (11)	395	1/14 (1) 2/16 (3) 3/96 (2) (3 wkts)	177

Bonus points – Hampshire 4, Somerset 3.

In the first innings Smith, when 7, retired hurt at 191 and resumed at 300.

Bowling: *First Innings*—McLean 21–6–68–2; Johnson 28–9–90–3; Jones 21.3–3–102–4; Laraman 23–5–71–0; Burns 4–0–27–0; Blackwell 9–5–20–1. *Second Innings*—McLean 8.3–2–37–2; Johnson 6–0–17–0; Laraman 2–0–6–0; Blackwell 18–3–48–1; Jones 7–1–31–0; Webley 1–0–16–0; Edwards 4.3–1–10–0; Bryant 1–0–8–0.

Somerset

M. J. Wood c Kenway b Tremlett	8
N. J. Edwards c Mascarenhas b Tomlinson	160
J. D. C. Bryant c Pothas b Kenway	73
*M. Burns c Mascarenhas b Udal	10
T. Webley b Tremlett	59
I. D. Blackwell c Tremlett b Prittipaul	189
A. W. Laraman run out	52
†R. J. Turner not out	67
P. S. Jones c Udal b Tremlett	20
R. L. Johnson c Crawley b Tremlett	19
B 14, l-b 2, w 4, n-b 28	48
1/26 (1) 2/173 (3) 3/189 (4) 4/304 (2) 5/448 (5) 6/564 (7) 7/616 (6) 8/663 (9) 9/705 (10) (9 wkts dec.)	705

N. A. M. McLean did not bat.

Bonus points – Somerset 5, Hampshire 2 (130 overs: 594-6).

Bowling: Tremlett 33–4–152–4; Mascarenhas 23–5–108–0; Tomlinson 28–4–142–1; Prittipaul 17–1–101–1; Udal 42–3–177–1; Kenway 2–0–9–1.

Umpires: M. J. Harris and T. E. Jesty.

At Leeds, September 3, 4, 5. SOMERSET lost to YORKSHIRE by nine wickets.

SOMERSET v DERBYSHIRE

At Taunton, September 10, 11, 12, 13. Somerset won by 27 runs. Somerset 22 pts, Derbyshire 8 pts. Toss: Somerset. First-class debut: J. C. Hildreth. County debut: Hasan Adnan.

This was Somerset's first Championship win since May, though it will be remembered principally for the stunning brilliance of Blackwell, who learned during his double-hundred that he had been named in England's one-day squad for Bangladesh and Sri Lanka. Somerset were 31 for four

BLACKWELL'S BLITZES

In the last three games at Taunton, Ian Blackwell's batting statistics were as follows:

	Runs	*Balls*	*Minutes*	*Fours*	*Sixes*
v Northamptonshire	140	149	176	22	4
	38	35	32	7	1
v Hampshire.	189	211	255	32	2
v Derbyshire.	247*	156	234	27	11
	4	16	19	0	0
Total	618	567	716	88	18

In these innings, Blackwell's average was 154.50 and his strike-rate 108.99. In all, 460 – or over 74% – came in boundaries.

when he went in, soon to be 75 for six. But against his old county Blackwell responded with an extraordinary *tour de force*, a display of such clean and mighty hitting that his power drew comparisons with that of Viv Richards. Blackwell's unbeaten 247 came from 156 deliveries, his second hundred smashed off just 41, and several of his 11 sixes disappeared out of sight, the balls never retrieved. The blitz lasted just under four hours, and included 27 fours and a county-record last-wicket stand of 163 with McLean (bettering 143 by Arthur Gibbs and Jim Bridges in 1919). His 200 came up in 207 minutes and 134 balls. In terms of balls faced, it was the fastest double-century on record by an Englishman (this statistic was not routinely noted until recent times). After McLean's 39, Somerset's next-highest score was 25; Cork took six wickets – and ten in the match without the aid of a fielder – but not the one that mattered. However, Derbyshire reached 400 themselves in their first innings, with a hundred from Gait and 93 by Stubbings, in only his second Championship match of the season. Somerset collapsed in their second innings to leave a target of 224 but Derbyshire tumbled badly too, from 178 for four to 196 all out. It was Blackwell, now the bowler, who took four crucial wickets.

Close of play: First day, Derbyshire 32-0 (Gait 11, Di Venuto 20); Second day, Derbyshire 326-6 (Hasan Adnan 11, Dumelow 22); Third day, Somerset 214.

Somerset

M. J. Wood lbw b Dean	14 – b Mohammad Ali	72
N. J. Edwards b Cork	10 – b Havell	28
*M. Burns b Cork	0 – c Di Venuto b Mohammad Ali . . .	58
T. Webley lbw b Cork.	0 – b Dumelow	12
J. C. Hildreth b Cork	9 – b Cork	0
I. D. Blackwell not out	247 – c Havell b Dumelow	4
†R. J. Turner lbw b Dean	16 – not out	18
G. M. Andrew b Cork.	9 – c Adnan b Dumelow	0
R. L. Johnson lbw b Cork	25 – lbw b Cork	6
S. R. G. Francis c Gait b Mohammad Ali.	18 – lbw b Cork	4
N. A. M. McLean lbw b Mohammad Ali	39 – b Cork	0
B 4, l-b 7, w 1, n-b 10	22 B 5, l-b 1, n-b 6.	12
1/19 (1) 2/26 (3) 3/26 (4) 4/31 (2) 5/42 (5) 6/75 (7) 7/112 (8) 8/176 (9) 9/246 (10) 10/409 (11)	409 1/87 (2) 2/124 (1) 3/165 (4) 4/170 (5) 5/185 (6) 6/186 (3) 7/191 (8) 8/206 (9) 9/214 (10) 10/214 (11)	214

Bonus points – Somerset 5, Derbyshire 3.

Bowling: *First Innings*—Cork 20–3–92–6; Dean 22–4–118–2; Havell 7–0–66–0; Mohammad Ali 13–3–83–2; Dumelow 3–0–39–0. *Second Innings*—Cork 20.3–7–35–4; Dean 2–0–21–0; Havell 8–0–45–1; Mohammad Ali 17–9–38–2; Dumelow 29–7–69–3.

Derbyshire

	First innings			Second innings	
A. I. Gait b Francis	110	–	(2) lbw b Blackwell	49
M. J. Di Venuto c Turner b Johnson	46	–	(1) c Turner b Francis	23
R. M. Khan c Turner b Andrew	24	–	c Webley b Blackwell	22
S. D. Stubbings c Turner b Francis	93	–	c Andrew b Francis	9
Hasan Adnan not out	59	–	c Johnson b Francis	32
†L. D. Sutton c Turner b Francis	10	–	c Turner b Andrew	49
*D. G. Cork c Turner b Francis	0	–	st Turner b Blackwell	1
N. R. C. Dumelow c Wood b Johnson	26	–	b Andrew	6
Mohammad Ali c Turner b McLean	6	–	c Webley b Andrew	0
K. J. Dean b McLean	7	–	b Blackwell	1
P. M. R. Havell not out	7	–	not out	1
L-b 8, w 2, n-b 2	12		L-b 2, w 1	3
1/64 (2) 2/96 (3) 3/281 (1) 4/282 (4) 5/292 (6) 6/293 (7) 7/345 (8) 8/352 (9) 9/362 (10) (9 wkts dec.)	400		1/43 (1) 2/78 (3) 3/97 (4) 4/105 (2) 5/178 (6) 6/179 (7) 7/188 (8) 8/188 (9) 9/193 (10) 10/196 (5)	196

Bonus points – Derbyshire 5, Somerset 3.

Bowling: *First Innings*—McLean 27–6–86–2; Johnson 36–9–98–2; Andrew 12–2–42–1; Francis 23.3–4–94–4; Burns 3–1–14–0; Blackwell 22–6–58–0. *Second Innings*—McLean 9–1–25–0; Johnson 11–1–47–0; Blackwell 27–7–65–4; Francis 13–1–43–3; Andrew 4–0–14–3.

Umpires: G. I. Burgess and J. F. Steele.

DATES OF WINNING COUNTY CHAMPIONSHIP

The dates on which the County Championship has been settled since 1979 are as follows:

			Final margin
1979	Essex	August 21	77 pts
1980	Middlesex	September 2	13 pts
1981	Nottinghamshire	September 14	2 pts
1982	Middlesex	September 11	39 pts
1983	Essex	September 13	16 pts
1984	Essex	September 11	14 pts
1985	Middlesex	September 17	18 pts
1986	Essex	September 10	28 pts
1987	Nottinghamshire	September 14	4 pts
1988	Worcestershire	September 16	1 pt
1989	Worcestershire	August 31	6 pts
1990	Middlesex	September 20	31 pts
1991	Essex	September 19	13 pts
1992	Essex	September 3	41 pts
1993	Middlesex	August 30	36 pts
1994	Warwickshire	September 2	42 pts
1995	Warwickshire	September 16	32 pts
1996	Leicestershire	September 21	27 pts
1997	Glamorgan	September 20	4 pts
1998	Leicestershire	September 19	15 pts
1999	Surrey	September 2	56 pts
2000	Surrey	September 13	20 pts
2001	Yorkshire	August 24	16 pts
2002	Surrey	September 7	44.75 pts
2003	Sussex	September 18	34 pts

Note: The earliest date on which the Championship has been won since it was expanded in 1895 was August 12, 1910, by Kent.

SURREY

Invincible? Not exactly

DAVID LLEWELLYN

Winning is an exhausting business. Surrey made that plain, losing the last three Championship matches very wearily, as they staggered to the finish. In the wake of winning the inaugural Twenty20 Cup, and plodding on to win the National League, they lost their way in the one competition they really wanted – the County Championship – and finished third, below the prize money. Surrey's ultimately unsuccessful defence of their title became the focus of their whole season.

There were plenty prepared to label the summer a failure, despite an operating profit in excess of £400,000 and two of the four main trophies, which would have delighted any other county. Excuses included the usual suspects: injuries, the odd toss, the weather, loss of form, the occasional dodgy decision. But lurking among them were some less obvious ones.

Since he first took charge of Surrey, standing in for Alec Stewart in 1995, Adam Hollioake perhaps proved himself the county's best captain since Stuart Surridge more than 40 years earlier. His innovative, imaginative approach often produced seemingly impossible victories, when all others would have surrendered to the percentage result, the draw. But in 2003, his seventh season in sole charge, he looked a tired man, merely going through the motions during the last weeks.

On his own admission, Hollioake found it hard to motivate himself, let alone his team. That led to a secondary cause of their downfall – a lack of the famous team spirit which had helped them lift the Championship crown in three of the previous four seasons. It was hardly a surprise that, having announced he would retire after 2004, his benefit season, Hollioake relinquished the captaincy. At least he would be around to support his successor, Jon Batty, for the next year.

However, Keith Medlycott, the cricket manager and Hollioake's partner for the past six successful years, resigned in November "to pursue other opportunities", saying he had taken Surrey as far as he could. There were undercurrents suggesting senior players felt Batty, like Stewart before him, would find captaining, keeping wicket and opening too onerous. The task of repairing these cracks, as Medlycott's successor, now falls to the Australian Steve Rixon.

Everything had gone swimmingly until the tail-end of August. While Surrey might have liked more than six wins, still they were unbeaten in the Championship, which they had led since mid-May. Then came three gruelling away matches. Leicestershire kept them in the field for almost three days and a draining draw. Already feeling punchy, Surrey immediately got into the ring with title rivals Lancashire. Down they went for their first KO. They suffered another at Canterbury and, by the time they got home to face relegated Essex, they were completely reeling.

Jimmy Ormond

There were international calls for seven players; whatever the depth of a squad, that is a serious drain. A domestic accident to Saqlain Mushtaq early on (he fell downstairs while holding his baby) damaged his precious right wrist, reducing him to an ordinary spinner and an even more ordinary set of figures. Jimmy Ormond should have put his feet up to nurse his injuries – a fractured toe, a side injury and tendinitis in a knee. Instead, he played through the pain. Alex Tudor failed to overcome knee trouble and a persistent side strain. Azhar Mahmood suffered hamstring and shoulder problems. Martin Bicknell was injured early and called up by England late. Little wonder Surrey struggled to bowl out sides twice. None of the bowlers reached 50 Championship wickets, the valiant Ormond coming closest.

Runs were not a problem, even if they came from some unexpected quarters – only Mark Ramprakash topped four figures in the Championship. The usual rock, Alistair Brown, had a horrid season, and Ian Ward underperformed (he later left for Sussex). In a fistful of matches, the lower order and tail-enders had to knuckle down and scrabble for batting points.

Then there was selection which, when Surrey were close to full strength, inevitably caused trouble. Mark Butcher made a stand after being overlooked for the opening match and was reinstated until England claimed him. Graham Thorpe found his path back to the England team hampered by some early omissions, and Rikki Clarke was dropped for two games straight after a match-saving hundred against Lancashire. Unsurprisingly, he became disgruntled. Despite the injury list, Tim Murtagh played just five Championship games, and the signing of West Indian Franklyn Rose for three September fixtures sent an insensitive message to young thrusters. Scott Newman, who had shown his batting promise in 2002, was noticeable by his absence.

The most prominent absentee in 2004 will be Stewart, who announced his retirement in September. He had wanted one more year, but Surrey had been granted planning permission to develop the Vauxhall End, at a cost of £22m, and claimed there was no spare cash – or sentiment. Stewart was therefore denied a chance to add to the 14,440 Championship runs he had scored since 1981. He was, however, appointed the club's director of new business.

There was one other significant departure, that of head groundsman Paul Brind. He was reluctantly allowed to leave after a decade in charge, thus ending a Brind dynasty that started with the appointment of his father Harry in 1975. The job is hardly going to an outsider, though: Brind's deputy, Bill Gordon, took over, and he has been at The Oval for 38 years.

SURREY RESULTS

All first-class matches – Played 18: Won 6, Lost 3, Drawn 9.
County Championship matches – Played 16: Won 6, Lost 3, Drawn 7.

Frizzell County Championship, 3rd in Division 1; Cheltenham & Gloucester Trophy, q-f; National Cricket League, winners in Division 1; Twenty20 Cup, winners.

COUNTY CHAMPIONSHIP AVERAGES

BATTING AND FIELDING

Cap		*M*	*I*	*NO*	*R*	*HS*	*100s*	*50s*	*Avge*	*Ct/St*
2002	M. R. Ramprakash	14	22	4	1,239	279*	5	2	68.83	7
1996	M. A. Butcher	6	8	0	527	144	2	2	65.87	10
1985	A. J. Stewart	6	8	1	451	98	0	5	64.42	20
1991	G. P. Thorpe	11	18	2	880	156	1	7	55.00	8
2001	J. N. Batty	10	19	4	794	168*	2	4	52.93	25/2
	R. Clarke	9	14	2	513	139	2	1	42.75	9
	Azhar Mahmood§	10	13	2	441	98	0	4	40.09	17
1989	M. P. Bicknell	11	11	3	318	141	1	0	39.75	1
2000	I. J. Ward	15	24	1	856	158	3	2	37.21	8
1998	I. D. K. Salisbury	14	18	4	455	101*	1	1	32.50	6
1998	Saqlain Mushtaq§	14	15	2	421	69	0	4	32.38	4
1995	A. J. Hollioake	13	18	0	567	122	1	3	31.50	10
1999	A. J. Tudor	6	7	1	177	55	0	1	29.50	0
1994	A. D. Brown	12	19	2	481	74	0	5	28.29	10
2003	J. Ormond	12	14	5	198	47	0	0	22.00	2
1998	N. Shahid	2	4	0	72	67	0	1	18.00	0
	T. J. Murtagh	5	8	4	61	21	0	0	15.25	0

Also batted: J. G. E. Benning (1 match) 18, 47; S. A. Newman (1 match) 9, 0 (2 ct); F. A. Rose§ (1 match) 1, 36; N. C. Saker (1 match) 1, 0; P. J. Sampson (1 match) 3, 32*; B. J. M. Scott (1 match) 58*, 5 (6 ct).

§ *Overseas player.*

BOWLING

	O	*M*	*R*	*W*	*BB*	*5W/i*	*Avge*
M. P. Bicknell	326.4	83	1,023	39	5-42	3	26.23
Azhar Mahmood	262.2	48	994	34	5-78	1	29.23
J. Ormond	366.1	65	1,363	44	5-45	2	30.97
Saqlain Mushtaq	471	100	1,364	41	5-46	3	33.26
I. D. K. Salisbury	371.1	60	1,224	33	4-116	0	37.09
T. J. Murtagh	115	13	475	11	4-130	0	43.18
R. Clarke	130.1	13	607	12	4-21	0	50.58
A. J. Tudor	144	24	532	10	3-56	0	53.20

Also bowled: J. G. E. Benning 8–1–39–1; A. D. Brown 9.4–3–22–1; M. A. Butcher 12–1–44–3; A. J. Hollioake 68.2–8–265–4; M. R. Ramprakash 8–4–9–0; F. A. Rose 28–8–101–3; N. C. Saker 20.1–1–103–1; P. J. Sampson 19.5–1–101–4; A. J. Stewart 2.3–0–23–0; G. P. Thorpe 11–1–73–1; I. J. Ward 16.3–0–76–0.

COUNTY RECORDS

Highest score for:	357*	R. Abel v Somerset at The Oval	1899
Highest score against:	366	N. H. Fairbrother (Lancashire) at The Oval	1990
Best bowling for:	10-43	T. Rushby v Somerset at Taunton	1921
Best bowling against:	10-28	W. P. Howell (Australians) at The Oval	1899
Highest total for:	811	v Somerset at The Oval	1899
Highest total against:	863	by Lancashire at The Oval	1990
Lowest total for:	14	v Essex at Chelmsford	1983
Lowest total against:	16	by MCC at Lord's	1872

SURREY DIRECTORY

ADDRESS

The Oval, Kennington, London SE11 5SS (020 7582 6660; fax 020 7735 7769; email enquiries@surreyccc.co.uk). **Website** www.surreycricket.com.

GROUNDS

The Oval: In South London on A23 just N of A202 Camberwell New Road and ½ mile S of Vauxhall Bridge. Nearest stations: Oval (Northern Line Underground) (adjacent) and Vauxhall (Victoria Line Underground and mainline) (⅓ mile).

Guildford: ½ mile N of town centre in Woodbridge Road at junction with Wharf Road. Nearest station: Guildford (¾ mile).

Whitgift School: 1 mile S of Croydon town centre at junction of A23 Brighton Road and Nottingham Road. Nearest station: South Croydon (½ mile).

OFFICIALS

Captain 2003 – A. J. Hollioake;
2004 – J. N. Batty
Cricket manager 2003 – K. T. Medlycott
2004 – S. J. Rixon
President B. G. K. Downing
Chairman D. Stewart
Chief executive P. C. J. Sheldon
Cricket administration manager S. B. Howes
Head groundsman 2003 – P. D. Brind
2004 – W. Gordon
Scorer K. R. Booth

PLAYERS

Players expected to reappear in 2004

	Former counties	*Country*	*Born*	*Birthplace*
***Azhar Mahmood**		P	28.2.1975	*Rawalpindi*
Batty Jonathan Neil		E	18.4.1974	*Chesterfield*
Benning James Graham Edward		E	4.5.1983	*Mill Hill*
***Bicknell** Martin Paul		E	14.1.1969	†*Guildford*
Brown Alistair Duncan		E	11.2.1970	*Beckenham*
***Butcher** Mark Alan		‡E	23.8.1972	†*Croydon*
***Clarke** Rikki		E	29.9.1981	*Orsett*
Dernbach Jade		E	3.3.1986	*Johannesburg, SA*
***Hollioake** Adam John		E	5.9.1971	*Melbourne, Aus.*
Murtagh Timothy James		E	2.8.1981	*Lambeth*
Newman Scott Alexander		E	3.11.1979	†*Epsom*
***Ormond** James	Leics	E	20.8.1977	*Walsgrave*
***Ramprakash** Mark Ravin	Middx	E	5.9.1969	*Bushey*
Saker Neil Clifford		E	20.9.1984	*Tooting*
***Salisbury** Ian David Kenneth	Sussex	E	21.1.1970	*Northampton*
Sampson Philip James		E	6.9.1980	*Manchester*
***Saqlain Mushtaq**		P	29.12.1976	*Lahore*
Scott Ben James Matthew		E	4.8.1981	*Isleworth*
Shahid Nadeem	Essex	E	23.4.1969	*Karachi, Pak.*
***Thorpe** Graham Paul		E	1.8.1969	†*Farnham*
Todd Matthew Julian		E	25.5.1983	†*Chertsey*
***Tudor** Alex Jeremy		E	23.10.1977	*Kensington*

Player due to join in 2004

Hodd Andrew John	Sussex	E	12.1.1984	*Chichester*

* *Test player.* † *Born in Surrey.* ‡ *12-month ECB contract.*

SURREY v LANCASHIRE

At The Oval, April 18, 19, 20, 21. Drawn. Surrey 7 pts, Lancashire 12 pts. Toss: Lancashire. County debuts: M. B. Loye, I. J. Sutcliffe.

Champions Surrey were outplayed for three-quarters of this match, but recovered on the final day to save the game. After they had been forced to follow on for the first time since September 1998, Ward picked up where he left off in 2002 with a six-hour hundred, and towed Clarke in his wake, helping him to a third century in his 13th first-class game. They combined just after lunch, with Surrey 169 behind and five second-innings wickets left, and put on 144. The architect of Surrey's original downfall was 20-year-old Anderson, who claimed the top five, including four internationals, bowling at a good tempo with an air of aggression. Lancashire's batting assault echoed 1990, when 1,650 runs were amassed in the equivalent fixture. Two winter signings, Sutcliffe and Loye, flourished; the former Northamptonshire batsman Loye was the fourth player, and the first since Ralph Whitehead in 1908, to score a century on first-class debut for Lancashire, and added 282 with Law. The home batsmen initially fell short, despite a genial track, but Ward and Clarke, plus the loss of nearly 80 overs to weather, saved them. To his intense disappointment, Butcher, the regular England No. 3, was omitted from the Surrey team, a situation unthinkable at any other county.

Close of play: First day, Lancashire 391-2 (Loye 104, Law 129); Second day, Lancashire 599; Third day, Surrey 61-2 (Ward 40, Thorpe 4).

Lancashire

A. J. Swann run out	57
I. J. Sutcliffe lbw b Saqlain Mushtaq	70
M. B. Loye lbw b Clarke	126
S. G. Law b Clarke	169
M. J. Chilton lbw b Salisbury	28
A. Flintoff c Batty b Salisbury	43
G. Chapple c and b Salisbury	32
C. P. Schofield c Batty b Tudor	1
*†W. K. Hegg b Murtagh	14
K. W. Hogg c Hollioake b Salisbury	16
J. M. Anderson not out	3
L-b 4, n-b 36	40
	599

1/108 (1) 2/169 (2) 3/451 (3) 4/460 (4) 5/523 (6) 6/534 (5) 7/565 (8) 8/565 (7) 9/593 (10) 10/599 (9)

Bonus points – Lancashire 5, Surrey 1 (130 overs: 523-4).

Bowling: Tudor 37–7–137–1; Murtagh 21.4–2–100–1; Hollioake 8–0–27–0; Clarke 21–0–137–2; Saqlain Mushtaq 22–5–78–1; Salisbury 42–10–116–4.

Surrey

I. J. Ward c Hegg b Anderson	49	– c Sutcliffe b Anderson	158
†J. N. Batty b Anderson	13	– c Swann b Chapple	4
M. R. Ramprakash c Hegg b Anderson	50	– c Hegg b Flintoff	13
G. P. Thorpe c Loye b Anderson	15	– c Anderson b Flintoff	35
A. D. Brown lbw b Anderson	2	– run out	0
R. Clarke c Chilton b Schofield	38	– (7) not out	127
*A. J. Hollioake c Flintoff b Chapple	42	– (6) c Chilton b Hogg	10
A. J. Tudor c Chilton b Schofield	9	– not out	11
I. D. K. Salisbury c Hegg b Flintoff	18		
Saqlain Mushtaq c Anderson b Schofield	23		
T. J. Murtagh not out	0		
B 4, l-b 5, n-b 12	21	B 11, l-b 6, w 2, n-b 2	21
	280	(6 wkts)	379

1/35 (2) 2/106 (1) 3/123 (3) 4/129 (5) 5/140 (4) 6/204 (7) 7/227 (8) 8/230 (6) 9/268 (9) 10/280 (10)

1/8 (2) 2/48 (3) 3/124 (4) 4/131 (5) 5/150 (6) 6/294 (1)

Bonus points – Surrey 2, Lancashire 3.

Bowling: *First Innings*—Anderson 13–2–61–5; Chapple 15–2–52–1; Flintoff 13–2–42–1; Hogg 9–1–39–0; Schofield 17.4–4–77–3. *Second Innings*—Anderson 22–7–72–1; Chapple 20–1–100–1; Flintoff 19–5–47–2; Schofield 25–8–86–0; Hogg 12–3–46–1; Swann 2–0–11–0.

Umpires: V. A. Holder and N. A. Mallender.

SURREY v LOUGHBOROUGH UCCE

At The Oval, April 23, 24, 25. Drawn. Toss: Loughborough UCCE. First-class debut: P. D. Lewis.

Four Surrey batsmen scored centuries in one innings for the first time since 1947, a feat owing more to them fielding an unusually strong team for a student fixture than any particular weakness in the attack. Ramprakash got there first and, as with his last two first-class hundreds, made it a double. He hit 30 fours and three sixes in 258 balls and 376 minutes. Hollioake smacked five sixes, one bouncing over the roof of the Barrington Centre, in an 87-ball hundred before retiring; Batty was the third centurion, and Hollioake resumed to help No. 10 Bicknell complete the second hundred of his career. The sum of the parts made Surrey's seventh-highest total, and the biggest against non-county opposition. Earlier, Ormond had returned his best figures for Surrey. But the students made a better fist of it second time around. When rain closed in at tea on the final day, the promising Vikram Atri was 18 short of a hundred.

Close of play: First day, Surrey 176-4 (Ramprakash 92, Hollioake 17); Second day, Loughborough UCCE 26-0 (White 10, Adams 8).

Loughborough UCCE

R. A. White c Brown b Ormond	76	– c Brown b Ormond	14
*J. H. K. Adams c Shahid b Ormond	4	– b Clarke	23
J. D. Francis c Batty b Ormond	0	– c Bicknell b Hollioake	57
V. Atri c Batty b Clarke	26	– not out	82
C. D. Nash c Hollioake b Bicknell	54	– lbw b Shahid	16
Z. K. Sharif lbw b Ormond	5	– not out	22
R. E. King c Batty b Ormond	0		
†L. J. Goddard c Batty b Ormond	0		
P. D. Lewis not out	10		
J. E. Anyon c and b Clarke	0		
R. A. G. Cummins c Batty b Azhar Mahmood	1		
L-b 6, n-b 24	30	B 6, l-b 6, w 3, n-b 6	21
1/8 (2) 2/8 (3) 3/94 (4) 4/151 (1) 5/181 (6) 6/181 (7) 7/181 (8) 8/193 (5) 9/201 (10) 10/206 (11)	206	1/31 (1) 2/66 (2) 3/156 (3) 4/193 (5)	(4 wkts) 235

Bowling: *First Innings*—Bicknell 15–3–58–1; Ormond 14–8–34–6; Azhar Mahmood 9.3–1–58–1; Clarke 9–2–42–2; Hollioake 4–2–6–0; Butcher 2–0–2–0. *Second Innings*—Bicknell 10–2–30–0; Ormond 12–1–31–1; Azhar Mahmood 12–3–45–0; Clarke 7–2–24–1; Ramprakash 10–2–31–0; Hollioake 8–1–29–1; Shahid 9–2–33–1.

Surrey

M. A. Butcher lbw b Cummins	45
N. Shahid c White b Anyon	4
M. R. Ramprakash c Anyon b King	205
G. P. Thorpe b Cummins	15
A. D. Brown lbw b Sharif	3
*A. J. Hollioake not out	121
R. Clarke c Nash b Adams	0
Azhar Mahmood lbw b Adams	4
†J. N. Batty lbw b Lewis	123
M. P. Bicknell not out	103
J. Ormond b Sharif	28
B 6, l-b 1, w 5	12
1/13 (2) 2/86 (1) 3/114 (4) 4/135 (5) 5/307 (7) 6/315 (8) 7/480 (3) 8/557 (9) 9/647 (11)	(9 wkts dec.) 663

Hollioake, when 112, retired hurt at 307-4 and resumed at 647.

Bowling: Anyon 24–3–139–1; King 21–3–108–1; Lewis 16–2–77–1; Cummins 16–2–108–2; Sharif 19–3–101–2; Nash 18.4–1–99–0; Adams 8–1–24–2.

Umpires: R. J. Bailey and J. H. Hampshire.

SURREY v WARWICKSHIRE

At The Oval, April 30, May 1, 2, 3. Drawn. Surrey 11 pts, Warwickshire 12 pts. Toss: Warwickshire.

With their embarrassment of riches, Surrey made five changes from their last Championship game and fielded an all-international side. Thorpe and Clarke missed out, Stewart made his first appearance, and Butcher, who had fussed about being left out, returned – promptly dropping a simple chance from Frost, who scored 52 more on a superb pitch. Wagh completed an excellent century, reviving chatter about his Test prospects, during a last-wicket stand of 70 with Richardson. Butcher and Stewart retaliated with fifties, but were eclipsed by Hollioake's power play. He should have been stumped on 49, when he stepped boldly down the pitch to Giles, missed the ball, then watched Frost take it in Super Slo-Mo, giving him all the time he needed to regain his ground. Hollioake went on to a dazzling 122 in 137 balls. Rain, permitting a pitiful 29 overs on the third day, dictated a draw, although Tudor and Saqlain Mushtaq sent a tremor through Warwickshire – six down, 140 ahead, 41 overs to go – until Knight dug in for an unbeaten hundred.

Close of play: First day, Warwickshire 342-8 (Wagh 91, Smith 20); Second day, Surrey 237-4 (Stewart 29, Hollioake 87); Third day, Surrey 349-7 (Tudor 25, Bicknell 1).

Warwickshire

N. V. Knight c Ward b Bicknell	58	– not out	103
†T. Frost c Hollioake b Bicknell	78	– b Tudor	5
M. A. Wagh b Ormond	136	– c Azhar Mahmood b Tudor	19
I. R. Bell c sub b Tudor	4	– b Saqlain Mushtaq	13
J. O. Troughton hit wkt b Tudor	17	– b Tudor	0
D. P. Ostler b Tudor	0	– c Hollioake b Saqlain Mushtaq	25
D. R. Brown c Stewart b Saqlain Mushtaq	8	– c Hollioake b Saqlain Mushtaq	0
*A. F. Giles c Azhar Mahmood b Ormond	25	– c Stewart b Brown	33
M. A. Sheikh c Stewart b Ormond	14	– not out	4
N. M. K. Smith c Stewart b Azhar Mahmood	20		
A. Richardson not out	20		
L-b 10, w 1, n-b 22	33	B 4, l-b 3, w 2, n-b 10	19
1/153 (2) 2/158 (1) 3/180 (4) 4/215 (5) 5/215 (6) 6/237 (7) 7/288 (8) 8/310 (9) 9/343 (10) 10/413 (3)	413	1/28 (2) 2/48 (3) 3/71 (4) 4/72 (5) 5/117 (6) 6/117 (7) 7/169 (8) (7 wkts dec.)	221

Bonus points – Warwickshire 5, Surrey 3.

Bowling: *First Innings*—Bicknell 20–9–62–2; Ormond 25.2–4–83–3; Azhar Mahmood 15–3–72–1; Tudor 23–3–92–3; Saqlain Mushtaq 26–4–86–1; Hollioake 3–1–8–0. *Second Innings*—Ormond 11–3–41–0; Tudor 14–2–56–3; Saqlain Mushtaq 19–9–29–3; Azhar Mahmood 9–1–34–0; Ramprakash 8–4–9–0; Brown 9–3–11–1; Ward 4–0–11–0; Stewart 2.3–0–23–0.

Surrey

M. A. Butcher b Richardson	64
I. J. Ward c Frost b Brown	2
M. R. Ramprakash b Sheikh	45
†A. J. Stewart c Knight b Brown	50
A. D. Brown c Sheikh b Richardson	2
*A. J. Hollioake c Frost b Brown	122
Azhar Mahmood c Wagh b Sheikh	25
A. J. Tudor c Knight b Brown	55
M. P. Bicknell retired hurt	1
Saqlain Mushtaq b Brown	5
J. Ormond not out	5
L-b 8, n-b 6	14
1/12 (2) 2/113 (3) 3/115 (1) 4/121 (5) 5/292 (4) 6/309 (6) 7/347 (7) 8/375 (10) 9/390 (8)	390

Bonus points – Surrey 4, Warwickshire 3.

Bicknell retired hurt at 349.

Bowling: Richardson 24–4–89–2; Brown 27.3–4–96–5; Sheikh 23–6–91–2; Giles 16–2–53–0; Smith 13–1–53–0.

Umpires: J. H. Evans and P. Willey.

At Nottingham, May 9, 10, 11. SURREY beat NOTTINGHAMSHIRE by an innings and six runs.

SURREY v LEICESTERSHIRE

At The Oval, May 14, 15, 16, 17. Drawn. Surrey 12 pts, Leicestershire 7 pts. Toss: Leicestershire. Championship debut: V. Sehwag.

The loss of all but half a day's play out of the last two cruelly denied Surrey after they had dominated proceedings completely. The ageing warhorse DeFreitas rescued Leicestershire from 70 for seven in the first innings, and Sehwag marked his Championship debut with a muscular 81 in the second, but there was precious little else on offer from the visitors. Surrey declared after equalling their second-highest total against Leicestershire. Stewart made it three fifties in a row, and Brown hammered his way back into form with a belligerent half-century; there was a fabulous hundred from Ramprakash and an unlikely one from Salisbury – only the second of his career – brought up with a six off Snape. On the second evening, Bicknell had figures of 4–4–0–2, but his Pakistani team-mates, Azhar Mahmood and Saqlain Mushtaq, also worked their magic: Azhar picked up five wickets on the first day, Saqlain five on the last. For the third Championship game running, Surrey could find no place for Thorpe, still widely regarded as just about the best batsman in England.

Close of play: First day, Surrey 182-2 (Ramprakash 59, Stewart 58); Second day, Leicestershire 14-2 (Sehwag 14, Maddy 0); Third day, Leicestershire 32-2 (Sehwag 32, Maddy 0).

Leicestershire

First innings		Second innings	
T. R. Ward c Stewart b Azhar Mahmood	14	– c Butcher b Bicknell	0
V. Sehwag c Brown b Azhar Mahmood	2	– lbw b Saqlain Mushtaq	81
D. L. Maddy c Stewart b Bicknell	1	– (4) b Saqlain Mushtaq	40
B. J. Hodge lbw b Azhar Mahmood	14	– (5) c Ward b Saqlain Mushtaq	47
D. I. Stevens c Brown b Azhar Mahmood	0	– (6) lbw b Salisbury	0
†P. A. Nixon c Brown b Butcher	22	– (7) c Hollioake b Saqlain Mushtaq	1
J. N. Snape c Ward b Butcher	10	– (8) not out	5
*P. A. J. DeFreitas b Saqlain Mushtaq	65	– (9) c Hollioake b Saqlain Mushtaq	0
D. D. Masters c Clarke b Azhar Mahmood	33	– (3) c Azhar Mahmood b Bicknell	0
C. E. Dagnall not out	23		
D. E. Malcolm c Butcher b Saqlain Mushtaq	3		
B 2, l-b 2, w 5, n-b 4	13	L-b 1, n-b 10	11
1/14 (2) 2/19 (1) 3/25 (3) 4/26 (5) 5/47 (4) 6/68 (6) 7/70 (7) 8/155 (9) 9/167 (8) 10/200 (11)	200	1/0 (1) 2/6 (3) 3/107 (2) 4/168 (4) 5/171 (6) 6/172 (7) 7/183 (5) 8/185 (9)	(8 wkts) 185

Bonus points – Leicestershire 1, Surrey 3.

Bowling: *First Innings*—Bicknell 17–2–64–1; Azhar Mahmood 19–5–78–5; Butcher 6–0–20–2; Clarke 4–2–14–0; Saqlain Mushtaq 5.3–0–20–2. *Second Innings*—Bicknell 12–5–40–2; Azhar Mahmood 14–3–65–0; Saqlain Mushtaq 15.2–3–46–5; Salisbury 13–3–33–1.

Surrey

M. A. Butcher c Stevens b Malcolm	39
I. J. Ward b DeFreitas	19
M. R. Ramprakash c Stevens b Dagnall	152
†A. J. Stewart c Snape b DeFreitas	71
A. D. Brown c Maddy b Snape	73
*A. J. Hollioake c Nixon b DeFreitas	41
R. Clarke c Nixon b DeFreitas	0
Azhar Mahmood c Maddy b Snape	27
I. D. K. Salisbury not out	101
Saqlain Mushtaq not out	20
B 6, l-b 5, n-b 6	17
1/39 (2) 2/80 (1) 3/204 (4) 4/345 (5) 5/408 (3) 6/408 (6) 7/423 (7) 8/461 (8)	(8 wkts dec.) 560

M. P. Bicknell did not bat.

Bonus points – Surrey 5, Leicestershire 2 (130 overs: 500-8).

Bowling: DeFreitas 36–9–101–4; Dagnall 28–8–95–1; Masters 20–4–93–0; Malcolm 16–4–58–1; Maddy 9–2–23–0; Sehwag 4–1–26–0; Stevens 5–3–11–0; Hodge 7–0–50–0; Snape 20.2–2–92–2.

Umpires: B. Dudleston and N. A. Mallender.

At Chelmsford, May 21, 22, 23, 24. SURREY beat ESSEX by 258 runs.

SURREY v SUSSEX

At The Oval, May 30, 31, June 1, 2. Surrey won by 113 runs. Surrey 22 pts, Sussex 6 pts. Toss: Surrey.

Hollioake waived the follow-on, lost half a day to weather, and still completed a victory that increased Surrey's first division lead to 28 points. It was touch and go: 33 balls remained when, with nine fielders around the bat and Ormond steaming in with the new ball, Yardy stepped back and edged to second slip. In his first Championship match since July 2002, Yardy resisted more than five hours while Saqlain Mushtaq worked through his team-mates. Ormond had done the damage first time round, after Bicknell pulled a hamstring – a factor in Hollioake's choosing to bat again. Ward and Batty wasted little time extending a lead of 173, and Sussex were eventually set 407. It looked a mountain, but Surrey had scored almost that on the opening day, when Hollioake won only his second toss in 13 games. Thorpe batted 325 minutes for a century which demonstrated that he had refocused on cricket after a long period of family troubles, and there were sizzling contributions from Brown and Hollioake himself.

Close of play: First day, Surrey 401-8 (Salisbury 10, Saqlain Mushtaq 2); Second day, Surrey 22-0 (Ward 16, Batty 6); Third day, Sussex 12-0 (Goodwin 10, Montgomerie 0).

Surrey

First innings		Second innings	
I. J. Ward c Ambrose b Kirtley	9	c Goodwin b Innes	135
†J. N. Batty c Adams b Taylor	12	b Mushtaq Ahmed	56
M. R. Ramprakash c Yardy b Mushtaq Ahmed	37	c Prior b Innes	23
G. P. Thorpe c Adams b Mushtaq Ahmed	156	not out	18
A. D. Brown c Goodwin b Kirtley	74	not out	1
*A. J. Hollioake lbw b Martin-Jenkins	77		
Azhar Mahmood c Adams b Kirtley	0		
M. P. Bicknell b Martin-Jenkins	11		
I. D. K. Salisbury c Ambrose b Mushtaq Ahmed	45		
Saqlain Mushtaq c Montgomerie b Martin-Jenkins	32		
J. Ormond not out	1		
B 4, l-b 17, w 1, n-b 4	26		
1/22 (1) 2/22 (2) 3/132 (3) 4/263 (5) 5/359 (4) 6/360 (7) 7/379 (8) 8/394 (6) 9/469 (10) 10/480 (9)	480	1/137 (2) 2/192 (3) 3/219 (1) (3 wkts dec.)	233

Bonus points – Surrey 5, Sussex 3.

Bowling: *First Innings*—Kirtley 33–5–122–3; Taylor 7.2–2–15–1; Martin-Jenkins 23.4–8–86–3; Innes 12–4–59–0; Mushtaq Ahmed 36.5–1–159–3; Yardy 7–1–18–0. *Second Innings*—Kirtley 14–3–49–0; Martin-Jenkins 19–3–66–0; Mushtaq Ahmed 11–1–47–1; Innes 14–1–64–2; Yardy 2–0–7–0.

"Worcestershire's tactics prompted Northamptonshire coach Kepler Wessels to complain that the spirit of cricket had been lost. But some thought Northamptonshire were in no position to invoke the spirit of cricket."

Northamptonshire in 2003, page 655.

Sussex

R. R. Montgomerie c Ward b Ormond	5	– (2) c sub b Saqlain Mushtaq	31
M. W. Goodwin b Saqlain Mushtaq	60	– (1) b Azhar Mahmood	26
M. H. Yardy c Thorpe b Ormond	0	– c Azhar Mahmood b Ormond	69
*C. J. Adams c Batty b Azhar Mahmood	5	– b Saqlain Mushtaq	0
T. R. Ambrose c Ramprakash b Ormond	75	– b Saqlain Mushtaq	1
R. S. C. Martin-Jenkins lbw b Azhar Mahmood	61	– b Azhar Mahmood	88
†M. J. Prior b Saqlain Mushtaq	6	– c Ramprakash b Azhar Mahmood	14
K. J. Innes b Salisbury	2	– c Azhar Mahmood b Saqlain Mushtaq	1
Mushtaq Ahmed lbw b Ormond	41	– (10) lbw b Saqlain Mushtaq	36
R. J. Kirtley run out	21	– (9) c sub b Salisbury	7
B. V. Taylor not out	4	– not out	0
L-b 9, w 2, n-b 16	27	B 9, l-b 3, w 2, n-b 6	20
1/5 (1) 2/13 (3) 3/24 (4) 4/98 (2) 5/189 (6) 6/217 (7) 7/220 (8) 8/279 (5) 9/282 (9) 10/307 (10)	307	1/45 (1) 2/83 (2) 3/83 (4) 4/85 (5) 5/198 (6) 6/218 (7) 7/221 (8) 8/242 (9) 9/293 (10) 10/293 (3)	293

Bonus points – Sussex 3, Surrey 3.

Bowling: *First Innings*—Bicknell 3–1–9–0; Ormond 15.1–2–81–4; Azhar Mahmood 16–1–57–2; Salisbury 14–1–67–1; Saqlain Mushtaq 21–4–68–2; Hollioake 4–0–16–0. *Second Innings*—Ormond 19.4–3–65–1; Azhar Mahmood 21–4–76–3; Salisbury 21–5–67–1; Saqlain Mushtaq 34–15–73–5.

Umpires: A. A. Jones and R. Palmer.

At Lord's, June 27, 28, 29, 30. SURREY drew with MIDDLESEX.

SURREY v KENT

At The Oval, July 2, 3, 4, 5. Surrey won by 186 runs. Surrey 20 pts, Kent 7 pts. Toss: Surrey. County debut: R. S. Ferley.

The game hinged on Fulton's declaration, 49 runs behind. Weather had cost nearly 80 overs and, still searching for Kent's first Championship win, he took a positive approach. Butcher, standing in for Hollioake, whose father was ill, responded in kind. He smashed a brutal 74-ball 90 on the third evening, then set Kent 301 in 90 overs. Since June 1995, only one county visiting The Oval had managed 200 in the fourth innings to win, and Kent collapsed. Typically, Saqlain Mushtaq had the last word, passing 700 wickets in all first-class cricket. Kent were without four front-line bowlers, including Sheriyar, who had cut his hand washing up. Butcher punished the remaining attack for his 25th hundred, though Trott and Ferley, a left-arm spinner from Durham University, held their nerve to take four wickets each. In reply, Smith set up Fulton's gamble by following up a pair at Chelmsford with what was to be the first of five hundreds in six innings.

Close of play: First day, Surrey 245-3 (Butcher 117, Brown 0); Second day, Kent 101-2 (Smith 33, Symonds 33); Third day, Surrey 249-3 (Brown 63, Stewart 24).

Surrey

I. J. Ward c Fulton b Trott	33		
*M. A. Butcher c Jones b Trott	144	– (1) c Smith b Carberry	90
M. R. Ramprakash c Ealham b Mohammad Sami	6	– (2) c Symonds b Trott	22
G. P. Thorpe c Jones b Ferley	68	– (3) c Jones b Ferley	46
A. D. Brown c Symonds b Ferley	27	– (4) not out	64
†A. J. Stewart c and b Ealham	1	– (5) not out	25
A. J. Tudor c Ealham b Trott	18		
M. P. Bicknell c Jones b Ferley	22		
I. D. K. Salisbury not out	34		
Saqlain Mushtaq b Trott	4		
J. Ormond c Tredwell b Ferley	15		
B 5, l-b 10, w 2, n-b 12	29	B 2, l-b 2	4
1/73 (1) 2/105 (3) 3/243 (4) 4/293 (2) 5/305 (5) 6/305 (6) 7/336 (8) 8/355 (7) 9/359 (10) 10/401 (11)	401	1/72 (2) 2/130 (1) 3/208 (3)	(3 wkts dec.) 251

Bonus points – Surrey 5, Kent 3.

Bowling: *First Innings*—Mohammad Sami 22–3–83–1; Trott 18–5–73–4; Ealham 21–3–67–1; Symonds 10–0–55–0; Tredwell 8–1–32–0; Ferley 16.2–0–76–4. *Second Innings*—Mohammad Sami 3–0–10–0; Trott 7–0–37–1; Tredwell 6–2–35–0; Ferley 11.2–2–53–1; Carberry 8–0–45–1; Symonds 5–0–28–0; Walker 4–0–25–0; Smith 3–1–14–0.

Kent

*D. P. Fulton lbw b Bicknell	14	– b Ormond	11
M. A. Carberry c Stewart b Saqlain Mushtaq	16	– c Stewart b Saqlain Mushtaq	24
E. T. Smith c Brown b Salisbury	135	– c Butcher b Ormond	0
A. Symonds c Butcher b Bicknell	53	– c Salisbury b Tudor	30
M. J. Walker not out	82	– c Stewart b Saqlain Mushtaq	7
M. A. Ealham c Thorpe b Ormond	5	– c Butcher b Saqlain Mushtaq	5
†G. O. Jones not out	38	– c Saqlain Mushtaq b Salisbury	8
J. C. Tredwell (did not bat)		– lbw b Salisbury	17
R. S. Ferley (did not bat)		– b Saqlain Mushtaq	2
Mohammad Sami (did not bat)		– lbw b Salisbury	0
B. J. Trott (did not bat)		– not out	9
B 1, l-b 5, w 1, n-b 2	9	L-b 1	1
1/25 (2) 2/40 (1) 3/151 (4) 4/275 (3) 5/286 (6)	(5 wkts dec.) 352	1/21 (1) 2/21 (3) 3/61 (2) 4/67 (4) 5/73 (5) 6/78 (6) 7/92 (7) 8/94 (9) 9/95 (10) 10/114 (8)	114

Bonus points – Kent 4, Surrey 1.

Bowling: *First Innings*—Bicknell 18–4–65–2; Ormond 16–4–60–1; Saqlain Mushtaq 23–5–63–1; Salisbury 29–5–111–1; Tudor 8–1–47–0; Butcher 1–1–0–0. *Second Innings*—Bicknell 11–5–26–0; Ormond 9–3–23–2; Tudor 10–2–26–1; Saqlain Mushtaq 14–5–27–4; Salisbury 5.4–1–11–3.

Umpires: D. J. Constant and I. J. Gould.

At Birmingham, July 9, 10, 11, 12. SURREY beat WARWICKSHIRE by 135 runs.

At The Oval, July 15, 16, 17. SURREY drew with INDIA A (see India A tour section).

SURREY v MIDDLESEX

At Guildford, July 23, 24, 25, 26. Drawn. Surrey 12 pts, Middlesex 11 pts. Toss: Middlesex.

Ramprakash was disciplined over a last-day incident. After a bouncer from occasional seamer Joyce hit his helmet, prompting mirth among his old Middlesex team-mates, he asked the umpires, less than politely, why he had to bat in the drizzle. Ramprakash earned a three-point penalty for a level two offence (obscene or insulting language or gestures) under the ECB code of conduct. Ormond had happier memories of this rain-ruined match. He made his best score for Surrey, and a last-wicket stand of 89 with Saqlain Mushtaq ensured a fifth batting point, undreamed of at 131 for five. Then, with Middlesex 163 for one, he dismissed four left-handers in one amazing over. His first ball had Strauss lbw, Hutton offered a leg-side catch off the fourth, Joyce was lbw to the fifth, and Weekes bowled when the sixth dipped in late. It was the third hat-trick at Woodbridge Road, after Jim Laker in 1953 and Pat Pocock in 1971, and apparently the first composed purely of left-handers in any first-class match in Britain. When Bicknell dismissed the right-handed Shah, Middlesex had lost five for two in nine balls. But Abdul Razzaq and Nash added 155, and the third day was washed out. The captains could not agree a target so Guildford saw its first draw since 1992.

Close of play: First day, Surrey 375-9 (Saqlain Mushtaq 40, Ormond 32); Second day, Middlesex 346-8 (Nash 69, Cook 1); Third day, No play.

Surrey

*I. J. Ward b Noffke	10	– not out	33
†J. N. Batty b Keegan	2	– retired hurt	25
M. R. Ramprakash c Nash b Cook	33	– not out	28
G. P. Thorpe c Weekes b Cook	51		
A. D. Brown c Strauss b Cook	8		
R. Clarke b Noffke	85		
A. J. Tudor c Strauss b Keegan	27		
M. P. Bicknell b Keegan	11		
I. D. K. Salisbury c Nash b Noffke	40		
Saqlain Mushtaq not out	61		
J. Ormond c Weekes b Keegan	47		
B 7, l-b 15, n-b 14	36	N-b 8	8
1/16 (2) 2/20 (1) 3/113 (3) 4/126 (4) 5/131 (5) 6/210 (7) 7/232 (8) 8/283 (6) 9/322 (9) 10/411 (11)	411		(no wkt) 94

Bonus points – Surrey 5, Middlesex 3.

In the second innings Batty retired hurt at 45.

Bowling: *First Innings*—Noffke 24–3–91–3; Keegan 28.5–3–114–4; Abdul Razzaq 5–1–17–0; Cook 22–4–77–3; Hutton 3–0–18–0; Weekes 19–3–72–0. *Second Innings*—Noffke 6–1–21–0; Keegan 8–1–29–0; Cook 6–1–21–0; Hutton 5–0–20–0; Joyce 1–0–3–0.

Middlesex

*A. J. Strauss lbw b Ormond	87
S. G. Koenig c Batty b Tudor	42
O. A. Shah c Batty b Bicknell	22
B. L. Hutton c Batty b Ormond	2
E. C. Joyce lbw b Ormond	0
P. N. Weekes b Ormond	0
Abdul Razzaq c Ward b Bicknell	78
†D. C. Nash not out	96
A. A. Noffke c and b Saqlain Mushtaq	18
S. J. Cook lbw b Bicknell	4
C. B. Keegan b Bicknell	4
B 8, l-b 10, n-b 14	32
1/101 (2) 2/163 (1) 3/165 (4) 4/165 (5) 5/165 (6) 6/165 (3) 7/320 (7) 8/343 (9) 9/377 (10) 10/385 (11)	385

Bonus points – Middlesex 4, Surrey 3.

Bowling: Bicknell 29.3–3–102–4; Ormond 26–5–106–4; Tudor 11–4–28–1; Clarke 17–2–74–0; Saqlain Mushtaq 16–3–33–1; Salisbury 5–0–24–0.

Umpires: M. R. Benson and P. J. Hartley.

At Hove, July 30, 31, August 1, 2. SURREY drew with SUSSEX.

SURREY v NOTTINGHAMSHIRE

At Whitgift School, August 13, 14, 15. Surrey won by an innings and 211 runs. Surrey 22 pts, Nottinghamshire 4 pts. Toss: Surrey.

Leaders Surrey rolled over bottom-placed Nottinghamshire for the eighth time in nine Championship meetings, and the second time by an innings in 2003. Despite a painful blow to his knee on 21, Ramprakash scored a classy double-hundred, his ninth. An eventual career-best 279, lasting 517 minutes and 400 balls with four sixes and 40 fours, was a record between these sides. Surrey's previous best was 235 not out by Darren Bicknell, now with Nottinghamshire. Ramprakash added 241 with Thorpe, and shared century stands with Salisbury and Saqlain Mushtaq, as Surrey passed their score against Loughborough early in the season and again posted their seventh-highest first-class total. Martin Bicknell dismissed his brother lbw for the second successive innings, and his 40th five-wicket haul forced Nottinghamshire to follow on 453 behind on the third morning. Within an hour, they were 45 for six; only Read emerged with much credit. This was the maiden first-class fixture at Whitgift School, near the centre of Croydon, and represented Surrey's first home Championship game away from The Oval and Guildford since they were sent to Lord's when The Oval was requisitioned in August 1914. A Whitgift pupil, Sam Woodward, already on Surrey's books, fielded as a substitute after collecting his A-level results (an A and two Bs), and caught Darren Bicknell. The facilities were as uneven as the cricket: Surrey commandeered the pleasant school pavilion while the Nottinghamshire dressing-room comprised a set of Portakabins in which the players' showers, before the third day, were as visible to the spectators as the actual game.

Close of play: First day, Surrey 488-8 (Ramprakash 191, Salisbury 13); Second day, Nottinghamshire 224-8 (Smith 0).

HIGHEST SURREY TOTALS

811	v Somerset at The Oval	1899
742	v Hampshire at The Oval	1909
707-9 dec.	v Lancashire at The Oval	1990
706-4 dec.	v Nottinghamshire at Nottingham	1947
701-9 dec.	v Glamorgan at Cardiff	2001
698	v Sussex at The Oval	1888
693	**v Nottinghamshire at Whitgift School**	**2003**
663-9 dec.	**v Loughborough UCCE at The Oval**	**2003**
652-9 dec.	v Durham at The Oval	1995
650	v Hampshire at The Oval	1883
650	v Oxford University at The Oval	1888

Surrey

I. J. Ward b Shreck	17
†J. N. Batty c Warren b Smith	17
M. R. Ramprakash not out	279
G. P. Thorpe c Read b Cairns	99
R. Clarke st Read b MacGill	36
A. D. Brown c Read b Franks	32
*A. J. Hollioake c Read b Franks	0
Azhar Mahmood c Pietersen b Smith	25
M. P. Bicknell c and b Cairns	9
I. D. K. Salisbury c Smith b Franks	65
Saqlain Mushtaq c Read b Smith	50
B 16, l-b 13, w 5, n-b 30	64
1/33 (2) 2/41 (1) 3/282 (4) 4/345 (5) 5/392 (6) 6/392 (7) 7/442 (8) 8/457 (9) 9/586 (10) 10/693 (11)	693

Bonus points – Surrey 5, Nottinghamshire 3 (130 overs: 632-9).

Bowling: Smith 27.3–7–110–3; Shreck 25–4–112–1; Franks 22–2–91–3; Cairns 27–3–133–2; MacGill 35–3–196–1; Pietersen 4–0–22–0.

Nottinghamshire

D. J. Bicknell lbw b Bicknell	14	– c sub b Azhar Mahmood	3
G. E. Welton c Thorpe b Bicknell	0	– c Clarke b Azhar Mahmood	0
U. Afzaal c Azhar Mahmood b Bicknell	4	– lbw b Bicknell	5
R. J. Warren lbw b Salisbury	76	– c Batty b Azhar Mahmood	9
K. P. Pietersen c Clarke b Saqlain Mushtaq	79	– c Clarke b Bicknell	16
*C. L. Cairns b Bicknell	26	– c Hollioake b Azhar Mahmood	9
†C. M. W. Read c Batty b Bicknell	4	– c Azhar Mahmood b Salisbury	93
P. J. Franks c Thorpe b Saqlain Mushtaq	8	– b Hollioake	27
G. J. Smith c Clarke b Saqlain Mushtaq	6	– c Brown b Saqlain Mushtaq	42
S. C. G. MacGill st Batty b Salisbury	9	– c Brown b Saqlain Mushtaq	7
C. E. Shreck not out	0	– not out	2
B 5, l-b 5, n-b 4	14	B 16, l-b 8, w 1, n-b 4	29
1/1 (2) 2/11 (3) 3/20 (1) 4/133 (5) 5/186 (6) 6/196 (7) 7/224 (4) 8/224 (8) 9/237 (9) 10/240 (10)	240	1/0 (2) 2/6 (3) 3/18 (1) 4/19 (4) 5/35 (6) 6/45 (5) 7/129 (8) 8/233 (7) 9/239 (9) 10/242 (10)	242

Bonus points – Nottinghamshire 1, Surrey 3.

Bowling: *First Innings*—Bicknell 15–3–42–5; Azhar Mahmood 11–3–32–0; Saqlain Mushtaq 21–4–80–3; Clarke 7–0–32–0; Salisbury 18–6–44–2. *Second Innings*—Bicknell 8–2–19–2; Azhar Mahmood 9–1–45–4; Clarke 4–0–22–0; Saqlain Mushtaq 15–1–49–2; Hollioake 8–0–41–1; Salisbury 11–2–42–1.

Umpires: V. A. Holder and N. J. Llong.

At Leicester, August 21, 22, 23, 24. SURREY drew with LEICESTERSHIRE.

At Manchester, August 26, 27, 28, 29. SURREY lost to LANCASHIRE by eight wickets.

At Canterbury, September 4, 5, 6. SURREY lost to KENT by an innings and 155 runs.

SURREY v ESSEX

At The Oval, September 17, 18, 19. Essex won by eight wickets. Essex 22 pts, Surrey 6 pts. Toss: Surrey. Championship debuts: J. G. E. Benning, N. C. Saker, B. J. M. Scott.

Surrey's third successive Championship defeat made a dismal finish to their title defence. Earlier in the season, they had Test stars queuing for a game; now, departures plus a seven-man injury list left only four regulars. All Surrey were playing for was second-place prize money, but Essex, already relegated, looked far more positive. Flower amassed an unbeaten 201, in 297 balls and 419 minutes, with 20 fours, and fluent strokeplay by the exciting Pettini and Cook, who scored his third half-century in three first-class matches, showed the young Surrey quicks that nothing comes easily. Batty was Surrey's top-scorer; he had passed the gloves to 22-year-old Ben Scott, who responded with a fifty and six catches but ended the season wondering whether to return to Middlesex. On the third day, Surrey were swept aside by the stunning pace bowling of Pakistan's Mohammad Akram, who claimed a career-best eight for 49, the final indignity for the dethroned champions.

Close of play: First day, Essex 112-1 (Cook 63, Flower 47); Second day, Essex 464.

Surrey

S. A. Newman c Foster b Napier	9	– c Cook b Mohammad Akram	0
J. N. Batty b Napier	87	– c Foster b Mohammad Akram	47
N. Shahid c Pettini b Middlebrook	67	– c Cook b Mohammad Akram	0
R. Clarke b Middlebrook	4	– b Mohammad Akram	18
A. D. Brown c Bopara b Middlebrook	17	– b Mohammad Akram	0
J. G. E. Benning hit wkt b Mohammad Akram	18	– c Foster b Mohammad Akram	47
†B. J. M. Scott not out	58	– c Foster b Mohammad Akram	5
*I. D. K. Salisbury c Flower b Bopara	14	– lbw b Napier	29
T. J. Murtagh c Napier b Mohammad Akram	21	– b Mohammad Akram	0
P. J. Sampson lbw b Middlebrook	3	– not out	32
N. C. Saker b Napier	1	– b Napier	0
L-b 7, w 4, n-b 8	19	L-b 7, w 1, n-b 8	16
1/17 (1) 2/120 (3) 3/130 (4) 4/164 (5) 5/195 (6) 6/222 (2) 7/241 (8) 8/300 (9) 9/313 (10) 10/318 (11)	318	1/0 (1) 2/0 (3) 3/24 (4) 4/26 (5) 5/122 (2) 6/125 (6) 7/134 (7) 8/138 (9) 9/194 (8) 10/194 (11)	194

Bonus points – Surrey 3, Essex 3.

Bowling: *First Innings*—Mohammad Akram 21–5–93–2; Napier 18.3–4–58–3; Clarke 7–2–32–0; Middlebrook 28–3–93–4; Stephenson 2–0–12–0; Bopara 5–0–23–1. *Second Innings*—Mohammad Akram 21–9–49–8; Napier 12.3–1–54–2; Clarke 7–1–19–0; Stephenson 12–2–39–0; Middlebrook 5–0–26–0.

Essex

W. I. Jefferson c Brown b Sampson	0	– c Scott b Sampson	22
A. N. Cook c Scott b Saker	84	– c Scott b Sampson	18
*A. Flower not out	201		
M. L. Pettini c Newman b Benning	70	– (3) not out	4
R. S. Bopara c Newman b Salisbury	31	– (4) not out	2
†J. S. Foster lbw b Clarke	36		
J. D. Middlebrook c Scott b Clarke	3		
G. R. Napier b Murtagh	1		
J. P. Stephenson c Scott b Murtagh	1		
A. J. Clarke c Scott b Clarke	8		
Mohammad Akram lbw b Sampson	0		
B 1, l-b 5, w 1, n-b 22	29	L-b 1, n-b 2	3
1/0 (1) 2/157 (2) 3/272 (4) 4/343 (5) 5/429 (6) 6/433 (7) 7/440 (8) 8/442 (9) 9/457 (10) 10/464 (11)	464	1/36 (1) 2/47 (2)	(2 wkts) 49

Bonus points – Essex 5, Surrey 3.

Bowling: *First Innings*—Sampson 14.5–1–85–2; Clarke 20–1–104–3; Murtagh 27–4–89–2; Saker 16–1–71–1; Salisbury 21–1–70–1; Benning 8–1–39–1. *Second Innings*—Sampson 5–0–16–2; Saker 4.1–0–32–0.

Umpires: A. G. T. Whitehead and P. Willey.

GROUNDSMEN OF THE YEAR

In his last year as Surrey's head groundsman, Paul Brind, assisted by Bill Gordon, repeated his double success of 2002 in the ECB's Groundsman of the Year awards. The Oval won both the four-day and the one-day titles for 2003. Mick Hunt at Lord's was runner-up for his four-day pitches, and Philip Frost of Taunton in the one-day category. Cheltenham, now in the care of Bob McInroy, was the best county outground for the third year running, ahead of Shenley, managed by Andy Atkinson. The award for the best UCCE ground was won by Craig Thompson for the Racecourse Ground, Durham, with Chris Cay second for Park Avenue, home of Bradford/Leeds.

SUSSEX

164 years of hurt, never stopped believing

ANDY ARLIDGE AND BRUCE TALBOT

Sussex had to wait 164 years for their first Championship title but, when the moment of history arrived, it was perfect. They made certain of their triumph during a crushing victory in the last game of the season, at their Hove headquarters. Some of those present spoke of a dreamlike atmosphere. But for Sussex supporters, for years the butt of jokes about their love of dozing in deckchairs regardless of events in the middle, it was glorious reality. When Murray Goodwin pulled Leicestershire's Phil DeFreitas for four to earn the bonus point that clinched the title, play halted for several minutes. A lap of honour by the squad, accompanied over the loudspeakers by "Sussex by the Sea", gave a packed house a memory to treasure.

Sussex were hardly tipped as Championship contenders. Three years earlier, they had claimed the wooden spoon, but they shot to the top of Division Two the following season. In 2002, they just held on to first-division status, but the captain, Chris Adams, hailed that as a greater accomplishment than promotion. Evidently, they had been doing the right things to succeed in the modern game for a couple of seasons, and in 2003 it all came right. A youngish side with tremendous belief, who had been playing together for three or four years, performed above themselves to win ten Championship matches, a superlative effort. After seven weeks in second place, behind defending champions Surrey, they inched ahead in late August; they might have secured the title in their penultimate game, at Old Trafford, but Lancashire, by then their likeliest challengers, took it to the wire – which set up the dream finish at Hove.

The key ingredient was the signing of Mushtaq Ahmed, the Pakistani leg-spinner, who took 103 Championship wickets and undoubtedly won games that Sussex would have drawn without him. Mushtaq collected ten or more in a match five times, all of them leading to victory. His remarkable success had been indirectly predicted by his old international captain, Imran Khan, who said on leaving Hove in the 1980s that his replacement should have been an accomplished leg-spinner. Mushtaq rose to the challenge by becoming the first bowler for five years to take 100 first-class wickets in the English season. He was the first to do it for Sussex since Tony Buss in 1967, and the first to take 100 Championship wickets for Sussex since Buss and John Snow the year before that. It was a profitable season in more ways than one for Mushtaq, who earned a bonus of more than £10,000 through an incentive scheme rewarding him for every wicket he took over 50. No time was wasted in offering him a fresh two-year contract. Adams described Mushtaq's season as "awesome" and said: "The most important signings we made were two world-class overseas players. They should have been playing international cricket, and we were lucky that they didn't."

Mushtaq Ahmed

The other overseas player was Goodwin, the former Zimbabwean Test batsman. He had joined Sussex in 2001, when he contributed more than 1,500 runs to their successful bid for promotion. This time, his Championship aggregate was 1,496 and his average just under 60. He crowned Sussex's day of title glory in spectacular fashion, hitting 335 not out against Leicestershire, beating Duleepsinhji's 73-year-old county record. He boasted three other Championship hundreds, including a double against Essex, as well as four in the National League.

Adams, who had taken over the captaincy when he arrived from Derbyshire in 1998, proclaimed that winning the Championship was more special to him even than playing for England. He had no doubt that a greater desire and collective spirit had proved decisive in Sussex beating off Surrey and Lancashire. "We won it because we wanted it more," he said. "Sides like that are used to winning, but we had never won it before and that was the difference." On an individual level, Adams had to fight his way out of the worst run of form of his Sussex career. By late July, he was averaging 18 from ten Championship games. Then he scored 107 in a home draw with Surrey and, in the next match, followed up with twin hundreds to beat Lancashire. A fourth century, in the final victory over Leicestershire, left him only 34 short of 1,000 runs in his benefit season; his average for the last six games was 64. His determination typified Sussex's knack of finding someone to come to the rescue as players went in and out of form. Matt Prior also hit four centuries, and Tony Cottey three; both passed 1,000 runs, while Tim Ambrose, who shared wicket-keeping duties with Prior, fell just short, and all three averaged over 40. Richard Montgomerie and Robin Martin-Jenkins scored over 800 runs apiece, and Martin-Jenkins combined that with 31 wickets.

James Kirtley led the pace attack with distinction. He had taken 49 wickets in 11 Championship matches by early August, when he finally broke into the Test team, after several disappointments when he was named in the squad but omitted on the morning of the game. He bowled England to victory with eight wickets on his Test debut at Nottingham, and took five more at Leeds, but missed the final Test and the Championship run-in because of shin splints. He joined England's one-day squad for the winter tours, and was promoted to the Test squad in Sri Lanka. Though the loss of Kirtley for the last six weeks of the Championship campaign was rough luck after he had played such a key role in the Sussex revival, the blow to the county was cushioned by the return to fitness of left-armer Jason Lewry. He had only 13

MUSHTAQ AHMED'S BOWLING IN THE CHAMPIONSHIP, 2003

		First Innings	*Second Innings*
1	lost to Middlesex at Lord's	3 for 16	1 for 97
2	beat Kent at Hove	3 for 44	3 for 42
3	lost to Warwickshire at Birmingham	6 for 157	0 for 69
4	beat Nottinghamshire at Horsham	6 for 163	6 for 81
5	lost to Surrey at The Oval	3 for 159	1 for 47
6	beat Kent at Tunbridge Wells	5 for 70	4 for 56
7	beat Warwickshire at Hove	4 for 55	7 for 85
8	beat Essex at Arundel	2 for 102	1 for 92
9	beat Leicestershire at Leicester	5 for 93	5 for 96
10	drew with Nottinghamshire at Nottingham	2 for 87	0 for 41
11	drew with Surrey at Hove	4 for 123	0 for 26
12	beat Lancashire at Hove	6 for 124	5 for 49
13	beat Essex at Colchester	4 for 87	3 for 83
14	beat Middlesex at Hove	6 for 145	4 for 80
15	lost to Lancashire at Manchester	0 for 99	
16	beat Leicestershire at Hove	4 for 71	

For the season

O	*M*	*R*	*W*	*BB*	*5W/i*	*10W/m*	*Avge*
836.3	163	2,539	103	7-85	10	5	24.65

Championship wickets by the end of June, then took 28 in his last six games, capping a strong finish with a career-best eight for 106 against Leicestershire.

That form earned Lewry a new one-year contract, but three other seamers left Hove. Billy Taylor moved to Hampshire after failing to get assurances about his long-term future; Paul Hutchison, who had a year left on his contract, felt he could not afford another season in the second team and joined Middlesex; and Shaun Rashid, who failed to break into the first team, was released. Dutch batsman Bas Zuiderent also chose to seek another club. In October, Sussex recruited left-handed opener Ian Ward from Surrey; he hoped a new challenge at Hove might help him add to his five England caps.

Sussex's one-day record remained dismal. Since losing their place in Division One of the National League in 2000, they have won only 18 League matches in three seasons. In 2003, understandably distracted by the Championship, they lost 15 of their 25 limited-overs games. They went down to Middlesex in the fourth round of the C&G Trophy, and in the Twenty20 Cup three late wins, in front of packed houses at Hove, were not enough for them to progress to the semi-finals. Peter Moores, who has proved himself a fine coach in the modern idiom, needs to improve their one-day game in 2004, as well as making a stout defence of the long-awaited Championship title. But whatever lies ahead, the warmth of that September day will glow in the memory for many summers.

SUSSEX IN 2003

Back row: S. Osborne (*physiotherapist*), J. Carmichael (*physiotherapist*), C. D. Hopkinson, B. V. Taylor, S. Rashid, P. M. Hutchison, K. Greenfield (*academy director*). *Middle row:* M. J. G. Davis, B. Zuiderent, M. J. Prior, T. R. Ambrose, M. H. Yardy, R. R. Montgomerie, K. J. Innes. *Front Row:* J. D. Lewry, Mushtaq Ahmed, M. A. Robinson (*coach*) R. J. Kirtley, C. J. Adams, R. S. C. Martin-Jenkins, P. Moores (*director of cricket*), M. W. Goodwin, P. A. Cottey.

SUSSEX RESULTS

All first-class matches – Played 17: Won 10, Lost 4, Drawn 3.
County Championship matches – Played 16: Won 10, Lost 4, Drawn 2.

Frizzell County Championship, winners in Division 1; Cheltenham & Gloucester Trophy, 4th round; National Cricket League, 8th in Division 2; Twenty20 Cup, 2nd in South Group.

COUNTY CHAMPIONSHIP AVERAGES

BATTING AND FIELDING

Cap		*M*	*I*	*NO*	*R*	*HS*	*100s*	*50s*	*Avge*	*Ct/St*
2001	M. W. Goodwin§	16	28	3	1,496	335*	4	5	59.84	10
2003	M. J. Prior	16	24	3	1,006	153*	4	3	47.90	28
1999	P. A. Cottey	15	25	0	1,149	188	3	7	45.96	8
2003	T. R. Ambrose	15	26	3	931	93*	0	9	40.47	29/7
2000	R. S. C. Martin-Jenkins	16	25	3	811	121*	1	5	36.86	7
1998	C. J. Adams	16	27	0	966	190	4	2	35.77	18
1998	R. J. Kirtley	11	13	7	207	40*	0	0	34.50	3
1999	R. R. Montgomerie	16	28	2	884	105	1	7	34.00	22
2003	Mushtaq Ahmed§	16	19	2	456	60	0	3	26.82	3
2002	M. J. G. Davis	10	12	2	259	168	1	0	25.90	4
	K. J. Innes	7	11	3	182	103*	1	0	22.75	1
	B. V. Taylor	7	7	4	55	35*	0	0	18.33	0
1996	J. D. Lewry	11	15	3	215	70	0	1	17.91	4

Also batted: P. M. Hutchison (4 matches) 18, 5, 0; M. H. Yardy (2 matches) 0, 69, 47 (3 ct).

§ *Overseas player.*

BOWLING

	O	*M*	*R*	*W*	*BB*	*5W/i*	*Avge*
Mushtaq Ahmed	836.3	163	2,539	103	7-85	10	24.65
J. D. Lewry	315.2	71	1,020	41	8-106	3	24.87
R. J. Kirtley	430.2	95	1,403	49	6-26	2	28.63
B. V. Taylor	214.1	60	617	21	4-42	0	29.38
R. S. C. Martin-Jenkins	364	82	1,258	31	3-9	0	40.58
M. J. G. Davis	220	42	703	14	3-44	0	50.21

Also bowled: C. J. Adams 1–0–1–0; P. A. Cottey 13–1–59–0; M. W. Goodwin 3–0–17–0; P. M. Hutchison 77–12–311–3; K. J. Innes 74–11–297–7; R. R. Montgomerie 3–0–9–1; M. H. Yardy 27–3–89–0.

COUNTY RECORDS

Highest score for:	335*	M. W. Goodwin v Leicestershire at Hove	2003
Highest score against:	322	E. Paynter (Lancashire) at Hove	1937
Best bowling for:	10-48	C. H. G. Bland v Kent at Tonbridge	1899
Best bowling against:	9-11	A. P. Freeman (Kent) at Hove	1922
Highest total for:	705-8 dec.	v Surrey at Hastings	1902
Highest total against:	726	by Nottinghamshire at Nottingham	1895
Lowest total for:	19	v Surrey at Godalming	1830
	19	v Nottinghamshire at Hove	1873
Lowest total against:	18	by Kent at Gravesend	1867

SUSSEX DIRECTORY

ADDRESS

County Ground, Eaton Road, Hove BN3 3AN (01273 827100; fax 01273 771549; email fran.watson@sussexcricket.co.uk). **Website** www.sussexcricket.co.uk.

GROUNDS

Hove: ½ mile from seafront and 1 mile W of Brighton town centre in Eaton Road, Hove. Nearest station: Hove (½ mile).

Horsham: 1 mile S of town centre. From A281 Worthing Road, turn L into Cricketfield Road. Nearest station: Horsham (1 mile).

Arundel: 1 mile N of town centre within grounds of Arundel Park N of Castle. From A284 London Road follow signs for castle and cricket ground. Nearest station: Arundel (1 mile).

OFFICIALS

Captain C. J. Adams
Director of cricket P. Moores
President J. M. Parks
Chairman D. E. Green
Chief executive H. H. Griffiths
Chairman, cricket committee J. R. T. Barclay
Head groundsman D. J. Traill
Scorer J. Hartridge

PLAYERS

Players expected to reappear in 2004

	Former counties	*Country*	*Born*	*Birthplace*
***Adams** Christopher John	Derbys	E	6.5.1970	*Whitwell*
Ambrose Timothy Raymond		A (EU)	1.12.1982	*Newcastle*
Cottey Phillip Anthony	Glam	E	2.6.1966	*Swansea*
Davis Mark Jeffrey Gronow		SA (EU)	10.10.1971	*Port Elizabeth*
***Goodwin** Murray William		Z/A	11.12.1972	*Salisbury, Rhodesia*
Hopkinson Carl Daniel		E	14.9.1981	†*Brighton*
Innes Kevin John	Northants	E	24.9.1975	*Wellingborough*
***Kirtley** Robert James		E	10.1.1975	†*Eastbourne*
Lewry Jason David		E	2.4.1971	†*Worthing*
Martin-Jenkins Robin Simon Christopher		E	28.10.1975	*Guildford*
Montgomerie Richard Robert	Northants	E	3.7.1971	*Rugby*
***Mushtaq Ahmed**	Somerset, Surrey	P	28.6.1970	*Sahiwal*
Prior Matthew James		E	26.2.1982	*Johannesburg, SA*
Turk Neil Richard Keith		E	28.4.1983	†*Cuckfield*
Yardy Michael Howard		E	27.11.1980	*Pembury*

Players due to join in 2004

***Mohammad Akram**	Northants, Essex	P (EU)	10.9.1974	*Islamabad*
Voros Jason Alexander		A (EU)	31.12.1976	*Canberra*
***Ward** Ian James	Surrey	E	30.9.1972	*Plymouth*
Wright Luke James	Leics	E	7.3.1985	*Grantham*

* *Test player.* † *Born in Sussex.*

At Hove, April 18, 19 (not first-class). **Sussex won by an innings and 280 runs.** Toss: Cardiff UCCE. **Cardiff UCCE 116** (Mushtaq Ahmed 6-20) **and 133** (Mushtaq Ahmed 5-29); **Sussex 529-8 dec.** (R. R. Montgomerie 116, P. A. Cottey 110, C. J. Adams 100, R. S. C. Martin-Jenkins 112).

County debut: Mushtaq Ahmed, who took 11 for 49 in the match.

At Lord's, April 23, 24, 25, 26. SUSSEX lost to MIDDLESEX by three wickets.

SUSSEX v KENT

At Hove, April 30, May 1, 2. Sussex won by 133 runs. Sussex 19 pts, Kent 3 pts. Toss: Kent.

Kirtley exploited an old-fashioned seaming pitch to wrap up Sussex's first Championship victory of 2003 on the third afternoon. Needing 293, Kent were well placed at 97 for two. But once Mushtaq Ahmed had Blewett caught at silly point, Kirtley tore through the middle order. In one dramatic Kirtley over, Cottey badly bruised his thumb parrying a pull from Smith, who fell two balls later; two balls after that, Lewry took an outstanding one-handed catch to dismiss Jones, but collided with Cottey's substitute, Hopkinson, and broke his own nose. First-day honours had gone to Sheriyar, who broke the back of the Sussex innings, though Mushtaq, hitting seven fours, helped earn a second batting point. Kent's reply was on course at 105 for three, but Mushtaq's exemplary control eventually forced mistakes and their remaining seven fell for 80. Goodwin contributed a crucial 96 to Sussex's second innings, but lost four team-mates for eight on the second evening and, perhaps fearing being left high and dry, played across the line to the day's last delivery – and cursed himself all the way back to the pavilion.

Close of play: First day, Kent 81-3 (Blewett 21, Walker 30); Second day, Sussex 174-9 (Kirtley 0).

Sussex

R. R. Montgomerie b Sheriyar	22	– (2) b Sheriyar	12
M. W. Goodwin b Saggers	9	– (1) lbw b Tredwell	96
P. A. Cottey c Ealham b Sheriyar	19	– lbw b Sheriyar	2
*C. J. Adams c Blewett b Sheriyar	54	– st Jones b Tredwell	11
T. R. Ambrose c Jones b Saggers	41	– c Blewett b Saggers	10
R. S. C. Martin-Jenkins c Jones b Sheriyar	16	– b Ealham	34
†M. J. Prior c Jones b Ealham	40	– st Jones b Tredwell	4
K. J. Innes c Walker b Ealham	9	– lbw b Ealham	1
Mushtaq Ahmed c Jones b Saggers	37	– c Blewett b Ealham	0
R. J. Kirtley not out	7	– not out	14
J. D. Lewry b Sheriyar	22	– c Jones b Tredwell	10
B 1, n-b 2	3	L-b 4	4
1/25 (2) 2/42 (1) 3/83 (3) 4/134 (4) 5/158 (6) 6/166 (5) 7/193 (8) 8/242 (7) 9/256 (9) 10/279 (11)	279	1/28 (2) 2/34 (3) 3/55 (4) 4/84 (5) 5/166 (6) 6/171 (7) 7/174 (8) 8/174 (9) 9/174 (1) 10/198 (11)	198

Bonus points – Sussex 2, Kent 3.

Bowling: *First Innings*—Saggers 20–3–77–3; Trott 9–0–53–0; Sheriyar 20.2–5–65–5; Ealham 14–4–45–2; Tredwell 9–2–38–0. *Second Innings*—Saggers 13–4–49–1; Sheriyar 14–3–34–2; Ealham 10–3–34–3; Trott 8–2–29–0; Tredwell 19.1–4–48–4.

Kent

	First innings		Second innings	
M. A. Carberry	c Prior b Lewry	3	c Prior b Kirtley	3
R. W. T. Key	b Kirtley	0	b Lewry	28
E. T. Smith	c Adams b Innes	23	c Ambrose b Kirtley	33
G. S. Blewett	c Prior b Kirtley	41	c Montgomerie b Mushtaq Ahmed	37
M. J. Walker	c Montgomerie b Kirtley	40	b Mushtaq Ahmed	11
*M. A. Ealham	lbw b Mushtaq Ahmed	24	lbw b Mushtaq Ahmed	15
†G. O. Jones	b Lewry	2	c Lewry b Kirtley	0
J. C. Tredwell	not out	32	lbw b Kirtley	10
M. J. Saggers	lbw b Mushtaq Ahmed	9	c Prior b Kirtley	1
B. J. Trott	b Innes	0	b Kirtley	0
A. Sheriyar	lbw b Mushtaq Ahmed	2	not out	7
	L-b 7, n-b 2	9	B 9, l-b 4, w 1	14
	1/2 (2) 2/10 (1) 3/29 (3) 4/105 (5) 5/114 (4) 6/119 (7) 7/163 (6) 8/181 (9) 9/182 (10) 10/185 (11)	185	1/31 (2) 2/35 (1) 3/97 (4) 4/111 (5) 5/123 (3) 6/124 (7) 7/145 (8) 8/147 (9) 9/147 (10) 10/159 (6)	159

Bonus points – Sussex 3.

Bowling: *First Innings*—Lewry 13–2–44–2; Kirtley 17–6–41–3; Innes 7–1–18–2; Martin-Jenkins 12–2–31–0; Mushtaq Ahmed 19–3–44–3. *Second Innings*—Lewry 14–1–59–1; Kirtley 15–4–26–6; Martin-Jenkins 4–2–5–0; Innes 3–0–14–0; Mushtaq Ahmed 13.5–2–42–3.

Umpires: J. H. Hampshire and P. J. Hartley.

At Birmingham, May 9, 10, 11, 12. SUSSEX lost to WARWICKSHIRE by 234 runs.

At Hove, May 15, 16, 17, 18. SUSSEX drew with ZIMBABWEANS (see Zimbabwean tour section).

SUSSEX v NOTTINGHAMSHIRE

At Horsham, May 21, 22, 23, 24. Sussex won by ten wickets. Sussex 22 pts, Nottinghamshire 7 pts. Toss: Sussex.

History was made at Cricketfield Road when Innes became the first twelfth man in first-class cricket to score a century. Under new ECB regulations, Kirtley, released from England's squad, could replace a nominated player. But before Kirtley could arrive from Lord's, his replacement, Innes, was needed at the crease. He made a thoroughly deserved maiden hundred as Sussex piled up 619, a ground record, against a dispirited attack on the second morning. Kirtley was there in time to see his alter ego reach 100. The situation was so unusual that the ECB computers – and at least one daily paper – credited the runs to Kirtley, who did take over in the field. On the first day, Montgomerie had ended a lean spell with his third successive Horsham century. Innes's job was to support Prior, who dashed off 124 runs on the second morning, slamming six sixes and bounding from 98 to 133 in ten balls. He later twisted an ankle and passed the gloves to Ambrose, while Kirtley took over from Innes in the field. All the bowlers found a slow pitch demanding, and even Mushtaq Ahmed took some stick from Pietersen, whose power and timing gave him three figures in 75 balls. But Mushtaq, varying his flight and speed, demolished Nottinghamshire to enforce the follow-on. Gallian and Bicknell brought the draw in reach, scoring 103 on the third evening, but there was no stopping Mushtaq or the latecomer Kirtley on the final day. Six wickets fell in an hour; despite a brief fightback, Sussex were left with a small target, which they knocked off before tea. Mushtaq's figures of 12 for 244 were the best by a Sussex spinner for ten years, since 44-year-old Eddie Hemmings took 12 for 58, also at Horsham.

Close of play: First day, Sussex 330-5 (Ambrose 36, Prior 9); Second day, Nottinghamshire 85-1 (Welton 45, Afzaal 0); Third day, Nottinghamshire 103-0 (Bicknell 61, Gallian 38).

Sussex

R. R. Montgomerie c Gallian b MacGill	105	– (2) not out	25
M. W. Goodwin c Pietersen b Elworthy	38	– (1) not out	23
P. A. Cottey lbw b MacGill	58		
*C. J. Adams c Gallian b MacGill	9		
T. R. Ambrose c Read b Elworthy	55		
R. S. C. Martin-Jenkins c Welton b Harris	49		
†M. J. Prior c sub b Elworthy	133		
K. J. Innes not out	103		
M. J. G. Davis not out	32		
B 2, l-b 20, w 1, n-b 14	37	L-b 2, n-b 2	4
1/87 (2) 2/210 (3) 3/227 (1) 4/232 (4) 5/312 (6) 6/378 (5) 7/535 (7) (7 wkts dec.)	619	(no wkt)	52

Mushtaq Ahmed, B. V. Taylor and R. J. Kirtley did not bat.

Bonus points – Sussex 5, Nottinghamshire 2 (130 overs: 557-7).

Bowling: *First Innings*—Smith 24–2–97–0; Harris 20–2–102–1; Gallian 12–2–45–0; Elworthy 30–3–107–3; MacGill 50–12–172–3; Shafayat 4–0–39–0; Pietersen 7–0–35–0. *Second Innings*—Elworthy 5–1–22–0; MacGill 4–1–13–0; Pietersen 1–0–9–0; Harris 0.2–0–6–0.

Nottinghamshire

G. E. Welton lbw b Mushtaq Ahmed	50	– (3) st Ambrose b Mushtaq Ahmed	12
*J. E. R. Gallian c Prior b Taylor	36	– c Montgomerie b Mushtaq Ahmed	44
U. Afzaal c Ambrose b Kirtley	35	– (4) c Ambrose b Kirtley	18
D. J. Bicknell lbw b Kirtley	9	– (1) c and b Kirtley	61
K. P. Pietersen st Ambrose b Mushtaq Ahmed	166	– c Cottey b Mushtaq Ahmed	1
B. M. Shafayat lbw b Mushtaq Ahmed	71	– b Mushtaq Ahmed	0
†C. M. W. Read lbw b Mushtaq Ahmed	0	– lbw b Kirtley	42
S. Elworthy c Ambrose b Martin-Jenkins	28	– c Ambrose b Mushtaq Ahmed	45
G. J. Smith b Mushtaq Ahmed	9	– not out	5
A. J. Harris b Mushtaq Ahmed	5	– st Ambrose b Mushtaq Ahmed	1
S. C. G. MacGill not out	4	– c sub b Kirtley	2
B 1, l-b 1, n-b 6	8	L-b 5, w 1, n-b 10	16
1/71 (2) 2/109 (1) 3/126 (4) 4/139 (3) 5/332 (6) 6/332 (7) 7/369 (8) 8/390 (9) 9/398 (10) 10/421 (5)	421	1/103 (1) 2/111 (2) 3/132 (4) 4/133 (5) 5/142 (3) 6/143 (6) 7/237 (8) 8/239 (7) 9/242 (10) 10/247 (11)	247

Bonus points – Nottinghamshire 5, Sussex 3.

Bowling: *First Innings*—Kirtley 21–7–85–2; Martin-Jenkins 17–0–87–1; Mushtaq Ahmed 37.1–3–163–6; Taylor 11–3–32–1; Davis 7–0–52–0. *Second Innings*—Kirtley 24.2–4–74–4; Taylor 13–3–36–0; Davis 9–1–26–0; Martin-Jenkins 6–1–25–0; Mushtaq Ahmed 30–9–81–6.

Umpires: N. G. Cowley and N. J. Llong.

At The Oval, May 30, 31, June 1, 2. SUSSEX lost to SURREY by 113 runs.

At Tunbridge Wells, June 4, 5, 6, 7. SUSSEX beat KENT by 191 runs.

At Hove, June 20 (day/night). SUSSEX lost to SOUTH AFRICANS by 153 runs (see South African tour section).

SUSSEX v WARWICKSHIRE

At Hove, June 27, 28, 29. Sussex won by an innings and 59 runs. Sussex 22 pts, Warwickshire 3 pts. Toss: Sussex.

Sussex's gathering momentum carried them to their first Championship win over Warwickshire since 1992, and second place in the table. The platform was laid by Cottey, whose six-hour 188 was his biggest century for Sussex, and his first at Hove for four years. On a true pitch, he caned some ordinary bowling with powerful off-side drives and fleet-footed accumulation. Prior, relieved of wicket-keeping, followed up with a stylish hundred, and the last two wickets put on 106. On a pitch taking only slow turn, Mushtaq Ahmed soon got to work, claiming four wickets in the first innings, as nine tumbled for 97. When Warwickshire followed on during the third morning, 344 behind, Knight and Powell built a purposeful century stand, but Mushtaq removed both after lunch. This time, bowling in tandem with off-spinner Davis, he collected seven wickets, which took him to 52 in seven matches. In contrast, Warwickshire's two spinners bowled 33 wicketless overs for 129 between them.

Close of play: First day, Sussex 395-5 (Martin-Jenkins 25, Prior 15); Second day, Warwickshire 194-8 (Brown 36, Waqar Younis 7).

Sussex

R. R. Montgomerie c Frost b Brown	66
M. W. Goodwin c Frost b Waqar Younis	0
P. A. Cottey c Frost b Richardson	188
*C. J. Adams c Bell b Waqar Younis	31
†T. R. Ambrose b Richardson	50
R. S. C. Martin-Jenkins b Waqar Younis	28
M. J. Prior c Frost b Brown	100
M. J. G. Davis b Waqar Younis	6
Mushtaq Ahmed c Trott b Waqar Younis	2
R. J. Kirtley not out	40
J. D. Lewry b Brown	6
B 1, l-b 9, n-b 18	28
1/3 (2) 2/168 (1) 3/239 (4) 4/342 (3) 5/357 (5) 6/407 (6) 7/431 (8) 8/439 (9) 9/519 (7) 10/545 (11)	545

Bonus points – Sussex 5, Warwickshire 2 (130 overs: 478-8).

Bowling: Waqar Younis 24–2–99–5; Betts 20–1–91–0; Brown 31.1–8–95–3; Richardson 34–6–92–2; Bell 3–0–24–0; Obuya 19–1–89–0; Wagh 14–1–40–0; Trott 2–1–5–0.

Warwickshire

*M. J. Powell c Ambrose b Martin-Jenkins	60	– c Adams b Mushtaq Ahmed	80
N. V. Knight lbw b Lewry	11	– c Prior b Mushtaq Ahmed	64
M. A. Wagh c Prior b Mushtaq Ahmed	39	– c Prior b Mushtaq Ahmed	2
I. R. Bell lbw b Mushtaq Ahmed	0	– c Martin-Jenkins b Mushtaq Ahmed	37
I. J. L. Trott c Goodwin b Kirtley	6	– lbw b Davis	31
†T. Frost run out	1	– b Davis	4
D. R. Brown not out	42	– c Adams b Mushtaq Ahmed	20
C. O. Obuya lbw b Kirtley	2	– (9) not out	8
M. M. Betts c Davis b Mushtaq Ahmed	21	– (8) c Adams b Lewry	15
Waqar Younis c Ambrose b Kirtley	8	– c Kirtley b Mushtaq Ahmed	14
A. Richardson b Mushtaq Ahmed	0	– c Ambrose b Mushtaq Ahmed	0
B 1, l-b 9, w 1	11	B 2, l-b 7, w 1	10
1/22 (2) 2/104 (1) 3/105 (4) 4/122 (3) 5/124 (6) 6/131 (5) 7/140 (8) 8/171 (9) 9/198 (10) 10/201 (11)	201	1/135 (2) 2/139 (3) 3/146 (1) 4/185 (5) 5/196 (6) 6/236 (4) 7/249 (7) 8/267 (8) 9/284 (10) 10/285 (11)	285

Bonus points – Warwickshire 1, Sussex 3.

Bowling: *First Innings*—Kirtley 15–2–57–3; Lewry 10–2–35–1; Mushtaq Ahmed 22.5–6–55–4; Martin-Jenkins 10–1–40–1; Davis 2–1–4–0. *Second Innings*—Kirtley 16–2–62–0; Lewry 9–2–41–1; Mushtaq Ahmed 32.4–9–85–7; Martin-Jenkins 12–4–38–0; Davis 23–6–50–2.

Umpires: V. A. Holder and M. J. Kitchen.

SUSSEX v ESSEX

At Arundel, July 9, 10, 11, 12. Sussex won by six wickets. Sussex 21 pts, Essex 6 pts. Toss: Essex.

Sussex kept in touch with leaders Surrey, reaching the halfway stage with five wins and growing self-belief. Stalemate threatened when Essex started the final day 235 ahead with four men left, but by lunch both sides had a chance: Lewry's tenth wicket finished off Essex, Sussex slid to 32 for three. For the second time running, Cottey and Ambrose rescued them, putting on 172. Cottey fell two short of a third successive hundred, but Ambrose saw it through. A duel between Mushtaq Ahmed and Hussain, on a slow, true pitch, was the first-day highlight. Mushtaq finally won, and Essex tumbled to 215 for eight before a pugnacious 89 from Napier. Sussex were a troubled 53 for three, then Cottey and Ambrose's first rescue act added 178: Cottey gave a masterclass against spin, Ambrose drove fluidly through the arc. Slow left-armer Grayson claimed four when belatedly introduced, but Davis emerged from Mushtaq's shadow to keep Sussex in it with his controlled off-breaks. Warm weather boosted the crowds: 3,000 attended each of the first three days.

Close of play: First day, Essex 305-8 (Napier 62, ten Doeschate 26); Second day, Sussex 282-8 (Mushtaq Ahmed 16, Kirtley 0); Third day, Essex 254-6 (Middlebrook 23, ten Doeschate 5).

Essex

First innings		Second innings	
A. P. Grayson c Ambrose b Kirtley	0	b Davis	71
N. Hussain c Montgomerie b Mushtaq Ahmed	95	c Mushtaq Ahmed b Lewry	22
†J. S. Foster c Montgomerie b Lewry	12	run out	1
A. Flower lbw b Kirtley	37	lbw b Davis	54
A. Habib c Ambrose b Lewry	0	c Ambrose b Lewry	53
*R. C. Irani c Adams b Lewry	15	c Adams b Davis	6
J. D. Middlebrook lbw b Martin-Jenkins	14	c Adams b Lewry	23
J. M. Dakin c Kirtley b Lewry	35	(9) b Lewry	0
G. R. Napier not out	89	(10) not out	10
R. N. ten Doeschate b Lewry	31	(8) lbw b Mushtaq Ahmed	6
S. A. Brant c Prior b Mushtaq Ahmed	3	b Lewry	2
B 2, l-b 7	9	L-b 19, w 5, n-b 2	26
1/0 (1) 2/23 (3) 3/95 (4) 4/97 (5) 5/115 (6) 6/149 (7) 7/203 (2) 8/215 (8) 9/331 (10) 10/340 (11)	340	1/49 (2) 2/50 (3) 3/140 (1) 4/187 (4) 5/193 (6) 6/243 (5) 7/258 (7) 8/262 (8) 9/262 (9) 10/274 (11)	274

Bonus points – Essex 3, Sussex 3.

Bowling: *First Innings*—Kirtley 24–4–88–2; Lewry 29–7–72–5; Mushtaq Ahmed 36.5–10–102–2; Martin-Jenkins 17–3–44–1; Davis 8–0–25–0. *Second Innings*—Kirtley 17–2–48–0; Lewry 19.4–6–52–5; Mushtaq Ahmed 30–4–92–1; Martin-Jenkins 8–3–19–0; Davis 19–3–44–3.

Sussex

First innings		Second innings	
M. W. Goodwin b Brant	11	(2) b Dakin	18
R. R. Montgomerie c Hussain b Brant	1	(1) c Foster b Dakin	1
P. A. Cottey c Middlebrook b Dakin	107	c Foster b Dakin	98
*C. J. Adams c Foster b Napier	20	c Habib b Middlebrook	0
†T. R. Ambrose c Flower b Grayson	88	not out	93
R. S. C. Martin-Jenkins lbw b Grayson	6	not out	21
M. J. Prior lbw b Brant	13		
M. J. G. Davis c Habib b Grayson	12		
Mushtaq Ahmed c Dakin b Grayson	34		
R. J. Kirtley not out	35		
J. D. Lewry c Flower b Middlebrook	22		
L-b 3, w 3, n-b 4	10	B 7, l-b 4, w 15	26
1/4 (2) 2/13 (1) 3/53 (4) 4/231 (5) 5/233 (3) 6/250 (6) 7/254 (7) 8/280 (8) 9/323 (9) 10/359 (11)	359	1/1 (1) 2/31 (2) 3/32 (4) 4/204 (3)	(4 wkts) 257

Bonus points – Sussex 4, Essex 3.

Bowling: *First Innings*—Dakin 25–5–67–1; Brant 25–4–90–3; ten Doeschate 10–1–53–0; Napier 16–2–45–1; Middlebrook 17.5–1–54–1; Grayson 17–2–47–4. *Second Innings*—Brant 7–0–27–0; Dakin 16–2–54–3; Middlebrook 23.1–1–78–1; Napier 7–0–24–0; Grayson 24–7–63–0.

Umpires: D. J. Constant and B. Leadbeater.

At Leicester, July 15, 16, 17, 18. SUSSEX beat LEICESTERSHIRE by five wickets.

At Nottingham, July 25, 26, 27, 28. SUSSEX drew with NOTTINGHAMSHIRE.

SUSSEX v SURREY

At Hove, July 30, 31, August 1, 2. Drawn. Sussex 12 pts, Surrey 11 pts. Toss: Sussex.

This top-of-the-table contest attracted record receipts for a Championship match at Hove, but Adams ended it defending a declaration delayed until ten minutes before tea, leaving Surrey 36 overs to get 377. The more vocal element of a usually placid crowd felt Sussex had missed their chance by coming off for bad light on the third day with 37 overs to go. But they squandered an earlier opportunity when Surrey were 126 for six, 303 behind. The last four put on 229, thanks to a hundred from Ramprakash, and Saqlain Mushtaq slapped Mushtaq Ahmed for two sixes in three balls. The tide was turning. Sussex began the final day 143 ahead, but Adams seemed intent on protecting what he had. Protests ranged from Salisbury and Saqlain bowling seam-up to a slow handclap from the deckchairs. Sussex had punished some wayward first-day bowling: Montgomerie and Goodwin shared their first century stand of 2003, and Adams got his first hundred for 15 months. But Surrey fought back next day to take the last six for 66, after Adams walked in the first over, indicating he had gloved it. Neither Ormond, the bowler, nor umpire Benson, who commended his sportsmanship, was convinced.

Close of play: First day, Sussex 362-4 (Adams 107, Martin-Jenkins 12); Second day, Surrey 212-6 (Ramprakash 74, Bicknell 42); Third day, Sussex 69-2 (Goodwin 21, Adams 1).

Sussex

R. R. Montgomerie b Salisbury	90	– (2) lbw b Bicknell	2
M. W. Goodwin b Ormond	75	– (1) c Ward b Saqlain Mushtaq	29
P. A. Cottey lbw b Saqlain Mushtaq	1	– c Ramprakash b Azhar Mahmood	41
*C. J. Adams c Batty b Ormond	107	– lbw b Saqlain Mushtaq	23
†T. R. Ambrose c Azhar Mahmood b Salisbury	43	– not out	76
R. S. C. Martin-Jenkins b Bicknell	40	– b Salisbury	45
M. J. Prior c Thorpe b Ormond	0	– not out	50
M. J. G. Davis c Clarke b Ormond	0		
Mushtaq Ahmed c Batty b Azhar Mahmood	26		
P. M. Hutchison c Ward b Bicknell	5		
R. J. Kirtley not out	1		
B 6, l-b 13, n-b 22	41	B 9, l-b 8, n-b 14, p 5	36
1/149 (2) 2/150 (3) 3/232 (1) 4/330 (5) 5/363 (4) 6/363 (7) 7/367 (8) 8/415 (6) 9/423 (9) 10/429 (10)	429	1/7 (2) 2/67 (3) 3/89 (1) 4/108 (4) 5/228 (6) (5 wkts dec.)	302

Bonus points – Sussex 5, Surrey 3.

Bowling: *First Innings*—Bicknell 26–5–94–2; Ormond 25–6–106–4; Hollioake 7–3–23–0; Azhar Mahmood 18–5–61–1; Saqlain Mushtaq 36–5–84–1; Salisbury 14–0–42–2. *Second Innings*—Bicknell 16–5–54–1; Ormond 10–3–17–0; Saqlain Mushtaq 35–7–97–2; Azhar Mahmood 4–1–3–1; Salisbury 22–0–98–1; Hollioake 0.5–0–11–0.

Surrey

I. J. Ward lbw b Kirtley	20	– lbw b Davis	33
†J. N. Batty c Ambrose b Hutchison	12	– not out	65
M. R. Ramprakash c Ambrose b Kirtley	104	– not out	14
G. P. Thorpe c Davis b Martin-Jenkins	23		
R. Clarke c Mushtaq Ahmed b Martin-Jenkins	12		
*A. J. Hollioake lbw b Mushtaq Ahmed	13		
Azhar Mahmood lbw b Mushtaq Ahmed	9		
M. P. Bicknell lbw b Mushtaq Ahmed	42		
I. D. K. Salisbury st Ambrose b Mushtaq Ahmed	1		
Saqlain Mushtaq b Martin-Jenkins	68		
J. Ormond not out	42		
B 1, l-b 6, n-b 2	9	L-b 2	2
1/32 (1) 2/32 (2) 3/75 (4) 4/89 (5) 5/116 (6) 6/126 (7) 7/215 (8) 8/217 (9) 9/301 (3) 10/355 (10)	355	1/82 (1)	(1 wkt) 114

Bonus points – Surrey 4, Sussex 3.

Bowling: *First Innings*—Kirtley 28–4–90–2; Hutchison 16–2–58–1; Mushtaq Ahmed 38–7–123–4; Martin-Jenkins 17.3–3–67–3; Davis 3–0–10–0. *Second Innings*—Kirtley 6–1–23–0; Hutchison 7–1–30–0; Martin-Jenkins 3–0–17–0; Mushtaq Ahmed 6–1–26–0; Davis 4–1–16–1.

Umpires: M. R. Benson and M. J. Harris.

SUSSEX v LANCASHIRE

At Hove, August 14, 15, 16, 17. Sussex won by 252 runs. Sussex 21 pts, Lancashire 7 pts. Toss: Sussex.

Sussex pulled further ahead of third-placed Lancashire, completing a breathless victory with 12 minutes to spare after four enthralling days of cut and thrust. Adams appeared to err on caution's side again, delaying his declaration until 12.35 to leave a target of 392, but he was spot on. Lancashire's only option was to bat for a draw, while Sussex attacked. Taylor, an admirable stand-in for Kirtley, delivered 17 overs unchanged from lunch to tea, seizing four in 33 balls, before leaving the stage to Mushtaq, who bowled 17.2–10–23–5 after tea, often with seven expectant fielders round the bat. With time running out, the Sussex coaches patrolled the boundary to return balls more quickly, but Lancashire gave them little cause to fret. Mushtaq collected 11 victims, while Adams was the fourth batsman to score twin hundreds for Sussex more than once – joining C. B. Fry, Duleepsinhji and John Langridge. He batted over ten hours, a tremendous physical effort in temperatures that passed 90°C. With Kirtley finally making his Test debut, it was Chapple who was sent back from Nottingham, replacing nominated substitute Hogg; his bowling was profligate, but he helped Law ensure first-innings parity. Sussex wobbled in the second innings when Martin struck in his first two overs, but vintage strokeplay by Adams took the game away from Lancashire.

Close of play: First day, Lancashire 12-0 (Chilton 8, Sutcliffe 4); Second day, Lancashire 351-8 (Hegg 24, Wood 12); Third day, Sussex 265-3 (Adams 147, Ambrose 42).

"In 1956, bowling for Somerset II at Trowbridge, Biddulph slowed the over-rate down to prevent a Wiltshire win; more than 40 years later he wrote to Wiltshire to apologise, saying it had been on his conscience all his life."

Obituaries, page 1535.

Sussex

R. R. Montgomerie c Law b Martin	72	– (2) c Sutcliffe b Martin	70
M. W. Goodwin c Hegg b Wood	9	– (1) c Sutcliffe b Martin	1
P. A. Cottey c Schofield b Hogg	18	– c Hegg b Martin	0
*C. J. Adams lbw b Schofield	140	– c and b Chapple	190
†T. R. Ambrose c Sutcliffe b Wood	18	– c and b Chapple	44
R. S. C. Martin-Jenkins c Law b Wood	18	– lbw b Chapple	13
M. J. Prior c Hegg b Keedy	9	– c Sutcliffe b Wood	35
M. J. G. Davis lbw b Hooper	3	– not out	16
Mushtaq Ahmed lbw b Schofield	60		
P. M. Hutchison lbw b Schofield	0		
B. V. Taylor not out	13		
B 8, l-b 6, w 1, n-b 10	25	B 2, l-b 8, n-b 4	14
1/12 (2) 2/60 (3) 3/132 (1) 4/156 (5) 5/190 (6) 6/252 (7) 7/257 (8) 8/332 (4) 9/332 (10) 10/385 (9)	385	1/2 (1) 2/2 (3) 3/155 (2) 4/268 (5) 5/313 (6) 6/348 (4) 7/383 (7) (7 wkts dec.)	383

Bonus points – Sussex 4, Lancashire 3.

Bowling: *First Innings*—Martin 15–2–64–1; Wood 17–2–64–3; Chilton 12–2–33–0; Hogg 8–2–24–1; Keedy 24–6–76–1; Hooper 12–2–48–1; Chapple 7–0–48–0; Schofield 5.3–2–14–3. *Second Innings*—Martin 21–5–61–3; Chapple 21–3–89–3; Hooper 22–4–65–0; Wood 17.4–2–72–1; Keedy 19–3–61–0; Schofield 4–0–25–0.

Lancashire

M. J. Chilton c Montgomerie b Davis	65	– b Taylor	9
I. J. Sutcliffe c Prior b Mushtaq Ahmed	43	– c Montgomerie b Taylor	12
M. B. Loye c Goodwin b Taylor	2	– lbw b Mushtaq Ahmed	33
S. G. Law c Montgomerie b Mushtaq Ahmed	96	– c Adams b Taylor	7
C. L. Hooper c and b Mushtaq Ahmed	23	– c Adams b Taylor	1
C. P. Schofield b Mushtaq Ahmed	3	– b Davis	18
G. Chapple c Goodwin b Taylor	54	– lbw b Mushtaq Ahmed	7
*†W. K. Hegg c Montgomerie b Mushtaq Ahmed	31	– c Montgomerie b Mushtaq Ahmed	25
P. J. Martin b Taylor	9	– c Prior b Mushtaq Ahmed	0
J. Wood lbw b Mushtaq Ahmed	30	– lbw b Mushtaq Ahmed	0
G. Keedy not out	0	– not out	2
B 10, l-b 3, n-b 8	21	B 6, l-b 7, n-b 12	25
1/99 (2) 2/102 (3) 3/150 (1) 4/189 (5) 5/192 (6) 6/289 (4) 7/307 (7) 8/321 (9) 9/358 (8) 10/377 (10)	377	1/27 (2) 2/28 (1) 3/56 (4) 4/64 (5) 5/97 (3) 6/109 (6) 7/128 (7) 8/132 (9) 9/132 (10) 10/139 (8)	139

K. W. Hogg did not bat.

Bonus points – Lancashire 4, Sussex 3.

Bowling: *First Innings*—Hutchison 14–2–50–0; Taylor 24–8–56–3; Mushtaq Ahmed 48–10–124–6; Martin-Jenkins 9–1–48–0; Davis 26–2–86–1. *Second Innings*—Hutchison 2–0–20–0; Taylor 26–12–42–4; Mushtaq Ahmed 33.2–14–49–5; Davis 12–6–15–1.

Umpires: B. Dudleston and A. A. Jones.

At Colchester, August 20, 21, 22. SUSSEX beat ESSEX by an innings and 120 runs.

Rearguard rally: Matt Prior (*left*) and Mark Davis added 195 for the seventh wicket to resurrect Sussex's first innings against Middlesex.

Pictures by Mike Hewitt, Getty Images.

SUSSEX v MIDDLESEX

At Hove, September 5, 6, 7, 8. Sussex won by seven wickets. Sussex 22 pts, Middlesex 7 pts. Toss: Middlesex. Championship debut: C. T. Peploe.

Sussex supporters finally began to believe they could win the title after a remarkable fightback clinched their seventh win in nine games. On the second afternoon, they were 107 for six, 136 short of saving the follow-on. A new scoreboard clock had just been unveiled in memory of their late team-mate, Umer Rashid; perhaps minds had wandered. A day later, however, Davis walked off with a career-best 168, and Sussex's last four had added 430. The game was transformed by a seventh-wicket stand of 195. Prior reached his fourth century of 2003 with aggressive strokeplay; Davis accumulated patiently; even last man Taylor made his highest score. Middlesex lost four wickets wiping out arrears of 145, and only Weekes resisted long on the final day. Relishing a turning pitch, Mushtaq Ahmed collected his fifth ten-wicket haul of the season before Montgomerie guided Sussex home. Middlesex had also squandered a mighty first-day position after Strauss and Shah made entertaining centuries. Mushtaq went wicketless for 26 overs, then the floodgates opened – he took four of the last five for three runs in 17 balls. Players on both sides wore black armbands after the death of the former Sussex scorer Len Chandler earlier in the week.

Close of play: First day, Middlesex 392; Second day, Sussex 401-8 (Davis 97, Lewry 0); Third day, Middlesex 157-5 (Weekes 15, Peploe 0).

Middlesex

*A. J. Strauss c Prior b Martin-Jenkins	138	– c Ambrose b Lewry	4
S. G. Koenig b Lewry	5	– lbw b Martin-Jenkins	16
B. L. Hutton lbw b Lewry	1	– c Martin-Jenkins b Taylor	36
O. A. Shah lbw b Mushtaq Ahmed	140	– st Ambrose b Davis	34
E. C. Joyce lbw b Mushtaq Ahmed	22	– b Mushtaq Ahmed	31
P. N. Weekes c Ambrose b Mushtaq Ahmed	31	– c Prior b Mushtaq Ahmed	65
†D. C. Nash c Adams b Mushtaq Ahmed	15	– (8) b Lewry	5
S. J. Cook b Davis	11	– (9) b Mushtaq Ahmed	11
C. T. Peploe not out	0	– (7) lbw b Lewry	13
C. B. Keegan c Adams b Mushtaq Ahmed	3	– not out	3
J. H. Dawes c Prior b Mushtaq Ahmed	0	– lbw b Mushtaq Ahmed	2
B 7, l-b 13, n-b 6	26	B 11, l-b 11, n-b 8	30
1/17 (2) 2/33 (3) 3/252 (1) 4/309 (5) 5/334 (4) 6/374 (7) 7/387 (6) 8/387 (8) 9/390 (10) 10/392 (11)	392	1/4 (1) 2/42 (2) 3/79 (3) 4/124 (5) 5/152 (4) 6/201 (7) 7/215 (8) 8/241 (9) 9/244 (6) 10/250 (11)	250

Bonus points – Middlesex 4, Sussex 3.

Bowling: *First Innings*—Lewry 20–6–53–2; Taylor 15–2–66–0; Mushtaq Ahmed 40–4–145–6; Martin-Jenkins 14–2–46–1; Davis 11–0–62–1. *Second Innings*—Lewry 25–8–73–3; Taylor 10–1–30–1; Martin-Jenkins 7–3–12–1; Mushtaq Ahmed 35.2–8–80–4; Davis 19–4–33–1.

Sussex

M. W. Goodwin lbw b Dawes	14	– (2) lbw b Dawes	4
R. R. Montgomerie c Nash b Dawes	21	– (1) not out	54
P. A. Cottey c Hutton b Keegan	15	– lbw b Dawes	7
*C. J. Adams c Nash b Cook	20	– c Hutton b Weekes	30
†T. R. Ambrose c Hutton b Keegan	12	– not out	11
R. S. C. Martin-Jenkins c Hutton b Dawes	8		
M. J. Prior c Shah b Weekes	148		
M. J. G. Davis c Dawes b Keegan	168		
Mushtaq Ahmed c Shah b Weekes	57		
J. D. Lewry c Peploe b Keegan	21		
B. V. Taylor not out	35		
B 5, l-b 2, w 7, n-b 4	18	B 1, l-b 1	2
1/26 (1) 2/37 (2) 3/66 (3) 4/70 (4) 5/82 (5) 6/107 (6) 7/302 (7) 8/399 (9) 9/431 (10) 10/537 (8)	537	1/10 (2) 2/22 (3) 3/92 (4) (3 wkts)	108

Bonus points – Sussex 5, Middlesex 3 (130 overs: 469-9).

Bowling: *First Innings*—Dawes 35–2–126–3; Keegan 32.2–4–120–4; Cook 30–7–83–1; Peploe 28–2–100–0; Weekes 27–3–101–2. *Second Innings*—Keegan 7–2–29–0; Dawes 7–3–25–2; Cook 2–0–9–0; Peploe 6–2–20–0; Weekes 5.5–0–23–1.

Umpires: J. W. Holder and R. Palmer.

At Manchester, September 10, 11, 12, 13. SUSSEX lost to LANCASHIRE by an innings and 19 runs.

SUSSEX v LEICESTERSHIRE

At Hove, September 17, 18, 19. Sussex won by an innings and 55 runs. Sussex 22 pts, Leicestershire 1 pt. Toss: Leicestershire. First-class debut: L. J. Wright.

Sussex's long wait for their first Championship finally ended at 1.44 on the second afternoon. Goodwin pulled DeFreitas for four to secure their sixth bonus point, which ensured Lancashire could not catch them. The rest of the squad flooded on to the outfield, and play halted for eight minutes as they did a lap of honour while the county anthem "Sussex by the Sea" echoed around the old ground. It was an unforgettable moment for a near-full house bathed in late summer sunshine. Lengthier celebrations began after Sussex completed their tenth victory, with over a day to spare. There were several outstanding performances. Goodwin amassed an unbeaten 335, beating Duleepsinhji's 333 against Northamptonshire in 1930 as the highest score for Sussex. He batted eight hours nine minutes, striking 52 fours and a six in 390 balls; while the bowling often left a lot to be desired, it was a monumental effort of concentration and a glorious exhibition of back-foot strokeplay. Goodwin added 267 in three hours with Adams, who reached his fourth hundred in six games. And with the last ball before lunch on the opening day, Mushtaq Ahmed had bowled Hodge to become the first bowler since 1998 to reach 100 first-class wickets in a season. That wicket transformed the match. Leicestershire seemed in a mood to delay Sussex on another excellent pitch but, once Mushtaq broke through, they fell in a heap, losing nine for 68. Sussex scored 614 in little over three sessions against demoralised opponents. But Leicestershire's determination revived when the injured Mushtaq rested. Left-hander Sadler equalled his highest score and put on 208 with night-watchman Masters, who reached a maiden century. Then Lewry, making the old ball swing prodigiously, took five for six in 25 deliveries on his way to a career-best eight. A few minutes later, Adams was holding the trophy aloft and the party was in full swing.

Close of play: First day, Sussex 137-1 (Goodwin 71, Cottey 47); Second day, Leicestershire 38-2 (Masters 14, Walker 4).

Leicestershire

First innings		Second innings	
J. K. Maunders c Lewry b Martin-Jenkins	21	– c Martin-Jenkins b Lewry	15
D. L. Maddy c Cottey b Taylor	55	– (7) lbw b Lewry	29
B. J. Hodge b Mushtaq Ahmed	36	– (5) c Ambrose b Lewry	1
J. L. Sadler st Ambrose b Mushtaq Ahmed	0	– (6) b Lewry	145
†P. A. Nixon c Ambrose b Taylor	1	– (8) c Goodwin b Lewry	0
L. J. Wright c Montgomerie b Mushtaq Ahmed	0	– (9) not out	11
J. N. Snape c Ambrose b Lewry	13	– (2) c Adams b Taylor	1
*P. A. J. DeFreitas b Martin-Jenkins	23	– (10) b Lewry	0
V. C. Drakes c Ambrose b Martin-Jenkins	8	– (11) c Ambrose b Lewry	0
G. W. Walker not out	4	– (4) c sub b Lewry	21
D. D. Masters b Mushtaq Ahmed	2	– (3) c Martin-Jenkins b Taylor	119
B 5, l-b 6, w 1, n-b 4	16	B 8, l-b 14, n-b 16	38
1/42 (1) 2/111 (3) 3/117 (4) 4/117 (2) 5/118 (6) 6/118 (5) 7/142 (7) 8/167 (8) 9/174 (9) 10/179 (11)	179	1/16 (2) 2/20 (1) 3/65 (4) 4/69 (5) 5/277 (3) 6/353 (7) 7/353 (8) 8/370 (6) 9/370 (10) 10/380 (11)	380

Bonus points – Sussex 3.

Bowling: *First Innings*—Lewry 15–4–37–1; Taylor 18–6–40–2; Martin-Jenkins 12–6–20–3; Mushtaq Ahmed 24.5–3–71–4. *Second Innings*—Lewry 24.1–3–106–8; Taylor 21.2–6–84–2; Martin-Jenkins 9.4–0–60–0; Davis 25–9–75–0; Cottey 4–0–15–0; Goodwin 3–0–17–0; Adams 1–0–1–0.

Sussex

R. R. Montgomerie c Nixon b DeFreitas	10
M. W. Goodwin not out	335
P. A. Cottey c Nixon b DeFreitas	56
*C. J. Adams c Drakes b Walker	102
†T. R. Ambrose c Sadler b Hodge	82
B 12, l-b 9, n-b 8	29
1/24 (1) 2/151 (3) 3/418 (4) 4/614 (5) (4 wkts dec.)	614

R. S. C. Martin-Jenkins, M. J. Prior, M. J. G. Davis, Mushtaq Ahmed, J. D. Lewry and B. V. Taylor did not bat.

Bonus points – Sussex 5, Leicestershire 1.

Bowling: DeFreitas 28–4–94–2; Drakes 19–2–64–0; Masters 18–0–88–0; Maddy 4–0–21–0; Wright 19–0–95–0; Snape 12–0–72–0; Walker 19–1–92–1; Hodge 6–0–51–1; Maunders 1–0–16–0.

Umpires: T. E. Jesty and M. J. Kitchen.
(L. J. Lenham deputised for Kitchen on the second day.)

WARWICKSHIRE

Middling and muddling

Paul Bolton

The feeling that Warwickshire had overachieved in 2002 was confirmed by a season of moderate cricket and baffling selection policy, culminating in the resignation of their captain, Michael Powell. The county retained first-division status in both Championship and National League, albeit with a struggle, finishing mid-table in both, and reached the final of the inaugural Twenty20 Cup. Some teams would have considered this a satisfactory year, but not Warwickshire.

Powell bowed out with a Championship century at Canterbury, only his third in as many seasons in charge, but stepped down a few days later, citing his deteriorating batting form. Nick Knight was named as the sixth captain in nine seasons. The surprise was that Powell's was the only resignation. Warwickshire reported a record loss of £370,000 at the start of the year, which led to a series of cost-cutting measures. The second-largest playing staff in the country was pruned, and a proposal to make the players pay a contribution towards a pre-season trip to Portugal was dropped only after a threatened dressing-room revolt. Crisis management was evident on the field. A rotational selection policy, designed to keep as many players as possible involved in the first-team squad, meant Warwickshire rarely fielded their strongest available side.

John Inverarity, the former Australian all-rounder, spent his first season as director of coaching assessing the squad and the political situation at Edgbaston. He adopted a low profile, but sometimes Warwickshire would have preferred him to be more assertive. Inverarity inherited a squad that lacked bowling depth, and failed to find an adequate replacement for Shaun Pollock, a huge influence on and off the pitch in 2002. They had some bad luck: Shane Bond, the New Zealand fast bowler, was forced to withdraw by a back injury, and attempts to sign Anil Kumble, Muttiah Muralitharan, Brad Hogg, Adam Dale or Zaheer Khan came to nothing (though Hogg, the Australian left-arm wrist-spinner, later agreed to join in 2004).

But the gamble of recruiting Kenyan leg-spinner Collins Obuya backfired spectacularly. Obuya spent much of his three months in England in the second team before returning home with a knee injury. He had been signed because Warwickshire wanted a mystery spinner: the mystery was why they thought a player with such a moderate career record would be a match-winner. Michael Clark, a left-arm seamer from Western Australia standing in for Bond, broke down with a stress fracture of the back after just one match, and Corey Collymore, the West Indian seamer, lacked penetration when he replaced Obuya.

Clark, Collymore and Obuya took 14 Championship wickets between them, but Waqar Younis, the ageing Pakistan swing bowler, redeemed the

Dougie Brown

overseas players' record. He finished as the leading wicket-taker with 39, including 23 in his last three matches, which set up three of the season's four wins. Waqar's was a chance signing; he was visiting friends at Edgbaston when news of Bond's injury broke. Slower and more round-armed than in his previous stints in county cricket, for Surrey and Glamorgan, he still produced some devastating spells.

Alan Richardson was the most consistent of the English-qualified seamers, Dougie Brown the most productive. Brown's bowling became less effective as the season progressed – 18 wickets in his first five matches, another 18 in the next 11 – but his place was never under threat because he contributed 1,000 first-class runs for the first time. In one purple patch, he passed 50 eight times in ten Championship innings. His extra runs suggested some of the specialist batsmen did not spend long enough at the crease.

Knight and Mark Wagh, the other batsmen to pass 1,000, scored consistently, as did Jonathan Trott, an English-qualified South African, when he was given his chance. Powell missed five of the first six Championship matches with a broken toe. Jim Troughton began with centuries in the first three home games, but his form tailed off after he was called up for England's one-day squad. He looked uncomfortable at international level and was out of sorts after his return. Ian Bell failed to build on a century in May, in the win over eventual champions Sussex, and again saved his best efforts for one-day cricket. Tony Frost, preferred as wicket-keeper in the Championship for most of the season, failed to score sufficient runs and lost his place to Keith Piper in the closing stages.

Once again, Warwickshire's weak hand was spin bowling after Ashley Giles departed for England duty. Obuya's shortcomings and the failure of Jamie Spires, who suffered injury and run-up problems, meant that the former captain Neil Smith was recalled for six Championship matches, even though he was contracted for one-day cricket only.

Smith was eventually released after 17 years with the county, along with seamers Melvyn Betts, who moved to Middlesex, and Mohammad Sheikh. Betts appeared to have regained form after a miserable 2002 when he bowled Warwickshire to an early victory over Sussex, but fell away again. The decision to recall him for a farewell appearance against Lancashire, when he had already cleared his locker after being told he would not be offered a new contract, typified a summer of muddled thinking.

WARWICKSHIRE RESULTS

All first-class matches – Played 17: Won 4, Lost 5, Drawn 7, Tied 1.
County Championship matches – Played 16: Won 4, Lost 5, Drawn 6, Tied 1.

Frizzell County Championship, 5th in Division 1; Cheltenham & Gloucester Trophy, q-f; National Cricket League, 4th in Division 1; Twenty20 Cup, finalists.

COUNTY CHAMPIONSHIP AVERAGES

BATTING AND FIELDING

Cap		*M*	*I*	*NO*	*R*	*HS*	*100s*	*50s*	*Avge*	*Ct/St*
	C. O. Obuya§	2	4	2	95	55	0	1	47.50	1
1995	D. R. Brown	16	26	4	1,028	140*	3	7	46.72	10
2000	M. A. Wagh	16	30	3	1,228	138	3	7	45.48	15
1995	N. V. Knight	14	26	3	1,012	146	3	5	44.00	11
2002	J. O. Troughton	12	20	2	748	129*	3	2	41.55	5
	I. J. L. Trott	9	17	0	685	134	2	4	40.29	4
1996	A. F. Giles	6	10	1	338	96	0	2	37.55	0
	Waqar Younis§	8	13	5	268	61	0	2	33.50	1
1999	M. J. Powell	11	21	0	686	110	1	5	32.66	2
	M. A. Sheikh	5	7	3	129	57*	0	1	32.25	2
2001	M. M. Betts	9	13	2	327	73	0	2	29.72	2
2001	I. R. Bell	16	29	2	779	107	1	4	28.85	4
1999	T. Frost	12	20	1	401	84	0	3	21.10	31/2
	N. M. Carter	4	6	0	118	38	0	0	19.66	1
1992	K. J. Piper	4	7	0	137	42	0	0	19.57	12/1
1993	N. M. K. Smith	6	8	0	138	57	0	1	17.25	2
1991	D. P. Ostler	4	7	0	109	58	0	1	15.57	2
2002	A. Richardson	14	19	5	158	47	0	0	11.28	1
	C. D. Collymore§	5	8	3	25	11*	0	0	5.00	2

Also batted: M. W. Clark§ (1 match) 2*, 2; T. L. Penney (cap 1994) (1 match) 19, 2 (1 ct); G. G. Wagg (1 match) 11, 4.

§ *Overseas player.*

BOWLING

	O	*M*	*R*	*W*	*BB*	*5W/i*	*Avge*
Waqar Younis	244.2	39	917	39	5-40	3	23.51
D. R. Brown	377.5	81	1,274	36	5-72	2	35.38
M. A. Wagh	193.3	28	730	20	7-222	1	36.50
M. M. Betts	214.2	24	885	24	5-43	1	36.87
M. A. Sheikh	151	37	454	12	4-60	0	37.83
A. Richardson	453	104	1,314	33	4-37	0	39.81
A. F. Giles	198.5	36	577	13	5-115	1	44.38

Also bowled: I. R. Bell 78.3–10–346–5; N. M. Carter 103–13–443–8; M. W. Clark 33–7–110–3; C. D. Collymore 138–24–475–8; N. V. Knight 6–3–39–0; C. O. Obuya 36–2–180–3; D. P. Ostler 2–0–33–0; M. J. Powell 6–0–28–0; N. M. K. Smith 90.3–9–408–4; I. J. L. Trott 37.1–3–168–7; J. O. Troughton 13–0–85–0; G. G. Wagg 31–2–189–3.

COUNTY RECORDS

Highest score for:	501*	B. C. Lara v Durham at Birmingham	1994
Highest score against:	322	I. V. A. Richards (Somerset) at Taunton	1985
Best bowling for:	10-41	J. D. Bannister v Combined Services at Birmingham	1959
Best bowling against:	10-36	H. Verity (Yorkshire) at Leeds	1931
Highest total for:	810-4 dec.	v Durham at Birmingham	1994
Highest total against:	887	by Yorkshire at Birmingham	1896
Lowest total for:	16	v Kent at Tonbridge	1913
Lowest total against:	15	by Hampshire at Birmingham	1922

WARWICKSHIRE DIRECTORY

ADDRESS

County Ground, Edgbaston, Birmingham B5 7QU (0121 446 4422; fax 0121 446 4544; email info@thebears.co.uk). **Website** www.thebears.co.uk.

GROUNDS

Birmingham (Edgbaston): 1¼ miles S of city centre in B4217 Edgbaston Road at junction with A441 Pershore Road. Close to A38 Bristol Road. Nearest stations: Birmingham New Street (1¾ miles), Birmingham Moor Street (1¾ miles) and Birmingham Snow Hill (2¼ miles).

Stratford-on-Avon: ½ mile SE of town centre and bounded by River Avon to W. From A41 London Road L into Swan's Nest Lane before bridge over canal and river. Nearest station: Stratford-on-Avon (1½ miles).

OFFICIALS

Captain 2003 – M. J. Powell; 2004 – N. V. Knight
Director of coaching J. Inverarity
President The Rt Hon. Lord Guernsey
Chairman W. N. Houghton
Chief executive D. L. Amiss
Chairman, cricket committee T. A. Lloyd
Head groundsman S. J. Rouse
Scorer D. Wainwright

PLAYERS

Players expected to reappear in 2004

	Former counties	*Country*	*Born*	*Birthplace*
Bell Ian Ronald		E	11.4.1982	†*Walsgrave*
Brown Douglas Robert		E/SCO	29.10.1969	*Stirling*
Carter Neil Miller		SA (EU)	29.1.1975	*Cape Town*
Frost Tony		E	17.11.1975	*Stoke-on-Trent*
***Giles** Ashley Fraser		‡E	19.3.1973	*Chertsey*
***Knight** Nicholas Verity	Essex	E	28.11.1969	*Watford*
Ostler Dominic Piers		E	15.7.1970	†*Solihull*
Penney Trevor Lionel		E	12.6.1968	*Salisbury, Rhodesia*
Piper Keith John		E	18.12.1969	*Leicester*
Powell Michael James		E	5.4.1975	*Bolton*
Richardson Alan	Derbys	E	6.5.1975	*Newcastle-under-Lyme*
Trott Ian Jonathan Leonard		SA (EU)	22.4.1981	*Cape Town*
Troughton Jamie Oliver		E	2.3.1979	*Camden*
Wagg Graham Grant		E	28.4.1983	†*Rugby*
Wagh Mark Anant		E	20.10.1976	†*Birmingham*
Warren Nicholas Alexander		E	26.6.1982	†*Moseley*
Westwood Ian James		E	13.7.1982	†*Birmingham*

Player due to join in 2004

***Hogg** George Bradley		A	6.2.1971	*Narrogin*

** Test player. † Born in Warwickshire. ‡ 12-month ECB contract.*

At Nottingham, April 18, 19, 20, 21. WARWICKSHIRE lost to NOTTINGHAMSHIRE by three wickets.

WARWICKSHIRE v ESSEX

At Birmingham, April 23, 24, 25, 26. Tied. Warwickshire 12 pts, Essex 9 pts. Toss: Warwickshire.

Contrivance resuscitated a moribund contest and produced the first Championship tie in ten years as well as the first ever in the 1,207 first-class matches staged at Edgbaston. After nearly two days were washed out, a forfeiture and four overs of joke bowling opened up the game. Irani sustained the Essex pursuit of what would have been the highest fourth-innings total to beat Warwickshire, with a belligerent 87 including four sixes, while Giles posted attacking fields to keep them interested and absorbed some heavy punishment, notably when Irani and Flower put on 132 in 26 overs. But Giles kept chipping away and finally yorked Napier, charging down the pitch when Essex required a single from eight balls. On the first day, Troughton and Brown had rescued Warwickshire from a sticky start on a flat pitch, adding 201. Brown, the main aggressor, completed his first century for 20 months.

Close of play: First day, Warwickshire 411-7 (Troughton 107, Sheikh 17); Second day, Warwickshire 446-7 (Troughton 129, Sheikh 28); Third day, No play.

Warwickshire

N. V. Knight lbw b Irani	26
†T. Frost c Foster b Brant	59
M. A. Wagh c Foster b Brant	32
I. R. Bell lbw b Brant	18
J. O. Troughton not out	129
D. P. Ostler lbw b Dakin	18
D. R. Brown lbw b Napier	120
*A. F. Giles b Irani	1
M. A. Sheikh not out	28
B 5, l-b 6, n-b 4	15
1/44 (1) 2/122 (3) 3/135 (2) 4/154 (4) 5/176 (6) 6/377 (7) 7/386 (8)	(7 wkts dec.) 446

M. M. Betts and A. Richardson did not bat.

Bonus points – Warwickshire 5, Essex 2.

Bowling: Brant 30.1–5–133–3; Dakin 23–5–79–1; Irani 19–5–51–2; Napier 13–1–62–1; Middlebrook 19–4–62–0; Grayson 10–1–48–0.

Warwickshire forfeited their second innings.

Essex

	First innings	Second innings	
D. D. J. Robinson not out	42	– c Frost b Betts	56
W. I. Jefferson not out	20	– lbw b Sheikh	49
A. P. Grayson (did not bat)		– b Betts	28
A. Flower (did not bat)		– c Betts b Giles	55
A. Habib (did not bat)		– lbw b Giles	0
*R. C. Irani (did not bat)		– lbw b Giles	87
†J. S. Foster (did not bat)		– c Frost b Betts	24
J. M. Dakin (did not bat)		– lbw b Richardson	23
J. D. Middlebrook (did not bat)		– lbw b Giles	25
G. R. Napier (did not bat)		– b Giles	9
S. A. Brant (did not bat)		– not out	1
N-b 4	4	B 9, l-b 6, w 6, n-b 2	23
	(no wkt dec.) 66	1/88 (2) 2/128 (3) 3/147 (1) 4/148 (5) 5/280 (4) 6/300 (6) 7/330 (7) 8/365 (8) 9/379 (9) 10/380 (10)	380

Bowling: *First Innings*—Ostler 2–0–33–0; Knight 2–0–33–0. *Second Innings*—Betts 20–2–82–3; Richardson 17–0–70–1; Sheikh 18–5–54–1; Brown 7–0–44–0; Giles 27.5–3–115–5.

Umpires: R. Palmer and J. F. Steele.

At The Oval, April 30, May 1, 2, 3. WARWICKSHIRE drew with SURREY.

WARWICKSHIRE v SUSSEX

At Birmingham, May 9, 10, 11, 12. Warwickshire won by 234 runs. Warwickshire 22 pts, Sussex 7 pts. Toss: Warwickshire. County debut: I. J. L. Trott.

Jonathan Trott, an English-qualified South African and reputedly a distant relative of Victorian cricketers Albert and Harry Trott, put Warwickshire in control with an imperious maiden century. Trott, who had previously played for Boland and Western Province, became the first batsman since Brian Lara in 1994 to score a hundred on Warwickshire debut, and failed by only three runs to do it before lunch. Mushtaq Ahmed was made to work hard for his six wickets, before Warwickshire's last pair contributed 74 runs and two batting points. Sussex appeared to believe a defiant 125-run partnership between Ambrose and Prior had insured them against defeat; their out-cricket on the final morning was apathetic. Bell, with his first first-class century since September 2001, and Troughton had other ideas. An aggressive stand of 182 set up the declaration with 55 overs to go. On a pitch of increasingly low bounce, only Cottey resisted long against Betts and Brown.

Close of play: First day, Warwickshire 350-9 (Sheikh 39, Richardson 1); Second day, Sussex 116-3 (Cottey 12); Third day, Warwickshire 79-3 (Bell 35, Troughton 0).

Warwickshire

†T. Frost b Kirtley	37	– (2) c Prior b Lewry	0
I. J. L. Trott c Montgomerie b Mushtaq Ahmed	134	– (1) lbw b Lewry	5
M. A. Wagh b Mushtaq Ahmed	43	– lbw b Martin-Jenkins	38
I. R. Bell c Prior b Mushtaq Ahmed	3	– lbw b Davis	107
J. O. Troughton c Prior b Kirtley	41	– c sub b Davis	105
D. P. Ostler lbw b Mushtaq Ahmed	1	– b Martin-Jenkins	7
D. R. Brown c Ambrose b Mushtaq Ahmed	0	– c Montgomerie b Martin-Jenkins	0
*A. F. Giles lbw b Mushtaq Ahmed	22	– not out	13
M. A. Sheikh not out	57		
M. M. Betts c Cottey b Kirtley	20		
A. Richardson b Martin-Jenkins	47		
B 6, l-b 7, n-b 4	17	B 8, l-b 2	10
1/86 (1) 2/194 (3) 3/198 (4) 4/233 (2) 5/239 (6) 6/239 (7) 7/269 (5) 8/307 (8) 9/348 (10) 10/422 (11)	422	1/5 (1) 2/18 (2) 3/64 (3) 4/246 (4) 5/271 (6) 6/271 (7) 7/285 (5) (7 wkts dec.)	285

Bonus points – Warwickshire 5, Sussex 3.

Bowling: *First Innings*—Lewry 11–2–41–0; Kirtley 30–4–107–3; Martin-Jenkins 6.3–1–46–1; Mushtaq Ahmed 48–7–157–6; Davis 22–7–58–0. *Second Innings*—Kirtley 14–2–48–0; Lewry 9–1–51–2; Mushtaq Ahmed 13–0–69–0; Martin-Jenkins 13–3–57–3; Davis 9–0–50–2.

Sussex

R. R. Montgomerie lbw b Sheikh	41	– (2) lbw b Betts	0
M. W. Goodwin c Troughton b Sheikh	28	– (1) lbw b Betts	10
P. A. Cottey c Frost b Richardson	41	– lbw b Brown	55
*C. J. Adams b Sheikh	22	– b Betts	0
R. J. Kirtley c Brown b Giles	31	– (9) c Frost b Richardson	6
T. R. Ambrose lbw b Sheikh	85	– (5) lbw b Betts	0
R. S. C. Martin-Jenkins c Frost b Brown	7	– (6) b Betts	11
†M. J. Prior c Ostler b Betts	84	– (7) b Brown	5
M. J. G. Davis c Frost b Betts	1	– (8) lbw b Brown	0
Mushtaq Ahmed not out	2	– not out	7
J. D. Lewry b Betts	1	– b Brown	0
B 4, l-b 17, w 1, n-b 2	24	B 5, l-b 7	12
1/67 (2) 2/74 (1) 3/116 (4) 4/165 (3) 5/216 (5) 6/235 (7) 7/360 (8) 8/364 (9) 9/364 (6) 10/367 (11)	367	1/12 (1) 2/17 (2) 3/21 (4) 4/21 (5) 5/37 (6) 6/43 (7) 7/43 (8) 8/82 (9) 9/106 (3) 10/106 (11)	106

Bonus points – Sussex 4, Warwickshire 3.

Bowling: *First Innings*—Betts 23.4–2–83–3; Richardson 29–12–65–1; Brown 23–7–76–1; Sheikh 28–11–60–4; Giles 23–5–60–1; Wagh 2–1–2–0. *Second Innings*—Betts 13–2–43–5; Richardson 13–6–19–1; Sheikh 6–2–15–0; Brown 9–4–17–4; Giles 2–2–0–0.

Umpires: G. I. Burgess and I. J. Gould.

At Abergavenny, May 14, 15, 16 (not first-class). WARWICKSHIRE drew with CARDIFF UCCE (see Other UCCE Matches).

WARWICKSHIRE v KENT

At Birmingham, May 21, 22, 23, 24. Drawn. Warwickshire 10 pts, Kent 11 pts. Toss: Warwickshire.

Only Troughton and Walker gleaned any satisfaction from a game blighted by rain: Troughton scored his sixth Championship hundred in 12 months, Walker his first in almost two years. Powell took first use of a decent batting pitch, but survived a mere nine balls in his first first-class innings of the season after recovering from a broken toe, and Warwickshire slid to six for three inside half an hour. But Troughton rescued them with a majestic century, his third in consecutive home matches, and Smith followed up with a lively 57 in 69 balls spread over three days. On the final day, the captains opted to play for bonus points, and Walker took full advantage of perfunctory bowling and fielding.

Close of play: First day, Warwickshire 195-7 (Sheikh 5, Smith 2); Second day, Warwickshire 280-9 (Smith 38, Richardson 0); Third day, Kent 196-3 (Blewett 30, Walker 38).

Warwickshire

First innings		Second innings	
*M. J. Powell c Jones b Saggers	0	– c Jones b Ealham	30
†T. Frost c Tredwell b Trott	6		
M. A. Wagh c Ealham b Saggers	0	– not out	50
I. R. Bell c Blewett b Sheriyar	31	– not out	12
J. O. Troughton c Tredwell b Sheriyar	120		
I. J. L. Trott run out	9	– (2) c Ealham b Trego	31
D. R. Brown c Blewett b Saggers	18		
M. A. Sheikh c Walker b Saggers	5		
N. M. K. Smith c Tredwell b Saggers	57		
M. M. Betts c and b Trego	46		
A. Richardson not out	10		
B 1, l-b 3, w 1, n-b 4	9	W 1	1
1/4 (1) 2/6 (3) 3/6 (2) 4/77 (4) 5/113 (6) 6/170 (7) 7/193 (5) 8/195 (8) 9/275 (10) 10/311 (9)	311	1/50 (1) 2/98 (2) (2 wkts)	124

Bonus points – Warwickshire 3, Kent 3.

Bowling: *First Innings*—Saggers 23–5–62–5; Trott 17–2–90–1; Sheriyar 17–2–66–2; Ealham 12–2–39–0; Trego 8–0–43–1; Tredwell 1–0–7–0. *Second Innings*—Walker 4–0–25–0; Ealham 9–3–35–1; Blewett 6–0–27–0; Carberry 6–1–11–0; Trego 5–0–26–1.

Kent

Batsman	Runs
M. A. Carberry c Smith b Sheikh	58
J. C. Tredwell lbw b Betts	10
E. T. Smith b Sheikh	43
G. S. Blewett lbw b Brown	71
M. J. Walker b Richardson	106
*M. A. Ealham c Sheikh b Brown	9
†G. O. Jones c Frost b Brown	12
P. D. Trego c Wagh b Sheikh	13
M. J. Saggers not out	24
A. Sheriyar b Brown	2
B. J. Trott c Powell b Brown	0
L-b 9, w 5, n-b 14	28
1/13 (2) 2/102 (3) 3/129 (1) 4/273 (4) 5/295 (6) 6/308 (7) 7/327 (8) 8/371 (5) 9/374 (10) 10/376 (11)	376

Bonus points – Kent 4, Warwickshire 3.

Bowling: Betts 15–2–55–1; Richardson 23–3–91–1; Sheikh 36–4–110–3; Bell 3–0–10–0; Brown 19.5–5–72–5; Smith 8–2–26–0; Wagh 2–1–3–0.

Umpires: D. J. Constant and T. E. Jesty.

WARWICKSHIRE v NOTTINGHAMSHIRE

At Birmingham, June 4, 5, 6, 7. Drawn. Warwickshire 9 pts, Nottinghamshire 12 pts. Toss: Warwickshire. Championship debut: C. O. Obuya.

Pietersen, a Warwickshire triallist in 2000, plundered his third double-century in three years. He faced 270 balls in 337 minutes, and struck 27 fours and four sixes, one of which sailed over the pavilion and narrowly missed the car of the Warwickshire chief executive, Dennis Amiss. Pietersen and Cairns pulverised the attack to add 273, the centrepiece of Nottinghamshire's highest total since 1947 and the biggest conceded by Warwickshire since 1928. After three heavy defeats, Nottinghamshire – 295 ahead on first innings – scented their first Championship win since beating Warwickshire in the opening game. But Knight defied them for nearly five hours before falling to MacGill's persistent leg-spin, and Collins Obuya, more impressive as a batsman than as a leg-spinner, also supervised spirited resistance. Nottinghamshire finally needed 111 in 12 overs; Waqar Younis, on Championship debut for his third county, had them five down after ten.

Close of play: First day, Warwickshire 351-9 (Obuya 55, Waqar Younis 15); Second day, Nottinghamshire 389-3 (Pietersen 140, Cairns 52); Third day, Warwickshire 138-1 (Knight 85, Wagh 15).

Warwickshire

N. V. Knight c Noon b Smith	33	– lbw b MacGill	146
I. J. L. Trott c Franks b Smith	63	– b Pietersen	28
M. A. Wagh b Smith	58	– lbw b MacGill	39
I. R. Bell c Noon b Franks	21	– b MacGill	64
J. O. Troughton c Shafayat b Franks	0	– lbw b Pietersen	5
†T. Frost run out	11	– c Gallian b MacGill	15
*D. R. Brown c Pietersen b MacGill	40	– c Welton b Smith	20
M. A. Sheikh c Noon b Pietersen	13	– b MacGill	8
C. O. Obuya c Noon b Smith	55	– not out	30
M. M. Betts c Smith b Malik	6	– b Pietersen	11
Waqar Younis not out	15	– lbw b MacGill	8
B 2, l-b 13, w 1, n-b 20	36	B 13, l-b 6, n-b 12	31
1/104 (1) 2/109 (2) 3/184 (4) 4/184 (5) 5/198 (6) 6/216 (3) 7/238 (8) 8/298 (7) 9/309 (10) 10/351 (9)	351	1/113 (2) 2/198 (3) 3/270 (1) 4/297 (5) 5/312 (6) 6/317 (4) 7/329 (8) 8/350 (7) 9/385 (10) 10/405 (11)	405

Bonus points – Warwickshire 4, Nottinghamshire 3.

Bowling: *First Innings*—Smith 15.3–4–60–4; Malik 19–1–102–1; Franks 20–2–80–2; MacGill 28–4–75–1; Pietersen 5–2–19–1. *Second Innings*—Smith 21–4–85–1; Malik 5–0–24–0; MacGill 47.4–10–117–6; Franks 13–1–57–0; Pietersen 29–3–95–3; Shafayat 2–0–8–0.

Nottinghamshire

G. E. Welton c Knight b Bell	99	– (2) b Waqar Younis	11
*J. E. R. Gallian c Wagh b Betts	6	– (5) not out	6
U. Afzaal b Wagh	72	– (1) c Troughton b Waqar Younis	28
K. P. Pietersen c and b Obuya	221	– (3) c sub b Waqar Younis	6
C. L. Cairns c Frost b Sheikh	104		
B. M. Shafayat b Waqar Younis	11	– b Waqar Younis	8
P. J. Franks not out	62	– (4) c Frost b Sheikh	1
†W. M. Noon c Frost b Bell	25	– (7) not out	0
M. N. Malik c Knight b Obuya	10		
G. J. Smith c Knight b Obuya	0		
S. C. G. MacGill c and b Bell	0		
B 12, l-b 5, w 4, n-b 15	36	B 5, l-b 1, w 1	7
1/14 (2) 2/160 (3) 3/244 (1) 4/517 (4) 5/536 (6) 6/564 (5) 7/616 (8) 8/639 (9) 9/639 (10) 10/646 (11)	646	1/25 (2) 2/52 (3) 3/52 (1) 4/55 (4) 5/66 (6)	(5 wkts) 67

Bonus points – Nottinghamshire 5, Warwickshire 1 (130 overs: 537-5).

Bowling: *First Innings*—Waqar Younis 25–3–84–1; Betts 4–1–7–1; Sheikh 36–9–94–1; Brown 25–2–127–0; Obuya 17–1–91–3; Wagh 21–3–93–1; Bell 14.3–1–79–3; Trott 12–0–54–0. *Second Innings*—Waqar Younis 6–1–30–4; Sheikh 4–0–30–1; Wagh 1–0–1–0.

Umpires: B. Dudleston and M. J. Kitchen.

At Hove, June 27, 28, 29. WARWICKSHIRE lost to SUSSEX by an innings and 59 runs.

At Leicester, July 2, 3, 4, 5. WARWICKSHIRE drew with LEICESTERSHIRE.

WARWICKSHIRE v SURREY

At Birmingham, July 9, 10, 11, 12. Surrey won by 135 runs. Surrey 21 pts, Warwickshire 4 pts. Toss: Surrey.

Wayward bowling and slipshod fielding handed Surrey the initiative, and Warwickshire were barracked by disgruntled supporters as they fell to defeat. In all, they conceded 805 runs – 526 in boundaries. On the first day, Stewart scored his sixth fifty in nine first-class innings and Hollioake made a run-a-ball 88. Their stand of 150 sustained Surrey between two eventful overs from Carter which brought five wickets – though he also went for nearly five an over in his first Championship match of the season. Warwickshire put down four catches, and their batsmen squandered a promising start when a burst of three wickets in eight balls from Azhar Mahmood helped Surrey to a 110-run lead. Butcher and Ramprakash extended that with some vivid strokeplay, adding 187 in 35 overs of increasingly dispirited bowling. Challenged to score 561 in 173 overs, Warwickshire batted far more credibly, reached their highest-ever fourth-innings total (beating the Kallicharran-inspired 417 for two against Glamorgan in 1983) but, with the pitch turning for Saqlain Mushtaq, it was nowhere near enough.

Close of play: First day, Warwickshire 85-1 (Knight 37, Wagh 9); Second day, Surrey 282-3 (Ramprakash 121, Stewart 27); Third day, Warwickshire 304-5 (Frost 8, Brown 2).

Surrey

I. J. Ward c Knight b Wagg	23	– c Frost b Waqar Younis	9
M. A. Butcher c Trott b Waqar Younis	28	– c Frost b Smith	118
M. R. Ramprakash c Frost b Carter	18	– not out	182
G. P. Thorpe lbw b Carter	30	– c and b Smith	4
†A. J. Stewart c Frost b Carter	74	– b Brown	45
*A. J. Hollioake c Wagh b Brown	88	– lbw b Wagg	30
Azhar Mahmood c Frost b Wagg	13	– not out	50
M. P. Bicknell not out	25		
I. D. K. Salisbury c Frost b Carter	0		
Saqlain Mushtaq c Trott b Carter	0		
J. Ormond b Brown	33		
B 4, l-b 3, w 4, n-b 12	23	B 3, l-b 7, n-b 2	12
1/47 (2) 2/56 (1) 3/102 (4) 4/103 (3) 5/253 (6) 6/288 (7) 7/288 (5) 8/288 (9) 9/288 (10) 10/355 (11)	355	1/20 (1) 2/207 (2) 3/219 (4) 4/319 (5) 5/364 (6)	(5 wkts dec.) 450

Bonus points – Surrey 4, Warwickshire 3.

Bowling: *First Innings*—Waqar Younis 17–7–65–1; Carter 17–0–75–5; Wagg 18–2–101–2; Brown 17.2–4–59–2; Smith 7–0–34–0; Bell 3–0–14–0. *Second Innings*—Waqar Younis 14–1–81–1; Wagg 13–0–88–1; Carter 20–3–81–0; Brown 12–0–74–1; Smith 22–1–111–2; Bell 1–0–5–0.

Warwickshire

*M. J. Powell c Azhar Mahmood b Salisbury	27	– b Ormond	91
N. V. Knight c Ormond b Azhar Mahmood	42	– lbw b Bicknell	8
M. A. Wagh lbw b Azhar Mahmood	34	– c Stewart b Hollioake	51
I. R. Bell c Stewart b Bicknell	1	– c Salisbury b Saqlain Mushtaq	71
I. J. L. Trott lbw b Azhar Mahmood	1	– lbw b Hollioake	51
†T. Frost c Butcher b Azhar Mahmood	24	– b Saqlain Mushtaq	12
D. R. Brown lbw b Ormond	61	– c Thorpe b Saqlain Mushtaq	56
G. G. Wagg c Stewart b Bicknell	11	– c sub b Saqlain Mushtaq	4
N. M. K. Smith c sub b Bicknell	1	– c Salisbury b Saqlain Mushtaq	8
N. M. Carter c Thorpe b Ormond	20	– lbw b Salisbury	11
Waqar Younis not out	0	– not out	30
L-b 4, w 5, n-b 14	23	B 8, l-b 14, n-b 10	32
1/62 (1) 2/114 (2) 3/116 (3) 4/120 (5) 5/120 (4) 6/195 (6) 7/224 (7) 8/224 (8) 9/245 (10) 10/245 (9)	245	1/39 (2) 2/138 (3) 3/188 (1) 4/293 (5) 5/296 (4) 6/321 (6) 7/327 (8) 8/351 (9) 9/387 (10) 10/425 (7)	425

Bonus points – Warwickshire 1, Surrey 3.

Bowling: *First Innings*—Bicknell 21.2–4–62–3; Ormond 15–3–57–2; Azhar Mahmood 16–4–61–4; Salisbury 6–2–20–1; Saqlain Mushtaq 10–0–41–0. *Second Innings*—Bicknell 11–5–31–1; Ormond 17–3–83–1; Hollioake 11–2–32–2; Azhar Mahmood 10–0–53–0; Salisbury 29–2–70–1; Saqlain Mushtaq 35.1–3–134–5.

Umpires: J. H. Hampshire and M. J. Harris.

At Southgate, July 15, 16, 17, 18. WARWICKSHIRE drew with MIDDLESEX.

At Manchester, July 23, 24, 25, 26. WARWICKSHIRE drew with LANCASHIRE.

At Birmingham, July 30, 31, August 1, 2. WARWICKSHIRE drew with INDIA A (see India A tour section).

WARWICKSHIRE v LEICESTERSHIRE

At Birmingham, August 14, 15, 16. Warwickshire won by eight wickets. Warwickshire 19 pts, Leicestershire 5.5 pts (after 0.5 pt penalty). Toss: Warwickshire. County debut: C. D. Collymore.

Leicestershire surrendered control with a collapse on the second evening and wasteful bowling on the third afternoon. A fifth defeat left them rooted in the relegation zone. Waqar Younis sparked their downfall in both innings, with two bursts of three wickets in two overs, but his 61 in 55 balls, only the sixth fifty of a 16-year career, proved equally decisive. On the opening day, Leicestershire reached 228 for two but a vintage spell of reverse swing from Waqar ended their hopes of a huge score and his aggression with the bat saved Warwickshire from following on. Set a potentially testing target, they made light of it with Knight's third century of the season. Leicestershire helped Warwickshire accelerate to their first Championship victory since May by conceding 70 in ten overs when Knight and Wagh were at their most dominant.

Close of play: First day, Warwickshire 15-1 (Powell 2, Richardson 5); Second day, Leicestershire 121-6 (Nixon 5, Masters 0).

Leicestershire

J. K. Maunders c Knight b Bell	38	– c Brown b Carter	10
D. L. Maddy c Waqar Younis b Collymore	51	– c Carter b Wagh	44
B. J. Hodge lbw b Waqar Younis	70	– lbw b Waqar Younis	35
T. R. Ward b Waqar Younis	42	– (9) lbw b Waqar Younis	0
J. L. Sadler not out	59	– (4) lbw b Wagh	4
†P. A. Nixon lbw b Waqar Younis	0	– (7) not out	33
D. G. Brandy lbw b Richardson	6	– (5) c Bell b Waqar Younis	0
*P. A. J. DeFreitas c Frost b Richardson	0	– (10) lbw b Wagh	37
V. C. Drakes lbw b Richardson	17	– (11) lbw b Wagh	0
D. D. Masters st Frost b Wagh	9	– (8) b Richardson	3
M. J. A. Whiley b Brown	16	– (6) c Wagh b Waqar Younis	4
B 4, l-b 21, w 9, n-b 4	38	B 2, l-b 18, w 1, n-b 4	25
1/103 (1) 2/107 (2) 3/228 (3) 4/235 (4) 5/235 (6) 6/252 (7) 7/252 (8) 8/277 (9) 9/301 (10) 10/346 (11)	346	1/29 (1) 2/98 (2) 3/112 (4) 4/112 (3) 5/116 (6) 6/117 (5) 7/128 (8) 8/129 (9) 9/195 (10) 10/195 (11)	195

Bonus points – Leicestershire 3, Warwickshire 3.

Bowling: *First Innings*—Waqar Younis 18–2–52–3; Carter 16–5–53–0; Richardson 16–3–55–3; Collymore 18–4–71–1; Bell 3–0–11–1; Brown 11–4–31–1; Wagh 15–5–48–1. *Second Innings*—Waqar Younis 13–1–37–4; Carter 8–3–11–1; Collymore 10–2–36–0; Richardson 17–5–34–1; Brown 13–2–37–0; Wagh 10.4–2–20–4.

Warwickshire

*M. J. Powell c Maddy b Masters	28	– b DeFreitas	13
N. V. Knight b Drakes	0	– not out	122
A. Richardson b Drakes	12		
M. A. Wagh lbw b Masters	3	– (3) lbw b Maddy	58
I. R. Bell c Hodge b Masters	4	– (4) retired hurt	7
J. O. Troughton c Hodge b Whiley	41	– (5) not out	55
†T. Frost c Nixon b Whiley	10		
D. R. Brown not out	56		
N. M. Carter c Nixon b Maddy	30		
Waqar Younis b Maddy	61		
C. D. Collymore lbw b Maddy	2		
L-b 12, w 6, n-b 12	30	B 5, l-b 2, w 1, n-b 4	12
1/1 (2) 2/35 (3) 3/54 (4) 4/58 (5) 5/63 (1) 6/86 (7) 7/138 (6) 8/180 (9) 9/272 (10) 10/277 (11)	277	1/20 (1) 2/127 (3)	(2 wkts) 267

Bonus points – Warwickshire 2, Leicestershire 3.

In the second innings Bell retired hurt at 161.

Bowling: *First Innings*—Drakes 15–4–42–2; Whiley 16–1–77–2; Masters 10–1–40–3; DeFreitas 16–1–67–0; Maddy 9.2–3–29–3; Brandy 2–0–10–0. *Second Innings*—Drakes 12–5–31–0; Whiley 7–0–59–0; DeFreitas 14–3–40–1; Masters 13–2–59–0; Maddy 12–1–51–1; Sadler 0.5–0–20–0.

Umpires: J. W. Holder and P. Willey.

WARWICKSHIRE v MIDDLESEX

At Birmingham, August 26, 27, 28, 29. Warwickshire won by 31 runs. Warwickshire 18 pts (after 1 pt penalty), Middlesex 5 pts. Toss: Middlesex.

Tentative batting on a pitch of variable bounce cost Middlesex victory. They needed only 88 on the final day with eight wickets standing, but surrendered their last seven for 30. Richardson culled three in an over and Waqar Younis produced some devastating swing to finish with nine in the match. Both sides' batting was as uneven as the wicket. On the opening day, Powell and Wagh played pleasantly, while Brown passed 50 for the sixth time running, but none of their team-mates managed 30. Middlesex, without an official overseas player, found it no easier, until Joyce returned to form with a brave hundred, achieved with the help of Bloomfield, who held out with him for 13 overs. Leading by four, Warwickshire were back in trouble before a resourceful stand between Troughton, showing a glimpse of the form that attracted the England selectors, and Piper, in his first Championship game of 2003, gave them a chance. Strauss took Middlesex halfway to their target, and Shah had just hit Wagh for six when they went off for bad light. The mood on the final day was very different.

Close of play: First day, Middlesex 78-2 (Weston 29, Shah 36); Second day, Warwickshire 113-6 (Troughton 29, Piper 10); Third day, Middlesex 115-2 (Hutton 36, Shah 6).

Warwickshire

First innings		Second innings	
*M. J. Powell c Shah b Hutton	73	lbw b Keegan	1
N. V. Knight b Keegan	10	b Cook	9
M. A. Wagh st Nash b Weekes	62	lbw b Bloomfield	46
I. R. Bell c Weekes b Keegan	27	b Keegan	0
J. O. Troughton b Cook	0	c Nash b Bloomfield	64
D. R. Brown c Strauss b Cook	71	b Bloomfield	0
A. F. Giles b Hutton	7	c and b Weekes	9
†K. J. Piper c Dalrymple b Keegan	8	c Cook b Keegan	42
Waqar Younis c Cook b Weekes	0	not out	13
C. D. Collymore not out	11	c Cook b Bloomfield	1
A. Richardson run out	0	c Dalrymple b Keegan	4
B 1, l-b 7, w 1, n-b 12	21	B 4, l-b 5	9
1/21 (2) 2/117 (1) 3/155 (4) 4/156 (5) 5/230 (3) 6/251 (7) 7/261 (8) 8/264 (9) 9/288 (6) 10/290 (11)	290	1/12 (2) 2/12 (1) 3/20 (4) 4/75 (3) 5/75 (6) 6/99 (7) 7/180 (5) 8/182 (8) 9/184 (10) 10/198 (11)	198

Bonus points – Warwickshire 2, Middlesex 3.

Bowling: *First Innings*—Keegan 23.5–5–76–3; Bloomfield 12–0–74–0; Cook 22–9–46–2; Hutton 10–0–43–2; Joyce 2–0–15–0; Weekes 11–2–28–2. *Second Innings*—Keegan 25–4–67–4; Cook 17–5–53–1; Bloomfield 15–1–57–4; Weekes 5–2–8–1; Dalrymple 2–0–4–0.

Middlesex

First innings		Second innings	
*A. J. Strauss b Waqar Younis	0	lbw b Wagh	61
R. M. S. Weston c Piper b Collymore	31	b Waqar Younis	6
B. L. Hutton lbw b Waqar Younis	5	lbw b Collymore	37
O. A. Shah lbw b Collymore	54	c Piper b Richardson	25
E. C. Joyce c and b Wagh	107	b Waqar Younis	9
P. N. Weekes lbw b Brown	23	lbw b Richardson	7
†D. C. Nash c Brown b Giles	4	c Piper b Waqar Younis	5
J. W. M. Dalrymple c Piper b Collymore	12	b Richardson	0
S. J. Cook c Troughton b Waqar Younis	9	lbw b Waqar Younis	0
C. B. Keegan c Wagh b Waqar Younis	9	not out	3
T. F. Bloomfield not out	9	b Waqar Younis	9
B 4, l-b 8, w 5, n-b 6	23	L-b 1, n-b 8	9
1/0 (1) 2/24 (3) 3/98 (4) 4/99 (2) 5/151 (6) 6/166 (7) 7/199 (8) 8/232 (9) 9/242 (10) 10/286 (5)	286	1/17 (2) 2/109 (1) 3/118 (3) 4/141 (5) 5/151 (4) 6/154 (6) 7/154 (8) 8/158 (7) 9/159 (9) 10/171 (11)	171

Bonus points – Middlesex 2, Warwickshire 3.

Bowling: *First Innings*—Waqar Younis 18–5–69–4; Collymore 14–1–42–3; Richardson 10–1–50–0; Giles 28–9–69–1; Bell 2–0–14–0; Wagh 3–0–12–1; Brown 11–2–18–1. *Second Innings*—Waqar Younis 13.5–2–40–5; Collymore 15–5–39–1; Richardson 18–4–40–3; Brown 4–1–14–0; Wagh 8–1–30–1; Giles 6–2–7–0.

Umpires: J. H. Evans and N. J. Llong.

WARWICKSHIRE v LANCASHIRE

At Birmingham, September 3, 4, 5, 6. Lancashire won by an innings and 145 runs. Lancashire 21 pts, Warwickshire 6 pts. Toss: Warwickshire. Championship debut: S. P. Crook.

This was a game for statisticians, Lancastrians and lovers of brilliant strokeplay. Lancashire's 781 was the season's highest total, their third-biggest ever and the third-best at Edgbaston. Chilton, Loye, Law and Hooper made history as the first four batsmen to score hundreds in the same innings twice; a fortnight earlier, they did it against Middlesex. Chilton and Loye added 222, Law and Hooper 360 – a county fifth-wicket record and 11 short of their all-wicket best. Hooper was the most spectacular, with eight sixes and 16 fours, one of which umpire Constant signalled from the floor after diving for safety. With Brown unfit to bowl, a heavy burden fell on Wagh, whose off-breaks earned a career-best seven wickets, though he was one run short of Warwickshire's most expensive analysis. Among totals at Edgbaston, the 781 failed to match only Yorkshire's 107-year-old 887 and the Lara-led 810 for four declared by Warwickshire against Durham in 1994. Lancashire's exploits on a featherbed pitch overshadowed first-day centuries from Trott and Brown, who was interrupted when he strained a calf muscle. Second time round, Warwickshire were demoralised: even a thunderstorm, which cost two and a half hours when they were six down, could not save them. The Lancashire players, scorer and coach driver helped to mop up, then Chapple struck three times in four balls. Brown, with a runner, and last man Richardson resisted for 13 overs but, with four to go, Anglo-Australian Steven Crook completed a win that just kept Lancashire's title hopes alive.

Close of play: First day, Warwickshire 342-6 (Piper 14, Betts 0); Second day, Lancashire 278-4 (Law 11, Hooper 1); Third day, Lancashire 781.

HIGHEST PARTNERSHIPS FOR LANCASHIRE

371 for 2nd	F. Watson and E. Tyldesley v Surrey at Manchester	1928
368 for 1st	A. C. MacLaren and R. H. Spooner v Gloucestershire at Liverpool	1903
364 for 3rd	M. A. Atherton and N. H. Fairbrother v Surrey at The Oval	1990
363 for 2nd	A. C. MacLaren and A. Paul v Somerset at Taunton	1895
360 for 5th	**S. G. Law and C. L. Hooper v Warwickshire at Birmingham**	**2003**
358 for 4th	S. P. Titchard and G. D. Lloyd v Essex at Chelmsford	1996
350* for 1st	C. Washbrook and W. Place v Sussex at Manchester	1947

LOTS FOR PLENTY

Seven or more wickets in a first-class innings at a cost of more than 200 runs:

8-287	G. Giffen	South Australia v New South Wales at Adelaide	1899-1900
8-218	E. J. Tyler	Somerset v Gloucestershire at Bristol	1898
7-254	P. Thakur	Haryana v Bombay at Faridabad	1993-94
7-227	Shahid Aziz	Punjab B v PIA at Karachi	1975-76
7-223	J. H. Pennington	Nottinghamshire v South Africans at Nottingham	1904
7-222	**M. A. Wagh**	**Warwickshire v Lancashire at Birmingham**	**2003**
7-220	Kapil Dev	India v Pakistan at Faisalabad	1982-83
7-220	Saeed Ajmal	Faisalabad v Karachi Whites at Karachi	1996-97
7-216	G. H. S. Trott	Victoria v South Australia at Adelaide	1887-88
7-207	C. L. Townsend	Gloucestershire v Yorkshire at Bristol	1897
7-204	A. E. Trott	Middlesex v Sussex at Hove	1900
7-202	A. S. Kennedy	Hampshire v Middlesex at Lord's	1919
7-201	C. H. Ellis	Sussex v Surrey at Hove	1863

Research: Philip Bailey

Warwickshire

*M. J. Powell c Hegg b Chapple	0 – c Law b Chapple	4
N. V. Knight lbw b Chapple	28 – b Chapple	3
M. A. Wagh b Chapple	20 – c Crook b Wood	16
I. J. L. Trott b Hogg	126 – c Loye b Keedy	43
I. R. Bell c Hooper b Hogg	3 – b Keedy	46
T. L. Penney lbw b Wood	19 – b Hogg	2
D. R. Brown not out	140 – b Crook	44
†K. J. Piper c Hooper b Wood	15 – c Sutcliffe b Chapple	6
M. M. Betts lbw b Crook	73 – b Chapple	0
C. D. Collymore c Hegg b Keedy	0 – b Chapple	0
A. Richardson c Hooper b Keedy	2 – not out	4
B 1, l-b 14, w 2, n-b 6	23 L-b 2, w 1, n-b 16	19
1/0 (1) 2/46 (3) 3/55 (2) 4/64 (5) 5/101 (6) 6/317 (4) 7/357 (8) 8/446 (9) 9/447 (10) 10/449 (11)	449 1/6 (1) 2/11 (2) 3/39 (3) 4/111 (4) 5/114 (6) 6/126 (5) 7/143 (8) 8/143 (9) 9/143 (10) 10/187 (7)	187

Bonus points – Warwickshire 5, Lancashire 2 (130 overs: 446-8).

In the first innings Brown, when 112, retired hurt at 338 and resumed at 357.

Bowling: *First Innings*—Chapple 28–6–92–3; Wood 23–3–101–2; Hogg 24–7–66–2; Crook 12–1–52–1; Keedy 26.5–4–84–2; Hooper 7–0–16–0; Chilton 10–4–15–0; Law 2–0–8–0. *Second Innings*—Chapple 20–7–86–5; Wood 9–1–32–1; Hogg 7–3–24–1; Keedy 18–9–33–2; Hooper 2–0–4–0; Crook 1.1–0–6–1.

Lancashire

M. J. Chilton b Richardson	121
I. J. Sutcliffe c Piper b Collymore	16
M. B. Loye c Richardson b Wagh	102
G. Keedy c Penney b Wagh	0
S. G. Law c Wagh b Richardson	168
C. L. Hooper c Collymore b Wagh	177
G. Chapple st Piper b Wagh	60
*†W. K. Hegg c Trott b Wagh	12
K. W. Hogg c Collymore b Wagh	31
S. P. Crook c sub b Wagh	27
J. Wood not out	0
B 8, l-b 5, w 6, n-b 48	67
1/42 (2) 2/264 (3) 3/264 (4) 4/266 (1) 5/626 (6) 6/669 (5) 7/716 (8) 8/730 (7) 9/764 (10) 10/781 (9)	781

Bonus points – Lancashire 5, Warwickshire 1 (130 overs: 546-4).

Bowling: Betts 26–2–151–0; Collymore 30–5–99–1; Richardson 45–8–128–2; Bell 16–5–70–0; Wagh 39.5–2–222–7; Trott 12–0–70–0; Powell 6–0–28–0.

Umpires: D. J. Constant and A. A. Jones.

At Chelmsford, September 11, 12, 13, 14. WARWICKSHIRE beat ESSEX by nine wickets.

At Canterbury, September 17, 18, 19. WARWICKSHIRE lost to KENT by an innings and 70 runs.

WORCESTERSHIRE

Giving no quarter

JOHN CURTIS

Tom Moody achieved his prime objective for 2003 by guiding Worcestershire to the first division of the County Championship for the first time. After drawing their opening three games, they won ten of their next 12 to guarantee promotion before their meeting with Northamptonshire, the only side that could deny them the second division title, in the last Championship match of the summer.

In a controversial game, Ben Smith declared, still 24 behind, at the fall of the eighth wicket, so depriving Northamptonshire of the chance of a third bowling point, which could have seen them squeeze past Worcestershire by a mere quarter-point. Smith's side later succumbed to their only first-class defeat of the season, but took the title, initially by three-quarters of a point – and then by another eight after Northamptonshire were penalised for preparing a pitch that took spin pretty much from the word go.

However, the celebrations were tempered by relegation in the National League, just 12 months after finishing as runners-up. A dire run of eight defeats gave their limited-overs season a depressing end, undoing some earlier outstanding performances in the C&G that had seen Worcestershire to their first one-day final in nine years. But an embarrassing Lord's defeat by Gloucestershire formed part of that unhappy sequence.

Those setbacks aside, the overall signs were encouraging: slowly but surely, Moody seemed to have gathered a side that could gel together – and might yet rekindle some of the success of the Botham–Dilley era. Before that, however, some questions must be answered, especially concerning the batting. Graeme Hick, a foot soldier again after being relieved of the captaincy, experienced his leanest season in living memory, while Vikram Solanki could not manage 500 Championship runs from 20 innings.

The key to Worcestershire's four-day success, though, was an attack not reliant on a single bowler. Four of them – the pacemen Nantie Hayward, Matt Mason and Kabir Ali, and the off-spinner Gareth Batty (who made his Test debut in the autumn) – picked up 50-plus first-class wickets by making intelligent use of Worcester's bowler-friendly conditions. Of the six home Championship wins, five came within three days' playing time. Inconsistent bounce was a major worry – a familiar, unwelcome side-effect of attempts to quicken the New Road wickets – and Worcestershire twice survived visits from ECB pitch inspectors. Within 48 hours of the curtain coming down on the season, Tim Packwood and his groundstaff began remedial work across the entire square.

After upsetting the South Africa selectors by declaring his unwillingness to play international cricket, Hayward had a mixed season. Not the most sociable of players, it took him a while to fit into the dressing-room. But he bowled with genuine fire and pace in unsettling the top order, and had the useful knack of polishing off the tail. He was perhaps flattered by his 67 wickets, and proved expensive in one-day games. In February, the county decided they would rather have the whole-hearted Australian Andy Bichel for 2004, alongside Hayward's compatriot, Andrew Hall, whose dramatic last over in the C&G semi-final against Lancashire made him an instant hero.

Kabir Ali

If a lack of trust in the wickets contributed to Hick not recapturing his touch after returning in late July from breaking a bone in his hand, it did not hold back Ben Smith. He proved that application would bring its rewards by accumulating 1,289 runs – his best yet – with 14 scores of 50 or more. For the first time, Stephen Peters completed 1,000 runs, though in 2004 he will have a new opening partner after Anurag Singh asked to be released, and joined Nottinghamshire. Much is expected of Kadeer Ali, who fell one short of a maiden hundred against Yorkshire, and joined the England Academy over the winter.

His cousin, Kabir, continued to make progress and was rewarded with an international debut, against Zimbabwe, though rain meant he never touched the ball. However, he managed five South African wickets in his first Test, at Headingley, before his form faded in the final month of the season. Much to his disappointment, Kabir missed out on the overseas tours, but the England management insisted he remained in their plans.

But it was Mason, described by Smith as our "Rock of Gibraltar", who made biggest strides after admitting he had found county cricket's punishing schedule difficult to cope with in 2002. He was the only bowler to perform consistently in the Championship and in the one-day game, where Worcestershire often struggled to bowl a consistent line and length.

They could perhaps point to a crippling injury list, which – together with international call-ups – at one stage in June cost them the services of at least six front-line players. For the Championship match at Cardiff, there were four making one form of debut or another, including Shaftab Khalid, a 20-year-old off-break bowler who joined Kadeer in the ECB Academy.

WORCESTERSHIRE RESULTS

All first-class matches – Played 18: Won 10, Lost 1, Drawn 6, Tied 1.
County Championship matches – Played 16: Won 10, Lost 1, Drawn 5.

Frizzell County Championship, winners in Division 2; Cheltenham & Gloucester Trophy, finalists; National Cricket League, 9th in Division 1; Twenty20 Cup, 3rd in Midlands/Wales/West Group.

COUNTY CHAMPIONSHIP AVERAGES

BATTING AND FIELDING

Cap/Colours		*M*	*I*	*NO*	*R*	*HS*	*100s*	*50s*	*Avge*	*Ct/St*
2002	B. F. Smith	16	26	2	1,155	110	2	10	48.12	3
2002	D. J. Pipe	3	6	2	163	104*	1	0	40.75	14/1
2002	S. D. Peters	16	27	1	1,009	165	2	7	38.80	11
2002	Kadeer Ali	6	11	0	375	99	0	3	34.09	2
2003	S. J. Adshead	2	4	1	102	63	0	1	34.00	7/1
1986	G. A. Hick	13	23	3	670	155	1	3	33.50	19
2003	S. C. Moore	2	4	1	97	28*	0	0	32.33	2
2003	A. J. Hall§	6	7	0	222	104	1	1	31.71	2
2002	Kabir Ali	12	16	4	371	84*	0	2	30.91	2
2002	A. Singh	14	24	1	628	105	1	3	27.30	6
2003	J. M. Kemp§	6	11	0	290	90	0	1	26.36	9
1986	S. J. Rhodes	11	14	2	309	81*	0	2	25.75	38/2
1998	V. S. Solanki	13	20	1	464	79	0	3	24.42	18
1994	D. A. Leatherdale	4	7	0	164	61	0	2	23.42	2
2002	G. J. Batty	16	25	3	497	60	0	3	22.59	14
2002	M. S. Mason	13	18	3	237	52	0	1	15.80	2
2003	M. Hayward§	16	21	5	123	28	0	0	7.68	5
2003	M. A. Harrity	5	7	5	14	5*	0	0	7.00	0

Also batted: S. A. Khalid (colours 2003) (4 matches) 13, 8 (1 ct); D. H. Wigley (colours 2003) (1 match) 15, 8.

§ *Overseas player.*

Since 2002, Worcestershire have awarded county colours to all players making their Championship debut.

BOWLING

	O	*M*	*R*	*W*	*BB*	*5W/i*	*Avge*
A. J. Hall	110	29	297	17	3-10	0	17.47
M. S. Mason	385.3	101	1,038	49	6-68	2	21.18
J. M. Kemp	102.1	17	319	14	5-48	1	22.78
M. Hayward	427.3	83	1,533	67	5-46	2	22.88
Kabir Ali	336.2	57	1,279	54	8-53	2	23.68
G. J. Batty	515.2	121	1,436	53	6-88	1	27.09

Also bowled: M. A. Harrity 120.5–29–423–9; G. A. Hick 21–5–63–0; S. A. Khalid 77–13–275–8; D. A. Leatherdale 39–6–142–4; V. S. Solanki 2–1–9–0; D. H. Wigley 29.1–9–95–3.

COUNTY RECORDS

Highest score for:	405*	G. A. Hick v Somerset at Taunton	1988
Highest score against:	331*	J. D. Robertson (Middlesex) at Worcester	1949
Best bowling for:	9-23	C. F. Root v Lancashire at Worcester	1931
Best bowling against:	10-51	J. Mercer (Glamorgan) at Worcester	1936
Highest total for:	670-7 dec.	v Somerset at Worcester	1995
Highest total against:	701-4 dec.	by Leicestershire at Worcester	1906
Lowest total for:	24	v Yorkshire at Huddersfield	1903
Lowest total against:	30	by Hampshire at Worcester	1903

WORCESTERSHIRE DIRECTORY

ADDRESS

County Ground, New Road, Worcester WR2 4QQ (01905 748474; fax 01905 748005; email joan.grundy@wccc.co.uk). **Website** www.wccc.co.uk.

GROUND

Worcester (New Road): ¼ mile SW of city centre S of River Severn on L side of New Road one-way system. Nearest stations: Worcester Foregate Street (½ mile) and Worcester Shrub Hill (1 mile).

OFFICIALS

Captain B. F. Smith
Director of cricket T. M. Moody
Academy director D. B. D'Oliveira
President 2003 – M. G. Jones; 2004 – N. H. Whiting

Chairman J. W. Elliott
Chief executive M. S. Newton
Head groundsman T. R. Packwood
Scorers W. Clarke; N. Smith

PLAYERS

Players expected to reappear in 2004

	Former counties	*Country*	*Born*	*Birthplace*
***Ali** Kabir*		E	24.11.1980	*Moseley*
Ali Kadeer		E	7.3.1983	*Moseley*
***Batty** Gareth Jon	Yorks, Surrey	E	13.10.1977	*Bradford*
***Bichel** Andrew John		A	27.8.1970	*Laidley*
***Hall** Andrew James		SA	31.7.1975	*Johannesburg*
Harrity Mark Andrew		A (EU)	9.3.1974	*Semaphore*
***Hick** Graeme Ashley		E	23.5.1966	*Salisbury, Rhodesia*
Khalid Shaftab Ahmed		E	6.10.1982	*Lahore, Pak.*
Leatherdale David Antony		E	26.11.1967	*Bradford*
Liptrot Christopher George		E	13.2.1980	*Wigan*
Mason Matthew Sean		A (EU)	20.3.1974	*Claremont, Aus.*
Moore Stephen Colin		E	4.11.1980	*Johannesburg*
Peters Stephen David	Essex	E	10.12.1978	*Harold Wood*
Pipe David James		E	16.12.1977	*Bradford*
***Rhodes** Steven John	Yorks	E	17.6.1964	*Bradford*
Smith Benjamin Francis	Leics	E	3.4.1972	*Corby*
Solanki Vikram Singh		E	1.4.1976	*Udaipur, India*
Taylor David Kenneth		E	17.12.1974	*Oxford*
Wigley David Harry	Yorks	E	26.10.1981	*Bradford*

Player due to join in 2004

Malik Muhammad Nadeem	Notts	E	6.10.1982	*Nottingham*

* *Test player*

WORCESTERSHIRE v HAMPSHIRE

At Worcester, April 18, 19, 20, 21. Drawn. Worcestershire 11 pts, Hampshire 10 pts. Toss: Worcestershire. County debuts: M. A. Harrity, M. Hayward; E. S. H. Giddins, Wasim Akram.

In a nerve-shredding climax, Hampshire's last pair of Mullally and Giddins survived eight balls to scrape a draw, after Nantie Hayward had threatened to mark his debut by bowling Worcestershire to victory. Hayward overcame a seaming but slow pitch with raw pace and took five wickets in the second innings – and nine in the match. In improbable opening-day heat, a crowd of 2,412, the best in the Championship at New Road since computerised records began in 1999, saw the new Worcestershire captain, Ben Smith, crunch an attacking century. Hampshire slumped to 81 for four in reply, but Crawley and Pothas rallied, and held the lead down to 49. Smith again led the way for Worcestershire before a well-judged declaration set Hampshire 314 at just above four an over. Crawley and Robin Smith were on course before tea, but Hayward came roaring back with a fiery spell and took his side within a sniff of victory.

Close of play: First day, Worcestershire 318-7 (Rhodes 5, Ali 12); Second day, Hampshire 267-5 (Pothas 110, Mascarenhas 0); Third day, Worcestershire 187-5 (Leatherdale 7, Batty 0).

Worcestershire

S. D. Peters c Smith b Mullally	52	– c Pothas b Wasim Akram	24
A. Singh lbw b Wasim Akram	8	– c Adams b Wasim Akram	8
G. A. Hick c Crawley b Mullally	72	– lbw b Giddins	4
*B. F. Smith lbw b Giddins	104	– c Pothas b Mullally	82
V. S. Solanki c and b Udal	22	– c Kenway b Mascarenhas	45
D. A. Leatherdale b Giddins	4	– c Kenway b Wasim Akram	12
G. J. Batty lbw b Wasim Akram	12	– c sub b Mullally	14
†S. J. Rhodes c Mullally b Giddins	22	– not out	20
Kabir Ali b Giddins	40	– b Udal	25
M. Hayward c Mullally b Wasim Akram	22	– c sub b Udal	6
M. A. Harrity not out	2	– not out	0
B 5, l-b 6, w 7, n-b 18	36	L-b 7, n-b 17	24
1/25 (2) 2/102 (1) 3/175 (3) 4/244 (5) 5/267 (6) 6/289 (4) 7/299 (7) 8/345 (8) 9/369 (10) 10/396 (9)	396	1/29 (2) 2/34 (3) 3/78 (1) 4/175 (5) 5/185 (4) 6/204 (6) 7/210 (7) 8/257 (9) 9/263 (10)	(9 wkts dec.) 264

Bonus points – Worcestershire 4, Hampshire 3.

Bowling: *First Innings*—Wasim Akram 26–5–102–3; Mullally 23–6–61–2; Mascarenhas 22–11–40–0; Giddins 24.5–3–88–4; Udal 20.3–2–80–1; Kendall 3–1–14–0. *Second Innings*—Wasim Akram 18–5–45–3; Giddins 12–2–48–1; Mullally 21–6–69–2; Mascarenhas 17–4–47–1; Udal 11–1–48–2.

Hampshire

D. A. Kenway b Hayward	5	– c Rhodes b Hayward	1
J. H. K. Adams c Rhodes b Ali	11	– b Hayward	9
*J. P. Crawley lbw b Batty	93	– c Rhodes b Ali	67
R. A. Smith lbw b Ali	22	– lbw b Leatherdale	77
W. S. Kendall c Rhodes b Hayward	16	– b Batty	13
†N. Pothas not out	146	– c Leatherdale b Hayward	48
A. D. Mascarenhas c Batty b Ali	20	– c Rhodes b Hayward	38
Wasim Akram c Solanki b Ali	5	– c Solanki b Batty	5
S. D. Udal c Rhodes b Hayward	1	– lbw b Hayward	4
A. D. Mullally lbw b Hayward	7	– not out	5
E. S. H. Giddins b Harrity	10	– not out	0
L-b 1, w 2, n-b 8	11	L-b 2, w 1, n-b 6	9
1/10 (1) 2/24 (2) 3/60 (4) 4/81 (5) 5/263 (3) 6/305 (7) 7/311 (8) 8/312 (9) 9/326 (10) 10/347 (11)	347	1/5 (1) 2/13 (2) 3/135 (3) 4/160 (5) 5/186 (4) 6/246 (6) 7/262 (8) 8/267 (7) 9/276 (9)	(9 wkts) 276

Bonus points – Hampshire 3, Worcestershire 3.

Bowling: *First Innings*—Hayward 31–9–95–4; Ali 26–8–74–4; Harrity 24.4–7–90–1; Leatherdale 13–1–47–0; Batty 25–9–40–1. *Second Innings*—Ali 17–1–78–1; Hayward 18–2–70–5; Harrity 12–3–32–0; Batty 22–4–71–2; Leatherdale 5–0–23–1.

Umpires: J. H. Hampshire and N. J. Llong.

At Oxford, April 23, 24, 25. WORCESTERSHIRE drew with OXFORD UCCE.

WORCESTERSHIRE v NORTHAMPTONSHIRE

At Worcester, April 30, May 1, 2, 3. Drawn. Worcestershire 6 pts, Northamptonshire 10 pts. Toss: Northamptonshire.

Northamptonshire dominated when snatches of cricket interrupted the rain. Showers docked the first day, washed out the third and continually interrupted the fourth. And on the second, which was dry, groundstaff discovered that water had oozed under the cover protecting one of the run-ups. Play failed to start until late afternoon and only 32 overs were bowled, prompting Worcestershire's chief executive, Mark Newton, to tour the ground, apologising to disgruntled supporters. On the first day, Blain and Phillips – formerly of Kent and making his first Championship appearance in nearly five years – took advantage of a pacy and unpredictable pitch and grabbed nine wickets between them. The rest of the match belonged to Jaques, born in Australia of English parents. He began his innings on the first day and was 149 not out at the end of the fourth, after more than five hours of application.

Close of play: First day, Northamptonshire 108-1 (Hussey 39, Jaques 27); Second day, Northamptonshire 196-3 (Jaques 86, Sales 14); Third day, No play.

Worcestershire

S. D. Peters b Blain	17
A. Singh b Blain	6
G. A. Hick c Hussey b Phillips	37
*B. F. Smith lbw b Cook	50
V. S. Solanki c Bailey b Blain	79
D. A. Leatherdale c Bailey b Phillips	2
G. J. Batty lbw b Phillips	0
†S. J. Rhodes c Cook b Blain	4
Kabir Ali c Brophy b Blain	6
M. Hayward c Bailey b Phillips	6
M. S. Mason not out	0
B 4, l-b 1, n-b 24	29
1/27 (1) 2/36 (2) 3/99 (3) 4/142 (4) 5/156 (6) 6/164 (7) 7/191 (8) 8/221 (9) 9/236 (5) 10/236 (10)	236

Bonus points – Worcestershire 1, Northamptonshire 3.

Bowling: Nel 17–7–46–0; Blain 15–0–84–5; Phillips 14.3–6–45–4; Cook 8–1–37–1; Panesar 3–0–19–0.

Northamptonshire

*M. E. K. Hussey c Rhodes b Mason	45
M. J. Powell run out	31
P. A. Jaques not out	149
J. W. Cook b Ali	2
D. J. Sales b Ali	33
G. L. Brophy st Rhodes b Batty	6
†T. M. B. Bailey not out	12
L-b 16, n-b 18	34
1/57 (2) 2/133 (1) 3/140 (4) 4/248 (5) 5/284 (6)	(5 wkts) 312

B. J. Phillips, A. Nel, J. A. R. Blain and M. S. Panesar did not bat.

Bonus points – Northamptonshire 3, Worcestershire 1.

Bowling: Ali 25–6–65–2; Hayward 19–2–81–0; Mason 26–5–80–1; Leatherdale 9–0–43–0; Batty 15–2–27–1.

Umpires: M. J. Harris and V. A. Holder.

At Worcester, May 9, 10, 11, 12. WORCESTERSHIRE tied with ZIMBABWEANS (see Zimbabwean tour section).

At Stockton-on-Tees, May 14, 15, 16, 17. WORCESTERSHIRE drew with DURHAM.

WORCESTERSHIRE v GLOUCESTERSHIRE

At Worcester, May 21, 22, 23, 24. Worcestershire won by 111 runs. Worcestershire 17 pts, Gloucestershire 3 pts. Toss: Gloucestershire.

Worcestershire won for the first time in the 2003 Championship, thanks chiefly to a stubborn unbeaten 83 by Singh on another seamer-friendly New Road wicket. The momentum was with Gloucestershire at the end of the third day, with their opponents 95 for five, just 92 ahead. But although his normally fluent opening partnership with Peters had ground out just 33 in 22 overs, the out-of-form Singh clung on, helped by two dropped catches. Gloucestershire came to rue the misses: on the fourth day, he went on to share the only fifty partnership of the match with Hall, gleaned support from the lower order and carried his bat. Left 210 to chase, Gloucestershire were never in the hunt after Hayward decapitated the innings, and Kabir Ali finished them off. On the interrupted first two days the pitch proved ideal for Smith to get movement. Gloucestershire fared little better in their own first innings.

Close of play: First day, Worcestershire 72-4 (Solanki 11, Hall 2); Second day, Gloucestershire 66-3 (Weston 30, Windows 2); Third day, Worcestershire 95-5 (Singh 36, Hall 13).

Worcestershire

S. D. Peters c Rhodes b Lewis	8	– c Alleyne b Butler	20
A. Singh c Spearman b Smith	26	– not out	83
G. A. Hick c Hancock b Lewis	20	– c Spearman b Alleyne	5
*B. F. Smith lbw b Butler	1	– lbw b Smith	5
V. S. Solanki c Russell b Smith	34	– b Smith	15
A. J. Hall c Russell b Smith	4	– (7) c Windows b Butler	35
G. J. Batty not out	32	– (8) b Butler	0
†S. J. Rhodes lbw b Smith	3	– (9) c Fisher b Smith	9
Kabir Ali c Spearman b Smith	0	– (6) lbw b Smith	0
M. S. Mason b Butler	30	– c Rhodes b Lewis	29
M. Hayward b Lewis	2	– b Butler	1
L-b 9, n-b 6	15	L-b 10	10
1/26 (1) 2/40 (2) 3/41 (4) 4/70 (3) 5/83 (6) 6/112 (5) 7/124 (8) 8/126 (9) 9/172 (10) 10/175 (11)	175	1/33 (1) 2/38 (3) 3/57 (4) 4/75 (5) 5/75 (6) 6/135 (7) 7/136 (8) 8/174 (9) 9/211 (10) 10/212 (11)	212

Bonus points – Gloucestershire 3.

Bowling: *First Innings*—Lewis 18.3–8–37–3; Smith 22–4–70–5; Butler 16–4–59–2. *Second Innings*—Lewis 23–7–64–1; Smith 18–5–41–4; Butler 20–3–74–4; Alleyne 13–6–23–1.

Gloucestershire

W. P. C. Weston b Hayward	42	– (2) c Solanki b Hayward	6
C. M. Spearman b Hayward	19	– (1) c Solanki b Ali	24
T. H. C. Hancock lbw b Hayward	0	– c Rhodes b Hayward	0
J. N. Rhodes lbw b Mason	14	– run out	13
M. G. N. Windows c Hall b Mason	14	– lbw b Hall	3
*M. W. Alleyne b Batty	19	– b Mason	11
†R. C. Russell lbw b Ali	38	– lbw b Hall	0
I. D. Fisher c Batty b Ali	15	– not out	11
J. Lewis b Hayward	0	– b Ali	5
I. G. Butler b Ali	0	– c Rhodes b Ali	0
A. M. Smith not out	0	– b Ali	2
L-b 9, w 4, n-b 4	17	B 4, l-b 5, w 6, n-b 8	23
1/37 (2) 2/37 (3) 3/62 (4) 4/93 (1) 5/93 (5) 6/134 (6) 7/171 (8) 8/178 (7) 9/178 (10) 10/178 (9)	178	1/15 (2) 2/19 (3) 3/52 (4) 4/52 (1) 5/60 (5) 6/60 (7) 7/75 (6) 8/96 (9) 9/96 (10) 10/98 (11)	98

Bonus points – Worcestershire 3.

Bowling: *First Innings*—Hayward 21.1–5–58–4; Ali 14–3–51–3; Mason 22–9–31–2; Hall 10–4–18–0; Batty 5–1–11–1. *Second Innings*—Hayward 9–3–30–2; Ali 13–5–39–4; Hall 7–1–15–2; Mason 3–1–5–1.

Umpires: R. Palmer and P. Willey.

At Derby, May 30, 31, June 1. WORCESTERSHIRE beat DERBYSHIRE by nine wickets.

At Bath, June 4, 5, 6, 7. WORCESTERSHIRE beat SOMERSET by nine wickets.

At Worcester, June 25. WORCESTERSHIRE lost to SOUTH AFRICANS by 69 runs (see South African tour section).

At Cardiff, June 27, 28, 29, 30. WORCESTERSHIRE drew with GLAMORGAN.

WORCESTERSHIRE v DURHAM

At Worcester, July 2, 3, 4. Worcestershire won by 31 runs. Worcestershire 18 pts, Durham 3 pts. Toss: Worcestershire. Championship debut: Shoaib Akhtar.

With five wickets standing and 68 needed, Durham were sniffing victory until Adshead held a brilliant catch off Pratt's inside edge and tipped the match decisively Worcestershire's way. Despite the ball jagging around, Pratt had made a stylish, Championship-best 85, but after he went Durham disintegrated. Mason, an Australian-bred component of Worcestershire's rather unEnglish seam attack, took a career-best six for 68. Indeed, bowlers had held sway from the start. The Pakistan fast bowler Shoaib Akhtar, making his Championship debut, and Harmison formed the quickest opening pair in Durham's first-class history, with lateral movement making them more awkward still – 73 from Smith was worth a century on a normal day. But sloppy shots led to a swift collapse – and also helped the pitch escape censure, despite 18 first-day wickets. Harrity's best bowling of 2003 undermined Durham's reply and gave Worcestershire a lead of 98. Smith then stretched the advantage with another high-quality fifty, but it was a crucial eighth-wicket stand of 61 between Adshead and Mason that took the target just beyond Durham.

Close of play: First day, Durham 110-8 (Wells 36, Shoaib Akhtar 0); Second day, Durham 145-3 (Pratt 46, Muchall 10).

Worcestershire

S. D. Peters c Mustard b Harmison	0	– run out	0
A. Singh b Harmison	15	– c Mustard b Shoaib Akhtar	8
Kadeer Ali c Mustard b Plunkett	35	– b Harmison	13
*B. F. Smith b Phillips	73	– c Pratt b Plunkett	60
J. M. Kemp c Mustard b Shoaib Akhtar	32	– lbw b Harmison	5
S. C. Moore c Mustard b Harmison	28	– b Plunkett	17
G. J. Batty c Wells b Plunkett	11	– lbw b Shoaib Akhtar	15
†S. J. Adshead c and b Phillips	5	– c Mustard b Plunkett	31
M. S. Mason c Mustard b Harmison	0	– c Mustard b Phillips	27
M. A. Harrity not out	0	– not out	5
M. Hayward c Love b Phillips	2	– c Wells b Phillips	0
B 5, l-b 5, w 5, n-b 2	17	B 8, l-b 3, n-b 6	17
1/7 (1) 2/16 (2) 3/93 (3) 4/135 (5) 5/188 (4) 6/207 (7) 7/212 (6) 8/212 (9) 9/216 (8) 10/218 (11)	218	1/5 (1) 2/17 (2) 3/21 (3) 4/41 (5) 5/86 (6) 6/110 (7) 7/127 (4) 8/188 (8) 9/198 (9) 10/198 (11)	198

Bonus points – Worcestershire 1, Durham 3.

Bowling: *First Innings*—Shoaib Akhtar 13–5–28–1; Harmison 13–3–50–4; Wells 6–1–35–0; Plunkett 13–4–55–2; Phillips 11–1–40–3. *Second Innings*—Shoaib Akhtar 13–2–33–2; Harmison 14–3–53–2; Plunkett 13–0–61–3; Phillips 11.5–2–40–2.

Durham

*J. J. B. Lewis lbw b Hayward	0	– b Batty	53
M. A. Gough c Adshead b Mason	4	– c Adshead b Mason	26
M. L. Love c Adshead b Mason	28	– c Peters b Mason	0
G. J. Pratt b Harrity	23	– c Adshead b Mason	85
G. J. Muchall b Harrity	3	– c Peters b Mason	11
V. J. Wells c Adshead b Mason	36	– b Batty	18
†P. Mustard c Batty b Harrity	7	– b Batty	20
L. E. Plunkett c Peters b Kemp	3	– (9) not out	15
N. C. Phillips b Kemp	0	– (10) c Kemp b Mason	8
Shoaib Akhtar c Kemp b Harrity	5	– (8) c Kemp b Batty	2
S. J. Harmison not out	5	– c Batty b Mason	10
L-b 1, w 1, n-b 4	6	B 1, l-b 9, w 1, n-b 6	17
1/0 (1) 2/6 (2) 3/42 (4) 4/50 (5) 5/84 (3) 6/100 (7) 7/106 (8) 8/108 (9) 9/110 (6) 10/120 (10)	120	1/53 (2) 2/53 (3) 3/120 (1) 4/149 (5) 5/195 (6) 6/229 (4) 7/229 (7) 8/234 (8) 9/243 (10) 10/265 (11)	265

Bonus points – Worcestershire 3.

Bowling: *First Innings*—Hayward 4.5–2–10–1; Mason 16–3–48–3; Kemp 8.1–2–15–2; Harrity 11.1–2–39–4; Batty 5–1–7–0. *Second Innings*—Mason 30.4–6–68–6; Kemp 15–5–41–0; Harrity 14–1–68–0; Batty 26–4–78–4.

Umpires: B. Dudleston and G. Sharp.

WORCESTERSHIRE v DERBYSHIRE

At Worcester, July 15, 16, 17, 18. Worcestershire won by an innings and 42 runs. Worcestershire 19.75 pts (after 0.25 pt penalty), Derbyshire 3 pts. Toss: Derbyshire.

With bowlers having dominated Worcestershire's last home match, an ECB pitch inspector was present from the start. Again wickets tumbled on the opening day, 16 in all, and they went on to win inside two days' playing time. But the inspector, John Jameson, said indifferent batting was as culpable as the surface. Derbyshire, skittled inside 45 overs, were also desperately short of self-belief, and Mason capitalised with five for 43. But Worcestershire's reply looked like going the same way against a fired-up Cork, before the last four wickets added an unlikely 197, with Rhodes the fulcrum. Having taken a lead of 138, Worcestershire did not have to bat again. On the second evening Kabir Ali grabbed three wickets, having been given his family's blessing to stay at the ground rather than leave to attend the funeral of his infant nephew. After a near-washout on day three, he destroyed a demoralised Derbyshire on day four, taking the last five wickets inside an hour. Even Kabir himself was slightly sheepish about his career-best eight for 58: "It was one of those days," he said. Worcestershire's win was their fifth in six Championship games; Derbyshire's defeat their seventh in succession – the county's worst run since 1921.

Close of play: First day, Worcestershire 155-6 (Batty 23, Rhodes 26); Second day, Derbyshire 27-4 (Kaif 12); Third day, Derbyshire 51-5 (Kaif 26, Welch 2).

Derbyshire

First innings		Second innings	
C. W. G. Bassano c Rhodes b Mason	16	(2) lbw b Kabir Ali	4
M. J. Di Venuto b Kabir Ali	12	(1) lbw b Kabir Ali	2
R. M. Khan c Peters b Mason	15	lbw b Kabir Ali	0
M. Kaif lbw b Mason	31	lbw b Kabir Ali	30
S. A. Selwood c Peters b Mason	0	c Rhodes b Hayward	0
*D. G. Cork c Solanki b Hall	12	c Rhodes b Hayward	7
G. Welch c Batty b Mason	28	not out	11
†K. M. Krikken c Rhodes b Hall	14	b Kabir Ali	1
K. J. Dean c Solanki b Hayward	4	b Kabir Ali	0
Mohammad Ali b Hayward	11	c Rhodes b Kabir Ali	0
L. J. Wharton not out	5	b Kabir Ali	30
B 4, l-b 7, w 2, n-b 2	15	L-b 3, n-b 8	11
1/33 (2) 2/41 (1) 3/56 (3) 4/56 (5) 5/86 (6) 6/121 (4) 7/136 (8) 8/142 (7) 9/155 (9) 10/163 (10)	163	1/2 (1) 2/4 (3) 3/19 (2) 4/27 (5) 5/39 (6) 6/56 (4) 7/58 (8) 8/58 (9) 9/58 (10) 10/96 (11)	96

Bonus points – Worcestershire 3.

Bowling: *First Innings*—Kabir Ali 7–1–25–1; Hayward 11.2–4–46–2; Mason 14–4–43–5; Hall 12–3–38–2. *Second Innings*—Kabir Ali 15.4–3–58–8; Mason 12–7–16–0; Hayward 3–0–10–2; Batty 1–1–0–0; Solanki 1–0–9–0.

Worcestershire

Batsman	Runs
S. D. Peters c Di Venuto b Cork	5
A. Singh c Di Venuto b Cork	8
Kadeer Ali lbw b Cork	18
*B. F. Smith c Selwood b Welch	22
V. S. Solanki b Welch	28
A. J. Hall c Mohammad Ali b Dean	6
G. J. Batty lbw b Dean	37
†S. J. Rhodes not out	81
Kabir Ali c Krikken b Mohammad Ali	68
M. S. Mason b Mohammad Ali	0
M. Hayward b Cork	0
B 5, l-b 9, n-b 14	28
1/21 (2) 2/26 (1) 3/58 (4) 4/83 (3) 5/98 (6) 6/104 (5) 7/190 (7) 8/294 (9) 9/294 (10) 10/301 (11)	301

Bonus points – Worcestershire 3, Derbyshire 3.

Bowling: Cork 26.2–8–60–4; Dean 30–8–95–2; Welch 28–7–81–2; Mohammad Ali 18–6–51–2.

Umpires: G. I. Burgess and N. G. Cowley.

At Cheltenham, July 23, 24, 25, 26. WORCESTERSHIRE drew with GLOUCESTERSHIRE.

WORCESTERSHIRE v GLAMORGAN

At Worcester, July 31, August 1, 2, 3. Worcestershire won by 14 runs. Worcestershire 18 pts, Glamorgan 3 pts. Toss: Glamorgan.

To jubilation from Worcestershire, Kabir Ali broke a last-wicket stand of 56 to leave Glamorgan an agonising 15 short of victory. The chase, like the match, had twisted and turned. Opener Maher proved determined, and he and Wallace took Glamorgan to 210 for four, 129 short. Then, inside three balls, both perished. But Croft came in and found an unexpected partner in the last man Harrison, who hit six defiant boundaries in his 27 before driving uppishly to backward point. On the first day, Harrison had whipped out four of Worcestershire's top five inside 22 balls, before Leatherdale, a late replacement when Andrew Hall was called up by South Africa, and Batty put on 101. Glamorgan's batsmen coped even less well with a capricious pitch, and Smith produced another fighting innings when most needed to give Worcestershire a lead of 338. Leatherdale, who had not expected to play, had a benefit function in London on the first night and was whisked away by helicopter – piloted by Reuben Spiring, a former Worcestershire team-mate.

Close of play: First day, Glamorgan 0-2 (Hughes 0, I. J. Thomas 0); Second day, Worcestershire 120-4 (Smith 30); Third day, Glamorgan 174-4 (Maher 84, Wallace 32).

Worcestershire

First innings		Second innings	
S. D. Peters c Wallace b Harrison	29	– b Croft	56
A. Singh c Wallace b S. D. Thomas	30	– c Maher b Wharf	10
G. A. Hick c Wharf b Harrison	1	– b Wharf	6
*B. F. Smith c Powell b Harrison	0	– b Harrison	87
V. S. Solanki c Maynard b Harrison	4	– c I. J. Thomas b Croft	8
D. A. Leatherdale c I. J. Thomas b Wharf	50	– b Wharf	15
G. J. Batty c I. J. Thomas b Wharf	60	– lbw b Kasprowicz	5
†S. J. Rhodes c Powell b Croft	0	– c Hughes b Croft	20
Kabir Ali not out	38	– not out	28
M. S. Mason c Croft b Wharf	16	– c Kasprowicz b Croft	1
M. Hayward b Wharf	0	– b Kasprowicz	4
L-b 9	9	B 1, l-b 10, w 4, n-b 2	17
1/45 (2) 2/46 (3) 3/46 (4) 4/64 (5) 5/65 (1) 6/166 (7) 7/175 (8) 8/183 (6) 9/237 (10) 10/237 (11)	237	1/28 (2) 2/40 (3) 3/106 (1) 4/120 (5) 5/147 (6) 6/163 (7) 7/216 (4) 8/222 (8) 9/228 (10) 10/257 (11)	257

Bonus points – Worcestershire 1, Glamorgan 3.

Bowling: *First Innings*—Kasprowicz 16–3–48–0; Wharf 16–3–63–4; Croft 9–2–43–1; S. D. Thomas 6–0–22–1; Harrison 16–5–52–4. *Second Innings*—Kasprowicz 19.4–5–46–2; Wharf 15–4–38–3; S. D. Thomas 9–0–38–0; Harrison 20–5–55–1; Croft 20–2–69–4.

Glamorgan

First innings		Second innings	
J. P. Maher c Rhodes b Hayward	0	– c Hick b Mason	95
J. Hughes b Mason	24	– c Batty b Ali	30
D. S. Harrison b Hayward	0	– (11) c Batty b Ali	27
I. J. Thomas c Solanki b Leatherdale	53	– (3) c Hick b Mason	1
M. J. Powell b Mason	0	– (4) b Ali	3
M. P. Maynard c Peters b Mason	12	– (5) c Peters b Hayward	19
†M. A. Wallace c Solanki b Batty	29	– (6) b Batty	55
*R. D. B. Croft lbw b Leatherdale	0	– (7) not out	51
S. D. Thomas lbw b Ali	21	– (8) lbw b Batty	10
M. S. Kasprowicz b Ali	9	– b Ali	0
A. G. Wharf not out	0	– (9) lbw b Leatherdale	13
L-b 3, n-b 5	8	B 8, l-b 10, n-b 2	20
1/0 (1) 2/0 (3) 3/56 (2) 4/70 (5) 5/90 (6) 6/106 (4) 7/106 (8) 8/146 (9) 9/156 (10) 10/156 (7)	156	1/51 (2) 2/65 (3) 3/72 (4) 4/119 (5) 5/210 (6) 6/210 (1) 7/229 (8) 8/262 (9) 9/268 (10) 10/324 (11)	324

Bonus points – Worcestershire 3.

Bowling: *First Innings*—Hayward 11–2–34–2; Ali 13–2–55–2; Mason 12–3–22–3; Batty 10.1–2–24–1; Leatherdale 5–2–18–2. *Second Innings*—Ali 29–6–96–4; Hayward 15–1–75–1; Mason 23–6–58–2; Batty 23–3–66–2; Leatherdale 7–3–11–1.

Umpires: J. H. Evans and G. Sharp.

At Scarborough, August 13, 14. WORCESTERSHIRE beat YORKSHIRE by five wickets.

WORCESTERSHIRE v SOMERSET

At Worcester, August 20, 21, 22. Worcestershire won by eight wickets. Worcestershire 20 pts, Somerset 5 pts. Toss: Somerset.

The unwavering belief Worcestershire had built up over the season was evident as they overcame a disastrous first morning to win with more than a day to spare. By lunch Somerset had raced to 150 for one, hitting 29 boundaries against some distinctly ordinary bowling. But the pendulum slowly but surely swung Worcestershire's way. Better line and length kept Somerset to 296, and in reply Peters produced batting of the highest quality. The recurring New Road problem of unreliable bounce was again obvious but he surpassed his 165 at Bath earlier in 2003 with a better century in worse conditions. By the end of the second day the contest was effectively decided: Somerset, still three runs behind, were four wickets down. On the third morning, Hayward, who reached 50 Championship victims for the season, continued the blitz and from 49 for six there was no way back for Somerset, despite some late resistance.

Close of play: First day, Worcestershire 86-2 (Peters 44, Rhodes 0); Second day, Somerset 32-4 (Burns 10, Blackwell 1).

Somerset

M. J. Wood c Rhodes b Batty	53	– run out	6
N. J. Edwards c Hick b Mason	45	– b Hayward	1
*M. Burns c Hick b Hayward	89	– c Hick b Hayward	13
J. Cox c Rhodes b Mason	0	– lbw b Mason	0
T. Webley c Rhodes b Harrity	20	– c Hick b Hayward	4
I. D. Blackwell lbw b Batty	21	– c Hick b Hayward	9
A. W. Laraman c Rhodes b Mason	29	– lbw b Harrity	35
†R. J. Turner c Rhodes b Hayward	4	– lbw b Batty	26
P. S. Jones c Kemp b Hayward	0	– lbw b Hayward	25
R. L. Johnson c Hayward b Batty	24	– c Batty b Harrity	0
N. A. M. McLean not out	4	– not out	7
W 3, n-b 4	7	B 6, l-b 10, w 5	21
1/63 (2) 2/154 (1) 3/155 (4) 4/201 (5) 5/235 (6) 6/239 (3) 7/263 (8) 8/263 (9) 9/284 (7) 10/296 (10)	296	1/3 (2) 2/18 (1) 3/18 (4) 4/31 (5) 5/48 (6) 6/49 (3) 7/90 (8) 8/134 (7) 9/134 (10) 10/147 (9)	147

Bonus points – Somerset 2, Worcestershire 3.

Bowling: *First Innings*—Mason 19–1–56–3; Hayward 11–2–53–3; Harrity 15–5–53–1; Kemp 5–0–23–0; Batty 24.4–3–111–3. *Second Innings*—Hayward 13.5–3–46–5; Mason 14–4–31–1; Harrity 7–2–26–2; Batty 6–1–28–1.

Worcestershire

S. D. Peters c and b Johnson	103	– lbw b Jones	54
A. Singh c Turner b Laraman	14	– c Laraman b Blackwell	44
G. A. Hick b Laraman	23	– not out	13
†S. J. Rhodes lbw b Jones	25		
*B. F. Smith b McLean	48	– (4) not out	2
V. S. Solanki lbw b Laraman	2		
J. M. Kemp c Turner b Johnson	32		
G. J. Batty not out	52		
M. S. Mason c Jones b Blackwell	13		
M. A. Harrity lbw b Blackwell	5		
M. Hayward c Laraman b Blackwell	0		
B 5, l-b 5, n-b 4	14	L-b 3	3
1/38 (2) 2/68 (3) 3/143 (4) 4/198 (1) 5/223 (6) 6/229 (5) 7/286 (7) 8/301 (9) 9/331 (10) 10/331 (11)	331	1/94 (1) 2/102 (2) (2 wkts)	116

Bonus points – Worcestershire 3, Somerset 3.

Bowling: *First Innings*—McLean 21–9–60–1; Johnson 21–7–43–2; Laraman 18–5–49–3; Jones 15–4–65–1; Blackwell 24.5–6–91–3; Burns 4–0–13–0. *Second Innings*—McLean 8–2–29–0; Johnson 5–1–15–0; Blackwell 14–3–39–1; Laraman 3–1–10–0; Jones 6–2–6–1; Edwards 2.2–0–14–0.

Umpires: R. J. Bailey and B. Leadbeater.

At Southampton, September 3, 4, 5, 6. WORCESTERSHIRE beat HAMPSHIRE by 101 runs.

WORCESTERSHIRE v YORKSHIRE

At Worcester, September 12, 13, 14, 15. Worcestershire won by 71 runs. Worcestershire 21 pts, Yorkshire 7 pts (after 1 pt penalty). Toss: Yorkshire.

On the last afternoon Hayward produced one of the most penetrative spells of his up-and-down summer to force Worcestershire's tenth win in 12 Championship games. With limited back-up, Hayward bowled with sustained pace, accuracy and aggression, and took four for 37. Batty, recently named in England's winter touring squad, also took four, as Yorkshire fell 72 short. Before the bounce became more variable on the last day, the bat had generally held sway. Smith passed 1,000 Championship runs for Worcestershire during a century full of front-foot charm, and Kadeer Ali, who suppressed his attacking instincts, fell one run short of a maiden hundred. The match then seemed to be going Yorkshire's way: an eighth-wicket stand of 104 between White and Dawson gave them a slender lead, Worcestershire's reply dwindled from 134 for two to 251 all out and Kabir Ali was left unable to bowl after being struck on the instep. But the inspired Hayward soon changed the tone. Defeat left Yorkshire's promotion hopes hanging on victory in their last match.

Close of play: First day, Worcestershire 309-5 (Kemp 8, Batty 5); Second day, Yorkshire 266-5 (Kirby 2, White 5); Third day, Worcestershire 208-6 (Batty 7, Pipe 0).

Worcestershire

S. D. Peters b Dawson	44	– c and b Silverwood	0
G. A. Hick c Dawson b Hoggard	7	– b Craven	57
Kadeer Ali c Blakey b Silverwood	99	– c Blakey b Hoggard	21
*B. F. Smith lbw b Kirby	110	– b Craven	57
A. Singh b Kirby	17	– c Blakey b Silverwood	14
J. M. Kemp c Dawson b Kirby	20	– lbw b Kirby	33
G. J. Batty c McGrath b Hoggard	34	– lbw b Silverwood	21
†D. J. Pipe c McGrath b Craven	10	– b Silverwood	1
Kabir Ali c Blakey b Kirby	0	– lbw b Silverwood	3
D. H. Wigley c Blakey b Kirby	15	– c Blakey b Kirby	8
M. Hayward not out	6	– not out	7
B 10, l-b 5, w 6, n-b 6	27	B 9, l-b 13, w 3, n-b 4	29
1/15 (2) 2/82 (1) 3/264 (4) 4/292 (3) 5/304 (5) 6/323 (6) 7/361 (8) 8/365 (7) 9/370 (9) 10/389 (10)	389	1/2 (1) 2/58 (3) 3/134 (2) 4/155 (4) 5/185 (5) 6/203 (6) 7/222 (8) 8/227 (7) 9/229 (9) 10/251 (10)	251

Bonus points – Worcestershire 4, Yorkshire 3 (130 overs: 388-9).

Bowling: *First Innings*—Hoggard 26–6–85–2; Silverwood 28–9–56–1; Kirby 32.3–4–122–5; Dawson 29–12–61–1; McGrath 7–0–25–0; Craven 8–1–25–1. *Second Innings*—Silverwood 21–7–63–5; Kirby 28.1–7–62–2; Hoggard 13–4–41–1; Dawson 6–0–34–0; Craven 9–1–29–2.

Yorkshire

C. R. Taylor c Batty b Kemp	40	– lbw b Hayward	14
M. J. Wood c Kadeer Ali b Kabir Ali	37	– c Pipe b Hayward	14
*A. McGrath c Pipe b Hayward	47	– lbw b Wigley	6
M. J. Lumb c and b Kemp	61	– lbw b Batty	23
V. J. Craven b Batty	45	– c Kemp b Batty	24
S. P. Kirby c Pipe b Hayward	2	– (10) lbw b Batty	8
C. White lbw b Wigley	66	– (6) lbw b Hayward	9
†R. J. Blakey c Pipe b Hayward	3	– (7) not out	31
R. K. J. Dawson b Kabir Ali	60	– (8) c Hick b Hayward	18
C. E. W. Silverwood c Batty b Wigley	1	– (9) c Hick b Batty	6
M. J. Hoggard not out	0	– run out	1
B 14, l-b 11, w 2, n-b 16	43	L-b 6, n-b 4	10
1/69 (2) 2/127 (1) 3/151 (3) 4/254 (5) 5/258 (4) 6/285 (6) 7/289 (8) 8/393 (7) 9/405 (9) 10/405 (10)	405	1/18 (1) 2/33 (3) 3/35 (2) 4/73 (4) 5/98 (5) 6/98 (6) 7/130 (8) 8/137 (9) 9/163 (10) 10/164 (11)	164

Bonus points – Yorkshire 5, Worcestershire 3.

Bowling: *First Innings*—Kabir Ali 23–2–108–2; Hayward 28–10–74–3; Wigley 19.1–5–56–2; Kemp 12–0–62–2; Batty 34–10–80–1. *Second Innings*—Hayward 19–5–37–4; Wigley 10–4–39–1; Batty 20–4–57–4; Kemp 7–1–25–0.

Umpires: R. J. Bailey and D. J. Constant.

At Northampton, September 17, 18, 19. WORCESTERSHIRE lost to NORTHAMPTONSHIRE by 92 runs.

YORKSHIRE

In debt and the dungeons

DAVID WARNER

Yorkshire's new management board got half the job right. The four-man executive team, formed in August 2002 to replace an unwieldy general committee, eased the pressure of debt that had threatened to crush the club in 2002. But they failed by a whisker to satisfy the county's burning desire for an immediate return to the top division of the Championship.

Promotion would have put a different complexion on the summer, and Yorkshire came close – maybe within one late-September shower. Going into their last match, their hopes hung on victory against Gloucestershire, while their opponents needed only a draw to cement third place. However, with Gloucestershire tottering on the last day, autumnal gloom and drizzle descended. But Yorkshire refused to use the weather as an excuse. The captain, Anthony McGrath, admitted that his side, rich in individual talent, had simply not played well enough across the season. Relegation in the National League, and the early surrender of the C&G Trophy, made it a summer to forget.

At least there was still a functioning club at the end of it all. The escalating costs of redeveloping Headingley, and what the club treasurer called an "abysmal failure to conduct business properly", prompted serious fears of bankruptcy in 2002, and in March 2003 Yorkshire announced a yearly loss of nearly £1.3m – with total debts of £7m. Having squeezed expenditure, most publicly when the club's most famous names were asked to pay for their own hospitality during the Headingley Test, the management board hoped to have cut total debts to £5m by early 2004.

The team could not be blamed for some of the other troubles, either. The balance was disrupted when the hero of the 2002 C&G final, Matthew Elliott, returned to Australia before playing a game to rest a knee injury and be closer to his terminally ill brother-in-law. He never came back. His replacement, Yuvraj Singh of India, was below par, while the New Zealand captain, Stephen Fleming, brought wisdom and experience but lacked the consistency with the bat to make a big impact.

Both left at the end of August, and Yorkshire called in the Australian Damien Martyn – who had a brief but astonishing stay. Having reached 87 in his debut innings, he edged a hook, and ended up in hospital with a broken and gashed nose. Martyn insisted on playing in the decisive Championship match, when he plundered a breathtaking 238, including the fastest first-class century of the season, off 65 balls.

Not having a genuine all-rounder was another big handicap. It had been hoped that both Craig White and Gavin Hamilton would be back bowling again but White missed the early season after a rib operation and was always struggling to bowl, and Hamilton never recovered his lost confidence.

Despite these problems, Yorkshire could – and should – have done better. In the Championship, they won 101 batting and bowling points for performances in the first innings – 11 more than anyone else in the second division. But a total of only four wins showed how they lacked the killer touch. With the Championship-winning Australian coach, Wayne Clark, having left before the season, Geoff Cope, the director of cricket, brought in Kevin Sharp as batting (later, head) coach and Anthony McGrath was made captain. Dedicated as this pair undoubtedly were, they lacked the extensive experience of Clark and Darren Lehmann, McGrath's predecessor.

Matthew Wood

There were individual compensations. Despite being thrust into the captaincy when McGrath was suddenly elevated to the England Test team, Matthew Wood maintained his form. He scored 1,339 richly deserved Championship runs, with five centuries including a double, at an average of 53.56. The only regular batsman to come close was Michael Lumb, son of the former Yorkshire opener, Richard, whose fluency was a joy to behold.

And in an attack crammed with internationals, the undisputed king was a man with no caps at all. Fast bowler Steve Kirby took 67 Championship wickets at 26.40, twice grabbed ten or more in a match and, in one golden period, picked up 46 in six games. Chris Silverwood, the second-highest wicket-taker, managed 48 all season. Ryan Sidebottom had 35 by late July, injured his ankle and could not regain his place. Sidebottom, like Hamilton, was released; they moved to Nottinghamshire and Durham respectively.

That was just the start of a winter of major upheaval even by Yorkshire standards. In December David Byas, who quit the club after being dropped as captain after the 2001 Championship triumph, came back as director of cricket in place of Cope, who became operations director. Soon after that, McGrath opted out of the captaincy after being chosen for England's one-day games in the West Indies, which will eat heavily into the 2004 season. Craig White, whose international days seemed over, was named to replace him. Byas is likely to bring discipline back into the club; and the appointment of the experienced White will command widespread respect.

In February Darren Gough, after some years of speculation that he would move south for family reasons, finally signed for Essex. Gough's England record has long been better than his Yorkshire record, which is perhaps inevitable for a modern fast bowler. Byas regretted his departure, but he will have two Australians to lead the charge for him: Lehmann again, and – solving the all-rounder problem, everyone hopes – Ian Harvey, snapped up from Gloucestershire.

YORKSHIRE RESULTS

All first-class matches – Played 17: Won 4, Lost 5, Drawn 8.
County Championship matches – Played 16: Won 4, Lost 5, Drawn 7.

Frizzell County Championship, 4th in Division 2; Cheltenham & Gloucester Trophy, 4th round; National Cricket League, 8th in Division 1; Twenty20 Cup, 2nd in North Group.

COUNTY CHAMPIONSHIP AVERAGES

BATTING AND FIELDING

Cap		*M*	*I*	*NO*	*R*	*HS*	*100s*	*50s*	*Avge*	*Ct/St*
1995	M. P. Vaughan.	3	6	2	263	103	1	1	65.75	1
2001	M. J. Wood.	16	31	6	1,339	207	5	2	53.56	8
1993	C. White	9	14	2	592	173*	2	3	49.33	4
1999	A. McGrath	10	18	3	649	127*	1	5	43.26	5
2003	M. J. Lumb	16	25	2	917	115*	2	5	39.86	7
	S. P. Fleming§.	7	14	2	469	98	0	3	39.08	13
	A. K. D. Gray.	8	11	1	366	104	1	1	36.60	11
1987	R. J. Blakey	12	17	2	447	223*	1	0	29.80	30/1
	R. K. J. Dawson . . .	12	18	2	467	77	0	2	29.18	11
	V. J. Craven	5	9	1	208	47	0	0	26.00	0
2000	M. J. Hoggard.	6	7	5	49	21*	0	0	24.50	2
1993	D. Gough.	7	10	1	199	83	0	2	22.11	1
	G. M. Fellows.	5	6	0	114	53	0	1	19.00	0
	S. A. Richardson . . .	3	6	0	103	50	0	1	17.16	3
	Yuvraj Singh§	7	12	2	145	56	0	1	14.50	12
2000	R. J. Sidebottom . . .	9	11	2	122	28	0	0	13.55	4
1996	C. E. W. Silverwood.	12	18	4	152	53	0	1	10.85	2
	S. M. Guy	6	8	0	73	26	0	0	9.12	16/2
2003	S. P. Kirby	14	18	4	113	33	0	0	8.07	5

Also batted: T. T. Bresnan (3 matches) 7, 3, 19 (1 ct); G. M. Hamilton (cap 1998) (1 match) 68 (1 ct); D. R. Martyn§ (2 matches) 87*, 238, 17 (2 ct); P. J. Swanepoel (1 match) 17, 2 (1 ct); C. R. Taylor (2 matches) 16, 40, 14 (1 ct).

§ *Overseas player*

BOWLING

	O	*M*	*R*	*W*	*BB*	*5W/i*	*Avge*
R. J. Sidebottom	222.2	37	710	35	7-97	2	20.28
C. E. W. Silverwood. . . .	351.4	73	1,177	48	5-63	2	24.52
S. P. Kirby	463	80	1,769	67	8-80	5	26.40
A. McGrath	117.1	20	347	13	3-26	0	26.69
M. J. Hoggard.	192.3	44	547	18	7-49	1	30.38
D. Gough.	218.1	46	651	19	3-40	0	34.26
R. K. J. Dawson	241.5	47	840	17	3-119	0	49.41
A. K. D. Gray.	207.2	43	628	12	3-43	0	52.33

Also bowled: T. T. Bresnan 58–12–171–4; V. J. Craven 72–18–239–8; G. M. Fellows 14–1–27–1; M. J. Lumb 12–0–66–1; P. J. Swanepoel 34–11–70–3; M. P. Vaughan 1–0–5–0; C. White 21–3–64–0; M. J. Wood 2–0–4–1; Yuvraj Singh 34.3–5–130–3.

COUNTY RECORDS

Highest score for:	341	G. H. Hirst v Leicestershire at Leicester	1905
Highest score against:	318*	W. G. Grace (Gloucestershire) at Cheltenham. . . .	1876
Best bowling for:	10-10	H. Verity v Nottinghamshire at Leeds	1932
Best bowling against:	10-37	C. V. Grimmett (Australians) at Sheffield	1930
Highest total for:	887	v Warwickshire at Birmingham	1896
Highest total against:	681-7 dec.	by Leicestershire at Bradford	1996
Lowest total for:	23	v Hampshire at Middlesbrough	1965
Lowest total against:	13	by Nottinghamshire at Nottingham	1901

YORKSHIRE DIRECTORY

ADDRESS

Headingley Cricket Ground, Leeds LS6 3BU (0113 278 7394; fax 0113 278 4099; email cricket@yorkshireccc.org.uk). **Website** www.yorkshireccc.org.uk.

GROUNDS

Leeds (Headingley): 2¼ miles NW of city centre and ¼ mile SW of Headingley centre. From city centre take A660 to Headingley High Street for Kirkstall Lane and St Michael's Lane. Nearest stations: Headingley (½ mile), Burley Park (¾ mile) or Leeds (2½ miles).

Scarborough: 1 mile N of town centre in North Marine Road, close to seafront. From A165 Coastal Road, L into Peasholm Road for North Marine Road and signs for cricket ground. Nearest station: Scarborough (¾ mile).

OFFICIALS

Captain 2003 – A. McGrath
2004 – C. White
Director of cricket 2003 – G. Cope
2004 – D. Byas
First-team coach K. Sharp

President R. A. Smith
Chief executive C. J. Graves
Operations director G. Cope
Head groundsman A. W. Fogarty
Scorer J. T. Potter

PLAYERS

Players expected to reappear in 2004

	Former counties	*Country*	*Born*	*Birthplace*
***Blakey** Richard John		E	15.1.1967	†*Huddersfield*
Bresnan Timothy Thomas		E	28.2.1985	†*Pontefract*
Craven Victor John		E	31.7.1980	†*Harrogate*
***Dawson** Richard Kevin James		E	4.8.1980	†*Doncaster*
Gray Andrew Kenneth Donovan		E	19.5.1974	*Armadale, Aus.*
Guy Simon Mark		E	17.11.1978	†*Rotherham*
***Hoggard** Matthew James		E	31.12.1976	†*Leeds*
Kirby Steven Paul		E	4.10.1977	*Bury*
***Lehmann** Darren Scott		A	5.2.1970	*Gawler*
Lumb Michael John		E	12.2.1980	*Johannesburg, SA*
***McGrath** Anthony		E	6.10.1975	†*Bradford*
Sayers Joseph John		E	5.11.1983	†*Leeds*
***Silverwood** Christopher Eric Wilfred		E	5.3.1975	†*Pontefract*
Swanepoel Pieter Johannes		SA (EU)	30.3.1977	*Paarl*
Taylor Christopher Robert		E	21.2.1981	†*Leeds*
Thornicroft Nicholas David		E	23.1.1985	†*York*
***Vaughan** Michael Paul		‡E	29.10.1974	*Manchester*
***White** Craig		E	16.12.1969	†*Morley*
Wood Matthew James		E	6.4.1977	†*Huddersfield*

Player due to join in 2004

Harvey Ian Joseph	Glos	A	10.4.1972	*Wonthaggi*

** Test player.* *† Born in Yorkshire.* *‡ 12-month ECB contract.*

YORKSHIRE v NORTHAMPTONSHIRE

At Leeds, April 18, 19, 20. Yorkshire won by an innings and 343 runs. Yorkshire 22 pts, Northamptonshire 2 pts. Toss: Northamptonshire. County debuts: P. A. Jaques, A. Nel.

Yorkshire dominated their lacklustre opponents at every stage and won the third-biggest innings victory in their history. In his first completed Championship match in nearly two seasons, Gough bowled menacingly to pick up six wickets and suggest that he had recovered from serious knee problems. With the bat, Wood put his wretched form in 2002 behind him with a powerful 157 in Yorkshire's only innings, but the *tour de force* came from Blakey, who hit an unbeaten 223 at better than a run a ball. His second double-century for the county came 16 years after his first, and the innings took him only 206 balls and 291 minutes, with 35 fours, many of them from cuts and cover-drives. McGrath delayed the declaration until Blakey had reached his career-best score and by then Yorkshire had piled up 673 – a lead of 489 and the fourth-largest total in their history. Andre Nel, making his Northamptonshire debut early after being thrown off South Africa A's tour of Australia for drink-driving, endured a difficult introduction, becoming one of four bowlers to concede over 100. During the two Northamptonshire innings, the Australian-born batsmen Cook and Phil Jaques made 171 runs, while the rest contributed a pathetic 103. It was a misleading guide to the season.

YORKSHIRE'S BIGGEST INNINGS VICTORIES

Inns and 397 runs	v Northamptonshire at Harrogate	1921
Inns and 387 runs	v Derbyshire at Chesterfield	1898
Inns and 343 runs	**v Northamptonshire at Leeds**	**2003**
Inns and 321 runs	v Leicestershire at Leicester (Aylestone Road)	1908
Inns and 314 runs	v Northamptonshire at Northampton *Yorkshire's first match v Northamptonshire.*	1908

YORKSHIRE'S BIGGEST TOTALS

887	v Warwickshire at Birmingham	1896
704	v Surrey at The Oval	1899
681-5 dec.	v Sussex at Sheffield (Bramall Lane)	1897
673-8 dec.	**v Northamptonshire at Leeds**	**2003**
662	v Derbyshire at Chesterfield	1898

Close of play: First day, Yorkshire 210-2 (Wood 109, Lumb 33); Second day, Northamptonshire 20-1 (Powell 0, Jaques 14).

Northamptonshire

First innings		Second innings	
R. A. White c Wood b Silverwood	2	c Taylor b Gough	0
M. J. Powell c Blakey b Gough	0	c Lumb b Silverwood	4
P. A. Jaques lbw b Silverwood	9	c and b Sidebottom	60
J. W. Cook c Wood b Dawson	74	c Blakey b Silverwood	28
*D. J. Sales lbw b Gough	12	lbw b McGrath	1
G. L. Brophy lbw b Gough	2	lbw b McGrath	0
G. P. Swann lbw b Sidebottom	10	b Silverwood	0
†T. M. B. Bailey lbw b Silverwood	31	lbw b Silverwood	0
C. G. Greenidge c Blakey b Hoggard	1	not out	9
A. Nel b Sidebottom	17	b Gough	8
J. A. R. Blain not out	1	lbw b Gough	5
B 1, l-b 10, w 2, n-b 12	25	B 18, l-b 7, n-b 6	31
1/2 (2) 2/8 (1) 3/15 (3) 4/45 (5) 5/53 (6) 6/101 (7) 7/147 (4) 8/163 (8) 9/181 (9) 10/184 (10)	184	1/0 (1) 2/36 (2) 3/84 (4) 4/85 (5) 5/85 (6) 6/86 (7) 7/86 (8) 8/123 (3) 9/132 (10) 10/146 (11)	146

Bonus points – Yorkshire 3.

Bowling: *First Innings*—Gough 12–1–40–3; Silverwood 10–2–45–3; Hoggard 14–3–37–1; Sidebottom 5.1–1–14–2; McGrath 3–0–10–0; Dawson 4–1–27–1. *Second Innings*—Gough 11.4–1–41–3; Silverwood 13–4–39–4; Sidebottom 7–1–28–1; McGrath 7–3–9–2; Fellows 2–0–4–0.

Yorkshire

C. R. Taylor c Brophy b Greenidge	16
M. J. Wood c White b Swann	157
*A. McGrath run out	35
M. J. Lumb c Bailey b Blain	42
†R. J. Blakey not out	223
G. M. Fellows b Nel	30
R. K. J. Dawson c Sales b Blain	38
C. E. W. Silverwood c Brophy b White	53
D. Gough c Sales b Blain	3
R. J. Sidebottom not out	24
B 4, l-b 10, w 3, n-b 35	52
1/46 (1) 2/99 (3) 3/230 (4) 4/330 (2) 5/405 (6) 6/489 (7) 7/604 (8) 8/621 (9)	(8 wkts dec.) 673

M. J. Hoggard did not bat.

Bonus points – Yorkshire 5, Northamptonshire 2 (130 overs: 654-8).

Bowling: Nel 29–3–120–1; Blain 26.2–3–153–3; Greenidge 27–1–164–1; Cook 22–3–79–0; Swann 26–1–108–1; White 4–0–35–1.

Umpires: M. J. Kitchen and J. W. Lloyds.

At Southampton, April 30, May 1, 2, 3. YORKSHIRE drew with HAMPSHIRE.

YORKSHIRE v DERBYSHIRE

At Leeds, May 9, 10, 11, 12. Derbyshire won by 166 runs. Derbyshire 22 pts, Yorkshire 4 pts. Toss: Derbyshire.

Derbyshire's win was thoroughly deserved because they batted with far greater resolve and exploited swinging conditions more effectively. However, they nearly failed to make the advantage count. After winning a first-innings lead of 192 by the third morning, Cork chose not to enforce the follow-on – despite heavy rain in the area and a grim forecast. The decision was widely questioned, but Cork got away with it – just. Di Venuto's 77 helped stretch Derbyshire's lead to 406, a circle of blue stationed itself over Headingley for most of the final day and Derbyshire took the last wicket by 5 p.m. Earlier, it had been Sutton's diligence which put them on top. His disciplined, seven-hour 127 was very much in the Boycott mould, and a chalk-and-cheese stand with Cork added 159 for the sixth wicket. Yorkshire's only outstanding bowler was Sidebottom, who jagged the ball around and took a career-best seven for 97. Dean and Welch responded in kind, wreaking havoc in both Yorkshire innings. Welch twice dismissed Vaughan when he looked set.

Close of play: First day, Derbyshire 297-5 (Sutton 79, Cork 39); Second day, Yorkshire 203-4 (Blakey 21, Richardson 10); Third day, Yorkshire 12-0 (Wood 6, Vaughan 2).

Derbyshire

A. I. Gait b Sidebottom	32	– (2) lbw b Dawson	25
M. J. Di Venuto c Blakey b Sidebottom	50	– (1) c McGrath b Dawson	77
C. W. G. Bassano c Richardson b Sidebottom	23	– not out	53
S. A. Selwood c Blakey b Sidebottom	2	– c Blakey b Sidebottom	14
D. R. Hewson run out	57	– lbw b Sidebottom	3
†L. D. Sutton b Dawson	127	– not out	22
*D. G. Cork lbw b McGrath	92		
T. Lungley lbw b Sidebottom	7		
G. Welch lbw b Sidebottom	0		
Mohammad Ali c Richardson b Sidebottom	5		
K. J. Dean not out	0		
B 3, l-b 18, w 2, n-b 4	27	B 7, l-b 3, w 6, n-b 4	20
1/75 (1) 2/84 (2) 3/86 (4) 4/116 (3) 5/217 (5) 6/376 (7) 7/408 (8) 8/408 (9) 9/416 (10) 10/422 (6)	422	1/109 (1) 2/120 (2) 3/147 (4) 4/155 (5) (4 wkts dec.)	214

Bonus points – Derbyshire 5, Yorkshire 3 (130 overs: 416-9).

Bowling: *First Innings*—Silverwood 23–3–75–0; Hoggard 27–4–80–0; Kirby 24–4–90–0; Sidebottom 31–3–97–7; Dawson 17.4–3–38–1; McGrath 10–3–21–1. *Second Innings*—Hoggard 9–2–26–0; Silverwood 6–0–23–0; Kirby 7–0–37–0; Sidebottom 10–2–24–2; Dawson 25.2–4–72–2; McGrath 6–1–15–0; Lumb 1–0–7–0.

Yorkshire

M. J. Wood c Sutton b Dean	9	– lbw b Mohammad Ali	32
M. P. Vaughan c Cork b Welch	47	– b Welch	38
*A. McGrath c Hewson b Cork	61	– lbw b Welch	4
M. J. Lumb lbw b Cork	38	– lbw b Mohammad Ali	86
†R. J. Blakey c Gait b Welch	29	– run out	11
S. A. Richardson c Bassano b Welch	10	– c Sutton b Welch	6
R. K. J. Dawson c Di Venuto b Dean	0	– lbw b Dean	13
C. E. W. Silverwood c Sutton b Dean	2	– c Selwood b Dean	2
R. J. Sidebottom lbw b Welch	9	– c Di Venuto b Welch	4
M. J. Hoggard not out	1	– not out	13
S. P. Kirby c Di Venuto b Dean	0	– lbw b Mohammad Ali	4
L-b 2, w 2, n-b 20	24	B 5, l-b 2, n-b 20	27
1/15 (1) 2/97 (2) 3/152 (3) 4/174 (4) 5/204 (6) 6/205 (7) 7/209 (8) 8/224 (9) 9/229 (5) 10/230 (11)	230	1/58 (2) 2/66 (3) 3/103 (1) 4/124 (5) 5/148 (6) 6/163 (7) 7/165 (8) 8/196 (9) 9/236 (4) 10/240 (11)	240

Bonus points – Yorkshire 1, Derbyshire 3.

Bowling: *First Innings*—Cork 21–5–69–2; Dean 12.3–1–39–4; Welch 16–4–39–4; Mohammad Ali 8–0–48–0; Lungley 8–2–33–0. *Second Innings*—Cork 16–3–44–0; Dean 23–8–63–2; Welch 20–3–74–4; Lungley 5–0–26–0; Mohammad Ali 7.4–0–26–3.

Umpires: B. Dudleston and M. J. Kitchen.

At Northampton, May 14, 15, 16, 17. YORKSHIRE drew with NORTHAMPTONSHIRE.

YORKSHIRE v GLAMORGAN

At Leeds, May 21, 22, 23, 24. Drawn. Yorkshire 7.75 pts (after 0.25 pt penalty), Glamorgan 10 pts. Toss: Yorkshire. County debut: Yuvraj Singh.

During this rain-ravaged match the total amount of play Yorkshire had lost in the month rose to more than 36 hours, making it their wettest May in over ten years. At the start, the pitch looked damp at the football-stand end and Glamorgan's pace attack took advantage, none more so than

Bradford-born Wharf. After the second day was washed out, Silverwood also bowled with venom during Glamorgan's reply, while Blakey held six catches, giving him 800 first-class dismissals for Yorkshire. But from 157 for eight, Wallace mastered some untidy bowling and helped build stands of 94 and 64 for the last two wickets. Despite the lively pitch, more interruptions on the last two days meant any prospects of a result disappeared. Yuvraj Singh arrived in Yorkshire from India the day before the match, and began to acclimatise during a solid 25 not out in the second innings. Yorkshire remained third in the table.

Close of play: First day, Yorkshire 190-9 (Sidebottom 24, Kirby 4); Second day, No play; Third day, Glamorgan 248-8 (Wallace 77, Kasprowicz 34).

Yorkshire

First innings		Second innings	
*M. J. Wood c Dale b Harrison	9	– not out	73
S. A. Richardson c and b Harrison	1	– c Wallace b Harrison	50
Yuvraj Singh c Powell b Kasprowicz	11	– not out	25
M. J. Lumb b Kasprowicz	39		
†R. J. Blakey c Powell b Wharf	1		
G. M. Fellows c Wallace b Wharf	53		
T. T. Bresnan c Maynard b Kasprowicz	3		
R. K. J. Dawson c and b Kasprowicz	20		
C. E. W. Silverwood c Powell b Harrison	10		
R. J. Sidebottom b Wharf	28		
S. P. Kirby not out	13		
B 1, l-b 9, w 1, n-b 10	21	L-b 3, n-b 8	11
1/4 (2) 2/19 (3) 3/43 (1) 4/46 (5) 5/85 (4) 6/90 (7) 7/126 (8) 8/141 (9) 9/183 (6) 10/209 (10)	209	1/105 (2) (1 wkt dec.)	159

Bonus points – Yorkshire 1, Glamorgan 3.

Bowling: *First Innings*—Kasprowicz 21–7–51–4; Harrison 22–8–58–3; Wharf 15.4–4–63–3; Croft 9–3–21–0; Dale 2–0–6–0. *Second Innings*—Kasprowicz 6–0–23–0; Harrison 12–5–32–1; Croft 15–2–50–0; Wharf 6–0–39–0; Dale 2–0–12–0.

Glamorgan

A. Dale c Blakey b Silverwood	0
I. J. Thomas c Blakey b Silverwood	25
D. L. Hemp c Blakey b Silverwood	0
M. J. Powell c Lumb b Kirby	11
M. P. Maynard c Yuvraj Singh b Sidebottom	51
J. Hughes c Blakey b Kirby	10
†M. A. Wallace c Sidebottom b Bresnan	94
*R. D. B. Croft lbw b Kirby	9
D. S. Harrison c Blakey b Sidebottom	1
M. S. Kasprowicz c Blakey b Silverwood	36
A. G. Wharf not out	29
B 8, l-b 12, w 3, n-b 26	49
1/4 (1) 2/6 (3) 3/35 (2) 4/57 (4) 5/95 (6) 6/141 (5) 7/152 (8) 8/157 (9) 9/251 (10) 10/315 (7)	315

Bonus points – Glamorgan 3, Yorkshire 3.

Bowling: Silverwood 20–4–57–4; Sidebottom 16–3–51–2; Bresnan 11.4–0–51–1; Kirby 22–3–89–3; Dawson 10–1–44–0; Fellows 2–0–3–0.

Umpires: J. W. Holder and V. A. Holder.

YORKSHIRE v DURHAM

At Leeds, May 30, 31, June 1. Durham won by 167 runs. Durham 19 pts, Yorkshire 4 pts. Toss: Durham. First-class debut: P. J. Swanepoel. Championship debuts: P. Mustard, L. E. Plunkett.

Coach Martyn Moxon was overjoyed to beat his old county, in Durham's first Championship win over Yorkshire, at the 11th attempt. And another, younger, native of the Broad Acres also wore a smile: on his Championship debut, 18-year-old Middlesbrough-born Liam Plunkett took five for 53 in the first innings, including a burst of four wickets in nine balls, and crushed Yorkshire's spirit. Sandwiching Plunkett's achievements were two unyielding innings from his captain, Lewis, who batted over 11 hours in total on an untrustworthy pitch. It was an object lesson in the art of surviving and thriving, and during his first-innings century he became Durham's top-scorer in first-class cricket, passing John Morris's 5,670. Lewis's efforts left Yorkshire chasing 261 to win but they collapsed to 93 all out, a defeat that sent them out of the top three and even inspired a death threat to the executive board – politely signed by the former member who sent it. Martin Love broke his thumb shortly before the match, and Pattison dislocated his right shoulder during it, adding to Durham's long injury list.

Close of play: First day, Durham 267-7 (Lewis 120, Phillips 17); Second day, Durham 99-3 (Lewis 43, Phillips 0).

Durham

*J. J. B. Lewis lbw b Silverwood	124	– c Lumb b Silverwood	66
M. A. Gough c Blakey b Gough	10	– lbw b Lumb	43
G. J. Muchall c Blakey b Kirby	10	– c and b Swanepoel	4
G. J. Pratt c Blakey b Swanepoel	4	– c Blakey b Silverwood	0
N. Peng c Richardson b Gough	2	– (6) st Blakey b Dawson	29
I. Pattison lbw b Fellows	62	– absent hurt	
†P. Mustard c Blakey b Dawson	23	– c Yuvraj Singh b Silverwood	20
L. E. Plunkett lbw b Kirby	4	– lbw b Gough	0
N. C. Phillips c Blakey b Silverwood	19	– (5) lbw b Swanepoel	9
N. Killeen lbw b Silverwood	0	– (9) not out	2
D. Pretorius not out	1	– (10) c Yuvraj Singh b Silverwood	2
B 1, l-b 12, n-b 8	21	B 7, l-b 3, w 1, n-b 14	25
1/29 (2) 2/41 (3) 3/46 (4) 4/51 (5) 5/183 (6) 6/220 (7) 7/230 (8) 8/275 (1) 9/279 (10) 10/280 (9)	280	1/79 (2) 2/84 (3) 3/99 (4) 4/117 (5) 5/169 (6) 6/191 (7) 7/192 (8) 8/194 (1) 9/200 (10)	200

Bonus points – Durham 2, Yorkshire 3.

Bowling: *First Innings*—Gough 23–5–55–2; Silverwood 21.3–1–80–3; Kirby 20–4–40–2; Swanepoel 18–9–30–1; Dawson 16–7–27–1; Fellows 10–1–20–1; Lumb 3–0–15–0. *Second Innings*—Gough 15–2–36–1; Silverwood 15–2–40–4; Kirby 12–5–29–0; Swanepoel 16–2–40–2; Lumb 6–0–29–1; Dawson 2–0–16–1.

Yorkshire

*M. J. Wood lbw b Pretorius	0	– b Pretorius	0
S. A. Richardson b Pattison	18	– lbw b Killeen	18
Yuvraj Singh c Mustard b Pretorius	56	– b Plunkett	1
M. J. Lumb b Phillips	105	– c Gough b Pretorius	9
†R. J. Blakey c Mustard b Plunkett	3	– lbw b Muchall	8
G. M. Fellows c Killeen b Plunkett	9	– c Pretorius b Muchall	4
R. K. J. Dawson c Phillips b Plunkett	0	– lbw b Muchall	21
D. Gough c Pretorius b Plunkett	4	– b Pretorius	9
C. E. W. Silverwood b Plunkett	0	– b Pretorius	8
P. J. Swanepoel c and b Pretorius	17	– b Plunkett	2
S. P. Kirby not out	0	– not out	0
L-b 5, w 1, n-b 2	8	B 1, l-b 8, n-b 4	13
1/0 (1) 2/66 (2) 3/84 (3) 4/89 (5) 5/111 (6) 6/111 (7) 7/115 (8) 8/115 (9) 9/194 (10) 10/220 (4)	220	1/4 (1) 2/9 (3) 3/18 (4) 4/39 (2) 5/39 (5) 6/52 (6) 7/71 (8) 8/85 (7) 9/91 (10) 10/93 (9)	93

Bonus points – Yorkshire 1, Durham 3.

Bowling: *First Innings*—Pretorius 16–2–54–3; Plunkett 12–1–53–5; Killeen 15–2–46–0; Pattison 5.4–3–7–1; Muchall 4.2–0–13–0; Phillips 7.4–0–42–1. *Second Innings*—Pretorius 9.4–1–15–4; Plunkett 7–1–21–2; Killeen 6–1–22–1; Muchall 8–2–26–3.

Umpires: B. Dudleston and B. Leadbeater.

At Bradford, June 4, 5, 6. YORKSHIRE drew with BRADFORD/LEEDS UCCE.

At Taunton, June 27, 28, 29, 30. YORKSHIRE beat SOMERSET by ten wickets.

At Derby, July 2, 3, 4, 5. YORKSHIRE beat DERBYSHIRE by ten wickets.

At Leeds, July 9, 10, 11. YORKSHIRE drew with INDIA A (see India A tour section).

At Chester-le-Street, July 15, 16, 17, 18. YORKSHIRE lost to DURHAM by three wickets.

YORKSHIRE v HAMPSHIRE

At Scarborough, July 23, 24, 25, 26. Drawn. Yorkshire 11 pts, Hampshire 9 pts. Toss: Yorkshire. Championship debut: I. Brunnschweiler.

Anxious to keep the game alive following the third-day washout, Yorkshire set a target of 307 in what became 71 overs – a generous declaration given the good pitch and Sidebottom's absence with a twisted ankle. Craven undid the two best batsmen, Katich and Crawley, with his increasingly useful medium-pace, and Hampshire were in some trouble at 111 for six. But Hamblin and Udal survived the last 77 minutes. The first-day crowd of 3,000 had endured a slow start before Wood increased the tempo, hitting a splendid 155. Hampshire avoided the follow-on thanks to Katich: after arriving in the first over, he survived a sharp slip chance before scoring but ended up unbeaten on 143. The rest of the top six managed nine between them. On the final day, Yorkshire thrashed 188 in 112 minutes to set up their declaration, but the draw was a just conclusion.

Close of play: First day, Yorkshire 326-5 (Yuvraj Singh 6, Guy 13); Second day, Yorkshire 23-0 (Wood 14, Fleming 9); Third day, No play.

Yorkshire

Batsman	First innings		Second innings	
*M. J. Wood c Crawley b Tremlett	155	–	lbw b Mascarenhas	43
S. P. Fleming c Tremlett b Bruce	16	–	c Francis b Bruce	53
V. J. Craven lbw b Mascarenhas	47	–	c Mascarenhas b Udal	38
M. J. Lumb lbw b Mascarenhas	64	–	c Tremlett b Udal	59
Yuvraj Singh c Francis b Udal	26	–	not out	0
C. White lbw b Mascarenhas	0			
†S. M. Guy c Brunnschweiler b Tremlett	13			
A. K. D. Gray lbw b Udal	30			
C. E. W. Silverwood not out	4			
R. J. Sidebottom c Tremlett b Bruce	0			
S. P. Kirby c Adams b Udal	0			
L-b 8, w 1, n-b 20	29		B 3, l-b 3, n-b 12	18
1/55 (2) 2/149 (3) 3/303 (1) 4/303 (4) 5/303 (6) 6/326 (7) 7/380 (5) 8/380 (8) 9/383 (10) 10/384 (11)	384		1/89 (1) 2/109 (2) 3/211 (3) 4/211 (4) (4 wkts dec.)	211

Bonus points – Yorkshire 4, Hampshire 3.

Bowling: *First Innings*—Tremlett 27–5–94–2; Mascarenhas 31–9–51–3; Hamblin 8–0–35–0; Bruce 23–4–101–2; Udal 33–11–70–3; Katich 8–1–25–0. *Second Innings*—Tremlett 8–2–32–0; Mascarenhas 9–2–39–1; Udal 10.5–1–42–2; Bruce 7–0–65–1; Hamblin 5–0–27–0.

Hampshire

D. A. Kenway b Kirby	0	– lbw b Kirby	5
J. H. K. Adams c Gray b Silverwood	0	– c and b Gray	47
S. M. Katich not out	143	– b Craven	4
*J. P. Crawley c Guy b Kirby	0	– c Wood b Craven	32
J. D. Francis lbw b Silverwood	9	– c Wood b Gray	2
J. R. C. Hamblin b Silverwood	0	– not out	35
A. D. Mascarenhas c Fleming b Sidebottom	4	– c Wood b Gray	0
S. D. Udal b Craven	26	– not out	33
†I. Brunnschweiler b Silverwood	34		
C. T. Tremlett c Fleming b Sidebottom	19		
J. T. A. Bruce c Guy b Gray	2		
B 4, l-b 5, n-b 43	52	L-b 9, w 1, n-b 12	22
1/2 (1) 2/4 (2) 3/7 (4) 4/96 (5) 5/96 (6) 6/107 (7) 7/159 (8) 8/232 (9) 9/284 (10) 10/289 (11)	289	1/12 (1) 2/30 (3) 3/83 (4) 4/96 (5) 5/105 (2) 6/111 (7)	(6 wkts) 180

Bonus points – Hampshire 2, Yorkshire 3.

Bowling: *First Innings*—Kirby 16–1–79–2; Silverwood 15–1–86–4; Sidebottom 11–1–28–2; Gray 16–0–49–1; Craven 9–1–38–1. *Second Innings*—Silverwood 16–3–40–0; Kirby 13–1–59–1; Craven 11–4–25–2; Gray 26–12–43–3; Yuvraj Singh 4.4–1–4–0.

Umpires: J. H. Evans and B. Leadbeater.

At Cheltenham, July 30, 31, August 1, 2. YORKSHIRE drew with GLOUCESTERSHIRE.

YORKSHIRE v WORCESTERSHIRE

At Scarborough, August 13, 14. Worcestershire won by five wickets. Worcestershire 17 pts, Yorkshire 3 pts. Toss: Yorkshire.

The match was over inside two days after a thunderstorm earlier in the week had left damp in the pitch. But despite 25 wickets falling on the first day – the result of good full-pitched bowling, seam movement and late swing – the ECB inspector left satisfied. Bowling with superb control, Kabir Ali took Yorkshire's first seven wickets, and finished with eight for the second time in a month. His figures were the best in the Championship at Scarborough since Bill Bowes's nine for 121 against Essex in 1932, and, for two days, the best of the 2003 Championship. In reply, Ali's rival for a Test place, Kirby, took six and, helped by Silverwood, despatched Worcestershire for 91 in less than a session. After the carnage, conditions eased on day two. But despite the first fifty of the match, by White, Yorkshire batted disappointingly, leaving Worcestershire to chase 278, and 273 overs to get them. At 188 for five it was touch and go, but a lack of support meant Kirby and Silverwood were bowled into the ground, allowing Smith and Batty (released by England on the first afternoon and thus replacing Khalid in the Worcestershire team) to settle the issue with an unbroken stand of 90.

Close of play: First day, Yorkshire 137-5 (White 42, Kirby 6).

Yorkshire

M. J. Wood lbw b Ali	4	– c and b Hayward	16
S. P. Fleming lbw b Ali	31	– c Rhodes b Kemp	35
*A. McGrath lbw b Ali	11	– lbw b Mason	15
M. J. Lumb lbw b Ali	0	– c Rhodes b Kemp	0
V. J. Craven b Ali	7	– c Solanki b Kemp	17
C. White c Solanki b Ali	12	– lbw b Mason	54
†S. M. Guy c Rhodes b Ali	0	– (8) lbw b Mason	26
A. K. D. Gray b Mason	11	– (9) c Hick b Hayward	27
R. K. J. Dawson not out	42	– (10) c Solanki b Kemp	24
C. E. W. Silverwood c Khalid b Ali	7	– (11) not out	0
S. P. Kirby b Hayward	4	– (7) c Solanki b Ali	15
L-b 1	1	L-b 2, w 1, n-b 6	9
1/4 (1) 2/26 (3) 3/26 (4) 4/34 (5) 5/57 (2) 6/57 (7) 7/72 (6) 8/80 (8) 9/93 (10) 10/130 (11)	130	1/21 (1) 2/67 (3) 3/67 (2) 4/78 (4) 5/124 (5) 6/150 (6) 7/168 (7) 8/197 (8) 9/238 (10) 10/238 (9)	238

Bonus points – Worcestershire 3.

Bowling: *First Innings*—Ali 16–4–53–8; Hayward 7.2–2–39–1; Mason 8–1–37–1. *Second Innings*—Ali 12–2–51–1; Hayward 8.2–0–48–2; Kemp 18–6–44–4; Mason 19–6–53–3; Batty 13–2–40–0.

Worcestershire

S. D. Peters c Fleming b Kirby	6	– c McGrath b Kirby	15
A. Singh lbw b Silverwood	1	– c Gray b Silverwood	41
G. A. Hick c Dawson b Kirby	16	– b Kirby	47
*B. F. Smith c Guy b Silverwood	2	– not out	87
V. S. Solanki lbw b Silverwood	0	– st Guy b Gray	2
J. M. Kemp c and b Kirby	5	– b Dawson	23
†S. J. Rhodes c Gray b Kirby	10		
G. J. Batty c Guy b Craven	5	– (7) not out	54
Kabir Ali c Guy b Kirby	6		
M. S. Mason b Kirby	25		
M. Hayward not out	1		
L-b 1, w 1, n-b 12	14	B 1, l-b 5, w 1, n-b 2	9
1/3 (2) 2/17 (1) 3/22 (4) 4/24 (5) 5/36 (3) 6/38 (6) 7/53 (8) 8/53 (7) 9/70 (9) 10/91 (10)	91	1/21 (1) 2/96 (3) 3/115 (2) 4/134 (5) 5/188 (6)	(5 wkts) 278

Bonus points – Yorkshire 3.

S. A. Khalid did not bat.

Bowling: *First Innings*—Silverwood 10–4–33–3; Kirby 14–5–51–6; Craven 4–2–6–1. *Second Innings*—Silverwood 18–3–59–1; Kirby 22–6–79–2; Craven 4–1–26–0; McGrath 11–2–39–0; Gray 14.2–3–52–1; Dawson 7–0–17–1.

Umpires: M. J. Harris and B. Leadbeater.

At Colwyn Bay, August 25, 26, 27, 28. YORKSHIRE drew with GLAMORGAN.

YORKSHIRE v SOMERSET

At Leeds, September 3, 4, 5. Yorkshire won by nine wickets. Yorkshire 22 pts, Somerset 3 pts. Toss: Somerset. County debut: D. R. Martyn.

Yorkshire, who had not won in the Championship since July 5, outplayed Somerset, winless since May 24, to move into third and rekindle their fading promotion hopes. They did so despite losing Kirby for the second day – he lost consciousness after McLean hit a fierce return drive straight at him. On top of that, the Australian Test player Damien Martyn had to retire hurt during his debut innings for Yorkshire after top-edging a hook into his face. On a good Headingley pitch, Hoggard, returning from a cartilage operation in late May, settled straight into a rhythm and whittled through Somerset's first innings: his seven for 49 was a career-best. After a patient 93 by White and Martyn's retirement on 87, a boisterous seventh-wicket stand of 108 between Dawson and Gough helped Yorkshire to a lead of 182. Off-side hitting by Edwards then left a token target of 132, which Wood and McGrath – who plundered eight boundaries off Andrew's four overs – reached before the end of the third day.

Close of play: First day, Yorkshire 86-3 (White 36, Martyn 6); Second day, Somerset 94-2 (Edwards 55).

Somerset

M. J. Wood lbw b Hoggard	3	– lbw b Gough	1
N. J. Edwards c Dawson b Hoggard	7	– c and b Kirby	90
*M. Burns c Lumb b Hoggard	28	– c sub b Wood	34
J. Cox c Blakey b Gough	11	– lbw b Kirby	59
T. Webley c Kirby b Hoggard	22	– lbw b McGrath	12
I. D. Blackwell b Hoggard	0	– c Kirby b Dawson	48
†R. J. Turner b Hoggard	11	– lbw b Gough	13
G. M. Andrew c Dawson b Gough	11	– c Gough b Dawson	9
P. S. Jones not out	61	– c and b Hoggard	15
R. L. Johnson c Hoggard b Kirby	30	– not out	14
N. A. M. McLean c McGrath b Hoggard	15	– lbw b Hoggard	2
B 2, l-b 5, w 1, n-b 21	29	L-b 3, w 1, n-b 12	16
1/7 (1) 2/13 (2) 3/45 (4) 4/75 (3) 5/75 (6) 6/91 (7) 7/108 (8) 8/120 (5) 9/199 (10) 10/228 (11)	228	1/1 (1) 2/94 (3) 3/157 (2) 4/180 (5) 5/231 (4) 6/266 (6) 7/278 (8) 8/291 (7) 9/301 (9) 10/313 (11)	313

Bonus points – Somerset 1, Yorkshire 3.

Bowling: *First Innings*—Gough 20–8–42–2; Hoggard 22.4–9–49–7; Kirby 14.5–1–82–1; Dawson 3–0–35–0; Craven 2–0–13–0. *Second Innings*—Hoggard 20.5–2–57–2; Gough 19–2–58–2; Craven 12–3–28–0; McGrath 14–2–43–1; Dawson 18–2–59–2; Wood 2–0–4–1; Kirby 13–0–61–2.

"A common criticism of Tendulkar has been that, at the crunch, he crumbles. As if to counter that, he has transformed himself from a spontaneous marauder to a purposeful builder."

West Indians in India and Bangladesh, page 1117.

Yorkshire

C. White b Jones	93	– b Johnson	8
M. J. Wood c Turner b Andrew	40	– not out	53
*A. McGrath c Turner b Andrew	0	– not out	67
M. J. Lumb c Turner b Johnson	2		
D. R. Martyn retired hurt	87		
V. J. Craven c Turner b Johnson	3		
†R. J. Blakey c Turner b Jones	27		
R. K. J. Dawson c and b Burns	47		
D. Gough c Cox b Johnson	83		
M. J. Hoggard not out	11		
S. P. Kirby absent hurt			
B 4, l-b 10, w 1, n-b 2	17	L-b 4	4
1/72 (2) 2/72 (3) 3/79 (4) 4/225 (1) 5/248 (6) 6/264 (7) 7/372 (8) 8/410 (9)	410	1/29 (1)	(1 wkt) 132

Bonus points – Yorkshire 5, Somerset 2.

In the first innings Martyn retired hurt at 225-4.

Bowling: *First Innings*—McLean 19–1–90–0; Johnson 27.4–8–92–3; Jones 18–0–86–2; Andrew 11–2–48–2; Blackwell 14–1–53–0; Edwards 1–0–6–0; Burns 2–0–21–1. *Second Innings*—McLean 6–1–21–0; Johnson 6–0–31–1; Jones 6–1–28–0; Andrew 4–0–36–0; Edwards 3–0–6–0; Wood 1.1–0–6–0.

Umpires: V. A. Holder and P. Willey.

At Worcester, September 12, 13, 14, 15. YORKSHIRE lost to WORCESTERSHIRE by 71 runs.

YORKSHIRE v GLOUCESTERSHIRE

At Leeds, September 17, 18, 19, 20. Drawn. Yorkshire 12 pts, Gloucestershire 10 pts. Toss: Yorkshire.

The battle for the last promotion place came down to this: Yorkshire needed to win; a draw was enough for Gloucestershire. At tea on the last afternoon Gloucestershire were tottering at 93 for five, chasing 254, but gloom and rain descended and Yorkshire were denied. However, even McGrath admitted his side had not done enough over the summer to feel hard done by. The match will be remembered for a sensational career-best 238 from Martyn, who stroked the season's fastest first-class century – 65 balls, four sixes and 15 text-book fours. He then surged to 200 in 128 balls and 176 minutes, 38 minutes quicker than Bradman on the way to his famous 309-in-a-day against England on this ground in 1930. When he finally played across a ball from Gidman, after 222 minutes and 159 balls of startlingly pure strokeplay, Martyn had hit seven sixes and 38 fours. Together with Wood – who hit a fine 116 – he added a Yorkshire-record 330 for the fourth wicket (beating 312 between David Denton and George Hirst at Southampton in 1914). It was also the highest Championship stand for Yorkshire at Headingley. However, their grip loosened when a crucial ninth-wicket partnership of 97 between Fisher, formerly on their staff, and Lewis took Gloucestershire past the follow-on target of 327. Bad weather, which allowed less than eight overs on day three, further darkened Yorkshire's prospects. On the fourth morning, they tried to make up lost time, hurtling to the declaration, but the Leeds murk rescued Gloucestershire.

Close of play: First day, Gloucestershire 5-0 (Weston 4, Spearman 1); Second day, Yorkshire 4-0 (White 2, Wood 2); Third day, Yorkshire 29-2 (Wood 17, Lumb 4).

Yorkshire

C. White c Harvey b Smith	0	– c sub b Lewis	2
M. J. Wood c sub b Gidman	116	– c Russell b Lewis	25
*A. McGrath c Hancock b Harvey	28	– c Hancock b Harvey	1
M. J. Lumb lbw b Harvey	4	– b Harvey	31
D. R. Martyn b Gidman	238	– c Gidman b Lewis	17
†R. J. Blakey b Fisher	9	– c Spearman b Lewis	21
R. K. J. Dawson not out	48	– b Harvey	5
D. Gough c Weston b Fisher	10	– not out	2
C. E. W. Silverwood c Russell b Lewis	4	– not out	7
S. P. Kirby c Rhodes b Lewis	5		
M. J. Hoggard b Harvey	2		
L-b 6, n-b 6	12	L-b 6, n-b 4	10
1/0 (1) 2/47 (3) 3/51 (4) 4/381 (2) 5/396 (5) 6/408 (6) 7/436 (8) 8/445 (9) 9/467 (10) 10/476 (11)	476	1/4 (1) 2/7 (3) 3/43 (2) 4/69 (5) 5/82 (4) 6/100 (7) 7/108 (6)	(7 wkts dec.) 121

Bonus points – Yorkshire 5, Gloucestershire 3.

Bowling: *First Innings*—Smith 10–1–57–1; Lewis 22–5–91–2; Harvey 20–4–91–3; Gidman 20–1–121–2; Fisher 28–5–110–2. *Second Innings*—Lewis 12–1–71–4; Harvey 11–1–44–3.

Gloucestershire

W. P. C. Weston b Silverwood	84	– (2) lbw b Hoggard	4
*C. M. Spearman c Martyn b Hoggard	41	– (1) c Martyn b Kirby	8
T. H. C. Hancock c Dawson b Silverwood	6	– c Dawson b McGrath	48
J. N. Rhodes b Silverwood	5	– b McGrath	16
M. G. N. Windows lbw b Silverwood	0	– b Gough	4
A. P. R. Gidman b Gough	8	– not out	9
I. J. Harvey b McGrath	70	– not out	1
†R. C. Russell c Dawson b McGrath	0		
I. D. Fisher c sub b McGrath	71		
J. Lewis b Silverwood	36		
A. M. Smith not out	0		
B 8, l-b 7, n-b 8	23	B 1, n-b 2	3
1/79 (2) 2/94 (3) 3/100 (4) 4/108 (5) 5/116 (6) 6/209 (1) 7/210 (8) 8/247 (7) 9/344 (10) 10/344 (9)	344	1/4 (2) 2/25 (1) 3/63 (4) 4/78 (5) 5/92 (3)	(5 wkts) 93

Bonus points – Gloucestershire 3, Yorkshire 3.

Bowling: *First Innings*—Hoggard 21–3–72–1; Silverwood 25.1–7–75–5; Kirby 13.5–3–63–0; Gough 22–4–83–1; McGrath 11.2–2–26–3; Dawson 3–0–10–0. *Second Innings*—Silverwood 9–4–19–0; Hoggard 10–5–26–1; Gough 10–5–17–1; Kirby 8–2–19–1; McGrath 4–1–11–2.

Umpires: N. G. Cowley and J. W. Lloyds.

WALTER LAWRENCE TROPHY

The Walter Lawrence Trophy for the fastest first-class century in 2003 was won by Damien Martyn of Yorkshire, who reached 100 in 65 balls against Gloucestershire at Leeds on September 17, in the last first-class match of the season. His nearest rival was Bilal Shafayat of Nottinghamshire, who reached his hundred in 73 balls against Durham UCCE at Nottingham on April 13, the second day of the season. Martyn, who went on to 200 in 128 balls and finished on 238 from 159, received £5,000 from the trophy's sponsors, Aon.

CHELTENHAM & GLOUCESTER TROPHY, 2003

REVIEW BY LAWRENCE BOOTH

Mike Smith

As parting shots go, it was hard to beat. The one-day revolution that John Bracewell had set in motion in 1999, when Gloucestershire lifted both the Benson and Hedges Cup and the NatWest Trophy, came full circle on a sun-kissed day at Lord's. Victory in the final against Worcestershire was numbingly straightforward, but Bracewell was hardly complaining: this was his sixth major one-day trophy in six years as coach – a glittering farewell before he headed off to take charge of his native New Zealand, and a reminder to everyone else that Gloucestershire, ageing personnel and all, remained the slickest limited-overs outfit in the land.

Even so, the soggy soufflé of a final was a letdown after two mouth-wateringly moreish semi-finals. Gloucestershire were thankful for the cool head of their tailender, James Averis, after they were pushed all the way by Derbyshire, the surprise package of the competition. Two days later, Worcestershire were celebrating one of the most nerveless overs in one-day history. Lancashire needed seven from six balls with four wickets in hand, but were scuppered by Andrew Hall, the never-say-die South African all-rounder, who produced a string of inch-perfect yorkers. It was just a shame for the neutrals that, when Worcestershire arrived at Lord's, they had left their pizzazz at New Road. Like many a side before them, they had no answer to the most intelligently varied one-day attack in the country: Mike Smith's economy – he conceded just 3.43 an over throughout the competition – Ian Harvey's cunning, Averis's bustle and Martyn Ball's bounce made an irresistible mix.

If there was an element of predestination about Gloucestershire's triumph – their name, after all, was almost literally on the cup from the start – then no one could have predicted Derbyshire's derring-do. Their early progress was memorable for the feats of Chris Bassano. In 27 one-day innings before the third-round clash with Kent Cricket Board, he had never scored more than 61. Now, Bassano, a diabetic, hit two hundreds in successive rounds, with the innings against Glamorgan coming just three days after he had been in hospital on a drip. Derbyshire's real day in the sun, however, came in the quarter-finals. Amid the ruins of a run of seven Championship defeats, they came up against the Division One leaders Surrey, who were unbeaten in all cricket since August 2002. But Derbyshire tore up the form book with ease, before coming within one agonising wicket of surprising Gloucestershire too.

Elsewhere, the romance was limited. In a first-round game played in August 2002, David Taylor, a building contractor, dismantled Suffolk with 140 in 77 balls out of a Buckinghamshire total of 424 for five – comfortably the highest by a minor team in the competition's history. He went on to represent Worcestershire in the Twenty20 Cup.

But no non-first-class team made it past the third round, even if several came close. Nottinghamshire were on the ropes at 125 for five in pursuit of 280 against Lincolnshire only to wriggle free, while Staffordshire gave the Surrey all-stars a run for their money before falling nine runs short. Warwickshire squeezed past Bedfordshire by just 15 runs, and Leicestershire recovered well after totalling only 182 against Northumberland. Perhaps the most surprising moment of the third round came in one of the two all-first-class clashes, at the Rose Bowl, where Wasim Akram, a veteran of 356 one-day internationals for Pakistan, was smashed for 20 off the second-last over by Chris Adams as Sussex fought back to beat Hampshire.

In the fourth round, the defending champions, Yorkshire, threw away a promising position to crash out at Worcester, but Warwickshire did it the other way round. At 83 for six in pursuit of Essex's 256 for five at Edgbaston, they were dead and buried, only to rise again with a record stand of 170 between Dougie Brown and Ashley Giles. It was the comeback of this – and many another – competition. Lancashire bundled out Durham for 86, then made short work of Middlesex in the quarter-finals, where Worcestershire ran through Leicestershire thanks to some typically thrifty incisions from Matt Mason, an Australian-born seamer with an Irish passport who bowled 42 overs in the competition for just 124 runs. Harvey's bag of tricks helped Gloucestershire ease past Warwickshire into the last four.

A Lancashire–Gloucestershire final would have brought together the best one-day team at the start of the 1990s with the best at the end. But Lancashire had developed a phobia of semi-finals, while Gloucestershire, it seemed, did not know how to lose. When Worcestershire reached 64 for no wicket in the final at Lord's, you began to wonder. But this was the team that John built, and there was no way he was going back to New Zealand without leaving one more trophy on the mantelpiece.

Prize money

£43,000 for winners: GLOUCESTERSHIRE.
£22,000 for runners-up: WORCESTERSHIRE.
£12,000 for each losing semi-finalist: DERBYSHIRE, LANCASHIRE.
£8,000 for each losing quarter-finalist: LEICESTERSHIRE, MIDDLESEX, SURREY, WARWICKSHIRE.

For the 2003 competition, man of the match award winners received £1,500 in the final, £550 in the semi-finals, £500 in the quarter-finals, £400 in the fourth round, £300 in the third round, £325 in the second round (played in 2002) and £300 in the first round (also played in 2002). For the first round of the 2004 competition (played in 2003), match award winners received £200.

FIRST ROUND

Note: All matches played in 2002.

At Luton, August 29, 2002. **Bedfordshire won by eight wickets.** Toss: Hertfordshire. **Hertfordshire 167** (45.4 overs) (S. G. Cordingley 58, M. R. Evans 37; M. W. Patterson 3-39, R. J. Pack 3-20); **Bedfordshire 169-2** (26.1 overs) (D. R. Clarke 73*, S. Young 50*).
Man of the Match: R. J. Pack.

At Finchampstead, August 29, 2002. **Berkshire won by four wickets.** Toss: Ireland. **Ireland 113** (35 overs) (N. A. Denning 3-22, T. Henderson 3-30, S. P. Naylor 3-28); **Berkshire 114-6** (27 overs) (P. J. Prichard 51*; G. J. Neely 3-40).
Man of the Match: P. J. Prichard.

At Dinton, August 29, 2002. **Buckinghamshire won by 230 runs.** Toss: Buckinghamshire. **Buckinghamshire 424-5** (50 overs) (D. K. Taylor 140, P. D. Atkins 110, P. R. Sawyer 50, J. D. Batty 36*); **Suffolk 194** (40 overs) (R. J. Catley 65, A. D. Mawson 65; Z. A. Sher 3-50, A. R. Clarke 5-36).
Man of the Match: D. K. Taylor.
Buckinghamshire's total was the third-highest in all "List A" limited-overs cricket, after Surrey's 438 for five and Glamorgan's 429, made in the same match in the fourth round of the C&G in 2002. David Taylor, who went on to play for Worcestershire in the Twenty20 Cup, reached his century in 47 balls, believed to be the county's fastest; in all he faced 77.

At Toft, August 29, 2002. **Cheshire won by 12 runs.** Toss: Cheshire. **Cheshire 230-5** (50 overs) (A. J. Hall 38, A. J. Batterley 43, R. G. Hignett 32, K. E. A. Upashantha 59*); **Huntingdonshire 218** (49 overs) (P. C. Strydom 37, N. J. Adams 31; R. G. Hignett 3-21).
Man of the Match: K. E. A. Upashantha.
Eric Upashantha, who had played for Sri Lanka against England earlier in 2002, faced 36 balls.

At Camborne, August 29, 30, 2002. **Cornwall won by two runs.** Toss: Somerset Board XI. **Cornwall 301-8** (50 overs) (B. P. Price 50, T. G. Sharp 60, J. P. Kent 80, J. C. J. Stephens 31*; M. Parsons 3-70); **Somerset Board XI 299** (50 overs) (K. J. Parsons 33, K. G. Sedgbeer 37, W. J. Durston 50, A. V. Suppiah 70, R. T. Timms 38*, Extras 34; J. C. J. Stephens 3-54).
Man of the Match: J. P. Kent.
The match went into a reserve day after rain stopped play 13.1 overs into the Somerset Board XI innings. Somerset Board XI needed three from the last ball, but Michael Parsons was stumped off Justin Stephens.

At Keswick, August 29, 2002. **Cumberland won by 86 runs.** Toss: Nottinghamshire Board XI. **Cumberland 280-5** (50 overs) (S. T. Knox 108*, A. A. Metcalfe 71, S. A. Twigg 63); **Nottinghamshire Board XI 194** (50 overs) (M. W. Creed 37, Z. Iqbal 56*; D. B. Pennett 3-30, I. D. Austin 4-25).
Man of the Match: S. T. Knox.
Steven Knox added 122 with Ashley Metcalfe, formerly of Yorkshire, and 114 with Simon Twigg.

At Bristol, August 29, 2002. **Surrey Board XI won by 17 runs.** Toss: Gloucestershire Board XI. **Surrey Board XI 290-4** (50 overs) (S. V. Bahutule 105, J. J. Porter 96, Extras 46; J. W. White 3-32); **Gloucestershire Board XI 273-8** (50 overs) (M. A. Coombes 97, B. R. F. Staunton 56, Extras 31; J. J. Porter 4-51).
Man of the Match: S. V. Bahutule.
Bahutule, a former Indian Test player, added 199 for the third wicket with Joe Porter. Mark Coombes and Ben Staunton put on 164 for Gloucestershire Board XI's second wicket.

At Winchester, August 29, 2002. **Hampshire Board XI won by 84 runs.** Toss: Hampshire Board XI. **Hampshire Board XI 280-6** (50 overs) (D. C. Shirazi 101, R. T. P. Miller 32, L. Ronchi 78, Extras 30; J. Hibberd 4-48); **Wiltshire 196** (41.4 overs) (M. R. Hobson 3-54, R. T. P. Miller 3-26).

Man of the Match: D. C. Shirazi.

Damian Shirazi shared a second-wicket stand of 154 with Luke Ronchi.

At Ratcliffe College, Leicester, August 29, 2002. **Leicestershire Board XI won by four wickets.** Toss: Leicestershire Board XI. **Denmark 249-6** (50 overs) (B. Singh 43, B. E. McGain 51, Aftab Ahmed 77, Extras 35; N. J. Pullen 4-36); **Leicestershire Board XI 253-6** (46.1 overs) (M. D. R. Sutliff 97, N. J. Pullen 65*).

Man of the Match: N. J. Pullen.

Neil Pullen took his tally to 20 wickets at 11.60 in six List A games; he faced only 43 balls.

At Southgate, August 29, 2002. **Middlesex Board XI won by 38 runs.** Toss: Derbyshire Board XI. **Middlesex Board XI 239-9** (50 overs) (S. K. Ranasinghe 36, P. E. Wellings 59, K. H. A. Powell 42, Extras 32; Naeem Akhtar 3-40); **Derbyshire Board XI 201** (47.5 overs) (D. Smit 38, J. E. H. Owen 48; K. H. A. Powell 3-34, J. P. Rodham 4-23).

Man of the Match: K. H. A. Powell.

Kirk Powell played first-class cricket for Jamaica.

At Northampton, August 29, 2002. **Yorkshire Board XI won by 57 runs.** Toss: Yorkshire Board XI. **Yorkshire Board XI 233-8** (50 overs) (S. Widdup 90, S. Clark 52; D. J. Capel 3-35); **Northamptonshire Board XI 176** (43.2 overs) (D. J. Capel 32, T. M. Baker 63; N. S. Gill 3-24, S. A. Patterson 3-11).

Man of the Match: S. Widdup.

Seamers Neil Gill (10–2–24–3) and Steven Patterson (7.2–3–11–3) helped reduce Northamptonshire to 58 for six.

At Bodicote, August 29, 2002. **Lancashire Board XI won by 31 runs.** Toss: Oxfordshire. **Lancashire Board XI 229-8** (50 overs) (P. Green 63, S. E. Dearden 67*; A. P. Cook 3-40); **Oxfordshire 198** (48.2 overs) (S. V. Laudat 39, G. P. Savin 33, R. Lynch 39; A. J. Mercer 4-26).

Man of the Match: S. E. Dearden.

At Coventry, August 29, 2002. **Herefordshire won by 73 runs.** Toss: Herefordshire. **Herefordshire 276-6** (50 overs) (P. S. Lazenbury 71, I. Dawood 60, C. W. Boroughs 39); **Warwickshire Board XI 203** (47.5 overs) (D. A. T. Dalton 46, L. J. Marland 39; Naved-ul-Hasan 4-49, P. S. Lazenbury 3-49).

Man of the Match: P. S. Lazenbury.

Naved-ul-Hasan went on to make his one-day debut for Pakistan in April 2003.

At Kidderminster, August 29, 2002. **Worcestershire Board XI won by five wickets.** Toss: Worcestershire Board XI. **Dorset 227** (49.4 overs) (G. R. Treagus 76, S. W. D. Rintoul 55; I. Jamshed 5-36, G. J. Williams 3-61); **Worcestershire Board XI 228-5** (46 overs) (D. Manning 80, G. S. Kandola 53).

Man of the Match: D. Manning.

Dorset collapsed from 193 for three.

SECOND ROUND

Note: All matches played in 2002.

At Luton, September 12, 2002. **Bedfordshire won by ten wickets.** Toss: Holland. **Holland 96** (34.4 overs) (S. Rashid 4-30, R. J. Pack 3-1); **Bedfordshire 97-0** (15.3 overs) (D. J. Roberts 31*, N. A. Stanley 56*).

Man of the Match: S. Rashid.

Holland's First XI were in Sri Lanka, preparing for the ICC Champions Trophy. Two weeks later, Shaun Rashid was signed by Sussex.

At Reading, September 12, 2002. **Berkshire won by six wickets.** Toss: Norfolk. **Norfolk 119** (40.5 overs) (S. C. Goldsmith 35; S. D. Myles 4-8); **Berkshire 123-4** (27.1 overs) (P. J. Prichard 45*).

Man of the Match: S. D. Myles.

Simon Myles's full figures were 10–5–8–4.

At Beaconsfield, September 12, 2002. **Buckinghamshire won by 11 runs.** Toss: Buckinghamshire. **Buckinghamshire 160** (49.5 overs) (P. D. Atkins 38, J. D. Batty 36); **Shropshire 149** (48.5 overs) (A. Saleem 3-24, A. R. Clarke 4-28).

Man of the Match: J. D. Batty.

Jeremy Batty, the ex-Yorkshire off-spinner, also took two for 16 from ten overs.

At Neston, September 12, 2002. **Lincolnshire won by four runs.** Toss: Lincolnshire. **Lincolnshire 281-7** (50 overs) (M. C. Dobson 90, R. W. J. Howitt 31, J. Trower 67); **Cheshire 277-8** (50 overs) (M. R. Currie 94, P. R. J. Bryson 59, R. G. Hignett 84; M. A. Fell 4-20).

Man of the Match: R. G. Hignett.

Richard Hignett faced 56 balls. Cheshire collapsed from 244 for one, and needed five from the last ball, but Simon Marshall was bowled by Mark Fell.

At Exmouth, September 12, 2002. **Devon won by 127 runs.** Toss: Cumberland. **Devon 285-6** (50 overs) (M. P. Hunt 70, R. I. Dawson 138); **Cumberland 158** (43.5 overs) (D. B. Pennett 51*; M. A. E. Richards 4-22, T. S. Anning 3-40).

Man of the Match: R. I. Dawson.

Matthew Hunt and Robert Dawson, who scored three first-class centuries for Gloucestershire, put on 172 for Devon's second wicket.

At Darlington, September 12, 2002. **Durham Board XI won by 50 runs.** Toss: Herefordshire. **Durham Board XI 274-8** (50 overs) (S. J. Birtwisle 32, A. Worthy 53, Q. J. Hughes 51, G. M. Scott 100; N. M. Davies 4-72); **Herefordshire 224** (47.2 overs) (I. Dawood 37, C. W. Boroughs 72, R. S. Nagra 37, K. Pearson 30; S. Humble 3-33).

Man of the Match: G. M. Scott.

Eighteen-year-old Gary Scott faced 65 balls, hitting ten fours and five sixes.

At Chelmsford, September 12, 2002. **Essex Board XI won by 49 runs.** Toss: Surrey Board XI. **Essex Board XI 302-8** (50 overs) (Tauseef Ali 65, G. D. James 51*, Saad Janjua 91; R. B. Bowers 3-50, D. E. Gorrod 3-37); **Surrey Board XI 253** (45.5 overs) (R. J. Mansfield 40, J. A. W. Fry 69, D. E. Gorrod 49, Extras 37; A. P. Palladino 3-56, Tauseef Ali 4-66).

Man of the Match: Saad Janjua.

At Winchester, September 12, 2002. **Staffordshire won by 105 runs.** Toss: Hampshire Board XI. **Staffordshire 249-6** (50 overs) (G. D. Franklin 63, G. F. Archer 58, D. R. Womble 31*, M. I. Humphries 33*); **Hampshire Board XI 144** (36.4 overs) (R. T. P. Miller 34, I. Brunnschweiler 37; M. J. R. Rindel 4-21, R. J. Bailey 3-16).

Man of the Match: G. F. Archer.

Mike Rindel played 22 one-day internationals for South Africa.

At Maidstone, September 12, 2002. **Kent Board XI won by seven wickets.** Toss: Kent Board XI. **Leicestershire Board XI 175** (47.4 overs) (C. P. Crowe 35, N. G. Patel 33); **Kent Board XI 176-3** (40.4 overs) (J. D. P. Bowden 38, M. R. M. Bennett 31, H. Iqbal 30*).

Man of the Match: A. Tutt.

For Kent Board XI, Andrew Tutt's figures were 10–2–21–2.

At Southgate, September 12, 2002. **Cambridgeshire won by seven wickets.** Toss: Middlesex Board XI. **Middlesex Board XI 194** (44 overs) (S. K. Ranasinghe 75; T. S. Smith 3-35, P. M. Such 3-37); **Cambridgeshire 200-3** (44.3 overs) (I. N. Flanagan 45, S. A. Kellett 79, Nasim Khan 47*).

Man of the Match: S. A. Kellett.

Keerthi Ranasinghe played four one-day internationals for Sri Lanka in 1985-86.

At Jesmond, September 12, 2002. **Northumberland won by 126 runs.** Toss: Yorkshire Board XI. **Northumberland 352** (49.4 overs) (S. Chapman 44, M. P. Speight 30, C. J. Hewison 69, B. Parker 108, J. B. Windows 33; N. S. Gill 3-62); **Yorkshire Board XI 226** (47.1 overs) (A. J. Bethel 38, S. Widdup 46, Extras 39; L. J. Crozier 3-44).

Man of the Match: B. Parker.

For Northumberland, Shahid Nazir conceded 19 runs from ten overs. Bradley Parker's hundred was his first in 78 "List A" games for Yorkshire and Northumberland.

At Aberdeen, September 12, 13, 2002. **Scotland won by three wickets.** Toss: Scotland. **Lancashire Board XI 175-7** (50 overs) (S. E. Dearden 48); **Scotland 177-7** (42.4 overs) (C. J. O. Smith 36; D. R. Snellgrove 3-23).

Man of the Match: S. E. Dearden.

Stephen Dearden also took one for 44.

At Sully, September 12, 2002. **Cornwall won by 24 runs.** Toss: Cornwall. **Cornwall 248-7** (50 overs) (J. M. Hands 61, T. G. Sharp 41, G. D. Edwards 31*); **Wales 224** (48.2 overs) (J. P. J. Sylvester 37, P. V. Simmons 59, S. E. Morris 46, Extras 35; J. M. Hands 3-40).

Man of the Match: J. M. Hands.

At Kidderminster, September 12, 2002. **Worcestershire Board XI won by six wickets.** Toss: Worcestershire Board XI. **Sussex Board XI 225** (48.5 overs) (C. M. Mole 66, Extras 39; S. H. Cook 3-35, I. Jamshed 3-34); **Worcestershire Board XI 227-4** (43.5 overs) (Kadeer Ali 66, G. S. Kandola 40, G. R. Hill 56*, R. K. Illingworth 53*).

Man of the Match: I. Jamshed.

Simon Cook played two Tests for Australia in 1997-98.

THIRD ROUND

Note: All subsequent matches played in 2003.

At Luton, May 7. **Warwickshire won by 15 runs.** Toss: Warwickshire. **Warwickshire 233-8** (50 overs) (T. Frost 47, I. R. Bell 41, J. O. Troughton 38, D. R. Brown 30; W. E. Sneath 4-38); **Bedfordshire 218-9** (50 overs) (T. W. Roberts 48, A. R. Roberts 38; M. A. Wagh 3-35).

Man of the Match: W. E. Sneath.

At Reading, May 7. **Durham won by eight wickets.** Toss: Berkshire. **Berkshire 110** (44.2 overs) (V. J. Wells 6-20); **Durham 111-2** (23 overs) (V. J. Wells 63*).

Man of the Match: V. J. Wells.

Berkshire were 58 for eight. For Durham, Killeen returned figures of 8–0–9–1.

At Wing, May 7. **Gloucestershire won by 324 runs.** Toss: Gloucestershire. **Gloucestershire 401-7** (50 overs) (C. M. Spearman 76, T. H. C. Hancock 135, J. N. Rhodes 87); **Buckinghamshire 77** (25.1 overs) (J. M. M. Averis 6-23).

Man of the Match: T. H. C. Hancock.

Spearman faced 41 balls, Hancock 118 and Rhodes 73; for Buckinghamshire, Russell Lane's figures were 6–0–70–1. Buckinghamshire lost their last eight wickets for 35.

At March, May 7. **Yorkshire won by 85 runs.** Toss: Yorkshire. **Yorkshire 299-5** (50 overs) (M. J. Lumb 82, M. J. Wood 118*, A. McGrath 56; Ajaz Akhtar 3-53); **Cambridgeshire 214-8** (50 overs) (E. J. Wilson 33, N. T. Gadsby 53, Ajaz Akhtar 46; A. K. D. Gray 3-37, M. J. Wood 3-45).

Man of the Match: M. J. Wood.

McGrath faced 33 balls; Yorkshire used nine bowlers.

At Truro, May 7. **Kent won by five wickets.** Toss: Kent. **Cornwall 140** (46.1 overs) (C. A. Hunkin 30; B. J. Trott 3-16, J. P. Hewitt 3-26); **Kent 141-5** (38.4 overs) (G. O. Jones 30*).

Man of the Match: C. A. Hunkin.

At Exmouth, May 7. **Lancashire won by nine wickets.** Toss: Lancashire. **Devon 180** (49.1 overs) (N. D. Hancock 73*; J. Wood 4-33, A. Flintoff 3-54); **Lancashire 182-1** (40.4 overs) (M. J. Chilton 51, I. J. Sutcliffe 89*, Extras 36).

Man of the Match: N. D. Hancock.

Chilton and Sutcliffe put on 166 for the first wicket.

At Darlington, May 7. **Glamorgan won by 86 runs.** Toss: Durham Board XI. **Glamorgan 312-9** (50 overs) (I. J. Thomas 93, M. P. Maynard 115; L. E. Plunkett 3-63); **Durham Board XI 226** (47.4 overs) (A. Worthy 59, P. Mustard 33, K. J. Coetzer 30, M. J. North 46; R. D. B. Croft 3-54).

Man of the Match: M. P. Maynard.

Maynard faced 86 balls.

At Chelmsford, May 7. **Essex won by 42 runs.** Toss: Essex Board XI. **Essex 315-6** (50 overs) (D. D. J. Robinson 70, W. I. Jefferson 132, R. C. Irani 38); **Essex Board XI 273** (49.3 overs) (Adnan Akram 61, M. Akhtar 71, Saad Janjua 37; S. A. Brant 3-54, G. R. Napier 3-47).

Man of the Match: M. Akhtar.

Robinson and Jefferson added 170 for the first wicket.

HAMPSHIRE v SUSSEX

At Southampton, May 7. Sussex won by four wickets. Toss: Hampshire.

When Wasim Akram began the penultimate over with Sussex still 27 short of victory, the match looked beyond their reach. But Adams chose the moment to launch an astonishing assault. He smashed Wasim's first delivery over long-off for six, stole two runs next ball after surviving the toughest of caught-and-bowled chances, then crashed the third delivery to the cover fence. A pair of twos was followed by a four through mid-wicket to make it 20 off the over. As Wasim stood disbelieving at mid-off, Davis completed an unlikely win with three balls to spare. Earlier, Katich's unbeaten 82 on a sluggish pitch provided the basis for a competitive Hampshire total, and at 160 for six in reply, Sussex needed something special from their captain. They duly got it.

Man of the Match: C. J. Adams.

Hampshire

*J. P. Crawley b Kirtley	4
†N. Pothas run out	40
R. A. Smith c Ambrose b Taylor	13
S. M. Katich not out	82
Wasim Akram run out	38
J. R. C. Hamblin c Prior b Martin-Jenkins	4
A. D. Mascarenhas run out	1
W. S. Kendall b Taylor	21
S. D. Udal not out	3
L-b 4, w 3	7
1/21 (1) 2/51 (3) 3/73 (2) 4/133 (5) 5/155 (6) 6/156 (7) 7/204 (8) — (7 wkts, 50 overs)	213

C. T. Tremlett and A. D. Mullally did not bat.

Bowling: Martin-Jenkins 10–3–28–1; Kirtley 10–2–38–1; Taylor 10–1–52–2; Yardy 2–0–16–0; Mushtaq Ahmed 10–1–33–0; Davis 8–0–42–0.

Sussex

R. R. Montgomerie c Kendall b Mascarenhas	8
†T. R. Ambrose c Katich b Mullally	43
M. W. Goodwin c Pothas b Mullally	21
*C. J. Adams not out	80
R. S. C. Martin-Jenkins c Kendall b Udal	8
M. H. Yardy b Mascarenhas	12
M. J. Prior c Kendall b Mascarenhas	0
M. J. G. Davis not out	21
B 3, l-b 8, w 10	21
1/15 (1) 2/68 (3) 3/98 (2) 4/119 (5) 5/156 (6) 6/160 (7) — (6 wkts, 49.3 overs)	214

Mushtaq Ahmed, R. J. Kirtley and B. V. Taylor did not bat.

Bowling: Wasim Akram 10–1–47–0; Mascarenhas 10–2–31–3; Tremlett 9.3–1–47–0; Mullally 10–1–44–2; Udal 10–0–34–1.

Umpires: D. J. Constant and I. J. Gould.

At Canterbury, May 7. **Derbyshire won by 171 runs.** Toss: Kent Board XI. **Derbyshire 299-5** (50 overs) (D. G. Cork 59, C. W. G. Bassano 101, D. R. Hewson 69); **Kent Board XI 128** (45.2 overs) (K. J. Dean 3-6).

Man of the Match: C. W. G. Bassano.

Hewson faced 43 balls. Dean's figures were 6–4–6–3. Kent Board XI collapsed to 38 for six.

At Lincoln, May 7. **Nottinghamshire won by four wickets.** Toss: Nottinghamshire. **Lincolnshire 279-7** (50 overs) (M. A. Fell 77, J. Clarke 53, R. J. Chapman 53*, Extras 33); **Nottinghamshire 280-6** (48.1 overs) (D. J. Bicknell 33, U. Afzaal 71, P. J. Franks 84*; J. R. Davies 3-40).

Man of the Match: P. J. Franks.

Lincolnshire included four former Nottinghamshire players: Mark Fell, Mathew Dowman, Paul Pollard and Robert Chapman, whose innings took only 44 balls. Nottinghamshire were 125 for five and 210 for six, but Franks, who faced 70 balls, saved the day.

NORTHAMPTONSHIRE v MIDDLESEX

At Northampton, May 7. Middlesex won by 26 runs. Toss: Middlesex. County debut: Imran Tahir.

On a pitch that had yielded 589 runs in a National League fixture three days earlier, Middlesex were indebted to Joyce, whose thoughtful, patient innings earned him the match award. Strauss had already helped out with an important, if less solid, half-century, while Cook's robust hitting down the order pushed Middlesex past 200. Their seemingly modest total quickly assumed daunting proportions as the Northamptonshire top order crumbled against Keegan and Dawes; Hutton's diving catch at backward point to account for Jaques was magnificent. From 29 for four, Cook and Swann laid the foundations for a recovery, but when Swann pulled a long-hop to Imran Tahir – the 24-year-old leg-spinner from Pakistan called in to replace Abdul Razzaq – at deep square leg, Northamptonshire's best chance of victory had gone.

Man of the Match: E. C. Joyce.

Middlesex

P. N. Weekes c Hussey b Cawdron	10	†D. Alleyne c Phillips b Swann	3
*A. J. Strauss lbw b Cook	53	C. B. Keegan not out	10
O. A. Shah b Cawdron	8	L-b 4, w 4	8
E. C. Joyce st Bailey b Swann	72		——
D. C. Nash c Bailey b Swann	16	1/27 (1) 2/53 (3) (7 wkts, 50 overs)	214
B. L. Hutton st Bailey b Swann	1	3/89 (2) 4/137 (5)	
S. J. Cook not out	33	5/145 (6) 6/178 (4) 7/195 (8)	

Imran Tahir and J. H. Dawes did not bat.

Bowling: Nel 10–2–36–0; Cawdron 10–2–26–2; Phillips 7–0–38–0; Brown 8–0–37–0; Cook 7–0–33–1; Swann 8–0–40–4.

Northamptonshire

*M. E. K. Hussey lbw b Keegan	5	A. Nel b Keegan	14
G. L. Brophy c Shah b Keegan	13	J. F. Brown not out	2
P. A. Jaques c Hutton b Dawes	5		
D. J. Sales b Dawes	4	B 6, l-b 3, w 7, n-b 2	18
J. W. Cook c Nash b Cook	57		——
G. P. Swann c Imran Tahir b Cook	24	1/19 (1) 2/24 (3) 3/28 (2) (48.4 overs)	188
†T. M. B. Bailey run out	19	4/29 (4) 5/95 (6) 6/131 (5)	
B. J. Phillips c Nash b Keegan	19	7/142 (7) 8/171 (9)	
M. J. Cawdron run out	8	9/173 (8) 10/188 (10)	

Bowling: Keegan 9.4–1–35–4; Dawes 10–1–30–2; Imran Tahir 10–2–41–0; Cook 10–0–29–2; Weekes 9–0–44–0.

Umpires: P. J. Hartley and M. J. Kitchen.

At Jesmond, May 7. **Leicestershire won by 90 runs.** Toss: Leicestershire. **Leicestershire 182-9** (50 overs) (P. A. Nixon 57, J. N. Snape 30; S. Chapman 3-40); **Northumberland 92** (25.4 overs) (D. D. Masters 4-15).

Man of the Match: P. A. Nixon.

At Edinburgh, May 7. **Somerset won by ten wickets.** Toss: Scotland. **Scotland 138-9** (50 overs) (D. R. Lockhart 51, C. M. Wright 45*; K. A. Parsons 3-29); **Somerset 142-0** (19.2 overs) (J. Cox 39*, M. E. Trescothick 103*).

Man of the Match: M. E. Trescothick.

Trescothick faced 70 balls, hitting 13 fours and five sixes.

At Stone, May 7. **Surrey won by nine runs.** Toss: Staffordshire. **Surrey 273** (49.3 overs) (I. J. Ward 108, R. Clarke 47, A. J. Hollioake 33; G. Bulpitt 3-39); **Staffordshire 264-4** (50 overs) (G. D. Franklin 39, D. R. Womble 49, G. F. Archer 65, P. F. Shaw 55*, Extras 30).

Man of the Match: I. J. Ward.

Ward, who faced 87 balls and hit 11 fours and seven sixes, scored his first one-day century: he moved from 82 to 100 with three successive sixes off Richard Cooper. For Staffordshire, Graeme Archer, formerly of Nottinghamshire, and Paul Shaw added 112 for the fourth wicket. Both men hit four sixes. Richard Harvey finished unbeaten on 14 from four balls, including two sixes.

At Worcester, May 7. **Worcestershire won by 170 runs.** Toss: Worcestershire Board XI. **Worcestershire 311-4** (50 overs) (V. S. Solanki 164*, B. F. Smith 44, Extras 37); **Worcestershire Board XI 141-9** (50 overs).

Man of the Match: V. S. Solanki.

Solanki faced 170 balls, hitting 20 fours and three sixes.

FOURTH ROUND

DURHAM v LANCASHIRE

At Chester-le-Street, May 28. Lancashire won by 143 runs. Toss: Durham.

Perhaps demoralised by the loss of Love, who broke a thumb while attempting a slip catch, Durham subsided to their lowest score in the competition as a first-class club. Only the 82 they made against Worcestershire in 1968, while they were still a minor county, stood between them and history of the wrong kind. The game was all but over when they slumped to 26 for six, with three wickets each for Martin, who bowled well, and Anderson, who benefited from some rash strokeplay. Only Peng, who scored more than half Durham's total, and Killeen reached double figures. Lancashire had sprung a surprise by recalling Flintoff, who had been suffering with a back injury. While he and Hooper were building on Law's brisk start by adding 61 in nine overs, Lancashire were on course for a decent total. But they could only add 36 off their last ten overs as Durham clawed their way back. The recovery did not last long.

Man of the Match: S. G. Law.

Lancashire

M. J. Chilton c Mustard b Harmison	22
M. B. Loye b Pretorius	1
S. G. Law c sub b Phillips	59
C. L. Hooper c and b Harmison	61
A. Flintoff c Mustard b Pretorius	31
A. J. Swann run out	20
G. Chapple c Harmison b Pretorius	6
*†W. K. Hegg b Killeen	4
P. J. Martin b Killeen	1
S. I. Mahmood not out	5
J. M. Anderson not out	7
B 4, l-b 3, w 5	12
1/7 (2) 2/76 (1) 3/97 (3) 4/158 (5) 5/203 (4) 6/206 (6) 7/215 (8) 8/217 (7) 9/219 (9) (9 wkts, 50 overs)	229

Bowling: Pretorius 10–1–32–3; Killeen 10–1–42–2; Harmison 10–0–37–2; Pattison 6–0–38–0; Phillips 10–0–50–1; Muchall 4–0–23–0.

Durham

N. Peng c Law b Mahmood 44
†P. Mustard c Flintoff b Anderson 0
G. J. Muchall c Chilton b Anderson. . . . 4
G. J. Pratt c Hegg b Martin 1
*J. J. B. Lewis lbw b Martin 0
I. Pattison c and b Anderson 5
N. C. Phillips c Hegg b Martin. 1
N. Killeen b Chapple 18
D. Pretorius c Hooper b Mahmood 2
S. J. Harmison not out 0
M. L. Love absent hurt
B 1, l-b 1, w 7, n-b 2 11

1/1 (2) 2/15 (3) 3/16 (4) (26.3 overs) 86
4/16 (5) 5/23 (6) 6/26 (7)
7/79 (8) 8/86 (1) 9/86 (9)

Bowling: Anderson 5–1–14–3; Martin 6–1–22–3; Chapple 8–1–25–1; Mahmood 2.3–0–8–2; Hooper 5–0–15–0.

Umpires: I. J. Gould and J. F. Steele.

GLAMORGAN v DERBYSHIRE

At Cardiff, May 28. Derbyshire won by seven wickets. Toss: Derbyshire.

A heroic century from Bassano condemned Glamorgan to their first one-day defeat of the season. Three days after being discharged from hospital, where he had been undergoing treatment for a diabetes-related illness, Bassano made light work of a challenging Glamorgan total to inspire Derbyshire to victory with almost nine overs to spare. His second successive hundred in the competition came up in 89 balls and included three straight sixes in six balls off the left-arm spin of Cosker. By the time he was bowled by Kasprowicz, Bassano had faced 100 balls, hit ten fours and four sixes, and shared a third-wicket stand of 191 in 30 overs with Gait. Glamorgan's innings was a thing of fits and starts. Nine men got into double figures but only Hughes, a late replacement for the ailing Hemp, made a half-century. Kasprowicz struck twice to reduce Derbyshire to 54 for two, but Gait and Bassano ensured there would be no more wobbles.

Man of the Match: C. W. G. Bassano.

Glamorgan

*R. D. B. Croft c Hewson b Welch 21
I. J. Thomas run out 34
M. J. Powell c Sutton b Welch 22
M. P. Maynard c Sutton b Afridi 27
J. Hughes c Welch b Hewson 51
A. Dale c Cork b Afridi 13
†M. A. Wallace c Hewson b Dean. 11
M. S. Kasprowicz c Hewson b Welch. . . 18
A. G. Wharf b Cork 18
A. P. Davies not out 5
D. A. Cosker not out. 2
L-b 6, w 8, n-b 12. 26

1/47 (1) 2/83 (3) (9 wkts, 50 overs) 248
3/85 (2) 4/125 (4)
5/157 (6) 6/190 (7)
7/209 (5) 8/236 (9) 9/242 (8)

Bowling: Cork 10–0–46–1; Dean 8–0–56–1; Welch 10–1–47–3; Lungley 8–0–30–0; Shahid Afridi 10–0–45–2; Hewson 4–0–18–1.

Derbyshire

A. I. Gait not out. 87
Shahid Afridi c Wallace b Kasprowicz . . 23
M. J. Di Venuto c Wallace b Kasprowicz 11
C. W. G. Bassano b Kasprowicz 121
S. A. Selwood not out. 1
L-b 4, w 2, n-b 2 8

1/37 (2) 2/54 (3) (3 wkts, 41.1 overs) 251
3/245 (4)

D. R. Hewson, *D. G. Cork, T. Lungley, G. Welch, †L. D. Sutton and K. J. Dean did not bat.

Bowling: Kasprowicz 10–2–43–3; Davies 4–0–38–0; Wharf 9–0–55–0; Dale 4.1–0–25–0; Croft 8–0–42–0; Cosker 6–0–44–0.

Umpires: N. G. Cowley and P. Willey.

KENT v GLOUCESTERSHIRE

At Canterbury, May 28. Gloucestershire won by five wickets. Toss: Kent.

A fine team display with the ball and a gutsy innings from Rhodes helped Gloucestershire gain revenge for their quarter-final defeat by Kent in 2002. Batting with a runner because he had pulled a hamstring earlier in his innings, Rhodes hustled Gloucestershire home with more than four overs to spare after Spearman had made the initial thrusts with an aggressive 71. Earlier, Kent were looking good at 101 for two, but Key's flat-footed steer to slip sparked a collapse of eight for 93. On his 29th birthday, Averis struck twice in an over to remove Blewett, for 50, and Fulton, playing his first senior game of the season following a serious eye injury, third ball. The ever-economical Smith returned to help apply the finishing touches, and Gloucestershire were never in serious trouble after that.

Man of the Match: A. M. Smith.

Kent

M. A. Ealham c Hancock b Smith	15
R. W. T. Key c Ball b Alleyne	32
E. T. Smith c Russell b Smith	14
G. S. Blewett c Rhodes b Averis	50
M. J. Walker lbw b Ball	22
*D. P. Fulton c Rhodes b Averis	0
†G. O. Jones c Russell b Smith	34
J. C. Tredwell c Ball b Alleyne	9
J. P. Hewitt c Russell b Smith	2
M. J. Saggers not out	2
B. J. Trott b Averis	3
L-b 4, w 3, n-b 4	11
1/18 (1) 2/42 (3) 3/101 (2) 4/128 (4) 5/128 (6) 6/148 (5) 7/169 (8) 8/185 (9) 9/187 (7) 10/194 (11) (47.4 overs)	194

Bowling: Smith 10–1–35–4; Butler 9–0–40–0; Averis 9.4–0–39–3; Alleyne 10–1–33–2; Ball 9–0–43–1.

Gloucestershire

W. P. C. Weston c Tredwell b Saggers	7
C. M. Spearman c Ealham b Trott	71
T. H. C. Hancock b Ealham	9
J. N. Rhodes not out	45
M. G. N. Windows c Walker b Saggers	15
†R. C. Russell c Walker b Saggers	30
*M. W. Alleyne not out	2
L-b 9, w 7	16
1/20 (1) 2/56 (3) 3/103 (2) 4/130 (5) 5/187 (6) (5 wkts, 45.4 overs)	195

I. G. Butler, J. M. M. Averis, M. C. J. Ball and A. M. Smith did not bat.

Bowling: Saggers 9.4–1–45–3; Trott 10–1–35–1; Hewitt 8–0–49–0; Ealham 8–1–17–1; Blewett 1–0–11–0; Tredwell 9–2–29–0.

Umpires: D. J. Constant and M. J. Kitchen.

LEICESTERSHIRE v NOTTINGHAMSHIRE

At Leicester, May 28. Leicestershire won by 99 runs. Toss: Nottinghamshire. County debut: J. K. Maunders.

At the age of 37, DeFreitas turned back the clock with a performance reminiscent of his days as an up-and-coming England all-rounder. He began by hitting 22 off 23 balls at the end of the Leicestershire innings, but it was his bowling that settled the match. In conditions conducive to seam and swing, DeFreitas was a class act: after conceding ten runs in his first two overs, he went for just ten in his next eight and picked up three wickets into the bargain. Dagnall and Grove provided excellent support and although a belligerent 67 from Cairns delayed the inevitable, Nottinghamshire were bowled out with almost ten overs remaining. Earlier, Sehwag clouted ten fours and a six in his attractive 51-ball 56, but Nottinghamshire made life easy for their opponents by gifting 49 extras, of which 29 were wides and no-balls. Franks, who conceded seven wides in four overs and also overstepped twice, was particularly guilty.

Man of the Match: P. A. J. DeFreitas.

Leicestershire

J. K. Maunders c MacGill b Clough . . . 14
V. Sehwag c Cairns b Clough 56
D. I. Stevens lbw b Gallian 18
B. J. Hodge b Franks 0
D. L. Maddy c Cairns b Clough 35
†P. A. Nixon c Pietersen b Smith 26
J. N. Snape b Smith 24
J. L. Sadler run out. 8
*P. A. J. DeFreitas c Clough b Logan. . . 22
C. E. Dagnall not out 4
J. O. Grove not out. 2

B 7, l-b 13, w 21, n-b 8. 49

1/61 (1) 2/88 (2) 3/97 (4) 4/118 (3) 5/174 (5) 6/188 (6) 7/209 (8) 8/250 (7) 9/253 (9) (9 wkts, 50 overs) 258

Bowling: Smith 10–0–45–2; Logan 10–1–56–1; Clough 10–1–47–3; Franks 4–0–19–1; Gallian 6–0–33–1; MacGill 10–0–38–0.

Nottinghamshire

J. E. R. Gallian c Stevens b Dagnall . . . 16
G. D. Clough c Nixon b DeFreitas 11
U. Afzaal c Nixon b DeFreitas 14
K. P. Pietersen c Maddy b DeFreitas . . . 5
B. M. Shafayat lbw b Dagnall 0
*C. L. Cairns c Snape b Grove. 67
P. J. Franks b Maddy 4
†W. M. Noon c Nixon b Grove. 9
R. J. Logan c Stevens b Grove 9
G. J. Smith not out. 4
S. C. G. MacGill b Dagnall 0

L-b 8, w 8, n-b 4 20

1/23 (1) 2/34 (2) 3/40 (4) 4/46 (5) 5/62 (3) 6/84 (7) 7/107 (8) 8/142 (9) 9/157 (6) 10/159 (11) (40.2 overs) 159

Bowling: DeFreitas 10–2–20–3; Dagnall 8.2–0–39–3; Maddy 7–1–17–1; Grove 10–0–43–3; Stevens 5–0–32–0.

Umpires: P. J. Hartley and J. W. Lloyds.

MIDDLESEX v SUSSEX

At Lord's, May 28. Middlesex won by 17 runs. Toss: Middlesex.

Middlesex reached the quarter-finals almost in spite of themselves. A jumbled batting line-up – Cook came in at No. 5, Joyce at No. 7, and Nash, picked for his batting while Alleyne kept wicket, mysteriously low at No. 10 – almost contrived to throw the game away after Weekes and the classy Strauss had started with 139 in 29 overs. At that stage, 280 looked the bare minimum, but five wickets fell for eight runs in the last four overs of the innings and Middlesex had to settle for 258. Sussex were kept afloat by Adams and Martin-Jenkins, but when Noffke held on to a sharp return catch to see off Martin-Jenkins, the innings subsided. Davis and Kirtley biffed gamely towards the end but Sussex could not match the heroics of the previous round: 27 off the final over was beyond them.

Man of the Match: A. J. Strauss.

Middlesex

P. N. Weekes c Innes b Taylor. 73
*A. J. Strauss c Adams b Mushtaq Ahmed . 75
O. A. Shah c Innes b Kirtley 29
Abdul Razzaq c Martin-Jenkins b Kirtley 30
S. J. Cook c Prior b Kirtley 16
B. L. Hutton b Kirtley. 0
E. C. Joyce b Taylor 6
†D. Alleyne b Kirtley 0
C. B. Keegan not out 6
D. C. Nash not out. 5

L-b 12, w 6 18

1/139 (2) 2/175 (1) 3/212 (3) 4/238 (4) 5/239 (6) 6/246 (7) 7/246 (5) 8/246 (8) (8 wkts, 50 overs) 258

A. A. Noffke did not bat.

Bowling: Kirtley 10–0–41–5; Martin-Jenkins 2–0–20–0; Taylor 10–0–47–2; Innes 8–0–53–0; Davis 10–0–39–0; Mushtaq Ahmed 10–0–46–1.

Sussex

R. R. Montgomerie c and b Razzaq	36	Mushtaq Ahmed b Cook	11
†T. R. Ambrose c Alleyne b Keegan	5	R. J. Kirtley not out	30
M. W. Goodwin b Cook	32	L-b 7, w 2, n-b 2	11
*C. J. Adams b Weekes	39		
R. S. C. Martin-Jenkins c and b Noffke	38	1/12 (2) 2/72 (3) (8 wkts, 50 overs)	241
M. J. Prior c Noffke b Razzaq	3	3/76 (1) 4/148 (5)	
K. J. Innes b Cook	4	5/153 (6) 6/164 (7)	
M. J. G. Davis not out	32	7/168 (4) 8/183 (9)	

B. V. Taylor did not bat.

Bowling: Keegan 10–1–47–1; Noffke 10–1–47–1; Abdul Razzaq 10–0–49–2; Cook 9–0–37–3; Weekes 8–0–38–1; Hutton 3–0–16–0.

Umpires: V. A. Holder and T. E. Jesty.

SOMERSET v SURREY

At Taunton, May 28. Surrey won by six runs. Toss: Somerset.

An exquisite century from Thorpe was just enough to see off Somerset, the 2002 beaten finalists. After Surrey had stuttered to 169 for six, he found a lively ally in Batty, who helped add 112 match-turning runs. Thorpe timed the ball perfectly to reach his hundred from 102 deliveries in the last over of the innings, while Batty's maiden one-day half-century came from just 44 balls. It left the Somerset attack, with the exception of McLean, looking ordinary and tired. When Trescothick mistimed a pull, Somerset were up against it at 51 for three, but Parsons steadied the ship with Burns, then sailed full steam ahead with the muscular Blackwell. Hollioake, however, came to Surrey's rescue with three late overs – and three crucial wickets. Twelve off Azhar Mahmood's final over was too big a task for Turner and Jones.

Man of the Match: G. P. Thorpe.

Surrey

M. A. Butcher c Turner b Jones	14	†J. N. Batty not out	55
A. D. Brown b McLean	5		
M. R. Ramprakash c Dutch b Burns	32	L-b 14, w 14, n-b 2	30
G. P. Thorpe not out	102		
R. Clarke c Turner b Parsons	10	1/8 (2) 2/34 (1) (6 wkts, 50 overs)	281
*A. J. Hollioake lbw b Johnson	33	3/86 (3) 4/106 (5)	
Azhar Mahmood lbw b Johnson	0	5/169 (6) 6/169 (7)	

M. P. Bicknell, Saqlain Mushtaq and J. Ormond did not bat.

Bowling: Johnson 10–0–58–2; McLean 10–0–29–1; Jones 10–1–80–1; Burns 10–0–51–1; Parsons 10–0–49–1.

Somerset

J. Cox lbw b Ormond	7	†R. J. Turner not out	13
M. E. Trescothick c Hollioake b Azhar Mahmood	17	R. L. Johnson b Hollioake	3
J. D. C. Bryant b Bicknell	9	N. A. M. McLean b Hollioake	6
*M. Burns c Batty b Clarke	47	P. S. Jones not out	8
K. A. Parsons c Thorpe b Saqlain Mushtaq	83	L-b 13, w 14, n-b 2	29
I. D. Blackwell c Butcher b Saqlain Mushtaq	39	1/7 (1) 2/25 (3) (9 wkts, 50 overs)	275
K. P. Dutch lbw b Hollioake	14	3/51 (2) 4/148 (4)	
		5/222 (6) 6/231 (5)	
		7/247 (7) 8/254 (9) 9/262 (10)	

Bowling: Bicknell 10–2–23–1; Ormond 8–0–53–1; Azhar Mahmood 10–1–43–1; Butcher 2–0–15–0; Saqlain Mushtaq 10–1–58–2; Clarke 7–0–51–1; Hollioake 3–0–19–3.

Umpires: M. J. Harris and B. Leadbeater.

WARWICKSHIRE v ESSEX

At Birmingham, May 28. Warwickshire won by three wickets. Toss: Warwickshire. County debut: Waqar Younis.

Warwickshire owed everything to a competition-record seventh-wicket stand of 170 between Brown, who hit his maiden one-day century, and Giles. Essex appeared to be heading for the quarter-finals when they reduced Warwickshire to 83 for six, but their change bowlers failed to support the impressive Brant and Dakin. By the time they returned to the attack, the game was already over. Brown struck four sixes and nine fours from 99 deliveries before losing his middle stump, and Giles's seventh boundary completed victory with five balls to spare. Essex had made a disastrous start, losing two wickets in Waqar Younis's first over: Hussain was run out first ball after being called for an improbable single, before Jefferson carved to slip. But they were revived by a resourceful fifth-wicket stand of 107 between the grafting Flower and Pettini, who was back from Cardiff University and played with maturity and composure to make his highest one-day score from 81 balls. Pettini seemed destined for the match award – then came Brown and Giles.

Man of the Match: D. R. Brown.

Essex

N. Hussain run out 0
W. I. Jefferson c Knight b Waqar Younis 0
†J. S. Foster c Ostler b Brown 22
A. Flower c Knight b Giles 82
*R. C. Irani c Knight b Brown 11
M. L. Pettini not out. 92
A. P. Grayson not out 41
L-b 4, w 4. 8

1/0 (1) 2/0 (2) 3/49 (3) 4/71 (5) 5/178 (4) (5 wkts, 50 overs) 256

G. R. Napier, J. M. Dakin, A. J. Clarke and S. A. Brant did not bat.

Bowling: Waqar Younis 10–1–61–1; Wagg 5–1–29–0; Sheikh 10–1–40–0; Brown 10–1–37–2; Giles 10–0–49–1; Bell 2–0–14–0; Wagh 3–0–22–0.

Warwickshire

M. A. Wagh c Hussain b Dakin 4
N. V. Knight c Grayson b Brant 2
G. G. Wagg c Pettini b Irani. 19
I. R. Bell c Jefferson b Dakin. 0
J. O. Troughton b Dakin 17
D. P. Ostler c Jefferson b Napier 18
D. R. Brown b Brant. 108
*A. F. Giles not out 71
M. A. Sheikh not out 0
L-b 5, w 7, n-b 6 18

1/6 (2) 2/20 (1) 3/23 (4) 4/49 (3) 5/52 (5) 6/83 (6) 7/253 (7) (7 wkts, 49.1 overs) 257

†K. J. Piper and Waqar Younis did not bat.

Bowling: Brant 10–1–45–2; Dakin 8.1–1–30–3; Irani 10–1–51–1; Napier 7–0–41–1; Grayson 9–0–47–0; Clarke 5–0–38–0.

Umpires: B. Dudleston and R. Palmer.

WORCESTERSHIRE v YORKSHIRE

At Worcester, May 28. Worcestershire won by 67 runs. Toss: Yorkshire.

A gutsy all-round performance from Leatherdale and fiery bowling from Hayward dug Worcestershire out of trouble and propelled them into the quarter-finals. Despite a pugnacious 60 from 56 balls from Solanki, Yorkshire's decision to bowl first looked justified as Worcestershire folded to 130 for six. But Hoggard, who had Hick caught at third man with his first ball, managed just two more deliveries before leaving the field with a knee injury, and Leatherdale began to turn the innings around with the help of his fellow Yorkshireman Rhodes. Leatherdale finally fell for 80, his highest score in 15 years of limited-overs cricket, and was soon in the action again, holding four catches as Yorkshire lost eight for 77 after reaching 100 for two. Batty, yet another Yorkshire exile, strangled the middle of the innings, while Hayward returned to complete a five-wicket haul.

Man of the Match: D. A. Leatherdale.

Worcestershire

S. D. Peters c Craven b Gough 5	Kabir Ali not out 8
V. S. Solanki c Vaughan b Gray 60	M. S. Mason not out. 3
G. A. Hick c Lumb b Hoggard 19	B 1, l-b 8, w 3, n-b 2 14
*B. F. Smith lbw b Silverwood 0	——
A. J. Hall lbw b Bresnan 12	1/13 (1) 2/50 (3) (8 wkts, 50 overs) 244
D. A. Leatherdale b Gough 80	3/59 (4) 4/92 (5)
G. J. Batty lbw b Bresnan 14	5/107 (2) 6/130 (7)
†S. J. Rhodes st Blakey b Vaughan 29	7/209 (8) 8/235 (6)

M. Hayward did not bat.

Bowling: Silverwood 10–1–49–1; Gough 10–2–43–2; Hoggard 0.3–0–0–1; Craven 0.3–0–8–0; Bresnan 10–0–53–2; Gray 10–1–37–1; Yuvraj Singh 6–0–27–0; Vaughan 3–0–18–1.

Yorkshire

M. J. Lumb c Batty b Hayward. 0	D. Gough lbw b Hayward 0
M. P. Vaughan c Leatherdale b Batty . . . 47	M. J. Hoggard not out 7
C. E. W. Silverwood b Hayward 17	
*M. J. Wood c Leatherdale b Mason . . . 29	L-b 3, w 7, n-b 2 12
Yuvraj Singh b Hayward 27	——
†R. J. Blakey c Solanki b Hayward 23	1/0 (1) 2/26 (3) 3/100 (4) (41.1 overs) 177
V. J. Craven c Leatherdale b Batty. 1	4/108 (2) 5/145 (5)
T. T. Bresnan c Leatherdale b Hall 14	6/150 (7) 7/156 (6)
A. K. D. Gray run out. 0	8/157 (9) 9/157 (10) 10/177 (8)

Bowling: Hayward 10–0–49–5; Ali 7–0–47–0; Hall 6.1–1–31–1; Mason 8–1–22–1; Batty 10–1–25–2.

Umpires: A. Clarkson and N. A. Mallender.

QUARTER-FINALS

LEICESTERSHIRE v WORCESTERSHIRE

At Leicester, June 10, 11. Worcestershire won by 75 runs. Toss: Worcestershire.

Rain brought the reserve day into play, and when Sehwag was trapped on the back foot by Mason's first ball of the second morning, shock waves reverberated right through the Leicestershire ranks. The previous evening, a target of 217 had seemed reachable, even on a sluggish pitch, but five wickets fell for 16 runs in ten overs and Worcestershire were on course. For the home supporters it was a bitterly disappointing performance after Worcestershire's batsmen had been reasonably contained. At one stage Maddy took three wickets in five balls, but a stand of 111 for the fifth wicket between Singh and Leatherdale, who hit the game's only half-centuries, ultimately proved decisive.

Close of play: Leicestershire 5-0 (5.3 overs) (Maunders 2, Sehwag 2).

Man of the Match: A. Singh.

Worcestershire

V. S. Solanki c DeFreitas b Dagnall. . . . 4	†S. J. Rhodes not out 17
A. Singh run out 74	M. S. Mason not out. 1
Kadeer Ali c Snape b Maddy 30	L-b 10, w 10 20
*B. F. Smith c Brignull b Maddy 0	——
A. J. Hall c Brignull b Maddy 0	1/9 (1) 2/62 (3) (8 wkts, 50 overs) 216
D. A. Leatherdale run out 62	3/62 (4) 4/62 (5)
G. J. Batty run out 1	5/173 (2) 6/176 (7)
Kabir Ali c Hodge b Dagnall 7	7/184 (8) 8/215 (6)

M. A. Harrity did not bat.

Bowling: DeFreitas 10–2–21–0; Dagnall 10–3–20–2; Brignull 7–0–44–0; Maddy 8–1–44–3; Grove 3–0–14–0; Stevens 5–0–24–0; Snape 7–0–39–0.

Leicestershire

J. K. Maunders c Harrity b Mason	11	C. E. Dagnall not out	24
V. Sehwag lbw b Mason	2	D. S. Brignull c Smith b Mason	5
D. I. Stevens lbw b Hall	34	J. O. Grove c Rhodes b Harrity	2
B. J. Hodge lbw b Harrity	4	B 1, l-b 4, w 5	10
D. L. Maddy lbw b Hall	0		
†P. A. Nixon c Smith b Leatherdale	17	1/5 (2) 2/44 (1) 3/48 (3) (43.5 overs)	141
J. N. Snape b Harrity	2	4/48 (5) 5/54 (4) 6/60 (7)	
*P. A. J. DeFreitas c Kabir Ali b Leatherdale	30	7/98 (8) 8/129 (6)	
		9/137 (10) 10/141 (11)	

Bowling: Kabir Ali 6–1–20–0; Mason 10–3–28–3; Hall 7–3–11–2; Harrity 7.5–0–23–3; Leatherdale 9–0–42–2; Batty 4–0–12–0.

Umpires: T. E. Jesty and A. A. Jones.

DERBYSHIRE v SURREY

At Derby, June 11. Derbyshire won by 137 runs. Toss: Surrey.

On his first appearance at the County Ground, the Indian Test player Mohammad Kaif set up the most unexpected county result of the season – it was Surrey's first defeat in 22 matches in all competitions, and one as comprehensive as it was surprising. Derbyshire started well before Kaif, helped by the brisk-scoring Hewson, lifted the innings with an irresistible mix of urgent running and graceful strokeplay. Surrey's bowling, with the exception of Azhar Mahmood and Saqlain Mushtaq, who never conceded more than a single, was poor. Cork bowled Brown in the first over to set the tone for the Surrey innings as he and Dean reduced them to 26 for four. Thorpe, put down by Sutton on nine, became Surrey's main hope, but when he fell in an excellent spell by Welch, Derbyshire were in control. They did not relinquish it. Before the start, the teams lined up as a mark of respect for the former Derbyshire captain Guy Willatt, who had died earlier that morning.

Man of the Match: M. Kaif.

Derbyshire

A. I. Gait c Batty b Azhar Mahmood	0	T. Lungley c Sampson b Hollioake	0
M. J. Di Venuto c Azhar Mahmood b Ormond	51	†L. D. Sutton not out	1
C. W. G. Bassano b Ormond	33	K. J. Dean b Azhar Mahmood	2
M. Kaif c Ramprakash b Hollioake	81	L-b 12, w 18	30
D. R. Hewson c Batty b Ormond	34	1/15 (1) 2/75 (3) 3/99 (2) (50 overs)	271
*D. G. Cork run out	10	4/187 (5) 5/238 (6) 6/254 (7)	
N. R. C. Dumelow b Azhar Mahmood	15	7/260 (4) 8/261 (9)	
G. Welch c Brown b Azhar Mahmood	14	9/268 (8) 10/271 (11)	

Bowling: Azhar Mahmood 10–2–49–4; Sampson 6–0–33–0; Saqlain Mushtaq 10–0–24–0; Ormond 10–2–53–3; Clarke 7–0–51–0; Hollioake 7–0–49–2.

Surrey

I. J. Ward c Lungley b Dean	6	J. Ormond c Cork b Lungley	2
A. D. Brown b Cork	0	P. J. Sampson not out	5
M. R. Ramprakash c Di Venuto b Dean	7		
G. P. Thorpe c Sutton b Welch	37	L-b 1, w 2, n-b 8	11
R. Clarke lbw b Cork	0		
*A. J. Hollioake c Lungley b Welch	20	1/1 (2) 2/12 (1) 3/23 (3) (33.4 overs)	134
Azhar Mahmood b Welch	16	4/26 (5) 5/66 (4) 6/83 (6)	
†J. N. Batty c Sutton b Lungley	28	7/97 (7) 8/103 (9)	
Saqlain Mushtaq c Dean b Welch	2	9/113 (10) 10/134 (8)	

Bowling: Cork 7–0–17–2; Dean 8–1–26–2; Welch 7–0–26–4; Lungley 8.4–1–45–2; Dumelow 3–0–19–0.

Umpires: D. J. Constant and A. G. T. Whitehead.

LANCASHIRE v MIDDLESEX

At Manchester, June 11. Lancashire won by 57 runs. Toss: Lancashire.

A patient innings from Loye and one of unadulterated violence from Chapple helped Lancashire towards a win that was never in doubt once Martin and Anderson had reduced Middlesex to 22 for three in reply. Loye, badly missed at second slip by Weekes off Keegan's second ball, dropped anchor, before Chapple provided a late surge with 45 in 25 balls, including three sixes, two of them over extra cover off Weekes in the final over. Martin, passed fit just before the start, pegged Middlesex back with two for ten in his first six overs, and when Abdul Razzaq and Strauss both fell at 86, Lancashire were all but through. Flintoff, in particular, was all smiles, having bowled for the first time in a month to prove he had recovered from a shoulder injury to the watching England one-day captain, Vaughan.

Man of the Match: M. B. Loye.

Lancashire

M. B. Loye c Noffke b Weekes	74
I. J. Sutcliffe c Cook b Hutton	32
S. G. Law c Hutton b Weekes	25
C. L. Hooper c and b Keegan	11
A. Flintoff c Hutton b Razzaq	13
M. J. Chilton b Razzaq	34
G. Chapple not out	45
*†W. K. Hegg run out	7
K. W. Hogg not out	0
B 1, l-b 4, w 6	11
1/69 (2) 2/103 (3) 3/120 (4) 4/141 (5) 5/180 (1) 6/213 (6) 7/246 (8) — (7 wkts, 50 overs)	252

P. J. Martin and J. M. Anderson did not bat.

Bowling: Keegan 10–2–30–1; Noffke 10–1–37–0; Cook 8–0–60–0; Abdul Razzaq 10–1–51–2; Hutton 2–0–14–1; Weekes 10–0–55–2.

Middlesex

P. N. Weekes c Chilton b Anderson	8
*A. J. Strauss c Law b Martin	32
O. A. Shah lbw b Martin	1
E. C. Joyce c Hegg b Martin	6
D. C. Nash c Hegg b Chapple	13
Abdul Razzaq lbw b Flintoff	18
B. L. Hutton b Hooper	27
S. J. Cook b Hooper	8
A. A. Noffke c Loye b Martin	19
†D. Alleyne c and b Flintoff	19
C. B. Keegan not out	29
L-b 9, w 6	15
1/13 (1) 2/14 (3) 3/22 (4) 4/55 (5) 5/86 (6) 6/86 (2) 7/104 (8) 8/139 (7) 9/147 (9) 10/195 (10) — (49.1 overs)	195

Bowling: Martin 10–2–34–4; Anderson 10–0–33–1; Hogg 7–0–34–0; Chapple 8–0–34–1; Flintoff 6.1–1–22–2; Hooper 8–0–29–2.

Umpires: J. H. Evans and B. Leadbeater.

WARWICKSHIRE v GLOUCESTERSHIRE

At Birmingham, June 11. Gloucestershire won by five wickets. Toss: Warwickshire.

Warwickshire, who handicapped themselves by selecting only two specialist seamers, had no answer to the sublime one-day skills of Harvey. The Australian all-rounder ran out Bell with a brilliant left-handed throw from mid-wicket and then ruthlessly dismantled the lower order to finish with five wickets, including a spell of three for one in nine balls. In between, Knight and Troughton gave Warwickshire a chance with a fourth-wicket stand of 92, but the last five wickets fell for just 14, and their total was at least 50 below par on a good pitch. With Brown unable to bowl because of a groin strain – an injury Warwickshire were aware of before they picked their side –

their attack lacked depth and penetration. Weston, overlooked by Worcestershire for one-day cricket in 2002, anchored Gloucestershire's reply with an unflustered 88 and Warwickshire's theory that the pitch would turn – they included three spinners – was found wanting.

Man of the Match: I. J. Harvey.

Warwickshire

N. V. Knight c Windows b Ball	88
M. A. Wagh c Ball b Harvey	2
I. R. Bell run out	9
D. P. Ostler c Russell b Harvey	0
J. O. Troughton lbw b Smith	52
D. R. Brown c Russell b Ball	10
*A. F. Giles run out	28
N. M. K. Smith c Windows b Harvey	0
M. A. Sheikh c Windows b Harvey	2
†K. J. Piper st Russell b Harvey	0
Waqar Younis not out	1
B 4, l-b 5, w 3	12
1/12 (2) 2/26 (3) 3/30 (4) 4/122 (5) 5/141 (6) 6/190 (1) 7/192 (8) 8/201 (9) 9/202 (10) 10/204 (7) (47.4 overs)	204

Bowling: Smith 10–2–37–1; Harvey 9–0–23–5; Averis 6.4–0–39–0; Alleyne 10–0–41–0; Ball 10–0–44–2; Gidman 2–0–11–0.

Gloucestershire

W. P. C. Weston not out	88
C. M. Spearman b Waqar Younis	5
I. J. Harvey c Brown b Giles	12
J. N. Rhodes c Smith b Giles	24
M. G. N. Windows lbw b Waqar Younis	29
†R. C. Russell run out	15
A. P. R. Gidman not out	22
L-b 3, w 8	11
1/20 (2) 2/56 (3) 3/102 (4) 4/157 (5) 5/181 (6) (5 wkts, 40.5 overs)	206

*M. W. Alleyne, M. C. J. Ball, J. M. M. Averis and A. M. Smith did not bat.

Bowling: Waqar Younis 8.5–1–41–2; Sheikh 5–1–30–0; Bell 3–0–17–0; Giles 10–1–52–2; Smith 8–0–39–0; Wagh 6–0–24–0.

Umpires: G. I. Burgess and N. J. Llong.

SEMI-FINALS

GLOUCESTERSHIRE v DERBYSHIRE

At Bristol, August 7. Gloucestershire won by one wicket. Toss: Derbyshire.

Dominic Cork's assertive captaincy almost lifted the underdogs Derbyshire to a famous victory in front of a full house. And Gloucestershire supporters' early sniggers when Cork appeared wearing an Alice band, in the manner of David Beckham, almost turned to tears. As a grassy outfield quickened and a low wicket baked, Gloucestershire reached 193 for five in pursuit of a modest 220, only for their innings to unravel suddenly. Alleyne and Russell fell in the same over to Wharton, and Cork, who had been uneasy about his decision to bat first, called his players into a soccer-style huddle, sensing an improbable victory. His first three overs had cost 31, but now, with Gloucestershire needing just three runs, Cork struck back. Shoaib Malik misjudged a bouncer to fall for a cultured 74, and Ball was acrobatically held in the gully by Di Venuto. But Averis kept his head, and played out four deliveries from Welch before instinctively clipping a leg-side full toss to the boundary. Gloucestershire were through to their sixth final in five years and Shoaib, who returned to Pakistan after the game, picked up the match award. He gave the champagne to the dressing-room but, in view of his imminent departure, was allowed to take the cheque rather than add it to the players' pool. Derbyshire's innings was undermined by three run-outs, and it needed a calm innings from Kaif to keep them in contention.

Man of the Match: Shoaib Malik.

Derbyshire

M. J. Di Venuto lbw b Smith	14	K. J. Dean c Averis b Shoaib Malik	2
S. A. Selwood c Ball b Smith	10	L. J. Wharton not out	0
C. W. G. Bassano c Russell b Gidman	10		
M. Kaif c Windows b Ball	72	B 1, l-b 10, w 10, n-b 2	23
D. R. Hewson run out	37		——
†L. D. Sutton run out	13	1/28 (1) 2/29 (2) 3/59 (3) (49.3 overs)	219
*D. G. Cork c and b Ball	6	4/134 (5) 5/157 (6)	
G. Welch run out	22	6/171 (7) 7/193 (4)	
N. R. C. Dumelow c Alleyne b Averis	10	8/206 (9) 9/211 (10) 10/219 (8)	

Bowling: Smith 10–1–35–2; Averis 9.3–1–41–1; Alleyne 7–1–23–0; Gidman 4–0–19–1; Ball 10–0–44–2; Shoaib Malik 9–0–46–1.

Gloucestershire

W. P. C. Weston c Cork b Welch	14	J. M. M. Averis not out	4
C. M. Spearman c Sutton b Welch	27	A. M. Smith not out	0
A. P. R. Gidman lbw b Hewson	41		
J. N. Rhodes lbw b Dean	0	B 1, l-b 4, w 11, n-b 4	20
M. G. N. Windows b Dean	7		——
Shoaib Malik c Dean b Cork	74	1/48 (2) 2/57 (1) (9 wkts, 45.5 overs)	221
*M. W. Alleyne c Kaif b Wharton	27	3/58 (4) 4/78 (5)	
†R. C. Russell c Sutton b Wharton	0	5/134 (3) 6/193 (7)	
M. C. J. Ball c Di Venuto b Cork	7	7/194 (8) 8/217 (6) 9/217 (9)	

Bowling: Cork 9–0–50–2; Dean 10–0–37–2; Welch 9.5–0–49–2; Wharton 6–0–31–2; Dumelow 7–0–28–0; Hewson 4–0–21–1.

Umpires: M. R. Benson and B. Dudleston.

WORCESTERSHIRE v LANCASHIRE

At Worcester, August 9. Worcestershire won by six runs. Toss: Lancashire.

Hall, granted permission to play by the South African tourists, produced one of one-day cricket's unforgettable final overs to pull off a remarkable victory for Worcestershire and condemn Lancashire to their fifth defeat in a semi-final in four years. Lancashire had needed just seven from the final over but, with the centurion Loye watching helplessly from the non-striker's end, Hall bowled Hegg with the first ball, Martin with the third and ran out Wood with the fifth. An exhausted Loye, who faced 154 balls, and hit nine fours and four sixes – three of them with outrageous sweep shots off the quicker bowlers – could not even bring himself to run a single from the final ball. Hall, who had earlier dismissed Hooper and Flintoff cheaply, held a smart slip catch to remove Law and biffed 26 off 20 balls, was carried shoulder-high from the field. Worcestershire's total centred on a second-wicket stand of 155 in 32 overs between a restrained Singh and Hick, in his first major contribution since breaking a bone in his hand. Lancashire then struggled against the accuracy of Mason, before Loye's improvisation appeared to turn the match in their favour. He added 63 with Schofield and 76 with Chapple, who was bowled by Kabir Ali with eight needed. Lancashire were still favourites – but Hall had the final say and received the match award ahead of Loye, who had been on the field all through one of the hottest days of a hot summer. He was so dehydrated – "as dry as a cornflake," said Lancashire manager Mike Watkinson – that he struggled to provide a urine sample for a routine drugs test.

Man of the Match: A. J. Hall.

Worcestershire

V. S. Solanki c Hegg b Anderson	2	G. J. Batty not out	9
A. Singh c Schofield b Flintoff	63	L-b 8, w 3, n-b 6	17
G. A. Hick c Hooper b Chapple	97		—
*B. F. Smith c Anderson b Flintoff	36	1/4 (1) 2/159 (2) (5 wkts, 50 overs)	254
A. J. Hall c Chilton b Anderson	26	3/191 (3) 4/237 (5)	
D. A. Leatherdale not out	4	5/240 (4)	

†S. J. Rhodes, Kabir Ali, M. S. Mason and M. Hayward did not bat.

Bowling: Martin 10–2–39–0; Anderson 9–1–48–2; Chapple 10–1–57–1; Wood 6–0–31–0; Flintoff 8–0–33–2; Hooper 7–0–38–0.

Lancashire

M. B. Loye not out	116	J. Wood run out	0
M. J. Chilton lbw b Hayward	6	J. M. Anderson not out	0
S. G. Law c Hall b Mason	8		
C. L. Hooper lbw b Hall	1	L-b 5, w 14, n-b 6	25
A. Flintoff lbw b Hall	15		—
C. P. Schofield c Hayward b Leatherdale	32	1/15 (2) 2/70 (3) (9 wkts, 50 overs)	248
G. Chapple b Ali	44	3/81 (4) 4/108 (5)	
*†W. K. Hegg b Hall	1	5/171 (6) 6/247 (7)	
P. J. Martin b Hall	0	7/248 (8) 8/248 (9) 9/248 (10)	

Bowling: Ali 10–1–46–1; Hayward 8–1–55–1; Mason 10–3–23–1; Hall 10–2–36–4; Batty 8–1–46–0; Leatherdale 4–0–37–1.

Umpires: J. H. Hampshire and J. W. Holder.

FINAL

GLOUCESTERSHIRE v WORCESTERSHIRE

MIKE WALTERS

At Lord's, August 30. Gloucestershire won by seven wickets. Toss: Gloucestershire.

Despite the window-dressing of a violent half-century by Harvey and Gloucestershire's latest triumph of teamwork over ego trips, another Lord's showpiece receded quickly into a one-horse race. Ever since Warwickshire scored 15 runs from the final over to scramble past Sussex's 321 for six back in 1993, English cricket's blue-riband cup final had been crying out for a cliff-hanger. But in a summer in which crowds had flocked to the gimmicks and gusto of 20-over slogfests, the C&G Trophy final had the appearance of a neglected child. The 6,000 empty seats winked at the ECB's marketing gurus like lightbulbs on Blackpool Illuminations, and Worcestershire's feeble performance gave those who did turn up scant value for money.

THE BRACEWELL BOYS

Gloucestershire's one-day successes since John Bracewell took over as coach in 1998:

Benson and Hedges Super Cup, 1999
NatWest Trophy, 1999
Benson and Hedges Cup, 2000
NatWest Trophy, 2000
National League, 2000
National League (Division 2), 2002
C&G Trophy, 2003

Under azure skies and on a dry pitch, Worcestershire gave themselves a formidable basis for negotiation by reaching 64 without loss, but within ten overs they had slumped to 99 for six. Solanki, whose county form had dipped alarmingly since his successful one-day sabbatical with England, hinted at a return to prolific ways with seven boundaries. But when he was run out by a combination of Singh's indecision and Rhodes's peerless handiwork, Worcestershire's fortunes went downhill fast.

Hick, back on the big stage for the first time since England's selectors had cut him adrift two and a half years earlier, made an appearance worthy of the catwalk: he marched out, gave a twirl, wafted wantonly to extra cover fourth ball and shuffled off again. This accelerated Worcestershire's collapse, and even the seventh-wicket stand of 34 between Rhodes and Batty, which briefly suspended the abject capitulation, carried a prohibitive premium as Rhodes pulled a muscle in his side. Alleyne agreed to allow James Pipe, a specialist gloveman who had been watching from the crowd with his girlfriend, to keep wicket during the Gloucestershire reply, but he was merely afforded a front-row view of the one-way traffic.

Weston gave the Gloucestershire innings irresistible impetus with eight fours in 50 balls, before Harvey brutalised Worcestershire by unfurling a series of withering off-side strokes. Launching Batty for 20 runs in his first over, mainly over extra cover, he smashed 61 from 36 balls to demoralise Worcestershire's attack and earn the match award by a landslide. Batty extracted a token of revenge by having Harvey stumped, but in all Gloucestershire needed only 92 minutes and a little more than 20 overs to take the chequered flag. It was all over by 4.10 p.m.

For Gloucestershire's departing coach John Bracewell, heading home to take charge as New Zealand's drill sergeant, the county's seventh one-day triumph in five seasons was a fitting send-off. Under his tutelage, they had become unquestionably the most dynamic limited-overs outfit in the country. In a touching gesture of self-deprecation, his players (average age: nearly 32) whistled the theme tune from TV's wartime sitcom, Dad's Army, which somehow seemed appropriate: for the most part, it was men against boys.

Man of the Match: I. J. Harvey. *Attendance:* 20,624; *receipts* £554,585.

Worcestershire

V. S. Solanki run out	40
A. Singh c Ball b Harvey	28
G. A. Hick c Windows b Harvey	0
*B. F. Smith run out	12
A. J. Hall lbw b Gidman	11
D. A. Leatherdale c Ball b Gidman	2
G. J. Batty lbw b Lewis	20
†S. J. Rhodes c Ball b Lewis	15
Kabir Ali not out	5
M. S. Mason st Russell b Ball	0
M. Hayward c sub b Ball	4
L-b 6, w 4, n-b 2	12
1/64 (1) 2/65 (3) 3/72 (2) 4/92 (4) 5/96 (6) 6/99 (5) 7/133 (7) 8/134 (8) 9/136 (10) 10/149 (11) (46.3 overs)	149
15 overs: 62-0	

Bowling: Smith 5–0–24–0; Lewis 10–2–28–2; Harvey 10–1–37–2; Alleyne 7–0–21–0; Gidman 7–1–12–2; Ball 7.3–0–21–2.

Gloucestershire

C. M. Spearman c Smith b Ali	10
W. P. C. Weston c Hall b Mason	46
I. J. Harvey st sub b Batty	61
A. P. R. Gidman not out	12
J. N. Rhodes not out	7
B 4, l-b 3, w 3, n-b 4	14
1/30 (1) 2/108 (2) 3/132 (3) (3 wkts, 20.3 overs)	150
15 overs: 130-2	

M. G. N. Windows, *M. W. Alleyne, †R. C. Russell, M. C. J. Ball, J. Lewis and A. M. Smith did not bat.

Bowling: Ali 4–0–25–1; Hayward 3–0–20–0; Mason 7–0–38–1; Hall 3–0–33–0; Batty 3.3–0–27–1.

Umpires: M. R. Benson and J. H. Hampshire.

CHELTENHAM & GLOUCESTER TROPHY RECORDS

(Including Gillette Cup, 1963–80, and NatWest Trophy, 1981–2000)

65-over games in 1963; 60-over games 1964–98; 50-over games 1999–2003.

The first two rounds of the 2002 competition, played in 2001, are designated as 2001-02; similarly 2002-03 and 2003-04.

Batting

Highest individual scores: 268, A. D. Brown, Surrey v Glamorgan, The Oval, 2002; 206, A. I. Kallicharran, Warwickshire v Oxfordshire, Birmingham, 1984; 201, V. J. Wells, Leicestershire v Berkshire, Leicester, 1996; 180*, T. M. Moody, Worcestershire v Surrey, The Oval, 1994; 179, J. M. Dakin, Leicestershire v Wales, Swansea, 2001; 177, C. G Greenidge, Hampshire v Glamorgan, Southampton, 1975; 177, A. J. Wright, Gloucestershire v Scotland, Bristol, 1997; 176*, D. R. Clarke, Bedfordshire v Derbyshire Board XI, Dunstable, 2001-02; 173*, M. J. Di Venuto, Derbyshire v Derbyshire Board XI, Derby, 2000; 172*, G. A. Hick, Worcestershire v Devon, Worcester, 1987; 165*, V. P. Terry, Hampshire v Berkshire, Southampton, 1985; 164*, V. S. Solanki, Worcestershire v Worcestershire Board XI, Worcester, 2003; 162*, C. J. Tavaré, Somerset v Devon, Torquay, 1990; 162*, I. V. A. Richards, Glamorgan v Oxfordshire, Swansea, 1993. *In the final:* 146, G. Boycott, Yorkshire v Surrey, 1965. (409 hundreds have been scored in the competition. The most hundreds in one tournament was 29 in 2002.)

Most runs: G. A. Gooch 2,547; R. A. Smith 2,377; G. A. Hick 2,277; K. J. Barnett 2,215; M. W. Gatting 2,148; A. J. Lamb 1,998; D. L. Amiss 1,950.

Fastest hundred: G. D. Rose off 36 balls, Somerset v Devon, Torquay, 1990.

Most hundreds: R. A. Smith 8; G. A. Hick and C. L. Smith 7; G. A. Gooch 6; D. I. Gower, I. V. A. Richards and G. M. Turner 5.

Highest totals: 438-5, Surrey v Glamorgan, The Oval, 2002; 429, Glamorgan v Surrey, The Oval, 2002; 424-5, Buckinghamshire v Suffolk, Dinton, 2002-03; 413-4, Somerset v Devon, Torquay, 1990; 406-5, Leicestershire v Berkshire, Leicester, 1996; 404-3, Worcestershire v Devon, Worcester, 1987; 401-7, Gloucestershire v Buckinghamshire, Wing, 2003; 392-5, Warwickshire v Oxfordshire, Birmingham, 1984; 387-4, Ireland v Hertfordshire, Bishop's Stortford, 2003-04; 386-5, Essex v Wiltshire, Chelmsford, 1988; 384-6, Kent v Berkshire, Finchampstead, 1994; 384-9, Sussex v Ireland, Belfast, 1996; 381-3, Lancashire v Hertfordshire, Radlett, 1999. *In the final:* 322-5, Warwickshire v Sussex, Lord's, 1993.

Highest total by a side batting first and losing: 327-8 (60 overs), Derbyshire v Sussex, Derby, 1997. *In the final:* 321-6 (60 overs), Sussex v Warwickshire, 1993.

Highest totals by a side batting second: 429 (49.5 overs), Glamorgan lost to Surrey, The Oval, 2002; 350 (59.5 overs), Surrey lost to Worcestershire, The Oval, 1994; 339-9 (60 overs), Somerset lost to Warwickshire, Birmingham, 1995; 339 (49.1 overs), Kent lost to Somerset, Taunton, 2002; 329-5 (59.2 overs), Sussex beat Derbyshire, Derby, 1997; 326-9 (60 overs), Hampshire lost to Leicestershire, Leicester, 1987; 323-8 (50 overs), Sussex lost to Surrey, Hove, 2002; 322-5 (60 overs), Warwickshire beat Sussex, Lord's, 1993 (*in the final*); 319-9 (59.5 overs), Essex beat Lancashire, Chelmsford, 1992.

Lowest completed totals: 39 (26.4 overs), Ireland v Sussex, Hove, 1985; 41 (20 overs), Cambridgeshire v Buckinghamshire, Cambridge, 1972; 41 (19.4 overs), Middlesex v Essex, Westcliff, 1972; 41 (36.1 overs), Shropshire v Essex, Wellington, 1974. *In the final:* 57 (27.2 overs), Essex v Lancashire, 1996.

Lowest total by a side batting first and winning: 98 (56.2 overs), Worcestershire v Durham, Chester-le-Street, 1968.

Shortest innings: 10.1 overs (60-1), Worcestershire v Lancashire, Worcester, 1963.

Matches rearranged on a reduced number of overs are excluded from the above.

Record partnerships for each wicket

311	for 1st	A. J. Wright and N. J. Trainor, Gloucestershire v Scotland at Bristol . .	1997
286	for 2nd	I. S. Anderson and A. Hill, Derbyshire v Cornwall at Derby	1986
309*	for 3rd	T. S. Curtis and T. M. Moody, Worcestershire v Surrey at The Oval . . .	1994
234*	for 4th	D. Lloyd and C. H. Lloyd, Lancashire v Gloucestershire at Manchester .	1978
166	for 5th	M. A. Lynch and G. R. J. Roope, Surrey v Durham at The Oval	1982
226	for 6th	N. J. Llong and M. V. Fleming, Kent v Cheshire at Bowdon	1999
170	for 7th	D. R. Brown and A. F. Giles, Warwickshire v Essex at Birmingham . . .	2003
112	for 8th	A. L. Penberthy and J. E. Emburey, Northamptonshire v Lancashire at Manchester	1996
87	for 9th	M. A. Nash and A. E. Cordle, Glamorgan v Lincolnshire at Swansea . .	1974
81	for 10th	S. Turner and R. E. East, Essex v Yorkshire at Leeds	1982

Bowling

Most wickets: A. A. Donald 88; G. G. Arnold 81; C. A. Connor 80; J. Simmons 79.

Best bowling (12 overs unless stated): 8-21 (10.1 overs), M. A. Holding, Derbyshire v Sussex, Hove, 1988; 8-31 (11.1 overs), D. L. Underwood, Kent v Scotland, Edinburgh, 1987; 7-15, A. L. Dixon, Kent v Surrey, The Oval, 1967; 7-15 (9.3 overs), R. P. Lefebvre, Somerset v Devon, Torquay, 1990; 7-19, N. V. Radford, Worcestershire v Bedfordshire, Bedford, 1991; 7-27 (9.5 overs), D. Gough, Yorkshire v Ireland, Leeds, 1997; 7-30, P. J. Sainsbury, Hampshire v Norfolk, Southampton, 1965; 7-32, S. P. Davis, Durham v Lancashire, Chester-le-Street, 1983; 7-33, R. D. Jackman, Surrey v Yorkshire, Harrogate, 1970; 7-35 (10.1 overs), D. E. Malcolm, Derbyshire v Northamptonshire, Derby, 1997; 7-37, N. A. Mallender, Northamptonshire v Worcestershire, Northampton, 1984. *In the final:* 6-18 (6.2 overs), G. Chapple, Lancashire v Essex, 1996.

Most economical analysis: 12–9–3–1, J. Simmons, Lancashire v Suffolk, Bury St Edmunds, 1985.

Most expensive analysis: 9–0–108–3, S. D. Thomas, Glamorgan v Surrey, The Oval, 2002.

Hat-tricks (13): J. D. F. Larter, Northamptonshire v Sussex, Northampton, 1963; D. A. D. Sydenham, Surrey v Cheshire, Hoylake, 1964; R. N. S. Hobbs, Essex v Middlesex, Lord's, 1968; N. M. McVicker, Warwickshire v Lincolnshire, Birmingham, 1971; G. S. le Roux, Sussex v Ireland, Hove, 1985; M. Jean-Jacques, Derbyshire v Nottinghamshire, Derby, 1987; J. F. M. O'Brien, Cheshire v Derbyshire, Chester, 1988; R. A. Pick, Nottinghamshire v Scotland, Nottingham, 1995; J. E. Emburey, Northamptonshire v Cheshire, Northampton, 1996; A. R. Caddick, Somerset v Gloucestershire, Taunton, 1996; D. Gough, Yorkshire v Ireland, Leeds, 1997; P. J. Swanepoel, Yorkshire Board XI v Somerset, Scarborough, 2002; B. V. Taylor, Sussex v Leicestershire, Leicester, 2002.

Four wickets in five balls: D. A. D. Sydenham, Surrey v Cheshire, Hoylake, 1964.

Wicket-keeping and Fielding

Most dismissals: R. C. Russell 104 (87 ct, 17 st); S. J. Rhodes 75 (65 ct, 10 st); R. W. Taylor 66 (58 ct, 8 st); A. P. E. Knott 65 (59 ct, 6 st).

Most dismissals in an innings: 8 (all ct), D. J. Pipe, Worcestershire v Hertfordshire, Hertford, 2001; 7 (all ct), A. J. Stewart, Surrey v Glamorgan, Swansea, 1994.

Most catches by a fielder: W. Larkins and J. Simmons 27; M. W. Gatting and G. A. Gooch 26; G. Cook and G. A. Hick 25; N. H. Fairbrother and P. J. Sharpe 24.

Four catches by a fielder in an innings: A. S. Brown, Gloucestershire v Middlesex, Bristol, 1963; G. Cook, Northamptonshire v Glamorgan, Northampton, 1972; C. G. Greenidge,

Hampshire v Cheshire, Southampton, 1981; D. C. Jackson, Durham v Northamptonshire, Darlington, 1984; T. S. Smith, Hertfordshire v Somerset, St Albans, 1984; H. Morris, Glamorgan v Scotland, Edinburgh, 1988; C. C. Lewis, Nottinghamshire v Worcestershire, Nottingham, 1992; G. Yates, Lancashire v Essex, Manchester, 2000; D. P. Fulton, Kent v Northamptonshire, Canterbury, 2001; D. A. Leatherdale, Worcestershire v Yorkshire, Worcester, 2003.

Results

Largest victories in runs: Somerset by 346 runs v Devon, Torquay, 1990; Gloucestershire by 324 runs v Buckinghamshire, Wing, 2003; Sussex by 304 runs v Ireland, Belfast, 1996; Worcestershire by 299 runs v Devon, Worcester, 1987; Essex by 291 runs v Wiltshire, Chelmsford, 1988; Worcestershire by 267 runs v Hertfordshire, Hertford, 2001.

Victories by ten wickets (25): By Bedfordshire, Essex, Glamorgan, Hampshire (twice), Holland, Lancashire (twice), Middlesex, Northamptonshire, Nottinghamshire, Scotland, Somerset (twice), Surrey (twice), Sussex (twice), Warwickshire (twice), Yorkshire (five times).

Earliest finishes: both at 2.20 p.m. Worcestershire beat Lancashire by nine wickets at Worcester, 1963; Essex beat Middlesex by eight wickets at Westcliff, 1972.

Scores level (13): Nottinghamshire 215, Somerset 215-9 at Taunton, 1964; Surrey 196, Sussex 196-8 at The Oval, 1970; Somerset 287-6, Essex 287 at Taunton, 1978; Surrey 195-7, Essex 195 at Chelmsford, 1980; Essex 149, Derbyshire 149-8 at Derby, 1981; Northamptonshire 235-9, Derbyshire 235-6 at Lord's, 1981 (*in the final*); Middlesex 222-9, Somerset 222-8 at Lord's, 1983; Hampshire 224-8, Essex 224-7 at Southampton, 1985; Essex 307-6, Hampshire 307-5 at Chelmsford, 1990; Hampshire 204-9, Leicestershire 204-9 at Leicester, 1995; Cheshire 204, Lincolnshire 204-9 at Chester, 2000; Norfolk 245-3, Holland 245 at Horsford, 2001-02; Essex 283-9, Yorkshire 283-5 at Chelmsford, 2002.

Under competition rules the side which lost fewer wickets won; at Leicester in 1995, Leicestershire won by virtue of their higher total after 30 overs.

Match Awards

Most awards: G. A. Gooch and R. A. Smith 9; C. H. Lloyd and C. L. Smith 8.

WINNERS 1963–2003

Gillette Cup

		Man of the Match
1963	SUSSEX* beat Worcestershire by 14 runs.	N. Gifford†
1964	SUSSEX beat Warwickshire* by eight wickets.	N. I. Thomson
1965	YORKSHIRE beat Surrey* by 175 runs.	G. Boycott
1966	WARWICKSHIRE* beat Worcestershire by five wickets.	R. W. Barber
1967	KENT* beat Somerset by 32 runs.	M. H. Denness
1968	WARWICKSHIRE beat Sussex* by four wickets.	A. C. Smith
1969	YORKSHIRE beat Derbyshire* by 69 runs.	B. Leadbeater
1970	LANCASHIRE* beat Sussex by six wickets.	H. Pilling
1971	LANCASHIRE* beat Kent by 24 runs.	Asif Iqbal†
1972	LANCASHIRE* beat Warwickshire by four wickets.	C. H. Lloyd
1973	GLOUCESTERSHIRE* beat Sussex by 40 runs.	A. S. Brown
1974	KENT* beat Lancashire by four wickets.	A. P. E. Knott
1975	LANCASHIRE* beat Middlesex by seven wickets.	C. H. Lloyd
1976	NORTHAMPTONSHIRE* beat Lancashire by four wickets.	P. Willey
1977	MIDDLESEX* beat Glamorgan by five wickets.	C. T. Radley
1978	SUSSEX* beat Somerset by five wickets.	P. W. G. Parker
1979	SOMERSET beat Northamptonshire* by 45 runs.	I. V. A. Richards
1980	MIDDLESEX* beat Surrey by seven wickets.	J. M. Brearley

NatWest Trophy

		Man of the Match
1981	DERBYSHIRE* beat Northamptonshire by losing fewer wickets with the scores level.	G. Cook†
1982	SURREY* beat Warwickshire by nine wickets.	D. J. Thomas
1983	SOMERSET beat Kent* by 24 runs.	V. J. Marks
1984	MIDDLESEX beat Kent* by four wickets.	C. T. Radley
1985	ESSEX beat Nottinghamshire* by one run.	B. R. Hardie
1986	SUSSEX* beat Lancashire by seven wickets.	D. A. Reeve
1987	NOTTINGHAMSHIRE* beat Northamptonshire by three wickets.	R. J. Hadlee
1988	MIDDLESEX* beat Worcestershire by three wickets.	M. R. Ramprakash
1989	WARWICKSHIRE beat Middlesex* by four wickets.	D. A. Reeve
1990	LANCASHIRE* beat Northamptonshire by seven wickets.	P. A. J. DeFreitas
1991	HAMPSHIRE* beat Surrey by four wickets.	R. A. Smith
1992	NORTHAMPTONSHIRE* beat Leicestershire by eight wickets.	A. Fordham
1993	WARWICKSHIRE* beat Sussex by five wickets.	Asif Din
1994	WORCESTERSHIRE* beat Warwickshire by eight wickets.	T. M. Moody
1995	WARWICKSHIRE beat Northamptonshire* by four wickets.	D. A. Reeve
1996	LANCASHIRE beat Essex* by 129 runs.	G. Chapple
1997	ESSEX* beat Warwickshire by nine wickets.	S. G. Law
1998	LANCASHIRE* beat Derbyshire by nine wickets.	I. D. Austin
1999	GLOUCESTERSHIRE beat Somerset* by 50 runs.	R. C. Russell
2000	GLOUCESTERSHIRE* beat Warwickshire by 22 runs (D/L method).	A. A. Donald†

Cheltenham & Gloucester Trophy

2001	SOMERSET* beat Leicestershire by 41 runs.	K. A. Parsons
2002	YORKSHIRE beat Somerset* by six wickets.	M. T. G. Elliott
2003	GLOUCESTERSHIRE* beat Worcestershire by seven wickets.	I. J. Harvey

* *Won toss.* † *On losing side.*

TEAM RECORDS 1963–2003

	Rounds reached				*Matches*		
	W	*F*	*SF*	*QF*	*P*	*W*	*L*
Derbyshire	1	3	5	14	85*	45	40
Durham	0	0	0	2	51	18	33
Essex	2	3	6	16	91	52	39
Glamorgan	0	1	4	16	88	47	41
Gloucestershire	4	4	8	18	95	57	38
Hampshire	1	1	10	22	102	62	40
Kent	2	5	8	17	96	57	39
Lancashire	7	10	18	24	120	86	34
Leicestershire	0	2	5	17	89	48	41
Middlesex	4	6	13	22	107	70	37
Northamptonshire	2	7	10	21	102	63	39
Nottinghamshire	1	2	3	13	85	45	40
Somerset	3	7	12	20	105	67	38
Surrey	1	4	12	25	107*	67	40
Sussex	4	8	13	20	104	67	37
Warwickshire	5	11	18	24	120	84	36
Worcestershire	1	5	11	17	96	56	40
Yorkshire	3	3	8	19	93	55	38

* Derbyshire and Surrey totals each include a bowling contest after their first-round matches were abandoned in 1991; Derbyshire lost to Hertfordshire and Surrey beat Oxfordshire.

MINOR COUNTY RECORDS

From 1964 to 1979 the previous season's top five Minor Counties were invited to take part in the competition. In 1980 these were joined by Ireland, and in 1983 the competition was expanded to embrace 13 Minor Counties, Ireland and Scotland. The number of Minor Counties dropped to 12 in 1992 when Durham attained first-class status, and 11 in 1995 when Holland were admitted to the competition.

Between 1964 and 1991 Durham qualified 21 times, including 15 years in succession from 1977–91. They reached the second round a record six times.

Up to the 1998 tournament, Staffordshire qualified most among the remaining Minor Counties, 20 times, followed by Devon, 19. Only Hertfordshire have ever reached the quarter-finals, in 1976.

From 1999, the competition was reformed and two preliminary rounds introduced, in which 42 teams competed for the right to join the first-class counties in the third round. They were all 20 Minor Counties (including Wales), plus Huntingdonshire Board XI, the first-class county Board XIs (excluding Glamorgan, covered by Wales) and the national teams of Denmark, Holland, Ireland and Scotland. These four national teams did not take part in the 2001 Trophy because of the forthcoming ICC Trophy. The Board XIs were dropped for the 2004 competition.

Wins by a minor team over a first-class county (11)**:** Durham v Yorkshire (by five wickets), Harrogate, 1973; Lincolnshire v Glamorgan (by six wickets), Swansea, 1974; Hertfordshire v Essex (by 33 runs), 2nd round, Hitchin, 1976; Shropshire v Yorkshire (by 37 runs), Telford, 1984; Durham v Derbyshire (by seven wickets), Derby, 1985; Buckinghamshire v Somerset (by seven runs), High Wycombe, 1987; Cheshire v Northamptonshire (by one wicket), Chester, 1988; Hertfordshire v Derbyshire (2–1 in a bowling contest after the match was abandoned), Bishop's Stortford, 1991; Scotland v Worcestershire (by four runs), Edinburgh, 1998; Holland v Durham (by five wickets), Amstelveen, 1999; Herefordshire v Middlesex (by three wickets), Kingsland, 2001.

COUNTY CAPS AWARDED IN 2003

Essex	S. A. Brant, J. M. Dakin, J. D. Middlebrook, G. R. Napier.
Glamorgan	M. A. Wallace.
Hampshire	S. M. Katich, N. Pothas.
Kent	G. O. Jones, M. Muralitharan.
Lancashire	C. L. Hooper, M. B. Loye, I. J. Sutcliffe, J. Wood.
Leicestershire	B. J. Hodge, V. Sehwag.
Middlesex	S. J. Cook, J. H. Dawes, B. L. Hutton, C. B. Keegan, A. A. Noffke.
Northamptonshire	T. M. B. Bailey, J. W. Cook, P. A. Jaques.
Somerset	N. A. M. McLean.
Surrey	J. Ormond.
Sussex	T. R. Ambrose, Mushtaq Ahmed, M. J. Prior.
Yorkshire	S. P. Kirby, M. J. Lumb.

Note: Worcestershire have abolished caps and award "colours" to all Championship players.

No caps were awarded by Derbyshire, Durham, Gloucestershire, Nottinghamshire or Warwickshire.

CHELTENHAM & GLOUCESTER TROPHY, 2004

For 2004, the C&G Trophy has been reduced from 60 teams to 42 by the removal of the county board XIs from the competition. The 42 comprise the 18 first-class counties, the 20 Minor Counties, Ireland, Scotland, Holland and Denmark.

Ten first-round matches were played in August 2003. The winners join four minor teams granted byes plus the first-class counties in the second round in May 2004.

FIRST ROUND

Note: Matches played in 2003.

At Luton, August 28. **Cheshire won by 39 runs.** Toss: Bedfordshire. **Cheshire 241-8** (50 overs) (S. A. Twigg 68, R. G. Hignett 36, N. A. Din 75; A. R. Roberts 4-38); **Bedfordshire 202** (47.3 overs) (A. D. Patterson 38, J. A. Knott 38, A. R. Roberts 38, Extras 30; J. P. Whittaker 3-29, S. J. Renshaw 3-50).

Man of the Match: S. A. Twigg.

At Exmouth, August 28. **Devon won by 88 runs.** Toss: Devon. **Devon 333-6** (50 overs) (M. P. Hunt 74, D. F. Lye 121, R. I. Dawson 55; P. Joubert 4-82); **Suffolk 245-9** (50 overs) (R. J. Catley 33, P. Joubert 46, P. J. Caley 31, I. S. Morton 31; A. J. Procter 3-36, R. J. Newman 3-48).

Man of the Match: D. F. Lye.

Matthew Hunt and David Lye put on 185 for Devon's first wicket.

At Bournemouth, August 28, 29. **No result.** Toss: Buckinghamshire. **Buckinghamshire 272-6** (48 overs) (R. P. Lane 95, D. J. Barr 51, H. J. H. Marshall 66*) **v Dorset.**

Man of the Match: R. P. Lane.

Russell Lane and David Barr put on 137 for the second wicket. Dorset won the match on a bowl-out 4–1.

At Bishop's Stortford, August 28, 29. **Ireland won by 75 runs.** Toss: Hertfordshire. **Ireland 387-4** (50 overs) (J. A. M. Molins 84, A. C. Botha 139, G. Dros 124; N. G. E. Walker 3-49); **Hertfordshire 312** (43.2 overs) (G. P. Butcher 126, S. G. Cordingley 58; P. J. K. Mooney 3-81, R. L. Eagleson 3-56, A. C. Botha 4-37).

Man of the Match: A. C. Botha.

Ireland's total was the second-highest by a minor team in the competition's history. Andre Botha, formerly of Griqualand West, shared stands of 157 for the second wicket with Jason Molins and 146 for the third with Gerald Dros, of Northerns (South Africa). For Hertfordshire, Gary Butcher, formerly of Glamorgan and Surrey, added 116 for the sixth wicket with Stephen Cordingley.

At Amstelveen, August 28. **Holland won by 12 runs.** Toss: Cornwall. **Holland 237-5** (50 overs) (C. Smith 48, D. L. S. van Bunge 36, T. B. M. de Leede 42, M. P. Mott 45*, D. J. Reekers 33); **Cornwall 225** (49.3 overs) (J. M. Hands 37, S. C. Pope 74, B. P. Price 30; J. F. Kloppenburg 3-34).

Man of the Match: S. C. Pope.

Cornwall collapsed from 136 for three.

At Horsford, August 28. **Lincolnshire won by 52 runs.** Toss: Lincolnshire. **Lincolnshire 228-9** (50 overs) (P. R. Pollard 40, M. A. Higgs 50, M. C. Dobson 52; P. J. Bradshaw 3-37, J. P. Marquet 3-55, P. G. Newman 3-38); **Norfolk 176** (44 overs) (S. C. Goldsmith 47; J. R. Davies 3-45, M. P. Dowman 4-30).

Man of the Match: M. A. Higgs.

At Oswestry, August 28, 29. **Shropshire won on scoring-rate.** Toss: Shropshire. **Northumberland 139** (39 overs) (T. J. Mason 5-17); **Shropshire 131-1** (20.1 overs) (S. J. Adshead 77*, C. J. L. Rogers 49).

Man of the Match: S. J. Adshead.

Under C&G playing conditions, rain-shortened matches are decided on run-rate rather than Duckworth/Lewis in rounds before the first-class counties enter the competition.

At Abergavenny, August 28. **Wales won by seven wickets.** Toss: Denmark. **Denmark 189-8** (50 overs) (B. Singh 58, A. Lambert 38*); **Wales 190-3** (48.2 overs) (A. J. Jones 93, A. W. Evans 60).

Man of the Match: A. J. Jones.

Andrew Jones and Alun Evans began the Wales reply with a stand of 137.

At Bodicote, August 31. **Herefordshire won by 126 runs.** Toss: Herefordshire. **Herefordshire 267-9** (50 overs) (H. V. Patel 49, I. Dawood 53, M. J. Rawnsley 61); **Oxfordshire 141** (31.4 overs) (A. P. Cook 66; F. A. Rose 5-19, M. J. Rawnsley 3-8).

Man of the Match: F. A. Rose.

Franklyn Rose, who played the most recent of his 19 Tests for West Indies at Old Trafford in 2000, took three wickets in four balls to reduce Oxfordshire to two for three, and struck again in his next over to make it seven for four. Matthew Rawnsley, formerly of Worcestershire, added 100 for Herefordshire's fifth wicket with another ex-Worcestershire player, Ismail Dawood, before returning figures of 6.4–2–8–3.

At Edinburgh, August 31. **Scotland won by four wickets.** Toss: Cumberland. **Cumberland 237-9** (50 overs) (A. A. Metcalfe 39, G. D. Lloyd 123; J. G. Williamson 3-38); **Scotland 239-6** (46.4 overs) (J. G. Williamson 77, C. J. O. Smith 56, C. M. Wright 30*).

Man of the Match: J. G. Williamson.

Graham Lloyd, who won six one-day caps for England, rescued Cumberland from 112 for six.

I ZINGARI RESULTS, 2003

Matches 23: Won 12, Lost 2, Drawn 9. Abandoned 1.

April 24	Eton College	Lost by six wickets
April 29	Charterhouse School	Lost by four wickets
May 4	Hampshire Hogs	Won by 146 runs
May 11	Stragglers of Asia	Drawn
May 17	Eton Ramblers	Drawn
May 24	Royal Armoured Corps	Abandoned
June 1	Earl of Carnarvon's XI	Won by 106 runs
June 8	Defence Academy CC	Drawn
June 14	RMA Sandhurst	Won by 82 runs
June 21	Guards CC	Won by 13 runs
June 24	Winchester College	Won by 114 runs
June 29	Hagley CC	Won by four wickets
June 29	Harrow School	Drawn
July 6	Old Wykehamists	Won by 31 runs
July 12	Green Jackets CC	Won by seven wickets
July 20	Sir John Starkey's XI	Won by 38 runs
July 26	Willow Warblers	Drawn
July 27	Duke of Norfolk's XI	Drawn
August 2	Hurlingham CC	Won by three wickets
August 3	Band of Brothers	Drawn
August 10	Lord Vestey's XI	Drawn
August 30	South Wales Hunts	Won by 186 runs
August 31	J. H. Pawle's XI	Drawn
September 14	Sir Paul Getty's XI	Won by four wickets

NATIONAL LEAGUE, 2003

Mark Ramprakash

In a year generally regarded as disappointing for county cricket's dominant club, Surrey completed a double – which would have delighted any other team – by winning the National League. It was only their second success in the tournament's 35-year history.

Surrey ensured victory with a week to spare when they beat Glamorgan at Cardiff. It was a turnaround almost as remarkable as the one that gave Sussex their first ever County Championship. In 1998, the last year before the old Sunday League was split into two divisions, Surrey finished stone last.

Previous generations at The Oval had been inclined to treat this competition with some disdain, but Mark Ramprakash's hunger for runs at every opportunity spearheaded their challenge. Adam Hollioake's gift for captaincy in this form of cricket, and his occasionally devastating bowling – he took five wickets in 15 balls at Canterbury – were other factors. So was the competition for first-team places. With even England stars being left out of the side, no one could spurn the chance to make an impression whatever the occasion.

Surrey put together two separate sequences of six successive wins (one interrupted by a washout) to finish four points clear of Gloucestershire, who crucially lost at The Oval. The rest trailed a long way back, but Essex came third meaning the three promoted teams filled the top three places. Glamorgan, the reigning champions, began with five successive wins, which took their record since July 2002 to 12 out of 13 – then they collapsed.

Lancashire won the second division, winning a crucial final-day showdown with Northamptonshire; Mal Loye, returning to his old home ground for the first time since he left Northampton a year earlier, sealed a nine-wicket win with an unbeaten century. Northamptonshire also went up along with Hampshire; these three replaced Leicestershire, Yorkshire and Worcestershire.

Lancashire actually went unbeaten between May 25 and September 14. They were evidently galvanised by losing to Scotland, who made a remarkable start to their debut season, winning their first two matches – against Durham and Somerset. In the Somerset game, Ryan Watson scored a century in 43 balls. Victory at Old Trafford made it three wins and a washout out of five even before their overseas star, Rahul Dravid, arrived. But when Dravid got there, and began scoring runs – 600 of them – the rest of the team lost their edge and 12 of the remaining 13 games, to finish last.

Total attendances for the two divisions went back over 400,000 for the first time since 1999: the total was 410,536 compared to 358,667 in 2002. The addition of Scotland meant there were 162 matches instead of 144. However, the Scots played most of their home games on weekday afternoons and averaged barely 1,000, so the figures would probably have risen slightly anyway.

NATIONAL LEAGUE

Division One

	M	*W*	*L*	*T*	*NR*	*Pts*	*Net run-rate*
1 – Surrey Lions (*2*)	16	12	3	0	1	50	2.99
2 – Gloucestershire Gladiators (*1*)	16	11	4	0	1	46	4.48
3 – Essex Eagles (*3*)	16	8	7	1	0	34	3.80
4 – Warwickshire Bears (**3**)	16	8	8	0	0	32	–0.57
5 – Glamorgan Dragons (**1**)	16	8	8	0	0	32	–0.94
6 – Kent Spitfires (**5**)	16	7	8	1	0	30	3.51
7 – Leicestershire Foxes (**6**)	16	7	9	0	0	28	–3.82
8 – Yorkshire Phoenix (**4**)	16	5	11	0	0	20	–6.95
9 – Worcestershire Royals (**2**)	16	4	12	0	0	16	–1.16

Division Two

	M	*W*	*L*	*T*	*NR*	*Pts*	*Net run-rate*
1 – Lancashire Lightning (*5*)	18	14	3	0	1	58	5.81
2 – Northamptonshire Steelbacks (*6*)	18	12	5	0	1	50	10.99
3 – Hampshire Hawks (*7*)	18	11	7	0	0	44	4.79
4 – Middlesex Crusaders (*9*)	18	10	7	0	1	42	–0.27
5 – Nottinghamshire Outlaws (**9**)	18	9	9	0	0	36	–0.61
6 – Derbyshire Scorpions (*4*)	18	8	8	0	2	36	–0.36
7 – Durham Dynamos (**8**)	18	7	10	0	1	30	4.24
8 – Sussex Sharks (*8*)	18	6	12	0	0	24	–8.16
9 – Somerset Sabres (**7**)	18	5	12	0	1	22	–4.12
10 – Scottish Saltires (–)	18	4	13	0	1	18	–14.03

2002 positions are shown in brackets: Division One in bold, Division Two in italic.

The bottom three teams in Division One are relegated for 2004, the top three teams in Division Two are promoted. The bottom four counties in Division Two (excluding Scotland) play each other in the second round of the 2004 Cheltenham and Gloucester Trophy.

When two or more teams finished with an equal number of points, the positions were decided by a) most wins, b) higher net run-rate (runs scored per 100 balls minus runs conceded per 100 balls).

Prize money

Division One
£54,000 for winners: SURREY.
£27,000 for runners-up: GLOUCESTERSHIRE.

Division Two
£20,000 for winners: LANCASHIRE.
£11,000 for runners-up: NORTHAMPTONSHIRE.

Winners of each match (both divisions): £600.

Leading run-scorers: *M. E. K. Hussey* 820, *P. A. Jaques* 803, *K. P. Pietersen* 776, *P. N. Weekes* 746, *M. W. Goodwin* 731, *S. M. Katich* 728, C. M. Spearman 717, *J. P. Crawley* 692, M. R. Ramprakash 686, N. V. Knight 684, *M. J. Di Venuto* and *O. A. Shah* 655.

Leading wicket-takers: *A. D. Mascarenhas* 34, G. R. Napier 33, *M. J. Cawdron* and *R. S. C. Martin-Jenkins* 26, *G. Chapple*, *N. Killeen* and *C. M. Wright* 25, *P. J. Martin* 24, *D. G. Cork*, A. J. Hollioake, *C. B. Keegan* and *S. D. Udal* 23, Kabir Ali and *A. Nel* 22.

Most economical bowlers (runs per over, minimum 50 overs): *A. Nel* 3.54, *Wasim Akram* 3.62, A. M. Smith 3.70, D. Gough 3.72, *Mushtaq Ahmed* 3.76, G. J. Batty 3.86, *N. Killeen* 3.87, *A. M. Davies* 3.89, *P. J. Martin* 3.93, M. Muralitharan 3.95.

Leading wicket-keepers: G. O. Jones 33 (27 ct, 6 st), *W. K. Hegg* 29 (26 ct, 3 st), M. A. Wallace 24 (21 ct, 3 st), J. N. Batty 23 (19 ct, 4 st), *L. D. Sutton* 22 (21 ct, 1 st), S. J. Rhodes 20 (15 ct, 5 st).

Leading fielders: *C. L. Hooper*, *S. M. Katich* and *O. A. Shah* 13, *M. B. Loye* 12, *G. J. Pratt* and D. I. Stevens 11, *E. C. Joyce* and N. V. Knight 10.

Players who appeared in Division Two are shown in italics.

SUMMARY OF RESULTS, 2003

DIVISION ONE

	Essex	Glamorgan	Gloucestershire	Kent	Leicestershire	Surrey	Warwickshire	Worcestershire	Yorkshire
Essex	–	W	L	W	W	L	L	W	W
Glamorgan	W	–	W	W	L	L	W	W	W
Gloucestershire	W	W	–	L	W	N	W	L	W
Kent	T	W	L	–	W	L	W	W	W
Leicestershire	W	L	L	L	–	L	L	W	W
Surrey	W	W	W	W	L	–	W	L	W
Warwickshire	L	W	L	W	W	W	–	W	L
Worcestershire	L	W	L	W	L	L	L	–	L
Yorkshire	L	L	L	W	L	L	W	W	–

DIVISION TWO

	Derbyshire	Durham	Hampshire	Lancashire	Middlesex	Northamptonshire	Nottinghamshire	Scotland	Somerset	Sussex
Derbyshire	–	L	W	L	L	W	L	W	W	W
Durham	N	–	W	L	W	L	L	L	L	W
Hampshire	W	W	–	L	L	W	L	W	W	W
Lancashire	W	W	W	–	W	L	W	L	N	L
Middlesex	W	W	W	L	–	L	W	W	W	L
Northamptonshire	N	W	L	L	L	–	W	W	W	W
Nottinghamshire	W	L	L	L	L	L	–	W	W	W
Scotland	L	L	L	L	N	L	L	–	W	L
Somerset	L	L	L	L	W	L	W	W	–	L
Sussex	L	W	L	L	W	L	L	L	L	–

Home teams listed on left, away teams across top; results are for home teams. W = Won, L = Lost, T = Tied, N = No result.

DIVISION ONE

ESSEX

At Chelmsford, April 27. **Surrey won by 15 runs.** Toss: Essex. **Surrey 268-8** (45 overs) (A. J. Hollioake 77, Azhar Mahmood 98; J. M. Dakin 3-51, G. R. Napier 3-50); **Essex 253** (43 overs) (W. I. Jefferson 47, R. C. Irani 64, J. S. Foster 41; A. J. Tudor 3-57, Saqlain Mushtaq 3-27). *Surrey 4 pts.*

On a seaming pitch, Surrey recovered from 82 for six, thanks to a seventh-wicket stand of 154 between Hollioake and Azhar Mahmood, who hit three sixes in 98 balls. Jefferson gave Essex a sparkling start but his opening partner, the England captain Hussain, scored a scratchy seven, and Essex could not keep up with the rate.

At Chelmsford, May 10. **Essex won by three wickets.** Toss: Kent. **Kent 176** (45 overs) (M. A. Carberry 37; G. R. Napier 3-9); **Essex 179-7** (43 overs) (W. I. Jefferson 35, A. P. Grayson 40, J. S. Foster 36, J. D. Middlebrook 32*; B. J. Trott 3-22). *Essex 4 pts.*

Essex prevailed despite losing three of their batsmen to Trott, who dismissed Hussain, Jefferson and Flower in the space of five balls. But they revived to clinch victory with two overs to spare. Napier had rocked Kent to leave them 33 for five before a recovery.

At Chelmsford, June 15. **Warwickshire won by 125 runs.** Toss: Essex. **Warwickshire 307-5** (45 overs) (I. J. L. Trott 59, I. R. Bell 125, T. L. Penney 36*, G. G. Wagg 32); **Essex 182** (27.5 overs) (G. R. Napier 52; I. R. Bell 5-41). *Warwickshire 4 pts.*

Warwickshire hit their highest League score and dismayed a crowd of 4,000 to score an overwhelming win after losing their first four games. They were indebted to career-best performances by their highly rated 21-year-old, Bell. Speculation that Bell might soon be chosen for England intensified after he stroked an authoritative 125 in 109 balls. The force being with him, his unprepossessing seam bowling was then too good for Essex, who were hitting out recklessly in the face of a daunting total.

At Chelmsford, July 17 (day/night). **Gloucestershire won by seven wickets.** Toss: Gloucestershire. **Essex 252-8** (45 overs) (A. Flower 39, N. Hussain 98, A. Habib 31; M. A. Hardinges 3-40); **Gloucestershire 255-3** (35 overs) (C. M. Spearman 101, I. J. Harvey 96). *Gloucestershire 4 pts.*

Gloucestershire reached what had appeared to be a formidable target with ten overs to spare thanks to devastating batting from Spearman and Harvey, who plundered 145 in 18 overs on a benign pitch. Earlier, Hussain was yorked by Harvey just short of his second successive League hundred.

At Southend, July 27. **Essex won by 37 runs.** Toss: Essex. **Essex 203-6** (45 overs) (W. I. Jefferson 61, R. C. Irani 36, R. S. Bopara 32*; J. N. Snape 3-14); **Leicestershire 166** (42.2 overs) (P. A. Nixon 40). *Essex 4 pts.*

Essex ended a run of four successive League defeats thanks to vibrant fielding: three run-outs put paid to Leicestershire's attempt to recover from 87 for five. The Essex batsmen had struggled against Snape, who bowled beautifully for figures of 9–1–14–3, thwarting their hopes of acceleration after a stand of 101 between Jefferson and Irani.

At Chelmsford, August 5 (day/night). **Essex won by 145 runs.** Toss: Essex. **Essex 298-5** (45 overs) (A. Flower 57, N. Hussain 161*, J. M. Dakin 40*; D. A. Cosker 5-54); **Glamorgan 153** (26.1 overs) (M. P. Maynard 50; A. P. Palladino 3-32, G. R. Napier 4-26). *Essex 4 pts.*

Hussain, a late addition to the scorecard at No. 11, actually opened and took his second League century in a month off Glamorgan. As he did the previous time, he reached his best-ever one-day score. Hussain completed his hundred, in 91 balls, before his opening partner, Flower, reached 50. Wharf conceded 39 from his second and third overs, and Harrison 23 from his first two. Cosker took five wickets in six overs, but it was all too much for the Glamorgan batsmen.

At Colchester, August 28 (day/night). **Essex won by two wickets** (D/L method). Toss: Essex. **Worcestershire 141-3** (25 overs) (A. Singh 43, J. M. Kemp 31*); **Essex 86-8** (9.5 overs) (M. A. Harrity 3-27). *Essex 4 pts.*

Essex's target revised to 83 in ten overs.

In a match reduced initially to 25 overs a side, Essex won at 10.40 p.m. with a ball to spare. There were two lengthy interruptions through rain, and the outfield was very greasy: Darren Robinson fell on it awkwardly while fielding, injured his groin severely, and was stretchered to hospital.

At Chelmsford, September 10 (day/night). **Essex won by four wickets.** Toss: Essex. **Yorkshire 174** (43.5 overs) (V. J. Craven 31, R. J. Blakey 30, D. Gough 33; A. J. Clarke 4-28); **Essex 177-6** (42.5 overs) (M. L. Pettini 59, J. D. Middlebrook 46*). *Essex 4 pts.*

Reduced to 44 overs a side. Pettini and Middlebrook put on 88 for the sixth wicket to bring Essex victory on a seaming pitch, ensuring their survival in the League's first division but consigning Yorkshire to second-division status in both main competitions. Their defeat came despite an inspirational performance from Gough, who hit 33 off 41 balls, bowled a testing opening spell and dismissed Foster with an athletic catch at long-on.

GLAMORGAN

At Cardiff, May 5. **Glamorgan won by seven wickets.** Toss: Kent. **Kent 192-9** (45 overs) (R. W. T. Key 68, E. T. Smith 33, G. O. Jones 31; R. D. B. Croft 3-33); **Glamorgan 195-3** (36.2 overs) (R. D. B. Croft 59, M. J. Powell 58, M. P. Maynard 39*). *Glamorgan 4 pts.*

League champions Glamorgan completed their second win in the competition in two days, as their spinners, Croft and Cosker, thrived on a slow pitch. Croft and Powell then took control with the bat, though both were dropped in a sub-par fielding performance.

At Cardiff, May 18. **Glamorgan won by ten wickets** (D/L method). Toss: Glamorgan. **Gloucestershire 133-9** (26 overs) (M. G. N. Windows 32; A. P. Davies 3-31, A. G. Wharf 4-18); **Glamorgan 135-0** (21.2 overs) (R. D. B. Croft 60*, I. J. Thomas 71*). *Glamorgan 4 pts.*

Glamorgan's target revised to 133 in 26 overs.

Glamorgan's third win out of three gave them their best League start since 1980 and was achieved in spectacular style, with Thomas setting the tone by hoisting three sixes in the first seven overs. Earlier, Windows had hit Croft for six into the river.

At Swansea, June 8. **Glamorgan won by 31 runs.** Toss: Glamorgan. **Glamorgan 215-9** (39 overs) (M. J. Powell 46, D. L. Hemp 59, A. Dale 60; Kabir Ali 4-38); **Worcestershire 184** (36.2 overs) (A. Singh 37, A. J. Hall 35, D. A. Leatherdale 32; A. G. Wharf 4-24, R. D. B. Croft 3-33). *Glamorgan 4 pts.*

Reduced to 39 overs a side. Glamorgan's fifth League win out of five was their 12th out of 13 in a sequence dating back to August 2002. Worcestershire were undermined by Wharf's bowling and six penalty runs for a slow over-rate. Glamorgan recovered from a poor start thanks to a fifth-wicket stand of 112 between Hemp and Dale.

At Cardiff, July 13. **Glamorgan won by eight wickets.** Toss: Essex. **Essex 267-6** (45 overs) (N. Hussain 144*, R. C. Irani 63, A. Habib 35); **Glamorgan 269-2** (38.1 overs) (R. D. B. Croft 64, J. P. Maher 142, M. J. Powell 31*). *Glamorgan 4 pts.*

Hussain's highest one-day score was overshadowed by Maher, who shared an opening stand of 181 with Croft and smashed 20 in an over off Nick Denning, making his League debut.

At Cardiff, August 10. **Glamorgan won by seven wickets.** Toss: Warwickshire. **Warwickshire 196** (43.5 overs) (M. J. Powell 39, T. L. Penney 64*; A. Dale 3-16, D. A. Cosker 3-44); **Glamorgan 198-3** (40.5 overs) (R. D. B. Croft 70, M. P. Maynard 47*, D. L. Hemp 41*). *Glamorgan 4 pts.*

Having lost five successive away games, Glamorgan maintained their 100% record at home and gave themselves a slim chance of retaining their title with a workmanlike performance against weakened opposition. Only Penney managed to dominate an accurate attack, and Croft then gave Glamorgan the edge with his fourth fifty of the season.

At Colwyn Bay, August 24. **Glamorgan won by one run.** Toss: Yorkshire. **Glamorgan 238-8** (45 overs) (J. P. Maher 53, M. J. Powell 61, D. L. Hemp 37); **Yorkshire 237** (45 overs) (M. J. Lumb 92; M. S. Kasprowicz 3-39, D. A. Cosker 4-37). *Glamorgan 4 pts.*

Yorkshire needed two to win from the final ball, but Hoggard's drive was gathered by Kasprowicz, the bowler, who then ran out Gough with a direct throw at the batsman's end. It was Glamorgan's narrowest margin of victory in the competition for 21 years. Earlier, Yorkshire had slumped to 150 for seven, but recovered thanks to Lumb. Gough was sportingly recalled by Wallace after he had been given run out, as the Glamorgan wicket-keeper indicated to the umpire that his glove had dislodged a bail before the ball struck the stumps. Cosker bowled an accurate spell of left-arm spin, not conceding anything more than a single until his final over.

At Cardiff, September 2 (day/night). **Leicestershire won by three wickets.** Toss: Glamorgan. **Glamorgan 226-7** (45 overs) (M. J. Powell 91*; D. S. Brignull 3-48); **Leicestershire 227-7** (45 overs) (T. R. Ward 104, P. A. Nixon 67*; D. S. Harrison 4-44). *Leicestershire 4 pts.*

Leicestershire pulled off a remarkable victory after collapsing to 52 for five when Harrison claimed four for three in 14 balls. Ward and Nixon then put on 125. After Snape was out to the third ball of the final over, Leicestershire still needed five to win, but Nixon settled the issue with a boundary and a single. Powell had been the mainstay of Glamorgan's innings, achieving a career-best score – his third successive half-century in the competition – and passing 500 runs for the season.

GLAMORGAN v SURREY

At Cardiff, September 14. Surrey won by eight runs. Toss: Surrey.

Surrey made certain of succeeding Glamorgan as National League champions when Clarke bowled Harrison. Their win distracted the players from their failure in the Championship and growing signs of internal dissent. Ramprakash and Hollioake rescued Surrey after a poor start on a slow pitch. Powell fell two runs short of 600 runs for the season and, with Maynard absent through injury, no other batsman was able to master an accurate attack, led by Clarke.

Surrey

S. A. Newman lbw b Kasprowicz	10
A. D. Brown b Harrison	12
M. R. Ramprakash c Wharf b Dale	53
G. P. Thorpe c Maher b Kasprowicz	9
R. Clarke b Wharf	4
*A. J. Hollioake b Croft	51
†J. N. Batty c Maher b Dale	18
I. D. K. Salisbury c Maher b Dale	19
M. P. Bicknell not out	12
F. A. Rose c Wharf b Dale	1
T. J. Murtagh not out	0
B 1, l-b 1, w 7	9
1/27 (2) 2/31 (1) 3/49 (4) 4/61 (5) 5/137 (6) 6/159 (3) 7/176 (7) 8/189 (8) 9/192 (10) (9 wkts, 45 overs)	198

Bowling: Kasprowicz 8–2–25–2; Harrison 6–0–33–1; Dale 9–0–35–4; Wharf 4–1–18–1; Cosker 9–0–49–0; Croft 9–0–36–1.

Glamorgan

J. P. Maher c Batty b Bicknell	21
I. J. Thomas c Batty b Rose	18
A. G. Wharf run out	0
M. J. Powell b Murtagh	40
D. L. Hemp c Batty b Murtagh	21
A. Dale c Thorpe b Hollioake	12
†M. A. Wallace c Batty b Clarke	1
*R. D. B. Croft c Bicknell b Hollioake	20
M. S. Kasprowicz b Murtagh	20
D. S. Harrison b Clarke	14
D. A. Cosker not out	2
L-b 6, w 11, n-b 4	21
1/29 (1) 2/29 (3) 3/51 (2) 4/100 (4) 5/111 (5) 6/114 (7) 7/130 (6) 8/161 (8) 9/184 (9) 10/190 (10) (43.4 overs)	190

Bowling: Bicknell 6–1–32–1; Rose 9–0–45–1; Murtagh 9–1–44–3; Clarke 8.4–0–19–2; Hollioake 8–0–29–2; Salisbury 3–0–15–0.

Umpires: N. G. Cowley and B. Dudleston.

GLOUCESTERSHIRE

At Bristol, April 27. **Worcestershire won by 35 runs** (D/L method). Toss: Worcestershire. **Gloucestershire 143** (43.3 overs) (M. G. N. Windows 38; M. S. Mason 4-35); **Worcestershire 98-2** (24.4 overs) (G. A. Hick 52*). *Worcestershire 4 pts.*

Gloucestershire never recovered after being put in on a damp pitch and struggling to 96 for five. Windows and Hardinges put on a bright 48, but the last five wickets fell for five runs. A confident 52 off 56 balls from Hick put Worcestershire well ahead of the run-rate when the rain arrived.

At Bristol, May 5. **Gloucestershire won by 57 runs.** Toss: Gloucestershire. **Gloucestershire 311-4** (45 overs) (C. M. Spearman 89, W. P. C. Weston 92, T. H. C. Hancock 82; C. E. Dagnall 3-52); **Leicestershire 254** (43.5 overs) (D. I. Stevens 65, J. N. Snape 39, P. A. J. DeFreitas 90; M. C. J. Ball 3-59). *Gloucestershire 4 pts.*

Gloucestershire made their highest League score at Bristol after racing to 239 for one; Hancock hit 80 out of 100 in his second-wicket stand with Weston, and his 82 came off 57 balls with six sixes. DeFreitas and Snape put on 110 for the sixth wicket in a vain attempt to get close.

At Bristol, May 25. **No result** (abandoned). **Gloucestershire v Surrey**. *Gloucestershire 2 pts, Surrey 2 pts.*

At Gloucester, June 8. **Gloucestershire won by 78 runs.** Toss: Gloucestershire. **Gloucestershire 307-8** (45 overs) (C. M. Spearman 153, W. P. C. Weston 61, Extras 31); **Warwickshire 229** (40.2 overs) (N. V. Knight 70, I. R. Bell 50, J. O. Troughton 53; A. P. R. Gidman 3-26). *Gloucestershire 4 pts.*

Spearman was in brilliant form as he delighted a large festival crowd by racing to Gloucestershire's highest League score in 123 balls with five sixes and 15 fours.

At Cheltenham, July 27. **Gloucestershire won by seven wickets.** Toss: Glamorgan. **Glamorgan 197** (37.2 overs) (J. Hughes 30, M. P. Maynard 39, A. Dale 39; J. M. M. Averis 3-34, M. A. Hardinges 3-43); **Gloucestershire 199-3** (36.5 overs) (W. P. C. Weston 36, A. P. R. Gidman 49, M. G. N. Windows 54*). *Gloucestershire 4 pts.*

Reduced to 38 overs a side.

Gloucestershire went top of the league on run-rate, winning comfortably enough after a mid-innings wobble when the spinners, Croft and Cosker, slowed the scoring-rate.

At Cheltenham, August 3. **Gloucestershire won by eight wickets.** Toss: Yorkshire. **Yorkshire 183** (41.5 overs) (M. J. Wood 38; J. M. M. Averis 4-50); **Gloucestershire 184-2** (32.4 overs) (W. P. C. Weston 62, C. M. Spearman 93*). *Gloucestershire 4 pts.*

The first-division leaders crushed the bottom club, with another blazing innings from Spearman, the League's top-scorer, who took his total for the season to 566. He put on 143 for the first wicket with Weston and was especially harsh on Kirby, who had figures of 4–0–42–0.

At Bristol, August 27 (day/night). **Kent won by 36 runs.** Toss: Kent. **Kent 251-7** (45 overs) (E. T. Smith 59, M. J. Walker 101; I. J. Harvey 4-55); **Gloucestershire 215** (43 overs) (I. J. Harvey 33, A. P. R. Gidman 40, M. W. Alleyne 35; M. Muralitharan 5-34). *Kent 4 pts.*

Kent had an unexpected win after Ed Smith and Walker put on 152 for the third wicket. They took command after Kent suffered patiently through an opening spell of 9–0–16–1 from Mike Smith. Gloucestershire, possibly distracted with the C&G final only three days away, put down several catches and were unable to get the innings going against Muralitharan.

At Bristol, September 7. **Gloucestershire won by five runs.** Toss: Essex. **Gloucestershire 232-7** (45 overs) (I. J. Harvey 43, J. N. Rhodes 38, M. G. N. Windows 83*; G. R. Napier 3-40); **Essex 227** (45 overs) (A. Flower 90, R. C. Irani 61; I. J. Harvey 5-38). *Gloucestershire 4 pts.*

At 168 for one, Essex were congratulating themselves on their decision to bat second: then Harvey transformed the game. In three overs, he took four wickets and ran out Mohammad Akram. His match-winning ball, a yorker, uprooted the off stump as Middlebrook shaped for a winning six.

KENT

At Canterbury, April 27. **Kent won by 54 runs.** Toss: Leicestershire. **Kent 254-4** (45 overs) (M. A. Ealham 41, R. W. T. Key 31, G. S. Blewett 46, M. J. Walker 82*, P. D. Trego 31*); **Leicestershire 200** (39.2 overs) (T. R. Ward 45, J. L. Sadler 33, P. A. Nixon 41; P. D. Trego 4-39). *Kent 4 pts.*

County debuts: P. D. Trego (Kent); B. J. Hodge (Leicestershire).

In his first week as Kent's first-choice wicket-keeper, Geraint Jones equalled the League record by dismissing six batsmen, all caught. Ealham, promoted to pinch-hitter by Kent, hit three sixes off Masters, who gave away 31 runs in his opening two overs against his former club.

At Tunbridge Wells, June 8. **Kent won by 22 runs.** Toss: Yorkshire. **Kent 208-7** (45 overs) (G. S. Blewett 46, M. J. Walker 31; R. J. Sidebottom 3-39); **Yorkshire 186-9** (45 overs) (M. J. Lumb 77, R. J. Blakey 41; B. J. Trott 3-19). *Kent 4 pts.*

Kent ended a four-match losing streak thanks to Trott, who bowled nine overs straight through in which time Yorkshire dropped further and further behind the rate on a sluggish pitch. Play was held up for several minutes when a straight six by Symonds hit a member of the groundstaff in the face.

At Beckenham, June 15. **Gloucestershire won by six wickets.** Toss: Kent. **Kent 222-8** (45 overs) (A. Symonds 56, G. O. Jones 74*); **Gloucestershire 223-4** (41.2 overs) (C. M. Spearman 43, M. G. N. Windows 58*, A. P. R. Gidman 49*). *Gloucestershire 4 pts.*

First-team debut: M. J. Dennington (Kent).

Kent's first game on the ground for 49 years produced a large crowd, whose only disappointment was the result. Kent made a terrible start on a lovely batting pitch, losing three quick wickets. Symonds, leading Kent against his former county, began a recovery, continued by Jones and the 20-year-old debutant Matthew Dennington, who shared a stand of 49 in five overs. But Gloucestershire's one-day specialists saw them home in comfort.

At Maidstone, July 6. **Kent won by 52 runs.** Toss: Glamorgan. **Kent 291-4** (45 overs) (E. T. Smith 122, R. W. T. Key 40, A. Symonds 45, M. A. Ealham 50*); **Glamorgan 239** (41.4 overs) (M. P. Maynard 72, A. Dale 36, M. S. Kasprowicz 35*; Mohammad Sami 3-30, R. S. Ferley 3-59). *Kent 4 pts.*

Smith continued his superb form with his first League hundred, in front of another big crowd. Ealham maintained the momentum with a 22-ball fifty and Sami took charge with the ball, removing both Croft and Maher, who had returned to England only hours earlier.

At Canterbury, August 3. **Tied.** Toss: Kent. **Kent 254-9** (45 overs) (R. W. T. Key 36, M. J. Walker 32, G. O. Jones 58, M. A. Ealham 73, Extras 36); **Essex 254-9** (45 overs) (W. I. Jefferson 58, A. Flower 100; M. J. Saggers 4-36). *Kent 2 pts, Essex 2 pts.*

County debut: Mohammad Akram (Essex).

Mohammad Akram, Essex's new overseas player, began nervously with a flurry of no-balls and wides, then almost won the game with the bat. Flower gave Essex a strong start towards their target but they collapsed from 197 for two and still needed 32 off the last three overs, with Muralitharan bowling two of them. They were five short with a ball to go but Akram's attempted six to long-on landed just short and went for four.

At Canterbury, August 11 (day/night). **Kent won by eight wickets.** Toss: Worcestershire. **Worcestershire 225-8** (45 overs) (V. S. Solanki 70, B. F. Smith 34; M. Muralitharan 3-45, J. C. Tredwell 3-38); **Kent 226-2** (36.2 overs) (M. A. Carberry 79, A. Symonds 93*, M. J. Walker 30*). *Kent 4 pts.*

Kent's decision to play three spinners paid off as they completed a comfortable victory in this relegation battle in front of a 7,000 crowd. Solanki could find little support in Worcestershire's innings, but Symonds shrugged off a flu bug to share a stand of 130 in 16 overs with Carberry. Play was held up for several minutes when one floodlight failed.

At Canterbury, September 3 (day/night). **Surrey won by five wickets.** Toss: Kent. **Kent 142** (31.4 overs) (A. Symonds 53; A. J. Hollioake 6-17); **Surrey 143-5** (37 overs) (M. R. Ramprakash 42*, A. J. Hollioake 38). *Surrey 4 pts.*

County debut: F. A. Rose (Surrey).

Surrey almost wrapped up the title thanks to a blazing performance by Hollioake. He had a burst of five for nine in 15 balls as Kent collapsed, losing their last seven wickets for 33. There was another hold-up due to floodlight failure.

At Canterbury, September 21. **Kent won by 104 runs.** Toss: Kent. **Kent 267-7** (45 overs) (E. T. Smith 74, A. Symonds 49, M. J. Walker 37, Extras 31; D. R. Brown 3-44); **Warwickshire 163** (37.2 overs) (M. J. Powell 48; A. Khan 3-31). *Kent 4 pts.*

Kent retained first-division status to the delight of a 5,500 crowd on an unseasonably hot day. Amjad Khan took three early wickets and Powell, in his last match as Warwickshire captain, could not quite hold the innings together.

LEICESTERSHIRE

At Leicester, May 4. **Glamorgan won by 44 runs.** Toss: Leicestershire. **Glamorgan 249-5** (45 overs) (M. J. Powell 40, M. P. Maynard 43, D. L. Hemp 83*); **Leicestershire 205** (41.3 overs) (D. L. Maddy 80; R. D. B. Croft 3-39). *Glamorgan 4 pts.*

County debut: V. Sehwag (Leicestershire).

Glamorgan scored steadily rather than spectacularly, before Hemp and Wallace plundered 59 off the last 32 balls. Only Maddy showed conviction in reply, and there was no way back from 75 for five after 15 overs. Following an early-morning sprint from Heathrow, Indian Test batsman Sehwag reeled off a cameo of 23 on his Leicestershire debut.

At Leicester, May 18. **Leicestershire won by 66 runs.** Toss: Leicestershire. **Leicestershire 247-8** (45 overs) (V. Sehwag 54, D. I. Stevens 63, B. J. Hodge 47, D. L. Maddy 36; R. J. Sidebottom 5-42); **Yorkshire 181** (44.2 overs) (V. J. Craven 35, A. K. D. Gray 30*, Extras 30; C. E. Dagnall 4-41). *Leicestershire 4 pts.*

On a seaming pitch, Dagnall took four wickets in 15 balls as Yorkshire plunged to 28 for five. Only the tail took them beyond their lowest one-day score of 54, set in their last League match. A sparkling stand of 97 between Sehwag and Stevens had set up the win – and delighted the many Indians in the crowd. Of Sidebottom's five wickets, three came late in the innings.

At Leicester, June 1. **Gloucestershire won by three wickets.** Toss: Leicestershire. **Leicestershire 234-6** (45 overs) (B. J. Hodge 63, J. N. Snape 39*, Extras 46); **Gloucestershire 235-7** (43.4 overs) (C. M. Spearman 34, C. G. Taylor 47, M. G. N. Windows 76). *Gloucestershire 4 pts.*

First-team debut: L. J. Wright (Leicestershire).

Gloucestershire feasted on a generous supply of long-hops and half-volleys to win an exciting game and disappoint the large crowd. On a helpful pitch, Leicestershire had successfully rebuilt their innings from 63 for three, against niggardly bowling from Smith (9–3–29–2) and Alleyne (9–0–24–2).

At Oakham School, July 13. **Leicestershire won by 76 runs.** Toss: Leicestershire. **Leicestershire 295-7** (45 overs) (T. R. Ward 68, V. Sehwag 76, B. J. Hodge 38, D. L. Maddy 58; G. J. Batty 3-51); **Worcestershire 219** (41.5 overs) (S. D. Peters 82, A. Singh 44, B. F. Smith 35; J. N. Snape 3-35, D. S. Brignull 3-40). *Leicestershire 4 pts.*

Under azure skies and on a flawless pitch, Leicestershire openers Ward (44 balls, 56 in boundaries) and Sehwag (59 balls, 50 in boundaries) hit 129 in 15 exciting overs to set up the county's eighth successive win in competitive one-day games, after their impressive run in the Twenty20 Cup. Hayward's six overs went for 64. In reply, Worcestershire lost their last eight wickets for just 41.

At Leicester, August 3. **Warwickshire won by four wickets.** Toss: Warwickshire. **Leicestershire 172** (45 overs) (P. A. Nixon 51; Waqar Younis 4-37); **Warwickshire 173-6** (41.5 overs) (N. V. Knight 50, I. R. Bell 43). *Warwickshire 4 pts.*

County debut: V. C. Drakes (Leicestershire).

Leicestershire slumped to 23 for three and spent the rest of the innings trying to consolidate, failing to score off 150 of their 276 deliveries. Mohamed Sheikh (9–2–20–2) capitalised on their caution. A stand of 81 between Knight and Bell put Warwickshire on course, despite struggling to score from the off-spinner, Snape, who had figures of 9–0–14–1.

At Leicester, August 10. **Leicestershire won by six wickets** (D/L method). Toss: Leicestershire. **Essex 212-6** (43.3 overs) (A. Flower 103, D. D. J. Robinson 35); **Leicestershire 90-4** (15.4 overs). *Leicestershire 4 pts.*

As thunderclouds loomed, Flower accumulated superbly to reach a second League century in eight days, from 107 balls. But it proved in vain: rain ended Essex's innings after 43.3 overs and Leicestershire, whose innings was interrupted several times, scrambled to a revised target of 89 in 16 overs. Needing eight off the last six balls, Maddy hit the winning boundary with two deliveries left.

At Leicester, August 20 (day/night). **Surrey won by seven wickets.** Toss: Leicestershire. **Leicestershire 217-8** (45 overs) (P. A. J. DeFreitas 39, B. J. Hodge 46, D. L. Maddy 66; A. J. Hollioake 4-35); **Surrey 218-3** (28.2 overs) (I. J. Ward 70*, A. D. Brown 89). *Surrey 4 pts.*

Surrey stormed home before the floodlights hit full power. The comfortable win, with more than 16 overs spare, took them eight points clear at the top of the first division. Brown, dropped at slip on one, smashed 89 from 65 balls during an opening stand of 131 with Ward. Leicestershire had been strangled mid-innings by Hollioake and Salisbury.

At Leicester, September 14. **Kent won by eight wickets.** Toss: Kent. **Leicestershire 98** (35.1 overs) (P. A. Nixon 32; A. Khan 4-26, M. A. Ealham 4-19); **Kent 101-2** (19.2 overs) (R. W. T. Key 44*, A. Symonds 45*). *Kent 4 pts.*

A Leicestershire win would have guaranteed their first-division survival and condemned Kent to relegation. But Leicestershire's nerve failed. Poor shots and a green pitch helped Khan grab four wickets in 13 balls and Ealham's cutters were also dangerous. Leicestershire were 61 for six before Muralitharan even got a bowl, and only three batsmen reached double figures. Kent blazed to victory in less than 20 overs.

SURREY

At The Oval, May 4. **Surrey won by 25 runs.** Toss: Surrey. **Surrey 281-8** (45 overs) (I. J. Ward 47, M. R. Ramprakash 63, G. P. Thorpe 58); **Warwickshire 256** (43.1 overs) (N. V. Knight 105, G. G. Wagg 31*; A. J. Tudor 4-45). *Surrey 4 pts.*

Warwickshire, seemingly down and out at 127 for seven, flickered back to life but could not make 26 from the last two overs. Knight, who had recently announced his retirement from one-day internationals, hit a magnificent hundred at better than a run a ball, and Wagg smashed 31 off 11 deliveries from No. 10. Earlier, Surrey had slowed after taking 111 from their first 14 overs.

At The Oval, May 18. **Surrey won by six runs.** Toss: Kent. **Surrey 322-7** (45 overs) (I. J. Ward 31, A. D. Brown 44, M. R. Ramprakash 107*, G. P. Thorpe 36, Azhar Mahmood 70; P. D. Trego 4-66); **Kent 316-7** (45 overs) (R. W. T. Key 39, E. T. Smith 99, G. S. Blewett 36, M. J. Walker 80*). *Surrey 4 pts.*

The match aggregate of 638 was the highest in the competition's history, beating 631 by Nottinghamshire and Surrey at The Oval in 1993. Azhar's 70 in 41 balls made Ramprakash (107 not out in 99) look pedestrian, and four of Surrey's ten sixes sailed out of the ground. But Kent's batsmen were equally savage. Smith (99 from 86 balls) and Walker (80 not out from 62) kept up with the rate, and Hollioake (5–0–52–1) was despatched at will. Kent needed 35 off five overs with six wickets remaining – a breeze given the previous scoring-rates – but they could not feed Walker enough of the strike.

At The Oval, June 8. **Surrey won by three wickets.** Toss: Surrey. **Essex 220** (44.2 overs) (D. D. J. Robinson 78, A. P. Grayson 37; Azhar Mahmood 6-37); **Surrey 221-7** (42.5 overs) (M. R. Ramprakash 38, G. P. Thorpe 79*). *Surrey 4 pts.*

As Essex looked to accelerate in their final 11 overs, a series of devastating yorkers from Azhar Mahmood forced them to concentrate on survival. His burst of five wickets in 16 balls left Surrey a relatively straightforward target, and Thorpe paced the chase well, making an unbeaten and untroubled 79.

At The Oval, July 6. **Surrey won by seven wickets.** Toss: Yorkshire. **Yorkshire 199** (41.5 overs) (S. P. Fleming 90; I. D. K. Salisbury 3-40, A. J. Hollioake 3-7); **Surrey 200-3** (38.1 overs) (M. A. Butcher 104, M. R. Ramprakash 60*). *Surrey 4 pts.*

England Test batsman Butcher hit his first-ever one-day century, 12 years after his limited-overs debut and nearly two seasons after his last League appearance. His beautiful innings lasted 107 deliveries. Surrey won with 41 balls spare: they remained unbeaten in the first division, while Yorkshire remained bottom.

At Guildford, July 27. **Worcestershire won by 79 runs.** Toss: Surrey. **Worcestershire 219-6** (45 overs) (B. F. Smith 93*, A. J. Hall 32; J. Ormond 3-46); **Surrey 140** (37.1 overs) (A. J. Hollioake 33; Kabir Ali 4-30, M. S. Mason 4-34). *Worcestershire 4 pts.*

Kabir Ali found some zip off the pitch and removed four of Surrey's top five in his opening five overs. The rest of an under-strength batting line-up then fell away. Busy running from Smith had helped take Worcestershire to a competitive 219; Martin Bicknell's near-pristine figures (9–4–17–1) reflected his immaculate control. Surrey were knocked off top spot – but only temporarily.

At The Oval, August 5 (day/night). **Surrey won by 66 runs.** Toss: Surrey. **Surrey 297-6** (45 overs) (A. D. Brown 84, M. R. Ramprakash 83, G. P. Thorpe 36, R. Clarke 36); **Gloucestershire 231** (40 overs) (C. M. Spearman 85; R. Clarke 3-48). *Surrey 4 pts.*

Surrey won this top-of-the-table clash thanks to their dead-eyed fielding: after Spearman hit the first over of the innings for 22, Gloucestershire, with only one wicket down, reached 100 even more quickly than their opponents had. But they then suffered five run-outs, two direct hits by Clarke. Brown's 84 from 61 balls had helped Surrey to an intimidating total.

At Whitgift School, Croydon, August 17. **Surrey won by 58 runs.** Toss: Surrey. **Surrey 298-5** (45 overs) (I. J. Ward 44, M. R. Ramprakash 101, G. P. Thorpe 77*, A. J. Hollioake 41; J. P. Maher 3-29); **Glamorgan 240** (39.4 overs) (R. D. B. Croft 31, M. J. Powell 60, M. P. Maynard 41, D. L. Hemp 30; A. J. Hollioake 3-22). *Surrey 4 pts.*

On this intimate school ground, Ramprakash and Thorpe played innings of true quality, adding 120 in 19 overs. Hollioake's sizzling 41 off 16 deliveries was less elegant, but it gave Surrey another formidable score. Glamorgan's reply stalled when Maynard was afflicted with cramp.

At The Oval, September 21. **Leicestershire won by 168 runs.** Toss: Surrey. **Leicestershire 283-9** (45 overs) (D. L. Maddy 69, B. J. Hodge 43, J. L. Sadler 35, V. C. Drakes 43*; P. J. Sampson 3-68, J. G. E. Benning 4-43); **Surrey 115** (22 overs) (P. A. J. DeFreitas 5-40, C. E. Dagnall 3-21). *Leicestershire 4 pts.*

Surrey had already secured the title, but their heaviest-ever League defeat took the edge off the trophy presentation. After 20 overs Leicestershire's top order had already flown to 162 for three, on their way to 283; by contrast, Surrey were all out in 22 overs. DeFreitas's swing and seam emphasised his enduring quality, and his figures (9–1–40–5) were the second-best of an 18-year League career. Despite victory, Leicestershire were relegated.

WARWICKSHIRE

At Birmingham, April 27. **Yorkshire won by six wickets** (D/L method). Toss: Yorkshire. **Warwickshire 158-9** (42 overs) (M. A. Wagh 32, A. F. Giles 61*); **Yorkshire 160-4** (35 overs) (M. J. Lumb 61, A. McGrath 41). *Yorkshire 4 pts.*

Yorkshire's target revised to 158 in 42 overs.

Lumb scored 61 in an opening partnership of 76, overcoming a two-paced pitch to launch a 40-ball assault. That blitz made Yorkshire's task much easier and they cruised home with seven overs to spare. Earlier, their accurate attack had pinned Warwickshire down, during an innings briefly interrupted by rain.

At Birmingham, May 18. **Essex won by eight wickets.** Toss: Essex. **Warwickshire 143** (18.4 overs) (I. J. L. Trott 40, D. R. Brown 37; R. C. Irani 3-21); **Essex 146-2** (19.1 overs) (W. I. Jefferson 50, A. Flower 49*). *Essex 4 pts.*

Reduced to 20 overs a side.

A lunchtime cloudburst provided an unscheduled and chaotic rehearsal for the forthcoming Twenty20 Cup. But Warwickshire failed to bat out even 20 overs: only Trott (40 in 28 balls) and Brown (37 in 25) played sensibly and six batsmen were caught on the boundary. Jefferson and Flower paced Essex's chase perfectly.

At Birmingham, June 22. **Warwickshire won by two wickets** (D/L method). Toss: Glamorgan. **Glamorgan 193** (44 overs) (R. D. B. Croft 42, D. L. Hemp 41; D. R. Brown 4-37); **Warwickshire 179-8** (38.5 overs) (N. V. Knight 75, D. R. Brown 49; M. S. Kasprowicz 3-20, A. G. Wharf 3-27). *Warwickshire 4 pts.*

Reduced to 44 overs a side. Warwickshire's target later revised to 179 in 39 overs.

Having reduced Warwickshire to 44 for four, Glamorgan looked as if they might yet preserve their unbeaten record. Knight and Brown steadied things, adding 82 for the next wicket, but Knight fell with three still needed and Warwickshire scrambled home off the penultimate ball. Earlier, Croft had given Glamorgan a breezy start, while Hemp held them together towards the end.

At Birmingham, July 13. **Warwickshire won by six wickets.** Toss: Surrey. **Surrey 242-9** (45 overs) (M. R. Ramprakash 57, I. D. K. Salisbury 33; Waqar Younis 4-35, C. O. Obuya 3-65); **Warwickshire 244-4** (42.1 overs) (N. V. Knight 74, I. J. L. Trott 51, I. R. Bell 59*). *Warwickshire 4 pts.*

Surrey suffered their first defeat in 11 League matches, a run that stretched back 11 months. Waqar took three important wickets in his first spell and, apart from Ramprakash and three last-over sixes from Salisbury, Surrey laboured. On a good batting pitch, Knight and Trott added 131 for Warwickshire's second wicket. Bell, recently overlooked for England's one-day side, did the rest, scoring at better than a run a ball.

At Birmingham, August 13 (day/night). **Warwickshire won by eight wickets.** Toss: Leicestershire. **Leicestershire 178** (40.4 overs) (B. J. Hodge 55, Extras 34; I. R. Bell 3-25); **Warwickshire 182-2** (30.5 overs) (N. M. Carter 75, M. A. Wagh 42*, I. R. Bell 54*). *Warwickshire 4 pts.*

Leicestershire withered in the face of a barrage of slogs from Carter, a tailender in the Championship but opening here. His 75 came from 37 balls, and included six leg-side sixes. After the storm, Bell provided calm and ensured the win. Bell had also nipped out three of Leicestershire's middle order with his medium-paced seamers on a grassy, bouncing pitch. Wicket-keeper Piper equalled the League record with six catches.

At Birmingham, August 24. **Warwickshire won by four wickets.** Toss: Warwickshire. **Kent 212** (44.5 overs) (M. J. Walker 72, G. O. Jones 40, M. A. Ealham 37; Waqar Younis 4-20); **Warwickshire 213-6** (42.2 overs) (N. M. Carter 31, M. A. Wagh 66, I. R. Bell 30). *Warwickshire 4 pts.*

Kent saw the worst of a pitch that helped seamers early on and then flattened out. Waqar and Wagh took advantage: Waqar's accuracy was rewarded with four cheap wickets, while Wagh's punishing strokeplay entertained a crowd of 5,000 (let in free on Edgbaston's open day) and helped Warwickshire to a routine win.

At Birmingham, September 1. **Gloucestershire won by two runs.** Toss: Warwickshire. **Gloucestershire 246-6** (45 overs) (W. P. C. Weston 33, I. J. Harvey 33, A. P. R. Gidman 73, J. N. Rhodes 45); **Warwickshire 244-7** (45 overs) (T. L. Penney 88*, D. R. Brown 48). *Gloucestershire 4 pts.*

A brilliant unbeaten 88 by Penney, from 92 balls, gave Gloucestershire a fright but could not deny them a victory which kept the title race alive. Warwickshire needed 95 off their last ten overs, then 20 off one, and Penney took 16 from Alleyne's first five balls. But he could only scramble a single from the last. It was a busy match for Jonty Rhodes: first he and Gidman rescued Gloucestershire after a slow start then, during the tea interval, he claimed a new world record for accurate throwing at a set of stumps after beating Warwickshire's Trevor Penney in a head-to-head contest. Each had to pick up and throw from five fielding positions, all 20 metres away. Rhodes hit the stumps ten times out of 20 and Penney eight.

At Birmingham, September 9 (day/night). **Warwickshire won by 18 runs** (D/L method). Toss: Warwickshire. **Warwickshire 250-4** (45 overs) (N. V. Knight 122, M. A. Wagh 35, I. J. L. Trott 51*); **Worcestershire 173-6** (35.3 overs) (A. Singh 36, J. M. Kemp 36*; C. D. Collymore 3-26). *Warwickshire 4 pts.*

County debut: D. H. Wigley (Worcestershire).

Knight batted for all but five balls of Warwickshire's innings, setting up the win which guaranteed their first-division survival. His 122 at nearly a run a ball took him beyond Dennis Amiss's county record for runs in a League season: 594 in 1981. Worcestershire were behind the rate throughout, which proved fatal when rain arrived. This was their sixth successive League defeat.

WORCESTERSHIRE

At Worcester, May 5. **Surrey won by one wicket.** Toss: Worcestershire. **Worcestershire 244-5** (45 overs) (S. D. Peters 48, V. S. Solanki 40, G. A. Hick 81, Kadeer Ali 52); **Surrey 247-9** (41.3 overs) (A. D. Brown 81, M. R. Ramprakash 67, G. P. Thorpe 38; Kabir Ali 3-43, M. Hayward 3-66). *Surrey 4 pts.*

After Brown's 68-ball 81, Surrey looked to be home. But six wickets fell in seven chaotic overs and they ended up staggering over the line, with their last man, Ormond, hitting four through the covers. Seamers Kabir Ali and Hayward took five wickets during the collapse. Hick also made 81, but Worcestershire's total always looked vulnerable.

At Worcester, May 25. **Worcestershire won by 139 runs.** Toss: Kent. **Worcestershire 271-4** (45 overs) (S. D. Peters 43, G. A. Hick 108, B. F. Smith 51, A. J. Hall 47*); **Kent 132** (31.5 overs) (D. A. Leatherdale 5-36). *Worcestershire 4 pts.*

Hick hit with glorious disdain despite an untrustworthy pitch, reaching fifty in 35 balls and his century in exactly 100. In conditions ideally suited to medium-pace, Leatherdale's accuracy was rewarded with five wickets as Kent lost seven in nine overs. They failed to make even half their target.

At Worcester, June 15. **Leicestershire won by two wickets.** Toss: Worcestershire. **Worcestershire 193-7** (45 overs) (S. D. Peters 50, B. F. Smith 37; B. J. Hodge 3-34); **Leicestershire 198-8** (42.1 overs) (P. A. J. DeFreitas 68, D. L. Maddy 56, T. R. Ward 31*; M. S. Mason 3-26, D. A. Leatherdale 4-41). *Leicestershire 4 pts.*

Leicestershire's chase was transformed from routine to nerve-racking as Leatherdale sent them tumbling from 142 for three to 172 for eight. That left the ninth-wicket pair needing 22. But Ward, batting at No. 7 after straining a hamstring, edged them home against a depleted Worcestershire side.

At Worcester, July 6. **Warwickshire won by eight wickets.** Toss: Worcestershire. **Worcestershire 218-8** (45 overs) (A. Singh 97, G. J. Batty 31); **Warwickshire 219-2** (41.1 overs) (N. M. Carter 33, I. J. L. Trott 56*, I. R. Bell 97*). *Warwickshire 4 pts.*

Penney made a crucial contribution in the unlikely role of wicket-keeper. When he took over from the injured Piper at the end of the 14th over, Worcestershire had blazed to 96 for no wicket; almost immediately he held an edge from Peters, then took a stunning airborne catch to remove Kadeer Ali. Worcestershire never recovered their momentum. In reply, a chalk-and-cheese stand of 158 between the sparky Bell and the resolute Trott was decisive.

At Worcester, July 29 (day/night). **Worcestershire won by three runs** (D/L method). Toss: Glamorgan. **Worcestershire 117-5** (18 overs) (B. F. Smith 43*; M. S. Kasprowicz 3-23); **Glamorgan 122-7** (18 overs) (M. P. Maynard 32, M. J. Powell 33). *Worcestershire 4 pts.*

Glamorgan's target revised to 126 in 18 overs.

A bright start by Worcestershire was interrupted first by three wickets from Kasprowicz and then by rain. Resuming at 84 for four, they were allotted only 15 more balls, from which they hit 33. Glamorgan laboured to keep up with the rate and failed to score the ten needed from the final over. It was Worcestershire's second League win in three days.

At Worcester, August 24. **Gloucestershire won by four wickets.** Toss: Worcestershire. **Worcestershire 146** (44.2 overs) (J. M. Kemp 50; M. W. Alleyne 4-26); **Gloucestershire 148-6** (40.5 overs) (C. M. Spearman 37, A. P. R. Gidman 67*; M. Hayward 3-32). *Gloucestershire 4 pts.*

A poor surface with erratic bounce was exploited by an expert Gloucestershire attack. Mike Smith (9–2–22–2) set the tone, taking two wickets before a run was scored, before Alleyne and Harvey strangled the Worcestershire innings. Gloucestershire hit out aggressively to try and close the game quickly.

At Worcester, September 7. **Yorkshire won by seven wickets.** Toss: Worcestershire. **Worcestershire 223-7** (45 overs) (V. S. Solanki 32, G. A. Hick 52, J. M. Kemp 46, B. F. Smith 42*; M. J. Hoggard 3-29); **Yorkshire 227-3** (43.4 overs) (C. White 40, M. J. Wood 91, M. J. Lumb 62*). *Yorkshire 4 pts.*

Two days after clinching promotion in the Championship, Worcestershire were relegated in the League. Both Solanki and Hick fell to poor shots when well set and Worcestershire's total was far from intimidating. Yorkshire's opening stand of 75 included 60 in boundaries, and Wood continued to produce powerful drives as he and Lumb put on 114, which took Yorkshire to the cusp of victory.

At Worcester, September 21. **Essex won by four wickets.** Toss: Worcestershire. **Worcestershire 213** (42.4 overs) (Kabir Ali 92; A. J. Clarke 3-30); **Essex 217-6** (42 overs) (W. I. Jefferson 74, M. L. Pettini 36). *Essex 4 pts.*

In late-September sunshine and in front of a crowd of nearly 3,000, Worcestershire lost their seventh League match in succession. Kabir Ali was promoted to No. 3 and hit 92 from 93 balls but Worcestershire, typically, could not keep up the rate. On a grudging pitch, Essex's openers added 69 in 11 overs in reply, and Essex were handed a comfortable victory by some very ordinary bowling.

YORKSHIRE

At Leeds, May 5. **Essex won by 157 runs.** Toss: Yorkshire. **Essex 211-6** (45 overs) (D. D. J. Robinson 35, W. I. Jefferson 57, A. Habib 50, M. L. Pettini 32; T. T. Bresnan 3-29); **Yorkshire 54** (20.2 overs) (S. A. Brant 4-25, G. R. Napier 4-18). *Essex 4 pts.*

County debut: A. G. A. M. McCoubrey (Essex).

Accurate bowling from Brant and Napier, as well as poor shot selection, sent Yorkshire crashing to their worst one-day score (the previous low was 56 at Edgbaston in 1995). In fact, 54 all out marked a recovery: Yorkshire had been 24 for seven, with only Sidebottom reaching double figures. On a seaming pitch, Essex managed 211 thanks to some heavy hitting from Jefferson and a fifty from Habib, who overcame a pulled hamstring.

At Leeds, May 25. **Glamorgan won by four wickets** (D/L method). Toss: Glamorgan. **Yorkshire 153-7** (32 overs) (C. E. W. Silverwood 37, Yuvraj Singh 34); **Glamorgan 165-6** (27.1 overs) (M. J. Powell 47, M. P. Maynard 37; C. E. W. Silverwood 4-45). *Glamorgan 4 pts.*

Glamorgan's target revised to 164 in 32 overs.

Sidebottom ended the match with figures of 0.1–0–11–0: after bowling two wides, one short ball hooked for six, and three more leg-side wides, he retired with a tight hamstring. Despite Silverwood taking wickets in each of his first two overs, Powell hurried Glamorgan home. Earlier, two wickets in six balls from Dale undermined Yorkshire's rain-interrupted innings.

At Leeds, June 22. **Leicestershire won by 18 runs.** Toss: Leicestershire. **Leicestershire 251-8** (45 overs) (V. Sehwag 65, B. J. Hodge 104); **Yorkshire 233** (44.4 overs) (Yuvraj Singh 50, M. J. Wood 30, T. T. Bresnan 61; D. D. Masters 3-33, P. A. J. DeFreitas 3-33). *Leicestershire 4 pts.*

Hodge plundered 104 from 119 balls with 13 fours – five off consecutive deliveries from Yuvraj Singh – as Yorkshire slipped to a fifth successive League defeat. Yuvraj hit back with a 46-ball 50 but Yorkshire lost wickets regularly, and even a late blast from Bresnan, who made 61 in 51 balls from No. 9, could not save them.

At Scarborough, July 27. **Yorkshire won by 18 runs.** Toss: Kent. **Yorkshire 197-8** (45 overs) (C. White 47, R. J. Blakey 35, T. T. Bresnan 36*; B. J. Trott 3-39); **Kent 179** (43.5 overs) (E. T. Smith 36, D. P. Fulton 48; V. J. Craven 4-22). *Yorkshire 4 pts.*

County debut: M. Muralitharan (Kent).

With Kent needing 20 from their last two overs, Craven proved the unlikely hero, taking two wickets with his medium-pace to ensure Yorkshire edged home. Yorkshire had recovered from 76 for five (including two disputed decisions), with their ninth-wicket pair adding 54 in the last seven overs. In reply, Kent, at 40 for no wicket after five, were strolling, before Silverwood and Craven struck. After an ill-tempered game, umpire Leadbeater said several players had come very close to disciplinary action.

At Leeds, August 6 (day/night). **Yorkshire won by seven wickets.** Toss: Warwickshire. **Warwickshire 273-6** (45 overs) (N. V. Knight 95, I. R. Bell 36, J. O. Troughton 77, T. L. Penney 45); **Yorkshire 274-3** (38.2 overs) (M. J. Wood 65, S. P. Fleming 139*). *Yorkshire 4 pts.*

Despite facing the highest League total made by a team visiting Headingley, Yorkshire sailed to their target with nearly seven overs to spare – thanks to a thrilling century from Fleming. Under the floodlights, he and Wood put on 167 in 21 overs for the first wicket, and Fleming reached fifty off 23 deliveries. His 139 not out (104 balls) was Yorkshire's third-highest League score. Knight and Troughton had both played fluently, but were later overshadowed.

At Scarborough, August 17. **Yorkshire won by three wickets.** Toss: Worcestershire. **Worcestershire 170** (44.5 overs) (B. F. Smith 56, S. J. Rhodes 35*; S. P. Kirby 3-27, R. K. J. Dawson 3-26); **Yorkshire 171-7** (42 overs) (M. J. Wood 60; Kabir Ali 3-59, M. Hayward 3-35). *Yorkshire 4 pts.*

Yorkshire's third successive home win raised hopes of dodging relegation. Both Kirby's pace and Dawson's off-spin found help in the pitch, and Worcestershire were tied down. Mason was trying to provide a late boost when he lifted Dawson toward the boundary; Wood went for the catch and, as his momentum carried him over the rope, he off-loaded the ball to Lumb, who was credited with the dismissal. Wood, despite being relentlessly sledged by Hayward and restricted by Mason (9–5–15–1) and Batty (9–3–17–0), provided the backbone of Yorkshire's reply.

At Leeds, August 31. **Surrey won by two runs.** Toss: Yorkshire. **Surrey 202** (44.2 overs) (A. D. Brown 50, R. Clarke 46*, Extras 31; A. McGrath 4-41); **Yorkshire 200-8** (45 overs) (M. P. Vaughan 90, V. J. Craven 47). *Surrey 4 pts.*

The late run-outs of both Craven and Vaughan began a remarkable turnaround. Yorkshire still needed only five runs from 11 balls but, struggling to put bat to ball in fading light, they managed just two. Surrey had also wavered after a confident start but were steadied by Clarke who came in at 93 for three and eventually ran out of partners.

At Leeds, September 21. **Gloucestershire won by three wickets.** Toss: Gloucestershire. **Yorkshire 213-7** (45 overs) (J. J. Sayers 62, T. T. Bresnan 33; M. C. J. Ball 5-33); **Gloucestershire 214-7** (44.1 overs) (M. G. N. Windows 91*, A. P. R. Gidman 48; N. D. Thornicroft 5-42). *Gloucestershire 4 pts.*

County debut: J. J. Sayers (Yorkshire).

After 19-year-old Joe Sayers had helped hold Yorkshire's innings together on debut, 18-year-old Thornicroft swept through Gloucestershire's top order (including Rhodes for a duck in his last innings before retirement) and it looked as if Yorkshire's young side would win. But Windows (118 balls) stamped his authority, and Gloucestershire fought back from 37 for four.

DIVISION TWO

DERBYSHIRE

At Derby, May 4. **Derbyshire won by 15 runs.** Toss: Derbyshire. **Derbyshire 220-7** (45 overs) (C. W. G. Bassano 57, S. A. Selwood 88*); **Somerset 205** (41.1 overs) (I. D. Blackwell 40, R. L. Johnson 53; G. Welch 3-44). *Derbyshire 4 pts.*

On a slow pitch, Bassano and Selwood added 88 for the fourth wicket, and a final assault from Welch plundered 60 in the last six overs. Somerset slipped to 53 for five before a brief charge by Blackwell; later, Johnson's 53 in 47 balls kept them interested, but too many wickets had gone.

At Derby, June 15. **Lancashire won by five runs.** Toss: Lancashire. **Lancashire 251-6** (45 overs) (M. B. Loye 63, I. J. Sutcliffe 43, S. G. Law 46, C. L. Hooper 37); **Derbyshire 246-9** (45 overs) (L. D. Sutton 83, D. G. Cork 49; G. Chapple 4-37). *Lancashire 4 pts.*

Lancashire won their sixth successive game in all competitions, despite failing to build properly on an imposing 169 for two. Derbyshire were 61 for five in 17 overs, but Sutton, No. 11 in the previous day's Twenty20 match, made a one-day best 83 in 85 balls, adding 114 in 19 overs with Cork. With ten runs needed from the last over, Martin conceded four singles.

At Derby, July 23 (day/night). **Nottinghamshire won by five wickets** (D/L method). Toss: Nottinghamshire. **Derbyshire 244-9** (42 overs) (M. J. Di Venuto 76, S. A. Selwood 35, C. W. G. Bassano 41, Extras 30; P. J. Franks 4-12); **Nottinghamshire 245-5** (41 overs) (J. E. R. Gallian 30, U. Afzaal 33, C. L. Cairns 66*, C. M. W. Read 39*). *Nottinghamshire 4 pts.*

Cairns chose to bat second under lights and in what turned out to be pouring rain, which had revised Nottinghamshire's target to 245 in 42 overs. He responded with a 41-ball 66, hitting three sixes and six fours; needing 100 from the last ten overs, Nottinghamshire used only nine. Di Venuto gave Derbyshire a flying start – 100 in 13 overs – but did not capitalise.

At Derby, August 3. **Middlesex won by four wickets.** Toss: Middlesex. **Derbyshire 259-8** (45 overs) (M. J. Di Venuto 106, L. D. Sutton 39, D. G. Cork 41, Extras 33; T. F. Bloomfield 4-25); **Middlesex 260-6** (44 overs) (P. N. Weekes 54, A. J. Strauss 57, O. A. Shah 66, D. C. Nash 38). *Middlesex 4 pts.*

Di Venuto's first League century helped Derbyshire to their highest 45-overs total of 2003, despite another competition-best, from Bloomfield, who dismissed their first four in an unbroken nine-over spell. But Shah (dropped on 14) and Nash (nearly run out) added 82 in 13 overs to take Middlesex to the brink of victory.

At Derby, August 10. **Derbyshire won by six wickets** (D/L method). Toss: Derbyshire. **Sussex 160-6** (32 overs) (P. A. Cottey 36, M. J. Prior 60*); **Derbyshire 163-4** (30.5 overs) (M. Kaif 55*, D. R. Hewson 39). *Derbyshire 4 pts.*

Prior scored 60 in 55 balls, but Sussex were twice interrupted by rain, and Derbyshire's target was revised to 163 in 32 overs. Kaif made his third consecutive one-day fifty before Sutton completed victory with seven balls to spare, leaving Sussex bottom of the League.

At Derby, August 24. **Derbyshire won by three wickets.** Toss: Northamptonshire. **Northamptonshire 251-5** (45 overs) (M. E. K. Hussey 103, M. J. Powell 70); **Derbyshire 254-7** (43 overs) (M. J. Di Venuto 130, C. W. G. Bassano 41; A. Nel 3-33). *Derbyshire 4 pts.*

Hussey's 103 in 130 balls took him to 825 runs in six innings in all cricket (five centuries and one fifty); he added 127 with Powell, who scored a one-day best 70. But Hussey's fellow-Australian Di Venuto responded with 130 in 104 balls, and Derbyshire won with two overs in hand.

At Derby, August 31. **Durham won by 11 runs.** Toss: Derbyshire. **Durham 216-7** (45 overs) (M. L. Love 48, G. J. Muchall 39, A. M. Thorpe 34, P. D. Collingwood 54; D. G. Cork 3-28); **Derbyshire 205** (44.1 overs) (M. J. Di Venuto 63, C. W. G. Bassano 51, S. D. Stubbings 45; G. D. Bridge 4-39). *Durham 4 pts.*

County debut: C. Z. Harris (Derbyshire).

Di Venuto and Bassano took Derbyshire to 113 for one but, after Di Venuto was messily stumped off Bridge's left-arm spin, they folded to 150 for eight. Only Stubbings, with 45 in 56 balls, kept them in the game. Cork restricted Durham though their top order all made solid starts.

At Derby, September 7. **Derbyshire won by eight wickets.** Toss: Derbyshire. **Scotland 201-8** (45 overs) (R. R. Watson 70, R. M. Haq 35, I. M. Stanger 42*; D. G. Cork 3-15); **Derbyshire 202-2** (38.4 overs) (D. G. Cork 31, C. W. G. Bassano 108*). *Derbyshire 4 pts.*

Cork and Dean reduced Scotland to 25 for five in the tenth over, with Colin Smith retired hurt after being hit on the helmet; despite concussion, he later kept wicket. His team-mates, led by Watson, made a spirited recovery, adding a further 176. Bassano replied with his fourth one-day hundred of the season. His 15th four (he also hit a six) won the game with 38 balls to spare.

At Derby, September 21. **Derbyshire won by nine runs.** Toss: Derbyshire. **Derbyshire 172-7** (45 overs) (S. D. Stubbings 33, C. W. G. Bassano 44; J. R. C. Hamblin 3-20); **Hampshire 163** (44.3 overs) (S. M. Katich 56, D. A. Kenway 33). *Derbyshire 4 pts.*

Di Venuto led Derbyshire to an unlikely victory, the day before he was appointed captain for 2004. This was Hampshire's fourth defeat since beating Derbyshire on August 17, but they scraped promotion as Middlesex lost. Dimitri Mascarenhas finished with 34 wickets, the most in the 2003 League, and Katich reached 728 runs, beating Chris Smith's Hampshire record of 720 in 1984. They seemed in control at 143 for three, but lost their last seven for 20 in eight overs.

DURHAM

DURHAM v SCOTLAND

At Chester-le-Street, May 4. Scotland won by four wickets. Toss: Scotland.

The kilted fans in a crowd of 2,000 danced for joy as Scotland triumphed on their National League debut – their fourth win over an English county in senior one-day cricket. On a slow pitch, 19-year-old off-spinner Majid Haq, born in Paisley, bowled beautifully, claiming three wickets in four balls on his way to figures of four for 36. He was backed by a naggingly accurate quartet of medium-pacers. For the home side, Harmison bowled with extra pace – but the Scots exploited it to flash anything short and wide to the boundary behind point. Lockhart and Watson opened with 75, and South African Jon Kent, their one professional, drove successive balls from Gough for four, six and six. There were hiccoughs, but Scotland's task was greatly eased when Harmison returned and bowled two wides in the first three balls of an over which cost 12. Smith eased them home with four balls to spare.

Durham

N. Peng run out	14	J. Srinath st Smith b Hoffmann	16
M. A. Gough lbw b Wright	15	N. Killeen not out	8
G. J. Muchall st Smith b Haq	46	L-b 2, w 6	8
G. J. Pratt b Haq	34		—
*J. J. B. Lewis b Haq	1	1/20 (1) 2/46 (2) (7 wkts, 45 overs)	167
D. R. Law lbw b Haq	0	3/106 (4) 4/113 (5)	
†A. Pratt not out	25	5/113 (6) 6/116 (3) 7/144 (8)	

D. Pretorius and S. J. Harmison did not bat.

Bowling: Brinkley 9–2–28–0; Hoffmann 9–1–35–1; Kent 9–0–41–0; Wright 9–1–25–1; Haq 9–1–36–4.

Scotland

D. R. Lockhart c A. Pratt b Gough	44	N. J. MacRae not out	6
R. R. Watson b Killeen	25		
J. G. Williamson b Harmison	20	L-b 8, w 9, n-b 6	23
J. C. Kent c A. Pratt b Pretorius	25		—
†C. J. O. Smith not out	15	1/75 (2) 2/88 (1) (6 wkts, 44.2 overs)	168
I. M. Stanger c A. Pratt b Pretorius	0	3/104 (3) 4/132 (4)	
*C. M. Wright c Gough b Harmison	10	5/132 (6) 6/151 (7)	

P. J. C. Hoffmann, J. E. Brinkley and R. M. Haq did not bat.

Bowling: Pretorius 8.2–2–23–2; Srinath 9–1–14–0; Harmison 9–0–43–2; Killeen 9–0–28–1; Gough 9–1–52–1.

Umpires: B. Leadbeater and A. G. T. Whitehead.

At Chester-le-Street, May 5. **Lancashire won by five wickets** (D/L method). Toss: Durham. **Durham 186-8** (44 overs) (G. J. Pratt 66*; A. Flintoff 3-46); **Lancashire 188-5** (42.2 overs) (A. J. Swann 73*, A. Flintoff 42). *Lancashire 4 pts.*

Pratt took his League aggregate for the season to 201 in three innings (for one dismissal), but Durham suffered their second home defeat in two days. Lancashire were 78 for four at the halfway mark, chasing 187 in 44 overs (Duckworth/Lewis was invoked, but did not change the target). Then Flintoff thrashed 42 in 24 balls, and added 64 in eight overs with Swann, who picked off the remaining runs at leisure.

At Chester-le-Street, May 25. **No result** (abandoned). **Durham v Derbyshire.** *Durham 2 pts, Derbyshire 2 pts.*

At Chester-le-Street, July 13. **Northamptonshire won by 49 runs.** Toss: Northamptonshire. **Northamptonshire 215-7** (45 overs) (M. E. K. Hussey 112*, T. M. B. Bailey 31*); **Durham 166** (43 overs) (V. J. Wells 47; B. J. Phillips 3-25, R. S. G. Anderson 3-42). *Northamptonshire 4 pts.*

Hussey batted throughout Northamptonshire's innings, harvesting 112 in 123 balls while the rest floundered in perfect conditions. They were 150 for seven before Bailey joined him and made a run-a-ball 31, while Hussey reached his hundred with a six off Killeen. Phillips grabbed Durham's first three wickets and, once Wells top-edged Anderson to third man, the innings faded away.

At Chester-le-Street, August 3. **Somerset won by four wickets.** Toss: Durham. **Durham 187** (44.2 overs) (M. L. Love 42, P. Mustard 41; P. S. Jones 3-27, G. M. Andrew 3-38); **Somerset 189-6** (39 overs) (K. A. Parsons 31, I. D. Blackwell 79*; Shoaib Akhtar 5-35). *Somerset 4 pts.*

Two days earlier, Durham had dismissed Somerset for 56 in the Championship. Shoaib Akhtar took his haul of Somerset wickets to 13 in three innings, rattling the stumps with four perfect yorkers, but could not dismiss Blackwell – dropped on 35 – who struck three sixes in an 81-ball 79 to secure Somerset's first win in 13 games since June 18.

At Chester-le-Street, August 5. **Nottinghamshire won by four wickets.** Toss: Durham. **Durham 199** (43.1 overs) (N. Peng 42, M. L. Love 32, J. J. B. Lewis 30; P. J. Franks 3-36, G. D. Clough 3-48); **Nottinghamshire 203-6** (38.3 overs) (K. P. Pietersen 72, C. M. W. Read 46*, P. J. Franks 31*). *Nottinghamshire 4 pts.*

Pietersen became the first batsman to clear the Don Robson Pavilion in nine seasons of cricket at the Riverside. It was one of three sixes in Bridge's first over, which cost 24. Pietersen rescued Nottinghamshire from 56 for five in a 59-run stand with Read, who contributed three, but went on to see their team home.

At Chester-le-Street, August 24. **Durham won by seven wickets.** Toss: Hampshire. **Hampshire 131** (39.5 overs) (S. J. Harmison 3-31, G. D. Bridge 4-20); **Durham 132-3** (25.3 overs) (N. Peng 56*, P. D. Collingwood 48). *Durham 4 pts.*

Durham ended a run of five League defeats by beating Hampshire, who had won ten of their last 11. The pace of Harmison and Plunkett reduced Hampshire to 58 for five, then Bridge returned a one-day best four for 20; the highest stand was 30 for the last wicket. Collingwood, in his second game of the season, scored a 50-ball 48 as Durham swept home with nearly half their overs left.

At Chester-le-Street, August 26 (day/night). **Durham won by four wickets.** Toss: Sussex. **Sussex 137** (38.5 overs) (S. J. Harmison 4-43); **Durham 141-6** (36.2 overs) (A. M. Thorpe 37, P. D. Collingwood 45; M. J. G. Davis 3-16). *Durham 4 pts.*

Harmison, omitted from the Fourth Test, demonstrated his fitness by bowling at his fastest before the Sky TV cameras and a crowd of 4,000. His first five overs cost 20, including seven wides, but he later took four wickets to equal his one-day best analysis. Collingwood hit 45 in 52 balls as Durham won with eight overs to spare.

At Chester-le-Street, September 21. **Durham won by nine wickets.** Toss: Durham. **Middlesex 112-9** (30 overs) (B. L. Hutton 43*, C. B. Keegan 36; Shoaib Akhtar 4-21, N. Killeen 3-16); **Durham 114-1** (15.4 overs) (N. Peng 66*, V. J. Wells 33*). *Durham 4 pts.*

Defeat cost Middlesex promotion. In a match reduced to 30 overs a side by rain, they collapsed to 27 for seven; Killeen induced three edged catches and Shoaib Akhtar's sheer pace claimed four for 21 in six overs. Peng and Wells went for their shots, adding 63 in five overs; Durham needed less than 16 overs to win their fourth League game in five.

HAMPSHIRE

At Southampton, May 4. **Hampshire won by 43 runs.** Toss: Hampshire. **Hampshire 144-9** (45 overs) (R. A. Smith 44, N. Pothas 30*; B. V. Taylor 3-25, K. J. Innes 3-31); **Sussex 101** (36.4 overs) (C. T. Tremlett 3-17, S. D. Udal 3-11). *Hampshire 4 pts.*

On a difficult pitch, Hampshire were indebted to Smith, who batted for a painstaking 21 overs, and Pothas. A meagre target of 145 looked comfortably in reach when Sussex were 50 for one, but Tremlett and Udal induced a collapse of nine for 51.

At Southampton, May 5. **Middlesex won by four wickets.** Toss: Hampshire. **Hampshire 198-5** (45 overs) (R. A. Smith 92, J. R. C. Hamblin 33); **Middlesex 201-6** (45 overs) (P. N. Weekes 53, Abdul Razzaq 30, Extras 32; Wasim Akram 3-17). *Middlesex 4 pts.*

Middlesex needed seven off Tremlett's final over, and two off the last ball: Hutton cut it for four. Wasim Akram (9–4–17–3) had restricted them, but Abdul Razzaq seized the initiative with three sixes in Udal's final over. Smith hit 11 fours, some redolent of his England past.

At Southampton, May 25. **Hampshire won by 99 runs.** Toss: Hampshire. **Hampshire 248-3** (45 overs) (D. A. Kenway 115, J. P. Crawley 66, S. M. Katich 51*); **Somerset 149** (39.2 overs) (A. D. Mascarenhas 4-33). *Hampshire 4 pts.*

Kenway hit his first one-day hundred, including 13 fours, on a flat track, putting on 138 in 29 overs with Crawley to set up an easy win. Katich followed up with a run-a-ball fifty, adding a running catch and two wickets to wrap up Somerset's innings inside 40 overs.

At Southampton, June 8. **Hampshire won by seven runs.** Toss: Hampshire. **Hampshire 203-5** (45 overs) (J. P. Crawley 102, S. M. Katich 34, N. Pothas 30*); **Durham 196-8** (45 overs) (N. Peng 44, J. J. B. Lewis 43, G. J. Muchall 38; A. D. Mascarenhas 4-44). *Hampshire 4 pts.*

Crawley won his 11th toss in 13 games, then scored only his second hundred in 12 seasons in the League. Once Mascarenhas dismissed Peng for a 47-ball 44, on his way to four wickets, Durham fell behind the asking-rate. Mullally bowled 9–1–15–1 and Durham managed only eight of the 16 required off Giddins's final over.

At Southampton, July 13. **Nottinghamshire won by five wickets.** Toss: Nottinghamshire. **Hampshire 208-7** (45 overs) (S. M. Katich 56, J. D. Francis 34, N. Pothas 45*); **Nottinghamshire 212-5** (44.4 overs) (J. E. R. Gallian 60, C. L. Cairns 57*, C. M. W. Read 33*). *Nottinghamshire 4 pts.*

Nottinghamshire ended Hampshire's run of four wins when Cairns and Read added 55 in seven overs. Read, who had played for England in the NatWest Series final the previous day, hit two fours off Wasim Akram to complete victory with two balls to spare.

At Southampton, July 30 (day/night). **Hampshire won by 54 runs.** Toss: Hampshire. **Hampshire 216-8** (45 overs) (J. R. C. Hamblin 32, D. A. Kenway 78; M. J. Cawdron 4-52); **Northamptonshire 162** (42.4 overs) (D. J. Sales 73; A. D. Mascarenhas 4-22, S. D. Udal 4-40). *Hampshire 4 pts.*

Hampshire's meeting with division leaders Northamptonshire attracted their biggest attendance for a floodlit match, over 6,200. Kenway scored a carefully paced 78, though Cawdron's four wickets prevented acceleration. Then, under lights, Northamptonshire groped to 50 for five as Mascarenhas exploited a pitch suddenly infused with life; he destroyed the top order and Udal the tail. Only Sales, last out, prevented a rout.

At Southampton, August 4. **Hampshire won by seven wickets.** Toss: Hampshire. **Scotland 225-5** (45 overs) (R. R. Watson 37, R. Dravid 81, J. C. Kent 78*); **Hampshire 226-3** (44 overs) (S. M. Katich 45, J. P. Crawley 83*, J. D. Francis 62*; C. M. Wright 3-25). *Hampshire 4 pts.*

County debut: W. P. U. J. C. Vaas (Hampshire).

India's Dravid and Kent, a South African, put on 103 in 18 overs for Scotland's fourth wicket. Wright took all three Hampshire wickets to fall, including two in consecutive balls, before Crawley and Francis added 126 in 21 overs on a fine track to return their side to second place.

At Southampton, August 17. **Hampshire won by six wickets.** Toss: Hampshire. **Derbyshire 158-9** (45 overs) (D. G. Cork 49; C. T. Tremlett 4-26); **Hampshire 162-4** (35.4 overs) (J. R. C. Hamblin 31, J. P. Crawley 33*). *Hampshire 4 pts.*

Hampshire's tenth win in 11 matches lifted them to the head of Division Two. Derbyshire slid to 73 for six before Cork's 52-ball 49. Mascarenhas returned figures of 9–5–11–2, then played a flurry of bold off-side shots to help Crawley to victory with nearly ten overs in hand.

At Southampton, September 7. **Lancashire won by 45 runs.** Toss: Hampshire. **Lancashire 204-5** (45 overs) (C. L. Hooper 73, G. Chapple 66*); **Hampshire 159** (41.3 overs) (N. Pothas 58; C. L. Hooper 3-18). *Lancashire 4 pts.*

Lancashire's 11th win in 11 completed League games set back Hampshire's hopes of joining them in Division One. Hooper scored an 88-ball 73 and added 124 in 22 overs with Chapple, rescuing Lancashire from 52 for four; he later took three wickets, including Pothas whose dismissal triggered the loss of Hampshire's last six wickets for 43.

LANCASHIRE

At Manchester, April 27. **Northamptonshire won by 45 runs.** Toss: Northamptonshire. **Northamptonshire 196-2** (37 overs) (M. E. K. Hussey 84*, M. J. Powell 30, P. A. Jaques 65); **Lancashire 151** (33.4 overs) (M. J. Chilton 35; G. P. Swann 3-15). *Northamptonshire 4 pts.*

Hussey, who had flown in from Australia two days before, batted throughout the innings (reduced by rain to 37 overs a side), adding 152 in 24 overs with Jaques thanks to some sharp-witted running between the wickets. He later swooped from mid-on to run out Flintoff, who had just struck Cook for six, with a backward flick. This sparked a collapse of seven for 34, with Swann picking up three.

At Manchester, May 18. **Lancashire won by 70 runs** (D/L method). Toss: Hampshire. **Lancashire 231-4** (30 overs) (M. B. Loye 41, S. G. Law 98, C. L. Hooper 51*); **Hampshire 150** (23.3 overs) (J. P. Crawley 37, A. D. Mascarenhas 37; M. J. Chilton 3-20). *Lancashire 4 pts.*

Hampshire's target revised to 221 in 28 overs.

First-team debut: S. P. Crook (Lancashire).

Former Lancashire captains Wasim Akram, who announced his retirement from international cricket, and Crawley returned to Old Trafford. In a match reduced to 30 overs a side, Law hit an 81-ball 98, adding 102 in 15 overs with Loye and 91 in ten with Hooper. Hampshire lost their top five in 17 balls, with Chilton claiming his best figures for Lancashire.

At Manchester, May 25. **Scotland won by 41 runs.** Toss: Lancashire. **Scotland 192-8** (45 overs) (J. G. Williamson 60, C. J. O. Smith 60; S. I. Mahmood 3-41); **Lancashire 151** (42.1 overs) (M. B. Loye 38; C. M. Wright 3-27, R. R. Watson 3-11). *Scotland 4 pts.*

Scotland's third win in five matches was easily their best and put them second in the table. The margin might have been even bigger but for four dropped catches. Williamson set the tone with three sixes in a 71-ball 60, and medium-pacers Watson and Wright took three wickets each. Wright, the captain, said "to beat a team with such a reputation in one-day cricket on one of the most famous grounds is something special".

At Manchester, June 8. **Lancashire won by seven wickets** (D/L method). Toss: Lancashire. **Nottinghamshire 100-6** (17 overs) (J. E. R. Gallian 36); **Lancashire 114-3** (15.3 overs) (C. L. Hooper 40*, A. Flintoff 43*). *Lancashire 4 pts.*

Lancashire's target revised to 112 in 17 overs.

Rain during Nottinghamshire's innings reduced the match to 17 overs a side. Though Lancashire stumbled to 26 for three, Flintoff and Hooper cruised home with 88 in 11 overs against an attack missing Cairns, whose hand was broken. Flintoff ended it with a huge six into the pavilion.

At Manchester, June 22. **Lancashire won by three wickets.** Toss: Durham. **Durham 197-7** (45 overs) (M. L. Love 53, G. J. Pratt 39, J. J. B. Lewis 37; G. Chapple 3-38); **Lancashire 198-7** (43.5 overs) (G. Chapple 77*, W. K. Hegg 39; L. E. Plunkett 3-38). *Lancashire 4 pts.*

Sutcliffe retired hurt when a delivery from Liam Plunkett, an 18-year-old seamer making his League debut, fractured his cheekbone; Plunkett also took three for three in ten balls. Lancashire fought back from 58 for five thanks to a handful of dropped catches and a 74-run stand between Hegg and Chapple, who also bowled superbly. Earlier, Love scored his third successive fifty. Lancashire jumped to second.

At Manchester, July 28 (day/night). **No result.** Toss: Somerset. **Lancashire 129-8** (20 overs) (M. J. Chilton 37, S. G. Law 32; I. D. Blackwell 3-27) **v Somerset.** *Lancashire 2 pts, Somerset 2 pts.*

First-team debut: J. C. Hildreth (Somerset).

The game was reduced to 20 overs a side by a series of showers, but rain prevented Somerset's reply.

At Manchester, August 4 (day/night). **Lancashire won by eight wickets.** Toss: Derbyshire. **Derbyshire 197** (43.4 overs) (M. J. Di Venuto 40, M. Kaif 70; C. L. Hooper 3-30); **Lancashire 199-2** (35.3 overs) (M. B. Loye 62*, S. G. Law 39, C. L. Hooper 79*). *Lancashire 4 pts.*

Lancashire's second win in two days took them six points clear at the top of Division Two. Despite a decent pitch and 70 from Kaif, Derbyshire lost their last six for 40, with Hooper claiming three in nine balls; he then hit four sixes in a 70-ball 79, adding 106 with Loye to steer Lancashire home in front of a crowd of 8,500.

At Manchester, August 19 (day/night). **Lancashire won by seven wickets.** Toss: Middlesex. **Middlesex 278-4** (45 overs) (A. J. Strauss 127, E. C. Joyce 70); **Lancashire 281-3** (43.3 overs) (I. J. Sutcliffe 71, S. G. Law 78, C. L. Hooper 51*, M. J. Chilton 43*). *Lancashire 4 pts.*

Strauss scored his maiden one-day century and added 157 in 25 overs with Joyce, but Lancashire trumped them. They won their third successive floodlit run-chase with nine balls to spare, thanks to a stand of 155 in 24 overs between Sutcliffe and Law, and 92 from Hooper and Chilton. Hooper was caught by Joyce on the mid-wicket boundary, only for Joyce to fall over the rope, making it six. Lancashire were held up for seven minutes when the umpires found some of the 30-metre discs had disappeared during the interval.

At Manchester, September 14. **Sussex won by nine wickets.** Toss: Lancashire. **Lancashire 125** (41 overs) (M. J. Chilton 43, C. P. Schofield 32; B. V. Taylor 3-32, M. J. G. Davis 4-14); **Sussex 128-1** (18.2 overs) (R. R. Montgomerie 66*, M. W. Goodwin 59). *Sussex 4 pts.*

The previous day, Lancashire had crushed Sussex to delay their Championship title; now Sussex spoiled Lancashire's party. Victory would have made them Division Two champions, but the trophy had to be taken away until they met second-placed Northamptonshire the next week. Hutchison and Taylor found early help in the pitch, and Davis claimed four as Lancashire were bowled out for their lowest League total of the season; then Goodwin and Montgomerie blasted 121 inside 16 overs and Sussex won with 26 overs to go.

MIDDLESEX

At Lord's, April 27. **Middlesex won by five wickets.** Toss: Middlesex. **Derbyshire 203** (45 overs) (M. J. Di Venuto 61, C. W. G. Bassano 52; S. J. Cook 4-30, P. N. Weekes 3-45); **Middlesex 205-5** (43.5 overs) (P. N. Weekes 76, O. A. Shah 48; T. Lungley 3-47). *Middlesex 4 pts.*

Middlesex, last in the League in 2002, began with a comfortable win. On a true pitch, Cook claimed career-best one-day figures as Derbyshire stumbled from 156 for three to 167 for seven. Weekes then took the last three Derbyshire wickets before sharing an opening partnership of 96 in 19 overs with Strauss.

At Shenley Park, May 25. **Northamptonshire won by eight wickets.** Toss: Middlesex. **Middlesex 200-7** (45 overs) (E. C. Joyce 61, D. C. Nash 50, S. J. Cook 38); **Northamptonshire 204-2** (44.3 overs) (M. E. K. Hussey 86*, D. J. Sales 75*). *Northamptonshire 4 pts.*

Both sides began this match unbeaten. Middlesex scored slowly, barely exceeding two an over for the first half of their innings, before Joyce and Nash picked up the rate in a fourth-wicket stand of 84. Cook needed just 27 deliveries for his 38; Hutton, after hitting his first ball, from Andre Nel, for six, was then floored by a bouncer. Dazed, he was run out off his third ball. Northamptonshire kept wickets in hand, but still needed 59 from their last ten overs.

At Lord's, June 8. **Sussex won by 49 runs** (D/L method). Toss: Sussex. **Sussex 161-7** (39 overs) (M. W. Goodwin 81*, T. R. Ambrose 44; Abdul Razzaq 3-45); **Middlesex 133** (33.2 overs) (A. J. Strauss 57; K. J. Innes 5-41). *Sussex 4 pts.*

Middlesex's target revised to 183 in 39 overs.

On a low pitch, Sussex won their first League match of the summer, despite reeling at three for three in the third over, later 23 for four. Goodwin and Ambrose then put on 112 in Sussex's rain-affected innings. In reply, Middlesex seemed well set after Innes conceded 35 in his first four overs. But from 115 for three, they fell apart dramatically, Innes taking five for six in 15 balls as the last seven wickets added just 18. Mushtaq Ahmed had figures of 8–1–14–1.

At Richmond, June 17. **Middlesex won by 112 runs.** Toss: Scotland. **Middlesex 255-9** (45 overs) (P. N. Weekes 80, E. C. Joyce 59*; R. M. Haq 3-39); **Scotland 143** (30.1 overs) (P. J. C. Hoffmann 33; C. B. Keegan 5-48). *Middlesex 4 pts.*

In a shoddy fielding performance, Scotland put down five catches, including Weekes, who went on to 80 from 77 balls, off the first ball of the match. Dravid fell lbw to one that seemed high, leaving Scotland 36 for five. Hoffmann faced just 14 balls for his 33. Dravid was no luckier off the pitch. He had £200 and a gold bangle stolen from the dressing-room.

At Lord's, July 6. **Lancashire won by five wickets.** Toss: Middlesex. **Middlesex 255-6** (45 overs) (E. C. Joyce 32, D. C. Nash 62, Abdul Razzaq 61*); **Lancashire 257-5** (43.4 overs) (M. B. Loye 78, S. G. Law 37, C. L. Hooper 88*; Abdul Razzaq 3-48). *Lancashire 4 pts.*

Lancashire moved to within two points of Northamptonshire at the top of the division after their fourth straight win. Given such a true pitch, Middlesex had dawdled to 199 from 41 overs, but then Abdul Razzaq, who faced just 31 balls, helped ensure a testing total, as 56 came from the last four overs. Hooper, who needed just 68 balls for an unbeaten 88, languidly steered them home.

At Southgate, July 13. **Middlesex won by 32 runs.** Toss: Middlesex. **Middlesex 337-5** (45 overs) (P. N. Weekes 65, A. J. Strauss 74, O. A. Shah 74, Abdul Razzaq 79; N. A. M. McLean 3-76); **Somerset 305-9** (45 overs) (J. Cox 39, K. P. Dutch 65, I. D. Blackwell 64, W. J. Durston 51*; C. B. Keegan 3-46, J. W. M. Dalrymple 3-55). *Middlesex 4 pts.*

Middlesex hit their highest one-day total thanks to half-centuries from their top four. All were brisk, but Abdul Razzaq was brutal: his 79 came from 49 balls, with six fours and five sixes. Somerset, bottom of the division, needed their highest total chasing, but despite more violent fifties, especially from Blackwell (50 balls) and Durston (43), they were never up with the rate, though a match aggregate of 642 beat the League record of 638 by Surrey and Kent in May. Middlesex moved into third place.

At Lord's, August 10. **Middlesex won by seven runs.** Toss: Middlesex. **Middlesex 210-8** (45 overs) (E. C. Joyce 77, S. J. Cook 67*; N. Killeen 5-33); **Durham 203-6** (45 overs) (N. Peng 41, G. J. Muchall 44, G. J. Pratt 63*; T. F. Bloomfield 4-36). *Middlesex 4 pts.*

With three overs and six wickets in hand, Durham required just 19 runs. But Bloomfield maintained his nerve – and the form that now brought him four wickets in a League game for the third time in a week – to give Middlesex a tense win. Earlier, Killeen had reduced Middlesex to 66 for six before Joyce and Cook, who made his unbeaten 67 at a run a ball, added 116.

At Lord's, August 17. **Middlesex won by 37 runs.** Toss: Nottinghamshire. **Middlesex 300-4** (45 overs) (P. N. Weekes 72, C. B. Keegan 50, O. A. Shah 91*); **Nottinghamshire 263** (43.1 overs) (P. J. Franks 34, B. M. Shafayat 38, G. D. Clough 38, K. P. Pietersen 33, C. M. W. Read 31; C. B. Keegan 3-38). *Middlesex 4 pts.*

Weekes and Strauss hit their sixth opening stand of 50 or more in the League in 2003, paving the way for a superb 56-ball unbeaten 91 by Shah which guided Middlesex to 300 for the second time in six League games. Cairns's nine overs cost 78. In reply, six of Nottinghamshire's top seven reached 29, but none passed 38 as they lost wickets too regularly to mount a serious threat. Victory kept Middlesex's promotion hopes alive.

At Lord's, September 14. **Middlesex won by six wickets.** Toss: Middlesex. **Hampshire 277-7** (45 overs) (N. Pothas 78, S. M. Katich 106; P. N. Weekes 4-45); **Middlesex 278-4** (44.5 overs) (P. N. Weekes 104, A. J. Strauss 34, C. B. Keegan 46, O. A. Shah 49). *Middlesex 4 pts.*

A Hampshire win would have assured them a place in Division One; a Middlesex victory would mean these two sides would have to wait till the last day of the season to see which would go up. In a thrilling conclusion, Middlesex triumphed with one ball to spare. After Pothas and Katich put on 144 for the first wicket, Hampshire struggled against the off-spin of Weekes. When Middlesex batted, Weekes passed 50 in the League for the ninth time in 2003, this time converting it into only his second League hundred. Hampshire did not field well: Hamblin dropped Shah when ten were needed off seven balls, and the next Shah walloped for six.

NORTHAMPTONSHIRE

At Northampton, May 4. **Northamptonshire won by five wickets.** Toss: Nottinghamshire. **Nottinghamshire 294-8** (45 overs) (C. M. W. Read 119*, J. E. R. Gallian 42, K. P. Pietersen 77; J. W. Cook 3-69); **Northamptonshire 295-5** (44.3 overs) (P. A. Jaques 68, D. J. Sales 133*; S. Elworthy 3-37). *Northamptonshire 4 pts.*

A maiden one-day century by Read – who shared a fourth-wicket stand of 116 with Pietersen – was the cornerstone of the Nottinghamshire innings. Read faced 108 balls and hit three sixes and 15 fours, but his effort was trumped by another maiden limited-overs hundred, this one from Sales. He added 149 at seven an over with Jaques, hit 14 fours and a six off 120 balls, and ended unbeaten on 133, the highest one-day score for Northamptonshire since Wayne Larkins larruped 172 against Warwickshire at Luton in 1983.

At Northampton, May 18. **No result** (D/L method). Toss: Northamptonshire. **Northamptonshire 131-9** (33 overs) (M. J. Cawdron 37*; D. G. Cork 3-22); **Derbyshire 5-0** (3 overs). *Northamptonshire 2 pts, Derbyshire 2 pts.*

Derbyshire's target was revised to 131 in 33 overs before play was called off.

The rain was kinder to Northamptonshire than Derbyshire, who had restricted them to a poor score, even allowing for a pitch of uncertain bounce. Cawdron, who came in at 61 for seven and shared a partnership of 43 with Penberthy, ensured a modicum of respectability.

At Northampton, June 15. **Northamptonshire won by 13 runs.** Toss: Northamptonshire. **Northamptonshire 148** (44.3 overs) (G. L. Brophy 31); **Sussex 135** (42.2 overs) (M. J. Cawdron 3-33). *Northamptonshire 4 pts.*

No one fully came to terms with a slow, testing pitch, but the result was an absorbing, low-scoring contest. Mushtaq Ahmed had figures of 9–3–16–2 as Northamptonshire laboured. In the Sussex reply, Cawdron and Nel made early inroads, reducing them to 45 for five. Sussex had plummeted to 98 for eight before rallying through Davis and Hutchison, who took them to within 15 of their target. Hutchison was then run out for 20, and Lewry lasted just three balls. Northamptonshire's sixth win in six completed games kept them top.

At Northampton, July 6. **Hampshire won by four wickets.** Toss: Northamptonshire. **Northamptonshire 228-8** (45 overs) (P. A. Jaques 117; A. D. Mascarenhas 3-47); **Hampshire**

229-6 (44.3 overs) (S. M. Katich 54, R. A. Smith 33, J. P. Crawley 77*, A. D. Mascarenhas 31). *Hampshire 4 pts.*

This was Northamptonshire's first League defeat of the summer. Jaques hit his maiden one-day hundred, in all facing 113 balls, but of his team-mates only Swann reached 20, and the last nine overs produced just 29 runs. Katich followed four catches and three wickets with a quickfire fifty. Hampshire paced their innings perfectly, especially Crawley, who faced 72 balls.

At Northampton, July 27. **Middlesex won by five wickets.** Toss: Northamptonshire. **Northamptonshire 234-8** (45 overs) (T. W. Roberts 64, D. J. Sales 56, G. L. Brophy 33; S. J. Cook 3-40); **Middlesex 238-5** (43.4 overs) (A. J. Strauss 41, O. A. Shah 83*). *Middlesex 4 pts.*

Middlesex went third after beating the leaders. On a slow pitch, Roberts and Sales helped steer Northamptonshire to 135 for two, but thereafter the bowlers regained control: 59 came from the last ten overs. In the Middlesex reply, Shah – who had dawdled to 35 off 59 balls when he was dropped by Phillips at long-off – then crashed 48 from his next 27 as he and Hutton added an unbeaten 81 at nine an over.

At Northampton, August 6. **Northamptonshire won by 75 runs.** Toss: Northamptonshire. **Northamptonshire 319-7** (45 overs) (M. E. K. Hussey 123, P. A. Jaques 76, D. J. Sales 53; C. M. Wright 3-55); **Scotland 244** (43.4 overs) (N. J. MacRae 38, R. Dravid 114, G. I. Maiden 33). *Northamptonshire 4 pts.*

In searing heat and on a dry pitch that spun significantly, Hussey hit his highest one-day score as Northamptonshire made their best League total. Hussey faced 115 balls and shared a second-wicket stand of 138 with Jaques. Sales flogged his 53 from 37 balls. For Scotland, Dravid alone looked comfortable in the subcontinental conditions as he stroked his third League hundred of the summer. He put on 86 for the third wicket with McRae and 72 with Maiden for the ninth.

At Northampton, August 12 (day/night). **Northamptonshire won by four wickets.** Toss: Somerset. **Somerset 202-9** (45 overs) (C. M. Gazzard 42, K. P. Dutch 33; J. F. Brown 3-28); **Northamptonshire 206-6** (43.3 overs) (M. E. K. Hussey 53, P. A. Jaques 73). *Northamptonshire 4 pts.*

Somerset, unable to build so much as a fifty partnership, never gained momentum, despite an enterprising 38-ball innings from Gazzard. Northamptonshire were strolling to victory while Hussey and Jaques put on 104 for the second wicket, but wobbled en route to their target. Five of the six Northamptonshire batsmen to fall were caught behind by Gazzard.

At Northampton, September 7. **Northamptonshire won by 27 runs.** Toss: Northamptonshire. **Northamptonshire 241-6** (45 overs) (M. E. K. Hussey 55, P. A. Jaques 67); **Durham 214** (42.3 overs) (A. M. Thorpe 76, P. D. Collingwood 43, G. J. Pratt 40; G. P. Swann 4-57). *Northamptonshire 4 pts.*

Northamptonshire guaranteed promotion with this win. Their two Australian left-handers, Hussey and Jaques, added 84 for the second wicket, and the middle order maintained the momentum. Durham lurched to 15 for two, but were rescued by Thorpe, another Australian-born left-hander. He fell at 168 for four, the first of four wickets in four overs for Swann, as Durham crumbled. Two days earlier, Northamptonshire had ensured promotion in the Championship by beating Durham.

NORTHAMPTONSHIRE v LANCASHIRE

At Northampton, September 21. Lancashire won by nine wickets. Toss: Northamptonshire.

The match to determine the second-division champions was decided by Mal Loye on his first return to Wantage Road since leaving a year earlier. He faced 99 balls for his unbeaten 104 and shared century partnerships with Sutcliffe and Law as Lancashire eased to their target with more than eight overs to spare. It was an afternoon of mixed emotions for Hussey, the Northamptonshire captain, who was making perhaps his final appearance for them. He received a standing ovation and two player of the year awards, and ended the League season with 820 runs, a club record and the best in the country… but he also dropped Loye at slip on 11. Jaques, No. 2 in the League scoring list, had dominated the Northamptonshire innings with 107 from 109 balls, only to see the initiative pass to Lancashire as the last 15 overs brought just 63 runs.

Northamptonshire

*M. E. K. Hussey c Hegg b Hooper	35	M. J. Cawdron c Hegg b Wood	2
T. W. Roberts c Law b Martin	10	J. F. Brown run out	0
P. A. Jaques c Wood b Keedy	107		
D. J. Sales b Hooper	23	B 1, l-b 2, w 7	10
G. L. Brophy st Hegg b Schofield	1		
J. W. Cook c Hegg b Chapple	18	1/13 (2) 2/85 (1) 3/126 (4) (44.5 overs)	240
G. P. Swann b Chapple	7	4/127 (5) 5/186 (6)	
†T. M. B. Bailey not out	27	6/196 (7) 7/216 (3)	
B. J. Phillips run out	0	8/223 (9) 9/239 (10) 10/240 (11)	

Bowling: Martin 9–0–45–1; Chapple 7–0–36–2; Wood 5.5–0–34–1; Hooper 9–0–33–2; Keedy 9–0–57–1; Schofield 5–0–32–1.

Lancashire

M. B. Loye not out	104
I. J. Sutcliffe c Brophy b Swann	54
S. G. Law not out	79
L-b 2, w 4	6
1/112 (2) (1 wkt, 36.4 overs)	243

M. J. Chilton, C. L. Hooper, *†W. K. Hegg, C. P. Schofield, G. Chapple, G. Keedy, P. J. Martin and J. Wood did not bat.

Bowling: Phillips 8–0–62–0; Cawdron 7–0–45–0; Cook 5–0–36–0; Swann 7.4–0–42–1; Brown 7–0–39–0; Hussey 2–0–17–0.

Umpires: A. Clarkson and R. Palmer.

NOTTINGHAMSHIRE

At Nottingham, May 5. **Nottinghamshire won by one wicket.** Toss: Nottinghamshire. **Derbyshire 252** (45 overs) (S. A. Selwood 67, D. R. Hewson 50, D. G. Cork 35, T. Lungley 30, Extras 32; S. Elworthy 4-41, G. J. Smith 3-48); **Nottinghamshire 254-9** (44.2 overs) (K. P. Pietersen 130*, C. L. Cairns 40; G. Welch 3-48). *Nottinghamshire 4 pts.*

Derbyshire recovered from a precarious 23 for four thanks to Selwood and Hewson, who added 96 to help set a demanding target. Nottinghamshire in turn tottered to 29 for three, then 140 for six before Pietersen cut loose. He had taken 69 balls over his first 50 runs, but his next 40 yielded 80. Derbyshire had appeared on the brink of success when Nottinghamshire required 103 from ten overs, but Pietersen – who mauled five sixes and 13 fours – was undeterred.

At Nottingham, June 15. **Durham won by seven runs.** Toss: Durham. **Durham 183** (44.5 overs) (M. L. Love 55, Extras 34; G. J. Smith 3-16, S. C. G. MacGill 3-26); **Nottinghamshire 176** (44.5 overs) (G. E. Welton 39, G. D. Clough 42*; N. Killeen 5-22, I. D. Hunter 3-34). *Durham 4 pts.*

Killeen bowled Durham to victory on a low, cracked wicket that made run-scoring awkward. He dismissed Gallian, Pietersen and Shafayat before returning to take two lower-order wickets – and snuff out Nottinghamshire hopes boosted by a late surge from Clough, whose unbeaten 42 was a career-best. The Durham innings had been held together by a resolute innings from Love.

At Nottingham, June 22. **Middlesex won by one run.** Toss: Middlesex. **Middlesex 234** (44 overs) (P. N. Weekes 40, O. A. Shah 106; R. J. Logan 4-44); **Nottinghamshire 233-8** (45 overs) (G. E. Welton 50, K. P. Pietersen 82, R. J. Warren 36*). *Middlesex 4 pts.*

County debut: R. J. Warren (Nottinghamshire).

Nottinghamshire, who lost to Leicestershire off the last ball of the previous day's Twenty20 game, repeated the trick. Shah hit a brisk hundred – the first for Middlesex against Nottinghamshire in the League's 35 seasons – to set a challenging total. Pietersen picked up the pace of the Nottinghamshire reply, and while he was in, they were favourites. But his wicket was quickly followed by two more, and in the end Warren, on county debut, ran out Logan attempting the single that would have tied the match.

At Nottingham, July 21 (day/night). **Hampshire won by six wickets.** Toss: Nottinghamshire. **Nottinghamshire 249-6** (45 overs) (R. J. Warren 91, K. P. Pietersen 58, C. M. W. Read 38*; A. D. Mascarenhas 3-46); **Hampshire 250-4** (45 overs) (S. M. Katich 67, D. A. Kenway 50, J. P. Crawley 58). *Hampshire 4 pts.*

This was the fourth consecutive League match at Trent Bridge decided in the last over – and Nottinghamshire's third last-ball defeat in three home one-day games. Warren, with his first League fifty since arriving from Northampton, and Pietersen laid down the bedrock of the Nottinghamshire total. In the Hampshire reply, Katich was kept waiting for three minutes to learn from the third umpire, Barrie Leadbeater, that he had been run out. Crawley then reached the fastest fifty of the game before Francis scrambled the required two off the last ball.

At Cleethorpes, August 3. **Lancashire won by 25 runs.** Toss: Lancashire. **Lancashire 210-9** (45 overs) (S. G. Law 47, C. L. Hooper 71, G. Chapple 37; G. J. Smith 3-44); **Nottinghamshire 185** (42.2 overs) (K. P. Pietersen 54, U. Afzaal 51; P. J. Martin 3-18). *Lancashire 4 pts.*

A crowd approaching 3,000 welcomed Nottinghamshire back to Chichester Road after four years. Lancashire began well, but after Hooper hit MacGill into a neighbouring garden for six, the ball was changed – and the replacement offered far greater seam movement. Hooper held the innings together with his 105-ball 71. Nottinghamshire then stumbled to 34 for three before Pietersen pulled them round with a punchy fifty. No one else could sustain the required rate. Lancashire went top of Division Two.

At Nottingham, August 24. **Nottinghamshire won by 71 runs.** Toss: Nottinghamshire. **Nottinghamshire 292-5** (45 overs) (P. J. Franks 38, C. L. Cairns 91*, C. M. W. Read 79*; R. S. C. Martin-Jenkins 4-50); **Sussex 221** (44.3 overs) (P. A. Cottey 36, B. Zuiderent 47; D. S. Lucas 3-52, C. L. Cairns 3-48). *Nottinghamshire 4 pts.*

Cairns and Read put on an unbroken 167 for the sixth wicket – a League record – including 126 from the last ten overs. They undid the good work of Martin-Jenkins, who had dismantled the Nottinghamshire top order to leave them 99 for four. An under-strength Sussex steadily lost wickets and never threatened to make a game of it. They were now top of the Championship's first division and bottom of the League's second.

At Nottingham, August 31. **Northamptonshire won by 212 runs.** Toss: Northamptonshire. **Northamptonshire 296-5** (45 overs) (M. E. K. Hussey 59, T. W. Roberts 131; D. S. Lucas 3-59); **Nottinghamshire 84** (21 overs) (S. R. Patel 33*; A. Nel 3-22, C. G. Greenidge 3-24, M. J. Cawdron 3-23). *Northamptonshire 4 pts.*

Northamptonshire's win was the third-biggest in League history in terms of runs. When Nottinghamshire were 18 for six, however, the margin looked set to be much larger. They were rescued from total ignominy by Patel, the England Under-19 captain, who managed a mature 42-ball 33 not out. Earlier, Roberts, who faced 112 balls, hit his first century in county cricket, almost outscoring in boundaries (15 fours and three sixes) the whole of the Nottinghamshire innings.

At Nottingham, September 7. **Nottinghamshire won by 35 runs.** Toss: Nottinghamshire. **Nottinghamshire 279-5** (45 overs) (B. M. Shafayat 35, K. P. Pietersen 141*, S. R. Patel 44); **Somerset 244-8** (45 overs) (C. M. Gazzard 76, K. A. Parsons 39). *Nottinghamshire 4 pts.*

Pietersen made the highest innings of the summer in the second division, and his third hundred in his last four League games against Somerset. Initially, he worked the singles before opening up in the later overs. Somerset were in with a shout while Gazzard and Blackwell were together – they took the Somerset reply to 189 for three – but not thereafter. Blackwell belted one six over the main Trent Bridge scoreboard.

At Nottingham, September 14. **Nottinghamshire won by seven wickets.** Toss: Scotland. **Scotland 183** (44.1 overs) (J. E. Brinkley 67; S. C. G. MacGill 3-27); **Nottinghamshire 185-3** (37.4 overs) (J. E. R. Gallian 43*, C. L. Cairns 76*). *Nottinghamshire 4 pts.*

A sixth successive League defeat for Scotland condemned them to the wooden spoon. For Nottinghamshire, the win meant they would avoid first-class opponents in the second round of the 2004 C&G Trophy. Brinkley made 67, his highest in all competitions, but no one else passed 25 as Scotland lost their last six wickets for 44. Cairns survived a chance on 19 and went on to a run-a-ball 76.

SCOTLAND

SCOTLAND v SOMERSET

At Edinburgh, May 9. Scotland won by six wickets (D/L method). Toss: Somerset.

The Scots had been trounced by Somerset in the C&G match two days earlier, but now an unmatched spirit resulted in a sensational victory and the third-fastest hundred recorded in one-day cricket. Rain interrupted Somerset's innings for four hours, reducing them to 16 overs. Resuming with 11 overs left, Trescothick went berserk, bombarding nearby gardens and tennis courts with sixes to reach 80 in 44 balls. With another over cut, the Scots needed 180 in 15 – an asking-rate of 12 an over. But the openers were undaunted, running up 99 by the time Brinkley was stumped in the ninth over. Meanwhile, Ryan Watson, a 26-year-old Rhodesian-born right-hander, plundered Somerset's attack with a ferocity never before witnessed in Scotland. With an apparently impossible 43 needed from three overs, he walloped six deliveries from Dutch for six. He reached Scotland's most amazing century in just 43 balls, smashing seven sixes and ten fours, and took the Saltires to their second successive League win with three balls to spare.

FASTEST ONE-DAY HUNDREDS BY BALLS

36	G. D. Rose (110)	Somerset v Devon at Torquay	1990
37	Shahid Afridi (102)	Pakistan v Sri Lanka at Nairobi	1996-97
43	**R. R. Watson (103*)**	**Scotland v Somerset at Edinburgh**	**2003**
44	M. A. Ealham (112)	Kent v Derbyshire at Maidstone	1995
45	B. C. Lara (117)	West Indies v Bangladesh at Dhaka	1999-2000
46	G. D. Rose (148)	Somerset v Glamorgan at Neath	1990
47	M. P. Speight (126)	Sussex v Somerset at Taunton	1993
48	S. T. Jayasuriya (134)	Sri Lanka v Pakistan at Singapore	1995-96
48	A. J. Lamb (120)	Northamptonshire v Sussex at Northampton	1992

Somerset

J. Cox b Brinkley	17
M. E. Trescothick not out	80
J. D. C. Bryant c Lockhart b Wright	13
I. D. Blackwell c Kent b Watson	34
*M. Burns not out	29
L-b 2, w 4	6
1/23 (1) 2/54 (3) 3/133 (4) (3 wkts, 16 overs)	179

K. A. Parsons, †R. J. Turner, K. P. Dutch, R. L. Johnson, N. A. M. McLean and S. R. G. Francis did not bat.

Bowling: Brinkley 4–1–42–1; Hoffmann 3–0–5–0; Wright 2–0–30–1; Kent 1–0–17–0; Watson 3–0–45–1; Haq 3–0–38–0.

Scotland

R. R. Watson not out	103
J. G. Williamson c Dutch b Johnson	6
J. E. Brinkley st Turner b Blackwell	48
J. C. Kent run out	5
†C. J. O. Smith b Francis	5
*C. M. Wright not out	6
L-b 5, w 3	8
1/15 (2) 2/99 (3) 3/133 (4) 4/166 (5) (4 wkts, 14.3 overs)	181

D. R. Lockhart, I. M. Stanger, N. J. MacRae, P. J. C. Hoffmann and R. M. Haq did not bat.

Bowling: McLean 3–0–22–0; Johnson 3–0–30–1; Blackwell 3–0–33–1; Francis 3–0–34–1; Dutch 2–0–48–0; Burns 0.3–0–9–0.

Umpires: B. Leadbeater and N. A. Mallender.

At Edinburgh, May 19. **No result.** Toss: Scotland. **Middlesex 88-4** (20.2 overs) **v Scotland.** *Scotland 2 pts, Middlesex 2 pts.*

The Scots, who had to fancy their chances of chasing 115 in 20 overs after the Somerset game, were deeply disappointed by Middlesex's reluctance to continue after two showers; the umpires cited a damp run-up. Scotland remained unbeaten, and rose to second place in the second-division table.

At Edinburgh, May 20. **Derbyshire won by six wickets** (D/L method). Toss: Derbyshire. **Scotland 206** (44 overs) (D. R. Lockhart 37, J. C. Kent 85, C. J. O. Smith 33; D. R. Hewson 4-25); **Derbyshire 139-4** (22.2 overs) (A. I. Gait 37, Shahid Afridi 35; C. M. Wright 3-25). *Derbyshire 4 pts.*

Scotland lost for the first time in their fourth League game. Kent scored a run-a-ball half-century and added 108 with Lockhart, but Hewson tore the heart out of their batting, and Shahid Afridi slogged 35 in 19 balls, depositing one six in a large rubbish bin five yards behind the boundary. Rain revised Derbyshire's target to a comfortable 139 in 27 overs; they usurped Scotland in second place.

At Edinburgh, June 1. **Hampshire won by six wickets.** Toss: Hampshire. **Scotland 201-8** (45 overs) (J. G. Williamson 37, J. C. Kent 57; Wasim Akram 3-32, S. D. Udal 3-43); **Hampshire 202-4** (43 overs) (D. A. Kenway 51, R. A. Smith 82*). *Hampshire 4 pts.*

Scotland debut: R. Dravid.

Watched by Sky TV cameras and Scotland's new patron, Ian Botham, Dravid found himself batting in the first over and managed 25 in his first competitive innings since the World Cup final. Robin Smith, dropped on 39, guided his side home with a run-a-ball 82 which took him past 7,000 League runs and Hampshire into third place – two points behind Scotland.

At Edinburgh, July 6. **Nottinghamshire won by four wickets.** Toss: Scotland. **Scotland 222-7** (45 overs) (R. Dravid 129*, C. J. O. Smith 44; R. J. Logan 4-32); **Nottinghamshire 224-6** (42.1 overs) (P. J. Franks 55, C. L. Cairns 65*, G. D. Clough 37*; C. M. Wright 3-31). *Nottinghamshire 4 pts.*

Dravid scored his second regal, unbeaten hundred in three innings, building Scotland's recovery from nine for three with the help of a 136-run stand with Smith. He distributed 14 fours and four sixes to all points of the compass; spinners MacGill and Pietersen went for 72 in nine overs. Cairns, dropped on 23, calmly dashed Scottish hopes with a 56-ball 65.

At Edinburgh, July 7. **Durham won by 114 runs.** Toss: Durham. **Durham 267-7** (45 overs) (N. Peng 46, V. J. Wells 41, G. J. Muchall 87, G. J. Pratt 37; J. C. Kent 3-38); **Scotland 153** (36 overs) (C. M. Wright 43, R. M. Haq 55*; Shoaib Akhtar 4-34, N. C. Phillips 3-41). *Durham 4 pts.*

Durham claimed convincing revenge for their May defeat. Muchall scored a one-day best 87, though Kent picked up his best return of 2003. Shoaib Akhtar blew four Scots away and when Killeen nipped one back to bowl Dravid they were six for five, then 32 for seven. Wright and Haq – the division's leading wicket-takers with 14 each – added 90 in 18 overs to avoid humiliation.

At Edinburgh, July 9. **Lancashire won by ten wickets** (D/L method). Toss: Scotland. **Scotland 168-7** (39 overs) (C. M. Wright 46*; J. Wood 4-22); **Lancashire 170-0** (29 overs) (M. B. Loye 88*, M. J. Chilton 69*). *Lancashire 4 pts.*

Lancashire's target revised to 170 in 39 overs.

Lancashire's fifth successive win since losing to Scotland at Old Trafford took them to the top of the second division. It was Scotland's sixth successive League defeat, and third in four days at Raeburn Place. They were 57 for five, though Wright battled to respectability. Loye and Chilton survived some confident lbw shouts in the Lancashire innings, scoring nearly six an over to win with ten overs in hand.

At Edinburgh, August 26. **Northamptonshire won by eight wickets.** Toss: Northamptonshire. **Scotland 119** (40.2 overs) (C. M. Wright 31; A. Nel 3-20); **Northamptonshire 123-2** (21.5 overs) (M. E. K. Hussey 36, P. A. Jaques 49*). *Northamptonshire 4 pts.*

Scotland debut: S. T. Knox.

Third-placed Northamptonshire boosted their promotion hopes, while Scotland remained ninth. Ex-Cumberland opener Steven Knox lasted only six balls against South African pace bowler Nel, and Scotland barely survived 40 overs; Northamptonshire needed only 22 overs to win. Jaques's unbeaten 49 was the match's highest score.

At Edinburgh, August 28. **Sussex won by one wicket** (D/L method). Toss: Sussex. **Scotland 191-9** (39 overs) (R. R. Watson 48, C. J. O. Smith 38; P. M. Hutchison 4-29, C. D. Hopkinson 3-19); **Sussex 173-9** (31 overs) (C. D. Hopkinson 67*; C. M. Wright 3-28). *Sussex 4 pts.*

Sussex's target revised to 170 in 31 overs.

Two career-bests from 21-year-old Carl Hopkinson helped bottom-placed Sussex to a last-ball victory over Scotland, one place higher, in a match of 39 overs a side. First, Hopkinson took three wickets, ending a useful stand by Watson, who lifted a six on to the press tent, and Smith. Sussex slumped to 69 for six before Hopkinson staged the recovery with 67 not out from 48 balls. With two needed off the last over, Watson bowled Hutchison, last man Taylor ran one off the penultimate delivery, and Hopkinson hit the winning boundary to end a run of six League defeats.

SOMERSET

At Taunton, April 27. **Durham won by seven wickets** (D/L method). Toss: Durham. **Somerset 233-9** (45 overs) (M. E. Trescothick 74, K. A. Parsons 35, K. P. Dutch 39; D. Pretorius 4-31); **Durham 215-3** (32.4 overs) (N. Peng 92, G. J. Pratt 101*). *Durham 4 pts.*

First-team debuts: D. Pretorius; G. M. Andrew (Somerset).

Durham's target revised to 215 in 40 overs.

Trescothick made a handsome 86-ball 74, but was overshadowed by two of Durham's young prospects, Peng and Pratt, who together put on 164 for the third wicket. Peng scored a run-a-ball 92, Pratt reached his first hundred for Durham from just 79 deliveries, equalling the Durham record for the fastest one-day hundred, set by Dean Jones, in their first-ever League match, against Lancashire in 1992.

At Taunton, May 18. **Somerset won by 49 runs** (D/L method). Toss: Nottinghamshire. **Somerset 293-4** (35 overs) (J. Cox 110, C. M. Gazzard 58, J. D. C. Bryant 56*); **Nottinghamshire 265** (33 overs) (J. E. R. Gallian 69, U. Afzaal 105; S. R. G. Francis 3-50, G. M. Andrew 3-56). *Somerset 4 pts.*

Nottinghamshire's target revised to 315 in 35 overs.

Somerset's huge total was the more daunting since it came from just 35 overs after rain had twice disrupted their innings. Cox and Gazzard began with 131 from 16 overs, and Cox hared to his hundred from just 81 balls. Nottinghamshire's revised target asked them to score at nine an over, and at 201 for two after 23, they were on course. But then the wickets fell – including Afzaal for a 71-ball 105 – and the innings became one of heroic failure. Eleven of the 12 bowlers used in this match conceded seven or more an over; the exception was Parsons (5–0–28–1).

At Bath, June 8. **Northamptonshire won by seven wickets** (D/L method). Toss: Somerset. **Somerset 143** (32.3 overs) (K. A. Parsons 32, K. P. Dutch 50; M. J. Cawdron 4-31); **Northamptonshire 131-3** (27.3 overs) (M. E. K. Hussey 54, D. J. Sales 33*). *Northamptonshire 4 pts.*

Northamptonshire's target revised to 131 in 35 overs.

The Somerset innings was interrupted by a thunderstorm after four wickets from Cawdron had helped reduce them to 35 for five. Parsons and Dutch then rallied Somerset with a sixth-wicket stand of 71, but they could not bat out their 35 overs. It was all rather easy for Northamptonshire when they batted, though Blackwell – who had figures of 7–3–14–2 – caused a problem or two. Kevin Shine, the Somerset coach, called their one-day performances "embarrassing"; Northamptonshire's fifth win (plus one no-result) took them to the head of the division.

At Taunton, June 15. **Somerset won by one wicket.** Toss: Scotland. **Scotland 296-4** (45 overs) (D. R. Lockhart 30, R. R. Watson 75, R. Dravid 120*, J. C. Kent 48; S. R. G. Francis 3-53); **Somerset 299-9** (44.1 overs) (C. M. Gazzard 81, J. Cox 82, K. P. Dutch 32, M. Burns 34*; J. E. Brinkley 3-50, R. M. Haq 3-39). *Somerset 4 pts.*

Somerset almost fell to a second League defeat to Scotland in five weeks, but on this gorgeous pitch, last man Francis – who had taken three of the four Scotland wickets – hit the first ball of the last over for four. Earlier, Dravid made an impeccable unbeaten hundred that guided Scotland to their highest League score. It seemed nothing like enough while Gazzard and Cox were compiling a second-wicket stand of 160, but Haq and Brinkley hauled Scotland back into the match.

At Taunton, July 6. **Sussex won by 90 runs.** Toss: Sussex. **Sussex 286-5** (45 overs) (M. W. Goodwin 123, P. A. Cottey 41, C. J. Adams 69*); **Somerset 196** (38.3 overs) (K. P. Dutch 32, K. A. Parsons 74; R. J. Kirtley 3-33). *Sussex 4 pts.*

Michael Parsons, an 18-year-old from Taunton, removed Prior with the first ball of the match, his first wicket in senior cricket. But Goodwin shared hundred stands with Cottey and Adams, and hit his first century of the season in any cricket – he would manage another seven after this – as Sussex reached their highest League total for four years. At 45 for four inside ten overs, Somerset were out of the hunt, though Keith Parsons saved face with a resolute 74. Somerset replaced Sussex at the foot of the table.

At Taunton, August 5. **Somerset won by 67 runs.** Toss: Somerset. **Somerset 283-8** (45 overs) (J. Cox 130, K. A. Parsons 38, W. J. Durston 30; T. F. Bloomfield 4-58); **Middlesex 216** (39.1 overs) (R. M. S. Weston 34, O. A. Shah 31, E. C. Joyce 59, J. W. M. Dalrymple 38; I. D. Blackwell 3-48). *Somerset 4 pts.*

Cox made his highest one-day score, from 120 balls, and steered Somerset to a useful total on another glorious Taunton pitch. He gained encouraging support from Hildreth (27 runs) and Durston, two of the younger members of the Somerset squad. Bloomfield was the pick of a modest Middlesex attack. Joyce and Dalrymple scored briskly to keep the Middlesex innings on course, but when they fell in quick succession, the late batting folded.

At Taunton, August 10. **Hampshire won by 116 runs.** Toss: Hampshire. **Hampshire 335-6** (45 overs) (S. M. Katich 106, D. A. Kenway 35, J. P. Crawley 92, J. D. Francis 50; N. A. M. McLean 3-51); **Somerset 219** (36.1 overs) (K. P. Dutch 36, I. D. Blackwell 43, K. A. Parsons 46; S. D. Udal 3-36). *Hampshire 4 pts.*

Fine attacking batting from Katich (88 balls) and Crawley (64) saw Hampshire to 329 for six, already their highest League total before gaining an extra six penalty runs because of Somerset's slow over-rate. Needing around seven and a half an over, Somerset lost both openers almost immediately, and although the middle order threw the bat, there was never any prospect of keeping up with the rate.

At Taunton, September 1 (day/night). **Lancashire won by 24 runs.** Toss: Somerset. **Lancashire 310-7** (45 overs) (M. J. Chilton 103, S. G. Law 51, C. L. Hooper 82, C. P. Schofield 38*; N. A. M. McLean 3-61); **Somerset 286** (42.5 overs) (K. A. Parsons 90, J. C. Hildreth 30, A. W. Laraman 33, Extras 31; G. Chapple 4-60). *Lancashire 4 pts.*

Lancashire had the best of the conditions after Burns surprisingly inserted them and, as Hampshire had in the last game at Taunton, made their highest League total. Hooper, dropped on 14, scored 82 from 78 balls and put on 155 in 23 overs with Chilton, who hit his first League hundred, in all facing 109 balls. Somerset's "fifth" bowler – a combination of Blackwell, Parsons, Burns and Dutch – had figures of 9–0–97–1. Despite plummeting to 87 for five, Somerset made a match of it, thanks to a fighting innings from Parsons. Lancashire returned to the top of the table.

At Taunton, September 14. **Derbyshire won by two wickets.** Toss: Somerset. **Somerset 243-9** (45 overs) (M. J. Wood 58, I. D. Blackwell 60, S. R. G. Francis 33*; D. G. Cork 3-44, N. R. C. Dumelow 3-26); **Derbyshire 249-8** (44.5 overs) (M. J. Di Venuto 113; R. L. Johnson 3-41). *Derbyshire 4 pts.*

On another billiard-table surface, Somerset should have made more: Wood, in his first League appearance of the season, and Blackwell added 90 for the fourth wicket, but Somerset depended on big-hitting from the tail to lift them from 181 for eight. Derbyshire, at 190 for two, seemed home and dry, but they lost five wickets for 20 – and then six for 34 when Di Venuto fell to his 117th ball.

SUSSEX

At Hove, May 5. **Northamptonshire won by four wickets.** Toss: Sussex. **Sussex 217-3** (45 overs) (C. J. Adams 109*, R. S. C. Martin-Jenkins 68*); **Northamptonshire 221-6** (44.4 overs) (P. A. Jaques 68, J. W. Cook 49, G. L. Brophy 35*). *Northamptonshire 4 pts.*

On a slow, awkward pitch, Sussex subsided to 34 for three before Adams crafted a classy century from 116 balls, sharing an unbeaten stand of 183 in 30 overs with Martin-Jenkins. Two of Adams's four sixes came off Nel, with whom he exchanged heated words. Jaques then hit his third sixty in three League outings, and with useful contributions from the middle order, Northamptonshire maintained their 100% record. The 3,000 or so spectators were admitted free.

At Horsham, May 25. **Nottinghamshire won by 97 runs** (D/L method). Toss: Sussex. **Nottinghamshire 258-6** (40 overs) (U. Afzaal 83, K. P. Pietersen 39, C. L. Cairns 53*); **Sussex 150** (31.3 overs) (C. D. Hopkinson 31; G. D. Clough 4-32). *Nottinghamshire 4 pts.*

Reduced to 40 overs a side. Sussex's target later revised to 248 in 37 overs.

Two hours before play, Cairns stepped off a plane from Colombo. He reached the ground late, but in time to put the finishing touches to an impressive batting performance that included an elegant 83 from Afzaal. Cairns hit a massive six into the River Arun, reputedly the first batsman to do so since Viv Richards. Three rain delays reduced Sussex's target slightly, but they could not handle the medium-pace of Clough, who ended with career-best figures.

At Arundel, July 13. **Derbyshire won by six wickets.** Toss: Sussex. **Sussex 232-6** (45 overs) (M. W. Goodwin 129*; D. R. Hewson 4-40); **Derbyshire 235-4** (41.4 overs) (C. W. G. Bassano 126*, M. Kaif 44, D. R. Hewson 34). *Derbyshire 4 pts.*

Bassano shrugged off dire Championship form to stroke his highest one-day score – an unbeaten 126 off 129 balls. He and Kaif added 126 on a slow pitch as Derbyshire made light of what had seemed a reasonable Sussex total. Goodwin batted from start to finish in the Sussex innings, hitting 18 of his 130 balls for four, but no one else could reach 25. Hewson's slowish medium-pace proved the most destructive.

At Hove, July 22 (day/night). **Sussex won by eight runs.** Toss: Sussex. **Sussex 169-9** (45 overs) (M. J. G. Davis 30); **Durham 161** (44 overs) (G. J. Muchall 58, P. Mustard 32; P. M. Hutchison 3-30, B. V. Taylor 3-26). *Sussex 4 pts.*

Another cussedly slow pitch brought about a tense, low-scoring game. Sussex might not have recovered from 125 for eight if injury had not prevented Shoaib Akhtar from bowling his last three overs, though when the Durham reply staggered to 26 for five, that seemed irrelevant. But Muchall, showing great maturity, oversaw Durham's own recovery, battling 112 balls before being run out by a direct hit for 58.

At Hove, August 3. **Scotland won by six wickets.** Toss: Sussex. **Sussex 270-4** (45 overs) (M. W. Goodwin 106, C. J. Adams 95*; P. J. C. Hoffmann 3-40); **Scotland 272-4** (43.3 overs) (R. R. Watson 43, R. Dravid 69, J. C. Kent 115*; R. S. C. Martin-Jenkins 3-43). *Scotland 4 pts.*

Scotland halted a run of six successive League defeats and sent Sussex to the bottom of the table when they won with nine balls to spare. A third League hundred in four innings by Goodwin, backed up by some hard hitting from Adams, propelled Sussex to 270. When Scotland lost three wickets at 57, the contest seemed over, but their overseas players, Dravid and Kent – who compiled an unbeaten 115 from 113 balls – put on 167 in 29 overs.

At Hove, August 5 (day/night). **Hampshire won by 62 runs** (D/L method). Toss: Hampshire. **Hampshire 250-6** (45 overs) (J. R. C. Hamblin 53, S. M. Katich 57, J. P. Crawley 55, J. D. Francis 38); **Sussex 181** (35.3 overs) (M. H. Yardy 36, M. J. G. Davis 37; A. D. Mascarenhas 4-24, J. T. A. Bruce 3-45). *Hampshire 4 pts.*

Sussex's target revised to 244 in 41 overs.

On one of the hottest days of the year, Duckworth/Lewis recalculations were required after four of the eight floodlights failed for around 20 minutes during the Sussex reply. The delay made their task all the more difficult, but since they were 28 for four, it was already almost impossible. Mascarenhas, the highest League wicket-taker, had grabbed three, and ended with four for the fourth time in the League season. Earlier, three separate fifties guided Hampshire to an imposing score; their eighth win in nine games left them two points behind the leaders, Lancashire.

At Hove, August 13 (day/night). **Lancashire won by seven wickets.** Toss: Sussex. **Sussex 112** (32.1 overs) (R. S. C. Martin-Jenkins 36; P. J. Martin 3-31, K. W. Hogg 4-24); **Lancashire 113-3** (26.5 overs) (M. B. Loye 58). *Lancashire 4 pts.*

Clammy conditions helped Lancashire's seamers, but so did the misguided shots of the Sussex batsmen on a largely guileless pitch. Hogg was the pick of the bowlers, though Wood also returned figures of 9–3–19–2. Loye then batted imperiously for his fifth fifty in eight League innings as Lancashire returned to the top of the table. The match was over at 8.40, before the floodlights had taken full effect.

At Hove, September 3 (day/night). **Sussex won by eight wickets.** Toss: Middlesex. **Middlesex 248-6** (45 overs) (P. N. Weekes 91, O. A. Shah 33, E. C. Joyce 40; R. S. C. Martin-Jenkins 4-46); **Sussex 249-2** (43.2 overs) (M. W. Goodwin 118*, C. J. Adams 115*). *Sussex 4 pts.*

Middlesex, in need of a win to maintain their promotion push, set a challenging target – especially under lights – thanks to a well-paced innings from Weekes. However, Martin-Jenkins bowled tightly at the death, took his best League figures and helped restrict Middlesex to 68 off the last ten overs. Sussex lost two early wickets to Keegan before Goodwin, who pulled handsomely on his way to his fourth League hundred of the summer, and Adams joined forces. Together they set a competition-record third-wicket stand of 228, beating the 223 set by Graham Rose and Jimmy Cook for Somerset against Glamorgan in 1990.

At Hove, September 21. **Somerset won by 191 runs.** Toss: Somerset. **Somerset 377-9** (45 overs) (M. Burns 91, K. P. Dutch 44, K. A. Parsons 40, I. D. Blackwell 111; B. V. Taylor 3-56); **Sussex 186** (30.2 overs) (M. H. Yardy 32*; I. D. Blackwell 3-57, K. P. Dutch 4-34). *Somerset 4 pts.*

Sussex played as if hung over from celebrating their first Championship. Blackwell, whose late-season form had been astounding, had no complaints, blitzing 111 from just 56 balls. His second fifty came from 18, and in all he lashed 13 fours and five sixes to speed up a scoring-rate already healthy from Burns's 81-ball 91. Sussex contributed six penalty runs for a slow over-rate to Somerset's 377, the highest total in the League, beating 375 for four by Surrey against Yorkshire in 1994. Sussex never looked like getting close. Blackwell and Dutch rounded off the game with seven wickets between them.

NATIONAL LEAGUE RECORDS

40 overs available in all games up to 1998, except for 1993, when teams played 50 overs; 45 overs 1999–2003.

Batting

Highest individual scores: 203, A. D. Brown, Surrey v Hampshire, Guildford, 1997; 191, D. S. Lehmann, Yorkshire v Nottinghamshire, Scarborough, 2001; 176, G. A. Gooch, Essex v Glamorgan, Southend, 1983; 175*, I. T. Botham, Somerset v Northamptonshire, Wellingborough School, 1986.

Most runs: K. J. Barnett 9,002; G. A. Gooch 8,573; G. A. Hick 8,420; C. W. J. Athey 7,526; W. Larkins 7,499; M. P. Maynard 7,415; P. Johnson 7,225; D. W. Randall 7,062; R. A. Smith 7,050; D. L. Amiss 7,048; R. J. Bailey 7,031. **In a season:** T. M. Moody 917 for Worcestershire, 1991.

Most hundreds: W. Larkins 14; G. A. Hick 13; A. D. Brown and G. A. Gooch 12; C. J. Adams and C. G. Greenidge 11; T. M. Moody and R. A. Smith 10. 743 hundreds have been scored in the League. The most in one season is 59 in 2003.

Most sixes in an innings: I. T. Botham, 13, Somerset v Northamptonshire, Wellingborough School, 1986. **By a team in an innings:** 18, Derbyshire v Worcestershire, Knypersley, 1985, and Surrey v Yorkshire, Scarborough, 1994. **In a season:** I. V. A. Richards, 26, Somerset, 1977.

Highest total: 377-9, Somerset v Sussex, Hove, 2003 (45-overs match). **By a side batting second:** 317-6, Surrey v Nottinghamshire, The Oval, 1993 (50-overs match).

Highest match aggregate: 642-14, Middlesex (337-5) v Somerset (305-9), Southgate, 2003 (45-overs match).

Lowest total: 23 (19.4 overs), Middlesex v Yorkshire, Leeds, 1974.

Shortest completed innings: 16 overs (59), Northamptonshire v Middlesex, Tring, 1974.

Record partnerships for each wicket

239	for 1st	G. A. Gooch and B. R. Hardie, Essex v Nottinghamshire at Nottingham . .	1985
273	for 2nd	G. A. Gooch and K. S. McEwan, Essex v Nottinghamshire at Nottingham .	1983
228*	for 3rd	M. W. Goodwin and C. J. Adams, Sussex v Middlesex at Hove	2003
219	for 4th	C. G. Greenidge and C. L. Smith, Hampshire v Surrey at Southampton . .	1987

220* for 5th	C. C. Lewis and P. A. Nixon, Leicestershire v Kent at Canterbury	1999
167* for 6th	C. L. Cairns and C. M. W. Read, Notts v Sussex at Nottingham	2003
164 for 7th	J. N. Snape and M. A. Hardinges, Gloucestershire v Notts at Nottingham	2001
116* for 8th	N. D. Burns and P. A. J. DeFreitas, Leicestershire v Northants at Leicester	2001
105 for 9th	D. G. Moir and R. W. Taylor, Derbyshire v Kent at Derby	1984
82 for 10th	G. Chapple and P. J. Martin, Lancashire v Worcestershire at Manchester	1996

Bowling

Most wickets: J. K. Lever 386; J. E. Emburey 368; D. L. Underwood 346; J. Simmons 307; S. Turner 303; N. Gifford 284; E. E. Hemmings 281; R. K. Illingworth 273; J. N. Shepherd 267; G. C. Small 261; A. C. S. Pigott 260; I. T. Botham 256; M. V. Fleming 250. **In a season:** A. J. Hollioake, 39 for Surrey, 1996.

Best bowling: 8-26, K. D. Boyce, Essex v Lancashire, Manchester, 1971; 7-15, R. A. Hutton, Yorkshire v Worcestershire, Leeds, 1969; 7-16, S. D. Thomas, Glamorgan v Surrey, Swansea, 1998; 7-30, M. P. Bicknell, Surrey v Glamorgan, The Oval, 1999; 7-39, A. Hodgson, Northamptonshire v Somerset, Northampton, 1976; 7-41, A. N. Jones, Sussex v Nottinghamshire, Nottingham, 1986.

Most economical analysis: 8–8–0–0, B. A. Langford, Somerset v Essex, Yeovil, 1969.

Most expensive analyses: 9–0–99–1, M. R. Strong, Northamptonshire v Gloucestershire, Cheltenham, 2001; 8–0–96–1, D. G. Cork, Derbyshire v Nottinghamshire, Nottingham, 1993; 8–0–94–2, P. N. Weekes, Middlesex v Leicestershire, Leicester, 1994; 9–0–91–1, M. J. Cawdron, Northamptonshire v Gloucestershire, Bristol, 2002.

Hat-tricks: There have been 32 hat-tricks, four of them for Glamorgan.

Four wickets in four balls: A. Ward, Derbyshire v Sussex, Derby, 1970; V. C. Drakes, Nottinghamshire v Derbyshire, Nottingham, 1999.

Wicket-keeping and Fielding

Most dismissals: S. J. Rhodes 395 (303 ct, 92 st); W. K. Hegg 297 (255 ct, 42 st); R. C. Russell 292 (232 ct, 60 st); R. J. Blakey 285 (239 ct, 46 st); D. L. Bairstow 257 (234 ct, 23 st). **In a season:** G. O. Jones 33 (27 ct, 6 st) for Kent, 2003.

Seven dismissals in an innings: (6 ct, 1 st), R. W. Taylor, Derbyshire v Lancashire, Manchester, 1975.

Six catches in an innings: K. Goodwin, Lancashire v Worcestershire, Worcester, 1969; R. W. Taylor, Derbyshire v Lancashire, Manchester, 1975; K. M. Krikken, Derbyshire v Hampshire, Southampton, 1994; P. A. Nixon, Leicestershire v Essex, Leicester, 1994; G. O. Jones, Kent v Leicestershire, Canterbury, 2003; K. J. Piper, Warwickshire v Leicestershire, Birmingham, 2003.

Four stumpings in an innings: S. J. Rhodes, Worcestershire v Warwickshire, Birmingham, 1986, N. D. Burns, Somerset v Kent, Taunton, 1991 and R. J. Turner, Somerset v Kent, Taunton, 2002.

Most catches by a fielder: K. J. Barnett 107; C. J. Adams 105; M. W. Alleyne† and V. P. Terry 103; J. F. Steele 101; G. A. Gooch 100. **In a season:** J. M. Rice, 16 for Hampshire, 1978.

† *M. W. Alleyne also took four catches as a wicket-keeper.*

Five catches in an innings: J. M. Rice, Hampshire v Warwickshire, Southampton, 1978.

Results

Largest victory in runs: Somerset by 220 runs v Glamorgan, Neath, 1990.

Victories by ten wickets (36): By Derbyshire, Durham, Essex (four times), Glamorgan (three times), Hampshire (twice), Kent, Lancashire (twice), Leicestershire (twice), Middlesex (twice), Northamptonshire, Nottinghamshire, Somerset (twice), Surrey (three times), Warwickshire (twice), Worcestershire (six times) and Yorkshire (three times).

This does not include those matches in which the side batting second was set a reduced target but does include matches where both sides faced a reduced number of overs.

Ties: There have been 59 tied matches. Essex and Worcestershire have both tied 11 times.

Shortest match: 1 hr 53 min (26.3 overs), Surrey v Leicestershire, The Oval, 1996.

WINNERS 1969–2003

John Player's County League

1969 Lancashire

John Player League

1970 Lancashire
1971 Worcestershire
1972 Kent
1973 Kent
1974 Leicestershire
1975 Hampshire
1976 Kent
1977 Leicestershire
1978 Hampshire
1979 Somerset
1980 Warwickshire
1981 Essex
1982 Sussex
1983 Yorkshire

John Player Special League

1984 Essex
1985 Essex
1986 Hampshire

Refuge Assurance League

1987 Worcestershire
1988 Worcestershire
1989 Lancashire
1990 Derbyshire
1991 Nottinghamshire

Sunday League

1992 Middlesex

AXA Equity & Law League

1993 Glamorgan
1994 Warwickshire
1995 Kent
1996 Surrey

AXA Life League

1997 Warwickshire

AXA League

1998 Lancashire

CGU National League

1999 Lancashire

Norwich Union National League

2000 Gloucestershire

Norwich Union League

2001 Kent
2002 Glamorgan

National League

2003 Surrey

MATCH RESULTS 1969–2003

	Matches					*League positions*		
	P	*W*	*L*	*T*	*NR*	*1st*	*2nd*	*3rd*
Derbyshire	569	230	277	5	57	1	0	1
Durham	201	62	115	3	21	0	0	0
Essex	567	285	226	11	45	3	5*	5
Glamorgan	567	219	284	8	56	2	0	0
Gloucestershire	567	212	285	4	66	1	2	1
Hampshire	569	267	250	7	45	3	1	3
Kent	567	304	202	9	52	5	4	5
Lancashire	569	294	201	10	64	5	2	3
Leicestershire	567	249	247	5	66	2	3*	2
Middlesex	569	247	252	10	60	1	1	3
Northamptonshire	569	230	276	6	57	0	0	2
Nottinghamshire	569	242	273	4	50	1	3	1
Somerset	569	265	247	4	53	1	6*	0
Surrey	567	259	245	5	58	2	0	1
Sussex	569	240	265	6	58	1	2*	1
Warwickshire	567	252	250	7	58	3	2	3
Worcestershire	567	277	226	11	53	3	5	2
Yorkshire	567	255	259	3	50	1	2	1
Scotland	18	4	13	0	1	0	0	0

* *Includes one shared 2nd place in 1976.*

TWENTY20 CUP, 2003

HUGH CHEVALLIER

Azhar Mahmood

At 9.30 p.m. precisely on Saturday July 19, the longest day of cricket anyone could remember ended, almost 11 hours after it began. It was a paradoxical conclusion for a competition whose very *raison d'être* was to be over quickly. In fact, finals day of the Twenty20 Cup – with the first semi beginning at 10.45 a.m. and the winner not due to be decided till 10 p.m. – was far from the star turn of the venture. Even so, the 15,000 who spent the day in the Nottingham sunshine seemed to go home satisfied. Such was the popularity of what the ECB termed short-form cricket that its rationale could be turned on its head and it would still work.

Attendances were the key. In 1998, the ECB, concerned at dwindling gates for county matches, had mooted a reduced form of cricket. The First-Class Forum – the game's powerbase, comprising the 18 first-class counties and MCC – had not taken to the idea, and it was shelved. By 2001, though, attendances were still falling, concern had become alarm, and the scheme was resurrected. And this time, it was backed by substantial investment in market research.

More than 30 focus groups later, the ECB knew a great deal more about why the public were spurning county cricket: they did not know how, when or even where to watch the game; and they thought the grounds were intimidating, like private members' clubs that met only when most people were at work or school. A programme of 4,000 15-minute, face-to-face interviews revealed that about two-thirds of the population either hated or had zero interest in cricket. Prominent among the rejectors were children, young people aged 16–34, women, ethnic minorities and lower social strata. But when these rejectors were offered a game that went like the clappers, was wrapped up in well under three hours on a weekday evening and included some intriguing innovations, around half flocked to join the middle-aged, middle-class white males in the tolerators' camp. Faced with these findings, the First-Class Forum voted in April 2002 by 11–7 (with MCC abstaining) in favour of short-form cricket. The great experiment had begun.

Not that there was carte blanche to redefine how the game was played. As Stuart Robertson, marketing manager at the ECB during the genesis of the project, put it: "The Twenty20 is not an end in itself, but a means to an end. The hope is that a 20-over game after work or school will be the first rung on a cricket-watching ladder that has a Championship game at its top." And so some of the more creative ideas were discarded. (At one stage, there were *It's A Knockout*-style plans for captains to play a joker – a "golden over" in which all runs counted double.)

Alternative attraction: Jenny Frost of Atomic Kitten, the warm-up act before the final at Trent Bridge.
Picture by Nigel Davies.

There was no watering down of the format's philosophy of speed, though: limit each side to 20 overs, allow just 15 minutes between innings, give the incoming batsman a maximum of 90 seconds to reach the crease after the fall of a wicket, and come down like a ton of bricks on a slow over-rate. Critics had long accused cricket of being far too slow a game, but here was a version that fizzed like a Shoaib Akhtar yorker – very, very fast, but would it be well directed? Would the ECB show a decent return on their research budget of £200,000?

They wisely stacked the odds in their favour by spending another £250,000 on marketing. The contrast with the Twenty20's near-invisible predecessor, sponsored by the tobacco pariah, Benson and Hedges (who, towards the end, were legally barred from poking their head above the parapet), could hardly have been greater. Shoppers at Sainsbury's were encouraged to redeem their loyalty vouchers for tickets, and countless newspaper adverts pushed the tournament hard. For all the hype, though, the ECB had failed to find a name sponsor for the competition, and there were plenty who would delight in the brash, profligate new kid on the block coming an embarrassing cropper.

So it was a brave move to launch the tournament on Friday 13th. Brave – or foolhardy – to trust the British weather, too; there were provisions for Duckworth/Lewis to step in, though even a short weather delay could scupper a game already pared to the bone, timewise. But in glorious midsummer sunshine, the Twenty20 made a faultless debut. Everything went right, and the wails of the Jeremiahs were soon drowned by the appreciative roar of the hordes, who couldn't seem to get enough.

TWENTY20: HOW THE PLAYERS SAW IT

SIMON BRIGGS

There was a revealing moment in Surrey's first Twenty20 Cup match when Azhar Mahmood, fielding at the third-man boundary, started waving at new-ball bowler Phil Sampson and miming a back-foot defensive shot.

Azhar's sign-language highlighted the urgency of this ultra-speed contest. End-of-over pow-wows suddenly looked outmoded: even if there had been time for them in a 75-minute innings, the key to Twenty20 success was to react *at once*, not in a few balls time.

In this case, Azhar was urging Sampson to bowl a few lifters at his fellow Pakistani, Abdul Razzaq of Middlesex. Sampson had been getting the treatment from Razzaq, who is among the best in the world at what the professionals call "clearing the leg", when the batsman steps away to mid-wicket with his front foot, opening up the body for a baseball-style swing.

Casting his mind back to that first game, Middlesex captain Andrew Strauss said: "I was surprised how quickly everything happened, and how important it was to think on our feet. As the tournament went on, we started chopping and changing the bowling, using one-over spells to break up the batsman's rhythm, and constantly moving the fielders to try to stem the tide.

"But what we didn't do was jig the batting order around too much. In the first six overs, there were fielding restrictions that created gaps for orthodox strokeplayers. Then, as the ball got softer, it was useful to have your hitters coming in down the order."

Nick Knight of Warwickshire said he went into his first match with little idea how to approach it. "We batted first at Taunton and I blocked the first four balls. Then I thought, 'I can't be doing this,' so I slogged the next ball for six and the one after for four. I could easily have been out on either shot. We soon realised that 20 overs is quite a long time – and you can play proper cricket.

"When we bowled, we would start off with two slips, and try to hit the top of off stump. You don't want to get too smart early on: if you try a yorker it might end up as a half-volley that goes crashing to the boundary. It was only when the batting side got on top of the situation that we'd start changing plans and mucking about. As a batter I know that when you're in, there's nothing better than facing someone who keeps serving up length – you just smack it out of the park."

According to Worcestershire off-spinner Gareth Batty: "Spin was the surprise package in the tournament. People thought the spinners would get walloped, but game after game they were able to frustrate the batter.

"I got wickets just bowling length when someone decided to have a hack, but I also had the option to go underneath him. It's very difficult to hit a spinner out of the blockhole because there's no pace on the ball."

Even so, Batty's view is that the shorter the game gets, the more it favours the batsman. "The key is to work out your method. Even if you're facing Ian Harvey, who is probably the best in the business, you know what he's going to bowl: either a length ball, aimed at the top of off, or a yorker or slower ball."

Initially, there was some doubt about quite what it was that the crowds couldn't get enough of. "The acid test," wrote Mike Selvey in *The Guardian*, "will come when the cricket rather than the peripheral attractions are perceived to be the main event." He had a point. In the ECB's understandable desire to make sure things started with a bang, the cricket was in danger of being forgotten. Jacuzzis, fairground rides, bouncy castles, face-painting, barbecue zones, boy bands, girl bands – you name it, it was there as a sideshow. Rather more in your face were the banks of loudspeakers blaring out frequent musical snatches – "I don't like cricket, I love it!" from 10cc (remixed for our times by the United Colours of Sound) greeted boundaries, while Queen's "Another one bites the dust" taunted dismissed batsmen as they sprinted for the dug-out.

The dug-out and loudspeakers were symbols of two important tenets of the Twenty20 concept. To demystify the game and to bring play closer to the paying public, batsmen rejoined their colleagues beside the boundary rather than retreat into the confines of a dark pavilion to do who knew what. For the glitzy opening match, between Hampshire and Sussex at Southampton and televised on Sky, the dug-out was a sophisticated affair, all smoked curving glass; for the next game at the Rose Bowl, this had become a couple of garden benches.

The players stuggled to make themselves heard over the din

The loudspeakers – to the relief of the fuddy-duddier members of the crowd – also diminished in size when the television cameras weren't there. For that first game, some were oddly pointing toward the square, and the players struggled to make themselves heard over the din. Snatches of song were a fundamental part of the Twenty20 package, which was designed to bring sport and music together, a move seemingly welcomed by many, especially the younger ticket-holders. But in a sign that Selvey did not have too much to worry about, Mis-teeq, a high-profile girl band hired to pep up the opening fixture at the Rose Bowl, saw more than half the substantial crowd filter out of the ground after the game – and before their set had begun.

All seemed to agree that, with or without Mis-teeq, they had been well entertained. The pace had indeed been fast and furious, the batting blistering, the fielding phenomenal, the bowling hittable (but occasionally devastating), the innovations lapped up by a crowd unusually representative of the population at large. Here were women, girls, teenagers, boys and, yes, a few regular cricket-goers, too. Reception from press and public alike was massively positive. Some children even admitted they found it more exciting than football, and nobody was in the mood to take issue. Surely something had to go wrong, but just as the sun seemed to shimmer all summer long, so the Twenty20 went from strength to strength.

At Edgbaston, advance ticket sales were so encouraging that Warwickshire rushed to lay on extra car park space. For the Roses clash at Old Trafford, an astonishing crowd of almost 15,000 turned out. No one could remember

Beats homework: starting Twenty20 matches at tea-time brought in younger spectators.

Picture by Patrick Eagar.

an occasion outside Lord's when so many had paid to see a county match. The comparison with the old B&H from the previous year was not entirely fair, but irresistible. By sensibly retaining the zonal groups, the ECB ensured that local derbies lived on, and in all 45 group games, the gates were up on 2002, often gigantically. Fifteen matches were sell-outs, and the total attendance mushroomed from under 67,000 for the B&H to around 240,000.

The 16th sell-out of the tournament was the finals day. In another break with tradition, this was not held at Lord's – ruled out because their application for a concert licence was turned down by Westminster Council – but at Trent Bridge. It certainly made sense for an occasion scheduled to last until ten at night to be located close to a motorway hub. The finals day was arguably the least pleasing part of the whole jamboree. Playing both semi-finals and the final on the same pitch meant scores became progressively lower, and having four sets of supporters ensured at least half the audience were always neutral. And there were endless hiatuses, despite two more bands – Atomic Kitten and United Colours of Sound – playing to a moderately enthusiastic crowd before the final began.

As luck would have it, the best game of the day – between the two strongest sides, Gloucestershire and Surrey – was a semi rather than the final. Still, it felt right that Surrey lifted the first Twenty20 Cup after defeating Warwickshire. They had the deepest resources and played the most ruthless cricket, though it was a shame that, in a contest designed to eliminate the drabness of a one-sided limited-overs game, that was how the final turned out. There was talk of abandoning the three-game format for 2004, but the ECB decided to stick with it, at least for one more year.

For both the finals and the group games, England's leading lights were elsewhere, either taking part in the NatWest Challenge against Pakistan, or enjoying enforced rest. More's the pity: Lancashire could have done with Andrew Flintoff, for whom this competition could have been made. The stars still shone, though, particularly those from the southern hemisphere. Time and again, the dominant figures, especially with the bat, were Australian. Ian Harvey hit the competition's only hundred, a feat made all the more astounding by the fact that Gloucestershire, habitually batting second after winning the toss, were chasing just 135 against Warwickshire. He took just 50 balls for his century, but would probably have been upstaged by Andrew Symonds had Kent been set a stiffer target by Hampshire. Symonds, who ended unbeaten on 96 from 37 balls, was thwarted by his colleagues scoring too quickly. Symonds didn't quite fire on all cylinders again, but his meteoric strike-rate of 226 per 100 balls was comfortably the best. Mike Hussey, from Northamptonshire, and Essex's Andy Flower never appeared to miss out, and Brad Hodge sneaked past 300 runs for the competition during Leicestershire's semi-final defeat by Warwickshire.

England-qualified players produced only one of the five heaviest scorers, Nick Knight, and won only 25 of the 48 match awards. Overseas players did not have things quite so much their own way in the bowling. Medium-pace was the order of the day, and those who took the pace off the ball often proved more penetrative than their fierier counterparts. Adam Hollioake, the Surrey captain, and Derbyshire's Dominic Hewson, with 16 and ten wickets respectively, were cases in point.

Surrey, in fact, had three of the four most successful bowlers in terms of wickets. Azhar Mahmood picked up a dozen (and hit 114 runs), while James Ormond demolished Warwickshire in the final. Jason Brown and Collins Obuya, from Northamptonshire and Warwickshire, showed that spinners could be a potent weapon by taking 21 wickets between them. But arguably as important was economy. Gloucestershire's Mike Smith averaged a fraction more than four an over; respectable enough in 50-over cricket but truly outstanding in Twenty20.

For that, he could in part thank the most agile fielding of all 18 counties. Following the example of Jonty Rhodes, Gloucestershire took standards of catching, stopping, diving and throwing to new heights. In fact, every team fielded with an athleticism and commitment unseen only a few years before – one of the thngs which made Twenty20 cricket so good to watch. Less obvious but just as remarkable was the trend for wicket-keepers to stand up to the stumps for all but the quickest bowlers.

Once the counties realised quite what a financial success they had on their hands, there was a huge temptation to increase the number of games. Some argued for two groups of nine, raising the preliminary games from 45 to 72, while others warned of killing the goose that laid the golden egg. The ECB sagely decided to leave largely alone, the two substantial changes being the introduction of quarter-finals and the removal of the whole competition into July. The first should reduce the number of dead matches in the later zonal rounds, the second should prevent Twenty20 from disappearing from

The Lions purr: Surrey destroyed Warwickshire in the inaugural final to land their fifth trophy in four years.

Picture by Patrick Eagar.

sight during the media frenzy expected to surround the Euro 2004 football championships. All that was needed now was major sponsorship. For contractural reasons, a name-sponsor was unlikely. But it was no secret that the ECB were hoping for what the marketing people call an FMCG (fast-moving consumer goods) brand to get involved. They have hoped this before. This time they might get lucky.

Prize money

£42,000 for winners: SURREY.
£21,000 for runners-up: WARWICKSHIRE.
£10,000 for losing semi-finalists: GLOUCESTERSHIRE, LEICESTERSHIRE.

The following awards were made at the end of the group stages. In each category, the leading player received £1,500; when a second player is listed, he received £1,000.

Most runs: M. E. K. Hussey (Northamptonshire) 279; A. Flower (Essex) 266.
Most sixes: M. J. Lumb (Yorkshire) 13.
Best strike-rate (minimum 48 balls faced): A. Symonds (Kent) 226.66.
Best all-rounder: G. J. Batty (Worcestershire); I. J. Harvey (Gloucestershire).
Best wicket-keeper: T. R. Ambrose (Sussex).
Most wickets: A. J. Hollioake (Surrey) 13; J. F. Brown (Northamptonshire) 11.
Best economy-rate (minimum 48 balls bowled): A. J. Hall (Worcestershire) 4.25; A. M. Smith (Gloucestershire) 4.30.

Note: Performances in the semi-finals and final had no bearing on these awards.

Match award winners received £1,000 in the final, £500 in the semi-finals and £200 in the group games.

FINAL GROUP TABLES

Midlands/Wales/West Group	*Played*	*Won*	*Lost*	*Points*	*Net run-rate*
GLOUCESTERSHIRE	5	5	0	10	2.18
WARWICKSHIRE*	5	4	1	8	1.07
Worcestershire	5	2	3	4	−0.45
Northamptonshire	5	2	3	4	−0.24
Somerset	5	1	4	2	−1.41
Glamorgan	5	1	4	2	−1.09

North Group	*Played*	*Won*	*Lost*	*Points*	*Net run-rate*
LEICESTERSHIRE	5	5	0	10	0.86
Yorkshire	5	3	2	6	0.45
Derbyshire	5	3	2	6	0.60
Lancashire	5	2	3	4	−0.12
Durham	5	1	4	2	−1.02
Nottinghamshire	5	1	4	2	−0.88

South Group	*Played*	*Won*	*Lost*	*Points*	*Net run-rate*
SURREY	5	5	0	10	1.06
Sussex	5	3	2	6	0.61
Kent	5	2	3	4	0.25
Middlesex	5	2	3	4	0.19
Essex	5	2	3	4	−0.81
Hampshire	5	1	4	2	−1.32

* *Warwickshire qualified as the most successful second-placed team.*

Where two or more counties finished with an equal number of points, the positions were decided by (a) most wins (b) most points in head-to-head matches (c) net run-rate (runs scored per over minus runs conceded per over) (d) most wickets taken per balls bowled in matches achieving a result.

MIDLANDS/WALES/WEST GROUP

At Taunton, June 13. **Warwickshire won by 19 runs.** Toss: Somerset. **Warwickshire 188-7** (20 overs) (T. L. Penney 52, C. O. Obuya 34*; W. J. Durston 3-31); **Somerset 169** (20 overs) (J. Cox 47, K. P. Dutch 70; G. G. Wagg 3-33, C. O. Obuya 3-16). *Warwickshire 2 pts.*

Man of the Match: G. G. Wagg. *Attendance:* 4,211.

Penney faced 28 balls for his 52.

At Worcester, June 13. **Worcestershire won by one wicket.** Toss: Northamptonshire. **Northamptonshire 150-9** (20 overs) (M. E. K. Hussey 67, P. A. Jaques 33; C. G. Liptrot 3-32); **Worcestershire 151-9** (19.4 overs) (D. K. Taylor 46, S. C. Moore 39*; R. S. G. Anderson 4-29). *Worcestershire 2 pts.*

First-team debuts: S. C. Moore, D. K. Taylor (Worcestershire).

Man of the Match: D. K. Taylor. *Attendance:* 4,005.

David Taylor, a 28-year-old club cricketer from High Wycombe, was recruited specifically for this competition: his 46 from 20 balls showed why. Worcestershire collapsed from 77 for one to 84 for six before Stephen Moore, an Exeter University student and one of only three Worcestershire batsmen to reach double figures, guided them home.

At Bristol, June 14. **Gloucestershire won by four wickets.** Toss: Gloucestershire. **Worcestershire 122** (19.5 overs) (A. J. Hall 46); **Gloucestershire 126-6** (19.1 overs) (J. N. Rhodes 42). *Gloucestershire 2 pts.*

Man of the Match: M. W. Alleyne. *Attendance:* 2,854.

Alleyne had figures of 4–1–25–1 (including a wicket maiden), held a catch, made a run-out and hit an unbeaten 19.

At Cardiff, June 16. **Northamptonshire won by 23 runs.** Toss: Northamptonshire. **Northamptonshire 159-5** (20 overs) (M. E. K. Hussey 79*, P. A. Jaques 31); **Glamorgan 136** (18.4 overs) (R. D. B. Croft 53). *Northamptonshire 2 pts.*

Man of the Match: M. E. K. Hussey. *Attendance:* 3,519.

Four Glamorgan batsmen were run out.

At Cardiff, June 18. **Somerset won by seven wickets.** Toss: Glamorgan. **Glamorgan 193-7** (20 overs) (M. P. Maynard 39, D. L. Hemp 49*); **Somerset 197-3** (18 overs) (J. Cox 53, K. P. Dutch 49*). *Somerset 2 pts.*

Man of the Match: J. Cox. *Attendance:* 1,640.

In persistent mizzle that hampered the bowlers, Glamorgan made the highest Twenty20 score so far, but were still comfortably beaten. Cox hit 11 fours and a six from 21 balls, and Somerset had reached 86 for two when he fell at the beginning of the sixth over. Kasprowicz conceded 54 runs from his three overs.

At Worcester, June 18. **Warwickshire won by 20 runs.** Toss: Warwickshire. **Warwickshire 175** (19.4 overs) (N. V. Knight 89; G. J. Batty 3-45); **Worcestershire 155-5** (20 overs) (Kadeer Ali 53, B. F. Smith 40*; N. M. Carter 3-19). *Warwickshire 2 pts.*

Man of the Match: N. V. Knight. *Attendance:* 4,591.

Knight hit nine fours and three sixes off 58 balls. Steve Rhodes made three stumpings in the Warwickshire innings, all off Batty.

At Bristol, June 19. **Gloucestershire won by five wickets.** Toss: Gloucestershire. **Northamptonshire 128-5** (20 overs) (M. E. K. Hussey 32; I. J. Harvey 3-28); **Gloucestershire 129-5** (19.3 overs) (I. J. Harvey 41). *Gloucestershire 2 pts.*

Man of the Match: I. J. Harvey. *Attendance:* 3,494.

In their reply, Gloucestershire stumbled from 60 without loss to 89 for five.

At Northampton, June 20. **Northamptonshire won by 15 runs.** Toss: Northamptonshire. **Northamptonshire 166-6** (20 overs) (M. E. K. Hussey 88); **Somerset 151** (20 overs) (C. M. Gazzard 39, M. Burns 33; M. J. Cawdron 3-24, J. F. Brown 5-27). *Northamptonshire 2 pts.*

Man of the Match: M. E. K. Hussey. *Attendance:* 5,123.

Somerset used eight bowlers in the Northamptonshire innings, but none could subdue Hussey: his 58-ball 88 took his Twenty20 record to 266 runs at a strike-rate of 123.72 and an average of 88.66.

At Birmingham, June 20. **Warwickshire won by 68 runs.** Toss: Warwickshire. **Warwickshire 181-9** (20 overs) (N. M. Carter 47, N. V. Knight 54; R. D. B. Croft 3-42); **Glamorgan 113** (16.2 overs) (M. P. Maynard 50; C. O. Obuya 5-24). *Warwickshire 2 pts.*

Man of the Match: C. O. Obuya. *Attendance:* 10,431.

Warwickshire's third successive win in the Twenty20 was Glamorgan's third straight defeat, leaving them as the only side without a win in the competition. Obuya, the Kenya leg-spinner, returned the best figures in the competition thus far.

At Taunton, June 21. **Gloucestershire won by ten wickets.** Toss: Gloucestershire. **Somerset 119-9** (20 overs); **Gloucestershire 120-0** (10.2 overs) (C. M. Spearman 43*, I. J. Harvey 75*). *Gloucestershire 2 pts.*

Man of the Match: I. J. Harvey. *Attendance:* 4,938.

Martyn Ball had figures of 4–0–11–1, the most economical four overs of the competition, before Spearman and Harvey, who crashed an unbeaten 75 from 34 balls, with ten fours and four sixes, produced the Twenty20's first hundred partnership. Gloucestershire now had three wins out of three.

At Cardiff, June 23. **Glamorgan won by 56 runs.** Toss: Glamorgan. **Glamorgan 170-4** (20 overs) (M. P. Maynard 72, M. J. Powell 66*); **Worcestershire 114** (19 overs) (S. C. Moore 34*; R. D. B. Croft 3-32). *Glamorgan 2 pts.*

First-team debut: R. E. Watkins (Glamorgan). County debut: S. J. Adshead (Worcestershire).

Man of the Match: M. P. Maynard. *Attendance:* 3,466.

A Glamorgan victory, at the fourth attempt, meant neither side could progress to the semi-finals.

At Birmingham, June 23. **Gloucestershire won by eight wickets.** Toss: Gloucestershire. **Warwickshire 134-7** (20 overs) (I. J. L. Trott 65*); **Gloucestershire 135-2** (13.1 overs) (I. J. Harvey 100*). *Gloucestershire 2 pts.*

Man of the Match: I. J. Harvey. *Attendance:* 6,861.

Both sides came into the game undefeated, but it was Gloucestershire who strolled through to the semi-finals with a clinical win. Trott became the first player to bat through all 20 overs, Jon Lewis equalled the record for the most niggardly four overs in the Twenty20 when he conceded just 11, but both were overshadowed by Harvey, who won his third match award in four starts. His hundred, the competition's first, came off 50 balls and contained 13 fours and four sixes; it constituted more than 74% of the Gloucestershire total.

At Bristol, June 24. **Gloucestershire won by 53 runs.** Toss: Gloucestershire. **Gloucestershire 221-7** (20 overs) (C. M. Spearman 88, C. G. Taylor 36, A. P. R. Gidman 36); **Glamorgan 168-7** (20 overs) (M. P. Maynard 69, M. S. Kasprowicz 31). *Gloucestershire 2 pts.*

Man of the Match: C. M. Spearman. *Attendance:* 5,292.

Mark Alleyne won his fifth consecutive toss, but for the first time chose to bat. Spearman crashed seven fours and seven sixes in a 39-ball 88 as Gloucestershire became the first side to pass 200 in the Twenty20. Maynard responded with similar ferocity – his 69 came from 36 balls – but had scant support.

At Northampton, June 24. **Warwickshire won by 54 runs.** Toss: Warwickshire. **Warwickshire 202-5** (20 overs) (N. V. Knight 69*, T. L. Penney 42, Extras 37); **Northamptonshire 148-7** (20 overs) (G. P. Swann 42*). *Warwickshire 2 pts.*

Man of the Match: N. V. Knight. *Attendance:* 4,986.

Victory ensured Warwickshire qualified for the semi-finals as best runners-up. Knight became the second player, after his colleague Trott, to bat through all 20 overs, and Warwickshire became the second side – just moments after Gloucestershire – to pass 200 in the Twenty20.

At Worcester, June 24. **Worcestershire won by 37 runs.** Toss: Somerset. **Worcestershire 161-5** (20 overs) (S. C. Moore 33, G. J. Batty 87); **Somerset 124** (18.2 overs) (W. J. Durston 34; M. Hayward 3-21). *Worcestershire 2 pts.*

Man of the Match: G. J. Batty. *Attendance:* 2,348.

Batty's 87 came from 48 balls, including six sixes and five fours. One of his sixes earned Kevin Kolb, a spectator and Droitwich Second XI player, £1,000 for making a clean catch beyond the boundary rope.

NORTH GROUP

At Chester-le-Street, June 13. **Durham won by six wickets.** Toss: Durham. **Nottinghamshire 157-7** (20 overs) (J. E. R. Gallian 62; V. J. Wells 3-39); **Durham 160-4** (19.1 overs) (N. Peng 49, A. M. Thorpe 35*). *Durham 2 pts.*

Man of the Match: J. E. R. Gallian. *Attendance:* 3,703.

Ian Hunter bowled the competition's first wicket maiden; his three other overs cost 21.

At Leeds, June 14. **Yorkshire won by 45 runs.** Toss: Derbyshire. **Yorkshire 186-5** (20 overs) (Yuvraj Singh 44, M. J. Lumb 42, R. J. Blakey 30*; M. J. Di Venuto 3-19); **Derbyshire 141** (18.1 overs) (M. J. Di Venuto 67). *Yorkshire 2 pts.*

County debut: S. P. Fleming (Yorkshire).

Man of the Match: M. J. Di Venuto. *Attendance:* 5,342.

Fleming, the New Zealand captain making his Yorkshire debut, was dismissed first ball.

At Leicester, June 16. **Leicestershire won by 16 runs.** Toss: Leicestershire. **Leicestershire 174-6** (20 overs) (B. J. Hodge 97, P. A. Nixon 43); **Yorkshire 158** (20 overs) (Yuvraj Singh 71; J. O. Grove 3-23, J. N. Snape 3-14, B. J. Hodge 3-6). *Leicestershire 2 pts.*

Man of the Match: B. J. Hodge. *Attendance:* 4,160.

Hodge missed out on the first hundred in the Twenty20 when he was lbw to the final ball of the innings. His 97 came from 61 balls, the last 47 from just 17. Two overs of off-spin from Andy Gray cost 40 as Leicestershire blitzed 74 from their last 30 balls. Yuvraj Singh responded in kind, hammering 71 off 37, but had little help. The off-spinners Snape and Hodge had combined figures of six for 20 from six overs.

At Nottingham, June 16. **Nottinghamshire won by seven wickets.** Toss: Nottinghamshire. **Lancashire 120** (19.2 overs) (W. K. Hegg 45; R. J. Logan 5-26); **Nottinghamshire 124-3** (19.1 overs) (K. P. Pietersen 58). *Nottinghamshire 2 pts.*

Man of the Match: R. J. Logan. *Attendance:* 4,388.

Logan matched the best figures in the competition, set by James Ormond for Surrey against Middlesex. Lancashire, who recovered from 42 for six, still recorded the lowest total so far. The game was advertised locally as a "Girls' Night Out", and posters featured four Nottinghamshire players stripped to the waist.

At Chester-le-Street, June 18. **Leicestershire won by 46 runs.** Toss: Durham. **Leicestershire**

THE SUFFERERS

Most expensive bowling analysis

4-0-58-0	G. Welch	Derbyshire v Yorkshire at Leeds.
4-0-56-0	B. J. Phillips	Northamptonshire v Warwickshire at Northampton.
3-0-54-0	M. S. Kasprowicz	Glamorgan v Someset at Cardiff.

Most runs conceded in an over

27	S. R. Patel	Nottinghamshire v Yorkshire at Leeds.
26	N. C. Phillips	Durham v Yorkshire at Leeds.
24	W. J. Durston	Somerset v Gloucestershire at Taunton.
24	M. S. Kasprowicz	Glamorgan v Somerset at Cardiff.

Most runs conceded in boundaries in the competition

114	S. A. Brant (Essex)	102	P. S. Jones (Somerset)
110	G. Welch (Derbyshire)	102	N. M. Carter (Warwickshire)
102	C. O. Obuya (Warwickshire)		

168-9 (20 overs) (B. J. Hodge 64); **Durham 122-9** (20 overs) (V. Sehwag 3-14). *Leicestershire 2 pts.*

Man of the Match: B. J. Hodge. *Attendance:* 3,275.

Hodge, playing against his former county, faced 44 balls.

At Derby, June 19. **Derbyshire won by nine wickets.** Toss: Nottinghamshire. **Nottinghamshire 94** (19.1 overs) (T. Lungley 4-13); **Derbyshire 95-1** (11.3 overs) (M. J. Di Venuto 35*). *Derbyshire 2 pts.*

Man of the Match: T. Lungley. *Attendance:* 3,595.

No Nottinghamshire batsman passed 17 as they became the first side to fail to make three figures in the competition. However, the pitch was marked as "poor" by the umpires, and an ECB Pitch Panel later ruled that any further transgression by Derbyshire in a one-day game within a year would result in a points penalty.

At Manchester, June 19. **Lancashire won by seven wickets.** Toss: Yorkshire. **Yorkshire 102-8** (20 overs) (R. J. Blakey 32; P. J. Martin 3-20); **Lancashire 104-3** (13.1 overs) (M. B. Loye 45). *Lancashire 2 pts.*

Man of the Match: M. B. Loye. *Attendance:* 14,862.

A huge crowd watched what two-division cricket had left as the only Roses Match of the season. Dismissal to the first legitimate ball of the match meant Stephen Fleming had faced only four balls in his first three innings for Yorkshire, who were soon two for three. When Gavin Hamilton was out for a second successive golden duck, Yorkshire were 28 for five. None of the Lancashire bowlers conceded as much as a run a ball; all bar Gray did for Yorkshire.

At Leicester, June 20. **Leicestershire won by 22 runs.** Toss: Leicestershire. **Leicestershire 178-7** (20 overs) (D. I. Stevens 32, D. L. Maddy 46; P. J. Martin 3-29); **Lancashire 156-8** (20 overs) (G. Chapple 55*). *Leicestershire 2 pts.*

Man of the Match: D. L. Maddy. *Attendance:* 5,112.

Leicestershire's third win in three starts put them top of their group. Maddy followed up his 28-ball 46 with two wickets – the openers, Mal Loye and Stuart Law – in five balls. Chapple restored some honour after Lancashire plummeted to 70 for seven.

At Leeds, June 20. **Yorkshire won by 55 runs.** Toss: Yorkshire. **Yorkshire 198-4** (20 overs) (S. P. Fleming 58, M. J. Lumb 50, M. J. Wood 37*); **Durham 143-8** (20 overs) (M. L. Love 51; R. J. Sidebottom 3-20, Yuvraj Singh 3-20). *Yorkshire 2 pts.*

Man of the Match: S. P. Fleming. *Attendance:* 9,136.

Fleming hit 58 from 35 deliveries, 31 more than his first three Twenty20 innings had lasted in total. Two balls into his final over, Phillips had unremarkable figures of one for 27; Lumb then smashed his last four for consecutive sixes to reach a 30-ball half-century. Yorkshire's total was the highest in the competition so far. Sidebottom reduced Durham to 15 for three, which became 17 for four, before Love oversaw a recovery of sorts.

At Manchester, June 21. **Derbyshire won by seven wickets.** Toss: Derbyshire. **Lancashire 91** (17.4 overs) (D. R. Hewson 4-18, N. R. C. Dumelow 3-8); **Derbyshire 95-3** (15.5 overs) (M. J. Di Venuto 52*). *Derbyshire 2 pts.*

Man of the Match: M. J. Di Venuto. *Attendance:* 7,025.

Only three Lancashire batsmen made it into double figures as they were dismissed for 91, the lowest total of the competition. Derbyshire's Neil Gunter had figures of 4–1–12–1, at the time, the competition's most economical four overs.

At Nottingham, June 21. **Leicestershire won by one wicket.** Toss: Nottinghamshire. **Nottinghamshire 158-5** (20 overs) (G. E. Welton 39); **Leicestershire 159-9** (20 overs) (D. L. Maddy 53). *Leicestershire 2 pts.*

Man of the Match: D. L. Maddy. *Attendance:* 5,739.

Leicestershire, with three wickets in hand, needed 12 from the last two overs to preserve their 100% record. Two wickets for Richard Logan left Jamie Grove and Damien Brandy needing nine from seven balls; a scrambled single off the last saw them home.

At Derby, June 23. **Derbyshire won by six runs.** Toss: Durham. **Derbyshire 157** (19.5 overs) (M. J. Di Venuto 36, D. R. Hewson 36; N. Killeen 4-32); **Durham 151-5** (20 overs) (N. Peng 32, G. J. Pratt 62*). *Derbyshire 2 pts.*

Man of the Match: D. R. Hewson. *Attendance:* 2,966.

Dominic Cork, unable to bowl because of an injured ankle, kept wicket in place of Luke Sutton, who had pulled a muscle while batting. To retain a chance of reaching the finals day, Durham needed 25 from the last over, then eight off two deliveries. Pratt hit an unbeaten 62 off 44 balls, but in a losing cause.

At Manchester, June 24. **Lancashire won by four runs.** Toss: Lancashire. **Lancashire 144-8** (20 overs) (A. J. Swann 56; A. M. Thorpe 3-20); **Durham 140-9** (20 overs) (P. Mustard 61; C. L. Hooper 4-18). *Lancashire 2 pts.*

County debuts: G. I. Maiden (Lancashire); Shoaib Akhtar (Durham).

Man of the Match: A. J. Swann. *Attendance:* 5,162.

Durham required eight from the final over to win this dead match, but could manage just three. Shoaib Akhtar bowled Law for 22, but otherwise had a debut to forget, yielding 31 from his four overs and, as a pinch-hitting No. 3, falling for a first-ball duck. Gregor Maiden also played against Lancashire twice in 2003, in the National League.

At Leicester, June 24. **Leicestershire won by one run.** Toss: Leicestershire. **Leicestershire 171-8** (20 overs) (B. J. Hodge 37; D. R. Hewson 3-25); **Derbyshire 170-9** (20 overs) (M. Kaif 53, C. W. G. Bassano 43; P. A. J. DeFreitas 3-39). *Leicestershire 2 pts.*

Man of the Match: P. A. J. DeFreitas. *Attendance:* 4,800.

With the winners guaranteed progress to the finals day – and the losers likely to be eliminated – this crunch match boiled over from excitement into acrimony. In the penultimate over of the Derbyshire reply, Steve Selwood was caught on the long-on boundary by Hodge. Umpire Roy Palmer consulted with the fielder and ruled that the wicket should stand. But Derbyshire lodged an appeal, arguing that Hodge had stepped on the rope before *he had the ball under control and that the result be reversed. Alan Fordham, the ECB cricket operations manager, rejected the claim, which led Dominic Cork, the Derbyshire captain, to call Hodge a "cheat" and Tim Lamb, chief executive of the ECB, "pathetic". At a subsequent disciplinary hearing at Lord's, Cork was given a three-match ban, suspended for 12 months, fined £500 and ordered to pay another £500 towards costs. Derbyshire had come very close to winning without recourse to appeals. They needed 14 from the last over, bowled by DeFreitas, which came down to six off the last ball, hit for four by Gunter.*

At Leeds, June 24. **Yorkshire won by 18 runs.** Toss: Yorkshire. **Yorkshire 196-5** (20 overs) (M. J. Wood 57, M. J. Lumb 55, G. M. Hamilton 41*; S. C. G. MacGill 3-42); **Nottinghamshire 178** (18.1 overs) (J. E. R. Gallian 34, K. P. Pietersen 44; T. T. Bresnan 3-31, M. J. Lumb 3-32). *Yorkshire 2 pts.*

Man of the Match: M. J. Lumb. *Attendance:* 10,176.

Over 10,000 people crammed into Headingley and saw Yorkshire win, but other results prevented them from squeezing into the semis. Lumb's 26-ball 55 contained five sixes and four fours. Nottinghamshire were well placed at 169 for five, but then lost five wickets for nine runs.

SOUTH GROUP

At Southampton, June 13. **Hampshire won by five runs.** Toss: Sussex. **Hampshire 153** (19.4 overs) (J. R. C. Hamblin 34, D. A. Kenway 35; M. J. G. Davis 3-13); **Sussex 148-7** (20 overs) (T. R. Ambrose 54*). *Hampshire 2 pts.*

Man of the Match: J. R. C. Hamblin. *Attendance:* 8,500.

In warm evening sunshine, the televised inaugural Twenty20 match was played to a gripping finish. Sussex needed 22 from two overs and, after Ambrose and Mushtaq Ahmed took 12 from the penultimate, ten off the last. Ed Giddins, playing against one of his three former counties, bowled Mushtaq with the third ball and conceded just four off the over.

At The Oval, June 13. **Surrey won by four wickets.** Toss: Surrey. **Middlesex 155** (20 overs) (A. J. Strauss 52, R. M. S. Weston 30; J. Ormond 5-26); **Surrey 158-6** (19.2 overs) (I. J. Ward 31). *Surrey 2 pts.*

Man of the Match: J. Ormond. *Attendance:* 8,500.

Ormond became the first bowler to take five wickets in a Twenty20 game.

At Imber Court, June 14. **Surrey won by 44 runs.** Toss: Essex. **Surrey 182-9** (20 overs) (I. J. Ward 30, G. P. Thorpe 50, Azhar Mahmood 43); **Essex 138** (18.5 overs) (A. Flower 30, M. L. Pettini 31; Azhar Mahmood 4-20). *Surrey 2 pts.*

First-team debut: R. N. ten Doeschate (Essex).

Man of the Match: Azhar Mahmood. *Attendance:* 2,677.

Azhar Mahmood faced 18 balls for his 43.

At Beckenham, June 16. **Kent won by six wickets.** Toss: Kent. **Hampshire 145-6** (20 overs) (J. R. C. Hamblin 38, S. M. Katich 59*); **Kent 147-4** (12 overs) (A. Symonds 96*). *Kent 2 pts.*

Man of the Match: A. Symonds. *Attendance:* 5,594.

Symonds, who faced just 37 balls for his unbeaten 96, reached fifty from 16 balls; only Adam Hollioake, who needed 15 for Surrey against Yorkshire in the Sunday League in 1994, had hit a faster half-century. Symonds pummelled 14 fours and three sixes. Two of those came in Giddins's only over, which cost 24.

At Imber Court, June 16. **Surrey won by four wickets.** Toss: Sussex. **Sussex 143-8** (20 overs) (B. Zuiderent 35, C. J. Adams 36; A. J. Hollioake 4-31); **Surrey 145-6** (18.1 overs). *Surrey 2 pts.*

Man of the Match: A. J. Hollioake. *Attendance:* 2,804.

This was Surrey's third successive win in the competition. The match's two leg-spinners, Ian Salisbury and Mushtaq Ahmed, had identical figures of 4–0–20–2.

At Southampton, June 18. **Essex won by four runs.** Toss: Hampshire. **Essex 155-6** (20 overs) (A. Flower 49, M. L. Pettini 32*); **Hampshire 151-3** (20 overs) (D. A. Kenway 40, S. M. Katich 59*). *Essex 2 pts.*

Man of the Match: A. Flower. *Attendance:* 3,000.

Flower hit his 49 from 33 balls. Hampshire needed 12 from the last over, bowled by Jon Dakin, but managed only seven.

At Hove, June 18 (day/night). **Sussex won by 41 runs.** Toss: Middlesex. **Sussex 177-9** (20 overs) (M. J. Prior 46, R. S. C. Martin-Jenkins 47*; C. B. Keegan 3-34); **Middlesex 136** (19.3 overs) (P. N. Weekes 39, R. M. S. Weston 34*; R. S. C. Martin-Jenkins 4-20). *Sussex 2 pts.*

Man of the Match: R. S. C. Martin-Jenkins. *Attendance:* 3,092.

In the first floodlit match of the tournament, Martin-Jenkins faced 34 balls for his unbeaten 47 and took a wicket in each of his four overs.

At Richmond, June 19. **Middlesex won by seven wickets.** Toss: Middlesex. **Kent 161-8** (20 overs) (J. C. Tredwell 34, M. J. Walker 35; A. A. Noffke 3-29); **Middlesex 165-3** (17.2 overs) (A. J. Strauss 60, O. A. Shah 40*). *Middlesex 2 pts.*

Man of the Match: A. J. Strauss. *Attendance:* 3,700.

Strauss faced 37 balls and hit ten fours.

At Chelmsford, June 20 (day/night). **Kent won by three wickets.** Toss: Essex. **Essex 116** (18.4 overs) (A. Flower 33; M. J. Dennington 4-28); **Kent 120-7** (16.1 overs) (A. Symonds 32, J. C. Tredwell 31; G. R. Napier 3-20). *Kent 2 pts.*

Man of the Match: M. J. Dennington. *Attendance:* 7,374.

A sell-out crowd saw Dennington, a 20-year-old South African with a British passport, rip the heart out of the Essex middle order. Symonds then smashed 32 from 15 balls.

At Hove, June 21. **Sussex won by seven runs.** Toss: Sussex. **Sussex 180-6** (20 overs) (M. W. Goodwin 38, R. S. C. Martin-Jenkins 56*); **Essex 173-4** (20 overs) (A. Flower 71, R. C. Irani 39). *Sussex 2 pts.*

Man of the Match: A. Flower. *Attendance:* 3,243.

Both teams had to win in order to retain a chance of qualifying for the finals day.

At Canterbury, June 23. **Surrey won by 18 runs.** Toss: Kent. **Surrey 186-8** (20 overs) (M. R. Ramprakash 53, Azhar Mahmood 57*); **Kent 168-9** (20 overs) (E. T. Smith 56; T. J. Murtagh 3-37). *Surrey 2 pts.*

County debut: Mohammad Sami (Kent).

Man of the Match: Azhar Mahmood. *Attendance:* 6,782.

Surrey guaranteed progress to the semi-finals with a fourth consecutive win. Azhar Mahmood's 57 came from 31 balls with two fours and five sixes, and his clumping helped reap 52 from the last three overs. Only Smith passed 20 in Kent's reply.

At Uxbridge, June 23. **Middlesex won by eight wickets.** Toss: Middlesex. **Hampshire 134-7** (20 overs) (J. R. C. Hamblin 30, A. D. Mascarenhas 39; A. A. Noffke 3-22, S. J. Cook 3-14); **Middlesex 136-2** (14.5 overs) (P. N. Weekes 56, A. J. Strauss 36, C. B. Keegan 31*). *Middlesex 2 pts.*

Man of the Match: P. N. Weekes. *Attendance:* 3,900.

A third defeat in four games removed Hampshire's last chance of reaching the semi-finals. They subsided from 35 for no wicket to 48 for four as the Middlesex bowlers found the right line. Ed Joyce was unable to play after being held up in traffic.

At Chelmsford, June 24 (day/night). **Essex won by two runs.** Toss: Middlesex. **Essex 175-5** (20 overs) (A. Flower 83, R. C. Irani 30, A. P. Grayson 34*); **Middlesex 173-7** (20 overs) (P. N. Weekes 35, Abdul Razzaq 33, E. C. Joyce 31). *Essex 2 pts.*

Man of the Match: A. Flower. *Attendance:* 6,335.

The ground was packed for a match that had no bearing on the finals. Play was held up for five minutes after umpire Allan Jones, standing at square leg, was struck on the arm by a full-blooded pull from Flower. John Emburey, the Middlesex coach, took over at square leg until Per Brekkeflat, a local umpire, emerged from the crowd after the interval. Flower won his third match award in his fifth game.

At Southampton, June 24. **Surrey won by 19 runs.** Toss: Surrey. **Surrey 140-9** (20 overs) (S. A. Newman 59, A. D. Brown 33; J. R. C. Hamblin 3-31); **Hampshire 121** (20 overs) (S. M. Katich 45; A. J. Hollioake 5-21). *Surrey 2 pts.*

Man of the Match: A. J. Hollioake. *Attendance:* 6,500.

Hollioake's five for 21, the best return of the competition, helped Surrey, who were fielding a below-strength team, to their fifth successive win.

At Hove, June 24 (day/night). **Sussex won by five wickets.** Toss: Kent. **Kent 114** (18.5 overs) (J. D. Lewry 3-34); **Sussex 115-5** (15.5 overs) (B. Zuiderent 42, C. J. Adams 34). *Sussex 2 pts.*
Man of the Match: B. Zuiderent. *Attendance:* 4,259.
For Sussex, Mushtaq Ahmed had figures of 4–0–12–2. Zuiderent and Adams put on 80 in nine overs after Sussex had slipped to six for two. Kent's Andrew Symonds bowled four wides in his one over, which cost 18.

SEMI-FINALS

LEICESTERSHIRE v WARWICKSHIRE

At Nottingham, July 19. Warwickshire won by seven wickets. Toss: Leicestershire.

Leicestershire fans who made the short journey to Nottingham in the hope of shouting themselves hoarse during the floodlit final found themselves disinterested spectators by lunchtime. And although Warwickshire won with just four balls to spare, the game was up for the Foxes sooner than that suggests. Hodge maintained his phenomenal Twenty20 form with a 50-ball 66 that made him the only player to pass 300 runs for the tournament, but there was little else in the Leicestershire kitty, and on a decent pitch 162 felt below par. Carter began the reply with his usual array of improvised shots, and after five overs, including a nervy one from Grove that lasted 11 balls and cost 20 runs, Warwickshire, at 61 without loss, could afford to ease off the accelerator. Penney and Troughton then combined to see them home.

Man of the Match: B. J. Hodge.

Leicestershire

T. R. Ward run out	5
V. Sehwag c Knight b Waqar Younis	5
B. J. Hodge c Brown b Waqar Younis	66
D. I. Stevens b Wagg	14
D. L. Maddy c Carter b Obuya	26
†P. A. Nixon c Obuya b Brown	7
*P. A. J. DeFreitas c Obuya b Waqar Younis	11
J. N. Snape not out	9
J. L. Sadler not out	2
L-b 5, w 8, n-b 4	17
1/12 (2) 2/12 (1) 3/38 (4) 4/97 (5) 5/125 (6) 6/137 (7) 7/160 (3) (7 wkts, 20 overs)	162

D. D. Masters and J. O. Grove did not bat.

Bowling: Carter 4–0–27–0; Waqar Younis 4–0–21–3; Wagg 2–0–24–1; Brown 3–0–30–1; Obuya 4–0–35–1; Smith 3–0–20–0.

Warwickshire

N. M. Carter c Grove b Sehwag	35
*N. V. Knight run out	32
I. R. Bell lbw b Hodge	4
†T. L. Penney not out	43
J. O. Troughton not out	33
L-b 2, w 9, n-b 8	19
1/67 (1) 2/83 (3) 3/99 (2) (3 wkts, 19.2 overs)	166

I. J. L. Trott, D. R. Brown, G. G. Wagg, C. O. Obuya, N. M. K. Smith and Waqar Younis did not bat.

Bowling: Maddy 3.2–0–28–0; DeFreitas 1–0–13–0; Grove 1–0–20–0; Masters 4–0–35–0; Sehwag 4–0–17–1; Hodge 4–0–27–1; Snape 2–0–24–0.

Umpires: J. W. Holder and G. Sharp.

GLOUCESTERSHIRE v SURREY

At Nottingham, July 19. Surrey won by five runs. Toss: Surrey.

Many had hoped that these teams – widely considered the strongest one-day outfits in the country – would contest the final. As neither had been in any real danger of losing in the group stages, something had to give. It proved to be Gloucestershire, but only after the best match of the day. A score of 49 at just over a run a ball is not the usual anchor role, but Twenty20 was in the business of redefining cricket, and Ward, apparently unencumbered by a helmet with built-in camera, kept Surrey from drifting. Smith, the tightest of them all in this game, went wicketless, but allowed only 11 runs from his four overs. Gloucestershire had packed their top order with their destructive overseas talent, and when Azhar Mahmood and Ormond reduced them to five for two, then 17 for three, a less resilient team would have buckled. Not Gloucestershire, who rallied valiantly through Gidman and Hardinges. They came close, but Azhar effectively settled matters when he returned to york Gidman for a resolute 61.

Man of the Match: Azhar Mahmood.

Surrey

I. J. Ward b Harvey	49
A. D. Brown c Windows b Lewis	18
R. Clarke st Pope b Hardinges	15
*A. J. Hollioake c Gidman b Hardinges	15
Azhar Mahmood c Rhodes b Hardinges	13
G. P. Thorpe b Harvey	4
M. R. Ramprakash c and b Ball	8
†J. N. Batty not out	10
I. D. K. Salisbury b Ball	0
Saqlain Mushtaq run out	5
B 2, l-b 2, w 2, n-b 4	10
1/26 (2) 2/55 (3) 3/91 (4) 4/112 (5) 5/116 (6) 6/129 (1) 7/137 (7) 8/137 (9) 9/147 (10) (9 wkts, 20 overs)	147

J. Ormond did not bat.

Bowling: Smith 4–0–11–0; Lewis 4–0–37–1; Hardinges 4–0–37–3; Ball 4–0–26–2; Harvey 4–0–32–2.

Gloucestershire

*C. M. Spearman b Ormond	1
I. J. Harvey c Saqlain Mushtaq b Azhar Mahmood	7
J. N. Rhodes c Batty b Azhar Mahmood	0
A. P. R. Gidman b Azhar Mahmood	61
M. G. N. Windows b Saqlain Mushtaq	3
M. A. Hardinges b Hollioake	24
C. G. Taylor not out	21
M. C. J. Ball not out	11
L-b 5, w 3, n-b 6	14
1/4 (1) 2/5 (3) 3/17 (2) 4/35 (5) 5/87 (6) 6/120 (4) (6 wkts, 20 overs)	142

†S. P. Pope, J. Lewis and A. M. Smith did not bat.

Bowling: Ormond 4–0–21–1; Azhar Mahmood 4–0–28–3; Saqlain Mushtaq 4–0–24–1; Salisbury 4–0–34–0; Hollioake 4–0–30–1.

Umpires: B. Dudleston and G. Sharp.

FINAL

SURREY v WARWICKSHIRE

At Nottingham, July 19 (day/night). Surrey won by nine wickets. Toss: Warwickshire.

Surrey had around three hours less recovery time than Warwickshire, but no one would have guessed. In tricky crepuscular light, Ormond charged in as though running on fresh batteries and utterly wrecked the Warwickshire innings. Finding movement and bounce on a pitch beginning to show its age, he put the ball on or short of a length and even risked a little width – pretty much as he would in a Championship match. He may have been helped by one or two ropy shots, but this was a beautiful, match-winning spell that would have tested the finest batsman. When Ormond finished his fourth over, the seventh of the game, he had figures of four for 11 and Warwickshire,

33 for five, were dead in the water. No one had bowled better – or more frugally – throughout the tournament. Penney and Frost dug deep, but few believed 115 would trouble Surrey. It didn't. Four boundaries boomed from Ward's bat in the opening over as they rushed pell-mell toward their target. Even the explosive Ali Brown was outscored as the runs came thick, fast and handsome, the 100 coming up to the second ball of the tenth over. Warwickshire had failed to use their last couple of overs, which pros consider disgraceful. Surrey didn't need their last nine, which was disdainful.

Man of the Match: J. Ormond.

Attendance (for all three matches on finals day): 14,961; receipts £236,111.

Warwickshire

N. M. Carter b Ormond	8
*N. V. Knight b Ormond	8
I. R. Bell c Clarke b Azhar Mahmood	5
J. O. Troughton c Brown b Ormond	1
T. L. Penney b Hollioake	33
D. R. Brown c Batty b Ormond	0
†T. Frost c Ormond b Saqlain Mushtaq	31
G. G. Wagg b Hollioake	5
C. O. Obuya c Ward b Saqlain Mushtaq	17
N. M. K. Smith run out	1
Waqar Younis not out	0
W 2, n-b 4	6
1/16 (1) 2/20 (2) 3/22 (4) 4/32 (3) 5/33 (6) 6/63 (5) 7/83 (8) 8/112 (7) 9/115 (9) 10/115 (10)	(18.1 overs) 115

Bowling: Ormond 4–0–11–4; Azhar Mahmood 3–0–22–1; Saqlain Mushtaq 4–0–35–2; Clarke 4–0–20–0; Hollioake 3.1–0–27–2.

Surrey

I. J. Ward c Waqar Younis b Wagg	50
A. D. Brown not out	55
M. R. Ramprakash not out	4
L-b 4, w 2, n-b 4	10
1/100 (1)	(1 wkt, 10.5 overs) 119

R. Clarke, *A. J. Hollioake, Azhar Mahmood, G. P. Thorpe, †J. N. Batty, I. D. K. Salisbury, Saqlain Mushtaq and J. Ormond did not bat.

Bowling: Carter 2–0–20–0; Waqar Younis 4–0–29–0; Brown 2–0–24–0; Obuya 1–0–18–0; Wagg 1–0–20–1; Knight 0.5–0–4–0.

Umpires: B. Dudleston and J. W. Holder.

CAREER FIGURES

Players not expected to appear in county cricket in 2004.

BATTING

	M	*I*	*NO*	*R*	*HS*	*100s*	*Avge*	*1,000r/ season*
M. J. Banes	11	18	1	388	69	0	22.82	0
J. A. R. Blain	20	22	8	150	34	0	10.71	0
I. Brunnschweiler	6	8	1	91	34	0	13.00	0
R. J. Cunliffe	68	114	7	2,542	190*	3	23.75	0
G. M. Fellows	48	74	6	1,592	109	1	23.41	0
B. W. Gannon	32	37	17	188	28	0	9.40	0
E. S. H. Giddins	147	175	74	534	34	0	5.28	0
M. A. Gough	67	119	3	2,952	123	2	25.44	0
J. B. Grant	29	35	14	165	36*	0	7.85	0
J. O. Grove	25	31	9	204	33	0	9.27	0
N. G. Hatch	18	25	12	157	24	0	12.07	0
J. P. Hewitt	61	82	13	1,264	75	0	18.31	0
T. A. Hunt	3	1	0	3	3	0	3.00	0
I. D. Hunter	21	32	4	577	65	0	20.60	0
S. P. James	245	424	33	15,890	309*	47	40.63	9
K. M. Krikken	214	323	60	5,725	104	1	21.76	0
D. R. Law	108	170	8	3,298	115	2	20.35	0
D. S. Lucas	22	28	8	436	49	0	21.80	0
A. C. McGarry	15	18	13	28	11*	0	5.60	0
D. E. Malcolm	304	366	113	1,985	51	0	7.84	0
A. C. Morris	62	81	12	1,392	65	0	20.17	0
O. T. Parkin	41	48	20	228	24*	0	8.14	0
D. E. Paynter	5	9	2	268	146	1	38.28	0
A. L. Penberthy	181	270	30	7,212	132*	10	30.05	0
N. C. Phillips	77	118	27	1,410	58*	0	15.49	0
S. P. Pope	5	8	3	65	17*	0	13.00	0
S. A. Richardson	13	23	2	377	69	0	17.95	0
M. A. Sheikh	20	27	7	572	58*	0	28.60	0
N. M. K. Smith	205	289	34	6,783	161	4	26.60	1
R. A. Smith	426	717	87	26,155	209*	61	41.51	11
A. J. Stewart	447	734	81	26,165	271*	48	40.06	8
A. M. Thorpe	9	16	0	321	95	0	20.06	0
P. D. Trego	15	22	3	534	140	1	28.10	0
T. R. Ward	248	425	22	13,876	235*	29	34.43	6
V. J. Wells	196	306	22	9,314	224	18	32.79	2
G. E. Welton	73	133	5	3,299	200*	2	25.77	0
R. M. S. Weston	62	104	6	2,841	156	7	28.98	0
L. J. Wharton	38	59	30	173	30	0	5.96	0
M. J. A. Whiley	18	24	6	72	16	0	4.00	0
B. Zuiderent	19	30	1	679	122	1	23.41	0

BOWLING AND FIELDING

	R	W	BB	Avge	5W/i	10W/m	Ct/St
M. J. Banes	175	3	3-65	58.33	–	–	4
J. A. R. Blain	2,313	49	6-42	47.20	2	–	5
I. Brunnschweiler	–	–	–	–	–	–	20
R. J. Cunliffe	3	0	–	–	–	–	53
G. M. Fellows	1,228	32	3-23	38.37	–	–	23
B. W. Gannon	2,832	85	6-80	33.31	3	–	8
E. S. H. Giddins	13,562	478	6-47	28.37	22	2	22
M. A. Gough	1,350	30	5-66	45.00	1	–	57
J. B. Grant	2,247	63	5-38	35.66	1	–	7
J. O. Grove	2,089	43	5-90	48.58	1	–	2
N. G. Hatch	1,795	48	4-61	37.39	–	–	4
J. P. Hewitt	4,948	170	6-14	29.10	5	–	23
T. A. Hunt	285	7	3-43	40.71	–	–	0
I. D. Hunter	1,894	45	4-55	42.08	–	–	6
S. P. James	3	0	–	–	–	–	173
K. M. Krikken	121	1	1-54	121.00	–	–	526/31
D. R. Law	7,000	213	6-53	32.86	8	–	55
D. S. Lucas	1,909	52	5-104	36.71	1	–	3
A. C. McGarry	1,386	27	5-27	51.33	1	–	3
D. E. Malcolm	31,973	1,054	9-57	30.33	46	9	45
A. C. Morris	4,119	156	5-39	26.40	5	1	34
O. T. Parkin	3,014	108	5-24	27.90	2	–	12
D. E. Paynter	26	0	–	–	–	–	2
A. L. Penberthy	9,051	231	5-37	39.18	4	–	108
N. C. Phillips	7,074	162	6-97	43.66	5	1	44
S. P. Pope	–	–	–	–	–	–	10/1
S. A. Richardson	–	–	–	–	–	–	11
M. A. Sheikh	1,391	36	4-36	38.63	–	–	3
N. M. K. Smith	13,968	374	7-42	37.34	18	–	73
R. A. Smith	993	14	2-11	70.92	–	–	233
A. J. Stewart	446	3	1-7	148.66	–	–	721/32
A. M. Thorpe	32	0	–	–	–	–	5
P. D. Trego	1,272	29	4-84	43.86	–	–	6
T. R. Ward	694	9	2-10	77.11	–	–	226
V. J. Wells	7,920	302	5-18	26.22	5	–	134
G. E. Welton	5	0	–	–	–	–	43
R. M. S. Weston	104	2	1-15	52.00	–	–	37
L. J. Wharton	2,167	54	6-62	40.12	3	–	14
M. J. A. Whiley	1,797	27	3-60	66.55	–	–	3
B. Zuiderent	–	–	–	–	–	–	19

THE UNIVERSITIES, 2003

REVIEW BY GRENVILLE HOLLAND

The Loughborough UCCE squad for their match against MCC Young Cricketers at Lord's: *Standing:* Z. K. Sharif, S. Clark, J. Anyon, D. H. Wigley, P. Lewis, R. A. G. Cummins, R. M. Wilkinson. *Seated:* C. D. Nash, L. J. Goddard, J. H. K. Adams (*captain*), R. A. White, V. Atri.

In order to meet ECB requirements and justify their financial support, as well as meet a first-class fixture list, the University Centres of Cricketing Excellence are becoming artificial creations detached from their traditional bases. As the high academic demands for admission have closed doors to gifted cricketers, Oxford and Cambridge have begun to rely on affiliated institutions, Oxford Brookes and Anglia Polytechnic University, to bridge the gap.

Durham is also moving down this path, strengthening its focus on research ratings and academic excellence, but lacks the option of an ex-polytechnic affiliate to shore up its sporting traditions. Cardiff, in the longer run, may find the balance, but Bradford/Leeds has still to put together an effective structure from its scattered campuses. Only Loughborough, now host to the ECB National Academy, has the right ingredients for long-term success.

Loughborough remained the dominant team in university cricket. They became the fourth UCCE to be granted first-class status, joining Oxford, Cambridge and Durham, and they headed the inter-UCCE two-day league, as they had done since it began in 2001. But defeat by Exeter – a non-UCCE side – in the semi-finals of the British Universities Championship opened the way for Durham to regain that title.

Loughborough and Durham each lost one of their three first-class matches against the counties and drew the rest; Oxford drew all three, but Cambridge, usually regarded as the weakest of the first-class university teams, sprang a surprise by beating Northamptonshire. Oxford reasserted themselves by winning both first-class and one-day Varsity matches, thanks to outstanding performances by Jamie Dalrymple. Cardiff, despite a heavy defeat by Sussex, continued to look a stronger side than Bradford/Leeds, some of whose players were as young as 16.

OXFORD

RALPH DELLOR

President: A. C. Smith (Brasenose)
Chairman: Dr S. R. Porter (St Cross College)

Oxford UCCE Captain: J. J. Sayers (St Mary's RC Menston and Worcester)
Oxford University Captain: J. W. M. Dalrymple (Radley and St Peter's)
Captain (both) for 2004: P. J. McMahon (Trinity RC Nottingham and Wadham)

Oxford cricket enjoyed a highly satisfactory season. The University finished in style, with convincing wins over Cambridge in both first-class and one-day encounters. Meanwhile, the UCCE side, which also draws on Oxford Brookes University, were unbeaten in three games against the first-class counties – in 2002, they lost all three – reached the semi-finals of the British Universities Championship for the fourth year running, were second in the two-day inter-UCCE league and shared the UCCE Challenge Trophy (thanks to the weather).

These results underlined their overall achievement, though results were not the sole purpose of the campaign. The UCCE system was established to further the development of players, and there was discernible progress. The bowlers never allowed first-class opponents to go on the rampage; the batsmen showed strength of character and resilience against county attacks keen to make an impression.

Early in the season, the opposition tends to be near full strength, with county cricketers looking to play themselves into form. Hampshire brought a young side to The Parks in mid-May, but appeared set on a competitive match, which made the UCCE's respectable performances the more admirable.

The UCCE captain, Joe Sayers, made a hundred in the Hampshire match, when Australian batsman Ed Cowan was out for 99. Omar Anwar had succumbed to the same unfortunate fate on his first-class debut, against Middlesex. All three, as well as Stuart Airey and wicket-keeper William Howard, averaged over 30 against the counties, and Cowan managed over 50.

Two spinners led the way in bowling, with seven wickets apiece against the counties. Off-spinner Paul McMahon, who bowled nearly 108 overs, had captained England Under-19 in 2002, when he also appeared for Nottinghamshire; it showed, and he was named Oxford captain for 2004. Leg-spinner Michael Munday was more expensive but had a better strike-rate. The pair claimed another 13 wickets between them against Cambridge.

Two-thirds of the UCCE side came from Brookes, but a couple of players from the original University were unavailable because of academic activities until the end of term. When he returned, Jamie Dalrymple made a massive impact against Cambridge, leading Oxford to an innings victory by scoring 236 not out, then claiming five for

49 with his off-breaks. He followed up with another hundred in the one-day Varsity game at Lord's. Neil Millar also scored a century at Cambridge, in his only first-class match of the season, and his medium-pace took five wickets at Lord's.

Oxford were on the brink of the British Universities final when they reduced Durham to 114 for seven in the semi, but lost out yet again. For the second year running, they reached the UCCE Challenge match, effectively the final of the inter-UCCE competition, but persistent rain at Trent Bridge meant they shared the Challenge Trophy with Loughborough, cementing their place as one of the four strongest university teams in the country.

OXFORD UCCE/UNIVERSITY RESULTS

First-class matches – Played 4: Won 1, Drawn 3.

OXFORD UCCE v MIDDLESEX

At Oxford, April 12, 13, 14. Drawn. Toss: Middlesex. First-class debuts: S. J. Airey, O. S. Anwar, E. J. M. Cowan, S. J. Lowe, M. K. Munday. UCCE debut: P. J. McMahon. County debut: J. H. Dawes.

The season made a familiar start, with Middlesex enjoying batting practice on a flat pitch, against an attack that stuck to its task without threatening. Koenig made the most of it, striking 23 fours and a six before retiring with a neck strain. In reply, Oxford's batsmen held out for six and a half hours. Omar Anwar, a 19-year-old with experience of Middlesex youth teams, was last out, only a single short of a hundred on first-class debut. The county had to work for runs in their second innings, when another debutant, wicket-keeper Stephen Lowe, had a hand in all five wickets, stumping two and catching three. Set a nominal 275, Oxford batted out time with a funereal 48 in 32 overs, but secured the draw with only one wicket lost.

Close of play: First day, Oxford UCCE 25-1 (Sayers 3, Cowan 7); Second day, Middlesex 23-0 (Hutton 10, Nash 8).

Middlesex

*A. J. Strauss b Munday	76	– (7) not out	3
S. G. Koenig retired hurt	166		
O. A. Shah c and b Munday	73		
†D. C. Nash c Lowe b Mees	12	– (2) st Lowe b McMahon	27
E. C. Joyce b Airey	12	– (3) not out	50
P. N. Weekes not out	8	– (4) st Lowe b Munday	17
B. L. Hutton (did not bat)		– (1) c Lowe b Airey	27
S. J. Cook (did not bat)		– (5) c Lowe b Sharpe	12
C. B. Keegan (did not bat)		– (6) c Lowe b Airey	26
B 5, l-b 6, w 2, n-b 4	17	B 5, l-b 4	9
1/126 (1) 2/268 (3) 3/344 (4) 4/364 (5)	(4 wkts dec.) 364	1/58 (2) 2/62 (1) 3/101 (4) 4/121 (5) 5/158 (6)	(5 wkts dec.) 171

J. H. Dawes and T. F. Bloomfield did not bat.

In the first innings Koenig retired hurt at 339.

Bowling: *First Innings*—Mees 18–3–60–1; Sharpe 12–1–64–0; Airey 12.1–1–5'. 31–8–90–0; Munday 14–0–82–2. *Second Innings*—Mees 15–3–47–0; Sharpe McMahon 16.5–3–52–1; Airey 12–3–32–2; Munday 2–1–4–1.

Oxford UCCE

G. R. Butcher c Nash b Dawes	7	– b Bloomfield	7
*J. J. Sayers lbw b Weekes	19	– not out	15
E. J. M. Cowan run out	40	– not out	21
H. R. Jones b Keegan	35		
O. S. Anwar b Keegan	99		
†S. J. Lowe c and b Weekes	2		
S. J. Airey lbw b Weekes	3		
T. Mees c Nash b Weekes	9		
P. J. McMahon b Dawes	14		
M. K. Munday c Hutton b Keegan	0		
T. J. Sharpe not out	10		
B 3, l-b 18, w 2	23	B 4, l-b 1	5
1/10 (1) 2/68 (2) 3/89 (3) 4/151 (4) 5/176 (6) 6/186 (7) 7/200 (8) 8/243 (9) 9/248 (10) 10/261 (5)	261	1/12 (1)	(1 wkt) 48

Bowling: *First Innings*—Dawes 27–11–63–2; Keegan 21.5–8–27–3; Cook 18–4–46–0; Bloomfield 14–3–49–0; Weekes 23–12–55–4. *Second Innings*—Bloomfield 8–3–9–1; Cook 9–5–7–0; Weekes 13–5–26–0; Joyce 2–1–1–0.

Umpires: D. J. Constant and R. T. Robinson.

OXFORD UCCE v WORCESTERSHIRE

At Oxford, April 23, 24, 25. Drawn. Toss: Oxford UCCE. First-class debuts: J. A. Allen; S. A. Khalid.

In a positive statement of intent, Oxford batted first. Initially, their confidence seemed misplaced, as the Worcestershire bowlers extracted the first five for 79. But the lower order added 152, led by Howard, whose only previous first-class appearance had brought him one run. Called up as wicket-keeper because Lowe was on a field trip, he went on the attack with 72 in only 59 balls, including 12 fours and a six. The county openers accumulated 155 in 37 overs and Smith scored his third successive fifty, but McMahon collected three wickets, bowling his off-breaks with impressive control. Rain on the second and third days consigned the match to a draw.

Close of play: First day, Worcestershire 37-0 (Peters 12, Singh 25); Second day, Worcestershire 256-3 (Smith 29, Ali 4).

Oxford UCCE

E. J. M. Cowan b Mason	8
*J. J. Sayers c Pipe b Mason	15
J. A. Allen lbw b Liptrot	0
H. R. Jones c Solanki b Batty	19
O. S. Anwar b Mason	26
S. J. Airey c Peters b Liptrot	38
†W. O. F. Howard c Solanki b Batty	72
T. Mees c Liptrot b Khalid	18
P. J. McMahon c Liptrot b Khalid	21
T. J. Sharpe c Pipe b Liptrot	5
M. K. Munday not out	0
B 4, l-b 5	9
1/24 (1) 2/31 (2) 3/35 (3) 4/63 (4) 5/79 (5) 6/172 (7) 7/200 (6) 8/210 (8) 9/219 (10) 10/231 (9)	231

Bowling: Mason 16–10–22–3; Harrity 11–1–31–0; Liptrot 20–8–47–3; Batty 26–9–63–2; [illegible]d 13.5–1–59–2.

Worcestershire

S. D. Peters c Jones b McMahon	87	†D. J. Pipe not out	0
A. Singh c Sayers b Airey	77		
V. S. Solanki b McMahon	41	B 9, l-b 15, w 3, n-b 6	33
*B. F. Smith c Airey b Munday	63		
Kadeer Ali b McMahon	27	1/155 (2) 2/192 (1) (5 wkts)	348
G. J. Batty not out	20	3/246 (3) 4/317 (4) 5/342 (5)	

C. G. Liptrot, S. A. Khalid, M. S. Mason and M. A. Harrity did not bat.

Bowling: Mees 24–1–99–0; Airey 16–3–63–1; Munday 8–2–34–1; McMahon 26–7–93–3; Sharpe 14–3–35–0.

Umpires: T. E. Jesty and K. Shuttleworth.

OXFORD UCCE v HAMPSHIRE

At Oxford, May 9, 10, 11. Drawn. Toss: Oxford UCCE. First-class debut: T. E. Linley. County debuts: J. T. A. Bruce, D. A. Clapp, M. Thorburn.

Again Sayers chose to bat, and this time he was rewarded with a maiden first-class hundred – an excellent, if careful, innings lasting nearly six hours, which testified to his concentration. Kendall, his opposite number and a former Blue, scored a rather quicker century, just over three hours, then declared 19 behind. Cowan, who had made his own maiden hundred a week earlier, for British Universities against the Zimbabweans, was one short of a second on the last day when a ball from Udal that hardly bounced got him lbw. Oxford set Hampshire 291 in what would have been 52 overs, and the openers raised three figures in a mere 19. Then wickets started to fall, and so did the rain, ruining a potentially interesting finish.

Close of play: First day, Hampshire 36-0 (Kenway 13, Hamblin 19); Second day, Oxford UCCE 72-1 (Lowe 22, Cowan 39).

Oxford UCCE

*J. J. Sayers c Hamblin b Udal	122	– c Morris b Thorburn	3
S. J. Lowe lbw b Thorburn	19	– lbw b Udal	38
E. J. M. Cowan c Prittipaul b Thorburn	45	– lbw b Udal	99
H. R. Jones c Brunnschweiler b Mascarenhas	22	– c Kenway b Bruce	8
O. S. Anwar lbw b Hamblin	3	– c Brunnschweiler b Bruce	0
†W. O. F. Howard lbw b Prittipaul	6	– c Bruce b Udal	19
S. J. Airey c Brunnschweiler b Bruce	13	– not out	46
P. J. McMahon c Brunnschweiler b Udal	6	– c Brunnschweiler b Udal	7
T. Mees b Udal	9	– not out	36
T. E. Linley c Morris b Udal	7		
M. K. Munday not out	0		
B 5, l-b 3, w 5, n-b 16	29	L-b 5, n-b 10	15
1/39 (2) 2/114 (3) 3/160 (4) 4/176 (5)	281	1/3 (1) 2/120 (2) (7 wkts dec.)	271
5/200 (6) 6/231 (7) 7/252 (8)		3/137 (4) 4/143 (5)	
8/262 (9) 9/273 (1) 10/281 (10)		5/171 (3) 6/190 (6) 7/201 (8)	

Bowling: *First Innings*—Bruce 19–9–42–1; Thorburn 17–5–53–2; Mascarenhas 11–3–28–1; Hamblin 16–4–53–1; Prittipaul 13–3–47–1; Udal 10.2–0–50–4. *Second Innings*—Bruce 14–1–61–2; Thorburn 14–1–67–1; Hamblin 11–5–24–0; Mascarenhas 11–3–37–0; Prittipaul 1–1–0–0; Udal 18–5–58–4; Kendall 1.3–0–19–0.

Hampshire

First innings		Second innings	
D. A. Kenway lbw b Mees	35	– b Munday	68
J. R. C. Hamblin c Lowe b Mees	20	– b Munday	34
*W. S. Kendall c Munday b McMahon	114		
A. C. Morris st Howard b McMahon	1	– (3) lbw b McMahon	20
L. R. Prittipaul not out	69		
A. D. Mascarenhas (did not bat)		– (4) not out	16
D. A. Clapp (did not bat)		– (5) st Howard b Munday	4
S. D. Udal (did not bat)		– (6) not out	0
B 3, l-b 8, w 2, n-b 10	23	L-b 4, w 2, n-b 2	8
1/46 (2) 2/98 (1) 3/101 (4) 4/262 (3)	(4 wkts dec.) 262	1/105 (1) 2/114 (2) 3/143 (3) 4/150 (5)	(4 wkts) 150

†I. Brunnschweiler, M. Thorburn and J. T. A. Bruce did not bat.

Bowling: *First Innings*—Mees 18–4–68–2; Airey 9–0–50–0; McMahon 23.4–5–70–2; Linley 5–1–40–0; Munday 7–0–23–0. *Second Innings*—Mees 7–0–39–0; Airey 4–1–16–0; Linley 5–1–23–0; McMahon 10.2–0–35–1; Munday 9–0–33–3.

Umpires: S. A. Garratt and V. A. Holder.

At Cambridge, June 26, 27, 28. OXFORD UNIVERSITY beat CAMBRIDGE UNIVERSITY by an innings and 71 runs (see The University Matches, 2003).

At Nottingham, June 30. LOUGHBOROUGH UCCE v OXFORD UCCE. Abandoned.

At Lord's, July 2. OXFORD UNIVERSITY beat CAMBRIDGE UNIVERSITY by 73 runs (D/L method) (see The University Matches, 2003).

CAMBRIDGE

DAVID HALLETT

President: Professor A. D. Buckingham (Pembroke)

Cambridge UCCE Captain: S. J. Marshall (Birkenhead and Pembroke)
Cambridge University Captain for 2003 and 2004: A. Shankar (Bedford and Queens')
Cambridge UCCE Captain for 2004: T. Webley (King's College Taunton and Anglia Polytechnic University)

Cambridge had struggled to adapt in the first two seasons of the new University Centres of Cricketing Excellence but they put that right in 2003. Such was the transformation that Cambridge became the first of the six UCCEs to defeat a first-class county, when they beat Northamptonshire in a fourth-innings run-chase. They were also the first to get the better of Loughborough, the strongest of the six UCCEs, in a two-day UCCE championship game, which they won on first innings. They might have beaten Durham, too, but for the weather. In the British Universities Championship, Cambridge were third in the Northern Premier league, and made it into the revamped Premier League of six for 2004. It seemed they were turning the corner.

The principal reason for this turnaround was the emergence of players from Anglia Polytechnic University, the junior partner in the UCCE, for the first time. Unrepresented in the first two years, they provided five key players in 2003. Two of them, seamer Tony Palladino and all-rounder Tom Webley, went on to make debuts for Essex and Somerset respectively. In addition, there were the Akram twins, Adnan and Arfan, plus the talented sportsman Gary Park. Arfan Akram scored 110 against Kent, while his brother contributed a match-winning 98 in the run-chase against Northamptonshire, building on a century by Webley earlier in the game. Both Akrams, Webley and Vikram Kumar, from the older university, averaged over 40 against the counties. Still, much of the credit for improving fortunes was down to the recruiting work of coach Chris Scott, and his ability to weld players into a cohesive unit.

While the UCCE began to flourish, Cambridge University struggled, despite a core of experienced players including Tom Savill, a seam bowler awarded a summer contract by Middlesex. They fell to the all-round talents of Oxford's captain, Jamie Dalrymple, in both the four-day Varsity Match, played at Fenner's, and the one-day game at Lord's. Cambridge were handicapped throughout by the absence of Jamie Parker, who led them in 2002 but was prevented from playing by his medical studies. This left Simon Marshall, the UCCE captain, to carry much of the load, but not even his fighting second-innings century in the Varsity Match could save them from an innings defeat.

With all the 2003 players returning, and promising recruits joining both universities, Cambridge hoped to maintain an upward curve towards their old pre-eminence in university cricket. During the winter, a new cricket school was being built at Fenner's, and was expected to be fully operational by the start of the 2004 season. The building, housing three indoor practice lanes, is sited in the corner of the ground by the tennis club. With student accommodation for Hughes Hall being constructed opposite the school, the face of Fenner's is changing for ever.

CAMBRIDGE UCCE/UNIVERSITY RESULTS

First-class matches – Played 4: Won 1, Lost 1, Drawn 2.

CAMBRIDGE UCCE v ESSEX

At Cambridge, April 12, 13, 14. Drawn. Toss: Essex. First-class debuts: Adnan Akram, Arfan Akram, R. J. Mann, A. P. Palladino, G. T. Park, T. Webley. County debut: S. A. Brant.

Cambridge batted with assurance through the final two sessions to draw a game that had seen the Essex batsmen run rampant. Jefferson and Robinson piled up 240 in 35 overs, and Jefferson had scored 125 in 122 balls, with 21 fours, when he retired at lunch. Flower kept up the momentum, and the county declared at 497 – scored at more than five an over. McGarry wrecked the students' top order, with a career-best five wickets, but Irani chose to bat again, allowing himself and Habib to complete their own centuries before retiring. Set a theoretical target of 677, Cambridge batted sensibly, surviving with only four wickets down. Five of their six debutants were from Anglia Polytechnic University; three of those had already played for Essex's Second Eleven.

Close of play: First day, Cambridge UCCE 31-1 (Shankar 18, Mann 4); Second day, Essex 190-1 (Habib 72, Irani 18).

Essex

D. D. J. Robinson c Kumar b Adnan Akram	89		
W. I. Jefferson retired hurt	125		
A. P. Grayson c Marshall b Adnan Akram	11	– (1) c Kumar b Arfan Akram	90
A. Flower c Heath b Webley	91		
A. Habib c Arfan Akram b Savill	37	– (2) retired hurt	102
*R. C. Irani c Shankar b Savill	45	– (3) retired hurt	102
†J. S. Foster c Heath b Savill	41		
J. M. Dakin not out	8	– (5) c Palladino b Savill	13
J. D. Middlebrook (did not bat)		– (4) c Marshall b Palladino	16
A. C. McGarry (did not bat)		– (6) not out	2
B 8, l-b 9, w 8, n-b 25	50	B 13, l-b 4, n-b 10	27
1/240 (1) 2/304 (3) 3/395 (5) 4/400 (4) 5/484 (6) 6/497 (7)	(6 wkts dec.) 497	1/153 (1) 2/327 (4) 3/352 (5)	(3 wkts dec.) 352

S. A. Brant did not bat.

In the first innings Jefferson retired hurt at 243; in the second Habib retired hurt at 274 and Irani at 337.

Bowling: *First Innings*—Palladino 19–1–110–0; Savill 13.5–0–86–3; Park 12–0–53–0; Adnan Akram 20–1–85–2; Marshall 20–2–91–0; Webley 9–0–55–1. *Second Innings*—Palladino 14–0–71–1; Savill 13.1–1–51–1; Park 13–1–70–0; Marshall 14–1–55–0; Adnan Akram 8–0–38–0; Webley 8–0–31–0; Arfan Akram 5–0–19–1.

Cambridge UCCE

First innings		Second innings	
A. Shankar c Foster b Irani	38	lbw b Middlebrook	40
D. R. Heath c Foster b Dakin	6	b Middlebrook	21
R. J. Mann b McGarry	21	b Grayson	43
Adnan Akram c Robinson b McGarry	3		
Arfan Akram c Foster b McGarry	0	(4) b Flower	30
*S. J. Marshall c Middlebrook b McGarry	10	not out	0
T. Webley c Jefferson b Brant	10	(5) not out	19
G. T. Park c Foster b McGarry	21		
†V. H. Kumar c Jefferson b Middlebrook	41		
T. E. Savill c Robinson b Middlebrook	10		
A. P. Palladino not out	3		
L-b 7, w 1, n-b 2	10	L-b 6, n-b 4	10
1/19 (2) 2/64 (1) 3/67 (4) 4/73 (5) 5/80 (3) 6/87 (6) 7/98 (7) 8/149 (8) 9/166 (10) 10/173 (9)	173	1/35 (2) 2/98 (1) 3/116 (3) 4/151 (4)	(4 wkts) 163

Bowling: *First Innings*—Brant 19–7–57–1; Dakin 17–5–38–1; Irani 8–4–12–1; McGarry 16–7–27–5; Middlebrook 12.3–4–29–2; Grayson 3–1–3–0. *Second Innings*—Dakin 5–0–12–0; McGarry 12–4–29–0; Middlebrook 21–4–61–2; Irani 5–1–10–0; Grayson 11–6–18–1; Robinson 3–0–22–0; Flower 2–0–5–1.

Umpires: B. Dudleston and A. Hill.

CAMBRIDGE UCCE v KENT

At Cambridge, April 18, 19, 20. Drawn. Toss: Kent. County debuts: G. S. Blewett, M. A. Carberry, A. Sheriyar.

Kent openers Carberry and Key plundered the Cambridge bowling for 258 in the first 54 overs, setting up a total of 408 for three. But this time, the university batsmen replied strongly. Shankar and Heath scored more than four an over on the first evening and, though they fell to Sheriyar next morning, Cambridge batted throughout the second day (shortened to 78 overs by rain) and up to lunch on the third. Arfan Akram, at No. 7, played carefully for five and a half hours, struck 15 fours in a maiden century, and shared hundred partnerships with Park and Kumar. They declared just 13 short of Kent's first-innings total. The rain, however, meant there was no time to contrive a result.

Close of play: First day, Cambridge UCCE 56-0 (Shankar 22, Heath 21); Second day, Cambridge UCCE 271-7 (Arfan Akram 57, Kumar 9).

Kent

First innings		Second innings	
M. A. Carberry c Palladino b Webley	137		
R. W. T. Key b Adnan Akram	129		
E. T. Smith not out	61		
G. S. Blewett b Savill	11	(1) c Kumar b Heath	47
M. J. Walker not out	32	(3) c Mann b Webley	92
*M. A. Ealham (did not bat)		(2) c Mann b Webley	64
†G. O. Jones (did not bat)		(4) not out	43
J. C. Tredwell (did not bat)		(5) not out	0
L-b 1, w 1, n-b 36	38	B 1, l-b 1, n-b 8	10
1/258 (1) 2/309 (2) 3/332 (4)	(3 wkts dec.) 408	1/63 (1) 2/168 (2) 3/249 (3)	(3 wkts dec.) 256

A. Khan, M. J. Saggers and A. Sheriyar did not bat.

Bowling: *First Innings*—Savill 15–0–88–1; Palladino 16–1–71–0; Park 8–0–38–0; Marshall 23–1–84–0; Webley 22–0–103–1; Adnan Akram 6–0–23–1. *Second Innings*—Palladino 10–1–53–0; Park 8–0–46–0; Heath 7–1–27–1; Marshall 17–1–71–0; Webley 15–2–57–2.

Cambridge UCCE

A. Shankar c Jones b Sheriyar	29
D. R. Heath c Jones b Sheriyar	30
R. J. Mann b Sheriyar	2
Adnan Akram lbw b Saggers	38
T. Webley c and b Tredwell	28
*S. J. Marshall b Saggers	0
Arfan Akram b Tredwell	110
G. T. Park lbw b Walker	43
†V. H. Kumar not out	62
A. P. Palladino not out	1
B 8, l-b 17, w 7, n-b 20	52
1/67 (1) 2/71 (3) 3/86 (2) 4/149 (5) 5/149 (4) 6/154 (6) 7/261 (8) 8/394 (7) (8 wkts dec.)	395

T. E. Savill did not bat.

Bowling: Saggers 28–7–70–2; Sheriyar 22–3–101–3; Khan 20–1–93–0; Blewett 9–3–29–0; Tredwell 26–13–38–2; Walker 8–2–24–1; Ealham 7–3–15–0.

Umpires: R. A. Kettleborough and A. G. T. Whitehead.

CAMBRIDGE UCCE v NORTHAMPTONSHIRE

At Cambridge, May 9, 10, 11. Cambridge UCCE won by four wickets. Toss: Northamptonshire. First-class debuts: J. J. N. Heywood; T. B. Huggins, A. J. Shantry.

A brave last-ball victory was the first by a UCCE over a first-class county. Cambridge's seam attack continued to struggle: David Paynter, great-grandson of Test player Eddie, scored a maiden hundred in his fourth first-class match, putting on 153 with Powell and 104 with Brophy. But when the eighth bowler came on, leg-spinner Arfan Akram, he picked up three wickets in 14 balls. Then it was Webley's turn for a maiden century, with 15 fours, supported by Park. Cambridge declared 88 behind, and Northamptonshire accepted the challenge, setting a target of 263 from 48 overs. The students started badly, Blain taking their first two for 17, but Adnan Akram and Webley added a rapid 139. Adnan finished with 98 in 89 balls and captain Marshall raised the tempo with 59 in 40 balls. With six wickets down, Arfan scrambled the winning single from the bowling of Greenidge.

Close of play: First day, Cambridge UCCE 26-1 (Adnan Akram 13, Park 0); Second day, Northamptonshire 7-1 (Penberthy 0, Panesar 4).

Northamptonshire

M. J. Powell lbw b Palladino	64	– b Palladino	3
D. E. Paynter c Arfan Akram b Webley	146	– (6) not out	33
†G. L. Brophy not out	102	– (5) not out	45
*A. L. Penberthy c Heath b Arfan Akram	45	– (2) b Savill	16
T. B. Huggins c and b Arfan Akram	0	– (4) b Palladino	40
R. S. G. Anderson c Heywood b Arfan Akram	0		
A. J. Shantry not out	17		
M. S. Panesar (did not bat)		– (3) lbw b Webley	28
B 1, l-b 5, w 3, n-b 4	13	B 5, l-b 1, w 1, n-b 2	9
1/153 (1) 2/257 (2) 3/344 (4) 4/345 (5) 5/353 (6) (5 wkts dec.)	387	1/3 (1) 2/37 (2) 3/77 (3) 4/108 (4) (4 wkts dec.)	174

J. A. R. Blain, C. G. Greenidge and J. F. Brown did not bat.

Bowling: *First Innings*—Palladino 14–3–37–1; Savill 12.4–2–70–0; Park 9–0–54–0; Heath 13–2–44–0; Adnan Akram 3–0–14–0; Marshall 21–2–73–0; Webley 14–2–48–1; Arfan Akram 9–0–41–3. *Second Innings*—Savill 15–2–52–1; Palladino 14–4–37–2; Webley 8–3–24–1; Marshall 9–1–32–0; Arfan Akram 2–0–23–0.

Cambridge UCCE

Adnan Akram c Powell b Greenidge	23	– c Powell b Brown	98
D. R. Heath c Brophy b Blain	11	– lbw b Blain	4
G. T. Park c Brophy b Greenidge	68	– lbw b Blain	0
T. Webley c Powell b Panesar	104	– c Brophy b Panesar	59
*S. J. Marshall not out	28	– b Anderson	59
Arfan Akram lbw b Shantry	27	– not out	24
V. H. Kumar not out	15	– lbw b Anderson	4
T. E. Savill (did not bat)		– not out	1
B 4, l-b 1, n-b 18	23	B 1, l-b 7, n-b 6	14
1/23 (2) 2/50 (1) 3/193 (3) 4/245 (4) 5/274 (6)	(5 wkts dec.) 299	1/17 (2) 2/17 (3) 3/156 (1) 4/198 (4) 5/252 (5) 6/256 (7)	(6 wkts) 263

A. Shankar, A. P. Palladino and †J. J. N. Heywood did not bat.

In the first innings Marshall, when 0, retired hurt at 195 and resumed at 245.

Bowling: *First Innings*—Blain 18.5–2–61–1; Shantry 15–4–40–1; Anderson 13–2–47–0; Greenidge 17.1–2–64–2; Brown 20–7–37–0; Panesar 19–5–45–1. *Second Innings*—Blain 6–2–22–2; Greenidge 8–0–48–0; Penberthy 6–1–28–0; Panesar 11–1–65–1; Anderson 7–1–33–2; Brown 10–1–59–1.

Umpires: N. L. Bainton and M. R. Benson.

At Cambridge, June 26, 27, 28. CAMBRIDGE UNIVERSITY lost to OXFORD UNIVERSITY by an innings and 71 runs (see The University Matches, 2003).

At Lord's, July 2. CAMBRIDGE UNIVERSITY lost to OXFORD UNIVERSITY by 73 runs (D/L method) (see The University Matches, 2003).

DURHAM

GRENVILLE HOLLAND

President: Dr J. G. Holland (St Hild & St Bede)
Hon. Treasurer: B. R. Lander (Hatfield)

Captain: A. G. R. Loudon (Eton and St Hild & St Bede)
Secretaries: P. W. Howells (Yarm School and St Aidan's)
J. D. Holland (Durham Johnston and St Cuthbert's)

Durham regained the British Universities title after a three-year gap, but had a mixed season, falling victim to injuries and examinations. Tim Phillips, the chosen captain, never played: he tore knee ligaments attempting a sliding pick-up in practice. Alex Loudon took over and proved a fine leader. For the second year running, Justin Bishop – the former England Under-19 opening bowler, now with Essex – was injured when most needed. Examinations also took their toll. In a university seeking academic excellence, cricketers are at a particular disadvantage. For home games, invigilated dawn exams are an option; away, they are not. Durham's substandard results in the ECB's inter-UCCE competition owed much to unfortunate timing, and the fixture with Lancashire, despite pleas, was scheduled in the very heart of examinations. Most students in the six UCCEs will not make a career in cricket, and their academic needs should be respected.

The season began with an innings defeat by Nottinghamshire at Trent Bridge; the two remaining county games were played at the Racecourse in May. Both produced draws: a thrilling one against Durham county, when the students narrowly missed a target of 299, and a duller one against Lancashire.

Loudon scored 317 first-class runs – more than any other UCCE batsman in 2003 – at 52.83, thanks to a superb 172 against Durham. Ferley, who scored a 70-ball 78 in the same game, was also outstanding. His left-arm spin bore the burden of the attack, bowling 85 first-class overs. Bishop was the most successful bowler with seven wickets, striking every 38 balls. Freshmen David Brown and Will Smith made valuable contributions with the bat and Sean Polley proved a useful all-rounder. But the season's find was Simon Hawk, who made runs with style and grace when most needed: his half-centuries in the British Universities semi-final and final were crucial.

Durham were disappointing in the two-day UCCE competition, where they finished fifth of six. They had got off to a bad start against Oxford, and made a hash of their first innings against Loughborough: 60 all out in 31 overs. But they triumphed in the senior British Universities competition, after losing the last three finals to Loughborough. Durham also won the women's championship, beating Loughborough in a low-scoring semi before destroying Brighton by 123 runs. Juliet Tetley had an inspired season with bat and ball, well supported by Emma Barnes and Ruth Barron.

At the end of the academic year Durham University began a restructuring exercise, culling departments deemed too small or producing too little research. Many of Durham's best cricketers were studying for one of two sports-related degrees; one was to be dropped, and the other absorbed into Social Sciences. It remains to be seen whether Durham's well-established tradition of success in sport, and cricket in particular, will be a casualty.

DURHAM UCCE RESULTS

First-class matches – Played 3: Lost 1, Drawn 2.

At Nottingham, April 12, 13, 14. DURHAM UCCE lost to NOTTINGHAMSHIRE by an innings and 168 runs.

DURHAM UCCE v DURHAM

At Durham, May 9, 10, 11. Drawn. Toss: Durham. First-class debuts: S. L. J. M. Hawk, J. W. Somerville-Hendrie; L. E. Plunkett.

An exhilarating game was a credit to both teams. On the first day, Peng came in with three down in the ninth over, and raced to 103 before lunch. He finished with a career-best 158 from 138 balls, and Gary Pratt just missed a maiden century. Next day, Loudon responded superbly, with gritty support from Maiden. Loudon, whose previous first-class best was 48, batted serenely for more than five hours to reach 172 off 243 balls, finally misjudging a flighted ball from Phillips. He declared 118 behind, and Durham rattled up a brisk 180 to set a challenge of 299 in 52 overs. The students accepted, accelerating to more than a run a ball: Ferley finished on 78 not out from 70, and they were just 14 short of the target.

Close of play: First day, Durham 450-8 (Plunkett 25, Phillips 9); Second day, Durham UCCE 332-5 (Ferley 29, Polley 12).

Durham

*J. J. B. Lewis c Loudon b Bishop	6	– retired out	58
M. A. Gough b Daggett	5	– c Maiden b Somerville-Hendrie	0
G. J. Muchall c Polley b Bishop	19	– not out	101
G. J. Pratt c Hanson b Daggett	96		
N. Peng c Brown b Bishop	158		
D. R. Law b Ferley	74		
†A. Pratt c Smith b Polley	1	– (4) not out	13
I. D. Hunter c Hanson b Loudon	47		
L. E. Plunkett not out	25		
N. C. Phillips not out	9		
B 2, l-b 4, n-b 4	10	B 4, l-b 2, w 2	8
1/10 (2) 2/28 (1) 3/35 (3) 4/259 (4) 5/303 (5) 6/304 (7) 7/391 (8) 8/433 (6)	(8 wkts dec.) 450	1/0 (2) 2/140 (1)	(2 wkts dec.) 180

N. Killeen did not bat.

Bowling: *First Innings*—Bishop 15–1–56–3; Daggett 16–1–95–2; Somerville-Hendrie 15–1–55–0; Polley 11–1–54–1; Ferley 28–5–129–1; Loudon 11.4–0–55–1. *Second Innings*—Daggett 8–3–21–0; Somerville-Hendrie 6–0–34–1; Ferley 15.4–3–52–0; Polley 8–0–36–0; Loudon 6–1–31–0.

Durham UCCE

A. J. Maiden c Gough b Phillips	53	– c Peng b Muchall	51
S. L. J. M. Hawk c A. Pratt b Plunkett	8	– c A. Pratt b Killeen	7
*A. G. R. Loudon c Law b Phillips	172	– c A. Pratt b Law	40
W. R. Smith lbw b Hunter	5	– c and b Phillips	15
D. O. Brown c Phillips b Killeen	33	– c Muchall b Phillips	46
R. S. Ferley not out	29	– not out	78
S. R. Polley not out	12	– run out	39
†W. T. D. Hanson (did not bat)		– b Killeen	0
L. M. Daggett (did not bat)		– not out	3
L-b 9, w 3, n-b 8	20	B 5, l-b 1	6
1/21 (2) 2/168 (1) 3/173 (4) 4/225 (5) 5/314 (3)	(5 wkts dec.) 332	1/15 (2) 2/77 (3) 3/104 (4) 4/136 (1) 5/192 (5) 6/274 (7) 7/277 (8)	(7 wkts) 285

J. E. Bishop and J. W. Somerville-Hendrie did not bat.

Bowling: *First Innings*—Hunter 23–3–90–1; Plunkett 14–7–36–1; Killeen 12–4–35–1; Law 13–1–43–0; Phillips 29–8–86–2; Gough 11–1–33–0. *Second Innings*—Killeen 11–3–63–2; Law 14–4–54–1; Hunter 4–0–25–0; Phillips 15–1–85–2; Muchall 3–0–23–1; Gough 5–0–29–0.

Umpires: A. Clarkson and R. T. Robinson.

DURHAM UCCE v LANCASHIRE

At Durham, May 21, 22, 23. Drawn. Toss: Durham UCCE. First-class debuts: S. P. Crook, P. J. Horton, O. J. Newby.

Taking first use of an easy-paced wicket, Durham UCCE batted sensibly throughout the opening day, with determined fifties from Hawk and Brown providing the springboard for a more rapid one from Bishop. But Bishop later broke down in his sixth over, and an otherwise modest attack offered some easy runs. Swann and Currie opened with a stand of 215, before Hooper completed a maiden century for Lancashire. The county led by 105 at the start of the final day, but ran up another 70 in 11 overs. Mahmood reduced the students to 40 for four, on his way to nine in the match, before Brown and the indomitable Ferley, who batted for three hours, held Lancashire at bay for an honourable draw.

Close of play: First day, Durham UCCE 285-6 (Bishop 41, Polley 15); Second day, Lancashire 432-3 (Chilton 57, Schofield 29).

Durham UCCE

A. J. Maiden c Haynes b Mahmood	5	– b Mahmood	0
S. L. J. M. Hawk c Currie b Schofield	59	– c Chilton b Mahmood	7
*A. G. R. Loudon c Schofield b Newby	27	– b Mahmood	18
W. R. Smith c Chilton b Mahmood	31	– c Hooper b Mahmood	8
D. O. Brown lbw b Schofield	54	– c sub b Mahmood	59
R. S. Ferley c Currie b Schofield	32	– not out	61
J. E. Bishop c and b Mahmood	50		
S. R. Polley c Chilton b Schofield	41	– (7) c Horton b Chilton	2
L. M. Daggett c Swann b Mahmood	1	– (8) not out	3
†W. T. D. Hanson not out	4		
J. W. Somerville-Hendrie not out	1		
B 1, l-b 9, n-b 12	22	L-b 8, w 1, n-b 8	17
1/8 (1) 2/57 (3) 3/123 (4) 4/137 (2) 5/217 (6) 6/234 (5) 7/302 (7) 8/310 (9) 9/326 (8)	(9 wkts dec.) 327	1/1 (1) 2/30 (2) 3/31 (3) 4/40 (4) 5/135 (5) 6/164 (7)	(6 wkts) 175

Bowling: *First Innings*—Mahmood 24–3–76–4; Crook 16–3–62–0; Newby 18–4–41–1; Keedy 20–1–50–0; Schofield 31–10–64–4; Chilton 2–0–13–0; Hooper 6–0–11–0. *Second Innings*—Mahmood 14–4–37–5; Crook 8–0–35–0; Newby 11–3–41–0; Schofield 5–1–10–0; Keedy 4–0–11–0; Hooper 12–3–31–0; Chilton 2–1–2–1.

Lancashire

A. J. Swann st Hanson b Ferley	137
M. R. Currie c Smith b Brown	97
C. L. Hooper c Polley b Somerville-Hendrie	101
*M. J. Chilton c Maiden b Somerville-Hendrie	89
C. P. Schofield c Hanson b Daggett	47
†J. J. Haynes c Hanson b Somerville-Hendrie	13
P. J. Horton not out	2
S. I. Mahmood not out	5
B 2, l-b 3, w 2, n-b 4	11
1/215 (1) 2/263 (2) 3/388 (3) 4/469 (5) 5/495 (4) 6/495 (6)	(6 wkts dec.) 502

S. P. Crook, G. Keedy and O. J. Newby did not bat.

Bowling: Bishop 5.2–0–31–0; Daggett 27–3–110–1; Somerville-Hendrie 24.4–3–124–3; Ferley 17–0–105–1; Loudon 11–0–69–0; Polley 2–0–20–0; Brown 9–1–38–1.

Umpires: M. R. Benson and A. Hill.

"The match ended with a scene out of John le Carré, when Henry Olonga was spirited to a safe house amid rumours that a snatch-squad from Zimbabwe's secret police had arrived."

The World Cup, page 1025.

LOUGHBOROUGH

GUY JACKSON

Director of Cricket: Dr G. A. M. Jackson
Head Coach: G. R. Dilley

Loughborough UCCE Captain: J. H. K. Adams
Loughborough Club Captain: D. H. Wigley

Loughborough University entered their maiden first-class season without the services of several players who had helped secure this status, most notably Mark Powell, who had joined Northamptonshire, Stephen Selwood, with Derbyshire, influential Australian opening bowler Mark Tournier, and Monty Panesar, who spent the winter with the ECB National Academy and then rejoined Northamptonshire.

It was testament to Loughborough's strength that the new captain, James Adams (on Hampshire's books), was still able to lead a team with several county prospects, including Robert White (Northamptonshire), John Francis (Hampshire), Zoheb Sharif (Essex), Chris Nash (Sussex), David Wigley (Worcestershire) and Vikram Atri (Nottinghamshire). Another Nottinghamshire player, Chris Read, was also a Loughborough student, but his only contribution in a season which saw him recalled by England came in a coaching capacity.

Loughborough had dominated university cricket since the inception of the University Centres of Cricketing Excellence in 2001, with successive clean sweeps in all three senior competitions: the two-day UCCE Championship and one-day UCCE Challenge, plus the British Universities Championship, which they had also won in 2000. This comprehensive success and their player development programme under head coach Graham Dilley earned them promotion.

Their first-class career began with draws at Taunton and The Oval, before they succumbed to an innings defeat by neighbours Leicestershire. The bowling, weakened by injuries, struggled to contain the county batsmen – the lowest total they conceded was 413 for three by Somerset, Surrey recorded four centuries in one innings, and Darren Maddy and Brad Hodge plundered 436, a Leicestershire all-wicket record. The batting was far more convincing. Adams scored a maiden first-class hundred, to follow his twin centuries in the previous season's non-first-class match with Kent. Atri twice held firm for unbeaten fifties to force draws with Somerset and Surrey, and averaged 56.25. White made an aggressive 76 against Surrey, and Sharif scored two half-centuries in difficult circumstances at Leicester. No bowler exceeded three wickets, though they had their moments: James Anyon had a hand in all three first-innings wickets at Taunton – he took two and caught one. Against his native Surrey, Ryan Cummins claimed two Test victims, Mark Butcher and Graham Thorpe.

Loughborough's supremacy on the university circuit slipped very slightly. They headed the two-day UCCE league for the third year running, effectively clinching the title with the competition's only outright win, by an innings and 49, against Bradford/Leeds, though their best session was probably dismissing arch-rivals Durham for 60 before lunch at the Racecourse. The one-day Challenge Shield was shared with Oxford because of a washout at Trent Bridge. But Loughborough missed the British Universities final, for only the second time in eight years, when they went out in the semis at the hands of a highly motivated Exeter University side.

But with player development Loughborough's primary goal, there was equal satisfaction later in the summer when Adams returned to his role as opening bat at Hampshire, Atri made his Championship debut for Nottinghamshire and Wigley for Worcestershire.

LOUGHBOROUGH UCCE RESULTS

First-class matches – Played 3: Lost 1, Drawn 2.

At Taunton, April 12, 13, 14. LOUGHBOROUGH UCCE drew with SOMERSET.

At The Oval, April 23, 24, 25. LOUGHBOROUGH UCCE drew with SURREY.

At Leicester, May 9, 10, 11. LOUGHBOROUGH UCCE lost to LEICESTERSHIRE by an innings and 35 runs.

THE UNIVERSITY MATCHES, 2003

CAMBRIDGE UNIVERSITY v OXFORD UNIVERSITY

At Cambridge, June 26, 27, 28. Oxford University won by an innings and 71 runs. Toss: Oxford University. First-class debuts: A. Singh; S. R. Daley, C. W. Free.

Everything went right for Dalrymple from the moment he won the toss. After watching a century opening stand, he and Millar, in their first first-class game of the summer because of exams, added 263, a third-wicket Varsity Match record. Dalrymple completed his second successive century in the fixture with a six off John Heath; next day, he reached a maiden double-hundred with a six off Heath's brother Duncan. He hit one more six, and 23 fours, in 266 balls, batting six hours 12 minutes before he declared, unaware that he was two short of the Varsity record, 238 not out by the Nawab of Pataudi senior in 1931. Oxford's total of 522 for seven was their highest against Cambridge. Dalrymple gave off-spinner McMahon the new ball, but his own off-breaks claimed five wickets and forced the home side to follow on. Cambridge rallied, thanks to an unbeaten 126 from Marshall lasting nearly five hours. This time the leg-spinner, Munday, dismissed five men. Oxford secured an innings win, their 50th victory in first-class Varsity cricket, with a day to spare.

Close of play: First day, Oxford University 415-5 (Dalrymple 153, Evans 0); Second day, Cambridge University 181.

Oxford University

J. J. Sayers (*St Mary's RC Menston and Worcester*) c Savill b J. A. Heath	69
S. J. Hawinkels (*St Stithians, Island School Hong Kong and University*) lbw b McGrath	49
*J. W. M. Dalrymple (*Radley and St Peter's*) not out	236
N. Millar (*Fettes and Christ Church*) c Heywood b Savill	108
J. A. Allen (*Bede Polding, Sydney U. of Tech and University*) c D. R. Heath b Savill	0
G. R. Butcher (*Wallington CGS and Oriel*) c Heywood b Marshall	0
†P. P. Evans (*Eton and Keble*) c Savill b J. A. Heath	14
P. J. McMahon (*Trinity RC Nottingham and Wadham*) b McGrath	7
B 7, l-b 10, w 4, n-b 18	39
1/119 (2) 2/151 (1) 3/414 (4) 4/414 (5) 5/415 (6) 6/489 (7) 7/522 (8) (7 wkts dec.)	522

S. R. Daley (*Nudgee C., Queensland U. and Magdalen*), C. W. Free (*Sydney High, UNSW and Balliol*) and M. K. Munday (*Truro and Corpus Christi*) did not bat.

Bowling: Savill 28–3–113–2; McGrath 20–7–90–2; Marshall 26–3–76–1; Noble 11–2–49–0; D. R. Heath 17–2–75–0; J. A. Heath 21–1–83–2; Singh 4–0–19–0.

Cambridge University

Batsman	First innings		Second innings	
*A. Shankar (*Bedford and Queens'*)	lbw b McMahon	7	lbw b Free	6
D. R. Heath (*Sir John Nelthorpe S, Brigg SFC and Pembroke*)	b Dalrymple	32	c Dalrymple b McMahon	0
R. J. Mann (*Ipswich and St John's*)	lbw b McMahon	52	c and b McMahon	63
S. J. Marshall (*Birkenhead and Pembroke*)	c Evans b Dalrymple	6	not out	126
A. Singh (*King Edward's Birmingham and Gonville & Caius*)	c Evans b Munday	0	lbw b Munday	22
V. H. Kumar (*Dulwich and St John's*)	c Evans b Dalrymple	50	b Munday	0
T. E. Savill (*Fernwood and Homerton*)	c Dalrymple b Munday	7	lbw b Munday	4
J. A. Heath (*Sir John Nelthorpe S, Brigg SFC and Pembroke*)	lbw b McMahon	2	lbw b Dalrymple	6
D. J. Noble (*Rugby and Emmanuel*)	not out	8	b Munday	1
†J. J. N. Heywood (*Worth and Homerton*)	c Evans b Dalrymple	3	c Dalrymple b Munday	8
D. E. T. McGrath (*St Joseph's, Queensland U. of Tech and St Edmund's*)	lbw b Dalrymple	1	lbw b McMahon	4
	B 4, w 3, n-b 6	13	B 12, l-b 4, w 10, n-b 4	30
	1/8 (1) 2/50 (2) 3/66 (4) 4/67 (5) 5/136 (3) 6/143 (7) 7/156 (8) 8/171 (6) 9/177 (10) 10/181 (11)	181	1/6 (1) 2/8 (2) 3/151 (3) 4/194 (5) 5/194 (6) 6/198 (7) 7/221 (8) 8/233 (9) 9/259 (10) 10/270 (11)	270

Bowling: *First Innings*—Free 5–0–23–0; McMahon 29–7–59–3; Dalrymple 22.1–7–49–5; Munday 15–4–46–2. *Second Innings*—Free 10–1–32–1; McMahon 26.5–12–54–3; Daley 9–1–31–0; Munday 25–1–83–5; Dalrymple 22–4–43–1; Millar 2–0–11–0.

Umpires: M. Dixon and B. Leadbeater.

OXFORD v CAMBRIDGE, NOTES

The University Match dates back to 1827. Altogether there have been 158 official matches, Cambridge winning 56 and Oxford 50, with 52 drawn. Since the war Cambridge have won ten times (1949, 1953, 1957, 1958, 1972, 1979, 1982, 1986, 1992 and 1998) and Oxford 11 (1946, 1948, 1951, 1959, 1966, 1976, 1984, 1993, 1995, 2001 and 2003). All other matches have been drawn; the 1988 fixture was abandoned without a ball being bowled. The first-class fixture was moved from its traditional venue at Lord's in 2001, to be staged alternately at Cambridge and Oxford, and a one-day game was played instead at Lord's.

One hundred and fourteen three-figure innings have been played in the University matches, 54 for Oxford and 60 for Cambridge. For the fullest lists see the 1940 and 1993 *Wisdens*. There have been three double-centuries for Cambridge (211 by G. Goonesena in 1957, 201 by A. Ratcliffe in 1931 and 200 by Majid Khan in 1970) and three for Oxford (238* by Nawab of Pataudi, sen. in 1931, 236* by J. W. M. Dalrymple in 2003 and 201* by M. J. K. Smith in 1954). Ratcliffe's score was a record for the match for only one day, before being beaten by Pataudi's. M. J. K. Smith and R. J. Boyd-Moss (Cambridge) are the only players to score three hundreds.

The highest totals in the fixture are 604 in 2002 by Cambridge, and 522-7 in 2003, 513-6 in 1996, 503 in 1900, 457 in 1947, 453-8 in 1931 and 453-9 in 1994, all by Oxford. The lowest totals are 32 by Oxford in 1878 and 39 by Cambridge in 1858.

F. C. Cobden, in the Oxford v Cambridge match in 1870, performed the hat-trick by taking the last three wickets and won an extraordinary game for Cambridge by two runs. Other hat-tricks, all for Cambridge, have been achieved by A. G. Steel (1879), P. H. Morton (1880), J. F. Ireland (1911) and R. G. H. Lowe (1926). S. E. Butler, in the 1871 match, took all ten wickets in the Cambridge first innings.

D. W. Jarrett (Oxford 1975, Cambridge 1976), S. M. Wookey (Cambridge 1975-76, Oxford 1978) and G. Pathmanathan (Oxford 1975-78, Cambridge 1983) gained Blues for both Universities.

A full list of Blues from 1837 may be found in Wisdens *published between 1923 and 1939. The lists thereafter were curtailed, covering more recent years only, and dropped after 1992.*

†At Lord's, July 2. **Oxford University won by 73 runs (D/L method).** Toss: Oxford University. **Cambridge University 190** (49.5 overs) (N. Millar 5-23); **Oxford University 162-1** (31 overs) (J. W. M. Dalrymple 105*).

Dalrymple followed up his 236 in the first-class Varsity match with 105* in 104 balls, including ten fours and four sixes. Rain ended play when Oxford were 73 runs ahead of the D/L par score of 89 in 31 overs; they took a 5–4 lead in the one-day Varsity series.*

OTHER UCCES, 2003

The elevation of Loughborough, the strongest team since the introduction of the University Centres of Cricketing Excellence in 2001, left only two non-first-class UCCEs – Cardiff (made up of Cardiff University, UWIC and the University of Glamorgan) and Bradford/Leeds (Bradford University, Bradford College, Leeds University and Leeds Metropolitan University). They had both lost all their county matches the previous season, but improved on that in 2003: Bradford/Leeds, whose captain, Ismail Dawood, scored a century against his old club Yorkshire, drew all three games, and Cardiff lost only to Sussex. Cardiff, however, appeared the stronger side overall. They finished third, for the third year running, in the UCCE's two-day league, and beat Bradford/Leeds in a play-off to win a place in the British Universities' revamped six-strong Premier League in 2004.

Note: Matches in this section were not first-class. UCCE away games appear in the county sections.

At Cardiff, April 12, 13, 14. CARDIFF UCCE drew with GLAMORGAN.

At Bristol, April 12, 13, 14. BRADFORD/LEEDS UCCE drew with GLOUCESTERSHIRE.

At Hove, April 18, 19. CARDIFF UCCE lost to SUSSEX by an innings and 280 runs.

At Derby, April 23, 24, 25. BRADFORD/LEEDS UCCE drew with DERBYSHIRE.

At Abergavenny, May 14, 15, 16. **Drawn.** Toss: Warwickshire. **Warwickshire 367-4 dec.** (M. J. Powell 140, I. J. L. Trott 69, I. J. Westwood 63*) **and 132-1**; **Cardiff UCCE 251** (A. N. French 67; I. R. Bell 4-13).

County debut: C. O. Obuya. First-team debut: I. J. Westwood.

At Bradford, June 4, 5, 6. **Drawn.** Toss: Bradford/Leeds UCCE. **Yorkshire 409-3 dec.** (M. J. Wood 63, C. White 65, R. J. Blakey 117, G. M. Hamilton 143*) **and 140-2 dec.** (S. M. Guy 55*, M. J. Wood 63*); **Bradford/Leeds UCCE 241** (I. Dawood 125; P. J. Swanepoel 4-50) **and 113-4.**

Two men were absent hurt in Bradford/Leeds' first innings.

THE INTER-UCCE CHAMPIONSHIP, 2003

GRENVILLE HOLLAND

Loughborough continued to dominate the ECB's UCCE competitions. They headed the two-day league, as they had done since its introduction in 2001, and secured the only outright, two-innings win when they crushed Bradford/Leeds in the penultimate round.

They bowled them out for 127 on the first day, then piled up 309 thanks to half-centuries from James Adams and John Francis, before medium-pacer Steve Clarke, claiming five for 31, wrapped up the Bradford/Leeds second innings in 36 overs, to complete victory by an innings and 49 runs. Loughborough also recorded first-innings wins over Cardiff and Durham, bowled out in a morning at the Racecourse. For the second year running, Oxford came in second and Cardiff third. As usual, Bradford/Leeds were never in contention.

The two leading individual performances both came for Loughborough in their match with Cardiff, when James Anyon took six for 54 and then John Francis eased them into the lead with an unbeaten 150. Cardiff's Mark Pettini scored 102 in the same game; Adrian Shankar of Cambridge and Oxford's Australian batsman, Ed Cowan, also scored centuries. For Cambridge, Tony Palladino had five-wicket returns against both Cardiff and Oxford.

Note: Matches in this section were not first-class.

INTER-UCCE CHAMPIONSHIP, 2003

					1st-inns	*Bonus points*		
	Played	*Won*	*Lost*	*Drawn*	*points*	*Batting*	*Bowling*	*Points*
Loughborough	5	1	0	4	28	16	24	77†
Oxford	5	0	0	5	36	11	16	63
Cardiff	5	0	0	5	20	19	18	57
Cambridge	5	0	0	5	23	11	19	53
Durham	5	0	0	5	23	12	11	46
Bradford/Leeds	5	0	1	4	3	8	11	22

† 1 pt deducted for slow over-rate.

Outright win = 10 pts; 1st-innings lead in a match reaching an outright result = 5 pts; 1st-innings win in a drawn match = 10 pts; draw or no result on 1st innings = 3 pts.

Up to four bonus points for batting and bowling were available in each innings, though in the first innings batting points were available only for the first 102 overs (or 50 per cent of the total overs in a shortened match).

ONE-DAY UCCE CHALLENGE

At Nottingham, June 30. **Loughborough v Oxford. Abandoned.**
Loughborough and Oxford shared the Trophy.

"You would think 'Where is he?'. Then all of a sudden he would jump out from behind the umpire and the ball would come up like a whirlwind."
Angus Fraser on Wasim Akram, page 1589.

THE BRITISH UNIVERSITIES CHAMPIONSHIP, 2003

GRENVILLE HOLLAND

The usual suspects carved up the British Universities Championships in 2003. Durham took their 17th outright senior title, but their first since 1999, and retained the women's championship; Loughborough's second and third teams won the men's minor titles.

Durham were on top from the moment they overcame Loughborough UCCE in their first, rain-affected, match in late April. They headed the Northern Premier League with four wins and a washout. The Southern leaders were Exeter, perennial applicants for UCCE status, who also won four matches, though they lost to Oxford UCCE, who were unlucky with the weather, and finished a point behind.

That meant that the same four teams reached the semi-finals for the fourth season running. It looked as if Oxford might be first-time finalists when they sent Durham sliding to 114 for seven in the 33rd over, chasing 198, but the imperturbable Simon Hawk steered Durham home. The run of Durham–Loughborough finals was broken, however, when a lacklustre Loughborough team fell easy prey to Exeter, who triumphed by a handsome eight wickets to enter their first final since 1995.

In that final, Durham had crushed Exeter by 239 runs, and the outcome was the same, though without the humiliation. Batting first, Durham accumulated 251, thanks to valuable fifties from Will Smith and, yet again, Hawk, while off-spinner Paul James collected four wickets. Exeter made a confident start in reply, with Simon Moore and Neil Turk adding 118 for the second wicket, but Durham captain Alex Loudon's off-spin removed both, the later order succumbed to the pressure, and they were dismissed with 11 balls to spare.

In 2004, the British Universities Sports Association planned a new structure for the men's senior championship. The top six teams – the 2003 semi-finalists, plus Cambridge UCCE and Cardiff UCCE, who won play-offs against Bradford/Leeds and St Mary's College, Twickenham – would form a national Premier League, a first in any BUSA competition.

Note: Matches in this section were not first-class.

BRITISH UNIVERSITIES PREMIER LEAGUES

Northern	*Played*	*Won*	*Lost*	*No result*	*Points*
DURHAM UCCE	5	4	0	1	13
LOUGHBOROUGH UCCE	5	4*	1	0	12
Cambridge UCCE	5	2	1	2	8
Bradford/Leeds UCCE	5	1	2	2	5
Liverpool	5	0	4	1	1
Nottingham	5	1	4*	0	0

* *Nottingham conceded their match with Loughborough and lost their three points.*

Southern	*Played*	*Won*	*Lost*	*No result*	*Points*
EXETER	5	4	1	0	12
OXFORD UCCE	5	3	0	2	11
St Mary's	5	2	2	1	7
Cardiff UCCE	5	2	2	0*	6
Bristol	5	1	2	1*	4
Reading	5	0	5	0	0

* *The match between Cardiff and Bristol was void.*
Win = 3pts; no result = 1pt.

SEMI-FINALS

At Sheffield, June 9. **Durham UCCE won by three wickets.** Toss: Oxford UCCE. **Oxford UCCE 197-8** (50 overs); **Durham UCCE 198-7** (46.5 overs) (S. L. J. M. Hawk 57*).

Durham recovered from 114-7 in the 33rd over after losing five wickets for 26.

At Bournemouth, June 9. **Exeter won by eight wickets.** Toss: Exeter. **Loughborough UCCE 161-9** (50 overs); **Exeter 162-2** (41.4 overs) (C. Coulson 59, I. Haley 66*).

FINAL

At Southampton, June 16. **Durham UCCE won by 58 runs.** Toss: Exeter. **Durham UCCE 251-7** (50 overs) (W. R. Smith 62, S. L. J. M. Hawk 73; P. B. C. James 4-50); **Exeter 193** (48.1 overs) (S. Moore 55, N. R. K. Turk 57).

WINNERS 1927–2003

The UAU Championship was replaced by the British Universities Championship from 1995.

1927 Manchester
1928 Manchester
1929 Nottingham
1930 Sheffield
1931 Liverpool
1932 Manchester
1933 Manchester
1934 Leeds
1935 Sheffield
1936 Sheffield
1937 Nottingham
1938 Durham
1939 Durham
1946 Not completed
1947 Sheffield
1948 Leeds
1949 Leeds
1950 Manchester
1951 Manchester
1952 Loughborough Colls.
1953 Durham
1954 Manchester
1955 Birmingham
1956 Null and void
1957 Loughborough Colls.
1958 Null and void
1959 Liverpool
1960 Loughborough Colls.
1961 Loughborough Colls.
1962 Manchester
1963 Loughborough Colls.
1964 Loughborough Colls.
1965 Hull
1966 { Newcastle / Southampton }
1967 Manchester
1968 Southampton
1969 Southampton
1970 Southampton
1971 Loughborough Colls.
1972 Durham
1973 { Leicester / Loughborough Colls. }
1974 Durham
1975 Loughborough Colls.
1976 Loughborough
1977 Durham
1978 Manchester
1979 Manchester
1980 Exeter
1981 Durham
1982 Exeter
1983 Exeter
1984 Bristol
1985 Birmingham
1986 Durham
1987 Durham
1988 Swansea
1989 Loughborough
1990 Durham
1991 Durham
1992 Durham
1993 Durham
1994 Swansea
1995 Durham
1996 Loughborough
1997 Durham
1998 { Durham / Loughborough }
1999 Durham
2000 Loughborough
2001 Loughborough
2002 Loughborough
2003 Durham

Durham have won the Championship outright 17 times, Loughborough 14, Manchester 11, Sheffield 4, Exeter, Leeds and Southampton 3, Birmingham, Liverpool, Nottingham and Swansea 2, Bristol and Hull 1. Loughborough have shared the title twice; Durham, Leicester, Newcastle and Southampton once each.

MCC MATCHES, 2003

ERIC MIDWINTER

Those who witnessed the incursions of the bulldozers at the end of 2002 scarcely dared believe that the re-laying of the Lord's outfield would be finished in time for the next season. For much of the winter, the ground resembled a ploughed field: 21,500 square yards of turf was pulled up and two miles of new drainage laid.

But on a sunny morning on May 7, MCC stepped on to a pristine surface to face the club's Young Cricketers. With a stalwart 82, Maurits van Nierop, from Holland, helped the Young Cricketers to a 13-run win. In June, they enjoyed another impressive success at Lord's, beating Loughborough UCCE – recently made a first-class side. Loughborough would be swept aside by big margins twice more during the summer, as the Young Cricketers went unbeaten against university teams, including Cambridge UCCE, Oxford UCCE and English Universities.

With no flagship first-class fixture, the senior side's match against the ECB Amateur XI was perhaps the most testing. In a 50-over game at Lord's, Owais Shah of Middlesex and James Hudson both scored fifties for MCC, but a late and lively partnership secured the ECB's second successive win in the fixture, with nine balls left. Among the other major Lord's matches, MCC Home Counties beat a combined side from MCC Ireland, Scotland and Wales on August 18. Bill Hubbick's 82 for the Home Counties was the best of several resplendent innings, in a match that saw 539 runs scored in 105 overs. The following day, Ireland came to Lord's, and won by seven

Hallowed turf? Lord's in the winter of 2002-03.

Picture courtesy of MCC.

wickets. MCC struggled to set a competitive target and Ireland knocked off the runs with ten of their 50 overs left. Jeremy Bray's 94 was outstanding for Ireland, while all their bowlers plied away diligently.

In 2003, MCC men's teams played 408 games against schools and clubs, winning 187, drawing 83 and losing 90. All told, 48 were abandoned because of the weather – fewer than in 2002, but more than might have been suspected, as happy memories of spectacular midsummer sunshine supplanted those of early-season rain. To these matches must be added the fast-developing MCC Women's list. They played 18 games over the season, won the Durham Women's Cricket Festival and defeated a national touring side – the South Africans – for the first time.

Fixtures in 2003 included tours to countries as far-flung as Nigeria and Nepal. This autumn also marked the 100th anniversary of the club's first overseas trip, in 1903-04. Then, a side led by Plum Warner sailed for Australia to face the likes of Victor Trumper and Warwick Armstrong; in September 2003 MCC encountered slightly less intimidating opposition, on an anniversary tour of Greece. It is sometimes forgotten, amid the pomp of the major occasions at Lord's, that MCC remains the largest playing cricket club on the planet.

PRESIDENTS OF MCC SINCE 1946

1946	General Sir Ronald Adam, Bt.
1947	Captain Lord Cornwallis
1948	Brig.-Gen. The Earl of Gowrie
1949	HRH The Duke of Edinburgh
1950	Sir Pelham Warner
1951-52	W. Findlay
1952-53	The Duke of Beaufort
1953-54	The Earl of Rosebery
1954-55	Viscount Cobham
1955-56	Field Marshal Earl Alexander of Tunis
1956-57	Vis. Monckton of Brenchley
1957-58	The Duke of Norfolk
1958-59	Marshal of the RAF Viscount Portal of Hungerford
1959-60	H. S. Altham
1960-61	Sir Hubert Ashton
1961-62	Col. Sir William Worsley, Bt.
1962-63	Lt-Col. Lord Nugent
1963-64	G. O. B. Allen
1964-65	R. H. Twining
1965-66	Lt-Gen. Sir Oliver Leese, Bt.
1966-67	Sir Alec Douglas-Home
1967-68	A. E. R. Gilligan
1968-69	R. Aird
1969-70	M. J. C. Allom
1970-71	Sir Cyril Hawker
1971-72	F. R. Brown
1972-73	A. M. Crawley
1973-74	Lord Caccia
1974-75	HRH The Duke of Edinburgh
1975-76	C. G. A. Paris
1976-77	W. H. Webster
1977-78	D. G. Clark
1978-79	C. H. Palmer
1979-80	S. C. Griffith
1980-81	P. B. H. May
1981-82	G. H. G. Doggart
1982-83	Sir Anthony Tuke
1983-84	A. H. A. Dibbs
1984-85	F. G. Mann
1985-86	J. G. W. Davies
1986-87	M. C. Cowdrey
1987-88	J. J. Warr
1988-89	Field Marshal The Lord Bramall
1989-90	The Hon. Sir Denys Roberts
1990-91	The Rt Hon. The Lord Griffiths
1991-92	M. E. L. Melluish
1992-94	D. R. W. Silk
1994-96	The Hon. Sir Oliver Popplewell
1996-98	A. C. D. Ingleby-Mackenzie
1998-2000	A. R. Lewis
2000-01	Lord Alexander of Weedon
2001-02	E. R. Dexter
2002-03	Sir Timothy Rice
2003-04	C. A. Fry

Since 1951, Presidents of MCC have taken office on October 1. Previously they took office immediately after the annual general meeting at the start of the season. From 1992 to 2000, Presidents were eligible for two consecutive years of office; since then the period has reverted to one year.

OTHER MATCHES, 2003

Note: Matches in this section were not first-class.

At Canterbury, April 29, 30, May 1, 2. **Drawn.** England Under-19 batted first by mutual agreement. **England Under-19 471** (A. N. Cook 82, R. S. Bopara 50, S. R. Patel 104, L. J. Wright 57, Extras 83; P. M. R. Havell 4-92) **and 233-6** (A. W. Gale 50); **Kent Second Eleven 335** (M. J. Dennington 99, N. O'Brien 72).

This was the annual fixture between the previous season's Second Eleven champions and England Under-19. Over three innings, the two teams between them conceded 119 in no-balls. The last day was washed out.

At Cardiff, June 14. **England XI won by eight runs.** Toss: England XI. **England XI 235-8** (50 overs) (M. E. Trescothick 55, A. McGrath 50); **Wales 227** (48.4 overs) (R. D. B. Croft 59).

Michael Vaughan began his reign as England's one-day captain with a narrow win over Wales (essentially Glamorgan, including their Australian overseas player Michael Kasprowicz plus Steffan Jones of Somerset) in a warm-up for the NatWest Challenge with Pakistan. Trescothick was Man of the Match.

ZONE6 CITY CRICKET

All matches in the Zone6 City Cricket tournament were played at Hove, on August 8.

Group A

Cape Town won by 31 runs. Toss: Cape Town. **Leeds 152; Cape Town 183**. *Cape Town 7 pts, Leeds 1 pt.*

London won by 34 runs. Toss: London. **Leeds 184** (C. White 79); **London 218** (M. J. Walker 60, A. D. Brown 52). *London 8 pts, Leeds 2 pts.*

London won by 22 runs. Toss: Cape Town. **London 199** (A. D. Brown 58); **Cape Town 177.** *London 6 pts, Cape Town 3 pts.*

London 14 pts, Cape Town 10 pts, Leeds 3 pts.

Group B

Brighton & Hove won by 38 runs. Toss: Brighton & Hove. **Birmingham 162; Brighton & Hove 200.** *Brighton & Hove 8 pts, Birmingham 1 pt.*

Colombo won by 65 runs. Toss: Birmingham. **Colombo 226** (S. T. Jayasuriya 98); **Birmingham 161.** *Colombo 8 pts, Birmingham 1 pt.*

Colombo won by 13 runs. Toss: Brighton & Hove. **Colombo 179** (S. T. Jayasuriya 62); **Brighton & Hove 166.** *Colombo 6 pts, Brighton & Hove 2 pts.*

Colombo 14 pts, Brighton & Hove 10 pts, Birmingham 2 pts.

Final

Colombo won by 39 runs. Toss: Colombo. **Colombo 187; London 148** (M. Muralitharan 4-27).

The Zone6 tournament was organised by the PCA. Brighton & Hove, Cape Town and Colombo replaced Bristol, Manchester and Southampton from the previous year's competition, played at Birmingham and won by Leeds. The city teams fielded eight players, who could bat or bowl but not both. Matches were eight overs a side, with bowlers limited to three overs each. Teams started with a total of 100 runs, and lost six for every wicket; dismissed batsmen could return after two more wickets had fallen. Runs were doubled for boundaries hit through one of six "scoring zones". Results were calculated on runs, with no allowance for wickets. Four points were awarded for a win, with bonus points available. In nine overs during the day, Muttiah Muralitharan took seven wickets for 67.

THE MINOR COUNTIES, 2003

PHILIP AUGUST

Mathew Dowman

Lincolnshire became the first outright Minor Counties champions since the experiment with three-day matches began in 2001. The previous two finals, between the winners of the Eastern and Western Divisions, ended in draws; this time, Lincolnshire fought back after trailing Devon on first innings, bowled them out for 97, and completed an eight-wicket victory. They had been joint champions with Cheshire in 2001, but their only previous outright title had been in 1966.

Lincolnshire were confirmed as Eastern Division champions with a round to go, but there was an exciting climax in the Western Division; second-placed Devon met leaders Berkshire in the last match needing a win to make up a 12-point deficit. Their positive play and the captaincy of Bobby Dawson, who just missed a century, saw them home by 162 runs.

The quality of cricket improved during the first three years of three-day matches, and it was agreed that the format should continue. It does have a downside, however. There is time for only six divisional matches a side, so it is not possible for each team to play all the other nine in their division in one season. In 2003 the top three in the Eastern Division, Lincolnshire, Staffordshire and Bedfordshire, never played one another. It takes three years for a full round-robin, with each team playing the others home and away, to be completed; it is interesting, though, to note that, when the combined points were totted up for this first full three-year cycle, the divisional winners were the 2003 finalists: Lincolnshire and Devon.

The one-day knockout competition, which had been contested by the Minor Counties and the Board XIs of the first-class counties and known as the ECB 38-County Cup for the previous four seasons, reverted to Minor Counties only, for financial reasons. Cambridgeshire defeated Shropshire in the final at Lord's.

MINOR COUNTIES CHAMPIONSHIP, 2003

Eastern Division	P	W	L	D	*Bonus Points* Batting	Bowling	*Total* Points
Lincolnshire	6	5	0	1	21	24	127*
Staffordshire	6	3	1	2	20	20	96
Bedfordshire	6	3	1	2	16	15	87
Cambridgeshire	6	3	3	0	12	19	79
Suffolk	6	2	1	3	13	19	76
Cumberland	6	2	3	1	13	24	73
Norfolk	6	2	3	1	17	19	72
Hertfordshire	6	1	2	3	8	23	59
Northumberland	6	0	3	3	13	19	44
Buckinghamshire	6	0	4	2	6	18	32

Western Division	P	W	L	D	*Bonus Points* Batting	Bowling	*Total* Points
Devon	6	3	0	3	20	20	100
Berkshire	6	3	1	2	17	21	94
Cornwall	6	2	0	4	17	24	89
Wiltshire	6	3	2	1	16	20	88
Shropshire	6	2	0	4	18	20	86
Cheshire	6	2	1	3	16	20	80
Herefordshire	6	1	1	4	16	22	68*
Wales	6	1	4	1	9	16	45
Dorset	6	0	4	2	10	22	40
Oxfordshire	6	0	4	2	10	20	38

Final: Lincolnshire beat Devon by eight wickets.

Win = 16 points; draw = 4 points.

* *Two points deducted for a slow over-rate.*

Lincolnshire won five of their six divisional matches and took the Eastern Division before the last round – despite the loss of their captain, Mark Fell, after a serious knee injury in July. A sixth victory, in the final, gave them the title. They owed their dominance to two former Nottinghamshire batsmen, Paul Pollard and Mathew Dowman, who joined Lincolnshire in 2003 after spells with Worcestershire and Derbyshire respectively. Pollard shared an all-wicket county record stand when he and Martyn Dobson added 331 for the second wicket against Northumberland at Grantham; in all, he scored 702 runs at 78, and Dowman 690 at 69 – the two highest aggregates for any county in 2003. Dowman also collected 24 wickets, but the leading wicket-taker was Elliot Wilson with 30 at 24.03. Eleven bowlers took 126 wickets between them at an economical rate, and the strength of the attack was reflected in the figures of wicket-keeper Oliver Burford, who completed 33 catches and three stumpings.

The former England batsman Kim Barnett, who turned 43 during the season, returned to his native county, **Staffordshire**, and headed the overall averages with 689 at 86, including three centuries, the highest being 198 not out against Suffolk. That was trumped by two double-hundreds, from Paul Shaw, 200 not out against Buckinghamshire, and Graeme Archer, an unbeaten 201 against Norfolk. There had been only five previous double-centuries for the county. David Follett took 39 wickets, more than anyone else in the Championship, and was instrumental in each of the three victories that lifted Staffordshire into second place in the Eastern Division. Wicket-keeper Mark Humphries retired after 114 games in 14 seasons and, in the last innings of his 22nd season, 42-year-old Steve Dean completed 10,000 Championship runs.

David Mercer, 18 months younger than Dean, finished just over 500 short of that landmark. Rediscovering his appetite for runs, he helped **Bedfordshire** improve on their fourth place in 2002, and his 116 on a poor pitch against Northumberland must rank as one of his best innings. James Knott scored 535 at 59 – his lowest average in three seasons with Bedfordshire is 57.50 – including a maiden hundred when he and Adrian Shankar added a third-wicket county record 191 against Norfolk. Having lost Shaun Rashid to Sussex, the bowling relied heavily on captain Andy Roberts, whose leg-spin claimed 25 wickets, and Irishman Mark Patterson, who bowled 192 overs of genuine pace for 23 wickets.

Cambridgeshire's season was one of brilliant batting. It began when 19-year-old John Mann scored 147 on his county debut, against Suffolk, and in the same innings captain Ajaz Akhtar reached his first century in his 103rd game. In August, opener Chris Jones batted throughout a fourth-innings run-chase for an unbeaten 162, to beat Buckinghamshire in the last over. In the one-day knockout, Simon Kellett scored two hundreds and in the Lord's final shared a 131-run opening stand with Michael Sutliff to set up Cambridgeshire's win.

Phil Caley completed his tenth season as captain of **Suffolk** but a mid-table finish reflected some modest performances. Seven batsmen reached 200 runs without going on to 300, and nobody scored a century. Tim Catley's 269 was the highest aggregate, though he averaged only 24. Seamers Trevor Smith and Paul King were the leading wicket-takers, with 21 and 17 respectively; eight other bowlers took 22 wickets between them.

The appointment of Steve O'Shaughnessy as captain improved the fortunes of **Cumberland**, who rose from the bottom of the division to sixth place, though the runs of Ashley Metcalfe and Graham Lloyd, newly retired from Lancashire, proved the key factor. They shared a third-wicket stand of 212 against Bedfordshire, a county record, and Metcalfe later made Cumberland's highest individual score, 172 against Northumberland at Jesmond. In all, he scored 680 at 85, and Lloyd 541 at 54. A 20-year-old seamer from Loughborough UCCE, James Anyon, returned match figures of ten for 134 on his county debut to set up victory over Cambridgeshire.

Steve Goldsmith announced his retirement after 11 seasons with **Norfolk**, who will find him hard to replace. Aged 38, he was their leading run-scorer with 599 at 66, which took him to 6,063 runs, plus 181 wickets, since he joined from Derbyshire in 1993. Norfolk, the previous year's joint champions, also had a new captain, Paul Bradshaw, who led them to two wins during the festival at Manor Park: they beat Hertfordshire by an innings in two days, and Staffordshire at the end of a run-feast – 1,241 for only 22 wickets.

Another new captain, David Ward of **Hertfordshire**, secured victory over Buckinghamshire in their first match, but it proved a false dawn. They never won again and finished a lowly eighth for the second season running. Ward, the former Surrey batsman, scored 678 runs at 75, in an explosive style which may have backfired when opposing captains were considering declarations; he could make any target look achievable.

Phil Nicholson, the **Northumberland** captain and wicket-keeper, injured himself in practice and missed all but the first Championship game. His experience was badly missed: the side never won a match. The acting-captain, Bradley Parker, scored 491 runs and all-rounder Steve Chapman produced another solid performance with 302 runs and 15 wickets.

Buckinghamshire had a season best forgotten. They lost four games, did not manage a single victory and recorded the lowest points total in either division. David Barr stood out among the batsmen, with 373 at 74; leg-spinner Andrew Clarke took 19 wickets and seamer Simon Stanway 18.

After Peter Roebuck's 11-year reign at **Devon**, former Gloucestershire batsman Bobby Dawson took charge in 2003, and led from the front with 614 runs at 55. Heading the Western Division – thanks to their third win, against Berkshire in the last round, when Dawson scored 99 – was a real team achievement for a relatively young and inexperienced side, even if losing the Championship final to Lincolnshire removed the gloss. Richard Foan, a 20-year-old opener, scored 453 runs, and Ian Bishop was the leading wicket-taker with 36, having got off to a near-perfect start with eight for 99 in the first innings he bowled, against Cornwall.

Berkshire also had three victories in a fine season, but losing the last match to Devon meant they slipped to second place. Seamer James Theunissen took five in each innings against Oxfordshire to set up their opening win, while spinners Carl Crowe and James Morris took seven apiece to defeat Wiltshire. In between, three men scored centuries in a total of 466 for five against Cheshire: Lee Nurse, Richard Howitt and Paul Prichard. Howitt, who had joined from Lincolnshire, followed up a career-best 170 not out in that innings with an unbeaten 125 in the next game to secure a seven-wicket victory over Dorset. Crowe took 33 wickets in all, and also averaged 43 with the bat.

Cornwall were considerably strengthened by the return of two batsmen born in Truro, Dave Roberts and Ryan Driver: third place was their highest finish since the Championship split into two divisions in 1983. Roberts, who played his first-class cricket for Northamptonshire but appeared for Bedfordshire in 2002, scored 465 runs and averaged 66, while Driver, formerly of Worcestershire and Lancashire, was impressive with bat and ball, averaging 67 and taking 22 wickets. Off-spinner Tom Sharp headed the averages, and was the leading wicket-taker with 23 at 15.

Wiltshire, in Russell Rowe's first year as captain, had their most successful season since the introduction of three-day cricket: after two years without a win, they managed three and finished fourth. The signing of former England spinner Richard Illingworth proved to be an asset both on and off the field; he scored 208 runs and claimed 20 wickets. Kevin Blackburn was the leading run-scorer despite playing only three matches, with 368 including two hundreds.

Yet another new captain, **Shropshire's** Guy Home, made a successful start. His team never lost a Championship match and reached the knockout final at Lord's, only to lose to Cambridgeshire. Shropshire's strength lay in their batting. Four players averaged over 60 in the Championship, with Stephen Adshead's 433 the leading aggregate. All-rounder Tim Mason collected 32 wickets with his off-spin and scored 211 runs.

Cheshire finished sixth for the second season running under Andy Hall's leadership, but it was a much-improved year. Their positive style gave them a chance of heading the Western Division; they entered the last round 14 points behind leaders Berkshire, but were pushed down the table when they lost to Shropshire. Hall himself scored 414 runs, including a career-best 175 in their win against Wales. Another career-best came from all-rounder Jason Whittaker, who took seven for 31 against Herefordshire. Dave Pennett was the leading wicket-taker with 17 and left-arm spinner Robin Fisher had 16.

Despite retaining most of the squad which brought them a shared Championship title in 2002, **Herefordshire** did not enjoy the same success, finishing seventh with a single win, over Wiltshire. Captain Chris Boroughs was the leading run-scorer, with 410 including two centuries; Harshad Patel and Rob Hughes scored a hundred each. Former England pace bowler Martin McCague was the leading wicket-taker with 28, and took seven in an innings against Wiltshire and Cheshire. Kevin Cooper, dogged by injury, announced his retirement; the county's leading wicket-taker with 219 victims in eight seasons, he will be very difficult to replace.

No fewer than 29 players represented **Wales**, who seemed to be heading for a second successive wooden spoon until the final round, when the tail helped to haul them up to eighth place. Replying to Oxfordshire's first-innings 378, they were 163 for seven until a county-record eighth-wicket 104 by Owen Dawkins and Matthew Mason. Then, in the last-day run-chase, Nos 10 and 11, Ian Capon and Colin Metson, added 23 to steer them home with five balls to spare. Earlier in the season, Wales fought back from a 246-run first-innings deficit by scoring their highest total yet, 407 for five, against Cornwall at Swansea, boosted by a maiden century from 18-year-old Gareth Rees.

Dorset have yet to win a Championship match in the three seasons of three-day cricket, despite some good individual performances. There were four hundreds, all in losing causes. Darren Cowley scored centuries against Berkshire and mighty Devon, when he was joined by Stuart Rintoul, the retiring captain; Glyn Treagus made a career-best 152 out of 293 during a ten-wicket defeat by Wiltshire. In the Berkshire match, Damian Worrad returned a career-best seven for 71.

Oxfordshire plummeted from third to bottom in the Western Division, with four defeats and a solitary win; in a hot summer, they fell foul of whatever wet weather was around, and captain Keith Arnold lost the toss in four games out of six. On both occasions when he did win, Charlie Knightley scored centuries; in their best match of the season, the one-wicket defeat by Wales, he was joined by Rob Williams in a 210-run stand, while Arnold took nine wickets in the match. Arnold, now 43, was the most successful bowler, with 16 wickets in all in an attack that lacked both accuracy and penetration.

LEADING AVERAGES, 2003

BATTING

(Qualification: 8 completed innings, average 35.00)

	M	*I*	*NO*	*R*	*HS*	*100s*	*Avge*
K. J. Barnett (*Staffordshire*)	6	10	2	689	198*	3	86.12
A. A. Metcalfe (*Cumberland*)	5	10	2	680	172	2	85.00
P. R. Pollard (*Lincolnshire*)	7	12	3	702	184	2	78.00
D. M. Ward (*Hertfordshire*)	6	11	2	678	150*	1	75.33
M. P. Dowman (*Lincolnshire*)	7	11	1	690	179	2	69.00
S. C. Goldsmith (*Norfolk*)	6	10	1	599	118	2	66.55
G. F. Archer (*Staffordshire*)	6	10	2	502	201*	1	62.75
P. J. Prichard (*Berkshire*)	5	9	1	496	101	1	62.00
J. A. Knott (*Bedfordshire*)	6	11	2	535	158	1	59.44
R. W. J. Howitt (*Berkshire*)	6	12	3	507	170*	2	56.33
R. I. Dawson (*Devon*)	7	12	1	614	140*	2	55.81
G. D. Lloyd (*Cumberland*)	6	11	1	541	130	2	54.10
J. R. Wood (*Berkshire*)	6	11	1	503	158	1	50.30
D. J. M. Mercer (*Bedfordshire*)	5	9	1	395	116	1	49.37
A. T. Heather (*Northumberland*)	5	9	0	444	106	2	49.33
B. Parker (*Northumberland*)	6	11	1	491	175	1	49.10
M. P. Hunt (*Devon*)	5	9	1	384	94*	0	48.00
P. F. Shaw (*Staffordshire*)	6	10	1	398	200*	2	44.22
C. Amos (*Norfolk*)	6	10	0	438	107	1	43.80
C. Jones (*Cambridgeshire*)	6	12	3	391	162*	1	43.44
N. A. Din (*Cheshire*)	4	8	0	347	160	2	43.37
M. C. Dobson (*Lincolnshire*)	7	11	2	385	161*	1	42.77
M. D. R. Sutliff (*Cambridgeshire*)	4	8	0	332	118	1	41.50
A. J. Hall (*Cheshire*)	6	11	1	414	175	1	41.40
C. J. Rogers (*Norfolk*)	6	10	1	368	78*	0	40.88
G. R. Treagus (*Dorset*)	5	10	1	364	152	1	40.44
A. J. Pugh (*Devon*)	4	8	0	321	76	0	40.12
R. J. Rowe (*Wiltshire*)	6	9	0	355	128	1	39.44
R. D. Hughes (*Herefordshire*)	6	11	2	346	103*	1	38.44
J. Clarke (*Lincolnshire*)	5	9	1	303	118	1	37.87
R. J. Foan (*Devon*)	7	12	0	453	130	1	37.75
S. Chapman (*Northumberland*)	5	9	1	302	107	1	37.75
D. G. Court (*Devon*)	7	11	3	298	75	0	37.25
N. J. Thurgood (*Dorset*)	5	10	1	329	79	0	36.55
A. R. Roberts (*Bedfordshire*)	6	10	1	326	78	0	36.22

BOWLING

(Qualification: 10 wickets, average 25.00)

	O	*M*	*R*	*W*	*BB*	*5W/i*	*Avge*
T. G. Sharp (*Cornwall*)	134.5	35	352	23	6-26	1	15.30
S. Oakes (*Lincolnshire*)	65.1	14	179	10	5-37	1	17.90
M. S. Coles (*Wiltshire*)	64.5	19	220	12	5-39	1	18.33
J. C. J. Stephens (*Cornwall*)	137.2	52	360	19	5-59	2	18.94
I. E. Bishop (*Devon*)	262.3	73	708	36	8-99	2	19.66
C. D. Crowe (*Berkshire*)	223.2	56	657	33	6-93	3	19.90
J. E. Anyon (*Cumberland*)	105	17	430	21	6-31	1	20.47
J. R. Davies (*Lincolnshire*)	81.3	16	273	13	4-28	0	21.00
T. J. Mason (*Shropshire*)	258.3	86	676	32	6-66	2	21.12
K. A. Arnold (*Oxfordshire*)	121	38	340	16	6-46	1	21.25
R. P. Lane (*Buckinghamshire*)	65	14	213	10	3-35	0	21.30
R. K. Illingworth (*Wiltshire*)	204.1	63	428	20	5-46	2	21.40
R. J. Bates (*Wiltshire*)	151	38	407	19	6-72	1	21.42
M. P. Dowman (*Lincolnshire*)	160.1	40	524	24	4-43	0	21.83
R. C. Driver (*Cornwall*)	168	49	481	22	5-49	2	21.86
J. C. Morris (*Berkshire*)	85	25	244	11	5-30	1	22.18
T. M. Smith (*Suffolk*)	164.1	45	467	21	5-46	2	22.23
C. W. Boroughs (*Herefordshire*)	80.2	20	295	13	5-121	1	22.69
M. C. Dobson (*Lincolnshire*)	153	64	298	13	4-35	0	22.92
M. A. Sharp (*Cumberland*)	229	81	529	23	4-40	0	23.00
A. R. Roberts (*Bedfordshire*)	201.5	47	589	25	5-48	2	23.56
S. J. Airey (*Lincolnshire*)	89	20	286	12	4-25	0	23.83
D. Follett (*Staffordshire*)	264.2	47	932	39	8-87	3	23.89
O. A. Dawkins (*Wales*)	87.2	13	312	13	5-38	1	24.00
J. M. Fielding (*Cumberland*)	85.3	18	240	10	5-88	1	24.00
E. J. Wilson (*Lincolnshire*)	204.5	31	721	30	4-24	0	24.03
M. J. Rawnsley (*Herefordshire*)	192.2	61	486	20	6-79	2	24.30
B. J. Frazer (*Hertfordshire*)	128.2	28	417	17	5-51	1	24.52

CHAMPIONSHIP FINAL

DEVON v LINCOLNSHIRE

At Cleethorpes, September 7, 8, 9. Lincolnshire won by eight wickets. Toss: Devon.

After taking a first-innings lead of 101, Devon lost control of this match with the title at their mercy. On the second day, they collapsed for their lowest total of the season; seamers Elliot Wilson and Stuart Airey grabbed four wickets each. With thunder rumbling, Lincolnshire's most successful batsmen of 2003, Paul Pollard and Mathew Dowman, hurried past a target of 199 on the third afternoon. Devon openers Matthew Hunt and Richard Foan had made a perfect start, putting on 153 in the first two hours of the match, and Devon reached 371 for three in the 70 overs allotted for the first innings. In reply, Lincolnshire slumped to 147 for five before a run-a-ball century stand between Simon Webb and Oliver Burford hauled them back into the game.

Man of the Match: E. J. Wilson.

Close of play: First day, Lincolnshire 92-2 (Dobson 25, Dowman 30); Second day, Lincolnshire 32-1 (Pollard 20, Dobson 10).

Devon

M. P. Hunt not out	94	– c Burford b Wilson	40
R. J. Foan c Burford b Wilson	84	– c Dowman b Davies	0
*R. I. Dawson c Dowman b Davies	36	– lbw b Wilson	12
A. J. Pugh st Burford b Christmas	40	– lbw b Wilson	0
†C. M. Mole not out	57	– c Burford b Airey	1
D. F. Lye (did not bat)		– c Webb b Airey	3
D. G. Court (did not bat)		– c Burford b Airey	10
R. J. Newman (did not bat)		– c Burford b Airey	4
D. J. Burke (did not bat)		– b Dobson	8
I. E. Bishop (did not bat)		– b Wilson	2
A. Jones (did not bat)		– not out	0
B 7, l-b 12, w 11, n-b 6, pen 24	60	B 4, l-b 1, w 4, n-b 8	17
1/153 (2) 2/201 (3) 3/265 (4)	(3 wkts) 371	1/0 (2) 2/15 (3) 3/15 (4) 4/34 (5) 5/47 (6) 6/57 (7) 7/69 (8) 8/88 (9) 9/91 (1) 10/97 (10)	97

Bowling: *First Innings*—Wilson 16–1–41–1; Davies 9–1–37–1; Airey 11–1–43–0; Christmas 11–1–76–1; Dowman 18–3–114–0; Dobson 5–1–17–0. *Second Innings*—Wilson 10.4–3–24–4; Davies 5–2–9–1; Dobson 19–8–34–1; Airey 14–6–25–4.

Lincolnshire

*J. Clarke c Mole b Bishop	16	– b Bishop	1
P. R. Pollard b Burke	15	– not out	85
M. C. Dobson c Pugh b Bishop	31	– lbw b Dawson	27
M. P. Dowman c Lye b Bishop	65	– not out	70
J. Trower c Court b Bishop	9		
S. Webb not out	56		
†O. E. Burford b Pugh	58		
D. A. Christmas not out	8		
L-b 6, w 2, n-b 4	12	B 4, l-b 11, n-b 4	19
1/30 (2) 2/38 (1) 3/102 (3) 4/142 (5) 5/147 (4) 6/254 (7)	(6 wkts) 270	1/6 (1) 2/78 (3)	(2 wkts) 202

S. J. Airey, E. J. Wilson and J. R. Davies did not bat.

Bowling: *First Innings*—Bishop 29–6–88–4; Burke 9–3–29–1; Jones 18–4–66–0; Newman 7–0–35–0; Pugh 5–0–28–1; Dawson 2–0–18–0. *Second Innings*—Bishop 18–5–49–1; Burke 19–3–32–0; Court 6–0–32–0; Dawson 6–1–29–1; Pugh 5–0–19–0; Jones 3–0–13–0; Mole 2–0–13–0.

Umpires: K. Coburn and W. E. Smith.

THE MINOR COUNTIES CHAMPIONS

1895	Norfolk / Durham / Worcestershire	1901	Durham	1912	In abeyance
1896	Worcestershire	1902	Wiltshire	1913	Norfolk
1897	Worcestershire	1903	Northamptonshire	1914	Staffordshire†
1898	Worcestershire	1904	Northamptonshire	1920	Staffordshire
1899	Northamptonshire / Buckinghamshire	1905	Norfolk	1921	Staffordshire
1900	Glamorgan / Durham / Northamptonshire	1906	Staffordshire	1922	Buckinghamshire
		1907	Lancashire II	1923	Buckinghamshire
		1908	Staffordshire	1924	Berkshire
		1909	Wiltshire	1925	Buckinghamshire
		1910	Norfolk	1926	Durham
		1911	Staffordshire	1927	Staffordshire

Year	County
1928	Berkshire
1929	Oxfordshire
1930	Durham
1931	Leicestershire II
1932	Buckinghamshire
1933	Undecided
1934	Lancashire II
1935	Middlesex II
1936	Hertfordshire
1937	Lancashire II
1938	Buckinghamshire
1939	Surrey II
1946	Suffolk
1947	Yorkshire II
1948	Lancashire II
1949	Lancashire II
1950	Surrey II
1951	Kent II
1952	Buckinghamshire
1953	Berkshire
1954	Surrey II
1955	Surrey II
1956	Kent II
1957	Yorkshire II
1958	Yorkshire II
1959	Warwickshire II
1960	Lancashire II
1961	Somerset II
1962	Warwickshire II
1963	Cambridgeshire
1964	Lancashire II
1965	Somerset II
1966	Lincolnshire
1967	Cheshire
1968	Yorkshire II
1969	Buckinghamshire
1970	Bedfordshire
1971	Yorkshire II
1972	Bedfordshire
1973	Shropshire
1974	Oxfordshire
1975	Hertfordshire
1976	Durham
1977	Suffolk
1978	Devon
1979	Suffolk
1980	Durham
1981	Durham
1982	Oxfordshire
1983	Hertfordshire
1984	Durham
1985	Cheshire
1986	Cumberland
1987	Buckinghamshire
1988	Cheshire
1989	Oxfordshire
1990	Hertfordshire
1991	Staffordshire
1992	Staffordshire
1993	Staffordshire
1994	Devon
1995	Devon
1996	Devon
1997	Devon
1998	Staffordshire
1999	Cumberland
2000	Dorset
2001	Cheshire / Lincolnshire
2002	Herefordshire / Norfolk
2003	Lincolnshire

† *Disputed. Most sources claim the Championship was never decided.*

MCCA KNOCKOUT TROPHY FINAL

At Lord's, September 2. Cambridgeshire won by three wickets. Toss: Cambridgeshire. **Shropshire 266-9** (50 overs) (S. J. Adshead 59, M. A. Downes 56); **Cambridgeshire 267-7** (47.5 overs) (M. D. R. Sutliff 99).

Shropshire failed to capitalise after reaching 129 with only one wicket down. Sutliff and Simon Kellett responded with an opening stand of 131 and their team-mates got Cambridgeshire home with two overs to spare.

WINNERS 1983–2003

Year	County
1983	Cheshire
1984	Hertfordshire
1985	Durham
1986	Norfolk
1987	Cheshire
1988	Dorset
1989	Cumberland
1990	Buckinghamshire
1991	Staffordshire
1992	Devon
1993	Staffordshire
1994	Devon
1995	Cambridgeshire
1996	Cheshire
1997	Norfolk
1998	Devon
1999	Bedfordshire
2000	Herefordshire
2001	Norfolk
2002	Warwickshire Board XI
2003	Cambridgeshire

Note: Staged as the ECB 38-County Competition from 1999 to 2002.

SECOND ELEVEN CHAMPIONSHIP, 2003

REVIEW BY MICHAEL VOCKINS

Yorkshire won the 2003 Second Eleven Championship, after near misses in the previous two years. Seven victories from ten games edged them ahead of Kent, the 2002 champions, who went unbeaten and again battled determinedly.

Yorkshire's worthy victory came at the eleventh hour and by the narrowest of margins. Facing Lancashire in their last match, they had to win, and also earn sufficient bonus points. They did both – though the win was by just one run – to give them their first title since 1991.

In a season when there was, for the first time, no first-class Roses match, the old enemies' second teams made up for it by producing an extraordinary finish at Old Trafford. Lancashire, needing 274 to win, began well – opener Alec Swann scored a century – before losing five wickets for 40. The ninth wicket fell at 266, when their most experienced player, Gary Yates, was joined by Oliver Newby. They started getting them in singles before Peter Swanepoel came on to bowl at the Stretford End, and produced a short ball that was fended off to a diving Tim Bresnan at backward square-leg. Coach Arnie Sidebottom raced on to join his players in the celebrations.

In the one-day Trophy, last year's finalists Hampshire swept through all their ten games unbeaten. Warwickshire's total of 190 in the final always looked inadequate, and so it proved.

SECOND ELEVEN CHAMPIONSHIP, 2003

					Bonus points			
	P	*W*	*L*	*D*	*Batting*	*Bowling*	*Points*	*Avge*
1 – Yorkshire (3)	10	7	1	2	29	32	167	16.70
2 – Kent (1)	10	6	0	4	31	34	165	16.50
3 – Hampshire (8)	10	5	3	2	24	34	136	13.60
4 – Northamptonshire (6)	12	5	2	5	30	43	163	13.58
5 – Durham (9)	11	5	4	2	36	35	149	13.55
6 – Surrey (11)	13	4	4	5	45	39	160	12.31
7 – Somerset (15)	10	3	3	4	31	31	120	12.00
8 – Lancashire (7)	14	5	4	5	38	36	164	11.71
9 – Nottinghamshire (13)	11	3	4	4	30	39	127	11.55
10 – Gloucestershire (16)	10	2	2	6	31	32	115	11.50
11 – Leicestershire (17)	10	2	1	7	31	27	114	11.40
12 – Warwickshire (5)	12	4	4	4	31	33	136	11.33
13 – Essex (18)	10	2	3	5	30	33	111	11.10
14 – Sussex (14)	12	2	6	4	28	41	113	9.42
15 – Middlesex (10)	10	0	3	7	23	35	86	8.60
16 – Glamorgan (4)	11	1	5	5	21	37	92	8.36
17 – Worcestershire (12)	10	0	4	6	32	24	80	8.00
18 – Derbyshire (2)	10	0	3	7	31	19	78	7.80

2002 positions are shown in brackets.

Win = 14 pts; draw = 4 pts.

More young players – in some cases very young – were given second-team opportunities in 2003. Middlesex fielded some who were just 14. Unsurprisingly, those counties with more full-time professionals generally did better than those relying on triallists and youngsters.

Yorkshire, for example, regularly fielded both Gavin Hamilton, once an England all-rounder, and Richard Dawson, who played in the Ashes the previous winter. Hamilton began a slow recovery from the yips, taking 12 wickets at 20, and scored 821 runs. Dawson took 22 cheap wickets and looked out of place at this level. Chris Taylor also scored heavily, while England Under-19 leg-spinner Mark Lawson, in his first full county summer, equalled Dawson's haul.

At the other end of the table, three teams failed to achieve a single win. A lack of experience – combined with some poor early-season weather – cost Derbyshire, who often fielded just two contracted players. Like their first team, they finished last. Second-bottom Worcestershire used 40 players in ten matches, Steven Moore scoring 931 runs at 66 in eight games. And Middlesex, another county with a small first-team squad, struggled too. But impressive seam bowling by Chris Whelan, a 17-year-old, hinted he might have a bright future.

Batsmen generally fared better than bowlers. Surrey players alone hit four double-hundreds, two in the highest-ever partnership in the Second Eleven Championship. Scott Newman and Nadeem Shahid put on 552 against Derbyshire (see below), and went on to become the two heaviest scorers of the year.

Shahid hit another double in his next game, but still made only two first-team Championship appearances. By contrast, Newman's career seemed to be on the up, and he won an ECB Academy place. Steve Paulsen, an Australian at Essex, and Ian Westwood of Warwickshire also hit big double-hundreds. And at Nottinghamshire, three young batsmen – Samit Patel, Will Smith and Vikram Atri – got off to a flying start, with centuries on debut.

Three of the sides who doggedly pursued Yorkshire unearthed new batsmen in the process. Kent owed much to 17-year-old Joe Denly, who ended on a high with two centuries. Meanwhile, another 17-year-old, Kevin Latouf from Hampshire, impressed, as did Tom Huggins of Northamptonshire. Huggins played in all 12 games and hit a double-century against Worcestershire. The other chasing side, Durham, relied more heavily on established players.

The long dry summer also encouraged slow bowlers. Shaftab Khalid, Worcestershire's 20-year-old off-spinner, joined Newman at the Academy on the back of an impressive first season; there were also rumours that he could bowl the "wrong 'un". Left-armer Rob Ferley made a key contribution to Kent's challenge – 22 inexpensive wickets and an average of 65 with the bat. And Surrey's match against Sussex was won thanks to 13 wickets from off-spinner Noel Brett. But with several counties producing good, true pitches bowlers had to work hard, rightly forcing them to learn all the skills of their craft.

Behind the stumps, Surrey looked at first to have found an able deputy for their new captain, Jon Batty. The glovework of Ben Scott was described by his coach, Alan Butcher, as "sublime", but Middlesex will get the benefit in 2004, as Scott moved there, and Surrey signed Andrew Hodd, the England Under-19 keeper, who arrived from Sussex in the close season. Jamie Haynes of Lancashire also kept outstandingly, with 27 catches and seven stumpings.

For 2004, the minimum number of Championship matches played by each county has been cut from ten to six. But all counties have been asked to play at least six games after July 1 – these will be a mix of three and four day contests. Some, influenced by financial pressures, have readily opted for the bare minimum: for them, second-eleven cricket will mean late-summer games (after the school and university terms) and a greater focus on developing non-staff players, enabling them to employ fewer professionals.

To provide early-season matches for their contracted cricketers, some counties will team up with their neighbours and form combined sides to play friendlies. But a joint Lancashire–Yorkshire side is not on the cards. In 2003, Lancashire played 14 games, more than any other county. Despite the financial appeal of cutting matches, they are one of several counties who intend to keep a full programme.

SURREY v DERBYSHIRE

At The Oval, August 13, 14, 15. Drawn. Toss: Derbyshire.

This historic match will be remembered for broken records and a bizarre stoppage. After Derbyshire declared their first innings on 580 for seven, Surrey openers Scott Newman and Nadeem Shahid hammered their way past 500, in 74 overs. At this point, New Zealand Test umpire Billy Bowden, renowned for the originality of his hand signals, added to his aura of eccentricity by producing a camera. He halted play to snap the grinning batsmen in front of the scoreboard, which showed 501 for nought. Bowden, getting his eye in before standing in the Fourth Test, took more photos at the close of play, by which time 547 had been plundered in just over two sessions. His sense of occasion was justified: the partnership of 552 was the best in the history of the Second XI Championship: Newman finally made 284 off 292 balls, with three sixes and 49 fours, Shahid 266 from 271 balls, with three sixes and 41 fours. After waiting padded-up for nearly a day, Surrey's No. 3, Christopher Murtagh, made one. Surrey lost their last nine wickets for 130, with Derbyshire's Paul Havell emerging with a respectable six for 97.

Close of play: First day, Derbyshire 475-3 (Flanagan 144, Kerr 1); Second day, Surrey 547-0 (Newman 266, Shahid 266).

Derbyshire

A. I. Gait b Saker	34	– (2) c Scott b Saker	1
S. D. Stubbings c Scott b Benning	53	– (1) not out	39
I. N. Flanagan c and b Saker	152		
R. S. Clinton c C. P. Murtagh b Newman	213	– c sub (M. J. Todd) b Miller	16
*J. I. D. Kerr c Sampson b T. J. Murtagh	60	– (6) not out	27
N. Perry-Taylor b Saker	1	– (5) b T. J. Murtagh	4
†L. J. Goddard c Scott b T. J. Murtagh	9	– (3) b Sampson	1
A. Parker not out	6		
J. P. Tucker not out	17		
B 8, l-b 2, w 3, n-b 22	35	B 4, l-b 11, n-b 4	19
1/75 2/103 3/474 4/500 5/502 6/515 7/560 (7 wkts dec.)	580	1/4 2/5 3/50 4/57 (4 wkts)	107

C. Windmill and P. M. R. Havell did not bat.

Bowling: *First Innings*—Sampson 22.2–5–84–0; T. J. Murtagh 18–2–94–2; Saker 21–3–94–3; Miller 20–2–90–0; Brett 34–4–140–0; Benning 9.4–1–43–1; Newman 5–1–25–1. *Second Innings*—Sampson 5–1–9–1; T. J. Murtagh 8–3–16–1; Saker 8–2–41–1; Miller 6–1–26–1; Brett 1–1–0–0.

Picture by Billy Bowden.

Caught by the umpire: when Surrey passed 500 without losing a wicket, Billy Bowden briefly stopped play to record the occasion on film. The openers – Nadeem Shahid (*left*) and Scott Newman – went on to 552 before they were parted. This time, Bowden posed in front of the scoreboard, passing the camera to his fellow-umpire, Bob McLeod.

Picture by Bob McLeod.

Surrey

S. A. Newman b Havell 284
*N. Shahid c Kerr b Tucker 266
C. P. Murtagh c Stubbings b Havell 1
J. G. E. Benning lbw b Havell 8
†B. J. M. Scott c Flanagan b Havell . . . 35
C. J. Salmons lbw b Clinton 5
T. J. Murtagh c Havell b Tucker 46
P. J. Sampson b Havell 0
N. C. Saker c Clinton b Tucker 8
D. J. Miller c Goddard b Havell 2
N. A. Brett not out 4
B 5, l-b 11, w 3, n-b 4 23

1/552 2/553 3/574 4/575 5/586 6/664 7/664 8/664 9/670 — 682

Bowling: Havell 24–7–97–6; Tucker 22–3–109–3; Parker 7–0–51–0; Windmill 27–1–160–0; Clinton 10–1–66–1; Flanagan 25–5–94–0; Stubbings 2–0–24–0; Perry-Taylor 12–0–65–0.

Umpires: B. F. Bowden (New Zealand) and R. McLeod.

LEADING AVERAGES, 2003

BATTING

(Qualification: 300 runs, average 50.00)

	M	*I*	*NO*	*R*	*HS*	*100s*	*50s*	*Avge*	*Ct/St*
E. J. Wilson (*Middx*)	3	5	2	353	206*	1	1	117.67	3
D. A. Leatherdale (*Worcs*)	4	6	2	374	166*	2	0	93.50	2
C. P. Schofield (*Lancs*)	5	5	0	448	210	2	1	89.60	3
G. M. Hamilton (*Yorks*)	7	11	1	821	219*	3	4	82.10	2
C. R. Taylor (*Yorks*)	9	14	2	972	205	3	6	81.00	10
A. N. Cook (*Essex*)	4	6	0	482	143	2	2	80.33	4
G. D. Bridge (*Durham*)	5	7	2	353	113	2	1	70.60	4
M. L. Pettini (*Essex*)	4	7	1	422	217	1	2	70.33	4
A. M. Thorpe (*Durham*)	7	11	1	698	186	3	1	69.80	10
D. R. Law (*Durham*)	8	11	2	611	115	2	3	67.88	5
N. Shahid (*Surrey*)	12	20	1	1,269	272	5	1	66.78	18
S. C. Moore (*Worcs*)	8	14	0	931	144	5	1	66.50	2
C. P. Murtagh (*Surrey*)	6	8	3	329	150	2	0	65.80	2
I. J. Thomas (*Glam*)	6	10	0	658	267	1	3	65.80	1
R. S. Ferley (*Kent*)	5	7	2	329	154*	1	2	65.80	3
R. J. Cross (*Lancs*)	6	9	4	323	61*	0	3	64.60	3
J. D. C. Bryant (*Somerset*)	3	6	1	319	121	1	2	63.80	4
A. Singh (*Worcs*)	4	7	1	382	179	1	2	63.67	2
S. J. Adshead (*Glos, Leics & Worcs*)	3	5	0	318	161	2	0	63.60	0/1
K. P. Dutch (*Somerset*)	5	9	1	502	105	1	5	62.75	7
T. R. Ward (*Leics*)	5	9	1	572	157	2	2	61.50	4
A. J. Hodd (*Sussex*)	7	11	4	417	100*	1	2	59.57	18/2
C. G. Taylor (*Glos*)	6	11	2	527	117*	1	5	58.56	5
S. A. Newman (*Surrey*)	13	22	1	1,228	284	4	4	58.47	15
M. J. Wood (*Somerset*)	3	6	0	350	124	1	3	58.33	1
G. D. Clough (*Notts*)	5	9	1	462	173	1	2	57.75	4
I. J. Westwood (*Warwicks*)	10	14	1	739	250*	2	3	56.85	6
R. M. Khan (*Derbys*)	5	6	0	338	137	1	3	56.33	1
R. A. White (*Northants*)	6	9	1	450	119	2	2	56.25	2
J. G. E. Benning (*Surrey*)	13	20	3	933	220	4	2	54.88	7

	M	I	NO	R	HS	100s	50s	Avge	Ct/St
S. J. Paulsen (*Essex*)	4	6	0	329	237	1	1	54.83	4
I. J. L. Trott (*Warwicks*)	6	9	0	481	248	1	2	53.44	4
L. J. Wright (*Leics*)	7	12	3	480	184	1	3	53.33	7
A. D. Shaw (*Glam*)	11	18	4	734	127*	4	1	52.43	28/4
J. L. Denly (*Kent*)	6	11	2	468	164*	2	0	52.00	7
P. J. Horton (*Lancs*)	13	20	3	861	177	1	7	50.65	3

BOWLING

(Qualification: 10 wickets, average 23.00)

	O	M	R	W	BB	5W/i	Avge
A. Richardson (*Warwicks*)	131	45	309	26	9-41	3	11.88
C. G. Greenidge (*Northants*)	99.1	31	253	20	5-36	1	12.65
N. G. Hatch (*Durham*)	76	25	204	15	5-44	1	13.60
R. S. Ferley (*Kent*)	136.2	41	305	22	4-45	0	13.86
A. K. D. Gray (*Yorks*)	59	10	147	10	6-88	1	14.70
A. J. Shantry (*Northants*)	100.4	17	299	19	6-41	1	15.73
J. C. Tredwell (*Kent*)	82.5	23	200	12	5-49	1	16.67
R. K. J. Dawson (*Yorks*)	155.1	46	377	22	6-22	3	17.13
S. D. Thomas (*Glam*)	121.2	15	404	23	6-48	1	17.57
R. M. Pyrah (*Yorks*)	118.1	29	363	19	4-64	0	19.10
P. D. Trego (*Kent*)	71.2	12	235	12	5-42	1	19.58
P. D. Lewis (*Somerset*)	69.3	15	235	12	5-17	1	19.58
K. P. Dutch (*Somerset*)	163.4	16	406	20	4-54	0	20.30
G. M. Hamilton (*Yorks*)	57.4	8	245	12	4-34	0	20.41
S. M. J. Cusden (*Kent*)	59	7	247	12	7-80	1	20.58
M. S. Panesar (*Northants*)	341.2	100	876	42	6-42	3	20.85
G. Onions (*Durham*)	177.5	39	676	32	6-62	3	21.12
G. M. Andrew (*Somerset*)	71	17	254	12	5-50	1	21.16
N. C. Phillips (*Durham*)	206.4	60	519	24	5-66	1	21.62
D. R. Law (*Durham*)	108	27	352	16	4-13	0	22.00
P. J. McMahon (*Notts*)	166.1	49	402	18	6-40	2	22.33
A. G. A. M. McCoubrey (*Essex*)	83.2	18	247	11	4-46	0	22.45
J. T. A. Bruce (*Hants*)	235.2	48	789	35	6-26	1	22.54
R. S. G. Anderson (*Northants*)	198.5	39	589	26	4-43	0	22.65
C. P. Schofield (*Lancs*)	131.1	32	342	15	6-43	1	22.80

SECOND ELEVEN CHAMPIONS 1959–2003

1959 Gloucestershire
1960 Northamptonshire
1961 Kent
1962 Worcestershire
1963 Worcestershire
1964 Lancashire
1965 Glamorgan
1966 Surrey
1967 Hampshire
1968 Surrey
1969 Kent
1970 Kent
1971 Hampshire
1972 Nottinghamshire
1973 Essex
1974 Middlesex
1975 Surrey
1976 Kent
1977 Yorkshire
1978 Sussex
1979 Warwickshire
1980 Glamorgan
1981 Hampshire
1982 Worcestershire
1983 Leicestershire
1984 Yorkshire
1985 Nottinghamshire
1986 Lancashire
1987 { Kent / Yorkshire
1988 Surrey
1989 Middlesex
1990 Sussex
1991 Yorkshire
1992 Surrey
1993 Middlesex
1994 Somerset
1995 Hampshire
1996 Warwickshire
1997 Lancashire
1998 Northamptonshire
1999 Middlesex
2000 Middlesex
2001 Hampshire
2002 Kent
2003 Yorkshire

SECOND ELEVEN TROPHY, 2003

A Zone

	Played	Won	Lost	No result	Points	Net run-rate
DERBYSHIRE	8	4	2	2	10	9.03
Yorkshire	8	3	2	3	9	4.27
Nottinghamshire	8	3	2	3	9	2.13
Durham	8	2	2	4	8	7.09
Lancashire	8	1	5	2	4	-18.65

B Zone

	Played	Won	Lost	No result	Points	Net run-rate
WARWICKSHIRE	8	5	1	2	12	27.29
Middlesex	8	4	3	1	9	8.52
Leicestershire	8	3	3	2	8	-27.11
Minor Counties	8	2	4	2	6	-2.89
Northamptonshire	8	2	5	1	5	-8.81

C Zone

	Played	Won	Lost	No result	Points	Net run-rate
HAMPSHIRE	8	8	0	0	16	7.26
Gloucestershire	8	4	2	2	10	17.20
Glamorgan	8	2	3	3	7	1.56
Worcestershire	8	1	5	2	4	-21.81
Somerset	8	1	6	1	3	-4.36

D Zone

	Played	Won	Lost	No result	Points	Net run-rate
SUSSEX	8	6	2	0	12	10.24
Surrey	8	4	3	1	9	-1.29
Essex	8	3	3	2	8	1.08
Kent	8	3	4	1	7	-5.34
MCC Young Cricketers	8	2	6	0	4	-4.53

Semi-finals

At Derby, August 11. **Warwickshire won by 28 runs.** Toss: Derbyshire. **Warwickshire 253-4** (50 overs) (L. C. Parker 37, M. A. Wagh 85, D. P. Ostler 64); **Derbyshire 225** (48.4 overs) (R. M. Khan 31, N. R. C. Dumelow 39, L. J. Goddard 33; T. Mees 4-50, J. A. Spires 3-46).

At Southampton, August 11. **Hampshire won by 41 runs.** Toss: Hampshire. **Hampshire 225** (49.1 overs) (J. R. C. Hamblin 56, G. A. Lamb 53, L. R. Prittipaul 37; C. D. Hopkinson 4-28); **Sussex 184** (44.2 overs) (C. D. Hopkinson 48, B. Zuiderent 51; L. R. Prittipaul 3-24, G. A. Lamb 3-42).

Final

At Southampton, September 8. **Hampshire won by eight wickets.** Toss: Warwickshire. **Warwickshire 190** (49 overs) (N. A. Warren 40; J. T. A. Bruce 3-22, G. A. Lamb 3-35; **Hampshire 191-2** (33.2 overs) (J. H. K. Adams 97*, W. S. Kendall 46).

LEAGUE CRICKET IN ENGLAND AND WALES IN 2003

GEOFFREY DEAN

The fifth year of Premier League cricket was the first in which no new leagues were assimilated. Only one, Leicestershire, had been accepted in 2002, and no new converts were expected in 2004. With several leagues in Lancashire, Yorkshire and South Wales still unwilling to meet the criteria for premier status, the prospect of further additions looked distant. While the ECB would like to increase the number of premier leagues, every region in the country is represented, and the current figure of 25 possesses a nicely symmetrical ring. The family may have reached capacity.

The ECB was more disappointed by the increasing opposition of premier league clubs to playing 120 overs a day – or even 110. Originally regarded as a centrepiece of premiership doctrine, the longer form of the game has lost its appeal: only six premier leagues – East Anglia, Essex, Home Counties, Middlesex, North-East and Surrey – played 120 overs a day in 2003, and several were discussing a reduction to 100, which could lead to a loss of premiership status and funding.

Frank Kemp, the ECB's operations manager for recreational cricket, revealed that about half the other club captains canvassed preferred 100 to 110 overs. "The board's panel saw a minimum of 110 overs as non-negotiable for the 2003 season," Kemp said. "But there's been real pressure to discuss a reduction for 2004. While that may be regrettable, you can only push a snowball uphill for so long."

Unsurprisingly in view of the ECB's financial problems, no increase in funding was due for premier leagues in 2004. Of the clubs embracing 120 overs, those in the Middlesex and Essex Leagues would still benefit to the tune of £1,250, while the three regional leagues, East Anglia, North-East and Home Counties, would receive £2,000 each because of higher travel expenses. The grant for clubs playing the shorter format remained at £750, the same amount offered to the Southern League, who compromised on 50 overs a side for half the season and 120-over declaration cricket for the other half.

One of the hottest summers on record assisted several batsmen to beat records, notably the Southern League's highest aggregate by an individual. Back in 1982, when he was qualifying for Hampshire, Robin Smith had scored 1,015 runs for Trojans, but Neal Parlane, a 25-year-old New Zealander, reached 1,074 as he helped BAT Sports regain the title from Havant. At the other end of the country, in the Yorkshire League, Castleford captain Andrew Bourke scored 1,421 to beat David Byas's record of 1,394 for Scarborough in 1984; his team finished joint third, behind Cleethorpes and Harrogate, who were level on points. Yorkshire supremacists were not pleased when Cleethorpes, a Lincolnshire side, were proclaimed champions on the basis of more outright victories. Meanwhile, Indian all-rounder Dodda Ganesh became the first player to pass 1,000 runs in the Lincolnshire Premier

League. Outside the premier circle, in the West Riding, South African-born Brandon Nash raised the Huddersfield League record to 1,522 runs and steered Delph & Dobcross to their first title.

An outstanding all-round performance by Gary Yates helped Bowdon clinch the Cheshire County League for the third time in four years. Yates, the Lancashire Second Eleven captain, scored 930 runs and took 77 wickets with his off-spin. Bootle were crowned Liverpool & District champions, after Cheshire spinner Robin Fisher took 19 wickets in the last three matches to finish with 63 at 19 apiece. In the non-premier Bolton Association, Walshaw's professional, Jon Fielding, claimed 113 wickets to mastermind the club's fourth title in five years.

There was a controversial finish in the Essex League: Saffron Walden had to wait until October to be confirmed as champions after an appeal by runners-up Gidea Park & Romford. The dispute went back to May, when both teams claimed five points too many from a match between Gidea Park and South Woodford that was ended by bad light. The mistake was not noticed until just before the final round, when Gidea Park had the points deducted and were held to a draw by Hainault, while Saffron Walden beat Ilford to finish two points clear. Gidea Park argued that they would have employed different tactics in their closing games had the mistake been spotted earlier, but officials were unmoved. The League was also rocked by allegations of match-fixing involving a relegation-haunted clash between Wanstead and Fives & Heronians, a game which Fives won by one wicket to stay up. Officials eventually concluded there was no case to answer.

There was confusion too in East Anglia, where bottom club Fakenham escaped relegation after it emerged that neither of the two sides eligible for promotion wanted it. Fakenham were due to play off against the winners of the Cambs & Hunts League, Ramsey, whom they had replaced the previous season, but Ramsey's senior players decided that a return to 120-over cricket did not appeal. Nor did Halstead, relegated from the East Anglian League in 2001 and now the Two Counties champions, wish to apply for promotion. Evidently, neither side had relished their experience of premier league cricket.

There were tense finishes in both Surrey and Devon. Reigate Priory and Weybridge were level on points at the top of the Surrey Championship when they met on the final Saturday. Seeking their first title, Reigate managed only 187 for nine, and Weybridge comfortably overhauled them with five wickets to spare. In Devon, Sandford needed only a draw from their last match, against Plympton, to beat Barton to the championship, but collapsed to 99 for eight chasing 142. Matt Theedom and James Gibson, who made a single run, held out heroically for an hour and a half to give Sandford the title.

Wellington, promoted at the end of 2002, became the first Shropshire club to win the Birmingham & District League. Their unexpected triumph underlined how the balance of cricketing power had changed in the West Midlands: since the introduction of a pyramid structure, a year before premier league status in 1998, only one of the six different champions, Walsall, were founder members of the Birmingham League, the oldest in the world.

Chris Aspin writes: More runs were scored in the Lancashire League than ever before. East Lancashire became champions after a 13-year gap and also reached the Worsley Cup final, which they lost to Rawtenstall. Their South African professional, Johann Louw, hit 1,127 runs at 51. His team-mate, Paul Turner, and Rawtenstall's Andrew Payne became the eighth and ninth amateurs to pass 1,000 in a season. Payne hammered 173 in the last game, against Nelson. The highest score, however, was by New South Wales batsman Greg Mail, who hit 180 including 11 sixes in a cup match for Church against Rishton. The leading scorer was South Australian Ben Higgins, with 1,614 for Colne; Bacup's Tasmanian pro, Shaun Young, headed the averages with 1,385 at 81.47.

Michael Ingham, who has played for Haslingden since 1974, took his league aggregate to 15,245, passing the record of 14,951 reached by Peter Wood of Rawtenstall in 1996. Ingham and Graham Knowles shared the highest stand in the league's 111 years, 273 for the second wicket against Church, in July; a month later, Knowles's brother Barry and Steve Dearden set a sixth-wicket league record with 203 against Enfield. Haslingden beat five Central Lancashire League sides on their way to the Inter League Trophy.

Though it was a batsman's season, 16-year-old Jonathan Clare, who learned his cricket alongside James Anderson at Burnley, claimed nine Church wickets for 15, the best amateur return in league history, and topped the averages with 26 at 11, though he missed many games through injury. Bacup amateur David Ormerod was the leading wicket-taker, with 74.

Runs also flowed in the Central Lancashire League, won by Rochdale, while Heywood took the Wood Cup. More than 600 were scored in an afternoon when Crompton replied with 301 to Werneth's 326 for five. Sajith Fernando, the Werneth pro, scored 183 and took six for 84; he finished the league's leading wicket-taker with 106 at 11, and headed the averages. Heywood pro Johan Botha combined 1,432 runs with 102 wickets, while Asif Mujtaba scored 1,436 for Norden. The league is to gain a 16th member in 2005: seven clubs applied for the vacancy, with Monton & Weaste, from the Manchester Association, the successful candidate.

ECB PREMIER LEAGUE TABLES, 2003

Birmingham & District Premier Cricket League

	P	*W*	*L*	*Pts*
Wellington	22	10	1	289
Barnt Green	22	9	3	274
Knowle & Dorridge	22	8	4	271
Halesowen	22	7	4	260
Walsall	22	9	5	248
Old Hill	22	9*	6	247
Moseley	22	7	6	236
Himley	22	5	8	214
Cannock	22	5	8	188
Coventry & N. Warwicks	22	3	7	170
Wolverhampton	22	1*	10	131
Shrewsbury	22	1	12	111

* *Plus one tie.*

Cheshire County Cricket League

	P	*W*	*L*	*Pts*
Bowdon	22	15	2	416
Nantwich	22	13	5	352
Oulton Park	22	12	6	326
Alderley Edge	22	8	7	326
Chester Boughton Hall	22	9	7	300
Neston	22	9	6	299
Hyde	22	7	7	270
Oxton	22	7	10	265
Macclesfield	22	6	10	263
Didsbury	22	4	8	255
Urmston	22	5	13	227
Bramhall	22	2	16	189

Cornwall Premier League

	P	W	L	Pts
Newquay	22	14	2	331
St Buryan	22	10	4	300
Falmouth	22	12	6	293
Truro	22	8	6	264
Grampound Road	22	6	5	256
St Just	22	7	8	253
Callington	22	7*	5	249
Troon	22	2	10	189
Menheniot	22	3*	12	175
Mullion	22	2	13	135

* *Plus one tie.*

Derbyshire Premier League

	P	W	L	Pts
Clifton	20	13	2	359
Sandiacre Town	20	8	3	336
Sawley & Long Eaton Park	20	10	5	322
Denby	20	8	5	295
Ockbrook & Borrowash	20	6	5	277
Chesterfield	20	7	6	272
Ilkeston Rutland	20	4	6	249
Quarndon	20	4	8	228
Wirksworth	20	4	8	205
Alvaston & Boulton	20	3	12	181
Dunstall	20	2	9	181

Devon Cricket League

	P	W	L	Pts
Sandford	17	12	2	270
Barton	17	12	3	268
Exeter	17	12	4	259
Paignton	18	8	6	234
Torquay	17	7	6	214
Plympton	17	7	5	213
Sidmouth	18	5	9	185
North Devon	17	2	11	132
Abbotskerswell	17	1	9	121
Bovey Tracey	17	0	11	94

East Anglian Premier Cricket League

	P	W	L	Pts
Vauxhall Mallards	18	13	1	349
Maldon	18	9	2	291
Norwich	18	7	3	247
Cambridge Granta	18	7	4	237
Cambridge & Godmanchester	18	7	6	233
Clacton-on-Sea	18	6	7	211
Swardeston	18	6	10	197
Bury St Edmunds	18	3	8	139
Mildenhall	18	2	9	130
Fakenham	18	1	11	92

Essex Premier League

	P	W	L	Pts
Saffron Walden	18	8	3	237
Gidea Park & Romford	18	8	2	235
Loughton	18	8	2	234
Hainault & Clayhall	18	6	4	206
Ilford	18	6	4	203
South Woodford	18	6	9	182
Wanstead	18	5	8	179
Fives & Heronians	18	5	8	171
Colchester & East Essex	18	3	6	160
Hadleigh & Thundersley	18	3	12	131

Home Counties Premier Cricket League

	P	W	L	Pts
High Wycombe	18	10	2	334
Reading	18	8	6	275
Slough	18	7	4	275
Radlett	18	5	5	247
Basingstoke & N. Hants	18	7	7	243
Banbury	17	6	4	238
Oxford & Horspath	17	5	4	221
Henley	18	4	6	185
Beaconsfield	18	2	7	179
Hemel Hempstead	18	4	13	178

Kent Cricket League

	P	W	L	Pts
St Lawrence	18	11	2	236
Sevenoaks Vine	18	8	4	217
Whitstable	18	8	6	202
Bromley	18	6	3	188
Lordswood	18	7	8	176
Folkestone	18	5	8	170
Bexley	18	5	5	165
Broadstairs	18	5	10	148
Tunbridge Wells	18	6	9	146
The Mote	18	2	8	141

Lincolnshire Cricket Board Premier League

	P	W	L	Pts	Avge
Bracebridge Heath	21	17	1	377	17.95
Bourne	17	10	3	262	15.41
Market Deeping	19	9*	6	244	12.84
Messingham	20	10	5	255	12.75
Lindum	18	8	6	226	12.56
Grimsby Town	21	9*	4	259	12.33
Owmby	21	11	4	251	11.95
Market Rasen	18	5	6	192	10.67
Sleaford	20	6	10	181	9.05
Long Sutton	21	4	14	135	6.43
Boston	20	2	15	89	4.45
Grantham	18	0	17	47	2.61

* *Plus one tie.*

Leicestershire County Cricket League

	P	W	L	Pts
Loughborough Town	22	17	0	452
Market Harborough	22	11	4	393
Kibworth	22	12	2	387
Lutterworth	22	12	6	369
Syston Town	22	7	7	307
Leicester Ivanhoe	22	7	7	295
Barrow	22	5	10	260
Billesdon	22	5	12	257
Broomleys	22	3	8	254
Barwell	22	6	12	252
Leicester Banks	22	4	11	235
Stoughton & Thurnby	22	2	12	210

Liverpool & District Cricket Competition

	P	W	L	Pts
Bootle	22	15	4	389
Huyton	22	11*	7	297
Wallasey	22	10	11	276
Lytham	22	11	5	271
New Brighton	22	10	5	267
Ormskirk	22	9	6	252
Leigh	22	6	5	207
Northern	22	6	6	195
Maghull	22	5*	10	181
Northop Hall	22	5	10	176
Wigan	22	4	11	155
Newton-le-Willows	22	4	16	137

** Plus one tie.*

Middlesex County Cricket League

	P	W	L	Pts
Brondesbury	18	10	0	123
Stanmore	18	8	4	95
Ealing	18	9	2	90
Teddington	18	7	3	84
Finchley	18	6	6	72
Richmond	18	5	6	69
Southgate	18	4	7	53
Barnes	18	3	7	53
Eastcote	18	1	8	25
Wembley	18	0	10	17

Northamptonshire Cricket Championship

	P	W	L	Pts
Finedon Dolben	22	18	0	545
Northants Cricket Academy	22	13	3	445
Peterborough Town	22	14	2	444
Bedford Town	22	11	9	343
Old Northamptonians	22	9	8	327
Brixworth	22	7	10	279
Rushden Town	22	6	11	259
Northampton Saints	22	5	9	258
Stony Stratford	22	6	11	250
Horton House	22	5	13	247
Rothwell Town	22	7	14	243
Wellingborough Town	22	4	15	200

North East Premier Cricket League

	P	W	L	Pts
South Northumberland	22	13	0	447
Durham Cricket Board	22	10	1	382
Stockton	22	10	5	352
Chester-le-Street	22	9	6	323
Sunderland	22	9	7	321
Blaydon	22	8	7	275
Philadelphia	22	8	9	264
Newcastle	22	4	6	258
Benwell Hill	22	5	11	207
Norton	22	5	11	192
Tynemouth	22	2	10	184
Gateshead Fell	22	2	12	168

Northern Cricket League

	P	W	L	Pts
Darwen	22	13	2	215
St Annes	22	11	2	198
Netherfield	22	10	4	192
Kendal	22	8	6	181
Morecambe	22	10	7	175
Preston	22	8	10	167
Chorley	22	6	6	160
Lancaster	22	6	6	151
Leyland Motors	22	4	12	130
Fleetwood	22	5	11	129
Leyland & Farington	22	4	11	128
Blackpool	22	3	11	120

North Staffs & South Cheshire League

	P	W	L	Pts
Longton	22	15	2	370
Audley	22	11	3	323
Norton-in-Hales	22	11	7	310
Moddershall	22	11	4	307
Checkley	22	9	5	290
Little Stoke	22	8	6	248
Caverswall	22	4	10	198
Leek	22	4	6	175
Meir Heath	22	4	11	173
Porthill Park	22	5	8	172
Betley	22	3	11	164
Barlaston	22	2	14	140

North Wales Premier League

	P	W	L	Pts
Hawarden Park	22	13	2	348
Bangor	22	11*	2	340
Mochdre	22	9	5	311
Pontblyddin	22	9*	4	303
Marchwiel & Wrexham	22	8	5	285
Llandudno	22	9	6	273
Mold	22	8	7	254
Brymbo	22	3	7	230
St Asaph	22	7	10	224
Northop	22	3	11	165
Halkyn	22	3	11	164
Dolgellau	22	1	14	95

** Plus one tie.*

Nottinghamshire Cricket Board Premier League

	P	W	L	Pts
West Indian Cavaliers	22	16	1	378
Kimberley Institute	22	14	3	339
Welbeck Colliery	22	12	3	318
Caythorpe	22	13	7	302
Collingham & District	22	7	6	250
Notts Unity Casuals	22	9	10	228
Wollaton	22	8	11	217
Papplewick & Linby	22	7	11	217
Southwell	22	8	7	210
Clifton Village	22	5	11	200
Bridon	22	2	14	124
Blidworth Colliery Welfare	22	1	18	79

Southern Premier Cricket League

	P	W	L	Pts	Avge
BAT Sports	14	11	1	263	18.79
Bournemouth	15	11	3	254	16.93
Hampshire Academy	15	9	4	231	15.40
Havant	16	8	5	232	14.50
Bashley	16	7*	5	222	13.88
South Wiltshire	15	6*	4	190	12.67
Andover	16	6	7	179	11.19
Liphook & Ripsley	16	3	12	120	7.50
Portsmouth	15	2	11	106	7.07
Calmore Sports	16	2	13	102	6.38

** Plus one tie.*

South Wales Cricket League

	P	W	L	Pts	Avge
Sully Centurions	13	9	2	221	17.00
Cardiff	13	6	1	216	16.62
Newport	13	7	3	199	15.31
Sudbrook	14	7	3	205	14.64
St Fagans	13	4	4	164	12.62
Usk	14	4	6	152	10.86
Penarth	14	4	5	130	9.29
Pentyrch	13	3	8	116	8.92
Chepstow	13	1	8	106	8.15
Pontypridd	14	2	7	106	7.57

Surrey Championship

	P	W	L	Pts
Weybridge	18	10	3	144
Reigate Priory	18	9	4	131
Wimbledon	18	9	4	125
Guildford	18	8	4	116
Esher	18	6	4	99
Normandy	18	6	5	94
Banstead	18	4	7	66
Malden Wanderers	18	4	8	61
Cheam	18	3	11	45
Sutton	18	1	10	20

Sussex Cricket League

	P	W	L	Pts
Hastings & St Leonard's	19	14	1	467
Horsham	19	11	6	400
Brighton & Hove	19	9	3	355
Three Bridges	19	8	6	338
East Grinstead	19	6	4	315
Steyning	19	7	9	300
Sussex Development XI	10	3	3	279†
Chichester Priory Park	19	6	8	274
Eastbourne	19	6	7	271
Worthing	19	2	11	212
Stirlands	19	1	15	119

† Sussex Development XI played only ten games; their actual points total, 147, was multiplied by 1.9.

West of England Premier League

	P	W	L	Pts	Avge
Bath	15	10	2	223	14.87
Cheltenham	15	9	1	210	14.00
Optimists & Clifton	16	7	4	159	9.94
Taunton St Andrews	14	5	6	119	8.50
Corsham	15	5	6	127	8.47
Keynsham	15	6	7	125	8.33
Taunton	16	4	7	102	6.38
Thornbury	15	3	6	95	6.33
Bristol West Indians	15	3	8	80	5.33
Weston-super-Mare	14	3	8	74	5.29

Yorkshire ECB County Premier League

	P	W	L	Pts
Cleethorpes	26	19	5	138
Harrogate	26	17	7	138
York	26	17	7	132
Castleford	26	17	8	132
Sheffield Collegiate	26	17	7	127
Scarborough	26	17	7	123
Doncaster Town	26	13	12	100
Driffield Town	26	13	12	94
Sheffield United	26	11	13	92
Barnsley	26	9*	14	83
Hull	26	10	15	76
Yorkshire Academy	26	7	16	67
Appleby Frodingham	26	1*	23	20
Rotherham Town	26	1	23	15

** Plus one tie.*
Cleethorpes won the title by virtue of more outright wins than Harrogate.

The following leagues do not have ECB Premier League status:

LANCASHIRE LEAGUES

Lancashire League

	P	W	L	Pts
East Lancashire	26	21	5	231
Haslingden	26	19	7	227
Nelson	26	16*	8	204
Bacup	26	17	9	199
Enfield	26	15	11	183
Ramsbottom	26	15	11	183
Todmorden	26	13*	11	169
Lowerhouse	26	13	13	167
Burnley	26	12	13	157
Church	26	10	16	146
Colne	26	10	16	143
Rawtenstall	26	10	15	135
Accrington	26	6	20	89
Rishton	26	2	24	49

* *Plus one tie.*

Central Lancashire League

	P	W	L	Pts
Rochdale	28	21	1	109
Radcliffe	28	20	4	103
Werneth	28	18	6	100
Heywood	28	17	9	92
Walsden	28	14	10	76
Littleborough	28	13	11	73
Norden	28	13	10	70
Middleton	28	12	12	70
Royton	28	11	13	66
Crompton	28	10	13	64
Oldham	28	9	16	58
Milnrow	28	7	14	50
Ashton	28	7	17	43
Unsworth	28	4	21	30
Stand	28	3	22	26

OTHER LEAGUE WINNERS, 2003

Airedale & Wharfedale	Bilton
Bolton Association	Walshaw
Bolton League	Walkden
Bradford	Pudsey Congs
Cambs & Hunts	Ramsey
Central Yorkshire	Wrenthorpe
Durham County	Evenwood
Durham Senior	Horden
Hertfordshire	Potters Bar
Huddersfield	Delph & Dobcross
Lancashire County	Denton West
Merseyside Competition	Rainhill
North Lancs & Cumbria League	Millom
Northumberland & Tyneside Senior	Lanchester
North Yorks & South Durham	Guisborough
Pembrokeshire	Carew
Ribblesdale	Read
Saddleworth	Flowery Field
South Wales Association	Swansea
Two Counties	Halstead
West Wales Association	Llangennech
West Wales Conference	Llanybydder
York Senior	Dunnington

NATIONAL CLUB CHAMPIONSHIP, 2003

The National Club Championship reached its most gripping climax in years as Sandiacre pinched a match they always looked like losing. Derbyshire's first finalists fielded like dervishes and held their nerve; Bath's last pair, needing two from the final four balls, lost theirs.

Bath were fresh from winning the West of England Premier League and almost throughout the final at Lord's they must have expected to complete the double. Instead they collected an unwanted treble: this was the third Championship final, after 1998 and 2001, that they had lost in the last over. But neither of those matches were as tight, or as memorable, as this.

But did Sandiacre's win really make them the best club side in Britain? The question becomes harder to answer conclusively as the numbers of Championship entrants falls. Several times in the 1980s the organisers hit their ceiling of 512 clubs. Excluding a blip in 1995, when many sides withdrew over an eligibility dispute, the average entry in the 1990s was 441. By 2003, the figure had dropped to 335. Unless the decline is reversed, the competition will struggle to match its billing as British club cricket's showpiece.

Roger Chown, the editor of *Extra Cover*, the Club Cricket Conference magazine, said: "The decline *must* have something to do with the fact that there is no sponsor, and scant promotion or support by the ECB." Mark Campkin, the ECB competitions manager, said that, though numbers were declining, standards were going up: "The better clubs are still entering but the weaker ones, who were often knocked out early, are not."

Sandiacre certainly beat strong semi-final opposition to get to Lord's. West Indian Cavaliers had won the 2002 Nottinghamshire Premier League by a massive 92 points. But after hopping across the Erewash the few miles into Derbyshire, they were beaten by 51 runs. Bath beat Teddington from Middlesex by three wickets.

But neither semi-final got as much national press attention as the South-East group match between Banbury and Bromsgrove. A key moment in the bad-tempered game came when Bromsgrove's Jon Farrow, contracted to Worcestershire, was caught out of his ground backing up. Farrow, so the bowler claimed, turned and said "Go on then mate, take the bails off if you like." He did – and Banbury won, by 21 runs.

FINAL

BATH v SANDIACRE TOWN

At Lord's, September 4. Sandiacre won by one run. Toss: Bath.

Sandiacre's captain John Trueman summed it up best when he said, with a smile, "We weren't winning it at any stage were we?" And, right until the last ball, he was probably right. With ten overs to face and six wickets in hand, Bath needed 54. Quick bowler Irfan-ul-Haq – known in Sandiacre as "Cyril" – scattered the stumps of the key remaining batsman, Tom Hankins. But Stuart Barnes hit two successive fours: 26 needed from four overs. Barnes ran himself out: ten needed from 12 balls. Two more wickets fell to Irfan: two runs from four balls. Even with the last pair at the crease, Bath were favourites. But in the final twist Simon Gwilliam set off for what looked, and proved, a suicidal single – and, after one of the best finals in the competition's

35-year history, Sandiacre had pickpocketed a win. It all looked very different when Sandiacre, from Derbyshire, had crawled to 124 in 35 overs, on a pitch with none of the usual September-at-Lord's zip. But Trueman picked up the pace, Rob Attwood swung at everything and Sandiacre managed 90 from their last ten overs. It proved just enough.

Man of the Match: J. F. Trueman.

Sandiacre Town

*J. F. Trueman run out	88	A. R. Taylor not out	4
I. N. Hopkins c Swinney b Barnes	13		
C. R. Attwood c McComish b Gwilliam	16	B 4, l-b 10, w 17, n-b 2	33
Imtiaz Ahmed run out	1		
R. D. Attwood c Staunton b Stayt	39	1/34 2/92 3/96 (7 wickets, 45 overs)	214
J. R. Jordison c Owen b Barnes	3	4/171 5/187	
Irfan-ul-Haq c Hankins b Stayt	17	6/205 7/214	

†S. J. Kinselle, S. N. Guerra and P. Standring did not bat.

Bowling: Stayt 9–1–48–2; McComish 9–2–35–0; Barnes 9–1–42–2; Gwilliam 9–0–38–1; Swinney 7–0–25–0; Murrie 2–0–12–0.

Bath

A. S. Owen b Irfan-ul-Haq	5	P. J. McComish c Kinselle b Irfan-ul-Haq	0
W. D. Murrie lbw b Jordison	38	T. P. G. Stayt not out	1
B. R. F. Staunton c Kinselle b Standring	33	S. A. Gwilliam run out	2
G. R. Swinney c Imtiaz Ahmed b Trueman	43	L-b 3, w 7, n-b 3	13
†T. E. Hankins b Irfan-ul-Haq	37		
*G. Brown c Trueman b Guerra	15	1/8 2/62 3/118 4/128 (44.3 overs)	213
N. G. Potter b Irfan-ul-Haq	13	5/173 6/188 7/201	
S. N. Barnes run out	13	8/205 9/213	

Bowling: Irfan-ul-Haq 9–0–41–4; Jordison 9–0–50–1; Guerra 8.3–0–48–1; Standring 9–1–28–1; Trueman 9–0–43–1.

Umpires: M. Dade and C. T. Puckett.

WINNERS 1969–2003

1969	Hampstead	1981	Scarborough	1993	Old Hill
1970	Cheltenham	1982	Scarborough	1994	Chorley
1971	Blackheath	1983	Shrewsbury	1995	Chorley
1972	Scarborough	1984	Old Hill	1996	Walsall
1973	Wolverhampton	1985	Old Hill	1997	Eastbourne
1974	Sunbury	1986	Stourbridge	1998	Doncaster Town
1975	York	1987	Old Hill	1999	Wolverhampton
1976	Scarborough	1988	Enfield	2000	Sheffield Collegiate
1977	Southgate	1989	Teddington	2001	Bramhall
1978	Cheltenham	1990	Blackpool	2002	Saffron Walden
1979	Scarborough	1991	Teddington	2003	Sandiacre Town
1980	Moseley	1992	Optimists		

NATIONAL VILLAGE CHAMPIONSHIP, 2003

In the September final at Lord's, Shipton-under-Wychwood from Oxfordshire became the fourth village side to retain the 40-over National Championship. Their opponents, Astwood Bank, founded in the 19th century by Worcestershire's needle-makers, were routed for just 79 by Chris Panter, a glazier, and Paul Snell, a former rally driver. The win thrust Shipton into some exalted company: the only other teams to win twice at Lord's in the preceding 12 months were Middlesex, MCC Young Cricketers and England.

However, an eligibility controversy dispelled a touch of the romance. In both the semi-final and the final, Jason Constable made important runs for Shipton – which came as a surprise to the Cherwell League, who had only just banned him for his part in an on-field bust-up. Shipton claimed that the village competition's organisers had cleared Constable to play; the organisers denied any such conversation. Either way, the Cherwell League called the lack of support for their punishment "gobsmacking".

Shipton's route to Lord's had been strewn with narrow escapes. In the third round, they successfully defended 118 against Sandford, with spinner Shaun Miller taking five for three; in their next game they tied with Dumbleton, scraping through by having lost fewer wickets; and in the semi-final against Findon of Sussex, only Snell's 26 from the last over left Shipton a defensible total. Despite the scares, they ended the season unbeaten in home Championship matches since 1995.

By contrast, Astwood's progress through a starting field of more than 500 villages was more serene. In six of the first eight rounds they left their opponents staring at daunting totals of 200-plus. However, their semi-final was a touch more nervy. Watched by a crowd of 800 – bigger than many in the County Championship – 18-year-old Peter Alexander took a memorable catch at long leg and, at the last gasp, turned the game against Streethouse of West Yorkshire.

Elsewhere, Paul Gillett of Overbury in Worcestershire hit 212 in the second round – the highest score of the year and the fourth-highest in the competition's 31-year history. A flock of invading sheep briefly succeeded where the bowlers of Mishaps CC failed, by halting the onslaught. In reply, Mishaps were dismissed for 61. The summer's best bowling came in the South Yorkshire and Humberside group, where Tom Glover took nine for 24 for Bardsley against Thornton.

For 2004 and 2005, a new deal with npower, also sponsors of England's home Test matches, ended a period of uncertainty about the future of the Village Championship, now organised by *The Wisden Cricketer*. So in 2004, Shipton will have the opportunity to go for an unprecedented hat-trick.

FINAL

ASTWOOD BANK v SHIPTON-UNDER-WYCHWOOD

At Lord's, September 7. Shipton-under-Wychwood won by 67 runs. Toss: Astwood Bank.

Despite a docile pitch, and a Tavern Stand boundary just a gentle clip away, Shipton-under-Wychwood successfully defended a vulnerable 40-over total of 146, to become Britain's champion village for the second year running. Astwood Bank's chase began slowly – 29 for no wicket after ten overs – and was soon catatonic: the next nine overs produced six runs and three wickets. In the game's crucial phase, Astwood could hardly get the ball off the square against seamer Chris Panter and left-arm spinner Shaun Miller, who conceded only six runs in a nine-over spell – three from edges. With 68 needed from the last ten overs, batsmen swished and wickets fell. The last five went with the total stuck on 79 – the lowest in a Village final. Earlier, after a brisk opening partnership of 63, Shipton also suffered a mid-innings lull. From 93 for five after 30 overs, Ian Lewis did a decent salvage job.

Shipton-under-Wychwood

J. M. Constable lbw b Summers	34
S. Bates c Robinson b Sealey	24
S. P. Gillett c Robinson b Sealey	1
*P. Hemming run out	24
A. Hemming c Robinson b Sealey	9
C. P. Panter st Robinson b Boycott	1
I. Lewis c Freeman b Clarke	23
S. Miller b Boycott	3
P. Snell b Clarke	5
C. Lambert not out	4
†C. Brain not out	6
L-b 3, w 5, n-b 4	12
1/63 2/66 3/74 4/90 5/93 6/120 7/123 8/130 9/136 (9 wkts, 40 overs)	146

Bowling: Bowes 6–1–35–0; Freeman 4–0–21–0; Summers 9–2–11–1; Sealey 9–0–22–3; Boycott 7–0–31–2; Clarke 5–0–23–2.

Astwood Bank

D. Sealey c P. Hemming b Panter	16
A. Clayton c Brain b Panter	13
S. Jagielski c Brain b Panter	3
S. Churchley c Brain b Panter	0
*†A. Robinson c Brain b Snell	16
S. Clarke lbw b Snell	17
P. Boycott b Snell	1
P. Alexander b Snell	0
J. Summers run out	0
I. Bowes not out	0
D. Freeman b Snell	0
B 1, l-b 5, w 5, n-b 2	13
1/31 2/34 3/34 4/52 5/68 6/79 7/79 8/79 9/79 (32.5 overs)	79

Bowling: Constable 6–2–12–0; Snell 6.5–1–24–5; Miller 9–4–6–0; Panter 9–4–26–4; P. Hemming 2–1–5–0.

Umpires: B. Ireton and T. Wilson.

WINNERS 1972–2003

1972 Troon (Cornwall)
1973 Troon (Cornwall)
1974 Bomarsund (Northumberland)
1975 Gowerton (Glamorgan)
1976 Troon (Cornwall)
1977 Cookley (Worcestershire)
1978 Linton Park (Kent)
1979 East Bierley (Yorkshire)
1980 Marchwiel (Clwyd)
1981 St Fagans (Glamorgan)
1982 St Fagans (Glamorgan)
1983 Quarndon (Derbyshire)
1984 Marchwiel (Clwyd)
1985 Freuchie (Fife)
1986 Forge Valley (Yorkshire)
1987 Longparish (Hampshire)
1988 Goatacre (Wiltshire)
1989 Toft (Cheshire)
1990 Goatacre (Wiltshire)
1991 St Fagans (Glamorgan)
1992 Hursley Park (Hampshire)
1993 Kington (Herefordshire)
1994 Elvaston (Derbyshire)
1995 Woodhouse Grange (Yorkshire)
1996 Caldy (Cheshire)
1997 Caldy (Cheshire)
1998 Methley (Yorkshire)
1999 Linton Park (Kent)
2000 Elvaston (Derbyshire)
2001 Ynystawe (Glamorgan)
2002 Shipton-under-Wychwood (Oxfordshire)
2003 Shipton-under-Wychwood (Oxfordshire)

IRISH CRICKET, 2003

DEREK SCOTT

Although there were no trophies at stake, 2003 was one of the Irish team's best years. They played 14 games, all limited-overs, and won ten, including nine in succession, their best run ever. And for the first time since the famous 1969 match against the West Indians, when Basil Butcher's side were skittled for 25 on an emerald-green Londonderry pitch, Ireland beat a Test nation. If this year's Zimbabwean opposition was not as formidable, the thumping win, by ten wickets, was almost as comprehensive. Defeats by Zimbabwe and South Africa later in the summer could not dampen the glow of satisfaction. All told, the only recent season to rival 2003 was 1996, when Ireland won the UK Triple Crown and the European Championship.

Highlights were many and varied. On a tour of England, the Irish won four matches in four days, bowling out the Duke of Norfolk's XI, MCC, Free Foresters (all fielding at least a handful of first-class players) and the Club Cricket Conference. Then, in the opening round of the 2004 Cheltenham & Gloucester Trophy, played in August 2003, they plundered 387 for four against Hertfordshire. That set up a win – plus a high-profile second-round match in May 2004 against Surrey's international all-stars. The only minor hiccough was losing 2–1 at home to the ECB's amateur XI.

To top it all, back in Dublin, Ireland buried Denmark under another pile of runs to clinch a best-of-three series. The Irish won more than kudos: victory qualified them for the European Zone of the new ICC Intercontinental Cup, a tournament designed to give those teams one rank below full international standard more three-day experience.

The season provided much for the players to be proud of. The total of four centuries (including Ireland's third against Test opposition, 107 not out by captain Jason Molins against the Zimbabweans) was the highest ever, as was the 34.95 runs the side averaged per wicket. The leading run-scorer and wicket-taker was Andre Botha, born in Johannesburg and recently qualified by residence. He became the first to hit 500 runs and take 20 wickets in a season. Great credit also accrued to another South African, Adrian Birrell, in his second year as coach.

Remarkably, Ireland's bowlers took 118 wickets of a possible 140 across the summer. Kyle McCallan passed both 100 career wickets and 2,000 runs – only the third Irish player to do so, after Garfield Harrison and Alec O'Riordan. In a season of records, Eoin Morgan, a left-handed batsman, became Ireland's youngest-ever player, at 16; despite being run out on both of his first appearances he was later snapped up by Middlesex.

It was a happy year at all levels. The Under-19s qualified for the 2004 World Cup in Bangladesh, while the Under-15s and Under-13s also won their versions of the European championship. The women qualified for their first World Cup, in South Africa, by winning all five of their qualifying matches in the Netherlands. Barbara McDonald was named Woman of the Tournament.

Of Ireland's 19 international players in 2003, five came from Dublin's North County club. Undoubtedly, North County were club of the year, pulling off an impressive treble – the Royal Liver Irish Senior Cup, along with the major local league and cup competitions.

Winners of Irish Leagues and Cups
Royal Liver Irish Senior Cup: North County; **Ulster Cup:** Brigade; **Dublin Senior League:** North County; **Dublin Senior Cup:** North County; **Munster League:** Cork County; **Munster Cup:** Cork County; **Northern Union:** North Down; **Northern Union Cup:** North Down; **North-West League:** Donemana; **North-West Cup:** Limavady.

SCOTTISH CRICKET, 2003

NEIL LEITCH

Craig Wright

Ryan Watson

Scotland made their debut alongside English counties in a League competition in 2003, appearing as the Scottish Saltires in the National League. But the scheme was very nearly still-born. The original plan, to establish a group of full-time professionals throughout the season, was not viable: there was no money for the Scottish-qualified cricketers.

South African international Jon Kent was secured for one of the two permitted overseas berths, with most of his salary met by his club in Edinburgh, but serious thought was given to pulling out. Thankfully, Scotland pressed on, swayed partly by Glasgow's Indian community, who funded the star signing of Rahul Dravid.

Dravid had to miss the first five fixtures, and expectations were low when the campaign commenced, against Durham on May 4. The almost unprecedented sight of Scotland wholly outplaying county professionals changed everything. That victory boosted confidence, and two more followed before Dravid arrived – making three Scottish wins over first-class counties in 22 days, after three in the previous 23 years. Victory at home to Somerset was secured by the innings of a lifetime from Ryan Watson; his brutal century, from 44 balls, was the third-fastest in one-day history. But there was even more satisfaction in a fine team performance to beat Lancashire at Old Trafford.

Almost inevitably, the expectations thus raised were not realised. While Dravid was the model professional, he played in only one win, at Hove. Still, Scotland were usually competitive. Captain Craig Wright rose to the challenge with some telling all-round performances and was ably, though not consistently, supported by most of his team-mates. The contribution of charismatic coach Tony Judd (another part-time appointment, due to funding constraints) was immense.

A one-day match against Pakistan in June very nearly provided the most historic win of all. In 138 years of international cricket, Scotland had beaten only one Test side – Australia, in a hastily arranged fixture in 1882. Despite a first-ball dismissal for Dravid, Pakistan only just scrambled home, by one wicket. In the Cheltenham & Gloucester Trophy, Scotland were hammered by Somerset two days before their National League encounter, but overcame Cumberland in the 2004 preliminaries. A Scotland Development side comfortably beat MCC over three days.

Scottish Cricket's management continued to suffer a high turnover. Assistant coach Mike Hendrick asked to be released, and Peter Drinnen took over. Hendrick will be missed: his work with age-group teams helped the Under-19s qualify for the 2004 World Cup. Chief executive Gwynne Jones, instrumental in securing the National League debut, also left.

Grange were the club to beat in the Scottish National League. Victory over 2002 champions Greenock made them early leaders, though they were less steady in the Scottish Cup and the Plate. Uddingston, spurred on by Paul Hoffmann, perhaps the quietest opening bowler Australia has ever produced, were surprise Cup victors, beating West of Scotland.

Edinburgh, who finished on top of the East of Scotland League, had 35 points docked – which cost them their title and their promotion – for fielding an ineligible player. An appeals panel ruled that the player billed as Asad Rehman, who appeared in seven games, was really Rana Jahanzaib, a 27-year-old Pakistani all-rounder with first-class experience for Gujranwala.

Winners of Scottish Leagues and Cups

Scottish National Cricket League: *Premier Division* – Grange; *First Division* – Ferguslie; *Second Division* – Penicuik. **Scottish Cup:** Uddingston. **SCL Trophy:** Edinburgh. **Small Clubs' Cup:** Holy Cross Academicals. **Border League:** Kelso. **East of Scotland League:** Grange II. **Strathmore Union:** St Modan's High School FP. **Western Union:** Weirs. **North of Scotland League:** Buckie. **Perthshire League:** Rossie Priory. **West League Cup:** 2002 – Greenock; 2003 – Greenock. **Rowan Cup:** Clydesdale. **Masterton Trophy:** Watsonians.

SOUTH AFRICA UNDER-19 IN ENGLAND, 2003

GARETH A. DAVIES

While their elders endured a tour of mixed fortunes, a South African squad of great maturity and professionalism defeated England Under-19 in both Test and one-day series in August 2003, going unbeaten throughout their tour.

"It was a huge, invaluable learning curve," said tour manager Morgan Pillay. "Our boys prepared very well, and bonded well during the tour. There is a future for all of them in the game in South Africa."

Pillay had managed South Africa Under-19's previous tour in 1995; four of that party – Mark Boucher, Neil McKenzie, Makhaya Ntini and Boeta Dippenaar – were back in England with the senior Test squad, and he had no doubt, given the recent appointment of 22-year-old Graeme Smith as South African captain, that many of his latest charges would reach the top. Pillay has also administered the annual Khaya Majola week, which brings together South Africa's best schoolboy cricketers. "We have a very strong schools structure – with a great deal of coaching and financial support," he said. South Africa's national academy, and the 11 provincial academies, help to maintain strength in depth, and cricket in the townships continues to grow: several of the tour party came from those areas.

It was self-evident that this was a group who gelled well, but their most potent collective asset lay in their ability to see matches through to success at the slightest scent of weakness in the opposition. Nor did they crack under pressure, as England did at times. The players' maturity had much to do with their age. All but four players were already over 19; they just qualified for the ICC's definition of Under-19, but would become ineligible before the World Cup in February 2004. They looked like men rather than boys.

Their determined performances enabled them to dominate the Tests, winning the First and the Third, and recovering strongly from an apparently disastrous position in the Second. They won the only completed one-day international by a single wicket; the last two were washed out.

The South Africans scored the highest total in Under-19 Test cricket during the last match at Chelmsford, and nine of their batsmen averaged 40 or more during the series. The leading run-scorer was Francois du Plessis, with 226. Rieel de Kock and Abraham de Villiers also passed 200, and de Villiers added 200 more in the one-day internationals. Three seamers led the attack: William Hantam collected 16 Test wickets, with 14 for Vernon Philander and 11 for Heinrich le Roux.

England's tendency to juggle players worked against them, with 18 used over five international games. A run of injuries did not help, and the counties were calling back some of their players by the end of the series, including the captain, Bilal Shafayat of Nottinghamshire. He ended his England Under-19 career looking like a batsman to watch out for in the future. A century in the Second Test at Worcester gave him four in Under-19 Test cricket, equalling Marcus Trescothick, and he averaged 42 in the series. The leading scorers were his Nottinghamshire team-mate, Samit Patel, who scored 175 Test runs and another 122 in his only one-day innings, and Yorkshire's Joe Sayers, who made 186. Tim Bresnan, another Yorkshireman, was the most successful bowler, with nine wickets in the two Tests he played.

SOUTH AFRICA UNDER-19 TOURING PARTY

I. Khan (KwaZulu-Natal) (*captain*), F. du Plessis (Northerns) (*vice-captain*), J. Booysen (Easterns), R. de Kock (Free State), A. B. de Villiers (Northerns), J-P. Duminy (Western Province), W. C. Hantam (Western Province), H. W. le Roux (Northerns), F. G. Nkuna (Northerns), V. Pennazza (Boland), A. M. Phangiso (Northerns), V. Philander (Western Province), D. Smit (KwaZulu-Natal), E. T. Springer (KwaZulu-Natal), C. A. Thyssen (Eastern Province).

B. L. Reddy (Easterns) withdrew due to injury and was replaced by Pennazza.

Coach: D. O. Nosworthy. *Assistant coach:* N. Matoti. *Manager:* M. Pillay. *Physiotherapist:* B. Jackson.

SOUTH AFRICA UNDER-19 TOUR RESULTS

Played 9: Won 6, Drawn 2, No result 1, Abandoned 1.

Note: Matches in this section were not first-class.

At Bradfield College, Reading, July 27, 28, 29. **South Africa Under-19 won by an innings and three runs.** Toss: South Africa Under-19. **Development of Excellence (South) XI 207** (V. Pennazza 4-33) **and 149** (I. Khan 6-22); **South Africa Under-19 359-9 dec.** (F. du Plessis 151, J-P. Duminy 79; N. C. Saker 4-63).

ENGLAND v SOUTH AFRICA

First Under-19 Test

At Leeds, August 1, 2, 3, 4. South Africa Under-19 won by four wickets. Toss: South Africa Under-19.

One day after South Africa's seniors won the Lord's Test, the Under-19s made it a double – though this game was less one-sided. Asked to bat, England were allowed to run up 327, thanks to half-centuries from Sayers and Patel and late hitting by Liam Plunkett of Durham. It took a seventh-wicket stand of 85 between Smit and le Roux to steer South Africa out of trouble against Bresnan, who picked up five. In the second innings, England lost their last four for 25, leaving South Africa to chase 228. It was in the balance overnight at 113 for three, but England's attack was handicapped on the last day when Plunkett and Michael Parsons of Somerset succumbed to muscle strains and Adam Harrison of Glamorgan bowled with an upset stomach. De Villiers thumped 65 in 70 balls to see his team to the brink of victory.

Close of play: First day, England Under-19 298-9 (Plunkett 32, Parsons 14); Second day, South Africa Under-19 288-8 (le Roux 74, Philander 11); Third day, South Africa Under-19 113-3 (Duminy 0, de Villiers 4).

England Under-19

N. J. Edwards c Hantam b Philander	41	– c Duminy b Nkuna	34
J. J. Sayers c and b Hantam	60	– lbw b Hantam	26
*B. M. Shafayat c Duminy b Nkuna	6	– c and b Hantam	0
R. S. Bopara b Hantam	4	– c Smit b Hantam	19
S. R. Patel c and b Hantam	61	– c de Villiers b Philander	55
L. J. Wright b Philander	24	– lbw b Philander	18
†A. J. Hodd c de Villiers b le Roux	14	– c de Villiers b Philander	0
T. T. Bresnan lbw b Philander	1	– c Khan b Philander	16
L. E. Plunkett not out	48	– c Smit b Philander	1
A. J. Harrison c de Villiers b Hantam	6	– not out	8
M. Parsons c de Villiers b Hantam	24	– c and b Hantam	9
L-b 1, w 6, n-b 31	38	B 1, l-b 6, n-b 4	11
1/106 (1) 2/122 (3) 3/128 (4) 4/154 (2) 5/179 (6) 6/228 (5) 7/229 (8) 8/252 (7) 9/275 (10) 10/327 (11)	327	1/65 (2) 2/65 (3) 3/65 (1) 4/115 (4) 5/153 (5) 6/158 (7) 7/172 (6) 8/179 (8) 9/182 (9) 10/197 (11)	197

Bowling: *First Innings*—le Roux 26–7–76–1; Nkuna 25–2–81–1; Hantam 26.4–8–86–5; Philander 21–7–65–3; Khan 13–5–17–0; du Plessis 2–1–1–0. *Second Innings*—le Roux 15–3–48–0; Nkuna 13–4–50–1; Philander 20–5–50–5; Hantam 13.5–5–27–4; de Villiers 2–0–11–0; Khan 3–2–4–0.

South Africa Under-19

*I. Khan c Patel b Harrison	61	– c Patel b Bopara	27
R. de Kock lbw b Bresnan	14	– lbw b Harrison	59
F. du Plessis lbw b Bresnan	17	– lbw b Bresnan	20
J-P. Duminy c Shafayat b Bresnan	0	– c sub b Patel	13
A. B. de Villiers c Wright b Harrison	10	– c Hodd b Shafayat	65
J. Booysen lbw b Plunkett	25	– c Hodd b Harrison	3
†D. Smit lbw b Patel	51	– not out	27
H. W. le Roux c Hodd b Bresnan	74	– not out	6
W. C. Hantam b Plunkett	8		
V. Philander not out	16		
F. G. Nkuna b Bresnan	4		
B 6, l-b 2, w 2, n-b 7	17	L-b 6, n-b 2	8
1/23 (2) 2/63 (3) 3/63 (4) 4/101 (5) 5/117 (1) 6/138 (6) 7/223 (7) 8/253 (9) 9/291 (8) 10/297 (11)	297	1/51 (1) 2/108 (2) 3/108 (3) 4/138 (4) 5/153 (6) 6/208 (5)	(6 wkts) 228

Bowling: *First Innings*—Bresnan 23–4–81–5; Harrison 17–7–32–2; Parsons 9–2–36–0; Plunkett 22–5–82–2; Bopara 2–0–8–0; Shafayat 6–1–15–0; Patel 15–7–27–1; Wright 1–0–8–0. *Second Innings*—Plunkett 3–2–6–0; Bresnan 19–7–42–1; Harrison 12–4–49–2; Shafayat 7–0–37–1; Bopara 5–0–26–1; Patel 13.3–3–62–1.

Umpires: B. Dudleston and P. J. Hartley.

At Sleaford, August 6, 7, 8. **Drawn.** Toss: Development of Excellence (North) XI. **South Africa Under-19 354-9 dec.** (R. de Kock 133; M. K. Munday 4-77) **and 333-8 dec.** (I. Khan 91, F. du Plessis retired out 103; D. L. Broadbent 4-100); **Development of Excellence (North) XI 300-7 dec.** (J. C. Hildreth 170*; F. du Plessis 4-67) **and 149-6**.

ENGLAND v SOUTH AFRICA

Second Under-19 Test

At Worcester, August 11, 12, 13, 14. Drawn. Toss: England Under-19.

England were ideally placed to level this series on the third afternoon, when South Africa were three down second time round and 207 behind. But Duminy and de Villiers put on 220 – a fourth-wicket record against England Under-19, beating 212 by Greg Blewett and Adam Gilchrist for Australia in 1991. Harrison went off with a hand injury needing eight stitches, and it was Cook's occasional off-spin that broke through after 73 overs. He held a return catch off Duminy, who had struck 18 fours and two sixes, and bowled de Villiers, looking to work a single for his hundred. South Africa led by 26, with 59 overs left, but Springer ensured they took their advantage to Chelmsford. Alastair Cook of Essex had launched his England debut by scoring 51 out of an opening stand of 68, and Shafayat completed his fourth Under-19 hundred, equalling the record of Marcus Trescothick and Pakistan's Hasan Raza. Finally, last man Nick Thornicroft of Yorkshire smashed four sixes in one Khan over, reaching 42 in 11 balls. South Africa got only halfway to England's formidable 523 at their first attempt. Bresnan seized three for 16 in his opening spell; de Kock batted four and a half hours but could not avert the follow-on.

Close of play: First day, England Under-19 289-2 (Shafayat 107, Bopara 68); Second day, South Africa Under-19 112-5 (de Kock 22, Smit 34); Third day, South Africa Under-19 166-3 (Duminy 69, de Villiers 38).

England Under-19

A. N. Cook c le Roux b Thyssen	51
J. J. Sayers st Smit b Khan	53
*B. M. Shafayat b Hantam	121
R. S. Bopara c Smit b Hantam	69
S. R. Patel c Khan b le Roux	14
L. J. Wright c Smit b Philander	54
†A. J. Hodd c du Plessis b Philander	31
T. T. Bresnan c Smit b Philander	6
G. M. Andrew c Springer b Khan	32
A. J. Harrison b Hantam	29
N. D. Thornicroft not out	42
B 5, l-b 2, w 4, n-b 10	21
1/68 (1) 2/141 (2) 3/291 (4) 4/319 (5) 5/319 (3) 6/399 (6) 7/414 (7) 8/415 (8) 9/472 (9) 10/523 (10)	523

Bowling: le Roux 33–9–88–1; Hantam 32.4–7–96–3; Philander 34–12–89–3; Thyssen 22–4–84–1; du Plessis 9–0–51–0; Khan 26–7–101–2; Springer 6–1–7–0.

South Africa Under-19

First innings		Second innings	
*I. Khan c Sayers b Bresnan	0	c Hodd b Wright	30
R. de Kock b Patel	82	c Andrew b Thornicroft	16
F. du Plessis c and b Bresnan	8	c Wright b Andrew	4
J-P. Duminy lbw b Harrison	14	c and b Cook	116
A. B. de Villiers lbw b Bresnan	5	b Cook	99
E. T. Springer b Thornicroft	24	c sub b Cook	79
†D. Smit b Thornicroft	44	b Patel	21
H. W. le Roux b Patel	20	not out	37
C. A. Thyssen c Patel b Andrew	45	c Hodd b Shafayat	10
W. C. Hantam lbw b Patel	4		
V. Philander not out	0	(10) not out	4
B 6, l-b 6, w 1, n-b 3	16	B 8, l-b 18, w 4, n-b 7	37
1/0 (1) 2/8 (3) 3/23 (4) 4/28 (5) 5/65 (6) 6/126 (7) 7/172 (8) 8/256 (2) 9/262 (10) 10/262 (9)	262	1/26 (2) 2/54 (1) 3/54 (3) 4/274 (4) 5/287 (5) 6/333 (7) 7/411 (6) 8/439 (9)	(8 wkts) 453

Bowling: *First Innings*—Bresnan 17–3–41–3; Thornicroft 15–3–52–2; Harrison 4.2–1–18–1; Andrew 11.3–1–47–1; Patel 17.4–8–55–3; Shafayat 5–1–25–0; Cook 2–0–12–0. *Second Innings*—Bresnan 27–9–69–0; Thornicroft 19–2–83–1; Andrew 18–4–59–1; Wright 23–6–59–1; Patel 24–5–87–1; Cook 24–10–50–3; Bopara 6–1–15–0; Shafayat 4–2–5–1.

Umpires: I. J. Gould and M. J. Kitchen.

ENGLAND v SOUTH AFRICA

Third Under-19 Test

At Chelmsford, August 16, 17, 18, 19. South Africa Under-19 won by an innings and 163 runs. Toss: England Under-19.

South Africa clinched the series on an excellent pitch. They batted England – who had lost Shafayat and Bresnan to their counties – out of the match, with 415 runs on the second day. Their eventual 646 for nine declared was the biggest total in Under-19 Tests, beating England's 620 for nine against West Indies in 2001. Du Plessis made a monumental 177, battering the hoardings with 26 fours and three sixes, though South Africa were an unconvincing 147 for four in reply to England's unconvincing 229 before he began to find allies and the bowlers wilted in the heat. An unbroken stand of 123 was a last-wicket record in England Under-19 Tests: No. 9 Thyssen reached a century and last man Hantam 71 in 80 balls. Hantam and le Roux had undone England's first innings, when several batsmen got starts but none reached 40. Resuming 417 behind, England Under-19 went down to their heaviest defeat; only Cook and debutant James Hildreth, from Somerset, with an unbeaten 116, resisted long.

Close of play: First day, South Africa Under-19 48-1 (de Kock 22, du Plessis 23); Second day, South Africa Under-19 463-8 (Thyssen 23, Philander 8); Third day, England Under-19 137-4 (Hildreth 43, Wright 8).

England Under-19

First innings		Second innings	
A. N. Cook lbw b le Roux	2	c Springer b du Plessis	46
*J. J. Sayers c Springer b Philander	30	lbw b Hantam	17
R. S. Bopara lbw b le Roux	38	c Smit b le Roux	10
S. R. Patel c de Villiers b Hantam	37	c Smit b Philander	8
J. C. Hildreth c Smit b le Roux	14	not out	116
L. J. Wright c Smit b le Roux	0	lbw b le Roux	17
†A. J. Hodd lbw b Philander	33	c de Villiers b le Roux	5
L. E. Plunkett not out	25	run out	0
M. L. Turner b Hantam	22	c Hantam b du Plessis	6
N. D. Thornicroft c Smit b Hantam	4	st Smit b du Plessis	15
M. A. K. Lawson lbw b le Roux	1	c du Plessis b le Roux	5
L-b 5, w 3, n-b 15	23	L-b 6, n-b 3	9
1/2 (1) 2/63 (2) 3/117 (3) 4/117 (4) 5/118 (6) 6/157 (5) 7/182 (7) 8/219 (9) 9/225 (10) 10/229 (11)	229	1/26 (2) 2/42 (3) 3/65 (4) 4/91 (1) 5/151 (6) 6/161 (7) 7/167 (8) 8/219 (9) 9/245 (10) 10/254 (11)	254

Bowling: *First Innings*—le Roux 24.2–6–59–5; Hantam 24–8–51–3; Philander 24–3–60–2; Thyssen 13–2–41–0; Khan 2–0–13–0. *Second Innings*—le Roux 19.2–2–60–4; Hantam 20–7–49–1; Philander 15–4–47–1; du Plessis 17–3–39–3; Thyssen 7–3–19–0; Khan 9–2–34–0.

South Africa Under-19

*I. Khan lbw b Thornicroft	0
R. de Kock c Bopara b Lawson	31
F. du Plessis c Hodd b Thornicroft	177
J-P. Duminy lbw b Wright	5
A. B. de Villiers c Patel b Plunkett	23
E. T. Springer c Turner b Lawson	77
†D. Smit b Patel	52
H. W. le Roux hit wkt b Turner	49
C. A. Thyssen not out	100
V. Philander c Hodd b Thornicroft	27
W. C. Hantam not out	71
B 13, l-b 12, w 4, n-b 5	34
1/0 (1) 2/84 (2) 3/111 (4) 4/147 (5) 5/285 (6) 6/336 (3) 7/407 (7) 8/447 (8) 9/523 (10) (9 wkts dec.)	646

Bowling: Thornicroft 28–2–142–3; Plunkett 32–9–111–1; Turner 20–1–82–1; Lawson 26–7–91–2; Wright 18–5–70–1; Patel 29–11–66–1; Cook 7–0–29–0; Bopara 6–0–30–0.

Umpires: T. E. Jesty and G. Sharp.

At Billericay, August 21. **South Africa Under-19 won by nine wickets. Development of Excellence XI 190-6** (50 overs) (B. W. Harmison 55*); **South Africa Under-19 193-1** (25.5 overs) (A. B. de Villiers 78, R. de Kock 87*).

At Billericay, August 22. **South Africa Under-19 won by two wickets. Development of Excellence XI 188** (47.3 overs) (C. P. Murtagh 52); **South Africa Under-19 189-8** (31.4 overs) (J. Booysen 88).

At Arundel, August 26. **First one-day international: South Africa Under-19 won by one wicket.** Toss: England Under-19. **England Under-19 267-8** (50 overs) (S. R. Patel 122, T. J. New 50); **South Africa Under-19 270-9** (49.5 overs) (A. B. de Villiers 143).

Patel scored 122 in 112 balls, with 16 fours and a six; de Villiers 143 in 153 balls, with 18 fours.

At Hove, August 28. **Second one-day international: No result.** Toss: England Under-19. **South Africa Under-19 190-7** (32 overs) (A. B. de Villiers 59; L. J. Wright 5-46); **England 8-0** (2 overs).

Rain and bad light reduced the match to 32 overs an innings, and ended it as England began their reply. Medium-pacer Wright took a hat-trick during South Africa's collapse from 112 for nought to 119 for five.

At Hove, August 29. **Third one-day international: England Under-19 v South Africa Under-19. No result (abandoned).**

Rain washed out the game without a ball bowled. South Africa won the one-day series 1–0.

UMPIRES FOR 2004

FIRST-CLASS UMPIRES

M. R. Benson, G. I. Burgess, A. Clarkson, D. J. Constant, N. G. Cowley, B. Dudleston, J. H. Evans, I. J. Gould, J. H. Hampshire, M. J. Harris, P. J. Hartley, J. W. Holder, V. A. Holder, T. E. Jesty, A. A. Jones, M. J. Kitchen, B. Leadbeater, N. J. Llong, J. W. Lloyds, N. A. Mallender, R. Palmer, G. Sharp, D. R. Shepherd, J. F. Steele, A. G. T. Whitehead, P. Willey. *Reserves:* R. J. Bailey, N. L. Bainton, S. A. Garratt, R. K. Illingworth, R. A. Kettleborough, R. T. Robinson.

MINOR COUNTIES UMPIRES

N. L. Bainton, T. Beale, S. F. Bishopp, S. Boulton, P. Brown, A. Bullock, D. L. Burden, P. D. Clubb, K. Coburn, D. Davis, M. Dixon, R. Dowd, H. Evans, J. Ilott, J. H. James, J. S. Johnson, R. Johnson, P. W. Joy, P. W. Kingston-Davey, S. W. Kuhlmann, G. Maddison, S. Z. Marszal, C. Martin, C. Megennis, M. P. Moran, C. G. Pocock, C. T. Puckett, G. P. Randall-Johnson, P. L. Ratcliffe, J. G. Reed, K. S. Shenton, W. E. Smith, R. M. Sutton, D. G. Tate, J. M. Tythcott, M. C. White, J. Wilkinson.

SCHOOLS CRICKET, 2003

REVIEW BY PAUL COUPAR

Coloured clothing, white balls and black sightscreens lie just over the horizon, but for 2003, what happened on the genteel grounds of the United Kingdom's cricket-playing schools was familiar. Whites were worn, exams stole more time than ever and, for the second year running, slow bowlers prospered. From a field of around 2,500 players (most, but not all, boys – see for instance South Craven School) two familiar names rose to the top. Alastair Cook, a left-handed opening bat from Bedford School, and Tom Woolsey, an accurate left-arm spinner from St Peter's, York, remained, as they were in 2002, the heaviest run-scorer, and the leading wicket-taker among those schools reporting to *Wisden*.

Cook went on to hallmark his talent by hitting fifties in his first three County Championship matches for Essex. But it now takes good fortune in your choice of school, as well as talent, to reach the top of the tables. Fewer and fewer first teams play a significant amount of cricket. In 1983, 22% of schools listed in *Wisden* arranged more than 20 matches. Ten years later, that figure was 19%. By 2003, it had tumbled to 7%. As the exam season gets longer – now nearly seven weeks in some schools – the downward trend continues. On average, schools cut half a game from their fixture card for 2003. This summer almost certainly saw the fewest scheduled matches for many years.

At least more escaped the rain than in 2002 – although the azure skies and record temperatures so entrenched in the memories of cricket watchers did not arrive until term was over.

Despite grey clouds in May it was a good season for batsmen. In 2003, scoreboards didn't tick; they whirred, and 14 schools reported new batting records. Among schools reaching their highest-ever totals were University College School, who scorched to 334 for four against Highgate, and Tiffin, who managed just two fewer against Reigate Grammar School. In that match, Kapilan Balasubramaniam hit 204 not out, including 13 sixes, then completed five stumpings – four off quick bowlers. Nick Howell took 11 balls to reach the fastest fifty on record for The Oratory, Daniel Howes hit his 665 runs for Repton off 522 balls, and an incredible 180 of Robin Gaymer's 632 for Berkhamsted came in sixes.

But Cook stood alone. He began the season revising for A-levels and ended it in the Essex first team. In between, he scored 1,287 runs for Bedford, 263 more than 16-year-old Stephen Bilboe managed for King's, Worcester. Cook also topped the national averages – with 160.87. His concentration was immense – seven hundreds, two unbeaten double-centuries, and one opening partnership (with Will Notley) of 333 in 50 overs. Even compared with exceptional schoolboys of the past, Cook stood tall. Bedford's last outstanding player, Toby Bailey, now of Northamptonshire, made five hundreds during his school career; Cook hit 17. Another Cook, Paul of

Alastair Cook of Bedford hit the most runs in schools cricket and enjoyed further success in the Essex first team.

Malvern College, was his nearest rival, averaging over 106 and scoring 961 runs.

No bowler stood out so obviously. Woolsey, with 50 wickets, took just one more than James Hay, a swing bowler from Oundle. Hay's total included four Stamford batsmen, all bowled, in four balls. With another year at school, Woolsey, an open-side flanker for England's Under-16 rugby side, still has a chance to complete an unprecedented hat-trick. Three of the six leading wicket-takers bowled spin, and two – Michael Swartz of Lord Wandsworth College and Wian Potgieter of Merchiston Castle – were scholars visiting from South Africa. It is not just in county cricket that teams are turning to imports. A slow bowler led the averages too – Chetan Depala, a leg-spinner for Christ's, Finchley, who took 28 wickets at six. Another Depala, Chetan's cousin Mayur, ended third in the list.

In a good season for Sussex, a truly dominant schools team emerged on the South Coast. Brighton College blazed through the summer, winning 15 of their 16 games. In 1999, they won 20 out of 24, but this was the highest proportion of victories in a long season (16 games or more) recorded in *Wisden* since at least 1980.

Before running into Eton, Brighton had won 19 in a row, a sequence stretching back to 2002. Nor were all of the matches limited-overs. Positive captaincy, 48 wickets from spinner Ronak Sekhri and 831 runs from the

Tom Woolsey of St Peter's (*left*) was leading wicket-taker in the country for the second year running, while Chris Grammer of Brighton College captained the country's most successful side.

captain Chris Grammer added up to what the school's coach, John Spencer, called a "golden era." And when Brighton entered the new Ben Hollioake memorial tournament, a seven-a-side, five-over bash at The Oval, they won that too. No other school could quite match their record, but Hampton, Leeds Grammar, Lord Williams's, Woodbridge and Wyggeston all went unbeaten.

Wisden covers cricket in all schools of a sufficient cricketing standard who send in reports, whether they are in the independent or state sector. But outside the small group of traditional cricket schools, the vast majority of young players are still learning the game in clubs. The ECB claim that 85% of state secondary schools provide cricket but that is based on a very loose definition of what constitutes "cricket". The definitions are debatable; what is certain is that with teachers overstretched and the Government having approved 210 playing field sales since October 1998 (only six applications were turned down), the amount of organised, competitive cricket in state schools is unlikely to rise soon.

Additional Reporting by Gareth A. Davies.

> "Once at Bradford he declined to give David Bairstow stumped off a wide until a small boy ran on with a scorebook containing the Laws and pointed to the relevant passage."
>
> Obituaries, page 1561.

ETON v HARROW

At Lord's, July 1. Eton won by 36 runs. Toss: Harrow.

Eton beat their old rivals for the second year running, with Ben Thompson again the top-scorer, unfurling eight fours in a run-a-ball half-century. In the 50 overs allotted – down from 55 in 2002 – Eton built on a brisk opening stand, reached three figures with one wicket down, and quickly recovered from losing four for 18 either side of a rain-hastened lunch-break. By contrast, Harrow slumped to 95 for seven, despite steady batting from Peter Dunbar, and struggled to score against a trio of spinners. Michael Davidson hit out late on, but they succumbed with three balls to spare.

Eton

Batsman	Runs
A. W. A. Barker b Morrison	30
†G. D. G. George c Davidson b Dunbar	42
C. P. A. Nissen run out	19
*B. R. Thompson c Turner b Davidson	50
E. F. J. Nissen c Howe b Spencer	0
E. C. A. Bruce b Roditi	5
A. H. Ball c Dunbar b Davidson	31
G. O. A. Scott-Hayward c Dunbar b Roditi	10
J. P. Sherrard not out	2
W. T. Dobson not out	1
L-b 9, w 9, n-b 3	21
1/58 2/105 3/106 4/112 5/123 6/181 7/206 8/208 (8 wkts, 50 overs)	211

N. C. R. Westoll did not bat.

Bowling: Roditi 10–1–35–2; Travers 5–0–22–0; Morrison 10–2–22–1; Spencer 10–0–46–1; Dunbar 8–0–29–1; Davidson 7–0–48–2.

Harrow

Batsman	Runs
N. E. Defty c Thompson b Bruce	12
J. H. Walker b Bruce	1
H. R. Howe st George b Sherrard	17
*P. R. Dunbar c Thompson b Sherrard	43
C. G. M. Travers c Bruce b Sherrard	11
E. J. Turner lbw b Dobson	3
H. M. Morrison b Dobson	23
†R. T. de Oliveira lbw b Dobson	0
M. R. Davidson b Westoll	35
W. J. Spencer not out	11
J. B. K. Roditi c Barker b Westoll	0
B 1, l-b 3, w 12, n-b 3	19
1/6 2/30 3/37 4/58 5/69 6/93 7/95 8/125 9/172 (49.3 overs)	175

Bowling: Thompson 10–0–38–0; Bruce 10–0–43–2; Sherrard 10–0–32–3; Dobson 10–3–19–3; Westoll 9.3–0–39–2.

Umpires: G. Cooper and A. V. Farnfield.

Of the 165 matches played between the two schools since 1805, Eton have won 54, Harrow 45 and 66 have been drawn. Matches during the two world wars are excluded from the reckoning. The fixture was reduced from a two-day, two-innings-a-side match to one day in 1982, and became a limited-overs fixture from 1999. Forty-nine centuries have been scored, the highest being 183 by D. C. Boles of Eton in 1904; M. C. Bird of Harrow is the only batsman to have made two hundreds in a match, in 1907. The highest score since the First World War is 161 not out by M. K. Fosh of Harrow in 1975, Harrow's last victory before 2000. Since then Eton have won in 1977, 1985, 1990, 1991, 2002 and 2003, Harrow in 2000, the 1997, 1999 and 2001 matches were abandoned and all others have been drawn. A full list of centuries since 1918 and results from 1950 can be found in Wisdens *prior to 1994.*

Note: The following five tables cover only those schools listed in the Schools A–Z section.

BATTING

BEST AVERAGE IN SCHOOLS CRICKET

(Qualification: 150 runs, 3 completed innings, average 70.00)

	I	*NO*	*Runs*	*HS*	*100s*	*Avge*
A. N. Cook (*Bedford School*)	14	6	1,287	206*	7	160.87
P. G. Cook (*Oakham School*)	14	5	961	130*	4	106.77
W. M. Gifford (*Malvern College*)	17	7	942	158	1	94.20
I. K. Lodhi (*Wyggeston & QE I College*)	9	3	555	118*	2	92.50
D. G. Roots (*Warwick School*)	14	6	724	125*	1	90.50
P. Harman (*Colfe's School*)	6	3	234	70	0	78.00
R. Bhome (*Chigwell School*)	11	4	544	135*	1	77.71
E. Buxton (*Forest School*)	12	3	693	133	1	77.00
M. E. Westwood (*Brentwood School*)	16	6	760	119*	2	76.00
A. J. Blakeborough (*Leeds GS*)	5	2	225	107*	1	75.00
J. A. Chervak (*Ashville College*)	10	2	588	153*	3	73.50
T. G. Burrows (*Reading School*)	7	1	438	125*	2	73.00
J. L. T. Bolam (*Pocklington School*)	10	3	504	141*	2	72.00
C. Nelson (*RGS, Guildford*)	11	4	503	105	2	71.85
A. Wynd (*Lord Williams's School*)	9	2	502	134*	2	71.71
A. Mace (*Repton School*)	13	7	429	119*	1	71.50
N. J. Lamb (*St Albans School*)	10	2	569	107	1	71.12

MOST RUNS IN SCHOOLS CRICKET

(Qualification: 800 runs)

	I	*NO*	*Runs*	*HS*	*100s*	*Avge*
A. N. Cook (*Bedford School*)	14	6	1,287	206*	7	160.87
S. P. Bilboe (*King's School, Worcester*)	21	2	1,024	130*	2	53.89
P. G. Cook (*Oakham School*)	14	5	961	130*	4	106.77
W. M. Gifford (*Malvern College*)	17	7	942	158	1	94.20
S. M. Butler (*Radley College*)	17	3	931	125*	2	66.50
J. N. Butler (*King's School, Rochester*)	18	2	883	115*	1	55.18
R. M. Fahrenheim (*Oundle School*)	22	2	840	125	2	42.00
C. M. Grammer (*Brighton College*)	17	3	831	114*	3	59.35
C. J. Wake (*Oundle School*)	26	3	810	84	0	35.21
J. W. K. Beeny (*Tonbridge School*)	17	2	809	193*	2	53.93

BOWLING

BEST AVERAGE IN SCHOOLS CRICKET

(Qualification: 10 wickets, average 9.00)

	O	*M*	*R*	*W*	*BB*	*Avge*
C. C. Depala (*Christ's College, Finchley*)	75.2	22	168	28	6-5	6.00
J. W. Potgieter (*Merchiston Castle School*)	133	41	260	41	6-24	6.34
M. R. Depala (*Christ's College, Finchley*)	96.4	26	270	37	5-16	7.29
T. A. R. Dilnot-Smith (*Sir Roger Manwood's*)	40	15	81	11	4-5	7.36
S. M. Martin (*Chigwell School*)	52.2	9	164	22	6-8	7.45
T. Markham (*RGS, Guildford*)	52.1	10	155	20	3-14	7.75

	O	M	R	W	BB	Avge
R. J. Browning (*Wolverhampton GS*)	59	16	133	17	4-15	7.82
S. Ahmed (*Christ's College, Finchley*)	63	11	205	26	4-7	7.88
A. Shahzad (*Woodhouse Grove*)	85.5	22	205	25	7-9	8.20
K. Hodnett (*Downside School*)	43.5	5	108	13	5-14	8.30
J. L. Cluett (*Reading School*)	24	3	84	10	4-37	8.40
C. J. P. Howland (*Newcastle-under-Lyme School*)	43	12	101	12	3-15	8.41
P. Towner (*Cranbrook School*)	95.5	22	214	24	5-25	8.91
N. J. Lamb (*St Albans School*)	63.4	15	162	18	4-7	9.00

MOST WICKETS IN SCHOOLS CRICKET

(Qualification: 35 wickets)

	O	M	R	W	BB	Avge
T. J. Woolsey (*St Peter's, York*)	233.4	74	594	50	6-27	11.88
J. I. Hay (*Oundle School*)	204	46	705	49	5-19	14.38
R. Sekhri (*Brighton College*)	118.4	38	545	46	6-75	11.84
F. Khalid (*Malvern College*)	192	41	638	42	5-20	15.19
J. W. Potgieter (*Merchiston Castle School*)	133	41	260	41	6-24	6.34
M. M. T. Swartz (*Lord Wandsworth College*)	180	32	674	40	5-50	16.85
P. J. Foster (*Oundle School*)	245	55	706	40	4-17	17.65
N. S. Coles (*RGS, Colchester*)	203.3	27	854	39	6-27	21.89
M. R. Depala (*Christ's College, Finchley*)	96.4	26	270	37	5-16	7.29
S. N. Dave (*Merchant Taylors', Northwood*)	196	40	524	37	6-21	14.16
J. C. Douglas-Hughes (*Felsted School*)	208.3	41	706	37	7-54	19.08
O. M. Griffiths (*Malvern College*)	178	38	538	36	5-24	14.94
P. E. Short (*Wellington School*)	151.4	20	600	36	6-68	16.66
T. Giles (*Exeter School*)	134.4	33	374	35	6-18	10.68
R. Gnanendran (*Tiffin School*)	150.1	22	584	35	6-28	16.68

OUTSTANDING SEASONS, 2003

(Qualification: played eight matches)

	P	W	L	D	A	%W
Blundell's School	11	10	1	0	0	90.9
Brighton College	16	15	1	0	3	93.7
Christ's College, Finchley	17	14	1	2	0	82.3
Hampton School	14	11	0	3	1	78.5
Leeds Grammar School	10	5	0	5	5	50.0
Lord Williams's School	12	8	0	4	0	66.6
Merchiston Castle School	18	16	2	0	2	88.8
Oakham School	16	9	0	7	2	56.2
Royal Grammar School, Guildford	17	14	1	2	0	82.3
St Albans School	10	9	1	0	2	90.0
Watford Grammar School	11	6	0	5	1	54.5
Wellington College	16	14	1	1	1	87.5
Woodbridge School	12	6	0	6	1	50.0
Wyggeston and Queen Elizabeth I College	10	8	0	2	0	80.0

SCHOOLS A–Z

Qualification for averages: 150 runs or ten wickets.

Abingdon School P20 W7 L11 D2 A1

Master i/c S. P. G. Spratling **Professional** G. Palmer

The Stern brothers scored their maiden centuries for the first team in the same innings, putting on 216 for the third wicket against University College School, albeit in a losing cause. Jonathon Watkins scored 557 runs in his final season.

Batting J. A. D. Watkins* 557 at 34.81; S. M. T. Florey 170 at 28.33; P. T. R. Stern 480 at 28.23; S. Kapoor 207 at 25.87; G. W. A. Stern 335 at 20.93; J. E. Mugnaioni 165 at 18.33.

Bowling A. M. McKenzie-Husband 20 at 18.70; S. M. T. Florey 11 at 21.36; J. E. Mugnaioni 14 at 24.14; S. M. Holland 13 at 24.69; A. U. Rehman 11 at 32.18; G. W. A. Stern 17 at 34.17.

Aldenham School P12 W5 L6 D1 A3

Master i/c A. P. Stephenson **Professional** D. Goodchild

The season included several closely fought games and the younger squad members ended the summer as better players.

Batting S. F. Gray* 348 at 38.66; A. Sharma 186 at 18.60.

Bowling S. F. Gray 17 at 17.17; A. Sharma 13 at 17.30; J. Thakrar 10 at 27.00.

Alleyn's School P12 W8 L2 D2 A2

Master i/c R. Ody **Professional** P. H. Edwards

Batting A. L. Fuller 342 at 42.75; C. E. Morris 269 at 33.62; F. A. D. Baird 163 at 20.37.

Bowling A. L. Fuller 12 at 12.16; A. M. F. Johnson 15 at 12.20; C. J. McGill 18 at 12.50; T. A. Matthews* 14 at 15.14; C. O. Greenwood 13 at 17.61.

Ampleforth College P18 W5 L7 D6 A2

Master i/c G. D. Thurman

Ampleforth struggled with the bat but shone with the ball. Toby Fitzherbert formed a formidable opening bowling partnership with Archie Woodhead. Between them they took 44 wickets.

Batting A. H. J. Kisielewski 422 at 28.13; C. A. Woodhead 215 at 26.87; J. E. N. Brennan 254 at 23.09; T. F. Fitzherbert 227 at 17.46; L. A. Codrington 185 at 14.23; J. R. W. Pawle 203 at 13.53.

Bowling C. A. Woodhead 19 at 17.68; A. C. M. Faulkner 23 at 17.91; T. F. Fitzherbert 25 at 21.40; J. E. N. Brennan 26 at 24.65; A. H. J. Kisielewski 19 at 28.26.

Arnold School P12 W1 L 3 D8 A1

Master i/c M. Evans

Batting B. J. G. Taylor 356 at 29.66; J. Patel 225 at 20.45; T. Muir 264 at 20.30; P. Storey 178 at 17.80.

Bowling T. Muir 10 at 11.50; M. Patel 11 at 20.00; J. Patel 11 at 25.54; B. J. G. Taylor 13 at 26.30.

Ashville College P10 W7 L2 D1 A8

Master i/c I. M. Walker

James Chervak beat the College record for the highest individual score, when he hit an unbeaten 153 against the XL Club. He averaged an impressive 73, as he led his side to seven wins in ten matches.

Batting J. A. Chervak* 588 at 73.50; J. I. Townsend 161 at 23.00; T. Rowlay 150 at 18.75.

Bowling G. N. Randle 15 at 22.13; N. R. Gupta 13 at 23.61.

Bancroft's School P20 W13 L4 D3 A1

Master i/c J. K. Lever

Simon Miller performed with distinction throughout a highly successful season – with bat, ball and as a positive and effective captain. However, all of the side contributed. The team scored 266 for seven against Highgate, believed to be a school record.

Batting S. C. Miller* 541 at 36.06; J. H. T. Curran 269 at 33.62; P. D. MacLeod 326 at 23.28; C. P. Smith 386 at 22.70; J. K. Lever 153 at 21.85; A. Wilkinson 240 at 20.00; F. S. Khan 204 at 18.54.

Bowling M. Rowland 21 at 15.23; F. S. Khan 27 at 16.44; J. K. Lever 17 at 16.58; S. C. Miller 22 at 20.77.

Bangor Grammar School
P17 W11 L2 D4 A3

Master i/c D. J. Napier **Professional** C. C. J. Harte

Scott Cooper, composed and thoughtful throughout, led his team by example. A cheerful, positive approach made for a notably enjoyable, and largely successful, season.

Batting S. Cooper* 589 at 49.08; C. S. Cook 277 at 25.18; R. McLarnon 326 at 23.28; G. S. J. Watterson 209 at 20.90; C. J. Cargo 323 at 20.18; J. A. Goldthorpe 165 at 16.50.

Bowling G. S. J. Watterson 27 at 13.92; S. P. Connell 16 at 14.37; T. B. G. Speers 20 at 14.65; H. R. Haston 11 at 15.45; P. J. S. Speers 27 at 15.88.

Bedford School
P17 W8 L4 D5 A1

Master i/c J. J. Farrell **Professional** D. W. Randall

Alastair Cook was the pick of the batsmen in schools cricket in 2003, captaining Bedford through another successful summer. His 1,287 runs – including two unbeaten double-hundreds – was a school record. He and Will Notley shared four stands of over 150 and one of 333 unbeaten, from 50 overs. Cook later played three games for the Essex first team, passing 50 in all of them.

Batting A. N. Cook* 1,287 at 160.87; W. H. Notley 605 at 40.33; A. G. Wakely 395 at 39.50.

Bowling T. D. B. Coleman 28 at 14.85; T. M. R. Elliott 15 at 19.60; W. H. Notley 14 at 23.57; R. V. R. Patel 20 at 24.50; D. J. Binnington 13 at 26.38.

Bedford Modern School
P14 W8 L2 D4

Master i/c N. J. Chinneck

The school had a decent summer which should have been even better. David Myers, a very able all-rounder, made 600 runs and took 17 wickets.

Batting D. N. Myers 600 at 50.00; N. K. Choudhury 510 at 42.50; R. W. Cruickshank 191 at 27.28; B. N. Campbell 271 at 27.10; L. J. Steeden 150 at 25.00; A. L. Chinneck 193 at 24.12.

Bowling A. Devnani 21 at 14.00; A. M. Walker 16 at 18.06; R. A. Kemp 24 at 18.08; B. N. Campbell 15 at 26.46; D. N. Myers 17 at 32.58.

Berkhamsted Collegiate School
P14 W4 L8 D2

Master i/c S. J. Dight **Professional** D. Fortescue

The bowling lacked penetration and too often the batting relied upon the captain, Robin Gaymer. Of his 632 runs, 180 came in sixes. In his first year, David Sidebottom made a huge difference with his left-arm spin.

Batting R. Gaymer* 632 at 45.14; B. Ramsden 336 at 33.60; R. Bartholomew 296 at 32.88; D. Cooke 154 at 19.25.

Bowling F. Rodwell 17 at 29.82; I. Dent 15 at 30.06; D. Sidebottom 10 at 30.40; T. Chesters 18 at 32.77; C. Ayres 14 at 34.07.

Bloxham School
P11 W0 L4 D7

Master i/c N. C. W. Furley **Professional** R. Kaufmann

Batting A. Baig 208 at 18.90; K. A. Rahman 165 at 16.50.

Bowling H. Ahmad 11 at 17.36; A. Baig 15 at 18.93; K. A. Rahman 14 at 24.78.

Blundell's School
P11 W10 L1 D0

Master i/c C. L. L. Gabbittas

One of the best seasons in the school's history was based upon excellent team spirit and significant contributions from each member of the side. The only defeat came against Millfield.

Batting M. Lancelles 177 at 59.00; L. Lewis 360 at 45.00; S. Harding 215 at 30.71; S. Sobclak 194 at 27.71; S. Wright* 212 at 26.50; W. Gingell 196 at 24.50; T. Beard 167 at 20.87; J. Menhenestt 187 at 20.77.

Bowling A. Gingell 18 at 14.55; L. Lewis 13 at 15.07; S. Wright 19 at 16.05; M. Lancelles 11 at 20.63; L. Loveridge 15 at 21.00.

Bradfield College
P14 W1 L6 D7

Master i/c D. Clark **Professional** J. Wood

The season started slowly but gradually improved. While the batting was sometimes disappointing, the bowling often excelled. In four drawn matches, the opposition were nine down at the end. James Morris led by example, and his batting average was almost four times higher than his bowling. George Trewby proved the worth of a genuine off-spinner.

Batting J. C. Morris* 537 at 44.75; D. J. Plume 255 at 23.18; W. H. Chaloner 270 at 22.50; N. S. Woodroffe 151 at 12.58.

Bowling J. C. Morris 31 at 11.90; G. W. Trewby 23 at 19.69; R. K. Morris 15 at 20.40; D. J. Plume 10 at 38.20.

Bradford Grammar School P19 W7 L7 D5 A5

Master i/c A. G. Smith

The Mahomed brothers were the most consistent performers. Sarfaraaz scored 436 runs and took 29 wickets; Uzair 636 and 19. The team began to play to their full potential on a two-week tour to the West Indies in July.

Batting U. Mahomed 636 at 37.41; S. Mahomed 436 at 36.33; J. A. S. Benzafar* 421 at 32.38; J. A. Robinson 160 at 20.00; T. D. Ambepitiya 343 at 19.05; L. Stochill 153 at 11.76.

Bowling S. Mahomed 29 at 13.06; F. L. Parish 20 at 15.35; J. L. Dangerfield 20 at 20.50; U. Mahomed 19 at 21.73.

Brentwood School P16 W8 L4 D4 A1

Master i/c B. R. Hardie

It was a summer of big run-chases on good wickets. The Westwood twins hit all of the team's centuries. Christopher smashed 136 in 61 balls against Framlingham and 123 from 79 against Colfe's. Matthew's unbeaten hundreds guided the school to substantial targets set by Felsted and Ipswich. He also managed two five-wicket hauls.

Batting M. E. Westwood* 760 at 76.00; C. J. Westwood 476 at 43.27; O. T. Allen 241 at 34.42; C. G. Prowting 356 at 32.36; T. M. Gamby 341 at 31.00; W. Harrison 160 at 22.85; K. Sohal 222 at 22.20; J. Harrison 154 at 22.00.

Bowling S. J. Mair 15 at 24.73; M. E. Westwood 32 at 26.62.

Brighton College P16 W15 L1 D0 A3

Master i/c M. J. Edmunds **Professionals** J. Spencer/R. G. Halsall

Brighton won their first 13 matches – a sequence of 19 straight wins stretching back to 2002 – and were named *The Wisden Cricketer's* team of the season. Chris Grammer was a dynamic leader, prepared to gamble with early declarations, who also scored three centuries. Ronak Sekhri took 46 wickets with his flighty slow left-arm.

Batting C. M. Grammer* 831 at 59.35; R. Sekhri 240 at 40.00; R. L. Young 486 at 34.71; M. N. Waller 447 at 34.38; M. Gardner 361 at 32.81; J. S. Gatting 300 at 25.00.

Bowling R. Sekhri 46 at 11.84; M. N. Waller 11 at 12.54; M. J. Wood 22 at 14.27; C. M. Grammer 24 at 14.41; M. T. Sleep 10 at 15.40.

Bristol Grammar School P12 W4 L4 D4 A1

Masters i/c K. R. Blackburn/R. S. Jones **Professional** C. Baxter

After a poor start, a well-balanced side found form. Among the bowlers only Tom Westray showed any consistency. But a good nucleus of young players remains, promising much for the future.

Batting J. L. H. Williams 232 at 33.14; M. W. Leonard 301 at 30.10; T. M. Parnell 233 at 29.12; J. D. Butt* 262 at 29.11.

Bowling T. D. Westray 16 at 22.68; M. W. Leonard 10 at 31.50; J. D. Butt 11 at 35.81.

Bromsgrove School P12 W7 L2 D3

Master i/c P. Mullan **Professional** P. Greetham

A very young side improved dramatically as the summer progressed: only one squad member was due to leave. A successful season included wins against MCC, Worcestershire Under-16s, King's, Worcester and Dean Close, and was based on all-round contributions by the whole team. However, the fielding could be sharpened up.

Batting S. P. Robinson 461 at 46.10; R. P. Young 331 at 36.77; M. J. Mullan 325 at 36.11; P. Mann 347 at 31.54.

Bowling P. Mann 23 at 17.86; J. G. Jones 16 at 25.93; R. P. Young 16 at 30.18.

Bryanston School P19 W4 L12 D3 A2

Master i/c T. J. Hill **Professional** P. J. Norton

This inexperienced side, often fielding five Under-16s and at least one Under-15, showed their lack of years when it came to crafting victories, undoing the work of a good and varied bowling attack. Tom Turney scored 455 runs, including a magnificent century, and returns in 2004.

Batting T. A. C. Turney 455 at 35.00; M. W. Pritchard 291 at 20.78; L. C. Bettesworth 269 at 15.82; J. R. H. Gibbs 199 at 15.30.

Bowling N. Canning 20 at 20.35; I. C. Bettesworth 12 at 31.50; J. G. Scott Bolton 15 at 33.53.

Campbell College
P9 W5 L4 D0 A2

Master i/c B. F. Robinson **Professional** G. Fry

Hamilton Coulter represented both Ulster and Irish Schools.

Batting H. J. Coulter 211 at 26.37.

Bowling H. J. Coulter 12 at 14.91; B. J. Clements 15 at 18.73.

Charterhouse
P16 W10 L1 D5 A2

Master i/c P. J. Deakin **Professional** R. V. Lewis

The highlights were a historic victory over Harrow – the first in 40 years – and the successful pursuit of 265 against MCC. Nick Wood, who reached 155 against Harrow, and Harry Hooper both hit two hundreds.

Batting J. H. P. Hooper 568 at 63.11; N. A. Wood 569 at 40.64; J. R. Wood 373 at 28.69; M. St H. Stimpson 191 at 19.10; L. E. Carpenter 240 at 17.14.

Bowling D. V. D. Moger 16 at 18.62; J. B. Hunter 19 at 18.78; G. F. Palley 29 at 21.10; R. J. Aldridge 12 at 22.25; L. E. Carpenter 16 at 22.50.

Cheltenham College
P14 W7 L4 D3 A2

Master i/c M. W. Stovold **Professional** M. P. Briers

The side was well captained by Tom Brierley and contained seven players who will return for 2004. They again reached the final of the Chesterton Cup but were soundly beaten by a good Malvern side. Remarkably, the fixture against St Edward's, Oxford ended with the scores level for the second year running.

Batting D. C. Hall 507 at 46.09; T. M. B. Brierley* 411 at 41.10; E. J. L. Richardson 361 at 36.10; R. D. Mace 161 at 32.20; C. J. L. Sandbach 329 at 25.30.

Bowling A. J. Brooksbank 12 at 9.41; C. S. Luckock 24 at 16.54; C. B. Kemp 12 at 22.00; N. J. Abendanon 11 at 27.63; T. M. B. Brierley 17 at 32.35.

Chigwell School
P14 W7 L 3 D4 A1

Master i/c D. N. Morrison **Professional** F. A. Griffith

Seven wins in a transitional season was a commendable result. Most of the first team will be back next year. The outstanding memory will be of the young opening batsmen, the right-and-left combination of Rahul Bhome (Essex Under-12) and Nikunj Amin (Essex Under-16).

Batting R. Bhome 544 at 77.71; N. Amin 521 at 52.10; S. Ditta 212 at 26.50; V. Skandakumar 152 at 21.71.

Bowling S. M. Martin 22 at 7.45; T. J. Russell 14 at 15.57; J. Chandrakumar 16 at 22.50; V. Skandakumar 13 at 29.92; R. Bhome 11 at 31.63.

Chislehurst and Sidcup Grammar School
P12 W4 L6 D2 A2

Another positive, encouraging season, with David Meeking leading a young side by example. He topped both batting and bowling averages.

Master i/c R. A. Wallbridge

Batting No batsman scored 150 runs. The leading batsman was D. G. Meeking who scored 149 at 21.30.

Bowling D. G. Meeking* 19 at 12.36; J. Ahmed 10 at 21.60.

Christ College, Brecon
P11 W5 L4 D2 A2

Masters i/c N. C. Blackburn/J. R. Williams

The side's strength lay in its batting, and became particularly adept at chasing big targets. Four times they successfully scored more than 210 to win, leading to some very exciting and enjoyable matches. Five out of six schools matches were won.

Batting R. G. Davies 305 at 38.12; M. D. Wolfe 378 at 37.80; C. S. D. James* 233 at 33.28; D. R. L. Jones 174 at 29.00; H. C. I. Rich 176 at 22.00; M. B. D. Powell 152 at 16.88.

Bowling H. C. I. Rich 10 at 28.70; M. D. Wolfe 10 at 28.90; T. M. R. Cleland 11 at 31.36; J. P. Vaughan 12 at 40.08.

Christ's College, Finchley
P17 W14 L1 D2

Master i/c S. S. Goldsmith

In all their 14 wins, the college's bowling attack dismissed their opposition, with Aldenham skittled for just 34. Leg-spinner Chetan Depala represented Middlesex Under-17s, while his brother, Darshan, and their cousin, Mayur, bowled with blistering pace. Timothy Percival, the captain of the visiting MCC side, said Christ's had "the best school attack I've played against".

Cousins Chetan (*left*) and Mayur Depala, both of Christ's, Finchley, came first and third respectively in the national bowling averages.

Batting D. C. Depala* 676 at 42.25; C. C. Depala 437 at 36.41; M. R. Depala 328 at 29.81; N. C. Depala 237 at 23.70; R. A. Barney 280 at 20.00.
Bowling C. C. Depala 28 at 6.00; M. R. Depala 37 at 7.29; S. Ahmed 26 at 7.88; R. A. Barney 14 at 11.85; D. C. Depala 15 at 13.40.

Christ's Hospital P13 W4 L4 D5

Master i/c H. P. Holdsworth **Professional** L. J. Lenham

This young side did not sparkle, but they played tough, competitive cricket under the sympathetic leadership of Paul Rider. The eleven lost just two matches against other schools, but struggled to bowl teams out.
Batting R. J. J. Hawke 291 at 29.10; G. K. Chamberlin 300 at 25.00; J. B. Mitra 218 at 18.16; J. G. Maxwell 162 at 18.00; P. W. Rider* 182 at 16.54.
Bowling S. C. Crocker 17 at 15.70; J. T. Maddren 13 at 18.69; P. C. P. Boardman 12 at 28.00.

Clayesmore School P11 W6 L3 D2 A3

Master i/c D. Rimmer **Professional** P. Warren

Batting W. J. Harding* 161 at 32.20; E. J. B. Lack 310 at 31.00; A. O. Allen 175 at 21.87; J. D. Morton 158 at 17.55.
Bowling A. G. Merson 22 at 14.59; S. J. Hughes 19 at 17.00.

Clifton College P15 W4 L7 D4 A2

Master i/c D. C. Henderson **Professional** P. W. Romaines

This was very much a year for rebuilding, with the College fielding an exceptionally young side. The accomplished captain Simon Read scored two centuries and made 553 runs; when he failed the side crashed. Three of the seven losses ended in nail-biting finishes.
Batting S. J. Read* 553 at 55.30; P. E. Bliss 276 at 25.09; C. A. Jenkins 245 at 24.50; T. Read 192 at 12.80.
Bowling G. H. C. Robinson 16 at 17.06; C. A. Jenkins 17 at 20.94; J. J. Innes 14 at 22.64; C. A. Lincoln 10 at 28.70.

Colfe's School P10 W7 L2 D1 A4

Master i/c G. S. Clinton

Batting P. Harman 234 at 78.00; S. Cullum* 336 at 48.00; G. Houghton 154 at 38.50; Y. Khan 202 at 33.66; B. White 204 at 20.40; T. Holmes 151 at 18.87.

Bowling P. Harman 16 at 21.00; N. Patel 10 at 21.00; G. Houghton 13 at 25.92.

Cranbrook School P13 W10 L2 D1 A1

Master i/c A. J. Presnell

This was an excellent season, with no defeats in matches against other schools. Peter Towner, the captain who returns next year, has now taken 97 first-team wickets, already a school record. The season's highlight was a rare win for an English side over an Australian one – against Westminster College, Adelaide.

Batting C. Marriott 414 at 37.63; M. Roberts 178 at 35.60; P. Towner* 318 at 28.90; J. Burgess 338 at 28.16; A. Fullwood 209 at 26.12; O. Reynolds 150 at 16.66.

Bowling P. Towner 24 at 8.91; R. Lawless 14 at 10.21; T. Cullen 27 at 10.44; R. Roberts-Thomson 16 at 17.43.

Cranleigh School P17 W4 L7 D6 A1

Master i/c D. C. Williams

A lack of consistency cost the team, though the younger players gained valuable experience, and the distinct promise of two 14-year-olds, Alan Cope and Stuart Meaker, augurs well for the future. The captain, Jonathan Gates, stuck to his task well in leading an inexperienced side and scored 606 runs, including one century.

Batting J. R. Gates* 606 at 40.40; A. C. Cope 349 at 38.77; S. Meaker 150 at 30.00; H. P. C. Jupp 362 at 22.62; D. A. C. Lewis 170 at 21.25; R. H. Jones 248 at 20.66; J. A. Finnigan 159 at 17.66; T. I. Merry 160 at 13.33.

Bowling A. C. Cope 13 at 16.07; D. A. C. Lewis 23 at 19.56; E. P. C. Prince 13 at 22.92; S. Meaker 13 at 23.46; A. E. Kendrick 20 at 23.55; N. J. W. Pritchard 11 at 23.72; R. H. Jones 10 at 38.10.

Culford School P12 W3 L4 D5 A3

Master i/c N. A. Wheedon **Professional** D. Cousins

The first team left their best till last, winning three of their final four games. Fifteen-year-old Oliver Wade scored most runs and Max Fronicke made an impressive all-round contribution. Eight of the regular first team, including these two, should be back next year.

Batting M. T. Fronicke 306 at 43.71; O. W. Wade 376 at 37.60; L. E. J. Cousins 252 at 22.90; R. J. Hobley 228 at 22.80.

Bowling M. T. Fronicke 14 at 20.42; M. J. Feczko 18 at 20.72; R. E. H. Dennis 11 at 24.54; M. Burchett* 10 at 25.70.

Dauntsey's School P17 W5 L8 D4

Master i/c A. J. Palmer **Professional** R. Chaudhuri

Dauntsey's season started in March, with a win in a floodlit match – believed to be the first in schools cricket in the country – on an astroturf pitch against Prior Park. The first half of the season was disappointing: the batsmen failed to build innings and the bowlers delivered too many wides, but results improved as the summer wore on.

Batting S. E. Blackford 393 at 28.07; J. L. Thompson 224 at 14.93; S. S. Chaudhry* 153 at 11.76; C. H. Kemp 158 at 10.53.

Bowling W. P. J. Whyte 20 at 18.85; K. S. Chaudhry 19 at 20.47; S. J. Cowen 16 at 21.37; C. T. J. Jones 15 at 21.60; S. S. Chaudhry 15 at 28.13.

Dean Close School P17 W7 L8 D2

Master i/c C. J. Townsend **Professional** D. Trist

Despite a weak batting line-up, Dean Close managed a respectable seven wins. It was not until the final game, with a total of 270 against Malvern, that the batting came together. Joe Jenkins completed 1,000 runs in his first-team career and, with 84 wickets, was close to a notable double.

Batting J. Jenkins* 480 at 34.28; R. Brignull 337 at 24.07; W. Pearce 153 at 21.85; N. Ball 242 at 17.28; J. Miles 179 at 14.91; A. Carlisle 207 at 12.93.

Bowling J. Jenkins 27 at 20.00; B. Gibbons 12 at 20.25; A. Carlisle 22 at 26.00; T. Knights Johnson 12 at 28.00.

Denstone College P14 W5 L3 D6 A1

Master i/c S. J. Dean

David Soar took 34 wickets, including seven for 60 against Wickersley and seven for 14 against Abbotsholme. Matthew Gouldstone's batting oozed class and Alistair Whiston's wicket-keeping was at times outstanding. Denstone convincingly beat Staffordshire Under-16s and Trinity GS from Australia.

Batting M. A. Gouldstone 299 at 37.37; M. A. R. Ovens 181 at 25.85; S. J. F. Grosvenor 175 at 19.44; A. J. Whiston 176 at 17.60.

Bowling D. G. Soar* 34 at 12.20; J. W. D. Sharp 16 at 17.62; J. W. Bevington 10 at 21.60.

Dollar Academy P13 W6 L6 D1 A1

Master i/c J. G. Frost

Batting G. Wilson 407 at 33.91; J. Allen* 242 at 26.88; E. Batson 271 at 22.58.

Bowling E. Batson 20 at 10.45; G. Wilson 20 at 14.25; J. Barber-Fleming 15 at 15.73; J. Allen 14 at 21.14.

Dover College P4 W0 L2 D2 A3

Master i/c D. C. Butler

A disappointingly reduced programme was further curtailed by bad weather.

Batting No batsman scored 150 runs. The leading batsman was J. T. Last*, who scored 88 at 22.00.

Bowling No bowler took ten wickets. The leading bowler was J. T. Last, who took six at 22.16.

Downside School P7 W5 L1 D1 A1

Master i/c N. Bryars **Professional** G. Kenness

Downside's cricket improved markedly in 2003. The season was dominated by South African scholars: Kyle Hodnett, who took five for 14, Dean Bleasdale and Sean Dixon. Oliver Mellotte scored the school's first hundred for some years.

Batting S. Dixon 190 at 47.50.

Bowling K. Hodnett 13 at 8.30; S. Dixon 12 at 12.16; O. Mellotte 11 at 13.27; D. Bleasdale 14 at 13.35.

Duke of York's Royal Military School P10 W4 L3 D3 A6

Master i/c S. Salisbury **Professional** N. J. Llong

Sixteen-year-old Richard Kaye starred with both bat and ball, and was named the team's cricketer of the year. Opener Sebastian Cripps demonstrated his clean hitting with a firecracker of a century against the XL Club, while Ben Inshaw batted with maturity and kept wicket skilfully.

Batting B. M. W. Inshaw 216 at 54.00; S. B. Cripps 269 at 38.42; M. I. Gilbert 229 at 28.62; R. H. Kaye 167 at 23.86.

Bowling R. H. Kaye 16 at 15.68; D. Malla 16 at 18.00.

Dulwich College P20 W10 L4 D6 A1

Master i/c D. J. Cooper **Professional** C. W. J. Athey

Hard work before the season paid off, and Dulwich's trouncing of MCC, who were bowled out for 76, will live long in the memory. Ruel Brathwaite showed real pace on a Dulwich track that gets better each year. Surprisingly, Tommy Roy's unbeaten 142 against Incogniti was the only century.

Batting T. D. Roy 682 at 37.88; M. Kafle 312 at 28.36; T. T. Askew* 441 at 23.21; V. Patel 185 at 23.12; C. J. Owen 391 at 23.00; V. L. Cella 320 at 22.85; R. Brathwaite 313 at 22.37.

Bowling W. J. Charnley 23 at 17.86; R. Brathwaite 30 at 18.96; G. P. Porter 26 at 19.46; L. P. Furst 14 at 25.64; C. J. Owen 20 at 26.55.

Durham School P16 W7 L3 D6

Master i/c M. Hirsch

The captain, Tim Stonock, hit 685 runs, including a century. His replacement for next year, Ben Embleton, made the season's top score – 122 not out – while Paul Muchall, brother of Durham CCC's Gordon, was the leading wicket-taker.

Batting T. C. Stonock* 685 at 48.92; J. R. McCredie 396 at 36.00.

Bowling T. C. Stonock 30 at 13.93; P. J. Dias 25 at 16.64; P. B. Muchall 26 at 17.69; J. R. McCredie 21 at 24.28.

Eastbourne College P18 W10 L5 D3

Master i/c N. L. Wheeler **Professional** D. Keulder

After enjoying Namibia's World Cup adventure as a batsman, Daniel Keulder proved a highly popular Eastbourne coach. While results were not quite as good as in 2002, the side were prepared to risk defeat in search of victory. James Farley hit 401 runs and took 32 wickets with his left-arm spin; Howard Hassen, the captain, batted with aggression.

Batting J. C. Farley 401 at 36.45; H. C. Hassen* 527 at 32.93; J. P. Reid 269 at 29.88; C. B. Chisholm 175 at 29.16; J. A. M. Toy 378 at 27.00; W. J. Ripley 188 at 17.09.

Bowling H. C. Hassen 18 at 12.22; J. C. Farley 32 at 13.21; L. M. Winter 12 at 18.41; P. J. Morgan 17 at 19.29; W. J. Ripley 18 at 19.83; C. B. Chisholm 19 at 20.84.

The Edinburgh Academy P18 W6 L10 D2 A2

Master i/c M. Allingham

A good season, with many competitive performances, though the batting was disappointing. Only David Blair scored regularly and dominated attacks. The Academy reached the final of the Lothian Schools Cup and nearly pulled off a surprise win against Merchiston.

Batting D. W. Blair* 448 at 40.72; J. A. Zegleman 217 at 18.08; S. G. Cosh 282 at 15.66; P. D. M. Loudon 250 at 15.62; T. A. Clark 184 at 14.15; A. J. Cosh 180 at 12.00.

Bowling A. J. Cosh 14 at 14.78; N. J. Lyell 22 at 15.81; T. A. Clark 11 at 16.63; H. Paton 21 at 17.38; S. G. Cosh 26 at 20.03; P. D. M. Loudon 16 at 23.56.

Elizabeth College, Guernsey P15 W2 L7 D6

Master i/c M. E. Kinder **Professional** A. Bannerjee

A young side, led by all-rounder Luke Gallienne, tried to play positive cricket. James Warr dominated the batting.

Batting J. D. Warr 563 at 56.30; J. A. J. Nussbaumer 269 at 22.41; L. J. Gallienne* 252 at 19.38; C. M. McClymont 239 at 18.38; T. N. Le Tissier 173 at 15.72.

Bowling L. J. Gallienne 22 at 26.36; J. D. Warr 16 at 28.25; S. E. De La Rue 10 at 43.30; C. M. McClymont 11 at 45.00.

Ellesmere College P10 W2 L3 D5 A4

Master i/c P. J. Hayes

Jasmeet Bhamra provided the highlight of the season. After completing a run-out, he then took five wickets in four overs to send Hurstpierpoint crashing to defeat. They lost their last seven wickets for 11 runs. Eight of this side return next year and prospects are good.

Batting R. A. M. Baxter* 239 at 39.83; B. Shyamal 290 at 32.22.

Bowling J. Bhamra 20 at 13.60; N. D. Watson Jones 14 at 27.21.

Eltham College P14 W4 L9 D1 A1

Master i/c I. Latham **Professional** R. Hills

Batting R. J. Malcolm 641 at 58.27; J. Ratnarajan 203 at 33.83; T. J. Goodyear 281 at 28.10; J. G. Harris 163 at 18.11.

Bowling R. J. Malcolm 23 at 15.56; B. Patel 10 at 26.50.

Enfield Grammar School P13 W5 L6 D2

Master i/c M. Alder

Enfield won the Middlesex Under-19 Cup.

Batting T. Ansari 260 at 37.14; B. Watts 265 at 26.50; R. Najib 190 at 19.00; S. Nabi 161 at 16.10.

Bowling J. Schott 12 at 13.58; A. Barrell 11 at 22.90; T. Ansari 10 at 29.40; T. Tyler* 10 at 29.60.

Epsom College P10 W3 L7 D0 A1

Master i/c P. Williams **Professional** D. Campbell

The first team were found wanting in the batting department. On no fewer than five occasions Epsom lost when chasing a total of under 150. However, the bowling was impressive throughout. The experience gained should stand the ten players who return for 2004 in good stead.

Batting C. Poutney 206 at 22.88; J. Laidler 236 at 21.45; R. Lammiman* 222 at 20.18.

Bowling D. Hastings 25 at 10.64; R. Pooley 21 at 15.95; A. Maurice 21 at 18.61.

Eton College P20 W14 L3 D3

Master i/c R. D. Oliphant-Callum

This side equalled 2002's record 14 wins – and won all 12 of their limited-overs matches against schools. Both the Cowdrey Cup (a round-robin involving Tonbridge, Harrow, Charterhouse and Wellington) and the Silk Trophy were retained. And Eton were also the only side to beat the otherwise all-conquering Brighton College. The strengths were in the depth of the batting and in the spin bowling. Ben Thompson was again one of the dominant batsmen in schools cricket.

Batting B. R. Thompson* 725 at 48.33; A. W. A. Barker 646 at 34.00; E. C. A. Bruce 361 at 27.76; E. F. J. Nissen 466 at 27.41; G. O. A. Scott-Hayward 257 at 25.70; H. W. Annandale 150 at 25.00; C. P. A. Nissen 346 at 23.06; G. D. G. George 287 at 17.93; A. H. Ball 271 at 16.93.

Bowling E. C. A. Bruce 32 at 16.90; B. R. Thompson 29 at 18.72; N. C. R. Westoll 33 at 21.84; A. H. Ball 10 at 21.90; J. P. Sherrard 19 at 28.21; W. T. Dobson 22 at 30.86.

Exeter School P18 W12 L4 D2

Master i/c W. Hughes

Toby Giles played 58 times for the First XI over five seasons and he bowed out in style, taking 26 wickets in his last eight games. Harry Trick led the side superbly, and kept wicket with equal skill.

Batting C. Horne 325 at 46.42; R. Hooper 493 at 29.00; J. Cooke 269 at 26.90; T. Giles 321 at 22.92; S. Barlow 233 at 19.41; H. Trick* 182 at 15.16.

Bowling T. Giles 35 at 10.68; M. Chandler 14 at 13.64; O. Kernick 23 at 15.43; S. Barlow 10 at 15.50; S. Chappell 20 at 17.05; B. Cadoux-Hudson 17 at 19.70; A. Phillips 18 at 19.94.

Felsted School P18 W9 L6 D3

Master i/c C. S. Knightley **Professional** N. J. Lockhart

The season's highlights were a second-wicket partnership of 239 between Joseph Buttleman and "GB" Ladipo; an elegant 139 not out from Christopher Huntington; and a seven-wicket haul from Charles Douglas-Hughes. Both the team spirit and the fielding were excellent.

Batting J. E. L. Buttleman 615 at 41.00; G. Ladipo* 497 at 35.50; D. Edwards 183 at 30.50; C. J. Huntington 381 at 27.21; N. J. R. Adams 309 at 25.75; J. C. Douglas-Hughes 280 at 23.33; N. P. M. Harrison 216 at 16.61.

Bowling P. H. M. Ward 20 at 14.10; N. J. R. Adams 23 at 17.52; J. C. Douglas-Hughes 37 at 19.08; J. L. Harmon 11 at 24.63; J. E. L. Buttleman 12 at 30.08.

Fettes College P16 W5 L10 D1 A1

Master i/c C. Thomson **Professional** B. Russell

The season started brightly but batting inadequacies were cruelly exposed towards the end, when the side slipped to seven defeats in eight games. There were cheap five-wicket hauls for Matthew Boyd, Louis Vieilledent, and Edward Philip. However, the batting relied far too heavily on Craig Samuel, the captain, and Scott MacLennan

Batting S. K. MacLennan 300 at 23.07; C. B. Samuel* 263 at 15.47; R. G. Edington 165 at 11.00.

Bowling L. G. M. Vieilledent 19 at 15.47; A. P. Cadzow 23 at 16.52; M. R. Boyd 13 at 20.15; E. C. R. Philip 14 at 22.85; D. N. R. Philip 14 at 25.07.

Forest School P12 W9 L1 D2 A4

Master i/c S. Turner

Edward Buxton, in his final season, once again scored heavily. He also took 24 wickets. Wicket-keeper/batsman Chris Swainland is part of the Essex Academy and he, along with Gordon Whorlow, represented Essex Under-16s.

Batting E. Buxton* 693 at 77.00; G. Whorlow 184 at 26.28; C. Swainland 202 at 25.25; M. Declaiterosse 174 at 21.75; N. Rotsey 188 at 20.88; J. Palmer 249 at 20.75; A. Palmer 151 at 18.87.

Bowling M. Declaiterosse 16 at 13.93; A. Ryatt 17 at 15.82; J. Palmer 15 at 16.33; E. Buxton 24 at 16.95; G. Whorlow 11 at 21.09.

Framlingham College P12 W5 L4 D3 A2

Master i/c R. Curtis **Professionals** M. Robinson/M. Bennett-King

Spencer Veevers-Chorlton was top run-scorer and wicket-taker for Framlingham. He also played for Suffolk Under-21, the senior Suffolk Second XI and in the ECB Schools Under-19 trial.

Batting S. Veevers-Chorlton* 580 at 64.44; M. J. Stacpoole 406 at 40.60; A. J. Wybar 247 at 22.45; R. W. Sprake 174 at 19.33.

Bowling M. J. Stacpoole 18 at 22.44; S. Veevers-Chorlton 23 at 26.39.

Giggleswick School — P12 W5 L5 D2 A3

Master i/c P. Humphreys — **Professional** D. Fallows

Batting I. H Canaway 253 at 31.62; G. T. Crosby 231 at 19.25; A. H. MacDonald 151 at 16.77.
Bowling N. C Hird 17 at 13.76; M. C Hughes 20 at 17.80; G. T Crosby 10 at 24.90; S. D Christian* 11 at 25.09.

Glasgow Academy — P8 W5 L2 D1 A2

Master i/c A. G. Lyall — **Professional** V. Hariharan

The outstanding feature of a short season was the excellent bowling of Michael Hopkins and Gautham Hariharan.
Batting J. W. Beattie* 178 at 29.66.
Bowling M. W. J. Hopkins 12 at 14.75; G. Hariharan 11 at 15.00.

Glenalmond College — P17 W7 L8 D2 A1

Master i/c A. Norton

Batting M. R. Harvey 470 at 33.57; W. A. Rodger 424 at 26.50; A. J. M. Elder 380 at 23.75; A. F. H. Murray 230 at 20.90; T. F. Harper 179 at 19.88.
Bowling W. A. Rodger 31 at 17.93; P. A. D. Stoll 27 at 18.81; J. D. Brunton 15 at 23.46.

Gordonstoun School — P10 W3 L4 D3

Master i/c G. Broad — **Professional** J. Rufey

Batting C. Begg 290 at 41.42; D. Thompson 227 at 32.42; M. Gregory 175 at 21.87.
Bowling M. Gregory 15 at 20.06.

Gresham's School — P16 W7 L4 D5 A1

Master i/c A. M. Ponder

Fifteen-year-old Felix Flower immediately made a big impression, opening the batting with composure and assurance. New partnership records were set for the third, fourth and sixth wickets.
Batting W. J. F. Stebbings 371 at 46.37; A. C. G. Groom 487 at 37.46; F. J. Flower 472 at 33.71; T. J. Farrow* 301 at 30.10; R. M. K. Steward 269 at 19.21.
Bowling R. M. K. Steward 25 at 18.36; J. O. Elliott 13 at 20.69; H. G. Flower 20 at 24.70; A. C. R. Peaston 11 at 30.54; F. J. Flower 13 at 39.53.

Haberdashers' Aske's School — P22 W8 L9 D5 A1

Master i/c S. D. Charlwood — **Professional** M. W. Patterson

A young side experienced a mixed season. Fourteen-year-old Gavin Baker made 111 not out against Doug Yeabsley's XI to become the youngest recorded century-maker for the school. Leg-spinner Mark Gray, with 34 wickets in his first full season, also performed with distinction.
Batting S. Vieira 225 at 45.00; G. C. Baker 256 at 32.00; A. M. Theivendra* 328 at 25.23; J. S. T. Williams 475 at 25.00; E. G. Clements 254 at 21.16; A. M. Patel 318 at 19.87; P. Sirimanna 277 at 17.31; G. E. B. Fitzgerald 190 at 14.61; R. Pandya 173 at 13.30.
Bowling R. G. Clements 15 at 13.13; A. M. Patel 27 at 20.92; M. F. Gray 34 at 23.67; E. G. Clements 20 at 30.05.

Haileybury — P14 W5 L7 D2 A1

Master i/c C. Igolen-Robinson — **Professional** G. P. Howarth

This was set to be a difficult season for a young First XI. But the players gave their all, and team spirit took the side a long way. There were memorable victories against Uppingham and, in front of a packed house on speech day, against MCC. Wicket-keeper Tom Stewart, a fifth-former, hit a fluent 98.
Batting B. Wilson 411 at 45.66; G. George 168 at 28.00; A. C. M. Morgan 218 at 27.25; J. Melvill* 178 at 25.42; T. Stewart 315 at 24.23.
Bowling L. Mason 18 at 17.94; J. Melvill 16 at 20.68.

Hampton School — P14 W11 L0 D3 A1

Master i/c E. M. Wesson

An extremely strong team won 11 games from 14 and ended the season unbeaten. As comfortable chasing as setting a target, the batting was dominated by two outstanding school cricketers, Neil Khanna and Oliver Roland-Jones. Tight seam bowling throttled the opposition, while the spinners, Roland-Jones and Akbar Ansari, took 50 wickets. Shimir Patel's all-round efforts were impressive.

Batting O. G. K. Roland-Jones 639 at 58.09; N. Khanna* 688 at 57.33; S. Patel 220 at 31.42; W. M. Gaines 193 at 24.12; N. E. Baker 183 at 22.87; T. S. Roland-Jones 165 at 20.62.
Bowling O. G. K. Roland-Jones 26 at 13.96; A. S. Ansari 24 at 16.75; P. J. Sellick 15 at 18.86; W. M. Gaines 13 at 22.00; N. Khanna 11 at 23.90; S. Patel 12 at 25.00; T. H. A. Ayers 11 at 25.81.

Harrow School — P16 W8 L5 D3 A1

Master i/c S. J. Halliday — **Professional** R. K. Sethi
Harrow had success in declaration games, but struggled in overs matches. The annual game at Lord's against Eton was lost by 36 runs. James Roditi, the spearhead of a good attack, was player of the season.
Batting R. H. Symes 155 at 51.66; P. R. Dunbar 537 at 41.30; C. G. M. Travers 362 at 32.90; H. R. Howe 298 at 27.09; N. E. Defty 360 at 24.00; W. J. Spencer 163 at 23.28; H. M. Morrison 237 at 21.54.
Bowling J. B. K. Roditi 27 at 11.44; M. R. Davidson 17 at 19.05; W. J. Spencer 23 at 20.34; H. M. Morrison 14 at 24.64; C. G. M. Travers 11 at 29.90.

Harvey Grammar School — P22 W11 L9 D2 A2

Master i/c P. J. Harding
An excellent season saw the captain, Paul Goddard, scoring the highest number of runs for the first team since 1976.
Batting P. W. Goddard* 600 at 40.00; B. Washer 445 at 34.23; P. Ireland 330 at 25.38; S. Howland 170 at 24.28; P. Owen 262 at 18.71.
Bowling W. Storer 12 at 11.33; B. Washer 16 at 12.43; P. Owen 23 at 12.47; P. W. Goddard 17 at 17.47; S. Ireland 17 at 18.17.

Hereford Cathedral School — P16 W2 L10 D4 A1

Master i/c A. Connop
Batting G. J. B. Jacobs 551 at 50.09; B. R. Owens 323 at 21.53; N. A. Townson 289 at 20.64; M. A. Lowden* 259 at 18.50.
Bowling G. J. B. Jacobs 15 at 29.26; M. A. Parry 12 at 32.33.

Highgate School — P11 W1 L6 D4 A2

Master i/c R. W. Halstead — **Professional** R. Farrow
Though this was a young side, they should have won more than one game, given their basic talent. The main batsmen failed too often, while the bowling was steady but not penetrating. Both fielding and team spirit were excellent. The match against University College School saw a remarkable 609 runs scored in a day.
Batting D. C. Goldschmidt 169 at 28.16; J. S. Williams 215 at 23.88; J. Mallinson 236 at 21.45; N. A. W. Bell 179 at 19.88; J. A. Whybrow* 174 at 19.33.
Bowling J. A. Whybrow 16 at 19.37; J. D. M. Atchinson 15 at 24.80; J. Mallinson 11 at 26.00; N. A. W. Bell 12 at 27.16.

Hurstpierpoint College — P17 W8 L5 D4 A2

Master i/c C. W. Gray — **Professional** D. J. Semmence
The top-order batting was strong, Tom Harrison making 131 not out against Worth School, but the bowling lacked consistency. Derek Semmence, who played for Sussex in the 1950s and 60s, retires after 28 years as professional.
Batting T. J. Jarvis 556 at 50.54; D. K. Harris 426 at 30.42; T. P. Harrison 491 at 28.88; J. Andrews* 415 at 25.93; N. Singh 254 at 16.93.
Bowling A. W. Gordon-Stewart 19 at 19.63; N. J. Jessup 16 at 25.62; L. B. Tarr 22 at 27.36; D. K. Harris 19 at 34.05; N. Singh 15 at 35.80.

Ipswich School — P13 W2 L9 D2 A2

Master i/c A. K. Golding — **Professional** R. E. East
Batting C. W. Flather 408 at 45.33; H. J. Knights* 359 at 27.61; P. W. Hughes 223 at 20.30; J. R. Green 164 at 16.40.
Bowling M. J. Hilton 15 at 10.40; J. C. Daunt 23 at 21.04; C. W. Flather 16 at 25.87; B. J. Payne 10 at 29.60.

The John Lyon School P16 W7 L5 D4

Master i/c I. R. Parker

Under-16 bowler Krunal Desai took 33 wickets in his first season. Rhodri James led the side admirably.

Batting R. T. James* 476 at 43.27; N. Rughani 322 at 23.00; D. N. Patel 186 at 16.90.

Bowling K. Desai 33 at 10.54; P. R. Johnson 15 at 11.66; T. Cook 20 at 17.95; R. T. James 13 at 22.84; N. Rughani 12 at 25.16.

Kimbolton School P15 W4 L9 D2 A2

Master i/c A. G. Tapp **Professional** T. Huggins

Oliver Huggins, a fifth-former, scored over 600 runs, including six fifties and one hundred in 15 innings.

Batting O. J. Huggins 630 at 45.00; M. J. Ralph* 384 at 29.53; C. D. Nobles 276 at 19.71; D. W. Payne 209 at 16.07; R. B. Howcroft 175 at 13.46.

Bowling H. M. Gillam 19 at 25.21; S. A. Bird 10 at 27.30; M. J. Ralph 18 at 27.83; R. B. Howcroft 12 at 43.00.

King Edward VI College, Stourbridge P9 W2 L6 D1 A3

Masters i/c M. L. Ryan/R. A. Williams

Douglas Northover was the outstanding player, batting with supreme confidence and bowling with commendable accuracy.

Batting D. Northover 282 at 40.28; A. R. Bingham 238 at 26.44; R. S. Musk* 166 at 23.71.

Bowling No bowler took ten wickets. The leading bowler was D. Northover, who took nine at 24.55.

King Edward VI School, Southampton P24 W13 L8 D3 A4

Master i/c R. J. Putt

Following a successful tour of South Africa (including a day/night match), the school played some good cricket. A memorable tied match on the Hampshire Rose Bowl Nursery Ground saw King Edward's and Barton Peveril Sixth Form College share the county-wide Altham Trophy.

Batting G. H. Noble* 640 at 37.64; M. D. Boydx 207 at 34.50; A. P. Richardson 477 at 29.81; T. W. Carter 356 at 27.38; B. Anderson 301 at 23.15; R. N. Miller 366 at 21.52; W. Bebb 302 at 18.87; J. R. Hale 164 at 14.90.

Bowling G. H. Noble 24 at 14.08; W. A. Fleming 15 at 15.00; W. Bebb 21 at 18.23; A. P. Richardson 20 at 21.90; B. S. Gardner 13 at 22.92; M. J. Gurd 15 at 24.73; T. W. Carter 18 at 24.83.

King Edward VII & Queen Mary School, Lytham P16 W1 L8 D7 A1

Master i/c S. J. Williams **Professional** W. McSkimming

With all bar three of the players returning next year, the school hopes to improve on the season's solitary win.

Batting B. P. Hall* 388 at 48.50; J. Kelliher 164 at 41.00; D. R Hartley 255 at 23.18; R. J. Openshaw 256 at 19.69; T. E. Shillito 195 at 16.25.

Bowling R. J. Openshaw 19 at 18.89; J. A. Atherton 10 at 19.10; S. T. Pitman 11 at 25.90; P. A. Jackson 10 at 25.90.

King Edward's School, Birmingham P20 W10 L6 D4

Master i/c M. D. Stead **Professional** D. Collins

A young team – only Ravi Tiwari was leaving – did better than expected.

Batting S. P. G. Chase 408 at 40.80; A. P. S. Holmes 366 at 36.60; R. D. Tiwari 483 at 28.41; J. W. Neale 450 at 28.12; N. R. Chase 262 at 20.15; A. Gatrad 151 at 15.10; V. Katyal 167 at 12.84.

Bowling J. R. Botha 19 at 11.78; J. W. Neale 19 at 13.47; N. R. Chase 25 at 16.48; A. P. S. Holmes 19 at 17.73; V. Katyal 20 at 18.80; R. D. Tiwari 17 at 18.82.

King Edward's School, Witley P13 W5 L6 D2 A1

Master i/c D. H. Messenger **Professional** A. Jan

Robert Ledger and Bhabatosh Bogi, the mainstays of the batting, became the first players to pass 500 runs for the season. Sean Shuker, a promising youngster, swung the ball and was usefully supported by the spinner, Ben Copeman.

Batting B. Bogi 507 at 56.33; R. C. Ledger* 517 at 43.08; S. E. B. Shuker 225 at 20.45; A. M. W. Manley 174 at 13.38.

Bowling S. E. B. Shuker 14 at 19.78; B. P. T. Copeman 12 at 22.41; B. Bogi 13 at 22.84; A. B. Fitzgerald 12 at 31.91; J. J. Wooldridge 12 at 35.00; A. M. W. Manley 10 at 39.90.

King Henry VIII School, Coventry

P9 W4 L4 D1 A4

Master i/c A. M. Parker **Professional** A. W. McAllister

Batting R. Shah 219 at 43.80; B. Fleming 174 at 43.50; S. Humphrey 209 at 34.63.

Bowling S. Hennessey 10 at 24.10.

King's College, Taunton

P11 W7 L4 D0 A1

Master i/c H. R. J. Trump

George Webber began with a bang, making his first century in the first match of the season, against the XL Club. King's seven wins included victories over MCC and local rivals Taunton School.

Batting S. C. Whittaker 299 at 29.90; G. W. Webber 319 at 29.00; C. A. Sheppard* 264 at 26.40; J. W. Excell 152 at 25.33.

Bowling C. J. W. Boyle 17 at 15.47; S. C. Whittaker 12 at 17.08; J. W. Excell 17 at 17.47; J. W. Corrick 11 at 20.36; M. J. Worden 10 at 23.30.

King's College School, Wimbledon

P16 W10 L5 D1

Master i/c T. Howland

Batting T. W. Eaves 670 at 47.85; G. E. Peck 518 at 47.09; N. J. E. Burberry 347 at 38.55; J. J. Bensohn 345 at 28.75; J. D. Hearne 217 at 24.11.

Bowling N. J. E. Burberry 33 at 15.54; M. B. Howard 16 at 23.25; N. P. Lister 19 at 23.36; J. J. Bensohn 21 at 25.23; S. H. Shandro 10 at 39.

King's School, Bruton

P16 W6 L7 D3

Master i/c J. D. Roebuck

Batting T. R. Browne 450 at 37.50; C. R. Masters 329 at 23.50; T. L. Martin 300 at 20.00; D. J. Ball 239 at 17.07; S. M. Smyth 153 at 15.30; D. J. Green 169 at 12.07; G. A. Ridout 155 at 10.33.

Bowling D. J. Ball 24 at 13.95; C. J. Stevenson 15 at 18.33; M. C. R. Masters 23 at 21.52.

The King's School, Canterbury

P16 W6 L4 D6

Master i/c R. White **Professional** A. G. E. Ealham

Wicket-keeper/batsman Paul Dixey took 12 catches, made three stumpings and hit 402 runs.

Batting J. D. E. Stubbs* 452 at 37.66; P. G. Dixey 402 at 30.92; M. E. B. Humphrey 315 at 22.50; T. C. V. Wilson 207 at 20.70; P. R. Archer 248 at 19.07.

Bowling T. J. L. Humphrey 24 at 14.54; A. L. Thorne 12 at 16.83; J. D. E. Stubbs 16 at 18.06; D. H. Johnston 12 at 27.41.

The King's School, Chester

P10 W5 L3 D2 A3

Master i/c S. Neal **Professional** A. L. Shillinglaw

Batting F. G. Owen 322 at 46.00; C. B. Sanderson 227 at 32.42; A. C. J. Sissons 150 at 21.42; E. A. N. Whittaker 151 at 18.87.

Bowling R. A. Batey 10 at 21.40; G. N. Hughes* 11 at 24.36; B. E. Turner 11 at 25.27.

The King's School, Ely

P9 W1 L6 D2 A2

Master i/c T. Arrand/J. Marshall

Batting R. N. W. Ransom 223 at 31.85; H. C. Sperling 175 at 25.00; B. H. N. Howgego 174 at 21.75; A. Vincent 155 at 19.37.

Bowling No bowler took ten wickets. The leading bowler was H. C. Sperling, who took eight at 31.25.

The King's School, Macclesfield

P15 W9 L4 D2 A4

Master i/c S. Moores

After eight wins from the first ten games, King's faltered. The opening batsmen, Oliver Kenyon and Alan Day, enjoyed another fine season – their fourth and last. Day's 791 runs represented a fine effort in a season much hampered by rain.

Batting A. Day 791 at 60.84; O. D. Kenyon 543 at 41.76; T. Parfett-Manning 275 at 30.55; S. Allday 260 at 23.63.

Bowling J. Barratt 30 at 18.86; A. Day 19 at 19.00; O. D. Kenyon 18 at 19.27; A. Jackson 15 at 24.66.

King's School, Rochester

P18 W9 L7 D2 A2

Master i/c G. R. Williams

Once again, the school had a talented batting side but simply could not take wickets. The bowling was often wayward; there was no real strike bowler, and much depended on the only accurate spinner, Chris Maurice.

Batting J. N. Butler 883 at 55.18; C. A. Maurice 617 at 41.13; B. D. Phillips 497 at 31.06; S. G. Wakeman 347 at 28.91; C. P. Deane 299 at 23.00.
Bowling R. K. Singh 19 at 17.89; J. A. W. Warner 12 at 21.83; C. A. Maurice 21 at 26.80; J. A. O'Connor 14 at 31.35.

King's School, Tynemouth P10 W2 L4 D4 A1

Masters i/c W. Ryan/P. J. Nicholson
Tom Pollock was the leading run-scorer, as he was in 2002, and he will captain the side next year. Wicket-keeper Michael Conn improved both behind and in front of the stumps, but the bowling lacked penetration.
Batting T. J. Pollock 303 at 33.66; M. P. Conn 163 at 27.16.
Bowling B. C. Telfer 11 at 18.36; C. J. Simpson 11 at 20.00.

King's School, Worcester P22 W9 L6 D7

Master i/c D. P. Iddon **Professional** A. A. D. Gillgrass
Although the fielding was always sharp, the bowling often struggled to break through. At 16, Stephen Bilboe became the youngest King's boy to score 1,000 runs. In his last 12 innings he passed fifty nine times. Oliver Mathew kept him company in many good partnerships.
Batting S. P. Bilboe 1,024 at 53.89; O. J. Mathew 593 at 32.94; O. Fiaz* 317 at 28.81; O. J. Bendall 331 at 22.06; T. H. Weston 374 at 20.77.
Bowling W. M. Smith 21 at 13.90; T. P. Cullen 27 at 17.14; S. Cullen 15 at 18.86; J. A. Kelly 11 at 21.36; O. Fiaz 24 at 27.12; K. M. McNally 12 at 36.33.

Kingston Grammar School P10 W1 L7 D2 A1

Master i/c D. Wethey **Professional** T. Smith
Batting B. C. Collier 206 at 20.60; H. J. Mir* 180 at 18.00; B. R. Trivedi 171 at 17.10.
Bowling B. C. Collier 22 at 15.68; H. J. Mir 20 at 18.45.

Lancing College P11 W4 L6 D1 A1

Master i/c P. Richardson **Professional** R. J. Davies
After a promising start, the rest of term proved disappointing. Runs were the main problem: indifferent batting provided a sharp contrast to some competitive bowling and fielding.
Batting A. G. Dodsworth 307 at 38.37; B. J. M. Hanley 275 at 30.55; J. A. G. Green* 178 at 19.77; G. J Cowell 152 at 19.00.
Bowling L. T. Griffith-Wilkin 19 at 17.00; J. A. G. Green 10 at 27.20; B. J. M. Hanley 10 at 31.00.

Langley Park School for Boys P9 W6 L3 D0 A1

Master i/c T. Booth **Professional** C. H. Williams
May rains and exams meant another disrupted season. But the most successful season for several years showed cricket is alive and kicking in this comprehensive school.
Batting J. Smedley 226 at 45.20; J. Couldrey 266 at 33.25; S. Bagnall 186 at 26.57; B. Couldrey 180 at 22.50; P. Kennedy 153 at 19.12.
Bowling T. Briggs 10 at 9.50; J. Smedley 10 at 13.80; D. Walshe 10 at 17.70.

Leeds Grammar School P10 W5 L0 D5 A5

Master i/c R. Hill
Although it was disappointing to have five matches abandoned, a very young XI had an outstanding season. The highlight was a last-over, one-wicket win over Bradford GS.
Batting A. J. Blakeborough 225 at 75.00; T. R. E. James 256 at 42.66; D. J. Stokoe 202 at 40.40; D. T. Syers 240 at 40.00; A. M. Guest 162 at 27.00.
Bowling D. I. Sweeting 21 at 13.04; S. Siddiqui 15 at 14.26; T. J. Jacklin* 14 at 27.07.

The Leys School, Cambridge P14 W6 L6 D2 A1

Master i/c A. Batterham **Professional** P. B. Ediriweera
Batting M. J. Sanders 454 at 41.27; J. Webb 271 at 33.87; J. Waters 366 at 30.50; T. Hoy 333 at 25.61; C. Yeoman 157 at 17.44.
Bowling W. Turner 32 at 11.71; J. Webb 17 at 21.29; G. Musson 10 at 36.50.

Llandovery College P6 W3 L3 D0 A5

Master i/c T. Marks **Professional** A. Jones
Batting B. Esterhuizen* 339 at 67.80.
Bowling D. George 10 at 16.00.

Will Gifford of Malvern (*left*) scored 942 runs at 94.20, while Stephen Bilboe of King's, Worcester hit 1,024 – one of just two batsmen to pass 1,000.

Lord Wandsworth College P17 W5 L8 D4

Master i/c M. C. Russell **Professional** S. J. Power

The college made some reasonable scores but were unable to defend them, due to wayward bowling and poor catching. The star was 16-year-old Michael Swartz, an exchange student from Cape Town. Once he became used to slow English pitches he dominated attacks and scored three fine centuries. His slow left-arm bowling was also impressive, as was that of Nick Priggen.

Batting M. M. T. Swartz 707 at 44.18; J. D. Irving* 541 at 36.06; M. D. Feeney 197 at 16.41; P. K. Knight 223 at 14.86.

Bowling P. K. Knight 33 at 14.84; M. M. T. Swartz 40 at 16.85; N. I. Priggen 16 at 33.31.

Lord Williams's School P12 W8 L0 D4

Master i/c J. E. Fulkes

Chris Wynd hit a superb hundred against Wellingborough, while his brother, Andrew, hit two – against Magdalen College School and Aylesbury GS. The highlight though, was Will Eason's astounding eight for seven against Aylesbury Grammar, which included an all-bowled hat-trick.

Batting A. Wynd 502 at 71.71; W. Eason 285 at 57.00; J. Hewitt 294 at 36.75; A. Jewell 175 at 35.00; C. Wynd* 266 at 29.55.

Bowling J. Hewitt 11 at 10.72; W. Eason 18 at 13.88; J. Shirley 13 at 16.07; C. Watling 11 at 23.09.

Loughborough Grammar School P14 W5 L8 D1 A1

Master i/c H. T. Tunnicliffe **Professional** M. Scott

With key players either injured or unavailable throughout the season, the team struggled for consistency.

Batting F. B. Baker 397 at 49.62; S. J. Underwood 219 at 36.50; R. M. Worrall 185 at 30.83; C. Ashcroft 294 at 29.40; C. M. Krarup 223 at 20.27.

Bowling S. J. Bird 18 at 15.94; F. B. Baker 19 at 18.05; H. F. Gurney 18 at 19.55; M. Ashcroft 11 at 29.81.

Malvern College P20 W10 L2 D8

Master i/c A. J. Murtagh **Professional** R. W. Tolchard

Malvern still play declaration games – and of 20 matches just eight were drawn. Will Gifford had a highest score of 158 and looks to have a future in the game. Arum Ayyavooraju, scorer of two hundreds and 630 runs, is from France.

Batting W. M. Gifford* 942 at 94.20; C. W. Tolchard 515 at 51.50; A. Ayyavooraju 630 at 37.05; W. A. Murtagh 324 at 23.14; B. C. Raymond 175 at 17.50; F. Khalid 174 at 17.40.
Bowling O. M. Griffiths 36 at 14.94; F. Khalid 42 at 15.19; A. Ayyavooraju 26 at 18.38; M. J. G. King 11 at 24.09; R. D. K. Price 13 at 34.61.

Manchester Grammar Schoool — P12 W5 L2 D5 A2

Master i/c D. Moss
Few sides have an Under-15 and an Under-14 in their regular top three, but Imran Azam and David Leeming justified their selection. Daniel Woods, still only in the fourth-form, was again the leading wicket-taker. David Madden, an opening batsman, continued to be most reliable.
Batting D. C. Madden 367 at 33.36; T. M. Wildig* 263 at 26.30; D. T. G. Leeming 205 at 25.62; I. S. Azam 209 at 23.22; N. T. Reid 188 at 20.89.
Bowling N. T. Reid 20 at 17.35; D. A. Woods 33 at 17.96; E. R. Simpson 12 at 22.33; J. G. Williams 11 at 23.63; C. J. Hemmings 10 at 29.20; J. J. Squires 10 at 31.30.

Marlborough College — P14 W5 L2 D7

Master i/c N. E. Briers — **Professional** B. M. Ratcliffe
A very successful pre-season tour to Cape Town helped to mould this relatively young side into a competitive and committed unit. They also supported the Ben Hollioake Memorial Fund by competing in a seven-a-side tournament at The Oval.
Batting H. A. Adair 397 at 44.11; J. A. Bill 333 at 23.78; J. A. Sinclair 198 at 19.80; A. W. Montagu-Pollock 235 at 18.07.
Bowling R. E. M. Williams 27 at 13.11; T. J. Forsythe 20 at 18.10; A. E. G. Marigold 10 at 26.50; P. A. Clague 22 at 27.45; R. D. Hartley 11 at 34.00.

Merchant Taylors' School, Crosby — P9 W3 L2 D4 A2

Master i/c Rev. D. A. Smith — **Professional** P. A. Strang
Batting C. R. Firth 223 at 27.87; J. Cole* 190 at 27.14.
Bowling S. Cole 13 at 17.76; A. D. Fraser 12 at 24.58.

Merchant Taylors' School, Northwood — P18 W10 L4 D4 A1

Master i/c C. Evans-Evans
Shivan Dave, in the first team for a third season, led the side well. Dave remained a quality opening bowler and ended his school career with 99 wickets. Ashish Mehta was a useful wicket-keeper/batsman and Jack O'Sullivan a talented all-rounder.
Batting J. P. P. O'Sullivan 637 at 57.90; A. Mehta 616 at 47.38; M. Patel 364 at 24.26; V. Le Vesconte 295 at 22.69; D. Jennings 154 at 12.83.
Bowling S. N. Dave 37 at 14.16; K. H. Patel 17 at 18.58; V. Paul 18 at 22.83.

Merchiston Castle School — P18 W16 L2 D0 A2

Master i/c C. W. Swan — **Professional** C. English
For the first time in the school's 170-year history, the first team won all their matches against other schools – 12 in all. James Crosthwaite scored 797 runs, but South African Wian Potgieter had a phenomenal all-round season. Both scored centuries against Gordonstoun.
Batting J. W. Potgieter 675 at 67.50; J. L. Crosthwaite 797 at 46.88; R. J. C. Windle* 445 at 31.78; W. J. H. Quin 295 at 21.07; D. I. McKerchar 157 at 17.44; R. J. Holroyd 202 at 14.42.
Bowling J. W. Potgieter 41 at 6.34; O. J. Stephens 13 at 12.61; R. J. C. Windle 23 at 12.95; R. J. Holroyd 19 at 13.00; W. G. H. Quin 10 at 14.50; R. M. S. Legget 22 at 15.00; D. J. W. Smith 17 at 17.23.

Millfield School — P18 W13 L3 D2 A1

Master i/c R. M. Ellison — **Professional** M. R. Davis
James Hildreth played ten times for the Somerset first team, and Rory Hamilton-Brown captained the England Under-15s. Robin Lett had an excellent first season in the side.
Batting J. C. Hildreth* 563 at 62.55; R. J. Lett 606 at 43.28; R. J. Hamilton-Brown 321 at 40.12; R. T. Timms 462 at 33.00; S. C. Taylor 227 at 32.42; L. R. Wilson 178 at 29.66; S. J. P. Parry 224 at 24.88; O. S. R. Norris 178 at 19.77.
Bowling N. A. Williams 29 at 11.62; J. C. Hildreth 23 at 14.08; S. J. P. Parry 25 at 21.88; C. N. Haley 16 at 21.93.

Monkton Combe P11 W7 L1 D3 A4

Master i/c N. D. Botton **Professional** P. R. Wickens

The school's best season for several years included a first win against MCC since 1971.

Batting T. C. R. Moore 208 at 23.11; D. R. Spear 204 at 22.66; H. J. H. Williams 170 at 21.25; P. Auld 208 at 20.80; J. A. Lowde 155 at 15.50.

Bowling H. J. H. Williams 16 at 13.68; P. Auld 16 at 13.75; R. N. B. Baddeley 21 at 15.00; N. R. Wilsher 11 at 19.27.

Monmouth School P14 W8 L5 D1 A2

Master i/c A. Jones **Professional** G. I. Burgess

Batting L. S. Cronk 340 at 37.77; M. T. Knight 278 at 30.88; J. A. Richards 268 at 26.80; A. T. Seymour 265 at 24.09; W. A. Jacks 198 at 19.80; M. L. Robinson 155 at 17.22; J. D. D. Osbourne 201 at 16.75.

Bowling M. L. Robinson 17 at 14.35; L. S. Cronk 18 at 18.44; G. W. Lloyd 11 at 19.27; J. D. D. Osbourne 18 at 19.27; D. R. Wilson 13 at 19.30; H. E. J. Molyneux 11 at 30.36.

Newcastle-under-Lyme School P10 W3 L2 D5 A4

Master i/c P. S. J. Goodwin

A tight-knit side included four of the school's finest players in many years, so there was real disappointment when rain blighted six of the 14 scheduled matches.

Batting A. Merali 219 at 43.80; V. Kumar 177 at 29.50; J. D. Wright 198 at 28.28.

Bowling C. J. P. Howland* 12 at 8.41; C. D. Whalley 20 at 14.40.

Norwich School P9 W4 L3 D2 A3

Master i/c T. J. W. Day **Professionals** R. A. Bunting/M. E. Parlane

After many of last season's outstanding team had left, much responsibility fell on Edward Foster. He played for the ECB Schools East against the West.

Batting M. J. Kelly 203 at 25.37; A. J. Kelly 173 at 19.22.

Bowling E. J. Foster 13 at 14.30.

Nottingham High School P14 W9 L5 D0 A2

Master i/c J. Lamb **Professional** K. E. Cooper

Batting C. P. Saxton 575 at 47.91; T. R. Chalkley* 489 at 44.45; J. A. Coupland 282 at 20.14; C. C. J. Nembhard 249 at 19.15.

Bowling T. R. Chalkley 23 at 15.86; C. J. Harrison 14 at 17.00; J. C. Sharpe 13 at 20.84; M. W. Hallam 23 at 21.00; D. J. Howell 13 at 22.76.

Oakham School P16 W9 L0 D7 A2

Master i/c F. C. Hayes **Professional** D. S. Steele

Oakham School had one of the most successful seasons in its history. The side were unbeaten in all games, including a win against Eton, who were also unbeaten at the time. Paul Cook scored 961 runs at a remarkable 106.77. Leg-spinner Bhargav Modha took 28 wickets.

Batting P. G. Cook* 961 at 106.77; M. W. Smith 213 at 42.60; M. A. G. Boyce 547 at 36.46; S. C. J. Broad 281 at 31.22; B. Modha 223 at 20.27; R. I. Cummine 176 at 19.55.

Bowling B. Modha 28 at 19.21; P. G. Cook 10 at 25.70; J. D. Huq 17 at 27.88; M. C. Collier 11 at 28.36; S. C. J. Broad 14 at 37.64.

The Oratory School P17 W10 L4 D3

Master i/c J. B. K. Howell

The season exceeded all expectations. Among others, the school beat a strong Eton side and MCC. Nick Howell scored the fastest fifty on record for the school – in an astonishing 11 balls. The innings turned the match against Berkshire Gentlemen.

Batting D. M. Housego 764 at 58.76; B. A. C. Howell 344 at 38.22; A. J. H. Thomson 250 at 35.71; N. J. K. Howell 379 at 31.58.

Bowling R. G. Ashton 31 at 13.77; S. C. Boughton 14 at 14.64; E. A. S. Fraser 15 at 14.93; R. E. Greenland 12 at 22.08.

Oswestry School P3 W0 L3 D0 A5

Master i/c P. S. Jones

Batting No batsman scored 150 runs. The leading batsman was M. S. Leonard*, who scored 69 at 23.00.

Bowling No bowler took ten wickets. The leading bowler was M. S. Leonard, who took two at 15.00.

Paul Cook of Oakham (*left*) averaged over 106 with the bat, second in the country; James Hay of Oundle had the second-highest tally of wickets – 49.

Oundle School — P26 W14 L7 D5

Master i/c J. R. Wake — **Professional** A. Howorth

James Hay, who bowled four Stamford batsman in four balls, and Cameron Wake both played for ECB representative sides. Robert Fahrenheim was a powerful stroke-maker and hit two hundreds.

Batting R. M. Fahrenheim 840 at 42.00; C. J. Wake 810 at 35.21; M. J. Phythian 641 at 30.52; M. L. Austin 628 at 28.54; E. J. Clough 442 at 26.00; W. B. Wilson 310 at 18.23; C. M. Morris 291 at 18.18; M. K. Outar 288 at 16.94.

Bowling J. I. Hay 49 at 14.38; P. J. Foster 40 at 17.65; M. K. Outar 26 at 21.00; C. M. Morris 34 at 23.64; E. J. Clough 27 at 28.81; C. J. Wake 15 at 36.60.

The Perse School, Cambridge — P14 W8 L4 D2 A3

Master i/c M. A. Judson

A pre-season tour to Cyprus was the prelude to a fine season. The first team retained the Cambridgeshire County Cup.

Batting P. M. Frenay 448 at 40.72; B. A. Apperly 429 at 35.75; D. E. Howells 213 at 23.66; C. D. Rogers 198 at 18.00; O. J. Bassett 194 at 16.16; R. M. Bourne 199 at 15.30.

Bowling D. E. Howells 26 at 16.57; A. R. Harris 16 at 18.12; R. G. Ayton 12 at 23.91; J. A. M. Crawford 17 at 23.94; R. M. Bourne 12 at 24.00; R. L. Hesket 11 at 32.27.

Plymouth College — P14 W4 L4 D6

Master i/c G. C. Roderick

Captain Phillip Wass scored his maiden century in the match against Wellington.

Batting A. G. Trevarthan 446 at 31.85; P. W. Wass* 345 at 28.75; C. M. Hockin 171 at 24.42; P. J. Garland 276 at 23.00; W. G. B. Gates 222 at 18.50.

Bowling T. Trevarthan 13 at 20.23; B. D. Vince 24 at 20.58; C. M. Hockin 14 at 20.92; J. D. Whitehead 10 at 21.60.

Pocklington School — P13 W5 L4 D4 A4

Master i/c D. Watton

Batting J. L. T. Bolam 504 at 72.00; P. Van Dijk 453 at 37.75; C. L. Johnson 214 at 30.57; T. P. Nettleton* 270 at 22.50; R. J. Bradley 165 at 20.62.

Bowling C. L. Johnson 11 at 16.54; D. A. Suddaby 15 at 21.33; D. Mays 19 at 24.21; I. R. L. Gladstone 17 at 27.70.

Portsmouth Grammar School P14 W6 L7 D1 A2

Master i/c G. D. Payne

A young side relied heavily on Ben Morgan for runs and wickets. He was backed up by Edward Dixon-Lowe who, in his first season, took 20 wickets. With many young players used, the season, despite only six wins, was encouraging.

Batting B. Morgan* 450 at 50; D. Neville 173 at 24.71; M. Saunders 224 at 18.66; S. Khoyratty 204 at 17.

Bowling E. Dixon-Lowe 20 at 17.65; A. Jessop 14 at 21.64; B. Morgan 11 at 24.45; M. Saunders 10 at 44.80.

Prior Park College P14 W4 L6 D4

Master i/c D. R. Holland **Professional** M. Browning

An inexperienced team made good progress, achieving some notable results. Simon Williams was named best bowler in the Bath and District Schools' Cricket League. The fact that no match was lost to the weather was a credit to the groundstaff.

Batting J. M. Dann 163 at 20.37; S. L. Williams 214 at 19.45; J. R. Campbell 194 at 19.40; B. J. Todd* 166 at 12.76; H. D. Shepperd 157 at 12.07.

Bowling J. M. Dann 15 at 12.33; S. M. Williams 29 at 13.58; O. P Lawson 11 at 26.81.

Queen Elizabeth's Hospital, Bristol P8 W3 L3 D2 A2

Master i/c P. E. Joslin

The season was disappointing. Good batting was let down by average bowling.

Batting E. J. Humphreys 282 at 56.40; D. P. Chapman 248 at 41.33; A. T. Hamid* 171 at 34.20; H. M. Zaidi 170 at 24.28.

Bowling A. T. Hamid 13 at 16.00.

Queen's College, Taunton P13 W5 L5 D3 A3

Master i/c A. S. Free

Calum Doutch led the side with great skill and by excellent example. He was well supported by the all-round talents of Oliver Stewart, Robert Dickins and Robert Palmer – and by Richard Catchpole with the bat. Fraser Campbell-Wilson hit a hundred on first-team debut against a strong Old Queenians attack.

Batting R. L. F. Palmer 301 at 30.10; C. H. Doutch* 309 at 25.75; R. P. Dickins 213 at 23.66; R. S. E. Catchpole 221 at 22.10; O. J. Stewart 191 at 21.22.

Bowling C. H. Doutch 21 at 14.61; O. J. Stewart 13 at 19.23; J. A. Kelly 17 at 20.05; R. P. Dickins 11 at 21.90.

Radley College P18 W6 L2 D10

Master i/c W. J. Wesson **Professionals** A. R. Wagner/A. G. Robinson

With a bit more luck, five of the ten draws might have been wins – the opposition were nine down on each occasion. Simon Butler was the leading batsman in a largely young side and finished his school career with nearly 2,500 runs. Charlie Dufell was one of the best wicket-keepers on Radley's circuit.

Batting S. M. Butler* 931 at 66.50; A. J. Cama 472 at 42.90; C. B. R. Duffell 299 at 29.90; D. P. R. Clements 435 at 27.18; W. P. Clarkson 168 at 24.00; T. A. D. Davies 191 at 17.36; D. R. Dancy 193 at 16.08.

Bowling T. A. D. Davies 31 at 17.41; A. J. Cama 26 at 20.34; S. M. Butler 14 at 22.14; D. J. W. Mooney 18 at 23.16; J. A. C. Bridcut 15 at 25.60.

Ratcliffe College P8 W1 L3 D4 A5

Master i/c R. M. Hughes **Professional** M. J. Deane

Batting T. Cabrelli* 302 at 43.14.

Bowling A. J. Smith 20 at 18.65.

Reading School P11 W8 L1 D2 A2

Master i/c A. D. Walder **Professional** J. E. Bonneywell

Batting T. G. Burrows 438 at 73.00; G. J. Duncan 352 at 44.00; J. E. Lloyd 188 at 37.60.

Bowling J. L. Cluett 10 at 8.40; T. J. H. Jacob* 21 at 10.42; T. S. Vaal 14 at 10.85; M. D. Jubb 12 at 14.08; R. S. Mendhir 11 at 22.27.

Reed's School P12 W5 L4 D3 A4

Master i/c M. R. Dunn

Joe Worrall hit 34 off one over – and 40 off seven deliveries – against Christ's Hospital. The flighted off-spin of Nick Davies took 27 wickets. On their successful tour of Barbados, the school won four matches from seven.

Batting J. D. Worrall 319 at 39.87; S. J. Day 369 at 33.54; J. I. Morrison* 329 at 32.90; J. Dodd 185 at 30.83; N. J. Davies 228 at 20.72; M. P. Wakefield 168 at 16.80.

Bowling M. P. Wakefield 17 at 17.05; N. J. Davies 27 at 23.77; J. I. Morrison 18 at 25.77; J. Dodd 10 at 37.80.

Reigate Grammar School P17 W6 L5 D6 A1

Master i/c P. J. O'Brien **Professional** J. Benjamin

This was a successful year for a young side. The batting revolved around the consistently excellent wicket-keeper, Stuart Mills, whose 693 runs came at a school-record 69.30. Oli Wassell played more aggressively. The captain, Alex Mendis, is nephew of the former Lancashire opener, Gehan.

Batting S. Mills 693 at 69.30; J. Halton 172 at 43.00; O. Wassell 430 at 33.07; O. Tame 203 at 20.30; A. Mendis* 157 at 15.70.

Bowling A. Norrie 10 at 9.90; M. Chesterton 12 at 16.66; O. Wassell 11 at 20.27; A. Mendis 17 at 28.23; T. Davies 11 at 30.27.

Repton School P16 W12 L3 D1 A3

Master i/c F. P. Watson **Professional** M. E. Kettle

Daniel Howes's aggression ensured several flying starts. His 665 runs came from only 522 balls as the team scored at 4.6 per over across the summer. Scott Chilman, playing his fourth season in the side, claimed his 100th schools wicket.

Batting A. Mace 429 at 71.50; D. W. R. Howes 665 at 47.50; A. J. Whiteley* 406 at 40.60; J. E. Lamb 198 at 39.60; B. D. Bridgen 426 at 30.42.

Bowling S. K. Chilman 27 at 18.14; A. Mace 17 at 21.82; C. D. Paget 20 at 23.50; J. E. L. Jordan 11 at 30.09; J. M. D. Wilson 10 at 38.80.

Rossall School P10 W2 L6 D2

Master i/c A. Brunt

Batting F. Hameed 299 at 49.83; P. Heald 320 at 35.55; J. Preston 188 at 20.88; I. Swaine 164 at 20.50.

Bowling P. Heald 17 at 21.52; R. Dingle 22 at 22.40.

The Royal Grammar School, Colchester P18 W5 L11 D2 A2

Master i/c R. L. Bayes

A bright start was undermined by inconsistency mid-term. Two senior players led by example: Tom George's 780 runs included 110 against an MCC side managed by his father, Philip, and Neil Coles's 39 wickets included three six-fors. Omar Ahmed was a promising 13-year-old. Eleven players with first-team experience return next season.

Batting T. W. R. George 780 at 43.33; J. W. E. Carvell 273 at 30.33; J. Warner 465 at 25.83; S. J. E. George 400 at 23.52; T. G. Glasby 208 at 23.11; S. Hummerstone 279 at 15.50; G. G. Tuck 169 at 15.36.

Bowling N. S. Coles 39 at 21.89; R. A. Lomer 19 at 28.21; S. J. E. George 17 at 31.76; T. W. R. George 17 at 36.29.

The Royal Grammar School, Guildford P17 W14 L1 D2

Master i/c S. B. R. Shore **Professional** M. A. Lynch

This was a magnificent season: four consecutive wins at the RGS Festival and 14 victories in total – matching the school record. Scores of over 250 were commonplace and the bowlers did well too.

Batting C. Nelson 503 at 71.85; W. Sabey 493 at 49.30; S. Coomer 177 at 44.25; T. Markham 423 at 42.30; T. Barford 274 at 27.40; N. Symonds-Baig 239 at 26.55; R. Colville 254 at 21.16.

Bowling T. Markham 20 at 7.75; W. Sabey 32 at 10.15; A. Wilson 24 at 18.00; M. Ackroyd* 16 at 21.62; S. Ackroyd 12 at 27.25.

Royal Grammar School, Newcastle P12 W5 L6 D1 A3

Master i/c O. L. Edwards

A mixed season, though hosting the annual RGS Festival – where the school played some of their best cricket – was a highlight.

Batting M. C. Phillips 417 at 46.33; G. R. Applegarth 372 at 37.20; B. M. Ahmad 162 at 18.00.

Bowling R. P. Malcolm 17 at 12.52; V. Chandra 12 at 18.41.

Royal Grammar School, Worcester — P19 W7 L12 D0 A3

Master i/c M. D. Wilkinson — **Professional** P. J. Newport

An excellent Easter tour to India did not quite lead on to the season anticipated. A very young side struggled to score heavily enough to give the promising bowlers a decent chance. When the captain, James Watkins, scored runs the result was usually a win, but he had little support. Dominic Harris took 27 wickets with his out-swing; Miles Illingworth followed in his father Richard's footsteps bowling niggardly left-arm spin.

Batting J. R. Watkins* 582 at 36.67; D. P. Harris 363 at 30.25; G. W. R. Broadfield 234 at 26.00; W. J. F. O'Driscoll 309 at 23.76; M. J. R. Illingworth 336 at 22.40; N. A. Newport 293 at 20.92; S. C. Howell 223 at 14.86.

Bowling D. P. Harris 27 at 19.85; O. J. Haines 10 at 27.50; T. J. R. Ohlson 14 at 29.64; M. J. R. Illingworth 16 at 32.25; T. J. Lewis 10 at 48.20.

Rugby School — P15 W1 L10 D4 A1

Master i/c P. J. Rosser — **Professionals** J. J. Whitaker/R. A. Cobb

Batting S. C. V. Greaves* 318 at 19.87; R. L. H. Crawford 312 at 19.50; G. W. Price 166 at 18.44; A. D. Martin 238 at 18.30; O. Benzie 156 at 14.18.

Bowling R. C. R. Hardwick 17 at 23.82; O. Benzie 12 at 28.41; H. A. Woodruff 10 at 41.10; S. C. V. Greaves 13 at 45.55.

Rydal Penrhos, Colwyn Bay — P8 W4 L2 D2 A1

Master i/c M. T. Leach

A team including five sons of former Rydalians proved an asset to the school. Captain David Watkins and Craig Stock put on 241 for the fourth wicket against Liverpool College, beating a school record set in 1937.

Batting D. M. Watkins* 344 at 57.33; C. D. R. Stock 326 at 46.57; P. J. H. Leach 230 at 46.00.

Bowling P. J. H. Leach 14 at 15.42; S. J. Wilson 11 at 20.90; C. D. R. Stock 12 at 23.83.

St Albans School — P10 W9 L1 D0 A2

Master i/c C. C. Hudson — **Professional** M. Hill

After a match against Queens Park on a Caribbean tour, the team were invited home by Brian Lara, who lived nearby. Nick Lamb was a powerful batting force. In ten innings, he scored 569 runs, and in the one-run victory over Queen Elizabeth's Barnet, Lamb also took a decisive hat-trick. The only defeat came against Latymer Upper.

Batting N. J. Lamb* 569 at 71.12; C. D. Rayner 194 at 24.25; M. S. Searle 230 at 23.00; J. D. Colmans 152 at 19.00.

Bowling N. J. Lamb 18 at 9.00; S. A. McIntyre 14 at 13.57.

St Edmund's College, Ware — P7 W0 L7 D0

Master i/c J. Faithfull

Batting No batsman took ten wickets. The leading batsman was S. Bratu, who scored 96 at 16.00.

Bowling No bowler took ten wickets. The leading bowler was A. K. Butt, who took eight at 27.62.

St Edmund's School, Canterbury — P11 W5 L2 D4 A3

Master i/c M. C. Dobson

During the season, St Edmund's combined excellent wins and frustrating defeats in almost equal measure.

Batting S. S. Barda 317 at 35.22; J. J. Reed-Ashton 255 at 25.50; R. Waitt* 219 at 24.33.

Bowling E. P. Curry 12 at 11.66; C. E. Densham 20 at 13.80; B. M. Holmes 15 at 17.40.

St Edward's School, Oxford — P15 W6 L3 D6

Master i/c J. Cope — **Professional** R. O. Butcher

The team worked very hard and played more positive and professional cricket as the season progressed. Alastair Simmie's strokeplay was a highlight, along with Jonathan Gabriel's bowling.

Batting M. R. Smith 368 at 30.66; A. J. Simmie 412 at 29.42; J. W. Barrett 290 at 29.00; D. R. Brewer 232 at 23.20; C. E. Arber 271 at 20.84; J. W. Gabriel* 266 at 19.00.

Bowling M. R. Smith 24 at 17.50; J. W. Gabriel 28 at 17.92; R. T. Hazelton 18 at 19.00; F. R. Hustler 14 at 28.64; M. E. Cunningham 14 at 31.21.

St George's College, Weybridge — P15 W3 L3 D9 A1

Master i/c R. S. Ambrose — **Professional** D. Ottley

Batting D. O. J. Holman 485 at 44.09; T. Grant* 636 at 42.40; T. N. J. Doran 480 at 40.00; J. D. Hardman 235 at 21.36; M. J. Ford 224 at 18.66; D. W. McGahon 159 at 13.25.

Bowling P. L. Haydon 15 at 17.13; T. C. A. Reynolds 13 at 21.00; H. Grant 28 at 21.53; B. Williams 17 at 29.64; D. W. McGahon 14 at 36.42; T. Grant 15 at 38.26.

St John's School, Leatherhead — P17 W12 L3 D2

Master i/c A. B. Gale

Batting P. C. F. Scott 681 at 48.64; K. D. S. Burge 292 at 41.71; D. J. Balcombe 520 at 37.14; W. J. Kim 166 at 33.20; G. D. Littlejohns 507 at 29.82; P. D. Anderson 310 at 22.14.

Bowling K. de Beer 16 at 11.87; A. J. M. Price 18 at 16.72; D. J. Balcombe 14 at 16.78; P. D. Anderson 27 at 17.66; P. N. Barrett 15 at 23.60; J. R. Amos 19 at 24.26.

St Paul's School — P14 W3 L7 D4

Master i/c M. G. Howat — **Professional** A. G. J. Fraser

Jake Lofdahl again impressed as a wicket-keeper/batsman. David Newsome took 17 wickets in three games at the Monkton Combe Festival.

Batting J. J. Lofdahl 494 at 41.16; M. Maini 292 at 32.44; I. M. R. Ladak 224 at 28.00; R. J. D. Kyle 189 at 23.62; M. B. Kiernan 266 at 22.16; M. E. Harries 202 at 20.20; F. W. H. Abrahams* 241 at 17.21.

Bowling D. M. Newsome 21 at 18.04; N. S. Kokri 11 at 21.90; E. R. H. Poland 18 at 25.00; I. M. R. Ladak 14 at 29.35.

St Peter's School, York — P18 W11 L3 D4 A2

Master i/c D. Kirby

St Peter's had an outstanding season, with a school-record 11 wins. The batting was strong, with Ben Hough excellent, while the bowling was steady. The attack relied heavily on left-arm spinner, Tom Woolsey, the highest wicket-taker in 2003 schools cricket.

Batting B. R. M. Hough 579 at 44.53; A. J. Chalmers 470 at 39.16; T. B. Cleminson 342 at 34.20; T. S. Bartram* 359 at 29.91; J. M. Wackett 282 at 25.63; T. J. Woolsey 245 at 24.50; M. S. Hodsdon 312 at 22.28; P. E. M. Puxon 156 at 19.50.

Bowling T. J. Woolsey 50 at 11.88; M. S. Hodsdon 20 at 16.80; M. B. Spalding 16 at 17.06; T. S. Bartram 24 at 18.79.

Sedbergh School — P15 W5 L4 D6

Master i/c J. C. Bobby — **Professional** D. Fallows

An opening stand of 259 between Chris Barrington and George Mosey against Giggleswick is believed to be a school record.

Batting C. Barrington 585 at 41.78; G. A. Mosey 472 at 36.30; D. G. Ford 272 at 24.72; A. J. Cowperthwaite 164 at 23.42; E. C. Parker 301 at 23.15.

Bowling G. A. Mosey 19 at 20.52; C. Barrington 22 at 26.13; A. J. Cowperthwaite 10 at 26.20.

Sevenoaks School — P14 W5 L7 D2 A1

Master i/c C. J. Tavaré

After just one win in 2002, this was a much better season. Most of the team returns for 2004.

Batting S. Sharma* 390 at 32.50; H. S. R. Florry 399 at 30.69; G. E. R. Alexander 152 at 15.20.

Bowling N. J. Tunnell 11 at 16.36; D. L. C. Walker 12 at 23.50; H. S. R. Florry 14 at 28.85; G. E. R. Alexander 12 at 31.66.

Shebbear College — P7 W3 L3 D1 A4

Master i/c A. Bryan

Batting C. A. Jenn 208 at 41.60; O. D. Wickett* 290 at 41.42.

Bowling O. D. Wickett 12 at 12.41; J. J. Corry 13 at 15.46.

Sherborne School — P18 W10 L5 D3

Master i/c M. D. Nurton — **Professional** A. Willows

A side of senior players and promising youngsters toured the West Indies in July. Mike Nurton retired after 15 years as master-in-charge.

Batting S. A. Crawford 462 at 51.33; T. P. Cracknell 554 at 34.62; H. M. G. Goldschmidt 327 at 29.72; H. P. Lamb 278 at 19.85; F. J. Mead 210 at 16.15.

Ajmal Shahzad of Woodhouse Grove (*left*) was a leading all-rounder with 595 runs at 66 and 25 wickets at 8.20, while Nick Lamb of St Albans averaged 71 with the bat and nine with the ball, both figures among the best in the country.

Bowling H. P. Lamb 27 at 13.59; W. R. B. Dawson 27 at 20.48; T. P. Cracknell 11 at 22.45; F. J. Mead 17 at 22.47; N. W. V. Southwell 14 at 24.35.

Shrewsbury School — P18 W9 L4 D5 A3

Master i/c M. J. Lascelles **Professional** A. P. Pridgeon

Tom Cox hit three hundreds, including one on tour in Sri Lanka. Both he and Ian Massey return next year, when Massey will be captain.

Batting T. W. P. Cox 645 at 43.00; I. R. Massey 629 at 41.93; B. R. G. Marlow 319 at 35.44; F. C. Argyle 288 at 22.15; A. M. McKeever* 226 at 18.83; A. M. Evans 159 at 14.45.

Bowling C. E. Tustain 24 at 15.33; B. R. G. Marlow 24 at 18.75; A. M. McKeever 20 at 23.55; R. D. T. Nichols 11 at 30.54.

Simon Langton Grammar School — P5 W3 L1 D1 A3

Master i/c R. H. Green

Batting No batsman scored 150 runs. The leading batsman was A. McNeil*, who scored 92 at 23.00.

Bowling No bowler took ten wickets. The leading bowler was M. Farrer, who took five at 15.40.

Sir Roger Manwood's School — P9 W4 L3 D2 A3

Master i/c G. Gayton

The performances of the side never quite matched their potential during a season interrupted by both exams and rain.

Batting M. J. van Poppel 163 at 27.16.

Bowling T. A. R. Dilnot-Smith* 11 at 7.36; M. J. van Poppel 12 at 12.66; B. C. Stephens 10 at 18.00.

Solihull School — P15 W6 L8 D1

Master i/c S. Morgan **Professionals** C. Borroughs/L. Pearson

Some good individual performances did not translate into team results. Justin Hemming was a laudable captain who showed real heart and passion for the game and always encouraged his players. However, his bowling attack was a little thin.

Batting J. D. Hemming* 590 at 49.16; B. J. Pugh 375 at 31.25; S. J. Reddish 341 at 22.73; C. S. Bartley 284 at 20.28; J. Sammons 213 at 15.21.

Bowling J. D. Hemming 15 at 17.93; A. J. Madeley 19 at 21.26; Q. A. S. Tchakhotine 11 at 23.54; C. S. Bartley 11 at 33.18.

South Craven School P8 W3 L2 D3 A3

Master i/c D. M. Birks **Professional** D. A. Batty

Anna Spragg, the school's 15-year-old wicket-keeper, was selected for the England Women's Under-19 squad. The side enjoyed a rare victory over MCC. Matthew Shuttleworth and Andrew Sewell broke the school record for an opening partnership with 134 against Grange Technology College.

Batting M. Shuttleworth 201 at 40.20.

Bowling A. Hussain 10 at 17.70; M. Shuttleworth 10 at 23.90.

Stamford School P10 W2 L7 D1 A4

Master i/c A. N. Pike **Professional** T. Roberts

A young team worked hard throughout and genuine progress was made. They will return next year with increased confidence and expectations are high. William Clough proved a talented all-rounder and Hugh Jackson produced some match-winning performances with the ball.

Batting W. R. Clough 414 at 59.14; S. Harris 154 at 22.00.

Bowling H. X. Jackson 14 at 20.35; N. P. Wells* 11 at 31.90.

Stockport Grammar School P12 W3 L5 D4 A3

Masters i/c R. Young/C. Wright **Professional** D. J. Makinson

This was a season of high endeavour but mixed reward. Bad weather and several draws where Stockport were on top created frustration. Captain Simon Elliott hit two hundreds, and the batting had depth; Charles Mercer's bowling was exceptional. The July tour to Malta, including a match against the national side, was again a success.

Batting S. Elliott* 524 at 52.40; M. Wood 227 at 37.83; M. Howarth 236 at 29.50; J. Davenport 211 at 21.10.

Bowling C. Mercer 22 at 15.63; S. Elliott 12 at 25.83.

Stowe School P8 W0 L5 D3 A1

Master i/c G. A. Cottrell **Professional** J. A. Knott

This was a disappointing season. Although an untried batting line-up managed to score sufficient runs, the bowlers struggled for consistency and never managed to bowl out the opposition.

Batting G. G. White 337 at 42.12; A. G. F. Leon 219 at 31.28; W. J. H. Gallimore* 160 at 22.85; H. J. Cussins 175 at 21.87; E. H. Prince 152 at 21.71.

Bowling G. G. White 22 at 20.86.

Strathallan School P9 W5 L1 D3 A1

Master i/c R. H. Fitzsimmons **Professional** K. Pillay

After a washout in 2002, this was a very successful year. Ross Andrews created a good team spirit and lots of individuals made substantial contributions. Five batsmen scored at least one half-century. Jono Becks, in his first season in the XI, took 19 wickets at 15.

Batting S. Blood 448 at 64.00; R. Anders* 166 at 20.75; T. W. F. Hine 167 at 18.55; D. Hoffmann 158 at 17.55.

Bowling J. F. Becks 19 at 15.26; R. Anders 18 at 20.33; S. Blood 14 at 28.57.

Tiffin School P17 W12 L2 D3 A2

Master i/c M. J. Williams

This was another terrific season for Tiffin. The small number of draws is testament to the attacking cricket encouraged by captain Ravi Uthayashanker. But one player stole the limelight: Kapilan Balasubramaniam hit a breathtaking double-century in a 50-over match with Reigate GS, before putting on the gloves and completing five stumpings, four of them off pace bowlers. Five new school records were set during the game, including Tiffin's highest-ever total – 331 for two declared.

Batting K. Balasubramaniam 719 at 59.91; A. Harinath 449 at 49.88; M. M. Patel 307 at 34.11; R. Uthayashanker* 294 at 26.72; H. M. Vanderman 280 at 25.45; N. L. Desai 315 at 22.50.

Bowling R. Gnanendran 35 at 16.68; M. M. Patel 29 at 17.10; R. Kumarasuriyar 13 at 19.69; J. R. Anderson 10 at 21.50.

Tonbridge School P17 W6 L7 D4

Master i/c N. Leamon **Professional** D. Chadwick

Batting J. W. K. Beeny 809 at 53.93; S. Kapila 482 at 34.43; E. J. Bonner 366 at 26.14; O. G. K. Howick 392 at 26.13; A. O. J. Shales 229 at 25.44; D. H. Odds* 359 at 21.11; A. C. Howeson 153 at 13.90.

Bowling A. C. Howeson 10 at 17.20; H. S. C. Thomson 16 at 20.31; C. F. Young 13 at 22.46; O. G. K. Howick 27 at 23.11; C. M. M. Hill 23 at 25.26; A. J. R. Collier 15 at 26.26; J. W. K. Beeny 12 at 44.25.

Against Reigate Grammar School, Kapilan Balasubramaniam of Tiffin hit an unbeaten 204, the season's second-highest score, then completed five stumpings.

Trent College — P11 W4 L7 D0 A3

Master i/c J. T. Jordison **Professional** J. A. Afford

Many of the defeats were very close. The outstanding batting came from Damien Jones, with two centuries. But the bowling lacked control.

Batting D. L Jones* 581 at 52.81; D.J Cupit 274 at 30.44; J. E. Acton 204 at 25.50; P. T. Robinson 227 at 22.70; A. S. G. Marshall 210 at 19.09.

Bowling G. Johnston 12 at 23.00; J. E. Acton 12 at 28.58.

Trinity School, Croydon — P13 W4 L7 D2 A1

Master i/c B. Widger

Batting M. W. Stoneman 332 at 27.66; B. T. Shorten 259 at 19.92; J. P. May 226 at 17.38.

Bowling N. R. Cook 10 at 22.60; D. G. Whitehair 14 at 30.42; B. T. Shorten 12 at 33.83; J. P. May 10 at 43.90.

Truro School — P12 W5 L6 D1

Master i/c A. Lawrence

The pick of the games was a win against MCC early in the season. After the visitors set a sporting total, Truro won with seven balls remaining. Captain Tom Glover ended the game unbeaten on 100.

Batting M. Lockwood 318 at 31.80; T. Glover* 314 at 28.54; S. De Gruchy 242 at 20.16.

Bowling S. De Gruchy 22 at 14.68; T. Glover 19 at 23.89.

University College School — P14 W5 L5 D4

Masters i/c C. P. Mahon/S. M. Bloomfield

In an exciting season a number of school batting records were broken. James Floyd's 188 against Highgate was the highest-ever individual innings, with Nick Jones's 175 against Abingdon the second-highest.

Batting N. Jones* 421 at 42.10; J. Floyd 561 at 40.07; D. Patel 178 at 25.42; V. Nair 254 at 21.16; G. Gedroyc 218 at 18.16.

Bowling B. Kirmani 26 at 14.19; N. Jones 15 at 16.20; V. Nair 19 at 19.26; B. Bloom 11 at 24.45.

Uppingham School P15 W8 L4 D3

Master i/c C. C. Stevens **Professional** B. T. P. Donelan

Duncan Wood, the captain, and Josh Branson, the wicket-keeper, can look back with pride on 32 wins in four seasons of first-team cricket. Wood took a school-record 116 wickets at 11.59, while Branson has completed 69 dismissals, and scored 1,189 runs. Of the three draws, two were matches ended by rain.

Batting J. C. J. Sharrock 403 at 31.00; D. C. Wood* 217 at 31.00; D. M. Abbott 189 at 27.00; S. W. Peters 240 at 26.66; J. T. Branson 244 at 24.40; H. M. C. Judd 252 at 22.91.

Bowling D. C. Wood 33 at 13.54; T. J. Burwell 11 at 17.63; J. C. J. Sharrock 14 at 18.14; B. R. Crowder 19 at 21.10; T. H. Higgs 11 at 36.72.

Victoria College, Jersey P18 W8 L4 D6

Master i/c M. Smith **Professional** C. Minty

After leading the college through a successful season, Peter Gough went on to captain Jersey's Under-21 and Under-25 sides. He also hit two centuries, though the six draws highlighted a lack of cutting edge among the bowlers.

Batting P. Gough* 781 at 48.81; R. Mohanty 410 at 41.00; T. Minty 425 at 35.41; J. Gough 489 at 32.60; S. Warren 163 at 32.60; O. Hughes 374 at 23.37; S. Dewhurst 153 at 15.30.

Bowling S. Warren 21 at 14.19; T. McAuiney 13 at 14.46; J. Gough 24 at 21.70; T. Minty 23 at 22.08; H. MacLachlan 12 at 23.25; P. Gough 15 at 29.13.

Warwick School P15 W11 L2 D2 A2

Master i/c G. A. Tedstone **Professional** F. Klopper

Batting D. G. Roots 724 at 90.50; K. Chhibber 277 at 55.40; A. R. Wilkinson 367 at 52.42; O. C. Higgens 471 at 36.23; T. F. Rigby 262 at 32.75; C. M. Wilson 278 at 30.88.

Bowling B. E. A. Carr 17 at 17.58; A. E. Wilkinson 22 at 19.72; P. M. Rowe 11 at 20.00; C. J. Carr 13 at 26.76.

Watford Grammar School P11 W6 L0 D5 A1

Masters i/c J. Williams/G. Welch **Professional** A. Needham

The best results for many years were still not a fair reflection: three of the five draws were nearly won. Zawar Hussein scored an unbeaten 102 out of the 136 made against Old Fullerians. With the ball, Matthew Corbridge did the most consistent damage, though Robin Willis was dangerous in the early matches.

Batting Z. I. Hussein 430 at 61.42; J. G. H. England 225 at 25.00.

Bowling R. H. Willis 18 at 11.00; M. I. Corbridge 24 at 13.70; R. H. Mukherjee 13 at 20.84.

Wellingborough School P10 W4 L5 D1 A 3

Master i/c L. M. Hilton

Batting G. D. Evans 316 at 31.60; J. D. Warwick 183 at 20.33.

Bowling W. J. Chudley 18 at 17.94; D. C. Leach 11 at 19.00; J. D. Warwick 13 at 19.76.

Wellington College P16 W14 L1 D1 A1

Masters i/c C. M. Oliphant-Callum/R. I. H. B. Dyer **Professionals** P. J. Lewington/N. A. Brett

Hugo Shephard's captaincy was exceptional, and the 14 wins a school record. Shephard hit a swashbuckling unbeaten 165 against Haileybury.

Batting H. T. Y. Shephard* 784 at 56.00; G. R. Tysoe 517 at 43.08; P. J. W. Young 502 at 38.61; A. A. Shelley 329 at 32.90; R. H. St J. Huckin 177 at 29.50; A. G. Walker 176 at 25.14; J. D. Atkinson 199 at 24.87.

Bowling C. J. Rylatt 29 at 12.10; H. T. Y. Shephard 21 at 14.80; A. A. Shelley 31 at 14.96; G. R. Tysoe 29 at 15.17; J. R. Coyne 19 at 26.89.

Wellington School P15 W3 L5 D7

Master i/c M. H. Richards

A young and very inexperienced team gelled well under the retiring captain Paul Short, the school's outstanding spin bowler over the last four seasons. Four of the final five matches went to the last over.

Batting J. D. Crowther 206 at 25.75; P. E. Short* 297 at 21.21; T. Collard 283 at 18.86; S. C. Marsh 195 at 16.25; P. Shepherd 162 at 14.72.

Bowling T. Collard 22 at 16.04; P. E. Short 36 at 16.66; A. D. Leach 12 at 21.91; R. J. Tuer 11 at 32.54.

Wells Cathedral School P13 W5 L5 D3 A1

Master i/c M. Stringer

Batting G. Oram* 330 at 30.00; J. Sellick 238 at 23.80; T. Tapfield 190 at 23.75.

Bowling G. Oram 27 at 12.70; M. Brandon 15 at 15.80; W. Lewis 10 at 27.20; M. Taylor-Maughan 18 at 28.00.

West Buckland School P14 W3 L6 D5 A1

Master i/c L. Whittal-Williams **Professional** M. T. Brimson

Batting D. J. Bowser 568 at 56.80; A. M. Laugharne 320 at 29.09; S. F. Bowen 202 at 22.44; J. D. Wallace* 248 at 20.66; J. C. Chickman 172 at 17.20; M. A. Stevens 188 at 17.09.

Bowling J. D. Wallace 16 at 23.93; C. A. Boulden 16 at 24.18; J. M. Robinson 10 at 30.50; A. D. Hobbs 11 at 36.63.

Westminster School P14 W4 L4 D6 A2

Master i/c J. Kershan

A very good bowling and fielding team would have won more often if the batsmen performed more consistently. William Yell's five for 13 against St. Dunstan's were comfortably the best bowling figures. The best team performances came in reaching the semi-finals of the Ben Hollioake Memorial seven-a-side at The Oval.

Batting O. Butler 264 at 24.00; A. J. Hall 203 at 20.30; W. N. J. Yell* 171 at 19.00; W. B. J. Stevenson 206 at 18.72; D. C. R. Bamford 256 at 18.28; R. K. Clark 173 at 15.72.

Bowling R. H. C. Low 10 at 15.20; W. N. J. Yell 20 at 15.25; G. W. D. Gilmore 13 at 24.30; N. R. Manners 10 at 31.20.

Whitgift School P11 W6 L3 D2

Master i/c D. M. Ward **Professional** N. M. Kendrick

Batting M. N. W. Spriegel 493 at 61.62; S. J. Woodward* 431 at 53.87; A. P. Clarke 198 at 33.00; S. Ratnayake 179 at 29.83; A Bailey 169 at 28.16.

Bowling M. D. A. Fielder 12 at 12.75; A. P. Clarke 17 at 19.82; S. J. Woodward 11 at 24.36; N. A. C. Grant 10 at 36.50.

Winchester College P16 W6 L9 D1

Master i/c C. J. Good **Professional** B. Reed

Batting J. R. Irvine-Fortescue 335 at 27.91; J. M. Burridge 276 at 25.09; C. M. Walters 250 at 22.72; J. H. Walters* 163 at 12.53.

Bowling J. S. Pringle 30 at 14.36; H. Mohammed 12 at 16.83; J. H. Walters 16 at 21.62; J. A. Kenyon 17 at 24.23; R. L. Harding 12 at 26.25; T. L. Hemmingway 11 at 38.45.

Wolverhampton Grammar School P14 W7 L3 D4

Master i/c N. H. Crust **Professional** T. King

Positive batting and tight bowling led to the most successful season for some time. Christian Mulvilhill and Chris Lowe led the way with bat and ball, while 15-year-old fast-bowler Richard Browning showed real potential.

Batting C. J. Mulvihill 434 at 54.25; C. J. Brook 389 at 32.41; C. W. Lowe 346 at 28.83; A. J. Whitby 168 at 24.00; J. R. Acaster 185 at 16.81.

Bowling R. J. Browning 17 at 7.82; S. T. Jackson 10 at 10.00; C. S. Adey 19 at 14.36; C. J. Mulvihill 14 at 17.14; A. J. Cuthbert 10 at 17.40; C. W. Lowe 16 at 19.18.

Woodbridge School P12 W6 L0 D6 A1

Master i/c S. Carlisle **Professional** C. Rutterford

Woodbridge's first undefeated season in living memory. All-round team performances, rather than individual feats, stood out. Mark Fernley's 116 against King's School, Ely included 100 in boundaries.

Batting M. K. Fernley* 477 at 59.62; W. C. Nicholls 217 at 43.40; J. R. Ayris 199 at 24.87; J. P. McNally 195 at 21.66.

Bowling C. W. Tunstall 13 at 18.92; J. P. McNally 21 at 20.57; W. C. Nicholls 14 at 28.07.

Woodhouse Grove P11 W3 L6 D2 A5

Master i/c R. I. Frost **Professional** G. R. J. Roope

This was a tough year for a young team. But Ajmal Shahzad, in his first season, was outstanding. He made 122 on debut, then scored 133 and took seven for nine in a magnificent performance against Arnold School. Ajmal is with the Yorkshire Academy and played for ECB Schools.

Batting A. Shahzad 595 at 66.11; R. H. Haslam* 369 at 41.00; A. Silley 160 at 16.00.
Bowling A. Shahzad 25 at 8.20.

Worksop College P16 W8 L3 D5 A1

Master i/c N. R. Gaywood **Professional** R. A. Kettleborough

The college's ability to build the tempo of an innings was impressive: Bhavesh Patel and Sam Ogrizovic invariably produced a good start and excellent running between the wickets maintained the momentum. The fielding was always aggressive and the college's spin bowlers caused batsmen problems.

Batting B. Patel 738 at 52.71; S. Patel 368 at 40.88; S. E. Ogrizovic 528 at 37.71; R. M. Davies 368 at 33.45; T. Corbyn 307 at 25.58.
Bowling B. Patel 22 at 12.36; O. Rossington 12 at 12.75; S. Patel 19 at 13.10; T. Corbyn 16 at 18.00; R. M. Davies 11 at 24.27.

Wrekin College P15 W7 L2 D6

Master i/c M. de Weymarn **Professional** P. Dawson

Seven wins was the college's best total in recent memory, and all but one of the victories came in declaration games.

Batting J. D. Pee* 302 at 43.14; A. Sultan 344 at 43.00; M. R. Rosslee 415 at 37.72; R. J. W. Whitehouse 279 at 31.00.
Bowling J. D. R. Zonko 22 at 16.54; A. Sultan 17 at 18.41; J. D. Pee 22 at 18.63; J. P. Andrews 10 at 27.50.

Wycliffe College P8 W5 L3 D0

Master i/c D. Pemberton **Professional** M. Kimber

To win more than half their matches represented a good performance for one of the youngest first teams Wycliffe have ever fielded.

Batting S. Russell 190 at 38.00; G. Harding 246 at 30.75; H. Clemett* 171 at 21.37.
Bowling S. Russell 11 at 12.81; T. Williams 16 at 13.43.

Wyggeston and Queen Elizabeth I College P10 W8 L0 D2

Master i/c J. P. Murphy

The college was unbeaten for the second year in a row. Kunal Jogia, the captain, was again selected for Leicestershire's Second Eleven, while Imran Lodhi's 92.50 was the highest batting average for several decades. The first team retained the Leicestershire Schools Under-19 County Cup.

Batting I. K. Lodhi 555 at 92.50; M. Contractor 217 at 43.40; J. Jogia* 226 at 28.25.
Bowling J. Jogia 13 at 11.53; I. K. Lodia 13 at 11.84; L. C. Berriman 16 at 12.87.

Notes: In the result line, A = abandoned without a ball bowled. An asterisk next to a name indicates captain. Schools provide their own comments.

TEST MATCH SPECIAL UNDER-15 YOUNG CRICKETER OF THE YEAR

Ben Wright, from Cowbridge in Glamorgan, won the fourth BBC Test Match Special Under-15 Young Cricketer of the Year Award, decided by a panel of ECB national judges. An outstanding cover fielder and middle-order batsman, he scored 411 at 102.75 for England Under-15 in the 2003 season, including 138 in 121 balls against Scotland. The previous winners were Samit Patel (Nottinghamshire), Adam Harrison (Glamorgan) and Phillip Holdsworth (Yorkshire).

YOUTH CRICKET, 2003

PAUL COUPAR

The last three ECB-approved county academies opened their doors in 2003. Every first-class county now provides their best 13 to 18-year-old cricketers with a closely managed development programme, a short cut to the top covering everything from technique and fitness to psychology and lifestyle. But some counties report an unexpected gap in the curriculum – cricket matches.

There is now no organised representative cricket for county players over 17. The ECB scrapped the two-day Under-19 County Championship after the summer of 2002. Instead, the 38-County Cup was revamped as an Under-21 tournament. That too has now gone, as the financial ramifications of England's refusal to play in Harare during the World Cup hit home.

And for 2004, two more stepping-stones to first-class cricket are being removed or threatened. No county board sides will play in the Cheltenham & Gloucester Trophy. And some counties will organise just six second-team games, down from a previous minimum of ten. Steve Watkin, director of the Glamorgan academy, summed up the predicament of some counties. "Players spend a lot of time over the winter doing technical work and physical training", he said, "but it comes to summer and there's not enough cricket to be played."

Many Academies field a side in local league cricket. But Lancashire (one of the few counties still playing two-day Under-19 cricket) do not see that as a stand-alone solution. "You go from Under-17 two-day cricket back to one-day League cricket," said their academy director John Stanworth, "which is not right for development."

Those counties who still fund Under-19 friendlies and full second-team fixture cards deny there is a problem. So do the ECB. Others claim bluntly that if you're not good enough for the second team by your late teens, you're not good enough for first-class cricket. But with most second-team fixture lists getting shorter not longer, it looks increasingly as if a rung in the ladder into four-day first-class cricket is missing.

Another problem facing youth cricket is more straightforward. *Wisden 2003* mentioned Travis Binnion (page 1090), a teenage wicket-keeper attached to Nottinghamshire who had been picked out as a special talent from the age of 12. He has just signed youth terms – for Sheffield United FC.

UNDER-21 CRICKET

For what turned out to be just one season, the old ECB 38-County Cup became an Under-21 competition, with each side allowed two over-age players. It was won by Lancashire, who beat Devon in a rain-marred final at Derby. A subdued 50 from Neil Bettiss and a more punchy 45 by Trevor Anning gave Devon 205 in 50 overs. After stumbling to 36 for three, Lancashire then sauntered towards their target. Rain brought an early halt and again ruined the reserve day. Lancashire ended up 134 for three after 30.4 overs, and won on a faster scoring-rate. The ECB later announced they were abolishing the tournament.

Faces of the future? England Under-15 batsmen Ben Wright (Wales) (*left*) and Karl Brown (Lancashire) dominated bowlers – and impressed coaches.

Pictures by Steve Watkin and David Dawson.

UNDER-17 CRICKET

Lancashire also won the Under-17 County Championship, beating last year's runners-up Surrey by 78 runs in the final at Grace Road. Although Karl Brown, whose batting caused carnage in England Under-15 games over the summer, failed in the final, Jack Kelliher, with 77, and Tom Smith, with 64, gave Lancashire a foundation. They finally reached 336 for nine in their maximum 100 overs. On the second day, Surrey never built the big partnership they needed. Stephen Parry grabbed five for 48 with his left-arm spin. For the first time, the regional groups were divided into three divisions, with promotion and relegation.

UNDER-15 CRICKET

Rod Marsh's summary of the 17th ESCA/Bunbury Under-15 Festival was equivocal: plenty of talent, said the Director of the ECB Academy, but no one at the "genius level". Showers blighted two of the six group games and washed out the final. In between, Adil Rashid, a leg-spinner from Bradford, took 14 wickets in three games, building on his work with Australian guru Terry Jenner in the ECB's Wrist Spin programme. The programme aims to have a leg-spinner in the England Test side by 2007. Daniel Housego of Oxfordshire (now with the Gloucestershire Academy) scored 198 runs at 99, which helped the successful Midlands side squeak two wins in three games.

The *Daily Telegraph*/Bunbury scholarships went to Rashid, Mervyn Westfield (a fast bowler from Essex) and two more England Under-15 team-mates – wicket-keeper Paul Dixey from Kent and all-rounder Rory Hamilton-Brown from Surrey. All four joined the full ECB Academy in Loughborough for a week. "He might have cut me up," said Hamilton-Brown after facing recuperating England pace bowler Simon Jones, "but he didn't get me out."

England fielded one of their strongest Under-15 sides for several years. They twice swept aside Ireland Under-17 – Karl Brown racing to 64 in the first and 120 in the second – and repeated the 2–0 scoreline in a one-day series against Scotland Under-17. England also had much the better of a drawn three-day game against the Scots; their only defeat was against England Under-16. The side flew to South Africa in February 2004, searching for stronger opposition to test the likes of Ben Wright (a Wales batsman who averaged 102 for England in 2003) and Westfield, both seen as outstanding prospects.

Surrey won the Under-15 County Championship finals at Oundle School. Runners-up in the mini-league were Yorkshire and Devon. For the first time the Championship was played to a declaration format. Needing to win (or dominate a draw) in their last game against Devon, Surrey declared after making 172 for six in 54 overs. In reply, Devon plodded towards safety but never made it – all out for 110 in the 50th over. Spinners Akbar Ansari and Simon King took four wickets each.

The Under-15 County Cup was won by Wales. They were captained by batsman Ben Wright, winner of the Cricket Society award for the country's best Under-16 prospect.

Yet again, Millfield School lifted the Colts Trophy at Trent Bridge. This was their eighth outright win in 15 years (they have also shared the trophy once). In every round before the final they batted first, scored more than 250 in their 40 overs and won by at least 75 runs. Loughborough pushed them harder but it was still not close. James Fear batted for most of Millfield's innings, hitting a commanding 94, then took two crucial wickets with his medium-pace.

UNDER-14 CRICKET

No one side or individual stamped their mark on the Under-14 Festival at Oundle. Both Midlands and West beat North, but the other four matches were drawn. Alex Wakely of Midlands was the heaviest run-scorer with 204; Tom Maynard, son of Glamorgan's Matthew, hit the only other century. Christopher Morgan, a left-armer from Hampshire who puts plenty of spin on the ball, took most wickets with 11. He was later selected, among boys more than two years older, to tour South Africa in February 2004 with an England squad.

UNDER-13 CRICKET

The Under-13 regional festival at Taunton uncovered more depth in batting than in bowling. South triumphed, winning all three of their declaration games by burying their opponents under a pile of runs. Against North, Luc Durandt and Hamza Riazuddin both made centuries; against West, Robert Newton hit with startling power to reach 109 in fewer than 50 balls. The South's 321 for six declared was the highest-ever score at the Festival. Christopher Morgan again shone for West, taking eight for 87 against North.

The 40-over Under-13 County Cup was held alongside the Under-15 version at Oundle. Akhil Patel's 72 swung a low-scoring final Nottinghamshire's way; they beat Wales by 33 runs. In Nottinghamshire's semi-final, against Essex, Husnain Riaz was the hero, with four wickets for five runs. The other semi-finalists were Staffordshire. For the first time, counties played declaration games too – an attempt to encourage wicket-taking bowlers.

The former sponsors of the Under-13 schools cup, the drinks firm Calypso, pulled out for 2003, concerned that a state school had never reached the final. Ironically, a state school *did* make it this year. But John Taylor School from Barton-under-Needwood, Staffordshire, fell just short of chasing down Whitgift's 169.

UNDER-11 CRICKET

Christ Church Primary School from Ealing in London won the National Under-11 BBC Kwik Cricket tournament. While plenty of the other 5,500 schools were coached by women, Christ Church were probably the only side trained by a female Sorbonne graduate with a French passport. Marie Holt was born in Paris, arrived in England in 1972 and developed an interest in cricket when her son David showed promise. The national hard-ball competition was won by Eagle House from Berkshire, who beat Harlands School from Sussex in the final.

Additional reporting by Gareth A. Davies.

WOMEN'S CRICKET, 2003

CAROL SALMON

SOUTH AFRICAN WOMEN IN ENGLAND, 2003

England enjoyed their most productive season since their World Cup triumph in 1993. Runs flowed from their often brittle batting line-up and the attack maintained excellent control, as the new coach, former Nottinghamshire spinner Richard Bates, quickly stamped his authority.

Seven players from the winter touring party to Australasia were dropped, but the changes were vindicated. One surprise selection, Sussex teenager Rosalie Birch, had a dream debut with bat and ball. Wicket-keeper Jane Smit (who has dropped her former married name of Cassar) returned after a year and a half out of favour. Another teenager, Lydia Greenway, who had been called up to bolster the squad in Australia, made some solid contributions. Claire Taylor had barely scraped a run at the County Championship in July, but burst back into form with back-to back centuries. The decision to seek batting stability by sticking to the same top five throughout the hot summer paid off. England passed 450 in both Tests, and won that series 1–0 – their first home win for 24 years – plus the one-day internationals 2–1. A crowd of 1,500 witnessed the one-day game at Chelmsford, the first day/night women's international in England.

South Africa included seven teenagers in their party and were, by their own admission, under-prepared. Only Daleen Terblanche had been on South Africa's first tour of England in 1997; three others, including captain Alison Hodgkinson, had come with her in 2000. The squad had to be revised to meet their board's requirement of six "players of colour", and had not assembled before arriving at the airport. Still, lacking in experience, fitness and organisation as they were, they had some potential stars. Johmari Logtenberg, aged just 14, scored Test and one-day fifties; 19-year-old Charlize van der Westhuizen was their leading scorer in the Tests; Cri-Zelda Brits and Alicia Smith demonstrated further promise. Clearly, South Africa have plenty of talent waiting to be harvested.

SOUTH AFRICAN TOURING PARTY

A. L. Hodgkinson (Western Province) (*captain*), Y. van der Merwe (Northerns) (*vice-captain*), J. Barnard (Western Province), C-Z. Brits (Western Province), C. J. Cowan (Western Province), S. A. Fritz (Western Province), L. J. Jacobs (Western Province), A. P. C. Kilowan (Boland), J. Logtenberg (KwaZulu-Natal), N. Ndzundzu (Border), A. E. Smith (Boland), C. S. Terblanche (Eastern Province), M. Terblanche (Gauteng), C. van der Westhuizen (Northerns), S. S. D. van Zyl (Western Province).

Coach: R. Booi. *Manager:* A. Connolly. *Physiotherapist:* S. Vallabhjee.

SOUTH AFRICAN TOUR RESULTS

Matches – Played 9: Won 2, Lost 6, Drawn 1.

Note: Matches in this section were not first-class.

At Cambridge, July 31. **Sussex won by 24 runs.** Toss: South Africans. **Sussex 188-6** (45 overs) (C. J. Connor 97*); **South Africans 164-9** (45 overs) (C. J. Connor 4-24).

Sussex, crowned county champions the previous day, won a match reduced to 45 overs a side by rain.

At Stokenchurch, August 3. **MCC Women's Invitational XI won by 45 runs.** Toss: MCC. **MCC Women's Invitational XI 157** (45.5 overs); **South Africans 112** (45.2 overs).

At Marston College, Oxford, August 4. **South Africans won by ten runs.** Toss: South Africans. **South Africans 179** (49.3 overs); **ECB Under-21 Development XI 169-8** (50 overs).

At Marston College, Oxford, August 5. **ECB England Development XI won by seven wickets.** Toss: South Africans. **South Africans 167-8** (50 overs) (A. L. Hodgkinson 56); **ECB England Development XI 168-3** (45 overs) (A. Thompson 84*).

ENGLAND v SOUTH AFRICA

First Test Match

At Shenley Park, August 7, 8, 9, 10. Drawn. Toss: South Africa. Test debuts: R. A. Birch, L. Spragg; C. S. Cowan, L. Z. Jacobs, J. Logtenberg, A. E. Smith, C. van der Westhuizen.

A broiling sun and a friendly batting surface saw England come within six runs of their highest Test total, while South Africa exceeded their previous best – 266 for eight against England, in their very first series in 1960-61 – in both innings. In only their second Test since readmission, and their ninth in all, South Africa batted with far greater determination than their early tour outings had suggested. Still, England would have won had they accepted all their catches. The first day was dominated by 14-year-old Johmari Logtenberg and 19-year-old Charlize van der Westhuizen, who added 138 for the fifth wicket, a women's Test record. Then England's Claire Taylor claimed centre stage, striking 22 fours in a career-best 177 occupying six and a half hours. She added 103 with Clare Connor and 203 – England's fourth-wicket best – with Lydia Greenway, a left-hander from Kent who celebrated her 18th birthday the day before the Test. England led by 181, and had South Africa four down and 95 behind on the final day, but Alison Hodgkinson saved them with a four-hour 95.

Player of the Match: S. C. Taylor.

Close of play: First day, South Africa 213-5 (Logtenberg 70, van der Merwe 0); Second day, England 209-3 (S. C. Taylor 89, Greenway 21); Third day, South Africa 18-0 (Cowan 3, Barnard 13).

South Africa

Batter	First innings		Second innings	
C. S. Cowan	c Smit b Wardlaw	6	c Wardlaw b Pearson	23
J. Barnard	lbw b Connor	22	c Greenway b Edwards	13
†M. Terblanche	c Guha b Wardlaw	4	lbw b Edwards	12
*A. L. Hodgkinson	lbw b Pearson	21	c Greenway b Birch	95
J. Logtenberg	c Connor b Pearson	74	lbw b Pearson	0
C. van der Westhuizen	c Greenway b Wardlaw	83	c Edwards b Birch	25
Y. van der Merwe	c Edwards b Guha	1	not out	52
C-Z. Brits	run out	32	c Smit b Wardlaw	11
S. S. D. van Zyl	b Pearson	37	lbw b Birch	18
A. E. Smith	lbw b Birch	20	not out	10
L. Z. Jacobs	not out	3		
	B 5, l-b 3, w 1, n-b 4	13	B 7, l-b 15, w 1, n-b 3	26
	1/20 (1) 2/24 (3) 3/57 (4) 4/57 (2) 5/195 (6) 6/218 (5) 7/218 (7) 8/277 (8) 9/292 (9) 10/316 (10)	316	1/22 (2) 2/36 (3) 3/86 (1) 4/86 (5) 5/137 (6) 6/214 (4) 7/235 (8) 8/264 (9)	(8 wkts dec.) 285

Bowling: *First Innings*—Pearson 36–12–83–3; Guha 21–13–28–1; Wardlaw 32–10–53–3; Spragg 19–5–60–0; Connor 25–14–26–1; Newton 11–3–35–0; Birch 9.2–2–23–1. *Second Innings*—Pearson 22–10–36–2; Guha 4–3–4–0; Wardlaw 36–14–60–1; Newton 5–2–15–0; Edwards 26–6–81–2; Connor 6–4–10–0; Birch 22–4–57–3.

England

C. M. Edwards c Terblanche b Brits	18	H. Wardlaw b van der Westhuizen	36
L. K. Newton lbw b Smith	7	L. Spragg c van der Merwe b Barnard	2
S. C. Taylor b Logtenberg	177	I. T. Guha run out	15
*C. J. Connor c Terblanche b Brits	61	B 6, l-b 15, w 11, n-b 2	34
L. Greenway b Jacobs	70		—
R. A. Birch run out	18	1/19 (1) 2/34 (2) 3/137 (4) 4/340 (5)	497
†J. Smit not out	56	5/358 (3) 6/385 (6) 7/397 (8)	
L. C. Pearson c Cowan b Jacobs	3	8/453 (9) 9/456 (10) 10/497 (11)	

Bowling: Brits 18–2–68–2; Smith 13–2–37–1; van Zyl 13–4–47–0; van der Merwe 23–5–74–0; Jacobs 26–2–106–2; van der Westhuizen 25–5–67–1; Logtenberg 17–2–47–1; Barnard 4.5–0–30–1.

Umpires: L. E. Elgar and P. J. Hartley.

At Chelmsford, August 13 (day/night). **First one-day international: England won by 175 runs.** Toss: England. **England 273-8** (50 overs) (C. M. Edwards 64, S. C. Taylor 51; S. A. Fritz 4-36); **South Africa 98** (34.5 overs) (M. Terblanche 51).

One-day international debuts: R. A. Birch, L. Greenway; S. A. Fritz, J. Logtenberg, A. E. Smith, C. S. Terblanche, C. van der Westhuizen.

This was the first floodlit women's international in England.

At Bristol, August 16. **Second one-day international: South Africa won by 11 runs.** Toss: South Africa. **South Africa 210-6** (50 overs) (J. Logtenberg 61, M. Terblanche 79); **England 199** (47.4 overs) (L. K. Newton 68).

One-day international debut: A. P. C. Kilowan.

Johmari Logtenberg (aged 14) and Daleen Terblanche (aged 33) added 136 for the second wicket, a South African record.

At Cardiff, August 17. **Third one-day international: England won by nine wickets.** Toss: South Africa. **South Africa 147** (50 overs) (A. L. Hodgkinson 52*; R. A. Birch 4-22); **England 148-1** (34.4 overs) (L. K. Newton 77*).

England won the series 2–1. Laura Newton, the leading scorer with 172 runs, was named Player of the Series.

ENGLAND v SOUTH AFRICA

Second Test Match

At Taunton, August 20, 21, 22. England won by an innings and 96 runs. Toss: South Africa. Test debut: N. Ndzundzu.

England, fresh from their one-day series victory, followed up by taking the Test series 1–0, ramming home their advantage against the tired and increasingly dispirited tourists. It was their first Test win since they beat India by two runs at Jamshedpur in November 1995 – only Jane Smit survived from that side – and their first on home soil since 1979, when they defeated West Indies. Lucy Pearson and off-spinner Helen Wardlaw dismissed South Africa by the first afternoon, and England were already 59 ahead by the close. Claire Taylor went on to a second successive century, with 23 fours, and shared another big fourth-wicket stand, this time 164, with Greenway; a maiden fifty from Rosalie Birch steered England past 400 again. Needing 325 to avoid an innings defeat, South Africa were overwhelmed. Clare Taylor (not to be confused with her batting namesake, Claire) took three wickets for just five runs in 13 overs. Brits scored a lively 61, but the moment of victory was an anticlimax, as Nolubabalo Ndzundzu limped off with over four sessions to spare.

Player of the Match: S. C. Taylor. *Player of the Series:* S. C. Taylor.

Close of play: First day, England 189-3 (S. C. Taylor 78, Greenway 37); Second day, South Africa 67-3 (Logtenberg 18, Hodgkinson 2).

South Africa

First innings		Second innings	
J. Barnard c Smit b Guha	3	(2) c Birch b Guha	5
J. Logtenberg c Wardlaw b Pearson	4	(4) lbw b C. E. Taylor	18
†M. Terblanche c Connor b Birch	41	lbw b Birch	19
*A. L. Hodgkinson lbw b Newton	1	(5) lbw b Edwards	37
C. van der Westhuizen c Newton b Pearson	29	(6) lbw b Edwards	22
C. S. Cowan b Wardlaw	11	(1) c Newton b C. E. Taylor	14
Y. van der Merwe c Edwards b Pearson	1	c S. C. Taylor b Birch	22
C-Z. Brits lbw b Pearson	0	c Guha b C. E. Taylor	61
A. E. Smith not out	24	c S. C. Taylor b Guha	11
N. Ndzundzu c C. E. Taylor b Wardlaw	8	retired hurt	0
L. Z. Jacobs c S. C. Taylor b Wardlaw	0	not out	1
L-b 4, w 4	8	B 10, l-b 7, w 2	19
1/7 (1) 2/22 (2) 3/33 (4) 4/66 (3) 5/95 (5) 6/97 (6) 7/97 (7) 8/97 (8) 9/130 (10) 10/130 (11)	130	1/19 (2) 2/28 (1) 3/59 (3) 4/73 (4) 5/120 (6) 6/133 (5) 7/182 (7) 8/220 (8) 9/224 (9)	229

In the second innings Ndzundzu retired hurt at 229.

Bowling: *First Innings*—Pearson 16–11–25–4; Guha 6–2–19–1; Newton 5–2–8–1; C. E. Taylor 5–1–15–0; Wardlaw 13.3–3–35–3; Birch 5–0–18–1; Edwards 1–0–6–0. *Second Innings*—Pearson 8–3–13–0; Guha 9.5–4–14–2; Wardlaw 22–6–59–0; C. E. Taylor 13–11–5–3; Birch 19–5–51–2; Edwards 15–2–54–2; Connor 8–4–16–0.

England

C. M. Edwards lbw b van der Merwe	37
L. K. Newton c and b Brits	5
S. C. Taylor c Hodgkinson b van der Westhuizen	131
*C. J. Connor c Hodgkinson b Jacobs	24
L. Greenway c Barnard b Jacobs	66
R. A. Birch c Terblanche b van der Westhuizen	62
†J. Smit lbw b Brits	33
H. Wardlaw c Hodgkinson b van der Merwe	16
C. E. Taylor c sub (C. S. Terblanche) b Barnard	43
I. T. Guha lbw b Barnard	0
L. C. Pearson not out	18
B 3, l-b 8, w 6, n-b 3	20
1/40 (2) 2/60 (1) 3/107 (4) 4/271 (5) 5/275 (3) 6/329 (7) 7/366 (8) 8/421 (6) 9/424 (10) 10/455 (9)	455

Bowling: Brits 31–5–96–2; Smith 17–2–81–0; van der Merwe 21–5–81–2; Jacobs 20–2–72–2; Ndzundzu 6–1–24–0; Logtenberg 4–1–16–0; van der Westhuizen 15–2–49–2; Barnard 6.3–0–25–2.

Umpires: M. R. Benson and G. D. Cooper.

ENGLISH WOMEN'S CRICKET, 2003

Like their male counterparts, Sussex's women won the County Championship for the first time in 2003. It could not have been closer: when Sussex, led by England captain Clare Connor, lost to Surrey on Duckworth/Lewis in the final round of a rain-affected tournament in Cambridge, they were left just half a point ahead of Nottinghamshire.

Defending champions Yorkshire, who had won in 11 of the past 12 seasons, unexpectedly found themselves in a relegation struggle. In the last game, they had to beat Berkshire – runners-up a year earlier – to survive, and duly did. Berkshire were replaced by Division Two champions Lancashire, while Durham won promotion from Division Three. But there was to be a change of format in 2004: Division Three was disbanded, and its teams, plus relegated Hertfordshire and the Emerging Counties entries, were to contest a County Challenge Cup on a regional basis over the season. The winner would be promoted to the 2005 County Championship.

For the first time, the county champions earned the right to play the international tourists the following day. Sussex beat the South Africans too, courtesy of Connor's all-round form: an unbeaten 97 plus four wickets. After leading England to triumph in the one-day and Test series, she rounded off a golden season when she captained the victorious Brighton & Hove club in the National League final. Yorkshire did retain their Under-19 title, with Sussex becoming Under-17 champions and Warwickshire winning the Under-15 competition.

There were still worries. Richard Bates, the former Nottinghamshire off-spinner appointed England's first full-time coach in June, was one of those expressing concern over pitches at the County Championship. As rain intervened again, batting sometimes became a lottery; covers must surely be a basic requirement for a competition of this status.

The Super Fours in June had also suffered from the weather. The first round was washed out and, with no spare dates available, only five were played. This tournament was established in 2002, and aimed to raise standards by assembling the country's best players to compete against each other. Allowing for a few changes of personnel, the four teams retained their membership from the previous season, when Connor's Braves were champions, but this was one title she missed in 2003. The Knight Riders, led by Charlotte Edwards, fought off a strong challenge from the Super Strikers, captained by Claire Taylor, who lost to her namesake Clare Taylor's V Team in a last-round upset. For the second year running, Edwards scored most runs – 199 at 49 – while her team-mate Lucy Pearson was the leading bowler, with ten wickets.

A large crowd enjoyed a charity match at Lord's Nursery Ground marking the tenth anniversary of England's World Cup victory: the team of 1993 lost to their 2003 successors. But an otherwise outstanding English season was marred when Surrey club Wallington, home to a host of international players down the years, decided to fold for lack of numbers.

Note: Matches in this section were not first-class.

FRIZZELL COUNTY CHAMPIONSHIP, 2003

Division One	*Played*	*Won*	*Lost*	*No result*	*Points*
Sussex	5	4	1	0	86.5
Nottinghamshire	5	4	1	0	86
Kent	5	3	2	0	68.5
Yorkshire	5	2	3	0	58.5
Surrey	5	2	3	0	54.5
Berkshire	5	0	5	0	32

Division Two	*Played*	*Won*	*Lost*	*No result*	*Points*
Lancashire	5	4	0	1	93
Middlesex	5	4	1	0	86.5
Staffordshire	5	3	1	1	74.5
Somerset	5	2	3	0	56.5
Hampshire	5	1	4	0	38
Hertfordshire	5	0	5	0	19.5

Division Three	*Played*	*Won*	*Lost*	*No result*	*Points*
Durham	5	3	1	1	82.5
Derbyshire	5	3	1	1	80.5
Warwickshire	5	3	1	1	74
Cheshire	5	2	2	1	66
Essex	5	0	3	2	42
Northamptonshire	5	1	4	0	33.5

Berkshire and Hertfordshire were relegated from their respective divisions; Lancashire and Durham were promoted. Division Three was to be replaced in 2004 by a County Challenge Cup.

SUPER FOURS, 2003

	Played	*Won*	*Lost*
Knight Riders	5	4	1
Super Strikers	5	3	2
Braves	5	2	3
V Team	5	1	4

ECB NATIONAL KNOCKOUT FINAL, 2003

At Aldershot, September 6. **Wakefield won by 124 runs.** Toss: Reading Ridgeway. **Wakefield 187-9** (40 overs) (C. M. J. Atkins 52); **Reading Ridgeway 63** (27.5 overs) (C. E. Taylor 4-26).

ECB NATIONAL LEAGUE FINAL, 2003

At Slough, September 7. **Brighton & Hove won by 97 runs.** Toss: Brighton & Hove. **Brighton & Hove 200** (49.5 overs) (M. C. Godliman 60, S. Price 59; D. Holden 4-40); **Thrumpton 103-8** (50 overs).

IWCC TROPHY, 2003

Ireland and West Indies qualified to compete in the 2005 World Cup in South Africa, as the two leading teams in the International Women's Cricket Council Trophy in July. They will join the top six from the last competition – holders New Zealand, Australia, India, South Africa, England and Sri Lanka – when the event is staged in February and March next year.

The host nation, Holland, had appeared in the previous four World Cups, and possessed a powerful batting line-up headed by Pauline te Beest, who scored 317 runs, more than twice as many as anyone else. But they missed out after a surprise seven-wicket defeat by West Indies in their second game. Ireland won all their five matches, thanks to a strong attack led by seamer Barbara McDonald and off-spinner Catherine O'Neill, who took 11 wickets apiece. Japan's international debut produced five heavy defeats; Sajjida Shah, Pakistan's 15-year-old off-spinner, claimed seven Japanese wickets for four runs, the best figures in women's one-day internationals.

Ireland 10 pts, West Indies 8 pts, Holland 6 pts, Pakistan 4 pts, Scotland 2 pts, Japan 0 pts.

Opposite: Watching from on high.
Test cricket at Kandy during England's
tour of Sri Lanka, 2003-04
Picture by Tom Shaw, Getty Images.

PART SIX

Overseas Cricket

FEATURES OF 2002-03 AND 2003

Double-Hundreds (41)

301*†	P. G. Fulton	Canterbury v Auckland at Christchurch.
290	H. H. Kanitkar	Maharashtra v Bihar at Jamadoba.
274*	S. P. Fleming	New Zealand v Sri Lanka (First Test) at Colombo.
267	S. Sriram	Tamil Nadu v Punjab at Mohali.
250	J. L. Langer	Australia v England (Fourth Test) at Melbourne.
250‡	M. L. Love	Queensland v England XI at Brisbane.
247	M. H. Parmar	Gujarat v Assam at Ahmedabad.
240	Yashpal Singh	Services v Tripura at Delhi.
237*	B. M. Rowland	Karnataka v Jammu and Kashmir at Bangalore.
237	A. R. Khurasiya	Madhya Pradesh v Maharashtra at Indore.
234*	J. D. C. Bryant	Eastern Province v North West at Potchefstroom.
233*	G. Gambhir	Delhi v Railways at Delhi.
230*	P. Dharmani	Punjab v Gujarat at Ahmedabad.
228*	C. N. Evans	Mashonaland v Manicaland at Mutare.
228‡	H. H. Gibbs	South Africa v Pakistan (Second Test) at Cape Town.
224	C. T. Perren	Queensland v South Australia at Brisbane.
223	A. Kanhai	West Indies B v Trinidad & Tobago at Couva.
222*	J. A. Rudolph	South Africa v Bangladesh (First Test) at Chittagong.
222	S. Somasunder	Kerala v Tripura at Kochi.
220*	W. M. B. Perera	Moors v Colombo at Colombo.
220	L. A. Roberts	Trinidad & Tobago v West Indies B at Couva.
219*	S. V. Carlisle	Mashonaland v Manicaland at Harare.
216	M. P. Mott	Victoria v New South Wales at Melbourne.
212	G. M. Ewing	Matabeleland v Midlands at Kwekwe.
211	S. R. Waugh	New South Wales v Victoria at Melbourne.
210†	A. T. Rayudu	Hyderabad v Andhra at Secunderabad.
209*	Rizwan Aslam	Lahore Whites v Gujranwala at Lahore.
209	B. C. Lara	West Indies v Sri Lanka (First Test) at Gros Islet, St Lucia.
207*	D. P. Viljoen	Midlands v Manicaland at Mutare.
207	Yasir Hameed	PIA v KRL at Karachi.
206	R. T. Ponting	Australia v West Indies (Second Test) at Port-of-Spain.
204†	R. W. Sims	Manicaland v Matabeleland at Bulawayo.
204	M. J. Slater	New South Wales v Western Australia at Perth.
203*	A. Gupta	Jammu and Kashmir v Bihar at Jamshedpur.
203‡	H. H. Gibbs	Western Province v KwaZulu-Natal at Durban.
201*	M. G. Bevan	New South Wales v Tasmania at Sydney.
201*	M. N. Hart	Northern Districts v Auckland at Auckland.
201*‡	M. L. Love	Australia A v England XI at Hobart.
201*	W. A. D. A. P. Perera	Chilaw Marians v Police at Colombo.
200	Hasanuzzaman	Khulna v Chittagong at Dhaka.
200	G. C. Smith	South Africa v Bangladesh (First Test) at East London.

† *Maiden first-class hundred.*
‡ *Gibbs and Love both scored two double-hundreds.*

Hundred on First-Class Debut

106	E. T. Nkwe	Gauteng v Easterns at Johannesburg.
100*	L. Pawar	Gujarat v Assam at Ahmedabad.
115	S. S. Salaria	Jammu and Kashmir v Bihar at Jamshedpur.
102	Sukhbinder Singh	Orissa v Uttar Pradesh at Lucknow.

Three Hundreds in Successive Innings

Misbah-ul-Haq (KRL)	101*	v ZTBL at Rawalpindi;
	144	v Karachi Blues at Rawalpindi;
	110	v Rawalpindi at Rawalpindi.
Yasir Hameed (PIA and Pakistan) . . .	108	v Rawalpindi at Karachi;
	207	v KRL at Karachi;
	170 } 105 }	v Bangladesh (First Test) at Karachi.

Hundred in Each Innings of a Match

J. L. Arnberger	172*	102*	Victoria v Tasmania at Melbourne.
M. L. Hayden	197	103	Australia v England (First Test) at Brisbane.
J. M. Henderson	122	110*	North West v Gauteng at Potchefstroom.
G. J. Hopkins	113	175*	Canterbury v Auckland at Auckland.
A. V. Kale	108	104*	Maharashtra v Haryana at Rohtak.
G. F. J. Liebenberg . .	115	110*	Free State v KwaZulu-Natal at Bloemfontein.
A. T. Rayudu	210	159*	Hyderabad v Andhra at Secunderabad.
Yasir Hameed	170	105	Pakistan v Bangladesh (First Test) at Karachi.

Carrying Bat through Completed Innings

Babar Naeem	91*	Rawalpindi (133) v ZTBL at Rawalpindi.
H. M. P. Fernando . .	102*	Moratuwa (172) v Air Force at Katunayake.
I. H. Jan	42*	Carib Beer XI (132) v Australians at Georgetown.
Mohammad Ramzan .	110*	KRL (267) v National Bank at Karachi.
P. H. D. Premadasa . .	106*	Ragama (304) v Kandy at Katunayake.
B. H. Tucker	182*	Griqualand West (369) v Boland at Kimberley.
Zeeshan Mohsin	64*	Peshawar (144) v PIA at Peshawar.

Hundred before Lunch

Inzamam-ul-Haq	103*	Pakistan v Zimbabwe (First Test) at Harare (3rd day).
D. P. Viljoen . . .	57* to 178*	Midlands v Manicaland at Mutare (3rd day).

Hundred by No. 11 Batsman

C. Macmillan	109	Midlands v Manicaland at Mutare.

Long Innings

Mins		
653	S. P. Fleming (274*)	New Zealand v Sri Lanka (First Test) at Colombo.
636	B. M. Rowland (237*) . . .	Karnataka v Jammu and Kashmir at Bangalore.
624	Z. de Bruyn (169)	Easterns v Western Province at Benoni.
613	G. Gambhir (233*)	Delhi v Railways at Delhi.
608	M. P. Mott (216)	Victoria v New South Wales at Melbourne.

An Hour without Scoring a Run

Mins		
96	D. J. Watson (129)	KwaZulu-Natal v Boland at Durban (on 0*).
88	B. A. Nash (34)	Queensland v Tasmania at Hobart (on 0*).
69	Aqeel Abbas (0*)	Bahawalpur v Dadu at Bahawalpur (on 0*).

Unusual Dismissal

Timed Out

V. C. Drakes . . . . Border v Free State at East London.

The second instance in first-class cricket.

First-Wicket Partnership of 100 in Each Innings

106	174	J. A. Rudolph/A. N. Petersen, Northerns v North West at Centurion.

Highest Partnerships

First Wicket

368 G. C. Smith/H. H. Gibbs, South Africa v Pakistan (Second Test) at Cape Town.
314† N. R. Ferreira/R. W. Sims, Manicaland v Matabeleland at Bulawayo.
263 G. J. Mail/M. J. Slater, New South Wales v Western Australia at Perth.
260 R. A. Lawson/Mohammad Wasim, Otago v Northern Districts at Dunedin.

Second Wicket

441† C. C. Bradfield/J. D. C. Bryant, Eastern Province v North West at Potchefstroom.
274 M. E. K. Hussey/S. M. Katich, Australia A v South Africa A at Perth.
272 G. C. Smith/G. Kirsten, South Africa v Bangladesh (First Test) at East London.
272 M. L. Hayden/R. T. Ponting, Australia v England (First Test) at Brisbane.
260 B. A. Johnson/G. S. Blewett, South Australia v Victoria at Adelaide.
253 G. Kirsten/A. G. Prince, Western Province v Boland at Bellville.

Third Wicket

429*† J. A. Rudolph/H. H. Dippenaar, South Africa v Bangladesh (First Test) at Chittagong.
336 G. Gambhir/M. Manhas, Delhi v Railways at Delhi.
315 R. T. Ponting/D. S. Lehmann, Australia v West Indies (Second Test) at Port-of-Spain.
279 H. H. Kanitkar/A. V. Kale, Maharashtra v Bihar at Jamadoba.
256 H. H. Dippenaar/N. D. McKenzie, South Africa A v Sri Lankans at Kimberley.
279 were added by W. A. D. A. P. Perera, C. S. Fernando, K. H. R. K. Fernando and R. S. A. Palliyaguruge, Chilaw Marians v Police at Colombo; Perera retired hurt after 191 runs were added and C. S. Fernando also retired hurt after a further 77 runs.

Fourth Wicket

369 C. J. L. Rogers/M. J. North, Western Australia v New South Wales at Perth.
284 D. D. Ebrahim/C. N. Evans, Mashonaland v Manicaland at Mutare.
281* B. M. Rowland/V. S. T. Naidu, Karnataka v Jammu and Kashmir at Bangalore.
272 G. W. Flower/A. Flower, Mashonaland v Matabeleland at Harare.
250 D. S. Lehmann/S. R. Waugh, Australia v Bangladesh (Second Test) at Cairns.

Fifth Wicket

245 Raja Ali/Abhay Sharma, Railways v Andhra at Vijayawada.
235* G. P. Sulzberger/J. D. Ryder, Central Districts v Canterbury at Napier.
228 H. H. Kanitkar/R. D. Khirid, Maharashtra v Bihar at Jamadoba.
228 D. J. Gandhi/Y. Venugopal Rao, Elite Group A v Plate Group B at Bangalore.
226* C. N. Evans/T. Taibu, Mashonaland v Manicaland at Mutare.

Seventh Wicket

228 Afsar Nawaz/Riaz Sheikh, PWD v Multan at Multan.
227 Asif Hussain/Farooq Iqbal, Faisalabad v Service Industries at Faisalabad.
222* N. Deonarine/C. S. Baugh, Carib Beer XI v Australians at Georgetown.

Eighth Wicket

268† S. Sriram/M. R. Srinivas, Tamil Nadu v Punjab at Mohali.
222 M. C. Miller/B. E. Young, South Australia v Queensland at Adelaide.
204 D. A. Chougule/D. Ganesh, Karnataka v Vidarbha at Nagpur.
155 Umair Hasan/Ahmed Hayat, Sargodha v Service Industries at Sargodha.

Ninth Wicket

198*† V. Nagamootoo/R. L. Griffith, Guyana v West Indies B at Christiansted.
168 S. Narwal/D. Phagna, Haryana v Bihar at Gurgaon.

Tenth Wicket

144† D. P. Viljoen/C. Macmillan, Midlands v Manicaland at Kwekwe.
102 Usman Arshad/Jibran Khan, Sargodha v Lahore Whites at Peshawar.
101 R. B. Elahi/R. Mishra, Uttar Pradesh v Baroda at Varanasi.

† *National record.*

Eight Wickets in an Innings (12)

9-29	F. Shaikh	Goa v Services at Delhi.
9-111	C. R. B. Mudalige	Colombo v Panadura at Panadura.
8-43	M. V. Sane	Maharashtra v Jammu and Kashmir at Pune.
8-46	B. C. N. Amarasinghe	Moratuwa v Antonians at Katunayake.
8-59	J. E. Taylor	Jamaica v Trinidad & Tobago at Port-of-Spain.
8-64	N. O. Perry	Jamaica v Windward Islands at Kingston.
8-78	R. W. Price	Midlands v Matabeleland at Bulawayo.
8-86	Arshad Khan	Allied Bank v Bahawalpur at Bahawalpur.
8-101	I. J. Harvey	Australia A v South Africa A at Adelaide.
8-111	F. Shaikh	Goa v Vidarbha at Nagpur.
8-112	A. W. Ekanayake	Kurunegala Youth v Kandy at Kurunegala.
8-180	Sarandeep Singh	Elite Group A v Plate Group B at Bangalore.

Twelve Wickets in a Match (7)

15-111	Arshad Khan	Allied Bank v Bahawalpur at Bahawalpur.
13-79	B. C. N. Amarasinghe	Moratuwa v Antonians at Katunayake.
12-89	D. Ganesh	Karnataka v Haryana at Faridabad.
12-89	Kamran Hussain	Bahawalpur v PWD at Bahawalpur.
12-133	N. O. Perry	Jamaica v Windward Islands at Kingston.
12-137	S. B. Joshi	Karnataka v Kerala at Bangalore.
12-200	N. D. Hirwani	Plate Group B v Plate Group A at Bangalore.

Hat-Tricks (7)

Alok Kapali	Bangladesh v Pakistan (Second Test) at Peshawar.
Gagandeep Singh	Punjab v Uttar Pradesh at Mohali.
S. M. Harwood	Victoria v Tasmania at Melbourne (*on first-class debut*).
C. M. Hathurusinghe	Moratuwa v Kandy at Moratuwa.
Kashif Raza	WAPDA v Sargodha at Sargodha.
J. J. C. Lawson	West Indies v Australia (Third Test) at Bridgetown (*across two innings*).
K. R. Pushpakumara	Nondescripts v Panadura at Colombo (*the first three balls of the match*).

Outstanding Spell of Bowling

Wkts/Balls		
6 in 15	J. J. C. Lawson	West Indies v Bangladesh (First Test) at Dhaka.

Six Wicket-Keeping Dismissals in an Innings

7 ct.	Wasim Ahmed	Dadu v PWD at Karachi.
6 ct.	T. R. Arasu	Goa v Saurashtra at Rajkot.
6 ct.	W. Bossenger	Griqualand West v Western Province at Kimberley.
6 ct.	V. Dahiya	Delhi v Rajasthan at Jaipur.
6 ct.	T. M. Dilshan	Bloomfield v Panadura at Colombo.
6 ct.	C. S. Fernando	Sri Lanka A v BCCSL Club XI at Colombo.
6 ct.	D. Jennings	Easterns v Eastern Province at Port Elizabeth.
6 ct.	Mohammad Fazil	Multan v Allied Bank at Multan.
5 ct, 1 st	Mohammad Fazil	Multan v PWD at Multan.
6 ct.	S. J. Palframan	Boland v Border at Paarl.
6 ct.	T. Taibu	Mashonaland v Midlands at Harare.
6 ct.	Tasawwar Hussain	Rawalpindi v KRL at Rawalpindi.
6 ct.	R. A. Young	Auckland v Wellington at Wellington.

Nine Wicket-Keeping Dismissals in a Match

11 ct†	Wasim Ahmed	Dadu v PWD at Karachi.
9 ct.	D. S. Berry	Victoria v Tasmania at Hobart.
9 ct.	T. M. Dilshan	Bloomfield v Panadura at Colombo.
9 ct.	C. S. Fernando	Sri Lanka A v BCCSL Club XI at Colombo.
9 ct.	P. A. Patel	Elite Group C v Plate Group A at Secunderabad.

† *Equalled national record.*

Five Catches in an Innings in the Field

S. Jayantha	Bloomfield v Galle at Galle.

Six Catches in a Match in the Field

U. L. K. D. Fernando	Sebastianites v Ragama at Moratuwa.

No Byes Conceded in Total of 500 or More

S. G. Clingeleffer	Tasmania v South Australia (500-6 dec.) at Adelaide.
J. S. Foster	England v Australia (551-6 dec.) (Fourth Test) at Melbourne.
Khaled Masud	Bangladesh v West Indies (536) (First Test) at Dhaka.
Khaled Masud	Bangladesh v Australia (556-4 dec.) (Second Test) at Cairns.
M. S. K. Prasad	Andhra v Railways (505-7 dec.) at Vijayawada.

Highest Innings Totals

715-8 dec.†	Midlands v Manicaland at Mutare.
653-6 dec.	Maharashtra v Bihar at Jamadoba.
650-8 dec.	Manicaland v Matabeleland at Bulawayo.
640-4 dec.	Mashonaland v Manicaland at Mutare.
620-7 dec.	South Africa v Pakistan (Second Test) at Cape Town.
607-9 dec.	Karnataka v Vidarbha at Nagpur.
606-4	West Indians v Indian Board President's XI at Bangalore.
605-9 dec.	Australia v West Indies (Third Test) at Bridgetown.
600-8 dec.	Allied Bank v Dadu at Karachi.

† *National record.*

Lowest Innings Totals

53	Pakistan v Australia (Second Test) at Sharjah (2nd innings) (*One batsman retired hurt*).
57	Pakistan A v Sri Lanka A at Multan.
58	Nondescripts v Galle at Colombo (1st innings).
59	Pakistan v Australia (Second Test) at Sharjah (1st innings).
62	Tamil Union v Sinhalese at Colombo.
62	Colts v Bloomfield at Colombo.
66	Dadu v PWD at Karachi.
68	Madhya Pradesh v Haryana at Rohtak.
73	Dadu v Allied Bank at Karachi.
73	Nondescripts v Galle at Colombo (2nd innings).

Highest Fourth-Innings Totals

418-7 . . . . . . West Indies v Australia (Fourth Test) at St John's (set 418).
402-6 . . . . . . Carib Beer XI v Australians at Georgetown (set 442).

Match Aggregate of 1,500 Runs

1,567-35 . . . . Manicaland (650-8 dec. and 134-7) v Matabeleland (432 and 351) at Bulawayo.
1,510-27 . . . . Australia (576-4 dec. and 238-3 dec.) v West Indies (408 and 288) (Second Test) at Port-of-Spain.
1,504-28 . . . . Manicaland (381 and 369) v Midlands (715-8 dec. and 39-0) at Mutare.

Large Margin of Victory

Karnataka (364 and 607-9 dec.) beat Vidarbha (236 and 270) at Nagpur by 465 runs.
Allied Bank (600-8 dec.) beat Dadu (102 and 73) at Karachi by an innings and 425 runs.

Most Extras in an Innings

	b	*l-b*	*w*	*n-b*	
73	28	11	5	29	Sargodha (374) v Service Industries at Sargodha.
63	5	6	5	47	West Indies B (388) v India A at Bridgetown.
62	16	10	5	31	South Africa (386) v Sri Lanka (First Test) at Johannesburg.
60	11	6	2	41	PIA (395) v Rawalpindi at Rawalpindi.

Career Aggregate Milestones

15,000 runs . . . . G. S. Blewett, D. J. Cullinan, S. P. Fleming, G. Kirsten, Sajid Ali.
10,000 runs . . . . S. Chanderpaul, M. E. K. Hussey, M. L. Love.
500 wickets . . . . A. W. Ekanayake, S. M. Pollock.

PETER SMITH MEMORIAL AWARD, 2003

The Peter Smith Memorial Award, awarded by the Cricket Writers' Club in memory of its former chairman for services to the presentation of cricket to the public, was won in 2003 by Andy Flower and Henry Olonga. The award was instituted in 1992. Previous winners were David Gower, John Woodcock, Brian Lara, Mark Taylor, the Sri Lankan 1996 World Cup squad, Dickie Bird, Angus Fraser, Courtney Walsh and Jack Russell. There was no award in 2001.

THE 2003 WORLD CUP

REVIEW BY SIMON WILDE

The hosts of the eighth World Cup wanted it to be the greatest yet. In financial terms, it was – profits of $US194m represented a huge increase on the $51m made in 1999 – but in other respects, it fell short. Indeed, this traditional organisers' boast rather came back to haunt the South Africans, who headed a pan-African triumvirate also including Zimbabwe and Kenya. A great tournament needs dramatic tension, and the brilliance of the Australians never allowed it. In winning all their 11 matches, the champions repeatedly displayed talent, audacity – and a superiority over all rivals. Not since West Indies ran away with the prize in 1979 (like Australia, to retain the trophy they had won four years earlier) had anyone won the World Cup with such élan.

The nearest Ricky Ponting's side came to losing was in their final group match, at Port Elizabeth, when England had them 135 for eight needing 205. Doing no more than was necessary to keep up with an asking-rate that only once crept above six an over, Michael Bevan and Andy Bichel saw them home with breathtaking coolness. Ponting was outspokenly critical of the St George's Park square, and no wonder: its slow surface hinted at one way the gap between Australia and the others might be narrowed and, as Ponting feared, the favourites again hit trouble in two subsequent games on the ground. Even so, they still ran out decisive winners in both, against New Zealand in the Super Six and Sri Lanka in the semi-final.

On true surfaces – and these were in the majority – Australia were unstoppable. Runs poured from their bats while disciplined bowling drew opposing batsmen to their ruin; out of a possible 110 wickets, Australia claimed 101. Never was this truer than in the final at the Wanderers, one of the most bountiful grounds for batsmen. With the two strongest batting sides on show, including the player of the tournament, Sachin Tendulkar, there were high hopes of a taut, run-filled finale. But Australia, surprisingly put in by Sourav Ganguly in a move that betrayed Indian nerves, ran up too many runs. Ponting himself led the way with an unbeaten 140 from 121 balls that was a masterpiece in measured ferocity: off his last 47 balls he hit eight sixes and 90 runs in all. This was a record individual score for a World Cup final, as was Australia's team effort of 359 for two. Tendulkar fell in the first over of the reply and India, though they hit spiritedly, were never in the game.

Ganguly's side nevertheless emerged from the tournament in credit. Not fancied to do well in the conditions, they steadily grew in confidence after a shaky batting performance in their opener with Holland and put together a winning streak of eight matches – including one in their first meeting with Pakistan for almost three years – with some of the most entertaining cricket on show. An eleventh-hour decision to restore Tendulkar to the opener's role

A firm grasp: the World Cup stays with Australia, easily the most potent force in international cricket.

Picture by Patrick Eagar.

he favoured proved inspired. He ran up a record run aggregate of 673, more than 200 ahead of his nearest challengers – his own captain, Ganguly, and Australia's captain, Ponting.

Australia would have beaten a Rest of the World XI had they been asked. They swatted away difficulties like troublesome flies. Predictions that the middle order was suspect, and that they would regret selecting Andrew Symonds ahead of Steve Waugh, proved unfounded. As well as a crucial innings in the semi-final, Symonds played the innings of his life – an unbeaten 143 off 125 balls – to carry his side from a precarious 86 for four to 310 in their opening encounter against Pakistan. It set up a resounding victory in a game that began with Australia at their most vulnerable.

Hours earlier, Shane Warne, their match-winner in the semi-final and final of 1999, had returned home after failing a drugs test taken during the VB Series in Australia the previous month. Warne's "A" sample – later confirmed by the "B" – showed he had taken two banned diuretics, hydrochlorothiazide and amiloride. Warne said he got them from his mum and took them out of vanity, wanting to lose weight before his return to the Australia side after injury. But diuretics can also mask steroids, which could have expedited Warne's swift recovery from a dislocated shoulder. A fortnight into the tournament, he was handed a one-year ban. It was the highest-profile drugs

THE TEAMS' WORLD CUP RECORDS

The leading teams' records in the eight World Cups held so far are:

	Winners	*Reached final*	*Reached semi-final*
Australia	3	5	5
West Indies	2	3	4
Pakistan	1	2	5
India	1	2	4
Sri Lanka	1	1	2
England	–	3	5
New Zealand	–	–	4
South Africa	–	–	2
Kenya	–	–	1

case to afflict cricket and sent shock waves through the game but, as with everything else, the Australians rode them well.

Then, before the second phase, Australia lost another key bowler when Jason Gillespie's right heel succumbed to tendon damage. Nathan Bracken became the second addition to the party (and the second Nathan, after Hauritz had replaced Warne), but Gillespie's place in the eleven had already gone to Bichel, an experienced and pugnacious character who never doubted his worth. No other attack could have coped with two such losses; Australia simply continued on their all-conquering way, Bichel's staunch contributions epitomising their supremacy better than anything else. He bowled his heart out to finish pretty much top of the averages and the economy ratings; played three vital innings and brilliantly ran out Aravinda de Silva in the semi-final. Australia may not have liked Port Elizabeth, but to their immense gratitude Bichel, wise to low seaming pitches after two seasons with Worcestershire, did.

If Bichel epitomised Australia's depth of resources, Brett Lee illustrated their brilliance. Despite being rested against the Dutch, Lee finished with 22 wickets in ten matches, second only to Chaminda Vaas, whose 23 – a record for any World Cup – included nine against Bangladesh and Canada. Beforehand, Lee was targeted by Shoaib Akhtar, the fastest bowler in 1999. "Lee is not a match-winner," he said. "Only when he starts winning matches will he be compared with me." But, although Shoaib won the race to break

Definite article or death threat? In Afrikaans, it means simply "The Aussies". In English, it means a jingoistic ad for local TV coverage.

Picture by David Gray, Reuters.

cricket's speed-barrier with a 100mph delivery against England, he was proved wrong.

Lee was a match-winner, time and again. Growing in confidence and stature as the event unfolded, he was devastating in the Super Six, claiming 11 wickets in three games before adding three more in the semi-final (bowling Marvan Atapattu with a delivery a fraction under 100mph) and two in the final. He probed everyone's resolve: Sri Lanka's was tested when Sanath Jayasuriya retired after being struck on thumb and forearm, as was Kenya's when he performed a second-over hat-trick. No wonder Ganguly put off facing Lee in the final by fielding first.

It is a tribute to Australia that the tournament will be remembered for their cricket rather than the off-field disputes that plagued it. These were rarely out of the headlines; indeed, the drawn-out schedule meant they were latched on to as talking points more lively than much of the cricket. There were really only two brief periods when the cricket held the stage. The first was towards the end of the pool matches, as teams fought for qualification and four enthralling games unfolded in as many days. The second was in the lead-up to the final, which to the relief of sponsors and television companies involved two high-profile teams. Prize money was much greater than before – Australia took $2m for winning the final – but there was a suspicion that the real financial winners were the lawyers, who were rarely out of action and, unlike the players, never succumbed to fatigue.

The run-up to the tournament was fraught with problems, with countries courting damages claims from the ICC for failing to fulfil contractual commitments. An intractable dispute between the Indian board and their players, over product endorsement, threatened their participation, while the issue of whether it was safe to play in Zimbabwe and Kenya – and whether it was morally right to do so in Zimbabwe, given the violent and repressive nature of President Robert Mugabe's regime – spilled over into the event itself.

The heat could have been taken out of these disputes had the ICC shown more imagination and willingness to compromise, but Mal Speed, overseeing his first World Cup as ICC chief executive, stuck to the disingenuous line that the ICC were concerned only with cricket-related issues, not politics. His background as a Melbourne lawyer seemingly made Speed wary of setting precedents that might unpick the delicate political tapestry of world cricket, not to mention a rich television deal with the Global Cricket Corporation that extended to the 2007 tournament. Overall, his was the least impressive performance by an Australian at the event.

In the end, India took part, with the ICC withholding their share of revenue until the contracts problem was resolved. However, the issue of safety and security was more complex. The ICC strove to convince doubtful participants that it was safe to play in Kenya, where there had been recent terrorist atrocities, and Zimbabwe, where economic and social conditions were seemingly deteriorating by the week. Inspection delegations, made up of senior ICC officials and board representatives from teams due to play there, were sent to both countries, and a security directorate was appointed to monitor the day-to-day situation. Kroll, an independent risk assessment firm, were called in to review procedure. It would have been logistically simpler and unarguably better for the tournament as a spectacle had the six matches scheduled for Zimbabwe and the two in Kenya been moved to South Africa, but the ICC feared it would set an awkward precedent and betray promises made years earlier.

In the event, New Zealand refused to play in Nairobi, and England in Harare. The ICC appeals committee predictably rejected their cases and awarded "victory" to the hosts – "results" that skewed the tournament off its axis. Had England gone to Harare and avoided defeat they, rather than Zimbabwe, would have reached the second phase. By winning four of the five pool matches they actually played, New Zealand reached the Super Six anyway, but the forfeiture enabled Kenya – the surprise package of the tournament and the second-most memorable participants – to go through at the expense of the improving West Indies and eventually qualify for the semi-finals.

New Zealand dealt with the crisis more smoothly than England. Their board decided against playing without consulting the players, whose response was to keep their prospects alive by unexpectedly routing South Africa. England's withdrawal was far more tortured. They had a noble record of fulfilling fixtures in political hotspots, but a vigorous public and media campaign proved too much for Tim Lamb, chief executive of the ECB. The turning point came when the players issued a statement through their

Vox pop: a South African supporter enjoys the latest controversial chapter in Shane Warne's career, while Indian fans during the game against Pakistan wrestle with weightier issues.

Pictures by Hamish Blair and Mike Hewitt, Getty Images.

high-profile representative, Richard Bevan, asking for the match to be relocated on "moral, political and contractual" grounds. Mindful that they would be liable if they sent their players into danger against their will, the ECB had little choice but to support their request.

Any appeal was likely to be expensively futile, but the process proved more damaging than anyone could have imagined. The day after England's first appeal failed on February 6, Patrick Ronan, head of the World Cup security directorate, personally assured players that Harare was safe: he dismissed a letter from a group calling itself the Sons and Daughters of Zimbabwe, which threatened to send England players "back to Britain in wooden coffins", as a hoax. This was undermined by evidence from an official from Kroll, Pete Richer. Asked to provide evidence that the letter was indeed a hoax, Ronan eventually produced an email which, when it arrived, only convinced Lamb and David Morgan, the ECB's chairman, that their concerns were indeed justified. England formally withdrew from the game. For some people, the ICC's integrity was now as much an issue as security, a point highlighted when Nasser Hussain, the England captain, rounded on Speed during a meeting in Cape Town and accused him of having let down his team. Speed later admitted the two forfeitures damaged the credibility of the cup. The ICC believed the ECB had completely mishandled the situation.

England and New Zealand both faced compensation claims for lost television and sponsorship revenue, with the ICC withholding \$3.5m from England's share of revenue and \$2.5m from New Zealand's, pending settlement of the cases. In England's case, this led directly to the ECB reducing their financial support for the domestic game – and the counties soon felt the draught.

The ICC's hope of keeping cricket and politics separate did not survive the second day of the tournament, when two prominent Zimbabwe players, Andy Flower and Henry Olonga, one white, the other black, took the field against Namibia in Harare wearing black armbands after issuing a statement "mourning the death of democracy in our beloved Zimbabwe". The ICC asked them to desist from making political gestures; Flower said he was not making a political statement but a humanitarian plea. For what turned out to be Zimbabwe's next match – against India nine days later, after England's game was abandoned – the pair wore black wristbands, Olonga in his capacity as twelfth man, having been dropped in what looked like retaliation. He was also expelled from his club, Takashinga CC.

As the tournament continued, it became plain Zimbabwe's team selection had become highly politicised, with preference given to those not critical of Mugabe's regime. Andy Pycroft, a selector, resigned after being told the team was "non-negotiable". Unsurprisingly, the team failed to ignite as a unit and it was no great surprise when they lost to Kenya. It was also clear Flower and Olonga's days as Zimbabwe players were numbered. For Flower, at 34, this was little hardship; indeed, he had already arranged to play for Essex and South Australia. But Olonga, eight years his junior, lost much more. Perhaps the most disturbing development concerned the South African board, which discarded Errol Stewart, a wicket-keeper (and trained lawyer) who had refused to tour Zimbabwe with their A team on moral grounds. So much for no politics in sport.

The ICC's prediction that Zimbabwe's home matches would be trouble-free looked equally awry. A human rights organisation, Solidarity Peace Trust, reported that in three matches in Bulawayo 80 protesters were arrested and detained in inhumane conditions for up to six days.

All this served to fracture the African dream of staging a glorious sporting spectacle in which an African team (presumably South Africa) emerged victors, so paving the way for the staging of an even bigger prize such as the football World Cup or Olympic Games. Africa was desperate to show itself a safe and attractive place for tourists, hence a lavish opening ceremony in Cape Town that came across as a glorified travel commercial.

Public expectations of a home victory were sky high long before South Africa's opening encounter with West Indies – graced by an accomplished hundred from Brian Lara – was lost by three runs. Allan Donald, the fast bowler who retired from international cricket after his team's early exit, said beforehand that the whole build-up was making the pressure unbearable.

The outcome for South Africa could hardly have been worse. Crippled by a shortage of back-up bowling and rumours of disharmony in the ranks, South Africa failed to beat any major opposition and went out – in the cruellest fashion – at the first hurdle. They were trounced by New Zealand in a rain-affected match in Johannesburg, and the elements also had a say in their do-or-die affair with Sri Lanka in Durban. With South Africa needing 269 under lights, the contest was on a knife-edge when rain, which had been falling for a while, became heavier. The dressing-room sent word to the batsmen, Mark Boucher and Lance Klusener, that the Duckworth/Lewis target at the end of the next over – the 45th – was 229, provided they lost no more wickets. Boucher achieved this by hitting the fifth ball from Muttiah Muralitharan for six and then blocking the last.

The umpires debated whether to carry on, but the rain was falling hard and the players came off – never, as it happened, to return. By now, the South Africans had realised their mistake: 229 would *tie* the match, as Duckworth/Lewis clearly stated. While a tie was fine for Sri Lanka, it wasn't for South Africa, who had to win. So, astonishingly, for the second World Cup in a row, South Africa went out on a cock-up and a tie, and with Klusener at the crease. As Andrew Hudson put it on TV: "42 million South Africans are going to go to bed tonight hoping it is a bad dream." But it wasn't, and the sacrificial sacking of Shaun Pollock as captain was only a matter of time.

HERE TODAY...

2003 World Cup captains and what became of them.

Australia	R. T. Ponting	in post, end 2003
Bangladesh	Khaled Masud	resigned, March
Canada	J. V. Harris	in post, end 2003
England	N. Hussain	resigned, March
Holland	R. P. Lefebvre	retired, March
India	S. C. Ganguly	in post, end 2003
Kenya	S. O. Tikolo	in post, end 2003
Namibia	D. B. Kotze	in post, end 2003
New Zealand	S. P. Fleming	in post, end 2003
Pakistan	Waqar Younis	sacked, March
South Africa	S. M. Pollock	sacked, March
Sri Lanka	S. T. Jayasuriya	resigned, April
West Indies	C. L. Hooper	sacked, March
Zimbabwe	H. H. Streak	in post, end 2003

In fact, an African team did make it to the semi-finals. Kenya, one of four non-Test nations, enjoyed the greatest giant-killing run in international cricket and survived for 40 of the competition's 43 days. However, had they played, and lost to, New Zealand they would not have made the second phase. The enthusiasm of their players, coached by Sandeep Patil, a World Cup winner with India in 1983, and of their red-white-and-green-painted supporters, were among the most vivid memories.

In contrast to media scrums surrounding bigger fish, the Kenyans were greeted on their arrival by just one journalist and when they lost to South Africa by ten wickets, this seemed about right. But 12 days later, everything changed. With some ease Kenya defended a score of 210 to beat Sri Lanka in Nairobi. Collins Obuya, who was inspired to bowl leg-spin by watching Mushtaq Ahmed on television in the 1996 World Cup, took five for 24 against a team normally accomplished at playing slow bowling. Jayasuriya labelled his players "amateurs".

MASS HYSTERIA AND MORNING SICKNESS

The world reacts to the Cup

After India's embarrassing early performances against Holland and Australia, both Sourav Ganguly, the captain, and Mohammad Kaif had their homes attacked. In the town of Pathalgaon, about 50 youths staged a mock-funeral procession, burning Ganguly in effigy and torching Sachin Tendulkar's picture. One placard read: "Let them do only ads, no need for them to play."

This sentiment was echoed by the president of the Indian Olympic Association, Suresh Kalmadi. "They are spending more time in studios for ad shoots than on the pitch. I have always said that there is too much money involved in cricket." Another fan went to court, filing a claim that the players' commercial activities should be restricted because their "dismal performance" had brought discredit and disrespect to the country.

Even success brought no respite. When India beat Pakistan, a teenager was killed and 12 others injured in the state of Gujarat after Hindu youths subjected Muslim youths and their families to volleys of stones and acid to "teach a lesson" to Pakistan followers. There were similar incidents in other areas: four policemen were hurt by stones in Bangalore.

In Kolkata, Sarathi Biswas killed herself by drinking poison, having felt slighted by the way her husband was ignoring her in favour of the game. In Karnataka, one man was killed and three workmates injured when a boiler exploded at a dairy. In their eagerness to watch the match on television, said police, they raised the heating level to facilitate faster production. Outside Ganguly's house, crowds massed again, this time chanting "Long live India".

India's passage to the final and defeat there led to yet another tragedy: a father in Kolkata killed his 14-year-old son by striking him on the head with a bat because the boy refused to part with the money he had saved to celebrate if India won. But the team's near-success was wonderful news for the flagging bat-making industry of Jammu & Kashmir, which reported a huge increase in sales. "Our business had died," said saw-mill owner Farooq Ahmad Dar, "but the World Cup has come as a blessing."

The streets in Pakistan were said to be silent after the India game, but there were protests in several cities following the defeat by England. Elsewhere, extremist reaction to failure was mostly confined to the media. Back in South Africa, Daryll Illbury, presenter of the breakfast show on East Coast Radio, reacted to the home team's exit by denouncing the Sri Lankan players, saying among other things: "their mothers are men," "they have long stupid names" and "their willies are too small to fit into South African condoms". Illbury was suspended.

In Britain, response moved on to post-modern irony. On the Guardian Unlimited website, Scott Murray, reporting on the India–New Zealand game from TV coverage, asked his readers: "What sort of life is this and what the hell am I doing boarding a train for Moorgate at 6.30 in the morning?... I know cricket's good and all that but I've got out of the wrong side of bed this morning and in any case it's not as if I'll write a cracking match report and then get rewarded by being sent on a wonderful assignment around the world because I'll be very surprised if any of my bosses will read any of this..." His reports rapidly acquired a cult following.

Less than a week later, the Kenyans – whose strategy was based on tight fielding and disciplined bowling conceding few extras – confirmed a Super Six place with an altogether less surprising victory over Bangladesh. The points from the New Zealand "win" were carried forward to the second stage, meaning that Kenya began the Super Sixes second only to Australia, and they sealed a semi-final spot with victory over Zimbabwe, their third genuine victory over Test opposition. But India, whom they momentarily frightened in the Super Six, outplayed them in the semi-finals.

BIGGER AND BETTER?

HOW CRICKET WORLD CUPS HAVE EXPANDED...

Year	*Main venue(s)*	*Teams*	*Days*	*Matches*
1975	England	8	15	15
1979	England	8	15	15
1983	England	8	17	27
1987	India and Pakistan	8	32	27
1992	Australia and New Zealand	9	33	39
1996	India, Pakistan and Sri Lanka	12	33	37
1999	England	12	38	42
2003	**South Africa**	**14**	**43**	**54**
2007	West Indies	16	?	51

...AND HOW OTHER SPORTS DO IT

	Teams	*Days*	*Matches*
Football World Cup 2002 (Japan and South Korea)	32	31	64
Hockey World Cup 2002 (Malaysia)	16	14	72
Rugby World Cup 2003 (Australia)	20	44	48
Netball World Championship 2003 (Jamaica)	24	11	100

Kenya's romantic journey brought huge benefits. The ICC brought forward their application for full-member status by one year to 2005 and earmarked more than £1m for development. Kenya were also invited to take part in the Busta Cup in the West Indies. Moreover, the players, who threatened strike action over pay beforehand, picked up $530,000 in prize money, having at one point anticipated a mere fraction of that.

South Africa's exit contributed to the event failing to capture the imagination of the country's majority. A broadening of cricket's appeal had been one aim of Ali Bacher's organising committee. To this end, sponsor companies were required to have a black empowerment element and a total of 50,000 tickets were reserved for black children to attend every game. However, a survey revealed only 11% of Nguni and Sotho speakers (i.e. most black South Africans) expressing an interest in the World Cup.

Political and sponsorship disputes were not the only problems. Large tournaments always have imperfections, but this one suffered profound structural and organisational faults. It was simply too big and too long. The decision to allow two more minor teams to join in took the participants to

End of the dream: Kenya's amazing journey through the World Cup stopped when they ran into India in the semi-finals. Sachin Tendulkar, the man of the tournament, here lofts Steve Tikolo for six.

Picture by Michael Steele, Getty Images.

14, the games to 54 (12 more than in 1999) and the duration to six weeks and a day. Moreover, the 42 pool matches were spread across 24 days in an indecent kowtowing to television. Bacher later conceded the event might have been better had it not been "of biblical proportions". And the ICC eventually announced a new system for 2007: two more teams but three fewer fixtures with a format designed to let the weak make a quick, graceful exit and the top eight to go through to a round robin.

The pool stage might have been even longer had reserve days not been dumped, a decision which cost West Indies dear. Their game with Bangladesh in Benoni was rained off when they were in a dominant position; had it been completed, West Indies, and not Kenya, would have gone through to the Super Six. Out of fairness to all parties, the final pool matches should have been played on the same day. Sri Lanka rightly pointed out that by forfeiting their last match with South Africa they could have all but guaranteed themselves a Super Six place, but agreed to fulfil the fixture in the wider interests of the game. The staging of day/night matches in the coastal cities of Durban and Cape Town was also questioned. The ball certainly seemed to swing more for the sides bowling second, though the results were not unduly skewed. India asked for their Durban semi-final to be switched to a wholly daytime game but their appeal to the ICC met with no more joy than anyone else's.

And while the South African camp were justly criticised for misreading the Duckworth/Lewis charts, the fact remains that if the electronic scoreboard at Kingsmead had carried the par score (as commonly happens in England), the mistake might not have occurred – and South Africa would probably have gone through. Even before the tournament was over, the organisers of the 2007 event in the West Indies were hinting at changes to the format.

That said, two things did work out. The umpiring was generally good, and the controversial decision not to continue the experiment with Hawkeye, the ball-tracking system, caused few problems; perhaps its absence actually removed an unwelcome spotlight from the decision-making. Nor was there any serious whiff of match-fixing. The biggest security operation mounted by the ICC led Lord Condon, head of the Anti-Corruption Unit, to declare the tournament – the first World Cup since the Cronje scandal – clean.

Consumed by the Zimbabwe row, England unsurprisingly failed to make a serious impression for the third time in a row. Unlike in 1996 and 1999 however, they played some compelling cricket, roundly beating Pakistan and running Australia close. Had they played, and beaten, Zimbabwe they would have reached the Super Six with reasonable prospects of making the semi-finals. And had the injured Darren Gough been present, they might have won the match with Australia too. Apart from Andrew Caddick, who cut a swathe through the top order, England lacked another proven wicket-taker, which made Hussain's decision to hand the crucial penultimate over in Port Elizabeth to the inexperienced James Anderson, who was having an off-day, all the more peculiar. It cost England the game and two days later Hussain, exhausted by an arduous winter, was making his resignation speech as one-day captain to cameras down the road at the team's hotel.

Anderson was England's prime discovery. Without even a full season with Lancashire behind him, he showed few qualms about stepping on to the big stages by walking off with two match awards, one for a stunning display of swing bowling against quality Pakistan opposition under the Cape Town lights. He faded in the defeats by India and Australia, but there was no doubting his potential. Another Lancastrian stepped out of the shadows. Plagued by a slow recovery from hernia surgery that cast his involvement into doubt, Andrew Flintoff turned in some of his most mature performances to date. He scored important runs against India and Australia and by bowling a relentless high-bouncing off-stump line finished as the most economical bowler in the tournament. Paul Collingwood, who ran more singles than a dating agency, also enhanced his reputation. After an exhausting winter, England's players probably returned home with a mixture of disappointment and relief. One of the chief regrets was that the tournament – the Zimbabwe row aside – went virtually unnoticed by those in Britain without satellite television because Channel Four went back on an earlier plan to show nightly highlights.

Hussain and Pollock were not the only leaders to jump or fall. In the now customary post-World Cup captaincy clear-out, so too did Jayasuriya (despite

Sri Lanka surprising many by making the semi-finals), Carl Hooper of West Indies, Waqar Younis of Pakistan and Khaled Masud of Bangladesh.

The Pakistanis were the biggest disappointment. They won no match of consequence and slid into rapid decline after losing their eagerly anticipated opener against Australia, which showed them in all their undisciplined glory. Shoaib's pre-match jibes at Lee were just the start. Waqar himself was ordered out of the attack for bowling two beamers and Adam Gilchrist subsequently launched a racial abuse charge against Rashid Latif that was turned down by match referee Clive Lloyd. Shahid Afridi was suspended and fined by his own board for sledging during the politically sensitive match with India. No wonder their cheerleader Abul Jalil, now sponsored by the Pakistan board, was so much quieter than in 1999.

DON'T REMIND ME...

	Career at the start		*World Cup, 2003*	
	Runs	*Avge*	*Runs*	*Avge*
D. P. M. D. Jayawardene (SL)	3,586	32.01	21	3.00
Inzamam-ul-Haq (P)	8,938	39.20	19	3.16
N. Hussain (E)	2,308	31.18	24	8.00
J. H. Kallis (SA)	5,902	44.04	63	15.75
	Wkts	*Avge*	*Wkts*	*Avge*
A. A. Donald (SA)	271	21.37	1	133.00
D. L. Vettori (NZ)	82	39.30	2	129.50
J. H. Kallis (SA)	164	29.73	3	64.33

For all the greyness of the political squabbles, the tournament threw up its share of glorious colour. There was John Davison, Canada's 32-year-old Australian recruit, astonishing West Indies and the world by smashing the fastest century in World Cup history only four days after his team had been dismissed for 36. There was Namibia's merry Jan-Berrie Burger applying his beefy blade to England's attack in Port Elizabeth and the exemplary glovework of Jeroen Smits, the Dutch keeper who conceded only five byes in six matches, earning the praise of Ian Healy.

And there was Shoaib swinging boundaries on his way to the highest score by a No. 11 batsman in one-day internationals; Ramnaresh Sarwan returning from hospital after being felled by a bouncer to take the field to a standing ovation; and Aasif Karim, a 39-year-old on his second career with Kenya, bowling maiden after maiden to Australia.

In a tournament short of technical innovation, one – relay-throwing, in which two fielders chased balls hit into the deep to hasten its return – turned a match when Lara was run out through the joint efforts of Lou Vincent and Chris Cairns of New Zealand.

But the best story came in Durban on the third day of the competition, when a Canadian team made up of salesmen, teachers, graphic artists, students, a dreadlocked plumber and only three people born in the world's second-largest country beat the game's newest Test nation, Bangladesh, by 60 runs. Until the warm-up games, the Canadians had not played together for five months, and were the lowest-ranked of the competing sides. The Bangladeshis may have been guilty of an unfamiliar sin – overconfidence.

The result created front-page headlines back home. The *Ottawa Citizen* proclaimed "Canada's Miracle on Grass" to countrymen more familiar with sport played on ice. It added: "Spunky Canadians Beat Top-Ranking Bangladesh," thus showing that everything is relative, and explaining "This is the equivalent of Tonga beating Canada in curling or the Jamaican bobsled team winning gold". The *National Post* stated simply: "Stunning Win Puts Canada on Cricket Map." In pursuing a long-term vision to globalise the game, it looked as though the ICC had got one thing right.

NATIONAL SQUADS

POOL A

Australia *R. T. Ponting, M. G. Bevan, A. J. Bichel, A. C. Gilchrist, J. N. Gillespie, I. J. Harvey, M. L. Hayden, G. B. Hogg, B. Lee, D. S. Lehmann, G. D. McGrath, J. P. Maher, D. R. Martyn, A. Symonds, †S. K. Warne. *Coach:* J. M. Buchanan.

Shortly after the tournament started, Warne was sent home for testing positive for a banned substance, and was later replaced by †N. M. Hauritz. Gillespie, suffering from a heel injury, returned to Australia at the end of the group stage, and was replaced by †N. W. Bracken.

England *N. Hussain, J. M. Anderson, I. D. Blackwell, A. R. Caddick, P. D. Collingwood, A. Flintoff, A. F. Giles, †S. J. Harmison, †M. J. Hoggard, R. C. Irani, N. V. Knight, A. J. Stewart, M. E. Trescothick, M. P. Vaughan, C. White. *Coach:* D. A. G. Fletcher.

Holland *R. P. Lefebvre, Adeel Raja, T. B. M. de Leede, J-J. Esmeijer, J. F. Kloppenburg, H-J. C. Mol, †R. G. Nijman, E. Schiferli, R. H. Scholte, J. Smits, N. A. Statham, D. L. S. van Bunge, K-J. J. van Noortwijk, L. P. van Troost, B. Zuiderent. *Coach:* E. N. Trotman.

India *S. C. Ganguly, †A. B. Agarkar, †S. B. Bangar, R. Dravid, Harbhajan Singh, M. Kaif, A. Kumble, D. Mongia, A. Nehra, †P. A. Patel, V. Sehwag, J. Srinath, S. R. Tendulkar, Yuvraj Singh, Zaheer Khan. *Coach:* J. G. Wright.

Namibia *D. B. Kotze, A. J. Burger, L. J. Burger, S. F. Burger, M. Karg, D. Keulder, B. L. Kotze, J. L. Louw, G. B. Murgatroyd, G. Snyman, S. J. Swanepoel, B. O. van Rooi, †M. van Schoor, R. J. van Vuuren, R. Walters. *Coach:* D. R. Brown.

During the group stage, Walters was replaced by †J. M. van der Merwe.

Pakistan *Waqar Younis, Abdul Razzaq, Azhar Mahmood, Inzamam-ul-Haq, Mohammad Sami, Rashid Latif, Saeed Anwar, Salim Elahi, Saqlain Mushtaq, Shahid Afridi, Shoaib Akhtar, Taufeeq Umar, Wasim Akram, Younis Khan, Yousuf Youhana. *Coach:* R. A. Pybus.

Zimbabwe *H. H. Streak, A. M. Blignaut, D. D. Ebrahim, S. M. Ervine, A. Flower, G. W. Flower, T. J. Friend, D. T. Hondo, D. A. Marillier, B. A. Murphy, H. K. Olonga, T. Taibu, M. A. Vermeulen, G. J. Whittall, C. B. Wishart. *Coach:* G. R. Marsh.

During the Super Six, A. D. R. Campbell was called up in place of Vermeulen, who had a hairline fracture above his left eye, and S. Matsikenyeri in place of Murphy, who had a calf injury.

POOL B

Bangladesh *Khaled Masud, Alok Kapali, Al Sahariar, Ehsanul Haque, Habibul Bashar, Hannan Sarkar, Khaled Mahmud, Manjurul Islam, Mashrafe bin Mortaza, Mohammad Ashraful, Mohammad Rafiq, Sanwar Hossain, Talha Jubair, Tapash Baisya, Tushar Imran. *Coach:* Mohsin Kamal.

Akram Khan was called up for Mortaza, who tore ligaments in his ankle during training before the match against West Indies.

Canada *J. V. Harris, A. Bagai, I. S. Billcliff, D. Chumney, A. Codrington, J. M. Davison, N. A. De Groot, N. Ifill, D. Joseph, I. Maraj, A. Patel, A. M. Samad, A. F. Sattaur, B. B. Seebaran, S. Thuraisingam. *Coach:* A. L. Logie.

Kenya *S. O. Tikolo, J. O. Angara, A. Y. Karim, H. S. Modi, C. O. Obuya, D. O. Obuya, T. M. Odoyo, M. O. Odumbe, P. J. Ongondo, K. O. Otieno, B. J. Patel, R. D. Shah, M. A. Suji, T. O. Suji, †A. V. Vadher. *Coach:* S. M. Patil.

New Zealand *S. P. Fleming, A. R. Adams, N. J. Astle, S. E. Bond, C. L. Cairns, C. Z. Harris, B. B. McCullum, C. D. McMillan, K. D. Mills, J. D. P. Oram, M. S. Sinclair, S. B. Styris, D. R. Tuffey, D. L. Vettori, L. Vincent. *Coach:* D. C. Aberhart.

South Africa *S. M. Pollock, N. Boje, M. V. Boucher, H. H. Dippenaar, A. A. Donald, H. H. Gibbs, A. J. Hall, J. H. Kallis, G. Kirsten, L. Klusener, C. K. Langeveldt, M. Ntini, R. J. Peterson, J. N. Rhodes, M. Zondeki. *Coach:* E. O. Simons.

G. C. Smith replaced Rhodes after he broke a bone in his right hand in the game against Kenya.

Sri Lanka *S. T. Jayasuriya, R. P. Arnold, M. S. Atapattu, P. A. de Silva, C. R. D. Fernando, †T. C. B. Fernando, P. W. Gunaratne, D. A. Gunawardene, D. P. M. D. Jayawardene, J. Mubarak, M. Muralitharan, R. A. P. Nissanka, K. C. Sangakkara, H. P. Tillekeratne, W. P. U. J. C. Vaas. *Coach:* D. F. Whatmore.

West Indies *C. L. Hooper, S. Chanderpaul, P. T. Collins, C. D. Collymore, M. Dillon, V. C. Drakes, C. H. Gayle, W. W. Hinds, R. D. Jacobs, B. C. Lara, J. J. C. Lawson, N. A. M. McLean, R. L. Powell, M. N. Samuels, R. R. Sarwan. *Coach:* R. A. Harper.

* *Captain.* † *Did not play in World Cup.*

2002-03 WORLD CUP STATISTICS

† *World Cup record.*

Leading run-scorers

S. R. Tendulkar (I) 673†; S. C. Ganguly (I) 465; R. T. Ponting (A) 415; A. C. Gilchrist (A) 408; H. H. Gibbs (SA) 384; M. S. Atapattu (SL) 382; A. Flower (Z) 332; M. L. Hayden (A) 328; A. Symonds (A) 326; D. R. Martyn (A) 323; S. P. Fleming (NZ) 321; S. T. Jayasuriya (SL) 321; R. Dravid (I) 318.

Hundreds

172*	C. B. Wishart	Z v N	at Harare
152	S. R. Tendulkar	I v N	at Pietermaritzburg
143*	A. Symonds	A v P	at Johannesburg
143	H. H. Gibbs	SA v NZ	at Johannesburg
141	S. B. Styris	NZ v SL	at Bloemfontein
140*	R. T. Ponting	A v I	at Johannesburg
134*	S. P. Fleming	NZ v SA	at Johannesburg
134*	K-J. J. van Noortwijk	H v N	at Bloemfontein
124	M. S. Atapattu	SL v SA	at Durban
121	J. F. Kloppenburg	H v N	at Bloemfontein

120	S. T. Jayasuriya	SL v NZ	at Bloemfontein
119	C. H. Gayle	WI v K	at Kimberley
116	B. C. Lara	WI v SA	at Cape Town
114	R. T. Ponting	A v SL	at Centurion
112*	S. C. Ganguly	I v N	at Pietermaritzburg
111*	S. C. Ganguly	I v K	at Durban
111	J. M. Davison	C v WI	at Centurion
107*	S. C. Ganguly	I v K	at Cape Town
103*	M. S. Atapattu	SL v Z	at East London
102*	N. J. Astle	NZ v Z	at Bloemfontein
101	Saeed Anwar	P v I	at Centurion

Ganguly scored three hundreds, Atapattu and Ponting two each.

Most runs scored per 100 balls

156.94	R. L. Powell (WI)	103.43	M. O. Odumbe (K)
138.20	A. M. Blignaut (Z)	101.90	S. B. Styris (NZ)
118.94	J. M. Davison (C)	100.78	H. H. Gibbs (SA)
114.01	Rashid Latif (P)	100.50	A. J. Burger (N)
105.15	A. C. Gilchrist (A)		

Minimum 100 runs.

Leading wicket-takers

W. P. U. J. C. Vaas (SL) 23†; B. Lee (A) 22; G. D. McGrath (A) 21; Zaheer Khan (I) 18; S. E. Bond (NZ) and M. Muralitharan (SL) 17; A. J. Bichel (A), V. C. Drakes (WI) and J. Srinath (I) 16; A. Nehra (I) 15.

Five wickets in an innings

7-15†	G. D. McGrath	A v N	at Potchefstroom
7-20	A. J. Bichel	A v E	at Port Elizabeth
6-23	A. Nehra	I v E	at Durban
6-23	S. E. Bond	NZ v A	at Port Elizabeth
6-25	W. P. U. J. C. Vaas	SL v B	at Pietermaritzburg
5-24	C. O. Obuya	K v SL	at Nairobi
5-27	A. Codrington	C v B	at Durban
5-28	Wasim Akram	P v N	at Kimberley
5-33	V. C. Drakes	WI v K	at Kimberley
5-42	B. Lee	A v NZ	at Port Elizabeth
5-43	R. J. van Vuuren	N v E	at Port Elizabeth
5-44	V. C. Drakes	WI v C	at Centurion

Drakes took five in an innings twice.

Best strike-rate – balls per wicket

19.43	V. C. Drakes (WI)	25.00	T. B. M. de Leede (H)
21.37	A. J. Bichel (A)	25.20	J. M. Davison (C)
22.68	B. Lee (A)	27.52	S. E. Bond (NZ)
22.95	W. P. U. J. C. Vaas (SL)	27.66	A. Nehra (I)
23.75	Wasim Akram (P)	28.20	J. M. Anderson (E)
24.00	Shoaib Akhtar (P)	29.44	Zaheer Khan (I)
24.85	G. D. McGrath (A)		

Minimum ten wickets.

Most economical bowlers – runs per over

2.87	A. Flintoff (E)	3.52	R. P. Lefebvre (H)
2.95	A. Y. Karim (K)	3.56	G. D. McGrath (A)
3.26	J. N. Gillespie (A)	3.58	S. M. Pollock (SA)
3.37	M. Ntini (SA)	3.63	M. Muralitharan (SL)
3.45	A. J. Bichel (A)	3.68	C. Z. Harris (NZ)

Minimum 20 overs.

Leading wicket-keepers

A. C. Gilchrist (A) 21† (all ct); K. C. Sangakkara (SL) 17 (15 ct, 2 st); R. Dravid (I) 16 (15 ct, 1 st); K. O. Otieno (K) 12 (8 ct, 4 st); M. V. Boucher (SA) 11 (all ct); A. Bagai (C) 10 (8 ct, 2 st).

Four dismissals in an innings

6 ct	A. C. Gilchrist	A v N at Potchefstroom
2 ct, 2 st	K. O. Otieno	K v B at Johannesburg
3 ct, 1 st	K. O. Otieno	K v Z at Bloemfontein
3 ct, 1 st	K. C. Sangakkara	SL v NZ at Bloemfontein
3 ct, 1 st	K. C. Sangakkara	SL v A at Port Elizabeth

Leading fielders

R. T. Ponting (A) 11; B. Lee (A), D. Mongia (I), D. O. Obuya (K) and V. Sehwag (I) 8; L. J. Burger (N), P. A. de Silva (SL) and Zaheer Khan (I) 6; C. L. Hooper (WI), S. T. Jayasuriya (SL), M. Kaif (I), D. R. Martyn (A), S. B. Styris (NZ) and B. Zuiderent (H) 5.

Highest totals

359-2	Australia v India at Johannesburg	310-8	Australia v Pakistan at Johannesburg
340-2	Zimbabwe v Namibia at Harare	306-6	South Africa v New Zealand at Johannesburg
319-5	Australia v Sri Lanka at Centurion	301-6	Australia v Namibia at Potchefstroom
314-4	Holland v Namibia at Bloemfontein	301-8	Zimbabwe v Holland at Bulawayo
311-2	India v Namibia at Pietermaritzburg		

Lowest completed totals

36†	Canada v Sri Lanka at Paarl	108	Bangladesh v South Africa at Bloemfontein
45	Namibia v Australia at Potchefstroom	109	Sri Lanka v India at Johannesburg
84	Namibia v Pakistan at Kimberley	112	New Zealand v Australia at Port Elizabeth
104	Kenya v West Indies at Kimberley	120	Bangladesh v Canada at Durban

Match reports by Tanya Aldred, Rahul Bhattacharya, Lawrence Booth, Paul Coupar, David Hopps, Andrew Radd, Rob Steen and John Stern.

POOL A

ZIMBABWE v NAMIBIA

At Harare, February 10, 2003. Zimbabwe won by 86 runs (D/L method). Toss: Namibia. One-day international debuts: Namibia (all).

In one of the World Cup's most enduring moments, Andy Flower and Henry Olonga issued a powerful statement mourning "the death of democracy in our beloved Zimbabwe", and took the field wearing black armbands in protest at human rights abuses by the Mugabe regime. Olonga was expelled by his club, Takashinga, and soon left Zimbabwe, while Flower would later be chosen against Australia only after his team-mates revolted against the selectors. The match itself belonged to Wishart, who hit a brutal and unbeaten 172 in 151 balls, driving with strength and timing. His first fifty took 55 deliveries, his second 46 and his third 36, as he accelerated smoothly to the highest score for Zimbabwe in a one-day international. Wishart's hectic and unbroken stand of 166 in 117 balls with Grant Flower – whose 78 needed just 55 deliveries – lifted Zimbabwe to 340, their best total in 223 one-day matches. Namibia promptly lost a wicket to their first ball they faced in international cricket when Riaan Walters nibbled at Streak, before a brief flurry of hitting from Jan-Berrie Burger. By the 26th over, when rain stopped play for the second time, this time for good, Namibia were 104 for five and on the ropes. Zimbabwe breathed a huge sigh of relief: if the game had been abandoned two balls earlier, it would have been declared a draw.

Man of the Match: C. B. Wishart. *Attendance:* 3,889.

Zimbabwe

C. B. Wishart not out	172
M. A. Vermeulen c and b Louw	39
A. Flower c Karg b A. J. Burger	39
G. W. Flower not out	78
L-b 7, w 4, n-b 1	12
1/107 (2) 2/174 (3) (2 wkts, 50 overs)	340
15 overs: 62-0	

D. D. Ebrahim, G. J. Whittall, †T. Taibu, *H. H. Streak, B. A. Murphy, H. K. Olonga and D. T. Hondo did not bat.

Bowling: Snyman 10–0–49–0; L. J. Burger 10–1–70–0; B. L. Kotze 10–1–75–0; Louw 10–0–60–1; D. B. Kotze 7–0–56–0; A. J. Burger 3–0–23–1.

Namibia

R. Walters c Taibu b Streak	0
S. J. Swanepoel c Streak b Whittall	23
A. J. Burger c A. Flower b Streak	26
D. Keulder c Ebrahim b Whittall	27
G. B. Murgatroyd c Wishart b G. W. Flower	10
L. J. Burger not out	4
*D. B. Kotze not out	5
L-b 1, w 8	9
1/0 (1) 2/40 (3) 3/80 (2) 4/94 (4) 5/98 (5) (5 wkts, 25.1 overs)	104
15 overs: 71-2	

†M. Karg, G. Snyman, J. L. Louw and B. L. Kotze did not bat.

Bowling: Streak 5–0–35–2; Hondo 6–1–20–0; Olonga 3–1–8–0; Murphy 1–0–7–0; G. W. Flower 5.1–1–13–1; Whittall 5–0–20–2.

Umpires: D. L. Orchard (South Africa) and S. J. A. Taufel (Australia).
Third umpire: D. B. Hair (Australia). Referee: Wasim Raja (Pakistan).

AUSTRALIA v PAKISTAN

At Johannesburg, February 11, 2003. Australia won by 82 runs. Toss: Pakistan.

This match provided a reminder, if any were needed, of why Australia began the tournament as prohibitively-priced favourites. Although Pakistan had spent the winter turning capriciousness into an art, the holders looked vulnerable: Darren Lehmann was suspended for racial abuse, Michael Bevan was injured and, on the morning of the game, Shane Warne announced he would be returning home to face drugs charges. But Symonds, a player many Australians would have left out of the squad after just two fifties in 54 one-day internationals, hit a free-flowing and unbeaten 143, from 125 balls, and two other lesser-known Australians, Harvey and Hogg, provided the main support act. They shared seven wickets and each made a nuggety contribution to a valuable stand. Australia commanded at every stage, except the first hour, when Wasim Akram had Gilchrist caught off a miscued pull in his second over, then struck with consecutive balls in his sixth. Symonds entered at 86 for four and, after jogging in Ponting's slipstream, revealed the range of muscular strokes he previously reserved for county cricket. Waqar Younis's dismissal from the attack in the 49th over, for a second beamer at Symonds, encapsulated his frustration; he could not bring himself to apologise. Pakistan's hopes of chasing 311, with an over docked, were gone by the halfway mark. Shahid Afridi flashed, Taufeeq Umar mis-hooked, Inzamam-ul-Haq edged lazily and the chase ground to a halt when Symonds dashed from the leg-side boundary and plunged to catch the menacing Yousuf Youhana.

Man of the Match: A. Symonds. *Attendance:* 27,075.

Australia

†A. C. Gilchrist c Waqar Younis b Wasim Akram . 1
M. L. Hayden b Wasim Akram 27
*R. T. Ponting c Taufeeq Umar b Shoaib Akhtar . 53
D. R. Martyn b Wasim Akram 0
J. P. Maher c Rashid Latif b Waqar Younis . 9
A. Symonds not out 143
G. B. Hogg run out 14
I. J. Harvey c Waqar Younis b Shoaib Akhtar . 24
B. Lee c Inzamam-ul-Haq b Waqar Younis . 2
J. N. Gillespie not out 6
B 1, l-b 9, w 12, n-b 9. 31

1/10 (1) 2/52 (2) 3/52 (4) 4/86 (5) 5/146 (3) 6/216 (7) 7/270 (8) 8/292 (9) (8 wkts, 50 overs) 310

15 overs: 86-3

G. D. McGrath did not bat.

Bowling: Wasim Akram 10–0–64–3; Shoaib Akhtar 10–0–45–2; Waqar Younis 8.3–1–50–2; Abdul Razzaq 6–0–42–0; Shahid Afridi 9.3–0–63–0; Younis Khan 6–0–36–0.

Pakistan

Taufeeq Umar c Hogg b Lee 21
Shahid Afridi c Gilchrist b Gillespie . . . 1
Salim Elahi c Lee b Harvey. 30
Inzamam-ul-Haq c Gilchrist b McGrath . 6
Yousuf Youhana c Symonds b Harvey . . 27
Younis Khan c Ponting b Hogg. 19
Abdul Razzaq c and b Hogg 25
†Rashid Latif b Hogg 33
Wasim Akram c Ponting b Harvey. 33
*Waqar Younis c McGrath b Harvey . . . 6
Shoaib Akhtar not out 0
B 3, l-b 9, w 10, n-b 5. 27

1/9 (2) 2/38 (1) 3/49 (4) 4/81 (3) 5/103 (5) 6/125 (6) 7/147 (7) 8/201 (8) 9/223 (9) 10/228 (10) (44.3 overs) 228

14 overs: 45-2

Bowling: McGrath 10–2–39–1; Gillespie 8–1–28–1; Lee 7–0–37–1; Harvey 9.3–0–58–4; Hogg 10–0–54–3.

Umpires: E. A. R. de Silva (Sri Lanka) and D. R. Shepherd (England).
Third umpire: B. F. Bowden (New Zealand). Referee: C. H. Lloyd (West Indies).

HOLLAND v INDIA

At Paarl, February 12, 2003. India won by 68 runs. Toss: India. One-day international debut: J. Smits.

India won all right but their batting line-up, the most lustrous in the tournament, was skittled for 204 by a team who train by skating on frozen ponds. And it was a very good day for Tim de Leede (formerly of various county Second XIs), who snared Tendulkar as his first World Cup wicket and celebrated by taking three more. During his innings of 52, Tendulkar overtook Javed Miandad as the highest run-scorer in World Cups, but Dutch captain Lefebvre was able to be humorously patronising: "Tendulkar looked very tame to me," he said. Yuvraj Singh and Mongia prevented a disastrously low total and early wickets prevented an embarrassing result, but it was not until the penultimate over on a day of extreme heat that India bowled Holland out. Daan van Bunge, a student from The Hague, scored 62. India reflected on their performance, looked at their next fixture, and gulped.

Man of the Match: T. B. M. de Leede. *Attendance:* 3,674.

India

*S. C. Ganguly c Smits b Lefebvre	8
S. R. Tendulkar c Smits b de Leede	52
V. Sehwag c Zuiderent b Kloppenburg	6
†R. Dravid b de Leede	17
Yuvraj Singh c and b Adeel Raja	37
M. Kaif c Lefebvre b Adeel Raja	9
D. Mongia run out	42
Harbhajan Singh b de Leede	13
A. Kumble run out	9
Zaheer Khan lbw b de Leede	0
J. Srinath not out	0
L-b 2, w 8, n-b 1	11
1/30 (1) 2/56 (3) 3/81 (2) 4/91 (4) 5/114 (6) 6/169 (5) 7/186 (8) 8/203 (9) 9/204 (7) 10/204 (10) (48.5 overs)	204

15 overs: 56-2

Bowling: Schiferli 10–2–49–0; Lefebvre 9–1–27–1; de Leede 9.5–0–35–4; Kloppenburg 10–0–40–1; Adeel Raja 9–0–47–2; van Troost 1–0–4–0.

Holland

J. F. Kloppenburg c Sehwag b Srinath	0
D. L. S. van Bunge b Srinath	62
H-J. C. Mol c Dravid b Srinath	2
B. Zuiderent c Sehwag b Zaheer Khan	0
T. B. M. de Leede c Dravid b Harbhajan Singh	0
L. P. van Troost c Dravid b Kumble	1
R. H. Scholte lbw b Kumble	1
*R. P. Lefebvre lbw b Kumble	3
E. Schiferli c Mongia b Kumble	13
†J. Smits c Sehwag b Srinath	26
Adeel Raja not out	0
B 2, l-b 6, w 18, n-b 2	28
1/0 (1) 2/29 (3) 3/31 (4) 4/38 (5) 5/42 (6) 6/44 (7) 7/54 (8) 8/82 (9) 9/131 (2) 10/136 (10) (48.1 overs)	136

15 overs: 39-4

Bowling: Srinath 9.1–1–30–4; Zaheer Khan 8–1–17–1; Harbhajan Singh 10–1–20–1; Kumble 10–1–32–4; Ganguly 4–0–14–0; Tendulkar 4–0–9–0; Sehwag 3–0–6–0.

Umpires: D. J. Harper (Australia) and P. Willey (England).
Third umpire: Nadeem Ghauri (Pakistan). Referee: D. T. Lindsay (South Africa).

ENGLAND v ZIMBABWE

At Harare, February 13, 2003. Zimbabwe awarded match by default after England withdrew.

On February 11, after a series of failed appeals for a relocation to South Africa, the ECB announced their decision not to travel to Harare, citing safety fears. The ICC cancelled the game and awarded the points to Zimbabwe.

AUSTRALIA v INDIA

At Centurion, February 15, 2003. Australia won by nine wickets. Toss: India.

This was the Australia the rest of the world had been dreading: an unstoppable force, which blasted away one of their most highly-fancied rivals through force of reputation and a swinging ball. India, uneasy against Holland, were quivering here – all nervous edges and twitches, with no vivacious strokeplay until Harbhajan Singh briefly revelled in the freedom of a lost cause. McGrath's probing line and Lee's waspish pace created the nervy mood but it was Gillespie who snuffed out India's hopes. Instead of respite, he provided mean accuracy at first change, bowling ten overs straight through and taking three for 13. India's last hope evaporated with Tendulkar, removed by a magical slow off-cutter from Gillespie. Their top six had made 51 between them. It took Australia just 22.2 overs to overtake India's lowest-ever World Cup total, as Gilchrist and Hayden entertained those of the crowd who were not burying their heads in their hands, and despairing at the apparent inevitability of it all.

Man of the Match: J. N. Gillespie. *Attendance:* 17,730.

India

*S. C. Ganguly c Gilchrist b Lee	9
S. R. Tendulkar lbw b Gillespie	36
V. Sehwag c Gilchrist b Lee	4
†R. Dravid b Gillespie	1
Yuvraj Singh lbw b McGrath	0
M. Kaif c Symonds b Gillespie	1
D. Mongia c Symonds b Lee	13
A. Kumble not out	16
Harbhajan Singh lbw b Hogg	28
Zaheer Khan lbw b Lehmann	1
J. Srinath run out	0
L-b 5, w 10, n-b 1	16
1/22 (1) 2/41 (3) 3/44 (4) 4/45 (5) 5/50 (6) 6/78 (2) 7/80 (7) 8/120 (9) 9/125 (10) 10/125 (11) — (41.4 overs)	125
15 overs: 45-4	

Bowling: McGrath 8–3–23–1; Lee 9–1–36–3; Gillespie 10–2–13–3; Symonds 6–0–25–0; Hogg 4.4–0–16–1; Lehmann 4–0–7–1.

Australia

†A. C. Gilchrist st Dravid b Kumble	48
M. L. Hayden not out	45
*R. T. Ponting not out	24
L-b 3, w 8	11
1/100 (1) — (1 wkt, 22.2 overs)	128
15 overs: 91-0	

D. R. Martyn, D. S. Lehmann, M. G. Bevan, A. Symonds, G. B. Hogg, B. Lee, J. N. Gillespie and G. D. McGrath did not bat.

Bowling: Srinath 4–0–26–0; Zaheer Khan 4–0–26–0; Harbhajan Singh 7.2–0–49–0; Kumble 7–0–24–1.

Umpires: E. A. R. de Silva (Sri Lanka) and D. R. Shepherd (England).
Third umpire: B. G. Jerling (South Africa). Referee: C. H. Lloyd (West Indies).

ENGLAND v HOLLAND

At East London, February 16, 2003. England won by six wickets. Toss: England. One-day international debut: N. A. Statham.

Game but outgunned, Holland paid for England's pent-up frustrations. While this was the tournament's 13th match, the boycott of Zimbabwe meant it was England's first, and they began it desperate to forget the politicking and get on with the cricket. Faced with an undemanding target, Trescothick, over-eager to assert, was soon bowled on the charge, but Knight and Vaughan then did much as they pleased before both played unseemly shots against van Bunge, a part-time leg-spinner. Earlier, England's bowlers had performed a thoroughly professional dissection of Holland's top order. Anderson bowled ten overs off the reel, grabbed the first four wickets and displayed an old-fashioned consistency of line and length. From 31 for five, the patient de Leede kept England in the field for the remaining 33 overs – Hussain later admitted he was relieved to get the extra practice.

Man of the Match: J. M. Anderson. *Attendance:* 4,840.

Holland

L. P. van Troost lbw b Anderson	8
D. L. S. van Bunge c White b Anderson	4
N. A. Statham lbw b Flintoff	7
B. Zuiderent c Hussain b Anderson	2
K-J. J. van Noortwijk c Stewart b Anderson	0
T. B. M. de Leede not out	58
J. F. Kloppenburg c Knight b Blackwell	10
E. Schiferli st Stewart b Blackwell	12
*R. P. Lefebvre b White	6
Adeel Raja lbw b White	2
†J. Smits not out	17
L-b 10, w 4, n-b 2	16
(9 wkts, 50 overs)	142

1/15 (2) 2/22 (1) 3/31 (4) 4/31 (5) 5/31 (3) 6/67 (7) 7/90 (8) 8/108 (9) 9/112 (10) — 15 overs: 28-2

Bowling: Caddick 10–4–19–0; Anderson 10–1–25–4; Flintoff 10–2–29–1; White 10–3–22–2; Blackwell 10–0–37–2.

England

M. E. Trescothick b Schiferli	12
N. V. Knight c Zuiderent b van Bunge	51
M. P. Vaughan c de Leede b van Bunge	51
A. Flintoff c Lefebvre b van Bunge	0
I. D. Blackwell not out	22
P. D. Collingwood not out	5
W 3	3
(4 wkts, 23.2 overs)	144

1/18 (1) 2/107 (3) 3/107 (4) 4/126 (2) — 15 overs: 86-1

*N. Hussain, †A. J. Stewart, C. White, A. R. Caddick and J. M. Anderson did not bat.

Bowling: Schiferli 5–0–33–1; Lefebvre 5–0–18–0; de Leede 4–0–29–0; Adeel Raja 5–0–34–0; van Bunge 3–0–16–3; Kloppenburg 1.2–0–14–0.

Umpires: D. B. Hair (Australia) and R. E. Koertzen (South Africa).
Third umpire: T. H. Wijewardene (Sri Lanka). Referee: M. J. Procter (South Africa).

NAMIBIA v PAKISTAN

At Kimberley, February 16, 2003. Pakistan won by 171 runs. Toss: Pakistan. One-day international debuts: M. van Schoor, R. J. van Vuuren.

Shoaib Akhtar bowled one of the fastest spells in history, touching 99mph, Wasim Akram found his zip again, and together they shredded Namibia. Chasing 256, Namibia were three for three before they knew it, with Wasim – in his record-breaking 34th World Cup appearance – bending the ball late and fast into the pads, Shoaib sprinting in, and six slips waiting with open hands. There was, as the captain Deon Kotze admitted, "a bit of a rush to put the pads on". Only a last-wicket stand of 42 took Namibia past the lowest World Cup total (45 by Canada against England in 1979) and the innings lasted less than 18 overs. Earlier, Namibia had constricted a sluggish Pakistan with agile fielding and controlled bowling – much to the disappointment of the Pakistani supporters. But they found their voice later.

Man of the Match: Wasim Akram. *Attendance:* 2,943.

Pakistan

Saeed Anwar c L. J. Burger b B. L. Kotze	23
Salim Elahi c D. B. Kotze b A. J. Burger	63
Younis Khan c van Schoor b L. J. Burger	28
Inzamam-ul-Haq b D. B. Kotze	4
Yousuf Youhana c L. J. Burger b B. L. Kotze	43
†Rashid Latif b Snyman	36
Wasim Akram not out	20
Abdul Razzaq c van Schoor b Snyman	4
*Waqar Younis run out	8
Saqlain Mushtaq run out	1
Shoaib Akhtar not out	3
L-b 11, w 10, n-b 1	22
1/47 (1) 2/105 (3) 3/118 (4) 4/150 (2) 5/208 (5) 6/223 (6) 7/227 (8) 8/247 (9) 9/248 (10) — 15 overs: 60-1	(9 wkts, 50 overs) 255

Bowling: Snyman 8–0–51–2; van Vuuren 10–1–47–0; B. L. Kotze 10–1–51–2; L. J. Burger 10–0–45–1; D. B. Kotze 8–0–32–1; A. J. Burger 4–0–18–1.

Namibia

R. Walters c Rashid Latif b Wasim Akram	0
S. J. Swanepoel c Inzamam-ul-Haq b Shoaib Akhtar	1
A. J. Burger c Younis Khan b Shoaib Akhtar	14
D. Keulder b Shoaib Akhtar	0
G. B. Murgatroyd lbw b Wasim Akram	4
L. J. Burger lbw b Wasim Akram	0
*D. B. Kotze lbw b Wasim Akram	8
G. Snyman lbw b Shoaib Akhtar	0
†M. van Schoor lbw b Wasim Akram	2
B. L. Kotze not out	24
R. J. van Vuuren c Waqar Younis b Saqlain Mushtaq	14
L-b 9, w 4, n-b 4	17
1/1 (1) 2/3 (2) 3/3 (4) 4/17 (5) 5/17 (6) 6/32 (3) 7/32 (8) 8/35 (9) 9/42 (7) 10/84 (11) — 15 overs: 61-9	(17.4 overs) 84

Bowling: Wasim Akram 9–1–28–5; Shoaib Akhtar 8–1–46–4; Saqlain Mushtaq 0.4–0–1–1.

Umpires: N. A. Mallender (England) and D. L. Orchard (South Africa).
Third umpire: S. J. A. Taufel (Australia). Referee: D. T. Lindsay (South Africa).

ENGLAND v NAMIBIA

At Port Elizabeth, February 19, 2003. England won by 55 runs. Toss: Namibia. One-day international debut: S. F. Burger.

Nine thousand increasingly pro-Namibian fans watched Jan-Berrie Burger set hearts thumping nervously across England. If the technique was simple – move into line, hit as far as possible – the end result was certainly effective. Burger smashed 85 in 86 balls, and the England fielders threatened to join Nasser Hussain, laid up with a stiff neck, as they watched the ball fly over their heads. With the clouds thickening over Port Elizabeth, Namibia were ahead on Duckworth/Lewis for nearly 12 overs, though it later transpired that England were blissfully unaware of their peril: Stewart, their stand-in captain, said he had entrusted the crib sheet to Trescothick, who botched the maths and kept insisting England were ahead. A diving catch from Collingwood ended the Burger menace, but the Namibians kept fighting and when van Vuuren hit the last ball of the match for a huge six his team-mates rushed on to the field to celebrate a gutsy display. Earlier, van Vuuren, also a Namibian rugby international, had finished off the England innings, striking three times in the last over. Trescothick, Stewart and White all batted pugnaciously, but the match award could only go to one man.

Man of the Match: A. J. Burger. *Attendance:* 9,756.

England

M. E. Trescothick c L. J. Burger b A. J. Burger	58
N. V. Knight c L. J. Burger b van Vuuren	6
M. P. Vaughan c L. J. Burger b van Vuuren	14
*†A. J. Stewart c B. L. Kotze b D. B. Kotze	60
P. D. Collingwood c Keulder b Snyman	38
A. Flintoff c Keulder b Snyman	21
I. D. Blackwell c van Schoor b Snyman	16
C. White c S. F. Burger b van Vuuren	35
R. C. Irani c D. B. Kotze b van Vuuren	12
A. R. Caddick b van Vuuren	4
J. M. Anderson not out	0
L-b 1, w 4, n-b 3	8
1/26 (2) 2/43 (3) 3/121 (1) 4/159 (4) 5/202 (5) 6/205 (6) 7/242 (7) 8/264 (8) 9/268 (9) 10/272 (10)	(50 overs) 272
	15 overs: 59-2

Bowling: Snyman 10–0–69–3; van Vuuren 10–2–43–5; L. J. Burger 9–0–45–0; B. L. Kotze 3–0–24–0; D. B. Kotze 10–0–35–1; A. J. Burger 2–0–23–1; S. F. Burger 6–0–32–0.

Namibia

S. J. Swanepoel c Vaughan b Anderson	8
A. J. Burger c Collingwood b White	85
L. J. Burger c and b Flintoff	5
D. Keulder run out	46
G. B. Murgatroyd b Irani	24
G. Snyman b White	0
*D. B. Kotze b Flintoff	7
S. F. Burger c Collingwood b Irani	5
†M. van Schoor not out	11
B. L. Kotze lbw b Irani	0
R. J. van Vuuren not out	12
L-b 5, w 6, n-b 3	14
1/12 (1) 2/42 (3) 3/139 (2) 4/174 (4) 5/174 (6) 6/188 (5) 7/190 (7) 8/200 (8) 9/200 (10)	(9 wkts, 50 overs) 217
	15 overs: 56-2

Bowling: Caddick 8–2–28–0; Anderson 8–0–44–1; Flintoff 10–2–33–2; White 10–0–46–2; Vaughan 6–0–31–0; Irani 8–0–30–3.

Umpires: S. J. A. Taufel (Australia) and S. Venkataraghavan (India).
Third umpire: Nadeem Ghauri (Pakistan). Referee: M. J. Procter (South Africa).

ZIMBABWE v INDIA

At Harare, February 19, 2003. India won by 83 runs. Toss: Zimbabwe.

This was a game India dared not lose. Their limp start to the competition had sparked effigy-burning and stone-throwing back home, but the players responded with a pumped-up performance that kept the critics at arm's length. India were given the ideal platform by a blistering run-a-ball stand of 99 between Sehwag and Tendulkar, but the innings faltered against the nagging left-arm spin of Grant Flower. First he frustrated Mongia, who made just 12 in 36 deliveries before chipping to long-on; two balls later, he bamboozled Tendulkar with a beauty that pitched on middle-and-off and straightened. Had Flower not been forced out of the attack with a finger injury, India's total might have been less daunting. In the event, 255 was ample. Srinath quickly fired out the openers, and the best efforts of the black-sweatbanded Andy Flower to disrupt the bowlers' concentration – at one point he tried a truly remarkable one-handed reverse sweep against Harbhajan Singh – never quite succeeded. The real damage was done by Ganguly, who took three for two in six balls, and at 87 for six, Zimbabwe's main concern was their net run-rate; Taibu helped them to respectability. A random inspection by the ICC found that bats belonging to players on both sides were marginally wider than the Laws allowed.

Man of the Match: S. R. Tendulkar. *Attendance:* 5,800.

India

V. Sehwag c Taibu b Whittall	36
S. R. Tendulkar b G. W. Flower	81
D. Mongia c Hondo b G. W. Flower	12
*S. C. Ganguly c Streak b Blignaut	24
†R. Dravid not out	43
Yuvraj Singh c Taibu b Murphy	1
M. Kaif lbw b Hondo	25
Harbhajan Singh c Murphy b Streak	3
Zaheer Khan not out	13
B 4, l-b 4, w 9	17
1/99 (1) 2/142 (3) 3/142 (2) 4/182 (4) 5/184 (6) 6/227 (7) 7/234 (8) — (7 wkts, 50 overs)	255
15 overs: 91-0	

J. Srinath and A. Nehra did not bat.

Bowling: Streak 9–0–46–1; Blignaut 10–0–54–1; Hondo 9–1–56–1; Whittall 6–0–37–1; G. W. Flower 6–0–14–2; Murphy 10–0–40–1.

Zimbabwe

C. B. Wishart b Srinath	12
M. A. Vermeulen c Dravid b Srinath	0
A. Flower b Harbhajan Singh	22
G. W. Flower c Harbhajan Singh b Ganguly	23
D. D. Ebrahim c sub (A. B. Agarkar) b Ganguly	19
A. M. Blignaut c Mongia b Ganguly	2
†T. Taibu not out	29
G. J. Whittall c Zaheer Khan b Sehwag	28
*H. H. Streak c Kaif b Harbhajan Singh	20
B. A. Murphy b Zaheer Khan	2
D. T. Hondo b Zaheer Khan	2
B 4, l-b 2, w 5, n-b 2	13
1/1 (2) 2/23 (1) 3/48 (3) 4/83 (4) 5/83 (5) 6/87 (6) 7/124 (8) 8/160 (9) 9/165 (10) 10/172 (11) — (44.4 overs)	172
15 overs: 43-2	

Bowling: Srinath 8–1–14–2; Zaheer Khan 7.4–0–23–2; Nehra 7–0–35–0; Harbhajan Singh 10–0–42–2; Ganguly 5–1–22–3; Sehwag 3–0–14–1; Mongia 4–0–16–0.

Umpires: E. A. R. de Silva (Sri Lanka) and R. E. Koertzen (South Africa).
Third umpire: D. B. Hair (Australia). Referee: C. H. Lloyd (West Indies).

AUSTRALIA v HOLLAND

At Potchefstroom, February 20, 2003. Australia won by 75 runs (D/L method). Toss: Holland.

Holland, 1,000 to 1 for the tournament, met the 5 to 4 favourites, and there were no prizes for guessing the outcome. The biggest threat to Australia came from the weather, which constantly looked poised to snatch away victory. Australia's innings was twice interrupted, leaving Holland an inflated target of 198 in 36 overs, and as Dutch wickets clattered, ominous dark clouds loomed. In a desperate effort to rattle through 25 overs – the minimum needed to ensure a result – before the heavens opened, Ponting ignored ideal seam conditions and had his part-time spinners on by the seventh over. That he could pay more attention to the length of a bowler's run than his effectiveness said it all about the gulf between the teams. Earlier, play had begun an hour late after the ground staff slopped rainwater on to the pitch as they removed the covers, prompting the police to help with a blow-dry from the rotor blades of their helicopter. On a greasy strip the ball darted wickedly, and even the fearsome Australian batting line-up laboured. Helped by Smits, razor-sharp standing up to the seamers, Lefebvre bowled eight overs for 19. But Martyn blocked the straight and swung at the wide for an unbeaten 67, the rain held off long enough, and the Australians ploughed relentlessly onwards.

Man of the Match: D. R. Martyn. *Attendance:* 4,376.

Australia

†J. P. Maher c van Bunge b de Leede	26
M. L. Hayden c Schiferli b de Leede	33
D. R. Martyn not out	67
D. S. Lehmann not out	29
B 4, l-b 3, w 8	15
1/52 (1) 2/103 (2) (2 wkts, 36 overs)	170
14 overs: 52-1	

*R. T. Ponting, M. G. Bevan, A. Symonds, I. J. Harvey, A. J. Bichel, J. N. Gillespie and G. D. McGrath did not bat.

Bowling: Schiferli 7–0–42–0; Lefebvre 8–2–19–0; de Leede 7–0–34–2; Kloppenburg 7–0–32–0; Esmeijer 5–0–16–0; van Bunge 2–0–20–0.

Holland

L. P. van Troost c Bichel b Lehmann	23
D. L. S. van Bunge c Martyn b Gillespie	1
B. Zuiderent c Maher b Gillespie	5
K-J. J. van Noortwijk lbw b Lehmann	13
T. B. M. de Leede c Maher b Bichel	24
R. H. Scholte lbw b Bichel	8
E. Schiferli b Harvey	9
J. F. Kloppenburg c Ponting b Bichel	9
*R. P. Lefebvre not out	14
†J. Smits c Maher b Harvey	0
J-J. Esmeijer c Ponting b Harvey	0
L-b 4, w 11, n-b 1	16
1/8 (2) 2/18 (3) 3/42 (1) 4/59 (4) 5/85 (5) 6/90 (6) 7/96 (7) 8/112 (8) 9/118 (10) 10/122 (11) (30.2 overs)	122
10 overs: 40-2	

Bowling: McGrath 3–1–10–0; Gillespie 3–0–7–2; Lehmann 8–0–27–2; Symonds 7–0–36–0; Bichel 5–0–13–3; Harvey 4.2–0–25–3.

Umpires: D. L. Orchard (South Africa) and P. Willey (England).
Third umpire: Aleem Dar (Pakistan). Referee: R. S. Madugalle (Sri Lanka).

ENGLAND v PAKISTAN

At Cape Town, February 22, 2003 (day/night). England won by 112 runs. Toss: England.

This was England's most heartening World Cup performance for more than a decade. They had to win – defeat would have left them only a glimmer of making the Super Six – and thanks to a precocious display of controlled swing by Anderson they did. Many thought the toss decided the game by forcing Pakistan to bat on a dewy evening. But Anderson's bowling was exceptional. In any case, it was Pakistan who dominated the early stages. Vaughan, caught off his first delivery, a no-ball, reeled off a sparkling if frantic fifty, but at 118 for five England were clinging on by a fingernail. Then Collingwood, putting placement before power and turning ones into twos, marshalled the lower order so adroitly that England scampered 246. To all intents and purposes, Anderson's second over settled matters: Inzamam-ul-Haq sliced an out-swinger to slip, and Yousuf Youhana also went first ball, castled by an impeccable swinging yorker. Another two-wicket Anderson over – the 18th – made doubly sure: Saeed Anwar shuffled in front, Rashid Latif gloved a lifter and a star had been born. Pakistan's impotence was symbolised by Shoaib Akhtar, who bowled the first ball officially timed at 100mph (comfortably repulsed by Knight) but went for seven an over. Later, Shoaib blazed 43 off 16 balls but it was already too late to matter.

Man of the Match: J. M. Anderson. *Attendance:* 22,796.

FASTER THAN A SPEEDING BULLET...

		mph
The fastest games:	pelota/jai-alai – ball speeds up to	**188**
	golf – ball speeds up to	**170**
The fastest Formula 1 race:	Peter Gethin (Britain) won the 1971 Italian Grand Prix at Monza at an average	**151**
The fastest tennis serve:	Andy Roddick (USA), 2004, measured at	**150**
The fastest baseball pitch:	Nolan Ryan (USA), 1974, measured at	**100.9†**
The fastest Derby winner:	Lammtarra, 1995	**35.39**
The fastest man:	Tim Montgomery (USA), 100m record-holder (9.78 seconds), 2002	**22.87**

† Baseball pitchers are regularly clocked at over 100mph, but stadium timings are regarded as unreliable and unofficial. No one has beaten Ryan's time in controlled circumstances.

Research: Ian Morrison

England

M. E. Trescothick c Rashid Latif b Wasim Akram	1
N. V. Knight c Abdul Razzaq b Waqar Younis	15
M. P. Vaughan c Younis Khan b Shoaib Akhtar	52
*N. Hussain c Rashid Latif b Waqar Younis	8
†A. J. Stewart b Shahid Afridi	30
P. D. Collingwood not out	66
A. Flintoff st Rashid Latif b Saqlain Mushtaq	26
C. White c Younis Khan b Shahid Afridi	15
A. F. Giles c Shahid Afridi b Saqlain Mushtaq	17
A. R. Caddick not out	3
L-b 1, w 7, n-b 5	13
1/7 (1) 2/45 (2) 3/59 (4) 4/110 (3) 5/118 (5) 6/160 (7) 7/194 (8) 8/223 (9) — (8 wkts, 50 overs)	246
15 overs: 64-3	

J. M. Anderson did not bat.

Bowling: Wasim Akram 10–1–37–1; Shoaib Akhtar 9–1–63–1; Waqar Younis 7–0–37–2; Saqlain Mushtaq 10–0–44–2; Shahid Afridi 8–0–36–2; Abdul Razzaq 6–0–28–0.

Two down, two to go: James Anderson bowls Pakistan's Yousuf Youhana, on his way to four match-winning wickets.

Picture by Tom Shaw, Getty Images.

Pakistan

Saeed Anwar lbw b Anderson	29	*Waqar Younis c Knight b White	2
Shahid Afridi c Stewart b Caddick	6	Shoaib Akhtar b Flintoff	43
Inzamam-ul-Haq c Knight b Anderson	0		
Yousuf Youhana b Anderson	0	B 4, l-b 4, w 11	19
Younis Khan c Stewart b Flintoff	5		
Abdul Razzaq b White	11	1/13 (2) 2/17 (3) 3/17 (4) (31 overs)	134
†Rashid Latif c Stewart b Anderson	0	4/52 (5) 5/59 (1) 6/59 (7)	
Wasim Akram c Giles b White	7	7/71 (6) 8/78 (8)	
Saqlain Mushtaq not out	12	9/80 (10) 10/134 (11) 15 overs: 53-4	

Bowling: Caddick 7–0–27–1; Anderson 10–2–29–4; Flintoff 9–2–37–2; White 5–0–33–3.

Umpires: B. G. Jerling (South Africa) and R. E. Koertzen (South Africa).
Third umpire: S. A. Bucknor (West Indies). Referee: M. J. Procter (South Africa).

"When Hussain referred to Graeme Smith as 'wotsisname' Smith expressed irritation, then imposed an authority so crushing that no one on the field is likely to forget his name as long as they live."

South Africans in England, page 427.

INDIA v NAMIBIA

At Pietermaritzburg, February 23, 2003. India won by 181 runs. Toss: Namibia. One-day international debut: B. O. van Rooi.

India's batting blasted off at last, propelling them to their biggest victory in the World Cup (at least until they thrashed Sri Lanka in the Super Six). Earlier in the week, the team had been greeted rapturously when they helped unveil a plaque at Pietermaritzburg station where, in 1893, Mahatma Gandhi had been thrown off a train because of his colour. Here at the cricket ground, their support was equally fervent. To shouts of "Sachin, Sachin", Tendulkar eased his way to 152 – his 34th one-day century – without ever producing that familiar, resounding crack of the bat. Namibia, who had chosen to field first, had the despair of dropping him on 32, although Ganguly played, if anything, with more freedom and found his form with hoisted fours and sixes. Together they added 244, their third stand of more than 200 in one-day internationals. Jan-Berrie Burger then injected some fire to Namibia's reply – hitting four fours and a six – but after he had gone their biggest success was managing to bat out more than 42 overs. India's main setback came when Nehra slipped and damaged his ankle attempting his second delivery.

Man of the Match: S. R. Tendulkar. *Attendance:* 4,805.

India

V. Sehwag c Keulder b van Vuuren	24
S. R. Tendulkar b van Vuuren	152
*S. C. Ganguly not out	112
Yuvraj Singh not out	7
L-b 2, w 13, n-b 1	16
1/46 (1) 2/290 (2) (2 wkts, 50 overs)	311
15 overs:	77-1

D. Mongia, †R. Dravid, M. Kaif, Harbhajan Singh, Zaheer Khan, J. Srinath and A. Nehra did not bat.

Bowling: Snyman 10–0–57–0; van Vuuren 10–1–53–2; L. J. Burger 6–0–49–0; van Rooi 6–0–36–0; B. L. Kotze 10–0–64–0; D. B. Kotze 8–0–50–0.

Namibia

S. J. Swanepoel lbw b Zaheer Khan	9
A. J. Burger b Mongia	29
L. J. Burger lbw b Zaheer Khan	0
D. Keulder c Mongia b Harbhajan Singh	4
G. B. Murgatroyd lbw b Harbhajan Singh	0
*D. B. Kotze c and b Mongia	27
†M. van Schoor c Dravid b Yuvraj Singh	24
B. O. van Rooi c Mongia b Yuvraj Singh	17
B. L. Kotze c Dravid b Yuvraj Singh	3
G. Snyman c Srinath b Yuvraj Singh	5
R. J. van Vuuren not out	0
L-b 1, w 8, n-b 3	12
1/19 (1) 2/21 (3) 3/43 (4) 4/47 (2) 5/47 (5) 6/98 (6) 7/99 (7) 8/124 (8) 9/124 (9) 10/130 (10) (42.3 overs)	130
15 overs:	47-5

Bowling: Srinath 6–0–25–0; Nehra 0.1–0–0–0; Zaheer Khan 7.5–0–24–2; Harbhajan Singh 10–1–34–2; Mongia 10–1–24–2; Sehwag 4–0–16–0; Yuvraj Singh 4.3–2–6–4.

Umpires: Aleem Dar (Pakistan) and D. R. Shepherd (England).
Third umpire: K. C. Barbour (Zimbabwe). Referee: Wasim Raja (Pakistan).

ZIMBABWE v AUSTRALIA

At Bulawayo, February 24, 2003. Australia won by seven wickets. Toss: Zimbabwe.

This should have been one of Zimbabwean cricket's greatest occasions but politics dominated the game. The selectors tried to drop Andy Flower for "not trying" against India until his team-mates threatened to boycott the match; Olonga remained out of the side, although spectators sang his favourite song in a show of solidarity. The information secretary of the ruling Zanu-PF party bizarrely announced, "Olonga is not a Zimbabwean, he is a Zambian. Flower is also not a Zimbabwean. He is British." On the pitch, Flower somehow put the machinations to one side and top-scored with 62, before being bamboozled by Hogg's flipper. Blignaut then launched into Gillespie and Hogg, crashing eight fours and two sixes in a blistering 28-ball 54, as Zimbabwe stood up to Australia. In reply, a smash-and grab fifty from Gilchrist, part of a rapid opening stand of 89, removed any pressure. Martyn and Lehmann cantered home and Australia made a swift exit from Bulawayo – and a game they had been urged to boycott. The English umpire Peter Willey was originally due to stand in this match, with Neil Mallender as third umpire, but both withdrew because they were unwilling to visit Zimbabwe.

Man of the Match: A. M. Blignaut. *Attendance:* 5,000.

Zimbabwe

C. B. Wishart b Gillespie	10
G. J. Whittall c Hogg b Gillespie	1
A. Flower b Hogg	62
G. W. Flower run out	37
D. D. Ebrahim b Hogg	15
†T. Taibu b McGrath	23
D. A. Marillier c Ponting b Hogg	0
A. M. Blignaut c and b Lee	54
*H. H. Streak not out	28
B. A. Murphy b McGrath	1
D. T. Hondo not out	1
B 4, l-b 3, w 3, n-b 4	14
(9 wkts, 50 overs)	246

1/13 (2) 2/28 (1) 3/113 (4) 4/121 (3) 5/142 (5) 6/142 (7) 7/208 (8) 8/242 (6) 9/244 (10) 15 overs: 52-2

Bowling: McGrath 9–2–24–2; Gillespie 9–1–50–2; Symonds 10–1–35–0; Lee 10–0–63–1; Hogg 8–0–46–3; Martyn 4–0–21–0.

Australia

†A. C. Gilchrist c sub (S. M. Ervine) b Marillier	61
M. L. Hayden c G. W. Flower b Hondo	34
*R. T. Ponting c and b Murphy	38
D. R. Martyn not out	50
D. S. Lehmann not out	56
L-b 1, w 8	9
(3 wkts, 47.3 overs)	248

1/89 (2) 2/113 (1) 3/156 (3) 15 overs: 92-1

M. G. Bevan, A. Symonds, G. B. Hogg, B. Lee, J. N. Gillespie and G. D. McGrath did not bat.

Bowling: Streak 6–0–38–0; Blignaut 10–0–54–0; Hondo 9–0–49–1; Whittall 3.3–0–26–0; Marillier 10–1–32–1; Murphy 9–0–48–1.

Umpires: B. F. Bowden (New Zealand) and D. L. Orchard (South Africa).
Third umpire: B. G. Jerling (South Africa). Referee: G. R. Viswanath (India).

500 not out: after taking his 500th wicket in one-day internationals during the match against Holland, Wasim Akram marks the occasion in unconventional style.
Picture by Clive Mason, Getty Images.

HOLLAND v PAKISTAN

At Paarl, February 25, 2003. Pakistan won by 97 runs. Toss: Holland.

With the result never in serious doubt, the spotlight centred on Wasim Akram, who began the match needing just one wicket to become the first to 500 in one-day internationals. The 36-year-old Wasim, playing his 354th game, admitted that, "like any youngster", he had been unable to sleep the previous night. But when Holland set off in pursuit of an improbable 254, he did not have to wait long: with his seventh ball he bowled Statham for a duck and wheeled away, whooping. His 500th wicket came 18 years and a day after his first, Robbie Kerr of Australia. Holland quickly subsided to 43 for four, and although van Bunge chipped in with a feisty 31, including a swat for six off Saqlain Mushtaq, they needed a generous helping of extras (the top-scorer, with 40) to take them past 150. Earlier, Yousuf Youhana dug a lackadaisical Pakistan out of a spot of bother with a run-a-ball 58, after Inzamam-ul-Haq had failed yet again. That set the stage for Wasim.

Man of the Match: Yousuf Youhana. *Attendance:* 5,508.

Pakistan

Taufeeq Umar run out	48
Saeed Anwar c Esmeijer b de Leede	25
Abdul Razzaq c Smits b van Bunge	47
Inzamam-ul-Haq lbw b de Leede	0
Yousuf Youhana b Lefebvre	58
Salim Elahi c Zuiderent b van Bunge	5
†Rashid Latif c van Bunge b Schiferli	24
Wasim Akram run out	1
Shoaib Akhtar not out	26
*Waqar Younis c and b Mol	1
Saqlain Mushtaq not out	3
B 1, l-b 8, w 6	15
1/61 (2) 2/106 (1) 3/108 (4) 4/143 (3) 5/153 (6) 6/192 (7) 7/196 (8) 8/238 (5) 9/245 (10) (9 wkts, 50 overs)	253
15 overs: 69-1	

Bowling: Schiferli 10–1–48–1; Lefebvre 10–1–39–1; de Leede 10–0–53–2; van Troost 2–0–18–0; Esmeijer 10–0–35–0; van Bunge 4–0–27–2; Mol 4–0–24–1.

Holland

N. A. Statham b Wasim Akram 0
E. Schiferli c Abdul Razzaq b Shoaib Akhtar . 9
B. Zuiderent lbw b Waqar Younis 8
K-J. J. van Noortwijk c Rashid Latif b Wasim Akram . 7
T. B. M. de Leede c Shoaib Akhtar b Saqlain Mushtaq . 15
D. L. S. van Bunge c Rashid Latif b Abdul Razzaq . 31
L. P. van Troost c Rashid Latif b Shoaib Akhtar . 22
H-J. C. Mol b Shoaib Akhtar 13
J-J. Esmeijer lbw b Saeed Anwar 0
*R. P. Lefebvre not out 4
†J. Smits lbw b Wasim Akram 7
B 6, l-b 11, w 17, n-b 6 40

1/6 (1) 2/31 (2) 3/35 (3) (39.3 overs) 156
4/43 (4) 5/78 (5)
6/108 (6) 7/135 (8)
8/136 (9) 9/138 (7)
10/156 (11) 15 overs: 58-4

Bowling: Wasim Akram 8.3–2–24–3; Shoaib Akhtar 7–0–26–3; Waqar Younis 6–1–19–1; Saqlain Mushtaq 8–2–32–1; Abdul Razzaq 6–0–23–1; Saeed Anwar 4–0–15–1.

Umpires: S. A. Bucknor (West Indies) and S. Venkataraghavan (India).
Third umpire: T. H. Wijewardene (Sri Lanka). Referee: C. H. Lloyd (West Indies).

ENGLAND v INDIA

At Durban, February 26, 2003 (day/night). India won by 82 runs. Toss: India.

This time it was England who fell foul of the toss of a coin and a zesty young fast bowler. Beginning the match with a dicky ankle and 30 wickets in 32 one-day internationals, Nehra snatched six for 23 and wiped out England's chase with searing pace and swing – much as Anderson had done to Pakistan. It was, at the time, the third-best analysis in World Cup history – and the best away from the green fields of Headingley. It was also a kick in the guts for England, who had earlier managed to subdue India after a booming overture worth 75 from the first 11 overs. It was Flintoff who silenced the innings: Sehwag got a leading edge and Tendulkar, in ineffable form and hitting with silky ferocity, cut to point just after drinks. After that, the next ten overs produced 21 runs; Flintoff, straight and fast, leaked just nine in his first eight overs. However, Dravid and Yuvraj Singh broke loose, adding a run-a-ball 62, and though England filched four wickets from the last four balls, their spirits were soon flagging again. Knight underestimated Kaif's agility and was run out in the second over of the reply, Trescothick mis-hooked, and as the ball swung under the lights, Vaughan barely survived a mesmeric spell from Zaheer Khan. Nehra then made the key thrusts: in his third over, he induced a bottom-edge from Hussain, then trapped Stewart with an in-swinger; in his fourth, he had Vaughan caught behind with something equally unanswerable. The top six had made 62 between them, and only Flintoff, in his best all-round performance for England, prevented a massacre.

Man of the Match: A. Nehra. *Attendance:* 18,353.

India

V. Sehwag c and b Flintoff 23
S. R. Tendulkar c Collingwood b Flintoff 50
*S. C. Ganguly c Trescothick b White . . 19
D. Mongia lbw b Collingwood 32
†R. Dravid c Collingwood b Caddick . . . 62
Yuvraj Singh c Hussain b Anderson 42
M. Kaif c Flintoff b Caddick 5
Harbhajan Singh not out 0
Zaheer Khan run out 0
J. Srinath c Trescothick b Caddick 0
B 1, l-b 4, w 9, n-b 3 17

1/60 (1) 2/91 (2) (9 wkts, 50 overs) 250
3/107 (3) 4/155 (4)
5/217 (6) 6/250 (7) 7/250 (5)
8/250 (9) 9/250 (10) 15 overs: 91-1

A. Nehra did not bat.

Bowling: Caddick 10–0–69–3; Anderson 10–0–61–1; Flintoff 10–2–15–2; White 10–0–57–1; Irani 6–0–28–0; Collingwood 4–0–15–1.

England

M. E. Trescothick c Tendulkar b Zaheer Khan	8
N. V. Knight run out	1
M. P. Vaughan c Dravid b Nehra	20
*N. Hussain c Dravid b Nehra	15
†A. J. Stewart lbw b Nehra	0
P. D. Collingwood c Sehwag b Nehra	18
A. Flintoff c Sehwag b Srinath	64
C. White c Dravid b Nehra	13
R. C. Irani c Sehwag b Nehra	0
A. R. Caddick not out	13
J. M. Anderson lbw b Zaheer Khan	2
L-b 5, w 7, n-b 2	14
1/6 (2) 2/18 (1) 3/52 (4) 4/52 (5) 5/62 (3) 6/93 (6) 7/107 (8) 8/107 (9) 9/162 (7) 10/168 (11) (45.3 overs)	168
15 overs: 45-2	

Bowling: Zaheer Khan 9.3–1–29–2; Srinath 10–0–37–1; Nehra 10–2–23–6; Ganguly 6–0–34–0; Harbhajan Singh 10–0–40–0.

Umpires: R. E. Koertzen (South Africa) and S. J. A. Taufel (Australia).
Third umpire: E. A. R. de Silva (Sri Lanka). Referee: R. S. Madugalle (Sri Lanka).

AUSTRALIA v NAMIBIA

At Potchefstroom, February 27, 2003. Australia won by 256 runs. Toss: Australia.

As expected, this was the biggest mismatch of the tournament: Namibia's collection of part-timers against the world's best. Australia thundered to a forbidding 301, led by Hayden's ruthless 88, but even he was eclipsed by Lehmann, who began the last over on 22 and ended it by launching a soaring leg-side six to bring up his fifty. Van Vuuren had gone for 28 – the most expensive over in World Cup history. More history followed

BIGGEST WORLD CUP WINS BY RUNS

256	**Australia (301-6) beat Namibia (45)**	**Potchefstroom**	**2002-03**
202	England (334-4) beat India (132-3)	Lord's	1975
196	England (290-5) beat East Africa (94)	Birmingham	1975
192	Pakistan (330-6) beat Sri Lanka (138)	Nottingham	1975
191	West Indies (360-4) beat Sri Lanka (169-4)	Karachi	1987-88
183	**India (292-6) beat Sri Lanka (109)**	**Johannesburg**	**2002-03**
181	New Zealand (309-5) beat East Africa (128-8)	Birmingham	1975
181	**India (311-2) beat Namibia (130)**	**Pietermaritzburg**	**2002-03**
171	**Pakistan (255-9) beat Namibia (84)**	**Kimberley**	**2002-03**

Three of the six ten-wicket wins in World Cups were also in the 2002-03 tournament.

soon afterwards, when Namibia were bowled out in 14 overs and lost by 256 runs – the heaviest defeat in one-day internationals. Only Deon Kotze (plus Extras) made it into double figures. By doing little more than bowling accurately, McGrath took seven for 15, another World Cup record, beating Winston Davis's seven for 51 at Headingley in 1983, and the second-best in any one-day international. Afterwards he nonchalantly claimed that he had bowled better earlier in the tournament. "I'll feel better when I take eight against England," he added. Eight months later, Namibia would lose to Australia by a record 142–0 in a rugby World Cup game held, appropriately enough for a cricket score, at the Adelaide Oval. Van Vuuren, though in the rugby squad, managed to escape playing in that.

Man of the Match: G. D. McGrath. *Attendance:* 5,966.

Australia

†A. C. Gilchrist b van Rooi	13	D. S. Lehmann not out	50
M. L. Hayden b L. J. Burger	88	G. B. Hogg not out	19
M. G. Bevan c and b L. J. Burger	17	L-b 8, w 6, n-b 4	18
A. Symonds run out	59		
*R. T. Ponting c D. B. Kotze b L. J. Burger	2	1/26 (1) 2/104 (3) 3/140 (2) 4/146 (5) 5/230 (4) 6/231 (6)	(6 wkts, 50 overs) 301
D. R. Martyn b B. L. Kotze	35		15 overs: 66-1

B. Lee, A. J. Bichel and G. D. McGrath did not bat.

Bowling: van Vuuren 10–0–92–0; van Rooi 6–0–24–1; B. L. Kotze 10–0–62–1; L. J. Burger 10–1–39–3; D. B. Kotze 10–0–54–0; A. J. Burger 4–0–22–0.

Namibia

A. J. Burger c Ponting b McGrath	4	B. O. van Rooi not out	0
S. J. Swanepoel c Ponting b Lee	2	R. J. van Vuuren c Gilchrist b Bichel	0
M. Karg c Gilchrist b McGrath	4		
D. Keulder c Gilchrist b McGrath	3	L-b 4, w 6, n-b 5	15
G. B. Murgatroyd lbw b McGrath	0		
*D. B. Kotze c Gilchrist b McGrath	10	1/5 (1) 2/14 (2) 3/16 (3) 4/17 (5) 5/28 (4) 6/34 (7) 7/45 (6) 8/45 (9) 9/45 (8) 10/45 (11)	(14 overs) 45
L. J. Burger c Gilchrist b McGrath	1		
†M. van Schoor c Gilchrist b Bichel	6		
B. L. Kotze b McGrath	0		

Bowling: McGrath 7–4–15–7; Lee 6–1–26–1; Bichel 1–1–0–2.

Umpires: B. F. Bowden (New Zealand) and R. B. Tiffin (Zimbabwe).
Third umpire: N. A. Mallender (England). Referee: G. R. Viswanath (India).

ZIMBABWE v HOLLAND

At Bulawayo, February 28, 2003. Zimbabwe won by 99 runs. Toss: Holland.

Two spectators, one black, one white, who unfurled a banner reading "Zimbabwe Needs Justice" – and, once out of camera shot, were led away by the police – put any heroics on the field in stark perspective. Not that there were many. Andy Flower caressed, glided and reverse-swept his way to 71, an artist among artisans; and Blignaut and Streak biffed a very biffable attack, both scoring freely as Zimbabwe flicked on the afterburners and blazed 165 in the last 20 overs. In reply, Holland never looked like getting the win that would have smoothed England's path to the Super Six. Van Bunge and Lefebvre played a sprinkling of boisterous shots, but the biggest cheer was for Henry Olonga – now emerging as cricket's conscience, and fielding as substitute in place of his co-protester, Andy Flower.

Man of the Match: H. H. Streak. *Attendance:* 4,850.

Zimbabwe

C. B. Wishart c Smits b Lefebvre	21	†T. Taibu not out	7
M. A. Vermeulen b Kloppenburg	27		
A. Flower c Esmeijer b Schiferli	71	L-b 3, w 7	10
G. J. Whittall c Zuiderent b Kloppenburg	30		
D. D. Ebrahim b de Leede	32	1/24 (1) 2/82 (2) 3/135 (4) 4/165 (3) 5/245 (6) 6/274 (5) 7/281 (8) 8/301 (7)	(8 wkts, 50 overs) 301
A. M. Blignaut c Kloppenburg b Schiferli	58		
*H. H. Streak c Esmeijer b de Leede	44		
D. A. Marillier lbw b Lefebvre	1		15 overs: 61-1

B. A. Murphy and D. T. Hondo did not bat.

Bowling: Schiferli 10–2–43–2; Lefebvre 8–0–38–2; de Leede 7–0–69–2; Kloppenburg 10–0–40–2; Esmeijer 9–0–60–0; van Bunge 3–0–22–0; Mol 3–0–26–0.

Holland

J. F. Kloppenburg c Streak b Hondo	18	*R. P. Lefebvre b Marillier	30
E. Schiferli b Streak	22	†J. Smits not out	8
B. Zuiderent run out	15	J-J. Esmeijer not out	3
D. L. S. van Bunge lbw b Whittall	37	B 1, l-b 7, w 3, n-b 1	12
T. B. M. de Leede lbw b Murphy	1		
L. P. van Troost c Hondo b Murphy	26	1/41 (2) 2/49 (1) (9 wkts, 50 overs)	202
R. H. Scholte c Blignaut b Murphy	7	3/80 (3) 4/85 (5)	
H-J. C. Mol c sub (H. K. Olonga) b Marillier	23	5/127 (6) 6/128 (4) 7/148 (7)	
		8/190 (9) 9/191 (8) 15 overs: 46-1	

Bowling: Blignaut 10–1–30–0; Streak 10–1–36–1; Hondo 6–1–16–1; Murphy 10–3–44–3; Marillier 9–0–49–2; Whittall 5–1–19–1.

Umpires: S. A. Bucknor (West Indies) and T. H. Wijewardene (Sri Lanka).
Third umpire: Nadeem Ghauri (Pakistan). Referee: C. H. Lloyd (West Indies).

INDIA v PAKISTAN

At Centurion, March 1, 2003. India won by six wickets. Toss: Pakistan.

Though the players played down the first clash between India and Pakistan since June 2000, it remained the tournament's most feverishly talked-up match. Almost incredibly, the cricket lived up to the hype. Under a hot sun and in front of a crammed stadium (and a TV audience implausibly guesstimated at a billion) Tendulkar played an astounding innings – perhaps the best of the tournament, and undoubtedly one of his best in one-day internationals. Chasing 274, on a shirtfront but against a testosterone-propelled pace attack, he hit a vivid and memorable stream of shots, none so perfect as the cut six and the two fours – one swirled into the leg side, one pushed down the ground – which concluded Shoaib Akhtar's first over. By the 12th, India had reached 100; Tendulkar, missed on 32 and struggling with cramp, went on to 98 from 75 balls. After the storm came calm, as Dravid and Yuvraj Singh eased home to maintain India's pristine World Cup record (four wins out of four) against Pakistan. All along it had been a batsman's match, started by Saeed Anwar, whose century, full of dextrous, angle-batted shots, contained only seven boundaries. It took the ball of the game – a rapid Nehra yorker – to remove him. Younis Khan provided a late, impish flourish, along with Rashid Latif, who was hit on the helmet and could not keep wicket. But the 28 extras in India's innings were not so much an indictment of Taufeeq Umar's keeping as of the experienced fast bowlers who billowed in with passion but not discipline. The win guaranteed India's progress and nudged the door further open for England.

Man of the Match: S. R. Tendulkar. *Attendance:* 19,679.

Pakistan

Saeed Anwar b Nehra	101	†Rashid Latif not out	29
Taufeeq Umar b Zaheer Khan	22	Wasim Akram not out	10
Abdul Razzaq c Dravid b Nehra	12	B 2, l-b 7, w 11, n-b 7	27
Inzamam-ul-Haq run out	6		
Yousuf Youhana c Zaheer Khan b Srinath	25	1/58 (2) 2/90 (3) (7 wkts, 50 overs)	273
Younis Khan c Mongia b Zaheer Khan	32	3/98 (4) 4/171 (5)	
Shahid Afridi c Kumble b Mongia	9	5/195 (1) 6/208 (7) 7/256 (6) 15 overs: 72-1	

Shoaib Akhtar and *Waqar Younis did not bat.

Bowling: Zaheer Khan 10–0–46–2; Srinath 10–0–41–1; Nehra 10–0–74–2; Kumble 10–0–51–0; Ganguly 3–0–14–0; Sehwag 4–0–19–0; Mongia 3–0–19–1.

India

S. R. Tendulkar c Younis Khan b Shoaib Akhtar	98	†R. Dravid not out	44
V. Sehwag c Shahid Afridi b Waqar Younis	21	Yuvraj Singh not out	50
*S. C. Ganguly lbw b Waqar Younis	0	B 1, l-b 3, w 19, n-b 5	28
M. Kaif b Shahid Afridi	35	1/53 (2) 2/53 (3) 3/155 (4) 4/177 (1) (4 wkts, 45.4 overs)	276
		15 overs: 120-2	

D. Mongia, A. Kumble, Zaheer Khan, J. Srinath and A. Nehra did not bat.

Bowling: Wasim Akram 10–0–48–0; Shoaib Akhtar 10–0–72–1; Waqar Younis 8.4–0–71–2; Shahid Afridi 9–0–45–1; Abdul Razzaq 8–0–36–0.

Umpires: R. E. Koertzen (South Africa) and D. R. Shepherd (England).
Third umpire: B. F. Bowden (New Zealand). Referee: M. J. Procter (South Africa).

AUSTRALIA v ENGLAND

At Port Elizabeth, March 2, 2003. Australia won by two wickets. Toss: England.

As Bichel and Bevan ran off delirious, England stood still. Hussain was on his knees, his head in his hands; Stewart stood with his back to his team-mates: both would later announce their retirement from one-day matches. How had this happened? How had Australia – chasing 205, in terrible trouble at 48 for four, and again at 135 for eight – won with two balls to spare? "Bichel" was the short answer. First, he took seven for 20 on a slow pitch and strangled England's innings; then he struck a granite-willed 34 not out from No. 10 to end their fightback – and, as it turned out, their World Cup. With Australia needing 14 from two overs, Hussain threw the ball not to Caddick (9–2–35–4 at the time) but Anderson (8–0–54–0). It was a hunch he later came to regret: Bichel swung the second ball for six, a four followed, and the game was gone. It was the final twist in a match full of them. England's openers had the Barmy Army in raptures with a stand of 66 in nine overs – milking, seemingly at will, a furious McGrath. In response, Ponting brought on Bichel; half an hour later he had four for ten, having found just enough seam movement to reward his accuracy. Flintoff and Stewart played sensibly, if slowly, adding 90 in just under 25 overs, before Bichel returned and made sure there would be no late surge. In reply, Caddick made early incisions, but it was Bichel and Bevan, with a magnificent 74, who made the headlines. Australia had won their 12th successive one-day international – a record – beating West Indies' 11 between June 1984 and February 1985. Defeat was not necessarily disastrous for England – there were tortuous mathematical calculations that suggested it might, in some circumstances, even help their chances of reaching the Super Six. In the event, it did prove their undoing. And it was yet another chapter in the 14-year saga of humiliation against their oldest cricketing enemy.

Man of the Match: A. J. Bichel. *Attendance:* 15,987.

No worries mate: Andy Bichel (*left*) and Michael Bevan celebrate after dragging Australia from a seemingly hopeless 135 for eight to victory against England. Marcus Trescothick sees it otherwise.

Picture by Darren Staples, Reuters.

England

Batsman	Runs
M. E. Trescothick c Martyn b McGrath	37
N. V. Knight c Martyn b Bichel	30
M. P. Vaughan c Gilchrist b Bichel	2
*N. Hussain b Bichel	1
†A. J. Stewart b Bichel	46
P. D. Collingwood c Gilchrist b Bichel	10
A. Flintoff c Gilchrist b Bichel	45
C. White not out	16
A. F. Giles c Bevan b Bichel	2
A. R. Caddick not out	5
L-b 3, w 3, n-b 4	10
1/66 (2) 2/72 (3) 3/74 (4) 4/74 (1) 5/87 (6) 6/177 (7) 7/180 (5) 8/187 (9) — (8 wkts, 50 overs)	204

15 overs: 75-4

J. M. Anderson did not bat.

Bowling: McGrath 9–2–41–1; Lee 9–0–58–0; Bichel 10–0–20–7; Hogg 10–1–28–0; Lehmann 10–0–34–0; Symonds 2–0–20–0.

Australia

Batsman	Runs
†A. C. Gilchrist c Vaughan b Caddick	22
M. L. Hayden c Giles b Caddick	1
*R. T. Ponting c Giles b Caddick	18
D. R. Martyn lbw b Caddick	0
D. S. Lehmann c Stewart b White	37
M. G. Bevan not out	74
A. Symonds c and b Giles	0
G. B. Hogg c Stewart b Giles	1
B. Lee run out	6
A. J. Bichel not out	34
B 4, l-b 4, w 4, n-b 3	15
1/15 (2) 2/33 (1) 3/33 (4) 4/48 (3) 5/111 (5) 6/112 (7) 7/114 (8) 8/135 (9) — (8 wkts, 49.4 overs)	208

15 overs: 60-4

G. D. McGrath did not bat.

Bowling: Caddick 9–2–35–4; Anderson 9–0–66–0; Flintoff 9.4–1–26–0; White 10–2–21–1; Giles 10–0–42–2; Vaughan 2–0–10–0.

Umpires: Aleem Dar (Pakistan) and R. B. Tiffin (Zimbabwe).
Third umpire: D. L. Orchard (South Africa). Referee: Wasim Raja (Pakistan).

Raising their game: Tim de Leede, Jan Smits (both Holland) and Jan-Berrie Burger (Namibia) showed that smaller stars could shine brightly too.
Pictures by Getty Images.

HOLLAND v NAMIBIA

At Bloemfontein, March 3, 2003. Holland won by 64 runs. Toss: Holland.

Holland swept home in this clash of the club cricketers. Revelling in some beatable opposition at last, they won their first World Cup match in 11 attempts; sadly, a hamstring injury meant their captain, Roland Lefebvre, could only watch what was supposed to be his last game. Feiko Kloppenburg and the unbeaten Klaas-Jan van Noortwijk entered uncharted waters for Dutch cricket as they became the first batsmen to make one-day international centuries for Holland, and they added 228 for the second wicket. Holland's final total of 314 was 13 more than the Australians had managed against the same opposition four days earlier. Namibia's brave run-chase was led by a typically strong-armed 41 from Jan-Berrie Burger, matched by his opening partner Morne Karg. But Kloppenburg's medium-pace maintained control, and Namibia flew home without a win. Unlike Bangladesh, they went home happy.

Man of the Match: J. F. Kloppenburg. *Attendance:* 2,939.

Holland

J. F. Kloppenburg c van Schoor b Snyman	121
E. Schiferli b van Vuuren	10
K-J. J. van Noortwijk not out	134
B. Zuiderent b L. J. Burger	5
T. B. M. de Leede b L. J. Burger	0
*L. P. van Troost not out	16
B 4, l-b 2, w 18, n-b 4	28
1/25 (2) 2/253 (1) 3/270 (4) 4/270 (5) — (4 wkts, 50 overs)	314
15 overs: 73-1	

D. L. S. van Bunge, H-J. C. Mol, J-J. Esmeijer, †J. Smits and Adeel Raja did not bat.

Bowling: Snyman 10–0–55–1; van Vuuren 10–1–63–1; van Rooi 8–0–59–0; L. J. Burger 10–1–49–2; A. J. Burger 3–0–18–0; Kotze 4–0–29–0; S. F. Burger 5–0–35–0.

Namibia

A. J. Burger c sub (R. G. Nijman) b Kloppenburg	41
M. Karg c sub (R. G. Nijman) b de Leede	41
D. Keulder b Kloppenburg	52
G. B. Murgatroyd c Zuiderent b Mol	52
*D. B. Kotze lbw b Adeel Raja	25
L. J. Burger b Kloppenburg	1
G. Snyman c de Leede b Kloppenburg	0
S. F. Burger st Smits b Adeel Raja	6
†M. van Schoor b Adeel Raja	15
B. O. van Rooi not out	9
R. J. van Vuuren c Mol b Adeel Raja	0
L-b 5, w 2, n-b 1	8
1/76 (1) 2/87 (2) 3/179 (3) 4/209 (4) 5/213 (6) 6/213 (7) 7/224 (8) 8/237 (5) 9/250 (9) 10/250 (11) — (46.5 overs)	250
15 overs: 78-1	

Bowling: Schiferli 7–0–46–0; Esmeijer 7–0–43–0; de Leede 8–0–33–1; Kloppenburg 10–0–42–4; Adeel Raja 8.5–0–42–4; Mol 6–0–39–1.

Umpires: D. J. Harper (Australia) and Nadeem Ghauri (Pakistan).
Third umpire: D. B. Hair (Australia). Referee: G. R. Viswanath (India).

ZIMBABWE v PAKISTAN

At Bulawayo, March 4, 2003. No result. Toss: Pakistan.

The fate of three teams, scrapping for one place in the Super Six, hinged on the outcome here, and after persistent drizzle limited play to just 14 overs, it was Zimbabwe who emerged smiling. England would almost certainly have qualified had Pakistan won. Pakistan themselves had a faint hope, which rested on winning by a margin large enough to overhaul England's vastly superior net run-rate. But, in the event, Zimbabwe picked up two points for the no-result and pulled clear in third place. While they celebrated a spot in the second phase for the second World Cup in a row, England and Pakistan were left to rue the controversial decision not to set aside a reserve day for group matches. When Pakistan chose to bat, they needed at least 300 to give themselves a remote chance but by the second over the rain had arrived. Then, with Pakistan 73 for three, the players were driven off for the third, and final, time. The miserable Inzamam-ul-Haq was one of the batsmen to fall; he ended the competition with 19 runs in six innings. Nasser Hussain responded to England's elimination by resigning the one-day captaincy.

Attendance: 3,964.

Pakistan

Saeed Anwar not out	40
Salim Elahi lbw b Hondo	4
Yousuf Youhana c Taibu b Streak	17
Inzamam-ul-Haq c Whittall b Ervine	3
Younis Khan not out	0
B 1, l-b 6, w 2	9
1/4 (2) 2/55 (3) 3/72 (4) — (3 wkts, 14 overs)	73
11 overs: 55-2	

Azhar Mahmood, †Rashid Latif, Wasim Akram, Shoaib Akhtar, *Waqar Younis and Mohammad Sami did not bat.

Bowling: Streak 7–1–25–1; Hondo 4–0–22–1; Ervine 3–0–19–1.

Zimbabwe

C. B. Wishart, D. D. Ebrahim, A. Flower, G. W. Flower, G. J. Whittall, †T. Taibu, A. M. Blignaut, *H. H. Streak, S. M. Ervine, D. A. Marillier and D. T. Hondo.

Umpires: B. F. Bowden (New Zealand) and E. A. R. de Silva (Sri Lanka).
Third umpire: R. E. Koertzen (South Africa). Referee: R. S. Madugalle (Sri Lanka).

POOL B

SOUTH AFRICA v WEST INDIES

At Cape Town, February 9, 2003 (day/night). West Indies won by three runs. Toss: West Indies.

After the South African board's evangelical campaign and Olympic-standard opening ceremony the previous night (a world away from the half-hearted fiasco at Lord's four years earlier), the opening game needed to be great – and it was, thanks to a masterful performance from a great player. Unfortunately for the organisers, though, he was not South African. It was Lara: he lit up Newlands with a century that transformed a terrible West Indies start when Pollock reduced them to seven for two. Playing his first competitive innings since mysteriously falling ill in Sri Lanka five months earlier, Lara was almost out first ball when Kallis dropped a hard chance at second slip. At first he seemed to be over-cautious: it was 30 for two after 15 overs and still 67 for two after 25. But then he tore into Donald and Klusener with a bat as swift as a scimitar to reach 116 off 134 balls. With Powell and Sarwan scoring even more spectacularly – Pollock's penultimate over cost 23 runs – 110 came off the last ten, and West Indies amazed themselves by reaching 278. With one over docked because of their slow over-rate, South Africa were up against it. But Kirsten held on, Boucher hit out and then came Klusener, dragging the bittersweet memories of the 1999 tournament with him. His bat still as broad, his jaw still as set, he set out to improve a World Cup average of 140.50. He might have gone when Collins carried a catch over the boundary, but when his fifth six took him to his fifty, South Africa were favourites. However, with four balls remaining and eight needed, Klusener was caught by Hooper at deep mid-wicket. He and Boje failed to cross, leaving the tailenders exposed to Drakes.

Man of the Match: B. C. Lara. *Attendance:* 24,180.

West Indies

C. H. Gayle b Pollock	2
W. W. Hinds c Boucher b Pollock	0
B. C. Lara c Pollock b Ntini	116
S. Chanderpaul c Boucher b Klusener	34
*C. L. Hooper c Kallis b Ntini	40
R. L. Powell not out	40
R. R. Sarwan not out	32
L-b 6, w 4, n-b 4	14
1/4 (2) 2/7 (1) 3/109 (4) 4/198 (5) 5/215 (3) (5 wkts, 50 overs)	278
15 overs: 30-2	

†R. D. Jacobs, V. C. Drakes, M. Dillon and P. T. Collins did not bat.

Bowling: Pollock 10–2–52–2; Ntini 10–1–37–2; Donald 9–0–54–0; Kallis 10–2–52–0; Klusener 8–0–53–1; Boje 3–0–24–0.

South Africa

H. H. Gibbs c Jacobs b Dillon	24
G. Kirsten c and b Dillon	69
H. H. Dippenaar st Jacobs b Hooper	20
J. H. Kallis c Jacobs b Collins	13
J. N. Rhodes b Hooper	2
†M. V. Boucher b Gayle	49
*S. M. Pollock c Hooper b Gayle	4
L. Klusener c Hooper b Drakes	57
N. Boje not out	25
M. Ntini c Sarwan b Drakes	0
A. A. Donald not out	0
L-b 4, w 5, n-b 3	12
1/46 (1) 2/79 (3) 3/104 (4) 4/117 (5) 5/155 (2) 6/160 (7) 7/204 (6) 8/271 (8) 9/271 (10) (9 wkts, 49 overs)	275
14 overs: 62-1	

Bowling: Dillon 10–0–47–2; Collins 9–0–54–1; Drakes 8–1–33–2; Hooper 10–0–63–2; Gayle 10–1–60–2; Powell 2–0–14–0.

Umpires: D. J. Harper (Australia) and S. Venkataraghavan (India).
Third umpire: P. Willey (England). Referee: R. S. Madugalle (Sri Lanka).

NEW ZEALAND v SRI LANKA

At Bloemfontein, February 10, 2003. Sri Lanka won by 47 runs. Toss: New Zealand.

A courageous lone hand from Styris was not enough to prevent an easy Sri Lankan win, which revolved around a run-a-ball second-wicket stand of 170 between Jayasuriya and Tillekeratne. But the result could have been different if umpire Mallender had spotted a thin edge off Tuffey when Jayasuriya had 18. After that, only a sharp chance on 86 to Vincent, chosen as wicket-keeper ahead of McCullum, marred Jayasuriya's path to his 16th one-day century, which came up in 111 balls with a characteristically raucous upper cut to the third-man boundary. Sri Lanka were heading for 300, but Astle applied the brakes, and Tillekeratne, who hit just five fours in his patient 106-ball innings, was hindered when forced to use a runner after an attack of cramp. On a pudding of a pitch, New Zealand quickly made a meal of their reply. But from 15 for three, Styris responded in style, crashing 141 in 125 balls, including six sixes, three courtesy of Popeye-forearm slog-sweeps off Muralitharan. His team-mates, however, struggled against Sri Lanka's battery of slow bowlers – Fleming later admitted it had been an error to leave out their left-arm spinner, Vettori – and by the time Styris was last out, he had scored 63% of his side's runs. Only Glenn Turner, with an unbeaten 171 against East Africa at Edgbaston in 1975, had made more for New Zealand in a one-day international.

Man of the Match: S. T. Jayasuriya. *Attendance:* 3,766.

Sri Lanka

M. S. Atapattu c Styris b Bond	6
*S. T. Jayasuriya lbw b Astle	120
H. P. Tillekeratne not out	81
D. P. M. D. Jayawardene lbw b Adams	1
P. A. de Silva c Styris b Astle	12
†K. C. Sangakkara c Adams b Astle	13
R. P. Arnold b Bond	12
W. P. U. J. C. Vaas b Adams	5
M. Muralitharan not out	4
B 3, l-b 6, w 4, n-b 5	18
1/23 (1) 2/193 (2) 3/196 (4) 4/213 (5) 5/240 (6) 6/256 (7) 7/263 (8) (7 wkts, 50 overs)	272

15 overs: 83-1

C. R. D. Fernando and P. W. Gunaratne did not bat.

Bowling: Tuffey 5–0–36–0; Bond 10–1–44–2; Oram 10–0–37–0; Adams 9–0–58–2; Harris 4–0–26–0; Styris 5–0–28–0; Astle 7–0–34–3.

New Zealand

*S. P. Fleming c Sangakkara b Gunaratne	1
N. J. Astle run out	0
C. D. McMillan c Sangakkara b Gunaratne	3
S. B. Styris c Vaas b Arnold	141
C. L. Cairns c and b de Silva	32
†L. Vincent c Muralitharan b Jayasuriya	1
C. Z. Harris b Muralitharan	13
J. D. P. Oram st Sangakkara b Muralitharan	12
A. R. Adams c sub (J. Mubarak) b Arnold	1
D. R. Tuffey c Sangakkara b Arnold	4
S. E. Bond not out	2
L-b 10, w 5	15
1/1 (2) 2/2 (1) 3/15 (3) 4/93 (5) 5/94 (6) 6/150 (7) 7/179 (8) 8/182 (9) 9/200 (10) 10/225 (4) (45.3 overs)	225

15 overs: 63-3

Bowling: Vaas 7–0–22–0; Gunaratne 5–0–24–2; Fernando 3–1–19–0; Muralitharan 9–1–42–2; Jayasuriya 8–0–32–1; de Silva 5–0–29–1; Arnold 8.3–0–47–3.

Umpires: S. A. Bucknor (West Indies) and N. A. Mallender (England).
Third umpire: R. B. Tiffin (Zimbabwe). Referee: M. J. Procter (South Africa).

BANGLADESH v CANADA

At Durban, February 11, 2003 (day/night). Canada won by 60 runs. Toss: Canada. One-day international debuts: Canada (all).

Nearly four years after tearing up the World Cup form-book against Pakistan at Northampton, Bangladesh were themselves humbled by a Canadian side playing their first full international since 1979 and containing players born in eight different countries. Canada's hero was Austin Codrington, a 27-year-old apprentice plumber from Jamaica with flopping dreadlocks and an open-chested action, who unplugged the Bangladeshi batting with his wobbly medium-pace. His five for 27 was the third-best by a player on one-day international debut (behind Tony Dodemaide of Australia with five for 21 against Sri Lanka in 1987-88 and S. H. U. Karnain of Sri Lanka with five for 26 against New Zealand in 1983-84). At 106 for four in the 21st over, Bangladesh were on course, only for the last six wickets to tumble for 14 in 44 balls amid a flurry of panicky strokes. The Canadians, keen as mustard, celebrated each wicket with disbelieving leaps and hugs; the Bangladeshis, who had won none of their 43 Tests and one-day internationals since Northampton, simply looked stunned. Back in Canada, people were stunned as well, and the two national papers – the *National Post* and the *Globe and Mail* – made the result front-page news. After choosing to bat, Canada were given a decent start thanks to a clumping cameo from the St Kitts-born David Chumney, and a more patient 42 from Ian Billcliff, raised in New Zealand and the scorer of a first-class century for Otago. But from 70 for two, the innings petered out, and only a last-wicket stand of 21 lifted them to 180. It should not have been enough.

Man of the Match: A. Codrington. *Attendance:* 10,482.

Canada

Batsman	Runs
I. Maraj c Sanwar Hossain b Tapash Baisya	24
J. M. Davison b Mashrafe bin Mortaza	8
D. Chumney run out	28
I. S. Billcliff run out	42
*J. V. Harris c Khaled Masud b Sanwar Hossain	4
N. A. De Groot c Alok Kapali b Sanwar Hossain	0
A. F. Sattaur lbw b Alok Kapali	13
†A. Bagai b Mashrafe bin Mortaza	7
S. Thuraisingam lbw b Mohammad Rafiq	6
A. Codrington c Tapash Baisya b Manjurul Islam	16
D. Joseph not out	9
L-b 7, w 14, n-b 2	23
1/18 (2) 2/47 (1) 3/70 (3) 4/92 (5) 5/104 (6) 6/130 (7) 7/134 (4) 8/146 (8) 9/159 (9) 10/180 (10) (49.1 overs)	180

15 overs: 71-3

Bowling: Manjurul Islam 8.1–1–30–1; Mashrafe bin Mortaza 8–0–38–2; Tapash Baisya 3–0–26–1; Mohammad Rafiq 10–2–34–1; Sanwar Hossain 10–0–26–2; Alok Kapali 10–0–19–1.

Bangladesh

Batsman	Runs
Hannan Sarkar c Bagai b Codrington	25
Al Sahariar c sub (A. M. Samad) b Joseph	9
Habibul Bashar c Bagai b Thuraisingam	0
Ehsanul Haque c Bagai b Joseph	13
Sanwar Hossain lbw b Davison	25
Alok Kapali lbw b Codrington	19
*†Khaled Masud c sub (A. M. Samad) b Davison	1
Mohammad Rafiq c Davison b Codrington	12
Tapash Baisya c Sattaur b Codrington	0
Mashrafe bin Mortaza c Sattaur b Codrington	0
Manjurul Islam not out	0
L-b 2, w 14	16
1/33 (2) 2/44 (3) 3/46 (1) 4/76 (4) 5/106 (5) 6/108 (6) 7/108 (7) 8/119 (9) 9/119 (10) 10/120 (8) (28 overs)	120

15 overs: 76-3

Bowling: Joseph 8–1–42–2; Thuraisingam 6–0–34–1; Codrington 9–3–27–5; Davison 5–1–15–2.

Umpires: Aleem Dar (Pakistan) and B. G. Jerling (South Africa).
Third umpire: A. V. Jayaprakash (India). Referee: G. R. Viswanath (India).

SOUTH AFRICA v KENYA

At Potchefstroom, February 12, 2003. South Africa won by ten wickets. Toss: Kenya.

South Africa made up for their narrow opening-day defeat by West Indies with a clinical win against an overwhelmed Kenya. But victory came at a price: Rhodes, South Africa's effervescent talisman, broke a hand while failing to catch a fierce drive by Odumbe. Two days later, he announced his retirement from international cricket. In his absence, his team-mates still cantered home. Faced with a target of just 141, Gibbs pummelled a ferocious 87 off just 66 balls with 12 fours and four sixes – including 20 off an over of Odumbe off-breaks – while Kirsten finished with a measured 52 off 63 balls. The winning boundary came with more than 28 overs to spare. Earlier, Kenya's top order had struggled against the accuracy of Pollock and Ntini, although Shah, a shining exception, played attractively all round the wicket. When he was run out by Klusener after being sent back by Odumbe, Shah had hit all seven of Kenya's boundaries and almost two-thirds of their runs. Without him, Kenya folded: only three others reached double figures while Klusener, cleverly varying his pace, mopped up the tail to claim his best one-day-international figures for nearly three years.

Man of the Match: L. Klusener. *Attendance:* 7,364.

Kenya

Batsman	Runs
†K. O. Otieno run out	1
R. D. Shah run out	60
B. J. Patel c Boucher b Pollock	1
*S. O. Tikolo c Kirsten b Pollock	3
H. S. Modi c Pollock b Boje	9
M. O. Odumbe c Gibbs b Klusener	16
T. M. Odoyo c Boucher b Ntini	22
C. O. Obuya lbw b Klusener	0
M. A. Suji c Pollock b Klusener	0
P. J. Ongondo c Kirsten b Klusener	13
A. Y. Karim not out	0
B 1, l-b 3, w 7, n-b 4	15
1/4 (1) 2/7 (3) 3/26 (4) 4/62 (5) 5/92 (2) 6/105 (6) 7/105 (8) 8/120 (9) 9/139 (10) 10/140 (7)	(38 overs) 140
	15 overs: 51-3

Bowling: Pollock 6–2–15–2; Ntini 7–1–14–1; Kallis 3–0–23–0; Langeveldt 5–0–24–0; Boje 9–1–44–1; Klusener 8–2–16–4.

South Africa

Batsman	Runs
H. H. Gibbs not out	87
G. Kirsten not out	52
W 2, n-b 1	3
(no wkt, 21.2 overs)	142
15 overs: 84-0	

H. H. Dippenaar, J. H. Kallis, J. N. Rhodes, †M. V. Boucher, *S. M. Pollock, L. Klusener, N. Boje, M. Ntini and C. K. Langeveldt did not bat.

Bowling: Suji 4–0–21–0; Odoyo 6–1–34–0; Karim 2–0–17–0; Obuya 5–1–32–0; Odumbe 2–0–21–0; Ongondo 2.2–0–17–0.

Umpires: K. C. Barbour (Zimbabwe) and T. H. Wijewardene (Sri Lanka).
Third umpire: N. A. Mallender (England). Referee: R. S. Madugalle (Sri Lanka).

NEW ZEALAND v WEST INDIES

At Port Elizabeth, February 13, 2003. New Zealand won by 20 runs. Toss: West Indies.

New Zealand's win was largely the handiwork of Andre Adams, who produced four wickets, a run-out and the key innings. The ploy of promoting Vettori to open proved only moderately productive and, despite a counter-attack from Astle and Cairns, New Zealand's innings was mostly a struggle, especially when Hinds struck three times in successive overs, doubling his tally of victims at this level. When Harris missed a straight ball from Gayle, West Indies seemed to start celebrating. Instead, Adams, who was dropped on 14 by Samuels, the substitute, took a fancy to Gayle's bowling. He and McCullum piled on 45 in the last five overs, Adams driving and pulling 15 from the last. When they reversed roles and Gayle opened the batting, his riposte was three fours in a row off Adams. But the next over from Adams resolved the personal contest. Fleming expertly held Gayle's carve at slip, the first of three incisions by Adams in as many overs. To make things worse, Lara was run out too. He flicked to backward square and turned confidently for a third. Vincent sprawled to intercept and threw to Cairns, stationed at square leg; his aim was true and Lara was short: a training ground move, pilfered from baseball and honed to perfection. West Indies had sagged to 80 for six before Sarwan and Jacobs reinjected some tension with a seventh-wicket stand of 98, a tournament record, but Adams had long since reduced his St Vincentian father to glum silence.

Man of the Match: A. R. Adams. *Attendance:* 9,659.

New Zealand

*S. P. Fleming c and b Dillon	25
D. L. Vettori b Drakes	13
N. J. Astle c Jacobs b Hinds	46
S. B. Styris c Powell b Drakes	5
C. L. Cairns c Dillon b Hinds	37
L. Vincent c Hooper b Hinds	9
C. Z. Harris b Gayle	19
†B. B. McCullum not out	36
A. R. Adams not out	35
L-b 10, w 4, n-b 2	16
1/42 (1) 2/58 (2) 3/66 (4) 4/130 (3) 5/141 (5) 6/147 (6) 7/188 (7) — 15 overs: 61-2	(7 wkts, 50 overs) 241

J. D. P. Oram and S. E. Bond did not bat.

Bowling: Dillon 10–1–30–1; McLean 6–0–38–0; Drakes 10–1–49–2; Hinds 10–0–35–3; Hooper 9–0–42–0; Gayle 5–0–37–1.

West Indies

C. H. Gayle c Fleming b Adams	22
W. W. Hinds c Styris b Adams	14
B. C. Lara run out	2
S. Chanderpaul lbw b Oram	2
*C. L. Hooper c Bond b Adams	3
R. R. Sarwan b Vettori	75
R. L. Powell b Oram	14
†R. D. Jacobs c Oram b Styris	50
V. C. Drakes not out	16
N. A. M. McLean run out	5
M. Dillon b Adams	8
B 1, l-b 3, w 5, n-b 1	10
1/34 (1) 2/36 (3) 3/42 (2) 4/46 (5) 5/46 (4) 6/80 (7) 7/178 (6) 8/191 (8) 9/200 (10) 10/221 (11) — 15 overs: 50-5	(49.4 overs) 221

Bowling: Bond 10–2–43–0; Adams 9.4–1–44–4; Oram 10–2–26–2; Cairns 1–0–21–0; Vettori 10–0–38–1; Astle 4–0–14–0; Styris 5–0–31–1.

Umpires: D. B. Hair (Australia) and R. E. Koertzen (South Africa).
Third umpire: S. Venkataraghavan (India). Referee: M. J. Procter (South Africa).

BANGLADESH v SRI LANKA

At Pietermaritzburg, February 14, 2003. Sri Lanka won by ten wickets. Toss: Sri Lanka.

The classic one-day pattern is for the result to be in doubt until the final over; this was the match in which victory was secured in the first. Vaas, Sri Lanka's nippy left-arm seamer, woke up with a sore back, but the morning damp was just what he needed to soothe the pain. With the first ball of the Bangladesh innings he castled Hannan Sarkar, aiming a wildly ambitious drive. With the second, he clasped a simple return catch off Mohammad Ashraful. And with the third, he forced Ehsanul Haque to edge to second slip. For the first time ever, an international match had begun with a hat-trick. Vaas's celebration was appropriately wild: he looked like an aeroplane piloted by a drunkard. There was more turbulence for Bangladesh when umpire Tiffin gave Sanwar Hossain out leg-before: at five for four after one over, the game was up. But Vaas was still not finished. Al Sahariar lifted a limp catch to de Silva, playing his 300th one-day international, at mid-off. Then, after some gutsy resistance from Alok Kapali and Khaled Masud, and three cheap wickets for Muralitharan, Vaas returned to have Mashrafe bin Mortaza taken at gully. His figures of six for 25 were then the third-best in a World Cup. Sri Lanka's reply was dominated by the elegant Atapattu, who pulled and cover-drove his way to a classy, unbeaten 69, and became the fourth Sri Lankan (after de Silva, Jayasuriya and Arjuna Ranatunga) to pass 6,000 one-day international runs.

Man of the Match: W. P. U. J. C. Vaas. *Attendance:* 2,900.

Bangladesh

Hannan Sarkar b Vaas 0
Al Sahariar c de Silva b Vaas 10
Mohammad Ashraful c and b Vaas 0
Ehsanul Haque c Jayawardene b Vaas. . . 0
Sanwar Hossain lbw b Vaas 4
Alok Kapali c Jayasuriya b Fernando . . . 32
*†Khaled Masud lbw b Muralitharan . . . 20
Mohammad Rafiq c Sangakkara b Muralitharan . 6
Tapash Baisya c Arnold b Muralitharan . 5
Mashrafe bin Mortaza c Muralitharan b Vaas . 28
Manjurul Islam not out 3
B 1, l-b 4, w 9, n-b 2 16

1/0 (1) 2/0 (3) 3/0 (4) 4/5 (5) 5/25 (2) 6/70 (6) 7/82 (8) 8/88 (7) 9/98 (9) 10/124 (10) (31.1 overs) 124

15 overs: 70-6

Bowling: Vaas 9.1–2–25–6; Nissanka 5–0–22–0; Fernando 7–0–47–1; Muralitharan 10–4–25–3.

Sri Lanka

M. S. Atapattu not out 69
*S. T. Jayasuriya not out 55
W 1, n-b 1. 2

(no wkt, 21.1 overs) 126
15 overs: 81-0

H. P. Tillekeratne, P. A. de Silva, D. P. M. D. Jayawardene, †K. C. Sangakkara, R. P. Arnold, W. P. U. J. C. Vaas, R. A. P. Nissanka, M. Muralitharan and C. R. D. Fernando did not bat.

Bowling: Manjurul Islam 6–1–22–0; Mashrafe bin Mortaza 5–0–38–0; Tapash Baisya 3–0–21–0; Mohammad Rafiq 4.1–1–22–0; Sanwar Hossain 2–0–14–0; Alok Kapali 1–0–9–0.

Umpires: B. F. Bowden (New Zealand) and R. B. Tiffin (Zimbabwe).
Third umpire: Aleem Dar (Pakistan). Referee: G. R. Viswanath (India).

CANADA v KENYA

At Cape Town, February 15, 2003 (day/night). Kenya won by four wickets. Toss: Canada.

Canada came close to pulling off their second upset of the competition, but were denied by a robust all-round peformance from Odoyo. First he topped and tailed Canada's innings to record career-best figures with his bustling fast-medium. Then, as the apparent Kenyan cakewalk crumbled, he applied the icing with a patient unbeaten 27 to guide them home with nine balls to spare. After Shah – crucially dropped on one by the wicket-keeper Bagai down the leg side – and Tikolo had taken Kenya to 99 for one, they stuttered against the unassuming off-breaks of Davison, who rattled through his ten overs to take three for 15 and help reduce Kenya to 154 for five; Modi had become so bogged down that he spent more than an hour and a quarter scoring six, but Kenya got away with it. Earlier, Billcliff became the first Canadian to score a half-century in a one-day international when he biffed a muscular 71. But from 134 for three the innings declined and Odoyo got to work on the tail. His job, though, was only half done.

Man of the Match: T. M. Odoyo. *Attendance:* 12,627.

Canada

I. Maraj b Odoyo	5
J. M. Davison c C. O. Obuya b Ongondo	31
D. Chumney c Shah b C. O. Obuya	10
I. S. Billcliff b T. O. Suji	71
*J. V. Harris c T. O. Suji b C. O. Obuya	31
A. F. Sattaur b Odumbe	7
N. A. De Groot lbw b Odumbe	0
†A. Bagai c D. O. Obuya b Odoyo	12
S. Thuraisingam c D. O. Obuya b Odoyo	13
A. Codrington b Odoyo	5
D. Joseph not out	4
L-b 2, w 5, n-b 1	8
(49 overs)	197

1/18 (1) 2/47 (2) 3/48 (3) 4/134 (5) 5/158 (4) 6/159 (7) 7/162 (6) 8/186 (9) 9/186 (8) 10/197 (10) — 15 overs: 58-3

Bowling: M. A. Suji 7–1–23–0; Odoyo 10–1–28–4; Ongondo 6–1–12–1; C. O. Obuya 10–1–46–2; Odumbe 9–0–41–2; T. O. Suji 7–0–45–1.

Kenya

K. O. Otieno b Thuraisingam	4
R. D. Shah c Maraj b Thuraisingam	61
*S. O. Tikolo lbw b Davison	42
H. S. Modi c Harris b Davison	6
M. O. Odumbe lbw b Davison	26
T. M. Odoyo not out	27
P. J. Ongondo b Codrington	16
†D. O. Obuya not out	4
L-b 3, w 9	12
(6 wkts, 48.3 overs)	198

1/15 (1) 2/99 (3) 3/116 (2) 4/148 (5) 5/154 (4) 6/192 (7) — 15 overs: 61-1

C. O. Obuya, T. O. Suji and M. A. Suji did not bat.

Bowling: Joseph 10–1–39–0; Thuraisingam 10–1–53–2; Codrington 10–1–44–1; Davison 10–3–15–3; De Groot 4–0–22–0; Maraj 4.3–0–22–0.

Umpires: A. V. Jayaprakash (India) and Nadeem Ghauri (Pakistan).
Third umpire: K. C. Barbour (Zimbabwe). Referee: R. S. Madugalle (Sri Lanka).

SOUTH AFRICA v NEW ZEALAND

At Johannesburg, February 16, 2003. New Zealand won by nine wickets (D/L method). Toss: South Africa.

An innings of rumbustious flamboyance from Gibbs was upstaged by one of graceful power by Fleming, who hit a career-best unbeaten 134 to stun a capacity crowd into near silence. In 191 previous one-day internationals, Fleming had managed just three centuries, but now, when his team needed him most, he played the innings of his life: after defeat to Sri Lanka and with their game in Kenya likely to be forfeited, New Zealand simply had to win. They did it in style, to leave the hosts on the brink of elimination. New Zealand's first one-day away win against South Africa (at the ninth attempt) had looked a distant prospect after Gibbs – mixing dash with luck – raced to 143 in 141 balls, before a 21-ball whirlwind from Klusener helped South Africa to 306. On an ideal batting pitch, Fleming moved to a run-a-ball fifty with four consecutive fours off Kallis before surviving a simple chance high to Boucher's left on 53. McMillan fell soon after, but Fleming made South Africa pay with a string of exquisite on-drives and less characteristic cuts. A 15-minute power failure was followed by two rain breaks, which brought Duckworth/Lewis into play at 182 for one in the 31st over. The recalculation meant New Zealand needed 44 in eight and a half overs for a famous win. Astle, almost anonymous, finished unbeaten on 54, but this was Fleming's match. By the time he had crashed the winning four off the ailing Donald, Fleming had faced 132 balls and hit 21 of New Zealand's 27 boundaries. He had never played better.

Man of the Match: S. P. Fleming. *Attendance:* 31,326.

South Africa

G. C. Smith c McCullum b Bond	23	G. Kirsten not out	5
H. H. Gibbs c McMillan b Oram	143		
N. Boje b Styris	29	L-b 6, w 11, n-b 3	20
J. H. Kallis c Vincent b Vettori	33		
†M. V. Boucher c Cairns b Oram	10	1/60 (1) 2/126 (3) (6 wkts, 50 overs)	306
L. Klusener not out	33	3/193 (4) 4/243 (5)	
*S. M. Pollock c Oram b Adams	10	5/260 (2) 6/287 (7) 15 overs: 92-1	

H. H. Dippenaar, M. Ntini and A. A. Donald did not bat.

Bowling: Bond 10–0–73–1; Adams 9–0–57–1; Oram 8–0–52–2; Styris 10–0–44–1; Vettori 10–0–58–1; Astle 3–0–16–0.

New Zealand

C. D. McMillan c Boucher b Donald	25
*S. P. Fleming not out	134
N. J. Astle not out	54
L-b 8, w 8	16
1/89 (1) (1 wkt, 36.5 overs)	229
15 overs: 97-1	

S. B. Styris, C. L. Cairns, L. Vincent, †B. B. McCullum, J. D. P. Oram, A. R. Adams, D. L. Vettori and S. E. Bond did not bat.

Bowling: Pollock 8–0–36–0; Ntini 8–1–33–0; Donald 5.5–0–52–1; Kallis 8–0–47–0; Boje 2–0–16–0; Klusener 5–0–37–0.

Umpires: S. A. Bucknor (West Indies) and P. Willey (England).
Third umpire: D. J. Harper (Australia). Referee: Wasim Raja (Pakistan).

BANGLADESH v WEST INDIES

At Benoni, February 18, 2003. No result. Toss: Bangladesh.

Bangladesh picked up their first points of the World Cup by default, but the chief beneficiaries of the bad weather were South Africa: because West Indies, one of their main rivals in an increasingly complex race for Super Six qualification, had lost two points, South Africa's fate was back in their own hands. The hopes of West Indies, meanwhile, now rested on their showdown with Sri Lanka. On a sporting pitch and under cloudy skies, the Bangladesh bowlers put in their most disciplined performance of the competition: they wilted only when Powell launched a late, withering assault, reaching a 30-ball half-century with his fourth six and helping West Indies add 73 in the last seven overs. The Bangladesh reply lasted just 49 deliveries, but included two wickets and three dropped slip catches, two by Hooper.

Attendance: 4,323.

West Indies

W. W. Hinds c Al Sahariar b Khaled Mahmud	18
C. H. Gayle c Sanwar Hossain b Manjurul Islam	0
B. C. Lara c Al Sahariar b Ehsanul Haque	46
S. Chanderpaul lbw b Ehsanul Haque	29
*C. L. Hooper c and b Alok Kapali	45
R. R. Sarwan c and b Khaled Mahmud	13
R. L. Powell c Sanwar Hossain b Manjurul Islam	50
†R. D. Jacobs not out	6
V. C. Drakes run out	0
M. Dillon c Mohammad Ashraful b Manjurul Islam	10
C. D. Collymore not out	0
B 1, l-b 6, w 13, n-b 7	27
1/19 (2) 2/40 (1) 3/108 (4) 4/130 (3) 5/158 (6) 6/217 (5) 7/231 (7) 8/231 (9) 9/242 (10) (9 wkts, 50 overs)	244

15 overs: 61-2

Bowling: Manjurul Islam 10–0–62–3; Talha Jubair 8–0–46–0; Khaled Mahmud 10–1–48–2; Ehsanul Haque 10–0–34–2; Mohammad Rafiq 10–0–44–0; Alok Kapali 2–1–3–1.

Bangladesh

Al Sahariar c Gayle b Drakes	5
Ehsanul Haque b Dillon	12
Mohammad Ashraful not out	8
Sanwar Hossain not out	2
L-b 2, w 3	5
1/19 (1) 2/19 (2) (2 wkts, 8.1 overs)	32

Tushar Imran, Alok Kapali, *†Khaled Masud, Khaled Mahmud, Mohammad Rafiq, Manjurul Islam and Talha Jubair did not bat.

Bowling: Dillon 4.1–0–13–1; Drakes 4–1–17–1.

Umpires: B. G. Jerling (South Africa) and R. B. Tiffin (Zimbabwe).
Third umpire: B. F. Bowden (New Zealand). Referee: G. R. Viswanath (India).

CANADA v SRI LANKA

At Paarl, February 19, 2003. Sri Lanka won by nine wickets. Toss: Sri Lanka. International debut: B. B. Seebaran.

When Joe Harris, the Canada captain, said his side had not been able to handle the pressure, he was verging on comic understatement. Canada had been blown away for the lowest total in one-day international history; no one reached double figures; and Sri Lanka needed just 28 balls to knock off the runs. The whole match lasted under two hours – just 23.2 overs were bowled – making it comfortably the shortest in World Cup history. Inserted on a lively track, Canada were undone by the swing of Vaas and the pace and bounce of Nissanka (only playing because Gunaratne was injured), who returned

SHORTEST VICTORY CHASES IN ONE-DAY INTERNATIONALS

4.2 overs	Sri Lanka (40-1) v Zimbabwe (38) at Colombo (SSC)	2001-02
4.4 overs	**Sri Lanka (37-1) v Canada (36) at Paarl**	**2002-03**
10.1 overs	West Indies (70-2) v Scotland (68) at Leicester	1999
11.3 overs	India (91-0) v Kenya (90) at Bloemfontein	2001-02
12 overs	**South Africa (109-0) v Bangladesh (108) at Bloemfontein**	**2002-03**
12.2 overs	**Australia (118-0) v England (117) at Sydney**	**2002-03**
12.3 overs	West Indies (45-3) v Pakistan (43) at Cape Town	1992-93

Shortened matches are excluded.

career-best figures of four for 12. The high point of Canada's innings came when Harris hit Vaas for successive fours; three balls later, he hit his own wicket after being struck in the ribs by Nissanka. A total of 36 represented a minor recovery from the depths of 12 for six, but it was still two short of the 38 Zimbabwe made, also against Sri Lanka, in Colombo in December 2001. The Sri Lankan-born Sanjayan Thuraisingam prevented a ten-wicket win by removing Jayasuriya; it was scant consolation.

Man of the Match: R. A. P. Nissanka. *Attendance:* 3,298.

Canada

D. Chumney c Sangakkara b Vaas	9
J. M. Davison c Sangakkara b Nissanka	0
A. F. Sattaur lbw b Vaas	0
I. S. Billcliff lbw b Vaas	1
N. A. De Groot lbw b Nissanka	0
*J. V. Harris hit wkt b Nissanka	9
I. Maraj lbw b Nissanka	0
†A. Bagai c Jayawardene b Fernando	6
S. Thuraisingam lbw b Fernando	6
A. Codrington b Muralitharan	0
B. B. Seebaran not out	0
L-b 2, w 2, n-b 1	5
1/0 (2) 2/6 (3) 3/11 (1) 4/12 (4) 5/12 (5) 6/12 (7) 7/21 (6) 8/31 (9) 9/36 (8) 10/36 (10) — (18.4 overs)	36

15 overs: 30-7

Bowling: Vaas 7–4–15–3; Nissanka 7–1–12–4; Muralitharan 2.4–0–3–1; Fernando 2–0–4–2.

Sri Lanka

M. S. Atapattu not out	24
*S. T. Jayasuriya lbw b Thuraisingam	9
†K. C. Sangakkara not out	4
1/23 (2) — (1 wkt, 4.4 overs)	37

H. P. Tillekeratne, P. A. de Silva, D. P. M. D. Jayawardene, R. P. Arnold, W. P. U. J. C. Vaas, R. A. P. Nissanka, M. Muralitharan and C. R. D. Fernando did not bat.

Bowling: Thuraisingam 2.4–0–22–1; Davison 2–0–15–0.

Umpires: N. A. Mallender (England) and D. R. Shepherd (England).
Third umpire: K. C. Barbour (Zimbabwe). Referee: Wasim Raja (Pakistan).

KENYA v NEW ZEALAND

At Nairobi, February 21, 2003. Kenya awarded match by default after New Zealand withdrew.

New Zealand chose not to play in Nairobi because of security fears. The four points awarded to Kenya put them second in the Pool B table, behind Sri Lanka and ahead of New Zealand.

SOUTH AFRICA v BANGLADESH

At Bloemfontein, February 22, 2003. South Africa won by ten wickets. Toss: South Africa.

South Africa kept alive their hopes of qualifying for the Super Six with a bloodless victory, achieved without Donald, who was omitted from the side on his home ground. They managed well enough without him. Spearheaded by Pollock, South Africa reduced Bangladesh to 33 for five, then 56 for six, Dippenaar helping out with three sharp catches in the slips. Khaled Masud and Khaled Mahmud did their best to ensure a measure of respectability, adding 35 before Ntini mopped up to leave South Africa a straightforward task. They completed it in only 12 overs as Gibbs and Kirsten successfully set about boosting their team's net run-rate. It was their ninth century opening stand in one-day internationals. As far as Bangladesh's confidence was concerned, their captain's post-match verdict – "This defeat is really bad for us" – was not overstating the case.

Man of the Match: M. Ntini. *Attendance:* 7,672.

Bangladesh

Al Sahariar c Peterson b Pollock	0
Ehsanul Haque c Zondeki b Pollock	3
Mohammad Ashraful c Boucher b Ntini	6
Sanwar Hossain c Kallis b Hall	11
Alok Kapali c Dippenaar b Zondeki	2
Tushar Imran c Dippenaar b Hall	9
*†Khaled Masud c Boucher b Ntini	29
Khaled Mahmud c Klusener b Ntini	23
Mohammad Rafiq run out	1
Manjurul Islam c Dippenaar b Ntini	0
Talha Jubair not out	4
L-b 4, w 8, n-b 8	20
1/3 (1) 2/14 (3) 3/21 (2) 4/33 (4) 5/33 (5) 6/56 (6) 7/91 (7) 8/93 (9) 9/99 (10) 10/108 (8)	(35.1 overs) 108
	15 overs: 36-5

Bowling: Pollock 6–2–8–2; Ntini 7.1–1–24–4; Zondeki 5–1–17–1; Hall 6–2–15–2; Kallis 5–0–19–0; Peterson 6–0–21–0.

South Africa

H. H. Gibbs not out	49
G. Kirsten not out	52
L-b 1, w 7	8
(no wkt, 12 overs)	109

J. H. Kallis, H. H. Dippenaar, †M. V. Boucher, L. Klusener, *S. M. Pollock, A. J. Hall, R. J. Peterson, M. Ntini and M. Zondeki did not bat.

Bowling: Manjurul Islam 4–0–26–0; Talha Jubair 2–0–24–0; Khaled Mahmud 2–0–20–0; Mohammad Rafiq 2–0–20–0; Alok Kapali 2–0–18–0.

Umpires: B. F. Bowden (New Zealand) and S. Venkataraghavan (India).
Third umpire: T. H. Wijewardene (Sri Lanka). Referee: C. H. Lloyd (West Indies).

Getting there the quick way: Canada's John Davison on his way to a 67-ball hundred against West Indies, the fastest in World Cup history.

Picture by Andy Clark, Reuters.

CANADA v WEST INDIES

At Centurion, February 23, 2003. West Indies won by seven wickets. Toss: West Indies. One-day international debut: N. Ifill.

If the result came as no surprise, John Davison's batting was a complete shock. In 37 first-class matches in Australia, he averaged under 11; representing the country of his birth, however, he batted like a millionaire, clobbering a sensational hundred in just 67 balls – a World Cup record – and briefly giving Canada a glimmer of hope. By the time he was out to a stunning one-handed catch at long-on by Drakes, back-pedalling furiously, Davison had made 111 from 76 balls and struck six sixes and eight fours, many of them one-bounce. There were moments of luck – he was dropped twice, and even watched open-mouthed as the ball trickled on to leg stump without dislodging a bail – but this was clean hitting par excellence. At 155 for one in the 21st over, Canada were motoring, but the departure of Chumney and, more importantly, Davison caused a terminal splutter: the last nine wickets fell for 47, five to Drakes. Taking their cue from Davison – and with an eye on net run-rate – Hinds and Lara cruised to 100 in the tenth over. For all of five minutes Hinds held the record for the fastest World Cup fifty before Lara snatched it from him and West Indies raced home with nearly 30 overs to spare.

Man of the Match: J. M. Davison. *Attendance:* 11,630.

FASTEST WORLD CUP HUNDREDS

Balls			
67	**J. M. Davison**	**Canada v West Indies at Centurion**	**2002-033**
72	Kapil Dev	India v Zimbabwe at Tunbridge Wells	1983
82	C. H. Lloyd	West Indies v Australia at Lord's	1975
83	B. C. Lara	West Indies v South Africa at Karachi	1995-96
84	S. R. Tendulkar	India v Kenya at Bristol	1999
85	S. M. Gavaskar	India v New Zealand at Nagpur	1987-88

FASTEST WORLD CUP FIFTIES

Balls			
23	**B. C. Lara**	**West Indies v Canada at Centurion**	**2002-03**
24	**W. W. Hinds**	**West Indies v Canada at Centurion**	**2002-03**
25	**A. M. Blignaut**	**Zimbabwe v Australia at Bulawayo**	**2002-03**
25	**J. M. Davison**	**Canada v New Zealand at Benoni**	**2002-03**
28	T. M. Moody	Australia v Bangladesh at Chester-le-Street	1999
29	A. Ranatunga	Sri Lanka v Kenya at Kandy	1995-96

Note: At Centurion, Davison also became the fifth player to hit a World Cup fifty from 30 balls.

Canada

I. Maraj c Hooper b Collins	16
J. M. Davison c Drakes b Hinds	111
D. Chumney c Gayle b Hinds	19
I. S. Billcliff c Jacobs b Drakes	16
N. Ifill c Jacobs b Drakes	9
*J. V. Harris c Hooper b Drakes	6
N. A. De Groot run out	11
†A. Bagai run out	2
A. Codrington c Jacobs b Drakes	0
B. B. Seebaran lbw b Drakes	0
D. Joseph not out	0
L-b 3, w 3, n-b 6	12
1/96 (1) 2/155 (3) 3/156 (2) 4/174 (5) 5/185 (4) 6/190 (6) 7/197 (8) 8/202 (9) 9/202 (10) 10/202 (7)	(42.5 overs) 202
	15 overs: 112-1

Bowling: Dillon 5–0–41–0; Collins 7–1–35–1; Drakes 9.5–1–44–5; Hooper 8–1–31–0; Gayle 9–1–29–0; Hinds 4–0–19–2.

West Indies

C. H. Gayle c Bagai b Joseph	8
W. W. Hinds st Bagai b Davison	64
B. C. Lara b De Groot	73
R. R. Sarwan not out	42
*C. L. Hooper not out	5
L-b 5, w 8, n-b 1	14
1/32 (1) 2/134 (2) 3/177 (3)	(3 wkts, 20.3 overs) 206
	15 overs: 163-2

S. Chanderpaul, R. L. Powell, †R. D. Jacobs, V. C. Drakes, M. Dillon and P. T. Collins did not bat.

Bowling: Joseph 4–0–47–1; Codrington 4–0–25–0; Ifill 4–0–46–0; Seebaran 1–0–26–0; Davison 5–0–36–1; De Groot 2.3–0–21–1.

Umpires: E. A. R. de Silva (Sri Lanka) and D. B. Hair (Australia).
Third umpire: Nadeem Ghauri (Pakistan). Referee: R. S. Madugalle (Sri Lanka).

KENYA v SRI LANKA

At Nairobi, February 24, 2003. Kenya won by 53 runs. Toss: Sri Lanka.

A World Cup bloated by too many one-sided games needed this like a desert explorer needs a cold beer. Kenya's shock victory was memorable enough, but the style, all wide-grinning, grassy-kneed enthusiasm, was unforgettable: Kenya chased like lion cubs, backed up in gangs and jigged after every wicket. Sri Lanka, by contrast, simply moped. "The worst game of my career," admitted Jayasuriya. Violent hitting by Otieno helped Kenya to 46 for one in the seventh over but they never really hit the balance between big shots and blocking, especially mid-innings, when Muralitharan found drift and turn. In reply to 210, Sri Lanka almost sleepwalked to defeat. Only when they lost their fifth wicket for 105 in the 28th over did they finally seem to wake to their predicament. And when de Silva went soon afterwards, it was too late to do much about it. He at least had stuck around for a while, and of five who fell to Obuya's accurate but unthreatening leg-spin, only he could plead not guilty. Kenya's lap of honour ended up more a half-marathon.

Man of the Match: C. O. Obuya. *Attendance:* 8,218.

Kenya

†K. O. Otieno c Muralitharan b de Silva	60
R. D. Shah lbw b Vaas	0
B. J. Patel c Sangakkara b Vaas	12
*S. O. Tikolo lbw b Muralitharan	10
H. S. Modi b Muralitharan	26
M. O. Odumbe c Arnold b Muralitharan	26
T. M. Odoyo c Sangakkara b Vaas	6
C. O. Obuya not out	13
T. O. Suji b Muralitharan	6
P. J. Ongondo b Jayasuriya	20
M. A. Suji not out	3
B 5, l-b 11, w 10, n-b 2	28
1/1 (2) 2/46 (3) 3/75 (4) 4/112 (1) 5/152 (5) 6/163 (7) 7/163 (6) 8/173 (9) 9/205 (10) — (9 wkts, 50 overs)	210
15 overs: 75-2	

Bowling: Vaas 10–1–41–3; Nissanka 7–2–29–0; Fernando 7–0–33–0; Muralitharan 10–1–28–4; Jayasuriya 9–1–30–1; de Silva 5–1–23–1; Arnold 2–0–10–0.

Sri Lanka

M. S. Atapattu b Odoyo	23
*S. T. Jayasuriya c Patel b M. A. Suji	3
H. P. Tillekeratne c T. O. Suji b Obuya	23
P. A. de Silva c Otieno b Obuya	41
D. P. M. D. Jayawardene c and b Obuya	5
†K. C. Sangakkara c Otieno b Obuya	5
R. P. Arnold not out	25
W. P. U. J. C. Vaas c and b Obuya	4
R. A. P. Nissanka c Odoyo b Tikolo	2
M. Muralitharan c T. O. Suji b Tikolo	10
C. R. D. Fernando b Odumbe	7
B 2, w 6, n-b 1	9
1/13 (2) 2/39 (1) 3/71 (3) 4/87 (5) 5/105 (6) 6/112 (4) 7/119 (8) 8/131 (9) 9/149 (10) 10/157 (11) — (45 overs)	157
15 overs: 57-2	

Bowling: M. A. Suji 8–1–24–1; Odoyo 7–0–33–1; Obuya 10–0–24–5; Ongondo 5–0–22–0; Odumbe 10–0–39–1; Tikolo 5–1–13–2.

Umpires: D. J. Harper (Australia) and R. B. Tiffin (Zimbabwe).
Third umpire: A. V. Jayaprakash (India). Referee: D. T. Lindsay (South Africa).

BANGLADESH v NEW ZEALAND

At Kimberley, February 26, 2003. New Zealand won by seven wickets. Toss: Bangladesh.

After forfeiting their fixture in Kenya, New Zealand needed the reassurance of a no-nonsense win. A margin of seven wickets with more than 16 overs to spare looked good, but there were signs of rust after their ten-day break. The youngster Mohammad Ashraful audaciously swung Bond for six over long leg during a classy, career-best 56 – Bangladesh's only half-century of the competition – before the captain, Khaled Masud, and Mohammad Rafiq rescued another apparently hopeless position with an unbroken stand of 70 for the eighth wicket. A nervy display by New Zealand's seamers was compounded by several dropped catches. But McMillan, in his new role as opener, whacked a quick 75 off 83 balls in reply, and the finishing touches were applied in a hurry by Styris and Cairns, who added 61 in 41. In the scissors–paper–stone world of Group B, where all the major teams, plus Kenya, were capable of beating one another, New Zealand were not yet guaranteed a place in the Super Six.

Man of the Match: C. D. McMillan. *Attendance:* 3,712.

Bangladesh

Hannan Sarkar c McCullum b Bond	9
Mohammad Ashraful c and b Bond	56
Sanwar Hossain b Oram	5
Habibul Bashar c McCullum b Oram	0
Alok Kapali c Bond b Adams	9
Akram Khan c Fleming b Bond	13
*†Khaled Masud not out	35
Khaled Mahmud c McCullum b Oram	12
Mohammad Rafiq not out	41
B 1, l-b 4, w 10, n-b 3	18
1/19 (1) 2/37 (3) 3/37 (4) 4/71 (5) 5/105 (6) 6/107 (2) 7/128 (8) — (7 wkts, 50 overs)	198
15 overs: 52-3	

Tapash Baisya and Manjurul Islam did not bat.

Bowling: Bond 10–1–33–3; Mills 6–0–32–0; Adams 10–0–50–1; Oram 10–1–32–3; Cairns 3–0–17–0; Vettori 10–0–19–0; Styris 1–0–10–0.

New Zealand

C. D. McMillan b Khaled Mahmud	75
*S. P. Fleming c and b Khaled Mahmud	32
A. R. Adams c Mohammad Ashraful b Khaled Mahmud	18
S. B. Styris not out	37
C. L. Cairns not out	33
W 3, n-b 1	4
1/71 (2) 2/99 (3) 3/138 (1) — (3 wkts, 33.3 overs)	199
15 overs: 73-1	

M. S. Sinclair, †B. B. McCullum, J. D. P. Oram, K. D. Mills, D. L. Vettori and S. E. Bond did not bat.

Bowling: Manjurul Islam 7–1–37–0; Tapash Baisya 8–0–56–0; Khaled Mahmud 10–0–46–3; Alok Kapali 6–0–38–0; Sanwar Hossain 2–0–19–0; Mohammad Ashraful 0.3–0–3–0.

Umpires: D. B. Hair (Australia) and D. R. Shepherd (England).
Third umpire: B. G. Jerling (South Africa). Referee: M. J. Procter (South Africa).

SOUTH AFRICA v CANADA

At East London, February 27, 2003. South Africa won by 118 runs. Toss: Canada. One-day international debut: A. Patel.

This match ended with neither team covered in glory: the South Africans, eager for an emphatic victory before their crucial game against Sri Lanka, were less than convincing, while Canada made few friends with their grim determination to bat out the overs. Davis Joseph and Ashish Patel had stunned South Africa by grabbing three wickets with only 23 on the board, and Dippenaar could have been caught in the slips on 12. He celebrated his escape by helping Smith add 109 for the fourth wicket, before some late hitting completed the recovery. Canada's hopes of making a serious challenge were fatally wounded by the departure of Davison in the second over, and once Zondeki removed Billcliff with his first ball, there was little to play for. This did not prevent Ishwar Maraj – dropped at least four times – taking root to reach a laborious fifty. Maraj became the eighth player to bat out a full allotment of World Cup overs (a sequence started by Sunil Gavaskar's notorious 36 not out at Lord's in 1975). For Donald, who would be surplus to requirements for the showdown with Sri Lanka, it proved an unglamorous end to a phenomenal career which produced more than 600 international wickets, though none against Canada.

Man of the Match: H. H. Dippenaar. *Attendance:* 9,279.

South Africa

G. C. Smith b Davison	63
H. H. Gibbs c Bagai b Patel	8
G. Kirsten c Bagai b Joseph	0
J. H. Kallis c Ifill b Patel	1
H. H. Dippenaar c Seebaran b De Groot	80
†M. V. Boucher b De Groot	21
*S. M. Pollock c Bagai b Joseph	32
A. J. Hall not out	22
M. Ntini b Patel	14
M. Zondeki not out	1
L-b 3, w 8, n-b 1	12
1/19 (2) 2/22 (3) 3/23 (4) 4/132 (1) 5/174 (6) 6/197 (5) 7/227 (7) 8/249 (9) — 15 overs: 59-3	(8 wkts, 50 overs) 254

A. A. Donald did not bat.

Bowling: Joseph 9–1–42–2; Patel 7–0–41–3; Ifill 7–0–35–0; Davison 10–1–45–1; Seebaran 10–0–43–0; De Groot 7–0–45–2.

Canada

I. Maraj not out	53
J. M. Davison c Zondeki b Ntini	1
D. Chumney c Smith b Pollock	2
I. S. Billcliff b Zondeki	9
N. A. De Groot c Boucher b Hall	16
*J. V. Harris c Boucher b Ntini	15
†A. Bagai not out	28
L-b 6, w 4, n-b 2	12
1/2 (2) 2/8 (3) 3/28 (4) 4/58 (5) 5/84 (6) — 15 overs: 28-2	(5 wkts, 50 overs) 136

N. Ifill, A. Patel, B. B. Seebaran and D. Joseph did not bat.

Bowling: Pollock 8–5–13–1; Ntini 10–2–19–2; Donald 10–2–27–0; Zondeki 9–1–24–1; Hall 7–1–26–1; Kallis 5–1–11–0; Smith 1–0–10–0.

Umpires: K. C. Barbour (Zimbabwe) and D. J. Harper (Australia).
Third umpire: Aleem Dar (Pakistan). Referee: Wasim Raja (Pakistan).

Walking wounded: Ramnaresh Sarwan is welcomed back to the crease by Sri Lanka's Aravinda de Silva, having been hit on the head and sent to hospital by a bouncer. Sarwan ended the match 47 not out, but West Indies still lost.

Picture by Andy Clark, Reuters.

SRI LANKA v WEST INDIES

At Cape Town, February 28, 2003 (day/night). Sri Lanka won by six runs. Toss: Sri Lanka.

Like the opening match almost three weeks earlier, this was a Cape Town classic whose outcome was in doubt until the final over. West Indies looked as though they would sneak through again, but after 27 runs had flowed from the two previous overs, Muralitharan returned to concede just two from the 49th. His tight hold on the purse strings – 14 from the last six balls proved too much – took the game, and the Super Six, away from West Indies, who exited at the first opportunity, just as in 1999. Vaas won the match award for his four wickets, including Lara, caught behind for one, but the truly heroic performance came from Sarwan. Knocked out by a Fernando bouncer and stretchered off to hospital, blood pouring from the wound, he was not expected to add to his ten runs. But with West Indies in desperate trouble at 169 for seven in the 43rd over, back he came – in a maroon cap and to a whooping standing ovation. He batted from that moment with no fear, laying in to both Jayasuriya and de Silva, and being dropped by Atapattu. But this was no fairy tale. West Indies fell just short, and Hooper was too desolate to praise him. "I don't think it is too big a deal," he said. "We've seen blood shed before."

Man of the Match: W. P. U. J. C. Vaas. *Attendance:* 19,382.

Sri Lanka

M. S. Atapattu run out	3	†K. C. Sangakkara c Lara b Drakes	24
*S. T. Jayasuriya c Chanderpaul b Gayle	66	W. P. U. J. C. Vaas not out	28
H. P. Tillekeratne b Hinds	36	L-b 5, w 8, n-b 2	15
P. A. de Silva run out	13		—
D. P. M. D. Jayawardene c Powell b Hooper	9	1/11 (1) 2/96 (3) 3/113 (4) 4/131 (5) 5/139 (2) 6/178 (7) (6 wkts, 50 overs)	228
R. P. Arnold not out	34	15 overs: 54-1	

M. Muralitharan, C. R. D. Fernando and P. W. Gunaratne did not bat.

Bowling: Dillon 10–0–30–0; Collins 10–0–62–0; Drakes 10–1–32–1; Hooper 6–0–30–1; Hinds 4–0–27–1; Gayle 10–0–42–1.

West Indies

C. H. Gayle lbw b Vaas	55	M. Dillon run out	4
W. W. Hinds c Jayasuriya b Vaas	2	P. T. Collins not out	1
B. C. Lara c Sangakkara b Vaas	1	L-b 6, w 12, n-b 3	21
R. R. Sarwan not out	47		—
*C. L. Hooper lbw b Fernando	0	1/10 (2) 2/27 (3) 3/62 (5) 4/121 (1) (9 wkts, 50 overs)	222
S. Chanderpaul c Atapattu b de Silva	65	5/121 (7) 6/122 (8)	
†R. D. Jacobs c Sangakkara b Vaas	0	7/169 (6) 8/186 (9)	
R. L. Powell b Muralitharan	1	9/219 (10)	
V. C. Drakes c Vaas b Jayasuriya	25	15 overs: 67-3	

Sarwan, when 10, retired hurt at 62-2 and resumed at 169.

Bowling: Vaas 10–3–22–4; Gunaratne 6–1–41–0; de Silva 10–0–48–1; Fernando 6–0–33–1; Muralitharan 10–1–26–1; Jayasuriya 8–0–46–1.

Umpires: D. L. Orchard (South Africa) and S. Venkataraghavan (India).
Third umpire: B. G. Jerling (South Africa). Referee: D. T. Lindsay (South Africa).

"Play up in the Tropics started at 9.30, so lunch was at 11.30. George Gunn, who insisted on lunching at 1.30 whatever the hours of play, would not have approved."

Bangladeshis in Australia, page 1218.

BANGLADESH v KENYA

At Johannesburg, March 1, 2003. Kenya won by 32 runs. Toss: Kenya.

Joy was unconfined as Kenya celebrated qualification for the Super Six, thanks largely to an outstanding all-round contribution from Odumbe. First, his unbeaten 52 from 46 balls – building on the foundations laid carefully by Shah and Patel – gave the Kenyans a competitive total. Then he claimed four for 38 to undermine Bangladesh's middle order, secure the match award and trigger his team's victory dance. If delight was the prevailing emotion for Kenya and most of the spectators in the crowd, it was another day of despair for Bangladesh, who had lost all of their last 30 completed one-day internationals. Despite testing spells from Manjurul Islam and Tapash Baisya with the new ball, they let their opponents off the hook, dropping at least three catches, and later slipped badly from 151 for five when, with 12 overs left, victory should have been within their grasp. Fittingly, it fell to Tikolo, the captain, to capture the last wicket as Kenya recorded their sixth success in seven games against Bangladesh, this far and away the most significant.

Man of the Match: M. O. Odumbe. *Attendance:* 17,897.

Kenya

†K. O. Otieno c Khaled Masud b Manjurul Islam	0
R. D. Shah c Akram Khan b Mohammad Rafiq	37
B. J. Patel c Manjurul Islam b Khaled Mahmud	32
*S. O. Tikolo b Sanwar Hossain	27
H. S. Modi c and b Sanwar Hossain	12
M. O. Odumbe not out	52
T. M. Odoyo lbw b Sanwar Hossain	19
C. O. Obuya b Tapash Baisya	22
P. J. Ongondo not out	2
B 1, l-b 2, w 11	14
1/1 (1) 2/68 (3) 3/80 (2) 4/116 (4) 5/124 (5) 6/164 (7) 7/197 (8) (7 wkts, 50 overs)	217
15 overs: 52-1	

T. O. Suji and M. A. Suji did not bat.

Bowling: Manjurul Islam 7–0–30–1; Tapash Baisya 8–1–22–1; Khaled Mahmud 10–1–39–1; Mohammad Rafiq 7–0–35–1; Sanwar Hossain 10–0–49–3; Alok Kapali 2–0–9–0; Mohammad Ashraful 6–0–30–0.

Bangladesh

Al Sahariar c Otieno b M. A. Suji	14
Mohammad Ashraful lbw b M. A. Suji	1
Tushar Imran c sub (J. O. Angara) b Odumbe	48
*†Khaled Masud c Shah b Obuya	14
Alok Kapali c Otieno b Odumbe	18
Akram Khan c sub (J. O. Angara) b Tikolo	44
Sanwar Hossain c M. A. Suji b Odumbe	16
Khaled Mahmud st Otieno b Odumbe	3
Mohammad Rafiq c Modi b Tikolo	5
Tapash Baisya not out	2
Manjurul Islam st Otieno b Tikolo	2
B 2, l-b 3, w 10, n-b 3	18
1/16 (1) 2/17 (2) 3/53 (4) 4/99 (5) 5/111 (3) 6/151 (7) 7/158 (8) 8/180 (9) 9/180 (6) 10/185 (11) (47.2 overs)	185
15 overs: 49-2	

Bowling: M. A. Suji 8–1–27–2; Odoyo 4–0–9–0; Ongondo 7–0–29–0; Obuya 9–0–40–1; T. O. Suji 4–0–23–0; Odumbe 10–0–38–4; Tikolo 5.2–0–14–3.

Umpires: E. A. R. de Silva (Sri Lanka) and N. A. Mallender (England).
Third umpire: S. J. A. Taufel (Australia). Referee: R. S. Madugalle (Sri Lanka).

CANADA v NEW ZEALAND

At Benoni, March 3, 2003. New Zealand won by five wickets. Toss: New Zealand. One-day international debut: A. M. Samad.

New Zealand did not know it at the time, but victory by any margin would prove enough to take them through to the next phase. South Africa's fatal Duckworth/Lewis blunder was still several hours away, so New Zealand approached the match in the belief that their best hope was to win as quickly as possible and squeeze through on net run-rate. Not for the first time in the competition, however, Davison was in the mood to ruin reputations. While his team-mates struggled against the pace of Bond and the accuracy of Oram, Davison blasted 75 in 62 balls, including nine fours and four sixes, three pulled high over mid-wicket in one Oram over. New Zealand set themselves the target of winning in just 16 overs, but lost three cheap wickets to Davison, opening the bowling with his off-breaks, and were in trouble at 114 for five in the 14th over. Styris and Harris, however, kept their heads to share a match-winning partnership of 83 in just 58 balls, and New Zealand were home, seven overs behind their self-imposed schedule.

Man of the Match: J. M. Davison. *Attendance:* 5,114.

Canada

I. Maraj lbw b Bond	0	A. Patel b Styris	25
J. M. Davison c Cairns b Harris	75	B. B. Seebaran not out	4
N. Ifill c McCullum b Oram	7		
I. S. Billcliff c Fleming b Styris	8	L-b 1, w 12, n-b 1	14
N. A. De Groot lbw b Oram	17		—
*J. V. Harris c McCullum b Bond	26	1/21 (1) 2/43 (3) 3/80 (4) (47 overs)	196
†A. Bagai b Oram	1	4/98 (2) 5/123 (5) 6/129 (7)	
A. M. Samad lbw b Bond	12	7/152 (8) 8/153 (6)	
A. Codrington b Oram	7	9/173 (9) 10/196 (10)	15 overs: 81-3

Bowling: Bond 10–3–29–3; Adams 6–0–38–0; Oram 10–1–52–4; Vettori 10–0–34–0; Styris 4–0–23–2; Harris 7–1–19–1.

New Zealand

C. D. McMillan c Bagai b Davison	14	C. Z. Harris not out	38
*S. P. Fleming run out	5		
N. J. Astle st Bagai b Davison	11	L-b 3, w 5	8
C. L. Cairns c Maraj b Davison	31		—
A. R. Adams c sub (S. Thuraisingam) b Seebaran	36	1/19 (2) 2/31 (3) (5 wkts, 23 overs)	197
		3/32 (1) 4/97 (5)	
S. B. Styris not out	54	5/114 (4)	15 overs: 129-5

†B. B. McCullum, J. D. P. Oram, D. L. Vettori and S. E. Bond did not bat.

Bowling: Patel 3–0–32–0; Davison 10–0–61–3; Codrington 2–0–33–0; Seebaran 7–0–61–1; Ifill 1–0–7–0.

Umpires: A. V. Jayaprakash (India) and B. G. Jerling (South Africa).
Third umpire: T. H. Wijewardene (Sri Lanka). Referee: D. T. Lindsay (South Africa).

SOUTH AFRICA v SRI LANKA

At Durban, March 3, 2003 (day/night). Tied (D/L method). Toss: Sri Lanka.

Sydney 1992, Edgbaston 1999, and now Durban 2003: South Africa have certainly acquired an unhappy knack of exiting World Cups in bizarre fashion. Late in the South African innings, with rain falling steadily, it had become a question of when – not if – Duckworth/Lewis would come into play. And so, when Boucher swung the penultimate ball of the 45th – and, as had begun to seem inevitable, final – over for six, he pumped his right fist, believing the job done. The last soggy ball of the match he pushed casually to leg, and stayed put. Crucially, though, the South Africans had misread the fine print: they had needed 229 to *tie*, when only a win would do. The match might not have happened at all. Sri Lanka disputed the interpretation of the rules for separating teams tied on points, and there was talk of them forfeiting the fixture, until the prospect of a fine and disqualification did wonders for obedience. Jayasuriya embodied such navel-gazing: when an over-cautious Atapattu declined an early single, he mooched back to his crease and was run out. Eschewing his habitual orthodoxy, Atapattu atoned with a superlative 124, adding 152 in 22 overs with the lyrical de Silva to hand the hosts a daunting task. Smith and Gibbs galloped away until Smith heaved de Silva's first ball to deep mid-wicket. Muralitharan bowled Gibbs behind his legs as the spinners made deep inroads, before Pollock and Boucher rallied. Their stand ended when Murali speculatively flicked the ball on to the stumps – and Pollock, after endless replays, was given out by what must have been a millimetre. Klusener laboured to a single off eight balls as the rain grew heavier, but had Boucher been given the right information, it might not have mattered. As it was, Sri Lanka progressed – and South Africa's world fell apart. Jayasuriya draped an arm around Pollock's shoulders as they awaited the media inquisition, compassion supplanting his own relief, however briefly.

Man of the Match: M. S. Atapattu. *Attendance:* 19,744.

Sri Lanka

M. S. Atapattu c sub (R. J. Peterson) b Hall	124
*S. T. Jayasuriya run out	16
H. P. Tillekeratne c Boucher b Kallis	14
D. P. M. D. Jayawardene c Boucher b Hall	1
P. A. de Silva c Smith b Ntini	73
R. P. Arnold b Pollock	8
†K. C. Sangakkara c Pollock b Kallis	6
W. P. U. J. C. Vaas run out	3
M. Muralitharan b Kallis	4
C. R. D. Fernando not out	1
L-b 2, w 11, n-b 5	18
(9 wkts, 50 overs)	268

1/37 (2) 2/77 (3) 3/90 (4) 4/242 (1) 5/243 (5) 6/258 (7) 7/261 (6) 8/266 (9) 9/268 (8) 15 overs: 62-1

P. W. Gunaratne did not bat.

Bowling: Pollock 10–1–48–1; Ntini 10–0–49–1; Zondeki 6–0–35–0; Kallis 10–0–41–3; Hall 10–0–62–2; Klusener 4–0–31–0.

South Africa

G. C. Smith c Gunaratne b de Silva	35
H. H. Gibbs b Muralitharan	73
G. Kirsten b de Silva	8
J. H. Kallis b Jayasuriya	16
H. H. Dippenaar lbw b Jayasuriya	8
†M. V. Boucher not out	45
*S. M. Pollock run out	25
L. Klusener not out	1
L-b 4, w 12, n-b 2	18
(6 wkts, 45 overs)	229

1/65 (1) 2/91 (3) 3/124 (4) 4/149 (2) 5/149 (5) 6/212 (7) 15 overs: 79-1

A. J. Hall, M. Ntini and M. Zondeki did not bat.

Bowling: Vaas 7–1–33–0; Gunaratne 6–0–26–0; Fernando 1–0–14–0; de Silva 8–0–36–2; Arnold 4–0–16–0; Muralitharan 9–0–51–1; Jayasuriya 10–0–49–2.

Umpires: S. A. Bucknor (West Indies) and S. Venkataraghavan (India).
Third umpire: P. Willey (England). Referee: C. H. Lloyd (West Indies).

A Duckworth disaster: Mark Boucher (*left*) and Lance Klusener leave the field at Kingsmead, believing South Africa have done enough to beat Sri Lanka and qualify for the Super Six. Shaun Pollock (*below*) soon discovers otherwise.
Pictures by Shaun Botterill, Getty Images, and Mike Hutchings, Reuters.

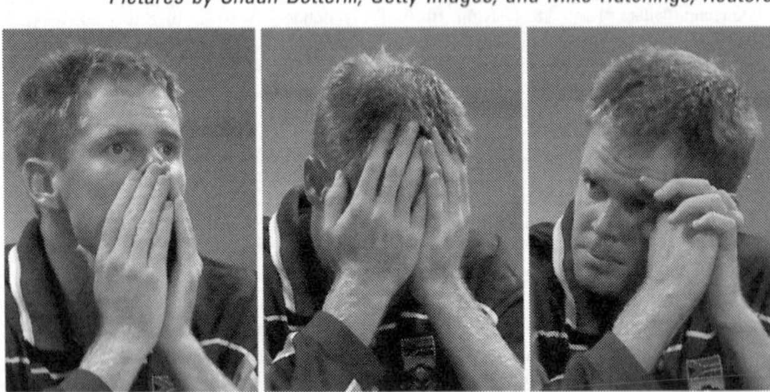

KENYA v WEST INDIES

At Kimberley, March 4, 2003. West Indies won by 142 runs. Toss: West Indies.

Kenya were already through to the Super Sixes, West Indies were already going home – this was a game with no fuse to light. West Indies certainly looked uninspired when batting, though a century from Gayle – who shared a first-wicket stand of 122 with Chanderpaul – contained moments of delight, especially two exquisite sixes. But once Lara was caught by David Obuya, the innings petered out. The West Indian bowling, however, was a revelation, driven by Drakes but sparked by Lawson, the seriously quick bowler who until now had seemingly been forgotten by the selectors, despite pleas from West Indian journalists. He bowled accurately and fast – about 95mph when knocking Odumbe on to his stumps for a duck. Drakes, who bowled his ten overs straight through, taking out five of the top seven in the process, lifted his tally of wickets against Bangladesh and the non-Test nations in one-day internationals to 23 wickets at 9.08.

Man of the Match: V. C. Drakes. *Attendance:* 4,587.

West Indies

C. H. Gayle c D. O. Obuya b Angara	119
S. Chanderpaul c Angara b C. O. Obuya	66
B. C. Lara c D. O. Obuya b Tikolo	10
M. N. Samuels c Patel b Odumbe	14
R. L. Powell c Otieno b Odumbe	8
*C. L. Hooper st Otieno b Angara	6
W. W. Hinds b Suji	10
†R. D. Jacobs not out	9
V. C. Drakes not out	1
W 3	3
1/122 (2) 2/158 (3) 3/182 (4) 4/196 (5) 5/222 (1) 6/224 (6) 7/245 (7) (7 wkts, 50 overs)	246

15 overs: 68-0

M. Dillon and J. J. C. Lawson did not bat.

Bowling: Suji 10–1–38–1; Angara 7–0–53–2; Ongondo 5–0–17–0; Odumbe 10–0–62–2; C. O. Obuya 10–0–48–1; Tikolo 8–0–28–1.

Kenya

†K. O. Otieno c Dillon b Drakes	3
R. D. Shah c Gayle b Dillon	12
B. J. Patel c Lara b Drakes	11
*S. O. Tikolo lbw b Drakes	12
H. S. Modi c Jacobs b Drakes	0
M. O. Odumbe hit wkt b Lawson	0
D. O. Obuya c Powell b Drakes	4
C. O. Obuya c Powell b Lawson	13
P. J. Ongondo b Powell	24
M. A. Suji c Chanderpaul b Hinds	13
J. O. Angara not out	0
L-b 3, w 8, n-b 1	12
1/8 (1) 2/26 (2) 3/34 (3) 4/34 (5) 5/43 (4) 6/43 (6) 7/54 (7) 8/62 (8) 9/102 (9) 10/104 (10) (35.5 overs)	104

15 overs: 35-4

Bowling: Dillon 10–1–31–1; Drakes 10–2–33–5; Lawson 8–0–16–2; Powell 4–2–8–1; Chanderpaul 2–0–6–0; Hinds 1.5–0–7–1.

Umpires: D. R. Shepherd (England) and S. J. A. Taufel (Australia).
Third umpire: K. C. Barbour (Zimbabwe). Referee: M. J. Procter (South Africa).

POOL A FINAL TABLE

	Played	*Won*	*Lost*	*Tied*	*No result*	*Points*	*Net run-rate*
AUSTRALIA	6	6	0	0	0	24	2.04
INDIA	6	5	1	0	0	20	1.10
ZIMBABWE	6	3	2	0	1	14	0.50
England	6	3	3	0	0	12	0.82
Pakistan	6	2	3	0	1	10	0.22
Holland	6	1	5	0	0	4	–1.45
Namibia	6	0	6	0	0	0	–2.95

POOL B FINAL TABLE

	Played	*Won*	*Lost*	*Tied*	*No result*	*Points*	*Net run-rate*
SRI LANKA	6	4	1	1	0	18	1.20
KENYA	6	4	2	0	0	16	–0.69
NEW ZEALAND	6	4	2	0	0	16	0.99
West Indies	6	3	2	0	1	14	1.10
South Africa	6	3	2	1	0	14	1.73
Canada	6	1	5	0	0	4	–1.98
Bangladesh	6	0	5	0	1	2	–2.04

Where teams finished with equal points, the positions were decided by a) most wins, b) results of head-to-head matches, c) higher net run-rate (calculated by subtracting runs conceded per over from runs scored per over) in completed matches.

SUPER SIX STARTING TABLE

	Played	*Won*	*Lost*	*Tied*	*No result*	*Points*	*Net run-rate*
Australia	2	2	0	0	0	12	1.67
Kenya	2	2	0	0	0	10	1.06
India	2	1	1	0	0	8	–0.35
Sri Lanka	2	1	1	0	0	7.5	–0.06
New Zealand	2	0	2	0	0	4	–0.94
Zimbabwe	2	0	2	0	0	3.5	–0.98

Super Six teams carried forward four points each for wins against fellow Super Six qualifiers, and one point each for wins (half a point for a tie or no result) against teams eliminated at the Pool stage.

SUPER SIX

AUSTRALIA v SRI LANKA

At Centurion, March 7, 2003. Australia won by 96 runs. Toss: Australia.

This was supposed to be South Africa's big day in the battle of the group winners, but history had turned a different corner and Sri Lanka were the sacrificial lambs instead. They had been the last team to beat the Australians – back in January – but by the 20th over Australia were already in the distance, 131 for one and cruising into the future; this win was enough to see them into the semi-finals. Sri Lanka had to cope with a conveyor-belt of run-a-ball partnerships – 75, 106 and 112 for the first three wickets. Gilchrist pounded 14 fours and two sixes before walking back distraught, only the third man run out for 99 in one-day internationals (after Graeme Smith of South Africa and Jayasuriya), all three involving Sri Lanka and in the last five months. It wasn't even his run. But Ponting did get his hundred, moving from 52 to 101 in 30 balls. Sangakkara, who should have run him out on 35, could only watch. Lee took out Sri Lanka's talisman Jayasuriya – chipping his thumb, then bruising his forearm – in his first over. Sri Lanka lost four wickets in the forties and, though de Silva did enough to wreck Lee's figures, there was no contest.

Man of the Match: R. T. Ponting. *Attendance:* 14,273.

Australia

†A. C. Gilchrist run out 99
M. L. Hayden c Tillekeratne b Muralitharan . 22
*R. T. Ponting c Sangakkara b Fernando. 114
D. R. Martyn b Fernando. 52
D. S. Lehmann c de Silva b Fernando . . 10
I. J. Harvey not out 5
M. G. Bevan not out. 1
L-b 4, w 5, n-b 7 16

1/75 (2) 2/181 (1) 3/293 (3) 4/313 (4) 5/314 (5) (5 wkts, 50 overs) 319
15 overs: 99-1

G. B. Hogg, A. J. Bichel, B. Lee and G. D. McGrath did not bat.

Bowling: Vaas 8–0–59–0; Gunaratne 6–0–46–0; de Silva 5–0–36–0; Muralitharan 10–0–47–1; Arnold 2–0–21–0; Fernando 9–0–47–3; Jayasuriya 10–0–59–0.

Sri Lanka

M. S. Atapattu c and b Lee 16
*S. T. Jayasuriya retired hurt 1
H. P. Tillekeratne b McGrath 21
D. P. M. D. Jayawardene c Gilchrist b Lee . 0
P. A. de Silva c and b Hogg. 92
R. P. Arnold lbw b Lee 1
†K. C. Sangakkara run out. 20
W. P. U. J. C. Vaas lbw b Hogg. 21
M. Muralitharan c Lee b Lehmann 4
C. R. D. Fernando lbw b McGrath. 9
P. W. Gunaratne not out. 15
B 6, l-b 8, w 6, n-b 3 23

1/42 (1) 2/46 (4) 3/47 (3) 4/48 (6) 5/100 (7) 6/144 (8) 7/149 (9) 8/203 (5) 9/223 (10) (47.4 overs) 223
15 overs: 49-4

Jayasuriya retired hurt at 6.

Bowling: McGrath 9.4–1–25–2; Lee 10–1–52–3; Harvey 7–0–29–0; Bichel 7–1–32–0; Hogg 9–1–45–2; Lehmann 5–0–26–1.

Umpires: B. F. Bowden (New Zealand) and D. R. Shepherd (England).
Third umpire: B. G. Jerling (South Africa). Referee: M. J. Procter (South Africa).

INDIA v KENYA

At Cape Town, March 7, 2003 (day/night). India won by six wickets. Toss: Kenya.

This was only the second victory chasing under lights, in the tournament's eighth day/nighter, and it was a hard-earned one. Kenya played to their carefully cultivated strengths – good fielding, paceless bowling, and the will to bat 50 overs – and it required a dutiful century from Ganguly to take his team home. India's catching was embarrassing: three regulation chances were dropped in the first hour, all off Nehra, and Otieno benefited from two of them to top-score with a long-drawn-out 79. Committed swing bowling in a nippy evening breeze, and a swooping catch by Tony Suji off Tendulkar's superbly timed flick, reduced India to 24 for three in the tenth over. But Ganguly found partners in Dravid and, more decisively, Yuvraj Singh, whose energetic leg-side attack on the spinners provided a much-needed thrust. Ganguly's 21st hundred in one-day internationals took him past Saeed Anwar to No. 2 on the all-time list headed by Tendulkar on 34. At the post-match press conference, he was asked whether India ever contemplated tanking the game, to improve their chances of meeting Kenya again in the semi-final. However, South Africa's fate showed what happens to teams who attempt higher mathematics and fail.

Man of the Match: S. C. Ganguly. *Attendance:* 17,866.

Kenya

†K. O. Otieno b Harbhajan Singh	79
R. D. Shah run out	34
*S. O. Tikolo c Zaheer Khan b Harbhajan Singh	3
T. M. Odoyo lbw b Mongia	32
M. O. Odumbe not out	34
C. O. Obuya c Mongia b Srinath	8
P. J. Ongondo c Tendulkar b Srinath	8
M. A. Suji not out	11
B 4, l-b 8, w 4	16
1/75 (2) 2/81 (3) 3/157 (1) 4/165 (4) 5/191 (6) 6/206 (7) (6 wkts, 50 overs)	225
15 overs: 48-0	

B. J. Patel, H. S. Modi and T. O. Suji did not bat.

Bowling: Zaheer Khan 10–1–53–0; Srinath 10–0–43–2; Nehra 10–2–30–0; Harbhajan Singh 10–0–41–2; Mongia 8–0–37–1; Yuvraj Singh 2–0–9–0.

India

V. Sehwag c Tikolo b Odoyo	3
S. R. Tendulkar c T. O. Suji b M. A. Suji	5
*S. C. Ganguly not out	107
M. Kaif lbw b Odoyo	5
†R. Dravid c and b Obuya	32
Yuvraj Singh not out	58
L-b 5, w 8, n-b 3	16
1/5 (1) 2/11 (2) 3/24 (4) 4/108 (5) (4 wkts, 47.5 overs)	226
15 overs: 53-3	

D. Mongia, Harbhajan Singh, Zaheer Khan, J. Srinath and A. Nehra did not bat.

Bowling: M. A. Suji 10–3–27–1; Odoyo 7–0–27–2; Ongondo 5–0–31–0; T. O. Suji 7–0–25–0; Obuya 9.5–2–50–1; Odumbe 3–0–25–0; Tikolo 6–0–36–0.

Umpires: D. J. Harper (Australia) and P. Willey (England).
Third umpire: S. J. A. Taufel (Australia). Referee: Wasim Raja (Pakistan).

NEW ZEALAND v ZIMBABWE

At Bloemfontein, March 8, 2003. New Zealand won by six wickets. Toss: Zimbabwe.

This match will be remembered for an apocalyptic late blitz by Streak and Ervine. It was not enough to secure victory for Zimbabwe in a game both sides needed to win, but it injected a skip and a jump into what was threatening to be a boring procession. After taking first use of a bland surface, Zimbabwe spent most of their innings consolidating, and began the 48th over modestly placed at 190 for seven. That was the cue for complete mayhem. Making liberal use of the long handle, Streak and Ervine belted the last three overs – bowled by Harris, whose first nine had cost just 22, Vettori and Adams – for 62, including eight fours and three sixes. The previously sedate Streak advanced from 37 to 72, Ervine from six to 31. "Things went a bit pear-shaped," Fleming later remarked. Suddenly faced with a challenging chase, New Zealand were teetering at 97 for three. But Astle embarked on a careful stand of 121 with Cairns, dropped at backward square leg on 21, and completed his 13th one-day century as he steered New Zealand home with 16 balls to spare. Earlier, Zimbabwe lost Andy Flower to a superb direct hit from Astle at mid-on, and were grateful for a maiden one-day fifty from Taibu, which kickstarted the recovery.

Man of the Match: N. J. Astle. *Attendance:* 3,551.

Zimbabwe

C. B. Wishart c Styris b Cairns	30
D. D. Ebrahim b Adams	0
A. Flower run out	37
G. W. Flower c Cairns b Oram	1
G. J. Whittall c McCullum b Cairns	0
†T. Taibu lbw b Harris	53
A. M. Blignaut run out	4
*H. H. Streak not out	72
S. M. Ervine not out	31
L-b 9, w 13, n-b 2	24
1/5 (2) 2/59 (1) 3/63 (4) 4/65 (5) 5/98 (3) 6/106 (7) 7/174 (6) (7 wkts, 50 overs)	252
15 overs: 61-2	

B. A. Murphy and D. T. Hondo did not bat.

Bowling: Bond 10–1–37–0; Adams 5–0–54–1; Oram 10–4–28–1; Cairns 4–0–16–2; Vettori 10–0–52–0; Harris 10–0–45–1; Astle 1–0–11–0.

New Zealand

C. D. McMillan c Taibu b Hondo	8
*S. P. Fleming lbw b Blignaut	46
N. J. Astle not out	102
S. B. Styris c sub (T. J. Friend) b Blignaut	13
C. L. Cairns b Ervine	54
C. Z. Harris not out	14
L-b 5, w 10, n-b 1	16
1/27 (1) 2/72 (2) 3/97 (4) 4/218 (5) (4 wkts, 47.2 overs)	253
15 overs: 77-2	

†B. B. McCullum, J. D. P. Oram, A. R. Adams, D. L. Vettori and S. E. Bond did not bat.

Bowling: Streak 10–0–59–0; Hondo 8.2–0–52–1; Blignaut 10–0–41–2; G. W. Flower 10–0–33–0; Whittall 3–0–19–0; Ervine 6–0–44–1.

Umpires: D. B. Hair (Australia) and R. E. Koertzen (South Africa).
Third umpire: E. A. R. de Silva (Sri Lanka). Referee: G. R. Viswanath (India).

INDIA v SRI LANKA

At Johannesburg, March 10, 2003. India won by 183 runs. Toss: Sri Lanka.

Jayasuriya arrived with a bad thumb and a bruised forearm; from the moment he inserted India on a decent pitch, he had a colossal headache as well. Sri Lanka's fast bowlers – Vaas apart – were ill equipped for the task, leaving Tendulkar and Sehwag to put on 153, the third and highest century stand they had shared in ten innings opening together. Tendulkar met Vaas judiciously, Muralitharan introspectively, and regally dismissed the rest from his presence. He fell just short of a hundred for the second time in ten days, but passed 500 runs for the second World Cup running. Sehwag played with a responsibility often lacking before his late blitz ended at long-on. India's 292 for six looked insurmountable and, by the fourth over of their reply, a misconceived Sri Lankan batting order had proved as much. Atapattu, Mubarak, a static and inexperienced No. 3, Jayawardene, hopelessly bereft of form, and de Silva all went for nought. When Jayasuriya scooped Srinath to Kaif at cover it told of his handicap. Kaif finished with four catches – a World Cup fielding record – but Srinath's four wickets deservedly won the match award and made all India's labours to tempt him out of retirement worthwhile. India's zest and skill had ensured their place in the semi-finals; Sri Lanka could still get there, but they began to wonder quite how.

Man of the Match: J. Srinath. *Attendance:* 23,050.

India

S. R. Tendulkar c Sangakkara b de Silva	97
V. Sehwag c de Silva b Muralitharan	66
*S. C. Ganguly b Vaas	48
M. Kaif b Muralitharan	19
Yuvraj Singh b Vaas	5
†R. Dravid not out	18
D. Mongia c de Silva b Muralitharan	9
Harbhajan Singh not out	7
B 4, l-b 9, w 7, n-b 3	23
1/153 (2) 2/214 (1) 3/243 (3) 4/251 (5) 5/265 (4) 6/277 (7) (6 wkts, 50 overs)	292
15 overs: 84-0	

Zaheer Khan, J. Srinath and A. Nehra did not bat.

Bowling: Vaas 10–2–34–2; Nissanka 6–0–49–0; Fernando 10–1–61–0; Muralitharan 10–0–46–3; Jayasuriya 3–0–27–0; de Silva 6–0–32–1; Arnold 5–0–30–0.

Sri Lanka

M. S. Atapattu c Kaif b Srinath	0
*S. T. Jayasuriya c Kaif b Srinath	12
J. Mubarak c Dravid b Srinath	0
D. P. M. D. Jayawardene lbw b Zaheer Khan	0
P. A. de Silva lbw b Srinath	0
†K. C. Sangakkara c Yuvraj Singh b Nehra	30
R. P. Arnold lbw b Zaheer Khan	8
W. P. U. J. C. Vaas c Tendulkar b Nehra	9
R. A. P. Nissanka c Kaif b Nehra	0
C. R. D. Fernando not out	13
M. Muralitharan c Kaif b Nehra	16
B 1, l-b 5, w 14, n-b 1	21
1/2 (1) 2/2 (3) 3/3 (4) 4/15 (5) 5/40 (2) 6/59 (6) 7/75 (7) 8/78 (8) 9/78 (9) 10/109 (11) (23 overs)	109
15 overs: 60-6	

Bowling: Zaheer Khan 7–0–33–2; Srinath 9–1–35–4; Nehra 7–1–35–4.

Umpires: D. R. Shepherd (England) and S. J. A. Taufel (Australia).
Third umpire: D. J. Harper (Australia). Referee: C. H. Lloyd (West Indies).

No. 29, your time is up: Shane Bond uproots Ian Harvey's middle stump to leave Australia reeling at 84 for seven – yet they won by 96 runs.

Picture by Patrick Eagar.

AUSTRALIA v NEW ZEALAND

At Port Elizabeth, March 11, 2003. Australia won by 96 runs. Toss: New Zealand.

Strong, straight and vividly justifying his billing as one of the world's fastest bowlers, Bond concluded with a spell of 4–2–3–3 to emerge with six for 23, the best one-day international return yet for New Zealand. Yet, once again, Australia showed that great teams like nothing better than a hole to escape from. Bond's analysis thus became the most individually fruitful, yet collectively fruitless, in World Cup annals. Having won four of their last six one-day games against Australia, New Zealand were optimistic about slaying the dragon even before the St George's pitch, a muddy shade of pale, shortened the odds. Defying local wisdom by fielding first, Fleming shuffled his attack with a quiet flourish and made seven changes by the 24th over. Australia were in desperate trouble at 84 for seven. Bond's allocation, though, was all but spent and, in a virtual replay of their stand against England on the same ground, Bevan and Bichel added 97, with Bevan contributing the lamb's share of 36. His high-risk strategy having paid off less profitably than hoped, Fleming fought alone as McGrath slipped through the top order. Cairns began with four, four and six, but his slice to third man prefaced an almighty clatter and New Zealand's lowest World Cup total: Lee plucked out the last five in 15 balls, a vulture bent on supper.

Man of the Match: S. E. Bond. *Attendance:* 11,104.

Australia

†A. C. Gilchrist lbw b Bond	18
M. L. Hayden c McCullum b Bond	1
*R. T. Ponting c Fleming b Bond	6
D. R. Martyn c McCullum b Bond	31
D. S. Lehmann c Astle b Adams	4
M. G. Bevan c Vincent b Oram	56
G. B. Hogg lbw b Bond	0
I. J. Harvey b Bond	2
A. J. Bichel c Cairns b Oram	64
B. Lee not out	15
G. D. McGrath not out	3
L-b 1, w 4, n-b 3	8
1/17 (2) 2/24 (1) 3/31 (3) 4/47 (5) 5/80 (4) 6/80 (7) 7/84 (8) 8/181 (6) 9/192 (9) — (9 wkts, 50 overs)	208
15 overs: 55-4	

Bowling: Bond 10–2–23–6; Adams 9–2–46–1; Vettori 10–1–40–0; Oram 7–0–48–2; Harris 10–1–24–0; Styris 3–0–18–0; Astle 1–0–8–0.

New Zealand

D. L. Vettori c Gilchrist b McGrath	10
*S. P. Fleming c Gilchrist b Lee	48
N. J. Astle c Ponting b McGrath	0
S. B. Styris lbw b McGrath	3
C. L. Cairns c Lee b Bichel	16
L. Vincent c Martyn b Harvey	7
C. Z. Harris not out	15
†B. B. McCullum lbw b Lee	1
J. D. P. Oram b Lee	0
A. R. Adams b Lee	0
S. E. Bond c and b Lee	3
L-b 4, w 5	9
1/14 (1) 2/14 (3) 3/33 (4) 4/66 (5) 5/84 (6) 6/102 (2) 7/104 (8) 8/104 (9) 9/108 (10) 10/112 (11) — (30.1 overs)	112
15 overs: 67-4	

Bowling: McGrath 6–1–29–3; Lee 9.1–2–42–5; Harvey 6–3–11–1; Bichel 5–0–15–1; Hogg 4–0–11–0.

Umpires: S. A. Bucknor (West Indies) and E. A. R. de Silva (Sri Lanka).
Third umpire: B. G. Jerling (South Africa). Referee: R. S. Madugalle (Sri Lanka).

One-way traffic: Andy Flower (*hidden*) and Andy Blignaut both charge towards the striker's end while Kennedy Otieno, ball in glove, sprints down the pitch. Blignaut is out, and the Kenyans head for the semis.

Picture by Nick Laham, Getty Images.

KENYA v ZIMBABWE

At Bloemfontein, March 12, 2003. Kenya won by seven wickets. Toss: Zimbabwe.

The Kenyan safari became ever more adventurous as they beat Zimbabwe for the first time in 15 attempts to become the least fancied side ever to reach the World Cup semi-finals. "Today is the biggest day in every Kenyan's life," enthused Tikolo. It was their third win over Test opponents in the competition – and their most convincing. On another anodyne pitch, Martin Suji's bustling, accurate medium-pace accounted for three early wickets – including Campbell, summoned hastily from the commentary box because of Zimbabwe's injury list – before Obuya's leg-breaks baffled the middle order. Only Andy Flower, with a patient 63 including five of Zimbabwe's nine boundaries, batted with any common sense. With history beckoning, Kenya stuttered; they were 62 for three when Olonga, picked for the first time since his black-armband protest during Zimbabwe's opening game, trapped Otieno. But Odoyo and Odumbe launched a thrilling counter-attack. Odoyo was merciless off the back foot, while Odumbe repeatedly used his feet to hit inside-out over extra cover. When the two of them combined to hit six consecutive deliveries to the boundary, Zimbabwe knew their World Cup was over.

Man of the Match: M. A. Suji. *Attendance:* 2,727.

> "Vaughan had not been thrown in at the deep end so much as tossed into the Pacific without a life jacket."
>
> South Africans in England, page 430.

Zimbabwe

C. B. Wishart c Otieno b M. A. Suji	5	H. K. Olonga c Odumbe b Tikolo	3
A. D. R. Campbell lbw b M. A. Suji	7	D. T. Hondo not out	0
A. Flower b Odoyo	63		
G. W. Flower c Otieno b M. A. Suji	7	L-b 1, w 4, n-b 2	7
†T. Taibu c Otieno b Obuya	3		
D. D. Ebrahim st Otieno b Obuya	13	1/8 (1) 2/26 (2) 3/45 (4) (44.1 overs)	133
A. M. Blignaut run out	4	4/66 (5) 5/85 (6) 6/95 (7)	
*H. H. Streak c Shah b Obuya	0	7/97 (8) 8/114 (3)	
D. A. Marillier b Tikolo	21	9/129 (10) 10/133 (9)	15 overs: 45-3

Bowling: M. A. Suji 8–2–19–3; Odoyo 10–0–43–1; Ongondo 5–2–16–0; Obuya 10–0–32–3; Karim 9–0–20–0; Tikolo 2.1–0–2–2.

Kenya

†K. O. Otieno lbw b Olonga	19
R. D. Shah run out	14
*S. O. Tikolo c Streak b Blignaut	2
T. M. Odoyo not out	43
M. O. Odumbe not out	38
L-b 4, w 6, n-b 9	19
1/24 (2) 2/33 (3) (3 wkts, 26 overs)	135
3/62 (1)	15 overs: 48-2

H. S. Modi, C. O. Obuya, P. J. Ongondo, T. O. Suji, M. A. Suji and A. Y. Karim did not bat.

Bowling: Streak 6–0–24–0; Blignaut 9–1–36–1; Olonga 4–0–21–1; Hondo 3–1–14–0; G. W. Flower 3–0–27–0; Marillier 1–0–9–0.

Umpires: Aleem Dar (Pakistan) and S. Venkataraghavan (India).
Third umpire: B. F. Bowden (New Zealand). Referee: Wasim Raja (Pakistan).

INDIA v NEW ZEALAND

At Centurion, March 14, 2003. India won by seven wickets. Toss: India.

India – already in the semis – displayed their growing confidence, won their seventh game in succession and achieved sweet revenge for their recent defeat in New Zealand. As Kaif hit Styris for two consecutive fours to polish off the match, New Zealand had to sleep on their fate – hoping Zimbabwe could conjure an unlikely victory over Sri Lanka. They were in trouble immediately after the national anthems: Zaheer Khan launched into his run-up, and his second and third balls took out McMillan and Astle while Fleming stood dazed at the non-striker's end like a jilted lover. After that, Ganguly's bowling changes were touched by stardust, and only the tail made the total respectable. So it was down to Bond. When Sehwag edged his sixth ball to second slip, Ganguly was yorked and Tendulkar holed out to Tuffey after flaying him for three consecutive fours, New Zealand were quivering with hope. But once Dravid was dropped on one – a simple chance to the keeper – the heads went down and so did the match. He and Kaif steered India to easy victory with nine overs to go.

Man of the Match: Zaheer Khan. *Attendance:* 16,124.

New Zealand

C. D. McMillan c Harbhajan Singh b Zaheer Khan . 0
*S. P. Fleming c Tendulkar b Srinath . . . 30
N. J. Astle lbw b Zaheer Khan 0
S. B. Styris c Dravid b Nehra. 15
†B. B. McCullum b Zaheer Khan 4
C. L. Cairns c Zaheer Khan b Harbhajan Singh . 20
C. Z. Harris lbw b Zaheer Khan 17
J. D. P. Oram b Sehwag. 23
D. L. Vettori c Ganguly b Harbhajan Singh . 13
D. R. Tuffey c and b Mongia 11
S. E. Bond not out 0
L-b 5, w 4, n-b 4 13

1/0 (1) 2/0 (3) 3/38 (4) (45.1 overs) 146
4/47 (5) 5/60 (2) 6/88 (6)
7/96 (7) 8/129 (9)
9/144 (8) 10/146 (10) 15 overs: 52-4

Bowling: Zaheer Khan 8–0–42–4; Srinath 8–0–20–1; Nehra 10–3–24–1; Harbhajan Singh 10–2–28–2; Ganguly 2–0–4–0; Tendulkar 5–0–20–0; Sehwag 2–1–3–1; Mongia 0.1–0–0–1.

India

V. Sehwag c Styris b Bond. 1
S. R. Tendulkar c Oram b Tuffey. 15
*S. C. Ganguly b Bond 3
M. Kaif not out 68
†R. Dravid not out 53
W 8, n-b 2. 10

1/4 (1) 2/9 (3) (3 wkts, 40.4 overs) 150
3/21 (2) 15 overs: 65-3

Yuvraj Singh, D. Mongia, Harbhajan Singh, Zaheer Khan, J. Srinath and A. Nehra did not bat.

Bowling: Tuffey 10–1–41–1; Bond 8–2–23–2; Oram 5–0–20–0; Vettori 5–0–18–0; McMillan 2–1–4–0; Styris 6.4–0–29–0; Harris 4–1–15–0.

Umpires: D. J. Harper (Australia) and P. Willey (England).
Third umpire: D. B. Hair (Australia). Referee: R. S. Madugalle (Sri Lanka).

SRI LANKA v ZIMBABWE

At East London, March 15, 2003. Sri Lanka won by 74 runs. Toss: Sri Lanka.

The tangled story of black and white in southern Africa once again had a sad impact on the cricket field as Andy Flower said a premature goodbye to international competition. As so often, his dismissal changed the tone of Zimbabwe's chase from cautious optimism to resignation. After a brief but brutal opening partnership and some authoritative nurdling from Flower, they needed 117 from 130 balls, with seven wickets left. But, on 38, Flower got the woodiest of inside edges on to pad, only to be given lbw. He was aghast, Zimbabwe's self-belief evaporated, and the last six tumbled for 32, giving Sri Lanka's win a flattering veneer. Needing victory to reach the semi-finals, their strategy – accumulate, preserve wickets, bash – was simple and, on a sluggish pitch, Zimbabwe had neither the firepower nor the finesse to disrupt it. Atapattu did the accumulating, finding gaps and running hard throughout the innings, Sangakkara the bashing – 35 in 25 balls – as Sri Lanka added 73 in the last eight overs. The match ended with a scene out of John le Carré, when Henry Olonga was spirited to a safe house amid rumours that a seven-man snatch squad from Zimbabwe's secret police had arrived. He too announced a sad, and premature, retirement.

Man of the Match: M. S. Atapattu. *Attendance:* 6,380.

Sri Lanka

M. S. Atapattu not out	103	W. P. U. J. C. Vaas not out	11
*S. T. Jayasuriya c Taibu b Streak	22		
D. A. Gunawardene c and b Marillier	41	L-b 3, w 15	18
P. A. de Silva c Taibu b Ervine	25		
†K. C. Sangakkara c G. W. Flower b Streak	35	1/41 (2) 2/124 (3) 3/175 (4) 4/227 (5) 5/233 (6)	(5 wkts, 50 overs) 256
R. P. Arnold c G. W. Flower b Hondo	1		15 overs: 52-1

H. P. Tillekeratne, M. Muralitharan, C. R. D. Fernando and P. W. Gunaratne did not bat.

Bowling: Streak 10–0–40–2; Blignaut 8–0–40–0; Friend 2–0–13–0; Hondo 5–0–36–1; G. W. Flower 10–0–44–0; Marillier 10–0–43–1; Matsikenyeri 2–0–13–0; Ervine 3–0–24–1.

Zimbabwe

C. B. Wishart b Jayasuriya	43	S. Matsikenyeri not out	1
D. A. Marillier c Jayasuriya b Gunaratne	19	D. T. Hondo b Vaas	0
T. J. Friend b Gunaratne	21	L-b 5, w 4, n-b 3	12
A. Flower lbw b de Silva	38		
G. W. Flower c and b Jayasuriya	31	1/36 (2) 2/68 (3)	(41.5 overs) 182
†T. Taibu b Muralitharan	2	3/111 (1) 4/140 (4)	
A. M. Blignaut c de Silva b Fernando	1	5/150 (6) 6/151 (7)	
S. M. Ervine b Vaas	12	7/178 (8) 8/181 (9)	
*H. H. Streak c Atapattu b Jayasuriya	2	9/181 (5) 10/182 (11)	15 overs: 88-2

Bowling: Vaas 9.5–0–46–2; Gunaratne 7–0–33–2; de Silva 9–1–36–1; Muralitharan 7–0–22–1; Jayasuriya 6–0–30–3; Fernando 3–0–10–1.

Umpires: B. G. Jerling (South Africa) and R. E. Koertzen (South Africa).
Third umpire: S. Venkataraghavan (India). Referee: C. H. Lloyd (West Indies).

AUSTRALIA v KENYA

At Durban, March 15, 2003 (day/night). Australia won by five wickets. Toss: Australia.

Another Kenyan match, another fantasy. This was the night they imagined they might beat the world's most powerful cricketing nation thanks to the exploits of a middle-aged spinner who had retired after the last World Cup but now made a Brett Lee hat-trick seem insignificant. Aasif Karim's greatest claims to fame amounted to five wickets against Bangladesh in 1997-98 and some Davis Cup tennis. After this, he could also regale his grandchildren with the tale of how, at 39, he reduced the great Australians to impotence. Karim's style on delivery suggested that he might be about to serve, not bowl. He never remotely turned a ball, but in his first two overs he had Ponting lbw, Lehmann caught at the wicket by David Obuya (deputising for the injured Otieno) and then stooped for a low return catch off Hogg. Called out of retirement barely a month before the tournament began, Karim had reduced Australia to 117 for five; Gilchrist's withering assault, that had brought 98 within 12 overs, was quite forgotten. Karim had figures of 8–6–2–3 before Symonds and Harvey took five from his last two balls to achieve victory. Ponting professed himself "bemused" that Lee's thrilling hat-trick, which had reduced Kenya to three for three, had not earned the match award. For once, world-class athleticism had to give way to the romantic choice. Australia had won quite enough.

Man of the Match: A. Y. Karim. *Attendance:* 14,769.

Kenya

†K. O. Otieno b Lee 1
R. D. Shah c sub (N. M. Hauritz) b Hogg 46
B. J. Patel c Ponting b Lee 0
D. O. Obuya b Lee 0
*S. O. Tikolo c Bichel b Lehmann 51
H. S. Modi not out 39
C. O. Obuya c Gilchrist b Bichel 3
P. J. Ongondo c Gilchrist b Bichel 1
T. O. Suji c Ponting b Lehmann 1
M. A. Suji not out 15
L-b 10, w 6, n-b 1 17

1/3 (1) 2/3 (3) 3/3 (4) 4/82 (2) 5/131 (5) 6/139 (7) 7/141 (8) 8/144 (9) (8 wkts, 50 overs) 174

15 overs: 46-3

A. Y. Karim did not bat.

Bowling: McGrath 10–1–32–0; Lee 8–3–14–3; Bichel 9–1–42–2; Hogg 10–1–31–1; Harvey 7–0–23–0; Lehmann 6–0–22–2.

Australia

†A. C. Gilchrist c D. O. Obuya b Ongondo . 67
M. L. Hayden c sub (J. O. Angara) b Ongondo . 20
*R. T. Ponting lbw b Karim 18
A. Symonds not out 33
D. S. Lehmann c D. O. Obuya b Karim . 2
G. B. Hogg c and b Karim 0
I. J. Harvey not out 28
B 4, l-b 1, w 4, n-b 1 10

1/50 (2) 2/98 (1) 3/109 (3) 4/117 (5) 5/117 (6) (5 wkts, 31.2 overs) 178

15 overs: 109-2

D. R. Martyn, A. J. Bichel, B. Lee and G. D. McGrath did not bat.

Bowling: M. A. Suji 3–0–36–0; Ongondo 10–0–44–2; T. O. Suji 2–0–24–0; C. O. Obuya 8–0–62–0; Karim 8.2–6–7–3.

Umpires: B. F. Bowden (New Zealand) and S. A. Bucknor (West Indies).
Third umpire: E. A. R. de Silva (Sri Lanka). Referee: M. J. Procter (South Africa).

SUPER SIX

	Played	*Won*	*Lost*	*Tied*	*No result*	*Points*	*Net run-rate*
AUSTRALIA	5	5	0	0	0	24	1.85
INDIA	5	4	1	0	0	20	0.88
KENYA	5	3	2	0	0	14	0.35
SRI LANKA	5	2	3	0	0	11.5	–0.84
New Zealand	5	1	4	0	0	8	–0.89
Zimbabwe	5	0	5	0	0	3.5	–1.25

Super Six teams carried forward four points each for wins against fellow Super Six qualifiers, and one point each for wins (half a point for a tie or no result) against teams eliminated at the Pool stage.

SEMI-FINALS

AUSTRALIA v SRI LANKA

At Port Elizabeth, March 18, 2003. Australia won by 48 runs (D/L method). Toss: Australia.

This was Gilchrist's match, not for what he did with bat or gloves but for his decision to walk, which astonished everyone unused to such Australian magnanimity. Despite being reprieved by umpire Koertzen, Gilchrist knew he had edged an attempted sweep that was caught off his pad. His departure, swiftly followed by Ponting's, gave Sri Lanka their chance to beat Australia: they blew it. Sangakkara missed a simple chance to stump Symonds, on 33, off Jayasuriya, who later removed Lehmann and Bevan with successive balls, but Symonds was not to be dismissed. He adapted well to another difficult St George's Park surface and his innings was defined by patience rather than brute force. Sri Lanka needed only 213, but their optimism had gone. Atapattu, their form batsman, was dropped by Hogg at cover on 14, but had his off stump ripped out by Lee's next ball, which was measured at 99.4mph. Jayasuriya hit Lee for six before being caught at square leg. Then Bichel, in his follow-through, swooped left-handed to pick up a defensive push from Sangakkara, turned, and threw down the batsman's stumps, stranding de Silva, who trudged off into retirement. The late-afternoon rain halted Sri Lanka's first decent partnership – 47 for the eighth wicket between Sangakkara and Vaas – but no one complained about Duckworth/Lewis. Australia had deservedly reached their fifth World Cup final and their third in succession.

Man of the Match: A. Symonds. *Attendance:* 14,525.

Australia

†A. C. Gilchrist c Sangakkara b de Silva	22	(20)
M. L. Hayden c Tillekeratne b Vaas	20	(38)
*R. T. Ponting c Jayasuriya b Vaas	2	(8)
D. S. Lehmann b Jayasuriya	36	(66)
A. Symonds not out	91	(118)
M. G. Bevan c Sangakkara b Jayasuriya	0	(1)
G. B. Hogg st Sangakkara b de Silva	8	(19)
I. J. Harvey c Sangakkara b Vaas	7	(10)
A. J. Bichel not out	19	(21)
L-b 3, w 3, n-b 1	7	
1/34 (1) 2/37 (3) 3/51 (2) 4/144 (4) 5/144 (6) 6/158 (7) 7/175 (8) (7 wkts, 50 overs)	212	

15 overs: 64-3

B. Lee and G. D. McGrath did not bat.

Bowling: Vaas 10–1–34–3; Gunaratne 8–0–60–0; de Silva 10–0–36–2; Muralitharan 10–0–29–0; Jayasuriya 10–0–42–2; Arnold 2–0–8–0.

Sri Lanka

M. S. Atapattu b Lee	14	(17)
*S. T. Jayasuriya c Symonds b McGrath	17	(24)
H. P. Tillekeratne c Gilchrist b Lee	3	(15)
D. A. Gunawardene c Ponting b Lee	1	(4)
P. A. de Silva run out	11	(16)
†K. C. Sangakkara not out	39	(70)
D. P. M. D. Jayawardene c Gilchrist b Hogg	5	(8)
R. P. Arnold c Lee b Hogg	3	(27)
W. P. U. J. C. Vaas not out	21	(50)
B 4, l-b 1, w 2, n-b 2	9	
1/21 (1) 2/37 (2) 3/37 (3) 4/43 (4) 5/51 (5) 6/60 (7) 7/76 (8) (7 wkts, 38.1 overs)	123	

15 overs: 60-5

M. Muralitharan and P. W. Gunaratne did not bat.

Bowling: McGrath 7–1–20–1; Lee 8–0–35–3; Bichel 10–4–18–0; Hogg 10–1–30–2; Harvey 2.1–0–11–0; Lehmann 1–0–4–0.

Umpires: R. E. Koertzen (South Africa) and D. R. Shepherd (England).
Third umpire: B. F. Bowden (New Zealand). Referee: C. H. Lloyd (West Indies).

INDIA v KENYA

At Durban, March 20, 2003 (day/night). India won by 91 runs. Toss: India.

The steel instilled into the Indian team and distilled by Ganguly, drop by steady drop, ensured there were no Disneyfied endings for Kenya. Captaining India for the 99th time in a one-day international, Ganguly re-emphasised his batting mastery against modest attacks to guide his team to an imposing if not unanswerable total, then sat back as his pace trio did the needful. India equalled their record for consecutive successes, set in 1985, with win No. 8. India began carefully enough but Ganguly was in no mood to accept dictation. After five runs had been squeezed from leg-spinner Collins Obuya's opening two overs, he darted out to launch a six off the first ball of his third, then repeated the message four balls later; the chastened Obuya lasted just six overs. Tendulkar seemed destined for a hundred until he pulled Tikolo to deep mid-wicket. But Ganguly matched Mark Waugh's 1996 feat of three centuries in a World Cup tournament, getting there with his fifth six, the product of a golfer's swing and that unmistakable superiority complex. Arms aloft, he drank in the acclaim. His opposite number, Tikolo, also top-scored in the Kenyan reply, before his men took a weary lap of honour, smiles intact, their place in the pantheon assured.

Man of the Match: S. C. Ganguly. *Attendance:* 18,111.

India

Batting	Runs	Balls
V. Sehwag c Odumbe b Ongondo	33	(56)
S. R. Tendulkar c D. O. Obuya b Tikolo	83	(101)
*S. C. Ganguly not out	111	(114)
M. Kaif run out	15	(20)
Yuvraj Singh c D. O. Obuya b Odoyo	16	(10)
†R. Dravid not out	1	(1)
W 9, n-b 2	11	
(4 wkts, 50 overs)	270	

1/74 (1) 2/177 (2) 3/233 (4) 4/267 (5) — 15 overs: 56-0

D. Mongia, Harbhajan Singh, Zaheer Khan, J. Srinath and A. Nehra did not bat.

Bowling: Suji 10–1–62–0; Odoyo 10–1–45–1; Ongondo 10–1–38–1; Karim 4–0–25–0; Tikolo 10–0–60–1; C. O. Obuya 6–0–40–0.

Kenya

Batting	Runs	Balls
†K. O. Otieno c Dravid b Srinath	15	(43)
R. D. Shah lbw b Zaheer Khan	1	(17)
P. J. Ongondo c Zaheer Khan b Nehra	0	(5)
T. M. Odoyo c Sehwag b Nehra	7	(15)
*S. O. Tikolo b Tendulkar	56	(83)
M. O. Odumbe c Zaheer Khan b Yuvraj Singh	19	(16)
H. S. Modi c Dravid b Zaheer Khan	9	(25)
D. O. Obuya run out	3	(23)
C. O. Obuya lbw b Tendulkar	29	(42)
M. A. Suji b Zaheer Khan	1	(8)
A. Y. Karim not out	0	(1)
B 16, l-b 8, w 15	39	
(46.2 overs)	179	

1/20 (2) 2/21 (3) 3/30 (1) 4/36 (4) 5/63 (6) 6/92 (7) 7/104 (8) 8/161 (5) 9/179 (9) 10/179 (10) — 15 overs: 36-4

Bowling: Zaheer Khan 9.2–2–14–3; Srinath 7–1–11–1; Nehra 5–1–11–2; Harbhajan Singh 10–1–32–0; Yuvraj Singh 6–0–43–1; Sehwag 3–1–16–0; Tendulkar 6–0–28–2.

Umpires: S. A. Bucknor (West Indies) and D. J. Harper (Australia).
Third umpire: S. J. A. Taufel (Australia). Referee: M. J. Procter (South Africa).

FINAL

AUSTRALIA v INDIA

JOHN STERN

At Johannesburg, March 23, 2003. Australia won by 125 runs. Toss: India.

Ricky Ponting played a captain's innings to deliver Australia their third title. His 140, the highest individual score in a World Cup final, and his leadership through the tournament completed his ascent from under-achieving Tasmanian devil to cornerstone of Australian dominance.

Just like Nasser Hussain at Brisbane a few months earlier, Ganguly raised eyebrows by putting Australia in. He was acting from fear of Australia's bowlers rather than on aggressive intent: against any other opponents, he would surely have batted first. Yet it had been 71 matches and three years since Australia last failed to defend a total of 200 or more.

Ganguly was right to think that the pitch would offer movement and bounce, but his in-form seamers were now under pressure to perform. They buckled. The first over from Zaheer Khan contained ten deliveries and 15 runs, and there was no coming back. Gilchrist and Hayden chanced their arms, as they do: after nine overs, Australia were 74 without loss. "Intent and intimidate – that has been our motto," said Ponting afterwards. The grammar was dubious; the effectiveness beyond question.

Ganguly turned to spin in the tenth over, and Harbhajan Singh did send back both openers. But Australia were not reined in for long. The partnership of 234 between Ponting and Martyn was Australia's highest for any wicket in one-day internationals. So was their total. Martyn's performance was the more remarkable because he had missed the semi-final with a finger injury and was not expected to play. His batting

Off the meat: Ricky Ponting flails the Indian attack to reach the highest score in a World Cup final.

Picture by Patrick Eagar.

was the perfect foil for Ponting – selfless, intelligent and perfectly tuned to the situation. Martyn actually reached his fifty first, despite a six-over handicap. Ponting was just warming up. He started slowly, his first 50 taking 74 balls to Martyn's 46, and containing a single four. Off his next 47 balls, he scored 90 runs and hit three more fours and eight sixes – the most in a World Cup innings, beating seven by Viv Richards and Ganguly – all on the leg side.

The gear-change occurred when Harbhajan returned in the 39th over. Ponting completed his fifty with a single – then hit him out of the attack with two successive sixes over mid-wicket. Harbhajan was replaced by Nehra; Ponting responded with a remarkable one-handed slog-sweep off a low full toss that also disappeared over mid-wicket. Off the penultimate ball of the innings, he drove Srinath for six over long-on into the second deck of the stand at the Golf Course End. Australia's acceleration had been breathtaking: 109 off the last ten overs, 64 off the last five. Srinath conceded 87 runs, the most in a final.

SIMPLY THE BEST

"As improbable as it might seem, this team has lifted the bar yet again."

Mike Coward, *The Australian*

"It's great to be a part of the Australian side like it is at the moment. It's awesome. Everyone's challenging each other to become better. You definitely feel the presence or the aura of being a part of a side like this."

Michael Bevan

"The pleasing thing... is that we've done it all fairly quietly, just gone about our business right the way through the World Cup."

Ricky Ponting

"It was the most compelling, destructive cricket performance I have ever seen."

Former captain Greg Chappell

"The Australian team cannot be faulted for its brilliance, but it would be to cricket's benefit if the rest of the world provided some competition."

Greg Baum, *The Age*

The army of Indian supporters – many from the UK – had been bemused when Ganguly asked Australia to bat. By the interval, they had all but given up hope. The dream was shattered entirely when Tendulkar tried to pull McGrath's fifth ball and was caught by the bowler off a top edge. Sehwag, who was caught off a Lee no-ball on four, did his best to keep India in it with a bullish run-a-ball 82, including ten fours and three sixes. But he was run out by a direct hit from Lehmann at deep mid-off, ending a promising stand of 88 with Dravid.

Rain had briefly threatened the unsatisfactory prospect of a replay the following day, with Australia's record-breaking performances consigned to history – so every sign of precipitation was greeted uproariously by India's fans. Knowing his side had to bowl 25 overs to ensure a result, Ponting brought on his spinners: there was a surreal period where Hogg and Lehmann were being thrashed to all parts as Indian supporters cheered and the fielders, running to their positions to speed up the over-rate, got wet. Then the umpires called a drinks break. After drinks, Bichel and McGrath returned, the lights came on, and the rain became heavy enough for the players to leave the field, with India on 103 for three. They returned 25 minutes later – no overs were deducted – and the formality of Australia's third World Cup (and 17th consecutive one-day victory) was completed under darkening skies to the sound of frequent thunderclaps.

Man of the Match: R. T. Ponting. *Attendance:* 31,827.

Man of the Tournament: S. R. Tendulkar.

The one they wanted: the Indian reply is just five balls old, but the cup already seems destined for Australia once Glenn McGrath holds on to a return catch from Sachin Tendulkar.

Picture by Patrick Eagar.

Australia

†A. C. Gilchrist c Sehwag b Harbhajan Singh	57	(48)
M. L. Hayden c Dravid b Harbhajan Singh	37	(54)
*R. T. Ponting not out	140	(121)
D. R. Martyn not out	88	(84)
B 2, l-b 12, w 16, n-b 7	37	
1/105 (1) 2/125 (2) (2 wkts, 50 overs)	359	
15 overs: 107-1		

D. S. Lehmann, A. Symonds, M. G. Bevan, G. B. Hogg, A. J. Bichel, B. Lee and G. D. McGrath did not bat.

Bowling: Zaheer Khan 7–0–67–0; Srinath 10–0–87–0; Nehra 10–0–57–0; Harbhajan Singh 8–0–49–2; Sehwag 3–0–14–0; Tendulkar 3–0–20–0; Mongia 7–0–39–0; Yuvraj Singh 2–0–12–0.

India

S. R. Tendulkar c and b McGrath	4	(5)
V. Sehwag run out	82	(81)
*S. C. Ganguly c Lehmann b Lee	24	(25)
M. Kaif c Gilchrist b McGrath	0	(3)
†R. Dravid b Bichel	47	(57)
Yuvraj Singh c Lee b Hogg	24	(34)
D. Mongia c Martyn b Symonds	12	(11)
Harbhajan Singh c McGrath b Symonds	7	(8)
Zaheer Khan c Lehmann b McGrath	4	(8)
J. Srinath b Lee	1	(4)
A. Nehra not out	8	(4)
B 4, l-b 4, w 9, n-b 4	21	
1/4 (1) 2/58 (3) 3/59 (4) 4/147 (2) 5/187 (5) 6/208 (6) 7/209 (7) 8/223 (8) 9/226 (10) 10/234 (9) (39.2 overs)	234	
15 overs: 88-3		

Bowling: McGrath 8.2–0–52–3; Lee 7–1–31–2; Hogg 10–0–61–1; Lehmann 2–0–18–0; Bichel 10–0–57–1; Symonds 2–0–7–2.

Umpires: S. A. Bucknor (West Indies) and D. R. Shepherd (England).
Third umpire: R. E. Koertzen (South Africa). Referee: R. S. Madugalle (Sri Lanka).

Figures in brackets in semi-final and final scorecards are balls received.

ENGLAND IN AUSTRALIA, 2002-03

REVIEW BY SCYLD BERRY

As in 1989 and the six subsequent Ashes series, so it was in 2002-03. The standard of Australia's cricket was so superior that England never came close, and lost for the eighth time running. When the series was alive, in the first three Tests, Australia won by mountainous margins – once by 384 runs, twice by an innings – and so swift was their despatch of England that only 11 days of play were necessary for the destiny of the Ashes to be decided.

After the First Test in Brisbane, the main debate centred not on the outcome of the series, which was taken for granted, but on whether this was the best Australian team of all time. There was plenty of support for the motion, so long as Glenn McGrath and Shane Warne were fit. By the Second Test, in Adelaide, Alec Stewart, who had played in seven of the eight disasters, said the gap between England and Australia was the largest he had known. Perhaps the most objective assessment came from Keith Miller, one of the 1948 Invincibles, the other main contenders for the all-time title; Miller accorded it to Steve Waugh's side. In full flight, Australia's cricketers were wondrous to behold, most particularly in the Third Test, in Perth, when Brett Lee replaced Andy Bichel. After that match, England's captain Nasser Hussain said his team had played "poorly", but a fairer summary would have been that Australia had played superlatively. While the Ashes were still at stake, the only time England were in the game was the first day at Adelaide, when Michael Vaughan hit 177.

In only two respects were the Australians anything less than magnificent. Strangely enough, it was not one of their better fielding sides. Adam Gilchrist tired as a wicket-keeper as the series went on, although his batting remained phenomenal until the end (his strike-rate was 102 runs per 100 balls). Before the series, Mark Waugh was dropped and announced his retirement from Test cricket; Ricky Ponting filled the vacancy at second slip to the pace bowlers, but there was no adequate replacement when Warne was bowling. Damien Martyn, who tried his hand there, dropped more than he caught. Only when Martin Love was given his debut in the Fourth Test, in Melbourne, did the slip fielding return to exalted standards.

The second respect was behaviour. So long as Australia were winning, everything was fine, but as soon as England got on top in the final Test, in Sydney, the game got bad-tempered. Matthew Hayden, after a debated lbw, was fined 20% of his match fee for breaking the glass of a pavilion door, and Gilchrist received an official reprimand for swearing after his appeal for a catch was turned down. Throughout the series some of the sledging, led by Hayden and Justin Langer, was all too obvious. If Waugh's team generated the same admiration as the Invincibles, they did not prompt quite the same public affection.

For the rest, Australia were superlative. Either their top three batsmen, led by Hayden, captured the initiative, with strokes of demoralising power, or their attack did. It was either intimidating batting or intimidating bowling which took England apart. But if one statistic summarised the difference between the two sides, it was that Australia's bowlers earned 91 wickets in the series, England's 63. Hussain was widely criticised, not least by himself, for sending Australia in at Brisbane rather than playing to the relative strength of England's batting. But it was hard to see how his depleted attack could have dismissed the home line-up twice at any time while the series was alive.

When Australia fielded their first-string attack, however, there was no such thing as a free run. On the generally true pitches which prevailed – in spite of a drought – until the second half of the Sydney Test, their virtue was unrelenting accuracy. England's batsmen, as usual, tried to dominate, but they did not get on top until the first innings at Sydney, when Mark Butcher and Hussain did so only by means of accumulation. McGrath and Gillespie set the tone with the new ball, rarely trying bouncers or experiments, just giving the batsmen six balls an over a fraction outside off stump. Gillespie bowled a fuller length than McGrath, and was considered by England's batsmen to be the pick of the opposing bowlers, but seldom had the figures to prove it. Hitting the pitch at greater pace, he beat the bat and was gone; McGrath "stayed in the pitch" a fraction longer and found the edge. After them came Lee with pace that was devastating on Perth's fast pitch but otherwise relatively straightforward until he was given the new ball in Sydney and swung it away. Warne was still the master until he dislocated his right shoulder in a one-day international between the Third and Fourth Tests. England's playing of spin was a huge improvement on their two previous performances in Australia, thanks to the coaching of Duncan Fletcher, but still Warne maintained control from one end, allowing Waugh to rotate his three pace bowlers from the other.

England were a rabble compared to Australia's sleek efficiency. If the eleven who took the field looked as though they had never played together before, this was usually true

In the first three Tests, England were a rabble compared to Australia's sleek efficiency. If the eleven who took the field looked as though they had never played together before, this was usually true. The injury list was the longest on any England tour, disrupting planning and damaging morale. When the management should have been thinking about the game in hand, they had to select replacements and fly home casualties. When they should have been bringing the Test eleven to the boil, they had to give some players a game to see if they were match-fit or not. Serious questions were raised about the competence of England's medical set-up, and only partly answered by the appointment of a full-time medical officer, Dr Peter Gregory, after the tour had started. The chief question was whether injured players had been given proper rehabilitation after surgery: the only possible answer seemed to be no.

The captain's downfall: Ricky Ponting gets both hands to an edge from Nasser Hussain, and England lurch towards defeat in the opening Test at the Gabba.
Picture by Graham Morris.

For England to have had any chance of extending Australia when it mattered, they had to hit the ground running, not stumbling as they did. On arrival in Perth in October, they found that instead of one player less than match-fit – Darren Gough – they had so many that their reputation was risibly undermined in the eyes of the Australian media and public. Mustering what players they could, England were beaten in their opening game by the ACB Chairman's side, by 58 runs. Their image as perennial losers to Australia – and perhaps their self-image – was thus reinforced from the outset.

Vaughan had had a simple knee operation after the Oval Test in September and was due to be fit from the start of the Australian tour, but he needed an injection in Perth, managed only one warm-up innings before the series, and could not bowl until the VB one-day series in mid-January. Simon Jones arrived with a rib injury, then warmed up to the extent that he was bowling flat out by the first day of the Brisbane Test, when he twisted his right knee while diving in the field and ruptured his cruciate ligaments.

At the start of the tour, Marcus Trescothick could not throw because of his right shoulder. Most unexpected of all, Andrew Flintoff could not even run. Medical opinion had said that he should recover from his double hernia operation in time, but he had to be sent straight off to Adelaide for rehabilitation at the ECB's National Academy. For months, the question of his fitness dragged on; he was sent home in mid-December, to return only for the second final of the VB Series.

Gough's case was exceptional in that medical opinion had never said his right knee would recover before the tour. But as he was the only bowler in the original party who had taken a Test wicket in Australia before, he was judged to be worth the risk. He bowled in the nets, and was due to play in a Brisbane grade match during the First Test, but broke down again before the game. He went home and, with him, went England's only hope of dismissing well-set batsmen with a soft ball on flat pitches, either in Australia or in the World Cup.

In addition to all these, there were injuries to: John Crawley (bruised hip and torn muscle which ruled him out of the Second and Third Tests); Stewart (bruised hand, which ruled him out of the Fourth); Ashley Giles (left wrist broken in the nets by Steve Harmison before the Second Test; sent home until January); Harmison himself (sore shins, which ruled him out of the First Test); and Andrew Caddick (sore back, which ruled him out of the Third).

Then there were the injuries to the replacements, like Chris Silverwood who was called up to replace Jones; his ankle ligaments gave way after he had bowled four overs in the Perth Test. (If England had employed a larger pool of 20 or more players on central contracts, he might have been readier for match action.) Craig White, called up a week into the tour, bowled as well as anyone in the first three Tests and prompted England's revival with 85 not out in the Fourth, but then suffered a rib strain and missed the Sydney victory. Alex Tudor, who replaced Gough, suffered one of the impact injuries which have to be budgeted for in Australia: a nasty blow to his left temple from a bouncer Brett Lee bowled with the second new ball in Perth. The *reductio ad absurdum* was reached when Jeremy Snape arrived with the one-day party and could not survive a single delivery in one piece: Lee, playing for New South Wales, broke his thumb first ball in a warm-up game.

Jeremy Snape arrived with the one-day party and could not survive a single delivery; Lee broke his thumb first ball

Given all the toings and froings, which required the astonishing total of 31 Test and one-day players combined, England could have fallen into complete chaos: it was thanks to the management that a veneer of organisation was maintained, which kept them in good enough shape to become the first visiting team to win a Test in Australia since they themselves had done so four years before. Nobody pretended that a fully fit England would have regained the Ashes but, as Hussain remarked, they might have lost the first three Tests in five full days apiece.

For certain, England went into the series undercooked, at least one if not two four-day matches short of readiness (the first-class games they did play were limited to three days). Their pace bowlers never did emulate McGrath and Gillespie by delivering six accurate balls an over. Their fielding on the opening day in Brisbane was beset with tension, but by the Sydney Test nine chances out of nine were caught in Australia's first innings. To make up for only nine days of cricket before the First Test – any more and they would have had no break at all after the English season and the Champions

Finishing on a high: England at last found something to celebrate when their triumph at the SCG ended Australia's four-year unbeaten run in home Tests. *Standing:* James Foster, Ian Blackwell, Andrew Caddick, Steve Harmison, Richard Dawson, Alex Tudor, Rob Key, John Crawley, Paul Collingwood. *Kneeling:* Matthew Hoggard, Nasser Hussain, Marcus Trescothick, Mark Butcher, Michael Vaughan, Alec Stewart.
Picture by Graham Morris.

Trophy in Sri Lanka – England held an extraordinarily long team meeting on the eve of it, and it was counter-productive. From the second ball, which Vaughan let trickle through his legs at gully, their confidence seemed to shatter; it was not only their supporters who sighed: "Here we go again."

In the Second Test at Adelaide came England's chance at least of holding the line. Had they survived an hour or so longer on the fourth day, they would have drawn: the final day would have been washed out. Some of Graham Thorpe's tenacity could have made the difference, but he had pulled out in September on the grounds that his private life was still in such turmoil that he could not have given the tour his full attention. In three Tests, Crawley occupied Thorpe's place and batted for considerable time, but solely in defensive style: he had cured his former weakness outside off stump by bringing his bat down straighter, but at the expense of missing out on leg-stump balls. At Adelaide, when neither Thorpe nor Crawley was available, Robert Key was introduced on the strength of a match-saving 174 not out against Australia A and scored a single in each innings. There was nothing England could have done about the Perth Test though, where, on the hard surface, they continued an even sorrier record than they have had post-war in Brisbane.

It was in Melbourne that England came into the series at last, a process that culminated at Sydney. Step by step, England improved as Australia passed their peak. First, White attacked Warne's replacement, Stuart MacGill, driving him for three sixes: it demonstrated that, in the master's absence, one end was open, a great relief after being tied down at both. MacGill had the same sort of career strike-rate as Warne but not the control and accuracy in between taking wickets. This was the difference between the great and the good. Steve Waugh then enforced the follow-on when the game was only halfway through its course in stifling heat. His decision allowed England to manoeuvre Australia into batting fourth, the position from which four of England's last six Ashes victories had come. Under the pressure of batting last in Melbourne, Australia wobbled and England, for a change, took regular wickets.

At Sydney, they continued to do so: it was the one ground where the ball swung for Matthew Hoggard (and Lee), while Caddick used the uneven bounce to the full in the second innings. But in the first three Tests, when it mattered, and at Melbourne in the first innings, England never looked like dismissing Australia for less than 450. How Australia would have played in the absence of McGrath and Warne if the Ashes had still been at stake can only be speculation. The goal of becoming only the second Australian side to win an Ashes series 5–0, after Warwick Armstrong's in 1920-21, proved to be insufficient motivation.

Vaughan was chosen as Man of the Series for his three large hundreds, following four in the English summer. Sooner than his opening partner, Trescothick, he learned to make a clear distinction between defence and attacking shots, rather than blurring the two with open-faced nudges which might have succeeded in England but not on pitches of Australian bounce. His driving all round the wicket was reminiscent of Peter May; his pulling was equally brilliant. Vaughan's footwork had always been outstanding in a generation of English batsmen who either played on the crease or pushed half-forward. Now he used it to move into position to pull the short ball, as perhaps no tall batsman has done better.

Earlier, though, Hayden was the dominant batsman. He set the tone for the series with his pair of hundreds in Brisbane, standing outside his crease to England's pace bowlers after their new-ball overs and sending them cowering into submission. On the first morning at Melbourne, he ran down the pitch to drive White for six. With Ponting in the first three Tests, and Langer in Melbourne, Hayden made sure Australia's top three scored most of the necessary runs, and at a rattling pace: his 496 runs came at a strike-rate of 70 per 100 balls. Martyn at No. 4 was passive by comparison with his predecessor, Mark Waugh. At No. 5, Steve Waugh played significant innings of 77 in Melbourne and 102 in Sydney, after the Australian selectors announced that he had to make runs to stay in the side. His hundred, reached off the last ball of the day, made one of the great moments in Ashes history – it was even called Australia's most famous innings – as a great cricketer fought for his place.

Of England's batsmen apart from Vaughan, only Hussain maintained his reputation: no century, but his fifth good series in a row, in spite of the strain

MOST RUNS IN A TEST SERIES AGAINST AUSTRALIA

	T	*I*	*NO*	*R*	*HS*	*100s*	*Avge*	*Series*	
W. R. Hammond . . .	5	9	1	905	251	4	113.12	A v E	1928-29
C. L. Walcott	5	10	0	827	155	5	82.70	WI v A	1954-55
H. Sutcliffe	5	9	0	734	176	4	81.55	A v E	1924-25
G. A. Faulkner	5	10	0	732	204	2	73.20	A v SA	1910-11
D. I. Gower	6	9	0	732	215	3	81.33	E v A	1985
G. A. Gooch	6	12	0	673	133	2	56.08	E v A	1993
J. B. Hobbs	5	9	1	662	187	3	82.75	A v E	1911-12
G. Boycott.	5	10	3	657	142*	2	93.85	A v E	1970-71
J. H. Edrich	6	11	2	648	130	2	72.00	A v E	1970-71
M. P. Vaughan	**5**	**10**	**0**	**633**	**183**	**3**	**63.30**	**A v E**	**2002-03**
D. T. Lindsay	5	7	0	606	182	3	86.57	SA v A	1966-67
E. J. Barlow	5	10	2	603	201	3	75.37	A v SA	1963-64

of captaining a losing and injured team. Trescothick and Butcher paid the price for minimalist footwork, while Trescothick was also troubled on the back foot by the steeper bounce as he had never been on pitches elsewhere. As the pace bowlers normally disposed of Trescothick, a superb player of spin, Warne had a far easier time against England's remaining batsmen. Key justified his selection ahead of an older player, like Mark Ramprakash, but did not cement his place. Stewart, after a pair in Brisbane, scored enough runs to edge his Test average back above 40, including a vital 71 in Sydney, but the best display of wicket-keeping from either side was considered to be James Foster's when he stood in for Stewart at Melbourne.

Hussain's decision to send Australia in to bat in Brisbane was not consistent with the logic of Test cricket or recent history at the Gabba, but it was consistent with the logic of England's tour: they never looked like bowling any side out without something in the pitch to help them. Browbeaten by Hayden, and unable to swing the ball, Hoggard faded before returning off a shorter run in Sydney. Caddick, who turned 34 on his first senior tour of Australia, was his usual enigmatic self: harmless when the batsmen came after him on flat pitches with the series at stake, yet as formidable as any of the Australians by the second innings in Sydney, when the bounce was uneven and the advantage had only to be rammed home. When the going was toughest, Harmison was the likeliest of the England pace bowlers to take a wicket, but never had the figures to show for his pace and bounce until the end. England had thought he was learning to eradicate the balls he speared down leg side until, after hitting a rollicking 20 not out in Sydney, his direction went haywire again.

In spite of the one-sided nature of the contest, the crowds were large enough for the Australian Cricket Board to announce that the Ashes would remain their only five-Test home series. Several thousand members of the "Barmy Army" – the best-behaved to date – were further swelled after Christmas, and helped to save the last two Tests from anticlimax. Nothing, however, could disguise the fact that, when it mattered, Australia were far superior to England – and, arguably, superior to all other cricket teams there have been save the West Indians of the early to mid-1980s.

ENGLAND TOURING PARTY

N. Hussain (Essex) (*captain*), M. A. Butcher (Surrey), A. R. Caddick (Somerset), J. P. Crawley (Hampshire), R. K. J. Dawson (Yorkshire), A. Flintoff (Lancashire), J. S. Foster (Essex), A. F. Giles (Warwickshire), D. Gough (Yorkshire), S. J. Harmison (Durham), M. J. Hoggard (Yorkshire), S. P. Jones (Glamorgan), R. W. T. Key (Kent), A. J. Stewart (Surrey), M. E. Trescothick (Somerset), M. P. Vaughan (Yorkshire).

G. P. Thorpe (Surrey) was originally selected but withdrew for personal reasons and was replaced by Key. C. White (Yorkshire) was added to the party after two matches as cover for injuries. A. J. Tudor (Surrey) replaced the injured Gough, C. E. W. Silverwood (Yorkshire) the injured Jones. Flintoff (unfit) and Giles (injured) went home in early December, but returned in January; A. J. Hollioake (Surrey) joined the party as cover. I. D. Blackwell (Somerset), P. D. Collingwood (Durham), R. C. Irani (Essex), R. J. Kirtley (Sussex), N. V. Knight (Warwickshire), O. A. Shah (Middlesex) and J. N. Snape (Gloucestershire) joined for the one-day international series. J. M. Anderson (Lancashire) arrived as cover for Caddick and G. J. Batty (Worcestershire) replaced the injured Snape. National Academy players Kabir Ali (Worcestershire) and C. M. W. Read (Nottinghamshire) each played in one warm-up match.

Coach: D. A. G. Fletcher. *Operations manager:* P. A. Neale. *Assistant coach:* G. R. Dilley. *Team analyst:* M. N. Ashton. *Physiotherapist:* K. A. Russell. *Physiologist:* N. P. Stockill. *Media relations managers:* A. J. Walpole and D. A. Clarke.

For the one-day international series, T. J. Boon took over from Dilley as assistant coach, and D. O. Conway replaced Russell as physiotherapist.

ENGLAND TOUR RESULTS

Test matches – Played 5: Won 1, Lost 4.
First-class matches – Played 8: Won 1, Lost 4, Drawn 3.
Win – Australia.
Losses – Australia (4).
Draws – Western Australia, Queensland, Australia A.
One-day internationals – Played 10: Won 3, Lost 7. *Wins* – Sri Lanka (3). *Losses* – Australia (6), Sri Lanka.
Other non-first-class matches – Played 6: Lost 5, Drawn 1. *Losses* – ACB Chairman's XII, New South Wales, Australia A, Prime Minister's XI, Sir Donald Bradman XII. *Draw* – Western Australia.

TEST MATCH AVERAGES

AUSTRALIA – BATTING

	T	*I*	*NO*	*R*	*HS*	*100s*	*50s*	*Avge*	*Ct/St*
†M. L. Hayden	5	8	0	496	197	3	0	62.00	8
J. N. Gillespie	5	5	4	61	31*	0	0	61.00	0
†A. C. Gilchrist	5	8	2	333	133	1	2	55.50	23/2
†J. L. Langer	5	8	0	423	250	1	0	52.87	2
R. T. Ponting	5	8	0	417	154	2	1	52.12	6
M. L. Love	2	4	2	95	62*	0	1	47.50	4
D. R. Martyn	5	8	0	320	95	0	3	40.00	2
S. R. Waugh	5	8	0	305	102	1	2	38.12	2
†D. S. Lehmann	3	4	1	97	42	0	0	32.33	2
A. J. Bichel	3	4	0	101	49	0	0	25.25	2

Played in four Tests: G. D. McGrath 0, 8* (2 ct). Played in three Tests: B. Lee 41, 0, 46; S. K. Warne 57, 25, 35 (1 ct). Played in two Tests: S. C. G. MacGill 1, 1.

† *Left-handed batsman.*

BOWLING

	Style	O	M	R	W	BB	5W/i	Avge
G. D. McGrath.	RFM	162.2	53	380	19	4-36	0	20.00
J. N. Gillespie	RF	181.5	53	492	20	4-25	0	24.60
S. K. Warne	LBG	131.1	29	347	14	4-93	0	24.78
A. J. Bichel.	RFM	94.3	14	351	10	3-86	0	35.10
S. C. G. MacGill	LBG	169	36	486	12	5-152	1	40.50
B. Lee	RF	144.4	26	536	13	3-78	0	41.23

Also bowled: D. S. Lehmann (SLA) 5–0–11–0; D. R. Martyn (RM) 6–2–23–1; S. R. Waugh (RM) 25–8–43–2.

ENGLAND – BATTING

	T	I	NO	R	HS	100s	50s	Avge	Ct
M. P. Vaughan	5	10	0	633	183	3	0	63.30	0
A. J. Stewart	4	8	2	268	71	0	3	44.66	11
J. P. Crawley	3	6	2	162	69*	0	1	40.50	3
N. Hussain	5	10	0	382	75	0	4	38.20	3
†M. A. Butcher	5	10	0	318	124	1	1	31.80	6
†M. E. Trescothick	5	10	0	261	72	0	1	26.10	5
C. White.	4	8	1	154	85*	0	1	22.00	0
R. W. T. Key	4	8	0	141	52	0	1	17.62	1
R. K. J. Dawson.	4	8	2	87	19*	0	0	14.50	2
S. J. Harmison	4	8	2	47	20*	0	0	7.83	1
A. R. Caddick	4	8	1	52	17	0	0	7.42	3
M. J. Hoggard	3	6	1	12	6	0	0	2.40	1

Played in one Test: J. S. Foster 19, 6 (3 ct); A. F. Giles 13, 4 (2 ct); C. E. W. Silverwood 10; A. J. Tudor 0, 3* (2 ct). †S. P. Jones played in one Test but did not bat.

† *Left-handed batsman.*

BOWLING

	Style	O	M	R	W	BB	5W/i	Avge
A. F. Giles	SLA	53.2	5	191	6	4-101	0	31.83
A. R. Caddick	RFM	171	28	690	20	7-94	1	34.50
C. White.	RFM	122.1	14	532	14	5-127	1	38.00
S. J. Harmison.	RF	132.3	28	455	9	3-70	0	50.55
M. J. Hoggard	RFM	103.3	17	375	6	4-92	0	62.50
R. K. J. Dawson.	OB	96	5	398	5	2-121	0	79.60

Also bowled: M. A. Butcher (RM) 25–3–104–0; S. P. Jones (RF) 7–0–32–1; C. E. W. Silverwood (RF) 4–0–29–0; A. J. Tudor (RFM) 29–2–144–2.

"'When the temperature is 51°C and the humidity is high, you shouldn't be outside,' said Waugh, 'let alone playing sport.'"

Pakistan v Australia in Sharjah, page 1106.

ENGLAND TOUR AVERAGES – FIRST-CLASS MATCHES

BATTING

	M	*I*	*NO*	*R*	*HS*	*100s*	*50s*	*Avge*	*Ct*
M. P. Vaughan	7	13	0	782	183	4	0	60.15	0
J. P. Crawley	6	11	4	312	69*	0	2	44.57	6
N. Hussain	7	13	1	534	117	1	4	44.50	3
R. W. T. Key	6	12	2	443	174*	1	2	44.30	3
A. J. Stewart	6	11	3	353	71	0	3	44.12	16
†M. A. Butcher	8	15	0	466	124	1	1	31.06	7
†M. E. Trescothick	8	15	0	388	72	0	1	25.86	9
C. White	6	12	1	179	85*	0	1	16.27	0
R. K. J. Dawson	5	9	2	87	19*	0	0	12.42	2
J. S. Foster	2	4	1	33	19	0	0	11.00	4
A. R. Caddick	6	9	2	58	17	0	0	8.28	6
A. F. Giles	3	4	1	24	13	0	0	8.00	2
S. J. Harmison	6	10	2	54	20*	0	0	6.75	1
M. J. Hoggard	4	7	1	13	6	0	0	2.16	1

Played in three matches: †S. P. Jones 4. Played in two matches: A. Flintoff 3, 1, 15 (2 ct); A. J. Tudor 12, 0, 3* (2 ct). Played in one match: C. E. W. Silverwood 10.

† *Left-handed batsman.*

BOWLING

	Style	*O*	*M*	*R*	*W*	*BB*	*5W/i*	*Avge*
A. F. Giles	SLA	121.2	16	410	13	4-101	0	31.53
A. R. Caddick	RFM	239.5	50	859	27	7-94	1	31.81
S. P. Jones	RF	66	6	255	8	5-78	1	31.87
C. White	RFM	159.3	19	690	17	5-127	1	40.58
S. J. Harmison	RF	166.3	34	567	11	3-70	0	51.54
M. J. Hoggard	RFM	132.3	21	487	7	4-92	0	69.57
R. K. J. Dawson	OB	112	9	468	6	2-121	0	78.00

Also bowled: M. A. Butcher (RM) 31–3–141–0; A. Flintoff (RFM) 36–1–174–2; C. E. W. Silverwood (RF) 4–0–29–0; A. J. Tudor (RFM) 48–5–223–3.

Note: Matches in this section which were not first-class are signified by a dagger.

†At Lilac Hill, Perth, October 22, 2002. **ACB Chairman's XII won by 58 runs.** Toss: England XIII. **ACB Chairman's XII 301-7** (50 overs) (M. E. K. Hussey 69, K. M. Harvey 114); **England XIII 243** (48.5 overs) (R. W. T. Key 68, N. Hussain 65; G. B. Hogg 5-33).

The Chairman's team named 12 players and England 13; only 11 could bat and 11 bowl on each side. Harvey scored 114 in 88 balls with ten fours and six sixes.

†At Perth, October 24, 25, 2002. **Drawn.** Toss: Western Australia. **England XI 221** (A. R. Caddick 62*; C. D. Thorp 4-58); **Western Australia 313-6** (C. J. L. Rogers 57, S. E. Marsh 92).

WESTERN AUSTRALIA v ENGLAND XI

At Perth, October 28, 29, 30, 2002. Drawn. Toss: England XI.

A convincing all-round performance lifted England's spirits, though they fell just short chasing 135 in 20 overs. Key, who hit 59 in 49 balls, needed six from the final delivery, but missed a Williams yorker. On the first day, interrupted four times by showers, Caddick bowled into a stiff wind to reduce Western Australia to 54 for four inside 27 overs; it took a three-hour innings from North to see them past 200. Then Key and Trescothick ran up six an over under floodlights on a gloomy evening. The next day sometimes seemed like a replay of the same fixture four years earlier: Hussain scored 117 before falling to Nicholson, who collected six victims (respectively one run and one wicket fewer than these two achieved in 1998-99). Starting with Hussain, Nicholson grabbed the last five in 22 balls. Langer and Rogers continued the home fightback, adding 141, but Jones claimed four wickets either side of tea, helping to set up the whirlwind finish.

Close of play: First day, England XI 54-0 (Trescothick 21, Key 33); Second day, Western Australia 16-1 (Hussey 14, Rogers 0).

Western Australia

*J. L. Langer c Crawley b Caddick	13	– (4) c Stewart b White	68
S. W. Meuleman c Stewart b Harmison	21	– lbw b Caddick	1
C. J. L. Rogers c Stewart b Caddick	7	– lbw b Jones	86
M. E. K. Hussey c Trescothick b Caddick	0	– (1) c Caddick b Jones	14
M. J. North not out	71	– c Stewart b White	0
†R. J. Campbell c Caddick b Harmison	37	– c Crawley b Jones	25
G. B. Hogg lbw b Giles	22	– c Trescothick b Jones	18
M. J. Nicholson c Key b Jones	19	– lbw b Jones	2
S. J. Karppinen b Giles	1	– (11) not out	3
B. A. Williams lbw b Giles	3	– (9) c Crawley b Giles	13
J. Angel c Key b Caddick	4	– (10) run out	10
B 2, l-b 7, w 2, n-b 4	15	L-b 4, n-b 4	8
1/34 (1) 2/51 (3) 3/52 (2) 4/54 (4) 5/120 (6) 6/163 (7) 7/194 (8) 8/197 (9) 9/202 (10) 10/213 (11)	213	1/9 (2) 2/23 (1) 3/164 (4) 4/164 (5) 5/178 (3) 6/203 (7) 7/219 (8) 8/222 (6) 9/240 (9) 10/248 (10)	248

Bowling: *First Innings*—Caddick 19.5–9–49–4; Jones 14–3–49–1; Harmison 11–3–30–2; White 10–3–34–0; Giles 11–0–42–3. *Second Innings*—Caddick 18–7–31–1; Jones 19–1–78–5; Harmison 7–0–28–0; White 13.2–1–54–2; Giles 17–4–53–1.

England XI

M. E. Trescothick c Hussey b Nicholson	46	– b Williams	19
R. W. T. Key c Nicholson b Williams	33	– not out	59
M. A. Butcher lbw b Angel	29	– (4) st Campbell b Hogg	7
*N. Hussain c Campbell b Nicholson	117	– (7) not out	7
J. P. Crawley b Karppinen	45	– c Angel b Hogg	0
†A. J. Stewart c Hussey b Angel	29	– c Campbell b Nicholson	26
C. White b Nicholson	7	– (3) run out	12
A. F. Giles lbw b Nicholson	0		
A. R. Caddick not out	6		
S. P. Jones c Hussey b Nicholson	4		
S. J. Harmison c North b Nicholson	4		
L-b 5, n-b 2	7		
1/55 (2) 2/94 (1) 3/153 (3) 4/232 (5) 5/288 (6) 6/312 (4) 7/312 (8) 8/313 (7) 9/319 (10) 10/327 (11)	327	1/52 (1) 2/64 (3) 3/80 (4) 4/80 (5) 5/121 (6)	(5 wkts) 130

Bowling: *First Innings*—Williams 23–5–71–1; Karppinen 18–5–61–1; Nicholson 19.5–6–79–6; Angel 22–8–62–2; Hogg 20–5–49–0. *Second Innings*—Williams 8–1–41–1; Angel 5–0–37–0; Hogg 4–0–26–2; Nicholson 3–0–26–1.

Umpires: I. H. Lock and R. G. Patterson.

QUEENSLAND v ENGLAND XI

At Allan Border Field, Brisbane, November 2, 3, 4, 2002. Drawn. Toss: Queensland.

Two convalescent Englishmen had their first outings of the tour. Vaughan confirmed his fitness for the Brisbane Test with a century, in his first game since he made 195 against India at The Oval two months earlier; Flintoff managed to bowl 26 overs, but scored only three runs. The match's dominant figure was Love, who batted most of five sessions for his fifth double-hundred. He hit 27 fours and a six from 414 balls in 542 minutes, and shared consecutive century stands with Law, Symonds and Carseldine. England dropped him four times on the second day, before Queensland's innings finally drew to a conclusion after tea. The pitch remained perfectly true as Vaughan and Trescothick hurried to 100 in 17 overs that evening. Vaughan was almost run out early on, and offered two chances off Noffke's bowling, but survived to enjoy nearly five hours in the middle. Only 17 wickets had fallen when thunderstorms brought an early finish to the final day.

Close of play: First day, Queensland 333-4 (Love 124, Carseldine 14); Second day, England XI 106-1 (Vaughan 49, Hoggard 1).

Queensland

*J. P. Maher c Butcher b Caddick 41
B. P. Nash c Trescothick b Caddick 18
M. L. Love lbw b Hoggard 250
S. G. Law c and b Flintoff. 68
A. Symonds c Stewart b Flintoff. 47
L. A. Carseldine c Flintoff b Giles 51
†W. A. Seccombe lbw b Giles 2
A. A. Noffke c Caddick b Giles 30
N. M. Hauritz c Trescothick b Jones . . . 31
M. S. Kasprowicz run out 7
D. R. MacKenzie not out. 3
B 2, l-b 10, w 2, n-b 20. 34

1/60 (2) 2/65 (1) 3/193 (4) 582
4/298 (5) 5/423 (6) 6/431 (7)
7/515 (8) 8/570 (3) 9/570 (9) 10/582 (10)

Bowling: Caddick 31–6–89–2; Hoggard 29–4–112–1; Jones 26–2–96–1; Flintoff 26–1–112–2; Giles 40–7–124–3; Butcher 6–0–37–0.

England XI

M. E. Trescothick run out 46
M. P. Vaughan lbw b Hauritz 127
M. J. Hoggard c Seccombe b Kasprowicz 1
M. A. Butcher c Seccombe b Noffke . . . 45
*N. Hussain c Kasprowicz b Hauritz . . . 28
J. P. Crawley c Law b Hauritz. 7
†A. J. Stewart not out 30
A. Flintoff c Maher b Carseldine. 3
A. F. Giles not out 7
L-b 8, n-b 20 28

1/100 (1) 2/107 (3) 3/199 (4) (7 wkts) 322
4/259 (5) 5/275 (2)
6/292 (6) 7/308 (8)

A. R. Caddick and S. P. Jones did not bat.

Bowling: Kasprowicz 20–0–106–1; Noffke 21–6–58–1; MacKenzie 16–1–62–0; Symonds 11–2–26–0; Hauritz 24–7–48–3; Carseldine 10–4–14–1.

Umpires: D. L. Orchard and P. D. Parker.

AUSTRALIA v ENGLAND

First Test Match

TREVOR MARSHALLSEA

At Brisbane, November 7, 8, 9, 10, 2002. Australia won by 384 runs. Toss: England.

It will go down as one of the costliest decisions in Test history. England captain Nasser Hussain had forecast in his last pre-Ashes newspaper column that "the worst nightmare" would be working out what to do if he won the toss. Despite the fact opening batsmen Vaughan and Trescothick were clearly his side's most potent weapons, Hussain sent Australia in. At stumps on day one, Australia were 364 for two. There went the match and the momentum.

Hussain's choice will rank up there with David Gower's invitation to the 1989 Australians to bat at Headingley, a gesture repaid by a first-innings score of 601 for

Staring into the abyss: Alec Stewart completes his first pair in 123 Tests, England lurch towards disaster at 35 for five, and the humiliation is almost complete.
Picture by Graham Morris.

seven declared. Australia went on to win that Ashes series 4–0, and have been winning them ever since.

Hussain later admitted his mistake, saying it had been based on a belief there would be enough early life in the green-tinged pitch to help his inexperienced seam attack restrict the Australian batting. The pitch quickly dried out into the proverbial belter, and Hayden and Ponting feasted. They put on 272 for the second wicket in 253 minutes, Hayden continuing his incredible 2002 by marching imperiously to 186 not out at stumps, while Ponting fell in the final hour of the day for 123. By then, the young pace bowler Simon Jones had tumbled out of the attack – and the series – when he horribly ruptured knee ligaments in the field. He bowled only seven overs, and dismissed Langer with his ninth ball.

Both captains pointed out that, whatever a team does with the toss, they still have to execute their plans well. While Australia surged, England did not help their own chances. The tourists put down four catches on the opening day; Hayden survived on 40, when the luckless Jones held a catch on the fine-leg boundary but cancelled it by falling over the rope.

Hayden, dropped also on 102, 138 and 149, moved to within three runs of a double-century early on the second morning before gloving a leg-side catch off Caddick. There began a substandard batting performance from the new-look Australian middle order, now bereft of Mark Waugh, sacked after 107 consecutive Tests. They lost four for 37, with Martyn, Steve Waugh and Gilchrist all failing, and helping to reduce England's target from mammoth to merely daunting. Waugh, who was still on four after an hour at the crease, fell to a clever leg-gully trap set by Hussain, the first chapter of an intriguing battle between the captains over the series. It was left to Warne, with some lusty hitting, to scramble a total of 492.

England began their reply well against an attack missing Brett Lee, who had been sent back to state cricket to find form, a move which would pay off handsomely later. Vaughan showed glimpses of what lay ahead in the series with a quickfire 33, then Trescothick and Butcher saw their side through to stumps at 158 for one. It was Australia's turn to underperform in the field, with each batsman dropped once and Butcher surviving a stumping chance.

Both men were out in the same McGrath over next morning, but Hussain – dropped on 12 as the fielding mishaps continued – and Crawley continued to take the game to the feared Australian attack, adding 97 for the fourth wicket. Once Hussain was removed for 51, however, the familiar England collapse began – from 268 for three to 325.

Facing a deficit of 167, Hussain went on the attack, and his aggressive fields were rewarded when Australia quickly lost Langer and Ponting to Caddick. Normal order was soon restored, however, and the following day, the awe-inspiring Hayden cracked 60 off as many balls to reach his second hundred of the match, his seventh in ten Tests, and his sixth in seven Tests on home soil. He fell for 103, but with Martyn and the quick-scoring Gilchrist reaching half-centuries, Waugh was able to declare on 296 for five, scored in just 71 overs against an attack both undermanned and unimaginative.

TWIN HUNDREDS IN ENGLAND–AUSTRALIA TESTS

W. Bardsley (Australia)	136 and 130	at The Oval	1909
H. Sutcliffe (England)	176 and 127	at Melbourne	1924-25
W. R. Hammond (England)	119* and 177	at Adelaide	1928-29
D. C. S. Compton (England)	147 and 103*	at Adelaide	1946-47
A. R. Morris (Australia)	122 and 124*	at Adelaide	1946-47
S. R. Waugh (Australia)	108 and 116	at Manchester	1997
M. L. Hayden (Australia)	**197 and 103**	**at Brisbane**	**2002-03**

In contrast with their first-innings resistance, now came the darkest hour for England. Needing to make a fanciful 464 to win or bat for 47 overs and a day to avert defeat, Hussain's men lost Vaughan, again to McGrath, off the third ball of the innings, and went on to capitulate pathetically for 79 in just 28.2 overs. That Butcher scored 40 of them says much about his colleagues. It was one of the worst England batting efforts since Tests began, with the last seven wickets (Jones was absent) falling inside 13 overs, and the innings lasting little more than two hours. The final result was their fourth-heaviest defeat by runs; it was also a 50th defeat in 123 Tests for Stewart, who completed his first Test pair. McGrath claimed four more wickets and would have made a deserving man of the match, but for the broad-shouldered Hayden who scored 300 over both innings on his home ground. It would take a phenomenal effort for England to rebound from here.

Man of the Match: M. L. Hayden. *Attendance:* 81,277.

Close of play: First day, Australia 364-2 (Hayden 186, Martyn 9); Second day, England 158-1 (Trescothick 63, Butcher 51); Third day, Australia 111-2 (Hayden 40, Martyn 40).

Australia

J. L. Langer c Stewart b Jones	32	– c Stewart b Caddick	22
M. L. Hayden c Stewart b Caddick	197	– c and b Giles	103
R. T. Ponting b Giles	123	– c Trescothick b Caddick	3
D. R. Martyn c Trescothick b White	26	– c Hussain b Giles	64
*S. R. Waugh c Crawley b Caddick	7	– (6) c Trescothick b Caddick	12
D. S. Lehmann c Butcher b Giles	30	– (7) not out	20
†A. C. Gilchrist c Giles b White	0	– (5) not out	60
S. K. Warne c Butcher b Caddick	57		
A. J. Bichel lbw b Giles	0		
J. N. Gillespie not out	0		
G. D. McGrath lbw b Giles	0		
B 1, l-b 11, w 1, n-b 7	20	B 3, l-b 5, n-b 4	12
1/67 (1) 2/339 (3) 3/378 (2) 4/399 (4) 5/408 (5) 6/415 (7) 7/478 (6) 8/478 (9) 9/492 (8) 10/492 (11)	492	1/30 (1) 2/39 (3) 3/192 (2) 4/213 (4) 5/242 (6)	(5 wkts dec.) 296

Bowling: *First Innings*—Caddick 35–9–108–3; Hoggard 30–4–122–0; Jones 7–0–32–1; White 27–4–105–2; Giles 29.2–3–101–4; Butcher 2–0–12–0. *Second Innings*—Caddick 23–2–95–3; Hoggard 13–2–42–0; White 11–0–61–0; Giles 24–2–90–2.

England

M. E. Trescothick c Ponting b McGrath	72	– c Gilchrist b Gillespie	1
M. P. Vaughan c Gilchrist b McGrath	33	– lbw b McGrath	0
M. A. Butcher c Hayden b McGrath	54	– c Ponting b Warne	40
*N. Hussain c Gilchrist b Gillespie	51	– c Ponting b McGrath	11
J. P. Crawley not out	69	– run out	0
†A. J. Stewart b Gillespie	0	– c Hayden b Warne	0
C. White b McGrath	12	– c Hayden b McGrath	13
A. F. Giles c Gilchrist b Bichel	13	– c Gilchrist b McGrath	4
A. R. Caddick c Ponting b Bichel	0	– c Lehmann b Warne	4
M. J. Hoggard c Hayden b Warne	4	– not out	1
S. P. Jones absent hurt		– absent hurt	
B 2, l-b 8, n-b 7	17	L-b 1, n-b 4	5
1/49 (2) 2/170 (3) 3/171 (1) 4/268 (4) 5/270 (6) 6/283 (7) 7/308 (8) 8/308 (9) 9/325 (10)	325	1/1 (2) 2/3 (1) 3/33 (4) 4/34 (5) 5/35 (6) 6/66 (7) 7/74 (8) 8/74 (3) 9/79 (9)	79

Bowling: *First Innings*—McGrath 30–9–87–4; Gillespie 18–4–51–2; Bichel 23–4–74–2; Warne 26.5–4–87–1; Waugh 4–2–5–0; Lehmann 5–0–11–0. *Second Innings*—McGrath 12–3–36–4; Gillespie 6–1–13–1; Warne 10.2–3–29–3.

Umpires: S. A. Bucknor (West Indies) and R. E. Koertzen (South Africa).
Third umpire: S. J. A. Taufel. Referee: Wasim Raja (Pakistan).

AUSTRALIA A v ENGLAND XI

At Hobart, November 15, 16, 17, 2002. Drawn. Toss: England XI.

Acting-captain Trescothick emulated Hussain at Brisbane by putting Australia A in, hoping the bowlers contending for a place at Adelaide would exploit early life in the pitch. But after Tudor's opening burst – his first ball struck Elliott painfully on the elbow – they could make nothing of it. Two expensive spells proved Flintoff still well short of fitness. Love took his second double-hundred off the English attack in a fortnight, batting a minute over five hours and hitting 25 fours from 243 balls. Controlled bowling from Williams removed both England openers, and he later mopped up with three wickets in successive overs. Following on, England were three down and still 74 behind by the close. But they were saved when Crawley, unbeaten first time round, joined Key. Although Crawley needed a runner after his hip was badly bruised, they added 176 before the pain drove him off. He missed the next two Tests; his place went to Key, who scored a career-best 174 here, hitting 18 fours in nearly seven hours.

Close of play: First day, England XI 50-1 (Trescothick 5, Butcher 30); Second day, England XI 96-3 (Key 38, Crawley 6).

Australia A

M. T. G. Elliott retired hurt	0
*J. P. Maher c Foster b Tudor	6
M. L. Love not out	201
G. S. Blewett b White	25
M. J. Clarke c sub (C. E. W. Silverwood) b Dawson	50
M. J. North not out	33
B 2, l-b 16, w 5, n-b 15	38
1/13 (2) 2/153 (4) 3/275 (5) (3 wkts dec.)	353

†B. J. Haddin, N. M. Hauritz, A. A. Noffke, S. R. Clark and B. A. Williams did not bat.

Elliott retired hurt at 0.

Bowling: Tudor 19–3–79–1; Harmison 16–3–54–0; Flintoff 10–0–62–0; White 14–1–70–1; Dawson 16–4–70–1.

England XI

*M. E. Trescothick c Haddin b Williams	5	– b Noffke	11
M. P. Vaughan b Williams	8	– b Clark	14
M. A. Butcher c Love b Clark	42	– c Haddin b Blewett	25
R. W. T. Key c Hauritz b Noffke	36	– not out	174
J. P. Crawley not out	43	– retired hurt	55
A. Flintoff b Clark	1	– c and b Hauritz	15
C. White c Clarke b Clark	4	– c Williams b Hauritz	2
†J. S. Foster c Love b Noffke	7	– not out	1
A. J. Tudor lbw b Williams	12		
R. K. J. Dawson lbw b Williams	0		
S. J. Harmison lbw b Williams	3		
B 6, l-b 9, w 3, n-b 4	22	B 8, l-b 1, n-b 4	13
1/11 (2) 2/51 (1) 3/85 (3) 4/108 (4) 5/109 (6) 6/122 (7) 7/131 (8) 8/173 (9) 9/179 (10) 10/183 (11)	183	1/16 (1) 2/28 (2) 3/74 (3) 4/291 (6) 5/299 (7)	(5 wkts dec.) 310

In the second innings Crawley retired hurt at 250.

Bowling: *First Innings*—Williams 18.2–5–52–5; Clark 24–7–60–3; Noffke 17–4–31–2; Blewett 3–0–6–0; Hauritz 8–2–19–0. *Second Innings*—Noffke 19–6–45–1; Clark 25–4–78–1; Williams 17–5–46–0; Blewett 11–5–17–1; Hauritz 40–16–75–2; Clarke 15–2–38–0; Maher 1–0–2–0.

Umpires: R. L. Parry and J. H. Smeaton.

AUSTRALIA v ENGLAND

Second Test Match

JOHN ETHERIDGE

At Adelaide, November 21, 22, 23, 24, 2002. Australia won by an innings and 51 runs. Toss: England.

When England reached 295 for three with four balls of the first day remaining, they appeared for once to be offering a genuine challenge to Australia. Then, however, Vaughan's magnificent if controversial innings of 177 was ended and, in little more than seven further sessions, England descended to a crushing defeat. Australia's superiority in every facet was again obvious and, despite Hussain's insistence to the contrary, they dominated the touring team mentally as well as technically. Already, with three Tests of the series to go, the bookmakers were rating a 5–0 whitewash as odds-on.

Vaughan's dismissal in the 90th over of the opening day was a microcosm of why Australia are so good. He had batted sublimely and, metaphorically at least, his head was touching the pillow after a full day's labour. Yet Australia never relent. Steve Waugh brought back Bichel, an honest toiler alongside three wonderful craftsmen, for a single over; he ran in as hard as if it was his first spell, nudged one away from Vaughan's bat and Warne held the catch at slip. It was the turning point of the match.

Bichel did it again when Waugh turned to him for the final over of the third evening, and he breached Hussain's defences. Equally revealing, and even more spectacular,

Silver lining: England went down to another hefty defeat at Adelaide, but Michael Vaughan restored some pride with a sublime innings.

Picture by Patrick Eagar.

was Vaughan's second-innings dismissal: a running, diving, stunning catch by McGrath at deep square leg. McGrath, who was in the middle of a spell at the time, is a six-and-a-half-foot quick bowler and as such meant to be a lumberer in the field. It is unlikely that any of England's bowlers would have even contemplated a catch, let alone possessed the athleticism actually to reach the ball.

England's preparation was even more chaotic than usual. Giles's left wrist was broken by Harmison in the nets two days before the game – just after he had been measured for a new, longer armguard – and he became the third player, following Jones and Gough, to fly home. Flintoff and Crawley were also still unfit and, when Vaughan tweaked his knee during pre-match fielding practice, England's problems had become almost comical. Hussain decided Vaughan had to play: the alternative was recruiting a batsman from the National Academy, whose winter quarters were conveniently nearby.

In fact, Vaughan batted superbly, driving and pulling and punching his trademark backfoot shots behind square on the off side, often from good length balls. When he had scored 19, the naked eye insisted he was caught by Langer at point and TV replays appeared to provide corroboration. But Vaughan, like most batsmen these days, stood his ground and Steve Davis, like most third umpires these days, judged him not out. Once more, debate raged about the efficacy of TV decisions for catches.

Vaughan gave two more chances, at 56 and 151, and Hussain was also reprieved twice as they put on 140 together. In the afternoon, Vaughan reached his fifth Test century of 2002, and he went on to what was then England's highest innings in a Test in Australia since Mike Denness scored 188 in Melbourne 28 years earlier. But once he was dismissed, the remainder of the batting subsided meekly; next morning, England lost their final six wickets for 47. Gillespie, operating with pace and intelligence, turned in a spell of four for ten in 32 balls.

Hayden and Langer responded with their seventh century opening stand in Tests, at nearly five and a half an over – Caddick's initial spell of seven overs cost 40 runs – and then Ponting made his second century of the series. Although he was not as commanding as at Brisbane, there was a feeling of inevitability as he cruised to three figures, with dazzling footwork, certainty of stroke and hard running between the wickets – he struck only nine boundaries. England suffered a gruelling time in the field. Caddick was restricted by a back problem and Harmison, fast enough to cause some unsettling moments, was so drained by the end that he struggled to reach the stumps. With Vaughan unable to field after being struck on the right shoulder by Gillespie while batting, England used four different substitutes. Catches continued to go down – five, including Martyn, who was badly spilled by Stewart on 37 as he and Ponting added 242 for the third wicket. White collected four wickets, including his brother-in-law, Lehmann. Australia's lower order continued to plunder the weary attack, extending the first-innings lead to 210.

Tired and dejected by their toil in the field, England lost three wickets inside 12 overs on the third evening. Although Vaughan and Stewart added 74 next morning, Australia's march to victory was not long delayed. Stewart reached 8,000 Test runs when 52, and Dawson had the temerity to strike McGrath for three off-side boundaries in as many balls, but McGrath, as usual, had the final word, finishing with four wickets, plus his astonishing catch. By then it was occasionally spitting with rain; on what would have been the fifth day it poured, taunting a demoralised team.

So, for the second successive Test, England enjoyed one day when they matched Australia, but were ruthlessly punished for their inability to sustain such standards. At 2–0 down, pressure was building on Hussain. That well-known voice of reason, Merv Hughes, suggested he should be sacked at once. Hussain himself knew Australia would not let up: "They want to beat us 5–0. They'll be completely cut-throat, they'll show no mercy at all."

Man of the Match: R. T. Ponting. *Attendance:* 78,508.

Close of play: First day, England 295-4 (Butcher 22); Second day, Australia 247-2 (Ponting 83, Martyn 48); Third day, England 36-3 (Vaughan 17).

England

M. E. Trescothick b McGrath	35	–	lbw b Gillespie	0
M. P. Vaughan c Warne b Bichel	177	–	c McGrath b Warne	41
R. W. T. Key c Ponting b Warne	1	–	(5) c Lehmann b Bichel	1
*N. Hussain c Gilchrist b Warne	47	–	b Bichel	10
M. A. Butcher c Gilchrist b Gillespie	22	–	(3) lbw b McGrath	4
†A. J. Stewart lbw b Gillespie	29	–	lbw b Warne	57
C. White c Bichel b Gillespie	1	–	c sub (B. Lee) b McGrath	5
R. K. J. Dawson lbw b Warne	6	–	c Gilchrist b McGrath	19
A. R. Caddick b Warne	0	–	(11) not out	6
M. J. Hoggard c Gilchrist b Gillespie	6	–	(9) b McGrath	1
S. J. Harmison not out	3	–	(10) lbw b Warne	0
L-b 7, n-b 8	15		B 3, l-b 4, n-b 8	15
1/88 (1) 2/106 (3) 3/246 (4) 4/295 (2) 5/295 (5) 6/308 (7) 7/325 (8) 8/325 (9) 9/337 (6) 10/342 (10)	342		1/5 (1) 2/17 (3) 3/36 (4) 4/40 (5) 5/114 (2) 6/130 (7) 7/130 (6) 8/132 (9) 9/134 (10) 10/159 (8)	159

Bowling: *First Innings*—McGrath 30–11–77–1; Gillespie 26.5–8–78–4; Bichel 20–2–78–1; Warne 34–10–93–4; Waugh 5–1–9–0. *Second Innings*—McGrath 17.2–6–41–4; Gillespie 12–1–44–1; Warne 25–7–36–3; Bichel 5–0–31–2.

Australia

J. L. Langer c Stewart b Dawson	48
M. L. Hayden c Caddick b White	46
R. T. Ponting c Dawson b White	154
D. R. Martyn c Hussain b Harmison	95
*S. R. Waugh c Butcher b White	34
D. S. Lehmann c sub (A. Flintoff) b White	5
†A. C. Gilchrist c Stewart b Harmison	54
S. K. Warne c and b Dawson	25
A. J. Bichel b Hoggard	48
J. N. Gillespie not out	0
B 1, l-b 17, w 7, n-b 18	43
1/101 (2) 2/114 (1) 3/356 (4) 4/397 (3) 5/414 (6) 6/423 (5) 7/471 (8) 8/548 (9) 9/552 (7) (9 wkts dec.)	552

G. D. McGrath did not bat.

Bowling: Caddick 20–2–95–0; Hoggard 26–4–84–1; Harmison 28.2–8–106–2; White 28–2–106–4; Dawson 37–2–143–2.

Umpires: S. A. Bucknor (West Indies) and R. E. Koertzen (South Africa).
Third umpire: S. J. Davis. Referee: Wasim Raja (Pakistan).

AUSTRALIA v ENGLAND

Third Test Match

VIC MARKS

At Perth, November 29, 30, December 1, 2002. Australia won by an innings and 48 runs. Toss: England.

England's quest for the Ashes came to an end before those back home had opened a door on their Advent calendars. They were thrashed again, and there was barely a redeeming feature for the 4,000 diehard English supporters who swelled the crowd at the WACA to record proportions.

It had taken 11 days for the Australians to dismantle the English team; for the fundamentalists it took only six to make the world. By these standards alone England had been obdurate in this series. But it was difficult to regard this team as fundamentalist in approach. Hussain may have preached a "back to basics" doctrine, but no one in his ranks seemed to pay much attention. Indeed there were times when Hussain himself, through eccentric bowling plans or the odd wild hook shot, deserted his own philosophy.

Dangerous weapon: Alex Tudor falls to the ground after ducking into a short delivery from Brett Lee. The ball squeezed through the visor, and Tudor was forced to retire.

Picture by Patrick Eagar.

By now the side was disorientated – by two thumping defeats at Brisbane and Adelaide and by a catalogue of injuries which had reached ridiculous proportions. For this game Caddick was absent, having failed to recover from his back spasms in Adelaide, and so was Crawley.

Even so, a measure of desperation was evident in England's selection. They decided to drop Hoggard and to replace him with Silverwood, who had flown out as a replacement when Jones was injured and had not bowled a ball in the middle. He shared the new ball with another recent arrival, Tudor. Dawson was retained even though orthodox spinners are usually redundant at Perth: there was no one else around. Almost inevitably, Silverwood bowled only four overs before his ankle gave way. An ECB press release quickly pointed out "This is a new injury and not related to the joint inflammation he experienced in the same ankle at the end of the English season." Which convinced nobody. The Ashes campaign had been a shambles.

There were plenty of examples of England's disintegration in Perth, but the most obvious were two run-outs, one scarring each innings. Both involved Vaughan and Butcher in dismissals which would have left primary school coaches aghast; both times, the needless sacrifice of a wicket led to the rest of the batting subsiding.

England's ineptitude tended to mask Australia's ruthless efficiency. After the game, Waugh acknowledged that some of their recent victories had been "a bit hollow" because they had been so one-sided. Apart from some fallibility in their close catching, the Australians were routinely brilliant here, but they were never put under any sort of pressure.

Losing the toss for the third time running hardly inconvenienced them. Given recent history and a patchwork bowling attack, Hussain had to bat first but, on the paciest wicket seen even at Perth for years, batting would present unique challenges. When the WACA pitch is fast, it bears no relation to any other in the world – and Australia's fastest bowler, Lee, had returned in place of Bichel.

At 69 for one, England appeared to be competing well, but then came the first mix-up between Vaughan and Butcher. Waugh, from cover, unerringly hit the stumps at the non-striker's end with Butcher yards adrift, a self-inflicted blow from which England never recovered. Soon there were ill-judged pulls and hooks from Hussain, Vaughan and Stewart, all caught behind as they failed to come to terms with exceptional bounce and pace. Only Key, in a stout, mostly passive knock, resisted long, and he was duped by the introduction of Martyn's gentle medium-pacers just before tea.

Run-scoring was a more straightforward occupation for Australia. Silverwood soon limped off, though not before his throw from the leg-side boundary had accounted for Langer, seeking an ambitious third run. Thereafter, all the Australians settled and sparkled briefly, though none of them managed a major innings. Ponting, in sublime form, looked set for his third century of the series until he played on to White. Martyn's measured 71 was the highest score, a modest contribution for a match award winner.

White snaffled five wickets, which flattered him, Harmison just one, which didn't. Harmison bowled with pace, usually short, and he often tested both the batsmen and a sprawling Stewart behind the stumps. He overcame a minor attack of the yips with impressive grit. On the second morning, he consistently lost his run-up, stuttering as he approached his delivery stride. Even so, he kept going and was still faster and more threatening than the other bowlers.

ALL OVER BY CHRISTMAS...

Dates when the Ashes winner was decided in Australia

Series	*Winner*	*Test*	*Date*	*Days*
2002-03	A	Third	December 1	11
1998-99	A	Third	December 15	13
1994-95	A	Third	January 5	15
1990-91	A	Third	January 8	13
1986-87	E	Fourth	December 28	18

With a lead of 271, there was never much chance of Australia suffering the indignity of having to bat twice. Again, England folded after a masochistic run-out. This time, Vaughan was the victim, but Butcher was so ruffled by a second running aberration that he missed his next ball, from McGrath, was patently lbw, and swiped the bails with his bat to earn a fine. Having started the third day on 33 for one, England should have been 34 for five when Warne dropped a straightforward catch at first slip from Hussain's first ball.

A battling innings from Hussain, another stubborn one from Key and a flighty, though futile, effort from Stewart enabled England to reach 223, their highest second-innings score in the series so far. Just before the end, Tudor received a sickening blow to the head as he ducked into a bouncer from Lee. He was stretchered off and for a moment thought he had lost an eye. Fortunately, he suffered just a nasty gash, which required stitches, and a terrible headache.

Lee justified his return by bowling with fierce pace throughout. He looked briefly concerned by the damage he had caused to Tudor, but it did not deter him from bowling a vicious bouncer at the hapless Harmison second ball. Soon after that, Lee splattered Harmison's stumps and it was all over. The Australians had retained the Ashes, even though the little urn, to their dismay, was still locked away in St John's Wood.

Man of the Match: D. R. Martyn. *Attendance:* 56,974.

Close of play: First day, Australia 126-2 (Ponting 43, Martyn 20); Second day, England 33-1 (Vaughan 8, Dawson 8).

England

First innings		Second innings	
M. E. Trescothick c Gilchrist b Lee	34	– c Gilchrist b Lee	4
M. P. Vaughan c Gilchrist b McGrath	34	– run out	9
M. A. Butcher run out	9	– (4) lbw b McGrath	0
*N. Hussain c Gilchrist b Lee	8	– (5) c Gilchrist b Warne	61
R. W. T. Key b Martyn	47	– (6) lbw b McGrath	23
†A. J. Stewart c Gilchrist b McGrath	7	– (7) not out	66
C. White c Martyn b Lee	2	– (8) st Gilchrist b Warne	15
A. J. Tudor c Martyn b Warne	0	– (9) retired hurt	3
R. K. J. Dawson not out	19	– (3) c Waugh b Gillespie	8
C. E. W. Silverwood c Hayden b Gillespie	10	– absent hurt	
S. J. Harmison b Gillespie	6	– (10) b Lee	5
L-b 2, n-b 7	9	B 8, l-b 5, w 1, n-b 15	29
1/47 (1) 2/69 (3) 3/83 (4) 4/101 (2) 5/111 (6) 6/121 (7) 7/135 (8) 8/156 (5) 9/173 (10) 10/185 (11)	185	1/13 (1) 2/33 (3) 3/34 (2) 4/34 (4) 5/102 (6) 6/169 (5) 7/208 (8) 8/223 (10)	223

In the second innings Tudor retired hurt at 214.

Bowling: *First Innings*—McGrath 17–5–30–2; Gillespie 17.2–8–43–2; Lee 20–1–78–3; Warne 9–0–32–1; Martyn 1–1–0–1. *Second Innings*—Lee 18.1–3–72–2; McGrath 21–9–24–2; Gillespie 15–4–35–1; Warne 26–5–70–2; Martyn 2–0–9–0.

Australia

J. L. Langer run out	19
M. L. Hayden c Tudor b Harmison	30
R. T. Ponting b White	68
D. R. Martyn c Stewart b Tudor	71
D. S. Lehmann c Harmison b White	42
*S. R. Waugh b Tudor	53
†A. C. Gilchrist c Tudor b White	38
S. K. Warne run out	35
B. Lee c Key b White	41
J. N. Gillespie b White	27
G. D. McGrath not out	8
B 4, l-b 5, n-b 15	24
1/31 (1) 2/85 (2) 3/159 (3) 4/226 (5) 5/264 (4) 6/316 (7) 7/348 (6) 8/416 (8) 9/423 (9) 10/456 (10)	456

Bowling: Silverwood 4–0–29–0; Tudor 29–2–144–2; Harmison 28–7–86–1; White 23.1–3–127–5; Butcher 10–1–40–0; Dawson 5–0–21–0.

Umpires: S. A. Bucknor (West Indies) and R. E. Koertzen (South Africa).
Third umpire: D. J. Harper. Referee: Wasim Raja (Pakistan).

†At Sydney, December 6, 2002 (day/night). **New South Wales won by eight wickets.** Toss: England XI. **England XI 206** (49.2 overs) (R. C. Irani 81); **New South Wales 211-2** (42 overs) (M. J. Slater 115, M. G. Bevan 54).

Jeremy Snape had his thumb broken by Brett Lee in his first match of the tour.

†At Sydney, December 8, 2002 (day/night). **Australia A won by 23 runs.** Toss: Australia A. **Australia A 205-9** (50 overs) (J. L. Langer 62); **England XI 182** (47 overs).

†At Canberra, December 10, 2002 (day/night). **Prime Minister's XI won by four wickets.** Toss: England XI. **England XI 152** (40.4 overs); **Prime Minister's XI 153-6** (31.4 overs).

Mark Waugh, who had retired from international cricket in October, led the Prime Minister's XI. The match was reduced to 42 overs a side by the weather.

England's matches against Australia and Sri Lanka in the VB Series (December 13–20) appear on pages 1268–1281.

AUSTRALIA v ENGLAND

Fourth Test Match

STEVEN LYNCH

At Melbourne, December 26, 27, 28, 29, 30, 2002. Australia won by five wickets. Toss: Australia. Test debut: M. L. Love.

With the Ashes already surrendered yet again, England made a better fist of matters at the MCG – but still lost. On an exciting final day, Australia wobbled, showing signs of their old fallibility when chasing small targets, but finally made it 4–0 with five wickets to spare.

It might have been closer: after the on-song Harmison had grabbed two wickets in his sixth over, Waugh came in, suffering from a migraine, and somehow survived a manic over from Harmison, in which he was beaten, caught behind (but no one appealed because the racket from the Barmy Army drowned out the noise of the ball kissing the bat-face), then caught off a no-ball. Waugh hadn't heard the call, and was halfway to the pavilion before he realised. The spell was broken with an emphatically driven four and, although Waugh really was out a few overs later, the moment had passed.

MOST EXPERIENCED DEBUTANTS FOR EACH TEST COUNTRY

Figures shown are first-class matches played before Test debut.

W. E. Astill (England)	424	**M. L. Love (Australia)**	**129**
R. G. A. Headley (West Indies)	392	D. R. Doshi (India)	122
P. N. Kirsten (South Africa)	270	M. N. Nawaz (Sri Lanka)	93
D. N. Patel (New Zealand)	254	D. L. Houghton (Zimbabwe)	79
Khalid Ibadulla (Pakistan)	217	Mohammad Salim (Bangladesh)	24

Research: Philip Bailey

All this drama seemed unthinkable as Australia racked up another huge first-innings total. Langer and Hayden combined in an opening stand of 195, then a blitzkrieg from Waugh lifted Australia to 356 for three, the highest first-day score by one side in any Melbourne Test. Again, it might have been different: Hayden hooked his first ball from Caddick, which ballooned to long leg. But Hussain had brought Harmison in off the rope, and the ball sailed over his head for four. Hayden never looked back, clattering ten fours and three sixes – two off White into the stands over long-on – in his 12th Test hundred and his ninth in the last 14 months.

Langer rolled on to a massive 250, the highest of his 13 Test centuries. It took him 578 minutes and 407 balls, and included 30 fours; he reached his hundred with a six over long-on off Dawson. After Waugh celebrated the 17th anniversary of his Test debut with a staccato 77, studded with 15 fours – several cracked through the covers with a whipped follow-through as he sprinted to 50 in 49 balls – there was time for a mature innings from Martin Love. Fresh from two double-centuries against these tourists, for Queensland and Australia A, Love had played an Australian-record 129 first-class matches before his first Test. And, among Australians, only Lehmann, whose poisoned leg allowed the upright Love in here, had scored more runs before his debut.

Warne was also absent, after dislocating his shoulder in a one-day international on this ground on December 15, prompting a recall for his understudy, MacGill. Injuries affected England too: they had to reshuffle their side, including only four bowlers, when Stewart dropped out with a bruised hand. This meant that, for the fourth Ashes

Pulling power: Justin Langer keeps his eye on the ball on his way to 250, his highest Test score.

Picture by Patrick Eagar.

tour running, he did not keep wicket in the Melbourne Test (he played as a batsman in the previous three). Foster, his tidy replacement, did not concede a bye in Australia's big first innings, but he was quieter than Stewart might have been when that final-day catch skimmed through from Waugh. Crawley and Caddick were fit again and returned to the side.

Some spineless batting condemned England to follow on. McGrath, playing in his 54th consecutive Test to pass Courtney Walsh's record for a specialist fast bowler, removed Vaughan, then a Lee screamer accounted for Trescothick. Hussain, reprieved by the third umpire after seemingly being caught by Gillespie at mid-on when 14, added only ten more before MacGill had his revenge.

With Hussain's dismissal on the third morning, England slumped to 118 for six. But then White, playing his maiden first-class match on the ground where he cheered England on as a displaced Pommie schoolboy, collared the bowling. His 85 not out included nine fours and three sixes (all off MacGill), and almost doubled his previous aggregate against Australia – 86 runs in 11 completed innings. But it was a bittersweet knock: White batted in the painful knowledge that he had twanged an intercostal muscle while bowling. Apart from his second innings, he played no further part in the tour.

Following on 281 behind, England faced an unprecedented third successive innings defeat. They lost Trescothick for his second promising 37 of the match, one of five wickets for the persevering MacGill and one of several dubious decisions from umpire Tiffin. But Vaughan ploughed on, pulling imperiously and cover-driving as if he had been studying videos of Colin Cowdrey. He purred to 145, with 19 fours and three sixes, out of 236. On the way, he eclipsed Dennis Amiss's England record of 1,379 runs in a calendar year, and he finished with 1,481, an annual aggregate exceeded only by Viv Richards (1,710 in 1976) and Sunil Gavaskar (1,555 in 1979). Vaughan's second century of the series, like Hayden's his sixth of 2002, stamped him as a player of the utmost class. The Australians paid him their highest compliment: they stopped sledging him.

A plucky maiden half-century from Key swelled the total, but a characteristic collapse, in which the last five tumbled for only 45, meant Australia's target was a seemingly simple 107. But Langer seemed unable to time a thing, and Caddick – ineffective in the first innings, as so infuriatingly often – suddenly clicked into top gear. Hayden swung the first ball of the final day to Tudor, the substitute, on the square-leg boundary. Later, Caddick had Waugh gloving into the slips, and wrung another dubious decision out of Tiffin to trap Langer leg-before.

In between, Harmison worked up a head of steam, beating Ponting and Martyn for pace in the space of four balls. But Gilchrist stopped the rot, popping the winning four over point in the 24th over. The thrilling last morning was fine fare – and free – for a crowd of 18,666. The match total was an impressive 177,658, despite the loss of a chunk of the stands on the railway side of the MCG as rebuilding rumbled on.

There was one final Australian record: this was Waugh's 33rd win in just 44 Tests as captain, passing Allan Border's 32 wins in 93 matches, and closing in on the all-time record of 36 in 74 by Clive Lloyd.

Man of the Match: J. L. Langer. *Attendance:* 177,658.

Close of play: First day, Australia 356-3 (Langer 146, Waugh 62); Second day, England 97-3 (Hussain 17, Dawson 0); Third day, England 111-2 (Vaughan 55, Hussain 8); Fourth day, Australia 8-0 (Langer 4, Hayden 1).

Australia

J. L. Langer c Caddick b Dawson	250	– lbw b Caddick	24
M. L. Hayden c Crawley b Caddick	102	– c sub (A. J. Tudor) b Caddick	1
R. T. Ponting b White	21	– c Foster b Harmison	30
D. R. Martyn c Trescothick b White	17	– c Foster b Harmison	0
*S. R. Waugh c Foster b White	77	– c Butcher b Caddick	14
M. L. Love not out	62	– not out	6
†A. C. Gilchrist b Dawson	1	– not out	10
L-b 11, w 5, n-b 5	21	B 8, l-b 5, n-b 9	22
1/195 (2) 2/235 (3) 3/265 (4) 4/394 (5) 5/545 (1) 6/551 (7) (6 wkts dec.)	551	1/8 (2) 2/58 (3) 3/58 (4) 4/83 (5) 5/90 (1) (5 wkts)	107

B. Lee, J. N. Gillespie, S. C. G. MacGill and G. D. McGrath did not bat.

Bowling: *First Innings*—Caddick 36–6–126–1; Harmison 36–7–108–0; White 33–5–133–3; Dawson 28–1–121–2; Butcher 13–2–52–0. *Second Innings*—Caddick 12–1–51–3; Harmison 11.1–1–43–2.

England

M. E. Trescothick c Gilchrist b Lee	37	– lbw b MacGill	37
M. P. Vaughan b McGrath	11	– c Love b MacGill	145
M. A. Butcher lbw b Gillespie	25	– c Love b Gillespie	6
*N. Hussain c Hayden b MacGill	24	– c and b McGrath	23
R. K. J. Dawson c Love b MacGill	6	– (9) not out	15
R. W. T. Key lbw b Lee	0	– (5) c Ponting b Gillespie	52
J. P. Crawley c Langer b Gillespie	17	– (6) b Lee	33
C. White not out	85	– (7) c Gilchrist b MacGill	21
†J. S. Foster lbw b Waugh	19	– (8) c Love b MacGill	6
A. R. Caddick b Gillespie	17	– c Waugh b MacGill	10
S. J. Harmison c Gilchrist b Gillespie	2	– b Gillespie	7
B 3, l-b 10, n-b 14	27	B 3, l-b 21, w 2, n-b 6	32
1/13 (2) 2/73 (1) 3/94 (3) 4/111 (5) 5/113 (6) 6/118 (4) 7/172 (7) 8/227 (9) 9/264 (10) 10/270 (11)	270	1/67 (1) 2/89 (3) 3/169 (4) 4/236 (2) 5/287 (5) 6/342 (6) 7/342 (7) 8/356 (8) 9/378 (10) 10/387 (11)	387

Bowling: *First Innings*—McGrath 16–5–41–1; Gillespie 16.3–7–25–4; MacGill 36–10–108–2; Lee 17–4–70–2; Waugh 4–0–13–1. *Second Innings*—McGrath 19–5–44–1; Gillespie 24.4–6–71–3; MacGill 48–10–152–5; Lee 27–4–87–1; Waugh 2–0–9–0.

Umpires: D. L. Orchard (South Africa) and R. B. Tiffin (Zimbabwe).
Third umpire: D. B. Hair. Referee: Wasim Raja (Pakistan).

AUSTRALIA v ENGLAND

Fifth Test Match

CHRISTIAN RYAN

At Sydney, January 2, 3, 4, 5, 6, 2003. England won by 225 runs. Toss: England.

England carried over their Melbourne momentum to inflict Australia's first home defeat in four years. It was tempting to blame it on dead-rubber syndrome, but this was a hard-fought, fair-dinkum English victory. Their two previous Test wins against Australia hinged on a miraculous spell by Dean Headley and an even more miraculous innings by Mark Butcher. This time, they played grinding cricket for five days. They did it under a hot sun and an unflinching leader. And maybe, just maybe, they exposed the first crack in a mighty empire.

The match was witnessed by the second-biggest Sydney crowd in history. A further 2.1 million TV viewers – one in nine Australians – tuned in for the gripping second evening. And yet, for all of them, this was about one man. Steve Waugh's 102 was not, contrary to local hyperbole, the greatest century in Ashes folklore; next day, Gilchrist and Vaughan produced a couple every bit as good. But few, if any, have hit hundreds with such a sense of inevitability.

The looming US invasion of Iraq dominated the New Year, but Australians were preoccupied with a different Waugh. Should he stay or should he go? Waugh entered the Test – his 156th, matching Allan Border's record – knowing it could be his last. He entered the final over of the second day needing five runs for 100. Then came the magical bit. Dawson's first three balls were dead-batted down the pitch. Waugh square-drove his fourth for three, but Gilchrist did the right thing and pushed a single. One ball left, two runs needed. Unflustered, Waugh leaned back and drilled a flattish delivery

Arms and the men: Steve Waugh (*left*) accepts the applause after reaching his 29th Test hundred from the last ball of the second day. Andrew Caddick, expensive in Australia's first innings, caught fire in the second; Ricky Ponting holds his stroke, but Caddick has his number.

Pictures by Patrick Eagar and Graham Morris.

through extra cover for four, sparking a roar that the writer David Frith reckoned was the loudest he had heard in 52 years' watching at the SCG. Pink-skinned revellers at the nearby Captain Cook Hotel were still chanting Waugh's name two hours later.

For the first time since November 1992, Australia started with neither McGrath (side strain) nor Warne (shoulder). Without those two, as many had long suspected, they were half the side. Still, a half-strength Australia is troublesome enough. After Hussain chose to bat on a true pitch, England were soon in a familiar fiddle. Lee swung the ball both ways at high speed, before Butcher and Hussain combined for what was briefly England's highest third-wicket stand at Sydney. They were dropped three times, underlining how much Australia missed their superslipper, Mark Waugh, who made a lunchtime lap of honour round his home ground atop a 1967 Mustang. But few begrudged Hussain, in particular, his luck. Gone were the frazzled, manic starts of earlier innings. Instead, he seemed to smile more. Butcher's 124, peppered with delicious cover-drives and neat tucks off his body, was the performance he had hinted at all series. As with Headingley 2001, however, it was only once the Ashes were lost that he loosened up enough to produce it.

Steve Waugh eventually brought himself on, mesmerically trapping Key lbw with an innocuous half-volley. But it was another endangered old-timer who swung things England's way. Stewart had been restored after his Melbourne injury, only to be taken to Sydney's Clinic of Infectious Diseases before the match with a mysterious rash across his face. The rash proved undiagnosable and Stewart unflappable, swiping 15 boundaries; with his eighth, he eclipsed Geoff Boycott (8,114) as England's third-highest run-scorer. Though Bichel, standing in for McGrath, bowled him on 71, England stretched the total to 362.

The Australians went one run better, thanks largely to Waugh's Bradman-equalling 29th Test hundred. This was not the methodical, crablike Waugh of recent years, but the footloose version of the late 1980s, thriving on crunching cover-drives and meaty slashes over the slips. He became the third man to scale 10,000 Test runs, after Gavaskar and Border, and took only 130 balls over his hundred. (The next morning was an anticlimax; Hoggard, recalled to the team because of White's injury, removed him in his first over.) Yet Waugh looked almost pedestrian beside Gilchrist, who required only 94 balls for his century, despite barely hazarding an unconventional stroke. The exception was the shot that got him there: instead of ducking a Harmison bouncer, Gilchrist lifted his bat vertically above his head and swatted the ball tennis-style into the empty expanses of mid-on for three.

Even more praiseworthy, and only slightly more prosaic, was Vaughan's seventh hundred in eight months. This was his best yet. He erupted in the third over of the innings, swinging Gillespie for a glorious six off his hips, before settling into an almost flawless rhythm, which brought 27 fours in 278 balls. Trescothick became Lee's 100th victim, nudging an armpit rocket on to his stumps, but Vaughan, ever methodical but never monotonous, sailed on. He sat on MacGill's stock big-turner and feasted on his plentiful loose offerings. MacGill appeared over-anxious, too eager to impress, while Gillespie, always deadlier at the start of a series, conspicuously failed to lead the attack. Vaughan put on 189 with Hussain – an upgrade on the first day's third-wicket record – before succumbing to a recklessly idiosyncratic lbw decision, one of several by umpire Tiffin. But as the bowlers wilted, the lower order, better late than never, took advantage; when Hussain declared on the fourth evening, Stewart and last man Harmison had added 43 unbeaten runs in seven overs.

> Australia don't do draws. Batting seven hours to save a match was beyond them

That set Australia 452. Fat chance turned swiftly to no chance. Langer, Hayden and Ponting were despatched leg-before on a tense fourth evening, Langer Tiffined by a ball pitching eight inches outside leg. Hayden inadvertently smashed a glass panel on his stomp back to the dressing-room and was fined $A2,200. Bichel was mystifyingly sent in 18 overs before stumps – a pinch-watchman, perhaps? – and swung sensibly before falling to Caddick, that other golden oldie rumoured to be past his use-by date, at the start of the final morning. Banging the ball in purposefully, Caddick made the most of some uneven bounce and undisciplined batting to collect ten wickets in a Test for the first time. Martyn and Love lingered briefly but the rest went down swinging. Waugh's men have achieved many wondrous feats; they don't, however, do draws. Batting seven hours to save a match proved hopelessly beyond them.

Their whitewash ambitions scuppered, it completed an irksome few days for the Australians. The previous day, thanks to a mathematical quirk, they had bequeathed their No. 1 ranking in the ICC Test Championship to South Africa. Hussain, long-sleeved white shirt buttoned to his throat and wrists, was his usual gloomy self at the post-match press conference. But he had glimpsed a new world, a brighter world, a world without McGrath and Warne. It was hard to shake the feeling that, after 14 years of ritual Ashes humiliation, the worst for England might finally be over.

Man of the Match: M. P. Vaughan. *Attendance:* 174,357.

Man of the Series: M. P. Vaughan.

Close of play: First day, England 264-5 (Crawley 6, Stewart 20); Second day, Australia 237-5 (Waugh 102, Gilchrist 45); Third day, England 218-2 (Vaughan 113, Hussain 34); Fourth day, Australia 91-3 (Bichel 49, Martyn 19).

England

M. E. Trescothick c Gilchrist b Bichel	19	– b Lee	22
M. P. Vaughan c Gilchrist b Lee	0	– lbw b Bichel	183
M. A. Butcher b Lee	124	– c Hayden b MacGill	34
*N. Hussain c Gilchrist b Gillespie	75	– c Gilchrist b Lee	72
R. W. T. Key lbw b Waugh	3	– c Hayden b Lee	14
J. P. Crawley not out	35	– lbw b Gillespie	8
†A. J. Stewart b Bichel	71	– not out	38
R. K. J. Dawson c Gilchrist b Bichel	2	– c and b Bichel	12
A. R. Caddick b MacGill	7	– c Langer b MacGill	8
M. J. Hoggard st Gilchrist b MacGill	0	– b MacGill	0
S. J. Harmison run out	4	– not out	20
B 6, l-b 3, n-b 13	22	B 9, l-b 20, w 2, n-b 10	41
1/4 (2) 2/32 (1) 3/198 (4) 4/210 (5) 5/240 (3) 6/332 (7) 7/337 (8) 8/348 (9) 9/350 (10) 10/362 (11)	362	1/37 (1) 2/124 (3) 3/313 (4) 4/344 (5) 5/345 (2) 6/356 (6) 7/378 (8) 8/407 (9) 9/409 (10) (9 wkts dec.)	452

Bowling: *First Innings*—Gillespie 27–10–62–1; Lee 31–9–97–2; Bichel 21–5–86–3; MacGill 44–8–106–2; Waugh 4–3–2–1. *Second Innings*—Gillespie 18.3–4–70–1; Lee 31.3–5–132–3; MacGill 41–8–120–3; Bichel 25.3–3–82–2; Martyn 3–1–14–0; Waugh 6–2–5–0.

Australia

J. L. Langer c Hoggard b Caddick	25	– lbw b Caddick	3
M. L. Hayden lbw b Caddick	15	– lbw b Hoggard	2
R. T. Ponting c Stewart b Caddick	7	– (4) lbw b Caddick	11
D. R. Martyn c Caddick b Harmison	26	– (5) c Stewart b Dawson	21
*S. R. Waugh c Butcher b Hoggard	102	– (6) b Caddick	6
M. L. Love c Trescothick b Harmison	0	– (7) b Harmison	27
†A. C. Gilchrist c Stewart b Harmison	133	– (8) c Butcher b Caddick	37
A. J. Bichel c Crawley b Hoggard	4	– (3) lbw b Caddick	49
B. Lee c Stewart b Hoggard	0	– c Stewart b Caddick	46
J. N. Gillespie not out	31	– not out	3
S. C. G. MacGill c Hussain b Hoggard	1	– b Caddick	1
B 2, l-b 6, w 2, n-b 9	19	B 6, l-b 8, w 3, n-b 3	20
1/36 (2) 2/45 (3) 3/56 (1) 4/146 (4) 5/150 (6) 6/241 (5) 7/267 (8) 8/267 (9) 9/349 (7) 10/363 (11)	363	1/5 (1) 2/5 (2) 3/25 (4) 4/93 (3) 5/99 (6) 6/109 (5) 7/139 (7) 8/181 (8) 9/224 (9) 10/226 (11)	226

Bowling: *First Innings*—Hoggard 21.3–4–92–4; Caddick 23–3–121–3; Harmison 20–4–70–3; Dawson 16–0–72–0. *Second Innings*—Hoggard 13–3–35–1; Caddick 22–5–94–7; Harmison 9–1–42–1; Dawson 10–2–41–1.

Umpires: D. L. Orchard (South Africa) and R. B. Tiffin (Zimbabwe).
Third umpire: S. J. A. Taufel. Referee: Wasim Raja (Pakistan).

At Bowral, January 8, 2003. **Sir Donald Bradman XII won by six wickets.** Toss: Sir Donald Bradman XII. **England XI 279-8** (50 overs) (O. A. Shah 127, A. J. Hollioake 53); **Sir Donald Bradman XII 285-4** (46.3 overs) (M. E. Waugh 108*).

The Bradman team named 12 players, of whom only 11 could bat and 11 bowl; they were led by Waugh, who scored 108 from 99 balls, and won the game with his fifth six.

England's matches against Australia and Sri Lanka in the VB Series (January 11–25) appear on pages 1268–1281.

ENGLAND IN BANGLADESH AND SRI LANKA, 2003-04

REVIEW BY ANDREW MILLER

England were under no illusions about the challenge they faced on an intensive 11-week tour of Bangladesh and Sri Lanka. Perhaps they should have been. That way the players might have retained the mental reserves to survive a cruelly conceived itinerary, and been allowed the freedom of expression to conquer a pair of utterly polarised opponents.

Against Bangladesh, a team that had lost 23 of their 24 Tests, England were such cast-iron favourites that the slightest slip-up invited ridicule. In Sri Lanka, however, they were competing not only against formidable opposition, but also with the legacy of their astonishing series victory in 2000-01 – arguably England's best performance of the past decade. If that were not enough, another England team 5,000 miles away were adding to the pressure by stealing every available plaudit in winning the rugby World Cup in Australia.

As a consequence, the team were dogged by the fear of failure. For ten gruelling weeks they ploughed a lonely and unspectacular furrow, but were nonetheless beginning to tick off their winter's objectives. At the 11th hour, however, their resolve snapped, and in the defining Test in Colombo they tumbled to defeat by an innings and 215 runs. It was England's third-worst beating ever; after that, it was almost impossible to haul any positives out of the wreckage.

The difference between the sides was simple. For the first time since his 16 wickets at The Oval in 1998, Muttiah Muralitharan was fit and ready to face England on his own terms. The groin and shoulder injuries that had hindered his mobility in 2000-01 and 2002 were gone, and instead he introduced a wickedly illegible ball known as the "doosra" that spat back into the left-hander and made England's pad-dominated tactics fraught with danger. At the age of 31, and with 459 Test wickets to his name already, Murali had become the most complete bowler in world cricket.

The doosra – meaning "second" or "the other one" in Hindi and Urdu – is the off-spinner's leg-break, first introduced by Pakistan's Saqlain Mushtaq in the mid-1990s, but not yet seriously mastered by any non-subcontinental bowler. This new weapon had England in a quandary, and drove a timid squad so deep into their shells that they lost the power to reply. In particular, Murali established a stranglehold over his former nemesis Graham Thorpe, who he dismissed five times out of six to attacking and defensive strokes alike. As Thorpe demonstrated in Colombo, where he was stumped like a novice as he charged down the track, taking on Murali was like trying to tweak a cobra's tail. It was all very well to think positively about doing so, but putting those thoughts into practice required the sort of confidence that bordered on insanity.

One man did attempt to take Murali on – but not with the bat. When Nasser Hussain, who appeared frustrated in his new role of elder statesman, allegedly chose the midpoint of the Kandy Test to cast aspersions about Murali's action, his remarks were tossed to the media and turned into front-page headlines. The England team muttered darkly that comments made on the field should remain on the field, but Murali won that particular propaganda battle hands down. Even an apparent weakness had been converted into a strength. The Barmy Army made their feelings known with their song to the tune of "Row, Row, Row your Boat":

Throw, throw, throw the ball
Gently down the seam.
Murali, Murali, Murali, Murali
Chucks it like a dream.

Other than that, England had nothing in their armoury with which to retaliate. Their own No. 1 spinner, Ashley Giles, provided the success story of the Sri Lanka tour, clinging to Murali's coat-tails and picking up 18 wickets to atone for a miserable Bangladesh series, but with Darren Gough retired and Andrew Caddick in plaster, the lack of firepower was all too apparent. The one man who had the pace to make a difference was Steve Harmison. But after terrorising the Bangladeshis on a dead pitch in Dhaka, he limped out of the series with a back strain, and was not invited back amid murmurings about his attitude.

In Harmison's absence, England got through their seamers like disposable nappies. In all, four different new-ball partnerships were used in the five Tests – the only pairing to feature in consecutive matches was that of Richard Johnson, who grabbed nine wickets at Chittagong, and Matthew Hoggard, who was named England's Man of the Series in Bangladesh, presumably for lasting the distance. But after one more ineffectual outing at Galle, England purged their front line entirely. For Kandy, they promoted Andrew Flintoff from first-change and James Kirtley from nowhere; at Colombo, James Anderson completed the merry-go-round, having recovered from a twisted ankle – an injury sustained playing against Kirtley on the squash court.

This slash-and-burn selection policy was partly in response to a brutal itinerary. Cramming the three most important Tests into the final 21 days of the tour was as cruel to the players, and their prospects of glory, as it was kind to the families who would have their loved ones home for Christmas. England managed to pull off back-to-back heroics in saving the first two Tests, with Michael Vaughan leading the way at Kandy with a seven-and-a-half-hour century, his first as captain. But, as he admitted shortly after the Colombo surrender, his team had been on the ropes all series and simply could not withstand any more punches.

John Dyson, Sri Lanka's Australian coach, was unsympathetic. He suggested after the Kandy draw that England's tactics were 20 years out of date, and that any other side would have thrown some punches of their own. Initially, the timing of his comments seemed absurd – all accusations of

England cricketers celebrate winning the World Cup... the rugby World Cup. Michael Vaughan, the England cricket captain, had to make do with the trophy for defeating Bangladesh.

Pictures by Graham Morris.

negativity were being directed at Dyson's own captain, Hashan Tillekeratne, whose field placings in the closing stages of the game had been extraordinarily defensive. Five days after the match, £7,000 worth of rupees were discovered in a hotel room that had been used by Marvan Atapattu. Though the ICC's anti-corruption unit found no evidence of wrongdoing on Atapattu's part, cricket's experiences over the past ten years inevitably make such incidents alarming.

By the end of the Third Test, however, such suspicions had been put to one side and Dyson had been proved right. England allowed the euphoria of their escapes to cloud their judgment, and dared to believe that the series was in their grasp. At Colombo, Vaughan even won his first toss of the series, and with it a rare opportunity to dictate the pace of the game. But as they shuffled out of their foxholes to engage in open warfare, England's inadequacies were laid bare.

MASTER OF ALL HE SURVEYED

Muttiah Muralitharan took 26 wickets at an average of 12.30 in the three Tests against England:

	First innings	*Second innings*
Galle	31.4–15–46–7	37–18–47–4
Kandy	40–18–60–4	56–28–64–4
Colombo (SSC)	40–21–40–3	27–9–63–4

The manner of England's capitulation was particularly unfortunate, given the tactics they had been advocating all tour. Three years earlier, under the attritional, emotional leadership of Hussain, they had scrapped for every inch of every session, and never veered from their course until the job was fully completed. "Stay in the game at all costs," had been Hussain's mantra. It became Vaughan's as well – partly because it had been so successful, partly because he had finished a confusing summer none the wiser as to what type of leader he wanted to be. But it was an out-of-character approach for a man who had used his feet, as well as his head, to carry the fight to Australia the previous winter. By the end of that final Test, it seemed that Hussain's war of attrition had been interpreted as a siege mentality.

In hindsight, England probably expended too much energy in the early weeks of the tour, much of it fretting over the Bangladeshi challenge. But the lessons learned on their horror tour to Zimbabwe seven years earlier – the last time they had travelled as such overwhelming favourites – meant they had no choice but to train like Trojans and perform with the utmost professionalism throughout. Three years earlier, England had turned down the chance to play in Bangladesh's inaugural Test. Now they were pitched against an improving side that had just run Pakistan unspeakably close in a Test in Multan and, under the astute guidance of Dav Whatmore, were looking for all the world like an embarrassment waiting to happen. Until the arrival of Flintoff for the one-day series, caution dogged England's every move. They were outplayed on two of the five days of the Dhaka Test and, though they won comfortably at Chittagong, they were shaken by two dramatic first-innings collapses.

If England had been apprehensive about what mysteries awaited them in Bangladesh, then their first impressions merely added to that sense of foreboding. They arrived in the midst of a spectacular downpour that barely let up for the first week and, with every practice pitch in Dhaka under water, were reduced to commuting north for one and a quarter hours every day, to the Bangladesh Institute of Sport and its four lanes of indoor nets – the only such facility in the whole country.

But the rains relented as suddenly as they had arrived and, after England has splashed through two drawn warm-up games, the inaugural Test stuttered into life amid the Dhaka puddles. At this early stage of the tour, England's seamers looked like browbeaten world-beaters – Hoggard and Harmison sweated buckets in the humid conditions, but shared 16 wickets at Dhaka to ease the pain. However the spinners were a constant source of worry, and were even denounced as "very much ordinary" by Nafis Iqbal, the captain of the Bangladeshi Under-19s, after he had eased to a century in the second practice match.

Giles, who had gambled on a complete deconstruction of his bowling action, was struggling for balance in his new, straighter run-up, and tottered to a series haul of one for 112. His partner Batty just about kept his head above water, metaphorically in Bangladesh, and literally in Sri Lanka, where he came close to drowning in a surfing accident near Galle. But by the end of the tour, Giles and Batty were attracting more attention for their batting, in particular their match-saving performances at Galle and Kandy. Robert Croft had been hustled back into the squad as back-up for the Sri Lanka leg, but Batty's batting kept him at bay and he retired from international cricket for a second time after Christmas.

The rains pursued England to Sri Lanka as well, though not – unfortunately for them – as far north as Dambulla, the venue of the only one-day match to survive an extended monsoon. Fresh from a 3–0 victory over the Bangladeshis, England were bundled out for 88, their lowest total overseas, and battered by ten wickets inside 14 overs. Meanwhile, the Sri Lanka Cricket officials looked on from the stands, panicking that their newly installed floodlights would not even be required. Among them was the board president, Thilanga Sumathipala, who was subsequently arrested on fraud charges. Local press speculation about the affair cast another odd shadow over the entire series.

England were denied the chance to come back when the following two one-day matches were washed out without a ball being bowled, so the squad settled down in the team hotel to watch the rugby World Cup final. Patriotic delight about the result must have been accompanied by a certain wistfulness.

ENGLAND TOURING PARTY

M. P. Vaughan (Yorkshire) (*captain*), J. M. Anderson (Lancashire), G. J. Batty (Worcestershire), M. A. Butcher (Surrey), R. Clarke (Surrey), P. D. Collingwood (Durham), A. Flintoff (Lancashire), A. F. Giles (Warwickshire), S. J. Harmison (Durham), M. J. Hoggard (Yorkshire), N. Hussain (Essex), G. O. Jones (Kent), C. M. W. Read (Nottinghamshire), G. P. Thorpe (Surrey), M. E. Trescothick (Somerset).

I. D. Blackwell (Somerset), R. L. Johnson (Somerset), R. J. Kirtley (Sussex), A. McGrath (Yorkshire), V. S. Solanki (Worcestershire) and A. J. Strauss (Middlesex) replaced Butcher, Harmison, Hoggard, Hussain, Jones and Thorpe for the two one-day series.

Johnson replaced Anderson (knee injury) for the Test series in Bangladesh and Harmison (back) for the Tests in Sri Lanka. M. J. Saggers (Kent) replaced Flintoff, who withdrew with a groin injury, for the Bangladesh Tests. R. D. B. Croft (Glamorgan) was added to the squad in Sri Lanka and Kirtley was kept on after the one-day series in Sri Lanka as cover for Anderson, who injured his ankle playing squash with Kirtley.

Coach: D. A. G. Fletcher. *Assistant coach* (*Test squad*)*:* M. Watkinson. *Assistant coach* (*one-day squad*)*:* T. J. Boon. *Operations manager:* P. A. Neale. *Team analyst:* M. N. Ashton. *Physiotherapist* (*Test squad*)*:* K. A. Russell. *Physiotherapist* (*one-day squad*)*:* D. O. Conway. *Physiologist:* N. P. Stockill. *Team doctor* (*Bangladesh*)*:* M. Ridgewell. *Media manager* (*Bangladesh*)*:* A. J. Walpole. *Media manager* (*Sri Lanka*)*:* M. C. K. Hodgson.

ENGLAND TOUR RESULTS

Test matches – Played 5: Won 2, Lost 1, Drawn 2.
First-class matches – Played 6: Won 2, Lost 1, Drawn 3.
Wins – Bangladesh (2).
Loss – Sri Lanka.
Draws – Sri Lanka (2), Sri Lanka Cricket President's XI.
One-day internationals – Played 4: Won 3, Lost 1, Abandoned 2. *Wins* – Bangladesh (3). *Loss* – Sri Lanka. *Abandoned* – Sri Lanka (2).
Other non-first-class matches – Played 4: Won 1, Drawn 2, No result 1. *Win* – BCB Development Squad. *Draws* – Bangladesh Cricket Board President's XII, Bangladesh A. *No result* – Sri Lanka Cricket President's XI.

TEST MATCH AVERAGES – BANGLADESH v ENGLAND

BANGLADESH – BATTING AND FIELDING

	T	*I*	*NO*	*R*	*HS*	*100s*	*50s*	*Avge*	*Ct/St*
Mushfiqur Rahman	2	4	1	114	46*	0	0	38.00	1
Hannan Sarkar	2	4	0	111	59	0	1	27.75	1
Habibul Bashar	2	4	0	99	58	0	1	24.75	0
Khaled Masud	2	4	0	73	51	0	1	18.25	7/1
Khaled Mahmud	2	4	0	70	33	0	0	17.50	1
†Mohammad Rafiq	2	4	1	45	32	0	0	15.00	1
Rajin Saleh	2	4	0	60	32	0	0	15.00	2
Alok Kapali	2	4	0	59	28	0	0	14.75	0
Javed Omar	2	4	0	50	27	0	0	12.50	0
Enamul Haque, jun.	2	4	2	10	9	0	0	5.00	0
Mashrafe bin Mortaza	2	3	0	13	11	0	0	4.33	0

† *Left-handed batsman.*

BOWLING

	Style	O	M	R	W	BB	5W/i	Avge
Mashrafe bin Mortaza .	RFM	66	19	170	8	4-60	0	21.25
Mohammad Rafiq. . . .	SLA	114.5	27	310	10	3-84	0	31.00
Mushfiqur Rahman . . .	RFM	43.3	13	162	4	2-50	0	40.50
Enamul Haque, jun. . .	SLA	67	17	201	4	2-53	0	50.25

Also bowled: Alok Kapali (LB) 7–1–16–0; Khaled Mahmud (RM) 57–19–169–1; Rajin Saleh (OB) 7–1–27–0.

ENGLAND – BATTING AND FIELDING

	T	I	NO	R	HS	100s	50s	Avge	Ct
M. P. Vaughan	2	4	1	208	81*	0	2	69.33	2
†M. E. Trescothick	2	4	1	206	113	1	1	68.66	4
N. Hussain	2	4	0	188	95	0	2	47.00	1
†G. P. Thorpe.	2	4	1	136	64	0	2	45.33	0
C. M. W. Read.	2	3	1	76	38*	0	0	38.00	10
R. Clarke	2	3	0	96	55	0	1	32.00	1
†M. A. Butcher	2	4	0	56	42	0	0	14.00	3

Played in two Tests: A. F. Giles 19, 6; M. J. Hoggard 6*, 0* (1 ct). Played in one Test: G. J. Batty 19; S. J. Harmison 0; R. L. Johnson 6; M. J. Saggers 1 (1 ct).

† *Left-handed batsman.*

BOWLING

	Style	O	M	R	W	BB	5W/i	Avge
S. J. Harmison.	RF	46.5	17	79	9	5-35	1	8.77
R. L. Johnson	RFM	33.1	7	93	9	5-49	1	10.33
R. Clarke	RFM	29	11	60	4	2-7	0	15.00
M. J. Saggers	RFM	19.1	4	62	3	2-29	0	20.66
M. J. Hoggard	RFM	82	23	204	9	4-48	0	22.66

Also bowled: G. J. Batty (OB) 41–8–108–2; A. F. Giles (SLA) 39–7–112–1.

TEST MATCH AVERAGES – SRI LANKA v ENGLAND

SRI LANKA – BATTING AND FIELDING

	T	I	NO	R	HS	100s	50s	Avge	Ct/St
D. P. M. D. Jayawardene . .	3	5	1	334	134	1	2	83.50	7
T. M. Dilshan	2	3	0	246	100	1	2	82.00	3
T. T. Samaraweera.	3	5	1	214	142	1	0	53.50	0
†S. T. Jayasuriya.	3	5	0	209	85	0	1	41.80	3
U. D. U. Chandana	2	3	0	116	76	0	1	38.66	0
†K. C. Sangakkara	3	5	0	165	71	0	1	33.00	9/4
M. Muralitharan	3	4	1	91	38	0	0	30.33	1
K. A. D. M. Fernando	2	3	1	56	51*	0	1	28.00	0
†W. P. U. J. C. Vaas	3	5	1	102	32	0	0	25.50	1
H. D. P. K. Dharmasena. . .	2	4	1	65	29	0	0	21.66	0
M. S. Atapattu	3	4	0	83	35	0	0	20.75	3
†H. P. Tillekeratne.	3	5	0	78	45	0	0	15.60	4

Played in one Test: C. R. D. Fernando 1*.

† *Left-handed batsman.*

BOWLING

	Style	*O*	*M*	*R*	*W*	*BB*	*5W/i*	*Avge*
M. Muralitharan	OB	231.4	109	320	26	7-46	1	12.30
C. R. D. Fernando	RFM	24	7	82	4	3-27	0	20.50
W. P. U. J. C. Vaas	LFM	103.2	24	273	13	4-77	0	21.00
S. T. Jayasuriya	SLA	90	22	158	5	2-5	0	31.60
H. D. P. K. Dharmasena	RM/OB	87	19	228	4	1-36	0	57.00

Also bowled: U. D. U. Chandana (LBG) 63–18–148–2; T. M. Dilshan (OB) 3–1–10–0; K. A. D. M. Fernando (RFM) 21–2–107–1; T. T. Samaraweera (OB) 8–3–20–0; H. P. Tillekeratne (OB) 1–0–1–0.

ENGLAND – BATTING AND FIELDING

	T	*I*	*NO*	*R*	*HS*	*100s*	*50s*	*Avge*	*Ct/St*
M. P. Vaughan	3	6	0	221	105	1	1	36.83	2
†G. P. Thorpe	3	6	0	183	57	0	1	30.50	1
†M. A. Butcher	3	6	0	175	54	0	2	29.16	1
†M. E. Trescothick	3	6	0	167	70	0	1	27.83	6
A. Flintoff	3	6	0	143	77	0	1	23.83	0
G. J. Batty	3	6	1	117	38	0	0	23.40	0
P. D. Collingwood	2	4	0	89	36	0	0	22.25	6
A. F. Giles	3	5	1	74	18	0	0	18.50	0
C. M. W. Read	3	6	2	49	18*	0	0	12.25	5/2
N. Hussain	2	4	0	46	17	0	0	11.50	0
R. J. Kirtley	2	3	1	16	12	0	0	8.00	1

Played in one Test: †J. M. Anderson 1, 1*; M. J. Hoggard 6*, 0*; R. L. Johnson 26, 3.

† *Left-handed batsman.*

BOWLING

	Style	*O*	*M*	*R*	*W*	*BB*	*5W/i*	*Avge*
A. Flintoff	RFM	97	20	221	9	3-42	0	24.55
A. F. Giles	SLA	197.3	49	539	18	5-116	1	29.94
R. J. Kirtley	RFM	81	18	302	6	2-62	0	50.33
G. J. Batty	OB	124.2	20	396	6	3-55	0	66.00

Also bowled: J. M. Anderson (RFM) 24–5–85–0; P. D. Collingwood (RM) 16–3–37–0; M. J. Hoggard (RFM) 29–6–82–1; R. L. Johnson (RFM) 24–7–82–1; M. E. Trescothick (RM) 2–0–10–0; M. P. Vaughan (OB) 10–0–27–0.

ENGLAND TOUR AVERAGES – FIRST-CLASS MATCHES

	M	*I*	*NO*	*R*	*HS*	*100s*	*50s*	*Avge*	*Ct/St*
M. P. Vaughan	5	10	1	429	105	1	3	47.66	4
†M. E. Trescothick	5	10	1	373	113	1	2	41.44	10
†M. A. Butcher	6	11	1	382	151*	1	2	38.20	4
†G. P. Thorpe	6	11	1	354	64	0	3	35.40	2
A. Flintoff	4	7	0	190	77	0	1	27.14	0
N. Hussain	5	9	0	234	95	0	2	26.00	2
P. D. Collingwood	2	4	0	89	36	0	0	22.25	6
G. J. Batty	5	8	1	144	38	0	0	20.57	2

	M	I	NO	R	HS	100s	50s	Avge	Ct/St
A. F. Giles	6	8	1	129	30	0	0	18.42	0
C. M. W. Read	6	10	3	128	38*	0	0	18.28	16/2
M. J. Hoggard	4	5	4	16	6*	0	0	16.00	1
R. J. Kirtley	3	4	2	16	12	0	0	8.00	2

Played in two matches: R. Clarke 14, 55, 27 (1 ct); R. L. Johnson 6, 26, 3. Played in one match: †J. M. Anderson 1, 1*; R. D. B. Croft 0; S. J. Harmison 0; G. O. Jones 5 (2 ct, 2 st); M. J. Saggers 1 (1 ct).

† *Left-handed batsman.*

BOWLING

	Style	O	M	R	W	BB	5W/i	Avge
S. J. Harmison	RF	46.5	17	79	9	5-35	1	8.77
R. L. Johnson	RFM	57.1	14	175	10	5-49	1	17.50
A. Flintoff	RFM	111	22	262	10	3-42	0	26.20
A. F. Giles	SLA	259.3	66	707	23	5-116	1	30.73
M. J. Hoggard	RFM	127	32	330	10	4-48	0	33.00
R. J. Kirtley	RFM	101	22	365	11	4-41	0	33.18
G. J. Batty	OB	190.1	32	564	11	3-55	0	51.27

Also bowled: J. M. Anderson (RFM) 24–5–85–0; R. Clarke (RFM) 29–11–60–4; P. D. Collingwood (RM) 16–3–37–0; R. D. B. Croft (OB) 14–3–41–1; M. J. Saggers (RFM) 19.1–4–62–3; M. E. Trescothick (RM) 2–0–10–0; M. P. Vaughan (OB) 10–0–27–0.

Notes: Matches in this section which were not first-class are signified by a dagger.
Figures in brackets in one-day internationals are balls received.

†At Dhaka, October 12, 13, 14, 2003. **Drawn.** Toss: Bangladesh Cricket Board President's XII. **England 253** (M. E. Trescothick 90; Enamul Haque, jun. 4-59) **and 69-1 dec.**; **Bangladesh Cricket Board President's XII 57** (M. J. Hoggard 6-13) **and 143-9**.

Each side fielded 12 players, of whom 11 could bat and 11 field. Only Aftab Ahmed (10) and Extras (14) reached double figures in the President's XI's first innings.

†At Savar, October 16, 17, 18, 2003. **Drawn.** Toss: Bangladesh A. **Bangladesh A 242** (Nafis Iqbal 118) **and 81-4**; **England XII 333** (M. E. Trescothick 96, C. M. W. Read 82, G. J. Batty 50).

Each side fielded 12 players, of whom 11 could bat and 11 field.

BANGLADESH v ENGLAND

First Test Match

MATTHEW ENGEL

At Dhaka, October 21, 22, 23, 24, 25, 2003. England won by seven wickets. Toss: Bangladesh. Test debuts: Enamul Haque, jun.; G. J. Batty, R. Clarke.

The inaugural Test between Bangladesh and England – the last unplayed fixture between any of the ten full members of the ICC – came close to providing an earthquake that would have surpassed anything on the seismograph of England's embarrassments down the years. With a day to go, Bangladesh (previous Test record: P 24 L 23 D1) had a distinct chance of victory.

Waiting for the light: play on the third afternoon of the Dhaka Test ended early when the floodlights failed. Michael Vaughan kept his England team on the field, but the Bangladesh batsmen knew better, and headed for the pavilion.
Picture by Graham Morris.

In the end, England came through comfortably enough and, objectively, Bangladesh's performance was no more than a logical continuation of their improved form since the World Cup and their near miss in Multan six weeks earlier. However, defeat would have caused derision both at home and across the cricketing world. As it was, in a contest billed locally as Tigers v Lions, the home-grown cubs at least managed to inflict some scratches on opponents who – certainly on days three and four – looked both mangy and toothless.

The game also came only six weeks after one of England's most remarkable victories, against South Africa at The Oval. But, as so often, the team showed little continuity, with nearly half the Oval team gone: Stewart (retired), Smith and Bicknell (not selected), and Anderson and Flintoff (unfit). At The Oval, England came back from an apparently impossible position; this time, they flirted with defeat from a near-impregnable one.

After the first day was almost entirely rained off (the actual rain only lasted 15 minutes, but it stair-rodded, and the outfield turned to mush), England made up for lost time and swept towards command on the second. They only fielded two specialist seamers, which was a mistake. But Harmison and Hoggard, neither with a reputation for robustness, gamely shouldered the burden of the attack. This was unenviable work, because of the humidity, because the sessions were lengthened to make up lost time and because Giles, England's only experienced spinner, was very publicly remodelling his action and was short on control.

When Khaled Masud and Mushfiqur Rahman dug in at 72 for five, it became especially tough. But Harmison polished off Bangladesh with the new ball, and their

203 soon looked paltry. Trescothick came in and blazed away and Vaughan, still searching for his first worthwhile score as England captain, survived an early struggle in a manner that suggested he might soon put aside all the doubts about whether responsibility was harming his batting.

But next morning, on 48, Vaughan swept on to his stumps and England contrived to collapse from 137 for nought to 295 all out. This happened despite Trescothick making his way to 113, and Thorpe joining him in a shorter and rather less exuberant rerun of their great stand at The Oval. Thorpe was left to shepherd the tail which, as usual with England, proved a thankless task.

On a pitch that was not slow by subcontinental standards but was never either trustworthy or favourable to strokeplay, most of the batsmen struggled against the two left-arm spinners, the aggressive Mohammad Rafiq and Enamul Haque (no relation to the player of the same name who appeared in ten previous Tests for Bangladesh). This Enamul was officially listed as still being 16; he said on TV he was 17; reliable local sources said he was probably at least 18. Anyway, he looked about 12 – and bowled like a mature and confident cricketer.

England still hoped to make inroads on the batting that night, and the two seamers were raring to go. But with less than four overs bowled, the floodlights – which had helped keep the show on the road during a sunless week – failed. England sat themselves in a circle in the forlorn hope of a restart. Investigations into the mysteries of the Dhaka power supply, including one after the fact by the ICC's Anti-Corruption and Security Unit, failed to produce a coherent explanation.

The next morning, the mood had changed. Harmison and Hoggard had their worst session of the match, and Habibul Bashar and Hannan Sarkar eased Bangladesh into the lead with a second-wicket stand of 108. To the delight of the game's largest crowd – about 15,000 – Bangladesh frustrated England all day. By the close, they were 153 ahead with four wickets standing and their hopes were sky-high.

Then England got their act together. Harmison – who finished with nine for 79 in the match – and Hoggard whipped through the remaining batsmen with the newish ball in nine overs on the fifth morning. Faced with 164 to win, Vaughan led from the front and England charged to victory. Bangladesh blew their best chance by failing to bowl their spinners early enough, and there was a sense afterwards that they might struggle to get so close to England another time. Asked to name his preferred line-up for the Chittagong Test, Bangladesh coach Dav Whatmore replied: "Eight batsmen and six bowlers."

Man of the Match: S. J. Harmison.

Close of play: First day, Bangladesh 24-2 (Hannan Sarkar 18, Rajin Saleh 0); Second day, England 111-0 (Trescothick 77, Vaughan 30); Third day, Bangladesh 12-1 (Hannan Sarkar 4, Habibul Bashar 0); Fourth day, Bangladesh 245-6 (Mushfiqur Rahman 43, Khaled Mahmud 17).

Bangladesh

Hannan Sarkar b Hoggard	20	– c Trescothick b Hoggard	59
Javed Omar c Clarke b Harmison	3	– (7) lbw b Hoggard	27
Habibul Bashar c Trescothick b Harmison	2	– c Trescothick b Batty	58
Rajin Saleh c Read b Harmison	11	– (2) c Read b Harmison	8
Alok Kapali b Batty	28	– (4) c Butcher b Harmison	12
Mushfiqur Rahman lbw b Hoggard	34	– (5) not out	46
†Khaled Masud lbw b Clarke	51	– (6) c Hussain b Giles	7
*Khaled Mahmud lbw b Hoggard	4	– lbw b Harmison	18
Mohammad Rafiq b Harmison	32	– c Read b Harmison	1
Mashrafe bin Mortaza b Harmison	11	– c Trescothick b Hoggard	1
Enamul Haque, jun. not out	0	– lbw b Hoggard	0
B 2, l-b 3, n-b 2	7	L-b 10, n-b 3, p 5	18
1/12 (2) 2/24 (3) 3/38 (1) 4/40 (4) 5/72 (5) 6/132 (6) 7/148 (8) 8/182 (7) 9/198 (9) 10/203 (10)	203	1/12 (2) 2/120 (3) 3/140 (4) 4/148 (1) 5/176 (6) 6/219 (7) 7/248 (8) 8/254 (9) 9/255 (10) 10/255 (11)	255

COW CORNER: The generation who might transform Bangladesh's cricketing fortunes practise outside Dhaka, October 2003.

Picture by Michael Steele, Getty Images.

GAME WITHOUT BOUNDARIES: Saima Yousuf, 21, plays in a women's tournament in Srinagar, Kashmir, August 2003.

Picture by Fayaz Kabli, Reuters.

HAIR TODAY: Following the route to stardom chosen by David Beckham, cricketers' hair became increasingly eccentric in 2003. Jason Gillespie and Ian Harvey (*top*) went for the 1970s retro-look; James Anderson (*left*) opted for red highlights; Chad Keegan bravely chose an Alice band.

*Pictures by Hamish Blair, Getty Images (*top*) and Graham Morris.*

PALMY DAYS: Michael Vaughan batting during his epic century at the Kandy Test in Sri Lanka, December 2003.

Picture by Philip Brown.

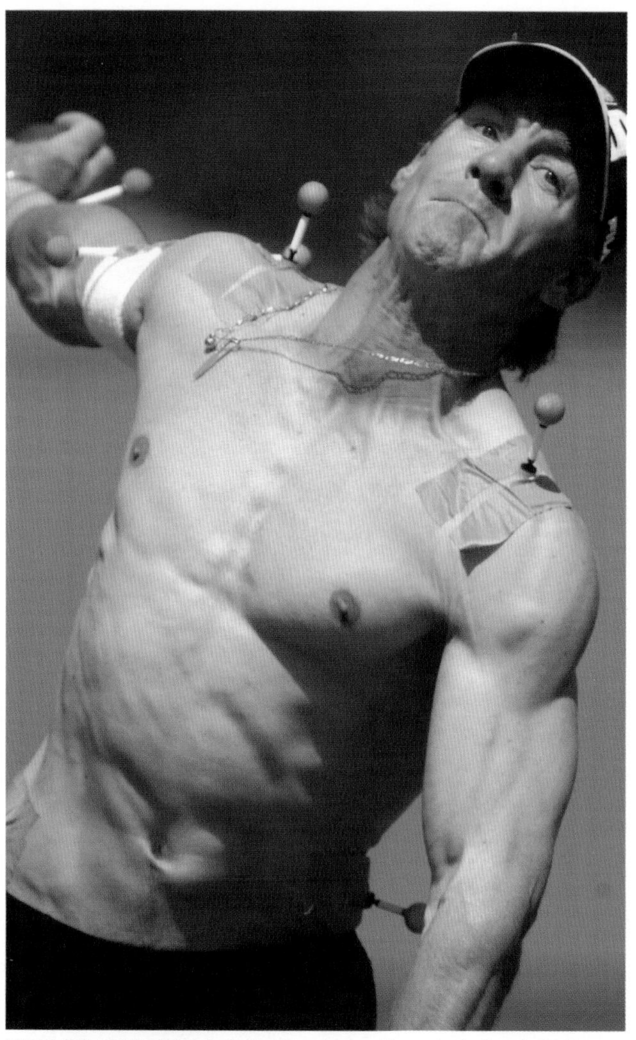

WIRED FOR SOUNDNESS: Andy Bichel undergoes biomechanical analysis during a net session at Perth, October 2003.

Picture by Hamish Blair, Getty Images.

OLYMPIC CRICKET: New South Wales play their inaugural game at the Sydney Olympic Stadium, against South Australia in an ING Cup tie, February 2003. A crowd of 25,763 turned up, encouraging the idea of soon using the stadium for one-day internationals.

Picture by Daniel Berehulak, Getty Images.

THAT'S THE ONE THEY WANTED: Ed Smith joins Martin Bicknell in jubilation at the Oval Test. Bicknell gets Graeme Smith lbw for 19 – and England are on the way to victory.

Picture by Tom Jenkins.

THE FUN OF THE FAIR: Hampshire v Sussex on the opening day of the inaugural Twenty20 competition at the Rose Bowl, Southampton, June 2003.
Picture by Patrick Eagar.

Bowling: *First Innings*—Hoggard 23–6–55–3; Harmison 21.5–9–35–5; Clarke 6–1–18–1; Batty 21–6–43–1; Giles 12–1–47–0. *Second Innings*—Hoggard 27–11–48–4; Harmison 25–8–44–4; Batty 20–2–65–1; Giles 20–4–52–1; Clarke 15–6–31–0.

England

First innings		Second innings	
M. E. Trescothick c Khaled Mahmud b Enamul Haque	113	– st Khaled Masud b Mohammad Rafiq	32
*M. P. Vaughan b Mohammad Rafiq	48	– not out	81
M. A. Butcher lbw b Mushfiqur Rahman	0	– lbw b Mohammad Rafiq	8
N. Hussain c Khaled Masud b Mushfiqur Rahman	0	– lbw b Mashrafe bin Mortaza	17
G. P. Thorpe c Rajin Saleh b Mashrafe bin Mortaza	64	– not out	18
R. Clarke b Mohammad Rafiq	14		
†C. M. W. Read c Khaled Masud b Enamul Haque	1		
G. J. Batty c Khaled Masud b Mashrafe bin Mortaza	19		
A. F. Giles c sub (Aftab Ahmed) b Mohammad Rafiq	19		
S. J. Harmison lbw b Mashrafe bin Mortaza	0		
M. J. Hoggard not out	6		
L-b 4, w 2, n-b 5	11	B 1, l-b 1, w 1, n-b 5	8
1/137 (2) 2/140 (3) 3/140 (4) 4/175 (1) 5/224 (6) 6/225 (7) 7/266 (8) 8/267 (5) 9/267 (10) 10/295 (9)	295	1/64 (1) 2/86 (3) 3/128 (4)	(3 wkts) 164

Bowling: *First Innings*—Mashrafe bin Mortaza 23–6–41–3; Mushfiqur Rahman 17–6–55–2; Khaled Mahmud 17–7–45–0; Mohammad Rafiq 35.3–9–84–3; Enamul Haque 23–8–53–2; Rajin Saleh 2–0–9–0; Alok Kapali 3–1–4–0. *Second Innings*—Mashrafe bin Mortaza 11–2–46–1; Mushfiqur Rahman 3–1–16–0; Khaled Mahmud 3–1–14–0; Mohammad Rafiq 13.2–0–57–2; Enamul Haque 7–0–27–0; Rajin Saleh 2–0–2–0.

Umpires: Aleem Dar (Pakistan) and E. A. R. de Silva (Sri Lanka).
Third umpire: A. F. M. Akhtaruddin. Referee: Wasim Raja (Pakistan).

BANGLADESH v ENGLAND

Second Test Match

ANDREW MILLER

At Chittagong, October 29, 30, 31, November 1, 2003. England won by 329 runs. Toss: Bangladesh. Test debut: M. J. Saggers.

For six consecutive Tests, coinciding with the arrival of Dav Whatmore as coach, Bangladesh had displayed a slow but steady improvement, and seemed at last to be coming to terms with Test cricket. At Chittagong, however, they were sent scurrying back to the drawing board, as England wrapped up a 2–0 sweep of the series with an emphatic 329-run victory.

It was not the heaviest defeat of Whatmore's brief reign (Australia had twice beaten them by an innings in July) but it was the most dispiriting. Bangladesh had competed eagerly for seven of the nine days in the series, including the first half of this match, but fell away badly as England brought their discipline and fitness to bear.

England's enforcer was Johnson, playing in only his second Test. On debut, against Zimbabwe in June, he had bowled a full, pad-rapping length to pluck out six wickets for 33. Here, he realigned his radar to buzz around the Bangladeshis' midriffs, and gained match figures of nine for 93, becoming the first English bowler since Nick Cook in 1983 to pick up five-wicket hauls in his first two Tests.

Johnson had not been an original selection for the tour party. He abandoned his honeymoon in the Maldives when Anderson withdrew with a knee injury, and stepped up to the Test team when Harmison's back gave way after his match-winning efforts at Dhaka. His reward was a fright of a pitch – all green and tufty, like a Martian's chest hair – quite unlike any other that England had encountered on tour. It gave ample assistance to the seamers and no end of problems to Bangladesh's brittle batsmen, who mustered 290 in two innings.

Bangladesh's captain, Khaled Mahmud, had betrayed his batsmen's anxieties at the toss, when he opted to bowl first despite the selection of two spinners, Enamul Haque and Mohammad Rafiq, who had been his most prized assets in the closeish encounter at Dhaka. England, by contrast, had packed their side with seamers – Johnson, Hoggard and the debutant Martin Saggers – while retaining the off-colour Giles, who contributed only seven overs in the entire match, apparently on humanitarian grounds.

Quite apart from avoiding England's pace men, Mahmud had gambled on exploiting what little moisture there might have been in the wicket. When Trescothick and Vaughan eased to another century opening stand, that line of optimism was quashed. But then, quite without warning, England lost four wickets in five overs to tumble to 134 for four. Trescothick flapped loosely to point, Butcher was suckered by Rafiq's arm-ball, and when Vaughan and Thorpe fell in three balls to the highly promising pace man, Mashrafe bin Mortaza, the apparent standard of the opposition counted for little.

But England had the perfect combination of young and old to dig themselves out of trouble. Hussain later described his funereal 76 as one of the best innings of his career; that might have been over-egging it, but in loitering for nearly six hours and 266 balls he approached the Bangladeshi bowlers as if he were trying to recreate his Durban epic of 1999-2000 against Allan Donald and Shaun Pollock.

At the other end of the experience scale was Rikki Clarke, given his opportunity by Flintoff's absence, and discovering there was no time like the present for making his mark. The pair added 116 for the fifth wicket to calm the jitters, only for England to surrender their last five for 13. But Clarke, who struggled with a virus throughout the match, revealed a happy wicket-taking knack as well, grabbing two in consecutive deliveries as Bangladesh tottered to 93 for four at the close of the second day.

That marked the end of Bangladesh's resistance – for this match, and for the remainder of England's visit. Their last six wickets tumbled in 24 overs: four for Johnson and his alarming bounce, and a brace for Saggers, another man who had dumped his holiday plans to answer the call. If Saggers was to be England's latest one-cap wonder, he did at least make his big day out a memorable one – especially in the second innings, when he pulled off an astonishing one-handed, back-pedalling catch at fine leg to remove Alok Kapali.

England launched their second innings without Trescothick, who had bruised his thumb while attempting a slip catch, so Butcher stepped out to open with Vaughan, and responded with his first fluent innings of the tour. His impetus even rubbed off on Hussain, who took 34 deliveries to get past his first run, but then warmed to the theme by slapping a merry 95 from 144 balls.

Bangladesh's last vestige of hope vanished when Mortaza – easily their classiest bowler – fell awkwardly in his follow-through and limped out of the match with a twisted knee. Vaughan declared at the close of the third day with a lead of 467 and, though defeat for Bangladesh may have been inevitable, surrender was not a foregone conclusion. Two early run-outs, however, sealed their fate. Clarke found the strength to grab a wicket in his only over before returning to his sickbed, and Saggers pulled off that catch. Only Mahmud hung around with any intent, but when he paddled a simple catch off Johnson, Vaughan gratefully accepted the offering at square leg to complete his first series victory as England captain.

Man of the Match: R. L. Johnson. *Man of the Series:* M. J. Hoggard.

Close of play: First day, England 237-4 (Hussain 47, Clarke 53); Second day, Bangladesh 93-4 (Rajin Saleh 24, Mushfiqur Rahman 16); Third day, England 293-5 (Read 38, Trescothick 1).

Over and out: Martin Saggers, on his England debut, hurls himself at the ball and clings on one-handed. Alok Kapali has gone, and England close in on victory at Chittagong.

Picture by Graham Morris.

England

M. E. Trescothick c Mushfiqur Rahman b Khaled Mahmud	60	– (7) not out	1
*M. P. Vaughan c Khaled Masud b Mashrafe bin Mortaza	54	– run out	25
M. A. Butcher b Mohammad Rafiq	6	– (1) c Khaled Masud b Mohammad Rafiq	42
N. Hussain c Khaled Masud b Mashrafe bin Mortaza	76	– (3) c and b Mohammad Rafiq	95
G. P. Thorpe b Mashrafe bin Mortaza	0	– (4) lbw b Mohammad Rafiq	54
R. Clarke c Hannan Sarkar b Mashrafe bin Mortaza	55	– lbw b Enamul Haque	27
†C. M. W. Read c Rajin Saleh b Enamul Haque	37	– (5) not out	38
A. F. Giles lbw b Mushfiqur Rahman	6		
R. L. Johnson c Khaled Masud b Mushfiqur Rahman	6		
M. J. Saggers lbw b Mohammad Rafiq	1		
M. J. Hoggard not out	0		
B 8, l-b 5, w 7, n-b 5	25	B 4, w 1, n-b 6	11
1/126 (1) 2/133 (3) 3/134 (2) 4/134 (5) 5/250 (6) 6/313 (7) 7/313 (4) 8/321 (9) 9/326 (10) 10/326 (8)	326	1/66 (1) 2/70 (2) 3/208 (4) 4/231 (3) 5/290 (6) (5 wkts dec.)	293

Bowling: *First Innings*—Mashrafe bin Mortaza 28–11–60–4; Mushfiqur Rahman 18.3–6–50–2; Khaled Mahmud 23–8–46–1; Mohammad Rafiq 37–15–63–2; Enamul Haque 23–4–81–1; Alok Kapali 4–0–12–0; Rajin Saleh 2–1–1–0. *Second Innings*—Mashrafe bin Mortaza 4–0–23–0; Mushfiqur Rahman 5–0–41–0; Mohammad Rafiq 29–3–106–3; Khaled Mahmud 14–3–64–0; Enamul Haque 14–5–40–1; Rajin Saleh 1–0–15–0.

Bangladesh

Batsman	First innings		Second innings	
Hannan Sarkar	lbw b Clarke	28	c Read b Johnson	4
Javed Omar	c Vaughan b Johnson	2	c Read b Saggers	18
Habibul Bashar	c Butcher b Hoggard	18	run out	21
Rajin Saleh	c Read b Johnson	32	c Read b Clarke	9
Alok Kapali	c Butcher b Clarke	0	(6) c Saggers b Johnson	19
Mushfiqur Rahman	c Read b Saggers	28	(5) run out	6
†Khaled Masud	c sub (P. D. Collingwood) b Johnson	0	c Read b Johnson	15
*Khaled Mahmud	c sub (P. D. Collingwood) b Johnson	15	c Vaughan b Johnson	33
Mohammad Rafiq	not out	12	c Read b Hoggard	0
Mashrafe bin Mortaza	b Johnson	1	absent hurt	
Enamul Haque, jun.	c Hoggard b Saggers	9	(10) not out	1
	L-b 1, n-b 6	7	B 4, l-b 5, w 1, n-b 2	12
	1/6 (2) 2/44 (3) 3/61 (1) 4/63 (5) 5/107 (4) 6/110 (7) 7/126 (8) 8/138 (6) 9/139 (10) 10/152 (11)	152	1/5 (1) 2/33 (3) 3/51 (2) 4/58 (5) 5/70 (4) 6/91 (6) 7/108 (7) 8/126 (9) 9/138 (8)	138

Bowling: *First Innings*—Hoggard 20–3–64–1; Johnson 21–6–49–5; Clarke 7–4–7–2; Saggers 12.1–3–29–2; Giles 2–1–2–0. *Second Innings*—Hoggard 12–3–37–1; Johnson 12.1–1–44–4; Giles 5–1–11–0; Saggers 7–1–33–1; Clarke 1–0–4–1.

Umpires: Aleem Dar (Pakistan) and E. A. R. de Silva (Sri Lanka).
Third umpire: Mahbubur Rahman. Referee: Wasim Raja (Pakistan).

†At Dhaka, November 5, 2003. **England XI won by 167 runs.** Toss: BCB Development Squad. **England XI 328** (49.3 overs) (V. S. Solanki 79, A. J. Strauss 51, I. D. Blackwell 62); **BCB Development Squad 161** (47.4 overs).

†BANGLADESH v ENGLAND

First One-Day International

At Chittagong, November 7, 2003. England won by seven wickets. Toss: Bangladesh. One-day international debuts: Jamaluddin Ahmed, Manjurul Islam Rana, Nafis Iqbal.

After missing the Tests with a groin injury, Flintoff marked his return with an irresistible all-round display, taking a career-best four for 14 from 9.4 splice-hitting overs, before belting 55 not out from just 52 deliveries. His contribution ensured that a comfortable victory turned into a rout, and at the post-match presentations Bangladesh's captain, Khaled Mahmud, was booed by home fans. The victory had never been in doubt after an extraordinary 14-ball spell midway through Bangladesh's innings. After easing to 65 for two, they lost five wickets for one run, three of them to a rejuvenated Giles. By reverting to Test-match tactics, the tail did well to grind along to 143, although they were helped by 29 extras. England in reply shed three careless wickets, but Flintoff and Collingwood sealed the match with almost 25 overs to spare.

Man of the Match: A. Flintoff.

Bangladesh

Batsman	Dismissal	Runs	Balls
Hannan Sarkar	c Read b Flintoff	30	(55)
Nafis Iqbal	c Trescothick b Anderson	9	(19)
Habibul Bashar	c Read b Flintoff	10	(22)
Rajin Saleh	c Clarke b Giles	2	(8)
Alok Kapali	lbw b Giles	0	(3)
*Khaled Mahmud	c Read b Flintoff	0	(2)
Mushfiqur Rahman	c and b Giles	0	(2)
Manjurul Islam Rana	run out	18	(60)
†Khaled Masud	c Vaughan b Clarke	13	(45)
Jamaluddin Ahmed	not out	18	(28)
Tapash Baisya	c and b Flintoff	14	(28)
	B 4, l-b 14, w 8, n-b 3	29	
	1/16 (2) 2/50 (3) 3/65 (4) 4/65 (1) 5/65 (6) 6/65 (5) 7/66 (7) 8/100 (9) 9/107 (8) 10/143 (11) — (44.4 overs)	143	

Bowling: Anderson 10–2–33–1; Johnson 8–2–23–0; Flintoff 9.4–4–14–4; Giles 10–1–29–3; Clarke 6–0–24–1; Blackwell 1–0–2–0.

England

M. E. Trescothick c Hannan Sarkar b Mushfiqur Rahman .	28	(29)	P. D. Collingwood not out.	34	(49)
V. S. Solanki c Jamaluddin Ahmed b Mushfiqur Rahman .	10	(15)	A. Flintoff not out.	55	(52)
*M. P. Vaughan st Khaled Masud b Manjurul Islam Rana .	9	(9)	B 1, l-b 4, w 1, n-b 2 . .	8	
			1/39 (2) (3 wkts, 25.3 overs)	144	
			2/39 (1) 3/55 (3)		

R. Clarke, I. D. Blackwell, †C. M. W. Read, A. F. Giles, R. L. Johnson and J. M. Anderson did not bat.

Bowling: Tapash Baisya 5–0–29–0; Mushfiqur Rahman 6–1–34–2; Manjurul Islam Rana 8–1–33–1; Jamaluddin Ahmed 4–1–28–0; Alok Kapali 2.3–1–15–0.

Umpires: Aleem Dar (Pakistan) and Mahbubur Rahman.
Third umpire: A. F. M. Akhtaruddin. Referee: Wasim Raja (Pakistan).

†BANGLADESH v ENGLAND

Second One-Day International

At Dhaka, November 10, 2003 (day/night). England won by seven wickets. Toss: Bangladesh. One-day international debut: Moniruzzaman.

For the fourth one-day international in five, Flintoff walked off with the match award, as Bangladesh were overwhelmed in a carbon-copy of their defeat at Chittagong. Once again, they won the toss, chose to bat, and floundered after a wretched top-order collapse. Johnson and Anderson grabbed two wickets each in the first ten overs, and at seven for four the match looked over. Rajin Saleh and Mushfiqur Rahman, however, compiled a safety-first partnership of 53 in 20 overs, and Bangladesh batted out their full quota of overs for the only time in the series. But a target of 135 was small change for Flintoff. After three early wickets, he thumped an unbeaten 70 from 47 balls, and in the process equalled Botham's England one-day record of 44 sixes. As yet another defeat unfolded in front of them, the crowd found alternative entertainment in bonfires and food fights.

Man of the Match: A. Flintoff.

Bangladesh

Hannan Sarkar c Collingwood b Anderson .	0	(7)	Manjurul Islam Rana run out . . .	8	(25)
Nafis Iqbal c Read b Johnson . . .	4	(20)	Mohammad Rafiq not out	27	(33)
Moniruzzaman c Read b Anderson	0	(6)	Tapash Baisya not out	12	(13)
Rajin Saleh c Giles b Clarke	37	(77)	B 5, l-b 1, w 7, n-b 1 . .	14	
Alok Kapali c Read b Johnson . .	2	(3)	1/1 (1) 2/3 (3) (9 wkts, 50 overs)	134	
Mushfiqur Rahman b Johnson . . .	22	(93)	3/5 (2) 4/7 (5)		
*Khaled Mahmud lbw b Giles . . .	4	(15)	5/60 (4) 6/69 (7)		
†Khaled Masud c Read b Flintoff .	4	(9)	7/77 (8) 8/80 (6) 9/112 (9)		

Bowling: Anderson 10–4–17–2; Johnson 10–0–22–3; Flintoff 10–2–17–1; Clarke 10–3–35–1; Giles 9–2–32–1; Blackwell 1–0–5–0.

England

M. E. Trescothick b Mushfiqur Rahman .	9	(18)	A. Flintoff not out.	70	(47)
V. S. Solanki lbw b Tapash Baisya	0	(9)	B 4, l-b 2, w 2, n-b 2 . .	10	
*M. P. Vaughan not out	37	(69)	1/5 (2) (3 wkts, 27.4 overs)	137	
P. D. Collingwood b Tapash Baisya	11	(25)	2/19 (1) 3/37 (4)		

R. Clarke, I. D. Blackwell, †C. M. W. Read, A. F. Giles, R. L. Johnson and J. M. Anderson did not bat.

Bowling: Tapash Baisya 7–0–35–2; Mushfiqur Rahman 10–4–28–1; Mohammad Rafiq 5–0–39–0; Khaled Mahmud 3.4–0–22–0; Manjurul Islam Rana 2–0–7–0.

Umpires: Aleem Dar (Pakistan) and A. F. M. Akhtaruddin.
Third umpire: Mahbubur Rahman. Referee: Wasim Raja (Pakistan).

†BANGLADESH v ENGLAND

Third One-Day International

At Dhaka, November 12, 2003 (day/night). England won by seven wickets. Toss: Bangladesh.

Bangladesh's best showing of the series ended in familiar fashion, as Flintoff wrapped up a seven-wicket win for the third match in succession. Once again the contest was an unequal one, but England were at least forced to work for their wickets after they had lost the toss for the eighth time out of eight on tour. The talking point of the innings came in the 34th over, when Bangladesh's besieged captain, Khaled Mahmud, was given out by the third umpire after he and his batting partner, Mushfiqur Rahman, had dived for the same end of the pitch. The decision was greeted with glee by an otherwise subdued crowd. England's target of 183 seemed a long way off when Solanki fell to complete a series tally of 11 runs, but Trescothick eased to 50 before Flintoff strode out to the middle with malice aforethought. He duly crashed a 39-ball half-century, and completed the match and his milestone with successive sixes.

Man of the Match: A. Flintoff.

Man of the Series: A. Flintoff.

ENGLAND'S LEADING SIX-HITTERS IN ONE-DAY INTERNATIONALS

	Sixes	*Matches*		*Sixes*	*Matches*
A. Flintoff	48	66	G. A. Hick	41	120
I. T. Botham	44	116	A. J. Lamb	30	122

Bangladesh

Hannan Sarkar run out	21	(33)
Moniruzzaman c and b Anderson	1	(14)
Habibul Bashar lbw b Clarke	21	(65)
Rajin Saleh c Read b Batty	19	(42)
Mushfiqur Rahman lbw b Flintoff	36	(37)
Alok Kapali b Clarke	2	(7)
*Khaled Mahmud run out	11	(24)
†Khaled Masud b Flintoff	16	(36)
Manjurul Islam Rana not out	20	(21)
Mohammad Rafiq b Kirtley	13	(10)
Tapash Baisya c Collingwood b Kirtley	7	(8)
L-b 2, w 11, n-b 2	15	
1/6 (2) 2/35 (1) 3/66 (3) 4/75 (4) 5/83 (6) 6/103 (7) 7/139 (5) 8/152 (8) 9/172 (10) 10/182 (11) (49.1 overs)	182	

Bowling: Anderson 10–2–36–1; Kirtley 9.1–1–33–2; Flintoff 10–3–32–2; Blackwell 4–0–16–0; Batty 10–0–35–1; Clarke 6–0–28–2.

England

M. E. Trescothick b Khaled Mahmud	50	(70)
V. S. Solanki c Khaled Masud b Mushfiqur Rahman	1	(4)
*M. P. Vaughan lbw b Mushfiqur Rahman	29	(46)
P. D. Collingwood not out	46	(79)
A. Flintoff not out	52	(39)
L-b 3, w 3, n-b 1	7	
1/5 (2) 2/66 (3) 3/102 (1) (3 wkts, 39.3 overs)	185	

R. Clarke, I. D. Blackwell, †C. M. W. Read, G. J. Batty, R. J. Kirtley and J. M. Anderson did not bat.

Bowling: Tapash Baisya 8–0–41–0; Mushfiqur Rahman 10–0–29–2; Khaled Mahmud 10–2–32–1; Manjurul Islam Rana 5–0–33–0; Mohammad Rafiq 6–0–34–0; Hannan Sarkar 0.3–0–13–0.

Umpires: Aleem Dar (Pakistan) and Mahbubur Rahman.
Third umpire: A. F. M. Akhtaruddin. Referee: Wasim Raja (Pakistan).

†At Moratuwa, November 15, 2003. **No result.** Toss: England XI. **England XI 237-8** (38 overs) (A. J. Strauss 83, I. D. Blackwell 63); **Sri Lanka Cricket President's XI 76-1** (17.1 overs)

Anthony McGrath captained the England XI in a match first reduced to 38 overs per side by rain, then abandoned completely.

†SRI LANKA v ENGLAND

First One-Day International

At Dambulla, November 18, 2003 (day/night). Sri Lanka won by ten wickets. Toss: England. One-day international debuts: K. A. D. M. Fernando, K. M. D. N. Kulasekara; A. J. Strauss.

This was an unmitigated disaster for England. After being skittled for 88, their second-lowest total in 385 one-day internationals, they were destroyed by the Sri Lankan openers, who raced to victory in little more than an hour. "We were in it for about 1.2 overs," admitted a sheepish Vaughan. On a pitch that was sluggish but far from unplayable, and against an attack that contained two debutant seamers, England needed a last-wicket stand of 21 between Giles and Anderson to squeeze past their all-time one-day nadir of 86, against Australia at Old Trafford in 2001. It was not the only near-miss in the record books: the 83 balls required by Jayasuriya and Kaluwitharana to knock off the runs represented England's second-fastest defeat, behind the 74-ball sprint by Gilchrist and Hayden for Australia at Sydney ten months earlier. England replaced the out-of-touch Solanki with Strauss, but he provided his fellow-debutant Dinusha Fernando with a return catch in the fourth over, and the rest followed amid a flurry of misjudgments, over-ambition, and world-class fielding, with Jayawardene outstanding; only Collingwood and Giles reached double figures. England managed just four boundaries in 46.1 overs, but Jayasuriya and Kaluwitharana equalled that tally inside three, and went on to smash 13 fours and a six between them to romp home with more than 36 overs to spare. In the steamy Dambulla jungle, the two one-day trophies of the English summer felt a world away.

Man of the Match: W. P. U. J. C. Vaas.

England

M. E. Trescothick c Kulasekara b Vaas	9	(22)
A. J. Strauss c and b Fernando	3	(9)
*M. P. Vaughan b Fernando	2	(19)
P. D. Collingwood c and b Chandana	31	(96)
A. Flintoff c Sangakkara b Vaas	3	(7)
R. Clarke b Kulasekara	2	(19)
I. D. Blackwell c Dilshan b Kulasekara	3	(12)
†C. M. W. Read c Jayawardene b Chandana	0	(11)
A. F. Giles c Jayawardene b Vaas	21	(54)
R. L. Johnson b Muralitharan	6	(12)
J. M. Anderson not out	4	(16)
W 4	4	
1/8 (2) 2/12 (1) 3/17 (3) 4/26 (5) 5/36 (6) 6/44 (7) 7/45 (8) 8/59 (4) 9/67 (10) 10/88 (9)	(46.1 overs) 88	

Bowling: Vaas 9.1–2–15–3; Fernando 7–2–13–2; Muralitharan 10–0–15–1; Kulasekara 9–1–19–2; Chandana 10–1–23–2; Jayasuriya 1–0–3–0.

Sri Lanka

S. T. Jayasuriya not out	46	(41)
†R. S. Kaluwitharana not out	36	(42)
W 7	7	
(no wkt, 13.5 overs)	89	

*M. S. Atapattu, K. C. Sangakkara, D. P. M. D. Jayawardene, T. M. Dilshan, U. D. U. Chandana, W. P. U. J. C. Vaas, K. A. D. M. Fernando, M. Muralitharan and K. M. D. N. Kulasekara did not bat.

Bowling: Anderson 5–0–25–0; Johnson 3–1–17–0; Flintoff 3.5–0–27–0; Clarke 2–0–20–0.

Umpires: D. J. Harper (Australia) and T. H. Wijewardene.
Third umpire: M. G. Silva. Referee: C. H. Lloyd (West Indies).

†SRI LANKA v ENGLAND

Second One-Day International

At R. Premadasa Stadium, Colombo, November 21, 2003 (day/night). No result.

The folly of staging cricket during Colombo's wet season was all too evident when the teams arrived at the Premadasa Stadium to find that parts of the outfield had been rendered a boggy mess by rain in the preceding week. Attempts to get the game under way were wrecked by further showers. Any chance of holding the match the following day had already fallen by the wayside after a disagreement between the two boards: Sri Lanka had insisted that any new game start afresh, while England wanted a continuation of whatever play might have been possible. It left Vaughan expressing concern about the scheduling of the series and the quality of the pitch covering.

†SRI LANKA v ENGLAND

Third One-Day International

At R. Premadasa Stadium, Colombo, November 23, 2003 (day/night). No result.

Following the twice-aborted final of the ICC Champions Trophy between Sri Lanka and India in September 2002, this was the fourth time in four one-day internationals at the Premadasa Stadium that the monsoon had had the final say. Hopes of a prompt start were dashed when steady drizzle began to fall at lunchtime. Then the shower turned into an apocalyptic electrical storm. Sri Lanka's 1–0 series win gave Vaughan his first failure in four one-day series as captain.

SRI LANKA CRICKET PRESIDENT'S XI v ENGLAND XI

At Maitland Crescent, Colombo, November 26, 27, 28, 2003. Drawn. Toss: Sri Lanka Cricket President's XI.

Butcher's unbeaten 151 was the centrepiece of a game that was never allowed to develop, as Sri Lanka's regular-as-clockwork weather prevented any play after tea on each of the three days. Butcher had been in shaky form throughout the Bangladesh series, but put that behind him with a superb array of strokes that bore all the hallmarks of his finest touch and timing. The first day of the match, however, belonged to Kirtley, a bowler who would not even have remained on tour had Anderson not twisted his ankle playing squash. He grabbed four for six in his first six overs, with a fine display of skiddy, wicket-to-wicket fast bowling of which Darren Gough would have approved. The second innings was a three-way shootout between England's spinners. Giles, Batty and Croft all picked up a wicket apiece before the rains arrived, but for Croft it proved to be the final act of his England career – he would announce his retirement after being overlooked for all three Tests. In the absence of Vaughan and Trescothick, England were captained for the first time in first-class cricket by Flintoff, and gave a representative debut to Read's understudy, Geraint Jones, who responded with two smart stumpings.

Close of play: First day, Sri Lanka Cricket President's XI 142-8 (Perera 29); Second day, England XI 225-5 (Butcher 105, Jones 4).

> "Players are given stern pre-match warnings against hitting the throne for reasons of cultural sensitivity."
>
> Cricket Round the World, page 1438.

Sri Lanka Cricket President's XI

Batsman	First innings		Second innings	
M. G. Vandort	lbw b Kirtley	1	c Kirtley b Batty	42
T. K. D. Sudarshana	c Jones b Kirtley	5	lbw b Kirtley	19
L. P. C. Silva	c Jones b Kirtley	0	c Thorpe b Giles	31
*R. P. Arnold	c Batty b Kirtley	27		
T. T. Samaraweera	c Hussain b Batty	32	(4) not out	18
W. M. B. Perera	not out	55	(5) c Read b Croft	1
†T. R. Peiris	lbw b Giles	27	(6) not out	19
D. G. R. Dhammika	st Jones b Giles	0		
C. R. D. Fernando	lbw b Giles	5		
M. K. G. C. P. Lakshitha	c Batty b Flintoff	5		
P. N. Ranjith	st Jones b Batty	8		
	L-b 7, n-b 9	16	B 2, l-b 2, n-b 1	5
	1/3 (1) 2/6 (3) 3/19 (2) 4/69 (4) 5/86 (5) 6/128 (7) 7/128 (8) 8/142 (9) 9/152 (10) 10/181 (11)	181	1/57 (2) 2/62 (1) 3/103 (3) 4/110 (5)	(4 wkts) 135

Bowling: *First Innings*—Hoggard 11–3–22–0; Kirtley 14–3–41–4; Giles 15–8–25–3; Flintoff 9–1–32–1; Batty 11.5–2–31–2; Croft 7–1–23–0. *Second Innings*—Hoggard 5–0–22–0; Kirtley 6–1–22–1; Batty 13–2–29–1; Giles 8–2–31–1; Flintoff 5–1–9–0; Croft 7–2–18–1.

England XI

M. A. Butcher	not out	151
N. Hussain	b Fernando	0
G. P. Thorpe	c Peiris b Fernando	35
*A. Flintoff	c Lakshitha b Perera	47
C. M. W. Read	run out	3
G. J. Batty	run out	8
†G. O. Jones	b Fernando	5
A. F. Giles	b Lakshitha	30
R. D. B. Croft	lbw b Dhammika	0
M. J. Hoggard	lbw b Lakshitha	4
R. J. Kirtley	not out	0
	B 4, l-b 11, n-b 16	31
	1/3 (2) 2/96 (3) 3/189 (4) 4/200 (5) 5/211 (6) 6/229 (7) 7/284 (8) 8/285 (9) 9/294 (10)	(9 wkts dec.) 314

Bowling: Fernando 21–6–79–3; Ranjith 7–0–57–0; Lakshitha 13–4–47–2; Samaraweera 14–4–51–0; Dhammika 14.3–2–58–1; Perera 2–1–7–1.

Umpires: A. G. Dissanayake and C. B. C. Rodrigo.

SRI LANKA v ENGLAND

First Test Match

LAWRENCE BOOTH

At Galle, December 2, 3, 4, 5, 6, 2003. Drawn. Toss: Sri Lanka. Test debuts: K. A. D. M. Fernando; P. D. Collingwood.

Drawn Test matches rarely set the pulse racing. This one nearly induced several coronaries. At tea on the final day, Sri Lanka were three wickets away from completing a sixth successive victory at Galle. Instead, England's tailenders launched one of the most improbable rearguards in Test history. When, after much agonising, the umpires offered the light to the final pair at 5.42 p.m., a huge English cheer echoed off the walls of the old Dutch fort that guards the stadium. It was a mixture of relief and disbelief, but not necessarily in that order.

Next one, please: Muttiah Muralitharan spun out seven Englishmen at a cost of 46 in their first innings at Galle, the best bowling figures at the ground.
Picture by Graham Morris.

England's week had ended as it began: with a heroic rescue act. Two days before the start of the Test, their off-spinner Gareth Batty was saved from drowning by lifeguards after he was caught in a strong cross-current while body-surfing. Back on terra firma six days later, Batty was one of the saviours himself, although by that stage he was used to swimming against the tide.

The Sri Lankans were devastated. As Giles and Hoggard marched briskly to the pavilion, where the England balcony was awash with hugs and high-fives, the fielders lingered in the middle, urging the umpires to double-check their light meters. They had enjoyed the best of the game, but the worst of the umpiring; one home estimate made the error count ten–two in England's favour. Placatory in public, the Sri Lankans were furious in private.

Sri Lanka were favourites from the moment Tillekeratne won a crucial toss. They packed their side with five spinners, and handed a Test debut to the fast bowler Dinusha Fernando. England played just two spinners – Giles and Batty – and gave a first Test cap to Paul Collingwood, a last-minute replacement for Hussain, who was suffering from flu and missed his first overseas Test for 41 matches.

Three wickets from the rejuvenated Giles helped England shade a rain-affected first day after Sri Lanka's openers had put on a studious 76. The classy Sangakkara fought back with 71, but when Flintoff struck in consecutive overs before lunch on the second day to make it 239 for seven, the initiative was England's. Tail-end resistance, however, was to become a theme of the series. Dharmasena and Vaas added 40, before Muralitharan made hay with an agricultural run-a-ball 38.

But his work for the day was not done. Trescothick and Vaughan raced to fifty, only for Muralitharan to have Trescothick caught behind – fortuitously, replays suggested. Soon afterwards, he bowled Vaughan through his legs as he attempted to pad away a big off-break. It was a huge psychological blow, and the effects reverberated for the rest of the series.

On the third morning, Butcher, dropped by the bowler Muralitharan on 18, and Thorpe, given not out when he edged Jayasuriya to slip on 29, somehow extended their partnership to 75. But when the resourceful Vaas removed Thorpe, England crumbled, losing eight for 93. Muralitharan embarrassed an inexperienced middle order with liberal use of the wrong'un, then mopped up a swishing tail to finish with seven for 46, Galle's best Test figures. Butcher said later he and Thorpe had read him only half the time.

Sri Lanka led by 96, but were in danger of throwing away their advantage when they slipped to 85 for five. But Jayawardene shared in a succession of middle-sized stands, including 46 with Muralitharan, whose two Keystone Cops innings had helped tack 86 on to England's eventual target of 323. Jayawardene batted for more than five hours of selfless grind and was the only player who showed any confidence handling Giles, whose Test-best match haul of eight for 132 represented something of a rebirth.

He was not, however, the No. 1 spinner in the match, although England's task of keeping out Murali was made easier when rain ended the fourth day early, enabling them to enter the final day, delayed by half an hour because of a wet patch on the outfield, with all ten wickets intact. But Vaughan edged a leaden-footed drive, and Trescothick and Thorpe fell to slogs that would have been more at home in a one-day game.

Lunch was taken at 84 for three, yet it could have been worse. In the final over of the session, the third umpire, Gamini Silva, was asked to rule on whether Collingwood's deflection to silly point was a bump-ball. It was not – but Silva strayed beyond his brief by deciding that Collingwood, four at the time, had not touched the ball. Crucially, he would frustrate Sri Lanka for another 44 overs.

Even so, the decision did not seem to matter when Vaas removed Butcher, for another gutsy half-century, and Flintoff in successive overs; nor when Read and Collingwood followed before tea. But Batty hung around for an hour, and although he spoiled things by heaving across the line to give Muralitharan ten wickets in a Test for the 12th time, Sri Lanka's bowlers were fading, and so was the light.

As England tried every trick in the book to slow down the over-rate, and the umpires tested the light with over-officious regularity, the Sri Lankans became increasingly exasperated, particularly at umpire Venkat's refusal to uphold a series of stomach-churning shouts for leg-before.

Johnson kept Giles company for 41 minutes before agonisingly playing on, and it was left to Hoggard, trudging slowly out amid the catcalls, to play out a tense maiden from Muralitharan, who finished with 11 for 93. One more over from Jayasuriya to Giles and, with four overs remaining, the umpires consulted for the last time. Moments later, heavy rain began to fall.

Man of the Match: M. Muralitharan.

Close of play: First day, Sri Lanka 138-4 (Sangakkara 39, Samaraweera 1); Second day, England 97-2 (Butcher 15, Thorpe 20); Third day, Sri Lanka 99-5 (Jayawardene 14, Vaas 6); Fourth day, England 4-0 (Trescothick 4, Vaughan 0).

Sri Lanka

First innings		Second innings	
M. S. Atapattu c Read b Flintoff	29	st Read b Batty	35
S. T. Jayasuriya c Collingwood b Giles	48	c Trescothick b Giles	17
†K. C. Sangakkara lbw b Johnson	71	run out	19
D. P. M. D. Jayawardene c Collingwood b Giles	17	not out	86
*H. P. Tillekeratne c Read b Giles	0	lbw b Batty	1
T. T. Samaraweera c Read b Flintoff	45	c Trescothick b Giles	1
U. D. U. Chandana lbw b Flintoff	21	(8) lbw b Giles	19
H. D. P. K. Dharmasena lbw b Batty	27	(9) lbw b Hoggard	2
W. P. U. J. C. Vaas not out	22	(7) c Collingwood b Giles	19
K. A. D. M. Fernando c Collingwood b Batty	4	c Trescothick b Flintoff	1
M. Muralitharan c Read b Giles	38	c Collingwood b Batty	13
B 5, l-b 2, w 1, n-b 1	9	B 4, l-b 9	13
1/76 (2) 2/88 (1) 3/132 (4) 4/132 (5) 5/202 (3) 6/238 (6) 7/239 (7) 8/279 (8) 9/291 (10) 10/331 (11)	331	1/26 (2) 2/72 (3) 3/72 (1) 4/78 (5) 5/85 (6) 6/123 (7) 7/163 (8) 8/179 (9) 9/180 (10) 10/226 (11)	226

Bowling: *First Innings*—Hoggard 20–4–49–0; Johnson 17–5–54–1; Flintoff 23–7–42–3; Collingwood 4–0–12–0; Batty 31–5–98–2; Giles 32.5–9–69–4. *Second Innings*—Hoggard 9–2–33–1; Johnson 7–2–28–0; Flintoff 17–5–32–1; Giles 40–14–63–4; Batty 23.2–7–55–3; Vaughan 1–0–2–0.

England

First innings		Second innings	
M. E. Trescothick c Sangakkara b Muralitharan	23	b Jayasuriya	24
*M. P. Vaughan b Muralitharan	24	c Tillekeratne b Fernando	8
M. A. Butcher c Sangakkara b Jayasuriya	51	c Sangakkara b Vaas	54
G. P. Thorpe lbw b Vaas	43	c Vaas b Muralitharan	10
P. D. Collingwood c Jayasuriya b Muralitharan	1	c Tillekeratne b Dharmasena	36
A. Flintoff lbw b Muralitharan	1	c Tillekeratne b Vaas	0
†C. M. W. Read c Tillekeratne b Muralitharan	0	c Jayawardene b Muralitharan	14
G. J. Batty c Jayasuriya b Dharmasena	14	b Muralitharan	26
A. F. Giles c Atapattu b Muralitharan	18	not out	17
R. L. Johnson c Atapattu b Muralitharan	26	b Muralitharan	3
M. J. Hoggard not out	6	not out	0
B 12, l-b 8, n-b 8	28	B 10, l-b 1, n-b 7	18
1/56 (1) 2/67 (2) 3/142 (4) 4/143 (5) 5/151 (6) 6/155 (7) 7/177 (3) 8/183 (8) 9/208 (9) 10/235 (10)	235	1/16 (2) 2/62 (1) 3/73 (4) 4/125 (3) 5/125 (6) 6/148 (7) 7/170 (5) 8/204 (8) 9/208 (10) (9 wkts)	210

Bowling: *First Innings*—Vaas 12–2–25–1; Fernando 3–1–21–0; Dharmasena 24–6–55–1; Muralitharan 31.4–15–46–7; Chandana 13–2–24–0; Jayasuriya 17–2–44–1. *Second Innings*—Vaas 14–4–23–2; Fernando 4–0–29–1; Samaraweera 3–1–9–0; Jayasuriya 21–5–31–1; Muralitharan 37–18–47–4; Chandana 11–2–24–0; Dharmasena 18–8–36–1.

Umpires: D. J. Harper (Australia) and S. Venkataraghavan (India).
Third umpire: M. G. Silva. Referee: C. H. Lloyd (West Indies).

“‘There were at least two outbreaks of cannibalism among the spectators... which I am convinced were responsible for the loss of our most promising young leg-spinner, M. M. Rudman-Stott.’”

Obituaries, page 1559.

SRI LANKA v ENGLAND

Second Test Match

ANDREW MILLER

At Kandy, December 10, 11, 12, 13, 14, 2003. Drawn. Toss: Sri Lanka.

Maybe familiarity breeds contempt, but England's second great escape in consecutive matches somehow failed to capture the imagination in the manner of their magnificent rearguard at Galle. Maybe that is doing a gross disservice to Vaughan, who exuded such an inhumanly calm aura in compiling his first century as England captain that he made it all look too easy. But Sri Lanka themselves added to the anticlimax, with field placings on the final day that were defensive in the extreme and transmitted an air of indifference.

Vaughan later described his match-saving 105, from 448 minutes and 333 balls, as the finest innings of his career. He had gone 15 innings as captain without adding to his tally of nine centuries, but responded to the wagging tongues with an effort that evoked memories of Mike Atherton's legendary performance at Johannesburg in December 1995. England's hopes of victory had ended on the second day of the match, and they were eventually left with four sessions to survive and a nominal target of 368. But Vaughan exuded his trademark cool under fire, and nonchalantly led his side to safety.

In fact, it was all so serene that Sri Lanka's coach, John Dyson, said he was "staggered" England did not push for victory on a fifth-day wicket that had not deteriorated dramatically. But the negative approach – if it could be labelled as such – was merely in keeping with a strangely muted match. The most explosive moments centred around Vaughan's predecessor Hussain, and what he may or may not have said to Muralitharan; the most intriguing episode came five days later, when a stash of banknotes – worth around £7,000 – were found in a hotel room that had earlier been occupied by Atapattu.

Right from the start of the match, a draw had been the upper limit of England's ambitions. Hussain's return from illness, coupled with Collingwood's impressive debut at Galle, meant that six specialist batsmen were shoehorned into the team at the expense of a seam bowler. Neither Hoggard nor Johnson deserved to be singled out, but both were given the heave-ho in favour of the willing understudy Kirtley, who was thrust in ahead of the more mercurial Anderson.

For two sessions, the motley crew made hay. As if on cue, Vaughan lost the toss for the seventh time in eight Tests, but Kirtley buzzed and Flintoff bulldozed with the new ball, and Sri Lanka slid to 206 for six. England did, however, owe their position to several moments of good luck, not least a dreadful mix-up that resulted in Sangakkara's run-out. And in picking up the wickets of Jayasuriya and Samaraweera en route to a five-wicket haul, Giles twice benefited from umpire Harper's generosity, which so incensed the Sri Lankan management that they complained to the ICC.

By the time that letter was sent, however, Sri Lanka were 277 for seven, and the initiative had been stolen from England's tiring attack. A stroke-filled 63 from Dilshan had hinted at the scoring opportunities on offer, but it was a seventh-wicket stand of 64 between Tillekeratne and Vaas that really took the game away from England. When the usually mild-mannered Kirtley snared Vaas in the dying overs of the day, his in-your-face celebration was an indication of England's struggles; it earned him a date with Clive Lloyd, the match referee, as well.

Lloyd was a busy man on the second afternoon, when the match reached its false summit of excitement. A ninth-wicket partnership of 76 had already pushed Sri Lanka's total into the realms of the unreachable, when Muralitharan strolled out to join the unheralded Dinusha Fernando, who was fast approaching his maiden half-century. In what was later assumed to have been a premeditated strike, Hussain was alleged to have

Kandy is dandy: the Sri Lankans are cock-a-hoop at dismissing Michael Vaughan for a defiant hundred, but the England tail hung on – again.
Picture by Graham Morris.

sworn at Murali, calling him an "effing cheat and an effing chucker". The TV evidence was inconclusive and, for that reason alone, Hussain escaped without penalty. But the incident soured relations between the teams and reduced Hussain's personal standing in a country that had previously held him in the highest regard. An editorial in one local paper warned him: "Tread lightly, old boy, tread lightly and mind your manners."

In response, the England camp attempted to ridicule Murali for "telling tales out of school", as Thorpe put it. It all added to the tension as they prepared to face him. Although Vaughan and Trescothick launched England's reply with panache, Murali accounted for both before pinning Thorpe with a deliciously disguised doosra that sent tremors through the England dressing-room. He finished with four for 60 from 40 overs, and Sri Lanka had secured a potentially decisive first-innings lead of 88.

With just over two days remaining, Sri Lanka had a window of opportunity, and in Dilshan, they had just the man to jump through it. Dilshan's only previous Test century had come four years earlier, against Zimbabwe, but you would not have known it from the way he bombarded the off-side boundary with furious cuts and free-flowing drives. After the tentative tempo of the first three days, Dilshan's 100 from 129 balls represented a sudden breakout.

Despite Dyson's claims, an English victory was an absurd notion – their highest winning fourth-innings total was a mere 332 for seven, a record that had stood for 75 years. But with Vaughan in such wonderful form, no figure was beyond the bounds of feasibility as far as Tillekeratne was concerned. Even when Hussain fell to the fourth ball of the final morning, he persisted with a solitary slip and five men on the boundary. It was a baffling tactic, one that enabled England to block to their hearts' content.

All the same, it took every shred of England's collective will to see off Murali, who twirled his way through another 56 overs in the second innings for match figures of 96–46–124–8. Though he tired towards the end, his fielders were unstinting in their enthusiasm, not least Sangakkara, who earned himself a ticking-off for excessive appealing, but not before he had successfully completed the stumping of Butcher for the second time in the match – something that had happened only once in a Test since 1956.

STUMPED TWICE IN A TEST

Mark Butcher was the 16th player in Test history to be stumped in both innings of a Test. Instances since the Second World War:

Batsman	*Wicket-keeper*		
W. Place	C. L. Walcott	England v West Indies at Kingston	1947-48
H. J. Tayfield	R. A. Saggers	South Africa v Australia at Port Elizabeth	1949-50
F. M. M. Worrell	T. G. Evans	West Indies v England at Manchester	1950
M. J. Hilton	P. Sen	England v India at Madras	1951-52
R. J. Christiani	P. G. Joshi	West Indies v India at Bridgetown	1952-53
B. Sutcliffe	C. C. Depeiza	New Zealand v India at Christchurch	1955-56
P. J. L. Dujon	K. S. More	West Indies v India at Madras	1987-88
M. A. Butcher	**K. C. Sangakkara**	**England v Sri Lanka at Kandy**	**2003-04**

Thorpe's second important innings of the match ended unluckily, caught behind off his front pad, and when Vaughan himself fell to the slightest of misjudgments with 25 overs remaining, Sri Lanka's patient approach seemed sure to pay off. But Batty and Read manned the barriers for the final hour of England's resistance, aided to the bitter end by Tillekeratne's peculiar reticence.

Man of the Match: M. P. Vaughan.

Close of play: First day, Sri Lanka 277-7 (Tillekeratne 45, Dharmasena 1); Second day, England 163-4 (Thorpe 20, Collingwood 19); Third day, Sri Lanka 39-1 (Jayasuriya 25, Sangakkara 1); Fourth day, England 89-2 (Vaughan 50, Hussain 17).

Sri Lanka

M. S. Atapattu lbw b Kirtley	11	– lbw b Giles	8
S. T. Jayasuriya c Read b Giles	32	– b Kirtley	27
†K. C. Sangakkara run out	34	– c Collingwood b Giles	10
D. P. M. D. Jayawardene c Kirtley b Giles	45	– b Flintoff	52
T. M. Dilshan c Trescothick b Flintoff	63	– st Read b Batty	100
*H. P. Tillekeratne c Butcher b Flintoff	45	– c Thorpe b Giles	20
T. T. Samaraweera lbw b Giles	3	– not out	23
W. P. U. J. C. Vaas lbw b Kirtley	32	– c Vaughan b Kirtley	20
H. D. P. K. Dharmasena lbw b Giles	29	– not out	7
K. A. D. M. Fernando not out	51		
M. Muralitharan b Giles	19		
B 1, l-b 15, n-b 2	18	L-b 6, w 1, n-b 5	12
1/20 (1) 2/76 (3) 3/84 (2) 4/187 (4) 5/201 (5) 6/206 (7) 7/270 (8) 8/278 (6) 9/354 (9) 10/382 (11)	382	1/33 (1) 2/41 (2) 3/53 (3) 4/206 (5) 5/212 (4) 6/243 (6) 7/272 (8) (7 wkts dec.)	279

Bowling: *First Innings*—Kirtley 33–10–109–2; Flintoff 24–5–60–2; Giles 37.4–7–116–5; Collingwood 9–3–13–0; Batty 18–3–59–0; Vaughan 5–0–9–0. *Second Innings*—Kirtley 17–4–62–2; Flintoff 15–3–40–1; Giles 22–3–101–3; Batty 11–1–47–1; Vaughan 3–0–11–0; Collingwood 3–0–12–0.

England

M. E. Trescothick c Dilshan b Muralitharan	36	– c Jayawardene b Vaas	14
*M. P. Vaughan c Jayawardene b Muralitharan	52	– c Dilshan b Muralitharan	105
M. A. Butcher st Sangakkara b Dharmasena	4	– st Sangakkara b Muralitharan	6
N. Hussain lbw b Vaas	10	– c Sangakkara b Vaas	17
G. P. Thorpe lbw b Muralitharan	57	– c Sangakkara b Muralitharan	41
P. D. Collingwood c Sangakkara b Vaas	28	– c Jayawardene b Dharmasena	24
A. Flintoff b Muralitharan	16	– lbw b Muralitharan	19
†C. M. W. Read lbw b Jayasuriya	0	– not out	18
G. J. Batty c Dilshan b Vaas	38	– not out	25
A. F. Giles c Jayawardene b Vaas	16		
R. J. Kirtley not out	3		
B 16, l-b 10, n-b 8	34	B 5, l-b 6, n-b 5	16
1/89 (1) 2/100 (3) 3/119 (2) 4/119 (4) 5/177 (6) 6/202 (7) 7/205 (8) 8/256 (5) 9/279 (10) 10/294 (9)	294	1/24 (1) 2/50 (3) 3/90 (4) 4/167 (5) 5/208 (6) 6/233 (7) 7/239 (2) (7 wkts)	285

Bowling: *First Innings*—Vaas 24.2–4–77–4; Fernando 7–0–36–0; Dharmasena 19–3–63–1; Muralitharan 40–18–60–4; Jayasuriya 24–6–32–1. *Second Innings*—Vaas 29–7–59–2; Fernando 7–1–21–0; Dharmasena 26–2–74–1; Muralitharan 56–28–64–4; Jayasuriya 17–2–45–0; Tillekeratne 1–0–1–0; Samaraweera 1–1–0–0; Dilshan 3–1–10–0.

Umpires: Aleem Dar (Pakistan) and D. J. Harper (Australia).
Third umpire: P. T. Manuel. Referee: C. H. Lloyd (West Indies).

SRI LANKA v ENGLAND

Third Test Match

LAWRENCE BOOTH

At Sinhalese Sports Club, Colombo, December 18, 19, 20, 21, 2003. Sri Lanka won by an innings and 215 runs. Toss: England.

England arrived in Colombo full of optimism. They left dazed and confused, having suffered their third-heaviest defeat in 127 years of Test cricket and their first series loss under Vaughan's captaincy. After the energy-sapping escape acts of the first two Tests, they played with as much edge as a lump of plasticine.

For Sri Lanka – and not least for their captain, Tillekeratne, whose conservative brand of leadership had roused the critics – it was a delightful surprise. After failing to beat anyone but Bangladesh since March 2002, they pulled off the most crushing win in their history. To beat England in a proper series for the first time was merely a bonus.

There was little sign of the grim fate that awaited Vaughan's men when he won England's first toss in Sri Lanka for ten years, then helped bring up a freewheeling fifty in only the ninth over. In the pre-match build-up, the Sri Lanka coach, John Dyson, had accused England of rekindling a duller, more defensive era of Test cricket. But for the first hour at least, that accusation seemed absurd.

Then it all went wrong. Vaughan nicked a leg-break, and Trescothick, who had crashed 11 fours in a 39-ball half-century, edged the last ball before lunch to slip. Less than an hour later, on a pitch that should have reduced the bowlers to tears, England were an eye-watering 139 for five: Butcher thin-edged Dilhara Fernando, who had replaced his namesake Dinusha; Hussain, who had been lucky to squeeze Collingwood out of the team, was less fortunate when Vaas won a dubious lbw decision; and Thorpe misread Muralitharan's doosra.

Outside the ground there was chaos too, as police prevented a group of Buddhist monks from storming the stadium. The monks were furious that the cricket had not

Colombo epic: Thilan Samaraweera faced 408 balls for his career-best 142, and with Mahela Jayawardene batted England out of the Third Test.
Picture by Graham Morris.

been halted out of respect for a well-known colleague, the Venerable Gangodavila Soma Thera, who had died the previous week. Deprived of spiritual assistance, England had to make do with Flintoff and Batty, who now embarked on a damage-limitation stand of 87.

Flintoff, averaging less than seven in Asia, dealt patiently with the impossibly economical Muralitharan but showed scant regard for the rest. He mowed Chandana over mid-wicket, reached his half-century with a flick-pull off Vaas for six more, then launched Chandana down the ground for a third. But in the same over, the otherwise patient Batty pulled a long-hop straight to mid-wicket, where Atapattu held on, splitting the webbing in his left hand in the process. After Flintoff gave Muralitharan a simple return catch to depart for a 109-ball 77 containing four sixes and ten fours, resistance was minimal. When Vaas wrapped up the tail on the second morning, the last five wickets had fallen for 39.

England's 265 was quickly put into perspective. Jayasuriya and Sangakkara waltzed to fifty, and although Sangakkara edged Kirtley to slip soon afterwards, it proved an illusory breakthrough. Jayasuriya, back to his swashbuckling best, added 67 with Samaraweera before edging a full-length delivery from Flintoff to Trescothick at slip. But English heads were already drooping. Two overs earlier, Trescothick had missed Samaraweera on 12. And as England's limited attack toiled in the afternoon heat, he did it again, this time on 46. After two days, Sri Lanka trailed by a single run, and Samaraweera and Jayawardene were doing as they pleased.

Even the night-time provided no respite. The hotel management allowed a noisy party to go on till the early hours, infuriating the England players, and on the third morning they duly fielded like insomniacs. Giles dropped Jayawardene at fine leg on 74, before Trescothick completed a hat-trick of slip fumbles off Samaraweera, then on 98. The fluent Jayawardene had just completed his tenth Test hundred, from 206 balls, and two overs later Samaraweera registered his third – all three at the SSC – from 345. By the time Jayawardene pulled the deserving Flintoff to deep square leg, the pair had added 262. Dilshan and Chandana then danced on English graves with a light-hearted stand of 126.

The declaration came at 628 for eight, Sri Lanka's second-highest Test score, which left England needing 363 to avoid an innings defeat – or five and a half sessions to survive. They held out for just over two. Trescothick steered Vaas's sixth ball to point, Vaughan mistimed Fernando to cover, and when Hussain was given out caught behind to make it 44 for three, Muralitharan became the first bowler to take 100 wickets at a single Test venue.

The rest followed like lost sheep. Thorpe (on the charge) and Batty (the victim of a marginal call by the third umpire) were stumped off successive balls from Muralitharan, who would have had a hat-trick had Flintoff's inside edge not cannoned off his pad over the head of silly point. But it was merely delaying the inevitable, and when Kirtley was bowled through the gate to give Muralitharan his 26th wicket of the series, Sri Lanka were home and dry with more than a day to spare. It was no more than they deserved.

Man of the Match: T. T. Samaraweera.

Man of the Series: M. Muralitharan.

Close of play: First day, England 259-8 (Read 13, Kirtley 1); Second day, Sri Lanka 264-2 (Samaraweera 68, Jayawardene 60); Third day, Sri Lanka 563-5 (Dilshan 72, Chandana 54).

England

First innings		Second innings	
M. E. Trescothick c Jayawardene b Muralitharan	70	c sub (M. G. Vandort) b Vaas	0
*M. P. Vaughan c Jayawardene b Chandana	18	c Jayasuriya b Fernando	14
M. A. Butcher c Sangakkara b Fernando	23	b Jayasuriya	37
N. Hussain lbw b Vaas	8	c Sangakkara b Muralitharan	11
G. P. Thorpe lbw b Muralitharan	13	st Sangakkara b Muralitharan	19
A. Flintoff c and b Muralitharan	77	(7) c Sangakkara b Fernando	30
G. J. Batty c Atapattu b Chandana	14	(6) st Sangakkara b Muralitharan	0
†C. M. W. Read not out	17	lbw b Jayasuriya	0
A. F. Giles run out	10	b Fernando	13
R. J. Kirtley lbw b Vaas	1	b Muralitharan	12
J. M. Anderson lbw b Vaas	1	not out	1
B 4, l-b 8, n-b 1	13	B 2, l-b 8, n-b 1	11
1/78 (2) 2/108 (1) 3/114 (3) 4/135 (4) 5/139 (5) 6/226 (7) 7/236 (6) 8/258 (9) 9/259 (10) 10/265 (11)	265	1/0 (1) 2/22 (2) 3/44 (4) 4/82 (5) 5/82 (6) 6/84 (3) 7/84 (8) 8/124 (9) 9/137 (7) 10/148 (10)	148

Bowling: *First Innings*—Vaas 17–5–64–3; Fernando 12–3–55–1; Samaraweera 4–1–11–0; Chandana 26–7–82–2; Muralitharan 40–21–40–3; Jayasuriya 2–1–1–0. *Second Innings*—Vaas 7–2–25–1; Fernando 12–4–27–3; Chandana 13–7–18–0; Muralitharan 27–9–63–4; Jayasuriya 9–6–5–2.

Sri Lanka

†K. C. Sangakkara c Trescothick b Kirtley 31
S. T. Jayasuriya c Trescothick b Flintoff . 85
T. T. Samaraweera run out 142
D. P. M. D. Jayawardene
c sub (P. D. Collingwood) b Flintoff . 134
T. M. Dilshan b Giles 83
*H. P. Tillekeratne b Giles 12
U. D. U. Chandana c Vaughan b Kirtley . 76
W. P. U. J. C. Vaas run out. 9
M. Muralitharan not out 21
C. R. D. Fernando not out 1

B 7, l-b 16, w 5, n-b 6. 34

1/71 (1) 2/138 (2) (8 wkts dec.) 628
3/400 (4) 4/428 (3)
5/456 (6) 6/582 (5)
7/605 (8) 8/606 (7)

M. S. Atapattu did not bat.

Bowling: Kirtley 31–4–131–2; Anderson 24–5–85–0; Flintoff 18–0–47–2; Giles 65–16–190–2; Batty 41–4–137–0; Vaughan 1–0–5–0; Trescothick 2–0–10–0.

Umpires: Aleem Dar (Pakistan) and S. A. Bucknor (West Indies).
Third umpire: T. H. Wijewardene. Referee: C. H. Lloyd (West Indies).

THE BANGLADESHIS IN SOUTH AFRICA, 2002-03

MARCUS PRIOR

On the eve of South Africa's fateful World Cup game against Sri Lanka at Durban in March 2003 – the rain-affected tie that threw them ignominiously out of the tournament – the Sri Lankans were unamused to see a poster outside their dressing-room. "When little dogs play with big dogs," it read, "it's better they stay indoors." If the patronising sentiment proved wholly misplaced at Kingsmead, it did perhaps have some relevance during Bangladesh's visit five months earlier.

True, the tourists were up against one of the wolfhounds of world cricket, but they never came close to mounting a credible challenge during three one-day internationals or two horribly one-sided Tests.

Perhaps it really would have been better if they had stayed indoors. As soon as Bangladesh emerged from the pavilion, they were mercilessly, predictably and often tediously put to the sword. Time and again, from both sides, came the mantra that they would learn from the experience, that they could only improve by playing against the best, that there was genuine talent in the squad. But it wore thin.

South Africa took the opportunity to blood two players and two Test grounds. Martin van Jaarsveld appeared in both forms of the game, while Ashwell Prince made his one-day debut; their performances were inconclusive. Meanwhile, Buffalo Park in East London and the North West Cricket Stadium in Potchefstroom became Test cricket's 85th and 86th venues but they did not enjoy the financial benefits of higher-profile opposition.

Still, several South Africans cashed in, record-wise, and gave their statistics a healthy if questionable boost. Herschelle Gibbs was denied a record fourth consecutive one-day hundred by a wild wide from leg-spinner Alok Kapali, Gary Kirsten became the first batsman to score hundreds against all nine Test opponents, and Jacques Kallis ground on, scoring 214 unbeaten runs in the two five-day games, which altogether lasted less than six.

For Bangladesh, comfort came in crumbs rather than chunks. There were encouraging signs from their young seam bowlers, Talha Jubair and Tapash Baisya, as well as welcome signs of solidity in the batting. But they all struggled against the accuracy and hostility of Makhaya Ntini.

BANGLADESHI TOURING PARTY

Khaled Masud (Rajshahi) (*captain*), Alok Kapali (Sylhet), Al Sahariar (Dhaka), Anwar Hossain Monir (Dhaka), Habibul Bashar (Biman), Hannan Sarkar (Barisal), Javed Omar (Dhaka), Khaled Mahmud (Dhaka), Manjurul Islam (Khulna), Mohammad Rafiq (Dhaka), Rafiqul Islam (Rajshahi), Sanwar Hossain (Barisal), Talha Jubair (Bangladesh A), Tapash Baisya (Sylhet), Tushar Imran (Khulna).

Coach: Mohsin Kamal. *Manager:* A. S. M. Faruque.
Assistant coach: Ali Zia. *Physiotherapist:* J. Gloster.

BANGLADESHI TOUR RESULTS

Test matches – Played 2: Lost 2.
One-day internationals – Played 3: Lost 3.
Other non-first-class matches – Played 4: Won 3, Lost 1. *Wins* – N. F. Oppenheimer's XI, South African Country Districts (2). *Loss* – South Africa A.

Note: Matches in this section which were not first-class are signified by a dagger.

†At Randjesfontein, September 27, 2002. **Bangladeshis won by six wickets**. N. F. Oppenheimer's XI batted first by mutual agreement. **N. F. Oppenheimer's XI 195** (48.4 overs); **Bangladeshis 196-4** (46 overs) (Hannan Sarkar 81).

†At Nelspruit, September 29, 2002. **Bangladeshis won by 22 runs** (D/L method). Toss: Bangladeshis. **South African Country Districts 227-8** (50 overs) (J. Krynauw 53*); **Bangladeshis 177-5** (37.2 overs) (Tushar Imran 64, Sanwar Hossain 58*).

Sanwar Hossain also took three for 39. Rain cut short the Bangladeshi innings; the D/L par score was 155 in 37.2 overs.

†At Soweto, October 1, 2002. **South Africa A won by 72 runs**. Toss: Bangladeshis. **South Africa A 279-5** (50 overs) (A. G. Prince 87, M. van Jaarsveld 50, N. D. McKenzie 77; Tapash Baisya 4-49); **Bangladeshis 207-8** (50 overs) (D. J. Terbrugge 4-23).

†SOUTH AFRICA v BANGLADESH

First One-Day International

At Potchefstroom, October 3, 2002 (day/night). South Africa won by 168 runs. Toss: South Africa.

Gibbs became only the third batsman, after Pakistan's Zaheer Abbas and Saeed Anwar, to score hundreds in three consecutive one-day internationals as South Africa claimed the first of a series of crushing victories. Gibbs was imperious, reaching his highest one-day score before holing out to deep square leg. He faced 130 balls and hit 17 fours and three sixes. Bangladesh were never likely to threaten South Africa's huge total – certainly not from 26 for five – and settled for drawing small comforts, notably a partnership of 60, their eighth-wicket best, between the captain, Khaled Masud, and Tapash Baisya. Then Kallis wrapped up the match with three wickets in five balls.

Man of the Match: H. H. Gibbs. *Attendance:* 2,168.

South Africa

G. C. Smith c Javed Omar b Talha Jubair . 28
H. H. Gibbs c Al Sahariar b Tapash Baisya . 153
*S. M. Pollock c Al Sahariar b Talha Jubair . 5
J. H. Kallis c Manjurul Islam b Khaled Mahmud . 47
H. H. Dippenaar c Khaled Mahmud b Talha Jubair . 41
D. M. Benkenstein c Khaled Mahmud b Tapash Baisya . 2
J. L. Ontong c Khaled Masud b Tapash Baisya . 2
L. Klusener c Javed Omar b Talha Jubair . 9
†E. L. R. Stewart not out 4
A. A. Donald not out 1
B 1, l-b 3, w 3, n-b 2 9

1/63 (1) 2/79 (3) 3/186 (4) 4/267 (2) 5/283 (6) 6/285 (7) 7/287 (5) 8/299 (8) (8 wkts, 50 overs) 301

M. Ntini did not bat.

Bowling: Manjurul Islam 10–1–61–0; Tapash Baisya 10–1–50–3; Talha Jubair 10–1–65–4; Alok Kapali 5–0–43–0; Khaled Mahmud 10–1–52–1; Sanwar Hossain 5–0–26–0.

Bangladesh

Javed Omar run out	8
Hannan Sarkar c Kallis b Ntini	2
Al Sahariar c Kallis b Ntini	1
Tushar Imran c Gibbs b Ntini	1
Sanwar Hossain c Benkenstein b Donald	4
Alok Kapali c Stewart b Donald	25
*†Khaled Masud not out	34
Khaled Mahmud c Donald b Kallis	24
Tapash Baisya c Pollock b Kallis	24
Manjurul Islam c Stewart b Kallis	0
Talha Jubair b Kallis	0
L-b 3, w 7	10
1/8 (2) 2/10 (3) 3/12 (4) 4/12 (1) 5/26 (5) 6/43 (6) 7/73 (8) 8/133 (9) 9/133 (10) 10/133 (11) (41.5 overs)	133

Bowling: Pollock 5–2–6–0; Ntini 10–4–18–3; Donald 7–0–22–2; Kallis 8.5–1–33–4; Klusener 6–0–27–0; Ontong 5–0–24–0.

Umpires: B. F. Bowden (New Zealand) and B. G. Jerling.
Third umpire: S. Wadvalla. Referee: R. S. Madugalle (Sri Lanka).

HIGHEST SCORES FOR SOUTH AFRICA IN ONE-DAY INTERNATIONALS

188*	G. Kirsten v United Arab Emirates at Rawalpindi	1995-96
169*	D. J. Callaghan v New Zealand at Verwoerdburg	1994-95
161	A. C. Hudson v Holland at Rawalpindi	1995-96
153	**H. H. Gibbs v Bangladesh at Potchefstroom**	**2002-03**
143	**H. H. Gibbs v New Zealand at Johannesburg**	**2002-03**
133*	G. Kirsten v India at Johannesburg	2001-02

†SOUTH AFRICA v BANGLADESH

Second One-Day International

At Benoni, October 6, 2002. South Africa won by ten wickets. Toss: South Africa. One-day international debut: M. van Jaarsveld.

This was another rout, though it was at least enlivened by a moment's controversy. With 30 overs to go, South Africa six short of victory and Gibbs a boundary from an unprecedented fourth consecutive one-day international century, leg-spinner Alok Kapali speared a delivery down the leg side. It beat the wicket-keeper and crossed the ropes to concede five wides, levelling the scores. Gibbs then drove down the ground for a single. The Bangladeshis denied they had deliberately deprived him of the record. Whatever the intention, it could not detract from another magnificently explosive innings: Gibbs's undefeated 97 included 19 fours and came off just 66 balls. Had he reached his hundred, it would have been comfortably South Africa's fastest.

Man of the Match: H. H. Gibbs. *Attendance:* 3,130.

Bangladesh

Javed Omar c Boucher b Klusener	24
Hannan Sarkar c Boucher b Ntini	7
Al Sahariar b Ntini	0
Sanwar Hossain lbw b Donald	8
Tushar Imran c Boucher b Benkenstein	23
Alok Kapali c Pollock b Klusener	0
*†Khaled Masud b Ntini	15
Khaled Mahmud c Boucher b Pollock	18
Tapash Baisya not out	35
Manjurul Islam run out	13
Talha Jubair not out	0
L-b 5, w 6	11
1/26 (2) 2/26 (3) 3/46 (1) 4/46 (4) 5/57 (6) 6/74 (5) 7/102 (8) 8/117 (7) 9/154 (10) (9 wkts, 50 overs)	154

Bowling: Pollock 10–0–16–1; Ntini 10–5–28–3; Klusener 9–2–23–2; Donald 10–2–38–1; Ontong 7–0–27–0; Benkenstein 4–0–17–1.

South Africa

G. C. Smith not out 48
H. H. Gibbs not out 97
L-b 1, w 7, n-b 2 10

(no wkt, 20.2 overs) 155

M. van Jaarsveld, H. H. Dippenaar, D. M. Benkenstein, J. L. Ontong, L. Klusener, †M. V. Boucher, *S. M. Pollock, A. A. Donald and M. Ntini did not bat.

Bowling: Manjurul Islam 7–1–46–0; Tapash Baisya 6–0–37–0; Talha Jubair 3–0–33–0; Alok Kapali 2.2–0–19–0; Khaled Mahmud 2–0–19–0.

Umpires: B. F. Bowden (New Zealand) and I. L. Howell.
Third umpire: S. Wadvalla. Referee: R. S. Madugalle (Sri Lanka).

†SOUTH AFRICA v BANGLADESH

Third One-Day International

At Kimberley, October 9, 2002 (day/night). South Africa won by seven wickets. Toss: Bangladesh. One-day international debuts: A. G. Prince; Anwar Hossain Monir, Rafiqul Islam.

South Africa completed a clean sweep with an easy, unremarkable win. Habibul Bashar, playing his first game of the series, hit a determined half-century, but otherwise it was another poor batting effort. Pollock, coming on first-change, mopped up with four for 24, and South Africa needed just 26 overs to canter home. Their reply was very much a team effort: van Jaarsveld, who had earlier taken a wicket with his only ball in one-day internationals, top-scored with a rapid 42 after the openers fell to the young bowlers, Tapash Baisya and Talha Jubair. When the winning runs came, Rhodes, playing in his 234th one-day international, was batting with Ashwell Prince, making his debut.

Man of the Match: S. M. Pollock. *Attendance:* 3,949.
Man of the Series: H. H. Gibbs.

Bangladesh

Javed Omar c Boucher b Elworthy. 3
Rafiqul Islam c van Jaarsveld b Elworthy 0
Habibul Bashar c Rhodes b Ntini 51
Sanwar Hossain lbw b Pollock 23
Tushar Imran lbw b Pollock 0
Alok Kapali lbw b Peterson 20
*†Khaled Masud c and b Pollock 23
Khaled Mahmud b Peterson 17
Tapash Baisya c Gibbs b Pollock 1
Anwar Hossain Monir not out. 0
Talha Jubair b van Jaarsveld. 0
B 1, l-b 1, w 10, n-b 1. 13

1/5 (1) 2/15 (2) 3/83 (4) (43.1 overs) 151
4/83 (5) 5/93 (3) 6/113 (6)
7/150 (8) 8/150 (7)
9/151 (9) 10/151 (11)

Bowling: Elworthy 8–1–25–2; Ntini 8–1–25–1; Pollock 9–3–24–4; Donald 8–0–36–0; Peterson 10–1–39–2; van Jaarsveld 0.1–0–0–1.

South Africa

G. C. Smith c Sanwar Hossain
b Talha Jubair . 21
H. H. Gibbs b Tapash Baisya 15
M. van Jaarsveld c Javed Omar
b Talha Jubair . 42
A. G. Prince not out. 14
J. N. Rhodes not out. 30
L-b 8, w 10, n-b 12. 30

1/33 (2) 2/73 (1) (3 wkts, 25.4 overs) 152
3/103 (3)

†M. V. Boucher, *S. M. Pollock, R. J. Peterson, S. Elworthy, A. A. Donald and M. Ntini did not bat.

Bowling: Tapash Baisya 6–0–33–1; Anwar Hossain Monir 8–0–45–0; Talha Jubair 6–1–41–2; Khaled Mahmud 3.4–0–17–0; Alok Kapali 2–0–8–0.

Umpires: B. F. Bowden (New Zealand) and B. G. Jerling.
Third umpire: S. Wadvalla. Referee: R. S. Madugalle (Sri Lanka).

†At Bedford, October 12, 13, 14, 15, 2002. **Bangladeshis won by 100 runs**. Toss: South African Country Districts. **Bangladeshis 260** (Sanwar Hossain 114; P. Wiltshire 4-62) **and 164** (P. Wiltshire 5-48); **South African Country Districts 174** (M. Stuurman 61; Tapash Baisya 4-32) **and 150** (Manjurul Islam 4-46).

SOUTH AFRICA v BANGLADESH

First Test Match

At East London, October 18, 19, 20, 21, 2002. South Africa won by an innings and 107 runs. Toss: Bangladesh. Test debut: M. van Jaarsveld.

Given the three thrashings Bangladesh had just suffered in the one-day series and their dire Test record – one draw and 12 defeats – they cannot have been brimful of confidence. It might have been unkind of one South African journalist to report that Bangladesh won the toss and "refused to bat". Even so, the timid gesture spoke volumes about their frame of mind.

In his defence, Khaled Masud could cite a humid morning and a green pitch at Buffalo Park, hosting its first Test, though critics might have countered that Shaun Pollock's absence with a knee injury left the South African attack vulnerable. However, the Bangladesh bowlers struggled to exploit the helpful, swinging conditions and, by the first-day close, South Africa were in complete command at 369 for two. Graeme Smith had just converted his first Test hundred into a double when, having faced 287 balls in 338 minutes and hit precisely half his runs in fours, he lofted to mid-on. By then, Kirsten had become the first batsman to score centuries against nine Test opponents. He and Smith had added 272 for the second wicket as batting eased to the extremely comfortable. The benign conditions also allowed debutant Martin van Jaarsveld to settle himself into Test cricket, and he had scored an unfussy 39 not out by the time Boucher, standing in as captain on his home ground, declared at 529 for four.

Ntini, Boucher's Border team-mate, then precipitated Bangladesh's rapid spiral towards defeat. He produced a fiery spell of pace and bounce, taking three for 13 in ten overs as Bangladesh hobbled to stumps. By the time the innings ended at 170 early on the third morning, Ntini had five for 19, and Bangladesh were about to bat again, 359 behind.

Their second innings was a grittier, more determined effort, and they succeeded in frustrating the South Africans by taking the match into a fourth day. Opener Al Sahariar hit a career-best 71, and Sanwar Hossain also made the bowlers work for his wicket before falling within spitting distance of a maiden Test fifty. But the frustrater-in-chief was Masud, who held out for nearly three and a half hours. He departed as soon as the flame-haired Terbrugge took the second new ball on the fourth morning, on his way to collecting five in a Test innings for the first time. South Africa were soon celebrating a straightforward win.

Man of the Match: G. C. Smith. *Attendance:* 11,698.

Close of play: First day, South Africa 369-2 (Kirsten 113, Kallis 1); Second day, Bangladesh 153-7 (Mohammad Rafiq 10, Tapash Baisya 1); Third day, Bangladesh 209-5 (Khaled Masud 32, Alok Kapali 9).

South Africa

G. C. Smith c Manjurul Islam b Sanwar Hossain	200
H. H. Gibbs c Tushar Imran b Tapash Baisya	41
G. Kirsten c Alok Kapali b Talha Jubair	150
J. H. Kallis not out	75
A. G. Prince c Alok Kapali b Talha Jubair	2
M. van Jaarsveld not out	39
B 2, l-b 1, w 4, n-b 15	22
1/87 (2) 2/359 (1) 3/440 (3) 4/448 (5) (4 wkts dec.)	529

*†M. V. Boucher, D. J. Terbrugge, C. W. Henderson, M. Ntini and M. Hayward did not bat.

Bowling: Manjurul Islam 29–3–104–0; Tapash Baisya 30–3–148–1; Talha Jubair 26–5–108–2; Mohammad Rafiq 23–2–85–0; Alok Kapali 18–0–72–0; Sanwar Hossain 3–0–9–1.

Bangladesh

Javed Omar lbw b Terbrugge	7	– c Gibbs b Hayward	10
Al Sahariar b Hayward	18	– b Ntini	71
Habibul Bashar c Boucher b Ntini	38	– c Terbrugge b Hayward	21
Sanwar Hossain c Boucher b Ntini	31	– lbw b Terbrugge	49
Tushar Imran b Ntini	0	– (6) c van Jaarsveld b Henderson	8
Alok Kapali c Kallis b Henderson	35	– (7) lbw b Terbrugge	10
*†Khaled Masud c van Jaarsveld b Hayward	4	– (5) lbw b Terbrugge	33
Mohammad Rafiq not out	17	– b Terbrugge	19
Tapash Baisya c Boucher b Ntini	2	– c Kirsten b Terbrugge	10
Manjurul Islam b Ntini	4	– c sub (A. C. Thomas) b Ntini	8
Talha Jubair c Boucher b Terbrugge	3	– not out	4
L-b 9, w 1, n-b 1	11	B 3, l-b 3, n-b 3	9
1/21 (1) 2/25 (2) 3/91 (4) 4/97 (5) 5/100 (3) 6/130 (7) 7/149 (6) 8/155 (9) 9/161 (10) 10/170 (11)	170	1/22 (1) 2/78 (3) 3/121 (2) 4/158 (4) 5/176 (6) 6/211 (7) 7/212 (5) 8/231 (8) 9/244 (9) 10/252 (10)	252

Bowling: *First Innings*—Hayward 15–3–50–2; Terbrugge 11.4–3–43–2; Henderson 9–2–23–1; Ntini 15–9–19–5; Kallis 8–2–26–0. *Second Innings*—Ntini 18.5–6–55–2; Terbrugge 15–1–46–5; Hayward 16–2–65–2; Kallis 10–3–22–0; Henderson 28–8–58–1.

Umpires: D. J. Harper (Australia) and R. B. Tiffin (Zimbabwe).
Third umpire: S. Wadvalla. Referee: R. S. Madugalle (Sri Lanka).

SOUTH AFRICA v BANGLADESH

Second Test Match

At Potchefstroom, October 25, 26, 27, 2002. South Africa won by an innings and 160 runs. Toss: Bangladesh. Test debut: Rafiqul Islam.

As at East London a week earlier, Bangladesh won the toss – and were steamrollered. A desperately one-sided contest came to a merciful close on the third afternoon with South Africa completing a comprehensive and entirely predictable 2–0 rout.

To give the Bangladeshis their due, though, they punched above their weight for an entire session. After deciding to bat on a flat track at North West Stadium – like Buffalo Park making its Test debut – they went to lunch on the first day on 124 for one. The rollicking start was provided by openers Al Sahariar and Hannan Sarkar, who struck a Test-best 65, and continued by perhaps their only batsman of genuine class, Habibul Bashar. It was stirring stuff and, as boundaries blazed from Bangladeshi bats, South Africa's bowling and fielding dropped well below their usual standards.

Lunch changed everything. The South Africans, whose attention had wandered in the morning, emerged refocused. Pollock, back as captain after missing the First Test with an injured knee, led the resurgence, but wickets were shared around as they skittled Bangladesh for 215. Kirsten, again at No. 3 to allow Smith to continue his opening partnership with Gibbs, provided the backbone of the reply, with his 16th Test century. Gibbs, however, laid the foundations in flamboyant style. He revelled in picking off a Bangladesh attack who, despite showing vastly greater application and discipline than at East London, fared little better. Kallis became the third South African centurion before the third-morning declaration, five down and 267 ahead.

Pollock set his bowlers the target of finishing the game off that day, and they obliged, in less than 31 overs. It was thanks largely to Kallis, who careered through the bottom order with five wickets in 12 balls. His figures were impressive in themselves, but what turned the eye was his ability to conjure sharp lift from a pitch that appeared to have breathed its last on day one. The Bangladeshis were flummoxed, and all five of Kallis's victims were caught, either by the keeper or at mid-wicket from mistimed pull shots.

Asked afterwards about Bangladesh's progress, the South African coach, Eric Simons, tried to find crumbs of comfort for them amid the carnage: "They themselves keep on saying this is all part of a learning process for them, and I've certainly felt that they've learned," he said. "But they're struggling a bit at the moment."

Man of the Match: J. H. Kallis. *Attendance:* 2,879.

Man of the Series: J. H. Kallis.

Close of play: First day, South Africa 61-1 (Gibbs 36); Second day, South Africa 414-2 (Kirsten 154, Kallis 107).

Bangladesh

First innings		Second innings	
Hannan Sarkar c Kallis b Ntini	65	– b Ntini	17
Al Sahariar c Smith b Hayward	30	– c Kallis b Hayward	27
Habibul Bashar c Boucher b Pollock	40	– c Boucher b Ntini	7
Sanwar Hossain lbw b Ntini	0	– c Kallis b Ntini	6
*†Khaled Masud c van Jaarsveld b Kallis	20	– (6) c Boucher b Kallis	9
Rafiqul Islam c Gibbs b Kallis	6	– (8) c Kirsten b Kallis	1
Tushar Imran c Boucher b Pollock	8	– (5) c Prince b Hayward	0
Alok Kapali not out	38	– (7) c Boucher b Kallis	23
Tapash Baisya c van Jaarsveld b Hayward	2	– c Gibbs b Kallis	0
Manjurul Islam c Smith b Henderson	0	– c Gibbs b Kallis	5
Talha Jubair run out	0	– not out	1
B 4, n-b 2	6	L-b 8, n-b 3	11
1/52 (2) 2/136 (1) 3/136 (4) 4/140 (3) 5/162 (6) 6/169 (5) 7/184 (7) 8/197 (9) 9/202 (10) 10/215 (11)	215	1/33 (1) 2/43 (3) 3/52 (4) 4/60 (2) 5/61 (5) 6/95 (7) 7/101 (8) 8/101 (6) 9/104 (9) 10/107 (10)	107

Bowling: *First Innings*—Pollock 16–6–38–2; Ntini 21–4–69–2; Hayward 14–3–64–2; Kallis 13–4–26–2; Henderson 5.5–2–14–1. *Second Innings*—Pollock 6–0–25–0; Ntini 12–1–37–3; Hayward 8–3–16–2; Kallis 4.3–1–21–5.

South Africa

G. C. Smith c Khaled Masud b Sanwar Hossain	24
H. H. Gibbs run out	114
G. Kirsten c Khaled Masud b Talha Jubair	160
J. H. Kallis not out	139
A. G. Prince c Khaled Masud b Talha Jubair	0
M. van Jaarsveld lbw b Tapash Baisya	11
†M. V. Boucher not out	14
B 13, l-b 2, n-b 5	20
1/61 (1) 2/202 (2) 3/436 (3) 4/436 (5) 5/452 (6) (5 wkts dec.)	482

*S. M. Pollock, C. W. Henderson, M. Ntini and M. Hayward did not bat.

Bowling: Manjurul Islam 26–7–80–0; Tapash Baisya 28–3–103–1; Talha Jubair 26–3–109–2; Alok Kapali 20–2–75–0; Sanwar Hossain 20–1–98–1; Habibul Bashar 1–0–2–0.

Umpires: D. J. Harper (Australia) and R. B. Tiffin (Zimbabwe).
Third umpire: S. Wadvalla. Referee: R. S. Madugalle (Sri Lanka).

PAKISTAN v AUSTRALIA, 2002-03

MARTIN BLAKE

Pakistan's proximity to trouble-torn Afghanistan, and the aftermath of the Karachi suicide bombing that cut short New Zealand's tour in May, had a lingering impact on Pakistani cricket later in 2002. In August, after months of discontented murmuring from their players, the Australian Cricket Board finally pulled out of their scheduled three-Test tour, citing government advice and security concerns.

Confronted with a choice between finding a neutral venue and cancelling the tour, the Pakistani board discussed grounds in Morocco and Bangladesh. But they finally chose Colombo for the First Test and Sharjah (where they had played West Indies in similar circumstances earlier in the year) for the last two. There were no one-day games. Even then, in the midst of the gathering storm over Iraq, the selection of a Middle Eastern venue caused concern among the Australians. The relocation was a blow to Pakistan; with home advantage seized from their grasp and several key players missing, they were crushed 3–0. Steve Waugh wanted a whitewash and his men delivered.

HOME FROM HOME

Only nine Test matches have ever been played on neutral grounds.

		Venues	*Reason*
1912	Australia v South Africa	Manchester, Lord's, Nottingham	Triangular Tournament
1998-99	Pakistan v Sri Lanka	Dhaka	Asian Test Championship
2001-02	Pakistan v West Indies	Sharjah (2)	Political problems in Pakistan
2002-03	**Pakistan v Australia**	**Colombo, Sharjah (2)**	**Political problems in Pakistan**

Pakistan's biggest failing was to field a team that was far from their strongest, a fatal flaw against a unit of Australia's quality. The experienced Saeed Anwar and Wasim Akram withdrew, claiming they needed rest, yet bobbed up in a hit-and-giggle tournament in Wales. Both were later called before the board to explain themselves. Injuries to Inzamam-ul-Haq and Yousuf Youhana kept them out too, and in each of the matches at least four of the top six had fewer than nine Tests' experience. Glenn McGrath announced that he would target the newcomers and, despite the emergence of Faisal Iqbal as a batsman of quality, the inexperienced line-up was exposed by a ruthless attack.

Still, Pakistan competed to the end in the First Test, as Shoaib Akhtar bowled a couple of gale-force spells and twice dragged them back into the game. But, ultimately, they were beaten by the genius of Shane Warne and the cool-headedness of his colleagues. Needing just 86 to win on the last morning, with six wickets in hand, Pakistan were bowled out 42 short. Warne went on to enjoy a vintage series, taunting the Pakistanis with his sleight of hand and taking 27 wickets. Thirteen were lbws, evidence of the effectiveness of his "slider", a new delivery that skidded straight on.

During the Second Test, in the sledgehammer heat of Sharjah, Pakistan unravelled pitifully. Bowled out for 59 and 53, they managed fewer runs in two innings than Matthew Hayden made in one, and slumped to a humiliating innings defeat inside two days. The chairman of the board, Lieutenant General Tauqir Zia, immediately offered his resignation, though it was not accepted. The Australians were equally merciless in the Third Test. Shoaib withdrew with what officials called a "minor back niggle" and Pakistan were thrashed by an innings once again. The recriminations would come, but only after the embarrassment was compounded by a poor World Cup.

Despite Australia's handsome win, the series was played against a clamour of speculation about the future of the Waugh twins. Mark averaged only 20 and missed several regulation chances at slip. His final innings at Sharjah proved his last before withdrawing from Test cricket. By the end of the month, he was dropped, and he then chose to retire.

The captain, Steve, also had his difficult moments, but an unbeaten 103 in the Third Test, clinched with consecutive sixes from Danish Kaneria's leg-spin, kept the wolves at bay for a while longer. In any event, cricket's most accomplished twins were hardly needed: Ricky Ponting and Hayden both had superb series. Combined with Warne's magic and McGrath's accuracy, it proved more than enough for the Australians to maintain their ascendancy.

PAKISTANI TOURING PARTY

Waqar Younis (National Bank) (*captain*), Younis Khan (Habib Bank) (*vice-captain*), Abdul Razzaq (ADBP), Danish Kaneria (Habib Bank), Faisal Iqbal (PIA), Hasan Raza (Habib Bank), Imran Farhat (Habib Bank), Imran Nazir (National Bank), Misbah-ul-Haq (KRL), Mohammad Sami (National Bank), Mohammad Zahid (PIA), Naved-ul-Hasan (WAPDA), Rashid Latif (Allied Bank), Saqlain Mushtaq (PIA), Shoaib Akhtar (KRL), Taufeeq Umar (Habib Bank).

Shahid Afridi (Habib Bank) replaced Abdul Razzaq, who broke his wrist during the Second Test.

Coach: R. A. Pybus. *Manager:* Brigadier Mohammad Nasir. *Batting consultant:* Hanif Mohammad. *Team analyst:* Sikander Bakht. *Physiotherapist:* D. J. M. Waight. *Doctor:* Riaz Ahmed.

AUSTRALIAN TOURING PARTY

S. R. Waugh (New South Wales) (*captain*), A. C. Gilchrist (Western Australia) (*vice-captain*), A. J. Bichel (Queensland), J. N. Gillespie (South Australia), N. M. Hauritz (Queensland), M. L. Hayden (Queensland), J. L. Langer (Western Australia), B. Lee (New South Wales), D. S. Lehmann (South Australia), G. D. McGrath (New South Wales), D. R. Martyn (Western Australia), R. T. Ponting (Tasmania), S. K. Warne (Victoria), M. E. Waugh (New South Wales).

B. A. Williams (Western Australia) replaced Gillespie when he went home injured.

Coach: J. M. Buchanan. *Manager:* S. R. Bernard. *Assistant manager/cricket analyst:* M. K. Walsh. *Physiotherapists:* E. L. Alcott/S. Partridge. *Physical performance manager:* J. A. Campbell.

AUSTRALIAN TOUR RESULTS

Test matches – Played 3: Won 3.
Wins – Pakistan (3).

TEST MATCH AVERAGES

PAKISTAN – BATTING

	T	*I*	*NO*	*R*	*HS*	*100s*	*50s*	*Avge*	*Ct*
Faisal Iqbal	3	6	0	144	83	0	1	24.00	2
Rashid Latif	3	6	1	115	66	0	1	23.00	4
Younis Khan	3	6	0	123	58	0	2	20.50	4
†Taufeeq Umar	3	6	0	94	88	0	1	15.66	5
Imran Nazir	2	4	0	56	40	0	0	14.00	3
Mohammad Sami	2	4	2	28	22	0	0	14.00	0
Abdul Razzaq	2	4	1	40	21	0	0	13.33	0
Danish Kaneria	2	4	2	26	15	0	0	13.00	0
Misbah-ul-Haq	3	6	0	69	17	0	0	11.50	1
Saqlain Mushtaq	3	6	0	65	44	0	0	10.83	1
Waqar Younis	3	6	0	45	24	0	0	7.50	0
Shoaib Akhtar	2	4	0	14	6	0	0	3.50	0

Played in one Test: Hasan Raza 54*, 68; †Imran Farhat 29, 18.

† *Left-handed batsman.*

BOWLING

	Style	*O*	*M*	*R*	*W*	*BB*	*5W/i*	*Avge*
Shoaib Akhtar	RF	43	10	114	9	5-21	1	12.66
Abdul Razzaq	RFM	27.1	3	100	4	3-22	0	25.00
Saqlain Mushtaq	OB	135.4	13	424	14	4-46	0	30.28
Waqar Younis	RFM	49.3	10	189	6	4-55	0	31.50
Danish Kaneria	LB	62	10	244	4	3-128	0	61.00

Also bowled: Mohammad Sami (RF) 54–9–187–1; Taufeeq Umar (OB) 6–1–18–0.

AUSTRALIA – BATTING

	T	*I*	*NO*	*R*	*HS*	*100s*	*50s*	*Avge*	*Ct/St*
R. T. Ponting	3	4	0	342	150	2	0	85.50	2
†M. L. Hayden	3	4	0	246	119	1	1	61.50	0
S. R. Waugh	3	4	1	134	103*	1	0	44.66	4
†A. C. Gilchrist	3	4	1	122	66*	0	1	40.66	10/1
†J. L. Langer	3	4	0	138	72	0	1	34.50	1
D. R. Martyn	3	4	0	121	67	0	1	30.25	3
M. E. Waugh	3	4	0	80	55	0	1	20.00	8
S. K. Warne	3	4	0	30	19	0	0	7.50	2
B. Lee	3	4	0	27	12	0	0	6.75	0
G. D. McGrath	3	4	1	12	5*	0	0	4.00	2

Played in two Tests: A. J. Bichel 2*, 9 (1 ct). Played in one Test: J. N. Gillespie 0, 1.

† *Left-handed batsman.*

BOWLING

	Style	*O*	*M*	*R*	*W*	*BB*	*5W/i*	*Avge*
G. D. McGrath	RFM	75.2	27	152	14	4-41	0	10.85
S. K. Warne	LBG	124	29	342	27	7-94	2	12.66
A. J. Bichel	RFM	33.2	4	106	8	3-43	0	13.25
J. N. Gillespie	RF	35.3	10	117	3	2-62	0	39.00
B. Lee	RF	66.5	13	234	5	2-15	0	46.80

Also bowled: R. T. Ponting (RM/OB) 1–0–5–0; M. E. Waugh (RM/OB) 19–4–71–0.

Note: Matches in this section which were not first-class are signified by a dagger.

†At Police Park, Colombo, September 27, 28, 29, 2002. **Drawn.** Toss: West Indians. **West Indians 300** (S. Chanderpaul 83*) **and 230-7 dec.** (R. O. Hinds 54); **Pakistanis 248-9 dec.** (Misbah-ul-Haq 129*) **and 124-2** (Taufeeq Umar 64*).

The West Indians, on their way to India, joined the Pakistanis in a warm-up match; each side named 16 players, of whom only 11 could bat and 11 bowl.

PAKISTAN v AUSTRALIA

First Test Match

At P. Saravanamuttu Stadium, Colombo, October 3, 4, 5, 6, 7, 2002. Australia won by 41 runs. Toss: Australia.

A marvellous contest fell Australia's way on the last day after a feisty young Pakistan team almost conjured a miracle. The Australians had dominated until, in their second innings, a breathtaking spell of five wickets in 15 balls by Shoaib Akhtar turned the tide. Set a difficult 316 to win on the final two days, Pakistan were in striking distance at 187 for three. But against unremitting bowling they fell short.

The Australians had shown a touch of paranoia over the pitch after Waqar Younis said he hoped it would be prepared to suit Pakistan. Steve Waugh insisted this was disgraceful – he would never ask for a certain type of surface, let alone admit to it in public. But there were no demons in it, anyway.

Batting first after winning the toss, Australia piled on a formidable 467 after an inspired, chanceless 141 from Ponting, who enjoyed the relative anonymity of merely batting at first-drop after his stint as captain in the preceding Champions Trophy. Only Shoaib's characteristic old-ball assault prevented a score well above 500; under the blowtorch of reverse swing at nearly 100mph, the last five wickets fell for ten runs.

In reply, the inexperienced openers did not contribute a single run and, with Warne showing the benefits of his new fitness regime, Pakistan only just avoided the follow-on. Faisal Iqbal danced down the wicket to carve Warne through the off side on his way to a run-a-ball 83, which went some way to vindicating Pakistan's youth policy. Rashid Latif backed him up with 66, but Warne, indefatigable, wheeled away in the heat to take seven for 94.

The third day belonged to a very different bowler. At one point Australia had reached 61 without loss, and seemingly had the match in hand. But the charismatic Shoaib returned to bowl an unplayable second spell. He ripped the heart out of the innings, grabbing three prize wickets in four balls – Ponting and the Waughs – and in his next over a yorker from round the wicket smashed Gilchrist's stumps before he could complete his stroke. The contest was re-ignited. With Saqlain Mushtaq spinning his way to four for 46, Australia were humbled for 127. Of Shoaib's memorable five for 21, three were bowled, two trapped lbw. It was one of Test cricket's greatest short spells.

By tea on the fourth day – before the last session was lost to rain – Pakistan needed only 137 more for a famous victory. Their left-handed opener Taufeeq Umar, a young player unfamiliar to the Australians, had hammered 88 with a string of delightful drives and pulls, while Australia suffered a fit of uncharacteristically error-riddled fielding. They would spill seven catches in the match, and even the lithe Mark Waugh could not handle relatively simple slip chances. The lapses added to the growing pressure on him, though his first-innings 55 had made him the 11th batsman to pass 8,000 Test runs.

But Australia called on their renowned toughness. At 230 for four, needing just 86, Pakistan were within a breath of triumph. However, their opponents simply piled on the pressure until the dam wall burst. The pivotal moment was Warne's dismissal of Younis Khan for an elegant 51. Five wickets then tumbled for 26 to McGrath and Gillespie with the new ball. Though Gillespie broke down with a calf strain, a few balls later Faisal spooned a catch to Ponting at backward point and it was all over. Once again, Australia's old firm of Warne, who took 11 wickets in total, and McGrath had performed heroically when it mattered most.

Man of the Match: S. K. Warne.

Close of play: First day, Australia 330-5 (Martyn 6, Gilchrist 1); Second day, Pakistan 210-5 (Faisal Iqbal 78, Rashid Latif 30); Third day, Australia 127; Fourth day, Pakistan 179-3 (Younis Khan 32, Misbah-ul-Haq 4).

Australia

First innings		Second innings	
J. L. Langer c Rashid Latif b Abdul Razzaq	72	– c Taufeeq Umar b Saqlain Mushtaq	25
M. L. Hayden c Imran Nazir b Waqar Younis	4	– c Taufeeq Umar b Saqlain Mushtaq	34
R. T. Ponting c Younis Khan b Waqar Younis	141	– b Shoaib Akhtar	7
M. E. Waugh c and b Saqlain Mushtaq	55	– b Shoaib Akhtar	0
*S. R. Waugh c Younis Khan b Saqlain Mushtaq	31	– lbw b Shoaib Akhtar	0
D. R. Martyn c Younis Khan b Saqlain Mushtaq	67	– c Imran Nazir b Saqlain Mushtaq	20
†A. C. Gilchrist not out	66	– b Shoaib Akhtar	5
S. K. Warne c Faisal Iqbal b Shoaib Akhtar	0	– lbw b Shoaib Akhtar	0
B. Lee b Shoaib Akhtar	2	– c Misbah-ul-Haq b Saqlain Mushtaq	12
J. N. Gillespie lbw b Shoaib Akhtar	0	– lbw b Mohammad Sami	1
G. D. McGrath lbw b Saqlain Mushtaq	4	– not out	5
B 4, l-b 16, n-b 5	25	B 4, l-b 12, n-b 2	18
1/5 (2) 2/188 (1) 3/272 (3) 4/302 (4) 5/329 (5) 6/457 (6) 7/458 (8) 8/462 (9) 9/462 (10) 10/467 (11)	467	1/61 (1) 2/74 (3) 3/74 (4) 4/74 (5) 5/74 (2) 6/85 (7) 7/89 (8) 8/107 (9) 9/112 (10) 10/127 (6)	127

Bowling: *First Innings*—Waqar Younis 16–2–86–2; Shoaib Akhtar 21–5–51–3; Mohammad Sami 20–3–93–0; Abdul Razzaq 17–0–78–1; Saqlain Mushtaq 40.5–6–136–4; Taufeeq Umar 2–1–3–0. *Second Innings*—Waqar Younis 8–1–23–0; Shoaib Akhtar 8–2–21–5; Saqlain Mushtaq 15.5–0–46–4; Taufeeq Umar 2–0–8–0; Mohammad Sami 6–0–13–1.

Pakistan

First innings		Second innings	
Imran Nazir lbw b McGrath	0	– c McGrath b Warne	40
Taufeeq Umar c Ponting b Gillespie	0	– c M. E. Waugh b Lee	88
Abdul Razzaq c Gilchrist b Warne	11	– lbw b Warne	4
Younis Khan c Langer b Lee	58	– lbw b Warne	51
Misbah-ul-Haq c M. E. Waugh b Warne	17	– c S. R. Waugh b Warne	10
Faisal Iqbal c M. E. Waugh b Warne	83	– c Ponting b McGrath	39
†Rashid Latif c Martyn b Warne	66	– c Gilchrist b Gillespie	11
Saqlain Mushtaq lbw b Warne	1	– c S. R. Waugh b McGrath	1
*Waqar Younis lbw b Warne	14	– c Gilchrist b Gillespie	1
Shoaib Akhtar c McGrath b Warne	5	– lbw b McGrath	6
Mohammad Sami not out	0	– not out	6
B 11, l-b 10, n-b 3	24	B 3, l-b 6, n-b 8	17
1/2 (1) 2/4 (2) 3/45 (3) 4/75 (4) 5/116 (5) 6/219 (6) 7/239 (8) 8/267 (9) 9/274 (7) 10/279 (10)	279	1/91 (1) 2/117 (3) 3/173 (2) 4/187 (5) 5/230 (4) 6/248 (7) 7/251 (8) 8/252 (9) 9/259 (10) 10/274 (6)	274

Bowling: *First Innings*—McGrath 15–3–40–1; Gillespie 12–2–55–1; Lee 11–3–49–1; Warne 24.3–7–94–7; M. E. Waugh 3–0–20–0. *Second Innings*—McGrath 24.2–12–38–3; Gillespie 23.3–8–62–2; Lee 14–1–63–1; Warne 30.3–3–94–4; M. E. Waugh 2–1–8–0.

Umpires: S. A. Bucknor (West Indies) and S. Venkataraghavan (India).
Third umpire: Aleem Dar (Pakistan). Referee: C. H. Lloyd (West Indies).

PAKISTAN v AUSTRALIA

Second Test Match

At Sharjah, October 11, 12, 2002. Australia won by an innings and 198 runs. Toss: Pakistan.

Pakistan arrived in Sharjah comfortable with the familiar conditions and buoyed by their competitive performance in Colombo. But their mood would quickly darken as they slumped to a display that, even allowing for their reputation for spasmodic performances, could only be described as a shocker. In 125 years, Test cricket had produced only 16 two-day defeats; here, on a slow, flat pitch and against an Australian attack weakened by the absence of the injured Gillespie, Pakistan subsided to the 17th.

After Waqar Younis was granted his wish to bat first on one of world cricket's most benign strips, the Pakistanis were rolled over for their lowest-ever score, a pathetic 59, three below their previous worst at Perth in 1981-82. They had lasted less than 32 overs. The openers Imran Nazir and Taufeeq Umar repeated the pair of ducks they managed in the first innings in Colombo, and only Abdul Razzaq, who endured almost two hours for 21, reached double figures. Warne caused the damage again, taking four for 11 and bewitching the batsmen with his new "slider". Pushing forward, they found themselves trapped lbw by deliveries that were doing precisely nothing.

LOWEST AGGREGATE BY ONE TEAM IN A TEST

81	(36 and 45)	South Africa v Australia (153†) at Melbourne	1931-32
90	(47 and 43)	South Africa v England (292) at Cape Town	1888-89
96	(42 and 54)	New Zealand v Australia (199-8 dec.) at Wellington	1945-46
112	**(59 and 53†)**	**Pakistan v Australia (310) at Sharjah**	**2002-03**
115	(53 and 62)	England v Australia (116 and 60) at Lord's	1888
121	(47 and 74)	New Zealand v England (269) at Lord's	1958
123	(93 and 30)	South Africa v England (185 and 226) at Port Elizabeth	1895-96
124	(42 and 82)	Australia v England (113 and 137) at Sydney	1887-88
137	(65† and 72†)	England v Australia (284) at Sydney	1894-95
140	(58 and 82)	India v England (347-9 dec.) at Manchester	1952

† *One man absent or retired hurt. All matches ended in defeat for the first-named team.*

TEST BATSMAN OUTSCORES OPPOSITION AGGREGATE IN SINGLE INNINGS

R. Abel	120	England v South Africa (47 and 43) at Cape Town	1888-89
L. Hutton	364	England v Australia (201‡ and 123‡) at The Oval	1938
D. G. Bradman	185	Australia v India (58 and 98) at Brisbane	1947-48
Inzamam-ul-Haq	329	Pakistan v New Zealand (73 and 246) at Lahore	2002
M. L. Hayden	**119**	**Australia v Pakistan (59 and 53†) at Sharjah**	**2002-03**

† *One man retired hurt.* ‡ *Two men absent.*

Two balls after tea on the first day, the Australians were already in front. With the temperature pushing 50°C in the middle, Hayden likened it to batting in an oven and wondered whether hell was any hotter. But his sheer hunger for runs came to the fore. While Ponting looked ready to expire by the time he was out for 44, Hayden ground his way relentlessly to 119, showing his opponents the determination that the conditions demanded. Dropped twice, he never truly dominated – though he reached

Horror story: Shane Warne outwits Waqar Younis, and the slaughter comes to an end. Waqar's second duck was Pakistan's eighth.

Picture by Hamish Blair, Getty Images.

three figures with a six off Danish Kaneria – but the seven-hour vigil was exactly what Australia needed. Afterwards, Steve Waugh would label Hayden the best batsman in the world.

Following their mauling in Colombo, the Australians had spent a lot of time devising strategies to counter Shoaib Akhtar's speed and reverse swing. In fact Shoaib could not cope with the heat and proved ineffectual, managing only 14 overs. Waqar Younis bowled just eight, and the batsmen pummelled Kaneria, the young leg-spinner who had come into the team in place of the seamer Mohammad Sami. It meant that Pakistan leaned heavily on Saqlain Mushtaq, who toiled for 34 overs and was rewarded with four for 83, including the Waughs with consecutive balls. Pressure on the twins remained as intense as the heat. The Australians had toasted Steve on the eve of the match to celebrate his 150th Test; a first-ball duck scarcely crowned the event, and meant Waugh beat Mike Atherton's record for an established batsman of 20 Test ducks.

Australia were aiming for 500; although they managed only 310, it proved more than enough. After Nazir simply turned his back on Taufeeq as he charged through for a run in Pakistan's first over, and Razzaq's wrist was broken by Lee in the sixth, their resolve fractured too. Warne once again imposed his authority, taking four for 13, and the quick bowlers mopped up. Pakistan had survived less than 25 overs, and were routed for 53. Their record low had lasted only one day.

Man of the Match: M. L. Hayden.

Close of play: First day, Australia 191-4 (Hayden 74, Martyn 19).

Pakistan

Imran Nazir c Warne b McGrath	0	– c Gilchrist b Warne	16
Taufeeq Umar b Lee	0	– run out	0
Abdul Razzaq c Martyn b Warne	21	– retired hurt	4
Younis Khan c Bichel b McGrath	5	– lbw b McGrath	0
Misbah-ul-Haq c M. E. Waugh b Bichel	2	– c S. R. Waugh b Bichel	12
Faisal Iqbal lbw b Warne	4	– c M. E. Waugh b Warne	7
†Rashid Latif not out	4	– c M. E. Waugh b Bichel	0
Saqlain Mushtaq lbw b Warne	0	– c Warne b Lee	9
Shoaib Akhtar c Gilchrist b Bichel	1	– c S. R. Waugh b Warne	2
*Waqar Younis lbw b Warne	0	– lbw b Warne	0
Danish Kaneria b Lee	8	– not out	1
B 8, l-b 2, n-b 4	14	N-b 2	2
1/0 (1) 2/1 (2) 3/8 (4) 4/23 (5) 5/41 (6) 6/46 (3) 7/46 (8) 8/49 (9) 9/50 (10) 10/59 (11)	59	1/0 (2) 2/13 (4) 3/32 (1) 4/34 (5) 5/36 (7) 6/50 (6) 7/52 (8) 8/52 (9) 9/53 (10)	53

In the second innings Abdul Razzaq retired hurt at 11.

Bowling: *First Innings*—McGrath 7–4–10–2; Lee 7.5–1–15–2; Bichel 6–2–13–2; Warne 11–4–11–4. *Second Innings*—McGrath 6–2–5–1; Lee 5–2–16–1; Bichel 7–1–19–2; Warne 6.5–2–13–4.

Australia

J. L. Langer run out	37
M. L. Hayden c Imran Nazir b Saqlain Mushtaq	119
R. T. Ponting lbw b Danish Kaneria	44
M. E. Waugh lbw b Saqlain Mushtaq	2
*S. R. Waugh c sub (Imran Farhat) b Saqlain Mushtaq	0
D. R. Martyn c Taufeeq Umar b Abdul Razzaq	34
†A. C. Gilchrist c Taufeeq Umar b Shoaib Akhtar	17
S. K. Warne c Younis Khan b Saqlain Mushtaq	19
B. Lee lbw b Abdul Razzaq	12
A. J. Bichel not out	2
G. D. McGrath lbw b Abdul Razzaq	0
B 15, l-b 7, n-b 2	24
1/55 (1) 2/145 (3) 3/148 (4) 4/148 (5) 5/224 (6) 6/252 (7) 7/285 (8) 8/304 (9) 9/310 (2) 10/310 (11)	310

Bowling: Waqar Younis 8–2–25–0; Shoaib Akhtar 14–3–42–1; Danish Kaneria 26–2–116–1; Abdul Razzaq 10.1–3–22–3; Saqlain Mushtaq 34–2–83–4.

Umpires: S. A. Bucknor (West Indies) and S. Venkataraghavan (India).
Third umpire: Nadeem Ghauri (Pakistan). Referee: C. H. Lloyd (West Indies).

PAKISTAN v AUSTRALIA

Third Test Match

At Sharjah, October 19, 20, 21, 22, 2002. Australia won by an innings and 20 runs. Toss: Australia.

This was a triumphant match for the Australians, collectively and individually. Pakistan were again comprehensively beaten, only just dragging the game into a fourth day; Glenn McGrath became the eighth man in Test history to reach 400 wickets; and Steve Waugh achieved redemption by hitting a thrilling century.

After the early finish to the Second Test, the Australians tried to have this match brought forward, but it did not suit the TV broadcasters, so they were kept in the heat of Sharjah a few days longer. However, the referee, Clive Lloyd, did agree to a loosening of the usual over-rate requirements and to extra drinks breaks, during which players could return to the dressing-rooms. Waugh had complained that "When the temperature is 51°C and the humidity is high, you shouldn't even be outside, let alone playing sport."

As temperatures rose, tempers frayed. Pakistan's coach, Richard Pybus, ruffled Australian feathers by suggesting that all was "not well" within the camp, and that Waugh's team was "at the end of an era". The second statement had some merit but might have been better timed, given Pakistan's capitulation in the Second Test. "If I was him," retorted Allan Border, an Australian selector, "I'd be keeping my mouth shut. Let's see if they can score 60 next time they bat. Most second-grade sides could do better than his national side."

Ultimately, Australia would make Pybus cringe. After lining up for a minute's silence to commemorate the victims of the Bali terrorist bombing – in which many Australian tourists died – a week earlier, they were straight to work – and on their way to 444. Hayden launched into his favourite slog-sweeps from the outset, and it took a brilliant catch at bat-pad to deny him a hundred. While Hayden made light of the conditions, Ponting battled heat exhaustion during another brilliant century. Despite having to put on an ice vest at each drinks break – and suffering a gashed jaw from a Mohammad Sami bouncer, when he was wearing only the baggy green because his helmet was too hot – he remained in charge during a chanceless 150, dancing down the track to the spinners and punishing a pace attack diluted by a back injury to Shoaib Akhtar. Meanwhile, Mark Waugh's dismissal for 23, stumbling forward and caught behind off Saqlain Mushtaq, would prove to be the ungainly last chapter of a graceful Test career.

His twin brother was another matter. Beginning the second day on 33, he crawled along until it looked as though he would run out of partners in search of a momentous century. He was on 82 when Australia's last man, McGrath, trudged through the gate. Steve Waugh was not about to dither. He promptly smashed 20 off one Danish Kaneria over, slogging consecutive sixes to leg and punching the air, head bowed, before raising his bat to celebrate his first century in 12 Tests.

In reply, Pakistan soon fell under Warne's spell again. He mesmerised batsmen and took five wickets with his combination of sharp spin and disguised straighter balls. McGrath grabbed four, the last of which was his 400th in Tests – and 650th in first-class cricket. Having pinned Waqar Younis in front, he raised the ball to the crowd in celebration. Pakistan fell for 221 and the match seemed destined for another vastly abbreviated finish.

Following on, the Pakistanis were teetering at 176 for eight when bad light and the stubbornness of Hasan Raza, who had hit his second half-century of the match, halted the Australian charge. But victory next morning was a formality. Not many captains complete a whitewash away from home and hold on to their place by the skin of their teeth. That Steve Waugh did says something about the dominance of this Australian side.

Man of the Match: S. K. Warne. *Man of the Series:* S. K. Warne.

Close of play: First day, Australia 298-3 (Ponting 142, S. R. Waugh 33); Second day, Pakistan 163-6 (Hasan Raza 37, Saqlain Mushtaq 27); Third day, Pakistan 176-8 (Hasan Raza 56, Mohammad Sami 12).

Australia

Batsman	Runs
J. L. Langer b Waqar Younis	4
M. L. Hayden c Faisal Iqbal b Saqlain Mushtaq	89
R. T. Ponting b Waqar Younis	150
M. E. Waugh c Rashid Latif b Saqlain Mushtaq	23
*S. R. Waugh not out	103
D. R. Martyn lbw b Waqar Younis	0
†A. C. Gilchrist c Rashid Latif b Danish Kaneria	34
S. K. Warne lbw b Danish Kaneria	11
B. Lee run out	1
A. J. Bichel c Taufeeq Umar b Danish Kaneria	9
G. D. McGrath c Rashid Latif b Waqar Younis	3
B 4, l-b 10, n-b 3	17
1/4 (1) 2/188 (2) 3/233 (4) 4/308 (3) 5/308 (6) 6/363 (7) 7/403 (8) 8/404 (9) 9/418 (10) 10/444 (11)	444

Bowling: Waqar Younis 17.3–5–55–4; Mohammad Sami 28–6–81–0; Saqlain Mushtaq 45–5–159–2; Danish Kaneria 36–8–128–3; Taufeeq Umar 2–0–7–0.

Pakistan

Taufeeq Umar lbw b McGrath	5	– c Gilchrist b McGrath	1
Imran Farhat lbw b Warne	29	– c Gilchrist b Bichel	18
Younis Khan c Gilchrist b McGrath	5	– lbw b McGrath	4
Faisal Iqbal c Gilchrist b Warne	9	– run out	2
Misbah-ul-Haq lbw b Bichel	11	– lbw b Warne	17
Hasan Raza not out	54	– c Gilchrist b Bichel	68
†Rashid Latif c M. E. Waugh b Warne	17	– lbw b Warne	17
Saqlain Mushtaq b McGrath	44	– lbw b Warne	10
*Waqar Younis lbw b McGrath	6	– c M. E. Waugh b McGrath	24
Mohammad Sami lbw b Warne	0	– c Martyn b Bichel	22
Danish Kaneria st Gilchrist b Warne	15	– not out	2
B 3, l-b 10, w 2, n-b 11	26	L-b 9, n-b 9	18
1/22 (1) 2/50 (3) 3/50 (2) 4/70 (5) 5/76 (4) 6/100 (7) 7/191 (8) 8/198 (9) 9/199 (10) 10/221 (11)	221	1/6 (1) 2/12 (3) 3/18 (4) 4/30 (2) 5/58 (5) 6/86 (7) 7/102 (8) 8/157 (9) 9/197 (6) 10/203 (10)	203

Bowling: *First Innings*—McGrath 16–4–41–4; Lee 11–1–47–0; Warne 30.1–10–74–5; Bichel 9–0–31–1; M. E. Waugh 4–0–10–0; Ponting 1–0–5–0. *Second Innings*—McGrath 7–2–18–3; Lee 18–5–44–0; Bichel 11.2–1–43–3; Warne 21–3–56–3; M. E. Waugh 10–3–33–0.

Umpires: S. A. Bucknor (West Indies) and S. Venkataraghavan (India).
Third umpire: Asad Rauf (Pakistan). Referee: C. H. Lloyd (West Indies).

THE WEST INDIANS IN INDIA AND BANGLADESH, 2002-03

AMIT VARMA AND UTPAL SHUVRO

How absurd it would have been, two decades ago, to imagine that West Indies could be relieved to lose a three-Test series against India 2–0. Yet that is how it was. Their decline of the 1990s had accelerated into an alarming freefall. Of their last 27 overseas Tests, West Indies had lost 23, and they had just suffered a humiliating home defeat by New Zealand. In India, they began with more of the same, as they were drubbed in the first two Tests. But they salvaged some pride at Kolkata, where they might have won until Sachin Tendulkar and V. V. S. Laxman saved the day, fought back to take the one-day series, and of course gained predictable consolation afterwards on their first tour of Bangladesh.

In India, West Indies remained stuck in a vicious circle: every loss eroded their self-belief, and their lack of self-belief kept losing them games. The first two Tests were from a familiar template. They were diffident and lacklustre on the field; their batsmen threw away starts; their bowlers never believed they could get wickets. Carl Hooper was a square peg in a deep round hole – the calm and composed captain of a team which really needed an inspirational leader who could lift them to play, if not above themselves, at least to their potential. Hooper summed up their despair after the Second Test: "It's a shame that we've come to this level."

At times, West Indian cricket again seemed worthy of a calypso, not a dirge

How far could they fall? Viv Richards, the chairman of selectors, didn't want to find out. In their first bold move, West Indies became the first team to enter a Test at Kolkata without a specialist spinner. Jermaine Lawson and Darren Powell, raw pacemen both, joined journeymen Mervyn Dillon and Cameron Cuffy to form, once again, a West Indian pace quartet. They were backing their strengths.

West Indies played like a team rejuvenated. The batsmen applied themselves, the bowlers bent their backs, the fielders threw themselves around, and actually believed it mattered. Shivnarine Chanderpaul, their most consistent batsman throughout, was rewarded with a big hundred. At times – when Lawson and Powell were humming, or Marlon Samuels stroking the ball around with disdainful ease – West Indian cricket again seemed worthy of a calypso, not a dirge.

The tourists carried their new confidence into the one-day series, which was played on flat tracks that were dream pitches for the stick-front-foot-out-and-thwack school of batsmanship. The average first-innings score was 285, yet the side chasing won the first six matches before Samuels played one of the great one-day innings to win the decider.

West Indies were without Brian Lara, suffering from a mysterious illness contracted in Sri Lanka. Hooper also pulled out of the Bangladesh leg, so he could have surgery on a troublesome knee before the World Cup, as did their most experienced fast bowler Mervyn Dillon. Ridley Jacobs led the team.

India's success did little to solve the central mystery of Indian cricket: the difference between the team's home and away form. The opening combination of Virender Sehwag and Sanjay Bangar averaged 78 here, but only seven in New Zealand a few weeks later. Harbhajan Singh and Anil Kumble initially seemed a world-class spin duo, collecting 36 Test wickets between them, but their ineffectiveness at Kolkata underscored their reliance on favourable conditions.

The Test pitches presented a different problem. The Indian board had embarked on a long-awaited programme to re-lay its main pitches to make them more competitive. But the cure merely aggravated the symptoms. These were worse than the originals, which had staged the enthralling Tests between India and Australia in 2000-01. The board stated that they needed time to settle in, and deserved the benefit of the doubt.

The umpiring was awful. It was shocking to see two of the best umpires in the game, David Shepherd and Asoka de Silva, make a slew of mistakes. This did not reflect on their abilities or intent, but on the insanely crowded schedule of the ICC's elite panel of umpires – in its first year, the elite eight were each scheduled to stand in an average of 80 days of international cricket.

The one-day series drew large crowds, most there for the revelry more than the cricket. The first three one-day internationals were all interrupted by crowd trouble, and the third had to be called off early; controversially, the game was awarded to India on Duckworth/Lewis calculations. Politics ensured that no action was taken against the venues – the host associations were part of the powerbase maintained by Jagmohan Dalmiya, the board president, and the ICC had too many battles on its hands to take on another.

Bangladesh provided West Indies with their first Test series win in the subcontinent for eight years. It also produced happy memories for Ramnaresh Sarwan, who finally hit maiden hundreds in both one-day internationals and Tests, and for Lawson, who seized six wickets in 15 balls to inflict on Bangladesh their biggest Test defeat yet.

WEST INDIAN TOURING PARTY

C. L. Hooper (Guyana) (*captain*), R. D. Jacobs (Leeward Islands) (*vice-captain*), G. R. Breese (Jamaica), S. Chanderpaul (Guyana), P. T. Collins (Barbados), C. E. Cuffy (Windward Islands), M. Dillon (Trinidad & Tobago), D. Ganga (Trinidad & Tobago), C. H. Gayle (Jamaica), R. O. Hinds (Barbados), W. W. Hinds (Jamaica), J. J. C. Lawson (Jamaica), M. V. Nagamootoo (Guyana), D. B. Powell (Jamaica), M. N. Samuels (Jamaica), R. R. Sarwan (Guyana).

B. C. Lara (Trinidad & Tobago) withdrew through illness during the preceding ICC Champions Trophy and was replaced by Ganga. C. D. Collymore (Barbados), V. C. Drakes (Barbados) and R. L. Powell (Jamaica) replaced Breese, Lawson and D. B. Powell for the one-day series in India and the tour of Bangladesh. Lawson was recalled after injuries to Cuffy and R. O. Hinds. Hooper, Dillon and Hinds left the party because of injuries before the Bangladesh leg, when D. B. Powell returned and R. D. Jacobs took over the captaincy.

Coach: R. A. Harper. *Manager:* R. O. Skerritt. *Sports therapist:* R. Rogers. *Statistician:* G. S. Smith.

WEST INDIAN TOUR RESULTS

Test matches – Played 5: Won 2, Lost 2, Drawn 1.
First-class matches – Played 7: Won 2, Lost 2, Drawn 3.
Wins – Bangladesh (2).
Losses – India (2).
Draws – India, Indian Board President's XI, Railways.
One-day internationals – Played 10: Won 6, Lost 3, No result 1. *Wins* – India (4), Bangladesh (2). *Losses* – India (3). *No result* – Bangladesh.
Other non-first-class match: Drew v Pakistanis.

TEST MATCH AVERAGES

INDIA – BATTING

	T	*I*	*NO*	*R*	*HS*	*100s*	*50s*	*Avge*	*Ct/St*
V. V. S. Laxman	3	4	1	271	154*	1	0	90.33	1
S. R. Tendulkar	3	5	1	306	176	1	0	76.50	2
V. Sehwag	3	5	0	286	147	1	1	57.20	5
R. Dravid	3	5	2	148	100*	1	0	49.33	2
†P. A. Patel	3	4	1	118	47	0	0	39.33	4/1
S. B. Bangar	3	5	0	192	77	0	2	38.40	1
J. Srinath	3	4	0	137	46	0	0	34.25	0
Harbhajan Singh	3	4	0	69	37	0	0	17.25	5
†S. C. Ganguly	3	4	0	49	29	0	0	12.25	9
A. Kumble	3	4	2	24	12*	0	0	12.00	3

Played in two Tests: Zaheer Khan 0, 4. Played in one Test: A. Nehra 0*.

† *Left-handed batsman.*

BOWLING

	Style	*O*	*M*	*R*	*W*	*BB*	*5W/i*	*Avge*
Zaheer Khan	LFM	42.4	12	111	8	4-41	0	13.87
Harbhajan Singh	OB	166	54	335	20	7-48	2	16.75
A. Kumble	LBG	153.2	35	387	16	5-30	1	24.18
J. Srinath	RFM	53	19	127	4	2-16	0	31.75

Also bowled: S. B. Bangar (RM) 18–7–63–0; A. Nehra (LFM) 23–9–66–1; V. Sehwag (OB) 10–0–51–1; S. R. Tendulkar (RM/OB/LB) 8–0–35–0.

WEST INDIES – BATTING

	T	*I*	*NO*	*R*	*HS*	*100s*	*50s*	*Avge*	*Ct/St*
†S. Chanderpaul	3	5	1	260	140	1	1	65.00	3
†W. W. Hinds	3	5	0	220	100	1	1	44.00	1
†C. H. Gayle	3	5	0	160	88	0	1	32.00	4
R. R. Sarwan	3	5	0	138	78	0	1	27.60	1
C. L. Hooper	3	5	0	124	46	0	0	24.80	5
†R. D. Jacobs	3	5	1	34	22*	0	0	8.50	5/3
†R. O. Hinds	2	4	0	34	16	0	0	8.50	0
P. T. Collins	2	4	2	15	8	0	0	7.50	0
M. Dillon	3	5	0	29	21	0	0	5.80	0
J. J. C. Lawson	2	3	0	7	5	0	0	2.33	0
C. E. Cuffy	2	3	1	4	4*	0	0	2.00	0

Played in one Test: G. R. Breese 5, 0 (1 ct); †M. V. Nagamootoo 9, 18; D. B. Powell 0; M. N. Samuels 104.

† *Left-handed batsman.*

BOWLING

	Style	*O*	*M*	*R*	*W*	*BB*	*5W/i*	*Avge*
M. Dillon	RFM	109.2	30	275	11	3-44	0	25.00
C. E. Cuffy.	RF	70.4	13	224	6	2-52	0	37.33
D. B. Powell	RFM	41.2	8	115	3	2-62	0	38.33
M. V. Nagamootoo . . .	LBG	47	12	132	3	3-132	0	44.00
C. L. Hooper.	OB	59.5	12	190	4	2-32	0	47.50
J. J. C. Lawson	RFM	64	10	206	4	2-63	0	51.50

Also bowled: G. R. Breese (OB) 31.2–3–135–2; S. Chanderpaul (LB) 3–0–9–1; P. T. Collins (LFM) 53–12–142–1; C. H. Gayle (OB) 27–6–79–0; R. O. Hinds (SLA) 15–1–49–0; W. W. Hinds (RM) 4–0–11–0; M. N. Samuels (OB) 16–3–21–1; R. R. Sarwan (LB) 10–1–49–0.

Note: Matches in this section which were not first-class are signified by a dagger.

†At Police Park, Colombo, September 27, 28, 29, 2002. WEST INDIANS drew with PAKISTANIS (see Pakistan v Australia).

At Bangalore, October 4, 5, 6, 2002. **Drawn.** Toss: Indian Board President's XI. **Indian Board President's XI 275-8 dec.** (H. K. Badani 67, D. Mongia 101*); **West Indians 606-4** (C. H. Gayle 62, W. W. Hinds 147, R. R. Sarwan 140 retired hurt, C. L. Hooper 67, R. O. Hinds 74 retired hurt, R. D. Jacobs 50*).

INDIA v WEST INDIES

First Test Match

At Mumbai, October 9, 10, 11, 12, 2002. India won by an innings and 112 runs. Toss: India.

The writing was on the pitch. The Wankhede Stadium's newly relaid surface had none of its predecessor's liveliness, and was underprepared – the match had been brought forward by two weeks so that Tendulkar could play his 101st Test on his home ground, where a stand was renamed in his honour. It was a consolation prize, as his 100th had come at The Oval a month earlier. The wicket heralded no brave new age, but harked back to the 1990s, when India won repeatedly on dustbowls that never gave visitors a chance. West Indies duly crumbled in three and a half days.

Not that the Indians needed help. They were charged up, eager to banish the demons of losing in the Caribbean five months earlier. It was an overwhelming team performance: they fired in every department, with an intensity in stark contrast to their opponents. They seized the initiative early and never let go. When Ganguly opted to bat, Sehwag and Bangar shared India's first 200-run opening partnership since Gavaskar's final series in 1986-87, and their best opening stand against West Indies. Bangar was patient, playing a compact game, making the bowlers do all the work; Sehwag gave the first hour to the bowlers and then took the breath away with his belligerence. His 147, off 206 balls, was studded with 24 fours and three sixes.

India ended the day on 278 for two, but the second day was not the run-fest it promised to be. Tendulkar and Ganguly were out early, and Dravid and Laxman added

Opening statement: at Mumbai, Virender Sehwag dominated both the West Indian bowlers and the double-century opening stand with Sanjay Bangar.
Picture by Arko Datta, Reuters.

a dour 105 in 53 overs. Rather than push home the advantage, they tried to avoid losing it; along with the momentum, the pitch deteriorated.

Laxman was stumped just before tea, and just after it Dravid completed his hundred. It was his fourth consecutive Test century, one behind Everton Weekes's record. The four innings spanned 29 hours, and combined resolute, orthodox defence with elegant, classical strokeplay. Through it all, his mind never wavered – though his body finally gave way to dehydration. He was struck with cramp during his 99th run, but limped back for another one, thanks to Patel's exhortations, before he was helped off. Patel's next three partners fell in eight balls. Then Srinath, who had revoked his retirement, helped him lift India to 457.

With the pitch fast falling apart, Harbhajan Singh and Kumble looked like the men to watch on the third day. Instead, it was Zaheer Khan who bowled the key spell. After West Indies slid to 59 for four, Hooper, in his 100th Test, and Chanderpaul threatened a recovery. Ganguly then made an inspired post-lunch move, bringing back Zaheer. On a humid afternoon with the pitch offering no assistance, he wrenched out three crucial wickets in 21 balls.

West Indies followed on that evening, 300 behind, and had no chance on the fourth morning, when the pitch appeared more suited to beach cricket than a Test match. Now Harbhajan and Kumble were unplayable, and took all ten second-innings wickets between them. Seven went to Harbhajan, who belied his reputation as a man relying more on surface than on air, flighting the ball beautifully. His guile would have delighted his one-time critic, that perfectly classical off-spinner, Erapalli Prasanna.

MOST HUNDREDS IN CONSECUTIVE TEST INNINGS

5	E. D. Weekes (West Indies)	1 v England 1947-48	4 v India 1948-49
4	J. H. W. Fingleton (Australia)	3 v South Africa 1935-36	1 v England 1936-37
	A. Melville (South Africa)	1 v England 1938-39	3 v England 1947
	R. Dravid (India)	**3 v England 2002**	**1 v West Indies 2002-03**

The following have achieved three consecutive centuries: W. Bardsley, G. Boycott, D. G. Bradman, D. C. S. Compton, P. A. de Silva (twice), S. M. Gavaskar (twice), G. A. Gooch, C. G. Greenidge, D. L. Haynes, V. S. Hazare, G. A. Headley, A. H. Jones, V. G. Kambli, C. G. Macartney, A. R. Morris, Mudassar Nazar, G. S. Sobers, H. Sutcliffe, P. R. Umrigar, E. D. Weekes, Zaheer Abbas.

Chanderpaul had been last man out in the first innings and was last man standing in the second. By the end of the game, he averaged 89 against India and was handling their spinners magnificently. With an ungainly shuffle across the wicket, he played the ball late, with soft hands and perfect balance, and neutered the bowling instead of demolishing it. In this game, he was a near-immovable object, batting six and a half hours. But Harbhajan and Kumble were the irresistible forces that blew away his colleagues to ensure India's first-ever innings victory over West Indies.

Man of the Match: V. Sehwag.

Close of play: First day, India 278-2 (Dravid 28, Tendulkar 35); Second day, West Indies 33-2 (Sarwan 20, Dillon 4); Third day, West Indies 91-1 (Gayle 34, Sarwan 9).

India

S. B. Bangar c Sarwan b Dillon	55
V. Sehwag c Jacobs b Dillon	147
R. Dravid retired hurt	100
S. R. Tendulkar c Jacobs b Dillon	35
*S. C. Ganguly lbw b Cuffy	4
V. V. S. Laxman st Jacobs b Nagamootoo	45
†P. A. Patel not out	21
Harbhajan Singh c Jacobs b Cuffy	0
A. Kumble c Hooper b Nagamootoo	0
Zaheer Khan lbw b Nagamootoo	0
J. Srinath c Jacobs b Hooper	31
L-b 7, w 3, n-b 9	19
1/201 (1) 2/213 (2) 3/281 (4) 4/296 (5) 5/401 (6) 6/407 (8) 7/408 (9) 8/408 (10) 9/457 (11)	457

Dravid retired hurt at 407-5.

Bowling: Dillon 31.2–9–54–3; Collins 28–7–76–0; Cuffy 28.4–6–88–2; Nagamootoo 47–12–132–3; Hooper 11.5–3–40–1; W. W. Hinds 4–0–11–0; R. O. Hinds 10–0–40–0; Gayle 2–1–3–0; Sarwan 1–0–6–0.

West Indies

First innings		Second innings	
C. H. Gayle lbw b Zaheer Khan	7	c Ganguly b Harbhajan Singh	42
W. W. Hinds c sub (S. S. Das) b Harbhajan Singh	1	b Harbhajan Singh	40
R. R. Sarwan lbw b Kumble	22	c Tendulkar b Kumble	17
M. Dillon b Srinath	21	(9) c Dravid b Harbhajan Singh	0
S. Chanderpaul c and b Kumble	54	(4) not out	36
*C. L. Hooper c Bangar b Zaheer Khan	23	(5) c and b Harbhajan Singh	1
R. O. Hinds lbw b Zaheer Khan	9	(6) c Sehwag b Kumble	2
†R. D. Jacobs c Ganguly b Zaheer Khan	0	(7) c Ganguly b Kumble	0
M. V. Nagamootoo c Harbhajan Singh b Kumble	9	(8) c Ganguly b Harbhajan Singh	18
P. T. Collins lbw b Kumble	0	c Dravid b Harbhajan Singh	8
C. E. Cuffy not out	4	c and b Harbhajan Singh	0
L-b 5, n-b 2	7	B 8, l-b 15, n-b 1	24
1/7 (1) 2/27 (2) 3/43 (3) 4/59 (4) 5/103 (6) 6/119 (7) 7/123 (8) 8/145 (9) 9/146 (10) 10/157 (5)	157	1/60 (2) 2/105 (1) 3/107 (3) 4/110 (5) 5/117 (6) 6/117 (7) 7/158 (8) 8/158 (9) 9/184 (10) 10/188 (11)	188

Bowling: *First Innings*—Srinath 11–5–16–1; Zaheer Khan 16–4–41–4; Harbhajan Singh 21–8–37–1; Kumble 24.5–5–51–4; Sehwag 2–0–7–0. *Second Innings*—Srinath 4–2–19–0; Zaheer Khan 4–0–26–0; Bangar 6–1–20–0; Harbhajan Singh 28.3–12–48–7; Kumble 25–8–50–3; Tendulkar 1–0–2–0.

Umpires: E. A. R. de Silva (Sri Lanka) and D. R. Shepherd (England).
Third umpire: I. Sivaram. Referee: M. J. Procter (South Africa).

INDIA v WEST INDIES

Second Test Match

At Chennai, October 17, 18, 19, 20, 2002. India won by eight wickets. Toss: West Indies. Test debuts: G. R. Breese, J. J. C. Lawson.

At the end of this match, Hooper summed it up by saying: "We didn't play cricket." Pithy, and apt. The West Indian batting lacked application, their bowling lacked discipline and their fielding lacked motivation. India won on autopilot to claim their first Test series victory over West Indies in nearly 24 years; unlike the First Test, they had their moments of frailty – but the tourists were already down, and almost out.

The saga of relaid-pitches-gone-wrong continued at Chennai. The fast bowlers got little assistance and not much bounce, while the spinners extracted plenty of turn and often got the ball to rear up viciously. On the first day, West Indies ground to 45 for one by lunch, but that was one of their best sessions. Oddly, in a move reeking of bad strategy and low confidence, too many of the top order tried to bat out time rather than score runs – Hinds had a mere 18 to his name after facing 97 balls in more than two hours. The pitch would deteriorate, but it wasn't quite that bad yet. Only Hooper counter-attacked and, on his 32nd birthday, Kumble picked up four for ten in 8.3 overs after tea to finish with five in a Test innings for the 20th time.

Sehwag and Bangar were batting by the close, and gave India another solid start. Sehwag was dropped twice in the 40s, but played with refreshing freedom. Once he was out at 93, though, the Indians lost their way. Dillon bowled with uncharacteristic accuracy, but wasn't backed up by his fielders; Jermaine Lawson, on Test debut, bowled with raw pace but little control. Still, they reduced India to 190 for five by the end of a second day cut to 62 overs by rain and bad light. Tendulkar made a subdued 43, Ganguly got a doubtful decision first ball, and Dravid was beaten by sheer pace – Lawson's first Test wicket thus protecting Everton Weekes's record of five Test centuries in a row.

When the third day began under floodlights, off-spinner Gareth Breese claimed the last recognised batsman, Laxman, as his own maiden wicket. But India's tail wagged viciously. Harbhajan Singh, perfecting his helicopter-rotor swing, and Srinath, baring all three stumps with exhibitionist frenzy, played entertaining cameos to create a lead of 149.

Sarwan was the rock for the West Indian second innings, but his colleagues sank around him. He made an elegant, five-hour 78, playing the spinners with deft footwork and solid defence. He added 96 with Hinds and 72 with Hooper, both of whom attacked with gusto. But the cause was desperate – no other man reached double figures. On another floodlit morning, Sarwan saw West Indies to 200 for the first time in this series but, once he went, they lost their last six for 21. Harbhajan took three in a single over, and the only setback came when Ganguly collided with Kumble attempting a catch, and was carried off on a stretcher.

Ganguly's batting was not needed. Sehwag celebrated his 24th birthday with a 30-ball blast, and India reached their target of 81 in light drizzle just before the clouds opened up to rain literally, as well as metaphorically, on a battered West Indian side. They had lost the series in less than seven days' playing time.

Man of the Match: Harbhajan Singh.

Close of play: First day, India 31-0 (Bangar 6, Sehwag 24); Second day, India 190-5 (Laxman 18, Patel 1); Third day, West Indies 186-4 (Sarwan 62, R. O. Hinds 1).

West Indies

C. H. Gayle c Tendulkar b Harbhajan Singh	23	– c Kumble b Srinath	0
W. W. Hinds lbw b Kumble	18	– c Ganguly b Harbhajan Singh	61
R. R. Sarwan b Srinath	19	– lbw b Zaheer Khan	78
S. Chanderpaul c Patel b Kumble	27	– c Harbhajan Singh b Srinath	3
*C. L. Hooper c Ganguly b Zaheer Khan	35	– c Patel b Kumble	46
R. O. Hinds lbw b Kumble	16	– c Kumble b Harbhajan Singh	7
†R. D. Jacobs c Sehwag b Harbhajan Singh	9	– c Patel b Zaheer Khan	3
G. R. Breese c Sehwag b Harbhajan Singh	5	– c Ganguly b Harbhajan Singh	0
M. Dillon b Kumble	4	– lbw b Harbhajan Singh	4
P. T. Collins not out	1	– not out	6
J. J. C. Lawson c Ganguly b Kumble	0	– b Zaheer Khan	2
B 8, l-b 1, n-b 1	10	B 12, l-b 3, w 1, n-b 3	19
1/40 (1) 2/46 (2) 3/62 (3) 4/117 (5) 5/135 (4) 6/142 (6) 7/161 (8) 8/166 (9) 9/166 (7) 10/167 (11)	167	1/0 (1) 2/96 (2) 3/107 (4) 4/179 (5) 5/208 (3) 6/210 (6) 7/210 (8) 8/214 (9) 9/222 (7) 10/229 (11)	229

Bowling: *First Innings*—Srinath 10–5–14–1; Zaheer Khan 10–3–21–1; Bangar 6–3–29–0; Harbhajan Singh 29–13–56–3; Kumble 23.3–10–30–5; Sehwag 1–0–8–0. *Second Innings*—Srinath 9–4–16–2; Zaheer Khan 12.4–5–23–3; Harbhajan Singh 30–6–79–4; Kumble 26–3–87–1; Sehwag 2–0–9–0.

India

S. B. Bangar c Hooper b Dillon	40	– c Gayle b Hooper	20
V. Sehwag b Collins	61	– st Jacobs b Hooper	33
R. Dravid b Lawson	11	– not out	6
S. R. Tendulkar b Lawson	43	– not out	16
*S. C. Ganguly lbw b Dillon	0		
V. V. S. Laxman c and b Breese	24		
†P. A. Patel st Jacobs b Breese	23		
Harbhajan Singh b Dillon	37		
J. Srinath run out	39		
A. Kumble not out	12		
Zaheer Khan run out	4		
B 4, l-b 10, w 1, n-b 7	22	L-b 3, n-b 3	6
1/93 (2) 2/109 (3) 3/155 (1) 4/155 (5) 5/180 (4) 6/204 (6) 7/255 (8) 8/281 (7) 9/305 (9) 10/316 (11)	316	1/50 (2) 2/61 (1)	(2 wkts) 81

Bowling: *First Innings*—Dillon 26–11–44–3; Collins 23–5–59–1; Lawson 20–4–63–2; Breese 26.1–3–108–2; Hooper 6–2–19–0; R. O. Hinds 5–1–9–0. *Second Innings*—Dillon 5–1–10–0; Collins 2–0–7–0; Lawson 2–0–2–0; Breese 5.1–0–27–0; Hooper 7–1–32–2.

Umpires: E. A. R. de Silva (Sri Lanka) and D. R. Shepherd (England).
Third umpire: K. Hariharan. Referee: M. J. Procter (South Africa).

At Pune, October 24, 25, 26, 2002. **Drawn.** Toss: West Indians. **West Indians 449-8 dec.** (C. H. Gayle 154, W. W. Hinds 50, D. Ganga 71, G. R. Breese 57*; K. S. Parida 4-107) **and 35-0; Railways 402** (S. N. Khanolkar 102, M. Kartik 72, Y. Gowda 107; C. E. Cuffy 4-84).

Railways were the reigning Ranji champions.

INDIA v WEST INDIES

Third Test Match

At Kolkata, October 30, 31, November 1, 2, 3, 2002. Drawn. Toss: India.

There was no better venue for a turnaround. The last Test at Kolkata had seen one of the most dramatic fightbacks of all time, when Laxman had scored 281 and Harbhajan Singh had spun India to victory over Australia after following on. Here, West Indies sprung a surprise even before the toss: they named a side without a specialist spinner, something unprecedented in almost 70 years of Test cricket at Eden Gardens. The positive intent was followed by spirited cricket, and they might have won but for a backs-to-the-wall stand between Tendulkar and, once again, Laxman.

India batted more like the West Indians had been doing. Eight got starts, but only Bangar crossed 50; partnerships sprang up, only to be uprooted against the run of play. The only dismissal actually plotted was Tendulkar's, frustrated into indiscretion by the familiar geometry of a 7–2 field and a negative line outside off. The brightest moments came from a 77-run stand between Bangar and Laxman straight after tea. Bangar moved up a couple of gears, pulling and driving with elegant ease to match Laxman himself. Still, it took 46 off 40 balls from Srinath next morning to get India past 300.

Gayle and Hinds responded with grim determination and an opening stand of 172, perhaps feeling in their guts what Hooper had articulated beforehand: that the West Indians were "playing for pride". They used their feet superbly against Harbhajan Singh and Kumble, and easily nullified their leg-stump line of attack.

But the partnership of the innings belonged to Chanderpaul and Samuels, who moved West Indies into the lead while adding 195. Chanderpaul equalled his highest Test score, batting with customary assurance against spin – first the grind, then the blast. He smashed Kumble for four fours and a six in two overs, and reduced Harbhajan to an outside-leg line of containment. Samuels had almost been sent home after breaking a curfew at a disco, but now he danced to his maiden Test century. Circumspect at first, he opened out with some gorgeous drives and pulls, his effortless flair evoking West Indian batting of an earlier era.

The last five wickets tumbled in an hour on the fourth morning, and a 139-run lead did not look much on a good pitch – until India slid to 49 for three before lunch. The collapse was in part manufactured: Dravid was given out leg-before off an inside edge for the second time in the match, and after the interval Ganguly got his third doubtful lbw decision in four innings. With India four down and 52 behind, an upset seemed in the offing. Then, Tendulkar stepped up.

A common criticism of Tendulkar has been that, at the crunch, he crumbles. As if to counter that, he has transformed himself from a spontaneous marauder to a purposeful innings builder. His average has not suffered, but his aura has diminished. In this daunting situation, would he dig in or hit out? He did both, imperiously progressing to 176, his maiden Test century at Kolkata, and occupied the crease for seven hours to save the match. He did this with minimum risk and to maximum effect: unlike lesser batsmen, he looked least likely to get out when most dominant. This was the Tendulkar of old, re-emerging when India most needed him.

Kolkata cut: Sachin Tendulkar hits another boundary during his key partnership with V. V. S. Laxman. Together they added 214 to bat West Indies out of contention in the Third Test.

Picture by Sucheta Das, Reuters.

The Old Tendulkar was accompanied by the New Laxman. After his legendary 281, Laxman had nearly lost his place, playing one graceful cameo after another without building any more monuments. But he had re-invented himself as a dependable No. 6, and here he put together another Kolkata masterclass. He was the perfect support act in a stand of 214 spanning 70 overs, an Indian fifth-wicket record against West Indies.

The last afternoon was a disappointment. As India's lead climbed towards 200, Ganguly might have declared and gone for a win. With the series secure, he let it drift. After the outstanding efforts of Tendulkar and Laxman, who remained unbeaten after nearly nine hours, the end was not worthy of the means.

Man of the Match: S. R. Tendulkar. *Man of the Series:* Harbhajan Singh.

Close of play: First day, India 275-6 (Patel 18, Harbhajan Singh 3); Second day, West Indies 189-3 (Gayle 80, Chanderpaul 1); Third day, West Indies 446-5 (Chanderpaul 136, Samuels 89); Fourth day, India 195-4 (Tendulkar 114, Laxman 30).

India

S. B. Bangar c Hinds b Cuffy	77	– c Chanderpaul b Dillon	0
V. Sehwag lbw b Dillon	35	– c Chanderpaul b Dillon	10
R. Dravid lbw b Powell	14	– lbw b Powell	17
S. R. Tendulkar c Gayle b Lawson	36	– c Gayle b Cuffy	176
*S. C. Ganguly c Jacobs b Hooper	29	– lbw b Cuffy	16
V. V. S. Laxman c Gayle b Dillon	48	– not out	154
†P. A. Patel c Chanderpaul b Lawson	47	– run out	27
Harbhajan Singh b Cuffy	6	– c Hooper b Samuels	26
J. Srinath c Hooper b Dillon	46	– c Hooper b Chanderpaul	21
A. Kumble lbw b Powell	4	– not out	8
A. Nehra not out	0		
L-b 7, w 1, n-b 8	16	B 8, l-b 7, n-b 1	16
1/49 (2) 2/72 (3) 3/116 (4) 4/165 (5) 5/242 (1) 6/271 (6) 7/280 (8) 8/353 (7) 9/358 (9) 10/358 (10)	358	1/0 (1) 2/11 (2) 3/49 (3) 4/87 (5) 5/301 (4) 6/373 (7) 7/407 (8) 8/458 (9) (8 wkts dec.)	471

Bowling: *First Innings*—Dillon 22–3–82–3; Cuffy 25–4–84–2; Lawson 20–3–76–2; Powell 16.2–4–62–2; Hooper 15–5–36–1; Gayle 2–0–6–0; Sarwan 1–0–5–0. *Second Innings*—Dillon 25–6–85–2; Cuffy 17–3–52–2; Lawson 22–3–65–0; Powell 25–4–53–1; Hooper 20–1–63–0; Gayle 23–5–70–0; Sarwan 8–1–38–0; Samuels 16–3–21–1; Chanderpaul 3–0–9–1.

West Indies

C. H. Gayle c Sehwag b Kumble	88
W. W. Hinds c Ganguly b Harbhajan Singh	100
R. R. Sarwan st Patel b Harbhajan Singh	2
M. Dillon b Harbhajan Singh	0
S. Chanderpaul c Harbhajan Singh b Sehwag	140
*C. L. Hooper c Patel b Nehra	19
M. N. Samuels c Sehwag b Harbhajan Singh	104
†R. D. Jacobs not out	22
D. B. Powell lbw b Kumble	0
J. J. C. Lawson lbw b Kumble	5
C. E. Cuffy c Laxman b Harbhajan Singh	0
B 4, l-b 7, n-b 6	17
1/172 (2) 2/186 (3) 3/186 (4) 4/213 (1) 5/255 (6) 6/450 (5) 7/469 (7) 8/470 (9) 9/496 (10) 10/497 (11)	497

Bowling: Srinath 19–3–62–0; Nehra 23–9–66–1; Harbhajan Singh 57.3–15–115–5; Kumble 54–9–169–3; Bangar 6–3–14–0; Tendulkar 7–0–33–0; Sehwag 5–0–27–1.

Umpires: E. A. R. de Silva (Sri Lanka) and D. R. Shepherd (England).
Third umpire: A. V. Jayaprakash. Referee: M. J. Procter (South Africa).

†INDIA v WEST INDIES

First One-Day International

At Jamshedpur, November 6, 2002. West Indies won by four wickets. Toss: India. One-day international debut: Jai P. Yadav.

This opening game set a pattern. Batting first, India made 283 but still lost; bottle-throwing halted play for ten minutes with West Indies 13 short of victory; and Sarwan saw them home with an immaculate 83. Agarkar was India's star. Experimentally promoted to No. 3, he plundered 95 off 102 balls before Kaif exploded to 31 in 18 at the end. For West Indies, Hinds made a belligerent 93 having been dropped twice, and Samuels a cultured fifty before becoming Kumble's 300th wicket in one-day internationals. The players were called off the field after Harbhajan had conceded 17 in the 47th over. TV commentators announced that referee Mike Procter had awarded the game to West Indies under Duckworth/Lewis but, when the crowd calmed down, the game resumed and the batsmen stumbled. They needed six off the last over and three off the final ball. But an ice-cool Sarwan hit a full toss from Agarkar for four over extra cover.

Man of the Match: R. R. Sarwan.

India

V. Sehwag c and b Drakes	28
*S. C. Ganguly b Collins	16
A. B. Agarkar c Gayle b Collins	95
V. V. S. Laxman b Nagamootoo	47
†R. Dravid not out	46
Yuvraj Singh c Gayle b Hooper	4
Jai P. Yadav b Dillon	0
M. Kaif not out	31
B 4, l-b 6, w 5, n-b 1	16
1/43 (1) 2/49 (2) 3/147 (4) 4/222 (3) 5/235 (6) 6/236 (7) (6 wkts, 50 overs)	283

Harbhajan Singh, A. Kumble and A. Nehra did not bat.

Bowling: Dillon 10–0–64–1; Collins 10–1–40–2; Drakes 10–1–62–1; Hooper 10–2–46–1; Nagamootoo 8–0–45–1; Gayle 2–0–16–0.

West Indies

W. W. Hinds c Dravid b Nehra	93
C. H. Gayle c Yadav b Agarkar	7
M. N. Samuels b Kumble	51
R. R. Sarwan not out	83
*C. L. Hooper c Yadav b Sehwag	4
S. Chanderpaul c Ganguly b Nehra	23
†R. D. Jacobs run out	0
M. V. Nagamootoo not out	1
B 2, l-b 5, w 16	23
1/28 (2) 2/114 (3) 3/201 (1) 4/206 (5) 5/277 (6) 6/279 (7) (6 wkts, 50 overs)	285

V. C. Drakes, M. Dillon and P. T. Collins did not bat.

Bowling: Nehra 9–1–50–2; Agarkar 9–1–42–1; Yadav 4–0–22–0; Harbhajan Singh 9–0–68–0; Kumble 7–0–48–1; Sehwag 10–0–37–1; Yuvraj Singh 2–0–11–0.

Umpires: E. A. R. de Silva (Sri Lanka) and A. V. Jayaprakash.
Third umpire: I. Sivaram. Referee: M. J. Procter (South Africa).

†INDIA v WEST INDIES

Second One-Day International

At Nagpur, November 9, 2002. West Indies won by seven wickets (D/L method). Toss: West Indies.

India paid the price for playing an extra bowler on yet another batsman's pitch. West Indies timed their chase of a 280-run target perfectly, with Gayle scoring an aggressive century. Ganguly had given India a solid start, passing 8,000 one-day runs en route, but, despite a 105-run stand in 85 balls between Laxman and Dravid, India fell at least 20 short of par on this pitch. Once again, the crowd stopped play, bombarding the West Indian fielders; this interruption, plus a late start because of dew, reduced the game to 47 overs a side.

Man of the Match: C. H. Gayle.

India

*S. C. Ganguly c Drakes b Nagamootoo	78
V. Sehwag c Dillon b Drakes	1
A. B. Agarkar c Sarwan b Dillon	6
V. V. S. Laxman st Jacobs b Gayle	99
Harbhajan Singh c sub (R. L. Powell) b Nagamootoo	2
†R. Dravid run out	51
Yuvraj Singh c Chanderpaul b Drakes	1
M. Kaif not out	12
J. Srinath run out	2
A. Kumble b Drakes	2
A. Nehra not out	2
L-b 5, w 8, n-b 10	23
1/3 (2) 2/20 (3) 3/148 (1) 4/155 (5) 5/260 (6) 6/260 (4) 7/262 (7) 8/267 (9) 9/272 (10) (9 wkts, 47 overs)	279

Bowling: Dillon 10–0–59–1; Drakes 9–0–55–3; Collymore 4–0–35–0; Hooper 9–1–42–0; Nagamootoo 10–0–49–2; Gayle 5–0–34–1.

West Indies

C. H. Gayle b Srinath	103
W. W. Hinds c Agarkar b Srinath	27
M. N. Samuels c Kaif b Sehwag	52
R. R. Sarwan not out	39
S. Chanderpaul not out	39
B 6, l-b 6, w 7, n-b 1	20
1/42 (2) 2/176 (3) 3/221 (1) (3 wkts, 46.2 overs)	280

*C. L. Hooper, †R. D. Jacobs, M. V. Nagamootoo, V. C. Drakes, M. Dillon and C. D. Collymore did not bat.

Bowling: Srinath 9.2–1–35–2; Nehra 10–0–67–0; Agarkar 7–0–47–0; Sehwag 8–0–51–1; Harbhajan Singh 6–0–35–0; Kumble 6–0–33–0.

Umpires: E. A. R. de Silva (Sri Lanka) and K. Hariharan.
Third umpire: A. V. Jayaprakash. Referee: M. J. Procter (South Africa).

†INDIA v WEST INDIES

Third One-Day International

At Rajkot, November 12, 2002. India won by 81 runs (D/L method). Toss: India.

A chucking controversy ruined this game, but for the third time running the chuckers were in the stands. Water bottles hit Drakes and narrowly missed substitute Ryan Hinds, while Pedro Collins, who was not even playing, was struck by a small sandbag. Jacobs, acting-captain because Hooper was injured, led the West Indians off the field. After an hour and 20 minutes, the game was abandoned. India were then awarded the match on Duckworth/Lewis – they were 81 ahead of par – a decision to which West Indies understandably but unsuccessfully objected. Local rumour was that bookmakers had sabotaged the match to stop India winning, and had been floored by the outcome. India were put on course by Sehwag, who scored a glorious 114 in 82 balls.

Man of the Match: V. Sehwag.

West Indies

C. H. Gayle b Harbhajan Singh	72
W. W. Hinds c Laxman b Srinath	10
M. N. Samuels c Dravid b Ganguly	16
R. R. Sarwan c Dravid b Nehra	84
S. Chanderpaul c Yadav b Harbhajan Singh	74
R. L. Powell not out	19
*†R. D. Jacobs not out	9
L-b 3, w 9, n-b 4	16
1/36 (2) 2/93 (3) 3/119 (1) 4/268 (5) 5/272 (4) (5 wkts, 50 overs)	300

M. V. Nagamootoo, V. C. Drakes, M. Dillon and C. E. Cuffy did not bat.

Bowling: Srinath 9–0–46–1; Nehra 10–0–56–1; Agarkar 6–0–63–0; Yadav 2–0–14–0; Ganguly 7–0–30–1; Harbhajan Singh 10–0–59–2; Sehwag 6–0–29–0.

India

*S. C. Ganguly c Chanderpaul b Drakes	72
V. Sehwag not out	114
V. V. S. Laxman not out	0
L-b 6, w 4, n-b 4	14
1/196 (1) (1 wkt, 27.1 overs)	200

†R. Dravid, A. B. Agarkar, Yuvraj Singh, M. Kaif, Jai P. Yadav, Harbhajan Singh, J. Srinath and A. Nehra did not bat.

Bowling: Dillon 6–0–40–0; Drakes 6–0–36–1; Cuffy 6–0–41–0; Gayle 1–0–18–0; Nagamootoo 5–0–43–0; Samuels 3.1–1–16–0.

Umpires: E. A. R. de Silva (Sri Lanka) and A. V. Jayaprakash.
Third umpire: K. Hariharan. Referee: M. J. Procter (South Africa).

†INDIA v WEST INDIES

Fourth One-Day International

At Ahmedabad, November 15, 2002 (day/night). India won by five wickets. Toss: India.

India pulled level in the series when they reached 325 with 14 balls to spare – the third-highest run-chase in a one-day international. All three occurred in 2002, and India had also been responsible for the second: 326 to overtake England at Lord's in July (Australia had scored 330 against South Africa in April). Earlier, 140 from Gayle, with five sixes in 127 balls, and an enterprising 99 not out from Sarwan – still chasing his maiden international hundred – seemed to have made West Indies unchallengeable. But Dravid's nerves of steel guided India to the finish as Bangar, that epitome of Test match stodge, finally lived up to his name with a breathtaking 57 off 41 balls. Ahmedabad, a city infamous for communal violence, produced the first trouble-free game of the series.

Man of the Match: C. H. Gayle.

West Indies

C. H. Gayle c Kartik b Sehwag 140	*C. L. Hooper not out. 36
W. W. Hinds c Dravid b Srinath 26	
M. N. Samuels run out 5	L-b 5, w 9, n-b 1 15
R. R. Sarwan not out 99	——
S. Chanderpaul c sub (D. Mongia) b Harbhajan Singh . 3	1/80 (2) 2/90 (3) 3/238 (1) 4/258 (5) (4 wkts, 50 overs) 324

†R. D. Jacobs, M. V. Nagamootoo, V. C. Drakes, M. Dillon and P. T. Collins did not bat.

Bowling: Srinath 9–1–71–1; Nehra 5–0–53–0; Harbhajan Singh 10–1–30–1; Kartik 10–0–46–0; Ganguly 1–0–9–0; Sehwag 8–0–49–1; Yuvraj Singh 6–0–48–0; Bangar 1–0–13–0.

India

*S. C. Ganguly c Jacobs b Collins 28	S. B. Bangar not out. 57
V. Sehwag c Hooper b Dillon 4	L-b 2, w 8, n-b 13. 23
V. V. S. Laxman run out 66	——
†R. Dravid not out 109	1/5 (2) 2/45 (1) (5 wkts, 47.4 overs) 325
Yuvraj Singh c Hooper b Dillon 30	3/148 (3) 4/209 (5)
M. Kaif c sub (R. L. Powell) b Drakes. . 8	5/231 (6)

M. Kartik, Harbhajan Singh, J. Srinath and A. Nehra did not bat.

Bowling: Dillon 10–0–65–2; Collins 9–0–60–1; Drakes 9.4–0–60–1; Hooper 9–0–61–0; Nagamootoo 9–0–62–0; Gayle 1–0–15–0.

Umpires: E. A. R. de Silva (Sri Lanka) and K. Hariharan.
Third umpire: I. Sivaram. Referee: M. J. Procter (South Africa).

†INDIA v WEST INDIES

Fifth One-Day International

At Vadodara (formerly Baroda), November 18, 2002. West Indies won by five wickets. Toss: West Indies. One-day international debut: L. Balaji.

This was no day to be a ball. Both sides battered the leather at the start, consolidated, and then hiccoughed before accelerating at the end. The side that knew the target won. Sehwag mauled the bowling, helping India gain 290 even though two overs had been lost to dew. Like the Indian openers, Gayle and Hinds set off at eight an over. Hinds pummelled five sixes in a 61-ball 80, one hitting a female spectator (she reappeared, bandaged but waving cheerfully), and Gayle hustled his third hundred in four games. The bowlers might as well have been spectators, too, bar Kartik, who flighted the ball generously and was the only man to go for less than four an over.

Man of the Match: W. W. Hinds.

India

*S. C. Ganguly b Hooper 53	J. Srinath not out 3
V. Sehwag c Chanderpaul b Collymore. . 52	Harbhajan Singh not out 1
V. V. S. Laxman c Hooper b Collins . . . 71	B 2, l-b 7, w 6, n-b 5 20
†R. Dravid c Gayle b Samuels 33	——
M. Kaif c Sarwan b Collins 4	1/88 (2) 2/134 (1) (8 wkts, 48 overs) 290
Yuvraj Singh c Hooper b Collymore . . . 15	3/212 (4) 4/223 (5)
S. B. Bangar run out. 27	5/232 (3) 6/254 (6)
M. Kartik c Jacobs b Collins 11	7/285 (8) 8/286 (7)

L. Balaji did not bat.

Bowling: Collins 9–0–60–3; Drakes 3–0–17–0; Collymore 10–0–56–2; Hinds 1–0–16–0; Hooper 9–1–41–1; Gayle 8–0–44–0; Samuels 8–0–47–1.

West Indies

C. H. Gayle c Dravid b Harbhajan Singh 101
W. W. Hinds c Ganguly b Sehwag 80
M. N. Samuels c Ganguly b Harbhajan Singh . 1
R. R. Sarwan c Ganguly b Kartik 34
S. Chanderpaul run out 8
R. L. Powell not out 30
*C. L. Hooper not out. 21
L-b 3, w 9, n-b 4 16

1/132 (2) 2/135 (3) (5 wkts, 46.5 overs) 291
3/218 (4) 4/239 (5)
5/239 (1)

†R. D. Jacobs, V. C. Drakes, P. T. Collins and C. D. Collymore did not bat.

Bowling: Srinath 6–0–42–0; Balaji 4–0–44–0; Bangar 1–0–6–0; Harbhajan Singh 10–1–53–2; Sehwag 9.5–0–55–1; Kartik 10–0–38–1; Yuvraj Singh 3–0–18–0; Laxman 1–0–8–0; Ganguly 2–0–24–0.

Umpires: E. A. R. de Silva (Sri Lanka) and A. V. Jayaprakash.
Third umpire: I. Sivaram. Referee: M. J. Procter (South Africa).

†INDIA v WEST INDIES

Sixth One-Day International

At Jodhpur, November 21, 2002. India won by three wickets. Toss: India.

At last, the bowlers claimed their revenge. The Indians bowled with aggression and guile to dismiss West Indies for 201, the first all-out total in this series: Agarkar and Kartik collected three wickets apiece. Dravid, the acting-captain while Ganguly rested, was the mainstay of the run-chase, adding 99 with Yuvraj Singh, but a mini-collapse of three in 11 balls removed them both and blew the match right open again. Bangar kept his head to steer India to a victory that squared the series with one match to go.

Man of the Match: A. B. Agarkar.

West Indies

C. H. Gayle lbw b Kartik 27
W. W. Hinds c Mongia b Agarkar 1
M. N. Samuels b Kartik 3
R. R. Sarwan b Kartik 14
S. Chanderpaul c Dravid b Agarkar 58
R. L. Powell lbw b Sehwag 29
*C. L. Hooper c and b Bangar 38
†R. D. Jacobs run out 9
V. C. Drakes b Bangar 0
P. T. Collins c Bangar b Agarkar 2
C. D. Collymore not out 2
B 1, l-b 8, w 7, n-b 2 18

1/34 (2) 2/42 (1) 3/47 (3) (46.3 overs) 201
4/74 (4) 5/135 (6) 6/183 (5)
7/193 (7) 8/193 (9)
9/197 (10) 10/201 (8)

Bowling: Srinath 8.3–1–28–0; Agarkar 9–1–24–3; Bangar 10–2–39–2; Kartik 10–1–36–3; Mongia 3–0–24–0; Sehwag 6–0–41–1.

India

D. Mongia c Jacobs b Drakes 5
V. Sehwag c Samuels b Drakes 18
V. V. S. Laxman c Gayle b Collins 7
*†R. Dravid c Powell b Drakes 58
Yuvraj Singh c Powell b Collymore 54
M. Kaif c Powell b Collins 15
R. S. Sodhi c Jacobs b Collymore 1
S. B. Bangar not out 32
A. B. Agarkar not out 6
W 2, n-b 4 6

1/19 (1) 2/26 (2) (7 wkts, 46.2 overs) 202
3/48 (3) 4/147 (5)
5/147 (4) 6/148 (7) 7/187 (6)

M. Kartik and J. Srinath did not bat.

Bowling: Collins 10–1–38–2; Drakes 10–0–38–3; Collymore 9.2–0–42–2; Hooper 4–0–19–0; Gayle 4–0–28–0; Samuels 9–0–37–0.

Umpires: E. A. R. de Silva (Sri Lanka) and K. Hariharan.
Third umpire: I. Sivaram. Referee: M. J. Procter (South Africa).

†INDIA v WEST INDIES

Seventh One-Day International

At Vijayawada, November 24, 2002. West Indies won by 135 runs. Toss: India.

Two young West Indians stepped forward to revive the spirit of an earlier, greater generation. Their career-best performances enabled their side to buck the series trend, thrashing India despite batting first. Just as he did in the final Test, Samuels scored a maiden hundred, an astonishing 108 off 75 balls. He lashed five sixes and 11 fours, destroying the bowlers with a flair and a swagger recalling Viv Richards – though the red handkerchief he waved in celebration was a gift from Steve Waugh. West Indies scored 120 in their last ten overs. Then Lawson, summoned back from the Caribbean as injury cover, tore through India, seizing four wickets in seven new-ball overs – a blast of *déjà vu* from the days of Marshall and Holding. West Indies secured the series with 13 overs in hand, a remarkable end to a tour that had begun in such despair.

Man of the Match: M. N. Samuels. *Man of the Series:* C. H. Gayle.

West Indies

C. H. Gayle c Kaif b Srinath	5
W. W. Hinds b Sehwag	58
S. Chanderpaul c Kartik b Agarkar	6
R. R. Sarwan lbw b Agarkar	83
M. N. Samuels not out	108
R. L. Powell st Dravid b Sehwag	30
*C. L. Hooper c Kaif b Sehwag	13
†R. D. Jacobs not out	0
L-b 6, w 1, n-b 5	12
1/8 (1) 2/16 (3) 3/132 (2) 4/182 (4) 5/291 (6) 6/307 (7) (6 wkts, 50 overs)	315

V. C. Drakes, J. J. C. Lawson and C. D. Collymore did not bat.

Bowling: Srinath 9–0–55–1; Agarkar 10–1–56–2; Bangar 5–0–39–0; Kartik 9–0–69–0; Sarandeep Singh 10–0–31–0; Sehwag 7–0–59–3.

India

V. Sehwag c Hooper b Lawson	12
D. Mongia b Lawson	20
V. V. S. Laxman c Jacobs b Lawson	22
*†R. Dravid c Sarwan b Lawson	3
Yuvraj Singh b Gayle	68
M. Kaif b Collymore	10
S. B. Bangar lbw b Collymore	2
A. B. Agarkar c Collymore b Gayle	4
M. Kartik b Gayle	2
Sarandeep Singh c sub (M. V. Nagamootoo) b Drakes	19
J. Srinath not out	3
B 3, l-b 2, w 9, n-b 1	15
1/23 (1) 2/56 (3) 3/59 (2) 4/67 (4) 5/99 (6) 6/107 (7) 7/121 (8) 8/126 (9) 9/158 (10) 10/180 (5) (36.5 overs)	180

Bowling: Drakes 7–0–44–1; Lawson 10–0–57–4; Collymore 7–0–30–2; Hooper 6–0–22–0; Gayle 6.5–0–22–3.

Umpires: E. A. R. de Silva (Sri Lanka) and A. V. Jayaprakash.
Third umpire: K. Hariharan. Referee: M. J. Procter (South Africa).

†BANGLADESH v WEST INDIES

First One-Day International

At Chittagong, November 29, 2002. No result. Toss: Bangladesh.

Rain put a stop to Bangladesh's streak of 23 one-day defeats since they beat Pakistan in the 1999 World Cup. In what became the pattern for this series, West Indies started slowly, stumbling to 142 for four in the first 36 overs – and then blasted their way through the closing stages. Of 133 runs scored in the last 14 overs, 88 came from a Ricardo Powell blitz lasting a mere 50 balls, and studded with seven fours and six sixes. Drakes, playing the tenth game of his international comeback, took all the wickets as Bangladesh reached 90 for four. Then the rain came down hard.

West Indies

C. H. Gayle run out 38
W. W. Hinds c Hannan Sarkar b Manjurul Islam . 30
M. N. Samuels c Manjurul Islam b Mohammad Rafiq . 9
R. R. Sarwan c Alok Kapali b Mohammad Ashraful . 39
D. Ganga c Hannan Sarkar b Alok Kapali 44
R. L. Powell c Al Sahariar b Tapash Baisya . 88
*†R. D. Jacobs c Tapash Baisya b Mohammad Ashraful . 10
M. V. Nagamootoo not out 6
V. C. Drakes not out 0
L-b 5, w 4, n-b 2 11

1/49 (2) 2/75 (3) 3/103 (1) 4/142 (4) 5/209 (5) 6/261 (7) 7/271 (6) (7 wkts, 50 overs) 275

J. J. C. Lawson and C. D. Collymore did not bat.

Bowling: Manjurul Islam 9–3–46–1; Tapash Baisya 7–1–43–1; Mohammad Rafiq 10–0–45–1; Naimur Rahman 10–1–30–0; Mohammad Ashraful 9–0–71–2; Alok Kapali 5–0–35–1.

Bangladesh

Hannan Sarkar c Jacobs b Drakes 5
Al Sahariar b Drakes 10
Mohammad Ashraful c Gayle b Drakes . 29
Habibul Bashar c Jacobs b Drakes. 2
Sanwar Hossain not out. 16
Alok Kapali not out 20
L-b 1, w 3, n-b 4 8

1/15 (1) 2/34 (2) 3/48 (4) 4/52 (3) (4 wkts, 17 overs) 90

*†Khaled Masud, Naimur Rahman, Mohammad Rafiq, Tapash Baisya and Manjurul Islam did not bat.

Bowling: Drakes 8–2–26–4; Lawson 3–0–26–0; Collymore 3–0–18–0; Nagamootoo 2–0–17–0; Gayle 1–0–2–0.

Umpires: D. R. Shepherd (England) and A. F. M. Akhtaruddin.
Third umpire: Showkatur Rahman. Referee: R. S. Madugalle (Sri Lanka).

†BANGLADESH v WEST INDIES

Second One-Day International

At Dhaka, December 2, 2002 (day/night). West Indies won by 84 runs. Toss: West Indies. One-day international debut: Ehsanul Haque.

West Indies struggled to 77 for two by the halfway mark on a wicket of low bounce that discouraged strokeplay. Manjurul Islam conceded only 20 in a single ten-over spell. But Samuels and Sarwan dug deep and gained momentum, adding 146. Sarwan, whose highest international score in 74 innings – 27 Tests and 27 one-day games – was 99 not out, reached a long-awaited century at a run a ball off the very last delivery, with a thick outside edge to the third-man boundary. His celebration was as spectacular as his batting. Drakes then bowled Al Sahariar with his first ball, struck twice more in his fifth over and finished with four in all. A 71-run stand between Khaled Masud and Naimur Rahman helped Bangladesh save face.

Man of the Match: R. R. Sarwan.

West Indies

C. H. Gayle c Khaled Masud b Manjurul Islam . 21
W. W. Hinds lbw b Tapash Baisya 0
M. N. Samuels b Naimur Rahman. 82
R. R. Sarwan not out 102
R. L. Powell b Ehsanul Haque 10
D. Ganga not out 21
B 5, l-b 20, w 4, n-b 1. 30

1/0 (2) 2/37 (1) 3/183 (3) 4/214 (5) (4 wkts, 50 overs) 266

*†R. D. Jacobs, M. V. Nagamootoo, V. C. Drakes, J. J. C. Lawson and C. E. Cuffy did not bat.

Bowling: Manjurul Islam 10–3–20–1; Tapash Baisya 10–1–42–1; Ehsanul Haque 10–0–57–1; Mohammad Rafiq 10–2–41–0; Naimur Rahman 7–0–53–1; Alok Kapali 3–0–28–0.

Bangladesh

Al Sahariar b Drakes 0
Ehsanul Haque c Gayle b Drakes 9
Mohammad Ashraful c Hinds b Nagamootoo . 44
Habibul Bashar b Drakes 0
Sanwar Hossain lbw b Lawson 13
Alok Kapali st Jacobs b Nagamootoo . . . 12
*†Khaled Masud b Cuffy 41
Naimur Rahman run out 37
Mohammad Rafiq c Sarwan b Drakes . . 0
Tapash Baisya not out 2
Manjurul Islam b Cuffy 0
L-b 7, w 14, n-b 3 24

1/0 (1) 2/34 (2) 3/34 (4) (48 overs) 182
4/59 (5) 5/84 (3) 6/94 (6)
7/165 (8) 8/179 (9)
9/182 (7) 10/182 (11)

Bowling: Drakes 9–4–18–4; Lawson 10–1–42–1; Cuffy 9–1–33–2; Nagamootoo 10–1–32–2; Gayle 8–1–38–0; Samuels 2–0–12–0.

Umpires: D. R. Shepherd (England) and Mahbubur Rahman.
Third umpire: Showkatur Rahman. Referee: R. S. Madugalle (Sri Lanka).

†BANGLADESH v WEST INDIES

Third One-Day International

At Dhaka, December 3, 2002 (day/night). West Indies won by 86 runs. Toss: West Indies. One-day international debuts: Anwar Hossain Piju; D. B. Powell.

For the third match running, Drakes claimed four wickets – this time they came in two successive overs. Bangladesh fought back as the youngster Alok Kapali joined debutant Anwar Hossain Piju to add 67, and Alok – originally regarded as a leg-spinner – continued to wage a lone battle with a wonderful 92-ball 89 not out, the third-highest one-day international score for Bangladesh. Again, the West Indian batsmen saved their best until last, smashing 180 in the final 25 overs. Spinners Naimur Rahman and Mohammad Rafiq bowled well earlier, but Gayle and Samuels gave West Indies the platform on which to build 281.

Man of the Match: V. C. Drakes. *Man of the Series:* V. C. Drakes.

West Indies

C. H. Gayle c Khaled Masud b Sanwar Hossain . 73
W. W. Hinds b Tapash Baisya 16
M. N. Samuels b Mohammad Rafiq 77
R. R. Sarwan c Mohammad Rafiq b Naimur Rahman . 28
R. L. Powell not out 36
*†R. D. Jacobs run out 23
M. V. Nagamootoo not out 9
B 1, l-b 10, w 7, n-b 1 19

1/46 (2) 2/154 (1) (5 wkts, 50 overs) 281
3/200 (4) 4/208 (3)
5/270 (6)

D. Ganga, V. C. Drakes, D. B. Powell and C. E. Cuffy did not bat.

Bowling: Manjurul Islam 10–0–77–0; Tapash Baisya 10–0–55–1; Mohammad Rafiq 10–0–45–1; Naimur Rahman 10–0–32–1; Ehsanul Haque 3.3–0–22–0; Sanwar Hossain 3.3–0–16–1; Mohammad Ashraful 3–0–23–0.

Bangladesh

Ehsanul Haque lbw b Drakes 20
Anwar Hossain Piju c Hinds b D. B. Powell . 42
Mohammad Ashraful c Hinds b Drakes . 1
Sanwar Hossain c Jacobs b Drakes 5
Tushar Imran lbw b Drakes 0
Alok Kapali not out 89
*†Khaled Masud b Gayle 16
Naimur Rahman c and b Gayle 7
Mohammad Rafiq lbw b Gayle 0
Tapash Baisya lbw b Cuffy 0
Manjurul Islam not out 2
B 1, l-b 2, w 7, n-b 3 13

1/29 (1) 2/32 (3) (9 wkts, 50 overs) 195
3/42 (4) 4/42 (5)
5/109 (2) 6/151 (7)
7/171 (8) 8/171 (9) 9/172 (10)

Bowling: Drakes 10–1–33–4; Cuffy 10–0–43–1; D. B. Powell 10–2–34–1; Nagamootoo 10–0–45–0; Gayle 10–2–37–3.

Umpires: D. R. Shepherd (England) and A. F. M. Akhtaruddin.
Third umpire: Showkatur Rahman. Referee: R. S. Madugalle (Sri Lanka).

BANGLADESH v WEST INDIES

First Test Match

At Dhaka, December 8, 9, 10, 2002. West Indies won by an innings and 310 runs. Toss: West Indies. Test debuts: Anwar Hossain Piju; V. C. Drakes.

Bangladesh hit several new lows on the third day: their lowest innings total, their lowest match aggregate, and the biggest defeat in their 16 Tests. It was all due to Jermaine Lawson, the 20-year-old Jamaican fast bowler, who had made his Test debut at Chennai in October. He propelled himself into the record books with scarcely believable figures of 6.5–4–3–6, the most economical six-wicket haul in Test history. Only Australia's Ernie Toshack had taken five or more for fewer runs, when he claimed five for two against India at Brisbane in 1947-48. All Lawson's six wickets came in a devastating 15-ball spell, in which he did not concede a single run; in one over, he took three in four deliveries. Bangladesh collapsed from 80 for three, losing their final seven for as many runs as the last five all made ducks. They had lasted 31.5 overs, only eight balls more than their shortest innings, against South Africa at Potchefstroom a few weeks earlier.

SIX DUCKS IN A TEST INNINGS

Pakistan (128) v West Indies at Karachi	1980-81
South Africa (105) v India at Ahmedabad	1996-97
Bangladesh (87) v West Indies at Dhaka	**2002-03**

There have been 28 instances of five batsmen out without scoring.

Research: Philip Bailey and M. L. Fernando

In South Africa, Bangladesh had only once succumbed for less than 170, so a much better show was expected at home against a bowling attack which was hardly fearsome by West Indian standards. But it started to go wrong when they were inserted and lost opener Hannan Sarkar to the first ball of the match, a perfect yorker from left-arm pacer Collins. He and Vasbert Drakes were too hot for the batsmen to handle; Bangladesh were tottering at 44 for five by the 16th over. Alok Kapali carried forward his one-day form, scoring his first Test fifty, and stabilised the innings, adding 73 with captain Khaled Masud. But when both departed inside nine balls there was little further resistance: the innings folded for 139. Collins was the chief destroyer, with five; Vasbert Drakes, making his Test debut at the ripe age of 33, after 142 first-class matches, took four, just as he had in each of the one-day games. Other than Alok and Masud, only Habibul Bashar reached double figures, which made him the first Bangladeshi to score 1,000 Test runs.

West Indian openers Gayle and Hinds almost matched the home side's total with a 131-run partnership. But both fell on the second morning, in the same over from Tapash Baisya. Chanderpaul soon followed, but Bangladesh's joy evaporated when Sarwan and Samuels shared a fine stand of 176. Sarwan, who had got his first international century in the one-day game a week earlier, added a maiden Test hundred, after passing the fifty mark 14 times in his previous 48 innings. Samuels fell nine short of his second successive Test century, and Jacobs was stranded on the same score when West Indies were finally bowled out for a huge 536. That meant a lead of 397 and, thanks to Lawson, they completed the seventh-largest victory in all Tests on the third evening.

Man of the Match: J. J. C. Lawson.

Close of play: First day, West Indies 118-0 (Gayle 44, Hinds 73); Second day, West Indies 400-5 (Ganga 34, Jacobs 14).

Six and all out: Jermaine Lawson is mobbed by exultant team-mates after snatching the last six Bangladesh wickets – five without assistance and all without conceding a run.

Picture by Rafiqur Rahman, Reuters.

Bangladesh

Hannan Sarkar b Collins	0	– c Ganga b Drakes	25
Anwar Hossain Piju c Jacobs b Drakes	2	– b Drakes	12
Mohammad Ashraful c Jacobs b Collins	6	– b Drakes	0
Habibul Bashar c Ganga b Collins	24	– lbw b Collins	22
Aminul Islam lbw b Lawson	5	– lbw b Lawson	12
Alok Kapali lbw b Drakes	52	– lbw b Lawson	0
*†Khaled Masud b Drakes	22	– lbw b Lawson	0
Naimur Rahman c Gayle b Collins	1	– not out	5
Enamul Haque b Collins	6	– c Jacobs b Lawson	0
Tapash Baisya c Jacobs b Drakes	7	– b Lawson	0
Talha Jubair not out	4	– b Lawson	0
L-b 6, w 1, n-b 3	10	B 4, l-b 3, n-b 4	11
1/0 (1) 2/4 (2) 3/25 (3) 4/40 (4) 5/44 (5) 6/117 (7) 7/118 (6) 8/124 (8) 9/135 (10) 10/139 (9)	139	1/30 (1) 2/30 (3) 3/44 (2) 4/80 (4) 5/80 (5) 6/80 (7) 7/81 (6) 8/83 (9) 9/87 (10) 10/87 (11)	87

Bowling: *First Innings*—Collins 17.1–7–26–5; Drakes 18–2–61–4; Lawson 9–2–24–1; Powell 10–2–22–0. *Second Innings*—Collins 9–2–30–1; Drakes 9–3–19–3; Powell 7–1–28–0; Lawson 6.5–4–3–6.

West Indies

C. H. Gayle c Khaled Masud b Tapash Baisya	51
W. W. Hinds c Naimur Rahman b Tapash Baisya	75
R. R. Sarwan c Naimur Rahman b Talha Jubair	119
S. Chanderpaul c Khaled Masud b Enamul Haque	4
M. N. Samuels lbw b Talha Jubair	91
D. Ganga run out	40
*†R. D. Jacobs not out	91
V. C. Drakes c sub (Al Sahariar) b Naimur Rahman	15
D. B. Powell st Khaled Masud b Mohammad Ashraful	16
P. T. Collins c Habibul Bashar b Mohammad Ashraful	13
J. J. C. Lawson lbw b Talha Jubair	1
L-b 8, w 3, n-b 9	20
1/131 (1) 2/132 (2) 3/150 (4) 4/326 (5) 5/377 (3) 6/417 (6) 7/453 (8) 8/493 (9) 9/527 (10) 10/536 (11)	536

Bowling: Tapash Baisya 34–3–117–2; Talha Jubair 31–3–135–3; Naimur Rahman 36–5–118–1; Enamul Haque 46–13–101–1; Mohammad Ashraful 13–0–57–2.

Umpires: D. L. Orchard (South Africa) and D. R. Shepherd (England).
Third umpire: A. F. M. Akhtaruddin. Referee: R. S. Madugalle (Sri Lanka).

BANGLADESH v WEST INDIES

Second Test Match

At Chittagong, December 16, 17, 18, 2002. West Indies won by seven wickets. Toss: Bangladesh.

Bangladesh suffered their eighth three-day defeat in 17 Tests – but this was actually one of their better performances. They put up a brave fight, and the cricket played had an intensity rarely seen in their matches. It was only the second time they had picked as many as three seamers in a home Test, but the decision was vindicated: those three bowled their hearts out on a lifeless pitch, making the West Indians sweat for every run.

As usual, however, Bangladesh had too few runs to defend. They had made very little of winning the toss in perfect batting conditions, going under for 194. Al Sahariar and Hannan Sarkar started well enough, but Drakes separated them on the stroke of the first drinks break, and Darren Powell followed up next ball. Sanwar Hossain and Mohammad Ashraful raised hopes, adding 64, but the rot really began when Ashraful fell to an outstanding one-handed catch by a leaping Powell at mid-off. Sanwar departed in the next over, and only Khaled Masud hung around after that, batting more than two hours.

The match seemed to be on a familiar course, as West Indies looked for a huge lead. To date, the average first-innings total against Bangladesh was 468, the average first-innings lead 282. But the home seamers decided to write a different script, removing the West Indian top five with only 127 on the board. It took a 99-run stand between Ganga and Jacobs to tug the tourists into the lead, and they were eventually restricted to 296, the lowest all-out total by any Test side against Bangladesh. Tapash Baisya led the three-pronged pace attack, taking three wickets in his last spell to finish with four for 72 – almost doubling his career total.

Bangladesh's deficit was 102, and by stumps on the second day the openers had wiped off 40 and promised more. But both were victims of the vagaries of the pitch: Hannan bowled by a straight, low ball from Drakes, and Al Sahariar trapped plumb in front when Powell cut one back from a crack outside off stump. In between, their best batsman, Habibul Bashar, gloved a snorter from Collins to the keeper. Before long, Bangladesh were a precarious 137 for six.

They were salvaged by Alok Kapali, pulling and flicking gracefully while finding an ally in Enamul Haque, who contributed just nine to their 73-run fightback. Alok hit 12 fours and two sixes, advancing to 85 in 111 balls, but fell mistiming a hook just before tea on the third day. That was the end of Bangladesh's resistance; the last four went in 21 deliveries.

Needing 111, West Indies were determined to get them that evening. They rattled up the runs inside 22 overs, thanks to Gayle, with 37 in 31 balls, though the seamers grabbed three quick wickets. Bangladesh found further satisfaction when Alok became only their third player, after Javed Omar and Mohammad Ashraful, to win the match award in a Test.

Man of the Match: Alok Kapali. *Man of the Series:* J. J. C. Lawson.

Close of play: First day, West Indies 38-1 (Gayle 10, Sarwan 14); Second day, Bangladesh 40-0 (Hannan Sarkar 12, Al Sahariar 21).

Bangladesh

First innings		Second innings	
Hannan Sarkar c Gayle b Powell	15	b Drakes	13
Al Sahariar lbw b Drakes	25	lbw b Powell	34
Habibul Bashar c Jacobs b Powell	3	c Jacobs b Collins	0
Sanwar Hossain c Jacobs b Lawson	36	c Gayle b Lawson	24
Mohammad Ashraful c Powell b Collins	28	c Sarwan b Lawson	15
Alok Kapali c Gayle b Collins	2	c Jacobs b Powell	85
*†Khaled Masud c Sarwan b Drakes	32	lbw b Drakes	5
Enamul Haque c Samuels b Lawson	8	not out	11
Tapash Baisya hit wkt b Powell	5	c Chanderpaul b Powell	0
Manjurul Islam b Collins	21	b Collins	0
Talha Jubair not out	4	c Jacobs b Collins	0
L-b 5, n-b 10	15	B 1, l-b 12, w 3, n-b 9	25
1/43 (2) 2/43 (1) 3/48 (3) 4/112 (5) 5/116 (4) 6/125 (6) 7/144 (8) 8/153 (9) 9/189 (7) 10/194 (10)	194	1/44 (1) 2/45 (3) 3/76 (2) 4/100 (4) 5/126 (5) 6/137 (7) 7/210 (6) 8/210 (9) 9/210 (10) 10/212 (11)	212

Bowling: *First Innings*—Collins 16.1–3–60–3; Drakes 9–3–23–2; Powell 16–4–51–3; Lawson 22–9–55–2. *Second Innings*—Collins 23–8–58–3; Drakes 18–6–52–2; Lawson 18–5–53–2; Powell 13–2–36–3.

West Indies

First innings		Second innings	
C. H. Gayle b Talha Jubair	38	b Tapash Baisya	37
W. W. Hinds c Khaled Masud b Tapash Baisya	14	lbw b Tapash Baisya	26
R. R. Sarwan c Khaled Masud b Manjurul Islam	17	c Enamul Haque b Manjurul Islam	13
S. Chanderpaul c Khaled Masud b Enamul Haque	16	not out	19
M. N. Samuels c Al Sahariar b Talha Jubair	31	not out	15
D. Ganga c Tapash Baisya b Sanwar Hossain	63		
*†R. D. Jacobs c Khaled Masud b Tapash Baisya	59		
V. C. Drakes run out	26		
D. B. Powell b Tapash Baisya	1		
P. T. Collins not out	12		
J. J. C. Lawson c Habibul Bashar b Tapash Baisya	6		
B 8, l-b 4, n-b 1	13	L-b 1	1
1/16 (2) 2/53 (3) 3/74 (1) 4/99 (4) 5/127 (5) 6/226 (6) 7/264 (7) 8/278 (9) 9/279 (8) 10/296 (11)	296	1/52 (1) 2/77 (2) 3/81 (3) (3 wkts)	111

Bowling: *First Innings*—Manjurul Islam 21–11–34–1; Tapash Baisya 21.3–2–72–4; Talha Jubair 20–5–58–2; Enamul Haque 19–3–62–1; Mohammad Ashraful 5–0–29–0; Sanwar Hossain 7–1–29–1. *Second Innings*—Manjurul Islam 8–2–38–1; Tapash Baisya 9–0–45–2; Talha Jubair 3–0–20–0; Mohammad Ashraful 1–0–3–0; Alok Kapali 0.3–0–4–0.

Umpires: D. L. Orchard (South Africa) and D. R. Shepherd (England)
Third umpire: Mahbubur Rahman. Referee: R. S. Madugalle (Sri Lanka).

THE SRI LANKANS IN SOUTH AFRICA, 2002-03

CHARLIE AUSTIN

Sri Lanka's two previous Test tours of South Africa had brought four defeats and a draw. This time, their coach, Dav Whatmore, had identified two areas in which he and his side needed to sharpen their act: preparation and "mental presence" on the pitch. Each went up a notch or two, but the results did not. Both Tests and all bar one of the five one-day internationals were lost. Yet it was difficult to draw watertight conclusions from the tour: was this yet another example of Sri Lanka's weakness away from home – or did the series, particularly a heart-pounding final day at Centurion, signal the end of their overseas fallibility? Matters weren't much clearer for South Africa: were these performances indicative of their emergence from behind the post-Cronje cloud – or was it an inevitable and irrelevant triumph against another side with subcontinental homesick blues?

"Who is Jacques Kallis? Jacques Kallis means nothing to me"

There was no doubt that Sri Lanka played a poor hand at Johannesburg. True, they had been given warm-up games on flat, honest pitches where runs came thick and fast, only to be confronted by a Wanderers strip so grassy that South Africa fielded no spinner for the first time in three years. The strategy was plain: negate the power of Muttiah Muralitharan, destroyer of the South Africans on their last Sri Lankan trip. They rightly reckoned that the gulf between the sides yawned widest when it came to the seam attack. While South Africa's fast bowlers, especially Shaun Pollock and the effervescent Makhaya Ntini, were energetic and menacing throughout, Sri Lanka's quicks were frustratingly wayward. The batting had a ghastly time, too, with only two players reaching 50 in the Tests.

Losing their captain, Sanath Jayasuriya, to a training injury before the Centurion match might have tipped Sri Lanka over the edge. Instead, under the acting-captain, Marvan Atapattu, they came close to squaring the series in a glorious contest where fortunes ebbed and flowed until the final session. They wriggled and kicked and punched and generally irritated their opponents so much that the largely unflappable Pollock grabbed Mahela Jayawardene by the helmet and shook him – a sign of frustration rather than malice. Tempers threatened to boil over, though no one was disciplined. By and large, the spirited fightback – in distinct contrast to previous tours, when they had been cowed and intimidated – was praised: "The Sri Lankans raised eyebrows with their performance and combative approach," noted one paper. "A Sri Lanka side that refused to lie down and die," applauded another.

They couldn't sustain the intensity in the five limited-overs internationals that followed, partly because Murali flew to Australia at the end of the Centurion Test for a hernia operation. The series was dominated by Jacques

Kallis, who was the highest run-scorer on either side, just as he had been in the Tests (where he also picked up ten wickets). It was the perfect riposte to the controversial South African sports minister, Ngconde Balfour, who before the First Test had been quoted by the UCBSA as saying he didn't go to cricket to watch the likes of Kallis and Mark Boucher ("Who is Jacques Kallis? Jacques Kallis means nothing to me.") but to see Ntini and Paul Adams, both players of colour.

SRI LANKAN TOURING PARTY

S. T. Jayasuriya (Bloomfield) (*captain*), M. S. Atapattu (Sinhalese) (*vice-captain*), R. P. Arnold (Nondescripts), W. R. S. de Silva (Galle), C. R. D. Fernando (Sinhalese), K. H. R. K. Fernando (Chilaw Marians), D. P. M. D. Jayawardene (Sinhalese), H. A. P. W. Jayawardene (Colombo), A. B. T. Lakshitha (Bloomfield), M. K. G. C. P. Lakshitha (Air Force), M. T. T. Mirando (Nondescripts), J. Mubarak (Colombo), M. Muralitharan (Tamil Union), P. D. R. L. Perera (Sinhalese), K. C. Sangakkara (Nondescripts), H. P. Tillekeratne (Nondescripts), W. P. U. J. C Vaas (Colts).

U. D. U. Chandana (Tamil Union), P. A. de Silva (Nondescripts), P. W. Gunaratne (Tamil Union), D. A. Gunawardene (Sinhalese), R. A. P. Nissanka (Bloomfield) and T. T. Samaraweera (Sinhalese) replaced W. R. S. de Silva, H. A. P. W. Jayawardene, A. B. T. Lakshitha, Mirando, Muralitharan (who flew to Australia for a hernia operation) and Perera for the one-day series.

Coach: D. F. Whatmore. *Manager:* Air Commodore A. Jayasekara.
Cricket adviser: L. R. D. Mendis. *Physiotherapist:* A. Kontouri.

SRI LANKAN TOUR RESULTS

Test matches – Played 2: Lost 2.
First-class matches – Played 4: Lost 2, Drawn 2.
Losses – South Africa (2).
Draws – South Africa A, Rest of South Africa.
One-day internationals – Played 5: Won 1, Lost 4.
Other non-first-class match – Lost v South Africa A.

Note: Matches in this section which were not first-class are signified with a dagger.

At Kimberley, October 25, 26, 27, 28, 2002. **Drawn.** Toss: South Africa A. **South Africa A 483-8 dec.** (H. H. Dippenaar 134, N. D. McKenzie 160) **and 220-9 dec.**; **Sri Lankans 272-9 dec.** (M. S. Atapattu 104, D. P. M. D. Jayawardene 60; R. J. Peterson 4-58) **and 239-4** (M. S. Atapattu 88, K. C. Sangakkara 70).

At Lenasia, November 1, 2, 3, 4, 2002. **Drawn.** Toss: Sri Lankans. **Sri Lankans 336-5 dec.** (D. P. M. D. Jayawardene 76, H. P. Tillekeratne 79*, K. H. R. K. Fernando 57*) **and 265-2** (M. S. Atapattu 81, R. P. Arnold 98, K. C. Sangakkara 61*); **Rest of South Africa 392** (D. J. Jacobs 146).

SOUTH AFRICA v SRI LANKA

First Test Match

At Johannesburg, November 8, 9, 10, 2002. South Africa won by an innings and 64 runs. Toss: Sri Lanka. Test debut: K. H. R. K. Fernando.

The Sri Lankans were brimming with optimism on the first morning of the series. Their coach, Dav Whatmore, believed them better prepared than at any time during his tenure, and he sensed an opportunity to unsettle South Africa. Two and a half days and eight sessions later, his side had been routed – overawed and overpowered by a five-pronged pace attack who bowled with sustained hostility on a trampoline-like Wanderers pitch.

Not that the game began smoothly for South Africa. Their regular opener, Herschelle Gibbs, developed back spasms during the warm-up and, as the captains walked out to toss, the SOS had still not gone out to his replacement, Martin van Jaarsveld, who was in Pretoria. Jayasuriya boldly chose to bat on a green-tinged surface, allowing the South African top order time to regroup.

The Sri Lankan batting also had a slightly unfamiliar look: Jayasuriya slunk back into the middle order while Arnold opened – and promptly wafted lamely into the slips. The rest of the top six made starts only to waste them. Sangakkara played positively before being caught on the back foot when he should have gone forward, and Atapattu played on. Even so, Jayawardene and Jayasuriya were guiding Sri Lanka towards recovery at 137 for three.

However, Kallis, maybe thinking more of the sports minister's attempt to belittle him than of his hamstring injury, took three wickets in six balls: Jayawardene feathered an out-swinger, Jayasuriya fended off a short ball into the slips and Hasantha Fernando, a medium-pace all-rounder making his debut, betrayed his nerves with an ill-advised pull. When Vaas was caught in the gully, Sri Lanka had slumped to 141 for seven. Tillekeratne grafted and Muralitharan swatted an entertaining first-ball six, but Sri Lanka's 192 was well below par.

By the close, Kirsten and Smith had sailed to 51 without loss. Next morning, they cruised to 133, relishing the width offered by undisciplined seamers. Dilhara Fernando repeatedly overstepped, conceding 21 in no-balls, while the left-armer, Perera, back after remedial work on his action, ran straight back into trouble. Umpire Harper banned him from bowling after he repeatedly followed through on to the pitch. Even Muralitharan was treated harshly, especially by the left-handed Smith, who time and again drilled him through the off side. But South Africa were suddenly derailed by a triple strike from Hasantha Fernando, who broke through with his second ball in Test cricket. With Vaas seeing off Prince and McKenzie, South Africa were teetering at 180 for five, still 12 behind. Kallis glued the innings together with a painstaking, five-hour 75, taking his run in Test cricket between dismissals to 909 minutes, and squeezed vital runs out of a deep batting order. A total of 62 extras – then the seventh-highest in Test history – also boosted the South African cause.

Trailing by 194, Sri Lanka crumbled against Ntini and Pollock. This time Arnold lasted one ball, which he poked feebly to the slips for a second time, completing a pair, as did Hasantha Fernando. By the 13th over, Sri Lanka had crashed to 25 for four. Atapattu stayed two hours and Tillekeratne batted stubbornly to carry Sri Lanka past 71, their lowest Test total, but the game ended in a rush as the last four wickets fell for just eight. Disappointing crowds led to a renewed suggestion from former UCBSA head Ali Bacher that Tests should not be shown on TV within 100km of the stadium, at least at weekends.

Man of the Match: J. H. Kallis. *Attendance:* 20,859.

Close of play: First day, South Africa 51-0 (Smith 15, Kirsten 21); Second day, South Africa 378-7 (Kallis 75, Hall 31).

Sri Lanka

M. S. Atapattu b Pollock	34	–	c Smith b Elworthy	43
R. P. Arnold c Smith b Ntini	0	–	c Kallis b Ntini	0
†K. C. Sangakkara c Smith b Elworthy	26	–	c Boucher b Ntini	7
D. P. M. D. Jayawardene c Boucher b Kallis	39	–	c Kirsten b Pollock	1
*S. T. Jayasuriya c Smith b Kallis	32	–	b Pollock	0
H. P. Tillekeratne run out	24	–	c Elworthy b Hall	27
K. H. R. K. Fernando c Kirsten b Kallis	0	–	lbw b Elworthy	0
W. P. U. J. C. Vaas c Kallis b Hall	1	–	c Kirsten b Ntini	32
C. R. D. Fernando b Pollock	7	–	not out	4
M. Muralitharan c Ntini b Hall	10	–	b Hall	0
P. D. R. L. Perera not out	11	–	b Hall	4
B 4, l-b 2, w 1, n-b 1	8		B 4, l-b 7, w 1	12
1/2 (2) 2/46 (3) 3/86 (1) 4/137 (4) 5/140 (5) 6/140 (7) 7/141 (8) 8/152 (9) 9/165 (10) 10/192 (6)	192		1/2 (2) 2/16 (3) 3/21 (4) 4/25 (5) 5/77 (1) 6/81 (7) 7/122 (8) 8/122 (6) 9/122 (10) 10/130 (11)	130

Bowling: *First Innings*—Pollock 18–8–45–2; Ntini 14–5–45–1; Elworthy 15.3–3–42–1; Kallis 17–8–35–3; Hall 11–6–19–2. *Second Innings*—Pollock 8–3–17–2; Ntini 10–4–22–3; Kallis 11–3–40–0; Elworthy 10–3–39–2; Hall 2–1–1–3.

South Africa

G. C. Smith c Tillekeratne b K. H. R. K. Fernando	73
G. Kirsten c Muralitharan b K. H. R. K. Fernando	55
M. van Jaarsveld b K. H. R. K. Fernando	3
J. H. Kallis c Sangakkara b Vaas	75
A. G. Prince c Perera b Vaas	3
N. D. McKenzie lbw b Vaas	0
†M. V. Boucher c Sangakkara b Muralitharan	38
*S. M. Pollock c Sangakkara b C. R. D. Fernando	38
A. J. Hall lbw b Muralitharan	31
S. Elworthy lbw b Muralitharan	6
M. Ntini not out	2
B 16, l-b 10, w 5, n-b 31	62
1/133 (1) 2/148 (3) 3/175 (2) 4/179 (5) 5/180 (6) 6/249 (7) 7/329 (8) 8/378 (9) 9/378 (4) 10/386 (10)	386

Bowling: Vaas 22–2–79–3; Perera 10.2–2–40–0; C. R. D. Fernando 20–2–95–1; Muralitharan 31.2–8–83–3; K. H. R. K. Fernando 21–2–63–3.

Umpires: D. J. Harper (Australia) and R. B. Tiffin (Zimbabwe).
Third umpire: S. Wadvalla. Referee: G. R. Viswanath (India).

SOUTH AFRICA v SRI LANKA

Second Test Match

At Centurion, November 15, 16, 17, 18, 19, 2002. South Africa won by three wickets. Toss: South Africa.

Sri Lanka had only four days to pick themselves up after their mauling in the First Test and, to make matters worse, lost Jayasuriya to torn ankle ligaments. But they confounded expectations and made a real fight of things, eventually losing a classic tussle by just three wickets. Fiercely contested, often acrimonious and richly entertaining, the match wound itself up to a compelling conclusion.

South Africa, preferring brawn to subtlety, again omitted the spinner, Claude Henderson, and stuck with a five-man battery of pace. Pollock opted to bowl, but no one could find much movement on an easy-paced pitch, and Sri Lanka should have made more of their opponents' lack of variety. Each time they poked their noses in front, South Africa edged past them again. Tillekeratne conjured up a trademark

No hard feelings: Shaun Pollock (*right*) and Makhaya Ntini head for the pavilion with Pollock left high and dry on 99 not out.

Picture by Getty Images.

obdurate, stonewalling innings spanning five and a half hours, and Sri Lanka looked well placed. But Ntini tore in with the second new ball like an Olympic sprinter and, in the blink of an eye, 263 for five became 281 for nine. Tillekeratne, on 91, must have seen the prospect of a hundred fade as Muralitharan grinned his way to the crease with Ntini on a hat-trick. But he did become the fourth Sri Lankan to hit ten Test centuries, and the first to score one in South Africa. The comic last-wicket stand, which included a Murali six off Ntini, dragged Sri Lanka to a respectable 323.

Dilhara Fernando plucked out two wickets to put early pressure on South Africa before Gibbs and Kallis plodded soporifically through the second afternoon. Next morning, though, the game burst back into life. Gibbs, calling for a suicidal single, was run out for 92, and Kallis missed a perfect leg-cutter from Hasantha Fernando – to be dismissed for the first time in 1,138 minutes spread over five Tests. The score slid from 211 for two to 264 for six. However, South Africa bat deep: Boucher was patient, Pollock bold. Had it not been for a wild slog by Ntini, the No. 11, Pollock would doubtless have completed a third Test century rather than become the fourth batsman stranded on 99 not out. Pollock, who had been talking to Ntini to try to encourage him, jerked his head back in dismay. Even so, the lead was a healthy 125. Earlier, Muralitharan, who had toiled into his 50th over for his first wicket, sneaked past Kapil Dev to become the third-highest wicket-taker in Tests.

Ntini took two wickets before the close to appease his captain ("All is forgiven," said Pollock). But, despite three poor decisions and a thunderstorm that cost valuable time, Sri Lanka played positively, racing to build a lead. Sangakkara dominated the fourth afternoon, batting majestically and adding 119 in 34 overs with Jayawardene. They were rattling along so fluently that they twice declined offers of bad light. The floodlit cricket was exhilarating – Ntini surging in to bowl as lightning carved up the skies – but foolhardy. Sangakkara was snared down the leg side moments before the ground was awash. Sri Lanka's advantage was a slender 55.

Day five was tumultuous and tense – and began in controversy. A shocking decision by umpire Tiffin saw Jayawardene lbw to its first delivery, and four more wickets tumbled for 29. A ninth-wicket partnership stretched the lead to 120, but that hardly looked enough. Far from fizzling out, though, the contest intensified. Vaas struck first ball to pin Smith lbw, and Dilhara Fernando created panic with four quick wickets after lunch. South Africa were a precarious 44 for five, and at 73, Hall was snapped up at bat-pad. It was left to McKenzie, with a precious 39, and Boucher to wrest back the initiative. Muralitharan bowled McKenzie with nine needed, but that was the final twist.

Man of the Match: S. M. Pollock. *Attendance:* 27,351.

Man of the Series: J. H. Kallis.

Close of play: First day, Sri Lanka 263-6 (Tillekeratne 82, Vaas 0); Second day, South Africa 183-2 (Gibbs 76, Kallis 69); Third day, South Africa 421-9 (Pollock 78, Ntini 3); Fourth day, Sri Lanka 180-3 (Jayawardene 40, Tillekeratne 0).

Sri Lanka

Batsman	First innings	Runs	Second innings	Runs
*M. S. Atapattu	c Kirsten b Kallis	17	c Boucher b Kallis	22
J. Mubarak	c Smith b Pollock	48	c Boucher b Ntini	15
†K. C. Sangakkara	c Pollock b Hall	35	c Boucher b Ntini	89
D. P. M. D. Jayawardene	b Pollock	44	lbw b Ntini	40
H. P. Tillekeratne	not out	104	c Boucher b Kallis	6
R. P. Arnold	c Boucher b Kallis	2	lbw b Pollock	4
K. H. R. K. Fernando	c Kallis b Ntini	24	c Hall b Ntini	14
W. P. U. J. C. Vaas	c Boucher b Ntini	7	lbw b Kallis	17
M. K. G. C. P. Lakshitha	c Kirsten b Ntini	2	c Pollock b Kallis	0
C. R. D. Fernando	c Boucher b Ntini	0	c Boucher b Elworthy	14
M. Muralitharan	b Kallis	27	not out	0
	L-b 10, w 1, n-b 2	13	B 13, l-b 1, w 7, n-b 3	24
	1/34 (1) 2/90 (3) 3/108 (2) 4/189 (4) 5/207 (6) 6/263 (7) 7/277 (8) 8/281 (9) 9/281 (10) 10/323 (11)	323	1/23 (2) 2/60 (1) 3/179 (3) 4/180 (4) 5/185 (6) 6/205 (7) 7/209 (5) 8/209 (9) 9/245 (10) 10/245 (8)	245

Bowling: *First Innings*—Pollock 29–11–51–2; Ntini 29–6–86–4; Elworthy 21–4–71–0; Kallis 15.5–2–71–3; Hall 14–3–34–1. *Second Innings*—Pollock 17–7–45–1; Ntini 22–5–52–4; Elworthy 12–1–54–1; Hall 8–0–29–0; Kallis 14.2–5–39–4; Smith 4–2–12–0.

South Africa

Batsman	First innings	Runs	Second innings	Runs
G. C. Smith	lbw b C. R. D. Fernando	15	lbw b Vaas	0
H. H. Gibbs	run out	92	c Sangakkara b C. R. D. Fernando	7
G. Kirsten	c K. H. R. K. Fernando b C. R. D. Fernando	11	c Mubarak b C. R. D. Fernando	11
J. H. Kallis	b K. H. R. K. Fernando	84	b C. R. D. Fernando	6
A. G. Prince	c Sangakkara b Vaas	20	c Sangakkara b C. R. D. Fernando	5
N. D. McKenzie	lbw b Lakshitha	28	(7) b Muralitharan	39
†M. V. Boucher	c and b Lakshitha	63	(8) not out	22
*S. M. Pollock	not out	99	(9) not out	6
A. J. Hall	lbw b Muralitharan	0	(6) c Arnold b Muralitharan	16
S. Elworthy	c Tillekeratne b Muralitharan	5		
M. Ntini	c Arnold b Vaas	8		
	B 4, l-b 10, w 4, n-b 5	23	B 5, l-b 1, n-b 6	12
	1/45 (1) 2/71 (3) 3/211 (2) 4/219 (4) 5/258 (5) 6/264 (6) 7/396 (7) 8/400 (9) 9/408 (10) 10/448 (11)	448	1/0 (1) 2/13 (2) 3/23 (3) 4/31 (4) 5/44 (5) 6/73 (6) 7/112 (7)	(7 wkts) 124

Bowling: *First Innings*—Vaas 33.3–7–81–2; Lakshitha 22–2–71–2; C. R. D. Fernando 27–0–91–2; Muralitharan 57–10–133–2; K. H. R. K. Fernando 18–5–45–1; Mubarak 2–0–6–0; Jayawardene 2–1–2–0; Arnold 5–2–5–0. *Second Innings*—Vaas 8–2–28–1; C. R. D. Fernando 12–0–49–4; Muralitharan 13.3–1–35–2; Lakshitha 2–1–6–0.

Umpires: D. J. Harper (Australia) and R. B. Tiffin (Zimbabwe).
Third umpire: S. Wadvalla. Referee: G. R. Viswanath (India).

†At Potchefstroom, November 23, 2002. **South Africa A won by 65 runs** (D/L method). Toss: South Africa A. **South Africa A 221** (47.4 overs) (R. J. Peterson 61; P. W. Gunaratne 4-44); **Sri Lankans 111-8** (32 overs).

The Sri Lankans began their innings chasing a revised target of 203 from 42 overs; after further interruptions, this was revised to 189 from 34 and 177 from 32.

†SOUTH AFRICA v SRI LANKA

First One-Day International

At Johannesburg, November 27, 2002. South Africa won by six wickets. Toss: South Africa. One-day international debut: J. Mubarak.

This was organised as a dress rehearsal for the World Cup final, to be held here four months later, though neither team would then be present. Traffic cones ringed the Wanderers and security men pored over supporters' cool-boxes, but no amount of planning could prepare an adequate pitch after a series of mechanical failures left the curator without a roller. The nets were dangerous and the strip a minefield. Sri Lanka collapsed to 30 for five in 13 overs and, after a brief rally by Jayawardene and Arnold, the last five went for 33. They were all out for just 128, and the new-ball pair, Pollock and Ntini, had combined figures of seven for 40. South Africa's top order also wobbled, sinking to 56 for four, but Kallis and Boucher motored home at five an over against an attack weakened by the absence of Muralitharan.

Man of the Match: S. M. Pollock. *Attendance:* 13,944.

Sri Lanka

M. S. Atapattu c Boucher b Ntini	1
*S. T. Jayasuriya c Dippenaar b Ntini	7
J. Mubarak lbw b Pollock	2
†K. C. Sangakkara c Ontong b Pollock	7
P. A. de Silva c Boucher b Pollock	12
D. P. M. D. Jayawardene c Gibbs b Donald	31
R. P. Arnold c Hall b Ntini	28
W. P. U. J. C. Vaas not out	19
C. R. D. Fernando c Boucher b Donald	0
R. A. P. Nissanka run out	5
P. W. Gunaratne lbw b Pollock	2
B 2, l-b 5, w 7	14
1/3 (1) 2/6 (3) 3/10 (2) 4/25 (4) 5/30 (5) 6/95 (7) 7/104 (6) 8/105 (9) 9/125 (10) 10/128 (11) (46.4 overs)	128

Bowling: Pollock 8.4–2–18–4; Ntini 10–1–22–3; Kallis 6–0–21–0; Donald 10–0–32–2; Hall 5–0–15–0; Boje 7–0–13–0.

South Africa

G. C. Smith c Sangakkara b Gunaratne	3
H. H. Gibbs c Sangakkara b Vaas	0
H. H. Dippenaar c Gunaratne b Nissanka	23
J. H. Kallis not out	38
J. L. Ontong c Sangakkara b Nissanka	6
†M. V. Boucher not out	45
L-b 5, w 5, n-b 4	14
1/1 (2) 2/11 (1) 3/50 (3) 4/56 (5) (4 wkts, 29.3 overs)	129

*S. M. Pollock, A. J. Hall, N. Boje, A. A. Donald and M. Ntini did not bat.

Bowling: Vaas 8–0–23–1; Gunaratne 6–0–25–1; Nissanka 7–0–33–2; Fernando 5.3–0–31–0; Jayasuriya 3–0–12–0.

Umpires: R. B. Tiffin (Zimbabwe) and B. G. Jerling.
Third umpire: S. Wadvalla. Referee: G. R. Viswanath (India).

†SOUTH AFRICA v SRI LANKA

Second One-Day International

At Centurion, November 29, 2002. South Africa won by 177 runs. Toss: South Africa.

South Africa overwhelmed Sri Lanka in every department. Smith and Dippenaar reached their highest one-day international scores, and Kallis bludgeoned his fifty in 24 balls, the second-fastest for South Africa. The air of command vanished only when Smith got to 99, pushed a ball from Jayasuriya just right of mid-wicket, hesitated, then went for the single that would have given him a century… He was the first man run out for 99 in a one-day international. The total of 317 was their best against Sri Lanka, who were punished for fielding just three front-line bowlers – 106 runs flooded from the last ten overs – and were fined a further over for their slow rate. Jayasuriya launched a thrilling counter-attack against the new ball, smacking 46 from 32 deliveries, but any hopes of squaring the series faded when three wickets fell in 14 balls. Ntini destroyed the middle order, and Sri Lanka were humbled for just 140.

Man of the Match: J. H. Kallis. *Attendance:* 11,435.

South Africa

G. C. Smith run out	99
H. H. Gibbs b Gunaratne	16
N. Boje c Chandana b C. R. D. Fernando	28
H. H. Dippenaar c Jayawardene b Gunaratne	89
J. H. Kallis run out	53
†M. V. Boucher run out	1
*S. M. Pollock not out	15
J. N. Rhodes not out	6
L-b 6, w 3, n-b 1	10
1/20 (2) 2/67 (3) 3/201 (1) 4/289 (5) 5/293 (6) 6/296 (4) — (6 wkts, 50 overs)	317

A. J. Hall, A. A. Donald and M. Ntini did not bat.

Bowling: Vaas 10–1–48–0; Gunaratne 10–1–61–2; C. R. D. Fernando 9–0–66–1; de Silva 5–0–26–0; Jayasuriya 5–0–25–0; Chandana 7–1–47–0; K. H. R. K. Fernando 4–0–38–0.

Sri Lanka

M. S. Atapattu c Rhodes b Pollock	6
*S. T. Jayasuriya b Hall	46
†K. C. Sangakkara c Gibbs b Donald	10
P. A. de Silva c and b Donald	8
D. P. M. D. Jayawardene c Kallis b Ntini	32
R. P. Arnold c Boucher b Ntini	12
W. P. U. J. C. Vaas c Boucher b Kallis	3
U. D. U. Chandana c Boucher b Ntini	6
K. H. R. K. Fernando st Boucher b Boje	1
C. R. D. Fernando not out	7
P. W. Gunaratne lbw b Boje	2
L-b 4, w 3	7
1/51 (1) 2/59 (2) 3/63 (3) 4/91 (4) 5/117 (5) 6/124 (7) 7/125 (6) 8/130 (8) 9/134 (9) 10/140 (11) — (33.2 overs)	140

Bowling: Pollock 5–0–28–1; Ntini 10–0–38–3; Hall 4–0–20–1; Donald 6–0–27–2; Kallis 6–0–16–1; Boje 2.2–0–7–2.

Umpires: R. B. Tiffin (Zimbabwe) and I. L. Howell.
Third umpire: S. Wadvalla. Referee: G. R. Viswanath (India).

†SOUTH AFRICA v SRI LANKA

Third One-Day International

At Benoni, December 1, 2002. Sri Lanka won by seven wickets. Toss: Sri Lanka.

A stylish, unbeaten run-a-ball hundred from Atapattu, who ended the game with a six, guided Sri Lanka home and kept the series alive. Vaas and Lakshitha had made early inroads to reduce South Africa to 35 for four. Kallis put the innings back on course with 87 from 117 balls, and Klusener, who replaced Hall, bounced back into form. He clubbed 60 from 57 at the death, his first half-century for 12 one-day internationals. A target of 254 appeared competitive, but Atapattu joined forces with de Silva, who played industriously for his 71, and together they added 140 for the third wicket, paving the way for a comfortable win.

Man of the Match: M. S. Atapattu. *Attendance:* 6,156.

South Africa

G. C. Smith b Vaas. 16
H. H. Gibbs lbw b Vaas 0
H. H. Dippenaar b Lakshitha 5
J. H. Kallis c Jayawardene b Nissanka . . 87
J. N. Rhodes c Sangakkara b Lakshitha . 0
†M. V. Boucher b Nissanka 14
*S. M. Pollock c Jayawardene b Jayasuriya . 39
L. Klusener not out 60
N. Boje not out 11
B 4, l-b 2, w 12, n-b 3. 21

1/3 (2) 2/15 (3) (7 wkts, 50 overs) 253
3/28 (1) 4/35 (5)
5/71 (6) 6/152 (7) 7/209 (4)

A. A. Donald and M. Ntini did not bat.

Bowling: Vaas 10–1–39–2; Lakshitha 7–0–37–2; Fernando 9–0–58–0; Nissanka 10–0–61–2; Jayasuriya 10–1–37–1; de Silva 4–0–15–0.

Sri Lanka

M. S. Atapattu not out 123
*S. T. Jayasuriya c Rhodes b Ntini 22
†K. C. Sangakkara c Boje b Donald . . . 10
P. A. de Silva b Pollock. 71
D. P. M. D. Jayawardene not out 15
B 4, l-b 4, w 8, n-b 1 17

1/40 (2) 2/73 (3) (3 wkts, 41.4 overs) 258
3/213 (4)

H. P. Tillekeratne, R. P. Arnold, W. P. U. J. C. Vaas, R. A. P. Nissanka, M. K. G. C. P. Lakshitha and C. R. D. Fernando did not bat.

Bowling: Pollock 10–0–42–1; Ntini 10–0–56–1; Donald 7–1–45–1; Klusener 7–0–38–0; Boje 3.4–0–35–0; Kallis 4–0–34–0.

Umpires: R. B. Tiffin (Zimbabwe) and B. G. Jerling.
Third umpire: S. Wadvalla. Referee: G. R. Viswanath (India).

†SOUTH AFRICA v SRI LANKA

Fourth One-Day International

At Kimberley, December 4, 2002 (day/night). South Africa won by eight wickets. Toss: South Africa.

South Africa clinched the series with 19 overs in hand. Asked to bat, Sri Lanka had threatened a high score, racing to 57 without loss in ten overs, with Atapattu continuing his glorious form. But he failed to ground his bat when a speculative backhanded flick from Boucher broke the stumps, Jayasuriya fell to a wonderful airborne catch by McKenzie, and the innings subsided to 97 for five. Arnold marshalled some lower-order resistance, but not enough. South Africa's reply got off to a jittery start before Gibbs and Kallis stamped their authority in an unbroken stand of 172. Early on, Gibbs played awkwardly, but he finished with a stream of magnificent boundaries: his third six lifted him to his century and South Africa to an emphatic victory.

Man of the Match: H. H. Gibbs. *Attendance:* 4,488.

Sri Lanka

M. S. Atapattu run out	39	C. R. D. Fernando c Boucher b Donald	2
*S. T. Jayasuriya c McKenzie b Donald	27	P. W. Gunaratne not out	13
†K. C. Sangakkara c McKenzie b Kallis	1		
P. A. de Silva c Ntini b Kallis	0	B 4, l-b 8, w 6, n-b 2	20
D. P. M. D. Jayawardene lbw b Donald	9		
H. P. Tillekeratne b Pollock	18	1/58 (1) 2/61 (3) 3/64 (4) (47.3 overs)	184
R. P. Arnold c McKenzie b Pollock	50	4/78 (2) 5/97 (5) 6/131 (6)	
W. P. U. J. C. Vaas lbw b Pollock	4	7/146 (8) 8/152 (9)	
R. A. P. Nissanka c Boucher b Klusener	1	9/155 (10) 10/184 (7)	

Bowling: Pollock 9.3–0–40–3; Ntini 9–1–35–0; Kallis 5–0–25–2; Donald 10–4–18–3; Klusener 9–0–29–1; Peterson 5–0–25–0.

South Africa

H. H. Gibbs not out	108	J. H. Kallis not out	64
A. J. Hall lbw b Vaas	2	B 4, w 5	9
N. D. McKenzie c Sangakkara b Gunaratne	7	1/7 (2) 2/18 (3) (2 wkts, 30.5 overs)	190

J. N. Rhodes, †M. V. Boucher, *S. M. Pollock, L. Klusener, R. J. Peterson, A. A. Donald and M. Ntini did not bat.

Bowling: Vaas 9–2–42–1; Gunaratne 6–0–46–1; Nissanka 5–0–29–0; Fernando 5–0–30–0; Jayasuriya 4.5–0–29–0; Jayawardene 1–0–10–0.

Umpires: R. B. Tiffin (Zimbabwe) and I. L. Howell.
Third umpire: B. G. Jerling. Referee: G. R. Viswanath (India).

†SOUTH AFRICA v SRI LANKA

Fifth One-Day International

At Bloemfontein, December 6, 2002 (day/night). South Africa won by six wickets. Toss: Sri Lanka. One-day international debut: M. Zondeki.

South Africa confirmed their supremacy, even though with the series already won and the World Cup looming, they took the opportunity to experiment. In came Monde Zondeki, a lithe, fresh-cheeked Xhosa fast bowler, the nephew and foster son of the late sports minister Steve Tshwete. His first delivery in international cricket provided the enduring image of the game when his extra bounce ended a fine fifty from Atapattu. Thereafter, Sangakkara held the innings together with 77 from 115 balls. But a target of 229 proved little obstacle for South Africa: Gibbs blazed 47 from 45 balls at the start and McKenzie eased to 70 at the end.

Man of the Match: S. M. Pollock. *Attendance:* 5,235.
Man of the Series: J. H. Kallis.

Sri Lanka

M. S. Atapattu c Hall b Zondeki	53	R. A. P. Nissanka run out	0
*S. T. Jayasuriya c Rhodes b Donald	2	M. K. G. C. P. Lakshitha not out	3
P. A. de Silva c Boucher b Pollock	0		
D. P. M. D. Jayawardene c Boucher b Pollock	3	B 2, l-b 6, w 10, n-b 3	21
†K. C. Sangakkara not out	77	1/6 (2) 2/7 (3) (8 wkts, 50 overs)	228
R. P. Arnold c Pollock b Hall	36	3/48 (4) 4/84 (1)	
T. T. Samaraweera run out	33	5/145 (6) 6/201 (7)	
W. P. U. J. C. Vaas c Gibbs b Donald	0	7/208 (8) 8/208 (9)	

P. W. Gunaratne did not bat.

Bowling: Pollock 10–4–23–2; Donald 9–0–64–2; Hall 10–0–37–1; Klusener 5–0–24–0; Zondeki 8–1–37–1; Peterson 8–0–35–0.

South Africa

H. H. Gibbs b Lakshitha	47	J. N. Rhodes not out	25
A. J. Hall c Sangakkara b Gunaratne	18	L-b 10, w 16, n-b 2	28
R. J. Peterson c Sangakkara b Vaas	5		—
N. D. McKenzie not out	70	1/44 (2) 2/53 (3) (4 wkts, 45.1 overs)	229
H. H. Dippenaar run out	36	3/87 (1) 4/175 (5)	

†M. V. Boucher, *S. M. Pollock, L. Klusener, A. A. Donald and M. Zondeki did not bat.

Bowling: Vaas 10–0–37–1; Lakshitha 10–1–52–1; Gunaratne 8.1–0–40–1; Nissanka 10–0–48–0; Samaraweera 4–0–25–0; Jayasuriya 3–0–17–0.

Umpires: R. B. Tiffin (Zimbabwe) and B. G. Jerling.
Third umpire: I. L. Howell. Referee: G. R. Viswanath (India).

PWC TEST RATINGS

Introduced in 1987, the PricewaterhouseCoopers (PwC) Ratings (originally the Deloitte Ratings, and later the Coopers & Lybrand Ratings) rank Test cricketers on a scale up to 1,000 according to their performances in Test matches. The ratings take into account playing conditions, the quality of the opposition and the result of the matches. In August 1998, a similar set of ratings for one-day internationals was added (see page 1237).

The leading 20 batsmen and bowlers in the Test ratings after the 2003-04 Test series between South Africa and West Indies which ended on January 20, 2004, were:

	Batsmen	*Rating*		*Bowlers*	*Rating*
1	B. C. Lara (*West Indies*)	895	1	M. Muralitharan (*Sri Lanka*)	908
2	R. T. Ponting (*Australia*)	891	2	Shoaib Akhtar (*Pakistan*)	861
3	R. Dravid (*India*)	884	3	S. M. Pollock (*South Africa*)	859
4	M. L. Hayden (*Australia*)	881	4	G. D. McGrath (*Australia*)	798
5	J. H. Kallis (*South Africa*)	839	5	M. Ntini (*South Africa*)	766
6	H. H. Gibbs (*South Africa*)	828	6	J. N. Gillespie (*Australia*)	751
7	Inzamam-ul-Haq (*Pakistan*)	811	7	A. Kumble (*India*)	748
8	S. R. Tendulkar (*India*)	783	8	D. R. Tuffey (*New Zealand*)	721
9	M. H. Richardson (*New Zealand*)	775	9	Harbhajan Singh (*India*)	655
10	V. V. S. Laxman (*India*)	756	10	W. P. U. J. C. Vaas (*Sri Lanka*)	629
11	D. P. M. D. Jayawardene (*Sri Lanka*)	754	11	Saqlain Mushtaq (*Pakistan*)	623
12	M. E. Trescothick (*England*)	735	12	J. H. Kallis (*South Africa*)	611
13	G. Kirsten (*South Africa*)	734	13	A. Nel (*South Africa*)	599
14	M. P. Vaughan (*England*)	726	14	Zaheer Khan (*India*)	595
15	Yousuf Youhana (*Pakistan*)	719	15	H. H. Streak (*Zimbabwe*)	593
16	G. C. Smith (*South Africa*)	710	16	C. L. Cairns (*New Zealand*)	592
17	A. C. Gilchrist (*Australia*)	702	17	S. E. Bond (*New Zealand*)	589
18	S. R. Waugh (*Australia*)	693	17	Shabbir Ahmed (*Pakistan*)	589
19	K. C. Sangakkara (*Sri Lanka*)	692	19	S. C. G. MacGill (*Australia*)	587
20	Taufeeq Umar (*Pakistan*)	686	20	S. J. Harmison (*England*)	558

The following players have topped the ratings since they were launched on June 17, 1987. The date shown is that on which they first went top; those marked by an asterisk have done so more than once.

Batting: D. B. Vengsarkar, June 17, 1987; Javed Miandad*, February 28, 1989; R. B. Richardson*, November 20, 1989; M. A. Taylor, October 23, 1990; G. A. Gooch*, June 10, 1991; D. L. Haynes, May 6, 1993; B. C. Lara*, April 21, 1994; S. R. Tendulkar*, December 5, 1994; J. C. Adams, December 14, 1994; S. R. Waugh*, May 3, 1995; Inzamam-ul-Haq, December 3, 1997; A. Flower, September 11, 2001; A. C. Gilchrist, May 5, 2002; M. L. Hayden*, October 12, 2002; M. P. Vaughan, April 13, 2003; R. T. Ponting, December 30, 2003.

Bowling: R. J. Hadlee*, June 17, 1987; M. D. Marshall*, June 21, 1988; Waqar Younis*, December 17, 1991; C. E. L. Ambrose*, July 26, 1992; S. K. Warne*, November 29, 1994; G. D. McGrath*, December 3, 1996; A. A. Donald*, March 30, 1998; S. M. Pollock*, November 1, 1999; M. Muralitharan*, January 7, 2002.

THE PAKISTANIS IN SOUTH AFRICA AND ZIMBABWE, 2002-03

NEIL MANTHORP AND JOHN WARD

The most notoriously unpredictable team in international cricket stretched even their own extremes on this tour. In Zimbabwe, they were all-conquering. In South Africa, many of their performances were bad enough to be laughable, yet somehow they produced a single day of brilliance, scoring 335 for six at Port Elizabeth to inflict South Africa's heaviest one-day defeat.

But Pakistan still lost that limited-overs series 4–1, and the two Test matches in South Africa were so one-sided that in a different sport they would have been stopped early. The bowling was routinely tired, and the batting – barring that one rousing day and two gritty but hopeless efforts by Taufeeq Umar in the Second Test – uncommitted. In general, Pakistan were depressingly uninspired. Their form in Zimbabwe on the first part of the trip, when they swept the board against a side wracked by injuries, most importantly to their captain and inspiration, Heath Streak, seemed irrelevant: their humiliation by Australia just beforehand did not.

Even to the naked eye the Pakistani team lacked cohesion and harmony but, in case anyone doubted it, the tour was awash with stories of infighting and argument. Wasim Akram, inevitably, was involved in most of them, and his decision to return home after the one-dayers was greeted with relief among some of his colleagues. The camp was clearly split. Shoaib Akhtar, one of Wasim's acolytes, expressed his contempt for management and team spirit during the First Test in Durban. Having decided he was carrying a knee injury and unable to play, Shoaib revelled in the attention of Durban's big Asian population, boogieing the night away in carefree fashion at a Bollywood extravaganza. Certainly beats bowling 20 overs a day in the heat.

Throughout this disintegrating mess, the captain Waqar Younis remained outwardly calm, but he was clearly resigned to having little influence and even less control. Damage limitation seemed to be the main priority, which led to a highly conservative approach to selection: Pakistan entered the opening Test with just three bowlers plus an all-rounder, with disastrous results, and still fielded only a four-man attack in the Second Test at Cape Town. This time, South Africa piled up 620 for seven, and the bowlers' futile and exhausted efforts were rewarded only by a whopping fine – 100% of the match fee – for a slow over-rate. Had a team ever emerged from a Test so utterly empty-handed?

By way of partial explanation, Pakistan's coach, Richard Pybus, revealed that some members of the squad were "mentally and physically exhausted" and had spent as few as five days at home during the preceding six months. But the end result was a heartless, soulless and headless display that was unworthy of Pakistan's proud reputation and history.

The series win temporarily lifted South Africa over Australia to No. 1 in the ICC Test Championship, which prompted two reactions: ridicule from most countries, particularly Australia – given the freshness of Australia's back-to-back series wins over South Africa – and a decision by the ICC to review the method by which Test-playing countries were rated.

Few people believed that South Africa were the best team in the world. But you can only beat what turns up, and on this occasion the South Africans – then excitedly anticipating the 2003 World Cup – did so with an unusual sense of exhilaration. N. M.

PAKISTANI TOURING PARTY

Waqar Younis (National Bank) (*captain*), Inzamam-ul-Haq (National Bank) (*vice-captain*), Abdul Razzaq (ZTBL), Faisal Iqbal (PIA), Hasan Raza (Habib Bank), Kamran Akmal (National Bank), Mohammad Sami (National Bank), Mohammad Zahid (PIA), Rashid Latif (Allied Bank), Salim Elahi (Habib Bank), Saqlain Mushtaq (PIA), Shahid Afridi (Habib Bank), Shoaib Akhtar (KRL), Taufeeq Umar (Habib Bank), Wasim Akram (PIA), Younis Khan (Habib Bank), Yousuf Youhana (ZTBL).

Rashid Latif pulled out injured before the First Test in Zimbabwe but returned for the one-day series in South Africa. Abdul Razzaq joined the party at the start of the South African leg of the tour. Azhar Mahmood (PIA) and Misbah-ul-Haq (KRL) were selected only for the one-day internationals, and Wasim Akram, who arrived after the Tests, chose to return home with them. Shoaib Akhtar also left after being declared unfit during the one-day games, and Fazl-e-Akbar (PIA) was called up as cover. Hasan Raza joined the squad for the Tests only.

Coach: R. A. Pybus. *Manager:* Brigadier Mohammad Nasir. *Batting consultant:* Hanif Mohammad. *Team analyst:* Sikander Bakht. *Physiotherapist:* D. J. M. Waight. *Doctor:* Riaz Ahmed.

PAKISTANI TOUR RESULTS

Test matches – Played 4: Won 2, Lost 2.
First-class matches – Played 6: Won 2, Lost 2, Drawn 2.
Wins – Zimbabwe (2).
Losses – South Africa (2).
Draws – Zimbabwe A, South Africa A.
One-day internationals – Played 10: Won 6, Lost 4. *Wins* – Zimbabwe (5), South Africa. *Losses* – South Africa (4).
Other non-first-class matches – Played 3: Won 1, Lost 1, Drawn 1. *Win* – South Africa A. *Loss* – Border Invitation XI. *Draw* – N. F. Oppenheimer's XI.

Note: Matches in this section which were not first-class are signified by a dagger.

At Harare Country Club, Harare, November 4, 5, 6, 2002. **Drawn.** Toss: Pakistanis. **Pakistanis 456-6 dec.** (Taufeeq Umar 86, Younis Khan 84, Inzamam-ul-Haq 63, Hasan Raza 64*); **Zimbabwe A 200-5** (G. J. Whittall 67*).

The third day was washed out.

ZIMBABWE v PAKISTAN

First Test Match

At Harare, November 9, 10, 11, 12, 2002. Pakistan won by 119 runs. Toss: Zimbabwe. Test debuts: N. B. Mahwire; Kamran Akmal.

This match set the tone for the Zimbabwe leg of the tour: Pakistan overcame initial nerves to take advantage of Zimbabwe's weak bowling and gain a confidence that – until they crossed the Limpopo into South Africa – never left them. With Rashid Latif injured, they gave a debut to wicket-keeper Kamran Akmal. Zimbabwe called up Masakadza from his South African university, but he was short of quality practice, and it showed. They also introduced the seamer Blessing Mahwire; he hit his first ball, a long-hop from Saqlain Mushtaq, for four, but thereafter appeared overawed.

There was some fascinating, if not always first-rate, cricket on the first day, when Pakistan failed to take advantage of an inaccurate attack. Campbell, deputising as captain for Streak (injured in an auto-rickshaw crash in Sri Lanka that kept him out of the entire series), optimistically put them in, but if there was any early life in the pitch the bowlers failed to exploit it. The best was Blignaut – also recovering from a road accident – who took the first three wickets. After Taufeeq Umar scored an impressive 75, Inzamam-ul-Haq and Yousuf Youhana threatened to take the match away from Zimbabwe.

But after Inzamam's dismissal, skying a pull off Olonga on the stroke of tea, Zimbabwe pulled back, thanks to a testing spell from medium-pacer Whittall, who tied down the batsmen enough to take wickets for the other bowlers. The last six wickets fell for only 39.

Zimbabwe got into early difficulties and the Flower brothers were setting the innings back on an even keel when Andy was unfortunately given out by umpire Venkat, caught at the wicket down the leg side off his thigh pad. But Taibu held out for three hours and a maiden Test fifty, while Blignaut bludgeoned 50 in 33 balls – his last 17 in five from Saqlain – to keep Pakistan's lead down to 60. There seemed little room for complacency when Olonga took two early wickets.

But Zimbabwe's bowlers, far from pressing home their advantage, were wayward. Inzamam achieved the rare feat of a Test century before lunch, albeit in an extended 150-minute session, after bad light shortened the previous day. He got off the mark fortuitously, with a snick for four that just cleared the slips, and was perhaps lucky to survive an lbw appeal on 40. Otherwise he punished some wild bowling, plundering 112 from 107 balls with 20 fours. When 32, Inzamam became the second Pakistani after Javed Miandad to pass 6,000 Test runs. Taufeeq, who helped him add 180, batted six hours for a responsible century, and the lower order did enough to set Zimbabwe 430 in just over two days.

They did reach the more-than-respectable total of 310 – their previous best in the fourth innings of a Test was 246 – but no one reached three figures or threatened to bat on into the fifth day. Shoaib Akhtar collected seven wickets in the match; it emerged afterwards that he had been severely reprimanded for ball-tampering, but referee Clive Lloyd imposed no fine.

Man of the Match: Taufeeq Umar.

Close of play: First day, Pakistan 285; Second day, Pakistan 14-1 (Taufeeq Umar 14, Younis Khan 0); Third day, Zimbabwe 19-1 (Ebrahim 9, Campbell 9).

Pakistan

First innings		Second innings	
Taufeeq Umar c A. Flower b Blignaut	75	c Taibu b Blignaut	111
Salim Elahi c Campbell b Blignaut	2	c Campbell b Olonga	0
Younis Khan c Ebrahim b Blignaut	40	c Campbell b Olonga	8
Inzamam-ul-Haq c sub (M. A. Vermeulen) b Olonga	39	c G. W. Flower b Olonga	112
Yousuf Youhana lbw b Price	63	c Taibu b Blignaut	0
Hasan Raza c Campbell b Mahwire	46	c Blignaut b Price	11
†Kamran Akmal b Price	0	b Price	38
Saqlain Mushtaq c A. Flower b Whittall	2	not out	29
*Waqar Younis lbw b Blignaut	2	b Blignaut	0
Shoaib Akhtar c G. W. Flower b Blignaut	1	c Taibu b Olonga	16
Mohammad Sami not out	0	c G. W. Flower b Olonga	17
L-b 2, w 4, n-b 9	15	B 4, l-b 3, w 11, n-b 9	27
1/7 (2) 2/122 (3) 3/125 (1) 4/217 (4) 5/246 (5) 6/251 (7) 7/262 (8) 8/271 (9) 9/274 (10) 10/285 (6)	285	1/10 (2) 2/25 (3) 3/205 (4) 4/207 (5) 5/238 (6) 6/292 (7) 7/318 (1) 8/318 (9) 9/339 (10) 10/369 (11)	369

Bowling: *First Innings*—Blignaut 21–4–79–5; Olonga 16–2–46–1; Mahwire 14.5–2–58–1; Price 16–4–56–2; Whittall 22–10–44–1. *Second Innings*—Blignaut 20–1–81–3; Olonga 17.5–1–93–5; Mahwire 14–4–60–0; Whittall 14–5–62–0; Price 24–5–66–2.

Zimbabwe

First innings		Second innings	
D. D. Ebrahim c Inzamam-ul-Haq b Mohammad Sami	31	– b Shoaib Akhtar	69
H. Masakadza c Kamran Akmal b Mohammad Sami	9	– c Salim Elahi b Shoaib Akhtar	0
*A. D. R. Campbell b Shoaib Akhtar	2	– c Kamran Akmal b Mohammad Sami	30
G. W. Flower lbw b Waqar Younis	31	– c Kamran Akmal b Saqlain Mushtaq	69
A. Flower c Kamran Akmal b Mohammad Sami	29	– c and b Shoaib Akhtar	67
G. J. Whittall b Shoaib Akhtar	7	– c Younis Khan b Saqlain Mushtaq	2
†T. Taibu not out	51	– lbw b Waqar Younis	28
A. M. Blignaut c Hasan Raza b Mohammad Sami	50	– c Younis Khan b Saqlain Mushtaq	12
N. B. Mahwire c Younis Khan b Saqlain Mushtaq	4	– lbw b Waqar Younis	3
R. W. Price c Younis Khan b Saqlain Mushtaq	2	– not out	5
H. K. Olonga b Shoaib Akhtar	3	– b Shoaib Akhtar	5
L-b 1, w 2, n-b 3	6	B 8, l-b 6, w 1, n-b 5	20
1/36 (2) 2/41 (3) 3/43 (1) 4/76 (5) 5/93 (6) 6/136 (4) 7/199 (8) 8/203 (9) 9/209 (10) 10/225 (11)	225	1/4 (2) 2/51 (3) 3/162 (1) 4/201 (4) 5/203 (6) 6/256 (7) 7/280 (8) 8/291 (9) 9/301 (5) 10/310 (11)	310

Bowling: *First Innings*—Waqar Younis 14–3–58–1; Shoaib Akhtar 14.5–1–43–3; Mohammad Sami 19–3–53–4; Saqlain Mushtaq 19–5–70–2. *Second Innings*—Waqar Younis 16–1–73–2; Shoaib Akhtar 18.3–4–75–4; Mohammad Sami 15–3–50–1; Saqlain Mushtaq 31–5–98–3; Taufeeq Umar 1–1–0–0.

Umpires: D. L. Orchard (South Africa) and S. Venkataraghavan (India).
Third umpire: I. D. Robinson. Referee: C. H. Lloyd (West Indies).

ZIMBABWE v PAKISTAN

Second Test Match

At Bulawayo, November 16, 17, 18, 19, 2002. Pakistan won by ten wickets. Toss: Zimbabwe. Test debut: M. A. Vermeulen.

Pakistan became only the second touring team to win both Tests of a two-match series on Zimbabwean soil, and they did it in eight days, to New Zealand's ten in 2000-01. In contrast to the First Test, they took a grip from the opening session that they never relinquished.

Zimbabwe replaced Whittall, who had aggravated his knee injury at Harare, with debutant opener Mark Vermeulen, and Mahwire with Nkala, who proved little more successful, despite greater experience. Pakistan were unchanged. They swiftly seized the initiative on a lifeless pitch, removing both openers by the fifth over. A determined partnership between Campbell and Grant Flower temporarily stemmed the tide, but Saqlain Mushtaq was finding spin by the first afternoon. Once he had despatched these two, Zimbabwe never looked like saving the match. They lost their last five for 23 after tea: Shoaib Akhtar produced a superb spell at one end, with little help from the pitch, while Saqlain bamboozled them from the other to finish with seven wickets. The batting crumbled under the relentless pressure of Pakistan at their best.

The following day, Zimbabwe's bowling was at least more accurate than in Harare, but it was never threatening. Still, Pakistan's top order endangered their position by over-adventurousness. The man who managed to cash in was Yousuf Youhana. While Younis Khan grafted his way to a painstaking four-hour fifty, Youhana, after a cautious start, cruised to 159 off 282 balls; he batted just over six hours and hit 21 fours, surviving four chances. He shared century partnerships with Younis and wicket-keeper Kamran Akmal, who showed pleasing fluency in a maiden Test fifty, and also impressed behind the stumps. Zimbabwe had little luck, but they did not make any.

Nine Zimbabweans reached double figures in the second innings, but none made the major contribution needed. After Saqlain bowled a single over with the new ball, Vermeulen played a brief cameo, striking five fours off nine balls from Shoaib, but Campbell alone reached fifty. For once, he applied himself thoroughly to the task in hand, sharing another gritty stand with Grant Flower. Later, Blignaut played a typical attacking 41 off 32 balls before throwing his wicket away: his approach appeared to be "Let's have a bash" rather than "Let's make a fight of it."

Saqlain had to toil harder for his wickets the second time round, but deservedly finished with ten in the match. Pakistan raced to a target of 57 in only 8.3 overs, and all but nine of their runs came in boundaries.

Man of the Match: Yousuf Youhana. *Man of the Series:* Saqlain Mushtaq.

Close of play: First day, Pakistan 29-0 (Taufeeq Umar 16, Salim Elahi 13); Second day, Pakistan 295-5 (Yousuf Youhana 116, Kamran Akmal 27); Third day, Zimbabwe 171-5 (A. Flower 13).

Zimbabwe

First innings		Second innings	
D. D. Ebrahim lbw b Waqar Younis	5	lbw b Waqar Younis	7
M. A. Vermeulen lbw b Shoaib Akhtar	2	lbw b Waqar Younis	26
*A. D. R. Campbell c Kamran Akmal b Saqlain Mushtaq	46	b Mohammad Sami	62
G. W. Flower lbw b Saqlain Mushtaq	54	b Shoaib Akhtar	43
A. Flower c Inzamam-ul-Haq b Shoaib Akhtar	30	lbw b Waqar Younis	13
H. Masakadza c Kamran Akmal b Saqlain Mushtaq	0	c Yousuf Youhana b Saqlain Mushtaq	16
†T. Taibu c Kamran Akmal b Saqlain Mushtaq	15	c Yousuf Youhana b Waqar Younis	37
A. M. Blignaut c Taufeeq Umar b Saqlain Mushtaq	0	st Kamran Akmal b Saqlain Mushtaq	41
M. L. Nkala not out	10	c Kamran Akmal b Saqlain Mushtaq	14
R. W. Price b Saqlain Mushtaq	1	b Mohammad Sami	12
H. K. Olonga b Saqlain Mushtaq	8	not out	3
L-b 3, w 1, n-b 3	7	L-b 5, n-b 2	7
1/4 (2) 2/8 (1) 3/94 (3) 4/119 (4) 5/119 (6) 6/155 (7) 7/159 (8) 8/161 (5) 9/170 (10) 10/178 (11)	178	1/28 (1) 2/37 (2) 3/125 (4) 4/146 (3) 5/171 (6) 6/171 (5) 7/226 (8) 8/248 (9) 9/265 (10) 10/281 (7)	281

Bowling: *First Innings*—Waqar Younis 13–6–20–1; Shoaib Akhtar 16–3–39–2; Mohammad Sami 15–3–38–0; Saqlain Mushtaq 25.5–2–66–7; Taufeeq Umar 2–0–12–0. *Second Innings*—Waqar Younis 21.2–4–78–4; Saqlain Mushtaq 38–9–89–3; Shoaib Akhtar 12–4–61–1; Mohammad Sami 19–6–47–2; Hasan Raza 1–0–1–0.

Pakistan

Taufeeq Umar c Taibu b Olonga	34	– not out	21
Salim Elahi b Olonga	27	– not out	30
Younis Khan lbw b Blignaut	52		
Inzamam-ul-Haq b Price	11		
Yousuf Youhana b Price	159		
Hasan Raza b Olonga	4		
†Kamran Akmal lbw b Nkala	56		
Saqlain Mushtaq c sub (C. K. Coventry) b Price	14		
Mohammad Sami c Campbell b Blignaut	1		
*Waqar Younis c Ebrahim b Price	6		
Shoaib Akhtar not out	9		
B 10, l-b 5, w 2, n-b 8, p 5	30	B 1, w 1, n-b 4	6
1/63 (2) 2/64 (1) 3/82 (4) 4/209 (3) 5/225 (6) 6/346 (7) 7/374 (5) 8/387 (8) 9/387 (9) 10/403 (10)	403	(no wkt)	57

Bowling: *First Innings*—Blignaut 22.4–5–75–2; Olonga 20–4–69–3; Price 51.3–14–116–4; Nkala 25–5–93–1; G. W. Flower 12–4–26–0; A. Flower 0.2–0–4–0. *Second Innings*—Olonga 4.3–0–35–0; Price 4–1–21–0.

Umpires: D. L. Orchard (South Africa) and S. Venkataraghavan (India).
Third umpire: M. A. Esat. Referee: C. H. Lloyd (West Indies).

†ZIMBABWE v PAKISTAN

First One-Day International

At Bulawayo, November 23, 2002. Pakistan won by seven runs. Toss: Pakistan. One-day international debuts: S. Matsikenyeri, B. G. Rogers, R. W. Sims; Kamran Akmal.

This match appeared completely one-sided as Pakistan took apart another incompetent attack and then reduced Zimbabwe to 32 for four – chasing 303. The home side, fielding three debutants, looked way out of their depth against Wasim Akram and Waqar Younis. But the innings was transformed when Evans, in his first international for three years after a prolific run for Mashonaland, joined Andy Flower. Together, they added 135 and created an outside chance of victory, but 19 off the final over was too much for the last pair. Earlier, Yousuf Youhana scored a superb, one-day best 141 – from 147 balls with 13 fours and three sixes. It was only a taste of what was to come from his bat.

Man of the Match: Yousuf Youhana.

Pakistan

Taufeeq Umar lbw b Ervine	1
Salim Elahi c Sims b G. W. Flower	53
Yousuf Youhana not out	141
Inzamam-ul-Haq c Blignaut b Olonga	55
Shahid Afridi c Evans b G. W. Flower	4
Younis Khan not out	33
L-b 4, w 10, n-b 1	15
1/1 (1) 2/127 (2) 3/236 (4) 4/241 (5) (4 wkts, 50 overs)	302

†Kamran Akmal, Wasim Akram, Azhar Mahmood, *Waqar Younis and Shoaib Akhtar did not bat.

Bowling: Blignaut 10–0–52–0; Ervine 10–0–71–1; Olonga 5–0–46–1; G. W. Flower 10–0–33–2; Sims 9–0–49–0; Rogers 4–0–30–0; Evans 2–0–17–0.

Zimbabwe

*A. D. R. Campbell b Waqar Younis	4
S. Matsikenyeri c Kamran Akmal b Wasim Akram	1
A. Flower c Taufeeq Umar b Wasim Akram	77
G. W. Flower run out	0
B. G. Rogers b Waqar Younis	13
C. N. Evans run out	68
A. M. Blignaut c Shahid Afridi b Shoaib Akhtar	55
†T. Taibu b Waqar Younis	35
S. M. Ervine run out	0
R. W. Sims not out	7
H. K. Olonga not out	13
L-b 5, w 13, n-b 4	22
1/11 (2) 2/16 (1) 3/17 (4) 4/32 (5) 5/167 (6) 6/185 (3) 7/257 (7) 8/261 (9) 9/276 (8)	(9 wkts, 50 overs) 295

Bowling: Wasim Akram 10–1–57–2; Waqar Younis 10–0–50–3; Azhar Mahmood 9–0–48–0; Shoaib Akhtar 10–0–57–1; Shahid Afridi 7–0–50–0; Taufeeq Umar 4–0–28–0.

Umpires: D. L. Orchard (South Africa) and K. C. Barbour.
Third umpire: I. D. Robinson. Referee: C. H. Lloyd (West Indies).

†ZIMBABWE v PAKISTAN

Second One-Day International

At Bulawayo, November 24, 2002. Pakistan won by 104 runs (D/L method). Toss: Pakistan. One-day international debut: W. Mwayenga.

After their scare the previous day, Pakistan raised their sights. Some thrilling batting brought them the second-highest one-day total conceded by Zimbabwe – now missing all of their four top pace bowlers after Blignaut injured his leg. Taufeeq Umar and Salim Elahi opened with 159 in 32 overs, but the highlight was a stunning unbeaten 76 off just 34 balls by Yousuf Youhana, unfurling strokes of incredible daring; his fifty took only 23 balls and altogether he hit three fours and eight sixes. Zimbabwe crumbled to 20 for four in Wasim Akram's new-ball spell, but Taibu exuded defiance, and Ervine battered 61 not out in 41 balls before rain ended the match, and Duckworth/Lewis set a retrospective target of 245 in 33 overs.

Man of the Match: Salim Elahi.

Pakistan

Taufeeq Umar c Rogers b Evans	76
Salim Elahi b G. W. Flower	107
Shahid Afridi c A. Flower b G. W. Flower	30
Yousuf Youhana not out	76
Wasim Akram c G. W. Flower b Evans	1
Azhar Mahmood c G. W. Flower b Ervine	18
†Kamran Akmal not out	24
L-b 1, w 10, n-b 1	12
1/159 (2) 2/204 (3) 3/252 (1) 4/270 (5) 5/310 (6)	(5 wkts, 50 overs) 344

Inzamam-ul-Haq, Faisal Iqbal, Saqlain Mushtaq and *Waqar Younis did not bat.

Bowling: Nkala 9–0–76–0; Ervine 10–0–61–1; Mwayenga 9–0–74–0; Sims 10–0–60–0; G. W. Flower 10–0–54–2; Evans 2–0–18–2.

Zimbabwe

*A. D. R. Campbell c Faisal Iqbal b Shahid Afridi	32
S. Matsikenyeri lbw b Wasim Akram	0
A. Flower b Wasim Akram	0
G. W. Flower b Wasim Akram	1
B. G. Rogers c Kamran Akmal b Wasim Akram	0
C. N. Evans c Inzamam-ul-Haq b Waqar Younis	4
†T. Taibu not out	30
S. M. Ervine not out	61
L-b 2, w 8, n-b 2	12
1/1 (2) 2/3 (3) 3/20 (4) 4/20 (5) 5/27 (6) 6/64 (1)	(6 wkts, 33 overs) 140

M. L. Nkala, R. W. Sims and W. Mwayenga did not bat.

Bowling: Wasim Akram 7–0–22–4; Waqar Younis 6–2–20–1; Shahid Afridi 10–1–43–1; Saqlain Mushtaq 6–1–30–0; Azhar Mahmood 4–0–23–0.

Umpires: D. L. Orchard (South Africa) and M. A. Esat.
Third umpire: K. C. Barbour. Referee: C. H. Lloyd (West Indies).

†ZIMBABWE v PAKISTAN

Third One-Day International

At Harare, November 27, 2002. Pakistan won by 48 runs. Toss: Zimbabwe.

Heavy security operated for this match, in a dress rehearsal for the World Cup. Yet again, Pakistan enjoyed a run feast and Zimbabwe's batsmen fought back, but the tourists still won comfortably to secure the series. Despite a slightly improved attack, Salim Elahi scored his second successive hundred after another stand of 150-plus with Taufeeq Umar, while Yousuf Youhana hit the final ball for six to reach another century himself – though at 68 balls it was actually less spectacular than his previous outing. Vermeulen starred for Zimbabwe with 79 off 81 deliveries, and they had a faint chance while the Flowers were adding 105; but both fell to Saqlain Mushtaq, and their side had to settle for another defeat with honour.

Man of the Match: Yousuf Youhana.

Pakistan

Taufeeq Umar c Vermeulen b G. W. Flower . 68
Salim Elahi run out 108
Yousuf Youhana not out 100
Shahid Afridi c Nkala b Brent 0
†Kamran Akmal not out 24
L-b 8, w 14, n-b 1. 23

1/154 (1) 2/246 (2) 3/246 (4) (3 wkts, 50 overs) 323

Inzamam-ul-Haq, Faisal Iqbal, Wasim Akram, Saqlain Mushtaq, *Waqar Younis and Mohammad Zahid did not bat.

Bowling: Hondo 10–1–58–0; Ervine 10–1–65–0; Brent 10–0–60–1; Nkala 10–0–80–0; G. W. Flower 10–0–52–1.

Zimbabwe

M. A. Vermeulen lbw b Shahid Afridi . . 79
D. D. Ebrahim run out 7
*A. D. R. Campbell c Taufeeq Umar b Mohammad Zahid . 6
A. Flower c Inzamam-ul-Haq b Saqlain Mushtaq . 63
G. W. Flower b Saqlain Mushtaq. 54
S. M. Ervine c Shahid Afridi b Saqlain Mushtaq . 1
C. N. Evans b Taufeeq Umar 17
†T. Taibu not out 19
M. L. Nkala not out 9
B 4, l-b 2, w 7, n-b 7 20

1/40 (2) 2/89 (3) 3/108 (1) 4/213 (5) 5/224 (6) 6/226 (4) 7/257 (7) (7 wkts, 50 overs) 275

G. B. Brent and D. T. Hondo did not bat.

Bowling: Wasim Akram 8–0–23–0; Waqar Younis 5–0–37–0; Mohammad Zahid 10–0–68–1; Saqlain Mushtaq 10–0–41–3; Shahid Afridi 10–1–51–1; Taufeeq Umar 7–0–49–1.

Umpires: D. L. Orchard (South Africa) and K. C. Barbour.
Third umpire: I. D. Robinson. Referee: C. H. Lloyd (West Indies).

"Most onlookers feared for Bangladesh: a press sweepstake on their likely total returned only two three-figure predictions."

Bangladeshis in Australia, page 1219.

†ZIMBABWE v PAKISTAN

Fourth One-Day International

At Harare, November 30, 2002. Pakistan won by eight wickets. Toss: Zimbabwe.

With the series settled, Pakistan rested their opening batsmen and bowlers, and for once Zimbabwe tried batting first. The tactic backfired: a hideous top-order display sent them sprawling to 13 for four, and then 41 for six, against the revamped new-ball attack. Fortunately, Grant Flower, having kept out Mohammad Sami's hat-trick ball, played one of his most defiant innings – his sixth one-day century – with good support from Friend; nobody else reached double figures. Then it was the turn of a fresh group of batsmen to gorge themselves on the Zimbabwean bowling. Kamran Akmal made a dashing start, surviving three hard chances, while Faisal Iqbal, beginning more circumspectly, just had time to record his first century for Pakistan, off 97 balls.

Man of the Match: Faisal Iqbal.

Zimbabwe

M. A. Vermeulen lbw b Shoaib Akhtar . . 9
D. D. Ebrahim b Shoaib Akhtar 2
*A. D. R. Campbell c Misbah-ul-Haq b Mohammad Sami . 0
A. Flower c Inzamam-ul-Haq b Mohammad Sami . 0
G. W. Flower not out 105
S. M. Ervine c Younis Khan b Mohammad Zahid . 5
†T. Taibu c Kamran Akmal b Mohammad Sami . 0
T. J. Friend b Shahid Afridi 48
G. B. Brent b Mohammad Sami 8
B. A. Murphy c Kamran Akmal b Mohammad Zahid . 7
D. T. Hondo c Mohammad Zahid b Saqlain Mushtaq . 5
L-b 7, w 11, n-b 3. 21

1/11 (1) 2/13 (3) 3/13 (4) 4/13 (2) 5/36 (6) 6/41 (7) 7/123 (8) 8/149 (9) 9/164 (10) 10/210 (11) (49.5 overs) 210

Bowling: Shoaib Akhtar 10–1–41–2; Mohammad Sami 10–0–41–4; Mohammad Zahid 10–1–35–2; Shahid Afridi 10–0–41–1; Saqlain Mushtaq 9.5–0–45–1.

Pakistan

†Kamran Akmal c Taibu b Hondo 44
Faisal Iqbal not out. 100
Younis Khan run out. 56
Misbah-ul-Haq not out 1
L-b 2, w 7, n-b 1 10

1/58 (1) 2/209 (3) (2 wkts, 35.4 overs) 211

*Inzamam-ul-Haq, Yousuf Youhana, Shahid Afridi, Saqlain Mushtaq, Shoaib Akhtar, Mohammad Sami and Mohammad Zahid did not bat.

Bowling: Friend 8–0–47–0; Hondo 5–0–43–1; Ervine 2.4–0–14–0; Brent 7–3–34–0; Murphy 10–0–50–0; G. W. Flower 3–0–21–0.

Umpires: D. L. Orchard (South Africa) and M. A. Esat.
Third umpire: I. D. Robinson. Referee: C. H. Lloyd (West Indies).

†ZIMBABWE v PAKISTAN

Fifth One-Day International

At Harare, December 1, 2002. Pakistan won by 70 runs. Toss: Zimbabwe.

Unexpectedly, Pakistan's top order struggled, but their colleagues still reached 300 for the fourth game in five to set up a series whitewash. Friend and Olonga bowled impressively with the new ball, demolishing the first three for 39, and Hondo also caused problems. But Yousuf Youhana, inevitably, and Younis Khan came to the rescue, adding 129 before Youhana was dismissed for the only time in the series, run out backing up. Andy Flower led the home side's chase but, once he was third out, the middle order caved in feebly, though Olonga and Hondo put on 47, a Zimbabwean last-wicket record. Younis held four catches and pulled off two run-outs. It was also a memorable match for Shoaib Akhtar: he bowled a venomous spell which touched 99.3 mph, but sledged the batsmen and threw a plastic bottle towards some hecklers, for which he received a fine and a one-match suspension.

Man of the Match: Younis Khan. *Man of the Series:* Yousuf Youhana.

Pakistan

†Kamran Akmal c Taibu b Friend	3
Faisal Iqbal c G. W. Flower b Olonga	25
Misbah-ul-Haq c and b Friend	0
*Inzamam-ul-Haq c and b Murphy	27
Yousuf Youhana run out	88
Younis Khan c A. Flower b Hondo	90
Shahid Afridi run out	8
Wasim Akram not out	24
Saqlain Mushtaq not out	13
L-b 2, w 19, n-b 1	22
1/15 (1) 2/16 (3) 3/39 (2) 4/90 (4) 5/219 (5) 6/238 (7) 7/267 (6) (7 wkts, 50 overs)	300

Shoaib Akhtar and Mohammad Sami did not bat.

Bowling: Friend 10–0–57–2; Olonga 10–0–53–1; Hondo 10–1–58–1; Murphy 10–0–64–1; G. W. Flower 8–0–49–0; Evans 2–0–17–0.

Zimbabwe

M. A. Vermeulen c Younis Khan b Shoaib Akhtar	5
D. D. Ebrahim run out	36
A. Flower c Wasim Akram b Saqlain Mushtaq	72
G. W. Flower c Misbah-ul-Haq b Shahid Afridi	28
*A. D. R. Campbell c Younis Khan b Saqlain Mushtaq	3
C. N. Evans c Younis Khan b Shahid Afridi	8
†T. Taibu c Younis Khan b Shahid Afridi	6
T. J. Friend c sub (Taufeeq Umar) b Younis Khan	6
B. A. Murphy run out	4
H. K. Olonga c and b Mohammad Sami	31
D. T. Hondo not out	15
L-b 4, w 11, n-b 1	16
1/14 (1) 2/117 (2) 3/134 (3) 4/140 (5) 5/162 (6) 6/171 (4) 7/171 (7) 8/181 (9) 9/183 (8) 10/230 (10) (45.3 overs)	230

Bowling: Wasim Akram 7–1–14–0; Shoaib Akhtar 7–0–34–1; Mohammad Sami 8.3–1–51–1; Shahid Afridi 10–0–45–3; Saqlain Mushtaq 10–1–41–2; Younis Khan 2–0–24–1; Faisal Iqbal 1–0–17–0.

Umpires: D. L. Orchard (South Africa) and K. C. Barbour.
Third umpire: I. D. Robinson. Referee: C. H. Lloyd (West Indies).

†At Randjesfontein, December 3, 2002. **Drawn.** Toss: N. F. Oppenheimer's XI. **Pakistanis 229-9 dec.** (Abdul Razzaq 63*); **N. F. Oppenheimer's XI 187-9** (Z. de Bruyn 83*; Mohammad Sami 4-52).

†At Benoni, December 5 (day/night), 2002. **Pakistanis won by three wickets** (D/L method). Toss: South Africa A. **South Africa A 206-6** (50 overs) (J. A. Rudolph 95); **Pakistanis 158-7** (28.4 overs) (Faisal Iqbal 59).

The Pakistani target was revised to 157 from 29 overs because of rain.

†SOUTH AFRICA v PAKISTAN

First One-Day International

At Durban, December 8, 2002. South Africa won by 132 runs. Toss: Pakistan.

Rhodes and Pollock rescued South Africa from a precarious 151 for six and effectively won the match with an energetic stand of 99 in just 16 overs. Rhodes hustled 98 in 92 balls before top-edging an attempted pull and becoming Waqar Younis's 400th one-day victim; Pollock's bat sounded more like a rifle as he launched three sixes in the last two overs in a 51-ball 57. The South Africans' stifling respect for Wasim Akram – the only other man with 400 wickets – played a part in his three for 19 in ten overs; back-up seamers Mohammad Sami and Abdul Razzaq both conceded over 70. In reply, Salim Elahi emerged with respect intact, making 31 out of Pakistan's 140, but the rest were abysmal. Pollock failed to bowl a bad ball and claimed three for 12.

Man of the Match: J. N. Rhodes. *Attendance:* 13,748.

South Africa

G. C. Smith b Wasim Akram	56
H. H. Gibbs c Rashid Latif b Wasim Akram	0
N. D. McKenzie c Yousuf Youhana b Mohammad Sami	11
N. Boje c Waqar Younis b Mohammad Sami	20
J. H. Kallis c Mohammad Sami b Abdul Razzaq	6
J. N. Rhodes c Rashid Latif b Waqar Younis	98
†M. V. Boucher b Wasim Akram	0
*S. M. Pollock not out	57
L. Klusener not out	4
L-b 5, w 6, n-b 9	20
1/6 (2) 2/33 (3) 3/63 (4) 4/86 (5) 5/151 (1) 6/151 (7) 7/250 (6) (7 wkts, 50 overs)	272

A. A. Donald and M. Ntini did not bat.

Bowling: Wasim Akram 10–1–19–3; Waqar Younis 10–1–59–1; Mohammad Sami 10–0–71–2; Abdul Razzaq 10–0–77–1; Saqlain Mushtaq 10–0–41–0.

Pakistan

Taufeeq Umar b Ntini	7
Salim Elahi c Kallis b Ntini	31
Yousuf Youhana c Pollock b Donald	8
Inzamam-ul-Haq b Kallis	11
Younis Khan c Smith b Boje	17
Abdul Razzaq c Donald b Boje	15
†Rashid Latif c Boucher b Pollock	12
Wasim Akram c McKenzie b Pollock	14
Saqlain Mushtaq c Pollock b Boje	1
*Waqar Younis not out	0
Mohammad Sami c McKenzie b Pollock	2
B 3, l-b 2, w 16, n-b 1	22
1/19 (1) 2/36 (3) 3/55 (4) 4/78 (2) 5/100 (5) 6/116 (6) 7/134 (8) 8/136 (9) 9/136 (7) 10/140 (11) (42.5 overs)	140

Bowling: Pollock 9.5–1–12–3; Ntini 8–0–35–2; Kallis 6–0–16–1; Donald 6–0–20–1; Klusener 6–0–23–0; Boje 7–1–29–3.

Umpires: N. A. Mallender (England) and I. L. Howell.
Third umpire: S. Wadvalla. Referee: C. H. Lloyd (West Indies).

†SOUTH AFRICA v PAKISTAN

Second One-Day International

At Port Elizabeth, December 11, 2002 (day/night). Pakistan won by 182 runs. Toss: Pakistan.

Mr Hyde became Dr Jekyll for the only time on the South African tour. Pakistan showed they could be very, very good as well as very bad as Salim Elahi and Abdul Razzaq made the bowlers toil on a red-hot batting strip, putting on 257. Confused by chirpy pace and bounce from a surface usually slow and low, South Africa bowled the wrong length, and Elahi and Razzaq feasted on a procession of silver-plattered long-hops and half-volleys. Elahi took just 94 balls to gallop to his third century in four internationals; Razzaq, relishing promotion, needed 111 to reach his first. All the South African bowlers conceded a run a ball, and their fielding cracked under the pressure. In reply, a rollicking opening stand of 57 in eight overs, dominated by Gibbs, was ended by a Waqar Younis in-swinger, and South Africa went down in 29 overs, for their heaviest defeat by runs in a one-day international.

Man of the Match: Salim Elahi. *Attendance:* 9,901.

Pakistan

Salim Elahi c Pollock b Kallis	135	†Rashid Latif not out	2
Shahid Afridi c Gibbs b Ntini	13		
Abdul Razzaq c Ntini b Klusener	112	L-b 5, w 11, n-b 1	17
Yousuf Youhana b Ntini	9		
Inzamam-ul-Haq not out	36	1/15 (2) 2/272 (3) (6 wkts, 50 overs)	335
Younis Khan b Donald	11	3/284 (4) 4/288 (1)	
Wasim Akram b Donald	0	5/333 (6) 6/333 (7)	

*Waqar Younis, Saqlain Mushtaq and Mohammad Sami did not bat.

Bowling: Pollock 10–0–61–0; Ntini 10–1–65–2; Donald 10–0–60–2; Kallis 9–0–60–1; Boje 6–0–45–0; Klusener 5–0–39–1.

South Africa

G. C. Smith b Waqar Younis	18	L. Klusener not out	29
H. H. Gibbs b Waqar Younis	40	A. A. Donald c Rashid Latif b Shahid Afridi	2
N. Boje c Yousuf Youhana b Mohammad Sami	7	M. Ntini c and b Saqlain Mushtaq	5
N. D. McKenzie lbw b Waqar Younis	4		
J. H. Kallis c Rashid Latif b Mohammad Sami	12	L-b 2, w 9, n-b 2	13
J. N. Rhodes b Mohammad Sami	1	1/57 (2) 2/61 (1) 3/67 (3) (29 overs)	153
†M. V. Boucher c Rashid Latif b Shahid Afridi	4	4/77 (4) 5/82 (6) 6/90 (7) 7/100 (5) 8/136 (8)	
*S. M. Pollock b Shahid Afridi	18	9/146 (10) 10/153 (11)	

Bowling: Wasim Akram 6–0–37–0; Waqar Younis 7–2–45–3; Mohammad Sami 5–1–26–3; Shahid Afridi 7–0–35–3; Saqlain Mushtaq 4–1–8–1.

Umpires: N. A. Mallender (England) and B. G. Jerling.
Third umpire: I. L. Howell. Referee: C. H. Lloyd (West Indies).

†SOUTH AFRICA v PAKISTAN

Third One-Day International

At East London, December 13, 2002 (day/night). South Africa won by 62 runs. Toss: South Africa.

Pollock played the lead role in a show with more drama than quality. In his first game of the series, Shoaib Akhtar bowled as fast as ever and his threat was unmistakably responsible for the steady fall of wickets – not just at his own end. However, there were some very ordinary shots. Dippenaar tried to hold things together with an obdurate 47, and Pollock scored a composed 32, but the innings never caught fire. Early wickets were crucial to defend a modest 182, and South Africa succeeded spectacularly, snaring five within 13 overs. As the evening dew settled, Pollock swung and seamed the ball prodigiously, while Ntini was fast and intimidating. From a hopeless 55 for eight, Wasim Akram and Waqar Younis gave the total a veneer of respectability without suggesting a miraculous resurrection. Boucher, behind the stumps, and Kallis, razor-sharp in the slips, clung on to three catches each.

Man of the Match: S. M. Pollock. *Attendance:* 9,059.

South Africa

G. C. Smith c Rashid Latif b Shoaib Akhtar	44	L. Klusener c Waqar Younis b Wasim Akram	4
H. H. Gibbs c Abdul Razzaq b Waqar Younis	13	A. J. Hall b Wasim Akram	3
H. H. Dippenaar c and b Shahid Afridi	47	A. A. Donald b Shoaib Akhtar	3
J. H. Kallis lbw b Saqlain Mushtaq	4	M. Ntini b Waqar Younis	0
J. N. Rhodes c Inzamam-ul-Haq b Saqlain Mushtaq	0	L-b 5, w 12	17
†M. V. Boucher lbw b Shoaib Akhtar	15	1/28 (2) 2/70 (1) 3/76 (4) 4/81 (5) 5/129 (6) 6/145 (3) 7/154 (8) 8/160 (9) 9/174 (10) 10/182 (11) (47.5 overs)	182
*S. M. Pollock not out	32		

Bowling: Wasim Akram 9–0–28–2; Waqar Younis 8.5–0–47–2; Saqlain Mushtaq 10–1–28–2; Shoaib Akhtar 10–0–50–3; Shahid Afridi 10–0–24–1.

Pakistan

Salim Elahi c Kallis b Pollock	6	*Waqar Younis c Kallis b Hall	18
Shahid Afridi c Boucher b Pollock	16	Shoaib Akhtar run out	1
Abdul Razzaq c Kallis b Ntini	6		
Yousuf Youhana b Pollock	5	L-b 8, w 5	13
Inzamam-ul-Haq c Boucher b Ntini	0		
Younis Khan c Boucher b Donald	5	1/20 (1) 2/27 (2) 3/33 (3) 4/33 (5) 5/39 (4) 6/48 (6) 7/49 (7) 8/55 (9) 9/101 (10) 10/120 (11) (36.2 overs)	120
†Rashid Latif c Smith b Donald	6		
Wasim Akram not out	43		
Saqlain Mushtaq c Hall b Kallis	1		

Bowling: Pollock 8–3–23–3; Ntini 7–2–12–2; Kallis 7–1–21–1; Donald 7–2–23–2; Hall 4–0–17–1; Klusener 3.2–0–16–0.

Umpires: N. A. Mallender (England) and I. L. Howell.
Third umpire: B. G. Jerling. Referee: C. H. Lloyd (West Indies).

†At Fort Hare University, Alice, December 14, 2002. **Border Invitation XI won by five wickets.** Toss: Border Invitation XI. **Pakistanis 135-9** (25 overs) (L. Graham 5-20); **Border Invitation XI 136-5** (25 overs) (C. B. Sugden 55*).

Team analyst Sikander Bakht played in the Pakistani team.

†SOUTH AFRICA v PAKISTAN

Fourth One-Day International

At Paarl, December 16, 2002. South Africa won by nine wickets. Toss: Pakistan.

Kirsten won the match, and thus the series, with a century that was well timed in more ways than one. Left out of South Africa's last 15 one-day internationals, he seemed certain to miss the World Cup. But the experimental opening partnership of Smith and Gibbs was seen as flimsy (despite Smith averaging nearly 40 in Kirsten's absence) and a commanding 102 from 118 balls gave the prevaricating selectors no choice but to include Kirsten. He was fortunate to make it that far: on two, he survived a raucous lbw appeal from Waqar Younis, and on 30 he was badly dropped at cover. Pakistan's innings was a study in their inability to adapt to conditions. A slow pitch and outfield are part and parcel of this picturesque ground but, apart from Yousuf Youhana, no batsman looked comfortable.

Man of the Match: G. Kirsten. *Attendance:* 4,808.

Pakistan

†Kamran Akmal b Ntini	31	*Waqar Younis not out	13
Salim Elahi lbw b Kallis	26	Shoaib Akhtar c and b Pollock	0
Abdul Razzaq lbw b Donald	5		
Yousuf Youhana run out	61	L-b 1, w 7	8
Inzamam-ul-Haq lbw b Peterson	34		
Younis Khan c Boucher b Ntini	20	1/54 (1) 2/65 (3) 3/67 (2) (48.4 overs)	213
Faisal Iqbal run out	9	4/129 (5) 5/166 (6)	
Shahid Afridi b Kallis	0	6/183 (7) 7/190 (8)	
Saqlain Mushtaq b Pollock	6	8/196 (4) 9/213 (9) 10/213 (11)	

Bowling: Pollock 9.4–1–39–2; Ntini 10–2–44–2; Donald 8–0–35–1; Kallis 9–0–35–2; Peterson 7–0–29–1; Klusener 5–0–30–0.

South Africa

H. H. Gibbs b Abdul Razzaq	52
G. Kirsten not out	102
H. H. Dippenaar not out	47
L-b 4, w 4, n-b 5	13
1/111 (1) (1 wkt, 42 overs)	214

J. H. Kallis, J. N. Rhodes, †M. V. Boucher, *S. M. Pollock, L. Klusener, R. J. Peterson, A. A. Donald and M. Ntini did not bat.

Bowling: Waqar Younis 8–0–47–0; Shoaib Akhtar 7–0–35–0; Saqlain Mushtaq 10–0–52–0; Abdul Razzaq 7–0–32–1; Shahid Afridi 10–0–44–0.

Umpires: N. A. Mallender (England) and B. G. Jerling.
Third umpire: I. L. Howell. Referee: C. H. Lloyd (West Indies).

†SOUTH AFRICA v PAKISTAN

Fifth One-Day International

At Cape Town, December 18, 2002 (day/night). South Africa won by 34 runs. Toss: South Africa.

The last match was the closest of the series and Pakistan had every chance when they needed 79 in 11 overs with six wickets in hand. But a series of Kallis away-swingers made sure they finished with a stagger rather than a sprint. Earlier, South Africa had slumped to an uncertain 61 for three, before Dippenaar and Rhodes took charge. Dippenaar pushed and prodded with his usual caution, but Rhodes ran him hard between the wickets, and runs piled up steadily, especially against the spinners. Boucher inflicted the worst of the late damage, belting 34 from 16 balls, with four sixes. Pakistan looked destined for another routine defeat at 81 for four, before Inzamam-ul-Haq and Younis Khan added 108.

Man of the Match: J. N. Rhodes. *Attendance:* 15,772.
Man of the Series: S. M. Pollock.

South Africa

H. H. Gibbs c Younis Khan b Waqar Younis	0	*S. M. Pollock c Abdul Razzaq b Saqlain Mushtaq	0
G. Kirsten b Waqar Younis	12	A. J. Hall not out	0
H. H. Dippenaar c Mohammad Sami b Waqar Younis	93	M. Zondeki not out	3
J. H. Kallis c Salim Elahi b Saqlain Mushtaq	8	B 1, l-b 8, w 10, n-b 4	23
J. N. Rhodes b Saqlain Mushtaq	81		
R. J. Peterson c Inzamam-ul-Haq b Waqar Younis	11	1/0 (1) 2/22 (2) (8 wkts, 50 overs)	265
†M. V. Boucher c Kamran Akmal b Saqlain Mushtaq	34	3/61 (4) 4/195 (5)	
		5/212 (6) 6/258 (3)	
		7/262 (8) 8/262 (7)	

M. Ntini did not bat.

Bowling: Waqar Younis 10–2–41–4; Mohammad Sami 10–1–46–0; Abdul Razzaq 10–1–32–0; Saqlain Mushtaq 10–0–68–4; Shahid Afridi 10–0–69–0.

Pakistan

†Kamran Akmal c Kirsten b Zondeki	15	Saqlain Mushtaq not out	3
Salim Elahi b Pollock	0	Mohammad Sami b Kallis	2
Faisal Iqbal lbw b Ntini	0		
Yousuf Youhana b Kallis	46	L-b 3, w 2, n-b 2	7
Inzamam-ul-Haq c Pollock b Kallis	63		
Younis Khan run out	72	1/1 (2) 2/2 (3) 3/42 (1) (47.4 overs)	231
Abdul Razzaq c Boucher b Kallis	2	4/81 (4) 5/189 (5) 6/201 (7)	
Shahid Afridi b Kallis	17	7/205 (6) 8/224 (9)	
*Waqar Younis b Ntini	4	9/229 (8) 10/231 (11)	

Bowling: Pollock 9–0–26–1; Ntini 10–0–45–2; Zondeki 6–0–36–1; Kallis 8.4–1–41–5; Hall 9–0–44–0; Peterson 5–0–36–0.

Umpires: N. A. Mallender (England) and I. L. Howell.
Third umpire: B. G. Jerling. Referee: C. H. Lloyd (West Indies).

At Pietermaritzburg, December 21, 22, 23, 2002. **Drawn.** Toss: Pakistanis. **Pakistanis 174** (R. J. Peterson 6-72) **and 174-8** (Taufeeq Umar 89*; R. J. Peterson 4-61); **South Africa A 206** (J. A. Rudolph 92; Mohammad Zahid 5-43).

SOUTH AFRICA v PAKISTAN

First Test Match

At Durban, December 26, 27, 28, 29, 2002. South Africa won by ten wickets. Toss: Pakistan.

On the first afternoon, Pakistan's hopes were raised when South Africa were struggling slightly at 214 for five. It was their only moment of optimism in the two-Test series before South Africa's depth and resilience proved decisive.

The first morning had been typically hard work for batsmen on the country's greenest wicket, but Pakistan had picked only three seamers, and they wasted the bounce and seam movement with a series of wide, harmless deliveries. Even their two early successes owed something to good fortune: Smith flapped at a wide Mohammad Sami half-volley that was swinging wider still, while Gibbs slapped a Waqar Younis long-hop to backward point. A couple more edges and a classic Waqar in-swinger later, and South Africa were nervous.

But Kallis was in stubborn mood, taking no chances and waiting for the limited attack to blow itself out. He treated every delivery with the respect it deserved, and when respect was inappropriate he belted it to the boundary. Long periods of dishearteningly solid defence drained the bowlers, and Kallis was nourished by their despair, completing a 205-ball hundred shortly before bad light ended play. On the second morning, Boucher emulated Kirsten's composed, unhurried half-century of the first day, and South Africa reached 368. Saqlain Mushtaq worked admirably hard for his four wickets in conditions offering him little encouragement, while Waqar and Sami finished with three each but could – and should – have done better.

In reply, Pakistan openers Taufeeq Umar, a revelation in both Tests, and Salim Elahi put on 77, and neither looked remotely threatened. It was a glimpse of what was possible on a pitch that routinely plays well on days two and three. But after the 21-year-old Taufeeq edged a lifter from Hayward, the rest of the batsmen whimpered like scolded dogs.

There may be no such thing as a bad century or five-wicket haul, but there are certainly lucky ones. Hayward bowled fast, but was wilder than a Karoo ostrich. Charging in, hair peroxide blond, he sprayed bouncers ad nauseam in the approximate direction of batsmen's heads. Sadly, the Pakistanis appeared happy enough to back away and offer catching practice. In between the many dreadful deliveries, Hayward filched five for 56 inside 11 eventful overs. Ntini, on the other hand, was no less rapid and a good deal more accurate for his three wickets. On the third morning, Waqar hit 28 in 19 balls, but was last out just eight short of saving the follow-on.

Asked to bat again, Pakistan managed 89 more in their second innings, but without application. Although Taufeeq again tried to weld things together, four of his colleagues wafted catches to the keeper, and their collective approach was best summed up when Yousuf Youhana flailed yet another Hayward bouncer straight to third man.

The fourth and final morning was a mixed experience for several of the South Africans. As Gibbs and Smith completed a ten-wicket win before lunch, the team already knew the 15-man squad for the World Cup, due to be announced publicly in a televised ceremony after the match. Among those to miss out was Smith, who later admitted to feeling gloomier than at any other time in his career. Little did he know: seven weeks on, he was called into the squad to replace the injured Jonty Rhodes; a month after that, he was captain of South Africa.

Man of the Match: J. H. Kallis. *Attendance:* 14,503.

Close of play: First day, South Africa 250-5 (Kallis 104, Boucher 13); Second day, Pakistan 120-8 (Kamran Akmal 0, Waqar Younis 0); Third day, Pakistan 218-8 (Kamran Akmal 21, Waqar Younis 2).

South Africa

Batsman	First innings		Second innings	
G. C. Smith c Kamran Akmal b Mohammad Sami	16	–	not out	13
H. H. Gibbs c Faisal Iqbal b Waqar Younis	11	–	not out	25
G. Kirsten c Younis Khan b Saqlain Mushtaq	56			
J. H. Kallis b Mohammad Sami	105			
H. H. Dippenaar c Kamran Akmal b Saqlain Mushtaq	1			
N. D. McKenzie b Waqar Younis	24			
†M. V. Boucher c Faisal Iqbal b Saqlain Mushtaq	55			
*S. M. Pollock c Kamran Akmal b Waqar Younis	21			
N. Boje not out	37			
M. Ntini c Taufeeq Umar b Saqlain Mushtaq	0			
M. Hayward b Mohammad Sami	10			
B 4, l-b 5, n-b 23	32		L-b 1, n-b 6	7
1/27 (1) 2/33 (2) 3/155 (3) 4/159 (5) 5/214 (6) 6/252 (4) 7/286 (8) 8/344 (7) 9/344 (10) 10/368 (11)	368		(no wkt)	45

Bowling: *First Innings*—Waqar Younis 25–3–91–3; Mohammad Sami 26–5–92–3; Abdul Razzaq 19–3–57–0; Saqlain Mushtaq 37–4–119–4. *Second Innings*—Mohammad Sami 5–0–36–0; Saqlain Mushtaq 4–2–8–0.

Pakistan

Taufeeq Umar c Smith b Hayward	39	– lbw b Boje	39
Salim Elahi c McKenzie b Ntini	39	– c Smith b Ntini	18
Younis Khan lbw b Pollock	1	– c Boucher b Kallis	30
Inzamam-ul-Haq c and b Ntini	18	– c Gibbs b Boje	13
Yousuf Youhana c Smith b Ntini	12	– c McKenzie b Hayward	42
Faisal Iqbal run out	6	– b Kallis	17
Abdul Razzaq c McKenzie b Hayward	1	– c Boucher b Hayward	22
†Kamran Akmal c Pollock b Hayward	12	– c Boucher b Ntini	29
Saqlain Mushtaq b Hayward	0	– c Boucher b Pollock	4
*Waqar Younis b Hayward	28	– c Kirsten b Pollock	15
Mohammad Sami not out	0	– not out	11
L-b 1, w 1, n-b 3	5	L-b 2, w 1, n-b 7	10
1/77 (1) 2/83 (3) 3/83 (2) 4/107 (4) 5/119 (6) 6/120 (5) 7/120 (7) 8/120 (9) 9/145 (8) 10/161 (10)	161	1/50 (2) 2/64 (1) 3/88 (4) 4/132 (3) 5/156 (6) 6/184 (5) 7/199 (7) 8/216 (9) 9/226 (8) 10/250 (10)	250

Bowling: *First Innings*—Pollock 14–5–23–1; Ntini 18–4–59–3; Hayward 10.4–1–56–5; Kallis 6–0–22–0. *Second Innings*—Ntini 21–2–73–2; Pollock 17.3–4–29–2; Kallis 17–5–30–2; Hayward 13–1–63–2; Boje 19–2–53–2.

Umpires: S. A. Bucknor (West Indies) and S. Venkataraghavan (India).
Third umpire: I. L. Howell. Referee: G. R. Viswanath (India).

SOUTH AFRICA v PAKISTAN

Second Test Match

At Cape Town, January 2, 3, 4, 5, 2003. South Africa won by an innings and 142 runs. Toss: South Africa.

Gibbs and Smith destroyed Pakistan's demoralised bowling with an opening stand of 368, at the time South Africa's best for any wicket. Gibbs, in particular, played shots that caused grown men in the stands to miss their mouths with their sandwiches. South Africa reached 445 by the first-day close, more than they had ever before managed in a day.

Having lost a toss he desperately needed to win, Waqar Younis ran in to bowl the first ball looking like a fun-runner completing the last mile of a charity marathon. Like so many that followed, it was wide and harmless. Despite a sad flogging for an understaffed attack in Durban, the selectors had not dipped into their reserves for reinforcement. The injured Abdul Razzaq was replaced by the tall medium-pacer Mohammad Zahid, playing his first Test in over four years, following major back surgery. He was a very different bowler from the one who took 11 for 130 on debut against New Zealand in November 1996, producing two spells of long-hops and leaking 61 in his first 11 overs.

Gibbs skipped down to hit all the bowlers, inside out, over extra cover, while Smith hooked, pulled and hooked again. Length became increasingly inconsequential as they tried to outdo each other, complete with toothy grins.

After tea, Eddie Barlow and Graeme Pollock's 341 for the third wicket at Adelaide in 1963-64 was erased as South Africa's highest partnership. Soon afterwards, Gibbs reached his double-hundred, from 211 deliveries, the second-fastest ever recorded in terms of balls. He couldn't help dreaming, he later said, of the records that lay within his grasp. But ten overs before the close, he pushed forward with a hint of tiredness to Saqlain Mushtaq, the ball looped off his pad to slip and umpire Venkat raised his finger – to the disbelief of Gibbs and dismay of the crowd. His 228 had lasted six hours 23 minutes and 240 balls, and included 29 fours and six sixes. It was the highest Test score at Newlands.

Next day, Dippenaar and McKenzie helped themselves to very deliberate half-centuries, but it was akin to looting in the aftermath of violent conflict. It seemed impossible that such an innings could end in disappointment, yet it came close when Pollock declared at 620 for seven to have a bowl before tea. Alas, he did not understand how the timings worked, and tea was taken anyway. His declaration left South Africa two short of their highest total, 622 for nine against Australia at Durban in 1969-70. "I didn't know," admitted a sheepish Pollock. His uncle Graeme could have reminded him: he scored 274 that day.

By now, most of the Pakistanis seemed to have lost all will to fight, and they would later be fined their entire match fee for a funereal over-rate. The exception was the determined Taufeeq Umar, who led them to 152 for one. On the third morning, though, Pollock trapped Younis Khan lbw, Ntini backed him up and nine wickets fell for 100. Taufeeq, however, had made a serious impression amid the collapse. Short, left-handed and well balanced, with quick feet and even quicker hands, he clearly had more time to play the ball than any of his team-mates and thoroughly deserved his 135, which occupied five and three-quarter hours with a six and 20 fours – most sweetly timed through the covers.

Taufeeq showed more guts during the follow-on, and not just on the field. Having top-scored again, with a classy 67, he watched from the pavilion as Yousuf Youhana launched a frenzied assault. But for a couple of miscues, he would have hit the fastest recorded Test fifty in balls, although 27, with six fours and two sixes, was still second-quickest. It was also inappropriate to the situation and Taufeeq, in broken English, let it be known how he felt: "I will not speak of that," he seethed through clenched teeth. "I have no comment."

Once Youhana went in the final over of the third day, the rest folded compliantly. And so it was with his second successive massive four-day win – which took South Africa to the top of the ICC Championship – that Shaun Pollock's reign as Test captain ended. Two months later he was sacked. For Gibbs and Smith, memories were not so bittersweet.

Man of the Match: H. H. Gibbs. *Attendance:* 35,485.

Man of the Series: M. Ntini.

Close of play: First day, South Africa 445-3 (Kallis 19, Dippenaar 8); Second day, Pakistan 141-1 (Taufeeq Umar 85, Younis Khan 44); Third day, Pakistan 184-5 (Faisal Iqbal 2).

South Africa

Batsman	Runs
G. C. Smith b Mohammad Zahid	151
H. H. Gibbs c Younis Khan b Saqlain Mushtaq	228
G. Kirsten c Younis Khan b Waqar Younis	19
J. H. Kallis lbw b Mohammad Sami	31
H. H. Dippenaar c Kamran Akmal b Saqlain Mushtaq	62
N. D. McKenzie c Kamran Akmal b Mohammad Zahid	51
†M. V. Boucher b Saqlain Mushtaq	7
*S. M. Pollock not out	36
N. Boje not out	7
B 1, l-b 5, w 1, n-b 21	28
1/368 (1) 2/413 (2) 3/414 (3) 4/463 (4) 5/548 (6) 6/557 (7) 7/594 (5)	(7 wkts dec.) 620

M. Ntini and M. Hayward did not bat.

Bowling: Waqar Younis 28–4–121–1; Mohammad Sami 28–2–124–1; Mohammad Zahid 25–3–108–2; Saqlain Mushtaq 50–3–237–3; Younis Khan 4–0–24–0.

Pakistan

Taufeeq Umar c Kallis b Ntini	135	– c Boucher b Pollock	67
Salim Elahi c Smith b Pollock	10	– c Dippenaar b Ntini	0
Younis Khan lbw b Pollock	46	– c McKenzie b Kallis	2
Inzamam-ul-Haq c Dippenaar b Hayward	32	– st Boucher b Boje	60
Yousuf Youhana c Boucher b Hayward	0	– c Kallis b Boje	50
Faisal Iqbal b Ntini	24	– c Pollock b Ntini	11
†Kamran Akmal lbw b Pollock	0	– lbw b Ntini	4
Saqlain Mushtaq c Boucher b Ntini	1	– run out	9
*Waqar Younis c Kallis b Pollock	0	– lbw b Hayward	9
Mohammad Sami not out	0	– not out	9
Mohammad Zahid c Smith b Ntini	0	– c Pollock b Ntini	0
L-b 1, n-b 3	4	L-b 1, w 1, n-b 3	5
1/36 (2) 2/152 (3) 3/208 (4) 4/208 (5) 5/240 (1) 6/247 (7) 7/251 (6) 8/252 (9) 9/252 (8) 10/252 (11)	252	1/0 (2) 2/9 (3) 3/130 (4) 4/130 (1) 5/184 (5) 6/190 (7) 7/203 (6) 8/216 (9) 9/221 (8) 10/226 (11)	226

Bowling: *First Innings*—Pollock 23–6–45–4; Ntini 20.4–7–62–4; Kallis 12–2–35–0; Hayward 15–2–56–2; Boje 17–2–53–0. *Second Innings*—Pollock 12–5–32–1; Ntini 15.1–2–33–4; Kallis 6–1–34–1; Hayward 11–3–44–1; Boje 15–0–82–2.

Umpires: S. A. Bucknor (West Indies) and S. Venkataraghavan (India).
Third umpire: B. G. Jerling. Referee: G. R. Viswanath (India).

THE KENYANS IN ZIMBABWE, 2002-03

JOHN WARD

A week after Zimbabwe's comprehensive defeat by Pakistan in both Test and limited-overs series, they were offered a pick-me-up in the form of three one-day internationals against the Kenyans in advance of the World Cup. Kenya arrived during the wet season, and though they did win one rain-affected game against Zimbabwe A, they never seriously threatened the senior side; their bowlers took only four wickets between them in the 71 overs they delivered. Zimbabwe were still missing their captain, Heath Streak, but some of their injured bowlers – Douglas Hondo, Travis Friend and finally Andy Blignaut – returned from injury during the series, and all of them prospered. Unusually for a modern one-day international series, there was no TV umpire: the series was not televised.

KENYAN TOURING PARTY

S. O. Tikolo (*captain*), T. M. Odoyo (*vice-captain*), J. O. Angara, J. K. Kamande, H. S. Modi, C. O. Obuya, D. O. Obuya, P. Ochieng, M. O. Odumbe, K. O. Otieno, M. A. Ouma, B. J. Patel, R. D. Shah, M. A. Suji, T. O. Suji.

Coach: S. M. Patil.

KENYAN TOUR RESULTS

One-day internationals – Played 3: Lost 2, No result 1.
Other non-first-class matches – Played 3: Won 1, Lost 2. *Win* – Zimbabwe A. *Losses* – Zimbabwe A (2).

Note: Matches in this section were not first-class.

At Harare Country Club, Harare, December 4, 2002. **Zimbabwe A won by 18 runs.** Toss: Kenyans. **Zimbabwe A 204-9** (50 overs) (D. A. Marillier 113*); **Kenyans 186** (41.4 overs) (T. M. Odoyo 69).

Zimbabwe A recovered from 26 for five.

At Harare Sports Club, Harare, December 7, 2002. **Kenyans won by six wickets (D/L method).** Toss: Kenyans. **Zimbabwe A 225-8** (50 overs) (M. A. Vermeulen 54, D. A. Marillier 56; S. O. Tikolo 4-44); **Kenyans 176-4** (33.4 overs) (K. O. Otieno 71).

The Kenyan innings was interrupted by rain and their target was revised to 176 from 39 overs.

ZIMBABWE v KENYA

First One-Day International

At Harare, December 8, 2002. No result. Toss: Kenya.

Kenya suffered a serious blow when their captain and top batsman, Steve Tikolo, had to withdraw with bronchitis. They still chose to bat, and Patel played some impressive strokes, including three fours in an over from Hondo. Modi shared good partnerships with Patel and acting-captain Odoyo, but Kenya's total seemed insufficient. Campbell ran himself out before rain drove the players off; they returned briefly, but a thunderstorm prevented further progress.

Kenya

K. O. Otieno c G. W. Flower b Hondo	18
R. D. Shah c Campbell b Friend	0
B. J. Patel b Murphy	44
M. O. Odumbe c Campbell b Friend	5
H. S. Modi c Olonga b Marillier	55
*T. M. Odoyo run out	37
†D. O. Obuya c Friend b Murphy	9
J. K. Kamande b Marillier	18
T. O. Suji c Wishart b Marillier	2
M. A. Suji c G. W. Flower b Hondo	8
J. O. Angara not out	4
B 1, l-b 3, w 5, n-b 2	11
1/1 (2) 2/36 (1) 3/41 (4) 4/96 (3) 5/165 (5) 6/176 (6) 7/184 (7) 8/199 (9) 9/199 (8) 10/211 (10) (50 overs)	211

Bowling: Friend 7–2–19–2; Olonga 4–0–25–0; Hondo 9–0–50–2; Murphy 10–3–28–2; G. W. Flower 10–0–46–0; Marillier 10–2–39–3.

Zimbabwe

*A. D. R. Campbell run out	2
M. A. Vermeulen not out	7
A. Flower not out	8
1/7 (1) (1 wkt, 5.1 overs)	17

G. W. Flower, C. B. Wishart, D. A. Marillier, †T. Taibu, T. J. Friend, B. A. Murphy, H. K. Olonga and D. T. Hondo did not bat.

Bowling: M. A. Suji 3–1–8–0; Odoyo 2.1–0–9–0.

Umpires: Aleem Dar (Pakistan) and M. A. Esat.
Third umpire: K. C. Barbour. Referee: D. T. Lindsay (South Africa).

ZIMBABWE v KENYA

Second One-Day International

At Kwekwe, December 11, 2002. Zimbabwe won by 47 runs (D/L method). Toss: Kenya.

This was the first Zimbabwean one-day international held outside Harare and Bulawayo, and the Midlands authorities were blessed with slightly drier weather than most of the country. Campbell batted slowly at first to regain his form, but opened up later, while Kwekwe-born Friend, sent in as a pinch-hitter, attacked from the start to score 91 at a run a ball. The one bowler nobody could dominate was Martin Suji, who bowled ten overs without a break for 17 runs and the wicket of Vermeulen. Despite an aggressive fifty from Otieno, who survived several chances, Kenya were never in the hunt; when bad light and rain halted them, six overs from the end, they were 181 for six against a par score of 228.

Man of the Match: T. J. Friend.

Zimbabwe

*A. D. R. Campbell c Odoyo b Odumbe	71
M. A. Vermeulen c Patel b M. A. Suji	8
T. J. Friend run out	91
A. Flower not out	58
G. W. Flower c Angara b Tikolo	14
C. B. Wishart not out	22
L-b 3, w 3, n-b 3	9
1/11 (2) 2/157 (3) 3/195 (1) 4/223 (5) (4 wkts, 50 overs)	273

D. A. Marillier, †T. Taibu, B. A. Murphy, H. K. Olonga and D. T. Hondo did not bat.

Bowling: M. A. Suji 10–2–17–1; Odoyo 8–1–38–0; T. O. Suji 5–0–29–0; Odumbe 9–0–73–1; Obuya 4–0–30–0; Tikolo 10–0–49–1; Angara 4–0–34–0.

Kenya

†K. O. Otieno c Friend b G. W. Flower	54	M. A. Suji not out	16
R. D. Shah c Vermeulen b Hondo	8		
T. M. Odoyo c Marillier b Friend	1	B 2, w 8, n-b 6	16
*S. O. Tikolo run out	20		
H. S. Modi b Marillier	26	1/55 (2) 2/60 (3) (6 wkts, 44 overs)	181
M. O. Odumbe lbw b Murphy	12	3/94 (1) 4/94 (4)	
B. J. Patel not out	28	5/122 (6) 6/145 (5)	

C. O. Obuya, T. O. Suji and J. O. Angara did not bat.

Bowling: Friend 7–0–33–1; Olonga 3–0–25–0; Hondo 5–0–28–1; Murphy 10–1–30–1; G. W. Flower 10–1–27–1; Marillier 7–0–29–1; Campbell 2–0–7–0.

Umpires: Aleem Dar (Pakistan) and M. A. Esat.
Third umpire: K. C. Barbour. Referee: D. T. Lindsay (South Africa).

At Bulawayo, December 14, 2002. **Zimbabwe A won by 74 runs.** Toss: Zimbabwe A. **Zimbabwe A 251** (49.5 overs) (A. D. R. Campbell 56, C. B. Wishart 70); **Kenyans 177** (39.4 overs).

ZIMBABWE v KENYA

Third One-Day International

At Bulawayo, December 15, 2002. Zimbabwe won by nine wickets. Toss: Kenya.

Zimbabwe rapidly sealed the series with their best performance. Kenya won their third toss, but slipped to 23 for three before Tikolo and Odumbe put together a superb stand of 83, which might have led to a challenging total had they not risked a second run to Blignaut. Tikolo was run out and the remaining six wickets tumbled for 27, all of them to Olonga, who returned his second-best analysis for Zimbabwe. After Campbell fell in the second over, Vermeulen and Blignaut matched each other stroke for stroke, racing to victory with an unbroken stand of 130. A storm which extended the lunch-break by nearly an hour provided the only tension.

Man of the Match: H. K. Olonga. *Man of the Series:* T. J. Friend.

Kenya

K. O. Otieno c Taibu b Hondo	11	P. J. Ongondo c Vermeulen b Olonga	0
R. D. Shah c Taibu b Blignaut	0	J. O. Angara lbw b Olonga	2
B. J. Patel c Wishart b Blignaut	8		
*S. O. Tikolo run out	34	B 4, l-b 2, w 5, n-b 3	14
M. O. Odumbe c Campbell b Olonga	48		
H. S. Modi c Taibu b Olonga	0	1/3 (2) 2/17 (1) 3/23 (3) (29 overs)	133
T. M. Odoyo b Olonga	4	4/106 (4) 5/107 (6) 6/116 (5)	
†D. O. Obuya not out	8	7/122 (7) 8/129 (9)	
M. A. Suji lbw b Olonga	4	9/129 (10) 10/133 (11)	

Bowling: Blignaut 6–0–29–2; Hondo 7–1–37–1; Olonga 9–2–28–6; Murphy 7–0–33–0.

Zimbabwe

*A. D. R. Campbell c Obuya b Suji	5
M. A. Vermeulen not out	62
A. M. Blignaut not out	63
W 2, n-b 4	6
1/6 (1) (1 wkt, 16 overs)	136

A. Flower, G. W. Flower, C. B. Wishart, D. A. Marillier, †T. Taibu, B. A. Murphy, H. K. Olonga and D. T. Hondo did not bat.

Bowling: Ongondo 4–0–34–0; Suji 7–0–50–1; Angara 2–0–21–0; Patel 1–0–17–0; Otieno 1–0–5–0; Modi 1–0–9–0.

Umpires: Aleem Dar (Pakistan) and K. C. Barbour.
Third umpire: I. D. Robinson. Referee: D. T. Lindsay (South Africa).

THE INDIANS IN NEW ZEALAND, 2002-03

LAWRENCE BOOTH

India's tour of New Zealand was an unmitigated disaster for them. The Tests were surrendered in the blink of an eye, and the seven-match limited-overs series was decided almost as quickly. India saved some face by scraping home in the fifth and sixth one-day internationals, but this was merely cosmetic. New Zealand completed a 5–2 drubbing at Hamilton to ensure that India's trip ended as it began: in total disarray. The chance to make amends at the World Cup could not come quickly enough.

New Zealand's cricket fraternity wondered whether this was the worst side ever to visit; Bangladesh had been guests the previous year, so that was stretching a point. But on some measures India were indeed worse: they averaged 13.37 runs per wicket against the Bangladeshis' 14.50. A fairer contention was that, for sustained misery, the tour ranked alongside India's disastrous visits to Australia in 1991-92 and 1999-2000, when they lost 4–0 and 3–0 respectively. It worsened an already awful record outside India – just six wins in 65 Tests since beating England in 1986.

New Zealand's cricket fraternity wondered whether this was the worst side ever to visit

The batsmen had to take much of the blame, although the pitches were hardly beyond reproach. New Zealand Cricket had directed the groundsmen to produce fast, bouncy tracks, but a wet summer left them thankful to produce anything at all. The inevitable result was a sequence of greentops which led to criticism from NZC's chief executive, Martin Snedden, and cluelessness from India's batsmen. In 11 international innings, they never passed 219, and a wicket fell every four and a half overs. Out of 120 individual innings, there were just two hundreds, both by Sehwag, and three fifties. And on 25 occasions a batsman failed to score. For all the efforts of their seamers – Zaheer Khan was outstanding in the Tests, Javagal Srinath in the one-dayers – the batsmen simply didn't fancy the fight.

Their travails were epitomised by the captain, Sourav Ganguly, who prodded and poked his way to 87 runs in those 11 innings. He did his best to smile his way through the carnage, and cheerfully admitted that this was the worst his side had played since he took charge in early 2000. But he looked worn out, and so did his team-mates. Since the beginning of December 2001, India had played 19 Tests. New Zealand, by contrast, had appeared in just 11.

Whether New Zealand derived any real benefit from such easy pickings was another matter. The public grew disenchanted with India's collapses, and Stephen Fleming took the unusual step of batting first in tricky conditions in the Wellington one-dayer simply to provide his side with a test. In truth, his own batsmen struggled too – scraping together only five fifties – and his seamers were not made to work hard enough for their wickets, although Daryl Tuffey and Shane Bond were at times irresistible. Daniel Vettori, the experienced left-arm spinner, did not bowl at all in the Tests.

Even so, New Zealand's 2–0 victory – the first time they had won more than one Test in a series against India – maintained their unlikely position, under the ICC ranking system, as the third-best side in the world. Dodgy pitches or not, that was worth celebrating.

INDIAN TOURING PARTY

S. C. Ganguly (Bengal) (*captain*), R. Dravid (Karnataka) (*vice-captain*), A. B. Agarkar (Mumbai), S. B. Bangar (Railways), S. S. Das (Orissa), Harbhajan Singh (Punjab), M. Kaif (Uttar Pradesh), M. Kartik (Railways), V. V. S. Laxman (Hyderabad), A. Nehra (Delhi), P. A. Patel (Gujarat), A. Ratra (Haryana), V. Sehwag (Delhi), S. R. Tendulkar (Mumbai), T. Yohannan (Kerala), Zaheer Khan (Baroda).

The one-day squad was reinforced by A. Kumble (Karnataka), R. B. Patel (Baroda), J. Srinath (Karnataka) and Yuvraj Singh (Punjab), replacing Das, Kartik, Ratra and Yohannan (though Das played in the first one-day international because of injuries). D. Mongia (Punjab) joined the squad for the second half of the one-day series.

Coach: J. G. Wright. *Manager:* N. R. Chowdhury.
Physiotherapist: A. Leipus. *Trainer:* A. le Roux.

INDIAN TOUR RESULTS

Test matches – Played 2: Lost 2.
First-class matches – Played 3: Lost 2, Drawn 1.
Losses – New Zealand (2).
Draw – Central Districts.
One-day internationals – Played 7: Won 2, Lost 5.
Other non-first-class match – Lost v New Zealand XI.

Note: Matches in this section which were not first-class are signified by a dagger.

†At Christchurch, December 4, 2002. **New Zealand XI won by 21 runs.** Toss: New Zealand XI. **New Zealand XI 123-5** (10 overs) **and 118-7** (10 overs) (B. B. McCullum 60); **Indians 133-5** (10 overs) (S. R. Tendulkar 72) **and 87-6** (10 overs).

This match took place under Super Max rules. Despite never having played this form of the game before, Tendulkar hit 72 from only 27 balls.

At Napier, December 6, 7, 8, 2002. **Drawn.** Toss: Central Districts. **Indians 209 and 191-3** (S. B. Bangar 70, V. Sehwag 61, S. R. Tendulkar 52*); **Central Districts 295-9 dec.** (C. M. Spearman 58, M. S. Sinclair 52, B. B. J. Griggs 100*; A. B. Agarkar 4-50).

NEW ZEALAND v INDIA

First Test Match

At Basin Reserve, Wellington, December 12, 13, 14, 2002. New Zealand won by ten wickets. Toss: New Zealand. Test debut: J. D. P. Oram.

The two anti-war protesters who broke into the ground at 2 a.m. on the second morning were clearly on to something. They were using petrol to burn six-foot-high letters into the outfield, protesting against the expected American invasion of Iraq. They got as far as "NO WA" before they were arrested. India's batsmen, though, got the message: a fight was not on their agenda either.

Already skittled for 161 in the first innings, they were bundled out for 121 in their second, in under three hours. The match was all over by 4.30 on the third afternoon, but interruptions for rain meant that New Zealand's 300th Test had lasted the equivalent of just over two days' play.

Fleming admitted that winning the toss had been crucial. The pitch changed from green to brown during the game, yet never lost its spongy quality and offered seam movement and bounce throughout. The batsmen needed to graft rather than glitter but, with the exception of Dravid and Tendulkar, India did neither. Charging into a back-breaking nor'wester that transformed the pohutakawa trees outside the ground into a billowing sea of red, Tuffey quickly removed the openers. Then came the big one, as the debutant Jacob Oram got the ball to cut back at Tendulkar, who perished lbw playing no stroke to a delivery heading over the stumps. Either side of lunch, Bond hurried out Ganguly, already dropped twice in the slips, and Laxman to leave India in disarray at 55 for five.

They were saved from annihilation by the wristy expertise of Dravid, who took his chances outside off and peppered the boundary between third man and extra cover before he was ninth out, beaten by a Styris nip-backer. Styris had already removed Agarkar and Harbhajan Singh – to a hare-brained short-arm pull – in successive balls, only to be denied a hat-trick when Zaheer Khan edged just in front of third slip.

In reply, New Zealand were grateful for the unfussy application of Richardson, who shouldered arms like an automaton and forced the bowlers to aim straighter. The result was a series of leg-side nudges, with the odd slash and drive to complete his nuggety repertoire. At 181 for three, New Zealand were cruising towards a big lead, but Zaheer kept things tight to finish with his first Test haul of five, Harbhajan – brought on surprisingly late by Ganguly – caused a mid-innings flutter with his turn and bounce, and the last seven fell for 66. Richardson, dropped in the slips on 63 and 83, finally fell to the first delivery with the second new ball. He was typically modest about his 407-minute, 245-ball vigil: "I just fought and scrapped and poked and pushed, really," he shrugged.

India began their second innings shortly before noon on the third day – and were hit by a hurricane. Tearing in with the wind behind him, Bond trapped Sehwag on the crease, bowled Dravid with a booming in-swinger – Bond later claimed it was the only ball he had got to swing all day – and had Ganguly feathering to the keeper. At lunch, his figures read 8–5–8–3 and, for a brief moment after the break, joy was unconfined when he bowled Tendulkar, on three, off an inside edge. But umpire de Silva harshly called no-ball. No matter: Tuffey, supported by razor-sharp catching, chipped away at a compliant lower order, and Bond bowled Tendulkar off the inside edge again, this time legitimately, to complete match figures of seven for 99. India simply failed to live with his venom and bounce.

New Zealand were left to make 36, and Richardson cut the winning runs with a whoop of delight and a punch of the air. It was New Zealand's 11th win at the Basin Reserve, which officially made it their happiest hunting-ground; India, by contrast, had now lost four Tests there in a row.

Man of the Match: M. H. Richardson.

Close of play: First day, New Zealand 53-1 (Richardson 27, Fleming 11); Second day, New Zealand 201-7 (Richardson 83, Vettori 0).

India

First innings		Second innings	
S. B. Bangar c Styris b Tuffey	1	lbw b Oram	12
V. Sehwag b Tuffey	2	lbw b Bond	12
R. Dravid b Styris	76	b Bond	7
S. R. Tendulkar lbw b Oram	8	b Bond	51
*S. C. Ganguly c Vincent b Bond	17	c Hart b Bond	2
V. V. S. Laxman c Hart b Bond	0	c Fleming b Oram	0
†P. A. Patel c Vincent b Oram	8	c Fleming b Tuffey	10
A. B. Agarkar c Astle b Styris	12	c McMillan b Tuffey	9
Harbhajan Singh c McMillan b Styris	0	c Styris b Tuffey	1
Zaheer Khan c Oram b Bond	19	c Styris b Oram	9
A. Nehra not out	10	not out	0
L-b 1, w 1, n-b 6	8	L-b 1, n-b 7	8
1/2 (2) 2/9 (1) 3/29 (4) 4/51 (5) 5/55 (6) 6/92 (7) 7/118 (8) 8/118 (9) 9/147 (3) 10/161 (10)	161	1/23 (2) 2/31 (1) 3/31 (3) 4/33 (5) 5/36 (6) 6/76 (7) 7/88 (8) 8/96 (9) 9/121 (10) 10/121 (4)	121

Bowling: *First Innings*—Bond 18.4–4–66–3; Tuffey 16–7–25–2; Oram 15–4–31–2; Styris 6–0–28–3; Astle 3–1–10–0. *Second Innings*—Bond 13.1–5–33–4; Tuffey 9–3–35–3; Oram 12–3–36–3; Styris 4–0–16–0.

New Zealand

First innings		Second innings	
M. H. Richardson lbw b Zaheer Khan	89	not out	14
L. Vincent c Patel b Bangar	12	not out	21
*S. P. Fleming b Zaheer Khan	25		
C. D. McMillan lbw b Bangar	9		
N. J. Astle c Harbhajan Singh b Zaheer Khan	41		
S. B. Styris st Patel b Harbhajan Singh	0		
J. D. P. Oram lbw b Harbhajan Singh	0		
†R. G. Hart lbw b Zaheer Khan	6		
D. L. Vettori c Patel b Zaheer Khan	21		
D. R. Tuffey not out	9		
S. E. Bond b Agarkar	2		
B 6, l-b 12, w 2, n-b 8, p 5	33	W 1	1
1/30 (2) 2/96 (3) 3/111 (4) 4/181 (5) 5/182 (6) 6/186 (7) 7/201 (8) 8/228 (1) 9/237 (9) 10/247 (11)	247		(no wkt) 36

Bowling: *First Innings*—Zaheer Khan 25–8–53–5; Nehra 19–4–50–0; Agarkar 13.1–1–54–1; Bangar 15–4–23–2; Harbhajan Singh 17–4–33–2; Ganguly 2–0–11–0. *Second Innings*—Zaheer Khan 3–0–13–0; Nehra 4.3–0–21–0; Harbhajan Singh 2–1–2–0.

Umpires: E. A. R. de Silva (Sri Lanka) and D. J. Harper (Australia).
Third umpire: B. F. Bowden. Referee: M. J. Procter (South Africa).

> "This match was the 2,000th one-day international. It had taken 24 years to reach 1,000 but only eight more to reach 2,000."
>
> Cherry Blossom Cup, page 1288.

NEW ZEALAND v INDIA

Second Test Match

At Hamilton, December 19, 20, 21, 22, 2002. New Zealand won by four wickets. Toss: New Zealand.

If the game at Wellington ended with indecent haste, this one had even less time for niceties. Never before in 1,632 Tests had both sides been dismissed for under 100 in their first innings; by the time New Zealand scraped home on the fourth afternoon of another rain-soaked match and sealed a 2–0 series win, there had been just 176 overs – nearly 21 fewer than in the First Test. Like the blade of the helicopter that

---

NO INDIVIDUAL FIFTY IN A COMPLETED TEST

Top score		
24 W. G. Grace†	England v Australia at Lord's	1888
33 J. Briggs	England v Australia at Sydney (1st Test)	1886-87
38 W. G. Grace	England v Australia at Manchester	1888
39 G. H. S. Trott†	Australia v England at The Oval	1890
39 R. Dravid†	**India v New Zealand at Hamilton**	**2002-03**
42 A. F. Kippax	Australia v South Africa at Melbourne	1931-32
42* R. G. Barlow	England v Australia at Sydney (2nd Test)	1886-87
44 A. Shrewsbury	England v Australia at Sydney	1887-88
44 G. A. Headley†	West Indies v England at Bridgetown	1934-35
46 R. Abel	England v South Africa at Port Elizabeth	1888-89
47 J. Darling†	Australia v England at The Oval	1896
48 J. M. Brearley	England v Australia at Birmingham	1981
49 K. S. Duleepsinhji	England v New Zealand at Christchurch	1929-30

† *On losing side.*

Research: Charlie Wat and M. L. Fernando

---

hovered over the ground on the second morning in an attempt to blow away the damp, the cricket was fast, furious and strangely compelling.

Torrential downpours had wreaked havoc with the groundsman's preparations and, when the game finally got under way at 4.30 on day two, the excessive sideways movement sowed doubt in the batsmen's minds and turned run-making into Russian roulette. It was Ganguly's misfortune to lose another crucial toss against an unchanged New Zealand side still buzzing after their walkover at Wellington. For India, Yohannan replaced Agarkar.

The Indian innings was a gruesome catalogue of playing and missing, groping and hoping, with the giant Tuffey an unerring destroyer. By the time he conceded his first run, from his 39th delivery, he had disposed of Bangar and Tendulkar, both trapped in the slips. When Ganguly and Dravid followed, Tuffey had an eye-catching four for eight from eight overs and India were an eye-watering 40 for five.

Bond returned to bowl the gritty Laxman, then got his own back on Harbhajan Singh, who had sliced, skewed and slogged his way to 20 in nine balls, which in the circumstances seemed as good a way to bat as any. Oram yorked Zaheer Khan and India staggered off at 92 for eight. Next morning, they lasted seven more balls.

In reply, Vincent soon nicked Zaheer to slip, but New Zealand were chugging along at 39 for one when the wheels fell off. Richardson's leave-alone for once proved fatal, and when Nehra removed McMillan and Astle in a single over it was 48 for four. Fleming, possibly distracted by a long delay caused by a fidgety spectator next to the sightscreen, chipped a simple return catch, Harbhajan struck twice in an over, and the incisive Zaheer polished things off to finish with a five-for for the second match running, and Test-best figures. New Zealand trailed by five runs, after losing nine for 55. Two local journalists, who had placed bets on each side failing to reach 100, didn't know whether to laugh or cry.

India had never dismissed New Zealand for less, but their joy was short-lived as Tuffey made quick work of Patel, promoted to open after resisting for 69 minutes in the first innings, and Bangar; at that point, he had match figures of six for 13. Dravid and Tendulkar responded with the most fluent batting of the game to add 49, but Tendulkar's adrenalin got the better of him when he reached for a drive against Tuffey and was once again bowled off the inside edge.

MOST TEST WICKETS IN A DAY

W	*R*		
27	157	England (18-3 to 53 and 62) v Australia (60) at Lord's (2nd day)	1888
25	221	Australia (112 and 48-5) v England (61) at Melbourne (1st day)	1901-02
24	255	England (69-1 to 145 and 60-5) v Australia (119) at The Oval (2nd day)	1896
22	197	Australia (92 and 5-2) v England (100) at The Oval (1st day)	1890
22	207	Australia (82 and 20-2) v West Indies (105) at Adelaide (1st day)	1951-52
22	195	England (292-7 to 347-9 dec.) v India (58 and 82) at Manchester (3rd day)	1952
22	229	England (175-4 to 249 and 74-6) v Sri Lanka (81) at Colombo (SSC) (3rd day)	2000-01
22	**279**	**India (92-8 to 99 and 154) v New Zealand (94 and 24-0) at Hamilton (3rd day)**	**2002-03**
21	278	England (185 and 0-1) v South Africa (93) at Port Elizabeth (1st day)	1895-96
21	236	England (0-0 to 126 and 3-1) v New Zealand (107) at Birmingham (2nd day)	1999
21	188	West Indies (267-9 to 267 and 54) v England (134 and 0-0) at Lord's (2nd day)	2000

Research: Charlie Wat

After that, only a flashy cameo from Sehwag, who creamed 25 in 18 balls, delayed New Zealand, and Oram docked the tail to leave a target of 160. Twenty-two wickets had fallen in the day – a number matched only once in the previous 50 years of Tests – and it would have been 23 had Bangar not dropped a sitter at short leg before Vincent had scored.

But New Zealand got to the close unscathed. At 8.30 the following morning, their batsmen were studiously honing their techniques in the nets. At 89 for two, with the runs flowing, their diligence was paying off, but Nehra weighed in once more with two quick wickets and Patel pulled off a miraculous leg-side catch to send back Astle and bring a spellbound crowd to life. When Styris edged a cut off Harbhajan, New Zealand needed 24 more with four wickets left. However, Oram kept his cool, and the local boy Hart shovelled the winning single to fine leg to provoke a minor eruption from an enthralled crowd. Epics don't come much shorter.

Man of the Match: D. R. Tuffey.

Close of play: First day, No play; Second day, India 92-8 (Patel 8); Third day, New Zealand 24-0 (Richardson 18, Vincent 6).

> "Almost every Australian made a start, Waugh and Ponting made hundreds, and the entire line-up made a mockery of West Indies."
>
> Australians in the West Indies, page 1187.

India

S. B. Bangar c Oram b Tuffey	1	– c and b Tuffey	7
V. Sehwag c Richardson b Bond	1	– (7) c Tuffey b Bond	25
R. Dravid c Hart b Tuffey	9	– c sub (M. J. Mason) b Oram	39
S. R. Tendulkar c Styris b Tuffey	9	– b Tuffey	32
*S. C. Ganguly c Fleming b Tuffey	5	– c Hart b Oram	5
V. V. S. Laxman b Bond	23	– b Astle	4
†P. A. Patel c Hart b Oram	8	– (2) b Tuffey	0
Harbhajan Singh b Bond	20	– c Hart b Tuffey	18
Zaheer Khan b Oram	0	– c Astle b Oram	0
A. Nehra c Fleming b Bond	7	– c Hart b Oram	10
T. Yohannan not out	0	– not out	8
L-b 12, n-b 4	16	L-b 1, w 2, n-b 3	6
1/1 (1) 2/11 (2) 3/26 (4) 4/34 (5) 5/40 (3) 6/70 (6) 7/91 (8) 8/92 (9) 9/93 (7) 10/99 (10)	99	1/2 (2) 2/8 (1) 3/57 (4) 4/64 (5) 5/85 (6) 6/110 (7) 7/130 (3) 8/131 (9) 9/136 (8) 10/154 (10)	154

Bowling: *First Innings*—Bond 14.2–7–39–4; Tuffey 9–6–12–4; Oram 10–1–22–2; Styris 2–0–10–0; Astle 3–2–4–0. *Second Innings*—Bond 10–0–58–1; Tuffey 16–3–41–4; Oram 12.5–2–41–4; Astle 5–1–13–1.

New Zealand

M. H. Richardson lbw b Zaheer Khan	13	– c Patel b Nehra	28
L. Vincent c Dravid b Zaheer Khan	3	– c Patel b Yohannan	9
*S. P. Fleming c and b Zaheer Khan	21	– c Zaheer Khan b Nehra	32
C. D. McMillan c Dravid b Nehra	4	– lbw b Nehra	18
N. J. Astle c Harbhajan Singh b Nehra	0	– c Patel b Zaheer Khan	14
S. B. Styris lbw b Harbhajan Singh	13	– c Patel b Harbhajan Singh	17
J. D. P. Oram c Tendulkar b Harbhajan Singh	3	– not out	26
†R. G. Hart lbw b Zaheer Khan	3	– not out	11
D. L. Vettori c Laxman b Zaheer Khan	6		
D. R. Tuffey run out	13		
S. E. Bond not out	0		
B 1, l-b 4, n-b 10	15	L-b 4, n-b 1	5
1/7 (2) 2/39 (1) 3/47 (4) 4/48 (5) 5/60 (3) 6/64 (7) 7/69 (6) 8/79 (8) 9/94 (10) 10/94 (9)	94	1/30 (2) 2/52 (1) 3/89 (3) 4/90 (4) 5/105 (5) 6/136 (6)	(6 wkts) 160

Bowling: *First Innings*—Zaheer Khan 13.2–4–29–5; Yohannan 9–4–16–0; Nehra 8–3–20–2; Bangar 2–1–4–0; Harbhajan Singh 6–0–20–2. *Second Innings*—Zaheer Khan 13–0–56–1; Yohannan 16–5–27–1; Nehra 16.2–4–34–3; Harbhajan Singh 11–0–39–1.

Umpires: E. A. R. de Silva (Sri Lanka) and D. J. Harper (Australia).
Third umpire: D. B. Cowie. Referee: M. J. Procter (South Africa).

†NEW ZEALAND v INDIA

First One-Day International

At Auckland, December 26, 2002 (day/night). New Zealand won by three wickets. Toss: New Zealand.

A gutsy all-round display from Oram inspired New Zealand to a nail-biting win on a grassy and greasy drop-in wicket. First, he found bounce and movement to run through India's frail lower-middle order for a career-best five for 26. Then, after Srinath and Nehra reduced New Zealand to 52 for six, he shepherded them home, aided by Mills. On Christmas Day, Tendulkar had sprained his ankle in the nets; without him, India lost their last eight for 45 as they made their lowest one-day total against New Zealand. Only Das – due to leave after the Tests, but asked to play because of injuries – and Dravid lasted longer than 21 balls. Both captains were scathing about the quality of a two-paced pitch.

Man of the Match: J. D. P. Oram.

India

S. S. Das c Fleming b Mills	30	Zaheer Khan lbw b Vettori	14
V. Sehwag b Bond	0	A. Nehra not out	0
V. V. S. Laxman c Mills b Tuffey	9		
*S. C. Ganguly b Oram	14	L-b 6, w 5, n-b 2	13
†R. Dravid c Vettori b Tuffey	20		
Yuvraj Singh c Astle b Oram	2	1/5 (2) 2/28 (3) 3/63 (1) (32.5 overs)	108
M. Kaif c Fleming b Oram	6	4/63 (4) 5/65 (6) 6/74 (7)	
A. Kumble lbw b Oram	0	7/74 (8) 8/74 (9)	
J. Srinath c Sinclair b Oram	0	9/108 (10) 10/108 (5)	

Bowling: Tuffey 6.5–0–23–2; Bond 7–0–32–1; Mills 8–2–20–1; Oram 10–4–26–5; Vettori 1–0–1–1.

New Zealand

*S. P. Fleming lbw b Nehra	12	K. D. Mills c Dravid b Srinath	21
N. J. Astle c Laxman b Srinath	0	D. L. Vettori not out	5
M. S. Sinclair c Ganguly b Zaheer Khan	15	L-b 2, w 3, n-b 3	8
C. D. McMillan c Dravid b Srinath	4		
L. Vincent lbw b Nehra	13	1/1 (2) 2/29 (1) (7 wkts, 37.4 overs)	109
†B. B. McCullum c Dravid b Srinath	4	3/29 (3) 4/48 (4)	
J. D. P. Oram not out	27	5/52 (6) 6/52 (5) 7/86 (8)	

D. R. Tuffey and S. E. Bond did not bat.

Bowling: Srinath 10–3–23–4; Zaheer Khan 9–1–43–1; Nehra 10–3–16–2; Kumble 7–1–15–0; Ganguly 1.4–0–10–0.

Umpires: E. A. R. de Silva (Sri Lanka) and B. F. Bowden.
Third umpire: D. B. Cowie. Referee: R. S. Madugalle (Sri Lanka).

†NEW ZEALAND v INDIA

Second One-Day International

At Napier, December 29, 2002. New Zealand won by 35 runs. Toss: India.

A stunning 108 in 119 balls from Sehwag could not save India from paying for a geriatric display in the field and another batting collapse, on the flattest track of the tour. Sehwag and Kaif had given them hope at 182 for four but, with 73 needed at a run a ball (a slow over-rate had cost them 12 balls), they lost six for 37. When Sehwag was run out trying to pinch a single, the game was up. New Zealand's 254 centred on a stand of 136 between Astle, bowled by a Zaheer Khan no-ball on one, and Sinclair, who was finally held off a gloved reverse sweep after being dropped twice during a painful but patient 78.

Man of the Match: V. Sehwag.

New Zealand

*S. P. Fleming c Kaif b Srinath 1
N. J. Astle c Zaheer Khan b Ganguly. . . 76
M. S. Sinclair c Dravid b Harbhajan Singh . 78
C. D. McMillan lbw b Srinath 5
L. Vincent b Srinath 34
J. D. P. Oram run out 4
†B. B. McCullum c Yuvraj Singh b Zaheer Khan . 7
K. D. Mills b Zaheer Khan 5
D. L. Vettori not out 9
D. R. Tuffey b Zaheer Khan 5
P. A. Hitchcock not out 2
B 9, l-b 9, w 6, n-b 4 28

1/10 (1) 2/146 (2) 3/157 (4) 4/199 (3) 5/204 (6) 6/224 (5) 7/233 (7) 8/237 (8) 9/252 (10) (9 wkts, 50 overs) 254

Bowling: Srinath 10–0–34–3; Zaheer Khan 10–0–47–3; Nehra 8–0–42–0; Harbhajan Singh 10–0–56–1; Bangar 7–0–34–0; Ganguly 5–0–23–1.

India

*S. C. Ganguly b Tuffey 0
V. Sehwag run out 108
V. V. S. Laxman c McCullum b Mills. . . 20
†R. Dravid run out. 18
Yuvraj Singh st McCullum b Vettori . . . 0
M. Kaif c McCullum b Tuffey 24
S. B. Bangar c McCullum b Oram 4
Harbhajan Singh c McCullum b Hitchcock . 14
Zaheer Khan c McMillan b Mills 11
J. Srinath c Oram b Mills 3
A. Nehra not out 0
L-b 3, w 7, n-b 7 17

1/0 (1) 2/57 (3) 3/104 (4) 4/104 (5) 5/182 (6) 6/187 (7) 7/204 (2) 8/206 (8) 9/217 (10) 10/219 (9) (43.4 overs) 219

Bowling: Tuffey 10–2–35–2; Mills 9.4–0–45–3; Oram 8–0–50–1; Vettori 8–0–48–1; Hitchcock 8–0–38–1.

Umpires: E. A. R. de Silva (Sri Lanka) and D. B. Cowie.
Third umpire: B. F. Bowden. Referee: R. S. Madugalle (Sri Lanka).

†NEW ZEALAND v INDIA

Third One-Day International

At Christchurch, January 1, 2003 (day/night). New Zealand won by five wickets. Toss: India.

On another seamer's dream, India's nightmare continued: they equalled their record low against New Zealand set six days earlier. Only Extras passed 20 as Fleming's medium-pacers kept their discipline and let the pitch and India's disorientated batsmen do the rest. McCullum clung on five times behind the stumps to complete an unprecedented ten dismissals in two games. Astle then rocket-fired New Zealand's reply by flaying five fours in Srinath's third over. Agarkar chipped away at the middle order, but it was too late.

Man of the Match: D. R. Tuffey.

India

V. Sehwag c McCullum b Mills 7
*S. C. Ganguly c McCullum b Tuffey . . 4
V. V. S. Laxman c McCullum b Hitchcock . 10
†R. Dravid c Vettori b Hitchcock 20
M. Kaif c McCullum b Oram. 17
Yuvraj Singh run out 12
S. B. Bangar c McCullum b Tuffey 1
A. B. Agarkar c Hitchcock b Astle 6
Zaheer Khan not out. 8
Harbhajan Singh c Vincent b Hitchcock . 0
J. Srinath c Fleming b Oram 1
L-b 8, w 9, n-b 5 22

1/10 (1) 2/15 (2) 3/38 (3) 4/67 (4) 5/82 (5) 6/83 (7) 7/90 (8) 8/100 (6) 9/102 (10) 10/108 (11) (41.1 overs) 108

Bowling: Tuffey 10–2–11–2; Mills 10–2–26–1; Oram 8.1–1–22–2; Hitchcock 8–0–30–3; Astle 5–1–11–1.

New Zealand

*S. P. Fleming c Kaif b Zaheer Khan . . . 4
N. J. Astle c Ganguly b Srinath 32
M. S. Sinclair c and b Agarkar 0
C. D. McMillan c Kaif b Agarkar 22
L. Vincent lbw b Agarkar 15
†B. B. McCullum not out 10
J. D. P. Oram not out 10
L-b 6, w 9, n-b 1 16

1/37 (1) 2/39 (3) 3/50 (2) 4/83 (5) 5/92 (4) (5 wkts, 26.5 overs) 109

K. D. Mills, D. L. Vettori, D. R. Tuffey and P. A. Hitchcock did not bat.

Bowling: Srinath 8–0–44–1; Zaheer Khan 9–2–26–1; Agarkar 8.5–1–26–3; Bangar 1–0–7–0.

Umpires: E. A. R. de Silva (Sri Lanka) and D. B. Cowie.
Third umpire: A. L. Hill. Referee: R. S. Madugalle (Sri Lanka).

†NEW ZEALAND v INDIA

Fourth One-Day International

At Queenstown, January 4, 2003. New Zealand won by seven wickets. Toss: New Zealand.

Queenstown's Events Centre was hosting its first one-day international, but for New Zealand it was business as usual. While India's openers were adding 38, a contest looked possible, but Adams, recovered from a back injury, struck four times in his first five overs, and Ganguly irresponsibly cut Tuffey to third man. Adams returned to finish with five for 22, then the joint second-best one-day figures for New Zealand, before Fleming played himself back into form with some handsome pulls. His team cruised to an unassailable – but anticlimactic – 4–0 lead inside 26 overs, prompting Fleming to reflect that such a one-sided triumph had left them feeling "a bit flat".

Man of the Match: A. R. Adams.

India

V. Sehwag c Astle b Adams 23
R. Dravid b Adams 18
D. Mongia c Vettori b Adams 12
M. Kaif c McMillan b Adams 0
*S. C. Ganguly c Mills b Tuffey 2
Yuvraj Singh c Tuffey b Styris 25
†P. A. Patel b Mills 13
A. B. Agarkar run out 0
Zaheer Khan c McCullum b Tuffey 1
J. Srinath not out 10
A. Nehra c McCullum b Adams 0
L-b 1, w 11, n-b 6 18

1/38 (1) 2/55 (2) 3/57 (4) 4/67 (3) 5/69 (5) 6/94 (7) 7/100 (8) 8/107 (9) 9/118 (6) 10/122 (11) (43.4 overs) 122

Bowling: Tuffey 10–0–36–2; Mills 10–2–28–1; Oram 10–1–28–0; Adams 8.4–1–22–5; Styris 3–1–5–1; Vettori 2–0–2–0.

New Zealand

*S. P. Fleming c Sehwag b Srinath 47
N. J. Astle c Dravid b Srinath 15
M. S. Sinclair not out 32
C. D. McMillan b Srinath 0
S. B. Styris not out 8
B 1, l-b 3, w 14, n-b 3 21

1/28 (2) 2/101 (1) 3/103 (4) (3 wkts, 25.4 overs) 123

J. D. P. Oram, †B. B. McCullum, A. R. Adams, K. D. Mills, D. L. Vettori and D. R. Tuffey did not bat.

Bowling: Srinath 9.4–1–35–3; Zaheer Khan 2–0–21–0; Nehra 10–1–37–0; Agarkar 4–0–26–0.

Umpires: E. A. R. de Silva (Sri Lanka) and D. B. Cowie.
Third umpire: A. L. Hill. Referee: R. S. Madugalle (Sri Lanka).

†NEW ZEALAND v INDIA

Fifth One-Day International

At WestpacTrust Stadium, Wellington, January 8, 2003 (day/night). India won by two wickets. Toss: New Zealand.

India averted a whitewash with their first win of the tour. Set 169, they lost the benighted Ganguly to a flat-footed swish at the first ball, soon followed by a fit-again Tendulkar for a duck. When Kumble dislodged his bails after making a mess of a delivery that bounced two yards in front of the bowler, India were 116 for seven, and the innings had a depressingly familiar look. However, the lower order finally showed unexpected grit: Yuvraj Singh made a responsible half-century, Zaheer Khan rode his luck but finished the job. New Zealand welcomed back Cairns for the first time since March 2002, and, with the series safe, took first use of a testing pitch. Zaheer quickly reduced them to three for three, and they were always vulnerable.

Man of the Match: Zaheer Khan.

New Zealand

*S. P. Fleming c Dravid b Nehra	19
N. J. Astle lbw b Zaheer Khan	0
M. S. Sinclair b Zaheer Khan	0
C. Z. Harris lbw b Zaheer Khan	1
C. L. Cairns b Srinath	25
S. B. Styris b Nehra	13
†B. B. McCullum b Kumble	35
A. R. Adams c Kaif b Ganguly	35
D. L. Vettori not out	16
D. R. Tuffey b Srinath	4
S. E. Bond lbw b Kumble	0
B 4, l-b 7, w 3, n-b 6	20
1/0 (2) 2/0 (3) 3/3 (4) 4/48 (5) 5/51 (1) 6/92 (6) 7/140 (8) 8/158 (7) 9/167 (10) 10/168 (11) — (42.4 overs)	168

Bowling: Srinath 10–2–24–2; Zaheer Khan 8–0–30–3; Nehra 9–1–38–2; Ganguly 6–0–27–1; Kumble 9.4–0–38–2.

India

*S. C. Ganguly c McCullum b Tuffey	0
V. Sehwag c Fleming b Styris	45
D. Mongia b Bond	2
S. R. Tendulkar lbw b Bond	0
†R. Dravid c McCullum b Styris	7
Yuvraj Singh c Harris b Vettori	54
M. Kaif c Fleming b Adams	1
A. Kumble hit wkt b Adams	2
Zaheer Khan not out	34
J. Srinath not out	1
L-b 5, w 16, n-b 2	23
1/0 (1) 2/19 (3) 3/25 (4) 4/66 (2) 5/91 (5) 6/114 (7) 7/116 (8) 8/160 (6) — (8 wkts, 43.2 overs)	169

A. Nehra did not bat.

Bowling: Tuffey 10–2–40–1; Bond 10–0–34–2; Adams 9.2–0–47–2; Styris 9–1–29–2; Vettori 5–1–14–1.

Umpires: D. J. Harper (Australia) and B. F. Bowden.
Third umpire: D. B. Cowie. Referee: R. S. Madugalle (Sri Lanka).

†NEW ZEALAND v INDIA

Sixth One-Day International

At Auckland, January 11, 2003 (day/night). India won by one wicket. Toss: India.

At 182 for three in pursuit of 200, India were home and dry. But the dismissal of Sehwag for a glorious 112, his second century of the series, sparked blind panic as six wickets tumbled for 16, two of them to chaotic run-outs. With three balls left (they had been fined one over) and nine wickets down, India still needed two. Srinath ran a leg-bye and then Nehra clubbed the winning single. Defeat would have been cruel on Sehwag, who was dropped twice but struck 11 clean-as-a-whistle fours and three breathtaking sixes in 139 balls. In the end, it was cruel on Bond, who had rescued New Zealand with a helter-skelter 15-ball 31 not out, and added 52 in 20 deliveries for the last wicket with Vincent. But for the parsimony of Srinath, however, New Zealand might have been out of sight.

Man of the Match: V. Sehwag.

New Zealand

*S. P. Fleming c Dravid b Nehra	14	D. R. Tuffey run out	1
M. S. Sinclair b Srinath	18	S. E. Bond not out	31
C. Z. Harris lbw b Agarkar	0		
C. L. Cairns b Srinath	13	B 4, l-b 11, w 2, n-b 8	25
S. B. Styris c Bangar b Ganguly	42		
L. Vincent not out	53	1/26 (1) 2/28 (3) (9 wkts, 50 overs)	199
†B. B. McCullum run out	0	3/47 (2) 4/50 (4)	
K. D. Mills c Dravid b Srinath	0	5/130 (5) 6/131 (7)	
A. R. Adams b Zaheer Khan	2	7/134 (8) 8/144 (9) 9/147 (10)	

Bowling: Srinath 10–2–13–3; Zaheer Khan 10–0–53–1; Nehra 10–1–31–1; Agarkar 8–0–34–1; Bangar 4–0–22–0; Ganguly 8–2–31–1.

India

*S. C. Ganguly c McCullum b Adams	23	J. Srinath not out	0
V. Sehwag c Fleming b Mills	112	A. Nehra not out	1
†R. Dravid lbw b Styris	21		
S. R. Tendulkar c McCullum b Tuffey	1	L-b 4, w 12, n-b 9	25
Yuvraj Singh c Fleming b Harris	8		
M. Kaif b Adams	7	1/70 (1) 2/142 (3) (9 wkts, 48.5 overs)	200
S. B. Bangar lbw b Adams	1	3/159 (4) 4/182 (2)	
A. B. Agarkar run out	0	5/187 (5) 6/194 (7)	
Zaheer Khan run out	1	7/194 (8) 8/197 (6) 9/198 (9)	

Bowling: Tuffey 10–0–46–1; Bond 6–1–20–0; Adams 9.5–0–41–3; Mills 10–0–43–1; Styris 10–1–40–1; Harris 3–0–6–1.

Umpires: D. J. Harper (Australia) and B. F. Bowden.
Third umpire: A. L. Hill. Referee: R. S. Madugalle (Sri Lanka).

†NEW ZEALAND v INDIA

Seventh One-Day International

At Hamilton, January 14, 2003 (day/night). New Zealand won by six wickets. Toss: New Zealand.

After two face-saving wins, India ended the tour as they began it – with a gruesome batting collapse. Tuffey and Mills did the early damage on yet another untrustworthy pitch, before three wickets fell on 44. Adams took two of them, and added two more after Yuvraj Singh and Kumble had wrung some life from the tail. Srinath and Zaheer Khan fought back with the ball, causing a New Zealand wobble, and the result might have been closer had Srinath, looking for his 300th one-day wicket, not spilled a dolly off his own bowling when Styris had six. Styris was to add a match-winning 84 with the stylish Fleming as New Zealand romped to a 5–2 series victory.

Man of the Match: S. P. Fleming. *Man of the Series:* D. R. Tuffey.

India

*S. C. Ganguly b Adams	15		J. Srinath lbw b Adams	15
V. Sehwag c McCullum b Mills	4		A. Nehra not out	2
S. R. Tendulkar c Fleming b Tuffey	1			
D. Mongia c Fleming b Tuffey	0		L-b 5, w 6, n-b 3	14
†R. Dravid c Styris b Mills	12			
Yuvraj Singh c Vincent b Styris	33		1/14 (2) 2/17 (3) 3/17 (4) (44.5 overs)	122
M. Kaif c McCullum b Adams	0		4/44 (5) 5/44 (1) 6/44 (7)	
A. Kumble c Fleming b Adams	21		7/93 (6) 8/99 (9)	
Zaheer Khan c McCullum b Styris	5		9/117 (8) 10/122 (10)	

Bowling: Tuffey 10–1–26–2; Mills 10–1–29–2; Adams 8.5–3–21–4; Styris 10–4–23–2; Vettori 6–0–18–0.

New Zealand

*S. P. Fleming not out	60		L. Vincent not out	5
M. S. Sinclair b Srinath	3		L-b 6, w 6, n-b 1	13
†B. B. McCullum lbw b Zaheer Khan	4			
C. L. Cairns b Srinath	11		1/5 (2) 2/12 (3) (4 wkts, 28.4 overs)	125
S. B. Styris b Kumble	29		3/32 (4) 4/116 (5)	

C. Z. Harris, K. D. Mills, A. R. Adams, D. L. Vettori and D. R. Tuffey did not bat.

Bowling: Srinath 8.4–2–28–2; Zaheer Khan 9–2–38–1; Nehra 5–0–28–0; Kumble 4–0–16–1; Ganguly 2–0–9–0.

Umpires: D. J. Harper (Australia) and D. B. Cowie.
Third umpire: B. F. Bowden. Referee: R. S. Madugalle (Sri Lanka).

THE SRI LANKANS IN AUSTRALIA, 2002-03

After a mostly unsuccessful tour of South Africa, Sri Lanka arrived in Australia for the triangular VB Series hoping to find some form before the World Cup. They had little success, winning only two of their internationals and being routed for 65 in a warm-up against Australia A. But when they did start winning, they did it in style, crushing Australia in their only defeat of the tournament.

SRI LANKAN TOURING PARTY

S. T. Jayasuriya (Bloomfield) (*captain*), M. S. Atapattu (Sinhalese) (*vice-captain*), R. P. Arnold (Nondescripts), K. S. C. de Silva (Burgher), C. R. D. Fernando (Sinhalese), P. W. Gunaratne (Tamil Union), D. P. M. D. Jayawardene (Sinhalese), R. S. Kaluwitharana (Colts), J. Mubarak (Colombo), M. Muralitharan (Tamil Union), R. A. P. Nissanka (Bloomfield), T. T. Samaraweera (Sinhalese), K. C. Sangakkara (Nondescripts), W. P. U. J. C. Vaas (Colts), D. N. T. Zoysa (Sinhalese).

Muralitharan was unfit during the first half of the tour. P. A. de Silva (Nondescripts) was unavailable for personal reasons until the end of December, when he, T. C. B. Fernando (Panadura), D. A. Gunawardene (Sinhalese) and H. P. Tillekeratne (Nondescripts) replaced K. S. C. de Silva, Kaluwitharana, Samaraweera and Zoysa. M. K. G. C. P. Lakshitha (Air Force) replaced Muralitharan when he injured his leg in January.

Coach: D. F. Whatmore. *Manager:* Air Commodore A. Jayasekara.

Cricket adviser: L. R. D. Mendis. *Physiotherapist:* A. Kontouri. *Computer officer:* N. de Alwis.

SRI LANKAN TOUR RESULTS

One-day internationals – Played 8: Won 2, Lost 6. *Wins* – Australia, England. *Losses* – England (3), Australia (3).

Other non-first-class matches – Played 5: Won 2, Lost 3. *Wins* – Victoria Country XIII, Australia A. *Losses* – Australia A (3).

Note: Matches in this section were not first-class.

At Brisbane, December 14, 2002 (day/night). **Australia A won by 102 runs.** Toss: Australia A. **Australia A 312-8** (50 overs) (J. P. Maher 106, M. J. Clarke 79; C. R. D. Fernando 4-57); **Sri Lankans 210-6** (48 overs) (R. P. Arnold 86*).

The Sri Lankans were fined two overs for a slow over-rate.

Sri Lanka's matches against England and Australia in the VB Series (December 17–22 and January 9–21) appear on pages 1268–1281.

At Hastings, December 29, 2002. **Sri Lankans won by 80 runs.** Toss: Sri Lankans. **Sri Lankans 219-7** (40 overs) (T. T. Samaraweera 58); **Victoria Country XIII 139** (39.5 overs).

Each team named 13 players of whom only 11 could bat and 11 bowl; 11 Sri Lankans bowled, including Muttiah Muralitharan (3–0–13–0) in his first match after a hernia operation. This was the Sri Lankans' first win of the tour, and profits were donated to a Colombo cancer hospital.

At Melbourne, January 1, 2003 (day/night). **Sri Lankans won by five wickets.** Toss: Australia A. **Australia A 210-8** (50 overs) (R. J. Campbell 61); **Sri Lankans 211-5** (48.4 overs) (M. S. Atapattu 101*).

At Adelaide, January 7, 2003 (day/night). **Australia A won by ten wickets.** Toss: Sri Lankans. **Sri Lankans 65** (25 overs); **Australia A 66-0** (11.5 overs).

For the Sri Lankans, only Hashan Tillekeratne (11) and Wides (17) reached double figures.

At Adelaide, January 7, 2003 (day/night). **Australia A won by 25 runs.** Toss: Sri Lankans. **Australia A 171** (23 overs) (A. Symonds 81; P. A. de Silva 4-22); **Sri Lankans 146-8** (25 overs) (K. C. Sangakkara 72; N. M. Hauritz 4-25).

After Sri Lanka's earlier rout, a 25-over match was held to entertain a 10,000 crowd.

THE AUSTRALIANS IN THE WEST INDIES, 2002-03

ANDREW RAMSEY

As usually happens when Australia tour the Caribbean, the Test series contained cussedness, controversy, a clattering of records and some cracking cricket. All, however, were squeezed into the final Test in Antigua, and the other three were as predictable, flat and lifeless as the shamefully benign pitches on which they were played. The quick, bouncy tracks which once characterised West Indian cricket have gone the way of the phalanx of fearsome fast bowlers who so ruthlessly exploited them.

As the Australian captain, Steve Waugh, adroitly noted, ground authorities in the region had to take heed of the connection. Until they produced pitches that encouraged pace bowlers and challenged batsmen, the stagnation of the game in the West Indies would continue. Waugh, whose unquenchable thirst for success stemmed from those enervating days in the Caribbean 12 years earlier, when he and his team-mates were battered into submission by a relentless pace barrage, refused to let his own goals deflect his commitment to strengthening cricket around the world. "I have played 159 Tests," he said after being confronted by yet another inert strip of earth for the Third Test, in Barbados, "and this is the slowest, lowest wicket I have ever played on. All the wickets have been really slow and it's a major problem for cricket in the Caribbean. They're not going to produce any quick bowlers if they keep putting pitches out like that. There's no encouragement for them; it's too much hard work."

West Indies' ambitions were never high for this series, and they seemed convinced the best hope was to play on bare pitches and hang on for a handful of honourable draws. Blunting the rampant Australian pace attack – which during his 12-month ban had to cope without the support of Shane Warne's leg-spin – seemed to be the summit of their aspirations.

It was no accident that the best-fought game of a lopsided series came at Antigua on a genuine cricket wicket. No accident, either, that its preparation was overseen by the former fast bowler, Andy Roberts. The match offered real cause for optimism, especially given the phenomenal outcome: West Indies won by mounting the highest successful run-chase in Test history. It is imperative that Caribbean groundsmen build on this and back their own players, rather than try to stymie the opposition.

But stymieing the opposition was effectively confirmed as policy by Brian Lara, reinstated as captain three years after resigning amid much acrimony. Not that his return to the post was much less traumatic. Even allowing for the poisonous political undercurrents that permeate Caribbean cricket, West Indies' lead-up to the Test series was farcical. When Lara was asked to take over from Carl Hooper in the wake of their poor World Cup campaign, Hooper waited until three days before the First Test to declare he was unavailable.

Leading men: Brian Lara – ecstatic at hitting his first Test hundred on his home ground – and Ricky Ponting both totalled over 500 runs for the series.
Pictures by Hamish Blair, Getty Images.

Around the same time, the West Indies Cricket Board proudly trumpeted that Bennett King, head of the Australian cricket academy, was their new national coach. Unfortunately, they told the press before contractual negotiations had been completed, and – though King denied his decision had been influenced by a glimpse of the workings of the WICB – he announced he was no longer interested.

On top of these embarrassments, the outstanding young opener, Chris Gayle, was omitted from the First Test team after he preferred a lucrative double-wicket tournament in St Lucia to turning out for Jamaica in the final of the Carib Beer Challenge, the region's first-class competition. In what looked for all the world to be disciplinary action, he missed the first two Tests, though the selection panel, headed by Sir Vivian Richards, muddied the waters by stating that Gayle had been considered, but simply wasn't picked.

It all added up to the kind of backstage buffoonery that might have unsettled a team heading into a series against lowly Bangladesh. Against the ultra-professional world champions, it was suicide. By lunch on the opening day of the First Test West Indies, having opted to bat, were battling for survival at 89 for five.

They went on battling, gamely but with limited success, throughout that Test, again in Trinidad and on to Barbados, where not even the most benign of pitches could prevent them losing 20 wickets and slipping to a third heavy defeat. Indeed the docile pitches, instead of diminishing Australia's attack, encouraged Waugh to implement a plan he and the Australian selectors had been hatching for some time: to employ a five-man specialist bowling line-up and play Adam Gilchrist as a front-line batsman at No. 6, rather than No. 7. The decision was made easier by the absence of Damien Martyn, a regular in the top order, who had fractured his right index finger during the World Cup. The plan proved a resounding success. In each of the first three batsman-friendly Tests, the Australians – minus Glenn McGrath for the first two because his wife was ill – dismissed West Indies twice to take an unassailable 3–0 lead.

The bland surfaces also allowed Australia's slightly shortened batting to score freely. Gilchrist, whose career average topped 59 at the end of the Tests, repaid the faith placed in him, but so did all the top six, and they averaged between 58 and 130 for the series. Ricky Ponting's form was especially remarkable: he had amassed 523 from five innings – including three centuries – before a virus prevented him from wreaking further havoc in Antigua. (The series' top-scorer, Lara, managed ten runs more against stiffer bowling, though from another three innings.)

The epic Antigua Test was decided as much by fatigue as courageous batting

Australia's modus operandi in retaining the Frank Worrell Trophy, which they had held since 1994-95, was as familiar as it was punishing. During the first three Tests, they averaged 550-plus in their first innings at a rate of more than four an over, giving their bowlers enough time and ammunition to knock over a West Indian batting line-up containing more talent than application. A major beneficiary of the Australians' approach was Stuart MacGill, who proved himself the perfect understudy to Warne: the 20 wickets he prised out with his leg-spin were the most by a bowler on either side.

In the end, the epic Fourth Test, which so nearly brought about Australia's first Caribbean whitewash, was decided perhaps as much by the fatigue of the Australian bowlers – enforcing the follow-on at Barbados subjected them to 244 overs off the reel – and by the absence of Ponting as by the courageous and mature batting from Lara's young players.

Boosted by the arrival of fresh reinforcements, Ponting led his World Cup-winning side to four straight victories in the one-day games, taking Australia's record to an astounding 21 consecutive wins. Either a lack of appetite on their part or the brilliance of Wavell Hinds – perhaps both – then let West Indies claw back three consolation victories at the end of a seemingly interminable series. For Ponting, Gilchrist and the others who played in both Test and one-day sides, it signalled some long-overdue rest at home before the arrival of Bangladesh in July.

AUSTRALIAN TOURING PARTY

S. R. Waugh (New South Wales) (*captain*), R. T. Ponting (Tasmania) (*vice-captain*), A. J. Bichel (Queensland), M. J. Clarke (New South Wales), A. C. Gilchrist (Western Australia), J. N. Gillespie (South Australia), M. L. Hayden (Queensland), G. B. Hogg (Western Australia), J. L. Langer (Western Australia), B. Lee (New South Wales), D. S. Lehmann (South Australia), M. L. Love (Queensland), S. C. G. MacGill (New South Wales), G. D. McGrath (New South Wales), A. A. Noffke (Queensland), B. A. Williams (Western Australia).

Before the tour party left, D. R. Martyn (Western Australia) withdrew through injury from the first-class leg of the tour and was replaced by Clarke, who was later asked to stay on for the one-day games. Soon after the beginning of the tour, McGrath flew back to Australia to be with his sick wife and did not rejoin the squad until after the Second Test. Williams, called up as cover for McGrath, returned home after the Third Test. J. P. Maher (Queensland), originally selected only for the one-day games, was added to the party as cover for Gilchrist after the Second Test. M. G. Bevan (New South Wales), I. J. Harvey (Victoria), N. M. Hauritz (Queensland) and A. Symonds (Queensland) replaced Waugh, Langer, Love, MacGill, Noffke and Williams for the one-day series that followed the Tests, when Ponting took over the captaincy.

Coach: J. M. Buchanan. *Manager:* S. R. Bernard.

Assistant coach/performance analyst: T. J. Nielsen. *Physiotherapist:* E. L. Alcott.

Physical performance manager: J. A. Campbell. *Massage therapist:* L. J. Frostick.

Media manager: J. D. Rose.

AUSTRALIAN TOUR RESULTS

Test matches – Played 4: Won 3, Lost 1.
First-class matches – Played 6: Won 4, Lost 1, Drawn 1.
Wins – West Indies (3), University of West Indies Vice-Chancellor's XI.
Loss – West Indies.
Draw – Carib Beer XI.
One-day internationals – Played 7: Won 4, Lost 3.

TEST MATCH AVERAGES

WEST INDIES – BATTING

	T	*I*	*NO*	*R*	*HS*	*100s*	*50s*	*Avge*	*Ct/St*
†B. C. Lara	4	8	0	533	122	2	3	66.62	4
O. A. C. Banks	2	4	2	119	47*	0	0	59.50	1
R. R. Sarwan	3	6	0	287	105	1	1	47.83	1
†S. Chanderpaul	3	6	0	257	104	2	0	42.83	2
†C. H. Gayle	2	4	0	146	71	0	2	36.50	1
D. Ganga	4	8	0	278	117	2	0	34.75	1
†R. D. Jacobs	2	4	1	91	54*	0	1	30.33	4
†D. S. Smith	4	8	0	189	62	0	2	23.62	2
V. C. Drakes	4	8	2	123	27*	0	0	20.50	1
M. N. Samuels	2	4	0	76	68	0	1	19.00	1
†W. W. Hinds	2	4	0	72	35	0	0	18.00	2
C. S. Baugh	2	4	0	62	24	0	0	15.50	2/1
M. Dillon	3	5	0	42	20	0	0	8.40	1
P. T. Collins	2	4	2	16	7*	0	0	8.00	0
J. J. C. Lawson	3	5	1	20	14	0	0	5.00	1

Played in one Test: D. E. Bernard 7, 4; T. L. Best 20*, 0.

† *Left-handed batsman.*

BOWLING

	Style	O	M	R	W	BB	5W/i	Avge
J. J. C. Lawson	RF	88.4	8	370	14	7-78	1	26.42
M. Dillon	RFM	123.1	7	490	11	4-112	0	44.54
V. C. Drakes	RFM	151.1	17	513	11	5-93	1	46.63
O. A. C. Banks	OB	98	9	421	6	3-204	0	70.16

Also bowled: D. E. Bernard (RFM) 11–1–61–0; T. L. Best (RFM) 20–1–99–0; P. T. Collins (LFM) 61–6–263–1; D. Ganga (OB) 5–0–10–0; C. H. Gayle (OB) 44.3–6–111–1; W. W. Hinds (RM) 7–0–20–0; M. N. Samuels (OB) 77.1–10–266–1; R. R. Sarwan (LB) 3–0–8–0.

AUSTRALIA – BATTING

	T	I	NO	R	HS	100s	50s	Avge	Ct/St
R. T. Ponting	3	5	1	523	206	3	0	130.75	3
S. R. Waugh	4	4	1	226	115	1	0	75.33	1
†A. C. Gilchrist	4	5	1	282	101*	1	2	70.50	12/3
†J. L. Langer	4	8	1	483	146	2	2	69.00	3
†M. L. Hayden	4	8	2	379	177	2	0	63.16	7
†D. S. Lehmann	4	7	1	353	160	1	2	58.83	2
A. J. Bichel	4	4	0	144	71	0	1	36.00	5
B. Lee	4	4	0	58	20	0	0	14.50	4
J. N. Gillespie	4	4	1	36	18*	0	0	12.00	0
S. C. G. MacGill	4	4	1	6	4*	0	0	2.00	0

Played in two Tests: †G. B. Hogg 3, 17*; G. D. McGrath 5*, 14. Played in one Test: M. L. Love 36, 2 (1 ct).

† *Left-handed batsman.*

BOWLING

	Style	O	M	R	W	BB	5W/i	Avge
J. N. Gillespie	RFM	168.4	53	353	17	5-39	1	20.76
B. Lee	RF	144.3	33	490	17	4-63	0	28.82
A. J. Bichel	RFM	103	21	346	11	3-21	0	31.45
S. C. G. MacGill	LBG	204.1	46	679	20	5-75	1	33.95
G. B. Hogg	SLC	58	5	264	5	2-40	0	52.80

Also bowled: D. S. Lehmann (SLA) 21–2–56–2; G. D. McGrath (RFM) 78–27–158–3; R. T. Ponting (RM/OB) 2–0–6–0; S. R. Waugh (RM) 24–4–76–0.

Note: Matches in this section which were not first-class are signified with a dagger.

At Everest CC, Georgetown, April 5, 6, 7, 2003. **Drawn.** Toss: Australians. **Australians 377-3 dec.** (J. L. Langer 60, M. L. Hayden 102, M. L. Love 56, S. R. Waugh 106*) **and 196** (M. L. Love 59); **Carib Beer XI 132** (G. B. Hogg 4-23) **and 402-6** (N. Deonarine 141*, C. S. Baugh 115*; G. B. Hogg 5-112).

In the Carib Beer XI's first innings, Imran Jan carried his bat for 42. In the second, Deonarine and Baugh shared an unbroken stand of 222 for the seventh wicket as they ended 40 from victory.*

WEST INDIES v AUSTRALIA

First Test Match

At Georgetown, April 10, 11, 12, 13, 2003. Australia won by nine wickets. Toss: West Indies. Test debut: D. S. Smith.

Understandably, given what had happened on their last Caribbean tour four years earlier, Australia were wary of the phenomenal, if sporadic, brilliance of a small, dynamic West Indian left-hander. It took less than two sessions for their fears to be realised, but this time it was the normally introverted Chanderpaul, rather than his exuberant captain, Lara, who briefly set the Australians on their heels.

Chanderpaul's century – off 69 deliveries, it was the third-fastest Test hundred in terms of balls faced – was both a sublime sideshow to start the series, and an innings of glorious cavalier defiance that foreshadowed how it would end. By the time Chanderpaul had reached six, half his team had been dismissed for 53 even though the Australians were without Glenn McGrath, who was at home with his sick wife, and speculation that Australia would crush their rivals appeared dishearteningly accurate. But in 108 minutes, Chanderpaul proved the calypso spirit was far from dead, as he launched himself at fast and slow bowling alike to lift West Indies to a respectable, if ultimately inadequate, 237. He gained invaluable support from Jacobs, who battled courageously after yanking a thigh muscle, an injury which required Hinds to keep wicket in both innings.

The Australians, many clearly still jaded after their World Cup success not three weeks before, then showed how batting should be approached on a flat, slow Bourda pitch. Langer and Ponting bettered West Indies' total in a single partnership of 248 and hinted at the dominance they would exert throughout almost all the series. Most of the middle order failed to cash in, but a typically robust 77 from Gilchrist at No. 6 helped Australia to a lead of 252.

A return of five for 93 from Drakes underscored what was wrong with the inexperienced West Indies attack. A journeyman professional, Drakes rarely threatened, though he did at least bowl a consistent line and length. West Indies badly missed Carl Hooper, sacked as captain and now apparently sulking, whose absence disturbed the balance of the attack. But their batsmen made up lost ground and at 295 for two in the second innings were thinking about possible safety. Lara had completed his 19th Test century on his return to the captaincy – an innings of growing authority that won over the hostile elements in the Bourda crowd who had jeered him for displacing the local hero, Hooper. But then came two crucial breakthroughs by Australia's left-arm spinners.

First the wrist-spinner, Hogg, removed Lara in bizarre fashion. One of Lara's hands came off the bat handle in an attempted sweep, and in a flailing of body and blade, the bat came down on to his leg stump. Australia struck an equally fortuitous blow near the close after Ganga, a surprise inclusion at No. 3, had broken through for his first Test century in his 18th appearance. After playing a patient hand, he tried a lazy drive against Lehmann's occasional finger-spin and was caught at short mid-wicket. West Indies went to stumps at 381 for five – 129 ahead with two days remaining.

Their last hopes vanished on the fourth morning when Gillespie unleashed a telling spell on the unresponsive pitch. West Indies lost their remaining five wickets – four to Gillespie – for 16 in just 45 balls. Another meticulously executed stand between Langer and Ponting clinched victory before tea. "Brian Lara can have a hundred every match," said Waugh "if we win by nine wickets." Waugh, had become Test cricket's most capped player in his 157th match, and there still seemed no stopping him and his team.

Man of the Match: J. L. Langer.

Close of play: First day, Australia 120-1 (Langer 55, Ponting 46); Second day, West Indies 16-0 (Hinds 2, Smith 13); Third day, West Indies 381-5 (Chanderpaul 26, Drakes 14).

West Indies

W. W. Hinds c Langer b Hogg	10	lbw b MacGill	7
D. S. Smith lbw b Lee	3	c Gilchrist b Gillespie	62
D. Ganga b Gillespie	0	c Lee b Lehmann	113
*B. C. Lara lbw b Bichel	26	hit wkt b Hogg	110
M. N. Samuels c Hayden b Hogg	0	c Ponting b MacGill	7
S. Chanderpaul lbw b Bichel	100	c Gilchrist b Gillespie	31
†R. D. Jacobs not out	54	(9) c Lehmann b MacGill	11
V. C. Drakes c Gilchrist b Bichel	0	(7) lbw b Gillespie	14
M. Dillon lbw b MacGill	20	(8) lbw b Gillespie	0
P. T. Collins st Gilchrist b MacGill	3	not out	1
J. J. C. Lawson b Lee	0	lbw b Gillespie	0
B 10, l-b 2, w 3, n-b 6	21	B 6, l-b 13, w 1, n-b 22	42
1/9 (2) 2/10 (3) 3/47 (1) 4/47 (5) 5/53 (4) 6/184 (6) 7/184 (8) 8/222 (9) 9/236 (10) 10/237 (11)	237	1/52 (1) 2/110 (2) 3/295 (4) 4/303 (5) 5/354 (3) 6/382 (7) 7/384 (8) 8/391 (6) 9/397 (9) 10/398 (11)	398

Bowling: *First Innings*—Lee 10.3–1–41–2; Gillespie 12–3–40–1; Bichel 8–1–55–3; Hogg 8–1–40–2; MacGill 12–4–49–2. *Second Innings*—MacGill 31–5–140–3; Hogg 15–0–68–1; Lee 14–4–57–0; Gillespie 20.2–5–39–5; Bichel 13–4–40–0; Waugh 8–1–29–0; Lehmann 4–0–6–1.

Australia

J. L. Langer c Hinds b Drakes	146	not out	78
M. L. Hayden run out	10	c sub (N. Deonarine) b Lawson	19
R. T. Ponting c Samuels b Drakes	117	not out	42
D. S. Lehmann c sub (D. E. Bernard) b Drakes	6		
*S. R. Waugh lbw b Dillon	25		
†A. C. Gilchrist c and b Lawson	77		
G. B. Hogg lbw b Collins	3		
A. J. Bichel c Hinds b Drakes	39		
B. Lee c Dillon b Drakes	20		
J. N. Gillespie b Lawson	7		
S. C. G. MacGill not out	4		
B 18, l-b 5, w 2, n-b 10	35	B 1, l-b 2, w 2, n-b 3	8
1/37 (2) 2/285 (3) 3/300 (4) 4/319 (1) 5/349 (5) 6/362 (7) 7/447 (8) 8/473 (6) 9/485 (10) 10/489 (9)	489	1/77 (2)	(1 wkt) 147

Bowling: *First Innings*—Dillon 23–1–116–1; Collins 23–1–96–1; Lawson 21–0–111–2; Drakes 26.1–5–93–5; Samuels 21–6–49–0; Ganga 1–0–1–0. *Second Innings*—Dillon 6–0–21–0; Drakes 8–0–28–0; Collins 6–2–14–0; Lawson 9–2–31–1; Samuels 9.1–1–41–0; Ganga 4–0–9–0.

Umpires: E. A. R. de Silva (Sri Lanka) and R. E. Koertzen (South Africa).
Third umpire: E. A. Nicholls. Referee: M. J. Procter (South Africa).

WEST INDIES v AUSTRALIA

Second Test Match

At Port-of-Spain, April 19, 20, 21, 22, 23, 2003. Australia won by 118 runs. Toss: Australia. Test debuts: C. S. Baugh, D. E. Bernard.

It's the sort of question likely to crop up in pub quizzes: who took seven wickets in the Second Test at Trinidad in 2002-03? Answer: West Indies. It's a fair bet that the moment the Australians caught a glimpse of their opponents' team sheet, they firmed up arrangements for the Worrell Trophy's return to Australia. This Test was decided even before the toss.

West Indies had already lost tearaway young quick Jermaine Lawson to chicken-pox, and were hamstrung further when Chanderpaul and Jacobs were ruled out through injuries they sustained at Georgetown: Chanderpaul had a badly bruised knee while Jacobs's damaged thigh would sideline him till the Fourth Test. He was replaced by 20-year-old Carlton Baugh from Jamaica. Uncapped off-spinner Omari Banks had been added to the squad, but even though the Queen's Park Oval was obviously dry and bare they opted instead for a decidedly thin, second-rate seam attack.

The out-of-form pair, Dillon and Collins, were to share the new ball, with back-up from Drakes. If they failed to make inroads, it would be up to another young Jamaican, the untried all-rounder Dave Bernard, only 21, and the part-time off-spinner, Samuels, one year older. Everything unravelled on the first day: by then Australia had reached 391 for three – and two of those three wickets came courtesy of lamentable leg-before decisions from umpire de Silva, who seemed to have trouble with the law about balls pitching outside leg. In fact, de Silva, after an indifferent game in Georgetown, was the only man to look like making a breakthrough all day. Ponting and Lehmann compiled an Australian-record third-wicket stand of 315, including an overdue maiden Test century from Lehmann, in his tenth match.

The ritual slaughter continued next morning as Ponting, in the form of his life, blazed his way to his first Test double-hundred. He batted eight hours 11 minutes, faced 362 balls and hit 24 fours and a six. Gilchrist, meanwhile, celebrated his latest promotion, to No. 5, with another unbeaten century. Waugh declared at 576 for four, and his hard-working bowlers grabbed three wickets by the end of the second day, including the key scalp of Lara, bowled around his legs within sight of a first Test hundred on his home ground. By completing back-to-back Test centuries, Ganga enabled his beleaguered team to pass the follow-on mark, though it was unlikely Waugh would have asked his bowlers to start again after 100-plus gruelling overs.

Instead, he instructed his batsmen to add quick runs, which they did – if not quite at the rate of their first-innings sprint – with Hayden becoming Australia's fourth centurion of the game. To achieve his pre-match aim of a draw, Lara needed his team to bat out more than four sessions, or score 407 at a little more than three an over to snatch an improbable win. By lunch on the last day, local hopes were swollen by Lara and Sarwan batting, largely untroubled, through the morning session to narrow the deficit to 197 with seven wickets left. Lara had reached a breakthrough home-town century despite an inspired spell of brutish fast bowling from Lee, which the former West Indian pace bowler, Ian Bishop, rated the fastest he had seen in the Caribbean. But that was followed by something almost as quick: West Indies went into free fall to lose their last seven wickets for 75 in 23 overs – and the Worrell Trophy stayed with Australia.

Man of the Match: R. T. Ponting.

Close of play: First day, Australia 391-3 (Ponting 146, Gilchrist 14); Second day, West Indies 186-3 (Ganga 69, Sarwan 1); Third day, Australia 31-1 (Hayden 15, Ponting 10); Fourth day, West Indies 107-3 (Lara 52, Sarwan 0).

Australia

J. L. Langer lbw b Dillon	25	– lbw b Drakes	3
M. L. Hayden lbw b Dillon	30	– not out	100
R. T. Ponting st Baugh b Samuels	206	– c Baugh b Dillon	45
D. S. Lehmann c Baugh b Drakes	160	– b Dillon	66
†A. C. Gilchrist not out	101		
G. B. Hogg not out	17		
B 11, l-b 7, w 7, n-b 12	37	B 13, l-b 5, w 1, n-b 5	24
1/49 (1) 2/56 (2) 3/371 (4) 4/542 (3)	(4 wkts dec.) 576	1/12 (1) 2/118 (3) 3/238 (4)	(3 wkts dec.) 238

*S. R. Waugh, A. J. Bichel, B. Lee, J. N. Gillespie and S. C. G. MacGill did not bat.

Bowling: *First Innings*—Dillon 28.5–1–124–2; Collins 25–2–123–0; Drakes 33–3–112–1; Samuels 26–2–111–1; Bernard 11–1–61–0; Sarwan 2–0–7–0; Hinds 7–0–20–0. *Second Innings*—Dillon 18.2–0–64–2; Drakes 20–4–61–1; Samuels 21–1–65–0; Collins 7–1–30–0.

West Indies

W. W. Hinds c Hayden b Lee	20	– b MacGill	35
D. S. Smith c Gilchrist b Gillespie	0	– lbw b Gillespie	0
D. Ganga c Hayden b Lee	117	– c Hayden b Gillespie	2
*B. C. Lara b Hogg	91	– c Hayden b MacGill	122
R. R. Sarwan b Lee	26	– c Lehmann b Bichel	34
M. N. Samuels c Bichel b MacGill	68	– lbw b Bichel	1
D. E. Bernard b Gillespie	7	– c Hayden b Bichel	4
†C. S. Baugh hit wkt b MacGill	19	– c Langer b Hogg	1
V. C. Drakes lbw b Lee	24	– not out	26
M. Dillon lbw b Gillespie	0	– c Bichel b Lee	13
P. T. Collins not out	7	– lbw b Gillespie	5
B 4, l-b 15, w 2, n-b 8	29	B 25, l-b 7, w 3, n-b 10	45
1/4 (2) 2/25 (1) 3/183 (4) 4/258 (5) 5/279 (3) 6/300 (7) 7/367 (8) 8/376 (6) 9/384 (10) 10/408 (9)	408	1/2 (2) 2/12 (3) 3/107 (1) 4/213 (5) 5/222 (6) 6/228 (7) 7/238 (4) 8/238 (8) 9/270 (10) 10/288 (11)	288

Bowling: *First Innings*—Lee 23–4–69–4; Gillespie 28–9–50–3; Bichel 12–1–58–0; MacGill 27–4–98–2; Hogg 22–3–98–1; Waugh 7–2–16–0. *Second Innings*—Lee 19–4–68–1; Gillespie 17.2–3–36–3; Bichel 13–3–21–3; Lehmann 7–0–20–0; MacGill 20–6–53–2; Hogg 13–1–58–1.

Umpires: E. A. R. de Silva (Sri Lanka) and R. E. Koertzen (South Africa).
Third umpire: B. R. Doctrove. Referee: M. J. Procter (South Africa).

At Bridgetown, April 26, 27, 28, 2003. **Australians won by six wickets.** Toss: Vice-Chancellor's XI. **University of West Indies Vice-Chancellor's XI 290** (C. H. Gayle 129, J. A. M. Haynes 58; S. C. G. MacGill 5-40) **and 162** (P. A. Wallace 53; S. C. G. MacGill 5-45); **Australians 358-6 dec.** (J. L. Langer 96, J. P. Maher 142) **and 95-4**.

WEST INDIES v AUSTRALIA

Third Test Match

At Bridgetown, May 1, 2, 3, 4, 5, 2003. Australia won by nine wickets. Toss: West Indies. Test debuts: O. A. C. Banks, T. L. Best.

Despite rating the Kensington pitch as the slowest and flattest he had come across in almost two decades of international cricket, Waugh managed to wring out of it his 30th Test century, another Test win – his 36th as captain, equalling the record held by Clive Lloyd – and yet another series success, his tenth in charge. It also restored Waugh's Australians to the top of the ICC Test championship, whose reputation, rather than Australia's, had been badly dented when they were deposed by South Africa in January.

Lara, his opposite number, would not have such happy memories of Barbados 2003. He again found his health the subject of speculation and controversy after he was reported to be suffering from a mystery virus on the second day, his 34th birthday, and was too ill next morning to bat at his usual No. 4. The confusion was heightened by initial suggestions he might have contracted chicken-pox, though this was never confirmed.

Nor was there any confirmation that Lara was fevered and delirious at the toss, but it is hard to conjure any other explanation why – at 2–0 down and armed with the greenest of seam attacks who, all told, had nine previous caps – he invited the world's most relentless batting team to put on their pads. It was, at best, an act of pure negativity which fitted West Indies' publicly stated aim of being hell-bent on a draw. Waugh,

Onwards and upwards: Stuart MacGill snatches the wicket of Ramnaresh Sarwan, and Australia are soon 3–0 up in the series.
Picture by Hamish Blair, Getty Images.

meanwhile, welcomed McGrath back into the side in place of Hogg. McGrath, who had missed the first two Tests to be with his sick wife in Australia, had a quiet return, and went wicketless for the first time in 26 Tests.

Lara appeared to rely on Waugh to set up the game with a couple of sporting declarations, as he had in Trinidad, but as Waugh wryly noted during the match: "my generosity is not going to go that far, especially on this pitch". Lara's benevolence at the toss, however, was gratefully received. Every Australian bar MacGill made a start, Waugh and Ponting made hundreds and the entire line-up made a mockery of the revamped West Indian attack. They plundered 605 for nine before declaring. Neither debutant had an entirely happy introduction to Test cricket: Tino Best, a fiery seam bowler from Barbados, had figures of none for 99, while Omari Banks, an off-spinner from the Leewards, did take three wickets, though at a cost of 204. West Indies' disarray was best illustrated by Sarwan, briefly acting-captain while Lara was confined to his sick bed. He admitted it was not until prompted by Gayle that he remembered it had become his duty to set the field.

The fact that Lara, batting at No. 8 because of ill health, came in not long after tea on the third day suggested even a draw was a forlorn hope. It became less likely still when Lara was dismissed, shortly before stumps, to another howler of an lbw decision, umpire Venkat missing a big inside edge.

When the West Indies innings finished early on the fourth day 277 behind, Waugh had little option but to enforce the follow-on if his bowlers were to have enough time to capture ten wickets on the featherbed. West Indies started the final day just 90 adrift with seven wickets in hand and, as so often, much rested on Lara, now apparently restored to health, and on Sarwan, who had together taken their stand to 93. But both fell during the first few minutes, Sarwan to another strange leg-before call from Venkat first ball of the day. The rest was attritional but the result inevitable: MacGill took five for 75, giving him nine in the match.

Even in the midst of a third hefty defeat, however, Caribbean cricket fans had something to cheer. By removing Langer with the first ball of Australia's second innings – they needed eight runs to win – Lawson became the first West Indian to take a Test hat-trick on home soil. His name was barely out of the headlines in the coming week.

Man of the Match: S. C. G. MacGill.

Close of play: First day, Australia 320-3 (Lehmann 89, Waugh 7); Second day, West Indies 89-0 (Gayle 47, Smith 34); Third day, West Indies 291-8 (Drakes 4); Fourth day, West Indies 187-3 (Sarwan 58, Lara 41).

Australia

Batsman	First innings	Runs	Second innings	Runs
J. L. Langer	c Chanderpaul b Banks	78	lbw b Lawson	0
M. L. Hayden	c Gayle b Drakes	27	not out	2
R. T. Ponting	run out	113		
D. S. Lehmann	lbw b Drakes	96	(3) not out	4
*S. R. Waugh	b Lawson	115		
†A. C. Gilchrist	c Smith b Banks	65		
A. J. Bichel	c Lara b Banks	71		
B. Lee	b Lawson	11		
J. N. Gillespie	not out	18		
S. C. G. MacGill	b Lawson	0		
	B 3, l-b 3, w 3, n-b 2	11	B 2	2
	1/43 (2) 2/151 (1) 3/292 (3) 4/331 (4) 5/444 (6) 6/568 (7) 7/580 (5) 8/605 (8) 9/605 (10) (9 wkts dec.)	605	1/0 (1) (1 wkt)	8

G. D. McGrath did not bat.

Bowling: *First Innings*—Lawson 32.3–2–131–3; Best 20–1–99–0; Drakes 30–2–85–2; Banks 40–2–204–3; Gayle 31–5–79–0; Sarwan 1–0–1–0. *Second Innings*—Lawson 1–0–2–1; Banks 1–0–2–0; Gayle 0.3–0–2–0.

West Indies

Batsman	First innings	Runs	Second innings	Runs
C. H. Gayle	b Gillespie	71	st Gilchrist b MacGill	56
D. S. Smith	c Gilchrist b Gillespie	59	lbw b Lee	5
D. Ganga	c Bichel b Lehmann	26	lbw b Lee	6
R. R. Sarwan	c Gilchrist b Lee	40	lbw b MacGill	58
S. Chanderpaul	c Lee b MacGill	0	(6) c Gilchrist b Gillespie	21
O. A. C. Banks	c Ponting b Gillespie	24	(7) c Hayden b MacGill	32
†C. S. Baugh	c Ponting b MacGill	24	(8) run out	18
*B. C. Lara	lbw b Bichel	14	(5) lbw b Bichel	42
V. C. Drakes	c Lee b MacGill	11	b MacGill	0
T. L. Best	not out	20	c Bichel b MacGill	0
J. J. C. Lawson	st Gilchrist b MacGill	1	not out	5
	B 11, l-b 16, n-b 11	38	B 13, l-b 25, w 1, n-b 2	41
	1/139 (1) 2/142 (2) 3/205 (3) 4/206 (5) 5/245 (4) 6/245 (6) 7/281 (8) 8/291 (7) 9/324 (9) 10/328 (11)	328	1/14 (2) 2/31 (3) 3/94 (1) 4/187 (4) 5/195 (5) 6/256 (7) 7/256 (6) 8/261 (9) 9/265 (10) 10/284 (8)	284

Bowling: *First Innings*—McGrath 18–7–25–0; Gillespie 21–9–31–3; Lee 25–8–77–1; MacGill 39.5–8–107–4; Lehmann 9–2–26–1; Bichel 16–3–35–1. *Second Innings*—McGrath 18–4–39–0; Gillespie 28–11–37–1; MacGill 36–11–75–5; Lee 15–6–44–2; Bichel 12–2–35–1; Ponting 2–0–6–0; Waugh 4–1–6–0; Lehmann 1–0–4–0.

Umpires: D. R. Shepherd (England) and S. Venkataraghavan (India).
Third umpire: E. A. Nicholls. Referee: M. J. Procter (South Africa).

Beyond dispute: Vasbert Drakes is jubilant after West Indies reach 418, the highest score to win a Test.

Picture by Hamish Blair, Getty Images.

WEST INDIES v AUSTRALIA

Fourth Test Match

At St John's, May 9, 10, 11, 12, 13, 2003. West Indies won by three wickets. Toss: Australia.

Many expected the final Test to bring a disappointing series to a historic conclusion with Australia's first Caribbean clean sweep. Few, though, could have imagined the controversies that the game would bring and still less that West Indies would etch their names in the record books by achieving the largest successful run-chase in 1,645 Tests.

The talking-point on the opening day was in fact more of a whisper. Presented with the most sporting pitch of the tour, Lawson could scarcely hide his excitement – and exposed hitherto unseen weaknesses in the Australian batting, which was without Ponting, suffering from a viral infection. Lawson, fast and furious, pocketed career-best figures of seven for 78 in Australia's modest 240. But by the end of the day the word was spreading around the Recreation Ground: to many, Lawson's action, which had first drawn the attention of the series referee, Mike Procter, during the First Test in Guyana, looked dubious. The murmurs grew louder when umpires David Shepherd and Venkat called for video evidence. By the fourth day, Procter confirmed that Lawson had been reported to the ICC for a suspect action.

By then, other storm clouds had gathered over St John's. On the second morning, Lara walked out to bat in a bellicose frame of mind, had exchanges with three Australians before he faced his first ball, from Lee, and duly hammered it over point for six. Lara spent the first half-hour of his innings arguing furiously with his tormentors, and at one stage stood toe to toe with Waugh, who had moved to short cover to pepper him with more chat, causing umpire Shepherd to intervene briefly.

It was an unedifying spectacle, though no further action was taken by umpires or referee. The game, however, continued to simmer, partly due to the closeness of the contest. West Indies also scored 240, the seventh instance of precise first-innings

Ongoing dispute: Glenn McGrath locks horns with Ramnaresh Sarwan before making his point to umpire Shepherd.

Pictures by Hamish Blair, Getty Images.

equality in Test history, and then – with Lawson ostensibly sidelined by a back strain – Dillon finally lived up to his billing as bowling spearhead to keep his team in the match. The importance of his four for 112 cannot be overstated, particularly after Australia raced to 242 from 55 overs on the strength of Langer and Hayden's fifth double-century opening stand, more than any other pair in Test history.

By restricting Australia to 417, about 150 fewer than Waugh had envisaged, West Indies had left themselves a target which, though unlikely, was not impossible now that the pitch had lost its juice if not its bounce. With more than two days available, time at least was on their side. But when West Indies wobbled to 74 for three on the fourth morning, the existing record score to win a Test – the 406 India hit against West Indies in Trinidad 27 years earlier – appeared safe. And hope was all but extinguished when Lara was fourth out at 165, trying to belt MacGill for a fourth huge six down the ground.

But Sarwan and Chanderpaul, who was nursing a broken finger, got on with the task – and under the skin of the Australians, especially McGrath. As Sarwan approached a mature hundred, there were signs that Australia were losing the plot. McGrath, who started the verbal war, became utterly incensed at Sarwan's riposte – he apparently referred to McGrath's wife. After a set-to with the batsman, he wagged his finger at umpire Shepherd, demanding he get involved. Despite this, no official action was taken, though once pictures were beamed round the world both the ACB and ICC castigated the Australians and called on them immediately to mend their ways.

When Sarwan had taken his score to 105 and his stand with Chanderpaul to 123, he mishooked Lee to leave the game perfectly poised: at 288 for five, either 130 runs or five wickets would settle it. The first-ball dismissal of Jacobs, caught behind though he was struck on the elbow, initially tilted things Australia's way. The crowd were furious, and disrupted play by throwing bottles on to the outfield. Through all this –

and a rain delay – Chanderpaul kept his concentration to reach a magnificent hundred. By the close, Australia needed four wickets for the clean sweep; West Indies 47 runs to prevent it.

On the final morning, Chanderpaul added only one to his overnight 103 before Lee prised him out, too, leaving West Indies to rely on Banks and Drakes, neither really an all-rounder. But they coolly took care of the 46 needed to reach a stunning, unparalleled victory. The Australian bowlers, having worked themselves into the ground to set up the series win, now made history as the attack to concede most runs to lose a Test. Lara reckoned the win the zenith of his career.

Man of the Match: S. Chanderpaul. *Man of the Series:* R. T. Ponting.

Close of play: First day, West Indies 47-2 (Smith 22, Drakes 12); Second day, Australia 171-0 (Langer 80, Hayden 79); Third day, West Indies 47-0 (Gayle 19, Smith 21); Fourth day, West Indies 371-6 (Chanderpaul 103, Banks 28).

Australia

First innings		Second innings	
J. L. Langer c Banks b Lawson	42	– c Lara b Gayle	111
M. L. Hayden c Drakes b Lawson	14	– run out	177
M. L. Love b Banks	36	– (4) c sub (M. N. Samuels) b Banks	2
D. S. Lehmann c Jacobs b Lawson	7	– (5) b Dillon	14
*S. R. Waugh c Jacobs b Dillon	41	– (6) not out	45
†A. C. Gilchrist c Chanderpaul b Dillon	33	– (3) c sub (M. N. Samuels) b Banks	6
A. J. Bichel c sub (M. N. Samuels) b Lawson	34	– c Smith b Dillon	0
B. Lee c Jacobs b Lawson	9	– c sub (S. C. Joseph) b Dillon	18
J. N. Gillespie c Jacobs b Lawson	6	– c Lara b Drakes	5
S. C. G. MacGill c Sarwan b Lawson	2	– c Lara b Dillon	0
G. D. McGrath not out	5	– c Ganga b Drakes	14
B 2, l-b 3, w 2, n-b 4	11	B 4, l-b 9, n-b 12	25
1/27 (2) 2/80 (1) 3/93 (4) 4/128 (3) 5/181 (5) 6/194 (6) 7/224 (7) 8/231 (8) 9/233 (10) 10/240 (9)	240	1/242 (1) 2/273 (3) 3/285 (4) 4/330 (5) 5/338 (2) 6/343 (7) 7/373 (8) 8/385 (9) 9/388 (10) 10/417 (11)	417

Bowling: *First Innings*—Dillon 18–2–53–2; Lawson 19.1–3–78–7; Drakes 15–2–42–0; Banks 20–2–62–1. *Second Innings*—Lawson 6–1–17–0; Dillon 29–3–112–4; Banks 37–5–153–2; Drakes 19–1–92–2; Gayle 13–1–30–1.

West Indies

First innings		Second innings	
C. H. Gayle b McGrath	0	– c Waugh b Lee	19
D. S. Smith c Gilchrist b Lee	37	– c Gilchrist b Gillespie	23
D. Ganga c Gilchrist b Bichel	6	– lbw b McGrath	8
V. C. Drakes lbw b Lee	21	– (9) not out	27
*B. C. Lara c Langer b Bichel	68	– (4) b MacGill	60
R. R. Sarwan c and b Bichel	24	– (5) c and b Lee	105
S. Chanderpaul b McGrath	1	– (6) c Gilchrist b Lee	104
†R. D. Jacobs run out	26	– (7) c Gilchrist b Lee	0
O. A. C. Banks not out	16	– (8) not out	47
M. Dillon b Lee	9		
J. J. C. Lawson c Love b MacGill	14		
L-b 8, w 3, n-b 7	18	B 9, l-b 9, w 1, n-b 6	25
1/1 (1) 2/30 (3) 3/73 (2) 4/80 (4) 5/137 (6) 6/140 (7) 7/185 (8) 8/197 (5) 9/224 (10) 10/240 (11)	240	1/48 (1) 2/50 (2) 3/74 (3) 4/165 (4) 5/288 (5) 6/288 (7) 7/372 (6) (7 wkts)	418

Bowling: *First Innings*—McGrath 17–6–44–2; Gillespie 17–3–56–0; Bichel 14–4–53–3; Lee 15–2–71–3; MacGill 2.3–0–8–1. *Second Innings*—McGrath 25–10–50–1; Gillespie 25–10–64–1; Lee 23–4–63–4; MacGill 35.5–8–149–1; Bichel 15–3–49–0; Waugh 5–0–25–0.

Umpires: D. R. Shepherd (England) and S. Venkataraghavan (India).
Third umpire: B. R. Doctrove. Referee: M. J. Procter (South Africa).

†WEST INDIES v AUSTRALIA

First One-Day International

At Kingston, May 17, 2003. Australia won by two runs (D/L method). Toss: West Indies. One-day international debuts: O. A. C. Banks, C. S. Baugh, D. S. Smith.

Suggestions that Australia would be lacking motivation in the wake of their World Cup triumph were scotched within moments of their taking the field. Sent in to bat, they slipped into world champion mode without missing a stride and, thanks to Ponting and Lehmann, rattled on at more than five an over. The elevation of the big-hitting Powell to opener gave West Indies' assault on 271 an immediate kick-start and, at 114 for two in the 24th over, they were on course. An hour was then lost to rain, and the target reduced to 208 off 37 overs. West Indian hopes were doused immediately after the break when Lara and Devon Smith both fell to Harvey who, despite an undefeated 30-ball 48 and three for 37, was overlooked for the match award. Sarwan kept West Indies in the frame, but in the end the gap between the sides was wider than the margin implied. Australia extended their unbeaten run in one-day internationals to 18.

Man of the Match: R. T. Ponting.

Australia

†A. C. Gilchrist c Samuels b Dillon	21
M. L. Hayden c Gayle b Dillon	7
*R. T. Ponting c Collymore b Gayle	59
D. S. Lehmann c Powell b Banks	55
A. Symonds c Dillon b Banks	18
M. G. Bevan not out	43
I. J. Harvey not out	48
L-b 6, w 9, n-b 4	19
1/35 (1) 2/47 (2) 3/133 (3) 4/169 (4) 5/183 (5) (5 wkts, 50 overs)	270

G. B. Hogg, A. J. Bichel, B. Lee and G. D. McGrath did not bat.

Bowling: Dillon 9–1–53–2; Drakes 8–0–50–0; Collymore 10–0–49–0; Samuels 6–0–26–0; Gayle 9–0–42–1; Banks 8–0–44–2.

West Indies

C. H. Gayle c Hogg b Lee	37
R. L. Powell c Gilchrist b Lee	37
D. S. Smith c Gilchrist b Harvey	26
*B. C. Lara c Gilchrist b Harvey	23
R. R. Sarwan not out	47
M. N. Samuels c Symonds b Harvey	2
O. A. C. Banks run out	12
†C. S. Baugh b McGrath	7
V. C. Drakes b Symonds	1
M. Dillon not out	8
L-b 2, w 1, n-b 2	5
1/75 (1) 2/75 (2) 3/124 (4) 4/133 (3) 5/137 (6) 6/161 (7) 7/176 (8) 8/185 (9) (8 wkts, 37 overs)	205

C. D. Collymore did not bat.

Bowling: McGrath 8–1–34–1; Lee 8–2–52–2; Bichel 7–1–38–0; Harvey 7–0–37–3; Symonds 7–0–42–1.

Umpires: D. R. Shepherd (England) and B. R. Doctrove.
Third umpire: E. A. Nicholls. Referee: R. S. Madugalle (Sri Lanka).

†WEST INDIES v AUSTRALIA

Second One-Day International

At Kingston, May 18, 2003. Australia won by eight wickets. Toss: West Indies.

The second match was as one-sided as the first was intriguing. It was effectively decided during the opening 90 minutes, when the Australian pace attack levelled the West Indian top order; by the 22nd over they were floundering at 75 for five. From there, 163 all out was a decent recovery. Australia had once been vulnerable chasing small targets, but Ponting's side confirmed this was a thing of the past. Hayden and Ponting, still not fully recovered from the virus that kept him out of the Fourth Test, hit fifties as Australia sauntered home with all but 15 overs unused.

Man of the Match: G. D. McGrath.

West Indies

C. H. Gayle c Gilchrist b Bichel 28
D. S. Smith c and b Lee 1
M. N. Samuels c Gilchrist b McGrath . . 6
*B. C. Lara c Gilchrist b Bichel 5
R. R. Sarwan c Hayden b Gillespie 14
R. L. Powell c McGrath b Hogg 32
O. A. C. Banks c Gilchrist b Lee 29
†C. S. Baugh b McGrath 29
V. C. Drakes b McGrath 1
M. Dillon not out 3
C. D. Collymore lbw b McGrath 0
B 2, l-b 4, w 9 15

1/4 (2) 2/21 (3) 3/43 (4) 4/50 (1) 5/75 (5) 6/103 (6) 7/157 (7) 8/160 (8) 9/163 (9) 10/163 (11) (49 overs) 163

Bowling: McGrath 10–2–31–4; Lee 7–0–22–2; Gillespie 9–0–28–1; Bichel 5–0–27–2; Hogg 10–3–27–1; Symonds 8–0–22–0.

Australia

†A. C. Gilchrist c Samuels b Collymore . 27
M. L. Hayden c Collymore b Banks . . . 51
*R. T. Ponting not out 57
A. Symonds not out 17
L-b 10, w 3, n-b 1 14

1/50 (1) 2/120 (2) (2 wkts, 35.1 overs) 166

M. G. Bevan, I. J. Harvey, G. B. Hogg, A. J. Bichel, B. Lee, J. N. Gillespie and G. D. McGrath did not bat.

Bowling: Dillon 10–1–45–0; Collymore 8.1–1–35–1; Banks 10–0–42–1; Drakes 1–0–6–0; Gayle 6–0–28–0.

Umpires: D. R. Shepherd (England) and E. A. Nicholls.
Third umpire: B. R. Doctrove. Referee: R. S. Madugalle (Sri Lanka).

†WEST INDIES v AUSTRALIA

Third One-Day International

At Gros Islet, St Lucia, May 21, 2003. Australia won by 25 runs. Toss: West Indies.

The Australians were taken with the lavish new Beausejour stadium in St Lucia, but perhaps not as impressed as the St Lucians must have been with Australia's 22-year-old batting prodigy Michael Clarke. In his first full international outing of the tour, Clarke, a former Australian Under-19 captain, stroked a composed unbeaten 75 from 100 balls to lift his team to a daunting 258. And then, each time West Indies looked on track, Clarke hung on to crucial outfield catches. The third and last dismissed Samuels, and signalled a limp end to any serious run-chase. Despite Clarke's success, he was, said Ponting, far from commanding a permanent place in the Australian one-day side.

Man of the Match: M. J. Clarke.

Australia

†J. P. Maher c Smith b Banks 17
M. L. Hayden c Baugh b Dillon 20
*R. T. Ponting run out 32
A. Symonds b Gayle 75
M. J. Clarke not out 75
M. G. Bevan not out 32
L-b 2, w 2, n-b 3 7

1/25 (2) 2/48 (1) 3/79 (3) 4/178 (4) (4 wkts, 50 overs) 258

G. B. Hogg, A. J. Bichel, N. M. Hauritz, J. N. Gillespie and G. D. McGrath did not bat.

Bowling: Dillon 10–1–36–1; Collymore 10–0–52–0; Banks 7–0–38–1; Hinds 7–0–42–0; Gayle 10–0–50–1; Samuels 6–0–38–0.

West Indies

C. H. Gayle c Clarke b Hauritz	43
D. S. Smith c Maher b McGrath	9
R. R. Sarwan c Gillespie b Hauritz	15
*B. C. Lara b Bichel	4
W. W. Hinds run out	42
M. N. Samuels c Clarke b Gillespie	37
R. L. Powell c Clarke b Gillespie	26
O. A. C. Banks run out	3
†C. S. Baugh not out	24
M. Dillon run out	4
C. D. Collymore not out	8
L-b 3, w 14, n-b 1	18
1/20 (2) 2/67 (3) 3/70 (1) 4/85 (4) 5/150 (5) 6/181 (7) 7/181 (6) 8/186 (8) 9/197 (10) (9 wkts, 50 overs)	233

Bowling: McGrath 10–1–35–1; Gillespie 10–1–48–2; Bichel 10–1–44–1; Hauritz 10–1–50–2; Hogg 10–0–53–0.

Umpires: D. R. Shepherd (England) and B. R. Doctrove.
Third umpire: E. A. Nicholls. Referee: R. S. Madugalle (Sri Lanka).

†WEST INDIES v AUSTRALIA

Fourth One-Day International

At Port-of-Spain, May 24, 2003. Australia won by 67 runs. Toss: Australia. One-day international debut: R. O. Hurley.

Australia, with their 21st consecutive one-day international victory, wrapped up the seven-match series 4–0. The two main contributors had some good fortune: Gilchrist, after sitting out the previous game, was dropped twice en route to 84, while Clarke, bowled by a Collymore no-ball on 41 and reprieved by Powell at deep mid-wicket on 47, also rode his luck to hit an unbeaten 55 from 40 balls. West Indies were eventually set 287, more than any team had successfully chased at Port-of-Spain, and though they had an outside chance at 146 for three in the 35th over, typically purposeful bowling and suicidal run-outs ensured a comfortable Australian win. One of those run-outs saw the end of the debutant, Hurley (first names Ryan O'Neal), without facing a ball. A 27-year-old off-spinning all-rounder from Barbados, he had given up first-class cricket in 2000 only to return for the 2002-03 season with the express intention of playing international cricket.

Man of the Match: A. C. Gilchrist.

Australia

†A. C. Gilchrist b Hurley	84
M. L. Hayden c Hurley b Drakes	44
*R. T. Ponting c Hurley b Powell	38
A. Symonds b Collymore	24
M. J. Clarke not out	55
M. G. Bevan c Lara b Drakes	21
L-b 9, w 10, n-b 1	20
1/78 (2) 2/148 (3) 3/200 (1) 4/223 (4) 5/286 (6) (5 wkts, 50 overs)	286

I. J. Harvey, G. B. Hogg, B. Lee, J. N. Gillespie and G. D. McGrath did not bat.

Bowling: Dillon 10–0–46–0; Collymore 9–1–58–1; Gayle 10–0–52–0; Hurley 10–0–57–1; Drakes 10–0–62–2; Powell 1–0–2–1.

West Indies

C. H. Gayle lbw b Harvey 84
R. L. Powell c Ponting b Gillespie. 8
W. W. Hinds lbw b Lee. 3
R. R. Sarwan lbw b McGrath 16
*B. C. Lara c Hayden b Symonds 40
M. N. Samuels c Hogg b Harvey 27
†R. D. Jacobs run out 13
R. O. Hurley run out. 0
V. C. Drakes lbw b Gillespie 9
M. Dillon not out. 0
C. D. Collymore run out 2

B 4, l-b 4, w 8, n-b 1 17

1/20 (2) 2/33 (3) 3/77 (4) 4/146 (5) 5/174 (1) 6/197 (6) 7/201 (8) 8/217 (7) 9/217 (9) 10/219 (11) (45.3 overs) 219

Bowling: Lee 8–1–30–1; Gillespie 8–0–30–2; McGrath 7–0–21–1; Hogg 9–1–41–0; Harvey 9.3–0–58–2; Symonds 4–0–31–1.

Umpires: R. E. Koertzen (South Africa) and E. A. Nicholls.
Third umpire: B. R. Doctrove. Referee: R. S. Madugalle (Sri Lanka).

†WEST INDIES v AUSTRALIA

Fifth One-Day International

At Port-of-Spain, May 25, 2003. West Indies won by 39 runs. Toss: West Indies. One-day international debut: D. E. Bernard.

At last, after 21 matches spanning four and a half months and ten different opponents, Australia lost a one-day international. The defeat also ended a run of 11 one-day victories over West Indies, whose last win had come over four years previously. Lara admitted after the match that his team remained in awe of Australia's ultra-professional approach. On this occasion, though, their preparation and professionalism were little help after Lara and Hinds put on 178 for the second wicket and provided the perfect foundation for a late assault which lifted West Indies to a commanding 290. For once, there was no response from Australia, and although all their batsmen made starts, only Symonds passed 50. Lara could not resist crowning the moment by bowling the final over.

Man of the Match: B. C. Lara.

West Indies

C. H. Gayle lbw b Lee 5
W. W. Hinds c Gilchrist b Bichel. 79
*B. C. Lara c Gilchrist b Bichel 80
R. R. Sarwan c Gilchrist b Lee. 32
M. N. Samuels lbw b Lee 42
R. L. Powell not out 20
†R. D. Jacobs not out 7

B 1, l-b 11, w 11, n-b 2. 25

1/5 (1) 2/183 (2) 3/192 (3) 4/263 (4) 5/264 (5) (5 wkts, 50 overs) 290

R. O. Hurley, D. E. Bernard, M. Dillon and C. D. Collymore did not bat.

Bowling: McGrath 10–1–46–0; Lee 10–2–56–3; Harvey 10–1–46–0; Bichel 10–0–67–2; Hauritz 6–0–38–0; Clarke 4–0–25–0.

Australia

†A. C. Gilchrist c Hinds b Collymore . . 11
J. P. Maher c Bernard b Collymore 21
*R. T. Ponting c Hinds b Dillon 10
A. Symonds b Samuels 77
M. J. Clarke c Lara b Dillon 39
M. G. Bevan c Samuels b Dillon 31
I. J. Harvey b Gayle 2
A. J. Bichel b Samuels 7
B. Lee c Gayle b Sarwan. 6
N. M. Hauritz not out 20
G. D. McGrath not out 3

L-b 15, w 8, n-b 1. 24

1/18 (1) 2/43 (2) 3/57 (3) 4/149 (5) 5/182 (4) 6/189 (7) 7/202 (8) 8/219 (9) 9/229 (6) (9 wkts, 50 overs) 251

Bowling: Collymore 8–0–25–2; Dillon 9–0–40–3; Hinds 1–0–3–0; Powell 1–0–8–0; Gayle 10–0–44–1; Sarwan 10–0–53–1; Samuels 10–0–48–2; Lara 1–0–15–0.

Umpires: R. E. Koertzen (South Africa) and B. R. Doctrove.
Third umpire: E. A. Nicholls. Referee: R. S. Madugalle (Sri Lanka).

†WEST INDIES v AUSTRALIA

Sixth One-Day International

At St George's, Grenada, May 30, 2003. West Indies won by three wickets. Toss: Australia.

As if to prove Trinidad was no fluke, West Indies did it again in Grenada in the most exciting game of the series. Despite several days' rest and relaxation before the game, the Australians still appeared jaded as they entered the last few days of a gruelling eight-month playing schedule. (To make matters worse, they arrived in Grenada without several items of kit, including bats, pads, shoes and sunglasses, stolen by a Trinidadian taxi driver.) But while their weariness may have contributed to some reckless batting – and they were making do without both Bevan and McGrath – nothing could detract from a brilliantly crafted undefeated 125 from Hinds which carried West Indies to a rousing triumph. Hinds, a late inclusion in the one-day squad after Chanderpaul withdrew with a broken finger, remained unflappable, despite taking 13 overs to reach double figures. He eventually exploded into an array of punishing strokes – including six sixes – and proved the difference between the teams.

Man of the Match: W. W. Hinds.

Australia

†A. C. Gilchrist c Lara b Samuels	64
M. L. Hayden c Hinds b Collymore	29
*R. T. Ponting run out	2
A. Symonds c Lara b Sarwan	16
D. S. Lehmann c and b Gayle	43
J. P. Maher c and b Gayle	19
G. B. Hogg c Gayle b Samuels	0
A. J. Bichel c Lara b Gayle	41
B. Lee c Powell b Collymore	14
N. M. Hauritz run out	2
J. N. Gillespie not out	1
L-b 8, w 10, n-b 3	21
1/90 (2) 2/105 (3) 3/105 (1) 4/149 (4) 5/177 (5) 6/178 (7) 7/193 (6) 8/243 (8) 9/250 (9) 10/252 (10) (50 overs)	252

Bowling: Collymore 10–1–46–2; Dillon 8–0–52–0; Samuels 10–1–39–2; Drakes 6–0–21–0; Bernard 2–0–17–0; Sarwan 4–0–32–1; Gayle 10–1–37–3.

West Indies

C. H. Gayle c Gilchrist b Lee	18
W. W. Hinds not out	125
*B. C. Lara c and b Symonds	15
R. R. Sarwan c Symonds b Lee	50
M. N. Samuels b Lee	0
R. L. Powell c and b Lehmann	1
†R. D. Jacobs c Maher b Bichel	8
D. E. Bernard lbw b Gillespie	7
V. C. Drakes not out	0
B 4, l-b 15, w 8, n-b 3	30
1/23 (1) 2/67 (3) 3/181 (4) 4/181 (5) 5/193 (6) 6/213 (7) 7/244 (8) (7 wkts, 48.4 overs)	254

M. Dillon and C. D. Collymore did not bat.

Bowling: Lee 9.4–2–50–3; Gillespie 9–2–33–1; Bichel 10–0–52–1; Symonds 4–0–19–1; Hogg 10–1–35–0; Hauritz 5–0–35–0; Lehmann 1–0–11–1.

Umpires: R. E. Koertzen (South Africa) and E. A. Nicholls.
Third umpire: B. E. W. Morgan. Referee: R. S. Madugalle (Sri Lanka).

†WEST INDIES v AUSTRALIA

Seventh One-Day International

At St George's, Grenada, June 1, 2003. West Indies won by nine wickets. Toss: Australia.

Although this last game contained some fine individual performances, its true significance was to highlight how tedious such prolonged bilateral series could be. Australia, confirmed victors eight days and three matches earlier, struggled to stir their competitive juices, before a nimble-footed hundred from Lehmann – his second on this ground – saw them to a respectable 247. But

50 RUNS AND FIVE WICKETS IN A ONE-DAY INTERNATIONAL

I. V. A. Richards (119 and 5-41) West Indies v New Zealand at Dunedin	1986-87
K. Srikkanth (70 and 5-27) India v New Zealand at Visakhapatnam	1988-89
M. E. Waugh (57 and 5-24) Australia v West Indies at Melbourne	1992-93
L. Klusener (54 and 6-49) South Africa v Sri Lanka at Lahore	1997-98
Abdul Razzaq (70* and 5-48) Pakistan v India at Hobart	1999-2000
G. A. Hick (80 and 5-33) England v Zimbabwe at Harare	1999-2000
Shahid Afridi (61 and 5-40) Pakistan v England at Lahore	2000-01
S. C. Ganguly (71* and 5-34) India v Zimbabwe at Kanpur	2000-01
S. B. Styris (63* and 6-25) New Zealand v West Indies at Port-of-Spain	2002
R. C. Irani (53 and 5-26) England v India at The Oval	2002
C. H. Gayle (60 and 5-46) West Indies v Australia at St George's	**2002-03**

when Gayle, after taking five wickets for the first time, teamed up with Hinds to steer West Indies to their first century opening partnership against Australia in limited-overs internationals, Ponting's side were all but going through the motions. Hinds blasted another unbeaten hundred, and Lara ensured proceedings ended with more of a bang than a whimper by crashing Lehmann for three successive sixes. Afterwards, he and Ponting, who injured his hip while batting, suggested these series should be capped at five matches to prevent the meaningless, soulless cricket that blighted the end of Australia's tour.

Man of the Match: C. H. Gayle. *Man of the Series:* W. W. Hinds.

Australia

†A. C. Gilchrist b Samuels	5
M. L. Hayden c Bernard b Dillon	8
*R. T. Ponting not out	2
D. S. Lehmann c Samuels b Gayle	107
A. Symonds c Hinds b Gayle	48
M. J. Clarke st Jacobs b Gayle	1
I. J. Harvey run out	4
G. B. Hogg b Gayle	53
B. Lee c Samuels b Gayle	4
J. N. Gillespie not out	0
L-b 3, w 10, n-b 2	15
1/17 (2) 2/18 (1) 3/125 (5) 4/127 (6) 5/133 (7) 6/228 (4) 7/246 (9) 8/246 (8) — (8 wkts, 50 overs)	247

G. D. McGrath did not bat.

Ponting, on 1, retired hurt at 23 and resumed at 246-8.

Bowling: Samuels 7–0–39–1; Dillon 10–0–46–1; Collymore 9–0–39–0; Sarwan 4–1–22–0; Drakes 10–0–52–0; Gayle 10–0–46–5.

West Indies

C. H. Gayle b Symonds	60
W. W. Hinds not out	103
*B. C. Lara not out	75
L-b 2, w 7, n-b 2	11
1/116 (1) — (1 wkt, 43.3 overs)	249

R. R. Sarwan, M. N. Samuels, R. L. Powell, †R. D. Jacobs, D. E. Bernard, V. C. Drakes, M. Dillon and C. D. Collymore did not bat.

Bowling: Lee 6–0–36–0; Gillespie 10–1–41–0; McGrath 6–0–29–0; Symonds 5–0–36–1; Hogg 10–0–47–0; Harvey 5–0–31–0; Lehmann 1.3–0–27–0.

Umpires: R. E. Koertzen (South Africa) and B. R. Doctrove.
Third umpire: E. A. Nicholls. Referee: R. S. Madugalle (Sri Lanka).

THE NEW ZEALANDERS IN SRI LANKA, 2003

BRIAN MURGATROYD

This pair of dull draws offered a compelling case for the abolition of two-Test series. Neither side wanted to risk going one down with one to play by losing the opening match, leading to a safety-first approach by both teams. Then, nervous about the prospect of throwing away the series through one bad slip, Sri Lanka clammed up during the Second Test. The net result was two dire matches. As an advertisement for Test cricket, the series was a disaster.

In fairness, New Zealand and their captain, Stephen Fleming, tried hard to fashion a positive result in the second game, and rain in both matches did not help. But it was clear that if Sri Lanka continued to play so negatively they would win few Tests and even fewer admirers.

In bare statistical terms, the batting contributions of the recently-appointed Sri Lankan captain, Hashan Tillekeratne, could not be questioned – only Fleming, with 376 in the series, scored more heavily. But the way he gathered his 237 runs proved an ideal antidote to insomnia, which was sad because every so often he unveiled a delicious drive that showed he had the shots if only he chose to use them. With the ball, Muttiah Muralitharan was once again the leading wicket-taker in the series. He sent down more than a third of Sri Lanka's deliveries and took 13 of their 32 wickets.

For New Zealand, a drawn series was an excellent result. They were without key players in Chris Cairns, who chose to play county cricket instead, and Nathan Astle, recuperating from a knee operation. On top of that, they played no first-class warm-up games, and by the time most of their players were coming to terms with the sapping heat and high humidity the series was over.

NEW ZEALAND TOURING PARTY

S. P. Fleming (Wellington) (*captain*), S. E. Bond (Canterbury), I. G. Butler (Northern Districts), R. G. Hart (Northern Districts), M. J. Horne (Auckland), R. A. Jones (Wellington), J. D. P. Oram (Central Districts), M. H. Richardson (Auckland), M. S. Sinclair (Central Districts), S. B. Styris (Northern Districts), D. R. Tuffey (Northern Districts), D. L. Vettori (Northern Districts), L. Vincent (Auckland), P. J. Wiseman (Canterbury).

A. R. Adams (Auckland), C. L. Cairns (Canterbury), C. Z. Harris (Canterbury), B. B. McCullum (Otago), K. D. Mills (Auckland) and C. J. Nevin (Wellington) replaced Butler, Hart, Horne, Jones, Richardson and Sinclair for the one-day series.

Coach: D. J. Aberhart. *Manager:* J. J. Crowe.

NEW ZEALAND TOUR RESULTS

Test matches – Played 2: Drawn 2.
Draws – Sri Lanka (2).
One-day internationals – Played 5: Won 3, Lost 2. Wins – Pakistan (2), Sri Lanka. Losses – Sri Lanka, Pakistan.
Non-first-class matches – Played 2: Drawn 2. *Draws* – Sri Lanka Board President's XI, Sri Lanka A.

Note: Matches in this section which were not first-class are signified by a dagger.

†At Maitland Place, Colombo (NCC), April 19, 20, 2003. **Drawn.** Toss: Sri Lanka Board President's XI. **Sri Lanka Board President's XI 258** (D. P. M. D. Jayawardene 108, R. S. Kaluwitharana 55; D. R. Tuffey 5-54); **New Zealanders 396** (M. H. Richardson 106, S. P. Fleming 69, S. B. Styris 64).

†At Maitland Place, Colombo (NCC), April 21, 22, 2003. **Drawn.** Toss: Sri Lanka A. **Sri Lanka A 284** (U. D. U. Chandana 55); **New Zealanders 283** (M. H. Richardson 93; U. D. U. Chandana 5-98).

SRI LANKA v NEW ZEALAND

First Test Match

At P. Saravanamuttu Stadium, Colombo, April 25, 26, 27, 28, 29, 2003. Drawn. Toss: New Zealand. Test debuts: K. S. Lokuarachchi, R. A. P. Nissanka.

This otherwise dreary match will be remembered for the amazing tenacity of Stephen Fleming. In ferocious heat, he showed great stamina and unwavering concentration – and almost single-handedly earned his side a draw. Fleming was on the field for all but the first 44 minutes of the match; in total, he defied the Sri Lankan attack for 956 minutes, making an unbeaten 274 in the first innings and 69 not out in the second. It was the highest aggregate by a New Zealander in a Test, passing the 329 Martin Crowe made at Wellington in 1991, also against Sri Lanka. But the numbers did not tell the whole story. The first-innings 274 saved the game psychologically as well as statistically by calming his team-mates' fears that they would be torn apart by an attack boasting four spinners, including Muralitharan.

Those fears were never realised, partly because the pitch turned out to be a little too good, partly because more than 40 overs were lost to rain and bad light, and partly because Tillekeratne, Sri Lanka's new Test captain, was more concerned with avoiding defeat than pursuing victory. After New Zealand had declared at 515 for seven in their first innings, Sri Lanka reached 424 for six by the close of the fourth day. Tillekeratne could have piled on the pressure by declaring behind and letting his spinners loose on a still uncertain batting line-up. Instead, he chose to let Sri Lanka's innings drift aimlessly into the fifth day. As it turned out, Muralitharan created enough trouble on the last afternoon to leave spectators wondering what might have been.

One the first day, New Zealand's main focus was on not collapsing in a heap. They ground their way to 207 for two in 93 overs as Richardson and Fleming absorbed the pressure exerted by Sri Lanka. Both men relied on their front pad as much as their bat, but they stayed together until Richardson was bowled, just seven overs before the close, by Vaas's first delivery with the second new ball. Despite straining a hamstring and batting with a runner, Richardson made 85 and added 172 with Fleming.

New Zealand were noticeably more positive on the second morning. Fleming was helped by businesslike innings from Styris and Oram – and several dropped catches – and added 308 before declaring with Martin Crowe's New Zealand record 299 apparently at his mercy. He had batted 653 minutes for his 274, faced 476 balls, hit 28 fours and a six, and had long since left behind his own previous best Test score of 174.

But his decision to put the team ahead of any individual landmarks looked justified when Tuffey removed Atapattu with his fifth ball. And although Jayasuriya and Sangakkara compiled attractive fifties on the next day, New Zealand still had a chance of enforcing the follow-on after both fell in quick succession, Sangakkara to a wild slog. Those hopes receded in the face of obduracy from Jayawardene, back in the side after a terrible World Cup, and Tillekeratne, and then a dazzling 76 from Kaluwitharana, who in his first Test in more than two years, hit 14 fours in 90 balls, mainly by exploiting New Zealand's belief they could get him out cutting. This raised the possibility of a Sri Lankan declaration but Tillekeratne's approach suggested it was not in his mind in any way. In 53 overs on the fourth day he eked out 55 runs, and by the time he was bowled off the inside edge by Bond on the last morning he had batted for 456 minutes for 144.

But there was still no declaration. Sri Lanka's misjudgment in not declaring was thrown into sharp focus when New Zealand's middle order then failed to master the spin threat on a fifth-day pitch. But any hint of a crisis was averted by Fleming's continued diligence. Opening in place of Richardson (unable to bat until No. 7 after spending most of the Sri Lanka innings off the field), he batted for more than five hours and was, again, unbeaten. But it was not just a one-man effort, and New Zealand also gained satisfaction from their unexpected choice, Oram, whose often surprising bounce at medium-pace had put the Sri Lankans under consistent pressure.

Close of play: First day, New Zealand 207-2 (Fleming 112, Sinclair 4); Second day, Sri Lanka 4-1 (Jayasuriya 2, Vaas 2); Third day, Sri Lanka 267-4 (Jayawardene 58, Tillekeratne 71); Fourth day, Sri Lanka 424-6 (Tillekeratne 126, Dharmasena 19).

New Zealand

First innings		Second innings	
M. H. Richardson b Vaas	85	(7) not out	6
M. J. Horne c Dharmasena b Nissanka	4	(1) lbw b Lokuarachchi	42
*S. P. Fleming not out	274	(2) not out	69
M. S. Sinclair c Sangakkara b Dharmasena	17	(3) c sub (T. M. Dilshan) b Muralitharan	1
S. B. Styris c Vaas b Dharmasena	63	(4) lbw b Lokuarachchi	16
J. D. P. Oram c Lokuarachchi b Muralitharan	33	(5) c Kaluwitharana b Muralitharan	19
†R. G. Hart c Jayawardene b Muralitharan	9	(6) c Sangakkara b Muralitharan	0
D. L. Vettori lbw b Dharmasena	7		
P. J. Wiseman not out	16		
B 2, l-b 3, w 1, n-b 1	7	B 2, l-b 5, n-b 1	8
1/20 (2) 2/192 (1) 3/235 (4) 4/392 (5) 5/471 (6) 6/486 (7) 7/499 (8)	(7 wkts dec.) 515	1/71 (1) 2/76 (3) 3/108 (4) 4/133 (5) 5/133 (6)	(5 wkts dec.) 161

D. R. Tuffey and S. E. Bond did not bat.

Bowling: *First Innings*—Vaas 29–8–73–1; Nissanka 23–9–53–1; Dharmasena 40–7–132–3; Muralitharan 58.5–16–140–2; Lokuarachchi 18–2–83–0; Jayasuriya 6–0–29–0. *Second Innings*—Vaas 7–2–27–0; Nissanka 6–1–18–0; Muralitharan 30–15–41–3; Lokuarachchi 19–2–47–2; Dharmasena 16–7–21–0.

Sri Lanka

M. S. Atapattu lbw b Tuffey	0
S. T. Jayasuriya b Bond	50
W. P. U. J. C. Vaas c Fleming b Bond	4
K. C. Sangakkara c Oram b Wiseman	67
D. P. M. D. Jayawardene c Hart b Oram	58
*H. P. Tillekeratne b Bond	144
†R. S. Kaluwitharana c Sinclair b Wiseman	76
H. D. P. K. Dharmasena lbw b Vettori	31
K. S. Lokuarachchi not out	28
R. A. P. Nissanka lbw b Vettori	0
M. Muralitharan lbw b Vettori	0
L-b 21, w 1, n-b 3	25
1/0 (1) 2/11 (3) 3/114 (2) 4/134 (4) 5/267 (5) 6/374 (7) 7/444 (6) 8/483 (8) 9/483 (10) 10/483 (11)	483

Bowling: Tuffey 17–5–54–1; Bond 28–6–97–3; Oram 30–13–62–1; Vettori 33–8–94–3; Wiseman 41–13–127–2; Styris 3–0–28–0.

Umpires: D. J. Harper (Australia) and S. J. A. Taufel (Australia).
Third umpire: T. H. Wijewardene. Referee: G. R. Viswanath (India).

SRI LANKA v NEW ZEALAND

Second Test Match

At Kandy, May 3, 4, 5, 6, 7, 2003. Drawn. Toss: New Zealand.

Sri Lanka's crushingly negative approach on the last day condemned a rain-affected match to a draw, just when it seemed that a positive result – or at least a thrilling finish – was possible. The stalemate left many spectators bewildered and disappointed, and kept the series tied at 0–0.

After Sri Lanka grabbed six wickets before lunch on the last day, New Zealand were left precariously placed, just 151 ahead, with seven wickets down. But instead of attacking after the interval, Tillekeratne posted three fielders on the boundary. As a result, Hart and Wiseman were able to survive largely untroubled for 28 overs, and New Zealand extended their innings until tea before finally being dismissed. Even then, Sri Lanka's task of scoring 191 in 38 to win the series was stiff but by no means impossible: their side was full of talented strokemakers, the pitch was still sound and Vettori was only half-fit. After Jayasuriya blazed two early fours it looked like the chase was on, but when he was deceived by a slower ball and miscued to mid-on, the shutters came down. The good-sized crowd that had filtered in, hoping for some excitement, drifted away again.

The match had begun on a flat note too. No play was possible until mid-afternoon on the second day after heavy rain during the build-up made parts of the outfield into a bog, calling into question the wisdom of staging internationals at a rainy time of year. New Zealand then made a disastrous start, slumping to 11 for three as Vaas and the strapping and promising Nissanka (deputising in this series for the injured Dilhara Fernando) exploited early movement. New Zealand recovered, with Oram hitting a patient and assured maiden Test fifty. Vettori continued the good work. Against an increasingly frustrated attack, he hung in while 68 runs were added for the last two wickets, and had reached 55 when he was run out – in painful circumstances. Trying to pinch a quick single he clattered into Atapattu, who had charged in to make the run-out. The net result was a sprained ankle for Vettori, concussion for Atapattu and the end of New Zealand's innings of 305.

Jayasuriya launched the Sri Lanka reply in positive style but when he fell, edging Wiseman's off-spin to slip for 82, the innings slipped into a self-induced coma. Only Kaluwitharana and Vaas tried to play positively. By the time Tillekeratne was last out, missing an attempted cut late on the fourth day to become the persevering Wiseman's fourth victim, Sri Lanka were still seven runs behind.

At that point, with less than four sessions to play, the match seemed to have nowhere to go, but New Zealand tried their best to set up a run-chase, with Richardson scoring his third half-century in three completed innings. The plan came unstuck thanks to some excellent pre-lunch bowling by Sri Lanka which suggested a different sort of finish. However, their subsequent negative tactics ruined their own chances. Muralitharan took his 450th Test wicket when he dismissed Tuffey, and in the process completed his 37th five-wicket haul in Tests, passing Sir Richard Hadlee's record of 36.

Close of play: First day, No play; Second day, New Zealand 75-4 (Richardson 32, Oram 0); Third day, Sri Lanka 94-2 (Jayasuriya 53, Tillekeratne 10); Fourth day, New Zealand 92-1 (Richardson 51, Fleming 10).

"They awarded five penalty runs for tampering and, with no suitably aged ball to hand, replaced it with a new one."

Cricket in Bangladesh, page 1428.

New Zealand

First innings		Second innings	
M. H. Richardson c Sangakkara b Lokuarachchi	55	c Kaluwitharana b Nissanka	55
M. J. Horne c Kaluwitharana b Vaas	1	c Tillekeratne b Muralitharan	27
*S. P. Fleming lbw b Nissanka	0	c Kaluwitharana b Dharmasena	33
M. S. Sinclair lbw b Vaas	3	st Kaluwitharana b Muralitharan	0
S. B. Styris c Tillekeratne b Muralitharan	32	c Muralitharan b Vaas	1
J. D. P. Oram c Kaluwitharana b Lokuarachchi	74	lbw b Muralitharan	16
†R. G. Hart lbw b Muralitharan	31	c Kaluwitharana b Vaas	12
D. L. Vettori run out	55	b Muralitharan	0
P. J. Wiseman b Muralitharan	7	c Tillekeratne b Vaas	29
D. R. Tuffey c Jayawardene b Nissanka	15	c Jayasuriya b Muralitharan	1
S. E. Bond not out	10	not out	1
B 3, l-b 7, w 5, n-b 7	22	B 1, l-b 6, n-b 1	8
1/6 (2) 2/7 (3) 3/11 (4) 4/71 (5) 5/109 (1) 6/189 (7) 7/222 (6) 8/237 (9) 9/271 (10) 10/305 (8)	305	1/65 (2) 2/109 (1) 3/110 (4) 4/115 (5) 5/136 (3) 6/139 (6) 7/139 (8) 8/179 (7) 9/182 (10) 10/183 (9)	183

Bowling: *First Innings*—Vaas 22–8–48–2; Nissanka 16.5–5–41–2; Muralitharan 34–10–90–3; Jayasuriya 8–0–24–0; Dharmasena 15–5–40–0; Lokuarachchi 16–5–52–2. *Second Innings*—Vaas 15.3–6–31–3; Nissanka 10–4–18–1; Dharmasena 12–2–32–1; Lokuarachchi 14–3–26–0; Muralitharan 39–18–49–5; Jayasuriya 7–0–20–0.

Sri Lanka

First innings		Second innings	
K. C. Sangakkara c Hart b Tuffey	10	not out	27
S. T. Jayasuriya c Fleming b Wiseman	82	c Richardson b Bond	9
D. P. M. D. Jayawardene c Hart b Oram	15	not out	32
*H. P. Tillekeratne b Wiseman	93		
†R. S. Kaluwitharana c Tuffey b Bond	20		
H. D. P. K. Dharmasena c Fleming b Wiseman	5		
K. S. Lokuarachchi c Tuffey b Oram	20		
W. P. U. J. C. Vaas b Oram	22		
M. S. Atapattu retired hurt	2		
R. A. P. Nissanka b Wiseman	6		
M. Muralitharan not out	2		
B 6, l-b 11, n-b 4	21	L-b 4	4
1/30 (1) 2/69 (3) 3/126 (2) 4/169 (5) 5/189 (6) 6/234 (7) 7/264 (8) 8/285 (10) 9/298 (4)	298	1/14 (2)	(1 wkt) 72

In the first innings Atapattu retired hurt at 267.

Bowling: *First Innings*—Tuffey 20–6–45–1; Bond 25–6–78–1; Oram 20–2–54–3; Wiseman 32.3–4–104–4. *Second Innings*—Tuffey 9–3–18–0; Bond 6–1–19–1; Wiseman 9–4–20–0; Vettori 6–1–11–0.

Umpires: D. J. Harper (Australia) and S. J. A. Taufel (Australia).
Third umpire: P. T. Manuel. Referee: G. R. Viswanath (India).

New Zealand's matches against Pakistan and Sri Lanka in the Bank AlFalah Cup (May 11–23) appear on pages 1297–1304.

THE SOUTH AFRICANS IN BANGLADESH, 2003

A trip to Bangladesh, on the face of it an uninspiring prospect for the South Africans, took on major significance following their disastrous World Cup campaign. It offered a chance to lick wounds, regain confidence and knock into shape a new-look squad of inexperienced players, many of whom had not been traumatised by the debacle.

The fallout from South Africa's failure to reach the second stage of the tournament they hosted was dramatic. Graeme Smith, who had not even been selected in the original World Cup squad, replaced Shaun Pollock as captain and thus became the third-youngest Test captain of all time, at 22 years 82 days, behind the Nawab of Pataudi, junior, and Waqar Younis, whose exact age is in dispute. Allan Donald and Jonty Rhodes announced their retirement from the international stage and Lance Klusener was left out of the touring party. In addition, Jacques Kallis missed the tour on compassionate grounds due to his father's ill health.

The hosts were also starting over. Bangladesh's desperate World Cup campaign, in which they lost to both Canada and Kenya, also meant that change was inevitable. The captain Khaled Masud made way for Khaled Mahmud, and coach Mohsin Kamal for Sarwar Imran, a caretaker until Dav Whatmore could take over. With the terrifying prospect of a first Test tour to Australia on the horizon, they were in desperate need of improvement.

Predictably, the two Test matches highlighted the massive gulf between the two sides. South Africa's gifted young batsmen set records in the First Test at Chittagong – Jacques Rudolph, finally making a long-overdue Test debut, struck an unbeaten 222 and shared a stand of 429 with Boeta Dippenaar – and their bowlers showed tremendous stamina and discipline in the Second, which they ultimately won at a canter.

SOUTH AFRICAN TOURING PARTY

G. C. Smith (Western Province) (*captain*), P. R. Adams (Western Province), M. V. Boucher (Border), A. C. Dawson (Western Province), H. H. Dippenaar (Free State), H. H. Gibbs (Western Province), A. J. Hall (Easterns), N. D. McKenzie (Northerns), M. Ntini (Border), R. J. Peterson (Eastern Province), S. M. Pollock (KwaZulu Natal), J. A. Rudolph (Northerns), C. M. Willoughby (Western Province).

J. H. Kallis (Western Province), withdrew from the tour to spend time with his ailing father.

Coach: E. O. Simons. *Manager:* Goolam Rajah.

SOUTH AFRICAN TOUR RESULTS

Test matches – Played 2: Won 2.
First-class matches – Played 2: Won 2.
Wins – Bangladesh (2).
One-day internationals – Played 5: Won 3, Lost 1, No result 1. *Wins* – Bangladesh (2), India. *Loss* – India. *No result* – India.
Other non-first-class match – Won v Bangladesh Cricket Board XI.

Note: Matches in this section which were not first-class are signified by a dagger.

†At Bangladesh Krira Shikkha Protisthan Ground, Savar, April 11, 2003. **South Africans won by 127 runs. South Africans 294-6** (50 overs) (J. A. Rudolph 55 retired out, H. H. Dippenaar 52 retired out); **Bangladesh Cricket Board XI 167** (39.3 overs) (M. Ntini 4-49).

South Africa's matches against India and Bangladesh in the TVS Cup (April 13–21) appear on pages 1290–1296.

BANGLADESH v SOUTH AFRICA

First Test Match

At Chittagong, April 24, 25, 26, 27, 2003. South Africa won by an innings and 60 runs. Toss: Bangladesh. Test debuts: Mohammad Salim; A. C. Dawson, J. A. Rudolph, C. M. Willoughby.

Fifteen months earlier, he was selected to make his Test debut at Sydney, and then left out at the last minute because of South Africa's racial quota system. Two months before that, he played in the Test against India denied official status. Now, Jacques Rudolph finally made his Test debut – and he made quite an impression. Rudolph stroked a brilliant 222 not out and shared in an unbroken third-wicket partnership with Dippenaar of 429 that effectively ended the game as a contest on the second day. South Africa lost only two wickets in storming to an innings victory.

YOUNGEST TEST CAPTAINS

Years	*Days*			
21	77	Nawab of Pataudi, jun.	India v West Indies at Bridgetown	1961-62
22	15†	Waqar Younis	Pakistan v Zimbabwe at Karachi	1993-94
22	**82**	**G. C. Smith**	**South Africa v Bangladesh at Chittagong**	**2003**
22	194	I. D. Craig	Australia v South Africa at Johannesburg	1957-58
22	260	Javed Miandad	Pakistan v Australia at Karachi	1979-80
22	306	M. Bisset	South Africa v England at Johannesburg	1898-99
23	144	M. P. Bowden	England v South Africa at Cape Town	1888-89
23	169	S. R. Tendulkar	India v Australia at Delhi	1996-97
23	217	G. C. Grant	West Indies v Australia at Adelaide	1930-31
23	292	Hon. Ivo Bligh	England v Australia at Melbourne	1882-83
23	319	S. P. Fleming	New Zealand v England at Christchurch	1996-97
23	354	A. D. R. Campbell	Zimbabwe v Sri Lanka at Colombo	1996-97

† *Age in dispute.*

Aside from Rudolph, South Africa gave debuts to Alan Dawson, the 33-year-old seamer, and the left-arm swing bowler Charl Willoughby. Bangladesh introduced a new wicket-keeper in Mohammad Salim. Two of their more experienced players, the obdurate Javed Omar and the more aggressive Habibul Bashar, batted with determination on the first morning to go to lunch at 78 for one. But two hours later the scoreboard told a more familiar tale: Bangladesh were all out for 173, undone by a resurgent Adams, whose five for 37 included the usual mix of long-hops, full tosses and unplayable deliveries.

The early wickets of Smith and Gibbs gave Bangladesh some encouragement, but those were to be their only rewards as they toiled in intense heat for a further 123 overs while 429 runs were scored. In that time, Rudolph and Dippenaar became the first South African pair to bat through an entire day, taking the score from 84 to 364. Rudolph displayed a controlled aggression born of waiting his turn. He survived a stumping chance on 98 off Mohammad Ashraful; unperturbed, he stroked the next delivery through the covers to become the second South African after Andrew Hudson to make a century on Test debut.

Like Dippenaar, Rudolph is slightly built. He stands upright at the crease and has quick feet, sound balance and a superb eye – all of which served him well on a wearing pitch as he used sweet timing to pierce the field almost at will. Dippenaar, whose second hundred in Tests came two and a half years and 13 Tests after his first, was content to play second fiddle throughout the record-breaking stand. When the pair went past 368 they eclipsed the previous highest for any wicket by South Africa, set by Smith and Gibbs against Pakistan just four months earlier.

A flurry of hitting on the third morning saw the score advance by 106 in 19 overs. Rudolph was struck behind the ear by a bouncer from Mashrafe bin Mortaza, but was soon on his feet and brought up a memorable double-century with a sweetly struck cover-drive and a nudge for one. The declaration came shortly before lunch, leaving the sixth-largest partnership in Test history unbroken and Bangladesh needing 297 to avoid yet another innings defeat. Rudolph had also become the fifth player to score a double-century on Test debut. In all, he struck 29 fours and two sixes from 383 balls, in 521 minutes.

There was much to admire in Bangladesh's second innings. Once again Omar and Bashar showed resilience in a partnership of 131 in 39 overs. Bashar's aggression was refreshing, if a little ill-conceived at times, and he carved out his second half-century of the match before edging a drive off Pollock. Omar lasted four hours and 20 minutes before he was caught behind for 71. Adams then struck twice before the close of the third day to leave Bangladesh on 185 for five.

A brief cameo from Ashraful and a bruising half-hour for Akram Khan offered little hope on the fourth morning; Adams completed his first ten-wicket haul in Tests, and South Africa wrapped up the match within the first hour.

Man of the Match: J. A. Rudolph.

Close of play: First day, South Africa 84-2 (Rudolph 15, Dippenaar 16); Second day, South Africa 364-2 (Rudolph 170, Dippenaar 131); Third day, Bangladesh 185-5 (Mohammad Ashraful 12).

Bangladesh

Javed Omar lbw b Dawson	28	– c Boucher b Ntini	71
Mehrab Hossain c Boucher b Pollock	6	– lbw b Pollock	5
Habibul Bashar c Gibbs b Dawson	60	– c Boucher b Pollock	75
Mohammad Ashraful c Dippenaar b Adams	12	– c Smith b Willoughby	28
Akram Khan c Rudolph b Adams	13	– (7) c Dippenaar b Adams	16
Alok Kapali c Boucher b Adams	0	– (5) c Boucher b Adams	7
*Khaled Mahmud b Ntini	6	– (8) st Boucher b Smith	1
†Mohammad Salim not out	16	– (6) lbw b Adams	0
Tapash Baisya c Dippenaar b Ntini	4	– (10) not out	0
Enamul Haque b Adams	1	– (11) c and b Adams	11
Mashrafe bin Mortaza st Boucher b Adams	20	– (9) c Pollock b Adams	0
W 1, n-b 6	7	B 5, l-b 10, w 6, n-b 2	23
1/14 (2) 2/97 (1) 3/100 (3) 4/124 (5) 5/124 (6) 6/126 (4) 7/136 (7) 8/144 (9) 9/147 (10) 10/173 (11)	173	1/7 (2) 2/138 (3) 3/173 (1) 4/183 (5) 5/185 (6) 6/213 (4) 7/224 (7) 8/224 (9) 9/224 (8) 10/237 (11)	237

Bowling: *First Innings*—Pollock 11–2–22–1; Ntini 17–4–45–2; Dawson 13–3–37–2; Willoughby 12–5–32–0; Adams 12.3–3–37–5. *Second Innings*—Pollock 13–9–12–2; Willoughby 18–6–47–1; Ntini 16–4–37–1; Dawson 12–4–48–0; Adams 18.4–5–69–5; Smith 5–2–9–1.

South Africa

*G. C. Smith c Mohammad Salim b Tapash Baisya	16	H. H. Dippenaar not out	177
H. H. Gibbs c Mohammad Salim b Mashrafe bin Mortaza	17	B 9, l-b 6, w 2, n-b 21	38
J. A. Rudolph not out	222	1/38 (1) 2/41 (2) (2 wkts dec.)	470

N. D. McKenzie, †M. V. Boucher, S. M. Pollock, P. R. Adams, A. C. Dawson, C. M. Willoughby and M. Ntini did not bat.

Bowling: Mashrafe bin Mortaza 24–3–108–1; Khaled Mahmud 17–5–56–0; Tapash Baisya 23–8–70–1; Enamul Haque 33–10–81–0; Alok Kapali 18.5–2–71–0; Mohammad Ashraful 8–0–31–0; Habibul Bashar 7–0–38–0.

Umpires: B. F. Bowden (New Zealand) and S. A. Bucknor (West Indies).
Third umpire: Mahbubur Rahman. Referee: C. H. Lloyd (West Indies).

BANGLADESH v SOUTH AFRICA

Second Test Match

At Dhaka, May 1, 2, 3, 4, 2003. South Africa won by an innings and 18 runs. Toss: South Africa. Test debut: R. J. Peterson.

Encouraged by Adams's success in Chittagong, South Africa brought in a second spinner, giving a debut to the left-armer, Robin Peterson. Bangladesh swapped slow left-armers, recalling Mohammad Rafiq for Enamul Haque. The match followed a similar pattern to the first, and only rain on the second day prevented a three-day finish. Yet despite the lopsided result, Bangladesh had much to encourage them. They reduced South Africa to 63 for four on the first day, and with better support for Rafiq might have caused deeper embarrassment.

Rudolph and Boucher had the task of rebuilding South Africa's first innings, and they did so cautiously on a pitch that turned sharply from the outset. Rudolph took up where he left off in the First Test and stroked the ball around the ground with ease. Boucher, South Africa's best player of spin, used his feet to good effect in hitting down the ground as the pair added 107 for the fifth wicket. A confident Rafiq bowled most of the afternoon and was seldom dominated.

Some typically positive batting by Pollock helped nurse a nervous Peterson, and a relieved South Africa, to 264 for six at the close. Peterson was left to fend for himself after just two balls on the second day, however, when Pollock was trapped in front by Mashrafe bin Mortaza. He shouldered the responsibility with aplomb, cutting and driving his way to a half-century, and dragging the South African innings to respectability at 330. Rafiq finished with six for 77, the best Test figures by a Bangladeshi.

In reply, and not for the first time in their dismal Test history, the Bangladesh batsmen capitulated without resolve or resistance. Pollock and Ntini exploited the moist conditions to strike four times between them in the opening stages. The run-out of Alok Kapali with his side in dire straits at 62 for four typified the desperation. Only the captain Khaled Mahmud stood firm as Peterson and Dawson swept the tail away in eight overs. South Africa's dominance was illustrated by the fact that their First Test hero Adams bowled just one over.

The run-out of the out-of-touch Mehrab Hossain in the 22nd over of Bangladesh's follow-on hinted at further panic and frustration: five of the top six got sound starts only to squander their hard work. Akram Khan batted like a man on the verge of retirement as he smashed 23 from 23 balls, including three successive boundaries off Ntini, and Habibul Bashar battled for two hours in making 33. When Mahmud departed two overs later for a duck, the capitulation looked complete. But Kapali and Mohammad Salim applied themselves bravely as the South African bowlers showed signs of wilting in the heat, and by the close Bangladesh needed just 24 to make South Africa bat again.

The task proved too much and, with rain threatening, Pollock removed Salim and Mortaza in the third over of the day to consign Bangladesh to yet another innings defeat. There was just enough evidence to suggest that all was not totally lost for Bangladesh, but for a new-look South African team, under a youthful but bullishly confident captain, the series was an ideal work-out ahead of a gruelling three-month tour of England.

Man of the Match: Mohammad Rafiq. *Man of the Series:* J. A. Rudolph.

Close of play: First day, South Africa 264-6 (Pollock 41, Peterson 15); Second day, Bangladesh 4-0 (Javed Omar 3, Mehrab Hossain 0); Third day, Bangladesh 204-8 (Mohammad Salim 24, Tapash Baisya 8).

South Africa

*G. C. Smith c Mohammad Ashraful b Tapash Baisya	15
H. H. Gibbs c Tapash Baisya b Mohammad Rafiq	21
J. A. Rudolph st Mohammad Salim b Mohammad Ashraful	71
H. H. Dippenaar c Mehrab Hossain b Mohammad Rafiq	1
N. D. McKenzie lbw b Mohammad Rafiq	7
†M. V. Boucher b Mohammad Rafiq	71
S. M. Pollock lbw b Mashrafe bin Mortaza	41
R. J. Peterson c Akram Khan b Mohammad Ashraful	61
A. C. Dawson c Mohammad Salim b Mohammad Rafiq	10
P. R. Adams b Mohammad Rafiq	9
M. Ntini not out	0
B 6, l-b 6, w 1, n-b 5, p 5	23
1/30 (1) 2/49 (2) 3/51 (4) 4/63 (5) 5/170 (3) 6/219 (6) 7/264 (7) 8/294 (9) 9/330 (8) 10/330 (10)	330

Bowling: Tapash Baisya 19–5–67–1; Mashrafe bin Mortaza 20–3–53–1; Khaled Mahmud 14–6–36–0; Mohammad Rafiq 37.2–7–77–6; Alok Kapali 11–2–33–0; Mohammad Ashraful 10–0–42–2; Mehrab Hossain 2–0–5–0.

Bangladesh

First innings		Second innings	
Javed Omar c sub (A. J. Hall) b Ntini	11	c Pollock b Adams	27
Mehrab Hossain c Smith b Pollock	8	run out	14
Habibul Bashar lbw b Pollock	14	c Boucher b Peterson	33
Mohammad Ashraful c Pollock b Ntini	15	c Pollock b Peterson	23
Akram Khan c Boucher b Ntini	13	c Rudolph b Ntini	23
Alok Kapali run out	1	c Ntini b Dawson	23
*Khaled Mahmud not out	20	c sub (A. J. Hall) b Peterson	0
†Mohammad Salim c Boucher b Peterson	7	c Smith b Pollock	26
Mohammad Rafiq c Pollock b Dawson	0	c Boucher b Adams	18
Tapash Baisya b Dawson	4	not out	8
Mashrafe bin Mortaza c Dippenaar b Peterson	1	b Pollock	4
L-b 4, w 1, n-b 3	8	B 5, w 2, n-b 4	11
1/22 (2) 2/22 (1) 3/37 (3) 4/53 (5) 5/62 (6) 6/66 (4) 7/73 (8) 8/77 (9) 9/85 (10) 10/102 (11)	102	1/46 (2) 2/46 (1) 3/93 (4) 4/119 (5) 5/131 (3) 6/139 (7) 7/163 (6) 8/190 (9) 9/206 (8) 10/210 (11)	210

Bowling: *First Innings*—Pollock 8–3–21–2; Ntini 11–4–32–3; Dawson 7–2–20–2; Peterson 8.5–1–22–2; Adams 1–0–3–0. *Second Innings*—Pollock 8–1–21–2; Ntini 12–2–37–1; Peterson 27–13–46–3; Dawson 10–5–12–1; Adams 19–3–70–2; Smith 7–0–19–0.

Umpires: B. F. Bowden (New Zealand) and S. A. Bucknor (West Indies).
Third umpire: A. F. M. Akhtaruddin. Referee: C. H. Lloyd (West Indies).

THE SRI LANKANS IN THE WEST INDIES, 2003

FAZEER MOHAMMED

In keeping with the trend of recent years, West Indies finished the Caribbean season on a high note. Though the three-match limited-overs series ended in defeat, and the First Test was a soggy draw, the decisive Second Test was won in emphatic style. However, local celebrations were tempered by the painful memory of the past three seasons, when bright performances in the final home Test had been followed by gloomy, even disastrous, foreign campaigns.

The turnover of players during a protracted season was rapid, with 20 tried altogether, but Brian Lara's insistence on injecting more young talent eventually paid off. The most significant and encouraging improvement was in fast bowling: from a cupboard generally regarded as bare, inspired guess-work by Lara produced Fidel Edwards, a 21-year-old fast-medium bowler who had missed the whole domestic season, first injured, then ignored by the Barbados selectors. On the evidence of a few net sessions, Edwards was selected for the Second Test in Jamaica – his second first-class match – and the gamble came off. His slingy pace won him five for 36 on the first day, the third-best debut figures by a West Indian. A second fast bowler, Jerome Taylor, a lithe Jamaican who turned 19 during the First Test in St Lucia, took fewer wickets, but was hailed as a special talent by Courtney Walsh.

Lara rekindled his love affair with Sri Lanka's bowlers

The young prospects were joined by a rejuvenated face from the past. Four years after his only Test, Corey Collymore finally got another chance. Although he had lost much of his raw speed after a series of back injuries, he made a mockery of his tag as a one-day specialist, and his 14 wickets included a devastating seven for 57 in the second innings at Sabina Park, which set up the series win.

Lara made sure the victory was achieved in style, with a belligerent and unbeaten 80, to add to a double-century – his fifth in Tests – in the first game. It marked the rekindling of a love affair with Sri Lanka's bowlers. He now averaged 123.37 in his last five Tests against them, and although he never completely dominated Muttiah Muralitharan, his positive attitude made sure the opposition were never allowed to feel comfortable. Clearly enjoying his second stint as captain, he revelled in the status of idol and father figure.

Sri Lanka were too easily cowed by the aggression of confident opponents. Several players who regularly shine in the comfort of home conditions were virtually anonymous, not least the Test captain, Hashan Tillekeratne, who scored only 33 Test runs and was indecision personified in the field, with last-minute switches of bowlers and frequent confabs.

Marvan Atapattu compiled a fluent hundred on the opening day of the series but, like his team-mates, seemed uneasy on a Sabina Park pitch encouraging the faster bowlers. Prabath Nissanka made the most of that assistance with five first-innings wickets, yet the unhealthy over-reliance on Muralitharan, and to a lesser extent on Chaminda Vaas, persisted. Lacking confidence and depth, the Sri Lankans were in the end dominated by a West Indies team toughened by the earlier visit of Australia and eager to show the benefits of that experience to an impatient public.

SRI LANKAN TOURING PARTY

H. P. Tillekeratne (Nondescripts) (*captain*), M. S. Atapattu (Sinhalese), H. D. P. K. Dharmasena (Bloomfield), T. M. Dilshan (Bloomfield), K. A. D. M. Fernando (Sebastianites), S. T. Jayasuriya (Bloomfield), D. P. M. D. Jayawardene (Sinhalese), R. S. Kaluwitharana (Colts), K. S. Lokuarachchi (Bloomfield), M. T. T. Mirando (Nondescripts), M. Muralitharan (Tamil Union), H. G. D. Nayanakantha (Bloomfield), R. A. P. Nissanka (Bloomfield), T. T. Samaraweera (Sinhalese), K. C. Sangakkara (Nondescripts), W. P. U. J. C. Vaas (Colts).

U. D. U. Chandana (Tamil Union) and M. N. Nawaz (Nondescripts) were in the party for the one-day series when Atapattu led the side; for the Tests they were replaced by Mirando, Samaraweera and Tillekeratne.

Coach: L. R. D. Mendis. *Manager:* Air Commodore A. Jayasekera.

SRI LANKAN TOUR RESULTS

Test matches – Played 2: Lost 1, Drawn 1.
First-class matches – Played 3: Lost 1, Drawn 2.
Loss – West Indies.
Draws – West Indies, West Indian Cricket Board President's XI.
One-day internationals – Played 3: Won 2, Lost 1.
Other non-first-class match – Win v Shell Cricket Academy Invitational XI.

Note: Matches in this section which were not first-class are signified by a dagger.

†At St George's, Grenada, June 4, 2003. **Sri Lankans won by 115 runs.** Toss: Sri Lankans. **Sri Lankans 243-7** (50 overs) (M. S. Atapattu 99); **Shell Cricket Academy Invitational XI 128-9** (50 overs).

Muralitharan's figures were 7–5–5–3.

†WEST INDIES v SRI LANKA

First One-Day International

At Bridgetown, June 7, 2003. Sri Lanka won by 55 runs. Toss: West Indies.

After three consecutive victories at the end of their one-day series against Australia, West Indies were blown away by an opening burst from Vaas and Nissanka, who reduced West Indies to 19 for four in swinging conditions. In pursuit of a modest 202, Lara's unbeaten 64 was a lone effort and his team fell embarrassingly short as Muralitharan took three for 17 and stifled attempts at a late revival. Sri Lanka had also found scoring difficult after losing Jayasuriya in the first over, and needed an unusually subdued fifty from Kaluwitharana to reach respectability.

Man of the Match: M. Muralitharan.

Sri Lanka

S. T. Jayasuriya c Jacobs b Dillon	0	M. Muralitharan c Samuels b Collymore	3
†R. S. Kaluwitharana run out	54	R. A. P. Nissanka not out	7
*M. S. Atapattu c and b Samuels	22	H. G. D. Nayanakantha run out	1
K. C. Sangakkara c Sarwan b Bernard	15		
D. P. M. D. Jayawardene c Dillon b Hinds	8	W 11, n-b 3	14
T. M. Dilshan b Drakes	27	1/0 (1) 2/46 (3) 3/83 (4) (48.4 overs)	201
H. D. P. K. Dharmasena c Jacobs b Dillon	40	4/106 (5) 5/112 (2) 6/171 (6) 7/186 (8)	
W. P. U. J. C. Vaas b Dillon	10	8/192 (7) 9/193 (9) 10/201 (11)	

Bowling: Dillon 9.4–1–39–3; Collymore 9–0–44–1; Samuels 10–0–31–1; Drakes 10–0–43–1; Bernard 2–0–11–1; Hinds 6–0–17–1; Gayle 2–0–16–0.

West Indies

C. H. Gayle c Kaluwitharana b Vaas	0	V. C. Drakes run out	4
W. W. Hinds b Nissanka	0	M. Dillon c Atapattu b Muralitharan	2
R. L. Powell lbw b Vaas	5	C. D. Collymore lbw b Dilshan	3
R. R. Sarwan c Sangakkara b Nissanka	8		
*B. C. Lara not out	64	B 1, l-b 1, w 5, n-b 10	17
M. N. Samuels c Kaluwitharana b Nayanakantha	29	1/2 (2) 2/4 (1) 3/15 (3) (41 overs)	146
†R. D. Jacobs c Jayasuriya b Muralitharan	14	4/19 (4) 5/73 (6) 6/105 (7) 7/106 (8) 8/118 (9)	
D. E. Bernard b Muralitharan	0	9/121 (10) 10/146 (11)	

Bowling: Vaas 6–2–16–2; Nissanka 6–1–27–2; Nayanakantha 7–1–30–1; Dharmasena 8–1–31–0; Muralitharan 7–2–17–3; Jayasuriya 2–0–9–0; Dilshan 5–0–14–1.

Umpires: B. F. Bowden (New Zealand) and B. R. Doctrove.
Third umpire: E. A. Nicholls. Referee: Wasim Raja (Pakistan).

†WEST INDIES v SRI LANKA

Second One-Day International

At Bridgetown, June 8, 2003. Sri Lanka won by four wickets. Toss: West Indies.

What should have been a cruise for West Indies degenerated into chaos. Sri Lanka were chasing 313, the highest-ever total in a one-day international at Bridgetown, but a belligerent 89 off 71 balls from Chandana put the pressure back on West Indies. In the final overs, their bowlers buckled under the strain, their fielding grew ragged and Sri Lanka sneaked a series-clinching win with three balls to spare. West Indies' 312 for four had looked more than enough in light of the low-scoring match the day before. Gayle hit 94, and Lara first ticked along, then exploded, reaching 116 as the last 11 overs produced 136.

Man of the Match: U. D. U. Chandana.

West Indies

C. H. Gayle run out	94	R. L. Powell not out	9
W. W. Hinds lbw b Vaas	10	L-b 3, w 15, n-b 6	24
*B. C. Lara c Jayasuriya b Nissanka	116		
R. R. Sarwan run out	3	1/30 (2) 2/167 (1) (4 wkts, 50 overs)	312
M. N. Samuels not out	56	3/174 (4) 4/283 (3)	

†R. D. Jacobs, R. O. Hurley, V. C. Drakes, M. Dillon and C. D. Collymore did not bat.

Bowling: Vaas 10–4–33–1; Nissanka 10–0–67–1; Dharmasena 8–0–54–0; Muralitharan 10–1–53–0; Jayasuriya 6–0–51–0; Chandana 4–0–40–0; Dilshan 2–0–11–0.

Sri Lanka

†R. S. Kaluwitharana run out	34	H. D. P. K. Dharmasena not out	3
S. T. Jayasuriya c Drakes b Samuels	41		
*M. S. Atapattu run out	47	L-b 5, w 12, n-b 6	23
K. C. Sangakkara c Hinds b Drakes	31		
U. D. U. Chandana c Powell b Collymore	89	1/71 (2) 2/78 (1) (6 wkts, 49.3 overs)	313
D. P. M. D. Jayawardene c Lara b Drakes	32	3/153 (3) 4/192 (4)	
T. M. Dilshan not out	13	5/293 (5) 6/301 (6)	

W. P. U. J. C. Vaas, M. Muralitharan and R. A. P. Nissanka did not bat.

Bowling: Dillon 10–0–66–0; Collymore 9.3–0–51–1; Samuels 10–0–50–1; Hurley 5–0–29–0; Gayle 5–0–40–0; Drakes 7–1–49–2; Sarwan 1–0–5–0; Hinds 2–0–18–0.

Umpires: B. F. Bowden (New Zealand) and E. A. Nicholls.
Third umpire: B. R. Doctrove. Referee: Wasim Raja (Pakistan).

†WEST INDIES v SRI LANKA

Third One-Day International

At St Vincent, June 11, 2003. West Indies won by six wickets (D/L method). Toss: West Indies. One-day international debut: J. E. Taylor.

As in the Tests and one-dayers against Australia, West Indies finally won only when the series was already gone. Samuels topped and tailed Sri Lanka's innings with agile run-outs and Jerome Taylor, a slightly built 18-year-old with a rhythmic, fluent action, impressed on debut. On a sluggish pitch, Collymore's experience in limited-overs matches brought a deserved three for 28 against impatient batsmen. Jayawardene was the exception, his 51 occupying nearly 28 overs before he became Collymore's third wicket. In reply, Lara failed for the first time in the series, and Gayle scratched 21 in 75 balls, but Samuels's effortless big hitting made sure West Indies remained on course to reach their adjusted target of 160 off 42 overs, the result of two rain breaks.

Man of the Match: M. N. Samuels. *Man of the Series:* M. N. Samuels.

Sri Lanka

S. T. Jayasuriya run out	8	W. P. U. J. C. Vaas run out	6
†R. S. Kaluwitharana c Lara b Collymore	14	M. Muralitharan b Gayle	4
*M. S. Atapattu c Hurley b Taylor	25	H. G. D. Nayanakantha not out	2
K. C. Sangakkara c Lara b Hurley	11	L-b 4, w 11, n-b 1	16
U. D. U. Chandana lbw b Taylor	33		
D. P. M. D. Jayawardene b Collymore	51	1/10 (1) 2/28 (2) 3/55 (4) (50 overs)	191
T. M. Dilshan c and b Samuels	0	4/63 (3) 5/130 (5) 6/134 (7)	
H. D. P. K. Dharmasena c Samuels b Collymore	21	7/176 (8) 8/184 (6)	
		9/185 (9) 10/191 (10)	

Bowling: D. B. Powell 9–0–37–0; Collymore 10–0–28–3; Hurley 10–1–25–1; Taylor 10–0–39–2; Gayle 6–0–29–1; Samuels 5–0–29–1.

West Indies

C. H. Gayle b Chandana	21	R. L. Powell not out	16
W. W. Hinds c Dilshan b Vaas	19		
*B. C. Lara c Nayanakantha b Dharmasena	14	L-b 4, w 10, n-b 6	20
R. R. Sarwan c Jayasuriya b Muralitharan	25	1/36 (2) 2/54 (3) (4 wkts, 36.5 overs)	160
M. N. Samuels not out	45	3/81 (1) 4/126 (4)	

†R. D. Jacobs, R. O. Hurley, D. B. Powell, C. D. Collymore and J. E. Taylor did not bat.

Bowling: Vaas 8–1–25–1; Nayanakantha 3.5–0–27–0; Muralitharan 9–1–26–1; Dharmasena 7–0–27–1; Chandana 4–0–25–1; Dilshan 1–0–6–0; Jayasuriya 4–0–20–0.

Umpires: B. F. Bowden (New Zealand) and B. R. Doctrove.
Third umpire: E. A. Nicholls. Referee: Wasim Raja (Pakistan).

At St Vincent, June 14, 15, 16, 2003. **Drawn.** Toss: Sri Lankans. **Sri Lankans 299** (M. S. Atapattu 59) **and 66-1; West Indies Cricket Board President's XI 296** (D. Ganga 54, R. O. Hinds 83).

WEST INDIES v SRI LANKA

First Test Match

At Gros Islet, St Lucia, June 20, 21, 22, 23, 24, 2003. Drawn. Toss: Sri Lanka. Test debut: J. E. Taylor.

The wisdom of scheduling international cricket at the start of the Caribbean rainy season was again brought into question by the loss of more than half the third day and all of the fourth to the weather. The rain further dampened the spectators' already lukewarm response to St Lucia's first Test match. The president of the West Indies Cricket Board, Reverend Wes Hall, compared it with trying to play cricket in the English winter.

Despite being located in what is considered the driest part of the island, the new Beausejour Stadium – never more than half full – did not escape the showers for long, and a torrential downpour on the third afternoon left the ground waterlogged. Though the clouds lifted early on the fourth morning, it remained too soft underfoot for any play to be possible, which was a major blow to celebrations scheduled to mark the 75th anniversary of West Indies' first Test. Only a handful of fans watched the modest ceremony, at which relatives of the pioneering 1928 touring team to England were presented with a mounted photograph of the side.

Before the match was condemned to its watery grave, Atapattu batted serenely through the opening day to score the first hundred at the Caribbean's eighth Test venue. On the second morning, his dismissal for 118 by Hinds's part-time seamers triggered a collapse: four wickets fell for 22 runs, the other three to Collymore, who had lost pace but gained an out-swinger since his only previous Test four years earlier. On a placid pitch, Sri Lanka went on to make 354, although the painfully slow progress of their last three would not have impressed any St Lucians watching Test cricket for the first time.

However, the fans' patience was eventually rewarded. In reply, West Indies plundered 161 off 33 overs before the close, as Lara and Hinds belted anything remotely off line. They extended their partnership to 174 on the third morning, until Hinds was left stranded by his captain's error of judgment and run out for 113. Shortly afterwards, the controversial dismissal of Sarwan sparked another furious argument in the interminable technology debate. Had umpire Bowden been allowed to consult the third official, Sarwan's pull – which hit the ground and then the ankle of Sangakkara at short leg before being caught by Atapattu – would have been ruled not out. As it was, Sarwan was sent on his way.

Always mindful of an occasion, Lara hoped he would reach his 21st Test century on the fourth day, which marked 75 years exactly since West Indies' first Test. But the ground failed to dry quickly enough and, though only seven short, he had to wait until the last morning. Having survived a stumping chance off Muralitharan on 94, he duly reached his fifth hundred in as many Tests against Sri Lanka.

In a doomed attempt to put some pressure on the opposition in the last few hours, Lara then stepped up the pace, making a second hundred in two-and-a-half hours and celebrating with a huge six over long-on. However, his dismissal for 209 – after 452 minutes and 360 balls, with 24 fours and a six – stalled the quest for quick runs and delayed the declaration. Muralitharan spun his way to five for 138, his 38th five-wicket innings in 81 Tests. In reply, Atapattu and Jayasuriya comfortably cancelled out West Indies' lead of 123.

Man of the Match: B. C. Lara.

Close of play: First day, Sri Lanka 250-4 (Atapattu 108, Samaraweera 7); Second day, West Indies 161-2 (Hinds 74, Lara 36); Third day, West Indies 272-4 (Lara 93, Samuels 5); Fourth day, No play.

Sri Lanka

M. S. Atapattu c Lara b Hinds	118	– not out	50
S. T. Jayasuriya c Banks b Collymore	8	– not out	72
K. C. Sangakkara lbw b Gayle	56		
D. P. M. D. Jayawardene c Lara b Banks	45		
*H. P. Tillekeratne b Collymore	13		
T. T. Samaraweera c Jacobs b Collymore	11		
†R. S. Kaluwitharana lbw b Collymore	2		
K. S. Lokuarachchi c Lara b Collymore	15		
W. P. U. J. C. Vaas c Jacobs b Gayle	38		
M. Muralitharan lbw b Hinds	14		
R. A. P. Nissanka not out	12		
B 4, l-b 5, w 5, n-b 8	22	B 1, l-b 2, n-b 1	4
1/19 (2) 2/127 (3) 3/195 (4) 4/228 (5) 5/266 (1) 6/269 (7) 7/285 (8) 8/288 (6) 9/326 (10) 10/354 (9)	354		(no wkt) 126

Bowling: *First Innings*—Dillon 29–7–48–0; Collymore 29–5–66–5; Taylor 27–3–97–0; Hinds 11–4–28–2; Banks 33–8–74–1; Gayle 9.2–1–22–2; Samuels 3–0–9–0; Sarwan 2–1–1–0. *Second Innings*—Dillon 5–1–24–0; Collymore 3–0–8–0; Hinds 4–0–25–0; Taylor 6–1–19–0; Banks 10–0–28–0; Samuels 3–1–15–0; Sarwan 3–0–4–0.

West Indies

C. H. Gayle lbw b Muralitharan	27
D. Ganga lbw b Vaas	12
W. W. Hinds run out	113
*B. C. Lara c Kaluwitharana b Nissanka	209
R. R. Sarwan c Atapattu b Muralitharan	7
M. N. Samuels st Kaluwitharana b Muralitharan	8
†R. D. Jacobs lbw b Muralitharan	13
O. A. C. Banks not out	50
M. Dillon c Atapattu b Lokuarachchi	2
C. D. Collymore c and b Muralitharan	0
J. E. Taylor not out	9
B 4, l-b 4, w 2, n-b 17	27
1/18 (2) 2/66 (1) 3/240 (3) 4/262 (5) 5/279 (6) 6/305 (7) 7/441 (4) 8/447 (9) 9/448 (10)	(9 wkts dec.) 477

Bowling: Vaas 39–5–116–1; Nissanka 21.3–1–108–1; Samaraweera 8–0–53–0; Muralitharan 50–10–138–5; Lokuarachchi 20–6–54–1.

Umpires: B. F. Bowden (New Zealand) and D. J. Harper (Australia).
Third umpire: B. R. Doctrove. Referee: Wasim Raja (Pakistan).

WEST INDIES v SRI LANKA

Second Test Match

At Kingston, June 27, 28, 29, 2003. West Indies won by seven wickets. Toss: West Indies. Test debuts: F. H. Edwards; M. T. T. Mirando.

A Sabina Park pitch offering help to the bowlers – a rare sight since the farcical abandoned Test against England in 1997-98 – served as the stage for a spectacular Test debut by Fidel Edwards, and a confirmation of Collymore's quality. Together, they took 15 wickets as ball dominated bat, before a dramatic reversal on the third afternoon, when ultra-aggressive innings by Lara and Sarwan made West Indies' target of 212 – the highest total of the match – look easy.

The 21-year-old Edwards had been selected by Lara on the basis of a few net sessions, a move criticised by some as a reckless gamble. Edwards's performance made it look like inspired genius. No giant at just 5ft 8in, and playing only his second first-class game, he became the seventh West Indian to take five wickets in an innings on debut, carving through Sri Lanka's first effort with a slingy, roundarm action.

After Lara put the Sri Lankans in, Jayawardene became Edwards's first victim, caught by a diving Gayle at second slip, and, having been entrusted with the second new ball, Edwards took the last four wickets for only 16 runs. West Indies dropped four catches, including top-scorer Sangakkara, put down by Taylor in his follow-through on four and finally lbw offering no shot after an obdurate 75. Despite these slips, Sri Lanka still reached only 208.

The skimpy total was soon made to look more competitive by Sri Lanka's bowlers, spearheaded by Nissanka. Playing only his fourth Test, he took five wickets inside 13 overs, a performance that would have been even more impressive had he pounded the ball in less, and let a seaming pitch do the work. Nissanka removed both openers after a deceptive first-wicket partnership of 54, exposing a middle order still heavily reliant on Lara, who was soon trapped on the back foot by Muralitharan's straight ball. Pockets of lower-order resistance then lifted West Indies to within 17, an effort which grew in significance as Taylor – wicketless in the First Test – and Collymore worked through the Sri Lankan top order. On the long second day, 15 wickets had tumbled.

Concerned about leaving his side a target in excess of 250, Lara banked on Collymore on the third morning, and he delivered instantly. First, he bowled Tillekeratne playing across the line then, after a brief flurry from Dharmasena and Vaas, sliced through the rest of the lower order to finish with seven for 57. However, West Indies' task of making 212 still looked tricky, until Lara counter-attacked brilliantly. Continuing his battle with Muralitharan, he cracked his first ball from Murali to the rope for the third innings in a row, but also survived several close lbw appeals. Unperturbed, he continued going for his shots, gambling on inducing disarray. It worked. As boundaries flowed with increasing frequency from both Lara and Sarwan, Tillekeratne's body language betrayed panic. The last 92 runs came in less than 12 overs after tea, though Sarwan fell on the very cusp of victory, trying to end the match with another of the spectacular shots that characterised the 161-run stand with his resurgent captain.

Man of the Match: C. D. Collymore. *Man of the Series:* C. D. Collymore.

Close of play: First day, West Indies 4-0 (Gayle 3, Hinds 1); Second day, Sri Lanka 129-5 (Tillekeratne 2, Dharmasena 9).

Sri Lanka

First innings		Second innings	
M. S. Atapattu c Gayle b Drakes	15	c Jacobs b Taylor	28
S. T. Jayasuriya c Jacobs b Collymore	26	lbw b Collymore	13
K. C. Sangakkara lbw b Edwards	75	c Jacobs b Collymore	12
D. P. M. D. Jayawardene c Gayle b Edwards	10	c Jacobs b Edwards	32
*H. P. Tillekeratne c Lara b Banks	13	(6) b Collymore	7
†R. S. Kaluwitharana c Samuels b Banks	10	(5) b Taylor	23
H. D. P. K. Dharmasena c Samuels b Collymore	6	c Lara b Collymore	20
W. P. U. J. C. Vaas not out	12	c Lara b Collymore	21
M. T. T. Mirando c Lara b Edwards	11	c Lara b Collymore	13
M. Muralitharan b Edwards	0	c Sarwan b Collymore	6
R. A. P. Nissanka c Gayle b Edwards	0	not out	0
B 1, l-b 17, w 2, n-b 10	30	B 4, l-b 6, w 2, n-b 7	19
1/38 (2) 2/48 (1) 3/77 (4) 4/109 (5) 5/129 (6) 6/140 (7) 7/192 (3) 8/204 (9) 9/208 (10) 10/208 (11)	208	1/25 (2) 2/43 (3) 3/80 (1) 4/118 (4) 5/118 (5) 6/138 (6) 7/173 (7) 8/176 (8) 9/184 (10) 10/194 (9)	194

Bowling: *First Innings*—Collymore 15–6–28–2; Taylor 11–1–40–0; Drakes 18–3–54–1; Edwards 15.4–1–36–5; Banks 22–6–31–2; Gayle 4–3–1–0. *Second Innings*—Edwards 15–2–54–1; Collymore 16–2–57–7; Drakes 11–3–29–0; Taylor 10–1–38–2; Banks 2–0–6–0.

West Indies

C. H. Gayle c Sangakkara b Nissanka	31	– lbw b Vaas	0
W. W. Hinds c Kaluwitharana b Nissanka	19	– b Muralitharan	29
R. R. Sarwan b Vaas	31	– c Jayasuriya b Vaas	82
*B. C. Lara lbw b Muralitharan	10	– not out	80
M. N. Samuels c Tillekeratne b Nissanka	14	– not out	0
O. A. C. Banks c Tillekeratne b Nissanka	2		
†R. D. Jacobs lbw b Muralitharan	16		
V. C. Drakes b Muralitharan	30		
J. E. Taylor c Muralitharan b Dharmasena	1		
C. D. Collymore c Sangakkara b Nissanka	13		
F. H. Edwards not out	5		
B 5, l-b 3, w 6, n-b 5	19	B 8, l-b 3, w 4, n-b 6	21
1/54 (1) 2/59 (2) 3/85 (4) 4/107 (3) 5/110 (6) 6/123 (5) 7/162 (7) 8/163 (9) 9/175 (8) 10/191 (10)	191	1/1 (1) 2/50 (2) 3/211 (3) (3 wkts)	212

Bowling: *First Innings*—Vaas 15–4–33–1; Mirando 10–1–36–0; Nissanka 12.3–0–64–5; Muralitharan 11–3–23–3; Dharmasena 5–0–27–1. *Second Innings*—Vaas 12–2–54–2; Mirando 5–0–23–0; Nissanka 8–1–64–0; Muralitharan 15.4–1–48–1; Dharmasena 2–0–12–0.

Umpires: D. B. Hair (Australia) and R. B. Tiffin (Zimbabwe).
Third umpire: E. A. Nicholls. Referee: Wasim Raja (Pakistan).

CEAT CRICKETER OF THE YEAR

Ricky Ponting of Australia was named CEAT International Cricketer of the Year for 2002-03. The CEAT formula awarded him 105 points for his performances in Tests and limited-overs internationals to April 30, 2003. Chris Gayle of West Indies was second with 93 points. Previous winners were Brian Lara (West Indies), Venkatesh Prasad (India), Sanath Jayasuriya (Sri Lanka), Jacques Kallis (South Africa), Sourav Ganguly (India) and Muttiah Muralitharan (Sri Lanka), who won two years running. Ponting was also CEAT Batsman of the Year. Harbhajan Singh and Virender Sehwag of India won the Bowler and Fielder awards respectively. Sachin Tendulkar of India was named CEAT Cricketer of the World Cup. World Cup winners Australia retained the team title.

THE BANGLADESHIS IN AUSTRALIA, 2003

STEVEN LYNCH

On the face of it, Bangladesh's first foray into Australia as a fully fledged Test nation was a disaster: both Tests were lost by an innings, and all three one-day internationals by wide margins. Their one-day performances were indeed disappointing, but some encouraging signs of added application did emerge from the Tests and the warm-up games.

It was evident that the ministrations of Dav Whatmore, the Australian in his first major outing as Bangladesh's coach after parting company with Sri Lanka (whom he coached to World Cup success in 1996), were having some effect. Nerves took hold on the first day of the First Test, when Bangladesh were shot out for 97; apart from that, the batsmen performed above expectations, especially on the first day of the Second Test on what was expected to be a spiteful pitch.

Bangladesh unearthed a potential batting star in the young opener Hannan Sarkar, who collected two wristy, watchful half-centuries in the Second Test at Cairns. He was surely one of the batsmen Steve Waugh had in mind during that match when he said that the Australians had encountered batting in recent Tests – from Pakistan and West Indies – that was worse than Bangladesh's efforts. That said, there was a shortage of runs from the middle order. Habibul Bashar batted well, if in his customary over-adventurous style, but Mohammad Ashraful was one of several slightly-built players who found the tall Australian fast bowlers' bounce hard to negotiate. And the much-touted Alok Kapali, himself a wrist-spinner, could make little of the leg-spin of Stuart MacGill, whose 17 wickets as a stand-in for the banned Shane Warne brought him the Man of the Series award.

The Australians, most of whom had been inactive for two months since their Caribbean tour, were rusty at first. The openers were unusually subdued, but Darren Lehmann and Martin Love took the chance to boost their averages. And then there was Waugh himself: he pushed his Test average back above 50 with an unbeaten century at Darwin, which meant he had scored a hundred against all nine Test opponents, then went one better at Cairns by extending that record to 150 or more against all-comers.

The experiment of playing in Australia's Top End – at Darwin in the Northern Territory and Cairns in far-north Queensland – during their winter was a success from every point of view except attendance. The weather was perfect and the facilities first-class, but local support was disappointing, with the first days of both Tests attracting only around 6,000 spectators. The experiment is to be repeated in July 2004, with Sri Lanka as more bankable visitors, and the Northern Territory government – whose chief minister Clare Martin is a distant relative of the old Australian great Victor Trumper – is hopeful of securing Tests for Darwin in four of the next five winters.

BANGLADESH TOURING PARTY

Khaled Mahmud (Dhaka) (*captain*), Alok Kapali (Sylhet), Al Sahariar (Dhaka), Anwar Hossain Monir (Dhaka), Habibul Bashar (Biman), Hannan Sarkar (Barisal), Javed Omar (Dhaka), Khaled Masud (Rajshahi), Manjurul Islam (Khulna), Mashrafe bin Mortaza (Khulna), Mohammad Ashraful (Dhaka), Mohammad Rafiq (Dhaka), Sanwar Hossain (Barisal), Tapash Baisya (Sylhet), Tareq Aziz (Chittagong).

Hasibul Hussain (Sylhet) and Tushar Imran (Khulna) replaced Manjurul Islam and Tareq Aziz in the squad for the one-day internationals.

Coach: D. F. Whatmore. *Manager:* Latif Khan.

BANGLADESH TOUR RESULTS

Test matches – Played 2: Lost 2.
One-day internationals – Played 3: Lost 3.
Other non-first-class matches – Played 4: Won 3, Lost 1. *Wins* – Commonwealth Bank Cricket Academy, Northern Territory Chief Minister's XI, Queensland Academy of Sport. *Loss* – Queensland Academy of Sport Invitation XI.

Note: Matches in this section which were not first-class are signified with a dagger.

†At Brisbane (Allan Border Field), June 27, 28, 29, 2003. **Queensland Academy of Sport Invitation XI won by 29 runs.** Toss: Bangladeshis. **Queensland Academy of Sport Invitation XI 201** (L. A. Carseldine 92, J. R. Hopes 53) and **176** (D. M. Payne 52; Alok Kapali 4-27); **Bangladeshis 203-9 dec.** (Alok Kapali 55; J. R. Hopes 4-35) and **145**.

In this and the following two matches, each side fielded 12 players, of whom 11 could bat and 11 field.

†At Brisbane (Allan Border Field), July 3, 4, 5, 2003. **Bangladeshis won by two wickets.** Toss: Commonwealth Bank Cricket Academy. **Commonwealth Bank Cricket Academy 258-3 dec.** (M. L. Innes 128*, R. J. G. Lockyear 90) and **203-4 dec.** (A. J. Nye 89*); **Bangladeshis 232-7 dec.** (Javed Omar 59, Habibul Bashar 99) and **232-8** (Mohammad Ashraful 61).

Innes, a left-hander from Victoria, hit 14 fours and two sixes in his century, the day before his 19th birthday.

†At Darwin, July 10, 11, 12, 13, 2003. **Bangladeshis won by two wickets.** Toss: Northern Territory Chief Minister's XI. **Northern Territory Chief Minister's XI 189** (M. J. Clarke 79) and **136**; **Bangladeshis 139** and **187-8**.

Only 171 runs came in the second day's play: Bangladeshis 139 in 79.2 overs, Northern Territory Chief Minister's XI 32 for three in 16 overs.

AUSTRALIA v BANGLADESH

First Test Match

At Darwin, July 18, 19, 20, 2003. Australia won by an innings and 132 runs. Toss: Australia.

The first Test to be played at Darwin's Marrara Oval – the 89th Test venue, and the eighth in Australia – was done and dusted in less than half the scheduled playing time. Bangladesh's fate was sealed on the first day when, overwhelmed by the occasion and the reputation of the opposition, they collapsed to 97 all out on a drop-in pitch (prepared in Melbourne and airlifted to Darwin a month before the match), which proved to be slow and low.

The Bangladesh batsmen struggled most with their shot-selection. Only Javed Omar was beaten by the bounce, but no one other than Mohammad Ashraful, who pulled straight to deep square just before lunch for 23, and Khaled Masud batted for longer than an hour. The Bangladeshis' failure to apply themselves chagrined their coach, Dav Whatmore, who said: "A few players presented their wickets, and that's just the area we're trying to improve." Late on, Khaled Mahmud, the tourists' hard-pressed captain,

STARTING AT THE TOP

Grounds where the first first-class match was also a Test:

Port Elizabeth	South Africa v England	1888-89
The first first-class match in South Africa		
Cape Town	South Africa v England	1888-89
Lucknow (University Ground)	India v Pakistan	1952-53
The only first-class match ever played there		
Dacca (later Dhaka)	Pakistan v India	1954-55
Karachi (National Stadium)	Pakistan v India	1954-55
Lahore (Gaddafi Stadium)	Pakistan v Australia	1959-60
Ahmedabad	India v West Indies	1983-84
Sheikhupura	Pakistan v Zimbabwe	1996-97
Multan	Pakistan v Bangladesh	2001-02
Sharjah	Pakistan v West Indies	2001-02
Darwin	**Australia v Bangladesh**	**2003**

spanked three fours – it was as many as the other ten batsmen managed between them.

The Australians also found scoring difficult, at least until Gilchrist joined Waugh and upped the tempo. By then Lehmann had posted Darwin's first Test century; Waugh's own was just over an hour quicker at 177 minutes, and completed his set against all nine possible Test opponents, matching Gary Kirsten of South Africa.

Bangladesh started their second innings brightly, reaching 70 for the loss of Javed Omar by the second-day close. But, still prone to losing wickets in batches, they collapsed on the third morning as MacGill continued to turn the ball sharply. Alok Kapali completed a pair, courtesy of MacGill's wiles, and only a sensible innings from Al Sahariar – who was singled out for praise by Waugh after the match, then dropped for the next Test – delayed the inevitable. Finally, he skied a return catch to give MacGill his fifth wicket of the innings, and the match was over at 12.41 on the third day. (Play up in the Tropics started at 9.30, so lunch was at 11.30. George Gunn, who insisted on lunching at 1.30 whatever the hours of play, would not have approved.)

Man of the Match: S. R. Waugh. *Attendance:* 13,862.

Close of play: First day, Australia 121-2 (Langer 40, Lehmann 51); Second day, Bangladesh 70-1 (Hannan Sarkar 29, Habibul Bashar 26).

Bangladesh

Hannan Sarkar lbw b McGrath	0	– c Gilchrist b Gillespie	35
Javed Omar c Gilchrist b Gillespie	5	– lbw b McGrath	5
Habibul Bashar b Lee	16	– b MacGill	54
Mohammad Ashraful c MacGill b McGrath	23	– c Gilchrist b Lee	7
Al Sahariar b Lee	0	– c and b MacGill	36
Alok Kapali lbw b MacGill	0	– lbw b MacGill	0
†Khaled Masud lbw b McGrath	11	– c Gilchrist b MacGill	6
*Khaled Mahmud c Gilchrist b MacGill	21	– b Gillespie	5
Mashrafe bin Mortaza c Gilchrist b Gillespie	3	– (10) run out	15
Tapash Baisya not out	2	– (9) lbw b MacGill	4
Manjurul Islam c Langer b Lee	1	– not out	0
B 1, l-b 5, w 6, n-b 3	15	L-b 6, w 2, n-b 3	11
1/4 (1) 2/26 (2) 3/36 (3) 4/39 (5) 5/40 (6) 6/60 (4) 7/87 (7) 8/91 (8) 9/94 (9) 10/97 (11)	97	1/8 (2) 2/89 (1) 3/112 (4) 4/112 (3) 5/112 (6) 6/122 (7) 7/143 (8) 8/152 (9) 9/171 (10) 10/178 (5)	178

Bowling: *First Innings*—McGrath 13–6–20–3; Gillespie 8–1–27–2; Lee 8.2–2–23–3; MacGill 13–4–21–2. *Second Innings*—McGrath 10–0–25–1; Gillespie 16–3–48–2; Lee 12–5–34–1; MacGill 13.1–1–65–5.

Australia

J. L. Langer lbw b Alok Kapali	71
M. L. Hayden b Mashrafe bin Mortaza	11
R. T. Ponting c Javed Omar b Tapash Baisya	10
D. S. Lehmann c Javed Omar b Mashrafe bin Mortaza	110
*S. R. Waugh not out	100
M. L. Love b Mashrafe bin Mortaza	0
†A. C. Gilchrist b Manjurul Islam	43
B. Lee run out	23
J. N. Gillespie not out	16
B 5, l-b 8, w 7, n-b 3	23
1/13 (2) 2/43 (3) 3/184 (1) 4/243 (4) 5/244 (6) 6/313 (7) 7/377 (8) (7 wkts dec.)	407

S. C. G. MacGill and G. D. McGrath did not bat.

Bowling: Manjurul Islam 24–4–78–1; Mashrafe bin Mortaza 23–7–74–3; Tapash Baisya 21.5–4–69–1; Khaled Mahmud 28–2–98–0; Alok Kapali 18–2–65–1; Mohammad Ashraful 2–0–9–0; Habibul Bashar 1–0–1–0.

Umpires: R. E. Koertzen (South Africa) and D. R. Shepherd (England).
Third umpire: S. J. A. Taufel. Referee: M. J. Procter (South Africa).

AUSTRALIA v BANGLADESH

Second Test Match

At Cairns, July 25, 26, 27, 28, 2003. Australia won by an innings and 98 runs. Toss: Australia. Test debut: Anwar Hossain Monir.

Bangladesh put up a spirited performance in Cairns, where the Bundaberg Rum Stadium (formerly Cazaly's Oval) became Test cricket's 90th venue, but they still went down by an innings. Australia thus swept the short series 2–0.

In the lead-up to the match, rain had left question-marks about the quality of the pitch, which looked green and enticing for the Australian fast bowlers. When Waugh won the toss and decided to bowl, most onlookers feared for Bangladesh: a press sweepstake on their likely total returned only two three-figure predictions. But Bangladesh applied themselves well on a surface that played much better than expected. Hannan Sarkar batted beautifully for a wristy 76, including nine fours, before losing concentration after the dismissal of Mohammad Ashraful for the first half of what turned out to be a sorry pair.

Sarkar and Habibul Bashar put on 108 for the second wicket as the Australian bowlers struggled early on: McGrath lacked penetration – he missed the one-day series for an operation on his ankle – while Gillespie and Lee bowled too short to threaten the stumps. Another solid innings from Khaled Masud and a forthright 46 from Sanwar Hossain, who clattered eight fours, including three in succession off Lee, lifted Bangladesh to a competitive 289 for eight by the end of the first day. MacGill narrowly missed a hat-trick when a confident lbw appeal against Tapash Baisya was turned down after he had dismissed Sanwar and Khaled Mahmud with successive balls.

That was as good as it got for Bangladesh. They were all out in 13 balls on the second morning, and although their bowlers started brightly, pitching the new ball up more than the Australians and extracting more from the pitch as a result, the home batsmen proved difficult to shift after Langer carved the impressive Mashrafe bin Mortaza to point early on. Hayden and Ponting both reached fifty, and then Lehmann and Waugh repeated their Darwin centuries: Waugh's was his 32nd in Tests, putting him ahead of Sachin Tendulkar and behind only Sunil Gavaskar's 34.

Lehmann grabbed the honour of becoming the first Test centurion on both Australia's new grounds, and his 177 – his highest Test score – included 105 between tea and the close on the second day. When he was out, Love, after a scratchy start, put a first-ball duck at Darwin behind him and compiled a neat century, his first in Tests. The evocative partnership of Love and Waugh yielded 174, with Waugh giving lots of the strike away as Love's milestone approached. There was also time for Waugh, who hit 17 fours in seven hours at the crease, to stretch his record to a score of 150 or more against all nine Test opponents, and for Sanwar's jerky off-spinning action to be reported as doubtful to the ICC.

Bangladesh again started brightly in their second innings, but three quick wickets just before the close of the third day – including Sarkar to a wild swipe shortly after he had completed another classy fifty – sealed their fate. On the fourth morning MacGill completed his third five-wicket haul in successive innings, while Gillespie finally adjusted his radar, pitched the ball up, and took three wickets in eight balls. Bangladesh duly subsided to their 20th defeat in 21 Test matches.

Man of the Match: S. C. G. MacGill. *Attendance:* 13,279.

Man of the Series: S. C. G. MacGill.

Close of play: First day, Bangladesh 289-8 (Tapash Baisya 21, Mashrafe bin Mortaza 7); Second day, Australia 351-3 (Lehmann 156, Waugh 74); Third day, Bangladesh 106-4 (Sanwar Hossain 6, Alok Kapali 10).

Bangladesh

Hannan Sarkar lbw b MacGill	76	– c Hayden b MacGill	55
Javed Omar c Gilchrist b Lee	26	– lbw b Gillespie	8
Habibul Bashar c and b MacGill	46	– c Langer b Lee	25
Mohammad Ashraful c Gilchrist b Gillespie	0	– c Ponting b MacGill	0
Sanwar Hossain b MacGill	46	– c Ponting b MacGill	16
Alok Kapali c Love b MacGill	5	– c Langer b MacGill	17
†Khaled Masud c Love b Gillespie	44	– lbw b Gillespie	14
*Khaled Mahmud lbw b MacGill	0	– c Lee b MacGill	17
Tapash Baisya c Gilchrist b McGrath	25	– lbw b Gillespie	0
Mashrafe bin Mortaza c Lee b Gillespie	8	– not out	3
Anwar Hossain Monir not out	0	– b Gillespie	4
L-b 8, n-b 11	19	L-b 2, n-b 2	4
1/47 (2) 2/155 (3) 3/156 (4) 4/156 (1) 5/170 (6) 6/230 (5) 7/230 (8) 8/281 (7) 9/295 (10) 10/295 (9)	295	1/12 (2) 2/87 (1) 3/90 (4) 4/90 (3) 5/123 (6) 6/136 (5) 7/156 (7) 8/156 (9) 9/156 (8) 10/163 (11)	163

Bowling: *First Innings*—McGrath 17.1–2–57–1; Gillespie 25–7–57–3; Lee 18–1–88–1; MacGill 24–9–77–5; Waugh 5–3–4–0; Lehmann 3–1–4–0. *Second Innings*—McGrath 15–9–22–0; Gillespie 12.4–3–38–4; MacGill 20–3–56–5; Lee 11–2–45–1.

Australia

J. L. Langer c Javed Omar b Mashrafe bin Mortaza . 1
M. L. Hayden b Sanwar Hossain 50
R. T. Ponting c Mohammad Ashraful b Sanwar Hossain . 59
D. S. Lehmann c Mohammad Ashraful b Tapash Baisya . 177
*S. R. Waugh not out 156
M. L. Love not out. 100
L-b 11, w 1, n-b 1. 13

1/14 (1) 2/105 (2) 3/132 (3) 4/382 (4) (4 wkts dec.) 556

†A. C. Gilchrist, B. Lee, J. N. Gillespie, S. C. G. MacGill and G. D. McGrath did not bat.

Bowling: Mashrafe bin Mortaza 25–7–60–1; Tapash Baisya 26–5–96–1; Anwar Hossain Monir 21–4–95–0; Khaled Mahmud 19–3–75–0; Sanwar Hossain 30–2–128–2; Alok Kapali 14.2–0–69–0; Mohammad Ashraful 4–0–22–0.

Umpires: R. E. Koertzen (South Africa) and D. R. Shepherd (England).
Third umpire: S. J. Davis. Referee: M. J. Procter (South Africa)
(R. G. Archer of Australia deputised when Procter flew home after a family bereavement).

†At Innisfail, July 31, 2003. **Bangladeshis won by four wickets.** Toss: Queensland Academy of Sport. **Queensland Academy of Sport 175-7** (50 overs) (C. A. Philipson 67); **Bangladeshis 176-6** (46.2 overs).

Each side fielded 12 players, of whom 11 could bat and 11 field.

†AUSTRALIA v BANGLADESH

First One-Day International

At Cairns, August 2, 2003. Australia won by eight wickets. Toss: Australia.

Bangladesh failed to carry their improved Test form into the one-day arena, going down to their 35th successive defeat in completed one-day internationals since the 1999 World Cup. This match was all over in little more than half the scheduled playing time, as Australia knocked off the runs required in only 22.3 overs after putting Bangladesh in and bundling them out for 105. Once Hannan Sarkar was run out in the second over, Lee did the early damage, taking four wickets as Bangladesh slumped to 33 for five. He also broke Khaled Masud's thumb with a lifter. Masud was unable to take his place behind the stumps, and Sarkar stepped in for the rest of the series.

Man of the Match: B. Lee. *Attendance:* 8,308.

Bangladesh

Hannan Sarkar run out 1
Al Sahariar c Hayden b Lee. 8
Habibul Bashar c Gilchrist b Lee 0
Alok Kapali b Lee 0
Sanwar Hossain c Gilchrist b Lee 7
Tushar Imran c Ponting b Gillespie 28
†Khaled Masud lbw b Gillespie 18
*Khaled Mahmud not out 25
Mohammad Rafiq c Symonds b Gillespie 3
Hasibul Hussain c Gilchrist b Bichel . . . 6
Mashrafe bin Mortaza c Gilchrist b Bichel . 0
L-b 1, w 5, n-b 3 9

1/2 (1) 2/9 (3) 3/14 (2) 4/19 (4) 5/33 (5) 6/66 (6) 7/76 (7) 8/80 (9) 9/105 (10) 10/105 (11) (34 overs) 105

Bowling: Gillespie 10–3–23–3; Lee 8–1–25–4; Bichel 5–0–24–2; Hogg 10–0–27–0; Symonds 1–0–5–0.

Australia

†A. C. Gilchrist c Khaled Masud b Mashrafe bin Mortaza	18	D. R. Martyn not out	0
M. L. Hayden not out	46	W 6, n-b 8	14
*R. T. Ponting b Mohammad Rafiq	29	1/29 (1) 2/103 (3) (2 wkts, 22.3 overs)	107

D. S. Lehmann, M. G. Bevan, A. Symonds, G. B. Hogg, B. Lee, J. N. Gillespie and A. J. Bichel did not bat.

Bowling: Mashrafe bin Mortaza 7–0–40–1; Hasibul Hussain 5–0–31–0; Khaled Mahmud 5.3–0–29–0; Mohammad Rafiq 5–2–7–1.

Umpires: D. R. Shepherd (England) and S. J. A. Taufel.
Third umpire: P. D. Parker. Referee: G. R. Viswanath (India).

†AUSTRALIA v BANGLADESH

Second One-Day International

At Cairns, August 3, 2003. Australia won by nine wickets. Toss: Bangladesh.

Khaled Mahmud won the toss and decided to bat, but his side were outclassed again, despite a useful start to their innings. This time it was Australia's spinners who applied the brake: Hogg and Lehmann (who was playing in his 100th one-day international) took three wickets apiece with their contrasting slow left-armers. Australia sprinted to their target of 148 in only 89 minutes, at better than seven an over. Martyn, who missed the Tests in order to allow the finger he broke in the World Cup to heal completely, belted 92 not out from only 51 balls; his half-century came from just 22 deliveries.

Man of the Match: D. R. Martyn. *Attendance:* 7,654.

Bangladesh

†Hannan Sarkar c Gilchrist b Harvey	19	Mohammad Rafiq c Bevan b Lehmann	6
Javed Omar c Gilchrist b Bichel	11	Hasibul Hussain not out	0
Habibul Bashar c and b Symonds	31		
Sanwar Hossain c Ponting b Hogg	3	L-b 2, w 16, n-b 2	20
Al Sahariar c Martyn b Hogg	8		
Tushar Imran c Bichel b Hogg	2	1/37 (1) 2/46 (2) 3/52 (4) (45.1 overs)	147
Alok Kapali c Martyn b Lehmann	34	4/84 (5) 5/86 (6) 6/101 (3)	
*Khaled Mahmud run out	11	7/121 (8) 8/133 (9)	
Tapash Baisya c Bevan b Lehmann	2	9/144 (10) 10/147 (7)	

Bowling: Lee 9–2–24–0; Bichel 10–0–29–1; Harvey 7–1–21–1; Hogg 10–0–31–3; Symonds 5–0–24–1; Lehmann 4.1–0–16–3.

Australia

A. Symonds c Sanwar Hossain b Hasibul Hussain	7
M. G. Bevan not out	40
D. R. Martyn not out	92
W 4, n-b 5	9
1/17 (1) (1 wkt, 20.2 overs)	148

*R. T. Ponting, D. S. Lehmann, M. L. Hayden, †A. C. Gilchrist, G. B. Hogg, I. J. Harvey, B. Lee and A. J. Bichel did not bat.

Bowling: Tapash Baisya 5–0–31–0; Hasibul Hussain 6–0–37–1; Khaled Mahmud 3–0–34–0; Mohammad Rafiq 4–0–29–0; Sanwar Hossain 2.2–0–17–0.

Umpires: D. R. Shepherd (England) and S. J. Davis.
Third umpire: P. D. Parker. Referee: G. R. Viswanath (India).

†AUSTRALIA v BANGLADESH

Third One-Day International

At Darwin, August 6, 2003. Australia won by 112 runs. Toss: Australia.

Australia predictably swept the one-day series 3–0 with another convincing victory. Their sizable total owed much to Ponting's 14th one-day century, which peculiarly contained four sixes but only two fours. It was his 12th international century inside 12 months. Ponting and Bevan added 127 for the fifth wicket after Mohammad Rafiq, the left-arm spinner who was puzzlingly overlooked for the Test matches, dismissed both openers, and Martyn – the only Darwin-born player to have represented Australia – managed only a single in front of his home crowd. Australia's total proved more than enough as Bangladesh slumped again. Alok Kapali dropped anchor, grafting to 49, but there was no comeback from 36 for five as the others struggled against Harvey's patent, potent mixture of slower balls and swinging yorkers.

Man of the Match: R. T. Ponting. *Attendance:* 8,398.
Man of the Series: R. T. Ponting.

Australia

†A. C. Gilchrist c Hannan Sarkar b Mohammad Rafiq	31
M. L. Hayden c and b Mohammad Rafiq	42
*R. T. Ponting c Tushar Imran b Tapash Baisya	101
D. R. Martyn b Alok Kapali	1
A. Symonds run out	0
M. G. Bevan b Mashrafe bin Mortaza	57
I. J. Harvey c Mohammad Rafiq b Mashrafe bin Mortaza	5
G. B. Hogg not out	4
L-b 7, w 5, n-b 1	13
1/54 (1) 2/112 (2) 3/113 (4) 4/114 (5) 5/241 (6) 6/247 (3) 7/254 (7) (7 wkts, 50 overs)	254

A. J. Bichel, J. N. Gillespie and B. A. Williams did not bat.

Bowling: Mashrafe bin Mortaza 10–2–41–2; Tapash Baisya 10–0–63–1; Khaled Mahmud 8–0–57–0; Mohammad Rafiq 10–0–31–2; Alok Kapali 10–1–43–1; Sanwar Hossain 2–0–12–0.

Bangladesh

†Hannan Sarkar lbw b Gillespie	1
Javed Omar lbw b Harvey	16
Habibul Bashar c Ponting b Bichel	2
Sanwar Hossain c and b Hogg	27
Tushar Imran run out	1
Mohammad Ashraful b Harvey	4
Alok Kapali c and b Hogg	49
*Khaled Mahmud run out	5
Tapash Baisya c Ponting b Harvey	11
Mohammad Rafiq not out	8
Mashrafe bin Mortaza b Harvey	2
L-b 11, w 5	16
1/4 (1) 2/24 (3) 3/27 (2) 4/30 (5) 5/36 (6) 6/102 (4) 7/119 (8) 8/119 (7) 9/136 (9) 10/142 (11) (47.3 overs)	142

Bowling: Gillespie 10–6–16–1; Williams 10–2–32–0; Bichel 10–1–35–1; Harvey 6.3–0–16–4; Hogg 10–0–32–2; Symonds 1–1–0–0.

Umpires: D. R. Shepherd (England) and S. J. A. Taufel.
Third umpire: S. J. Davis. Referee: G. R. Viswanath (India).

ALLAN BORDER MEDAL

Wicket-keeper/batsman Adam Gilchrist won the Allan Border Medal in January 2003. Team-mates, umpires and journalists voted for the best Australian international player of the past 12 months; Gilchrist polled 88 votes, four ahead of Ricky Ponting. Previous winners were Glenn McGrath, Steve Waugh and Matthew Hayden. Gilchrist was also One-day International Player of the Year, though Ponting beat him to Test Cricketer of the Year. Martin Love of Queensland was State Player of the Year, and another Queenslander, Nathan Hauritz, won the Sir Donald Bradman Young Player of the Year award. Karen Rolton retained her title of Women's International Cricketer of the Year.

THE BANGLADESHIS IN PAKISTAN, 2003

UTPAL SHUVRO

Bangladesh embarked on their first full tour of Pakistan with the aim of playing good cricket. And good cricket they played. Their long losing streak continued – Pakistan won all three Tests and five one-dayers – but the scoreline concealed more than it revealed.

After enduring three years of humiliation since their elevation in 2000, Bangladesh at last actually looked like a proper international side. In the Second Test, they took a first-innings lead for the first time, and it took a great individual performance from fast bowler Shoaib Akhtar to defeat them. And in the Third, at Multan, they were staring a historic maiden victory full in the face. Before the fourth day, their captain, Khaled Mahmud, put the likelihood of a Bangladesh win at 80%. It did not seem over-optimistic. But they were denied by a monumental innings from Inzamam-ul-Haq. Despite that deep disappointment, Bangladesh ended the series – the first in Pakistan since a bomb blast cut short New Zealand's trip in May 2002 – having taken a big step forward.

It was all very different from the three previous Tests between the sides, where Pakistan's narrowest scrape was a victory by an innings and 169 runs. Two factors played a major part in the turnaround. Firstly, Bangladesh had just returned from Australia, their first tour with Dav Whatmore as coach, having exceeded all expectations, and with their self-belief boosted. By contrast, Pakistan were still rebuilding after an unceremonious exit from the first round of the World Cup.

As a result, their side never had a settled look. There were too many experiments, and arguments over selection between captain Rashid Latif and chief selector Aamir Sohail simmered behind the scenes. Perhaps the most controversial choice was Junaid Zia, the 19-year-old son of Tauqir Zia, chairman of the Pakistan board. It was generally believed that there were far more deserving candidates than Junaid. In four one-day internationals he took three moderately expensive wickets.

An even bigger controversy involved Latif himself. He had been given the captaincy in the shake-up after the World Cup but his second stint ended ingloriously. During the Multan Test he claimed a catch having actually dropped the ball. Subsequently, he was banned for the entire one-day series, which – unlike the Tests – Pakistan won at a canter. Soon afterwards, he resigned the captaincy, criticising Sohail, Tauqir Zia and the coach Javed Miandad.

Inzamam stood in for Latif as captain in the one-day games, while Kamran Akmal took over as wicket-keeper. Akmal's arrival from club cricket in Ireland was delayed because the manager of his club had mistakenly locked his passport in a locker before going abroad on holiday.

BANGLADESHI TOURING PARTY

Khaled Mahmud (Dhaka) (*captain*), Habibul Bashar (Biman) (*vice-captain*), Alamgir Kabir (Rajshahi), Alok Kapali (Sylhet), Anwar Hossain Monir (Dhaka), Hannan Sarkar (Barisal), Javed Omar (Dhaka), Khaled Masud (Rajshahi), Manjurul Islam (Khulna), Mashrafe bin Mortaza (Khulna), Mohammad Ashraful (Dhaka), Mohammad Rafiq (Dhaka), Rajin Saleh (Sylhet), Sanwar Hossain (Barisal), Tapash Baisya (Sylhet).

Hasibul Hussain (Sylhet), Mushfiqur Rahman (Rajshahi) and Tushar Imran (Khulna) replaced Anwar Hossain, Javed Omar and Manjurul Islam for the one-day series.

Coach: D. F. Whatmore. *Manager:* Latif Khan. *Physiotherapist:* J. Gloster. *Trainer:* D. Woodford. *Video analyst:* Nasir Ahmed.

BANGLADESHI TOUR RESULTS

Test matches – Played 3: Lost 3.
One-day internationals – Played 5: Lost 5.

TEST MATCH AVERAGES

PAKISTAN – BATTING

	T	*I*	*NO*	*R*	*HS*	*100s*	*50s*	*Avge*	*Ct/St*
Yousuf Youhana	2	3	2	125	64*	0	1	125.00	0
Inzamam-ul-Haq	3	5	2	226	138*	1	0	75.33	1
Yasir Hameed	3	6	1	373	170	2	0	74.60	1
Mohammad Hafeez	3	6	1	214	102*	1	1	42.80	2
†Taufeeq Umar	2	4	0	160	75	0	1	40.00	2
Rashid Latif	3	4	1	104	54*	0	1	34.66	17/1
Shabbir Ahmed	3	4	0	31	13	0	0	7.75	3
Umar Gul	3	4	0	10	5	0	0	2.50	1

Played in two Tests: Danish Kaneria 8, 0; Shoaib Akhtar 1, 15. Played in one Test: Farhan Adil 25, 8; Misbah-ul-Haq 13; †Salman Butt 12, 37 (1 ct); Saqlain Mushtaq 9, 11; Shoaib Malik 0; Yasir Ali 0*, 1*; Younis Khan 34, 0 (2 ct).

† *Left-handed batsman.*

BOWLING

	Style	*O*	*M*	*R*	*W*	*BB*	*5W/i*	*Avge*
Shoaib Akhtar	RF	77.5	18	195	13	6-49	1	15.00
Shabbir Ahmed	RFM	119	23	341	17	5-48	1	20.05
Umar Gul	RFM	117.5	21	375	15	4-58	0	25.00
Danish Kaneria	LB	110	32	280	9	3-58	0	31.11

Also bowled: Mohammad Hafeez (OB) 34–15–61–1; Saqlain Mushtaq (OB) 27.3–5–70–2; Shoaib Malik (OB) 12–4–27–0; Yasir Ali (RFM) 20–5–55–2.

BANGLADESH – BATTING

	T	*I*	*NO*	*R*	*HS*	*100s*	*50s*	*Avge*	*Ct/St*
Habibul Bashar	3	6	0	379	108	1	3	63.16	1
Javed Omar	3	6	0	187	119	1	0	31.16	2
Rajin Saleh	3	6	0	186	60	0	1	31.00	4
Mohammad Ashraful	2	4	0	99	77	0	1	24.75	0
Mashrafe bin Mortaza	2	4	2	43	14	0	0	21.50	2
Hannan Sarkar	3	6	0	100	41	0	0	16.66	1
Alok Kapali	3	6	0	100	46	0	0	16.66	1
Khaled Mahmud	3	6	0	87	28	0	0	14.50	1
Khaled Masud	3	6	0	72	29	0	0	12.00	5/1
Tapash Baisya	2	4	1	29	14*	0	0	9.66	0
†Mohammad Rafiq	3	6	1	44	14	0	0	8.80	1

Played in one Test: Alamgir Kabir 1*, 4; †Manjurul Islam 0*, 5; Sanwar Hossain 15, 3.

† *Left-handed batsman.*

BOWLING

	Style	*O*	*M*	*R*	*W*	*BB*	*5W/i*	*Avge*
Khaled Mahmud	RM	99	26	257	11	4-37	0	23.36
Mohammad Rafiq	SLA	162.4	43	405	17	5-36	2	23.82
Alok Kapali	LB	28.1	4	93	3	3-3	0	31.00
Tapash Baisya	RFM	51	9	176	3	1-34	0	58.66
Mashrafe bin Mortaza	RM	62	14	204	3	3-68	0	68.00

Also bowled: Alamgir Kabir (RM) 20.3–4–100–0; Manjurul Islam (LFM) 34–5–106–2; Mohammad Ashraful (LB) 3–0–16–0; Rajin Saleh (OB) 14–2–34–1; Sanwar Hossain (OB) 14–1–46–0.

Note: Matches in this section which were not first-class are signified by a dagger.

PAKISTAN v BANGLADESH

First Test Match

At Karachi, August 20, 21, 22, 23, 24, 2003. Pakistan won by seven wickets. Toss: Pakistan. Test debuts: Mohammad Hafeez, Shabbir Ahmed, Umar Gul, Yasir Hameed; Rajin Saleh.

Test cricket returned to Pakistan after a gap of nearly 16 months, but the spectators still stayed away. Although the official attendance was not counted, on each of the five days police and security men outnumbered the few hundred spectators. Unusually for a Test involving Bangladesh, those who turned up saw cricket which was generally competitive and sometimes riveting. Bangladesh showed remarkable tenacity, and the eventual seven-wicket margin of their defeat did not reflect the real picture.

At the end of the third day, the underdogs were 105 runs ahead with seven second-innings wickets in hand. Rashid Latif, the captain of Pakistan, admitted it was the worst sleepless night of his career. But on the next day, Bangladesh's inexperience showed. As the lead grew to 193, with five wickets left, an upset was still on the cards. But that soon changed: their last five wickets fell for only 23 runs.

Pakistan were left a victory target of 217, which they achieved without fuss. Along the way, Yasir Hameed, one of four Pakistan debutants, wrote his name in the record books by scoring his second century of the match. It was a pivotal performance.

In the first innings, Yasir saved Pakistan by scoring 170 – almost half the total. And, by taking his side to the brink of victory with 105 in the second, he joined Lawrence Rowe of West Indies (who hit 214 and 100 not out against New Zealand at Kingston in 1971-72) with two centuries on Test debut. On his first-class debut, made on this same ground in 1996-97, Yasir had bagged a pair.

He dedicated his achievements to his late father, a lawyer who used to say that, one day, his son would play for Pakistan and score a century on debut. Even a proud father's dreams hadn't stretched to two. Pencil-thin, and with all the shots in the book, Yasir was particularly strong through the off side on the back foot. Pakistan finally seemed to have found an answer to their long-standing problem at No. 3.

In the first innings, Bangladesh, who had never managed more than 160 in three previous Tests against Pakistan, had surprised their hosts by scoring 288 after being inserted on a green-tinged wicket. But the grass was misleading and the pitch turned out to be perfect for batting. Hannan Sarkar and Habibul Bashar laid a foundation with 114 for the second wicket, Habibul's 71 coming from only 72 balls. The best puller among the Bangladeshi batsmen, he took on Shoaib Akhtar and three of Shoaib's first six balls to him disappeared for four. Habibul continued to play audacious shots but he and Sarkar undid some of their good work by getting out in consecutive overs.

After Yasir helped to give Pakistan a 58-run first-innings lead, Habibul did even better in the second innings. Often referred to as "Mr Fifty" in Bangladesh for his inability to convert half-centuries into hundreds, he became the first Bangladesh batsman to make two Test centuries. The 21 months and 14 Tests since their last hundred had been an abject period for Bangladeshi cricket. After this battling performance, they could hold their heads a little higher.

Man of the Match: Yasir Hameed.

Close of play: First day, Bangladesh 278-9 (Mohammad Rafiq 10, Mashrafe bin Mortaza 4); Second day, Pakistan 301-5 (Misbah-ul-Haq 12, Rashid Latif 27); Third day, Bangladesh 163-3 (Habibul Bashar 82, Rajin Saleh 27); Fourth day, Pakistan 112-1 (Mohammad Hafeez 36, Yasir Hameed 68).

Bangladesh

First innings		Second innings	
Hannan Sarkar c Rashid Latif b Shabbir Ahmed	41	– lbw b Mohammad Hafeez	30
Javed Omar b Umar Gul	1	– lbw b Shoaib Akhtar	13
Habibul Bashar c Mohammad Hafeez b Shoaib Akhtar	71	– c Shabbir Ahmed b Danish Kaneria	108
Sanwar Hossain lbw b Shoaib Akhtar	15	– lbw b Shabbir Ahmed	3
Rajin Saleh c Umar Gul b Danish Kaneria	26	– c Rashid Latif b Shabbir Ahmed	60
Alok Kapali c Shabbir Ahmed b Danish Kaneria	46	– b Danish Kaneria	1
†Khaled Masud lbw b Umar Gul	19	– st Rashid Latif b Danish Kaneria	22
*Khaled Mahmud c Yasir Hameed b Danish Kaneria	14	– lbw b Shabbir Ahmed	0
Tapash Baisya c Taufeeq Umar b Shabbir Ahmed	10	– c Rashid Latif b Shabbir Ahmed	5
Mohammad Rafiq c Rashid Latif b Shabbir Ahmed	14	– lbw b Shabbir Ahmed	6
Mashrafe bin Mortaza not out	9	– not out	10
B 3, l-b 5, n-b 14	22	L-b 11, w 1, n-b 4	16
1/9 (2) 2/123 (1) 3/123 (3) 4/146 (4) 5/176 (5) 6/231 (6) 7/251 (8) 8/252 (7) 9/273 (9) 10/288 (10)	288	1/19 (2) 2/73 (1) 3/83 (4) 4/194 (3) 5/195 (6) 6/251 (5) 7/251 (8) 8/254 (7) 9/262 (9) 10/274 (10)	274

Bowling: *First Innings*—Shoaib Akhtar 18–4–56–2; Umar Gul 20–5–91–2; Shabbir Ahmed 20.3–3–61–3; Danish Kaneria 21–6–58–3; Mohammad Hafeez 7–2–14–0. *Second Innings*—Shoaib Akhtar 25–8–59–1; Umar Gul 19–3–57–0; Danish Kaneria 38–12–85–3; Shabbir Ahmed 18.1–2–48–5; Mohammad Hafeez 14–8–14–1.

Pakistan

Mohammad Hafeez c Javed Omar b Mashrafe bin Mortaza	2	– b Mohammad Rafiq	50
Taufeeq Umar c Javed Omar b Mohammad Rafiq	38	– c Rajin Saleh b Tapash Baisya	4
Yasir Hameed c Mohammad Rafiq b Mashrafe bin Mortaza	170	– b Mohammad Rafiq	105
Inzamam-ul-Haq c Rajin Saleh b Tapash Baisya	0	– not out	35
Yousuf Youhana c and b Rajin Saleh	46	– not out	15
Misbah-ul-Haq lbw b Mashrafe bin Mortaza	13		
*†Rashid Latif not out	54		
Shoaib Akhtar b Mohammad Rafiq	1		
Shabbir Ahmed c Rajin Saleh b Mohammad Rafiq	6		
Danish Kaneria c and b Khaled Mahmud	8		
Umar Gul run out	0		
L-b 4, n-b 4	8	L-b 7, w 1	8
1/5 (1) 2/102 (2) 3/103 (4) 4/234 (5) 5/270 (3) 6/304 (6) 7/307 (8) 8/323 (9) 9/338 (10) 10/346 (11)	346	1/10 (2) 2/144 (1) 3/170 (3)	(3 wkts) 217

Bowling: *First Innings*—Mashrafe bin Mortaza 19–3–68–3; Tapash Baisya 17–6–42–1; Khaled Mahmud 17–2–74–1; Mohammad Rafiq 32–9–76–3; Sanwar Hossain 9–0–23–0; Alok Kapali 18–3–50–0; Rajin Saleh 5–0–9–1. *Second Innings*—Mashrafe bin Mortaza 18–4–62–0; Tapash Baisya 11–1–34–1; Khaled Mahmud 6–3–8–0; Mohammad Rafiq 26–6–61–2; Alok Kapali 2–0–10–0; Rajin Saleh 2–0–12–0; Sanwar Hossain 5–1–23–0.

Umpires: S. A. Bucknor (West Indies) and T. H. Wijewardene (Sri Lanka).
Third umpire: Nadeem Ghauri. Referee: M. J. Procter (South Africa).

PAKISTAN v BANGLADESH

Second Test Match

At Peshawar, August 27, 28, 29, 30, 2003. Pakistan won by nine wickets. Toss: Bangladesh.

For the second Test running, Bangladesh dominated long periods, and even whole days, but left empty-handed. For much of the opening three days, they were on top. They even took a first-innings lead, for the first time in Tests. And, although humbled in the end, it took two devastating spells from a world-class fast bowler to beat them.

Faced with a last chance to prove himself before returning to county cricket, Shoaib Akhtar responded in style. In the first innings, when Bangladesh threatened to reach an imposing total, he skittled the lower order. In the second, with Pakistan contemplating a tricky fourth-innings chase, he sent Bangladesh careering towards 96 all out.

Throughout the match, conditions were extreme. The temperature hovered around 40°C and the humidity soared above 75%. Umpire Russell Tiffin suffered heat exhaustion on the second afternoon and was temporarily replaced by the TV umpire, Asad Rauf, who had never stood in a Test before. Pakistani off-spinner Shoaib Malik also suffered cramp while fielding on the first day. He returned for the second, only to injure his groin. Despite the conditions, spectators came in good numbers and were always in festive mood.

Bangladesh won the toss and made first use of a wicket that looked ideal for batsmen. So it proved. The Bangladeshis threatened to dwarf their best-ever total of 400, made in their inaugural Test, but eventually had to settle for 361. Javed Omar and Habibul Bashar forged a second-wicket partnership of 167 – a national record. Habibul fell three short of becoming the first Bangladeshi to make back-to-back centuries, but another hundred partnership followed his dismissal. Just after lunch on the second day, Bangladesh were 310 for two – the sort of score more often associated with Australia.

Then lightning struck, in the form of Shoaib. Although he had come from glorious August sunshine in England, these conditions were something else, and he clearly struggled to cope with the heat, bowling 11 overs on the first day and two three-over spells on the second morning. Wicketless, he looked anything but threatening. That all changed after lunch.

Following the break, Shoaib found rhythm, extreme pace and reverse swing. He started the demolition job by bowling Javed Omar, whose 119 lasted eight hours 13 minutes, with a full-length thunderbolt. Sixteen balls later, Shoaib had taken five wickets for five runs. Bangladesh, from a commanding 310 for two, were reduced to 320 for eight, and eventually bowled out for 361. Shoaib finished off the innings, and returned to the cool of the dressing-room with figures of six for 50.

Still, it was enough to give Bangladesh a 66-run lead, thanks to a remarkable show of stamina and persistence by their left-arm spinner, Mohammad Rafiq. On the third day, he sent down all but one of the 33 overs Bangladesh bowled from the Pavilion End. His reward for sustained accuracy and a wonderful arm ball was a second five-wicket haul, in only his fifth Test. More spectacularly, Alok Kapali docked the tail by taking Bangladesh's first hat-trick (spread across two overs), just after tea on the third day.

Bangladesh started their second innings hoping to set Pakistan a stiff target. They failed. Shoaib had removed both openers by the fifth over, and there was no respite on the fourth day. Another two victims gave Shoaib his first ten-wicket haul in Tests. When the eighth batsman fell, with the score 75, Bangladesh were flirting with their lowest Test total of 87. Mashrafe bin Mortaza hit Umar Gul for three consecutive fours to avert that danger but Bangladesh still scraped just 96. A target of 163 was never going to test Pakistan, and Mohammad Hafeez made it look easy, with a maiden Test century.

Man of the Match: Shoaib Akhtar.

Close of play: First day, Bangladesh 240-2 (Javed Omar 96, Mohammad Ashraful 34); Second day, Pakistan 134-2 (Taufeeq Umar 60, Inzamam-ul-Haq 24); Third day, Bangladesh 52-4 (Rajin Saleh 5, Alok Kapali 4).

Bangladesh

First innings		Second innings	
Hannan Sarkar c Rashid Latif b Umar Gul	6	c Mohammad Hafeez b Shoaib Akhtar	7
Javed Omar b Shoaib Akhtar	119	c Rashid Latif b Shoaib Akhtar	0
Habibul Bashar lbw b Shabbir Ahmed	97	lbw b Umar Gul	28
Mohammad Ashraful c Rashid Latif b Shoaib Akhtar	77	c Taufeeq Umar b Danish Kaneria	7
Rajin Saleh c Rashid Latif b Danish Kaneria	3	lbw b Shoaib Akhtar	6
Alok Kapali c Rashid Latif b Shoaib Akhtar	4	c Rashid Latif b Shabbir Ahmed	16
†Khaled Masud lbw b Shoaib Akhtar	0	lbw b Shoaib Akhtar	0
*Khaled Mahmud c Shabbir Ahmed b Shoaib Akhtar	25	lbw b Danish Kaneria	1
Mohammad Rafiq b Shoaib Akhtar	0	not out	9
Mashrafe bin Mortaza b Umar Gul	10	b Umar Gul	14
Alamgir Kabir not out	1	b Umar Gul	4
B 4, l-b 4, w 1, n-b 10	19	L-b 2, n-b 2	4
1/13 (1) 2/180 (3) 3/310 (2) 4/315 (5) 5/315 (4) 6/315 (7) 7/320 (6) 8/320 (9) 9/341 (10) 10/361 (8)	361	1/7 (2) 2/20 (1) 3/43 (4) 4/43 (3) 5/64 (5) 6/64 (7) 7/65 (8) 8/75 (6) 9/90 (10) 10/96 (11)	96

Bowling: *First Innings*—Shoaib Akhtar 22.5–4–50–6; Umar Gul 27–3–67–2; Shabbir Ahmed 25–7–73–1; Danish Kaneria 41–11–110–1; Shoaib Malik 12–4–27–0; Mohammad Hafeez 10–4–26–0. *Second Innings*—Shoaib Akhtar 12–2–30–4; Shabbir Ahmed 7–2–21–1; Umar Gul 4.5–1–16–3; Danish Kaneria 10–3–27–2.

Pakistan

Mohammad Hafeez c Khaled Masud b Khaled Mahmud	21	– not out	102
Taufeeq Umar c Khaled Masud b Mohammad Rafiq	75	– c Mashrafe bin Mortaza b Khaled Mahmud	43
Yasir Hameed b Mohammad Rafiq	23	– not out	18
Inzamam-ul-Haq lbw b Mohammad Rafiq	43		
Yousuf Youhana not out	64		
*†Rashid Latif st Khaled Masud b Mohammad Rafiq	40		
Shoaib Malik lbw b Mohammad Rafiq	0		
Shoaib Akhtar b Khaled Mahmud	15		
Shabbir Ahmed c Mashrafe bin Mortaza b Alok Kapali	8		
Danish Kaneria lbw b Alok Kapali	0		
Umar Gul lbw b Alok Kapali	0		
L-b 1, n-b 5	6	L-b 1, w 1	2
1/51 (1) 2/84 (3) 3/159 (2) 4/178 (4) 5/242 (6) 6/250 (7) 7/265 (8) 8/289 (9) 9/289 (10) 10/295 (11)	295	1/140 (2)	(1 wkt) 165

Bowling: *First Innings*—Mashrafe bin Mortaza 18–6–48–0; Alamgir Kabir 13–3–61–0; Khaled Mahmud 21–6–42–2; Mohammad Rafiq 45–13–118–5; Rajin Saleh 7–2–13–0; Mohammad Ashraful 2–0–9–0; Alok Kapali 2.1–1–3–3. *Second Innings*—Mashrafe bin Mortaza 7–1–26–0; Alamgir Kabir 7.3–1–39–0; Khaled Mahmud 14–5–28–1; Mohammad Rafiq 12–2–34–0; Alok Kapali 6–0–30–0; Mohammad Ashraful 1–0–7–0.

Umpires: S. A. Bucknor (West Indies) and R. B. Tiffin (Zimbabwe).
Third umpire: Asad Rauf. Referee: M. J. Procter (South Africa).

PAKISTAN v BANGLADESH

Third Test Match

At Multan, September 3, 4, 5, 6, 2003. Pakistan won by one wicket. Toss: Bangladesh. First-class debut: Yasir Ali. Test debuts: Farhan Adil, Salman Butt.

Inzamam-ul-Haq played one of the innings of his life to save Pakistan from humiliation and break Bangladeshi hearts. On the third afternoon, Bangladesh's first Test win, so desperately longed for during three years of demoralising defeat, was within touching distance. On a pitch helping seamers, Pakistan were 132 for six – still 129 short of victory.

But Inzamam stood firm for five hours 17 minutes, and his unbeaten 138 guided Pakistan home. It was only the tenth one-wicket win in Test history, and Inzamam had now been at the crease for two of them. While the 1994-95 victory over Mark Taylor's Australians came at Karachi, this triumph was in front of his home crowd, who showered him in rose petals as he left the field.

It was cruel for Bangladesh. They dominated from the word go, and despite Inzamam's heroics might still have won, given a bit more luck. But things went against them on the fourth morning. First, Hannan Sarkar at second slip dropped Shabbir Ahmed on nought. It was perhaps the most costly miss in Bangladesh's short Test history: Shabbir and Inzamam went on to add 41 for the eighth wicket. Later, with 49 now needed, eight wickets down and Inzamam farming the strike, the No. 10 Umar Gul survived a run-out despite being beaten by a direct hit. The crestfallen bowler, Mohammad Rafiq, had brushed the stumps and dislodged the bails before the ball struck. In the same over, Rafiq sportingly chose not to run out Gul when he was backing up too far. By the time Gul *was* finally run out, after a bad call from Inzamam, they had added 52. Gul's contribution was five.

Four runs were now needed, five balls remained in the over and the No. 11 coming to the striker's end was Yasir Ali – a 17-year-old on first-class debut, with only a handful of junior games and a hurried lunchtime batting lesson from Javed Miandad, the Pakistan coach, behind him. But Yasir kept out three balls and then tickled a single into the leg side. Off the last delivery of the over, Inzamam flicked the winning boundary. Ramiz Raja, the former Test batsman, now chief executive of the PCB, called it "one of the best Test innings of modern times". That might have been a little overblown, but Inzamam's concentration had been steely and his hitting authoritative. Supporters rushed on to the field to hug their local hero.

For this final Test, Pakistan had made five changes, three of them enforced: Shoaib Akhtar had returned to Durham, while Shoaib Malik and Taufeeq Umar were injured. But the decision to rest Yousuf Youhana and Danish Kaneria, and to include three debutants, raised a few eyebrows. Pakistan nearly paid the price.

ONE-WICKET WINS IN TEST MATCHES

England beat Australia at The Oval	1902
South Africa beat England at Johannesburg	1905-06
England beat Australia at Melbourne	1907-08
England beat South Africa at Cape Town	1922-23
Australia beat West Indies at Melbourne	1951-52
New Zealand beat West Indies at Dunedin	1979-80
Pakistan beat Australia at Karachi	1994-95
West Indies beat Australia at Bridgetown	1998-99
West Indies beat Pakistan at St John's	1999-2000
Pakistan beat Bangladesh at Multan	**2003**

After two placid wickets in Karachi and Peshawar, the Multan pitch had a hint of grass, and the pace bowlers found considerable movement. Given the conditions, Bangladesh's batsmen did very well to reach 281, after Khaled Mahmud made the brave decision to bat first. Habibul Bashar hit 72 – his fourth innings of fifty-plus in the series – and again led the way. However, Shabbir Ahmed took three wickets in six balls to mop up the tail rapidly.

The Bangladeshi bowlers did even better than their batsmen. Pakistan were restricted to 175: Mahmud, whose form had been lousy, seamed the ball around and took the first four wickets to fall. After that, Mohammad Rafiq, with another five-wicket haul, took over. Just before tea on the second day, Bangladesh had a lead of 106 runs – and every right to start dreaming of victory.

But Pakistan fought back, dismissing them for 154 in a second innings twice delayed by sand storms. However, the biggest tumult involved Pakistan's captain and wicket-keeper, Rashid Latif. After diving to catch an edge from Alok Kapali, Latif claimed a catch. The umpires, who were unsighted as Latif rolled over on landing, gave it out. But TV replays clearly showed the ball briefly dropping out of Latif's gloves and on to the ground as he tumbled. The Bangladesh team management lodged a complaint to match referee Mike Procter, and Latif was later banned for five one-day internationals.

His temporary replacement was – almost inevitably – Inzamam. Having begun the series battling for a place in the side, he ended it with his career revived.

Man of the Match: Inzamam-ul-Haq.

Close of play: First day, Bangladesh 248-6 (Khaled Masud 29, Khaled Mahmud 1); Second day, Bangladesh 77-4 (Rajin Saleh 29, Khaled Mahmud 2); Third day, Pakistan 148-6 (Inzamam-ul-Haq 53, Saqlain Mushtaq 3).

Bangladesh

First innings		Second innings	
Hannan Sarkar c Rashid Latif b Umar Gul	13	– c Rashid Latif b Umar Gul	3
Javed Omar c Younis Khan b Umar Gul	38	– c Inzamam-ul-Haq b Shabbir Ahmed	16
Habibul Bashar c Rashid Latif b Yasir Ali	72	– c Rashid Latif b Umar Gul	3
Mohammad Ashraful lbw b Saqlain Mushtaq	12	– c Salman Butt b Shabbir Ahmed	3
Rajin Saleh run out	49	– c Rashid Latif b Umar Gul	42
Alok Kapali b Umar Gul	11	– c Rashid Latif b Yasir Ali	22
†Khaled Masud c Rashid Latif b Umar Gul	29	– (8) lbw b Shabbir Ahmed	28
*Khaled Mahmud lbw b Shabbir Ahmed	19	– (7) lbw b Shabbir Ahmed	2
Mohammad Rafiq b Shabbir Ahmed	11	– lbw b Umar Gul	4
Tapash Baisya lbw b Shabbir Ahmed	0	– not out	14
Manjurul Islam not out	0	– c Younis Khan b Saqlain Mushtaq	5
B 4, l-b 10, n-b 13	27	B 5, l-b 2, w 2, n-b 3	12
1/28 (1) 2/102 (2) 3/136 (4) 4/166 (3) 5/179 (6) 6/241 (5) 7/248 (7) 8/278 (9) 9/278 (10) 10/281 (8)	281	1/4 (1) 2/9 (3) 3/23 (4) 4/41 (2) 5/77 (7) 6/91 (6) 7/111 (5) 8/127 (9) 9/137 (8) 10/154 (11)	154

In the second innings Alok Kapali, when 17, retired hurt at 71 and resumed at 77.

Bowling: *First Innings*—Shabbir Ahmed 25.2–3–70–3; Umar Gul 32–7–86–4; Yasir Ali 14–4–43–1; Saqlain Mushtaq 25–5–61–1; Mohammad Hafeez 3–1–7–0. *Second Innings*—Umar Gul 15–2–58–4; Shabbir Ahmed 23–6–68–4; Yasir Ali 6–1–12–1; Saqlain Mushtaq 2.3–0–9–1.

Pakistan

First innings		Second innings	
Mohammad Hafeez lbw b Khaled Mahmud	21	– (2) c sub (Mashrafe bin Mortaza) b Manjurul Islam	18
Salman Butt c Khaled Masud b Khaled Mahmud	12	– (1) c sub (Mashrafe bin Mortaza) b Manjurul Islam	37
Yasir Hameed b Mohammad Rafiq	39	– c sub (Mashrafe bin Mortaza) b Khaled Mahmud	18
Inzamam-ul-Haq c Hannan Sarkar b Khaled Mahmud	10	– not out	138
Younis Khan c Khaled Masud b Khaled Mahmud	34	– run out	0
Farhan Adil lbw b Mohammad Rafiq	25	– c Habibul Bashar b Mohammad Rafiq	8
*†Rashid Latif c Alok Kapali b Tapash Baisya	5	– lbw b Khaled Mahmud	5
Saqlain Mushtaq b Mohammad Rafiq	9	– c Khaled Masud b Khaled Mahmud	11
Shabbir Ahmed lbw b Mohammad Rafiq	4	– lbw b Mohammad Rafiq	13
Umar Gul b Mohammad Rafiq	5	– run out	5
Yasir Ali not out	0	– not out	1
B 1, l-b 5, n-b 5	11	L-b 4, w 4	8
1/27 (2) 2/36 (1) 3/50 (4) 4/121 (5) 5/135 (3) 6/152 (7) 7/154 (6) 8/166 (9) 9/170 (8) 10/175 (10)	175	1/45 (1) 2/62 (2) 3/78 (3) 4/81 (5) 5/99 (6) 6/132 (7) 7/164 (8) 8/205 (9) 9/257 (10)	(9 wkts) 262

Bowling: *First Innings*—Manjurul Islam 13–3–42–0; Tapash Baisya 11–2–54–1; Khaled Mahmud 13–1–37–4; Mohammad Rafiq 17.4–7–36–5. *Second Innings*—Manjurul Islam 21–2–64–2; Tapash Baisya 12–0–46–0; Khaled Mahmud 28–9–68–3; Mohammad Rafiq 30–6–80–2.

Umpires: E. A. R. de Silva (Sri Lanka) and R. B. Tiffin (Zimbabwe).
Third umpire: Aleem Dar. Referee: M. J. Procter (South Africa).

†PAKISTAN v BANGLADESH

First One-Day International

At Multan, September 9, 2003. Pakistan won by 137 runs. Toss: Pakistan. One-day international debuts: Junaid Zia; Rajin Saleh.

This Multan pitch was completely different to the greenish one used for the memorable Test. On a batsman's paradise, Pakistan made their highest one-day total against Bangladesh. Yasir Hameed, after two centuries on debut in the Test series, made another here, dancing down the pitch to attack the spinners. The final thrust then came from Younis Khan and Inzamam-ul-Haq, replacing the suspended Rashid Latif as captain. Younis was the more savage, and his 31-ball 59 included several astonishing sweep shots off the quicker bowlers. Pakistan scored 126 from the last 12 overs. Bangladesh lost a wicket in their first over, and were 52 for five by the 13th. Mushfiqur Rahman, one of three recently arrived one-day specialists, delayed the inevitable.

Man of the Match: Yasir Hameed.

Pakistan

Mohammad Hafeez run out	27
Yasir Hameed c Rajin Saleh b Alok Kapali	116
Yousuf Youhana run out	49
*Inzamam-ul-Haq not out	56
Younis Khan not out	59
L-b 4, w 3, n-b 9	16
1/62 (1) 2/182 (3) 3/211 (2) (3 wkts, 50 overs)	323

Shoaib Malik, Abdul Razzaq, †Kamran Akmal, Junaid Zia, Shabbir Ahmed and Umar Gul did not bat.

Bowling: Mashrafe bin Mortaza 9–1–63–0; Mushfiqur Rahman 8–0–59–0; Khaled Mahmud 10–1–65–0; Sanwar Hossain 6–0–33–0; Mohammad Rafiq 10–0–55–0; Alok Kapali 7–0–44–1.

Bangladesh

Habibul Bashar run out	6
Mohammad Ashraful lbw b Umar Gul	0
Rajin Saleh b Abdul Razzaq	25
Tushar Imran c Kamran Akmal b Shabbir Ahmed	0
Alok Kapali lbw b Abdul Razzaq	26
*Khaled Mahmud c Inzamam-ul-Haq b Abdul Razzaq	0
Sanwar Hossain c Shabbir Ahmed b Mohammad Hafeez	19
†Khaled Masud lbw b Mohammad Hafeez	14
Mushfiqur Rahman not out	36
Mashrafe bin Mortaza run out	8
Mohammad Rafiq b Mohammad Hafeez	19
B 8, l-b 2, w 15, n-b 8	33
1/3 (2) 2/28 (1) 3/39 (4) 4/52 (3) 5/52 (6) 6/78 (5) 7/100 (8) 8/120 (7) 9/140 (10) 10/186 (11) (43.2 overs)	186

Bowling: Umar Gul 8–0–51–1; Shabbir Ahmed 8–2–19–1; Abdul Razzaq 8–2–32–3; Junaid Zia 7–0–35–0; Shoaib Malik 6–1–22–0; Mohammad Hafeez 6.2–1–17–3.

Umpires: R. B. Tiffin (Zimbabwe) and Aleem Dar.
Third umpire: Nadeem Ghauri. Referee: M. J. Procter (South Africa).

†PAKISTAN v BANGLADESH

Second One-Day International

At Faisalabad, September 12, 2003. Pakistan won by 74 runs. Toss: Pakistan.

Bangladesh clung on tenaciously for far longer than during their previous thrashing. On a wicket where the ball sometimes stopped a little, Pakistan managed 243, thanks to Yousuf Youhana. He scripted his century in ones and twos, hitting just seven fours and one six, in the last over. Trying to repeat the shot next ball, he was caught at long-on. In fact, he should have gone on 77, but umpire Tiffin missed the nick. In reply, Bangladesh were cruising until Habibul Bashar fell in the

19th over. Rajin Saleh, Bangladesh's find of the tour, went nine overs later, after a fine 64, and the rest collapsed like a house of cards. This was the first-one day international at the Iqbal Stadium since Sri Lanka knocked England out of the 1996 World Cup.

Man of the Match: Yousuf Youhana.

Pakistan

Mohammad Hafeez c Khaled Masud b Mushfiqur Rahman	26
Yasir Hameed b Mushfiqur Rahman	15
Yousuf Youhana c Mushfiqur Rahman b Mashrafe bin Mortaza	106
*Inzamam-ul-Haq b Mohammad Rafiq	41
Younis Khan c Mashrafe bin Mortaza b Rajin Saleh	8
Shoaib Malik c Alok Kapali b Rajin Saleh	6
Abdul Razzaq c Khaled Masud b Mohammad Rafiq	4
†Kamran Akmal c Mohammad Ashraful b Rajin Saleh	26
Junaid Zia not out	2
Shabbir Ahmed not out	0
B 2, l-b 2, w 3, n-b 2	9
1/45 (2) 2/46 (1) 3/133 (4) 4/158 (5) 5/168 (6) 6/177 (7) 7/230 (8) 8/240 (3) (8 wkts, 50 overs)	243

Umar Gul did not bat.

Bowling: Hasibul Hussain 6–0–30–0; Mashrafe bin Mortaza 8–0–41–1; Khaled Mahmud 9–0–38–0; Mushfiqur Rahman 7–1–29–2; Mohammad Rafiq 10–0–45–2; Alok Kapali 1–0–8–0; Rajin Saleh 9–0–48–3.

Bangladesh

Mohammad Ashraful c Inzamam-ul-Haq b Umar Gul	3
Habibul Bashar lbw b Abdul Razzaq	25
Rajin Saleh c Umar Gul b Shoaib Malik	64
Tushar Imran b Abdul Razzaq	1
Alok Kapali c Younis Khan b Junaid Zia	37
Mashrafe bin Mortaza c Yousuf Youhana b Shoaib Malik	1
Mushfiqur Rahman lbw b Umar Gul	0
*Khaled Mahmud c Kamran Akmal b Shoaib Malik	4
†Khaled Masud b Junaid Zia	12
Mohammad Rafiq b Junaid Zia	3
Hasibul Hussain not out	4
L-b 1, w 8, n-b 6	15
1/5 (1) 2/87 (2) 3/90 (4) 4/128 (3) 5/133 (6) 6/133 (7) 7/138 (8) 8/160 (5) 9/164 (9) 10/169 (10) (42.1 overs)	169

Bowling: Umar Gul 8–0–29–2; Shabbir Ahmed 10–2–41–0; Abdul Razzaq 7–1–22–2; Mohammad Hafeez 3–0–21–0; Shoaib Malik 10–0–34–3; Junaid Zia 4.1–0–21–3.

Umpires: R. B. Tiffin (Zimbabwe) and Aleem Dar.
Third umpire: Asad Rauf. Referee: M. J. Procter (South Africa).

†PAKISTAN v BANGLADESH

Third One-Day International

At Lahore, September 15, 2003 (day/night). Pakistan won by 42 runs (D/L method). Toss: Pakistan.

It was hard luck for Bangladesh when one of the Gaddafi Stadium's six floodlight towers broke down, making their run-chase much more difficult. Because they had lost two early wickets to the hostile and accurate Umar Gul, a tricky 258 in 50 overs was revised to an improbable 244 in 44. Although Hannan Sarkar and Alok Kapali put on 95 they were really just batting out time. Sarkar was given run out on 36, and was halfway to the pavilion when called back: TV replays showed Shoaib Malik had touched the rope while throwing in from the cover boundary. Earlier, Yousuf Youhana made 65 after being let off three times in the 30s. In Pakistan's penultimate over, Tapash Baisya took three wickets – but by then it was too late.

Man of the Match: Umar Gul.

Pakistan

Mohammad Hafeez c Khaled Masud b Tapash Baisya	2
Yasir Hameed c Tapash Baisya b Mohammad Rafiq	40
Yousuf Youhana b Mushfiqur Rahman	65
Younis Khan c Rajin Saleh b Mohammad Rafiq	41
*Inzamam-ul-Haq not out	64
Shoaib Malik c Alok Kapali b Khaled Mahmud	21
Abdul Razzaq c Habibul Bashar b Tapash Baisya	15
†Kamran Akmal b Tapash Baisya	0
Junaid Zia c Khaled Masud b Tapash Baisya	0
Shabbir Ahmed c Mashrafe bin Mortaza b Khaled Mahmud	1
B 2, l-b 1, w 4, n-b 1	8
1/13 (1) 2/90 (2) 3/126 (3) 4/173 (4) 5/213 (6) 6/242 (7) 7/249 (8) 8/249 (9) 9/257 (10) (9 wkts, 50 overs)	257

Umar Gul did not bat.

Bowling: Mashrafe bin Mortaza 5–1–29–0; Tapash Baisya 9–0–56–4; Khaled Mahmud 10–0–67–2; Mushfiqur Rahman 10–0–30–1; Mohammad Rafiq 10–1–34–2; Rajin Saleh 6–0–38–0.

Bangladesh

Hannan Sarkar b Mohammad Hafeez	61
Mohammad Ashraful c Inzamam-ul-Haq b Umar Gul	0
Rajin Saleh c Kamran Akmal b Umar Gul	4
Habibul Bashar c Abdul Razzaq b Umar Gul	14
Alok Kapali c Younis Khan b Umar Gul	61
Mushfiqur Rahman run out	4
*Khaled Mahmud c Younis Khan b Shabbir Ahmed	16
Mashrafe bin Mortaza b Umar Gul	6
†Khaled Masud not out	4
Tapash Baisya run out	4
Mohammad Rafiq not out	7
L-b 4, w 15, n-b 1	20
1/1 (2) 2/9 (3) 3/42 (4) 4/137 (1) 5/163 (6) 6/175 (5) 7/183 (7) 8/186 (8) 9/194 (10) (9 wkts, 44 overs)	201

Bowling: Umar Gul 9–2–17–5; Shabbir Ahmed 9–1–53–1; Junaid Zia 7–1–25–0; Abdul Razzaq 4–0–15–0; Shoaib Malik 9–0–46–0; Mohammad Hafeez 6–0–41–1.

Umpires: R. B. Tiffin (Zimbabwe) and Nadeem Ghauri.
Third umpire: Asad Rauf. Referee: M. J. Procter (South Africa).

†PAKISTAN v BANGLADESH

Fourth One-Day International

At Rawalpindi, September 18, 2003 (day/night). Pakistan won by five wickets. Toss: Bangladesh.

Bangladesh gave Pakistan a real scare. Yousuf Youhana still needed one run from the penultimate ball, which, to the relief of Pakistan supporters, he hit through mid-wicket for four. Youhana's 94 not out showed superlative calm; however, costly fumbles by Bangladeshi fielders unfamiliar with tight finishes made scoring 36 from the final six overs a bit easier. Earlier, Khaled Mahmud had at last called right and Bangladesh made good use of his luck: a 70-run partnership for the third wicket laid the foundation, but Bangladesh's impetus came from Tushar Imran and Khaled Mahmud. The last ten overs brought 77 runs. Pakistan's reply was reduced from a stroll to a scramble when Mohammad Rafiq ended Youhana's 85-run stand with Younis Khan.

Man of the Match: Yousuf Youhana.

Bangladesh

Hannan Sarkar lbw b Abdul Razzaq	25	Mohammad Rafiq not out	2
†Khaled Masud lbw b Mohammad Sami	0	Mashrafe bin Mortaza not out	6
Rajin Saleh lbw b Mohammad Hafeez	47	B 1, l-b 8, w 5, n-b 6	20
Habibul Bashar run out	37		——
Alok Kapali b Abdul Razzaq	12	1/9 (2) 2/47 (1) (8 wkts, 50 overs)	222
Tushar Imran lbw b Umar Gul	33	3/117 (4) 4/126 (3)	
Mushfiqur Rahman b Umar Gul	22	5/144 (5) 6/193 (6)	
*Khaled Mahmud b Mohammad Sami	18	7/212 (7) 8/216 (8)	

Tapash Baisya did not bat.

Bowling: Mohammad Sami 10–0–41–2; Umar Gul 9–1–29–2; Shoaib Malik 10–0–32–0; Abdul Razzaq 9–0–43–2; Junaid Zia 6–0–46–0; Mohammad Hafeez 6–0–22–1.

Pakistan

Imran Nazir c Hannan Sarkar b Tapash Baisya	28	Shoaib Malik run out	17
Mohammad Hafeez c Rajin Saleh b Tapash Baisya	9	Abdul Razzaq not out	8
Yousuf Youhana not out	94	B 1, l-b 5, w 9	15
Younis Khan lbw b Mohammad Rafiq	37		——
*Inzamam-ul-Haq c Tapash Baisya b Mashrafe bin Mortaza	18	1/38 (2) 2/50 (1) (5 wkts, 49.5 overs)	226
		3/135 (4) 4/170 (5)	
		5/205 (6)	

†Kamran Akmal, Junaid Zia, Mohammad Sami and Umar Gul did not bat.

Bowling: Mashrafe bin Mortaza 10–1–51–1; Tapash Baisya 8.5–0–42–2; Mushfiqur Rahman 10–1–38–0; Khaled Mahmud 8–0–30–0; Mohammad Rafiq 10–0–41–1; Rajin Saleh 3–0–18–0.

Umpires: R. B. Tiffin (Zimbabwe) and Aleem Dar.
Third umpire: Asad Rauf. Referee: M. J. Procter (South Africa).

†PAKISTAN v BANGLADESH

Fifth One-Day International

At Karachi, September 21, 2003 (day/night). Pakistan won by 58 runs. Toss: Pakistan.

The series ended as it began – with Pakistan reaching a total above 300, and the result never in question. Yasir Hameed returned after being rested at Rawalpindi and provided the anchor. He scored 82 off 107 balls, sharing a solid partnership of 95 with Mohammad Hafeez and an explosive one of 74 with Yousuf Youhana. Youhana came out blazing and hit a carefree 52 from 32 balls, taking his tally for the series to 366. In reply, Bangladesh made their highest total of the five one-dayers without ever really expecting to reach their target.

Man of the Match: Yasir Hameed.

Pakistan

Mohammad Hafeez st Khaled Mahmud b Mohammad Rafiq	44	Shoaib Malik c Mohammad Rafiq b Khaled Mahmud	31
Yasir Hameed st Khaled Masud b Rajin Saleh	82	Abdul Razzaq not out	15
Yousuf Youhana lbw b Mashrafe bin Mortaza	52	L-b 3, w 6, n-b 1	10
*Inzamam-ul-Haq not out	59		——
Younis Khan lbw b Mashrafe bin Mortaza	9	1/95 (1) 2/169 (2) (5 wkts, 50 overs)	302
		3/181 (3) 4/199 (5)	
		5/260 (6)	

†Kamran Akmal, Shabbir Ahmed, Mohammad Sami and Umar Gul did not bat.

Bowling: Tapash Baisya 8–1–47–0; Mushfiqur Rahman 10–1–40–0; Mashrafe bin Mortaza 9–0–63–2; Khaled Mahmud 9–0–64–1; Mohammad Rafiq 10–0–65–1; Rajin Saleh 4–0–20–1.

Bangladesh

Hannan Sarkar c Younis Khan b Shoaib Malik	50	†Khaled Masud not out	2
Habibul Bashar run out	13	Mashrafe bin Mortaza not out	1
Rajin Saleh run out	71		
Alok Kapali b Umar Gul	69	L-b 3, w 13, n-b 4	20
Tushar Imran c Inzamam-ul-Haq b Mohammad Sami	2	1/43 (2) 2/93 (1) (7 wkts, 50 overs)	244
Mushfiqur Rahman run out	2	3/221 (3) 4/221 (4)	
*Khaled Mahmud c Abdul Razzaq b Mohammad Sami	14	5/227 (5) 6/227 (6) 7/243 (7)	

Mohammad Rafiq and Tapash Baisya did not bat.

Bowling: Mohammad Sami 9–0–50–2; Umar Gul 10–1–52–1; Shabbir Ahmed 7–0–20–0; Abdul Razzaq 5–0–26–0; Shoaib Malik 10–0–39–1; Mohammad Hafeez 9–0–54–0.

Umpires: Nadeem Ghauri and R. B. Tiffin (Zimbabwe).
Third umpire: Aleem Dar. Referee: M. J. Procter (South Africa).

PWC ONE-DAY INTERNATIONAL RATINGS

The PricewaterhouseCoopers (PwC) One-Day International Ratings, introduced in August 1998, follow similar principles to the Test Ratings (see page 1141).

The leading 20 batsmen and bowlers in the One-Day International Ratings on December 31, 2003 were:

	Batsmen	*Rating*		*Bowlers*	*Rating*
1	S. R. Tendulkar (*India*)	834	1	M. Muralitharan (*Sri Lanka*)	911
2	C. H. Gayle (*West Indies*)	803	2	S. M. Pollock (*South Africa*)	909
3	M. G. Bevan (*Australia*)	772	3	G. D. McGrath (*Australia*)	841
4	R. T. Ponting (*Australia*)	756	4	W. P. U. J. C. Vaas (*Sri Lanka*)	836
5	A. C. Gilchrist (*Australia*)	755	5	M. Ntini (*South Africa*)	799
6	Yousuf Youhana (*Pakistan*)	750	6	B. Lee (*Australia*)	779
7	B. C. Lara (*West Indies*)	749	7	J. N. Gillespie (*Australia*)	776
8	J. H. Kallis (*South Africa*)	736	8	A. Flintoff (*England*)	774
9	S. T. Jayasuriya (*Sri Lanka*)	723	9	Zaheer Khan (*India*)	724
10	D. R. Martyn (*Australia*)	702	10	Harbhajan Singh (*India*)	719
11	V. Sehwag (*India*)	698	11	S. E. Bond (*New Zealand*)	715
12	M. L. Hayden (*Australia*)	693	12	D. Gough (*England*)	710
13	M. E. Trescothick (*England*)	692	13	Mohammad Sami (*Pakistan*)	706
14	R. Dravid (*India*)	683	14	J. M. Anderson (*England*)	703
15	H. H. Gibbs (*South Africa*)	674	15	H. H. Streak (*Zimbabwe*)	688
16	H. H. Dippenaar (*South Africa*)	669	16	D. L. Vettori (*New Zealand*)	678
17	M. S. Atapattu (*Sri Lanka*)	657	17	I. J. Harvey (*Australia*)	675
18	Yasir Hameed (*Pakistan*)	650	18	C. H. Gayle (*West Indies*)	668
19	S. C. Ganguly (*India*)	648	19	M. Dillon (*West Indies*)	663
20	R. R. Sarwan (*West Indies*)	635	19	Shoaib Akhtar (*Pakistan*)	663

THE SOUTH AFRICANS IN PAKISTAN, 2003-04

BRIAN MURGATROYD

This was a tour that very nearly never happened. Just 48 hours before South Africa were due to arrive in Pakistan, a bomb blast in a deserted office block in Karachi sent shockwaves of concern back to Johannesburg. As knees jerked everywhere, the United Cricket Board of South Africa announced the tour was off.

It was an unnecessarily hasty decision for several reasons. Subsequent investigations revealed that the bombing was gang-related and had no connection to terrorism; more significantly, by calling off the trip the UCBSA contradicted itself, having accepted the report of its own security delegation that it was safe to tour just days earlier.

For the Pakistan Cricket Board, already financially crippled by the absence of touring teams in the wake of the bomb blast that cut short the New Zealand tour of 2002, it was the last straw. They threatened to seek compensation from the South Africans for loss of revenue and gained ICC support in an attempt to revive the tour. After several days of discussion, they succeeded. There was a changed itinerary of two Tests and five one-day internationals instead of the originally planned split of three and three, and with Karachi and the northern frontier city of Peshawar removed from the schedule. Security was also beefed up, and the trip passed off without incident. That was hardly a surprise given that more than 2,000 police and security personnel were on duty at each venue; during the Test series they often outnumbered the paying spectators, with Pakistani crowds once again showing their preference for the one-day game.

There was, at least, one positive aspect of the on–off start to the tour: the ICC proposed a checklist to be worked through before tours could be called off in the future, a move that was ratified soon afterwards. Once the tour got started, player behaviour – and the way the ICC dealt with it – became the major issue following a clash between Andrew Hall and Yousuf Youhana in the second one-day international. Hall was clearly out of order for adding physical contact to his usual aggressive approach but, inexplicably, the umpires did not report the matter to the referee. With both sides seemingly happy to let the matter slide for fear of getting one of their players banned, the issue festered for four days until ICC chief executive Malcolm Speed ordered a hearing. This eventually took place five days after the original incident, an unacceptable delay that cast a shadow over the rest of the one-day series.

Hall and his captain Graeme Smith, who waded into the clash verbally, were both suspended, which left the South Africans feeling persecuted, and they responded by reporting Shoaib Akhtar for verbally abusing Paul Adams during the First Test. Shoaib was banned too, which meant that the behaviour of both sides was impeccable for the last Test and a half, but it also had the effect of blurring the line between abuse and acceptable banter. Almost all chat – witty or otherwise – was removed from the game as players fought shy of risking a ban. It created a strange atmosphere on the field, with one South African player saying: "It just doesn't feel like a Test match out there."

At the start of the tour it was difficult to escape the impression that the South Africa players would rather be anywhere but Pakistan, particularly as they had just come off the back of a three-month tour of England and had series against West Indies and New Zealand to follow. Once they acclimatised, however, they played some typically competitive cricket, although the trip illuminated their deficiencies. Smith led the side from the front but was hamstrung by the lack of a consistently hostile bowler to support the accuracy of Shaun Pollock, with Makhaya Ntini showing only glimpses of his best form.

Once again, they had no high-class spinner, with Adams rarely looking like running through top-order batsmen, even though he did take his best Test figures. With the bat, Gary Kirsten was brilliant in the Test series while Boeta Dippenaar showed signs of advancement, especially as a one-day player, but Neil McKenzie had a poor tour. His shot selection, particularly his use of the sweep, was a major cause for concern.

Pakistan's loss of the one-day series from an apparently impregnable position suggested they were too reliant on Inzamam-ul-Haq's talismanic qualities, but they subsequently showed real steel to win the Lahore Test without him. That victory illustrated the importance of having bowlers capable of taking 20 wickets; in that department, Pakistan had a clear edge thanks to Shoaib and the leg-spinner, Danish Kaneria, who bowled beautifully throughout.

The form of Taufeeq Umar and Imran Farhat hinted that Pakistan had finally found a stable opening pair again. Against that, the performances of Moin Khan, brought back when Rashid Latif opted out of the Test series for personal reasons, and leg-spinner Mushtaq Ahmed, picked on the back of 103 wickets for county champions Sussex, suggested their international careers were rapidly drawing to a close.

SOUTH AFRICA TOURING PARTY

G. C. Smith (Western Province) (*captain*), M. V. Boucher (Border) (*vice-captain*), P. R. Adams (Western Province), H. H. Dippenaar (Free State), H. H. Gibbs (Western Province), A. J. Hall (Easterns), J. H. Kallis (Western Province), G. Kirsten (Western Province), C. K. Langeveldt (Boland), N. D. McKenzie (Northerns), A. Nel (Easterns) M. Ntini (Border), R. J. Peterson (Eastern Province), S. M. Pollock (KwaZulu Natal), J. A. Rudolph (Northerns).

A. C. Dawson (Western Province) appeared in the one-day internationals but was replaced by Adams and Kirsten for the Tests. M. N. van Wyk (Free State) joined the party as cover for Gibbs.

Coach: E. O. Simons. *Managers:* C. Docrat/T. Southey. *Assistant coach:* V. A. Barnes. *Physiotherapist:* S. Jabar.

SOUTH AFRICA TOUR RESULTS

Test matches – Played 2: Lost 1, Drawn 1.
One-day internationals – Played 5: Won 3, Lost 2.
Other non-first-class match – Won v City Nazim XI.

Note: Matches in this section which were not first-class are signified with a dagger.

†At Lahore, October 1, 2003 (day/night). **South Africans won by seven wickets.** Toss: City Nazim XI. **City Nazim XI 250-4** (50 overs) (Imran Farhat 64); **South Africans 253-3** (46 overs) (G. C. Smith 72, J. H. Kallis 55).

Each side fielded 12 players, of whom 11 could bat and 11 field.

†PAKISTAN v SOUTH AFRICA

First One-Day International

At Lahore, October 3, 2003 (day/night). Pakistan won by eight runs. Toss: Pakistan.

Dynamic hitting from Shoaib Malik and South Africa's lack of acclimatisation combined to edge a close encounter Pakistan's way. Malik transformed their final total from useful to formidable by hammering six fours and six sixes, mostly in the arc between square leg and long-off, in an innings lasting just 41 balls. In the face of that onslaught, South Africa's fielders wilted in the humidity. And then they wilted with the bat after Smith and Dippenaar replied with a rousing partnership of 138 in 27 overs. Dippenaar, drafted in to open in place of the injured Gibbs, scored a maiden one-day hundred in his 63rd match. But the combination of the heat exhaustion, which afflicted both Smith and McKenzie, and the ferocious pace of both Shoaib Akhtar and Mohammed Sami were too much for South Africa.

Man of the Match: Shoaib Malik.

Pakistan

Batsman	Runs
Mohammad Hafeez c Dippenaar b Pollock	5
Yasir Hameed run out	56
Yousuf Youhana c Boucher b Hall	68
Younis Khan run out	19
*Inzamam-ul-Haq b Kallis	37
Shoaib Malik not out	82
Abdul Razzaq c Pollock b Kallis	2
†Rashid Latif not out	1
L-b 4, w 3	7
1/18 (1) 2/100 (2) 3/142 (4) 4/167 (3) 5/231 (5) 6/257 (7) (6 wkts, 50 overs)	277

Shoaib Akhtar, Mushtaq Ahmed and Mohammad Sami did not bat.

Bowling: Pollock 10–3–46–1; Ntini 3–0–26–0; Kallis 10–1–53–2; Hall 10–1–53–1; Peterson 8–0–40–0; Dawson 9–0–55–0.

South Africa

Batsman	Runs
*G. C. Smith c Inzamam-ul-Haq b Shoaib Akhtar	71
H. H. Dippenaar not out	110
J. H. Kallis b Shoaib Akhtar	1
N. D. McKenzie c Mohammad Hafeez b Shoaib Akhtar	62
†M. V. Boucher b Shoaib Akhtar	1
S. M. Pollock c Inzamam-ul-Haq b Mohammad Sami	0
J. A. Rudolph run out	3
A. J. Hall not out	0
B 3, l-b 5, w 5, n-b 8	21
1/138 (1) 2/140 (3) 3/241 (4) 4/244 (5) 5/245 (6) 6/268 (7) (6 wkts, 50 overs)	269

A. C. Dawson, R. J. Peterson and M. Ntini did not bat.

Bowling: Shoaib Akhtar 10–0–49–4; Mohammad Sami 10–0–44–1; Mushtaq Ahmed 10–0–65–0; Abdul Razzaq 5–0–30–0; Mohammad Hafeez 5–1–26–0; Shoaib Malik 10–0–47–0.

Umpires: D. B. Hair (Australia) and Aleem Dar.
Third umpire: Nadeem Ghauri. Referee: C. H. Lloyd (West Indies).

†PAKISTAN v SOUTH AFRICA

Second One-Day International

At Lahore, October 5, 2003 (day/night). Pakistan won by 42 runs. Toss: South Africa.

A comfortable Pakistan win will be remembered for an ugly incident in the 13th over of the day, when Hall appeared to block Yousuf Youhana's path with his elbow as the batsman took a single. Youhana responded by pointing his bat in Hall's direction and the umpire Nadeem Ghauri was forced to step between the pair to stop the matter getting out of hand. Smith joined in with an expletive aimed at Youhana and, although neither umpire nor the teams reported the matter to referee Clive Lloyd, ICC chief executive Malcolm Speed ordered a hearing when he viewed a video of the incident four days later. Hall was given a tour-ending ban of one one-day international and two Tests, Smith was suspended for a single one-day international while Youhana, viewed more as sinned against than sinning, was fined 50% of his match fee. As for the cricket, South Africa self-destructed in pursuit of 268, with three batsmen falling to sweep shots and three more run out by direct hits, two of them from the dynamic Mohammad Sami. However, Inzamam-ul-Haq damaged his right hamstring while batting and Youhana led the side in the field. Both sets of players were fined 10% of their match fees for slow over-rates with Smith and Inzamam, the captains, receiving 20% fines.

Man of the Match: Mohammad Sami.

Pakistan

Mohammad Hafeez b Pollock 7
Yasir Hameed c Boucher b Ntini 16
Yousuf Youhana c Boucher b Kallis 65
*Inzamam-ul-Haq not out 33
Younis Khan c Boucher b Ntini 41
Shoaib Malik b Ntini 45
†Rashid Latif run out 19
Abdul Razzaq b Ntini 15
Shoaib Akhtar not out 11

B 5, l-b 3, w 7 15

1/19 (1) 2/37 (2) 3/138 (3) 4/163 (5) 5/201 (7) 6/225 (6) 7/236 (8) (7 wkts, 50 overs) 267

Mohammad Sami and Umar Gul did not bat.

Inzamam-ul-Haq retired hurt at 56 and resumed at 225.

Bowling: Pollock 10–2–39–1; Ntini 10–0–46–4; Hall 9–0–52–0; Kallis 10–1–56–1; Peterson 3–0–21–0; Dawson 8–0–45–0.

South Africa

*G. C. Smith c Younis Khan b Mohammad Sami . 6
H. H. Dippenaar b Mohammad Hafeez . . 58
J. H. Kallis lbw b Mohammad Hafeez . . . 42
N. D. McKenzie run out 3
†M. V. Boucher run out 5
J. A. Rudolph lbw b Mohammad Hafeez . 25
S. M. Pollock run out 11
A. J. Hall b Mohammad Sami 8
R. J. Peterson b Mohammad Sami 1
A. C. Dawson not out 23
M. Ntini not out 16

L-b 9, w 12, n-b 6 27

1/19 (1) 2/108 (3) 3/116 (4)4/121 (5) 5/138 (2) 6/163 (6) 7/168 (7) 8/174 (9) 9/187 (8) (9 wkts, 50 overs) 225

Bowling: Mohammad Sami 8–1–20–3; Umar Gul 9–0–54–0; Shoaib Akhtar 8–0–43–0; Abdul Razzaq 7–0–27–0; Mohammad Hafeez 10–0–37–3; Shoaib Malik 8–0–35–0.

Umpires: D. B. Hair (Australia) and Nadeem Ghauri.
Third umpire: Asad Rauf. Referee: C. H. Lloyd (West Indies).

†PAKISTAN v SOUTH AFRICA

Third One-Day International

At Faisalabad, October 7, 2003. South Africa won by 13 runs (D/L method). Toss: Pakistan.

Pakistan's slow over-rate and the strange tactics of Yousuf Youhana, their stand-in captain, combined to hand South Africa a series-turning win. With the visitors wobbling in the face of some furious fast bowling from Shoaib Akhtar, Youhana opted to take him out of the attack with two overs unused – even though the onset of bad light was sure to mean he would be unable to bowl again later. South Africa's batsmen, duly reprieved, scored 15 runs from the next three overs to ensure they were comfortably ahead of the Duckworth/Lewis par score when offered the light by the umpires at the scheduled close of play with Pakistan still five overs short of bowling their allocation. Nine no-balls – including six by Saqlain Mushtaq – and six wides did little to help Pakistan's cause, while Kallis produced the most assured batting of the day before he was spectacularly yorked by Shoaib the ball after gloving a waist-high beamer for four. It was another bad-tempered match, with Pollock fined his entire match fee for showing dissent when an appeal was turned down and Boucher cleared of a charge of using abusive language to Shoaib Malik.

Man of the Match: J. H. Kallis.

Pakistan

Mohammad Hafeez c Dippenaar b Hall	20
Yasir Hameed c Gibbs b Peterson	72
*Yousuf Youhana c Boucher b Ntini	18
Younis Khan c Ntini b Peterson	9
Faisal Iqbal c Boucher b Nel	22
Shoaib Malik c Gibbs b Ntini	18
Abdul Razzaq not out	46
†Rashid Latif c Kallis b Pollock	14
Shoaib Akhtar b Ntini	7
Saqlain Mushtaq not out	1
L-b 3, w 12, n-b 1	16
1/52 (1) 2/95 (3) 3/128 (2) 4/138 (4) 5/169 (5) 6/181 (6) 7/200 (8) 8/232 (9) (8 wkts, 50 overs)	243

Umar Gul did not bat.

Bowling: Pollock 10–0–35–1; Nel 10–0–58–1; Hall 8–1–37–1; Ntini 9–0–45–3; Kallis 6–0–39–0; Peterson 7–0–26–2.

South Africa

*G. C. Smith c Rashid Latif b Abdul Razzaq	51
H. H. Gibbs c Rashid Latif b Shoaib Akhtar	4
J. H. Kallis b Shoaib Akhtar	62
J. A. Rudolph c Abdul Razzaq b Shoaib Malik	46
H. H. Dippenaar b Mohammad Hafeez	3
†M. V. Boucher b Shoaib Akhtar	24
S. M. Pollock not out	4
A. J. Hall not out	10
L-b 2, w 6, n-b 9	17
1/10 (2) 2/110 (1) 3/146 (3) 4/157 (5) 5/206 (6) 6/206 (4) (6 wkts, 45 overs)	221

R. J. Peterson, A. Nel and M. Ntini did not bat.

Bowling: Shoaib Akhtar 8–0–31–3; Umar Gul 5–0–42–0; Abdul Razzaq 7–0–27–1; Saqlain Mushtaq 8–0–52–0; Shoaib Malik 10–0–42–1; Mohammad Hafeez 7–0–25–1.

Umpires: D. B. Hair (Australia) and Nadeem Ghauri.
Third umpire: Aleem Dar. Referee: C. H. Lloyd (West Indies).

†PAKISTAN v SOUTH AFRICA

Fourth One-Day International

At Rawalpindi, October 10, 2003 (day/night). South Africa won by six wickets. Toss: Pakistan.

South Africa took advantage of a Pakistan side at their insipid worst to level the series with one to play. Nel produced his best figures in one-day internationals to start the slide, although his success owed a great deal to poor strokes and, in Younis Khan's case, a brilliant diving leg-side catch by Boucher. Pakistan's problems were compounded by a hamstring injury to Yousuf Youhana, and they looked a shadow of the energetic side that had won the first two matches. Kallis, who faced 87 balls, expertly shepherded South Africa home.

Man of the Match: A. Nel.

Pakistan

Mohammad Hafeez c Boucher b Nel	1
Yasir Hameed c Boucher b Hall	30
Faisal Iqbal c Hall b Nel	0
*Yousuf Youhana c Pollock b Nel	60
Younis Khan c Boucher b Nel	13
Naved Latif b Pollock	4
Shoaib Malik b Ntini	5
†Rashid Latif b Kallis	18
Shoaib Akhtar c Boucher b Ntini	0
Mohammad Sami not out	16
Shabbir Ahmed b Ntini	2
L-b 2, w 6	8
1/11 (1) 2/16 (3) 3/59 (2) 4/105 (5) 5/114 (4) 6/120 (6) 7/122 (7) 8/122 (9) 9/150 (8) 10/157 (11) (47.4 overs)	157

Bowling: Pollock 10–4–9–1; Nel 10–0–39–4; Ntini 7.4–0–25–3; Hall 8–1–31–1; Peterson 5–0–31–0; Kallis 7–0–20–1.

South Africa

*G. C. Smith b Mohammad Sami	13
H. H. Gibbs b Shoaib Akhtar	41
J. H. Kallis not out	58
J. A. Rudolph c Rashid Latif b Mohammad Hafeez	20
H. H. Dippenaar c Mohammad Hafeez b Shoaib Malik	11
†M. V. Boucher not out	4
L-b 6, w 1, n-b 4	11
1/31 (1) 2/73 (2) 3/116 (4) 4/153 (5) (4 wkts, 38.5 overs)	158

S. M. Pollock, A. J. Hall, R. J. Peterson, A. Nel and M. Ntini did not bat.

Bowling: Shoaib Akhtar 7–2–23–1; Mohammad Sami 6–0–38–1; Shabbir Ahmed 6–1–36–0; Shoaib Malik 10–0–29–1; Mohammad Hafeez 9.5–1–26–1.

Umpires: D. B. Hair (Australia) and Aleem Dar.
Third umpire: Asad Rauf. Referee: C. H. Lloyd (West Indies).

†PAKISTAN v SOUTH AFRICA

Fifth One-Day International

At Rawalpindi, October 12, 2003 (day/night). South Africa won by seven wickets. Toss: Pakistan.

Despite the absence of the suspended Smith and Hall, South Africa secured the series with a win that was every bit as convincing as the margin suggests. Pakistan's decision to select the half-fit Inzamam backfired when, unable to run properly – even by his standards – he was the victim of an over-enthusiastic call from Younis Khan and a direct hit from Rudolph at mid-on. With too many batsmen out of form, Pakistan surrendered meekly in the face of disciplined bowling, and a modest target gave South Africa no alarms. Dippenaar, restored to the top of the order in Smith's absence, became the tenth South African to reach 2,000 one-day international runs.

Man of the Match: H. H. Dippenaar. *Man of the Series:* H. H. Dippenaar.

Pakistan

Yasir Hameed c Kallis b Nel	28
Mohammad Hafeez b Nel	0
Yousuf Youhana lbw b Pollock	0
Younis Khan b Peterson	24
*Inzamam-ul-Haq run out	17
Shoaib Malik c Nel b Peterson	20
Abdul Razzaq c Boucher b Ntini	38
†Rashid Latif b Pollock	25
Mohammad Sami c Kallis b Ntini	22
Shoaib Akhtar c sub (M. N. van Wyk) b Pollock	6
Danish Kaneria not out	1
B 1, l-b 4, w 6	11
1/3 (2) 2/16 (3) 3/35 (1) 4/75 (5) 5/80 (4) 6/116 (6) 7/152 (7) 8/180 (8) 9/186 (9) 10/192 (10) (49.3 overs)	192

Bowling: Pollock 9.3–0–33–3; Nel 8–0–36–2; Dawson 7–0–26–0; Ntini 9–1–38–2; Kallis 6–0–22–0; Peterson 10–0–32–2.

South Africa

H. H. Dippenaar lbw b Mohammad Sami . 74	N. D. McKenzie not out 9
H. H. Gibbs st Rashid Latif b Danish Kaneria . 34	B 1, l-b 4, w 11, n-b 7. 23
J. H. Kallis b Mohammad Sami 40	1/75 (2) (3 wkts, 45.5 overs) 193
J. A. Rudolph not out 13	2/168 (3) 3/170 (1)

*†M. V. Boucher, S. M. Pollock, A. C. Dawson, R. J. Peterson, A. Nel and M. Ntini did not bat.

Bowling: Shoaib Akhtar 8–0–33–0; Mohammad Sami 10–0–47–2; Abdul Razzaq 10–0–33–0; Mohammad Hafeez 3.5–0–18–0; Danish Kaneria 10–1–37–1; Shoaib Malik 4–0–20–0.

Umpires: D. B. Hair (Australia) and Aleem Dar.
Third umpire: Asad Rauf. Referee C. H. Lloyd (West Indies).

PAKISTAN v SOUTH AFRICA

First Test Match

At Lahore, October 17, 18, 19, 20, 21, 2003. Pakistan won by eight wickets. Toss: South Africa. Test debut: Asim Kamal.

Every match has pivotal moments but few are as dramatic and decisive as the one that occurred on the first day of this Test. South Africa were cruising at 159 for three midway through the afternoon session when Kirsten was forced to retire hurt after being struck by a Shoaib Akhtar bouncer. After that they were never again in control and Pakistan, showing the character so absent from their play in the second half of the one-day series, slowly, surely took charge.

This was a great Test with something for everyone: high-class batting, top-quality bowling from Danish Kaneria and Shoaib, bravery from Kirsten, the drama of Asim Kamal's agonising fall just short of a hundred on debut – and also controversy, with Shoaib being banned for the Second Test. The shame was that so few people watched it.

Anyone who did watch the first session and a half before Kirsten's injury would have been hard-pressed to believe Pakistan would end up winning the match with almost three sessions in hand. Without the injured Inzamam and with just one player – Yasir Hameed – remaining from their previous Test against Bangladesh six weeks earlier, they played like strangers and dropped three catches in the first session. South Africa, by contrast, looked largely untroubled.

Yet again, however, Shoaib demonstrated his ability to make things happen with his removal of Kirsten and the dismissal of McKenzie next ball, a wicked in-swinging yorker. Kirsten sustained a broken nose and left eye socket, and required ten stitches in his face when he missed an attempted hook shot. But the fractures were "undisplaced" and, amazingly, he was batting again on the fourth morning. "The pitches here are too good to go home," he joked afterwards. But with him out of action in the first innings, Pakistan ended the opening day the happier side despite Boucher's effort in taking the fight back to the bowlers.

The day also had a dramatic postscript. As Adams frustrated Pakistan's attempts to mop up the tail, he was sworn at by Shoaib and, although the remark was just routine playground language, South Africa decided, as a matter of tit for tat, to report the matter to the referee, Clive Lloyd. As the offence was captured by television cameras, Lloyd had little option but to ban Shoaib, a punishment that became more severe because it was his second offence within 12 months. It cost Shoaib one Test and two one-day internationals.

Pakistan's ascendancy grew on day two as, faced with a diet of innocuous seam bowling and Adams's assortment, the batsmen did much as they pleased. Chief among them was Taufeeq Umar, who registered his fourth Test hundred and his second in succession against South Africa on his return after a troublesome knee injury. He had a huge slice of luck on 17, when he played Pollock on to his stumps without dislodging the bails (one of three occasions it happened in the match). Otherwise Taufeeq looked immovable, driving and cutting impressively until deceived by Adams after batting for five hours and 22 minutes.

Kamal, who survived a massive lbw appeal from Nel first ball, settled quickly and seemed set to take Pakistan to an enormous lead until he edged an indeterminate steer on to his stumps to become only the third player to score 99 on debut (after A. G. Chipperfield of Australia in 1934 and R. J. Christiani of West Indies in 1947-48). And with Adams finally finding some semblance of control to return Test-best figures, Pakistan's lead was restricted to just 81.

It was a great effort by South Africa and, when they wiped off the deficit for the loss of just one wicket by the close, the match appeared to be back in the melting pot. Two collapses on the fourth day, however, tipped the balance decisively back to Pakistan. The first was induced by Shoaib, who stood tall in the first session to take three key wickets before limping off with a hamstring strain, and the second was the result of the persistence of Kaneria, who bowled unchanged for 28.3 overs from the University End and provided Pakistan with the priceless asset of control. None of South Africa's batsmen could read him with certainty and when he removed Kirsten, caught off a leading edge as he tried to work a wrong 'un to leg, it started a collapse in which the last four wickets went down for four runs in 13 balls.

Pakistan were left with a target of 161 and, after the openers had negotiated the new ball, they came close to securing victory that evening until bad light and Farhat's dismissal prompted discretion. Although Taufeeq was castled by an Adams shooter on the final morning, it was too little, too late for South Africa. By the end of the match, the bubble that swelled in the one-day series had well and truly burst.

Men of the Match: Taufeeq Umar and Danish Kaneria.

Close of play: First day, South Africa 320; Second day, Pakistan 275-4 (Asim Kamal 49, Shoaib Malik 27); Third day, South Africa 99-1 (Gibbs 56, Dippenaar 25); Fourth day, Pakistan 137-1 (Taufeeq Umar 61, Yasir Hameed 3).

South Africa

First innings		Second innings	
*G. C. Smith c Asim Kamal b Mohammad Sami	33	– c Taufeeq Umar b Shoaib Akhtar	12
H. H. Gibbs c Taufeeq Umar b Danish Kaneria	27	– c Taufeeq Umar b Shoaib Akhtar	59
G. Kirsten retired hurt	53	– (6) c Yousuf Youhana b Danish Kaneria	46
J. H. Kallis c Moin Khan b Danish Kaneria	29	– c Moin Khan b Shoaib Akhtar	18
H. H. Dippenaar c Imran Farhat b Shoaib Malik	24	– (3) c Yousuf Youhana b Shoaib Akhtar	27
N. D. McKenzie lbw b Shoaib Akhtar	0	– (5) b Danish Kaneria	14
†M. V. Boucher c Imran Farhat b Shoaib Malik	72	– c Imran Farhat b Danish Kaneria	15
S. M. Pollock b Shoaib Malik	28	– b Danish Kaneria	18
P. R. Adams not out	18	– lbw b Danish Kaneria	0
A. Nel lbw b Shoaib Akhtar	0	– b Mushtaq Ahmed	0
M. Ntini c Asim Kamal b Shoaib Malik	8	– not out	0
L-b 5, n-b 23	28	B 1, l-b 11, n-b 20	32
1/52 (1) 2/84 (2) 3/154 (4) 4/159 (6) 5/229 (5) 6/282 (7) 7/302 (8) 8/307 (10) 9/320 (11)	320	1/43 (1) 2/104 (3) 3/108 (2) 4/149 (4) 5/149 (5) 6/192 (7) 7/237 (6) 8/238 (9) 9/241 (10) 10/241 (8)	241

Kirsten retired hurt at 159-3.

Bowling: *First Innings*—Shoaib Akhtar 14–1–62–2; Mohammad Sami 13–2–66–1; Mushtaq Ahmed 18–1–80–0; Danish Kaneria 21–2–65–2; Shoaib Malik 17–4–42–4. *Second Innings*—Shoaib Akhtar 14.3–2–36–4; Mohammad Sami 19.3–0–77–0; Mushtaq Ahmed 8–1–18–1; Shoaib Malik 14–0–52–0; Danish Kaneria 28.3–8–46–5.

Pakistan

Taufeeq Umar c and b Adams	111	– b Adams	63
Imran Farhat b Adams	41	– c Gibbs b Smith	58
Yasir Hameed c Boucher b Pollock	16	– not out	20
*Yousuf Youhana c Boucher b Nel	8		
Asim Kamal b Nel	99		
Shoaib Malik b Adams	47	– (4) not out	8
†Moin Khan lbw b Adams	37		
Shoaib Akhtar st Boucher b Adams	1		
Mohammad Sami b Adams	0		
Mushtaq Ahmed not out	14		
Danish Kaneria c Smith b Adams	0		
B 2, l-b 17, w 2, n-b 6	27	L-b 6, w 5, n-b 4	15
1/109 (2) 2/151 (3) 3/160 (4) 4/223 (1) 5/322 (6) 6/363 (5) 7/366 (8) 8/366 (9) 9/401 (7) 10/401 (11)	401	1/134 (2) 2/141 (1)	(2 wkts) 164

Bowling: *First Innings*—Pollock 22–7–48–1; Ntini 28–4–88–0; Adams 45–11–128–7; Nel 27–5–67–2; Kallis 18–3–37–0; Smith 8–1–14–0. *Second Innings*—Pollock 7–2–21–0; Ntini 6–0–24–0; Nel 5–1–13–0; Kallis 6–1–30–0; Adams 11–1–57–1; Smith 5.1–2–13–1.

Umpires: D. B. Hair (Australia) and N. A. Mallender (England).
Third umpire: Nadeem Ghauri. Referee: C. H. Lloyd (West Indies).

PAKISTAN v SOUTH AFRICA

Second Test Match

At Faisalabad, October 24, 25, 26, 27, 28, 2003. Drawn. Toss: South Africa.

South Africa's fallibility in the field cost them the chance of squaring the series. Four catches were dropped as they pressed for victory on the final afternoon and, although three of them were not expensive, the other proved fatal.

Ntini and Pollock had struck with successive deliveries with the second new ball and were rampant. There was more than an hour left to play and Shoaib Malik and Moin Khan, Pakistan's last recognised batsmen, were at the crease. Twice Shoaib involuntarily fenced Ntini through the slips; then, surprised by a lifting ball that cut back sharply, he somehow fended it to fine leg off the shoulder of the bat. Kirsten, whose batting had helped get South Africa into a winning position, moved to his right but grassed a waist-high chance. With it went South Africa's hopes of victory.

Pakistan themselves had flirted with the win on the last afternoon as, after a painfully slow start to the day, their batsmen suddenly realised that the pitch was still good and that most of South Africa's attack held few terrors. But Ntini and Pollock closed down that avenue.

It could be argued that neither side deserved to win. Pakistan adopted unduly negative tactics on day four and South Africa had a horrific first day. Against an attack missing both the suspended Shoaib Akhtar and Mohammad Sami, who was ill, their batsmen fell to a series of indiscreet strokes on a blameless pitch. The honourable exception was Gibbs, who drove beautifully and showed admirable restraint until he was undone by Mushtaq Ahmed's googly.

The start of the Pakistan innings followed a similar pattern to the First Test, with Taufeeq Umar and Imran Farhat looking largely untroubled except by a toy kite, fluttering over deepish mid-off, which stopped play for a while. This time it was Farhat, strong square of the wicket and unafraid to use his feet, who went on to three figures. Having put aside many of his aggressive instincts, he was rewarded with his maiden hundred in his sixth match.

When Kallis dropped an edge from Inzamam – back in the side in place of the hamstring victim Yousuf Youhana – off Pollock on the second evening, South Africa appeared doomed. But as at Lahore they fought back admirably on day three. Ntini and Pollock raced in with the new ball with the former producing his first meaningful spell of the series and the latter claiming his 16th five-for in Tests. Pakistan's lead was just 70.

Three wickets that evening kept the match on a knife-edge. Pakistan's scalps included Smith, but only after he had become the fourth South African (after Hansie Cronje, Gibbs and Kallis) to score 1,000 Test runs in a calendar year when he reached 57. On day four, however, a combination of Kirsten's doggedness and Pakistani negativity tipped the match the way of the visitors. Kirsten was patience personified on the ground where he carried his bat six years earlier, and his 19th Test hundred was full of trademark cuts, clips off the hip and rock-solid defence. He eventually fell in identical fashion to the first innings, caught cutting at Abdul Razzaq to give Taufeeq his sixth catch of the match, a Pakistan record.

The home side were handicapped by an under-the-weather Danish Kaneria and an under-performing Razzaq, but they appeared content to sit back and wait for a declaration rather than take the match by the throat, slowing the over-rate and opting for defensive fields. When they batted again, they kept wickets in hand and the possibility of victory alive until the final session, aided by three missed chances, two by Boucher off Peterson, who outbowled his fellow left-arm spinner Adams.

Then Inzamam inexplicably shouldered arms to Ntini, and Razzaq did the same to the next ball, bowled by Pollock. Now only South Africa could win, and they might have done so if Kirsten had grabbed that chance at fine leg. With fading light also an issue, the South Africans' cause was not helped on the final day by the need to take drinks inside the dressing-room because of the religious festival of Ramadan. But although both Moin and Shoaib enjoyed some luck, they also showed admirable resolve.

Men of the Match: Taufeeq Umar and G. Kirsten.

Man of the Series: Taufeeq Umar.

Close of play: First day, South Africa 256-9 (Adams 3, Ntini 5); Second day, Pakistan 237-2 (Imran Farhat 123, Inzamam-ul-Haq 16); Third day, South Africa 140-3 (Kirsten 27, McKenzie 0); Fourth day, Pakistan 8-0 (Taufeeq Umar 6, Imran Farhat 1).

South Africa

*G. C. Smith c Inzamam-ul-Haq b Shabbir Ahmed	2	– lbw b Shabbir Ahmed	65
H. H. Gibbs lbw b Mushtaq Ahmed	98	– lbw b Danish Kaneria	20
H. H. Dippenaar c Taufeeq Umar b Shabbir Ahmed	4	– lbw b Shoaib Malik	21
J. H. Kallis c Taufeeq Umar b Danish Kaneria	10	– (6) lbw b Abdul Razzaq	43
G. Kirsten c Taufeeq Umar b Abdul Razzaq	54	– (4) c Taufeeq Umar b Abdul Razzaq	118
N. D. McKenzie c Mushtaq Ahmed b Shabbir Ahmed	27	– (5) c Taufeeq Umar b Danish Kaneria	35
†M. V. Boucher b Abdul Razzaq	27	– b Abdul Razzaq	0
S. M. Pollock run out	16	– not out	30
R. J. Peterson c sub (Misbah-ul-Haq) b Shabbir Ahmed	4	– c Inzamam–ul–Haq b Shabbir Ahmed	17
P. R. Adams c Taufeeq Umar b Danish Kaneria	14	– not out	9
M. Ntini not out	16		
L-b 1, w 1, n-b 4	6	B 1, l-b 7, w 2, n-b 3	13
1/6 (1) 2/20 (3) 3/40 (4) 4/148 (5) 5/195 (2) 6/212 (6) 7/236 (7) 8/247 (8) 9/250 (9) 10/278 (10)	278	1/42 (2) 2/93 (3) 3/128 (1) 4/213 (5) 5/303 (4) 6/303 (7) 7/325 (6) 8/358 (9) (8 wkts dec.)	371

Bowling: *First Innings*—Shabbir Ahmed 26–8–74–4; Abdul Razzaq 22–4–68–2; Danish Kaneria 33.1–10–68–2; Shoaib Malik 5–0–19–0; Mushtaq Ahmed 13–1–48–1. *Second Innings*—Shabbir Ahmed 34.3–10–70–2; Abdul Razzaq 18–3–70–3; Danish Kaneria 37–6–100–2; Shoaib Malik 26–5–70–1; Mushtaq Ahmed 12–3–53–0.

Pakistan

Taufeeq Umar c Gibbs b Adams	68	– c Smith b Peterson	71
Imran Farhat c Peterson b Pollock	128	– lbw b Kallis	8
Yasir Hameed c Gibbs b Pollock	21	– c Dippenaar b Ntini	17
*Inzamam-ul-Haq lbw b Pollock	23	– lbw b Ntini	60
Asim Kamal c Pollock b Ntini	1	– c Boucher b Adams	38
Shoaib Malik c Smith b Pollock	9	– (7) not out	23
Abdul Razzaq c sub (J. A. Rudolph) b Ntini	37	– (6) b Pollock	10
†Moin Khan c Gibbs b Kallis	18	– not out	9
Mushtaq Ahmed lbw b Pollock	6		
Shabbir Ahmed not out	24		
Danish Kaneria c Smith b Pollock	0		
B 3, l-b 8, w 1, n-b 1	13	B 1, l-b 1, n-b 4	6
1/137 (1) 2/178 (3) 3/248 (4) 4/251 (2) 5/257 (5) 6/261 (6) 7/293 (8) 8/309 (9) 9/339 (7) 10/348 (11)	348	1/18 (2) 2/46 (3) 3/125 (1) 4/187 (5) 5/209 (4) 6/209 (6)	(6 wkts) 242

Bowling: *First Innings*—Pollock 29.2–9–78–6; Ntini 29–9–64–2; Kallis 22–4–57–1; Peterson 8–1–40–0; Adams 25–5–82–1; Smith 3–0–16–0. *Second Innings*—Pollock 22–12–27–1; Ntini 20–7–45–2; Kallis 19–6–51–1; Adams 20–2–75–1; Peterson 15–6–21–1; Smith 2–0–21–0.

Umpires: D. J. Harper (Australia) and S. J. A. Taufel (Australia).
Third umpire: Asad Rauf. Referee: C. H. Lloyd (West Indies).

THE NEW ZEALANDERS IN INDIA, 2003-04

RICHARD BOOCK

New Zealand's preparations for their tour of India included practising on custom-made dirt pitches, having music blasted through earphones as they batted, and hiring people to shout abuse and rattle the sides of the nets. The Kiwis, who had risen to third in the ICC Test Championship, were desperate to consolidate their position with a strong performance on the subcontinent, a region in which they had previously struggled to be competitive.

Bolstered by the memory of their first series win in the West Indies a year earlier, New Zealand were talking up their chances of creating history by winning in India for the first time too, particularly after performing strongly in Sri Lanka five months earlier. But they had to do without the cutting edge of the raw pace bowler Shane Bond, who was suffering from a stress fracture of the back, and this was a major setback.

For India, the series was billed as a chance to exact revenge on the New Zealanders, who had prepared unplayable greentops in the previous summer's series in a move designed to nullify the Indians' batting strength. As it happened, the pitches for both Tests were more durable than most Indian roads, and neither India at Ahmedabad nor New Zealand at Mohali could capitalise on their hard-earned advantage to deliver a telling blow.

There were, however, pluses for both sides. New Zealand had arrived in India with question marks hanging over both their opening combination and middle order but, by the time the series was over, Lou Vincent had re-established his place beside Mark Richardson at the top of the order. The tour was a triumph for Vincent who, having been dropped for the previous series against Sri Lanka, had worked hard on his mental approach and emerged as a more patient, composed and effective batsman.

The same could be said of Craig McMillan, who bounced back from six months in the wilderness to score back-to-back half-centuries at Ahmedabad and a fighting unbeaten century in the Second Test.

It was generally an encouraging tour for New Zealand's caretaker coach, Ashley Ross, standing in ahead of John Bracewell's arrival. There were noticeable technical improvements, too. Daniel Vettori's new batting stance gave him a far better balance, possibly opening the door for him to bat at No. 7. New Zealand's bowling was also a revelation, especially the effort of Daryl Tuffey – who had previously struggled overseas – at Mohali, where he brought back memories of old-fashioned English seamers like Chris Old and Mike Hendrick.

India were undoubtedly frustrated at being unable to break through and land the vital blow at Ahmedabad, but they could at least reflect on some top-class batting from the usual suspects. But it was the exception to this rule who really caught the eye: Sachin Tendulkar scored just 71 runs in the two Tests.

NEW ZEALAND TOURING PARTY

S. P. Fleming (Wellington) (*captain*), N. J. Astle (Canterbury), I. G. Butler (Northern Districts), R. G. Hart (Northern Districts), R. A. Jones (Wellington), C. D. McMillan (Canterbury), M. J. Mason (Central Districts), J. D. P. Oram (Central Districts), M. H. Richardson (Auckland), S. B. Styris (Northern Districts), D. R. Tuffey (Northern Districts), D. L. Vettori (Northern Districts), L. Vincent (Auckland), P. J. Wiseman (Canterbury).

C. L. Cairns (Canterbury), C. Z. Harris (Canterbury), P. A. Hitchcock (Auckland), B. B. McCullum (Canterbury), K. D. Mills (Auckland) and C. J. Nevin (Wellington) replaced Astle (who was injured), Hart, Jones, Mason, Richardson and Wiseman for the one-day series.

Coach: A. Ross. *Assistant coach:* B. R. Blair. *Manager:* L. M. Crocker. *Physiotherapist:* D. F. Shackel.

NEW ZEALAND TOUR RESULTS

Test matches – Played 2: Drawn 2.
First-class matches – Played 4: Drawn 4.
Draws – India (2), Indian Board President's XI, India A.
One-day internationals – Played 6: Won 1, Lost 4, No result 1. *Win* – India. *Losses* – Australia (3), India. *No result* – India.

At Vishakhapatnam, September 26, 27, 28, 2003. **Drawn.** Toss: Indian Board President's XI. **Indian Board President's XI 227-1** (A. Chopra 103*, Yuvraj Singh 80*) **v New Zealanders**.

Rain and a damp outfield meant only 10.2 overs were bowled on the first day, and none on the second.

At Rajkot, October 2, 3, 4, 2003. **Drawn.** Toss: New Zealanders. **New Zealanders 375-7 dec.** (M. H. Richardson 128*, J. D. P. Oram 101*) **and 68-4**; **India A 403** (A. Chopra 66, S. Ramesh 110, H. K. Badani 127).

All four hundreds were scored by left-handers. Richardson retired hurt at the end of the first day, with New Zealand 299 for five.

INDIA v NEW ZEALAND

First Test Match

At Ahmedabad, October 8, 9, 10, 11, 12, 2003. Drawn. Toss: India. Test debuts: L. Balaji, A. Chopra.

Some peculiar tactics in the field from New Zealand gave India the initiative from the start of this Test but, under extreme pressure, the New Zealanders inched to safety. Even though they had no genuinely fast bowlers, they worked on the theory that Indian batsmen struggle against the bouncing ball. The approach was not exactly a success. India controlled the match on the back of a high-class 222 from Dravid, scored off 387 balls and punctuated with 28 fours and two sixes, which continued his rich vein of form against New Zealand. Ganguly chipped in with an unbeaten, even hundred before declaring to leave New Zealand needing 301 to avoid the follow-on.

They were already in dire straits on the second evening, having lost three top batsmen for 17 to the lively Zaheer Khan. But, on the third morning, Astle led a fightback with an accomplished 103, aided by a gritty half-century from McMillan. It was an innings of some courage: after recovering from knee surgery, Astle had had scant preparation. He went on to score the first hundred by a New Zealander in India since Glenn Turner at Kanpur in 1976-77.

Despite Astle's heroics, New Zealand were in real danger of following on, particularly when Oram poked to slip to give Kumble his 350th wicket, in his 77th Test. At that stage 74 were needed with three wickets in hand; thankfully for New Zealand, one of those was Vettori. With his new-found batting skills on show, he effected the first stage of New Zealand's jailbreak. His crucial 60, in baking temperatures and against two of the best spinners in the world, made Vettori only the fourth New Zealander – after

Richard Hadlee, Chris Cairns and John Bracewell – to score 1,000 runs and take 100 wickets in Tests.

With a lead of 160, India were not exactly urgent about their second-innings work, leading to questions about Ganguly's strategy too. He eventually called time after India took 45 overs to extend their lead to 369. Happily for New Zealand, their two most vulnerable batsmen picked the perfect day to deliver, and they hung on to save the Test and keep the series alive. McMillan and Vincent, both recalled to the Test arena after being dumped for the series against Sri Lanka, repaid the selectors' faith with match-saving half-centuries.

New Zealand never seriously threatened the target but earned credit for their never-say-die approach in temperatures topping 40°C, ending at 272 for six after 107 overs of rugged defiance. McMillan, who again demonstrated his ability against spin, built steadily on the foundation set by Vincent, whose innings ended after lunch for 67 when he dragged on an attempted cut off Kumble. But New Zealand were able to survive the next two sessions, thanks to another fighting effort from Astle, who by now was unwell, and some more baffling captaincy from Ganguly, who employed run-saving fields and all but emptied the slip cordon at a time when India desperately needed a breakthrough.

Man of the Match: R. Dravid.

Close of play: First day, India 249-3 (Dravid 110, Laxman 56); Second day, New Zealand 41-3 (Styris 10, Astle 13); Third day, New Zealand 282-8 (Vettori 28, Wiseman 8); Fourth day, New Zealand 48-1 (Vincent 21, Tuffey 0).

India

A. Chopra c and b Vettori	42	– c Styris b Vettori	31
V. Sehwag lbw b Tuffey	29	– c Hart b Oram	17
R. Dravid c Hart b Oram	222	– c Vincent b Wiseman	73
S. R. Tendulkar c Astle b Styris	8	– c Vettori b Wiseman	7
V. V. S. Laxman c Wiseman b Vettori	64	– c Vettori b Wiseman	44
*S. C. Ganguly not out	100	– b Wiseman	25
†P. A. Patel not out	29	– not out	5
B 2, l-b 3, n-b 1	6	B 4, l-b 3	7
1/35 (2) 2/107 (1) 3/134 (4) 4/264 (5) 5/446 (3)	(5 wkts dec.) 500	1/20 (2) 2/97 (1) 3/118 (4) 4/166 (3) 5/177 (5) 6/209 (6)	(6 wkts dec.) 209

A. Kumble, Harbhajan Singh, L. Balaji and Zaheer Khan did not bat.

Bowling: *First Innings*—Tuffey 31–6–103–1; Oram 33–8–95–1; Styris 26–5–83–1; Vettori 44–9–128–2; McMillan 4–1–6–0; Wiseman 21–0–80–0. *Second Innings*—Tuffey 9–2–18–0; Oram 8–0–39–1; Vettori 16–0–81–1; Wiseman 11.5–0–64–4.

New Zealand

M. H. Richardson b Zaheer Khan	6	– c Chopra b Kumble	21
L. Vincent c Patel b Zaheer Khan	7	– b Kumble	67
*S. P. Fleming b Zaheer Khan	1	– (4) c Laxman b Harbhajan Singh	8
S. B. Styris c Chopra b Harbhajan Singh	34	– (5) lbw b Kumble	0
N. J. Astle st Patel b Harbhajan Singh	103	– (8) not out	51
C. D. McMillan c Chopra b Sehwag	54	– not out	83
J. D. P. Oram c Dravid b Kumble	5	– c Dravid b Harbhajan Singh	7
†R. G. Hart lbw b Balaji	15		
D. L. Vettori c Dravid b Kumble	60		
P. J. Wiseman c Laxman b Zaheer Khan	27		
D. R. Tuffey not out	2	– (3) b Kumble	8
B 4, l-b 18, n-b 4	26	B 4, l-b 11, n-b 12	27
1/11 (1) 2/16 (2) 3/17 (3) 4/108 (4) 5/199 (6) 6/223 (5) 7/227 (7) 8/265 (8) 9/332 (10) 10/340 (9)	340	1/44 (1) 2/68 (3) 3/85 (4) 4/86 (5) 5/150 (2) 6/169 (7)	(6 wkts) 272

Bowling: *First Innings*—Zaheer Khan 23–3–68–4; Balaji 26–7–84–1; Kumble 35.1–11–58–2; Harbhajan Singh 36–8–86–2; Sehwag 8–2–17–1; Tendulkar 3–2–5–0. *Second Innings*—Zaheer Khan 10–1–36–0; Balaji 11–4–21–0; Harbhajan Singh 38–9–65–2; Kumble 39–12–95–4; Tendulkar 7–0–40–0; Sehwag 2–2–0–0.

Umpires: R. E. Koertzen (South Africa) and D. R. Shepherd (England).
Third umpire: K. Hariharan. Referee: R. S. Madugalle.

INDIA v NEW ZEALAND

Second Test Match

At Mohali, October 16, 17, 18, 19, 20, 2003. Drawn. Toss: New Zealand. Test debut: Yuvraj Singh.

There are times when John Wright, India's Kiwi coach, must feel like dropping to his knees and kissing the feet of V. V. S. Laxman. It was Laxman, after all, who saved Wright's skin at Kolkata in 2001, his epic 281 setting the scene for one of Test cricket's most famous wins. And he was at it again here at Mohali, first compiling an unbeaten century as India fell just seven short of the follow-on mark, and then defying New Zealand for most of the final day to consign the Second Test, and the series, to an honourable draw. Indian administrators are not known for their tolerance when their team lose at home, and Wright would have been in the firing line had the side folded.

After four days of relentless batting dominance, the final day threw up an absorbing arm-wrestle, and it was left to Laxman to guide India to safety. It had begun when a supercharged Tuffey produced by far his best performance outside New Zealand: he took four first-innings wickets, effected a brilliant run-out, and then had India reeling with three second-innings strikes before lunch.

Tuffey, whose record away from home had been mediocre, had Sehwag and Dravid caught behind, and then produced a peach of an off-cutter to rattle Tendulkar's stumps, reducing India to 18 for three. At that stage they were still 188 in arrears, but any thoughts that New Zealand were to gain a series win on Indian soil had to be put on hold as Laxman joined up with Chopra and frustrated them for the best part of five hours. Chopra, in only his second Test, produced a mature innings that dripped with application, hitting his second half-century of the match off 159 balls. Dravid led India in a Test for the first time because Ganguly needed minor surgery for an abscess on his thigh; his place went to Yuvraj Singh, making his Test debut on his home ground.

As for India's attack, it appeared flat for most of the series, although it was the local groundsmen who copped most of the flak, on account of two Test pitches that favoured the batsmen for all five days. After the stalemate at Ahmedabad, a stream of centuries, records and batting milestones blew away any hopes that the Second Test pitch might prove more challenging for run-scoring, leaving both teams in agreement over the need for change.

The consolation for New Zealand, at least, was that they were able to maintain control of the match after some compelling batting on the first two and a half days. Their first-innings total of 630 for six declared was studded with four centuries, the last from McMillan, who was unbeaten on 100 when Fleming ended the Indians' misery. Along with Richardson, Styris and Vincent, McMillan made batting look ridiculously easy. It was only the second time in New Zealand's Test history that four batsmen had scored centuries in the same innings, following Perth in 2001-02, when Vincent was again one of the four.

Records came and went: it was the first time that New Zealand's first three batsmen had hit centuries; it was New Zealand's highest overseas total; and only the second time a New Zealand side had scored more than 600 anywhere. Only three other touring sides had scored bigger totals in India. Just to emphasise the batting dominance, Sehwag still had time to romp to a century before stumps on the third day, at which stage more than 800 runs had been scored for the loss of just seven wickets. The bowlers upped the ante after that, but the batsmen – and the pitch – had the final say.

Man of the Match: D. R. Tuffey. *Man of the Series:* V. V. S. Laxman.

Close of play: First day, New Zealand 247-1 (Richardson 102, Styris 7); Second day, New Zealand 536-5 (McMillan 58, Hart 10); Third day, India 203-1 (Sehwag 128, Dravid 9); Fourth day, India 390-6 (Laxman 86, Kumble 1).

New Zealand

M. H. Richardson c Kumble b Harbhajan Singh	145
L. Vincent lbw b Kumble	106
S. B. Styris lbw b Kumble	119
*S. P. Fleming b Tendulkar	30
N. J. Astle c Patel b Harbhajan Singh	18
C. D. McMillan not out	100
†R. G. Hart b Kumble	11
D. L. Vettori not out	48
B 21, l-b 28, w 1, n-b 3	53
1/231 (2) 2/382 (1) 3/433 (4) 4/447 (3) 5/507 (5) 6/540 (7)	(6 wkts dec.) 630

P. J. Wiseman, D. R. Tuffey and I. G. Butler did not bat.

Bowling: Zaheer Khan 26–8–95–0; Balaji 30–10–78–0; Tendulkar 22–3–55–1; Kumble 66–18–181–3; Harbhajan Singh 48–7–149–2; Sehwag 5.3–1–22–0; Yuvraj Singh 1–0–1–0.

India

A. Chopra c Astle b Tuffey	60	c Richardson b Wiseman	52
V. Sehwag b Styris	130	c Fleming b Tuffey	1
*R. Dravid c Hart b Butler	13	c Fleming b Tuffey	5
S. R. Tendulkar c Richardson b Vettori	55	b Tuffey	1
V. V. S. Laxman not out	104	not out	67
Yuvraj Singh c Hart b Tuffey	20	not out	5
†P. A. Patel c Richardson b Vettori	18		
A. Kumble run out	5		
Harbhajan Singh run out	8		
L. Balaji c Hart b Tuffey	4		
Zaheer Khan c Hart b Tuffey	0		
B 2, l-b 1, w 2, n-b 2	7	L-b 4, w 1	5
1/164 (1) 2/208 (3) 3/218 (2) 4/330 (4) 5/364 (6) 6/388 (7) 7/396 (8) 8/408 (9) 9/424 (10) 10/424 (11)	424	1/6 (2) 2/12 (3) 3/18 (4) 4/128 (1)	(4 wkts) 136

Bowling: *First Innings*—Tuffey 29–5–80–4; Butler 35–7–116–1; Styris 19–7–40–1; Vettori 56–24–84–2; Wiseman 32–7–95–0; McMillan 1–0–6–0. *Second Innings*—Tuffey 14–4–30–3; Butler 5–1–12–0; Vettori 23–8–40–0; Styris 4–2–4–0; Wiseman 17–6–37–1; McMillan 6–3–9–0.

Umpires: R. E. Koertzen (South Africa) and D. R. Shepherd (England).
Third umpire: I. Sivaram. Referee: R. S. Madugalle (Sri Lanka).

New Zealand's matches against India and Australia in the TVS Cup (October 23–November 15) appear on pages 1305–1313.

THE ZIMBABWEANS IN AUSTRALIA, 2003-04

CHLOE SALTAU

Where no man has gone before: Matthew Hayden reaches 376 during the Perth Test.
Picture by Hamish Blair, Getty Images.

Australia roused themselves from a two-month hiatus to play a Test series at home in October, in a nation preoccupied with the rugby World Cup, and against one of the world's lowliest Test nations. It had all the makings of an unremarkable, predictable series. But Zimbabwe's first Test tour of Australia, one-sided as it was, was better than that. It was better because of Matthew Hayden.

Hayden cast a muscular shadow over the series. His Test-record 380 at Perth defined and elevated a contest that would otherwise have been lost among the more common pursuits of early Australian spring. The great shame was that only 8,062 people were at the WACA on October 10 – Hayden's day – to witness the 31-year-old Queenslander calmly yet powerfully etch his own number into cricket history, eating up milestones owned by such revered Australian figures as Mark Taylor and Sir Donald Bradman (334), and the West Indian Brian Lara (375), as he went. Not bad for a man repeatedly ignored as a young batsman.

Rejected by Australian cricket's grooming school, the Academy, rejected by those who selected an Under-19 team to tour England, Hayden reflected later on the countless hours spent on Queensland beaches plotting a path back into the Australian team after his attempts to bed down a position over a six-year period yielded only eight Tests.

The series was made better, too, by Zimbabwe's refusal to crawl away and cower after being on the end of an innings of such greatness. Heath Streak's squad – sadly depleted by the retirements of Andy Flower, Henry Olonga and Guy Whittall, and diminished by a finger injury to Grant Flower – arrived determined to leave the politics of their troubled nation behind. But their former Test batsman Murray Goodwin ensured a degree of background tension by claiming the Zimbabwe Cricket Union had a quota system under which non-white cricketers were being promoted to the national team for reasons other than merit.

Zimbabwe lost by an innings and 175 runs at Perth and by nine wickets at Sydney, but the extent of the defeats did not accurately reflect their accomplishments. In Perth they pushed the match into a fifth day, an inconvenience with which Australia had grown unfamiliar. Ray Price, in particular, provided a delightful subplot to the series. Price, the nephew of the golfer, Nick Price, rose to international cricket after overcoming meningitis and partial deafness as a child, and revealed himself as a left-arm spinner of great heart and skill with six for 121 in the Second Test. Stuart Carlisle scored his maiden Test hundred in the same match, while Mark Vermeulen, Trevor Gripper and Sean Ervine emerged as cricketers of talent, poise and potential.

The other centuries were scored by Hayden, again (this time at Sydney), Adam Gilchrist (whose 84-ball hundred in Perth was swallowed up by Hayden's mountainous achievement) and Ricky Ponting, with a sublime 169 at the SCG. By then, the scheduling and limited preparation had taken its toll, with several Australians nursing injuries. The public's reaction to the unseasonable Test series was tepid, with an aggregate crowd of 18,363 over four days at the SCG and 24,051 over five days at the WACA a week earlier. Hayden deserved much better.

"Most effective of all is Harvey's slower ball. It was to be the Great Deceiver."

David Foot on Ian Harvey, page 64.

ZIMBABWEAN TOURING PARTY

H. H. Streak (Matabeleland) (*captain*), T. Taibu (Mashonaland) (*vice-captain*), A. M. Blignaut (Mashonaland), G. B. Brent (Manicaland), S. V. Carlisle (Mashonaland), D. D. Ebrahim (Mashonaland), S. M. Ervine (Midlands), C. N. Evans (Mashonaland), G. M. Ewing (Matabeleland), T. R. Gripper (Manicaland), D. T. Hondo (Mashonaland), N. B. Mahwire (Manicaland), S. Matsikenyeri (Manicaland), R. W. Price (Midlands), M. A. Vermeulen (Matabeleland), C. B. Wishart (Midlands).

Coach: G. R. Marsh. *Manager:* M. A. Meman. *Bowling coach:* B. A. Reid. *Physiotherapist:* B. I. Robinson.

ZIMBABWEAN TOUR RESULTS

Test matches – Played 2: Lost 2.
First-class matches – Played 3: Lost 2, Drawn 1.
Losses – Australia (2).
Draw – Western Australia.
Other non-first-class matches – Played 2: Won 1, Drawn 1. *Win* – Cricket Australia Chairman's XI. *Draw* – Rockingham-Mandurah Invitational XI.

Note: Matches in this section which were not first-class are signified with a dagger.

†At Settlers Hill, Baldivis, September 28, 29, 30, 2003. **Drawn.** Toss: Rockingham-Mandurah Invitational XI. **Zimbabweans 149** (D. J. Wates 4-22) **and 255-9 dec.** (C. B. Wishart 116, S. M. Ervine 51); **Rockingham-Mandurah Invitational XI 123** (S. M. Ervine 5-37) **and 135-6** (R. W. Price 4-55).

Zimbabwe fielded 12 players, of whom 11 could bat and 11 field.

†At Lilac Hill, Perth, October 1, 2003. **Zimbabweans won by seven wickets.** Toss: Cricket Australia Chairman's XI. **Cricket Australia Chairman's XI 240** (49.5 overs) (R. J. Campbell 65; H. H. Streak 4-33); **Zimbabweans 241-3** (41.2 overs) (M. A. Vermeulen 61, S. V. Carlisle 89*, C. B. Wishart 63*).

Each side fielded 12 players, of whom 11 could bat and 11 field. Zimbabwean coach Geoff Marsh and his son, Western Australia's Shaun, both played for the Chairman's XI. Their team-mate, Damien Martyn scored 31 off eight balls. Carlisle and Wishart added an unbroken 137 in 20.5 overs.

At Perth, October 3, 4, 5, 2003. **Drawn.** Toss: Western Australia. **Zimbabweans 330** (C. B. Wishart 100, A. M. Blignaut 57; P. Wilson 4-41) **and 146-6 dec.** (T. R. Gripper 54); **Western Australia 207-6 dec.** (M. J. North 59) **and 266-4** (M. E. K. Hussey 79, R. J. Campbell 59).

Western Australia's target was 270 in 38 overs.

AUSTRALIA v ZIMBABWE

First Test Match

At Perth, October 9, 10, 11, 12, 13, 2003. Australia won by an innings and 175 runs. Toss: Zimbabwe.

Matthew Hayden went to work with a sore back. He wore a heavy vest to keep it warm, and hardly indulged in the sweep shots that have served him so well in the past. Instead he played blissfully, ruthlessly straight. He went to work on a wicket friendlier to batsmen than WACA pitches prepared at the height of summer, after Streak won the toss and invited Australia to bat… and bat. Hayden batted for ten hours and 22

HAYDEN MAKES HISTORY

"I would not trade Matthew Hayden for anybody else in world cricket. If anyone is going to break Brian Lara's world record Test score of 375, he is the man."

Steve Waugh, Australian captain, speaking in November 2002

"He was just timing the ball superbly, hitting some balls on the up that most batsmen would block back at us. The confidence grew and grew, and he just kept timing it better and better, harder and harder."

Heath Streak, Zimbabwean captain

"I'm just thrilled that I was wearing the baggy green cap when the record was broken."

Matthew Hayden

"A standard has been set which we must strive to achieve to pass. I wish Matthew and his family peace and happiness."

Brian Lara, former record-holder

"I can't believe this. I can't believe I'm actually here. Don't you feel sorry for anyone who isn't?"

Lisbeth from Perth, spectator

---

minutes, and – with apologies to Waugh, Martyn and particularly Gilchrist – his innings of 380 must be considered on its own. At the end of it Hayden, this muscle-bound, sun-loving Queenslander, sat in the dressing-room gripping a bottle of beer, wearing whites, baggy green cap and flip-flops; he also sat comfortably in the company of his era's other master batsmen, Sachin Tendulkar and Brian Lara.

Hayden played within himself at first. He gave the impression of being on the brink of destroying Zimbabwe's attack, but didn't. Not yet. He was 76 not out at tea on the first day and took 210 balls, and just over five hours, to bring up his hundred. The boundaries were hit hard and mostly straight, but until then Hayden employed caution and restraint. He had spent as much time "surfing, fishing and cooking, like I do" as batting in previous weeks, and now he made an effort to hold himself back.

Then he cut loose. At his most destructive, during the 35 minutes and 32 balls it took him to speed from 100 to 150, he was perfectly still in his stance but swift and brutal when he wielded his bat. He began by despatching Price and Gripper, Zimbabwe's gentle slow bowlers, over the mid-off fence for six, and as he grew bolder would do the same to the fast bowlers.

The cyclonic period before stumps on the first day produced three sixes. By then, Australia were 368 for three and Hayden was 183 not out, his sights firmly trained on the 203 that breathed fresh life into his career at Chennai in 2001. He had no intention of faltering on the verge of a double-century as he did after crushing English spirits at Brisbane in the first Ashes Test a year earlier, but the records were not in focus yet.

That happened early on day two. Hayden dispensed with the vest, as if to show that he had limbered up now, and in due course replaced his helmet with the emblematic olive cap. Streak was not bowling with his usual zing, while line and length periodically escaped Blignaut. Hayden's gesture announced that fast bowlers held no fear for him anyway, and lent a strong sense of history and tradition to what he was about to accomplish.

On his way from 200 to 300, he unleashed five enormous sixes, mistiming some of them, an incredulous Streak noted later. By now a curious calm had come over Hayden. His concentration did not waver until after he had passed the revered Australian number of 334, set by Don Bradman and equalled by Mark Taylor, by sending a floating full toss to the boundary.

At 335, he faltered, but so too did the hapless Gripper, who fumbled a catch at deep mid-wicket and allowed Hayden to cruise on towards Lara's record. After driving to

Runs on the board: Matthew Hayden makes history.

Picture by Hamish Blair, Getty Images.

long-off three balls before tea on the second day, Hayden celebrated lustily as he ambled through a single and into territory never before explored by a Test cricketer. He wheeled his bat in celebration and embraced his batting partner Gilchrist. There was also something reverent about his reaction – especially when he touched the black band wound around his bicep in remembrance of the 88 Australians killed in the Bali terrorist attacks a year earlier.

Three balls after tea Hayden was out, caught by Carlisle at deep backward square leg for 380. His runs came in 437 balls – so quickly that Australia could declare at 735 for six and still have three days and a session in which to bowl Zimbabwe out twice – and contained 11 ruthlessly bludgeoned sixes and 38 fours. By the time Hayden was engulfed by his team-mates as he headed for the WACA dressing-rooms, Zimbabwe were outclassed and out of the match. Ervine was the only bowler to keep things respectable, with the thoughtfully captured wickets of four of Australia's top six, Waugh and Lehmann tricked into spooning up return catches.

The rest of the Test followed an inevitable course, with Zimbabwe bowled out for 239, asked to follow on, and bowled out again for 321. A crushing Australian victory was only ever threatened by the rainstorms that rolled over Perth on the fourth afternoon and fifth morning, as a lingering last-wicket partnership of 74 between Streak and the stubborn Price added to the irritation.

The brittle nature of Zimbabwe's batting was exposed after Gillespie and MacGill broke down, and Lehmann, labouring with an Achilles injury, picked up three for 61 in the second innings with his part-time left-arm spin. Bichel and Lee shared ten wickets between them; Lee was denied a first-innings hat-trick by the unwavering Price, who calmly steered the hat-trick ball wide of a seven-man slip cordon.

Man of the Match: M. L. Hayden. *Attendance: 24,051.*

Close of play: First day, Australia 368-3 (Hayden 183, Waugh 61); Second day, Zimbabwe 79-1 (Gripper 37, Vermeulen 9); Third day, Zimbabwe 87-2 (Vermeulen 50, Carlisle 26); Fourth day, Zimbabwe 272-9 (Streak 42, Price 17).

Australia

J. L. Langer b Ervine	26
M. L. Hayden c Carlisle b Gripper	380
R. T. Ponting lbw b Ervine	37
D. R. Martyn c Wishart b Gripper	53
*S. R. Waugh c and b Ervine	78
D. S. Lehmann c and b Ervine	30
†A. C. Gilchrist not out	113
B 4, l-b 10, w 1, n-b 3	18
1/43 (1) 2/102 (3) 3/199 (4) 4/406 (5) 5/502 (6) 6/735 (2)	(6 wkts dec.) 735

A. J. Bichel, B. Lee, J. N. Gillespie and S. C. G. MacGill did not bat.

Bowling: Streak 26–6–131–0; Blignaut 28–4–115–0; Ervine 31–4–146–4; Price 36–5–187–0; Gripper 25.3–0–142–2.

Zimbabwe

D. D Ebrahim b Gillespie	29	– b Gillespie	4
T. R. Gripper c Lehmann b Lee	53	– c Gilchrist b Gillespie	0
M. A. Vermeulen c Hayden b MacGill	38	– c Gilchrist b Lee	63
S. V. Carlisle c Hayden b MacGill	2	– c Hayden b Lehmann	35
C. B. Wishart c Gilchrist b Bichel	46	– lbw b Bichel	8
C. N. Evans b Bichel	22	– b Lehmann	5
†T. Taibu lbw b Gillespie	15	– c Gilchrist b Bichel	3
*H. H. Streak b Lee	9	– (9) not out	71
S. M. Ervine c Waugh b Gillespie	6	– (8) b Bichel	53
A. M. Blignaut lbw b Lee	0	– st Gilchrist b Lehmann	22
R. W. Price not out	2	– c Waugh b Bichel	36
L-b 10, w 2, n-b 5	17	B 4, l-b 6, w 5, n-b 6	21
1/61 (1) 2/105 (2) 3/120 (4) 4/131 (3) 5/199 (5) 6/200 (6) 7/231 (7) 8/231 (8) 9/231 (10) 10/239 (9)	239	1/2 (2) 2/11 (1) 3/110 (3) 4/112 (4) 5/118 (5) 6/126 (7) 7/126 (6) 8/209 (8) 9/247 (10) 10/321 (11)	321

Bowling: *First Innings*—Lee 15–4–48–3; Gillespie 25.3–9–52–3; Bichel 21–2–62–2; MacGill 21–4–54–2; Lehmann 2–1–3–0; Waugh 5–1–10–0. *Second Innings*—Lee 35–8–96–1; Gillespie 3–0–6–2; MacGill 3.4–1–10–0; Bichel 28.2–15–63–4; Lehmann 31.2–15–61–3; Martyn 13–5–34–0; Waugh 8–2–26–0; Ponting 5–1–15–0.

Umpires: S. Venkataraghavan (India) and P. Willey (England).
Third umpire: S. J. Davis. Referee: G. R. Viswanath (India).

AUSTRALIA v ZIMBABWE

Second Test Match

At Sydney, October 17, 18, 19, 20, 2003. Australia won by nine wickets. Toss: Zimbabwe. Test debuts: B. A. Williams; G. M. Ewing.

The Sydney Test was a more even contest than the First, with Australia weakened by the absence of the injured Gillespie, MacGill, Lehmann and, by the end of the second day, Lee. It was a match in which spin – this time of the left-arm variety – worked its magic as it so often does at the SCG; in which Ponting produced some dazzling artistry of his own; in which Katich made a surprising, impressive return to Test cricket; and in which a Zimbabwean bowler, Blessing Mahwire, had to climb into a completely empty stand to fetch a ball hit with awesome power by Hayden as he completed an 84-ball century.

The whole stadium felt eerily vacant, as Sydney demonstrated its ambivalence towards Test cricket in October – the Australian captain Waugh was uncertain whether such an experiment should be repeated. But it was a worthwhile experience for some: Brad Williams, the hearty and brutally fast bowler who was effectively discarded by his home state of Victoria but journeyed to Western Australia to regenerate his career, made his Test debut at 28, while Hogg and Katich, each armed with left-arm wrist spin that was almost entirely alien to Zimbabwe's batsmen, played their first Tests on Australian soil. For Zimbabwe, Ervine succumbed to a knee injury and Evans was left out of the team. They were replaced by Gavin Ewing, a 22-year-old off-spinning all-rounder, and Mahwire.

The loss of so many experienced Australian bowlers did not seem so much of a problem by lunch on the first day, with Zimbabwe's top three batsmen all gone. Williams veered the new ball around at great speed, and captured Vermeulen lbw for his first Test wicket, but Carlisle was at the crease, and building. He began by unsettling Hogg, twice clubbing dubiously directed deliveries to the boundary, and scored steadily throughout, sharing healthy partnerships with Taibu, the young, feisty vice-captain, and Streak. Carlisle had reached 50 from 96 balls just before a brilliant googly from Hogg spat off the pitch, caught the edge of Taibu's bat and thudded into Gilchrist's gloves.

As Carlisle's innings blossomed he was furnished with reminders from the Australian fielders that he had not made a Test century, and used the voices to spur him forward to his first. He reached an accomplished 118 but, when Australia batted, Ponting eclipsed him, imposing his aggressive frame of mind on the Zimbabwe bowlers and bringing up his 18th Test century in only 113 balls, pulling, driving and cutting with abandon. He finally fell to Price, who looked far more comfortable on the turning SCG pitch than he had in Perth. Price was absorbing to watch and not at all intimidated by the reputations of Ponting or Waugh and co. He captured them both for 169 and 61 respectively, and carved out the heart of Australia's middle order with his thoughtful left-arm spin.

Another of that middle order, Katich, proved an inspired selection. He rattled up his maiden Test half-century as Australia achieved a 95-run lead, and, though a late developer as a bowler, extracted six second-innings wickets including three important middle-order scalps.

Although Ponting and Hayden easily devoured the 172 runs needed for victory, giving Waugh his ninth clean sweep in 16 series as captain, Zimbabwe headed home with their dignity intact. They had lost 11 consecutive Tests, but revealed a proud team with a proud captain and considerable promise.

Man of the Match: R. T. Ponting. *Attendance:* 18,363.

Man of the Series: M. L. Hayden.

Close of play: First day, Zimbabwe 256-8 (Blignaut 9, Price 7); Second day, Australia 245-3 (Ponting 137, Waugh 43); Third day, Zimbabwe 151-4 (Wishart 32, Taibu 13).

Zimbabwe

D. D Ebrahim b Lee	9	– c Katich b Williams	0
T. R. Gripper c Gilchrist b Bichel	15	– c Hayden b Katich	47
M. A. Vermeulen lbw b Williams	17	– c Waugh b Williams	48
S. V. Carlisle c Ponting b Bichel	118	– c Williams b Katich	5
C. B. Wishart c Gilchrist b Williams	14	– st Gilchrist b Katich	45
†T. Taibu c Gilchrist b Hogg	27	– c Ponting b Katich	35
*H. H. Streak lbw b Hogg	14	– run out	25
G. M. Ewing c Martyn b Lee	2	– c Gilchrist b Hogg	0
A. M. Blignaut not out	38	– c Williams b Katich	44
R. W. Price c Williams b Bichel	20	– lbw b Katich	0
N. B. Mahwire c Gilchrist b Bichel	6	– not out	1
B 4, l-b 12, w 3, n-b 9	28	B 6, l-b 5, w 1, n-b 4	16
1/15 (1) 2/45 (2) 3/47 (3) 4/95 (5) 5/151 (6) 6/218 (7) 7/222 (8) 8/243 (4) 9/296 (10) 10/308 (11)	308	1/0 (1) 2/93 (3) 3/103 (4) 4/114 (2) 5/176 (5) 6/212 (7) 7/216 (8) 8/230 (6) 9/244 (10) 10/266 (9)	266

Bowling: *First Innings*—Lee 23–5–78–2; Williams 23–6–58–2; Bichel 24.2–7–66–4; Hogg 23–8–49–2; Waugh 4–0–7–0; Katich 7–0–25–0; Martyn 3–1–9–0. *Second Innings*—Williams 16–8–56–2; Bichel 19–5–64–0; Hogg 31–9–70–1; Katich 25.5–3–65–6.

Australia

J. L. Langer c Streak b Blignaut	2	– c Taibu b Streak	8
M. L. Hayden c Carlisle b Blignaut	20	– not out	101
R. T. Ponting b Price	169	– not out	53
D. R. Martyn lbw b Price	32		
*S. R. Waugh c Carlisle b Price	61		
S. M. Katich b Price	52		
†A. C. Gilchrist b Streak	20		
G. B. Hogg c Ebrahim b Price	13		
A. J. Bichel c Wishart b Blignaut	5		
B. Lee not out	6		
B. A. Williams c and b Price	7		
L-b 2, w 1, n-b 13	16	B 3, l-b 3, n-b 4	10
1/7 (1) 2/51 (2) 3/148 (4) 4/283 (5) 5/306 (3) 6/347 (7) 7/375 (8) 8/384 (6) 9/394 (9) 10/403 (11)	403	1/21 (1)	(1 wkt) 172

Bowling: *First Innings*—Streak 21–3–83–1; Blignaut 20–2–83–3; Mahwire 10–1–61–0; Price 41.3–6–121–6; Ewing 11–1–53–0. *Second Innings*—Streak 9–1–46–1; Blignaut 4–0–35–0; Price 12.1–0–63–0; Gripper 1–0–2–0; Ewing 3–0–20–0.

Umpires: B. F. Bowden (New Zealand) and S. Venkataraghavan (India).
Third umpire: P. D. Parker. Referee: G. R. Viswanath (India).

SHEFFIELD SHIELD/PURA CUP FINALS

1982-83	NEW SOUTH WALES* beat Western Australia by 54 runs.
1983-84	WESTERN AUSTRALIA beat Queensland by four wickets.
1984-85	NEW SOUTH WALES beat Queensland by one wicket.
1985-86	NEW SOUTH WALES drew with Queensland.
1986-87	WESTERN AUSTRALIA drew with Victoria.
1987-88	WESTERN AUSTRALIA beat Queensland by five wickets.
1988-89	WESTERN AUSTRALIA drew with South Australia.
1989-90	NEW SOUTH WALES beat Queensland by 345 runs.
1990-91	VICTORIA beat New South Wales by eight wickets.
1991-92	WESTERN AUSTRALIA beat New South Wales by 44 runs.
1992-93	NEW SOUTH WALES beat Queensland by eight wickets.
1993-94	NEW SOUTH WALES beat Tasmania by an innings and 61 runs.
1994-95	QUEENSLAND beat South Australia by an innings and 101 runs.
1995-96	SOUTH AUSTRALIA drew with Western Australia.
1996-97	QUEENSLAND* beat Western Australia by 160 runs.
1997-98	WESTERN AUSTRALIA beat Tasmania by seven wickets.
1998-99	WESTERN AUSTRALIA* beat Queensland by an innings and 31 runs.
1999-2000	QUEENSLAND drew with Victoria.
2000-01	QUEENSLAND beat Victoria by four wickets.
2001-02	QUEENSLAND beat Tasmania by 235 runs.
2002-03	NEW SOUTH WALES* beat Queensland by 246 runs.

Note: The team that finished top of the table had home advantage over the runners-up. In a drawn final, the home team won the title.

* *Victory for the away team.*

THE NEW ZEALANDERS IN PAKISTAN, 2003-04

BRIAN MURGATROYD

New Zealand's short visit, with five one-day internationals crammed into just nine days, was another step towards the return of cricketing normality in Pakistan. Following the attacks on the United States by Islamic terrorists in September 2001, international sides had repeatedly dodged scheduled tours of Pakistan on safety grounds – to the growing frustration of the cricket board, which saw the fears as largely unfounded. On this occasion they were proved right. However, in cricketing terms, New Zealand's trip was hardly an unqualified success. After coming close to a shock win in the thrilling first match, they were crushed in front of small crowds in the other four.

The visitors' squad was simply not good enough. New Zealand's previous trip, in May 2002, had been cut short by a bomb blast in Karachi (this visit was, in part, an attempt to make good Pakistan's financial losses from that tour) and six of their preferred squad refused to travel this time. Indeed in November, when New Zealand Cricket received a threatening email warning them not to tour, it looked as though the whole trip could be cancelled. It was only confirmed after the Pakistan board said they would pull out of a forthcoming return tour in retaliation.

As well as the refuseniks, several key players, most importantly captain Stephen Fleming and fast bowler Shane Bond, were ruled out by injury. As a result, New Zealand's squad contained seven players who had never appeared in a one-day international. In Hamish Marshall they unearthed a batsman with a look of real quality. But, on the whole, the inexperienced team could not compete with a Pakistan team skilled at playing in home conditions.

Pakistan's opening batsmen, Yasir Hameed and Imran Farhat, produced an unprecedented four successive century stands, their seamers bowled with pace and accuracy, and in the first three matches Abdul Razzaq scored 123 runs in 54 balls, a display of power hitting the New Zealand bowlers had no answer to.

As so often, the selection of the Pakistan squad had been controversial. A 22-man list of "probables" was reconsidered when it was revealed that the chief selector, Aamir Sohail, had not consulted either coach Javed Miandad or captain Inzamam-ul-Haq; one of the new players selected in the revised squad was Junaid Zia, a 19-year-old seam bowler and son of Lt General Tauqir Zia, chairman of the Pakistan board. Amid whisperings of nepotism, Junaid spared himself and the selectors any further embarrassment by pulling out almost immediately, citing pressure of exams. His father resigned as chairman shortly afterwards, after four years. By the turbulent standards of Pakistan cricket, it had been a long stint.

Note: Matches in this section were not first-class.

PAKISTAN v NEW ZEALAND

First One-Day International

At Lahore, November 29, 2003 (day/night). Pakistan won by three wickets. Toss: New Zealand. One-day international debuts: C. D. Cumming, R. A. Jones, H. J. H. Marshall, M. J. Mason, M. D. J. Walker, K. P. Walmsley.

Blazing hitting by Abdul Razzaq and Mohammad Sami won this game for Pakistan after all seemed lost. Joining forces with Pakistan needing an improbable 65 from 39 balls, they used just 27 of them, as a shot-a-ball blitz overwhelmed a green New Zealand side. Sami hit two sixes from only eight balls; Razzaq – dropped twice, the second a horrendous mix-up as Cairns and wicket-keeper McCullum dithered under a skier – faced just 22 deliveries for his 47. New Zealand still had cause for some satisfaction: 291 was their highest total in one-day internationals against Pakistan. Marshall, making a one-day debut three years after his first Test, looked highly accomplished, and Cairns provided savage late hitting during an unbeaten 84, from 51 balls, with six sixes. But Pakistan topped this with their highest successful run-chase at home. A dispute over television rights meant this match was not broadcast.

Man of the Match: Abdul Razzaq.

New Zealand

C. D. Cumming c Imran Farhat b Shabbir Ahmed	25
R. A. Jones b Abdul Razzaq	16
M. S. Sinclair st Moin Khan b Shoaib Malik	55
H. J. H. Marshall lbw b Shabbir Ahmed	55
*C. L. Cairns not out	84
J. D. P. Oram c Misbah-ul-Haq b Abdul Razzaq	35
†B. B. McCullum not out	0
L-b 5, w 8, n-b 8	21
1/49 (1) 2/57 (2) 3/156 (3) 4/178 (4) 5/268 (6) (5 wkts, 50 overs)	291

D. L. Vettori, M. D. J. Walker, K. P. Walmsley and M. J. Mason did not bat.

Bowling: Mohammad Sami 10–0–67–0; Shabbir Ahmed 10–0–30–2; Abdul Razzaq 10–1–71–2; Danish Kaneria 10–0–76–0; Shoaib Malik 10–0–42–1.

Pakistan

Yasir Hameed c Sinclair b Oram	52
Imran Farhat c McCullum b Mason	0
Yousuf Youhana run out	42
*Inzamam-ul-Haq lbw b Cairns	49
†Moin Khan c McCullum b Vettori	43
Shoaib Malik c Walker b Walmsley	9
Misbah-ul-Haq c Cumming b Oram	21
Abdul Razzaq not out	47
Mohammad Sami not out	17
L-b 7, w 2, n-b 3	12
1/2 (2) 2/92 (3) 3/95 (1) 4/194 (4) 5/196 (5) 6/223 (7) 7/227 (6) (7 wkts, 48 overs)	292

Shabbir Ahmed and Danish Kaneria did not bat.

Bowling: Mason 9–0–61–1; Walmsley 10–0–64–1; Cairns 6–0–52–1; Oram 8–0–33–2; Vettori 10–0–50–1; Walker 5–0–25–0.

Umpires: D. L. Orchard (South Africa) and Nadeem Ghauri.
Third umpire: Aleem Dar. Referee: D. T. Lindsay (South Africa).

PAKISTAN v NEW ZEALAND

Second One-Day International

At Lahore, December 1, 2003 (day/night). Pakistan won by 124 runs. Toss: Pakistan. One-day international debut: T. K. Canning.

Straight, quick, full-pitched bowling by Mohammad Sami – and some co-operative batting by the New Zealand tail – gave the match a spectacular conclusion. But, in truth, it was all over even before Sami sent stumps cartwheeling, with New Zealand 155 for five and needing to score at a run and a half a ball for their last 14 overs. As it turned out, they managed to reach only 157, as Sami took five wickets, four of them bowled, in just 12 balls. Earlier, Pakistan's batsmen made light of the absence of Inzamam-ul-Haq with a sore throat. Imran Farhat reached his first one-day fifty, Salim Elahi made 70 at a run a ball in his first appearance for 24 one-day internationals and Abdul Razzaq faced just 16 deliveries for his unbeaten 42. Only Vettori troubled the batsmen.

Man of the Match: Mohammad Sami.

Pakistan

Yasir Hameed c Cumming b Vettori	53
Imran Farhat c Hitchcock b Vettori	68
Salim Elahi c Vettori b Hitchcock	70
*Yousuf Youhana c sub (C. Z. Harris) b Vettori	11
Misbah-ul-Haq c Cairns b Tuffey	4
Shoaib Malik run out	23
Abdul Razzaq not out	42
†Moin Khan not out	1
B 4, l-b 1, w 4	9
1/115 (1) 2/144 (2) 3/162 (4) 4/171 (5) 5/221 (6) 6/266 (3) (6 wkts, 50 overs)	281

Mohammad Sami, Danish Kaneria and Shabbir Ahmed did not bat.

Bowling: Tuffey 10–1–62–1; Oram 9–1–38–0; Cairns 8–0–44–0; Hitchcock 9–0–54–1; Canning 4–0–34–0; Vettori 10–0–44–3.

New Zealand

C. D. Cumming c Shoaib Malik b Shabbir Ahmed	6
R. A. Jones b Shoaib Malik	63
M. S. Sinclair b Shabbir Ahmed	5
H. J. H. Marshall b Abdul Razzaq	14
*C. L. Cairns run out	29
J. D. P. Oram b Mohammad Sami	14
†B. B. McCullum b Mohammad Sami	0
T. K. Canning b Mohammad Sami	0
D. L. Vettori c Imran Farhat b Mohammad Sami	0
P. A. Hitchcock b Mohammad Sami	0
D. R. Tuffey not out	1
B 1, l-b 9, w 11, n-b 4	25
1/24 (1) 2/36 (3) 3/51 (4) 4/119 (5) 5/155 (2) 6/155 (6) 7/155 (8) 8/155 (9) 9/155 (10) 10/157 (7) (38.5 overs)	157

Bowling: Shabbir Ahmed 7–1–26–2; Mohammad Sami 7.5–2–10–5; Abdul Razzaq 6–1–27–1; Danish Kaneria 10–0–48–0; Shoaib Malik 8–1–36–1.

Umpires: D. L. Orchard (South Africa) and Nadeem Ghauri.
Third umpire: Aleem Dar. Referee: D. T. Lindsay (South Africa).

PAKISTAN v NEW ZEALAND

Third One-Day International

At Faisalabad, December 3, 2003. Pakistan won by 51 runs. Toss: Pakistan.

Inzamam-ul-Haq, in his 300th one-day international, caused a few raised eyebrows when he chose to bat first in cool, misty conditions. But his team justified the decision, becoming the first side to pass 300 in a one-day international on this ground. The New Zealand attack failed to exploit the conditions, their cause not helped by several dropped catches. Walker took three wickets in the final over with his medium-pace but by then the damage had been done: Yasir Hameed and Imran Farhat batted the first 30 overs for 142, before Abdul Razzaq again hit out contemptuously. In reply, Marshall, who had never made a century for Northern Districts, scored an unbeaten 101 at nearly a run a ball. But 31 of his runs came off part-time bowling when the result was inevitable.

Man of the Match: Imran Farhat.

Pakistan

Yasir Hameed c Cumming b Walmsley	63	Mohammad Sami not out	1
Imran Farhat c Marshall b Vettori	91	Salim Elahi not out	4
Yousuf Youhana c Marshall b Walker	64	L-b 1, w 12, n-b 3	16
*Inzamam-ul-Haq b Cairns	25		
Abdul Razzaq c Marshall b Walker	34	1/142 (1) 2/183 (2) (7 wkts, 50 overs)	314
Shoaib Malik c and b Walker	15	3/236 (4) 4/289 (3)	
†Moin Khan c Cumming b Walker	1	5/308 (6) 6/309 (5) 7/309 (7)	

Shabbir Ahmed and Shoaib Akhtar did not bat.

Bowling: Mason 10–0–74–0; Walmsley 10–0–53–1; Cairns 8–0–48–1; Walker 7–0–49–4; Harris 5–0–21–0; Vettori 10–0–68–1.

New Zealand

C. D. Cumming c Moin Khan b Shoaib Akhtar	10	M. D. J. Walker st Moin Khan b Imran Farhat	10
R. A. Jones c Yasir Hameed b Abdul Razzaq	23	D. L. Vettori not out	9
M. S. Sinclair run out	32		
H. J. H. Marshall not out	101	B 1, l-b 9, w 5, n-b 7	22
C. Z. Harris b Mohammad Sami	46		
*C. L. Cairns c Shabbir Ahmed b Mohammad Sami	9	1/12 (1) 2/58 (2) (7 wkts, 50 overs)	263
†B. B. McCullum lbw b Mohammad Sami	1	3/81 (3) 4/188 (5) 5/206 (6) 6/213 (7) 7/226 (8)	

M. J. Mason and K. P. Walmsley did not bat.

Bowling: Shoaib Akhtar 7–2–30–1; Mohammad Sami 8–1–22–3; Abdul Razzaq 10–0–50–1; Shabbir Ahmed 10–1–42–0; Shoaib Malik 10–0–64–0; Imran Farhat 3–0–22–1; Salim Elahi 1–0–10–0; Yasir Hameed 1–0–13–0.

Umpires: D. L. Orchard (South Africa) and Aleem Dar.
Third umpire: Nadeem Ghauri. Referee: D. T. Lindsay (South Africa).

PAKISTAN v NEW ZEALAND

Fourth One-Day International

At Rawalpindi, December 5, 2003 (day/night). Pakistan won by seven wickets. Toss: New Zealand.

After the match, Chris Cairns said his team had been hammered, and he was spot-on. New Zealand were second best from the moment Shoaib Akhtar struck with the fifth ball of the day and, though Cairns tried his best, his side never had enough runs to bowl at on an excellent pitch. Two needless run-outs made matters worse and, with Pakistan 134 for nought, they looked odds-on to face the ignominy of a ten-wicket defeat. Yasir Hameed prevented that embarrassment, driving carelessly to long-on. New Zealand only managed to stretch Pakistan's chase into the 42nd over because Inzamam decided to promote his middle-order players and give them some time at the crease.

Man of the Match: Imran Farhat.

> “‘When I saw four teams out there but not playing, I think that's the darkest day ever in the West Indies.’”
>
> Cricket in the West Indies, page 1357.

New Zealand

C. D. Cumming lbw b Shoaib Akhtar	0
R. A. Jones run out	17
M. S. Sinclair lbw b Abdul Razzaq	7
H. J. H. Marshall b Azhar Mahmood	11
C. Z. Harris c Salim Elahi b Shoaib Malik	25
*C. L. Cairns b Shoaib Malik	48
†B. B. McCullum run out	10
T. K. Canning c Yousuf Youhana b Shoaib Akhtar	13
P. A. Hitchcock b Umar Gul	9
D. R. Tuffey lbw b Shoaib Akhtar	10
M. J. Mason not out	13
L-b 8, w 7, n-b 5	20
1/0 (1) 2/23 (3) 3/31 (2) 4/49 (4) 5/82 (5) 6/100 (7) 7/143 (6) 8/149 (8) 9/162 (10) 10/183 (9) (47.5 overs)	183

Bowling: Shoaib Akhtar 10–1–23–3; Umar Gul 8.5–0–36–1; Abdul Razzaq 10–0–38–1; Azhar Mahmood 9–1–32–1; Shoaib Malik 10–0–46–2.

Pakistan

Yasir Hameed c Tuffey b Canning	61
Imran Farhat run out	82
Azhar Mahmood c Tuffey b Canning	4
Salim Elahi not out	7
Shoaib Malik not out	16
W 6, n-b 8	14
1/134 (1) 2/153 (3) 3/162 (2) (3 wkts, 41.2 overs)	184

Yousuf Youhana, †Moin Khan, *Inzamam-ul-Haq, Abdul Razzaq, Shoaib Akhtar and Umar Gul did not bat.

Bowling: Tuffey 7–0–45–0; Mason 10–1–44–0; Hitchcock 10–0–51–0; Cairns 4–1–12–0; Canning 10–1–30–2; Harris 0.2–0–2–0.

Umpires: D. L. Orchard (South Africa) and Aleem Dar.
Third umpire: Nadeem Ghauri. Referee: D. T. Lindsay (South Africa).

PAKISTAN v NEW ZEALAND

Fifth One-Day International

At Rawalpindi, December 7, 2003 (day/night). Pakistan won by 49 runs. Toss: Pakistan.

A New Zealand side short on quality and confidence failed to break Pakistan's opening pair for nearly 40 long overs. After trying 12 different openers in 15 months, Pakistan finally seemed to have found two that clicked: Yasir Hameed and Imran Farhat shared their fourth successive century stand – a world record – and both hit centuries. Although New Zealand restricted Pakistan to 131 from the final 20 overs, the off-spinner Shoaib Malik then slowly strangled their middle order, three of whom fell to suicidal run-outs as they tried to inject momentum into the innings. New Zealand's seventh successive one-day defeat made this their worst run since 1994-95.

Men of the Match (and Series): Imran Farhat and Yasir Hameed.

Pakistan

Yasir Hameed not out	127
Imran Farhat c Oram b Canning	107
Abdul Razzaq c Hitchcock b Canning	2
Shoaib Malik run out	4
†Moin Khan c Canning b Hitchcock	14
Azhar Mahmood not out	8
B 6, l-b 2, w 5, n-b 2	15
1/197 (2) 2/204 (3) 3/209 (4) 4/249 (5) (4 wkts, 50 overs)	277

Salim Elahi, Yousuf Youhana, *Inzamam-ul-Haq, Shabbir Ahmed and Shoaib Akhtar did not bat.

Bowling: Tuffey 8–1–48–0; Oram 6–1–23–0; Cairns 7–0–38–0; Hitchcock 9–0–56–1; Walker 10–0–45–0; Canning 10–0–59–2.

New Zealand

C. D. Cumming lbw b Abdul Razzaq	17	†B. B. McCullum lbw b Azhar Mahmood	5
R. A. Jones run out	49	T. K. Canning not out	23
M. S. Sinclair run out	36	L-b 12, w 10, n-b 7	29
H. J. H. Marshall not out	62		
*C. L. Cairns c Shabbir Ahmed b Shoaib Akhtar	6	1/50 (1) 2/106 (2) 3/141 (3) (6 wkts, 50 overs)	228
J. D. P. Oram run out	1	4/155 (5) 5/158 (6) 6/179 (7)	

M. D. J. Walker, P. A. Hitchcock and D. R. Tuffey did not bat.

Bowling: Shoaib Akhtar 8–1–36–1; Shabbir Ahmed 10–1–34–0; Abdul Razzaq 9–0–46–1; Azhar Mahmood 10–0–42–1; Shoaib Malik 10–0–33–0; Imran Farhat 2–0–18–0; Yasir Hameed 1–0–7–0.

Umpires: D. L. Orchard (South Africa) and Nadeem Ghauri.
Third umpire: Aleem Dar. Referee: D. T. Lindsay (South Africa).

ONE HUNDRED YEARS AGO

From JOHN WISDEN'S CRICKETERS' ALMANACK for 1904

NOTES BY THE EDITOR (Sydney Pardon) – "First-class cricket has increased enormously since the promotion of various counties in 1894 and I am not alone in thinking that now-a-days we have too many matches. In my opinion, bowling and fielding would be better if the leading players were not so constantly kept at full tension six days a week. Not many years ago the leading bowlers were able to vary their serious cricket with a holiday match now and then and the relief did them good. Now they are hard at it from the first week in May till the first week in September, and in fine summers are very apt to get stale."

THE LEADING COUNTIES IN 1903 – "Never has County Cricket been so affected by rain as in 1903. The summer was the wettest within the experience of anyone now playing first-class cricket, worse even than in 1879… Middlesex, for the first time since the Championship assumed anything like its present proportions, came out at the top of the list… Sussex, in coming out second… were mainly indebted to C. B. Fry and Ranjitsinhji, the former's batting in such a summer being nothing less than marvellous… Surrey had a disastrous season, and dropped from the fourth place on the list to eleventh."

DEATHS IN 1903, ARTHUR SHREWSBURY – "As everyone interested in cricket is aware, Arthur Shrewsbury shot himself on the evening of May 19. Illness which he could not be induced to believe curable, together with the knowledge that his career in the cricket field was over, had quite unhinged his mind… It may fairly be claimed for Shrewsbury that he was the greatest professional batsman of his day… He seemed to see the ball closer up to the bat than any other player. More than that, there was such an easy grace of style and such a suggestion of mastery in everything that he did that… excepting of course W. G. Grace, it may be questioned if we have ever produced a more remarkable batsman."

FIVE CRICKETERS OF THE YEAR, MR P. F. WARNER, – "A more enthusiastic player it would be impossible to find anywhere. Cricket, if one may be permitted the expression, is the very breath of his nostrils. When our season is over, his greatest delight is to journey to some region in which the game is practicable during our winter months, and few men have travelled so far or played in so many different parts of the world… Of medium height, small boned and light of frame, he does not by any means fill the eye as a great batsman, but… when the sun shines and the ground is hard, he is one of the best of batsmen to look at, combining a most attractive style with a great variety of strokes… He has lately taken to writing a good deal about the game to which he is so devoted, and, when cricket is the topic, he can make a capital after-dinner speech."

For excerpts from Wisden *50 years ago, see page 1321.*

VB SERIES, 2002-03

NICK HOULT

The sight of Australia dominating England in a one-day series was familiar enough, but the fact that they did it without several leading figures from recent contests suggested future meetings could be just as one-sided. Injuries to Shane Warne, Jason Gillespie and Glenn McGrath meant the three bowled together only in the first two matches while, for the first time since 1985, England faced an Australian side without either Waugh twin. But it made little difference. The series ended with England's 13th consecutive defeat by Australia; their only successes came against Sri Lanka when they were missing their injured match-winner, Muttiah Muralitharan.

Australia's superiority was emphatic. They lost only one of their eight group games, and in the first of the best-of-three finals crushed England in barely half the time allotted. The second final was very different, with England competing for long periods of a thrilling match, but in the closing stages the Australians called on their steely resilience – and on Brett Lee, who delivered the telling blows.

The tournament was not an unblemished Australian success, however. Following his dismissal in a match against Sri Lanka, Darren Lehmann was overheard shouting a racist obscenity in the Gabba changing-rooms. Although he apologised immediately and pacified the Sri Lankans, the ICC insisted on a hard line on racial abuse and he was banned for five matches. It was an ugly, unnecessary episode reflecting badly on the Australian game.

Another black cloud emerged after the series had finished. On January 23, less than six weeks after dislocating his bowling shoulder while fielding against England, Warne made his comeback in the first final. The previous day, he had announced his decision to retire from the frenetic demands of the one-day game after the World Cup, in an effort to prolong his Test career. It was a move that sent a warning to those authorities intent on filling every day of the year with international cricket.

But the speed of Warne's recovery, originally seen as another example of his ability to bounce back from serious injury, was later tainted by suspicion. On February 11, as Australia began their first World Cup game, it was announced that a drugs test he had taken before the VB finals had shown positive for diuretics, known masking agents. Warne claimed he was masking nothing, his mother had given him the pills and he took them to look slim in front of the cameras while announcing his retirement. Though his motives remained shrouded in doubt, the Australian board's response was unambiguous – a 12-month ban from all cricket.

Warne's injury gave Brad Hogg, a left-arm wrist-spinner from Western Australia, the chance to prove himself a capable replacement, and the experience Hogg gained here proved useful in the World Cup after Warne was banned. His total of 12 wickets was bettered for Australia only by Lee, the tournament's leading wicket-taker with 18 at 18.77. Often the catalyst with the new ball, Lee successfully allied his pace to accuracy, and the result was devastating.

Of Australia's regular top six, only the fill-ins, Jimmy Maher and Andrew Symonds, averaged less than 43, but it was England's Nick Knight, with 461, who narrowly beat Matthew Hayden to be the leading run-scorer. His lack of consistent support was one of England's major failings; they were usually short of wickets going into the last ten overs. Of the other batsmen, only Paul Collingwood could feel a real sense of achievement. His hundred against Sri Lanka at Perth was built on determination; he often produced his best in adversity.

James Anderson started the tournament as one of the less well-known faces at the ECB's National Academy, but injuries forced his rapid promotion. His late swing and consistency won him 13 wickets – England's joint-highest – and his emergence was their greatest fillip. But, when it mattered most, only Australia could call on a truly destructive bowler.

Unlike England, Sri Lanka did beat the Australians, but it was not enough to take them to the finals. If the Lehmann episode was the low point of their tour, that Sydney win, where Sanath Jayasuriya carved the first of two successive centuries, was the peak. But they managed only one other victory. With Murali, their record read: played three, won two. Without him they played five, and won none.

Note: Matches in this section were not first-class.

AUSTRALIA v ENGLAND

At Sydney, December 13, 2002 (day/night). Australia won by seven wickets. Australia 5 pts, England 1 pt. Toss: England. One-day international debut: G. J. Batty.

For the third time, Australia succeeded in doing what no one else has achieved: scoring more than 250 to win under the Sydney lights. On a wearing pitch, they made it with ease. Hayden marshalled a frantic opening assault, depositing Caddick over long-on for six as he and Gilchrist crashed 101 inside 14 overs. He went on to a 92-ball 98, and Australia sauntered home. England's openers had begun almost as briskly, but there was no sign of panic from Australia: when Lee found Trescothick's edge at 101 for nought in the 17th over, Warne was still at slip to snaffle the chance. Knight defied a 7–2 field to score heavily through the off side and, despite cramp, he limped past three figures, finding support from Hussain, who hit a lone four plus one six in his fifty. But Lehmann, turning the ball out of the rough, took three wickets and kept England within Hayden's reach.

Man of the Match: M. L. Hayden. *Attendance:* 35,873.

England

M. E. Trescothick c Warne b Lee	60
N. V. Knight not out	111
R. C. Irani lbw b Warne	0
*N. Hussain c Gillespie b Lehmann	52
I. D. Blackwell c Gilchrist b Lehmann	0
O. A. Shah c Bevan b Lehmann	2
†A. J. Stewart lbw b Lee	4
C. White b Lee	15
G. J. Batty b Lee	0
A. R. Caddick not out	1
B 2, w 3, n-b 1	6
1/101 (1) 2/103 (3) 3/205 (4) 4/206 (5) 5/211 (6) 6/223 (7) 7/249 (8) 8/249 (9) (8 wkts, 50 overs)	251

R. J. Kirtley did not bat.

Bowling: McGrath 8–0–36–0; Gillespie 7–1–41–0; Watson 3–0–25–0; Lee 8–0–47–4; Warne 10–0–42–1; Lehmann 10–0–32–3; Martyn 4–0–26–0.

Australia

†A. C. Gilchrist c Shah b Irani	53
M. L. Hayden c Trescothick b Blackwell	98
*R. T. Ponting c Irani b Blackwell	18
D. R. Martyn not out	46
D. S. Lehmann not out	27
L-b 5, w 2, n-b 3	10
1/101 (1) 2/161 (3) 3/190 (2) (3 wkts, 45 overs)	252

M. G. Bevan, S. R. Watson, S. K. Warne, B. Lee, J. N. Gillespie and G. D. McGrath did not bat.

Bowling: Kirtley 7–1–53–0; Caddick 6–0–35–0; White 7–0–33–0; Irani 5–0–33–1; Blackwell 10–0–38–2; Batty 10–0–55–0.

Umpires: R. E. Koertzen (South Africa) and S. J. A. Taufel.
Third umpire: S. J. Davis. Referee: Wasim Raja (Pakistan).

AUSTRALIA v ENGLAND

At Melbourne, December 15, 2002 (day/night). Australia won by 89 runs. Australia 6 pts. Toss: Australia. One-day international debut: J. M. Anderson.

The image of a distraught Shane Warne leaving on a stretcher overshadowed another imperious Australian performance. Diving to try and save a single off his own bowling, he had dislocated his right shoulder. Within an hour, Warne was being checked by the surgeon who had operated on the same joint in 1998; scans confirmed ligament damage, which put his World Cup place in jeopardy, but Warne would be back before this tournament was over. Earlier, Gilchrist and Ponting had blazed 225 together, an Australian second-wicket record. An unfamiliar England attack included 20-year-old James Anderson, who had played only three one-day games for Lancashire. Preferred to Caddick, he bowled more tidily than his figures suggested. In reply, three slick run-outs undid Knight's fluent work, and Australia's second-highest one-day total in Melbourne was well beyond England.

Man of the Match: A. C. Gilchrist. *Attendance:* 34,887.

Out of joint: Shane Warne is carried off after dislocating his shoulder.
Picture by Hamish Blair, Getty Images.

Australia

†A. C. Gilchrist b Anderson	124	S. K. Warne not out	19
M. L. Hayden c Batty b Kirtley	4		
*R. T. Ponting c Shah b Blackwell	119	L-b 6, w 7	13
M. G. Bevan b Batty	3		
D. R. Martyn c Batty b White	9	1/15 (2) 2/240 (1) (6 wkts, 50 overs)	318
D. S. Lehmann not out	18	3/247 (4) 4/271 (3)	
S. R. Watson c White b Blackwell	9	5/271 (5) 6/286 (7)	

B. Lee, J. N. Gillespie and G. D. McGrath did not bat.

Bowling: Kirtley 9–0–62–1; Anderson 6–0–46–1; White 10–1–56–1; Irani 5–0–29–0; Blackwell 10–0–54–2; Batty 10–0–65–1.

England

M. E. Trescothick c Hayden b Gillespie	6	J. M. Anderson b Lee	6
N. V. Knight c Warne b Watson	70	R. J. Kirtley b Lee	1
R. C. Irani run out	0		
*N. Hussain b Warne	19	B 4, l-b 4, w 5, n-b 1	14
O. A. Shah c McGrath b Warne	7		
†A. J. Stewart run out	3	1/13 (1) 2/16 (3) 3/76 (4) (48 overs)	229
I. D. Blackwell run out	43	4/87 (5) 5/92 (6) 6/131 (2)	
C. White not out	57	7/203 (7) 8/208 (9)	
G. J. Batty b Lehmann	3	9/223 (10) 10/229 (11)	

Bowling: McGrath 6–1–31–0; Gillespie 10–0–55–1; Lee 9–0–31–2; Warne 7.5–0–39–2; Watson 7–0–31–1; Martyn 2.1–0–13–0; Lehmann 6–0–21–1.

Umpires: S. A. Bucknor (West Indies) and S. J. A. Taufel.
Third umpire: S. J. Davis. Referee: Wasim Raja (Pakistan).

ENGLAND v SRI LANKA

At Brisbane, December 17, 2002 (day/night). England won by 43 runs. England 5 pts, Sri Lanka 1 pt. Toss: England. One-day international debut: S. J. Harmison.

It took 61 days, 14 matches and much exasperation before England finally claimed a victory on their Australian tour. The introduction of new, more fallible, opposition renewed their vigour and they destroyed Sri Lanka by following a perfectly executed strategy. First the batsmen, in particular Hussain and Stewart, paced the innings delightfully to reach a big total; then the bowlers finally obeyed captain's orders – straight and fast. But Anderson slipped in a slower one to dismiss Jayasuriya which had Hussain shouting "You're the man, Jimmy, you're the man", as weeks of frustration gave way to joy. Harmison, previously considered too unpredictable for one-day cricket, was given a start with the sole intention of exploiting Sri Lankan weakness against pace and bounce. The gamble worked: his two for 39 was reward for sustained speed allied to a good length. Sri Lanka's batsmen settled for a quiet recovery and a bonus point rather than a quest for victory.

Man of the Match: A. J. Stewart. *Attendance:* 9,495.

England

M. E. Trescothick c Mubarak b Vaas	27	A. R. Caddick c Fernando b Gunaratne	11
N. V. Knight c Jayawardene b Fernando	29	J. M. Anderson b Fernando	0
R. C. Irani c Mubarak b Gunaratne	1	S. J. Harmison not out	2
*N. Hussain run out	79	L-b 1, w 11, n-b 5	17
P. D. Collingwood c Jayawardene b Arnold	37	1/47 (1) 2/48 (3) 3/73 (2) (50 overs)	292
†A. J. Stewart b Jayasuriya	64	4/155 (5) 5/227 (4) 6/278 (7)	
I. D. Blackwell c and b Fernando	24	7/278 (6) 8/280 (8)	
C. White run out	1	9/284 (10) 10/292 (9)	

Bowling: Vaas 10–1–49–1; Gunaratne 10–1–55–2; Fernando 10–0–68–3; Samaraweera 7–0–44–0; Jayasuriya 10–0–58–1; Arnold 3–0–17–1.

Sri Lanka

*S. T. Jayasuriya c Hussain b Anderson . 13
†R. S. Kaluwitharana c Stewart b Caddick . 6
M. S. Atapattu c Knight b Harmison . . . 38
K. C. Sangakkara c Collingwood b Harmison . 11
D. P. M. D. Jayawardene c Stewart b White . 71
R. P. Arnold not out 60
J. Mubarak c Harmison b Anderson 13
T. T. Samaraweera not out 28
L-b 3, w 4, n-b 2 9

1/19 (2) 2/25 (1) (6 wkts, 50 overs) 249
3/63 (4) 4/101 (3)
5/176 (5) 6/192 (7)

W. P. U. J. C. Vaas, C. R. D. Fernando and P. W. Gunaratne did not bat.

Bowling: Caddick 10–0–53–1; Anderson 10–1–48–2; Harmison 10–1–39–2; Irani 10–0–58–0; White 10–1–48–1.

Umpires: R. E. Koertzen (South Africa) and D. B. Hair.
Third umpire: S. J. Davis. Referee: Wasim Raja (Pakistan).

ENGLAND v SRI LANKA

At Perth, December 20, 2002 (day/night). England won by 95 runs. England 6 pts. Toss: England.

Collingwood's maiden international century stood alone as a highlight in a match characterised by ineptitude. The fiery WACA pitch was not a welcoming venue for the Sri Lankans, who had joined England as a target of Australian mirth, and their defeat chipped at already dwindling confidence. England's win was shaped by Collingwood whose batting, unlike that of his more experienced top-order colleagues, showed maturity and substance. His century contained just four fours and two sixes and, despite temperatures touching 40°C, he ran hard between the wickets, adding 110 with White, a seventh-wicket England record. Sri Lanka helped England recover from early losses by dropping five catches. Anderson again found the right line and, more importantly in Perth, the right length, to contain the Sri Lankans, and three wickets from Caddick set England on course for a second successive victory.

Man of the Match: P. D. Collingwood. *Attendance:* 8,219.

England

M. E. Trescothick c Gunaratne b Vaas . . 11
N. V. Knight c Fernando b Vaas 15
R. C. Irani lbw b Vaas 4
*N. Hussain c Sangakkara b Nissanka . . 25
P. D. Collingwood c Atapattu b Fernando 100
†A. J. Stewart c Jayawardene b Nissanka 4
I. D. Blackwell c Jayawardene b Fernando 19
C. White b Fernando. 48
A. R. Caddick c Arnold b Fernando. . . . 9
J. M. Anderson not out 1
B 5, l-b 5, w 5, n-b 7 22

1/26 (1) 2/26 (2) (9 wkts, 50 overs) 258
3/39 (3) 4/89 (4)
5/93 (6) 6/122 (7)
7/232 (8) 8/250 (9) 9/258 (5)

S. J. Harmison did not bat.

Bowling: Vaas 10–0–36–3; Gunaratne 8–0–45–0; Fernando 10–0–48–4; Nissanka 10–0–59–2; Jayasuriya 10–0–49–0; Samaraweera 2–0–11–0.

Sri Lanka

M. S. Atapattu c Knight b Caddick 3
*S. T. Jayasuriya c and b Caddick. 10
J. Mubarak c Hussain b Caddick. 14
†K. C. Sangakkara c Stewart b Anderson 7
D. P. M. D. Jayawardene c Knight b White . 30
R. P. Arnold c Stewart b Harmison 44
T. T. Samaraweera c Stewart b Blackwell 27
W. P. U. J. C. Vaas c Collingwood b Blackwell . 3
R. A. P. Nissanka not out. 7
C. R. D. Fernando c Harmison b Anderson . 1
P. W. Gunaratne b Harmison. 0
L-b 10, w 6, n-b 1. 17

1/14 (1) 2/19 (2) 3/42 (3) (43.4 overs) 163
4/46 (4) 5/91 (5) 6/144 (7)
7/149 (8) 8/162 (6)
9/163 (10) 10/163 (11)

Bowling: Caddick 10–3–30–3; Anderson 8–2–23–2; Harmison 9.4–0–45–2; White 8–1–25–1; Irani 5–1–16–0; Blackwell 3–0–14–2.

Umpires: S. A. Bucknor (West Indies) and S. J. A. Taufel.
Third umpire: D. B. Hair. Referee: Wasim Raja (Pakistan).

AUSTRALIA v SRI LANKA

At Perth, December 22, 2002 (day/night). Australia won by 142 runs. Australia 6 pts. Toss: Australia.

Lehmann had asked for a chance further up the order, got it because of an injury to Adam Gilchrist, and responded with a century against the beleaguered Sri Lankans. His run-a-ball 119 combined brute force and improvisation, setting the tone for a one-sided game which culminated in another Sri Lankan surrender on a fast pitch ideal for Lee. After an opening partnership of 162 had set Australia charging towards a daunting 305 for five, Sri Lanka needed a vibrant start, but instead batted abjectly, losing their top three for 25. Defeat left them winless after three games – and apparently out of the running for a place in the final. As the series paused for the last two Ashes Tests, their only hopes lay in the return to fitness of Muttiah Muralitharan and the arrival of Aravinda de Silva.

Man of the Match: D. S. Lehmann. *Attendance:* 20,421.

Australia

D. S. Lehmann b Nissanka	119
M. L. Hayden c Jayawardene b Jayasuriya	64
*R. T. Ponting b Nissanka	17
D. R. Martyn c Arnold b Nissanka	9
M. G. Bevan not out	40
†R. J. Campbell c Arnold b Fernando	16
S. R. Watson not out	25
W 13, n-b 2	15
1/162 (2) 2/202 (3) 3/219 (1) 4/223 (4) 5/253 (6) (5 wkts, 50 overs)	305

G. B. Hogg, A. J. Bichel, B. Lee and G. D. McGrath did not bat.

Bowling: Vaas 7–0–47–0; Gunaratne 4–0–30–0; Fernando 10–1–55–1; Nissanka 8–0–54–3; Arnold 9–0–46–0; Jayasuriya 7–0–44–1; Mubarak 5–0–29–0.

Sri Lanka

M. S. Atapattu c Campbell b McGrath	15
*S. T. Jayasuriya c Bichel b Lee	3
J. Mubarak c Hayden b McGrath	4
D. P. M. D. Jayawardene c and b Lehmann	21
R. P. Arnold c Bichel b Hogg	15
K. C. Sangakkara c Bevan b Watson	40
†R. S. Kaluwitharana c Bevan b Watson	35
W. P. U. J. C. Vaas c Martyn b Lee	7
R. A. P. Nissanka not out	5
C. R. D. Fernando b Lee	0
P. W. Gunaratne c Campbell b Watson	2
B 4, l-b 3, w 6, n-b 3	16
1/15 (2) 2/24 (1) 3/25 (3) 4/60 (4) 5/62 (5) 6/140 (7) 7/153 (6) 8/160 (8) 9/160 (10) 10/163 (11) (43 overs)	163

Bowling: McGrath 8–2–22–2; Lee 7–1–23–3; Hogg 10–0–43–1; Lehmann 5–1–13–1; Bichel 8–0–28–0; Watson 5–0–27–3.

Umpires: R. E. Koertzen (South Africa) and D. B. Hair.
Third umpire: S. J. A. Taufel. Referee: Wasim Raja (Pakistan).

AUSTRALIA v SRI LANKA

At Sydney, January 9, 2003 (day/night). Sri Lanka won by 79 runs. Sri Lanka 6 pts. Toss: Australia.

Just two days after being bowled out for 65 by Australia A, Sri Lanka produced the performance of the competition. They were inspired by Jayasuriya, who swatted an 87-ball century to lift his side's tour out of mediocrity and inject interest into a triangular series which, before the Christmas break, had been a two-horse race. This was the Jayasuriya of old, riding his luck to provide grand entertainment. In contrast to his bluster was an authoritative century from Atapattu, the more temperate half of a partnership of 237 – Sri Lanka's all-wicket best in one-day internationals. Together, they scored seven an over against an attack depleted by injuries, and Sri Lanka eventually reached 343, the highest one-day total ever conceded by Australia. Jayasuriya the spinner then took over and ended with Murali-like figures of four for 39. Muralitharan himself, returning from a hernia operation, took two. Australia, just beaten by England in the final Test on the same ground, would have lost even more heavily but for a record stand of their own – 63 by the last pair, Watson and Bichel.

Man of the Match: S. T. Jayasuriya. *Attendance:* 33,759.

Sri Lanka

M. S. Atapattu run out	101	W. P. U. J. C. Vaas not out	5
*S. T. Jayasuriya b Watson	122	L-b 12, w 20, n-b 8	40
P. A. de Silva b Watson	13		—
D. P. M. D. Jayawardene not out	37	1/237 (2) 2/267 (3) (5 wkts, 50 overs)	343
R. P. Arnold st Gilchrist b Symonds	0	3/283 (1) 4/284 (5)	
†K. C. Sangakkara c Maher b Bichel	25	5/329 (6)	

H. P. Tillekeratne, M. Muralitharan, C. R. D. Fernando and P. W. Gunaratne did not bat.

Bowling: Lee 7–0–41–0; Bichel 10–0–70–1; Watson 10–0–72–2; Symonds 9–0–50–1; Hogg 9–0–75–0; Martyn 5–0–23–0.

Australia

†A. C. Gilchrist b Vaas	6	G. B. Hogg st Sangakkara b Muralitharan	4
M. L. Hayden c Jayawardene b Fernando	35	A. J. Bichel c Sangakkara b Gunaratne	28
*R. T. Ponting c Tillekeratne b Gunaratne	15		
D. R. Martyn b Jayasuriya	40	L-b 12, w 4, n-b 5	21
M. G. Bevan c Tillekeratne b Jayasuriya	41		—
A. Symonds c Tillekeratne b Muralitharan	4	1/6 (1) 2/35 (3) 3/78 (2) (49.3 overs)	264
B. Lee b Jayasuriya	20	4/143 (4) 5/150 (5) 6/152 (6)	
J. P. Maher c Jayawardene b Jayasuriya	15	7/188 (8) 8/188 (7)	
S. R. Watson not out	35	9/201 (10) 10/264 (11)	

Bowling: Vaas 6–0–29–1; Gunaratne 8.3–0–54–2; Fernando 9–0–46–1; de Silva 6–0–40–0; Muralitharan 10–1–44–2; Jayasuriya 10–1–39–4.

Umpires: R. B. Tiffin (Zimbabwe) and S. J. A. Taufel.
Third umpire: D. B. Hair. Referee: C. H. Lloyd (West Indies).

AUSTRALIA v ENGLAND

At Hobart, January 11, 2003. Australia won by seven runs. Australia 5 pts, England 1 pt. Toss: Australia.

England lost momentum with both bat and ball, and faded to their tenth successive one-day defeat by Australia. "Sloppy" was Hussain's summary. Anderson created early impetus and looked dependable in just his fourth international, but Martyn exploited England's lack of a reliable third seamer, hitting his first hundred of the southern summer. Australia accelerated towards 271 – above par on a pitch of variable bounce. A vivacious opening stand of 165 between Trescothick and Knight kept England's required rate under six an over, but Australia squeezed an inexperienced middle order: the big hitter Blackwell, promoted to No. 3, shifted the tempo down rather than up, and England were left needing 74 from ten overs. Watson kept his nerve, as Hussain tried to slog his way out of trouble in the final over, and his home crowd, a mass of coloured sunhats, were soon cheering a win that England had let slip away.

Man of the Match: D. R. Martyn. *Attendance:* 16,719.

Australia

†A. C. Gilchrist lbw b Anderson	2
M. L. Hayden c and b Harmison	21
*R. T. Ponting c Stewart b Anderson	15
D. R. Martyn not out	101
M. G. Bevan b Blackwell	52
J. P. Maher not out	49
L-b 9, w 22	31
1/7 (1) 2/25 (3) 3/53 (2) 4/171 (5) (4 wkts, 50 overs)	271

S. R. Watson, G. B. Hogg, A. J. Bichel, B. Lee and G. D. McGrath did not bat.

Bowling: Caddick 10–0–54–0; Anderson 10–1–40–2; Harmison 8–0–58–1; Irani 9–0–55–0; Collingwood 3–0–14–0; Blackwell 10–1–41–1.

England

M. E. Trescothick c sub (A. Symonds) b Martyn	82
N. V. Knight b Bichel	85
I. D. Blackwell c Gilchrist b Hogg	12
*N. Hussain b Watson	43
O. A. Shah c Ponting b Hogg	8
P. D. Collingwood c Maher b Hogg	1
†A. J. Stewart c Martyn b Watson	16
R. C. Irani not out	3
A. R. Caddick not out	2
B 2, l-b 2, w 2, n-b 6	12
1/165 (2) 2/189 (1) 3/193 (3) 4/209 (5) 5/211 (6) 6/252 (7) 7/262 (4) (7 wkts, 50 overs)	264

J. M. Anderson and S. J. Harmison did not bat.

Bowling: McGrath 7–1–31–0; Lee 10–0–65–0; Watson 8–0–36–2; Bichel 10–0–39–1; Hogg 9–0–55–3; Martyn 6–0–34–1.

Umpires: D. L. Orchard (South Africa) and D. B. Hair.
Third umpire: S. J. Davis. Referee: C. H. Lloyd (West Indies).

ENGLAND v SRI LANKA

At Sydney, January 13, 2003 (day/night). Sri Lanka won by 31 runs. Sri Lanka 5 pts, England 1 pt. Toss: Sri Lanka.

Jayasuriya's second hundred in five days reawakened Sri Lankan hopes of reaching the finals – and left England perplexed by their persistent failings with the bat. Whereas Jayasuriya, who was at his dynamic best, upper-cutting and scoring freely through square leg, was supported by those lower down the order, England were again negligent after the parting of their two opening batsmen. Trescothick and Knight set off at a gallop as they chased 285, and their opening partnership of 115 in 20 overs suggested a remarkable win. But once Trescothick had been run out, England deflated. De Silva's four wickets punctured England's resolve, Muralitharan collected his 300th wicket at this level, and Sri Lanka were left just two points behind, with a game in hand.

Man of the Match: S. T. Jayasuriya. *Attendance:* 11,716.

Sri Lanka

M. S. Atapattu c Knight b Caddick	0
*S. T. Jayasuriya c Knight b Blackwell	106
H. P. Tillekeratne c Trescothick b Collingwood	44
P. A. de Silva c Stewart b Caddick	51
†K. C. Sangakkara c and b Anderson	10
D. P. M. D. Jayawardene c Collingwood b Anderson	33
R. P. Arnold run out	0
W. P. U. J. C. Vaas not out	6
M. Muralitharan not out	3
B 1, l-b 10, w 16, n-b 4	31
1/0 (1) 2/144 (3) 3/199 (2) 4/224 (5) 5/264 (4) 6/269 (7) 7/277 (6) (7 wkts, 50 overs)	284

T. C. B. Fernando and C. R. D. Fernando did not bat.

Bowling: Caddick 10–3–29–2; Anderson 9–0–58–2; Harmison 9–0–59–0; Irani 9–0–53–0; Blackwell 10–0–54–1; Collingwood 3–0–20–1.

England

M. E. Trescothick run out	85
N. V. Knight c Sangakkara b C. R. D. Fernando	42
*N. Hussain c Sangakkara b C. R. D. Fernando	13
O. A. Shah c Jayawardene b de Silva	39
P. D. Collingwood b Jayasuriya	2
†A. J. Stewart run out	6
I. D. Blackwell c Atapattu b de Silva	16
R. C. Irani c and b de Silva	2
A. R. Caddick not out	14
J. M. Anderson b Muralitharan	1
S. J. Harmison c Arnold b de Silva	7
B 1, l-b 13, w 7, n-b 5	26
1/115 (2) 2/146 (3) 3/161 (1) 4/167 (5) 5/179 (6) 6/217 (7) 7/227 (4) 8/227 (8) 9/234 (10) 10/253 (11)	(49.2 overs) 253

Bowling: Vaas 9–1–54–0; T. C. B. Fernando 7–0–36–0; de Silva 6.2–1–30–4; C. R. D. Fernando 7–0–38–2; Muralitharan 10–1–36–1; Jayasuriya 10–0–45–1.

Umpires: R. B. Tiffin (Zimbabwe) and D. B. Hair.
Third umpire: S. J. A. Taufel. Referee: C. H. Lloyd (West Indies).

AUSTRALIA v SRI LANKA

At Brisbane, January 15, 2003 (day/night). Australia won by four wickets. Australia 5 pts, Sri Lanka 1 pt. Toss: Sri Lanka.

Australia's victory was tainted by a dreadful outburst from Darren Lehmann. After being run out, Lehmann shouted a racist obscenity in the Australian dressing-room and was overheard by the Sri Lankans. They complained to the referee, Clive Lloyd, but after verbal and written apologies from Lehmann their anger was assuaged, which influenced Lloyd to restrict himself to a severe reprimand. But the ICC's chief executive, Malcolm Speed, decided to lay charges and, after a further hearing at Adelaide on January 18, Lloyd imposed a five-match ban – the first such penalty for a racist offence in international cricket. Out in the middle, the match was decided by a well-judged 45 from Bevan. Chasing a moderate total, Australia were in control at 76 for no wicket, but then lost four – three to Muralitharan – for 24 in the space of 11 overs. Lehmann and Bevan ate away at the target, however, and Sri Lanka were dealt a mortal blow when Murali suffered a thigh injury in the field. He returned to bowl his final two overs from a standing start and claimed a fourth wicket, but Bevan won the game with only his second four.

Man of the Match: M. G. Bevan. *Attendance:* 34,485.

Sri Lanka

M. S. Atapattu c Ponting b McGrath	70
*S. T. Jayasuriya run out	6
H. P. Tillekeratne run out	7
P. A. de Silva c Martyn b Lee	0
D. P. M. D. Jayawardene b Hogg	56
†K. C. Sangakkara not out	42
R. P. Arnold c Maher b Hogg	3
W. P. U. J. C. Vaas b Williams	0
T. C. B. Fernando run out	3
M. Muralitharan run out	0
C. R. D. Fernando not out	0
B 4, l-b 6, w 11, n-b 3	24
1/13 (2) 2/30 (3) 3/35 (4) 4/147 (1) 5/165 (5) 6/173 (7) 7/181 (8) 8/199 (9) 9/201 (10)	(9 wkts, 50 overs) 211

Bowling: McGrath 10–2–33–1; Williams 10–0–33–1; Lee 10–1–44–1; Hogg 10–1–38–2; Watson 8–0–36–0; Lehmann 2–0–17–0.

Australia

†J. P. Maher st Sangakkara b Muralitharan	30
M. L. Hayden c C. R. D. Fernando b Muralitharan	42
*R. T. Ponting st Sangakkara b de Silva	15
D. R. Martyn b Muralitharan	1
D. S. Lehmann run out	38
M. G. Bevan not out	45
S. R. Watson c Tillekeratne b Muralitharan	4
G. B. Hogg not out	14
B 5, l-b 4, w 11, n-b 5	25
1/76 (1) 2/94 (2) 3/98 (4) 4/100 (3) 5/172 (5) 6/182 (7)	(6 wkts, 48.5 overs) 214

B. Lee, B. A. Williams and G. D. McGrath did not bat.

Bowling: Vaas 10–1–38–0; T. C. B. Fernando 7–0–32–0; C. R. D. Fernando 10–0–48–0; de Silva 6.5–0–31–1; Muralitharan 10–1–27–4; Jayasuriya 3–0–17–0; Arnold 2–0–12–0.

Umpires: D. L. Orchard (South Africa) and S. J. A. Taufel.
Third umpire: D. B. Hair. Referee: C. H. Lloyd (West Indies).

ENGLAND v SRI LANKA

At Adelaide, January 17, 2003 (day/night). England won by 19 runs. England 5 pts, Sri Lanka 1 pt. Toss: England.

When Jayasuriya set off for his 100th run, Sri Lanka needed 122 at less than a run a ball, with six wickets left. However, a mid-pitch collision with Sangakkara changed the course of the match and left England virtually assured of a place in the finals. Jayasuriya's run-out for an 83-ball 99 – one short of his third century in four games – shook Sri Lanka from their stride and Caddick, enjoying a resurgence since the Sydney Test, did the rest. On a warm evening which drew the best out of England's bowlers, his awkward length distressed the Sri Lankans and he ended with four for 35. The roots of the win were Knight's carefully paced innings and a jaunty reminder of Stewart's gift for timing the ball. His fifty injected a zeal the middle order had recently lacked, and lifted England to a total that disguised the difficulties of a two-paced pitch.

Man of the Match: A. R. Caddick. *Attendance:* 9,912.

England

M. E. Trescothick b Lakshitha	39
N. V. Knight c Sangakkara b Vaas	88
M. P. Vaughan c Vaas b C. R. D. Fernando	28
*N. Hussain b Jayasuriya	18
†A. J. Stewart b Lakshitha	51
I. D. Blackwell lbw b Vaas	0
P. D. Collingwood c Tillekeratne b C. R. D. Fernando	18
R. C. Irani not out	13
A. R. Caddick not out	1
L-b 11, w 4, n-b 8	23
1/56 (1) 2/114 (3) 3/155 (4) 4/206 (2) 5/206 (6) 6/260 (7) 7/272 (5) (7 wkts, 50 overs)	279

J. M. Anderson and S. J. Harmison did not bat.

Bowling: Vaas 10–0–54–2; T. C. B. Fernando 4–0–27–0; Lakshitha 9–0–42–2; de Silva 8–0–45–0; C. R. D. Fernando 9–0–52–2; Jayasuriya 10–0–48–1.

Sri Lanka

M. S. Atapattu b Caddick	12
*S. T. Jayasuriya run out	99
H. P. Tillekeratne c Stewart b Caddick	9
P. A. de Silva c Stewart b Collingwood	15
D. P. M. D. Jayawardene c Vaughan b Irani	13
†K. C. Sangakkara c Blackwell b Caddick	56
R. P. Arnold c Blackwell b Caddick	35
W. P. U. J. C. Vaas c Collingwood b Vaughan	1
M. K. G. C. P. Lakshitha c Trescothick b Anderson	4
T. C. B. Fernando not out	1
C. R. D. Fernando b Anderson	0
B 2, l-b 4, w 8, n-b 1	15
1/19 (1) 2/53 (3) 3/119 (4) 4/150 (5) 5/158 (2) 6/251 (6) 7/254 (8) 8/257 (7) 9/260 (9) 10/260 (11) (49.2 overs)	260

Bowling: Caddick 10–0–35–4; Anderson 7.2–0–54–2; Harmison 2–0–27–0; Irani 10–0–36–1; Collingwood 3–0–23–1; Blackwell 10–0–44–0; Vaughan 7–0–35–1.

Umpires: R. B. Tiffin (Zimbabwe) and D. J. Harper.
Third umpire: S. J. Davis. Referee: C. H. Lloyd (West Indies).

AUSTRALIA v ENGLAND

At Adelaide, January 19, 2003 (day/night). Australia won by four wickets. Australia 5 pts, England 1 pt. Toss: England. One-day international debut: M. J. Clarke.

A slow pitch and ferociously hot weather produced a woeful match, and England qualified for the finals despite their worst performance so far. Bracken helped reduce England to 71 for six, before Collingwood led a partial recovery. In reply, Australia lost their openers cheaply, and grinding, attritional cricket set in. With even spectators being treated for heat exhaustion, Anderson

ENGLAND'S MOST ECONOMICAL ONE-DAY SPELLS

C. M. Old	10	5	8	4	v Canada at Manchester	1979
J. A. Snow	12	6	11	4	v East Africa at Birmingham	1975
D. L. Underwood	10	5	11	0	v East Africa at Birmingham	1975
R. G. D. Willis	10.3	3	11	4	v Canada at Manchester	1979
C. M. Old	11	4	12	2	v West Indies at Leeds	1980
P. A. J. DeFreitas	11	4	12	1	v South Africa at Manchester	1994
I. T. Botham	10	4	12	2	v Pakistan at Adelaide	1991-92
J. M. Anderson	**10**	**6**	**12**	**1**	**v Australia at Adelaide**	**2002-03**

Only spells of ten or more overs included. A. Flintoff took 10–2–15–2 v India at Durban 38 days after Anderson's performance.

Research: Philip Bailey

defied the conditions, bowled his overs straight off and conceded only 12 runs, England's cheapest ten-over spell since Ian Botham's two for 12 against Pakistan at the 1992 World Cup. Bevan and Martyn spurned attack, and Australia failed to win inside 40 overs – giving England the bonus point that guaranteed them, not Sri Lanka, a place in the finals – but Michael Clarke, making his debut in a heavily depleted side, played more positively to inch Australia towards victory.

Man of the Match: N. W. Bracken. *Attendance:* 26,045.

England

M. E. Trescothick c Gilchrist b Bracken	6
N. V. Knight c Gilchrist b Bracken	11
M. P. Vaughan c Gilchrist b Williams	21
*N. Hussain c and b Bracken	0
†A. J. Stewart c Maher b Watson	6
P. D. Collingwood not out	63
I. D. Blackwell b Watson	0
R. C. Irani c Bevan b Clarke	20
A. R. Caddick c Martyn b Hogg	6
J. M. Anderson lbw b Hogg	8
M. J. Hoggard run out	5
L-b 2, n-b 4	6
(48.3 overs)	152

1/13 (1) 2/38 (3) 3/39 (4) 4/40 (2) 5/67 (5) 6/71 (7) 7/116 (8) 8/122 (9) 9/136 (10) 10/152 (11)

Bowling: Williams 7–1–20–1; Bracken 7.3–2–21–3; Watson 7–2–18–2; Lee 10–2–28–0; Hogg 10–0–39–2; Clarke 7–0–24–1.

Australia

*†A. C. Gilchrist c Trescothick b Caddick	4
J. P. Maher c Stewart b Anderson	0
D. R. Martyn c Collingwood b Blackwell	59
M. G. Bevan c Knight b Blackwell	30
B. Lee c Collingwood b Vaughan	0
M. J. Clarke not out	39
A. Symonds st Stewart b Blackwell	0
S. R. Watson not out	13
L-b 4, w 2, n-b 2	8
(6 wkts, 47.3 overs)	153

1/4 (2) 2/5 (1) 3/96 (4) 4/97 (5) 5/104 (3) 6/104 (7)

G. B. Hogg, B. A. Williams and N. W. Bracken did not bat.

Bowling: Caddick 10–2–34–1; Anderson 10–6–12–1; Blackwell 10–2–26–3; Hoggard 7.3–0–35–0; Vaughan 5–0–20–1; Irani 5–0–22–0.

Umpires: D. L. Orchard (South Africa) and D. J. Harper.
Third umpire: S. J. Davis. Referee: C. H. Lloyd (West Indies).

AUSTRALIA v SRI LANKA

At Melbourne, January 21, 2003 (day/night). Australia won by nine wickets. Australia 6 pts. Toss: Sri Lanka.

Half an Australian first eleven was again more than good enough for a comfortable win. Sri Lanka's decision to select only three specialist bowlers for this dead match depended for success on the efforts of their batsmen. Atapattu and Gunawardene put on 64 inside 15 overs, but a mid-innings collapse – partly to Hogg's quirky left-arm wrist-spin – negated the brisk start. Ponting then played with the ease of a man enjoying the form of his life. He cruised to 106 in 97 balls, with 11 fours and a six, and shared an unbroken stand of 178 with Hayden to guide Australia to an easy victory.

Man of the Match: R. T. Ponting. *Attendance:* 41,601.

Sri Lanka

*M. S. Atapattu c Hogg b Bichel	26
D. A. Gunawardene lbw b Hogg	45
†K. C. Sangakkara c Watson b Hogg	43
P. A. de Silva c Watson b Bracken	44
D. P. M. D. Jayawardene st Gilchrist b Hogg	0
R. P. Arnold b Williams	14
W. P. U. J. C. Vaas run out	1
J. Mubarak lbw b Williams	15
H. P. Tillekeratne not out	9
L-b 5, w 11, n-b 1	17
1/64 (1) 2/100 (2) 3/134 (3) 4/135 (5) 5/166 (6) 6/170 (7) 7/201 (4) 8/214 (8) (8 wkts, 50 overs)	214

M. K. G. C. P. Lakshitha and R. A. P. Nissanka did not bat.

Bowling: Williams 10–0–57–2; Bracken 9–0–33–1; Bichel 10–0–33–1; Hogg 10–0–37–3; Watson 4–0–17–0; Symonds 7–0–32–0.

Australia

†A. C. Gilchrist b Vaas	26
M. L. Hayden not out	80
*R. T. Ponting not out	106
W 3	3
1/37 (1) (1 wkt, 34.3 overs)	215

J. P. Maher, M. G. Bevan, A. Symonds, S. R. Watson, G. B. Hogg, A. J. Bichel, B. A. Williams and N. W. Bracken did not bat.

Bowling: Vaas 8–0–45–1; Nissanka 7.3–0–61–0; de Silva 9–0–51–0; Lakshitha 3–0–23–0; Arnold 5–0–27–0; Jayawardene 2–0–8–0.

Umpires: R. B. Tiffin (Zimbabwe) and D. J. Harper.
Third umpire: S. J. A. Taufel. Referee: C. H. Lloyd (West Indies).

QUALIFYING TABLE

	Played	*Won*	*Lost*	*Bonus points*	*Points*	*Net run-rate*
Australia	8	7	1	3	38	0.73
England	8	3	5	5	20	–0.02
Sri Lanka	8	2	6	4	14	–0.70

Win = 5 pts. One bonus point awarded either to the winning team for achieving victory with a run-rate 1.25 times that of the opposition, or to the losing team for denying the winners a bonus point. Net run-rate is calculated by subtracting runs conceded per over from runs scored per over.

AUSTRALIA v ENGLAND

First Final Match

At Sydney, January 23, 2003 (day/night). Australia won by ten wickets. Toss: England.

This was an almighty beating. It took Australia only 12.2 overs to pass their paltry target as Gilchrist and Hayden mercilessly pounded the bowlers. Gilchrist's 69 was bludgeoned from 37 balls, 14 despatched to the boundary. Four board-rattling cuts and pulls plus one all-run four came in a single Caddick over; Hayden's 45, also off 37 balls, looked muted by contrast. The carnage had begun much earlier, when, after England had digested a threatening letter from "Zimbabwe freedom fighters" about their imminent World Cup fixture in Harare, their openers were confronted by Lee aiming for the jugular – literally. Both were caught behind off vicious short balls, and only a spirited 43 from Collingwood dragged England to three figures. He was finally stumped off Warne, making his comeback after his shoulder operation. Bichel, who had also recently returned from injury, produced his best performance of the series; Gilchrist equalled his own record of six dismissals in a one-day international. It hardly mattered that Australia were without McGrath, Gillespie and Watson: they displayed awesome strength against a jaded side.

Man of the Match: B. Lee. *Attendance:* 37,879.

England

M. E. Trescothick c Gilchrist b Lee	0
N. V. Knight c Gilchrist b Lee	5
M. P. Vaughan lbw b Bichel	21
*N. Hussain b Williams	1
†A. J. Stewart c Gilchrist b Williams	12
P. D. Collingwood st Gilchrist b Warne	43
I. D. Blackwell c Ponting b Bichel	0
R. C. Irani c Bichel b Lee	10
A. R. Caddick not out	12
J. M. Anderson c Gilchrist b Bichel	0
M. J. Hoggard c Gilchrist b Bichel	0
L-b 7, w 5, n-b 1	13
1/1 (1) 2/11 (2) 3/19 (4) 4/33 (5) 5/45 (3) 6/45 (7) 7/79 (8) 8/115 (6) 9/117 (10) 10/117 (11) (41 overs)	117

Bowling: Williams 10–2–22–2; Lee 10–1–29–3; Bichel 7–2–18–4; Warne 10–0–28–1; Hogg 4–0–13–0.

Australia

†A. C. Gilchrist not out	69
M. L. Hayden not out	45
L-b 2, w 2	4
(no wkt, 12.2 overs)	118

*R. T. Ponting, D. R. Martyn, M. G. Bevan, A. Symonds, G. B. Hogg, S. K. Warne, B. Lee, A. J. Bichel and B. A. Williams did not bat.

Bowling: Caddick 3–0–31–0; Anderson 4–0–35–0; Hoggard 3.2–0–36–0; Irani 2–0–14–0.

Umpires: D. L. Orchard (South Africa) and S. J. A. Taufel.
Third umpire: D. B. Hair. Referee: C. H. Lloyd (West Indies).

AUSTRALIA v ENGLAND

Second Final Match

At Melbourne, January 25, 2003 (day/night). Australia won by five runs. Toss: Australia.

It was almost the great comeback: after 12 straight one-day losses against Australia, including that thrashing two days earlier, England came within six runs of victory. Lee once again wrecked their hopes. Beginning the 48th over with 14 needed and four wickets standing, he fired out Flintoff and Blackwell; when he returned to bowl the last, six were required, but Collingwood was stranded at the non-striker's end, and Caddick was promptly castled by a yorker. The last man, Anderson, never had a hope against one of the world's finest fast bowlers. A desperate scramble to get off strike ended in a run-out, closing England's tour on an appropriately disappointing note. Earlier, Hogg's perseverance and neat improvisations had helped Australia score nine an over in the late stages: from 148 for six (effectively seven, after Bevan tore a groin muscle) they reached a defensible 229. It looked plenty when Lee removed England's openers for the second time running and, when Hussain was fourth out at 88, it seemed another Australian walkover was unfolding. But Vaughan gave the middle order solidity, and Stewart added a sprinkling of crisp strokes. In the end, Lee emerged triumphant – though it was Warne, in what he said would be his last one-day international at his MCG home, who was chaired from the field.

Man of the Match: B. Lee. *Attendance:* 23,107.
Man of the Series: B. Lee.

Australia

†A. C. Gilchrist c Anderson b Flintoff . . 26
M. L. Hayden c sub (O. A. Shah) b Irani 69
*R. T. Ponting c Flintoff b Caddick 1
D. R. Martyn c Stewart b Caddick. 11
M. G. Bevan retired hurt 10
A. Symonds b Irani 8
G. B. Hogg not out. 71
S. K. Warne c and b Irani 0
B. Lee c Blackwell b Anderson. 18
A. J. Bichel not out 11
B 3, w 1 4

1/39 (1) 2/40 (3) 3/56 (4) 4/98 (6) 5/147 (2) 6/148 (8) 7/196 (9) (7 wkts, 50 overs) 229

B. A. Williams did not bat.

Bevan retired hurt at 74.

Bowling: Caddick 10–2–23–2; Anderson 9–0–57–1; Flintoff 10–0–56–1; Blackwell 10–0–32–0; Irani 10–1–46–3; Vaughan 1–0–12–0.

England

M. E. Trescothick c Bichel b Lee 0
N. V. Knight c Symonds b Lee 5
R. C. Irani c Symonds b Williams. 7
M. P. Vaughan c Ponting b Warne 60
*N. Hussain b Hogg 28
†A. J. Stewart c Lee b Warne. 60
P. D. Collingwood not out 25
A. Flintoff b Lee 16
I. D. Blackwell c Martyn b Lee 1
A. R. Caddick b Lee. 4
J. M. Anderson run out 0
L-b 7, w 4, n-b 7 18

1/8 (1) 2/18 (3) 3/20 (2) 4/88 (5) 5/151 (4) 6/182 (6) 7/216 (8) 8/218 (9) 9/224 (10) 10/224 (11) (49.3 overs) 224

Bowling: Lee 9.3–0–30–5; Williams 10–1–46–1; Bichel 10–0–42–0; Hogg 10–1–41–1; Warne 10–0–58–2.

Umpires: R. B. Tiffin (Zimbabwe) and D. B. Hair.
Third umpire: S. J. A. Taufel. Referee: C. H. Lloyd (West Indies).

CHERRY BLOSSOM SHARJAH CUP, 2002-03

BRIAN MURGATROYD

Just 37 days after Pakistan's disastrous first-round exit from the World Cup, their enthusiastic new-look side stormed unbeaten to victory in a four-way tournament in Sharjah. However, the tournament produced little entertaining cricket. The pitches were slow and many quality players were injured or had recently retired. Some were simply resting – after all, the first match here started only 11 days after the World Cup ended.

It nearly didn't start at all. With the US-led war in Iraq in its early stages, South Africa withdrew on safety grounds less than a fortnight before the first game. In hindsight, it was an over-reaction. In terms of distance, it was like cancelling a tour of England because of events in Spain, and life went on as normal in Sharjah. Bizarrely, the chairman of the South African board, Gerald Majola, chose to visit to tournament while on leave. A last-minute search provided not one replacement team but two – Zimbabwe and Kenya.

Pakistan were the flair side of the competition and worthy winners. A new selection panel jettisoned nine of their World Cup squad, including former captain Waqar Younis; instead Rashid Latif was appointed for his second spell in charge, with former Test batsman Javed Miandad appointed coach for the fourth time. The result was a young squad (average age less than 25) full of enthusiasm and boasting the fastest – and best – bowler on view in Mohammad Sami. After playing just once (and not bowling) in the World Cup, he took nine wickets in four matches.

Sri Lanka, by contrast, played with little flair or confidence. Sanath Jayasuriya had tried to resign as captain after the World Cup but was persuaded to fill in here by the sports minister and the selectors. And the coach, Dav Whatmore, whose sacking was announced before the tournament, also knew he was on the way out. Originally, both star spinner Muttiah Muralitharan and wicket-keeper/batsman Kumar Sangakkara were controversially omitted from the squad, prompting the sports minister, Johnston Fernando, to wade in. In the ensuing wranglings, the selection panel were replaced and both Murali and Sangakkara were finally reinstated. But Sri Lanka's batting – Sangakkara apart – was poor, and injuries to front-line fast bowlers Chaminda Vaas and Dilhara Fernando crippled their campaign.

Zimbabwe, weakened by recent retirements, including that of Andy Flower, played with admirable determination and qualified for the final. The use of Doug Marillier as a pinch-hitter was crucial to their success. But World Cup semi-finalists Kenya could not recapture the sparkle they showed in southern Africa. Instead, they revealed a worrying lack of depth.

Stars of the desert: Mohammad Sami (*left*) and Doug Marillier both shone in Sharjah after having a forgettable World Cup.
Pictures by Ben Radford and Clive Mason, Getty Images.

Note: Matches in this section were not first-class.

PAKISTAN v ZIMBABWE

At Sharjah, April 3, 2003 (day/night). Pakistan won by 68 runs. Pakistan 6 pts. Toss: Pakistan. One-day international debuts: Mohammad Hafeez, Umar Gul.

Six of the last 12 balls of Pakistan's innings sailed over the rope, as Abdul Razzaq – one of seven players who did not play in the World Cup match against Zimbabwe – launched his side back into the game. A remarkable 69 were ransacked from the final four overs; Razzaq, who had laboured to 19, hit 57 from his last 17 balls. Of his seven sixes, three came in succession off Ervine. Blignaut, another victim, bowled 11 wides. The recovery had been started by Younis Khan, who stabilised the innings after an inexperienced top three fell cheaply. In reply, Marillier drove powerfully but Zimbabwe lost wickets at regular intervals to enthusiastic Pakistan bowling and impressive fielding. Grant Flower became the second Zimbabwean, after his brother Andy, to play 200 one-day internationals.

Man of the Match: Abdul Razzaq.

Pakistan

Taufeeq Umar b Streak	16
Mohammad Hafeez c Taibu b Streak	12
Naved Latif b Blignaut	3
Yousuf Youhana c Taibu b Ervine	17
Younis Khan c Ervine b Blignaut	67
Shoaib Malik run out	13
*†Rashid Latif run out	34
Abdul Razzaq not out	76
Mohammad Sami not out	11
L-b 4, w 24, n-b 1	29
1/32 (2) 2/38 (3) 3/50 (1) 4/69 (4) 5/101 (6) 6/159 (7) 7/203 (5) (7 wkts, 50 overs)	278

Danish Kaneria and Umar Gul did not bat.

Bowling: Streak 10–1–31–2; Blignaut 10–1–50–2; Hondo 10–0–60–0; Ervine 4–1–36–1; Marillier 7–0–43–0; Flower 4–0–27–0; Rennie 5–0–27–0.

Zimbabwe

C. B. Wishart c Rashid Latif b Umar Gul . . 8
D. A. Marillier b Danish Kaneria 59
T. J. Friend c Taufeeq Umar b Umar Gul . 9
G. W. Flower c Mohammad Hafeez b Danish Kaneria . 13
D. D. Ebrahim lbw b Abdul Razzaq. . . . 31
G. J. Rennie lbw b Mohammad Hafeez . 11
A. M. Blignaut b Mohammad Hafeez. . . 24
S. M. Ervine run out 30
†T. Taibu b Mohammad Sami. 1
*H. H. Streak c Rashid Latif b Abdul Razzaq . 7
D. T. Hondo not out 0
L-b 6, w 2, n-b 9 17

1/21 (1) 2/47 (3) 3/87 (4) 4/104 (2) 5/121 (6) 6/152 (7) 7/194 (8) 8/197 (9) 9/208 (10) 10/210 (5) (44.1 overs) 210

Bowling: Mohammad Sami 7–0–34–1; Umar Gul 7–2–25–2; Abdul Razzaq 7.1–1–36–2; Danish Kaneria 9–1–38–2; Mohammad Hafeez 10–0–41–2; Shoaib Malik 4–0–30–0.

Umpires: B. R. Doctrove (West Indies) and A. V. Jayaprakash (India).
Third umpire: K. C. Barbour (Zimbabwe). Referee: A. M. Ebrahim (Zimbabwe).

PAKISTAN v SRI LANKA

At Sharjah, April 4, 2003 (day/night). Pakistan won by seven wickets. Pakistan 5 pts, Sri Lanka 1 pt. Toss: Sri Lanka. One-day international debuts: Naved-ul-Hasan; H. A. P. W. Jayawardene.

An unbroken stand of 124 in 19 overs between Yousuf Youhana and Younis Khan took Pakistan to their second successive win. However, it might have been much closer had Mubarak at long-on not dropped Youhana on ten. Reprieved, Youhana and his partner ticked over at the run a ball they needed, against an attack handicapped by dew that made gripping the ball difficult. Earlier, Sangakkara finally made a century, in his 86th one-day international match, when he pushed a single from the penultimate delivery of the Sri Lankan innings. He had cantered at close to a run a ball, but the rest of Sri Lanka's batting was a let-down in the face of strong Pakistan bowling and fielding.

Man of the Match: K. C. Sangakkara.

Sri Lanka

M. S. Atapattu b Umar Gul 13
*S. T. Jayasuriya c Mohammad Hafeez b Mohammad Sami . 27
D. A. Gunawardene run out 17
K. C. Sangakkara not out. 100
J. Mubarak st Rashid Latif b Shoaib Malik . 20
H. P. Tillekeratne b Naved-ul-Hasan. . . . 11
†H. A. P. W. Jayawardene b Naved-ul-Hasan . 0
H. D. P. K. Dharmasena not out 23
L-b 5, w 5, n-b 2 12

1/26 (1) 2/44 (2) 3/84 (3) 4/126 (5) 5/166 (6) 6/166 (7) (6 wkts, 50 overs) 223

T. C. B. Fernando, M. Muralitharan and C. R. D. Fernando did not bat.

Bowling: Mohammad Sami 10–2–36–1; Umar Gul 9–0–47–1; Mohammad Hafeez 5–0–26–0; Naved-ul-Hasan 10–0–55–2; Abdul Razzaq 6–0–18–0; Shoaib Malik 10–0–36–1.

Pakistan

Mohammad Hafeez run out 50
Taufeeq Umar b C. R. D. Fernando 6
Faisal Iqbal run out 32
Yousuf Youhana not out 64
Younis Khan not out. 57
L-b 9, w 5, n-b 2 16

1/21 (2) 2/97 (1) 3/101 (3) (3 wkts, 47.2 overs) 225

Shoaib Malik, *†Rashid Latif, Abdul Razzaq, Naved-ul-Hasan, Mohammad Sami and Umar Gul did not bat.

Bowling: T. C. B. Fernando 10–1–41–0; C. R. D. Fernando 8–1–34–1; Dharmasena 9.2–0–51–0; Muralitharan 10–0–33–0; Jayasuriya 10–0–57–0.

Umpires: K. C. Barbour (Zimbabwe) and B. R. Doctrove (West Indies).
Third umpire: A. V. Jayaprakash (India). Referee: A. M. Ebrahim (Zimbabwe).

KENYA v ZIMBABWE

At Sharjah, April 5, 2003 (day/night). Zimbabwe won by five wickets. Zimbabwe 5 pts, Kenya 1 pt. Toss: Kenya.

Zimbabwe, humiliated by Kenya in their recent World Cup match, appeared to be cruising to a comfortable win as Marillier, who hit a maiden one-day international hundred, and Flower added 130. Together, they took Zimbabwe within 28. But the loss of both – and Blignaut – inside three overs set up a closer-than-expected finish. The captain, Streak, hit 14 off six balls to make sure. Earlier, David Obuya had reached his first fifty in one-day internationals as Streak juggled an eight-man attack. However, Kenya could make only 56 from their final ten overs: a little more might have made a big difference.

Man of the Match: D. A. Marillier.

Kenya

†K. O. Otieno c Taibu b Streak 0
D. O. Obuya c Rennie b Price 57
B. J. Patel b Hondo 18
*S. O. Tikolo c Marillier b Price 37
T. M. Odoyo c Marillier b Hondo 46
M. O. Odumbe c and b Rennie 17
H. S. Modi not out 27
P. J. Ongondo not out 10
L-b 1, w 12 13

1/3 (1) 2/55 (3) 3/114 (2) 4/131 (4) 5/161 (6) 6/201 (5) (6 wkts, 50 overs) 225

C. O. Obuya, M. A. Suji and T. O. Suji did not bat.

Bowling: Streak 10–3–28–1; Blignaut 4–0–27–0; Hondo 8–0–37–2; Price 10–0–36–2; Flower 3–0–20–0; Marillier 6–0–30–0; Ervine 4–0–26–0; Rennie 5–0–20–1.

Zimbabwe

C. B. Wishart c Tikolo b C. O. Obuya . . 15
D. A. Marillier c Patel b T. O. Suji 100
G. J. Rennie c and b C. O. Obuya 7
G. W. Flower c Otieno b T. O. Suji 59
S. M. Ervine not out 12
A. M. Blignaut c sub (J. O. Angara) b Odoyo . 2
*H. H. Streak not out 14
L-b 8, w 11, n-b 2 21

1/56 (1) 2/68 (3) 3/198 (4) 4/199 (2) 5/208 (6) (5 wkts, 49 overs) 230

D. D. Ebrahim, †T. Taibu, R. W. Price and D. T. Hondo did not bat.

Bowling: M. A. Suji 10–1–27–0; Odoyo 9–2–37–1; Ongondo 1–0–6–0; C. O. Obuya 10–0–31–2; Odumbe 10–1–50–0; Tikolo 6–0–41–0; T. O. Suji 3–0–30–2.

Umpires: B. R. Doctrove (West Indies) and A. V. Jayaprakash (India).
Third umpire: K. C. Barbour (Zimbabwe). Referee: A. M. Ebrahim (Zimbabwe).

KENYA v SRI LANKA

At Sharjah, April 6, 2003 (day/night). Sri Lanka won by 129 runs. Sri Lanka 6 pts. Toss: Sri Lanka. One-day international debuts: A. S. Luseno; K. S. Lokuarachchi.

Sri Lanka gained revenge, of a rather limited kind, for defeat by Kenya at the World Cup. The match seven weeks earlier had ended with Kenya singing and dancing; this time they subsided with barely a whimper. Sangakkara set Sri Lanka on course with his second hundred in three days, although again he left it late, straight-driving the last ball of the innings for four. In reply to 256, Kenya surrendered. Sri Lankan all-rounder Kaushal Lokuarachchi became the 12th player in one-day internationals to take a wicket with his first ball when Tikolo smashed a leg-break straight to short cover. Muralitharan rounded up the innings with three wickets in an over. During the game, Jayasuriya confirmed he would be standing down as captain after the tournament. Sri Lanka's win meant the following day's match was effectively a semi-final.

Man of the Match: K. C. Sangakkara.

Sri Lanka

*S. T. Jayasuriya lbw b Suji	36
D. A. Gunawardene c Otieno b Odoyo	24
M. S. Atapattu c Odumbe b C. O. Obuya	19
K. C. Sangakkara not out	103
H. P. Tillekeratne c Odumbe b C. O. Obuya	43
K. S. Lokuarachchi b Suji	8
H. D. P. K. Dharmasena not out	16
B 1, l-b 1, w 3, n-b 2	7
1/53 (2) 2/64 (1) 3/98 (3) 4/191 (5) 5/220 (6) (5 wkts, 50 overs)	256

†H. A. P. W. Jayawardene, T. C. B. Fernando, M. Muralitharan and R. A. P. Nissanka did not bat.

Bowling: Odoyo 10–3–39–1; Luseno 4–0–26–0; Ongondo 4–0–23–0; Suji 8–0–52–2; C. O. Obuya 10–1–38–2; Odumbe 10–0–56–0; Tikolo 4–0–20–0.

Kenya

†K. O. Otieno c Jayawardene b Fernando	2
D. O. Obuya c Tillekeratne b Nissanka	6
B. J. Patel c Tillekeratne b Nissanka	13
*S. O. Tikolo c Gunawardene b Lokuarachchi	10
T. M. Odoyo lbw b Dharmasena	21
M. O. Odumbe lbw b Jayasuriya	42
H. S. Modi c Muralitharan b Jayasuriya	4
C. O. Obuya c Nissanka b Muralitharan	10
T. O. Suji not out	3
P. J. Ongondo st Jayawardene b Muralitharan	4
A. S. Luseno b Muralitharan	0
L-b 2, w 7, n-b 3	12
1/8 (2) 2/8 (1) 3/35 (3) 4/35 (4) 5/97 (5) 6/105 (7) 7/111 (6) 8/123 (8) 9/127 (10) 10/127 (11) (37.5 overs)	127

Bowling: Fernando 5–1–17–1; Nissanka 6–0–26–2; Lokuarachchi 6–0–22–1; Muralitharan 6.5–2–16–3; Dharmasena 6–0–23–1; Jayasuriya 8–1–21–2.

Umpires: K. C. Barbour (Zimbabwe) and A. V. Jayaprakash (India).
Third umpire: B. R. Doctrove (West Indies). Referee: A. M. Ebrahim (Zimbabwe).

SRI LANKA v ZIMBABWE

At Sharjah, April 7, 2003 (day/night). Zimbabwe won by four wickets. Zimbabwe 5 pts, Sri Lanka 1 pt. Toss: Sri Lanka.

Zimbabwe ruined Jayasuriya's hopes of a winning finale as captain by dumping Sri Lanka out of the tournament. Instead, Zimbabwe's sixth win in 29 matches between the sides meant they themselves reached the final. Five of the Sri Lankan top order fell for between 24 and 31, two to sprawling catches by Ebrahim; for Jayasuriya, who became the sixth man to appear in 300 one-day internationals, there was the pain of a second-ball duck. Zimbabwe's win should have been more comfortable, but they first allowed the last-wicket pair to add 25, and then wobbled within sight of victory. Three middle-order wickets fell in 17 balls, and it took the nous of Flower and Streak to see them home.

Man of the Match: G. W. Flower.

Sri Lanka

*S. T. Jayasuriya b Streak	0
D. A. Gunawardene c Ebrahim b Blignaut	24
M. S. Atapattu c Taibu b Ervine	29
K. C. Sangakkara c Flower b Price	25
H. P. Tillekeratne c Blignaut b Streak	31
K. S. Lokuarachchi c Ebrahim b Hondo	28
H. D. P. K. Dharmasena c Streak b Rennie	16
†H. A. P. W. Jayawardene c Taibu b Blignaut	4
T. C. B. Fernando not out	14
M. Muralitharan c Taibu b Blignaut	0
R. A. P. Nissanka lbw b Streak	11
L-b 1, w 9, n-b 1	11
1/0 (1) 2/51 (2) 3/58 (3) 4/106 (4) 5/129 (5) 6/158 (7) 7/163 (6) 8/168 (8) 9/168 (10) 10/193 (11) (49.1 overs)	193

Bowling: Streak 7.1–1–36–3; Blignaut 10–0–33–3; Hondo 10–0–43–1; Ervine 8–1–20–1; Price 10–0–43–1; Rennie 4–0–17–1.

Zimbabwe

C. B. Wishart b Nissanka	14
D. A. Marillier c Tillekeratne b Muralitharan	32
G. J. Rennie c Jayawardene b Lokuarachchi	26
G. W. Flower not out	61
†T. Taibu c Jayawardene b Dharmasena	31
S. M. Ervine b Lokuarachchi	0
D. D. Ebrahim lbw b Lokuarachchi	1
*H. H. Streak not out	19
W 6, n-b 4	10
1/36 (1) 2/65 (2) 3/103 (3) 4/158 (5) 5/165 (6) 6/167 (7) (6 wkts, 48.4 overs)	194

A. M. Blignaut, R. W. Price and D. T. Hondo did not bat.

Bowling: Fernando 2–0–20–0; Nissanka 6.4–0–40–1; Dharmasena 10–0–33–1; Muralitharan 10–3–27–1; Lokuarachchi 10–2–37–3; Jayasuriya 10–1–37–0.

Umpires: B. R. Doctrove (West Indies) and A. V. Jayaprakash (India).
Third umpire: K. C. Barbour (Zimbabwe). Referee: A. M. Ebrahim (Zimbabwe).

KENYA v PAKISTAN

At Sharjah, April 8, 2003 (day/night). Pakistan won by 143 runs. Pakistan 6 pts. Toss: Pakistan.

A pepped-up Pakistan got in the mood for the final with a crushing win. Every member of their top order got in, only to get out soon afterwards, and it took a dynamic 76 off 58 balls from Shoaib Malik to propel Pakistan to the highest score of the tournament. As Kenya dropped catches and hurled overthrows, 106 came from the final ten overs. Kenya's reply began with a comical run-out and did not improve by much. They reached exactly half of Pakistan's score, as Mohammad Sami's impressive pace and control brought four for 25, his best figures at the time. Kenya only avoided total collapse thanks to a classy half-century from Odumbe, who took 18 runs from Umar Gul's first over.

Man of the Match: Shoaib Malik.

Pakistan

Mohammad Hafeez c Otieno b Ongondo	36
Taufeeq Umar b Angara	17
Faisal Iqbal c Odumbe b C. O. Obuya	23
Misbah-ul-Haq c Patel b Tikolo	42
Yousuf Youhana b Tikolo	18
Shoaib Malik c C. O. Obuya b Ongondo	76
*†Rashid Latif b Tikolo	38
Naved-ul-Hasan c D. O. Obuya b Odoyo	13
Mohammad Sami not out	12
Danish Kaneria not out	0
L-b 2, w 7, n-b 2	11
1/45 (2) 2/63 (1) 3/102 (3) 4/129 (5) 5/150 (4) 6/222 (7) 7/265 (6) 8/280 (8) (8 wkts, 50 overs)	286

Umar Gul did not bat.

Bowling: Odoyo 10–1–42–1; Ongondo 9–0–57–2; Angara 8–0–52–1; C. O. Obuya 9–0–56–1; Odumbe 6–0–35–0; Tikolo 8–0–42–3.

Kenya

†K. O. Otieno c Rashid Latif b Naved-ul-Hasan	9
D. O. Obuya run out	10
B. J. Patel b Mohammad Sami	0
*S. O. Tikolo c Rashid Latif b Mohammad Sami	7
T. M. Odoyo run out	22
M. O. Odumbe c Rashid Latif b Shoaib Malik	54
H. S. Modi c Rashid Latif b Mohammad Sami	27
C. O. Obuya lbw b Mohammad Hafeez	0
J. K. Kamande lbw b Umar Gul	3
P. J. Ongondo not out	0
J. O. Angara lbw b Mohammad Sami	0
L-b 1, w 5, n-b 5	11
1/17 (2) 2/18 (3) 3/31 (4) 4/31 (1) 5/84 (5) 6/137 (6) 7/138 (8) 8/143 (9) 9/143 (7) 10/143 (11) (31.4 overs)	143

Bowling: Mohammad Sami 6.4–0–25–4; Naved-ul-Hasan 6–1–32–1; Umar Gul 2–0–23–1; Danish Kaneria 6–2–16–0; Shoaib Malik 8–1–42–1; Mohammad Hafeez 3–1–4–1.

Umpires: K. C. Barbour (Zimbabwe) and A. V. Jayaprakash (India).
Third umpire: B. R. Doctrove (West Indies). Referee: A. M. Ebrahim (Zimbabwe).

QUALIFYING TABLE

	Played	*Won*	*Lost*	*Bonus Points*	*Points*	*Net Run-Rate*
Pakistan	3	3	0	2	17	1.51
Zimbabwe	3	2	1	0	10	–0.34
Sri Lanka	3	1	2	3	8	0.74
Kenya	3	0	3	1	1	–1.88

Win = 5 pts. One bonus point awarded either to the winning team for achieving victory with a run-rate 1.25 times that of the opposition, or to the losing team for denying the winners a bonus point. Net run-rate is calculated by subtracting runs conceded per over from runs scored per over.

FINAL

PAKISTAN v ZIMBABWE

At Sharjah, April 10, 2003 (day/night). Pakistan won by eight wickets. Toss: Zimbabwe.

Taufeeq Umar took the match award for his unbeaten 81, but the game had long since been settled by Mohammad Sami. His pacy opening spell reduced Zimbabwe to 22 for three on a blameless pitch, and from that point there was no way back. Taibu scampered fifty and gave the innings a gloss of respectability, but Taufeeq and Yousuf Youhana shut out the possibility of any miracle comeback. Taufeeq supplied the staying power, Youhana the majority of the strokeplay and together they added an unbroken 144 in 29 overs, the highest stand of the tournament. This match was the 2,000th one-day international. It had taken 24 years to reach 1,000, but only eight more to reach 2,000.

Man of the Match: Taufeeq Umar. *Man of the Series:* K. C. Sangakkara.

"Tufnell's book is mildly engaging, though you can understand that Angus Fraser's gracious tribute to his former team-mate, 'a pain in the arse at times', might be near the mark."

Barry Norman on Books, page 1575.

Zimbabwe

C. B. Wishart c Rashid Latif b Mohammad Sami . 0
D. A. Marillier b Mohammad Sami 14
G. J. Rennie c Rashid Latif b Mohammad Sami . 6
G. W. Flower c Younis Khan b Shoaib Malik . 7
†T. Taibu not out 74
S. M. Ervine c Rashid Latif b Shoaib Malik . 25
D. D. Ebrahim c Shoaib Malik b Danish Kaneria . 13
*H. H. Streak lbw b Mohammad Hafeez 0
A. M. Blignaut c and b Mohammad Hafeez . 3
R. W. Price lbw b Danish Kaneria 1
D. T. Hondo c Yousuf Youhana b Shoaib Malik . 9
L-b 4, w 8, n-b 4 16

1/0 (1) 2/19 (3) 3/22 (2) (49.1 overs) 168
4/36 (4) 5/82 (6) 6/122 (7)
7/123 (8) 8/127 (9)
9/133 (10) 10/168 (11)

Bowling: Mohammad Sami 10–0–44–3; Umar Gul 8–0–24–0; Shoaib Malik 9.1–1–29–3; Abdul Razzaq 6–0–21–0; Danish Kaneria 10–1–32–2; Mohammad Hafeez 6–0–14–2.

Pakistan

Mohammad Hafeez c Wishart b Streak . . 2
Taufeeq Umar not out 81
Faisal Iqbal c Rennie b Streak 6
Yousuf Youhana not out 61
L-b 5, w 16, n-b 1. 22

1/10 (1) 2/28 (3) (2 wkts, 35.2 overs) 172

Younis Khan, Shoaib Malik, *†Rashid Latif, Abdul Razzaq, Mohammad Sami, Danish Kaneria and Umar Gul did not bat.

Bowling: Streak 8–0–35–2; Blignaut 9–0–50–0; Ervine 3–0–18–0; Price 10–1–31–0; Hondo 2–0–14–0; Marillier 3–0–14–0; Ebrahim 0.2–0–5–0.

Umpires: B. R. Doctrove (West Indies) and A. V. Jayaprakash (India).
Third umpire: K. C. Barbour (Zimbabwe). Referee: A. M. Ebrahim (Zimbabwe).

TVS CUP IN BANGLADESH, 2003

The breathing space between the World Cup and this triangular tournament in Bangladesh was 19 days. The difference in significance was measured in light years. There was no side at full strength, no television or radio coverage in South Africa, and no sniff of Bangladesh breaking their 34-match one-day losing streak. And, to top it all, there was no result: the South Africa–India final was washed out – twice.

What media attention there was focused on how South Africa would recover from their humiliating first-round exit at the World Cup. Graeme Smith became officially the second-youngest captain in one-day internationals at 22 years 71 days (the youngest was Waqar Younis, whose age is disputed). Almost his first decision was to demote Shaun Pollock, his predecessor as captain, from opening bowler. It upset Pollock – "I *like* bowling with the new ball," he said later – and he looked impotent without the hard Kookaburra, conceding 54 in nine overs. India went on to crush South Africa by 153 runs, their second-heaviest one-day defeat in terms of runs.

But Smith and South Africa came back strongly. With Pollock given the harder ball again, they won three in a row, including their second match against India. Neil McKenzie scored 186 in the tournament, and the other major performances also came from players who did not play in the World Cup: Jacques Rudolph began his one-day career with style, and Alan Dawson's nagging swing went for just above three and a half an over and lured out 11 batsmen.

If this was a new beginning for South Africa, it was the end of 19 months (and 21 Tests and 63 one-day internationals) on a treadmill for India, whose players were about to have a six-month break. They were without Sachin Tendulkar and Rahul Dravid. At times the rest looked very end-of-term, particularly in their lackadaisical fielding.

While India and South Africa were keen to be considered the second-best side in the world, Bangladesh were content to prove that a World Cup defeat to Canada was a one-off: Akram Khan, Habibul Bashar and Khaled Mahmud, now captain, injected a little fight into a demoralised team. Reaching 200 twice in a row was an achievement; that it was cause for celebration was a measure of how low they had fallen.

Note: Matches in this section were not first-class.

BANGLADESH v INDIA

At Dhaka, April 11, 2003 (day/night). India won by 200 runs. India 6 pts. Toss: India. One-day international debuts: G. Gambhir, A. M. Salvi.

A 200-run win was India's biggest, though not their best, while 76 all out was Bangladesh's lowest total but not their lowest hour. After humiliation at the World Cup, Bangladesh at least posed some questions for the Indian middle order, reducing them to 172 for six. However, Yuvraj Singh again dug his side out of a hole by thumping 92 in ten overs with Agarkar, and reaching a muscular hundred, his first in one-day internationals, after 12 fifties. Bangladesh's response was less reply, more whimper. Even in home conditions their lack of confidence was striking.

Man of the Match: Yuvraj Singh.

India

G. Gambhir c Khaled Masud b Tapash Baisya . 11
V. Sehwag lbw b Mohammad Rafiq 63
*S. C. Ganguly c Mohammad Rafiq b Alok Kapali . 30
M. Kaif c Khaled Masud b Sanwar Hossain . 23
Yuvraj Singh not out. 102
D. Mongia lbw b Alok Kapali 3
†P. A. Patel c and b Sanwar Hossain . . . 4
A. B. Agarkar c Tushar Imran b Khaled Mahmud . 20
Harbhajan Singh b Tapash Baisya 3
Zaheer Khan b Tapash Baisya. 0
A. M. Salvi c Alok Kapali b Khaled Mahmud . 0
L-b 5, w 10, n-b 2. 17

1/46 (1) 2/82 (2) 3/132 (3) 4/144 (4) 5/162 (6) 6/172 (7) 7/264 (8) 8/271 (9) 9/271 (10) 10/276 (11) (49.3 overs) 276

Bowling: Manjurul Islam 6–0–31–0; Tapash Baisya 10–0–65–3; Khaled Mahmud 7.3–0–46–2; Mohammad Rafiq 8–0–52–1; Alok Kapali 10–0–42–2; Sanwar Hossain 8–0–35–2.

Bangladesh

Mohammad Ashraful c Sehwag b Salvi . 5
Mehrab Hossain lbw b Salvi 0
Tushar Imran b Zaheer Khan 2
Alok Kapali c Salvi b Zaheer Khan. . . . 5
†Khaled Masud lbw b Agarkar 12
Akram Khan c Patel b Agarkar. 9
Sanwar Hossain c Gambhir b Harbhajan Singh . 0
*Khaled Mahmud c Patel b Agarkar . . . 10
Mohammad Rafiq not out 18
Tapash Baisya c Patel b Zaheer Khan . . 2
Manjurul Islam c Harbhajan Singh b Zaheer Khan . 1
L-b 5, w 5, n-b 2 12

1/2 (2) 2/5 (3) 3/11 (1) 4/24 (4) 5/37 (5) 6/43 (6) 7/43 (7) 8/65 (8) 9/74 (10) 10/76 (11) (27.3 overs) 76

Bowling: Salvi 7–1–15–2; Zaheer Khan 7.3–1–19–4; Agarkar 7–2–18–3; Harbhajan Singh 6–2–19–1.

Umpires: Aleem Dar (Pakistan) and Mahbubur Rahman.
Third umpire: Showkatur Rahman. Referee: C. H. Lloyd (West Indies).

INDIA v SOUTH AFRICA

At Dhaka, April 13, 2003 (day/night). India won by 153 runs. India 6 pts. Toss: India. One-day international debuts: A. Mishra; J. A. Rudolph.

South Africa's new captain, Smith, stamped his sovereignty by leaving their old one, Pollock, stewing in the outfield for 19 overs before giving him a bowl. Having opened during the World Cup, Pollock was now third change. Leaving the side's most consistent bowler to face well-set batsmen with a pummelled ball, while opening with Willoughby's medium-pace, seemed to confound logic. Ganguly married his usual effortless straight hitting with a less characteristic pursuit of quick singles and, after he fell, Kaif and Mongia swung 110 in under 12 overs as a breathless South Africa hurled overthrows and grassed catches. In reply, Harbhajan Singh found biting turn from his first ball, and a brittle-looking batting line-up, shorn of Jacques Kallis, Jonty Rhodes and Gary Kirsten, skidded to 89 for six and crashed to South Africa's second-heaviest defeat by runs.

Man of the Match: M. Kaif.

India

G. Gambhir c Boucher b Ntini 18
V. Sehwag c Rudolph b Dawson 37
*S. C. Ganguly c McKenzie b Dawson. . 75
M. Kaif not out 95
Yuvraj Singh run out 11
D. Mongia not out 55
L-b 3, w 8, n-b 5 16

1/45 (1) 2/89 (2) 3/175 (3) 4/197 (5) (4 wkts, 50 overs) 307

†P. A. Patel, A. B. Agarkar, Harbhajan Singh, Zaheer Khan and A. Mishra did not bat.

Bowling: Willoughby 10–0–77–0; Ntini 10–0–51–1; Dawson 10–2–46–2; Peterson 8–0–56–0; Pollock 9–0–54–0; Smith 3–0–20–0.

South Africa

*G. C. Smith b Agarkar	1	A. C. Dawson not out	7
H. H. Gibbs c and b Harbhajan Singh	26	M. Ntini b Sehwag	5
J. A. Rudolph c Sehwag b Agarkar	4	C. M. Willoughby st Patel b Sehwag	0
H. H. Dippenaar c Yuvraj Singh b Ganguly	22	B 7, l-b 3, w 2, n-b 3	15
N. D. McKenzie c Patel b Mishra	12		
†M. V. Boucher c Kaif b Sehwag	48	1/5 (1) 2/13 (3) 3/55 (2) (34.5 overs)	154
S. M. Pollock c Mongia b Harbhajan Singh	2	4/57 (4) 5/86 (5) 6/89 (7) 7/129 (8) 8/148 (6)	
R. J. Peterson lbw b Ganguly	12	9/154 (10) 10/154 (11)	

Bowling: Zaheer Khan 4.5–1–8–0; Agarkar 6–0–27–2; Ganguly 8.1–0–30–2; Harbhajan Singh 7–0–22–2; Mishra 5–0–29–1; Sehwag 3.5–0–28–3.

Umpires: B. F. Bowden (New Zealand) and A. F. M. Akhtaruddin.
Third umpire: Mahbubur Rahman. Referee: C. H. Lloyd (West Indies).

BANGLADESH v SOUTH AFRICA

At Dhaka, April 14, 2003 (day/night). South Africa won by 83 runs. South Africa 6 pts. Toss: South Africa.

After four years of defeats and eight months without making 200, Bangladesh marked the first day in the Bengali calendar with a welcome glimmer of New Year's resolution. On a docile pitch, they managed 211, with Mohammad Ashraful lasting nearly 30 overs for 52 and giving another glimpse of the gumption that made him Test cricket's youngest century-maker. However, South Africa had already reached a total some way beyond Bangladesh's modest firepower. Their top three all got themselves in but got themselves out with big scores beckoning: Smith pretended to beat his head against his bat as he trudged off. From 189 for three in the 32nd over, South Africa were disappointed with 294, but it was plenty.

Man of the Match: Mohammad Ashraful.

South Africa

*G. C. Smith st Khaled Masud b Mohammad Rafiq	45	N. D. McKenzie not out	55
H. H. Gibbs run out	62	B 4, l-b 10, w 6, n-b 2	22
J. A. Rudolph c Tareq Aziz b Mohammad Rafiq	44	1/112 (1) 2/133 (2) (3 wkts, 50 overs)	294
H. H. Dippenaar not out	66	3/189 (3)	

†M. V. Boucher, S. M. Pollock, P. R. Adams, A. C. Dawson, M. Ntini and C. M. Willoughby did not bat.

Bowling: Tareq Aziz 7–0–50–0; Tapash Baisya 10–0–54–0; Khaled Mahmud 2–0–29–0; Mohammad Rafiq 10–0–43–2; Alok Kapali 10–0–45–0; Sanwar Hossain 4–0–23–0; Mohammad Ashraful 7–0–36–0.

Bangladesh

Javed Omar c Boucher b Ntini	9	Tapash Baisya b Pollock	3
Mohammad Ashraful c Boucher b Adams	52	Tareq Aziz not out	1
Habibul Bashar b Dawson	18		
Sanwar Hossain lbw b Pollock	1	L-b 1, w 14, n-b 4	19
Alok Kapali lbw b Pollock	27		
Akram Khan lbw b Pollock	15	1/24 (1) 2/82 (3) 3/83 (4) (49.3 overs)	211
†Khaled Masud c Smith b Dawson	11	4/112 (2) 5/140 (5) 6/141 (6)	
*Khaled Mahmud c McKenzie b Ntini	40	7/174 (7) 8/204 (9)	
Mohammad Rafiq b Dawson	15	9/210 (8) 10/211 (10)	

Bowling: Ntini 9–1–51–2; Willoughby 8–0–32–0; Pollock 9.3–0–36–4; Dawson 10–1–26–3; Adams 10–0–42–1; Smith 3–0–23–0.

Umpires: Aleem Dar (Pakistan) and Mahbubur Rahman.
Third umpire: Showkatur Rahman. Referee: C. H. Lloyd (West Indies).

BANGLADESH v INDIA

At Dhaka, April 16, 2003 (day/night). India won by four wickets. India 5 pts, Bangladesh 1 pt. Toss: Bangladesh. One-day international debut: A. V. Kale.

Again Bangladesh managed 200, and they followed that by taking six wickets. A gritty 50 in 94 balls by Habibul Bashar reminded the selectors of the fighting spirit they had thrown away when they left him out for much of the World Cup. In reply, Sehwag, one of just three survivors from the Indian side that played in the World Cup final, and captain while Ganguly rested a stiff back, cut and pulled with his usual power, before Gambhir took India to the cusp of victory with an elegant 71.

Man of the Match: G. Gambhir.

Bangladesh

Mohammad Ashraful b Agarkar 7	Tapash Baisya run out 15
Mehrab Hossain c Agarkar b Bangar . . . 30	Tareq Aziz not out 3
Habibul Bashar c Kaif b Agarkar 50	
Javed Omar c and b Sarandeep Singh . . 1	B 4, l-b 2, w 4, n-b 8 18
Alok Kapali c Mongia b Sarandeep Singh 9	—
Akram Khan lbw b Sehwag 35	1/15 (1) 2/49 (2) 3/53 (4) (49.4 overs) 207
†Khaled Masud c Patel b Mishra 12	4/78 (5) 5/124 (3) 6/139 (7)
*Khaled Mahmud c Sehwag b Agarkar . . 23	7/163 (6) 8/182 (9)
Mohammad Rafiq b Salvi 4	9/182 (8) 10/207 (10)

Bowling: Salvi 10–0–51–1; Agarkar 10–2–36–3; Bangar 8.4–0–31–1; Sarandeep Singh 10–0–34–2; Mishra 9–1–38–1; Sehwag 2–0–11–1.

India

*V. Sehwag c Tareq Aziz b Mohammad Rafiq . 43	D. Mongia not out 16
G. Gambhir c Khaled Masud b Alok Kapali . 71	A. B. Agarkar not out 4
†P. A. Patel lbw b Alok Kapali 27	L-b 1, w 7, n-b 2 10
M. Kaif run out 20	—
S. B. Bangar lbw b Mohammad Rafiq . . 7	1/69 (1) (6 wkts, 42.5 overs) 208
A. V. Kale c Khaled Mahmud b Mohammad Ashraful . 10	2/117 (3) 3/164 (4)
	4/178 (5) 5/178 (2)
	6/204 (6)

A. M. Salvi, A. Mishra and Sarandeep Singh did not bat.

Bowling: Tapash Baisya 8–0–42–0; Tareq Aziz 4–0–31–0; Mohammad Rafiq 10–0–42–2; Khaled Mahmud 7–0–22–0; Alok Kapali 8–1–41–2; Mohammad Ashraful 3.5–0–19–1; Mehrab Hossain 2–0–10–0.

Umpires: B. F. Bowden (New Zealand) and Mahbubur Rahman.
Third umpire: A. F. M. Akhtaruddin. Referee: C. H. Lloyd (West Indies).

BANGLADESH v SOUTH AFRICA

At Dhaka, April 17, 2003 (day/night). South Africa won by 93 runs. South Africa 6 pts. Toss: South Africa. One-day international debut: Mohammad Salim.

This was an efficient win with optional frills not included. Tapash Baisya struck early with his slingy fast-medium, and he and Manjurul Islam regularly zipped the ball past the outside edge. But Smith dealt clinically with the short and the wide, Rudolph stocked up on singles and South Africa ground to 183 after 40 overs. Pollock added his customary late boost, belting a 20-ball 38, and then bowled a precise six-over spell of two for 14 now he had the new ball. At 29 for four Bangladesh were finished, but Alok Kapali followed his impressive spell of floaty leg-spin with a compact, correct innings of 71, and Bangladesh reached respectability despite tight bowling and niggardly fielding.

Man of the Match: S. M. Pollock.

South Africa

*G. C. Smith b Sanwar Hossain	67	N. D. McKenzie not out	39
H. H. Gibbs b Tapash Baisya	0	S. M. Pollock not out	38
J. A. Rudolph c Mohammad Salim b Sanwar Hossain	81	L-b 4, w 3, n-b 1	8
H. H. Dippenaar c and b Alok Kapali	16	1/5 (2) 2/106 (1) 3/143 (4) 4/174 (5) 5/192 (3)	(5 wkts, 50 overs) 261
†M. V. Boucher c Mehrab Hossain b Alok Kapali	12		

A. J. Hall, P. R. Adams, A. C. Dawson and M. Ntini did not bat.

Bowling: Manjurul Islam 10–0–38–0; Tapash Baisya 8–0–57–1; Mohammad Rafiq 10–2–42–0; Khaled Mahmud 4–0–40–0; Sanwar Hossain 8–1–40–2; Alok Kapali 10–1–40–2.

Bangladesh

Mohammad Ashraful lbw b Pollock	13	Tapash Baisya c Smith b Dawson	7
Mehrab Hossain c Boucher b Ntini	6	Manjurul Islam not out	5
Habibul Bashar lbw b Pollock	1		
Akram Khan c Boucher b Dawson	3	L-b 2, w 9, n-b 6	17
Alok Kapali c Adams b Hall	71		
*Khaled Mahmud c Boucher b Hall	24	1/16 (2) 2/19 (3) 3/25 (1)	(49 overs) 168
Sanwar Hossain c and b Adams	9	4/29 (4) 5/84 (6) 6/104 (7)	
†Mohammad Salim c Boucher b Pollock	9	7/145 (8) 8/150 (9)	
Mohammad Rafiq c Boucher b Hall	3	9/157 (5) 10/168 (10)	

Bowling: Pollock 7–2–17–3; Ntini 8–1–22–1; Dawson 10–1–29–2; Hall 10–1–32–3; Adams 10–0–40–1; Rudolph 4–0–26–0.

Umpires: Aleem Dar (Pakistan) and A. F. M. Akhtaruddin.
Third umpire: Showkatur Rahman. Referee: C. H. Lloyd (West Indies).

INDIA v SOUTH AFRICA

At Dhaka, April 18, 2003 (day/night). South Africa won by five wickets. South Africa 5 pts, India 1 pt. Toss: India.

South Africa were spirited to the brink of victory by McKenzie. He arrived at 42 for three and wrought order from muddle, putting on 63 with Rudolph and 107 with Boucher. Playing like Michael Bevan in a green shirt, he swept neatly and filched singles to keep the asking-rate in sight and then struck the killer blows. Earlier, South Africa had maintained a cool-headed discipline in the field, despite temperatures hitting 45°C. The pressure built and Indian wickets finally fell in a clatter: from 146 for three they lost six for 46, proving equally clumsy against Ntini's hostile pace and Dawson's niggling swing. On a pitch with a touch of green, Salvi bowled with some hostility and Harbhajan Singh struck twice in his first four balls. But rather than set up a victory for India, it only set the scene for McKenzie.

Man of the Match: N. D. McKenzie.

India

V. Sehwag c Smith b Hall	25	Sarandeep Singh c Smith b Dawson	19
G. Gambhir c Hall b Ntini	2	A. M. Salvi not out	4
*S. C. Ganguly c Pollock b Adams	61		
M. Kaif b Dawson	30	L-b 2, w 2, n-b 8	12
D. Mongia c McKenzie b Dawson	29		
S. B. Bangar lbw b Ntini	9	1/7 (2) 2/96 (4) 3/124 (3)	(49.1 overs) 215
A. B. Agarkar c Hall b Ntini	17	4/146 (6) 5/160 (1) 6/182 (5)	
†P. A. Patel run out	6	7/184 (7) 8/186 (9)	
Harbhajan Singh c Boucher b Dawson	1	9/192 (8) 10/215 (10)	

Sehwag, when 14, retired hurt at 32 and resumed at 146.

Bowling: Pollock 10–1–48–0; Ntini 10–0–37–3; Dawson 9.1–1–49–4; Hall 10–0–36–1; Adams 10–0–43–1.

South Africa

*G. C. Smith c Patel b Salvi	2	S. M. Pollock not out	2
H. H. Gibbs lbw b Harbhajan Singh	25		
H. H. Dippenaar b Harbhajan Singh	11	L-b 1, w 6, n-b 8	15
J. A. Rudolph c Kaif b Sehwag	37		
N. D. McKenzie c Salvi b Harbhajan Singh	80	1/11 (1) 2/41 (3) 3/42 (2) 4/105 (4) 5/212 (5)	(5 wkts, 48.4 overs) 216
†M. V. Boucher not out	44		

A. J. Hall, P. R. Adams, A. C. Dawson and M. Ntini did not bat.

Bowling: Salvi 8.4–2–31–1; Agarkar 6–2–34–0; Harbhajan Singh 10–0–43–3; Sarandeep Singh 10–0–32–0; Ganguly 3–0–13–0; Sehwag 8–0–43–1; Mongia 3–0–19–0.

Umpires: B. F. Bowden (New Zealand) and A. F. M. Akhtaruddin.
Third umpire: Showkatur Rahman. Referee: C. H. Lloyd (West Indies).

QUALIFYING TABLE

	Played	*Won*	*Lost*	*Bonus points*	*Points*	*Net run-rate*
India	4	3	1	3	18	1.93
South Africa	4	3	1	2	17	0.15
Bangladesh	4	0	4	1	1	–2.07

Win = 5 pts. One bonus point awarded either to the winning team for achieving victory with a run-rate 1.25 times that of the opposition, or to the losing team for denying the winners a bonus point. Net run-rate is calculated by subtracting runs conceded per over from runs scored per over.

FINAL

INDIA v SOUTH AFRICA

At Dhaka, April 20, 2003 (day/night). Abandoned.

The downpour that caused the game to be washed out blacked out television coverage too: the rain was so heavy that the studio covering the match was inundated.

INDIA v SOUTH AFRICA

At Dhaka, April 21, 2003 (day/night). No result. Toss: India.

If rain had cost India victory in their last rained-off final, during the 2002 ICC Champions Trophy, plenty of South Africans would say it saved them here. Ntini's bowling was nasty, brutish and short, with Pollock slower and on the spot. India were staggering at 46 for three in the 18th over when torrents sent the players scuttling. This second interruption – winds strong enough to whip off the umpires' hats had already brought a halt – proved terminal. The downpour ended in late afternoon but the outfield was already saturated.

Man of the Series: A. C. Dawson.

India

V. Sehwag c Dawson b Pollock	8
G. Gambhir c McKenzie b Ntini	11
*S. C. Ganguly not out	11
M. Kaif c Rudolph b Ntini	5
Yuvraj Singh not out	2
L-b 2, w 1, n-b 6	9
1/19 (1) 2/35 (2) 3/41 (4) (3 wkts, 17.1 overs)	46

D. Mongia, †P. A. Patel, A. B. Agarkar, Harbhajan Singh, Zaheer Khan and A. Mishra did not bat.

Bowling: Pollock 6–0–15–1; Ntini 8–2–26–2; Dawson 3–1–3–0; Hall 0.1–0–0–0.

South Africa

H. H. Gibbs, *G. C. Smith, H. H. Dippenaar, N. D. McKenzie, J. A. Rudolph, A. J. Hall, †M. V. Boucher, S. M. Pollock, P. R. Adams, A. C. Dawson and M. Ntini.

Umpires: Aleem Dar (Pakistan) and Mahbubur Rahman.
Third umpire: Showkatur Rahman. Referee: C. H. Lloyd (West Indies).

ONE-DAY INTERNATIONAL COMPETITIONS

Only competitions involving three or more teams are included. Table covers period between start of 2002-03 season and December 2003.

Competition		*Winners*	*Runners-up*	*Others*
VB Series (A)	Dec 2002–Jan 2003	**Australia**	England	Sri Lanka
World Cup (SA, Z, K)	Feb–March 2003	**Australia**	India	All Full Members plus Canada, Holland, Kenya and Namibia
Cherry Blossom Cup (Sharjah)	April 2003	**Pakistan**	Zimbabwe	Kenya, Sri Lanka
TVS Cup (B)	April 2003	**†India/ South Africa**		Bangladesh
Bank AlFalah Cup (SL)	May 2003	**New Zealand**	Pakistan	Sri Lanka
NatWest Series (E)	June–July 2003	**England**	South Africa	Zimbabwe
TVS Cup (I)	Oct–Nov 2003	**Australia**	India	New Zealand

† *Final rained off.*

BANK ALFALAH CUP, 2003

BRIAN MURGATROYD

The Bank AlFalah Cup will linger mainly in the memories of New Zealand players and supporters – it was, after all, only their second tournament victory, following the 2000 ICC Knockout in Kenya. Their success was quite an achievement, given their injury list and the unfamiliar conditions. However, this trilateral tournament in Sri Lanka was every bit as drab as the Test series between Sri Lanka and New Zealand that preceded it. And even the addition of Pakistan, often international cricket's most colourful team, was unable to redeem it.

The problem lay in the pitches which, for most of the competition, offered the bowlers far too much help: attrition replaced entertainment, and the seven games produced just eight stands of 50 or more, four individual fifties, and neither a hundred partnership nor an individual century.

The only consolation was that play was taking place at all. Dambulla, where all the matches were held, had been scheduled for just the first three, but persistent downpours in Colombo prompted the Sri Lankan board to switch the remaining fixtures to the dry zone.

New Zealand triumphed through a combination of self-belief and teamwork. They were missing the injured Nathan Astle and the out-of-form Craig McMillan, and soon lost Shane Bond. Chris Cairns took part as a specialist batsman – an unfortunate move, considering the way the wickets played – and at least three other key members of the party operated at reduced capacity during the tournament. Daryl Tuffey, though, was a tower of strength, and he received staunch support from his fellow-bowlers. Stephen Fleming led in his usual calm manner, and in the final produced a vital innings when it counted.

Under Marvan Atapattu, their new one-day captain, Sri Lanka failed to reach the final of a home tournament for the first time, performing with neither confidence nor positive intent. Although they played poorly in the final, Pakistan could still take satisfaction that their young squad got that far. Had Shoaib Akhtar (banned for ball tampering) been available for the game, they might even have won. Shoaib Malik, overlooked for the World Cup, shone brightly with bat and ball, and won the series award.

Note: Matches in this section were not first-class.

SRI LANKA v PAKISTAN

At Dambulla, May 10, 2003. Pakistan won by 79 runs. Pakistan 6 pts. Toss: Sri Lanka.

This match set the tone for the tournament: the ball dominated the bat, boundaries were in short supply – just 18 fours and two sixes – and Sri Lanka crumpled under pressure. Pakistan's total owed much to the patience of Mohammad Hafeez, who faced 114 balls, and to a late flourish from the tail, who struck 64 from the last ten overs. In reply, despite losing Jayasuriya to his first ball, Sri Lanka were well placed, only to lose their last seven wickets for 22 in 15 overs. One of the seven, Lokuarachchi, survived a run-out appeal at one end only to be given out at the other as he attempted an extra run in the confusion. Both decisions had to be referred to the third umpire. Kaluwitharana claimed his 200th one-day dismissal when he stumped Rashid Latif, and Nissanka was fined 20% of his match fee for showing dissent when an appeal for a catch behind off Taufeeq Umar was turned down.

Man of the Match: Mohammad Hafeez.

Pakistan

Mohammad Hafeez c Sangakkara b Jayasuriya	53
Taufeeq Umar c Kaluwitharana b Nissanka	9
Faisal Iqbal c Jayawardene b Muralitharan	21
Yousuf Youhana c Jayawardene b Lokuarachchi	1
Younis Khan c Lokuarachchi b Muralitharan	29
Shoaib Akhtar run out	5
Shoaib Malik run out	20
Abdul Razzaq not out	24
*†Rashid Latif st Kaluwitharana b Muralitharan	14
Mohammad Sami not out	8
B 2, l-b 6, w 5, n-b 2	15
1/21 (2) 2/69 (3) 3/70 (4) 4/115 (5) 5/123 (6) 6/146 (1) 7/158 (7) 8/181 (9) (8 wkts, 50 overs)	199

Umar Gul did not bat.

Bowling: Vaas 8–1–22–0; Nissanka 9–0–26–1; Weeraratne 4–0–14–0; Lokuarachchi 10–0–40–1; Muralitharan 10–0–38–3; Jayasuriya 9–0–51–1.

Sri Lanka

*M. S. Atapattu lbw b Abdul Razzaq	26
S. T. Jayasuriya c Younis Khan b Shoaib Akhtar	0
K. C. Sangakkara c Shoaib Malik b Shoaib Akhtar	29
D. P. M. D. Jayawardene lbw b Mohammad Sami	22
R. P. Arnold c Faisal Iqbal b Mohammad Hafeez	13
†R. S. Kaluwitharana c Younis Khan b Shoaib Malik	0
K. S. Lokuarachchi run out	2
W. P. U. J. C. Vaas run out	1
K. Weeraratne c Mohammad Hafeez b Shoaib Malik	1
R. A. P. Nissanka not out	5
M. Muralitharan b Mohammad Sami	1
L-b 4, w 12, n-b 4	20
1/1 (2) 2/62 (1) 3/75 (3) 4/98 (4) 5/99 (6) 6/107 (7) 7/110 (8) 8/111 (5) 9/118 (9) 10/120 (11) (43.1 overs)	120

Bowling: Shoaib Akhtar 8–2–19–2; Mohammad Sami 7.1–1–19–2; Umar Gul 8–1–28–0; Abdul Razzaq 7–0–22–1; Shoaib Malik 10–1–23–2; Mohammad Hafeez 3–1–5–1.

Umpires: S. J. A. Taufel (Australia) and P. T. Manuel.
Third umpire: M. G. Silva. Referee: G. R. Viswanath (India).

NEW ZEALAND v PAKISTAN

At Dambulla, May 11, 2003. New Zealand won by seven wickets. New Zealand 6 pts. Toss: New Zealand.

In conditions heavily favouring the side bowling first, New Zealand won the toss and went on to a resounding win. Tuffey removed Mohammad Hafeez in his first over, four of Pakistan's top six failed to score, and at 17 for five in the 12th over, they were in utter disarray. When he bowled

Faisal Iqbal, Bond took his 50th one-day international wicket in his 27th game, making him the quickest New Zealander to the landmark. But he soon left the field with a back injury that would end his tour, and Rashid Latif and Shoaib Akhtar lifted the score past three figures. Even so, Pakistan were routed for their lowest total against New Zealand. Vincent, a late inclusion in the one-day squad, saw his side home in the face of a hostile examination by Shoaib Akhtar.

Man of the Match: D. R. Tuffey.

Pakistan

Mohammad Hafeez c Styris b Tuffey	0	Mohammad Sami not out	11
Taufeeq Umar c Nevin b Styris	21	Umar Gul c Vettori b Oram	2
Faisal Iqbal b Bond	0		
Yousuf Youhana b Bond	0	L-b 6, w 8, n-b 3	17
Younis Khan lbw b Tuffey	3		—
Abdul Razzaq c Styris b Oram	0	1/0 (1) 2/2 (3) 3/5 (4) (43.1 overs)	116
Shoaib Malik b Styris	9	4/12 (5) 5/17 (6) 6/42 (2)	
*†Rashid Latif c Styris b Vettori	26	7/51 (7) 8/96 (8)	
Shoaib Akhtar b Vettori	27	9/103 (9) 10/116 (11)	

Bowling: Tuffey 10–2–28–2; Bond 5–2–7–2; Oram 9.1–2–16–2; Styris 6–0–32–2; Vettori 9–3–18–2; Harris 4–0–9–0.

New Zealand

C. J. Nevin c Taufeeq Umar b Umar Gul	28	C. L. Cairns not out	18
*S. P. Fleming c Mohammad Hafeez b Abdul Razzaq	21	L-b 5, w 11, n-b 3	19
L. Vincent not out	25		—
S. B. Styris c Shoaib Malik b Abdul Razzaq	6	1/42 (1) 2/65 (2) 3/82 (4) (3 wkts, 27.3 overs)	117

J. D. P. Oram, C. Z. Harris, †B. B. McCullum, D. L. Vettori, D. R. Tuffey and S. E. Bond did not bat.

Bowling: Shoaib Akhtar 10–0–41–0; Mohammad Sami 7–1–23–0; Umar Gul 4.3–0–29–1; Abdul Razzaq 6–0–19–2.

Umpires: D. J. Harper (Australia) and E. A. R. de Silva.
Third umpire: T. H. Wijewardene. Referee: G. R. Viswanath (India).

SRI LANKA v NEW ZEALAND

At Dambulla, May 13, 2003. Sri Lanka won by five wickets. Sri Lanka 5 pts, New Zealand 1 pt. Toss: Sri Lanka. One-day international debut: H. G. D. Nayanakantha.

Timid batting cost Sri Lanka a bonus point – and almost the match. Requiring just 140, Jayasuriya and Kaluwitharana, reunited as an opening pair for the first time in five months, put on 68 in 17 overs. But once Jayasuriya had gone, Sri Lanka lost all momentum, their paralysis such that they needed 18 from the last four overs before Dilshan slogged four successive boundaries off Tuffey to ease the pressure. Fleming felt that play began too soon after the covers were removed – morning rain had reduced the match to 46 overs a side – but although conditions were again bowler-friendly, several batsmen brought about their own downfall. Nayanakantha, a 24-year-old seamer with a distinctive bald head, conceded ten runs to Cairns in his first over, but removed him in his second.

Man of the Match: R. S. Kaluwitharana.

New Zealand

C. J. Nevin run out . . . 12
*S. P. Fleming c Sangakkara b Nissanka . 2
L. Vincent lbw b Jayasuriya . . . 32
S. B. Styris c Sangakkara b Nissanka . . . 0
C. L. Cairns c and b Nayanakantha 14
J. D. P. Oram c and b Muralitharan 20
C. Z. Harris not out . . . 20
†B. B. McCullum lbw b Muralitharan . . 0
K. D. Mills b Dharmasena . . . 6
D. L. Vettori run out . . . 5
D. R. Tuffey lbw b Muralitharan . . . 2

B 4, l-b 12, w 9, n-b 1 . . . 26

1/6 (2) 2/18 (1) 3/18 (4) (43.1 overs) 139
4/46 (5) 5/94 (6) 6/102 (3)
7/108 (8) 8/127 (9)
9/135 (10) 10/139 (11)

Bowling: Vaas 9–2–23–0; Nissanka 5–0–11–2; Nayanakantha 5–1–26–1; Dharmasena 8–0–28–1; Muralitharan 8.1–1–16–3; Jayasuriya 8–1–19–1.

Sri Lanka

S. T. Jayasuriya c Vettori b Oram 33
†R. S. Kaluwitharana c McCullum b Oram . 48
K. C. Sangakkara hit wkt b Oram 1
*M. S. Atapattu c Vincent b Styris 18
D. P. M. D. Jayawardene c McCullum b Tuffey . 2
T. M. Dilshan not out . . . 18
W. P. U. J. C. Vaas not out . . . 5
B 2, l-b 8, w 2, n-b 6 . . . 18

1/68 (1) 2/69 (3) (5 wkts, 43.4 overs) 143
3/116 (2) 4/116 (4)
5/120 (5)

H. G. D. Nayanakantha, H. D. P. K. Dharmasena, R. A. P. Nissanka and M. Muralitharan did not bat.

Bowling: Tuffey 7–0–37–1; Mills 5–0–32–0; Oram 9–4–12–3; Vettori 9–1–19–0; Harris 10–0–27–0; Styris 3.4–2–6–1.

Umpires: S. J. A. Taufel (Australia) and T. H. Wijewardene.
Third umpire: P. T. Manuel. Referee: G. R. Viswanath (India).

SRI LANKA v PAKISTAN

At Dambulla, May 18, 2003. Sri Lanka won by 12 runs. Sri Lanka 5 pts, Pakistan 1 pt. Toss: Pakistan.

This awful match came to life only because Pakistan made a mess of reaching an achievable target. Strong winds forced the umpires to dispense with bails from the 12th over, but could not excuse Pakistan conceding 14 no-balls and 12 wides. And they were lucky not to be punished for a dilatory over-rate that saw 23 overs in the first two, torturous hours. Sri Lanka, in trouble at 53 for five, recovered through the diligence of Dilshan and Dharmasena, who added 79, the highest stand of the tournament. Muralitharan chipped in with his best one-day international score before revelling in favourable conditions to match his best figures against Pakistan. Even so, Rashid Latif looked to be steering his side home until he rashly swept high to deep mid-wicket. Pakistan were not helped by a strange decision from umpire Harper, who disallowed four overthrows when Lokuarachchi's throw ricocheted off Mohammad Hafeez's bat to the boundary.

Man of the Match: M. Muralitharan.

Sri Lanka

†R. S. Kaluwitharana c Shabbir Ahmed b Shoaib Akhtar . 1
S. T. Jayasuriya c Rashid Latif b Mohammad Sami . 6
*M. S. Atapattu c Rashid Latif b Shabbir Ahmed . 9
K. C. Sangakkara c Rashid Latif b Abdul Razzaq . 17
D. P. M. D. Jayawardene run out 0
T. M. Dilshan c Rashid Latif b Shoaib Malik . 46
H. D. P. K. Dharmasena c Mohammad Hafeez b Shoaib Malik . 26
K. S. Lokuarachchi c Rashid Latif b Shoaib Akhtar . 5
W. P. U. J. C. Vaas not out . . . 8
M. Muralitharan c and b Mohammad Sami . 19
R. A. P. Nissanka run out . . . 2

B 2, l-b 5, w 12, n-b 14 . . . 33

1/13 (2) 2/13 (1) 3/47 (3) (49.5 overs) 172
4/48 (5) 5/53 (4) 6/132 (7)
7/137 (6) 8/139 (8)
9/164 (10) 10/172 (11)

Bowling: Mohammad Sami 9.5–0–46–2; Shoaib Akhtar 10–1–32–2; Shabbir Ahmed 10–2–23–1; Abdul Razzaq 10–0–26–1; Shoaib Malik 8–1–30–2; Mohammad Hafeez 2–0–8–0.

Pakistan

Mohammad Hafeez c Sangakkara b Nissanka . 20
Taufeeq Umar run out 3
Faisal Iqbal c Sangakkara b Lokuarachchi . 13
Yousuf Youhana c and b Muralitharan . . 13
Younis Khan st Kaluwitharana b Jayasuriya . 26
Shoaib Malik hit wkt b Muralitharan . . . 33
Abdul Razzaq c Kaluwitharana b Muralitharan . 7
*†Rashid Latif c Sangakkara b Lokuarachchi . 20
Shoaib Akhtar st Kaluwitharana b Muralitharan . 5
Mohammad Sami not out. 3
Shabbir Ahmed c Jayawardene b Muralitharan . 1
L-b 4, w 9, n-b 3 16

1/21 (2) 2/33 (1) 3/57 (4) 4/66 (3) 5/112 (5) 6/129 (6) 7/142 (7) 8/154 (9) 9/156 (8) 10/160 (11) (47.4 overs) 160

Bowling: Vaas 6–1–25–0; Nissanka 7–0–13–1; Dharmasena 10–2–32–0; Muralitharan 9.4–2–23–5; Lokuarachchi 8–0–29–2; Jayasuriya 7–0–34–1.

Umpires: D. J. Harper (Australia) and T. H. Wijewardene.
Third umpire: M. G. Silva. Referee: G. R. Viswanath (India).

SRI LANKA v NEW ZEALAND

At Dambulla, May 19, 2003. New Zealand won by nine runs. New Zealand 5 pts, Sri Lanka 1 pt. Toss: Sri Lanka.

Another poor game was played on a pitch Fleming described as "rubbish", even though his side won and qualified for the final. A New Zealand victory was unlikely when they were 104 for six after 43 overs, but McCullum, who faced 63 balls for his unbeaten 47, showed what could be done. Vettori then adroitly exploited conditions to take four for 14, his best one-day figures, enabling New Zealand to defend just 156. Sri Lanka's tactics were bewildering. First they opted to bowl, despite including four front-line spinners on a pitch bound to take more turn as the day wore on; then, ignoring McCullum's example and brief positive intent from Kaluwitharana, they endured a slow death. With ten required from the final over, Jayawardene, who in all faced 102 balls, was last out to a desperate reverse sweep.

Man of the Match: D. L. Vettori.

New Zealand

C. J. Nevin c Sangakkara b Nissanka . . . 8
*S. P. Fleming lbw b Muralitharan 16
L. Vincent run out 12
S. B. Styris c Kaluwitharana b Muralitharan . 29
C. L. Cairns c Dilshan b Jayasuriya. . . . 9
C. Z. Harris run out 4
†B. B. McCullum not out 47
K. D. Mills c Jayawardene b Jayasuriya . 17
A. R. Adams run out 1
B 1, l-b 5, w 5, n-b 2 13

1/17 (1) 2/40 (3) 3/42 (2) 4/69 (5) 5/76 (6) 6/88 (4) 7/138 (8) 8/156 (9) (8 wkts, 50 overs) 156

D. L. Vettori and D. R. Tuffey did not bat.

Bowling: Vaas 8–2–11–0; Nissanka 8–1–19–1; Dharmasena 10–2–19–0; Muralitharan 10–2–41–2; Lokuarachchi 5–1–25–0; Jayasuriya 9–0–35–2.

Sri Lanka

S. T. Jayasuriya c McCullum b Tuffey . . 9	H. D. P. K. Dharmasena c McCullum b Harris . 11
†R. S. Kaluwitharana c McCullum b Adams . 18	K. S. Lokuarachchi lbw b Styris 8
*M. S. Atapattu c sub (M. J. Horne) b Vettori . 13	M. Muralitharan c Mills b Vettori 4
K. C. Sangakkara b Vettori. 11	R. A. P. Nissanka not out. 6
D. P. M. D. Jayawardene c Harris b Styris . 38	B 3, l-b 2, w 9, n-b 4 18
T. M. Dilshan c Fleming b Vettori 7	1/28 (2) 2/43 (1) 3/60 (4) (49.1 overs) 147
W. P. U. J. C. Vaas c McCullum b Mills . 4	4/63 (3) 5/79 (6) 6/87 (7) 7/101 (8) 8/121 (9) 9/136 (10) 10/147 (5)

Bowling: Tuffey 9–4–22–1; Mills 8–2–30–1; Adams 3–0–14–1; Styris 9.1–0–30–2; Vettori 10–4–14–4; Harris 10–2–32–1.

Umpires: S. J. A. Taufel (Australia) and P. T. Manuel.
Third umpire: E. A. R. de Silva. Referee: G. R. Viswanath (India).

NEW ZEALAND v PAKISTAN

At Dambulla, May 20, 2003. Pakistan won by 22 runs. Pakistan 5 pts, New Zealand 1 pt. Toss: New Zealand. One-day international debut: Yasir Hameed.

Shoaib Akhtar was banned for two matches and fined 75% of his match fee after the referee, Gundappa Viswanath, found him guilty of ball-tampering. Television showed Shoaib, who was warned for the same offence by Clive Lloyd in Zimbabwe before Christmas, apparently scratching the ball in his sixth and seventh overs. It certainly worked: he demolished the New Zealand tail after the middle order had looked capable of seeing them to victory. Pakistan's total owed most to Shoaib Malik, whose 72-ball innings was the best of the tournament so far. The leg-spinner, Danish Kaneria, bowled beautifully in the New Zealand reply to shackle the middle order, and his dismissals of Cairns, beaten by a googly, and Styris, brilliantly caught at long-off, were key wickets. Pakistan's win meant Sri Lanka missed out on the final.

Man of the Match: Shoaib Malik.

Pakistan

Mohammad Hafeez b Mills 3	Shoaib Akhtar not out 18
Taufeeq Umar b Tuffey 2	Mohammad Sami c Vincent b Styris . . . 0
Yasir Hameed c Styris b Harris. 25	Danish Kaneria not out 0
Yousuf Youhana lbw b Vettori 17	L-b 2, w 9, n-b 2 13
Younis Khan c sub (M. J. Horne) b Vettori . 26	1/8 (2) 2/10 (1) (9 wkts, 50 overs) 203
Shoaib Malik c McCullum b Vettori. . . . 74	3/57 (3) 4/61 (4)
*†Rashid Latif c Cairns b Wiseman. . . . 2	5/102 (5) 6/108 (7)
Abdul Razzaq c Mills b Tuffey 23	7/179 (6) 8/191 (8) 9/201 (10)

Bowling: Tuffey 9–1–32–2; Mills 10–0–36–1; Styris 5–0–31–1; Vettori 10–1–34–3; Harris 10–0–41–1; Wiseman 6–0–27–1.

New Zealand

C. J. Nevin c Mohammad Sami b Danish Kaneria . 28
*S. P. Fleming c Rashid Latif b Mohammad Sami . 17
L. Vincent lbw b Mohammad Hafeez . . . 2
S. B. Styris c Shoaib Malik b Danish Kaneria . 46
C. L. Cairns b Danish Kaneria 28
C. Z. Harris lbw b Mohammad Sami . . . 24
†B. B. McCullum c Younis Khan b Shoaib Akhtar . 0
K. D. Mills c Taufeeq Umar b Shoaib Akhtar . 11
D. L. Vettori c Rashid Latif b Shoaib Akhtar . 4
P. J. Wiseman b Mohammad Sami 2
D. R. Tuffey not out 2
L-b 3, w 11, n-b 3. 17

1/36 (2) 2/40 (3) 3/71 (1) 4/113 (5) 5/160 (6) 6/161 (7) 7/163 (4) 8/172 (9) 9/179 (10) 10/181 (8) (48.1 overs) 181

Bowling: Shoaib Akhtar 9.1–0–36–3; Mohammad Sami 9–0–34–3; Mohammad Hafeez 10–1–33–1; Danish Kaneria 10–1–31–3; Shoaib Malik 9–0–39–0; Abdul Razzaq 1–0–5–0.

Umpires: D. J. Harper (Australia) and P. T. Manuel.
Third umpire: M. G. Silva. Referee: G. R. Viswanath (India).

QUALIFYING TABLE

	Played	*Won*	*Lost*	*Bonus points*	*Points*	*Net run-rate*
New Zealand	4	2	2	3	13	0.27
Pakistan	4	2	2	2	12	0.06
Sri Lanka	4	2	2	1	11	−0.33

Win = 5 pts. One bonus point awarded either to the winning team for achieving victory with a run-rate 1.25 times that of the opposition, or to the losing team for denying the winners a bonus point. Net run-rate is calculated by subtracting runs conceded per over from runs scored per over.

FINAL

NEW ZEALAND v PAKISTAN

At Dambulla, May 23, 2003. New Zealand won by four wickets. Toss: Pakistan. One-day international debut: Faisal Athar.

New Zealand's comfortable win would have been even easier if they had not thrown away four wickets to reckless shots in sight of victory. Their success was founded on all-round disciplined bowling and then an aggressive innings from Fleming, who grabbed the initiative during his 111-ball innings and saw New Zealand to the highest 15-over score of the tournament, 70 for one. Pakistan did themselves no favours by conceding 44 extras, equalling the fifth-highest total in one-day internationals, and they ended the match without captain Rashid Latif after he injured his right hand: Yasir Hameed took over behind the stumps; Yousuf Youhana took charge. Earlier, Younis Khan had held Pakistan together, in all facing 85 balls, though just five from the last three overs. Tuffey ended the innings with a double-wicket maiden.

Man of the Match: S. P. Fleming. *Man of the Series:* Shoaib Malik.

Pakistan

Mohammad Hafeez c McCullum b Tuffey	0
Faisal Athar c McCullum b Oram	9
Yasir Hameed lbw b Mills	6
Yousuf Youhana run out	25
Younis Khan not out	70
Shoaib Malik b Vettori	34
Abdul Razzaq run out	10
*†Rashid Latif c Tuffey b Oram	20
Mohammad Sami c Harris b Oram	7
Shabbir Ahmed c McCullum b Tuffey	2
Danish Kaneria c McCullum b Tuffey	0
L-b 6, w 3, n-b 6	15
1/0 (1) 2/11 (3) 3/39 (2) 4/56 (4) 5/113 (6) 6/136 (7) 7/179 (8) 8/194 (9) 9/198 (10) 10/198 (11) (50 overs)	198

Bowling: Tuffey 9–2–32–3; Mills 8–0–36–1; Styris 10–2–34–0; Oram 10–1–38–3; Vettori 10–1–32–1; Harris 3–0–20–0.

New Zealand

C. J. Nevin c Shoaib Malik b Mohammad Sami	17
*S. P. Fleming c Younis Khan b Mohammad Sami	65
L. Vincent run out	13
S. B. Styris b Mohammad Sami	22
C. L. Cairns c Abdul Razzaq b Shabbir Ahmed	18
J. D. P. Oram c Younis Khan b Abdul Razzaq	12
C. Z. Harris not out	5
†B. B. McCullum not out	4
L-b 13, w 25, n-b 6	44
1/54 (1) 2/113 (3) 3/151 (2) 4/152 (4) 5/170 (6) 6/194 (5) (6 wkts, 45.2 overs)	200

K. D. Mills, D. L. Vettori and D. R. Tuffey did not bat.

Bowling: Mohammad Sami 10–0–42–3; Shabbir Ahmed 8.2–0–36–1; Abdul Razzaq 3–0–20–1; Mohammad Hafeez 7–1–24–0; Danish Kaneria 10–2–35–0; Shoaib Malik 7–0–30–0.

Umpires: D. J. Harper (Australia) and E. A. R. de Silva.
Third umpire: M. G. Silva. Referee: G. R. Viswanath (India).

TVS CUP IN INDIA, 2003-04

RICHARD BOOCK

Ricky Ponting suggested this triangular series would be tougher than the World Cup for his depleted squad, but as it happened the result was exactly the same – Australia beat India in the final with New Zealand some way down the track. It was a sobering reminder of Australia's depth of talent: they overcame the absence of Shane Warne, Glenn McGrath, Jason Gillespie, Brett Lee, Stuart MacGill and Darren Lehmann to take the tournament by storm, losing only once in seven matches.

Having arrived in India just three days before their first match, Ponting's side received a setback at Gwalior before embarking on a six-match winning streak, including a 37-run victory against the hosts in the final at Eden Gardens. Far from looking vulnerable, the Australians received excellent overall contributions from their senior batsmen and an enthusiastic response from their lesser-known pacemen, Nathan Bracken and Brad Williams. Bracken was the tournament's top wicket-taker, with 14, and had the lowest average (13.92); Williams was not far behind, taking nine wickets in the first two matches against New Zealand.

For India, the only consolation was the form of Sachin Tendulkar, who was the top run-scorer with 466 – at an average of 77.66 and a strike-rate of 89.10. Sourav Ganguly's leg infection meant he played only the last two qualifying games, and the spinners, Anil Kumble and Harbhajan Singh, were less penetrating than usual. Indeed, for a few days, India were in danger of missing out on their own tournament final. Then they came to life against New Zealand at Hyderabad, smashing 353 for five. The New Zealanders, who performed so strongly in the Test series just beforehand, hardly fired a shot during the one-day competition.

Injuries meant the side were a skeleton crew. But even so there were some sobering truths to emerge from the series, not least the waning influence of Chris Harris, the ineffectiveness of Chris Nevin and the inconsistency of Lou Vincent, who had earlier emerged as one of the success stories of the Test series.

Note: Matches in this section were not first-class.

INDIA v NEW ZEALAND

At Chennai, October 23, 2003 (day/night). No result. India 3 pts, New Zealand 3 pts. Toss: India.

The rain started falling shortly after the halfway point of India's innings, just as they were starting to recover from the loss of three wickets through an unbeaten 48-run fourth-wicket stand between Tendulkar and Yuvraj Singh. Sehwag and Tendulkar started with aggressive intent, putting on 53 inside the first nine overs, and when Sehwag departed Laxman carried on where he left off, collecting 25 off 23 balls before miscuing a hook. By the time the umpires took the players from the field, Tendulkar was poised to strike and Yuvraj was looking similarly threatening. The biggest concern for New Zealand was a hamstring strain suffered by Cairns, who bowled only three overs in his comeback match before leaving the field.

India

V. Sehwag b Cairns	31	Yuvraj Singh not out	29
S. R. Tendulkar not out	48	W 3, n-b 1	4
V. V. S. Laxman c sub (K. D. Mills) b Styris	25		
*R. Dravid c Styris b Vettori	4	1/53 (1) 2/88 (3) 3/93 (4) (3 wkts, 26.5 overs)	141

M. Kaif, A. Kumble, †P. A. Patel, Harbhajan Singh, A. B. Agarkar and Zaheer Khan did not bat.

Bowling: Tuffey 4–0–26–0; Oram 6–0–31–0; Cairns 3–0–16–1; Hitchcock 3–0–17–0; Styris 4–0–19–1; Vettori 4–0–21–1; Harris 2.5–0–11–0.

New Zealand

*S. P. Fleming, †B. B. McCullum, L. Vincent, S. B. Styris, C. D. McMillan, C. L. Cairns, C. Z. Harris, J. D. P. Oram, D. L. Vettori, D. R. Tuffey and P. A. Hitchcock

Umpires: D. R. Shepherd (England) and A. V. Jayaprakash.
Third umpire: I. Sivaram. Referee: R. S. Madugalle (Sri Lanka).

INDIA v AUSTRALIA

At Gwalior, October 26, 2003 (day/night). India won by 37 runs. India 5 pts, Australia 1 pt. Toss: India.

In their first meeting since the World Cup final in March, India showed few signs of any psychological baggage against Australia and galloped to 283 for five batting first, following centuries from Tendulkar and Laxman. After Sehwag went to the third ball of the game, they repaired the innings quickly with a second-wicket partnership of 190, which set the scene for a late onslaught – 89 runs came off the last ten overs. Tendulkar's was an innings of two halves: his first fifty came at a run a ball and was punctuated with nine boundaries, while his second took 67 balls and included one six but no fours. Laxman was more sedate but no less intent, and looked in complete command against all the bowlers except Hogg, who troubled him on off stump. Australia began their chase in familiar style: Hayden and Gilchrist – whose 50 took just 39 balls – putting on 132 for the first wicket. However, in an uncharacteristic collapse Australia lost seven wickets for 53, with Kumble taking the crucial wickets of Hayden and Ponting.

Man of the Match: S. R. Tendulkar.

India

V. Sehwag c Hayden b Bracken	0	M. Kaif not out	1
S. R. Tendulkar c Gilchrist b Bracken	100	L-b 8, w 6	14
V. V. S. Laxman run out	102		
Yuvraj Singh c Symonds b Williams	44	1/1 (1) 2/191 (2) 3/255 (3) 4/263 (4) 5/283 (5) (5 wkts, 50 overs)	283
A. B. Agarkar c Symonds b Bracken	22		

*R. Dravid, †P. A. Patel, Harbhajan Singh, A. Kumble and Zaheer Khan did not bat.

Bowling: Bracken 10–0–53–3; Williams 10–0–67–1; Bichel 7–0–38–0; Harvey 8–0–46–0; Hogg 10–0–47–0; Symonds 5–0–24–0.

Australia

†A. C. Gilchrist b Zaheer Khan	83	B. A. Williams not out	11
M. L. Hayden st Patel b Kumble	47	N. W. Bracken not out	7
*R. T. Ponting c and b Kumble	2		
D. R. Martyn b Sehwag	16	L-b 4, w 4, n-b 6	14
A. Symonds lbw b Zaheer Khan	1		
M. G. Bevan b Sehwag	18	1/132 (1) 2/135 (3) (9 wkts, 50 overs)	246
I. J. Harvey b Tendulkar	4	3/140 (2) 4/141 (5)	
G. B. Hogg st Patel b Harbhajan Singh	29	5/176 (4) 6/177 (6)	
A. J. Bichel c Kaif b Zaheer Khan	14	7/185 (7) 8/225 (8) 9/229 (9)	

Bowling: Zaheer Khan 10–0–49–3; Agarkar 6–0–42–0; Kumble 10–1–28–2; Harbhajan Singh 10–0–43–1; Tendulkar 6–0–39–1; Sehwag 7–0–36–2; Yuvraj Singh 1–0–5–0.

Umpires: N. A. Mallender (England) and K. Hariharan.
Third umpire: A. V. Jayaprakash. Referee: R. S. Madugalle (Sri Lanka).

AUSTRALIA v NEW ZEALAND

At Faridabad, October 29, 2003. Australia won by eight wickets. Australia 6 pts. Toss: New Zealand.

Suggestions that an injury-stricken Australia would struggle went awry with the second ball of the match, when Bracken trapped Nevin in front. From that point on, it was like exhibition dominoes for the New Zealand batting line-up, already missing Astle, and further weakened on the eve of the game by the unavailability of Cairns. Before the end of the sixth over, three men were out: two runs had come off the bat and the score was just 11. Despite brief resistance from McMillan, New Zealand were mostly clueless against Bracken and Williams, who shared seven wickets. They were fortunate that the Australians gave away 18 wides and two no-balls. Even so, New Zealand made their fifth-lowest total in one-day internationals. Any hopes that Australia might also struggle evaporated at once: Gilchrist smashed 29 off 18 balls, and Hayden was just as carefree.

Man of the Match: B. A. Williams.

New Zealand

C. J. Nevin lbw b Bracken	0	P. A. Hitchcock c Hayden b Williams	10
*S. P. Fleming c Gilchrist b Bracken	2	D. R. Tuffey not out	3
L. Vincent c Bichel b Williams	0		
S. B. Styris c Ponting b Williams	7	L-b 12, w 18, n-b 2	32
C. D. McMillan lbw b Bichel	24		
J. D. P. Oram c Gilchrist b Bracken	0	1/0 (1) 2/11 (2) (33.4 overs)	97
C. Z. Harris lbw b Harvey	14	3/11 (3) 4/20 (4) 5/21 (6)	
†B. B. McCullum c Martyn b Williams	5	6/73 (7) 7/77 (5) 8/80 (8)	
D. L. Vettori lbw b Harvey	0	9/80 (9) 10/97 (10)	

Bowling: Bracken 9–2–25–3; Williams 9.4–1–22–4; Bichel 7–0–29–1; Harvey 8–2–9–2.

Australia

†A. C. Gilchrist c and b Oram	29
M. L. Hayden not out	51
*R. T. Ponting c McCullum b Tuffey	12
D. R. Martyn not out	2
L-b 5, n-b 2	7
1/47 (1) 2/90 (3) (2 wkts, 16.4 overs)	101

A. Symonds, M. G. Bevan, I. J. Harvey, A. J. Bichel, G. B. Hogg, B. A. Williams and N. W. Bracken did not bat.

Bowling: Tuffey 6.4–0–51–1; Oram 7–1–31–1; Hitchcock 2–0–8–0; Vettori 1–0–6–0.

Umpires: D. R. Shepherd (England) and S. Venkataraghavan.
Third umpire: I. Sivaram. Referee: R. S. Madugalle (Sri Lanka).

INDIA v AUSTRALIA

At Mumbai, November 1, 2003 (day/night). Australia won by 77 runs. Australia 6 pts. Toss: Australia.

John Wright, India's New Zealand-born coach, said before the game that he expected Australia, having had extra time to acclimatise and a rare defeat to absorb, would be a much tougher proposition this time around. So they were. Dravid's experiment of opening the bowling with Zaheer Khan and Sehwag will not be remembered as a great success: Gilchrist smashed eight fours in his 30-ball 41, and was the principal aggressor as Australia opened their account with 54 off the first five overs. The impetus served Australia well throughout the innings. Martyn brought up his first fifty off 84 deliveries but cut loose as the overs started running down and needed just 34 more balls to reach his century. India's reply started badly, with Sehwag falling to the first ball of the innings. Tendulkar and Dravid did enough repair work to keep India in the game. However, Clarke's left-arm spin was the surprise package – he dismissed those two plus Yuvraj Singh and returned to end Kumble's lower-order defiance.

Man of the Match: D. R. Martyn.

Australia

†A. C. Gilchrist c Kaif b Harbhajan Singh	41
M. L. Hayden c Yuvraj Singh b Zaheer Khan	0
*R. T. Ponting lbw b Agarkar	31
D. R. Martyn b Agarkar	100
A. Symonds c Harbhajan Singh b Yuvraj Singh	48
M. G. Bevan c Kaif b Agarkar	42
M. J. Clarke run out	2
A. J. Bichel b Agarkar	1
G. B. Hogg not out	0
B 4, l-b 2, w 8, n-b 7	21
1/9 (2) 2/55 (1) 3/93 (3) 4/171 (5) 5/282 (4) 6/283 (6) 7/286 (7) 8/286 (8) — (8 wkts, 50 overs)	286

N. W. Bracken and B. A. Williams did not bat.

Bowling: Zaheer Khan 7–0–64–1; Sehwag 4–0–28–0; Harbhajan Singh 10–0–44–1; Kumble 8–0–50–0; Agarkar 9–0–37–4; Tendulkar 4–0–21–0; Yuvraj Singh 8–1–36–1.

India

V. Sehwag lbw b Bracken	0
S. R. Tendulkar b Clarke	68
V. V. S. Laxman c Gilchrist b Bichel	21
*R. Dravid c Bichel b Clarke	59
Yuvraj Singh c Gilchrist b Clarke	9
M. Kaif c Gilchrist b Bracken	10
A. B. Agarkar c Symonds b Bracken	2
†P. A. Patel c Clarke b Hogg	16
Harbhajan Singh c and b Bracken	6
A. Kumble b Clarke	6
Zaheer Khan not out	5
L-b 2, w 4, n-b 1	7
1/0 (1) 2/38 (3) 3/137 (2) 4/153 (5) 5/172 (4) 6/175 (6) 7/178 (7) 8/185 (9) 9/200 (10) 10/209 (8) — (46.2 overs)	209

Bowling: Bracken 10–2–29–4; Williams 5–0–20–0; Bichel 6–0–31–1; Symonds 10–0–57–0; Hogg 5.2–0–28–1; Clarke 10–0–42–4.

Umpires: N. A. Mallender (England) and A. V. Jayaprakash.
Third umpire: K. Hariharan. Referee: R. S. Madugalle (Sri Lanka).

AUSTRALIA v NEW ZEALAND

At Pune, November 3, 2003. Australia won by two wickets. Australia 5 pts, New Zealand 1 pt. Toss: Australia.

Australia scrambled to the target of 259 with a ball to spare, thanks to a whirlwind 70 from Clarke, another chess-like half-century from Bevan, and some appalling catching. If Vincent had not dropped a regulation chance at extra cover when Symonds was one, it might not have even been close: Symonds eventually led his team home with an unbeaten 37 off 39 balls: even the winning shot should have been caught by Styris. New Zealand lost their first four wickets to Williams within eight overs, and a repeat of the Faridabad fiasco looked distinctly likely. This time, however, help was at hand, through consolidation from Fleming and then courtesy of a superb rearguard from Oram and McCullum. Oram hit the Aussie attack to all corners and McCullum backed up his plea for promotion up the order with an inventive maiden half-century.

Man of the Match: B. A. Williams.

New Zealand

C. J. Nevin lbw b Williams	0
*S. P. Fleming c Harvey b Symonds	40
L. Vincent c Ponting b Williams	1
S. B. Styris lbw b Williams	0
C. D. McMillan b Williams	0
C. L. Cairns lbw b Bichel	27
J. D. P. Oram b Symonds	81
C. Z. Harris c Harvey b Williams	1
†B. B. McCullum not out	51
D. L. Vettori b Harvey	18
D. R. Tuffey not out	1
L-b 4, w 32, n-b 2	38
(9 wkts, 50 overs)	258

1/3 (1) 2/10 (3) 3/11 (4) 4/21 (5) 5/68 (6) 6/130 (2) 7/151 (8) 8/219 (7) 9/246 (10)

Bowling: Bracken 10–3–39–0; Williams 10–1–53–5; Bichel 9–0–59–1; Harvey 9–1–33–1; Symonds 10–2–56–2; Clarke 2–0–14–0.

Australia

†A. C. Gilchrist c Vettori b Tuffey	25
M. L. Hayden c Styris b Tuffey	9
*R. T. Ponting b Styris	16
D. R. Martyn b Tuffey	10
M. J. Clarke b Tuffey	70
M. G. Bevan c Harris b Cairns	50
A. Symonds not out	37
I. J. Harvey c Styris b Vettori	19
A. J. Bichel c McCullum b Vettori	9
B. A. Williams not out	3
L-b 2, w 8, n-b 1	11
(8 wkts, 49.5 overs)	259

1/34 (1) 2/40 (2) 3/54 (4) 4/65 (3) 5/173 (5) 6/204 (6) 7/231 (8) 8/244 (9)

N. W. Bracken did not bat.

Bowling: Tuffey 10–2–30–4; Oram 9.5–0–65–0; Cairns 10–0–48–1; Styris 7–1–31–1; Vettori 8–0–59–2; Harris 5–0–24–0.

Umpires: D. R. Shepherd (England) and K. Hariharan.
Third umpire: A. V. Jayaprakash. Referee: R. S. Madugalle (Sri Lanka).

INDIA v NEW ZEALAND

At Cuttack, November 6, 2003 (day/night). New Zealand won by four wickets. New Zealand 5 pts, India 1 pt. Toss: India.

Styris initially helped New Zealand with the ball and then rescued their innings with McMillan after the customary top-order collapse. His 68 was especially meritorious: the pitch was low and slow, the new Barabati Stadium lights seemed underpowered, there were insects everywhere, a jam-packed crowd, the occasional fire and a pitch invader or two. Styris probably would have been there at the end, too, had it not been for a woeful lbw decision from umpire Jayaprakash. Styris conveyed his feelings, which later cost him his match fee. McMillan looked unstoppable once he got going. His unbeaten 82 contained some tireless running between the wickets, the occasional lusty blow, and two of the sweetest imaginable reverse sweeps. Only 33 by Zaheer Khan off 13 balls at the end, including 20 off the final over, from Oram, kept India in the hunt at all.

Man of the Match: S. B. Styris.

India

V. V. S. Laxman c and b Styris	31	Zaheer Khan not out	33
S. R. Tendulkar lbw b Mills	14	M. Kartik not out	1
M. Kaif b Styris	64	B 4, l-b 2, w 2	8
*†R. Dravid c Styris b Vettori	31		
Yuvraj Singh c Mills b Vettori	0	1/27 (2) 2/77 (1) (9 wkts, 50 overs)	246
H. K. Badani c McCullum b Tuffey	41	3/136 (4) 4/136 (5)	
S. V. Bahutule lbw b Styris	11	5/169 (3) 6/193 (7)	
A. B. Agarkar c McMillan b Tuffey	7	7/205 (6) 8/206 (8)	
Harbhajan Singh b Tuffey	5	9/223 (9)	

Bowling: Tuffey 10–1–31–3; Mills 8–0–51–1; Oram 10–0–68–0; Styris 10–0–38–3; Vettori 10–0–39–2; Harris 2–0–13–0.

New Zealand

C. J. Nevin c Yuvraj Singh b Harbhajan Singh	29	J. D. P. Oram run out	6
*S. P. Fleming lbw b Agarkar	24	†B. B. McCullum not out	19
C. Z. Harris lbw b Zaheer Khan	0	B 1, l-b 6, w 12, n-b 1	20
L. Vincent lbw b Zaheer Khan	1	1/39 (2) 2/40 (3) (6 wkts, 47.3 overs)	249
S. B. Styris lbw b Kartik	68	3/44 (4) 4/68 (1)	
C. D. McMillan not out	82	5/195 (5) 6/214 (7)	

D. R. Tuffey, D. L. Vettori and K. D. Mills did not bat.

Bowling: Zaheer Khan 9–1–49–2; Agarkar 8–0–41–1; Harbhajan Singh 10–0–41–1; Kartik 10–1–34–1; Tendulkar 3–0–25–0; Bahutule 3–0–24–0; Badani 3.3–0–21–0; Yuvraj Singh 1–0–7–0.

Umpires: N. A. Mallender (England) and A. V. Jayaprakash.
Third umpire: I. Sivaram. Referee: R. S. Madugalle (Sri Lanka).

AUSTRALIA v NEW ZEALAND

At Guwahati, November 9, 2003. Australia won by 44 runs. Australia 5 pts, New Zealand 1 pt. Toss: New Zealand.

This was Australia's sixth consecutive win against New Zealand, who won the toss, seized an early advantage and then slowly but surely disintegrated against a line-up missing at least nine front-line players. Having reduced Australia to 61 for four, New Zealand were unable to find a way of stopping Ponting and Bevan on a sluggish pitch. Australia, already through to the final, opted to rest Hayden, Gilchrist and Williams, but still found a successful formula when it mattered, something their captain Ponting put down to experience – and Bevan. So often the architect of New Zealand's demise, Bevan top-scored with 84 and marshalled the tail intelligently, wringing every possible run out of the final five overs. New Zealand again struggled against the left-arm swing of Bracken, and the only batsman who seemed to have much of an idea was Styris, who followed up his man-of-the-match effort in Cuttack with a battling half-century.

Man of the Match: M. G. Bevan.

Australia

I. J. Harvey c Nevin b Tuffey	25	G. B. Hogg c Styris b Harris	9
†J. P. Maher lbw b Tuffey	3	A. J. Bichel not out	15
*R. T. Ponting c McMillan b Vettori	52	L-b 9, w 7, n-b 1	17
D. R. Martyn c McCullum b Mills	0		
A. Symonds c McCullum b Mills	18	1/33 (1) 2/33 (2) (7 wkts, 50 overs)	225
M. G. Bevan not out	84	3/34 (4) 4/61 (5)	
M. J. Clarke c McMillan b Vettori	2	5/139 (3) 6/141 (7) 7/164 (8)	

M. S. Kasprowicz and N. W. Bracken did not bat.

Bowling: Tuffey 10–1–60–2; Mills 8–0–36–2; Oram 10–0–47–0; Vettori 10–0–20–2; Styris 9–1–38–0; Harris 3–0–15–1.

New Zealand

C. J. Nevin c Ponting b Bracken	2	K. D. Mills c Maher b Bracken	4
*S. P. Fleming c and b Harvey	29	D. R. Tuffey not out	0
L. Vincent c Hogg b Bracken	12		
S. B. Styris c Ponting b Hogg	54	B 4, l-b 6, w 9, n-b 2	21
C. D. McMillan c Maher b Bichel	0		—
J. D. P. Oram lbw b Hogg	14	1/7 (1) 2/38 (3) 3/66 (2) (45.3 overs)	181
C. Z. Harris run out	38	4/68 (5) 5/88 (6) 6/143 (4)	
†B. B. McCullum c Maher b Kasprowicz	7	7/169 (8) 8/170 (9)	
D. L. Vettori run out	0	9/181 (7) 10/181 (10)	

Bowling: Bracken 7.3–0–34–3; Kasprowicz 8–0–28–1; Bichel 7–0–21–1; Harvey 4–0–14–1; Hogg 10–0–39–2; Symonds 4–0–14–0; Clarke 5–0–21–0.

Umpires: D. R. Shepherd (England) and K. Hariharan.
Third umpire: I. Sivaram. Referee: R. S. Madugalle (Sri Lanka).

INDIA v AUSTRALIA

At Bangalore, November 12, 2003 (day/night). Australia won by 61 runs. Australia 5 pts, India 1 pt. Toss: Australia.

India welcomed back Nehra, one of the success stories of the World Cup, from a seven-month injury lay-off, but Gilchrist hit three fours off his first over. Things got no better, and Nehra was dropped for the rest of the series. Gilchrist hit eight fours and a six in a 42-ball fifty, and added five more boundaries before his century arrived 52 balls later. He eventually fell to Kumble in the 34th over, having steered his side to 198 for two, and set the scene for an all-out assault. Ponting, who scratched and searched during the early stages of his innings, hit his straps after the departure of Gilchrist and took only 31 balls to go from fifty to a century. Chasing 348, India never seriously threatened, although Tendulkar batted well for his 89, and the others all chanced their arms as the required run-rate escalated.

Man of the Match: A. C. Gilchrist.

Australia

†A. C. Gilchrist c Zaheer Khan b Kumble	111	D. R. Martyn not out	61
M. L. Hayden run out	44	B 1, l-b 9, w 12, n-b 1	23
			—
*R. T. Ponting not out	108	1/119 (2) 2/198 (1) (2 wkts, 50 overs)	347

A. Symonds, M. G. Bevan, M. J. Clarke, I. J. Harvey, A. J. Bichel, M. S. Kasprowicz and B. A. Williams did not bat.

Bowling: Nehra 10–0–80–0; Zaheer Khan 10–0–67–0; Kumble 9–0–60–1; Sehwag 5–0–36–0; Kartik 10–2–51–0; Ganguly 2–0–10–0; Yuvraj Singh 4–0–33–0.

India

V. Sehwag b Harvey	39	A. Kumble not out	12
S. R. Tendulkar b Harvey	89	M. Kartik not out	4
V. V. S. Laxman c Symonds b Clarke	18	B 5, l-b 6, w 11, n-b 1	23
*S. C. Ganguly c Bichel b Symonds	37		—
†R. Dravid c and b Kasprowicz	34	1/103 (1) 2/148 (3) (8 wkts, 50 overs)	286
Yuvraj Singh lbw b Symonds	20	3/172 (2) 4/217 (4)	
M. Kaif b Symonds	8	5/254 (5) 6/254 (6)	
Zaheer Khan run out	2	7/258 (8) 8/277 (7)	

A. Nehra did not bat.

Bowling: Williams 8–0–43–0; Kasprowicz 10–0–37–1; Bichel 9–0–46–0; Symonds 9–0–42–3; Harvey 10–0–71–2; Clarke 4–0–36–1.

Umpires: D. R. Shepherd (England) and A. V. Jayaprakash.
Third umpire: K. Hariharan. Referee: R. S. Madugalle (Sri Lanka).

INDIA v NEW ZEALAND

At Hyderabad, November 15, 2003 (day/night). India won by 145 runs. India 6 pts. Toss: India.

New Zealand's chances were not good after Fleming withdrew injured, and they were even worse after India, batting first, skipped through to 353 for five. Fuelled by barnstorming centuries from Sehwag and Tendulkar – his 36th in one-day internationals – and an incandescent knock from Dravid, India qualified for the final in style. Tendulkar restrained himself early on, before accelerating to reach his hundred off 87 balls. There was still time for Dravid to unleash his party trick, an eye-popping half-century off just 22 balls – equalling the second fastest by an Indian batsman, and including five fours and three sixes. The New Zealanders never got near the target despite a quick-fire 54 off 49 balls from Styris and another mature innings from McCullum.

Man of the Match: V. Sehwag.

India

V. Sehwag c Vincent b Styris 130
S. R. Tendulkar c Oram b Harris. 102
*S. C. Ganguly c Tuffey b Styris. 33
Yuvraj Singh c Harris b Mills. 7
†R. Dravid not out 50
V. V. S. Laxman b Tuffey. 3
M. Kaif not out 15
L-b 6, w 6, n-b 1 13

1/182 (2) 2/256 (3) 3/283 (1) 4/284 (4) 5/303 (6) (5 wkts, 50 overs) 353

M. Kartik, A. B. Agarkar, A. Kumble and Zaheer Khan did not bat.

Bowling: Tuffey 9–1–69–1; Mills 10–0–54–1; Oram 7–0–67–0; Cairns 7–0–47–0; Styris 6–0–46–2; Vettori 6–0–35–0; Harris 5–0–29–1.

New Zealand

C. J. Nevin b Agarkar 1
L. Vincent lbw b Zaheer Khan 22
C. Z. Harris lbw b Agarkar 1
S. B. Styris c Agarkar b Kartik. 54
C. D. McMillan c Dravid b Kumble. . . . 20
*C. L. Cairns c Khan b Kumble 23
J. D. P. Oram st Dravid b Kartik 11
†B. B. McCullum lbw b Zaheer Khan . . 31
D. L. Vettori run out 19
K. D. Mills not out. 7
D. R. Tuffey lbw b Zaheer Khan 0
B 2, l-b 9, w 7, n-b 1 19

1/8 (1) 2/25 (3) 3/48 (2) 4/110 (5) 5/118 (4) 6/136 (7) 7/154 (6) 8/187 (9) 9/208 (8) 10/208 (11) (47 overs) 208

Bowling: Zaheer Khan 8–1–30–3; Agarkar 6–0–28–2; Tendulkar 8–0–40–0; Kumble 10–1–36–2; Kartik 10–0–38–2; Yuvraj Singh 5–0–25–0.

Umpires: D. R. Shepherd (England) and K. Hariharan.
Third umpire: I. Sivaram. Referee: R. S. Madugalle (Sri Lanka).

QUALIFYING TABLE

	Played	*Won*	*Lost*	*No result*	*Bonus points*	*Points*	*Net run-rate*
Australia	6	5	1	0	3	28	1.11
India	6	2	3	1	3	16	0.11
New Zealand.	6	1	4	1	2	10	–1.46

Win = 5 pts, no result = 3 pts. One bonus point awarded either to the winning team for achieving victory with a run-rate 1.25 times that of the opposition, or to the losing team for denying the winners a bonus point. Net run-rate is calculated by subtracting runs conceded per over from runs scored per over.

FINAL

INDIA v AUSTRALIA

At Kolkata, November 18, 2003 (day/night). Australia won by 37 runs. Toss: Australia.

Despite gaining the advantage at least twice, India were again consigned to second place by Australia, this time by the all-rounders, Harvey and Clarke. Clarke crashed 44 off 28 balls to stretch Australia's total to a barely adequate 235 for five, while Harvey's repertoire of slower balls accounted for four wickets and ruined India's reply just as they were gaining momentum. The Australians lost Gilchrist and Hayden inside the first eight overs and, against testing spin on a slow pitch, were unable to increase the run-rate with their usual ease. India seemed on track when Tendulkar got going, to the delight of the traditional raucous Eden Gardens full house, estimated at close to 100,000. But he was undone by Bichel, Clarke took two vital wickets and, with the tail exposed, Harvey returned from a shaky first spell and took two wickets with successive balls. He then removed Harbhajan and Salvi – and Australia had yet another trophy.

Man of the Match: M. J. Clarke. *Man of the Series:* S. R. Tendulkar.

Australia

†A. C. Gilchrist b Agarkar	7
M. L. Hayden c Laxman b Zaheer Khan	19
*R. T. Ponting c Laxman b Kartik	36
D. R. Martyn c Yuvraj Singh b Sehwag	61
A. Symonds c Badani b Harbhajan Singh	10
M. G. Bevan not out	40
M. J. Clarke not out	44
B 4, l-b 7, w 7	18
1/16 (1) 2/32 (2) 3/112 (3) 4/129 (5) 5/170 (4) (5 wkts, 50 overs)	235

I. J. Harvey, A. J. Bichel, N. W. Bracken and B. A. Williams did not bat.

Bowling: Agarkar 8–2–50–1; Zaheer Khan 6–0–29–1; Salvi 3–0–23–0; Kartik 10–1–30–1; Harbhajan Singh 10–1–34–1; Sehwag 8–0–35–1; Badani 5–0–23–0.

India

S. R. Tendulkar b Bichel	45
V. Sehwag c and b Bracken	5
V. V. S. Laxman b Williams	22
*†R. Dravid b Clarke	49
Yuvraj Singh c Hayden b Symonds	4
H. K. Badani c Symonds b Clarke	30
A. B. Agarkar not out	26
M. Kartik b Harvey	1
Zaheer Khan b Harvey	0
Harbhajan Singh c Symonds b Harvey	2
A. M. Salvi b Harvey	0
B 4, l-b 5, w 5	14
1/8 (2) 2/36 (3) 3/99 (1) 4/110 (5) 5/159 (6) 6/168 (4) 7/186 (8) 8/186 (9) 9/198 (10) 10/198 (11) (41.5 overs)	198

Bowling: Bracken 8–1–15–1; Williams 7–1–30–1; Bichel 8–0–51–1; Harvey 4.5–0–21–4; Symonds 7–0–36–1; Clarke 7–1–36–2.

Umpires: D. R. Shepherd (England) and A. V. Jayaprakash.
Third umpire: K. Hariharan. Referee: R. S. Madugalle (Sri Lanka).

ENGLAND ACADEMY IN AUSTRALIA AND SRI LANKA, 2002-03

England's second batch of young academicians split their winter between Australia, where they continued to make use of facilities in Adelaide while work was completed on their home-to-be in Loughborough, and Sri Lanka. The squad was a talented one. Three members of the original 15-man party – Chris Read, Alex Tudor and Ian Blackwell – had already played international cricket, and that number was boosted to five when Richard Dawson and Robert Key, who had been on Ashes duty, arrived for the Sri Lankan leg of the trip.

But the success of any Academy is better measured by the number of future internationals, and how well they do. Of the original squad that flew out to Australia, five – Kabir Ali, James Anderson, Gareth Batty, Rikki Clarke and Jim Troughton – would represent England by the end of 2003; Anderson and Batty, both called up by the injury-hit senior squad for the VB Series in Australia, would do so not long after arriving in Adelaide. Their performances were mixed.

The previous year's intake had spent the whole winter programme in Australia, but now the ECB decided to broaden the players' horizons by sending them to Sri Lanka as well, where unofficial Test and one-day international series helped them gain a vital taste of subcontinental conditions.

Having left Australia without losing to any of the local sides, the Academy were provided with tougher opposition in Sri Lanka, but still emerged with a 1–1 draw in the three-match unofficial Test series and a 2–1 victory in the one-day games. Gordon Muchall, Durham's highly rated 20-year-old, was the pick of the batsmen, along with Key, who hit two first-innings centuries. Leicestershire's Darren Stevens scored his runs quickly, while Troughton reached three figures in both forms of the game.

It was the performance of the Academy's slow bowlers, however, that was most pleasing. The off-spinner Batty shared 23 first-class wickets with Northamptonshire's slow left-armer Monty Panesar, who sealed victory in the one-day series with figures of five for 20 in the deciding game. The sight of young English spinners taking wickets on the subcontinent was obviously encouraging.

ECB NATIONAL ACADEMY SQUAD

Kabir Ali (Worcestershire), J. M. Anderson (Lancashire), G. J. Batty (Worcestershire), I. D. Blackwell (Somerset), R. Clarke (Surrey), K. W. Hogg (Lancashire), G. J. Muchall (Durham), M. S. Panesar (Northamptonshire), C. M. W. Read (Nottinghamshire), D. I. Stevens (Leicestershire), C. T. Tremlett (Hampshire), J. O. Troughton (Warwickshire), A. J. Tudor (Surrey), M. A. Wallace (Glamorgan).

G. G. Wagg (Warwickshire) was originally named but withdrew through injury. Anderson, Blackwell and Tudor all left to join the senior England tour of Australia by early December. Kadeer Ali (Worcestershire), M. J. Brown (Middlesex), M. J. Chilton (Lancashire), V. S. Solanki (Worcestershire) and M. J. Wood (Yorkshire) appeared for the Academy team as stand-ins. A. Flintoff (Lancashire) and A. F. Giles (Warwickshire), members of the senior England party, played one game. I. R. Bell (Warwickshire) joined the Academy at the end of January, while R. K. J. Dawson (Yorkshire) and R. W. T. Key (Kent), who had been in the England party, arrived for the tour of Sri Lanka in February and March, when Read was officially named as captain, and Batty and Wallace as vice-captains.

Academy director: R. W. Marsh. *Assistant coach:* J. Abrahams.
Academy manager: N. E. F. Laughton. *Physiotherapist:* S. Osborne.
Physiologist: R. Smith.

ECB NATIONAL ACADEMY RESULTS

First-class matches – Played 3: Won 1, Lost 1, Drawn 1.
Win – BCCSL Academy XI.
Loss – Sri Lanka A.
Draw – Sri Lanka A.
Non-first-class matches – Played 14: Won 7, Lost 6, Drawn 1. *Wins* – Australian Capital Territory Second XI (2), Australia Under-19, South Australia Cricket Academy, Malaysian Cricket Association, Sri Lanka A, BCCSL Academy XI. *Losses* – England ODI Select XI (2), England Test Select XI, England Under-19, Sri Lanka Under-19, Sri Lanka A. *Draw* – New South Wales Institute of Sport Colts.

Note: Matches in this section which were not first-class are signified by a dagger.

†At Henley Oval, Adelaide, December 2. **England ODI Select XI won by nine runs.** Toss: ECB National Academy. **England ODI Select XI 261** (49.5 overs) (O. A. Shah 74); **ECB National Academy 252-5** (50 overs).

†At Henley Oval, Adelaide, December 3. **England ODI Select XI won by 79 runs.** Toss: ECB National Academy. **England ODI Select XI 332-8** (50 overs) (J. N. Snape 53, A. Flintoff 98, Kabir Ali 81); **ECB National Academy 253** (46.4 overs) (R. Clarke 64).

†At Stirling Oval, Canberra, December 12. **ECB National Academy won by two wickets.** Toss: Australian Capital Territory Second XII. **Australian Capital Territory Second XII 174** (49.1 overs) (S. A. Holcombe 52); **ECB National Academy 175-8** (46.4 overs).

In this and the next game, the ACT named 12 players, of whom 11 could bat and 11 field; the Academy had 11.

†At Stirling Oval, Canberra, December 13. **ECB National Academy won by seven wickets.** Toss: Australian Capital Territory Second XII. **Australian Capital Territory Second XII 203-5** (50 overs) (D. J. Richards 57, D. G. Dawson 82*); **ECB National Academy 204-3** (42.4 overs) (R. Clarke 58*).

†At Richardson Park, Perth, December 16, 17, 18. **England Test Select XI won by six wickets.** Toss: ECB National Academy. **ECB National Academy 370** (V. S. Solanki 51, Kadeer Ali 100, C. M. W. Read 91; M. J. Hoggard 5-70) **and 142**; **England Test Select XI 311-6 dec.** (W. I. Jefferson 89, D. L. Maddy 112*) **and 202-4** (M. A. Butcher 96*, J. P. Crawley 55).

†At Parkinson Oval, Adelaide, January 17. **England Under-19 won by one wicket.** Toss: ECB National Academy. **ECB National Academy 239-9** (50 overs) (C. M. W. Read 95); **England Under-19 240-9** (49.2 overs) (S. R. Patel 73).

The Under-19s fielded 14 players, including Andrew Flintoff and Ashley Giles from England's one-day squad, and the Academy 12; 11 could bat and 11 field.

†At Henley Oval, Adelaide, January 20, 21, 22, 23. **ECB National Academy won by 174 runs.** Toss: ECB National Academy. **ECB National Academy 231** (A. Flintoff 91; M. J. Bright 4-29) **and 441** (M. A. Wallace 103, D. I. Stevens 66, A. Flintoff 56, C. M. W. Read 94*; M. J. Bright 4-101); **Australia Under-19 265** (M. Harrison 80, T. P. Doropoulos 92; Kabir Ali 4-54) **and 233** (T. P. Doropoulos 51; M. S. Panesar 6-109).

Flintoff and Giles appeared for the Academy. Each team named 12 players a side, of whom 11 could bat and 11 field.

†At Coogee Oval, Sydney, January 28, 29, 30, 31. **Drawn.** Toss: New South Wales Institute of Sport Colts. **ECB National Academy 342** (C. M. W. Read 180) **and 368** (D. I. Stevens 70, J. O. Troughton 129, Kabir Ali 54*); **New South Wales Institute of Sport Colts 444** (E. J. M. Cowan 87, S. J. Phillips 68, J. J. Krejza 51) **and 196-9** (E. J. M. Cowan 80).

Read hit 21 fours and five sixes in 182 balls, Troughton nine fours and five sixes in 178 balls. Each team named 12 players a side, of whom 11 could bat and 11 field.

†At Henley Oval, Adelaide, February 9, 10, 11, 12. **ECB National Academy won by an innings and eight runs.** Toss: ECB National Academy. **ECB National Academy 452** (M. A. Wallace 95, J. O. Troughton 63, G. J. Batty 85, C. M. W. Read 88); **South Australia Cricket Academy 161** (D. J. Harris 77; G. J. Batty 4-29) **and 283** (L. Stevens 59, R. J. Harris 97, B. P. Cameron 56; G. J. Batty 4-79).

†At Royal Selangor Club, Kuala Lumpur, February 15. **ECB National Academy won by 89 runs.** Toss: ECB National Academy. **ECB National Academy 235-9** (40 overs) (M. J. Wood 69, G. J. Muchall 68; W. S. P. Jayawardene 6-43); **Malaysian Cricket Association 146** (39.2 overs).

Each side named 12 players a side, of whom 11 could bat and 11 field. Sri Lankan all-rounder Sarath Jayawardene played for the Malaysian CA.

†At Police Park, Colombo, February 19, 20, 21. **Sri Lanka Under-19 won by four wickets.** Toss: ECB National Academy. **ECB National Academy 420-8 dec.** (G. J. Muchall 106, D. I. Stevens 109, R. W. T. Key 76, R. Clarke 53; P. U. M. Chanaka 4-73) **and 89-4 dec.; Sri Lanka Under-19 225** (J. K. Silva 108; K. W. Hogg 5-65) and **288-6** (M. S. R. Wijeratne 100*, M. F. Maharoof 100).

Stevens scored a century before lunch on the first day, in an opening stand of 197 with Muchall. The Academy waived the follow-on and set a target of 285 in four and a half hours, which Sri Lanka Under-19 achieved with the help of a 99-ball century from Maharoof.

BCCSL ACADEMY XI v ECB NATIONAL ACADEMY

At Maitland Place, Colombo (NCC), February 24, 25, 26, 27. ECB National Academy won by 177 runs. Toss: ECB National Academy.

Though the home side's name changed, this match and the next two were regarded as an unofficial Test series. The tourists went 1–0 up, after another huge first-day score. Key scored a run-a-ball 115, putting on 158 with Bell before three wickets fell in two overs, and when Read was last out next morning they had amassed 458. They made short work of the Sri Lankan first innings; the spinners hurried out the last five in 13 overs. Again ignoring the follow-on, the ECB team stumbled to 96 for seven, seeking quick runs, but Muchall and Hogg rescued them with 108 in 15 overs, and Read declared 482 ahead. With seven Sri Lankans out on the third evening, he claimed the extra half-hour. Two more fell at the same score, but the final pair resisted for 13 overs, taking the game into the fourth day. Panesar's slow left-armers and Batty's off-spin claimed nine wickets between them, and 14 in the match.

Close of play: First day, ECB National Academy 451-9 (Read 75, Panesar 3); Second day, ECB National Academy 71-5 (Clarke 1, Batty 0); Third day, BCCSL Academy XI 275-9 (Wijesiriwardene 17, Nayanakantha 4).

ECB National Academy

M. A. Wallace b Nayanakantha	27	– (2) c Ranatunga b Wijesiriwardene	15
G. J. Muchall c Fernando b Nayanakantha	30	– (8) c M. D. K. Perera b G. A. S. Perera	62
D. I. Stevens st Fernando b G. A. S. Perera	15	– (1) c Fernando b G. A. S. Perera	33
R. W. T. Key c and b M. D. K. Perera	115	– (3) st Fernando b G. A. S. Perera	5
I. R. Bell c Fernando b Nayanakantha	72	– (4) c Daniel b G. A. S. Perera	4
*†C. M. W. Read c Ranatunga b Wijesiriwardene	80	– (5) c Fernando b M. D. K. Perera	10
R. Clarke c Fernando b Nayanakantha	0	– (6) c Dilhara b Wijesiriwardene	6
G. J. Batty c Wijesiriwardene b Kandamby	49	– (7) c Daniel b Wijesiriwardene	5
K. W. Hogg c Fernando b Dilhara	22	– not out	50
Kabir Ali b Nayanakantha	11	– not out	2
M. S. Panesar not out	4		
L-b 6, w 1, n-b 26	33	B 3, l-b 1, w 1, n-b 10	15
1/54 2/66 3/118 4/276 5/280 6/280 7/374 8/416 9/437	458	1/41 2/51 3/57 4/69 5/71 6/77 7/96 8/204 (8 wkts dec.)	207

Bowling: *First Innings*—Nayanakantha 24–2–109–5; Dilhara 15–2–84–1; Wijesiriwardene 12.3–3–71–1; G. A. S. Perera 21–1–92–1; M. D. K. Perera 18–0–78–1; Kandamby 3–0–18–1. *Second Innings*—Nayanakantha 8–1–41–0; Dilhara 7–0–44–0; Wijesiriwardene 9–1–33–3; G. A. S. Perera 13–1–51–4; M. D. K. Perera 4–1–16–1; Kandamby 2–0–18–0.

BCCSL Academy XI

*M. G. Vandort c Read b Ali	5	– c Wallace b Panesar	51
G. I. Daniel b Hogg	15	– b Panesar	25
D. A. Ranatunga b Panesar	48	– c Clarke b Batty	51
B. M. A. J. Mendis b Clarke	8	– b Batty	53
S. H. T. Kandamby b Clarke	56	– c and b Batty	0
M. D. K. Perera lbw b Clarke	0	– lbw b Clarke	0
†C. S. Fernando lbw b Batty	10	– c Wallace b Panesar	27
G. A. S. Perera c Clarke b Batty	8	– c Clarke b Batty	27
L. H. D. Dilhara c Wallace b Batty	9	– c Clarke b Panesar	0
O. L. A. Wijesiriwardene not out	6	– not out	29
H. G. D. Nayanakantha c and b Batty	0	– st Read b Panesar	24
L-b 2, w 1, n-b 15	18	N-b 18	18
1/20 2/27 3/49 4/129 5/129 6/150 7/164 8/168 9/179	183	1/84 2/85 3/172 4/181 5/195 6/195 7/250 8/250 9/250	305

Bowling: *First Innings*—Ali 10–2–29–1; Hogg 9–1–39–1; Clarke 14–2–55–3; Batty 16–5–40–4; Stevens 6–4–8–0; Panesar 5–1–10–1. *Second Innings*—Ali 16–2–85–0; Clarke 10–0–59–1; Hogg 8–4–20–0; Panesar 25–12–77–5; Batty 24–9–64–4.

Umpires: A. G. Dissanayake and R. Martinesz.
Referee: A. M. de Silva.

SRI LANKA A v ECB NATIONAL ACADEMY

At Police Park, Colombo, March 2, 3, 4. Sri Lanka A won by nine wickets. Toss: ECB National Academy.

For once, taking first use of the pitch did not pay off for the Academy; instead of batting all day for 400-plus, they were bowled out for 263 by leg-spinner Lokuarachchi and slow left-armer Rupasinghe. Only Bell, batting three hours, hung around long. But Tremlett made some early strikes, and Sri Lanka A were a shaky 101 for five by lunch on the second day. However, Lokuarachchi and Warnapura more than doubled the total, Fernando steered them into the lead, and last man Rupasinghe slogged 34 to make sure they were on top. The English openers, Muchall and Stevens, reduced the deficit from 116 to 38, but they fell to consecutive deliveries, and there was little defiance after that. Chasing 92, Vandort won the game with successive fours off Dawson, and Sri Lanka A levelled the "series" with a day to spare.

Close of play: First day, Sri Lanka A 36-2 (Jayawardene 19, Polonowita 1); Second day, ECB National Academy 7-0 (Muchall 7, Stevens 0).

ECB National Academy

G. J. Muchall c and b Rupasinghe	58	– c Jayawardene b Rupasinghe	40
D. I. Stevens c Vandort b Mirando	6	– c Polonowita b Samaraweera	36
I. R. Bell st Jayawardene b Samaraweera	61	– c Warnapura b Samaraweera	5
R. W. T. Key st Jayawardene b Rupasinghe	0	– c Polonowita b Warnapura	37
J. O. Troughton c Jayawardene b Lokuarachchi	8	– c and b Samaraweera	13
*†C. M. W. Read c Fernando b Rupasinghe	21	– c Warnapura b Samaraweera	0
G. J. Batty c and b Mirando	15	– c Lokuarachchi b Rupasinghe	0
R. K. J. Dawson c Nawaz b Rupasinghe	43	– c Polonowita b Warnapura	30
Kabir Ali c Jayawardene b Lokuarachchi	32	– not out	26
C. T. Tremlett c Polonowita b Lokuarachchi	0	– b Warnapura	8
M. S. Panesar not out	0	– lbw b Mirando	3
B 6, l-b 2, w 1, n-b 10	19	B 3, l-b 1, n-b 5	9
1/17 2/89 3/89 4/106 5/135 6/164 7/189 8/252 9/261	263	1/78 2/78 3/85 4/105 5/105 6/106 7/160 8/177 9/187	207

Bowling: *First Innings*—de Silva 3.5–1–16–0; Mirando 11–0–43–2; Polonowita 0.1–0–0–0; Fernando 5–1–18–0; Lokuarachchi 28–2–66–3; Rupasinghe 19.3–1–81–4; Samaraweera 10–3–31–1. *Second Innings*—Mirando 8–1–22–1; de Silva 3–1–14–0; Rupasinghe 23–5–47–2; Lokuarachchi 16–1–46–0; Samaraweera 18–6–44–4; Warnapura 7–0–30–3.

Sri Lanka A

M. G. Vandort c Stevens b Tremlett	13	– not out	58
M. N. Nawaz c Read b Tremlett	0	– c Read b Tremlett	0
†H. A. P. W. Jayawardene b Tremlett	19	– not out	34
A. S. Polonowita c and b Batty	26		
*T. T. Samaraweera c Read b Panesar	33		
B. S. M. Warnapura c Troughton b Ali	86		
K. S. Lokuarachchi st Read b Panesar	64		
K. H. R. K. Fernando c Batty b Panesar	55		
M. T. T. Mirando c Stevens b Batty	25		
W. R. S. de Silva not out	6		
N. S. Rupasinghe c Muchall b Panesar	34		
B 3, l-b 10, w 2, n-b 3	18	W 1, n-b 1	2
1/9 2/21 3/38 4/93 5/101 6/210 7/295 8/331 9/331	379	1/9	(1 wkt) 94

Bowling: *First Innings*—Tremlett 20–3–94–3; Ali 13–1–59–1; Panesar 37.3–12–98–4; Batty 37–10–101–2; Dawson 2–0–14–0. *Second Innings*—Tremlett 4–2–13–1; Ali 3–0–15–0; Panesar 7–2–24–0; Batty 5–2–13–0; Dawson 3.2–0–21–0; Troughton 2–0–8–0.

Umpires: L. V. Jayasundera and P. T. Manuel.
Referee: M. A. W. R. Madurasinghe.

SRI LANKA A v ECB NATIONAL ACADEMY

At Dambulla, March 8, 9, 10, 11. Drawn. Toss: ECB National Academy.

Honours ended even in this unofficial series. The Academy were initially in trouble after electing to bat again, losing three wickets in the first hour. But Key and Troughton combined to add 179 in 46 overs; Key hit 14 fours, Troughton 15 plus a six, and both completed centuries. Clarke backed up with a fifty, before he fell in a collapse of five for 26 runs on the second morning. Unusually, it was the Sri Lankan seamers who did the damage. In reply, the home batsmen all made starts, but none went on to 50 until Lokuarachchi and Fernando shared a 101-run stand for the seventh wicket. Tremlett broke down in the later stages of the innings, as Sri Lanka A built a lead of 31. On the final day, Bell made the match safe for the Academy, batting nearly six hours for 87.

Close of play: First day, ECB National Academy 338-5 (Clarke 45, Wallace 9); Second day, Sri Lanka A 205-5 (Samaraweera 28, Lokuarachchi 9); Third day, ECB National Academy 65-1 (Muchall 19, Bell 19).

ECB National Academy

*C. M. W. Read c Vandort b Mirando	23	– c Jayawardene b Nayanakantha	19
G. J. Muchall lbw b Mirando	26	– c Samaraweera b Mirando	43
I. R. Bell c Jayawardene b Nayanakantha	0	– c Warnapura b Lokuarachchi	87
R. W. T. Key c Polonowita b Lokuarachchi	105	– c Jayawardene b Mirando	10
J. O. Troughton c Vandort b Mirando	109	– b Fernando	30
R. Clarke c Jayawardene b Mirando	52	– c Nawaz b Lokuarachchi	17
†M. A. Wallace c Jayawardene b Lakshitha	11	– not out	36
G. J. Batty c Jayawardene b Lakshitha	4	– not out	16
R. K. J. Dawson not out	10		
K. W. Hogg c Jayawardene b Mirando	0		
C. T. Tremlett b Lakshitha	4		
B 8, l-b 4, w 4, n-b 8	24	B 2, l-b 5, w 2, n-b 4	13
1/46 2/47 3/57 4/236 5/300 6/342 7/349 8/352 9/353	368	1/24 2/96 3/125 4/182 5/211 6/228	(6 wkts) 271

Bowling: *First Innings*—Lakshitha 19.5–3–88–3; Nayanakantha 12–0–57–1; Mirando 23–3–72–5; Lokuarachchi 20–4–38–1; Fernando 9–0–45–0; Samaraweera 8–1–37–0; Warnapura 8–2–19–0. *Second Innings*—Nayanakantha 8–0–31–1; Lakshitha 14–5–40–0; Fernando 11–3–16–1; Mirando 14–2–46–2; Lokuarachchi 32–15–49–2; Samaraweera 17–6–30–0; Warnapura 13–0–52–0; Nawaz 1–1–0–0.

Sri Lanka A

M. G. Vandort c Bell b Batty	40
M. N. Nawaz c Clarke b Dawson	45
†H. A. P. W. Jayawardene c Troughton b Batty	40
A. S. Polonowita c Wallace b Hogg	26
*T. T. Samaraweera c Dawson b Tremlett	37
B. S. M. Warnapura c Hogg b Dawson	15
K. S. Lokuarachchi lbw b Tremlett	89
K. H. R. K. Fernando b Bell	60
M. T. T. Mirando c and b Dawson	15
H. G. D. Nayanakantha c sub (M. S. Panesar) b Batty	20
A. B. T. Lakshitha not out	1
B 4, l-b 3, w 3, n-b 1	11
1/75 2/99 3/153 4/153 5/188 6/237 7/338 8/359 9/397	399

Bowling: Tremlett 27.4–7–78–2; Hogg 22–6–57–1; Batty 33.3–7–85–3; Clarke 23.2–6–61–0; Dawson 30–5–91–3; Bell 12–3–20–1.

Umpires: S. Amerasinghe and M. G. Silva.
Referee: S. D. Anurasiri.

†At Dambulla, March 14. **First one-day international: ECB National Academy won by five wickets.** Toss: Sri Lanka A. **Sri Lanka A 240** (49.4 overs) (M. G. Vandort 118, H. A. P. W. Jayawardene 59); **ECB National Academy 241-5** (41.1 overs) (D. I. Stevens 64).

†At Kurunegala, March 16. **Second one-day international: Sri Lanka A won by 40 runs (D/L method).** Toss: Sri Lanka A. **Sri Lanka A 222-9** (45 overs) (K. S. Lokuarachchi 63); **ECB National Academy 168** (37.2 overs) (T. T. Samaraweera 7-30).

The Academy's target was revised to 209 in 41 overs.

†At Maitland Place, Colombo (NCC), March 19. **Third one-day international: ECB National Academy won by 141 runs.** Toss: BCCSL Academy XI. **ECB National Academy 271-7** (50 overs) (G. J. Muchall 62, J. O. Troughton 100; W. J. M. R. Dias 4-42); **BCCSL Academy XI 130** (39.1 overs) (G. I. Daniel 60; M. S. Panesar 5-20).

Muchall and Troughton, who hit nine fours and three sixes in 112 balls, added 168 for the fourth wicket. The ECB National Academy won the one-day series 2–1.

A-TEAM TOURS

AUSTRALIA A IN SOUTH AFRICA, 2002-03

Australia A toured South Africa in September 2002, playing a seven-match one-day series against South Africa A. The Australians won 5–1, losing in the final fixture, with the fifth game abandoned. The squad of 14 was as follows: J. L. Langer (Western Australia) (*captain*), S. M. Katich (New South Wales) (*vice-captain*), G. S. Blewett (South Australia), N. W. Bracken (New South Wales), R. J. Campbell (Western Australia), M. J. Clarke (New South Wales), S. R. Clark (New South Wales), I. J. Harvey (Victoria), M. A. Higgs (South Australia), G. B. Hogg (Western Australia), M. E. K. Hussey (Western Australia), A. Symonds (Queensland), B. A. Williams (Western Australia), D. G. Wright (Tasmania). *Coach:* A. R. Border. *Manager:* T. J. Robertson. *Physiotherapist:* S. Partridge.

SRI LANKA A IN PAKISTAN, 2002-03

Sri Lanka A toured Pakistan in September–October 2002. They drew a two-match first-class series with Pakistan A 1–1, but lost a three-match one-day series 3–0. The squad of 16 was as follows: T. T. Samaraweera (Sinhalese) (*captain*), W. R. S. de Silva (Galle), C. S. Fernando (Chilaw Marians), D. A. Gunawardene (Sinhalese), C. U. Jayasinghe (Burgher), A. B. T. Lakshitha (Bloomfield), M. K. G. C. P. Lakshitha (Air Force), K. S. Lokuarachchi (Bloomfield), B. M. A. J. Mendis (Sinhalese), M. T. T. Mirando (Nondescripts), J. Mubarak (Colombo), M. N. Nawaz (Nondescripts), P. N. Ranjith (Moors), N. S. Rupasinghe (Colombo), K. P. P. B. Seneviratne (Colombo), M. G. Vandort (Colombo). *Coach:* R. S. Kalpage. *Manager:* D. C. Wickremasinghe.

At Faisalabad, September 17, 18, 19, 20, 2002. **Pakistan A won by nine wickets.** Toss: Sri Lanka A. **Sri Lanka A 183** (D. A. Gunawardene 60; Naved-ul-Hasan 4-49, Danish Kaneria 5-42) **and 223** (J. Mubarak 93*; Umar Gul 4-36); **Pakistan A 391-8 dec.** (Taufeeq Umar 73, Faisal Iqbal 54, Hasan Raza 119*; K. S. Lokuarachchi 4-112) **and 16-1**.

At Multan, September 23, 24, 25, 2002. **Sri Lanka A won by 186 runs.** Toss: Pakistan A. **Sri Lanka A 184** (Abdur Rauf 4-46, Umar Gul 4-70) **and 275** (M. G. Vandort 51, M. N. Nawaz 70, J. Mubarak 63; Mohammad Zahid 4-43); **Pakistan A 216** (Bazid Khan 59*; W. R. S. de Silva 4-64) **and 57** (W. R. S. de Silva 4-19, T. T. Samaraweera 5-16).

In the final innings, Pakistan A lost their last seven wickets for 16 runs.

SOUTH AFRICA A IN ZIMBABWE, 2002-03

South Africa A toured Zimbabwe in January 2003, playing a three-match one-day series against Zimbabwe A in Harare. Zimbabwe A came from behind to win the series 2–1. The squad of 13 was as follows: G. C. Smith (Western Province) (*captain*), A. M. Amla (KwaZulu-Natal), A. C. Dawson (Western Province), S. Elworthy (Northerns), J. C. Kent (KwaZulu-Natal), N. D. McKenzie (Northerns), J. A. Morkel (Easterns), A. Nel (Easterns), J. L. Ontong (Boland), A. G. Prince (Western Province), J. A. Rudolph (Northerns), T. L. Tsolekile (Western Province), M. van Jaarsveld (Northerns). *Coach:* V. A. Barnes. *Manager:* G. Nkagisang.

SOUTH AFRICA A IN AUSTRALIA, 2002-03

South Africa A toured Australia in April 2003, playing two first-class matches and five one-day games against Australia A. Both first-class matches were drawn; Australia A won the one-day series 3–1, with the third game abandoned. The squad of 15 was as follows: G. Dros (Northerns) (*captain*), A. M. Amla (KwaZulu-Natal), A. M. Bacher (Gauteng), N. Boje (Free State), Q. Friend (Western Province), J. M. Kemp (Eastern Province), C. K. Langeveldt (Boland), J. A. Morkel (Easterns), A. Nel (Easterns), J. L. Ontong (Boland), D. Pretorius (Free State), A. G. Prince (Western Province), T. L. Tsolekile (Western Province), M. van Jaarsveld (Northerns), M. N. van Wyk (Free State). *Coach:* V. A. Barnes. R. Telemachus (Western Province) was originally selected, but withdrew after failing to recover from injury and was replaced by Kemp. Nel left the tour early after a drink-driving incident on April 11; he was fined and banned for six matches by the South African board.

At Adelaide, April 13, 14, 15, 2003. **Drawn.** Toss: South Africa A. **Australia A 263** (A. Symonds 78; D. Pretorius 4-65, N. Boje 4-55) **and 296** (M. E. K. Hussey 84, A. Symonds 88; N. Boje 4-88); **South Africa A 387** (A. M. Amla 56, M. van Jaarsveld 110, M. N. van Wyk 63; I. J. Harvey 8-101) **and 78-3.**

At Perth, April 19, 20, 21, 2003. **Drawn.** Toss: South Africa A. **Australia A 251** (B. J. Hodge 160; C. K. Langeveldt 4-78) **and 307-2 dec.** (M. E. K. Hussey 145, S. M. Katich 134*); **South Africa A 253-7 dec.** (N. Boje 74) **and 301-7** (M. van Jaarsveld 140, M. N. van Wyk 56; D. G. Wright 4-60).

In Australia A's second innings, Hussey and Katich added 274 for the second wicket.

FIFTY YEARS AGO

From WISDEN CRICKETERS' ALMANACK for 1954

NOTES BY THE EDITOR (Norman Preston) – "It is a great pleasure to record in this issue the return of the Ashes to England during the Coronation year of our Queen. Unfortunately our joy changed to sorrow all too soon at the pitiable displays of our batsmen in the West Indies… I am writing at the conclusion of the second Test in Barbados where… on the third day England scored only 128 runs in five hours… I hope the M.C.C. players who went to the West Indies realise that they caused all cricket-lovers at home to seethe with indignation at the negative methods which were adopted at Kensington Oval."

FIVE CRICKETERS OF THE YEAR, K. R. MILLER – "Even the Golden Age of cricket would have been enriched by a character so colourful as KEITH ROSS MILLER… In the 1953 Test series with England, Miller emulated the hitherto unique achievement of Wilfred Rhodes with 2,000 runs and 100 wickets in international cricket. Yet figures are the last thing by which this unpredictable personality, a man with the instinctive flair for turning a crowd's annoyance into instant delight, should be assessed. Miller has always placed the fun of the game above every consideration… and provides something for cricket-lovers to remember in the dark winter months before the next summer sun."

THE COUNTY CHAMPIONSHIP IN 1953 – "Surrey won the Championship for the second year in succession, but they had to fight much harder than in 1952… Under the inspiring leadership of D. S. Sheppard, Sussex enjoyed a splendid summer, rising from thirteenth to second place. They lost only three matches, one less than Surrey, whom they beat by seven wickets at Guildford. A succession of drawn games during July and August lost them their chance of finishing top for the first time in their history."

SOMERSET v LANCASHIRE (H. T. F. BUSE'S BENEFIT MATCH), AT BATH, JUNE 6, 1953 – "Lancashire won by an innings and 24 runs. A newly-laid pitch brought financial disaster for Buse, the match ending before six o'clock on the first day when thirty wickets fell for 292 runs. Tattersall, the England and Lancashire off-spin bowler, carried everything before him, taking thirteen for 69… Ironical as it seemed, Buse proved Somerset's central figure with the ball. Although hit for 18 in one over, he dismissed six batsmen for 41 runs. Lancashire, who lost half their side for 46, were put in a winning position by Marner and Wharton, whose fierce hitting brought 70 for the sixth stand in twenty-five minutes."

NOTES BY THE EDITOR – "Cricket and particularly the professional player was honoured when in June the Queen bestowed the order of Knighthood on Jack Hobbs, the great England and Surrey batsman. Hobbs, always modest and a model sportsman, has worn his honours gracefully. When one looks back and recalls men who have enjoyed every minute of their cricket, Hobbs comes readily to mind. It is his approach to the game which is needed in this hard-headed age."

For excerpts from Wisden *100 years ago, see page 1267.*

ENGLAND UNDER-19 IN AUSTRALIA, 2002-03

The England Under-19 tour of Australia in January and February 2003 was as much an exercise in forward thinking as an attempt to beat the world champions in their own back yard. Of the 15-strong squad, all but five players – the captain Bilal Shafayat, Neil Edwards, Andrew Gale, Andrew Hodd and James Pearson – qualified for the Under-18 category too. But with the next Under-19 World Cup, in Bangladesh, only a year away, the England management decided to plan for the future, even if it meant picking their most inexperienced side ever.

In the short term, it was a calculated risk – and it almost worked. To the amazement of the locals, England won the First Test, then came within a whisker of winning the decisive Third before the Australians' greater know-how and self-belief came through. The one-day series was surrendered 4–1, a result that looked worse than it should have done after England's batsmen twice threw away strong positions. Despite the final balance sheet of wins and losses, they had not been outclassed.

In the early part of the tour, the 5ft 7in Shafayat stood head and shoulders above his team-mates. He almost single-handedly won the Adelaide Test, driving like a dream to make 108 and 66 and leading the attack with his lively medium-pace. Sensing a threat, the Australians were soon testing his reflexes against the short ball; Shafayat's returns faded, and he missed the last two one-day internationals with an injured thumb. The rest of the batting was a disappointment. Samit Patel played attractively at times but tended to place too cheap a price on his wicket, while the only player other than Shafayat to pass fifty in the Tests was Edwards, a left-handed opener fleetingly reminiscent of his Somerset team-mate Marcus Trescothick. Too often, however, the side missed a wise head to marshal tight run-chases: England batted second in all five one-day internationals after losing the toss each time, and won only once, in the rain-affected fourth game in Sydney.

David Stiff was the pick of the attack and was the fastest bowler on either side, even if he lacked consistency. Liam Plunkett added edge either as first change or with the new ball, and Patel chipped in with his slow left-armers, not to mention his outstanding slip fielding. With the right attitude, he looked a future Test prospect.

Apart from the Adelaide Test, the more experienced Australians – all but three of their players were at the top end of their age category – did just enough to stay on top. Their batting was led by the outstanding Michael Bright, who scored more runs at a higher average (340 at 56.66) in the Tests than anyone else. The bowling, meanwhile, centred on three seamers. Between them, Grant Sullivan, Aaron Bird and Trent Kelly claimed 41 Test wickets at 14.70. Not everyone was impressed with Bird's action, but England were not in the mood to look for excuses. Their young side had come close to pulling off a major upset. At the start of the tour, that was something their management would have settled for.

ENGLAND UNDER-19 TOURING PARTY

B. M. Shafayat (Nottinghamshire) (*captain*), R. S. Bopara (Essex), T. T. Bresnan (Yorkshire), D. L. Broadbent (Yorkshire), S. M. J. Cusden (Kent), N. J. Edwards (Somerset), A. W. Gale (Yorkshire), A. J. Hodd (Sussex), M. A. K. Lawson (Yorkshire), S. R. Patel (Nottinghamshire), J. A. Pearson (Gloucestershire), L. E. Plunkett (Durham), D. A. Stiff (Yorkshire), N. D. Thornicroft (Yorkshire), L. J. Wright (Leicestershire).
Coach: P. Farbrace. *Manager:* G. J. Saville. *Physiotherapist:* K. A. Russell.

ENGLAND UNDER-19 TOUR RESULTS

Matches – Played 14: Won 3, Lost 10, Drawn 1.

Note: Matches in this section were not first-class. In every match outside the Test series, each side named 12 players, of whom 11 could bat and 11 field. The exception was the game against the ECB National Academy, in which England Under-19 fielded 14, and the Academy 12.

At Price Memorial Oval, Adelaide, January 4, 2003. **Sturt won by 89 runs.** Toss: Sturt. **Sturt 221-5** (50 overs) (M. Golding 67); **England Under-19 132** (32.3 overs) (B. M. Shafayat 59).

At Price Memorial Oval, Adelaide, January 5, 2003. **Sturt won by 100 runs.** Toss: Sturt. **Sturt 297-8** (50 overs) (D. Heavyside 114*; S. R. Patel 4-29); **England Under-19 197** (41.4 overs) (S. R. Patel 78).

Sturt were 106 for seven before David Heavyside, batting at No. 8, added 89 for the eighth wicket with Jay Nash, and an unbeaten 102 for the ninth with Cullen Bailey. Heavyside faced 103 balls, hitting 14 fours and two sixes. England under-19's Simon Cusden and Neil Edwards appeared for Sturt.

At Adelaide Oval No. 2, January 7, 8, 9, 2003. **South Australia Invitation Under-19 won by seven wickets.** Toss: England Under-19. **England Under-19 157 and 220** (R. S. Bopara 65); **South Australia Invitation Under-19 340** (B. P. Cameron 81, K. J. Skewes 101, J. W. Plant 54) **and 38-3**.

AUSTRALIA v ENGLAND

First Under-19 Test

At St Peter's College, Adelaide, January 12, 13, 14, 15, 2003. England Under-19 won by 14 runs. Toss: England Under-19.

A glittering all-round performance from the England captain Bilal Shafayat inspired his side to a nail-biting victory, their first in Australia at this level. Set 284 to win on a pitch that encouraged strokeplay throughout, Australia were 15 runs short when Shafayat, whose contribution with the bat earlier amounted to 174 runs, had the No. 11 Matthew Gale caught behind to complete figures of six for 54 and spark jubilant scenes. It was a suitably dramatic finale to a game full of ebb and flow. Shafayat had given England a decent start with a classy hundred, but Australia established a first-innings lead of 83, thanks to 132 from Liam Davis, merciless off the back foot, and a muscular 97 from Michael Bright. Neil Edwards responded with 97 before being run out, but the turning point came on the final morning. Overnight, Australia had lost the services of their opening – and most effective – bowler Trent Kelly, called up along with Mark Cosgrave by South Australia. Two full playing substitutes replaced them, but England's last pair, the Yorkshiremen Tim Bresnan and Nick Thornicroft, took advantage to thrash 53 runs in 44 minutes. The flurry of runs proved crucial, and although Australia were in contention at 68 without loss and, later, 203 for five, Shafayat kept chipping away with his busy swingers to seal a famous win.

Close of play: First day, Australia Under-19 18-1 (Davis 18, Hunt 0); Second day, England Under-19 15-0 (Gale 2, Edwards 13); Third day, England Under-19 313-9 (Bresnan 7, Thornicroft 10).

England Under-19

A. W. Gale lbw b Bright	37	– c Crosthwaite b Cosgrove	32
N. J. Edwards lbw b Cullen	18	– run out	97
†A. J. Hodd c Cosgrove b Bird	0	– (7) c Crosthwaite b Kelly	27
*B. M. Shafayat b Kelly	108	– c Hunt b Gale	66
R. S. Bopara b Kelly	5	– lbw b Kelly	1
J. A. Pearson c Crosthwaite b Kelly	34	– c sub (L. R. Davis) b Kelly	5
S. R. Patel run out	34	– (3) c Hunt b Bright	36
L. J. Wright c Harrison b Gale	48	– c Crosthwaite b Kelly	0
T. T. Bresnan not out	27	– not out	33
L. E. Plunkett b Kelly	4	– lbw b Hunt	12
N. D. Thornicroft c Crosthwaite b Gale	4	– st Crosthwaite b Bright	37
B 4, l-b 1, w 6, n-b 1	12	B 6, l-b 7, w 5, n-b 2	20
1/36 2/37 3/71 4/84 5/145 6/228 7/250 8/321 9/326	331	1/64 2/135 3/187 4/188 5/206 6/264 7/271 8/276 9/294	366

Bowling: *First Innings*—Kelly 19–4–63–4; Bird 11–2–45–1; Cullen 18–6–54–1; Gale 15.4–3–59–2; Bright 16–2–65–1; Cosgrove 9–1–40–0. *Second Innings*—Kelly 23–12–52–4; Gale 27–8–102–1; Cosgrove 15–5–38–1; Cullen 27–9–67–0; Bright 18.3–3–75–2; Hunt 4–0–19–1.

Australia Under-19

L. M. Davis b Shafayat	132	– (2) b Shafayat	34
M. Harrison lbw b Bresnan	0	– (1) c Patel b Bresnan	32
*G. I. Hunt b Plunkett	15	– c Plunkett b Shafayat	2
M. J. Cosgrove c Shafayat b Plunkett	17		
T. P. Doropoulos b Patel	44	– lbw b Patel	40
M. J. Bright c Thornicroft b Bopara	97	– c Wright b Shafayat	65
†A. J. Crosthwaite b Patel	22	– c Bopara b Shafayat	8
A. C. Bird not out	65	– b Bresnan	30
D. J. Cullen c Hodd b Plunkett	0	– lbw b Shafayat	4
T. P. Kelly b Plunkett	0		
M. G. Gale lbw b Patel	1	– c Hodd b Shafayat	0
K. J. Skewes (did not bat)		– (4) lbw b Plunkett	19
L. R. Butterworth (did not bat)		– (10) not out	24
B 5, l-b 3, n-b 13	21	B 1, l-b 9, w 1	11
1/4 2/71 3/112 4/210 5/225 6/291 7/389 8/403 9/403	414	1/68 2/68 3/76 4/129 5/143 6/203 7/212 8/226 9/262	269

Bowling: *First Innings*—Plunkett 16–2–72–4; Bresnan 15–3–66–1; Thornicroft 16–3–97–0; Patel 31.3–7–89–3; Shafayat 13–2–58–1; Bopara 3–0–24–1. *Second Innings*—Plunkett 15–2–71–1; Thornicroft 8–0–41–0; Shafayat 16.2–4–54–6; Bresnan 14–0–57–2; Patel 12–3–36–1.

Umpires: J. S. Booth and S. D. Fry.

At Parkinson Oval, Adelaide, January 17, 2003. **England Under-19 beat ECB National Academy by one wicket.** (See page 1315.)

At St Peter's College, Adelaide, January 18, 2003. **First one-day international: Australia Under-19 won by 22 runs.** Toss: Australia Under-19. **Australia Under-19 216** (48.3 overs) (M. Harrison 64); **England Under-19 194** (44 overs) (B. M. Shafayat 82).

Shafayat faced 67 balls, hitting ten fours and two sixes.

At Junction Oval, Melbourne, January 21, 22, 2003. **Drawn.** Toss: Victoria Institute of Sport. **Victoria Institute of Sport 354** (M. L. Innes 75, T. Lamb 63, M. G. Simpson 74*; L. J. Wright 4-66); **England Under-19 335-8** (R. S. Bopara 54, L. J. Wright 77, A. J. Hodd 104*; P. M. Siddle 4-45).

At Junction Oval, Melbourne, January 23, 2003. **Victoria Institute of Sport won by two wickets.** Toss: Victoria Institute of Sport. **England Under-19 239-9** (50 overs) (R. S. Bopara 52, N. J. Edwards 54); **Victoria Institute of Sport 243-8** (49.4 overs) (M. D. Allen 60).

At Melbourne, January 26, 2003. **Second one-day international: Australia Under-19 won by 63 runs.** Toss: Australia Under-19. **Australia Under-19 253-7** (50 overs); **England Under-19 190** (43.5 overs) (N. J. Edwards 54, S. R. Patel 61).

England Under-19 reached 131 for one, then lost six for 11 in 56 balls.

AUSTRALIA v ENGLAND

Second Under-19 Test

At Jubilee Park, Melbourne, January 28, 29, 30, 31, 2003. Australia Under-19 won by 168 runs. Toss: Australia Under-19.

England were left to count the cost of two limp displays from their top order as Australia, inspired by their fast bowler Aaron Bird, gained revenge for the defeat in Adelaide. At 107 for eight halfway through the opening day, Australia were struggling to stay in the series. But their last two wickets added 57, then their bowlers ran through a tentative England line-up; without a seventh-wicket stand of 52 between Luke Wright and Bresnan, England would not even have passed 100. Second time round, Australia stuttered again, but were rescued by a stand of 126 between Bright, who batted nearly four hours for his 127, and Bird. Chasing an unlikely 365, England folded to 114 for nine, before Liam Plunkett and Dan Broadbent delayed the inevitable. Bird, who once forced the Australian Test opener Michael Slater to retire hurt after hitting him on the helmet during a first-grade game, finished with match figures of 41.1–21–57–8. Peter Nevill took three catches as a full substitute for wicket-keeper Adam Crosthwaite, called up by Victoria, in England's second innings.

Close of play: First day, England Under-19 98-7 (Bresnan 30, Plunkett 0); Second day, Australia Under-19 297-9 (Bright 113, Sullivan 6); Third day, England Under-19 22-2 (Stiff 1).

Australia Under-19

L. M. Davis b Plunkett	0	– (2) c Wright b Bresnan	28
M. Harrison c Hodd b Stiff	18	– (1) b Plunkett	4
*G. I. Hunt c Plunkett b Stiff	20	– c Hodd b Stiff	10
K. J. Skewes c Patel b Stiff	13	– c Plunkett b Wright	36
T. P. Doropoulos c Plunkett b Patel	23	– c Bopara b Stiff	32
M. J. Bright c and b Patel	25	– c Hodd b Plunkett	127
†A. J. Crosthwaite c Hodd b Bresnan	46	– lbw b Patel	6
A. C. Bird c Edwards b Patel	1	– c Wright b Shafayat	50
L. R. Davis c Hodd b Patel	0	– c Hodd b Plunkett	0
T. P. Kelly c Shafayat b Stiff	12	– b Shafayat	6
G. J. Sullivan not out	4	– not out	10
†P. M. Nevill (did not bat)			
L-b 1, n-b 1	2	B 1, l-b 3, w 1, n-b 1	6
1/2 2/34 3/47 4/52 5/94 6/101 7/107 8/107 9/156	164	1/5 2/35 3/59 4/91 5/121 6/147 7/273 8/276 9/285	315

Bowling: *First Innings*—Bresnan 10–3–33–1; Plunkett 10–3–26–1; Stiff 13.4–6–32–4; Shafayat 5–1–13–0; Patel 13–2–33–4; Broadbent 7–1–26–0. *Second Innings*—Bresnan 11–1–40–1; Plunkett 22–4–78–3; Stiff 14–4–36–2; Patel 17–3–71–1; Wright 5–0–29–1; Shafayat 12–3–25–2; Broadbent 5–1–32–0.

England Under-19

A. W. Gale c Harrison b Sullivan	9	– lbw b Bird	12
N. J. Edwards c Crosthwaite b Bird	6	– c Nevill b Bird	2
S. R. Patel c Harrison b Bird	11	– (4) c Harrison b Bird	1
*B. M. Shafayat c Crosthwaite b Sullivan	10	– (5) b Bright b Sullivan	0
R. S. Bopara c Crosthwaite b Bird	0	– (6) c Nevill b Bird	34
†A. J. Hodd c Crosthwaite b Sullivan	1	– (7) lbw b Sullivan	18
L. J. Wright b Kelly	25	– (8) lbw b Bright	3
T. T. Bresnan c Skewes b Bird	31	– (9) c Kelly b Bright	8
L. E. Plunkett c Crosthwaite b Kelly	0	– (10) c Doropoulos b Bright	49
D. L. Broadbent run out	7	– (11) not out	22
D. A. Stiff not out	8	– (3) c Nevill b Sullivan	2
B 1, l-b 4, w 1, n-b 1	7	B 19, l-b 16, w 5, n-b 5	45
1/18 2/26 3/35 4/35 5/41 6/42 7/94 8/100 9/100	115	1/20 2/22 3/24 4/30 5/30 6/73 7/82 8/96 9/114	196

Bowling: *First Innings*—Bird 14.1–7–26–4; Kelly 11–5–23–2; Sullivan 8–1–26–3; Bright 14–6–22–0; L. R. Davis 3–0–13–0. *Second Innings*—Bird 27–14–31–4; Kelly 19–5–22–0; Sullivan 21–7–36–3; L. R. Davis 13–6–22–0; Bright 29–16–41–3; Skewes 7–5–3–0; Doropoulos 3–0–6–0.

Umpires: A. J. Soulsby and J. D. Ward.

AUSTRALIA v ENGLAND

Third Under-19 Test

At Bankstown Oval, Sydney, February 3, 4, 5, 6, 2003. Australia Under-19 won by 15 runs. Toss: Australia Under-19.

Australia clinched the series in thrilling fashion, winning a low-scoring, see-sawing game on the final morning. England needed 191 for a series victory themselves, but, on a pitch of uneven bounce, kept losing wickets at crucial moments and began the final morning on a precarious 102 for five. Samit Patel fell in the sixth over of the day, and when Bird had Shafayat caught behind to make it 144 for eight, Australia were nearly there. Only a last-ditch stand of 21 between Mark Lawson and David Stiff threatened to get in their way. Earlier, Stiff had bowled with real speed and hostility to take five wickets as the sides scrapped for first-innings supremacy. Australia reasserted themselves in their second innings to reach 149 for two, before crumbling against the rangy pace of Plunkett and losing eight for 50. England needed at least two of their top order to make half-centuries, but although several batsmen made starts, none could finish the job.

Close of play: First day, England Under-19 57-1 (Edwards 23, Pearson 10); Second day, Australia Under-19 66-2 (Hunt 8, Doropoulos 0); Third day, England Under-19 102-5 (Patel 30, Shafayat 10).

Australia Under-19

L. M. Davis c Hodd b Stiff	13	– (2) lbw b Patel	30
M. Harrison c Patel b Stiff	62	– (1) lbw b Lawson	22
*G. I. Hunt c Hodd b Shafayat	1	– c sub (L. J. Wright) b Bresnan	49
T. P. Doropoulos b Patel	35	– c Hodd b Bopara	43
M. J. Bright c Hodd b Stiff	25	– c sub (L. J. Wright) b Bopara	1
†A. J. Crosthwaite not out	42	– b Plunkett	13
A. C. Bird lbw b Stiff	0	– c Bopara b Plunkett	0
T. P. Kelly c Edwards b Patel	0	– b Plunkett	0
G. J. Sullivan c Hodd b Plunkett	0	– b Plunkett	14
D. J. Cullen c Hodd b Lawson	9	– not out	7
L. R. Davis b Stiff	6	– lbw b Patel	0
B 8, l-b 6, w 2, n-b 12	28	B 8, l-b 7, n-b 5	20
1/27 2/43 3/104 4/149 5/153 6/153 7/169 8/169 9/191	221	1/49 2/63 3/149 4/153 5/172 6/173 7/173 8/176 9/197	199

Bowling: *First Innings*—Bresnan 14–1–61–0; Stiff 13.5–4–35–5; Plunkett 10–3–34–1; Shafayat 9–1–30–1; Patel 19–7–29–2; Lawson 3–0–18–1. *Second Innings*—Plunkett 17–6–57–4; Stiff 16–6–32–0; Bresnan 16–5–42–1; Patel 12.1–4–20–2; Lawson 7–3–21–1; Bopara 3–1–12–2.

England Under-19

A. W. Gale c Cullen b Bird	21	– run out	18
N. J. Edwards c Hunt b Kelly	36	– c Doropoulos b Bird	14
J. A. Pearson c Crosthwaite b Cullen	22	– c Doropoulos b Sullivan	12
*B. M. Shafayat c Bird b Sullivan	14	– (7) c Crosthwaite b Bird	20
R. S. Bopara c Crosthwaite b Sullivan	5	– (4) lbw b L. R. Davis	10
S. R. Patel b Kelly	22	– (5) lbw b Bird	49
†A. J. Hodd lbw b Kelly	11	– (6) lbw b Bright	6
T. T. Bresnan c Crosthwaite b Bird	39	– c Crosthwaite b Sullivan	5
L. E. Plunkett b Kelly	24	– lbw b Sullivan	6
M. A. K. Lawson c L. M. Davis b Sullivan	5	– not out	2
D. A. Stiff not out	4	– b Kelly	20
L-b 15, w 4, n-b 8	27	B 4, l-b 3, w 1, n-b 5	13
1/34 2/81 3/99 4/117 5/121 6/140 7/162 8/214 9/223	230	1/23 2/40 3/54 4/60 5/88 6/123 7/144 8/144 9/154	175

Bowling: *First Innings*—Bird 24–4–49–2; Kelly 24–7–53–4; Sullivan 16.4–4–44–3; Cullen 20–8–45–1; Bright 7–3–8–0; L. R. Davis 7–2–16–0. *Second Innings*—Bird 19–8–32–3; Kelly 17.5–5–56–1; Sullivan 12–2–45–3; Cullen 10–5–15–0; L. R. Davis 7–0–18–1; Bright 6–4–2–1.

Umpires: N. S. D. Fowler and S. A. Reed.

At Bankstown Oval, Sydney, February 8, 2003. **Third one-day international: Australia Under-19 won by 16 runs.** Toss: Australia Under-19. **Australia Under-19 260-8** (50 overs) (L. M. Davis 76, K. J. Skewes 52); **England Under-19 244-8** (50 overs) (N. J. Edwards 92).

England Under-19 collapsed from 200 for two in the 43rd over to 238 for eight in the 49th.

At Hurstville Oval, Sydney, February 10, 2003. **Fourth one-day international: England Under-19 won by eight runs (D/L method).** Toss: Australia Under-19. **Australia Under-19 212** (45.4 overs) (K. J. Skewes 62; L. E. Plunkett 4-24); **England Under-19 125-4** (29.5 overs).

When bad light and rain stopped play, England's score was 117.

At Hurstville Oval, Sydney, February 11, 2003. **Fifth one-day international: Australia Under-19 won by 84 runs.** Toss: Australia Under-19. **Australia Under-19 270-6** (50 overs) (T. P. Doropoulos 179*); **England Under-19 186** (36.2 overs) (L. J. Wright 54).

Australia Under-19 were ten for three and 75 for five, but Theo Doropoulos smashed 21 fours and three sixes from 155 balls, adding an unbroken 115 for the seventh wicket with Bird (29). Australia won the series 4–1.*

YOUNG CRICKETER OF THE YEAR, 2003

James Anderson, who was the first person to win the award unopposed, was voted Young Cricketer of the Year by members of the Cricket Writers' Club. Surrey players have won the award eight times, Middlesex and Lancashire seven, and Yorkshire six. Worcestershire and Durham are the only first-class counties that have not had a winner.

1950 R. Tattersall (Lancs)
1951 P. B. H. May (Surrey)
1952 F. S. Trueman (Yorks)
1953 M. C. Cowdrey (OU & Kent)
1954 P. J. Loader (Surrey)
1955 K. F. Barrington (Surrey)
1956 B. Taylor (Essex)
1957 M. J. Stewart (Surrey)
1958 A. C. D. Ingleby-Mackenzie (Hants)
1959 G. Pullar (Lancs)
1960 D. A. Allen (Glos)
1961 P. H. Parfitt (Middx)
1962 P. J. Sharpe (Yorks)
1963 G. Boycott (Yorks)
1964 J. M. Brearley (CU & Middx)
1965 A. P. E. Knott (Kent)
1966 D. L. Underwood (Kent)
1967 A. W. Greig (Sussex)
1968 R. M. H. Cottam (Kent)
1969 A. Ward (Derbys)
1970 C. M. Old (Yorks)
1971 J. Whitehouse (Warwicks)
1972 D. R. Owen-Thomas (CU & Surrey)
1973 M. Hendrick (Derbys)
1974 P. H. Edmonds (CU & Middx)
1975 A. Kennedy (Lancs)
1976 G. Miller (Derbys)
1977 I. T. Botham (Somerset)
1978 D. I. Gower (Leics)
1979 P. W. G. Parker (Sussex)
1980† G. R. Dilley (Kent)
1981 M. W. Gatting (Middx)
1982 N. G. Cowans (Middx)
1983 N. A. Foster (Essex)
1984 R. J. Bailey (Northants)
1985 D. V. Lawrence (Glos)
1986 A. A. Metcalfe (Yorks)
J. J. Whitaker (Leics)
1987 R. J. Blakey (Yorks)
1988 M. P. Maynard (Glam)
1989 N. Hussain (Essex)
1990 M. A. Atherton (Lancs)
1991 M. R. Ramprakash (Middx)
1992 I. D. K. Salisbury (Sussex)
1993 M. N. Lathwell (Somerset)
1994 J. P. Crawley (Lancs)
1995 A. Symonds (Glos)
1996 C. E. W. Silverwood (Yorks)
1997 B. C. Hollioake (Surrey)
1998 A. Flintoff (Lancs)
1999 A. J. Tudor (Surrey)
2000 P. J. Franks (Notts)
2001 O. A. Shah (Middx)
2002 R. Clarke (Surrey)
2003 J. M. Anderson (Lancs)

Teams are those played for at the time.

† An extra award, in memory of Norman Preston, Editor of *Wisden* 1951–1980, was made to C. W. J. Athey (Yorks).

ENGLAND WOMEN IN NEW ZEALAND AND AUSTRALIA, 2002-03

CAROL SALMON

England's last matches under the charge of coach John Harmer took place in his native Australia, where he was returning to take up a position with the Australian Cricket Academy. After an unsuccessful run in a one-day quadrangular tournament in New Zealand, England arrived in Australia to face the strongest side in women's cricket. Predictably, they lost the Test series, but not nearly as heavily as when the teams last met, in England in 2001.

They actually claimed first-innings lead in the two low-scoring games, and gave Australia a scare at Brisbane, dismissing them for 78, only to collapse themselves against the pace of Cathryn Fitzpatrick, now 35, but still threatening. At Sydney, an unbeaten century from Lisa Sthalekar set England a target of 207 which they never seriously pursued. Fitzpatrick was named Player of the Series for her 14 wickets at 9.92, though England left-armer Lucy Pearson ran her close, taking 15 at 10.66, thanks to 11 in the match at Sydney. Her team-mate Sarah Collyer bowled a remarkable 42 maidens in her 67 overs. Sthalekar's hundred made her the leading scorer, with 144 runs, and England's Charlotte Edwards totalled 140. Belinda Clark, the home captain, overtook Betty Wilson's Australian record of 862 runs in a Test career during the first game, and finished on 899.

ENGLAND TOURING PARTY

C. J. Connor (Sussex) (*captain*), C. M. Edwards (Kent) (*vice-captain*), S. V. Collyer (Lancashire), M. C. Godliman (Sussex), L. J. Harper (Somerset), D. Holden (Nottinghamshire), K. M. Leng (Yorkshire), L. K. Newton (Cheshire), L. C. Pearson (Staffordshire), N. J. Shaw (Nottinghamshire), L. Spragg (Yorkshire), C. E. Taylor (Yorkshire), S. C. Taylor (Berkshire), A. Thompson (Lancashire).

L. Greenway (Kent), who had just toured Australia with England Under-19 Women, joined the party after Godliman was injured during the one-day tournament in New Zealand.

Coach: J. Harmer. *Assistant coach:* J. Powell. *Physiotherapist:* K. Buckley.

ENGLAND TOUR RESULTS

Matches – Played 11: Won 2, Lost 7, Drawn 2.

Note: Matches in this section were not first-class.

At Lincoln Green, January 25, 2003. **New Zealand A won by one wicket.** Toss: England XII. **England XII 199-7** (50 overs) (A. Thompson 75); **New Zealand A 200-9** (49.4 overs) (M. L. Lynch 50, M. J. Kane 57).

England named 12 players, of whom only 11 could bat and 11 bowl.

England's matches against India, Australia and New Zealand in the Women's World Series (January 27–February 7) appear on pages 1333–1334.

At Allan Border Field, Brisbane, February 12, 13, 2003. **Drawn.** Toss: England XII. **England XII 202** (L. Greenway 88; L. Ebsary 4-35) **and 44-2; Australian Under-23 131** (I. Noack 50; L. J. Harper 5-30).

Each team named 12 players, of whom only 11 could bat and 11 bowl.

AUSTRALIA v ENGLAND

First Test Match

At Brisbane, February 15, 16, 17, 2003. Australia won by five wickets. Toss: Australia. Test debuts: A. J. Blackwell, L. C. Sthalekar, E. Twining; L. Greenway.

Australia came through to victory after an undistinguished batting display by both teams on a Gabba pitch that had some difficult bounce but was not especially treacherous. After labouring through a painful 108 overs for 124 runs on the first day, England stunned Australia by shooting them out for 78 on the second. It was Australia's third-lowest Test total, and the first time they had missed three figures in 47 Tests since 1957-58. Clare Connor gave the new ball to off-spinner Laura Harper, who swiftly removed the prolific Belinda Clark, and seamers Lucy Pearson and Laura Newton put the skids under Australia to earn a 46-run lead.

England, however, were eight down again by the close, on a day which saw 19 wickets fall. Australia had plenty of time to make 139, the biggest total of the match, though Sarah Collyer slowed them down with 18 maidens. The tide turned as Clark and Karen Rolton added 78, the game's highest stand, and Australia won with nearly four sessions in hand. The only other fifty partnership had come at the start, when Collyer and Kathryn Leng batted through the first morning. But ultimately England's batting fell short yet again. Australia were more relieved than euphoric: in her Ashes diary, their wicket-keeper Julia Price later described her team's batting as "appalling".

Player of the Match: C. L. Fitzpatrick.

Close of play: First day, England 124-9 (Harper 20, Pearson 0); Second day, England 87-8 (Newton 8).

England

S. V. Collyer c Rolton b Fitzpatrick	29	– b Fitzpatrick	5
K. M. Leng lbw b Rolton	26	– c Goszko b Fitzpatrick	6
C. M. Edwards lbw b Twining	6	– c Price b Hayes	27
A. Thompson lbw b Rolton	1	– lbw b Rolton	10
L. Greenway c Jones b McGregor	5	– (6) c Price b Hayes	1
†S. C. Taylor c Price b McGregor	14	– (7) c Price b Sthalekar	6
*C. J. Connor c Fitzpatrick b Sthalekar	7	– (8) b Fitzpatrick	19
L. K. Newton c Price b Fitzpatrick	5	– (9) c Price b Twining	11
L. J. Harper not out	20	– (5) c Goszko b Hayes	0
C. E. Taylor c Clark b Fitzpatrick	0	– c Sthalekar b Fitzpatrick	1
L. C. Pearson c Jones b Fitzpatrick	0	– not out	0
B 2, l-b 6, w 2, n-b 1	11	B 4, l-b 2	6
1/57 (1) 2/67 (3) 3/67 (2) 4/70 (4) 5/76 (5) 6/93 (7) 7/97 (6) 8/110 (8) 9/116 (10) 10/124 (11)	124	1/7 (2) 2/24 (1) 3/43 (3) 4/43 (5) 5/45 (6) 6/56 (7) 7/65 (4) 8/87 (8) 9/91 (10) 10/92 (9)	92

Bowling: *First Innings*—Fitzpatrick 29.3–14–32–4; Twining 20–11–17–1; McGregor 14–7–24–2; Blackwell 11–6–9–0; Hayes 15–9–20–0; Rolton 8–5–6–2; Sthalekar 11–6–8–1. *Second Innings*—Fitzpatrick 20–9–28–4; Twining 9.3–4–14–1; Rolton 8–4–17–1; Sthalekar 15–7–16–1; Hayes 10–8–9–3; McGregor 5–4–2–0.

Australia

L. C. Sthalekar lbw b Pearson	6	– (2) c Pearson b Harper	0
*B. J. Clark c Newton b Harper	4	– (1) c S. C. Taylor b Collyer	47
K. L. Rolton c and b Newton	14	– c Greenway b Harper	46
M. Jones c S. C. Taylor b Pearson	22	– c S. C. Taylor b Newton	4
M. A. J. Goszko lbw b Newton	0	– c Harper b Collyer	4
A. J. Blackwell c Harper b Newton	4	– not out	9
J. Hayes c C. E. Taylor b Pearson	12	– not out	18
C. L. Fitzpatrick c S. C. Taylor b Pearson	1		
†J. C. Price c S. C. Taylor b Connor	3		
T. A. McGregor lbw b Connor	9		
E. Twining not out	0		
L-b 2, n-b 1	3	B 1, l-b 8, w 1, n-b 1	11
1/8 (1) 2/14 (2) 3/36 (3) 4/40 (5) 5/50 (6) 6/55 (4) 7/65 (8) 8/69 (7) 9/69 (9) 10/78 (10)	78	1/22 (2) 2/100 (3) 3/104 (1) 4/104 (4) 5/111 (5)	(5 wkts) 139

Bowling: *First Innings*—Pearson 15–6–31–4; Harper 6–2–16–1; Collyer 4–2–8–0; Newton 6–4–10–3; C. E. Taylor 4–3–3–0; Connor 6.4–4–8–2. *Second Innings*—Pearson 10–4–22–0; Connor 3–0–12–0; Harper 18–7–26–2; Newton 5–1–18–1; Collyer 25–18–17–2; C. E. Taylor 2–0–18–0; Leng 5–0–17–0.

Umpires: N. S. McNamara and B. N. J. Oxenford.

AUSTRALIA v ENGLAND

Second Test Match

At Bankstown Oval, Sydney, February 22, 23, 24, 25, 2003. Drawn. Toss: England. Test debut: K. L. Britt.

England left-arm seamer Lucy Pearson claimed 11 for 107, the third-best match return in women's Test cricket, but Australia still took the series 1–0. The match was frequently interrupted by rain, and Australia did not open their innings until 12.45 on the first day. When they did, Pearson ran amok, grabbing seven for 51 in 25 overs. Charlotte Edwards and Claire Taylor helped England carve out a lead of 53, but their hopes of squaring the series foundered on a stand of 136, then a fifth-wicket Test record, between Lisa Sthalekar and Alex Blackwell, both in their second Test. Blackwell hit six fours, Sthalekar only four; she batted over six hours for 120 not out from 329 balls, indicating how tricky conditions were. England needed 207 to win but found Cathryn Fitzpatrick and company just too difficult to get away. Edwards scored their only fifty of the series without suggesting a serious assault on the target. England captain Clare Connor later admitted that both sides' batting was "not out of the top drawer".

Player of the Match: L. C. Pearson. *Player of the Series:* C. L. Fitzpatrick.

Close of play: First day, England 21-1 (Leng 12, Edwards 9); Second day, England 151-4 (Greenway 31, S. C. Taylor 45); Third day, Australia 163-4 (Sthalekar 65, Blackwell 51).

"It does seem that a malign fate deprived English cricket prematurely of someone rather exceptional with an extraordinary life story."

Barry Norman on Books, page 1575.

Australia

*B. J. Clark b Pearson	16	– c Collyer b Pearson	16
K. L. Britt lbw b Pearson	5	– lbw b Pearson	3
K. L. Rolton b Harper	0	– c Greenway b Newton	15
M. Jones b Pearson	58	– c S. C. Taylor b Pearson	4
L. C. Sthalekar c Collyer b Pearson	18	– not out	120
A. J. Blackwell c S. C. Taylor b Pearson	13	– b Pearson	58
J. Hayes c S. C. Taylor b Pearson	0	– run out	5
C. L. Fitzpatrick c Newton b Leng	18	– c S. C. Taylor b C. E. Taylor	11
†J. C. Price b Pearson	4	– not out	6
T. A. McGregor not out	0		
E. Twining b Leng	0		
L-b 1, n-b 1	2	B 9, l-b 6, w 2, n-b 4	21
1/20 (1) 2/21 (3) 3/25 (2) 4/90 (5) 5/99 (4) 6/103 (7) 7/124 (6) 8/134 (8) 9/134 (9) 10/134 (11)	134	1/15 (2) 2/20 (1) 3/36 (3) 4/49 (4) 5/185 (6) 6/200 (7) 7/246 (8)	(7 wkts dec.) 259

Bowling: *First Innings*—Pearson 25–10–51–7; Harper 15–3–38–1; Connor 9–4–10–0; Newton 3–0–14–0; C. E. Taylor 6–0–13–0; Collyer 6–4–2–0; Leng 3.1–1–5–2. *Second Innings*—Pearson 33–11–56–4; Harper 23–6–45–0; Collyer 32–18–21–0; Newton 13–3–36–1; Leng 17–5–28–0; Edwards 1–0–10–0; C. E. Taylor 11–3–27–1; Connor 14–6–21–0.

England

S. V. Collyer c Price b Fitzpatrick	0	– lbw b Twining	3
K. M. Leng run out	21	– lbw b Sthalekar	28
C. M. Edwards lbw b Hayes	40	– lbw b Fitzpatrick	67
A. Thompson lbw b Britt	2	– lbw b Fitzpatrick	4
L. Greenway b Twining	31	– b Fitzpatrick	0
†S. C. Taylor lbw b Twining	48	– not out	21
*C. J. Connor c Rolton b Twining	3	– b Fitzpatrick	0
L. K. Newton b Hayes	16	– not out	6
L. J. Harper c Price b Fitzpatrick	0		
C. E. Taylor not out	9		
L. C. Pearson lbw b Hayes	0		
L-b 16, w 1	17	B 2, l-b 1, w 1	4
1/0 (1) 2/48 (2) 3/70 (3) 4/70 (4) 5/154 (5) 6/155 (6) 7/166 (7) 8/167 (9) 9/187 (8) 10/187 (11)	187	1/5 (1) 2/58 (2) 3/65 (4) 4/69 (5) 5/116 (3) 6/116 (7)	(6 wkts) 133

Bowling: *First Innings*—Fitzpatrick 42–21–64–2; Twining 26–10–32–3; Sthalekar 10–2–21–0; Rolton 3–2–1–0; McGregor 6–4–4–0; Hayes 21.4–8–32–3; Britt 7–1–17–1. *Second Innings*—Fitzpatrick 19–9–15–4; Twining 14–5–18–1; Rolton 5–2–13–0; Hayes 14–4–30–0; McGregor 6–3–5–0; Sthalekar 18–8–26–1; Britt 7–0–23–0.

Umpires: N. S. D. Fowler and S. A. Reed.

WOMEN'S WORLD SERIES, 2002-03

CAROL SALMON

The Women's World Series, staged at Lincoln, near Christchurch, was organised to provide top-level competition outside the World Cup for the best women's teams. Australia dominated the tournament, winning all their six group matches, against hosts New Zealand, England and India. And the final brought revenge for the upset in the 2000-01 World Cup final, when New Zealand beat them by four runs at the same ground; this time, they thrashed them by 109 runs.

They were deserving champions: in captain Belinda Clark, hard-hitting No. 3 Karen Rolton and feisty quick bowler Cathryn Fitzpatrick, Australia had the tournament's three most influential players. New Zealand lost only to Australia, and a useful batting line-up included opener Rebecca Rolls, who scored a 30-ball fifty against India.

England were bowled out for 86 by India in their opening game, and went from bad to worse until they scraped a one-run win in the last group match; they reached 200 for the first time, but India needed only 25, with six wickets in hand and Mithali Raj approaching her century, until three run-outs brought about an astonishing collapse. The following day, a career-best 80 from Kathryn Leng helped England beat India again in the play-off for third place.

Note: Matches in this section were not first-class.

At Bert Sutcliffe Oval, Lincoln, January 26, 2003. **Australia won by 63 runs.** Toss: Australia. **Australia 223-6** (50 overs) (L. C. Sthalekar 59, K. L. Rolton 86; F. S. King 4-24); **New Zealand 160-9** (50 overs).

Karen Rolton became the fifth woman to pass 2,000 runs in one-day internationals, in her 61st match, and later took her 50th one-day international wicket.

At Bert Sutcliffe Oval, Lincoln, January 27, 2003. **India won by six wickets.** Toss: India. **England 86** (35.5 overs) (N. Al-Khadeer 5-14); **India 89-4** (29.5 overs).

The match was reduced to 45 overs a side by rain. Nooshin Al-Khadeer's analysis was the best for India in one-day internationals.

At Bert Sutcliffe Oval, Lincoln, January 28, 2003. **New Zealand won by 83 runs.** Toss: India. **New Zealand 248-5** (50 overs) (N. Payne 93, H. M. Tiffen 52); **India 165-5** (50 overs).

At Bert Sutcliffe Oval, Lincoln, January 29, 2003. **Australia won by seven wickets.** Toss: England. **England 156-8** (50 overs); **Australia 157-3** (39.3 overs) (K. L. Rolton 68*).

At Lincoln No. 3, Lincoln, January 30, 2003. **New Zealand won by four wickets.** Toss: England. **England 140** (46.4 overs); **New Zealand 141-6** (39.1 overs).

Clare Taylor played her 100th game for England (13 Tests and 87 one-day internationals).

At Lincoln No. 3, Lincoln, February 1, 2003. **Australia won by 59 runs.** Toss: Australia. **Australia 216-9** (50 overs) (K. L. Rolton 68); **India 157-9** (50 overs).

Australia's Cathryn Fitzpatrick became the first woman to take 100 one-day international wickets, in her 64th match.

At Lincoln No. 3, Lincoln, February 2, 2003. **Australia won by 106 runs.** Toss: Australia. **Australia 226-8** (50 overs) (B. J. Clark 81); **England 120** (50 overs) (K. L. Britt 4-16).

Australia recorded their 16th successive one-day win over England.

At Bert Sutcliffe Oval, Lincoln, February 2, 2003. **New Zealand won by 53 runs.** Toss: India. **New Zealand 239-9** (50 overs) (R. J. Rolls 59, E. C. Drumm 51, M. A. M. Lewis 50; N. Al-Khadeer 4-38); **India 186** (47.2 overs) (M. Raj 82).

Rebecca Rolls reached 50 in 30 balls with ten fours, believed to be the fastest 50 in women's one-day internationals; in all, she scored 59 in 37.

At Bert Sutcliffe Oval, Lincoln, February 3, 2003. **New Zealand won by seven wickets.** Toss: England. England **173-9** (50 overs); **New Zealand 174-3** (44.3 overs) (E. C. Drumm 93).

At Bert Sutcliffe Oval, Lincoln, February 4, 2003. **Australia won by nine wickets.** Toss: India. **India 134-7** (50 overs); **Australia 135-1** (28 overs) (L. C. Sthalekar 58*).

At Bert Sutcliffe Oval, Lincoln, February 6, 2003. **Australia won by six wickets.** Toss: New Zealand. **New Zealand 174** (49.1 overs) (C. L. Fitzpatrick 5-27); **Australia 175-4** (40 overs) (L. C. Sthalekar 53, B. J. Clark 67).

At Lincoln No. 3, Lincoln, February 6, 2003. **England won by one run.** Toss: India. **England 208-4** (50 overs) (C. M. Edwards 79*); **India 207** (50 overs) (M. Raj 98).

Charlotte Edwards and Arran Thompson (38) added 98 in 15 overs for the fourth wicket. India collapsed from 184 for four in the 44th over with three run-outs.

QUALIFYING TABLE

	Played	*Won*	*Lost*	*Bonus points*	*Points*	*Net run-rate*
Australia	6	6	0	6	36	1.39
New Zealand	6	4	2	3	23	0.34
India	6	1	5	2	7	−0.79
England	6	1	5	1	6	−0.93

Win = 5 pts. One bonus point awarded either to the winning team for achieving victory with a run-rate 1.25 times that of the opposition, or to the losing team for denying the winners a bonus point. Net run-rate is calculated by subtracting runs conceded per over from runs scored per over.

Third-place play-off

At Bert Sutcliffe Oval, Lincoln, February 7, 2003. **England won by 90 runs.** Toss: England. **England 191** (48.1 overs) (K. M. Leng 80); **India 101** (43.5 overs).

Final

At Bert Sutcliffe Oval, Lincoln, February 8, 2003. **Australia won by 109 runs.** Toss: Australia. **Australia 214** (49.5 overs) (B. J. Clark 80); **New Zealand 105** (30 overs).

Belinda Clark became the leading scorer in women's one-day internationals, reaching 4,077 in 89 matches; the previous record-holder, New Zealander Debbie Hockley who scored 4,064 in 118, was commentating on the match for television.

CRICKET IN AUSTRALIA, 2002-03

JOHN MACKINNON

Michael Clarke

Behind the glittering façade of Australian cricket, there are corners that have quietly gathered dust and one, surprisingly, was at the Sydney Cricket Ground. While New South Wales had supplied the nucleus of Australia's world-conquering team, the state side had fallen on hard times. The giants of domestic cricket endured eight seasons without a first-class title – their second-longest barren patch outside the war years – with three wooden spoons, and third place their best showing.

Since the return of Steve Rixon, who coached their last three Sheffield Shield-winning sides before moving to New Zealand, they had rediscovered their one-day form, while off the field a new chief executive, David Gilbert, introduced a more zestful administration. But in the Pura Cup – the Shield's successor – even Rixon seemed powerless. New South Wales's decline could not simply be explained by international call-ups: Queensland and Western Australia had flourished with supporting casts. But a youth policy produced few results. Meanwhile, the Sydney pitch was no longer the spinners' paradise of the 1980s, when home wins were expected and generally delivered; now, the seamers usually enjoyed a couple of sessions before the wicket flattened out.

In 2002-03, New South Wales emerged from the wilderness, winning the Pura Cup at last along with a third successive one-day title. Rixon put his commitment to youth on hold, pinning his immediate hopes on the return of senior cricketers, such as the Waughs, and imports, such as Simon Katich from Western Australia. Sure enough, the key players were Steve Waugh – who scored three hundreds in seven games between Tests – and Katich, who captained in Waugh's absence, made runs when most needed, fielded splendidly and showed unexpected form as a spinner.

Whether the revival could continue once such stalwarts moved on remained uncertain. New South Wales often looked brittle, and their route to both finals was precarious: twice, they qualified in the last preliminary round. Sometimes, their batting just caved in. They were lucky to beat Western

Australia twice – they could have lost both, and finished fifth. In the last qualifier, they had to beat leaders and defending champions Queensland, but folded for 102 early on the first afternoon. Then Stuart MacGill's leg-spin transformed the game and, once they had Queensland's measure, New South Wales stormed Fortress Brisbane in the final. A few weeks earlier, they had squeezed Queensland out of the one-day ING Cup final, and travelled to Perth to confront Western Australia. Steve Waugh, no longer required by Australia's one-day team, hit 88 in 55 balls as they won with 23 overs to spare.

Waugh inspired his team-mates to greater awareness of their responsibilities. The best prospect, 21-year-old Michael Clarke, blossomed, his game greatly enhanced by playing alongside Waugh and Katich. His exuberant batting earned accolades everywhere, not to mention four centuries; impetuosity cost him several more. Clarke made a successful one-day international debut in January. Mark Waugh, who retired from international cricket in October, may not have been intensely committed, but a calm 60 at Perth anchored a run-chase when all around were panicking, and he caught everything at slip. Michael Slater may never play for Australia again, either, but he produced some breathtaking innings. Michael Bevan averaged 76 before Christmas, when he was lost to Australia's one-day side.

Brett Lee's two matches yielded 21 wickets, a message the selectors received and understood

The bowling had less of a pedigree. Stuart MacGill bowled endlessly – 556 overs in all first-class cricket – and deserved his 60 wickets, 17 in the last two games against Queensland. Glenn McGrath never played, but Brett Lee's two matches yielded 21 wickets, a message the national selectors received and understood.

Queensland strolled effortlessly to their fifth successive final. Their fast bowlers held sway, home and away: in a run of five victories, the highest total they conceded was 228. Michael Kasprowicz and Joe Dawes terrorised batsmen and, along with Ashley Noffke, claimed more than 40 first-class victims each. Andy Bichel took nine in his one appearance, but was barely missed, especially once Adam Dale returned. Shoulder surgery had kept Dale out for 15 months; he bowled as frugally as ever, but retired in April.

The bowlers' success camouflaged batting weaknesses, partly caused by international calls. Matthew Hayden never played, Andrew Symonds scored one fifty in five Pura games and Jimmy Maher one in four. Stuart Law could not get going, and dropped out after a blow on the wrist. Brendan Nash made 257 runs in one match, then played ten without another fifty. Martin Love won his Test cap after two double-hundreds against England – one for Australia A – and 190 on a dreadful Hobart pitch; then the runs dried up. The gaps were often filled by Clinton Perren, named Pura Cup Player of the Year. But the New South Wales spinners finally found him wanting, and Queensland's proud run of three titles was ended.

Victoria tied on points with New South Wales, but had fewer outright wins. They had entrusted their fortunes to David Hookes, the third coach in 12 months (whose own reign would later be cut short by his tragic death in January 2004). Hookes had his critics; some wondered whether he could combine a high profile media career with running a state team, especially as he had done little coaching at this level. Hookes appointed Shane Warne captain (he would be available for two first-class games) and Matthew Elliott his deputy. An inauspicious opening defeat convinced Elliott that captaincy was a distraction, so the job passed, more logically, to wicket-keeper Darren Berry, Victoria's most experienced player. Berry had his lows: in January, he was fined $A1,000 for remarks about the umpiring in Hobart, and then suspended for missing a beach training session at 6.30 a.m., a few hours after the Border Medal Dinner. But he was confirmed as captain after the end of the season.

At Christmas, Victoria led the table with four wins, culminating at Sydney, where their pace attack twice demolished New South Wales. But their next three games yielded just four points. Victoria needed more from their premier batsmen, particularly Elliott and Brad Hodge, who had a dreadful year until he scored 183 in the last match. Jason Arnberger, who made twin unbeaten hundreds against Tasmania, was easily the highest scorer. A 28-year-old seamer from Ballarat, Shane Harwood, launched his first-class career with a hat-trick against Tasmania, while leg-spinner Cameron White, aged 19, collected ten wickets against Western Australia – a fortnight after the ACB banned Warne for 12 months for doping offences. All-rounder Jon Moss was voted the state's most valuable player.

The team were celebrating a one-day win just before Hookes died. Cricketing routine was forgotten in a national outpouring of grief for one of the game's great personalities. His funeral took place at the Adelaide Oval, his home ground, which he so often electrified.

For the fourth year in five, South Australia finished fourth. Their spasmodic form was summed up in their last three games: an innings win over Queensland, an eight-wicket loss to Tasmania, then an eight-wicket win in the return. They actually beat everyone except Western Australia, but the coach, Greg Chappell, decided five years' service was enough. The form of their young fast bowlers was encouraging. Paul Rofe was not always as effective as in 2001-02, but Mark Cleary, aged 22, and Shaun Tait, 20, made an immediate impact. Of the two bowling imports from Victoria, Damien Fleming was fit only twice, and John Davison departed to find World Cup fame – and dazzling batting form – with Canada. There was ample batting, even though Darren Lehmann played only twice. Greg Blewett led the run-scoring, captained the side and took wickets.

Western Australia had a forgettable season, ending with the release of coach Mike Veletta; Wayne Clark, who had coached them to two Sheffield Shields in the 1990s, agreed to return after being sacked by Yorkshire. They fielded a full side once, when they annihilated an injury-hit Victoria; their other success was in Adelaide, where Justin Langer and Murray Goodwin scored 164 apiece and Beau Casson, a 20-year-old left-arm spinner, took ten wickets in his second game. Chris Rogers started as he left off the previous season, with big scores against England and South Australia, then faded until the penultimate match. Left-arm pace bowler Michael Clark, son of Wayne, was a model of consistency, taking three or more wickets eight times, but Brad Hogg's transformation to international all-rounder was not reflected in his few state games.

Tasmania sank from second to sixth. They lost their first four matches and by Christmas had two points. Thereafter, they won a couple of games at Hobart, but problems with the pitch there came to a head when they forfeited a match to Western Australia. An ACB forum found that "proper precautions were not taken to ensure the pitch was properly prepared". Perversely, they awarded the visitors six points, rather than penalising the home team. For those like Jamie Cox who had thrived on the Bellerive shirtfront, there was little joy: Tasmania's batting suffered an endemic loss of confidence – Ricky Ponting played once, scoring seven and nought. The bowlers had a better time, not least Damien Wright.

Of 31 Pura Cup games, 26 achieved outright results, but it was worrying that 11 ended in three days, including the final, scheduled for five. This excludes the second-day abandonment at Hobart – the only case where the pitch was investigated. In spite of the cascade of wickets, the major centres attracted minimal crowds. But New South Wales found enthusiastic audiences outside the SCG. For Australia Day in January, they took a game to Newcastle, 75 miles up the coast; 16,192 fans witnessed four days of riveting cricket and a two-run home win. And in February, a one-day game at the Olympic stadium in Western Sydney pulled 25,763.

FIRST-CLASS AVERAGES, 2002-03

BATTING

(Qualification: 500 runs)

	M	*I*	*NO*	*R*	*HS*	*100s*	*Avge*	*Ct*
M. L. Love (*Queensland, Aus. A & Australia*)	13	22	5	1,120	250	3	65.88	20
†M. A. Higgs (*South Australia*)	9	16	3	651	134*	2	50.07	2
C. T. Perren (*Queensland & Australia A*)	9	16	1	741	224	2	49.40	8
J. L. Arnberger (*Victoria*)	10	18	3	724	172*	3	48.26	8
G. S. Blewett (*South Australia & Australia A*)	10	18	0	868	135	2	48.22	0
M. J. Clarke (*New South Wales & Australia A*)	11	18	1	813	134	4	47.82	11
S. R. Waugh (*New South Wales & Australia*)	12	21	0	964	211	4	45.90	10
†L. A. Carseldine (*Queensland*)	12	19	3	709	124*	1	44.31	12
D. A. Fitzgerald (*South Australia*)	10	19	1	774	153	3	43.00	8
M. J. Slater (*New South Wales*)	10	18	0	770	204	3	42.77	6
M. W. Goodwin (*Western Australia*)	9	16	0	674	176	2	42.12	5
†J. L. Langer (*Western Australia & Australia*)	12	19	0	797	250	2	41.94	6
†M. T. G. Elliott (*Victoria & Australia A*)	9	15	2	531	191	1	40.84	7
†C. J. L. Rogers (*W. Australia & Australia A*)	13	23	1	884	194	2	40.18	11
B. J. Hodge (*Victoria & Australia A*)	12	19	1	722	183	2	40.11	7
†S. M. Katich (*New South Wales & Australia A*)	13	22	2	778	134*	1	38.90	13
†M. E. K. Hussey (*W. Australia & Australia A*)	10	17	1	610	145	1	38.12	13
D. J. Marsh (*Tasmania*)	10	17	1	561	111	1	35.06	6
†M. J. Di Venuto (*Tasmania*)	10	18	0	596	101	1	33.11	16
†B. P. Nash (*Queensland*)	12	23	3	513	176	1	25.65	7

† *Left-handed batsman.*

BOWLING

(Qualification: 20 wickets)

	Style	*O*	*M*	*R*	*W*	*BB*	*5W/i*	*Avge*
D. A. Nash (*New South Wales*)	RFM	156.1	40	428	26	6-48	1	16.46
J. H. Dawes (*Queensland*)	RFM	296.2	87	807	43	7-67	3	18.76
M. W. H. Inness (*Victoria*)	LFM	259.2	83	622	28	5-61	1	22.21
S. W. Tait (*South Australia*)	RFM	125	22	451	20	5-68	1	22.55
A. A. Noffke (*Queensland & Australia A*)	RFM	331.4	80	929	41	6-24	2	22.65
M. W. Clark (*Western Australia*)	LFM	287	74	879	38	5-47	1	23.13
J. N. Gillespie (*Australia*)	RFM	181.5	53	492	20	4-25	0	24.60
M. S. Kasprowicz (*Queensland*)	RFM	414.3	109	1,188	48	5-36	3	24.75
C. L. White (*Victoria*)	LBG	238.5	54	701	28	6-66	1	25.03
B. Lee (*New South Wales & Australia*)	RF	238.5	49	865	34	7-114	3	25.44
D. G. Wright (*Tasmania & Australia A*)	RFM	383.2	118	975	38	6-39	1	25.65
A. R. Griffith (*Tasmania*)	RF	183	44	525	20	5-46	1	26.25
S. K. Warne (*Victoria & Australia*)	LBG	198.1	43	528	20	4-93	0	26.40
S. M. Harwood (*Victoria & Australia A*)	RFM	266.1	65	795	29	5-54	2	27.41
M. J. Nicholson (*Western Australia*)	RFM	228.5	44	772	27	6-79	1	28.59
M. L. Lewis (*Victoria & Australia A*)	RFM	290	57	1,037	36	6-64	1	28.80
B. A. Williams (*WA & Australia A*)	RF	222.5	54	702	24	5-38	3	29.25
P. C. Rofe (*South Australia*)	RFM	314	100	820	28	5-62	1	29.28
S. C. G. MacGill (*NSW & Australia*)	LBG	556.3	99	1,774	60	5-16	4	29.56
S. R. Clark (*NSW & Australia A*)	RFM	391.4	102	1,188	36	6-84	1	33.00
J. Angel (*Western Australia*)	RFM	255.5	65	746	22	6-35	1	33.90

Note: Averages exclude Bangladesh's tour in July 2003.

PURA CUP, 2002-03

	Played	*Won*	*Lost*	*Drawn*	*1st-inns Points*	*Points*	*Quotient*
Queensland	10	6	3	1	6	42	1.283
New South Wales	10	6	2	2	0	36	1.183
Victoria	10	5	4	1	6	36	1.104
South Australia	10	4	5	1	4	28	0.862
Western Australia	10	2	5	3	2	20*	0.939
Tasmania	10	2	6	2	2	14	0.727

Final: New South Wales beat Queensland by 246 runs.

New South Wales finished ahead of Victoria by virtue of winning one more match outright.
** Western Australia were awarded 6 pts when their match against Tasmania at Hobart was abandoned on the second day because of a dangerous pitch.*
Outright win = 6 pts; lead on first-innings in a drawn or lost game = 2 pts.
Quotient = runs per wicket scored divided by runs per wicket conceded.

Full scores, match reports and statistics of the 2002-03 Australian season can be found in *Wisden Cricketers' Almanack Australia* 2003-04.

At Adelaide, October 15, 16, 17, 18. **South Australia won by 208 runs.** Toss: South Australia. **South Australia 149** (W. N. Carr 4-42) **and 515-6 dec.** (B. A. Johnson 165, G. S. Blewett 103, M. A. Higgs 134*); **Victoria 153** (G. C. Rummans 69*; M. C. Miller 7-55) **and 303** (I. J. Harvey 63*, D. S. Berry 52; J. M. Davison 4-107). *South Australia 6 pts, Victoria 2 pts.*

Matthew Elliott resigned as acting-captain after one match, handing over to Darren Berry, who made his 500th dismissal for Victoria.

At Brisbane, October 16, 17, 18, 19. **Drawn.** Toss: New South Wales. **Queensland 507-5 dec.** (B. P. Nash 176, L. A. Carseldine 124*, W. A. Seccombe 56*) **and 216-1** (B. P. Nash 81*, J. P. Maher 60, M. L. Love 56*); **New South Wales 443** (M. J. Phelps 147, M. J. Clarke 134). *Queensland 2 pts.*

At Adelaide, October 25, 26, 27. **New South Wales won by an innings and 71 runs.** Toss: South Australia. **New South Wales 474-6 dec.** (M. J. Clarke 129, M. J. Slater 177, B. J. Haddin 78*); **South Australia 233** (J. M. Davison 72*; N. W. Bracken 5-47) **and 170** (G. S. Blewett 69; D. A. Nash 4-30). *New South Wales 6 pts.*

John Davison, who would win fame in February with the fastest century in World Cup history (for Canada against West Indies), hit a maiden fifty in his 33rd match.

At Melbourne, October 30, 31, November 1, 2. **Victoria won by 159 runs.** Toss: Victoria. **Victoria 353-9 dec.** (J. L. Arnberger 172*, C. L. White 56) **and 236-2 dec.** (J. L. Arnberger 102*, M. T. G. Elliott 80); **Tasmania 224** (S. M. Harwood 5-55) **and 206** (M. J. Di Venuto 55; C. L. White 4-51). *Victoria 6 pts.*

Darren Berry broke Dean Jones's record of 124 first-class matches for Victoria. On his first-class debut, Shane Harwood took a hat-trick in Tasmania's first innings, including fellow-debutant Graeme Cunningham for a first-ball duck, which he followed with a second-ball duck in the next innings. Jason Arnberger batted throughout both innings, but did not field the whole time.

At Sydney, November 8, 9, 10. **New South Wales won by an innings and eight runs.** Toss: Tasmania. **Tasmania 171** (M. G. Dighton 62; B. Lee 5-63, S. C. G. MacGill 4-42) **and 258** (B. Lee 5-86); **New South Wales 437-8 dec.** (M. G. Bevan 201*; S. R. Watson 4-85). *New South Wales 6 pts.*

Michael Bevan's 201, his fourth double-hundred, lasted 456 minutes and 378 balls and included 29 fours and two sixes.*

At Melbourne, November 8, 9, 10, 11. **Victoria won by four wickets.** Toss: Queensland. **Queensland 187** (A. Symonds 92; R. J. Cassell 4-33) **and 139** (M. L. Lewis 4-27); **Victoria 164** (M. T. G. Elliott 64; M. S. Kasprowicz 4-35) **and 163-6.** *Victoria 6 pts, Queensland 2 pts.*

Victoria's first outright win over Queensland since Allan Border's farewell game in March 1996. Their captain, Berry, criticised the drop-in pitch.

At Perth, November 8, 9, 10, 11. **Drawn.** Toss: South Australia. **South Australia 359** (G. S. Blewett 92, C. J. Davies 75, S. A. Deitz 71*; M. W. Clark 5-47) **and 271-8 dec.** (C. J. Davies 125, S. A. Deitz 52); **Western Australia 217** (C. J. L. Rogers 64; P. C. Rofe 4-55) **and 342-5** (M. W. Goodwin 52, C. J. L. Rogers 110*, G. B. Hogg 79*). *South Australia 2 pts.*

Chris Rogers scored his third unbeaten hundred in his last four innings against South Australia.

At Sydney, November 14, 15, 16, 17. **South Australia won by 27 runs.** Toss: New South Wales. **South Australia 397** (D. A. Fitzgerald 153, D. S. Lehmann 97; B. Lee 7-114) **and 181** (M. A. Higgs 70; B. Lee 4-66); **New South Wales 296-9 dec.** (S. R. Waugh 135, S. M. Katich 53; J. M. Davison 5-81) **and 255** (M. J. Slater 91, M. G. Bevan 114; M. A. Higgs 4-25). *South Australia 6 pts.*

Steve Waugh scored his 70th first-class hundred. Mark Waugh took his 100th catch for New South Wales, but was later reprimanded for dissent when given out caught behind for nought.

At Brisbane, November 14, 15, 16. **Queensland won by five wickets.** Toss: Queensland. **Tasmania 187** (J. Cox 51, M. J. Di Venuto 50; A. J. Bichel 4-46) **and 154** (S. R. Watson 57; A. J. Bichel 5-46); **Queensland 229** (L. A. Carseldine 79) **and 116-5.** *Queensland 6 pts.*

Jamie Cox played his 147th first-class match for Tasmania, a record for any Australian state (beating Peter Sleep's 146 for South Australia).

At Perth, November 14, 15, 16. **Western Australia won by an innings and 69 runs.** Toss: Victoria. **Victoria 110** (J. Angel 4-29, M. W. Clark 4-33) **and 237** (P. Wilson 6-76); **Western Australia 416** (M. E. K. Hussey 56, D. R. Martyn 66, R. J. Campbell 75, A. C. Gilchrist 79, G. B. Hogg 93; J. Moss 4-50). *Western Australia 6 pts.*

No Victorian reached 40 in either innings. Damien Martyn, who like Gilchrist was playing his only Pura Cup match of the season, and Jo Angel made their 100th first-class appearances for Western Australia.

At Hobart, November 22, 23, 24, 25. **New South Wales won by 22 runs.** Toss: Tasmania. **New South Wales 393** (M. G. Bevan 70, S. M. Katich 84, D. A. Nash 50) **and 86** (D. G. Wright 6-39, S. J. Jurgensen 4-29); **Tasmania 224** (M. G. Dighton 54; D. A. Nash 6-48) **and 233** (M. J. Di Venuto 52, S. R. Watson 75; S. R. Clark 6-84). *New South Wales 6 pts.*

New South Wales recorded their second-lowest total against Tasmania (after 84 at Hobart in 1999-2000). The highest scorer was Brad Haddin with 24.

At Melbourne, November 22, 23, 24, 25. **Victoria won by an innings and 77 runs.** Toss: South Australia. **South Australia 202** (M. C. Miller 63; M. L. Lewis 6-64) **and 250** (B. A. Johnson 51, M. A. Higgs 71); **Victoria 529-9 dec.** (M. T. G. Elliott 191, B. J. Hodge 96, J. Moss 103*). *Victoria 6 pts.*

Victoria scored 500 for the first time in five years.

At Brisbane, November 24, 25, 26. **Queensland won by ten wickets.** Toss: Western Australia. **Western Australia 228** (R. J. Campbell 62) **and 126; Queensland 331** (W. A. Seccombe 134*) **and 24-0.** *Queensland 6 pts.*

At Perth, December 8, 9, 10, 11. **Drawn.** Toss: Tasmania. **Western Australia 255** (C. J. L. Rogers 51, L. Ronchi 90) **and 405** (M. W. Goodwin 176; X. J. Doherty 4-92); **Tasmania 382** (M. J. Di Venuto 101, S. R. Mason 60, D. J. Marsh 88). *Tasmania 2 pts.*

Michael Di Venuto scored his first hundred on Australian soil since January 2000.

At Sydney, December 19, 20, 21. **Victoria won by nine wickets.** Toss: Victoria. **New South Wales 141** (S. M. Katich 59*) **and 150** (S. M. Harwood 5-54); **Victoria 269** (G. C. Rummans 67; D. Bollinger 4-50) **and 25-1.** *Victoria 6 pts.*

At Adelaide, December 19, 20, 21, 22. **Western Australia won by an innings and 33 runs.** Toss: South Australia. **South Australia 226** (D. A. Fitzgerald 63, S. A. Deitz 56; B. Casson 6-64) **and 261** (D. A. Fitzgerald 106, G. S. Blewett 54; B. A. Williams 5-38, B. Casson 4-112); **Western Australia 520-9 dec.** (J. L. Langer 164, M. W. Goodwin 164, M. E. K. Hussey 62). *Western Australia 6 pts.*

At Hobart, December 19, 20, 21, 22. **Queensland won by ten wickets.** Toss: Queensland. **Queensland 408-8 dec.** (M. L. Love 190, L. A. Carseldine 55) **and 3-0; Tasmania 191** (J. Cox 88) **and 219** (S. R. Mason 54). *Queensland 6 pts.*

Cox became the first man to play 150 first-class matches for an Australian state. On the first day, Queensland opener Brendan Nash did not score his first run for 88 minutes; he was 1 at lunch. Stuart Law took his 300th first-class catch.*

At Perth, January 4, 5, 6. **Queensland won by seven wickets.** Toss: Queensland. **Western Australia 107** (M. S. Kasprowicz 5-36) **and 201** (M. J. North 50; J. H. Dawes 5-75); **Queensland 151** (J. Angel 6-35) **and 160-3** (L. A. Carseldine 62*, C. T. Perren 79*). *Queensland 6 pts.*

Adam Dale of Queensland returned after a 15-month lay-off. Angel returned the best figures of his 12-year career.

At Hobart, January 15, 16, 17, 18. **Tasmania won by 87 runs.** Toss: Tasmania. **Tasmania 120** (D. J. Marsh 58*; S. M. Harwood 4-42) **and 396** (S. R. Mason 174, M. J. Di Venuto 79; M. L. Lewis 4-104); **Victoria 174** (J. Moss 76; D. G. Wright 4-61, A. R. Griffith 5-46) **and 255** (I. J. Harvey 74; A. G. Downton 4-53). *Tasmania 6 pts, Victoria 2 pts.*

Victorian wicket-keeper Berry held nine catches in the match, but was fined for alleging the umpires made "six or seven wrong decisions" on the second day.

At Brisbane, January 19, 20, 21, 22. **Queensland won by 208 runs.** Toss: South Australia. **Queensland 129 and 487-8 dec.** (C. T. Perren 224, S. G. Law 72, W. A. Seccombe 70; M. F. Cleary 4-85); **South Australia 208** (G. S. Blewett 66, S. A. Deitz 56*; J. H. Dawes 7-67) **and 200** (G. S. Blewett 135; M. S. Kasprowicz 5-44). *Queensland 6 pts, South Australia 2 pts.*

Queensland's fifth successive win. Clinton Perren's 224, his maiden double-hundred, lasted 501 minutes and 367 balls and included 33 fours. In South Australia's second innings, the next highest score after Blewett's 135 was 13 by Ben Higgins.

At Newcastle, January 23, 24, 25, 26. **New South Wales won by two runs.** Toss: Western Australia. **New South Wales 370** (M. J. Clarke 69, M. E. Waugh 73) **and 316-5 dec.** (S. M. Katich 50, M. J. Clarke 116, M. E. Waugh 83*); **Western Australia 388** (M. E. K. Hussey 90, S. E. Marsh 119; S. C. G. MacGill 4-100) **and 296** (C. J. L. Rogers 62, R. J. Campbell 70; S. C. G. MacGill 5-112, S. M. Katich 5-45). *New South Wales 6 pts, Western Australia 2 pts.*

This outground fixture attracted 16,192 spectators. Steve Waugh reached 22,000 first-class runs in the first innings, Mark Waugh 26,000 in the second. Set 299 in 72 overs, Western Australia needed 27 with six wickets and ten overs remaining, but lost all six for 24 with four balls to spare.

At Adelaide, February 4, 5, 6. **South Australia won by an innings and 125 runs.** Toss: South Australia. **South Australia 464** (M. J. Cosgrove 52, M. C. Miller 112, B. E. Young 115; A. A. Noffke 6-100); **Queensland 118** (M. F. Cleary 4-23) **and 221** (C. T. Perren 94). *South Australia 6 pts.*

Nos 8 and 9 Mick Miller and Brad Young added 222 in 224 minutes, a South Australian eighth-wicket record.

At Hobart, February 5, 6. **Drawn.** Toss: Tasmania. **Tasmania 179** (B. A. Williams 5-48); **Western Australia 52-3.** *Western Australia 6 pts.*

The first day started late because of rain, but the match was abandoned at lunch on the second day, because of a dangerous pitch. Western Australia were awarded six points, as for an outright win.

At Melbourne, February 5, 6, 7, 8. **Drawn.** Toss: New South Wales. **New South Wales 544-8 dec.** (G. J. Mail 57, S. R. Waugh 211, M. J. Clarke 78, B. J. Haddin 117) **and 113-4; Victoria 563-9 dec.** (J. L. Arnberger 105, M. P. Mott 216, P. J. Roach 108*; S. M. Katich 7-130). *Victoria 2 pts.*

Waugh's 211, his fifth double-hundred, lasted 517 minutes and 392 balls and included 21 fours and one six; Matthew Mott's 216, his first, lasted 608 minutes and 484 balls and included 24 fours and two sixes. Mott and Peter Roach were both playing their first match of the season, replacing Elliott (injured) and Berry (suspended). It was Roach's maiden hundred, but he did not play again.

At Brisbane, February 27, 28, March 1. **Queensland won by nine wickets.** Toss: Victoria. **Queensland 349** (C. T. Perren 136, A. A. Noffke 67*; M. W. H. Inness 5-61) **and 40-1; Victoria 159** (D. J. Hussey 62; M. S. Kasprowicz 5-50) **and 229** (J. Moss 66). *Queensland 6 pts.*

Martin Love of Queensland passed 1,000 first-class runs for the season. Queensland qualified for their fifth successive final.

At Hobart, February 27, 28, March 1, 2. **Tasmania won by eight wickets.** Toss: Tasmania. **Tasmania 285** (D. J. Marsh 111; P. C. Rofe 5-62) **and 65-2; South Australia 122** (G. J. Denton 5-40) **and 227** (M. A. Higgs 96*). *Tasmania 6 pts.*

Tasmania's Jamie Cox became the third player to reach 10,000 Shield/Pura runs, after Jamie Siddons and Darren Lehmann.

At Perth, February 27, 28, March 1, 2. **New South Wales won by two wickets.** Toss: Western Australia. **New South Wales 418-8 dec.** (G. J. Mail 90, M. J. Slater 204; M. J. Nicholson 4-96) **and 184-8** (M. E. Waugh 60*); **Western Australia 110** (G. J. Mail 4-18) **and 489** (C. J. L. Rogers 194, M. J. North 178; S. R. Clark 4-96). *New South Wales 6 pts.*

Michael Slater's 204, his fourth double-hundred but his first for New South Wales, lasted 301 minutes and 238 balls and included 26 fours and five sixes. Following on, Rogers and Marcus North added 369, a Western Australian fourth-wicket record, then seven wickets fell for 44. New South Wales needed 182 to win in a day plus ten overs, but collapsed to 92 for six before Mark Waugh saw them home.

At Sydney, March 6, 7, 8. **New South Wales won by 241 runs.** Toss: New South Wales. **New South Wales 102** (A. A. Noffke 6-24) **and 477-8 dec.** (S. M. Katich 60, S. R. Waugh 138, M. J. Clarke 120); **Queensland 190** (D. M. Payne 55; S. C. G. MacGill 5-52) **and 148** (S. C. G. MacGill 4-76, D. A. Nash 4-10). *New South Wales 6 pts, Queensland 2 pts.*

Michael Clarke scored 106 between tea and stumps on the second day, reaching 100 in 87 balls. Stuart MacGill took nine for 128 in the match, passing 50 wickets for the season, to see New South Wales to their first final in nine years.

At Adelaide, March 6, 7, 8, 9. **South Australia won by eight wickets.** Toss: South Australia. **South Australia 500-6 dec.** (D. A. Fitzgerald 147, S. A. Deitz 57, G. S. Blewett 88, M. A. Higgs 112*) **and 41-2; Tasmania 276** (M. J. Di Venuto 81, S. G. Clingeleffer 50, X. J. Doherty 52; S. W. Tait 5-68) **and 264** (M. J. Di Venuto 82, D. J. Marsh 58). *South Australia 6 pts.*

Blewett's 200th first-class match. Sean Clingeleffer did not concede a bye in South Australia's first innings.

At Melbourne, March 6, 7, 8, 9. **Victoria won by ten wickets.** Toss: Western Australia. **Western Australia 275** (C. J. L. Rogers 66, M. W. Goodwin 56, L. Ronchi 67; C. L. White 6-66) **and 253** (L. Ronchi 61; C. L. White 4-70); **Victoria 486** (J. L. Arnberger 54, M. P. Mott 61, B. J. Hodge 183) **and 45-0.** *Victoria 6 pts.*

FINAL

QUEENSLAND v NEW SOUTH WALES

At Brisbane, March 14, 15, 16. New South Wales won by 246 runs. Toss: Queensland. First-class debut: N. J. Kruger.

New South Wales had to win to deprive Queensland of a fourth successive title: they did it with more than two days in hand. Queensland had unleashed their strong seam attack in damp conditions on the opening day, when the floodlights were on after lunch. But after a two-hour rain-break, Slater reached a priceless hundred, and took his partnership with Katich to 191. Then Dawes struck three times in nine balls in the evening murk and, when Mark Waugh was out early next day, Queensland were on top. Only a cheerful stand of 49 in 36 minutes between Nash and Clark raised a decent total. But Queensland's reply lasted just two hours. After early damage by the seamers, MacGill's leg-spin caused havoc; in 32 balls, he claimed five for 16. Desperate slogging by Seccombe saved the follow-on. Though Slater lasted four balls second time around, his team-mates steadily built up the lead. Queensland needed 462 to win – or eight sessions' survival for the draw. Carseldine resisted over three hours, but wrist-spinners MacGill and Katich mopped up with six wickets.

Man of the Match: S. M. Katich. *Attendance:* 11,928.

Close of play: First day, New South Wales 223-6 (M. E. Waugh 1, Nash 7); Second day, New South Wales 166-4 (S. R. Waugh 47, M. E. Waugh 18).

New South Wales

M. J. Slater c Perren b Kasprowicz	100	– b Kasprowicz	2
G. J. Mail c Seccombe b Dale	2	– c Payne b Nash	47
S. M. Katich c Seccombe b Kasprowicz	82	– c Love b Dawes	36
*S. R. Waugh lbw b Dawes	9	– lbw b Kasprowicz	56
M. J. Clarke lbw b Dawes	0	– c Carseldine b Kasprowicz	11
M. E. Waugh c Love b Kasprowicz	1	– c Carseldine b Noffke	38
†B. J. Haddin lbw b Dawes	1	– c Seccombe b Noffke	0
D. A. Nash c Kasprowicz b Dawes	34	– c Love b Dawes	22
S. R. Clark c sub (M. A. Anderson) b Dawes	27	– b Dawes	32
S. C. G. MacGill not out	3	– not out	10
D. Bollinger b Kasprowicz	1	– c sub (M. A. Anderson) b Dale	3
L-b 13, w 1, n-b 8	22	L-b 4, n-b 2	6
1/2 (2) 2/193 (1) 3/213 (4) 4/213 (5) 5/213 (3) 6/215 (7) 7/225 (6) 8/274 (9) 9/281 (8) 10/282 (11)	282	1/2 (1) 2/61 (3) 3/115 (2) 4/130 (5) 5/193 (6) 6/193 (7) 7/193 (4) 8/236 (8) 9/251 (9) 10/263 (11)	263

Bowling: *First Innings*—Kasprowicz 23.2–4–102–4; Dale 18–3–41–1; Noffke 15–2–50–0; Dawes 21–4–66–5; Nash 3–1–10–0. *Second Innings*—Kasprowicz 26–8–70–3; Dale 25.2–10–72–1; Dawes 17–2–64–3; Nash 5–0–22–1; Perren 2–0–12–0; Noffke 5–2–19–2.

Queensland

D. M. Payne c and b Bollinger	13	– (2) c Mail b Clark	1
N. J. Kruger c M. E. Waugh b Nash	2	– (1) c Clark b Mail	34
*M. L. Love c Clarke b Nash	2	– c Haddin b Nash	13
L. A. Carseldine c Clarke b Mail	8	– lbw b Katich	65
C. T. Perren c M. E. Waugh b MacGill	15	– b MacGill	19
B. P. Nash c Mail b MacGill	8	– lbw b Katich	15
†W. A. Seccombe not out	24	– b Katich	13
A. C. Dale lbw b Mail	2	– c M. E. Waugh b MacGill	33
A. A. Noffke c S. R. Waugh b MacGill	0	– absent ill	
M. S. Kasprowicz c Haddin b MacGill	0	– (9) c Slater b MacGill	8
J. H. Dawes c M. E. Waugh b MacGill	0	– (10) not out	0
B 4, l-b 2, w 1, n-b 3	10	B 2, l-b 9, w 1, n-b 2	14
1/3 (2) 2/11 (3) 3/34 (4) 4/34 (1) 5/52 (6) 6/65 (5) 7/70 (8) 8/73 (9) 9/73 (10) 10/84 (11)	84	1/13 (2) 2/48 (1) 3/52 (3) 4/111 (5) 5/143 (6) 6/169 (7) 7/182 (4) 8/215 (9) 9/215 (8)	215

Bowling: *First Innings*—Clark 7–5–7–0; Nash 5–2–9–2; Bollinger 4–1–23–1; Mail 8–3–23–2; MacGill 5.2–0–16–5. *Second Innings*—Clark 13–1–45–1; Nash 9–0–37–1; Mail 7–2–15–1; MacGill 14–3–43–3; Bollinger 8–2–21–0; Katich 14–4–43–3.

Umpires: S. J. Davis and P. D. Parker.
Referee: R. G. Archer.

CHAMPIONS

Sheffield Shield

1892-93	Victoria
1893-94	South Australia
1894-95	Victoria
1895-96	New South Wales
1896-97	New South Wales
1897-98	Victoria
1898-99	Victoria
1899-1900	New South Wales
1900-01	Victoria
1901-02	New South Wales
1902-03	New South Wales
1903-04	New South Wales
1904-05	New South Wales
1905-06	New South Wales
1906-07	New South Wales
1907-08	Victoria
1908-09	New South Wales
1909-10	South Australia
1910-11	New South Wales
1911-12	New South Wales
1912-13	South Australia
1913-14	New South Wales
1914-15	Victoria
1915-19	No competition
1919-20	New South Wales
1920-21	New South Wales
1921-22	Victoria
1922-23	New South Wales
1923-24	Victoria
1924-25	Victoria
1925-26	New South Wales
1926-27	South Australia
1927-28	Victoria
1928-29	New South Wales
1929-30	Victoria
1930-31	Victoria
1931-32	New South Wales
1932-33	New South Wales
1933-34	Victoria
1934-35	Victoria
1935-36	South Australia
1936-37	Victoria
1937-38	New South Wales
1938-39	South Australia
1939-40	New South Wales
1940-46	No competition
1946-47	Victoria
1947-48	Western Australia
1948-49	New South Wales
1949-50	New South Wales
1950-51	Victoria
1951-52	New South Wales
1952-53	South Australia
1953-54	New South Wales
1954-55	New South Wales
1955-56	New South Wales
1956-57	New South Wales
1957-58	New South Wales
1958-59	New South Wales
1959-60	New South Wales
1960-61	New South Wales
1961-62	New South Wales
1962-63	Victoria

1963-64 South Australia
1964-65 New South Wales
1965-66 New South Wales
1966-67 Victoria
1967-68 Western Australia
1968-69 South Australia
1969-70 Victoria
1970-71 South Australia
1971-72 Western Australia
1972-73 Western Australia
1973-74 Victoria
1974-75 Western Australia
1975-76 South Australia
1976-77 Western Australia
1977-78 Western Australia
1978-79 Victoria
1979-80 Victoria
1980-81 Western Australia
1981-82 South Australia
1982-83 New South Wales
1983-84 Western Australia
1984-85 New South Wales
1985-86 New South Wales
1986-87 Western Australia
1987-88 Western Australia
1988-89 Western Australia
1989-90 New South Wales
1990-91 Victoria
1991-92 Western Australia
1992-93 New South Wales
1993-94 New South Wales
1994-95 Queensland
1995-96 South Australia
1996-97 Queensland
1997-98 Western Australia
1998-99 Western Australia

Pura Milk Cup
1999-2000 Queensland

Pura Cup
2000-01 Queensland
2001-02 Queensland
2002-03 New South Wales

New South Wales have won the title 43 times, Victoria 25, Western Australia 15, South Australia 13, Queensland 5, Tasmania 0.

ING CUP, 2002-03

Note: Matches in this section were not first-class.
Each side had 12 players of whom 11 could bat and 11 field.

	Played	*Won*	*Lost*	*Tied*	*Bonus points*	*Points*	*Net run-rate*
Western Australia . . .	10	7	3	0	2	30	0.29
New South Wales . . .	10	6	3	1	2	28	0.19
Queensland	10	6	4	0	3	27	0.67
Tasmania.	10	5	4	1	3	25	0.45
Victoria.	10	4	6	0	2	18	–0.38
South Australia.	10	1	9	0	0	4	–1.20

Final

At Perth, February 23. **New South Wales won by seven wickets.** Toss: Western Australia. **Western Australia 207** (49.5 overs); **New South Wales 211-3** (26.5 overs) (S. M. Katich 75*, S. R. Waugh 88).

Man of the Match Stuart Clark (3-34) reduced Western Australia to 65-5 in 16 overs; Peter Worthington (49) launched a recovery, but Waugh's 88 in 55 balls helped New South Wales to secure their third successive limited-overs title with 23 overs to spare.*

PURA CUP PLAYER OF THE YEAR

The Pura Cup Player of the Year Award for 2002-03 was won by Clinton Perren of Queensland, who was awarded 17 points despite playing only six qualifying games. His team-mate Michael Kasprowicz finished second with 14 points, one ahead of South Australia's David Fitzgerald. The Award, instituted in 1975-76, is adjudicated by the umpires over the course of the season. Each of the two umpires standing in each of the 30 Pura Cup matches (excluding the final) allocated marks of 3, 2 and 1 to the three players who most impressed them during the game. The ING Cup Player of the Year award, decided on similar lines, was won by Justin Langer of Western Australia.

CRICKET IN SOUTH AFRICA, 2002-03

COLIN BRYDEN AND ANDREW SAMSON

Andrew Hall

The 2003 World Cup dominated the South African season, severely truncating the domestic competitions. The first-class SuperSport Series was completed by early November; in previous seasons, it would just have got going. The one-day Standard Bank Cup was decided by mid-January, two weeks before the world's stars started to arrive in South Africa.

The United Cricket Board's controversial decision, in July 2002, to scrap racial quotas at national and senior provincial level had no discernible effect on selection policies. In 2001-02, provinces had been committed to fielding a minimum of three "players of colour" for all matches. This quota was replaced by guidelines, but provinces adhered to the spirit of transformation. Northerns felt it necessary to issue a lengthy statement in October, explaining how injuries had caused them to select only two players of colour for a match against Easterns, and soliciting everyone's understanding.

Meanwhile, the UCB's annual general meeting in August 2003 elected the board's first black African president, Ray Mali of Border, to succeed Percy Sonn. The following day, after two years of debate, the board's general council decided to introduce a new structure for South African cricket, effective from 2004-05. The aim was to improve the domestic game's playing standards and financial viability. In May, the 11 provincial unions had rejected a proposal to reduce the number of teams to seven, and supported the introduction of two divisions, with promotion and relegation.

But in August the general council settled on more drastic reform. From 2004-05, the first-class competition would be contested by six professional "franchises", to be awarded after a bidding process. It was expected that the teams would be based in the main Test centres, Johannesburg, Cape Town, Durban, Centurion, Port Elizabeth and Bloemfontein.

The 11 existing provinces would play in amateur competitions, which would serve as a feeder system for the professional teams, along with sides from the hitherto neglected areas of Limpopo, Mpumalanga, South Western Districts, Border-Kei (formerly Transkei) and KwaZulu-Natal Inland.

Ironically, the 2002-03 SuperSport Series, the penultimate first-class competition in its present form, was won for the first time by Easterns, one of the "minor" provinces. Easterns, whose headquarters in Benoni are a short drive from both Johannesburg and Centurion, were formerly part of North-Eastern Transvaal and were likely to be a minor partner in one of the two Gauteng franchises. They did not even have a sponsor.

Because of the World Cup, the second stage of the SuperSport Series – the Super Six, for the most successful sides, and the Shield for the weaker ones – was dropped, cutting three games for each team. Instead, the winners of the two preliminary pools advanced straight to the final.

After a draw with Gauteng, Easterns gained convincing wins in their three remaining games in Pool B, and even secured home advantage in the final, because of a better points-per-match average than Western Province, who topped Pool A. None the less, it was widely expected that Western Province would win their third first-class title in five seasons. They had all their international players available except Jacques Kallis, who had a sore knee, whereas Easterns, with more limited resources at the best of times, were crippled by the absence of three injured bowlers, including the UCB-contracted Andre Nel. But, despite losing five wickets in the final's first 15 overs, Easterns turned the game round in their second innings, rolled Western Province over for 128, and won by 273 runs.

Easterns benefited from their neighbours' personality clashes

Easterns had imported much of their talent from neighbouring Gauteng, including their influential coach, Ray Jennings, the captain, Derek Crookes, the player of the season, all-rounder Andrew Hall, who took 36 wickets in five matches, and their leading batsman, Zander de Bruyn. Jennings instilled a robust competitiveness, which was appropriate for a side representing a hardy gold community, although Easterns unquestionably benefited from the administrative difficulties and personality clashes suffered in recent years by their Gauteng neighbours.

There was consolation for Western Province when they trounced Griqualand West in the Standard Bank Cup final. They also supplied the bulk of the national team once again, with nine players representing South Africa during the season. But they seldom had a settled side. H. D. Ackerman, the appointed captain, played only one first-class match because of injury, was not selected for the knockout matches of the limited-overs campaign, and finally left Cape Town for Gauteng. Charl Willoughby, the left-arm opening bowler, stood out with a haul of 38 wickets in six matches, the most in the SuperSport Series; he and the experienced Alan Dawson won their first Test caps in Bangladesh in April. They were backed up by Quinton Friend, a promising fast bowler who became a regular for South Africa A, and two international left-arm spinners, in Claude Henderson and Paul Adams. Left-hander Ashwell Prince lost his place in the national side but had a fearsome season for the province, scoring 556 SuperSport runs at 111.20.

Free State lost heavily to Western Province in their first match, and Andy Moles, in his fifth season as coach, was immediately dismissed. Thereafter, Jimmy Adams, the former West Indian captain, led them to second place in the SuperSport Pool A, and to the brink of the one-day semi-finals – but he too was released after moderate form with the bat. Northerns lost only to eventual champions Easterns in the SuperSport Series, though they had a dreadful one-day campaign. They had four pace and swing bowlers out of action, but they had strong batting – another solid season finally won Jacques Rudolph a Test place – and promise for the future: the B team were finalists in the three-day UCB Bowl competition, and Northerns were Under-19 champions.

Border, now coached by ex-player Wayne Wiblin, won three of their five first-class games – up from one in eight in 2001-02 – and reached the one-day semi-finals, despite losing Mark Boucher and Makhaya Ntini to the South African team and Vasbert Drakes to West Indies. It was a major surprise when, at the end of the season, captain Pieter Strydom was replaced by the inexperienced Justin Kreusch. Monde Zondeki, the talented young fast bowler, was also part of the national squad for much of the season, but played in all Border's first-class matches, and was their leading wicket-taker with 18.

KwaZulu-Natal, double champions in 2001-02, made no impression in either competition. An administrative decision to persist with a quota of four players of colour reportedly caused some disenchantment, and mixed results indicated a lack of harmony. Nixon McLean, the West Indian strike bowler who starred in their double-winning season, had niggling hamstring problems. One of the few highlights was the fine all-round form of Jon Kent. Griqualand West did well to reach the Standard Bank Cup final. In the longer game, they could seldom muster enough bowling firepower; their batting was stronger, with Martyn Gidley and Brett Tucker both scoring over 350 runs.

Gauteng drew all their first-class matches, and David Terbrugge had to carry their bowling almost single-handedly, though the batting was much better. During the off-season, Gauteng made some important signings in a bid to regain the glories of the old Transvaal days, including Crookes from Easterns, and Ackerman from Western Province, who became captain.

Eastern Province, coached by former national captain Kepler Wessels, failed to maintain the promise of their opening match, against North West, in which James Bryant and his captain, Carl Bradfield, shared a South African record second-wicket stand of 441. North West never won a first-class match despite James Henderson's 576 runs in four SuperSport games. At least they lost only one; Boland lost four out of five, though they headed their one-day pool, only to succumb to Griquas in the semis. Namibia, who played in the one-day competition as part of their preparations for the World Cup, lost all their matches.

FIRST-CLASS AVERAGES, 2002-03

BATTING

(Qualification: 6 completed innings, average 40.00)

	M	*I*	*NO*	*R*	*HS*	*100s*	*Avge*	*Ct/St*
J. H. Kallis (*W. Province & South Africa*)	7	8	2	525	139*	2	87.50	10
H. H. Gibbs (*W. Province & South Africa*)	7	10	1	776	228	3	86.22	5
†J. M. Henderson (*North West & Rest*)	5	9	1	606	122	3	75.75	2
H. H. Dippenaar (*Free State, SA A & S. Africa*)	5	7	0	525	144	2	75.00	3
†G. C. Smith (*W. Province & South Africa*)	8	11	1	613	200	2	61.30	20
Z. de Bruyn (*Easterns*)	5	9	2	421	169	1	60.14	4
J. D. C. Bryant (*E. Province*)	4	8	1	403	234*	1	57.57	4
†G. Kirsten (*W. Province & South Africa*)	11	14	1	733	160	3	56.38	13
†C. C. Bradfield (*E. Province*)	4	8	0	448	196	1	56.00	4
A. M. Bacher (*Gauteng & Rest*)	5	9	1	433	146	2	54.12	4
†A. G. Prince (*W. Province, S. Africa & SA A*)	11	13	2	594	143	2	54.00	9
†J. A. Rudolph (*Northerns, S. Africa & SA A*)	7	12	0	647	106	3	53.91	6
G. F. J. Liebenberg (*Free State*)	5	8	1	370	115	2	52.85	6
J. C. Kent (*KwaZulu-Natal & Rest*)	7	12	0	580	162	2	48.33	7
D. J. Cullinan (*Gauteng & South Africa A*)	5	8	0	383	142	1	47.87	5
M. N. van Wyk (*Free State*)	5	8	1	323	80	0	46.14	16/2
†M. I. Gidley (*Griqualand W.*)	5	10	2	361	84*	0	45.12	4
D. J. Jacobs (*North West & Rest*)	5	9	1	359	146	1	44.87	6
P. de Bruyn (*Easterns*)	5	8	1	314	120	1	44.85	5
R. Munnik (*W. Province*)	5	7	1	265	87	0	44.16	4
C. D. de Lange (*Boland & Rest*)	7	12	3	397	73	0	44.11	2
B. H. Tucker (*Griqualand W.*)	5	10	1	394	182*	1	43.77	2
†N. C. Johnson (*W. Province*)	5	7	0	301	119	1	43.00	10
A. J. Seymore (*Easterns*)	5	10	1	377	147	1	41.88	4
A. N. Petersen (*Northerns, SA A & Rest*)	7	13	1	502	150*	2	41.83	7
N. D. McKenzie (*Northerns, SA A & SA*)	10	16	2	585	160	2	41.78	12

† *Left-handed batsman.*

BOWLING

(Qualification: 15 wickets)

	Style	*O*	*M*	*R*	*W*	*BB*	*5W/i*	*Avge*
A. J. Hall (*Easterns, SA A & S. Africa*)	RFM	296	97	599	42	6-77	4	14.26
A. N. W. Tweedie (*KwaZulu-Natal*)	RFM	89.2	19	273	17	5-50	1	16.05
M. Ntini (*Border & South Africa*)	RF	258.4	66	739	42	5-19	1	17.59
Z. de Bruyn (*Easterns*)	RFM	108	21	326	17	4-41	0	19.17
D. J. Terbrugge (*Gauteng, SA & SA A*)	RFM	153.3	27	434	22	5-46	1	19.72
P. V. Mpitsang (*Free State*)	RFM	159.5	44	400	20	3-37	0	20.00
J. H. Kallis (*W. Province & S. Africa*)	RFM	163.5	44	465	23	5-21	1	20.21
S. M. Pollock (*South Africa*)	RFM	160.3	55	350	17	4-45	0	20.58
C. M. Willoughby (*W. Province & Rest*)	LFM	308.1	93	835	38	5-49	4	21.97
N. A. M. McLean (*KwaZulu-Natal*)	RFM	104.2	18	366	16	4-47	0	22.87
R. J. Peterson (*E. Province & SA A*)	SLA	200.3	48	571	24	6-72	2	23.79
G. J. Kruis (*Griqualand W.*)	RFM	197.3	54	525	22	5-31	2	23.86
J. F. Venter (*Free State*)	OB	177.4	36	484	20	4-31	0	24.20
P. Joubert (*Northerns & Rest*)	RFM	188.2	64	391	16	5-65	1	24.43
C. W. Henderson (*W. Province & SA*)	SLA	284.3	95	625	25	7-99	1	25.00
M. Zondeki (*Border & SA A*)	RF	172.3	41	495	19	4-22	0	26.05
C. K. Langeveldt (*Boland & SA A*)	RFM	193	68	453	17	3-19	0	26.64
Z. A. Abrahim (*Griqualand W. & Rest*)	RFM	176.2	52	450	16	5-56	1	28.12

	Style	O	M	R	W	BB	5W/i	Avge
A. Nel (*Easterns & South Africa A*)	RFM	199	61	511	18	3-42	0	28.38
J. Louw (*Griqualand W.*)	RFM	179	44	599	21	6-108	1	28.52
A. C. Dawson (*W. Province & Rest*)	RFM	179	60	489	17	3-15	0	28.76
J. C. Kent (*KwaZulu-Natal & Rest*)	RFM	132.3	22	521	18	3-29	0	28.94
M. Hayward (*E. Province & S. Africa*)	RF	239.3	53	804	27	5-56	1	29.77
S. Elworthy (*Northerns, SA A & SA*)	RFM	172.1	44	546	18	4-50	0	30.33

SUPERSPORT SERIES, 2002-03

Pool A					Bonus Points		
	Played	*Won*	*Lost*	*Drawn*	*Batting*	*Bowling*	*Points*
Western Province	5	3	0	2	21.18	17	68.18
Free State	5	3	1	1	15.30	17	62.30
Border	5	3	1	1	12.62	15	57.62
KwaZulu-Natal	5	2	3	0	14.30	18	52.30
Griqualand West	5	1	3	1	17.84	12	39.84
Boland	5	0	4	1	14.68	10	24.68

Pool B					Bonus Points		
	Played	*Won*	*Lost*	*Drawn*	*Batting*	*Bowling*	*Points*
Easterns	4	3	0	1	12.76	14	56.76
Northerns	4	1	1	2	9.68	13	32.68
Gauteng	4	0	0	4	13.36	12	25.36
Eastern Province	4	0	2	2	13.30	10	23.30
North West	4	0	1	3	13.56	8	21.56

Final: Easterns beat Western Province by 273 runs.

Outright win = 10 pts.
Bonus points awarded for the first 100 overs of each team's first innings. One batting point was awarded for the first 150 runs and 0.02 of a point for every subsequent run. One bowling point was awarded for the third wicket taken and for every subsequent two.

Pool A

At Bloemfontein, September 20, 21, 22, 23. **Western Province won by an innings and 14 runs.** Toss: Free State. **Free State 164** (J. J. van der Wath 56; C. M. Willoughby 5-49) **and 198** (J. C. Adams 67*; C. M. Willoughby 5-54); **Western Province 376-9 dec.** (A. G. Prince 98, J. J. McLean 57, R. Munnik 87). *Western Province 17.92 pts, Free State 3.28 pts.*

At Kimberley, September 20, 21, 22. **Griqualand West won by eight wickets.** Toss: Griqualand West. **Boland 333** (V. G. Kambli 61, S. J. Palframan 95) **and 188** (C. D. de Lange 58; C. Pietersen 6-43); **Griqualand West 369** (B. H. Tucker 182*, W. Bossenger 50) **and 156-2** (M. I. Gidley 68*, P. P. J. Koortzen 67). *Griqualand West 19.06 pts, Boland 8.66 pts.*

Tucker's 182 was the highest score by a batsman carrying his bat in South African first-class cricket.

At Durban, September 20, 21, 22, 23. **Border won by 76 runs.** Toss: KwaZulu-Natal. **Border 181** (S. C. Pope 58; N. A. M. McLean 4-69) **and 286** (S. C. Pope 86; N. A. M. McLean 4-47); **KwaZulu-Natal 102** (M. Zondeki 4-22, A. A. W. Pringle 4-40) **and 289** (J. C. Kent 104; T. Henderson 4-55). *Border 15.62 pts, KwaZulu-Natal 4 pts.*

At East London, September 27, 28, 29. **Free State won by an innings and 41 runs.** Toss: Border. **Border 172** (P. C. Strydom 67, T. Henderson 53) **and 136** (D. Pretorius 5-65, J. F. Venter 4-31); **Free State 349** (J. A. Beukes 89, M. N. van Wyk 80). *Free State 16.88 pts, Border 3.44 pts.*

Vasbert Drakes was recorded as timed out – only the second instance in first-class cricket – in Border's first innings: he had not even reached the ground, having been delayed on a flight from Colombo, where he had been with the West Indian squad. He did arrive in time to bowl.

At Kimberley, September 27, 28, 29, 30. **Drawn.** Toss: Griqualand West. **Griqualand West 330** (L. L. Bosman 140, W. Bossenger 64; R. Telemachus 4-72, C. M. Willoughby 4-74) **and 345** (B. H. Tucker 67, M. I. Gidley 54, W. Bossenger 82; C. W. Henderson 7-99); **Western Province 351** (L. D. Ferreira 124, A. G. Prince 64, R. Munnik 67; G. J. Kruis 5-66) **and 108-2** (G. Kirsten 56*). *Griqualand West 7.04 pts, Western Province 7.32 pts.*

Griquas wicket-keeper Bossenger held six catches in Western Province's first innings.

At Durban, September 27, 28, 29, 30. **KwaZulu-Natal won by 69 runs.** Toss: Boland. **KwaZulu-Natal 325** (D. J. Watson 129) **and 153; Boland 244** (C. D. de Lange 73, L. J. Wilkinson 87) **and 165.** *KwaZulu-Natal 16.94 pts, Boland 4.88 pts.*

Watson took 96 minutes (53 balls) to score his first run, reached his century in 316 minutes (246 balls) and batted seven hours (313 balls) in all.

At East London, October 4, 5, 6, 7. **Border won by 71 runs.** Toss: Griqualand West. **Border 465-9 dec.** (M. L. Bruyns 153, S. C. Pope 87, P. C. Strydom 116; J. Louw 6-108) **and 107** (C. B. Sugden 50; G. J. Kruis 5-31, Z. A. Abrahim 4-39); **Griqualand West 334** (M. I. Gidley 71, W. Bossenger 54) **and 167** (L. L. Bosman 75; V. C. Drakes 6-47). *Border 16.22 pts, Griqualand West 4.78 pts.*

Bruyns and Strydom added 205, a Border fourth-wicket record. Bossenger made his 200th first-class dismissal.

At Bloemfontein, October 4, 5, 6, 7. **Free State won by five wickets.** Toss: Free State. **KwaZulu-Natal 211** (H. M. Amla 64; J. J. van der Wath 5-47) **and 341** (R. Gobind 63, A. M. Amla 64, J. C. Kent 57, H. M. Amla 78; J. F. Venter 4-74); **Free State 323** (G. F. J. Liebenberg 115, H. C. Bakkes 50; N. A. M. McLean 4-72) **and 232-5** (G. F. J. Liebenberg 110*, J. A. Beukes 56). *Free State 18.46 pts, KwaZulu-Natal 6.22 pts.*

Liebenberg became the seventh player to score a hundred in each innings for Free State.

At Bellville, October 4, 5, 6. **Western Province won by an innings and 20 runs.** Toss: Western Province. **Western Province 411-4 dec.** (G. Kirsten 121, A. G. Prince 133, H. D. Ackerman 59*); **Boland 191** (V. G. Kambli 68; P. R. Adams 4-25) **and 200** (C. D. de Lange 61*; C. W. Henderson 4-53). *Western Province 18.82 pts, Boland 2.82 pts.*

The P. P. Smit Stadium, a dozen miles east of Cape Town, hosted only its second first-class match (after a B team fixture in 1997-98). Kirsten and Prince added 253, a Western Province second-wicket record.

At Paarl, October 11, 12, 13, 14. **Border won by four wickets.** Toss: Boland. **Boland 276** (H. Davids 64, S. J. Palframan 72*) **and 183** (S. J. Palframan 51); **Border 339** (M. V. Boucher 112, P. C. Strydom 60, L. L. Gamiet 54; J. L. Ontong 4-66) **and 124-6** (M. L. Bruyns 60). *Border 15.88 pts, Boland 4.4 pts.*

Boland wicket-keeper Palframan held six catches in Border's first innings. Strydom broke Ian Howell's record for Border of 57 first-class catches in the field.

At Bloemfontein, October 11, 12, 13, 14. **Free State won by 240 runs.** Toss: Griqualand West. **Free State 322** (G. F. J. Liebenberg 71, H. H. Dippenaar 57, M. N. van Wyk 64; G. J. Kruis 4-77, Z. A. Abrahim 5-56) **and 269-9 dec.** (H. H. Dippenaar 94, M. N. van Wyk 71*); **Griqualand West 219** (J. Louw 56*) **and 132** (J. J. van der Wath 4-37). *Free State 18.18 pts, Griqualand West 5.38 pts.*

In his 100th match for Free State, Liebenberg overtook Louis Wilkinson's record of 5,790 first-class runs for the province.

At Durban, October 11, 12, 13, 14. **Western Province won by an innings and four runs.** Toss: Western Province. **KwaZulu-Natal 354** (H. M. Amla 75, L. Klusener 56, J. C. Kent 59) **and 236** (A. Mall 51); **Western Province 594-8 dec.** (G. C. Smith 56, H. H. Gibbs 203, A. G. Prince 143, N. C. Johnson 69). *Western Province 19.02 pts, KwaZulu-Natal 6.36 pts.*

Gibbs's 203, his third double-hundred, lasted 333 minutes and 259 balls and included 23 fours and five sixes. Johnson made his 200th first-class catch.

At Paarl, October 18, 19, 20, 21. **Drawn.** Toss: Boland. **Boland 289** (J. L. Ontong 104, V. G. Kambli 60) **and 200-7** (J. L. Ontong 50, V. G. Kambli 61); **Free State 474-7 dec.** (H. H. Dippenaar 144, J. F. Venter 111, M. N. van Wyk 59, H. C. Bakkes 62*). *Boland 3.92 pts, Free State 5.5 pts.*

At Kimberley, October 18, 19, 20, 21. **KwaZulu-Natal won by 151 runs.** Toss: KwaZulu-Natal. **KwaZulu-Natal 465** (A. M. Amla 85, J. C. Kent 162, D. M. Benkenstein 67, L. Klusener 65*) **and 206-6 dec.** (E. L. R. Stewart 51*, R. P. Symcox 68*); **Griqualand West 229** (B. H. Tucker 50; A. N. W. Tweedie 5-50) **and 291** (M. I. Gidley 84*). *KwaZulu-Natal 18.78 pts, Griqualand West 3.58 pts.*

Russel Symcox, son of Pat and grandson of Rodger, made his debut. The Symcoxes thus became the tenth family to produce three generations of South African first-class cricketers.

At Bellville, October 18, 19, 20, 21. **Drawn.** Toss: Western Province. **Border 348** (C. B. Sugden 121, I. Mitchell 59; Q. Friend 4-59) **and 335-9 dec.** (S. C. Pope 101; J-P. Duminy 4-89); **Western Province 255-8 dec.** (N. C. Johnson 119) **and 258-8.** *Western Province 5.1 pts, Border 6.46 pts.*

Pool B

At Johannesburg, September 20, 21, 22, 23. **Drawn.** Toss: Gauteng. **Gauteng 405-9 dec.** (D. J. Cullinan 142, E. T. Nkwe 106, S. Conrad 51*; J. A. Morkel 6-110) **and 145-7 dec.; Easterns 380** (A. J. Seymore 89, Z. de Bruyn 68; D. J. Terbrugge 4-59, G. D. Elliott 4-56) **and 108-5** (Z. de Bruyn 53*). *Gauteng 5.88 pts, Easterns 5.26 pts.*

Enoch Nkwe, aged 19, scored 106 on first-class debut.

At Potchefstroom, September 20, 21, 22, 23. **Drawn.** Toss: North West. **Eastern Province 442-2 dec.** (C. C. Bradfield 196, J. D. C. Bryant 234*) **and 219-3 dec.** (J. D. C. Bryant 88, W. R. Wingfield 51*); **North West 297** (J. M. Henderson 77, A. Jacobs 64) **and 271-9** (A. Jacobs 73, M. C. Venter 72). *North West 3.44 pts, Eastern Province 6.18 pts.*

Bryant's 234, his maiden double-hundred, lasted 484 minutes and 414 balls and included 39 fours. It was the highest score for Eastern Province in Currie Cup/SuperSport cricket. He added 441 with Bradfield, a South African second-wicket record, after Johan Botha was out in the first over.*

At Port Elizabeth, September 27, 28, 29, 30. **Northerns won by 82 runs.** Toss: Eastern Province. **Northerns 396** (J. A. Rudolph 60, A. N. Petersen 109, P. Joubert 50, C. F. K. van Wyk 64) **and 221-5 dec.; Eastern Province 315** (C. C. Bradfield 64, J. D. C. Bryant 50; P. Joubert 5-65) **and 220.** *Northerns 16.76 pts, Eastern Province 5 pts.*

In Northerns' second innings, Gerald Dros scored 43 in 21 balls, with four fours and four sixes.*

At Benoni, September 27, 28, 29, 30. **Easterns won by nine wickets.** Toss: North West. **Easterns 356** (D. N. Crookes 75, P. de Bruyn 72) **and 96-1; North West 187** (A. J. Hall 5-50, Z. de Bruyn 4-41) **and 264** (D. J. Jacobs 55, J. M. Henderson 64). *Easterns 17.68 pts, North West 4.74 pts.*

At Johannesburg, October 4, 5, 6, 7. **Drawn.** Toss: Eastern Province. **Eastern Province 380** (J. M. Kemp 67, R. J. Peterson 130, W. R. Wingfield 72; E. T. Nkwe 5-78) **and 172-4** (J. Botha 59*, W. R. Wingfield 54*); **Gauteng 388** (A. M. Bacher 146, W. A. Dugmore 72; J. M. Kemp 4-46, R. J. Peterson 5-120). *Gauteng 7.18 pts, Eastern Province 7.1 pts.*

At Centurion, October 4, 5, 6, 7. **Drawn.** Toss: Northerns. **Northerns 312-9 dec.** (A. N. Petersen 69) **and 327-4 dec.** (A. N. Petersen 150*, J. A. Rudolph 102; F. van der Merwe 4-119); **North West 401** (J. M. Henderson 122, A. Jacobs 71, A. C. Thomas 119*; S. Elworthy 4-50) **and 149-2** (D. J. Jacobs 68*). *Northerns 4.88 pts, North West 6.12 pts.*

Rudolph and Petersen added 106 and 174 for the first wicket in Northerns' two innings.

At Benoni, October 11, 12, 13, 14. **Easterns won by 146 runs.** Toss: Easterns. **Easterns 262 and 253** (A. J. Hall 64; G. M. Hampson 4-59); **Northerns 124** (A. J. Hall 4-37) **and 245** (M. van Jaarsveld 54; A. J. Hall 4-59). *Easterns 17.24 pts, Northerns 4 pts.*

Andre Nel became the first bowler to take 100 first-class wickets for Easterns.

At Potchefstroom, October 11, 12, 13, 14. **Drawn.** Toss: North West. **North West 415** (J. M. Henderson 122, A. C. Thomas 75, G. A. Roe 56; S. E. Andrews 5-97) **and 235-4 dec.** (J. M. Henderson 110*); **Gauteng 259-8 dec.** (S. C. Cook 76, A. M. Bacher 58) **and 298-7** (W. A. Dugmore 100, M. R. Street 58*; M. Strydom 4-77). *North West 7.26 pts, Gauteng 6.02 pts.*

Henderson was the first batsman to score a hundred in each innings for North West.

At Port Elizabeth, October 18, 19, 20, 21. **Easterns won by six wickets.** Toss: Easterns. **Eastern Province 151** (A. J. Hall 4-29) **and 305** (C. C. Bradfield 56, J. Botha 56, W. R. Wingfield 81*; A. J. Hall 5-72); **Easterns 229** (Z. de Bruyn 62, P. de Bruyn 63; M. P. Nienaber 4-25) **and 230-4** (A. M. van den Berg 76, A. J. Hall 56*). *Easterns 16.58 pts, Eastern Province 5.02 pts.*

Easterns wicket-keeper Dylan Jennings held six catches in Eastern Province's first innings.

At Centurion, October 18, 19, 20, 21. **Drawn.** Toss: Gauteng. **Gauteng 214** (A. M. Bacher 51; C. J. Karemaker 4-65) **and 387-8 dec.** (A. M. Bacher 107, D. J. Cullinan 79, M. R. Street 54; P. L. Harris 4-133); **Northerns 252** (J. A. Rudolph 100, C. F. K. van Wyk 52*; S. E. Andrews 5-47) **and 340-9** (J. A. Rudolph 68, N. D. McKenzie 102). *Northerns 7.04 pts, Gauteng 6.28 pts.*

FINAL

EASTERNS v WESTERN PROVINCE

At Benoni, November 1, 2, 3, 4, 5. Easterns won by 273 runs. Toss: Easterns.

First-time finalists Easterns pulled off a conclusive victory over Western Province, who had eight internationals. No giant-killing seemed in prospect on the first morning, when Easterns crashed to 27 for five. But the back-up bowlers were less impressive, and the former Northerns player Pierre de Bruyn (no relation to Zander) counter-attacked with a fine century. Western Province overtook them with four wickets down, but their Test batsmen failed to capitalise after playing themselves in, Hall bowled brilliantly, and the eventual lead was no more than 71. The match was transformed on the third day, when Seymore and Zander de Bruyn added 213, a second-wicket record for Easterns. It was tedious at times, but Easterns ground out 472 by the fourth evening, leaving Western Province 96 overs to chase 402 or bat out to share the trophy. Crookes's off-breaks and Botha's left-arm spin had them in trouble; Hall ripped out the tail to finish with a career-best 11 for 99.

Man of the Match: A. J. Hall. *Man of the Series:* A. J. Hall.

Close of play: First day, Western Province 84-1 (Smith 45, Kirsten 10); Second day, Western Province 282-7 (Munnik 46, Henderson 0); Third day, Easterns 265-2 (Z. de Bruyn 99, Jennings 5); Fourth day, Easterns 472.

Easterns

First innings		Second innings	
A. J. Seymore c Smith b Willoughby	7	lbw b Willoughby	147
A. M. van den Berg b Willoughby	7	c Tsolekile b Henderson	8
Z. de Bruyn c Smith b Willoughby	8	c Prince b Willoughby	169
A. G. Botha b Dawson	3	(10) st Tsolekile b Henderson	18
*D. N. Crookes c Smith b Willoughby	34	(6) c Johnson b Dawson	3
A. J. Hall c Johnson b Dawson	0	(7) lbw b Willoughby	16
P. de Bruyn c Kirsten b Henderson	120	(8) b Willoughby	0
G. Toyana c Tsolekile b Willoughby	41	(9) c Smith b Willoughby	29
†D. Jennings lbw b Dawson	7	(4) c Tsolekile b Dawson	47
M. R. Sekhoto b Henderson	3	(5) c Smith b Henderson	10
G. E. Flusk not out	3	not out	14
B 1, n-b 4	5	L-b 1, w 1, n-b 4, p 5	11
1/14 (1) 2/15 (2) 3/27 (3) 4/27 (4) 5/27 (6) 6/87 (5) 7/221 (8) 8/225 (7) 9/232 (9) 10/238 (10)	238	1/27 (2) 2/240 (1) 3/339 (4) 4/352 (5) 5/364 (6) 6/407 (7) 7/407 (8) 8/412 (3) 9/445 (9) 10/472 (10)	472

Bowling: *First Innings*—Dawson 18–7–50–3; Willoughby 17–4–55–5; Friend 10–3–52–0; Johnson 9–1–36–0; Henderson 16.1–5–44–2. *Second Innings*—Dawson 44–14–110–2; Willoughby 40–12–106–5; Henderson 73.3–26–156–3; Friend 8–3–21–0; Johnson 4–0–13–0; Smith 13–3–42–0; Munnik 5–1–18–0.

Western Province

G. C. Smith st Jennings b Crookes	62	– c Jennings b Hall	3
H. H. Gibbs c Seymore b Flusk	22	– c Hall b Crookes	33
*G. Kirsten lbw b Hall	17	– b Crookes	22
A. G. Prince c Jennings b Hall	79	– (5) not out	26
N. C. Johnson st Jennings b van den Berg	30	– (6) c Seymore b Botha	16
R. Munnik c Jennings b Hall	54	– (4) c Jennings b Botha	3
†T. L. Tsolekile c Jennings b Hall	9	– (8) c Sekhoto b Hall	3
A. C. Dawson c Crookes b Z. de Bruyn	1	– (9) c Z. de Bruyn b Hall	0
C. W. Henderson not out	12	– (7) lbw b Botha	0
Q. Friend c P. de Bruyn b Hall	0	– lbw b Hall	0
C. M. Willoughby b Hall	0	– b Hall	4
B 7, l-b 10, w 2, n-b 4	23	B 5, l-b 9, n-b 4	18
1/60 (2) 2/101 (3) 3/133 (1) 4/206 (5) 5/243 (4) 6/254 (7) 7/276 (8) 8/293 (6) 9/293 (10) 10/309 (11)	309	1/6 (1) 2/73 (2) 3/74 (3) 4/80 (4) 5/108 (6) 6/114 (7) 7/119 (8) 8/121 (9) 9/121 (10) 10/128 (11)	128

Bowling: *First Innings*—Hall 39–10–77–6; Z. de Bruyn 17–3–64–1; Flusk 8–2–30–1; Crookes 28–9–62–1; van den Berg 12–4–21–1; Botha 15–4–38–0. *Second Innings*—Hall 19.4–11–22–5; Z. de Bruyn 7–0–27–0; Botha 25–10–40–3; Crookes 14–7–17–2; P. de Bruyn 3–1–5–0; van den Berg 5–3–3–0.

Umpires: B. G. Jerling and S. B. Lambson. Third umpire: I. L. Howell.

CHAMPIONS

Currie Cup

1889-90	Transvaal
1890-91	Kimberley
1892-93	Western Province
1893-94	Western Province
1894-95	Transvaal
1896-97	Western Province
1897-98	Western Province
1902-03	Transvaal
1903-04	Transvaal
1904-05	Transvaal
1906-07	Transvaal
1908-09	Western Province
1910-11	Natal
1912-13	Natal
1920-21	Western Province
1921-22	Transvaal/Natal/W. Prov. (Tied)
1923-24	Transvaal
1925-26	Transvaal
1926-27	Transvaal
1929-30	Transvaal
1931-32	Western Province
1933-34	Natal
1934-35	Transvaal
1936-37	Natal
1937-38	Natal/Transvaal (Tied)
1946-47	Natal
1947-48	Natal
1950-51	Transvaal
1951-52	Natal
1952-53	Western Province
1954-55	Natal
1955-56	Western Province
1958-59	Transvaal
1959-60	Natal
1960-61	Natal
1962-63	Natal
1963-64	Natal
1965-66	Natal/Transvaal (Tied)
1966-67	Natal
1967-68	Natal
1968-69	Transvaal
1969-70	Transvaal/W. Province (Tied)
1970-71	Transvaal
1971-72	Transvaal
1972-73	Transvaal
1973-74	Natal
1974-75	Western Province
1975-76	Natal
1976-77	Natal
1977-78	Western Province
1978-79	Transvaal
1979-80	Transvaal
1980-81	Natal
1981-82	Western Province
1982-83	Transvaal
1983-84	Transvaal
1984-85	Transvaal
1985-86	Western Province
1986-87	Transvaal
1987-88	Transvaal
1988-89	Eastern Province
1989-90	E. Province/W. Province (Shared)

Castle Cup	
1990-91	Western Province
1991-92	Eastern Province
1992-93	Orange Free State
1993-94	Orange Free State
1994-95	Natal
1995-96	Western Province

SuperSport Series	
1996-97	Natal
1997-98	Free State
1998-99	Western Province
1999-2000	Gauteng
2000-01	Western Province
2001-02	KwaZulu-Natal
2002-03	Easterns

Transvaal/Gauteng have won the title outright 25 times, Natal/KwaZulu-Natal 21, Western Province 17, Orange Free State/Free State 3, Eastern Province 2, Easterns and Kimberley 1. The title has been shared five times as follows: Transvaal 4, Natal and Western Province 3, Eastern Province 1.

Other first-class match

At L. C. de Villiers Oval, Pretoria, February 19, 20, 21. **South Africa A won by eight wickets.** Toss: Rest of South Africa. **Rest of South Africa 250-9 dec.** (H. M. Amla 108, J. C. Kent 71) **and 44-2 dec.; South Africa A forfeited first innings and 295-2** (J. A. Rudolph 106, M. van Jaarsveld 140*).

This match was staged to provide practice for players not appearing in the World Cup but in the frame for forthcoming tours.

STANDARD BANK CUP, 2002-03

Note: Matches in this section were not first-class.

Pool A	*Played*	*Won*	*Lost*	*No Result*	*Bonus Points*	*Points*	*Net run-rate*
Border	5	5	0	0	1	21	0.62
Griqualand West	5	3	2	0	0	12	−0.19
KwaZulu-Natal	5	2	3	0	1	9	0.05
Easterns	5	2	3	0	0	8	0.09
North West	5	2	3	0	0	8	−0.32
Northerns	5	1	4	0	0	4	−0.21

Pool B	*Played*	*Won*	*Lost*	*No Result*	*Bonus Points*	*Points*	*Net run-rate*
Boland	5	4	1	0	3	19	1.14
Western Province	5	4	1	0	1	17	0.62
Free State	5	3	2	0	2	14	0.78
Eastern Province	5	2	2	1	1	11	0.19
Gauteng	5	1	3	1	1	7	−0.79
Namibia	5	0	5	0	0	0	−1.94

Semi-finals

At Paarl, January 10 (day/night). **Griqualand West won by 65 runs.** Toss: Griqualand West. **Griqualand West 243-6** (45 overs) (L. L. Bosman 70, M. I. Gidley 51); **Boland 178** (36.4 overs) (C. Baxter 85).

At East London, January 10 (day/night). **Western Province won by 23 runs.** Toss: Western Province. **Western Province 228-7** (45 overs) (J. H. Kallis 88, G. Kirsten 103); **Border 205** (44 overs) (C. B. Sugden 50).

Final

At Cape Town, January 15 (day/night). **Western Province won by nine wickets.** Toss: Griqualand West. **Griqualand West 125** (38.2 overs) (M. I. Gidley 59; C. W. Henderson 4-26); **Western Province 129-1** (12.4 overs) (H. H. Gibbs 67*).

Gibbs scored 67 in 44 balls with ten fours and two sixes, adding 118* in 11.2 overs with Gary Kirsten.*

CRICKET IN THE WEST INDIES, 2002-03

TONY COZIER

Jerome Taylor

At last, a chink of sunshine broke through the clouds hanging over West Indies cricket. Much remained in shadow but, at the end of the international season in July, the outlook was brightening.

One of West Indies' youngest teams, including six players in their early twenties, finished a difficult home series against mighty Australia by amassing Test cricket's highest fourth-innings winning total in the fourth and final Test, following thrashings in the first three. Subsequent victory over Sri Lanka was a confident climax. New beginning or false dawn? Time would tell.

There was further cause for optimism. After cumulative losses of $15m over three years, the West Indies Cricket Board predicted a $1m profit for the year ending September 2003, thanks to a 63% rise in international gate receipts, and new sponsors. As the board gave a vote of confidence to the Cricket Academy in Grenada, heavily criticised in a report by two Australians the previous year, similar institutions sprouted elsewhere: in Trinidad & Tobago, on the University of the West Indies campus in Barbados, and in Jamaica.

The belatedly encouraging Test results coincided with Brian Lara's reinstatement as captain, three years after he resigned and took a break from the game to seek psychological counselling. Carl Hooper was dismissed, as much for his lack of tactical enterprise as for West Indies' early elimination from the World Cup in South Africa; he turned down selection against Australia, effectively ending a long but unfulfilled Test career. A reluctant Lara was persuaded to resume by the WICB president, the Reverend Wes Hall, and said it would have been "a dereliction of duty" to decline. He promised "a different Brian Lara"; he was certainly more involved, and relaxed, than on his first attempt.

Winning round Lara was one of Hall's last acts as president. Aged 65, he stepped down in July, citing medical reasons. As energetic in the presidency as he was in his pomp as a fearsome fast bowler, Hall could point to the financial recovery as a major achievement of his two years in office. But he was understandably shaken by the militancy of the West Indies Players' Association, which threatened strike action over contracts for the ICC Champions Trophy and the World Cup; they actually did strike in March, on the first day of the first-class semi-finals. "When I saw four teams out there and not playing, I think that's the darkest day ever in the West Indies," Hall said. Within a couple of months, the players' domestic pay was increased.

The choice of Hall's successor and, earlier, Roger Harper's as senior coach were embarrassing episodes. After the World Cup, Harper moved to the Academy, and the WICB announced that Bennett King, from the Australian Academy, would be its first foreign coach. King responded that no terms had been negotiated and rejected the appointment. The former Test batsman Gus Logie was elevated from youth coach instead, and confirmed for a three-year term in July.

Replacing Hall was even more contentious. The executive recommended Chetram Singh, head of the Guyana board, as the sole nomination, but Jamaica and Barbados supported Willie Rodriguez, a former Trinidad captain and Test all-rounder, though he later withdrew. Then it emerged that, because Singh owned a (legal) bookmaking operation, he would be ineligible to sit on the ICC executive board. His status compromised, Singh pulled out the day before the AGM in July, and a new election was called. In September Teddy Griffith was elected on a 9-4 vote over the former vice-president Clarvis Joseph. Griffith, a former all-rounder for both Barbados and Jamaica, is the son of the pre-war fast bowler Herman Griffith.

Barbados's title was based on an army-style camp and assertive captaincy

In domestic cricket, normal service resumed. Barbados, who have won almost as many regional championships as all the other teams combined, had had their pride stung the previous season, when they lost the Busta Cup and could not even qualify for the Busta International Shield. Their response was to become the first side to win both trophies – renamed the Carib Beer Cup and Carib Beer International Challenge – in one season. It completed a triple triumph; in September, Barbados had secured their first limited-overs title since 1987-88, defeating Jamaica in the Red Stripe Bowl final.

Barbados's 17th outright title was based on diligent preparation, including a week-long, army-style camp, and assertive captaincy by wicket-keeper Courtney Browne. They were unbeaten, and won six of their seven victories with a day to spare. Several old hands were to the fore. The left-handed Floyd Reifer and opener Philo Wallace were the leading batsmen; left-arm seamer Ian Bradshaw collected 28 wickets, and Corey Collymore returned from the World Cup to claim five in an innings in both Challenge games. It was not all down to experience. Tino Best, a bowler of pace and charisma, was the competition's leading wicket-taker, with 39 at 18.25 each, while Sulieman Benn, a beanpole left-arm spinner, had 27. In the final, Kurt Wilkinson redeemed a modest season with a vital 125. All three were 21.

Guyana and Trinidad & Tobago took second and third places in the Cup, but it was fourth-placed Jamaica who won through to their fourth successive first-class final. The World Cup claimed five Jamaican players, but they kept in the hunt and, in the semi, overturned the result of the 2001-02 final, just heading Guyana in a high-scoring match. They were then comprehensively outplayed by Barbados in a final overshadowed by the absence of opener Chris Gayle, who preferred a privately-organised international double-wicket tournament in St Lucia. The upshot was that, after 24 consecutive Tests, Gayle was dropped for the first two against Australia.

Three young Jamaicans announced themselves. Dave Bernard, 21, finished with a tournament aggregate of 551 – including a maiden hundred in the semi-final – plus 26 wickets from his steady medium-pace. Bernard made his Test debut, as did Jerome Taylor, a fast bowler who turned 19 during his first Test. Opener Brenton Parchment confirmed his potential, averaging 43.90 in his first full season.

With Shivnarine Chanderpaul available for just two matches (he scored hundreds in both) and Hooper just for the semi-final (he scored an unbeaten 130), Guyana were hard-pressed to build significant totals. Their only victories were over the Leewards and the Windwards, whose batting was even weaker. Guyana's bowling revolved around the spin of Neil McGarrell and Mahendra Nagamootoo, who took 62 wickets between them.

Although they reached a second successive semi-final, it was a disappointing season for Trinidad & Tobago, twice crushed by arch-rivals Barbados. Victories over the last three teams in the standings were scant consolation. Their runs came principally from their captain, Daren Ganga, with 722 at 51.57. The left-handed opener, Asif Jan, batted solidly, but the long-serving Lincoln Roberts and 19-year-old Dwayne Bravo fell away steadily after Roberts recorded a maiden double-century and Bravo 114 against West Indies B. Lara inevitably marked his return from the World Cup with a match-winning hundred against the Leewards. Two weeks later, he was out for nought in the semi-final against Barbados. Fast bowler Marlon Black took 30 wickets. But, in spite of the pace of 18-year-old Ravi Rampaul, Merv Dillon, on World Cup duty, was clearly missed, while leg-spinner Dinanath Ramnarine was shifting his focus towards his presidency of the players' association.

India A were the third foreign team to enter West Indies' first-class competition, following English and Bangladeshi sides. It was an opportunity to come to terms with a different environment, the bane of Indian teams abroad. Their overall form was inconsistent and their vaunted captain, V. V. S. Laxman, averaged only 15, against 79 in the Test tour a year earlier. Yet there was encouragement from younger players.

For the second season running, the Leeward Islands captain, Stuart Williams, was the tournament's highest scorer – his 827 runs, at 75.18, included three hundreds – but this time there was no Test recall. The rest of the batting was too brittle to reach the semi-final again. There was joy when 20-year-old all-rounder Omari Banks became the first Test cricketer from tiny Anguilla. Unreliable batting left the Windwards languishing in a familiar lowly position. The 21-year-old opener Devon Smith earned his first Test cap but, once he and former Test keeper Junior Murray were out, a collapse was never far away. Leg-spinner Orlanzo Jackson claimed 31 wickets.

When the WICB introduced the B team of Under-23s, its purpose was to give young players earlier experience of first-class cricket; critics charged that it would diminish standards. Although West Indies B have still won only two of their 21 matches, their players have begun to graduate to the Test team: during this season, Jermaine Lawson and Bernard (both now with Jamaica) and wicket-keeper Carlton Baugh. Left-handers Narsingh Deonarine (who scored hundreds against both the Indians and the Australians) and Aneil Kanhai scored heavily, and paceman Jason Bennett gathered 30 wickets at under 20 apiece.

Keen to spread the game, the WICB used 22 venues for the Carib Beer series. First-class cricket returned to Montserrat for the first time since two-thirds of the island was rendered uninhabitable by the volcanic eruption in 1995; St Croix and St Thomas in the US Virgin Islands were among five new grounds.

Many of these venues will be vying to host matches when the World Cup comes to the West Indies in 2006-07. It is a massive undertaking, given the region's peculiar problems: a dozen small, independent nations, all separated by water and all with limited infrastructure. The WICB set up a company, Windies World Cup 2007, headed by Rawle Brancker, a former Barbados all-rounder and successful businessman, with the board's former marketing director Chris Dehring as chief executive, to plan and execute the largest, most complex sporting event ever to come to the Caribbean. It could be the financial bonanza West Indies cricket needs, but it is a daunting project.

FIRST-CLASS AVERAGES, 2002-03

BATTING

(Qualification: 400 runs)

	M	*I*	*NO*	*R*	*HS*	*100s*	*Avge*	*Ct/St*
†B. C. Lara (*Trinidad & Tobago & West Indies*)	8	15	1	1,074	209	4	76.71	16
S. C. Williams (*Leeward Islands*)	7	13	2	827	167	3	75.18	5
†S. Chanderpaul (*Guyana & West Indies*)	5	9	0	558	145	4	62.00	3
†F. L. Reifer (*Barbados*)	9	15	2	624	105	1	48.00	12
†G. Gambhir (*India A*)	7	13	0	617	108	1	47.46	3
R. R. Sarwan (*West Indies*)	5	9	0	407	105	1	45.22	2
D. Ganga (*Trinidad & Tobago & West Indies*)	14	26	2	1,066	117	3	44.41	14
B. A. Parchment (*Jamaica*)	7	10	0	439	95	0	43.90	8
†N. Deonarine (*WI B, Guyana & Carib Beer XI*)	10	18	2	686	141*	2	42.87	10
P. A. Wallace (*Barbados & UWI VC XI*)	10	17	1	678	140	2	42.37	8
A. Chopra (*India A*)	7	13	0	537	174	1	41.30	10
†R. O. Hinds (*Barbados*)	8	13	3	412	88	0	41.20	9
C. S. Baugh (*West Indies B, Carib Beer XI & WI*)	11	20	2	738	115*	2	41.00	20/2
†C. C. Williams (*India A*)	6	11	1	403	89*	0	40.30	4
†A. Haniff (*Guyana*)	7	12	2	402	93*	0	40.20	2
S. L. Campbell (*Barbados*)	9	16	2	553	135	2	39.50	11

	M	I	NO	R	HS	100s	Avge	Ct/St
J. R. Murray (*Windward Islands*)	7	14	2	471	121	1	39.25	15/2
F. A. Adams (*Leeward Islands*)	7	14	1	471	103*	1	36.23	8
D. E. Bernard (*Jamaica, UWI VC XI & WI*)	12	19	2	612	109	1	36.00	7
O. A. C. Banks (*Leeward I., Carib Beer XI & WI*)	12	19	6	461	75	0	35.46	9
†A. Kanhai (*West Indies B & Carib Beer XI*)	8	15	0	528	223	2	35.20	3
†A. I. Jan (*Trinidad & Tobago*)	8	16	0	563	94	0	35.18	3
†C. H. Gayle (*Jamaica, UWI VC XI & WI*)	7	13	0	420	129	1	32.30	6
†D. S. Smith (*Windward I., Carib Beer XI & WI*)	13	25	0	806	101	1	32.24	10
R. K. Currency (*Windward Islands*)	7	14	0	432	92	0	30.85	4
†A. S. Jackson (*Trinidad & Tobago*)	8	16	0	466	90	0	29.12	8
D. J. J. Bravo (*T&T & Carib Beer XI*)	10	19	0	500	114	1	26.31	5

† *Left-handed batsman.*

BOWLING

(Qualification: 20 wickets)

	Style	O	M	R	W	BB	5W/i	Avge
C. E. Cuffy (*Windward Islands*)	RF	132.2	41	284	21	5-54	2	13.52
C. D. Collymore (*Barbados, UWI VC XI & WI*)	RFM	162.1	42	444	30	7-57	4	14.80
A. M. Salvi (*India A*)	RM	172.2	46	538	29	5-39	3	18.55
S. J. Benn (*Barbados*)	SLA	223.2	76	517	27	5-68	2	19.14
J. P. Bennett (*West Indies B*)	RFM	176	25	582	30	5-51	3	19.40
I. D. R. Bradshaw (*Barbados*)	LFM	200.5	55	569	28	4-43	0	20.32
T. L. Best (*Barbados & West Indies*)	RFM	231.2	39	873	40	5-40	2	21.82
N. C. McGarrell (*Guyana*)	SLA	357	115	725	32	5-33	2	22.65
G. R. Breese (*Jamaica*)	OB	263.2	61	640	28	4-74	0	22.85
N. O. Perry (*Jamaica*)	OB	211.1	48	522	22	8-64	1	23.72
A. Mishra (*India A*)	LB	219.2	38	635	26	5-30	2	24.42
J. J. C. Lawson (*Jamaica & West Indies*)	RF	137.4	18	514	21	7-78	1	24.47
K. C. B. Jeremy (*Leeward Islands*)	RFM	183	43	541	22	5-34	2	24.59
J. E. Taylor (*Jamaica & West Indies*)	RF	210	35	639	25	8-59	2	25.56
I. O. Jackson (*Windward Islands*)	LBG	348.3	79	828	31	5-89	1	26.70
R. L. Griffith (*Guyana*)	RFM	170	31	592	22	4-49	0	26.90
A. Sanford (*Leeward I. & Carib Beer XI*)	RFM	264.1	52	847	31	6-43	1	27.32
D. E. Bernard (*Jam., UWI VC XI & WI*)	RFM	240.1	50	736	26	5-56	1	28.30
M. I. Black (*T & T & Carib Beer XI*)	RFM	240.1	29	995	31	5-88	1	32.09
V. C. Drakes (*Barbados & West Indies*)	RFM	237.1	40	746	22	6-31	2	33.90
D. B. Powell (*Jamaica*)	RFM	206	42	698	20	5-34	1	34.90
M. V. Nagamootoo (*Guyana*)	LBG	403.4	83	1,101	30	5-40	1	36.70
A. P. Richardson (*WI B & UWI VC XI*)	RM	237.1	35	830	22	3-50	0	37.72
O. A. C. Banks (*Leeward I., Carib Beer XI & West Indies*)	OB	530.4	97	1,611	37	6-57	2	43.54

Note: Averages include Sri Lanka's tour in June 2003.

CARIB BEER CUP, 2002-03

	Played	Won	Lost	Drawn	1st-inns Points	Points
Barbados	7	5	0	2	6	72
Guyana	7	2	0	5	9	48
Trinidad & Tobago	7	3	3	1	4	43
Jamaica	7	2	2	3	10	43
India A	7	2	2	3	3	36
Leeward Islands	7	2	3	2	4	34
Windward Islands	7	2	4	1	3	30
West Indies B	7	0	4	3	3	12

Win = 12 pts; draw = 3 pts; 1st-innings lead in a drawn match = 3 pts; 1st-innings lead in a lost match = 4 pts.

Barbados won the Carib Beer Cup and became regional champions. The top four teams qualified for the Carib Beer International Challenge. Trinidad & Tobago were placed ahead of Jamaica by virtue of winning more matches. Matches involving India A and West Indies B counted for points but neither of these teams could win the Carib Beer Cup.

At Ronald Webster Park, The Valley, Anguilla, January 31, February 1, 2, 3. **Drawn.** Toss: Jamaica. **Leeward Islands 357** (S. C. Williams 71, K. I. Tittle 68, O. A. C. Banks 75; D. E. Bernard 4-101) **and 167-3** (F. A. Adams 65, S. C. Joseph 56*); **Jamaica 444** (L. V. Garrick 58, D. E. Bernard 91, K. H. Hibbert 81). *Leeward Islands 3 pts, Jamaica 6 pts.*

At Guaracara Park, Pointe-à-Pierre, January 31, February 1, 2, 3. **Drawn.** Toss: Guyana. **Trinidad & Tobago 303** (A. I. Jan 52, D. Ganga 89; C. E. L. Stuart 4-94) **and 332-5 dec.** (D. Ganga 111*, N. I. Chan 66*); **Guyana 338** (A. Haniff 62, A. R. Percival 76; M. I. Black 5-88) **and 192-6** (A. Haniff 69). *Trinidad & Tobago 3 pts, Guyana 6 pts.*

At Arnos Vale, St Vincent, January 31, February 1, 2. **Barbados won by seven wickets.** Toss: Windward Islands. **Windward Islands 156** (D. S. Smith 86) **and 223** (D. S. Smith 55; S. J. Benn 5-68); **Barbados 232** (R. O. Hurley 116; I. O. Jackson 4-80) **and 150-3** (S. L. Campbell 66*). *Barbados 12 pts.*

At Sabina Park, Kingston, February 7, 8, 9, 10. **Windward Islands won by 20 runs.** Toss: Jamaica. **Windward Islands 281** (K. K. Sylvester 113, I. O. Jackson 54; D. E. Bernard 5-56, N. O. Perry 4-69) **and 168** (N. O. Perry 8-64); **Jamaica 144 and 285** (R. G. Samuels 57, N. O. Perry 76; C. E. Cuffy 5-70, I. O. Jackson 5-89). *Windward Islands 12 pts.*

Perry's match figures of 55.2–10–133–12 were the best of the season; he also top-scored in the second innings, but was still on the losing side.

At Edgar Gilbert Sporting Complex, Molyneux, St Kitts, February 7, 8, 9, 10. **Guyana won by three wickets.** Toss: Guyana. **Leeward Islands 275** (J. A. Mitchum 60, S. C. Williams 78; M. V. Nagamootoo 4-74) **and 158; Guyana 228** (O. A. C. Banks 6-57) **and 208-7** (A. Haniff 93*; A. Sanford 4-61). *Guyana 12 pts, Leeward Islands 4 pts.*

At National Cricket Centre, Couva, Trinidad, February 7, 8, 9, 10. **Trinidad & Tobago won by six wickets.** Toss: West Indies B. **Trinidad & Tobago 406** (D. J. J. Bravo 114, L. A. Roberts 220) **and 188-4** (D. Ganga 67*, L. A. Roberts 61); **West Indies B 205** (C. S. Baugh 61; R. Rampaul 5-53) **and 387** (A. Kanhai 223, C. S. Baugh 51; D. Ramnarine 4-95). *Trinidad & Tobago 12 pts.*

Couva became the West Indies' 50th first-class venue. Roberts's 220, his maiden double-hundred, lasted 450 minutes and 362 balls and included 26 fours and one six. Kanhai's 223, his maiden hundred in his fourth first-class match, lasted 497 minutes and 379 balls and included 27 fours and two sixes.

At Windward Park, Lucas Street, Barbados, February 8, 9, 10. **Barbados won by an innings and 77 runs.** Toss: Barbados. **India A 201** (G. Gambhir 65, Jai P. Yadav 55; I. D. R. Bradshaw 4-43) **and 185** (T. L. Best 5-60); **Barbados 463** (P. A. Wallace 90, S. L. Campbell 89, F. L. Reifer 105, I. D. R. Bradshaw 58*; M. Kartik 5-105). *Barbados 12 pts.*

At Mount Gay North Stars, Crab Hill, Barbados, February 14, 15, 16, 17. **Drawn.** Toss: Jamaica. **Barbados 325** (F. L. Reifer 61, C. O. Browne 103*) **and 262-6** (R. O. Hinds 88, F. L. Reifer 95); **Jamaica 272** (B. A. Parchment 59, D. E. Bernard 53). *Barbados 6 pts, Jamaica 3 pts.*

Crab Hill became the West Indies' 51st first-class venue.

At Grove Park, Charlestown, Nevis, February 14, 15, 16, 17. **Drawn.** Toss: Leeward Islands. **India A 450** (G. Gambhir 98, A. Chopra 79, A. T. Rayudu 84, A. V. Kale 80); **Leeward Islands 201** (F. A. Adams 54; A. Mishra 5-55, A. T. Rayudu 4-43) **and 232-4** (J. A. Mitchum 72*, O. A. C. Banks 51*). *Leeward Islands 3 pts, India A 6 pts.*

At Polly Joseph Stadium, Christiansted, St Croix, February 14, 15, 16, 17. **Drawn.** Toss: Guyana. **West Indies B 134** (R. D. King 5-41, N. C. McGarrell 5-33) **and 339** (M. A. Nurse 55, N. Deonarine 64, G. Mahabir 71, C. S. Baugh 50; N. C. McGarrell 5-105); **Guyana 354-8 dec.** (V. Nagamootoo 115*, R. L. Griffith 82*; R. Thomas 4-69) **and 106-9.** *West Indies B 3 pts, Guyana 6 pts.*

St Croix, in the US Virgin Islands, became the West Indies' 52nd first-class venue. This was the first first-class match on US soil since the Australians visited Philadelphia in 1913. Nagamootoo and Griffith added 198, a West Indian ninth-wicket record.*

At Queen's Park, St George's, February 14, 15, 16, 17. **Trinidad & Tobago won by 75 runs.** Toss: Windward Islands. **Trinidad & Tobago 204** (A. I. Jan 67; C. E. Cuffy 4-36) **and 240-9 dec.** (A. S. Jackson 60, L. M. P. Simmons 68; C. E. Cuffy 5-54); **Windward Islands 84** (M. I. Black 4-43, D. J. J. Bravo 6-11) **and 285** (R. K. Currency 92, J. Eugene 71; R. Rampaul 4-49). *Trinidad & Tobago 12 pts.*

In the Windwards' first innings, Bravo's full figures were 7.4–1–11–6.

At Albion, Berbice, February 21, 22, 23, 24. **Drawn.** Toss: Guyana. **Guyana 213 and 247** (T. M. Dowlin 77; S. J. Benn 5-77); **Barbados 323** (P. A. Wallace 74, C. O. Browne 58; N. C. McGarrell 4-65) **and 121-8** (M. V. Nagamootoo 5-40). *Guyana 3 pts, Barbados 6 pts.*

At Kaiser Sports Club, Discovery Bay, February 21, 22, 23. **Jamaica won by an innings and 76 runs.** Toss: Jamaica. **West Indies B 94** (C. S. Baugh 50; D. B. Powell 5-34) **and 131; Jamaica 301-7 dec.** (B. A. Parchment 69, G. R. Breese 70). *Jamaica 12 pts.*

At Wilson Road Recreation Ground, Peñal, Trinidad, February 21, 22, 23, 24. **India A won by six wickets.** Toss: Trinidad & Tobago. **Trinidad & Tobago 261** (A. I. Jan 94, A. S. Jackson 62, D. Ganga 68; L. Balaji 4-59, A. M. Salvi 4-58) **and 181** (M. Kartik 4-57, A. Mishra 5-30); **India A 215** (A. Chopra 58, A. Ratra 50*; D. Ramnarine 4-60) **and 231-4** (G. Gambhir 67, C. C. Williams 89*). *India A 12 pts, Trinidad & Tobago 4 pts.*

At Botanical Gardens, Roseau, Dominica, February 21, 22, 23, 24. **Leeward Islands won by six wickets.** Toss: Windward Islands. **Leeward Islands 385** (S. C. Williams 158, K. I. Tittle 54, O. A. C. Banks 73*) **and 93-4; Windward Islands 180** (D. S. Smith 74; A. Sanford 6-43) **and 297** (R. K. Currency 79, J. R. Murray 74; A. Sanford 4-61). *Leeward Islands 12 pts.*

At Kensington Oval, Bridgetown, February 28, March 1, 2. **Barbados won by an innings and 110 runs.** Toss: Barbados. **Trinidad & Tobago 147** (A. I. Jan 53; T. L. Best 4-36, S. J. Benn 4-36) **and 245** (D. J. J. Bravo 56, Z. R. Ali 52); **Barbados 502-9 dec.** (P. A. Wallace 140, S. L. Campbell 103; D. J. J. Bravo 5-95). *Barbados 12 pts.*

On the third day, Best was removed from the attack in his 17th over, after bowling two beamers to No. 11 Mukesh Prasad in Trinidad & Tobago's second innings.

At Enmore, Demerara, February 28, March 1, 2, 3. **Drawn.** Toss: Jamaica. **Jamaica 387** (L. V. Garrick 74, B. A. Parchment 95, R. G. Samuels 85; S. Chattergoon 4-9); **Guyana 236** (A. R. Percival 51*; G. R. Breese 4-74) **and 195-6** (T. M. Dowlin 50). *Guyana 3 pts, Jamaica 6 pts.*

At Salem, Montserrat, February 28, March 1, 2, 3. **Leeward Islands won by seven wickets.** Toss: Leeward Islands. **West Indies B 191** (C. S. Baugh 61; K. C. B. Jeremy 5-34) **and 268** (S. M. Jeffers 62, A. Kanhai 104; O. A. C. Banks 5-88); **Leeward Islands 233** (S. C. Joseph 91; J. P. Bennett 5-51) **and 227-3** (F. A. Adams 103*, S. C. Williams 90*). *Leeward Islands 12 pts.*

Salem became the West Indies' 53rd first-class venue.

At Beausejour Stadium, Gros Islet, St Lucia, February 28, March 1, 2. **Windward Islands won by seven wickets.** Toss: India A. **Windward Islands 339** (D. S. Smith 101, J. R. Murray 72) **and 51-3; India A 183 and 206** (A. Chopra 70; D. C. Butler 4-47). *Windward Islands 12 pts.*

At Kensington Oval, Bridgetown, March 7, 8, 9. **Barbados won by seven wickets.** Toss: Barbados. **Leeward Islands 249** (S. C. Williams 146; I. D. R. Bradshaw 4-69) **and 98** (T. L. Best 4-26); **Barbados 291** (S. L. Campbell 50, R. O. Hurley 65) **and 57-3.** *Barbados 12 pts.*

At Bourda, Georgetown, March 7, 8, 9, 10. **Drawn.** Toss: India A. **India A 249** (C. C. Williams 54, V. V. S. Laxman 70) **and 402-3** (A. Chopra 174, G. Gambhir 78, C. C. Williams 61, H. K. Badani 57*); **Guyana 375** (K. Arjune 60, T. M. Dowlin 78, N. C. McGarrell 88; A. M. Salvi 5-58, A. Mishra 4-123). *Guyana 6 pts, India A 3 pts.*

In India A's second innings, Chopra shared century stands with each of his three partners, and nine Guyanese bowled.

At Queen's Park Oval, Port-of-Spain, March 7, 8, 9, 10. **Jamaica won by five wickets.** Toss: Trinidad & Tobago. **Trinidad & Tobago 218 and 234** (A. S. Jackson 90; J. E. Taylor 8-59); **Jamaica 332** (G. R. Breese 98; D. Mohammed 5-63) **and 123-5.** *Jamaica 12 pts.*

In his third first-class match, Taylor's analysis of 20.5–4–59–8 was the best of the season.

At Botanical Gardens, Roseau, Dominica, March 7, 8, 9, 10. **Drawn.** Toss: Windward Islands. **Windward Islands 338** (D. S. Smith 53, J. R. Murray 121) **and 246-5 dec.** (J. R. Murray 68*, R. N. Lewis 88*; J. P. Bennett 4-57); **West Indies B 273** (N. Deonarine 77, D. James 62; I. O. Jackson 4-92) **and 165-2** (P. A. Browne 57, N. Deonarine 59*). *Windward Islands 6 pts, West Indies B 3 pts.*

At Kensington Oval, Bridgetown, March 14, 15, 16. **Barbados won by ten wickets.** Toss: Barbados. **West Indies B 115** (P. A. Browne 56; T. L. Best 5-40) **and 248** (C. S. Baugh 100*; R. O. Hurley 4-22); **Barbados 353-9 dec.** (S. L. Campbell 135, F. L. Reifer 57; J. P. Bennett 5-83) **and 13-0.** *Barbados 12 pts.*

At Albion, Berbice, March 14, 15, 16, 17. **Guyana won by 73 runs.** Toss: Guyana. **Guyana 412** (A. Haniff 54, S. Chanderpaul 145) **and 161-5 dec.; Windward Islands 307** (J. R. Murray 67, R. N. Lewis 117*; R. L. Griffith 4-75) **and 193** (D. J. G. Sammy 53). *Guyana 12 pts.*

At Sabina Park, Kingston, March 14, 15, 16, 17. **India A won by two wickets.** Toss: India A. **Jamaica 130** (A. M. Salvi 5-39) **and 273** (G. R. Breese 56; A. M. Salvi 5-95); **India A 119** (J. E. Taylor 5-39) **and 285-8** (A. T. Rayudu 66, A. V. Kale 55; D. E. Bernard 4-61). *India A 12 pts, Jamaica 4 pts.*

At Addelita Cancryn Ground, Charlotte Amalie, St Thomas, March 14, 15, 16. **Trinidad & Tobago won by 180 runs.** Toss: Trinidad & Tobago. **Trinidad & Tobago 303** (A. S. Jackson 51, D. J. J. Bravo 59, B. C. Lara 53; K. C. B. Jeremy 5-55) **and 379-7 dec.** (A. I. Jan 50, A. S. Jackson 55, B. C. Lara 152); **Leeward Islands 158 and 344** (S. C. Williams 167; D. Mohammed 4-90). *Trinidad & Tobago 12 pts.*

St Thomas, in the US Virgin Islands, became the West Indies' 54th first-class venue.

At Kensington Oval, Bridgetown, March 21, 22, 23, 24. **Drawn.** Toss: India A. **West Indies B 388** (S. M. Jeffers 60, N. Deonarine 100, A. Kanhai 64, Extras 63; A. Mishra 4-111) **and 175** (Jai P. Yadav 4-46); **India A 296** (A. Chopra 58, G. Gambhir 108; J. P. Bennett 5-73) **and 205-9** (C. C. Williams 75). *West Indies B 6 pts, India A 3 pts.*

REGIONAL CHAMPIONS

Shell Shield

1965-66	Barbados
1966-67	Barbados
1967-68	No competition
1968-69	Jamaica
1969-70	Trinidad
1970-71	Trinidad
1971-72	Barbados
1972-73	Guyana
1973-74	Barbados
1974-75	Guyana
1975-76	Trinidad / Barbados
1976-77	Barbados
1977-78	Barbados
1978-79	Barbados
1979-80	Barbados
1980-81	Combined Islands
1981-82	Barbados
1982-83	Guyana
1983-84	Barbados
1984-85	Trinidad & Tobago
1985-86	Barbados
1986-87	Guyana

Red Stripe Cup

1987-88	Jamaica
1988-89	Jamaica
1989-90	Leeward Islands
1990-91	Barbados
1991-92	Jamaica
1992-93	Guyana
1993-94	Leeward Islands
1994-95	Barbados
1995-96	Leeward Islands
1996-97	Barbados

President's Cup

1997-98	Leeward Islands / Guyana

Busta Cup

1998-99	Barbados
1999-2000	Jamaica
2000-01	Barbados
2001-02	Jamaica

Carib Beer Cup

2002-03	Barbados

Barbados have won the title outright 17 times, Jamaica 6, Guyana 5, Leeward Islands and Trinidad/Trinidad & Tobago 3, Combined Islands 1. Barbados, Guyana, Leeward Islands and Trinidad have also shared the title.

CARIB BEER INTERNATIONAL CHALLENGE, 2002-03

Semi-finals

At Kensington Oval, Bridgetown, March 29, 30, 31. **Barbados won by nine wickets.** Toss: Barbados. **Trinidad & Tobago 258** (D. Ganga 95; C. D. Collymore 5-65) **and 104** (V. C. Drakes 6-31); **Barbados 336** (P. A. Wallace 137, C. O. Browne 67; R. I. Sooklal 4-82) **and 30-1.**

Both semi-finals started a day later than scheduled because of a players' strike. Barbados won with a day to spare, which gave them two days off before the final.

At Albion, Berbice, March 29, 30, 31, April 1. **Drawn.** Toss: Jamaica. **Jamaica 486-7 dec.** (W. W. Hinds 58, M. N. Samuels 79, D. E. Bernard 109, G. R. Breese 79, R. G. Samuels 55) **and 78-5** (R. L. Griffith 4-49); **Guyana 462** (K. Arjune 56, N. Deonarine 55, S. Chanderpaul 109, C. L. Hooper 130*).

Deonarine, who had played for West Indies B during the Carib Beer Cup, joined his native Guyana for the International Challenge. Jamaica qualified for the final on first-innings lead, but had only one day to reach Bridgetown for the final.

FINAL

BARBADOS v JAMAICA

At Kensington Oval, Bridgetown, April 3, 4, 5, 6. Barbados won by seven wickets. Toss: Jamaica.

Barbados completed their treble shortly after lunch on the fourth day. Jamaica started on the wrong foot, with Chris Gayle citing another engagement, Darren Powell ill, and the others making a hurried journey from Guyana, where they had just spent most of two days in the field. But they chose to field again, and Barbados looked uneasy at 98 for three. Then Wilkinson, recalled after a month out, joined Reifer in a stand of 191, and nearly trebled his season's aggregate. Parchment steered Jamaica to 117 for one in reply, before Collymore and Collins ran through the order; they got only halfway to Barbados's 369. In recent finals, sides had tended to sit on a first-innings lead, which would be decisive in a draw. Browne was more positive, enforcing the follow-on. Though Parchment shone again in a century opening stand with Garrick, Jamaica's last seven fell quickly on the final morning. Barbados lost three cheap wickets chasing 35 before Hinds saw them home.

Man of the Match: K. J. Wilkinson.

Close of play: First day, Barbados 228-3 (Reifer 59, Wilkinson 74); Second day, Jamaica 79-1 (Parchment 26, Hinds 11); Third day, Jamaica 166-3 (Garrick 56, Bernard 5).

Barbados

P. A. Wallace c Bernard b Breese	35	– b Bernard	0
S. L. Campbell c Lawson b Taylor	11	– hit wkt b Lawson	5
R. O. Hinds c Bernard b Breese	38	– not out	21
F. L. Reifer b Breese	88	– c Parchment b Lawson	1
K. J. Wilkinson lbw b Bernard	125	– not out	0
*†C. O. Browne lbw b Powell	25		
R. O. Hurley b Taylor	14		
V. C. Drakes b Lawson	8		
P. T. Collins b Lawson	4		
C. D. Collymore c R. G. Samuels b Breese	4		
T. L. Best not out	2		
B 6, l-b 4, w 5	15	L-b 3, w 1, n-b 4	8
1/18 (2) 2/63 (1) 3/98 (3) 4/289 (4) 5/331 (5) 6/350 (7) 7/350 (6) 8/362 (8) 9/365 (9) 10/369 (10)	369	1/6 (1) 2/10 (2) 3/23 (4)	(3 wkts) 35

Bowling: *First Innings*—Lawson 20–6–56–2; Taylor 24–3–67–2; Bernard 28–7–59–1; Breese 41–12–97–4; M. N. Samuels 5–2–17–0; Hinds 9–1–21–0; Powell 18–4–42–1. *Second Innings*—Lawson 3–0–12–2; Bernard 3–0–20–1; Garrick 1–1–0–0; Parchment 0.1–0–0–0.

Jamaica

L. V. Garrick lbw b Collymore	30	– lbw b Drakes	75
B. A. Parchment c Wilkinson b Hurley	52	– c Wallace b Hurley	82
W. W. Hinds c Browne b Drakes	22	– c Collymore b Hurley	2
M. N. Samuels c Browne b Collymore	6	– c Browne b Collymore	13
D. E. Bernard c Drakes b Collymore	22	– c Hurley b Collins	20
R. L. Powell c Reifer b Collymore	4	– c Reifer b Collins	0
*R. G. Samuels lbw b Collins	6	– c Wilkinson b Drakes	8
G. R. Breese c Best b Collins	2	– c Reifer b Drakes	1
†K. H. Hibbert not out	7	– c Collins b Best	2
J. J. C. Lawson c Browne b Collins	8	– not out	2
J. E. Taylor b Collymore	0	– run out	0
L-b 4, w 1, n-b 20	25	B 1, l-b 3, n-b 10	14
1/56 (1) 2/117 (3) 3/126 (4) 4/130 (2) 5/140 (6) 6/165 (7) 7/167 (5) 8/169 (8) 9/182 (10) 10/184 (11)	184	1/111 (2) 2/125 (3) 3/144 (4) 4/187 (5) 5/194 (1) 6/206 (6) 7/212 (7) 8/215 (8) 9/217 (9) 10/219 (11)	219

Bowling: *First Innings*—Collins 15–3–36–3; Drakes 11–0–31–1; Best 10–2–36–0; Collymore 21–4–44–5; Hinds 1–0–3–0; Hurley 10–2–30–1. *Second Innings*—Best 5.5–1–13–1; Drakes 12–5–44–3; Hurley 17–3–43–2; Hinds 8–0–27–0; Collymore 12–3–46–1; Collins 12–1–42–2.

Umpires: B. E. W. Morgan and E. A. Nicholls. Referee: D. de Peiza.

RED STRIPE BOWL, 2002-03

Note: Matches in this section were not first-class.

Zone A (in Jamaica)	*Played*	*Won*	*Lost*	*No result*	*Points*	*Net run-rate*
Jamaica	4	4	0	0	8	1.79
Barbados	4	3	1	0	6	2.01
St Vincent	4	1	3	0	2	–0.64
Rest of Leeward Islands	4	1	3	0	2	–1.41
University of the West Indies	4	1	3	0	2	–2.05

Zone B (in St Lucia)	*Played*	*Won*	*Lost*	*No result*	*Points*	*Net run-rate*
Guyana	4	4	0	0	8	0.65
Trinidad & Tobago	4	3	1	0	6	1.08
Canada	4	2	2	0	4	–0.72
Antigua & Barbuda	4	1	3	0	2	–0.27
Rest of Windward Islands	4	0	4	0	0	–0.73

Net run-rate was calculated by subtracting runs conceded per over from runs scored per over.

Semi-finals

At Kaiser Sports Club, Discovery Bay, August 29. **Jamaica won by seven wickets.** Toss: Trinidad & Tobago. **Trinidad & Tobago 147** (48 overs) (D. B. Powell 5-23); **Jamaica 151-3** (29.1 overs) (C. H. Gayle 56, M. N. Samuels 57*).

At Kaiser Sports Club, Discovery Bay, August 30. **Barbados won by five wickets (D/L method).** Toss: Barbados. **Guyana 162** (44.5 overs) (C. L. Hooper 71); **Barbados 143-5** (34.4 overs).

Rain reduced Guyana's innings to 46 overs, and later revised Barbados's target to 143 in 36.

Final

At Kaiser Sports Club, Discovery Bay, September 1. **Barbados won by 33 runs.** Toss: Jamaica. **Barbados 241-8** (50 overs) (K. J. Wilkinson 63, F. L. Reifer 86*); **Jamaica 208** (46.2 overs) (W. W. Hinds 103).

CRICKET IN NEW ZEALAND, 2002-03

DON CAMERON

Tim McIntosh

As New Zealand's cricketers approached the 2003 World Cup in South Africa in 2002-03, a casual observer might have sensed an air of contentment. They stood third in the then ICC Test championship; they had recently completed an historic win in the West Indies, and looked forward to a visit from those uncertain travellers, the Indians, as a prelude to the World Cup, where they quietly fancied their chances.

Then came the shock, several notches up the Richter Scale. The Cricket Players Association, founded in June 2001, tested the sharpness of its sword against New Zealand Cricket over the issue of pay and, when the thrust was repelled, called its 128 members out on strike. There had been murmurings of discontent over contract negotiations before the West Indian tour. Then the players realised the extent to which profits from TV coverage of the World Cup and Champions Trophy would flow into the New Zealand game.

Scenting riches, the CPA demanded 60% pay rises for its members, from Test champions to domestic players. The struggle soon acquired a personal dimension with two hard-nosed antagonists – Martin Snedden, NZC's chief executive, against CPA executive director Rob Nichol.

The players went on strike from October 1, thus missing a pre-season training camp, until November 11. Three factors helped to end the strike and save the season. When the CPA put their case at a press conference, comments about NZC by Dion Nash, the players' representative – "they looked after three or four top players but the rest of us could go to hell" – rebounded badly and affected public support. Meanwhile, Indian board president Jagmohan Dalmiya announced that India would tour, even if NZC put out a team of club cricketers. The strikers had expected that, without them, the series would be abandoned. Finally, two senior players, national captain Stephen Fleming and Chris Cairns, collaborated with Snedden and Nichol to cobble together a treaty. A four-year contract system was drawn up, though NZC had the right to withdraw if the expected ICC income failed to materialise. The average pay rise was about 15%, and the six first-class associations agreed each would contract 11 players (excluding any internationals contracted to NZC), improving job security. Senior Test players achieved annual retainers of up to $NZ140,000 (about £50,000) with top domestic players on about $NZ37,500.

The ten-over Max tournament, scheduled for the following weekend, was cancelled, but the rest of the programme was saved. Sir Richard Hadlee, the chairman of selectors, was quick to point out he had only a few weeks to prepare a side to face the Indians. In fact, it was the preparation of the pitches – which turned out over-grassed and treacherous – that settled the series. India lost both Tests well inside the distance, a disappointment for spectators awaiting the regal batsmanship of Sachin Tendulkar and his court, a blow to gate-takings and to attempts to ready the team for the World Cup.

Nevertheless, New Zealand's campaign there had its moments and the team appeared on the brink of the semi-finals when the brilliant bowling of Shane Bond had Australia reeling at 84 for seven. Somehow, Australia turned it round; then India took their revenge, and knocked a dispirited New Zealand out of the tournament. Criticism back home centred on the frequent omission of pace bowler Daryl Tuffey and tinkering with the batting order, and much of it landed at Hadlee's feet. He had been invited by the World Cup organisers as an international cricketing celebrity, but operated virtually as a tour official, chairing an unwieldy group of eight selectors.

As New Zealand returned from South Africa, the first-class championship was coming to a climax. It had started slowly, back in November, but after Christmas struck sunshine and hard, true pitches: the result was some excellent cricket.

Under new coach Mark O'Donnell, Auckland retained their championship. With two rounds to go, it was between them and Wellington, separated by a single point after four wins apiece. The penultimate match, between the two contenders, was a draw, but Auckland gained first-innings points and became champions six days later when Wellington were crushed by Otago, even though Auckland lost too, a few hours later. Tim McIntosh, a sturdy left-hander, was the season's leading run-scorer with 820 at 58.57, and had solid support in Auckland's line-up from Matt Horne and Mark Richardson. Tama Canning was outstanding, combining 465 runs with 46 wickets – the season's most. Long-serving all-rounder Aaron Barnes was granted a benefit, but not one of the new contracts, and was omitted from the early first-class games. Once in, he averaged 57 over seven innings in one purple patch, was named Auckland batsman of the year, and agreed to return in 2003-04, having previously decided to settle in Wales. Meanwhile, Auckland's women won their own championship final, against Canterbury, for a fourth successive title.

As usual, Wellington were dominant at home: three of their four wins came at the Basin Reserve. Matthew Bell, one of a growing number of New Zealand discards, led from the front, while his opening partner Richard Jones scored 726 runs, and was picked for New Zealand's tour of Sri Lanka. Andrew Penn and Iain O'Brien headed a lively attack, but the man who constantly caught the eye was Matthew Walker, a burly 26-year-old who set out as a Central Districts opener, then moved to Wellington and became an accurate seamer and steady middle-order run-scorer. Walker took 45 wickets, one behind Canning, the only other man to bowl more than 400 overs.

Otago won their last two games by ten and nine wickets to finish with four victories, on a par with Auckland and Wellington – a complete turnaround after 2001-02, when they lost nine matches out of ten, and a triumph for the redoubtable Glenn Turner in his second year as coach. Mohammad Wasim, the former Pakistan batsman, scored two centuries, but yielded top batting honours to the captain, Craig Cumming. Equally important was the three-pronged attack of Shayne O'Connor, Kerry Walmsley and Warren McSkimming. O'Connor, a promising left-armer until injury wrecked his Test career, took 42 wickets – his best season return – at 18.71. Sadly, he announced that, since he was not offered an NZC contract, he had to retire, aged 29, to earn a living, while Walmsley decided to return to Auckland.

MAKE MINE A TREBLE...

The highest maiden centuries in first-class cricket are:

337*	Pervez Akhtar	Railways v Dera Ismail Khan at Lahore	1964-65
324	Waheed Mirza	Karachi Whites v Quetta at Karachi	1976-77
314*	Wasim Jaffer	Bombay v Saurashtra at Rajkot	1996-97
302*	A. Kripal Singh	Tamil Nadu v Goa at Panjim	1988-89
301*	**P. G. Fulton**	**Canterbury v Auckland at Christchurch (Hagley Oval)**	**2002-03**

Northern Districts claimed the one-day State Shield, after winning a play-off with Wellington and beating Auckland in the final – a tense battle on an over-lively wicket at North Harbour Stadium. But weak top-order batting meant that Northern Districts could not maintain their consistency in the four-day game. However, Matthew Hart, a former Test spinner who now barely bowled, moved up to No. 4 to finish in a blaze of glory: 111 against Central Districts and a match-winning 201 not out against Auckland. Ian Butler grew in stature and speed, and found an effective pace partner in Joseph Yovich.

Central Districts promised more than they delivered, but were never dull. Craig Spearman returned, having left them in 2001 to concentrate on playing for Gloucestershire. He later stood in as captain, and led them to victory over Auckland by scoring 117 not out in a run-chase. But the limelight soon shifted to Jamie How and 18-year-old left-hander Jesse Ryder. How ended with 163 not out and 158 in successive matches, while Ryder made his first-class debut in February, having an immediate impact with confident, powerful strokeplay. Michael Mason bowled himself back into the national selectors' notebooks, but Central Districts lacked wicket-taking pressure.

Canterbury have often succeeded when their many internationals are available, but in 2002-03 they had to dig deep into the second-tier talent, and it showed. The highlight of an otherwise modest season came at Hagley Oval against Auckland, when 24-year-old Peter Fulton converted his maiden first-class hundred into 301 not out: the sixth triple-century by a New Zealander but the first ever scored by a non-Otago player. It was the fifth highest maiden century in history.

His brave deed came in a losing cause. After Fulton's marvellous innings, a series of declarations allowed Horne to sweep Auckland home with an explosive 187. One spectator observed that he had seen more cricket of genuine quality in those four days at Christchurch than in the 14 India had played. The lively, competitive and at times accomplished cricket during the sunny second half of the summer conferred princely stature on some supposedly second-string players. It made it all the more ludicrous that cricket's real royal family – Tendulkar, Fleming and the rest – had had to grovel for runs on impossibly one-sided pitches.

FIRST-CLASS AVERAGES, 2002-03

BATTING

(Qualification: 400 runs)

	M	*I*	*NO*	*R*	*HS*	*100s*	*Avge*	*Ct/St*
†T. G. McIntosh (*Auckland*)	10	17	3	820	157	2	58.57	8
†M. N. Hart (*Northern Districts*)	9	14	4	546	201*	2	54.60	5
P. G. Fulton (*Canterbury*)	8	13	1	628	301*	1	52.33	5
M. J. Horne (*Auckland*)	9	14	0	671	187	2	47.92	2
R. J. Nicol (*Auckland*)	10	16	2	664	147*	1	47.42	8
C. D. Cumming (*Otago*)	10	18	2	751	128	3	46.93	4
R. A. Jones (*Wellington*)	10	20	4	726	128	2	45.37	8
†G. P. Sulzberger (*Central Districts*)	11	18	6	540	111*	2	45.00	4
J. M. How (*Central Districts*)	10	18	2	704	163*	2	44.00	9
Mohammad Wasim (*Otago*)	10	17	1	651	108	2	40.68	9
C. M. Spearman (*Central Districts*)	10	17	1	622	117*	1	38.87	9
T. K. Canning (*Auckland*)	9	14	2	465	113	1	38.75	8
†M. H. Richardson (*Auckland & NZ*)	11	19	2	638	113	1	37.52	8
†N. K. W. Horsley (*Northern Districts*)	10	16	0	582	159	1	36.37	7
C. J. Nevin (*Wellington*)	10	16	1	532	73	0	35.46	30/1
C. B. Gaffaney (*Otago*)	8	14	1	436	108	1	33.53	4
G. J. Hopkins (*Canterbury*)	10	15	1	451	175*	2	32.21	22/1
†J. E. C. Franklin (*Wellington*)	8	13	0	413	87	0	31.76	1
N. R. Parlane (*Wellington*)	10	17	2	474	75	0	31.60	17
G. R. Stead (*Canterbury*)	10	15	0	472	111	1	31.46	4
M. H. W. Papps (*Canterbury*)	10	15	0	469	114	1	31.26	7
M. D. Bell (*Wellington*)	10	20	2	499	114	1	27.72	6

† *Left-handed batsman.*

BOWLING

(Qualification: 15 wickets)

	Style	*O*	*M*	*R*	*W*	*BB*	*5W/i*	*Avge*
J. D. P. Oram (*Central Districts & NZ*)	RM	96.5	35	183	15	4-41	0	12.20
D. R. Tuffey (*Northern Districts & NZ*)	RFM	106.3	34	240	17	4-12	0	14.11
M. D. J. Walker (*Wellington*)	RM	402.3	135	810	45	6-114	2	18.00
A. J. Penn (*Wellington*)	RFM	233	72	523	29	6-33	1	18.03
I. E. O'Brien (*Wellington*)	RM	257	83	631	34	6-103	2	18.55

	Style	O	M	R	W	BB	5W/i	Avge
S. B. O'Connor (*Otago*)	LFM	374.2	136	786	42	5-55	2	18.71
M. J. Mason (*Central Districts*)	RFM	353.2	120	787	40	6-56	2	19.67
K. P. Walmsley (*Otago*)	RFM	308.2	84	777	37	6-74	1	21.00
S. E. Bond (*Canterbury & NZ*)	RF	120.4	29	384	18	4-33	0	21.33
T. K. Canning (*Auckland*)	RFM	410	133	1,011	46	5-62	1	21.97
J. E. C. Franklin (*Wellington*)	LFM	183.2	35	523	22	6-40	1	23.77
I. G. Butler (*Northern Districts*)	RFM	194.1	44	597	25	5-44	1	23.88
W. C. McSkimming (*Otago*)	RM	269.2	88	640	26	5-40	1	24.61
A. M. Schwass (*Central Districts*)	RFM	226	73	542	20	5-38	1	27.10
B. E. Hefford (*Central Districts*)	RM	321	118	684	25	4-53	0	27.36
W. A. Wisneski (*Canterbury*)	RM	177.3	35	558	19	5-69	2	29.36
C. R. Pryor (*Auckland*)	RM	325	70	1,023	31	5-59	1	33.00
J. A. F. Yovich (*Northern Districts*)	RFM	270	61	816	24	5-49	2	34.00
J. M. McMillan (*Otago*)	RFM	181	44	530	15	4-56	0	35.33
G. P. Sulzberger (*Central Districts*)	OB	341.1	102	851	22	4-52	0	38.68
L. J. Hamilton (*Central Districts*)	LFM	276.5	75	799	19	4-36	0	42.05
C. S. Martin (*Canterbury*)	RFM	298.4	78	807	19	4-69	0	42.47
P. J. Wiseman (*Canterbury*)	OB	346.2	90	937	19	4-122	0	49.31

STATE CHAMPIONSHIP, 2002-03

	Played	Won	Lost	Drawn	1st-inns Points	Points	Net avge runs per wkt
Auckland	10	4	2	4	10	34	2.89
Wellington	10	4	3	3	7	31	5.91
Otago	10	4	3	3	2	26	0.00
Northern Districts	10	3	3	4	4	22	–4.15
Central Districts	10	2	4	4	10	22	0.00
Canterbury	10	2	4	4	4	16	–6.36

Outright win = 6 pts; lead on first innings in a drawn or lost game = 2 pts; no result or tie on first innings = 1 pt each.
Net average runs per wicket is calculated by subtracting average runs conceded per wicket from average runs scored per wicket.

At Victoria Park, Wanganui, November 23, 24, 25, 26. **Drawn.** Toss: Otago. **Central Districts 234** (J. D. P. Oram 96; K. P. Walmsley 4-53, J. M. McMillan 4-56) **and 234-3 dec.** (M. S. Sinclair 79, G. P. Sulzberger 62*, J. D. P. Oram 52*); **Otago 163** (C. D. Cumming 68; L. J. Hamilton 4-58) **and 202-4** (B. B. McCullum 78*). *Central Districts 2 pts.*

At Harry Barker Reserve, Gisborne, November 29, 30, December 1, 2. **Drawn.** Toss: Northern Districts. **Northern Districts 358** (J. A. H. Marshall 74, H. J. H. Marshall 88*; H. T. Davis 4-93); **Auckland 361-6** (T. G. McIntosh 50, R. J. Nicol 147*, C. R. Pryor 55*). *Auckland 2 pts.*

At Carisbrook, Dunedin, November 29, 30, December 1. **Canterbury won by an innings and four runs.** Toss: Canterbury. **Otago 206** (B. B. McCullum 53) **and 183** (Mohammad Wasim 62; N. J. Astle 4-35); **Canterbury 393** (M. H. W. Papps 88, P. J. Wiseman 91, C. L. Cairns 76*, S. E. Bond 52; J. M. McMillan 4-86). *Canterbury 6 pts.*

At Basin Reserve, Wellington, November 29, 30, December 1. **Wellington won by ten wickets.** Toss: Wellington. **Central Districts 91** (J. E. C. Franklin 6-40) **and 192** (A. J. Penn 4-62, I. E. O'Brien 5-42); **Wellington 245** (S. P. Fleming 55, C. J. Nevin 70, M. D. J. Walker 58) **and 39-0.** *Wellington 6 pts.*

At Eden Park Outer Oval, Auckland, December 5, 6, 7, 8. **Auckland won by two wickets.** Toss: Auckland. **Wellington 113 and 219** (C. J. Nevin 73); **Auckland 113** (A. J. Penn 4-30, M. D. J. Walker 5-31) **and 223-8** (T. G. McIntosh 70*; M. D. J. Walker 4-84). *Auckland 6 pts, Wellington 1 pt.*

At Dudley Park, Rangiora, December 5, 6, 7, 8. **Drawn.** Toss: Canterbury. **Northern Districts 236** (D. L. Vettori 81) **and 163-6** (N. K. W. Horsley 57); **Canterbury 236.** *Canterbury 1 pt, Northern Districts 1 pt.*

At Dudley Park, Rangiora, December 10, 11, 12, 13. **Drawn.** Toss: Canterbury. **Wellington 399** (M. D. Bell 114, R. A. Jones 55, N. R. Parlane 75, M. R. Jefferson 53; W. A. Wisneski 4-126) **and 185-6; Canterbury 338** (M. H. W. Papps 87, C. Z. Harris 73*; I. E. O'Brien 6-103). *Wellington 2 pts.*

At Horton Park, Blenheim, December 10, 11, 12, 13. **Central Districts won by four wickets.** Toss: Central Districts. **Auckland 328** (R. J. Nicol 87, K. D. Mills 55, B. G. K. Walker 67*) **and 169** (A. M. Schwass 4-44); **Central Districts 246** (P. J. Ingram 66, M. S. Sinclair 60) **and 254-6** (C. M. Spearman 117*). *Central Districts 6 pts, Auckland 2 pts.*

At Carisbrook, Dunedin, December 10, 11, 12, 13. **Otago won by 70 runs.** Toss: Northern Districts. **Otago 453-8 dec.** (R. A. Lawson 146, Mohammad Wasim 104, B. B. McCullum 105) **and 8-2 dec.; Northern Districts 133-5 dec. and 258** (M. N. Hart 66, J. A. F. Yovich 52; K. P. Walmsley 4-48). *Otago 6 pts.*

Lawson and Mohammad Wasim put on 260 for the first wicket.

At North Harbour Stadium, Albany, Auckland, January 9, 10, 11, 12. **Drawn.** Toss: Otago. **Auckland 289** (T. G. McIntosh 157; S. B. O'Connor 4-34) **and 16-0; Otago 185** (T. K. Canning 4-58). *Auckland 2 pts.*

At Aorangi Park, Timaru, January 9, 10, 11, 12. **Drawn.** Toss: Central Districts. **Canterbury 245-9 dec.** (M. H. W. Papps 114; M. J. Mason 5-59) **and 183** (P. G. Fulton 65; M. J. Mason 6-56, B. E. Hefford 4-53); **Central Districts 273** (J. M. How 73; C. S. Martin 4-69) **and 36-1.** *Central Districts 2 pts.*

At Owen Delany Park, Taupo, January 9, 10, 11, 12. **Drawn.** Toss: Northern Districts. **Wellington 269** (R. A. Jones 56, N. R. Parlane 63; B. P. Martin 5-48) **and 57-1; Northern Districts 210** (M. E. Parlane 80; I. E. O'Brien 4-68). *Wellington 2 pts.*

At Colin Maiden Park, Auckland, February 7, 8, 9, 10. **Auckland won by five wickets.** Toss: Auckland. **Canterbury 252** (G. J. Hopkins 113; G. S. Shaw 5-73) **and 413** (A. J. Redmond 59, G. J. Hopkins 175*, P. J. Wiseman 59; T. K. Canning 4-89, B. G. K. Walker 4-77); **Auckland 478** (M. H. Richardson 82, M. J. Horne 72, R. J. Nicol 77, T. K. Canning 113; P. J. Wiseman 4-122) **and 190-5.** *Auckland 6 pts.*

Hopkins was the first wicket-keeper to score a century in each innings in New Zealand first-class cricket, and the second player for Canterbury.

At McLean Park, Napier, February 7, 8, 9, 10. **Northern Districts won by four wickets.** Toss: Central Districts. **Central Districts 195** (C. M. Spearman 83) **and 159** (G. P. Sulzberger 69*; I. G. Butler 5-44); **Northern Districts 150** (L. J. Hamilton 4-36) **and 208-6** (J. A. F. Yovich 53). *Northern Districts 6 pts, Central Districts 2 pts.*

At Basin Reserve, Wellington, February 7, 8, 9, 10. **Otago won by five wickets.** Toss: Otago. **Wellington 314** (R. A. Jones 126, L. J. Woodcock 59; S. B. O'Connor 4-82) **and 253-5 dec.** (R. A. Jones 64, J. E. C. Franklin 87, G. T. Donaldson 52*; S. B. O'Connor 4-53); **Otago 273** (C. D. Cumming 60, Mohammad Wasim 77, C. B. Gaffaney 55; M. D. J. Walker 4-68) **and 295-5** (C. B. Gaffaney 108, C. D. Cumming 56, R. A. Lawson 66*; M. D. J. Walker 4-80). *Otago 6 pts, Wellington 2 pts.*

Cumming shared opening partnerships of 141 with Mohammad Wasim in the first innings and 147 with Gaffaney in the second.

At Colin Maiden Park, Auckland, February 13, 14, 15, 16. **Drawn.** Toss: Auckland. **Central Districts 245** (J. M. How 54) **and 281-2** (C. M. Spearman 76, G. R. Todd 50*, G. P. Sulzberger 111*); **Auckland 475-9 dec.** (T. G. McIntosh 80, M. J. Horne 51, R. J. Nicol 69, A. C. Barnes 107). *Auckland 2 pts.*

At Seddon Park, Hamilton, February 13, 14, 15, 16. **Northern Districts won by six wickets.** Toss: Northern Districts. **Otago 229** (Mohammad Wasim 78; I. G. Butler 4-82, G. L. West 4-58) **and 229** (C. D. Cumming 102; J. A. F. Yovich 5-49); **Northern Districts 323** (N. K. W. Horsley 59, M. G. Orchard 50, R. G. Hart 72*; S. B. O'Connor 4-78) **and 136-4.** *Northern Districts 6 pts.*

At Basin Reserve, Wellington, February 13, 14, 15, 16. **Wellington won by 143 runs.** Toss: Canterbury. **Wellington 314** (M. D. Bell 53, J. E. C. Franklin 68, M. D. J. Walker 62; W. A. Wisneski 5-81, A. M. Ellis 4-81) **and 245-8 dec.** (N. R. Parlane 66); **Canterbury 169** (I. E. O'Brien 4-27) **and 247** (G. R. Stead 54). *Wellington 6 pts.*

At Queen Elizabeth Park, Masterton, February 25, 26, 27. **Wellington won by nine wickets.** Toss: Central Districts. **Central Districts 128** (A. J. Penn 6-33) **and 212** (J. D. Ryder 66); **Wellington 305** (R. A. Jones 128, G. T. Donaldson 57; G. P. Sulzberger 4-52) **and 36-1.** *Wellington 6 pts.*

At Seddon Park, Hamilton, February 25, 26, 27, 28. **Drawn.** Toss: Canterbury. **Northern Districts 142-5 v Canterbury.** *Northern Districts 1 pt, Canterbury 1 pt.*

Paul Wiseman of Canterbury took his 300th first-class wicket.

At Queenstown Events Centre, Queenstown, February 25, 26, 27, 28. **Auckland won by 86 runs.** Toss: Otago. **Auckland 272** (M. J. Horne 74; K. P. Walmsley 6-74) **and 247-9 dec.** (R. J. Nicol 50; W. C. McSkimming 4-87); **Otago 273-6 dec.** (C. D. Cumming 128; T. K. Canning 4-66) **and 160** (T. K. Canning 4-38). *Auckland 6 pts, Otago 2 pts.*

At Hagley Oval, Christchurch, March 3, 4, 5, 6. **Auckland won by four wickets.** Toss: Auckland. **Canterbury 514-6 dec.** (P. G. Fulton 301*; T. K. Canning 4-125) **and 129-7 dec.** (G. R. Stead 50); **Auckland 284-7 dec.** (T. G. McIntosh 64, R. J. Nicol 57, A. C. Barnes 79; W. A. Wisneski 5-69) **and 361-6** (M. J. Horne 187). *Auckland 6 pts, Canterbury 2 pts.*

Fulton's 301, his maiden first-class hundred in his 12th match, lasted 570 minutes and 445 balls and included 45 fours and three sixes. The next highest score in Canterbury's first innings was 49.*

At Queen's Park, Invercargill, March 3, 4, 5, 6. **Drawn.** Toss: Otago. **Central Districts 208** (C. M. Spearman 50) **and 127-1** (P. J. Ingram 54*, J. M. How 55); **Otago 184** (W. C. McSkimming 66*; M. J. Mason 4-63, A. M. Schwass 5-38). *Central Districts 2 pts.*

At Basin Reserve, Wellington, March 3, 4, 5, 6. **Wellington won by ten wickets.** Toss: Wellington. **Northern Districts 223** (N. K. W. Horsley 56; M. D. J. Walker 4-39) **and 266** (J. A. H. Marshall 112; M. D. J. Walker 4-60); **Wellington 403** (M. D. Bell 52, N. R. Parlane 64, J. E. C. Franklin 79, C. J. Nevin 73; J. A. F. Yovich 5-117) **and 87-0** (M. D. Bell 51*). *Wellington 6 pts.*

At Hagley Oval, Christchurch, March 11, 12, 13, 14. **Otago won by ten wickets.** Toss: Otago. **Canterbury 246** (G. R. Stead 75; W. C. McSkimming 5-40) **and 258** (G. R. Stead 53, N. T. Broom 63; S. B. O'Connor 5-55, K. P. Walmsley 4-55); **Otago 485-9 dec.** (Mohammad Wasim 108, M. N. McKenzie 100, J. W. Wilson 66) **and 23-0.** *Otago 6 pts.*

At Seddon Park, Hamilton, March 11, 12, 13, 14. **Central Districts won by eight wickets.** Toss: Northern Districts. **Northern Districts 392-5 dec.** (N. K. W. Horsley 159, M. N. Hart 111, M. G. Orchard 54*) **and forfeited second innings; Central Districts 54-4 dec. and 339-2** (P. J. Ingram 60, J. M. How 163*, G. R. Todd 61*). *Central Districts 6 pts, Northern Districts 2 pts.*

At Basin Reserve, Wellington, March 11, 12, 13, 14. **Drawn.** Toss: Wellington. **Wellington 226** (L. J. Woodcock 72, M. D. J. Walker 50; T. K. Canning 5-62) **and 331-8** (C. J. Nevin 68); **Auckland 298** (M. J. Horne 119; M. D. J. Walker 4-83). *Auckland 2 pts.*

Auckland wicket-keeper Reece Young held six catches in Wellington's first innings. Horne passed 7,000 first-class runs.

At Eden Park Outer Oval, Auckland, March 17, 18, 19, 20. **Northern Districts won by 16 runs.** Toss: Northern Districts. **Northern Districts 298** (G. G. Robinson 125*; T. K. Canning 4-96) **and 352-9 dec.** (H. J. H. Marshall 57, M. N. Hart 201*; C. R. Pryor 5-59); **Auckland 294-7 dec.**

(T. G. McIntosh 146*) **and 340** (M. H. Richardson 113, T. G. McIntosh 64, R. J. Nicol 56). *Northern Districts 6 pts.*

Hart's 201, his maiden double-hundred, lasted 401 minutes and 308 balls and included 33 fours. Richardson passed 8,000 first-class runs.*

At McLean Park, Napier, March 17, 18, 19, 20. **Canterbury won by two wickets.** Toss: Central Districts. **Central Districts 542-4 dec.** (P. J. Ingram 84, J. M. How 158, G. P. Sulzberger 107*, J. D. Ryder 114*) **and 109-3 dec.** (R. L. Taylor 56); **Canterbury 290-8 dec.** (G. R. Stead 111, N. T. Broom 63; M. J. Mason 4-40) **and 362-8** (S. L. Stewart 68, P. G. Fulton 91). *Canterbury 6 pts, Central Districts 2 pts.*

Sulzberger and Ryder added 235 for Central Districts' fifth wicket.*

At Molyneux Park, Alexandra, March 17, 18, 19, 20. **Otago won by nine wickets.** Toss: Otago. **Wellington 203** (C. J. Nevin 50; S. B. O'Connor 4-35) **and 244** (L. J. Woodcock 80; S. B. O'Connor 5-82); **Otago 383** (C. D. Cumming 114, Mohammad Wasim 65, C. B. Gaffaney 72; M. D. J. Walker 6-114) **and 65-1.** *Otago 6 pts.*

CHAMPIONS

Plunket Shield

1921-22 Auckland
1922-23 Canterbury
1923-24 Wellington
1924-25 Otago
1925-26 Wellington
1926-27 Auckland
1927-28 Wellington
1928-29 Auckland
1929-30 Wellington
1930-31 Canterbury
1931-32 Wellington
1932-33 Otago
1933-34 Auckland
1934-35 Canterbury
1935-36 Wellington
1936-37 Auckland
1937-38 Auckland
1938-39 Auckland
1939-40 Auckland
1940-45 No competition
1945-46 Canterbury
1946-47 Auckland
1947-48 Otago
1948-49 Canterbury
1949-50 Wellington
1950-51 Otago
1951-52 Canterbury
1952-53 Otago
1953-54 Central Districts
1954-55 Wellington
1955-56 Canterbury
1956-57 Wellington
1957-58 Otago
1958-59 Auckland
1959-60 Canterbury
1960-61 Wellington
1961-62 Wellington
1962-63 Northern Districts
1963-64 Auckland
1964-65 Canterbury
1965-66 Wellington
1966-67 Central Districts
1967-68 Central Districts
1968-69 Auckland
1969-70 Otago
1970-71 Central Districts
1971-72 Otago
1972-73 Wellington
1973-74 Wellington
1974-75 Otago

Shell Trophy

1975-76 Canterbury
1976-77 Otago
1977-78 Auckland
1978-79 Otago
1979-80 Northern Districts
1980-81 Auckland
1981-82 Wellington
1982-83 Wellington
1983-84 Canterbury
1984-85 Wellington
1985-86 Otago
1986-87 Central Districts
1987-88 Otago
1988-89 Auckland
1989-90 Wellington
1990-91 Auckland
1991-92 { Central Districts / Northern Districts
1992-93 Northern Districts
1993-94 Canterbury
1994-95 Auckland
1995-96 Auckland
1996-97 Canterbury
1997-98 Canterbury
1998-99 Central Districts
1999-2000 Northern Districts
2000-01 Wellington

State Championship

2001-02 Auckland
2002-03 Auckland

Auckland have won the title outright 20 times, Wellington 19, Canterbury 14, Otago 13, Central Districts 6, Northern Districts 4. Central Districts and Northern Districts also shared the title once.

STATE SHIELD, 2002-03

Note: This match was not first-class.

Final

At North Harbour Stadium, Albany, Auckland, February 1. **Northern Districts won by 17 runs.** Toss: Northern Districts. **Northern Districts 234-7** (50 overs) (J. A. H. Marshall 67, H. J. H. Marshall 65); **Auckland 217-7** (50 overs).

CRICKET IN INDIA, 2002-03

R. Mohan and Mohandas Menon

Ambati Rayudu

Change is the essence of life, proclaims a Hindu maxim – but India's domestic season suggested that the more things change, the more they stay the same. Both first-class tournaments underwent drastic changes, with the Ranji Trophy split into two divisions. The outcome, however, was that India's premier cricketing power, Mumbai, re-established their supremacy, while realities on the ground were little altered.

Previously, the Ranji and Duleep competitions had been constructed around five geographical zones. In 2002-03, the Ranji Trophy featured two divisions, the Elite and Plate Groups, based on the previous season's placings. Each was subdivided into two mini-leagues, leading to semi-finals. The Plate finalists were promoted to the Elite, replacing the two bottom teams. The Duleep Trophy retained its league format, but the five zonal sides were replaced by three drawn from the Elite Group and two from the Plate. The one competition played on the old zonal basis was the limited-overs Deodhar Trophy, won by North Zone.

The handsome Ranji Trophy remained the most sought-after prize, as the only inter-state first-class competition. The new structure gave players more chance to experience conditions in different parts of the country. The divisions were intended to raise standards by cutting out mismatches; in fact, competition did not seem much stiffer, though fear of relegation may have sharpened up some Elite teams.

But the gravest threat to Indian national cricket is neglect, underlined by three long-standing weaknesses. The domestic game was played on lifeless pitches, with no benefit from the re-laying of surfaces at the international venues; the Indian board paid scant regard to the teams' comfort on or off the field; and the best players continued to stay away. This time it was no fault of theirs, in a busy season overshadowed by the World Cup in South Africa, where India reached the final; even when the stars were available, fitting in domestic matches would have overloaded them. There were a few cosmetic gestures – Virender Sehwag delayed joining Leicestershire to make what proved his sole appearance for Delhi, in the Ranji semi-final: his 99 failed to avert defeat by Tamil Nadu.

The public stayed away too. An apt picture of domestic cricket's subsidiary role was presented by the empty Sachin Tendulkar stand during the Ranji final in Mumbai. Tendulkar himself – the World Cup's player of the tournament – was in the United States, tending a finger injury. It is a marketing myth that thousands of Indians watch their local teams, while millions tune in on television. But every ball of India's international programme is brought live to the small screen, which is one factor discouraging interest in national cricket.

Even without Tendulkar, Mumbai regained their form and glory after a couple of years of losing out to less fashionable sides. In their 39th Ranji final, they beat Tamil Nadu to notch up their 35th title. The match was staged in early May, in temperatures close to 40°C. Tamil Nadu became the first state side to fly business class and stay in a luxury hotel for both semi and final. But Mumbai, who had crushed Baroda in the semi-final, when temperatures soared to 45°C, showed their traditional guts and gumption after being outplayed on the first two days. Sairaj Bahutule spun Tamil Nadu to defeat, taking his season's aggregate to 62 first-class wickets – second only to 79 by his fellow leg-spinner and former Test player Narendra Hirwani of Madhya Pradesh. Bahutule ascribed his success to changing his bowling action, and to the flipper he had picked up in a session with Shane Warne.

Karnataka, whose six Ranji titles had been exceeded only by Mumbai, started the new-look competition in the Plate division, after poor results in 2001-02. They soon put that right, overwhelming Vidarbha in the Plate semi-final, and Kerala in the final, when 12 wickets from Sunil Joshi, another discarded Test spinner, helped them win with two days to spare.

The changes in the Duleep Trophy did not solve its flaws. Abandoning the geographical format did not quite eliminate all regional selection prejudices, although the national selectors who chose all five teams had a wide choice. The Trophy went to the unimaginatively named Elite Group C, who finished two points ahead of Plate Group B; no team won more than once in four matches; the games were played in the heat of March and April, on generally flat pitches. Though the Duleep Trophy is supposed to provide a step up towards the international game, it did not seem to count for much; when some regulars dropped out of India's side for a triangular series in Dhaka, players from India A's recent tour of the Caribbean were preferred.

The media continued to hype the first-class competitions as selection trials. It was perhaps true of the Irani Cup match, between the reigning Ranji champions and the Rest of India. For Railways, an unfashionable side who triumphed in 2001-02 despite notoriously poor travel and living conditions, Jai P. Yadav combined a century with six wickets. He earned an international debut four days later, in the one-day series with West Indies, but was soon dropped. That series also introduced Lakshmipathy Balaji of Tamil Nadu, whose international stint lasted four expensive overs. He went on to take 47 wickets at 14.21 in seven Ranji matches, but was not recalled by the senior side; no other player from his state was picked all season. For the other

Ranji finalists, Mumbai, only Ajit Agarkar was a regular in India's squad, though not always their final eleven, but the 21-year-old Aavishkar Salvi made his one-day debut in April. Half a dozen more international discards played in the Ranji final, including the season's two leading first-class run-scorers, Wasim Jaffer of Mumbai and Tamil Nadu's Sridharan Sriram; the only other batsman to reach 1,000 was Sujith Somasunder of Kerala.

The outstanding individual performance came from a prodigiously talented 17-year-old, Ambati Rayudu. In his third first-class match, Rayudu scored 210 and 159 not out for Hyderabad against Andhra, becoming the second-youngest double-centurion in Ranji history and the youngest player ever to score a double-hundred and hundred in the same game.

Overall, the season was an experimental one; the new format deserved another year before being judged. It did provide plenty of four and five-day cricket in varied conditions, and fears that the two-tier Ranji Trophy would engender a transfer market were not immediately borne out. The underlying neglect remained, but the Indian board could claim some credit for trying to give national cricket a new direction.

FIRST-CLASS AVERAGES, 2002-03

BATTING

(Qualification: 600 runs, average 45.00)

	M	*I*	*NO*	*R*	*HS*	*100s*	*Avge*	*Ct/St*
M. H. Parmar (*Gujarat*)	6	9	0	619	247	1	68.77	2
†K. R. Powar (*Assam & Elite C*)	7	10	0	685	175	2	68.50	12
†S. Sriram (*Tamil Nadu & Elite A*)	12	19	3	1,072	267	5	67.00	5
A. V. Kale (*Maharashtra, Rest & Plate A*)	7	13	1	791	150	4	65.91	13
†G. Gambhir (*Delhi, Elite A & Pres. XI*)	10	15	1	893	233*	3	63.78	4
Yashpal Singh (*Services & Plate A*)	9	17	2	939	240	2	62.60	6
P. Dharmani (*Punjab & Elite C*)	10	14	1	808	230*	3	62.15	34/1
J. Arun Kumar (*Karnataka & Plate B*)	11	16	0	942	178	3	58.87	5
S. Somasunder (*Kerala & Plate B*)	11	17	0	1,000	222	4	58.82	5
A. T. Rayudu (*Hyderabad & Elite B*)	9	15	2	763	210	3	58.69	5
Wasim Jaffer (*Mumbai, Rest & Elite B*)	14	26	5	1,207	117	4	57.47	17
M. Manhas (*Delhi*)	8	12	0	674	158	3	56.16	6
S. S. Parab (*Baroda & Elite C*)	11	18	2	895	141	3	55.93	7
A. Chopra (*Delhi, Rest & Elite A*)	10	14	1	676	105	1	52.00	15
†A. R. Khurasiya (*Madhya Pradesh & Plate B*)	9	14	0	717	237	2	51.21	12
V. S. T. Naidu (*Karnataka & Plate A*)	11	18	2	817	167*	1	51.06	34/5
†H. H. Kanitkar (*Maharashtra & Plate A*)	9	17	0	858	290	2	50.47	6
†A. A. Pagnis (*Railways & Elite B*)	12	22	2	989	184	3	49.45	11
†H. K. Badani (*Tamil Nadu, Elite C & Pres. XI*)	10	14	0	692	129	3	49.42	7
A. V. Deshpande (*Vidarbha & Plate B*)	9	14	1	617	157*	1	47.46	22/5
B. M. Rowland (*Karnataka & Plate A*)	11	19	2	802	237*	2	47.17	10
†D. S. Manohar (*Hyderabad & Elite A*)	9	17	2	700	119	3	46.66	3
Y. Venugopal Rao (*Andhra & Elite A*)	11	19	2	786	127	2	46.23	12
†C. Hemanth Kumar (*Kerala & Plate B*)	11	17	3	640	150	1	45.71	12

† *Left-handed batsman.*

BOWLING

(Qualification: 25 wickets, average 30.00)

	Style	*O*	*M*	*R*	*W*	*BB*	*5W/i*	*Avge*
L. Balaji (*Tamil Nadu & Pres. XI*)	RFM	287.2	65	726	48	6-26	7	15.12
A. M. Salvi (*Mumbai & Elite B*)	RM	228.5	78	478	29	5-39	2	16.48
K. N. A. Padmanabhan (*Kerala & Plate A*)	LBG	253.1	69	719	42	7-39	4	17.11
S. V. Bahutule (*Mumbai & Elite B*)	LB	468	106	1,068	62	6-41	5	17.22
N. D. Hirwani (*Madhya Pradesh & Plate B*)	LBG	552.5	135	1,439	79	7-129	8	18.21
S. B. Joshi (*Karnataka & Plate A*)	SLA	495	149	1,085	57	6-62	4	19.03
P. V. Gandhe (*Vidarbha*)	OB	295.3	85	630	32	5-33	3	19.68
U. Chatterjee (*Bengal*)	SLA	268.4	81	569	28	5-34	2	20.32
N. M. Kulkarni (*Mumbai & Elite C*)	SLA	259.1	60	641	30	5-104	2	21.36
A. Bhandari (*Delhi & Elite C*)	RFM	381.1	69	1,234	55	6-73	3	22.43
A. Mishra (*Haryana & Pres. XI*)	LB	224.3	54	728	32	6-86	1	22.75
F. Shaikh (*Goa & Plate A*)	OB	336.3	73	886	38	9-29	3	23.31
P. L. Mhambrey (*Mumbai*)	RM	239.5	64	590	25	5-64	1	23.60
A. Uniyal (*Punjab & Elite B*)	LFM	278.1	57	827	35	6-92	3	23.62
M. Acharya (*Vidarbha*)	SLA	261.5	72	742	30	5-84	1	24.73
R. J. Kanwat (*Rajasthan & Elite A*)	OB	342.3	65	931	37	5-37	3	25.16
A. W. Zaidi (*Uttar Pradesh*)	RFM	226.5	50	643	25	6-62	3	25.72
Y. A. Golwalkar (*Madhya Pradesh & Plate A*)	LB	235.1	54	705	27	5-57	1	26.11
J. S. Yadav (*Hyderabad*)	OB	234.2	45	732	28	6-51	2	26.14
N. P. Singh (*Hyderabad*)	RM	213.2	44	707	27	6-37	1	26.18
D. Ganesh (*Karnataka & Plate A*)	RM	315.1	60	1,022	39	7-36	2	26.20
J. P. Jobanputra (*Saurashtra & Plate A*)	LM	231	44	748	26	7-83	1	28.76
S. Santh (*Kerala & Plate B*)	RM	303.1	62	956	33	5-57	1	28.96

IRANI CUP, 2002-03

Ranji Trophy Champions (Railways) v Rest of India

At Karnail Singh Stadium, Delhi, October 29, 30, 31, November 1, 2. **Railways won by five wickets.** Toss: Rest of India. **Rest of India 266** (A. Chopra 92, Yuvraj Singh 50; K. S. Parida 5-90) **and 292** (A. Chopra 59, Wasim Jaffer 116; Jai P. Yadav 6-39); **Railways 316** (Jai P. Yadav 104, Harvinder Singh 59) **and 244-5** (Y. Gowda 87*).

Jai P. Yadav was the first player to score a hundred and take five in an innings in the Irani Cup.

RANJI TROPHY, 2002-03

Elite Group A	*Played*	*Won*	*Lost*	*Drawn*	*1st-inns Points*	*Bonus Points*	*Points*
Mumbai	7	5	0	2	1	2	13
Delhi	7	2	1	4	3	1	8
Andhra	7	2	2	3	1	0	5
Hyderabad	7	1	2	4	3	0	5
Rajasthan	7	2	2	3	0	0	4
Bengal	7	1	2	4	1	0	3
Railways	7	0	2	5	3	0	3
Himachal Pradesh	7	0	2	5	1	0	1

Elite Group B	Played	Won	Lost	Drawn	1st-inns Points	Bonus Points	Points
Tamil Nadu	6	2	0	4	3	1	8
Baroda	6	2	0	4	2	1	7
Punjab	6	2	0	4	3	0	7
Assam	6	1	2	3	1	1	4
Gujarat	6	0	1	5	2	0	2
Uttar Pradesh	6	0	2	4	1	0	1
Orissa	6	0	2	4	1	0	1

Baroda qualified for the semi-finals ahead of Punjab because of a better run-quotient.

Semi-finals

Mumbai beat Baroda by an innings and 138 runs; Tamil Nadu beat Delhi by 132 runs.

Final

Mumbai beat Tamil Nadu by 141 runs.

Plate Group A	Played	Won	Lost	Drawn	1st-inns Points	Bonus Points	Points
Kerala	5	4	0	1	1	2	11
Vidarbha	5	2	1	2	1	1	6
Goa	5	1	2	2	2	0	4
Saurashtra	5	0	2	3	3	0	3
Services	5	0	0	5	1	0	1
Tripura	5	0	2	3	0	0	0

Plate Group B	Played	Won	Lost	Drawn	1st-inns Points	Bonus Points	Points
Karnataka	5	3	0	2	1	2	9
Madhya Pradesh	5	3	1	1	1	2	9
Haryana	5	3	1	1	0	1	7
Maharashtra	5	2	1	2	1	1	6
Jammu and Kashmir	5	0	4	1	0	0	0
Bihar	5	0	4	1	0	0	0

Semi-finals

Kerala beat Madhya Pradesh by 68 runs; Karnataka beat Vidarbha by 465 runs.

Final

Karnataka beat Kerala by an innings and 11 runs.

Karnataka and Kerala were promoted to the Elite Groups, replacing Himachal Pradesh and Orissa.

Outright win = 2 pts; lead on first innings in a drawn match = 1 pt; win by an innings or ten wickets = 1 bonus pt.

Elite Group A

At Trishna Stadium, Visakhapatnam, November 9, 10, 11, 12. **Drawn.** Toss: Himachal Pradesh. **Himachal Pradesh 321** (N. Gaur 155, Amit Sharma 107*) **and 29-0; Andhra 455** (Y. Venugopal Rao 126, M. S. K. Prasad 130; V. Bhatia 4-110). *Andhra 1 pt.*

At Eden Gardens, Kolkata, November 9, 10, 11, 12. **Drawn.** Toss: Rajasthan. **Bengal 413** (A. P. Chakraborty 90, D. J. Gandhi 138, R. S. Gavaskar 58, S. G. Das 50; P. K. Krishnakumar 4-79); **Rajasthan 200-3** (N. S. Doru 77*, P. K. Krishnakumar 57*).

At Feroz Shah Kotla, Delhi, November 9, 10, 11, 12. **Drawn.** Toss: Delhi. **Railways 205** (S. N. Khanolkar 68, J. J. Martin 56) **and 272-2** (A. A. Pagnis 107*, T. P. Singh 57, Y. Gowda 86*); **Delhi 507-4 dec.** (G. Gambhir 233*, M. Manhas 158). *Delhi 1 pt.*

Gambhir's 233, his third double-hundred, lasted 613 minutes and 411 balls and included 32 fours; he added 336 for Delhi's third wicket with Manhas.*

At Gymkhana Ground, Secunderabad, November 9, 10, 11, 12. **Mumbai won by 69 runs.** Toss: Mumbai. **Mumbai 98** (N. P. Singh 6-37) **and 337** (V. R. Mane 83, R. R. Powar 57*); **Hyderabad 130** (A. M. Salvi 5-40) **and 236** (Anirudh Singh 60, J. S. Yadav 78*). *Mumbai 2 pts.*

At Eden Gardens, Kolkata, November 17, 18, 19, 20. **Drawn.** Toss: Bengal. **Himachal Pradesh 290** (V. Rathore 120; R. Bose 6-110) **and 254-8 dec.** (V. Rathore 91; R. Bose 4-58); **Bengal 171** (D. J. Gandhi 63, R. S. Gavaskar 58*; A. K. Thakur 4-77, A. R. Kapoor 5-25) **and 257-5** (R. S. Gavaskar 103*). *Himachal Pradesh 1 pt.*

At Gymkhana Ground, Secunderabad, November 17, 18, 19, 20. **Drawn.** Toss: Andhra. **Hyderabad 353** (A. T. Rayudu 210) **and 374-6 dec.** (A. Nandakishore 69, A. T. Rayudu 159*, D. Vinay Kumar 59); **Andhra 352** (A. S. Pathak 51, Y. Venugopal Rao 59, M. S. K. Prasad 130; N. P. Singh 4-90, J. S. Yadav 5-87) **and 211-5** (M. S. K. Prasad 69*). *Hyderabad 1 pt.*

Rayudu's 210, his maiden first-class hundred in his third match, lasted 333 minutes and 232 balls and included 26 fours and four sixes. On the first day, he became the second-youngest player to score a Ranji double-hundred, aged 17 years 55 days (after Reetinder Singh Sodhi, 17 years 17 days); three days later, he became the second-youngest player to score a hundred in each innings (after Aamer Malik, 17 years 10 days) and the youngest player ever to score a double-hundred and a hundred in the same first-class match, beating Don Bradman's 21 years 104 days.

At Wankhede Stadium, Mumbai, November 17, 18, 19. **Mumbai won by nine wickets.** Toss: Delhi. **Delhi 123** (A. B. Agarkar 5-40) **and 251** (A. Chopra 63, M. Manhas 83); **Mumbai 302** (Wasim Jaffer 106, A. B. Agarkar 69; Arun Singh 4-51) **and 76-1.** *Mumbai 2 pts.*

At K. L. Saini Ground, Jaipur, November 17, 18, 19, 20. **Drawn.** Toss: Railways. **Railways 384** (S. N. Khanolkar 50, A. A. Pagnis 89, T. P. Singh 95) **and 179-5 dec.** (R. J. Kanwat 5-49); **Rajasthan 311** (R. B. Jhalani 63; K. S. Parida 4-105) **and 99-1.** *Railways 1 pt.*

At Kanchanjungwa Krirangan, Siliguri, November 27, 28, 29, 30. **Bengal won by three wickets.** Toss: Railways. **Railways 246** (S. V. Wankhede 84*; U. Chatterjee 5-89, S. S. Lahiri 4-89) **and 129** (U. Chatterjee 5-34); **Bengal 222** (S. G. Das 62) **and 157-7** (K. S. Parida 5-55). *Bengal 2 pts.*

At Feroz Shah Kotla, Delhi, November 27, 28, 29, 30. **Drawn.** Toss: Himachal Pradesh. **Himachal Pradesh 244** (R. K. Panta 51; A. Bhandari 5-89) **and 336-8** (Sandeep Sharma 170); **Delhi 506-6 dec.** (A. Chopra 105, G. Gambhir 157, P. Chawla 66, M. Manhas 111; V. Bhatia 4-119). *Delhi 1 pt.*

At Wankhede Stadium, Mumbai, November 27, 28, 29, 30. **Mumbai won by an innings and 72 runs.** Toss: Andhra. **Mumbai 403** (R. F. Morris 52, V. R. Samant 84, R. R. Powar 104, N. M. Kulkarni 54); **Andhra 147** (A. M. Salvi 5-39) **and 184** (H. H. Watekar 75*; N. M. Kulkarni 4-42). *Mumbai 3 pts.*

At K. L. Saini Ground, Jaipur, November 27, 28, 29, 30. **Rajasthan won by four wickets.** Toss: Hyderabad. **Hyderabad 212** (G. Arvind Kumar 94; S. Mathur 5-56) **and 350** (D. S. Manohar 101, G. Arvind Kumar 50, A. T. Rayudu 55; R. J. Kanwat 5-37); **Rajasthan 371** (N. S. Doru 122*, Sanjeev Sharma 76; S. Vishnuvardhan 4-65) **and 195-6** (G. K. Khoda 51; S. L. V. Raju 4-47). *Rajasthan 2 pts.*

At Feroz Shah Kotla, Delhi, December 19, 20, 21. **Delhi won by seven wickets.** Toss: Delhi. **Andhra 198** (M. S. K. Prasad 59, K. S. Sahabuddin 71*; A. Bhandari 6-73) **and 97** (A. Bhandari 4-34, Sarandeep Singh 4-24); **Delhi 111** (K. S. Sahabuddin 7-35) **and 186-3** (A. Chopra 93*, M. Manhas 53). *Delhi 2 pts.*

At Gymkhana Ground, Secunderabad, December 19, 20, 21, 22. **Drawn.** Toss: Bengal. **Hyderabad 395** (D. S. Manohar 64, A. T. Rayudu 134, D. Vinay Kumar 63; S. S. Lahiri 5-66) **and 238-5 dec.** (D. S. Manohar 119, A. Nandakishore 100); **Bengal 313** (D. Dasgupta 65, L. R. Shukla 84*) **and 248-8** (D. J. Gandhi 72; J. S. Yadav 4-69). *Hyderabad 1 pt.*

At Karnail Singh Stadium, Delhi, December 19, 20, 21, 22. **Drawn.** Toss: Mumbai. **Mumbai 248** (R. V. Pawar 71, S. V. Bahutule 67; K. S. Parida 4-93) **and 242-9 dec.** (V. R. Mane 62, Wasim Jaffer 117; Jai P. Yadav 5-47); **Railways 282-8 dec.** (Jai P. Yadav 60, A. A. Pagnis 116, T. P. Singh 83; N. M. Kulkarni 4-56) **and 66-2.** *Railways 1 pt.*

At K. L. Saini Ground, Jaipur, December 19, 20, 21, 22. **Rajasthan won by six wickets.** Toss: Rajasthan. **Himachal Pradesh 166** (K. J. Choudhary 4-28) **and 195** (R. J. Kanwat 5-47); **Rajasthan 266** (G. K. Khoda 84, N. S. Doru 64; A. K. Thakur 5-73) **and 96-4.** *Rajasthan 2 pts.*

At Indira Gandhi Stadium, Vijayawada, December 28, 29, 30, 31. **Drawn.** Toss: Andhra. **Andhra 371** (A. S. Pathak 80, I. G. Srinivas 97) **and 180-3** (M. Suresh 52*, Y. Venugopal Rao 91); **Railways 505-7 dec.** (Jai P. Yadav 62, A. A. Pagnis 92, Raja Ali 115, Abhay Sharma 166*). *Railways 1 pt.*

Raja Ali and Abhay Sharma added 245 for Railways' fifth wicket. Andhra wicket-keeper M. S. K. Prasad did not concede a bye.

At Lohnu Cricket Ground, Bilaspur, December 28, 29, 30, 31. **Drawn.** Toss: Hyderabad. **Hyderabad 262** (D. S. Manohar 62, A. S. Yadav 72*; Shakti Singh 6-75) **and 91-0; Himachal Pradesh 168** (R. Nayyar 54; J. S. Yadav 6-51). *Hyderabad 1 pt.*

At Wankhede Stadium, Mumbai, December 28, 29, 30, 31. **Mumbai won by nine wickets.** Toss: Mumbai. **Bengal 190** (R. S. Gavaskar 52) **and 179** (L. R. Shukla 52; S. V. Bahutule 6-67); **Mumbai 322** (N. S. Shetty 123, V. R. Samant 54; U. Chatterjee 4-43) **and 51-1.** *Mumbai 2 pts.*

At K. L. Saini Ground, Jaipur, December 28, 29, 30. **Delhi won by an innings and 11 runs.** Toss: Delhi. **Rajasthan 145** (A. Bhandari 5-52, Sarandeep Singh 4-45) **and 224** (V. A. Saxena 52, A. S. Jain 50; S. Gill 6-33); **Delhi 380** (A. Chopra 73, M. Manhas 101, V. Dahiya 74). *Delhi 3 pts.*

Delhi wicket-keeper Dahiya held six catches in Rajasthan's first innings.

At Trishna Stadium, Visakhapatnam, January 23, 24, 25, 26. **Andhra won by five wickets.** Toss: Rajasthan. **Rajasthan 204** (V. A. Saxena 64, G. K. Khoda 56) **and 282** (G. K. Khoda 117, R. B. Jhalani 58; M. Faiq 6-92); **Andhra 263** (Y. Venugopal Rao 93, M. S. K. Prasad 77; R. J. Kanwat 4-76) **and 227-5** (M. S. K. Prasad 62*, I. G. Srinivas 66). *Andhra 2 pts.*

At Feroz Shah Kotla, Delhi, January 25, 26, 27, 28. **Drawn.** Toss: Delhi. **Delhi 164** (S. S. Lahiri 5-24) **and 343-7 dec.** (A. Chopra 94, G. Gambhir 96); **Bengal 169** (S. G. Das 66) **and 134-4.** *Bengal 1 pt.*

At Gymkhana Ground, Secunderabad, January 25, 26, 27. **Hyderabad won by nine wickets.** Toss: Railways. **Hyderabad 355** (D. S. Manohar 107, A. T. Rayudu 62, J. S. Yadav 59*; Harvinder Singh 5-90, M. Kartik 4-83) **and 70-1; Railways 131** (N. P. Singh 4-43, J. S. Yadav 4-34) **and 290** (S. N. Khanolkar 53, M. Kartik 64, Harvinder Singh 52; S. Vishnuvardhan 6-55). *Hyderabad 2 pts.*

At Wankhede Stadium, Mumbai, January 25, 26, 27, 28. **Mumbai won by ten wickets.** Toss: Mumbai. **Himachal Pradesh 254** (V. Rathore 108; P. L. Mhambrey 5-64) **and 287** (Sandeep Sharma 67, V. Rathore 82, R. Nayyar 54); **Mumbai 415** (V. R. Mane 59, V. R. Samant 76, R. R. Powar 85) **and 130-0** (V. R. Mane 72*). *Mumbai 3 pts.*

At Eden Gardens, Kolkata, February 1, 2, 3, 4. **Andhra won by eight wickets.** Toss: Andhra. **Bengal 189** (N. Haldipur 59) **and 237** (D. J. Gandhi 102, D. Dasgupta 66; H. H. Watekar 4-73); **Andhra 319** (A. S. Pathak 88, H. H. Watekar 67*) **and 109-2** (Fayaz Ahmed 54*). *Andhra 2 pts.*

At Feroz Shah Kotla, Delhi, February 1, 2, 3, 4. **Drawn.** Toss: Hyderabad. **Hyderabad 297-9 dec.** (D. Vinay Kumar 96, V. V. S. Laxman 76; A. Bhandari 4-80) **and 106-2; Delhi 492-8 dec.** (G. Gambhir 174, S. Oberoi 64, Varun Kumar 77, V. Dahiya 78). *Delhi 1 pt.*

At Karnail Singh Stadium, Delhi, February 1, 2, 3, 4. **Drawn.** Toss: Railways. **Railways 198-4** (A. A. Pagnis 64, T. P. Singh 82) **v Himachal Pradesh.**

Rain permitted only 46.3 overs, on the third and fourth afternoons.

At K. L. Saini Ground, Jaipur, February 1, 2, 3, 4. **Drawn.** Toss: Mumbai. **Mumbai 242** (S. V. Bahutule 52, R. R. Powar 51) **and 218** (Sanjeev Sharma 4-43); **Rajasthan 230** (Sanjeev Sharma 51*; R. F. Morris 6-39) **and 140-6.** *Mumbai 1 pt.*

Elite Group B

At North-East Frontier Railway Stadium, Maligaon, Guwahati, November 9, 10, 11, 12. **Drawn.** Toss: Orissa. **Orissa 347** (B. B. C. C. Mohapatra 107, P. M. Mullick 129; A. Konwar 6-53); **Assam 364-7** (M. V. Joglekar 103, K. R. Powar 111; A. Barik 4-72). *Assam 1 pt.*

At Lalabhai Contractor Stadium, Surat, November 9, 10, 11, 12. **Drawn.** Toss: Uttar Pradesh. **Uttar Pradesh 413** (G. K. Pandey 122, Javed Anwar 66, A. W. Zaidi 69; S. K. Trivedi 5-102) **and 263-8** (R. Shamshad 79, A. W. Zaidi 50); **Gujarat 464** (N. D. Modi 124, M. H. Parmar 88, K. A. Damani 54, B. N. Mehta 52; R. Mishra 5-110, N. Chopra 4-117). *Gujarat 1 pt.*

At PCA Stadium, Mohali, November 9, 10, 11, 12. **Drawn.** Toss: Punjab. **Punjab 220** (R. B. Patel 4-43) **and 327-8 dec.** (R. S. Ricky 103, P. Dharmani 59; V. N. Buch 5-67); **Baroda 191** (C. C. Williams 104; Gagandeep Singh 4-35) **and 197-6.** *Punjab 1 pt.*

At Sardar Vallabhai Patel Stadium, Ahmedabad, November 17, 18, 19, 20. **Drawn.** Toss: Assam. **Gujarat 465** (M. H. Parmar 247, K. A. Damani 103; M. J. V. Ingty 4-81) **and 236-6** (L. Pawar 100*, K. A. Damani 66); **Assam 357** (K. R. Powar 72, S. S. Viswanathan 56, Sukhvinder Singh 54*; L. A. Patel 4-75). *Gujarat 1 pt.*

Parmar's 247, his second double-hundred, lasted 577 minutes and 406 balls and included 31 fours and five sixes. Pawar scored 100 on first-class debut.*

At Barabati Stadium, Cuttack, November 17, 18, 19, 20. **Drawn.** Toss: Punjab. **Orissa 301** (B. B. C. C. Mohapatra 56, R. R. Parida 56, S. S. Raul 72; Navdeep Singh 5-66) **and 256-6** (R. R. Parida 126*); **Punjab 381** (R. S. Ricky 51, P. Dharmani 81, Harminder Singh 87; D. S. Mohanty 4-37). *Punjab 1 pt.*

At Guru Nanak College Ground, Chennai, November 17, 18, 19, 20. **Drawn.** Toss: Baroda. **Baroda 381** (S. S. Parab 61, A. C. Bedade 51, N. R. Mongia 70, I. K. Pathan 54) **and 250-5** (S. S. Parab 68, T. B. Arothe 66*); **Tamil Nadu 427** (S. Sriram 128, S. Sharath 101, J. Gokulakrishnan 50; A. P. Bhoite 4-84). *Tamil Nadu 1 pt.*

At Nehru Stadium, Guwahati, November 27, 28, 29, 30. **Punjab won by 89 runs.** Toss: Punjab. **Punjab 177** (A. Kakkar 75; P. K. Das 4-30) **and 338** (P. Dharmani 121, A. Kakkar 122; M. J. V. Ingty 4-61); **Assam 230** (A. Uniyal 5-65, Navdeep Singh 4-64) **and 196** (K. R. Powar 55; Navdeep Singh 5-59). *Punjab 2 pts.*

At Barabati Stadium, Cuttack, November 27, 28, 29. **Baroda won by an innings and 141 runs.** Toss: Orissa. **Baroda 407** (S. S. Parab 141, Extras 50; D. S. Mohanty 4-69); **Orissa 131** (I. K. Pathan 6-31) **and 135** (S. S. Raul 53*; R. B. Patel 4-47). *Baroda 3 pts.*

At M. A. Chidambaram Stadium, Chennai, November 27, 28, 29, 30. **Drawn.** Toss: Tamil Nadu. **Uttar Pradesh 304** (G. K. Pandey 99, N. Chopra 86; L. Balaji 6-51) **and 253** (Jyoti P. Yadav 66, N. Chopra 67*; L. Balaji 5-78); **Tamil Nadu 260** (K. K. D. Karthik 88*; A. W. Zaidi 6-62) **and 194-9** (S. Vidyuth 59; N. Chopra 5-65). *Uttar Pradesh 1 pt.*

At Sardar Patel (Gujarat) Stadium, Motera, Ahmedabad, December 19, 20, 21, 22. **Drawn.** Toss: Gujarat. **Baroda 498** (S. S. Parab 139, C. C. Williams 67, R. K. Solanki 90; S. G. Bhatt 4-96); **Gujarat 210** (T. B. Arothe 4-51, H. N. Bachani 5-47) **and 294-9** (M. H. Parmar 78, B. N. Mehta 51*). *Baroda 1 pt.*

At PCA Stadium, Mohali, December 19, 20, 21. **Punjab won by 47 runs.** Toss: Uttar Pradesh. **Punjab 208** (A. W. Zaidi 5-84) **and 199** (D. Mongia 86; M. B. Tripathi 6-62); **Uttar Pradesh 111** (Vineet Sharma 5-22) **and 249** (N. Chopra 64; Gagandeep Singh 4-69). *Punjab 2 pts.*

Gagandeep Singh took a hat-trick in Uttar Pradesh's second innings.

At M. A. Chidambaram Stadium, Chennai, December 19, 20, 21. **Tamil Nadu won by an innings and 36 runs.** Toss: Tamil Nadu. **Orissa 122** (L. Balaji 5-25) **and 156** (R. R. Parida 61; L. Balaji 6-26); **Tamil Nadu 314** (S. Sriram 94, H. K. Badani 86). *Tamil Nadu 3 pts.*

At GSFC Ground, Vadodara, December 28, 29, 30. **Baroda won by seven wickets.** Toss: Baroda. **Assam 188** (I. S. Pathan 5-44) **and 147; Baroda 237** (R. K. Solanki 60, T. B. Arothe 64) **and 102-3.** *Baroda 2 pts.*

At M. A. Chidambaram Stadium, Chennai, December 28, 29, 30. **Tamil Nadu won by nine wickets.** Toss: Gujarat. **Gujarat 161** (L. Balaji 5-26) **and 228** (M. H. Parmar 75, B. N. Mehta 68; L. Balaji 5-81); **Tamil Nadu 260** (S. Suresh 56; L. A. Patel 5-72, S. K. Trivedi 4-75) **and 130-1** (S. Suresh 65*). *Tamil Nadu 2 pts.*

At K. D. Singh Babu Stadium, Lucknow, December 28, 29, 30, 31. **Drawn.** Toss: Orissa. **Orissa 245** (Sukhbinder Singh 102, N. Behera 51; A. W. Zaidi 6-97); **Uttar Pradesh 180-6** (R. Shamshad 82).

At Nehru Stadium, Guwahati, January 25, 26, 27, 28. **Drawn.** Toss: Tamil Nadu. **Tamil Nadu 508** (S. Suresh 132, S. Ramesh 69, H. K. Badani 115, S. V. Saravanan 81; S. Ganesh Kumar 4-95, Sukhvinder Singh 5-129) **and 57-1; Assam 468** (S. B. Saikia 63, K. R. Powar 96, N. H. Bordoloi 53, S. Z. Zuffri 81, Sukhvinder Singh 79). *Tamil Nadu 1 pt.*

At Sardar Patel (Gujarat) Stadium, Motera, Ahmedabad, January 25, 26, 27, 28. **Drawn.** Toss: Gujarat. **Gujarat 306** (N. K. Patel 66, M. H. Parmar 55, B. N. Mehta 55; Vineet Sharma 4-92) **and 302-5** (K. A. Damani 73*, B. N. Mehta 60*); **Punjab 446** (R. S. Ricky 65, P. Dharmani 230*; L. A. Patel 5-87). *Punjab 1 pt.*

Dharmani's 230, his fifth double-hundred, lasted 495 minutes and 347 balls.*

At Dr Sampurnanda Stadium, Varanasi, January 25, 26, 27, 28. **Drawn.** Toss: Uttar Pradesh. **Uttar Pradesh 384** (R. B. Elahi 93*; A. P. Bhoite 5-106) **and 55-1; Baroda 530-7 dec.** (S. S. Parab 134, T. B. Arothe 150, N. R. Mongia 111*; R. Mishra 4-116). *Baroda 1 pt.*

Elahi and Rajneesh Mishra (44) added 101 for Uttar Pradesh's tenth wicket.

At Nehru Stadium, Guwahati, February 1, 2, 3, 4. **Assam won by an innings and 87 runs.** Toss: Uttar Pradesh. **Uttar Pradesh 211** (R. B. Elahi 50; Sukhvinder Singh 4-52) **and 171** (A. Konwar 6-46); **Assam 469-9 dec.** (S. B. Saikia 77, K. R. Powar 175, M. V. Joglekar 80*; G. K. Pandey 6-97). *Assam 3 pts.*

At Sardar Patel (Gujarat) Stadium, Motera, Ahmedabad, February 1, 2, 3, 4. **Drawn.** Toss: Orissa. **Orissa 589-5 dec.** (B. B. C. C. Mohapatra 175, S. S. Das 60, R. R. Parida 112, S. S. Raul 128*, P. M. Mullick 61) **and 201; Gujarat 453** (A. A. Christian 52, N. K. Patel 165, K. A. Damani 74, B. N. Mehta 53*; Bipin Singh 5-115) **and 34-0.** *Orissa 1 pt.*

At PCA Stadium, Mohali, February 1, 2, 3, 4. **Drawn.** Toss: Tamil Nadu. **Punjab 233** (M. R. Srinivas 4-71) **and 11-0; Tamil Nadu 509-9 dec.** (S. Sriram 267, M. R. Srinivas 93; Vineet Sharma 5-136). *Tamil Nadu 1 pt.*

Sriram's 267, his third double-hundred, lasted 547 minutes and 362 balls and included 27 fours; he added 268 with Srinivas, an Indian eighth-wicket record.

Semi-finals

At GSFC Ground, Vadodara, April 25, 26, 27. **Mumbai won by an innings and 138 runs.** Toss: Mumbai. **Baroda 130** (A. B. Agarkar 5-46) **and 122** (S. V. Bahutule 5-21); **Mumbai 390** (N. S. Shetty 74, B. J. Thakkar 76, A. B. Agarkar 65; Zaheer Khan 5-46).

At Feroz Shah Kotla, Delhi, April 25, 26, 27, 28, 29. **Tamil Nadu won by 132 runs.** Toss: Tamil Nadu. **Tamil Nadu 327** (S. Ramesh 82, H. K. Badani 63) **and 261** (S. Ramesh 55, S. Sharath 75*); **Delhi 256** (M. R. Srinivas 4-47) **and 200** (V. Sehwag 99; L. Balaji 5-49).

FINAL

MUMBAI v TAMIL NADU

At Wankhede Stadium, Mumbai, May 4, 5, 6, 7, 8. Mumbai won by 141 runs. Toss: Mumbai.

Mumbai played some inspired cricket in intense heat and humidity. After they chose to bat, only Wasim Jaffer reached 50, but Tamil Nadu opted to sit on the splice and grind out a big total. They had the advantage on the second evening – 37 behind, six wickets in hand – but Agarkar struck twice in four overs next morning, and all six were gone before lunch. That gave Mumbai the initiative. Jaffer and Shetty, a 30-year-old left-hander playing his first season of Ranji cricket, built a stand of 188, and there were positive half-centuries from Thakkar (finally felled by cramp) and Powar. The declaration gave Tamil Nadu a day and a half to score 377, or draw to claim the title on first-innings lead. Badani batted five and a half hours before holing out, one of five victims for Bahutule's leg-breaks. But only two of his team-mates reached double figures as Mumbai crushed their hopes.

Close of play: First day, Mumbai 259-9 (Samant 16, Salvi 0); Second day, Tamil Nadu 223-4 (Badani 46, Sharath 10); Third day, Mumbai 228-4 (Muzumdar 4); Fourth day, Tamil Nadu 102-3 (Badrinath 12, Badani 23).

Mumbai

First innings		Second innings	
V. R. Mane c Raju b Gokulakrishnan	13	lbw b Balaji	2
Wasim Jaffer c Ramesh b Srinivas	83	lbw b Srinivas	98
N. S. Shetty c Raju b Gokulakrishnan	21	c Suresh b Srinivas	100
A. A. Muzumdar c Sriram b Suresh	30	(5) c Raju b Suresh	7
B. J. Thakkar lbw b Srinivas	0	(6) retired hurt	66
S. V. Bahutule c Raju b Suresh	34	(7) run out	27
A. B. Agarkar c Raju b Suresh	26	(8) c Balaji b Sriram	4
*P. L. Mhambrey c Ramesh b Sriram	2	(10) not out	0
R. R. Powar c Suresh b Balaji	18	not out	53
†V. R. Samant not out	17	(4) c Badrinath b Srinivas	6
A. M. Salvi c Raju b Balaji	0		
L-b 7, n-b 9	16	B 5, l-b 11, w 2, n-b 6	24
1/37 (1) 2/100 (3) 3/142 (2) 4/142 (5) 5/160 (4) 6/213 (7) 7/222 (6) 8/229 (8) 9/250 (9) 10/260 (11)	260	1/22 (1) 2/210 (3) 3/217 (2) 4/228 (4) 5/239 (5) 6/287 (7) 7/298 (8)	(7 wkts dec.) 387

In the second innings Thakkar retired hurt at 380.

Bowling: *First Innings*—Balaji 18–3–37–2; Srinivas 14–4–44–2; Gokulakrishnan 19–3–46–2; Suresh 18–2–51–3; Dhandapani 12–3–44–0; Sriram 10–1–31–1. *Second Innings*—Balaji 27–3–69–1; Srinivas 21–5–73–3; Gokulakrishnan 17–3–55–0; Suresh 14–5–48–1; Sriram 13–0–60–1; Dhandapani 10–1–55–0; Badani 3–0–11–0.

Tamil Nadu

First innings		Second innings	
*S. Suresh c Samant b Agarkar	3	b Mhambrey	44
S. Ramesh c Muzumdar b Bahutule	85	c Wasim Jaffer b Agarkar	6
S. Sriram c Samant b Agarkar	26	lbw b Bahutule	5
S. Badrinath c Mane b Bahutule	42	c Mane b Powar	20
H. K. Badani lbw b Agarkar	56	c Shetty b Bahutule	109
S. Sharath c Wasim Jaffer b Agarkar	15	lbw b Bahutule	9
M. R. Srinivas c Samant b Mhambrey	0	lbw b Salvi	4
J. Gokulakrishnan lbw b Bahutule	15	c Shetty b Powar	5
†P. Raju c Samant b Salvi	5	lbw b Bahutule	0
L. Balaji b Mhambrey	8	not out	3
D. Dhandapani not out	0	c Mane b Bahutule	0
B 3, l-b 6, n-b 7	16	B 8, l-b 13, n-b 9	30
1/4 (1) 2/72 (3) 3/131 (4) 4/202 (2) 5/228 (6) 6/239 (5) 7/239 (7) 8/251 (9) 9/271 (8) 10/271 (10)	271	1/27 (2) 2/62 (3) 3/62 (1) 4/121 (4) 5/151 (6) 6/199 (7) 7/214 (8) 8/225 (9) 9/235 (5) 10/235 (11)	235

Bowling: *First Innings*—Agarkar 29–8–57–4; Salvi 25–9–50–1; Mhambrey 16.3–1–36–2; Powar 24–5–60–0; Bahutule 21–4–59–3. *Second Innings*—Agarkar 19–6–44–1; Salvi 13–3–23–1; Bahutule 30.4–4–70–5; Mhambrey 14–5–20–1; Powar 24–4–57–2.

Umpires: V. Chopra and N. N. Menon. Referee: B. Ganguly.

RANJI TROPHY WINNERS

1934-35	Bombay	1957-58	Baroda	1980-81	Bombay
1935-36	Bombay	1958-59	Bombay	1981-82	Delhi
1936-37	Nawanagar	1959-60	Bombay	1982-83	Karnataka
1937-38	Hyderabad	1960-61	Bombay	1983-84	Bombay
1938-39	Bengal	1961-62	Bombay	1984-85	Bombay
1939-40	Maharashtra	1962-63	Bombay	1985-86	Delhi
1940-41	Maharashtra	1963-64	Bombay	1986-87	Hyderabad
1941-42	Bombay	1964-65	Bombay	1987-88	Tamil Nadu
1942-43	Baroda	1965-66	Bombay	1988-89	Delhi
1943-44	Western India	1966-67	Bombay	1989-90	Bengal
1944-45	Bombay	1967-68	Bombay	1990-91	Haryana
1945-46	Holkar	1968-69	Bombay	1991-92	Delhi
1946-47	Baroda	1969-70	Bombay	1992-93	Punjab
1947-48	Holkar	1970-71	Bombay	1993-94	Bombay
1948-49	Bombay	1971-72	Bombay	1994-95	Bombay
1949-50	Baroda	1972-73	Bombay	1995-96	Karnataka
1950-51	Holkar	1973-74	Karnataka	1996-97	Mumbai
1951-52	Bombay	1974-75	Bombay	1997-98	Karnataka
1952-53	Holkar	1975-76	Bombay	1998-99	Karnataka
1953-54	Bombay	1976-77	Bombay	1999-2000	Mumbai
1954-55	Madras	1977-78	Karnataka	2000-01	Baroda
1955-56	Bombay	1978-79	Delhi	2001-02	Railways
1956-57	Bombay	1979-80	Delhi	2002-03	Mumbai

Bombay/Mumbai have won the Ranji Trophy 35 times, Delhi and Karnataka 6, Baroda 5, Holkar 4, Bengal, Hyderabad, Madras/Tamil Nadu and Maharashtra 2, Haryana, Nawanagar, Punjab, Railways and Western India 1.

Plate Group A

At Nehru Stadium, Kochi, November 12, 13, 14, 15. **Kerala won by 158 runs.** Toss: Kerala. **Kerala 212 and 272-5 dec.** (S. Somasunder 106, M. P. Sorab 54); **Goa 215** (S. B. Dahad 85; M. Suresh Kumar 5-70) **and 111** (K. N. A. Padmanabhan 5-55). *Kerala 2 pts.*

At Model Sports Complex, Palam, Delhi, November 12, 13, 14, 15. **Drawn.** Toss: Services. **Services 491-8 dec.** (Jasvir Singh 120, Yashpal Singh 240) **and 144-2 dec.** (Yashpal Singh 67*); **Tripura 350** (R. Jaiswal 83, G. H. Banik 56, S. Roy 57; S. Dhull 5-110) **and 125-3** (R. Jaiswal 59*). *Services 1 pt.*

Yashpal Singh's 240 – his second hundred, both doubles – lasted 478 minutes and 342 balls and included 26 fours and two sixes.

At VCA Ground, Nagpur, November 12, 13, 14, 15. **Drawn.** Toss: Vidarbha. **Vidarbha 300** (C. E. Atram 59) **and 218; Saurashtra 312** (J. N. Shah 76, F. U. Bambhaniya 50*, J. P. Jobanputra 52; M. S. Acharya 5-84) **and 200-8** (R. V. Dhruv 72*; C. E. Atram 4-40). *Saurashtra 1 pt.*

At Madhavrao Scindia Cricket Ground, Rajkot, November 19, 20, 21. **Kerala won by an innings and 91 runs.** Toss: Kerala. **Kerala 375** (A. N. Kudva 52, S. R. Nair 147; N. R. Odedra 5-109); **Saurashtra 151** (S. Santh 5-57) **and 133** (T. Yohannan 6-61). *Kerala 3 pts.*

At VCA Ground, Nagpur, November 19, 20, 21, 22. **Drawn.** Toss: Vidarbha. **Vidarbha 484** (A. V. Deshpande 86, V. C. Naidu 74, N. S. Gawande 63, C. E. Atram 78; Arun Sharma 4-146)

and 174-6 dec. (A. V. Deshpande 50; H. Naidu 4-69); **Services 344** (M. P. Reddy 53, Jasvir Singh 77, Yashpal Singh 68, Sarabjit Singh 77; M. S. Acharya 4-97, P. V. Gandhe 5-91) **and 159-9** (Jasvir Singh 69; P. V. Gandhe 5-66). *Vidarbha 1 pt.*

At Dr Rajendra Prasad Stadium, Margao, November 20, 21, 22, 23. **Drawn.** Toss: Tripura. **Tripura 296** (T. K. Chanda 134; S. B. Dahad 4-50) **and 246-5** (R. Jaiswal 90, C. Sachdev 104); **Goa 466-8 dec.** (S. K. Kamat 83, A. A. Swapnil 61, S. B. Jakati 61, S. B. Dahad 65, R. P. Rane 75*). *Goa 1 pt.*

At Nehru Stadium, Kochi, November 27, 28, 29, 30. **Kerala won by an innings and 148 runs.** Toss: Kerala. **Kerala 457** (S. Somasunder 222, A. N. Kudva 130; J. Debnath 6-101); **Tripura 170** (T. K. Chanda 61; K. N. A. Padmanabhan 7-39) **and 139** (R. Deb Burman 58). *Kerala 3 pts.*

Somasunder's 222, his maiden double-hundred, lasted 522 minutes and 434 balls and included 25 fours and two sixes.

At Madhavrao Scindia Cricket Ground, Rajkot, November 27, 28, 29, 30. **Drawn.** Toss: Services. **Services 372** (Yashpal Singh 162, C. D. Thomson 130; S. Maniar 4-64) **and 185-2** (Jasvir Singh 106*); **Saurashtra 415** (A. A. Merchant 78, F. U. Bambhaniya 92, A. Kamalia 85; Arun Sharma 4-87). *Saurashtra 1 pt.*

At VCA Ground, Nagpur, November 27, 28, 29, 30. **Vidarbha won by 203 runs.** Toss: Vidarbha. **Vidarbha 336** (V. C. Naidu 81, A. S. Naidu 84; F. Shaikh 8-111) **and 294-3 dec.** (A. V. Deshpande 157*); **Goa 262** (S. K. Kamat 58, S. B. Jakati 80*; P. V. Gandhe 4-76, M. S. Acharya 4-77) **and 165** (P. V. Gandhe 5-33). *Vidarbha 2 pts.*

At Madhavrao Scindia Cricket Ground, Rajkot, December 19, 20, 21, 22. **Goa won by 90 runs.** Toss: Goa. **Goa 311** (M. D. Phadke 125, A. N. Amonkar 52; J. P. Jobanputra 7-83) **and 231** (A. P. Dani 80); **Saurashtra 251** (R. V. Dhruv 65*; F. Shaikh 5-52) **and 201** (S. B. Jakati 5-61). *Goa 2 pts.*

Goa wicket-keeper Thirugnanasambandam Arasu held six catches in Saurashtra's second innings.

At Model Sports Complex, Palam, Delhi, December 19, 20, 21, 22. **Drawn.** Toss: Services. **Kerala 478-8 dec.** (C. Hemanth Kumar 150, S. C. Oasis 71, S. R. Nair 133; Arun Sharma 4-123) **and 155-4; Services 360** (K. G. Chawda 52, Yashpal Singh 61, S. V. Ghag 52). *Kerala 1 pt.*

At VCA Ground, Nagpur, December 19, 20, 21. **Vidarbha won by an innings and 173 runs.** Toss: Tripura. **Tripura 102 and 170** (R. Jaiswal 51); **Vidarbha 445** (A. V. Deshpande 51, V. C. Naidu 113, N. S. Gawande 50, C. E. Atram 61, M. S. Acharya 55; T. Saha 4-125, J. Debnath 4-102). *Vidarbha 3 pts.*

At Madhavrao Scindia Cricket Ground, Rajkot, December 28, 29, 30, 31. **Drawn.** Toss: Saurashtra. **Tripura 263** (R. Jaiswal 53, R. Saha 60; J. P. Jobanputra 4-61) **and 292-4** (R. Jaiswal 89, S. D. Chowdhury 62, R. Saha 50*); **Saurashtra 402** (A. Kamalia 84, R. V. Dhruv 117; C. Sachdev 5-95). *Saurashtra 1 pt.*

At Model Sports Complex, Palam, Delhi, December 28, 29, 30, 31. **Drawn.** Toss: Goa. **Goa 278** (M. D. Phadke 128; A. Hariprasad 4-60); **Services 119** (F. Shaikh 9-29) **and 303-7** (M. P. Reddy 96). *Goa 1 pt.*

Shaikh's analysis of 20.4–7–29–9 was the best of the season.

At VCA Ground, Nagpur, December 28, 29, 30, 31. **Kerala won by eight wickets.** Toss: Vidarbha. **Vidarbha 303** (A. S. Naidu 118; K. N. A. Padmanabhan 6-45) **and 248** (V. C. Naidu 62, C. E. Atram 65; S. Santh 4-89); **Kerala 402** (C. M. Deepak 116, S. Somasunder 50, S. R. Nair 50) **and 155-2** (S. Somasunder 75, C. Hemanth Kumar 60*). *Kerala 2 pts.*

Plate Group B

At Keenan Stadium, Jamshedpur, November 9, 10, 11, 12. **Drawn.** Toss: Jammu and Kashmir. **Jammu and Kashmir 532-8 dec.** (V. Taggar 57, Kavaljit Singh 55, A. Gupta 203*, S. S. Salaria 115; Shahid Khan 4-113); **Bihar 142-2.**

Gupta's 203, his second double-hundred, lasted 508 minutes and 368 balls and included 17 fours. Salaria scored 115 on first-class debut.*

At Vaish College Ground, Rohtak, November 9, 10, 11, 12. **Haryana won by 103 runs.** Toss: Haryana. **Haryana 333** (A. Mishra 84, Joginder Sharma 81; H. S. Sodhi 6-72) **and 110** (N. D. Hirwani 5-30); **Madhya Pradesh 272** (M. A. Pasha 85; Joginder Sharma 5-63) **and 68** (Joginder Sharma 6-21). *Haryana 2 pts.*

Madhya Pradesh's second-innings 68 was the lowest first-class total of the season.

At Nehru Stadium, Pune, November 9, 10, 11, 12. **Drawn.** Toss: Karnataka. **Karnataka 252** (V. S. T. Naidu 61, D. Ganesh 59*; K. R. Khadkikar 4-67) **and 373-5 dec.** (J. Arun Kumar 112, V. S. T. Naidu 98, D. A. Chougule 58*; R. D. Khirid 4-103); **Maharashtra 199** (B. K. V. Prasad 4-50) **and 209-5** (N. A. Godbole 57, A. V. Kale 91). *Karnataka 1 pt.*

At Mecon Sail Stadium, Ranchi, November 17, 18, 19, 20. **Karnataka won by eight wickets.** Toss: Bihar. **Bihar 114** (Tariq-ur-Rehman 56; D. Ganesh 4-51, S. B. Joshi 5-25) **and 331** (Rajiv Kumar 67, Manish Kumar 59, M. S. Dhoni 93, S. Panda 71; B. Akhil 4-76); **Karnataka 302** (J. Arun Kumar 73, V. S. T. Naidu 86, B. Akhil 68) **and 144-2.** *Karnataka 2 pts.*

At Molana Azad Stadium, Jammu, November 17, 18, 19. **Haryana won by seven wickets.** Toss: Jammu and Kashmir. **Jammu and Kashmir 121 and 128** (Kavaljit Singh 51; A. Mishra 4-44); **Haryana 168** (Shafiq Khan 51; A. Gupta 4-32) **and 85-3.** *Haryana 2 pts.*

At Maharani Usharaje Trust Cricket Ground, Indore, November 17, 18, 19, 20. **Madhya Pradesh won by eight wickets.** Toss: Maharashtra. **Maharashtra 334** (H. H. Kanitkar 114, A. V. Kale 109; N. D. Hirwani 4-70) **and 151** (H. H. Kanitkar 64; N. D. Hirwani 5-42); **Madhya Pradesh 379** (A. R. Khurasiya 237, D. S. Bundela 75; M. J. Dalvi 5-41) **and 109-2** (A. R. Khurasiya 60). *Madhya Pradesh 2 pts.*

Khurasiya's 237, his third double-hundred, lasted 440 minutes and 299 balls and included 31 fours.

At Vaish College Ground, Rohtak, November 27, 28, 29, 30. **Drawn.** Toss: Maharashtra. **Maharashtra 298** (H. H. Kanitkar 50, A. V. Kale 108; A. Mishra 4-71) **and 262-4 dec.** (H. H. Kanitkar 63, A. V. Kale 104*); **Haryana 285** (Shafiq Khan 107, Joginder Sharma 75*; M. J. Dalvi 4-39) **and 121-4** (N. Negi 55). *Maharashtra 1 pt.*

Kale scored a century in each innings.

At M. Chinnaswamy Stadium, Bangalore, November 27, 28, 29. **Karnataka won by an innings and 321 runs.** Toss: Jammu and Kashmir. **Karnataka 598-3 dec.** (J. Arun Kumar 73, B. M. Rowland 237*, D. A. Chougule 80, V. S. T. Naidu 167*); **Jammu and Kashmir 163 and 114** (S. S. Salaria 53). *Karnataka 3 pts.*

Rowland's 237, his maiden double-hundred, lasted 636 minutes and 455 balls and included 21 fours; he added 281* for Karnataka's fourth wicket with Naidu.*

At Maharani Usharaje Trust Cricket Ground, Indore, November 27, 28, 29. **Madhya Pradesh won by an innings and 38 runs.** Toss: Madhya Pradesh. **Madhya Pradesh 379** (A. R. Khurasiya 50, D. S. Bundela 59, S. Abbas Ali 55, N. A. Patwardhan 83); **Bihar 140** (Rajiv Kumar 63; N. D. Hirwani 4-38) **and 201** (Y. A. Golwalkar 5-57). *Madhya Pradesh 3 pts.*

At Nehru Stadium, Gurgaon, December 19, 20, 21, 22. **Haryana won by an innings and 48 runs.** Toss: Haryana. **Bihar 225** (M. S. Dhoni 85; A. Mishra 6-86) **and 218** (Rajiv Kumar 68; A. Mishra 4-104); **Haryana 491** (Jitender Singh 73, Joginder Sharma 80, S. Narwal 137, D. Phagna 54). *Haryana 3 pts.*

Haryana's Nos 9 and 10, Narwal and Phagna, added 168 for the ninth wicket.

At Captain Roop Singh Stadium, Gwalior, December 19, 20, 21, 22. **Drawn.** Toss: Madhya Pradesh. **Madhya Pradesh 314** (D. S. Bundela 72, S. Abbas Ali 52, B. Tomar 60; S. B. Joshi 4-51) **and 219** (S. Abbas Ali 120; D. Ganesh 4-54); **Karnataka 263** (D. A. Chougule 60; S. K. Pandey 4-73) **and 210-7** (B. Akhil 53, V. S. T. Naidu 67*). *Madhya Pradesh 1 pt.*

At Deccan Gymkhana Ground, Pune, December 19, 20, 21, 22. **Maharashtra won by five wickets.** Toss: Maharashtra. **Jammu and Kashmir 131** (M. V. Sane 8-43) **and 458** (V. Taggar 128, Kavaljit Singh 99, S. S. Salaria 99); **Maharashtra 397** (N. A. Godbole 68, R. D. Khirid 89; Surendra Singh 5-75) **and 195-5** (H. H. Kanitkar 81). *Maharashtra 2 pts.*

At Tata Digwadi Stadium, Jamadoba, December 28, 29, 30. **Maharashtra won by an innings and 283 runs.** Toss: Maharashtra. **Maharashtra 653-6 dec.** (N. A. Godbole 54, H. H. Kanitkar 290, A. V. Kale 150, R. D. Khirid 101*); **Bihar 184** (M. S. Dhoni 83; M. V. Sane 4-24) **and 186** (Rajiv Kumar 71). *Maharashtra 3 pts.*

Kanitkar's 290, his second double-hundred, lasted 596 minutes and 447 balls and included 31 fours and four sixes; he added 279 for Maharashtra's third wicket with Kale, and 228 for the fifth with Khirid. His score, and Maharashtra's total, were the highest of the season.

At Nahar Singh Stadium, Faridabad, December 28, 29, 30. **Karnataka won by an innings and 47 runs.** Toss: Karnataka. **Karnataka 372** (R. V. Bharadwaj 53, D. A. Chougule 66, S. B. Joshi 84; A. Mishra 4-123); **Haryana 147** (D. Ganesh 7-36) **and 178** (Jitender Singh 51; D. Ganesh 5-53). *Karnataka 3 pts.*

Ganesh took 12-89 – the best match analysis of the season.

At Maharani Usharaje Trust Cricket Ground, Indore, December 28, 29, 30. **Madhya Pradesh won by an innings and 121 runs.** Toss: Madhya Pradesh. **Madhya Pradesh 562-7 dec.** (S. M. Dholpure 131, A. R. Khurasiya 108, D. S. Bundela 102, N. A. Patwardhan 54*); **Jammu and Kashmir 122** (N. D. Hirwani 5-51) **and 319** (S. Khajuria 53; N. D. Hirwani 6-89). *Madhya Pradesh 3 pts.*

Plate Semi-finals

At Nehru Stadium, Kochi, January 18, 19, 20, 21. **Kerala won by 68 runs.** Toss: Kerala. **Kerala 156 and 185** (M. Suresh Kumar 58; N. D. Hirwani 4-58); **Madhya Pradesh 112 and 161** (A. R. Khurasiya 77; S. R. Nair 5-66).

At VCA Ground, Nagpur, January 27, 28, 29, 30, 31. **Karnataka won by 465 runs.** Toss: Karnataka. **Karnataka 364** (B. M. Rowland 124, R. V. Bharadwaj 78) **and 607-9 dec.** (J. Arun Kumar 78, D. A. Chougule 166, S. B. Joshi 99, D. Ganesh 119); **Vidarbha 236** (S. B. Joshi 5-45) **and 270** (R. S. Paradkar 70, R. D. Jadhav 51; U. B. Patel 4-100, S. B. Joshi 4-51).

Chougule and Ganesh added 204 for Karnataka's eighth wicket.

Plate Final

At M. Chinnaswamy Stadium, Bangalore, March 4, 5, 6. **Karnataka won by an innings and 11 runs.** Toss: Kerala. **Kerala 190** (S. B. Joshi 6-62) **and 204** (S. B. Joshi 6-75); **Karnataka 405** (J. Arun Kumar 84, S. P. Shinde 84, V. S. T. Naidu 59, D. Ganesh 50; K. N. A. Padmanabhan 5-118).

Joshi took 12-137 in the match.

DULEEP TROPHY, 2002-03

	Played	*Won*	*Lost*	*Drawn*	*1st-innings Points*	*Points*
Elite C	4	1	0	3	4	21
Plate B	4	1	0	3	2	19
Elite B	4	1	1	2	4	18
Elite A	4	1	0	3	0	17
Plate A	4	0	3	1	2	5

Outright win = 8 pts; draw = 3 pts; lead on first innings in a drawn match = 2 pts.

At M. A. Chidambaram Stadium, Chennai, March 12, 13, 14, 15. **Drawn.** Toss: Plate Group A. **Plate Group A 373** (R. Jaiswal 80, B. M. Rowland 75, S. B. Joshi 73, D. Ganesh 72; I. K. Pathan 5-88) **and 342** (V. S. T. Naidu 83, S. B. Joshi 66, D. Ganesh 63; I. K. Pathan 4-106); **Elite Group A 281** (S. Sriram 119) **and 102-3.** *Elite Group A 3 pts, Plate Group A 5 pts.*

At Guru Nanak College Ground, Chennai, March 12, 13, 14, 15. **Drawn.** Toss: Elite Group B. **Elite Group B 350** (A. S. Yadav 59, T. P. Singh 64; N. D. Hirwani 6-80) **and 434** (A. A. Pagnis 184, Wasim Jaffer 59, M. S. K. Prasad 79; N. D. Hirwani 4-129); **Plate Group B 332** (S. Somasunder 116, S. R. Nair 95; A. Uniyal 6-92) **and 4-0.** *Elite Group B 5 pts, Plate Group B 3 pts.*

At Gymkhana Ground, Secunderabad, March 20, 21, 22, 23. **Drawn.** Toss: Elite Group C. **Elite Group A 369** (S. Sriram 109, D. Vinay Kumar 125*; N. M. Kulkarni 5-104) **and 13-1; Elite Group C 398** (J. J. Martin 132, P. Dharmani 105; I. K. Pathan 4-101). *Elite Group A 3 pts, Elite Group C 5 pts.*

At M. Chinnaswamy Stadium, Bangalore, March 20, 21, 22, 23. **Plate Group B won by an innings and seven runs.** Toss: Plate Group A. **Plate Group A 247** (R. Jaiswal 63; S. Santh 4-90, N. D. Hirwani 5-71) **and 273** (R. Jaiswal 50, Yashpal Singh 84*; N. D. Hirwani 7-129); **Plate Group B 527** (J. Arun Kumar 178, R. V. Bharadwaj 91, C. Hemanth Kumar 88). *Plate Group B 8 pts.*

At M. Chinnaswamy Stadium, Bangalore, March 27, 28, 29, 30. **Drawn.** Toss: Plate Group B. **Plate Group B 569** (J. Arun Kumar 106, S. Somasunder 153, R. V. Bharadwaj 69, D. S. Bundela 101, S. R. Nair 58; Sarandeep Singh 8-180) **and 185-4 dec.** (S. Somasunder 51, A. R. Khurasiya 73); **Elite Group A 469** (D. J. Gandhi 131, Y. Venugopal Rao 127; N. D. Hirwani 6-182). *Elite Group A 3 pts, Plate Group B 5 pts.*

Gandhi and Venugopal Rao added 228 for the fifth wicket.

At Indira Gandhi Stadium, Vijayawada, March 27, 28, 29, 30. **Drawn.** Toss: Elite Group B. **Elite Group B 390** (Wasim Jaffer 76, S. V. Bahutule 61*; N. M. Kulkarni 5-115) **and 201-7 dec.** (Wasim Jaffer 102*); **Elite Group C 247** (N. S. Doru 60*; S. V. Bahutule 6-41) **and 155-2** (S. S. Parab 65*, J. J. Martin 55*). *Elite Group B 5 pts, Elite Group C 3 pts.*

At M. Chinnaswamy Stadium, Bangalore, April 3, 4, 5, 6. **Elite Group A won by seven wickets.** Toss: Elite Group B. **Elite Group B 219** (Wasim Jaffer 62) **and 220** (Sarandeep Singh 4-48); **Elite Group A 362-8 dec.** (S. B. Bangar 57, S. Sriram 130*, Y. Venugopal Rao 51; S. V. Bahutule 5-116) **and 78-3.** *Elite Group A 8 pts.*

At Gymkhana Ground, Secunderabad, April 3, 4, 5, 6. **Elite Group C won by nine wickets.** Toss: Elite Group C. **Plate Group A 263** (A. V. Kale 98, Rajiv Kumar 61; S. K. Trivedi 4-49) **and 182** (Rajiv Kumar 55, V. S. T. Naidu 75; A. B. Agarkar 4-40, S. K. Trivedi 4-41); **Elite Group C 278** (S. S. Das 73, N. S. Doru 74) **and 172-1** (S. S. Parab 95*, Y. Gowda 50*). *Elite Group C 8 pts.*

Wicket-keeper Parthiv Patel held nine catches for Elite Group C in the match.

At M. A. Chidambaram Stadium, Chennai, April 10, 11, 12. **Elite Group B won by nine wickets.** Toss: Plate Group A. **Plate Group A 135** (B. M. Rowland 51; A. Uniyal 5-21) **and 244** (Yashpal Singh 93; S. V. Bahutule 4-44); **Elite Group B 329** (V. R. Mane 76, A. A. Pagnis 55, A. T. Rayudu 52) **and 53-1.** *Elite Group B 8 pts.*

At Nehru Stadium, Kochi, April 10, 11, 12, 13. **Drawn.** Toss: Elite Group C. **Elite Group C 426** (H. K. Badani 129, P. Dharmani 73) **and 167-7** (K. R. Powar 50; N. D. Hirwani 4-49); **Plate Group B 322** (J. Arun Kumar 78, R. V. Bharadwaj 105; N. M. Kulkarni 4-103). *Elite Group C 5 pts, Plate Group B 3 pts.*

A list of past winners of the Duleep Trophy may be found in *Wisden 2003.*

DEODHAR TROPHY, 2002-03

Note: Matches in this tournament were not first-class.

A one-day league played by teams drawn from five geographical zones.

	Played	*Won*	*Lost*	*No result*	*Bonus Points*	*Points*
North Zone	4	3	1	0	1	13
West Zone.	4	3	1	0	0	12
South Zone	4	2	2	0	1	9
East Zone	4	1	2	1	1	7
Central Zone . . .	4	0	3	1	0	2

Win = 4 pts; no result = 2 pts. One bonus point awarded for achieving victory with a run-rate 1.25 times that of the opposition.

CRICKET IN PAKISTAN, 2002-03

ABID ALI KAZI

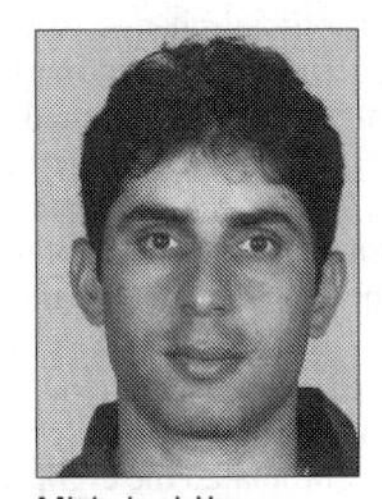

Misbah-ul-Haq

Pakistan's international fortunes continued to be a roller-coaster ride. In October 2002, they were bowled out for 59 and 53 – their two lowest Test totals – by Australia at Sharjah, and in March they were knocked out of the World Cup at the first stage. They had been semi-finalists or better in five of the previous seven World Cups, but this time their only wins came against ICC associates Namibia and Holland. Between these disasters, Pakistan enjoyed a clean sweep on a tour of Zimbabwe but lost heavily in South Africa. Afterwards, they had mixed results in one-day tournaments in Sharjah, Sri Lanka and England. And in September, Bangladesh very nearly inflicted a major embarrassment in the Third Test at Multan, where they were a single wicket short of their inaugural Test victory, though Pakistan finally completed another whitewash.

Australia had refused to play in Pakistan for security reasons, like the New Zealanders and West Indians the previous season, and South Africa threatened to stay away in October 2003, but they were eventually persuaded to come (and lost the Test series 1–0); even better news was that India said they were willing to return to Pakistan after politics had sabotaged their last scheduled visit in September 2001.

Problems on the field meant that heads rolled, though Tauqir Zia, the chairman of the Pakistan Cricket Board, remained in command for a fourth year. He offered his resignation in disgust at the Australian humiliation, but was persuaded to carry on by the national president, General Pervez Musharraf. He finally stepped down in December 2003. Well before that, the World Cup failure caused a massive overhaul. The captain, Waqar Younis, was one of nine players from the 15-strong World Cup squad dropped for the next one-day tournament. Richard Pybus, who had resumed as coach in October 2002 when Mudassar Nazar was dismissed, also went; Javed Miandad returned for his fourth stint in the job. Haroon Rashid became the fourth team manager in six months (following Yawar Saeed, Brigadier Mohammad Nasir, and diplomat Shaharyar Khan), and Ramiz Raja replaced Chishty

Mujahid as the board's chief executive. The new captain was Rashid Latif, who had filled the role before in 1997-98. He immediately led a young side to victory in the Cherry Blossom Sharjah Cup, but by September he had resigned after a selection row, to be replaced by Inzamam-ul-Haq. This was the 18th official change of captaincy in a decade.

Tampering with the domestic game's structure also continued. The Quaid-e-Azam Trophy was opened to both regional and "departmental" sides (i.e. commercial ones), a move last tried in 1999-2000 but abandoned after one season. When the regional and departmental teams compete in separate tournaments, the same players can appear for both; when the two are combined, the big companies can afford the best players, weakening the regional teams. In order to compensate, the Quaid-e-Azam format was revamped. The 14 regional sides plus ten departments from the previous year's Patron's Trophy were divided into four groups of six. These mini-leagues eliminated the eight weakest teams, while the remaining 16 advanced to a knockout.

But the next two rounds were structured to keep the top eight teams – those who had finished in first and second place in each group (mostly departments) – apart from those who had finished third and fourth (mostly regional) until the semi-finals. That meant two regional sides, Faisalabad and Rawalpindi, who had finished third in their respective groups, reached the semis, where they went out to two departments, PIA (the airline) and KRL (Khan Research Labs, based in Rawalpindi). PIA, who had won the Quaid-e-Azam the last time they were eligible three years earlier, won the final by a comfortable ten wickets with a day to spare thanks to a double-hundred from Yasir Hameed. Once again, however, the combined competition was a one-season wonder; in 2003-04, the regional teams and departments reverted to separate tournaments.

The Quaid-e-Azam's non-first-class Grade II was renamed the Cornelius Trophy, (after Justice A. R. Cornelius, a pioneer administrator in Pakistani cricket) and contested by 26 regional teams – including Afghanistan, whose debut had attracted much publicity the previous season. Islamabad beat Quetta by an innings in the final. Grade II of the Patron's Trophy (whose Grade I had disappeared with the expansion of the Quaid-e-Azam) was renamed the Kardar Trophy, after Pakistan's first Test captain, Abdul Hafeez Kardar, and contested by 11 departmental teams. Sui Gas Corporation won.

The national one-day tournament became the Patron's Cup, sponsored by National Bank. The teams were the same as those competing in the first-class Quaid-e-Azam Trophy, and produced a similar outcome: PIA added the cup to their first-class crown, beating WAPDA, who had crushed KRL in their semi-final.

The PCB initiated two further competitions. A Super League Ramzan Cup was played during the month of Ramadan by four teams selected by the board, labelled Greens, Whites, Blues and Reds. Initially, the tournament was scheduled to be not a day-nighter but an all-nighter – from 9 p.m. to 4.30 a.m. – but, because of the dew in Lahore, it moved to the daytime. In the final, Pakistan opener Imran Nazir led the Reds to victory over Moin

Khan's Whites. The other new tournament was the PCB Trophy, in which 28 new or weaker regional sides played two-day matches. Sahiwal won the three-day final against Mirpur Khas. In the Under-19 Grade I championships, Karachi Whites won the three-day and one-day titles; Grade II was won by Gujranwala and Grade III by Sahiwal.

The restructuring of first-class cricket meant fewer matches, so it was not surprising that no player crossed the 1,000-run mark in 2002-03. For the second successive season, Misbah-ul-Haq was the leading scorer and headed the batting averages, with 963 at 107. In 12 Quaid-e-Azam innings for finalists KRL, he scored four centuries – including three in succession – and five other fifties. The previous season, he had played 24 innings and totalled 1,386. The leading wicket-taker was 18-year-old pace bowler Umar Gul of PIA, who claimed 45 (including 11 against Sri Lanka A) in eight games, in his first full season, to win his international debut.

FIRST-CLASS AVERAGES, 2002-03

BATTING

(Qualification: 300 runs)

	M	*I*	*NO*	*R*	*HS*	*100s*	*Avge*	*Ct/St*
Misbah-ul-Haq (*KRL*)	8	12	3	963	167*	4	107.00	9
Yasir Hameed (*PIA*)	8	8	2	450	207	2	75.00	9
Ghulam Ali (*PIA*)	9	11	2	606	188	3	67.33	7
Aamer Hanif (*Allied Bank*)	6	7	2	321	97	0	64.20	3
Faisal Athar (*PWD*)	5	8	0	502	167	2	62.75	4
Ijaz Ahmed, jun. (*Allied Bank*)	6	6	0	372	125	1	62.00	8
†Usman Tariq (*Allied Bank*)	6	8	1	433	180	2	61.85	7
Aamer Sajjad (*Lahore Whites*)	4	5	0	303	153	1	60.60	1
Asif Hussain (*Faisalabad*)	7	10	1	516	198*	2	57.33	8
†Asif Mujtaba (*PIA*)	9	9	1	429	118	1	53.62	5
Wajahatullah Wasti (*Allied Bank*)	6	7	0	372	110	2	53.14	6
Maisam Hasnain (*Karachi Whites*)	5	9	0	454	148	2	50.44	2
Saeed Bin Nasir (*KRL*)	6	9	1	402	93*	0	50.25	1
Bazid Khan (*PIA & Pakistan A*)	10	10	1	450	91	0	50.00	9
Bilal Asad (*Allied Bank & Pakistan A*)	7	9	1	389	151	1	48.62	7
†Zeeshan Khan (*Multan*)	6	10	1	419	158	1	46.55	2
Mohammad Zaman (*Faisalabad*)	7	10	1	386	126	2	42.88	9/3
†Asim Kamal (*Karachi Whites & Pakistan A*)	7	13	2	465	164	2	42.27	5
†Sami-ul-Haq (*Faisalabad*)	7	10	2	336	63	0	42.00	2
Faisal Naved (*ZTBL*)	7	12	0	486	106	1	40.50	4
Hasan Adnan (*WAPDA*)	7	9	1	320	100*	1	40.00	3
Sheraz Khalid (*Rawalpindi*)	8	14	1	509	128	1	39.15	7
Mohammad Ramzan (*KRL*)	9	14	3	393	110*	1	35.72	11
Moin Khan (*PIA & Pakistan A*)	11	11	1	345	82	0	34.50	30/2
†Saeed Anwar, jun. (*KRL*)	9	14	1	408	93	0	31.38	2
†Nauman Aman (*Rawalpindi*)	8	14	2	343	142	1	28.58	7
Inam-ul-Haq (*ZTBL*)	7	13	1	342	129	1	28.50	3
†Babar Naeem (*Rawalpindi*)	8	14	1	354	91*	0	27.23	4
Zahoor Elahi (*ZTBL*)	7	12	0	319	84	0	26.58	5

† *Left-handed batsman.*

BOWLING

(Qualification: 20 wickets)

	Style	O	M	R	W	BB	5W/i	Avge
Farooq Iqbal (*Faisalabad*)	SLA	199	61	463	38	6-33	3	12.18
Kamran Hussain (*Bahawalpur*)	LM	119.1	34	287	23	7-46	2	12.47
Mohammad Zahid (*PIA & Pakistan A*)	RFM	110.2	19	358	25	7-26	1	14.32
Fahad Masood (*ZTBL*)	RFM	183.1	46	486	32	6-43	3	15.18
Jaffer Nazir (*KRL*)	RFM	258	62	675	44	7-104	7	15.34
Shabbir Ahmed (*National Bank*)	RFM	172.4	39	514	33	7-70	4	15.57
Arshad Khan (*Allied Bank*)	OB	236.1	65	620	39	8-86	2	15.89
Sajid Shah (*Habib Bank*)	RFM	114	18	323	20	4-37	0	16.15
Shoaib Malik (*PIA*)	OB	169.3	42	512	31	6-73	2	16.51
Mohammad Fayyaz (*Rawalpindi*)	RFM	152.4	32	483	29	6-65	3	16.65
Imran Ali (*Pakistan Customs*)	RFM	160.2	35	458	26	5-48	2	17.61
Danish Kaneria (*Habib Bank & Pakistan A*)	LB	167	44	402	22	5-42	3	18.27
Abdur Rauf (*Pakistan Customs & Pakistan A*)	RFM	119.2	18	407	22	7-55	2	18.50
Umar Gul (*PIA & Pakistan A*)	RFM	248.1	52	838	45	6-97	3	18.62
Tahir Mughal (*Sialkot*)	RFM	225.4	43	606	32	6-38	3	18.93
Ahmed Hayat (*Sargodha*)	RFM	143.3	20	524	27	6-57	1	19.40
Najaf Shah (*PIA*)	LFM	160.2	46	452	22	5-31	2	20.54
Mubashir Nazir (*ZTBL*)	RFM	173.1	45	509	24	5-39	1	21.20
Mohammad Asif (*KRL*)	RFM	201.1	34	645	28	5-100	1	23.03
Yasir Arafat (*KRL & Pakistan A*)	RM	245.5	41	876	38	5-57	4	23.05
Azhar Abbas (*Multan*)	RM	232.4	53	722	30	6-108	2	24.06
Zahid Saeed (*National Bank*)	LFM	172.1	32	524	21	6-77	2	24.95
Mohammad Akram (*Rawalpindi*)	RFM	200.5	41	598	22	4-78	0	27.18

Note: Averages do not include Bangladesh's tour in August–September 2003.

QUAID-E-AZAM TROPHY, 2002-03

Group I	Played	Won	Lost	Drawn	1st-inns Points	Points
National Bank	5	2	0	3	6	24
WAPDA	5	1	0	4	12	21
Faisalabad	5	1	1	3	6	15
Sargodha	5	1	1	3	6	15
Service Industries	5	0	2	3	3	3
Lahore Blues	5	0	1	4	0	0

Faisalabad were placed ahead of Sargodha on net run-rate.

Group II	Played	Won	Lost	Drawn	1st-inns Points	Points
Allied Bank	5	4	0	1	15	51
Bahawalpur	5	2	1	2	9	26*
PWD	5	1	0	4	9	18
Multan	5	1	2	2	3	12
Karachi Whites	5	0	1	4	9	9
Dadu	5	0	4	1	0	0

* *One point deducted due to non-submission of captain's report on umpires.*

Group III	*Played*	*Won*	*Lost*	*Drawn*	*1st-inns Points*	*Points*
Pakistan Customs	5	1	0	4	9	18
Habib Bank	5	1	0	4	3	12
Lahore Whites	5	1	0	4	3	12
Sialkot	5	0	1	4	6	6
Gujranwala	5	0	1	4	3	3
Sheikhupura	5	0	1	4	3	3

Habib Bank were placed ahead of Lahore Whites on net run-rate.

Group IV	*Played*	*Won*	*Lost*	*Drawn*	*1st-inns Points*	*Points*
PIA	5	4	0	1	12	48
KRL	5	3	0	2	15	42
Rawalpindi	5	2	2	1	6	24
ZTBL	5	1	2	2	6	15
Karachi Blues	5	1	3	1	3	12
Peshawar	5	0	4	1	3	3

ZTBL (Zarai Taraqiati Bank Ltd) were formerly known as ADBP (Agricultural Development Bank of Pakistan).

Outright win = 9 pts; lead on first innings in a won or drawn game = 3 pts.

Pre-quarter-finals: KRL beat Allied Bank on first-innings lead; Faisalabad beat Sialkot by an innings and seven runs; National Bank beat Habib Bank by an innings and 57 runs; Sargodha beat Lahore Whites by nine wickets; Rawalpindi beat Multan by seven wickets; WAPDA beat Pakistan Customs by two wickets; PIA beat Bahawalpur by an innings and 132 runs; ZTBL beat PWD on first-innings lead.

Quarter-finals: KRL beat National Bank on first-innings lead; PIA beat WAPDA on scoring-rate; Rawalpindi beat Sargodha on scoring-rate; Faisalabad beat ZTBL by five wickets.

Semi-finals: KRL beat Faisalabad by ten wickets; PIA beat Rawalpindi by an innings and 34 runs.

Final: PIA beat KRL by ten wickets.

Group I

At LCCA Ground, Lahore, December 21, 22, 23, 24. **Drawn.** Toss: Faisalabad. **Lahore Blues 195 and 28-0; Faisalabad 352** (Asif Hussain 121, Ijaz Mahmood 50; Sajid Ali 6-82). *Faisalabad 3 pts.*

At Sargodha Stadium, Sargodha, December 21, 22, 23, 24. **Drawn.** Toss: Sargodha. **National Bank 171** (Sajid Ali 57; Ahmed Hayat 4-50) **and 89-4; Sargodha 218** (Majid Saeed 62; Mushtaq Ahmed 5-54). *Sargodha 3 pts.*

At Gymkhana Ground, Okara, December 21, 22, 23. **WAPDA won by ten runs.** Toss: Service Industries. **WAPDA 136** (Tariq Aziz 64) **and 177** (Adil Nisar 69; Mohammad Irshad 4-38); **Service Industries 110** (Faisal Irfan 6-29) **and 193** (Rizwan Ahmed 51; Kashif Raza 4-48, Waqas Ahmed 4-58). *WAPDA 12 pts.*

At Iqbal Stadium, Faisalabad, December 27, 28, 29, 30. **National Bank won by two wickets.** Toss: National Bank. **Faisalabad 172** (Zeeshan Butt 59) **and 281** (Mohammad Zaman 126; Zahid Saeed 6-77); **National Bank 295** (Saeed Anwar, sen. 58, Qaiser Abbas 87, Mushtaq Ahmed 62; Farooq Iqbal 4-80) **and 159-8** (Naumanullah 54; Moazzam Ali 4-73, Farooq Iqbal 4-29). *National Bank 12 pts.*

At Sargodha Stadium, Sargodha, December 27, 28, 29, 30. **Sargodha won by eight wickets.** Toss: Sargodha. **Service Industries 286** (Bilal Khilji 58, Sufyan Munir 64, Asim Butt 67) **and 144** (Sufyan Munir 55; Ahmed Hayat 6-57); **Sargodha 374** (Ahmed Hayat 84, Extras 73; Mohammad Irshad 4-82) **and 58-2.** *Sargodha 12 pts.*

Umair Hasan (46) and Ahmed Hayat added 155 for Sargodha's eighth wicket.

At Gymkhana Ground, Okara, December 27, 28, 29, 30. **Drawn.** Toss: WAPDA. **WAPDA 243** (Hasan Adnan 100*; Mohammad Khalil 4-66) **and 284-6 dec.** (Atiq-ur-Rehman 99, Rizwan Malik 59*); **Lahore Blues 180** (Naved-ul-Hasan 5-49) **and 115-9** (Naved-ul-Hasan 4-49). *WAPDA 3 pts.*

At Iqbal Stadium, Faisalabad, January 2, 3, 4. **Faisalabad won by an innings and 137 runs.** Toss: Faisalabad. **Sargodha 122** (Farooq Iqbal 4-44) **and 110** (Farooq Iqbal 6-33, Adnan Rasool 4-38); **Faisalabad 369** (Mohammad Zaman 119, Tauqeer Hussain 55, Farooq Iqbal 55; Mohammad Hafeez 5-79). *Faisalabad 12 pts.*

At Gaddafi Stadium, Lahore, January 2, 3, 4, 5. **Drawn.** Toss: Lahore Blues. **Service Industries 252** (Sufyan Munir 67; Mohammad Khalil 5-109) **and 73-2; Lahore Blues 234** (Sohail Idrees 95; Imran Adil 6-79). *Service Industries 3 pts.*

At Lahore Country Club, Muridke, January 2, 3, 4, 5. **Drawn.** Toss: WAPDA. **National Bank 104-7** (Sarfraz Ahmed 4-32) **v WAPDA.**

Fog and bad light prevented all play except for 35 overs on the second day.

At Iqbal Stadium, Faisalabad, January 8, 9, 10, 11. **Drawn.** Toss: WAPDA. **Faisalabad 163** (Hasnain Haider 55; Aqeel Ahmed 5-46); **WAPDA 190-8** (Sarfraz Ahmed 52; Tauqeer Hussain 6-65). *WAPDA 3 pts.*

At Gaddafi Stadium, Lahore, January 8, 9, 10, 11. **Drawn.** Toss: National Bank. **Service Industries 150** (Kashif Nizami 55; Shabbir Ahmed 6-55); **National Bank 70-4.**

At Sargodha Stadium, Sargodha, January 8, 9, 10, 11. **Drawn.** Toss: Lahore Blues. **Sargodha 174** (Shehzad Butt 4-71); **Lahore Blues 88-7** (Ahmed Hayat 4-39).

At Iqbal Stadium, Faisalabad, January 14, 15, 16, 17. **Drawn.** Toss: Service Industries. **Faisalabad 361** (Asif Hussain 198*, Farooq Iqbal 91; Asim Butt 4-75); **Service Industries 71-1.**

Asif Hussain and Farooq Iqbal added 227 for Faisalabad's seventh wicket.

At Gymkhana Ground, Okara, January 14, 15, 16, 17. **National Bank won by 152 runs.** Toss: Lahore Blues. **National Bank 224** (Sajid Ali 50; Khurram Irshad 4-41) **and 231** (Shehzad Butt 4-87, Khurram Irshad 4-80); **Lahore Blues 125** (Shabbir Ahmed 7-70) **and 178** (Mushtaq Ahmed 4-59, Qaiser Abbas 4-36). *National Bank 12 pts.*

At Sargodha Stadium, Sargodha, January 14, 15, 16, 17. **Drawn.** Toss: WAPDA. **Sargodha 100** (Kashif Raza 4-39); **WAPDA 224-5** (Hasan Adnan 85; Sami Khan 4-57). *WAPDA 3 pts.*

Kashif Raza took a hat-trick.

Group II

At National Stadium, Karachi, December 21, 22, 23, 24. **Drawn.** Toss: Bahawalpur. **Bahawalpur 167 and 321-5** (Mohammad Rashid 80); **Karachi Whites 327** (Maisam Hasnain 116, Fahadullah Khan 85). *Karachi Whites 3 pts.*

At Multan Cricket Stadium, Multan, December 21, 22, 23, 24. **Allied Bank won by an innings and 33 runs.** Toss: Allied Bank. **Multan 158** (Arshad Khan 4-54) **and 251** (Mohammad Ali 82, Mohammad Fazil 91*); **Allied Bank 442-8 dec.** (Bilal Asad 151, Naved Latif 120, Aamer Hanif 50*; Azhar Abbas 4-114). *Allied Bank 12 pts.*

Multan wicket-keeper Mohammad Fazil held six catches in Allied Bank's innings.

At UBL Sports Complex, Karachi, December 21, 22, 23, 24. **PWD won by 97 runs.** Toss: Dadu. **PWD 116** (Saad Wasim 53*; Athar Laeeq 4-39, Kashif Ali 4-46) **and 196** (Athar Laeeq 6-35); **Dadu 66** (Shakeel-ur-Rehman 5-15) **and 149** (Mohammad Saleem 52*; Shakeel-ur-Rehman 4-52, Aftab Ahmed 4-13). *PWD 12 pts.*

Dadu wicket-keeper Wasim Ahmed held seven catches in PWD's second innings and 11 in the match, equalling Pakistan's first-class record for a match.

At Bahawal Stadium, Bahawalpur, December 27, 28, 29. **Allied Bank won by ten wickets.** Toss: Allied Bank. **Bahawalpur 81** (Arshad Khan 7-25) **and 257** (Kamran Hussain 54; Arshad Khan 8-86); **Allied Bank 324-9 dec.** (Ijaz Ahmed, jun. 75, Mohammad Zahid 50, Aamer Hanif 54; Faisal Elahi 4-74) **and 17-0.** *Allied Bank 12 pts.*

Arshad Khan took 15-111, the best match analysis of the season.

At National Stadium, Karachi, December 27, 28, 29, 30. **Drawn.** Toss: PWD. **Karachi Whites 302** (Agha Sabir 52; Rajesh Ramesh 5-91) **and 459-7** (Wasim Naeem 82, Mohammad Masroor 90, Fahadullah Khan 61, Amin-ur-Rehman 63); **PWD 343** (Faisal Athar 79, Saad Wasim 51, Iqbal Imam 53, Ahmer Saeed 74; Nasir Khan 4-104). *PWD 3 pts.*

At Multan Cricket Stadium, Multan, December 27, 28, 29. **Multan won by an innings and 11 runs.** Toss: Multan. **Dadu 149** (Mohammad Saleem 61; Naeem Iqbal 4-35) **and 164** (Shahid Qambrani 50; Farhan Abbasi 4-36); **Multan 324** (Mohammad Ali 84, Ali Rafi 53). *Multan 12 pts.*

At Bahawal Stadium, Bahawalpur, January 2, 3, 4, 5. **Bahawalpur won by 194 runs.** Toss: Bahawalpur. **Bahawalpur 241** (Bilal Rana 65; Athar Laeeq 4-58, Rizwan Ahmed 6-88) **and 262-8 dec.** (Maqsood Akbar 68, Mohammad Rashid 57, Kamran Hussain 54; Wasim Burfat 4-61); **Dadu 148 and 161** (Rizwan Ahmed 63*; Bilal Rana 5-45). *Bahawalpur 12 pts.*

Aqeel Abbas scored 0 in 69 minutes in Bahawalpur's first innings.*

At National Stadium, Karachi, January 2, 3, 4. **Allied Bank won by an innings and 45 runs.** Toss: Allied Bank. **Karachi Whites 195** (Aqib Javed 4-51) **and 209** (Tahir Khan 67*; Aqib Javed 6-54); **Allied Bank 449** (Bilal Asad 57, Ijaz Ahmed, jun. 66, Naved Latif 71, Aamer Hanif 97, Tanvir Ahmed 76). *Allied Bank 12 pts.*

At Multan Cricket Stadium, Multan, January 2, 3, 4, 5. **Drawn.** Toss: Multan. **PWD 365** (Afsar Nawaz 137, Riaz Sheikh 130; Azhar Abbas 6-108) **and 131-7** (Faisal Athar 63; Azhar Abbas 5-62); **Multan 289** (Zeeshan Khan 158; Rajesh Ramesh 4-71). *PWD 3 pts.*

Afsar Nawaz and Riaz Sheikh added 228 for the seventh wicket in PWD's first innings, when Multan wicket-keeper Mohammad Fazil made five catches and a stumping.

At Asghar Ali Shah Stadium, Karachi, January 8, 9, 10. **Allied Bank won by an innings and 425 runs.** Toss: Allied Bank. **Dadu 102** (Shahid Qambrani 50; Arshad Khan 4-23) **and 73** (Arshad Khan 4-29, Mohammad Zahid 4-17); **Allied Bank 600-8 dec.** (Usman Tariq 180, Wajahatullah Wasti 110, Ijaz Ahmed, jun. 58, Aaley Haider 100*, Aamer Hanif 65; Shahid Qambrani 4-137). *Allied Bank 12 pts.*

Usman Tariq outscored both Dadu innings single-handed.

At Bahawal Stadium, Bahawalpur, January 8, 9, 10, 11. **Drawn.** Toss: Bahawalpur. **PWD 146** (Saad Wasim 52*; Kamran Hussain 7-46) **and 272** (Faisal Athar 137; Kamran Hussain 5-43, Imranullah Aslam 4-103); **Bahawalpur 343-9 dec.** (Asif Iqbal 50, Ahsan Raza 60) **and 67-7** (Rauf Akbar 4-35). *Bahawalpur 3 pts.*

Chasing 76 in 14 overs, Bahawalpur finished nine runs short with three wickets left.

At UBL Sports Complex, Karachi, January 8, 9, 10, 11. **Drawn.** Toss: Multan. **Karachi Whites 376** (Maisam Hasnain 148, Iqbal Sheikh 53, Tahir Khan 85) **and 212-6 dec.** (Asif Zakir 51, Asim Kamal 104*); **Multan 287** (Kamran Ali 73; Tahir Khan 4-96, Arif Mahmood 4-84) **and 175-5** (Zeeshan Khan 84*). *Karachi Whites 3 pts.*

At UBL Sports Complex, Karachi, January 14, 15, 16, 17. **Drawn.** Toss: PWD. **PWD 279** (Saad Wasim 71; Bilal Asad 4-17) **and 77-2; Allied Bank 536** (Usman Tariq 104, Bilal Asad 77, Wajahatullah Wasti 108, Ijaz Ahmed, jun. 125; Rajesh Ramesh 4-125). *Allied Bank 3 pts.*

At Steel Mills Ground, Karachi, January 14, 15, 16, 17. **Drawn.** Toss: Karachi Whites. **Karachi Whites 380** (Asif Zakir 79, Asim Kamal 164, Iqbal Sheikh 54; Rizwan Ahmed 4-85) **and 164-5** (Arif Mahmood 55; Nawaz Ali 4-33); **Dadu 219** (Shahnawaz Baloch 54, Rizwan Ahmed 82; Tabish Khan 4-70) **and 350** (Mohammad Saleem 89, Zulfiqar Ali 76, Shahid Qambrani 53). *Karachi Whites 3 pts.*

First-class cricket returned to the Steel Mills ground after 16 years.

At Multan Cricket Stadium, Multan, January 14, 15, 16, 17. **Bahawalpur won by nine wickets.** Toss: Bahawalpur. **Multan 179** (Ali Rafi 55, Shahid Hameed 51; Kamran Hussain 4-58) **and 126** (Aqeel Abbas 7-69); **Bahawalpur 291** (Inam-ul-Haq Rashid 84; Naeem Iqbal 4-87) **and 18-1.** *Bahawalpur 12 pts.*

Group III

At Lahore Country Club, Muridke, December 21, 22, 23, 24. **Drawn.** Toss: Habib Bank. **Pakistan Customs 276** (Naseem Khan 92; Danish Kaneria 5-71) **and 165-8; Habib Bank 244** (Imran Ali 4-70). *Pakistan Customs 3 pts.*

At Gaddafi Stadium, Lahore, December 21, 22, 23, 24. **Drawn.** Toss: Sheikhupura. **Lahore Whites 353** (Aamer Sajjad 153, Mohammad Hussain 51; Waqas Chughtai 4-111); **Sheikhupura 397-6** (Saleem Mughal 146*, Mohammad Islam 69*, Extras 58). *Sheikhupura 3 pts.*

Saleem Mughal and Mohammad Islam added 183 for Sheikhupura's seventh wicket.*

At Saga Cricket Ground, Sialkot, December 21, 22, 23, 24. **Drawn.** Toss: Sialkot. **Gujranwala 280** (Iftikhar Ahmed 51, Kamran Younis 61; Imran Tahir 5-88) **and 275** (Khalid Butt 60; Tahir Mughal 4-89); **Sialkot 231** (Faisal Khan 88; Naved Arif 5-67) **and 10-1.** *Gujranwala 3 pts.*

At LCCA Ground, Lahore, December 27, 28, 29, 30. **Lahore Whites won by an innings and 57 runs.** Toss: Gujranwala. **Gujranwala 179** (Asim Munir 82; Wasim Khan 4-63) **and 203** (Mohammad Hussain 4-35); **Lahore Whites 439-9 dec.** (Rizwan Aslam 209*, Khurram Siddiq 63, Extras 55; Naved Arif 4-111). *Lahore Whites 12 pts.*

Rizwan Aslam's 209 lasted 540 minutes and 452 balls and included 27 fours.*

At Sheikhupura Stadium, Sheikhupura, December 27, 28, 29. **Habib Bank won by 90 runs.** Toss: Sheikhupura. **Habib Bank 155** (Irfan Fazil 53; Waqas Chughtai 6-65) **and 269** (Asadullah Butt 63, Atiq-uz-Zaman 66; Waqas Chughtai 4-73); **Sheikhupura 167** (Sajid Shah 4-37, Danish Kaneria 4-36) **and 167** (Sajid Shah 4-37, Shahid Nazir 4-62). *Habib Bank 9 pts.*

At Saga Cricket Ground, Sialkot, December 27, 28, 29, 30. **Pakistan Customs won by 54 runs.** Toss: Sialkot. **Pakistan Customs 255** (Aamer Bashir 75) **and 102** (Tahir Mughal 6-38); **Sialkot 179** (Extras 50; Nadeem Iqbal 4-46, Imran Ali 5-48) **and 124** (Abdur Rauf 7-55). *Pakistan Customs 12 pts.*

At Saga Cricket Ground, Sialkot, January 2, 3, 4, 5. **Drawn.** Toss: Pakistan Customs. **Gujranwala 173** (Saad Butt 55; Abdur Rauf 5-71); **Pakistan Customs 183-9** (Aamer Bashir 56*; Naved Arif 6-69). *Pakistan Customs 3 pts.*

At LCCA Ground, Lahore, January 2, 3, 4, 5. **Drawn.** Toss: Habib Bank. **Lahore Whites 188** (Danish Kaneria 5-72) **and 129-3** (Umar Javed 65*); **Habib Bank 303-6 dec.** (Farhan Adil 122*, Khaqan Arsal 66). *Habib Bank 3 pts.*

At Sheikhupura Stadium, Sheikhupura, January 2, 3, 4, 5. **Drawn.** Toss: Sialkot. **Sheikhupura 136** (Tahir Mughal 5-45, Zaman Haider 4-48) **and 67-9** (Tahir Mughal 4-44); **Sialkot 152** (Waqas Chughtai 5-48, Nadeem Javed 4-72). *Sialkot 3 pts.*

At Lahore Country Club, Muridke, January 8, 9, 10, 11. **Drawn.** Toss: Sheikhupura. **Gujranwala 54-2 v Sheikhupura.**

Bad light prevented all play except for 13 overs on the third day.

At LCCA Ground, Lahore, January 8, 9, 10, 11. **Drawn.** Toss: Pakistan Customs. **Pakistan Customs 309-5 dec.** (Azhar Shafiq 108, Kashif Siddiq 128); **Lahore Whites 255-4** (Fahad-ul-Haq 96).

At Saga Cricket Ground, Sialkot, January 8, 9, 10, 11. **Drawn.** Toss: Sialkot. **Habib Bank 201** (Shahid Khan 4-57, Sajjad-ul-Haq 5-44); **Sialkot 161-6** (Faisal Khan 84).

At Lahore Country Club, Muridke, January 14, 15, 16, 17. **Drawn.** Toss: Gujranwala. **Habib Bank 235-2** (Rafatullah Mohmand 61, Abdur Rehman 74*) **v Gujranwala.**

At LCCA Ground, Lahore, January 14, 15, 16, 17. **Drawn.** Toss: Sialkot. **Lahore Whites 264** (Khurram Chauhan 56, Aamer Sajjad 82; Tahir Mughal 4-82); **Sialkot 265-4** (Shaiman Anwar 106, Usman Mushtaq 67). *Sialkot 3 pts.*

At Sheikhupura Stadium, Sheikhupura, January 14, 15, 16, 17. **Drawn.** Toss: Pakistan Customs. **Sheikhupura 257-8 dec.** (Saleem Mughal 69, Mohammad Ayub 64); **Pakistan Customs 43-1.**

Group IV

At KRL Ground, Rawalpindi, December 21, 22, 23, 24. **Drawn.** Toss: KRL. **PIA 196** (Kamran Sajid 52; Jaffer Nazir 5-44) **and 1-0; KRL 238** (Saeed Anwar, jun. 93; Umar Gul 6-97). *KRL 3 pts.*

At Arbab Niaz Stadium, Peshawar, December 21, 22, 23, 24. **Drawn.** Toss: Karachi Blues. **Peshawar 414** (Jahangir Khan 168, Mohammad Fayyaz 68) **and 125** (Imranullah 4-48); **Karachi Blues 288** (Khurram Manzoor 73, Sajid Hanif 91, Imranullah 53; Nauman Habib 4-80) **and 7-1.** *Peshawar 3 pts.*

At Rawalpindi Cricket Stadium, Rawalpindi, December 21, 22, 23, 24. **Drawn.** Toss: ZTBL. **Rawalpindi 133** (Babar Naeem 91*; Iftikhar Anjum 4-37); **ZTBL 311-8** (Majid Jahangir 83, Faisal Naved 62, Javed Hayat 57). *ZTBL 3 pts.*

Babar Naeem carried his bat through Rawalpindi's innings.

At KRL Ground, Rawalpindi, December 27, 28, 29, 30. **Drawn.** Toss: ZTBL. **KRL 307** (Saeed Anwar, jun. 60, Saeed Bin Nasir 93*) **and 303-5 dec.** (Intikhab Alam 83, Misbah-ul-Haq 101*); **ZTBL 231** (Yasir Arafat 5-78) **and 278-9** (Inam-ul-Haq 129; Yasir Arafat 4-100). *KRL 3 pts.*

At Arbab Niaz Stadium, Peshawar, December 27, 28, 29. **PIA won by an innings and 167 runs.** Toss: PIA. **Peshawar 144** (Zeeshan Mohsin 64*; Shoaib Malik 5-27) **and 163** (Zeeshan Mohsin 51; Umar Gul 5-73); **PIA 474** (Ghulam Ali 138, Asif Mujtaba 61, Mahmood Hamid 108, Extras 51; Nauman Habib 4-133). *PIA 12 pts.*

Zeeshan Mohsin carried his bat through Peshawar's first innings.

At Rawalpindi Cricket Stadium, Rawalpindi, December 27, 28, 29, 30. **Rawalpindi won by 215 runs.** Toss: Karachi Blues. **Rawalpindi 281** (Sheraz Khalid 73, Nauman Aman 142; Imranullah 6-51) **and 220-7 dec.** (Babar Naeem 63; Ali Mohammad 5-88); **Karachi Blues 161** (Jaffar Qureshi 52; Mohammad Fayyaz 5-48) **and 125.** *Rawalpindi 12 pts.*

At KRL Ground, Rawalpindi, January 2, 3, 4, 5. **KRL won by an innings and 66 runs.** Toss: Karachi Blues. **Karachi Blues 115** (Jaffer Nazir 5-57) **and 215** (Mohammad Hasnain 59; Yasir Arafat 5-71); **KRL 396** (Saeed Anwar, jun. 51, Misbah-ul-Haq 144, Yasir Arafat 51). *KRL 12 pts.*

At Rawalpindi Cricket Stadium, Rawalpindi, January 2, 3, 4. **PIA won by an innings and 71 runs.** Toss: PIA. **PIA 400** (Kamran Sajid 50, Ghulam Ali 69, Bazid Khan 73, Shoaib Malik 100; Mubashir Nazir 4-74); **ZTBL 144** (Shoaib Malik 4-24) **and 185** (Shoaib Malik 6-73). *PIA 12 pts.*

At Arbab Niaz Stadium, Peshawar, January 2, 3, 4, 5. **Rawalpindi won by seven wickets.** Toss: Peshawar. **Rawalpindi 375** (Sheraz Khalid 128, Nadeem Abbasi 90*) **and 93-3; Peshawar 128 and 339** (Jahangir Khan 56, Sajjad Ahmed 106, Aftab Alam 63, Extras 50; Sheraz Khalid 4-59). *Rawalpindi 12 pts.*

At KRL Ground, Rawalpindi, January 8, 9, 10. **PIA won by an innings and 161 runs.** Toss: Karachi Blues. **PIA 460-9 dec.** (Ghulam Ali 188, Yasir Hameed 64, Asif Mujtaba 60, Shoaib Malik 57; Mohammad Hasnain 4-136); **Karachi Blues 165** (Khalid Latif 92; Najaf Shah 5-31) **and 134** (Sharjeel Ashraf 52; Umar Gul 4-49). *PIA 12 pts.*

At Arbab Niaz Stadium, Peshawar, January 8, 9, 10. **ZTBL won by 280 runs.** Toss: Peshawar. **ZTBL 240** (Atif Ashraf 71, Faisal Naved 61; Mohammad Siddiq 4-102, Abdul Nasir 4-51) **and 297** (Atif Ashraf 53, Zahoor Elahi 84); **Peshawar 144** (Mubashir Nazir 5-39) **and 113** (Mubashir Nazir 4-23, Fahad Masood 5-16). *ZTBL 12 pts.*

At Rawalpindi Cricket Stadium, Rawalpindi, January 8, 9, 10. **KRL won by an innings and 55 runs.** Toss: Rawalpindi. **Rawalpindi 158** (Jaffer Nazir 5-15) **and 197** (Yasir Arafat 5-57, Mohammad Asif 4-48); **KRL 410-8 dec.** (Mohammad Ramzan 84, Saeed Anwar, jun. 83, Misbah-ul-Haq 110; Junaid Zia 5-78). *KRL 12 pts.*

Misbah-ul-Haq scored his third hundred in successive innings. Rawalpindi wicket-keeper Tasawwar Hussain held six catches in KRL's innings.

At Arbab Niaz Stadium, Peshawar, January 14, 15. **KRL won by an innings and 43 runs.** Toss: Peshawar. **KRL 274** (Misbah-ul-Haq 98; Mohammad Siddiq 5-91); **Peshawar 124** (Jaffer Nazir 5-66, Mohammad Asif 4-44) **and 107** (Azhar Ali 4-34). *KRL 12 pts.*

Misbah-ul-Haq fell two runs short of a fourth successive hundred.

At Rawalpindi Cricket Stadium, Rawalpindi, January 14, 15, 16, 17. **PIA won by an innings and 163 runs.** Toss: PIA. **Rawalpindi 139** (Fazl-e-Akbar 5-41) **and 93** (Mohammad Zahid 7-26); **PIA 395** (Faisal Iqbal 56, Asif Mujtaba 62, Bazid Khan 91, Extras 60; Mohammad Akram 4-78). *PIA 12 pts.*

At KRL Ground, Rawalpindi, January 14, 15, 16, 17. **Karachi Blues won by 80 runs.** Toss: ZTBL. **Karachi Blues 182** (Fahad Masood 6-43) **and 244** (Mohammad Zafar 68; Fahad Masood 5-37); **ZTBL 157** (Mohammad Hasnain 6-69) **and 189** (Raheel Majeed 86; Mohammad Hasnain 4-55, Iftikhar Ali 4-92). *Karachi Blues 12 pts.*

Pre-quarter-finals

At UBL Sports Complex, Karachi, January 22, 23, 24, 25. **Drawn.** KRL were declared winners by virtue of their first-innings lead. Toss: Allied Bank. **KRL 212** (Misbah-ul-Haq 76) **and 453** (Mohammad Ramzan 60, Misbah-ul-Haq 167*; Arshad Khan 4-121, Mohammad Zahid 5-106); **Allied Bank 175** (Jaffer Nazir 5-45, Mohammad Asif 5-100) **and 213-5** (Usman Tariq 96, Wajahatullah Wasti 73; Mohammad Asif 4-40).

At Bahawal Stadium, Bahawalpur, January 22, 23, 24. **Faisalabad won by an innings and seven runs.** Toss: Faisalabad. **Sialkot 121** (Farooq Iqbal 4-19) **and 263** (Shaiman Anwar 83; Farooq Iqbal 6-67); **Faisalabad 391** (Sami-ul-Haq 63, Wasim Haider 101, Mohammad Zaman 52; Tahir Mughal 5-113).

At National Stadium, Karachi, January 22, 23, 24. **National Bank won by an innings and 57 runs.** Toss: Habib Bank. **National Bank 338** (Hanif-ur-Rehman 81, Imran Javed 66); **Habib Bank 109** (Zahid Saeed 5-41) **and 172** (Abdur Rehman 54; Shabbir Ahmed 5-43).

At Arbab Niaz Stadium, Peshawar, January 22, 23, 24, 25. **Sargodha won by nine wickets.** Toss: Sargodha. **Lahore Whites 131** (Ahmed Hayat 4-58) **and 192** (Khurram Chauhan 57*; Jibran Khan 5-51); **Sargodha 277** (Usman Arshad 92*, Extras 50; Khurram Chauhan 7-70) **and 50-1.**

Usman Arshad and Jibran Khan (29) added 102 for Sargodha's tenth wicket.

At Multan Cricket Stadium, Multan, January 22, 23, 24. **Rawalpindi won by seven wickets.** Toss: Rawalpindi. **Multan 172** (Zeeshan Khan 57; Mohammad Fayyaz 5-23) **and 161** (Shahid Nasim 67; Mohammad Fayyaz 6-65); **Rawalpindi 226** (Sheraz Khalid 66, Nadeem Abbasi 62; Azhar Abbas 4-68) **and 108-3** (Pervez Aziz 73*).

At KRL Ground, Rawalpindi, January 22, 23, 24, 25. **WAPDA won by two wickets.** Toss: WAPDA. **Pakistan Customs 212** (Azhar Shafiq 81; Aqeel Ahmed 4-38) **and 160** (Azhar Shafiq 51*, Aamer Bashir 53; Aqeel Ahmed 5-48); **WAPDA 183** (Tabish Nawab 6-48) **and 190-8** (Shahid Mansoor 63; Imran Ali 5-68).

At Rawalpindi Cricket Stadium, Rawalpindi, January 22, 23, 24. **PIA won by an innings and 132 runs.** Toss: PIA. **Bahawalpur 201** (Safdar Niazi 52, Arshad Ali 56; Mohammad Zahid 4-64) **and 147** (Aizaz Cheema 5-54); **PIA 480-7 dec.** (Kamran Sajid 54, Ghulam Ali 144, Faisal Iqbal 69, Asif Mujtaba 118, Bazid Khan 55).

At Aga Khan Gymkhana Ground, Karachi, January 22, 23, 24, 25. **Drawn.** ZTBL were declared winners by virtue of their first-innings lead. Toss: PWD. **ZTBL 510-9 dec.** (Raheel Majeed 87, Faisal Naved 106, Mubashir Nazir 54, Javed Hayat 115*, Khalid Mahmood 64) **and 40-0; PWD 420** (Faisal Athar 167, Rauf Akbar 58; Iftikhar Anjum 4-65).

Quarter-finals

At National Stadium, Karachi, January 28, 29, 30, 31. **Drawn.** KRL were declared winners by virtue of their first-innings lead. Toss: National Bank. **KRL 267** (Mohammad Ramzan 110*; Shabbir Ahmed 5-93) **and 169-4** (Misbah-ul-Haq 70*); **National Bank 251** (Naumanullah 67; Yasir Arafat 5-74).

Mohammad Ramzan carried his bat through KRL's first innings. The fourth day was lost to rain and bad light.

At Rawalpindi Cricket Stadium, Rawalpindi, January 28, 29, 30, 31. **Drawn.** PIA were declared winners on scoring-rate. Toss: PIA. **WAPDA 307** (Atiq-ur-Rehman 67, Hasan Adnan 61; Asif Mujtaba 4-74); **PIA 141-2.**

The last two days were lost to rain and bad light.

At Arbab Niaz Stadium, Peshawar, January 28, 29, 30, 31. **Drawn.** Rawalpindi were declared winners on scoring-rate. Toss: Rawalpindi. **Sargodha 365-3 dec.** (Mohammad Hafeez 106, Atiq Ahmed 83, Majid Saeed 105*); **Rawalpindi 170-4** (Sheraz Khalid 69*).

Part of the second day and all of the third were lost to rain.

At UBL Sports Complex, Karachi, January 28, 29, 30. **Faisalabad won by five wickets.** Toss: Faisalabad. **ZTBL 173** (Farooq Iqbal 5-63, Adnan Rasool 5-62) **and 209** (Tauqeer Hussain 4-40); **Faisalabad 290** (Zeeshan Butt 87, Hasnain Haider 93, Sami-ul-Haq 57*) **and 98-5.**

Semi-finals

At National Stadium, Karachi, February 3, 4, 5, 6. **KRL won by ten wickets.** Toss: Faisalabad. **KRL 336** (Saeed Bin Nasir 87, Misbah-ul-Haq 68) **and 51-0; Faisalabad 105** (Jaffer Nazir 6-31) **and 281** (Asif Hussain 85, Sami-ul-Haq 59).

At UBL Sports Complex, Karachi, February 6, 7, 8. **PIA won by an innings and 34 runs.** Toss: PIA. **PIA 392** (Yasir Hameed 108, Bazid Khan 82, Moin Khan 81; Junaid Zia 4-50); **Rawalpindi 79** (Nadeem Khan 5-16, Shoaib Malik 4-31) **and 279** (Pervez Aziz 94, Alamgir Khan 65*; Najaf Shah 5-88).

The match was moved from Peshawar because of worries about the weather.

FINAL

KRL v PIA

At National Stadium, Karachi, February 17, 18, 19, 20. PIA won by ten wickets. Toss: PIA.

PIA won with a day in hand, thanks to two men from Peshawar: Yasir Hameed contributed a maiden double-hundred, 18-year-old pace bowler Umar Gul seven wickets. Yasir's previous best, an unbeaten 171, had been for losing finalists Peshawar a year earlier; this time, he batted 544 minutes, hitting 27 fours in 345 balls. He shared century stands with Kamran Sajid and Moin

Khan, and just missed one with Asif Mujtaba. Disappointingly, barely 100 spectators watched his innings, finally ended by substitute Azhar Ali's throw from mid-on. Seven of his team-mates fell to Jaffer Nazir, who grabbed three in 34 balls on the fourth morning. PIA led by 203 over KRL, who had eventually made 263 after a rain-lopped opening day, with Ali Naqvi falling nine short of his hundred, and Misbah-ul-Haq reaching his ninth fifty in ten innings. But Umar ran through KRL's second innings, when only two batsmen passed 23. PIA squeezed 12 runs out of 14 overs to complete victory.

Man of the Match: Yasir Hameed.

Close of play: First day, KRL 157-3 (Ali Naqvi 82, Misbah-ul-Haq 19); Second day, PIA 131-1 (Kamran Sajid 38, Yasir Hameed 72); Third day, PIA 445-7 (Moin Khan 70, Mohammad Zahid 3).

KRL

First innings		Second innings	
*Ali Naqvi c Faisal Iqbal b Umar Gul	91	c Mohammad Zahid b Umar Gul	8
Mohammad Ramzan lbw b Mohammad Zahid	20	lbw b Umar Gul	0
Saeed Anwar, jun. lbw b Najaf Shah	5	c Mohammad Zahid b Najaf Shah	14
Saeed Bin Nasir lbw b Najaf Shah	16	c Moin Khan b Asif Mujtaba	65
Misbah-ul-Haq c Moin Khan b Ghulam Ali	55	lbw b Shoaib Malik	23
Intikhab Alam b Umar Gul	0	lbw b Shoaib Malik	9
Yasir Arafat c Moin Khan b Mohammad Zahid	30	c Yasir Hameed b Umar Gul	60
Naeem Akhtar b Mohammad Zahid	18	c Yasir Hameed b Umar Gul	18
†Zulfiqar Jan not out	5	lbw b Umar Gul	0
Jaffer Nazir c Faisal Iqbal b Najaf Shah	6	c Mohammad Zahid b Asif Mujtaba	5
Mohammad Asif b Najaf Shah	0	not out	4
B 4, l-b 10, n-b 3	17	L-b 3, n-b 5	8
1/76 (2) 2/81 (3) 3/117 (4) 4/186 (1) 5/186 (6) 6/224 (5) 7/245 (7) 8/252 (8) 9/259 (10) 10/263 (11)	263	1/3 (2) 2/12 (1) 3/30 (3) 4/116 (5) 5/120 (4) 6/127 (6) 7/178 (8) 8/178 (9) 9/183 (10) 10/214 (7)	214

Bowling: *First Innings*—Najaf Shah 29.3–7–108–4; Umar Gul 21–5–60–2; Mohammad Zahid 18–5–50–3; Asif Mujtaba 1–0–1–0; Ghulam Ali 6–1–15–1; Shoaib Malik 4–0–15–0. *Second Innings*—Umar Gul 14–0–69–5; Najaf Shah 11–0–42–1; Shoaib Malik 16–1–64–2; Asif Mujtaba 15–6–36–2.

PIA

First innings		Second innings	
Kamran Sajid c Zulfiqar Jan b Jaffer Nazir	43	not out	5
Ghulam Ali lbw b Jaffer Nazir	1	not out	4
Yasir Hameed run out	207		
Asif Mujtaba c Jaffer Nazir b Mohammad Asif	52		
Faisal Iqbal c Zulfiqar Jan b Jaffer Nazir	5		
Bazid Khan lbw b Jaffer Nazir	19		
*†Moin Khan lbw b Jaffer Nazir	82		
Shoaib Malik b Mohammad Asif	10		
Mohammad Zahid c Zulfiqar Jan b Jaffer Nazir	5		
Umar Gul not out	6		
Najaf Shah c and b Jaffer Nazir	0		
L-b 8, n-b 28	36	W 3	3
1/6 (2) 2/140 (1) 3/237 (4) 4/255 (5) 5/303 (6) 6/403 (3) 7/435 (8) 8/459 (9) 9/460 (7) 10/466 (11)	466	(no wkt)	12

Bowling: *First Innings*—Jaffer Nazir 34.4–8–104–7; Mohammad Asif 38–6–164–2; Yasir Arafat 37–9–106–0; Naeem Akhtar 14–3–44–0; Ali Naqvi 13–3–31–0; Saeed Anwar, jun. 4–0–9–0. *Second Innings*—Ali Naqvi 7–3–7–0; Saeed Anwar, jun. 6–5–2–0; Saeed Bin Nasir 0.4–0–3–0.

Umpires: Asad Rauf and Riazuddin. Referee: Ehtisham-ud-Din.

QUAID-E-AZAM TROPHY WINNERS

1953-54	Bahawalpur	1973-74	Railways	1988-89	ADBP
1954-55	Karachi	1974-75	Punjab A	1989-90	PIA
1956-57	Punjab	1975-76	National Bank	1990-91	Karachi Whites
1957-58	Bahawalpur	1976-77	United Bank	1991-92	Karachi Whites
1958-59	Karachi	1977-78	Habib Bank	1992-93	Karachi Whites
1959-60	Karachi	1978-79	National Bank	1993-94	Lahore City
1961-62	Karachi Blues	1979-80	PIA	1994-95	Karachi Blues
1962-63	Karachi A	1980-81	United Bank	1995-96	Karachi Blues
1963-64	Karachi Blues	1981-82	National Bank	1996-97	Lahore City
1964-65	Karachi Blues	1982-83	United Bank	1997-98	Karachi Blues
1966-67	Karachi	1983-84	National Bank	1998-99	Peshawar
1968-69	Lahore	1984-85	United Bank	1999-2000	PIA
1969-70	PIA	1985-86	Karachi	2000-01	Lahore City Blues
1970-71	Karachi Blues	1986-87	National Bank	2001-02	Karachi Whites
1972-73	Railways	1987-88	PIA	2002-03	PIA

The competition has been contested sometimes by regional teams, sometimes by departments, and sometimes by a mixture of the two. Karachi teams have won the Quaid-e-Azam Trophy 17 times, PIA 6, National Bank 5, Lahore teams and United Bank 4, Bahawalpur, Punjab and Railways 2, ADBP, Habib Bank and Peshawar 1.

Note: Matches in the following sections were not first-class.

SUPER LEAGUE RAMZAN CUP

Final

At Gaddafi Stadium, Lahore, November 28. **PCB Reds won by five wickets.** Toss: PCB Reds. **PCB Whites 223** (49.3 overs) (Farhan Adil 57); **PCB Reds 226-5** (44 overs) (Sufyan Munir 50, Naumanullah 50*).

NATIONAL BANK OF PAKISTAN PATRON'S CUP

Quarter-finals

At Gaddafi Stadium, Lahore, March 25. **KRL won by one wicket.** Toss: KRL. **Habib Bank 330** (50 overs) (Farhan Adil 70; Faisal Afridi 4-72); **KRL 334-9** (50 overs) (Saeed Bin Nasir 74, Mohammad Ramzan 114*, Shoaib Akhtar 56).

At UBL Sports Complex, Karachi, March 25. **Allied Bank won by six wickets.** Toss: Allied Bank. **Karachi Whites 236-9** (50 overs) (Sharjeel Ashraf 94*); **Allied Bank 238-4** (42.1 overs) (Ijaz Ahmed, jun. 86*, Naved Latif 70).

At National Stadium, Karachi, March 25. **PIA won by 129 runs.** Toss: PIA. **PIA 327-6** (50 overs) (Moin Khan 174, Faisal Iqbal 66); **Lahore Whites 198-4** (50 overs) (Musharaf Ali 55, Tariq Rasheed 66*).

At Gymkhana Ground, Okara, March 25. **WAPDA won by 127 runs.** Toss: WAPDA. **WAPDA 297-6** (50 overs) (Shahid Mansoor 54, Naved-ul-Hasan 67*); **Peshawar 170** (35 overs) (Adil Nisar 4-28).

Semi-finals

At National Stadium, Karachi, March 28. **PIA won by nine wickets.** Toss: Allied Bank. **Allied Bank 171** (44.2 overs) (Naved Latif 76); **PIA 173-1** (37 overs) (Ghulam Ali 54, Moin Khan 83*).

At Gaddafi Stadium, Lahore, March 28. **WAPDA won by 168 runs.** Toss: WAPDA. **WAPDA 298-8** (50 overs) (Adil Nisar 96, Rizwan Malik 74); **KRL 130** (33 overs) (Saeed Bin Nasir 50; Kashif Raza 4-34).

Final

At Gaddafi Stadium, Lahore, March 31. **PIA won by 55 runs.** Toss: PIA. **PIA 273-7** (50 overs) (Ghulam Ali 61, Yasir Hameed 102); **WAPDA 218-9** (50 overs) (Shahid Mansoor 60; Shoaib Malik 4-24).

CRICKET IN SRI LANKA, 2002-03

SA'ADI THAWFEEQ AND GERRY VAIDYASEKERA

Chandika Hathurusinghe

It was a year of change at the top of Sri Lankan cricket. After the World Cup, in which Sri Lanka lost to Australia in the semi-finals, the captain, Sanath Jayasuriya, and coach, Dav Whatmore, resigned – and, for the first time, different captains were appointed for Sri Lanka's Test and one-day sides. In June, the controversial Thilanga Sumathipala returned for another term as president of the Board of Control for Cricket in Sri Lanka, administered for the past two years by an interim committee appointed by the government.

This had replaced Sumathipala's previous administration in 2001, and a similar committee had replaced him in 1999. This time, he won a thumping 121 votes from the 144 clubs and associations forming the electorate. His rival Arjuna Ranatunga, who had led Sri Lanka to World Cup victory in 1996, received a mere seven. Ranatunga had been elected to parliament in 2001, but his cricketing background was not enough to convince these voters he would be a good administrator. Even the third candidate, Mohan de Silva, who stood in case Sumathipala was disqualified, got ten votes; he was also elected secretary. Sumathipala extended an olive branch to Ranatunga, citing the betterment of Sri Lankan cricket, but the offer was rejected. Ranatunga's long-time vice-captain, Aravinda de Silva, had no such qualms; he became a vice-president as well as a national selector.

Sumathipala immediately unveiled plans to transform the board into a professional body similar to Cricket Australia and New Zealand Cricket. It was renamed Sri Lanka Cricket, with a separate commercial arm, Sri Lanka Cricket Incorporated. Sumathipala aimed to make Sri Lanka "the most sought-after destination in world cricket" after Australia and England. He announced fund-raising initiatives, and upgrades to international venues and grassroots facilities. His first challenge was to reduce a $11m claim against the board by television company World Sports Group Nimbus, whose three-year contract had been cut short by the interim committee in 2001.

But by January 2004, Sumathipala had more pressing problems when he was arrested and held in custody over alleged serious passport offences. He remained president – for the moment, at least.

Jayasuriya, who had succeeded Ranatunga as captain after the 1999 World Cup, had had a running battle with the chairman of selectors, Guy de Alwis, which may have influenced his resignation. But de Alwis also quit, to be replaced by Lalith Kaluperuma, who had played in Sri Lanka's inaugural Test in 1981-82. Aravinda de Silva, who had retired after the World Cup, and two more ex-Test cricketers, Ashley de Silva and Roger Wijesuriya, made up the selection committee. With New Zealand about to arrive, they appointed Hashan Tillekeratne to lead in the Tests and Marvan Atapattu in the one-day internationals. Neither started well: the two Tests were drawn and Sri Lanka failed to reach the final of the triangular tournament which followed, the first time they had been squeezed out on home soil. Former Test captain Duleep Mendis was coach during New Zealand's visit and a subsequent Caribbean tour, but Australian John Dyson took charge in September.

There was hardly any international cricket played at home, with the national team mostly overseas; the only visitors were the ECB National Academy, the New Zealanders and Pakistan, who played in the one-day triangular. In domestic cricket, Moors Sports Club, founded in 1908, won their first national title, clinching the final of the Premier Trophy's Super League by one wicket in a low-scoring game. They were not a starry side, with only two ex-internationals: their captain, left-arm spinner Rangana Herath, and the seasoned player-coach Chandika Hathurusinghe, named man of the tournament. He was the only player to combine 500 runs and 50 wickets, finishing with 815 and 62. Colts No. 3 Sajith Fernando was named best batsman and Galle pace man Nuwan Kulasekara best bowler, in his first full season.

Moors were the only semi-finalists who had not been champions before. They had just qualified for the Super League, by winning their last preliminary group match, but a run of three wins in four games put them second to Bloomfield in the Super League itself. They came from behind to defeat Colombo in one semi-final, while Bloomfield beat a weakened Sinhalese side by an innings.

Chilaw Marians, who had achieved first-class status only the previous season, retained the Plate Championship for teams not qualifying for the Super League, with Kurunegala Youth a fraction of a point behind. The bottom three were relegated, reducing the first-class teams to 16; the 2003-04 Premier League was to be played on a simpler basis, with two qualifying groups leading straight to the semi-finals, and no Super League or Plate.

Once again, there was an Invitation Quadrangular, for Sri Lanka A, a Club XI, an Under-23 XI and a Schools side; the Club XI won all their three games. Bloomfield made up for their disappointment in the Premier final by winning the one-day Kandos final against Galle.

There was an alarming decline in discipline. One player, Sebastianites' Ajith Cooray, was banned for five years for assaulting an umpire. A couple of others received two-match bans for offensive language, and Panadura's coach was fined for threatening an umpire.

Performances on the field were below par. The absence of the international players provided an ideal opportunity to catch the selectors' eyes, but few did so. No batsman topped 1,000 runs or averaged 50; unusually, there were no totals of 500, but 18 under 100. Nandika Ranjith of Moors was the leading bowler with 69 wickets, including ten in the final. The batting figures rang alarm bells for the future of Sri Lankan cricket, urgently trying to replace retiring heavyweights such as Ranatunga and de Silva.

Part of the problem lies in the schools, the nurseries which feed the clubs. An over-emphasis on limited-overs cricket at this level is strangling the production of quality players. In September 2002, the Indian board banned limited-overs cricket for boys under 17. Sri Lanka Cricket and the Schools Cricket Association need to address the situation immediately, if Sri Lanka is not to emulate the decline of West Indies from their 1980s peak.

In schools cricket, the highest individual score was 281 by Thilina Dasun, of Piliyandala Central, against St Mary's, Dehiwela. The most violent hitting came from Sanath Sameera Silva, who plundered 124 in 43 balls for S. de S. Jayasinghe Vidyalaya Under-13 against Mahabodhi College; he hit 12 sixes and ten fours. Tharaka Kottahewa of Royal College performed the hat-trick against Jaffna Schools, but Nihal Vithanage went one better, with four wickets in four balls for Prince of Wales against Royal College.

FIRST-CLASS AVERAGES, 2002-03

BATTING

(Qualification: 500 runs)

	M	*I*	*NO*	*R*	*HS*	*100s*	*Avge*	*Ct/St*
C. N. Liyanage (*Police & Club XI*)	10	19	2	824	133	2	48.47	10
R. S. Kaluwitharana (*Colts, Club XI & SL*)	13	18	1	761	192	1	44.76	29/3
†S. I. Fernando (*Colts & Club XI*)	12	19	1	784	152	2	43.55	13
S. K. L. de Silva (*Colombo & Club XI*)	15	25	3	938	133	1	42.63	14
L. J. P. Gunaratne (*Chilaw M. & Under-23 XI*)	13	21	2	793	106*	1	41.73	11
R. S. A. Palliyaguruge (*Chilaw M. & Club XI*)	12	18	1	681	118	3	40.05	4
†M. N. Nawaz (*Nondescripts & Sri Lanka A*)	12	19	1	699	117*	3	38.83	8
S. Jayantha (*Bloomfield & Club XI*)	14	23	2	789	137	1	37.57	13
†W. M. G. Ramyakumara (*Tamil U. & SL A*)	10	19	1	675	116	1	37.50	5
E. F. M. U. Fernando (*Ragama*)	11	19	2	632	121	2	37.17	19
S. N. Wijesinghe (*Air Force*)	11	18	4	520	104	1	37.14	7
†M. G. Vandort (*Colombo, Academy & SL A*)	11	20	3	627	95	0	36.88	13
A. S. Polonowita (*Colombo & Sri Lanka A*)	17	27	3	885	127*	3	36.87	28
†C. S. Fernando (*Chilaw M., Academy & SL A*)	12	19	4	539	109	2	35.93	36
S. A. Perera (*Antonians*)	8	16	1	535	99	0	35.66	21/5
W. M. B. Perera (*Moors & Club XI*)	15	28	3	883	220*	1	35.32	15
†W. J. S. D. Perera (*Moratuwa*)	11	18	2	564	89	0	35.25	4
H. D. P. K. Dharmasena (*Bloomfield & SL*)	15	21	2	664	95	0	34.94	4
L. P. C. Silva (*Panadura & Club XI*)	14	24	1	788	130*	2	34.26	17
†S. E. D. R. Fernando (*Air Force*)	11	20	2	604	118	1	33.55	7
W. D. D. S. Perera (*Bloomfield & Under-23 XI*)	15	20	1	624	101	2	32.84	20
K. A. D. M. Fernando (*Sebastianites*)	11	16	0	523	91	0	32.68	11
†B. S. M. Warnapura (*Burgher & Sri Lanka A*)	17	22	1	663	109	1	31.57	15
N. S. Bopage (*Sebastianites*)	11	17	1	501	116	1	31.31	7
U. C. Hathurusinghe (*Moors & Club XI*)	17	29	2	816	78	0	30.22	17
K. H. R. K. Fernando (*Chilaw M. & SL A*)	14	19	1	543	92*	0	30.16	8

	M	*I*	*NO*	*R*	*HS*	*100s*	*Avge*	*Ct/St*
I. C. D. Perera (*Galle*)	12	21	1	553	153	1	27.65	14
†S. H. T. Kandamby (*Bloom., Acad. & U-23 XI*)	13	19	0	519	132	1	27.31	6
T. R. Peiris (*Air Force & Under-23 XI*)	14	24	3	572	103	1	27.23	29/5
G. I. Daniel (*Bloomfield, Acad. & Under-23 XI*)	15	25	2	625	156*	2	27.17	8
†R. H. T. A. Perera (*Panadura*)	12	21	1	535	74	0	26.75	5

† *Left-handed batsman.*

BOWLING

(Qualification: 35 wickets, average 25.00)

	Style	*O*	*M*	*R*	*W*	*BB*	*5W/i*	*Avge*
U. C. Hathurusinghe (*Moors & Club XI*)	RFM	371	94	929	62	5-32	2	14.98
K. Weeraratne (*Bloomfield & Under-23 XI*)	RFM	228.5	43	765	49	4-30	0	15.61
A. W. Ekanayake (*Kurunegala Youth*)	SLA	350.4	91	913	56	8-112	3	16.30
P. N. Ranjith (*Moors & Club XI*)	LFM	394.2	79	1,180	69	6-27	6	17.10
B. C. N. Amarasinghe (*Moratuwa*)	OB	237.4	30	719	40	8-46	4	17.97
H. M. Maduwantha (*Kurunegala Y. & U-23 XI*)	RFM	279.3	65	737	40	5-34	4	18.42
B. A. R. S. Priyadarshana (*Ragama*)	RFM	199.1	40	654	35	6-44	2	18.68
H. M. R. K. B. Herath (*Moors*)	SLA	321	92	731	38	6-46	2	19.23
H. D. P. K. Dharmasena (*Bloomfield & SL*)	RM/OB	300.1	69	775	40	4-52	0	19.37
A. P. Dalugoda (*Sebastianites*)	SLA	274.4	72	687	35	5-64	2	19.62
H. G. D. Nayanakantha (*Bloom., Acad. & SL A*)	RFM	268.2	51	853	43	5-38	2	19.83
M. R. C. N. Bandaratilleke (*Colts & Club XI*)	SLA	345.5	84	941	46	7-71	4	20.45
K. M. D. N. Kulasekara (*Galle & U-23 XI*)	RFM	336.3	40	1,285	61	5-25	3	21.06
M. S. Villavarayan (*Colombo & Club XI*)	RFM	383.4	83	1,140	54	5-56	2	21.11
N. S. Rupasinghe (*Colombo & Sri Lanka A*)	SLA	320.3	62	879	41	5-37	3	21.43
M. T. T. Mirando (*Nondescripts & SL A*)	LFM	227.2	29	751	35	5-60	3	21.45
L. H. D. Dilhara (*Galle, Academy & Club XI*)	RFM	259.3	47	911	42	5-28	2	21.69
K. S. Lokuarachchi (*Bloomfield, SL A & SL*)	LB	349.2	96	822	36	4-38	0	22.83

Note: Averages include New Zealand's tour in April–May 2003.

PREMIER TROPHY, 2002-03

SUPER LEAGUE

					1st-inns	*Bonus points*		
	Played	*Won*	*Lost*	*Drawn*	*lead*	*Batting*	*Bowling*	*Points*
Bloomfield C & AC	9	5	0	4	3	12.885	12.5	116.255
Moors SC	9	4	1	4	2	14.39	11.9	97.24
Colombo CC	9	4	1	4	1	12.96	11.5	87.225
Sinhalese SC	9	4	1	4	1	11.905	11.2	83.395
Galle CC	9	2	3	4	2	13.19	12.1	71.465
Burgher RC	9	1	2	6	3	12.56	11.8	67.36
Colts CC	9	1	2	6	3	12.925	9.0	64.48
Nondescripts CC	9	1	2	6	3	11.245	8.6	60.915
Tamil Union C & AC	9	1	3	5	1	12.44	9.6	47.435
Panadura SC	9	0	8	1	0	13.635	9.9	29.715

Super League teams carried forward results and points gained against fellow-qualifiers in the first round, but not those gained against the teams eliminated.

Semi-finals: Bloomfield beat Sinhalese by an innings and 24 runs; Moors beat Colombo by four wickets.

Final: Moors beat Bloomfield by one wicket.

PLATE CHAMPIONSHIP

	Played	Won	Lost	Drawn	1st-inns lead	Bonus points Batting	Bonus points Bowling	Points
Chilaw Marians CC	8	3	0	5	5	13.73	9.0	105.17
Kurunegala Youth CC	8	5	0	3	2	10.324	11.8	104.795
Air Force SC	8	3	1	4	3	12.67	11.0	90.505
Ragama CC	8	3	1	4	1	12.11	10.5	73.255
Police SC	8	3	3	2	1	15.325	13.7	73.025
Sebastianites C & AC	8	3	2	3	0	10.56	11.0	58.48
Moratuwa SC	8	1	1	6	2	11.345	10.3	55.245
Antonians SC	8	1	6	1	0	14.76	11.0	37.86
Kandy CC	8	0	8	0	0	13.89	11.4	25.29

Teams carried forward results and points gained against fellow group members in the first round, but not those gained against the teams who qualified for the Super League.

Outright win = 12 pts; lead on first innings in a drawn game = 8 pts. Bonus points were awarded as follows: 0.1 pt for each wicket taken and 0.005 pt for each run scored, up to 400 runs per innings.

Super Group

The Super Group was formed by the top four teams from the 2001-02 Super League. They were guaranteed entry to the 2002-03 Super League, and these results and points were carried forward.

At Nondescripts Cricket Club, Maitland Place, Colombo, October 11, 12, 13. **Drawn.** Toss: Colts. **Colts 270** (R. S. Kaluwitharana 71, M. R. C. N. Bandaratilleke 60) **and 63-1; Nondescripts 285** (H. P. Tillekeratne 141*; D. K. Liyanage 5-54).

At Sinhalese Sports Club, Maitland Place, Colombo, October 11, 12, 13. **Sinhalese won by an innings and 121 runs.** Toss: Tamil Union. **Sinhalese 294** (D. A. Gunawardene 50, D. P. M. D. Jayawardene 58, R. P. A. H. Wickremaratne 65*); **Tamil Union 62 and 111** (C. R. D. Fernando 4-22).

At Sinhalese Sports Club, Maitland Place, Colombo, October 18, 19, 20. **Drawn.** Toss: Colts. **Sinhalese 121-9** (K. E. A. Upashantha 5-40) **v Colts.**

At P. Saravanamuttu Stadium, Colombo, October 18, 19, 20. **Drawn.** Toss: Nondescripts. **Tamil Union 150; Nondescripts 66-5.**

At Colts Cricket Club, Havelock Park, Colombo, October 25, 26, 27. **Drawn.** Toss: Colts. **Tamil Union 126** (D. K. Liyanage 4-28, K. E. A. Upashantha 4-61) **and 250-6** (N. A. N. N. Perera 57, U. D. U. Chandana 81); **Colts 278** (C. Mendis 58, H. G. J. M. Kulatunga 61; U. D. U. Chandana 6-99).

At Sinhalese Sports Club, Maitland Place, Colombo, October 25, 26, 27. **Drawn.** Toss: Nondescripts. **Nondescripts 203-5 dec.** (R. R. Tissera 50, M. N. Nawaz 52); **Sinhalese 23-1.**

Sinhalese 16.69 pts, Colts 14.555 pts, Nondescripts 12.97 pts, Tamil Union 5.995 pts.

Group A

At Burgher Recreation Club, Havelock Park, Colombo, September 20, 21, 22. **Drawn.** Toss: Colombo. **Colombo 218** (A. S. Polonowita 119; S. H. S. M. K. Silva 5-48) **and 182-5** (S. K. L. de Silva 88*, H. A. P. W. Jayawardene 66); **Burgher 400-6 dec.** (B. C. M. S. Mendis 140, B. S. M. Warnapura 109, V. S. K. Waragoda 77*).

At FTZ Sports Complex, Katunayake, September 20, 21, 22. **Kurunegala Youth won by an innings and 38 runs.** Toss: Kurunegala Youth. **Kurunegala Youth 346** (C. L. Ediriweerage 64); **Ragama 140 and 168** (S. Arangalla 50; H. M. Maduwantha 5-35).

At Panadura Esplanade, Panadura, September 20, 21, 22. **Drawn.** Toss: Panadura. **Sebastianites 279** (W. J. M. Fernando 81, M. M. D. N. R. G. Perera 57, K. A. D. M. Fernando 91; M. D. K. Perera 4-23) **and 317** (H. G. P. Ranaweera 105*; G. A. S. Perera 4-82); **Panadura 323** (M. D. K. Perera 75, J. S. K. Peiris 63, T. C. B. Fernando 53*).

At Welagedera Stadium, Kurunegala, September 27, 28, 29. **Drawn.** Toss: Colombo. **Kurunegala Youth 178** (H. M. Maduwantha 72) **and 171** (M. S. Villavarayan 4-30); **Colombo 302-9 dec.** (A. S. Polonowita 102, D. F. Arnolda 53, I. S. Gallage 64; A. W. Ekanayake 4-97) **and 38-3.**

At Burgher Recreation Club, Havelock Park, Colombo, October 4, 5, 6. **Drawn.** Toss: Burgher. **Burgher 431-7 dec.** (U. Hettiarachchi 57, R. H. S. Silva 115, G. S. T. Perera 50*, K. S. C. de Silva 52*); **Panadura 213 and 185-5** (L. P. C. Silva 130*).

At Colombo Cricket Club, Maitland Crescent, Colombo, October 4, 5, 6. **Drawn.** Toss: Colombo. **Ragama 228** (E. F. M. U. Fernando 54; C. R. B. Mudalige 4-51) **and 176-4** (D. V. Gunawardene 50); **Colombo 347** (P. B. Ediriweera 79, A. S. Polonowita 80, J. W. H. D. Boteju 71; R. D. Dissanayake 4-86).

At Welagedera Stadium, Kurunegala, October 4, 5, 6. **Drawn.** Toss: Sebastianites. **Kurunegala Youth 308** (D. M. Ramanayake 111; K. A. D. M. Fernando 4-88) **and 80-3; Sebastianites 176** (K. A. D. M. Fernando 59).

At FTZ Sports Complex, Katunayake, October 11, 12, 13. **Panadura won by nine wickets.** Toss: Ragama. **Ragama 201** (K. N. S. Fernando 61; T. C. B. Fernando 4-50) **and 93** (G. A. S. Perera 4-7); **Panadura 220** (S. Arangalla 5-63) **and 78-1.**

At Tyronne Fernando Stadium, Moratuwa, October 11, 12, 13. **Drawn.** Toss: Burgher. **Sebastianites 120** (K. S. C. de Silva 5-46) **and 167-7** (S. H. S. M. K. Silva 4-33); **Burgher 317** (U. Hettiarachchi 78, R. H. S. Silva 63; A. P. Dalugoda 5-83).

At FTZ Sports Complex, Katunayake, October 18, 19, 20. **Drawn.** Toss: Ragama. **Ragama 38-3 v Burgher.**

At Colombo Cricket Club, Maitland Crescent, Colombo, October 18, 19, 20. **Drawn.** Toss: Sebastianites. **Colombo 196** (A. S. Polonowita 56) **v Sebastianites.**

At Panadura Esplanade, Panadura, October 18, 19, 20. **Drawn.** Toss: Panadura. **Kurunegala Youth 74-5 v Panadura.**

At Welagedera Stadium, Kurunegala, November 1, 2, 3. **Drawn.** Toss: Burgher. **Burgher 121-3** (C. U. Jayasinghe 59*) **v Kurunegala Youth.**

At Panadura Esplanade, Panadura, November 1, 2, 3. **Colombo won by seven wickets.** Toss: Colombo. **Panadura 214** (G. A. S. Perera 73; M. S. Villavarayan 4-26) **and 224** (S. D. C. Aravinda 64; C. R. B. Mudalige 9-111); **Colombo 247** (M. G. Vandort 95, D. K. Ranaweera 80; G. A. S. Perera 7-82) **and 192-3** (M. G. Vandort 50, K. P. P. B. Seneviratne 67*).

Mudalige's 21–2–111–9 was the best analysis of the season.

At Tyronne Fernando Stadium, Moratuwa, November 1, 2, 3. **Drawn.** Toss: Sebastianites. **Ragama 248** (B. A. R. S. Priyadarshana 58, H. S. S. M. K. Weerasiri 52*; A. P. Dalugoda 5-64) **and 373** (P. H. D. Premadasa 93, E. F. M. U. Fernando 121, D. V. Gunawardene 68; M. H. A. Jabbar 4-51); **Sebastianites 208** (M. M. D. N. R. G. Perera 62, K. A. D. M. Fernando 60; B. A. R. S. Priyadarshana 6-44).

Kalum (U. L. K. D.) Fernando of Sebastianites held six catches in the match in the field.

Colombo 42.61 pts, Burgher 35.19 pts, Panadura 33.785 pts, Kurunegala Youth 30.285 pts, Ragama 20.425 pts, Sebastianites 12.635 pts. Colombo, Burgher and Panadura qualified for the Super League.

Group B

At Air Force Ground, Katunayake, September 20, 21, 22. **Drawn.** Toss: Air Force. **Chilaw Marians 258** (L. J. P. Gunaratne 78, K. H. R. K. Fernando 67) **and 355** (R. S. A. Palliyaguruge 115; W. P. Wickrama 4-66); **Air Force 217** (S. E. D. R. Fernando 56, S. N. Wijesinghe 58; L. J. P. Gunaratne 7-79) **and 14-0.**

At Moors Sports Club, Braybrooke Place, Colombo, September 20, 21. **Bloomfield won by eight wickets.** Toss: Bloomfield. **Moors 179** (H. G. D. Nayanakantha 4-46) **and 113** (K. Weeraratne 4-42); **Bloomfield 148** (S. H. T. Kandamby 51; L. L. Fernando 5-36) **and 145-2** (S. Jayantha 71*).

At Tyronne Fernando Stadium, Moratuwa, September 20, 21. **Galle won by five wickets.** Toss: Galle. **Moratuwa 98 and 156** (W. J. S. D. Perera 73*; K. M. D. N. Kulasekara 4-33); **Galle 191 and 67-5.**

At Galle International Stadium, Galle, October 4, 5, 6. **Galle won by five wickets.** Toss: Galle. **Chilaw Marians 204 and 176** (L. J. P. Gunaratne 59; W. M. P. N. Wanasinghe 5-22); **Galle 230 and 152-5.**

At Moors Sports Club, Braybrooke Place, Colombo, October 4, 5, 6. **Drawn.** Toss: Moors. **Air Force 232** (M. G. N. A. Jayaratne 77; M. N. R. Cooray 4-24) **and 104** (U. C. Hathurusinghe 4-22); **Moors 100** (W. C. R. Tissera 6-26, K. C. A. Weerasinghe 4-42) **and 222-5** (M. A. M. Faizer 79, G. R. P. Peiris 51).

At Tyronne Fernando Stadium, Moratuwa, October 4, 5, 6. **Drawn.** Toss: Bloomfield. **Moratuwa 179** (B. D. A. P. Ranaweera 57; R. A. P. Nissanka 4-52) **and 202-4** (W. J. S. D. Perera 89, B. D. A. P. Ranaweera 70); **Bloomfield 433-8 dec.** (G. I. Daniel 100, H. D. P. K. Dharmasena 94, W. D. D. S. Perera 100*).

At Air Force Ground, Katunayake, October 11, 12, 13. **Drawn.** Toss: Moratuwa. **Air Force 196** (S. N. Wijesinghe 89*) **and 220** (B. C. N. Amarasinghe 6-80); **Moratuwa 172** (H. M. P. Fernando 102*; M. K. G. C. P. Lakshitha 4-44) **and 95-6.**

Fernando carried his bat through Moratuwa's first innings.

At Galle International Stadium, Galle, October 11, 12, 13. **Drawn.** Toss: Galle. **Bloomfield 257** (S. Jayantha 66, H. D. P. K. Dharmasena 73; L. H. D. Dilhara 5-31) **and 254** (G. I. Daniel 61; K. M. D. N. Kulasekara 5-56); **Galle 161** (I. C. D. Perera 75) **and 40-3.**

Saman Jayantha of Bloomfield held five catches in the field in Galle's first innings.

At Moors Sports Club, Braybrooke Place, Colombo, October 11, 12, 13. **Drawn.** Toss: Chilaw Marians. **Chilaw Marians 79** (P. N. Ranjith 6-27, U. C. Hathurusinghe 4-28) **and 220-9** (K. H. R. K. Fernando 92*; U. C. Hathurusinghe 5-42); **Moors 193-8 dec.** (M. N. R. Cooray 64).

At Air Force Ground, Katunayake, October 18, 19, 20. **Drawn.** Toss: Galle. **Air Force 78-3 v Galle.**

At Bloomfield Cricket and Athletic Club, Reid Avenue, Colombo, October 18, 19, 20. **Drawn.** Toss: Chilaw Marians. **Bloomfield 66-3 v Chilaw Marians.**

At Tyronne Fernando Stadium, Moratuwa, October 18, 19, 20. **Drawn.** Toss: Moors. **Moratuwa 144** (U. C. Hathurusinghe 5-32); **Moors 75-2.**

At Bloomfield Cricket and Athletic Club, Reid Avenue, Colombo, November 1, 2, 3. **Drawn.** Toss: Air Force. **Bloomfield 226** (M. S. G. Cooray 4-39) **and 150-6** (M. S. G. Cooray 4-62); **Air Force 125.**

At FTZ Sports Complex, Katunayake, November 1, 2, 3. **Drawn.** Toss: Chilaw Marians. **Moratuwa 237** (W. J. S. D. Perera 74, K. L. R. Fernando 58; L. D. I. Perera 4-47) **and 36-0; Chilaw Marians 275-9 dec.** (R. S. A. Palliyaguruge 62).

At Moors Sports Club, Braybrooke Place, Colombo, November 1, 2, 3. **Moors won by 184 runs.** Toss: Galle. **Moors 273** (G. R. P. Peiris 102, U. C. Hathurusinghe 67; W. M. P. N. Wanasinghe 4-56) **and 185-8 dec.** (H. M. R. K. B. Herath 71*, P. N. Ranjith 50*; K. M. D. N. Kulasekara 4-70); **Galle 189** (W. M. P. N. Wanasinghe 55; U. C. Hathurusinghe 4-60, M. N. R. Cooray 5-24) **and 85** (H. M. R. K. B. Herath 4-32).

Bloomfield 49.93 pts, Galle 36.975 pts, Moors 34.8 pts, Chilaw Marians 28.635 pts, Air Force 28.63 pts, Moratuwa 11.645 pts. Bloomfield, Galle and Moors qualified for the Super League.

Super League

At Burgher Recreation Club, Havelock Park, Colombo, January 3, 4, 5. **Drawn.** Toss: Burgher. **Colts 414** (S. I. Fernando 52, R. S. Kaluwitharana 93, S. Kalawithigoda 79, M. Pushpakumara 72; S. H. S. M. K. Silva 5-134) **and 368-6** (S. I. Fernando 82, R. S. Kaluwitharana 192); **Burgher 345** (B. C. M. S. Mendis 87, B. S. M. Warnapura 79, V. S. K. Waragoda 55, G. S. T. Perera 51).
Kaluwitharana scored 192 in 144 balls, with 19 fours and six sixes.

At Colombo Cricket Club, Maitland Crescent, Colombo, January 3, 4, 5. **Colombo won by ten wickets.** Toss: Colombo. **Sinhalese 116** (C. R. B. Mudalige 4-19) **and 215** (W. M. S. M. Perera 54; M. S. Villavarayan 5-65); **Colombo 313** (H. A. P. W. Jayawardene 61, A. S. Polonowita 51; P. D. R. L. Perera 4-88) **and 20-0.**

At Nondescripts Cricket Club, Maitland Place, Colombo, January 3, 4, 5. **Drawn.** Toss: Moors. **Nondescripts 371** (K. M. H. Perera 51, R. S. Kalpage 125, C. M. Bandara 71*; U. W. M. B. C. A. Welegedara 4-66) **and 19-0; Moors 187** (W. C. A. Ganegama 5-75, R. S. Kalpage 4-37) **and 306** (M. A. M. Faizer 61, H. M. R. K. B. Herath 71*; R. S. Kalpage 4-55).

At Panadura Esplanade, Panadura, January 3, 4, 5. **Galle won by 191 runs.** Toss: Panadura. **Galle 314** (I. C. D. Perera 153; P. U. M. Chanaka 4-59, G. A. S. Perera 5-56) **and 203** (M. D. K. Perera 7-71); **Panadura 179** (N. C. Komasaru 4-32) **and 147** (R. H. T. A. Perera 62; L. H. D. Dilhara 4-28, K. M. D. N. Kulasekara 4-31).

At P. Saravanamuttu Stadium, Colombo, January 3, 4, 5. **Drawn.** Toss: Bloomfield. **Tamil Union 321** (S. I. de Saram 52, U. D. U. Chandana 61, M. K. Gajanayake 54; H. G. D. Nayanakantha 4-65) **and 178** (W. M. G. Ramyakumara 74); **Bloomfield 279** (H. D. P. K. Dharmasena 95; W. J. M. R. Dias 5-69, U. D. U. Chandana 5-65).

At Bloomfield Cricket and Athletic Club, Reid Avenue, Colombo, January 10, 11. **Bloomfield won by ten wickets.** Toss: Bloomfield. **Bloomfield 256** (K. Weeraratne 59; M. R. C. N. Bandaratilleke 7-71) **and 27-0; Colts 62** (K. S. Lokuarachchi 4-38, H. G. D. Nayanakantha 4-7) **and 217** (S. Kalawithigoda 85, M. Pushpakumara 51*; K. S. Lokuarachchi 4-64).

At Burgher Recreation Club, Havelock Park, Colombo, January 10, 11, 12. **Drawn.** Toss: Galle. **Burgher 331** (C. U. Jayasinghe 86; N. C. Komasaru 4-66) **and 298-9 dec.** (B. S. M. Warnapura 51, C. U. Jayasinghe 122*; W. R. S. de Silva 4-71); **Galle 241** (A. Rideegammanagedera 63; R. C. R. P. Silva 4-58) **and 153-5** (T. K. D. Sudarshana 51).

At Colombo Cricket Club, Maitland Crescent, Colombo, January 10, 11, 12. **Colombo won by 14 runs.** Toss: Colombo. **Colombo 178** (W. J. M. R. Dias 6-41) **and 241** (M. G. Vandort 82; U. D. U. Chandana 4-62); **Tamil Union 176** (W. M. G. Ramyakumara 56, S. I. de Saram 52; N. S. Rupasinghe 5-37) **and 229** (N. S. Rupasinghe 5-70).

At Nondescripts Cricket Club, Maitland Place, Colombo, January 10, 11, 12. **Nondescripts won by six wickets.** Toss: Nondescripts. **Panadura 163** (L. P. C. Silva 61) **and 283** (R. H. T. A. Perera 74, J. S. K. Peiris 56); **Nondescripts 299** (R. P. Hewage 65, R. S. Kalpage 107) **and 148-4** (C. P. Mapatuna 81*).
Ravindra Pushpakumara took a hat-trick with the first three balls of the match.

At Sinhalese Sports Club, Maitland Place, Colombo, January 10, 11, 12. **Drawn.** Toss: Moors. **Sinhalese 377** (U. A. Fernando 107, R. P. A. H. Wickremaratne 50, T. T. Samaraweera 75; P. N. Ranjith 4-74) **and 149-6 dec.; Moors 239** (U. C. Hathurusinghe 78) **and 143-2** (B. M. P. D. Fernando 54).

At Burgher Recreation Club, Havelock Park, Colombo, January 17, 18, 19. **Drawn.** Toss: Burgher. **Nondescripts 298** (M. N. Nawaz 74, C. P. Mapatuna 72) **and 245-7 dec.** (R. S. Kalpage 54*, M. T. T. Mirando 103*); **Burgher 230** (C. U. Jayasinghe 56) **and 46-0.**

At Colombo Cricket Club, Maitland Crescent, Colombo, January 17, 18, 19. **Bloomfield won by an innings and 45 runs.** Toss: Bloomfield. **Colombo 130 and 139** (H. S. H. Alles 4-44); **Bloomfield 314** (T. M. Dilshan 78, H. D. P. K. Dharmasena 79; M. S. Villavarayan 4-74).

At Colts Cricket Club, Havelock Park, Colombo, January 17, 18, 19. **Moors won by two wickets.** Toss: Colts. **Colts 219** (U. C. Hathurusinghe 4-57) **and 87** (P. N. Ranjith 4-22); **Moors 151 and 158-8** (M. R. C. N. Bandaratilleke 5-57).

At Panadura Esplanade, Panadura, January 17, 18, 19. **Tamil Union won by four wickets.** Toss: Panadura. **Panadura 135 and 170** (R. H. T. A. Perera 50; K. L. S. L. Dias 7-37); **Tamil Union 164 and 146-6** (W. M. G. Ramyakumara 76*).

At Sinhalese Sports Club, Maitland Place, Colombo, January 17, 18, 19. **Sinhalese won by 244 runs.** Toss: Galle. **Sinhalese 287** (U. A. Fernando 120, W. L. P. Fernando 72*) **and 240-2 dec.** (N. T. Paranavitana 117*, R. P. A. H. Wickremaratne 58*); **Galle 134** (P. D. R. L. Perera 4-26) **and 149** (D. Hettiarachchi 5-48).

At Bloomfield Cricket and Athletic Club, Reid Avenue, Colombo, January 24, 25. **Bloomfield won by eight wickets.** Toss: Bloomfield. **Panadura 92** (A. B. T. Lakshitha 4-26, K. Weeraratne 4-30) **and 205** (L. P. C. Silva 50, G. A. S. Perera 50*, M. M. C. S. Perera 50; K. Weeraratne 4-55); **Bloomfield 223** (T. M. Dilshan 62, W. D. D. S. Perera 101; N. P. Navela 5-52) **and 75-2.**

Bloomfield wicket-keeper Dilshan held six catches in Panadura's first innings and nine in the match.

At Colombo Cricket Club, Maitland Crescent, Colombo, January 24, 25, 26. **Colombo won by seven wickets.** Toss: Colombo. **Galle 86** (N. S. Rupasinghe 4-21) **and 260** (A. Rideegammanagedera 52, W. M. P. N. Wanasinghe 56; I. S. Gallage 4-32); **Colombo 83** (W. M. P. N. Wanasinghe 5-12) **and 264-3** (S. K. L. de Silva 88*, J. Mubarak 68*).

At Moors Sports Club, Braybrooke Place, Colombo, January 24, 25, 26. **Moors won by 91 runs.** Toss: Burgher. **Moors 216** (W. M. B. Perera 62, U. C. Hathurusinghe 61; R. C. R. P. Silva 4-39, S. Weerakoon 4-42) **and 140** (R. C. R. P. Silva 5-22); **Burgher 159** (U. C. Hathurusinghe 4-37) **and 106.**

At Burgher Recreation Club, Havelock Park, Colombo, January 31, February 1, 2. **Drawn.** Toss: Bloomfield. **Bloomfield 347** (S. H. T. Kandamby 132; R. C. R. P. Silva 5-119) **and 255** (H. D. P. K. Dharmasena 63; S. Weerakoon 4-53); **Burgher 224** (S. H. S. M. K. Silva 57) **and 64-0.**

At Colombo Cricket Club, Maitland Crescent, Colombo, January 31, February 1, 2. **Drawn.** Toss: Colts. **Colombo 164** (M. R. C. N. Bandaratilleke 6-58) **and 190-3** (K. P. P. B. Seneviratne 61, S. K. L. de Silva 70*); **Colts 340** (S. I. Fernando 152).

At Nondescripts Cricket Club, Maitland Place, Colombo, January 31, February 1, 2. **Galle won by an innings and 275 runs.** Toss: Galle. **Nondescripts 58** (K. M. D. N. Kulasekara 5-25) **and 73** (L. H. D. Dilhara 5-28, K. M. D. N. Kulasekara 5-44); **Galle 406-7 dec.** (T. K. D. Sudarshana 58, D. D. Wickremasinghe 64, W. M. P. N. Wanasinghe 52, C. R. P. Galappathy 117*; M. T. T. Mirando 5-76).

Nondescripts lasted 21 overs in the first innings and 21.5 in the second.

At Panadura Esplanade, Panadura, January 31, February 1, 2. **Sinhalese won by eight wickets.** Toss: Sinhalese. **Sinhalese 385** (N. T. Paranavitana 116, R. P. A. H. Wickremaratne 70, T. T. Samaraweera 51) **and 133-2** (N. T. Paranavitana 64*); **Panadura 171** (L. P. C. Silva 76) **and 346** (R. H. T. A. Perera 69, S. D. C. Aravinda 147).

At P. Saravanamuttu Stadium, Colombo, January 31, February 1, 2. **Drawn.** Toss: Moors. **Tamil Union 101** (U. C. Hathurusinghe 4-18) **and 255** (U. C. Hathurusinghe 4-60); **Moors 213 and 87-5.**

At Burgher Recreation Club, Havelock Park, Colombo, February 7, 8, 9. **Burgher won by 114 runs.** Toss: Burgher. **Burgher 260** (B. S. M. Warnapura 59; W. J. M. R. Dias 4-54) **and 222-7 dec.** (R. H. S. Silva 68, V. S. K. Waragoda 82*); **Tamil Union 143** (S. Weerakoon 4-26) **and 225** (S. I. de Saram 51; S. Weerakoon 6-87).

At Colombo Cricket Club, Maitland Crescent, Colombo, February 7, 8, 9. **Drawn.** Toss: Nondescripts. **Colombo 261** (S. K. L. de Silva 80; M. T. T. Mirando 5-60) **and 254-9 dec.** (D. N. Hunukumbura 53, S. K. L. de Silva 77; C. P. Mapatuna 5-59); **Nondescripts 214** (R. R. Tissera 72*; N. S. Rupasinghe 5-60) **and 164-5.**

At Colts Cricket Club, Havelock Park, Colombo, February 7, 8, 9. **Drawn.** Toss: Galle. **Colts 237** (D. K. Liyanage 62*) **and 255-7 dec.** (M. R. C. N. Bandaratilleke 71, S. I. Fernando 73); **Galle 248 and 198-9** (T. K. D. Sudarshana 88; M. R. C. N. Bandaratilleke 6-69).

At Panadura Esplanade, Panadura, February 7, 8, 9. **Moors won by six wickets.** Toss: Moors. **Panadura 107** (P. N. Ranjith 5-34) **and 328** (L. P. C. Silva 114, S. D. C. Aravinda 50; H. M. R. K. B. Herath 5-115); **Moors 320** (W. M. B. Perera 64, W. R. Fernando 78*; M. D. K. Perera 4-106) **and 117-4.**

At Sinhalese Sports Club, Maitland Place, Colombo, February 7, 8, 9. **Drawn.** Toss: Sinhalese. **Bloomfield 191** (S. H. T. Kandamby 66; D. N. T. Zoysa 5-42) **and 249** (S. Jayantha 77, T. M. Dilshan 55; D. Hettiarachchi 4-44); **Sinhalese 102** (H. G. D. Nayanakantha 5-38) **and 169-5.**

At Bloomfield Cricket and Athletic Club, Reid Avenue, Colombo, February 21, 22. **Bloomfield won by nine wickets.** Toss: Nondescripts. **Nondescripts 106** (K. Weeraratne 4-48) **and 254** (M. N. Nawaz 117*; H. D. P. K. Dharmasena 4-52, D. M. G. S. Dissanayake 5-91); **Bloomfield 337** (W. D. D. S. Perera 80, S. Jayantha 137; W. C. A. Ganegama 5-80) **and 24-1.**

At Burgher Recreation Club, Havelock Park, Colombo, February 21, 22. **Sinhalese won by ten wickets.** Toss: Sinhalese. **Burgher 118** (D. N. T. Zoysa 4-33, T. T. Samaraweera 4-33) **and 89** (D. Hettiarachchi 4-21); **Sinhalese 182** (B. S. M. Warnapura 5-32) **and 26-0.**

At Colts Cricket Club, Havelock Park, Colombo, February 21, 22. **Colts won by an innings and 59 runs.** Toss: Colts. **Colts 460** (S. I. Fernando 115, H. G. J. M. Kulatunga 113, M. Pushpakumara 54; G. A. S. Perera 4-109); **Panadura 145** (D. K. Liyanage 4-21) **and 256** (M. T. P. Fernando 79; M. Pushpakumara 5-116).

At Moors Sports Club, Braybrooke Place, Colombo, February 21, 22, 23. **Drawn.** Toss: Moors. **Moors 357** (W. M. B. Perera 220*, U. C. Hathurusinghe 50) **and 244** (U. C. Hathurusinghe 76); **Colombo 203 and 152-3** (H. A. P. W. Jayawardene 72*).

Perera's 220, his maiden double-hundred, lasted 279 balls and included 21 fours and three sixes.*

At P. Saravanamuttu Stadium, Colombo, February 21, 22, 23. **Drawn.** Toss: Tamil Union. **Tamil Union 150** (K. M. D. N. Kulasekara 4-34) **and 467** (T. A. Weerappuli 52, W. M. G. Ramyakumara 116, M. K. Gajanayake 72, S. I. de Saram 65); **Galle 211** (U. D. U. Chandana 5-83) **and 41-4.**

Semi-finals

At Moors Sports Club, Braybrooke Place, Colombo, February 27, 28. **Bloomfield won by an innings and 24 runs.** Toss: Bloomfield. **Sinhalese 103 and 129** (T. M. Dilshan 5-49); **Bloomfield 256** (W. D. D. S. Perera 71, S. Jayantha 86; P. D. R. L. Perera 4-70, D. Hettiarachchi 4-52).

At R. Premadasa Stadium, Khettarama, Colombo, February 27, 28, March 1, 2. **Moors won by four wickets.** Toss: Colombo. **Colombo 241** (S. K. L. de Silva 99; P. N. Ranjith 5-49) **and 196** (D. N. Hunukumbura 66; H. M. R. K. B. Herath 6-46); **Moors 212** (W. M. B. Perera 84, W. T. Abeyratne 54; M. S. Villavarayan 5-56, C. R. B. Mudalige 4-91) **and 231-6** (G. R. P. Peiris 52).

FINAL

BLOOMFIELD v MOORS

At R. Premadasa Stadium, Khettarama, Colombo, March 6, 7, 8. Moors won by one wicket. Toss: Moors.

Moors beat favourites Bloomfield by a single wicket with a day to spare, to become champions for the first time in their 95-year history. The victory was set up by left-arm seamer Nandika Ranjith, who claimed five in each innings, but they were also indebted to 20-year-old Amila Wettasinghe, in his debut season. He came in on the first afternoon with Moors a precarious 96 for five, replying to Bloomfield's 121, and scored the game's only fifty, an unbeaten 62 in 75 balls, to steer his side to a lead of 67. Ranjith was soon back in business, reducing Bloomfield to 80 for five, and the eventual target was 106. Though Moors had two days to get there, it looked unlikely when they slumped to 16 for four inside six overs. Bathiya Perera pushed them forwards, and captain Rangana Herath took them to 97 for eight before he was run out. The last pair, Thamara Abeyratne and Chanaka Welegedara, scraped the remaining nine runs.

Man of the Match: P. N. Ranjith. *Man of the Tournament:* U. C. Hathurusinghe.

Close of play: First day, Moors 158-5 (Abeyratne 24, Wettasinghe 39); Second day, Bloomfield 172.

Bloomfield

†S. P. L. C. S. Perera b Ranjith	0	–	lbw b Ranjith	1
G. I. Daniel lbw b Ranjith	6	–	c Herath b Welegedara	1
T. M. Dilshan lbw b Welegedara	7	–	b Ranjith	18
W. D. D. S. Perera c Cooray b Ranjith	7	–	b Ranjith	1
S. Jayantha b Wettasinghe	19	–	c Abeyratne b Ranjith	47
*H. D. P. K. Dharmasena c Fernando b Hathurusinghe	28	–	lbw b Cooray	23
S. H. T. Kandamby c and b Hathurusinghe	17	–	b Herath	23
D. M. G. S. Dissanayake c Abeyratne b Ranjith	6	–	(9) c Peiris b Ranjith	21
K. Weeraratne c Herath b Hathurusinghe	14	–	(8) c Vitharana b Herath	20
H. S. H. Alles not out	7	–	not out	11
M. P. Ranasinghe b Ranjith	0	–	c Vitharana b Cooray	0
L-b 1, w 5, n-b 4	10		B 2, l-b 1, n-b 3	6
1/1 (1) 2/9 (3) 3/20 (4) 4/25 (2) 5/43 (5) 6/77 (7) 7/89 (8) 8/113 (9) 9/114 (6) 10/121 (11)	121		1/2 (1) 2/6 (2) 3/7 (4) 4/28 (3) 5/80 (5) 6/117 (7) 7/120 (6) 8/161 (9) 9/161 (8) 10/172 (11)	172

Bowling: *First Innings*—Ranjith 13.3–3–39–5; Welegedara 8–0–35–1; Wettasinghe 5–1–21–1; Hathurusinghe 9–1–19–3; Herath 2–0–6–0. *Second Innings*—Ranjith 13–2–38–5; Welegedara 9–2–34–1; Herath 13–3–30–2; Hathurusinghe 6–1–20–0; Wettasinghe 8–0–21–0; Cooray 9.5–1–26–2.

Moors

D. W. A. N. D. Vitharana c Dissanayake b Dharmasena	20	– c Dilshan b Ranasinghe	1
G. R. P. Peiris c Alles b Ranasinghe	7	– (7) c Daniel b Dharmasena	6
M. N. R. Cooray lbw b Ranasinghe	20	– (2) c Dilshan b Alles	0
W. M. B. Perera c W. D. D. S. Perera b Dharmasena	12	– b Dharmasena	31
U. C. Hathurusinghe lbw b Weeraratne	15	– (6) c W. D. D. S. Perera b Dharmasena	19
W. T. Abeyratne c Dilshan b Weeraratne	26	– (9) not out	25
A. C. Wettasinghe not out	62	– (8) c W. D. D. S. Perera b Weeraratne	1
†W. R. Fernando run out	2	– (3) lbw b Alles	5
*H. M. R. K. B. Herath c Dilshan b Ranasinghe	0	– (10) run out	8
P. N. Ranjith c W. D. D. S. Perera b Weeraratne	1	– (5) c Kandamby b Ranasinghe	0
U. W. M. B. C. A. Welegedara c Dissanayake b Weeraratne	0	– not out	0
B 7, l-b 3, n-b 13	23	B 4, l-b 2, n-b 4	10
1/13 (2) 2/55 (3) 3/64 (1) 4/83 (4) 5/96 (5) 6/164 (6) 7/170 (8) 8/179 (9) 9/188 (10) 10/188 (11)	188	1/1 (1) 2/6 (2) 3/11 (3) 4/16 (5) 5/60 (4) 6/65 (6) 7/66 (8) 8/79 (7) 9/97 (10)	(9 wkts) 106

Bowling: *First Innings*—Alles 3–1–12–0; Ranasinghe 10–0–60–3; Dilshan 5–1–15–0; Weeraratne 11–2–34–4; Dharmasena 14–3–37–2; Dissanayake 6–0–20–0. *Second Innings*—Alles 4–0–7–2; Ranasinghe 4–0–17–2; Dharmasena 13–2–38–3; Weeraratne 9.1–1–34–1; Dissanayake 2–0–4–0.

Umpires: A. G. Dissanayake and R. Martinaz.
Third umpire: C. B. C. Rodrigo. Referee: M. Devaraja.

CHAMPIONS

Lakspray Trophy

1988-89	Nondescripts CC / Sinhalese SC
1989-90	Sinhalese SC

P. Saravanamuttu Trophy

1990-91	Sinhalese SC
1991-92	Colts CC
1992-93	Sinhalese SC
1993-94	Nondescripts CC
1994-95	Bloomfield C and AC / Sinhalese SC
1995-96	Colombo CC
1996-97	Bloomfield C and AC
1997-98	Sinhalese SC

Premier Trophy

1998-99	Bloomfield C and AC
1999-2000	Colts CC
2000-01	Nondescripts CC
2001-02	Colts CC
2002-03	Moors SC

Sinhalese have won the title outright 4 times, Colts 3, Bloomfield and Nondescripts 2, Colombo and Moors 1. Sinhalese have also shared the title twice, and Bloomfield and Nondescripts once each.

PLATE CHAMPIONSHIP

The three top teams from the non-first-class Sara Trophy (Antonians, Kandy and Police) joined those teams who had not qualified for the Super League.

At FTZ Sports Complex, Katunayake, January 3, 4, 5. **Ragama won by three wickets.** Toss: Antonians. **Antonians 169** (S. A. Perera 66*; S. Arangalla 5-37) **and 228** (S. A. Perera 99; B. A. R. S. Priyadarshana 4-65); **Ragama 224** (D. A. Ranatunga 57; K. A. K. Janaka 6-56) **and 174-7** (K. N. S. Fernando 50; K. G. S. Sirisoma 4-42).

At Katugastota Oval, Kandy, January 3, 4, 5. **Chilaw Marians won by eight wickets.** Toss: Chilaw Marians. **Kandy 142** (R. S. A. Palliyaguruge 6-26) **and 183** (K. H. R. K. Fernando 6-38); **Chilaw Marians 198** (I. S. Baddegama 4-76, O. Mizran 4-80) **and 128-2** (W. A. D. A. P. Perera 57*).

At Welagedera Stadium, Kurunegala, January 3, 4, 5. **Kurunegala Youth won by an innings and nine runs.** Toss: Police. **Police 85** (H. M. Maduwantha 4-38, A. W. Ekanayake 4-10) **and 207** (C. N. Liyanage 69, R. R. Wimalasiri 55*; H. M. Maduwantha 5-54); **Kurunegala Youth 301** (D. P. S. Jayaratne 82; I. D. Gunawardene 4-82).

At Tyronne Fernando Stadium, Moratuwa, January 3, 4, 5. **Sebastianites won by five wickets.** Toss: Sebastianites. **Moratuwa 192** (H. A. H. U. Tillekeratne 53) **and 183** (K. S. D. Kumara 55*; W. J. M. Fernando 5-33); **Sebastianites 275** (N. S. Bopage 116; B. C. N. Amarasinghe 5-66) **and 102-5.**

At Air Force Ground, Katunayake, January 10, 11, 12. **Air Force won by three wickets.** Toss: Air Force. **Antonians 155** (M. Prasanga 65) **and 239** (D. U. Danthanarayana 61, C. V. Arulanandam 60; M. K. G. C. P. Lakshitha 4-67); **Air Force 260** (T. R. Peiris 77) **and 135-7.**

At FTZ Sports Complex, Katunayake, January 10, 11, 12. **Ragama won by 242 runs.** Toss: Ragama. **Ragama 304** (P. H. D. Premadasa 106*) **and 250-8 dec.** (E. F. M. U. Fernando 108; J. Y. S. T. de Silva 4-75); **Kandy 148 and 164** (D. C. P. D. Wickramanayake 84; B. A. R. S. Priyadarshana 5-28).

Premadasa carried his bat through Ragama's first innings.

At Tyronne Fernando Stadium, Moratuwa, January 10, 11, 12. **Drawn.** Toss: Moratuwa. **Kurunegala Youth 274** (R. H. Sureshchandra 53, G. S. P. Dharmapala 65*; R. G. D. Sanjeewa 4-52) **and 165; Moratuwa 153** (A. W. Ekanayake 6-66) **and 190-9** (H. A. H. U. Tillekeratne 54; A. W. Ekanayake 5-88).

At Police Park, Colombo, January 10, 11, 12. **Drawn.** Toss: Police. **Chilaw Marians 474-4 dec.** (W. A. D. A. P. Perera 201*, L. J. P. Gunaratne 57, C. S. Fernando 102*, K. H. R. K. Fernando 65) **and 342** (L. J. P. Gunaratne 106*, R. S. A. Palliyaguruge 101, K. H. R. K. Fernando 50); **Police 321** (C. N. Liyanage 51, I. D. Gunawardene 72; L. J. P. Gunaratne 5-74).

Perera's 201, his maiden hundred, lasted 293 balls and included 11 fours and three sixes. He retired hurt after adding 191 for the third wicket with Charith Sylvester Fernando, who also retired hurt later; in all, the third wicket added 279 runs.*

At FTZ Sports Complex, Katunayake, January 17, 18, 19. **Drawn.** Toss: Antonians. **Antonians 224** (B. Y. Arumathanthri 57; B. C. N. Amarasinghe 5-33) **and 179-9** (B. C. N. Amarasinghe 8-46); **Moratuwa 355** (B. D. A. P. Ranaweera 64, W. J. S. D. Perera 52).

Amarasinghe took 13-79, the best match analysis of the season.

At R. Premadasa Stadium, Khettarama, Colombo, January 17, 18, 19. **Drawn.** Toss: Ragama. **Ragama 358** (D. V. Gunawardene 135; K. H. R. K. Fernando 4-63) **and 23-0; Chilaw Marians 377** (L. J. P. Gunaratne 77, L. D. I. Perera 58; B. A. R. S. Priyadarshana 4-102, R. D. Dissanayake 4-101).

At Police Park, Colombo, January 17, 18, 19. **Air Force won by eight wickets.** Toss: Police. **Police 211** (C. N. Liyanage 69; P. L. U. Irandika 4-56) **and 121** (A. Rizan 6-23); **Air Force 190** (K. R. P. Silva 57) **and 144-2** (W. R. D. Dissanayake 52).

At Tyronne Fernando Stadium, Moratuwa, January 17, 18. **Sebastianites won by an innings and 136 runs.** Toss: Sebastianites. **Kandy 93 and 110; Sebastianites 339** (K. A. D. M. Fernando 84, M. P. A. Cooray 72; O. Mizran 5-95).

At Air Force Ground, Katunayake, January 24, 25, 26. **Kurunegala Youth won by 122 runs.** Toss: Air Force. **Kurunegala Youth 220** (H. M. Maduwantha 71*; W. C. R. Tissera 4-57) **and 114** (A. Rizan 6-38); **Air Force 135** (T. R. Peiris 57) **and 77** (A. W. Ekanayake 4-16, H. M. Maduwantha 5-34).

At FTZ Sports Complex, Katunayake, January 24, 25. **Chilaw Marians won by nine wickets.** Toss: Chilaw Marians. **Sebastianites 169** (L. D. I. Perera 6-40) **and 104** (K. H. R. K. Fernando 4-34, P. C. Jayasundera 4-28); **Chilaw Marians 245** (L. J. P. Gunaratne 77; M. M. D. N. R. G. Perera 5-61) **and 32-1.**

At Tyronne Fernando Stadium, Moratuwa, January 24, 25, 26. **Drawn.** Toss: Ragama. **Ragama 206** (E. F. M. U. Fernando 54; B. C. N. Amarasinghe 4-62) **and 218** (B. C. N. Amarasinghe 4-44); **Moratuwa 220** (H. M. P. Fernando 57, K. C. D. Fernando 57; S. Arangalla 5-91) **and 147-5** (H. M. P. Fernando 57*).

At Police Park, Colombo, January 24, 25, 26. **Police won by six wickets.** Toss: Police. **Antonians 207** (B. Y. Arumathanthri 56) **and 276** (D. U. Danthanarayana 52); **Police 360** (C. N. Liyanage 126, P. H. K. S. Nirmala 94) **and 126-4** (P. H. K. S. Nirmala 60).

At FTZ Sports Complex, Katunayake, January 31, February 1, 2. **Antonians won by 99 runs.** Toss: Kandy. **Antonians 254** (S. A. Perera 65; C. G. Wijesinghe 4-50) **and 198; Kandy 128** (D. S. Liyanage 5-51) **and 225** (K. G. S. Sirisoma 4-68).

At Bloomfield Cricket and Athletic Club, Reid Avenue, Colombo, February 7, 8. **Chilaw Marians won by nine wickets.** Toss: Chilaw Marians. **Antonians 106** (R. S. A. Palliyaguruge 5-16) **and 146** (S. A. Perera 59); **Chilaw Marians 195** (R. S. A. Palliyaguruge 67; S. D. Dissanayake 5-75) **and 59-1.**

At Welagedera Stadium, Kurunegala, February 7, 8, 9. **Kurunegala Youth won by eight wickets.** Toss: Kandy. **Kandy 97** (H. M. Maduwantha 5-35) **and 393** (C. G. Wijesinghe 146, W. A. S. N. B. Peiris 117; A. W. Ekanayake 8-112); **Kurunegala Youth 342** (C. L. Ediriweerage 50, D. P. S. Jayaratne 166; I. S. Baddegama 4-67, C. G. Wijesinghe 4-91) **and 149-2** (M. N. Jaymon 59*, I. P. Dharmawardene 65).

Ediriweerage and Jayaratne added 189 for Kurunegala's seventh wicket.

At Police Park, Colombo, February 7, 8, 9. **Drawn.** Toss: Police. **Moratuwa 217** (W. J. S. D. Perera 52) **and 213** (R. G. D. Sanjeewa 64; H. P. A. Priyantha 4-30); **Police 343-7 dec.** (C. N. Liyanage 75, R. R. Wimalasiri 103*) **and 37-2.**

At Tyronne Fernando Stadium, Moratuwa, February 7, 8, 9. **Drawn.** Toss: Sebastianites. **Air Force 289** (S. E. D. R. Fernando 59, W. C. R. Tissera 89*) **and 258** (W. C. R. Tissera 53; W. J. M. Fernando 4-71, M. M. D. N. R. G. Perera 4-87); **Sebastianites 238** (W. P. Wickrama 5-56) **and 182-8.**

Ajith Cooray of Sebastianites was banned from first-class cricket for five years for assaulting an umpire.

At Air Force Ground, Katunayake, February 14, 15, 16. **Drawn.** Toss: Air Force. **Air Force 321** (S. E. D. R. Fernando 118, T. R. Peiris 103) **and 254** (K. R. P. Silva 56, S. N. Wijesinghe 96); **Ragama 225** (S. Arangalla 53, B. A. R. S. Priyadarshana 73; M. K. G. C. P. Lakshitha 4-77) **and 33-2.**

At FTZ Sports Complex, Katunayake, February 14, 15. **Kurunegala Youth won by an innings and four runs.** Toss: Kurunegala Youth. **Antonians 100** (A. R. R. A. P. W. R. R. K. B. Amunugama 4-39) **and 121** (A. R. R. A. P. W. R. R. K. B. Amunugama 4-34, A. W. Ekanayake 4-18); **Kurunegala Youth 225** (K. G. S. Sirisoma 5-40).

Ekanayake passed 50 first-class wickets in his ninth match of the season.

At Tyronne Fernando Stadium, Moratuwa, February 14, 15, 16. **Moratuwa won by eight wickets.** Toss: Kandy. **Kandy 193** (K. U. N. Ratnayake 51; C. M. Hathurusinghe 4-57) **and 205** (C. G. Wijesinghe 77); **Moratuwa 348** (W. J. S. D. Perera 78, K. C. D. Fernando 58, K. L. R. Fernando 105; I. S. Baddegama 4-48) **and 51-2.**

Hathurusinghe took a hat-trick in Kandy's first innings.

At Nondescripts Cricket Club, Maitland Place, Colombo, February 14, 15, 16. **Police won by four wickets.** Toss: Police. **Sebastianites 94** (H. P. A. Priyantha 4-27) **and 258** (K. A. D. M. Fernando 53, A. S. N. Fernando 86); **Police 217** (C. N. Liyanage 58) **and 136-6** (M. M. D. N. R. G. Perera 4-61).

At Air Force Ground, Katunayake, February 21, 22, 23. **Police won by 256 runs.** Toss: Police. **Police 254** (H. P. A. Priyantha 93) **and 241-9 dec.** (C. N. Liyanage 133; C. G. Wijesinghe 4-91); **Kandy 117** (W. N. M. Soysa 6-17) **and 122.**

At Air Force Ground, Katunayake, February 28, March 1, 2. **Air Force won by nine wickets.** Toss: Air Force. **Kandy 327** (M. M. M. Rameez 54, D. T. B. Kolugala 61) **and 141** (C. G. Wijesinghe 74; G. S. Dananjaya 4-26); **Air Force 401** (S. E. D. R. Fernando 67, A. Rizan 68, K. R. P. Silva 72, S. N. Wijesinghe 104; M. M. M. Rameez 5-39) **and 71-1** (T. R. Peiris 52*).

At Welagedera Stadium, Kurunegala, February 28, March 1, 2. **Drawn.** Toss: Chilaw Marians. **Chilaw Marians 406** (L. J. P. Gunaratne 57, C. S. Fernando 109, D. T. de Zoysa 53, R. S. A. Palliyaguruge 70, Extras 55) **and 370-9** (D. T. de Zoysa 65, R. S. A. Palliyaguruge 118; A. S. Wewalwala 5-62); **Kurunegala Youth 275** (D. P. S. Jayaratne 74*; R. S. A. Palliyaguruge 5-52).

At FTZ Sports Complex, Katunayake, February 28, March 1, 2. **Ragama won by five wickets.** Toss: Ragama. **Police 154** (W. N. M. Soysa 82; S. Arangalla 7-44) **and 252** (C. N. Liyanage 71; S. Madanayake 4-49); **Ragama 201 and 206-5** (P. H. D. Premadasa 88).

At Tyronne Fernando Stadium, Moratuwa, February 28, March 1. **Sebastianites won by eight wickets.** Toss: Antonians. **Antonians 116** (K. A. D. M. Fernando 4-50) **and 234** (A. P. Dalugoda 4-59); **Sebastianites 233** (A. S. N. Fernando 97*; K. G. S. Sirisoma 5-60) **and 118-2** (N. S. Bopage 83*).

BCCSL INVITATION QUADRANGULAR TOURNAMENT

At Nondescripts Cricket Club, Maitland Place, Colombo, March 24, 25, 26. **BCCSL Club XI won by eight wickets.** Toss: BCCSL Club XI. **Sri Lanka Board Under-23 XI 170** (G. A. S. Perera 55; C. R. B. Mudalige 4-38) **and 171** (L. J. P. Gunaratne 67); **BCCSL Club XI 271** (R. S. Kaluwitharana 79, U. C. Hathurusinghe 61) **and 71-2.**

At Moors Sports Club, Braybrooke Place, Colombo, March 24, 25, 26. **Sri Lanka A won by eight wickets.** Toss: Sri Lanka Schools XI. **Sri Lanka Schools XI 131** (W. R. S. de Silva 5-43) **and 272** (W. U. Tharanga 58); **Sri Lanka A 359** (M. N. Nawaz 105; M. F. Maharoof 4-85, P. U. M. Chanaka 4-103) **and 48-2.**

At Police Park, Colombo, March 31, April 1, 2. **BCCSL Club XI won by one run.** Toss: BCCSL Club XI. **BCCSL Club XI 223** (U. C. Hathurusinghe 75; W. M. G. Ramyakumara 5-42) **and 108** (K. H. R. K. Fernando 5-28, T. T. Samaraweera 4-20); **Sri Lanka A 156 and 174** (P. N. Ranjith 4-48).

Sri Lanka A wicket-keeper Charith Sylvester Fernando held six catches in BCCSL Club XI's first innings and nine in the match.

At Nondescripts Cricket Club, Maitland Place, Colombo, March 31, April 1, 2, 3. **Sri Lanka Board Under-23 XI won by three wickets.** Toss: Sri Lanka Schools XI. **Sri Lanka Schools XI 117 and 352** (W. U. Tharanga 62, A. D. C. Kularatne 59, M. S. R. Wijeratne 108*); **Sri Lanka Board Under-23 XI 144** (M. F. Maharoof 4-36, R. S. R. de Zoysa 4-0) **and 326-7** (G. I. Daniel 156*, K. Weeraratne 51).

At Nondescripts Cricket Club, Maitland Place, Colombo, April 6, 7, 8, 9. **BCCSL Club XI won by 158 runs.** Toss: BCCSL Club XI. **BCCSL Club XI 233** (S. I. Fernando 59, S. K. L. de Silva 50, M. R. C. N. Bandaratilleke 52; P. U. M. Chanaka 4-62) **and 492** (S. K. L. de Silva 133, L. P. C. Silva 85, R. S. Kaluwitharana 91); **Sri Lanka Schools XI 231** (M. S. R. Wijeratne 59, G. T. de Silva 54; P. N. Ranjith 5-61) **and 336** (W. U. Tharanga 116, M. S. R. Wijeratne 69; L. H. D. Dilhara 4-47).

At Moors Sports Club, Braybrooke Place, Colombo, April 6, 7, 8. **Sri Lanka A won by 323 runs.** Toss: Sri Lanka A. **Sri Lanka A 186** (H. G. J. M. Kulatunga 50; M. Pushpakumara 4-27) **and 417-7 dec.** (M. N. Nawaz 115, W. M. G. Ramyakumara 65, A. S. Polonowita 127*); **Sri Lanka Board Under-23 XI 133** (A. B. T. Lakshitha 6-52) **and 147** (M. Pushpakumara 79; W. R. S. de Silva 7-49).

CRICKET IN ZIMBABWE, 2002-03

JOHN WARD

Sean Ervine

Zimbabwean cricket struggled under the shadow of the nation's political crisis. It should have been a season to rejoice in Zimbabwe's status as junior co-hosts of the 2003 World Cup; it was ruined by controversy over that status and the premature retirements of several senior cricketers, most notably Andy Flower.

The cancellation of Australia's tour in April 2002 was a foretaste. Somewhat belatedly – the political crisis dated back to 2000 – protests flooded in about playing World Cup matches in Zimbabwe. Objections centred on security, but many also brought up moral reasons. A boycott, however, threatened serious damage to Zimbabwean cricket without any impact on the government which was its target. Two ICC delegations declared Zimbabwe safe for visiting teams, and for the Zimbabwe Cricket Union security was never a concern. In the event, only England, after weeks of dithering, forfeited their match – which ultimately meant that Zimbabwe beat them to a place in the Super Six stage without defeating a Test side on the field. As in 1999, Zimbabwe lacked the temperamental fibre to do themselves justice in the Super Six, where the ultimate humiliation was their first defeat by Kenya, whose vibrant enthusiasm showed up the Zimbabweans' strained, careworn demeanour.

Zimbabwe's campaign is more likely to be remembered for the heroism of Andy Flower and Henry Olonga. Before their opening match, they issued a statement speaking out against the political situation, and wore black armbands in mourning for "the death of democracy in our beloved Zimbabwe". Flower had already planned to leave the country; Olonga was prepared to stay and face the consequences. However, rumours of secret police sent to escort him home after Zimbabwe's final game in South Africa forced him into exile.

Flower and Olonga felt they could no longer keep quiet, but this put the ZCU and the other players in a difficult position. They had deliberately not consulted their team-mates, so as not to put pressure on them, and none supported them openly, fearing for their careers and their families' safety.

The ZCU faced a serious dilemma. Failure to oppose the protest might be construed as treasonable and invite government interference, which could be disastrous to the game's well-being. Whatever the private views of individual administrators, they felt obliged in public to oppose Flower and Olonga, though they denied that this was why Olonga was promptly dropped – he played only one more game in the tournament. Naturally, the ZCU suffered worldwide condemnation. Next, they had to decide whether to pull out of their tour of England, knowing that the government might force them to do so. But the risk was averted when England promised undisclosed compensation for their World Cup withdrawal and said they would undertake their scheduled tour of Zimbabwe in 2004-05. By January 2004, however, it appeared increasingly likely that England would pull out anyway.

After the World Cup, the struggling Zimbabwe team was further weakened by the loss of some key players. The departure of Andy Flower, 35 in April and still at his peak, was the greatest blow. Besides him and Olonga, Guy Whittall gave up international cricket because of injury, while former captain Alistair Campbell retired after hearing he would not be picked for Sharjah and England; the convener of selectors, Ali Shah, cited a poor attitude to practice. Promising pace bowler Brighton Watambwa had already emigrated to the United States, following Everton Matambanadzo. Paul Strang retired because of injury, and his brother Bryan had moved to South Africa. They joined a long list of players lost to Zimbabwe over the years, from Graeme Hick to Murray Goodwin, losses that would have debilitated a much stronger team. On the positive side, dynamic all-rounder Andy Blignaut returned after a season's self-imposed absence.

Overall, Zimbabwe played less international cricket than in recent years, with tours by Pakistan (who won all seven games), Kenya and South Africa A. After the World Cup, they visited Sharjah for a four-way tournament with Pakistan, Sri Lanka and Kenya, and squeezed Sri Lanka out of the final. But they found little success in England.

The intermittent international programme allowed the top players to appear more often in domestic competitions. The Logan Cup was played on a home-and-away basis for the first time. Masvingo, who had been scheduled to replace the CFX Academy, and Mashonaland A dropped into a non-first-class division, joining the other second teams. With a surplus of top cricketers in Mashonaland (specifically, Harare), some were allocated to the other first-class provinces; it was not satisfactory, but it seemed the only way to ensure competitive cricket for all players of first-class standard.

The Logan Cup fell into two segments, in October and April. The gap meant not only a loss of momentum, but also a loss of personnel for all sides, thanks to retirements and injuries. For the most part, the matches were run-orgies by voracious and experienced batsmen against weak bowling on slow, flat pitches. Each side had at least one double-centurion, and Midlands became the first Zimbabwean team to pass 700 in a single innings, against Manicaland. The most successful bowlers tended to be spinners; the lack of quality seamers was alarming.

Mashonaland still tended to overawe their opponents, even after Andy Flower and Gus Mackay, who took up an administrative post at Leicestershire, departed. But when Midlands held them to a draw at Harare in October, it ended a run of 15 consecutive first-class victories. In April, they won two more games but had to fight to avoid defeat in Bulawayo. They extended their run to 27 Logan Cup matches since their last defeat. In February, they had also topped the Faithwear One-day Series, a new inter-provincial league, winning five of six matches; their one defeat, by Manicaland, was the first for the full Mashonaland side in any official match since 1995-96. The Flower brothers and Craig Evans remained their most consistent batsmen, though Stuart Carlisle clinched a place on the England tour with a double-century against Manicaland. Their most successful bowler was in fact opening batsman Trevor Gripper, who took 25 wickets with his off-breaks despite queries about his action. He did much to shed his dour image with the bat, without winning an international recall.

Matabeleland's weak batting line-up was fortified by their Mashonaland imports, with Gavin Rennie (also a useful left-arm spinner), Mark Vermeulen, Barney Rogers and Andre Hoffman all passing 400, as did local all-rounder Gavin Ewing, whose off-spin claimed 28 wickets, more than anyone else in the competition, but failed to win over the national selectors. Conversely, Matabeleland's strength in seam bowling declined; Heath Streak was available for only one game.

Manicaland suffered most from retirements, losing Campbell, Olonga and Whittall during the season, while Paul Strang played just twice. Neil Ferreira anchored their batting, while Gary Brent overcame a poor start to prove a tower of strength. Academy graduates Richie Sims and Guy Croxford (seven fifties in 12 innings) scored almost 600 runs each.

Midlands, Logan Cup runners-up in 2001-02, never clicked as a unit, apart from their record-breaking game against Manicaland. Sean Ervine prospered with bat and ball, scoring centuries against each of the other provinces, but fellow all-rounder Travis Friend struggled. Raymond Price was the leading wicket-taker, but found little help in the pitches in April. Another Academy graduate, Campbell Macmillan, became the first Zimbabwean to score a century at No. 11, and bowled well until injury curtailed his season.

A disturbing trend was the rise in player indiscipline, especially in club cricket. Sadly, many incidents involved the black Harare club Takashinga, whose fairytale rise turned sour. After problems the previous season, Olonga had joined the club, and exerted a moderating influence. But Takashinga suspended him after his World Cup protest. At all levels, dissent and verbal abuse increased, with players taking advantage of all but the strongest umpires with impunity, and the spirit of the game took a hammering. There was even one physical attack on an opposing player, but the authorities proved too weak to deal with the situation.

Unless problems within the country and in administration can be put to rights, the future of Zimbabwean cricket appears bleak. In the meantime, it needs the positive support and understanding of the rest of the cricketing world as never before.

FIRST-CLASS AVERAGES, 2002-03

BATTING

(Qualification: 350 runs)

	M	*I*	*NO*	*R*	*HS*	*100s*	*Avge*	*Ct/St*
†D. P. Viljoen (*Midlands*)	5	9	3	466	207*	1	77.66	6
†S. M. Ervine (*Midlands & Zimbabwe A*)	6	10	3	520	126	3	74.28	9
C. N. Evans (*Mashonaland*)	6	10	2	544	228*	1	68.00	2
†A. Flower (*Mashonaland & Zimbabwe*)	5	7	1	402	128*	2	67.00	5
G. W. Flower (*Mashonaland & Zimbabwe*)	6	10	0	645	150	2	64.50	9
D. A. Marillier (*Midlands*)	5	9	1	474	163	2	59.25	2
G. M. Croxford (*Manicaland*)	6	12	2	581	96*	0	58.10	3
S. V. Carlisle (*Mashonaland*)	5	10	3	398	219*	1	56.85	0
†A. D. R. Campbell (*Manicaland & Zimbabwe*)	5	10	0	513	95	0	51.30	9
†G. J. Rennie (*Matabeleland & Zimbabwe A*)	6	11	0	554	120	1	50.36	2
M. A. Vermeulen (*Matabeleland, Zim. & Zim. A*)	8	14	0	696	153	2	49.71	15
R. W. Sims (*Manicaland & Zimbabwe A*)	7	12	0	596	204	1	49.66	3
G. M. Ewing (*Matabeleland*)	6	11	0	543	212	2	49.36	4
A. P. Hoffman (*Matabeleland*)	6	11	1	463	102	1	46.30	5
†B. G. Rogers (*Matabeleland*)	6	11	0	467	141	2	42.45	4
G. B. Brent (*Manicaland*)	6	12	2	373	130	1	37.30	5
T. Taibu (*Mashonaland, Zimbabwe & Zim. A*)	8	13	2	410	114*	1	37.27	21/3
†N. R. Ferreira (*Manicaland*)	6	12	0	443	120	2	36.91	18/2
D. D. Ebrahim (*Mashonaland, Zim. & Zim. A*)	7	12	1	397	182	1	36.09	8
S. Matsikenyeri (*Manicaland & Zimbabwe A*)	6	11	0	368	80	0	33.45	5

† *Left-handed batsman.*

BOWLING

(Qualification: 10 wickets)

	Style	*O*	*M*	*R*	*W*	*BB*	*5W/i*	*Avge*
G. J. Rennie (*Matabeleland*)	SLA	94.5	22	200	12	5-55	1	16.66
A. J. Mackay (*Mashonaland*)	RFM	93	26	257	14	5-69	1	18.35
A. P. Hoffman (*Matabeleland*)	RM	57.3	13	187	10	5-25	1	18.70
G. W. Flower (*Mashonaland & Zim.*)	SLA	122.4	40	260	13	6-53	1	20.00
V. Sibanda (*Midlands*)	RM	60	9	235	10	4-30	0	23.50
T. R. Gripper (*Mashonaland*)	OB	190.4	37	623	25	5-40	2	24.92
G. B. Brent (*Manicaland*)	RFM	212.1	41	736	27	6-46	2	27.25
G. M. Ewing (*Matabeleland*)	OB	281	62	775	28	7-64	2	27.67
A. M. Blignaut (*Mashonaland & Zim.*)	RFM	169.3	37	567	20	5-79	1	28.35
C. Macmillan (*Midlands & Zimbabwe A*)	RM	130.3	29	475	15	4-97	0	31.66
N. B. Mahwire (*Manicaland, Zim. & Zim. A*)	RM	187.5	38	739	23	6-57	1	32.13
B. A. Murphy (*Mashonaland*)	LBG	148.5	30	555	17	4-127	0	32.64
R. W. Price (*Midlands & Zimbabwe*)	SLA	416.2	109	1,062	32	8-78	2	33.18
S. M. Ervine (*Midlands & Zimbabwe A*)	RM	172.5	31	664	18	6-82	2	36.88
M. L. Nkala (*Matabeleland, Zim. & Zim. A*)	RFM	199.2	41	776	17	4-53	0	45.64
H. K. Olonga (*Manicaland & Zimbabwe*)	RF	150.2	20	605	13	5-93	1	46.53
R. W. Sims (*Manicaland & Zimbabwe A*)	OB	261	34	1,046	17	3-81	0	61.52

LOGAN CUP, 2002-03

	Played	Won	Lost	Drawn	Bonus points Batting	Bonus points Bowling	Penalty	Points
Mashonaland	6	4	0	2	23	20	5	92
Matabeleland	6	2	2	2	16	14	0.5	59.5
Manicaland	6	2	4	0	19	19	4	58
Midlands	6	1	3	2	16	19	9.5	43.5

Outright win = 12 pts; drawn match = 3 pts.
Bonus points are awarded for the first 120 overs of each team's first innings. One batting point is awarded for the first 200 runs and for every subsequent 50, to a maximum of four points. One bowling point is awarded for the third wicket taken and for every subsequent two.
Penalty points are imposed for slow over-rates.

At Mutare Sports Club, Mutare, October 11, 12, 13, 14. **Mashonaland won by nine wickets.** Toss: Mashonaland. **Mashonaland 640-4 dec.** (D. D. Ebrahim 182, G. W. Flower 61, C. N. Evans 228*, T. Taibu 114*) **and 13-1; Manicaland 352** (A. D. R. Campbell 62, S. Matsikenyeri 80; B. A. Murphy 4-127) **and 299** (A. D. R. Campbell 92, S. Matsikenyeri 60, G. M. Croxford 53). *Mashonaland 18.5 pts, Manicaland 4 pts.*

Evans's 228, his second double-hundred, lasted 393 minutes and 302 balls and included 30 fours and six sixes. He added 284 for the fourth wicket with Ebrahim and 226* for the fifth with Taibu.*

At Queens Sports Club, Bulawayo, October 11, 12, 13, 14. **Drawn.** Toss: Matabeleland. **Matabeleland 462** (G. J. Rennie 120, A. P. Hoffman 93) **and 286** (G. J. Rennie 79, M. A. Vermeulen 55, C. K. Coventry 80; R. W. Price 8-78); **Midlands 348** (D. A. Marillier 69, S. M. Ervine 105; M. L. Nkala 4-83) **and 358-8** (V. Sibanda 82, D. A. Marillier 163; G. M. Ewing 4-95). *Matabeleland 10.5 pts, Midlands 8.5 pts.*

Price took 10-163 in the match.

At Harare Sports Club, Harare, October 18, 19, 20. **Mashonaland won by ten wickets.** Toss: Mashonaland. **Matabeleland 141** (B. G. Rogers 55) **and 279** (M. A. Vermeulen 153; G. W. Flower 4-70); **Mashonaland 415** (G. W. Flower 150, A. Flower 115; G. M. Ewing 5-109) **and 8-0.** *Mashonaland 20 pts, Matabeleland 3 pts.*

The Flower brothers added 272 for Mashonaland's fourth wicket.

At Kwekwe Sports Club, Kwekwe, October 18, 19, 20, 21. **Manicaland won by two wickets.** Toss: Midlands. **Midlands 292** (D. P. Viljoen 61*, C. Macmillan 109) **and 263** (T. J. Friend 69; N. B. Mahwire 6-57); **Manicaland 251** (R. W. Sims 72, A. D. R. Campbell 79; S. M. Ervine 4-38) **and 305-8** (G. M. Croxford 52, S. Matsikenyeri 65; R. W. Price 5-109). *Manicaland 16 pts, Midlands 6 pts.*

Viljoen and Macmillan, the first Zimbabwean to score a century at No. 11, added 144 for Midlands' last wicket, a Zimbabwean tenth-wicket record.

At Harare Sports Club, Harare, October 25, 26, 27, 28. **Drawn.** Toss: Midlands. **Mashonaland 516** (G. W. Flower 83, C. N. Evans 79, A. M. Blignaut 130; C. Macmillan 4-97, R. W. Price 4-136) **and 304-8 dec.** (A. Flower 128*); **Midlands 431** (T. Duffin 57, C. B. Wishart 118, D. A. Marillier 69, S. M. Ervine 119*; A. J. Mackay 5-69) **and 168-4** (D. A. Marillier 102*). *Mashonaland 4.5 pts, Midlands 1 pt.*

Tatenda Taibu held six catches in Midlands' first innings. By forcing a draw, Midlands brought to an end Mashonaland's run of 15 consecutive victories in first-class cricket, all Logan Cup matches. Poor over-rates cost Midlands nine penalty points in this match and Mashonaland 4.5.

At Queens Sports Club, Bulawayo, October 25, 26, 27, 28. **Manicaland won by three wickets.** Toss: Manicaland. **Manicaland 650-8 dec.** (N. R. Ferreira 120, R. W. Sims 204, G. J. Whittall 89, A. D. R. Campbell 95, G. M. Croxford 63*) **and 134-7** (M. L. Nkala 4-53); **Matabeleland 432** (G. J. Rennie 62, G. M. Ewing 148; G. B. Brent 4-71, N. B. Mahwire 4-109) **and 351** (M. A. Vermeulen 55, B. G. Rogers 100). *Manicaland 20 pts, Matabeleland 5 pts.*

Sims's 204, his maiden first-class hundred, lasted 344 minutes and 282 balls and included 32 fours and one six. He and Ferreira opened with 314, a Zimbabwean first-wicket record. 1,567 runs were scored in the match.

At Harare Sports Club, Harare, April 11, 12, 13. **Mashonaland won by four wickets.** Toss: Mashonaland. **Manicaland 397** (N. R. Ferreira 120, G. M. Croxford 80, G. B. Brent 130) **and 192** (G. M. Croxford 78; T. R. Gripper 5-66); **Mashonaland 431-9 dec.** (S. V. Carlisle 219*; G. B. Brent 5-102) **and 159-6.** *Mashonaland 20 pts, Manicaland 6 pts.*

Carlisle's 219, his maiden double-hundred and first first-class century since November 1996, lasted 387 minutes and 292 balls and included 29 fours and one six.*

At Kwekwe Sports Club, Kwekwe, April 11, 12, 13. **Matabeleland won by an innings and 77 runs.** Toss: Matabeleland. **Matabeleland 598** (M. A. Vermeulen 68, B. G. Rogers 52, A. P. Hoffman 102, G. M. Ewing 212); **Midlands 358** (D. P. Viljoen 95, A. Maregwede 105; H. P. Rinke 5-56) **and 163** (G. M. Ewing 7-64). *Matabeleland 18 pts, Midlands 5 pts.*

Ewing's 212, his maiden double-hundred, lasted 333 minutes and 267 balls and included 19 fours and five sixes.

At Mutare Sports Club, Mutare, April 18, 19, 20, 21. **Midlands won by ten wickets.** Toss: Manicaland. **Manicaland 381** (N. R. Ferreira 90, R. W. Sims 56) **and 369** (D. de Beer 74, G. M. Croxford 79, S. Matsikenyeri 59; S. M. Ervine 5-121, V. Sibanda 4-30); **Midlands 715-8 dec.** (C. B. Wishart 172, S. M. Ervine 126, D. P. Viljoen 207*, A. Maregwede 55, Extras 53) **and 39-0.** *Midlands 19 pts, Manicaland 6 pts.*

Viljoen's 207, his maiden double-hundred, lasted 323 minutes and 287 balls and included 25 fours and two sixes; he went from 57* to 178* before lunch on the third day. Midlands recorded the first total over 700 in any first-class match involving a Zimbabwean team.*

At Queens Sports Club, Bulawayo, April 18, 19, 20, 21. **Drawn.** Toss: Mashonaland. **Matabeleland 411** (G. J. Rennie 71, B. G. Rogers 141, G. M. Ewing 68; Douglas T. Hondo 4-90) **and 264** (G. J. Rennie 58; G. W. Flower 6-53); **Mashonaland 441** (T. R. Gripper 104, D. D. Ebrahim 59, G. W. Flower 122, T. Taibu 65; G. M. Ewing 4-111) **and 140-8** (G. J. Rennie 5-55). *Matabeleland 9 pts, Mashonaland 10 pts.*

At Mutare Sports Club, Mutare, April 25, 26, 27, 28. **Matabeleland won by 108 runs.** Toss: Manicaland. **Matabeleland 182** (A. P. Hoffman 78*; G. B. Brent 6-46) **and 416** (C. K. Coventry 67, M. A. Vermeulen 120, G. J. Rennie 68, A. P. Hoffman 60, M. L. Nkala 51*); **Manicaland 331** (G. M. Croxford 96*, T. K. Mawoyo 98) **and 159** (R. W. Sims 51; A. P. Hoffman 5-25). *Matabeleland 14 pts, Manicaland 6 pts.*

At Kwekwe Sports Club, Kwekwe, April 25, 26, 27. **Mashonaland won by 229 runs.** Toss: Mashonaland. **Mashonaland 326** (S. V. Carlisle 60, E. Chigumbura 67, B. A. Murphy 77; S. M. Ervine 6-82) **and 278-7 dec.** (B. A. Murphy 66*, Douglas T. Hondo 51*); **Midlands 148** (T. R. Gripper 5-40) **and 227** (T. Duffin 71, S. M. Ervine 52; T. R. Gripper 4-57). *Mashonaland 19 pts, Midlands 4 pts.*

LOGAN CUP WINNERS

1993-94	Mashonaland Under-24	1998-99	Matabeleland
1994-95	Mashonaland	1999-2000	Mashonaland
1995-96	Matabeleland	2000-01	Mashonaland
1996-97	Mashonaland	2001-02	Mashonaland
1997-98	Mashonaland	2002-03	Mashonaland

Mashonaland have won the title 7 times, Matabeleland 2 and Mashonaland Under-24 once.

CRICKET IN BANGLADESH, 2002-03

UTPAL SHUVRO

Manjurul Islam Rana

Life got worse for Bangladesh, who had not won a game since entering the Test arena in 2000. Between October 2002 and November 2003, they clocked up 13 more Test defeats, only two reaching the fifth day, and lost 25 one-day internationals, interrupted only by two washouts. Though there were chinks of light and two near-misses against Pakistan and England in late 2003, there was a growing feeling within the ICC, which Bangladesh could not ignore, that the country's promotion had been mishandled. The World Cup was the nadir. In 1999, their first World Cup, Bangladesh had won the most important victory in their cricketing history; beating Pakistan helped them gain Test status. Four years later, in South Africa, Bangladesh owed their only two points to rain, and endured humiliating defeats by Canada and Kenya.

The World Cup disaster evoked a sharp reaction. The Bangladesh Cricket Board set up an inquiry, which interviewed players, coach, manager, board officials past and present, and even journalists. Their explosive report condemned a lack of co-ordination between the captain, Khaled Masud, who was described as autocratic, coach Mohsin Kamal, the former Pakistan bowler, and manager A. S. M. Faruque. By then, all three had gone: Masud had always said he would quit the captaincy after the World Cup, while Mohsin and Faruque were sacked. But the report also pointed to the board's flawed management, criticising president Ali Asghar and cricket committee chairman Mahbubul Anam, and the circumstances of Mohsin's appointment. The most important recommendation was to keep politics out of cricket. The Bangladesh government has deliberately politicised the cricket board, to the detriment of sporting decisions.

After Test status came in 2000, steps had been taken to create a more professional board with elected directors and a general manager. Elections were held under this structure in 2001, but the general manager had not yet been appointed when the national government changed. The new ruling party installed their own nominee, Ali Asghar, as board president. Attempts to thwart this through the courts failed, as did an appeal to the International Cricket Council, which declined to interfere in a member's internal affairs. After the World Cup, however, an ICC official visited, recommended that the board appoint a chief executive from another country, and offered help in finding one. Maqbul Dudhia from Zimbabwe was appointed in October 2003.

Many believed the disorder on the board affected performances on the field. Poor planning was illustrated by the continued failure to ensure appropriate practice facilities for the national players. The Bangabandhu National Stadium, originally intended for cricket, now had to be shared with football, and the cricketers had nowhere else to practise in the football season. In June 2003, however, Bangladesh cricket was offered a new home at the Mirpur Stadium, designed for athletics and football. Plans were announced to convert it into a modern complex with a swimming pool, gymnasium and practice ground.

Another positive development was the appointment in April of Dav Whatmore, Bangladesh's fourth national coach in as many seasons. The popular South African, Eddie Barlow, had had to leave after a stroke; he was succeeded by an Australian, Trevor Chappell, who was replaced by Mohsin a year later. Neither was ideally suited to guide Bangladesh through the unknown world of international cricket, and the players sorely missed Barlow. Whatmore, a former Australian Test cricketer who had coached his native Sri Lanka from mediocrity to World Cup success in 1996, was welcomed. His first challenge was the most difficult imaginable – playing Australia in Australia. Almost inevitably, Bangladesh conceded innings defeats in both Tests before being thrashed in a one-day series, but Australian captain Steve Waugh pointed to signs of improvement in the Second Test. His remarks were justified on their next tour, of Pakistan, where their performance was so much stronger that they took first-innings lead twice and were a heart-stopping single wicket short of winning the final Test at Multan.

Back at home, domestic cricket had gone backwards in preparing players for international exposure, thanks to changes in the National Cricket League. Bangladesh's only first-class tournament had been established three years earlier, at the ICC's prompting, and had always featured home and away rounds. In 2002-03, it shrank to a single league round, followed by a final. Most cricketers played a mere five first-class games, down from ten, on largely substandard pitches, and the schedule clashed with West Indies' tour.

Despite the shortened format, there was a dramatic finale. With one day to go in the league, Chittagong and defending champions Dhaka looked certain finalists, until a sensational victory by Khulna over Sylhet. Khulna had to score 388 in 90 overs – having been bundled out for 197 in the first innings. Their last pair scraped home off the final ball.

That meant three teams – Khulna, Dhaka and Chittagong – finished on 14 points. The tie-breaker was runs per wicket, which put Khulna on top. Chittagong's 32.28 runs per wicket was fractionally ahead of Dhaka's 31.61 – but the regulations rounded those figures to the nearest whole number, which tied them on 32. An emergency meeting decided on a play-off, in which Dhaka outperformed an infuriated Chittagong. In the final, however, Dhaka's second-innings collapse allowed Khulna to emerge as first-time champions – though the tables were turned next day in the one-day final.

Khulna's first-class triumph was a real surprise; the previous season, they had finished fifth out of six, winning only one of their ten games. Their success was a team effort, but there were some notable individual performances. Captain Hasanuzzaman led from the front, with 444 runs, including 200 against Chittagong. Opening batsman Sajjadul Hasan had the season's highest aggregate, 447. The tournament's most valuable player, however, was Manjurul Islam Rana (not to be confused with Test player Manjurul Islam), who combined 390 runs at 48.75 with 27 wickets; his left-arm spin also earned 18 in the one-day tournament.

The annual national championship for district and corporation sides, discontinued after the founding of the National Cricket League, resumed in May 2003, with 59 teams. Biman Bangladesh Airlines and Rajshahi District were declared joint champions when the final was washed out. In the Dhaka Premier Cricket League, Victoria Sporting Club celebrated their centenary by retaining the title.

FIRST-CLASS AVERAGES, 2002-03

BATTING

(Qualification: 250 runs)

	M	*I*	*NO*	*R*	*HS*	*100s*	*Avge*	*Ct*
†Manjurul Islam Rana (*Khulna*)	6	10	2	390	78	0	48.75	2
Nafis Iqbal (*Chittagong*)	6	10	2	370	117	1	46.25	2
Rajin Saleh (*Sylhet*)	5	10	1	416	127	2	46.22	7
Aftab Ahmed (*Chittagong*)	6	10	1	415	129	1	46.11	10
Hasanuzzaman (*Khulna*)	6	11	1	444	200	1	44.40	4
Ali Arman (*Barisal*)	5	10	3	308	109*	1	44.00	2
Najimuddin (*Chittagong*)	5	9	2	291	140	1	41.57	3
Sajjadul Hasan (*Khulna*)	6	11	0	447	102	1	40.63	5
Akram Khan (*Chittagong & Bangladesh*)	6	10	0	404	105	1	40.40	3
Azam Iqbal (*Chittagong*)	6	9	2	279	130*	1	39.85	2
Rashidul Haque (*Dhaka*)	5	9	0	352	85	0	39.11	2
Raju Parvez (*Khulna*)	6	12	1	418	94	0	38.00	0
Jahurul Islam (*Rajshahi*)	4	8	1	257	86	0	36.71	3
Sajjad Ahmed (*Dhaka*)	5	8	0	293	90	0	36.62	4
Mazharul Haque (*Dhaka*)	7	12	1	393	119	1	35.72	4
Towhid Hossain (*Barisal*)	4	8	0	283	116	1	35.37	2
Jamaluddin Ahmed (*Khulna*)	5	10	1	311	121	1	34.55	2
Javed Omar (*Dhaka & Bangladesh*)	6	12	0	357	111	1	29.75	1
†Nahidul Haque (*Barisal*)	5	10	0	290	113	1	29.00	4
Fahim Muntasir (*Dhaka*)	7	12	2	284	60	0	28.40	7
Parvez Ahmed (*Sylhet*)	5	10	0	279	84	0	27.90	3
Jahangir Alam (*Dhaka*)	7	13	1	322	66	0	26.83	7
Imran Ahmed (*Barisal*)	5	10	0	250	93	0	25.00	0

† *Left-handed batsman.*

BOWLING

(Qualification: 10 wickets)

	Style	*O*	*M*	*R*	*W*	*BB*	*5W/i*	*Avge*
Hasanuzzaman (*Khulna*)	RFM	56.4	15	154	11	4-65	0	14.00
Arafat Sunny (*Dhaka*)	OB	213.1	56	542	31	6-62	4	17.48
Shafaq Al Zabir (*Rajshahi*)	LFM	152	40	429	24	5-42	1	17.87
Ahsanullah Hasan (*Chittagong*)	SLA	228.4	47	648	35	5-29	2	18.51
Anwar Hossain Monir (*Dhaka*)	RFM	184.4	39	520	27	6-58	1	19.25
Manjurul Islam Rana (*Khulna*)	SLA	212.5	42	540	27	7-82	2	20.00
Rezaul Haque (*Sylhet*)	LFM	121.1	28	355	17	5-41	1	20.88
Anisur Rahman (*Barisal*)	LFM	111	33	299	14	6-38	1	21.35
Parvez Ahmed (*Sylhet*)	RM/OB	97	22	271	11	3-39	0	24.63
Mosaddek Hossain (*Dhaka*)	LB	80.3	17	319	12	4-86	0	26.58
Enamul Haque, jun. (*Sylhet*)	SLA	155.5	25	510	19	5-41	1	26.84
Shafiuddin Ahmed (*Chittagong*)	RFM	136	40	324	12	5-84	1	27.00
Abdur Razzaq (*Khulna*)	SLA	182.1	36	568	19	4-60	0	29.89
Al Amin (*Khulna*)	RFM	184	44	557	18	5-78	1	30.94
Nadif Chowdhury (*Barisal*)	SLA	222	49	557	18	5-62	1	30.94
Fahim Muntasir (*Dhaka*)	OB	155.4	30	519	16	4-43	0	32.43
Shabbir Khan (*Chittagong*)	OB	241.3	50	760	23	5-102	1	33.04
Aminul Islam, jun. (*Rajshahi*)	RFM	131	36	405	11	3-71	0	36.81
Tapash Baisya (*Bangladesh*)	RFM	106.3	18	371	10	4-72	0	37.10
Naimur Rahman (*Dhaka & Bangladesh*)	OB	120.1	25	391	10	3-42	0	39.10
Ali Arman (*Barisal*)	OB	127.4	23	408	10	4-125	0	40.80

Note: Averages include South Africa's tour in April–May 2003.

ISPAHANI MIRZAPORE TEA NATIONAL CRICKET LEAGUE, 2002-03

	Played	*Won*	*Lost*	*Drawn*	*1st-inns Points*	*Points*	*Runs per wkt*
Khulna	5	3	0	2	2	14	35.59
Chittagong	5	3	0	2	2	14	32.28
Dhaka	5	3	0	2	2	14	31.61
Rajshahi	5	2	3	0	0	8	23.44
Barisal	5	0	4	1	2	2	24.15
Sylhet	5	0	4	1	0	0	21.75

Play-off: Dhaka beat Chittagong by 113 runs.

Final: Khulna beat Dhaka by three wickets.

Win = 4 pts; 1st-innings lead in a drawn match = 2 pts.
Teams tied on points were separated by dividing runs scored per wickets conceded; the figure was then rounded up or down to the nearest whole number, so that Chittagong and Dhaka tied on 32 runs per wicket and had to play off for the right to join Khulna in the final.
First innings were closed at 100 overs when the team had not been bowled out.

At Dhanmondi Cricket Stadium, Dhaka, December 10, 11, 12, 13. **Drawn.** Toss: Chittagong. **Khulna 221** (Raju Parvez 50) **and 415** (Salahuddin Ahmed 54, Hasanuzzaman 200; Ahsanullah Hasan 5-85); **Chittagong 310** (Nafis Iqbal 117, Azam Iqbal 75) **and 104-2** (Nafis Iqbal 53*). *Chittagong 2 pts.*

Hasanuzzaman's 200, his maiden double-hundred, lasted 481 minutes and 325 balls and included 24 fours and two sixes.

At Bangladesh Krira Shikkha Protisthan Ground, Savar, December 10, 11, 12, 13. **Dhaka won by three wickets.** Toss: Dhaka. **Barisal 196** (Nahidul Haque 61; Anwar Hossain Monir 4-46) **and 274** (Nahidul Haque 113, Ali Arman 72*; Arafat Sunny 5-45, Mosaddek Hossain 4-86); **Dhaka 324-9** (Javed Omar 111, Halim Shah 98; Ali Arman 4-125) **and 149-7** (Jahangir Alam 66). *Dhaka 4 pts.*

At Fatullah Khan Saheb Osman Ali Stadium, Dhaka, December 10, 11, 12. **Rajshahi won by ten wickets.** Toss: Rajshahi. **Sylhet 118** (Mushfiqur Rahman 4-45) **and 226** (Parvez Ahmed 57, Taqrimul Hadi 51; Shafaq Al Zabir 5-42); **Rajshahi 341-8** (Jahurul Islam 78, Anisur Rahman 54, Hasanuzzaman Rozel 57*; Enamul Haque, jun. 4-113) **and 4-0.** *Rajshahi 4 pts.*

At Fatullah Khan Saheb Osman Ali Stadium, Dhaka, December 17, 18, 19. **Chittagong won by ten wickets.** Toss: Chittagong. **Barisal 125** (Ahsanullah Hasan 4-21) **and 175** (Ahsanullah Hasan 4-41); **Chittagong 300** (Nafis Iqbal 71, Najimuddin 86, Aftab Ahmed 91; Nadif Chowdhury 4-85, Moinuzzaman 5-73) **and 4-0.** *Chittagong 4 pts.*

At Bangladesh Krira Shikkha Protisthan Ground, Savar, December 17, 18, 19. **Dhaka won by four wickets.** Toss: Dhaka. **Sylhet 175** (Rana Miah 74; Arafat Sunny 5-50) **and 144** (Taqrimul Hadi 50; Fahim Muntasir 4-43); **Dhaka 159** (Sajjad Ahmed 52, Fahim Muntasir 50) **and 163-6** (Mazharul Haque 57*). *Dhaka 4 pts.*

At Dhanmondi Cricket Stadium, Dhaka, December 17, 18, 19. **Khulna won by nine wickets.** Toss: Rajshahi. **Rajshahi 194** (Mushfiqur Rahman 55) **and 186** (Abdur Razzaq 4-60); **Khulna 260** (Raju Parvez 94) **and 121-1.** *Khulna 4 pts.*

At Dhanmondi Cricket Stadium, Dhaka, December 23, 24, 25, 26. **Rajshahi won by three wickets.** Toss: Rajshahi. **Barisal 221** (Prosenjit Joy 55) **and 315** (Imran Ahmed 93, Ali Arman 109*); **Rajshahi 198** (Jamiul Alam 92; Anisur Rahman 6-38) **and 339-7** (Jahurul Islam 86, Rafiqul Islam 87, Shamimul Haque 52*, Mahbub Alam 52). *Rajshahi 4 pts.*

At Bangabandhu National Stadium, Dhaka, December 23, 24, 25, 26. **Chittagong won by 46 runs.** Toss: Sylhet. **Chittagong 372** (Najimuddin 140, Akram Khan 105) **and 155** (Enamul Haque, jun. 5-41); **Sylhet 253** (Rajin Saleh 107*; Shafiuddin Ahmed 5-84) **and 228** (Nasirul Alam 56, Rana Miah 53; Shabbir Khan 4-90). *Chittagong 4 pts.*

At Bangladesh Krira Shikkha Protisthan Ground, Savar, December 23, 24, 25, 26. **Drawn.** Toss: Dhaka. **Khulna 310-5** (Sajjadul Hasan 102, Manjurul Islam Rana 55*) **and 86-3; Dhaka 298** (Rashidul Haque 61, Arafat Sunny 55; Manjurul Islam Rana 7-82). *Khulna 2 pts.*

Manjurul Islam Rana's figures of 37–7–82–7 were the best of the season.

At Dhanmondi Cricket Stadium, Dhaka, December 30, 31, January 1, 2. **Khulna won by four wickets.** Toss: Barisal. **Barisal 241** (Anisur Rahman 52) **and 318** (Kafi Khan 66, Towhid Hossain 116, Ali Arman 51*; Al Amin 5-78); **Khulna 392-8** (Sajjadul Hasan 75, Raju Parvez 84, Hasanuzzaman 55, Manjurul Islam Rana 59) **and 170-6.** *Khulna 4 pts.*

No. 11 Anisur Rahman top-scored in Barisal's first innings.

At Fatullah Khan Saheb Osman Ali Stadium, Dhaka, December 30, 31, January 1. **Chittagong won by an innings and eight runs.** Toss: Rajshahi. **Chittagong 343-7** (Aftab Ahmed 60, Azam Iqbal 130*); **Rajshahi 154** (Jahurul Islam 51; Ahsanullah Hasan 5-29) **and 181** (Aminul Islam, jun. 52; Ahsanullah Hasan 4-52). *Chittagong 4 pts.*

At Fatullah Khan Saheb Osman Ali Stadium, Dhaka, January 6, 7, 8, 9. **Drawn.** Toss: Sylhet. **Barisal 347-9** (Nayan Kumar 59, Prosenjit Joy 93, Nadif Chowdhury 51*) **and 179** (Imran Ahmed 57; Rezaul Haque 5-41); **Sylhet 212** (Parvez Ahmed 84; Nadif Chowdhury 5-62) **and 148-6** (Parvez Ahmed 56). *Barisal 2 pts.*

At Dhanmondi Cricket Stadium, Dhaka, January 6, 7, 8, 9. **Drawn.** Toss: Dhaka. **Dhaka 376-8** (Fahim Muntasir 60, Neeyamur Rashid 57*; Ahsanullah Hasan 4-97) **and 189-3 dec.** (Rashidul Haque 60, Aminul Islam 54*); **Chittagong 290** (Aftab Ahmed 129; Anwar Hossain Monir 6-58) **and 27-0.** *Dhaka 2 pts.*

At Fatullah Khan Saheb Osman Ali Stadium, Dhaka, January 13, 14, 15. **Dhaka won by eight wickets.** Toss: Dhaka. **Rajshahi 171 and 225** (Arafat Sunny 5-56); **Dhaka 361** (Rashidul Haque 85, Sajjad Ahmed 62, Neeyamur Rashid 72) **and 36-2.** *Dhaka 4 pts.*

At Dhanmondi Cricket Stadium, Dhaka, January 13, 14, 15, 16. **Khulna won by one wicket.** Toss: Khulna. **Sylhet 311** (Rajin Saleh 127) **and 273** (Rajin Saleh 78, Golam Mawla 50; Manjurul Islam Rana 5-52); **Khulna 197** (Manjurul Islam Rana 78) **and 391-9** (Raju Parvez 87, Hasanuzzaman 51, Manjurul Islam Rana 74). *Khulna 4 pts.*

Play-off

At Dhanmondi Cricket Stadium, Dhaka, January 20, 21, 22, 23. **Dhaka won by 113 runs.** Toss: Dhaka. **Dhaka 295** (Javed Omar 60, Jahangir Alam 51; Shabbir Khan 5-102) **and 215** (Rashidul Haque 58; Suja Irfan 4-57); **Chittagong 197** (Akram Khan 93; Arafat Sunny 6-62) **and 200** (Arafat Sunny 4-63).

The board ordered a play-off to decide which team should qualify for the final after Chittagong and Dhaka tied on points and on rounded runs per wicket.

FINAL

DHAKA v KHULNA

At Bangabandhu National Stadium, Dhaka, January 26, 27, 28, 29. Khulna won by three wickets. Toss: Khulna.

Asadullah Khan completed Khulna's victory with successive fours off Mazharul Haque. On the last morning, they had slipped to 42 for four against Dhaka's opening attack. Then the umpires noticed a spike mark on the ball. They awarded five penalty runs for tampering and, with no suitably aged ball to hand, replaced it with a new one. Dhaka complained that this forced them to keep their tired seamers going. The fielders grew ever more bad-tempered, challenging every decision, while Mohammad Salim and Asadullah put Khulna back on course. The first day had been dominated by a century from Mazharul, the second by one from Jamaluddin Ahmed in Khulna's reply. They conceded a 24-run lead, but Al Amin and Masudul Hasan swung the game round, reducing Dhaka to 74 for five. Despite a recovery launched by Sajjad Ahmed's efforts, they were bowled out on the third evening, and a target of 221 proved too low to defend.

Man of the Match: Jamaluddin Ahmed.

Close of play: First day, Dhaka 339-7 (Fahim Muntasir 15, Neeyamur Rashid 1); Second day, Khulna 271-7 (Monirul Islam 20, Abdur Razzaq 4); Third day, Dhaka 196.

Dhaka

Javed Omar b Abdur Razzaq	26	c Asadullah Khan b Masudul Hasan	8
Rashidul Haque c Mohammad Salim b Hasanuzzaman	50	c Jamaluddin Ahmed b Masudul Hasan	1
Jahangir Alam c Monirul Islam b Hasanuzzaman	27	c Mohammad Salim b Al Amin	10
Mazharul Haque c Jamaluddin Ahmed b Hasanuzzaman	119	b Al Amin	9
Sajjad Ahmed c Mohammad Salim b Hasanuzzaman	9	(6) b Abdur Razzaq	90
*Naimur Rahman c Sajjadul Hasan b Jamaluddin Ahmed	45	(7) lbw b Jamaluddin Ahmed	11
†Sajjad Kadir lbw b Manjurul Islam Rana	27	(9) run out	2
Fahim Muntasir lbw b Manjurul Islam Rana	18	(10) c sub (Niaz Morshed) b Abdur Razzaq	44
Neeyamur Rashid b Manjurul Islam Rana	4	(8) c Abdur Razzaq b Jamaluddin Ahmed	0
Arafat Sunny not out	5	(5) lbw b Al Amin	0
Anwar Hossain Monir lbw b Abdur Razzaq	4	not out	7
B 20, l-b 7, w 1	28	B 10, l-b 4	14
1/60 (1) 2/103 (3) 3/116 (2) 4/140 (5) 5/236 (6) 6/321 (7) 7/335 (4) 8/348 (8) 9/355 (9) 10/362 (11)	362	1/4 (2) 2/19 (1) 3/33 (3) 4/33 (5) 5/74 (4) 6/104 (7) 7/122 (8) 8/135 (9) 9/154 (6) 10/196 (10)	196

Bowling: *First Innings*—Al Amin 15–0–65–0; Masudul Hasan 7–0–30–0; Abdur Razzaq 21.4–5–70–2; Hasanuzzaman 20–5–65–4; Manjurul Islam Rana 24–2–68–3; Jamaluddin Ahmed 9–0–37–1. *Second Innings*—Al Amin 18–8–52–3; Masudul Hasan 17–5–46–2; Hasanuzzaman 2–0–13–0; Abdur Razzaq 8.1–3–18–2; Jamaluddin Ahmed 12–2–37–2; Manjurul Islam Rana 10–1–16–0.

Khulna

First innings	Runs	Second innings	Runs
Sajjadul Hasan c Neeyamur Rashid b Fahim Muntasir	68	lbw b Anwar Hossain Monir	15
Raju Parvez c Fahim Muntasir b Anwar Hossain Monir	0	b Anwar Hossain Monir	17
†Mohammad Salim lbw b Anwar Hossain Monir	6	(6) b Arafat Sunny	60
Jamaluddin Ahmed c Naimur Rahman b Anwar Hossain Monir	121	c Sajjad Kadir b Neeyamur Rashid	1
*Hasanuzzaman b Arafat Sunny	13	c Sajjad Kadir b Anwar Hossain Monir	12
Asadullah Khan c Sajjad Kadir b Naimur Rahman	12	(7) not out	72
Manjurul Islam Rana run out	7	(8) lbw b Naimur Rahman	8
Monirul Islam b Naimur Rahman	24	(3) b Neeyamur Rashid	6
Abdur Razzaq c Neeyamur Rashid b Naimur Rahman	43	not out	10
Masudul Hasan run out	3		
Al Amin not out	13		
B 2, l-b 17, w 9	28	B 6, l-b 4, w 7, p 5	22
1/1 (2) 2/29 (3) 3/157 (1) 4/183 (5) 5/218 (6) 6/230 (7) 7/264 (4) 8/281 (8) 9/306 (10) 10/338 (9)	338	1/31 (1) 2/36 (2) 3/41 (4) 4/42 (3) 5/88 (5) 6/161 (6) 7/186 (8)	(7 wkts) 223

Bowling: *First Innings*—Anwar Hossain Monir 31–6–93–3; Neeyamur Rashid 7–4–17–0; Naimur Rahman 30.1–9–104–3; Arafat Sunny 20–2–64–1; Fahim Muntasir 11–3–41–1. *Second Innings*—Anwar Hossain Monir 29–4–73–3; Neeyamur Rashid 20–5–42–2; Sajjad Ahmed 5–1–20–0; Arafat Sunny 12–5–22–1; Fahim Muntasir 3–1–10–0; Naimur Rahman 7–1–33–1; Mazharul Haque 0.4–0–8–0.

Umpires: A. F. M. Akhtaruddin and Syed Mahbubullah. Referee: Belayet Hossain.

NATIONAL CRICKET LEAGUE WINNERS

2000-01	Biman Bangladesh Airlines	2001-02	Dhaka	2002-03	Khulna

ISPAHANI MIRZAPORE TEA NATIONAL CRICKET ONE-DAY LEAGUE

Note: This match was not first-class.

Final

At Bangabandhu National Stadium, Dhaka, January 30 (day/night). **Dhaka won by 181 runs.** Toss: Dhaka. **Dhaka 236** (49.1 overs) (Anwar Hossain Piju 73, Naimur Rahman 50; Jamaluddin Ahmed 4-47); **Khulna 55** (23.3 overs).

CRICKET IN KENYA, 2003

JASMER SINGH

The year began in remarkable fashion for Kenya, who became the first non-Test-playing nation to reach the semi-finals of the World Cup. Only seven years after making their full one-day international debut, Kenya pulled off wins over Canada, Sri Lanka, Bangladesh and Zimbabwe to reach the last four, where they finally lost to India. By the end of the World Cup, Kenya had played 54 one-day internationals against Test-playing opposition and won six of them. Despite benefiting from the refusal of New Zealand to fulfil their group fixture in Nairobi because of security fears, Kenya had also won the hearts of the South African public.

The performance of Kenya's cricketers made them the county's best paid sportsmen after the top athletes; match earnings from the World Cup totalled $350,000. On their return to Kenya, the side was honoured with a visit to the State House to meet President Mwai Kibaki – the first time a cricket team had enjoyed such a privilege. Meanwhile, the leg-spinner Collins Obuya, who had taken five for 42 in the win over Sri Lanka, was signed by Warwickshire for the 2003 English county season.

Inevitably, perhaps, the rest of the year on the field was something of an anticlimax. In April, Kenya took part in the Cherry Blossom Sharjah Cup along with Pakistan, Sri Lanka and Zimbabwe, but lost all three matches comfortably. In October, Sri Lanka A visited to play five unofficial one-day internationals in the space of eight days – the Sri Lankans won the lot, with only Kennedy Otieno (218 runs at 43.60) averaging over 30 with the bat for Kenya. The following month, Kenya received their first invitation to play in the Hong Kong Sixes, where their lack of experience saw them lose to Sri Lanka, South Africa, England, and India, before they pulled off a consolation victory over the hosts.

The Under-19s toured the United Arab Emirates, where they won most of their games, and then came close to qualifying for the 2004 World Cup in Bangladesh. But, after group victories over Fiji (by a massive 320 runs), the hosts Namibia, and Tanzania, they lost in the semi-finals to Uganda by four wickets, and had to settle for third place. At the end of the year, the Under-19s visited India to take part in the Jawaharlal Nehru Commonwealth Tournament. They again reached the semi-finals, beating West Indies on the way, but went down to the eventual winners, South Africa.

Off the field, the ICC pledged two annual grants of $500,000 to Kenyan cricket to help lay the foundations for an application for full membership. The money was used in part to fund the Under-19 tour of India, as well as the senior side's trip to the West Indies at the start of 2004, when they took part in the first-class Carib Beer Cricket Series.

At the end of May, Kenya appointed Andy Moles as their new coach in place of Sandeep Patil, who, after four years in the job, was returning to his native India. Moles, a former Warwickshire opener who had previously coached Hong Kong at the 2001 ICC Trophy, was given a two-year contract and the responsibility of paving the way for Kenya's possible next promotion. The coaching department was further strengthened by the appointment of Mark Lane, formerly of Surrey, as development coach, and Mudassar Nazar, the former coach of Pakistan, as manager of the Kenya Cricket Association (KCA) Academy.

The development programme was also intensified at school level, while the Under-13 and Under-15 age groups received more attention and sponsorship from the corporate sector. The game's provincial structure, with Kisumu and Nakuru becoming vibrant centres, has helped spread cricket to all corners of the country. On the administrative front, the chairman of the KCA, Jimmy Rayani, was again elected to the ICC Board, and Harilal Shah to the ICC Cricket Committee – Playing. The game here is getting stronger, and the hope is that Kenya will join South Africa and Zimbabwe among Africa's leading cricket nations in the very near future.

CRICKET IN THE NETHERLANDS, 2003

David Hardy

The Dutch national team quickly shrugged off a very disappointing 2002 with an impressive 2003 World Cup. Changes in selection policy – the squad was largely home-born for the first time since the mid-1980s – were vindicated: team spirit was ebullient, bowling competitive and fielding committed. As expected, batting techniques were sometimes exposed. But none of the five defeats by Test countries was embarrassing, and the win over Namibia was a milestone.

It was Holland's first victory, in their 13th one-day international. Despite their inexperience, they beat the Namibians more comfortably than England did. Klaas-Jan van Noortwijk hit Holland's maiden century, to be joined moments later by Feiko Kloppenburg, who added four wickets to join a very select list of all-rounders. Against India, 20-year-old student Daan van Bunge outscored the opposition's glittering batsmen with 62; Tim de Leede won the match award for his four for 35. Meanwhile, some commentators judged Jeroen Smits, slick while standing up to the quick bowlers, the wicket-keeper of the tournament. The captain Roland Lefebvre bowed out of international cricket after 20 years calling himself "a very happy man".

Despite this success, Holland soon reverted to fielding more experienced Antipodean batsmen. With imports, they beat Denmark twice in July – on Scandinavia's only grass wicket – and Cornwall in August, in the first round of the 2004 Cheltenham & Gloucester Trophy.

Holland's next goal is full one-day international status. Before then, Dutch batsmen must improve against out-and-out fast bowling and spin, and bowlers must become more consistent in length and line. The former South African coach Bob Woolmer (who helped Holland as part of the ICC's High Performance Programme) said the facilities and talent were there but that more two- or three-day matches were needed. There are now three grass pitches in Holland, and two young Dutch batsmen, van Bunge and Maurits van Nierop, found a possible short cut into English first-class cricket with selection for the 2003 MCC Young Cricketers.

Despite the rousing performances by Holland, television coverage of the World Cup – and thus exposure to the wider public – was scant. It had been hoped that the arrival in October of Power Cricket, at the Ajax football stadium, would help. Star names and new rules, including rewards for big hits, were promised. But when Asian television pulled out, the event was cancelled.

In line with the trend, local clubs were happy to experiment in an attempt to brighten up cricket. The Hague's four premier league teams played a championship under floodlights in August, with music, bonus runs for consecutive boundaries, and designated hitters. In September, an "Eights" festival – eight teams, eight players, eight overs per innings – was played.

Meanwhile in the conventional game, VRA of Amstelveen won the Dutch league for the fourth time in six seasons. The top three bowlers in the averages – led by South African Test player Claude Henderson – were all from VRA. They were also all foreign-born. So was the top run-scorer, South African Grant Elliott of HBS (based in The Hague) who hit 776 at 51.73. Further down the premier league, another of the ever-improving ethnic minority teams, Bijlmer CC of Amsterdam, held their own in their first season. But the year's most memorable spectacle came in the second division. Esham Razaq hit an extraordinary 350 not out – including 222 in sixes – and eclipsed the previous highest score made in Holland. His side, Asian CC Second XI, hammered 503 for six in 50 overs.

CRICKET ROUND THE WORLD

EDITED BY TONY MUNRO

AFGHANISTAN

The boom in Afghan cricket – which began when the first refugees returned from their camps in Pakistan after the fall of the Taliban government – continued in 2003. There are now more than 2,500 players and leagues spread across 16 of the country's 21 provinces. Nearly all the players are Afghan with almost no expat participation except from the British forces team. The British Embassy, with support from several counties and sponsors, handed over a large quantity of kit, and the ECB donated six Kwik cricket sets which are now used on a regular basis in schools in Kabul. A new limited-over contest, the Olympia Lube Oil tournament, was held in May. It featured the first use of coloured clothing and white balls in Afghanistan: Khost beat 13 other teams to win a hard-fought competition. And in June, Afghanistan were made Associate Members of the Asia Cricket Council. The senior Afghan squad made several visits to Pakistan during the year, with mixed but encouraging results. Afghan government support for the development of cricket continues at all levels, and the president's advisor on tribal affairs, Shah Zada Masood, was elected as president of the cricket federation. Problems remain: for instance, Khost, near the Pakistan border, is a very keen cricketing province but is still troubled by fighting between Al-Qaeda and Coalition forces. However, cricket is helping provide hope in Afghanistan. Allah Dad Noori, the founder of the Afghanistan Cricket Federation, was playing one day in Kabul when a young man walked by carrying an AK47, watched for a while before being invited to join in. Afterwards, he asked if he could play next time. When he returned he was without the rifle. "Where's your AK47?" asked Noori. "Oh, I don't need that," the youth replied. "I'm playing cricket!" The aim of the ACF is to get all the men of Afghanistan to choose cricket instead of guns. KHALIL KHAN AND ANDREW BANKS

ARGENTINA

The 2002-03 season will be remembered for both its frenetic activity and a great loss. Argentina A won the South American Championship for the fifth time out of five, but only after a preliminary round defeat to Chile, a narrow win over Brazil and an exciting last-over win over Chile in the final, all of which reflected rising regional standards. Domestically, Lomas, the right blend of youth and experience, played exciting cricket to secure the first division championship. Belgrano, the traditional force in Argentine cricket, entered two teams as a development tool and still finished second and third. Their full-strength side beat St Albans to win the Robin Stuart Shield for the sixth successive year. The 104th North–South three-day game played at Hurlingham, ended in a draw. Fortunes swung throughout, but a shower on the final afternoon appeared to cost South victory. South left-arm spinner Hernan Pereyra took only the second hat-trick in the fixture's long history.

Amid all the joy, the season was marked by the loss of national team captain Guillermo Kirschbaum, who died tragically, aged 35 (see Obituaries, page 1545). He will be profoundly missed. GRANT DUGMORE

BELGIUM

Years of intensive junior development work paid off for Belgian officials when the national Under-15 squad enjoyed a highly successful year. The team performed highly creditably in the European Under-15B tournament in St Astier, France, finishing third against opposition from several Associate Member countries, and won preparatory matches against King's College, Rochester, Rotterdam's VOC club and a strong Dutch development side. Abhishek Mehta was named player of the tournament after taking five wickets in six balls against Spain, including a hat-trick with his last three deliveries. He finished with six for 15 and completed an unbeaten century after retiring in the middle of his innings through heat exhaustion. Domestically, a reinvigorated Royal Brussels won the league–cup double, snaring both trophies from Pakistan Greens. An influx of Pakistani-based teams in Flemish-speaking areas means the first and second Divisions will be expanded to six teams each in 2004. TED VORZANGER

BRUNEI DARUSSALAM

Fears that cricket would collapse in Brunei have proved unfounded. A fresh committee composed entirely of Bruneians has taken charge, the majority of them new to cricket. There are again six teams competing in the league championship, up from three last year. DEREK THURSBY

CANADA

Canada's development has again been compromised by financial shortfalls complicated by debts left over from the ICC Trophy in 2001, the abject failure of local fundraising efforts and the difficulty in bringing sponsors on board. The loss of the Sahara Cup fixtures between India and Pakistan has disrupted our plans. Canada's wonderful and historic victory over Bangladesh in the 2003 World Cup was a remarkable accomplishment and the culmination of wonderful performances in Sri Lanka, against West Indies A and in the Red Stripe Bowl. But the World Cup manager, Karam Gopaulsingh, reported that the team was held back by "the lack of self-discipline, a professional attitude, commitment to excellence and dedication to the cause". Gopaulsingh added: "We had the personnel: players, coach, physiotherapist who could have impressed the ICC to move us far forward on the road to one-day internationals, but the opportunity was lost at the 'altar of self.'" GEOFF EDWARDS

CHILE

Chile created a possible first in world cricket when it introduced an American-style player draft for the 2002-03 season. In an attempt to dilute the dominance of Las Condes CC and La Dehesa CC, the 47 available players were allotted a points value out of ten and the holders of the 2001-02 wooden spoon, Prince of Wales Country Club, given first choice. The system may require fine-tuning as La Dehesa remained unbeaten to win the Metropolitan Cup, defeating Las Condes in the final. La Dehesa player and national parachuting champion Anthony Adams jun. attracted everyone's attention when he arrived for a club game from the air, landing at fine leg, peeling off his gear and taking his place in the field at the very spot where he landed. Two new clubs joined the Metropolitan Cup for the 2003-04 season: Viña del Mar, comprising employees of an Australian-owned natural gas company, and San Bernardino, from the southern outskirts of Santiago. This club was formed when Miguel Angel Hernandez, a Chilean Christian missionary, visited India in his work and returned home converted to cricket. Both teams comprise only Chileans. JOSEPH WILLIAMS

CHINA

Cricket in Shanghai enjoyed another successful season. The catalyst for growth was the thriving season of indoor matches and coaching sessions, which act as a popular introduction point for beginners. Around 35 newcomers enjoyed their first taste, amongst them Chinese, Poles and Russians. The club's new outdoor net facilities, installed in September, attract inexperienced and established players alike. The annual Shanghai Sixes welcomed 12 teams from across the Far East; Shanghai Dragons won the Cup, defeating Japan in the final. Sadly, hopes of a concerted revival in Beijing floundered. JOE HEPWORTH

DENMARK

Celebrations marking the 50th anniversary of the foundation of the Dansk Cricket Forbund began positively when Denmark hosted and won the 12-team European Indoor Championships at Herning in February. Success was less forthcoming outdoors. Holland won both games of a commemorative series in July in Copenhagen. On the domestic scene, Skanderborg won their first title, ending Svanholm's record championship run of 12 successive titles. PETER S. HARGREAVES

EAST TIMOR

Sandwiched between the beach and mountains, around three kilometres from downtown Dili, is a small dirt road where once a month, cricket is played by a motley collection of expatriates, mainly Australian, and East Timorese. Play gets stopped by stray goats, pigs, children meandering across the "pitch" on the salt plain, and occasionally by people learning to drive. Sometimes, the children chasing the ball take off with it – when a child stops the ball, it's an automatic four. Kit was an issue (the bamboo stumps kept breaking) until we managed to acquire two large bags of cricket gear in return for 500kg of rice. Everyone was happy. Numbers vary and we have played six-a-side up to 21-a-side, especially during the period of reconstruction after post-independence violence, which brought an influx of Australians. In 2001, we played in the Bali Sixes, the organisers provocatively pitting us against the country's former rulers Indonesia in our first game. We hope to return this year, seeking revenge. The team has four East Timorese regulars, who are athletic fielders and deadly in throwing down a set of stumps. But our games are highly social and the few Portuguese and Americans who turn up are allowed to chuck. JIM RICHARDS

ECC TROPHY

Norway, who were admitted as ICC Affiliate Members only in 2000, were unbeaten just three years on to take the ECC Trophy in Vienna for European affiliates. The tournament featured 11 nations playing in three groups, with Malta, Greece and Norway emerging as group winners, and Austria, the best runners-up, qualifying for the second phase. No final was planned as such, but the match on the last day between Norway and Greece became a de facto final – and Norway won by 24 runs. Their margin of victory would have been greater had not five penalty runs been imposed for ball-tampering. The captain, Shammoon Chowdhury, was charged in the absence of an individual culprit and banned for one match. However, it later transpired that he was the guilty party and was subsequently given an extended ban by the Norwegian Cricket Board. Greece were pipped for third by Austria on run-rate. Remaining placings were, in order: Malta, Portugal, Belgium, Spain, Finland, Switzerland, Croatia, Luxembourg. STEPHEN LAMB

FIJI

The highlight of the year was the cricket section of the South Pacific Games, held in Fiji for the first time since 1979. In a thrilling final, Fiji lost by two runs to their old rivals, Papua New Guinea. Fiji qualified for the final through superior run-rate to Samoa and Cook Islands after a shock loss to Samoa in the round-robin. In an all-Fijian Dwarka Prasad tournament (the successor to the old Crompton Cup) held in Suva, Suva Crusaders beat Moce to win the trophy. The competition, which formerly attracted teams from Australia, New Zealand and the South Pacific, has not recovered since the 2000 coup. Generally, it was a difficult year as Fijian cricket struggled to regain old momentum. PETER KNIGHT

FRANCE

Highlight of the year was the six-day trip to Morocco in April, for the inaugural clash between cricket's leading Francophone powers. France won all three games at the Tangiers International Stadium against the fast-improving Moroccans, who were backed by a noisy crowd and an irrepressible stadium DJ, with Arab chart-toppers belting out across the ground throughout the day. It was even hotter at the European Under-15 championships in St Astier in the Dordogne in August, when temperatures of 42°C obliged one (hatless) umpire to retire with sunstroke. France won four games from five, inspired by wicket-keeper Jean-Luc Lambourdire, from

St Martin in the French West Indies, who averaged 80 with the bat. Another Frenchman with a colonial background, Pondicherry-born Arun Ayyavooraju, proved a hit on his one-term cricket scholarship to Malvern College in England, posting two centuries for the school, earning rave plaudits in the Daily Telegraph, and scoring 119 not out when he played for France Under-19s against Malvern – and beat them by 101 runs. The French also beat King's School, Worcester but were unable to repeat their form at the European Championships in Holland three weeks later. After violent incidents involving Stains CC players and supporters following their league game against Villepinte Al-Fatah, Stains were excluded from the championship. SIMON HEWITT

GERMANY

There was continued growth of clubs in all the cricketing regions of Germany in 2003: a new association, the North Rhine-Westphalia Cricket Union, was formed and got into its stride with the benefit of a new artificial pitch in Bonn. In the European B Under-15 tournament, Maxi Hook of Tegernsee CC became, at 14, the first native-born German ever to score a century at any level of international youth cricket when he made 103 not out in the group game against Spain. The German Championships were held in the Olympic Stadium Grounds in Berlin in September between Pak Orient Munich and first-time finalists Berlin Stragglers, who won their first national title by 185 runs. BRIAN FELL

GIBRALTAR

In contrast to the previous season, when UKCCC swept the board, the major honours were shared. UKCCC did retain the main prize, the weekend Senior League, but Grammarians regained the Wiggins Shield, and Gibraltar CC got into the act by taking the Murto Cup, a trophy contested since the early 1920s. New ground was broken in October when a GCA Development XI travelled to Tangier to play two matches against the Moroccan national side in the magnificent new facilities there, and won both. T. J. FINLAYSON

HONG KONG

Cricket continued to thrive in Hong Kong in 2002-03, despite the postponement of some competitions due to SARS. Hong Kong won the Plate competition at the Hong Kong Cricket Sixes and a new ground was opened at Po Kong Village Road. Internationally, the senior team retained the Tunku Ja'Afar Trophy held in Hong Kong but fell at the semi-final stage of the ACC Trophy in Singapore. Domestically, there were again 17 teams in the Saturday League and eight teams in the Sunday League. Nomads and St George's shared the Saturday championship while Mainlanders won the Saturday cup with Crusaders as runners up. There was also a full programme of leagues at every age group level from Under-19 down to Under-11. Little Sai Wan were winners in four of the five competitions. Hussain Butt was

Hit on the pad: Australian soldiers stationed in Baghdad baffle their American colleagues with their use of a military helipad.

Cricketer of the Year after a tremendous performance with both bat and ball. Irfan Ahmed and Nicholas Lau shared the Young Cricketer of the Year award and Billy Ko was the Wellcome most improved junior cricketer.
JOHN CRIBBIN

IRAQ

The Australian "Digger" in desert army fatigues takes strike with his red plastic bat, his rifle and pistol a handy arm's length away (making intimidation of batsmen a risky enterprise). When a dust storm blows up, the "pang" of the tennis ball hitting the empty ration drum which serves as stumps is his only way of knowing his fate, or even if a ball has been bowled, let alone picking what his British or American coalition comrades have bowled. That's if he's not running for cover to make way for an incoming chopper to land on the pitch, the American general's helipad. The threat of inconsistent bounce on the hessian cover is negated by the batsmen's love of the big hit, necessary because the ball decelerates quickly on the dusty outfield. This is especially true of the Americans, who make up the numbers if we are short for Australia v England. They are also the subject of accusations of chucking. Normal standards are further watered down at the indoor matches held in the cavernous 30-room North Palace in Baghdad, untouched by looters and occupied by troops of the Royal Australian Navy. Under the gaze of busts of Saddam Hussein in heroic poses, games are played in the ballroom-sized anteroom. A ball landing on the first landing of the massive marble staircase is a four, on the second level a six. Our bowlers take aim at the stumps, a garish reproduction 17th-century French reclining lounger placed end on, making wicket-keepers redundant. Players are given stern pre-match warnings against hitting the throne in the foyer for reasons of cultural sensitivity. At the time of writing, the Baghdad Ashes are to be inaugurated, comprising a 50-calibre bullet case containing the ashes of a broken leg from an equally tasteless reproduction

15th-century chair, used as the wicket for our first game. When the security situation improves, it is hoped we will play on the old cricket pitch, a remnant from the British days. LT MICHAEL MARLEY (Royal Australian Navy)

Latest from Iraq The Baghdad Ashes were abandoned owing to dangerous conditions – not from any hazards of war, but simply because temperatures were too high and the surface not up to it. The venue was within the grounds of the Palace of Abu Guyarb, now a helipad and the largest area we could find guaranteed free from mines or unexploded ordnance. The wicket was made up of some wooden doors from a nearby bombed-out building, which provided interesting bounce. And in the absence of protective gear other than combat helmets, it was decided to play for fun rather than putting national honour at stake. Worst of all, there was a total alcohol ban in force. COLIN MANSON

ISRAEL

Cricket in Israel is thriving, with more than 1,100 boys and girls actively involved in our youth programme on a weekly basis. In a country where soccer and basketball reign supreme, we have made inroads into major schools. The widening gap between Israel junior sides and the rest of Europe B division was evident at the Under-15 B division tournament in France where Israel swept away all five countries to take the gold medal: more than 98% of our youth players were born and bred in Israel. Lions Lod achieved the double for the second year running in the senior competitions. Opening batsmen Yefet Nagawkar and Mahendra Jaiswar scored more than 1,000 runs between them, while the Massil brothers took nearly 50 wickets. Tel Aviv were relegated for the first time, after their game in Beersheba was abandoned due to a sandstorm. STANLEY PERLMAN

ITALY

Pianoro retained the Championship with a remarkable comeback after Gallicano slumped, having won the first eight games of the 14-round event. Bologna finally won a major trophy, the Italian Cup, and again Gallicano were unlucky, losing the final by five runs. The national youth teams did not perform particularly well with the notable exception of the off-spinner and opening batsman, Francesco Scarponi, who starred with both bat and ball during the Under-19 World Cup qualifier in Holland. A five-year plan to introduce cricket in state schools all over the country was launched, and the Italian Cricket Academy in Hobart, run by Peter Di Venuto, Michael's older brother, was successfully inaugurated. SIMONE GAMBINO

JAPAN

The 2003 season was a combination of progress and frustration. The Fuji City Council approved the development of a ground to be used exclusively for cricket, and two suitable grounds were also found near Tokyo. Two teams with predominantly Japanese players and management (Millennium CC and Wyverns CC) dominated their respective divisions for 2003. The frustrating aspect however, was the weather. Dark clouds seemed to roll in every Friday afternoon, causing about half the Kanto Cricket League games to be washed out or rescheduled. Millennium CC and Giants CC were declared joint champions after the final too, was washed out. Fuji Far East won the women's title. MARK MCTAMNEY

LUXEMBOURG

An excellent summer allowed Luxembourg to enjoy an ever-increasing amount of cricket at all levels. Unfortunately, one of the few games to fall victim to the weather was the first of two home games against France, the visitors winning the second match. The other international played in Luxembourg in 2003, against Belgium, also ended in defeat. Star CC won both the indoor and outdoor LCF-CrossComm leagues in 2003. The search continues for a second ground to relieve the pressure on the Pierre Werner ground, which was in use almost every day between mid-April and early October. The season's highlight was the national team's debut at the 2003 ECC Trophy in Vienna, our first outing at an official international tournament. Luxembourg lost all six games, but perhaps provided the romance of the tournament. The squad ranged in age from 16-year-old Martin Thomas to 67-year-old Lancashire-born wicket-keeper Keith Glover, who completed three stumpings against Switzerland. Previously his greatest feat was obtaining David Gower's autograph. BRYAN ROUSE

MALTA

Malta remains a magnet for European touring sides; over 50 competitive matches were played in a season that attracted 26 visiting teams. This preparation helped the locals reach peak form at the ECC Trophy in Vienna, where they came second equal on points and fourth on run-rate. PIERRE NAUDI

NAMIBIA

The euphoria of World Cup participation has been tempered considerably by news that Namibian national teams at all levels have been excluded from all tournaments conducted by the United Cricket Board of South Africa (UCBSA), who decided they wanted to cut the number of teams to raise the standard. The senior national team last season competed in South Africa's premier one-day competition, the Standard Bank League, and in previous years played in the UCB Bowl for provincial second elevens. Just as cricket in Namibia was enjoying an upsurge in profile and participation (2,000 children are now playing mini-cricket in the country's northern regions), the Namibia Cricket Board must now look elsewhere. Already ties have been strengthened with the Zimbabwe and Kenya Cricket Associations. Namibia hosted Zimbabwe A in September, winning the three-match one-day series but losing the two three-day games. At one stage, Namibian and Zimbabwean players and umpires lay face down as a swarm of bees descended. LAURIE PIETERS

NAURU

Half Nauru's active cricketers are Nauruans, a fact that disguises the state of the game on this 21 sq km Pacific island (population: 12,000) formed from guano, and once made wealthy by phosphates. Two Sri Lankans, an Australian and three locals carry the flag with irregular net sessions in the world's smallest republic. Australian, Indian and Nauruan elevens used to play regularly on a coir matting wicket with a sandy outfield alongside the hospital. The Nauruans displayed high skill levels learnt through exposure to cricket in Victoria, where they worked in the phosphate company's headquarters. However, when phosphate revenues declined, the government slashed the expatriate-laden civil service, hence the recent collapse. However, the Sri Lankan organiser, Mervyn Weerasinghe, is confident player numbers can increase as long as he can hold on to the gear: recently, one of the coir mats was stolen; the other is now in hiding. TONY MUNRO

NORWAY

Norway's victory in the ECC Trophy in Vienna was the greatest event in the country's short cricketing history. It was a reward for much hard work and the first step on the road that in 2004 pits Norway against ICC Associate Members such as France and Germany and could (in theory, anyway) take Norway to a place in the 2007 World Cup. At home, it was the busiest year yet, but the increase in quantity did not dilute the quality. The first division winners were Sentrum CC, while Holmlia CC won the second division. We also found several foreign teams anxious to play us. One request for a tour of Norway purported to come from the Nigerian Cricket Association. There were, however, various aspects of the email that made us suspicious. Chief among them was the fact that they wanted to tour Norway in December when there is minimal daylight and the country is usually under several feet of snow. We believe it was an immigration scam. BOB GIBB

OMAN

Cricket in Oman only really became organised in 1979, but officials are proud of the indigenous participation. There are about 110 Omani nationals (most of them Arabs) playing amongst the 60 teams that compete in eight divisions. Teams are obliged to include one Omani, or otherwise field ten players, and the Omani must bat in the top five. Raha and Muscat are generally Oman's leading clubs, faring well in the United Arab Emirates' main domestic competitions, the Ramadan Floodlit tournament and the Bukhatir League. Although cricket's popularity has increased in recent years it still lags behind soccer, hockey and tennis in the hearts of Omanis. MADHU SAMPAT

PANAMA

The first individual century in a league match in more than 30 years highlighted a successful Panamanian 2003 season. Tarik Daya's 105 for Young Fighters against Kachalia CC was the stand-out individual performance. Interest amongst Panama's mainly Indian expatriate cricket community was bubbling by the time Dadabhai beat Muslim CC in the final by five wickets. Salim Jasat's 49 was the foundation of Dadabhai's win; it was the second year in succession Muslim CC had lost the final. SALEH AND MUSAJI BHANA

RWANDA

Rwanda is the most improbable of all cricketing countries. This small (and recently infamous) corner of East Africa has had minimal contact with Britain and has almost no unused areas of flat ground, let alone equipment or funding. Yet the Rwanda Cricket Association, led by law student Charles Haba, is alive and kicking. The initial five-team, 25-over, MTN league was held in 2003, and won by Kigali CC A – one of four Indian expatriate teams based in the capital – who also contended against Right Guards, drawn from Rwandan university students and Britsh expats. Promise has already been shown at international level when a Rwandan combined XI shared a two-game series against a Ugandan club team. Officials have been fortunate to secure a field at a Kigali secondary school; such is the competition for free space in the "Land of a Thousand Hills" that one of the first cricket matches was played on a lava field next to Mount Nyriangongo, which erupted in 2002. A sisal mat was rolled out after locals had cleared the worst of the rocks and pebbles. The game was held as part of British Week in the town of Gisenyi and attracted a crowd of several hundred. Two players learned about volcanic bounce the hard way: Richard Furama was struck on the cheek and one ball removed Charles Haba's helmet. There are other hazards in Rwanda. When the ICC donated a rubber matting wicket last year, officials refused to let it through customs, claiming it was a carpet and ineligible for the tax exemption on sporting goods. Only payment of an extortionate sum prevented it being auctioned to the highest bidder or perhaps ending up as a 22-yard rubber carpet in a Rwanda Revenue Authority employee's home. CHRIS FREAN

SPAIN

The future of Spanish cricket has never looked brighter, and our cherished goal of ICC associate membership has never seemed more vital. Spain's cricketing potential cannot be fulfilled while it remains an Affiliate, without the crucial funding given to Associates. New clubs have sprouted across Spain, primarily on the Costa del Sol. And the Festival of Cricket to celebrate the opening of the superb new La Manga cricket facility saw the national team compete in a Twenty20 tournament organised by the Club Cricket Conference. The experience for the players was invaluable. KEN SAINSBURY

SWEDEN

Sweden's 2003 season started in a heatwave. Everything is relative, though: the opening game was played on January 18 using a Flicx pitch on the frozen harbour in Stockholm. Players basked in the relative warmth of 3°C after several weeks of temperatures as low as –20°C. In a match played without boundaries between Guttsta Stockholm Exiles and Guttsta Nomads, the batsmen kept warm with several all-run sixes but, with the exception of one skated fielder who collected the ball 90% of the time, fielders were limited to small careful steps. A film of recently melted snow made the ice very slippery. Bowlers suffered mercilessly: Nomads scored 217 in their 15 overs in reply to Exiles' 230. The summer was less successful. Sweden withdrew at the last minute from the ECC Trophy in Vienna. And the national league was diminished, with two of the country's strongest clubs – Malmö CC and Malmöhuset – choosing to play their cricket in Danish competitions, with Malmöhuset winning the Danish Lower League Cup. PAUL EADE

UNITED STATES

Visitors to the annual re-enactments of Civil War battles throughout the United States would have noticed something unusual this year. There, next to the booming cannon and rifle volleys, were Yankees and Rebs playing mid-19th century cricket, resplendent in period costume with the equipment of the time. It was a pointed reminder of cricket's pre-eminence in American sporting culture at the time of the war, and what might have been. Cricket has, however, been experiencing a renaissance. Thanks in large part to waves of immigration from cricketing countries, there are around 15,000 regular cricketers in the US, playing in 600 cricket clubs and 40 leagues across the country – more than any other non-Test country. The numbers have more than doubled in the past decade. However, cricket's revival has been hampered by years of wretched organisation and internal strife: endless politics, questionable elections, accusations of corruption and "insider" deals, and a reluctance to deal with any matters of substance. In 2003, the ICC announced plans to fund the appointment of a chief executive who would be given the authority and funding to help American cricket fulfil its potential. Among the new appointee's first tasks would be to organise triangular tournaments, involving three full ICC members, in both 2005 and 2006, perhaps in the new stadium under construction in Fort Lauderdale, Florida. This could be the prelude to the US staging games in the 2007 World Cup, based in the West Indies, though that remains uncertain. An earlier plan to allow the US automatic qualification into the tournament has now been dropped. In the meantime, 2003 was marked by the old poor leadership. Even the second US National Championship, which had been USACA's successful showcase event the previous year, was marred by complaints about bad officiating and sloppy organisation. There were signs of hope for the future: the North Texas Cricket Association won the ICC's top award for innovative development of cricket; there was real progress at grassroots and junior level in several states; and Quickcricket, a derivative of New Zealand's Cricket Max, had its second full season in the North-west, playing under lights in football stadiums and attracting strong interest. DEB K. DAS

VANUATU

Vanuatu enjoyed another successful season with increased participation rates, particularly at the junior level. A five-team Under-19 competition was introduced while the Under-15 league rose from three to five teams. The main goal for the VCA is to obtain further grounds to cater for the increase in teams. We are hopeful of access to two new venues by next season. Mele Bulls won the BDO Club Championship, fielding an almost entirely indigenous squad. Paama Sharks scored 37 runs in an over (including a no-ball) bowled by Jonny Law of Berocca. MARK STAFFORD

TOURNAMENTS CONTESTED BY NON-TEST NATIONS, 2002-03 AND 2003

Competition	*Winners*	*Runners-up*	*Others*
Asian Cricket Council Emerging Nations (March, 2003)	**Nepal**	Maldives	Bhutan
Asian Cricket Council Emerging Nations (September, 2003)	**Nepal**	Maldives	Bhutan
European Cricket Council Trophy (August 2003)	**Norway**	Austria	Greece, Malta, Portugal, Belgium, Spain, Finland, Switzerland, Croatia, Luxembourg
South American Championships (December 2002)	**Argentina A**	Chile	Brazil, Andean Masters
South Pacific Games (June–July 2003)	**Papua New Guinea**	Fiji	Cook Islands, Samoa, Vanuatu, New Caledonia
Tuanku Ja'Afar Trophy (November–December 2002)	**Hong Kong**	Singapore	Malaysia
Tuanku Ja'Afar Trophy (September 2003)	**Hong Kong**	Malaysia	Singapore, Thailand
West African Championships (April–May 2003)	**Ghana**	Sierra Leone	Gambia

Opposite: Close of play. Father Time looks towards the setting sun, Lord's.
Picture by Patrick Eagar

PART SEVEN

History and Law

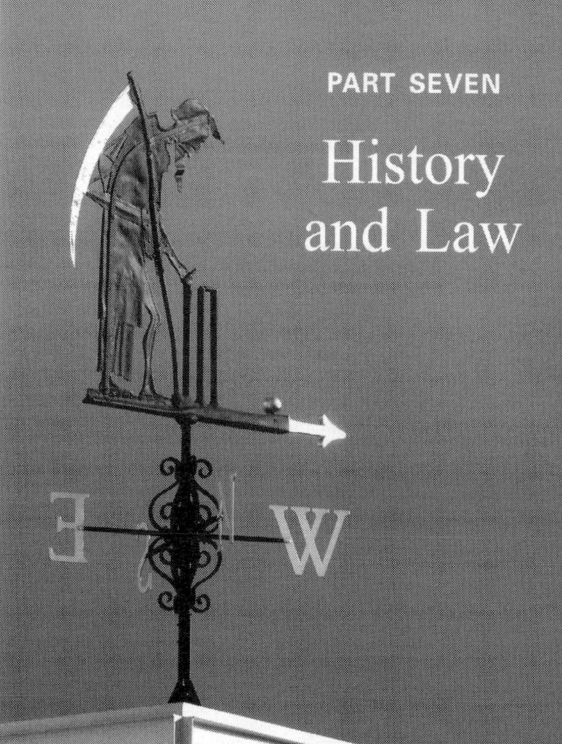

HISTORY OF CRICKET

What is cricket?

Cricket is a game played between two teams, generally of 11 members each. In essence, it is single combat, in which an individual batsman does battle against an individual bowler, who has helpers known as fielders. The bowler propels the ball with a straight arm from one end of the 22-yard pitch in an attempt to dismiss the batsman by hitting a target known as the wicket at the other end, or by causing the batsman to hit the ball into the air into a fielder's grasp, or by inducing one of a number of other indiscretions. The batsman attempts to defend the wicket with the bat and to score runs – the currency of the game – by striking the ball to the field boundary, or far enough from the fielders to allow the batsman to run to the other end of the pitch before the ball can be returned. At least two bowlers must take turns, from alternating ends; also, there are always two batsmen on the field, each to take a turn as required. When all but one of the batting team have been dismissed – or after an agreed period – the teams' roles are reversed. After all the players required to bat on both sides have done so either once or twice (which can take from a few hours to five days) the total number of runs accumulated determines the winner. But sometimes there isn't one.

Origins of the game

The origins of cricket lie somewhere in the Dark Ages – probably after the Roman Empire, almost certainly before the Normans invaded England, and almost certainly somewhere in Northern Europe. All research concedes that the game derived from a very old, widespread and uncomplicated pastime by which one player served up an object, be it a small piece of wood or a ball, and another hit it with a suitably fashioned club.

How and when this club–ball game developed into one where the hitter defended a target against the thrower is simply not known. Nor is there any evidence as to when points were awarded dependent upon how far the hitter was able to despatch the missile; nor when helpers joined the two-player contest, thus beginning the evolution into a team game; nor when the defining concept of placing wickets at either end of the pitch was adopted.

Etymological scholarship has variously placed the game in the Celtic, Scandinavian, Anglo-Saxon, Dutch and Norman-French traditions; sociological historians have variously attributed its mediaeval development to high-born country landowners, *emigré* Flemish cloth-workers, shepherds on the close-cropped downland of south-east England and the close-knit communities of iron- and glass-workers deep in the Kentish Weald. Most of these theories have a solid academic basis, but none is backed with enough evidence to establish a watertight case. The research goes on.

What is agreed is that by Tudor times cricket had evolved far enough from club–ball to be recognisable as the game played today; that it was well established in many parts of Kent, Sussex and Surrey; that within a few years it had become a feature of leisure time at a significant number of schools; and – a sure sign of the wide acceptance of any game – that it had become popular enough among young men to earn the disapproval of local magistrates.

Dates in cricket history

***c.* 1550** Evidence of cricket being played in Guildford, Surrey.

1598 Cricket mentioned in Florio's Italian–English dictionary.

1610 Reference to "cricketing" between Weald and Upland near Chevening, Kent.

1611 Randle Cotgrave's French–English dictionary translates the French word "crosse" as a cricket staff.
Two youths fined for playing cricket at Sidlesham, Sussex.

1624 Jasper Vinall becomes first man known to be killed playing cricket: hit by a bat while trying to catch the ball – at Horsted Green, Sussex.

1676 First reference to cricket being played abroad, by British residents in Aleppo, Syria.

1694 Two shillings and sixpence paid for a "wagger" (wager) about a cricket match at Lewes.

1697 First reference to "a great match" with 11 players a side for fifty guineas, in Sussex.

1700 Cricket match announced on Clapham Common.

1709 First recorded inter-county match: Kent v Surrey.

1710 First reference to cricket at Cambridge University.

1727 Articles of Agreement written governing the conduct of matches between the teams of the Duke of Richmond and Mr Brodrick of Peperharow, Surrey.

1729 Date of earliest surviving bat, belonging to John Chitty, now in the pavilion at The Oval.

1730 First recorded match at the Artillery Ground, off City Road, central London, still the cricketing home of the Honourable Artillery Company.

1744 Kent beat All England by one wicket at the Artillery Ground.
First known version of the Laws of Cricket, issued by the London Club, formalising the pitch as 22 yards long.

***c.* 1767** Foundation of the Hambledon Club in Hampshire, the leading club in England for the next 30 years.

1769 First recorded century, by John Minshull for Duke of Dorset's XI v Wrotham.

1771 Width of bat limited to 4 ¼ inches, where it has remained ever since.

1774 LBW law devised.

1776 Earliest known scorecards, at the Vine Club, Sevenoaks, Kent.

1780 The first six-seamed cricket ball, manufactured by Dukes of Penshurst, Kent.

1787 First match at Thomas Lord's first ground, Dorset Square, Marylebone – White Conduit Club v Middlesex.
Formation of Marylebone Cricket Club by members of the White Conduit Club.

1788 First revision of the Laws of Cricket by MCC.

1794 First recorded inter-schools match: Charterhouse v Westminster.

1795 First recorded case of a dismissal "leg before wicket".

1806 First Gentlemen v Players match at Lord's.

1807 First mention of "straight-armed" (i.e. round-arm) bowling: by John Willes of Kent.

1809 Thomas Lord's second ground opened at North Bank, St John's Wood.

1811 First recorded women's county match: Surrey v Hampshire at Ball's Pond, London.

1814 Lord's third ground opened on its present site, also in St John's Wood.

1827 First Oxford v Cambridge match, at Lord's. A draw.

1828 MCC authorise the bowler to raise his hand level with the elbow.

1833 John Nyren publishes his classic *Young Cricketer's Tutor* and *The Cricketers of My Time.*

1836 First North v South match, for many years regarded as the principal fixture of the season.

***c.* 1836** Batting pads invented.

1841 General Lord Hill, commander-in-chief of the British Army, orders that a cricket ground be made an adjunct of every military barracks.

1844 First official international match: Canada v United States.

1845 First match played at The Oval.

1846 The All-England XI, organised by William Clarke, begins playing matches, often against odds, throughout the country.

1849 First Yorkshire v Lancashire match.

***c.* 1850** Wicket-keeping gloves first used.

1850 John Wisden bowls all ten batsman in an innings for North v South.

1853 First mention of a champion county: Nottinghamshire.

1858 First recorded instance of a hat being awarded to a bowler taking three wickets with consecutive balls.

1859 First touring team to leave England, captained by George Parr, draws enthusiastic crowds in the US and Canada.

1864 "Overhand bowling" authorised by MCC.
John Wisden's *The Cricketer's Almanack* first published.

1868 Team of Australian aborigines tour England.

1873 W. G. Grace becomes the first player to record 1,000 runs and 100 wickets in a season.
First regulations restricting county qualifications, often regarded as the official start of the County Championship.

1877 First Test match: Australia beat England by 45 runs in Melbourne.

1880 First Test in England: a five-wicket win against Australia at The Oval.

1882 Following England's first defeat by Australia in England, an "obituary notice" to English cricket in the *Sporting Times* leads to the tradition of The Ashes.

1889 Present Lord's pavilion begun.
South Africa's first Test match.
Declarations first authorised, but only on the third day, or in a one-day match.

1890 County Championship officially constituted.

1895 W. G. Grace scores 1,000 runs in May, and reaches his 100th hundred.

1899 A. E. J. Collins scores 628 not out in a junior house match at Clifton College, the highest individual score in any match.
Selectors choose England team for home Tests, instead of host club issuing invitations.

1900 Six-ball over becomes the norm, instead of five.

1909 Imperial Cricket Conference (ICC – now the International Cricket Council) set up, with England, Australia and South Africa the original members.

1910 Six runs given for any hit over the boundary, instead of only for a hit out of the ground.

1912 First and only triangular Test series played in England, involving England, Australia and South Africa.

1915 W. G. Grace dies, aged 67.

1926 Victoria score 1,107 v New South Wales at Melbourne, the record total for a first-class innings.

1928 West Indies' first Test match.
A. P. Freeman of Kent and England becomes the only player to take more than 300 first-class wickets in a season: 304.

1930 New Zealand's first Test match.
Donald Bradman's first tour of England: he scores 974 runs in the five Ashes Tests, still a record for any Test series.

1931 Stumps made higher (28 inches not 27) and wider (nine inches not eight – this was optional until 1947).

1932 India's first Test match.
Hedley Verity of Yorkshire takes ten wickets for ten runs v Nottinghamshire, the best innings analysis in first-class cricket.

1932-33 The Bodyline tour of Australia in which England bowl at batsmen's bodies with a packed leg-side field to neutralise Bradman's scoring.

1934 Jack Hobbs retires, with 197 centuries and 61,237 runs, both records.
First women's Test: Australia v England at Brisbane.

1935 MCC condemn and outlaw Bodyline.

1947 Denis Compton of Middlesex and England scores a record 3,816 runs in an English season.

1948 First five-day Tests in England.
Bradman concludes Test career with a second-ball duck at The Oval and a batting average of 99.94 – four runs short of 100.

1952 Pakistan's first Test match.

1953 England regain the Ashes after a 19-year gap, the longest ever.

1956 Jim Laker of England takes 19 wickets for 90 v Australia at Manchester, the best match analysis in first-class cricket.

1957 Declarations authorised at any time.

1960 First tied Test, Australia v West Indies at Brisbane.

1963 Distinction between amateur and professional cricketers abolished in English cricket.
The first major one-day tournament begins in England: the Gillette Cup.

1969 Limited-over Sunday league inaugurated for first-class counties.

1970 Proposed South African tour of England cancelled: South Africa excluded from international cricket because of their government's apartheid policies.

1971 First one-day international: Australia v England at Melbourne.

1975 First World Cup: West Indies beat Australia in final at Lord's.

1976 First women's match at Lord's, England v Australia.

1977 Centenary Test at Melbourne, with identical result to the first match: Australia beat England by 45 runs.
Australian media tycoon Kerry Packer, signs 51 of the world's leading players in defiance of the cricketing authorities.

1978 Graham Yallop of Australia wears a protective helmet to bat in a Test match, the first player to do so.

1979 Packer and official cricket agree peace deal.

1980 Eight-ball over abolished in Australia, making the six-ball over universal.

1981 England beat Australia in Leeds Test, after following on with bookmakers offering odds of 500 to 1 against them winning.

1982 Sri Lanka's first Test.

1991 South Africa return, with a one-day international in India.

1992 Zimbabwe's first Test match.
Durham become the first county since Glamorgan in 1921 to attain first-class status.

1993 The ICC ceases to be administered by MCC, becoming an independent organisation with its own chief executive.

1994 Brian Lara of Warwickshire becomes the only player to pass 500 in a first-class innings: 501 not out v Durham.

2000 South Africa's captain Hansie Cronje banned from cricket for life after admitting receiving bribes from bookmakers in match-fixing scandal.
Bangladesh's first Test match.
County Championship split into two divisions, with promotion and relegation.
The Laws of Cricket revised and rewritten.

2001 Sir Donald Bradman dies, aged 92.

2003 Twenty20 Cup, a 20-over-per-side evening tournament, inaugurated in England.
Matthew Hayden of Australia scores highest individual Test innings: 380 v Zimbabwe.

OFFICIAL BODIES

INTERNATIONAL CRICKET COUNCIL

On June 15, 1909, representatives of cricket in England, Australia and South Africa met at Lord's and founded the Imperial Cricket Conference. Membership was confined to the governing bodies of cricket in countries within the British Commonwealth where Test cricket was played. India, New Zealand and West Indies were elected as members on May 31, 1926, Pakistan on July 28, 1952, Sri Lanka on July 21, 1981, Zimbabwe on July 8, 1992 and Bangladesh on June 26, 2000. South Africa ceased to be a member of the ICC on leaving the British Commonwealth in May, 1961, but was elected as a Full Member on July 10, 1991.

On July 15, 1965, the Conference was renamed the International Cricket Conference and new rules were adopted to permit the election of countries from outside the British Commonwealth. This led to the growth of the Conference, with the admission of Associate Members, who were each entitled to one vote, while the Foundation and Full Members were each entitled to two votes, on ICC resolutions. On July 12 and 13, 1989, the Conference was renamed the International Cricket Council and revised rules were adopted.

On July 7, 1993, the ICC ceased to be administered by MCC and became an independent organisation with its own chief executive, the headquarters remaining at Lord's. The category of Foundation Member, with its special rights, was abolished. On October 1, 1993, Sir Clyde Walcott became the first non-British chairman. On June 16, 1997, the ICC became an incorporated body, with an executive board and a president instead of a chairman.

Officers

President: Ehsan Mani (2003–05). *Chief Executive:* M. W. Speed.

Chairman of Committees: Cricket – Management: M. W. Speed; *Cricket – Playing:* S. M. Gavaskar; *Development:* M. W. Speed; *Audit Committee:* Sir John Anderson.

Executive Board: The president and chief executive sit on the board and all committees *ex officio*. They are joined by Ali Asghar (Bangladesh), Sir John Anderson (New Zealand), P. Chingoka (Zimbabwe), J. Dalmiya (India), E. H. C. Griffith (West Indies), R. F. Merriman (Australia), F. D. Morgan (England), J. Rayani (Kenya), Shaharyar Khan (Pakistan), P. H. F. Sonn (South Africa), T. Sumathipala (Sri Lanka), HRH Tunku Imran (Malaysia), R. van Ierschot (Netherlands).

General Manager – Cricket: D. J. Richardson. *Cricket Operations Manager:* C. D. Hitchcock. *Umpires and Referees Manager:* C. S. Kelly. *Development Manager:* M. R. Kennedy. *General Manager – Corporate Affairs:* B. F. Clements. *Commercial Manager:* D. C. Jamieson. *Chief Finance Officer:* F. Hasnain. *In-house Lawyer:* U. Naidoo.

Constitution

President: Each Full Member has the right, by rotation, to appoint ICC's president. In 1997, India named J. Dalmiya to serve until June 2000, when M. A. Gray of Australia took over. Ehsan Mani of Pakistan succeeded M. A. Gray in June 2003; he and subsequent presidents will serve for two years.

Chief Executive: Appointed by the Council. D. L. Richards served from 1993 to 2001, and was succeeded by M. W. Speed.

Membership

Full Members: Australia, Bangladesh, England, India, New Zealand, Pakistan, South Africa, Sri Lanka, West Indies and Zimbabwe.

Associate Members*: Argentina (1974), Bermuda (1966), Canada (1968), Cayman Islands (2002), Denmark (1966), East and Central Africa (1966), Fiji (1965), France (1998), Germany (1999), Gibraltar (1969), Hong Kong (1969), Ireland (1993), Israel (1974), Italy (1995), Kenya (1981), Malaysia (1967), Namibia (1992), Nepal (1996), Netherlands (1966), Nigeria (2002), Papua New Guinea (1973), Scotland (1994), Singapore (1974), Tanzania (2001), Uganda (1998), United Arab Emirates (1990), USA (1965), Zambia (2003).

Affiliate Members*: Afghanistan (2001), Austria (1992), Bahamas (1987), Bahrain (2001), Belgium (1991), Belize (1997), Bhutan (2001), Botswana (2001), Brazil (2002), Brunei (1992), Chile (2002), Cook Islands (2000), Costa Rica (2002), Croatia (2001), Cuba (2002), Cyprus (1999), Czech Republic (2000), Finland (2000), Gambia (2002), Ghana (2002), Greece (1995), Indonesia (2001), Iran (2003), Japan (1989), Kuwait (1998), Lesotho (2001), Luxembourg (1998), Malawi (2003), Maldives (2001), Malta (1998), Morocco (1999), Mozambique (2003), Norway (2000), Oman (2000), Panama (2002), Philippines (2000), Portugal (1996), Qatar (1999), Rwanda (2003), St Helena (2001), Samoa (2000), Saudi Arabia (2003), Sierra Leone (2002), South Korea (2001), Spain (1992), Suriname (2002), Sweden (1997), Switzerland (1985), Thailand (1995), Tonga (2000), Turks & Caicos Islands (2002) and Vanuatu (1995).

* *Year of election shown in parentheses.*

The following governing bodies for cricket shall be eligible for election.

Full Members: The governing body for cricket recognised by the ICC of a country, or countries associated for cricket purposes, or a geographical area, from which representative teams are qualified to play official Test matches.

Associate Members: The governing body for cricket recognised by the ICC of a country, or countries associated for cricket purposes, or a geographical area, which does not qualify as a Full Member but where cricket is firmly established and organised.

Affiliate Members: The governing body for cricket recognised by the ICC of a country, or countries associated for cricket purposes, or a geographical area (which is not part of one of those already constituted as a Full or Associate Member) where the ICC recognises that cricket is played in accordance with the Laws of Cricket. Affiliate Members have no right to vote or to propose or second resolutions at ICC meetings.

ICC: M. W. Speed, The Clock Tower, Lord's Cricket Ground, London NW8 8QN (020 7266 1818; fax 020 7266 1777; website www.icc.cricket.org; email icc@icc.cricket.org).

ENGLAND AND WALES CRICKET BOARD

The England and Wales Cricket Board (ECB) became responsible for the administration of all cricket – professional and recreational – in England and Wales on January 1, 1997. It took over the functions of the Cricket Council, the Test and County Cricket Board and the National Cricket Association which had run the game in England and Wales since 1968. The Management Board is answerable to the First-Class Forum on matters concerning the first-class game and to the Recreational Forum on matters concerning the non-professional game. The First-Class Forum elects five members to the Management Board and the Recreational Forum elects four.

Officers

Chairman: F. D. Morgan. *Chief Executive:* T. M. Lamb.

Management Board: F. D. Morgan *(chairman)*, D. L. Acfield, D. L. Amiss, R. G. Bransgrove, D. G. Collier, D. E. East, P. H. Edmonds, P. W. Gooden, R. Jackson, R. D. V. Knight, R. C. Moylan-Jones, J. B. Pickup, M. J. Soper, D. P. Stewart, D. Wilson.

Chairmen of Committees: First-Class Forum: M. J. Soper; *Recreational Forum:* J. B. Pickup; *Cricket Advisory Committee:* D. L. Acfield; *International Teams Management Group:* D. L.

Amiss; *Finance Advisory Committee:* D. P. Stewart; *Corporate Affairs and Marketing Advisory Committee:* D. Wilson; *Discipline Standing Committee:* G. Elias QC; *Registration and Contracts Standing Committee:* D. S. Kemp.

Finance Director: B. W. Havill; *Director of Cricket Operations:* J. D. Carr; *Commercial Director:* M. T. Sibley; *Director of Corporate Affairs:* J. C. Read; *Performance Director:* H. Morris; *National Development Director:* K. R. Pont; *Executive Director for Women's Cricket:* G. E. McConway; *Director of Legal Services and Business Development:* M. N. Roper-Drimie; *Cricket Operations Manager (First-Class):* A. Fordham; *Cricket Operations Manager (Recreational):* F. R. Kemp.

ECB: T. M. Lamb, Lord's Ground, London NW8 8QZ (020 7432 1200; fax 020 7289 5619; website www.ecb.co.uk).

THE MARYLEBONE CRICKET CLUB

The Marylebone Cricket Club evolved out of the White Conduit Club in 1787, when Thomas Lord laid out his first ground in Dorset Square. Its members revised the Laws in 1788 and gradually took responsibility for cricket throughout the world. However, it relinquished control of the game in the UK in 1968 and the International Cricket Council finally established its own secretariat in 1993. MCC still owns Lord's and remains the guardian of the Laws. It calls itself "a private club with a public function" and aims to support cricket everywhere, especially at grassroots level and in countries where the game is least developed.

Patron: HER MAJESTY THE QUEEN

Officers

President: 2003–04 – C. A. Fry.

Club Chairman: Lord Alexander of Weedon. *Chairman of Finance:* O. H. J. Stocken.

Trustees: A. C. D. Ingleby-Mackenzie, Sir Michael Jenkins, M. O. C. Sturt.

Hon. Life Vice-Presidents: Sir Alec Bedser, Lord Bramall, D. G. Clark, E. R. Dexter, G. H. G. Doggart, Lord Griffiths, D. J. Insole, M. E. L. Melluish, C. H. Palmer, D. R. W. Silk, J. J. Warr, J. C. Woodcock.

Secretary and Chief Executive: R. D. V. Knight. *Deputy Chief Executive:* D. N. Batts.

Head of Cricket: A. I. C. Dodemaide. *Assistant Secretary (Membership):* C. Maynard. *Personal Assistant to Secretary and Chief Executive:* Miss S. A. Lawrence. *Curator:* A. Chadwick.

MCC Committee: J. R. T. Barclay, P. H. Edmonds, D. J. C. Faber, M. W. Gatting, W. R. Griffiths, R. P. Hodson, P. L. O. Leaver, Rt Hon. J. Major, T. J. G. O'Gorman, N. M. Peters, J. A. F. Vallance, D. R. Walsh.

Chairmen of committees: A. R. Lewis (Cricket); M. J. de Rohan (Estates); C. A. Fry (Membership); A. W. Wreford (Marketing); *Additional Member of the cricket committee:* G. J. Toogood.

MCC: R. D. V. Knight, Lord's Ground, London NW8 8QN (020 7289 1611; fax 020 7289 9100. Tickets 020 7432 1066; fax 020 7432 1061).

PROFESSIONAL CRICKETERS' ASSOCIATION

The Professional Cricketers' Association was formed in 1967 (as the Cricketers' Association) to represent the first-class county playing staffs, and to promote and protect professional players' interests. During the 1970s, it succeeded in establishing pension schemes and a minimum wage. In 1995, David Graveney became the Association's general secretary and first full-time employee; in 1998, he became chief executive. In 1997, the organisation set up its own management company to raise regular revenue and fund improved benefits for members of the PCA during and after their playing careers.

President: M. W. Gatting. *Chairman:* M. C. J. Ball. *Group Chief Executive:* R. H. Bevan. *Group Chairman:* T. J. G. O'Gorman. *Group Directors:* S. A. Marsh, T. A. Munton, G. C. Small.

PCA: R. H. Bevan, 3rd Floor, 338 Euston Road, London NW1 3BT (020 7544 8668; fax 020 7544 8515; email admin@pcaml.co.uk).

FEDERATION OF INTERNATIONAL CRICKETERS' ASSOCIATIONS

The Federation of International Cricketers' Associations was established in 1998 to co-ordinate the activities of all national players' associations. It aims to protect the interests of professional cricketers throughout the world. In 2003 FICA was recognised as an official representative body by the ICC, and FICA representatives now sit on the ICC's Cricket Committee – Playing.

President: B. A. Richards. *Chief Executive:* T. B. A. May. *Secretary:* T. J. G. O'Gorman. *Director of Operations:* R. H. Bevan.

EUROPEAN CRICKET COUNCIL

On June 16, 1997, the eight-year-old European Cricket Federation was superseded by the European Cricket Council, bringing together all European ICC members, plus Israel. In February 2004, the Council consisted of England (Full Member); Denmark, France, Germany, Gibraltar, Ireland, Israel, Italy, Netherlands and Scotland (Associate Members); and Austria, Belgium, Croatia, Cyprus, Czech Republic, Finland, Greece, Luxembourg, Malta, Norway, Portugal, Spain, Sweden and Switzerland (Affiliate Members). The ECC also supports development initiatives in non-member countries Belarus, Bulgaria, Estonia, Iceland, Latvia, Lithuania, Macedonia, Moldova, Monaco, Poland, Romania, Russia, Slovakia, Slovenia, Turkey, Ukraine and Yugoslavia.

Chairman: D. J. Insole. *European Development Manager:* R. Holdsworth. *European Development Officer:* P. Hudson.

ECC: R. Holdsworth, Europe Office, Lord's Ground, London NW8 8QN (020 7616 8635; fax 020 7616 8634; website www.ecc-cricket.com).

ADDRESSES

INTERNATIONAL CRICKET COUNCIL

Full Members

Australia: Australian Cricket Board, J. Sutherland, 60 Jolimont Street, Jolimont, Victoria 3002 (00 61 3 9653 9999; fax 00 61 3 9653 9900; website www.acb.com.au).

Bangladesh: Bangladesh Cricket Board, Arafat Rahman, Navana Tower (5th Floor), 45 Gulshan Avenue, Dhaka 1212 (00 880 2 966 6805; fax 00 880 2 956 3844; email bcb@bangla.net).

England: England and Wales Cricket Board (see above).

India: Board of Control for Cricket in India, Kairali, GHS Lane, Manacaud, Trivandrum 695 009 (00 91 471 245 3307; fax 00 91 471 246 4620; email secbcci@sify.com).

New Zealand: New Zealand Cricket Inc., M. C. Snedden, PO Box 958, 109 Cambridge Terrace, Christchurch (00 64 3 366 2964; fax 00 64 3 365 7491; website www.nzcricket.org.nz).

Pakistan: Pakistan Cricket Board, C. Mujahid, Gaddafi Stadium, Ferozepur Road, Lahore 54600 (00 92 42 571 7231; fax 00 92 42 571 1860).

South Africa: United Cricket Board of South Africa, M. G. Majola, Wanderers Club, PO Box 55009, North Street, Illovo, Northlands 2116 (00 27 11 880 2810; fax 00 27 11 880 6578; website www.ucbsa.cricket.org; email ucbsa@ucb.co.za).

Sri Lanka: Board of Control for Cricket in Sri Lanka, L. R. D. Mendis, 35 Maitland Place, Colombo 7 (00 94 1 691439/689551; fax 00 94 1 697405; email: cricket@sri.lanka.net).

West Indies: West Indies Cricket Board, R. Brathwaite, Factory Road, PO Box 616 W, Woods Centre, St John's, Antigua (00 1 268 481 2450; fax 00 1 268 481 2498; email wicb@candw.ag).

Zimbabwe: Zimbabwe Cricket Union, V. Hogg, PO Box 2739, Josiah Tongogara Avenue, Harare (00 263 4 704616/8; fax 00 263 4 729370; website www.zcu.cricket.org; email zcu@mweb.co.zw).

Associate and Affiliate Members

Afghanistan Allah Dad Noori, afghan_cricket_fed@yahoo.com.
Argentina R. Lord, cricarg@hotmail.com.
Austria A. Simpson-Parker, simpson-parker@chello.at.
Bahamas G. T. Taylor, firstslip@hotmail.com.
Bahrain M. M. Osman, Osman@ramsis.com.bh.
Belgium T. Vorzanger, t.vorzanger@skynet.be.
Belize E. R. V. Wade Jr, juniorbest@btl.net.
Bermuda R. Pearman, rpearman@logic.bm.
Bhutan T. Tashi, bhutan_cricket_association@hotmail.com.
Botswana E. A. Bhamjee, chico@botsnet.bw.
Brazil J. N. Landers, john.landers@apis.com.br.
Brunei M. B. Ahmad, mirbash@brunet.bn.
Canada G. Edwards, Geoffed01@cs.com.
Cayman Islands C. Myles, cicaadmin@candw.ky.
Chile A. Adams, aadams@britanico.cl.
Cook Islands V. Henry, lily@oyster.net.ck.
Costa Rica R. Illingworth, trillingworth@yahoo.co.uk.
Croatia J. Butkovic, croatia@cricinfo.com.
Cuba L. I. Ford, leona@inder.co.uk.
Cyprus S. Carr, carrs@cylink.com.cy.
Czech Republic D. Talacko, talacko@vol.cz.
Denmark C. B. S. Hansen, dcf@cricket.dk.
East and Central Africa syusuf@globmw.net.
Fiji S. Yaqona, fijicrick@connect.com.fj.
Finland A. Armitage, fcachairman@cricketfinland.com.
France O. Dubaut, Olivier.dubaut@paris.pref.gouv.fr.
Gambia T. Manly-Rollings, sonnyann@qanet.gm.
Germany C. Hoefinghoff, hoefinghoff@adfontes.net.
Ghana W. Hackman, whackman@africaonline.com.gh.
Gibraltar T. J. Finlayson, gibarchives@gibnynex.gi.
Greece G. Sagiadinou, cricketadm@otenet.gr.
Hong Kong J. A. Cribbin, hkca@hkabc.net.
Indonesia M. K. Suresh, mksuresh1@yahoo.com.
Iran Mohammed B. Zolfagharian, mbzbaseballir@hotmail.com.
Ireland J. Wright, johnpwright@eircom.net.
Israel S. Perlman, israel@cricket.org.
Italy S. Gambino, segreteria@cricketitalia.org.
Japan T. Lto, takaoo804@aol.com.
Kenya H. Shah, kcricket@iconnect.co.ke.
Lesotho P. Maliehe, lesothosportcommission@ilesotho.com.
Luxembourg R. Fyfe, LCF@cricket.lu.

Malawi Shiraz Yusuf, syusuf@globemw.net.
Malaysia C. Sivanandan, crickmal@tm.net.my.
Maldives Ahmed Hassan Didi, ccbm@avasmail.com.mv.
Malta P. Naudi, maltacricket@yahoo.co.uk.
Morocco M. Boujil, marocricket@caramail.com.
Mozambique Angela Melo, fmc.moz@webmail.co.za.
Namibia L. Pieters, cricket@iway.na.
Nepal P. R. Pandey, prpandey52@hotmail.com.
Netherlands A. de la Mar, cricket@kncb.nl.
Nigeria John Abebe, segun_adeuk@yahoo.co.uk.
Norway R. Gibb, bobgibb@c2i.net.
Oman Madhu Sampat, latmad@omanteal.net.om.
Panama Ismael Patel, aptecpa@cwpanama.net.
Philippines C. Hartley, cjh@dls.com.ph.
Portugal P. D. Eckersley, mail@portugalcricket.org.
Qatar Manzoor Ahmad, afx@qatar.net.qa.
Rwanda Charles Haba, rwandacricket@yahoo.fr.
St Helena B. A. George, barbara@sainthelena.gov.sh.
Samoa U. L. Apelu, laki@samoa.ws.
Saudi Arabia Hasan Kabir, saudicricket@sps.net.sa.
Scotland C. Carruthers, admin@scottishcricket.co.uk.
Sierra Leone G. Fewry, hallelujahg@yahoo.com.
Singapore A. Kalaver, cricket@singnet.co.sg.
South Korea H. S. Kim, haksu@mac.com.
Spain K. Sainsbury, ksainsby@dragonet.es.
Suriname R. Hiralal, deloitte@sr.net.
Sweden J. Govindarajah, mohan_Sweden@hotmail.com.
Switzerland A. D. MacKay, alex.mackay@swisscricket.ch.
Tanzania Z. Rehmtulla, wizards@cats-net.com.
Thailand R. Sehgal, ravisehgall@hotmail.com.
Tonga S. Puloka, pmotrain@kalianet.to.
Turks & Caicos Islands H. Coalbrooke, mpapt@tciway.tc.
Uganda J. Bagabo, ugandacricket@utlonline.co.ug.
United Arab Emirates Mazhar Khan, cricket@emirates.net.ae.
USA G. Dainty, smxrefaie@aol.com.
Vanuatu M. Stafford, bdo@vanuatu.com.vu.
Zambia R. M. Patel, acricket@zamtel.zm.

Note: Full contact details for all Associate and Affiliate Members are available from the ICC.

ICC DEVELOPMENT PROGRAM GLOBAL AWARDS

Jai Kumar Nath Shah, president of the Cricket Association of Nepal for the last 30 years, won the first Lifetime Service Award in the ICC Development Program Global Awards for 2003. Laurie Pieters, president of the Namibian Cricket Board, was named Volunteer of the Year. Other awards were Best Overall Development Program – Indonesian Cricket Foundation; Best Junior Development Initiative – US Cricket Academy, New Jersey; Best Women's Cricket Initiative – Japan Cricket Association; Best Cricket Promotional Program – Vanuatu Cricket Association; Flicx Community Development Award – Chipata Community, Zambia; Best Spirit of Cricket Initiative – Glostrup CC, Denmark. The winners were selected by a panel including ICC president Ehsan Mani, his predecessor Malcolm Gray, World Cup executive director Dr Ali Bacher and MCC chief executive and secretary Roger Knight.

THE LAWS OF CRICKET

(2000 CODE)

INDEX OF THE LAWS

THE PREAMBLE – THE SPIRIT OF CRICKET

Cricket is a game that owes much of its unique appeal to the fact that it should be played not only within its Laws, but also within the Spirit of the Game. Any action which is seen to abuse this spirit causes injury to the game itself. The major responsibility for ensuring the spirit of fair play rests with the captains.

1. There are two Laws which place the responsibility for the team's conduct firmly on the captain.

Responsibility of captains

The captains are responsible at all times for ensuring that play is conducted within the Spirit of the Game as well as within the Laws.

Player's conduct

In the event of a player failing to comply with instructions by an umpire, or criticising by word or action the decisions of an umpire, or showing dissent, or generally behaving in a manner which might bring the game into disrepute, the umpire concerned shall in the first place report the matter to the other umpire and to the player's captain, and instruct the latter to take action.

2. Fair and unfair play

According to the Laws the umpires are the sole judges of fair and unfair play. The umpires may intervene at any time, and it is the responsibility of the captain to take action where required.

3. The umpires are authorised to intervene in cases of

- Time-wasting.
- Damaging the pitch.
- Dangerous or unfair bowling.
- Tampering with the ball.
- Any other action that they consider to be unfair.

4. The Spirit of the Game involves respect for

- Your opponents.
- Your own captain and team.
- The role of the umpires.
- The game's traditional values.

5. It is against the Spirit of the Game

- To dispute an umpire's decision by word, action or gesture.
- To direct abusive language towards an opponent or umpire.
- To indulge in cheating or any sharp practice, for instance:

(a) To appeal knowing that the batsman is not out.

(b) To advance towards an umpire in an aggressive manner when appealing.

(c) To seek to distract an opponent either verbally or by harassment with persistent clapping or unnecessary noise under the guise of enthusiasm and motivation of one's own side.

6. Violence

There is no place for any act of violence on the field of play.

7. Players

Captains and umpires together set the tone for the conduct of a cricket match. Every player is expected to make an important contribution to this.

The players, umpires and scorers in a game of cricket may be of either gender and the Laws apply equally to both. The use, throughout the text, of pronouns indicating the male gender is purely for brevity. Except where specifically stated otherwise, every provision of the Laws is to be read as applying to women and girls equally as to men and boys.

LAW 1. THE PLAYERS

1. Number of players

A match is played between two sides, each of 11 players, one of whom shall be captain. By agreement a match may be played between sides of more or less than 11 players, but not more than 11 players may field at any time.

2. Nomination of players

Each captain shall nominate his players in writing to one of the umpires before the toss. No player may be changed after the nomination without the consent of the opposing captain.

3. Captain

If at any time the captain is not available, a deputy shall act for him.

(a) If a captain is not available during the period in which the toss is to take place, then the deputy must be responsible for the nomination of the players, if this has not already been done, and for the toss. See 2 above and Law 12.4 (The toss).

(b) At any time after the toss, the deputy must be one of the nominated players.

4. Responsibility of captains

The captains are responsible at all times for ensuring that play is conducted within the spirit and traditions of the game as well as within the Laws. See The Preamble – The Spirit of Cricket and Law 42.1 (Fair and unfair play – responsibility of captains).

LAW 2. SUBSTITUTES AND RUNNERS; BATSMAN OR FIELDER LEAVING THE FIELD; BATSMAN RETIRING; BATSMAN COMMENCING INNINGS

1. Substitutes and runners

(a) If the umpires are satisfied that a player has been injured or become ill after the nomination of the players, they shall allow that player to have:

(i) A substitute acting instead of him in the field.

(ii) A runner when batting.

Any injury or illness that occurs at any time after the nomination of the players until the conclusion of the match shall be allowable, irrespective of whether play is in progress or not.

(b) The umpires shall have discretion, for other wholly acceptable reasons, to allow a substitute for a fielder, or a runner for a batsman, at the start of the match or at any subsequent time.

(c) A player wishing to change his shirt, boots, etc. must leave the field to do so. No substitute shall be allowed for him.

2. Objection to substitutes

The opposing captain shall have no right of objection to any player acting as a substitute on the field, nor as to where the substitute shall field. However, no substitute shall act as wicket-keeper. See 3 below.

3. Restrictions on the role of substitutes

A substitute shall not be allowed to bat or bowl nor to act as wicket-keeper or as captain on the field of play.

4. A player for whom a substitute has acted

A player is allowed to bat, bowl or field even though a substitute has previously acted for him.

5. Fielder absent or leaving the field

If a fielder fails to take the field with his side at the start of the match or at any later time, or leaves the field during a session of play:

(a) The umpire shall be informed of the reason for his absence.

(b) He shall not thereafter come on to the field during a session of play without the consent of the umpire. See 6 below. The umpire shall give such consent as soon as is practicable.

(c) If he is absent for 15 minutes or longer, he shall not be permitted to bowl thereafter, subject to (i), (ii) or (iii) below, until he has been on the field for at least that length of playing time for which he was absent.

(i) Absence or penalty for time absent shall not be carried over into a new day's play.

(ii) If, in the case of a follow-on or forfeiture, a side fields for two consecutive innings, this restriction shall, subject to (i) above, continue as necessary into the second innings but shall not otherwise be carried over into a new innings.

(iii) The time lost for an unscheduled break in play shall be counted as time on the field for any fielder who comes on to the field at the resumption of play. See Law 15.1 (An interval).

6. Player returning without permission

If a player comes on to the field of play in contravention of 5(b) above and comes into contact with the ball while it is in play:

(i) The ball shall immediately become dead and the umpire shall award five penalty runs to the batting side. See Law 42.17 (Penalty runs). The ball shall not count as one of the over.

(ii) The umpire shall inform the other umpire, the captain of the fielding side, the batsmen and, as soon as practicable, the captain of the batting side of the reason for this action.

(iii) The umpires together shall report the occurrence as soon as possible to the executive of the fielding side and any governing body responsible for the match, who shall take such action as is considered appropriate against the captain and player concerned.

7. Runner

The player acting as a runner for a batsman shall be a member of the batting side and shall, if possible, have already batted in that innings. The runner shall wear external protective equipment equivalent to that worn by the batsman for whom he runs and shall carry a bat.

8. Transgression of the Laws by a batsman who has a runner

(a) A batsman's runner is subject to the Laws. He will be regarded as a batsman except where there are specific provisions for his role as a runner. See 7 above and Law 29.2 (Which is a batsman's ground).

(b) A batsman with a runner will suffer the penalty for any infringement of the Laws by his runner as though he had been himself responsible for the infringement. In particular he will be out if his runner is out under any of Laws 33 (Handled the ball), 37 (Obstructing the field) or 38 (Run out).

(c) When a batsman with a runner is striker he remains himself subject to the Laws and will be liable to the penalties that any infringement of them demands.

Additionally, if he is out of his ground when the wicket is put down at the wicket-keeper's end, he will be out in the circumstances of Law 38 (Run out) or Law 39 (Stumped) irrespective of the position of the non-striker or of the runner. If he is thus dismissed, runs completed by the runner and the other batsman before the dismissal shall not be scored. However, the penalty for a no-ball or a wide shall stand, together with any penalties to be awarded to either side when the ball is dead. See Law 42.17 (Penalty runs).

(d) When a batsman with a runner is not the striker:

(i) He remains subject to Laws 33 (Handled the ball) and 37 (Obstructing the field) but is otherwise out of the game.

(ii) He shall stand where directed by the striker's end umpire so as not to interfere with play.

(iii) He will be liable, notwithstanding (i) above, to the penalty demanded by the Laws should he commit any act of unfair play.

9. Batsman leaving the field or retiring

A batsman may retire at any time during his innings. The umpires, before allowing play to proceed, shall be informed of the reason for a batsman retiring.

(a) If a batsman retires because of illness, injury or any other unavoidable cause, he is entitled to resume his innings subject to (c) below. If for any reason he does not do so, his innings is to be recorded as "Retired – not out".

(b) If a batsman retires for any reason other than as in (a) above, he may resume his innings only with the consent of the opposing captain. If for any reason he does not resume his innings it is to be recorded as "Retired – out".

(c) If after retiring a batsman resumes his innings, it shall be only at the fall of a wicket or the retirement of another batsman.

10. Commencement of a batsman's innings

Except at the start of a side's innings, a batsman shall be considered to have commenced his innings when he first steps on to the field of play, provided "Time" has not been called. The innings of the opening batsmen, and that of any new batsman at the resumption of play after a call of "Time", shall commence at the call of "Play".

LAW 3. THE UMPIRES

1. Appointment and attendance

Before the match, two umpires shall be appointed, one for each end to control the game as required by the Laws, with absolute impartiality. The umpires shall be present on the ground and report to the executive of the ground at least 45 minutes before the start of each day's play.

2. Change of umpire

An umpire shall not be changed during the match, other than in exceptional circumstances, unless he is injured or ill. If there has to be a change of umpire, the replacement shall act only as the striker's end umpire unless the captains agree that he should take full responsibility as an umpire.

3. Agreement with captains

Before the toss the umpires shall:

(a) Ascertain the hours of play and agree with the captains:

(i) The balls to be used during the match. See Law 5 (The ball).

(ii) Times and durations of intervals for meals and times for drinks intervals. See Law 15 (Intervals).

(iii) The boundary of the field of play and allowances for boundaries. See Law 19 (Boundaries).

(iv) Any special conditions of play affecting the conduct of the match.

(b) Inform the scorers of the agreements in (ii), (iii) and (iv) above.

4. To inform captains and scorers

Before the toss the umpires shall agree between themselves and inform both captains and both scorers:

(i) Which clock or watch and back-up timepiece is to be used during the match.

(ii) Whether or not any obstacle within the field of play is to be regarded as a boundary. See Law 19 (Boundaries).

5. The wickets, creases and boundaries

Before the toss and during the match, the umpires shall satisfy themselves that:

(i) The wickets are properly pitched. See Law 8 (The wickets).

(ii) The creases are correctly marked. See Law 9 (The bowling, popping and return creases).

(iii) The boundary of the field of play complies with the requirements of Law 19.2 (Defining the boundary – boundary marking).

6. Conduct of the game, implements and equipment

Before the toss and during the match, the umpires shall satisfy themselves that:

(a) The conduct of the game is strictly in accordance with the Laws.

(b) The implements of the game conform to the requirements of Laws 5 (The ball) and 6 (The bat), together with either Laws 8.2 (Size of stumps) and 8.3 (The bails) or, if appropriate, Law 8.4 (Junior cricket).

(c) (i) No player uses equipment other than that permitted.

(ii) The wicket-keeper's gloves comply with the requirements of Law 40.2 (Gloves).

7. Fair and unfair play

The umpires shall be the sole judges of fair and unfair play.

8. Fitness of ground, weather and light

The umpires shall be the final judges of the fitness of the ground, weather and light for play. See 9 below and Law 7.2 (Fitness of the pitch for play).

9. Suspension of play for adverse conditions of ground, weather or light

(a) (i) All references to ground include the pitch. See Law 7.1 (Area of pitch).

(ii) For the purpose of this Law the batsmen at the wicket may deputise for their captain at any appropriate time.

(b) If at any time the umpires together agree that the condition of the ground, weather or light is not suitable for play, they shall inform the captains and, unless

(i) in unsuitable ground or weather conditions both captains agree to continue, or to commence, or to restart play, or

(ii) in unsuitable light the batting side wish to continue, or to commence, or to restart play,

they shall suspend play, or not allow play to commence or to restart.

(c) (i) After agreeing to play in unsuitable ground or weather conditions, either captain may appeal against the conditions to the umpires before the next call of "Time". The umpires shall uphold the appeal only if, in their opinion, the factors taken into account when making their previous decision are the same or the conditions have further deteriorated.

(ii) After deciding to play in unsuitable light, the captain of the batting side may appeal against the light to the umpires before the next call of "Time". The umpires shall uphold the appeal only if, in their opinion, the factors taken into account when making their previous decision are the same or the condition of the light has further deteriorated.

(d) If at any time the umpires together agree that the conditions of ground, weather or light are so bad that there is obvious and foreseeable risk to the safety of any player or umpire, so that it would be unreasonable or dangerous for play to take place, then notwithstanding the provisions of 9(b)(i) and 9(b)(ii) above, they shall immediately suspend play, or not allow play to commence or to restart. The decision as to whether conditions are so bad as to warrant such action is one for the umpires alone to make.

Merely because the grass and the ball are wet and slippery does not warrant the ground conditions being regarded as unreasonable or dangerous. If the umpires consider the ground is so wet or slippery as to deprive the bowler of a reasonable foothold, the fielders of the power of free movement, or the batsmen of the ability to play their strokes or to run between the wickets, then these conditions shall be regarded as so bad that it would be unreasonable for play to take place.

(e) When there is a suspension of play it is the responsibility of the umpires to monitor the conditions. They shall make inspections as often as appropriate, unaccompanied by any of the players or officials. Immediately the umpires together agree that conditions are suitable for play they shall call upon the players to resume the game.

(f) If play is in progress up to the start of an agreed interval then it will resume after the interval unless the umpires together agree that conditions are or have become unsuitable or dangerous. If they do so agree, then they shall implement the procedure in (b) or (d) above, as appropriate, whether or not there had been any decision by the captains to continue, or any appeal against the conditions by either captain, prior to the commencement of the interval.

10. Exceptional circumstances

The umpires shall have the discretion to implement the procedures of 9 above for reasons other than ground, weather or light if they consider that exceptional circumstances warrant it.

11. Position of umpires

The umpires shall stand where they can best see any act upon which their decision may be required. Subject to this over-riding consideration the umpire at the bowler's end shall stand where he does not interfere with either the bowler's run-up or the striker's view.

The umpire at the striker's end may elect to stand on the off side instead of the on side of the pitch, provided he informs the captain of the fielding side, the striker and the other umpire of his intention to do so.

12. Umpires changing ends

The umpires shall change ends after each side has had one completed innings. See Law 14.2 (Forfeiture of an innings).

13. Consultation between umpires

All disputes shall be determined by the umpires. The umpires shall consult with each other whenever necessary. See also Law 27.6 (Consultation by umpires).

14. Signals

(a) The following code of signals shall be used by umpires.

(i) Signals made while the ball is in play:

Dead ball	– by crossing and re-crossing the wrists below the waist.
No-ball	– by extending one arm horizontally.
Out	– by raising the index finger above the head. (If not out the umpire shall call "Not out".)
Wide	– by extending both arms horizontally.

(ii) When the ball is dead, the signals above, with the exception of the signal for "Out", shall be repeated to the scorers. The signals listed below shall be made to the scorers only when the ball is dead.

Boundary 4	– by waving an arm from side to side finishing with the arm across the chest.
Boundary 6	– by raising both arms above the head.
Bye	– by raising an open hand above the head.
Commencement of last hour	– by pointing to a raised wrist with the other hand.
Five penalty runs awarded to the batting side	– by repeated tapping of one shoulder with the opposite hand.
Five penalty runs awarded to the fielding side	– by placing one hand on the opposite shoulder.
Leg-bye	– by touching a raised knee with the hand.
New ball	– by holding the ball above the head.
Revoke last signal	– by touching both shoulders, each with the opposite hand.

Short run – by bending one arm upwards and touching the nearer shoulder with the tips of the fingers.

(b) The umpires shall wait until each signal to the scorers has been separately acknowledged by a scorer before allowing play to proceed.

15. Correctness of scores

Consultation between umpires and scorers on doubtful points is essential. The umpires shall satisfy themselves as to the correctness of the number of runs scored, the wickets that have fallen and, where appropriate, the number of overs bowled. They shall agree these with the scorers at least at every interval, other than a drinks interval, and at the conclusion of the match. See Laws 4.2 (Correctness of scores), 21.8 (Correctness of result) and 21.10 (Result not to be changed).

LAW 4. THE SCORERS

1. Appointment of scorers

Two scorers shall be appointed to record all runs scored, all wickets taken and, where appropriate, number of overs bowled.

2. Correctness of scores

The scorers shall frequently check to ensure that their records agree. They shall agree with the umpires, at least at every interval, other than a drinks interval, and at the conclusion of the match, the runs scored, the wickets that have fallen and, where appropriate, the number of overs bowled. See Law 3.15 (Correctness of scores).

3. Acknowledging signals

The scorers shall accept all instructions and signals given to them by the umpires. They shall immediately acknowledge each separate signal.

LAW 5. THE BALL

1. Weight and size

The ball, when new, shall weigh not less than $5\frac{1}{2}$oz/155.9g, nor more than $5\frac{3}{4}$oz/163g, and shall measure not less than $8\frac{13}{16}$in/22.4cm, nor more than 9in/22.9cm in circumference.

2. Approval and control of balls

(a) All balls to be used in the match, having been approved by the umpires and captains, shall be in the possession of the umpires before the toss and shall remain under their control throughout the match.

(b) The umpire shall take possession of the ball in use at the fall of each wicket, at the start of any interval and at any interruption of play.

3. New ball

Unless an agreement to the contrary has been made before the match, either captain may demand a new ball at the start of each innings.

4. New ball in match of more than one day's duration

In a match of more than one day's duration, the captain of the fielding side may demand a new ball after the prescribed number of overs has been bowled with the old one. The governing body for cricket in the country concerned shall decide the number of overs applicable in that country, which shall not be less than 75 overs.

The umpires shall indicate to the batsmen and the scorers whenever a new ball is taken into play.

5. Ball lost or becoming unfit for play

If, during play, the ball cannot be found or recovered or the umpires agree that it has become unfit for play through normal use, the umpires shall replace it with a ball which has had wear comparable with that which the previous ball had received before the need for its replacement. When the ball is replaced the umpires shall inform the batsmen and the fielding captain.

6. Specifications

The specifications as described in 1 above shall apply to men's cricket only. The following specifications will apply to:

(i) *Women's cricket*
Weight – from 4 15/16oz/140g to 5 5/16oz/151g.
Circumference – from 8 1/4in/21.0cm to 8 7/8in/22.5cm.

(ii) *Junior cricket – Under-13*
Weight – from 4 11/16oz/133g to 5 1/16oz/144g.
Circumference – from 8 1/16in/20.5cm to 8 11/16in/22.0cm.

LAW 6. THE BAT

1. Width and length

The bat overall shall not be more than 38in/96.5cm in length. The blade of the bat shall be made solely of wood and shall not exceed 4 1/4in/10.8cm at the widest part.

2. Covering the blade

The blade may be covered with material for protection, strengthening or repair. Such material shall not exceed 1/16in/1.56mm in thickness, and shall not be likely to cause unacceptable damage to the ball.

3. Hand or glove to count as part of bat

In these Laws,

(a) Reference to the bat shall imply that the bat is held by the batsman.

(b) Contact between the ball and either

(i) the striker's bat itself, or

(ii) the striker's hand holding the bat, or

(iii) any part of a glove worn on the striker's hand holding the bat

shall be regarded as the ball striking or touching the bat, or being struck by the bat.

LAW 7. THE PITCH

1. Area of pitch

The pitch is a rectangular area of the ground 22yds/20.12m in length and 10ft/3.05m in width. It is bounded at either end by the bowling creases and on either side by imaginary lines, one each side of the imaginary line joining the centres of the two middle stumps, each parallel to it and 5ft/1.52m from it. See Laws 8.1 (Width and pitching) and 9.2 (The bowling crease).

2. Fitness of the pitch for play

The umpires shall be the final judges of the fitness of the pitch for play. See Laws 3.8 (Fitness of ground, weather and light) and 3.9 (Suspension of play for adverse conditions of ground, weather or light).

3. Selection and preparation

Before the toss the ground authority shall be responsible for the selection and preparation of the pitch. During the match the umpires shall control its use and maintenance.

4. Changing the pitch

The pitch shall not be changed during the match unless the umpires decide that it is unreasonable or dangerous for play to continue on it and then only with the consent of both captains.

5. Non-turf pitches

In the event of a non-turf pitch being used, the artificial surface shall conform to the following measurements:

Length – a minimum of 58ft/17.68m.
Width – a minimum of 6ft/1.83m.

See Law 10.8 (Non-turf pitches).

LAW 8. THE WICKETS

1. Width and pitching

Two sets of wickets shall be pitched opposite and parallel to each other at a distance of 22yds/20.12m between the centres of the two middle stumps. Each set shall be 9in/22.86cm wide and shall consist of three wooden stumps with two wooden bails on top.

2. Size of stumps

The tops of the stumps shall be 28in/71.1cm above the playing surface and shall be dome-shaped except for the bail grooves. The portion of a stump above the playing surface shall be cylindrical, apart from the domed top, with a circular section of diameter not less than $1\frac{3}{8}$in/3.49cm nor more than $1\frac{1}{2}$in/3.81cm.

3. The bails

(a) The bails, when in position on the top of the stumps:

(i) Shall not project more than $\frac{1}{2}$in/1.27cm above them.

(ii) Shall fit between the stumps without forcing them out of the vertical.

(b) Each bail shall conform to the following specifications.

Overall length	– $4\frac{5}{16}$in/10.95cm.
Length of barrel	– $2\frac{1}{8}$in/5.40cm.
Longer spigot	– $1\frac{3}{8}$in/3.49cm.
Shorter spigot	– $\frac{13}{16}$in/2.06cm.

4. Junior cricket

In junior cricket, the same definitions of the wickets shall apply subject to the following measurements being used:

Width	– 8in/20.32cm.
Pitched for Under-13	– 21yds/19.20m.
Pitched for Under-11	– 20yds/18.29m.
Pitched for Under-9	– 18yds/16.46m.
Height above playing surface	– 27in/68.58cm.

Each stump

Diameter	– not less than $1\frac{1}{4}$in/3.18cm nor more than $1\frac{3}{8}$in/3.49cm.

Each bail

Overall	– $3\frac{13}{16}$in/9.68cm.
Barrel	– $1\frac{13}{16}$in/4.60cm.
Longer Spigot	– $1\frac{1}{4}$in/3.18cm.
Shorter Spigot	– $\frac{3}{4}$in/1.91cm.

5. Dispensing with bails

The umpires may agree to dispense with the use of bails, if necessary. If they so agree then no bails shall be used at either end. The use of bails shall be resumed as soon as conditions permit. See Law 28.4 (Dispensing with bails).

LAW 9. THE BOWLING, POPPING AND RETURN CREASES

1. The creases

A bowling crease, a popping crease and two return creases shall be marked in white, as set out in 2, 3 and 4 below, at each end of the pitch.

2. The bowling crease

The bowling crease, which is the back edge of the crease marking, shall be the line through the centres of the three stumps at that end. It shall be 8ft 8in/2.64m in length, with the stumps in the centre.

3. The popping crease

The popping crease, which is the back edge of the crease marking, shall be in front of and parallel to the bowling crease and shall be 4ft/1.22m from it. The popping crease shall be marked to a minimum of 6ft/1.83m on either side of the imaginary line joining the centres of the middle stumps and shall be considered to be unlimited in length.

4. The return creases

The return creases, which are the inside edges of the crease markings, shall be at right angles to the popping crease at a distance of 4ft 4in/1.32m either side of the imaginary line joining the centres of the two middle stumps. Each return crease shall be marked from the popping crease to a minimum of 8ft/2.44m behind it and shall be considered to be unlimited in length.

LAW 10. PREPARATION AND MAINTENANCE OF THE PLAYING AREA

1. Rolling

The pitch shall not be rolled during the match except as permitted in (a) and (b) below.

(a) Frequency and duration of rolling
During the match the pitch may be rolled at the request of the captain of the batting side, for a period of not more than seven minutes, before the start of each innings, other than the first innings of the match, and before the start of each subsequent day's play. See (d) below.

(b) Rolling after a delayed start
In addition to the rolling permitted above, if, after the toss and before the first innings of the match, the start is delayed, the captain of the batting side may request to have the pitch rolled for not more than seven minutes. However, if the umpires together agree that the delay has had no significant effect on the state of the pitch, they shall refuse the request for the rolling of the pitch.

(c) Choice of rollers
If there is more than one roller available the captain of the batting side shall have the choice.

(d) Timing of permitted rolling
The rolling permitted (maximum seven minutes) before play begins on any day shall be started not more than 30 minutes before the time scheduled or rescheduled for play to begin. The captain of the batting side may, however, delay the start of such rolling until not less than ten minutes before the time scheduled or rescheduled for play to begin, should he so desire.

(e) Insufficient time to complete rolling
If a captain declares an innings closed, or forfeits an innings, or enforces the follow-on, and the other captain is prevented thereby from exercising his option of the rolling permitted (maximum seven minutes), or if he is so prevented for any other reason, the extra time required to complete the rolling shall be taken out of the normal playing time.

2. Sweeping

(a) If rolling is to take place the pitch shall first be swept to avoid any possible damage by rolling in debris. This sweeping shall be done so that the seven minutes allowed for rolling is not affected.

(b) The pitch shall be cleared of any debris at all intervals for meals, between innings and at the beginning of each day, not earlier than 30 minutes nor later than ten minutes before the time scheduled or rescheduled for play to begin. See Law 15.1 (An interval).

(c) Notwithstanding the provisions of (a) and (b) above, the umpires shall not allow sweeping to take place where they consider it may be detrimental to the surface of the pitch.

3. Mowing

(a) The pitch
The pitch shall be mown on each day of the match on which play is expected to take place, if ground and weather conditions allow.

(b) The outfield
In order to ensure that conditions are as similar as possible for both sides, the outfield shall be mown on each day of the match on which play is expected to take place, if ground and weather conditions allow.

If, for reasons other than ground and weather conditions, complete mowing of the outfield is not possible, the ground authority shall notify the captains and umpires of the procedure to be adopted for such mowing during the match.

(c) Responsibility for mowing
All mowings which are carried out before the match shall be the responsibility of the ground authority.

All subsequent mowings shall be carried out under the supervision of the umpires.

(d) Time of mowing

(i) Mowing of the pitch on any day of the match shall be completed not later than 30 minutes before the time scheduled or rescheduled for play to begin on that day.

(ii) Mowing of the outfield on any day of the match shall be completed not later than 15 minutes before the time scheduled or rescheduled for play to begin on that day.

4. Watering

The pitch shall not be watered during the match.

5. Re-marking creases

The creases shall be re-marked whenever either umpire considers it necessary.

6. Maintenance of footholes

The umpires shall ensure that the holes made by the bowlers and batsmen are cleaned out and dried whenever necessary to facilitate play. In matches of more than one day's duration, the umpires shall allow, if necessary, the re-turfing of footholes made by the bowler in his delivery stride, or the use of quick-setting fillings for the same purpose.

7. Securing of footholds and maintenance of pitch

During play, the umpires shall allow the players to secure their footholds by the use of sawdust provided that no damage to the pitch is caused and that Law 42 (Fair and unfair play) is not contravened.

8. Non-turf pitches

Wherever appropriate, the provisions set out in 1 to 7 above shall apply.

LAW 11. COVERING THE PITCH

1. Before the match

The use of covers before the match is the responsibility of the ground authority and may include full covering if required. However, the ground authority shall grant suitable facility to the captains to inspect the pitch before the nomination of their players and to the umpires to discharge their duties as laid down in Laws 3 (The umpires), 7 (The pitch), 8 (The wickets), 9 (The bowling, popping and return creases) and 10 (Preparation and maintenance of the playing area).

2. During the match

The pitch shall not be completely covered during the match unless provided otherwise by regulations or by agreement before the toss.

3. Covering bowlers' run-ups

Whenever possible, the bowlers' run-ups shall be covered in inclement weather, in order to keep them dry. Unless there is agreement for full covering under 2 above the covers so used shall not extend further than 5ft/1.52m in front of each popping crease.

4. Removal of covers

(a) If after the toss the pitch is covered overnight, the covers shall be removed in the morning at the earliest possible moment on each day that play is expected to take place.

(b) If covers are used during the day as protection from inclement weather, or if inclement weather delays the removal of overnight covers, they shall be removed promptly as soon as conditions allow.

LAW 12. INNINGS

1. Number of innings

(a) A match shall be one or two innings of each side according to agreement reached before the start of play.

(b) It may be agreed to limit any innings to a number of overs or by a period of time. If such an agreement is made then:

(i) In a one-innings match it shall apply to both innings.

(ii) In a two-innings match it shall apply to either
the first innings of each side, or
the second innings of each side, or
both innings of each side.

2. Alternate innings

In a two-innings match each side shall take their innings alternately except in the cases provided for in Law 13 (The follow-on) or Law 14.2 (Forfeiture of an innings).

3. Completed innings

A side's innings is to be considered as completed if:

(a) The side is all out, or

(b) At the fall of a wicket, further balls remain to be bowled, but no further batsman is available to come in, or

(c) The captain declares the innings closed, or

(d) The captain forfeits the innings, or

(e) In the case of an agreement under 1(b) above, either

(i) the prescribed number of overs has been bowled, or

(ii) the prescribed time has expired.

4. The toss

The captains shall toss for the choice of innings on the field of play not earlier than 30 minutes, nor later than 15 minutes, before the scheduled or any rescheduled time for the match to start. Note, however, the provisions of Law 1.3 (Captain).

5. Decision to be notified

The captain of the side winning the toss shall notify the opposing captain of his decision to bat or to field, not later than ten minutes before the scheduled or any rescheduled time for the match to start. Once notified the decision may not be altered.

LAW 13. THE FOLLOW-ON

1. Lead on first innings

(a) In a two-innings match of five days or more, the side which bats first and leads by at least 200 runs shall have the option of requiring the other side to follow their innings.

(b) The same option shall be available in two-innings matches of shorter duration with the minimum required leads as follows:

(i) 150 runs in a match of three or four days.

(ii) 100 runs in a two-day match.

(iii) 75 runs in a one-day match.

2. Notification

A captain shall notify the opposing captain and the umpires of his intention to take up this option. Law 10.1 (e) (Insufficient time to complete rolling) shall apply.

3. First day's play lost

If no play takes place on the first day of a match of more than one day's duration, 1 above shall apply in accordance with the number of days remaining from the actual start of the match. The day on which play first commences shall count as a whole day for this purpose, irrespective of the time at which play starts.

Play will have taken place as soon as, after the call of "Play", the first over has started. See Law 22.2 (Start of an over).

LAW 14. DECLARATION AND FORFEITURE

1. Time of declaration

The captain of the batting side may declare an innings closed, when the ball is dead, at any time during a match.

2. Forfeiture of an innings

A captain may forfeit either of his side's innings. A forfeited innings shall be considered as a completed innings.

3. Notification

A captain shall notify the opposing captain and the umpires of his decision to declare or to forfeit an innings. Law 10.1 (e) (Insufficient time to complete rolling) shall apply.

LAW 15. INTERVALS

1. An interval

The following shall be classed as intervals:

(i) The period between close of play on one day and the start of the next day's play.

(ii) Intervals between innings.

(iii) Intervals for meals.

(iv) Intervals for drinks.

(v) Any other agreed interval.

All these intervals shall be considered as scheduled breaks for the purposes of Law 2.5 (Fielder absent or leaving the field).

2. Agreement of intervals

(a) Before the toss:

(i) The hours of play shall be established.

(ii) Except as in (b) below, the timing and duration of intervals for meals shall be agreed.

(iii) The timing and duration of any other interval under 1(v) above shall be agreed.

(b) In a one-day match no specific time need be agreed for the tea interval. It may be agreed instead to take this interval between the innings.

(c) Intervals for drinks may not be taken during the last hour of the match, as defined in Law 16.6 (Last hour of match – number of overs). Subject to this limitation the captains and umpires shall agree the times for such intervals, if any, before the toss and on each subsequent day not later than ten minutes before play is scheduled to start. See also Law 3.3 (Agreement with captains).

3. Duration of intervals

(a) An interval for lunch or for tea shall be of the duration agreed under 2(a) above, taken from the call of "Time" before the interval until the call of "Play" on resumption after the interval.

(b) An interval between innings shall be ten minutes from the close of an innings to the call of "Play" for the start of the next innings, except as in 4, 6 and 7 below.

4. No allowance for interval between innings

In addition to the provisions of 6 and 7 below:

(a) If an innings ends when ten minutes or less remain before the time agreed for close of play on any day, there will be no further play on that day. No change will be made to the time for the start of play on the following day on account of the ten minutes between innings.

(b) If a captain declares an innings closed during an interruption in play of more than ten minutes duration, no adjustment shall be made to the time for resumption of play on account of the ten minutes between innings, which shall be considered as included in the interruption. Law 10.1(e) (Insufficient time to complete rolling) shall apply.

(c) If a captain declares an innings closed during any interval other than an interval for drinks, the interval shall be of the agreed duration and shall be considered to include the ten minutes between innings. Law 10.1(e) (Insufficient time to complete rolling) shall apply.

5. Changing agreed times for intervals

If for adverse conditions of ground, weather or light, or for any other reason, playing time is lost, the umpires and captains together may alter the time of the lunch interval or of the tea interval. See also 6, 7 and 9(c) below.

6. Changing agreed time for lunch interval

(a) If an innings ends when ten minutes or less remain before the agreed time for lunch, the interval shall be taken immediately. It shall be of the agreed length and shall be considered to include the ten minutes between innings.

(b) If, because of adverse conditions of ground, weather or light, or in exceptional circumstances, a stoppage occurs when ten minutes or less remain before the agreed time for lunch then, notwithstanding 5 above, the interval shall be taken immediately. It shall be of the agreed length. Play shall resume at the end of this interval or as soon after as conditions permit.

(c) If the players have occasion to leave the field for any reason when more than ten minutes remain before the agreed time for lunch then, unless the umpires and captains together agree to alter it, lunch will be taken at the agreed time.

7. Changing agreed time for tea interval

(a) (i) If an innings ends when 30 minutes or less remain before the agreed time for tea, then the interval shall be taken immediately. It shall be of the agreed length and shall be considered to include the ten minutes between innings.

(ii) If, when 30 minutes remain before the agreed time for tea, an interval between innings is already in progress, play will resume at the end of the ten-minute interval.

(b) (i) If, because of adverse conditions of ground, weather or light, or in exceptional circumstances, a stoppage occurs when 30 minutes or less remain before the agreed time for tea, then unless

either there is an agreement to change the time for tea, as permitted in 5 above,

or the captains agree to forgo the tea interval, as permitted in 10 below,

the interval shall be taken immediately. The interval shall be of the agreed length. Play shall resume at the end of this interval or as soon after as conditions permit.

(ii) If a stoppage is already in progress when 30 minutes remain before the time agreed for tea, 5 above will apply.

8. Tea interval – nine wickets down

If either nine wickets are already down when two minutes remain to the agreed time for tea, or the ninth wicket falls within these two minutes or at any later time up to and including the final ball of the over in progress at the agreed time for tea, then not withstanding the provisions of Law 16.5 (b) (Completion of an over) tea will not be taken until the end of the over in progress 30 minutes after the originally agreed time for tea, unless the players have cause to leave the field of play or the innings is completed earlier.

9. Intervals for drinks

(a) If on any day the captains agree that there shall be intervals for drinks, the option to take such intervals shall be available to either side. Each interval shall be kept as short as possible and in any case shall not exceed five minutes.

(b) (i) Unless both captains agree to forgo any drinks interval, it shall be taken at the end of the over in progress when the agreed time is reached. If, however, a wicket falls within five minutes of the agreed time then drinks shall be taken immediately. No other variation in the timing of drinks intervals shall be permitted except as provided for in (c) below.

(ii) For the purpose of (i) above and Law 3.9(a)(ii) (Suspension of play for adverse conditions of ground, weather or light) only, the batsmen at the wicket may deputise for their captain.

(c) If an innings ends or the players have to leave the field of play for any other reason within 30 minutes of the agreed time for a drinks interval, the umpires and captains together may rearrange the timing of drinks intervals in that session.

10. Agreement to forgo intervals

At any time during the match, the captains may agree to forgo the tea interval or any of the drinks intervals. The umpires shall be informed of the decision.

11. Scorers to be informed

The umpires shall ensure that the scorers are informed of all agreements about hours of play and intervals, and of any changes made thereto as permitted under this Law.

LAW 16. START OF PLAY; CESSATION OF PLAY

1. Call of "Play"

The umpire at the bowler's end shall call "Play" at the start of the match and on the resumption of play after any interval or interruption.

2. Call of "Time"

The umpire at the bowler's end shall call "Time" on the cessation of play before any interval or interruption of play and at the conclusion of the match. See Law 27 (Appeals).

3. Removal of bails

After the call of "Time", the bails shall be removed from both wickets.

4. Starting a new over

Another over shall always be started at any time during the match, unless an interval is to be taken in the circumstances set out in 5 below, if the umpire, after walking at his normal pace, has arrived at his position behind the stumps at the bowler's end before the time agreed for the next interval, or for the close of play, has been reached.

5. Completion of an over

Other than at the end of the match:

(a) If the agreed time for an interval is reached during an over, the over shall be completed before the interval is taken except as provided for in (b) below.

(b) When less than two minutes remain before the time agreed for the next interval, the interval will be taken immediately if either

(i) a batsman is out or retires, or

(ii) the players have occasion to leave the field

whether this occurs during an over or at the end of an over. Except at the end of an innings, if an over is thus interrupted it shall be completed on resumption of play.

6. Last hour of match – number of overs

When one hour of playing time of the match remains, according to the agreed hours of play, the over in progress shall be completed. The next over shall be the first of a minimum of 20 overs which must be bowled, provided that a result is not reached earlier and provided that there is no interval or interruption in play.

The umpire at the bowler's end shall indicate the commencement of this 20 overs to the players and the scorers. The period of play thereafter shall be referred to as the last hour, whatever its actual duration.

7. Last hour of match – interruptions of play

If there is an interruption in play during the last hour of the match, the minimum number of overs to be bowled shall be reduced from 20 as follows:

(a) The time lost for an interruption is counted from the call of "Time" until the time for resumption of play as decided by the umpires.

(b) One over shall be deducted for every complete three minutes of time lost.

(c) In the case of more than one such interruption, the minutes lost shall not be aggregated; the calculation shall be made for each interruption separately.

(d) If, when one hour of playing time remains, an interruption is already in progress:

(i) Only the time lost after this moment shall be counted in the calculation.

(ii) The over in progress at the start of the interruption shall be completed on resumption of play and shall not count as one of the minimum number of overs to be bowled.

(e) If, after the start of the last hour, an interruption occurs during an over, the over shall be completed on resumption of play. The two part-overs shall between them count as one over of the minimum number to be bowled.

8. Last hour of match – intervals between innings

If an innings ends so that a new innings is to be started during the last hour of the match, the interval starts with the end of the innings and is to end ten minutes later.

(a) If this interval is already in progress at the start of the last hour, then to determine the number of overs to be bowled in the new innings, calculations are to be made as set out in 7 above.

(b) If the innings ends after the last hour has started, two calculations are to be made, as set out in (c) and (d) below. The greater of the numbers yielded by these two calculations is to be the minimum number of overs to be bowled in the new innings.

(c) Calculation based on overs remaining:

(i) At the conclusion of the innings, the number of overs that remain to be bowled, of the minimum in the last hour, to be noted.

(ii) If this is not a whole number it is to be rounded up to the next whole number.

(iii) Three overs to be deducted from the result for the interval.

(d) Calculation based on time remaining:

(i) At the conclusion of the innings, the time remaining until the agreed time for close of play to be noted.

(ii) Ten minutes to be deducted from this time, for the interval, to determine the playing time remaining.

(iii) A calculation to be made of one over for every complete three minutes of the playing time remaining, plus one more over for any further part of three minutes remaining.

9. Conclusion of match

The match is concluded:

(a) As soon as a result, as defined in sections 1, 2, 3 or 4 of Law 21 (The result), is reached.

(b) As soon as both

(i) the minimum number of overs for the last hour are completed, and

(ii) the agreed time for close of play is reached

unless a result has been reached earlier.

(c) If, without the match being concluded either as in (a) or in (b) above, the players leave the field, either for adverse conditions of ground, weather or light, or in exceptional circumstances, and no further play is possible thereafter.

10. Completion of last over of match

The over in progress at the close of play on the final day shall be completed unless either

(i) a result has been reached, or

(ii) the players have occasion to leave the field. In this case there shall be no resumption of play except in the circumstances of Law 21.9 (Mistakes in scoring), and the match shall be at an end.

11. Bowler unable to complete an over during last hour of match

If, for any reason, a bowler is unable to complete an over during the last hour, Law 22.8 (Bowler incapacitated or suspended during an over) shall apply.

LAW 17. PRACTICE ON THE FIELD

1. Practice on the field

(a) There shall be no bowling or batting practice on the pitch, or on the area parallel and immediately adjacent to the pitch, at any time on any day of the match.

(b) There shall be no bowling or batting practice on any other part of the square on any day of the match, except before the start of play or after the close of play on that day. Practice before the start of play:

(i) Must not continue later than 30 minutes before the scheduled time or any rescheduled time for play to start on that day.

(ii) Shall not be allowed if the umpires consider that, in the prevailing conditions of ground and weather, it will be detrimental to the surface of the square.

(c) There shall be no practice on the field of play between the call of "Play" and the call of "Time", if the umpire considers that it could result in a waste of time. See Law 42.9 (Time-wasting by the fielding side).

(d) If a player contravenes (a) or (b) above he shall not be allowed to bowl until either at least one hour later than the contravention or until there has been at least 30 minutes of playing time since the contravention, whichever is sooner. If an over is in progress at the contravention he shall not be allowed to complete that over.

2. Trial run-up

No bowler shall have a trial run-up between the call of "Play" and the call of "Time" unless the umpire is satisfied that it will not cause any waste of time.

LAW 18. SCORING RUNS

1. A run

The score shall be reckoned by runs. A run is scored:

(a) So often as the batsmen, at any time while the ball is in play, have crossed and made good their ground from end to end.

(b) When a boundary is scored. See Law 19 (Boundaries).

(c) When penalty runs are awarded. See 6 below.

(d) When "Lost ball" is called. See Law 20 (Lost ball).

2. Runs disallowed

Notwithstanding 1 above, or any other provisions elsewhere in the Laws, the scoring of runs or awarding of penalties will be subject to any disallowance of runs provided for within the Laws that may be applicable.

3. Short runs

(a) A run is short if a batsman fails to make good his ground on turning for a further run.

(b) Although a short run shortens the succeeding one, the latter if completed shall not be regarded as short. A striker taking stance in front of his popping crease may run from that point also without penalty.

4. Unintentional short runs

Except in the circumstances of 5 below:

(a) If either batsman runs a short run, unless a boundary is scored the umpire concerned shall call and signal "Short run" as soon as the ball becomes dead and that run shall not be scored.

(b) If, after either or both batsmen run short, a boundary is scored, the umpire concerned shall disregard the short running and shall not call or signal "Short run".

(c) If both batsmen run short in one and the same run, this shall be regarded as only one short run.

(d) If more than one run is short then, subject to (b) and (c) above, all runs so called shall not be scored.

If there has been more than one short run the umpire shall inform the scorers as to the number of runs scored.

5. Deliberate short runs

Notwithstanding 4 above, if either umpire considers that either or both batsmen deliberately runs short at his end, the following procedure shall be adopted:

(a) (i) The umpire concerned shall, when the ball is dead, warn the batsmen that the practice is unfair, indicate that this is a first and final warning and inform the other umpire of what has occurred. This warning shall continue to apply throughout the innings. The umpire shall so inform each incoming batsman.

(ii) The batsmen shall return to their original ends.

(iii) Whether a batsman is dismissed or not, the umpire at the bowler's end shall disallow all runs to the batting side from that delivery other than the penalty for a no-ball or wide, or penalties under Laws 42.5 (Deliberate distraction or obstruction of batsman) and 42.13 (Fielders damaging the pitch), if applicable.

(iv) The umpire at the bowler's end shall inform the scorers as to the number of runs scored.

(b) If there is any further instance of deliberate short running by any batsman in that innings, when the ball is dead the umpire concerned shall inform the other umpire of what has occurred and the procedure set out in (a)(ii) and (iii) above shall be repeated. Additionally, the umpire at the bowler's end shall:

(i) Award five penalty runs to the fielding side. See Law 42.17 (Penalty runs).

(ii) Inform the scorers as to the number of runs scored.

(iii) Inform the batsmen, the captain of the fielding side and, as soon as practicable, the captain of the batting side of the reason for this action.

(iv) Report the occurrence, with the other umpire, to the executive of the batting side and any governing body responsible for the match, who shall take such action as is considered appropriate against the captain and player or players concerned.

6. Runs scored for penalties

Runs shall be scored for penalties under 5 above and Laws 2.6 (Player returning without permission), 24 (No-ball), 25 (Wide ball), 41.2 (Fielding the ball), 41.3 (Protective helmets belonging to the fielding side) and 42 (Fair and unfair play).

7. Runs scored for boundaries

Runs shall be scored for boundary allowances under Law 19 (Boundaries).

8. Runs scored for lost ball

Runs shall be scored when "Lost ball" is called under Law 20 (Lost ball).

9. Batsman dismissed

When either batsman is dismissed:

(a) Any penalties to either side that may be applicable shall stand but no other runs shall be scored, except as stated in 10 below.

(b) 12(a) below will apply if the method of dismissal is caught, handled the ball or obstructing the field. 12(a) will also apply if a batsman is run out, except in the circumstances of Law 2.8 (Transgression of the Laws by a batsman who has a runner) where 12(b) below will apply.

(c) The not out batsman shall return to his original end except as stated in (b) above.

10. Runs scored when a batsman is dismissed

In addition to any penalties to either side that may be applicable, if a batsman is:

(a) Dismissed handled the ball, the batting side shall score the runs completed before the offence.

(b) Dismissed obstructing the field, the batting side shall score the runs completed before the offence.

If, however, the obstruction prevents a catch from being made, no runs other than penalties shall be scored.

(c) Dismissed run out, the batting side shall score the runs completed before the dismissal. If however, a striker with a runner is himself dismissed run out, no runs other than penalties shall be scored. See Law 2.8 (Transgression of the Laws by a batsman who has a runner).

11. Runs scored when ball becomes dead

(a) When the ball becomes dead on the fall of a wicket, runs shall be scored as laid down in 9 and 10 above.

(b) When the ball becomes dead for any reason other than the fall of a wicket, or is called dead by an umpire, unless there is specific provision otherwise in the Laws, the batting side shall be credited with:

(i) All runs completed by the batsmen before the incident or call, and

(ii) the run in progress if the batsmen have crossed at the instant of the incident or call. Note specifically, however, the provisions of Law 34.4(c) (Runs permitted from a ball lawfully struck more than once) and 42.5(b)(iii) (Deliberate distraction or obstruction of batsman), and

(iii) any penalties that are applicable.

12. Batsman returning to wicket he has left

(a) If, while the ball is in play, the batsmen have crossed in running, neither shall return to the wicket he has left, except as in (b) below.

(b) The batsmen shall return to the wickets they originally left in the cases of, and only in the cases of:

(i) A boundary.

(ii) Disallowance of runs for any reason.

(iii) The dismissal of a batsman, except as in 9(b) above.

LAW 19. BOUNDARIES

1. The boundary of the field of play

(a) Before the toss, the umpires shall agree the boundary of the field of play with both captains. The boundary shall if possible be marked along its whole length.

(b) The boundary shall be agreed so that no part of any sightscreen is within the field of play.

(c) An obstacle or person within the field of play shall not be regarded as a boundary unless so decided by the umpires before the toss. See Law 3.4(ii) (To inform captains and scorers).

2. Defining the boundary – boundary marking

(a) Wherever practicable the boundary shall be marked by means of a white line or a rope laid along the ground.

(b) If the boundary is marked by a white line:

(i) The inside edge of the line shall be the boundary edge.

(ii) A flag, post or board used merely to highlight the position of a line marked on the ground must be placed outside the boundary edge and is not itself to be regarded as defining or marking the boundary. Note, however, the provisions of (c) below.

(c) If a solid object is used to mark the boundary, it must have an edge or a line to constitute the boundary edge.

(i) For a rope, which includes any similar object of curved cross section lying on the ground, the boundary edge will be the line formed by the innermost points of the rope along its length.

(ii) For a fence, which includes any similar object in contact with the ground, but with a flat surface projecting above the ground, the boundary edge will be the base line of the fence.

(d) If the boundary edge is not defined as in (b) or (c) above, the umpires and captains must agree, before the toss, what line will be the boundary edge. Where there is no physical marker for a section of boundary, the boundary edge shall be the imaginary straight line joining the two nearest marked points of the boundary edge.

(e) If a solid object used to mark the boundary is disturbed for any reason during play, then if possible it shall be restored to its original position as soon as the ball is dead. If this is not possible, then:

(i) If some part of the fence or other marker has come within the field of play, that portion is to be removed from the field of play as soon as the ball is dead.

(ii) The line where the base of the fence or marker originally stood shall define the boundary edge.

3. Scoring a boundary

(a) A boundary shall be scored and signalled by the umpire at the bowler's end whenever, while the ball is in play, in his opinion:

(i) The ball touches the boundary, or is grounded beyond the boundary.

(ii) A fielder, with some part of his person in contact with the ball, touches the boundary or has some part of his person grounded beyond the boundary.

(b) The phrases "touches the boundary" and "touching the boundary" shall mean contact with either

(i) the boundary edge as defined in 2 above, or

(ii) any person or obstacle within the field of play which has been designated a boundary by the umpires before the toss.

(c) The phrase "grounded beyond the boundary" shall mean contact with either

(i) any part of a line or a solid object marking the boundary, except its boundary edge, or

(ii) the ground outside the boundary edge, or

(iii) any object in contact with the ground outside the boundary edge.

4. Runs allowed for boundaries

(a) Before the toss, the umpires shall agree with both captains the runs to be allowed for boundaries. In deciding the allowances, the umpires and captains shall be guided by the prevailing custom of the ground.

(b) Unless agreed differently under (a) above, the allowances for boundaries shall be six runs if the ball having been struck by the bat pitches beyond the boundary, but otherwise four runs. These allowances shall still apply even though the ball has previously touched a fielder. See also (c) below.

(c) The ball shall be regarded as pitching beyond the boundary and six runs shall be scored if a fielder:

(i) Has any part of his person touching the boundary or grounded beyond the boundary when he catches the ball.

(ii) Catches the ball and subsequently touches the boundary or grounds some part of his person beyond the boundary while carrying the ball but before completing the catch. See Law 32 (Caught).

5. Runs scored

When a boundary is scored:

(a) The penalty for a no-ball or a wide, if applicable, shall stand together with any penalties under any of Laws 2.6 (Player returning without permission), 18.5(b) (Deliberate short runs) or Law 42 (Fair and unfair play) that apply before the boundary is scored.

(b) The batting side, except in the circumstances of 6 below, shall additionally be awarded whichever is the greater of:

(i) The allowance for the boundary.

(ii) The runs completed by the batsmen, together with the run in progress if they have crossed at the instant the boundary is scored. When these runs exceed the boundary allowance, they shall replace the boundary for the purposes of Law 18.12 (Batsman returning to wicket he has left).

6. Overthrow or wilful act of fielder

If the boundary results either from an overthrow or from the wilful act of a fielder the runs scored shall be:

(i) The penalty for a no-ball or a wide, if applicable, and any penalties under Laws 2.6 (Player returning without permission), 18.5(b) (Deliberate short runs) or Law 42 (Fair and unfair play) that are applicable before the boundary is scored, and

(ii) the allowance for the boundary, and

(iii) the runs completed by the batsmen, together with the run in progress if they have crossed at the instant of the throw or act.

Law 18.12(a) (Batsman returning to the wicket he has left) shall apply as from the instant of the throw or act.

LAW 20. LOST BALL

1. Fielder to call "Lost ball"

If a ball in play cannot be found or recovered, any fielder may call "Lost ball". The ball shall then become dead. See Law 23.1 (Ball is dead). Law 18.12(a) (Batsman returning to wicket he has left) shall apply as from the instant of the call.

2. Ball to be replaced

The umpires shall replace the ball with one which has had wear comparable with that which the previous ball had received before it was lost or became irrecoverable. See Law 5.5 (Ball lost or becoming unfit for play).

3. Runs scored

(a) The penalty for a no-ball or a wide, if applicable, shall stand, together with any penalties under any of Laws 2.6 (Player returning without permission), 18.5(b) (Deliberate short runs) or Law 42 (Fair and unfair play) that are applicable before the call of "Lost ball".

(b) The batting side shall additionally be awarded either

(i) the runs completed by the batsmen, together with the run in progress if they have crossed at the instant of the call, or

(ii) six runs,

whichever is the greater.

4. How scored

If there is a one-run penalty for a no-ball or for a wide, it shall be scored as a no-ball extra or as a wide as appropriate. See Laws 24.13 (Runs resulting from a no-ball – how scored) and 25.6 (Runs resulting from a wide – how scored). If any other penalties have been awarded to either side, they shall be scored as penalty extras. See Law 42.17 (Penalty runs).

Runs to the batting side in 3(b) above shall be credited to the striker if the ball has been struck by the bat, but otherwise to the total of byes, leg-byes, no-balls or wides as the case may be.

LAW 21. THE RESULT

1. A win – two-innings match

The side which has scored a total of runs in excess of that scored in the two completed innings of the opposing side shall win the match. Note also 6 below.

A forfeited innings is to count as a completed innings. See Law 14 (Declaration and forfeiture).

2. A win – one-innings match

The side which has scored in its one innings a total of runs in excess of that scored by the opposing side in its one completed innings shall win the match. Note also 6 below.

3. Umpires awarding a match

(a) A match shall be lost by a side which either

(i) concedes defeat, or

(ii) in the opinion of the umpires, refuses to play

and the umpires shall award the match to the other side.

(b) If an umpire considers that an action by any player or players might constitute a refusal by either side to play then the umpires together shall ascertain the cause of the action. If they then decide together that this action does constitute a refusal to play by one side, they shall so inform the captain of that side. If the captain persists in the action the umpires shall award the match in accordance with (a)(ii) above.

(c) If action as in (b) above takes place after play has started and does not constitute a refusal to play:

(i) Playing time lost shall be counted from the start of the action until play recommences, subject to Law 15.5 (Changing agreed times for intervals).

(ii) The time for close of play on that day shall be extended by this length of time, subject to Law 3.9 (Suspension of play for adverse conditions of ground, weather or light).

(iii) If applicable, no overs shall be deducted during the last hour of the match solely on account of this time.

4. A tie

The result of a match shall be a tie when the scores are equal at the conclusion of play, but only if the side batting last has completed its innings.

5. A draw

A match which is concluded, as defined in Law 16.9 (Conclusion of a match), without being determined in any of the ways stated in 1, 2, 3 or 4 above, shall count as a draw.

6. Winning hit or extras

(a) As soon as a result is reached, as defined in 1, 2, 3 or 4 above, the match is at an end. Nothing that happens thereafter, except as in Law 42.17(b), shall be regarded as part of it. Note also 9 below.

(b) The side batting last will have scored enough runs to win only if its total of runs is sufficient without including any runs completed before the dismissal of the striker by the completion of a catch or by the obstruction of a catch.

(c) If a boundary is scored before the batsmen have completed sufficient runs to win the match, then the whole of the boundary allowance shall be credited to the side's total and, in the case of a hit by the bat, to the striker's score.

7. Statement of result

If the side batting last wins the match without losing all its wickets, the result shall be stated as a win by the number of wickets still then to fall. If the side batting last has lost all its wickets but, as the result of an award of five penalty runs at the end of the match, has scored a total of runs in excess of the total scored by the opposing side, the result shall be stated as a win to that side by penalty runs. If the side fielding last wins the match, the result shall be stated as a win by runs.

If the match is decided by one side conceding defeat or refusing to play, the result shall be stated as "Match conceded" or "Match awarded" as the case may be.

8. Correctness of result

Any decision as to the correctness of the scores shall be the responsibility of the umpires. See Law 3.15 (Correctness of scores).

9. Mistakes in scoring

If, after the umpires and players have left the field in the belief that the match has been concluded, the umpires discover that a mistake in scoring has occurred which affects the result, then, subject to 10 below, they shall adopt the following procedure.

(a) If, when the players leave the field, the side batting last has not completed its innings, and either

(i) the number of overs to be bowled in the last hour has not been completed, or

(ii) the agreed finishing time has not been reached,

then unless one side concedes defeat the umpires shall order play to resume.

If conditions permit, play will then continue until the prescribed number of overs has been completed and the time remaining has elapsed, unless a result is reached earlier. The number of overs and/or the time remaining shall be taken as they were when the players left the field; no account shall be taken of the time between that moment and the resumption of play.

(b) If, when the players leave the field, the overs have been completed and time has been reached, or if the side batting last has completed its innings, the umpires shall immediately inform both captains of the necessary corrections to the scores and to the result.

10. Result not to be changed

Once the umpires have agreed with the scorers the correctness of the scores at the conclusion of the match – see Laws 3.15 (Correctness of scores) and 4.2 (Correctness of scores) – the result cannot thereafter be changed.

LAW 22. THE OVER

1. Number of balls

The ball shall be bowled from each wicket alternately in overs of six balls.

2. Start of an over

An over has started when the bowler starts his run-up or, if he has no run-up, his delivery action for the first delivery of that over.

3. Call of "Over"

When six balls have been bowled other than those which are not to count in the over and as the ball becomes dead – see Law 23 (Dead ball) – the umpire shall call "Over" before leaving the wicket.

4. Balls not to count in the over

(a) A ball shall not count as one of the six balls of the over unless it is delivered, even though a batsman may be dismissed or some other incident occurs before the ball is delivered.

(b) A ball which is delivered by the bowler shall not count as one of the six balls of the over:

(i) If it is called dead, or is to be considered dead, before the striker has had an opportunity to play it. See Law 23 (Dead ball).

(ii) If it is a no-ball. See Law 24 (No-ball).

(iii) If it is a wide. See Law 25 (Wide ball).

(iv) If it is called dead in the circumstances of Law 23.3(b)(vi) (Umpire calling and signalling "Dead ball").

(v) When five penalty runs are awarded to the batting side under any of Laws 2.6 (Player returning without permission), 41.2 (Fielding the ball), 42.4 (Deliberate attempt to distract striker) or 42.5 (Deliberate distraction or obstruction of batsman).

5. Umpire miscounting

If an umpire miscounts the number of balls, the over as counted by the umpire shall stand.

6. Bowler changing ends

A bowler shall be allowed to change ends as often as desired, provided only that he does not bowl two overs, or parts thereof, consecutively in the same innings.

7. Finishing an over

(a) Other than at the end of an innings, a bowler shall finish an over in progress unless he is incapacitated, or he is suspended under any of Laws 17.1 (Practice on the field), 42.7 (Dangerous and unfair bowling – action by the umpire), 42.9 (Time-wasting by the fielding side), or 42.12 (Bowler running on the protected area after delivering the ball).

(b) If for any reason, other than the end of an innings, an over is left uncompleted at the start of an interval or interruption of play, it shall be completed on resumption of play.

8. Bowler incapacitated or suspended during an over

If for any reason a bowler is incapacitated while running up to bowl the first ball of an over, or is incapacitated or suspended during an over, the umpire shall call and signal "Dead ball". Another bowler shall complete the over from the same end, provided that he does not bowl two overs, or parts thereof, consecutively in one innings.

LAW 23. DEAD BALL

1. Ball is dead

(a) The ball becomes dead when:

(i) It is finally settled in the hands of the wicket-keeper or the bowler.

(ii) A boundary is scored. See Law 19.3 (Scoring a boundary).

(iii) A batsman is dismissed.

(iv) Whether played or not it becomes trapped between the bat and person of a batsman or between items of his clothing or equipment.

(v) Whether played or not it lodges in the clothing or equipment of a batsman or the clothing of an umpire.

(vi) It lodges in a protective helmet worn by a member of the fielding side.

(vii) There is a contravention of Law 41.2 (Fielding the ball) or Law 41.3 (Protective helmets belonging to the fielding side).

(viii) This is an award of penalty runs under Law 2.6 (Player returning without permission).

(ix) "Lost ball" is called. See Law 20 (Lost ball).

(x) The umpire calls "Over" or "Time".

(b) The ball shall be considered to be dead when it is clear to the umpire at the bowler's end that the fielding side and both batsmen at the wicket have ceased to regard it as in play.

2. Ball finally settled

Whether the ball is finally settled or not is a matter for the umpire alone to decide.

3. Umpire calling and signalling "Dead ball"

(a) When the ball has become dead under 1 above, the bowler's end umpire may call "Dead ball", if it is necessary to inform the players.

(b) Either umpire shall call and signal "Dead ball" when:

(i) He intervenes in a case of unfair play.

(ii) A serious injury to a player or umpire occurs.

(iii) He leaves his normal position for consultation.

(iv) One or both bails fall from the striker's wicket before he has the opportunity of playing the ball.

(v) He is satisfied that for an adequate reason the striker is not ready for the delivery of the ball and, if the ball is delivered, makes no attempt to play it.

(vi) The striker is distracted by any noise or movement or in any other way while he is preparing to receive or receiving a delivery. This shall apply whether the source of the distraction is within the game or outside it. Note, however, the provisions of Law 42.4 (Deliberate attempt to distract the striker).
The ball shall not count as one of the over.

(vii) The bowler drops the ball accidentally before delivery.

(viii) The ball does not leave the bowler's hand for any reason other than an attempt to run out the non-striker before entering his delivery stride. See Law 42.15 (Bowler attempting to run out non-striker before delivery).

(ix) He is required to do so under any of the Laws.

4. Ball ceases to be dead

The ball ceases to be dead – that is, it comes into play – when the bowler starts his run-up or, if he has no run-up, his bowling action.

5. Action on call of "Dead ball"

(a) A ball is not to count as one of the over if it becomes dead or is to be considered dead before the striker has had an opportunity to play it.

(b) If the ball becomes dead or is to be considered dead after the striker has had an opportunity to play the ball, except in the circumstances of 3(b)(vi) above and Law 42.4 (Deliberate attempt to distract striker), no additional delivery shall be allowed unless "No-ball" or "Wide" has been called.

LAW 24. NO-BALL

1. Mode of delivery

(a) The umpire shall ascertain whether the bowler intends to bowl right-handed or left-handed, and whether over or round the wicket, and shall so inform the striker.
It is unfair if the bowler fails to notify the umpire of a change in his mode of delivery. In this case the umpire shall call and signal "No-ball".

(b) Underarm bowling shall not be permitted except by special agreement before the match.

2. Fair delivery – the arm

For a delivery to be fair in respect of the arm the ball must not be thrown. See 3 below.
Although it is the primary responsibility of the striker's end umpire to ensure the fairness of a delivery in this respect, there is nothing in this Law to debar the bowler's end umpire from calling and signalling "No-ball" if he considers that the ball has been thrown.

(a) If, in the opinion of either umpire, the ball has been thrown, he shall:

(i) Call and signal "No-ball".

(ii) Caution the bowler, when the ball is dead. This caution shall apply throughout the innings.

(iii) Inform the other umpire, the batsmen at the wicket, the captain of the fielding side and, as soon as practicable, the captain of the batting side of what has occurred.

(b) If either umpire considers that after such caution, a further delivery by the same bowler in that innings is thrown, the umpire concerned shall repeat the procedure set out in (a) above, indicating to the bowler that this is a final warning. This warning shall also apply throughout the innings.

(c) If either umpire considers that a further delivery by the same bowler in that innings is thrown:

(i) The umpire concerned shall call and signal "No-ball". When the ball is dead he shall inform the other umpire, the batsmen at the wicket and, as soon as practicable, the captain of the batting side of what has occurred.

(ii) The umpire at the bowler's end shall direct the captain of the fielding side to take the bowler off forthwith. The over shall be completed by another bowler, who shall neither have bowled the previous over nor be allowed to bowl the next over. The bowler thus taken off shall not bowl again in that innings.

(iii) The umpires together shall report the occurrence as soon as possible to the executive of the fielding side and any governing body responsible for the match, who shall take such action as is considered appropriate against the captain and bowler concerned.

3. Definition of fair delivery – the arm

A ball is fairly delivered in respect of the arm if, once the bowler's arm has reached the level of the shoulder in the delivery swing, the elbow joint is not straightened partially or completely from that point until the ball has left the hand. This definition shall not debar a bowler from flexing or rotating the wrist in the delivery swing.

4. Bowler throwing towards striker's end before delivery

If the bowler throws the ball towards the striker's end before entering his delivery stride, either umpire shall instantly call and signal "No-ball". See Law 42.16 (Batsmen stealing a run). However, the procedure stated in 2 above of caution, informing, final warning, action against the bowler and reporting shall not apply.

5. Fair delivery – the feet

For a delivery to be fair in respect of the feet, in the delivery stride:

(i) The bowler's back foot must land within and not touching the return crease.

(ii) The bowler's front foot must land with some part of the foot, whether grounded or raised, behind the popping crease.

If the umpire at the bowler's end is not satisfied that both these conditions have been met, he shall call and signal "No-ball".

6. Ball bouncing more than twice or rolling along the ground

The umpire at the bowler's end shall call and signal "No-ball" if a ball which he considers to have been delivered, without having previously touched the bat or person of the striker, either

(i) bounces more than twice, or

(ii) rolls along the ground

before it reaches the popping crease.

7. Ball coming to rest in front of striker's wicket

If a ball delivered by the bowler comes to rest in front of the line of the striker's wicket, without having touched the bat or person of the striker, the umpire shall call and signal "No-ball" and immediately call and signal "Dead ball".

8. Call of "No-ball" for infringement of other Laws

In addition to the instances above, an umpire shall call and signal "No-ball" as required by the following Laws.

Law 40.3 – Position of wicket-keeper.
Law 41.5 – Limitation of on-side fielders.
Law 41.6 – Fielders not to encroach on the pitch.
Law 42.6 – Dangerous and unfair bowling.
Law 42.7 – Dangerous and unfair bowling – action by the umpire.
Law 42.8 – Deliberate bowling of high full-pitched balls.

9. Revoking a call of "No-ball"

An umpire shall revoke the call of "No-ball" if the ball does not leave the bowler's hand for any reason.

10. No-ball to over-ride wide

A call of "No-ball" shall over-ride the call of "Wide ball" at any time. See Law 25.1 (Judging a wide) and 25.3 (Call and signal of "Wide ball").

11. Ball not dead

The ball does not become dead on the call of "No-ball".

12. Penalty for a No-ball

A penalty of one run shall be awarded instantly on the call of "No-ball". Unless the call is revoked this penalty shall stand even if a batsman is dismissed. It shall be in addition to any other runs scored, any boundary allowance and any other penalties awarded.

13. Runs resulting from a no-ball – how scored

The one-run penalty for a no-ball shall be scored as a no-ball extra. If other penalty runs have been awarded to either side, these shall be scored as in Law 42.17 (Penalty runs). Any runs completed by the batsmen or a boundary allowance shall be credited to the striker if the ball has been struck by the bat; otherwise they also shall be scored as no-ball extras.

Apart from any award of a five-run penalty, all runs resulting from a no-ball, whether as no-ball extras or credited to the striker, shall be debited against the bowler.

14. No-ball not to count

A no-ball shall not count as one of the over. See Law 22.4 (Balls not to count in the over).

15. Out from a no-ball

When "No-ball" has been called, neither batsman shall be out under any of the Laws except Laws 33 (Handled the ball), 34 (Hit the ball twice), 37 (Obstructing the field) or 38 (Run out).

LAW 25. WIDE BALL

1. Judging a wide

(a) If a bowler bowls a ball, not being a no-ball, the umpire shall adjudge it a wide if, according to the definition in (b) below, in his opinion the ball passes wide of the striker where he is standing and would also have passed wide of him in a normal guard position.

(b) The ball will be considered as passing wide of the striker unless it is sufficiently within his reach for him to be able to hit it with his bat by means of a normal cricket stroke.

2. Delivery not a wide

The umpire shall not adjudge a delivery as being a wide:

(a) If the striker, by moving, either

(i) causes the ball to pass wide of him, as defined in 1(b) above, or

(ii) brings the ball sufficiently within his reach to be able to hit it with his bat by means of a normal cricket stroke.

(b) If the ball touches the striker's bat or person.

3. Call and signal of "Wide ball"

(a) If the umpire adjudges a delivery to be a wide he shall call and signal "Wide ball" as soon as the ball passes the striker's wicket. It shall, however, be considered to have been a wide from the instant of delivery, even though it cannot be called wide until it passes the striker's wicket.

(b) The umpire shall revoke the call of "Wide ball" if there is then any contact between the ball and the striker's bat or person.

(c) The umpire shall revoke the call of "Wide ball" if a delivery is called a "No-ball". See Law 24.10 (No-ball to over-ride wide).

4. Ball not dead

The ball does not become dead on the call of "Wide ball".

5. Penalty for a wide

A penalty of one run shall be awarded instantly on the call of "Wide ball". Unless the call is revoked (see 3 above), this penalty shall stand even if a batsman is dismissed, and shall be in addition to any other runs scored, any boundary allowance and any other penalties awarded.

6. Runs resulting from a wide – how scored

All runs completed by the batsmen or a boundary allowance, together with the penalty for the wide, shall be scored as wide balls. Apart from any award of a five-run penalty, all runs resulting from a wide shall be debited against the bowler.

7. Wide not to count

A wide shall not count as one of the over. See Law 22.4 (Balls not to count in the over).

8. Out from a wide

When "Wide ball" has been called, neither batsman shall be out under any of the Laws except Laws 33 (Handled the ball), 35 (Hit wicket), 37 (Obstructing the field), 38 (Run out) or 39 (Stumped).

LAW 26. BYE AND LEG-BYE

1. Byes

If the ball, not being a no-ball or a wide, passes the striker without touching his bat or person, any runs completed by the batsmen or a boundary allowance shall be credited as byes to the batting side.

2. Leg-byes

(a) If a ball delivered by the bowler first strikes the person of the striker, runs shall be scored only if the umpire is satisfied that the striker has either

(i) attempted to play the ball with his bat, or

(ii) tried to avoid being hit by the ball.

If the umpire is satisfied that either of these conditions has been met, and the ball makes no subsequent contact with the bat, runs completed by the batsmen or a boundary allowance shall be credited to the batting side as in (b). Note, however, the provisions of Laws 34.3 (Ball lawfully struck more than once) and 34.4 (Runs permitted from ball lawfully struck more than once).

(b) The runs in (a) above shall

(i) if the delivery is not a no-ball, be scored as leg-byes.

(ii) if no-ball has been called, be scored together with the penalty for the no-ball as no-ball extras.

3. Leg-byes not to be awarded

If in the circumstances of 2(a) above the umpire considers that neither of the conditions (i) and (ii) therein has been met, then leg-byes will not be awarded. The batting side shall not be credited with any runs from that delivery apart from the one run penalty for a no-ball if applicable. Moreover, no other penalties shall be awarded to the batting side when the ball is dead. See Law 42.17 (Penalty runs). The following procedure shall be adopted.

(a) If no run is attempted but the ball reaches the boundary, the umpire shall call and signal "Dead ball", and disallow the boundary.

(b) If runs are attempted and if:

(i) Neither batsman is dismissed and the ball does not become dead for any other reason, the umpire shall call and signal "Dead ball" as soon as one run is completed or the ball reaches the boundary. The batsmen shall return to their original ends. The run or boundary shall be disallowed.

(ii) Before one run is completed or the ball reaches the boundary, a batsman is dismissed, or the ball becomes dead for any other reason, all the provisions of the Laws will apply, except that no runs and no penalties shall be credited to the batting side, other than the penalty for a no-ball if applicable.

LAW 27. APPEALS

1. Umpire not to give batsman out without an appeal

Neither umpire shall give a batsman out, even though he may be out under the Laws, unless appealed to by the fielding side. This shall not debar a batsman who is out under any of the Laws from leaving his wicket without an appeal having been made. Note, however, the provisions of 7 below.

2. Batsman dismissed

A batsman is dismissed if either

(a) he is given out by an umpire, on appeal, or

(b) he is out under any of the Laws and leaves his wicket as in 1 above.

3. Timing of appeals

For an appeal to be valid it must be made before the bowler begins his run-up or, if he has no run-up, his bowling action to deliver the next ball, and before "Time" has been called.

The call of "Over" does not invalidate an appeal made prior to the start of the following over provided "Time" has not been called. See Laws 16.2 (Call of "Time") and 22.2 (Start of an over).

4. Appeal "How's that?"

An appeal "How's that?" covers all ways of being out.

5. Answering appeals

The umpire at the bowler's end shall answer all appeals except those arising out of any of Laws 35 (Hit wicket), 39 (Stumped) or 38 (Run out) when this occurs at the striker's wicket. A decision "Not out" by one umpire shall not prevent the other umpire from giving a decision, provided that each is considering only matters within his jurisdiction.

When a batsman has been given not out, either umpire may, within his jurisdiction, answer a further appeal provided that it is made in accordance with 3 above.

6. Consultation by umpires

Each umpire shall answer appeals on matters within his own jurisdiction. If an umpire is doubtful about any point that the other umpire may have been in a better position to see, he shall consult the latter on this point of fact and shall then give his decision. If, after consultation, there is still doubt remaining the decision shall be "Not out".

7. Batsman leaving his wicket under a misapprehension

An umpire shall intervene if satisfied that a batsman, not having been given out, has left his wicket under a misapprehension that he is out. The umpire intervening shall call and signal "Dead ball" to prevent any further action by the fielding side and shall recall the batsman.

8. Withdrawal of an appeal

The captain of the fielding side may withdraw an appeal only with the consent of the umpire within whose jurisdiction the appeal falls and before the outgoing batsman has left the field of play. If such consent is given the umpire concerned shall, if applicable, revoke his decision and recall the batsman.

9. Umpire's decision

An umpire may alter his decision provided that such alteration is made promptly. This apart, the umpire's decision, once made, is final.

LAW 28. THE WICKET IS DOWN

1. Wicket put down

(a) The wicket is put down if a bail is completely removed from the top of the stumps, or a stump is struck out of the ground by:

(i) The ball.

(ii) The striker's bat, whether he is holding it or has let go of it.

(iii) The striker's person or by any part of his clothing or equipment becoming detached from his person.

(iv) A fielder, with his hand or arm, provided that the ball is held in the hand or hands so used, or in the hand of the arm so used.
The wicket is also put down if a fielder pulls a stump out of the ground in the same manner.

(b) The disturbance of a bail, whether temporary or not, shall not constitute its complete removal from the top of the stumps, but if a bail in falling lodges between two of the stumps this shall be regarded as complete removal.

2. One bail off

If one bail is off, it shall be sufficient for the purpose of putting the wicket down to remove the remaining bail, or to strike or pull any of the three stumps out of the ground, in any of the ways stated in 1 above.

3. Remaking the wicket

If the wicket is broken or put down while the ball is in play, the umpire shall not remake the wicket until the ball is dead. See Law 23 (Dead ball). Any fielder, however, may:

(i) Replace a bail or bails on top of the stumps.

(ii) Put back one or more stumps into the ground where the wicket originally stood.

4. Dispensing with bails

If the umpires have agreed to dispense with bails, in accordance with Law 8.5 (Dispensing with bails), the decision as to whether the wicket has been put down is one for the umpire concerned to decide.

(a) After a decision to play without bails, the wicket has been put down if the umpire concerned is satisfied that the wicket has been struck by the ball, by the striker's bat, person, or items of his clothing or equipment separated from his person as described in 1(a)(ii) or 1(a)(iii) above, or by a fielder with the hand holding the ball or with the arm of the hand holding the ball.

(b) If the wicket has already been broken or put down, (a) above shall apply to any stump or stumps still in the ground. Any fielder may replace a stump or stumps, in accordance with 3 above, in order to have an opportunity of putting the wicket down.

LAW 29. BATSMAN OUT OF HIS GROUND

1. When out of his ground

A batsman shall be considered to be out of his ground unless his bat or some part of his person is grounded behind the popping crease at that end.

2. Which is a batsman's ground?

(a) If only one batsman is within a ground:

(i) It is his ground.

(ii) It remains his ground even if he is later joined there by the other batsman.

(b) If both batsmen are in the same ground and one of them subsequently leaves it, (a)(i) above applies.

(c) If there is no batsman in either ground, then each ground belongs to whichever of the batsmen is nearer to it, or, if the batsmen are level, to whichever was nearer to it immediately prior to their drawing level.

(d) If a ground belongs to one batsman, then, unless there is a striker with a runner, the other ground belongs to the other batsman irrespective of his position.

(e) When a batsman with a runner is striker, his ground is always that at the wicket-keeper's end. However, (a), (b), (c) and (d) above will still apply, but only to the runner and the non-striker, so that that ground will also belong to either the non-striker or the runner, as the case may be.

3. Position of non-striker

The non-striker, when standing at the bowler's end, should be positioned on the opposite side of the wicket to that from which the ball is being delivered, unless a request to do otherwise is granted by the umpire.

LAW 30. BOWLED

1. Out Bowled

(a) The striker is out *Bowled* if his wicket is put down by a ball delivered by the bowler, not being a no-ball, even if it first touches his bat or person.

(b) Notwithstanding (a) above he shall not be out bowled if before striking the wicket the ball has been in contact with any other player or with an umpire. He will, however, be subject to Laws 33 (Handled the ball), 37 (Obstructing the field), 38 (Run out) and 39 (Stumped).

2. Bowled to take precedence

The striker is out bowled if his wicket is put down as in 1 above, even though a decision against him for any other method of dismissal would be justified.

LAW 31. TIMED OUT

1. Out Timed out

(a) Unless "Time" has been called, the incoming batsman must be in position to take guard or for his partner to be ready to receive the next ball within three minutes of the fall of the previous wicket. If this requirement is not met, the incoming batsman will be out, *Timed out*.

(b) In the event of protracted delay in which no batsman comes to the wicket, the umpires shall adopt the procedure of Law 21.3 (Umpires awarding a match). For the purposes of that Law the start of the action shall be taken as the expiry of the three minutes referred to above.

2. Bowler does not get credit

The bowler does not get credit for the wicket.

LAW 32. CAUGHT

1. Out Caught

The striker is out *Caught* if a ball delivered by the bowler, not being a no-ball, touches his bat without having previously been in contact with any member of the fielding side and is subsequently held by a fielder as a fair catch before it touches the ground.

2. Caught to take precedence

If the criteria of 1 above are met and the striker is not out bowled, then he is out caught even though a decision against either batsman for another method of dismissal would be justified. Runs completed by the batsmen before the completion of the catch will not be scored. Note also Laws 21.6 (Winning hit or extras) and 42.17(b) (Penalty runs).

3. A fair catch

A catch shall be considered to have been fairly made if:

(a) Throughout the act of making the catch:

(i) Any fielder in contact with the ball is within the field of play. See 4 below.

(ii) The ball is at no time in contact with any object grounded beyond the boundary.

The act of making the catch shall start from the time when a fielder first handles the ball and shall end when a fielder obtains complete control both over the ball and over his own movement.

(b) The ball is hugged to the body of the catcher or accidentally lodges in his clothing or, in the case of the wicket-keeper, in his pads. However, it is not a fair catch if the ball lodges in a protective helmet worn by a fielder. See Law 23 (Dead ball).

(c) The ball does not touch the ground, even though the hand holding it does so in effecting the catch.

(d) A fielder catches the ball after it has been lawfully struck more than once by the striker, but only if the ball has not touched the ground since first being struck.

(e) A fielder catches the ball after it has touched an umpire, another fielder or the other batsman. However, it is not a fair catch if the ball has touched a protective helmet worn by a fielder, although the ball remains in play.

(f) A fielder catches the ball in the air after it has crossed the boundary provided that:

(i) He has no part of his person touching, or grounded beyond, the boundary at any time when he is in contact with the ball.

(ii) The ball has not been grounded beyond the boundary.

See Law 19.3 (Scoring a boundary).

(g) The ball is caught off an obstruction within the boundary, provided it has not previously been decided to regard the obstruction as a boundary.

4. Fielder within the field of play

(a) A fielder is not within the field of play if he touches the boundary or has any part of his person grounded beyond the boundary. See Law 19.3 (Scoring a boundary).

(b) Six runs shall be scored if a fielder:

(i) Has any part of his person touching, or grounded beyond, the boundary when he catches the ball.

(ii) Catches the ball and subsequently touches the boundary or grounds some part of his person over the boundary while carrying the ball but before completing the catch.

See Laws 19.3 (Scoring a boundary) and 19.4 (Runs allowed for boundaries).

5. No runs to be scored

If the striker is dismissed caught, runs from that delivery completed by the batsmen before the completion of the catch shall not be scored, but any penalties awarded to either side when the ball is dead, if applicable, will stand. Law 18.12(a) (Batsman returning to wicket he has left) shall apply from the instant of the catch.

LAW 33. HANDLED THE BALL

1. Out Handled the ball

Either batsman is out *Handled the ball* if he wilfully touches the ball while in play with a hand or hands not holding the bat unless he does so with the consent of the opposing side.

2. Not out Handled the ball

Notwithstanding 1 above, a batsman will not be out under this Law if:

(i) He handles the ball in order to avoid injury.

(ii) He uses his hand or hands to return the ball to any member of the fielding side without the consent of that side. Note, however, the provisions of Law 37.4 (Returning the ball to a member of the fielding side).

3. Runs scored

If either batsman is dismissed under this Law, any runs completed before the offence, together with any penalty extras and the penalty for a no-ball or wide, if applicable, shall be scored. See Laws 18.10 (Runs scored when a batsman is dismissed) and 42.17 (Penalty runs).

4. Bowler does not get credit

The bowler does not get credit for the wicket.

LAW 34. HIT THE BALL TWICE

1. Out Hit the ball twice

(a) The striker is out *Hit the ball twice* if, while the ball is in play and it strikes any part of his person or is struck by his bat and, before the ball has been touched by a fielder, he wilfully strikes it again with his bat or person, other than a hand not holding the bat, except for the sole purpose of guarding his wicket. See 3 below and Laws 33 (Handled the ball) and 37 (Obstructing the field).

(b) For the purpose of this Law, "struck" or "strike" shall include contact with the person of the striker.

2. Not out Hit the ball twice

Notwithstanding 1(a) above, the striker will not be out under this Law if:

(i) He makes a second or subsequent stroke in order to return the ball to any member of the fielding side. Note, however, the provisions of Law 37.4 (Returning the ball to a member of the fielding side).

(ii) He wilfully strikes the ball after it has touched a fielder. Note, however, the provisions of Law 37.1 (Out obstructing the field).

3. Ball lawfully struck more than once

Solely in order to guard his wicket and before the ball has been touched by a fielder, the striker may lawfully strike the ball more than once with his bat or with any part of his person other than a hand not holding the bat.

Notwithstanding this provision, the striker may not prevent the ball from being caught by making more than one stroke in defence of his wicket. See Law 37.3 (Obstructing a ball from being caught).

4. Runs permitted from ball lawfully struck more than once

When the ball is lawfully struck more than once, as permitted in 3 above, only the first strike is to be considered in determining whether runs are to be allowed and how they are to be scored.

(a) If on the first strike the umpire is satisfied that either

(i) the ball first struck the bat, or

(ii) the striker attempted to play the ball with his bat, or

(iii) the striker tried to avoid being hit by the ball,

then any penalties to the batting side that are applicable shall be allowed.

(b) If the conditions in (a) above are met then, if they result from overthrows, and only if they result from overthrows, runs completed by the batsmen or a boundary will be allowed in addition to any penalties that are applicable. They shall be credited to the striker if the first strike was with the bat. If the first strike was on the person of the striker they shall be scored as leg-byes or no-ball extras, as appropriate. See Law 26.2 (Leg-byes).

(c) If the conditions of (a) above are met and there is no overthrow until after the batsmen have started to run, but before one run is completed:

- (i) Only subsequent completed runs or a boundary shall be allowed. The first run shall count as a completed run for this purpose only if the batsmen have not crossed at the instant of the throw.
- (ii) If in these circumstances the ball goes to the boundary from the throw then, notwithstanding the provisions of Law 19.6 (Overthrow or wilful act of fielder), only the boundary allowance shall be scored.
- (iii) If the ball goes to the boundary as the result of a further overthrow, then runs completed by the batsmen after the first throw and before this final throw shall be added to the boundary allowance. The run in progress at the first throw will count only if they have not crossed at that moment; the run in progress at the final throw shall count only if they have crossed at that moment. Law 18.12 (Batsman returning to wicket he has left) shall apply as from the moment of the final throw.

(d) If, in the opinion of the umpire, none of the conditions in (a) above has been met then, whether there is an overthrow or not, the batting side shall not be credited with any runs from that delivery apart from the penalty for a no-ball if applicable. Moreover, no other penalties shall be awarded to the batting side when the ball is dead. See Law 42.17 (Penalty runs).

5. Ball lawfully struck more than once – action by the umpire

If no runs are to be allowed, either in the circumstances of 4(d) above, or because there has been no overthrow and:

(a) If no run is attempted but the ball reaches the boundary, the umpire shall call and signal "Dead ball" and disallow the boundary.

(b) If the batsmen run and:

- (i) Neither batsman is dismissed and the ball does not become dead for any other reason, the umpire shall call and signal "Dead ball" as soon as one run is completed or the ball reaches the boundary. The batsmen shall return to their original ends. The run or boundary shall be disallowed.
- (ii) A batsman is dismissed, or if for any other reason the ball becomes dead before one run is completed or the ball reaches the boundary, all the provisions of the Laws will apply except that the award of penalties to the batting side shall be as laid down in 4(a) or 4(d) above as appropriate.

6. Bowler does not get credit

The bowler does not get credit for the wicket.

LAW 35. HIT WICKET

1. Out Hit wicket

(a) The striker is out *Hit wicket* if, after the bowler has entered his delivery stride and while the ball is in play, his wicket is put down either by the striker's bat or person as described in Law 28.1(a)(ii) and (iii) (Wicket put down) either

- (i) in the course of any action taken by him in preparing to receive or in receiving a delivery, or
- (ii) in setting off for his first run immediately after playing, or playing at, the ball, or
- (iii) if he makes no attempt to play the ball, in setting off for his first run, provided that in the opinion of the umpire this is immediately after he has had the opportunity of playing the ball, or
- (iv) in lawfully making a second or further stroke for the purpose of guarding his wicket within the provisions of Law 34.3 (Ball lawfully struck more than once).

(b) If the striker puts his wicket down in any of the ways described in Law 28.1(a)(ii) and (iii) (Wicket put down) before the bowler has entered his delivery stride, either umpire shall call and signal "Dead ball".

2. Not out Hit wicket

Notwithstanding 1 above, the batsman is not out under this Law should his wicket be put down in any of the ways referred to in 1 above if:

(a) It occurs after he has completed any action in receiving the delivery, other than as in 1(a)(ii), (iii) or (iv) above.

(b) It occurs when he is in the act of running, other than in setting off immediately for his first run.

(c) It occurs when he is trying to avoid being run out or stumped.

(d) It occurs while he is trying to avoid a throw-in at any time.

(e) The bowler, after entering his delivery stride, does not deliver the ball. In this case either umpire shall immediately call and signal "Dead ball". See Law 23.3 (Umpire calling and signalling "Dead ball").

(f) The delivery is a no-ball.

LAW 36. LEG BEFORE WICKET

1. Out LBW

The striker is out *LBW* in the circumstances set out below.

(a) The bowler delivers a ball, not being a no-ball, and

(b) the ball, if it is not intercepted full pitch, pitches in line between wicket and wicket or on the off side of the striker's wicket, and

(c) the ball not having previously touched his bat, the striker intercepts the ball, either full pitch or after pitching, with any part of his person, and

(d) the point of impact, even if above the level of the bails, either

(i) is between wicket and wicket, or

(ii) is either between wicket and wicket or outside the line of the off stump, if the striker has made no genuine attempt to play the ball with his bat, and

(e) but for the interception, the ball would have hit the wicket.

2. Interception of the ball

(a) In assessing points (c), (d) and (e) in 1 above, only the first interception is to be considered.

(b) In assessing point (e) in 1 above, it is to be assumed that the path of the ball before interception would have continued after interception, irrespective of whether the ball might have pitched subsequently or not.

3. Off side of wicket

The off side of the striker's wicket shall be determined by the striker's stance at the moment the ball comes into play for that delivery.

LAW 37. OBSTRUCTING THE FIELD

1. Out Obstructing the field

Either batsman is out *Obstructing the field* if he wilfully obstructs or distracts the opposing side by word or action. It shall be regarded as obstruction if either batsman wilfully, and without the consent of the fielding side, strikes the ball with his bat or person, other than a hand not holding the bat, after the ball has touched a fielder. See 4 below.

2. Accidental obstruction

It is for either umpire to decide whether any obstruction or distraction is wilful or not. He shall consult the other umpire if he has any doubt.

3. Obstructing a ball from being caught

The striker is out should wilful obstruction or distraction by either batsman prevent a catch being made.

This shall apply even though the striker causes the obstruction in lawfully guarding his wicket under the provisions of Law 34.3 (Ball lawfully struck more than once).

4. Returning the ball to a member of the fielding side

Either batsman is out under this Law if, without the consent of the fielding side and while the ball is in play, he uses his bat or person to return the ball to any member of that side.

5. Runs scored

If a batsman is dismissed under this Law, runs completed by the batsmen before the offence shall be scored, together with the penalty for a no-ball or a wide, if applicable. Other penalties that may be awarded to either side when the ball is dead shall also stand. See Law 42.17(b) (Penalty runs).

If, however, the obstruction prevents a catch from being made, runs completed by the batsmen before the offence shall not be scored, but other penalties that may be awarded to either side when the ball is dead shall stand. See Law 42.17(b) (Penalty runs).

6. Bowler does not get credit

The bowler does not get credit for the wicket.

LAW 38. RUN OUT

1. Out Run out

(a) Either batsman is out *Run out*, except as in 2 below, if at any time while the ball is in play

(i) he is out of his ground and

(ii) his wicket is fairly put down by the opposing side.

(b) (a) above shall apply even though "No-ball" has been called and whether or not a run is being attempted, except in the circumstances of Law 39.3(b) (Not out Stumped).

2. Batsman not Run out

Notwithstanding 1 above, a batsman is not out run out if:

(a) He has been within his ground and has subsequently left it to avoid injury, when the wicket is put down.

(b) The ball has not subsequently been touched again by a fielder, after the bowler has entered his delivery stride, before the wicket is put down.

(c) The ball, having been played by the striker, or having come off his person, directly strikes a helmet worn by a fielder and without further contact with him or any other fielder rebounds directly on to the wicket. However, the ball remains in play and either batsman may be run out in the circumstances of 1 above if a wicket is subsequently put down.

(d) He is out stumped. See Law 39.1(b) (Out Stumped).

(e) He is out of his ground, not attempting a run and his wicket is fairly put down by the wicket-keeper without the intervention of another member of the fielding side, if "No-ball" has been called. See Law 39.3(b) (Not out Stumped).

3. Which batsman is out

The batsman out in the circumstances of 1 above is the one whose ground is at the end where the wicket is put down. See Laws 2.8 (Transgression of the Laws by a batsman who has a runner) and 29.2 (Which is a batsman's ground).

4. Runs scored

If a batsman is dismissed run out, the batting side shall score the runs completed before the dismissal together with the penalty for a no-ball or wide, if applicable. Other penalties to either side that may be awarded when the ball is dead shall also stand. See Law 42.17 (Penalty runs).

If, however, a striker with a runner is himself dismissed run out, runs completed by the runner and the other batsman before the dismissal shall not be scored. The penalty for a no-ball or a wide and any other penalties to either side that may be awarded when the ball is dead shall stand. See Laws 2.8 (Transgression of the Laws by a batsman who has a runner) and 42.17(b) (Penalty runs).

5. Bowler does not get credit

The bowler does not get credit for the wicket.

LAW 39. STUMPED

1. Out Stumped

(a) The striker is out *Stumped* if

(i) he is out of his ground, and

(ii) he is receiving a ball which is not a no-ball, and

(iii) he is not attempting a run, and

(iv) his wicket is fairly put down by the wicket-keeper without the intervention of another member of the fielding side. Note Law 40.3 (Position of wicket-keeper).

(b) The striker is out stumped if all the conditions of (a) above are satisfied, even though a decision of run out would be justified.

2. Ball rebounding from wicket-keeper's person

(a) If the wicket is put down by the ball, it shall be regarded as having been put down by the wicket-keeper, if the ball

(i) rebounds on to the stumps from any part of his person, other than a protective helmet, or

(ii) has been kicked or thrown on to the stumps by the wicket-keeper.

(b) If the ball touches a helmet worn by the wicket-keeper, the ball is still in play but the striker shall not be out stumped. He will, however, be liable to be run out in these circumstances if there is subsequent contact between the ball and any member of the fielding side. Note, however, 3 below.

3. Not out Stumped

(a) If the striker is not out stumped, he is liable to be out run out if the conditions of Law 38 (Run out) apply, except as set out in (b) below.

(b) The striker shall not be out run out if he is out of his ground, not attempting a run, and his wicket is fairly put down by the wicket-keeper without the intervention of another member of the fielding side, if "No-ball" has been called.

LAW 40. THE WICKET-KEEPER

1. Protective equipment

The wicket-keeper is the only member of the fielding side permitted to wear gloves and external leg guards. If he does so, these are to be regarded as part of his person for the purposes of Law 41.2 (Fielding the ball). If by his actions and positioning it is apparent to the umpires that he will not be able to discharge his duties as a wicket-keeper, he shall forfeit this right and also the right to be recognised as a wicket-keeper for the purposes of Laws 32.3 (A fair catch), 39 (Stumped), 41.1 (Protective equipment), 41.5 (Limitation of on-side fielders) and 41.6 (Fielders not to encroach on the pitch).

2. Gloves

If, as permitted under 1 above, the wicket-keeper wears gloves, they shall have no webbing between fingers except joining index finger and thumb, where webbing may be inserted as a means of support. If used, the webbing shall be

(a) a single piece of non-stretch material which, although it may have facing material attached, shall have no reinforcement or tucks.

(b) such that the top edge of the webbing.

(i) does not protrude beyond the straight line joining the top of the index finger to the top of the thumb.

(ii) is taut when a hand wearing the glove has the thumb fully extended.

3. Position of wicket-keeper

The wicket-keeper shall remain wholly behind the wicket at the striker's end from the moment the ball comes into play until

(a) a ball delivered by the bowler either

(i) touches the bat or person of the striker, or

(ii) passes the wicket at the striker's end, or

(b) the striker attempts a run.

In the event of the wicket-keeper contravening this Law, the umpire at the striker's end shall call and signal "No-ball" as soon as possible after the delivery of the ball.

4. Movement by wicket-keeper

It is unfair if the wicket-keeper standing back makes a significant movement towards the wicket after the ball comes into play and before it reaches the striker. In the event of such unfair movement by the wicket-keeper, either umpire shall call and signal "Dead ball". It will not be considered a significant movement if the wicket-keeper moves a few paces forward for a slower delivery.

5. Restriction on actions of wicket-keeper

If in the opinion of either umpire the wicket-keeper interferes with the striker's right to play the ball and to guard his wicket, Law 23.3(b)(vi) (Umpire calling and signalling "Dead Ball") shall apply. If, however, the umpire concerned considers that the interference by the wicket-keeper was wilful, then Law 42.4 (Deliberate attempt to distract striker) shall apply.

6. Interference with wicket-keeper by striker

If, in playing at the ball or in the legitimate defence of his wicket, the striker interferes with the wicket-keeper, he shall not be out, except as provided for in Law 37.3 (Obstructing a ball from being caught).

LAW 41. THE FIELDER

1. Protective equipment

No member of the fielding side other than the wicket-keeper shall be permitted to wear gloves or external leg guards. In addition, protection for the hand or fingers may be worn only with the consent of the umpires.

2. Fielding the ball

A fielder may field the ball with any part of his person but if, while the ball is in play, he wilfully fields it otherwise:

(a) The ball shall become dead and five penalty runs shall be awarded to the batting side. See Law 42.17 (Penalty runs). The ball shall not count as one of the over.

(b) The umpire shall inform the other umpire, the captain of the fielding side, the batsmen and, as soon as practicable, the captain of the batting side of what has occurred.

(c) The umpires together shall report the occurrence as soon as possible to the executive of the fielding side and any governing body responsible for the match who shall take such action as is considered appropriate against the captain and player concerned.

3. Protective helmets belonging to the fielding side

Protective helmets, when not in use by fielders, shall only be placed, if above the surface, on the ground behind the wicket-keeper and in line with both sets of stumps. If a helmet belonging to the fielding side is on the ground within the field of play, and the ball while in play strikes it, the ball shall become dead. Five penalty runs shall then be awarded to the batting side. See Laws 18.11 (Runs scored when ball becomes dead) and 42.17 (Penalty runs).

4. Penalty runs not to be awarded

Notwithstanding 2 and 3 above, if from the delivery by the bowler the ball first struck the person of the striker and if, in the opinion of the umpire, the striker neither

(i) attempted to play the ball with his bat, nor

(ii) tried to avoid being hit by the ball,

then no award of five penalty runs shall be made and no other runs or penalties shall be credited to the batting side except the penalty for a no-ball if applicable. See Law 26.3 (Leg-byes not to be awarded).

5. Limitation of on-side fielders

At the instant of the bowler's delivery there shall not be more than two fielders, other than the wicket-keeper, behind the popping crease on the on side. A fielder will be considered to be behind the popping crease unless the whole of his person, whether grounded or in the air, is in front of this line.

In the event of infringement of this Law by the fielding side the umpire at the striker's end shall call and signal "No-ball".

6. Fielders not to encroach on the pitch

While the ball is in play and until the ball has made contact with the bat or person of the striker, or has passed the striker's bat, no fielder, other than the bowler, may have any part of his person grounded on or extended over the pitch.

In the event of infringement of this Law by any fielder other than the wicket-keeper, the umpire at the bowler's end shall call and signal "No-ball" as soon as possible after the delivery of the ball. Note, however, Law 40.3 (Position of wicket-keeper).

7. Movement by fielders

Any significant movement by any fielder after the ball comes into play and before the ball reaches the striker is unfair. In the event of such unfair movement, either umpire shall call and signal "Dead ball". Note also the provisions of Law 42.4 (Deliberate attempt to distract striker).

8. Definition of significant movement

(a) For close fielders anything other than minor adjustments to stance or position in relation to the striker is significant.

(b) In the outfield, fielders are permitted to move in towards the striker or striker's wicket, provided that 5 above is not contravened. Anything other than slight movement off line or away from the striker is to be considered significant.

(c) For restrictions on movement by the wicket-keeper see Law 40.4 (Movement by wicket-keeper).

LAW 42. FAIR AND UNFAIR PLAY

1. Fair and unfair play – responsibility of captains

The responsibility lies with the captains for ensuring that play is conducted within the spirit and traditions of the game, as described in The Preamble – The Spirit of Cricket, as well as within the Laws.

2. Fair and unfair play – responsibility of umpires

The umpires shall be sole judges of fair and unfair play. If either umpire considers an action, not covered by the Laws, to be unfair, he shall intervene without appeal and, if the ball is in play, shall call and signal "Dead ball" and implement the procedure as set out in 18 below. Otherwise the umpires shall not interfere with the progress of play, except as required to do so by the Laws.

3. The match ball – changing its condition

(a) Any fielder may:

(i) Polish the ball provided that no artificial substance is used and that such polishing wastes no time.

(ii) Remove mud from the ball under the supervision of the umpire.

(iii) Dry a wet ball on a towel.

(b) It is unfair for anyone to rub the ball on the ground for any reason, interfere with any of the seams or the surface of the ball, use any implement, or take any other action whatsoever which is likely to alter the condition of the ball, except as permitted in (a) above.

(c) The umpires shall make frequent and irregular inspections of the ball.

(d) In the event of any fielder changing the condition of the ball unfairly, as set out in (b) above, the umpires after consultation shall:

(i) Change the ball forthwith. It shall be for the umpires to decide on the replacement ball, which shall, in their opinion, have had wear comparable with that which the previous ball had received immediately prior to the contravention.

(ii) Inform the batsmen that the ball has been changed.

(iii) Award five penalty runs to the batting side. See 17 below.

(iv) Inform the captain of the fielding side that the reason for the action was the unfair interference with the ball.

(v) Inform the captain of the batting side as soon as practicable of what has occurred.

(vi) Report the occurrence as soon as possible to the executive of the fielding side and any governing body responsible for the match, who shall take such action as is considered appropriate against the captain and team concerned.

(e) If there is any further instance of unfairly changing the condition of the ball in that innings, the umpires after consultation shall:

(i) Repeat the procedure in (d)(i), (ii) and (iii) above.

(ii) Inform the captain of the fielding side of the reason for the action taken and direct him to take off forthwith the bowler who delivered the immediately preceding ball. The bowler thus taken off shall not be allowed to bowl again in that innings.

(iii) Inform the captain of the batting side as soon as practicable of what has occurred.

(iv) Report the occurrence as soon as possible to the executive of the fielding side and any governing body responsible for the match, who shall take such action as is considered appropriate against the captain and team concerned.

4. Deliberate attempt to distract striker

It is unfair for any member of the fielding side deliberately to attempt to distract the striker while he is preparing to receive or receiving a delivery.

(a) If either umpire considers that any action by a member of the fielding side is such an attempt, at the first instance he shall:

(i) Immediately call and signal "Dead ball".

(ii) Warn the captain of the fielding side that the action is unfair and indicate that this is a first and final warning.

(iii) Inform the other umpire and the batsmen of what has occurred.

Neither batsman shall be dismissed from that delivery and the ball shall not count as one of the over.

(b) If there is any further such deliberate attempt in that innings, by any member of the fielding side, the procedures, other than warning, as set out in (a) above shall apply. Additionally, the umpire at the bowler's end shall:

(i) Award five penalty runs to the batting side. See 17 below.

(ii) Inform the captain of the fielding side of the reason for this action and, as soon as practicable, inform the captain of the batting side.

(iii) Report the occurrence, together with the other umpire, as soon as possible to the executive of the fielding side and any governing body responsible for the match, who shall take such action as is considered appropriate against the captain and player or players concerned.

5. Deliberate distraction or obstruction of batsman

In addition to 4 above, it is unfair for any member of the fielding side, by word or action, wilfully to attempt to distract or to obstruct either batsman after the striker has received the ball.

(a) It is for either one of the umpires to decide whether any distraction or obstruction is wilful or not.

(b) If either umpire considers that a member of the fielding side has wilfully caused or attempted to cause such a distraction or obstruction he shall:

(i) Immediately call and signal "Dead ball".

(ii) Inform the captain of the fielding side and the other umpire of the reason for the call.

Additionally:

(iii) Neither batsman shall be dismissed from that delivery.

(iv) Five penalty runs shall be awarded to the batting side. See 17 below. In this instance, the run in progress shall be scored, whether or not the batsmen had crossed at the instant of the call. See Law 18.11 (Runs scored when ball becomes dead).

(v) The umpire at the bowler's end shall inform the captain of the fielding side of the reason for this action and, as soon as practicable, inform the captain of the batting side.

(vi) The ball shall not count as one of the over.

(vii) The batsmen at the wicket shall decide which of them is to face the next delivery.

(viii) The umpires shall report the occurrence as soon as possible to the executive of the fielding side and any governing body responsible for the match, who shall take such action as is considered appropriate against the captain and player or players concerned.

6. Dangerous and unfair bowling

(a) Bowling of fast short-pitched balls

(i) The bowling of fast short-pitched balls is dangerous and unfair if the umpire at the bowler's end considers that by their repetition and taking into account their length, height and direction they are likely to inflict physical injury on the striker, irrespective of the protective equipment he may be wearing. The relative skill of the striker shall be taken into consideration.

(ii) Any delivery which, after pitching, passes or would have passed over head height of the striker standing upright at the crease, although not threatening physical injury, shall be included with bowling under (i) both when the umpire is considering whether the bowling of fast short-pitched balls has become dangerous and unfair and after he has so decided. The umpire shall call and signal "No-ball" for each such delivery.

(b) Bowling of high full-pitched balls

(i) Any delivery, other than a slow-paced one, which passes or would have passed on the full above waist height of the striker standing upright at the crease is to be deemed dangerous and unfair, whether or not it is likely to inflict physical injury on the striker.

(ii) A slow delivery which passes or would have passed on the full above shoulder height of the striker standing upright at the crease is to be deemed dangerous and unfair, whether or not it is likely to inflict physical injury on the striker.

7. Dangerous and unfair bowling – action by the umpire

(a) As soon as the umpire at the bowler's end decides under 6(a) above that the bowling of fast short-pitched balls has become dangerous and unfair, or, except as in 8 below, there is an instance of dangerous and unfair bowling as defined in 6(b) above, he shall call and signal "No-ball" and, when the ball is dead, caution the bowler, inform the other umpire, the captain of the fielding side and the batsmen of what has occurred. This caution shall continue to apply throughout the innings.

(b) If there is any further instance of such dangerous and unfair bowling by the same bowler in the same innings, the umpire at the bowler's end shall repeat the above procedure and indicate to the bowler that this is a final warning.

Both the above caution and final warning shall continue to apply even though the bowler may later change ends.

(c) Should there be any further repetition by the same bowler in that innings, the umpire shall:

(i) call and signal "No-ball".

(ii) Direct the captain, when the ball is dead, to take the bowler off forthwith. The over shall be completed by another bowler, who shall neither have bowled the previous over nor be allowed to bowl the next over.

The bowler thus taken off shall not be allowed to bowl again in that innings.

(iii) Report the occurrence to the other umpire, the batsmen and, as soon as practicable, the captain of the batting side.

(iv) Report the occurrence, with the other umpire, as soon as possible to the executive of the fielding side and to any governing body responsible for the match, who shall take such action as is considered appropriate against the captain and bowler concerned.

8. Deliberate bowling of high full-pitched balls

If the umpire considers that a high full pitch which is deemed to be dangerous and unfair, as defined in 6(b) above, was deliberately bowled, then the caution and warning prescribed in 7 above shall be dispensed with. The umpire shall:

(a) Call and signal "No-ball".

(b) Direct the captain, when the ball is dead, to take the bowler off forthwith.

(c) Implement the remainder of the procedure as laid down in 7(c) above.

9. Time-wasting by the fielding side

It is unfair for any member of the fielding side to waste time.

(a) If the captain of the fielding side wastes time, or allows any member of his side to waste time, or if the progress of an over is unnecessarily slow, at the first instance the umpire shall call and signal "Dead ball" if necessary and:

(i) Warn the captain, and indicate that this is a first and final warning.

(ii) Inform the other umpire and the batsmen of what has occurred.

(b) If there is any further waste of time in that innings, by any member of the fielding side, the umpire shall either

(i) if the waste of time is not during the course of an over, award five penalty runs to the batting side (See 17 below), or

(ii) if the waste of time is during the course of an over, when the ball is dead, direct the captain to take the bowler off forthwith. If applicable, the over shall be completed by another bowler, who shall neither have bowled the previous over nor be allowed to bowl the next over. The bowler thus taken off shall not be allowed to bowl again in that innings.

(iii) Inform the other umpire, the batsmen and, as soon as practicable, the captain of the batting side, of what has occurred.

(iv) Report the occurrence, with the other umpire, as soon as possible to the executive of the fielding side and to any governing body responsible for the match, who shall take such action as is considered appropriate against the captain and team concerned.

10. Batsman wasting time

It is unfair for a batsman to waste time. In normal circumstances the striker should always be ready to take strike when the bowler is ready to start his run-up.

(a) Should either batsman waste time by failing to meet this requirement, or in any other way, the following procedure shall be adopted. At the first instance, either before the bowler starts his run-up or when the ball is dead, as appropriate, the umpire shall:

(i) Warn the batsman and indicate that this is a first and final warning. This warning shall continue to apply throughout that innings. The umpire shall so inform each incoming batsman.

(ii) Inform the other umpire, the other batsman and the captain of the fielding side of what has occurred.

(iii) Inform the captain of the batting side as soon as practicable.

(b) If there is any further time-wasting by any batsman in that innings, the umpire shall, at the appropriate time while the ball is dead:

(i) Award five penalty runs to the fielding side. See 17 below.

(ii) Inform the other umpire, the other batsman, the captain of the fielding side and, as soon as practicable, the captain of the batting side, of what has occurred.

(iii) Report the occurrence, with the other umpire, as soon as possible to the executive of the batting side and to any governing body responsible for the match, who shall take such action as is considered appropriate against the captain and player or players, or, if appropriate, the team concerned.

11. Damaging the pitch – area to be protected

(a) It is incumbent on all players to avoid unnecessary damage to the pitch. It is unfair for any player to cause deliberate damage to the pitch.

(b) An area of the pitch, to be referred to as "the protected area", is defined as that area contained within a rectangle bounded at each end by imaginary lines parallel to the popping creases and 5ft/1.52m in front of each and on the sides by imaginary lines, one each side of the imaginary line joining the centres of the two middle stumps, each parallel to it and 1ft/30.48cm from it.

12. Bowler running on the protected area after delivering the ball

(a) If the bowler, after delivering the ball, runs on the protected area as defined in 11(b) above, the umpire shall at the first instance, and when the ball is dead:

(i) Caution the bowler. This caution shall continue to apply throughout the innings.

(ii) Inform the other umpire, the captain of the fielding side and the batsmen of what has occurred.

(b) If, in that innings, the same bowler runs on the protected area again after delivering the ball, the umpire shall repeat the above procedure, indicating that this is a final warning.

(c) If, in that innings, the same bowler runs on the protected area a third time after delivering the ball, when the ball is dead the umpire shall:

(i) Direct the captain of the fielding side to take the bowler off forthwith. If applicable, the over shall be completed by another bowler, who shall neither have bowled the previous over nor be allowed to bowl the next over. The bowler thus taken off shall not be allowed to bowl again in that innings.

(ii) Inform the other umpire, the batsmen and, as soon as practicable, the captain of the batting side of what has occurred.

(iii) Report the occurrence, with the other umpire, as soon as possible to the executive of the fielding side and to any governing body responsible for the match, who shall take such action as is considered appropriate against the captain and bowler concerned.

13. Fielders damaging the pitch

(a) If any fielder causes avoidable damage to the pitch, other than as in 12(a) above, at the first instance the umpire shall, when the ball is dead:

(i) Caution the captain of the fielding side, indicating that this is a first and final warning. This caution shall continue to apply throughout the innings.

(ii) Inform the other umpire and the batsmen of what has occurred.

(b) If there is any further avoidable damage to the pitch by any fielder in that innings, the umpire shall, when the ball is dead:

(i) Award five penalty runs to the batting side. See 17 below.

(ii) Inform the other umpire, the batsmen, the captain of the fielding side and, as soon as practicable, the captain of the batting side of what has occurred.

(iii) Report the occurrence, with the other umpire, as soon as possible to the executive of the fielding side and any governing body responsible for the match, who shall take such action as is considered appropriate against the captain and player or players concerned.

14. Batsman damaging the pitch

(a) If either batsman causes avoidable damage to the pitch, at the first instance the umpire shall, when the ball is dead:

(i) Caution the batsman. This caution shall continue to apply throughout the innings. The umpire shall so inform each incoming batsman.

(ii) Inform the other umpire, the other batsman, the captain of the fielding side and, as soon as practicable, the captain of the batting side.

(b) If there is a second instance of avoidable damage to the pitch by any batsman in that innings:

(i) The umpire shall repeat the above procedure, indicating that this is a final warning.

(ii) Additionally he shall disallow all runs to the batting side from that delivery other than the penalty for a no-ball or a wide, if applicable. The batsmen shall return to their original ends.

(c) If there is any further avoidable damage to the pitch by any batsman in that innings, the umpire shall, when the ball is dead:

(i) Disallow all runs to the batting side from that delivery other than the penalty for a no-ball or a wide, if applicable.

(ii) Additionally award five penalty runs to the fielding side. See 17 below.

(iii) Inform the other umpire, the other batsman, the captain of the fielding side and, as soon as practicable, the captain of the batting side of what has occurred.

(iv) Report the occurrence, with the other umpire, as soon as possible to the executive of the batting side and any governing body responsible for the match, who shall take such action as is considered appropriate against the captain and player or players concerned.

15. Bowler attempting to run out non-striker before delivery

The bowler is permitted, before entering his delivery stride, to attempt to run out the non-striker. The ball shall not count in the over.

The umpire shall call and signal "Dead ball" as soon as possible if the bowler fails in the attempt to run out the non-striker.

16. Batsmen stealing a run

It is unfair for the batsmen to attempt to steal a run during the bowler's run-up. Unless the bowler attempts to run out either batsman – see 15 above and Law 24.4 (Bowler throwing towards striker's end before delivery) – the umpire shall:

(i) Call and signal "Dead ball" as soon as the batsmen cross in any such attempt.

(ii) Return the batsmen to their original ends.

(iii) Award five penalty runs to the fielding side. See 17 below.

(iv) Inform the other umpire, the other batsman, the captain of the fielding side and, as soon as practicable, the captain of the batting side of the reason for the action taken.

(v) Report the occurrence, with the other umpire, as soon as possible to the executive of the batting side and any governing body responsible for the match, who shall take such action as is considered appropriate against the captain and player or players concerned.

17. Penalty runs

(a) When penalty runs are awarded to either side, when the ball is dead the umpire shall signal the penalty runs to the scorers as laid down in Law 3.14 (Signals).

(b) Notwithstanding the provisions of Law 21.6 (Winning hit or extras), penalty runs shall be awarded in each case where the Laws require the award. Note, however, that the restrictions on awarding penalty runs in Laws 26.3 (Leg-byes not to be awarded), 34.4(d) (Runs permitted from ball struck lawfully more than once) and Law 41.4 (Penalty runs not to be awarded) will apply.

(c) When five penalty runs are awarded to the batting side, under either Law 2.6 (Player returning without permission) or Law 41 (The fielder) or under 3, 4, 5, 9 or 13 above, then:

(i) They shall be scored as penalty extras and shall be in addition to any other penalties.

(ii) They shall not be regarded as runs scored from either the immediately preceding delivery or the following delivery and shall be in addition to any runs from those deliveries.

(iii) The batsmen shall not change ends solely by reason of the five-run penalty.

(d) When five penalty runs are awarded to the fielding side, under Law 18.5(b) (Deliberate short runs), or under 10, 14 or 16 above, they shall be added as penalty extras to that side's total of runs in its most recently completed innings. If the fielding side has not completed an innings, the five penalty extras shall be added to its next innings.

18. Players' conduct

If there is any breach of the Spirit of the Game by a player failing to comply with the instructions of an umpire, or criticising his decisions by word or action, or showing dissent, or generally behaving in a manner which might bring the game into disrepute, the umpire concerned shall immediately report the matter to the other umpire.

The umpires together shall:

(i) Inform the player's captain of the occurrence, instructing the latter to take action.

(ii) Warn him of the gravity of the offence, and tell him that it will be reported to higher authority.

(iii) Report the occurrence as soon as possible to the executive of the player's team and any governing body responsible for the match, who shall take such action as is considered appropriate against the captain and player or players, and, if appropriate, the team concerned.

REGULATIONS OF THE INTERNATIONAL CRICKET COUNCIL

Extracts

1. Standard playing conditions

In 2001, the ICC Cricket Committee amended its standard playing conditions for all Tests and one-day internationals to include the new Laws of Cricket. The following playing conditions were to apply for three years from September 1, 2001:

Duration of Test Matches

Test matches shall be of five days' scheduled duration and of two innings per side. The two participating countries may:

(a) Provide for a rest day during the match, and/or a reserve day after the scheduled days of play.

(b) Play on any scheduled rest day, conditions and circumstances permitting, should a full day's play be lost on any day prior to the rest day.

(c) Play on any scheduled reserve day, conditions and circumstances permitting, should a full day's play be lost on any day. Play shall not take place on more than five days.

(d) Make up time lost in excess of five minutes in each day's play due to circumstances outside the game, other than acts of God.

Hours of Play and Minimum Overs in the Day in Test Matches

1. Start and cessation times shall be determined by the home board, subject to there being six hours scheduled for play per day (Pakistan a minimum of five and a half hours).

(a) Play shall continue on each day until the completion of a minimum number of overs or until the scheduled cessation time, whichever is the later. The minimum number of overs to be completed, unless an innings ends or an interruption occurs, shall be:

(i) on days other than the last day – a minimum of 90 overs (or a minimum of 15 overs per hour).

(ii) on the last day – a minimum of 75 overs (or 15 overs per hour) for playing time other than the last hour when a minimum of 15 overs shall be bowled. All calculations with regard to suspensions of play or the start of a new innings shall be based on one over for each full four minutes. (Fractions are to be ignored in all calculations except where there is a change of innings in a day's play, when the over in progress at the conclusion shall be rounded up.) If, however, at any time after 30 minutes of the last hour have elapsed both captains (the batsmen at the wicket may act for their captain) accept that there is no prospect of a result to the match, they may agree to cease play at that time.

(iii) Subject to weather and light, except in the last hour of the match, in the event of play being suspended for any reason other than normal intervals, the playing time on that day shall be extended by the amount of time lost up to a maximum of one hour. For the avoidance of doubt, the maximum of one hour shall be inclusive of any time that may have been added to the scheduled playing time due to time having been lost on previous days. The minimum number of overs to be bowled shall be in accordance with the provisions of this clause (i.e. a minimum of 15 overs per hour) and the cessation time shall be rescheduled accordingly.

(iv) If any time is lost and cannot be made up under (a)(iii), additional time of up to a maximum of one hour per day shall be added to the scheduled playing hours for the next day, and subsequent day(s) as required. Where appropriate, the first 30 minutes (or less) of this additional time shall be added before the scheduled start of the first session and the remainder to the last session. Where it is not possible to add this time before the scheduled start, the timing of the lunch and tea intervals will be adjusted to provide a scheduled two-and-a-half-hour session and not affect the start time. On any day's play, except the last day, when the scheduled hours have been completed but the required number of overs have not been bowled, and weather or bad light causes play to be abandoned, the remaining overs shall be made up on the next or subsequent days. On any one day, a maximum of 15 additional overs shall be permitted. When additional time is added to subsequent day(s), no scheduled day's play shall exceed seven hours. The length of each session is subject to Law 15. Timings can be altered at any time on any day if time is lost, not necessarily on that day. The captains, umpires and referee can agree different timings under those circumstances before play starts on any day.

(b) When an innings ends, a minimum number of overs shall be bowled from the start of the new innings. The number of overs to be bowled shall be calculated at the rate of one over for each full four minutes to enable a minimum of 90 overs to be bowled in a day. The last hour of the match shall be excluded from this calculation (see (a) (ii)).

Where a change of innings occurs during a day's play, in the event of the team bowling second being unable to complete its overs by the scheduled cessation time, play shall continue until the required number of overs have been completed.

2. The umpires may decide to play 30 minutes (a minimum eight overs) extra time at the end of any day (other than the last day) if requested by either captain if, in the umpires' opinion, it would bring about a definite result on that day. If the umpires do not believe a result can be achieved, no extra time shall be allowed. If it is decided to play such extra time, the whole period shall be played out even though the possibility of finishing the match may have disappeared before the full period has expired. Only the actual amount of playing time up to the maximum 30 minutes' extra time by which play is extended on any day shall be deducted from the total number of hours of play remaining and the match shall end earlier on the final day by that amount of time.

Use of Lights:

If, in the opinion of the umpires, natural light is deteriorating to an unfit level, they shall authorise the ground authorities to use the available artificial lighting so that the match can continue in acceptable conditions.

The lights are only to be used to enable a full day's play to be completed as provided for in Clause 1 above. In the event of power failure or lights malfunction, the existing provisions of Clause 1 shall apply.

Dangerous and Unfair Bowling: The Bowling of Fast, Short-Pitched Balls: Law 42.6

1. (a) A bowler shall be limited to two fast, short-pitched deliveries per over.

(b) A fast, short-pitched ball is defined as a ball which passes or would have passed above the shoulder height of the striker standing upright at the crease.

(c) The umpire at the bowler's end shall advise the bowler and the batsman on strike when each fast short-pitched ball has been bowled.

(d) For the purpose of this regulation, a ball that passes above head height of the batsman that prevents him from being able to hit it with his bat by means of a normal cricket stroke shall be called a wide.

(e) Any fast, short-pitched delivery called a wide under this condition shall count as one of the allowable short-pitched deliveries in that over.

(f) In the event of a bowler bowling more than two fast, short-pitched deliveries in an over, the umpire at the bowler's end shall call and signal "no-ball" on each occasion. The umpire shall call and signal "no-ball" and then tap the head with the other hand.

(g) If a bowler delivers a third fast, short-pitched ball in one over, the umpire must call no-ball and then invoke the procedures of caution, final warning, action against the bowler and reporting as set out in Law 42.7. The umpires will report the matter to the ICC referee who shall take such action as is considered appropriate against the captain and bowler concerned.

The above Regulation is not a substitute for Law 42.6 (as amended below), which umpires are able to apply at any time:

The bowling of fast, short-pitched balls is unfair if the umpire at the bowler's end considers that, by their repetition and taking into account their length, height and direction, they are likely to inflict physical injury on the striker, irrespective of the protective clothing and equipment he may be wearing. The relative skill of the striker shall also be taken into consideration.

The umpire at the bowler's end shall adopt the procedures of caution, final warning, action against the bowler and reporting as set out in Law 42.7. The ICC referee shall take any further action considered appropriate against the captain and bowler concerned.

New Ball: Law 5.4

The captain of the fielding side shall have the choice of taking a new ball any time after 80 overs have been bowled with the previous ball. The umpires shall indicate to the batsmen and the scorers whenever a new ball is taken into play.

Ball Lost or Becoming Unfit for Play: Law 5.5

The following shall apply in addition to Law 5.5

However, if the ball needs to be replaced after 110 overs for any of the reasons above, it shall be replaced by a new ball. If the ball is to be replaced, the umpires shall inform the batsmen.

Judging a Wide: Law 25.1

Law 25.1 will apply, but in addition

For bowlers attempting to utilise the rough outside a batsman's leg stump, not necessarily as a negative tactic, the strict limited-overs wide interpretation shall be applied. For bowlers whom umpires consider to be bowling down the leg side as a negative tactic, the strict limited-overs wide interpretation shall be applied.

Practice on the Field: Law 17

In addition to Law 17.1:

The use of the square for practice on any day of any match will be restricted to any netted practice area on the square set aside for that purpose.

Fieldsman Leaving the Field: Law 2.5

If a fielder fails to take the field with his side at the start of the match or at any later time, or leaves the field during a session of play, the umpire shall be informed of the reason for his absence, and he shall not thereafter come on to the field during a session without the consent of the umpire. The umpire shall give such consent as soon as practicable. If the player is absent from the field longer than eight minutes, he shall not be permitted to bowl in that innings after his return until he has been on the field for at least that length of playing time for which he was absent. This restriction will, if necessary, be carried over into a new day's play, and in the event of a follow-on or a forfeiture, it will continue into the second innings. Nor shall he be permitted to bat unless or until, in the aggregate, he has returned to the field and/or his side's innings has been in progress for at least that length of playing time for which he has been absent or, if earlier, when his side has lost five wickets. The restrictions shall not apply if he has suffered an external blow (as opposed to an internal injury such as a pulled muscle) while participating earlier in the match and consequently been forced to leave the field, nor if he has been absent for exceptional and acceptable reasons (other than injury or illness).

2. Classification of first-class matches

1. Definitions

A match of three or more days' duration between two sides of 11 players played on natural turf pitches on international standard grounds and substantially conforming with standard playing conditions shall be regarded as a first-class fixture.

2. Rules

(a) Full Members of the ICC shall decide the status of matches of three or more days' duration played in their countries.

(b) In matches of three or more days' duration played in countries which are not Full Members of the ICC, except Kenya (see 2.3 (l) below):

- (i) If the visiting team comes from a country which is a Full Member of the ICC, that country shall decide the status of matches.
- (ii) If the visiting team does not come from a country which is a Full Member of the ICC, or is a Commonwealth team composed of players from different countries, the ICC shall decide the status of matches.

Notes

(a) Governing bodies agree that the interest of first-class cricket will be served by ensuring that first-class status is not accorded to any match in which one or other of the teams taking part cannot on a strict interpretation of the definitions be adjudged first-class.

(b) In case of any disputes arising from these Rules, the Chief Executive of the ICC shall refer the matter for decision to the Council, failing unanimous agreement by postal communication being reached.

3. First-Class Status

The following matches shall be regarded as first-class, subject to the provisions of 2.1 (Definitions) being complied with:

(a) **In Great Britain and Ireland:** (i) County Championship matches. (ii) Official representative tourist matches from Full Member countries unless specifically excluded. (iii) MCC v any first-class county. (iv) Oxford, Cambridge, Durham and Loughborough University Centres of Excellence against first-class counties. (v) Oxford v Cambridge. (vi) Scotland v Ireland.

(b) **In Australia:** (i) Pura Cup matches. (ii) Matches played by Australia A or an Australian XI and teams representing states of the Commonwealth of Australia between each other or against opponents adjudged first-class.

(c) **In Bangladesh:** (i) Matches between Bangladesh and a Full Member. (ii) Matches between Full Member teams adjudged first-class and Bangladesh. (iii) Matches between teams adjudged first-class and a Full Member. (iv) Matches between Bangladesh and Kenya. (v) Matches between teams adjudged first-class and Kenya. (vi) National League three-day matches between the Divisions of Barisal, Chittagong, Dhaka, Khulna, Rajshahi and Sylhet.

(d) **In India:** (i) Ranji Trophy matches. (ii) Duleep Trophy matches. (iii) Irani Trophy matches. (iv) Matches played by teams representing state or regional associations affiliated to the Board of Control between each other or against opponents adjudged first-class. (v) Matches of three days or more against representative visiting sides.

(e) **In New Zealand:** (i) State Championship matches. (ii) Matches played by New Zealand A or major associations affiliated to New Zealand Cricket, between each other or against opponents adjudged first-class.

(f) **In Pakistan:** (i) Quaid-e-Azam Trophy (Grade 1) matches. (ii) Super League four-day games between provincial teams. (iii) Matches played by teams representing cricket associations and departments affiliated to the Pakistan Cricket Board, between each other or against teams adjudged first-class (organised by the PCB). (iv) A-team matches played in Pakistan between Pakistan and other Full Members and Kenya.

(g) **In South Africa:** (i) SuperSport Series four-day matches between Boland, Border, Eastern Province, Easterns, Free State, Gauteng, Griqualand West, KwaZulu-Natal, Northerns, North West, Western Province. (ii) Matches against touring teams from Full Member countries.

(h) **In Sri Lanka:** (i) Matches of three days or more against touring sides adjudged first-class. (ii) Premier League Division I matches played over three or more days for the Premier Trophy. (iii) Matches of three days or more against visiting A teams of Full Member countries by Sri Lanka A or senior development squad teams or BCCSL representative teams (except Under-19 and below).

(i) **In West Indies:** Matches played by teams representing Barbados, Guyana, Jamaica, the Leeward Islands, Trinidad & Tobago and the Windward Islands, either for the Busta Cup or against other opponents adjudged first-class.

(j) **In Zimbabwe:** (i) Logan Cup matches. (ii) Matches played by teams representing associations affiliated to the ZCU, between each other or against opponents adjudged first-class.

(k) **In all Full Member countries represented on the Council:** (i) Test matches and matches against teams adjudged first-class played by official touring teams. (ii) Official Test Trial matches. (iii) Special matches between teams adjudged first-class by the governing body or bodies concerned.

(l) **In Kenya:** (i) Matches between a Full Member and Kenya. (ii) Matches between teams adjudged first-class and Kenya.

3. Classification of Test matches

Any match of not more than five days' scheduled duration played between teams selected by Full Members as representatives of their member countries and accorded the status of Test match by the ICC.

Only Full Members of ICC can participate in Test matches.

4. Classification of one-day international matches

The following shall be classified as one-day internationals:

(a) All matches played in the official World Cup competition, including matches involving Associate Member countries.

(b) All matches played between the Full Member countries of the ICC as part of an official tour itinerary.

(c) All matches played as part of an official tournament between Full Member countries. These need not necessarily be held in a Full Member country.

(d) All matches between the Full Members and Kenya.

Note: Matches involving the A team of a Full Member country shall not be classified as one-day internationals.

5. Player qualification rules for ICC matches, series and competitions

(a) A cricketer is qualified to play in Tests, one-day internationals or any other representative cricket match for an ICC Member country of which he is a national or, in cases of non-nationals, in which he was born, provided that he has not played in Tests, one-day internationals or any other representative cricket match for any other Member country during the four immediately preceding years.

(b) Where the country is an Associate or Affiliate Member, the cricketer must satisfy one or more of the following additional Development Criteria:

(i) he shall have played 50 per cent or more of the scheduled games for his team in a national cricket competition in the relevant Member country in any three of the preceding five years.

(ii) he shall have spent a cumulative total of 100 days or more during the preceding five years coaching, playing or working in the administration or development of cricket in the relevant Member country.

(iii) he shall have played cricket at representative level for the relevant Member country.

(iv) he shall have dedicated a reasonable period of time to activities which, in the opinion of the Chairman of the Cricket Committee, constitute a sufficient demonstration of his genuine commitment to the development of cricket in the relevant Member country.

He must also satisfy the quota requirement for deemed nationals (see below).

(c) A player who has resided for a minimum of 183 days in a Member country in each of the four immediately preceding years shall be a "deemed national" of that country for the purpose of these rules. Affiliate and Associate Members may not field more than two players in any one team who are deemed nationals, but a player who has resided in an Affiliate or Associate Member country for a minimum of 183 days in each of the seven immediately preceding years shall be classified as a national rather than a deemed national of that Member country.

(d) Where an Associate or Affiliate Member country is fielding a team against a Full Member or in any tournament or competition involving teams from one or more Full Members, the requirements relating to having played a representative cricket match for any other Member country during the four immediately preceding years, the Development Criteria and the quota rules shall not apply.

(e) A cricketer qualified to play for a Member country can continue to represent that country without negating his eligibility or interrupting his qualification period for another Member country until he has played for the first Member country at Under-19 level or above.

(f) A cricketer qualified to play for an Associate or Affiliate Member can continue to represent that country without negating his eligibility or interrupting his qualification period for a Full Member country until he has played for the Full Member Country at Under-19 level or above.

(g) Associate and Affiliate Members shall be limited to two players per team who have formerly played Tests, one-day internationals or any other representative cricket match for a Full Member country, except when fielding a team against a Full Member or in any tournament or competition involving teams from one or more Full Members.

Notes: "Representative cricket match" means any cricket match in which a team representing a Member country at Under-19 level or above takes part, including Tests and one-day internationals.

The governing body for cricket of any Member country may impose more stringent qualification rules for that country.

ICC CODE OF CONDUCT

1. Players and/or team officials shall at all times conduct play within the spirit of the game as well as within the Laws of cricket, and the captains are responsible at all times for ensuring that this is adhered to.

2. Players and/or team officials shall at no time engage in conduct unbecoming to their status which could bring them or the game of cricket into disrepute.

3. Players and/or team officials shall be required to report to the captain and/or team manager or to a senior board official or to the Anti-Corruption and Security Unit any approach made to them by a bookmaker or any other corrupt approach or knowledge of such approach made to any other player or team official.

4. Players and/or team officials shall not bet on matches nor otherwise engage in any conduct of the nature described in the paragraphs below. For conduct in breach of this rule, the penalties to be considered are set out below, for individuals who have:

i. Bet on any match or series of matches, or on any connected event, in which such player, umpire, referee, team official or administrator took part or in which the Member country or any such individual was represented (penalty (a));

ii. Induced or encouraged any other person to bet on any match or series of matches or on any connected event or to offer the facility for such bets to be placed (penalty (b));

iii. Gambled or entered into any other form of financial speculation on any match or on any connected event (penalty (a));

iv. Induced or encouraged any other person to gamble or enter into any other form of financial speculation on any match or any connected event (penalty (b));

v. Was a party to contriving or attempting to contrive the result of any match or the occurrence of any connected event (penalty (c));

vi. Failed to perform on his merits in any match owing to an arrangement relating to betting on the outcome of any match or on the occurrence of any connected event (penalty (c));

vii. Induced or encouraged any other player not to perform on his merits in any match owing to any such arrangement (penalty (c));

viii. Received from another person any money, benefit or other reward (whether financial or otherwise) for the provision of any information concerning the weather, the teams, the state of the ground, the status of, or the outcome of, any match or the occurrence of any connected event unless such information has been provided to a newspaper or other form of media in accordance with an obligation entered into in the normal course and disclosed in advance to the cricket authority of the relevant Member country (penalty (b));

ix. Received any money, benefit or other reward (whether financial or otherwise) which could bring him or the game of cricket into disrepute (penalty (d));

x. Provided any money, benefit or other reward (whether financial or otherwise) which could bring the game of cricket into disrepute (penalty (d));

xi. Received any approaches from another person to engage in conduct such as that described above, and has failed to disclose the same to his captain or team manager, or to a senior board official or to the Anti-Corruption and Security Unit (penalty (e)); or

xii. Is aware that any other player or individual has engaged in conduct, or received approaches, such as described above, and has failed to disclose the same to his captain or team manager, or to a senior board official or to the Anti-Corruption and Security Unit (penalty (e));

xiii. Has received or is aware that any other person has received threats of any nature which might induce him to engage in conduct, or acquiesce in any proposal made by an approach, such as described above, and has failed to disclose the same to his captain or team manager, or to a senior board official or to the Anti-Corruption and Security Unit (penalty (e));.

xiv. Has engaged in any conduct which, in the opinion of the Executive Board, relates directly or indirectly to any of the above paragraphs (i to xiii) and is prejudicial to the interests of the game of cricket (penalty (e)).

Penalties:

(a) Ban for a minimum of two years and a maximum of five years. In addition, a fine may be imposed, the amount to be assessed in the circumstances.

(b) Ban for a minimum of two years and a maximum of five years if a bet was placed directly or indirectly for the benefit of the individual; otherwise, a ban for a minimum of 12 months. In addition, a fine may be imposed, the amount to be assessed in the circumstances.

(c) Ban for life (a minimum of 20 years).

(d) Ban for a minimum of two years and a maximum of life. In addition, a fine may be imposed, the amount to be assessed in the circumstances.

(e) Ban for a minimum of one year and a maximum of five years. In addition, a fine may be imposed, the amount to be assessed in the circumstances.

5. A valid defence may be made to a charge in respect of any prohibited conduct in paragraphs 4 (xi) to (xiii) above if a person proves that this conduct was the result of an honest and reasonable belief that there was a serious threat to the life or safety of himself or any member of his family.

6. Players and/or team officials shall not use or in any way be concerned in the use or distribution of illegal drugs. Illegal drugs shall mean those drugs which are classified as unlawful in the player's or team official's home country or in the country in which he is touring. Any such conduct shall constitute behaviour prohibited under paragraph 2 and shall be dealt with as such. Players and team officials shall also be subject to any doping policy which is applied by their home board and such policies which are introduced for ICC events. Any breach of such doping policy shall be dealt with under the terms of such policy itself and not under this code.

CRIME AND PUNISHMENT

ICC Code of Conduct – Breaches and Penalties in 2002-03 to 2003-04

G. W. Flower Zimbabwe v Pakistan, one-day international at Harare.
Obscene language and signalling to batsman to leave the field. Fined 50% of match fee and warned by C. H. Lloyd.

M. A. Butcher Australia v England, 3rd Test at Perth.
Dislodged the bails with his bat after given lbw. Fined 20% of match fee and reprimanded by Wasim Raja.

Shoaib Akhtar Zimbabwe v Pakistan, 1st Test at Harare.
Ball-tampering. Severely reprimanded by C. H. Lloyd.

Shoaib Akhtar Zimbabwe v Pakistan, one-day international at Harare.
Obscene gesture to crowd. Fined 50% of match fee and banned for one one-day international by C. H. Lloyd.

A. R. Caddick Australia v England, 4th Test at Melbourne.
Offensive gesture to the crowd after a no-ball. Reprimanded by Wasim Raja.

A. C. Gilchrist Australia v England, 5th Test at Sydney.
Dissent when appeal turned down. Reprimanded by Wasim Raja.

M. L. Hayden Australia v England, 5th Test at Sydney.
Broke glass in dressing-room door after given out. Fined 20% of match fee and warned by Wasim Raja.

D. S. Lehmann Australia v Sri Lanka, one-day international at Brisbane.
Heard to shout a racially offensive remark on return to the dressing-room when out. Banned for five one-day internationals by C. H. Lloyd.

Harbhajan Singh India v South Africa, one-day international at Dhaka.
Foul and abusive language to the umpire. Fined 50% of match fee by C. H. Lloyd.

Khaled Mahmud Bangladesh v South Africa, 2nd Test at Chittagong.
Inappropriate comments to a newspaper about match officials. Fined 50% of match fee by C. H. Lloyd.

R. A. P. Nissanka Sri Lanka v Pakistan, one-day international at Dambulla.
Dissent at umpire's decision. Fined 20% of match fee by G. R. Viswanath.

Shoaib Akhtar Pakistan v New Zealand, one-day international at Dambulla.
Ball-tampering. Fined 75% of match fee and banned for two one-day internationals by G. R. Viswanath.

Rashid Latif Pakistan v Bangladesh, 3rd Test at Multan.
Claimed catch after letting it touch ground. Banned for five one-day internationals by M. J. Procter.

A. J. Hall Pakistan v South Africa, one-day international at Lahore.
Inappropriate and deliberate contact with Yousuf Youhana; also speaking and behaving in aggressive and threatening manner. Banned for one one-day international plus two Tests by C. H. Lloyd.

G. C. Smith Pakistan v South Africa, one-day international at Lahore.
Obscene and offensive language. Fined 50% of match fee and banned for one one-day international by C. H. Lloyd.

Yousuf Youhana Pakistan v South Africa, one-day international at Lahore.
Raising bat to A. J. Hall during altercation. Fined 50% of match fee by C. H. Lloyd.

S. M. Pollock Pakistan v South Africa, one-day international at Faisalabad.
Dissent at umpire's decision. Fined 100% of match fee by C. H. Lloyd.

Shoaib Akhtar Pakistan v South Africa, 1st Test at Lahore.
Obscene and offensive language to P. R. Adams. Banned for one Test and two one-day internationals by C. H. Lloyd (His second breach on this count within 12 months meant the penalty was upgraded from Level 2 to Level 3).

R. Clarke Bangladesh v England, 1st Test at Dhaka.
Obscene, offensive and generally insulting language to Mushfiqur Rahman. Fined 50% of match fee by Wasim Raja.

Mohammad Rafiq Bangladesh v England, 2nd Test at Chittagong.
Pointed towards pavilion in aggressive manner after dismissing M. A. Butcher. Fined 50% of match fee and officially reprimanded by Wasim Raja.

S. B. Styris India v New Zealand, one-day international at Cuttack.
Shook head and used foul language when dismissed lbw. Fined 100% of match fee and officially reprimanded by R. S. Madugalle.

REGULATIONS FOR FIRST-CLASS MATCHES IN BRITAIN, 2003

Hours of play

1st, 2nd [and 3rd in 4-day matches] days. . . 11.00 a.m. to 6.30 p.m.
Final day . . . . 11.00 a.m. to 6.00 p.m.

Intervals

Lunch: 1.15 p.m. to 1.55 p.m. (1st, 2nd [3rd] days)
1.00 p.m. to 1.40 p.m. (final day)
Where an innings concludes or there is a break in play within ten minutes of the scheduled lunch interval, the interval will commence at that time and be limited to 40 minutes.

Tea: (Championship matches) A tea interval of 20 minutes shall normally be taken at 4.10 p.m. (3.40 p.m. on final day), or at the conclusion of the over in progress at that time, provided 32 overs or less remain to be bowled (except on the final day). The over in progress shall be completed unless a batsman is out or retires either within two minutes of, or after, the scheduled time for the interval. In the event of more than 32 overs remaining, the tea interval will be delayed.

If an innings ends or there is a stoppage caused by weather within 30 minutes of the scheduled time, the tea interval shall be taken immediately. There will be no tea interval if the scheduled timing for the cessation of play is earlier than 5.30 p.m.

(Other matches) 4.10 p.m. to 4.30 p.m. (1st, 2nd [3rd] days), 3.40 p.m. to 4.00 p.m. (final day).

Note: The hours of play, including intervals, are brought forward by half an hour for matches scheduled to start in September.

(i) Play shall continue on each day until the completion of a minimum number of overs or until the scheduled cessation time, whichever is the later. The minimum number of overs, unless an innings ends or an interruption occurs, shall be 104 (98 in tourist matches) on days other than the last day, and 80 (75) on the last day before the last hour.

(ii) Where there is a change of innings during a day's play (except during an interval or suspension of play or exceptional circumstances or during the last hour of domestic matches), two overs will be deducted from the minimum number, plus any over in progress at the end of the completed innings (in domestic matches).

(iii) If interruptions for weather or light occur, other than in the last hour of the match, the minimum number of overs shall be reduced by one over for each full 3¾ minutes (four minutes in tourist matches) of the aggregate playing time lost.

(iv) On the last day, if any of the minimum of 80 (75) overs, or as recalculated, have not been bowled when one hour of scheduled playing time remains, the last hour of the match shall be the hour immediately following the completion of those overs.

(v) Law 16.6, 16.7 and 16.8 will apply except that a minimum of 16 six-ball overs (15 in tourist matches) shall be bowled in the last hour, and all calculations with regard to suspensions of play or the start of a new innings shall be based on one over for each full 3¾ (four) minutes. If, however, at 5.30 p.m. both captains accept that there is no prospect of a result or (in Championship games) of either side gaining any further first-innings bonus points, they may agree to cease play at that time or at any time after 5.30 p.m.

(vi) (Domestic matches). The captains may agree or, in the event of disagreement, the umpires may decide to play 30 minutes (a minimum eight overs) extra time at the end of any day other than the last day if, in their opinion, it would bring about a definite result on that day. The whole period shall be played out even though the possibility of finishing the match may have disappeared before the full period has expired. The time by which play is extended on any day shall be deducted from the total number of hours remaining, and the match shall end earlier on the last day by the amount of time by which play was extended. If there is a change of innings immediately prior to the start of, or during the period of extra time, then two overs shall be deducted.

(vii) Notwithstanding any other provision, there shall be no further play on any day, other than the last day, if a wicket falls or a batsman retires, or if the players leave the field during the last minimum over within two minutes of the scheduled cessation time or thereafter.

(viii) An over completed on resumption of a new day's play shall be disregarded in calculating minimum overs for that day.

(ix) The scoreboard shall show the total number of overs bowled with the ball in use and the minimum number remaining to be bowled in a day. In Championship matches, it shall show the number of overs up to 130 in each side's first innings and subsequently the number bowled with the current ball, and the minimum remaining to be bowled. In addition it shall indicate the number of overs that the fielding side is ahead of or behind the over-rate.

Substitutes

(Domestic matches only) Law 2.1 will apply, but in addition:

No substitute may take the field until the player for whom he is to substitute has been absent from the field for five consecutive complete overs, with the exception that if a fieldsman sustains an obvious, serious injury or is taken ill, a substitute shall be allowed immediately. In the event of any disagreement between the two sides as to the authenticity of an injury or illness, the umpires shall adjudicate. A substitute shall be allowed immediately for all head or blood injuries. If a player leaves the field during an over, the remainder of that over shall not count in the calculation of the five complete overs.

The umpires shall have discretion, for other wholly acceptable reasons, to allow a substitute for a fielder, or a runner for a batsman, at the start of the match or at any subsequent time subject to consent being given by the opposing captain.

A substitute shall not be allowed to bat or bowl, or to act as captain. The opposing captain shall have no right of objection to any player acting as substitute, or to where the substitute shall field, with the exception of the position of wicket-keeper. However, with the agreement of both captains (not to be unreasonably withheld), any substitute may act as wicket-keeper. In the event of the captains' disagreement, the substitute shall not be allowed to act as wicket-keeper.

A substitute shall be allowed by right immediately in the event of a cricketer currently playing in a Championship match being required to join the England team for a Test match (or one-day international). Such a substitute may be permitted to bat or bowl in that match, subject to the approval of the ECB. If the cricketer substituted is batting at the time, he shall retire "not out" and his substitute may be permitted to bat later in that innings subject to the approval of the ECB. If the cricketer is subsequently not required by England then, subject to the approval of the ECB, he may return and resume a full part in the match, taking over from the player that substituted for him. If the substitute is batting, he shall complete his innings and the cricketer shall take over thereafter. If the substitute is bowling when the cricketer is ready to take the field, the substitute shall complete any unfinished over and the cricketer shall take the field thereafter.

If a player is released by England prior to the teams being named in his county match, his county may have a fielding-only substitute until the cricketer is able to join the Championship team. If a player is released by England after the teams have been named in his county match, then he may return to that match and take the place of a nominated player, who may or may not have already participated. Each county that has representation in the England squad must, if it wishes that a specified England player shall participate in a Championship match if released, specify which player will be replaced. This shall be done at the nomination of the teams to the umpires.

If the England player is released, then he must make all reasonable efforts to take his place in the county side at the earliest opportunity. No replacement will be allowed if the England player is not available to take his place in the county side until after the start of play on the third scheduled day. There is no option for the county to refuse the England player if they have nominated a player to be replaced.

If the nominated player is batting, he shall complete his innings and the England player shall take over thereafter. If the nominated player is bowling when the England player is ready to take the field, then the nominated player shall complete any unfinished over, and the England player shall take the field thereafter.

Fieldsman leaving the field

ICC regulations apply (see page 1507) but, in domestic matches, it is explained that "external blow" should include, but not be restricted to, collisions with boundary boards, clashes of heads, heavy falls etc and, in the case of "exceptional and acceptable reasons", consent for a substitute must be granted by the opposing captain.

New ball

The captain of the fielding side shall have the choice of taking the new ball after 90 overs (80 in tourist matches) have been bowled with the old one.

Covering of pitches and surrounding areas

The whole pitch shall be covered:

(a) The night before the match and, if necessary, until the first ball is bowled; and whenever necessary and possible at any time prior to that during the preparation of the pitch.

(b) On each night of the match and, if necessary, throughout any rest days.

(c) In the event of play being suspended on account of bad light or rain, during the specified hours of play.

The bowler's run-up shall be covered to a distance of at least ten yards, with a width of four yards, as will the areas 20 feet either side of the length of the pitch.

Declarations

Law 14 will apply, but if, due to weather conditions, play in a County Championship match has not started when less than eight hours' playing time remains, the first innings of each side shall automatically be forfeited and a one-innings match played.

MEETINGS AND DECISIONS, 2003

ICC TECHNICAL COMMITTEE

On February 6, the ICC Technical Committee declined a request from the ECB to reschedule England's World Cup match at Harare against Zimbabwe, due to take place on February 13. The ECB were concerned about the safety and security of their players, but the five-man Committee unanimously rejected the request. Two days later, the ICC Appeals Commissioner, Justice Albie Sachs, rejected the ECB's appeal, saying there were "neither procedural nor substantive grounds for overturning the decision". On February 11, the ECB announced that England would not be fulfilling the fixture because of safety concerns. On February 15, the Technical Committee awarded the full four points for the match to Zimbabwe.

ICC EXECUTIVE BOARD RULING

On February 20, the ICC decided not to reschedule the World Cup game between Kenya and New Zealand in Nairobi, due to be played the following day, and awarded the four points to Kenya. New Zealand Cricket had said on January 31 their team would not play in Nairobi because of security concerns.

ICC EXECUTIVE BOARD MEETING

At its meeting in Johannesburg on March 22, the ICC, anticipating compensation claims by its commercial partner, the Global Cricket Corporation, agreed to withhold distribution of some funds from the World Cup. It was agreed that India's full share of World Cup revenue – between $8m and $9m – would be withheld, in accordance with a decision made at the start of the competition, because of the refusal of India's players to sign the original tournament contracts. A total of $3.5m would be withheld from England, for its decision not to play in Zimbabwe; of $2.5m from New Zealand, for not playing in Kenya; and of $500,000 from Sri Lanka, for failing to meet the deadline for completion of its player contracts.

The board also agreed to a structured two-year programme to help Kenya achieve Full Member status. This included extra funding of $500,000 a year to the Kenya Cricket Association. The board accepted the recommendation of Michael Beloff QC, the Chairman of the ICC Code of Conduct Commission, that the following matters be considered closed: the Elliott Mottley Enquiry into allegations against Brian Lara; the United Arab Emirates Cricket Board Enquiry; and the ICC Anti-Corruption Unit Report on Asif Iqbal. The adoption of a new format for the ICC Test Championship, to start in June, was agreed.

ECB FIRST-CLASS FORUM

On April 1, it was agreed that a reduction of £4m would be made from the ECB's budgeted expenditure for 2003 – a direct consequence of the ECB's decision to withdraw England from their World Cup game in Zimbabwe.

ICC ELITE UMPIRES PANEL

On April 4, the ICC promoted three umpires to its elite panel, taking the number of elite umpires to 11. The three were: Billy Bowden of New Zealand, and Darrell Hair and Simon Taufel, both of Australia.

PCA ANNUAL GENERAL MEETING

On April 15, the Professional Cricketers' Association held its AGM at Edgbaston, where its members agreed two objectives: a reduction to one overseas player per county, and the presence of at least eight England-qualified players per side in any county match. The PCA also announced the formation of a new Cricket Advisory Group (CAG), comprising 14 senior county cricketers.

ENGLAND SUMMER CONTRACTS

Six-month summer contracts for the 2003 domestic season were awarded by the ECB to James Anderson and Steve Harmison on April 30. Anderson and Harmison joined nine other players already in possession of 12-month contracts: Nasser Hussain, Mark Butcher, Andrew Caddick, Andrew Flintoff, Ashley Giles, Matthew Hoggard, Alec Stewart, Marcus Trescothick and Michael Vaughan.

MCC ANNUAL GENERAL MEETING

The 216th AGM of the Marylebone Cricket Club was held on May 7, with the president, Sir Tim Rice, in the chair. He announced that his successor in October would be Charles Fry, formerly of Oxford University, Hampshire and Northamptonshire, and the grandson of C. B. Fry. The meeting discussed MCC's continuing membership of the ECB and other administrative issues. Membership of the club on December 31, 2002, totalled 21,903, made up of 17,749 full members, 3,629 associate members, 290 honorary members, 187 senior members and 48 out-match members. In 2002, 485 vacancies arose. Immediately after the AGM, a Special General Meeting was held to approve changes to the 2000 Code of the Laws of Cricket.

ECB MANAGEMENT BOARD

At its meeting on June 12, the ECB Management Board decided that the England coach, Duncan Fletcher, should report directly to the ECB's Director of Cricket Operations, John Carr, rather than to the chief executive. This was in line with a recommendation by Dennis Amiss, the chairman of the International Teams Management Group. Fletcher's role as manager (in addition to his position as head coach) was reinforced by the rejection of a new tour manager position.

ICC PRESIDENT

On June 19, Ehsan Mani was confirmed as the new President of the ICC for a two-year term. Mani, a 58-year-old Rawalpindi-born UK resident, replaced Malcolm Gray, who had been in office for three years. In a speech delivered at the ICC Cricket Business Forum at Lord's on the same date, the Chief Executive, Malcolm Speed, announced that the ICC would carry out a comprehensive review of the structure of international cricket. Six new member countries were admitted to the ICC: Zambia as associate members; Iran, Malawi, Mozambique, Rwanda and Saudi Arabia as affiliate members. ICC member countries now numbered 89.

ICC CRICKET COMMITTEE – MANAGEMENT

At their meeting on September 18–19 in Mumbai, the ICC Cricket Committee – Management (comprising national chief executives) confirmed that cricketing ties between India and Pakistan remained a bilateral issue between the two countries. The Committee also confirmed that it would continue planning for an ICC Super Series in

2005, probably in South Africa. The Series would consist of a Test match between the top-ranked Test side and a Rest of the World team, and a three-match one-day series between the top-ranked one-day side and a Rest of the World team. The Committee agreed to appoint a High-Performance Manager for umpires, as well as two additional Umpire Assessors to assist in the training and development of elite umpires.

ICC EXECUTIVE BOARD

On October 31, the ICC Executive Board, meeting in Barbados, adopted a new protocol to govern the cancellation of bilateral tours. It was agreed to set up a panel of security experts, who would, if asked by the board of any country, provide a report on the safety and security aspects of a particular tour. The ICC also introduced a new consultation period, during which any country considering cancelling a tour would have to consult the host board and the ICC before reaching a decision.

The board agreed to recognise the Federation of International Cricket Associations and any other players' association that is recognised by its home board. It was also decided not to return any money that had been withheld to deal with the claim for compensation from the Global Cricket Corporation until a series of strict conditions had been met. These conditions included countries agreeing to pay the money back if required.

ICC WORLD CUP 2007

The ICC announced on November 28 that the World Cup in the West Indies in 2007 would contain 16 teams, two more than in 2003, but 51 games, three fewer. After a first round involving four groups of four teams, the second round would contain eight sides – the top two from each of the first-round groups – playing six games each in a round-robin format. No team would play against the side it met in the first round, although points from this game would be carried forward into the second. The top four sides following the round-robin matches would qualify for the semi-finals.

Opposite: The latest from HQ.
Henry Blofeld commentates from Lord's
for *Test Match Special.*
Picture by Patrick Eagar.

PART EIGHT

The Wisden Review

CHRONICLE OF 2003

JANUARY

2 In Cape Town Test against Pakistan, Herschelle Gibbs and Graeme Smith put on 368, then a South African record for any wicket. **3** Steve Waugh hits memorable hundred in Sydney Ashes Test and becomes third man to 10,000 Test runs. **5** South Africa take series v Pakistan 2–0 and go top of ICC Test Championship. **6** England win Sydney Test, but lose eighth successive Ashes series, 4–1. **18** Darren Lehmann banned for five one-day internationals for racial abuse. **22** Shane Warne announces one-day retirement following World Cup **30** ICC confirm they will not relocate any World Cup matches. **31** New Zealand withdraw from their match in Kenya.

FEBRUARY

4 England call for relocation of their World Cup tie in Zimbabwe because of security fears. **6** World Cup technical committee refuse ECB's request. **9** World Cup opens in Johannesburg with exciting West Indies win over South Africa. **10** Andy Flower and Henry Olonga make protest against "death of democracy" in Zimbabwe. **11** Warne sent home after testing positive for diuretics. ECB announce decision not to travel to Harare; ICC say England will forfeit points. Canada record first-ever one-day international victory, by 60 runs over Bangladesh. **19** Sri Lanka bowl Canada out for 36, the lowest total in a one-day international. **22 Shane Warne banned for 12 months after positive drugs test.** Shoaib Akhtar bowls first officially recorded 100mph delivery, to Nick Knight of England. **23** Canada's John Davison hits the fastest World Cup hundred – 67 balls against West Indies. **24** Kenya beat Sri Lanka, one of the biggest upsets in World Cup history. **25** Wasim Akram becomes first bowler to 500 wickets in one-day internationals. **27** Australia beat Namibia by 256 runs – the biggest margin in one-day international history; Glenn McGrath records World Cup's best-ever figures, seven for 15.

MARCH

1 India and Pakistan meet for first time since June 2000; India win by six wickets. Kenya beat Bangladesh and reach Super Six. **2** England lose 14th successive one-day international to Australia. **3** Main hosts South Africa eliminated from World Cup after tied match with Sri Lanka. **4** England and Pakistan eliminated after Zimbabwe v Pakistan rained off: Zimbabwe through. Nasser Hussain resigns as England one-day captain. West Indies also go out. **8** Allan Donald retires from international cricket. **12** Kenya beat Zimbabwe and reach semi-finals. **15** Olonga announces international retirement. Shaun Pollock sacked as South Africa captain. **16** Graeme Smith named as Pollock's replacement. **18** Australia reach their third consecutive World Cup final after beating Sri Lanka. **19** Pakistan appoint Rashid Latif as captain and Javed Miandad as coach. **20** India reach final after beating Kenya. **22** ICC announce they will withhold over £2m from England because of Harare boycott. **23 Australia beat India by 125 runs and win World Cup**; Australia's 359 is their highest-ever one-day total. **29** Khaled Mahmud named new Bangladesh captain. **31** Brian Lara replaces Carl Hooper as West Indies captain. Sri Lanka announce that Dav Whatmore will be released as coach in May.

APRIL

10 In Guyana, Steve Waugh makes a world-record 157th Test appearance; Shivnarine Chanderpaul hits third-fastest Test hundred – in 69 balls. Phil Tufnell retires, to take part in celebrity TV show. **11** Sanath Jayasuriya stands down as Sri Lanka captain.

14 Michael Vaughan becomes first Englishman since Graham Gooch in 1993 to top Test batting ratings. **17** Sri Lanka appoint Hashan Tillekeratne Test captain and Marvan Atapattu one-day captain. **20** Whatmore appointed Bangladesh coach. **23** Australia win Trinidad Test, go 2–0 up and retain Frank Worrell Trophy. Warne offered ACB contract for 2003-04, despite drugs ban. **26** In First Test at Chittagong, debutant Jacques Rudolph and Boeta Dippenaar put on South African record 439, beating 368 by Gibbs and Smith in January.

MAY

1 In Bridgetown, Ricky Ponting hits his third hundred in successive Tests. **4** Scotland beat Durham in their first-ever National League game. **5** Jermaine Lawson completes hat-trick in Bridgetown but Australia win to go 3–0 up. **6** Vaughan appointed England's one-day captain. **13** In Antigua, West Indies complete the biggest successful fourth-innings run-chase in Test history, making 418 to win final Test; Australia win series 3–1. **17** At Hove, floodlights used for first time in first-class cricket in England. **18** Wasim Akram announces international retirement. **24** At Lord's, James Anderson takes five for 73 on Test debut as England beat Zimbabwe by innings and 92 runs. In Trinidad, Australia win 21st successive one-day international.

JUNE

5 Chester-le-Street becomes England's first new Test venue in 101 years. **7** England again beat Zimbabwe by an innings, to clinch series 2–0. **13** First Twenty20 Cup matches played, watched by large crowds. Ireland beat Zimbabwe by ten wickets. **19** Ehsan Mani succeeds Malcolm Gray as ICC President. **20** At The Oval against Pakistan, Anderson takes England's first one-day hat-trick. **29** Surrey's Mark Ramprakash becomes first to hit first-class hundreds against all 18 counties.

JULY

3 New Zealand appoint John Bracewell as coach. **12** At Lord's, England thrash South Africa to win one-day NatWest Series. **14** John Dyson appointed Sri Lanka coach. **16** Gus Logie appointed West Indies coach. **19** Surrey win inaugural Twenty20 Cup at a packed Trent Bridge. **20** Steve Waugh beats Clive Lloyd's record of 36 wins as a Test captain. **22** Alec Stewart announces retirement from international cricket at end of England's forthcoming series v South Africa. **26** In First Test at Edgbaston, Graeme Smith hits 277, a South African Test record. **27** Steve Waugh becomes first man to score 150 against nine Test teams. **28** England draw at Edgbaston; **Nasser Hussain resigns as England captain**, Vaughan replaces him.

AUGUST

2 At Lord's, Smith hits a double-hundred for second successive Test; South Africa reach their highest Test score – 682 for six. **3** England lose by an innings and 92. **5** Darren Gough retires from Tests. **15** Saeed Anwar retires. **18** At Trent Bridge, England square series at 1–1. **22** England women win their first Test for nearly eight years and take series against South Africa 1–0. **24** Yasir Hameed hits second century on debut for Pakistan, against Bangladesh. **25** England lose Fourth Test by 191 runs and go 2–1 down in the series. **30** Despite Bangladesh taking their first-ever first-innings lead, Pakistan win Second Test in Peshawar. Gloucestershire win C&G Trophy.

SEPTEMBER

4 Jonty Rhodes announces retirement from first-class cricket at end of English season. **6** In Multan Test, Bangladesh come within one wicket of first-ever win; instead Pakistan complete a 3–0 series victory, their first at home since 1997. **7** Pakistan captain Rashid Latif is banned for five one-day internationals for knowingly claiming a dropped catch during Multan Test. **8** At The Oval, England become seventh Test team to concede more than 450 in first innings and still win; their series against South Africa ends 2–2. **12** Robin Smith announces retirement. **14** Surrey win the National League. **15** Stewart announces first-class retirement. **17** Mushtaq Ahmed of Sussex becomes first man since 1998 to take 100 Championship wickets. **18** Sussex win their first-ever County Championship. **19** Mike Kasprowicz becomes first since Jim Laker in 1956 to take nine wickets in an innings twice in English season. **20** South Africa pull out of scheduled tour of Pakistan after bomb blast in Karachi. **23** South Africa accept revised tour itinerary. **24** Rashid Latif resigns as Pakistan captain. **25** Inzamam-ul-Haq replaces him. **26** England sponsors Vodafone call the prospect of England touring Zimbabwe in autumn 2004 "abhorrent".

OCTOBER

10 Matthew Hayden makes highest score in Test history – 380 against Zimbabwe in Perth, passing Lara's 375. **11** South African captain Graeme Smith is banned for one one-day international after clashing with Yousuf Youhana in a one-day game in Lahore. Andrew Hall also banned. **22** Indian government renew sporting ties with Pakistan. **25** In Dhaka, England win their inaugural Test against Bangladesh, by seven wickets. **31** World's oldest surviving Test cricketer, "Dad" Weir of New Zealand, dies aged 95.

NOVEMBER

13 In Bulawayo, Lara passes Viv Richards as West Indies' highest Test run-scorer. **14** Official opening of ECB Academy in Loughborough. **26** Steve Waugh announces retirement from international cricket after forthcoming series v India. **27** Ponting named as his successor. Keith Medlycott, who coached Surrey to seven major trophies in six years, resigns. **29** In Harare, Fidel Edwards takes six for 22 for West Indies, the best figures by a debutant in one-day internationals.

DECEMBER

1 Tauqir Zia resigns as chairman of Pakistan Cricket Board. Yorkshire appoint ex-captain David Byas as director of cricket. **6** England's last-wicket pair hold out to draw First Test against Sri Lanka in Galle; Muralitharan takes ten wickets in match for 12th time. **8** In Brisbane, first Australia–India Test ends in rain-blighted draw. **13** In Second Test in Adelaide, Ponting hits 242. **14** Dravid and Laxman put on 303 in reply. In Kandy, England sneak draw for second Test running. Lara hits Test-record 28 from one Robin Peterson over during First Test in Johannesburg. **16** In Adelaide, India win after conceding 556 in the first innings. Despite 202 from Lara, West Indies lose First Test. **21** England lose by an innings and 215 in Colombo, their heaviest Test defeat since 1973, Sri Lanka's biggest-ever win; Sri Lanka win series 1–0. World's oldest surviving Test cricketer, M. J. Gopalan of India, dies aged 94. **28** Ponting hits 257 during Third Test at Melbourne, becoming fifth batsman to hit double-hundreds in successive Tests. **29** In Second Test at Wellington, Pakistan take New Zealand's last seven wickets for eight runs. **30** Pakistan win to take series 1–0. Australia level series at 1–1. **31** Ponting ends 2003 as highest Test run-scorer of the year, South Africa's Makhaya Ntini as leading wicket-taker.

The following stories were also reported in the media during 2003:

The newest status symbols at the Sydney Ashes Test were "beer wenches", girls wearing hot pants and tight T-shirts hired for $A65 an hour to fetch the beers for groups of (male) spectators. "It's not too bad for the girls, they do get jostled and harassed a bit, but there are worse ways to spend your day," said a spokesman for their agency, Sex Bomb Promotions. (*Daily Telegraph*, Sydney, January 7)

A promising teenage cricketer was stabbed to death by fellow-students at Faridabad, near Delhi. Ajay Khurana, 16, a fast bowler hailed as "Faridabad's cricketing hope", was killed, apparently after a dispute involving a girl. Police arrested six "delinquents". (*Hindustan Times*, January 11)

An Australian judge rejected an attempt by a Sri Lankan-born Australian to stop umpire Darrell Hair officiating in games involving Muttiah Muralitharan. Viji De Alwis claimed Hair was biased against Muralitharan because he described the spinner's action as diabolical in his autobiography. De Alwis said Hair breached the disability discrimination provisions of the Human Rights and Equal Opportunity Act by no-balling the spinner during Sri Lanka's 1995-96 tour of Australia. Judge Robert French declared the matter "nonsensical" and "an utter waste of time". (*The Australian*, January 16)

During his televised induction into the Australian Cricket Hall of Fame, former Australian captain Ian Chappell said that Dick-a-Dick, Bullocky and other members of the Aboriginal team that toured England in 1868 should also be included. (*Sydney Morning Herald*, January 28)

Aamir Khan, who acted in and produced the Oscar-nominated film *Lagaan*, received a CEAT Cricket Award from Kapil Dev in Mumbai in recognition of the film's contribution to global promotion of the game. (*Asian Age*, January 30)

Ten promising Bangladeshi cricketers, all members of the Feringee Bazaar Masters Society team, were killed on their way to a tournament when their overloaded three-wheeled vehicle was involved in a head-on collision near Chittagong. (*The Independent*, Bangladesh, Feb 1)

Muslim militants arrested in Jammu, northern India, were found to have concealed cash, a wireless handset and 120 bullets inside cricket bats. (Associated Press, February 2)

Mudassar Sultan from Lahore, who was leading 22 Pakistani pilgrims on the haj to Mecca, carried a cricket bat aloft as identification to help the group stay together. "There are so many flags here and bamboo sticks with slippers or other objects tied on that I was searching for something unusual," he said. "Not surprisingly, pilgrims notice the bat and can often point out our direction." (Al-Jazeerah, February 13)

Former England women's captain Rachael Heyhoe-Flint was awarded an honorary doctorate of science by the University of Greenwich, where she studied. (University of Greenwich press release, February 15)

Simon Williams hit 40 and 28 in consecutive overs from the same (unnamed) bowler – the 40 comprised six sixes plus a four off a no-ball. Williams, who scored 100, was playing for Werribee South against Wyndhamvale in the Williamstown and District competition, Victoria. (*Herald Sun*, Melbourne, March 4)

Eleven people were arrested as police sought to quell mobs with tear gas following a riot stirred by a stray ball. Playing cricket in the road in Gomitpur near Ahmedabad, a boy hit one shot into an adjacent temple, whereupon those praying refused to return the ball, prompting the boys to throw missiles and set fire to two houses, two cars and a shop. (*Gujarat Samachar*, March 21)

Ramanlal Pathak, a Sanskrit scholar from Vadodara, India, has spent seven years assembling a cricket vocabulary to freshen the appeal of "a dying language". A batsman is *bat-dhar*, runs translate to *gaccha* or *dhavan*. *Pashya pashya chowka* means "another glorious shot for four", whereas "another four: the crowd is ecstatic" is *sahatu chowkra – sarvatra prekshaka mandalie anandasya vatavaranam*. (*Times of India*, March 22)

A 13-year-old Kandy schoolboy, Sachith Pathirana, scored 235 not out for Central Province against Uva Province in an Under-14 match. He reached his double-century in 88 balls, using a bat and gloves given to him by Sanath Jayasuriya, a friend of his family. (*Daily Mirror*, Colombo, March 27)

The first Steve Waugh medal for the outstanding New South Wales player of the season was won by – Steve Waugh. (*Sydney Morning Herald*, March 29)

On the eve of his marriage to Danielle Spencer, the actor Russell Crowe staged a cricket match between a Crowe XI (captained by his cousin Jeff, the former New Zealand captain) and a Spencer XI, captained by Shane Warne. (*Sun Herald*, Sydney, April 6)

Ellon Gordon CC, based near Aberdeen, fielded three generations of Barretts on a pre-season tour of Cumbria. Sam (grandson), Jon (son) and Hayden (grandfather) all played against Barrow. (*Ellon Times*, April 17)

Wade Jones, a ten-year-old boy, scored 26 off one ball playing for Baler against Port Hedland in a primary school match in Western Australia on April 17. The batsmen's hare-like running was credited with pressuring the fielders into a long sequence of overthrows (*Wisden Australia*, 2003-04)

In Cape Town, Ross Johnson, a left-arm spinner, took two hat-tricks in the same innings playing for Somerset College Under-14s against Plumstead High. (*District Mail*, Cape Town, April 19)

The Maharashtra state government said it wants to legalise betting on cricket to bolster its finances and weaken the underworld. The Mumbai police support the move, suggesting an amendment of sections 4 and 5 of the Bombay Prevention of Gambling Act, 1887. The government has also asked its lawyers to submit a report. (*Times of India*, April 24)

A fisherman from Batticaloa, Sri Lanka, died in hospital after an argument with young men playing cricket. The fisherman, S. Nesan, got into the dispute after he was hit by the ball. He was then attacked with the bats and stumps. (*Daily Mirror*, Colombo, April 28)

Dennis Lillee criticised Sir Vivian Richards for talking "a heap of bulldust" after his former on-field adversary called Lillee a "huff and puff" merchant. Richards said Lillee tempered his aggression when playing West Indies out of fear of the opposing fast bowlers. (*The West Australian*, April 30)

The Northern Premier League fixture between Darwen and Lancaster was abandoned because no umpires turned up. Ken Shenton, secretary of the umpires' federation, said it was a protest against the teams' poor disciplinary record. (*Sunday Sun*, Newcastle, May 4)

Curtly Ambrose and Richie Richardson's band, New Dread and The Baldhead, have released their latest CD, Back In Yur Face. Their seven-piece band features Richardson on rhythm guitar and Ambrose on bass. According to a correspondent who attended a gig in Antigua, the act is "slick, rocking the house with a mix of reggae, covers and some sing-along-able originals". (*Cricinfo*, May 11, *The Age*, Melbourne, June 1)

Former England player Phil Tufnell was voted by viewers as winner of the ITV programme *I'm a Celebrity, Get me out of Here* in which various people who had appeared on television were dumped in an Australian rain forest and obliged to survive with only a TV crew for company, while charming a regular audience of ten million viewers. Tufnell retired from cricket to take part. (*The Guardian*, May 13)

Eldine Baptiste, the former West Indies fast bowler, was released without charge three days after being arrested and remanded in Wandsworth prison on charges of attempting to import cocaine concealed in golf balls into Britain. His five-year-old daughter had to travel on alone to South Africa, where he was meant to be coaching, while Baptiste was in jail. Customs officials apologised "for the inconvenience". (*Daily Telegraph*, May 23)

Salil Ankola, the India Test-player-turned-actor, refused a film role that required him to play a cricketer who fixes matches. He said it was against his principles. (*Gujarat Samachar*, Ahmedabad, May 25)

Ezrafiq Andul Aziz scored 303 off 75 balls – including 30 sixes and 26 fours – to help Johore crush Labuan by 598 runs in a Malaysian Schools Sports Council match in Kota Baru. Labuan replied with 22 all out. (*New Straits Times*, Kuala Lumpur, May 26)

Darren Gough made his debut in *The Beano* comic, in a cartoon featuring the character Billy Whizz. The England fast bowler's walk-on role was confined to a single word: "Chortle". (*The Beano*, May 31)

Inspired by Donald Bradman's famous childhood regime, an old-fashioned water tank stand is being built at the New South Wales state training centre. Like the Don, youngsters will throw a golf ball against the brick base then attempt to hit the rebound with a stump. "Research identifies high-repetition skills as being a key," said the high performance manager of NSW Cricket, Alan Campbell, "along with a strongly competitive but unstructured framework – backyard cricket, if you like." (*The Observer*, June 1)

Bob Gallimore, former editor of the *Henley Standard*, died from a suspected heart attack on his return to cricket, poor health having necessitated a four-year break. After Gallimore, 61, had completed his innings for Sonning Common, a club he helped found, he walked off to applause but collapsed halfway to the pavilion. (*Henley Standard*, June 9)

Seven decades after his death, K. S. Ranjitsinhji, the Jam Sahib of Nawanagar, has caused controversy following the publication in India of a new biography. In *Battling for the Empire*, Mario Rodriguez describes the Sussex and England batsman as the "Raj's poster boy" and accuses him of conspiring against the struggle for freedom in his homeland. Descendants have rallied to his defence, including a granddaughter, Harshad Kumari. "Just because he was British in attitude did not mean he was anti-Indian," she said. "It is wrong to say he did nothing for Indian cricket," added Chhatrapalsinh Jadeja, a great-nephew. "He showed the British that an Indian can beat them at their own game." (*Times of India*, June 12)

Billy Whizz and the Dazzler: Darren Gough makes a cameo appearance in *The Beano.*

Interviewed on *Tonight*, the US TV chat show hosted by Jay Leno, the actor Keanu Reeves, fresh from filming in Australia, amazed both audience and compère by mounting a stirring defence of cricket. "But doesn't it go on for days and days?" wondered Leno to predictably uproarious studio laughter. "Cricket's cool," insisted Reeves. "In five days you have time to, like, get real into it." (*The Times*, June 14)

Playing for Chester-le-Street Under-13s against Eppleton, Anthony McMahon, 13, hit six sixes in an over, but still finished on the losing side. (*Sunday Telegraph*, June 15)

Thieves ransacked St Mary's CC in Birkenhead before burning down the pavilion, destroying trophies and memorabilia. (*Liverpool Echo*, June 16)

A school governor complained after watching a fellow spectator start marking GCSE exam papers at Chelmsford during an Essex–Warwickshire National League match. Carole Nadin said she saw him pass the papers to his friends, who laughed when they read the answers. (BBC News Online, June 17)

Mumbai police arrested a gang of 14-to-20-year-old boys for robbing the homes of the former India captains Sunil Gavaskar and Ajit Wadekar, recovering cash, jewellery and several awards from the pair's playing days. (*Sambhaav*, Ahmedabad, June 18)

Richard Smith, 29, of Queensbury CC, West Yorkshire, collapsed and died during a Halifax League game after hitting eight sixes in an innings of 98 against Bridgeholme. His father, David, had suffered the same fate 18 years earlier while bowling. (*The Times*, June 18)

Mali Richards, the 19-year-old son of Sir Vivian, hit 319, the highest score in the 90-year history of the Leeward Islands tournament, for Antigua & Barbuda in a three-day match against the US & British Virgin Islands at St John's. In reply to the hosts' 789, the Virgin Islands made 47. (Associated Press, June 24)

Cash-strapped Yorkshire told their honorary life members, including Fred Trueman, Ray Illingworth and Dickie Bird, that they would henceforth have to pay £75 for their seats at Headingley Test matches. Geoff Boycott, another of those affected, said the club was being run "like a supermarket". (*Daily Telegraph*, June 24)

In the list of the Hundred Sexiest Women in the World published in the South African edition of *FHM* magazine, South African Test batsman Neil McKenzie's model girlfriend, Kerry McGregor, a previous winner, came third. His sister, Megan, also a model, finished second. (*FHM*, July)

Schoolboy cricketers in Gazipur, northern Bangladesh, battered a team-mate to death after he accidentally smashed a newly won trophy. Identified solely as Rajiv, the teenager was waving the cup with one hand when it dropped on the pavement, whereupon fellow team members set about him with sticks. (*Ittefaq*, Bangladesh, July 2)

Rob Wade, captain of the South Wiltshire club in the Southern Premier League, was ruled out for the season after breaking his collarbone while competing in the fathers' sack race at a school sports day. (*Daily Telegraph*, July 4)

Javed Burki, the former Pakistan captain and ICC match referee, was released on bail from the Central Jail, Karachi, seven months after he was arrested. No charge had been laid against him. Burki, 65, who was also a former head of the Pakistan Automobile Corporation, was alleged to have embezzled funds while supplying trucks to the Pakistan army. Imran Khan has referred to Burki as "my hero" and it is thought his imprisonment might have been engineered by Imran's political opponents. (*The Times*, June 27, *The News*, Karachi, July 13)

Orkney beat Shetland by 36 runs in the first contest between Britain's two most northerly island groups since 1996. Orcadian Keith Keldie scored 90. (*Daily Telegraph*, July 21)

The Under-23 fixture between Rio and Singha in Ambalangoda was postponed as the ground was required for the cremation of a Buddhist priest. (*Daily Mirror*, Colombo, July 24)

When Gareth Lewis struck a six during a Beckett League game at Nawton Grange, North Yorkshire, the ball landed on a car radiator grille, continued up the A170, and wound up in a garage in Kirkbymoorside, three and a half miles from the ground. (*Wisden Cricket Monthly*, August)

Heather Willey, daughter of umpire Peter, finished runner-up in the girls' Under-18 section of the fast bowling challenge final at Lord's. (*Daily Telegraph*, August 1)

The Great Preston team has been fined £100 by the Wetherby League after Asian opponents were allegedly jeered as "al-Qaeda members" by supporters. The league chairman, Zahid Ali, resigned in protest at the leniency of the fine. (*The Guardian*, August 6)

A 21-year-old Herefordshire man drowned in the River Severn at Worcester after watching Worcestershire's one-day match against South Africa. Lee Muldowney of Dilwyn died after taking a £10 bet that he would jump in off the bridge, an inquest heard. But he was unable to climb out again because of a high brick wall and then got into difficulties as he tried to reach the far bank. His companions said he had drunk several lagers during the day. (*Hereford Times*, August 7)

Rodmersham CC's final pair, Chris Piesley, aged 11, and Christian Marsh, 12, defied the Sidcup bowlers for the last 22 overs to secure an improbable draw in an adult Kent League fixture. (*East Kent Gazette*, August 7)

The Judge's robes: Robin Smith (with parents) collects an honorary doctorate from the University of Portsmouth.
Picture by Dave Allen.

Former England batsman Robin Smith has been awarded an honorary doctorate of letters by the University of Portsmouth. (*Cricinfo*, August 11)

A South African woman claimed Shane Warne, currently banned from cricket after failing a drugs test, bombarded her with raunchy phone calls for more than a year after they had a brief fling. Helen Cohen-Alon, 45, also said she was offered £20,000 by an associate of Warne to keep quiet about their relationship. The Victoria coach David Hookes dismissed Warne's accuser as "some dopey hairy-backed Sheila". He later apologised. (*Sunday Times*, Johannesburg, August 10/*Sydney Morning Herald*, August 12)

Sibling rivalry: Steve Evans (*left*) and his twin brother Stuart captained opposing teams in a Marches League match between Ledbury and Bartestree & Lugwardine. *Picture by Derrick Jones.*

Mark Portsmouth, chairman of Mumbles CC in Swansea, offered £100 to the first player to hit a ball into the garden of the house soon to be owned by the privacy-obsessed actors Michael Douglas and Catherine Zeta Jones, 150 yards away. The money will be handed over provided the successful smiter asks for the ball to be returned. (*Daily Mirror*, August 14)

Meheniot gave St Buryan's a generous start in their Cornwall League Premier Division fixture, conceding 33 runs in the first over, though only eight in boundaries. J. Sedgley contributed 25 wides. (*The Cornishman*, August 14)

The Sri Lanka Test leg-spinner Kaushal Lokuarachchi, 21, was arrested after a fatal car crash in the Colombo suburb of Kadawatha. He allegedly lost control of his car while returning home late from a party, crashing through a wall and into a house, killing a woman and critically injuring her son. The player escaped with minor shoulder injuries and said he fell asleep at the wheel. He was subsequently banned from all cricket for four months. (BBC Online, August 17/*Cricinfo*, September 13)

Identical twins Steve and Stuart Evans, 33, captained the opposing teams in a Marches League match between Ledbury and Bartestree & Lugwardine. Steve is a right-handed batsman who bowls left-arm; Stuart is a left-handed batsman who bowls right-arm. (*Hereford Times*, August 21)

Malcolm Speed, the chief executive of the ICC, was named by Indian newspapers in connection with a police investigation into the death of a woman poet, Mudhumita Shukla, murdered in Lucknow in May. When Shukla's house was searched after her death, hotel swipe cards were found, apparently fitting the room that Speed occupied on a trip to Delhi. "I have no recollection of ever meeting this lady," Speed said. (*Cricinfo*, August 22)

A blind cricket team, the Eastern Vipers from March, Cambridgeshire, won £7,000 compensation for disability discrimination. A guest house turned them away when the owners realised the players had guide dogs. (*Daily Telegraph*, August 29)

Agencies are sprouting in India offering would-be migrants illegal entry to the UK via cricket tours. Five members of a women's side from Jalandhar, northern India, recently disappeared when supposedly playing in a tournament in Herefordshire. "We will attach you to a cricket club," one agent assured an undercover reporter. "All you need to do is slip out of the team once you land in the UK. Though I cannot assure you a job there, I have contacts among lawyers who can help." (*The Guardian*, August 20/*Times of India*, September 1)

The celebrity Tara Palmer-Tomkinson chose the footballer-turned-TV host Gary Lineker to help her answer a cricket question on a celebrity charity edition of the ITV show *Who Wants to be a Millionaire?* She was asked to name the decade in which England last won the Ashes. Lineker's correct reply won Ms Palmer-Tomkinson £32,000, which she donated to the Leukaemia Research Fund. (*The Times*, September 5)

Bookmakers William Hill said they took £500,000 in bets on the Oval Test between England and South Africa, their record for a cricket match. (*Financial Times*, September 9)

David Hare, the playwright and Sussex supporter, said the county's first-ever Championship triumph meant that his play, *Teeth and Smiles*, could never be revived in its current form. One of the characters, asked to cite "the most boring fact he can think of", mentions Sussex's failure to win the title. "The two things I never expected to happen in my lifetime were Sussex winning the Championship and a left-wing Labour government," said Hare. "As of today, a passionate Labour government is all that remains." (*The Guardian*, September 19)

Vandals broke into Leicestershire's ground, Grace Road, and did £7,000 worth of damage, leaving the message "Unseen, Unheard". (*The Guardian*, September 23)

Denis Streak, father of the Zimbabwean captain Heath, beat one of the favourites, Darren Burnett of Scotland, in the Champion of Champions bowls tournament in Perth, Australia. Streak, who has only been playing bowls seriously for five years, narrowly failed to reach the semi-final. (*Sunday Telegraph*, September 21/*Press & Journal*, Aberdeen, September 27)

Cricketers turned commentators Ian Botham and Bob Willis have lent their names to wines produced by the Australian winemaker Geoff Merrill. The BMW (Botham, Merrill, Willis) range, including a cabernet sauvignon and chardonnay, is being sold through an English supermarket. "Geoff didn't just point to a spare vat of wine and say 'Stick yer names on that, lads,'" said Willis. "These are the wines we like to drink." (*Daily Telegraph*, October 2)

Adam Hollioake of Surrey and England said he makes "a lot more" from running a property company in Western Australia than he does from cricket. (*Sunday Times*, October 5)

Parthiv Patel's uncle, Jagat Patel, has sworn to marry only after the wicket-keeper is performing consistently for India's Test XI, a tactic once tried, successfully, by Sachin Tendulkar's brother, Ajit. (*Rajasthan Patrika*, Ahmedabad, October 7)

West Indian Test player Mervyn Dillon of Trinidad and Fernix Thomas of the Windward Islands were both struck by lightning in a Red Stripe Bowl match at Kensington Park,

Jamaica. Witnesses said the lightning came from a clear blue sky. Both men were taken to hospital but were not seriously hurt. (*Cricinfo*, October 10)

Although MCC suspended him, Somerset CCC said they were happy to keep the membership of Jeffrey Archer, the author and peer recently released after being jailed for perjury. "He has been giving us a small donation by standing order for many years," said the club's chief executive, Peter Anderson. "There's nothing in the rules to say that people with criminal records can't join." (*Sunday Telegraph*, October 12)

Left-handed batsmen have a strategic advantage over right-handers, according to researchers from the University of New South Wales who analysed scores from the 2003 World Cup. Dr Rob Brooks and his colleagues said the advantage was particularly great against bowlers who were unused to left-handers. (*Daily Telegraph*, October 15)

A 52-year-old Exeter judge, Martin Meeke QC, armed himself with a cricket bat to prevent a burglar, Matthew Douglas-Fryer, 24, escaping from his basement. Douglas-Fryer was given a two-year community service order and told he was lucky to escape jail. (*Daily Telegraph*, October 22/Press Association, December 5)

Australian captain Steve Waugh turned down an invitation to meet President George W. Bush at a barbecue at the Prime Minister's residence in Canberra. His manager said Waugh was committed to attend the New South Wales team's seasonal launch. (*Herald Sun*, Melbourne, October 22)

George W. Bush: stood up.
Picture by Alex Wong, Getty Images.

Shaun Udal of Hampshire, the former England one-day player, has been banned from playing for his club side, Camberley, for three years, after what he admitted was "pushing and shoving" with Cranleigh's Australian leg-spinner Alex Wyatt. Udal said he heard one of his team-mates, who has a disability, being insulted while he was batting. He was previously banned after a post-match incident while playing for Camberley in 1996. (*Cricinfo*, October 22)

Between August 22 and September 8, Doug Robertson, a 60-year-old teacher from Bexhill, Sussex, visited each of the 18 first-class county headquarters in as many days – a unique feat, according to the Guinness Book of World Records. Rain at Derby and an early finish at Worcester prevented him from seeing cricket played every day, but in each instance the players signed a bat as evidence of his visit. Mr Robertson raised £6,000 for Friends of Tread, a charity for deprived children and families in southern India. (*The Wisden Cricketer*, November)

Villagers in Lynton, north Devon, have called for a cull of more than 50 goats in the Valley of Rocks after the herd had fouled local amenities, including the cricket pitch at one of England's most picturesque grounds. The breed is said to date back 6,000 years and is mentioned in the Domesday Book. Opponents condemned the proposal as "cruel and unnecessary" and suggested erecting a goat-proof fence around the village. (*Sunday Telegraph*, November 2)

Three people died and 35 were injured in a riot in the Indian state of Gujarat. Communal violence broke out after Muslim boys tried to get their cricket ball back from a Hindu temple in Viramgam. (*Daily Telegraph*, November 3)

A 13-year-old chinaman bowler, Sarfaraz Pothiyawala, took four for 15 for Christ Church against St Joseph in an inter-schools tournament in Mumbai. His right arm was left stunted by an accident when he was two. (*Mid-day*, Mumbai, November 20)

The commentator Henry Blofeld chose a selection including Noel Coward, Gilbert & Sullivan and Maurice Chevalier – plus the "Eton Boating Song" – when invited on to the BBC Radio Four programme *Desert Island Discs*. His luxury was a photograph album and his book was *A Pelican at Blandings* by P. G. Wodehouse. "Most of my life has been as close to the Bertie Wooster experience as I can get," he said. (BBC Online, November 30)

Anglo-Australian relations deteriorated amid a media-led squabble over the ball with which Jonny Wilkinson kicked the winning points in the rugby union World Cup final in Sydney. In London, *The Sun* urged readers to bombard the Australian High Commission in London until the missing ball, valued at up to £500,000, was returned to England; the *Sydney Daily Telegraph* (also owned by Rupert Murdoch) responded in trenchant fashion. "Want the ball? Then give us the Ashes." (*Daily Telegraph*, Sydney, December 6)

Local Shiv Sena activists, whose colleagues in Delhi dug up the Test ground pitch when Pakistan last toured India, inflicted similar damage at the stadium in Agra, scheduled venue for the third of a series of "Goodwill" veterans matches between the two nations. "We oppose the holding of cricket matches until Pakistan brings an end to terrorism," said a Sena spokesman after the arrival of police had prompted the protestors to flee just as they were poised to pour oil on the surface. (*Times of India*, December 18)

Gurjeet Sapal, 16, who plays for the Northamptonshire Academy, staged a 12-hour "bat-athon" to raise funds for Aiden Cox, a two-year-old local boy with cerebral palsy. (*Chronicle & Echo*, Northampton, December 18)

Channel Four announced that Geoff Boycott would join their regular commentary team for summer 2004. Boycott lost his contracts with BBC Radio and Sky after being convicted of assaulting a former girlfriend in France in 1998. More recently, he had been suffering from throat cancer. "Geoff Boycott is one of the great voices of cricket," said the station's head of sport, David Kerr. (*The Guardian*, December 19)

New Zealand Cricket officials were thrown into panic during the Hamilton Test against Pakistan when a rumour swept the city that the chief executive, Martin Snedden, had been killed in a road accident. Unable to contact him by phone, media liaison manager Simon Wilson forced his way into Snedden's hotel room – and found him asleep. (*New Zealand Herald*, December 22)

The Western Railway's Lower Parel and Matunga workshop team were recalled from a national tournament after the company's Vigilance Department discovered that only seven of the 15-man squad were railway employees. (*Mumbai Newsline*, December 28)

Chronicle is compiled by Rob Steen and Matthew Engel. We welcome contributions from readers, especially items from local or non-UK papers. Please send newspaper cuttings to Matthew Engel at Fair Oak, Bacton, Herefordshire HR2 0AT (always including the paper's name and date) and weblinks to copy@johnwisden.co.uk.

OBITUARIES

ABED, GASANT, died in April 2003, aged 72. One of four brothers who played under the auspices of the South African Cricket Board of Control (SACBOC) when opportunities for non-whites were restricted by the country's race laws, "Tiny" Abed learned his cricket on matting pitches and unmown outfields. He made his debut for Western Province Indians at 17 and, five years later, in 1953, was in the Western Province Federation team that travelled by lorry to Port Elizabeth and Durban to help pioneer the establishment of non-racial provincial cricket. Well over six feet tall, Abed bowled fast off a long run, varying away swing with a lively off-cutter, and was a forceful back-foot batsman. His inspiration was Keith Miller and he brought something of Miller's cavalier spirit to the drab grounds to which he was mostly confined. In South Africa's home-and-away series against Kenya, he took four for nine at Durban in 1956 and had match figures of eight for 80 at Nairobi in 1958. On the Kenyan tour – the first outside South Africa by a non-white side – he was Basil D'Oliveira's vice-captain and Abed's brother "Lobo" kept wicket. But whereas D'Oliveira went on to play in the Lancashire leagues, as did Abed's younger brother, "Dik", Tiny remained in South Africa, playing on in local cricket into his forties.

ADHIKARI, Lieutenant-Colonel HEMCHANDRA RAMACHANDRA, died on October 25, 2003, aged 84. Hemu Adhikari played in 21 Tests for India, bringing a military man's stay-at-your-post sense of duty to Indian cricket of the late 1940s and 1950s when the national team was frequently on the brink of rout and flight. His finest hour came in one of the darkest times of all, when India's batsmen were frightened by Wes Hall and Roy Gilchrist in the 1958-59 home series against West Indies and, at 39, he became the fourth captain in the five Tests. He was not even the obvious choice for this role – the selectors almost went for G. S. Ramchand – and Adhikari only accepted after prompting from his wife and his commanding officer. But he led by example with innings of 63 and 40, took three wickets with leg-breaks scarcely seen in Test cricket, and secured a draw to halt West Indies' three-match winning sequence. Despite his success, he did not make himself available for the 1959 tour of England which turned out even more disastrously. Adhikari had played only two Tests in the previous six years, partly because of army commitments, but his leadership qualities had been much in evidence as he guided Services to two successive Ranji Trophy finals. In his early days, he had won three

Hemu Adhikari: fourth-choice captain; first-class fighter.

Ranji Trophies with Baroda. At that stage he was renowned for his strokeplay, but in Test cricket he usually had to concentrate on crisis management: his only Test century came at Delhi in the maiden Test between India and West Indies in 1948-49 when his 114 not out just failed to save the follow-on; he again organised the resistance in the second innings with a prolonged 29 not out against a background chant of "Well played Ad-hi-ka-ri". He struggled as vice-captain in England in 1952 but against Pakistan that winter he tasted his only two Test wins, making 81 not out at Delhi in an 80-minute stand of 109 with Ghulam Ahmed, still India's highest last-wicket partnership. After retiring from the army, Adhikari became national coach and was manager of the triumphant 1971 tour of England. His style involved strict discipline, an emphasis on fielding and, in the words of Bapu Nadkarni, "not bothering about what anybody else thought". He was also occasionally heard as a radio summariser in a style the *Daily Telegraph* described as "somewhat Delphic".

ALLEN, ANTONY WILLIAM, died on December 21, 2003, a day before his 91st birthday. Tony Allen scored centuries in both the traditional Lord's showpiece games in the 1930s: 112 for Eton against Harrow in 1931, the first century before lunch in the fixture, and 115 for Cambridge against Oxford in 1934. On both occasions he shared in double-century opening stands. Tall and a fluent driver, Allen passed 1,000 runs that season, for Cambridge, MCC and Northamptonshire. But he went to work in insurance and played only twice for Northamptonshire after that, in 1936 when he was the first of their five captains in one season. He turned down the captaincy in 1937, causing *The Cricketer* to mourn that his "evanescent appearance only served to emphasise the recurrent loss of his beautiful batting".

ALLWORK, MATTHEW JULIAN, was killed in a helicopter crash in Dubai on March 26, 2003, aged 39, while filming a horse race. Allwork was an innovative cameraman, credited with the invention of the stump-cam.

AUSTIN, Wing Commander SIDNEY PETER, died on January 27, 2003, aged 89. A former RAF accountant who travelled the world to watch cricket, Peter Austin was Warwickshire's first-team scorer from 1982 to 1993. In 1986-87 he became the first county scorer to do the job on an England tour, and was reapponted for the next two trips. He was a courteous, self-effacing tourist.

BAIRD, JAMES GEORGE, died on November 4, 2003, aged 82. Jim Baird made his Sheffield Shield debut in March 1949 in Sir Donald Bradman's last hurrah, opening the bowling for Victoria against South Australia, and remained a regular through 1949-50 when their Test bowlers were in South Africa. He took 30 wickets for Victoria that season, second only to Jack Iverson's 46, with a mixture of swing and lift. Baird was also an outstanding all-round Australian Rules footballer for Carlton and briefly a professional runner, finishing third in the 1946 Stawell Gift sprint, Australia's most famous race.

BANERJEE, TATA, who died on September 5, 2003, played three Ranji Trophy games for Bihar as a medium-pace all-rounder in the 1950s. His son, Subroto, played one Test for India in 1991-92.

BIDDULPH, KENNETH DAVID, died after a heart attack on January 7, 2003, aged 70. Ken Biddulph was an Essex boy whose potential as a fast-medium bowler was spotted at Alf Gover's indoor school in London and taken up by Somerset. He had an awkward run-up, and never found the penetration to be a regular match-winner, but he was thoughtful in his work and willing to bowl all day if necessary. Biddulph served a lengthy apprenticeship before winning a regular first-team place in 1958, when his 40 wickets contributed to Somerset's climb to third place, and he managed to take around double that in both the next two years. Then he moved to become a club pro in the north-east and spent a decade playing Minor Counties cricket for Durham. Biddulph eventually returned to the West Country to coach, and his humorous anecdotes inspired Stephen Chalke to record the recollections of 1950s county cricketers in *Runs in the Memory*. His own attitude to the past was unusually reverent: in 1956, bowling for Somerset II at Trowbridge, Biddulph slowed the over-rate down to prevent a Wiltshire win; more than 40 years later he wrote to Wiltshire to apologise, saying it had been on his conscience all his life.

BIRRELL, HENRY BENSON, who died on September 18, 2003, aged 75, was a South African who won an Oxford Blue at both cricket and rugby in 1953 and 1954. As an opening bat, Harry Birrell made centuries against Yorkshire and Worcestershire in 1953 and the following year had an outstanding University match: he made 27 and 64 and then, moving the ball both ways at medium-pace, claimed five for 20 in 14 overs as Oxford just failed to secure victory. His batting – elegant rather than forceful – and bowling were eclipsed by his athleticism in the covers and outfield and his fast running between the wickets. Birrell later played for Eastern Province and Rhodesia, where he worked as a teacher, and was involved as a coach and selector for South African schools cricket. His son Adrian and nephew Warne Rippon both played for Eastern Province.

BISHOP, EDWARD BARRY, died on May 24, 2003, aged 79. Ted Bishop was a journalist and author whose main cricketing achievement was to "liberate" the Singapore Cricket Club after Britain recaptured the colony in 1945. The club had been used as the HQ of the Japanese secret police and Bishop found a bloodstained cricket bat on the steps. He took six wickets in the club's first post-war match and reportedly used the bat for several years thereafter.

BOLTON, ALAN, died on January 12, 2003, aged 63, after suffering from Alzheimer's disease. Bolton played 40 times for Lancashire between 1957 and 1961 after making his debut against Cambridge as a 17-year-old. Though a game and attractive batsman, he had limited opportunities and was regularly shifted up and down the order. His finest hour came when he scored a decisive 96 to lead a Lancashire recovery from 49 for six on a sporting Grace Road pitch in 1959.

BOYS, Commander CECIL, died on March 27, 2003, aged 84. A career Naval officer, educated at Dartmouth, Boys played seven first-class games for Combined Services between 1947 and 1951, scoring a career-best 84 against Essex in 1950, a performance which, along with ten wickets by Signalman Brian Close, almost secured victory.

BRICE, GORDON HARRY JOSEPH, who died in April 2003, aged 78, had 25 games for Northamptonshire between 1948 and 1952. Brice had a golden week in July 1951, when injuries gave him the chance to take the new ball, and he responded by taking eight for 124 in the first innings against Surrey and followed up with six for 84 in the next match against Nottinghamshire. However, he was unable to sustain such form and his batting promised more than it delivered. He played league football, mainly at centre-half, for several clubs including Wolves and Fulham.

BRIGGS, RONALD EDWARD, died on October 10, 2003, aged 74. Brought in to open New South Wales's batting in December 1952 when Arthur Morris was playing for Australia, Ron Briggs hit a debut hundred at Perth in the second innings and then scored fifties in his next five Shield games. Selected for the Australian XI against MCC in 1954-55, he top-scored with a three-hour 48, but a three-ball pair for New South Wales when he next met the tourists proved an ignominious finale to his state cricket.

CHANDLER, LEONARD VICTOR, died on September 2, 2003, aged 77, a fortnight before Sussex's long-awaited Championship triumph. He was the Sussex first-team scorer from 1982 to 2001, having previously worked in the building industry. His funeral was delayed so that the county's players could attend.

COLLIN, THOMAS, died on August 26, 2003, aged 92, a day after collapsing while reading a biography of Eric Hollies, his team-mate at Warwickshire. Tom Collin played the first of his 52 games for them as a left-handed batsman and occasional slow left-armer in 1933, and was capped in 1934. If a little uncertain in defence, he hit the ball hard, and his fielding was often spectacular. His square-leg catch to dismiss South Africa's Cyril Vincent in 1935 was so good Vincent dropped his bat and joined in the applause. Earlier that season, Collin made 105 not out against Gloucestershire at Edgbaston and, with Tom Dollery, put on 199 for the seventh wicket to save the game. This, however, was his only hundred and he returned to Durham, his home county, in 1937 to become professional at Durham School, a post he held, war service aside, until 1976.

CONSTANTINE, ELIAS, who died on May 22, 2003, his 91st birthday, was the son of Lebrun Constantine, who toured England in 1900 and 1906, and the younger brother by ten years of the great Learie, later Lord Constantine. Himself a talented all-rounder, Elias played 21 times for Trinidad in the 1940s and, on account of his brilliant fielding, was West Indies' twelfth man for the 1934-35 Trinidad Test against England. In the preceding MCC tour match, the brothers had opened the bowling together for the only time in first-class cricket, as well as adding 93 for the seventh wicket after Trinidad were 42 for six. Elias did not bowl as furiously as his famous brother, but he was so quick in the field that his team-mates reputedly congratulated him when he dropped a catch on his Trinidad debut, because no one else could have got close. His first-class career produced just 895 runs at 27.12, with one memorable hundred, against British Guiana in 1943-44, when he hit five sixes and, according to *Wisden,* pierced the field "with strokes reminiscent of his brother".

COWMAN, STANLEY CORBETT, who died on February 2, 2003, aged 79, was honorary curator of the New Zealand Cricket Museum at the Basin Reserve, Wellington – from its inauguration in 1987 until his death. The museum was a direct consequence of the public's interest in a display of cricketana that Cowman, an avid collector, had set out in a Basin tearoom during the Australia Test of February 1986. A Yorkshire-born dentist who emigrated to New Zealand in 1964, he umpired two one-day internationals in 1982-83.

Dickie Davis: five-county wanderer whose heart was always with Kent.

Picture by Patrick Eagar.

COWNLEY, JOHN MICHAEL, died on November 7, 1998, aged 69. Michael Cownley was a left-handed batsman and right-arm bowler of varying pace who played for Yorkshire against both universities in 1952 and was recruited by Lancashire to play twice ten years later. He was a Sheffield University graduate with a reputation as an amateur light-heavyweight boxer.

CROMPTON, COLIN NEIL, died on December 11, 2003, aged 66. Neil "Froggy" Crompton was a burly Melbourne club left-hander promoted to open the batting for Victoria in 1957-58, establishing himself with two centuries. He held his place, mostly batting down the order, for five seasons. He was still not finished with the MCG, however. Playing for Melbourne in front of 102,000 fans in the 1964 Australian Rules grand final, he kicked his first goal in eight seasons to bring Melbourne victory over arch-rivals Collingwood.

DAVIS, RICHARD PETER, who died on December 29, 2003, aged 37, had been suffering from a brain tumour since 2001, the season he became the first cricketer to play for five first-class counties. At 22, Dickie Davis, born in Margate, succeeded Derek Underwood as Kent's left-arm spinner, daunting enough even without the end of uncovered wickets, which made his task near-impossible. In 1992, he was the leading slow bowler in the country, taking 74 wickets and finishing sixth in the national averages. But that was the only year his average dipped below 30 and a year later the younger Min Patel was challenging for a place, so Davis, turning down a one-year contract, signed for Warwickshire. He appeared in most of their Championship matches in the county's miraculous 1994 season and played an important role by solving what had been the team's great weakness. But he quickly came under challenge from another young pretender, Ashley Giles, and moved on to Gloucestershire. Retirement from first-class cricket in 1997 (to become cricket development officer for Greater London) opened an even more peripatetic chapter. Likeable and sympathetic, he showed increasing promise as a coach, working with the England women's team, St Edmund's School, Canterbury and, as player-coach, Berkshire. Davis also played a few one-day games for Sussex in 1998 and in August 2001 relegation-rattled Leicestershire obtained a special registration so he could strengthen their meagre spin bowling on a Northampton dirt track; he repaid their confidence with a first-innings half-century and six for 73, his 17th five-for. Two weeks later he had a seizure and the tumour was diagnosed. "He was a pro's pro," said his Kent team-mate, Matthew Fleming, "unflashy, good in a crisis, a brilliant pair of hands, and a much better batsman than might have been obvious – he was the best hooker we had." As a bowler, however, he probably did not spin the ball enough to be truly effective in four-day cricket. Despite his wanderings, he remained close to his first county – ten days before he died, his wife's sister married the current captain David Fulton and Davis said grace. He was buried in his Kent blazer.

DEBNAM, ALEXANDER FREDERICK HENRY, died in January 2003, aged 81. Alec Debnam was a leg-spinning all-rounder who had four seasons of county cricket for Kent and Hampshire after the war. In 1949, he accounted for five of Gloucestershire's first six on a helpful pitch for Kent at Bristol, and Hampshire tried him as an opener after he hit a career-best 64 against Cambridge at Bournemouth. Then he went back into the RAF.

DEWS, GEORGE, who died on January 29, 2003, aged 81, was a Yorkshireman thwarted in his ambition to play for his own county, who instead became a Worcestershire stalwart of the 1950s. He could not have had a more inauspicious first-class debut, being bowled for a king pair by the Lancashire slow left-armer, Eric Price (see below, page 1551), in an innings defeat at Old Trafford in May 1946. But he persevered and dug himself into the county middle order for the entire 1950s, reaching his thousand runs 11 years out of 12, and if anything improving with age – he passed 1,500 in his last three seasons before retirement, aged 40, in 1961. Dews was strongest on the off side, but adaptable enough to switch his game as the situation demanded, and in 1951 he was at the heart of a batting performance that *Wisden* called "one of the most notable in the whole history of cricket". Nottinghamshire left Worcestershire ten minutes, plus a possible extra half-hour, to score 131 for victory. Don Kenyon promoted Dews to open the innings with him. After the ten minutes (in which time five overs were bowled) they had 54 on the board and went on to win by nine wickets with five minutes to spare. Dews made 43 not out. He was also a goal-scoring inside-forward for Middlesbrough, Plymouth Argyle and Walsall, and as a footballer earned the nickname of "Gentleman George", which was adopted at Worcester too. "He was a quiet, undemonstrative man, unfailingly courteous, with a gentle sense of humour and fun," according to former club secretary Mike Vockins.

DICKINSON, JOHN EDWARD, died on March 24, 2003, aged 88. Ted Dickinson was a left-handed batsman and slow bowler who played twice for Leicestershire in the 1930s. His parallel career in football was ended by a broken leg. After the war, Dickinson moved to Torquay, where he became a pillar of the town cricket club, occasionally played for Devon, and was a driving force behind the Torquay festival, which thrived in the 1950s as a rival to Scarborough and Hastings.

DIVECHA, RAMESH VITHALDAS, died on February 19, 2003, aged 75, having suffered from Alzheimer's disease. "Buck" Divecha played in India's first Test victory, against England at Madras in 1951-52, and 11 different first-class sides in all, but his golden days were spent at Oxford. He could swing the ball both ways at a brisk but accurate medium-pace, which had been honed under Alf Gover's tuition, and was an enthusiastic middle-order bat. Later, he added off-breaks to his repertoire, and used both bowling methods to remarkable effect in the 1950 and 1951 Varsity matches, culminating in 1951 when he took seven for 62 in the second innings and spun Oxford to a thrilling 21-run victory. Barely a week later he was back at Lord's taking five for 81 (including Compton and Hutton) for the Gentlemen against the Players. Divecha played four Tests against England over the next 13 months to less effect, but he took a hat-trick on the 1952 tour in a surprising win over the ultimate champions Surrey, swiftly followed by eight for 74 against Glamorgan. He was called up the following winter against Pakistan at Madras, where he trapped 18-year-old Hanif Mohammad lbw. Thereafter, his work as an oil company executive limited Divecha to a handful of Ranji Trophy appearances. "He was a cheerful and amusing character who loved to bowl," recalled his Oxford contemporary, Donald Carr.

DOWLING, DERECK FRANK, died on May 30, 2003, the day before his Natal team-mate, Billy Wade. He was 90. Dowling was a stylish left-handed bat and leg-spinner who played for Border and North-East Transvaal on either side of the war before starting an eight-year run with Natal in 1946-47. During that time they won the Currie Cup three times and Dowling was considered for tours of England and Australia. He remained involved with Natal cricket and was their president from 1974 till 1986. His father, Henry, and younger brother Justin also played Currie Cup cricket.

EDWARDS, Sir GEORGE ROBERT OM, CBE, FRS, DL, who died on March 2, 2003, aged 94, was one of the foremost aeronautical designers and administrators of the 20th century and chairman of the British Aircraft Corporation from 1963 to 1975. He was at the heart of almost every development in British aviation for 40 years from biplanes to Concorde. He was also a skilful leg-break bowler, playing alongside the Bedser twins in club cricket, and married his two interests by insisting on the importance of backspin in the design of Barnes Wallis's bouncing bombs used in the Dambusters raids of 1943. He was president of Surrey in 1980 and also an accomplished painter whose *Cricket at Guildford* was offered by *Wisden Cricket Monthly* in 1989 to support Surrey's appeal to save The Oval.

ENDEAN, WILLIAM RUSSELL, died on June 28, 2003, aged 79, having been suffering from Parkinson's disease. Like Jonty Rhodes in a later generation of South Africans, Russell Endean was an inspirational fielder, a dogged batsman, and a hockey international. Australians dubbed him "Endless Endean" for his long hours at the crease when Jack Cheetham's young side toured there in 1952-53

Russell Endean: dogged at the crease, devastating in the field.
Picture by Getty Images.

and, against every expectation, squared the series 2–2, largely due to Endean's chanceless seven-and-a-half-hour 162 not out that set up the first of South Africa's two wins at Melbourne. On arriving in Australia the South Africans practised fielding three to four hours a day, and Endean's brilliant catch in that first Test win at Melbourne was the embodiment of their commitment. Even as the crowd was rising to acclaim Keith Miller's six-bound blow over long-on, Endean was leaping in front of the MCG's iron boundary fence to clutch the ball one-handed. Endean had seen war service in Egypt and Italy when, still only 21, he announced himself with 95 opening for Transvaal at Bloemfontein in March 1946. Chosen as wicket-keeper/batsman for the 1951 tour of England, he struggled for runs in English conditions and played only when John Waite was injured at The Oval. But Endean's batting on harder pitches, where he could play square of the wicket with impunity, was sometimes devastating: playing for Transvaal at Ellis Park in 1954-55, he flayed Orange Free State for a world-record 197 not out before lunch, extraordinary, even allowing for a three-hour session. So he played in 27 more Tests without taking the gloves, and scored two more centuries, at Auckland in 1952-53 and at Headingley in 1955, though he continued his maddening form in England by following up with a pair in the decisive Oval Test. Endean was involved in two of the most bizarre dismissals in Test history: when he kept at The Oval in 1951, umpire Frank Chester ruled that Len Hutton, who instinctively flicked his bat when the ball ran off his arm and looked like dropping on his wicket, had impeded Endean's attempt to catch the ball and gave him out for obstruction. Against England at Cape Town in 1956-57, Endean himself became the first batsman out "handled the ball" in Test cricket when he tried to stop a top-edged paddle hitting his stumps. He said later: "I thought of heading it away, but that seemed too theatrical"; it might, however, have been legal. Endean represented Transvaal until 1960-61 then settled near London to work for BP as an accountant. He may not have liked the wickets, but his wife was English and he loved the opera and ballet. Endean played on for MCC in schools games and for many years captained Malden Wanderers in Surrey club cricket, making countless friends with his softly spoken, undemonstrative manner. "Whatever the passport is to be a gentleman," said John Waite, "Russell had that passport."

FERGUSON, Major RONALD IVOR, who died on March 16, 2003, aged 72, set up a thriving indoor cricket centre in a disused barn at Dummer in Hampshire, where he farmed after retiring from the Life Guards. The Dummer Centre, founded in 1995, rapidly became one of the most successful in the country. Ron Ferguson was better known as a polo player and administrator, and as the father of Sarah, former wife of Prince Andrew. Like his daughter, he acquired notoriety in the tabloid newspapers for his sexual indiscretions.

FRANK, JACK, died on June 5, 2003, aged 97 years 198 days, having been South Africa's oldest-known surviving first-class cricketer. He was a batsman who played six games for Griqualand West in the late 1920s.

GAEKWAD, HIRALAL GHASULAL, who died on January 2, 2003, aged 79, played only one official Test for India, against Pakistan at Lucknow in 1952-53. However, he was an important member of the great Holkar side that contested ten Ranji Trophy finals between 1945 and 1955, winning four. He bowled either left-arm medium-pace swing or orthodox spin, with exceptional accuracy and economy on the jute-matting pitches of the day. In a career of 101 games, spread over 22 years, he conceded little more than two runs an over, and in his Test he took nought for 47 in 37. Even more impressively, he had figures of 71–19–134–3 when Vijay Hazare and Gul Mahomed put on 577, the highest partnership of all time, for Baroda in the 1946-47 Ranji final. Match figures of nine for 109 against Bombay helped Holkar regain the title a year later.

GETTY, Sir JOHN PAUL KBE, who died on April 17, 2003, aged 70, described himself in *Who's Who* as simply a "philanthropist". Paul Getty inherited a fortune from the family oil business but, unlike his tycoon father, had little interest in adding to it. Instead, he settled in Britain and gave away huge chunks of his money to a vast array of beneficiaries, most of them institutions representing what he saw as the country's threatened heritage, including cathedrals, art galleries, the British Film Institute's archive and the Conservative Party. Cricket was close to the top of the list.

Born at sea off Italy and originally called Eugene Paul, he came to the game by an unbelievably circuitous route after an unhappy American childhood, a tumultuous youth and reclusive middle years. For nine years he worked for the Italian subsidiary of Getty Oil before being seduced by the distractions of the 1960s, divorcing his first wife, Gail, and marrying a Dutch beauty, Talitha, who died of a heroin overdose in Italy in 1971. He moved to London and lived as a recluse in Chelsea, subject to depression and his own drug dependence, a period that included the terrible kidnap of his eldest son Paul. During this period Mick Jagger, a friend since the 1960s, visited him, insisted on switching the TV over to the cricket and explained what was going on. Getty got the bug. Gubby Allen, *éminence grise* of MCC and at one time a fellow patient at the London Clinic, described by Getty as being "like a father", encouraged him into the cricketing community. Men like Brian Johnston and Denis Compton became friends, and he took delight in the game's history, traditions and etiquette, which were at one with the concept of Englishness that he embraced.

So he sprinkled cricket with some of the stardust that his wealth made possible. He gave an estimated £1.6 million to build the Mound Stand at Lord's, but this was the tip of an iceberg of donations: to every county, to countless clubs, to individuals fallen on hard times and to organisations like the Arundel Cricket Foundation, which received £750,000 from him to help disadvantaged youngsters play cricket. Even his pleasures were inclusive ones. At Wormsley, his estate nestling in the Chilterns, he created his own private cricketing Eden project: a square like a billiard table with a thatched pavilion. Getty built his field of dreams, and they really did come: the Queen Mother and the Prime Minister, John Major, attended Wormsley's inaugural match in 1992; touring teams made it a regular stopover; and cricketers ranging from the great to the gormless delighted in playing there or simply sharing the idyll. There was a touch of Scott Fitzgerald's West Egg about the place, but that was not inappropriate for a ground where the most coveted sidetrip was to the library to see the host's rare first editions. The Getty box at Lord's also became a London salon where celebrities, cricketing and otherwise, rubbed shoulders.

His ownership of *Wisden*, sealed in 1993, brought together the two great passions: cricket and books. In 1994 Getty sealed his own personal happiness by marrying Victoria, who had nursed him through the bad years, and four years later tied the knot with the country he had come to love, becoming a British citizen, which allowed him to use the knighthood that had been bestowed on him for his charitable services 12 years earlier. His presidency of Surrey, in 1996, was another honour he cherished. Those who knew him valued him as a generous spirit, a quality that has nothing to do with money. And cricket repaid him a little by giving him a sense of his own self-worth as a man, not just as a benefactor.

GHAZALI, Wing Commander MOHAMMAD EBRAHIM ZAINUDDIN, died on April 26, 2003, aged 78. Ebbu Ghazali was a tall, stroke-playing middle-order batsman and off-spinner who played in two Tests on Pakistan's first tour of England in 1954. He made his debut for Maharashtra in 1943, and soon established himself as one of Pakistan's leading players after Partition. He did not play in their inaugural Test series, against India in 1952-53, but a career-best 160 for Combined Services against Karachi a year later won him a place on the tour. He performed steadily round the counties but failed in the Tests, suffering a pair inside two hours on a spiteful pitch at Old Trafford. As manager of the Pakistan side to Australia and New Zealand in 1972-73, he ordered Saeed Ahmed and Mohammad Ilyas home because of "lack of fitness".

GOODWIN, KEITH, who died on August 19, 2003, aged 65, had his county career blighted by the relaxation of the rules governing imported players in the late 1960s. Goodwin, spotted keeping wicket for Oldham, made his Lancashire debut in 1960 but spent most of the next five years as deputy to Geoff Clayton. After Clayton was dismissed in 1964 for disciplinary reasons, Goodwin finally become No. 1 and was capped. Though a thoroughly competent keeper, he was an indifferent bat, and in 1968 Lancashire seized the chance to sign Farokh Engineer, the Indian Test player who was his superior in both departments. Goodwin returned to the Second XI, and, having declined offers from four other counties, was rewarded for his loyalty with a benefit in 1973. He later ran a post office in Hampshire.

GOONERATNE, GERRY, who died on September 24, 2003, aged 84, was revered as one of Sri Lanka's foremost coaches, establishing his reputation over 35 years at Nalanda College. He was appointed national coach in 1976 and also served as a Sri Lankan selector, sometimes as chairman. He was a stylish left-hand bat who hit 96 as a 21-year-old for All-Ceylon against India at Bombay in 1940-41 and captained Saracens for many years. While a schoolboy at St Joseph's, he is said to have shot a man-eating crocodile.

GOPALAN, MORAPPAKAM JOYSAM, his first name being his place of birth, died on December 21, 2003, aged 94 years and 198 days. M. J. Gopalan had been regarded as the oldest surviving Test cricketer since Lindsay Weir's death in October, although Gopalan and his family believed he was three years older than records show. "I don't know how the school where I studied listed my year of birth as 1909, but that stuck," M. J. told Cricinfo on his birthday in 2001. "I can confirm that I am 95 today." His Test career comprised just one match against England at Calcutta in 1933-34. And by touring England in 1936 he missed out on a hockey gold medal at the Berlin Olympics that summer, for he was already established as India's centre-half. But he was little more than a bystander on the tour and then returned home on the same ship as the victorious Olympians. Gopalan had 25 years of first-class cricket during which he captained Madras and South India. In taking ten wickets on debut, opening the Indians' bowling against the Europeans in 1926-27, he so impressed the former Kent and Cambridge batsman, C. P. Johnstone, that he found M. J. a job with Burmah Shell that allowed him to concentrate on cricket. In November 1934 Gopalan bowled the first ball in the inaugural Ranji Trophy match. Chepauk veterans would fondly recall him batting in a dark brown Homburg, or pausing at his bowling mark to knot his hair. He presented the Gopalan Trophy in 1952 for games between Madras and Ceylon, served as an Indian selector and was chairman of the Madras Cricket Association. With Gopalan's death, New Zealand's Don Cleverley became the oldest living Test cricketer, until his own death in February 2004, when the mantle passed to his compatriot Eric Tindill.

GRAY, DAVID ANTHONY ATHELSTAN DFC, died on November 9, 2003, aged 81. Gray was a slow left-armer who captained Winchester in 1941. After war service in Bomber Command, he appeared twice for Cambridge and once for Essex.

GUHA, SUBRATA, who died from a heart attack on November 5, 2003, aged 57, was a seam bowler who made headlines in December 1966 while a 20-year-old student at Calcutta University. He captured 11 West Indian wickets for 113 on an Indore green top when Central and East Zones inflicted the only defeat of their tour. But Guha took only two wickets in the four Tests he played: at

Headingley in 1967 and three times at home against Australia in 1969-70, where he was often just removing the shine for the spinners. In between, he missed several opportunities through knee trouble. But he represented Bengal for over a decade and took seven for 18 against Assam at Gauhati in 1972-73.

HARVEY, JOHN FRANK, died on August 20, 2003, aged 63, having been suffering from a brain tumour. Harvey was a steady middle-order performer in the sometimes fragile Derbyshire batting order of the 1960s. He joined the club from the Lord's groundstaff, and a century at Folkestone in his second Championship match suggested the county had found an opening batsman to replace Charlie Lee. Over the next three seasons *Wisden* downgraded him from "promising" to "inconsistent" to "could not command a regular place", but he eventually emerged as the regular No. 6, notable for his play through the covers, for his fielding there and his generally unselfish approach: a bonus point would always take precedence over his personal interest. Harvey's finest innings probably came at Chesterfield when he scored 92 as Derbyshire went down by only eight runs to the 1968 Australians. He was released in a shake-up in 1972, went on to play for Cambridgeshire and Berkshire (who he captained from 1982 to 1986) and to spend more than a quarter of a century as coach and groundsman at Bradfield College, where generations of boys adored the way he prepared both his pitches and his charges. "He allowed young cricketers to have their say," recalled Mark Nicholas, Bradfield's 1976 captain. "There was nothing schoolmasterly about it."

HATTON, LESLIE WALTER, died on February 28, 2003, aged 68. Les Hatton was Worcestershire's historian and statistician, and achieved a national reputation for his mastery of some of the more arcane statistical areas, notably the Sunday League and the Second XI Championship. He edited the ACS *Second Eleven Annual*, and contributed to *Wisden*. He was a cheerful soul, and formerly played the clarinet, flute and saxophone in the Royal Artillery Band and Midlands dance bands.

HAUGHTON, WILLIAM EDWARD, died on February 11, 2003, aged 79. Bill Haughton represented Ireland at both hockey and cricket, but bagged a pair in his only first-class match, against Glamorgan at Port Talbot in 1953.

HAWKINS, LAURENCE CYRIL, died in October 2003, aged 96. A prolific run-maker for Weston in club cricket, Laurie Hawkins played 46 times for Somerset as an amateur between 1928 and 1937. His best season was 1934, when he played 12 Championship games and his 96 at Lord's tided Somerset through a critical period to avoid defeat. His main contribution to cricket history was by not playing: he was injured for the game against Essex at Frome in 1935, which led to the call-up of 20-year-old Harold Gimblett and the most famous of all debut innings.

HOARE, WILFRED NORMAN STEWART, who died on August 28, 2003, aged 93, kept wicket for Cambridge for one match in 1931 after a good performance in Etceteras v Perambulators. From 1951 to 1970 Wilf Hoare was headmaster of Strathallan School where, the school history records, "His enthusiasm for the art of batting held an absolute priority… With an awe-inspiring bellow he would leave his audience open-mouthed as he stepped through the French window [of his study] on to the lawn and, wrestling the bat from the grasp of a boy, he would demonstrate the supreme importance of keeping up the left elbow."

HORNER, NORMAN FREDERICK, died on December 24, 2003, aged 77. Joining Warwickshire in their 1951 Championship season, after two games for his native Yorkshire in 1950, began a happy exile for Norman Horner. By 1953 he was established as Fred Gardner's opening partner and *Wisden* was praising his "readiness to punish the loose ball, no matter what time in the innings he received it". From then until 1964, his last full season, he never missed his thousand runs. The only time he batted down the order for any duration was when MCC asked Warwickshire to try M. J. K. Smith as an opener in 1958. Horner was a neat and nimble Little to Gardner's Large; Smith reckoned: "Norman would have run Fred's legs off him if he had been allowed." When Warwickshire adopted a quick-scoring policy in 1959, Horner was in his element and enjoyed his best three seasons. On an Oval belter in 1960 he scored a career-best 203 not out while putting on 377 with Billy Ibadulla on the first day, at the time the highest unbroken opening partnership anywhere in the world. Smith also bracketed him "with the very top cover fielders, particularly in saving the quick single." He retired in 1965 to concentrate on landscape gardening and work as a groundsman.

IVEY, ALFRED MICHAEL, died on August 10, 2001, aged 76. Michael Ivey was a grammar school boy from Leeds who played seven first-class matches for Oxford between 1949 and 1951 without being able to command a regular batting place.

JEFFREYS, Brigadier PETER JOHN, DSO (and bar), OBE, died on April 3, 2003, aged 93. Peter Jeffreys, decorated for his role on active service in Burma and Korea, was captain of cricket at Radley and also skippered Gold Coast in a four-day "Test" against Nigeria in 1947, scoring 51 in the second innings.

JONES, GAVIN WILLIAM, who died on July 17, 2002, aged 47, was a medium-pace all-rounder whose hard hitting enlivened the later batting. He helped Northern Transvaal win the inaugural Castle Bowl competition in his debut season, 1977-78, and retain it a year later. Jones later coached and managed Easterns and, at the time of his death, was Eastern Union's 2003 World Cup co-ordinator.

KING, FRANCES SARAH, died of meningococcal meningitis on September 11, 2003, aged 22. A skilful bat and seam bowler, she had played 15 one-day internationals for New Zealand's White Ferns, having forced her way into the national side after success at Under-21 and A-team level. She took four for 24 against Australia in the opening match of the 2002-03 World Series of Women's Cricket at Lincoln, and had looked a potential match-winner for the years ahead.

KIRSCHBAUM, GUILLERMO PATRICIO, died on April 13, 2003, aged 35, following a severe asthma attack. Kirschbaum was a star of the Belgrano club and an inspirational captain of the Argentine national side in more than 50 matches, including the 1997 and 2001 ICC Trophy tournaments. His typically flamboyant 34 not out off 18 balls against Malaysia in 2001 helped his side to victory and second place in their group. He was Argentina's highest ICC Trophy run-scorer, with 511.

KITSON, DAVID LEES, who died on May 17, 2002, aged 77, was one of several Yorkshiremen recruited by Somerset to bolster the side in the early 1950s. He spent three seasons at the club, often opening the batting but giving only glimpses of his Bradford League form.

KNOTT, CHARLES JAMES, died on February 27, 2003, aged 88. Charlie Knott was a beguiling and flighty amateur off-spinner for Hampshire in the years before and after the Second World War who went on to become one of the most important behind-the-scenes figures in the club's history. He began as a medium-pacer but in 1938, playing only his third game for Hampshire, Knott experimented with off-breaks on a turning pitch and took nine in the match for 114; the following year he took eight for 85 against Surrey and was capped. Stomach ulcers kept him from active war service – his close-of-play tipple was a pint of milk – but were not a handicap when Championship cricket resumed in 1946. Knott's 122 wickets at 18.47 were a record for a Hampshire amateur in a season and included ten against the touring Indians to warrant both a Test trial and his first invitation to play for the Gentlemen at Lord's. His hat-trick in the drawn 1950 fixture stopped the Players in their tracks when they were 36 runs from victory with seven wickets in hand. He reached 100 wickets that year for the fourth time in five seasons and might easily have been picked for a tour had his batting and fielding been better. After that, Knott began to devote more time to the family businesses: his father was in the fish trade at Southampton Docks and also owned the speedway and greyhound stadium next to the county ground at Northlands Road. But Knott's most important contribution to Hampshire was still to come. As chairman of the cricket committee from 1967 to 1988, he was instrumental in spotting and signing the stars who would lead the club to the 1973 Championship and a succession of one-day trophies. He lent Gordon Greenidge a pair of pyjamas when he arrived in Southampton as a 16-year-old; he insisted on plumping for the then little-known Barry Richards when thwarted in his attempt to sign Clive Lloyd, and also brought over Andy Roberts and Malcolm Marshall. Knott was also well-known in speedway and helped revive the sport in his role as promoter at Southampton, and later Poole. However, when the stadium closed, the land was sold off for housing and not to Hampshire, thus hemming in the ground and forcing the club, decades later, to move to the Rose Bowl.

LAY, STANLEY ARTHUR, died on July 27, 2003, aged 96. Stan Lay won the javelin gold medal for New Zealand in the first British Empire Games (now the Commonwealth Games) in Canada in 1930. Lay was also a cricketer, playing for Taranaki against the 1929-30 MCC team. He was advised to take up the javelin because his throwing arm was so good.

LUCAS, DOUGLAS CHARLES, died on October 28, 2003, aged 89. Doug Lucas was chairman of Northamptonshire from 1980 to 1985, during which time he oversaw a modernisation of the committee structure, and president from 1985 to 1990. He had a lifelong involvement with Horton House, one of the county's leading clubs, and was their president for nearly 30 years.

McCONNON, JAMES EDWARD, died on January 26, 2003, aged 80. Jim McConnon raised a few eyebrows in only his second season of county cricket, when a hat-trick and spell of six for 11 for Glamorgan brought down the 1951 South Africans as they chased 148 to win. He raised many more three years later when he was preferred to Jim Laker, for the 1954-55 Ashes tour. McConnon, from County Durham, had moved to South Wales after a knee injury had put paid to his hopes of a career as Aston Villa's centre-half. Glamorgan signed him in 1949 on the strength of his fast bowling and batting for Newport, but that winter coach George Lavis, observing McConnon's smooth action and long, strong fingers, made him an off-break bowler. Two seasons later he took 136 wickets. Over six feet tall, he flighted the ball beautifully and obtained sharp spin, those big hands held stunning gully catches and occasionally he could hit mightily: in the three years McConnon took 100 wickets (1951, 1954 and 1959) Glamorgan were in the top six. His brief elevation came after he outbowled Laker, taking seven for 23, when Glamorgan shocked Surrey at The Oval in July 1954. Two weeks later he was in the Test team as England experimented against Pakistan. Though he took three for 12 in a six-over spell at Old Trafford and kept his place at The Oval, his tour selection ahead of Laker was a shock, and not a success. "He was homesick by the time we got to Aden," noted MCC manager Geoffrey Howard. Three months into the tour he broke a finger fielding and returned home without playing a Test. The next summer, McConnon broke a bone in his left hand and walked out when Glamorgan insisted on a medical before issuing a new contract. However, after he took 52 wickets at 6.80 apiece to help Burnley win the Lancashire League, Glamorgan were back with the offer of both a contract and a benefit. There was also spin support from Don Shepherd, who was a great admirer: "Jim got so close to the stumps at delivery," he recalled, "he would often knock off the bails with his backside, and round the wicket he was still close." But after taking 113 wickets in 1959, the injuries returned and he went back north to play for Cheshire, coach at Stonyhurst College from 1966, and later work alongside Brian Statham as a sales rep for Guinness.

MALIN, FRANCIS, died on January 28, 2003, aged 73. Frank Malin was president of the Irish Cricket Union in 1985 and, from 1990 to 1992, its first chairman.

MARSH, FREDERICK ERIC, died on March 25, 2003, aged 82. Eric Marsh was an ex-miner who had four post-war seasons with Derbyshire as a left-handed batsman and slow bowler, and for the next 30 years was coach at Repton School, where he was regarded with great affection. "He had an infectious enthusiasm for the game and was unstinting in his attention," recalled one of his more gifted charges, Richard Hutton. At 17, Marsh was knocked unconscious in the Markham Colliery explosion of 1938 in which 79 died; on coming to, he helped in the rescue attempts. He made his debut for Derbyshire in 1946, alongside his uncle Stan Worthington, and over the next two seasons was a valued member of the team as an accurate rather than prodigious spinner. But he faded and, after a short-lived reincarnation as an opener, switched to coaching.

MASOOD IQBAL QURESHI died from kidney failure on October 31, 2003, aged 51. Known to his contemporaries as "Billa", Masood Iqbal was a controversial selection to understudy Wasim Bari as Pakistan's wicket-keeper on their 1972-73 tour of Australia and New Zealand. His batting was negligible, but he was an agile keeper and there were fewer quibbles when he went to England in 1978. "He owned the sweetest sense of timing – that was the key to his wicket-keeping," said Dr Nauman Niaz, a former cricket analyst for the PCB. By the time he played his only one-day international, though, against New Zealand at Multan in 1984-85, he was past his best and gave away 18 byes in 35 overs. Two years later he retired after 17 years of first-class cricket for Lahore teams and for Habib Bank, where he continued to work on completing his MBA. In the 1990s he returned to cricket as an administrator, A-team tour manager, referee and selector. In 2000 he was appointed a PCB groundsman.

Robert Mills with fellow-Yorkshireman Darren Gough before the 1999 World Cup. *Picture by Graham Morris.*

MILLING, HUGH, died in his sleep on February 17, 2003, aged 40, while in Austria with a party of boys from Hulme Grammar School, where he was master in charge of cricket. Earlier in the day he had suffered a blow to the head while skiing. A potent strike bowler in Irish university and club cricket, Milling played 26 times for Ireland and, in his only first-class match, against Scotland in 1987, had match figures of six for 98.

MILLS, ROBERT, who died of a heart attack on October 29, 2003, aged 51, was chief sports writer of the *Yorkshire Post* and had been its cricket correspondent since 1990. After joining the paper from the *Hull Daily Mail*, "Freddie" Mills proudly upheld the *Post's* long tradition of excellent cricket writing, dating back to J. M. Kilburn and beyond. He combined a sharp eye for a news story with a feel for the traditions of the game and his county, qualities that shone through his daily journalism and his book on Headingley, *Field of Dreams*. He was a pipe-smoker with a dry northern humour, much liked by his press box colleagues.

MOORE, DENIS NEVILLE, who died on October 2, 2003, aged 93, scored a double-century in his debut innings for Gloucestershire in 1930 and appeared to be on the verge of greatness. He hit 1,317 runs for Gloucestershire and Oxford University that year and in 1931 became the first man since 1863 to captain the university in his second year. But early that summer he split his thumb fielding in a minor match and, before he was fit again, fell seriously ill with pneumonia and then pleurisy, so missing the University Match and spending four months in bed. He never returned to Oxford, and his batting was never the same. Moore's exceptional talent came to the fore at Shrewsbury School, and he played twice for Oxford before being dropped for the Gloucestershire match at a time when the university's cricket was riddled by factions and dissent. Moore's response was to ask his own county captain, Bev Lyon, if he could play for Gloucestershire against the university. With forceful and attractive strokeplay, he made 206, sharing double-century partnerships of 219 with both "Charlie" Dipper and Wally Hammond out of a total of 627 for two declared; it remained the highest score on debut for a county until surpassed by David Sales of Northamptonshire in 1996. Oxford were obliged to recall him, and he was top-scorer in both innings of the University Match. He appeared occasionally for Gloucestershire between 1932 and 1936 but achieved little. Instead, he concentrated on running the family law firm in Croydon, but he remained a keen player for some of the grander roving clubs into his fifties.

MOORE, NIGEL HAROLD, died on December 24, 2003, aged 73. Moore was a golf Blue at Cambridge, but his first-class cricket there was limited to three early-season games in 1952. For Norfolk between 1947 and 1964 he was, Henry Blofeld said, "a jolly good competitor, an enormously strong man who was a formidable striker of the ball and bowled a sharpish fast-medium." Representing Minor Counties against the South Africans in 1960, he top-scored in the second innings with 59.

MUKHERJEE, SUJIT, who died on January 14, 2003, aged 72, played five Ranji Trophy games as a batsman for Bihar in the 1950s. He had a far greater reputation in India as a publisher, translator and prolific author whose work included five elegant cricket books. A selection of his writings, edited by Ramachandra Guha, was published as *An Indian Cricket Century* in 2002. He was a wry observer of both the game and academic pretentiousness. One essay, "Cricket in the Mother Tongue", combined the two by speculating on the possibilities for the teaching of cricket in a foreign language, with solemn professors churning out theses on "the effect of non-aspirated consonants on the off-drive of left-handed batsmen".

MUNAWWAR HUSSAIN KHAN died on March 26, 2003, aged 88. Popularly known as Mannay Khan, Munawwar Hussain umpired five Test matches in Pakistan between 1958-59 and 1969-70.

NAWAZ, M. E. M., who died on October 14, 2003, aged 70, was one of a select group of Ceylonese all-rounders to perform the double of 1,000 runs and 100 wickets in the Saravanamuttu Trophy. He played mainly for Moors SC and had a reputation as a devastating bowler of medium-pace leg-cutters on matting wickets.

NIAZ AHMED SIDDIQI, who died on April 12, 2000, aged 54, took the new ball for Pakistan in two Tests against England. Although sometimes said to be the only indigenous cricketer from East Pakistan (now Bangladesh) to play Test cricket for Pakistan, Niaz Ahmed was in fact born at Benares, in Uttar Pradesh, and taken to Dacca after Partition. When East Pakistan achieved independence as Bangladesh in 1972, he settled in Karachi. Niaz was on the 1967 tour of England and made his Test debut at Trent Bridge, taking two (Brian Close and Geoff Arnold) for 72. His second Test 18 months later was played against the background of East Pakistan's clamour for independence, and Niaz, the home-town bowler, was judiciously selected ahead of Asif Masood for the Dacca Test against Colin Cowdrey's beleaguered tourists. An engineer by profession, he played most of his domestic cricket for the Public Works Department (PWD), helping them reach the Quaid-e-Azam Trophy final in 1969-70 and captaining the side in 1973-74, his final season.

NICKEL, AARON, died on May 25, 2003, aged 79. Polish-born, Nickel played six games for Transvaal in the early 1950s, and in 1952-53 his fast-medium in-swing set up the vital win against Rhodesia that guaranteed Transvaal's immediate return to the Currie Cup A section after being relegated. Bowling unchanged on a damp Salisbury pitch he took seven for 43 as the home side were bowled out for 68. His match figures of ten for 87 were the best on the ground during Rhodesia's participation in South African domestic cricket. His nephew, Ali Bacher, captained South Africa and became a prominent administrator.

NIXON, Dr ROBERT GRAEME, died on June 27, 2003, aged 78. A Bulawayo dentist, Bob Nixon enjoyed a considerable reputation in southern Africa as a radio commentator. He also broadcast in England on World Cup matches and for the BBC while living there from 1986 to 1992. "Bob was the first to guide me in microphone technique," Robin Jackman said. "His was a gentle voice that belonged to a gentle man." When Rhodesia became Zimbabwe in 1980 Nixon entered parliament as an Independent.

NOREIGA, JACK MOLLINSON, who died on August 8, 2003, aged 67, after a stomach operation, was the only West Indian to take nine wickets in a Test innings. He did so against India at Queen's Park Oval in March 1971 in his second Test. Once Grayson Shillingford had bowled Ashok Mankad for 44, Noreiga wheeled away with his cleverly flighted off-spinners but was unable to prevent the Indians from establishing a match-winning lead. Eight of his victims were caught (two caught and bowled) and one was stumped. Noreiga, a clerk in Trinidad's Ministry of Works, was 34 at the time and before that season had played only one first-class game for the island – nine years earlier, and also against an Indian touring team. However, Trinidad called him up in 1970-71 on what *Wisden* called "the dubious pitches at the Queen's Park Oval", and with his sharp off-break and good control he immediately justified his inclusion: six for 50 in the innings win over Combined Islands was followed by 11 for 153 as Trinidad beat Barbados for the first time in 26 years. He was brought into the West Indies team because Lance Gibbs was out of form and played in four of the five Tests against India – taking 15 wickets in the two Tests at Queen's Park, but only two in his other two. Noreiga, a father of nine children, became a well-known coach and played club cricket up to the season before his death.

PHILLIPS, JOHN GORDON PICTON, died on February 24, 2003, aged 66. Gordon Phillips was a newspaper archivist and librarian, and a cricket-lover who joined Marcus Williams in compiling *The Wisden Book of Cricket Memorabilia* (1990). He was *Wisden's* cricketana correspondent from 1999 until his death. He emigrated from his native Rhodesia in 1965 and was archivist of *The Times* from 1970 to 1982.

POCOCK, HOWARD JOHN, died on August 10, 2003, aged 82. John Pocock played seven games for Kent as a batsman in the late 1940s. He was later a Maidstone businessman and a long-serving committee man who was Kent chairman from 1978 to 1985 and president in 1988.

PRICE, ERIC JAMES, died on July 13, 2002, aged 83. Eric Price was a left-arm spinner who in a short career in the late 1940s experienced some remarkable peaks and troughs. Price made a spectacular start with Lancashire after the war, with match figures of seven for 25 in his third match against Worcestershire, including George Dews (see above, page 1538) for a king pair. By the end of June Price had 40 wickets at 13.27 to earn a Test trial at Canterbury. Spinning and flighting the ball more than his Lancashire partner Bill Roberts, though less accurate, he finished the season with 87 wickets and was capped. There were fewer opportunities in 1947, though, and Essex enticed him south on a special registration. His first home game for them was a bowler's nightmare: he was the man treated most brutally (20–0–156–0) when Bradman's Australians ran up 721 in a day. Price had a better time in 1949, but, as Doug Insole recalled, "Essex wickets in those days were grassy and not really suited to a very slow left-armer like Eric." So he returned home to Middleton, took a job with the local authority, and played for the local club in the Central Lancashire League. In his four seasons of county cricket he had taken 215 wickets at 26.60. Never more than a tailender, Price had few strokes but a serene knack for survival that was occasionally endangered by his running between the wickets, a stagger described by the *Manchester Guardian's* T. C. F. Prittie as "a nervous febrile animation".

PRINS, VERNON GEORGE, who died on July 31, 2003, aged 79, captained Ceylon from 1956-57 to 1959-60. He was a seam-bowling all-rounder who led Nondescripts to the Saravanamuttu Trophy four times in the 1950s, and he was the club's patron when he died. Prins was a police inspector and also played hockey for Ceylon.

PROCTER, WOODROW COLLACOTT, who died on July 26, 2003, aged 81, was the father of South African all-rounder Mike Procter. As a 17-year-old schoolboy leg-spinner, he played for Eastern Province against Wally Hammond's 1938-39 MCC side, but his bowling was hammered: two for 114 in 13 overs. His only other first-class game was a friendly against Border the following season. Sons Anton and Mike played together for Natal in 1966-67.

RAMCHAND, GULABRAI SIPAHIMALANI, died on September 8, 2003, aged 76. "Ram" Ramchand captained India to their first Test win over Australia, at Kanpur in December 1959. Off-spinner Jasu Patel took 14 for 124 on a newly laid pitch and Ramchand "led us brilliantly to victory", Chandu Borde recalled, "always giving us the self-belief that we could beat them." Australia's captain, Richie Benaud, went to the Indian dressing-room afterwards and presented his counterpart with his Australian blazer. Born in Karachi, Ramchand played his first Ranji Trophy cricket for Sind and moved south to Bombay after Partition, helping them win six Ranji finals between 1948-49 and 1962-63. He hit hundreds in all but the first, when he made two unbeaten half-centuries: few contemporary Indians struck the ball harder. Add to that his robust fast-medium in-swing bowling and efficient fielding and it is easy to appreciate why English league clubs targeted him in the 1950s. He proved himself a useful utility player around the counties

Ram Ramchand at Lord's in 1952: in December 1959 he captained the first Indian team to beat Australia in a Test.

on India's 1952 tour but was less successful in the four Tests, spun out for a pair on debut and capturing only four wickets in the series. Given the new ball at Headingley and Lord's, he "looked every inch a fast bowler until he actually bowled," as Sujit Mukherjee put it. He probably lacked sufficient variety for Test cricket and only once managed a five-wicket return in his 33 Tests, getting six for 49 at his native Karachi in 1954-55. His middle-order batting, on the other hand, established him in the Test side and he made a sparkling 106 not out against New Zealand in 1955-56 and a watchful 109 against Australia at Bombay a year later. Hemu Adhikari was chosen ahead of him as India's fourth captain in the confused 1958-59 series against West Indies, and Ramchand was overlooked for the 1959 tour of England. Following that disaster, he was made captain against Australia and retired from Tests after the series, returning to winning Ranji Trophies for Bombay. In 1975, by now an executive at Air India, he was India's manager at the first World Cup.

REYNOLDS, ALFRED GEORGE, died on January 7, 2003, aged 95. Devon-born George Reynolds made his first-class debut for Orange Free State at 17 while still a schoolboy. Two seasons later, in 1926-27, he was opening their bowling and heading the averages when they were Currie Cup runners-up to Transvaal. His six for 27 in 12 overs at Newlands helped bowl out Western Province for a lowest-ever 44 after they had made the Free State follow on. The last of his ten games was against MCC in 1930-31. Reynolds also played provincial-level tennis and his daughter, Sandra, was runner-up to Maria Bueno at Wimbledon in 1960.

RICHARDSON, REGINALD MAXWELL, died on July 2, 2003, aged 80. Reg Richardson was one of five brothers who played first-class cricket for Tasmania, as did their father and uncle. Another four brothers also played first-grade. He later served as treasurer of the Tasmanian Cricket Association, and was chairman in 1986 when the committee was overthrown by a reformers' coup.

RING, DOUGLAS THOMAS, died on June 23, 2003, aged 84. Doug Ring was one of the spear-carriers for the 1948 Australian Invincibles, cheerfully describing himself as one of the "groundstaff bowlers" as he wheeled round the counties without getting near the Test team until the morning of the final Test, when Bradman asked Ring to sit alongside him in the taxi and told him he was playing. Ring was a wrist-spinner in an era when Australia had plenty of choice – Colin McCool, Bruce Dooland and fellow-Victorian George Tribe were all capped against England in 1946-47, and it was February 1948, the last Test against India, before Ring got a look-in. Match figures of six for 120 won him selection for England, and the captain's admiration, which he retained. Bradman said Ring bowled consistently well in England, and would have played far more but for the rule then in force permitting the new ball after only 55 overs. He won a regular place at home against West Indies and South Africa in 1951-52 and 1952-53, taking six for 72 against South Africa at Brisbane. He was also instrumental in one of the most thrilling of all Test wins. When last man Bill Johnston, his club-mate at Richmond, joined him at the MCG crease on the last day of the New Year Test in 1952, the Australians were 38 short of victory and the West Indians were one wicket away from squaring the series 2–2. Ring thumped 14 from one Valentine over, took 11 off another by Ramadhin and clinched the series. This was achieved with a borrowed bat – Ring never took himself or his batting seriously enough to acquire one – and accompanied by roars of "C'mon the Tigers", the nickname for Richmond. He played again in the Lord's Test of 1953, when Willie Watson and Trevor Bailey famously held out for a draw. Had Ray Lindwall caught Watson at short leg off Ring, Australia would probably have kept the Ashes. On that tour, he passed on the secret of his sliding top-spinner to the young Richie Benaud. Afterwards, he concentrated on captaining Richmond, working as a civil servant in a department run by Sir Robert Menzies's brother, Les, who in keeping with family tradition considered Ring's frequent absences to commentate on cricket for radio and TV entirely reasonable. He kept his cheerful, leg-spinner's disposition: "I never got mad about the game, because it *was* a game" he once said. Though the joke has persisted down the decades, there is no record that the famous scatological scorecard entry, Crapp c Hole b Ring, ever occurred.

Doug Ring after attending Don Bradman's memorial service in 2001.
Picture by Sean Garnsworthy, Getty Images.

ROGERS, NEVILLE HAMILTON, who died on October 7, 2003, aged 85, was a fixed point at the top of the Hampshire order for almost a decade after the war. He scored 1,000 runs nine times and in 1952 became the first post-war Hampshire batsman to reach 2,000. Rogers came from a cricketing family in Oxfordshire – his grandfather Charles appears in *Wisden* as the bowler in "Record Hit". He had a trial at Southampton before the war, rapidly established himself afterwards and several times came close to Test selection: he was twelfth man for both sides at the 1950 Test trial and for England at The Oval in 1951. He also played in the 1953 Test trial, only to damage his thumb next match, miss Hampshire's game against the Australians and suffer a dip in form at the wrong moment. Hampshire "never had a more technically and temperamentally complete and reliable opening batsman," wrote John Arlott. "He was at his best when his side was in trouble." This was illustrated in 1954 when Rogers carried his bat four times in the season, close to the record of five by C. J. B. Wood of Leicestershire in 1911 and matched only by R. G. Barlow of Lancashire in 1882. The following year Rogers announced he would retire to go into business, but there was one last challenge. Deputising as captain after Desmond Eagar was injured in early August, he led Hampshire to three wins, two draws and third place in the Championship, higher than ever before.

SARWATE, CHANDRASEKHAR TRIMBAK, died on December 23, 2003, aged 83. A diminutive spin-bowling all-rounder in the legendary Holkar team that contested ten Ranji Trophy finals in 11 seasons, Chandu Sarwate played nine Tests for India between 1946 and 1951-52. He is perhaps best remembered for his last-wicket partnership of 249 with Shute Banerjee against Surrey in 1946. As Banerjee walked out to join Sarwate, Oval groundsman Bert Lock went with him to ask the Surrey captain what roller he wanted between innings. Three hours ten minutes later both batsmen had hundreds, the only time the No. 10 and No. 11 have achieved this in the same innings. When Surrey followed on, Sarwate spun the Indians to victory with his mixture of off- and leg-breaks, finishing with five for 54. A week later he took a hat-trick against Scotland, but he was seen at his best only occasionally after that. *Wisden* said he "seemed to lack confidence". He had a horrid series as opener on the tour of Australia in 1947-48 and was disappointing again in England in 1952. Sarwate was simply more at home in domestic cricket, indulging his hard, straight hitting or bowling his varied spinners – the off-break reputedly turned more than the legger – with a jerky, but legitimate, action. Shortly before going to England in 1946 he hit 101 when opening Holkar's innings against Mysore – one of six centuries in their 912 for eight declared – and followed up with a career-best nine for 91 in Mysore's first innings. Sarwate's small stature and boyish smile led to him being called the Peter Pan of Indian cricket. His cricketing longevity made it even more appropriate. Having made his debut at 16 in 1936-37, he continued playing Ranji Trophy cricket until he was 48. He was a handwriting and fingerprint expert by profession, and in 1946 tricked fellow-tourist Gul Mahomed with a letter, purportedly from a female admirer, suggesting a romantic assignation. A national selector at the time India won the World Cup in 1983, he also served as secretary of Madhya Pradesh Cricket Association.

SCHOLES, WALTER JOHN, died from a heart attack on July 14, 2003, aged 53. Short, bandy-legged and unambiguously known as "Barrel", John Scholes was an influential figure in Victoria's cricket as player, selector and coach. He first played for the state at 19 when his footwork was compared to that of Neil Harvey, and became the state's youngest captain at 22, when he deputised in 1972-73 in the absence of Keith Stackpole and Paul Sheahan. Scholes marked the occasion with a century against New South Wales and went close to national recognition. Yet in other years he was in and out of the side, and for three seasons from 1976 could not get a game. When he did captain Victoria again, in 1981-82, they won only the wooden spoon and Scholes retired, but he went on to set records in local cricket and came back in 1996 as state coach. He soon instilled in his squad something of his own passion and a professional approach nurtured by his experience of Australian Rules football.

SHUJAUDDIN SIDDIQI, who died on July 21, 2003, aged 84, umpired in 22 Tests in Pakistan over a span of nearly a quarter of a century, starting in 1954-55. Some of those Tests required more than normal umpiring skills: on MCC's riot-racked tour in 1968-69, he stood in all three Tests, including the Karachi game when protesters stormed the gates.

SMITH, DAVID ROBERT, died on December 17, 2003, aged 69. For a decade Smith and Tony Brown carried the Gloucestershire seam attack, and in his 1968 benefit match Smith became the first fast bowler to take 1,000 wickets for the county. He was closer to medium-pace than fast, but had a classical action. "'Smudger' was much quicker than he looked," Brown said. "He held the ball seam-up, bowled an accurate off-stump line and hit the seam regularly. He didn't really swing it but batsmen were surprised by his movement and lift." Smith was also willing: in 1960, he bowled almost 1,300 overs and took 143 wickets. That winter he toured New Zealand with MCC, playing in 18 of their 21 games, and another 124 wickets in 1961 brought selection for the tour of India and Pakistan. He played in all five Tests in India, in conditions unsympathetic to his style. Later, he became more injury-prone but he had match figures of 11 for 92 against the West Indians a year later. And with Mike Procter spearheading the attack, Smith was still there to take 74 wickets in 1969 and help Gloucestershire finish second in the Championship. He retired in 1971 to help his wife run a fancy goods shop in Bristol. One of four League footballers at Gloucestershire in his early days (along with Arthur Milton, Barrie Meyer and Ron Nicholls), he played on the left wing for Bristol City and Millwall.

SMITH, NEIL, died of cancer on March 3, 2003, aged 53. Smith served a four-year apprenticeship as Yorkshire's Second Eleven wicket-keeper and seemed the natural successor to the long-serving Jimmy Binks in 1970 but, after a shaky start, was usurped in mid-season by 18-year-old David Bairstow, who took his A-Levels at 7 a.m. so he could play. Bairstow established himself, and Smith moved to Essex to succeed Brian Taylor in 1973 and spent the next eight years as a stalwart of that famously perky dressing-room. Technically, many thought him a better gloveman than Bairstow, but he was on the large side, and irritated Graham Gooch by eating a lot and getting larger. This helped his often beefy batting, which had minimal backlift but considerable power: Essex occasionally used him as a pinch-hitter long before the term was ever used. In 1981, he lost form and was again ousted in mid-season, this time by David East. Smith captained the second team for a season then went back north to go into business.

SOLANKY, JOHN WILLIAM, died of a heart attack on October 7, 2003, aged 61. Solanky was an all-rounder from Tanganyika who came to wider notice with a half-century and four wickets opening the bowling for East Africa against MCC

John Solanky: an all-rounder who made the long journey from his native Tanganyika to Glamorgan.

Picture by Patrick Eagar.

in Kampala in 1963. Political change encouraged him to move to England, and several counties noticed his wristy run-making and nagging medium-pace bowling when he played for Devon. Solanky joined Glamorgan in 1971, and was capped in 1973 although Glamorgan had to cope with a TCCB ruling that deemed him an overseas player until the end of 1974, the legacy of his two first-class games in East Africa. Solanky gave Glamorgan added value by mixing his seamers with off-breaks, and against Derbyshire at Cardiff in 1975 returned career-best figures of six for 63 on a turning pitch. But he failed to make a first-class century and left after a shake-up when Glamorgan finished bottom in 1976. He later coached and taught technology in Northern Ireland.

STEPHENSON, Lieutenant-Colonel JOHN ROBIN CBE, died on June 2, 2003, aged 72. He had been afflicted by a rare virus that attacked his spine. Known to staff, club members and public alike as "The Colonel", John Stephenson was secretary of MCC from 1987 to 1993, a position he once described as "tougher than commanding a battalion". Since he commanded a battalion in Northern Ireland at the height at the troubles, he spoke with some authority. After retiring from the army, Stephenson had gone to Lord's in 1979 as assistant secretary (cricket). He was in the Christ's Hospital XI in 1948 with both his predecessor as secretary, Jack Bailey, and a future MCC president in Dennis Silk; he was the only one of them not to play first-class cricket and the first MCC secretary not to do so in more than a century. He stepped into the job when he was already 56, just four years off the club's retirement age, after Bailey resigned in an acrimonious cross-Lord's dispute with the then Test and County Cricket Board about MCC's rights. Immediately after Stephenson took office, the members rebelled and rejected the club's annual report; and then Colin Cowdrey, a high-profile president in MCC's bicentenary year, underwent heart surgery. But "The Colonel" – then still also ex officio secretary of the ICC – took everything in his stride, bringing an air of calm to Lord's with the gifts of a natural conciliator. Though a mild figure of fun to the public, who most often saw him on wet days striding grandly across the Lord's outfield directing operations, he was a charming and unstuffy man, beloved by his staff. His most crusty-colonel remarks about modern cricketers ("I can't think why they want to kiss and hug and behave like association footballers, but they do") were made with a knowing air. But he was not a natural moderniser and, after his retirement, went on record against the admission of women into the club. MCC asked him to stay on for two more years after he reached 60, though he still felt underused in retirement. A congregation of 1,000 paid tribute to him in Salisbury Cathedral.

STUDD, SIR PETER MALDON GBE, KCVO, DL, who died on June 22, 2003, aged 86 was a handy batsman and the fourth member of his family to captain Cambridge University. Studd made a century for Harrow against Eton at Lord's in 1935 and slowly established himself in the Cambridge team in the years ahead. As secretary in 1938, Studd devised a number of measures to put the university's cricket on a less casual basis, but the following year still had to captain them through a second successive winless season. He became a senior executive at the printers De La Rue and in 1970 emulated one of his Cambridge great-uncles, Sir Kynaston Studd, by becoming Lord Mayor of London. As such, he officiated, in full regalia, at the reopening of London Bridge at Lake Havasu City, Arizona.

SYMCOX, CLAUDE WARREN, died in a road accident in South Africa on July 15, 2002, aged 38. Warren Symcox, a cousin of Test off-spinner Pat, was a medium-pace all-rounder who played 14 Castle Bowl games for Griqualand West after making his debut at 20 in 1984-85. He was an executive with the diamond company, De Beers.

THOMPSON, ROLAND GEORGE, died on May 16, 2003, aged 70. Although he first played for Warwickshire as a 16-year-old, and showed startling form as a teenage fast bowler, Roly Thompson never quite fulfilled his cricketing promise. He shared the new ball with Fred Trueman for the Combined Services against the 1952 Indians and went home on leave from the RAF to take nine for 65 for Warwickshire in Nottinghamshire's first innings at Edgbaston, surprising batsmen and team-mates alike with his pace off the pitch. Though he became a regular wicket-taker, there was strong competition for places and Thompson often found himself in the Second XI. In 1959, linking up with Ossie Wheatley, he took 97 wickets at 17.96 to finish sixth in the national averages and help Warwickshire climb from 16th to fourth in the Championship. But his place was soon threatened by younger bowlers. Increasingly injury-prone and disillusioned he turned down

The Colonel: Lt Col. John Stephenson was Secretary of MCC between 1987 and 1993, a position he described as 'tougher than commanding a battalion'.
Picture by Patrick Eagar.

a contract after the 1961 season and went to work at the Lockheed factory in Leamington. According to his former captain, M. J. K. Smith, "Roly probably shortened his career by trying to bowl too fast." Jack Bannister thought that Warwickshire did him no favours by preferring short-term prospects like Keith Dollery and Ossie Wheatley "just at a time when an extended run in the first team would have benefited club and player". He finished with a very respectable record of 479 wickets at 22.77.

THOMS, GEORGE RONALD, died on August 29, 2003, aged 76. Thoms played only two full seasons of Sheffield Shield cricket and in the first, 1951-52, he and Colin McDonald, his Melbourne University team-mate, formed such a successful opening partnership for Victoria that both made their Test debut in the final match of the West Indies series, as did Richie Benaud. It was Thoms's ninth first-class game. His batting was painstaking, and his future was decided when he trod on his wicket for 28 in the second innings. While McDonald went on to 47 Tests, Thoms had ten more games for Victoria before becoming a gynaecological surgeon and laser-surgery pioneer. He would certainly have played more Shield cricket but for his concern that a hand injury could jeopardise his future as a surgeon.

TINNISWOOD, PETER, who died of cancer on January 9, 2003, aged 66, was a prolific and original comic writer with an eye for the minutiae of English life. His genre was initially abrasive northern surrealism, but in the 1980s he turned his attention to cricket and through one character, a crusty cricket obsessive known as the Brigadier, created *Tales from a Long Room*, a fantasy on "our summer

The Brigadier: Peter Tinniswood holding court in the England dressing-room during the 1982-83 tour of Australia.

Picture by Graham Morris.

game" riddled with puns, verbal abuse and whimsical name-play. It began as a radio monologue with Robin Bailey, who had played Uncle Mort in Tinniswood's television masterpiece *I Didn't Know You Cared*, as the Brigadier, recalling the MCC tour of the Belgian Congo in 1914: "There were at least two outbreaks of cannibalism among spectators… which I am convinced were responsible for the loss of our most promising young leg-spinner, M. M. Rudman-Stott. He was sent out to field at deep third man in the match against an Arab Slavers' Country Eleven, and all we found of him after the tea interval was the peak of his Harlequins cap and half an indelible pencil." In time, Tinniswood transported listeners to the snug hamlet of Witney Scrotum, introducing them to Granny Roebuck who ran the cake shop, Mr Bruce Woodcock of *The Times*, E. W. "Gloria" Swanton, Winston Place, the former Lancashire batsman and one of Tinniswood's real-life heroes, and the recurrent Mr H. D. "Dickie" Bird. There was also romance. "Into my view she glided; a tall, slim sylphlike figure in purest white. My heart missed a beat. The sap rose in my loins. Dear God, she was the spitting image of Herbert Sutcliffe. Call it the impetuosity of youth if you will, but remember I had been out of the country for many years, serving my King and country in some of the remotest and most primitive outposts of his Empire. I had not seen a first-class cricketer for seven years." The monologues spawned several books, a stage play with Willie Rushton as the Brigadier, recalling army times in the Far East and the massive earthworks at Botham's Gut, a column in *The Cricketer*, even a short-lived television version. Though seriously ill, and able to communicate only through an electronic voicebox, Tinniswood continued to write prodigiously and was *Wisden's* book reviewer in 2000.

TOSHACK, ERNEST RAYMOND HERBERT, died on May 11, 2003, aged 88. Ernie Toshack – "the Black Prince" – had the briefest career of Don Bradman's 1948 Australian Invincibles. He was almost 31 when he made his debut for New South Wales, in November 1945, and his career was ended by a knee injury barely four years later. But in the years in between, he was integral to Australia's formidable attack, containing opposition batsmen with his accuracy and stamina while Ray Lindwall and Keith Miller drew breath. Toshack was a 6ft 2in left-arm swing bowler, who made himself a specialist on rain-affected wickets by reducing his pace from fast to brisk medium and developing an armoury that included off-cutters, in- and away-swingers, a quicker delivery and an orthodox left-arm spinner's leg-break to the right-hander. Bowling a leg-stump line from over the wicket to two short legs and a silly mid-on, he was almost impossible to get away in England in 1948. Bradman called him "unique in every way". Orphaned at six, Toshack had represented New South Wales Second XI before a ruptured appendix in 1938 left him in a wheelchair for months and kept him from active war service. After moving to Sydney, he made a slow but steady comeback and took six for 18, routing New Zealand in the March 1946 match at Wellington that was retrospectively elevated to Test status. In his first Test against England, on a Brisbane sticky in 1946-47, Toshack's line had been so leg-stump that Bradman took him out to the middle on the fifth morning to show him where he should be pitching the ball in such conditions. Without a wicket overnight, Toshack responded with nine that day as England followed on and were beaten by an innings. Two months later, in the heat of Adelaide, he bowled 66 eight-ball overs for match figures of five for 135. But later that year Toshack caught the Indians at Brisbane, wrapping up their first innings with five for two in 19 balls and taking six for 29 in the second. However, he was already having knee trouble, and he made the trip to England only on a 3–2 majority vote. By the time he broke down in the Fourth Test, Australia had retained the Ashes. In England's second innings at Lord's, with Miller unable to bowl, Toshack took five for 40. A born No. 11, he was the fifth Australian to average over 50 that series thanks to a series of not-outs. Toshack's rugged looks and dry humour made him a great favourite with the crowds, as did his theatrical appealing and equally theatrical off-field props (bowler hat, furled umbrella and large cigars). But when he retired, he joined a firm of builders and dropped out of sight. When the Invincibles held a reunion fifty years on, Toshack – his hair by then as white as it had once been dark – had to be reintroduced to some of his team-mates.

TUPPIN, ALFRED GEORGE, who died on July 20, 2003, aged 91, was a solidly built medium-pacer who played 23 games for Sussex before the war.

UNWIN, Lieutenant-Colonel ERNEST JAMES, died on November 23, 2003, aged 91. Better known as an England and 1938 British Lions rugby three-quarter, Unwin played most of his cricket for Army sides and had seven Championship games for Essex, bowling brisk medium, in the 1930s.

URQUHART, JOHN RANKIN, died on June 16, 2003, aged 82. A late selection by Cambridge for the 1948 University Match, Urquhart was a fast-medium swing bowler who pulled a back muscle in the nets on the second morning at Lord's and was unable to bowl in Oxford's only innings. He had earned his place with match figures of seven for 66 at Bristol, where he and Trevor Bailey bowled out Gloucestershire for 123.

VAN GELOVEN, JACK, who died on August 21, 2003, aged 69, was the last Yorkshireman to do the 1,000 runs-100 wickets double, a fact that is a staple of the more specialised type of cricket quiz since he was playing for Leicestershire at the time. Van Geloven achieved the feat in 1962 by taking his 100th wicket against Yorkshire, who were battling for yet another Championship, after plugging away for 52 overs in the match. Son of a Dutch professional footballer, young Jackie served apprenticeships with Yorkshire and Leeds United before choosing cricket over football, making his county debut in 1955 and a year later joining Leicestershire on a special registration. What he brought them were big in-swingers bowled from wide of the crease – he had opened the bowling in his three games for Yorkshire – and stolid concentration at the top of the order. He played on until 1966, by which time Grace Road was starting to favour spin, and then spent eight seasons with Northumberland. But from 1977 to 1983 he reappeared in the game as an umpire, and achieved a new kind of celebrity on the circuit. Van Geloven was not unlike Dickie Bird (though a much better player and a much inferior umpire), especially in the way in which he became the centrepiece of numerous anecdotes in which his role was always that a put-upon victim, usually in terror of being found out by Lord's. Though a brilliant, deadpan raconteur himself, especially over a pint or several, van Geloven never quite saw the humour in these situations, all of them well-attested though hard to pin down in place and time. On one occasion, Ray East – given out caught the ball before tea – insisted to Jack it was a bump ball and, with everyone else in on the joke, reappeared at the crease after the interval, loomed up to the umpire and said "You were joking, weren't you?" "Gerroff!" screamed a horrified Jack, "you'll get us all shot!" On a rainy day at Acklam Park, Middlesbrough, he was playfully pushed into the communal bath by a bored Graham Stevenson. Word got round, and van Geloven sought reassurance it would not get in the papers. Terry Brindle of the *Yorkshire Post* wound him up even more by saying he had already sent a paragraph but told him: "It's all right, Jack. I added the line 'Drink was in no way involved.'" Once at Bradford he declined to give David Bairstow stumped off a wide until a small boy ran on with a scorebook containing the Laws and pointed to the relevant passage. Van Geloven later spent 12 years as head groundsman and coach at Fettes College, where he was regarded with great affection, and the school helped him through a difficult last illness, when he suffered several heart attacks.

WADDINGTON, ALFRED, who died on December 10, 2002, aged 87, was a left-arm seamer and the older brother of the more famous Jack. Either side of World War II, Alfred played alongside him in all but three of his 22 games for Griqualand West. Against Rhodesia at Kimberley in 1946-47 they took 18 of the 20 wickets, with Alfred returning a career-best five for 52 in the first innings.

WADE, WALTER WAREHAM, died on May 31, 2003, aged 88, in the Durban house where he was born and had lived all his life. His 1932 Natal Schools team-mate and lifelong friend, Dereck Dowling, had died the day before. "Billy" Wade began and ended his first-class career as a wicket-keeper/batsman against Australian touring sides, making his provincial debut in 1935-36 alongside his older brother Herbie, then South Africa's captain. By the time MCC toured in 1938-39, however, he was playing purely as a batsman, with team-mate Bob Williams reckoned to be South Africa's premier wicket-keeper. But the selectors sprang a surprise by giving Wade the gloves, and his Test debut, to strengthen South Africa's batting. "In the event," he wrote, "although I kept pretty well in the First and Second Tests and most of the Third, I made no runs to speak of... Being the third man in Tom Goddard's hat-trick [in the First Test at Johannesburg] didn't help my confidence." Nor did it help that, being a naturally gifted, free-scoring batsman with time to play his strokes, he took Test match batting a shade conservatively. Conceding no byes as England compiled 559 for nine in just over two days at Cape Town confirmed his own assessment of his glove-work, but in the first of the two Durban Tests he failed to stump Eddie Paynter soon after he reached his half-century. Paynter went on to make 243 and Wade was dropped. It would be ten years before he next played Test cricket although, after being captured at Tobruk in 1942, he did captain South Africa in PoW "Tests" against Australia at Stalag 344, Lamsdorff. He opted out of cricket until late 1947 to concentrate on building up his accountancy practice, but once re-established as Natal's keeper, Wade hit form again, and kept in all five Tests against England in 1948-49. When the Australians toured a year later, the runs dried up, and after three Tests he was dropped and soon retired, although he returned as an umpire between 1966 and 1974. When he stood in the First Test at Cape Town in 1969-70 Wade became the first South African to play and umpire at this level.

WEEKES, DONALD RUDOLPH, died on November 29, 2003, aged 63. This Bajan blaster was never a first-class cricketer but a yarn-spinner of international calibre who was the subject of a lengthy profile in *The Cricketer* in 1975, headlined "The best batsman never to have played Test cricket?" Among various implausibilities, the description of his century "for Barbados against Trinidad" as "one of the most brilliant" seen on the Bridgetown ground omits the detail that it was for Barbados B. Tony Cozier, who worked with Weekes on the *Daily News* sports desk in Bridgetown in the mid-1960s, remembers him holding listeners spellbound with "descriptions of fantastic innings in far-flung places, a first-hand assessment of Muhammad Ali's cross [he claimed he had sparred with Ali in Tokyo] and analysis of the young Viv Richards." "I see a lot of Don Weekes in that boy," he would say. Certainly, they were similar in build, method and power. But Weekes's cavalier batting was given fullest expression outside the Caribbean. Living in California, he captained the United States against Canada in 1969 and 1970, and in 1972 hit their first hundred in the series since 1898. *Wisden* also records him making double-hundreds for American clubs touring British Columbia and England in 1970. But neither *Wisden*, nor any other source, authenticates his claims to have scored 700 not out in an innings in India, totalled 2,879 runs for Blackpool in his first English season, or played Othello in Moscow.

WEIR, GORDON LINDSAY, died on October 31, 2003, having been, at 95 years 151 days, considered the oldest surviving Test cricketer. That distinction passed to M. J. Gopalan of India (very briefly, see page 1543). Known as "Dad" for most of his adult life because, as his Auckland and New Zealand team-mate Merv Wallace put it, "his hair thinned out very quickly and he looked older than the rest of us", Weir played the first of his 11 Tests at 21 against England in 1929-30. He had made his Auckland debut two years earlier as a lower-order medium-pace all-rounder, but by the time he left for England with the 1931 New Zealanders he was arguably their leading right-hand batsman. As well as three half-centuries against the MCC tourists, he had hit four hundreds in his previous five Plunket Shield games. His defence was sound, he had a good selection of shots and, when he failed to score as freely as he expected on arriving in England, his tenacity helped him adjust to the different environment. But in an often overmatched team,

Lindsay "Dad" Weir: New Zealand all-rounder turned schoolmaster.
Picture by Photosport.

he was only a modest run-getter, and the gritty unbeaten 74 he scored as New Zealand went down by an innings at Christchurch against South Africa remained his best score. He did poorly in England in 1937. But Weir was a useful, adaptable cricketer, capable of opening the batting or bowling as required. He played on for Auckland and remained involved in his career as a schoolmaster, spending many years as selector-coach of Auckland's Under-20 teams for the national Brabin Cup tournament. In the early 1930s he also played rugby for Auckland.

WEST, PETER ANTHONY, who died on September 2, 2003, aged 83, was the beaming and unflustered front man for BBC's televised cricket coverage for nearly 20 years until his retirement in 1986. The smile was genuine: Peter West was a charming and courteous man with a boyish enthusiasm for sport that never left him. But he had an acute sense of the need to marry sport and commerce, and his most lasting contribution may well be as a pioneer of sporting sponsorship. At Cranbrook School he won colours at five games and was captain of cricket for three years: post-war employment as a sports reporter for the Exchange Telegraph agency seemed the perfect job. His break came in 1947 while covering cricket at Taunton. C. B. Fry's telephonist failed to materialise and West offered to phone his copy through. In return Fry, liking the clarity of the young man's voice, promised a recommendation to the BBC, with West wisely not letting on that he had already failed a newsreading audition. By August he was commentating on the South African tour and a year later was covering the London Olympics. He was in the commentary team when the BBC first televised Test cricket nationally in 1952 – he had been doing rugby since 1950 – and soon made his debut at Wimbledon. Aside from sport he hosted light entertainment programmes, and from 1957 to 1972, much to the amusement of the rugby fraternity, West was the dinner-jacketed compère of *Come Dancing*. There was even a stint presenting Miss World. He also set up the *Playfair* cricket and rugby annuals, editing the former until 1953, wrote books on the 1953 and 1956 Ashes, covered cricket for *The Times*, and was their rugby correspondent for 11 years. In 1970 he set up the sports marketing agency West Nally, which married the entrepreneurial vision of Patrick Nally with West's reputation and ambassadorial skills. The company were involved with the Benson and Hedges Cup from its start in 1972 and, five years later, managed Cornhill Insurance's ground-breaking sponsorship of Test matches in England. After retiring from television, West was offered the chance to cover the 1986-87 Ashes tour for the *Daily Telegraph*. He leapt at the chance to fill in one of the last gaps in his sporting CV, understandably imagining that the *Telegraph* expected him to cover the cricket in his own Corinthian and by then rather old-fashioned way. Instead, a tragi-comic few months ensued, with the *Telegraph*, which was in a confused period, sending increasingly testy messages demanding that West match the latest revelations or speculations in the tabloids. The experience did produce one last cricket book, *Clean Sweep*, to sit alongside his engaging memoir, *Flannelled Fool and Muddied Oaf*. West then headed for a happy retirement in the West Country, cultivating his garden.

WHITE, Brigadier WILLIAM MICHAEL EASTWOOD CBE, died on February 15, 2003, aged 89. Mike White was a medium-pace bowler who played occasionally for Cambridge in 1937 without winning a Blue. But he bowled well enough for Combined Services against Northamptonshire in 1947 to be asked to play for the county when available, and he removed three Somerset batsmen in six balls in both innings on his debut at Weston. He appeared in only four more county games, but achieved a footnote in cricket history by scoring two separate hundreds in a day, in a non-first-class game for Aldershot Services against MCC in 1949. He had bowled 41 overs unchanged the previous day. Brigadier White was aide-de-camp to the Queen from 1963 to 1969.

WILENKIN, BORIS CHARLES GREGORY, died on March 18, 2003, aged 69. Harrow's opening bat in his three years in the XI, Wilenkin played for Cambridge in the 1956 University match, making seven and 20. He played 16 first-class matches for Cambridge and Free Foresters.

WILLATT, GUY LONGFIELD, who died on June 11, 2003, aged 85, was one of Derbyshire's most successful captains when he was allowed the summer term off from teaching at Repton to lead them from 1951 to 1954. Willatt played some first-class cricket either side of the war for Cambridge, Nottinghamshire and Scotland, and in 1946 gained a soccer Blue as a no-nonsense wing-half. A similar philosophy was evident both in his left-handed batting, with his crouching stance, determined defence, strong driving and cutting, and in his captaincy. From 1952

Peter West: the beaming and unflappable front man of BBC TV cricket coverage. *Picture by Patrick Eagar.*

to 1954, when he left Repton to become headmaster at Heversham Grammar School in Westmorland, he hit a thousand Championship runs each season and Derbyshire finished fourth, sixth and third in the table. His leadership was distinguished by his willingness to press for victory and fixed on what he termed "method cricket" that was "gritty, purposive, combative, intensely competitive", without compromising his belief in fair play. Abolishing separate dressing-rooms for amateurs and professionals gained him the players' respect, as did winning the toss in 13 of their 15 home games in 1952. In 1969, aged 51 and headmaster of Pocklington School in Yorkshire, he opened the batting and scored 40 for their old boys' side, Pocklington Pixies, in the first-ever National Club Championship final against Hampstead. Guy Willatt returned to live near Repton in retirement, and was chairman of Derbyshire's cricket committee from 1985 to 1990, becoming a sagacious ally and mentor for their young captain, Kim Barnett, and later club president. One of his sons, Jonathan, was a Cambridge Blue in 1989.

WISHART, BRIAN CHARLES, was killed in a car crash in Harare on July 26, 2003, aged 55. He was the father of the Zimbabwean Test batsman, Craig Wishart, and had himself represented the country at various levels when it was Rhodesia.

WOODHOUSE, ANTHONY, died on January 17, 2003, aged 71. Tony Woodhouse was one of the most dedicated of all cricket followers. Until a serious road accident in 1992, he had attended every Yorkshire game at Headingley bar one since 1945, and had not missed a Yorkshire home game anywhere since 1957. He also had a cricket library with more than 12,000 titles along with a collection of cricket and football cards said to exceed 35,000. He represented Leeds district on the Yorkshire committee for 15 years from 1978, sat on its cricket committee and became a vice-president, as well as being curator and honorary librarian at Headingley. He wrote *The History of Yorkshire County Cricket Club* (1989) and *A Who's Who of Yorkshire County Cricket Club* (1992), contributed to *The Cricketer* on the Yorkshire leagues, and was a commonsense chairman of the Association of Cricket Statisticians from 1981 to 1993.

WRIGHT, GEOFFREY THOMAS, died on April 2, 2003, aged 74. Geoff Wright, father of New Zealand captain John Wright, was a batsman who played one game for Canterbury in 1955-56. His twin, Allan, was manager of the New Zealand team to England in 1983.

ZULFIQAR ALI, who died of cancer on May 10, 2003, aged 33, opened the bowling for Pakistan against Australia in the final of the 1988 World Youth Cup at Adelaide. He later played for Multan and PIA.

CAREER FIGURES OF TEST CRICKETERS

	Tests				*First-class*			
	Runs	*Avge*	*Wkts*	*Avge*	*Runs*	*Avge*	*Wkts*	*Avge*
Adhikari, H. R.	872	31.14	3	27.33	8,683	41.74	49	37.93
Divecha, R. V.	60	12.00	11	32.81	1,424	20.34	217	24.89
Endean, W. R.	1,630	33.95	–	–	7,757	37.83	2	36.50
Gaekwad, H. G.	22	11.00	0	–	2,487	19.42	375	23.62
Ghazali, M. E. Z.	32	8.00	0	–	1,701	27.43	61	34.27
Gopalan, M. J.	18	18.00	1	39.00	2,916	24.92	194	24.20
Guha, S.	17	3.40	3	103.66	1,067	12.70	299	20.29
McConnon, J. E.	18	9.00	4	18.50	4,661	14.38	819	19.88
Niaz Ahmed	17	–	3	31.33	466	14.56	62	38.38
Noreiga, J. M.	11	3.66	17	29.00	181	9.05	68	29.67
Ramchand, G. S.	1,180	24.58	41	46.31	6,026	36.30	255	29.48
Ring, D. T.	426	22.42	35	37.28	3,418	23.25	451	28.48
Sarwate, C. T.	208	13.00	3	124.66	7,430	32.73	494	23.54
Smith, D. R.	38	9.50	6	59.83	4,966	12.32	1,250	23.72
Thoms, G. R.	44	22.00	–	–	1,137	35.53	1	14.00
Toshack, E. R. H.	73	14.60	47	21.04	185	5.78	195	20.37
Wade, W. W.	511	28.38	–	–	2,859	48.45	–	–
Weir, G. L.	416	29.71	7	29.85	5,022	32.19	107	37.30

CRICKET BOOKS, 2003

Bragging Modestly

BARRY NORMAN

Let us begin, as selectors usually do, with the skipper: Michael Vaughan, a tyro about whose qualities the jury is, at the time of writing, still out. Never mind: the man's own book, **A Year in the Sun**, subtitled The Captain's Story, must shed some light on the subject.

Well, no, it doesn't actually, because apart from a hurried postscript – "It is 28 July, 2003, the day that this book goes to press, and a special day as it marks my appointment as captain of England" – the Vaughan story so far ends with England's exit from the World Cup and Nasser Hussain calling it a day. The book's subtitle, therefore, is a misnomer, and those eager to learn how Vaughan's keen cricketing brain plotted the downfall of mighty Bangladesh must wait.

On the general subject of leadership he takes an airy view. In the final chapter, written either in the knowledge or the expectation (it's hard to tell) that he would be appointed England's one-day captain, he says: "I think too much is made of captaincy. It is a huge job, but people make too much of it. I am sure at some stage I will buckle under the pressure, everybody does, but I am certainly not going to worry about it."

So a new kind of insouciant captain, then, not inclined, as Nasser was, "to kick the dirt or shake his head from time to time". Not that he has any quarrel with his predecessor. They had their "differences" but, he insists, "I respect him as a captain and understand what he has to put up with." The year in the sun of which Vaughan (or rather his collaborator, Martin Hardy) writes is 2002-03, that *annus mirabilis* in which his feats against Sri Lanka, India and Australia made him *Wisden's* first cover boy and, briefly, the world's leading batsman. These exploits are recounted with a mixture of modesty and mild bragging. In one innings he hits Stuart MacGill "all round the park" and was also "able to get on top of" McGrath, Gillespie and Lee. But then, yes, he did those things, so why shouldn't he brag a little?

This is a workmanlike book, giving the facts about the deeds but revealing little about the man. We learn that Vaughan admires Atherton, Tendulkar and Duncan Fletcher, thinks Yorkshire were wrong to let David Byas go (so, now, do Yorkshire), reckons Shane Warne's drug ban was excessively harsh (so do I) and doesn't like Justin Langer much because the latter, having had a catch off Vaughan disallowed at Adelaide, seemed to go into a permanent sulk. As to whether England should have played in Zimbabwe in the World Cup, he says: "I am a cricketer first and foremost." This is not exactly the same as saying that cricket and politics shouldn't mix but comes depressingly close. In the end he voted against the trip on security, rather than moral, grounds – which, for a future England captain, was a touch disappointing.

But then at least one of his predecessors, Alec Stewart, takes a similar view. In **Playing for Keeps** (in conjunction with Pat Murphy) he tells how "politics became inextricably linked with the World Cup and we, the naïve England players, got dragged into it". Which they did, and Stewart has a point when he says that the whole affair could have been resolved either by the British government, the ECB or the ICC. But pleading naïvety as a reason why grown men should have had difficulty reaching a decision on a political and moral issue hardly cuts the mustard.

Otherwise, there is a pleasingly disgruntled undertone to this memoir. Stewart feels he was harshly deprived of the England captaincy because of the cock-up of the 1999 World Cup and seems to have spent half his international career trying to persuade people that he was not too old to play for his country. Every time he tells of getting recalled after being dropped in favour of a younger man, he delights in reminding us how well he played. It's hard not to sympathise because he was undoubtedly England's finest all-rounder since Ian Botham; what's more, as Geoffrey Boycott told him, "if you'd been able to open… all the time, rather than getting distracted by your wicket-keeping, you'd have gone down as one of England's greatest openers". A comparison of Stewart's Test average as keeper (34.92) with that of his average as batsman alone (46.70) lends some credence to this view.

"I could be an outstanding professional for a couple of days a week"

The other great Stewart issue arose when M. K. Gupte, an Indian bookmaker, accused him of taking a bribe. Stewart devotes an indignant chapter to denying these allegations, although (am I the one being naïve here?) surely nobody ever believed them in the first place. Stewart bribed? He of the candid, childlike stare, the archetypal patriot who managed to score a 100 on his 100th Test appearance on the Queen Mother's 100th birthday? Never! No, no, this is a loyal NCO who, having served his time, now allows himself the liberty of taking a dig at the officers who had not always treated him too well.

On to another former England skipper, the great underachiever Tony Lewis. What, Tony Lewis, captain of Cambridge University, of Glamorgan's 1969 championship-winning team and of England? Rugby blue, president of MCC, BBC sports presenter, cricket correspondent of the *Sunday Telegraph*, chairman of the Welsh Tourist Board, not to mention damn nearly first violin for the Welsh Youth Orchestra – an underachiever?

In a cricketing sense, I think he was. And, in **Taking Fresh Guard**, he comes close to admitting it himself. His problem, he suggests, is that his interests were too varied. "When I look back," he writes, "I see that I could be an outstanding professional for a couple of days a week and a good one for another two but I lacked the focus to succeed all of the time." Indeed, he takes greater pride in the praise he received for his journalism than for anything he did on the cricket field which, to a mere journalist who would have given his eyeteeth, every other molar and even more vital bits as well to be a Test player, is both inexplicable and unsatisfactory. Does he really

Dominic Winter Book Auctions
Specialist Book Auctioneers
Twice-yearly sales of
SPORTS BOOKS & MEMORABILIA
including Cricket and Wisdens
Illustrated catalogues available by post
For advice without obligation,
please contact the Auction office.
Saleroom & Offices: The Old School, Maxwell Street, Swindon SN1 5DR
Tel: (01793) 611340. Fax: (01793) 491727.
Website: www.dominicwinter.co.uk
E-mail: info@dominicwinter.co.uk

not mind that his Test career (nine games, eight as captain) was so limited? He doesn't tell us. He doesn't even tell us what it was like to score his one Test century. But this is what the cricketer *manqué* wants to know – not the revelation that the controller of Radio 4 admired his reports on Kerry Packer's first World Series.

By comparison, of course, Don Bradman was an overachiever – by comparison with any other cricketer there has ever been, Bradman was an overachiever. Hence his position as the great Australian hero, a status that Brett Hutchins examines closely in **Don Bradman: Challenging the Myth**. Given that he was the very opposite of the stereotypical Australian male, being a small (5ft 6in), quiet, reclusive, non-smoking, non-gambling, monogamous teetotaller and an Anglophile to boot, the Don was a most unlikely national hero. So why, asks the puzzled Hutchins, did he become such an icon?

In this well-researched volume, he attempts to dissect the myths. Bradman, he says, was not – as the more romantic admirers would have it – the under-privileged "boy from the bush". On the contrary, he came from a modestly well-off family, and Bowral, where he was brought up, was only two hours from Sydney. Neither was he the family man of popular legend: he was estranged from his brother, neglected his ailing sister and failed to attend several important family funerals. He tended to play for himself, rarely bought a round, was involved in some possibly dodgy arrangements on the Adelaide Stock Exchange and, despite his own claims, was far from being an amateur – both during and after his career he made a great deal of money from cricket.

All these things may well be true but I can't see that they matter. The Don is not a national icon because his fellow Aussies – a notoriously cynical and sceptical lot – believe he was perfect. He became, and remains, a hero because he dominated cricket as nobody has ever dominated any other sport; he, above all, regularly stuffed the Poms and in an uneasy age, the 1930s and 1940s, made Australians feel good about themselves.

But what made him so great? Analysing his genius (not a word I use lightly) is like trying to grab a handful of mist, which is precisely what A. L. Shillinglaw has attempted in **Bradman Revisited**, another bid to demythologise the Don in that it dismisses the idea that Bradman was simply a law unto himself. His physique was unremarkable and his eyesight only average. Shillinglaw attributes Bradman's mastery to his self-taught technique: balance, grip, stance and the hours he spent as a boy hitting a fast-moving golf ball with a stump. It's an interesting theory and yet… if it were only a matter of copying the great man's approach why has nobody done it successfully? Can't we simply accept that some people are special?

Dennis Lillee was rather special, too. His autobiography, **Menace**, ghosted by Bob Harris, recounts his progress from innocent country boy, the butt of his team-mates' practical jokes, to one of the greatest of fast bowlers. It is a gutsy tale of horrendous injuries overcome (including a fractured spine) and the Establishment defied: he was one of the instigators of Packer's World Series Cricket.

About that he has no regrets, believing it introduced much-needed professionalism into the Australian game. And if he has still not quite come to terms with the Establishment, a mature, philosophical Lillee finally emerges, one who even likes the Poms – well, a few individual Poms anyway.

Interestingly, though, he worries about the future of the Australian game. Because playing Test cricket is now a lucrative business, he thinks people stay on too long. "Australia has to be careful," he says, "otherwise a few years down the line we may face a thin period, particularly with the batting, as I don't see a lot of players coming through." Now there's a heartening thought for an Englishman.

Wisden's book of the year: "the absorbing story of England's forgotten star of the 1954-55 Australian tour".

No Coward Soul, by Stephen Chalke and Derek Hodgson, is the absorbing story of Bob Appleyard, England's forgotten star of the 1954-55 Australian tour. Typhoon Tyson won the glory as England retained the Ashes but it was "the Applecart" with 11 wickets (all top-six batsmen) who headed the bowling averages. That was the peak of a brief but quite remarkable career, indeed of a remarkable life marked by almost Dickensian tragedy and hardship.

The son of John Appleyard, a railway fireman, Bob was born in Bradford in 1924. When he was seven his mother abandoned the family. Six years later his younger sister died of diphtheria. In the meantime, his father had remarried and had two more daughters. Then, in 1939, on the day war broke out, John Appleyard gassed himself and his new family to death in their home. Their bodies were discovered by the 15-year-old Bob.

Somehow he overcame this horror, was apprenticed as an engineer, served as a petty officer in the Navy during the war, became a salesman afterwards and, always a talented cricketer, was belatedly invited to play three games for Yorkshire in 1950 at the comparatively advanced age of 26. The following year, having added brisk off-breaks to his original fast-medium, he took 200 wickets. He was working on adding a leg-cutter, after a quick lesson on the subject from George Pope, when it was discovered that what a whisky-sozzled locum had diagnosed some time earlier as pleurisy was, in fact, tuberculosis.

Appleyard then spent five months in hospital before an operation to remove half a lung and thus missed nearly all the next two cricket seasons. In 1954, however, he made an astonishing comeback, took 154 wickets, celebrated his

Test debut with five wickets against Pakistan and was preferred to Jim Laker for the Australian tour. Then misfortune struck once more. He played one Test against South Africa in 1955 but arm and leg injuries curtailed his season. Thereafter he was never quite as effective again and by June 1958, his first-class career was over, Yorkshire informing him in a coldly impersonal letter that his services were no longer required.

"An awkward bugger" (Ray Illingworth) – but, clearly, one hell of a good bowler. Colin Cowdrey and Fred Trueman both placed him among the all-time greats. Who knows what he might have achieved, given normal luck and good health? It does seem that a malign fate deprived English cricket prematurely of someone rather exceptional with an extraordinary life story. This is my choice as *Wisden's* Book of the Year.

Stephen Chalke has an affinity with cricketers of the 1950s who never quite reached fulfilment. He has also covered, in **Guess My Story**, Appleyard's 1954-55 team-mate, the reserve wicket-keeper Keith Andrew of Northamptonshire. In the First Test, when Evans was ill, Andrew made his debut. But England got hammered and enough blame stuck for Andrew to be ignored by the selectors for a further nine years, even though he was commonly regarded as the best keeper in the country. He couldn't bat, and though he regrets that, he retains strong opinions about the importance of his craft, which he expresses to Chalke quietly but firmly.

And so to another England spinner – Philip Tufnell, the archetypal fag-puffing, beer-swilling, bird-pulling, bouncer-evading village cricketer who lurked, rather than fielded, in the deep yet somehow made it into the big time. **Phil Tufnell's A to Z of Cricket** (in conjunction with Adam Hathaway), emphasises the scatological Jack the Lad side of his character. It's mildly engaging and carefully uncontroversial though you can understand that Angus Fraser's gracious tribute to his former team-mate, "a pain in the arse at times", might be near the mark.

But as cricketing pains in the arse go, I imagine Javed Miandad takes some beating. Here, as he reveals in collaboration with Saad Shafqat in **Cutting Edge: My Autobiography**, is a man who never forgot a compliment or a slight. There is no false modesty in this book and, for that matter, no genuine modesty either. He has, he reveals, been described as "a cricketing genius" and he sees no reason to argue with that. Criticism he dismisses as "professional jealousy". Other players insult him, or try to intimidate him and the media dislike him, but Javed rises above it all. Furthermore, in any given contretemps – of which he was involved in many – he and Pakistan are always right, everyone else always wrong.

Inevitably, he figures largely in Lateef Jafri's **History of Pakistan Test Cricket**, for the most part, happily, as a player. Otherwise, in beguilingly eccentric English – "the gyrating balls of the West Indies trundlers" is a phrase that stands out – Jafri details the progress of his nation's cricketers, from Pakistan's foundation in 1947 to May 2002. The scorecard of every official match, Test records of the players, internal wranglings of various Pakistani boards, Shakoor Rana v Gatting – all is there in an engrossing record made the more enchanting by typographical errors and Jafri's turn of phrase. At one point "the Pakisatni (*sic*) batsmen defy the Indain (*sic*) attack with delightful tempo." And to add to the pleasure is a bizarre index.

Another cricketer with the knack of getting up people's noses is Sourav Ganguly, captain of India and known variously as "Maharaj", "the Prince of Calcutta" or, to his erstwhile Lancashire team-mates, "Lord Snooty". After an acrimonious tour of India three years ago, Steve Waugh said of him: "He was a prick, basically, and that's paying him a compliment." They appeared to get on better last winter in Australia but it's not hard to understand why people might dislike Ganguly. As Gulu Ezekiel says in his biography, **Sourav**, he was seen after India's victory in the NatWest final at Lord's in 2002, waving his shirt and "screaming obscenities in the direction of the despondent Englishmen". No doubt people have individual ways of celebrating a win but hurling obscenities at the vanquished does seem a little unconventional. Yet here, as in the two Pakistani books, you feel that decades of English condescension are being repaid.

Cricket, the Golden Age, compiled by Duncan Steer, offers 300 or so black and white illustrations, dating from 1859 to 1999, and conjures up a nostalgic image of a time when cricket, any kind of cricket, was mass entertainment, when all men wore hats, when everybody smoked, when kids batted and bowled in traffic-free streets and office workers arranged impromptu games on bomb sites during their lunch hours. There is even a photograph of a slim Mike Gatting, before he ate all the pies. The pictures, of the great and unknown alike, are captivating, but the effect is marred by

Cricket, the Golden Age captures Maurice Tate (Sussex and England) racing the Brighton Foot Beagles across the countryside in 1937.

Picture by Getty Images.

wayward caption-writing. As the eagle-eyed David Frith pointed out, the 1934 Australians are for some reason described as the Jaeger Works team. I'm also puzzled as to where exactly "the golden age" comes in. No explanation is offered. But all the pictures are of English cricketers, cricketers in England or matches involving England and even the enthusiastic Duncan Steer can hardly believe that the game in this country enjoyed an unbroken golden age lasting 140 years.

Lord's: Cathedral of Cricket, by Stephen Green, recently retired curator of the museum there, traces the history of the ground on its three different sites from 1787 through peace and war to the present. This, too, is rich in illustration, including reproductions of many of the Long Room's most famous paintings. It is a fitting and affectionate tribute to a London landmark, which, as Green points out, has been around for longer than Trafalgar Square. A nice companion piece is the thumpingly heavy and equally well-illustrated **Ground Rules: A Celebration of Test Cricket**, edited by Barney Spender, in which the likes of Waugh, Ganguly and Andy Flower provide personal reminiscences and histories of Test grounds from Sydney to Karachi.

A more scholarly work is Andre Odendaal's **The Story of an African Game**, with an introduction by Nelson Mandela. It details the development of cricket among black South Africans and disproves the canard that they have only recently produced international players because they have only recently developed an interest in the game. Nonsense. It was discrimination, pure and simple.

And finally this: we all remember, do we not, hearing Brian Johnston utter his famous clanger – "the bowler's Holding, the batsman's Willey"? Well, no we don't, actually. As Barry Johnston reveals in **Johnners: The Life of Brian**, the words were probably never broadcast at all but uttered as an off-air aside. Ah, well, there goes another illusion.

Barry Norman is a journalist and broadcaster, and formerly film critic for BBC television. As a "village offie", he is particularly proud of having dismissed two England captains, Colin Cowdrey and Mike Denness, on successive weekends while playing for the Lord's Taverners.

Matthew Engel writes: Two books from Australia should also be noted. The Bradman Museum in Bowral has produced **The Art of Bradman**, a sumptuously bound collection of the paintings that have been on display at the museum by the artist Brian Clinton. They depict Bradman at various stages of his life and career, and at times resemble iconography. They are unfailingly evocative.

At the other end of the publishing spectrum, the little Walla Walla Press in Sydney has produced **How Many More Are Coming?** Max Bonnell tells the story of the turn-of-the-century Aboriginal sprinter-turned-cricketer Jack Marsh who battled prejudice and accusations of throwing – and, almost inevitably, died tragically. It is beautifully written and deeply moving; I hope it gets a wide audience.

BOOKS RECEIVED IN 2003

GENERAL

Armstrong, Geoff and Russell, Ian **Top 10s of Australian Test Cricket** (ABC Books, $A29.95)
Baldwin, Mark **The History of the Cricket World Cup** (Sanctuary, £12.99)
Bevan, Michael **The Best of Bevan** The World's Finest One-Day Cricketer Recalls his Most Memorable Matches (Allen & Unwin, £8.99)
Blofeld, Henry **Cricket's Great Entertainers** (Hodder & Stoughton, £18.99)
Chapman, Jack **Cream Teas and Nutty Slack** A History of Club Cricket in County Durham (1751–2002) (available from Jack Chapman, 5 Park Road, Hebburn, NE31 2UI, £14.95)
Craven, Nico **That Darn'd Elusive Championship** Foreword by Grenville Simons, Illustrations by Frank Fisher (from the author, The Coach House, Ponsonby, Seascale, Cumbria CA20 1BX, Tel: 01946 41256, paperback, £9) *Another nostalgic effusion from the inveterate Gloucestershire supporter.*
Green, Stephen **Lord's** Cathedral of Cricket (Tempus, £25)
Hargreaves, Peter S. **An A to Z of Cricket Types** (available from I. R. Buxton, 44 Woolley Road, Matlock, Derbyshire, DE4 3HU, paperback, £5)
Haselhurst, Alan **Incidentally Cricket** More Cricket and Confusion from the Outcasts C.C. (Queen Anne Press, £16.99)
Hutchins, Brett **Don Bradman** Challenging the Myth (Cambridge University Press, £40)
Jones, Trevor **From Tragedy to Triumph** Surrey's Bittersweet Championship Success 2002 (Sporting Declarations, available from The Oval Shop, Kennington, London SE11 5SS, £13.99)
Jones, Trevor **268** The Blow-By-Blow Account Of Ali's Amazing Onslaught and the Day the Records Tumbled (Sporting Declarations, available from The Oval Shop, address as above, £6.99)
Lateef Jafri **History of Pakistan Test Cricket** Foreword by Omar Kureishi (Royal Book Company, Karachi, no price given)
Meher-Homji, Kersi **Heroes of 100 Tests** From Cowdrey and the Waughs to Warne, Tendulkar and Hooper (Rosenberg Publishers, Sydney, www.rosenbergpub.com.au, $A24.95 + p&p) *Profiles of the first 27 players to make a hundred Test appearances.*
Odendaal, Andre **The Story of an African Game** Black Cricketers and the Unmasking of one of Cricket's Greatest Myths, South Africa, 1850–2003 Foreword by Nelson Mandela (David Philip, from the Africa Book Centre 0845 458 1579, £30 + £6 p&p)
Paul, Jeremy **Sing Willow** The True Story of The Invalids CC, The Cricket Side Immortalised in A G Macdonell's *England, their England* Foreword by Simon Williams, Illustrated by Tim Jaques (The Book Guild, £16.95)
Rossiter, Tony **Only A Bloody Game** The Ins and Outs of Village Cricket (Sigma Leisure, £6.95)
Shillinglaw, A. L. **Bradman Revisited** The Legacy of Sir Donald Bradman (Parrs Wood Press, £15)
Shuja-ud-din Butt and Mohammed Salim Pervez **The Chequered History of Pakistan Cricket** Celebrating 50 Years of Test Nation (1952-53 to 2002-03) Foreword by Asif Iqbal (available from Mohammed Salim Pervez, 18 Lydford Avenue, Slough, Berkshire SL2 1NL)
Simm, Fraser **Echoes of a Summer Game** A Miscellany of Cricketing Memories (from the author, 5 Manor Park, Stow, Selkirkshire TD1 2RD, paperback, £10.99)
Spender, Barney ed. **Ground Rules** A Celebration of Test Cricket (Dakini Books, £45)
Tufnell, Phil **Phil Tufnell's A to Z of Cricket** (Sports Books, £8.99)
Vaughan, Michael **A Year In The Sun** (Hodder & Stoughton, £16.99)

AUTOBIOGRAPHY

Javed Miandad (with Saad Shafqat) **Cutting Edge** My Autobiography Foreword by Tony Greig (Oxford University Press, Rs495)
Lewis, Tony **Taking Fresh Guard** A Memoir (Headline, £18.99)
Lillee, Dennis **Menace** The Autobiography (Headline, £18.99)
Mortimer, Gerald **Are the Fixtures Out?** (Breedon Books, Derby, £14.99) *Engaging football and cricket memoirs of the chief sports correspondent of the Derby* Evening Telegraph *and* Wisden's *Derbyshire correspondent, reflecting on a lifetime of following Derbyshire sport.*
Stewart, Alec **Playing for Keeps** The Autobiography of Alec Stewart (BBC Consumer Publishing, £18.99)

BIOGRAPHY

Bonnell, Max **How Many More Are Coming?** The Short Life of Jack Marsh (Walla Walla Press, Sydney, www.asc.zipworld.com.au, $A27.45; available in UK from J. W. McKenzie, 12 Stoneleigh Park Road, Ewell, Epsom, Surrey KT19 0QT)

Bowen, Rowland et al. **Arthur Haygarth Remembered** Cricketer, Historian, Old Harrovian (from Roger Heavens, 2 Lowfields, Little Eversden, Cambridgeshire CB3 7HJ, Tel: 01223 262839, £4) *Pamphlet to mark the centenary of the historian's death.*

Bryden, Colin **Herschelle** A Biography (Spearhead, No price given)

Chalke, Stephen **Guess My Story** The Life and Opinions of Keith Andrew, Cricketer Foreword by Micky Stewart (Fairfield Books, 17 George's Road, Fairfield Park, Bath BA1 6EY, Tel: 01225 335813, £15)

Chalke, Stephen and Hodgson, Derek **No Coward Soul** The Remarkable Story of Bob Appleyard. Foreword by Dickie Bird (Fairfield Books, address as above, £16). Wisden's *Book of the Year*

Ezekiel, Gulu **Sourav** A Biography (Penguin Books India, Rs250)

Johnston, Barry **Johnners** The Life of Brian (Hodder & Stoughton, £20)

Winch, Jonty **England's Youngest Captain** The life and times of Monty Bowden and two South African journalists (Windsor Publishers, £10.99)

Wynne-Thomas, Peter **F. S. Ashley-Cooper** A Biographical Sketch & Bibliography (ACS, £3.50)

PICTORIAL

Bradman Museum **The Art of Bradman** Artwork by Brian Clinton, Text by Richard Mulvaney (Funtastic Ltd, publishing@fantastic.com.au, $A49.95)

Brooks, Gordon **Caught in Action** 20 Years of West Indies Cricket Photography (Paths International Ltd, £27.50)

Qamar Ahmed **An Artist's Impression of the Golden Greats of Pakistan's Cricket** Foreword by Patrick Eagar, Illustrations by Shafiq Ahmed (Deenar Design, available from Lord's Shop, Lord's Cricket Ground, St John's Wood, London NW8 8QN, £24.99)

Ray, Mark **Cricket Masala** (ABC Books, available from Wisden Books, Penguin Direct, Edinburgh Gate, Harlow, Essex CM20 2JE, £16.99)

Ryan, Christian ed. **The Unbreakables** Is this the greatest team ever? (ACP Publishing, Sydney, $A9.95)

Ryan, Christian ed. **The Hero** Farewell Steve Waugh (ACP Publishing, Sydney, $A9.95) *Two lavishly illustrated special issues of* Inside Edge, *the former Australian magazine, no longer in regular publication.*

Steer, Duncan **Cricket** The Golden Age Introduction by Graham Gooch, Picture Research by Ali Khoja (Cassell Illustrated, £30)

FICTION

Pankridge, Michael (with Lee, Brett) **Toby Jones and the Magic Cricket Almanack** (Harper Collins Australia, $A14.95)

REFERENCE

Abid Ali Kazi ed. **First-Class Cricket in Pakistan: Volume V 1970-71 to 1974-75** (Pakistan Association of Cricket Statisticians and Scorers; in UK from Limlow Books, Blue Bell House, 2–4 Main Street, Scredington, Sleaford, Lincs NG34 0AE, www.cricketarchive.co.uk, £33 inc. p&p)

Brannan, Laurie ed. **The Vodafone Dictionary of Cricket** (Sportsguide Press, £12.99)

Haygarth, Arthur **Cricket Scores and Biographies Volume XVI** (Roger Heavens, 2 Lowfields, Little Eversden, Cambridgeshire CB3 7HJ, Tel: 01223 262839, £65 inc. p&p) *Previously unpublished volume of statistics from 1879, obituaries and curiosities drawn from the manuscripts of Arthur Haygarth, to mark the centenary of his death.*

Somerset C. C. C. Players, Photographs & Statistics (Somerset Cricket Museum, 7 Priory Avenue, Taunton TA1 1XX, £30 + £5 p&p)

Wilson, Martin comp. **A Bibliography of Northamptonshire Cricket** (Bodyline Books, Tel: 020 7385 2176, limited edition of 75, £35)

STATISTICAL

Bailey, Philip comp. **First-Class Cricket Matches 1906** (Association of Cricket Statisticians (ACS)/Sport in Print, 3 Radcliffe Road, West Bridgford, Nottingham NG2 5FF, £16)
Carlaw, Derek **W. L. Murdoch** His Record Innings-by-Innings (ACS, address as above, £7.50)
Croudy, Brian **Bruce Mitchell** His Record Innings-by-Innings (ACS, £7.50)
Hart, Nigel **J. N. Crawford** His Record Innings-by-Innings (ACS, £7.50)
Harte, Wesley **Richard Hadlee** His Record Innings-by-Innings (ACS, £9.50)
Heavens, Roger **Arthur Haygarth** His Record Innings-by-Innings (ACS, £4)
Lodge, Derek **Bill Edrich** His Record Innings-by-Innings (ACS, £8.50)
Milton, Howard **Lord Cowdrey of Tonbridge, C.B.E.** His Record Innings-by-Innings (ACS, £9.50)
Percival, Tony comp. **Staffordshire Cricketers 1872-2002** (ACS, £4)
Sandiford, Keith A. P. **Sonny Ramadhin** His Record Innings-by-Innings (ACS, £7.50)

FIRST-CLASS COUNTY YEARBOOKS, 2003

Derbyshire £6, Durham £6, Essex £10, Glamorgan £5, Gloucestershire £6, Hampshire £8, Kent £5, Lancashire £10, Leicestershire £11.50, Middlesex £10, Northamptonshire £10, Nottinghamshire £7.50, Somerset £7.50, Surrey £7.50, Sussex £10, Warwickshire £5, Worcestershire £10, Yorkshire £20. 2004 prices may change. Some counties may add charges for p&p.

OTHER HANDBOOKS AND ANNUALS

ACS, comp. **First-Class Counties Second Eleven Annual 2003** (Association of Cricket Statisticians (ACS)/Sport in Print, 3 Radcliffe Road, West Bridgford, Nottingham NG2 5FF, £5.95)
Agnew, Jonathan **C&G Cricket Year 2003** 22nd edition (Bloomsbury, £22.50)
Bailey, Philip ed. **ACS International Cricket Year Book 2003** (ACS, address as above, £11.95)
Bryden, Colin ed. **Mutual & Federal South African Cricket Annual 2003** (UCBSA, available from cricket@mf.co.za, R95)

Franks, Warwick ed. **Wisden Cricketers' Almanack Australia 2003-04** Sixth edition (Hardie Grant, Victoria, $A49.95; in UK from Macmillan Wisden Direct, Brunel Road, Houndmills, Basingstoke, Hampshire RG21 6XS, Tel: 01256 302685, £22.50; abridged pocket paperback, $A14.95)

Frindall, Bill ed. **Playfair Cricket Annual 2003** (Headline, paperback, £5.99)

Irish Cricket Annual 2003 (from Dr E. M. Power, 5 Strangford Avenue, Belfast BT9 6PG or M. J. Ryan, 43 Biscayne, Malahide, Co. Dublin, £3/Euros 5)

Marshall, Chris ed. **The Cricketers' Who's Who 2003** (Queen Anne Press, £16.99)

Payne, Francis and Smith, Ian ed. **2003 New Zealand Cricket Almanack** (Hodder Moa Beckett, Auckland, no price given)

PCB Pepsi Cricket Annual 2002-03 Foreword by General Pervez Musharraf (from Limlow Books, Blue Bell House, 2–4 Main Street, Scredington, Sleaford, Lincolnshire NG34 0AE, www.cricketarchive.co.uk, £23 inc. p&p in UK)

Viswanath, G. comp. **Indian Cricket 2002** (Kasturi & Sons, Chennai, Rs100)

REPRINTS AND UPDATES

Agnew, Jonathan **Over to You Aggers** Life as a BBC Cricket Correspondent (revised paperback edition, Orion, £7.99)

Arthur Haygarth's/Marylebone Club Cricket Scores and Biographies Volumes XIII (1874–1876) and XIV (1877–1878) A continuation of Frederick Lillywhite's Scores and Biographies from 1772 to 1854 (facsimile edition, from Roger Heavens, 2 Lowfields, Little Eversden, Cambridgeshire CB3 7HJ; limited edition of 500, Volume XIII £68 inc. p&p, Volume XIV £73 inc. p&p)

Coldham, James P. **Lord Hawke** A Cricketing Legend (Tauris Parke Paperbacks, no price given)

Eastaway, Rob **What is a Googly?** The Mysteries of Cricket Explained (updated edition, Robson Books, £6.99)

Foot, David **Harold Gimblett** Tormented Genius of Cricket Foreword by John Arlott (new edition, Fairfield Books, 17 George's Road, Fairfield Park, Bath BA1 6EY, Tel: 01225 335813, £15)

Harte, Chris (with Whimpress, Bernard) **A History of Australian Cricket** Foreword by Richie Benaud (updated edition, Andre Deutsch, £25)

John Wisden's Cricketers' Almanack for 1920 and 1940 (facsimile editions, Willows Publishing, 17 The Willows, Stone, Staffordshire ST15 0DE, fax: 01785 615867, email: jenkins.willows@ntl.com, £53 inc. p&p in UK, £2 extra overseas postage; £5 extra for facsimile of original hard cloth cover)

Perry, Roland **Bradman's Best Ashes Teams** (Corgi, £8.99, paperback)

Powell, William A. **The Official ECB Guide to Cricket Grounds** (Sutton Publishing, £14.99)

Smith, E. T. **Playing Hard Ball:** A Kent County Cricketer's Journey into Big League Baseball (Abacus, £7.99, paperback)

Walmsley, Keith **Mosts Without in Test Cricket** Foreword by Christopher Martin-Jenkins (expanded edition, from the author, 1 Wheatley Close, Reading RG2 8LP, £14 inc. p&p in UK, £4 extra overseas)

PERIODICALS

The Cricketer Quarterly: Facts and Figures ed. Richard Lockwood (Wisden Cricketer Publishing, £3.50. Subscriptions: Ridge Farm, The Down, Lamberhurst, Kent TN3 8ER, 01892 893030, email subclub@wisdengroup.com)

Cricket Lore (ten per volume, frequency variable) ed. Richard Hill (Cricket Lore, 22 Grazebrook Road, London N16 0HS, £42.50 per volume)

The Cricket Statistician (quarterly) ed. Philip J. Bailey (ACS, £2, free to ACS members)

The Journal of the Cricket Society (twice yearly) ed. Clive W. Porter (from D. Seymour, 13 Ewhurst Road, Crofton Park, London, SE4 1AG, £5 to non-members)

The Scottish Cricketer (six newspapers per year) ed. Neil Leitch and Mike Stanger (Scottish Cricket Union, National Cricket Academy, Ravelston, Edinburgh EH4 3NT, 90p)

Wisden Asia Cricket (monthly) ed. Sambit Bal (208 Shalimar Morya Park, Andheri Link Road, Andheri West, Mumbai 400 053, India, Rs25. Subscriptions: 022 2496 0102, email subs.wac@wisdengroup.com, or via Ridge Farm, The Down, Lamberhurst, Kent TN3 8ER, 01892 893030, email subclub@wisdengroup.com)

The Wisden Cricketer (monthly) ed. John Stern (136 Bramley Road, London W10 6SR, 020 7565 3080, email twc@wisdengroup.com, £3.25. Subscriptions: Ridge Farm, Lamberhurst, Tunbridge Wells, Kent TN3 8ER, 01892 893030, email subclub@wisdengroup.com)

the complete cricket magazine

The Wisden Cricketer, which incorporates **The Cricketer International** and **Wisden Cricket Monthly**, launched in September 2003 covering the game at all levels from the Test match arena to the village green.

Edited by John Stern, **The Wisden Cricketer** offers unrivalled access to the best cricket writing and photography in the world each month. Regular contributors include Christopher Martin-Jenkins, Nasser Hussain, Angus Fraser, Scyld Berry, Peter Roebuck, Matthew Engel, Simon Wilde, Vic Marks and award-winning photographer Patrick Eagar.

For a special subscription offer, call

08707 879044

and quote WA04

CRICKET AND THE MEDIA, 2003

Pigeon English

ANDREW NICKOLDS

Besides being long and hot, 2003 was also the Summer of Sexing Up, and cricket dug out its rouge, false eyelashes and beauty spot in a strenuous attempt to persuade the public that the tough old mutton they'd been getting for years was in fact the freshest, most tender spring lamb. But would anybody buy it?

Judging from the media coverage, the answer was a resounding yes. England may have made an undistinguished exit from the World Cup in March, but within weeks a new hero had emerged from the swamps of the southern hemisphere. Flying the flag for the game was the winner of the ITV series *I'm a Celebrity, Get me out of Here!* Or more accurately, *Get me out of my Middlesex Contract!* Cricket's unlikely ambassador turned out to be Philip Tufnell wielding a toy bat.

His survival skills in an Australian rainforest impressed several million viewers – several million more than he would have impressed at Southgate – and almost overnight the former thorn in the side of the selectors had used his easy-going nature and his willingness to put disgusting objects (in

"And that, gentlemen, is lunch": Phil Tufnell sizes up a plate of witchetty grubs on his way to winning ITV's *I'm a Celebrity, Get me out of Here!*

Picture by Granada.

this case, witchetty grubs rather than cigarettes) in his mouth to acquire the status of lovable national hero.

This transformation caused a few raised eyebrows among Tufnell's former county and England team-mates turned media pundits, who remembered a somewhat different character and weren't afraid to say it. Mike Selvey and Angus Fraser, the Statler and Waldorf of the BBC commentary box, were particularly caustic as Tufnell was wheeled out (literally, on a red sofa, at Chester-le-Street) as the acceptable face of the game. But true to fair-weather form, the tabloid press rallied round their new best friend, and previously lurid front-page stories linking Tufnell with domestic violence were forgotten in the face of a bigger reconstruction job than the new Lord's outfield.

The *Daily Mail's* makeover was typical. Under the headline "The Secret of My Jungle Torment – Phil Tufnell tells of his desperate desire to meet the daughter he hasn't seen for eight years" we were introduced to a caring, sharing Tuffers who attributed the TV show victory to his experience of being a team player, a philosophy he was hoping to apply to his private life.

More immediate rewards were to be found on BBC Radio 5. *Phil Tufnell's Cricket Circus* was a particularly grim example of what is normally called "zoo" rather than circus radio, where everybody jabbers at once to little effect. Almost as raucous were Tufnell's appearances on the TV sports "quiz", *They Think It's All Over*, where, significantly enough, he replaced David Gower as a team captain and the game's prime-time public image.

Talking of quizzes, who said this and what was unusual about it?

"And there's the sound of a police siren hurtling up the Harleyford Road. I do hope nobody's in trouble. On the other hand they could be in pursuit of some desperado, in which case we wish them well."

The first part of the answer is, of course, Henry Blofeld, on Radio 4's *Test Match Special* during the Oval Test against South Africa, in that commentary style which Frank Keating, writing in *The Guardian*, affectionately called his "priceless rum-flummery". The odd thing is that Blofeld used almost the exact same phrase (with Wellington Road substituted for Harleyford) a few years ago during a broadcast from Lord's. I jotted it down then as an example of what set my teeth on edge about *TMS*.

I'm aware that to criticise "Blowers" for banging on about paraphernalia off the park like a latter-day Fotherington-Tomas ("Hello pigeons, hello buses") is as fruitless as attacking the Queen. No doubt there are many thousands out there, presumably the same cricket-book buyers who clamour for an ever more thinly cut slice of the late Brian Johnston, who adore this kind of thing.

But in a season which turned out to be pretty momentous, Blofeld's determinedly silly-ass approach – which now encompasses "Blowers' Test Chat Special Game" on the BBC cricket website, complete with "My dear old thing" catchphrases – seemed to me to be doing serious long-term damage to *TMS*, spreading to the rest of the team like wet rot.

Take the inaugural Test at Chester-le-Street against Zimbabwe. Admittedly this was a one-sided match in a half-hearted series, though had Blowers been there – to be unleashed on a new public transport system – the commentary at least might have gone into a fourth day. But the Zimbabweans were a demoralised side for a reason, the after-shocks from England's pulling out of the World Cup match in Harare were still being felt, and even as its cricketers were collapsing at the Riverside, the country's opposition leader was being arrested on charges of treason.

So was it absolutely necessary for the *TMS* team to spend quite so much time reporting excitedly on the hunt for a local ghost? Especially when they had access to the exiled Henry Olonga, an expert summariser if ever there was one – though by now he was learning to play this new game and seemed happiest telling listeners about his future in music, collaborating with the composer of the *Inspector Morse* theme.

Worse was to follow at Trent Bridge, where the enthralling and series-levelling Third Test against South Africa battled for equal airtime with the contest to name Jonathan Agnew's new dog. "Aggers" may be puppyish in his enthusiasm for new technology, but this brings with it a barmy army of texters and emailers, next to whom the Vikings and Elvis Presleys of Edgbaston are models of restraint. Cakes and pork pies I imagine are positively vetted before they reach the *TMS* box; spam seems not to be.

In 2003 the Elvises, not to mention the nuns, finally had something to sing about. James Anderson's five wickets in the first Lord's Test, his youth and looks, the connection with David Beckham (at the time they had Old Trafford and ever-changing hairstyles in common) all added up to an image-maker's dream. By the next Test, Anderson was running in to bowl with a red streak to match the Tufnell sofa, and the responsibility on his shoulders of being the new inspirational Darren Gough. He also had columns in the *Manchester Evening News* and on the BBC's cricket website, but these were short-lived, as the lad was still only 20 and no ghost-writer could do much with sentiments along the lines of "I owe it all to Mum and Dad".

Anderson was duly voted England's Sexiest Cricketer by readers of the *Daily Mirror* in July, but by the end of the season he was facing competition in the pages of *Wisden Cricket Monthly*. Its last issue reflected the current marketing-conscious mood of the game by printing a series of pin-ups ("The Hit Squad") of Vaughan, Trescothick, Flintoff, Harmison and various other England players sidelined through injury and with plenty of time to model cheesecloth shirts. Luckily, as a reminder that class is permanent, this was counterbalanced by a portfolio of wonderful Patrick Eagars, which included the famous scene at Headingley in 1981 of Ian Botham running off the pitch after his match-winning Ashes innings, surrounded by cheering boys.

The England captain Michael Vaughan (six years old at the time) might well look at this picture, reflect on his own relationship with the media in 2003 and conclude that a week in cricket is a long time, especially when it contains back-to-back Tests. After leading England to an apparently relaxed victory in the one-day series against South Africa, Vaughan's appointment when Nasser Hussain resigned after Edgbaston was widely welcomed in the press.

"Class is permanent": Patrick Eagar captures one of England's finest hours.

This was partly due to their increasingly prickly relationship with the ex-captain ("Tell someone who cares," he snarled at a broadsheet journalist, who had forewarned Hussain of a mildly critical piece around the time of his opaque behaviour during the World Cup boycott). Also, Hussain had his own column in the *Sunday Telegraph*, and could reasonably be expected to keep the best stuff, juiciest insights etc. for himself. Except that a week before his last Test in charge he wrote: "Captaining England is the best job I've ever had… I will keep doing the job, and enjoying it, until the selectors give me a call." Compare this to his column at the end of the season: "By Edgbaston I was running on empty, the red light was flashing and there was not a petrol station in sight…" Setting aside the strained imagery, here in a nutshell is surely an argument for letting captains do their talking on the field only, and saving their running commentaries for a time when they've retired to the comfort of the press box.

So the laid-back Vaughan was expected to usher in a more transparent and media-friendly era. This goodwill did not survive the first morning session at Lord's (94 for five, with Vaughan out); by the afternoon Statler and Waldorf were grumbling on *TMS* about England's over-relaxed attitude (Hussain had dropped Graeme Smith on eight, en route to 259); and next morning Derek Pringle, writing in the *Daily Telegraph*, was invoking the Iron Duke and Captains Hook and Pugwash in an effort to sum up Vaughan's leadership. As Martin Johnson commented in the same paper: "The life cycle of an England captain goes from caterpillar, to butterfly, to tasty meal for a garden predator. No sooner do you go on your honeymoon than they order your tombstone."

But this was also the summer of Twenty20 cricket, so it was little wonder that instant judgment was in the air when two semi-finals and the final of a competition could be played at Trent Bridge on the same day, with an Atomic Kitten set and a Dermot Reeve closing presentation thrown in. Much as this might have stuck in the craw of traditionalists, Twenty20 was as big a popular success in its way as Philip Tufnell – there was no real argument with packed stands.

The most persuasive opinions were expressed by converts sounding a note of caution, from Vic Marks writing in *The Observer* ("I would make a plea to the ECB and the administrators around the counties who smell a golden goose. Leave the punters wanting more. Cricket is not good at this.") to Simon Barnes in the last edition of *The Cricketer*: "What we need is what Catholics call a Conversion Experience – a rekindling of faith in cricket itself. What cricket is about is the battle between bat and ball. Everything else is garnish and gimmick and decoration, flumdiddle and money." The many thousands who turned up to see England beat South Africa on the fifth day of the Oval Test would have agreed with that, though the £10 reduced admission charge was welcome too.

Barnes's piece was one of several valedictions in *The Cricketer* and *Wisden Cricket Monthly*, before both magazines were amalgamated into *The Wisden Cricketer*. Among them was a striking reminiscence by Angus Fraser of the time when, not much older than James Anderson is now and playing in his second Test, he wept as he heard his team-mates planning to desert England and join the rebel tour to South Africa.

Here was a proper story, painful and stripped of rum-flummery and flumdiddle, and a useful reminder that not everything in cricket can be reduced to Blowers-style bromides.

Andrew Nickolds is a journalist and scriptwriter, and the back half of "Pod", a county cricketer almost as improbable as Tufnell.

RETIREMENTS IN 2003

The Cat, The Judge and The Invisible Man

ANGUS FRASER

Farewell tours have become the fashionable way for the great and the good to play out their final days as international cricketers. Steve Waugh and Alec Stewart, the most capped players Australia and England have produced, brought their careers to an emotional end at their home grounds. Wasim Akram and Saeed Anwar of Pakistan, Allan Donald and Jonty Rhodes of South Africa and Javagal Srinath of India all said goodbye to the topmost level of cricket at the 2003 World Cup. Only one of the seven went out as a winner. It is slightly ironic, in an era when England have won so little, that it should have been the Englishman.

Waugh (in the first week of 2004, to be exact) could only look on as Sourav Ganguly raised the Border–Gavaskar Trophy in Sydney. The two Pakistanis endured ignominious World Cup exits; the two South Africans were out of the team even before their country went out so bizarrely. Stewart, however, had the pleasure of celebrating a memorable victory over South Africa at The Oval.

Nasser Hussain reviews **Steve Waugh**'s career elsewhere in *Wisden* (see page 27). With Waugh in charge, Australia felt they could achieve almost anything. Draws were greeted like defeats, and the brand of cricket Australia played left opponents gasping for breath. They will find batsmen to score his runs; replacing his presence will be impossible.

But it was the crises that drew the best out of him. In his own cussed and slightly unconventional way, he would drag his side back into a match. Waugh was the type of player **Alec Stewart** admired most. In his formative years as a pro, Stewart spent several winters playing in Perth. It was here his game and respect for the Australian way developed.

The key to Stewart's career was his instinct for survival. He spent those early summers in the tough and cliquey atmosphere of the Surrey dressing-room, a place where self-preservation appeared as important as team spirit. That instinct kept him in the England side when others perished. His acquisition of a second skill, wicket-keeping, helped enormously – for his benefit as much as England's.

Famously, he was always immaculately turned out and he was certainly the most dedicated cricketer I ever played with. His corner of the dressing-room was as smart as a shop window in Bond Street. There would be three pairs of shoes, all with "AS" neatly written on the heel: full-spikes, half-spikes and rubbers. There would be nice piles of shirts, whites and gloves, and bats lined up, all numbered. Everyone else just had a heap of dirty washing.

And then there were two: (*clockwise, from top-left*) Jack Russell, Hugh Morris, Phillip DeFreitas, Chris Lewis, Phil Tufnell, Robin Smith, David Lawrence and Alec Stewart celebrate a 1991 victory over Sri Lanka at Lord's. Smith, Stewart and Tufnell all retired in 2003, leaving just Russell and DeFreitas in the first-class game. *Picture by Graham Morris.*

He was too regimented to be an inspiring captain: he couldn't make instinctive, off-the-cuff decisions. But his batting wasn't like his captaincy or his attitude to practice. He never looked a manufactured cricketer, and Stewart in full flow was a sensational sight. As his team-mates, we used to love watching him hook and cut opposing fast bowlers to the boundary. When he was timing the ball well, he made batting look as easy as David Gower.

Wasim Akram formed half of the most lethal bowling combination to hit cricket in recent times. Sarfraz Nawaz and Imran Khan were credited with inventing reverse swing, but it was Wasim and Waqar Younis who turned it into a destructive weapon. Together they changed the principles of bowling. The nature of the pitch was taken out of the equation by their ability to bowl fast, in-swinging yorkers, and it no longer mattered whether the ball was old or new.

If he was bowling round the wicket, you couldn't even see him, never mind the ball. You might come to the crease. The umpire would say "Left-arm round, two to come" or something and you would think "Where is he?" Then all of a sudden, he would jump out from behind the umpire and the ball would come up like a whirlwind. I tried to slog him in a one-day game once. It was a waste of time. My stumps were hanging out of the ground before I picked the bat up.

Javagal Srinath, the No. 1 Indian fast bowler of his generation, did not have Wasim's skills, but he never stopped trying. His reactions to a dropped catch or a misfield off his bowling were brilliant. The fielder was left in no doubt about how Srinath felt. He looked an unlucky bowler, because he often beat the bat, but he regularly bowled a yard too short. **Allan Donald**, in contrast, was the complete fast bowler. He had everything going for him. He was strong, athletic and possessed a beautiful action. There was a stage in his career when a few batsmen questioned his heart. They were wrong. Donald always gave it his all.

Saeed Anwar was 40 not out in Bulawayo when the rain came and Pakistan went out of the World Cup. At his best, he was a sublime left-hander – as easy on the eye as Lara. **Jonty Rhodes** was not in the same class as a batsman but he had a knack of putting the fielding side under pressure, getting under their skin. The single down to fine leg would be turned into two. He could muck a bowler's rhythm up: you felt you were playing at his pace.

He will be remembered most for his fielding, of course. Strangely, he never seemed to hit the stumps all that often, and he dropped catches as well as taking some magic ones. But he covered so much ground and he also chipped away at the batsmen verbally: a well-known Christian himself, he could make opponents feel pretty uncharitable.

English cricket also lost several of its brightest characters in 2003. If the mood was right **Devon Malcolm** could be as quick as anyone in the world. Like Donald he was fit and strong, but he failed to make the most of his talents. When he held his action together he was a real handful – no one will forget his nine for 57 against South Africa – but those days came along far too infrequently. A more open mind would have helped.

Philip Tufnell's antics on and off the field made him a celebrity but it would be a shame if his TV career overshadowed his achievements in cricket. He was a fine bowler, though his private life, which made *Eastenders* look tame, definitely affected his work. His insecurity, though, actually helped. "The Cat" always felt he had to impress because he doubted himself so much. Although he often looked as though he didn't care, he was always worried about what people would be saying. It stopped him letting himself down.

Tuffers could also be great fun, and nights out with him and **Robin Smith** were never dull. Robin was a superb player. Fielding in the gully or the covers was a life-threatening experience when he was really seeing it – few have cut or driven the ball with such power. As a bowler, you approached the wicket telling yourself not to drop it short and wide. But like a magnet the ball went there, and would come back to you with bits of concrete or advertising board in it. "The Judge" was fearless against pace, but fearful of spin. And it was this contradiction that defined Smith. I could never work it out. He was forever reading self-help books about mental strength. How could a man with so much going for him have so little belief in his ability? If anything, Robin was too nice a man.

Where did *he* come from? Wasim Akram appeared from nowhere to bowl – having been hidden by the umpire, in this case Steve Bucknor.

Picture by Patrick Eagar.

Ed Giddins, of four counties, four Test matches, a questionable action and a failed drugs test (and in February 2004 a betting allegation), could bowl all right, but I felt he was never really in love with the game. It was different with **Karl Krikken**, the Derbyshire wicket-keeper, the loudest voice in county cricket and another of the really nice guys.

All keepers have their own idiosyncratic ways but "Krikk" was a beauty. He was a fine keeper, especially when he stood up to Derbyshire's medium-pacers in one-day cricket. I didn't think that much of his batting. I lost my rag with him when he was facing me on a seaming wicket and missing everything. "Sorry," he called back. "I'm trying as hard as I can."

Angus Fraser, who played 46 Tests for England, is now cricket correspondent of The Independent.

CRICKET EQUIPMENT

Waving a Magic Wand

NORMAN HARRIS

By good fortune we can watch again and again the six consecutive sixes Garry Sobers hit at Swansea 36 years ago in a previously unremarkable match between Glamorgan and Nottinghamshire. BBC Wales were there that day and, although they were not in transmission mode when Sobers made his famous assault, the cameras, by happy chance, remained running. Very few other great county cricketing feats have been preserved for posterity.

Moves, however, are afoot that could change all that. Already, most counties tape all play using a distant video camera, often set up and managed by the coach, for "performance analysis". Durham are one of the few counties with the camera permanently installed, at the top of one sightscreen, while a couple of other grounds use one of their CCTV cameras, turned to the square rather than to the ground perimeter.

A camera at one end is clearly far from ideal, even for analysis purposes, though it might just about be good enough for a truly famous bit of cricket (six wickets in six balls, perhaps) to find its way on to our television screens. However, Surrey's plans to renovate The Oval include setting up a system that would follow all play, using cameras at both ends and also square of the wicket, with a mere mouse-click required to move the end-on cameras in line with the relevant strip.

The interests of coaches and spectators could come together here. This summer Surrey are intent on starting a daily video-streaming service for their supporters, with highlights and interviews, using their present equipment. This could be the precursor of something far more sophisticated once the new technology arrives. And the dream is that it could one day embrace all county grounds, allowing digital video to be streamed to clubs' websites and beyond.

It would also make coaches' lives easier: a coach at Taunton could view and download quality video output from Derby without needing to leave his desk. What pictures might be available to television is harder to say, such are the complexities of the contracts involved. But it is hard to imagine that a moment of real cricket history would not find its way on to the box.

Most of Andrew Flintoff's feats in 2003 were well televised, to the delight of Joe Sillett, founder of the Woodworm company. Sillett is an enthusiastic user of both video and statistics and was quick to tell the world how Flintoff's average had changed since the start of the year when he began using the "Wand", the novel-shaped bat with the pinched-in edges high up the blade.

Whether it was really the new bat that had changed everything for Flintoff, or the new Flintoff who changed everything for the bat (and the bat-maker), remained an open question. Sillett also went so far as to claim that the

Smashing shot, sir! Andrew Flintoff tests his bat to breaking point during the Lord's Test against South Africa.

Picture by Patrick Eagar.

narrower width near the splice (primarily intended to shift weight from where it isn't needed down to the critical hitting area) had meant fewer dismissals from snicks high on the blade. He cited two or three players who, on his analysis of video, had been out to edges that would have just escaped Flintoff's bat.

Whether this is fanciful or not, the summer of 2003 certainly marked an upward shift in the promotion of batsman-and-bat. Sillett said that Flintoff had "needed to be pulled away from the crowd, put on a pedestal, made to feel special, be the golden boy". Even two very public equipment failures – including a dramatically broken Wand held aloft at Lord's – were far from bad news for the bat-maker. "We couldn't have written a better script," Sillett said. "The PR is reckoned to be worth £100,000. The company line is: 'Flintoff hits the ball harder than any cricketer has hit it, and there's no guarantee the bat will survive the onslaught.'"

More happy hitting was seen in the new Twenty20 cricket, but the administrators missed a trick in not offering their new audience a new ball. To be fair to them, they would have liked an orange ball, which is said to be even easier to see than white (and is already used in some local evening leagues when sightscreens are not available) but Sky evidently vetoed it for technical reasons: orange does not show up well in the black-and-white monitors used by TV cameramen. Are there no colour monitors, then? Just a few, apparently: the BBC use them for orchestral concerts, among other things. Something to work on in the back room, then.

As for white balls, their rapid discoloration over 50 overs had prompted too many requests for a ball-change. Hence the adoption of the harder Kookaburra ball, which is more resistant to the scuffing and bruising that allows dirt to penetrate and discolour the surface. But a harder ball meant a more bowler-friendly one for the first ten overs or so, and some big games last summer were compromised by ruinous starts.

Thus did Kookaburra receive a request from on high: could they make what effectively would be a second-hand ball? An unusual request for any manufacturer, and the answer was no.

ERRATA

WISDEN, 1999

Page 432	Allan Donald scored 13 runs, there were six leg-byes and Sanath Jayasuriya conceded 37 runs.

WISDEN, 2001

Pages 1044 and 1404	Shoaib Mohammad did not carry his bat for PIA against WAPDA, as he retired hurt during the innings.

WISDEN, 2002

Page 440	Mark Waugh and Damien Martyn's second-innings partnership added 70 runs.
Page 1167	Craig McMillan hit his 26 runs in a Test over at Hamilton.

WISDEN, 2003

Page 486	Sangakkara was lbw b Trott.
Page 545	Gus Logie did not keep wicket for West Indies.
Pages 556–7	The order of counties at the top of the Summary of Results tables should match the order at the side.
Page 780	Bob Woolmer asks us to emphasise that he was offered a new contract by the Warwickshire cricket committee at the end of the 2002 season and that it was entirely his decision to leave the club at the end of his agreed term.
Page 973	Ian Harvey scored 68 not out v Sussex, as shown in the scorecard, not 63 as in the report.
Page 1019	In Oxford UCCE's first innings against Worcestershire, Huw Jones was caught by Ben Smith, not Graeme Hick.
Pages 1132–37	Ahmed Said carried his bat for 78* in Rest of NWFP's second innings v Rawalpindi at Rawalpindi, having been ninth out in the first innings. Zulfiqar Jan and Jaffer Nazir added 162 not 152 for KRL's ninth wicket v PWD at Sialkot (see also page 1508). Aamer Malik and Mohammad Asif added 109 for Lahore Whites' ninth wicket v Sheikhupura at Sheikhupura. T. T. Samaraweera completed the match double by scoring 100* and taking 4-76 and 6-101 for Sinhalese v Colombo at Colombo. Eastern Province wicket-keeper Z. Homani conceded no byes in Western Province's 504-8 dec. at Cape Town.
Page 1442	Greg Blewett is 20 months Darren Lehmann's junior, not his senior.
Page 1605	The Sydney Test in January 2002 may have been the first Test in Australia in which both official scorers were women, but it has been a frequent occurrence in South Africa, where the majority of scorers are female.
Page 1617	Bob Cristofani died in Fleet (Hampshire, England), not in Canberra.
Page 1636	Geoffrey Howard's first names were Cecil Geoffrey, not Geoffrey Cecil.
Page 1644	The players shown in the photograph are C. S. Nayudu, Shute Banerjee and Chandu Sarwate.

CRICKET AND THE WEATHER, 2003

A Different Kind of Century

PHILIP EDEN

Kent were not playing on Sunday August 10, 2003, the day when a new UK temperature record of 38.5ºC (101.3ºF) was established at Faversham, just ten miles from their Canterbury headquarters. Not that far away, though, Middlesex were entertaining Durham in a National League match at Lord's, and just after two o'clock in the afternoon the nearest weather-reporting stations at Clerkenwell and Hampstead recorded shade temperatures of 37.6ºC (99.7ºF) and 37.4ºC (99.4ºF) respectively. The temperature inside the ground at Lord's was probably fractionally higher, partly because it is more enclosed, and this may well have been the first time county cricketers in England have played in a ground where the shade temperature was over 100ºF.

That Sunday was hotter even than the hottest day of England's 2002-03 tour of Australia when 37ºC (99ºF) was reached on the Saturday of the Adelaide Test. Adelaide has the highest temperatures of all Australia's Test venues with an all-time record of 48ºC (118ºF), but even higher readings are obtained in India and Pakistan before the monsoon rains arrive and the recent habit of scheduling series there in April and May is extremely unwise, exposing players and spectators to the risk of sunstroke.

The ten-day heatwave in early August, and the drought that followed, have coloured our memories of 2003 in England, which some are already describing as a "long, hot summer". It was certainly consistently warm, but "episodic" is the word meteorologists use to describe a summer such as this, with lengthy spells of dry, sunny weather alternating with periods of persistent cloud and plentiful rain.

The season began promisingly enough after a very dry early spring, and there were some hot days in mid-April. But, just as in 2002, the dry spell broke around April 24, and the weather was decidedly cool and unsettled with frequent rain for exactly a month. Thereafter, further wet periods occurred from June 4 to 11, June 25 to July 4, and July 16 to 31. There was a time, towards the end of July, when national newspapers were asking what we had done to deserve a summer as bad as this.

The meteorological statistics, averaged over England and Wales, for the 2003 cricket season, were as follows:

	Average max temperature (°C)	*Difference from normal for 1971–2000*	*Total rainfall (mm)*	*% of normal*	*Total sunshine (hours)*	*% of normal*
April (second half)	15.2	+2.2	35	124	104	125
May	16.3	+0.7	78	121	195	98
June	20.9	+2.2	73	113	222	108
July	22.2	+1.3	76	130	189	99
August	23.5	+2.8	19	22	221	125
September (first half)	20.0	+1.2	13	23	96	133
2003 season	**20.1**	**+1.7**	**294**	**84**	**1,027**	**111**

Hot work: under a baking sun the Dorset village of Ibberton entertain touring side Badgers CC. But the summer of 2003 was not quite as glorious as some recall.
Picture by Graham Morris.

Each summer has slightly different regional variations although in most years northern and western counties are cooler, cloudier and damper than those in the east and south. The Wisden Summer Index allows us to compare the summer county by county. The index incorporates rainfall amount and frequency, sunshine, and temperature, in a single figure. The formula for the index is:

$$I = 20\ (Tx - 12) + (S - 400)/3 + 2Rd + (250 - R/3)$$

Tx is the mean maximum temperature, S is the total sunshine, Rd is the number of dry days, and R is the total rainfall, covering the period May 1 to August 31. The formula looks rather complicated, but it is designed so that temperature, sunshine, rainfall frequency and rainfall amount each contribute approximately 25% of the total. The final index ranges from zero for the theoretical worst possible summer to 1,000 for the theoretical best.

The score for an average recent summer ranges from 525 at Chester-le-Street and 530 at Old Trafford to 670 at Lord's and 675 at The Oval. Broadly speaking, an index over 650 indicates a good summer whereas one below 500 clearly describes a poor summer. Values for each county for the summer of 2003 against the average value for the standard reference period of 1971–2000 are given below:

	2003	Normal	Difference		2003	Normal	Difference
Derbyshire	623	580	+43	Middlesex	758	670	+88
Durham	587	525	+62	Northamptonshire	664	615	+49
Essex	746	640	+106	Nottinghamshire	637	590	+47
Glamorgan	615	555	+60	Somerset	699	620	+79
Gloucestershire	649	595	+54	Surrey	775	675	+100
Hampshire	706	645	+61	Sussex	723	665	+58
Kent	732	655	+77	Warwickshire	665	555	+110
Lancashire	587	530	+57	Worcestershire	721	615	+106
Leicestershire	671	585	+86	Yorkshire	632	560	+72

All counties had above-average scores, and Essex, Surrey, Warwickshire and Worcestershire exceeded the average by 100 points or more. Leicestershire's weather index was over 200 points higher than that for 2002. Derbyshire, Northamptonshire and Nottinghamshire had the smallest excesses, reflecting the heavy downpours which hit these counties in late June and both early and late in July.

Averaged nationally, last season's index of 647 was a massive 141 points above that of 2002, and the highest since 1996. It was not quite up there with the very best, but in the last 100 years there were only 19 better summers. But even in a good year, there is still a huge contrast between the figures for Sussex and Lancashire, which lends credence to the Lancastrian grumbles that they could have won the Championship themselves on a level climatic playing field.

In 2004, all the major cricket-playing nations may find out more about English weather if they gather as planned in September for the Champions Trophy. The final was scheduled to take place on September 25, which is actually after the autumnal equinox, and dangerously late in the year for a major tournament. The players may or may not escape the rain, but the extra hazards include equinoctial gales – and maybe leaves on the line of leg stump.

The Wisden Weather Index since 1992, together with the best and worst on record, is as follows:

1992	556	1995	777	1998	565	2001	632
1993	573	1996	663	1999	637	2002	506
1994	651	1997	601	2000	556	2003	647

Highest: 812 in 1976 Lowest: 309 in 1879

Philip Eden is weather expert for BBC Radio Five Live, and the Daily *and* Sunday Telegraph.

CRICKETANA IN 2003

Bradman first, the rest...

DAVID RAYVERN ALLEN

Whatever else changes in cricket, the Don is big business. At Christie's sale in London last summer, a Bradman 1930 tour bat was sold (including the buyer's premium) for £29,375, an extraordinary figure in itself. But one of his caps – minus a top button and with the dubious advantage of added ventilation through some small moth holes – fetched even more at £35,250.

The Bradman name was on it, but subsequently Keith Miller was quoted as saying that it was a cap Bradman wore for about a minute at the start of the 1946-47 Ashes series before it found a more comfortable perch on Miller's own head.

Even so, it is possible the buyer got a bargain, because in Australia Bradman caps were fetching even more extraordinary prices. In February a "mystery buyer" was reported to have paid $A160,500, about £70,000, for the cap Bradman wore against India in 1947-48. And in June the cap he wore on the 1948 tour was said to have fetched an unbelievable $A425,000 (about £178,000).

Green and gold-rush: Don Bradman in baggy green. Reported prices for Bradman caps soared through the roof in 2003.

Picture by EMPICS.

These figures were too unbelievable for some tastes. They came from private sales, which means that the figures were indeed private. The sales were conducted by a new Melbourne auction house, Ludgrove's, founded by Michael Ludgrove, a former Christie's employee, and chaired by Graham Halbish, former chief executive of the Australian Cricket Board. *The Age* in Melbourne ran stories casting doubt on the exact nature of the deals, which obviously lacked the transparency that comes from open bidding.

The 1948 sale followed a campaign to "Bring Home Bradman's Cap" in the Australian media. Whatever the truth, these numbers alarmed Richard Mulvaney, the director of the Bradman Museum in Bowral, who feared the museum would be priced out of bidding for further Bradman material and would have to rely on donations.

Leaving Bradman alone on his pedestal, there are few others who can trigger anywhere near that sort of response: Trumper, Hobbs, Sobers possibly, and perhaps Hammond. And this mania for holy relics was in total contrast to trends elsewhere in the collection market, with dealers noting sadly that once sought-after material was now finding it harder to attract buyers. "There used to be a loyal following at cricket auctions," said Rupert Neelands of Christie's in London. "That following is still there, but now it's much more changeable and inconsistent. And so it is difficult to evaluate what is going to happen, particularly with specialist items."

The results of Christie's summer sale in London emphasised the point. A number of unique Felix (Nicholas Wanostrocht) items, including two lovingly collected and "Grangerised" (illustrated with plates cut out of other books) copies of *Felix on the Bat*, failed to reach their admittedly high reserves. And in Australia, the same happened with an engraved silver tray given to William Clarke, president of the Melbourne Cricket Club, by captain Ivo Bligh and other members of the 1882-83 tour party. If Felix and Bligh no longer have the same cachet, the same goes for the more modest modern performers.

"The emphasis on personality has got more pronounced," said book dealer Christopher Saunders. "In selling terms, the gap between somebody who played county cricket and somebody who played Test cricket has widened and the gap between the average Test cricketer and the legends of the game has widened even more."

Saunders also notices another gap. The age differential of collectors on his mailing list is marked. "The vast majority are over 50 or 60 years old and the rest largely between 25 and 40. The younger group used occasionally to buy a reasonably expensive item, but that no longer happens – except perhaps for an early *Wisden*. They mostly want county team sheets for the last ten years and they don't really know who played before Botham – and even Botham they're a bit hazy about."

An uncertain financial climate generally is bound to be reflected by hesitant touches in the memorabilia market. For now, the only certainty is uncertainty. There lies opportunity.

CRICKET GROUNDS IN 2003

The Outer Limits

MATTHEW ENGEL

The decline of the English county outground – oh my Hinckley and my Buxton long ago! – has been going on for some time, and this almanack has often lamented the consequent loss of diversity, charm and spectators. However, an unexpected replacement has now appeared round the cricketing world: the Test match outground.

Seven new venues made their Test debut in the 13 months between June 2002 and July 2003, a surge unprecedented since Pakistan staged their first Tests nearly half a century ago. Though spread across four continents, ranging from the tropics to the edge of the cold North Sea, these grounds have much in common. All seven are a long way from the big metropolitan areas that have traditionally staged Test cricket; all were used for games against less attractive opposition on unseasonable dates. And none of them drew large crowds.

But there have also been paltry turnouts for Tests at Lord's against secondary opposition in May and for Australia's game against Zimbabwe at the SCG last October. The indifferent attendances at the new grounds had little to do with the where, something to do with the when, and a great deal to do with the what. Grenada, East London, Potchefstroom, Chester-le-Street, St Lucia, Darwin and Cairns are not necessarily the most sophisticated places on earth, but their inhabitants are not daft. Test matches against Bangladesh, the opposition in four of the fixtures, are considered unenticing everywhere.

Nonetheless, the game against Zimbabwe at Chester-le-Street, the first new Test ground in England for 101 years, was regarded as a modest success. And this year Australia have another "Top End" series, in the tropical north of the country in the depths of southern winter, this time against Sri Lanka, who might be more of a draw than Bangladesh. If the present much-derided, overblown international fixture list continues, so will the rush to find faraway places where people might be willing to fill the stands and make the TV pictures look better.

At least two more new English Test venues may be on the horizon: Hampshire's ground at the Rose Bowl could well get a game before long, at least if something can be done about the inadequate access. And an intriguing possibility arose in November when Lancashire announced they were considering an offer from Manchester City Council to help them build a ground next to the 2002 Commonwealth Games stadium (now used by Manchester City FC) on the city's east side. "This may be a chance in a lifetime opportunity," said chief executive Jim Cumbes.

Lancashire's historic home at Old Trafford has been looking increasingly dowdy and inadequate compared to rival Test grounds. And this may become

New setting, new time of year: midwinter Test matches come to Australia and Cairns makes its debut.

Picture by Hamish Blair, Getty Images.

even more true by 2005, when Surrey are due to complete rebuilding the Vauxhall End to increase ground capacity from 19,000 to 23,000. Glamorgan are planning a further upgrade at Cardiff. Somerset are another county with major plans. Fearful of being left behind if English cricket splits between Test clubs and the rest, they are plotting a redevelopment that could increase capacity to 15,000 and put Taunton in the frame for regular international fixtures. "There is no reason why Somerset people should have to take a train to London to watch Marcus Trescothick bat," said chairman Giles Clarke.

The day does seem to be coming when English county cricket will be staged in 18 increasingly well-appointed county headquarter grounds (if all 18 counties survive) plus Cheltenham, the one festival whose future seems assured. There was a chance that Twenty20 cricket might have led to a renewed spirit of adventure among the counties, some of whom did seem keen to show off their dynamic new form of the game to new spectators in new settings. But this idea was a victim of the tournament's success: with their main grounds often so close to full in the competition's first year, the counties became disinclined to move the games anywhere smaller.

However, the 2004 fixture list has produced one thoroughly romantic-sounding fixture. Warwickshire are playing a Championship match against Lancashire at Swan's Nest Lane, Stratford-on-Avon – hard by the river and the theatre – an apparently lovely ground that has not staged first-class cricket in 53 years. The weight of international cricket fixtures this summer has forced the county into one of its rare ventures away from Edgbaston. But this is precisely the sort of scheduling that can encourage newcomers to watch county cricket – confused American and Japanese tourists, even.

CRICKET PEOPLE IN 2003

Walking for Ben

SIMON BRIGGS

Just hours after announcing his resignation as Surrey captain, **ADAM HOLLIOAKE** set out on an epic fund-raising crusade in the Ian Botham mould. His goal was to travel from Edinburgh to Tangier in the company of four regular companions: his father John, Lancashire opener Iain Sutcliffe, former Worcestershire all-rounder Matt Church and former European heavyweight boxing champion Scott Welch. The route he chose – as befitting one of cricket's most innovative thinkers – was quite unique.

Hollioake and co. left Edinburgh on foot on October 2. As they walked south, covering around 20 miles per day, they notched up an eclectic bunch of supporters. Several current Test players made an appearance, as did the football manager Sir Bobby Robson, the Olympic gold medallist Jonathan Edwards, jump jockey Richard Guest and the entire Sale rugby union team.

Now things got really serious: the Hollioake four arrived in Brighton, and set out to tackle the 20-hour sail to Dieppe in a force-nine gale. "That was definitely the bit I enjoyed the least," Hollioake said. "It was so cold and windy – mainly an exercise in keeping warm. We did the sailing ourselves, but we were glad to have some people from the Ocean Youth Trust aboard, telling us how to go."

The travellers then switched to bicycles, covering the 1,400 miles to Gibraltar in 25 days. "That was quite mentally demanding, a bit like fielding every day for a month – though the roads and scenery were fantastic." For his final trick, Hollioake boarded another boat for a seven-hour row to Tangier, and the ensuing "two-day piss-up".

"I didn't have any time to prepare," Hollioake said afterwards. "Surrey were flat out trying to win the Championship, and just trying to get publicity for the walk took up the rest of my days. I struggled for the first week, while my body got used to it. But the whole thing was very fulfilling."

By the end of 2003, Hollioake's efforts had helped raise £200,000 towards the Ben Hollioake Fund, the charity he founded in memory of his brother (details, page 1613). His target is to reach £5 million in five years to build a children's hospice in South London.

The Music Man

JOHN ALTMAN, the composer and jazz musician, received an Emmy nomination for his work on the TV adaptation of Tennessee Williams's novella *The Roman Spring of Mrs Stone.* As a sideline, he also arranges songs for the Mark Butcher Band. According to Butcher, "John's our true professional, the man who makes sure everybody knows what they're supposed to be doing."

Altman's involvement in the band is not just chance. He has been fascinated by cricket since the 1950s, when his uncle, the trombonist Woolf Phillips, was not only the bandleader at the London Palladium but the captain of a celebrity cricket team along the lines of David English's modern Bunburys. "My first encounter with the sport came when Woolf turned up to take me down to a game in Surrey, and he had Terry Thomas and Peter Sellers in the car," Altman explains. "It could hardly fail to get my attention."

With his distinctive pointed bald pate, Altman is a regular spectator at Test matches – and even the odd county game. Derek Pringle remembers him as a diehard Essex supporter during the 1980s. "He always used to say he came up with his best jingles while he was watching us. And this is the man who arranged 'Always Look on the Bright Side of Life'."

These days, Altman follows Test cricket all around the world, but preferably in Australia, where he is particularly proud of his occasional invitations into the home dressing-room. But during the epic series against India this winter, he was exiled to Los Angeles, with only the internet to keep him up to date, while he worked on the score for the Jennifer Lopez–Richard Gere musical *Shall We Dance?*

Checking out of the Lord's B&B

On reaching the MCC's retirement age of 60, Lord's curator **STEPHEN GREEN** was interviewed for the occasion by *Daily Telegraph* sports writer Sue Mott. "She called me a Dickensian eccentric," Green chuckles. "I shall be suing any day now."

Underneath the façade, one suspects Green was rather flattered by the attention. And after 35 years spent sorting through some of the world's most arcane correspondence, he has earned it. "I would get around 20 letters a day," he says. "I was probably a bit of a soft touch, but I tried to remember that the MCC was paying for this research service. If a letter looked like it would take more than 20 minutes to answer, I would invite the author to come in and take a look at our books and magazines for themselves."

Away from this philanthropic service, Green's central task was to preserve and enhance the collection at Lord's: the art and artefacts as well as the books. One of his favourite acquisitions was the painting of Lord Winchelsea, the great patron of Thomas Lord, which now hangs in the Long Room. And one of his least favourite duties was overseeing the museum's regular renovations. "It was a little like running a seaside guest house," Green says. "You had to move things around during the winter, because the members and guests wouldn't have tolerated any building work going on.

"One of the things I'm looking forward to now is simply being able to enjoy the British spring. Whenever I saw the first snowdrop or daffodil, it would just make me realise there were another fifty things to do before the season started."

Green signed off with the publication of a book – *Lord's: The Cathedral of Cricket* – which explored "the history of the greatest and most evocative sports ground in the world". His retirement years, he said, would be dedicated to his passion for historic churches.

Verger of the Cathedral: Stephen Green, recently retired curator at Lord's and author of *Lord's: The Cathedral of Cricket.*

Picture by Graham Morris.

Bat it like Bradman

Long neglected by western film-makers, cricket made a triumphant return to the cinema when **PAUL MORRISON**'s coming-of-age drama *Wondrous Oblivion* won the main prize at the Giffoni Film Festival in Italy.

The film, due for release in the UK in April 2004, follows the story of a young Jewish boy, growing up in South London in the 1960s, whose passion for the game far exceeds his ability. Morrison said the idea for the screenplay began with the image of a small figure in whites, banished to field on the boundary, who can "still maintain his optimism and pleasure of it all while everybody's being so dismissive of him".

Morrison is keen to deflect any suggestion of autobiography, though he admits he is a) Jewish, b) no good at cricket, and c) enough of a fan to follow the international game on the TV. "I was just never a fanatic in the way David is," he says.

David Wiseman, the film's protagonist, finally gets his break when a West Indian family move in next door and put up a net in the back garden. Not only do David's new neighbours teach him how to bat, they also introduce him to Garry Sobers, who bowls a couple of balls at him during a Saturday-afternoon knockabout.

"We had a real problem when we shot that scene," Morrison said, "because Phil Simmons, our technical advisor, pointed out that Sobers was left-handed and the guy who was playing him was not. We considered flipping the film, but in the end we had to give him an hour to run away and learn to bowl left-handed, which he did very well. That's the magic of film."

Our Woman in Havana

Cricket is springing up in the shadow of the notorious Guantanamo Bay penal colony in Cuba, thanks to the industry of retired English professor **LEONA FORD**. Born in 1943, Ford is a second-generation Cuban whose Barbadian father founded the Guantanamo Cricket Club just before she was born.

"I grew up in that West Indian community and was involved in their social atmosphere," Ford said. "They maintained and taught us their tradition and cultural identity and this is what I am intending to rescue.

"I remember the players from here and from abroad and have the original photos. My initial objective was to write a book titled *Memoirs of Cricket in Cuba.* But then I became more actively involved."

In the late 1990s, Ford started a campaign to restore Cuban cricket to its former glory. Within five years, there were eight senior teams in action, and over a thousand juniors at 37 different schools. In April 2004, they were due to play an inaugural provincial tournament, perhaps the first stepping stone towards an international presence. As Ford says, "the natives of Cuba are very talented at ball sports, as their success in baseball has proved".

The temporary office of Cuban cricket is based at Ford's home, yet she still finds time to attend training every weekend and hold seminars all over the country. Her efforts were recently recognised by the ICC, which named her global volunteer of the year for 2002.

Livewire at Lord's

People with long memories of British political life might have done a double-take when they saw **DES WILSON** cropping up as author of the strategy document that appeared to pave the way for England to pull out of the 2004-05 Zimbabwe tour.

Wilson is not the normal figure associated with the English cricket establishment. For a start, he comes from New Zealand. Far more improbably, in a game supposedly run by buttoned-up conservatives, Wilson made his name over the years as a voluble campaigner on a variety of leftish causes.

He became well-known in the late 1960s as director of Shelter, when he brought an innovative campaigning approach to helping the homeless, using media-wise and sometimes daring strategies to attract attention. He went on to be involved with Friends of the Earth, the Campaign for Lead-Free Air, the Campaign for Freedom of Information and the fledgling Liberal Democrats, just missing election to parliament, but becoming the party's president – and vice-chairman of the funding body Sport England.

At 62, Wilson appeared to be winding down when someone suggested he applied for the (unpaid) vacancy as chairman of the ECB's corporate affairs and marketing committee. He jumped at the job and, characteristically, was in the thick of the action – the Zimbabwe crisis – within months.

He says he first developed a passion for cricket while listening to the famous Trevor Bailey–Willie Watson stand at Lord's in 1953: "One of the moments of my life was to meet them both at Lord's last year. Fifty years after the event, they are the link to where this all started for me."

Cricket match: Keith and Jennifer Booth share the Oval scorebox – and a passion for scoring.

Picture by Patrick Eagar.

Wedded to the Game

For the second year running, the official scorers for the Oval Test were a married couple – **KEITH BOOTH**, the regular Surrey scorer, and his wife **JENNIFER**, who is actually the senior scorer of the two. She met Keith at Reading University in the 1960s, when he played for the university team and she kept the scorecards.

"I was very much the junior partner," says Keith, "but then I took early retirement from my job in university administration. Computerised scoring had just come in, and a few of the counties were looking for people who didn't think of a menu as something you find hanging outside an Italian restaurant."

While Keith cranked up his new career, landing on Surrey via spells at Middlesex and *Test Match Special*, Jennifer stuck with her day job as head of the Tate Gallery archives. But having finally retired in October 2003, she now says she is ready to put cricket first.

"We have the occasional disagreement when we're scoring together," said Jennifer, "usually over the identity of fielders, but generally we keep pretty good control of ourselves. I don't think it makes much difference whether you're working with your husband or someone else from a different county – the fact is that you're there to do a job."

A Loon, MBE

DAVID ENGLISH, the founder of the Bunbury Cricket Club, was typically effusive after a brief audience with the Queen at Buckingham Palace. After a 25-year charity fund-raising career worth an estimated £8 million, an MBE was surely the least he deserved.

"It was just like being on a film set," said English, whose own acting career peaked with the delivery of two lines in Sir Richard Attenborough's *A Bridge Too Far*. "I love England – the chivalry, the castles. So many countries don't have that, do they?"

As a dyed-in-the-wool monarchist, English was proud to don the red, gold and mauve tie of the Royal Household Cricket Club, who play against the Bunburys every year at Windsor. "I asked Her Majesty if she recognised the tie," English said, "and she replied: 'Aren't the colours ghastly?'"

English also put out an autobiography, with a subtitle – *Confessions of a Loon* – that conjured entirely appropriate parallels with the Robin Askwith films of the late 1970s. He spent most of its 240-odd pages modestly reeling off details of his nocturnal conquests.

A serious business, this cricket: Eric Clapton (*left*) takes it easy as David English comes into bowl.

Picture by Philip Brown.

Going, Going...

David English was in the thick of it again as **ERIC CLAPTON**, the great blues guitarist, made a valedictory appearance in a Bunbury match at Ripley, the Surrey village where he grew up. Clapton, who says "I love watching cricket but I hate playing it," was finally dismissed for a tortuous 13, having been clean bowled twice by what conveniently turned out to be no-balls.

Unlike W. G. Grace, who once famously replaced his own bails with a cry of "They've come to watch me bat, not you bowl," Clapton was only too ready to leave the crease. "I know what they were trying to do," he told the *Daily Telegraph*. "Keep me out in 100 degrees for the entire innings. But I have to say that was one of my better performances, probably the best ever, in fact. I reckon that must have raised my average to... oh... two, maybe even three."

Thanks to English's inability to say no to anyone, the game was contested by two teams of 25. Clapton was nominally captaining one side; Alec Stewart was very definitely in charge of the other. As is traditional at a Bunbury game, Test cricketers crossed swords with stars of stage and screen, among them TV presenter Jamie Theakston and "art movie actress" Anoushka.

Clapton had already retired at least once from cricket, but said that he agreed to play after attending English's book launch. "As the afternoon went on and people began drifting off, I saw David sitting on his own looking quite crestfallen because his big day was over. I called him the following day and said 'Why don't I do it one more time for old times' sake?' The moment I uttered the words, I thought 'Oh, no, what have I done?'"

From Selector to Groundsman

Former England captain Ray Illingworth is said to have rolled the square at his home club ground of Farsley for decades, even during his controversial spell as England team supremo. But in 2003, **CHANDU BORDE** went one better. Borde, who has served India admirably in the various roles of national captain, chairman of selectors and team manager, made another bold career move when he took over as curator of the Nehru Stadium in Pune.

Borde said his interest in pitches had begun during a spell in the Lancashire Leagues in the 1960s. "Every season I used to assist the groundsmen and I picked up the fundamentals of making a wicket from there.

"I have been an all-rounder on and off the field," Borde added. "So this hunger for learning has always helped me in doing many interesting things. And preparing pitches is one of them."

In December 1984, Borde was asked to get a pitch together for Pune's first one-day international. It hosted an excellent contest, featuring hundreds from Dilip Vengsarkar and Mike Gatting, which England won by four wickets. Nineteen years later, his return to the middle brought an even closer finish: Australia inched past New Zealand's total of 258 for nine with just two wickets and one ball in hand.

CHARITIES IN 2003

Joint United Nations Programme on HIV/AIDS (UNAIDS)

In September 2003, the ICC entered into a strategic alliance with UNAIDS to help fight HIV/AIDS in cricket-playing countries. The partnership's primary aim is to use cricket to raise public awareness of the disease. Of the estimated 40 million people with HIV/AIDS worldwide, over 12 million live in the major cricket-playing countries. Teams playing internationals on or around World Aids Day (December 1, 2003) wore red ribbons as a sign of solidarity with victims of the disease. Each Full Member of the ICC has appointed a national co-ordinator to plan further projects.

ICC contact: Hilary Marshall, ICC, Lord's Cricket Ground, London NW8 8QN. Tel: 020 7266 7912; email: hilary.marshall@icc-cricket.com; website: www.icc.cricket.org/unaids.

The Cricket Foundation

The Foundation was reconstituted in 1996 and exists to plough money from the first-class game back into grassroots and youth cricket. Although the ECB provides much of its funding, it operates independently of the board, with Ossie Wheatley as chairman of trustees. Since 1996, the Foundation has handed out over £21m, paying for cricket development officers, county youth teams, club and schools cricket, and training of coaches, umpires, groundsmen and teachers. Within the next 18 months, the Foundation hopes to launch a highly ambitious campaign to regenerate competitive cricket in state schools.

Director: Nick Gandon, Lord's Cricket Ground, London NW8 8QZ. Tel: 0207 432 1200; email: nickgandon.cricketfoundation@ecb.co.uk.

The Lord's Taverners

The Lord's Taverners, founded in 1950, and accredited by the ECB as the official charity for recreational cricket, distributed £1.7m in 2003. This was raised to "give young people, particularly those with special needs, a sporting chance". Half the money was spent on youth cricket projects recommended by the ECB. The rest was used to provide young disabled people with sports equipment, and 52 specially adapted minibuses. And the Taverners began 2004 by raising a record £230,000 in a single night, with a party on the new Cunard liner, *Queen Mary 2*. Since it was begun 54 years ago, by a group of actors enjoying a pint in the old Lord's Tavern, the Club has raised more than £30m.

Chief Executive: Mark Williams, The Lord's Taverners, 10 Buckingham Place, London SW1E 6HX. Tel: 020 7821 2828; email: hq@lordstaverners.org; website: www.lordstaverners.org.

The Brian Johnston Memorial Trust

The Trust (run through the Lord's Taverners) was launched in 1995 to support causes dear to the late Brian Johnston: sport for the disabled, especially cricket for the blind, and scholarships for young cricketers of exceptional promise. Beneficiaries in 2003 included the ECB's wrist-spin programme, which aims to produce an England leg-spinner by 2007. Funded by the Trust, four young spinners flew to Adelaide to attend a clinic run by Terry Jenner. More than 15 other young players also benefited, as did the England blind team, whose kit is sponsored by the Trust.

Secretary: Richard Anstey, The Lord's Taverners, 10 Buckingham Place, London SW1E 6HX. Tel: 020 7821 2828; email: richard.anstey@lordstaverners.org; website: www.lordstaverners.org.

The Primary Club

The Primary Club began in 1955 when four club players, depressed by their poor performance with the bat, vowed to raise money for blind cricketers. The Club continues to provide sporting and recreational facilities for the blind and partially sighted. Membership is nominally restricted to those who have been dismissed first ball in any form of cricket, and there are currently 12,500 who admit to it. In total, the club has raised over £1.5m – through donations and members' events, and by selling its famous tie, popularised by *Test Match Special.* In 2003, donations included a canal boat for the Royal London Society for the Blind, an audio system for the visually impaired at Hove cricket ground and funding for after-school clubs to help introduce blind children to sport. In 2004, the Club intends to hand out around £180,000.

Hon. Secretary: Chris Larlham, PO Box 12121, Saffron Walden, Essex CB10 2ZF. Tel: 01799 586507; email: primaryclub@aol.com.

The Hornsby Professional Cricketers Fund

The Hornsby Professional Cricketers Fund was established in 1928, from the estate of J. H. J. Hornsby, who played for Middlesex, MCC and the Gentlemen. It provides money to assist "former professional cricketers [not necessarily first-class] or their wives, widows until remarriage, children and other dependants, provided the persons concerned shall be in necessitous circumstances". Assistance is given by monthly allowances, special grants or, in certain cases, loans. Donations, requests for help or information about potential recipients are all welcome.

Clerk to the Treasurers: Tony Brown, The Wickets, Badgers Drive, Brentry, Bristol BS10 6LZ. Tel: 0117 950 9225; email: asb@thewkts.demon.co.uk.

The Professional Cricketers' Association Charity

The PCA Charity was founded in 1983 by Harold Goldblatt. It aims to relieve financial hardship among present or former members of the Association, or anyone who has played cricket for a first-class county, along with their "wives, children, parents or dependants". At present the charity is helping more than 30 people. Donations are very welcome, as are requests for help, and information about cricketers who may be in need.

Chairman of Trustees: David Graveney, PCA, Third Floor, 338 Euston Road, London NW1 3BT. Tel: 020 7544 8660; email: david@graveney.thepca.net.

The Cricket Society Trust

The Trust was founded in 1958, and became a registered charity in 1992. It helps young cricketers by providing equipment for schools and clubs; the Trust also pays for children from deprived areas in London, including some who have never left the city, to spend a day playing various ball games at Arundel Castle, in rural Sussex. The aim is to target the specific small projects and problems often overlooked by bigger donors.

Hon. Secretary: Ken Merchant, 16 Louise Road, Rayleigh, Essex SS6 8LW. Tel: 01628 747414.

The Bunbury Cricket Club

The Bunbury Club was founded in 1986 by David English and, although not a registered charity, has raised £8m to help good causes and fund youth cricket. On August 10, 2003, the hottest day on record in England, a 25-a-side charity game, featuring Sir Viv Richards, Muttiah Muralitharan and Bill Wyman, raised £30,000 to help both Crossroads, a drug-rehabilitation centre in Richards's native Antigua, and the NSPCC. In total, the Bunbury Club raised around £400,000 in 2003.

Founder: David English, 1 Highwood Cottages, Nan Clark's Lane, London NW7 4HJ. Tel: 020 8959 0380; fax: 020 8959 2755.

Have bike, will travel: Adam Hollioake and the bicycle that carried him on the Dieppe–Gibraltar leg of his sponsored journey for the Ben Hollioake Fund.

Ben Hollioake Fund

The Fund was established in December 2002 by the family of the Surrey and England all-rounder Ben Hollioake, who had been killed in a car crash nine months earlier. By the end of 2007, they hope to have raised £5m to help build a new centre for CHASE, a Surrey-based charity caring for terminally ill children and their families. At the end of 2003, £200,000 had been raised. This included £125,000 in sponsorship raised by Ben's brother Adam, who walked, sailed and cycled 2,000 miles from Edinburgh to Tangier over the autumn. In 2004, the rock guitarist Eric Clapton plans to donate the proceeds of one of his May concerts at the Albert Hall.

Fund co-ordinator: Loraine Bicknell, CHASE, Loseley Park, Guildford, Surrey GU3 1HS. Tel: 08707 870353; email: loraine.bicknell@chasecare.org.uk; website: www.benhollioakefund.com.

NatWest Cricket with the Prince's Trust

Launched in May 2003, the project links groups of disadvantaged youngsters with county cricket clubs. The aim is to develop confidence and new skills, with a view to getting into work afterwards. Groups from the Prince's Trust, a charity providing self-development courses for young people, spent 12 weeks based at a county ground. The clubs provided work placements, motivational talks from players, ground tours, merchandise for auction, and cricket coaching for those who wanted it. Funded by NatWest and organised through the PCA, the scheme is particularly targeted at ethnic minorities. Twelve counties took part in the 2003 programme.

Prince's Trust contact: Joe Howes, Prince's Trust, 18 Park Square East, Regent's Park, London NW1 4LH. Tel: 020 7543 7340; email: joseph.howes@princes-trust.org.uk.

ACADEMIES IN 2003

Learning process

EMMA JOHN

After more than a decade of coveting the Australian youth academy and a year of building their own, England could finally claim one-up on their oldest rivals in 2003. The £4.5m chrome and glass edifice that sprang up at Loughborough University in Leicestershire was the world's largest and most comprehensive indoor cricket facility and the ECB's monument to the future.

Opened officially by the Queen on November 14, the National Academy gave its first 14-strong intake a grand start. But there was no escape from their rigid programme, or the eagle-eyed headmaster Rod Marsh, during ten subsequent weeks of live-in training. A custom-built gym housed early morning sweats; compulsory lectures on everything from captaincy to accountancy were held in the seminar rooms, while healthy eating, spa baths and medical care all came as standard.

The *pièce de résistance* was the massive cricket centre, incorporating six lanes of nets of varying speeds, each long enough for a wicket-keeper to stand back to a bowler with a 30-yard run up. Net-lane cameras tracked every move and replayed them on a giant plasma screen at ground level. From a gallery above, the director of cricket could watch his charges, surrounded by thousands of pounds of analysis equipment, some of it so futuristic that no one yet knew how to use it fully. Marsh's response to his new home was expectant and chilling: "There are no excuses now."

They were timely words – four years of peripatetic teaching at the Academy had, by the end of 2003, yet to produce a convincing Test player. Yet Marsh fever had already rampaged across the country; by the end of the domestic season, the ECB's network of centres of excellence was in place, with every first-class county able to boast its own ECB-accredited academy for 13-to-18-year-olds and a national coach, Keith Tomlins, to oversee the academy system.

Sri Lanka was another country to set up a base camp for protégés. In May 2003, the Sony Max Cricket Academy was opened at the Premadasa Stadium in Colombo, including dormitories, a gym and 16 lanes of outdoor nets to rival the Nursery at Lord's. The Indian board also agreed to move the National Cricket Academy, previously renting space at the Chinnaswamy Stadium in Bangalore, to a permanent home on a 15-acre site on the city's outskirts.

Private cricket academies, meanwhile, continued to be big business on the subcontinent. Rashid Latif, whose non-resident Karachi academy was established in 2000, announced his intention to plug a gap in Pakistan cricket by setting up a permanent "finishing school" for future international players.

The World Cricket Academy, a live-in training programme in Mumbai launched in December 2002 by former BCCI president Raj Singh Dungarpur, was quick to claim England's Ed Smith as an alumnus when he made his

Building for the future: the new ECB Academy at Loughborough University.
Picture by Graham Morris.

Test debut against South Africa (he had spent a few weeks there studying spin). Even Italy boasted its own academy, sending three youngsters to Hobart for an 11-week immersion course with Peter Di Venuto, Michael's brother.

There was still room for scepticism, however, at the worldwide scramble to emulate Australia's blue-chip success. "The Australian Academy was not responsible for the success of Australian cricket over the past decade," said the country's former captain and coach Bob Simpson. "Through self-publicity and an old mates system it has promoted itself beyond what it really has achieved."

In fact, of 226 students, only 20 (including the institution's most famous drop-out, Shane Warne) had played Test cricket for Australia by the end of 2003 and only 11 had played in more than 20 Tests. England, who by 2007 aim for 95% of Test players to be academy graduates, expect a more handsome return on their investment.

DIRECTORY OF BOOKSELLERS AND AUCTIONEERS

BOOKSELLERS

AARDVARK BOOKS, 19 Vanwall Drive, Waddington, Lincoln, Lincolnshire LN5 9LT. Tel/fax: 01522 722671. Peter Taylor specialises in *Wisdens*, including rare hardbacks and early editions. Quarterly catalogues sent on request. *Wisdens* purchased. Cleaning, gilding and restoration undertaken.

ACUMEN BOOKS, Nantwich Road, Audley, Staffordshire ST7 8DL. Tel: 01782 720753; fax: 01782 720798; email: wca@acumenbooks.co.uk; website: www.acumenbooks.co.uk. Everything for umpires, scorers and others; textbooks, equipment etc; import/export.

TIM BEDDOW, 66 Oak Road, Oldbury, West Midlands B68 0BD. Tel: 0121 421 7117; email: wisden1864@hotmail.com; website: www.edgbastonbooks.co.uk. Large stock of cricket/football books, programmes and signed material. Items purchased. Send SAE for catalogue. Stall at Thwaite Gate, Edgbaston, every first-team match.

BODYLINE BOOKS, 150a Harbord Street, London SW6 6PH. Tel: 020 7385 2176; fax: 020 7610 3314; email: info@bodylinebooks.com; website: www.bodylinebooks.com. We are the only specialist dealer in London for old copies of *Wisden Cricketers' Almanack*. Most years always in stock. Catalogue issued free on request.

BOUNDARY BOOKS LTD, 507 Castle Quay, Manchester M15 4NT. Fax: 01925 858237; email: mike@boundary-books.demon.co.uk. Publishers of high-quality limited-edition books and specialists in rare and hard-to-find books and memorabilia, particularly from great collectors of the past.

IAN DYER CRICKET BOOKS, 29 High Street, Gilling West, Richmond, North Yorkshire DL10 5JG. Tel: 01748 822786; fax: 0870 705 1561; email: iandyer@cricketbooks.co.uk; website: www.cricketbooks.co.uk. Cricketbooks.co.uk for *Wisdens*, annuals, books, programmes, tour guides, scorecards, benefit brochures, magazines, memorabilia. Keyword search; automatic postage calculation. *Paypal*/credit cards accepted.

K. FAULKNER, 65 Brookside, Wokingham, Berkshire RG41 2ST. Tel: 0118 978 5255. Email: kfaulkner@bowmore.demon.co.uk; website: www.bowmore.demon.co.uk. Book room open by appointment. Cricket books, *Wisdens*, memorabilia, bought and sold. Also at Gloucestershire CCC shop, Nevil Road, Bristol BS7 9EJ.

GEOFF FREEMAN, 51 Noah's Ark Lane, Lindfield, Haywards Heath, West Sussex RH16 2LU. Tel: 01444 484195; email: geoff.freeman@btinternet.com; website: www.geoff-freeman.com. Antiquarian books, *Wisdens*, 19th-century material, Australiana, postcards, photographs, letters, yearbooks, autographs, scrapbooks, albums, brochures, teamsheets and all signed material bought and sold. Catalogues issued.

GRACE BOOKS AND CARDS (TED KIRWAN), 3 Pine Garden, Oadby, Leicester LE2 5UT. Tel: 0116 271 6363 (weekdays) and 0116 271 4267 (evenings and weekends). Second-hand and antiquarian cricket books, *Wisdens*, autographed material and cricket ephemera of all kinds. Now also modern postcards.

ROGER HEAVENS, 2 Lowfields, Little Eversden, Cambridge CB3 7HJ. Tel: 01223 262839; fax: 01223 262033; mobile: 07967 096924; email: roger@ahaygarth.fsnet.co.uk. Cricket publisher specialising in the works of Arthur Haygarth and early history of cricket. Send for free catalogue. Order direct – all major credit cards accepted.

***J. W. McKENZIE, 12 Stoneleigh Park Road, Ewell, Epsom, Surrey KT19 0QT. Tel: 020 8393 7700; fax: 020 8393 1694; email: jwmck@netcomuk.co.uk; website: www.mckenziecricket.co.uk**. Specialists in antiquarian second-hand books, particularly *Wisdens*, and memorabilia. Established 1969. Catalogues issued. Publishers of cricket books. Shop premises open regular business hours.

MACMILLAN WISDEN DIRECT, Brunel Road, Houndmills, Basingstoke, Hampshire RG21 6XS. Tel: 01256 302685. New *Wisdens* for 1996–2004 and the first six editions of *Wisden Cricketers' Almanack Australia* available from Wisden's mail-order supplier. Prices from £19.99, including p&p.

ROGER PAGE, 10 Ekari Court, Yallambie, Victoria 3085, Australia. Tel: (03) 9435 6332; fax: (03) 9432 2050; email: rpcricketbooks@unite.com.au. Dealer in new and second-hand cricket books. Distributor of overseas cricket annuals and magazines. Agent for Association of Cricket Statisticians and Cricket Memorabilia Society.

RED ROSE BOOKS, 478 Bolton Road, Darwen, Lancashire BB3 2JR. Tel: 01254 776767; email: info@redrosebooks.co.uk; website: www.redrosebooks.co.uk. Specialist cricket booksellers and publishers. Catalogue sent on request.

WILLIAM H. ROBERTS, The Crease, 113 Hill Grove, Salendine Nook, Huddersfield, West Yorkshire HD3 3TL. Tel/fax: 01484 654463; email: william.roberts2@virgin.net; website: www.williamroberts-cricket.com. Second-hand/antiquarian cricket books, *Wisdens*, autograph material and memorabilia bought and sold. Catalogues sent on request.

ST MARY'S BOOKS & PRINTS, 9 St Mary's Hill, Stamford, Lincolnshire PE9 2DP. Tel: 01780 763033; email: cricket@stmarysbooks.com; website: www.stmarysbooks.com. Dealers in *Wisdens*, second-hand, rare cricket books and *Vanity Fair* prints. Also search service offered.

CHRISTOPHER SAUNDERS, Kingston House, High Street, Newnham-on-Severn, Gloucestershire GL14 1BB. Tel: 01594 516030; fax: 01594 517273; email: chrisbooks@aol.com. Office/bookroom open by appointment. Second-hand/antiquarian cricket books and memorabilia bought and sold. Regular catalogues issued containing selections from over 10,000 items in stock.

***SPORTS BOOKS DIRECT, Sportspages Bookshop at Caxton Walk, 94–96 Charing Cross Road, London WC2H 0JW. Tel: 020 7240 9604; and at Barton Square, St Ann's Square, Manchester M2 7HA. Tel: 0161 832 8530. Mail order – Sports Books Direct, tel: 020 7836 7817; fax: 020 7836 0104; website: www.sportsbooksdirect.co.uk.** New cricket books, especially Australian imports. Retail through Sportspages and worldwide mail-order service, including regular catalogues of new books, through Sports Books Direct.

STUART TOPPS, 40 Boundary Avenue, Wheatley Hills, Doncaster, South Yorkshire DN2 5QU. Tel: 01302 366044. Our 120-page plus catalogue of cricket books, *Wisdens*, booklets, brochures and county yearbooks is always available.

***WILLOWS PUBLISHING CO., 17 The Willows, Stone, Staffordshire ST15 0DE. Tel: 01785 814700; email: jenkins.willows@ntlworld.com.** *Wisden* reprints 1879–1889, 1900–1920 and 1940–1945. Send SAE for prices.

WISTERIA BOOKS, Wisteria Cottage, Birt Street, Birtsmorton, Malvern, Worcestershire WR13 6AW. Tel/Fax: 01684 833578. Visit our family-run stall at county grounds for new, second-hand, antiquarian cricket books and ephemera, or contact Grenville Simons at the address above.

MARTIN WOOD CRICKET BOOKS, 1c Wickenden Road, Sevenoaks, Kent TN13 3PJ. Tel/Fax: 01732 457205; email: martin@martinwoodcricketbooks.co.uk; website: www.martinwoodcricketbooks.co.uk. On-line catalogue lists all my cricket books which, standing, fill 160 yards of shelving. Established 1970.

AUCTIONEERS

***CHRISTIE'S, 85 Old Brompton Road, South Kensington, London SW7 3LD. Tel: 020 7752 3355; email: mdunbar@christies.com.** Christie's highly successful cricket memorabilia auctions have been held every year since the inaugural MCC Bicentenary sale in 1987. For enquiries, please contact Max Dunbar.

***T. VENNETT-SMITH, 11 Nottingham Road, Gotham, Nottinghamshire NG11 0HE. Tel: 0115 983 0541.** Auctioneers and valuers. Twice-yearly auctions of cricket and sports memorabilia. The cricket auction is run by cricketers for cricket-lovers worldwide.

***DOMINIC WINTER BOOK AUCTIONS, Specialist Book Auctioneers & Valuers, The Old School, Maxwell Street, Swindon, Wiltshire SN1 5DR. Tel: 01793 611340; fax: 01793 491727; email: info@dominicwinter.co.uk; website: www.dominicwinter.co.uk**. Twice-yearly auction sales of sports books and memorabilia, including *Wisdens*.

Asterisks indicate businesses that have display advertisements elsewhere in the Almanack. See Index of Advertisements for details.

DIRECTORY OF CRICKET SUPPLIERS

COACHING COURSES AND FESTIVALS

DURHAM SCHOOL, Durham DH1 4SZ. Tel: 0191 386 4783; email: enquiries@durhamschool.co.uk; website: www.durhamschool.co.uk. Cricket festivals and professional cricket coaching for young people aged 8–15 years. Residential and non-residential courses run during Easter and summer. Course Director: Mike Hirsch.

COACHING AIDS AND EQUIPMENT

CRAZY CATCH, Tel: 07789 915 345; email: rupes@crazycatch.com; website: www.crazycatch.com. Experience the unexpected! Unique, "insane" rebound catching device ensures an unpredictable ball response for healthy fun and skill development. A challenge for everyone!

CRICKET COACHING MATS LTD, Field Head, Whitegate, Halifax. Tel: 01422 244818; email: d.cooper20@ntlworld.com; website: www.cricketcoachingmats.com. I improve your batting. Use a coaching mat. Practice shots 100 times in ten minutes!! Comes with audio and video coaching tapes. A perfect gift.

THE ELIMINATOR – ROLAND BUTCHER CRICKET BOWLING TARGET. Tel: 01494 795100; website: www.bowlingtarget.com. Get more wickets – win more matches. Use the Eliminator Bowling Target. Contact us to order.

CRICKET EQUIPMENT

BOUNDARY SPORTS LTD, 206 Station Road, Kings Heath, Birmingham. Tel: 0121 444 2200; fax: 0121 444 4124; email: boundarysports@btconnect.com. Cricket equipment specialist, manufacturers and suppliers of quality cricket clothing and leisurewear to first-class and minor counties, clubs and schools. Suppliers to Somerset and Durham CCC.

DUKE SPORTSWEAR, Unit 4, Magdalene Road, Torquay, Devon TQ1 4AF. Tel/fax: 01803 292012. Test-standard sweaters to order in your club colours, using the finest yarns.

EXITO SPORTS COMPANY, Unit C1, Burley Heyes, Arley Road, Appleton Thorn, Warrington WA4 4RS. Tel: 01565 777300; email: info@exitosports.com; website: www.exitosports.com. Manufacturers and suppliers of quality cricket clothing and leisurewear to first-class and minor counties, amateur clubs, schools and colleges.

FORDHAM SPORTS LTD, 81/85 Robin Hood Way, Kingston Vale, London SW15 3PW. Tel: 020 8974 5654; email: fordham@fordhamsports.co.uk; website: www.fordhamsports.co.uk. Cricket equipment specialist with largest range of branded stock in London at discount prices. Mail order worldwide. Free catalogue.

GRAYS SPORTS, 36 Sidney Street, Cambridge CB2 3HX. Tel: 01223 362428. Specialist sports retailers offering a great range of products to cricketers of all levels.

GUNN & MOORE, Trent Lane, Colwick, Nottingham NG2 4DS. Tel: 0115 985 3500; fax: 0115 985 3501; email: assist@unicorngroup.com; website: www.gm-cricket.com. Gunn & Moore, established in 1885, is the world's most comprehensive provider of cricket bats, equipment, footwear and clothing. For full up-to-date information, visit www.gm-cricket.com.

NOMAD PLC. Tel: 01858 464878. Nomad manufacture coffins to suit all levels. The new "International" range has aluminium edging on all sides, wheels, and is available in ten different colours.

STUART & WILLIAMS (BOLA), 6 Brookfield Road, Cotham, Bristol BS6 5PQ. Email: info@bola.co.uk; website: www.bola.co.uk. Manufacturer of bowling machines and ball-throwing machines for all sports. Machines for recreational and commercial application for sale to the UK and overseas.

CRICKET TOURS

ALL WAYS SPORTS TOURS, 7 Whielden Street, Old Amersham, Buckinghamshire HP7 0HT. Tel: 01494 432747; email: sales@all-ways.co.uk; website: www.all-ways.co.uk. Specialist tour operators for supporters tours following rugby, cricket and golf world-wide and escorted and tailor made tours to New Zealand, Australia and South Pacific.

BARBADOS JOURNEYS. Tel: 0870 708 2010; email: barbadosjournies@wwj.uk.com. Specialist tour operators to the Caribbean. Schools, club sides, benefit tours, testimonials, intensive coaching academy – founders Sir Garry Sobers School Tournament.

GULLIVERS SPORTS TRAVEL, Fiddington Manor, Tewkesbury, Gloucester GL20 7BJ. Tel: 01684 293175; fax: 01684 297926; email: gullivers@gulliversports.co.uk; website: www.gulliversports.co.uk. The best value, quality, worldwide tours for supporters, schools and clubs – all ages and standards. ECB Official Tour Operator and fully bonded.

THE RED HOUSE HOTEL, 2 Whipton Village Road, Whipton, Exeter, Devon EX4 8AR. Tel: 01392 256104; email: info@redhousehotelexeter.co.uk; website: www.redhousehotelexeter.co.uk. Late bar, great prices, what more do you want! Give us a ring now and book early to avoid disappointment.

RIVERDALE HALL HOTEL, Bellingham, Near Hexham, Northumberland NE48 2JT. Tel: 01434 220254; fax: 01434 220457; email: iben@riverdalehall.demon.co.uk. Country House Hotel with cricket pitch, indoor pool, golf nearby, real ales, "Gold Plate" Les Routiers restaurant. Up to 20 visiting teams annually. Cocker family's 26th year.

SUN LIVING, 8a Milton Court, Ravenshead, Nottingham NG15 9BD. Tel: 01623 795365; fax: 01623 797421. Worldwide specialists for 25 years in tailor-made cricket tours for schools, clubs, counties, plus our ever-popular supporters tours. Fully ABTA and ATOL bonded.

SUNSPORT TOURS & TRAVEL, Hamilton House, 66 Palmerston Road, Northampton NN1 5EX. Tel (UK): 0870 742 7014; fax (UK): 01604 631628; email: paul@sunsport.co.uk; website: www.sunsport.co.uk. High-quality tailor-made tours to Kenya, South Africa, West Indies and subcontinent. Clients include counties, clubs, colleges, senior/prep schools. ATOL bonded. Contact Barry Dudleston/Paul Bush.

TITAN GROUPS LTD, HiTours House, Crossoak Lane, Redhill, Surrey RH1 5EX. Tel: 01293 450600; fax: 01293 450602; email: cricket@titantravel.co.uk; website: www.titangroups.co.uk. Tailor-made sports tours for supporters, schools, clubs, and universities to any destination in the world. ABTA, ATOL and IATA bonded. ECB official tour operator.

GIFTS AND MEMORABILIA

BUCKINGHAM COVERS, Church House, 136 Sandgate Road, Folkestone, Kent CT20 2BY. Tel: 01303 850672; fax: 01303 850687. Autographed cricket photographs and covers; if you collect memorabilia make sure we know your details so we can send you our FREE colour magazines.

DD DESIGNS, 62 St Catherine's Grove, Lincoln, Lincolnshire LN5 8NA. Tel: 01522 800298; email: ddprints@aol.com. Specialists in genuinely signed limited-edition prints. Official producers of *Wisden's* "Five Cricketers of the Year" sets, and other signed cricket portfolios. Free information leaflet available.

JOCELYN GALSWORTHY, 237 Chelsea Cloisters, Sloane Avenue, London SW3 3DT. Tel: 020 7591 0698; mobile: 07885 542652; fax: 01983 874182; email: theartist@jocelyngalsworthy.co.uk; website: www.jocelyngalsworthy.co.uk. Limited-edition cricket prints signed and numbered by the artist. Original cricket paintings for sale. Free catalogue.

THE WISDEN CRICKETER MAIL-ORDER SHOP, Ridge Farm, Lamberhurst, Tunbridge Wells, Kent TN3 8ER. Tel: 01892 893020; email: shophelp@cricketer.com; website: www.cricshop.com. A complete range of replica clothing, both UK and international, books, DVDs and videos, and wide variety of cricket gifts and memorabilia. Call for free catalogue.

PAVILION AND GROUND EQUIPMENT

AUTOGUIDE EQUIPMENT LTD, Stockley Road, Heddington, Nr Calne, Wiltshire SN11 0PS. Tel: 01380 850885; fax: 01380 850010; email: sales@autoguide.co.uk. Manufacturers of the world-famous Auto-Roller for cricket wickets. We now supply bolt-in Re-Power packs that include power steering for older rollers.

E. A. COMBS LTD, Quantum House, London E18 1BY. Tel: 020 8530 4216; website: www.eacombs.com. Pavilion clocks for permanent and temporary siting. Wide choice of sizes and styles to suit any ground.

COURTYARD DESIGNS, Suckley, Worcestershire WR6 5EH. Tel: 01886 884640; fax: 01886 884444; email: enquiries@courtyarddesigns.co.uk. Classic wooden pavilions made to the highest standards from weatherboard and clay tile roofs. Full colour brochure and testimonials.

CRICKET COVERS LTD, Carpenters Cottage, Forton, Longparish, Hampshire SP11 7AL. Tel: 01256 896574. Cricket Covers Ltd simply make the best mobile net, sightscreens and mobile covers in our opinion. For a better product give me a call.

CRICKET NETTING from ROMBULL (UK) LTD. Unit 1, Field End, Crendon Industrial Park, Long Crendon, Buckinghamshire HP18 9EJ. Tel: 01844 203870; fax: 01844 203871; email: enquiries@rombull.co.uk; website: www.rombull.co.uk. Wide range of durable, high-quality knotless polypropylene and knotted polyethylene netting products. Practise enclosures, ball-stop netting and boundary ropes.

ETC GRASS MACHINERY. Tel: 01829 733432; email: etc@grass-machinery.com; website: www.grass-machinery.com. For all your machinery requirements, from one of the largest suppliers of new and reconditioned machines to suit all budgets. Warranty and delivery included. UK and export welcome.

EXCLUSIVE LEISURE. 28 Cannock Street, Leicester LE4 9HR. Tel: 0116 233 2255; fax: 0116 246 1561; email: info@exclusiveleisure.co.uk; website: www.exclusiveleisure.co.uk. Installers of the "Tom Graveney" Cricketweave Artificial Pitch Systems, including ECB-approved Unique "T"-based system. "Probably the nearest to a natural wicket you'll ever play on."

FSL SCOREBOARDS. Tel: 028 8676 6131; website: www.fsl.ltd.uk. UK-designed and manufactured, FSL offer a complete range of electronic scoreboards in portable and self-install kits. Leasing options from less than £60/month.

HUCK NETS (UK) LTD, Gore Cross Business Park, Corbin Way, Bradpole, Bridport, Dorset DT6 3UX. Tel: 01308 425100; fax: 01308 458109; email: sales@hucknet.com; website: www.hucknet.com. Quality knotless netting. "Ultimate" range of mobile steel cages, sightscreens and pitch covers. Rolldown synthetic pitches. Slip cradles. Boundary ropes. Scorers. Spare numbers. Colour brochure.

JMS CRICKET LTD, Byeways, East Parade, Steeton, Keighley, West Yorkshire BD20 6RP. Tel: 0870 011 6144; fax: 0113 261 1444; email: sales@jmscricket.com; website: www.jmscricket.com. Buy direct from the manufacturer. Mobile covers, flat sheets, sightscreens, mobile nets, slip cradles plus much, much more. We've got cricket covered.

POWEROLL ROLLERS by Power Precision & Fabrication Ltd, Greenhill, Gunnislake, Cornwall PL18 9AS. Tel: 01822 832608; website: www.poweroll.com. Manufacturers of a comprehensive range of grass rollers to suit different budgets and applications.

PROCTOR NETS LTD of Worcester Park, Surrey. Tel: 020 8337 2554; fax: 020 8337 2558. For nets, artificial wickets, scoreboards and boxes, covers, sightscreens, ball-stop installations.

STUART CANVAS PRODUCTS, Warren Works, Hardwick Grange, Warrington, Cheshire WA1 4RF. Tel: 01925 814525; fax: 01925 831709; email: sales@stuartcanvas.freeserve.co.uk. Designers, manufacturers and suppliers of flat sheets, mobiles, roller and hover covers – sold throughout the world, including Test and county grounds.

TILDENET LTD, Hartcliffe Way, Bristol BS3 5RJ. Tel: 0117 966 9684; fax: 0117 923 1251; email: enquiries@tildenet.co.uk; website: www.tildenet.co.uk. An extensive range of equipment... grass germination sheets, ball-stop fencing, mobile practice nets, static nets and frames, sightscreens, layflat, mobile and automatic rain covers, practice netting.

PITCHES (TURF AND NON-TURF)

BOUGHTON LOAM LTD, Telford Way Industrial Estate, Telford Way, Kettering, Northamptonshire NN16 8UN. Tel: 01536 510515, fax: 01536 510691; email: enquiries@boughton-loam.co.uk; website: www.boughton-loam.co.uk. Boughton Loam offer the full range of cricket loams, grass seeds and fertilisers for construction and maintenance of cricket grounds, also contracting services including Koro "Field Topmaker".

CLUB SURFACES LTD, The Barn, Bisham Grange, Marlow, Buckinghamshire SL7 1RS. Tel: 01628 485969; fax: 01628 471944; email: clubsurfaces@uklinux.net. ClubTurf, world-leading non-turf pitch since 1978; top in independent Sports Council tests; 5,500+ installations, including Lord's; suppliers to ICC, ECB, MCC. Contact Derek Underwood for information pack.

FLICX UK LTD, Walltree House Farm, Steane, Brackley, Northamptonshire NN13 5NS. Tel: 01295 816765; fax: 01295 810298; email: flicxuk@flicx.com; website: www.flicx.com. Manufacturers and suppliers of portable cricketing equipment, including *Flicx* Cricket Pitches, *Brel* Bowling Machines, portable nets and coaching equipment. Call for brochure.

NOTTS SPORT®, Premier House, 18 Mandervell Road, Oadby, Leicester LE2 5LQ. Tel: 0116 272 0222; fax: 0116 272 0617; email: info@nottssport.com; website: www.nottssport.com. When all-round quality performance is a "must have", cricket centres and clubs throughout the world choose Notts Sport. Clients include ECC and ECB.

PEAK SPORTS LTD, Unit 4, Ford Street, Brinksway, Stockport SK3 0BT. Tel: 0161 480 2502; fax: 0161 480 1652; website: www.pscricket.com. Agents for Wimbledon Unreal Grass pitches. Glue to concrete, nail to tarmac or unroll on gym floor. Guaranteed ten years. Write for brochure. Installed at Radley, Winchester, Manchester GS, etc.

TECHNICAL SURFACES LTD, Whetstone House, High St, Whetstone, Leicester LE8 6LQ. Tel: 08702 400700; fax: 08702 400701; email: cricket@technicalsurfaces.co.uk; website: www.technicalsurfaces.co.uk. Nationwide maintenance to artificial cricket pitches. Over 20 years' experience of all types and systems. From block-hole repairs to complete resurfacing.

TOTAL TURF SOLUTIONS (tts), 21, Dunnock Lane, Grange Park, Northampton NN4 5DG. Tel: 01604 674368/07973 885775; email: enquiry@totalturfsolutions.co.uk; website: www.totalturfsolutions.co.uk. Independent consultants and lecturers to the sports turf industry. Specialist cricket contractors. Suppliers of "Climate Cover" a revolution in sports turf covering.

SCORESHEETS AND COMPUTER DATABASES

BILL FRINDALL, The Beeches, Blackboard Lane, Urchfont, Devizes, Wiltshire SN10 4RD. Tel/fax: 01380 840206; mobile: 07860 544221; email: beardedwonder@btinternet.com. Frindall linear scoring sheets and binders. Copies of his Test matches, limited-overs internationals and Lord's finals since 1966. Guest speaking.

***TASTATS, 214 Warwick Street, West Hobart, Tasmania, 7000, Australia. Tel/fax: (+61) 3 6231 0193; email: ricf@netspace.net.au; website: www.tastats.com.au.** CSW – a Windows-based interactive database of all Test cricket, ODIs, and Australian domestic first-class and one-day competitions, including full statistics and records. From £25.

GORDON VINCE, 5 Chaucer Grove, Camberley, Surrey GU15 2XZ. Email: gordon@gvince.demon.co.uk. Cricket Statistics System used worldwide to produce widest range of averages/statistics, from Test to village level. Available with extensive range of up-to-date databases of worldwide matches.

SPEAKERS AND SOCIETIES

CRICKET MEMORABILIA SOCIETY. Honorary Secretary: Steve Cashmore, 4 Stoke Park Court, Stoke Road, Bishops Cleeve, Cheltenham, Gloucestershire GL52 8US. Email: cms87@btinternet.com. For collectors worldwide – magazines, meetings, auctions, speakers, and – most of all – friendship.

LOOK WHO'S TALKING (Ian Holroyd), PO Box 3257, Ufton, Leamington Spa CV33 9YZ. Tel: 01926 614443; email: ian@look-whos-talking.co.uk; website: www.look-whos-talking.co.uk. A company specialising in providing first-class public speakers for cricket and other sporting events. Contact us to discuss the event and type of speaker.

Asterisks indicate businesses that have display advertisements elsewhere in the Almanack. See Index of Advertisements for details.

Opposite: Back to the beginning.
The title page of the first Almanack.

The Cricketer's Almanack,
FOR THE YEAR 1864,
BEING
Bissextile or Leap Year, and the 28th of the Reign of
HER MAJESTY QUEEN VICTORIA,
CONTAINING
The Laws of Cricket,
AS REVISED BY THE MARYLEBONE CLUB;
THE FIRST APPEARANCE AT LORD'S, AND NUMBER OF RUNS OBTAINED BY
MANY CRICKETING CELEBRITIES;
SCORES OF 100 AND UPWARDS, FROM 1850 TO 1863;
EXTRAORDINARY MATCHES;
ALL THE MATCHES PLAYED BETWEEN
THE GENTLEMEN AND PLAYERS,
AND
The All England and United Elevens,
With full and accurate Scores taken from authentic sources;
TOGETHER WITH
The Dates of the University Rowing Matches,
THE WINNERS OF THE
DERBY, OAKS, AND ST. LEGER;
RULES OF
BOWLS, QUOITS, AND KNUR AND SPELL,
AND OTHER INTERESTING INFORMATION.

LONDON:
PUBLISHED AND SOLD BY JOHN WISDEN AND CO.,
AT THEIR
CRICKETING AND BRITISH SPORTS WAREHOUSE,
2, NEW COVENTRY STREET, HAYMARKET, W.
May be had of all respectable Booksellers in the United Kingdom, or forwarded free by the Publisher to any part of Great Britain, for 13 Stamps.

1864. [One Shilling.

W. H. CROCKFORD, GREENWICH.

PART NINE

The Almanack

ANNIVERSARIES IN 2004-05

COMPILED BY STEVEN LYNCH

2004

April 11 Hugh Massie (Australia) born, 1854
Massie hit 55, easily the top score of the 1882 Oval Test, when Australia's seven-run win sparked the legend of the Ashes.

May 3 Austin Matthews (England) born, 1904
Northamptonshire and Glamorgan seam bowler who opened the bowling for England with Alf Gover against New Zealand at The Oval in 1937.

May 13 Tim Wall (Australia) born, 1904
Australia's fastest bowler during the 1930s.

June 10 Pakistan's first Test against England began at Lord's, 1954

June 11 John Dyson (Australia and coach of Sri Lanka) born, 1954

June 20 Allan Lamb (England) born, 1954

June 22 Middlesex tied with South Africans, 1904
The South Africans' last two wickets fell with the scores level in what Wisden *called "the sensational match of the tour".*

June 30 Tom Emmett (England) died, 1904
A left-hand round-arm bowler from Yorkshire who played in the first Test of all, at Melbourne in 1876-77.

July 5 John Wright (New Zealand and coach of India) born, 1954

July 7 American students beat MCC, 1904
Haverford College, a touring team from Pennsylvania, beat the Gentlemen of MCC at Lord's by 97 runs. Sir Arthur Conan Doyle top-scored for MCC with 41.

July 13 Ray Bright (Australia) born, 1954

July 19 Percy Perrin scored 343 not out, 1904...
...and finished on the losing side. Essex were bowled out for 97 in their second innings and Derbyshire won by nine wickets, "the most phenomenal performance ever recorded in first-class cricket," according to Wisden.

August 11 Yashpal Sharma (India) born, 1954

August 17 Pakistan beat England at The Oval, 1954
England fielded an experimental side at The Oval and lost by 24 runs as Fazal Mahmood took 12 wickets. This inaugural series was drawn 1–1.

October 27 Chris Tavaré (England) born, 1954

November 4 Jack Brown (England) died, 1904
The scorer of Test cricket's fastest half-century (28 minutes) on the way to a rapid match- and series-winning 140 at Melbourne in 1894-95, Brown was also a Yorkshire stalwart for many years. He was only 35 when he died, of "congestion of the brain and heart failure".

November 14 Harold Larwood (England) born, 1904
The leader of the Bodyline attack, Larwood demolished 33 batsmen in the infamous 1932-33 series, but never played for England again. He eventually settled in Sydney, and was the last survivor of the England players from the tour when he died in 1995.

December 11 Sylvester Clarke (West Indies) born, 1954
Famously aggressive fast bowler who died in 1999.

December 12 Wilf Slack (England) born, 1954
Middlesex and England left-handed opening batsman who collapsed and died at the crease in 1989.

2005

January 1 Hans Ebeling (Australia) born, 1905
The instigator of the triumphant Melbourne Centenary Test of 1977.

January 5 Frank Tyson (England) took seven for 27 v Australia, 1955
England won the Melbourne Test by 128 runs.

February 2 England won the Ashes, 1955
Spearheaded by Tyson, Len Hutton's team won the series 3–1.

February 25 George Bonnor (Australia) born, 1855
One of the biggest hitters cricket has known.

March 2 Ted Peate (England) born, 1855
The first in the line of famous Yorkshire slow left-armers.

March 15 Mohsin Khan (Pakistan) born, 1955

2004 FIXTURES

NWS	NatWest Series between England, New Zealand and West Indies
NWC	NatWest Challenge between England and India
ICC CT	ICC Champions Trophy
FCC Div 1/Div 2	Frizzell County Championship Division 1/Division 2
C&G	Cheltenham & Gloucester Trophy
NCL Div 1/Div 2	National Cricket League Division 1/Division 2
UCCE	University Centre of Cricketing Excellence
💡	Day/night game

Note: All matches of three days or more are first-class, except those involving Bradford/Leeds UCCE and Cardiff UCCE.

April 9–12	**Friendly**	MCC	v Sussex	Lord's
April 10–14	**England Tour 4th Test Match**			
		WEST INDIES	**v ENGLAND**	**St John's**
April 10–12	**Universities**	Cambridge UCCE	v Essex	Cambridge
		Durham UCCE	v Durham	Durham
		Oxford UCCE	v Surrey	Oxford
		Somerset	v Lough UCCE	Taunton
		Worcestershire	v Cardiff UCCE	Worcester
		Yorkshire	v Brad/Leeds UCCE	Leeds
April 16–18	**Universities**	Oxford UCCE	v Nottinghamshire	Oxford
April 16–19	**FCC Div 1**	Gloucestershire	v Kent	Bristol
		Northamptonshire	v Lancashire	Northampton
		Surrey	v Sussex	The Oval
		Warwickshire	v Middlesex	Birmingham
	FCC Div 2	Glamorgan	v Derbyshire	Cardiff
		Hampshire	v Durham	Southampton
April 18	**England Tour 1st ODI**			
		WEST INDIES	**v ENGLAND**	**Georgetown**
April 21–23	**Universities**	Cambridge UCCE	v Warwickshire	Cambridge
		Gloucestershire	v Lough UCCE	Bristol
		Northamptonshire	v Durham UCCE	Northampton
April 21–24	**FCC Div 1**	Kent	v Worcestershire	Canterbury
		Middlesex	v Surrey	Lord's
		Sussex	v Lancashire	Hove
	FCC Div 2	Durham	v Nottinghamshire	Chester-le-Street
		Leicestershire	v Glamorgan	Leicester
		Somerset	v Derbyshire	Taunton
		Yorkshire	v Essex	Leeds
April 24	**England Tour 2nd ODI**			
		WEST INDIES	**v ENGLAND**	**Port-of-Spain**
April 25	**England Tour 3rd ODI**			
		WEST INDIES	**v ENGLAND**	**Port-of-Spain**
April 25	**NCL Div 1**	Kent	v Gloucestershire	Canterbury
		Northamptonshire	v Lancashire	Northampton

Date	Competition	Home		Away	Venue
April 25	**NCL Div 1**	Surrey	v	Glamorgan	The Oval
		Warwickshire	v	Hampshire	Birmingham
	NCL Div 2	Durham	v	Nottinghamshire	Chester-le-Street
		Middlesex	v	Sussex	Lord's
		Somerset	v	Derbyshire	Taunton
		Yorkshire	v	Leicestershire	Leeds
April 28	**England Tour 4th ODI**				
		WEST INDIES	**v**	**ENGLAND**	**St George's**
April 28–30	**Universities**	Glamorgan	v	Cardiff UCCE	Cardiff
		Oxford UCCE	v	Kent	Oxford
Apr 28–May 1	**FCC Div 1**	Surrey	v	Northamptonshire	The Oval
		Warwickshire	v	Gloucestershire	Birmingham
		Worcestershire	v	Sussex	Worcester
	FCC Div 2	Derbyshire	v	Durham	Derby
		Essex	v	Somerset	Chelmsford
		Hampshire	v	Leicestershire	Southampton
		Nottinghamshire	v	Yorkshire	Nottingham
May 1	**England Tour 5th ODI**				
		WEST INDIES	**v**	**ENGLAND**	**Gros Islet**
May 2	**England Tour 6th ODI**				
		WEST INDIES	**v**	**ENGLAND**	**Gros Islet**
May 2	**NCL Div 1**	Gloucestershire	v	Glamorgan	Bristol
		Hampshire	v	Essex	Southampton
		Lancashire	v	Kent	Manchester
	NCL Div 2	Derbyshire	v	Durham	Derby
		Leicestershire	v	Scotland	Leicester
		Nottinghamshire	v	Yorkshire	Nottingham
		Worcestershire	v	Sussex	Worcester
May 3–6	**Tour Match**	British Universities	v	New Zealanders	Cambridge
May 3	**NCL Div 1**	Essex	v	Warwickshire	Chelmsford
		Glamorgan	v	Northamptonshire	Cardiff
		Surrey	v	Hampshire	The Oval
	NCL Div 2	Leicestershire	v	Derbyshire	Leicester
		Middlesex	v	Durham	Lord's
		Yorkshire	v	Scotland	Leeds
May 4	**NCL Div 2**	Worcestershire	v	Nottinghamshire	Worcester
May 5	**England Tour 7th ODI**				
		WEST INDIES	**v**	**ENGLAND**	**Bridgetown**
May 5	**C&G Trophy Round 2**	Berkshire	v	Kent	Reading
		Cambridgeshire	v	Northamptonshire	March
		Cheshire	v	Hampshire	Alderley Edge
		Derbyshire	v	Somerset	Derby
		Devon	v	Leicestershire	Exmouth
		Dorset	v	Yorkshire	Bournemouth
		Durham	v	Sussex	Chester-le-Street
		Herefordshire	v	Worcestershire	Luctonians

Date	Competition	Home		Away	Venue
May 5	**C&G Trophy Round 2**	Holland	v	Gloucestershire	Amsterdam
		Ireland	v	Surrey	Clontarf
		Lincolnshire	v	Glamorgan	Lincoln Lindum
		Scotland	v	Essex	Edinburgh
		Shropshire	v	Warwickshire	Wellington
		Staffordshire	v	Lancashire	Stone
		Wales	v	Middlesex	Lamphey
		Wiltshire	v	Nottinghamshire	Westbury
May 7–9	**Universities**	Brad/Leeds UCCE	v	Leicestershire	Bradford Park Ave
May 7–10	**Tour Match**	Worcestershire	v	New Zealanders	Worcester
May 7–10	**FCC Div 1**	Kent	v	Gloucestershire	Canterbury
		Middlesex	v	Lancashire	Lord's
		Northamptonshire	v	Sussex	Northampton
	FCC Div 2	Durham	v	Essex	Chester-le-Street
		Hampshire	v	Derbyshire	Southampton
		Nottinghamshire	v	Glamorgan	Nottingham
May 7	**NCL Div 2**	Scotland	v	Somerset	Edinburgh
May 9	**NCL Div 1**	Warwickshire	v	Surrey	Birmingham
	NCL Div 2	Somerset	v	Yorkshire	Taunton
May 12–14	**Universities**	Cambridge UCCE	v	Middlesex	Cambridge
		Sussex	v	Lough UCCE	Hove
May 12–15	**FCC Div 1**	Gloucestershire	v	Northamptonshire	Bristol
		Lancashire	v	Worcestershire	Manchester
		Warwickshire	v	Surrey	Birmingham
	FCC Div 2	Glamorgan	v	Essex	Cardiff
		Leicestershire	v	Nottinghamshire	Leicester
		Somerset	v	Durham	Taunton
		Yorkshire	v	Hampshire	Leeds
May 13–16	**Tour Match**	Kent	v	New Zealanders	Canterbury
May 16	**NCL Div 1**	Glamorgan	v	Essex	Cardiff
		Gloucestershire	v	Surrey	Bristol
		Lancashire	v	Hampshire	Manchester
	NCL Div 2	Leicestershire	v	Nottinghamshire	Leicester
		Scotland	v	Middlesex	Edinburgh
		Worcestershire	v	Durham	Worcester
		Yorkshire	v	Sussex	Leeds
May 18–21	**FCC Div 1**	Worcestershire	v	Gloucestershire	Worcester
May 19–21	**Universities**	Brad/Leeds UCCE	v	Lancashire	Bradford
		Hampshire	v	Cardiff UCCE	Southampton
May 19–22	**FCC Div 1**	Northamptonshire	v	Kent	Northampton
		Surrey	v	Middlesex	The Oval
		Sussex	v	Warwickshire	Horsham
	FCC Div 2	Derbyshire	v	Somerset	Derby
		Durham	v	Glamorgan	Chester-le-Street
		Essex	v	Leicestershire	Chelmsford
		Yorkshire	v	Nottinghamshire	Leeds

May 20–24	**1st npower Test Match**			
		ENGLAND	**v NEW ZEALAND**	**Lord's**
May 23	**NCL Div 1**	Gloucestershire	v Hampshire	Bristol
		Lancashire	v Glamorgan	Manchester
		Northamptonshire	v Kent	Northampton
		Surrey	v Essex	The Oval
	NCL Div 2	Derbyshire	v Somerset	Derby
		Nottinghamshire	v Middlesex	Nottingham
		Sussex	v Leicestershire	Horsham
		Yorkshire	v Worcestershire	Leeds
May 25–28	**FCC Div 1**	Lancashire	v Middlesex	Manchester
		Surrey	v Kent	The Oval
		Sussex	v Northamptonshire	Hove
		Warwickshire	v Worcestershire	Birmingham
	FCC Div 2	Derbyshire	v Glamorgan	Derby
		Nottinghamshire	v Durham	Nottingham
		Somerset	v Essex	Taunton
May 26	**C&G Rd 3**	Devon/Leics	v Dorset/Yorks	
May 28–31	**Tour Match**	Leicestershire	v New Zealanders	Leicester
May 29	**C&G Trophy Round 3**	Durham/Sussex	v Staffs/Lancs	
		Hereford/Worcs	v Derbys/Somerset	
		Holland/Glos	v Cheshire/Hants	
		Ireland/Surrey	v Cambs/Northants	
		Salop/Warwicks	v Berks/Kent	
		Wales/Middx	v Lincs/Glam	
		Wilts/Notts	v Scotland/Essex	
May 31	**NCL Div 1**	Hampshire	v Kent	Southampton
		Warwickshire	v Glamorgan	Birmingham
	NCL Div 2	Durham	v Derbyshire	Chester-le-Street
		Middlesex	v Somerset	Lord's
		Nottinghamshire	v Sussex	Nottingham
		Scotland	v Yorkshire	Edinburgh
June 2–5	**FCC Div 1**	Gloucestershire	v Surrey	Bristol
		Kent	v Lancashire	Tunbridge Wells
		Middlesex	v Warwickshire	Lord's
		Northamptonshire	v Worcestershire	Northampton
	FCC Div 2	Essex	v Yorkshire	Chelmsford
		Glamorgan	v Somerset	Swansea
		Hampshire	v Nottinghamshire	Southampton
		Leicestershire	v Derbyshire	Oakham School
June 3–7	**2nd npower Test Match**			
		ENGLAND	**v NEW ZEALAND**	**Leeds**
June 6	**NCL Div 1**	Glamorgan	v Gloucestershire	Swansea
		Hampshire	v Warwickshire	Southampton
		Kent	v Lancashire	Tunbridge Wells
		Northamptonshire	v Essex	Northampton
	NCL Div 2	Derbyshire	v Middlesex	Derby
		Durham	v Scotland	Chester-le-Street
		Leicestershire	v Worcestershire	Oakham School
		Sussex	v Somerset	Hove

Date	Competition	Home	Away	Venue
June 8–11	**FCC Div 2**	Durham	v Yorkshire	Chester-le-Street
June 8	**NCL Div 1**	Essex	v Hampshire	Chelmsford 💡
	NCL Div 2	Derbyshire	v Scotland	Derby
June 9–11	**Universities**	Derbyshire	v Durham UCCE	Derby
June 9–12	**FCC Div 1**	Gloucestershire	v Middlesex	Gloucester
		Lancashire	v Sussex	Manchester
		Warwickshire	v Northamptonshire	Birmingham
		Worcestershire	v Kent	Worcester
	FCC Div 2	Essex	v Hampshire	Chelmsford
		Glamorgan	v Leicestershire	Cardiff
		Somerset	v Nottinghamshire	Bath
June 10–14	**3rd npower Test Match**	**ENGLAND**	**v NEW ZEALAND**	**Nottingham**
June 13	**NCL Div 1**	Gloucestershire	v Northamptonshire	Gloucester
		Surrey	v Kent	The Oval
		Warwickshire	v Lancashire	Birmingham
	NCL Div 2	Middlesex	v Nottinghamshire	Lord's
		Somerset	v Leicestershire	Bath
		Worcestershire	v Yorkshire	Worcester
June 15	**C&G Trophy Quarter-Final**			
June 16	**Tour Matches**	Derbys or Worcs	v New Zealanders	Derby/Worcester
		Ireland	v West Indians	Belfast
June 16	**C&G Trophy Quarter-Finals**			
June 17	**Tour Match**	Ireland	v West Indians	Belfast
June 18–21	**FCC Div 1**	Middlesex	v Worcestershire	Lord's
		Surrey	v Gloucestershire	The Oval
		Warwickshire	v Lancashire	Stratford-on-Avon
	FCC Div 2	Hampshire	v Somerset	Southampton
		Nottinghamshire	v Derbyshire	Nottingham
		Yorkshire	v Leicestershire	Leeds
June 18	**Tour Match**	Essex	v New Zealanders	Chelmsford 💡
June 19	**Int'l Challenge**	Wales	v England	Cardiff
June 19	**Tour Match**	Sussex	v West Indians	Hove 💡
June 20	**NCL Div 2**	Scotland	v Durham	Edinburgh
June 20	**Tour Match**	Northamptonshire	v New Zealanders	Northampton
June 21	**Tour Match**	Kent	v West Indians	Beckenham
June 23–26	**FCC Div 1**	Kent	v Warwickshire	Beckenham
		Sussex	v Gloucestershire	Arundel
		Worcestershire	v Surrey	Worcester
	FCC Div 2	Derbyshire	v Essex	Derby
		Glamorgan	v Durham	Cardiff
		Hampshire	v Yorkshire	Southampton
		Somerset	v Leicestershire	Taunton

Date	Competition	Home	Away	Venue
June 23	**Tour Match**	Middlesex	v West Indians	Shenley Park
June 24	**Varsity Match**	Cambridge Univ	v Oxford Univ	Lord's
June 24	**NWS**	**ENGLAND**	**v NEW ZEALAND**	**Manchester**
June 25	**NCL Div 1**	Lancashire	v Northamptonshire	Manchester
June 26–29	**FCC Div 1**	Lancashire	v Northamptonshire	Liverpool
June 26	**NWS**	**NEW ZEALAND**	**v WEST INDIES**	**Birmingham**
June 27	**NWS**	**ENGLAND**	**v WEST INDIES**	**Nottingham**
June 27	**NCL Div 1**	Glamorgan	v Surrey	Cardiff
		Kent	v Warwickshire	Beckenham
	NCL Div 2	Derbyshire	v Worcestershire	Derby
		Leicestershire	v Middlesex	Leicester
		Scotland	v Nottinghamshire	Edinburgh
		Somerset	v Durham	Taunton
		Sussex	v Yorkshire	Arundel
June 28–July 1	**Varsity Match**	Oxford Univ	v Cambridge Univ	Oxford
June 28	**NCL Div 1**	Essex	v Gloucestershire	Chelmsford
June 29	**NWS**	**ENGLAND**	**v NEW ZEALAND**	**Chester-le-St**
June 30	**Tour Match**	British Universities	v Sri Lanka A	Leicester
June 30	**NCL Div 2**	Scotland	v Worcestershire	Edinburgh
		Sussex	v Durham	Hove
July 1	**NWS**	**ENGLAND**	**v WEST INDIES**	**Leeds**
July 2	**Twenty20 Cup**	Derbyshire	v Yorkshire	Derby
		Essex	v Hampshire	Chelmsford
		Kent	v Middlesex	Maidstone
		Lancashire	v Leicestershire	Manchester
		Northamptonshire	v Glamorgan	Northampton
		Nottinghamshire	v Durham	Nottingham
		Sussex	v Surrey	Hove
		Warwickshire	v Somerset	Birmingham
		Worcestershire	v Gloucestershire	Worcester
July 3	**Tour Match**	Yorkshire	v Sri Lanka A	Leeds
July 3	**NWS**	**NEW ZEALAND**	**v WEST INDIES**	**Cardiff**
July 3	**Twenty20 Cup**	Surrey	v Hampshire	The Oval
July 4	**NWS**	**ENGLAND**	**v NEW ZEALAND**	**Bristol**
July 4	**NCL Div 1**	Kent	v Essex	Maidstone
		Lancashire	v Gloucestershire	Manchester
		Warwickshire	v Northamptonshire	Birmingham

July 4	**NCL Div 2**	Durham	v Leicestershire	Chester-le-Street
		Nottinghamshire	v Derbyshire	Nottingham
		Sussex	v Scotland	Hove
		Worcestershire	v Somerset	Worcester
		Yorkshire	v Middlesex	Leeds
July 5	**NCL Div 2**	Middlesex	v Scotland	Richmond
July 5	**Tour Match**	Durham	v Sri Lanka A	Chester-le-Street
July 5	**Twenty20 Cup**	Kent	v Essex	Maidstone
		Northamptonshire	v Worcestershire	Luton
		Somerset	v Glamorgan	Taunton
July 6	**NWS**	**ENGLAND**	**v WEST INDIES**	**Lord's**
July 7	**Tour Match**	Worcestershire	v Sri Lanka A	Worcester
July 7	**Twenty20 Cup**	Essex	v Surrey	Chelmsford
		Leicestershire	v Durham	Leicester
		Middlesex	v Sussex	Richmond
		Nottinghamshire	v Yorkshire	Nottingham
July 8	**NWS**	**NEW ZEALAND**	**v WEST INDIES**	**Southampton**
July 8	**Twenty20 Cup**	Derbyshire	v Lancashire	Derby
		Glamorgan	v Warwickshire	Cardiff
		Northamptonshire	v Gloucestershire	Northampton
		Yorkshire	v Leicestershire	Leeds
July 9	**Tour Match**	Glamorgan	v Sri Lanka A	Cardiff
July 9	**Twenty20 Cup**	Durham	v Lancashire	Chester-le-Street
		Gloucestershire	v Somerset	Bristol
		Nottinghamshire	v Derbyshire	Nottingham
		Surrey	v Kent	The Oval
		Sussex	v Hampshire	Hove
		Warwickshire	v Worcestershire	Birmingham
July 10	**The NatWest Series Final**			**Lord's**
July 11	**NCL Div 1**	Hampshire	v Lancashire	Southampton
		Northamptonshire	v Glamorgan	Northampton
		Surrey	v Gloucestershire	The Oval
		Warwickshire	v Essex	Birmingham
	NCL Div 2	Durham	v Yorkshire	Chester-le-Street
		Leicestershire	v Sussex	Leicester
		Middlesex	v Derbyshire	Southgate
		Nottinghamshire	v Somerset	Nottingham
July 12	**Tour Match**	Sussex	v Sri Lanka A	Hove
July 12	**Twenty20 Cup**	Middlesex	v Essex	Southgate
		Warwickshire	v Northamptonshire	Birmingham
July 13–15	**Tour Match**	MCC	v West Indians	Arundel
July 13	**Twenty20 Cup**	Durham	v Derbyshire	Chester-le-Street
		Hampshire	v Middlesex	Southampton

Date	Competition	Team	Opponent	Venue
July 13	**Twenty20 Cup**	Kent	v Sussex	Canterbury
		Leicestershire	v Nottinghamshire	Leicester
		Somerset	v Worcestershire	Taunton
July 14	**Tour Match**	Kent	v Sri Lanka A	Canterbury
July 14	**Twenty20 Cup**	Glamorgan	v Gloucestershire	Cardiff
		Yorkshire	v Lancashire	Leeds
July 15	**Twenty20 Cup**	Derbyshire	v Leicestershire	Derby
		Durham	v Yorkshire	Chester-le-Street
		Essex	v Sussex	Chelmsford 💡
		Gloucestershire	v Warwickshire	Bristol
		Hampshire	v Kent	Southampton
		Lancashire	v Nottinghamshire	Manchester
		Middlesex	v Surrey	Lord's
		Somerset	v Northamptonshire	Taunton
		Worcestershire	v Glamorgan	Worcester
July 17	**C&G Trophy Semi-Finals**			
July 17–19	**Tour Match**	Sri Lanka A	v West Indians	Shenley
July 18	**NCL Div 1**	Glamorgan	v Warwickshire	Cardiff
		Hampshire	v Northamptonshire	Southampton
		Kent	v Surrey	Canterbury
		Lancashire	v Essex	Manchester
	NCL Div 2	Derbyshire	v Sussex	Derby
		Durham	v Middlesex	Chester-le-Street
		Somerset	v Worcestershire	Taunton
		Yorkshire	v Nottinghamshire	Leeds
July 19	**Twenty20 Cup Quarter-Finals**			
July 20	**NCL Div 1**	Kent	v Hampshire	Canterbury 💡
July 21–24	**Tour Match**	Glamorgan	v Sri Lanka A	†Swansea
July 21–24	**FCC Div 1**	Gloucestershire	v Lancashire	Cheltenham
		Surrey	v Warwickshire	Guildford
	FCC Div 2	Durham	v Derbyshire	Chester-le-Street
		Leicestershire	v Essex	Leicester
		Yorkshire	v Somerset	Scarborough
July 21	**NCL Div 2**	Sussex	v Nottinghamshire	Hove 💡
		Worcestershire	v Middlesex	Worcester 💡
July 22–26	**1st npower Test Match**	**ENGLAND**	**v WEST INDIES**	**Lord's**
July 22–25	**FCC Div 1**	Worcestershire	v Middlesex	Worcester
July 23–26	**FCC Div 1**	Sussex	v Kent	Hove
	FCC Div 2	Nottinghamshire	v Hampshire	Nottingham
July 25	**NCL Div 1**	Essex	v Northamptonshire	Southend
		Gloucestershire	v Lancashire	Cheltenham
		Surrey	v Warwickshire	Guildford
	NCL Div 2	Leicestershire	v Durham	Leicester
		Yorkshire	v Somerset	Scarborough
July 27–30	**Tour Match**	Somerset	v Sri Lanka A	Taunton

Date	Competition	Home	Away	Venue
July 27–30	**FCC Div 1**	Lancashire	v Warwickshire	Manchester
	FCC Div 2	Leicestershire	v Durham	Leicester
July 27	**NCL Div 1**	Surrey	v Northamptonshire	The Oval 💡
July 28–31	**1st U-19 Test**	England U-19	v Bangladesh U-19	Leeds
July 28–31	**FCC Div 1**	Gloucestershire	v Worcestershire	Cheltenham
		Middlesex	v Kent	Southgate
	FCC Div 2	Derbyshire	v Yorkshire	Derby
		Essex	v Nottinghamshire	Southend
July 28	**NCL Div 1**	Glamorgan	v Hampshire	Cardiff 💡
July 29–Aug 2	**2nd npower Test Match**	**ENGLAND**	**v WEST INDIES**	**Birmingham**
July 29–Aug 1	**FCC Div 1**	Northamptonshire	v Surrey	Northampton
	FCC Div 2	Glamorgan	v Hampshire	Cardiff
July 31	**NCL Div 1**	Lancashire	v Warwickshire	Manchester 💡
August 1	**NCL Div 1**	Gloucestershire	v Kent	Cheltenham
	NCL Div 2	Middlesex	v Yorkshire	Southgate
		Nottinghamshire	v Durham	Cleethorpes
		Scotland	v Leicestershire	Edinburgh
		Somerset	v Sussex	Taunton
		Worcestershire	v Derbyshire	Worcester
August 3–5	**FCC Div 1**	Kent	v Sussex	Canterbury
		Middlesex	v Gloucestershire	Lord's
		Surrey	v Worcestershire	The Oval
	FCC Div 2	Hampshire	v Essex	Southampton
		Somerset	v Glamorgan	Taunton
August 3	**NCL Div 2**	Derbyshire	v Leicestershire	Derby 💡
August 4	**NCL Div 1**	Northamptonshire	v Warwickshire	Northampton 💡
August 5–7	**Tour Match**	Dur/Lei/Der/Yor	v West Indians	
August 7	**Twenty20 Cup Semi-Finals and Final**			Birmingham 💡
August 8	**NCL Div 1**	Kent	v Glamorgan	Canterbury
		Northamptonshire	v Gloucestershire	Northampton
	NCL Div 2	Durham	v Worcestershire	Chester-le-Street
		Middlesex	v Leicestershire	Lord's
		Sussex	v Derbyshire	Hove
August 9	**NCL Div 1**	Essex	v Lancashire	Chelmsford 💡
		Hampshire	v Surrey	Southampton 💡
August 10	**NCL Div 2**	Yorkshire	v Derbyshire	Leeds 💡
August 10–13	**2nd U-19 Test**	England U-19	v Bangladesh U-19	Taunton
August 10–13	**FCC Div 1**	Middlesex	v Sussex	Lord's
August 11–14	**FCC Div 1**	Surrey	v Lancashire	Whitgift School
		Warwickshire	v Kent	Birmingham
		Worcestershire	v Northamptonshire	Worcester

Date	Competition	Home	Away	Venue
August 11–14	**FCC Div 2**	Hampshire	v Glamorgan	Southampton
		Nottinghamshire	v Leicestershire	Nottingham
August 11	**NCL Div 2**	Durham	v Somerset	Chester-le-Street
August 12–16	**3rd npower Test Match**	**ENGLAND**	**v WEST INDIES**	**Manchester**
August 12–15	**FCC Div 2**	Yorkshire	v Derbyshire	Leeds
August 13–16	**FCC Div 2**	Durham	v Somerset	Chester-le-Street
August 13	**NCL Div 1**	Gloucestershire	v Essex	Bristol
August 15	**NCL Div 1**	Hampshire	v Glamorgan	Southampton
		Surrey	v Lancashire	Whitgift School
		Warwickshire	v Kent	Birmingham
	NCL Div 2	Middlesex	v Worcestershire	Lord's
		Nottinghamshire	v Leicestershire	Nottingham
		Scotland	v Sussex	Edinburgh
August 17–20	**3rd U-19 Test**	England U-19	v Bangladesh U-19	Cardiff
August 17	**NCL Div 1**	Warwickshire	v Gloucestershire	Birmingham
	NCL Div 2	Sussex	v Worcestershire	Hove
August 18–21	**FCC Div 1**	Kent	v Surrey	Canterbury
		Northamptonshire	v Middlesex	Northampton
	FCC Div 2	Derbyshire	v Nottinghamshire	Derby
		Essex	v Durham	Colchester
		Somerset	v Hampshire	Taunton
August 18	**NCL Div 2**	Leicestershire	v Yorkshire	Leicester
August 19–23	**4th npower Test Match**	**ENGLAND**	**v WEST INDIES**	**The Oval**
August 19–22	**FCC Div 1**	Gloucestershire	v Warwickshire	Bristol
		Sussex	v Worcestershire	Hove
	FCC Div 2	Leicestershire	v Yorkshire	Leicester
August 22	**NCL Div 1**	Essex	v Kent	Colchester
		Glamorgan	v Lancashire	Colwyn Bay
		Northamptonshire	v Hampshire	Northampton
	NCL Div 2	Derbyshire	v Nottinghamshire	Derby
		Somerset	v Scotland	Taunton
August 24	**1st U-19 ODI**	England U-19	v Bangladesh U-19	Arundel
August 24–27	**FCC Div 1**	Lancashire	v Kent	Manchester
		Northamptonshire	v Gloucestershire	Northampton
		Warwickshire	v Sussex	Birmingham
	FCC Div 2	Derbyshire	v Leicestershire	Derby
		Durham	v Hampshire	Chester-le-Street
		Glamorgan	v Yorkshire	Colwyn Bay
August 24	**NCL Div 2**	Somerset	v Middlesex	Taunton
		Worcestershire	v Scotland	Worcester

Date	Competition	Home	Away	Venue
August 25	**NCL Div 1**	Essex	v Surrey	Chelmsford 💡
	NCL Div 2	Nottinghamshire	v Worcestershire	Nottingham 💡
August 26	**2nd U-19 ODI**	England U-19	v Bangladesh U-19	Hove
August 26	**Tour Match**	Somerset	v Indians	Taunton
August 26	**NCL Div 2**	Nottinghamshire	v Scotland	Nottingham
August 27	**3rd U-19 ODI**	England U-19	v Bangladesh U-19	Hove
August 28	**C&G Trophy Final**			**Lord's**
August 28	**Tour Match**	Leics/Glam/Essex	v Indians	
August 29	**NCL Div 1**	Glamorgan	v Kent	Cardiff
		Northamptonshire	v Surrey	Northampton
	NCL Div 2	Derbyshire	v Yorkshire	Derby
		Durham	v Sussex	Chester-le-Street
		Leicestershire	v Somerset	Leicester
August 30	**NCL Div 1**	Hampshire	v Gloucestershire	Southampton
Aug 31–Sept 3	**FCC Div 1**	Worcestershire	v Warwickshire	Worcester
August 31	**NCL Div 1**	Lancashire	v Surrey	Manchester 💡
Sept 1–4	**FCC Div 2**	Leicestershire	v Hampshire	Leicester
		Yorkshire	v Durham	Scarborough
Sept 1	**NWC**	**ENGLAND**	**v INDIA**	**Nottingham**
Sept 2–5	**FCC Div 1**	Lancashire	v Surrey	Manchester
	FCC Div 2	Essex	v Glamorgan	Chelmsford
Sept 2	**NCL Div 2**	Sussex	v Middlesex	Hove 💡
Sept 3–6	**FCC Div 1**	Kent	v Northamptonshire	Canterbury
	FCC Div 2	Nottinghamshire	v Somerset	Nottingham
Sept 3	**NWC**	**ENGLAND**	**v INDIA**	**The Oval**
Sept 4–7	**FCC Div 1**	Sussex	v Middlesex	Hove
Sept 4	**NCL Div 1**	Gloucestershire	v Warwickshire	Bristol
Sept 5	**NCL Div 2**	Scotland	v Derbyshire	Edinburgh
		Worcestershire	v Leicestershire	Worcester
		Yorkshire	v Durham	Scarborough
Sept 5	**NWC**	**ENGLAND**	**v INDIA**	**Lord's**
Sept 6	**NCL Div 1**	Essex	v Glamorgan	Chelmsford 💡
Sept 7	**NCL Div 1**	Kent	v Northamptonshire	Canterbury 💡
Sept 8	**NCL Div 2**	Somerset	v Nottinghamshire	Taunton 💡

Sept 9–12	**FCC Div 1**	Gloucestershire	v Sussex	Bristol
		Middlesex	v Northamptonshire	Lord's
		Worcestershire	v Lancashire	Worcester
	FCC Div 2	Durham	v Leicestershire	Chester-le-Street
		Essex	v Derbyshire	Chelmsford
Sept 10–13	**FCC Div 2**	Glamorgan	v Nottinghamshire	Cardiff
		Somerset	v Yorkshire	Taunton
Sept 10	**ICC CT**	**ENGLAND**	**v ZIMBABWE**	**Birmingham**
		NEW ZEALAND	**v QUALIFIER**	**The Oval**
Sept 11	**ICC CT**	**INDIA**	**v KENYA**	**Southampton**
Sept 12	**ICC CT**	**BANGLADESH**	**v SOUTH AFRICA**	**Birmingham**
Sept 13	**ICC CT**	**AUSTRALIA**	**v QUALIFIER**	**Southampton**
Sept 14	**ICC CT**	**KENYA**	**v PAKISTAN**	**Birmingham**
		SRI LANKA	**v ZIMBABWE**	**The Oval**
Sept 15	**ICC CT**	**BANGLADESH**	**v WEST INDIES**	**Southampton**
Sept 16	**ICC CT**	**AUSTRALIA**	**v NEW ZEALAND**	**The Oval**
Sept 16–19	**FCC Div 1**	Kent	v Middlesex	Canterbury
		Lancashire	v Gloucestershire	Manchester
		Northamptonshire	v Warwickshire	Northampton
		Sussex	v Surrey	Hove
	FCC Div 2	Derbyshire	v Hampshire	Derby
		Leicestershire	v Somerset	Leicester
		Nottinghamshire	v Essex	Nottingham
		Yorkshire	v Glamorgan	Leeds
Sept 17	**ICC CT**	**ENGLAND**	**v SRI LANKA**	**Southampton**
Sept 18	**ICC CT**	**SOUTH AFRICA**	**v WEST INDIES**	**The Oval**
Sept 19	**ICC CT**	**INDIA**	**v PAKISTAN**	**Birmingham**
Sept 21	**ICC CT First Semi-Final**			**Birmingham**
Sept 22	**ICC CT Second Semi-Final**			**Southampton**
Sept 25	**ICC CT Final**			**The Oval**

† *Venue unconfirmed.*

Notes: Directions to all home grounds used by first-class counties can be found on the directory page for each club.

All Champions Trophy (ICC CT) matches have a reserve day.

INTERNATIONAL SCHEDULE, 2004–2011

At an executive board meeting in Melbourne, in February 2001, the International Cricket Council unveiled a ten-year schedule of Tests and one-day internationals. The schedule initially runs from May 2001 to April 2011; all of the ICC's ten Test-playing members are intended to play each other in home and away Test series (with a minimum of two matches to a series) during each five-year period.

The programme is based around Test matches, but in most cases there will be associated one-day internationals. Countries may revise dates as long as they do not disrupt other series.

	Australia	Bangladesh	England	India	New Zealand	Pakistan	South Africa	Sri Lanka	West Indies	Zimbabwe
Australia	–	9/10	11/06 11/10	12/07	**11/04** 11/06	**12/04** 11/08	12/05 12/09	**7/04** 1/06	**11/05** 10/05	11/09
Bangladesh	4/06	–	2/07 2/11	**4/04** 10/06	**10/04** 10/07	1/10	3/08	**11/04** 2/08	10/09 11/10	1/09
England	**6/05** 6/09	**5/05** 5/10	–	6/07	**5/04** 5/09	6/06	6/08	5/06	**7/04** 6/10	5/08
India	**10/04** 10/10	**4/05** 12/10	2/06	–	10/09	1/06 1/11	**11/04** 10/08	11/05 12/09	2/08	10/07
New Zealand	**2/05** 12/05	12/06	2/08	2/07	–	12/08	2/11	**12/04** 12/07	2/06 12/09	12/05 2/10
Pakistan	2/08	9/09	11/05 11/09	**2/05** 3/09	10/08	–	10/07	**3/05** 2/10	12/06	**10/04** 10/06
South Africa	2/06 2/10	4/09	**12/04** 12/08	12/06 1/09	10/05 10/10	2/07 12/10	–	10/09	12/07	**2/05** 2/08
Sri Lanka	9/08	2/06	10/07	7/08	8/07	3/06 8/10	**8/04** 10/06	–	**7/05** 7/09	2/07
West Indies	2/07 2/11	**5/04** 11/08	**3/04** 2/09	5/06 3/10	4/08	**5/05** 4/10	**3/05** 4/11	5/08	–	4/06 4/09
Zimbabwe	**5/04** 9/06	12/07	**10/04** 10/09	10/05 3/11	9/05 9/10	9/07	8/06	**4/04** 12/08	9/08	–

Home teams listed on left, away teams across top. Tours between April 2004 and July 2005 shown in bold.

ENGLAND'S INTERNATIONAL SCHEDULE, 2004–2009

Home

2004	Tests and ODIs v New Zealand and West Indies; ICC Champions Trophy
2005	Tests and ODIs v Bangladesh and Australia
2006	Tests and ODIs v Sri Lanka and Pakistan
2007	Tests and ODIs v India
2008	Tests and ODIs v Zimbabwe and South Africa
2009	Tests and ODIs v New Zealand and Australia

Away

2004-05	Tests and ODIs v Zimbabwe and South Africa
2005-06	Tests and ODIs v Pakistan and India
2006-07	Tests and ODIs v Australia and Bangladesh WORLD CUP in the West Indies
2007-08	Tests and ODIs v Sri Lanka and New Zealand
2008-09	Tests and ODIs v South Africa and West Indies

All tours subject to confirmation.

TEST MATCHES, 2003-04

Full details of these Tests, and others too late for inclusion, will appear in *Wisden 2005*.

ZIMBABWE v WEST INDIES

First Test: At Harare, November 4, 5, 6, 7, 8, 2003. **Drawn.** Toss: Zimbabwe. **Zimbabwe 507-9 dec.** (T. R. Gripper 41, C. B. Wishart 47, S. Matsikenyeri 57, T. Taibu 83, H. H. Streak 127*, A. M. Blignaut 91; F. H. Edwards 5-133) **and 200-7 dec.** (C. B. Wishart 34, S. Matsikenyeri 46*; V. C. Drakes 4-67); **West Indies 335** (W. W. Hinds 79, D. Ganga 73, S. Chanderpaul 36, V. C. Drakes 31; R. W. Price 6-73) **and 207-9** (R. R. Sarwan 39, S. Chanderpaul 39, R. D. Jacobs 60*; R. W. Price 4-88).

Zimbabwe recovered from 154 for five, as Streak scored a maiden Test hundred, in his 56th match, and Blignaut helped him add 168, a Zimbabwean eighth-wicket Test record. Price took ten West Indian wickets before last man Edwards joined Jacobs, still 168 behind; they survived 71 balls to save the game. This ended Zimbabwe's run of 11 Test defeats.

Second Test: At Bulawayo, November 12, 13, 14, 15, 16, 2003. **West Indies won by 128 runs.** Toss: West Indies. **West Indies 481** (C. H. Gayle 47, W. W. Hinds 81, B. C. Lara 191, R. R. Sarwan 65; A. M. Blignaut 4-86, R. W. Price 5-199) **and 128** (H. H. Streak 3-39, A. M. Blignaut 3-29, R. W. Price 4-36); **Zimbabwe 377** (M. A. Vermeulen 118, C. B. Wishart 96, A. M. Blignaut 31, R. W. Price 35, Extras 37; C. D. Collymore 4-70) **and 104** (H. H. Streak 33*; O. A. C. Banks 3-35).

Lara scored his 22nd Test hundred and overtook Viv Richards (8,540) as West Indies' leading scorer in Test cricket. West Indies recorded their lowest total against Zimbabwe in the second innings, but bowled Zimbabwe out even more cheaply to take the series 1–0.

AUSTRALIA v INDIA

First Test: At Brisbane, December 4, 5, 6, 7, 8, 2003. **Drawn.** Toss: India. **Australia 323** (J. L. Langer 121, M. L. Hayden 37, R. T. Ponting 54, D. R. Martyn 42; Zaheer Khan 5-95, A. B. Agarkar 3-90) **and 284-3 dec.** (M. L. Hayden 99, R. T. Ponting 50, D. R. Martyn 66*, S. R. Waugh 56*); **India 409** (A. Chopra 36, V. Sehwag 45, S. C. Ganguly 144, V. V. S. Laxman 75, P. A. Patel 37; J. N. Gillespie 4-65, S. C. G. MacGill 4-86) **and 73-2** (R. Dravid 43*).

India scored 351 runs for six wickets on the fourth day. Hayden reached 1,000 Test runs for the third successive calendar year; in 2003, it took him ten Tests (17 innings).

Second Test: At Adelaide, December 12, 13, 14, 15, 16, 2003. **India won by four wickets.** Toss: Australia. **Australia 556** (J. L. Langer 58, R. T. Ponting 242, D. R. Martyn 30, S. R. Waugh 30, S. M. Katich 75, J. N. Gillespie 48*; A. Kumble 5-154) **and 196** (D. R. Martyn 38, S. R. Waugh 42, S. M. Katich 31, A. C. Gilchrist 43; A. B. Agarkar 6-41); **India 523** (V. Sehwag 47, R. Dravid 233, V. V. S. Laxman 148, P. A. Patel 31; A. J. Bichel 4-118) **and 233-6** (V. Sehwag 47, R. Dravid 72*, S. R. Tendulkar 37, V. V. S. Laxman 32).

Australia scored 400 for five on the opening day, but their eventual 556 was to be the third-highest Test total by a losing side, and Ponting's career-best 242 the highest individual score in a losing cause. Dravid's 233, also a career-best, helped him pass 6,000 runs in Tests; he and Laxman added 303 for the fourth wicket to help India recover from 85 for four. This was India's first Test win on Australian soil for 23 years.

Third Test: At Melbourne, December 26, 27, 28, 29, 30, 2003. **Australia won by nine wickets.** Toss: India. **India 366** (A. Chopra 48, V. Sehwag 195, R. Dravid 49, S. C. Ganguly 37; S. C. G. MacGill 3-70) **and 286** (R. Dravid 92, S. C. Ganguly 73, S. R. Tendulkar 44; B. A. Williams 4-53); **Australia 558** (M. L. Hayden 136, R. T. Ponting 257, D. R. Martyn 31, Extras 39; A. B. Agarkar 3-115, A. Kumble 6-176) **and 97-1** (M. L. Hayden 53*, R. T. Ponting 31*).

Sehwag scored 195 on the opening day. Ponting raised his career-best again as he became only the fifth player to score double-hundreds in consecutive Tests. He ended 2003 with 1,503 Test runs in the calendar year, a figure exceeded only by Viv Richards and Sunil Gavaskar.

The last farewell: a touching tribute to the former Australian Test batsman David Hookes, who died aged 48 on January 19, 2004, after becoming involved in a fight on a Melbourne street. His funeral drew more than 10,000 to the Adelaide Oval. His obituary will appear in *Wisden 2005*.

Picture by Hamish Blair, Getty Images.

Fourth Test: At Sydney, January 2, 3, 4, 5, 6, 2004. **Drawn.** Toss: India. **India 705-7 dec.** (A. Chopra 45, V. Sehwag 72, R. Dravid 38, S. R. Tendulkar 241*, V. V. S. Laxman 178, P. A. Patel 62, Extras 38; B. Lee 4-201, J. N. Gillespie 3-135) **and 211-2 dec.** (V. Sehwag 47, R. Dravid 91*, S. R. Tendulkar 60*); **Australia 474** (J. L. Langer 117, M. L. Hayden 67, S. R. Waugh 40, S. M. Katich 125, J. N. Gillespie 47, Extras 38; A. Kumble 8-141) **and 357-6** (J. L. Langer 47, M. L. Hayden 30, R. T. Ponting 47, D. R. Martyn 40, S. R. Waugh 80, S. M. Katich 77*; A. Kumble 4-138).

This was Steve Waugh's 168th and final Test. He finished with 10,927 runs, including 32 hundreds, beaten only by Sunil Gavaskar's 34 and equalled in this match by Tendulkar, who had been averaging 16 in the series, but regained form in a career-best unbeaten 241, becoming the fourth man to pass 9,000 Test runs. Tendulkar added 353 with Laxman, an Indian fourth-wicket record, to set up their highest total in all Tests. Ganguly waived the follow-on. The series was drawn 1–1, and India retained the Border-Gavaskar Trophy which they had won in 2000-01.

SOUTH AFRICA v WEST INDIES

First Test: At Johannesburg, December 12, 13, 14, 15, 16, 2003. **South Africa won by 189 runs.** Toss: South Africa. **South Africa 561** (G. C. Smith 132, H. H. Gibbs 60, J. H. Kallis 158, M. van Jaarsveld 73, S. M. Pollock 30; W. W. Hinds 3-79) **and 226-6 dec.** (G. C. Smith 44, J. A. Rudolph 44, J. H. Kallis 44); **West Indies 410** (D. Ganga 60, B. C. Lara 202, S. Chanderpaul 34, Extras 36; M. Ntini 5-94, A. Nel 3-78) **and 188** (S. Chanderpaul 74; S. M. Pollock 4-31, M. Ntini 4-53).

Lara hit one over from Robin Peterson for 28, a Test record, on his way to his sixth Test double-hundred and his second in a losing cause.

Second Test: At Durban, December 26, 27, 28, 29, 2003. **South Africa won by an innings and 65 runs.** Toss: South Africa. **West Indies 264** (B. C. Lara 72, R. D. Jacobs 58, V. C. Drakes 67; M. Ntini 5-66, A. Nel 3-43) **and 329** (R. R. Sarwan 114, S. Chanderpaul 109; M. Ntini 3-72, A. Nel 3-68); **South Africa 658-9 dec.** (H. H. Gibbs 142, J. A. Rudolph 36, J. H. Kallis 177, G. Kirsten 137, N. D. McKenzie 32, S. M. Pollock 38*, A. J. Hall 32, Extras 38; A. Sanford 3-170).

This was Lara's 100th Test. Gibbs reached 5,000 Test runs, and Kirsten 7,000; Kirsten and Kallis added 249 for South Africa's fourth wicket. West Indian wicket-keeper Jacobs did not concede a bye during the South African total of 658 for nine. Ntini finished 2003 as the year's leading wicket-taker in Tests, with 59.

Third Test: At Cape Town, January 2, 3, 4, 5, 6, 2004. **Drawn.** Toss: South Africa. **South Africa 532** (G. C. Smith 42, H. H. Gibbs 33, J. A. Rudolph 101, J. H. Kallis 73, N. D. McKenzie 76, M. V. Boucher 122*, Extras 38; F. H. Edwards 3-132, A. Sanford 4-132, D. Mohammed 3-112) **and 335-3 dec.** (H. H. Gibbs 142, J. H. Kallis 130*); **West Indies 427** (C. H. Gayle 116, R. R. Sarwan 44, B. C. Lara 115, D. Mohammed 36; A. Nel 5-87) **and 354-5** (C. H. Gayle 32, R. R. Sarwan 69, B. C. Lara 86, D. R. Smith 105*; M. Ntini 3-82).

Lara's 24th Test hundred made him the fifth batsman to reach 9,000 Test runs, two days after Sachin Tendulkar at Sydney. On the final day, 20-year-old Dwayne Smith scored an unbeaten run-a-ball 105 on Test debut, reaching his hundred from just 93 balls.

Fourth Test: At Centurion, January 16, 17, 18, 19, 20, 2004. **South Africa won by ten wickets.** Toss: West Indies. **South Africa 604-6 dec.** (G. C. Smith 139, H. H. Gibbs 192, J. A. Rudolph 37, J. H. Kallis 130*, N. D. McKenzie 40, Extras 42) **and 46-0; West Indies 301** (C. H. Gayle 77, B. C. Lara 34, S. Chanderpaul 42, D. R. Smith 39, V. C. Drakes 35, M. Dillon 30; M. Ntini 5-49, A. Nel 3-64) **and 348** (C. H. Gayle 107, R. R. Sarwan 119, Extras 30; S. M. Pollock 4-69, M. Ntini 3-99).

Smith and Gibbs opened with 301, becoming the first pair to share three 300-run partnerships in Tests. Kallis scored a hundred in every Test of the series, which South Africa won 3–0.

NEW ZEALAND v PAKISTAN

First Test: At Hamilton, December 19, 20, 21, 22, 23, 2003. **Drawn.** Toss: Pakistan. **New Zealand 563** (M. H. Richardson 44, S. P. Fleming 192, S. B. Styris 33, D. L. Vettori 137*, D. R. Tuffey 35, Extras 58; Shabbir Ahmed 5-117) **and 96-8** (Mohammad Sami 5-44); **Pakistan 463** (Yasir Hameed 80, Inzamam-ul-Haq 51, Abdul Razzaq 48, Moin Khan 137, Extras 36; D. R. Tuffey 5-87).

Fleming's 192 was New Zealand's second-highest score against Pakistan, and 563 their highest total against them. Vettori, batting at No. 9, scored a maiden Test hundred, as New Zealand's last three wickets added 249.

Second Test: At Basin Reserve, Wellington, December 26, 27, 28, 29, 30, 2003. **Pakistan won by seven wickets.** Toss: New Zealand. **New Zealand 366** (M. H. Richardson 82, S. B. Styris 36, J. D. P. Oram 97, D. L. Vettori 44, Extras 33; Shoaib Akhtar 5-48, Shabbir Ahmed 3-87) **and 103** (M. H. Richardson 41; Shoaib Akhtar 6-30); **Pakistan 196** (Yousuf Youhana 60, Inzamam-ul-Haq 34; I. G. Butler 6-46) **and 277-3** (Taufeeq Umar 34, Yasir Hameed 59, Yousuf Youhana 88*, Inzamam-ul-Haq 72*).

New Zealand led by 170 on first innings, but second time round lost their last seven for eight runs inside nine overs. Shoaib Akhtar took 11 for 78 in the match, a career-best. Pakistan won the series 1–0.

RECORD FOURTH-INNINGS TOTAL TO WIN A FIRST-CLASS MATCH

Less than a month after England declined to chase 368 for victory against Sri Lanka in the Kandy Test, a Sri Lankan provincial team achieved all that and more on the same ground.

On January 8, 2004, Central Province broke the 108-year-old world record for a fourth-innings run-chase by scoring 513 for nine to beat Southern Province by one wicket. The old record was held by Cambridge University, who scored 507 for seven to beat MCC and Ground at Lord's in 1896.

Central were set 512 to win. Sajith and Hasantha Fernando put on 198 for the third wicket before the Test wicket-keeper Kumar Sangakkara scored a rapid 101. But wickets tumbled after they reached 340 for three and the last pair, Nuwan Zoysa and Ruchira Perera, had to score 23 in the last three overs in fading light.

Full details will appear in *Wisden 2005*.

INDEX OF TEST MATCHES

INDEX OF ADVERTISEMENTS

INDEX OF FILLERS AND INSERTS

INDEX OF UNUSUAL OCCURRENCES

INDEX OF FILLERS AND INSERTS

INDEX OF UNUSUAL OCCURRENCES